What the ~~re~~ **sic Guide series:**

"It's a definit~~e~~

"Delivers on ~~All music guide to country~~ knowledge."

"This extremely valuable and exhaustive resource offers lively writing not only on recordings, but also style descriptions, history, profiles, reflective essays, music maps, and more."
— *The Christian Science Monitor*

"Anybody who owns a record collection should invest in the owners manual, *All Music Guide*."
— *San Francisco Chronicle*

"I can't imagine a serious music lover, record store, radio station or library without a copy."
— *Whole Earth Review*

"Quite an amazing reference volume, invaluable for the record collector."
— *DISCoveries*

"Don't visit a record store without it."
— *Guitar Player*

"A dream come true for contemporary record collectors . . . this book ought to be in every home that has a resident music enthusiast."
— *San Francisco Examiner*

"The sheer scope of the enterprise makes this volume the one indispensable book in a music reference library."
— *Addicted to Noise*

"Any library or individual who doesn't cough up the very reasonable bucks to own this tome will remain musically illiterate."
— *Small Press*

"A massive piece of work, and a very good value for the money."
— *Living Blues*

"This is the best overall record guide."
— *The Beat*

"A number of guides have appeared to help the neophyte wade through the maze of recordings. *The All Music Guide* is by far the best of these books. . . . The result is an informed (and informative), candid, and literate production."
— *Dirty Linen*

"A valuable resource and well worth its reasonable cover price for the music fan trying to make sense of the plethora of reissues and new releases."
— *Illinois Entertainer*

"In its scope, Miller Freeman's *All Music Guide* is without peer."
— *Publishers Weekly*

"A powerful informational tool—very condensed and rarely wishy-washy. . . . Such succinct summings-up, along with terse chronologies of career phases, and discussions of genre styles, make the book a true bargain."

—Puncture

"A treasure trove of concise informative reviews . . . an essential addition to any music lover's library."

—The Ithaca Journal

"Highly recommended references for discriminating music buyers."

—Reviewer's Bookwatch

"[The *All Music Guide to Jazz*] is one fun book for any fan of jazz, new or old. . . . This book represents the informational cornerstone to an understanding and appreciation of the genre . . . . So grab yourself a copy, flip on some Miles, pour a martini, and settle in for some cool fun."

—BAM Magazine

"An entertaining, informative and easy to access format. . . . Will easily become your number one reference book, if not replace all others."

—Small Press

"Easily the best guide to hit the market both as an encyclopedia and as a tool to help readers pick discs for purchase. Everyone needs one of these on their shelf."

—Real Blues

All
Music
Guide to
Country

All Music Guide to Country

The experts' guide to the best recordings in country music

Edited by
Michael Erlewine
Vladimir Bogdanov
Chris Woodstra
Stephen Thomas Erlewine

●AMG All Music Guide Series

Miller Freeman Books

San Francisco

Published by Miller Freeman Books
600 Harrison Street, San Francisco, CA 94107
Publishers of *Guitar Player, Bass Player* and *Keyboard* magazines
Miller Freeman, Inc. is a United News and Media Company

𝖀𝖓 Miller Freeman
A United News & Media company

Distributed to the book trade in the U.S. and Canada by
Publishers Group West, P.O. Box 8843, Emeryville, CA 94662

Distributed to the music trade in the U.S. and Canada by
Hal Leonard Publishing, P.O. Box 13819, Milwaukee, WI 53213

ISBN 0-87930-475-8

Cover Design: Nita Ybarra
Cover Photo: Hank Williams with Chet Atkins and Ernie Newton, onstage at the Grand Ole Opry c. 1950. Courtesy of the Country Music Hall of Fame.

Production: Dorothy Cox, Carolyn Keating, Linda Hager, Matt Kelsey, and Wendy Davis

Printed in the United States of America
97 98 99 00   5 4 3 2 1

CONTENTS

HOW TO USE THIS BOOK

ARTIST NAME (Alternate name in parentheses).

VITAL STATISTICS For indivdual performers, date and place of birth and death, if known.

INSTRUMENT(S) / STYLE Major instruments for each performer, followed by one or more styles of music associated with each performer or group.

BIOGRAPHY A quick view of the artist's life and musical career. For major performers, proportionately longer biographies are provided.

ALBUM REVIEWS These are the albums selected by our editors and contributors.

KEY TO SYMBOLS ● ☆ ★

☆ ESSENTIAL RECORDINGS Albums marked with a star should be part of any good collection of the genre. Often, these are also a good first purchase (filled star). By hearing these albums, you can get a good overview of the entire genre. These are must-hear and must-have recordings. You can't go wrong with them.

●★ FIRST PURCHASE Albums marked with either a filled circle or a filled star should be your first purchase. This is where to begin to find out If you like this particular artist. These albums are representative of the best this artist has to offer. If you don't like these picks, chances are this artist is not for you. In the case of an artist who has a number of distinct periods, you will find an essential pick marked for each period. Albums are listed chronologically when possible.

ALBUM RATINGS: ✦ TO ✦✦✦✦✦ In addition to the stars and circles used to distinguish exceptional noteworthy albums, as explained above, all albums are rated on a scale from one to five diamonds.

ALBUM TITLE The name of the album is listed in bold as it appears on the original when possible. Very long titles have been abbreviated, or repeated in full as part of the comment, where needed.

DATE The year of an album's first release, if known.

RECORD LABEL Record labels indicate the current (or most recent) release of this recording. Label numbers are not included because they change frequently.

REVIEWERS The name of each review's author are given at the end of the review. "AMG" indicates a review written by the *All Music Guide* staff.

Rosanne Cash

b. May 24, 1955, Memphis, TN
Guitar, Vocals / Contemporary Country

Reba McEntire sells more records, but Rosanne Cash, the daughter of Johnny Cash, may be the greatest woman currently working in country. Her brand of art, however, has never been confined to the cut-and-dried traditions of C&W, nor can she be pigeonholed as an "outlaw" upstart. Cash works within the context of country much as Bob Wills did: By bringing her unique perspectives to the genre, she has somehow eclipsed it, changing its patterns to suit her creative needs and tailoring it to encompass the complexities of her vision.

Her first hit, the self-penned "Seven Year Ache," was a crossover smash for several reasons: the sentiments of the song contradicted the roles enforced on female country artists, and the backbeat had more in common with Bonnie Raitt than Kitty Wells. Although many of her best personality-defining songs have come from outside writers, over the last few years Cash has blossomed into a clever and soul-searching songwriter. 1990's *Interiors*, produced and written entirely by Cash, uncompromisingly picked apart the disintegration of her marriage to Rodney Crowell. It remains a moody, unsettling masterpiece. Cash followed with *The Wheel* in 1993 and while sales were disappointing, the album received considerable critical acclaim. In 1996, she released *10 Song Demo*.

At her best, Cash sounds like a meeting of Patsy Cline, Joni Mitchell, and Chrissie Hynde: she has a full-bodied vocal style reminiscent of Cline's, she manifests her emotions with the persistence of Mitchell, and she has the confidence and attitude of Hynde. *–John Floyd*

★ **Seven Year Ache** / 1981 / Columbia ✦✦✦✦✦
Cash was arguably the most important artist to emerge in country music in the early '80s, and this was her breakthrough album, which introduced a new, assertive, passionate stance to women in country and also helped foster the crossover between folk, rock, and country. Cash's songwriting (the title track and "Blue Moon with a Heartache") was first-rate, and her choices from others, notably Leroy Preston's "My Baby Thinks He's a Train," were equally strong. *–William Ruhlmann*

Rhythm & Romance / 1985 / Columbia ✦✦✦
Cash expected criticism for this album, and got it but didn't deserve it. The orange hair and pink fingernails on the cover visually illustrate the musical risks she took in working with Eddie Rabbitt's former producer, David Malloy, and the result is a scorcher. Best cuts: Grammy-winner "I Don't Know Why You Don't Want Me" and "Halfway House." *–Tom Roland*

☆ **Interiors** / 1990 / Columbia ✦✦✦✦✦
What makes *Interiors* brilliant isn't that Cash produced herself for the first time nor that she wrote all the songs. It's that *Interiors*–the last album Cash made for Columbia's Nashville division–meticulously chronicles the unraveling of a terribly dysfunctional relationship, namely Cash's marriage to Rodney Crowell. Cash gets at the psychology behind country's cheating and drinking themes–the emotional anesthetic of addictions, the desperate grasping for love in affairs. The arrangements are stripped as bare as Cash's soul, but *Interiors* is country at its core. *–Brian Mansfield*

The Wheel / Jan. 19, 1993 / Columbia ✦✦✦✦
Like the dark, cathartic *Interiors, The Wheel* is an introspective, soul-searching set of confessional songs revolving around love and relationships. While many of the themes and emotions of *Interiors* are repeated on *The Wheel*, Roseanne Cash hasn't repeated herself, either lyrically or musically. Working from the same combination of folk and country that has fueled her songwriting throughout her career, she has created an album of subtle, melodic grace that helps convey the deep feelings of her lyrics. It's an immaculately produced album, but that never detracts from the emotional core of Cash's music. *–Stephon Thomas Erlewine*

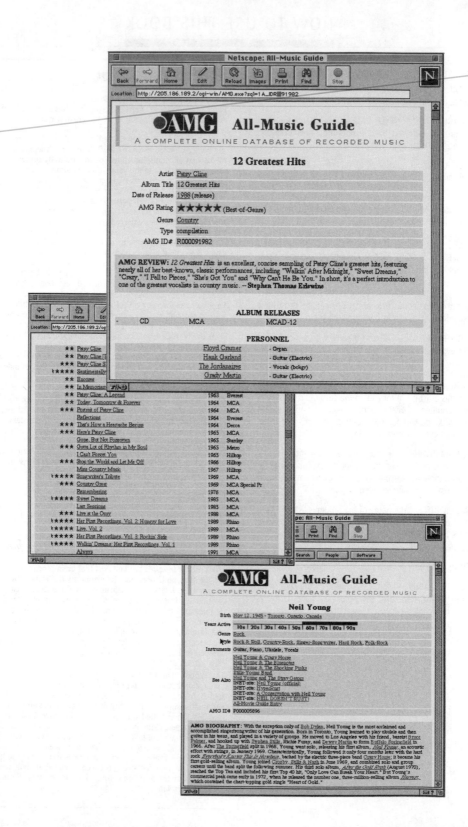

ALL MUSIC GUIDE WEBSITE

The *All Music Guide* reference books offer just a taste of the wealth of information to be discovered at our website (http://allmusic.com/), the largest and most comprehensive site of its kind on the Internet. Along with the same detailed biographical entries and album reviews found in the books, the AMG website offers much more, touching base with the one-hit wonders, session players, novelty artists, and studio technicians whom, for reasons of space, the book cannot.

Of course, the site doesn't replace the books, it complements them; while the books compile overviews of the superstars, the cult heroes and the true innovators into one handy volume, the AMG homepage fills in the gaps, taking full advantage of the seemingly boundless scope of the web to offer exhaustive coverage of thousands of other, more obscure artists and albums. In addition, it features even more detailed information on music's landmark performers and records, including recording information and hyperlinks to related artists; a click on your mouse allows quick access from, for example, our Neil Young biography to both the Buffalo Springfield or CSNY entries as well as less obvious—but no less important—links to the likes of Pearl Jam (with whom Young cut the 1995 LP *Mirror Ball*). At the same time, the site affords one luxury that the print format cannot; while published books cannot be updated until the next edition, the AMG website evolves and changes along with the music industry; if your favorite band releases a new album, or their drummer quits, you'll find it noted on-line long before you'll see it mentioned in book form. Information can be accessed through the All Music Guide site in one of three easy ways: to find what you're looking for, simply type the name of the particular artist, album or song in the appropriate space, click on the "search" button, and the available data will appear. You can also click on regular features like our music maps, essays and glossaries, or even help us grow by suggesting new artists and albums to cover.

ALL MUSIC GUIDE DATABASE

The All Music Guide is the most comprehensive database ever assembled and it is now available in many forms—books, kiosks, CD-ROMs, web sites, and commerical online services. The All Music Guide project continues to broaden its overall coverage and, at the same time, provide increasing detail for each artist. This book contains the most signficant subset of the database, the tip of the top (so to speak) of the very best country music of all time. We hope you will find it useful. The All Music Guide is also available in the following formats:

Books:
> *All Music Guide* (Miller Freeman Books, 3rd Edition, 1996)
> *All Music Guide to Jazz* (Miller Freeman Books, 2nd Edition, 1996)
> *All Music Guide to Rock* (Miller Freeman Books, 1995)
> *All Music Guide to the Blues* (Miller Freeman Books, 1996)
> *VideoHound & All-Movie Guide Stargazer* (Visible Ink, 1995)

Electronic Formats:
> All Music Guide CD-ROM (Corel, release date to be announced)
> All-Movie Guide CD-ROM (Corel)
> MusicRoms (music and data) for Blues, Jazz, R&B, Latin, etc. (Selectware/Compton's)
> All Music Guide (hard disk version) (Great Bear Technology)
> World Beat CD-ROM (Medio)

In Store Kiosks:
> Musicland's Soundsite
> Phonolog's the Source
> Sam Goody's

Internet AMG sites:
> ALLMUSIC.COM
> ALLMOVIE.COM
> THENEWAGE.COM

Other Internet Sites:
> CDNow! (CDNOW.COM)
> Entertainment Connection (ECONNECTION, BBS 914-426-2285)
> Music Boulevard (www.MusicBlvd.com)
> CDUniverse (www.CDUNIVERSE.COM)

Other Online Sites:
> Compact Disc Connection (BBS 408-730-9015)
> Billboard Online
> Dimple Records
> Reason Ware
> The Microsoft Network: New Age Forum: New Age Music

Since the All Music Guide is an ongoing project, we appreciate your feedback. Perhaps we have left out some of your favorite albums, and/or included ones that you don't consider essential. Let us know about it. We welcome criticism, suggestions, additions, and/or deletions. The All Music Guide is a work in progress. If you are knowledgeable on the recordings of a particular artist or group and would like to participate in future editions of the books and/or our larger electronic database, write or give us a call.

ALL MUSIC GUIDE
> 315 Marion Avenue
> Big Rapids, MI 49307

> 616-796-3437
> FAX 616-796-3060

> *A division of Alliance Entertainment Corp.*

FOREWORD

Although country music is one of the most popular music genres in the US, it boasts relatively few books and almost no comprehensive buyer guides. We hope the *All Music Guide to Country* will help to change all that and make this great music available to more people. This guide is more than a simple retrospective. We have taken the broadest possible definition of country music, covering "underground" artists and up-and-coming country trends as well as the classic stars. Almost 6,000 albums and more than 1,000 country artists are included along with dozens of essays, country MusicMaps, and other useful information.

I want to thank editor-in-chief Chris Woodstra and associate editor Stephen Thomas Erlewine for putting in the long hours necessary to research, organize, and edit a book of this size. Without their dedication and interest, a book of this quality would not have been possible. I would also like to thank Vladimir Bogdanov for the extensive database design and programming needed to complete this project.

Aside from this latest volume, the All Music Guide series includes our main *All Music Guide, All Music Guide to Jazz, All Music Guide to Rock,* and the *All Music Guide to the Blues.* Other books are in the works. The complete *All Music Guide* is available on CD-ROM from Corel Corporation. Also, the entire database is available on the Worldwide Web at: http://ALLMUSIC.com

The All Music Guide is an ongoing database project, the largest collection of substantive albums, ratings, and reviews ever assembled, and we welcome your feedback. Perhaps we have left out some of your favorite albums and/or included ones that you don't consider essential. Let us know about it. We welcome criticism, suggestions, and additions. Perhaps you are an expert on the complete output of a particular artist or group and would like to participate in future editions of this book and/or our larger computer database. We would be glad to hear from you.

Michael Erlewine
Executive Editor
All Music Guides

ABOUT THE EDITORS

Michael Erlewine

All Music Guide editor Michael Erlewine helped form the Prime Movers Blues Band in Ann Arbor, Michigan in 1965. He was the lead singer and played amplified harmonica in this pace-setting band (the first of its kind). The original band included a number of now well-known musicians including Iggy Pop (drums), "Blue" Gene Tyranny (piano; now a well-known avant-garde classical composer); Jack Dawson (bass; became bass player for Siegel-Schwall Blues Band); and Michael's brother Dan Erlewine (lead guitar; now monthly columnist for *Guitar Player* magazine). Michael has extensively interviewed blues performers, both in video and audio, and, along with his band, helped to shape the first few Ann Arbor Blues festivals. Today Michael is a systems programmer and director of Matrix Software. Aside from the company's work in music and film data, Matrix is the largest center for astrological programming and research in North America. Michael has been a practicing astrologer for more than 30 years and has an international reputation in that field.

Michael is also very active in Tibetan Buddhism and serves as the director of the Heart Center Karma Thegsum Choling, one of the main centers in North America for the translation, transcription, and publication of psychological texts and teachings of the Karma Kagyu Lineage of Tibetan Buddhism. Michael has been married for 25 years, and he and his wife Margaret live in Big Rapids, Michigan. They have four children.

Vladimir Bogdanov

Russian mathematician and programmer Vladimir Bogdanov has been involved in the design and development of *All Music Guide* databases since 1991. Having experience in many different fields such as nuclear physics, psychology, social studies and ancient chronology he now applies his knowledge to the construction of unique music reference tools utilizing the latest computer technologies. His personal interest lies in applying artificial intelligence and other mathematical methods to areas with complex semantic structures, like music, film, literature. Vladimir's ultimate goal is to provide people with the means to find what they need, even if they don't know what they are looking for.

Chris Woodstra

Chris Woodstra has had a lifelong obsession with music and is an avid record collector. He has worked many years in music retail, he was a DJ, hosting programs in every genre of music, and has been a contributing editor for several local arts and entertainment magazines. Working as an editor for the *All Music Guide* database has given him the opportunity to combine his technical skills, a B.S. in Physics and Mathematics, and his love of music for the first time in his life. Being a perfectionist by nature, Chris makes sure that that any information that goes into the database has been carefully researched and verified.

Stephen Thomas Erlewine

Stephen Thomas Erlewine studied English at the University of Michigan and was the arts editor of the school's newspaper, The Michigan Daily. In addition to editing the *All Music Guide*, Erlewine is a freelance writer and musician.

ACKNOWLEDGMENTS

This book would not have been possible without the guidance of Andrew Gun McIver and Ven. Khenpo Karthar, Rinpoche. Special thanks to Richie Unterberger, Cub Koda, Bruce Eder, Kurt Wolff, Jack Leaver, Jana Pendragon, Carl Bierling, and Holland Compact Disc.

To our production staff. . .
Jason Ankeny, Jonathan Ball, Sherry Batchelder, Nancy Beilfuss, Sandra Brennan, John Bush, Julie Clark, Grace Concepcion, Mark Donkers, Brandy Lynn Ellison, Elizabeth Carey Erlewine, Margaret Louise Erlewine, Sarah Morgen Erlewine, Clarke Fountain, Kevin Fowler, Yelena German, Yuriy German, Brenda Haney, Kristi Hassen, Mary Anne Henry, Jeanna Hopkins, Jennifer Hughes, Deborah Kirby, Katie Kuhns, Luda Lobenko, Jody Mitchell, Mary Prodger, Forest Ray, Bob Smith

and to all the Matrix staff. . .
Kyle Alexander, Irene Baldwin, Richard Batchelder, Susan Brownlee, Stephanie Clement, Walter Crockett, Tricia Davis, Phillip Erlewine, Stephen Erlewine, Iotis Erlewine, Thomas Goyett, Jeffrey Jawer, Mary E. King, Michael King, Madeline Koperski, Benjamin Slack, Teresa Swift-Eckert

All Music Guide to Country

Editors
Michael Erlewine
Vladimir Boganov
Chris Woodstra
Stephen Thomas Erlewine

Contributors
Jason Ankeny
George Bedard
Myles Boisen
Rob Bowman
Sandra Brennan
John Bush
Bil Carpenter
Kenneth M. Cassidy
James Chrispell
Rick Clark
Dan Cooper
Bill Dahl
Hank Davis
John Dougan
Bruce Eder
Michael Erlewine
Stephen Thomas Erlewine
John Floyd
Robert Gordon
Bob Gottlieb
Thom Granger
Jeff Hannusch
Brett Hartenbach
Dan Heilman
Bob Hinkle
Carl Hoyt
Steve Huey
Mark A. Humphrey
Alonso Jasso
Kit Kiefer
Cub Koda
Linda Kohanov
Larry Lapka
Jack Leaver
Richard Lieberson
Dennis MacDonald
Brian Mansfield
Michael McCall
Richard Meyer
David A. Milberg
Thom Owens
Roch Parisien
Dan Pavlides
Barry Lee Pearson
Jana Pendragon
Heather Phares
Larry Powell
Chip Renner
John Storm Roberts
Tom Roland
William Ruhlmann
Richard Skelly
Don Stevens
Jeff Tamarkin
Neal Umphred
Richie Unterberger
David Vinopal
Charles S. Wolfe
Kurt Wolff
Chris Woodstra
Jim Worbois
Ron Wynn
Scott Yanow

INTRODUCTION

Given its long history, a comprehensive overview of country music is somewhat difficult to achieve. After all, some of the genre's earliest artists weren't recorded frequently, if at all. Nevertheless, most of country's history has been well-documented, particularly since the 1920s, when the music was first recorded. Since that time, there have been a number of different styles from Western swing and bluegrass to Bakersfield country and countrypolitan that have developed, along with numerous country music stars. In other words, a wealth of great country music has been made over the course of the 20th century.

Unfortunately, that music hasn't always been well-presented. Despite its long, rich history, it wasn't until recently that country music has been treated with the same care and consideration as jazz, blues, and rock 'n' roll reissues. Furthermore, country has a history of poorly assembled studio albums, quickly recorded cash-in albums, budget-priced compilations, and rerecordings. Therefore, even the biggest artists in country music frequently have discographies that are convoluted and confusing, making the genre difficult to explore for listeners with only a little knowledge of the music and a limited budget.

With *The All Music Guide to Country,* we have created an overview of country music that will give both novices and experts an informative, single-volume encyclopedia of artist biographies, selected discographies, and capsule record reviews. We have also compiled a number of essays about various movements and subgenres in country's history, as well as music maps detailing the history and development of subgenres like Western swing.

The All Music Guide to Country is, first and foremost, a record-buyer's guide. It is designed to help record collectors sort out the myriad of albums on the market and in the used-record bin, as well as explain the place of individual artists in the history of country music. The artist biographies offer thorough and concise overviews of their careers, while the selected discographies highlight the artists' best albums and compilations. Often, a performer's discography is filled with budget-line hits compilations and rerecordings. That's because, at its core, country music is a single-driven medium where artists are identified by their signature songs, and they will rerecord that song every time they sign to a new label. Furthermore, the industry and its artists have never embraced the conceptual album like rock 'n' roll and jazz have. Sure, there have been several mavericks from Willie Nelson to Dwight Yoakam that have made conceptual, coherent albums, but the majority of country artists live and die by the hit single.

Consequently, studio albums have never been as important in country as they have been in rock. Therefore, original studio albums go in and out of print very quickly, yet hits collections stay in print. Often, these collections are supplanted several times each decade by new, slightly different compilations. And that means each major artist, as well as many minor ones, has a discography with literally hundreds of albums. By one estimation, there have been well over 300 George Jones albums alone.

As anyone who's tried to sort out the stacks of albums in used bins, or the piles of compact discs reissues will tell you, it's difficult to find out where all the good stuff is. *The All Music Guide to Country* is designed to help both the neophyte and the collector by showing which have all the original recordings, which budget-line collections are actually worthwhile, and what old records are worth searching for. Of course, space limitations prevent us from listing complete discographies and, for many artists, complete discographies would actually be a little confusing, since the appearance of many out-of-print albums and budget-line collections tend to obscure the worthwhile albums. Still, the selected discographies and reviews printed here are detailed and comprehensive, as are the accompanying biographies. Taken together, they present a thorough overview of an artist and their recorded work.

The question of "what is country music?" has plagued critics and fans for decades. Instead of subscribing to a narrow viewpoint, *The All Music Guide to Country* has adopted broadminded, far-reaching criteria geared toward inclusion. From string bands and old-timey country to new country and no depression country-rock, *The All Music Guide to Country* covers it all. Like any other book in *The All Music Guide* series, each artist's entry is arranged as a guide to the artist themselves. If you want to know all about Garth Brooks, Webb Pierce, Merle Haggard, or Jimmie Rodgers, and what albums of theirs to listen to, their entries are designed to help you out. Within each entry, to the right of the album's title, is a rating for the album itself, on a scale from one to five. These ratings are based according to the artist, not the overall worth of the album (for instance, a four-star Shania Twain album is not necessarily the same as a four-star Charlie Rich album). The only global rating in the book is a star, which signals an album that is the best of its genre—in other words, it's essential listening.

The All Music Guide to Country is helpful for country fans of all tastes. If you are an Alan Jackson fan who wants to explore classic honky tonk, this book will help you. If you are a Hank Williams fan intrigued by Gram Parsons or Wilco, this book will help. Some critics may argue whether certain artists in this book fit within the narrow definition of country, but the whole point of *The All Music Guide to Country* is to demonstrate the vast variety of country music and make it accessible to fans of all ages and tastes. Hopefully, it will help you discover some great music you may not have heard before.

—*Chris Woodstra and Stephen Thomas Erlewine*

STYLES

Alternative Country

Alternative country refers to country bands that play traditional country, but bend the rules slightly. They don't conform to Nashville's hit-making traditions, nor do they follow the accepted "outlaw" route to notoriety. Instead, Alternative Country bands work outside of the country industry's spotlight, frequently subverting musical traditions with singer/songwriter and rock 'n' roll lyrical and musical aesthetics.

Alternative Country-Rock

Alternative country-rock keeps the sound of Gram Parsons and Neil Young alive. Though the bands are all rock 'n' roll, their dedication to replicating the sound of Parsons and Young make them more traditionalist than either the alternative rock bands of the late '80s and '90s or the country bands of the same era. Though alternative country-rock bands occasionally have louder, grungier guitars than their idols, they are traditional in their songwriting style and dedication to keeping the actual sound of the early '70s alive through the use of vintage instruments. Occasionally some alternative country-rock bands stretch the boundaries of the form, but most are simply revivalists.

Americana

Much like its next-of-kin, alternative country-rock, the Americana genre developed during the 1990s as a roots-oriented reaction to the slick commercial sounds that dominated mainstream country during the decade. But while alternative country-rock developed as much out of punk and alternative rock as country, Americana sprang from less raw and edgy source material. In fact, much of what fell under the Americana umbrella was in fact a revival of dormant country styles, including Western swing and rockabilly. Though considered an alternative radio format, Americana did not break with country tradition. Instead, it embraced it—something, ironically enough, that the music hitting the Nashville charts throughout the era did not do.

Bakersfield Sound

Bakersfield was the first genre of country music to rely heavily on electric instrumentation, as well as a defined backbeat—in other words, it was the first to be significantly influenced by rock 'n' roll. Named after the town of Bakersfield, CA, where a great majority of the artists performed, the sound was pioneered by Wynn Stewart and popularized by Buck Owens and Merle Haggard. Using Telecaster guitars, the singers developed a clean, ringing sound that stood in direct opposition to the produced, string-laden Nashville sound. The Bakersfield sound became one of the most popular—and arguably the most influential—country genres of the '60s, setting the stage for country-rock and outlaw, as well as reviving the spirit of honky tonk.

Close Harmony

Close harmony is one of the most distinctive sounds in traditional country. The term refers to the keening two- (occasionally three-) part harmonies that acts like the Louvin Brothers and the Delmore Brothers popularized. The sound of close harmony grew out of the high, lonesome sound of bluegrass, yet most close harmony acts were closer to traditional country than bluegrass. During the late '40s and early '50s, close harmony acts became quite popular, thanks to a string of brother acts, who all sang in the style of close harmony. The Louvin Brothers, perhaps the definitive close harmony group, became popular at the tail end of the close harmony era. Their popularity was impeded by the emergence of rock 'n' roll, which cut the country audience dramatically. Ironically, close harmony acts in general and the Louvins in particular were an influence on the harmony style of the Everly Brothers, who happened to write the template for rock 'n' roll harmonies with their late '50s singles. The Everlys influence was as apparent in the Beatles' music as the Louvins' influence was in the Everlys' music, and that is just one testament to the depth of the influence of close harmony.

Contemporary Country

Contemporary country followed the urban cowboy movement and preceded the rise of Garth Brooks. It incorporated subtle pop production techniques, occasionally using synthesizers, but always sounding slick and polished. At times, the country roots of contemporary country were fairly well-hidden beneath pop trappings, but new traditionalists like George Strait and Randy Travis also fit into the genre.

Country Boogie

Country Boogie is a cross between the bluesy inflections of honky tonk and the polished style of the Nashville Sound. It has a rollicking beat and follows bluesy changes, but it is played with country instruments. In essence, the genre foreshadowed rockabilly with its uptempo beat and bluesy chords.

Country Gospel

Along with old-time, country gospel is the oldest genre in country music. Though it has changed somewhat with the times, country gospel remains the most simple and straightforward of all the country subgenres. The sound of country gospel is similar to traditional country—the only difference is that the subject matter is religious, not secular. Like traditional country, the sound of country gospel became smoother and more pop-oriented as the decades progressed, and by the early '70s, it became nearly indistinguishable from the lush sounds of mainstream pop. That trend continued throughout the rest of the '70s and '80s, and by the '90s, contemporary country gospel sounded identical to the adult contemporary inclinations of CCM. Nevertheless, that music was never widely recognized as country gospel, which will always be identified by its simple arrangements, small vocal choirs, and twangy instrumentation.

Country Humor

Like any kind of humor, country humor isn't suited to all tastes. For fans of more urbane music—including slickly produced country-pop—country humor is crude, simplistic, old-fashioned, and foolish. Nevertheless, the very squareness of the genre is what makes it appealing. Country humor grew directly out of vaudeville and burlesque, where comedians told silly jokes. Initially, country performers—including the Carter Family and Jimmie Rodgers—would perform comedy skits during their shows, and comedians like Minnie Pearl were major figures at the Grand Ole Opry. Often, country comedians were simply comedians, but there were several—like Grandpa Jones and Homer & Jethro—that were excellent musicians as well. From the late '40s to the mid-'60s, artists like Homer & Jethro were popular both as comedians and musicians, but by the beginning of the '70s, country comedy became the province of comedians. Of course, there were still novelty singles, but country humor was largely relegated to live performances, not records. In the mid-'90s, Jeff Foxworthy renewed country comedy as a viable commercial proposition with his series of "You Might Be a Redneck If..." records. In his wake, a number of other new country comedians, most notably Cledus T. Judd, also scaled the charts.

Country-Folk

Country-folk is a hybrid of country music and folk. Generally, the music is based on acoustic guitars and is gentler than most country music. Also, country-folk is dominated by singer/songwriters who write and record their own material in the manner of most folk singer/songwriters.

Country-Pop

Country-pop uses country instrumentation and song structures but has a greater inclination toward pop melody with a lusher, more orchestrated production.

Country-Rock

Essentially, country-rock is rock bands playing country music. Country-rock is country music informed by rock's counter-culture ideals, as well as rock's reliance on loud amplification, a prominent backbeat, and pop melodies. The first country-rock bands—the Flying Burrito Brothers, Gram Parsons, the Byrds, Neil Young—played straight country, inspired by the Bakersfield sound of Merle Haggard and Buck Owens, as well as honky tonkers like Hank Williams. As the genre moved into the '70s, the rougher edges were smoothed out as the Eagles, Poco, Pure Prairie League, and Linda Ronstadt made music that was smoother and more laidback. This became the predominant sound of country-rock in the '70s. In the late '80s, a small group of alternative rock bands began to revive the spartan sound of Gram Parsons and Neil Young.

Cowboy

Cowboy songs include both traditional Western songs and songs from Western movies. Most of the songs are performed on acoustic guitars (though movie songs have much more elaborate instrumentation, frequently featuring orchestras) and feature Western themes.

Hillbilly

"Hillbilly" was one of the first names applied to what would eventually become known as country music. Hillbilly was derived from the music of the hills of West Virginia, Virginia, southeastern Ohio, Kentucky, Tennessee, and other geographical locales associated with the South and hill country—i.e., the Southern Appalachians. As recorded music became a commercial enterprise in the 1920s, country music was sold as "hillbilly" music, with recordings by "Fiddlin John Carson," "Henry Whitter," and "Vernon Dahlert." By the 1940s innovations and commercial orientations had changed. Accordingly, the term "hillbilly" was dismissed as too rural and was supplanted by "bluegrass," "country," and "folk."

Honky Tonk

Honky tonk is the most recognizable genre of country music. It's spare and direct, featuring acoustic guitars, steel guitars, fiddles, and a high, lonesome vocal. Ernest Tubb was the first honky tonk musician to popularize the genre, but Hank Williams, George Jones, and Lefty Frizzell became the definitive artists in the '50s.

Instrumental Country

Instrumental country is exactly what it says it is—any form of country, from traditional honky tonk to country-rock, played strictly instrumentally and without any vocals.

Nashville Sound/CountrypolitanCountrypolitan—an outgrowth of the Nashville Sound of the '50s—is among the most commercially oriented genres of country music. The Nashville Sound emerged in the '50s as a way to bring country music to a broad pop audience. The movement was led by Chet Atkins, who was the head of RCA Records' country division. Atkins designed a smooth, commercial sound that relied on country song structures but abandoned all of the hillbilly and honky tonk instrumentation. He hired session musicians and coordinated pop-oriented, jazz-tinged productions. Similarly, Owen Bradley created music—most notably with Patsy Cline—using sophisticated production methods and smooth, textured instrumentation. Eventually, most records from Nashville featured this style of production and the Nashville Sound began to include strings and vocal choirs. In the late '60s, the Nashville Sound metamorphosed into countrypolitan, which emphasized these kinds of pop production flourishes. Featuring layers of keyboards, guitars, strings, and vocals, countrypolitan records were designed to cross over to pop radio, and they frequently did. The sound dominated the country charts in the '70s and stayed popular until the early '80s.

Neo-Traditionalist Country

Neo-traditionalist country refers to country artists who play hardcore, traditional country such as honky tonk, yet they are essentially revivalists. Since they are revivalists, they bring a variety of contemporary techniques—such as rock/pop or singer/songwriter influences—to their music, yet these are always subservient to the dominant strain of country music. Furthermore, where new traditionalists brought the sound of traditional country back to the mainstream, neo-traditionalists always operated on the fringes.

New Traditionalist

New traditionalist refers to the legions of young country singers that emerged in the late '80s. These artists reworked and updated the classic sounds of honky tonk and traditional country, adding contemporary production touches to make the music more commercially viable—yet even with the flourishes, the music was essentially hardcore country. After the first wave of new traditionalists (George Strait, Randy Travis, Dwight Yoakam), the genre became a bit slicker and demonstrated more overt rock influences, but the new traditionalists continued to dominate the country charts in one form or another until the mid-'90s.

Old-Time

Old-time (or old-timey) refers to the oldest form of country music ever recorded. First recorded in the early '20s, its style and sound remained consistent through the 1800s. Though it encompassed a number of different influences, the music's roots lay in British folk songs that were played on stringed instruments, such as the fiddle. By the late 1800s, rural Americans had begun playing the folk songs on Spanish guitars and African banjos as well, adding other instruments—dobro, bass, washboards—to the mix. During the early 1900s, this country folk music incorporated some contemporary influences, particularly the blues and vaudeville comedy. This rurally eclectic amalgamation was the sound of country music during the '20s, and it would forever be identified as "old-time" country, because it was the music that evoked country's roots. Although the music began to evolve in the '30s, as Jimmie Rodgers brought country into the industrial age, there were groups that performed old-time into the end of the century, frequently without changing the conventions of the genre at all. One major style within old-time was bluegrass, which developed in the late '40s as a reaction to the increasing modernization of country music.

Outlaw Country

Outlaw country was one of the more significant trends in country music in the '70s. During that decade, many of the most popular hardcore country singers of the '60s—from George Jones to Merle Haggard—softened their sound slightly, moving away from their honky tonk roots. While the outlaws weren't strictly honky tonk—they were as much storytellers in the tradition of folk songwriters as they were honky tonk vocalists—they kept that spirit alive. Outlaws didn't play by Nashville's rules. They didn't change their music to fit the heavily produced, pop-oriented Nashville sound, nor did they go out of their way to fit into the accepted conventions of country music. Instead, they created an edgy form of hardcore country that was influenced by rock 'n' roll, folk, and blues. Ironically, two of the leading figures of the movement—Waylon Jennings and Willie Nelson—had their roots in the music industry, but by the time they came into their own as recording artists in the mid-'70s, they had developed a unique, defiant way of performing. Several other musicians—including David Allan Coe, Billy Joe Shaver, and Tompall Glaser—followed in their footsteps, and the outlaws were quite popular for a period of three to four years. At the end of the '70s, the urban cowboy movement easily eclipsed the outlaw movement in terms of commercial appeal, but the outlaws had a lasting influence. During the '80s, certain neo-traditionalists owed a bit of their sound to the outlaws, while a whole breed of songwriters, led by Steve Earle, demonstrated a massive debt to the outlaws and their fusion of country, folk, and rock.

Progressive Bluegrass

Bluegrass is one of the most rigid music genres, one that steadfastly refuses to change its direction. Therefore, progressive bluegrass is viewed with skepticism at best, derision at worst, by some hardcore bluegrass fans. Progressive bluegrass expands the sonic palette of bluegrass either by adding elements of jazz, folk, country, and rock, or by amplifying the instruments. The subgenre developed in the late '60s, but it flourished in the '70s, when bands like the Dillards, Boone Creek, Country Gazette, and New Grass Revival began coming to the forefront of bluegrass and folk festivals. Throughout the '80s and '90s, progressive bluegrass continued to evolve, moving closer to folk and rock in some quarters and closer to jazz in others.

Progressive Country

Progressive country developed in the late '60s as a reaction to the increasingly polished and pop-oriented sound of mainstream, Nashville-based country. Inspired equally by the spare, twangy, hard-driving sound of Bakersfield country, the singer-songwriter introspection of Bob Dylan, classic honky tonk, and rock 'n' roll, progressive country was the first anti-Nashville movement to emerge since the dawn of rock 'n' roll. Progressive country was rootsier and more intellectual than many of its contemporary genres; it was more concerned with breaking boundaries than with scoring hits. The genre was also songwriter-based. Many of its key artists—Kris Kristofferson, Willie Nelson, Billy Joe Shaver, Tom T. Hall, Jimmie Dale Gilmore, Butch Hancock—were not "good" singers by conventional standards, yet they wrote distinctive, individual songs and had compelling voices. By the early '70s, such artists had developed a sizable cult following, and their songs began to inch their way into the mainstream, usually in the form of cover versions (Sammi Smith took Kristofferson's "Help Me Make It Through the Night" to the Country Top Ten). Progressive country also provided the basis for outlaw country, a harder-edged genre that shook country pop (briefly) off the top of the charts in the mid-'70s. Even after outlaw's five-year reign in the late '70s, progressive country continued to exist, until it eventually metamorphosed into alternative country in the '80s.

Rockabilly

Rockabilly was one of the earliest forms of rock 'n' roll and it has proved to be one of the most enduring. Where rock 'n' rollers like Chuck Berry, Little Richard, Jerry Lee Lewis, and Fats Domino emphasized the blues, R&B, and pop roots of rock 'n' roll, rocka-

billy was backwoods hillbilly music played to a boogie beat. The form emerged in the mid-'50s and it stayed the same for the next four decades, with new performers occasionally adding contemporary flairs but essentially sticking to the basic rockabilly formula.

Rockabilly Revival

Rockabilly revival refers to the legions of bands dedicated to replicating the style and sound of classic '50s rock 'n' roll. Though there have always been bands that have played rockabilly, the rockabilly revival didn't hit its stride until the post-punk era, when a number of new bands picked up the sounds of rockabilly; not only did they play the music, but they celebrated the kitschy pop culture that surrounded rockabilly. The first rockabilly revival culminated with the success of the Stray Cats in the early '80s. Following the Stray Cats' crossover success, a number of rockabilly bands appeared in the American underground during the late '80s. There were also a number of rockabilly bands that were associated with the roots-rock and blues-rock scenes, though not the alternative scene. The rockabilly revival continued to thrive into the '90s, when the most notable rockabilly band to emerge was the grunge-injected Reverend Horton Heat.

Roots-Rock

During the mid-'80s, a generation of bands reacted to the slick, pop-oriented sounds of new wave by reverting back to the traditional rock 'n' roll values of the '50s and '60s. By bringing rock back to its roots—whether that was rock 'n' roll, blues, or country—the groups managed to sound like a fresh alternative, which brought them critical praise and heavy airplay from American college radio stations. Most of the leading bands of the era—such as the Beat Farmers, Del Lords, Long Ryders, and Del Fuegos—filtered much of their traditional sound through the music of Creedence Clearwater Revival, but there were an equally large number of groups that simply worked in a "rootsy" fashion, without any direct influence outside of traditional rock and blues. In the late '80s, roots-rock ceased to be in the vanguard of the American underground, but most of the bands continued to record and perform into the '90s. Throughout the '90s, a small number of new roots-rockers emerged, although they weren't afforded the same exposure as their predecessors.

Singer-Songwriter

Although many vocalists sang their own songs, including early rock 'n' rollers like Chuck Berry and Buddy Holly, the term "singer/songwriter" refers to the legions of performers that followed Bob Dylan. Most of the original singer/songwriters performed alone with an acoustic guitar or a piano. Their lyrics were personal, although they were often veiled with layers of metaphors and obscure imagery. Singer/songwriters drew primarily from folk and country, although certain writers like Randy Newman and Carole King incorporated the songcraft of Tin Pan Alley pop. The main concern for any singer/songwriter was the song itself, not necessarily the performance. However, most singer/songwriter records have a similar sound, which is usually spare, direct, and reflective, placing the emphasis on the song itself. James Taylor, Jackson Browne, and Joni Mitchell were the quintessential singer/songwriters of the '70s and most of the songwriters that followed them imitated their styles, or Dylan. Singer/songwriters were at the height of their popularity in the early '70s, and although they faded away from the pop charts, they never disappeared. In the late '70s, Ricki Lee Jones and Joan Armatrading crossed over into the pop charts, as did Suzanne Vega and Tracy Chapman in the late '80s. Throughout the '80s and '90s, a number of songwriters—like John Gorka and Bill Morrissey—kept the tradition alive through a series of independently released albums.

String Band

With its intricate instrumental interplay and driving rhythms, string band was the most distinctive subgenre of old-time country. Though all old-time artists supported themselves with stringed instruments, string bands were notable because they emphasized the instrumentation, not the vocals. The popularity of string bands faded in the '30s after Jimmie Rodgers and the Carter Family became country's first stars, yet the groups provided the foundation for the harder sounds of bluegrass in the late '40s.

Traditional Bluegrass

Bluegrass music grew out of the traditional string band music that formed the roots of country music. In the '40s, country music began to split into different segments, as honky tonk and country-pop became genres of their own. Yet one group of country musicians continued playing traditional string music. Led by Bill Monroe, these musicians adhered to the songs, structures, and conventions of string bands, but they made the music faster, harder, and more technically demanding. The result was bluegrass; the genre was named after Bill Monroe's backing band, the Blue Grass Boys. After its inception in the mid-'40s, bluegrass didn't change for nearly 20 years. In the late '60s, a number of bluegrass groups began expanding the sound of the genre, much to the chagrin of many of the music's most popular artists and dedicated fans. Consequently, the new breed of bluegrass was dubbed progressive bluegrass while the music that adhered to its roots was tagged traditional bluegrass. Over the next three decades, progressive bluegrass changed frequently, while the sound of traditional bluegrass never varied.

Traditional Country

Traditional country is a nebulous term—it can refer to anything from Roy Acuff's simple songs to the electrified honky tonk of Johnny Paycheck—but it does evoke a specific sound, namely the longstanding tradition of simple country songs delivered with simple instrumentation and a distinct twang. The era of traditional country didn't begin until the early '30s, when Jimmie Rodgers became the first national country music star. Rodgers brought the formerly rural music into the industrial era by streamlining the music and lyrics; in the process, he made the genre a viable commercial property. Following Rodgers' success, old-time music faded in popularity and traditional country was born. For the next 40 years, most country music fell under the traditional country umbrella, regardless of whether it was the big-band dance music of Western swing or the driving roadhouse of honky tonk. The majority of the popular artists from the '30s and '40s—Roy Acuff, Eddy Arnold, Ernest Tubb, and Hank Williams—became the foundation of the Grand Ole Opry, a weekly radio broadcast that became the definitive word in country music. This generation of musicians inspired all the artists that emerged in the following two decades, who put their own spin on traditional country. Following the emergence of rock 'n' roll, country music began to incorporate more pop production techniques, and although this Nashville Sound was smoother than the music of the '40s and early '50s, it still conformed to the conventions of traditional country. During the '60s, mainstream country became progressively more pop-influenced, yet traditional country held strong until the early '70s, when country-pop became the dominant form of country music. Many fans of hard country turned toward the tougher sounds of progressive country and outlaw country, yet most of the country audience continued to listen to

country-pop, especially since traditional country singers like George Jones, Conway Twitty, and Loretta Lynn became part of that subgenre. By the late '70s, most new country singers were either raised on country-pop or pop-rock, and consequently, the reign of traditional country came to an end. During the mid-'80s, a wave of new traditionalist singers such as George Strait emerged, but their music tended to be influenced by their contemporaries as well, making the movement as much an evolution as a revival.

Urban Cowboy

Urban Cowboy was a 1979 film that romanticized the world of upscale, urban country fans and their lives and music. The music that comprised the soundtrack was modified outlaw and country-pop—it was slick, highly polished music that celebrated the outlaw mythology and honky tonk song structure, but with a glossy pop production. Consequently, the music appealed to a wider audience, even winning a number of pop music fans in the process. Following the success of *Urban Cowboy* and its soundtrack (which featured vocalists like Mickey Gilley and Johnny Lee), the country charts were dominated by acts that copied the style and sound of urban cowboy. Throughout the early '80s and well into the mid-'80s, urban cowboy was the sound of country music, and it wasn't until the late '80s, when the neo-traditionalists came along, that it disappeared from the charts.

Western Swing

Western swing was the most eclectic form of country music, and in its free-wheeling diversity, it set the stage for rock 'n' roll. Based in traditional string band music, Western swing also incorporated traditional pop melodies, jazz improvisation, blues, and folk, creating a wildly entertaining and eclectic form of American music. Bob Wills and Milton Brown popularized the genre in the '30s, and Wills became known as the father of the genre, since he had a remarkable string of hit singles. Although it sometimes faded from view, Western swing remained popular throughout the 20th century, occasionally experiencing upswings in popularity, such as in the early '70s and the early '90s.

Western Swing Revival

Musically, Western swing revival differs little from Western swing itself—it is still the same joyous, eclectic mix of big-band jazz, country songs, and pop melodies that was one of the most popular musical styles of the '40s. Western swing revival simply marks the moment when the genre reasserted itself as part of country's mainstream. Following World War II, Western swing slowly began to lose its fan base as honky tonk and country-pop won over the country audience. In the early '70s, the style reappeared thanks to the dedication of Merle Haggard and Asleep at the Wheel, two artists who incorporated Western swing into their sound and brought the music back to the top of the country charts. Throughout the '70s, '80s, and '90s, Western swing revival retained a popular cult following, occasionally slipping a hit single or two onto the charts.

A

Nathan Abshire

b. Jun. 23, 1913, Gueydcn, LA, **d.** May 13, 1981
Accordion, Vocals / Electric Louisiana Blues, Cajun, Electric Swamp Blues

Nathan Abshire helped bring the blues and honky tonk to Cajun music and re-popularized the accordion with his recordings during the 1950s and '60s, but still ncver managed a living from his music. Born in Gueyden, LA, on June 27, 1913, Abshire began playing professionally in the 1920s, and he first recorded in the early '30s with Happy Fats & the Rainbow Ramblers. Abshire went to work at the Basile, LA, town dump around that time, and he held the job for most of his working life.

His fortunes began looking bright by 1936, however, when the Rainbow Ramblers began backing him on sides for Bluebird. After serving in World War II, Abshire cut "Pine Grove Blues"—his most famous single and later his signature song—for D.T. Records. He recorded for Khoury/Lyric, Swallow and Kajun during the 1950s and '60s, meanwhile playing local dances and appearing on sessions by the Balfa Brothers. A renewal of interest in Cajun and folk music during the '70s gave Abshire a chance to play several festivals and colleges, and star in the 1975 PBS-TV Cajun documentary, *Good Times Are Killing Me*. The title proved prophetic, however, as Abshire fought alcoholism during his last years. Several sessions for Folkways and La Louisienne followed in the late '70s, but he died on May 13, 1981. —*John Bush*

Cajun Social Music / 1990 / Smithsonian/Folkways ✦✦✦✦
A summit meeting of Cajun stars yields outstanding renditions of classics and originals. —*Ron Wynn*

● **The Cajun Legend: Best of Nathan Abshire** / 1991 / Swallow ✦✦✦✦
With "The Good Times Are Killing Me" emblazoned on his accordion case, Abshire embodied the Cajun musician's ethos. There are 20 two-steps and waltzes here, some with the Balfa Brothers—includes a remake of the great "Pine Grove Blues" and a heartfelt "Tramp Sur La Rue" with wailing vocals from Nathan. —*Mark A. Humphrey*

Roy Acuff

b. Sep. 15, 1903, Maynardsville, TN, **d.** Nov. 23, 1992
Harmonica, Violin, Vocals / Traditional Country

Roy Acuff was called the King of Country Music, and for more than 60 years, he lived up to that title. If any performer embodied country music, it was Roy Acuff. Throughout his career, Acuff was a champion for traditional country values, enforcing his beliefs as a performer, a music publisher, and as the Grand Master of the Grand Ole Opry. Acuff was the first country music superstar after the death of Jimmie Rodgers, pioneering an influential vocal style that complemented the spare, simple songs he was performing. Generations of artists, from Hank Williams to George Jones, have been influenced by Acuff, and countless others have paid respect to him. At the time of his death in 1992, he was still actively involved in the Grand Ole Opry, and was as popular as ever.

Originally, Acuff didn't plan to be a singer. Born in the small town of Maynardville, TN, in 1903, Acuff sang in the church choir as a schoolboy, but he was more interested in sports, particularly baseball. Not only was he attracted to the sport, he had a wild streak—after his family moved to Knoxville, he was frequently arrested for fighting. Acuff continued to concentrate on playing ball, eventually becoming strong enough to earn a tryout for the Major Leagues. However, that tryout never took place. Before he had a chance to play, he was struck by severe sunstroke while he was on a fishing trip; after the sunstroke, Acuff suffered a nervous breakdown. While he was recovering, he decided that a career in baseball was no longer possible, so he decided to become an entertainer. He began to learn the fiddle and became an apprentice of Doc Hauer, a local medicine show man.

While traveling with the medicine show, Acuff learned how to be a performer—he learned how to sing, how to imitate, how to entertain, how to put on a show. Soon, Acuff joined the Tennessee Crackerjacks, who had a regular slot on the Knoxville radio station, WROL. Although he was performing frequently, he wasn't making any significant headway, failing to become a star in Tennessee. One song changed that situation—"The Great Speckled Bird," an old gospel tune that had become popular with the Church of God sect. After another radio entertainer wrote the words out to the song, Acuff began performing it in his shows. Quickly, he became popular throughout the eastern part of Tennessee and was asked to record the song by ARC, a record label with national distribution. Acuff headed north to Chicago for a recording session, which resulted in 20 different songs. In addition to "The Great Speckled Bird," he recorded "Steamboat Whistle Blues" and "The Wabash Cannonball," another Tennessee standard, which featured the singer imitating the sound of a train whistle; he also made a handful of risqué numbers during these sessions, which were released under the name the Bang Boys.

In 1938, the Grand Ole Opry invited Roy Acuff to audition for the show. During the show, he sang "The Great Speckled Bird," and became an instant hit, prompting the Opry to hire him full-time. Before he was given his regular slot, the Opry insisted that he change the name of his band to the Smokey Mountain Boys. The following year, Acuff reassembled his band, with the most notable addition being Bashful Brother Oswald (Pete Kirby), a Dobro player that sang high harmonies.

Roy Acuff became a national superstar during the '40s, scoring a long string of hit records, which included the classics "The Wreck on the Highway," "The Precious Jewel," and "Beneath That Lonely Mound of Clay," among many others. During this time, he discovered that there was a potential goldmine in music publishing. Acuff had printed his own songbook, which sold a staggering 100,000 copies. Publishers in New York tried to acquire the rights to his songs, but the success of the songbook convinced Acuff to hold on to the songs and seek out the help of Fred Rose, a professional songwriter and pianist working in Chicago. The pair founded Acuff-Rose Publications in October, 1942, using Acuff's songs as its base; Rose also added his songs, including "Faded Love," "Deep Water," and "Blue Eyes Crying in the Rain." Acuff-Rose was an immediate success and over the next two decades, many of the most popular songs and songwriters were the property of the company, including the songs of Hank Williams, the Louvin Brothers, Don Gibson, Roy Orbison, the Everly Brothers,

Roy Acuff

John D. Loudermilk, Boudleaux and Felice Bryant, and Redd Stewart and Pee Wee King's "Tennessee Waltz."

In the late '40s, Acuff continued to rule the country charts, as well as scoring a number of pop crossovers ("The Prodigal Son," "I'll Forgive You, But I Can't Forget"). For most of the '50s, he concentrated on touring—he didn't have a single charting record between 1947 and 1958—returning with the Top Ten hit "Once More," as well as two other Top 20 singles, "So Many Times" and "Come and Knock." The '60s yielded some hits, yet he continued to concentrate on touring; by the end of the decade, he decided to leave the road, staying at the Grand Ole Opry.

The beginning of the '80s was a difficult period for Acuff, as he experienced the death of his wife and several longtime band members, including pianist Jimmie Riddle and fiddler Howdy Forrester. In 1987, he released his final charting record, an inspirational duet with Charlie Louvin called "The Precious Jewel."

As his health began to decline in the late '80s, Acuff built a house near the Opry so he could greet friends and fans. In 1992, he became the first living performer to be inducted to the Country Music Hall of Fame. Several months later, he passed away, leaving behind a legacy that isn't limited to his music. Through his records, his performances and Acuff-Rose, Roy Acuff has had an enormous effect on shaping the role of country music in the 20th century; it is hard to imagine the music without him. —*Stephen Thomas Erlewine*

Fly Birdie Fly '39-41 / 1939 / Rounder ✦✦✦✦
The songs on *Fly Birdie Fly* were recorded in 1939-1941, as he was flying high as a new star of the Opry. Although these tracks are not his best-known, these blues and gospel songs are rowdier than his reputation and as good as his classics. —*Michael McCall*

Songs of the Smokey Mountains / 1955 / Capitol ✦✦✦
A nice assortment of re-recorded Acuff hits, including "The Great Speckled Bird," "Wabash Cannonball," "Wreck on the Highway," and "Precious Jewel." —*Barry Lee Pearson*

Greatest Hits [Columbia] / 1970 / Columbia ✦✦✦✦
Contains the original versions of Acuff's classic, groundbreaking work—"The Great Speckled Bird," "Wabash Cannonball," "Night Train to Memphis," "Were You There When They Crucified My Lord," and "Fire Ball Mail." —*Stephen Thomas Erlewine*

☆ **Columbia Historic Edition** / 1985 / Columbia ✦✦✦✦✦
This includes many of his early landmark recordings, including his first recording of "Wabash Cannonball," on which he blows the train whistle and bows the fiddle, but the vocals are by Dynamite Hatcher, a bandmember. Other cuts do feature a few of Acuff's earliest songs. It's a good representation of his initial string-band sound. —*Michael McCall*

☆ **Steamboat Whistle Blues** / 1985 / Rounder ✦✦✦✦✦
Steamboat Whistle Blues is a collection of fine early Roy Acuff band versions of blues, pop, and old-time country, recorded between 1936-1939. —*Barry Lee Pearson*

Best of Roy Acuff [Curb] / 1991 / Curb ✦✦✦
Curb's *The Best of Roy Acuff* is a selection of '60s hits and a number of re-recordings Acuff made in the '60s while signed to Hickory Records, a label he began with his publishing partner Fred Rose. By this point, Acuff's recording career was no longer successful; he concentrated on the Grand Ole Opry. Nevertheless, these re-recordings are entertaining, although they are considerably slicker and less affecting than his early, groundbreaking tracks. As a sampler of Acuff's '60s sound, *The Best of* is effective. Bear in mind, the disc only has ten tracks, so while it may be bargain-priced, it's not necessarily a bargain. —*Stephen Thomas Erlewine*

★ **The Essential Roy Acuff (1936-1949)** / 1992 / Columbia/Legacy ✦✦✦✦✦
The Essential Roy Acuff (1936-1949) contains the original versions of "The Great Speckled Bird," "Night Train to Memphis," "The Precious Jewel," and "Wabash Cannon Ball," and 16 other tracks that were cut for Columbia Records at the peak of his recording career. —*Stephen Thomas Erlewine*

Eddie Adcock

b. Jun. 21, 1938, Scottsville, VA
Banjo / Progressive Bluegrass
Among the major-league talent that emerged from the folk music boom of the late '50s were the Country Gentlemen, a DC-based quartet that introduced bluegrass to a generation of city folks and college students, people who had never heard of Flatt & Scruggs or Bill Monroe or the Stanley Brothers. The Gentlemen, in playing the old bluegrass standards but playing them "different," were in a sense the first newgrass group. Eddie Adcock was the band's banjo player and he was a player of distinction—his style was as innovative as Don Reno's. Adcock's considerable talent spread to other stringed instruments when he left the Gentlemen in 1970 and began exploring new musical genres. For the next three decades, Eddie Adcock remained one of the most popular musicians in bluegrass.

Adcock was born and raised in Scottsville, VA. He bought his first banjo as child and began performing with his brother Frank shortly afterward. The duo would sing in local churches and radio stations based in nearby Charlottesville. In his teens, he played in a band called the James River Playboys and worked at a theater in his hometown, where he had the opportunity to see major country artists of the day, including Wilma Lee & Stoney Cooper. At the age of 14, he left home after a family crisis and supported himself through semi-professional boxing. For the next seven years, he boxed and played music at nights. A few years later, he began racing cars. As a racer, Adcock racked up 34 straight wins with his car, which he named Mr. Banjo; he also set two track records at Manassas, VA. Not only did he box and race, he also performed various blue-collar jobs to pay the rent, and still continued to play music at night.

Eddie Adcock didn't begin his professional musical career until 1953, when he joined Smokey Graves and his Blue Star Boys, who had a regular show at a radio station in Crewe, VA. His exposure with Graves led to jobs with other musicians, including Mac Wiseman, Bill Harrell, and Buzz Busby. Between 1953 and 1957, he floated between different bands. Bill Monroe offered Adcock a job in 1957, and he played with the Blue Grass Boys for a short time—Monroe had to let him go because the band simply wasn't earning enough money to employ him. Adcock returned to working day jobs, but that was short-lived. After he started working in a sheet metal factory, Jim Cox, John Duffery, and Charlie Waller asked him to join their new band, the Country Gentlemen.

The Country Gentlemen became one of the most popular and respected bluegrass bands of the late '50s and '60s, as well as one of the most progressive. They expanded the repertoire of bluegrass bands to include contemporary country, folk, and rock songwriters, most notably Bob Dylan; usually they added this material at the urging of Adcock. The Country Gentlemen rode to popularity in the late '50s as part of the folk boom and continued to be one of the most popular bluegrass/folk bands in the country throughout the '60s.

At the end of the '60s, Adcock began to feel constrained by the Country Gentlemen. He wanted to experiment with different musical genres, which he felt the band wasn't willing to do. Consequently, he quit the Gentlemen and moved to California, where he formed a country-rock band called the Clinton Special. While he performed with the group, he used the pseudonym Clinton Codack. The band recorded only one single, "Just As You Are I Love You" / "Blackberry Fence," which was released on MGM Records; the A-side of the single was featured in the 1971 film, *The Horsemen.*

After the Clinton Special fell apart, Adcock headed back east, where he formed another group, II Generation, with Bob White, A.L. Wood, Wendy Thatcher, and Jimmy Gaudreau, who used to play with the Country Gentlemen. II Generation's lineup changed frequently during the '70s but it gelled around 1974 when Martha Hearon joined the group. Hearon played guitar for the band and wrote a good share of its material; she also married Adcock soon after she joined. II Generation was active throughout the '70s, releasing a handful of albums on the Rome, Rebel, and CMH labels.

Adcock and Hearon disbanded the group in 1980 and moved to Tennessee, where they formed a trio called Talk of the Town with bassist Missy Raines. In the mid-'80s, Adcock launched a solo career, releasing a series of cassette-only collections on CMH. In the '90s, he began releasing albums on compact disc, as well as performing with an all-star bluegrass outfit called the Masters. After nearly 40 years in the music business, Eddie Adcock remained as popular as he ever was, touring all around the world. —*Stephen Thomas Erlewine & David Vinopal*

● **Talk of the Town** / 1987 / CMH ◆◆◆◆
Backed by four women, Eddie is at his best here. The album features nice vocals. —*Chip Renner*

And His Guitar / 1988 / CMH ◆◆◆
Just Eddie and his guitar, no backup, and a very clean sound. Chet Atkins- and Merle Travis-influenced. —*Chip Renner*

The Acoustic Connection / 1988 / CMH ◆◆◆

Dixie Fried / 1991 / CMH ◆◆◆◆

Renaissance Man / 1996 / Pinecastle ◆◆◆

Trace Adkins

b. Jan. 13, 1962, Sarepta, LA
Guitar, Vocals / Contemporary Country
With one foot in the honky tonks and the other planted squarely in a gospel-quartet background, Trace Adkins and his warm baritone gained fans of Nashville's new-traditional movement in the mid-'90s. Born on January 13, 1962, in the small Louisiana town of Sarepta, Adkins grew up playing the guitar and listened to classic country, soul and rock 'n' roll. After high school, Adkins enrolled at Louisiana Tech; he studied music and played football while there, but found himself on an offshore oil rig for several years after graduation. Adkins decided to get back into music and joined a gospel quartet named the New Commitments. He toured the region and recorded two albums with the group, but became a solo performer in the early '90s. Adkins began playing honky tonks throughout Tennessee and Texas, and later moved to Nashville to make it in country music. At one gig, Capitol Nashville president Scott Hendricks approached him after a set and signed him to the label on the spot. Hendricks, the producer of Brooks & Dunn, Alan Jackson and Faith Hill, oversaw Trace Adkins' debut album *Dreamin' Out Loud.* Released in 1996, the album hit the

Alabama

Country Top 20, thanks to the No. 3 single, "Every Light in the House Is On." —*John Bush*

● **Dreamin' Out Loud** / 1996 / Capital ◆◆◆◆

Rhett Akins

Guitar, Vocals / Contemporary Country
With his Top Five single "That Ain't My Truck," Rhett Akins became a sensation, however briefly, in the summer of 1995. Like many new country singers, he wasn't able to follow the record up with an equally successful second record, but he managed to cultivate a following of dedicated fans.

Akins grew up in Valdosta, GA, learning to play guitar and forming his first band with his two younger brothers by the time he was 11. In 1992, he moved to Nashville, where he began singing on demos, as well as securing a publishing deal of his own. Eventually, Decca Records secured a demo of one of Akins' songs and the label offered him a contract.

A Thousand Memories, Akins' debut album, was released in 1994. After his first two singles—"What They're Talkin' About" and "I Brake for Brunettes"—cracked the Top 40, "That Ain't My Truck" became his breakthrough hit, rocketing to No. 3 in the summer of 1995. "That Ain't My Truck" became his signature song and helped the album become a hit. For most of 1995, he toured as Reba McEntire's opening act, performing a few dates as a headliner as well.

In the summer of 1996, Akins released his second album, *Somebody New.* Although the record sold well initially, it quickly fell out of the Top 40. —*Stephen Thomas Erlewine*

A Thousand Memories / 1995 / Decca ◆◆◆

● **Somebody New** / Jun. 1996 / Decca ◆◆◆◆

Alabama

Country-Rock, Country-Pop, Contemporary Country, Urban Cowboy
Before Alabama, bands were usually relegated to a supporting role in country music. In the first part of the century, bands were popular with audiences across the country, but as recordings became available, nearly every popular recording artist was a vocalist, not a group. Alabama was the group that made country bands popular again. Emerging in the late '70s, the band had roots in both country and rock; in fact, many of their musical concepts, particularly the idea of a performing band, owed more to rock and pop than hardcore country. However, there is no denying that Alabama is a country band—their pop instincts may come from rock, but their harmonies, songwriting, and approach are indebted to country, particularly the Bakersfield sound of Merle Haggard, bluegrass, and the sound of Nashville pop. Their sleek, country-rock sound made the group the most popular country

group in history, selling more records than any other artist of the '80s and earning stacks of awards.

First cousins Randy Owen (b. December 14, 1949; lead vocal, rhythm guitar) and Teddy Gentry (b. January 22, 1952; vocals, bass) form the core of Alabama. Owen and Gentry grew up on separate cotton farms on Lookout Mountain in Alabama, but the pair learned how to play guitar together; the duo also had sung in church together before they were six years old. On their own, Gentry and Owen played in a number of different bands during the '60s, playing country, bluegrass, and pop on different occasions. During high school, the duo teamed with another cousin, Jeff Cook (b. August 27, 1949; lead guitar, vocals, keyboards, fiddle), to form Young Country in 1969. Before joining his cousins, Cook had played in a number of bands and was a rock 'n' roll DJ. Young Country's first gig was at a high school talent contest, where they performed a Merle Haggard song; the band won first prize at the contest, a trip to the Grand Ole Opry. However, the group was fairly inactive when Owen and Cook went to college.

After Randy Owen and Jeff Cook graduated from college, they moved with Teddy Gentry to Anniston, AL, with the intention of keeping the band together. Sharing an apartment, the band practiced at night and performed manual labor during the day. They changed their name to Wildcountry in 1972, adding drummer Bennet Vartanian to the lineup. The following year, the band made the decision to become professional musicians, quitting their jobs and playing a number of bars in the Southeast. During this time, Wildcountry began writing their own songs, including "My Home's in Alabama." Vartanian left the band soon after they turned professional; after losing four more drummers, they added Rick Scott to the lineup in 1974.

Wildcountry changed their name to Alabama in 1977, the same year they signed a one-record contract with GRT. The resulting single, "I Wanna Be with You Tonight," was a minor success, peaking in the Top 80. Nevertheless, the single's performance was an indication that Alabama was one of the most popular bands in the Southeast; at the end of the decade, the group was playing over 300 shows a year. After "I Wanna Be with You Tonight," the group borrowed $4,000 from a Fort Payne bank, using the money to record and release their own records, which they sold at their shows. When GRT declared bankruptcy a year after the release of "I Wanna Be with You Tonight," Alabama discovered that they were forbidden from recording with another label because of a hidden clause in their contract. For two years, the band raised money to buy out their contract. In 1979, they were finally able to begin recording again. That same year, Scott left the band. Scott was replaced by Mark Herndon, a former rock drummer who helped give Alabama its signature sound.

Later in 1979, Alabama self-recorded and released an album, hiring an independent record promoter to help them get radio play for the single, "I Wanna Come Over." The band also sent hundreds of hand-written letters to program directors and DJs across the country. "I Wanna Come Over" gained the attention of MDJ Records, a small label based in Dallas. MDJ released the single, and it reached No. 33 on the charts. In 1980, MDJ released the group's "My Home's in Alabama," which made it into the Top 20. Based on the single's success, Alabama performed at the Country Music New Faces show, where they were spotted by an RCA Records talent scout, who signed them after the show.

Alabama released its first RCA single, "Tennessee River," late in 1980. Produced by Harold Shedd, the song began a remarkable streak of 21 No. 1 hits (interrupted by the 1982 holiday single, "Christmas in Dixie"), which ran until 1987; after one No. 7 hit, the streak resumed for another six singles, resulting in a total of 27 No. 1 singles during the decade. Taken alone, the amount of chart-topping singles is proof of Alabama's popularity, but they also won numerous awards, had seven multi-platinum albums, and crossed over to the pop charts nine times during the '80s.

In the '90s, their popularity declined somewhat, yet they were still having hit singles and gold and platinum albums with regularity. It's unlikely that any other country group will be able to surpass the success of Alabama. — Stephen Thomas Erlewine

My Home's in Alabama / 1980 / RCA ✦✦✦✦
This is the album that started it all for Alabama. Their Southern rock influences are obvious but encased in a country context. The title track's sentiment is overwhelming, whether you're from Alabama or Iowa. — Tom Roland

Feels So Right / 1981 / RCA ✦✦✦✦
On their second album, Alabama's apparently more comfortable with the studio. The harmonies are tighter than in the debut, but the material selection—heavy on uptempo tunes—shows that the club mentality developed at the Bowery is still very much intact. Three hits—the title track, "Love in the First Degree," "Old Flame"—but nearly all the extra cuts are strong as well. — Tom Roland

Mountain Music / 1982 / RCA ✦✦✦✦
This is their best effort. The group hadn't quite fallen into any formulas, and as a result, they cover the stylistic gamut pretty well. The title track practically defines what country groups have strived to accomplish, and the group slides easily from sentiment to social relevance to out-and-out partying. — Tom Roland

The Closer You Get / 1983 / RCA ✦✦✦✦
On their fourth album, Alabama shows signs that their hit-making approach is becoming a slick, well-produced formula, but when the formula produces hits like the title track and "Dixieland Delight," it's useless to complain. — Stephen Thomas Erlewine

Roll On / 1984 / RCA ✦✦✦
The title track and "If You're Gonna Play in Texas (You Gotta Have a Fiddle in the Band)" make this entertaining but slightly formulaic album worth pursuing. — Stephen Thomas Erlewine

Alabama Christmas / 1985 / RCA ✦✦✦✦
A must for your C&W Christmas, it contains the classic "Christmas in Dixie." — David A. Milberg

40 Hour Week / 1985 / RCA ✦✦✦✦
Opening with the driving title track, 40 Hour Week encapsulates why Alabama was the top country group of the '80s. Alternating between restrained rockers and well-crafted ballads, it captures the band at its peak. Nevertheless, it isn't quite as strong as their first albums—the performances and production are a bit too mannered—but its professionalism is appealing. And that professionalism made 40 Hour Week the group's most popular album, as it crossed over into the pop Top Ten. — Stephen Thomas Erlewine

The Touch / 1986 / RCA ✦
Although the album has a couple of worthwhile songs, particularly the title track, The Touch is the weakest record Alabama has put out to date. It follows the same formula as the band's previous records, but there aren't enough melodies or hooks to make the album memorable. — Stephen Thomas Erlewine

★ **Greatest Hits** / 1986 / RCA ✦✦✦✦✦
This batch of hits made them the most successful country act of the 1980s. More than the best available sampler of their much-imitated group sound, it also reflects the state-of-the-art Nashville sound the moment before Randy Travis hit. — Dan Cooper

Just Us / 1987 / RCA ✦✦
An improvement on the stilted Touch, Just Us has a number of fine moments, including the pining "(I Wish It Could Always Be) '55" and the K.T. Oslin duet "Face to Face," but it falls short of being a complete return to form, mainly because it is weighed down with too much mediocre material. — Stephen Thomas Erlewine

Live / 1988 / RCA ✦✦
Alabama have always been an entertaining live band, but Live simply doesn't capture the excitement of their concerts. — Stephen Thomas Erlewine

Southern Star / 1989 / RCA ✦✦✦✦
After eight very successful years with record producer Harold Shedd, Alabama wisely opts for change. Half the album is recorded with Josh Leo and Larry Lee, the other half with Barry Beckett, and the guys from Fort Payne attack the project with a little more energy than in some of their prior efforts. Get it on CD—three of the four "bonus" tracks are substantial. — Tom Roland

Pass It on Down / 1990 / RCA ✦✦✦
On the previous *Southern Star*, Alabama bounced out of their mid-'80s rut, and their winning streak continues on *Pass It On Down*. Like any of their albums, there is a fair share of filler, but that's outweighed by the best songs on the record, particularly the hit "Down Home." —*Stephen Thomas Erlewine*

Greatest Hits, Vol. 2 / 1991 / RCA ✦✦✦✦
Greatest Hits, Vol. 2 contains an 11-track cross-section of Alabama's hit singles from the mid- and late '80s, including the No. 1 singles "Dixieland Delight," "Lady Down on Love," "The Closer You Get," "Roll On (Eighteen Wheeler)," "Fallin' Again," "Song of the South," "High Cotton," and "Take Me Down." This second volume is even stronger than the first and represents some of the best mainstream rock-influenced country of the '80s. —*Thom Owens*

American Pride / 1992 / RCA ✦✦✦
So much happened between Alabama's arrival on the scene and the country boom of the early '90s that by the time the band released *American Pride*, they were among the genre's aging veterans. As such it was a little late to expect big surprises. So everything that Alabama's known for is here: full-group harmonies, small-town Southern virtues and common-sense patriotism. The group turned "I'm in a Hurry (And Don't Know Why)" into a big hit, but it's no surprise the best songs are about folks who settled in for the long haul, happily married parents ("Between the Two of Them"), and Richard Petty ("Richard Petty's Fans"). —*Brian Mansfield*

Gonna Have a Party...Live / 1993 / RCA ✦✦
Like the previous *Live*, *Gonna Have a Party...Live* suffers from a stiff performance and a tameness, failing to capture the fun of an Alabama concert. —*Stephen Thomas Erlewine*

Cheap Seats / 1993 / RCA ✦✦✦
A charming video helped sell the way-cute title track, which offers another context for Alabama's down-home brand of nostalgia. Not to be overlooked, however, is "A Better Word for Love," a quiet, mourning love song co-written by Gary Nicholson and former NRBQ guitarist Al Anderson. —*Dan Cooper*

Greatest Hits, Vol. 3 / 1994 / RCA ✦✦✦✦
Like most country artists, Alabama made better singles than albums, rarely releasing a bad song for a single. Their third greatest hits compilation collects their biggest and best hits of the late '80s and early '90s—including "I'm in a Hurry (And Don't Know Why)," "Tennessee River," "Angels Among Us," and "When We Make Love"—making it a worthwhile addition to a contemporary country library. —*Stephen Thomas Erlewine*

In Pictures / Aug. 15, 1995 / RCA ✦✦✦
Alabama's train hasn't run out of steam on *In Pictures*, their 13th album of original material. The group doesn't depart from their trademark sound at all, but as the single "She Ain't No Ordinary Girl" shows, that's a benefit. *In Pictures* may be merely another Alabama album, but the group's knack for turning out catchy, straightforward pop-inflected country has not diminished over the years. —*Stephen Thomas Erlewine*

Alabama Christmas, Vol. 2 / Sep. 17, 1996 / RCA ✦✦✦
Like its predecessor, *Alabama Christmas, Vol. 2* is a pleasant mix of traditional holiday carols ("Little Drummer Boy," "O Little Town of Bethlehem") and fine, but undistinguished, original carols like "New Year's Eve 1999" and "Christmas in Your Arms." There's not much about *Alabama Christmas, Vol. 2* for listeners that aren't already fans of the group, but for fans, it's a fine addition to their collection. —*Thom Owens*

Christine Albert

Progressive Bluegrass, Singer-Songwriter
Singer-songwriter Christine Albert drew on both her family's European heritage and the musical legacy of her adopted home state of Texas to create her unique sound. Born and raised in upstate New York, Albert moved to Santa Fe, NM, at the age of 16 and began to pursue a career in music. After settling in Austin in 1982, she became a fixture on the area's club scene, but did not release her first LP *You Are Gold* until 1990. Her next LP, 1992's

Texafrance, was a bilingual affair that explored her family's French roots while seeking a common ground between the music of Patsy Cline and Edith Piaf. 1993's *The High Road* marked a renewed focus on straightahead country, a trend further developed by 1995's *Underneath the Lone Star Sky*. —*Jason Ankeny*

You Are Gold / 1990 / Gambini ✦✦✦

Texafrance / 1992 / Gambini ✦✦✦

● **Underneath the Lone Star Sky** / Oct. 1995 / Dos ✦✦✦✦

Gary Allan

Vocals / Contemporary Country
Born and raised in Southern California, vocalist Gary Allan became infatuated with the Bakersfield country of Merle Haggard and the neo-traditionalist sounds of George Strait as a teenager. During his late teens and 20s, he worked the local Californian club circuit, developing a style of his own. By 1996, he landed a record contract with MCA. He released his debut album, *Used Heart for Sale*, in the fall of that year. —*Stephen Thomas Erlewine*

Used Heart for Sale / Sep. 24, 1996 / MCA ✦✦✦
Gary Allan's debut *Used Heart for Sale* is a competent set of new-traditionalist country that occasionally comes to life—such as on the single "Her Man"—but often is hampered by unimaginative material and timid performances. Allan's best moments suggest that he is capable of more, yet *Used Heart for Sale* doesn't give him enough opportunity to stretch out and showcase his talents. —*Thom Owens*

Allen Brothers

Old-Time, Traditional Country, Country Gospel
Allen Brothers Lee and Austin were among the most popular fraternal duets of the '20s and '30s, known for their fast-paced, upbeat blues and old-time music-influenced songs; with their contemporary, often bawdy and funny good-time music, they offered quite a change from the sedate gospel-oriented songs and sentimental ballads of such peers as the Blue Sky Boys. Between 1926 and 1934 they recorded 36 songs, some of which have become country standards.

The Allen Brothers were born five years apart (Austin was the eldest) at the turn of the century on Monteagle Mountain, 50 miles north of Chattanooga, to a sawyer and a trained violinist. During childhood they were influenced by a combination of contemporary and traditional music. The brothers hit the local music circuits around 1923, and were particularly popular in the isolated coal mining camps. While traveling, the Allens began collecting all sorts of local, traditional tunes. Soon they began writing their own songs, many of which contain references to their mountain home and the Chattanooga area. The Allens made their recording debut for Columbia in 1926. Their first single was a version of "Salty Dog Blues" titled "Bow Wow Blues." It became quite popular, but when the label accidentally released their bluesy tunes in the 1400 "Race" series instead of the 1500 "Hillbilly" series, the brothers were offended and threatened to sue the company if the records remained on the shelves. Later the Allens signed with Victor and met Ralph Peer, who was then handling Jimmie Rodgers. Peer was impressed by the brothers and thought they might do well singing good-time songs. During concerts the Allens sang a combination of uptempo and slower tunes, and became frustrated when Peer insisted that they record only the former. Still, they remained with Victor until 1938, recording such hits as "Skippin' and Flying" (1928) and "Jay Walk Blues" (1930).

During the Depression, the brothers turned to acting and appeared in a play, *Bushwhacker*. They continued to record, but despite their popularity, the Allens weren't earning enough to support their families and in 1933 Austin and his family moved to New York, where he became a radio announcer. Lee stayed in Tennessee and became a construction worker. They recorded their final session in 1934 for ARC. The recording contained updated versions of some of their best hits, but still they didn't make enough impact to justify a return to becoming full-time musicians. Austin later became a construction worker and engineer. He died in Williamston, SC, in 1959. In the late 1960s, there was a revival of old-time music and the Allen Brothers were rediscovered by a new generation. Their old recordings were reissued and later Lee was coerced into performing again. He appeared infrequently at local gigs near his home in Lebanon, TN. Lee Allen passed away in the 1980s. —*Sandra Brennan*

Are You Feeling It Too? / 1994 / Smithsonian/Folkways ✦✦✦✦
● **Clara's Boys** / Rounder ✦✦✦✦
Sweet Rumors / Rounder ✦✦
Allen Brothers with Banjo & Guitar / Old Timey ✦✦✦
The Chattanooga Boys / Old Timey ✦✦✦

Deborah Allen

b. Sep. 30, 1953, Memphis, TN
Vocals / Country-Pop, Urban Cowboy
An adventurous singer heavily influenced by Patsy Cline, Deborah Allen's work blended the punched-up swamp blues of her native Memphis with aggressive pop-country. Allen had wanted to be a country music singer since she was four. At age 17, she went to Nashville, where she worked as a waitress in a pancake house. Legend has it that one of her customers was Roy Orbison, who hired her on the spot as a backup singer after she convinced him of her singing ability. Allen then worked at Opryland on the General Jackson showboat and went on an international tour as a singer and dancer with Tennessee Ernie Ford's show. Jim Stafford then hired her to appear on his summer TV show in California and as an opening act for his concerts. She scored her first hits in 1979 when Mary Reeves selected her to dub her voice on three tracks by the late Jim Reeves. In 1980, she recorded her debut album, *Trouble in Paradise,* for Capitol; the album contained one Top 20 single, "You (Make Me Wonder Why)." In 1983, she released the mini-album *Cheat the Night,* which contained three major self-penned singles, including "Baby I Lied." Her success led to the full album *Let Me Be the First* in 1984. Afterwards, Allen stopped performing and became a songwriter, frequently collaborating with then-husband Rafe Van Hoy. Among her hits were Janie Fricke's "Don't Worry 'Bout Me Baby" and Tanya Tucker's "Can I See You Tonight." She came back to country singing in 1993 with the album *Delta Dreamland.* Her first single, "Rock Me," was released with a rather raw concept video. —*Sandra Brennan*

Trouble in Paradise / 1980 / Capitol ✦✦✦
Let Me Be the First / 1984 / RCA ✦✦✦
Working again with husband/producer/co-writer Rafe Van Hoy, Allen attempts an artful, electronic style of country-pop that proved too progressive for the country mainstream. —*Michael McCall*
● **Delta Dreamland** / 1993 / Warner Brothers ✦✦✦✦
Allen comes roaring back with another Van Hoy collaboration, this one produced before signing a record contract. Bluesy, sexy, and intimately powerful, it rocks harder than anything she previously offered. —*Michael McCall*

All That I Am / 1994 / Giant ✦✦✦✦
Allen pushes her steamy sensuality even more to the forefront here in another strong collection. —*Michael McCall*

Cheat the Night / RCA ✦✦✦✦
An EP features her two best-known hits of the 1980s, "Baby I Lied" and "I've Been Wrong Before." It's sweeter and softer-edged than her '90s work. —*Michael McCall*

Red Allen

b. Feb. 12, 1930, Perry County, KY, d. Apr. 3, 1993
Guitar, Vocals / Progressive Bluegrass, Traditional Bluegrass
Appalachia-born Red Allen had a voice that personified the "high lonesome sound" of traditional bluegrass music. He was born in Perry County, KY, and grew up influenced by the music of such performers as Charlie Monroe. After serving two years in the US Marine Corps, the 19-year-old Allen moved to Dayton, OH, in 1949. Many other musicians—including Frank Wakefield, the Osborne Brothers and Noah Crase—also relocated to Ohio, and together they all frequently played at local clubs and on the radio.

In 1954, Allen made his recording debut on an independent Kentucky label. Later he joined the Osborne Brothers, and the group became a mainstay on the *Wheeling Jamboree.* They began recording on MGM, where they made such classics as "Ruby" and "Wild Mountain Honey." Allen stayed with the Osbornes until 1958 and then left music for a time. In 1959, he moved to Washington, DC, where he formed the Kentuckians with Wakefield; over the years, the group included musicians like Bill and Wayne Yates and David Grisman.

In 1967, Allen moved to Nashville to temporarily replace a recuperating Lester Flatt in Flatt & Scruggs. The next year he and J.D. Crowe founded the Kentucky Mountain Boys. In 1969, Allen went back to Dayton and formed a band with his four teenaged sons. As Red Allen and the Allen Brothers, they began playing the *Wheeling Jamboree* and recording for King Bluegrass and Lemco. Throughout the '70s, he toured America and Europe, usually playing bluegrass and folk festivals. A decade later, Allen recorded two albums for Folkways. He continued to play clubs and festivals near Dayton until his death from cancer in 1993. —*Sandra Brennan*

● **Red Allen & The Kentuckians** / 1991 / County ✦✦✦✦
Red Allen & The Kentuckians is an album the bluegrass pioneer Red Allen recorded for County Records in 1966. The record is one of his best, capturing his pure and intense style through both instrumental showcases and a selection of fine material, such as "Milk Cow Blues," "I Wonder Where You Are Tonight," "Maiden's Prayer" and "If That's the Way You Feel." —*Thom Owens*

Rex Allen

b. Dec. 31, 1922, Wilcox, AZ
Guitar, Vocals / Cowboy
Better-known as the Arizona Cowboy, Rex Allen was the last of Hollywood's singing cowboys. Between 1950 and 1954, Allen starred in 19 movies for Republic Studios. The films launched a popular recording career for Allen, as he had several hit singles and albums in the early '50s, before the singing cowboys slowly disappeared from the charts.

The son of a fiddle player, Rex Allen was given his first guitar when he was 11 years old; his father intended Rex to support him at dances. Shortly afterwards, Rex began singing. After he finished high school, Allen was hired as a performer by a Phoenix radio station, but he only stayed there for a brief time. Instead, he hit the rodeo circuit. His career as a rodeo rider was short-lived, as he suffered an injury from a bull. The injury led Allen back to singing, and he was hired by WTTM in Trenton, NJ, in 1943.

After he left WTTM, Rex Allen joined the Sleepy Hollow Ranch gang in Pennsylvania. During the summer of 1946, Allen was spotted by Lulubelle and Scotty; impressed, the duo recommended that he try out for the National Born Dance and WLS in Chicago. Allen became a popular performer in the Windy City, which led him to become one of the first country-western artists signed by Mercury Records. Mercury released several of Allen's singles before he had a hit with "Afraid" in 1949. That same year, Allen went to Hollywood.

Bringing along a CBS Network radio program, Rex Allen approached Republic Pictures. The studio signed the singer to star in a film, *The Arizona Cowboy,* which was released in 1950. The movie was a success, beginning a string of 19 pictures that ran until February 1954. All of the movies were musical westerns, starring Allen with a rotating cast of sidekicks. Frequently, he would star with Slim Pickens, but Buddy Ebsen and Fuzzy Knight also made their appearances in Allen's films.

Allen's film successes led to a hit record in 1951, "Sparrow in the Tree Top." Released on Mercury Records, the single climbed into the country Top Ten and made it into the pop Top 30. Soon after its release, Allen signed with Decca Records, which released his biggest hit, 1953's "Crying in the Chapel"; the song peaked in the Top Five and reached the Top Ten pop charts. In the latter half of the decade, he made a number of albums composed of Western songs. During this time, he acted in 39 episodes of the television program, *Frontier Doctor.*

By the '60s, Rex Allen had re-signed with Mercury Records, which led to several minor hits and one major success—1962's "Don't Go Near the Indians," which returned the singer to the country Top Ten and the pop Top 20. On his '60s stint at Mercury, Allen had two other significant hits—1961's "Marines Let's Go" and "Tear After Tear" in 1964. In the late '60s, the singer went back to Decca Records, which resulted in one minor hit in 1968, "Tiny Bubbles." During this time and the early '70s, he recorded albums for Disneyland, Buena Vista, and JMI. However, he was more prominent in this era as a narrator for many Walt Disney films and television programs, as well as a voice in several Disney cartoons.

In the '80s, Allen's oldest son, Rex Allen Jr., became a star in his own right. A museum in his hometown of Willcox was dedicated to Rex Allen, and the Governor of Arizona honored him. Allen occasionally appeared at Western film fairs, where he remained as popular as ever. — *Stephen Thomas Erlewine*

Boney Kneed, Hairy Legged Cowboy Songs / 1984 / Bear Family ✦✦✦✦

Hawaiian Cowboy / Apr. 1986 / Bear Family ✦✦✦
This picture disc contains 16 cuts recorded by Allen for Mercury between 1946 and 1951. —*AMG*

Voice of the West / Aug. 1986 / Bear Family ✦✦✦✦
Voice of the West collects songs Rex Allen recorded in the early '70s with producer Jack Clement, who cut away the cinematic strings that dominated Allen's previous recordings. Instead, he leaves the singing cowboy with simple, straightforward production that accentuates the western roots of his music. Not only does he play tradtional cowboy classics, he does a handful of contemporary country numbers. It might not have his classic hits, but *Voice of the West* gives a good sense of the scope of Allen's talents. —*Stephen Thomas Erlewine*

● **Very Best of Rex Allen** / Nov. 8, 1994 / WEA ✦✦✦✦

Rosalie Allen (Julie Marlene Bedra)

b. Jun. 27, 1924, Old Forge, PA
Vocals / Cowboy
One of the first wave of female country stars, Rosalie Allen recorded several hits during the late '40s as a singing cowgirl and yodeler in the Patsy Montana tradition. Born Julie Marlene Bedra on June 27, 1924, she grew up in a large, poor Pennsylvania family. Inspired by the singing cowboys of the '30s, she taught herself to sing and play guitar, and began working on the radio in Wilkes-Barre, PA. She moved to New York in the early '40s, and sang with the Swing Billies and also with Zeke Manners, where she met her future duet partner Elton Britt. Allen's first hit came in 1946 with RCA Victor; the update of Patsy Montana's "I Want to Be a Cowboy's Sweetheart" hit No. 5 and was later trumped on the country charts by its B-side "Guitar Polka (Old Monterey)," which reached No. 3.

During the late '40s, Rosalie Allen became quite famous in New York as a major promoter of country music. She hosted a TV show in New York as well as the WOV radio program *Prairie Stars*, and her writing appeared in columns for *National Jamboree* and *Country Sound Roundup*. Her Rosalie Allen Hillbilly Music Center in New York was the first specifically country record store in the nation.

Allen's final two chart hits paired her with Elton Britt, the yodeler famous in the mid-'40s for "There's a Star-Spangled Banner Waving Somewhere." Their first single, "Beyond the Sunset," hit No. 7 in 1950; it was followed closely by the No. 3 "Quicksilver." The duo also recorded an album for Waldorf Records in the mid-'50s—now released as *Starring Elton Britt and Rosalie Allen* on the Grand Award label. Also, two albums of Allen's solo recordings are available as German imports. —*John Bush*

Rosalie Allen Sings Country & Western / 1957 / Waldorf Music ✦✦✦

● **Songs of the Golden West** / 1957 / Grand Award ✦✦✦✦

Rodeo / 1959 / Grand Award ✦✦✦

Rosalie Allen / 1961 / RCA ✦✦✦✦

Starring Elton Britt and Rosalie Allen / 1966 / Grand Award ✦✦✦

Queen of the Yodelers / 1983 / Cattle [Germany] ✦✦✦✦

The Cowboy's Sweetheart / 1990 / Cowgirlboy [Germany] ✦✦✦

Terry Allen

b. May 7, 1943, Wichita, KS
Keyboards, Vocals / Country-Rock, Alternative Country
There may be no greater maverick than Terry Allen in all of late-20th century country music. Along with Jimmie Dale Gilmore, Joe Ely, and Butch Hancock—all of whom he's known and collaborated with—Allen is a standardbearer of the Lubbock, TX, country scene. Though not widely heralded, this is perhaps the most progressive movement in all of contemporary country, digging into modern-day concerns with a gutsy, liberal perspective, while maintaining a firm musical grounding in regional country and folk traditions. Allen is perhaps the most ambitious of them all, writing complex song cycles that are performed with the help of fellow eclectics ranging from Lowell George to David Byrne.

Allen's audience, like those of the other Lubbock pioneers, is not the country mainstream. Indeed, his principal appeal may not lie with the country audience at all (though his music definitely *is* country), but with open-minded alternative folk and rock listeners. Unlike most current country artists, his words aim to question and confront hard day-to-day realities, rather than offer conservative cliches or maudlin comforts to shield listeners from those very day-to-day realities. He does so with a humor and irreverence that will also find little sympathy in Nashville or Middle America.

Country music is just one of Allen's artistic pursuits, perhaps accounting to some degree for his wide perspective. The renaissance man is also an internationally recognized artist with three NEA grants and a Guggenheim Fellowship to his credit. He's also a true multimedia performer, having done work in the mediums of painting, sculpture, film, video, installation, theater, and poetry. Just a few of his more interesting projects, for instance, were writing the music for *Amerasia*, a film about American servicemen living in Thailand after the Vietnam War; writing a new national anthem (with Ely, Hancock, and Gilmore) in conjunction with a book about Vietnam; and collaborating with his wife Jo Harvey Allen, Ely, and Hancock on the production of the acclaimed stage play *Chippy*.

But Allen is not a country music dilettante, having written songs for Bobby Bare and Robert Earl Keen. Outside of the strict country sphere, he wrote "New Delhi Freight Train" for Little Feat, and contributed a few songs to the soundtrack of David Byrne's *True Stories* film. The cinema has always been an inspiration and influence upon Allen's work. His first album, *Juarez* (from the mid-'70s), was a conceptual work that originated as a soundtrack to an imaginary film, evolving in performance to a set of songs inspired by Mexican imagery.

1979's *Lubbock (On Everything)* is considered his most significant album. Inspired by his experiences growing up in the Texan town, it won praise for observing the details of regional life and characters with a sensitivity and wit more akin to rock and folk singer-songwriters than country ones. Allen's music (if not his lyrics), however, remain very much in the Texan country tradition.

With many artistic projects always in the works, Allen has never had the need to record frequently. 1996's *Human Remains*, though, found his singing and songwriting prowess undimmed. He also expanded his musical horizons significantly with support from such noted stars and cult figures as David Byrne, Lucinda Williams, Ponty Bone, Lloyd Maines, and Joe Ely. —*Richie Unterberger*

Juarez / 1975 / Fate ✦✦✦

● **Lubbock on Everything** / 1979 / Fate ✦✦✦✦
In the view of most critics this is Allen's definitive statement, examining mundane and eccentric small town lives with a sympathetic but penetrating wit that is rare in country music. The musical arrangements are much plainer than the ones Allen would craft on his much more recent *Human Remains*. Still, you won't find songs about a wolfman of Del Rio, a football star who

ends up in the pen after a series of post-high school failures, or middle-aged women fighting fading beauty on many other country albums. —*Richie Unterberger*

Lubbock / 1979 / Fate ✦✦✦

Smokin' the Dummy / 1980 / Fate ✦✦

Bloodlines / 1983 / Fate ✦✦✦

Human Remains / Jan. 23, 1996 / Sugar Hill ✦✦✦✦
The conceptual scope of *Human Remains* is not nearly as ambitious as *Lubbock*. But the gutsier and more varied musical arrangements—crafted with help from Lloyd Maines, David Byrne, Joe Ely, Lucinda Williams, and many others—may make this a better introduction to Allen's world. There's certainly no shortage of interesting character sketches, like a one-legged dancing woman, memories of "flower children and their shit-eating grins," and 13-year-olds well on their way to reform school. "Gone to Texas" especially is a refreshing blast of true anti-establishment sentiment, Allen singing in even-mannered tones that he doesn't need a chickenshit (his term) business man telling him what to do, and dissing some country star who thinks that all it takes to be special is wear a hat and win Grammies. —*Richie Unterberger*

Shelly Lee Alley

b. Jul. 6, 1894, Alleyton, TX, **d.** 1964
Fiddle, Vocals / Western Swing
During the '30s and '40s, Shelly Lee Alley and his Alley Cats were one of the most prominent Western Swing bands in Texas. Born in Alleyton, TX, singer-songwriter/fiddle player Alley began his career as the leader of a San Antonio army camp orchestra during World War I. Following military service, he went on to lead several small orchestras, which played on radio stations throughout the Lone Star State. During the early '20s, Alley was primarily interested in pop and jazz music and belonged to several small combos, including the Dixie Serenaders, who played at a Dallas radio station. In addition to performing and conducting music, Alley was also a songwriter. One of his early songs, "Travelin' Blues," became a Depression-era hit for Jimmie Rodgers; its success turned Alley more towards country and western music, and he joined a Fort Worth radio show called "The Chuck Wagon Gang." He formed the Alley Cats in 1936 and played radio stations and local dances in the Houston and Beaumont area. The Alley Cats recorded several sessions for the American Record Corporation on the Vocalion label. Some Alley Cats members, such as Ted Daffan and Leon Selph, went on to form their own successful bands. In 1941, Alley cut a single for Bluebird, and also continued writing songs, many of which were recorded by Jimmie Davis. During World War II, the Alley Cats broke up and Alley began playing with Patsy and the Buckaroos. He got the Cats back together and cut a single for the Globe label, but the group disbanded for good around 1946. Alley still played his fiddle occasionally and wrote songs; his stepson, Clyde Brewer, went on to become a popular Western swing musician in his own right. —*Sandra Brennan*

Dave Alvin

b. 1955, Los Angeles, CA
Guitar, Vocals / Singer-Songwriter, Roots-Rock, Americana
Most neo-rockabilly artists merely mimic the music without expanding its vocabulary or its creative horizons. Dave Alvin is the exception that proves the rule. From his teeth-cutting days with the now-defunct Blasters (which featured Dave's brother Phil on vocals) up to his current solo career, Alvin has used rockabilly and country as a springboard (as opposed to sole inspiration) for his sympathetic and precise songwriting, which tackles some of the same issues as John Mellencamp's. He's also one hell of an axe slinger. —*John Floyd*

Every Night About This Time / 1987 / Demon ✦✦✦✦
This is Dave Alvin's solo debut, which was released initially in the UK, then picked up for US release by Epic Records, which changed the album title to *Romeo's Escape*. —*William Ruhlmann*

● **Romeo's Escape** / Dec. 1987 / Razor & Tie ✦✦✦✦
The former guitarist/songwriter of the Blasters has his solo debut, singing his own songs. As with the Blasters, it's the songs that impress most, notably here "Fourth of July" and "Border Radio." —*William Ruhlmann*

Blue Blvd / 1991 / Hightone ✦✦✦
Highlighted by an appearance by the legendary R&B saxophonist Lee Allen, Alvin's second solo album offers more of his revved-up mix of rockabilly, blues, and rock 'n' roll. —*Stephen Thomas Erlewine*

Museum of Heart / 1993 / Hightone ✦✦✦
Dave Alvin's third album contains more thoughtful story songs of hard living and romantic loss, set to rockabilly beats and overlaid with melodic guitar playing. If there's any criticism to be made of his approach, it's that he sometimes seems too satisfied with his obvious gifts to really push himself, which makes you think that there's a spark missing that would vault him into the big time. Maybe, maybe not. —*William Ruhlmann*

King of California / 1994 / Hightone ✦✦✦
Dave Alvin makes an "unplugged" album, reprising many of his familiar tunes, "Fourth of July," "Every Night About This Time," and "Border Radio" among them, in an acoustic setting that wouldn't be foreign to Woody Guthrie. Neither would the lower-class portraits of struggle that are Alvin's metier. The songs stand up well in this relatively unadorned, becalmed setting; in fact, some are even more poignant. —*William Ruhlmann*

Interstate City / Jul. 1996 / Hightone ✦✦✦✦
Recorded at the Continental Club in Austin, TX, with his backup band, the Guilty Men, *Interstate City* documents the nervy energy and gritty sound of Dave Alvin live in concert. Alvin tears through his back catalog with surprising gusto, touching on both the Blasters and his solo hits. Most enticing for fans, however, are the new songs he works into the set. Most of the newer numbers are on par with his finest material and they are delivered with an intoxicating rush. *Interstate City* is one of the rare live albums that actually improves on the original recordings. —*Thom Owens*

Phil Alvin

Vocals / Roots-Rock, Americana
Phil Alvin was the lead singer of the Blasters in the early '80s. He released an eclectic solo album, *Un "Sung" Stories*, in 1986, with backing from the Dirty Dozen Brass Band and Sun Ra & His Arkestra. —*William Ruhlmann*

● **Un "Sung" Stories** / 1986 / Slash ✦✦✦✦
Leaving the Blasters, lead singer Phil Alvin moved back in time from that band's rockabilly approach to jazz and jump-blues styles, employing the Dirty Dozen Brass Band and Sun Ra & His Arkestra on songs by Cab Calloway and others. —*William Ruhlmann*

County Fair 2000 / Oct. 25, 1994 / Hightone ✦✦✦

The Amazing Rhythm Aces

Country-Rock
A mainstream country-rock band similar in execution (if not commercial success) to the Eagles, the Amazing Rhythm Aces were formed in Memphis in 1974 by bassist Jeff Davis and drummer Butch McDade, who had earlier recorded and toured with the great singer-songwriter Jesse Winchester. After striking out on their own, Davis and McDade enlisted vocalist/guitarist Russell Smith, keyboardist Billy Earhart III, dobro player Barry Burton, and pianist James Hooker to develop a sound composed of equal parts pop, country and blue-eyed soul.
Stacked Deck, the Amazing Rhythm Aces debut album, appeared in 1975; it produced two significant crossover hits, "Third Rate Romance" and "Amazing Grace (Used to Be Her Favorite Song)," the group's lone Top Ten country single. A year later, the hit "The End Is Not in Sight (The Cowboy Tune)," from the LP *Too Stuffed to Jump*, won the Aces a Grammy for Country Vocal Performance by a Group. Following the release of 1977's *Toucan Do It Too*, Burton left the group, and was replaced by Duncan Cameron.

In 1978, the Aces released *Burning the Ballroom Down*, followed a year later by a self-titled effort featuring cameos by Joan Baez, Tracy Nelson, and the Muscle Shoals Horns; both were met with critical approval, but sold poorly. They released one final record, *How the Hell Do You Spell Rhythum*, before disbanding. While Smith went on to become a successful songwriter, Earhart joined Hank Williams, Jr.'s Bama Band, and Cameron joined Sawyer Brown—a group which, ironically enough, would find significant chart success in the 1980s with a sound similar to what the Amazing Rhythm Aces had created a decade earlier.

After a hiatus of some 15 years, the Aces reformed in 1994. The group, now comprised of Smith, Davis, McDade, Earhart, Hooker, and new guitarist/mandolinist Danny Parks, marked their return to duty by releasing *Born Again*, a collection of newly recorded renditions of their biggest hits. In addition, they also began composing new songs for a projected comeback album. —*Jason Ankeny*

● **Stacked Deck** / 1975 / ABC ✦✦✦✦
"Amazing" is certainly the word. In addition to "Third Rate Romance," which has been covered by artists as diverse as Earl Scruggs and Elvis Costello (and was a hit once again on the country chart in the mid-'90s), this album features a collection of amazing tunes by an incredibly hot band that sound fresh 20 years after they were recorded. Look for the single of "Third Rate Romance," which features the non-LP "Mystery Train" on the flip side. —*Jim Worbois*

Too Stuffed to Jump / 1976 / ABC ✦✦✦
Although *Too Stuffed to Jump* isn't quite as strong a record as the debut, the album features enough good material to recommend it. Some different influences come into play on this one, like the jazzy shuffle of "Same Ole Me." And who could not hear Leon Russell in "Typical American Boy"? —*Jim Worbois*

Toucan Do It Too / 1977 / ABC ✦✦
Compared to the first album, *Toucan Do It Too* just doesn't have life or joy. Still, it's a pleasant record from the Aces and the title track is particularly memorable. —*Jim Worbois*

Burning the Ballroom Down / 1978 / ABC ✦✦✦
This record is a bit more focused than the last and, for that reason, stands up a bit better over time. With the song "I Pity the Mother and Father," Smith explores territory not often examined in popular music; it will speak to anyone with kids who are growing up way too fast. — *Jim Worbois*

The Amazing Rhythm Aces / 1978 / Columbia ✦✦✦
By 1979, the Aces' recording career was winding down and their longtime label folded. As a result, this record was released on both ABC and Columbia with the only difference being the picture on the back cover. This album also saw the departure of guitarist/producer Barry Burton. Whatever the causes, this is their strongest album in some time. —*Jim Worbois*

How the Hell Do You Spell Rhythum? / 1980 / Warner Brothers ✦✦
The band goes out in tighter-than-tight style, covering "Futher on Down the Road," Delbert McClinton's "Object of My Affection," and Van Morrison's "Wild Night" and introducing the original version of "Big Ole Brew." —*Kit Kiefer*

Full House: Aces High / 1981 / MSS ✦✦

4 You 4 Ever: Best of Amazing Rhythm Aces / 1982 / M&R ✦✦✦✦

Eric Ambel

Guitar / Roots-Rock, Alternative Country-Rock
A Brooklyn-based artist known for his blistering guitar work, Eric "Roscoe" Ambel was one of the leading proponents of American roots rock both as a musician and producer. After serving in an early incarnation of Joan Jett's Blackhearts, in 1981 Ambel formed the Del-Lords with ex-Dictator Scott Kempner. One of the more successful bands to spring up from the "roots rock revival" of the early 1980s, the Del-Lords were essentially Kempner's baby, although Ambel did occasionally take over the lead vocal reins. After debuting in 1984 with the LP *Frontier Days*, the group issued three more albums—1985's *Johnny Comes Marching*

Home, 1988's *Based on a True Story*, and 1990's *Lovers Who Wander*—before Ambel's exit hastened the group's breakup.

Ambel left the Del-Lords to focus on a solo career, which he had begun in 1988 with *Roscoe's Gang*, a laid-back rock record cut with the aid of the Skeletons, Peter Holsapple, and other friends. The LP was a combination of originals as well as covers of Bob Dylan, Swamp Dogg, and Neil Young, the artist to whom Ambel has been most frequently compared throughout his career. He did not release another solo LP, however, until 1995, at which time he issued *Loud and Lonesome*. Throughout the 1990s, Ambel's greatest visibility was as a producer of like-minded musicians, including Nils Lofgren, the Bottle Rockets, Blue Mountain, the Blood Oranges, Go to Blazes and the Dog & Pony Show. In addition, he played with ex-Georgia Satellite Dan Baird in a raucous hillbilly side project called the Yay-Hoos. —*Jason Ankeny*

● **Roscoe's Gang** / 1988 / Enigma ✦✦✦✦
On his debut solo album, Del-Lord Eric Ambel cuts songs by buddies like Scott Kempner and Peter Holsapple, not to mention fave raves like Bob Dylan's "If You Gotta Go, Go Now," Swamp Dogg's "Total Destruction to Your Mind," and Neil Young's "Vampire Blues." "Recorded absolutely live in the studio. No overdubs, second takes or rehearsal," warns the record jacket, but that only contributes to the party atmosphere. Ambel is an authoritative singer, aided and abetted by Syd Straw, and he plays a vicious lead guitar, too. A worthy addition to the '80s roots rock library. —*William Ruhlmann*

Loud & Lonesome / 1995 / East Side Digital ✦✦✦

American Flyer

Country-Rock, Pop-Rock
American Flyer was a 1970s folk-rock quartet made up of former members of other groups: Craig Fuller was from Pure Prairie League, Eric Kaz had been a member of Blues Magoos, Steve Katz was in Blood, Sweat & Tears, and Doug Yule had played bass in the Velvet Underground. Together they charted with two albums on United Artists in the mid-'70s. —*William Ruhlmann*

● **American Flyer** / 1976 / United Artists ✦✦✦✦
American Flyer deserved better. Eric Kaz had written great love songs for Linda Ronstadt and Bonnie Raitt, and Craig Fuller was coming off his Top 40 hit "Amie" with Pure Prairie League. As it happened, Steve Katz's "Back in '57" turned out to be one of the album's highlights, but "Let Me Down Easy," by Kaz and Fuller, was a minor hit, and there was also Kaz's classic co-composition, "Love Has No Pride." But those were just the cream of an excellent set produced by George Martin. Add it all up, and it should have meant more than a chart peak in the lower reaches of the Top 100, an early indication that, for whatever reasons, American Flyer was not destined to become the next Crosby, Stills, Nash & Young. —*William Ruhlmann*

Spirit of a Woman / 1977 / United Artists ✦✦
Maybe there was only room for one really successful country-folkrock group with good songs and strong harmonies in the mid-'70s, and the job had already been taken by the Eagles. Who knows? American Flyer's second and final album didn't have as many great songs as the debut, and some of them were swamped by strings, but it was a pleasant work, notably featuring a version of Eric Kaz's "I'm Blowin' Away," which Bonnie Raitt had covered a couple of years earlier. —*William Ruhlmann*

Bill Anderson

b. Nov. 1, 1937, Columbia, SC

Vocals / Traditional Country, Country-Pop, Nashville Sound/ Countrypolitan
Singer Bill Anderson was one of the most enduring and talented songwriters in country music. He was born in South Carolina and raised in Georgia. He began writing songs for his own band while still in high school. Following his 1959 graduation from the University of Georgia, Anderson began working as a sportswriter; later, while working as a disc jockey in Commerce, GA, he began writing songs professionally. He wrote "City Lights" in 1958, and it became a major hit for Ray Price. Later that year he had his

own success with his debut single, "That's What It's Like to Be Lonesome."

Anderson came into his own during the 1960s when he had 24 hit songs on the national charts; among them was "Tips of My Fingers" (1960) and "Po Folks" (1961). He also continued writing hits for other singers; "I Missed Me" became a No. 3 hit for Jim Reeves. Anderson joined the Grand Ole Opry in 1961. He had his first No. 1 hit in 1962 with "Mama Sang a Song," which also became a minor pop hit. The next year he had a second crossover hit with "Still," which reached No. 1 on the country charts and made it to the Top Ten on the pop charts. During the early 1960s he was nicknamed "Whispering Bill" because of his quiet voice. His signature song became "Crook and Chase"; other major hits during the 1960s included "Five Little Fingers" (1964), "Bright Lights and Country Music" (1965), "My Life (Throw It Away If You Want To), and "But You Know I Love You" (1969). During the '60s, Anderson also hosted a syndicated music show.

During the 1970s, Anderson continued to find success with such hits as "Love Is a Sometimes Thing" (1970) and the No. 1 "World of Make Believe" (1973). He also cut a series of popular duets between 1966 and 1975 that included the smash "For Loving You" with Jan Howard in 1967; during the 1980s, he had success singing with David Allan Coe on "Get a Little Dirt on Your Hands" (1980) and with Roy Acuff on "I Wonder If God Likes Country Music" (1989). He also became a successful television producer and hosted ABC's game show *The Better Sex;* he later appeared regularly on that network's soap opera *One Life to Live.* Throughout his long career, Anderson won scores of awards including 50 songwriting awards from BMI. In a *Billboard* magazine poll he was named one of the "Three Greatest Country Music Songwriters" and in 1975 was inducted into the Nashville Songwriters Hall of Fame. In addition to releasing new material throughout the '90s, Anderson continued to appear regularly on the Grand Ole Opry and tour with his band Po Folks; he was also a spokesman for the Po Folks restaurant chain and wrote an autobiography. *— Sandra Brennan*

The Bill Anderson Story / Decca ✦✦✦✦
The 24-track collection *The Bill Anderson Story* contains the bulk of Anderson's major hits, including the No. 1 singles "Mama Sang a Song," "Still," and "I Get the Fever," as well as songs of his that were made famous by other performers. Several hits are missing, yet *The Bill Anderson Story* offers an effective introduction to the popular vocalist's easygoing, muted style. *— Thom Owens*

Still / 1963 / Decca ✦✦✦

Bill Anderson Showcase / 1964 / Decca ✦✦

Bright Lights and Country Music / 1965 / Decca ✦✦✦✦

Greatest Hits / 1971 / MCA ✦✦✦✦
Budget CD package of the absolute essential best, including the classic "Still." *— Cub Koda*

● **Bill Anderson's Greatest Hits** / 1996 / Varèse Vintage ✦✦✦✦
Bill Anderson's Greatest Hits contains 18 of his biggest hits and best-known songs, including "Mama Sang a Song," "Still," "I Get the Fever," "My Life (Throw It Away If You Want To)," "The Corner of My Life," and "8 X 10." Compiled by Anderson himself, the compilation hits almost all of the highlights, and represents the first thorough retrospective assembled on the country-pop crooner during the CD era. *— Stephen Thomas Erlewine*

John Anderson

b. Dec. 12, 1955, Apopka, FL
Guitar, Vocals / Honky Tonk, Outlaw Country, New Traditionalist
Growing up in Apopka, FL, John Anderson was enamored with the Beatles and the Rolling Stones, like most of his peers. But when he heard a Merle Haggard album at age 15, he found his true calling. Anderson headed for Nashville, where he showed up unannounced on his sister's doorstep. He took low-paying club jobs in Music City's Printer's Alley for experience, and worked a variety of places for money in the early '70s. In one of those jobs, he actually helped do roofing on the Grand Ole Opry House, before its opening in 1974. Signed to Warner Bros. in the late '70s, Anderson's first album hit the streets in 1980, bringing with it

critical acclaim for his attention to country tradition. Adding a vocal strain to the phrasing he picked up from Haggard and Lefty Frizzell, Anderson captured the Country Music Association's Horizon Award for 1983, given to an artist who makes the most career progress. "Swingin'," which, at 1.4 million in sales, is the best-selling country single in Warner history, also reeled in the CMA's Single of the Year trophy. Unfortunately Anderson fell out of favor with country radio within two years and future albums failed to capitalize on his earlier momentum.

Anderson began playing guitar when he was seven years old, learning the instrument from one of his sister's friends. Within five years, he had bought a Gibson guitar and began learning how to play British Invasion rock 'n' roll songs. When he was in seventh grade, he joined a garage band called the Weed Seeds, which later changed its name to the Living End. Anderson didn't begin playing country music until his older sister, Donna, joined a country band in Florida. Inspired by her change in direction, John started listening to the likes of Merle Haggard and George Jones, and he had soon decided what musical direction to pursue.

In 1971, he moved to Nashville, sharing an apartment with his sister Donna. The duo began playing local clubs together. John also landed a publishing deal with Al Callico, who helped him sign to the small independent label, Ace of Hearts, in 1974. Anderson released three singles on the label, including "What Did I Promise Her Last Night," but his hard country didn't make much of an impression within the country-pop confines of Nashville. After touring and working consistently for the next three years, he secured a contract with Warner Brothers in 1977, releasing his debut single "I Got a Feelin' (Somebody Stealin')," later in the year. The record became a minor hit, and over the next two years he had several small hits, including 1978's "The Girl at the End of the Bar," which was later covered by his idol, George Jones. It wasn't until late 1979 that he had a genuine hit record, when "Your Lying Blue Eyes" climbed to No. 15. Over the course of 1980, his star continued to rise, as "She Just Started Liking Cheatin' Songs" and "If There Were No Memories" both made the Top 40, helping him earn the Best New Artist award from the Academy of Country Music.

In 1981, John Anderson fulfilled his promise, as he had three Top Ten singles in a row: "1959," "I'm Just an Old Chunk of Coal (But I'm Gonna Be a Diamond Someday)," and "Chicken Truck." Later that year, he debuted on the Grand Ole Opry. The following year, he had his first country No. 1 single, "Wild and Blue," which followed two other Top Ten hits, "I Just Came Home to Count the Memories" and "Would You Catch a Falling Star." But the song that made John Anderson a household name was "Swingin'," a gently rocking tune co-written by Anderson and Lionel Delmore. "Swingin'" became a monster hit, peaking at No. 1 in early 1983 on the country charts, nearly making the pop Top 40 and eventually selling 1.4 million copies. Two other big hits, "Goin' Down Hill" and "Black Sheep," followed later that year, and Anderson stayed on top throughout 1984 with such hits as "Let Somebody Else Drive" and "She Sure Got Away with My Heart." Though he was very popular, Anderson was not getting along with Warner or his management, which resulted in his records slowly slipping down the charts over the course of 1986.

Anderson left Warner in 1987, signing with MCA, but his sales continued to decline. Four years later, he signed with the short-lived Universal label, but his lone record for the label was another failure. It wasn't until early 1992 that he bounced back into the charts with the surprise No. 1 hit "Straight Tequila Night." The single was his first for his new label BNA and it was pulled from the James Stroud-produced album *Seminole Wind.* The record revitalized Anderson's career, earning strong reviews and producing three other Top Ten hits—"When It Comes to You," "Seminole Wind," and "Let Go of the Stone." Upon the double-platinum success of *Seminole Wind,* Anderson was hailed as a trail-blazer for the new traditionalist movement of the late '80s and early '90s, and his new string of hits again made him a respected artist. The following year, he released *Solid Ground,* which produced the No. 1 single "Money in the Bank"; the album also went gold. His remaining albums for BNA weren't quite as popular, but they still sold well and John Anderson remained a popular concert attraction into the late '90s. — *Tom Roland*

John Anderson / 1980 / Warner Brothers ✦✦✦

John Anderson 2 / 1981 / Warner Brothers ✦✦✦✦
His second album (obviously), this traditionally minded package contrasted with the bulk of the material released in the same *Urban Cowboy*–influenced time period. His cover of Lefty Frizzell's "I Love You a Thousand Ways" shows his roots nicely, and "I'm Just an Old Chunk of Coal (But I'm Gonna Be a Diamond Someday)" is simply classic. — *Tom Roland*

Wild & Blue / 1982 / Warner Brothers ✦✦✦✦
The occasional use of strings in this album was probably masterminded by former Don Law protégé Frank Jones, who co-produced it. Twin fiddles and steel guitar dominate, though, especially in a remake of Ferlin Husky's "The Waltz You Saved for Me," featuring Emmylou Harris. It includes "Swingin'" and a new version of Lefty Frizzell's "Long Black Veil"—the very last track recorded in the legendary Columbia Studio B. — *Tom Roland*

★ **Greatest Hits** / 1984 / Warner Brothers ✦✦✦✦✦
Greatest Hits covers John Anderson's biggest hits from the early '80s, including the Top Ten singles "I Just Came Home to Count the Memories," "She Sure Got Away with My Heart," "Chicken Truck," "1959," "Would You Catch a Falling Star," "I'm Just an Old Chunk of Coal (But I'm Gonna Be a Diamond Someday)" and the No. 1 hits "Wild and Blue," "Swingin'," and "Black Sheep." — *Thom Owens*

Blue Skies Again / 1987 / MCA Special Products ✦✦

10 / 1988 / MCA ✦✦

Greatest Hits, Vol. 2 / 1990 / Warner Brothers ✦✦✦✦
Anderson keeps up the momentum. — *Dan Heilman*

Seminole Wind / 1992 / RCA ✦✦✦✦
A solid comeback album, it re-established Anderson as one of the most emotionally moving stylists of his generation. The title song features pointed social commentary about the ecological destruction of his native Florida. — *Michael McCall*

Solid Ground / Jun. 1993 / BNA ✦✦✦
Lighter in theme and impact than *Seminole Wind*, it's still a worthy and entertaining follow-up. — *Michael McCall*

Christmas Time / 1994 / BNA ✦✦
Some solid playing (most notably Paul Franklin on steel/dobro and Joe Spivey's fiddle work), but the self-penned title track has to carry too much of the originality weight. — *Roch Parisien*

Paradise / Jan. 30, 1996 / BNA ✦✦✦
Featuring guest appearances by Levon Helm and Mark Knopfler, John Anderson's *Paradise* is a typically consistent effort from the singer, featuring a handful of great songs that cancel out the fair amount of filler on the record. — *Thom Owens*

Greatest Hits / Oct. 15, 1996 /BNA ✦✦✦
Greatest Hits is a 15-track compilation that features John Anderson's '90s hits for BNA Records, as well as selections from his '80s work for RCA Records. The result is a career-spanning compilation that touches on most of Anderson's best work, including hit singles like "Swingin'" and "Money in the Bank." Consequently, it's the best place to get acquainted with one of the trailblazing new traditionalists of the '80s. — *Thom Owens*

Lynn Anderson (Lynn Rene Anderson)

b. Sep. 26, 1947, Grand Forks, ND
Vocals / Country-Pop, Nashville Sound/Countrypolitan
Vocalist, songwriter, and guitarist Lynn Anderson is best remembered for her gigantic 1971 crossover hit "Rose Garden." The daughter of songwriters Casey and Liz Anderson, she was born in North Dakota and raised in northern California. By the time she was a teen, Anderson was singing, dancing, and playing the guitar. In 1965 she joined *Country Corners* in Sacramento. When her mother Liz went to Nashville to collect a BMI Award (for writing Merle Haggard's first hit, "Strangers"), Anderson accompanied her; while she and her mother sang at a party during the Disc Jockey Convention, she was noticed by Slim Williamson of Chart Records, who signed her to his struggling label. She recorded her

first single at the end of 1965 with Jerry Lane; her first solo single, "In Person," followed in 1966, and a year later, Lawrence Welk invited her to become a regular on his show.

Anderson was named Most Promising Female Vocalist in a *Cash Box* deejay poll, which led to her debuting at the Grand Ole Opry and releasing her first album, *Ride, Ride, Ride*. In 1968 she married songwriter/producer Glenn Sutton. That year she was also named Best Female Vocalist by ACM and left the Welk show to record for Chart until 1970, by which time she had recorded over 100 songs; some of them, such as "Big Girls Don't Cry" (1968) and "That's a No-No," made it to the Top Ten. For Columbia, she released three singles before "Rose Garden," an international hit that topped both the country and pop charts. Anderson continued her affiliation with Columbia until 1981 and had numerous Top Ten hits; some of her tunes, such as "Even Cowboys Get the Blues" (1980), became country music standards. Anderson recorded *Back* for Permian in 1983, which produced two hits. One year later, Anderson released a single for MCA and then stopped recording for the next two years. In 1986, she signed with Mercury and staged a comeback with her album *What She Does Best*. In 1992, she issued *Cowboy's Sweetheart*. — *Sandra Brennan*

● **Greatest Hits** / 1972 / RCA ✦✦✦✦
With big pipes, big production, and big hits from the mid-to-late '60s, this includes "Rose Garden." — *Mark A. Humphrey*

Cowboy's Sweetheart / Jun. 1992 / Laserlight ✦✦
One of Anderson's stronger albums, *Cowboy's Sweetheart* is a collection of songs linked by their connection to Western mythos, including "Desperado," "Even Cowgirls Get the Blues" and "Happy Trails." A surprising cover of Cole Porter's "Don't Fence Me In" is also included. — *Jason Ankeny*

Country Spotlight / K-Tel ✦
Country Spotlight features inferior rerecordings instead of the original versions of Anderson's early-'70s hits. — *Stephen Thomas Erlewine*

Pete Anderson

Roots-Rock, Bakersfield Sound, Alternative Country
Pete Anderson was born in Detroit, and grew up to become the creative partner of one of the most significant country artists of the 1980s, Dwight Yoakam. An only child, Anderson's earliest musical memories revolve around the country and western music his father listened to and seeing Elvis on television. The sudden death of his father left the young prodigy to be raised by his mother, who also worked full time in one of Motor City's factories.

A natural athlete, Anderson vacillated between sports and music. His first instrument was a Hawaiian guitar, which he promptly knocked out of tune on a regular basis after imitating Elvis for the neighborhood kids, who loved to watch him perform. Still, he chose to participate in sports rather than spend his time practicing the guitar. But, as a teenager, music began to be more meaningful and Anderson joined several bands, including a jug band called the B-52 Blues when he was 17.

After high school, Anderson traveled the US by bus, went to art school, and got married. Shortly thereafter his then-wife gave birth to a son. Working in the factories, parenting, and playing music filled his life. Gigging around Detroit provided a solid education in the blues. Muddy Waters became the young father's hero. Still, he knew there was more to life than playing in bands in his hometown. As his marriage floundered, Anderson made up his mind to pursue his music at the next level. When his mother finally retired, she moved to Arizona, where the weather was not as severe as what she had known in Detroit. Both father and son followed and Anderson worked his way up the hierarchy of the Phoenix music scene. Again he knew that this was not his ultimate destination. With his son in the care of his ex-wife and his mother basking in the southwestern sunshine, Pete Anderson packed up and headed for California, and more specifically, L.A., in May of 1972.

A blues and rock player of some skill, the aggressive guitarist quickly made a name for himself. Wanting to record as much as play live gigs, the future producer honed his studio skills by making tapes and arranging songs. Working with various outfits, he was an important part of Hollywood Gumbo, which broke up on the road somewhere in Canada. He found that he could actually make a living playing the country music that had meant so much to his father. Developing his own rapid-fire style, Anderson was a working musician at night and painted houses when necessary during the daylight hours. His son and ex-wife came West and the small family tried to make a go of it one more time.

It was during this period that Boo Bernstein introduced Anderson to Dwight Yoakam, a struggling, skinny kid from Ohio who had a knack for writing real country songs. Needing a guitar player for a gig at the Cowboy in Orange Country, Yoakam remembered Anderson and asked him to do the date with him. That was the start of a partnership that resulted in numerous platinum records, sold out tours and some fine music in the Bakersfield and hillbilly traditions. Anderson became known as a top flight producer who could get the job done. Working not only in country, but also in other genres, he was responsible for some outstanding projects by Rosie Flores, Michelle Shocked, the Meat Puppets, the Backsliders, the Lonesome Strangers, and Thelonious Monster. He and Dusty Wakeman were responsible for volumes one and two of the compilation *Town South of Bakersfield*, a mid-'80s landmark that resulted in a resurgence of interest in the West Coast country scene and the Bakersfield Sound.

In 1993, along with Wakeman, Anderson joined Barbara Hein, a longtime Capitol Records executive with a history in the music business, and engineer Michael Dumas to form Little Dog Records. Recording his first solo CD on his own label in 1995, Anderson placed himself on the road in support of *Working Class*, a country-blues-rock-roots-music extravaganza produced by Wakeman. While continuing to work with Yoakam, being the president of a record label opened new worlds for Anderson. Signing artists that he and his partners believed in gave Anderson the creative freedom he craved. Having to be part businessman and part artist was a difficult part to play every day, but Anderson proved he was up to the challenge when he negotiated a distribution deal with Polygram in 1996. —*Jana Pendragon*

● **Working Class** / 1994 / Little Dog ◆◆◆
Before moving to California and beginning his successful association with country singer Dwight Yoakam, Anderson cut his musical teeth in Detroit playing rock 'n' roll and R&B. It comes as no surprise then, that on his first solo outing he would stray from the signature country string-bending style that has become his trademark. From the bluesy strut of Anderson's own "Working Class" to the gorgeous instrumental reading of the oft-covered Ruby & the Romantics classic "Our Day Will Come" along with the Texas blues-shuffle take on Jimi Hendrix's "Fire," Anderson's relaxed delivery—both vocally and with his always-captivating guitar playing—emits the feeling that there was little pressure in making this record. He and his band sound like they are having a great time. There are hints of country and folk (a solo cover of Dylan's "She Belongs to Me"), but primarily this is a blues record and a fine one at that. An enjoyable and insightful look at one of country music's most innovative and influential guitarists. —*Jack Leaver*

Terry Anderson

b. 1941
Roots-Rock, Alternative Country-Rock
North Carolina singer-songwriter Terry Anderson first gained local attention as the drummer and occasional vocalist of the bar bands the Woods and the Fabulous Knobs. His first widespread notice, however, came when his composition "Battleship Chains" was covered by the Georgia Satellites; later, the Satellites' frontman Dan Baird made his solo debut with Anderson's "I Love You Period." In 1994, Anderson cut his first solo effort, *You Don't Like Me; What Else Can Go Right*, a collection of no-frills rockers and rootsy acoustic numbers, followed two years later. —*Jason Ankeny*

You Don't Like Me / 1995 / ESD/REP ◆◆◆◆

Anglin Brothers

Traditional Country, Close Harmony
Red, Jim, and Jack Anglin were hailed as the South's favorite trio in the 1930s and were the predecessors of the successful 1940s duo Johnnie & Jack. The brothers were born in Franklin, TN, into a big family, which was raised in Athens, AL. Befriended and influenced by the Delmore Brothers while still growing up, the Anglins were inspired by the Delmores' performance on the Grand Ole Opry in 1930, three years after the Anglin family had moved to Nashville. Jack played guitar, Jim took up string bass, and all three shared vocal duties. During the mid-'30s, they debuted on a small Nashville radio station and performed for free. This led to a paying gig in Birmingham for the next two years, for which the Delmores recommended them. While there in 1937, the Anglins cut their first single for ARC, "They Are All Going Home but One," which became their most requested radio hit ever. In 1938, they had a second recording session at Columbia, SC; the brothers made 34 masters, but only released 14 for the Vocalion label. They went on to appear briefly on the radio in New Orleans and Atlanta until 1940, when Red was drafted. The brothers disbanded and never reunited, partly because Red was injured during the Allied invasion of France. Jim became one of the great songwriters of the 1940s and '50s, selling a great many compositions to Roy Acuff both before and after serving in the Navy. Of the three, Jack Anglin found the most success when he formed a duo with his brother-in-law Johnnie Wright in the early '40s. Johnnie & Jack produced numerous hits for RCA Victor until 1963, when Jack was killed in an auto wreck. In 1979, Old Homestead released a collector's edition containing all of the Anglin Brothers' released songs. —*Sandra Brennan*

Dave Apollon

b. 1898
Mandolin / Traditional Bluegrass
On the mandolin, Dave Apollon was, in a word, a virtuoso. The late Jethro Burns (of Homer and Jethro) said that Dave Apollon was the best that he had ever heard, and he ought to know, for Burns himself was the best mandolin player of the last quarter-century. Born in Russia, Apollon made many recordings, the first in 1932, and became a celebrity both through them and also through his movies. He was to the mandolin what Benny Goodman was to the clarinet. —*David Vinopal*

Mandolin Virtuoso / Yazoo ◆◆◆◆
A ragtime/vaudeville mandolin maestro. —*Mark A. Humphrey*

Amédée Ardoin

b. 1896, L'Anse Rougeau, LA, **d.** 1941
Accordion, Vocals / Blues, Cajun
One of the seminal names in recorded Lousiana music, Amédée Ardoin's high-pitched voice and great accordion playing influenced later developments in Cajun music, and he virtually invented what is now known as zydeco. Ardoin was born around 1896 in L'Anse Rougeau, LA, the son of former Creole slaves and sharecroppers. He formed a band in the 1910s with his brother Austin and the group played White dances around the area.

While sharecropping in 1921, Amédée Ardoin met White fiddler Dennis McGee; the two began playing together, and were often shuttled from dance to dance by landowner and music lover Celestin Marcantel. Ardoin and McGee won an accordion/fiddle contest in 1928, and Marcantel sponsored them to record for Columbia soon after. Among the first racially integrated recordings in history, the duo cut 12 sides in New Orleans in 1929 and 1930—with Ardoin billed alternately as Armadie and Anda Ardoin. Five years later, they played on six selections, and Ardoin traveled alone to New York later that year for 12 more sides—his final recordings. Ardoin continued to play dances around Louisiana until his death in 1941. —*John Bush*

★ **Louisiana Cajun Music, Vol. 6: Amédée Ardoin—His Original Recordings** / Mar. 1983 / Old Timey ◆◆◆◆◆
Amédée Ardoin's *His Original Recordings, 1928-1938* is divided between seven songs Ardoin recorded with Dennis McGee and

seven solo tracks. The duets with McGee are among the most legendary Cajun recordings; McGee's fiddle perfectly meshes with Ardoin's accordion and raw, bluesy voice. These are the recordings that laid the foundation of contemporary Cajun and zydeco. Ardoin's solo recordings are nearly as influential and exciting, capturing him alone with his accordion. While these aren't quite as kinetic as the duets, they are nevertheless enjoyable. —*Thom Owens*

☆ **The Roots of Zydeco** / 1995 / Arhoolie ✦✦✦✦✦
Amedée Ardoin was arguably the founder of zydeco music, incorporating blues into French folk. The songs on this collection were recorded in 1930 and 1934. Though the sound might be a bit harsh for some—these were taken from 78s, after all—these are important recordings and they continue to sound fresh and vital. —*Stephen Thomas Erlewine*

First Black Cajun Recording Artist / Arhoolie ✦✦✦
Violinist Dennis McGhee is featured on this 14-track album, which contains recordings from 1929, 1930, and 1934. —*AMG*

Armstrong Twins

Traditional Country, Close Harmony
The Armstrong Twins were one of the last duets to master the great harmonies of the traditional country music that came from the '30s and '40s. The twins, guitarist Lloyd and mandolin player Floyd, were born in DeWitt, AR, but were raised in Little Rock. They made their radio debut at age five and by the age of nine were hosting their own radio show. Greatly influenced by the Blue Sky Boys and the Bailes Brothers, the Armstrongs were appearing on two daily radio shows and on the *Arkansas Jamboree* by 1946. Between then and 1951, they cut over a dozen songs, most of which were bluegrass covers. Occasionally, they would also record instrumentals. The twins moved to Odessa, TX, in 1952 and began appearing on local radio and television programs. They then began touring with Johnny Horton and later worked on *Louisiana Hayride*.

In the late '50s, they moved to California and began appearing on the *Town Hall Party* in Compton. They were unique in that they were most popular on the West Coast at a time when local charts were dominated by Western swing and honky tonk tunes. After that, they moved back to Little Rock. Decades later, their old recordings were reissued, and the Armstrongs began a new series of festival and club engagements, even releasing a new album in 1980. Due to Floyd's ill health, the brothers had to curtail personal appearances and only played occasionally during the 1980s. —*Sandra Brennan*

Hillbilly Mandolin / 1979 / Old Timey ✦✦✦✦
● **Just Country Boys** / 1980 / Arhoolie ✦✦✦✦

Billy Armstrong

b. Mar. 18, 1930, Streator, IL
Fiddle / Western Swing
Billy Armstrong was one of country music's premiere fiddle players from 1965-1977, and was named Fiddle Player of the Year 13 years in a row by the ACM. He first played professionally in 1943 with Bob Lively's Dude Ranch Cowboys, quitting after four years to form Billy Armstrong and the Westerners, a group that included Don Hoag (drums), Bobby Wagoner (guitar), and Billy Strange (guitar). Armstrong began playing on the radio in 1948 on *Spade Cooley Presents;* the following year, he replaced "Lefty" Joe Holley in Tommy Duncan's Western All Stars. After playing on several of Duncan's recording sessions for the Intro label, he returned to L.A. and joined Hi Busse & the Frontiersmen, playing with them until 1951. Armstrong briefly played with another band until founding the Westernaires. Following their 1957 breakup, Armstrong joined Hank Thompson's Brazos Valley Boys for six months. Road life finally exhausted him and he quit, returned to L.A., and joined Cliffie Stone's *Hometown Jamboree*, and then Tex Williams' band. He released two singles, "Gloria" and "If You Leave While I'm Sleeping," in 1959. In 1965, Armstrong won his first ACM Fiddler of the Year award and also released the single "The Orange Blossom Special." He then played

with Gene Davis on the television series *Star Route* before joining the Sons of the Pioneers in 1966, with whom he sang lead and alternating tenor. He stayed with the Pioneers until early 1972, when he joined the Chaparral Brothers. During the 1970s, Armstrong also had a solo recording career, which produced three albums. —*Sandra Brennan*

● **World's Greatest Fiddle Player** / 1976 / Hillside ✦✦✦✦
Billy Don't Sell Your Fiddle / Hillside ✦✦✦

Eddy Arnold

b. May 15, 1918, Madisonville, TN
Guitar, Vocals / Traditional Country, Cowboy, Country Pop, Honky Tonk, Nashville Sound/Countrypolitan
Eddy Arnold moved hillbilly music to the city, creating a sleek sound that relied on his smooth voice and occasionally lush orchestrations. In the process, he became the most popular country performer of the century, spending more weeks at the top of the charts than any other artist. Arnold not only had 28 No. 1 singles, he has more charting singles than any other artist. More than any other country performer of the postwar era, he was responsible for bringing the music to the masses, to people that wouldn't normally listen to country music. Arnold was initially influenced by cowboy singers like Gene Autry, but as his career progressed, he shaped his phrasing in the style of Pete Cassell. Nevertheless, he was more of a crooner than a hillbilly singer, which is the main reason why he was embraced by the entertainment industry at large, and frequently crossed over to the pop charts. Arnold's career ran strong into the '90s. Although his records didn't dominate the charts like they did during the '40s and '50s, he continued to fill concert halls and reissues of his older recordings sold well.

Raised on a farm in Tennessee, Arnold was given a guitar at the age of ten by his mother. His father, who had played fiddle and bass, died the following year. Arnold left school so he could help out on the farm. However, he began playing dances whenever he had a chance. Several years later, he made his first radio appearance on a station in Jackson. Arnold then moved to St. Louis, where he played in night clubs with fiddler Speedy McNatt. In St. Louis, Arnold landed a regular spot on WMPS Memphis, spending six years at the radio station. Through the show, the singer earned a dedicated following of fans.

During World War II, Eddy Arnold became part of the R.J. Reynolds' Camel Caravan, which featured Redd Stewart, Pee Wee King's Golden West Cowboys, Minnie Pearl, and San Antonio Rose. The troupe performed for US troops throughout America, as well as some selected dates in Panama. After the Camel Caravan, Arnold became the featured singer in the Golden West Cowboys while they performed on the Grand Ole Opry. At first, he appeared under the name "The Tennessee Plowboy," a nickname that followed him throughout his career.

Arnold recorded his first single, "Mommy Please Stay Home with Me," in 1944 for RCA Victor. At RCA, the singer received the guidance of the label's A&R head, Steve Sholes, which proved to be invaluable help for his career.

Eddy Arnold pursued a solo career in 1945, the same year he got married to Sally Gayhart. "Each Minute Seems a Million Years," released on RCA's Bluebird division that same year, became his first charting record, peaking in the Top Five. Arnold's career really took off the following year, when "That's How Much I Love You" peaked in the Top Three, staying there for 16 weeks and selling over 650,000 copies; its flip side, "Chained to a Memory," also climbed into the Top Three. Arnold followed the single's success with two No. 1 hits in 1947, "What Is Life Without Love" and "It's a Sin." However, that didn't compare to the success of his next record, "I'll Hold You in My Heart (Till I Can Hold You in My Arms)." The single spent 46 weeks on the charts, with 21 of those weeks spent at the top; it also crossed over to the pop charts, reaching the Top 30. In the process, it became the No. 1 single of the decade.

"I'll Hold You in My Heart" confirmed that Arnold had become a country superstar, as did the performance of his 1948 singles. All of his nine singles went into the Top Five, and five of them

All Music Guide to Country

went to No. 1, including "Anytime," "What a Fool I Was," "Texarkana Baby," "Just a Little Lovin' (Will Go a Long, Long Way)," "My Daddy Is Only a Picture," and "Bouquet of Roses," which stayed at the top for 19 weeks. In total, Arnold racked up over 40 weeks on top of the charts during 1948, becoming the No. 1 country star in America. He headlined all the radio shows and concerts he appeared on, and he was in demand throughout the nation. By the end of the year, Colonel Tom Parker had become his manager; Parker would later become Elvis Presley's manager. Throughout 1949, he continued to dominate the charts, releasing a succession of Top Ten singles, including the No. 1 "Don't Rob Another Man's Castle," "One Kiss Too Many," "I'm Throwing Rice (At the Girl I Love)," and "Take Me in Your Arms and Hold Me."

Eddy Arnold became a familiar face not only to country fans, but to the general public in the early '50s. He toured all of the US, as well as several foreign countries. All of the major television shows of the era, including *The Perry Como Show* and *Arthur Godfrey's Talent Scouts*, featured the singer. Indeed, he became so popular that he was the first country star to have his own television show, *Eddy Arnold Time*. The show originally aired on NBC, but it later moved to ABC. Through all of this, his string of Top Ten hits remained unbroken, even though he didn't have another crossover pop hit until 1954. Nevertheless, the sheer amount of country hits was overwhelming: in 1950 he had seven, 13 in 1951 (including the No. 1s "There's Been a Change in Me," "Kentucky Waltz," "I Wanna Play House with You," "Easy on the Eyes," and "A Full Time Job"). The hits, including "Eddy's Song" (composed of the titles of previous hits), "How's the World Treating You?," "I Really Don't Want to Know," "My Everything," "The Cattle Call," "That Do Make It Nice," "Just Call Me Lonesome," and "The Richest Man (In the World)," continued to come in force until 1956.

Between 1956 and 1964, Arnold continued to chart, but he wasn't reaching the Top Ten at the same frequency of the previous decade. During this time, his style was beginning to change, as he was shedding his rootsy style for a slicker, more polished sound that was more appropriate for urban settings than rural territories. Arnold became a crooner, complete with subdued instrumental backings, highlighted by gentle steel guitars and the occasional orchestra. The change in musical direction was a major commercial success, sparking a new era of chart dominance that began in 1965 with "What's He Doing in My World." Not only did he return to the top of the country charts, he once again crossed over to the pop charts. Arnold's second streak of major hits ran until 1969. During this time, he earned several No. 1 and Top Ten singles, all of which were pop hits as well, including "Make the World Go Away," "I Want to Go with You," "The Last Word in Lonesome," "Somebody Like Me," "Lonely Again," "Turn the World Around," "Then You Can Tell Me Goodbye," "They Don't Make Love Like They Used To," and "Please Don't Go."

In the early '70s, Arnold continued to appear on the country charts, although his pop hits dried up. The singer signed with MGM in 1972, ending 27 straight years at RCA. Arnold spent only four years at MGM, landing only one major hit, 1974's "I Wish That I Had Loved You Better." Returning to RCA in 1976, he closed out the decade with two hits—"Cowboy" (1976) and "If Everyone Had Someone Like You" (1978). Arnold managed to put two songs into the Top Ten in 1980 ("Let's Get It While the Gettin's Good," "That's What I Get for Loving You"), making him one of the few artists that charted in five different decades. He continued to record in the '90s, although he has yet to chart a hit single. Nevertheless, his concert and television appearances remained popular.

Beginning in the '60s, Eddy Arnold was bestowed with a numerous amount of awards. In 1966, he was inducted into the Country Music Hall of Fame. The following year, he was the first "Entertainer of the Year" named by the CMA. The ACM gave him the Pioneer Award in 1984; three years later, the Songwriters Guild gave him the President's Award. Perhaps the truest gauge of his success is his record sales. Over the course of his career, he has sold over 85 million records, making him one of the most successful artists of the century. —*Stephen Thomas Erlewine*

Anytime/Eddy Arnold and His Guitar / 1952 / RCA ✦✦✦
The fine, early country material ("Bouquet of Roses," "Molly Darling") features Little Roy Wiggins on steel guitar. —*Richard Lieberson*

Have Guitar, Will Travel / 1959 / RCA ✦✦
Based around a loose "travel" concept, *Have Guitar, Will Travel* features a collection of songs with the names of states or cities in its title. It's a cute concept, but it wears thin fast, simply because the quality of the material is so drastically uneven. Within the album, there are some gems—like a beautiful "Carry Me Back to Old Virginny"—but the record is more interesting as an artifact than as an album. —*Stephen Thomas Erlewine*

Cattle Call/Thereby Hangs a Tale / 1963 / Bear Family ✦✦✦✦
Two of Eddy Arnold's early RCA/Victor albums, *Cattle Call* and *Thereby Hangs a Tale*, were combined on this single-disc from Bear Family. Though fans of Arnold's earliest records will find plenty of interest, the disc is primarily of historical interest—there are better places to listen to his early material. —*Stephen Thomas Erlewine*

Eddy's Songs / 1964 / RCA Camden ✦✦
Eddy's Songs may contain several fine tracks, including "Roll Along Kentucky Moon," "When My Blue Moon Turns to Gold Again," and "Kentucky Waltz," but the LP is burdened by uneven songs and performances, making it only a fitfully entertaining listen. (The stereo editions of *Eddy's Songs* are electronically reprocessed stereo, not true stereo.) —*Thom Owens*

★ **The Best of Eddy Arnold [RCA]** / 1967 / RCA ✦✦✦✦✦
His smooth, lushly produced crossover hits upset the traditional crowd, but they represent some of the most romantic country recordings of the era. Featured is "Make the World Go Away," "Anytime," "Bouquet of Roses," "The Last Word in Lonesome Is Me," and a re-recording of his classic "Cattle Call." —*Michael McCall*

Best of Eddy Arnold [Curb] / 1990 / Curb ✦✦
Best of Eddy Arnold is a somewhat misleading title. Although several of his greatest songs are included on this album, they are presented in re-recorded versions from the '70s. None of the new versions are particularly bad, but they aren't particularly good, either; stick with the RCA versions. —*Stephen Thomas Erlewine*

Last of the Love Singers: Then & Now / 1993 / RCA ✦✦✦✦
The double-disc box set *Last of the Love Song Singers: Then and Now* is a wasted opportunity. The first disc, called *Then*, is a quick overview of some of Arnold's biggest hits that doesn't offer enough songs. The second disc, titled *Now*, is a collection of new recordings. Though they aren't bad, the new recordings devalue the set's worth as a retrospective and as an introduction. —*Stephen Thomas Erlewine*

Essential Eddy Arnold / Jun. 18, 1996 / RCA ✦✦✦✦
The Essential Eddy Arnold contains the majority of Eddy Arnold's biggest hits, including "Make the World Go Away" and "Cattle Call." It's the only single-disc retrospective that offers a reasonably thorough overview of his hit singles, making it an ideal introduction and—considering that the two-disc box set *Last of the Love Song Singers* contained an entire disc of newly recorded material—the only currently available retrospective that could be considered definitive. —*Thom Owens*

Legendary Performer / RCA ✦✦✦
The double-LP, 24-track collection *Legendary Performer* contains many of Eddy Arnold's best-known hits—including "Anytime," "The Last Word in Lonesome Is Me," "Make the World Go Away," "Tennessee Stud," "The Kentuckian Song"—plus several lesser-known gems, giving a good overview of his entire career. A compilation of this size and quality should be available on compact disc, instead of languishing as an out-of-print LP. —*Thom Owens*

Jimmy Arnold

b. 1952, Fries, VA, **d.** Dec. 26, 1992
Fiddle, Guitar, Harmonica, Vocals / Traditional Bluegrass
Although Jimmy Arnold was never well-known—during his brief life, he recorded only a handful of albums—he remained one of the most acclaimed bluegrass musicians of the '70s and '80s. As a

child, Arnold became interested in music after hearing his friends practicing next door. His first instrument was a guitar, but he soon learned how to play the banjo and by age 12 had founded a bluegrass band, the Twin County Partners, with his cousin Tommy playing mandolin and his friend Wes Golden on guitar. The group became quite popular in their area, which led to appearances on local TV shows and even a single for Stark Records. They disbanded in 1965, and Arnold began performing at music festivals all over the South.

After graduating from high school, Arnold was invited by studio musician Joe Greene to play with him in Nashville. He next teamed up with Wes Golden to play with the Virginia Cut-ups, with whom he cut an album for Latco Records. Subsequently, Arnold joined many bands, including Keith Whitley and the New Tradition, but was frequently fired from the groups due to his excessive drinking. He recorded an album of banjo music, *Strictly Arnold*, in 1974. In 1977, he released his second album, *Jimmy Arnold Guitar*, followed six years later by *Southern Soul*. None of his albums were commercially successful, and Arnold abandoned music in 1984. He opened a tattoo parlor in North Carolina, but he soon fell into drug abuse and used the parlor as a front for selling narcotics. In 1985, he was arrested and briefly served a jail sentence. Following his release from prison, he was the resident artist at Martin Community College for a short time, but he soon returned to performing music. In 1992, he became a member of the Pentecostal Church and went completely sober. However, his body was irreparably damaged—he died of heart failure on Christmas Day in 1992. —*Sandra Brennan*

● **Southern Soul** / 1983 / Rebel ✦✦✦✦

Rainbow Ride / Rebel ✦✦✦✦

Strictly Arnold / Rebel ✦✦✦

Charline Arthur (Charline Highsmith)

b. Sep. 2, 1929, Henrietta, TX, **d.** 1987
Vocals / Honky Tonk, Country Boogie
Charline Arthur didn't play by the rules. During the '50s, country music wasn't particularly receptive of rowdy, racy material sung by females, much less one who refused to submit to the orders of her record company or promoters. No matter how much pressure Arthur received, she didn't change her ways. With a raging temper, she was difficult to work with, angering her producer, Chet Atkins, in particular. Nevertheless, her music was frequently impressive. In some ways, Arthur was a forerunner of rockabilly with her bluesy, raw hillbilly music and her wild stage shows. She was the first female singer in country music to perform in pants and she used the extra freedom to prowl the stage. While her career was extremely brief—she recorded for RCA for three years—her music gained a cult following over the years, as proved by the appearance of Bear Family's compilation, *Welcome to the Club*, in 1986.

The daughter of a Pentecostal preacher, Charline Arthur (born Charline Highsmith) began singing in church while she was in school. At the age of seven, she earned enough money collecting empty bottles to buy a guitar for six dollars. Influenced by the hardcore honky tonk of Ernest Tubb, she wrote her first song, "I've Got the Boogie Blues," when she was 12. By the time she was a teenager, she was performing on a local Texas radio show. Arthur won a spot on a traveling medicine show in the mid-'40s, yet her parents refused to let her leave home. She countered by marrying Jack Arthur, who would later play bass on her records.

In the late '40s, she began singing in honky tonks and nightclubs across Texas, which eventually led to a single with Bullet Records. "I've Got the Boogie Blues"/"Is Love a Game." After she recorded the single, she and Jack moved to Kermit, TX, where she was hired by a radio station as a DJ. Soon, Arthur assembled a band. Performing in local clubs and the radio, she gained a fan base. In 1950, she recorded a single for the small label, Imperial. During this time, Eddy Arnold and his manager Colonel Tom Parker heard Arthur perform. Impressed with what they heard, they directed Julian and Gene Aberbach, owners of the Hill and Range music publishing company, to the singer. The pair signed

her to a publishing deal and landed her a contract with RCA Records in 1953.

Charline Arthur made her first record for RCA early in 1953, recording with session musicians that included Floyd Cramer and Chet Atkins. Her contract with RCA led to appearances with the Louisiana Hayride, the Big D Jamboree, and the Ozark Jubilee. During this time, she frequently performed on the same stage as Elvis Presley, whose mother was a big fan of Arthur. All of her performances were gaining her acclaim—in 1955, she was the runner-up to Kitty Wells in *Country & Western Jamboree* magazine's DJ poll.

However, things weren't going smoothly for Arthur. Although she appeared on the "Prince Albert" portion of the Grand Ole Opry, her material was frequently rejected on the grounds it was too racy. At RCA, Chet Atkins followed Steve Sholes as her record producer, and the two musicians could not get along. Furthermore, she was having no success with any of her records. After her contract expired at the end of 1956, she left RCA for Colin, but she had a similar lack of success there. Shortly after her record label switch, she parted ways with her husband, Jack.

Arthur formed a trio with her sisters Betty Sue and Dottie, but the teaming was unsuccessful. By 1960, she was broke. Arthur moved to Salt Lake City, where she met Ray Pellum, a night club and record label owner that landed her a regular singing job in Chubbuck, ID. During this time, she also recorded for his Eldorado label. In 1965, Arthur headed out to California. Between 1965 and 1978, she recorded for three small labels—Rustic, Wytra, and Republic—with Alice M. Michaels as her manager. Suffering from a debilitating arthritis, she went back to Idaho in 1979, and stayed there until her death in 1987. Charline Arthur lived long enough to see her RCA material reissued by Germany's Bear Family Records in 1986. —*Stephen Thomas Erlewine*

Welcome to the Club / 1986 / Bear Family ✦✦✦✦
Unfortunately out of print, this excellent compilation is culled from Arthur's '50s recordings for RCA. Hard country, with hints of proto-rockabilly, it includes the infamous "Kiss the Baby Goodnight," a song more unforgettable than listenable. —*Dan Cooper*

Leon Ashley

b. May 18, 1936, Covington, GA
Vocals / Country-Pop, Nashville Sound/Countrypolitan
Leon Ashley has a small place in country music history as the first artist to write, record, release, distribute, and publish his own material. That record, "Laura (What's He Got That I Ain't Got)," is also part of Ashley's legacy, becoming a country standard of the '60s and '70s, as it was recorded by a variety of artists, including Marty Robbins and Kenny Rogers. In fact, Ashley had more influence as a songwriter, not a performer. Nevertheless, he had a modestly successful performing career as a country-pop singer that lasted through the '60s and '70s.

Ashley began performing at an early age. When he was nine, he performed on a Covington, GA, radio station, and by the time he was 11, he had his own show. In 1960, he recorded his first single, "He'll Never Go." Released on Goldband, the record didn't gain much attention. He signed for Imperial the following year, releasing "Teen Age Angel" and "It's Alright Baby" to a similar lack of attention. In 1962, he returned to Goldband and recorded one more single, "Not Going Home." Dot Records released his "You Gave Me Reason to Live" in 1964.

Leon Ashley was paired with Margie Singleton to record "How Can We Divide These Little Hearts" in 1966. The following year, the duo married; they continued working together for the rest of their marriage.

1967 was significant for Ashley for another reason—it was the year he founded his own record label, Ashley. Surprisingly, Leon's self-owned and operated record label was more successful for his career than any of the more-established labels he had previously recorded for. "Laura (What's He Got That I Ain't Got)," the third release on Ashley, rocketed to No. 1 on the country charts, and was followed by two other lesser hits later that year (a duet with Margie called "Hangin' On" and "Anna, I'm Taking You Home"). Leon had two more hits in 1968—the Top 15 "Mental Journey" and the duet "You'll Never Be Lonely Again"—and 1969 brought three more hits, "While Your Lover Sleeps," "Back to Birmingham," and "Ain't Gonna Worry." However, that was the end of his brief period of chart success. Leon had one more minor hit single, "Ease Up" in 1972. For the remainder of the decade, he toured with Margie and their manager, Linda G. Denny, and the Country Music Spectacular. Although he no longer had hits, other performers regularly recorded Leon Ashley's songs, including many co-written with Margie. — *Stephen Thomas Erlewine*

Laura (What's He Got That I Ain't Got) / 1967 / RCA Victor ✦✦✦✦

Ode to Bille Joe / 1968 / Hilltop ✦✦✦

Mental Journey / 1969 / Ashley ✦✦✦

A New Brand of Country / 1969 / Ashley ✦✦✦

● **The Best of Leon Ashley** / 1970 / Ashley ✦✦✦✦

Asleep at the Wheel

Neo-Traditionalist Country, Western Swing Revival
The Western swing revivalist band Asleep at the Wheel helped popularize the genre in the '70s and went on to enjoy an eclectic, freewheeling career that earned the group a dedicated following of both fans and critics. Over the course of their career, a number of musicians passed through the group—more than 80, to be precise—but throughout the years, the vision of vocalist/guitarist Ray Benson kept the band together.

Asleep at the Wheel was founded by Benson and Leroy Preston (drums, guitar, vocals) in 1970. Along with Benson's longtime friend Reuben "Lucky Oceans" Gosfield (steel guitar, drums), they played straightforward country at local bars and lodges in Virginia. They were soon joined by guitarist/singer Chris O'Connell, who had just graduated from high school. In 1971, Commander Cody saw the group performing in Washington, DC, and was impressed enough to send his manager Joe Kerr to meet with the band. They signed with Kerr, who convinced the band to move to San Francisco late in that year. Keyboardist Floyd Domino (born Jim Haber) joined the band following an inaugural 30-day tour with Stoney Edwards. After Domino joined the group, Asleep at the Wheel landed a permanent gig at the Longbranch Saloon in Berkeley. They soon cultivated a solid fan base and signed with United Artists Records. Their first album, *Comin' Right at Ya*, was released in 1973. In 1974, they moved to Austin, TX, which eventually became their home base. That year, they released an eponymous album on Epic Records and had their first minor hit, a remake of Louis Jordan's "Choo Choo Ch'Boogie."

Asleep at the Wheel added two members, fiddler Lisa Silver and trumpeter Bobby Womack, and moved to Capitol Records in 1975. Their first album for the label, *Texas Gold*, was their breakthrough, reaching the pop charts and spawning the hit single "The Letter That Johnny Walker Red." The album generated four more hits, and later that year they released *Wheelin' and Dealin'.* By that time four more members, including accordion player Jo-El Sonnier, had joined the lineup. For the rest of the decade, Asleep at the Wheel was one of the most popular country artists in America.

1980, however, was a year of setbacks; Lucky Oceans left the band, and the remaining members soon found that they were over $200,000 in debt. To keep afloat, the group performed TV commercials for Budweiser and worked on movie soundtracks. Shortly afterwards, the group lost Chris O'Connell, who quit to have a baby. In addition to their internal difficulties in the early '80s, Asleep at the Wheel had trouble selling records. The group had a hit album with *Framed* in 1980, but that was their last release for over half a decade. After their self-titled album for MCA-Dot flopped in 1985, Benson tried his hand at producing, working with such artists as Aaron Neville, Rob Wasserman, Willie Nelson, and Bruce Hornsby. By the time Asleep at the Wheel signed with Epic Records in 1987, the group had gone through a number of personnel changes, now consisting of Benson, O'Connell (who had returned from her leave of absence), fiddler Larry Franklin, fiddler Johnny Gimble, bassist Jon Mitchell, pianist/accordionist Tim Alexander, steel guitarist John Ely, saxo-

phonist Mike Francis, and David Sanger. *Asleep at the Wheel 10*, the group's first album for Epic, was released in 1987 and became the hit they needed: the album launched several hit singles, including "House of Blue Lights," "Way Down Texas Way," and the Grammy-winning "String of Pars." Their next Epic album, *Western Standard Time*, came out in 1988 and led to another Grammy for the instrumental "Sugarfoot Rag."

In 1990, Asleep at the Wheel signed with Arista and recorded *Keepin' Me Up Nights*. Two years later, they released *Greatest Hits Live and Kickin',* after which most of the band members left the group. In 1993, a re-formed lineup featuring Benson, fiddler Rickey Turpin, bassist David Earl Miller, drummer Tommy Beavers, and steel guitarist Cindy Cash-Dollar released *Tribute to the Music of Bob Wills and the Texas Playboys* on Liberty. Featuring a number of guest artists, including several original Texas Playboys, Merle Haggard, Willie Nelson, Chet Atkins, Brooks & Dunn, Dolly Parton, and Garth Brooks, the album received excellent reviews and became a big hit. The album *Still Swingin'* appeared in 1994, followed a year later by *Swing Time. — Sandra Brennan*

Comin' Right at Ya / 1973 / EMI America ✦✦✦✦

Asleep at the Wheel [Epic] / 1974 / Epic ✦✦✦
Texas guitarist and singer Ray Benson started this band in the early '70s as a "longhair" tribute to Bob Wills, and they've been swinging ever since. This is their first Columbia album. —*Mark A. Humphrey*

Texas Gold / 1975 / Capitol ✦✦✦
Texas Gold was the album that broke Asleep at the Wheel into the mainstream, and for good reason. Though the band has by no means abandoned their quirky take on Western swing and honky tonk, they opened their sound up on *Texas Gold*, focusing their energy into a series of ten tight, dazzling performances. They divided their energies between standards like "Trouble in Mind" and clever originals like "The Letter That Johnny Walker Red" and "Bump Bounce Boogie." There are a couple of weaker moments, but those are only when the band play by the rules—they sound good, but they sound conventional. Asleep at the Wheel are at their best when they are disregarding genres, and for the great majority of *Texas Gold*, that is exactly what they do. — *Thom Owens*

Asleep at the Wheel [Dot] / 1985 / Dot ✦✦✦✦
Benson by now is revealing a romantic baritone as well as his usual sublime swing. Guest appearances come from Bonnie Raitt and Willie Nelson. —*Michael McCall*

10 / 1987 / Epic ✦✦✦
They have a bodacious Western swing on their 10th Columbia album. —*Mark A. Humphrey*

Western Standard Time / 1988 / Epic ✦✦✦✦
Nicely done Western standards. —*Mark A. Humphrey*

● **Live & Kickin': Greatest Hits** / Aug. 1991 / Arista ✦✦✦✦
Recorded at an Austin roadhouse, *Live and Kickin': Greatest Hits* showcases Asleep at the Wheel running through their best-known material in a kinetic live setting. It's a great introduction to the band—they are never better than they are in concert, and the selection brings out the best in the musicians. —*Stephen Thomas Erlewine*

Best Of / 1992 / CEMA ✦✦✦✦
Features "Route 66," "Bump Bounce Boogie," "Texas, Me & You," and others. —*AMG*

The Swinging Best of Asleep at the Wheel / Oct. 27, 1992 / Epic ✦✦✦✦
The Swingin' Best collects the hits from Asleep at the Wheel's two tenures on the Epic label; in addition to their first hit, 1974's "Choo Choo Ch'Boogie," the album features "House of Blue Lights," "Way Down Texas Way" and "Blowin' Like a Bandit." —*Jason Ankeny*

Tribute to the Music of Bob Wills & The Texas Playboys / Oct. 25, 1993 / Liberty ✦✦✦✦
Benson and The Wheel invite a bus full of guests to pay homage to the King of Western Swing and do so with joyful, rollicking fun. Garth Brooks, Vince Gill, George Strait, Dolly Parton, Marty Stu-

art, and Suzy Bogguss are among those enjoying themselves on this exemplary album. —*Michael McCall*

The Wheel Keeps on Rollin' / 1995 / Capitol Nashville ✦✦✦
As the title suggests, *Wheel Keeps on Rollin'* doesn't offer anything new from Asleep at the Wheel, but that's not a bad thing at all. For over 20 years, the group has been the leading Western swing group in the United States, bringing the music to several new generations of fans. *Wheel Keeps on Rollin'* is another first-rate collection of music. It might not have the conceptual power of their previous *Tribute to the Music of Bob Wills & the Texas Playboys*, nor is it as raw as their earliest recordings, but it is an album that will satisfy their dedicated fans. —*Stephen Thomas Erlewine*

Chet Atkins (Chester Burton Atkins)

b. Jun. 20, 1924, Luttrell, TN
Fiddle, Guitar / Traditional Country, Country-Pop, Nashville Sound/Countrypolitan, Country Boogie
Without Chet Atkins, country music may never have crossed over into the pop charts in the '50s and '60s. Although he has recorded hundreds of solo records, Chet Atkins' largest influence came as a session musician and a record producer. During the '50s and '60s, he helped create the Nashville sound, a style of country music that owed nearly as much to pop as it did to honky tonk.

As a guitarist, he is without parallel. Atkins' style grew out of his admiration for Merle Travis, expanding Travis' signature syncopated thumb-and-fingers roll into new territory.

Interestingly, Chet Atkins didn't begin his musical career by playing guitar. On the recommendation of his older brother, Lowell, he began playing the fiddle as a child. However, Chet was still attracted to the guitar and at the age of nine, he traded a pistol for a guitar. Atkins learned his instrument rapidly, becoming an accomplished player by the time he left high school in 1941. Using a variety of contacts, he wound up performing on the *Bill Carlisle Show* on WNOX in Knoxville, TN, as well as becoming part of the Dixie Swingers. Atkins worked with Homer and Jethro while he was at the radio station. After three years, he moved to a radio station in Cincinnati.

Supporting Red Foley, Atkins made his first appearance at the Grand Ole Opry in 1946. That same year, he made his first records, recording for Bullet. Atkins also began making regular performances on the WRVA radio station in Richmond, VA, but he was repeatedly fired because his musical arrangements differed from the expectations of the station's executives. He eventually moved to Springfield, MO, working for the KWTO station. A tape of one of Atkins' performances was sent to RCA Victor's office in Chicago. Eventually, it worked its way to Steve Sholes, the head of country music at RCA. Sholes had heard Atkins previously and had been trying to find him for several years. By the time Sholes heard the tape, Atkins had moved to Denver, CO, and was playing with Shorty Thompson and His Rangers. Upon receiving the call from RCA, he moved to Nashville to record.

Once he arrived in Nashville, Chet recorded eight tracks for the label, five of which featured the guitarist singing. Impressed by his playing, Sholes made Atkins the studio guitarist for all of RCA studio's Nashville sessions in 1949. The following year, Mother Maybelle and the Carter Sisters hired him as a regular on the Grand Ole Opry, making his place in Nashville's musical community secure. While he worked for RCA, he played on many hit records and helped fashion the Nashville sound. RCA appreciated his work and made him a consultant to the company's Nashville division in 1953. That year, the label began to issue a number of instrumental albums that showcased Atkins' considerable talents. Two years later, he scored his first hit with a version of "Mr. Sandman"; it was followed by "Silver Bell," a duet with Hank Snow. By the late '50s, Chet Atkins was known throughout the music industry as a first-rate player. Not only did his records sell well, he designed guitars for Gibson and Gretsch; models of these instruments continued to sell in the '90s.

Steve Sholes left for New York in 1957 to act as head of pop A&R, leaving Atkins as the manager of RCA's Nashville division. However, the guitarist didn't abandon performing, and through-

Chet Atkins

out the early '60s his star continued to rise. He played the Newport Jazz Festival in 1960; in 1961, he performed at the White House. Atkins had his first Top Five hit in 1965 with a reworking of Boots Randolph's "Yakety Sax," retitled "Yakety Axe"; in addition to being a sizable country hit, the song crossed over to the pop charts. Atkins' role behind the scenes was thriving as well. He produced hits for the majority of RCA's Nashville acts, including Elvis Presley and Eddy Arnold, and discovered a wealth of talent, including Don Gibson, Waylon Jennings, Floyd Cramer, Charley Pride, Bobby Bare, and Connie Smith. Because of his consistent track record, Atkins was promoted to vice-president of RCA's country division when Steve Sholes died in 1968.

The following year, Atkins had his last major hit single, "Country Gentleman." In the late '60s and early '70s, several minor hits followed, but only one song, "Prissy" (1968), made it into the Top 40. Instead, the guitarist's major musical contribution in the early part of the '70s was with Homer and Jethro. Under the name the Nashville String Band, the trio released five albums between 1970 and 1972. Following Homer's death, Atkins continued to work with Jethro.

Atkins continued to record for RCA throughout the '70s, although he was creatively stifled by the label by the end of the decade. The guitarist wanted to record a jazz album, but he was met with resistance by the label. In 1982, he left RCA and signed with Columbia, releasing his first album for the label, *Work It Out with Chet Atkins*, in 1983. During his time at Columbia, Atkins departed from his traditional country roots, demonstrating that he was a bold and tasteful jazz guitarist as well. He did return to country on occasion, particularly on duet albums with Mark Knopfler and Jerry Reed, but by and large, Atkins' Columbia records demonstrated a more adventurous guitarist than was previously captured on his RCA albums.

Throughout his career, Chet Atkins earned numerous awards, including 11 Grammy awards and nine CMA "Instrumentalist of the Year" honors, as well as a Lifetime Achievement Award from NARAS. Although his award list is impressive, it only begins to convey his contribution to country music. —*Stephen Thomas Erlewine*

The Other Chet Atkins / 1960 / RCA ✦✦✦
The Other Chet Atkins is something of an unusual entry in Atkins' catalog—an entire album of the guitarist playing Spanish guitar, with no electric instruments or country music to be heard. It's a gentle, lilting album, featuring understated versions of "The Streets of Laredo," "Maria Elena," "Marcheta," and "Begin the Beguine." —*Thom Owens*

Teensville / 1960 / RCA ✦✦
As the title indicates, *Teensville* is Chet Atkins' attempt to cut a record that appealed to the teenage audience weaned on rock 'n'

roll. Though he records a fair amount of rock, rockabilly, R&B, and country songs—and the Everly Brothers, whom he produced, wrote the liner notes—he never captures the raw spark of rock 'n' roll. What shines through is Atkins' understated elegance. All of the numbers are arranged as pop instrumentals and his guitar playing is so tasteful that it makes the half-hearted execution almost forgivable. —*Stephen Thomas Erlewine*

Chet Atkins Picks on the Beatles / 1965 / RCA ✦✦
Chet Atkins Picks on the Beatles is an entertaining, if ultimately disposable, artifact. Atkins plays a cross-section of the Beatles' early hits, dressing them up as country-pop or light rockabilly. As always, his playing is subtle and tasteful, but the album doesn't provide enough inventive or energetic performances to be of lasting interest. —*Stephen Thomas Erlewine*

Pickin' My Way / 1970 / Mobile Fidelity ✦✦✦✦
Superior sound. Two previous Atkins albums on CD. —*Ron Wynn*

Stay Tuned / 1985 / Columbia ✦✦✦✦
This first-rate session teams Atkins with George Benson, Earl Klugh, Larry Carlton, and Mark Knopfler. —*Ron Wynn*

The Best of Chet Atkins & Friends / 1987 / RCA ✦✦✦
Atkins and his friends play "Avalon," "Twichy," "Terry on the Turnpike," "Sweet Georgia Brown," and other standards. —*AMG*

The Best of Chet Atkins & Friends, Vol. 2 / 1987 / RCA ✦✦✦
The second volume includes "Give the World a Smile," "Yakety Axe," "Alley Cat," "Que Sera, Sera," and others. —*AMG*

Neck & Neck / Feb. 1991 / Columbia ✦✦✦✦
Working with Dire Straits guitarist Mark Knopfler had a rejuvenating effect on Chet Atkins. Knopfler has Atkins moving toward his country roots, but both guitarists still play with a tasteful, jazzy sensibility. Atkins has, however, abandoned the overt jazz-fusion pretensions that sank most of his '80s records. With its direct, understated approach, *Neck and Neck* is the most focused and arguably the most rewarding record Atkins has released. —*Stephen Thomas Erlewine*

★ **The RCA Years** / Oct. 1992 / RCA ✦✦✦✦✦
The RCA Years—1947-1981 isn't quite a definitive compilation, but it is the closest attempt at a comprehensive retrospective to date. Chet Atkins compiled the set himself, which means it's filled with idiosyncratic selections that aren't necessarily his most representative. Nevertheless, *The RCA Years* does give a sense of Atkins' accomplishments and the breadth of his talents. —*Stephen Thomas Erlewine*

Galloping Guitar / 1993 / Bear Family ✦✦✦✦
A wonderful multi-disc boxed set retrospective of Atkins' earliest recordings. Casual fans will be surprised to hear that Chet was originally marketed as a vocalist/guitarist, much the same as then popular Merle Travis was on Capitol. His eventual move over to strict instrumentals doesn't come until the end of this box set, with guest vocalists flitting in and out of the picture, but Atkins' guitar is solid throughout. —*Cub Koda*

Almost Alone / Mar. 12, 1996 / Columbia ✦✦✦
On this album of nearly solo guitar instrumentals, Chet Atkins plays with his usual ease and dexterity, beginning with some tasty originals and gradually moving into such standards as "Mr. BoJangles" and "Cheek to Cheek." The most unusual track is the in-concert vocal performance "I Still Write Your Name in the Snow," which is a bit more risque than you might expect, but makes a welcome change of pace. —*William Ruhlmann*

Essential Chet Atkins / Jun. 18, 1996 / RCA ✦✦✦✦
Since *The Essential Chet Atkins* concentrates on his instrumental tracks—including hits like "Mr. Sandman" and "Yakety Axe"—it functions as the best single-disc retrospective of the guitarist. It is also one of the only collections that concisely demonstrates his subtly dazzling virtuosity. —*Thom Owens*

Mike Auldridge

b. Dec. 30, 1938, Washington, DC
Dobro / Progressive Bluegrass, Traditional Bluegrass
Generally considered one of the masters of bluegrass dobro, Mike Auldridge was raised in Kensington, MD, where he began playing

guitar at age 12, banjo at 16, and dobro at 17. In 1954, he made his first appearance on local radio, playing in a band with his brother Dave. In 1967, he graduated from the University of Maryland and became a commercial artist, continuing to play dobro occasionally at local clubs. In 1969 he joined the New Shades of Green; within a year, the bluegrass group had gained a stong following, and Auldridge was considered an innovator in the relatively new field of bluegrass dobro.

He became a member of the Seldom Scene in 1971, but still did session work, playing on albums by Emmylou Harris, Jonathan Edwards, Linda Ronstadt, and Jimmy Arnold. He also recorded several solo albums, including *Dobro* (1972), *Blues & Bluegrass* (1974), and *Eight-String Swing* (1982). Auldridge teamed with singer/mandolin player Lou Reid and bassist T. Michael Coleman in 1989 for the album *High Time*. Also in 1989, he released a solo album, *Treasures Untold*. Auldridge continued to play concerts and record as a session musician in the '90s. —*Sandra Brennan*

Blues & Bluegrass / 1974 / Takoma ✦✦✦✦
Dobro / 1974 / Takoma ✦✦✦
● **Dobro/Blues & Bluegrass** / 1974 / Takoma ✦✦✦✦
Two of Mike Auldridge's early '70s albums, *Dobro* and *Blues & Bluegrass*, are combined on this single disc, which provides an excellent introduction to the dobroist. —*Thom Owens*

Mike Auldridge / 1976 / Flying Fish ✦✦✦✦
On this one, the bluegrass dobroist is joined by apt accompanists. —*Mark A. Humphrey*

Mike Auldridge & Old Dog / 1978 / Flying Fish ✦✦✦
On this bluegrass album, Auldridge, a dobro legend, joins "Old Dog" for some fine picking and dulcet vocals. —*AMG*

Slidin' Smoke / 1979 / Flying Fish ✦✦✦✦
On this mellow album, Auldridge (dobro) and Newman (steel guitar) add a touch of jazz to their bluegrass sound. —*AMG*

Eight String Swing / 1988 / Sugar Hill ✦✦✦
As the title suggests, Mike Auldridge recorded *Eight String Swing* with a specially made, eight-string dobro, which helped him ease his music out of traditional bluegrass and into country, jazz, Western swing, and folk. Auldridge is joined by several of his Seldom Scene cohorts and fiddler Jimmy Arnold on the album, and the sympathetic support adds depth to both the originals and the eclectic covers (Duke Ellington's "Caravan," Willie Nelson's "Crazy," Benny Goodman's "Stompin' at the Savoy"). —*Stephen Thomas Erlewine*

Treasures Untold / 1989 / Sugar Hill ✦✦✦✦
Treasures Untold is comprised entirely of traditional Country & Western songs, ranging from cowboy standards ("Deep Water," "Shenandoah Waltz") to honky tonk ("Walking the Floor Over You," "Drivin' Nails in My Coffin"). Most of the record features lead vocals by Doc Watson, Tony Rice, and John Starling, while Auldridge simply plays some stunning dobro, but he does step to the mike for a couple of songs, including the title track. —*Thom Owens*

High Times / 1989 / Sugar Hill ✦✦✦

Austin Lounge Lizards

Progressive Bluegrass
The Austin Lounge Lizards are a country bluegrass band out of Austin. The Lizards are Hank Card (guitar, vocals), Conrad Deisler (guitar, mandolin), Tom Pittman (banjo, pedal steel, vocals), Michael Stevens (bass, vocals), and Tim Wilson (mandolin, fiddle, vocals). After the first album, Paul "Tex" Sweeney (mandolin) and Kirk Williams (bass, vocals) replaced Stevens and Wilson. They are known for the humor in their songs and live shows. The group's first album, *Creatures from the Black Saloon*, was released in 1984.—*Chip Renner*

● **Creatures from the Black Saloon** / 1984 / Watermelon ✦✦✦✦
Imagine tradition-steeped Texas swing fused to Monty Python, and you have an idea what's in store with the Austin Lounge Lizards. The Lizards can serve up the tastiest country licks imaginable while at the same time trashing every old West cliche/tradition in the book. The group's debut *Creatures from the Black*

Lagoon, revealed such classics as "The Car Hank Died In," "Kool Whip" (Devo meets the Bonzo Dog Band), and "Saguaro" (wailing pedal steel and mock heroic baritone rendering the tale of a twerpy urban cowpoke duelling a gang of desperado cacti—and losing). —*Roch Parisien*

The Highway Cafe of the Damned / 1988 / Watermelon ✦✦✦✦
Another good, solid, humor-packed CD featuring "The Highway Cafe of the Damned," "Industrial Strength Tranquilizer," "Ballad of Ronald Reagan," and more. —*Chip Renner*

Lizard Vision / 1991 / Flying Fish ✦✦✦
This very funny album was a Grammy nominee. It features the hit "Jesus Loves Me." —*Chip Renner*

Paint Me on Velvet / 1993 / Flying Fish ✦✦✦

Small Minds / 1995 / Watermelon ✦✦✦
The Lizards offer up a sly collection of country/R&B-flavored songs that range from a commentary on the singer's intelligence in "Shallow End of the Gene Pool" to "Truckload of Art," which blows New York's elitist art attitude all over the road. The playing is greasy and dynamic. These guys know how to play no matter how much genre hopping they do. One imagines that these songs function best in a crowded smoke-filled bar, but it is a testament to the Austin Lounge Lizards that such ephemeral material stands up on record. —*Richard Meyer*

Gene Autry (Orvin Gene Autry)

b. Sep. 29, 1907, Tioga Springs, TX
Guitar, Vocals / Cowboy
Gene Autry was more than a musician. His music, coupled with his careers in movies and on radio and television, made him a part of the mythos that has made up the American identity for the past hundred years—John Wayne with a little bit of Sam Houston and Davy Crockett all rolled into one, with a great singing voice and an ear for music added on. He defined country music for two generations of listeners, and cowboy songs for much of this century, and American music for much of the world. He was country music's first genuine "multimedia" star, the best known Country & Western singer on records, in movies, on radio, and television from the early '30s until the mid-'50s. His 300 songs cut between 1929 and 1964 include nine gold record awards and one platinum record; his 93 movies saved one big chunk of the movie industry, delighted millions, and made millionaires of several producers (as well as Autry himself); his radio and television shows were even more popular and successful; and a number of his songs outside of the Country & Western field have become American pop-culture touchstones.

The biggest selling Country & Western singer of the middle of the century was born Orvin Gene Autry on September 29, 1907, in the tiny Texas town of Tioga, the son of Delbert and Elnora Ozmont Autry. He was first taught to sing at age five by his grandfather, William T. Autry, a Baptist preacher and descendant of some of the earliest settlers in Texas, contemporaries of the Houstons and the Crocketts (an Autry had died at the Alamo). The boy's interest in music was encouraged by his mother, who taught him hymns and folk songs, and read psalms to him at night. Autry got his first guitar at age 12, bought from the Sears, Roebuck catalog for eight dollars (saved from his work as a hired hand on his uncle's farm baling and stacking hay). By the time he was 15, he had played anyplace there was to perform in Tioga, including school plays and the local cafe, but made most of his living working for the railroad as an apprentice at $35 a month. Later on, as a proper telegraph operator, he was making $150 a month which, in those days, was a comfortable income in their part of Texas.

He was working the four-to-midnight shift at the local telegraph office in Chelsea, OK, one summer night in 1927 when, to break up the monotony, he began strumming a guitar and singing quietly to himself. A customer came into the office; rather than insisting upon immediate service, he motioned for Autry to continue singing, then sat down to watch and listen while he looked over the pages he was preparing to send. At one point, the visitor asked him to sing another. Finally, after dropping his copy on the counter, the customer told Autry that with some hard

work, he might have a future on the radio, and should consider going to New York to pursue a singing career. The man, whom Autry had recognized instantly, was Will Rogers, the humorist, writer, movie actor, and one of the most popular figures in the entertainment world of that era.

Autry didn't immediately give up his job, but just over a year later, he was in New York auditioning for a representative of RCA-Victor. The judgment was that he had a good voice, but should stay away from pop hits, find his own kind of songs and his own sound, and get some experience. He was back six months later, on October 9, 1929, cutting his first record, "My Dreaming of You"/ "My Alabama Home," for Victor. Two weeks later, Autry was making a demo record for the Columbia label of Jimmie Rodgers' "Blue Yodel No. 5." Present that same day in the studio were two up-and-coming singers, Rudy Vallee and Kate Smith. Autry found himself being pressured to sign an exclusive contract with Victor, but chose instead to sign with the American Record Corporation. Their general manager, Arthur Sattherly (who would later record Leadbelly, among many other acts), persuaded Autry that while Victor was a large company and could offer more money and a better marketing apparatus, he would be lost at Victor amid its existing stable of stars, whereas ARC would treat him as their most important star. Additionally, Sattherly—through a series of arrangements involving major retail and chain stores across the country—now had the means to get Autry's records into people's hands as easily as Victor.

His first recordings had just been released when his mother, who'd been ill for months, died at the age of 45, apparently of cancer. Autry's father began drifting away soon afterward, and he became the head of the family and the main supporter of his two sisters and younger brother. In early December of 1929, Autry cut his first six sides for ARC. The music was a mix of hillbilly, blues, country, yodel songs, and cowboy ballads. His breakthrough record, "That Silver-Haired Daddy of Mine," co-written by Autry and his friend Jimmy Long one night at the railroad depot, was released in 1931. The song had sold 30,000 copies within a month, and by the end of a year 500,000 copies had been sold, an occasion that American Records decided to mark with the public presentation of a gold-plated copy of the record. Autry received a second gold record when sales later broke one million. And that was where the notion of the Gold Record Award was born. The record also led him into a new career on the radio as Oklahoma's Yodeling Cowboy on the *National Barn Dance* show sponsored by WLS out of Chicago. It was there that Autry became a major national star—his record sales rose, assisted by his exposure on radio.

During the early years of his career, Autry brought a number of important collaborators and musicians onboard. Among them were Fred Rose, the songwriter (later responsible for "Your Cheatin' Heart") with whom he collaborated on many of his hits; and fiddle player Carl Cotner (who also played sax, clarinet, and piano), who became his arranger. Autry had a knack for knowing a good song when he heard it (though he almost passed on the biggest hit of his career), and for knowing when a song needed something extra in its arrangement, but it was Cotner who was able to translate his sensibilities into musical notes and arrangements. Mary Ford, later of Les Paul fame, was in Autry's band at one time, and in 1936, Autry signed up a 17-year-old guitar player named Merle Travis, the future country star and songwriter.

By the early '30s, Autry became one of the most beloved singers in Country & Western music. By 1933, he was getting fan letters by the hundreds every week, and his record sales were only going up. Autry's career might've been made right there, but fate intervened again that year, in the form of the movie business. The Western—especially the "B" Western, the bottom-of-the-bill, low-budget action oater—had been hit very hard by the coming of sound in the years 1927 to 1929. Audiences expected dialogue in their movies, and most Western stars up to that time were a lot better at riding, roping, and shooting than reading lines. Not only did producers and directors need something to fill up the soundtracks of their movies, especially on the limited budgets of the B-Westerns, but something to substitute for violent action, which was being increasingly criticized by citizen groups.

Cowboy star Ken Maynard, who was a great trick rider and stuntman but no singer, had tried singing songs in a few of his movies, and the producers noticed that the songs had gone over well despite his vocal limitations. Maynard was making another Western, *In Old Santa Fe* (1934), for Mascot Pictures, and producer Nat Levine decided to try an experiment, putting in a musical number sung by a professional. By sheer chance, the American Record Company and Mascot Pictures were locked together financially, though indirectly, and with the help from the president of ARC, Levine was steered toward Autry.

A phone call brought the young singer and another ARC performer—multi-instrumentalist/comedian Smiley Burnette—out to Hollywood, where, after a quick meeting and screen test, the two were put into *In Old Santa Fe*. Autry had only one scene, singing a song and calling a square dance, but that scene proved to be one of the most popular parts of the movie.

Levine next stuck Autry and Burnette into a Ken Maynard serial, *Mystery Mountain*, in minor supporting roles. But Autry's next appearance was much more important, as the star of the highly successful 12-chapter serial *The Phantom Empire*. Perhaps recognizing that Autry was no "actor," and that he had an audience of millions already, he, the writers, and the producer agreed that he should simply play "Gene Autry," a good-natured radio singer and sometime cowboy. The success of Autry's early films was not enough to save Mascot Pictures, which collapsed under the weight of debts held by Consolidated Film Laboratories, which did Mascot's film processing. In 1935, Consolidated forced a merger of Mascot and a handful of other small studios and formed Republic Pictures, with Consolidated's president Herbert J. Yates at the helm. Republic thrived in the B-movie market, ultimately dominating the entire field for the next 20 years. And central to Republic's success were the Westerns of Gene Autry.

His first starring Western for the newly organized Republic Pictures, *Tumbling Tumbleweeds* (released Sept. 5, 1935), which also included the singing group the Sons of the Pioneers, was a huge hit, and was followed by *Melody Trail*, *The Sagebrush Troubador*, and *The Singing Vagabond*, all released during the final three months of 1935. Autry settled into a schedule of one movie every six weeks, or eight per year, at $5000 per movie, and a formula was quickly established. The production values on these movies were modest, in keeping with their low budgets and tight shooting schedules, but within the framework of B-Westerns, and the context of their music, they were first-rate productions. By 1937, and for five years after—a string that was only broken when he enlisted in the Army during World War II—Autry was rated in an industry survey of theater owners as one of the top ten box-office attractions in the country, alongside the likes of James Cagney and Clark Gable. Autry was the only cowboy star to make the list, and the only actor from B-movies on the list.

For Republic Pictures, his movies were such a cash cow, and so popular in the Southern, border, and Western states, that the tiny studio was able to use them as a way to force "block booking" on theater owners and chains—that is, theaters only got access to the Autry movies scheduled each season if they bought all of Republic's titles for that season. It was Autry's discovery of this policy (which, in fairness, was practiced by every major studio at the time, and led to the anti-trust suit by the government that ultimately forced the studios to give up their theater chains) in early 1938 that led to his first break with Republic. The problems had been brewing for some time, over Autry's unhappiness at never having gotten a raise from his original Mascot-era $5000-per-movie deal, and contractual clauses—which had never been exercised, but worried him nonetheless—giving Republic a share of his radio, personal appearance, and endorsement earnings. After trying unsuccessfully to work out the problems with Yates, Autry walked out of the studio chief's office and thereafter refused to report for the first day's shooting on a movie called *Washington Cowboy*, later retitled *Under Western Stars* when it became the debut of Roy Rogers.

After eight months of legal sparring, Autry was enjoined from making live appearances. Republic, however, found itself with an uprising of theater owners and chains on its hands—without a guarantee that they would have any Autry movies to release, the

studio's entire annual distribution plans were jeopardized. By the fall of 1938 the two sides had come to terms, with raises for Autry and freedom from the most onerous clauses in his old contract. Despite his best efforts, however, he couldn't help the theater owners over the block-booking policy, for it was now entrenched in the industry and an integral part of Republic's business plan.

Meanwhile, his recording career continued, often in tandem with the movies. Whenever Republic could, they licensed the rights to whatever hit song Autry had most recently recorded to use it as the title of his newest picture—when they did this, they always charged the theater owners somewhat more for the film, and they paid it, because the song had "pre-sold" the movie to the public. The songs kept coming, sometimes out of the movies themselves, and not always his own: Autry's friend Ray Whitley had written "Back in the Saddle Again" for a 1938 George O'Brien Western called *Border G-Man*, and when Autry was looking for a theme song for his own radio show, he went back to Whitley's song, made a few changes, and recorded it himself. Along with "That Silver-Haired Daddy of Mine," it was the song he would be most closely associated with.

Autry's career was interrupted by his service in the military during World War II, but when he returned to the recording and movie studios in 1945, he resumed both his singing and film careers without skipping a beat. He was still a name to be reckoned with at the box office, although he was never again ranked among the top ten money-making stars of movies. The cultural dislocations caused by World War II and their effect upon rural and small town America and on the movie business, as well as the impending arrival of television, had shrunk the B-movie market to a shadow of its 1930s glory. His movies still made money, however, and he kept making them right into the beginning of the 1950s, after which he moved into television production—Autry had already begun buying up radio stations before the war, and by the early '50s he was the owner of several television stations, a studio, and his own production company, where he made his own television program as well as others that he owned.

His singing career was bigger than ever, however. Even before the war, Autry had occasionally moved away from country music and scored big, as with his 1940 hit version of "Blueberry Hill," which predated Fats Domino's recording by 16 years. After the war, he still did cowboy and country songs such as "Silver Spurs" and "Sioux City Sue," sprinkled with occasional folk songs and pop numbers. In 1949, however, Autry scored the biggest single hit of his career—and possibly the second- or third-biggest hit song ever recorded up to that time—with "Rudolph the Red-Nosed Reindeer," a song by Johnny Marks that Autry had recorded only reluctantly, in a single take at the end of a session. That same year, he cut "(Ghost) Riders in the Sky," a number by a former forest ranger named Stan Jones, which became both a country and pop music standard, cut by everyone from Vaughan Monroe to Johnny Cash.

By the mid-'50s, Autry's career had slowed. Rock 'n' roll and rhythm & blues were attracting younger listeners, and a new generation of country music stars, heralded by Johnny Cash and Marty Robbins, were beginning to attract serious sales. Autry, then in his forties, still had his audience, but he gradually receded from the limelight to attend to his burgeoning business interests. —*Bruce Eder*

Country Music Hall of Fame / 1970 / Columbia ✦✦✦✦
Country's first hat act was the inspiration to a generation crooning, smooth and sincere, in the Roosevelt era. —*Mark A. Humphrey*

Back in the Saddle Again / 1977 / Sony ✦✦✦✦
This 12-song budget collection covers Autry's early career at Columbia Records, much of which is not usually included on compilations—not only the expected cowboy songs ("Way Out West in Texas," "The Dying Cowgirl" etc., which feature Autry yodeling), but blues as well. Going back to 1931 and "Mississippi Valley Blues," a duet with Jimmy Long, and other, less well remembered songs, the sound is rougher and less sophisticated than that which he subsequently achieved in the studio. Some of

the music almost has the texture of field recordings, Autry's basic, unaffected singing style and the relatively primitive recorded sound combining to give the music an authentic feel that is startling today. The version of "Back in the Saddle Again" featured here is also different from that usually included in Autry collections. The age and conditions of some of the masters has made this disc a little noisier than usual, but for fans who want to hear what Autry sounded like early in his career, add an extra notch to the rating. —*Bruce Eder*

Columbia Historic Edition / 1982 / Columbia ✦✦✦✦
This ten-song low—to mid-priced collection covers yet more Autry songs that aren't on the other budget Autry releases—and, like them, includes only minimal annotation. Originally released by the Vocalion, Okeh, Banner, and Columbia labels between 1935 and 1944, this is a chunk of an Autry best-of set, featuring his cover of Bob Nolan's "Tumbling Tumbleweeds," the gentle Western swing-styled "I'll Go Ridin' Down That Texas Trail," "Don't Fence Me In" (which is best remembered today as the title of a Roy Rogers B-Western), the ravishingly romantic "Amapola" (which makes "South of the Border" seem tepid), and the previously unreleased romantic ballad "There's a New Moon Over My Shoulder," one of the catchiest, bounciest, most well-played songs in Autry's output. In the absence of a complete Gene Autry set from Bear Family (which would require at least eight CDs), it's worth springing for this collection, which was prepared with the assistance of the Country Music Foundation, along with the others. —*Bruce Eder*

Golden Hits / 1985 / Good Music ✦✦✦✦
If this 20-song collection were easy to find, it would probably be a good starting point for Autry fans to start collecting him on CD. But it's not, being a product of the Good Music Company of Katonah, NY. It does, however, have the most popular versions of many of Autry's most familiar songs, including "Back in the Saddle Again," "That Silver-Haired Daddy of Mine," "You Are My Sunshine," "South of the Border," and "Goodbye, Little Darlin' Goodbye," grouped with such standards as "Tumbling Tumbleweeds," "Home on the Range," "Sioux City Sue," "Red River Valley," and "The Last Roundup," all with good sound. —*Bruce Eder*

Christmas Favorites / 1989 / CBS Special Products ✦✦✦✦
Beyond his work as a singer of cowboy songs and pop standards, Gene Autry also had a major career as a singer of novelty songs, including Christmas songs, recording the second biggest seller of them all after "White Christmas," "Rudolph, the Red-Nosed Reindeer," in 1948. He cut three other Christmas songs that day, plus a bunch more throughout his career, and 14 of them (including "Rudolph") are included here, among them such stylized pieces as "The Night Before Christmas (In Texas, That Is)" as well as familiar fare like "Here Comes Santa Claus" and "Santa Claus Is Coming to Town." The voice is so honest and unaffected, that you absolutely want to believe that Santa is somewhere out there, and the arrangements are top-notch, bright, and engaging in their own right. Two of them feature Autry in duets with Rosemary Clooney (mother of George, for any youngsters reading this) when she was in her prime. —*Bruce Eder*

Greatest Hits / 1992 / Sony ✦✦✦✦
Gene Autry was the greatest Western singer who ever stepped in front of a microphone, and if anyone doubts it, this budget-priced ten-song collection will change their minds. This 27-minute CD may not offer a lot in length, and any real Autry greatest hits collection could easily run 20 songs and still be skimpy. But the ten songs that are here are the ones for which audiences most loved Autry—"That Silver-Haired Daddy of Mine," "You Are My Sunshine," "Back in the Saddle Again," "Have I Told You Lately That I Love You," "Blueberry Hill" (he had the hit with it more than ten years before Fats Domino), "South of the Border," and Stan Jones' "(Ghost) Riders in the Sky," the latter in its most soulful and moving interpretation ever. The sound is excellent, and the particular versions (Autry recorded a couple of these numbers more than once) are definitive. There are no notes or recording dates, but the music is so beguiling that this is a must-own bargain volume. —*Bruce Eder*

★ **The Essential Gene Autry** / Aug. 18, 1992 / Columbia/Legacy ✦✦✦✦✦
This would be a perfect Autry collection but for the fact that it has only 18 songs, when there was room for about 25, and the producers evidently think that "South of the Border" and "Blueberry Hill" aren't "essential." But you do get "The Yellow Rose of Texas," "The Last Round-up," "Take Me Back to My Boots and Saddle," "The Call of the Canyon," "It Makes No Difference Now," "Deep in the Heart of Texas," "Tumbling Tumbleweeds" (featuring Jimmy Long and Smiley Burnette) and "Maria Elena," among others. And for a change, there are decent, detailed notes, though as soon as Bear Family gets around to it, their release will probably put all of these to shame. —*Bruce Eder*

South of the Border / 1994 / Castle ✦✦✦
This isn't a bad collection, mid-priced with 18 songs, also Mexican or Spanish theme material. There are no dates for the music listed, although all of it is in stereo, and dates from long after the classic Columbia recordings. Autry's voice is less rich and attractive than those classic sides, and the cover art is tacky, but there's a lot here that isn't easy to find elsewhere on compact disc, including "You Belong to My Heart," "El Rancho Grande," "In a Little Spanish Town," "My Adobe Hacienda," and "A Gay Ranchero," as well as his recordings of "Dixie Cannon Ball," "Serenade of the Bells," and "Down in the Valley." The material tends toward the more romantic pop side of Autry's repertory, and fans of his blues and cowboy songs may want to skip this release. But anyone who likes his voice or enjoys the romantic side of singing cowboy movies will love this collection—and his performance of "Under Fiesta Stars" by itself will prove worth the price. —*Bruce Eder*

● **Portrait of an Artist** / 1995 / Sound Exchange ✦✦✦✦
Now this is more like it—the notes still aren't much, but there are 22 songs here, including most of the best material of the existing budget collections, except for the early '30s-focused "Back in the Saddle Again" (yet another, different, even more lively version of that song is present here), and a few odd items like "Buttons and Bows" that just aren't around elsewhere. The sound is about as good as it gets, and this would be the collection to go out and buy, except that it's a mail-order item from Time Warner on its Sound Exchange imprint, and, thus, you can't find it in stores, except maybe as a used item. And who would sell anything this good? —*Bruce Eder*

Back in the Saddle Again / 1996 / ASV ✦✦✦✦
This is one of the more interesting and appealing of Autry's compact discs, covering his earliest hillbilly and blues numbers, including "High Steppin' Mama" and "Blue Yodel No. 5," as well as alternate versions of such standards as "You Are My Sunshine" and "South of the Border" (in versions utterly different from those on the various Sony compilations) and pop numbers like "Blueberry Hill" going right into the end of World War II. The 25 songs run from the late 1920s through the mid-1940s, and the sound is generally excellent, even on the older tracks, although "That Silver Haired Daddy of Mine" and a handful of others are pretty rough. —*Bruce Eder*

Blues Singer 1929-1931: Booger Rooger Saturday / Oct. 8, 1996 / ✦✦✦✦
If your concept of a blues singer embraces the sound of country music singer Jimmie Rodgers, as well as a Muddy Waters sideman like Jimmy Rogers, then this collection will make perfect sense to you. This superlative collection of Autry's earliest recordings for various Columbia budget labels like Melotone, Banner, Velvet Tone, Diva, and Oriole cast the latter-day cowboy hero in direct competition with Rodgers, sometimes recording covers of well known hits by the Singing Brakeman. While seven of the 23 tracks collected here are Rodgers tunes (and superlative covers they are, too), ten of them are from Autry's pen, an indication that he not only had his own ideas to impart but had figured the game out early from a business standpoint as well. On the majority of tracks, Autry is only accompanied by his yodeling and his acoustic guitar, but the addition on certain tracks of Roy Smeck on steel guitar or banjo certainly spices things up while allowing Gene to play some nifty fills in tandem. The biggest surprise, of course, is how comfortable Autry sounds on all of this material, clearly

enjoying himself while finding his own voice as the sessions progress toward his "cowboy singer" breakthrough, only a year away from the last of these recordings. Yes, Gene Autry sang the blues and was pretty good at it, too. A landmark in country music's history while clearly demonstrating the cross genre appeal of the blues as a musical form accessible to everyone. —*Cub Koda*

Sing, Cowboy, Sing! The Gene Autry Collection / Mar. 18, 1997 / Rhino ✦✦✦✦

Sing, Cowboy, Sing!: The Gene Autry Collection is a comprehensive overview of the most famous singing cowboy in Hollywood history. Spanning three CDs and 84 tracks, the box set contains every one of Autry's biggest hits, plus several unreleased cuts from his *Melody Ranch* radio show and a handful of rarities from his classic Columbia recordings. Though the set is far too exhaustive for the casual listener, *Sing, Cowboy, Sing!* is a loving tribute to Autry, and it is worth the investment of any devoted fan. —*Stephen Thomas Erlewine*

Hoyt Axton

b. Mar. 25, 1938, Duncan, OK
Guitar, Vocals / Traditional Country, Country-Pop
Hoyt Axton enjoyed an amazingly diverse career as a songwriter, recording artist and movie actor. While rooted equally in the folk and country traditions, his pop smarts enabled him to land substantial hits with numerous artists; as a performer, Axton released a string of remarkably consistent albums featuring his warm baritone and wry, earthy lyrical style. Born in Duncan, OK, Axton was inspired to become a songwriter and performer by his mother, who had abandoned a teaching career to become a distinguished songwriter; her best work, "Heartbreak Hotel," was immortalized by Elvis Presley in 1956. Axton's mother taught him much about traditional music; she also made him take classical piano lessons until he made clear his preference for boogie-woogie music. He learned to play guitar while a teenager, and while attending Oklahoma State University on a football scholarship, played music informally for his buddies. By the late '50s, Axton had served a stint in the Navy, and began an interest in folk music that led him to perform on the California coffeehouse circuit. He had his first real songwriting success in 1962 with "Greenback Dollar," a song he had co-written with Ken Ramsey. Though it didn't make much money for him, it did lead to his signing with Horizon Records. His debut album was *The Balladeer*. After recording another album for Horizon, Axton switched to Vee-Jay Records where he made four albums, including *Saturday's Child*. More albums for different labels followed, but Axton didn't really hit it big until he began opening for the pop group Three Dog Night in 1969. When they recorded his song "Joy to the World," he found himself with a gigantic international crossover hit. Among the other artists who recorded Axton's songs were The

Kingston Trio ("Greenback Dollar"), Steppenwolf ("The Pusher," "Snowblind Friend"), and Ringo Starr ("No No Song"), as well as Waylon Jennings, Glen Campbell, Tanya Tucker, John Denver, and Commander Cody.

Between 1969 and 1971, Axton recorded three albums, including *Joy to the World*. He first hit the charts in 1974 with two Top Ten tunes: "When the Morning Comes" and "Boney Fingers." He moved to MCA in 1977 where he produced one of his best albums, *Snowblind Friend*. He left the label to found his own Jeremiah Records in 1978. The following year, his *Rusty Old Halo* album produced two major hits, "Della and the Dealer" and the title track. He continued to record steadily. Axton made his acting debut in 1966, and has since appeared in many feature films and television shows, including 1979's *Black Stallion*. Other films included 1994's *Season of Change*. —*Sandra Brennan and Rick Clark*

Thunder & Lightnin' / 1963 / Horizon ✦✦✦

My Griffin Is Gone / 1969 / Columbia ✦✦✦
One of Axton's less interesting albums—though, considering the consistent quality of this fine songwriter's work, this shouldn't deter anyone interested in it. —*Jim Worbois*

Joy to the World / 1971 / Capitol ✦✦✦
Songwriter Hoyt Axton lets loose with a batch of original songs that have been heavily covered (resulting in hits) by artists as varied as Three Dog Night, Steppenwolf, and Waylon Jennings. Axton has a distinctive style that makes his original versions as interesting as the better-known covers. —*Jim Worbois*

Life Machine / 1974 / A&M ✦✦✦✦
Among Axton's many albums, *Life Machine* features some of his best writing. "When the Morning Comes" and "Boney Fingers" are highlights. —*Rick Clark*

Southbound / 1975 / A&M ✦✦✦✦
Another solid effort, it includes "Pride of Man" and "Lion in the Winter." —*Rick Clark*

Fearless / 1976 / A&M ✦✦✦
Included is "The Devil." —*Rick Clark*

Snowblind Friend / 1977 / MCA ✦✦✦
This is the fourth in a series of enjoyable album releases. The title track is one of Axton's better-known songs, having been recorded by Steppenwolf. —*Rick Clark*

● **Road Songs** / 1977 / A&M ✦✦✦✦
Featuring instrumental support from James Burton and backing vocals from Linda Ronstadt, *Road Songs* has a good cross-section of Axton's best-known songs, including "Boney Fingers" and "The No-No Song," making it a good introduction to the songwriter. —*Stephen Thomas Erlewine*

American Originals / Jan. 18, 1993 / Capitol ✦✦✦✦

B

The Backsliders

Roots-Rock, Alternative Country-Rock, Alternative Country
The Backsliders were an alternative-traditional country-rock band from North Carolina made up of guitarist Steve Howell, frontman and acoustic guitarist Chip Robinson, bassman Danny Kurtz, and drummer Jeff Dennis, with guitarist Brad Rice rounding things out. In 1994, inspired by Buck Owens, Webb Pierce, and the honky tonk life, Howell and Robinson put together the Backsliders and started playing the clubs in their area. Both Howell and Robinson were working with other acts at the time. Robinson was playing with a rock band and Howell was a member of the Shady Grove Band, a traditional bluegrass outfit that recorded for Flying Fish. *Mulberry Moon* was the Shady Grove release that included Howell's tune, "Mansion in the Sky."

Their North Carolina appearances resulted in a popular following for the band that was being compared to Gram Parsons, the Blasters, and Los Lobos, all pioneers in American roots music and all products of the wild West Coast. Just as wild, the Backsliders were a direct contradiction to the overly manufactured sounds coming out of Nashville, where '70s rock acts held more sway than Lefty Frizzell or George Jones. The Backsliders also provided a contrast to the whining, angry "woe is me" style of contemporary rock bands, and could more often than not rock the so-called rockers off any stage.

With a positive attitude and extolling the virtues of shuffle and twang, the Backsliders started touring regularly around the Southeast. Each homecoming to the Brewery in their hometown of Raleigh was met with a full house and a satisfied crowd who took great pleasure in seeing, and hearing, a band made up of their own homeboys. These live shows eventually resulted in what was to be their first release on Mammoth Records. A six-song EP, *From Raleigh, NC,* displayed all the power and intensity that made the Backsliders such a high-profile band. Their first full-length project on Mammoth was released in January 1997. *Throwing Rocks at the Moon,* produced by West Coast patriarch Pete Anderson, was recorded at Mad Dog Studios during the early fall of 1996. Stating that it was the quality of the songwriting that swayed him to take on the Backsliders, Anderson proceeded to pull out all the stops and extract every ounce of talent and sweat that the band had to give. *—Jana Pendragon*

From Raleigh, North Carolina / 1996 / Mammoth/Atlantic ♦♦♦
Rough-hewn vocals with the flavor of Billy Joe Shaver and the reckless spirit of Gram Parsons serving his rock 'n' roll apprenticeship with the Stones. The revved up country-honk backing is ragged, but definitely right. This six-song EP— recorded live on a hot summer night in a Southern college town—was released to give a taste of the band's fire. The result has a lot of charm, not to mention a liquid cover of the Flying Burrito Brothers' "High Fashion Queen." Cool! *—Jack Leaver*

● **Throwin' Rocks at the Moon** / 1997 / Mammoth/Atlantic ♦♦♦♦
The full-length debut, produced by Pete Anderson (Dwight Yoakam), of this Raleigh, NC, quintet. With a driving guitar sound that picks up where the New Riders of the Purple Sage left off in the '70s and what Jason & the Scorchers started in the '80s, the Backsliders will appeal to fans who like their country a little

rough around the edges. The songwriting and musical attitude comes off as honest and sincere, and Anderson does a great job of toughening the band's already muscular live-show attack, without messing with its charm. Adding a little Hammond B-3 on the soulful rockers, the country elements are in turn accentuated by occasional pedal steel and mandolin. Standout cuts include the heartfelt "Broken Wings," the melodic honky-tonk of "Lonesome Teardrops" and the rambunctious album closer "Cowboy Boots." *—Jack Leaver*

Bad Livers

Alternative Pop-Rock, Roots-Rock, Alternative Country-Rock
Danny Barnes (vocals, banjo, guitar) formed the hillbilly punk band Bad Livers in 1990, recruiting Mark Rubin (upright bass, tuba) and Ralph White (fiddle, accordion). Quarterstick Records released *Delusions of Banjer* in 1992. Two additional albums soon followed. *—John Bush*

● **Delusions of Banjer** / 1992 / Quarterstick ♦♦♦♦

Horses in the Mines / Quarterstick ♦♦♦

The Bailes Brothers

Traditional Country, Close Harmony
From the mid-'40s through the '50s the Bailes Brothers were among the most popular close-harmony duets. There were actually four brothers—Kyle, Johnnie, Walter, and Homer—but they seldom worked together as an entire group, instead pairing off for performances. The Bailes Brothers were born and raised in West Virginia, near Charleston. Their father, a minister, died when they were young and their impoverished mother had to struggle to keep them together. (Years later, Walter paid tribute to her trials with his song "Give Mother My Crown.") While working a variety of odd jobs during the Depression, the brothers were inspired to pursue music by the songs of such performers as Billy Cox and Buddy Starcher. They started out on a variety of radio programs, but didn't earn much recognition until 1942, when Johnnie and Walter began working as a duo at WSAZ Huntington. All four brothers played string instruments; after they became popular, they added other members to their group, among them Fiddlin' Arthur Smith.

It was Roy Acuff who got the Bailes Brothers their big break when he suggested to WSM Nashville executives that the brothers appear on the Grand Ole Opry. They made their debut on the show in 1944 and stayed in Nashville for two years. They made their recording debut in early 1945 for Columbia; among their first singles were their original songs "Dust on the Bible" and "The Drunkard's Grave." As they continued recording the brothers added more and more original songs, such as "Broken Marriage Vows." In 1947, Walter left to become a minister and Homer became the singing partner of their friend Dean Upson. They made their last recordings for Columbia at the end of the year, later becoming co-founders of the famous *Louisiana Hayride* show.

The original Bailes Brothers went their separate ways in 1949. Over the next decade, different combinations of Bailes Brothers appeared. In the early '50s Homer and Kyle teamed up to work at a Little Rock, AR, station. They also recorded a single. Later Johnnie and Walter reunited and began singing gospel in Texas. In 1953, they recorded three singles for King; Johnnie also cut a few solo records. During the 1960s, they continued the pattern, with Walter teaming up with Kyle and Homer at different times. Johnnie and Homer reunited during the early '70s, and from the mid-'70s through the '80s Walter, Kyle, and former band member Ernest Ferguson frequently played at churches and sometimes at festivals. Homer was busy working as a pastor while Johnnie ran three radio stations. Walter was also an evangelical preacher. In 1976 Walter and Kyle made an album; in 1977, all four reunited for a record, joined by their sister Minnie on a few cuts. Later, Walter recorded on his Starlit and White Dove labels, while Homer also recorded solo. Much of the Bailes Brothers' early works are available on anthologies, and some of their records have been reissued. —*Sandra Brennan*

Gospel Reunion / 1973 / Starday ✦✦✦

● **Yesterday and Today** / 1983 / White Dove ✦✦✦✦

Reunion / ✦✦✦

Early Radio Favorites / ✦✦✦✦

Early Radio Favorites, Vol. 2 / ✦✦✦✦

The Bailey Brothers

Traditional Bluegrass, Old-Time, Close Harmony

Charlie and Danny Bailey were extremely popular radio singers in West Virginia and Tennessee during the late '40s through the '50s, and were among the few fraternal duets to successfully make the transition from old-time music to bluegrass. The Baileys were born to a large, musically inclined family in Happy Valley, TN. Charlie made his professional singing debut in 1936 when he teamed up with Charlie Cope and began touring. He and brother Danny teamed up shortly after, and soon they were singing on local radio. In 1940 they went to Knoxville to play on WNOX and WROL, and soon gained a devoted following. But in 1941, just before they were to make their recording debut, Charlie was inducted into the Army. While he was gone Danny founded the Happy Valley Boys, and remained in Knoxville. By 1944, the Happy Valley Boys had moved to Nashville and were appearing on the Grand Ole Opry. The group changed personnel when two members were drafted. They were replaced by Charlie and Lester Cope. In 1946, Charlie returned and the Copes left to find their own fame.

Not long after, the Happy Valley Boys became a full-fledged bluegrass band; joined by fiddler L.E. White, banjo picker Wiley Birchfield, and bass player Jake Tullock, Charlie played mandolin and guitar while Danny played guitar. With this lineup they waxed six songs in late 1947, among them the first recorded version of "The Sweetest Gift," by J.B. Coates. They made two more singles before moving to a radio station in Raleigh, NC. There, fiddler Clarence "Tater" Tate and banjo player Hoke Jenkins joined the Happy Valley Boys.

The Baileys founded their own Canary label before moving to play on the *Wheeling Jamboree* at WWVA in Wheeling, WV, in 1952. Here the brothers were at their most popular; at one time, the Baileys and their band were even bigger than Bill Monroe and His Blue Grass Boys. About two years later, Danny began having health problems and, except for a few months in 1954, the Baileys stopped playing together. They reunited briefly between 1957 and 1958, but Danny basically remained in Knoxville after 1954 and continued working on radio and television on the *Farm and Home Hour* until the show was canceled in 1983. Meanwhile Charlie went to work in Richmond and then eventually returned to Wheeling, where he founded a band featuring members of the McCumbee Family and later the Osborne Brothers. He later teamed up with Jimmy Elrod, Chubby Collier, and Ray Meyers. With this lineup, he recorded a few songs at WWVA. Following his brief professional reunion with his brother in 1958, Charlie embarked upon a six-month tour of the Canadian Maritime Provinces. He retired in 1960 and went on to open an exterminating business in Delaware.

The Baileys briefly reunited in 1970 for a concert during the Smithsonian Festival of American Folklife; later in the decade they recorded two albums for Rounder. In 1975, they gathered for the old-timer reunion at Fan Fair, and in 1982 played at the Knoxville World's Fair. The Rounder label has reissued most of the Bailey Brothers recordings for Rich-R-Tone and Canary. —*Sandra Brennan*

Have You Forgotten / 1974 / Rounder ✦✦✦

Take Me Back to Happy Valley / 1975 / Rounder ✦✦✦

Just As the Sun Went Down / 1980 / Rounder ✦✦✦

Early Duet Stylings / 1981 / Old Homestead ✦✦✦✦

● **Early Days of Bluegrass, Vol. 6—Have You Forgotten?** / Rounder ✦✦✦✦

Bob Bailey

Vocals, Session Musician / Country Gospel

Gospel performer Bob Bailey was best known in country circles for his work as a backing vocalist, primarily on mainstream artists' excursions into spiritual and holiday territory. A popular session singer, he appeared on recordings for Reba McEntire (*Rumor Has It, For My Broken Heart*), Vince Gill (*Let There Be Peace on Earth, High Lonesome Sound*), Garth Brooks (*Beyond the Season*), Dolly Parton (*Home for Christmas*), and Sawyer Brown (*Buick*). He also recorded and toured with Wynonna, and performed with pop artists like Billy Joel and James Ingram. As a solo gospel artist, Bailey's most successful recording was *I'm Walkin,'* which was nominated for a Grammy award in the Best Male Gospel Performance category. —*Jason Ankeny*

Bob Bailey / 1989 / Airborne ✦✦✦

Bailey makes the leap from gospel to pop on his solo debut, which highlights his covers of R&B chestnuts like Marvin Gaye's "Inner City Blues" and Stevie Wonder's "Heaven Help Us All." —*Jason Ankeny*

● **I'm Walkin'** / Light ✦✦✦✦

Razzy Bailey (Rasie Bailey)

b. Feb. 14, 1939, Five Points, AL
Vocals / Rockabilly

A singer whose vocal style fused country with blue-eyed soul, Alabama-born Rasie Michael "Razzy" Bailey cut his first recordings in 1949 at the age of ten. By the age of 15, he was leading a string band, sponsored by the local chapter of the Future Farmers of America, which came in second in a talent contest held at Auburn University.

Bailey married and had children immediately after graduating high school; as a result, his career as a performer was sporadic and unsuccessful for a number of years. In 1966, he contributed a number of songs to Atlantic Records' Bill Lowery, among them "9,999,999 Tears," which Lowery agreed to produce. While the single, on which Bailey was backed by a studio band featuring Billy Joel, Joe South, and Freddy Weller, failed to chart, it renewed the singer's interest in pursuing a recording career full-time. As a result, he formed the pop-oriented trio Daily Bread in 1968, releasing a pair of albums on small labels. Another group, the Aquarians, followed in 1972; in 1974, Bailey recorded the album *I Hate Hate* simply as "Razzy."

After *I Hate Hate* failed to chart, Bailey again dropped out of music, but in 1976, singer Dickey Lee hit No. 3 with a cover of "9,999,999 Tears"; after Lee hit the Top 20 with another of his songs, "Peanut Butter," Bailey signed a new recording contract of his own. In 1978, he released the single "What Time Do You Have to Be Back in Heaven," the first of five consecutive Top Ten hits.

Between August 1980 and December 1981, Bailey reached his commercial peak with a string of five No. 1 hits—"Loving Up a Storm," "I Keep Coming Back," "Friends," "Midnight Hauler," and "She Left Love All Over Me"—and in 1981 was named *Billboard* magazine's Country Singles Artist of the Year. The albums *Razzy* (1980), *Makin' Friends* (1981), *Feelin' Right* and *A Little More Razzy* (both 1982) were also very successful.

By the mid-1980s, however, Bailey's hit-making days were largely over; his singles landed only in the lower rungs of the charts. In 1987, he began issuing his records through his own label, SOA (Sounds of America). In 1993, the release of the album *Razzy Bailey: Fragile, Handle with Care* was marred by the suicide of Bailey's wife, Sandra. —*Jason Ankeny*

Razzy / 1979 / RCA ✦✦✦

Makin' Friends / 1981 / RCA ✦✦✦

Feelin' Alright / 1982 / RCA ✦✦✦

● **Greatest Hits** / 1983 / RCA ✦✦✦✦

In the Midnight Hour / 1984 / RCA ✦✦✦

Baillie & the Boys

Contemporary Country

Though originally from New Jersey, Kathy Baillie and Michael Bonagura met in Delaware through a friend who gave Bonagura a tape that featured Baillie's vocals. Fans of artists like the Four Tops, the Beatles, the Supremes, Linda Ronstadt, and James Taylor, they developed a strong harmony—both on stage and off: they were married in 1977. Bonagura's buddy, bass player Alan LeBoeuf, joined them, and after a number of years on the Garden State's nightclub circuit, yet another friend—a driver with Allied Van Lines—persuaded them to join him on a trip to Nashville. They stayed in Music City, and in 1982 they got their first chance to appear on a record, singing backup on Ed Bruce's *My First Taste of Texas*. Bonagura co-wrote Marie Osmond's single "There's No Stopping Your Heart," and the trio sang backing vocals on a number of singles for Dan Seals and Randy Travis. Ultimately, they signed with RCA Records, making their debut in 1987. After completing their second album, LeBoeuf decided their touring schedule was too hectic and left. Baillie and Bonagura retained the original name, though Boys seems a bit misleading. —*Tom Roland*

Baillie & The Boys / 1987 / RCA ✦✦✦

Turn the Tide / 1989 / RCA ✦✦✦✦

Lights of Home / 1990 / RCA ✦✦✦

● **The Best of Baillie & The Boys** / 1991 / RCA ✦✦✦✦

This highlights the real strength of the act: tuneful melodies, pristine harmonies, and Kathy Baillie's infectious enunciations. Best cuts: "Oh Heart," "(Wish I Had A) Heart of Stone," "Long Shot," and "I Can't Turn the Tide." —*Tom Roland*

Lovin' Every Minute / 1996 / Intersound ✦✦

Baker & Myers

Contemporary Country

Baker & Myers are professional contemporary country songwriters based in Nashville. After Alabama had a hit with the duo's "Once in a Lifetime" and John Michael Montgomery took "I Swear" to No. 1 (the song was also a pop and R&B hit by All 4 One), Baker & Myers launched a performing career, releasing their eponymous debut on Curb Records in the fall of 1995. —*Stephen Thomas Erlewine*

Baker & Myers / Oct. 10, 1995 / Curb ✦✦✦

Though Baker & Myers are talented professional songwriters, they haven't quite developed into skilled performers of their own, as their eponymous debut proves. Neither has a very compelling voice, and the studio musicians make the music too polished to truly stick. Still, the duo's strong point is slickness, such as John Michael Montgomery's hit "I Swear," yet slickness has to be delivered with a little more flair than the pleasant, but dull, professionalism that comprises *Baker & Myers*. —*Stephen Thomas Erlewine*

Kenny Baker (Kenneth Baker)

b. Mar. 1, 1921, Withernsea, England

Fiddle, Trumpet, Fluegelhorn / Traditional Bluegrass

Longtime Bill Monroe fiddler Kenny Baker is considered one of the most influential players in contemporary bluegrass music. During his illustrious career, his many compositions greatly expanded the fiddler's repertoire, and his unique style influenced scores of aspiring players. He was born and raised in Jenkins, a coal-mining town in east Kentucky, the third generation in a fam-

ily of fiddle players and coal miners. Eight-year-old Baker was discouraged by his father's criticism of his fiddle playing, but he returned to the instrument in his late teens after joining the Navy. Following his honorable discharge, he returned to Jenkins to work as a coal loader and play at local events. Baker was most heavily influenced by Marion Summer's blend of traditional music with newer swing and pop sounds, as well as Django Reinhardt and Stephane Grappelli. In 1953, he began playing on Nashville's *Saturday Night Barn Dance* radio show with Don Gibson, who encouraged Baker to continue with his jazz fiddle playing. Meanwhile, he was approached by Bill Monroe about joining his Bluegrass Boys; after Gibson's departure for Nashville in 1957, Baker decided to rise to the challenge of the dramatically different genre and give it a shot. During the lean initial years, he quit the band twice to go back to the mines, but by 1967, bluegrass music had become increasingly popular, and he returned, remaining with Monroe's band until the early 1980s. He also occasionally recorded solo albums, the first being *Portrait of a Bluegrass Fiddler* in 1969; many were recorded in motel rooms during festivals. During the 1980s, Baker performed with the Masters, an all-star group, and worked with Josh Graves. During the 1990s, Baker appeared on a series of tours backed by the National Council on Traditional Arts called "Masters of the Folk Violin." He also continues to record and frequently works with colleagues Blaine Sprouse and Bobby Hicks. —*Sandra Brennan*

● **Master Fiddler** / County ✦✦✦✦

Master Fiddler compiles the highlights of Kenny Baker's albums recorded between 1968 and 1983. Throughout that 15-year span, Baker turned out a number of wonderful recordings, alive with his distinctive, fluid technique. Every cut on *Master Fiddler* demonstrates Baker's unique style and prodigious talent—the record proves that the musician is indeed a *Master Fiddler*. —*Thom Owens*

Butch Baldassari

Mandolin / Traditional Bluegrass

Butch Baldassari is a member of the bluegrass band Weary Hearts. He is one of the better mandolin players in his field. —*Chip Renner*

Evergreen / **Mandolin Music for Christmas** / 1990 / Cactus ✦✦✦

Butch Baldassari's *Evergreen / Mandolin Music for Christmas* is a charming collection of folky Christmas carols—such as "Away in a Manger," "Little Drummer Boy," and "The First Noel"—recorded with a variety of stringed instruments, from mandolin and guitar to viola and violin. —*Stephen Thomas Erlewine*

● **Old Town** / 1990 / Rebel ✦✦✦✦

One of the finer bluegrass albums of 1990—Butch Baldassari has five originals on the CD, plus strong material by Alison Krauss and Bill Monroe. Tom Adams (banjo) and Stuart Duncan (fiddle) are very good in support. —*Chip Renner*

Day in the Country / 1994 / Pinecastle ✦✦✦

The Balfa Brothers

Fiddle, Guitar / Cajun

The Balfa Brothers (Les Freres Balfas) helped keep traditional Cajun music alive in the 1960s, when it was in danger of disappearing. The sons, three of a family of six, were born to a poor southwest Louisiana sharecropper, from whom they learned about traditional Cajun lore and culture. Fiddler Dewey Balfa was heavily influenced by players such as J.B. Fusilier, Leo Soileau, Harry Choates, and Bob Wills. He and his brothers—Rodney, who sang and played guitar and harmonica, Will, the second fiddler, Harry, the accordion player, and Burkeman, who played triangle and spoons—began playing informally at family parties and local gatherings during the '40s. They achieved enough local popularity to play up to eight dances a week at local dance halls. The Balfas were later joined by neighbor Hadley Fontenot on accordion. They made their recording debut in 1951 with "La Valse de Bon Baurche" and "Le Two Step de Ville Platte," which were captured on a home recorder and released as a 78 rpm single. Dewey Balfa went on to a solo career playing with numerous Cajun artists and recording on such labels as Khoury, Kajun, and Swallow.

In 1967, Dewey, Rodney, Will and his daughter Nelda, along with Fontenot, formed the Balfa Brothers and began spreading the Cajun sound throughout Europe and at folk festivals across the US. In 1968, they played for the Olympics Festival in Mexico City. They made their first professional recording, "Le Valse de Bambocheurs/Indian on a Stomp," in 1967 for Swallow. This led to an album, *Balfa Brothers Play Traditional Cajun Music,* also on Swallow. After releasing another LP, the Balfas appeared in the 1972 Les Blank documentary *Spend It All,* which introduced a new generation to the lively Cajun sound. That year they also recorded *The Cajuns* on Sonet and another for Swallow, *The Good Times Are Killing Me,* which included the soundtrack for the documentary of the same name. Although most of their musical focus was on tradition, the Balfas were not averse to trying more modernized Cajun songs with a nightclub orchestra comprised of Dewey, Rodney, accordion player Nathan Menard, fiddler Dick Richard, J.W. Pelsia on steel guitar, Austin Broussard on drums and Rodney's son Tony on bass guitar.

Things went well for the band until February 1979, when Rodney and Will were killed in a car wreck. The next year, Dewey's wife died of trichinosis. Despite the tragedy, the Balfa Brothers continued (with a few personnel changes) even after Dewey's death in 1992. Through them, his rich and valuable legacy of Cajun music carries on. —*Sandra Brennan*

● **Play Trad. Cajun Music, Vols. 1 & 2** / 1987 / Swallow ◆◆◆◆
The Balfa Brothers Play Traditional Cajun Music, Vols. 1 & 2 combines both of the group's original *Play Traditional Cajun Music* albums onto one disc. The first volume was released on Swallow Records in 1965 and helped kick-start the Cajun revival of the '60s. It's an excellent album, featuring wonderful harmonies from Rodney, Will and Dewey, as well as stellar instrumental work. The second volume, recorded and released in 1974, isn't quite as strong as its predecessor, but it is still very good and is filled with terrific music. Both albums represent the Balfa Brothers at their peak. They may have a number of very good albums in their catalog, but *The Balfa Brothers Play Traditional Cajun Music, Vols. 1 & 2* effectively explains what they are all about. —*Thom Owens*

J'ai Vu Le Loup, Le Renard Et La Belette / 1988 / Rounder ◆◆◆◆
The Balfa Brothers' long heritage in traditional Cajun music has never been exemplified better than on this 13-cut CD recorded in 1975. These are mostly short songs (only one song is longer than four minutes), which are predominantly uptempo dance numbers with some two-steps, waltzes, and romantic pieces mixed in, as well as an interesting version of "Casey Jones." The session was produced and recorded by Gerard Dole and was originally issued on the Cezame label in France. True believers and purists couldn't find a better example of the vintage sound anywhere. —*Ron Wynn*

Let's Get Cajun / Flying Fish ◆◆◆
These modern Cajun sounds are played by young musicians. —*Jeff Hannusch*

David Ball

b. May 3, 1959, Rock Hill, SC
Guitar, Vocals / Contemporary Country
Distinguished singer-songwriter David Ball has been playfully dubbed the "human jukebox" by producer Blake Chancey for his inability to pass a guitar without picking it up and playing his upbeat music. A talented performer with a friendly, laidback attitude, Ball was born in Rock Hill, SC, the son of a Baptist minister. He was influenced by a Fred Kirby concert he saw at the age of five, and got his own start a few years later when he received a ukulele for Christmas and a guitar for his birthday. He made his formal debut singing a song he'd penned with his group the Strangers during a 7th grade talent show. After mastering the bass, the teenaged Ball began appearing on the folk festival circuit. Just after graduation, he founded the trio Uncle Walt's Band and moved to Austin, TX, playing "dance-hall music" through the

late '80s, when he landed a contract with Nashville producer Chancey. In between he and Uncle Walt's Band recorded two albums in the early '80s including *Girl on the Sunny Shore* (1980). A little while later, the A&R director at Warner Brothers requested that Ball audition for him. He was impressed, and Ball released his debut album for the label *Thinkin' Problem.* The album went gold, and the video made it to No. 1. He followed with *Starlite Lounge* in June of 1996. —*Sandra Brennan*

● **Thinkin' Problem** / 1994 / Warner Brothers ◆◆◆◆
This hard-country album has a cerebral twist, as the title song suggests. Ball, 41 when this album came out, had a craggy Texas face and a voice to match. When he has material to match, such as "Thinkin' Problem" or the ballad "When the Thought of You Catches up with Me," he's the kind of singer neo-traditional country fans dream about. —*Brian Mansfield*

Starlite Lounge / Jun. 25, 1996 / Warner Brothers ◆◆◆◆
Starlite Lounge is another set of gritty, contemporary honky tonk from David Ball, highlighted by his gutsy vocals and no-holds-barred approach. Ball doesn't treat honky tonk as a museum piece, but he has respect for its roots, as well—he just tears through the songs with energy and conviction, which means *Starlite Lounge* is simply an invigorating listen. —*Thom Owens*

E.C. and Orna Ball

Guitar, Vocals / Old-Time, Country Gospel
A fine old-time gospel singer and guitarist, Estil C. Ball (1913-1978) hailed from Rugby, VA, and performed with his wife Orna (b. 1907) and the Friendly Gospel Singers. First recorded for the Library of Congress in 1938, Ball was recorded extensively in his later years by the County and Rounder labels. His lively, Travis-style guitar was an unusual element in traditional gospel singing. —*Mark A. Humphrey*

Fathers Have a Home Sweet Home / Rounder ◆◆◆
● **E.C. Ball with Orna Ball & the Friendly Gospel Singers** / Rounder ◆◆◆◆
This is old-time mountain gospel as good as it gets. Ball's guitar virtuosity and powerful baritone blend beautifully. —*David Vinopal*

The Band

Rock & Roll, Country-Rock, Folk-Rock
Composed of four Canadians and one American, the Band first came together in Toronto in the early '60s as Ronnie Hawkins' backup group. Hawkins recorded nine 45s for Roulette between 1959 and 1963. Drummer Levon Helm plays on all nine, guitarist Robbie Robertson and bass player Rick Danko can be heard on the last three, pianist Richard Manuel on the last two, and organist Garth Hudson plays on the final outing only. Leaving Hawkins collectively in early 1964, they called themselves the Levon Helm Sextet, Levon and the Hawks, and (for a brief spell) the Canadian Squires, releasing two singles before becoming Bob Dylan's backup ensemble for his crazed electric tour of North America, Australia, and Europe from the fall of 1965 through the spring of 1966. (After a couple of gigs, Levon headed back to Arkansas.)

Playing with Dylan had a profound influence on the Band. Woodshedding for two years in Woodstock, NY, they released their debut album, *Music from Big Pink,* in the summer of 1968. Over the succeeding eight years, the Band stood completely apart from everything else happening in rock 'n' roll. There was no precedent for what they did and there have been no antecedents. Ironically, given that they were four-fifths Canadian, their music embodied an essence of Americana that no one else in rock 'n' roll has approached. Chief writer, Torontonian Robbie Robertson, wrote about the South, the land, rural America, tradition, and the value and richness of heritage and blood ties. The settings for his songs took place in cornfields, during the Civil War, and at carnivals at the edge of town. He was most concerned with displaced people and the passing of a way of life. Sonically, the Band was equally unique. Hudson played accordion, sax, and organ; drummer Levon Helm doubled on mandolin and guitar; pianist Manuel drummed whenever Helm was out front; bassist Rick Danko played fiddle when they needed a rural or "old-timey" feel; guitarist Robbie Robertson had a pinched, economical style that kept one teetering on the edge with its tension. As a unit, they quite consciously avoided any of the current trends. They didn't want their voices to blend, because that is what everyone else was doing; they wanted their piano to sound like a funky old upright, not like a brand spanking new Yamaha Grand; and so on. In the process they created some of the most ethereal and evocative music imaginable. — *Rob Bowman*

☆ **Music from Big Pink** / Jul. 1, 1968 / Capitol ✦✦✦✦✦
Everything about the Band's debut album, *Music from Big Pink*, flew in the face of the current ethos of rock 'n' roll in 1968. For example, the disc opens in an unusual fashion, with a ballad, the Richard Manuel/Bob Dylan composition "Tears of Rage." There is not a guitar solo on the album, and this was a time when Jeff Beck, Eric Clapton, and Jimi Hendrix ruled the world. There was a lot of harmony singing that was deliberately ragged: together but not together—the band was a community where the people that made it up could be individuals. And then there were the songs, enigmatic tales such as "The Weight," "Chest Fever," and the first released version of Bob Dylan's "I Shall Be Released." An unbelievably strong debut. — *Rob Bowman*

★ **The Band** / Sep. 22, 1969 / Capitol ✦✦✦✦✦
Big Pink had been a fine, even superior debut; *The Band* was their masterpiece. Robbie Robertson's songwriting had grown by leaps and bounds. As players, all five musicians had reached a completely new level of ensemble cohesion. The sum was very much greater than the parts, and the parts were as good as any that existed. The album's single, "Up on Cripple Creek," became the Band's first and only Top 30 release. It was one of several songs on the album that had an "old-timey" feel. Other highlights on this masterpiece include "Rag Mama Rag," "The Night They Drove Old Dixie Down," and "King Harvest." — *Rob Bowman*

Stage Fright / Aug. 17, 1970 / Capitol ✦✦✦
Stage Fright was a reaction to a level of adulation that the Band members were unprepared for. It was conceived as a lighter, less serious, more rock 'n' roll type of album. The final product ended up somewhat darker, as the Band themselves were going through a number of changes. "The Shape I'm In" and "Stage Fright" tell the story well. Some of the original feeling manifests itself in romps such as "Strawberry Wine" and "W.S. Walcott Medicine Show." — *Rob Bowman*

Cahoots / Sep. 15, 1971 / Capitol ✦✦
Cahoots was the first album recorded at Albert Grossman's Bearsville Studios in Woodstock. The sessions were difficult, as the studio was still having the bugs worked out and the Band was experiencing internal problems. Robertson's songs had become much more difficult; the structures, chord changes, and arrangements were increasingly complex. Despite these factors, the album has a number of gems, including "Life Is a Carnival" with its great Allen Toussaint horn arrangement, Dylan's "When I Paint My Masterpiece," a duet between Richard Manuel and Van Morrison entitled "4% Pantomime," "The River Hymn," and "Where Do We Go from Here?" — *Rob Bowman*

Rock of Ages / Aug. 15, 1972 / Capitol ✦✦✦✦
Recorded on New Year's Eve 1971/72, this was the Band's last gig for a year and a half. Allen Toussaint was brought in again to write horn arrangements for many of the Band's classics. The results were inspired. Highlights are many, but of particular note are a cover of Marvin Gaye's "Baby Don't Do It" and a live recording of a track that had earlier been relegated to B-side status only, "Get up Jake." — *Rob Bowman*

Moondog Matinee / Oct. 15, 1973 / Capitol ✦✦
The Band essentially went back to being The Hawks of the late 1950s and early '60s on this album of cover tunes. They demonstrated considerable expertise on their versions of rock 'n' roll and R&B standards like Clarence "Frogman" Henry's "Ain't Got No Home," Chuck Berry's "The Promised Land," and Fats Domino's "I'm Ready," but of course that didn't do much to satisfy the audience they had established with their original material and that, two years after the disappointing *Cahoots*, was waiting for something in the same league with their first three albums. — *William Ruhlmann*

Northern Lights Southern Cross / Nov. 1, 1975 / Capitol ✦✦✦✦
The first studio album of Band originals in four years, in many respects *Northern Lights, Southern Cross* was viewed as a comeback. It also can be seen as a swan song. The album is the Band's finest since their self-titled sophomore effort. Totaling eight songs in all, on this album the Band explores new timbres, utilizing for the first time 24 tracks and what was (then) new synthesizer technology. "Acadian Driftwood" stands out as one of Robertson's finest compositions, the equal to anything else the Band ever recorded. — *Rob Bowman*

The Best of the Band / Jul. 15, 1976 / Capitol ✦✦✦✦
With this album, Capitol Records began the inevitable process of repackaging the music of the Band, which the company would do at increasing length without solving the fundamental problem that the Band, despite the quality of their individual songs, was not a singles act and was hard to summarize in a compilation. That said, for the real neophyte, this single-disc, 11-song album may be as good as anything. It contains the Band's two most famous songs, "The Weight" and "The Night They Drove Old Dixie Down," as well as the group's only Top 30 hit, "Up on Cripple Creek," and such songs as "Tears of Rage" and "Stage Fright" that they probably played at nearly every show they performed. It's true that if you really want to understand the Band, you have to hear all of *Music from Big Pink* and *The Band*. But if you just want a snapshot, here it is. — *William Ruhlmann*

Islands / Mar. 15, 1977 / Capitol ✦✦
Theoretically, even though the Band had given up touring as of Thanksgiving 1976, they were going to keep making records, and *Islands* was the first album released in the new era. Only, it wasn't; it was the album they scraped together to complete their ten-LP contract with Capitol Records and the last new full-length album the original five members ever made. The playing, as ever, is impeccable, and the record has its moments, notably a Richard Manuel vocal on the chestnut "Georgia on My Mind" that had been released as a single in 1976 to boost Georgia Governor Jimmy Carter's successful run for the Presidency. But the songwriting quality is mediocre, and the Band had set such a standard for itself in that department that *Islands* couldn't help suffering enormously in comparison. — *William Ruhlmann*

Anthology / 1978 / Capitol ✦✦✦
Deciding 1976's *The Best of the Band* wasn't enough (or wanting to have a product out to compete with *The Last Waltz*), Capitol released the two-LP *Anthology*, a skimpy 20-track, two-LP set with liner notes by rock critic Robert Palmer. It's more complete than *The Best of the Band*, but shares the same problem—that the Band is best appreciated on their full-length albums rather than on any compilation. — *William Ruhlmann*

The Last Waltz / Apr. 1978 / Warner Brothers ✦✦✦✦
The Band's farewell gig was held at Winterland in San Francisco on Thanksgiving 1976. Guests from all periods of their career were invited to participate. The luminaries included Bob Dylan, Van Morrison, Neil Young, Joni Mitchell, Muddy Waters, Eric Clapton, and Paul Butterfield. The four-hour concert was one of the most spectacular in rock history. Two hours of it were released on this three-LP (now two-CD) set. Utilizing horns one more time, this was the gig of the Band's life and one of the greatest in rock history. — *Rob Bowman*

● **To Kingdom Come** / 1989 / Capitol ✦✦✦✦
If (and only if) you have it in your budget for just *one* Band set, *To Kingdom Come (The Definitive Collection)* provides a good collection of their best songs, presented in remastered form. Even though the sequencing is chronological, experiencing these songs out of the context of their original albums may be disconcerting for some. In other words, the best way to *hear* this great group is to start with their first two albums, then move on to *Rock of Ages*, and so on. Nevertheless, this is an exceptionally solid overview. — *Rick Clark*

Jericho / 1993 / Rhino ✦✦✦
A full 17 years after *The Last Waltz*, the Band reformed without
Robbie Robertson or the late Richard Manuel and recorded *Jericho*. Far from being an embarrassment, *Jericho* is their strongest
record since *Northern Lights, Southern Cross* and arguably their
best since *Stage Fright*. Without Robertson, the Band relies on a
variety of sources for their material (including Bob Dylan, Bruce
Springsteen and Jules Shear) and prove that they can interpret
nearly any song well. Musically, the Band can still juggle rock,
folk, blues, and country effortlessly, producing a rootsy sound distinctly their own. It sounds like the heyday of the group, which is
more than can be said of either of Robertson's solo albums.
—Stephen Thomas Erlewine

Across the Great Divide / 1994 / Capitol ✦✦✦
Capitol's 1989 Band compilation *To Kingdom Come* was subtitled
"The Definitive Collection," so what is this? Well, the other one
was only a two-disc set, and this is a three-disc set. As the CD reis-
sue/box set boom goes on, record companies have taken to redo-
ing acts they've already done once, so even though the Band has
one classy CD anthology (and a few tacky ones), Capitol gives us
another. In this case, they've divided it into two discs' worth of the
greatest hits, followed by a disc of rarities (some not so rare) and
unreleased tracks that includes pre-Band recordings by the
Hawks, collaborations with Bob Dylan, live tracks from the Woodstock and Watkins Glen festivals, and the like. All of which
pushes this set up a price point or two from the earlier one without adding anything substantial to the story. *—William Ruhlmann*

Live at Watkins Glen / 1995 / Capitol ✦✦
Along with the Allman Brothers and the Grateful Dead, the Band
were a featured act at the 1973 Watkins Glen festival, a half-for-
gotten event that attracted half a million spectators. This rather
brief (ten-song) excerpt from their set may be of interest to Band
fans. But it's really rather unnecessary in light of a much better
live album (*Rock of Ages*) and the fact that the performance itself
wasn't anything spectacular. It does have a couple of surprising
covers (Chuck Berry's "Back to Memphis" and the Four Tops'
"Loving You Is Sweeter Than Ever"), and a couple of jams, including one of Garth Hudson's patented strange instrumental organ
interludes. *—Richie Unterberger*

High on the Hog / Feb. 27, 1996 / Rhino ✦✦
Jericho was a surprise. The reunited Band, minus guitarist Robbie
Robertson, created an album that built on their strengths by using
carefully selected contemporary songwriters and covers. Although
it lacked the resonance of *Music from Big Pink* or even *Stage
Fright*, the group sounded fresh and it was a better album than
most of the Band's solo records. *High on the Hog*, the second
album by the reunited Band, isn't quite as good but it has a number of stellar moments. The key to the album's success isn't the
material—they're saddled with a couple of weak songs—but the
group's interplay. By now, the musicians have developed a sympathetic interaction that sounds ancient but still living, breathing,
and vital. It's a joy to hear them play and that's what carries *High
on the Hog* over its rough spots. *—Stephen Thomas Erlewine*

Moe Bandy

b. Feb. 12, 1944, Meridan, MS
*Guitar, Vocals / Traditional Country, Contemporary Country,
    Honky Tonk*

Moe Bandy was one of the most popular country singers of the
1970s, turning out a series of hits in the latter half of the decade
that made many fans and critics believe he was one of the great
honky tonk singers. Bandy's songs never strayed far from the traditional bar-room fare—delivered with a knowing sense of humor,
loving, cheating, drinking, and patriotic songs form the core of his
repertoire. Throughout the late '70s and early '80s, the singer
racked up hits. A decade after his career took off, his audience
declined somewhat, yet he remained a popular favorite in the
'90s, through his theater in Branson, MO.

Bandy was born in Meridian, MS, the birthplace of Jimmie
Rodgers. In fact, Bandy's grandfather worked with Rodgers on the
railroad, so it's no surprise that the singer first fell in love with

country music through the Jimmie Rodgers records that were
around his house, as well as the Hank Williams albums. Bandy's
family moved to San Antonio, TX, when he was six. During high
school, he was a rodeo rider, but his career came to a halt after
too many injuries. Once he left school, Bandy was a sheet metal
worker, singing in country night clubs at night. In 1964 he landed
a one-record deal with Satin Records. The label released Bandy's
original song "Lonely Lady," but the record made no impact. Nevertheless, he continued to perform at night in various Texan
honky tonks.

In 1972, Bandy met record producer Ray Baker on a hunting
trip and convinced him to listen to some demo tapes he had
made. Provided that Moe could pay for the recording sessions,
Baker agreed to produce the singer. Excited by his new prospect,
Bandy pawned his furniture and financed a session. Once they
were released, the records went nowhere. The following year, the
singer took out a loan to pay for another recording date. "I Just
Started Hatin' Cheatin' Songs Today" was the result of this session
and Baker released the single on Footprint Records, manufacturing only 500 copies. Unlike Bandy's previous records, the single
began to sell. GRC acquired the rights to the record and released
it nationally; it eventually became a Top 20 hit. Nevertheless,
Bandy kept his job as a sheet metal worker, uncertain of the end
result of his taste of success.

Bandy followed "I Just Started Hatin' Cheatin' Songs Today"
with several singles on GRC, including the Top Ten hits "It Was So
Easy to Find an Unhappy Woman" (1974) and "Bandy the Rodeo
Clown" (1975), which was written by Lefty Frizzell and Whitey
Shafer. Bandy signed with Columbia Records in 1975, keeping
Baker as a producer. "Hank Williams You Wrote My Life," his first
single for the label, was an instant No. 3 hit, leading to his "Most
Promising Male Vocalist" award from the Academy of Country
Music. Bandy's string of hit singles in 1976—including "Here I Am
Drunk Again" and "She Took More Than Her Share"— confirmed
that he was one of the most popular singers of the latter half of
the decade. The following two years were equally successful for
the singer, as he had hits with "I'm Sorry for You My Friend,"
"Cowboys Aren't Supposed to Cry," "She Just Loved the Cheatin'
Out of Me," "That's What Makes the Jukebox Play," and "Two
Lonely People."

Bandy's career reached a peak in 1979. During that year, he
teamed up with Janie Fricke in 1979 for "It's a Cheatin' Situation."
The song became a No. 3 hit and won the Song of the Year award
from ACM. Bandy had another successful duet that year with Joe
Stampley. The pair released *Just Good Ole Boys*, which became
one of the most popular albums of the year, spawning the No. 1
title tracks and the Top Ten "Holding the Bag." Like his pairing
with Fricke, the duet with Stampley was an award-winning combination, as the duo won the Country Music Association's "Duet of
the Year' and the ACM's "Duo of the Year" in 1980. Moe also had
a pair of major solo hits, with the No. 1 "I Cheated Me Right Out
of Her" and the Top Ten "Barstool Mountain."

During 1980, Moe Bandy's winning streak continued with the
Top Ten hits "Yesterday Once More" and "Following the Feeling,"
a duet with Judy Bailey. Bandy teamed up with Stampley again in
1981, which proved as successful as the duo's first outing. The
pair again reached the Top Ten with "Hey Moe Hey Joe," and
charted again with "Honky Tonk Queen." With "My Woman Loves
the Devil Out of Me" and "Rodeo Romeo," Bandy had a pair of
solo hits the same year. For the next two years, he regularly
charted in the Top 20, both as a solo act and with various duet
partners, including Becky Hobbs on the Top Ten 1983 hit "Let's
Get Over Them Together." However, none of his songs caused the
sensation that "Where's the Dress" did, a parody of Culture Club's
Boy George recorded with Joe Stampley. Although Boy George
sued the duo, the song was a major hit, winning an award for
Best Country Video from the American Video Awards and the
New York Film Festival.

Moe Bandy switched record labels in 1986, signing with MCA/
Curb. He also changed producers, abandoning his old collaborator
Ray Baker for Jerry Kennedy. Appropriately, the sound of the
singer's records changed as well. No longer modern-day honky
tonk, they were slicker and more pop-oriented. Ironically, the

change in sound didn't bring about more commercial success. For a brief time, Bandy continued to have Top Ten hits, including "Till I'm Too Old to Die Young" (1987) and "Americana" (1988), which became presidential candidate George Bush's campaign theme song; Bandy played Bush's Presidential Inauguration, as well as playing the White House twice in 1989. However, he wasn't faring as well on the country charts. His albums became increasingly safer and smoother, failing to reach the peaks of his rowdier early material.

Moe Bandy opened the Moe Bandy Americana Theatre in 1991, becoming one of many country performers to establish themselves in Branson, MO. Bandy frequently performs in the 900-seat venue with his Americana Band. In the '90s, his theater was more popular than his records, but for a time in the late '70s and early '80s he was one of the most popular and exciting singers recording. — *Stephen Thomas Erlewine*

I Just Started Hatin' Cheatin' Songs Today / 1974 / GRC ✦✦✦✦

It Was Always So Easy / 1975 / GRC ✦✦✦

Bandy, The Rodeo Clown / 1975 / GRC ✦✦✦✦

The Best of Moe Bandy, Vol. 1 / 1977 / Columbia ✦✦✦✦
Best of Moe Bandy, Vol. 1 covers the honky tonk singer's first big hits, including "It Was Always So Easy (To Find an Unhappy Woman)" and "Hank Williams, You Wrote My Life." Although it has a good song selection, it has since been replaced by the more comprehensive collection *Honky Tonk Amnesia*. — *Stephen Thomas Erlewine*

Greatest Hits [Moe Bandy & Joe Stampley] / 1982 / Columbia ✦✦✦✦
Carousing, drinking, and dodging wives are the order of the day here. "Holding the Bag" and "Tell Ole I Ain't Here, He Better Get on Home" are particularly amusing, but the biggest laughs come with the transvestite storyline of "Honky Tonk Queen." — *Tom Roland*

You Haven't Heard the Last of Me / 1987 / MCA ✦✦✦
Released nearly four years after his last previous Top Ten single, this album gave Bandy a brief return to the spotlight. Working with record-producer Jerry Kennedy for the first time, Bandy maintains more command of his delivery than on any previous album. — *Tom Roland*

Many Mansions / 1989 / Curb ✦✦✦
A fine title song about homelessness, among others. — *Mark A. Humphrey*

Greatest Hits [Curb] / 1992 / Curb ✦✦✦✦
Moe Bandy's late-'80s hits for Curb Records are collected on this brief album. By this time, he had tamed a lot of the rowdier aspects of his music, settling into a smoother rhythm. There are some genuine overlooked gems here—"Back in My Roarin' 20s" and "Till I'm Too Old to Die Young" are particularly noteworthy—but fans of his gut-level honky tonk might be disappointed. Nevertheless, it's a first-rate retrospective of a generally overlooked era. — *Stephen Thomas Erlewine*

★ **Honky Tonk Amnesia: The Best of Moe Bandy** / Feb. 20, 1996 / Razor & Tie ✦✦✦✦✦
Honky Tonk Amnesia is the first comprehensive collection of Moe Bandy's career, featuring all of his biggest hits on Columbia, plus a couple of his duets with Joe Stampley. Bandy's strength is his conviction—at his best, he was a straightahead, no-frills honky tonker and there is nothing but his best on this disc. It's the essential Bandy album. — *Stephen Thomas Erlewine*

Glenn Barber

b. Feb. 2, 1935, Hollis, OK
Banjo, Bass, Dobro, Guitar, Mandolin, Guitar (Steel) / Traditional Country
During the 1970s, the multi-talented performer Glenn Barber had 21 singles on the charts, but never really became a country music star. He was born in Hollis, OK, but was raised in Pasadena, TX. He began playing guitar as a child and turned out to be a prodigy who won numerous talent contests. In high school, Barber started his own band; he made his recording debut at age 16 with "Ring

Around the Moon" for the Stampede label. The owner of the label, "Pappy" Dailey, would be a key figure in the development of Barber's career, as he became the young singer's manager for the next two decades. Barber became a disc jockey and featured performer on KIKK Houston in 1962. He and his band the Western Swingmasters would appear there five times a week until 1968. Barber made his chart debut in 1964 with "How Can I Forget You," which made it to the Top 50. He then switched from Sims to Starday and scored a double-sided hit for his debut with "If Anyone Can Show Cause"/"Stronger Than Dirt." He signed with Hickory in 1968 and remained with them through 1974, and during that time, appeared on the Top 30 charts four times with songs such as "Kissed by the Rain, Warmed by the Sun" (1969) and "Unexpected Goodbye" (1972). After 1974, Barber had no chart action until 1978, when he had two Top 30 hits. He moved to MMI in late 1979 and had two more hits, including "Everybody Wants to Disco." During the 1970s he built the Orbit recording studio. In addition to performing and writing songs, Barber is also a noted portrait and mural painter. During the '90s he also turned to screenwriting. — *Sandra Brennan*

New Star / 1970 / Hickory ✦✦✦✦

● **Best of Glenn Barber** / 1972 / Hickory ✦✦✦✦

Glenn Barber / 1974 / MGM/Hickory ✦✦✦

First Love Feelings / 1983 / Tudor ✦✦✦

Saturday's Heros Are Gone / 1984 / Tudor ✦✦✦
Not a bad album. Many of the songs are quite good, and on a couple, it's difficult imagining anyone but Barber performing them. He doesn't have a great voice, but overall each song is done well. — *Jim Worbois*

Bobby Bare

b. Apr. 7, 1935, Irontown, OH
Guitar, Vocals / Traditional Country, Progressive Country, Country-Folk, Nashville Sound/Countrypolitan
Bobby Bare's story is nearly as fascinating as his music. Bare's mother died when he was five. His father couldn't earn enough money to feed his children, forcing the family to split up. Bare was working on a farm by the time he was 15 years old, later working in factories and selling ice cream to support himself. Building his first guitar, he began playing music in his late teens, performing with a local Ohio band in Springfield.

In the late '50s, he moved out to Los Angeles. Bare's first appearance on record was in 1958, when he recorded his own talking blues "The All American Boy," which was credited to "Bill Parsons." A number of labels refused the record before the Ohio-based Fraternity Records bought it for $50; the fee also included the publishing rights. "The All American Boy" was released in 1959 and it surprisingly became the second-biggest single in the US that December, crossing over to the pop charts and peaking at No. 3. The single was also a big hit in the UK, reaching No. 22.

Before Bobby Bare could capitalize on his success, he was drafted into the armed forces. While he was on duty, Fraternity hired another singer to become Bill Parsons and sent him out on tour. After Bare left the Army, he became roommates with Willie Nelson. During this time, he decided to become a pop singer. Soon, he was touring with rock/pop stars like Roy Orbison and Bobby Darin, recording records for a number of California labels. Meanwhile, his songs were being recorded by a number of artists; three of his tunes were featured in the Chubby Checker movie, *Teenage Millionaire*.

Even though he was having some modest success, Bare decided he wasn't fulfilled playing pop music. Instead, he turned back to country, developing a distinctive blend of country, folk, and pop. In 1962, Chet Atkins signed him to RCA Records. By the end of the year, he had a hit with "Shame on You," which was notable for being one of the first records out of Nashville to make concessions to the pop charts by featuring horns. The production worked, as the single broke into the pop charts. The following year, he recorded Mel Tillis and Danny Dill's "Detroit City," which became his second straight single to make both the country and pop charts. Bare followed up the single with a traditional folk song, "500 Miles from Home." It was another big hit for the singer, peaking in the Top Ten on both the country and pop charts. Bare continued to rack up hits in 1964 and 1965, as well as appearing in the Western movie *A Distant Trumpet*.

As the '60s progressed, Bobby Bare continued to blur the lines between country and folk, as he was influenced by songwriters like Bob Dylan, recording material by Dylan and several of his contemporaries. Along with exploring American folk, Bare traveled to England, where he was popular. In 1968, he recorded an album with a Liverpool country band called the Hillsiders, (*The English Country Side*), which signaled his artistic drive.

Bare switched record labels in 1970, signing with Mercury Records. He stayed at the label for two years, producing a string of Top Ten hits, including "How I Got to Memphis," "Please Don't Tell Me How the Story Ends," and "Come Sundown." Upon leaving Mercury, he recorded an album for United Artists called *This Is Bare Country*, which remained unreleased until 1976; instead, the label released a collection, *The Very Best of Bobby Bare*. After leaving UA, he re-signed with RCA in 1973.

Later in 1973, Bare released a double album of Shel Silverstein songs, *Bobby Bare Sings Lullabys, Legends and Lies*. Not only did the album represent the beginning of a collaboration with Silverstein, it was arguably the first country concept album, adding fire to the outlaw movement of the '70s in the process. The record was a hit with country audiences as well as rock fans, gaining airplay on FM radio stations. The following year, he had his first No. 1 single with "Marie Laveau." Bare released another record of Silverstein songs, *Bobby Bare and the Family Singin' in the Kitchen*, in 1975. Unfortunately, the singer's oldest daughter died shortly after recording the album; she was only 15.

In 1977, Bare received a major publicity push from Bill Graham, the legendary rock concert promoter. Graham signed the singer to his management company, proclaiming that Bare was the "Springsteen of country music." Soon, the singer found new audiences at college campuses and Canada. He switched record labels the same year, recording the self-produced *Bare* for Columbia. Two years later, he released *Sleeper Whenever I Fall*, which featured contributions from Rodney Crowell and rearranged rock 'n' roll songs like the Rolling Stones' "The Last Time" and the Byrds' "Feel a Whole Lot Better." Bare resumed his collaboration with Silverstein in 1980, releasing the live collection *Down and Dirty*, which spawned two humorous hits, "Numbers" and "Tequila Sheila." The following year, he released *As Is*, which showed that he was continuing to record a diverse selection of songwriters, including Townes Van Zandt, J.J. Cale, and Guy Clark.

Despite the fact that his work was consistently critically acclaimed, Bare's record sales began to slip in the early '80s, as the 1982 Silverstein collaboration *Drinkin' from the Bottle, Singin' from the Heart* and his 1985 record for EMI failed to launch any major hit singles. Nevertheless, Bobby Bare retained a devoted following in the US and the UK into the '90s, and his influence on contemporary country music is evident. —*Stephen Thomas Erlewine*

Detroit City / 500 Miles Away from Home / 1963 / RCA Victor ✦✦✦✦

Bobby Bare's first two albums, *Detroit City* and *500 Miles Away From Home*, are combined on this single disc. Though there are some weak tracks on the disc, this is one of the strongest and most exciting collections of Bare's music, showcasing the songwriter in his earliest stages. He might not have perfected his sound, but it is thrilling to hear him sort it out. —*Stephen Thomas Erlewine*

Lullabys, Legends and Lies / 1973 / Bear Family ✦✦✦
This two-album set features 14 Shel Silverstein songs, all performed in a room of rowdy friends who sing along and comment when the mood strikes. —*Michael McCall*

☆ **This Is Bobby Bare** / 1973 / RCA ✦✦✦✦✦
The best assortment of his '60s work includes such classic hits as "Detroit City," "500 Miles from Home" and "Streets of Baltimore" as well as country-folk versions of "Four Strong Winds," "Miller's Cave" and "Long Black Veil." —*Michael McCall*

Cowboys & Daddys / 1975 / RCA ✦✦✦✦
Instead of singing about outlaws and rhinestone cowboys, Bare's songs speak of the struggles and joys of those who truly make their home on the range. —*Michael McCall*

This Is Bobby Bare / 1976 / United Artists ✦✦✦✦

Sleeper Wherever I Fall / 1978 / Columbia ✦✦✦
Some of Bare's best albums barely registered on the radio charts, but they're rich in unusual songs and distinct performances. Selections here include a cover of the Rolling Stones' "The Last Time" and a Rodney Crowell gem, "On a Real Good Night." —*Michael McCall*

As Is / 1981 / Columbia ✦✦✦✦
Produced by Rodney Crowell, it's a solid collection of good songs in which Bare's sly, low-key charms shine. —*Michael McCall*

★ **Best of Bobby Bare** / 1994 / Razor & Tie ✦✦✦✦✦
The 21-track, single-disc collection *The Best of Bobby Bare* offers the first comprehensive overview of his big hits from the '60s and early '70s, including "Detroit City," "The Long Black Veil," and "500 Miles from Home." Featuring nearly all of his essential tracks, the disc is a near-definitive retrospective, and a perfect introduction to Bare's music. —*Stephen Thomas Erlewine*

The Mercury Years 1970-1972, Vol. 1 / 1994 / Bear Family ✦✦✦✦
Instead of packaging Bobby Bare's complete Mercury recordings in a box set, Bear Family released three individual discs entitled *The Mercury Years*. Bare was a part of Mercury's roster in the early '70s, nearly a full decade after he began a streak of country hits for RCA Records. In general, his Mercury records boasted fuller production than his RCA sides, but that didn't mean they were diluted—Bare continued to explore an intriguing fusion of traditional country, rock, folk and pop. *The Mercury Years* is presented chronologically, which means there is often as much filler as prime material on each volume. However, *Vol. 1* is the most consistent of the batch, boasting all three of his Top Ten hits for the label—"That's How I Got to Memphis," "Come Sundwon," "Please Don't Tell Me How the Story Ends"—plus a wealth of lesser-known, but equally fine, cuts like "For the Good Times," "It's Freezing in El Paso," "Don't It Make You Want to Go Home" and "Where Have All the Seasons Gone." —*Stephen Thomas Erlewine*

The Mercury Years 1970-1972, Vol. 2 / 1994 / Bear Family ✦✦✦✦
The second installment of Bear Family's three-volume retrospective of Bobby Bare's Mercury recordings covers 1971 and early 1972, and features the minor hit "Short and Sweet." Though there is a fair amount of mediocre material on *Vol. 2*, the best songs here—including "The World Is Weighing Heavy on My Mind," "Don't You Ever Get Tired of Hurting Me," "West Virginia Woman," "The Year That Clayton Delaney Died" and "Lonely Street"—rank among Bare's best. —*Stephen Thomas Erlewine*

The Mercury Years 1970-1972, Vol. 3 / 1994 / Bear Family ✦✦✦
The final volume of Bear Family's three-disc overview of Bobby Bare's Mercury recordings includes the minor hits "What Am I Gonna Do" and "Sylvia's Mother," plus a number of good, but overlooked cuts, such as "Footprints in the Sand of Time," "Even the Bad Times Are Good," "Laying Here Lyin' in Bed," "Lorena" and "Music City, USA." Though the overall quality of the disc isn't as strong as its two predecessors, *Vol. 3* remains a necessary purchase for Bobby Bare completists. —*Stephen Thomas Erlewine*

All-American Boy / 1994 / Bear Family ✦✦✦✦
The four-disc box set *The All-American Boy* contains all of Bobby Bare's RCA recordings between 1962 and 1970, including the Top Ten hits "Detroit City," "500 Miles Away from Home," "Miller's Cave," "Four Strong Winds," "A Dear John Letter," "It's Alright," "The Streets of Baltimore," "The Game of Triangles" and "(Margie's At) The Lincoln Park Inn." In addition to all of the master recordings, the set also includes several alternate takes, unreleased tracks, incomplete takes, duets and rarities. Certainly, box sets that are this comprehensive only appeal to dedicated fans, yet *The All-American Boy* is more listenable than the average all-encompassing Bear Family release because Bare's RCA recordings

were of consistently high quality. Of course, that doesn't mean casual fans should purchase the set—it means that the set is worthwhile for serious fans. —*Thom Owens*

Essential / Jan. 28, 1997 / RCA ✦✦✦✦
Like all the other volumes of RCA's *Essential* series, *The Essential Bobby Bare* contains a cross-section of Bare's hits, lesser-known singles, rarities, and album tracks. Though it is a useful and entertaining collection, Razor & Tie's compilation remains a more definitive retrospective. —*Thom Owens*

Mercury Years / Bear Family ✦✦✦✦
Bear Family has issued Bobby Bare's entire recordings for Mercury on a three-disc box set. Bare was only at Mercury for two years, but that time did produce a handful of his finest singles, including "How I Got to Memphis," "Please Don't Tell Me How the Story Ends," and "Come Sundown," a duet with Kris Kristofferson. Though the music is quite good, the set remains of interest only to completists, since there is simply too much music for casual listeners. Nevertheless, it's a necessary purchase for devoted Bare fans. —*Stephen Thomas Erlewine*

Greatest Hits / RCA ✦✦✦
His '70s chart songs are here, including the No. 1 hit "Marie Laveau," a sharp version of Billy Joe Shaver's "Ride Me Down Easy" and his best-known novelty song, "Dropkick Me, Jesus." —*Michael McCall*

Barefoot Jerry

Country-Rock, Southern Rock
Guitarist Wayne Moss remained the one constant member of Barefoot Jerry on the band's recordings for Capitol, Warner, and Monument during the '70s. Moss had played in several rock and R&B groups before he joined Brenda Lee's backing band in the early '60s. Session work in Nashville brought him a credit on Bob Dylan's *Blonde on Blonde* in 1966, and he also played with the Escorts during the late '60s before forming Area Code 615 with several other Dylan alumni. The group recorded a self-titled album in 1970 and *A Trip in the Country* the following year, but musical commitments prevented them from touring. Area Code 615 played its only live show in 1970 at the Fillmore West, and broke up soon after. Moss was back in action by 1971, though, forming Barefoot Jerry with two members of Area Code 615—vocalist/guitarist Mac Gayden and drummer Kenny Buttrey—plus keyboard player John Harris.

The group signed to Capitol and released *Southern Delight* in 1971. By the time of the following year's self-titled LP for Warner Bros., Russ Hicks and Kenny Malone had replaced Gayden and Buttrey. Another label change (to Monument) and additional lineup replacements (Si Edwards on drums, Dave Doran on bass, Fred Newell on vocals) characterized 1974's *Watchin' TV*, which featured Moss' friend Charlie McCoy. Barefoot Jerry returned the favor on McCoy's Country hits "Boogie Woogie" and "Summit Ridge Drive." The following year, after Barefoot Jerry recorded *You Can't Get Off with Your Shoes On*, Monument re-released both the Capitol and Warner Bros. albums on a double-LP set titled *Grocery*.

Moss assembled yet another group for Barefoot Jerry's 1976 update, *Keys to the Country*. His band included bassist Terry Bearmore, guitarist Jim Colvard, Warren Hartman on various keyboards and Charlie McCoy, who again made a guest appearance. The same members (sans McCoy) returned for a final album in 1977, *Barefootin'.* Wayne Moss has continued to play and produce, especially for his friend McCoy. —*John Bush*

Southern Delight / 1971 / Capitol ✦✦
Barefoot Jerry / 1972 / Warner Brothers ✦✦✦
Watchin' TV / 1974 / Monument ✦✦✦
The picking is hot but the songs leave something to be desired. For example: "Funky Lookin' Eyes" is based on the same lick as Cream's "Sunshine of Your Love" but isn't nearly as interesting. —*Jim Worbois*

You Can't Get off with Your Shoes on / 1975 / Monument ✦✦
● **Grocery** / 1976 / Monument ✦✦✦✦

Keys to the Country / 1976 / Monument ✦✦✦
Somewhat an outgrowth of Area Code 615, it's more interesting. Instead of just doing jams, this group does proper songs which include vocals. While not great by any stretch of the imagination, it's a nice-sounding record. —*Jim Worbois*

Barefootin' / 1976 / Monument ✦✦✦

Russ Barenberg

Guitar / Traditional Bluegrass
Russ Barenberg is a guitarist who played with the bluegrass band Country Cooking. He later went solo, playing a blend of jazz, funk, Latin, and bluegrass. *Chip Renner*

Cowboy Calypso / 1979 / Rounder ✦✦✦
A good album with Andy Statman and Jerry Douglas. —*Chip Renner*

Behind the Melodies / 1983 / Rounder ✦✦✦✦
A very good cast: Tony Trischka, Andy Statman. —*Chip Renner*

● **Halloween Rehearsal** / 1987 / Rounder ✦✦✦✦
Combines his *Cowboy Calypso* and *Behind the Melodies.* —*Chip Renner*

Moving Pictures / 1988 / Rounder ✦✦✦✦
The second choice, after *Halloween Rehearsal.* —*Chip Renner*

Randy Barlow

b. Mar. 29, 1943, Detroit, MI
Vocals / Country-Pop, Singer-Songwriter, Neo-Traditionalist Country
A singer-songwriter who reached his commercial peak in the late '70s, Randy Barlow was born in Detroit in 1943. By the age of ten, he was playing guitar with local rhythm & blues bands; at 14, he was performing professionally. After leaving college in 1965, he moved to California to become a Hollywood stuntman, but instead found work with Dick Clark's *Caravan of Stars*, serving as a promoter and emcee in addition to performing music and comedy.

In 1968, Barlow issued his first single, "Color Blind," which failed to chart. After years of struggle playing local clubs, he was awarded another shot at recording in 1974, making the best of it with the minor hit "Throw Away the Pages." After a string of other small successes, he reached the Top 20 in 1976 with a rendition of "Twenty-four Hours from Tulsa," which had been a Top Ten hit for Gene Pitney in 1963.

From 1978 to 1979, Barlow issued four back-to-back No. 10 singles—"Slow and Easy," "No Sleep Tonight," "Fall in Love with Me Tonight" and "Sweet Melinda"—and received notice for the 1977 album *Arrival*, its 1978 follow-up *Fall in Love with Me*, and a 1979 self-titled effort. However, subsequent singles and albums (like 1981's *Dimensions*) failed to garner much commercial or critical acclaim; in 1983, Barlow released his final chart single, "Don't Leave Me Lonely Loving You," which hit No. 67. —*Jason Ankeny*

Arrival / 1977 / Republic ✦✦✦
Fall in Love with Me / 1978 / Republic ✦✦✦
● **Randy Barlow** / 1979 / Republic ✦✦✦✦
Dimensions / 1981 / Paid ✦✦✦

Max D. Barnes

b. Jul. 24, 1936, Hardscratch, IA
Vocals / Contemporary Country, New Traditionalist
Max D. Barnes may not have released many records, but he left an important mark on contemporary country music. As a songwriter, Barnes composed many familiar songs of the '80s and '90s, receiving 42 songwriter awards in his career. Artists like George Jones ("Who's Gonna Fill Their Shoes"), Waylon Jennings ("Drinkin' and Dreamin'"), Conway Twitty ("Red Neckin' Love Makin' Night"), Keith Whitley ("Ten Feet Away"), Randy Travis ("I Won't Need You Anymore [Forever and Always]"), Vern Gosdin ("Way Down Deep," "Slow Burnin' Memory"), Pam Tillis ("Don't Tell Me What to Do"), and Vince Gill ("Look at Us") have recorded his songs, as have many others. Although he has had a couple of

minor hits himself (most notably "Allegheny Lady" in the mid-'70s), his true legacy lies in his songs, not his records.

Barnes grew up in Iowa, receiving his first guitar from his sister Ruthie Steele at age 11. Shortly afterward, his parents were divorced. He moved to Omaha, NE, with his mother and two younger brothers. At 16, he dropped out of school and began singing in a local nightclub. During this time, he formed a band called the Golden Rockets, which featured his future wife Patsy as lead singer. Max and Patsy quit playing clubs after the birth of their son, Patrick. At first, Barnes worked for an Omaha concrete company, but the family soon moved to Long Beach, CA, where he was the foreman at a lamp factory. After a while, he quit, spending his summers in Omaha and his winters singing in California. By 1962, he saved up enough money to buy a nightclub near Lake Okiboji, IA, but he sold it after eight months. Again, the Barnes family moved back to Omaha, where Max spent nine years working as a truck driver.

Barnes' musical career didn't really begin until 1971, when he recorded a single for Jed, "Ribbons of Steel"/"Hello Honky Tonk." He followed it with "You Gotta Be Putting Me On"/"Growing Old with Grace," which was released on Willex. Following some words of encouragement from songwriter Kent Westberry, Barnes moved to Nashville in 1973. He became a staff writer for Roz-Tense Music, which led to Charley Pride recording two of his songs. Soon, he moved to Gary S. Paxman Music, then to Danor Music. While he was with Danor, Barnes wrote nearly 30 songs recorded by other artists, including several hit singles; on one occasion, he had five of his songs on the charts simultaneously. He also co-wrote many songs with Troy Seals, one of the co-owners of the publishing company. Sadly, tragedy befell the Barnes' family, as the eldest son Patrick died in a car accident in 1975. Max wrote about the incident on "Chiseled in Stone," which was co-written with Vern Gosdin, who had a hit with the song in 1989.

In 1976, Max signed a publishing deal with Screen-Gems EMI, which helped him secure a recording contract with Polydor. Released the following year, *Rough Around the Edges* spawned the minor hit "Allegheny Lady," which scraped the bottom of the charts. If he didn't have hits with his own records, he did have hits with his songs, as Conway Twitty brought several of Max's songs to the charts, including the Loretta Lynn duets "I Can't Love You Enough" and "From Seven Till Ten," and the solo "Don't Take It Away," which hit No. 1. — *Stephen Thomas Erlewine*

● **Rough Around the Edges** / 1980 / Ovation ✦✦✦✦
Pieces of My Life / 1981 / Country Roads [UK] ✦✦✦

Mandy Barnett

b. Sep. 28, 1975, Crossville, TN
Contemporary Country
Born Amanda Carol Barnett, Mandy Barnett began singing as a child, winning the Best Country Act at Dollywood when she was only ten, and her mother started bringing her on trips to Nashville. As a teenager, she was signed by renowned talent scout and producer Jimmy Bowen, and eventually Asylum Records. An uncompromising singer whose style is rooted in the classic country of Patsy Cline, Jim Reeves, Webb Pierce, and Brenda Lee, Barnett's keen interpretative sense enables her to delve into a song, study the intricacies of its emotional content, and render a powerful performance through her full-bodied voice. Her torchy delivery on her contemporary, yet retro-sounding, country and pop-tinged material recalls Patsy Cline; it's no wonder then that while waiting to record her self-titled debut, she paid her bills by playing the legendary singer four nights a week, 26 weeks a year in the musical production *Always . . . Patsy Cline* at the Ryman Auditorium. — *Jack Leaver*

Mandy Barnett / 1996 / Asylum ✦✦✦✦
Tennessee native Mandy Barnett has already been busy bringing Patsy Cline back to life by playing (and singing the songs of) the rowdy, legendary vocalist in the stage production *Always . . . Patsy Cline*. Now Barnett, who's not yet even 21 years old, has taken that experience and used it to power her self-titled debut album for Asylum Records. Cline's influence is out front on Barnett's handling of Willie Nelson's 1962 classic "Three Days"

and the brand-new Kostas/Richard Bennett song "I'll Just Pretend." The downside of Barnett's album is that the production tends toward clean and safe territory (such as the overabundance of strings on the syrupy "Rainy Days"). The upside is that, even during her album's most middle-of-the-road moments, Barnett's voice remains strong, smooth, and confident. And a few of the songs shine with real promise—Barnett's delicate handling of Jim Lauderdale's "Planet of Love," for example, and the traditional "Wayfaring Stranger," which closes the album on a comfortable, unhurried note. — *Kurt Wolff*

Barrier Brothers

Traditional Bluegrass
The Barrier Brothers were pioneers of bluegrass music. All three, Herman, Ernest, and Henry, were born in Hardin, TN, where Herman and Ernest learned to play old-time music when they were young. They started out at a small radio station in Corinth, MS, during the early 1950s. Later, the whole Barrier family moved to South Bend, IN, to find work. There, when not working, they honed their musical skills: Ernest mastered the five-string banjo, while Herman became an adept bass player. The two taught young Henry to sing lead and play guitar. After Henry grew up, they formed a band that included fiddler Gene Dykes. The Barriers were a semi-professional weekend band, and during the '50s mostly played at parks, fairs, and minor jamborees throughout the Midwest. The brothers and their Ozark Mountain Boys finally cut their first record for Ray Earle's independent Armoneer label near the end of the decade. They had two singles and a gospel EP, which led to a major contract with Philips International, where they recorded three albums in as many years. The Barriers were a versatile band, but they didn't get to show it on these albums, as Philips executives insisted on their recording bluegrass standards. After their contract expired, Herman and Ernest returned to Tennessee and Henry remained in Indiana, where he continued to play in various bands. Following Herman's death in 1988, Ernest continued working in his welding business. He continued jamming with local musicians until his death in early 1994. — *Sandra Brennan*

● **Golden Bluegrass Hits** / 1962 / Philips ✦✦✦✦
More Golden Bluegrass Hits / 1962 / Philips ✦✦✦✦
Gospel Songs, Bluegrass Style / 1962 / Philips ✦✦✦
Pickin' and Singin' / 1977 / Old Homestead ✦✦✦

Bashful Brother Oswald (Beecher Kirby)

b. Dec. 26, 1911, Sevier County, TN
Banjo, Dobro, Guitar / Old-Time, Traditional Country
For nearly 60 years, Bashful Brother Oswald was one of the most influential and talented dobro players in country music. For the majority of his career, he was the dobroist for Roy Acuff's Smoky Mountain Boys, becoming the leading dobroist in country as well as one of the most popular members of the band. Over the course of his career, Oswald released only a handful of solo recordings, but left behind enough music to illustrate why he was one of the most influential players of his era.

Bashful Brother Oswald (born Beecher Ray Kirby) was the son of an Appalachian musician. As a child, he learned how to play dobro and banjo, as well as sing gospel music. When he was a teenager, he began playing square dances with various country groups. In the late '20s, Oswald moved to Flint, MI, to work in a Buick factory. After the Great Depression hit, he lost his job and became a musician at the radio station WFDF. Because Hawaiian music was very popular, the station manager decided to feature it prominently during regular programming, thus inspiring Oswald to buy his first steel guitar. In 1933, he performed at the Chicago World's Fair and found himself greatly influenced by the wide variety of music he heard there. The following year, he went to Knoxville and began playing dobro with several different bands, including Acuff's Crazy Tennesseans. Oswald became a permanent member of Acuff's band after the singer was invited to join the Grand Ole Opry in the late '30s.

As a vocalist, Oswald gained recognition for singing a few lines on Acuff's classic "Precious Jewel" (1940) and on "Wreck on the Highway" (1942). Acuff named his sideman "Brother Oswald" in a ruse to convince audiences that he was the brother of the band's singer, Rachel Veach, to obscure the fact that Veach was an unmarried woman. The dobroist happily complied in creating the Oswald character, and began wearing a floppy mountain hat, tattered overalls, and enormous shoes while adopting a braying horse laugh. The cartoonish character immediately became a favorite of audiences, and it stayed popular throughout his career.

Oswald continued performing and recording with Acuff until the '80s, but began a solo career in the '60s. After working as a session musician, he released a few albums of his own, beginning with 1962's *Bashful Brother Oswald*. In the early '70s, the Nitty Gritty Dirt Band had Oswald perform on their 1972 hit album, *Will the Circle Be Unbroken*. Also in 1972, guitarist and dobro player Tut Taylor produced Oswald's *Brother Oswald* album. In the late '70s, he began playing in the Opryland theme park with former Smoky Mountain bandmate Charlie Collins. During the 1980s, Oswald continued performing with Collins at Opryland and Acuff at the Opry. Following Acuff's death in 1992, he and Collins earned a regular slot on the Opry's main stage. —*Sandra Brennan*

Bashful Brother Oswald / 1962 / Starday ✦✦✦✦   .
● **Brother Oswald** / 1972 / ✦✦✦✦
Roy Acuff's dobroist since the '30s, in a pleasant set of Hawaiian-inspired old-time country songs. —*Mark A. Humphrey*

Don't Say Aloha / Rounder ✦✦✦

That's Country / Rounder ✦✦✦

Oz & Charlie / Rounder ✦✦

Molly Bee (Molly Beechwood)

b. Aug. 18, 1939, Oklahoma City, OK
Vocals / Traditional Country, Country-Pop, Rockabilly, Country Boogie
Molly Bee had several hits in the early '60s, crafting a showy stage persona, ideal for clubs. Raised in Beltbuckle, TN, Molly Bee didn't begin singing until her family moved to Tucson, AZ. Even then, she started her singing career much earlier than most—she was ten years old when she gained the attention of Rex Allen, the singing cowboy. Bee's mother took her to see the singer at a local concert, where she had her daughter sing for him. Impressed with her performance of "Lovesick Blues," Allen had the child sing on his radio show shortly afterward. A year later, her family moved to Hollywood, where she became a regular on *Hometown Jamboree*, a Los Angeles-based television show run by Cliffie Stone. Bee sang with the Jamboree throughout her teens, gaining a large following of fans; she was so popular, the program was occasionally called the "Molly Bee Show." During this time, she was also a regular on *The Pinky Lee Show*, appearing on the television program for three years.

When she was 13, Bee signed with Capitol Records, releasing her first single, "Tennessee Tango." However, it was "I Saw Mommy Kissing Santa Claus," released late in 1952, that was her first major success. In 1953, she recorded "Don't Start Courtin' in a Hot Rod Ford," a duet with Tennessee Ernie Ford. The following year, she left Pinky Lee's show for Ford's daytime television show. Bee's career continued to grow, as she had more hit singles—including "Young Romance," "Don't Look Back," and "Five Points of a Star"—and appeared on a variety of television shows. By the late '50s, her live shows were drawing large, record-breaking crowds.

In the early '60s, Molly Bee began to move her talents to other areas, acting in several musical plays (*The Boy Friend, Finian's Rainbow, Paint Your Wagon*) and movies (*Chartreuse Caboose, The Young Swingers*), as well as becoming a fixture in Las Vegas. However, her recording career began to decline after she signed to Liberty Records in 1962. After two unsuccessful years there, she moved to MGM in 1965, releasing the *It's Great... It's Molly Bee* album. Bee found her greatest success at MGM the following year with "Losing You/Miserable Me."

By the late '60s, Bee had fallen prey to drug addiction and had to take several years off the road as she rebuilt her life. She re-emerged in 1975 with *Good Golly Ms. Molly*, this time on Cliffie Stone's Granite record label. Her comeback was successful, producing two charting singles: "She Kept on Talking'" and "Right or Left at Oak Street." In 1982, she released her final album, *Sounds Fine to Me*, which failed to match the performance of *Good Golly*, although she remained a popular concert draw. —*Stephen Thomas Erlewine*

Young Romance / 1958 / Capitol ✦✦✦

It's Great, It's Molly Bee / 1965 / MGM ✦✦✦✦
● **Swingin' Country** / 1967 / MGM ✦✦✦✦

Carl Belew (Carl Robert Belew)

b. Apr. 21, 1931, Salina, OK, **d.** Oct. 31, 1990
Vocals / Nashville Sound/Countrypolitan
Despite recording eight albums between 1960 and 1972, Carl Belew is best remembered as a songwriter whose work was covered by an eclectic group of artists ranging from Patsy Cline to Gene Vincent to Andy Williams. Born in Oklahoma in 1931, Belew first entered the studio in 1955; by the following year, he gained his first widespread exposure thanks to appearances on a pair of California-based radio programs, *Town Hall Party* and *The Cliffie Stone Show*. In 1957, he performed on the *Louisiana Hayride*.

Belew's composition "Stop the World (and Let Me Off)" hit the Top Ten in 1958 in a rendition by Johnnie and Jack; the following year, Andy Williams hit the Top Five with "Lonely Street," a song which would become Belew's trademark tune thanks to subsequent covers by Cline, Vincent, and Rex Allen Jr. Later in 1959, the breakup of his marriage inspired Belew to write "Am I That Easy to Forget," a Top 40 pop hit for actress Debbie Reynolds, which was later recorded by Engelbert Humperdinck, Skeeter Davis, Don Gibson, Jim Reeves, and Leon Russell. Belew's own rendition hit the Top Ten in 1959.

In 1960, Belew released his self-titled debut LP; in the same year, he notched a Top 20 hit with the single "Too Much to Lose." Two years later, a label change prompted another eponymous effort; the single "Hello Out There" earned him another Top Ten hit, his last. Between 1964 and 1968, Belew released an album a year, beginning with *Hello Out There* and continuing with *Am I That Easy to Forget, Country Songs, Lonely Street*, and finally *Twelve Shades of Belew*. His last studio album, *When My Baby Sings His Song*, a record of duets with Betty Jean Robinson, was issued in 1972, while one final single, "Welcome Back to My World," appeared in 1974.

Throughout his career, Belew's songs continued to be popular with (and popularized by) other singers; Eddy Arnold hit No. 1 in 1965 with "What's He Doing in My World," while Jim Reeves scored a posthumous success in 1968 with "That's When I See the Blues (in Your Pretty Brown Eyes)." "Stop the World (and Let Me Off)" also reached the Top 20 twice more thanks to a 1965 cover by Waylon Jennings and a 1974 version by Susan Raye. Carl Belew died of cancer on Halloween, 1990, at the age of 59. —*Jason Ankeny*

Carl Belew / 1960 / Decca ✦✦

Hello out There / 1964 / RCA ✦✦✦

Am I That Easy to Forget? / 1965 / RCA ✦✦✦
● **Twelve Shades of Belew** / 1968 / RCA ✦✦✦✦

The Bellamy Brothers

Country-Rock, Country-Pop, Contemporary Country
Although the Bellamy Brothers are the most successful duo in country music history, they have never been favored by the critics. That doesn't mean their music was rote, by-the-books formulaic country-pop. More than most acts of the late '70s and '80s, the Bellamys pushed the borders of country music, adding strong elements of rock, reggae, and even rap. Nearly a decade after their first hit—the 1975 pop chart-topper, southern-rock-tinged "Let Your Love Flow"—the brothers had earned a stack of best-selling records, as well as critical respect by the late '80s. By that time,

The Bellamy Brothers

they had firmly established themselves as the top duo of the '80s, both in terms of popularity and musical diversity.

Howard and David Bellamy were raised in Florida. Their father, Homer, played traditional country music around the house and performed with a Western swing band on the weekends. In addition to the country music they heard in their house, the brothers were drawn to the calypso music of the neighboring Caribbean islands. However, nothing provided as much attraction as the rock 'n' roll they heard on their sister's records and the radio. From the Everly Brothers to the Beatles, the Bellamy Brothers soaked up the sounds of contemporary pop and rock. In their late teens and early 20s, they became reinfatuated with country music, thanks to the music of George Jones and Merle Haggard.

Both Howard and David learned how to play a variety of instruments in their childhood. Neither child had any formal training, but Howard managed to learn the guitar, banjo, and mandolin, while David learned the piano, accordion, fiddle, banjo, organ, and mandolin. Both brothers went to college at the University of Florida, with Howard earning a degree in veterinary medicine, and David one in psychology. While they were students, they had their first paying gig playing fraternity parties.

During the late '60s, the two performed in a number of bands, both together and separately. In 1968, they moved to Atlanta, forming Jericho. Performing in such a large number of bands meant that the duo perfected a number of different musical styles, since they were expected to please the tastes of many different club audiences. Yet playing in a never-ending series of bands and clubs proved tiring, and the brothers moved back home to work on their songwriting.

In a short time, the move paid off. In 1973, the brothers met a friend of singer Jim Stafford, who directed the vocalist to David's "Spiders and Snakes." Stafford was immediately taken with the tune, releasing it as his next single; the humorous retelling of David's boyhood farm experiences would eventually sell over three million copies. The success of "Spiders and Snakes" gave the Bellamy Brothers enough money to move out to Los Angeles, where they began to concentrate on a full-time musical career.

In 1975, the brothers signed to Curb/Warner, releasing their first single, David's "Nothing' Heavy." The song flopped. Dennis St. John, who was a friend of the Bellamys and Neil Diamond's drummer, suggested that the duo record a song written by Larry E. Williams, one of Diamond's roadies. After some encouragement, the Bellamy Brothers recorded and released Williams' song, "Let Your Love Flow." The song broke the doors wide open for the brothers, topping the pop charts and climbing into the country Top 30, as well as becoming a major hit in Britain, West Germany, and Scandinavia.

The Bellamy Brothers quickly released their debut album, also called *Let Your Love Flow,* which became nearly as successful as the single. Instead of concentrating on a domestic follow-up, the duo spent their time in Europe, touring off and on for the next two years, which led to a great deal of financial success. Soon, the duo was able to pay off their debts and install their mother Frances as their financial manager. Their second album, 1977's *Plain and Fancy,* was a major success in Sweden and Norway, but it didn't make much of an impact in America.

The next year, the Bellamy Brothers moved back to America and returned to the family farm in Darby, FL. Not only did they change their address, but they changed their musical direction, moving closer to a straight country sound. The shift in style paid off, even if "Slippin' Away," the second single they released after they returned to the US, only made it into the country Top 20.

The Bellamy Brothers' country breakthrough happened in 1979, with the tongue-in-cheek "If I Said You Had a Beautiful Body Would You Hold It Against Me." Initially, the song was a hit in Ireland, convincing the duo's American record company to release it as a single. The song rocketed to No. 1 on the country charts, which led to the Top Five success of "You Ain't Just Whistlin' Dixie." The Bellamys' success continued to roll forward in 1980, as they scored two straight No. 1 hits, "Sugar Daddy" and "Dancin' Cowboys." They earned a Grammy nomination for Best Country Performance by Duo or Group and the CMA named them the Most Promising Group of the Year. Throughout 1980 and 1981, the group continued to rack up the hits, including "Do You Love As Good As You Look" and "They Could Put Me in Jail."

Curb switched the Bellamys' distribution from Warner to Elektra at the end of 1981. The change in distribution coincided with the duo's desire to experiment with their music. After they released the No. 1 "For All the Wrong Reasons," the brothers followed with "Get into Reggae Cowboy," a groundbreaking country record that incorporated Jamaican rhythms. In 1982, the group was given a Lifetime Membership of the Federation of International Country Air Personalities, and was named Top Country Duo by *Billboard.*

Throughout 1983, the brothers logged a number of hits. The following year, Curb signed a distribution deal with MCA, which didn't compromise the continuing success of the Bellamy Brothers. For the next three years, the duo was at their peak, both popularly and artistically, scoring a number of hit singles that showcased their continuing musical development as well as their increasing lyrical sophistication, indicated by the Vietnam vet anthem "Old Hippie" and "Kids of the Baby Boom." The Bellamy Brothers continued to have hits on Curb/MCA until the end of the '80s.

By the end of the decade, their audience had begun to shrink, leading the duo to switch to Atlantic. After one album with Atlantic, 1991's *Rollin' Thunder,* the Bellamys left the label and founded their own record company, Bellamy Brothers Records. *The Latest and the Greatest* (1992) was their label's first release. Although the independent record label meant that the group wasn't charting as frequently as it used to, it was also a reflection of the shift in the country audience's taste. The duo still had minor hits, like the Top 25 "Cowboy Beat," which proved that the Bellamy Brothers could continue to hold on to a dedicated group of fans in their second decade of performing. *—Stephen Thomas Erlewine*

Let Your Love Flow / 1976 / Warner Brothers ✦✦✦✦

Plain & Fancy / 1977 / Warner Brothers ✦✦
If you stumble onto this record expecting to hear the group who had all the country hits, you may be sadly surprised. Produced by Phil Gernhard (who produced Lobo), this record has no direction, and probably wouldn't be mistaken as the same group that had a hit with "Let Your Love Flow" just a short time before. "Miss Misunderstood" was done again on *You Can Get Crazy* to much better effect. *—Jim Worbois*

Two & Only / 1979 / Warner Brothers ✦✦✦
The Bellamys explore a number of musical styles with success. In addition to the hits, check out "May You Never," written by the outstanding British folk artist John Martyn, the bluesy "Miss Mis-

understood," or "Why Did We Die So Young?" with a strong early-'60s pop influence. — *Jim Worbois*

You Can Get Crazy / 1980 / Warner Brothers ✦✦✦
These prolific brothers turn in another fine batch of tunes (and one non-original) for this record. Their harmonies are appealing, whether on the reggae-influenced "Dancin' Cowboys" or "Let Me Waltz into Your Heart," with not a weak track here. Not great, but highly enjoyable. — *Jim Worbois*

● **Greatest Hits** / 1982 / MCA ✦✦✦✦
This contains such hits as "Dancin' Cowboys," "Redneck Girl," "Let Your Love Flow," "Lovers Live Longer," and others. — *AMG*

When We Were Boys / 1982 / Elektra ✦✦✦✦
Michael Lloyd, probably best-known as the producer on Shaun Cassidy's "Da Doo Ron Ron," oversaw the brothers' cute, early country years. In this album, they were given the reins for the first time, leading to a more serious, reflective, and simple approach. Also for the first time, they recorded the album at their own home studio, located on their farm in Darby, FL. — *Tom Roland*

Greatest Hits, Vol. 2 / 1986 / MCA ✦✦✦✦
Picking up where the first installment left off, *Greatest Hits, Vol. 2* captures the Bellamy Brothers maturing, both in terms of music and message. *Greatest Hits, Vol. 2* collects ten of their biggest singles—including "Feelin' the Feelin'," "When I'm Away from You," "I Need More of You," "Old Hippie," "Lie to You for Your Love" and "Too Much Is Not Enough"—all of which hit the charts between 1982 and 1986. The production and arrangements on these songs borrow from soft-rock and folk-rock, taking away most of the duo's country edge. Of course, this is what their fans wanted to hear, and these singles dominated the charts during the '80s. — *Thom Owens*

Country Rap / 1987 / MCA ✦✦✦
"Kids of the Baby Boom," encapsulating images from JFK to Third World abusiveness, speaks out for an entire generation. But the album is dominated by experimental and infectious "fun stuff," including "D-D-D-D-Divorcee," "Country Rap" and their bopping group effort with the Forester Sisters, "Too Much Is Not Enough." — *Tom Roland*

Rebels Without a Clue / Sep. 19, 1988 / MCA ✦✦✦
David Bellamy shows the depth of his songwriting talents, particularly in "The Courthouse," "The Andy Griffith Show," and the autobiographical "When the Music Meant Everything." Firm images and lots of conviction are here. — *Tom Roland*

Greatest Hits, Vol. 3 / 1989 / MCA ✦✦✦✦
This member of the series contains "The Center of My Universe," "Big Love," "Hillbilly Hell," "Santa Fe," and other hits. — *AMG*

Rip off the Knob / Aug. 1, 1993 / Bellamy Brothers ✦✦✦
Featured is Freddie Fender and Flaco Jeminez on "Staying in Love." — *Dan Cooper*

Dancin' / Jul. 1996 / Intersound ✦✦✦
The Bellamy Brothers' *Dancin'* is a professional, immaculately produced latter-day album and that's part of its fault. It might sound high-tech, but its high-class production makes it sound lifeless. The Bellamys perform with some conviction, but they lack the songs to make it worth the effort to listen to the stale sound of the record. — *Thom Owens*

Boyd Bennett

b. Dec. 7, 1924, Muscle Shoals, AL
Vocals / Rock & Roll, Rockabilly
Boyd Bennett's music fell into the cracks between country and the early days of rock 'n' roll. Boyd never received much recognition from country circles while he was performing, possibly because his music sounded more like the emerging rockabilly than hardcore honky tonk.

Bennett was raised outside of Nashville, performing as a drummer and singer with a band led by Francis Craig. After a stint in the military at the end of World War II, he became a regular performer on a local radio station, assembling a band named the Southlanders. The Southlanders sounded similar to Western swing, with some additional honky tonk grit. Bennett signed with

King Records late in 1952, recording his first single in December. The resulting record, "Time," became a minor country hit the following year.

Later in 1953, Bennett revamped the Southlanders, renaming them the Rockets and adding R&B and blues elements to his music with the intention of gaining a younger audience. Not coincidentally, this occurred at the same time Bill Haley was reworking his sound and renaming his backing band the Comets. Early in 1955, Bennett and the Rockets recorded the rock 'n' roller "Seventeen." King Records was unsure of the record's commercial appeal, yet they eventually released it, which proved to be fortunate. "Seventeen" rocketed to No. 5 on the pop charts, eventually becoming one of the best-selling records in the label's history. Not only was the original successful, but the song spawned several cover versions, making Bennett and his co-author John Young several million dollars.

The Rockets' next single, "My Boy Flat-Top," was sung by the group's Big Moe (b. James Muzey), and it also made it into the pop Top 40. In 1956, the Rockets supported Moon Mullican on the classic rockabilly single "Seven Nights to Rock." One more Rockets single—a 1956 cover of Carl Perkins' "Blue Suede Shoes"—was a minor pop success, but the Rockets couldn't replicate their success with "Seventeen" no matter how many times they tried. And throughout 1957 and 1958 they tried a lot, recording several regional hits ("Hit That Jive," "High School Hop") that never made it nationally. While all of these songs touched on rockabilly, they were significantly tamer than most of their contemporaries; consequentially, the Rockets never developed much of a cult following.

Boyd Bennett left King Records in 1959, signing with Mercury Records. Late in '59, he had one minor hit on his new record label, "Boogie Bear." After a series of unsuccessful singles, Boyd realized that he was too old for the current rock 'n' roll audience and decided to retire from performing. With the money he earned from "Seventeen," he had already bought three nightclubs and co-owned a television station. A decade after his retirement, he founded Hardcast Manufacturing, which primarily constructed parts for air conditioning. For most of his musical retirement, Bennett lived in Dallas. With the exception of the occasional charity concert with Ray Price, Boyd Bennett never re-entered the music business. — *Stephen Thomas Erlewine*

Boyd Bennett / 1957 / King ✦✦✦✦
● **Tennessee Rock 'n' Roll** / Charly ✦✦✦✦

Stephanie Bentley

Contemporary Country
Georgia-born singer Stephanie Bentley earned her first taste of musical success at the age of nine, when she, her sister Camille, and a friend took top honors in a local talent contest. The young vocal trio's success won Bentley a slot in a music and drama troupe, where she remained for a number of years, singing everything from showtunes to modern dance pop and even performing at the White House for then-President Jimmy Carter. In 1984, she formed her own band, Special Delivery, which specialized in Top 40 music and oldies.

After a stint in Georgia singing demos and advertising jingles, Bentley reunited with sister Camille and, as the Bentley Sisters, signed a Nashville production deal which failed to pan out. Discouraged, she eventually relocated to Nashville on a permanent basis, and returned to recording demos; one, for a song called "Shake the Sugar Tree," was later used as a backing vocal when the tune was re-cut by Pam Tillis. Another developmental deal followed, but again proved fruitless. A third contract, however, resulted in a hit 1995 duet with Ty Herndon, "Heart Half Empty." Bentley's solo debut, *Hopechest*, followed in 1996. — *Jason Ankeny*

● **Hopechest** / 1996 / Columbia ✦✦✦✦

Matraca Berg

b. 1964, Nashville, TN
Vocals / Contemporary Country
The daughter of country songwriter and session singer Icee Berg, Matraca Berg has written songs for Reba McEntire ("The Last One

to Know"), Suzy Bogguss ("Hey Cinderella"), Trisha Yearwood ("Wrong Side of Memphis"), and Pam Tillis ("Calico Plains"). Matraca got her start while still a teen, when her mother took her to several music publishing houses. At Tree Publishing, Berg met and teamed up with Bobby Braddock. Their first song, "Faking Love," became a No. 1 hit in 1983 for T.G. Sheppard and Karen Brooks. She then became a keyboardist for the rock-oriented Kevin Stewart Band. Two years later, Berg returned to Nashville and continued to write songs, but never considered singing them herself until 1990, when she released her first album, *Lying to the Moon*, which spawned the Top 40 single "Baby, Walk On." The following year, four more singles from the album made respectable showings on the chart. RCA Nashville refused her second album, so the songwriter moved to the label's pop music division, releasing *Bittersweet Surrender* in 1991 and *The Speed of Grace* in 1993. —*Sandra Brennan*

● **Lying to the Moon** / 1990 / RCA ✦✦✦✦
An enchanting album from one of Nashville's best female songwriting voices, this album included two minor hits, "Baby, Walk On" and "The Things You Left Undone." The title track eventually became something of a Nashville standard, being recorded by Trisha Yearwood, Robin & Linda Williams and by Berg on *The Speed of Grace*. —*Brian Mansfield*

Bittersweet Surrender / 1991 / RCA ✦✦✦

The Speed of Grace / Nov. 1993 / RCA ✦✦✦
After RCA Nashville refused a second album, Berg moved to the label's pop division, recording an album primarily with such L.A. studio musicians as guitarist Michael Landau and drummer Jim Keltner. The results highlighted Berg's bluesy side, but, aside from a cover of Dolly Parton's "Jolene" recorded with her Nashville buddies, lacked the acoustic Southern mysticism of *Lying to the Moon*. —*Brian Mansfield*

Byron Berline

b. 194?, Caldwell, KS
Fiddle / Progressive Bluegrass, Instrumental
Like his contemporary Vassar Clements, fiddler Byron Berline expanded the sonic possibilities of bluegrass, adding elements of jazz, pop, blues, rock, and traditional country to the genre. In addition to being a popular solo act, he performed as a session musician on a number of albums, including records by the Flying Burrito Brothers, Stephen Stills, the Dillards, Gram Parsons, the Nitty Gritty Dirt Band, Emmylou Harris, Kris Kristofferson, and James Taylor.

Berline learned to play from his father, an old-time fiddler. After graduating from high school, he attended the University of Oklahoma, where he played music with a campus folk group. In 1963, the Dillards played a concert on the University of Oklahoma campus. A friend of Berline's arranged an audition for him with Doug Dillard, who was so impressed he invited the young fiddler to join them for a number. Berline then joined the Cleveland Country Ramblers, and in 1964, he appeared on the Dillards' *Pickin' and Fiddlin'* and won the National Fiddle Championship in Missoula, MO. He played the Newport Folk Festival in 1965, where he met Bill Monroe, who told Berline that he wanted him to join the Blue Grass Boys in the future. In 1967, he graduated with a BA in education, but chose to join Monroe; his first appearance with the band was a show at the Grand Ole Opry. Six months after he joined the Blue Grass Boys, he was drafted into the US Army.

Just before Berline was discharged from the Army in 1969, he was invited to join the Dillard and Clark Expedition. He remained with Dillard and Clark until 1971, when the group disbanded. While with them, he played sessions for a number of other artists, including the Flying Burrito Brothers' debut album, *The Gilded Palace of Sin*. Following the breakup of Dillard and Clark, Berline played with the Dillard Expedition. In 1970, Berline scored the ABC television movie, *Run Simon Run*, the first of many films he would score. In 1971, he toured with a revamped version of the Flying Burrito Brothers. Following the tour, Berline and fellow Burritos Roger Bush and Kenny Wertz formed the Country Gazette. During this time, he also continued with his session

work, appearing on albums by Gram Parsons, Bert Jansch, Ian Matthews and Southern Comfort, and Bill Wyman.

In 1975, Berline left Country Gazette and moved to Los Angeles with his family, where he intended to concentrate on songwriting, session work, and scoring films. Later that year, he founded Sundance with Dan Crary, Jack Skinner, John Hickman, Allen Wald, and Skip Conover; the following year, Vince Gill and Mark Cohen joined the band. Sundance recorded one eponymous album in 1976 before disbanding. In the late '70s, Berline recruited Crary and Hickman for a tour of Japan. Following the tour, the trio recorded three albums for Sugar Hill; concurrently, Berline also founded the LA Fiddle Band.

In 1980, Berline founded the production company BCH with Crary and Hickman, and released a solo album, *Outrageous*, on Flying Fish. In 1981, the LA Fiddle Band released an eponymous solo album for Sugar Hill. Berline worked on Chris Hillman's 1984 album *Desert Rose* and also an album of duets with fiddler Hickman in 1986. Two years later, Berline, Crary, and Hickman changed the name of their trio to BCH and added bassist Steve Spurgin to their lineup. The new incarnation of BCH released *Now They Are Four* in 1988. The group added mandolinist/guitarist John Moore in 1990; following his addition, the group renamed itself California, and released their first album, *Traveler*, in 1992. Berline also continued releasing solo efforts. —*Sandra Brennan*

Live at McCabes / 1978 / Takoma ✦✦✦

● **And the L.A. Fiddle Band** / 1980 / Sugar Hill ✦✦✦✦
Put together three fiddles and some great acoustic bluegrass music and you have *Byron Berline & the L.A. Fiddle Band*, a great album. Guests are Vince Gill and John Hickman. —*Chip Renner*

Outrageous / 1980 / Flying Fish ✦✦✦
Berline has a strong cast featuring Dan Crary, Albert Lee, James Burton, and John Hickman. —*Chip Renner*

Berline, Crary, Hickman / 1981 / Sugar Hill ✦✦✦✦
Nice songs: "Bonapart's Retreat," "Turkey in the Straw." —*Chip Renner*

Night Run / 1984 / Sugar Hill ✦✦✦
Fine bluegrass. Pistol Pete, Forked River, Berline, Dan Crary, and John Hickman will knock you out. —*Chip Renner*

B-C-H / 1986 / Sugar Hill ✦✦✦
Eclectic. This one's my favorite. —*Chip Renner*

Double Trouble / 1986 / Sugar Hill ✦✦✦✦
Berline and John Hickman feed off each other's talents. Very smooth. —*Chip Renner*

Now They Are Four / 1989 / Sugar Hill ✦✦✦
You'll love "Kodak 1955." A must-have for Berline fans. —*Chip Renner*

Fiddle & A Song / 1995 / Sugar Hill ✦✦✦
Fiddle & A Song is another first-rate album from fiddler Byron Berline, featuring guest contributions from Earl Scruggs, Bill Monroe, Vince Gill, and other musicians. —*AMG*

Jumpin' the Strings / Sugar Hill ✦✦✦
While the fiddle playing of Byron Berline sets him squarely within the realm of bluegrass, the melodic originality of his work seems to almost transcend the genre over the course of the 21 self-penned songs that make up *Jumpin' the Strings*. While Berline is the star attraction, a fine backing band comprised of banjoists Alan Munde and John Hickman, guitarists Howard Yearwood and Joe Carr and dobro player Skip Conover is also given the chance to cut loose on this fine release. —*Jason Ankeny*

Rod Bernard

b. Aug. 12, 1940, Opelousas, LA
Guitar, Vocals / Rock & Roll, Cajun, Tex-Mex
An enticing blend of Cajun, rock, and country, Rod Bernard's music is difficult to classify. He was born in Opelousas, LA, in the early '40s and made his professional debut on KSLO Opelousas when he was only ten. Two years later, Bernard was a deejay at the station, but in 1954, his family moved to Texas. There Bernard became accquainted with the town barber Huey Meaux, who later

became a major producer of Cajun recordings. By the time he was a teenager, Bernard formed his first band (the Twisters) and cut two records on Jake Graffagzino's Carl label.

They then recorded King Karl's "This Should Go on Forever" for the Jin label and took the records to Huey Meaux—who was now hosting a French music show on KPAC Port Arthur. Meaux had the song played throughout East Texas and took a copy to the Big Bopper, who played it at KTRN Beaumont, TX. It took seven months, but eventually the record made it to the Top 20 on the pop charts. Bernard then appeared on Dick Clark's *American Bandstand* (where he had to sanitize some of the lyrics for mainstream audiences) and signed with Mercury Records. After recording over 40 songs for the label, Bernard watched as only four sides were released. One of them,"One More Chance," made it to the pop charts as a minor hit.

By 1962, Bernard's Mercury contract had run out. He began working for Hall-Way Records, where many of his sessions were backed by Johnny and Edgar Winter. Disillusioned by the results, though, he became a deejay and musical director at KVOL and WLFY-TV in Lafayette. He also performed on television with the Shondels, a group he had co founded in 1963. In 1965, a compilation of 12 songs he and the Shondels sang on the show were released as *Saturday Hop* on the La Louisienne label. The group also released a single, "Our Teenage Love" for Teardrop. Bernard and Carol Ranchou of La Louisienne founded the Arbee label. During the '70s, Bernard only released a couple of albums. He moved to Fresno, CA, in 1979 and cut his first country single, "Love Me Tonight." —*Sandra Brennan*

Rod Bernard / 1978 / Jin ✦✦✦✦

Boogie in Black & White / 1979 / Jin ✦✦✦

Country Lovin' / 1979 / Jin ✦✦✦

Nights Lights & Love Songs / 1979 / Jin ✦✦✦

● **This Should Go on Forever** / 1985 / Ace ✦✦✦✦

Lot of Dominoes / 1992 / Jin ✦✦

John Berry

b. Sep. 14, 1959, Aiken, SC
Vocals / Contemporary Country
John Berry was born in South Carolina but raised in Atlanta, GA. Before signing to Liberty Records, he released a few solo albums; his 1993 eponymous major-label debut featured the Top 30 song "Kiss Me in the Car." In 1994, a hectic tour schedule was interrupted when Berry underwent brain surgery to remove a cyst. On the same day of the surgery, his single "Your Love Amazes Me" hit No. 1 on the country charts. Berry's next album, *Standing on the Edge*, appeared in 1995, as did a Christmas album, *O Holy Night. Faces* followed in 1996. —*Sandra Brennan*

John Berry / Jun. 7, 1993 / Liberty ✦✦✦
Though his eponymous debut shows promise, only a few cuts on *John Berry*—most notably the hit single "Kiss Me in the Car"—are completely successful. —*Thom Owens*

Saddle the Wind / Nov. 15, 1994 / Patriot ✦✦✦✦

Things Are Not the Same / Nov. 15, 1994 / Liberty ✦✦✦✦

● **Standing on the Edge** / 1995 / Patriot/Liberty ✦✦✦✦

Faces / Sep. 17, 1996 / Capitol ✦✦✦
John Berry's fifth album finds the singer's formula beginning to wear a bit thin, as he turns out the same blend of countrified MOR ballads and slick, rock-injected uptempo numbers. Berry still has enough skills to make a handful of tracks worthwhile—check out the single "Change My Mind"—but much of the album is a little too bland and predictable for comfort. —*Thom Owens*

Big Sandy & the Fly-Rite Trio

Alternative Country-Rock, Americana
Clad in vintage stage attire and travelling the country in a 1949 Flexible tour bus, Big Sandy and His Fly-Rite Boys were a latter-day update of the Western swing sound popularized by the likes of Bob Wills and Spade Cooley. A five-piece combo that conjured the spirit of postwar country music for appreciative pre-millen-

nium audiences, the Anaheim, CA, group was the brainchild of Robert Williams, also known as vocalist/guitarist/frontman Big Sandy and the leader of the band in its earlier incarnation as Big Sandy and the Fly-Rite Trio. Initially, they were a rockabilly unit in the tradition of Gene Vincent and His Bluecaps, but a lineup change that saw the core of Williams and bassist Wally Hersom joined by steel guitarist Lee Jeffries, guitar player Ashley Kingman, and drummer Bobby Trimble brought about not only an altered name but also a new, hillbilly bop-flavored sound.

Produced by the group's mentor, ex-Blaster Dave Alvin, Big Sandy and His Fly-Rite Boys' 1994 debut *Jumping from 6 to 6* straddled the line between rockabilly and swing; while cuts like "Hi-billy Music" and "Who, Tell Me Who?" stood as straightforward rave-ups, a cover of Hank Williams' "Weary Blues from Waitin'" pointed in the direction of the Fly-Rites' immediate future. The title alone of 1995's *Swingin' West* was indicative of the quintet's shift towards a more purist sensibility, recalling Hank Thompson, Lefty Frizzell and Faron Young in both attitude and execution. —*Jason Ankeny*

Jumping from 6 to 6 / 1994 / Hightone ✦✦✦✦
While others may suggest that this Western swing/rockabilly outfit's second Hightone release, *Swingin' West*, is a more definitive representation of the band's potential and brilliance, it is more likely that those who have watched their development will stand by this debut project as their defining work. Much in the same way *Guitars, Cadillacs, Etc., Etc.* gave Dwight Yoakam his calling card, *Jumpin' from 6 to 6* gives Big Sandy and the band their identity in the minds of listeners. An outstanding freshman effort with energy to spare, Big Sandy's voice is phenomenal. The band is tight, especially the teamwork displayed by steel man Lee Jeffriess and lead picker Ashley Kingman. As always, the king of California, Dave Alvin, is an impeccable producer who knows how to get the very best from each artist. The additions of guests Brantley Kearns on fiddle and Bobby Mizzell on piano on "Juiced" makes for a well-layered musical experience that is multidimensional. Their treatment of Hank Sr.'s "Weary Blues from Waitin'" is inspired, as is "Honky Tonk Queen," an E.G. Thornton tune. Jeffriess lends his skills as a songwriter to outstanding cuts like "Hi-Billy Music" and "This Ain't a Good Time." The significance of this debut was not lost on the many bands who followed in the wake of Sandy's success. A landmark recording that opened the floodgates for others seeking to bring Western swing back to prominence, *Jumpin' from 6 to 6* marks the birth of a new era in Country & Western music. —*Jana Pendragon*

● **Swingin' West** / Oct. 1995 / Hightone ✦✦✦✦
The follow-up to a strong 1994 debut, *Swingin' West* continues the Western swing and rockin' hillbilly assault that endeared the California-based Big Sandy and His Fly-Rite Boys to fans and critics alike. While many rockabilly outfits derive their sound primarily from artists from the 1950s, Big Sandy and his Fly-Rite Boys are a more accurate take on the style, venturing back into the '30s and '40s to tap the influences of legends such as Elvis Presley and Gene Vincent. With the lead guitar/steel guitar combination of Ashley Kingman and Lee Jeffries—both originally out of Britain's rockabilly scene—the five-piece band is fully empowered to explore Western swing, jump-blues and hillbilly-boogie, while still injecting originality to make the sound unique. Big Sandy (aka Robert Williams) possesses a big, rich, molasses-coated voice that is engaging throughout this 15-song set. Produced once again by Dave "everything-I-touch-turns-into-musical-gold" Alvin, the energy of the band's live show is captured intact. Highlights include the Latin-influenced rhythms of "Hey Muchachita," and the vintage dancehall-like, call-and-response vocalizing on "We Tried to Tell You." —*Jack Leaver*

Big Sandy & the Fly Rite Trio / Dionysus ✦✦

Black Tie

Country-Rock
Black Tie was a country-rock band featuring Billy Swan, Jimmy Griffith (Bread), and Randy Meisner (Eagles). They made one album before breaking up. They reunited in 1992 as The Remingtons. —*Chip Renner*

Clint Black

When the Night Falls / Bench ✦✦✦✦
Billy Swan, Jimmy Griffin, and Randy Meisner joined forces to put out an album that goes from rock to soul to honky tonk to ballads and back again. —*Chip Renner*

Clint Black
....
b. 1962, Long Branch, NJ
Guitar, Vocals / Contemporary Country, New Traditionalist
A country music traditionalist from Texas, Clint Black was one of the first artists to kick-start the mass-market popularity of country in the '90s. Black also is one of the first artists of a generation that was equally inspired by rock-oriented pop—like '70s singer-songwriters and '60s rock 'n' roll—as well as country artists like Merle Haggard, Bob Wills, and George Jones. He offered a shiny, marketable version of traditional country, and in the process paved the way for a new generation of country artists, particularly Garth Brooks. After Brooks broke through into the pop mainstream, Black's career began to fade somewhat, but he remained one of the most popular and acclaimed vocalists of the '90s.

Clint Black was born in New Jersey, but raised in Katy, TX, a suburb of Houston. As a child, he listened to both country and rock 'n' roll, but he didn't begin playing guitar until the age of 13, when he started playing harmonica. Two years later, he began writing songs, as well as performing in his brother Kevin's band, where he played bass and sang. In the early '80s, he began busking on the streets of Katy, eventually working his way into coffeehouses, bars, and nightclubs.

In 1987, Clint met Hayden Nicholas, a guitarist and songwriter that had a home studio. Nicholas and Black began collaborating together, writing songs and recording demos; Hayden would become the bandleader for Clint, playing lead guitar and co-writing a large majority of his hit singles. A tape of their songs made its way to Bill Ham, the manager of ZZ Top. Impressed with the tape, Ham became Black's manager; the singer had a contract with RCA Nashville by the end of 1988.

"A Better Man," Black's first single, was released early in 1989 and it went to No. 1—he was the first new male country artist to have a No. 1 hit with his debut single in 15 years. Black was an immediate sensation throughout country music and he played the Grand Ole Opry in April, one month before his debut album, *Killin' Time*, was released. *Killin' Time* was an immediate hit, going gold within six months and spawning four other hit singles, including the No. 1s "Killin' Time," "Nobody's Home," and "Walkin' Away." At the end of 1989, he won the Country Music Association's Horizon Award, as well as that organization's Best Male Vocalist award. He also won Best Album, Single, Best Male Vocalist, and Best New Male Vocalist awards from the Academy of Country Music and the NSAI Songwriter/Artists of the Year Award. By the end of 1990, *Killin' Time* had sold over two million copies in America.

Black released his second album, *Put Yourself in My Shoes*, in 1990. Like the debut, *Put Yourself in My Shoes* was a major success, spawning four Top Ten hits—"Put Yourself in My Shoes," "One More Payment," and the No. 1s "Loving Blind" and "Where Are You Now"—selling over two million copies and peaking at No. 18 on the pop charts. Even though it sold well, it didn't receive the same critical acclaim as the debut. Nevertheless, Black was named Best Male Vocalist that same year.

Throughout 1990, Black was on tour with Alabama and appeared on television shows across the country. In 1991, several singles from *Put Yourself in My Shoes* charted and he was inducted into the Grand Ole Opry. On New Year's Eve of 1991, he married the television actress Lisa Hartman.

Clint Black began 1992 in a lawsuit with his manager Bill Ham. Black claimed that his original contract gave Ham too large of a percentage of the singer's royalties and publishing rights. For seven months he was embroiled in the lawsuit, during which he was recording his third album. By the summer, the suit was settled and his new album, *The Hard Way*, finally was released. *The Hard Way* received positive reviews and became an immediate hit, peaking at No. 2 on the country charts and crossing over into the pop Top Ten. The first single from the album, "We Tell Ourselves," reached No. 1 that summer. Black began a lengthy world tour in June of 1992 to support *The Hard Way*.

Although it was a success, *The Hard Way* wasn't as popular as Black's first two records, selling no more than a million copies. *No Time to Kill*, his fourth album, released in 1993, continued the stagnation in his record sales, even though its sales were more than respectable—the album went platinum and spawned the hit single "When My Ship Comes In." —*Stephen Thomas Erlewine*

☆ **Killin' Time** / 1989 / RCA ✦✦✦✦✦
Black's accessible brand of Texas country burned up the charts upon its release, selling two million copies and yielding the hit singles "Better Man," "Killin' Time," "Nobody's Home," "Walkin' Away," and "Nothing's News." —*Brian Mansfield*

Put Yourself in My Shoes / 1990 / RCA ✦✦✦
Put Yourself in My Shoes never approaches the perfection of Black's debut, but it still produced a number of singles, including "Put Yourself in My Shoes," "Loving Blind," "Where Are You Now," and "This Nightlife." —*Brian Mansfield*

The Hard Way / 1992 / RCA ✦✦✦✦
Back to form, Black put some of his most exciting singles on his third album. "We Tell Ourselves" rocked without resorting to Southern boogie, and "When My Ship Comes In" contained a masterful chorus. The album also included the hit "Burn One Down." —*Brian Mansfield*

Clint Black / 1993 / RCA ✦✦
Not a proper album nor a greatest hits collection, the budget-priced *Clint Black* contains a selection of material from his first and second albums, *Killin' Time* and *Put Yourself in My Shoes*. Comprised entirely of album tracks, there are gems scattered throughout the record, but there is simply no reason for this album to exist—*Killin' Time* should be heard in its entirety, while not all of the good songs from *Put Yourself in My Shoes* are included. There is good music on *Clint Black*, but it's hard to call the album anything but a rip-off. —*Stephen Thomas Erlewine*

No Time to Kill / Jul. 1993 / RCA ✦✦✦
Black's albums seems to alternate between the remarkable and the merely pretty good. *No Time to Kill*, which plays off the title of his first album, is one of the latter. All of this is acceptable, though little matches the quality of the title track. Black does a duet with Wynonna Judd called "A Bad Goodbye." —*Brian Mansfield*

One Emotion / 1994 / RCA ✦✦✦

One Emotion continued Clint Black's streak of uneven albums, featuring a handful of exemplary tracks, including the Merle Haggard collaboration "Untanglin' My Mind," but just as many mediocre songs, like "You Made Me Feel," which was written with Michael McDonald. Nothing on *One Emotion* is particularly bad, but it doesn't sound like Black is pushing himself into new territories, either. —*Stephen Thomas Erlewine*

Looking for Christmas / Oct. 17, 1995 / RCA ✦✦✦

Clint Black's *Looking for Christmas* consists entirely of new seasonal songs that he wrote or co-wrote himself. This clearly breaks country music law, and the Nashville police must be in hot pursuit. Black often lets schmaltzy production overcome him, but the many fine songs include the killer ballad "The Kid" (co-written with Merle Haggard) and the back-porch bluegrasss of "The Coolest Pair." —*Roch Parisien*

★ **Greatest Hits** / Sep. 24, 1996 / RCA ✦✦✦✦✦

Clint Black's 16-song *Greatest Hits* is a comprehensive collection, featuring eight No. 1 hits—including "Killing Time," "Where Are You Now," and "Nobody's Home"—four additional hits, plus four new songs ("Like the Rain," "Half Way Up," "Cadillac Jack Favor," and a live version of the Eagles' "Desperado"). Though the collection is missing a handful of essential tracks, it still provides a convincing argument that Clint Black was one of the finest new traditionalist singers of the early '90s. —*Stephen Thomas Erlewine*

Blackhawk

Contemporary Country

Comprised of a trio of seasoned professional musicians, Blackhawk became one of the most successful new country groups of the mid-'90s, scoring a string of Top Ten hits from their first two albums. Featuring Henry Paul (lead vocals, mandolin), Van Stephenson (guitar, vocals), and Dave Robbins (keyboards, vocals), the band formed in the early '90s, releasing their first single, "Goodbye Says It All," on Arista Records in late 1993. "Goodbye Says It All" sailed to No. 1, quickly followed in 1994 by the No. 2 "Every Once in a While," the No. 9 "I Sure Can Smell the Rain," the No. 10 "Wherever You Go" and their eponymous debut album, which would eventually go platinum. *Strong Enough*, Blackhawk's second album, was released in the fall of 1995 and was equally successful, spawning the hit singles "I'm Not Strong Enough to Say No," "Like There Ain't No Yesterday," "Almost a Memory Now," and "King of the World." —*Stephen Thomas Erlewine*

Blackhawk / 1994 / Arista ✦✦✦

● **Strong Enough** / Sep. 12, 1995 / Arista ✦✦✦✦

After their debut album became a platinum success, Blackhawk decided to follow the same formula for their follow-up, *Strong Enough*. Not merely a reproduction of their self-titled debut, *Strong Enough* finds the group consolidating their strengths as songwriters and performers. Throughout the album, the group turns in first-rate songs and tight performances, distinguished by their strong harmonies. —*Stephen Thomas Erlewine*

The Blackwood Brothers

Country Gospel

The Blackwood Brothers have been singing gospel for over 60 years, and from the 1950s to the '70s, they were one of the most popular gospel groups in the US. One of their biggest fans was a young Elvis Presley, who auditioned—and was turned down—for the group in 1953. The quartet was formed in 1934 by brothers Roy (b. Dec. 24, 1900, Fentress, MS; d. Mar. 21, 1971), Doyle (b. Aug. 22, 1911, Ackerman, MS), and James Blackwood (b. Aug. 4, 1919, Ackerman, MS), along with Roy's 13-year-old son R.W. Blackwood (b. Oct. 23, 1921, Ackerman, MS; d. June 24, 1954). The Blackwoods sang at churches around their base of Ackerman, MS, during the mid-'30s. By 1937, however, they began working a radio show in Kosciusko, MS. The quartet moved to WJDX-Jackson later that year, singing pop and country in addition to gospel. After two years in Jackson, they were popular enough to move to

KWKH-Shreveport, LA, a regional superstation that broadcast over much of the South.

While working in Shreveport, the Blackwood Brothers were signed by V.O. Stamps, the largest Southern gospel publisher of the 1930s. The group worked for Stamps during the late '30s and early '40s, but broke up during World War II. When they reformed in 1946—without the Stamps affiliation—Doyle Blackwood had been replaced by Don Smith. The Blackwoods began their own record company, and became so popular that Doyle soon returned to start another group, the Blackwood Gospel Quartet.

By 1950, Roy had retired and was replaced by Bill Lyles. The Blackwoods then moved to Memphis and signed a contract with RCA Victor. They began recording in 1952, and the increased exposure led to national recognition and a spot on Arthur Godfrey's TV show in 1954. Less than a month later, however, R.W. Blackwood and Bill Lyles were killed in a plane crash. The Blackwoods immediately disbanded and vowed to never perform again. Fortunately they returned several years later, gradually adding J.D. Sumner (as a replacement for Lyles) plus Roy's son Cecil Blackwood (b. October 28, 1934, Ackerman, MS) and James' son James Blackwood, Jr. (b. July 31, 1943, San Diego).

The Blackwoods entered the LP era during the mid-'50s and eventually recorded many albums for RCA and Skylite throughout the 1950s and '60s. They won the first of their eight Grammy Awards for Best Gospel Performance in 1966, and James Blackwood won seven Dove Awards for Male Vocalist of the Year during the '70s. He was inducted into the Gospel Music Hall of Fame in 1974 and is still known as "Mr. Gospel Singer of America." —*John Bush*

The Best of the Blackwood Brothers Quartet / 1992 / RCA ✦✦✦

● **16 All Time Favorites** / Starday ✦✦✦✦

Blackwood Brothers / Arrival ✦✦

Nancy Blake

Vocals / Progressive Bluegrass, Traditional Bluegrass, Bluegrass

Nancy Blake has released albums with husband Norman Blake and solo. She is an accomplished musician whose musical styles include bluegrass, traditional, and classical. —*Chip Renner*

● **Grand Junction** / 1986 / Rounder ✦✦✦✦

A good album featuring Nancy Blake and her many instruments. —*Chip Renner*

Blind Dog / 1988 / Rounder ✦✦✦✦

Nancy and Norman Blake on traditional songs like "Wreck of the Old 197," "Black Mountain Rag," and a good cover of Woody Guthrie's "Grand Coulee Dam." —*Chip Renner*

Just Gimme Somethin' I'm Used To / 1992 / Shanachie ✦✦✦

More pleasant parlor traditionalist tunes by Norman and Nancy Blake. Fine guitar from both, plus Norman's fiddle and Nancy's cello. —*Mark A. Humphrey*

Norman Blake

b. Mar. 10, 1938, Chattanooga, TN

Dobro, Fiddle, Guitar, Mandolin, Vocals / Progressive Bluegrass, Traditional Bluegrass

Although he is proficient with a variety of stringed instruments, Norman Blake is famous for his acoustic guitar skills—he was one of the major bluegrass guitarists of the '70s. Blake came into view in the late '60s, when he began performing as a sideman with artists as diverse as June Carter and Bob Dylan. During the '70s, he began a solo career that quickly became one of the most popular and musically adventurous within bluegrass. He continued recording and performing—occasionally with his wife, Nancy—well into the '90s.

Blake began playing music professionally when he was 16 years old, joining the Dixieland Drifters as a mandolinist in 1954; the group debuted on *Tennessee Barn Dance*, a radio show based in Knoxville. After two years, he left the band and became a member of the Lonesome Travellers, which was led by banjoist Bob Johnson. By the end of the '50s, the Lonesome Travellers had added a second banjoist, Walter Forbes, and had made two records for RCA. Although he joined Hylo Brown and the Timber-liners in 1959, Blake continued to perform with Johnson. The following year, he also became a member of June Carter's touring band.

In 1961, Blake was drafted into the Army, and he was stationed in Panama. While he was in the service, he was a radio operator on the Panama Canal and formed a band called the Kobbe Mountaineers. The band became a popular attraction and was voted the best band in the Caribbean Command. In 1962, Blake recorded *12 Shades of Bluegrass* with the Lonesome Travellers while he was on leave. He was discharged from the Army the following year and moved to Nashville.

Once he was in Nashville, Blake joined Johnny Cash's band. That same year, he married Nancy Short and settled in Chattanooga, TN. For the next few years he played with Cash, both on recordings and concerts. In 1969, Bob Dylan hired Norman Blake to play on his country-rock album, *Nashville Skyline*, providing the guitarist with a whole new audience. That audience expanded even further when he became Cash's main guitarist on the singer's television show. Cash's program featured a wide array of musical guests, who were often impressed with Blake's talents. Kris Kristofferson asked him to join his touring band and Norman did so, playing both guitar and dobro; he also played on several of Kristofferson's records. Blake also played on several of Joan Baez's records, including her hit version of "The Night They Drove Old Dixie Down."

Following his folk and country-rock experiments, Blake returned to his bluegrass roots in 1971 when he joined John Hartford's band, Aeroplane, which also featured fiddler Vassar Clements. Aeroplane fell apart quickly, but Blake stayed with Hartford for a year and a half. In 1972, Norman recorded his first solo album, *Back Home in Sulphur Springs*, which began a long relationship with Rounder Records. —*Kurt Wolff*

Back Home in Sulphur Springs / 1972 / Rounder ✦✦✦
Norman Blake and Tut Taylor (dobro), basic and pure. —*Chip Renner*

Blackberry Blossom / 1974 / Flying Fish ✦✦✦
Norman and Nancy Blake. A little less bluegrass with the addition of Nancy Blake's cello. —*Chip Renner*

The Fields of November / 1974 / Flying Fish ✦✦✦✦
A first-class album. Tut Taylor, Charlie Collins, and Nancy Short come up strong. Features "Greycoat Soldiers," "Last Train to Poor Valley," and "The Fields of November." —*Chip Renner*

Norman Blake W/ Jethro Burns & Sam Bush / 1975 / Flying Fish ✦✦✦
A super jam session, it features Norman Blake with Sam Bush, Jethro Burns, David Holland, Butch Robbins, and Tut Taylor. —*AMG*

Old & New / 1975 / Flying Fish ✦✦✦
This fine collection of Blake's music was chosen by Blake himself. —*AMG*

Live at McCabe's / 1976 / Takoma ✦✦✦
Very good record features "Nine Pound Hammer" and "Arkansas Traveler." Good sound. —*Chip Renner*

Whiskey Before Breakfast / 1976 / Rounder ✦✦✦✦
Blake's best. He and Charlie Collins let their guitars do the talking. Perfect. —*Chip Renner*

Norman Blake and Red Rector / 1976 / County ✦✦✦
On these 12 cuts, Blake and Red Rector (on mandolin) are backed by Charlie Collins and Roy Huskie, Jr. —*Chip Renner*

Directions / 1978 / Takoma ✦✦✦✦

Rising Fawn String Ensemble / 1979 / Rounder ✦✦✦
More memorable acoustic instrumental work. —*Hank Davis*

Full Moon on the Farm / 1981 / Rounder ✦✦✦
This album features Norman Blake and the Rising Fawn String Ensemble—James Bryan, Charlie Collins, and Nancy Blake. It has a nice, well-rounded feeling. —*Chip Renner*

Original Underground Music / 1982 / Rounder ✦✦✦✦
Original Underground Music from the Mysterious South includes deceptively simple acoustic string music featuring multiple man-

dolins, mandolas, cellos, fiddles, and guitars for a hauntingly beautiful yet old-timey feel. —*Hank Davis & Chip Renner*

Nashville Blues / 1984 / Rounder ✦✦✦
Blake's vocals give this one more of an old-timey bluegrass feel. —*Hank Davis*

Lighthouse on the Shore / 1985 / Rounder ✦✦✦
Norman teams up with Nancy Blake, James Bryan, and Tom Jackson. Features "Hello Stranger," "President Garfield's Hornpipe," and "Wildwood Flower." —*Chip Renner*

The Norman & Nancy Blake Compact Disc / 1986 / Rounder ✦✦✦✦
The Norman & Nancy Blake Compact Disc combines Norman's *Lighthouse on the Shore* and Nancy's *Grand Junction* on one 21-track compact disc, offering neophytes a good introduction to the duo's distinctive style of acoustic country and bluegrass. —*Thom Owens*

Slow Train through Georgia / 1987 / Rounder ✦✦✦✦
Slow Train through Georgia collects 22 tracks from Norman Blake's early '70s albums, making it an excellent retrospective of the beginning of his solo career. —*Thom Owens*

★ **Natasha's Waltz** / 1987 / Rounder ✦✦✦✦✦
Natasha's Waltz is a compilation of highlights from the albums Norman and Nancy Blake recorded for Rounder during the '80s, giving an excellent overview of one of the finest bluegrass and new acoustic duos of the era. —*Thom Owens*

Blake & Rice / 1987 / Rounder ✦✦✦✦
Underrated but sprightly, these two fleet-fingered acoustic-guitar flatpickers flex their chops in these 14 cuts. —*Mark A. Humphrey*

Blind Dog / 1988 / Rounder ✦✦✦✦
Blind Dog is a fine summation of bluegrass guitarist Norman Blake's career and aesthetics, a largely instrumental collection of favorites from his own catalog as well as from his influences. The covers include songs by A.P. Carter and Woody Guthrie, while Blake dips into his own back pages to redo fan-favorite "Billy Gray." The focus of the record, however, is Blake's playing; a tasteful, economical picker, he shadows the melodies to allow the songs to speak for themselves. —*Jason Ankeny*

Blake & Rice No. 2 / 1990 / Rounder ✦✦✦✦
Blake & Rice No. 2 is every bit as enjoyable as the guitarists' first duet albums, featuring an astonishing array of flat-picking and harmonies. —*Thom Owens*

Just Gimme Somethin' I'm Used To / 1992 / Shanachie ✦✦✦
Just Gimme Somethin' I'm Used To is another charming album by Norman and Nancy Blake, featuring an excellent selection of old-timey country and traditional folk like "Wabash Cannonball" and "Georgia Railroad." There's not much that separates *Just Gimme Somethin' I'm Used To* from the rest of the duo's catalog, yet it remains a thoroughly enjoyable listen. —*Stephen Thomas Erlewine*

Live at McCabes/Directions / Takoma ✦✦✦✦

Blood Oranges

Folk, Alternative Country-Rock, Alternative Country
An alternative country band with a strong bluegrass background, the Blood Oranges were fronted by Jim Ryan, a singer-songwriter who led the group on a custom-produced electric mandolin. Born in New York in 1957, Ryan was first introduced to traditional American bluegrass and folk as a child through the state university in his hometown of Binghamton, where a local country and blues organization sponsored shows highlighting the nation's musical roots. After spending his formative years attending bluegrass festivals, he began honing his own skills as a performer by playing with fiddlers and pickers of all ages and musical backgrounds.

Ryan formed the Blood Oranges in the late 1980s with bassist/vocalist Cheri Knight, guitarist Mark Spencer, and drummer Ron Ward as a forum for fusing his love of traditional music along with his interest in rock 'n' roll; while Ryan's twangy vocals and bluegrass background were the dominant elements of their sound, the group's experimental nature aligned its music more strongly with the Americana movement of the 1990s than with any stripe of straightforward country. In 1991, the Blood Oranges issued their debut album, *Corn River*, a collection of bluegrass originals combined with renditions of classics like "Dig a Hole" and "Shady Grove." Both 1992's *Lone Green Valley* and 1994's *The Crying Tree* continued to refine the quartet's distinctive sound. In 1995, Spencer left the group to tour with Lisa Loeb, and the Blood Oranges promptly disbanded; Knight continued as a solo performer, while Ryan and Spencer ultimately reunited in Wooden Leg. —*Jason Ankeny*

● **Corn River** / 1990 / East Side Digital ✦✦✦✦
The Blood Oranges' debut offers both strong originals and well-chosen covers (including "Dig a Hole"), propelled by Jim Ryan's reedy twang and bassist Cheri Knight's impassioned backing vocals. —*Jason Ankeny*

Lone Green Valley / 1992 / East Side Digital ✦✦✦
In addition to a reprise of "Shady Grove" from their debut *Corn River*, this five-cut EP includes four original efforts, highlighted by the frenetic "Potters Field" and the mournful "All the Way Down." —*Jason Ankeny*

Crying Tree / 1994 / East Side Digital ✦✦✦✦

Blue Highway

Progressive Bluegrass, Traditional Bluegrass
A traditional bluegrass group comprised of five experienced musicians, the members of Blue Highway have played in the bands of such notable artists as Alison Krauss & Union Station, Ricky Skaggs, Larry Sparks, and Doyle Lawson. Guitarist and vocalist Tim Stafford played on the Grammy-winning album *Everytime You Say Goodbye*, by Alison Krauss & Union Station, while dobro player Rob Ickes earned one for his contribution to the various-artists project *The Great Dobro Sessions* and another for his playing on *I Know Who Holds Tomorrow*, the collaborative album project by Krauss & the Cox Family. Other Blue Highway members include: Shawn Lane on tenor vocals, mandolin and fiddle; bassist, vocalist, and songwriter Wayne Taylor; and Jason Burleson on banjo, mandolin, and vocals. The Tennessee-based group has been nominated for four International Bluegrass Music Association awards, including 1996 Album of the Year for their debut release *It's a Long, Long Road*, with both the title-track single and album staying at No. 1 on the national bluegrass chart for five months. —*Jack Leaver*

● **It's a Long Long Road** / Jul. 4, 1995 / Blind Pig ✦✦✦✦
Wind to the West / Jul. 1996 / Rebel ✦✦✦✦
Traditional bluegrass at its best, this album contains masterful playing, inspired singing and memorable songwriting. Blue Highway turns in an affecting vocal and instrumental performance on guitarist Tim Stafford's haunting "The Rounder," as well as ripping through a cover of Merle Haggard's "Huntsville," and showcasing their gospel side on a soul-stirring arrangement of the traditional "God Moves in a Windstorm." Shawn Lane's lonesome tenor is pleasing, as well as the harmony blend and the lead vocals of the rest of the band. Ace dobro player Rob Ickes—voted 1996 Dobro Player of the Year by the International Bluegrass Music Awards—shines throughout, rounding out this band's second effort and making it more than a worthwhile choice. —*Jack Leaver*

Blue Mountain

Alternative Country-Rock
Led by the husband-and-wife team of Cary Hudson and Laurie Stirratt, roots-rockers Blue Mountain drew their name from a small town near their home base of Oxford, MS, where the group's members first began soaking up the country, blues, and rock influences that lent the trio its distinct sound. Blue Mountain was formed in 1993 by vocalist/guitarist Hudson and bassist Stirratt after their previous band, the Los Angeles-based, punk-inspired Hilltops (which also included Stirratt's twin brother John, who would go on to join the band Wilco), dissolved following the release of their lone LP *Big Black River*.

Returning to Mississippi, the couple hooked up with drummer Matt Brennan, and began writing and performing live. After releasing a self-titled album—recorded for about $1,000—on their own label, 4-Barrel Records, Blue Mountain was signed to indie label Roadrunner, where in 1995 they released *Dog Days*, an album cut mostly live in the studio with new drummer Frank Coutch and producer Eric "Roscoe" Ambel. Reprising a number of songs from the first release, *Dog Days* ran the gamut of the group's influences, incorporating everything from country hoedowns to gentle acoustic numbers to a cover of the Skip James jam "Special Rider Blues." In 1996, they were back in the studio, recording tracks for a third LP as well as composing the score for an independent film. —*Jason Ankeny*

● **Dog Days** / Jul. 25, 1995 / Roadrunner ✦✦✦✦
Once you hear the songs on *Dog Days*, you will want to hear them over and over and over again. Anyone who likes roots-rock will feel right at home on Blue Mountain's turf. Great songs such as "Blue Canoe," "Soul Sister," "Eyes of a Child" and a cover of Skip James' "Special Rider Blues" sound familiar on first listening and soon grow to become good friends. This band has heart and is well worth your listening time. Enjoy! —*James Chrispell*

Blue Rodeo

Folk-Rock, Alternative Country-Rock, Americana
Blue Rodeo's style has drawn comparisons to a number of pop and rock icons, including the Beatles, Buffalo Springfield, the Band, and Bob Dylan. Formed in Toronto, the band is led by the songwriting team of vocalists/guitarists Jim Cuddy and Greg Keelor and also features bassist Bazil Donovan, drummer Glenn Milchem, and keyboardist Bob Wiseman, who also plays harmonica and accordion. Their debut album, 1987's *Outskirts*, showcased the group's harmonies and musical interplay in a classic, rootsy folk-rock style. 1989's punchier *Diamond Mine* covered more lyrical ground, bringing a bit of social commentary into Blue Rodeo's tales of loss and heartbreak, but the recording site (an empty hall in Toronto) dulled the songs' impact somewhat. In 1990, Wiseman recorded his own solo album, *Bob Wiseman Sings Wrench Tuttle: In Her Dreams*. Producer Pete Anderson (Michelle Shocked, Dwight Yoakam) accentuated the group's vocal harmonies on the following year's *Casino*, which was well-received. Even higher praise was reserved for *Lost Together*, which synthesized the previous albums' stylistic changes into a cohesive whole. —*Steve Huey*

Outskirts / 1987 / Discoveries ✦✦✦
A highly likeable debut featuring mid-tempo country-rockers fleshed out by a tasteful use of organ in the arrangements—a subtle touch that, along with the sheer quality of the material, distinguished Blue Rodeo from the hordes of other Gram Parsons devotees in the mid-'80s. —*Chris Woodstra*

Diamond Mine / 1989 / Discoveries ✦✦✦
Diamond Mine is a considerably more quiet affair. Beginning with the very Dylanesque "God and Country," a darker, introverted mood is set by their minimalist approach and slow tempos. —*Chris Woodstra*

● **Casino** / 1991 / Discoveries ✦✦✦✦
Casino is a more pop-oriented album. Blue Rodeo seem to have finally established their fine blend of harmonies and laid-back country-rock a la the Band and Bob Dylan. Produced by Pete Anderson (Dwight Yoakam, Michelle Shocked). —*Chris Woodstra*

Lost Together / 1992 / Discoveries ✦✦✦✦
Lost Together is easily the best Blue Rodeo album to date. Hit the random button on the disc player and no matter where the laser touches down, you're assured a worthwhile listening experience. Blue Rodeo have built a fortress on the foundation of their previous three outings. The straight pop song "Flying" and ballads "Already Gone" and the epic title track offer added depth and maturity without rehashing previous successes. "Willin' Fool" and "Angels" tackle the progressive elements of Blue Rodeo's second album, *Diamond Mine*, and sharpen them to a manic, cutting edge. "Fools Like You" spits out a defense of native rights, Greg

Keelor doing his best outraged-Bob Dylan impression. —*Roch Parisien*

Five Days in July / 1994 / Discoveries ✦✦✦
Each new Blue Rodeo album seems like the best one yet, and *Five Days in July* is no exception. Even the one cover (Rodney Crowell's "Til I Gain Control Again") ends up sounding like a Blue Rodeo original. Also, if you've been slow to embrace her as an artist, Sarah McLachlan's vocal contributions to songs like "What Is This Love" will totally captivate you. —*Jim Worbois*

Nowhere to Here / Sep. 5, 1995 / Discoveries ✦✦✦
Blue Rodeo continue to experiment on their latest release. Opening and closing with expansive mood pieces, it takes a little bit of listening to get into this album. But sandwiched in between lies the real meat of this record. Bluesy ballads such as "Sky" and "Train" are balanced by upbeat pop tunes like "What You Want" and "Better Off As We Are." The rockin', Beatlesque "Get through to You" shows them in top form. Every song here tends to evoke the pictorial majesty of the Canadian countryside while never sounding hokey. Once you let these tunes seep into your psyche, you'll find there isn't a bum tune in the bunch. Fantastic! —*James Chrispell*

Blue Rose

Traditional Bluegrass
This band features the talents of Laurie Lewis, Cathy Fink, Marcy Marxer, Molly Mason, and Sally Van Meter. —*Chip Renner*

Blue Rose / 1972 / Sugar Hill ✦✦✦✦
This is the women's bluegrass version of Blind Faith. Cathy Fink, Laurie Lewis, Marcy Marxer, Molly Mason, and Sally Van Meter combine for a fantastic sound. This was a supergroup. Highly recommended! —*Chip Renner*

The Blue Sky Boys

Old-Time, Bluegrass, Traditional Country, Close Harmony
In the '30s brother duets were common in country music. Among the better known were the Monroes, the Delmores, the Dixons, and the Carlisles. Bill and Earl Bolick, who in 1936 were ready to make their first recording, followed their producer's suggestion that they should be "different" by avoiding the word *brother*. From "Blue Ridge Mountains, Land of the Sky" they took two words and named their act. But the Bolicks would have been different without the new name. Their intricate yet simple harmonies, their perfectly matching voices, and their unadorned mandolin and guitar instrumental backing set them off from the competition, so much so that two generations of subsequent duet singers have echoed them, some without realizing it. The Everly Brothers and the Louvin Brothers, themselves recognized as exceptional vocal duets, acknowledge the influence of the Blue Sky Boys. In the '50s, when tastes in country music changed drastically, the Blue Sky Boys retired from music rather than forsake their love of old mountain ballads for the uptempo popularity of electric instruments, drums, and honky tonk. In the '60s they were coaxed out of retirement, playing an occasional college date during the hootenanny phenomenon and recording albums in 1963, 1965, and 1976.

Born and raised in East Hickory, NC, Bill and Earl Bolick—the fourth and fifth of six children by deeply religious parents—learned how to harmonize by singing hymns and gospel songs at home. Bill learned to play guitar and banjo from his neighbor, teaching Earl in the process. Earl had been given a mandolin, but he preferred guitar, so the two brothers switched instruments and began performing as a duo. Bill also performed with another local group, the Crazy Hickory Nuts, who happened to land a radio spot in Asheville, NC, in 1935. Shortly afterward, the siblings formed the JFG Coffee Boys with Homer Sherrill, a fiddler who played with the Crazy Hickory Nuts, and the new group also landed a regular spot on Asheville radio. The group stayed in Asheville for a while, before moving to Atlanta to play as the Blue Ridge Hillbillies. While in Atlanta, the Bolicks split away from Sherrill and recorded several sides for RCA Victor, which were released under the name the Blue Sky Boys.

Over the next four years, the Blue Sky Boys made nearly 100 recordings for RCA that made them one of the more popular brother duos of the period. The Bolicks' career was sidetracked in 1941, when both brothers entered the military to fight in World War II. Early in 1946, they were discharged, and they returned to playing radio in Atlanta and recording for RCA. Occasionally, the duo recorded with a fiddler, usually Sam "Curley" Parker, Joe Tyson, Leslie Keith, or Richard "Red" Hicks. Many of their records from 1946 and 1947, including "Kentucky," ranked among their biggest hits, but by the end of 1947 the duo was growing frustrated with the changing climates in country music, and their record label as well. Honky tonk music was beginning to take over the country market, and RCA asked them to add an electric guitar and try some newer songs, but the Bolicks steadfastly refused and didn't record again until 1949. Over the course of the following year, they made a handful of recordings, performing their final sessions for RCA in the spring of 1950.

Fed up with the changes in country music, the Blue Sky Boys disbanded and retired from music in 1951. For the next 11 years, Bill lived in North Carolina, working for the post office, and Earl made his residence in Georgia, working for Lockheed Aircraft. Then in 1962 Starday Records released an album of Blue Sky Boys radio transcriptions. The following year, Bill convinced Earl to come out of retirement and record two albums, the secular *Together Again* and the inspirational *Precious Moments*, for Starday. Over the next few years, they played the occasional concert and appeared at folk festivals. In 1965, Capitol released a live album capturing the duo at the UCLA Folk Festival. Yet by the end of the '60s, the Blue Sky Boys had retired again. However in 1975, they were persuaded to record an album for Rounder and play several bluegrass and folk festivals. Shortly afterward, Bill again retired and moved back to his hometown of East Hickory, while Earl settled in Tucker, GA.

No one in country music has done vocal duets better than the Blue Sky Boys. If your taste runs more to Conway & Loretta, George & Tammy, Wynonna & Naomi, listen to the effortless, exquisite singing of Bill and Earl Bolick. See where it all started. —*David Vinopal*

Blue Sky Boys on Radio, Vol. 1 / Copper Creek ✦✦✦✦
Blue Sky Boys on Radio, Vol. 1 contains a selection of the duo's radio transcriptions from 1946 and 1947, when the Blue Sky Boys were at the height of their career. Almost all of their most popular songs are included, as are some commercials, comedy routines, and instrumental solos, all of which help to effectively evoke the era. But the album is much more valuable than a mere artifact—it demonstrates what a tremendous duo Bill and Earl Bolick actually were, as well as how rich their music was. —*Thom Owens*

★ **There'll Come a Time / Can't You Hear That Nightbird** / 1936 / Blue Tone ✦✦✦✦✦
Sacred songs, weepers, and hillbilly heart-singing at its best. —*Mark A. Humphrey*

☆ **Within the Circle / Who Wouldn't Be Lonely** / 1937 / Blue Tone ✦✦✦✦✦
This genuine classic contains old-time recordings from 1937-1938. —*AMG*

In Concert '64 / Rounder ✦✦✦✦
The Blue Sky Boys in Concert, 1964 captures a reunion concert that Bill and Earl Bolick gave at the University of Illinois. The show was designed to be a mini-history of the group's career, since it was the first time the duo performed outside of the South. Consequently, the show features most of their biggest hits and functions as an excellent retrospective and introduction to their music; a delight for dedicated fans, since the group sounds as good as they ever have. —*Stephen Thomas Erlewine*

The Bluegrass Album Band

Progressive Bluegrass
The Bluegrass Album Band was a bluegrass supergroup formed in 1980. Originally, the band featured J.D. Crowe, Doyle Lawson, Tony Rice, Bobby Hicks, and Todd Phillips. All of the members were known as progressive bluegrass musicians, but the Bluegrass Album Band was designed to showcase the traditional side

of their talents. Their first album, *The Bluegrass Album*, was intended as a one-shot project, but it proved so successful the group recorded four other albums over the course of the decade. Over the years, the lineup of the Bluegrass Album Band shifted, but Crowe, Lawson, and Rice remained its core members. The group's final album, *The Bluegrass Album, Vol. 5: Sweet Sunny South*, was released in 1989 and featured Crowe, Lawson, Rice, Vassar Clements, Jerry Douglas, and Mark Schatz. —*Thom Owens*

The Bluegrass Album, Vol. 1 / 1981 / Rounder ✦✦✦✦
The debut from this superstar bluegrass band featuring Tony Rice, J. D. Crowe, Doyle Lawson, Bobby Hicks, Todd Phillips, and Jerry Douglas. —*Chip Renner*

The Bluegrass Album, Vol. 2 / 1982 / Rounder ✦✦✦✦
The Bluegrass Album Band's second record reiterates all of the strong points of their debut—the group's interaction and harmonies are so natural, they're breathtaking. —*Thom Owens*

The Bluegrass Album, Vol. 3 (California Connection) / 1983 / Rounder ✦✦✦✦
On their third album, the Bluegrass Album Band adds some more country-rock to the mix, in the form of the Flying Burrito Brothers' "Devil in Disguise," but they largely stick to bluegrass classics from the likes of Bill Monroe and Flatt & Scruggs. Like the group's two previous albums, *California Connection* is filled with graceful, stunning musicianship that continues to astonish after several listens. —*Thom Owens*

Bluegrass Album, Vol. 4 / 1984 / Rounder ✦✦✦✦
They get tighter as they go along. Any one of these records is gonna get you movin'. —*Chip Renner*

The Bluegrass Album, Vol. 5: Sweet Sunny South / 1989 / Rounder ✦✦✦

The Bluegrass Compact Disc / Rounder ✦✦✦✦
A full, classic bluegrass album. —*Chip Renner*

● **The Bluegrass Compact Disc, Vol. 2** / Rounder ✦✦✦✦
A collection of the group's first four releases. There are 21 songs in all. —*Chip Renner*

The Bluegrass Cardinals

Progressive Bluegrass, Traditional Bluegrass
During the '70s and '80s, the Bluegrass Cardinals were one of the premiere bluegrass bands in America, noted for performing both contemporary and traditional bluegrass with tight, intricate vocal harmonies and dynamic, precise musicianship. Banjoist Don Parmley and his then 15-year-old son David founded the Cardinals in 1974. Earlier, Don had played banjo for *The Beverly Hillbillies*, and had been part of the Golden State Boys and the Hillmen, both featuring the Gosdin Brothers. In 1976, the Cardinals,—which also featured Mike Hartgrove, Norman Wright, John Davis, and Dale Perry—moved from California to Virginia, where they recorded their eponymous debut album for Briar. The following year, they recorded *Welcome to Virginia*. The Bluegrass Cardinals eventually released five more albums, in addition to touring America and Europe. In 1991, Don and David Parmley left the group, and recorded *Parmley and McCoury* with Del McCoury and his two sons Ronnie and Robbie. Later, after some solo work, David Parmley performed in Continental Divide with Scott Vestal. —*Sandra Brennan*

The Bluegrass Cardinals / 1976 / Briar ✦✦✦✦

Welcome to Virginia / 1977 / Rounder ✦✦✦✦
The Bluegrass Cardinals' second album is as fine as their first, featuring wonderful, empathetic playing and pure, joyous vocals, as well as a good batch of originals and covers. —*Thom Owens*

Livin' in the Good Old Days / 1978 / CMH ✦✦✦
Twelve solid songs. —*Chip Renner*

Cardinal Soul / 1979 / CMH ✦✦✦
Early sound. Good. —*Chip Renner*

Live & on Stage / 1980 / CMH ✦✦✦✦
The double album has 29 songs. —*Chip Renner*

Sunday Mornin' Singin' / 1980 / CMH ✦✦✦
One of your better gospel albums. —*Chip Renner*

Where Rainbows Touch / 1982 / CMH ✦✦✦

● **Cardinal Class** / 1983 / Sugar Hill ✦✦✦✦
A very good, solid, tight album. The Cardinals at their best. Highly recommended. —*Chip Renner*

Home Is Where the Heart Is / 1984 / Sugar Hill ✦✦✦
A good mix of music. Jerry Douglas guests. —*Chip Renner*

The Shining Path / 1986 / Sugar Hill ✦✦✦✦
My favorite of their gospel releases. —*Chip Renner*

Ginger Boatwright

b. Sep. 21, 1944, Columbus, MS
Guitar, Vocals / Traditional Bluegrass
Ginger Boatwright (born Ginger Kay Hammond) was a talented bluegrass musician who became especially popular on the festival circuit. Known for her keen flat-picking, she learned to play guitar while attending the University of Alabama in the mid-'60s. In 1966, she attended a concert by Grant Boatwright, who invited her onstage to play. Following the concert, they formed a duo; eventually, her cousin Dale Whitcomb joined the group.

In 1969, Ginger was diagnosed with cancer. The treatment prevented her from graduating; consequently, she turned to a professional musical career—her trio with Boatwright and Whitcomb became Red, White & Blue(grass). Around this time she also married Boatwright. Ginger was still playing with Red, White & Blue(grass) when she signed to GRC Records as a solo act in 1972. Her first successful single, "The Lovin's Over," was a bluegrass hit. Red, White & Blue(grass) signed with Mercury in the mid-'70s. Simultaneously, Ginger signed to the label as a solo act. None of her records for Mercury gained much attention, nor did any of the band's. In 1979, the group disbanded and she divorced Grant.

Following the breakup, she and banjo player Susie Monick formed the all-female bluegrass group the Bushwhackers, along with bassist April Barros and fiddler Ingrid Reese. The Bushwhackers began playing the college circuit and released their eponymous debut in 1980. In 1981, the group broke up and Boatwright was prepared to quit the music business when Rodney Dillard informed her that his brother Doug was putting together a new band. Ginger joined Doug Dillard's group in 1982 and continued playing with him into the mid-'90s. She also released a handful of solo records, including 1991's *Fertile Ground* and 1994's *Sentimental Journey*. —*Sandra Brennan*

● **Fertile Ground** / 1991 / Flying Fish ✦✦✦✦
An excellent album. Ginger Boatwright brings her great vocals from the Red, White & Blue(grass) Band. She gets better with age. —*Chip Renner*

Sentimental Journey: Bluegrass / 1994 / Laserlight ✦✦✦

The Bushwackers / Laser Lady ✦✦✦

What's That / Flying Fish ✦✦✦

Suzy Bogguss

b. Dec. 30, 1956, Aledo, IL
Vocals / Country-Pop, Contemporary Country, New Traditionalist
Free-spirited Suzy Bogguss successfully straddled the line between traditional and mainstream country, and in the process became one of the most popular and critically acclaimed female country singers of the late '80s and early '90s. Born in Aledo, IL, Bogguss sang in the Aledo Presbyterian Church Angel Choir at age five. As a young adult, she became interested in the guitar and began singing, playing whenever and wherever she could find an audience; soon Bogguss had developed a sizable following throughout the Midwest, the Northeast, and Canada. She appeared on a Peoria public television station, and after a positive viewer response, came back to host and star in two more shows. Not long afterward, Bogguss was hired as an opener for such acts as Dan Seals and Asleep at the Wheel, and toured the West and Mexico.

In 1985, she headed for Nashville and got a job singing in a rib joint and doing session work. She recorded an album at Wendy Waldman's studio and began giving copies to local radio stations and magazines, receiving glowing reviews. She got a gig singing at Dolly Parton's Dollywood theme park in Pigeon Forge, TN, which led to a contract with Capitol Nashville and an appearance on TNN's *Nashville Now*, where Chet Atkins invited her to open a concert. Bogguss' first two singles, "I Don't Want to Set the World on Fire" and "Love Will Never Slip Away," were released in 1987 and became minor hits. In 1988, she demonstrated her prowess as a yodeler on "I Want to Be a Cowboy's Sweetheart," also a modest chart success. She and producer Wendy Waldman cut Bogguss' first major label album, *Somewhere Between*, in 1989, and several tracks became hits. Her next album, 1990's *Moment of Truth*, did fairly well, but her third, *Aces*, went gold in 1992, a year after it was released. *Voices in the Wind*, Bogguss' fourth album, was released that year; it too went gold and spawned a string of Top Ten singles, including the No. 2 hit "Drive South," written by John Hiatt. In 1994, she released her fifth album, *Simpatico*, as well as a greatest hits collection; in 1996 she released *Give Me Some Wheels*. —*Sandra Brennan*

★ **Somewhere Between** / 1988 / Liberty ◆◆◆◆◆
A fabulous, truly surprising debut, this album firmly plants one foot in the past and the other in the Nashville mainstream. The best songs here come from country legends. Merle Haggard penned the powerhouse title cut, "My Sweet Love Ain't Around" came from Hank Williams, and "I Want to Be a Cowboy's Sweetheart" was an old Patsy Montana tune. The new stuff is pretty danged good, too: "Cross My Heart," written by Verlon Thompson and Kye Fleming, was the album's highest-charting single. —*Brian Mansfield*

Moment of Truth / 1990 / Liberty ◆◆◆
Under the wing of producer and new label head Jimmy Bowen, Bogguss relinquished her cowboy's sweetheart role and began recording more polished records that often burnished singer-songwriter material. This album didn't do so well, though: it produced only two weakly performing singles, "Under the Gun" and "All Things Made New Again." —*Brian Mansfield*

Aces / 1991 / Liberty ◆◆◆◆
The new strategy paid off here: Bogguss took Cheryl Wheeler's "Aces" and Nanci Griffith's "Outbound Plane" into the Top Ten. She also hit with "Someday Soon" and "Letting Go." This is the album that won her the CMA's Horizon Award, five years after her first single. —*Brian Mansfield*

Voices in the Wind / 1992 / Liberty ◆◆◆
This sounds like one of those white-bread pop albums folks occasionally try to pawn off as country—until you start listening to the lyrics. *Voices in the Wind* may be bigger on string sections than twin fiddlers, but Bogguss' choice in covers remains just off-center enough to be exciting, with Cheryl Wheeler's "Don't Wanna" and Lowell George's "Heartache." She revives John Hiatt's "Drive South" for a hit. The more risky material—especially the bleary-eyed blues of "Eat at Joe's" and the troubled alcoholic haze of Bogguss' own "In the Day"—shows why the Country Music Association gave her its Horizon Award just before the release of this album. —*Brian Mansfield*

Somethin' up My Sleeve / Sep. 13, 1993 / Liberty ◆◆◆
Includes "Hey Cinderella," which Bogguss wrote with Matraca Berg; "Just Like the Weather," which she wrote with husband Doug Crider; and "Souvenirs," a remarkably understated indictment of materialism by Gretchen Peters. The title track is a duet with Billy Dean. —*Brian Mansfield*

Greatest Hits / Mar. 8, 1994 / Liberty ◆◆◆◆
Ten of Bogguss' best are included, from "I Want to Be a Cowboy's Sweetheart" to 1993's "Heartache." The album doesn't contain anything from *Something up My Sleeve*, but it does have "Hopelessly Yours," a duet with Lee Greenwood, that doesn't appear on any of Bogguss' other albums. —*Brian Mansfield*

Simpatico / Oct. 1994 / Liberty ◆◆◆
Simpatico is a laidback, charming duet album with Chet Atkins. The duo covers a lot of ground, beginning with Jimmie Rogers' "In the Jailhouse Now," running through Elton John's "Sorry Seems to Be the Hardest Word," and playing a couple of nice, understated originals. Although it isn't a strict country record—there's quite a bit of pop flourishes scattered throughout

the record—it's a charmingly low-key listen. —*Stephen Thomas Erlewine*

Give Me Some Wheels / Jul. 23, 1996 / Liberty ◆◆◆
In the three years between the release of Suzy Bogguss' fourth studio album of new material, *Something up My Sleeve*, and her fifth, *Give Me Some Wheels*, she released a greatest hits album and a duet album with Chet Atkins (*Simpatico*); her record company, Liberty, was reconfigured into Capitol Nashville; and she took time out to start a family. None of those factors may be as important as the sheer passage of time for an artist who had achieved a moderate level of success in a New Traditionalist vein and now faces a tough post-Garth country music environment defined by a new crop of female singers. *Give Me Some Wheels* is a sturdy album of well-performed, consistently written country songs. The title track, which Bogguss co-wrote with Matraca Berg and Gary Harrison, is a satisfying statement of purpose, and the album's second single, "No Way Out," is a pleasing uptempo love song. But neither became hits ("She Said, He Heard" would have made a better single choice), and the album was a commercial disappointment. If it had been released two years earlier, it probably would have done better, but coming back to a new climate in Nashville, Bogguss needed to make a bolder or more accomplished album than this to keep from losing ground. —*William Ruhlmann*

Johnny Bond (Cyrus Whitfield Bond)

b. Jun. 1, 1915, Enville, OK, **d.** Jun. 12, 1978, Burbank, CA
Guitar, Vocals / Cowboy, Bakersfield Sound
Johnny Bond played sidekick to cinema and radio cowboys such as Gene Autry and Jimmy Wakely, but also enjoyed a long music career with seven Country Top Ten hits. He was born in Enville, OK, on June 1, 1915, and early on was influenced by the Light Crust Doughboys and Jimmie Rodgers. After high school, he traveled to Oklahoma City to hit the big time in radio. With Jimmy Wakely and Scotty Harrell he formed the Bell Boys, and the trio found work for WKY. An appearance in the 1939 Western *Saga of Death Valley* with Roy Rogers inspired Bond and Wakely to move to Hollywood, where they joined Gene Autry's *Melody Ranch* radio show in late 1940.

Wakely had gained a Decca music contract in 1940, and Johnny Bond followed soon after, recording his initial sides for Columbia in August 1941. The singles weren't very successful, though, so Bond contented himself with his very busy schedule: regular appearances on the *Melody Ranch* show (until it was canceled in 1956) and the *Hollywod Barn Dance*, tours with Gene Autry, and over 40 films with Autry, Wakely, and Tex Ritter.

By 1947, the accumulated exposure broke him into the charts: he released the Top Five singles "Divorce Me C.O.D.," "So Round, So Firm, So Fully Packed" and "The Daughter of Jole Blon" within six months. The following year, "Oklahoma Waltz" reached the Top Ten. "Till the End of the World" and "Tennessee Saturday Night" were Top Ten near-misses in 1949, but Bond was back in the spotlight during 1950-51 with the No. 8 hit "Love Song in 32 Bars" and the No. 7 "Sick, Sober and Sorry."

Johnny Bond's chart success ended suddenly in late 1951, but he continued his previous radio and TV commitments, even adding Compton, CA's *Town Hall Party* in 1953. His Columbia contract ended in the late '50s, and Bond signed with Starday in 1961 after a short time on Gene Autry's Republic Records. His first Starday hit was the Top 30 "Three Sheets in the Wind" in 1963, but the novelty drinking song "10 Little Bottles" became his biggest mover two years later. The single, a re-recording of Bond's from 1954, spent four weeks at No. 2, but was his last major hit. He recorded many more albums for Starday until 1971, when he turned to writing. He had written an unpublished Gene Autry biography in 1970, but his biography of Tex Ritter and an autobiography, *Reflections*, were both released in the mid-'70s. He was writing a book on Western music at the time of his death in 1978. —*John Bush*

● **The Best of Johnny Bond** / 1969 / Starday ◆◆◆◆

Bonnie Lou (Bonnie Lou Kath)

Vocals / Cowboy

During the mid-'50s, yodeling cowgirl Bonnie Lou was one of the most popular female country singers in the US. She was born Mary Kath in central Illinois and learned yodeling from her Swiss grandmother; as a child she played violin, but switched to guitar at age 11. While a teen, she won a talent contest and decided she wanted a career in radio, getting a job at WMBD in Peoria. Soon after graduating high school, she became a regular on the *Brush Creek Follies* in Kansas City, singing solo and with the Rhythm Rangers under the name "Sally Carson." In 1945, she was hired at the powerful WLW station in Cincinnati. She soon became a staple on both the radio and television versions of *Midwestern Hayride* under the name Bonnie Lou, (suggested by station owner Bill McCluskey), and appeared on *Louisiana Hayride*, an NBC summer replacement television show. She began recording in 1953 on the King label with her first single, "Seven Lonely Nights," making it to the Top Ten on the country charts. Her next song, "Tennessee Wig Walk," also released in 1953, was an even bigger hit. Although she went on to record 22 more songs for King, none were as popular as the first two. She continued to appear on the *Hayride* shows throughout the mid-'60s. She has also appeared on several other television shows, most notably the *Paul Dixon Show,* where she was a regular until 1974. —*Sandra Brennan*

● **Bonnie Lou Sings** / 1958 / King ✦✦✦✦

Daddy-O / 1958 / King ✦✦✦

Boone Creek

Progressive Bluegrass, Traditional Bluegrass

Boone Creek was the first band Ricky Skaggs led after his apprenticeship with Ralph Stanley, Country Gentlemen, and J.D. Crowe & the New South. Skaggs formed the band in 1977, when he was only 23 years old. Even though he was quite young, he had already played with some of the most respected musicians in bluegrass, playing both traditional bluegrass with Stanley and progressive newgrass with the Country Gentlemen and Crowe. With Boone Creek, Skaggs wanted to create a music that approached traditional bluegrass with a progressive attitude. To achieve this sound, he added electric guitar, drums, and piano to the traditional bluegrass lineup.

Boone Creek released their eponymous debut in 1977. It was quickly followed by *One Way Track* in early 1978. After the release of *One Way Track*, Skaggs broke up the group and joined Emmylou Harris' Hot Band. Skaggs would achieve solo success after leaving Harris in the early '80s. —*Stephen Thomas Erlewine*

Boone Creek / 1977 / Rounder ✦✦✦

A fine album with great picking. —*Chip Renner*

● **One Way Track** / 1978 / Sugar Hill ✦✦✦✦

Boone Creek's second album *One Way Track* showcases the stunning instrumental skills of a young Ricky Skaggs, as well as his compatriots Jerry Douglas and Terry Baucom. The three musicians blend on tight, thrilling harmonies, but where they really shine is on their rampaging instrumentals, where they demonstrate their virtuosity. The emphasis on playing makes *One Way Track* a little uneven, yet when it's digested in small, individual bits, the album is quite enjoyable. —*Thom Owens*

Larry Boone

b. Jun. 7, 1956, Cooper City, FL

Vocals / Contemporary Country, New Traditionalist

Neo-traditional vocalist Larry Boone began playing guitar at a young age and was influenced by such singers as George Jones, Merle Haggard, Ray Charles, and B.B. King. He originally wanted to become a professional baseball player like his father, but, derailed by a knee injury, he turned to country music. While attending Florida Atlantic University, Boone played at nightclubs and restaurants. In 1976, he got his first paying gig at a steak house in Plantation, FL, and moved to Nashville in 1980, where he eked out a living from substitute teaching and the tips he got playing at the Country Music Wax Museum on Music Row. While in Nashville, he began honing his songwriting skills, and was

noticed by manager Gene Ferguson, whose clients included John Anderson and Charly McClain. Ferguson convinced McClain to record a song Larry had co-written, "Meet You in the Middle of the Bed," and MTM signed Boone as a writer. Some of his collaborations, such as "Until I Fall in Love Again," went on to minor success. Between 1985 and 1987, his tunes were recorded by close to 40 artists, and his "American Faces" was sung by John Conlee on NBC-TV during the 1988 Olympics.

In 1986, Boone signed with Mercury, and after five somewhat successful singles, debuted with an eponymous album. Three songs from the album did well on the charts, with "Don't Give Candy to a Stranger" reaching the Top Ten in 1988, the same year his song "Old Coyote Town" was a Top Ten hit for Don Williams and his "Burnin' Old Memories" provided Kathy Mattea with a No. 1 single. His 1989 album *Swingin' Doors, Sawdust Floors* contained the hit "I Just Called to Say Goodbye Again." His third album, *Down that River Road,* (1990) contained the minor hit "Everybody Wants to Be Hank Williams (But Nobody Wants to Die)." The following year, Boone moved to Columbia and hit the charts with two songs, "I Need a Miracle" and "To Be with You," which eventually appeared on his 1993 album *Get in Line. —Sandra Brennan*

One Way to Go / 1987 / Columbia ✦✦

This includes the singles "I Need a Miracle" and "To Be with You." —*Brian Mansfield*

Larry Boone / Dec. 1987 / Mercury ✦✦✦✦

Boone had had a number of small hits ("Stranger Things Have Happened," "Roses in December") when his debut album came out in the wake of such country hunks as Garth Brooks and Clint Black. Boone figured to tap into that market with his muscular voice, but didn't quite make it, though this album includes his biggest hit, "Don't Give Candy to a Stranger." —*Brian Mansfield*

Swingin' Doors, Sawdust Floors / 1988 / Mercury ✦✦✦

This album, currently out of print, contains three Top 40 hits: "I Just Called to Say Goodbye Again," "Wine Me Up" and "Fool's Paradise." —*Brian Mansfield*

Down That River Road / 1990 / Mercury ✦✦✦

"Everybody Wants to Be Hank Williams," a brutal song about the price singers pay for commercial success, is the best thing Boone has recorded. It's also the closest thing to a hit this now-out-of-print album produced. —*Brian Mansfield*

● **Get in Line** / Mar. 23, 1993 / Columbia ✦✦✦✦

Working with producer Don Cook (Brooks & Dunn, Mark Collie), Boone tried to retool his image into a tougher, leaner figure. Musically, he was fairly successful with rockers like "Call Me When the Sun Goes Down" and "I Still Got (What You Got Over)." Commercial success was another matter: "Get in Line," the album's only charting single, peaked at 65 in *Billboard. —Brian Mansfield*

Bottle Rockets

Roots-Rock, Alternative Country-Rock

Festus, MO's Bottle Rockets ranked as one of the leading lights of the 1990s roots-rock revival, thanks to a sound that bypassed the punk heritage proudly upheld by most of their contemporaries in favor of a redneck fusion of Southern boogie, country-folk, and crunching rock 'n' roll. The group was fronted by singer/guitarist Brian Henneman, a Missouri native who formed his first band, Waylon Van Halen and the Ernest Tubbadours, in 1977 with friends Tom and Bob Parr. After a succession of names and a steady rise in musical competence, the trio began landing club dates both locally and in Illinois, where they became friends with the young Jay Farrar and Jeff Tweedy, who would later start Uncle Tupelo.

In 1985, the trio was playing straightahead honky tonk under the moniker Chicken Truck (named in honor of the John Anderson song) with a new drummer, Mark Ortmann. Instead of giving in to local crowds, who wanted to hear covers instead of originals, the group focused solely on performing their own material, which they began roughing up with a Crazy Horse-like edge. Shortly after frequent tour mates Uncle Tupelo signed a 1990 record deal, however, internal problems led Chicken Truck to disband; while the Parrs returned to civilian jobs, Ortmann moved to Nashville to become a session player, and Henneman became a roadie with Uncle Tupelo, even playing on their *March 16-20, 1992* album.

During his roadie days, Henneman recorded a demo tape of new material, which Tupelo manager Tony Margherita began discreetly shopping around. After cutting a solo single backed by Farrar and Tweedy, he reformed his old band, replaced Bob Parr with bassist Tom Ray, and renamed the outfit the Bottle Rockets. After a 1993 self-titled effort, a year later the band issued their second independent LP, called *The Brooklyn Side,* after a bowling term. A portrait of life in rural, blue-collar America, *The Brooklyn Side* earned lavish critical praise, and was later re-released on a major label. *—Jason Ankeny*

Bottle Rockets / 1993 / East Side Digital ✦✦✦✦
If Neil Young had played guitar and written songs with Lynyrd Skynyrd, it might've come out something like the eponymous debut by Festus, MO's own Bottle Rockets. Raw and spirited, with a guitar attack that burns furiously, this record was recorded and mixed in a couple of days. Although it contains some strong material, overall it lacks the focus of the band's follow-up *The Brooklyn Side.* That's not to say that this one should be passed over; there's a satisfying mix of rockers and country-tinged numbers. Frontman and principal songwriter Brian Henneman's keen observations on everyday rural-redneck life and characters are explored with insightful detail in songs about convenience store clerks and trailer inhabitants. In the Southern rock-sounding "Wave That Flag," he takes an angry shot at rebel flag wavers, and the escape of a dead-end life in the ragged, breakneck-speed country-rocker "Rural Route." Before the Bottle Rockets, Henneman served a tenure as a guitar-technician and sometime instrumentalist for Uncle Tupelo, and both Jeff Tweedy and Jay Farrar make backup vocal appearances, with Farrar giving a particularly strong performance on the highlight ballad "Kerosene." *—Jack Leaver*

● **The Brooklyn Side** / 1995 / Atlantic ✦✦✦✦
While the Bottle Rockets' brand of Skynyrd-esque raunch 'n' roll is considerably more good-timey than most of the band's roots-rock brethren, their incisive, provocative songwriting skills set them squarely among the genre's elite. *The Brooklyn Side,* produced by Eric "Roscoe" Ambel, is fairly bursting with dead-on character studies exploring the realities and quiet desperation of rural Southern life, from the blackly humorous "Sunday Sports," about a family man who finds that watching TV in his underwear is "the only way to get away from everything else" in his life, to the poignant "Welfare Music," a depiction of the struggles facing a young single mother. The band also possesses a wickedly comic edge, as evidenced by "Idiot's Revenge," a diatribe against alt-rock rhetoric; "1000 Dollar Car," a eulogy for a used automobile; and the flamethrower single "Radar Gun," the tale of a sadistic, ticket-happy traffic cop. *—Jason Ankeny*

Jimmy Bowen

b. Nov. 30, 1937, Santa Rita, NM
Bass, Vocals / Rock & Roll, Rockabilly, Traditional Pop
Since the 1970s, Jimmy Bowen has been a powerful executive in the record industry, working for several labels. Since he joined MCA in 1986, he is acknowledged as one of the most influential figures in Nashville. Bowen entered the business as a teenage rockabilly singer, landing a Top 20 hit in 1957 with "I'm Stickin' with You," a basic song built around a thwacking bass riff, a sing-song melody, and Bowen's own nervous, boyish vocals. Possibly intended as nothing more than a demo, it was first released as a B-side to Buddy Knox's No. 1 hit, "Party Doll."

Bowen and Knox's careers were bound together in an unusually close fashion, making thumbnail sketches of their recording activities rather difficult. Knox (guitar, vocals) and Bowen (bass, vocals) met in the '50s and became the frontmen of a rockabilly combo, the Orchids. They were directed to Norman Petty's studio in Clovis, NM, by Roy Orbison, where they cut "Party Doll," with Knox on vocals, and "I'm Stickin' with You," with Bowen on bass. The tracks, both co-written by Knox and Bowen, were issued on

the small Triple D label, with the top side billed to Buddy Knox & the Orchids, and the flip side to Jimmy Bowen & the Orchids. When the single was leased to Roulette for nationwide distribution, the company shrewdly divided the product into two separate singles. When both became hits, it found itself with two separate new stars, although nominally they were still part of the same group (now renamed, to further confuse matters, the Rhythm Orchids).

Bowen and Knox embarked on simultaneous solo careers for Roulette, although each continued to use the Rhythm Orchids as their backup band for quite a while, which accounts for the similar mild rockabilly pop sound of each artist. Knox, however, was a far better singer, songwriter, and instrumentalist than Bowen; for that matter, he was far more successful, landing a string of smaller follow-up hits to "Party Doll." Bowen never entered the Top 20 again, although he did quite a bit of recording for Roulette in the late '50s. Finding it hard to recapture the unforced bounce of "I'm Stickin' with You," Bowen's Roulette sides rate as some of the tamest rockabilly of the '50s. Bowen was probably unsuited to be a frontman to begin with, despite his teen-idol looks; his range was narrow (sometimes he sounds like a gawky Johnny Cash), and his delivery sounded stiff and unsure. His material was fairly slight as well, and at the end of his stay with Roulette, he abandoned rock for a misguided and soggy stab at orchestrated pop.

Bowen made a few more records, but it was really more the beginning than the end when he moved into production. In the mid-'60s he worked with Frank Sinatra, Sammy Davis, Jr., and Dean Martin at Reprise; since then he's had high posts at Capitol, MGM, Elektra/Asylum, and MCA, concentrating mostly on country music in recent times. *—Richie Unterberger*

● **The Complete Roulette Recordings** / 1996 / Sequel ✦✦✦✦
Bowen has only half of this double CD; the other disc consists of Buddy Knox's complete Roulette recordings, not Bowen's. It may be an unwieldy way to pick up Bowen's material, but his disc, with 30 tracks, presents a thorough retrospective of his late-'50s rockabilly and pop recordings, including all the singles, LP cuts, and two previously unreleased tracks. It's more than anyone but the collector needs to hear, despite the meticulous quality of the packaging. Nothing else Bowen did matched the leadoff song, "I'm Stickin' with You," which is better heard as a track on various-artist '50s compilations. The rest of this mild rockabilly is pretty trivial, and the pop sides (with orchestration) are exactly the kinds of things rockabilly was reacting *against.* Though he couldn't have been considered one of rockabilly's leading lights either, Knox's half of the program outshines Bowen's by a considerable margin. *—Richie Unterberger*

Best of Jimmy Bowen / Collectables ✦✦

Bryan Bowers

b. Aug. 18, 1940, Yorktown, VA
Autoharp / Folk, Traditional Bluegrass, Old-Time
Folk artist Bryan Bowers, one of the great autoharp players, is known for his innovative five-finger picking style on an instrument that is typically strummed. While growing up in Yorktown, VA, Bowers listened to the call-and-answer songs of the field workers, which had a tremendous effect on his development as a musician. Though he majored in Spanish at a small Virginia college, he dropped out three credits shy of a degree when his parents died. Coping with his deep depression by playing guitar, Bowers was also introduced to the autoharp, which soon became his instrument of choice. After living in Seattle during 1971, he drove to Washington, DC, and got a regular gig playing between sets at a club. After meeting the Dillards at another local club, Bowers impressed the group with his playing and was invited to play at the Berryville Bluegrass Festival. His virtuosity, coupled with his humor and fascinating stories, made Bower an instant hit with the audience. He signed with Flying Fish Records in 1977 and recorded his debut album, *The View from Home.* Primarily a live artist, Bowers only recorded three more albums over the next 17 years. He was a charter member of *Frets* magazine's "First Gallery of Greats," a list of some of the finest string players in the world generated from a fan poll; his name appears beside such

greats as Chet Atkins, David Grisman, Stephane Grappelli, and Itzhak Perlman. —*Sandra Brennan*

● **The View from Home** / 1977 / Flying Fish ✦✦✦✦
This, the debut record of the autoharpist virtuoso, features backing from some of the country's best pickers. —*AMG*

By Heart / 1982 / Flying Fish ✦✦✦

For You / 1982 / Flying Fish ✦✦✦

Home, Home on the Road / 1982 / Flying Fish ✦✦✦
On this album Bowers plays the autoharp and sings a mixture of serious and comic songs. —*AMG*

Boxcar Willie (Lecil Travis Martin)

b. Sep. 1, 1931, Sterret, TX
Guitar, Vocals / Traditional Country, Country Humor
Boxcar Willie is perhaps the most successful invented character in the history of country music. With his kitschy persona and stage act—highlighted by his amazingly accurate impersonation of a train whistle—Willie played into the stereotype of the loveable, good-natured hobo, who spent his life riding the rails and singing songs. Since his popularity had more to do with his image than his music, it makes sense that he was massively successful in England, where he personified Americana. Willie's English success carried him over to American success in the early '80s, where he ironically was perceived as carrying the torch for traditional country, because he kept the stereotypes alive.

Born Lecil Travis Martin, Boxcar Willie never worked on the railroads—his father did. However, Willie loved the railroads and kept running away to ride the trains when he was a child. He also loved country music, particularly the songs of Jimmie Rodgers, Roy Acuff, and Ernest Tubb.

As a teenager, Boxcar Willie would perform under his given name, eventually becoming a regular on the Big D Jamboree in Dallas, Texas. In his early 20s, he served in the Air Force. After he left the service, he continued to sing in clubs and radio shows.

In the late '50s, he began performing as Marty Martin, while working blue collar jobs during the day. He released an album, *Marty Martin Sings Country Music and Stuff like That*, around 1958, but it was ignored.

In the mid-'60s, Willie wrote a song called "Boxcar Willie," based on a hobo he saw on a train. Willie continued to struggle in his musical career until the mid-'70s. By that time, he had become a DJ in Corpus Christi, TX. In 1975, he decided to risk everything he had on one final chance at stardom. He moved to Nashville and developed the Boxcar Willie character, using his song as the foundation.

Initially, Willie wasn't very successful, but he had a lucky break in 1976 when he was called in to replace a sick George Jones at a Nashville club. During that performance, he was spotted by Drew Taylor, a Scottish booking agent. Taylor brought Boxcar Willie over to England for a tour, where he was enthusiastically received. Later that year, he released his first album, which was a moderate success in the UK. Through the rest of the '70s, Willie toured Britain in a series of increasingly successful tours, culminating in a performance at the International Country Music Festival at Wembley in 1979. After his Wembley show, he received a standing ovation—the performance established Boxcar Willie as a star. His next album, *King of the Road*, became a humongous success in England, reaching No. 5 on the album charts; the record was helped immeasurably by its accompanying television advertisements, which sold the record through the mail.

By the end of 1980, Willie had become the most successful country artist in England, and his American success was just beginning. *King of the Road* was advertised on American television, "Train Medley" was a minor hit on the country charts, and he was becoming a popular attraction on US concert circuits. In 1981, he received a spot on the Country Music Hall of Fame's Walkway of the Stars and became a member of the Grand Ole Opry.

Boxcar Willie enjoyed his time in the spotlight, becoming a regular on the television show *Hee Haw* in 1982 and turning out albums as fast as he could make them. Yet "Bad News" became his only American country Top 40 hit in 1982. In 1985, he played

Boxcar Willie

a hobo in *Sweet Dreams*, a film about Patsy Cline. By the mid-'80s, his star had faded, but he remained a popular concert attraction, particularly in England, into the '90s. —*Stephen Thomas Erlewine*

Boxcar Willie / 1976 / MCA ✦✦✦✦
Never issued on compact disc, *Boxcar Willie* remains one of the hobo's best albums, highlighted by a guest appearance by Willie Nelson. —*Stephen Thomas Erlewine*

Marty Martin Sings Country Music / 1976 / AHMC ✦✦✦

● **The Collection** / 1987 / Castle ✦✦✦✦
Castle's *The Collection* is the best Boxcar Willie compilation ever assembled, featuring his signature hit, "Train Medley," as well as several other songs in a similar vein. Appropriately, *The Collection* was only released in England, the country that made Boxcar Willie famous. —*Stephen Thomas Erlewine*

Best Loved Favorites / 1989 / Vanguard ✦✦✦✦
Best Loved Favorites is not a greatest hits collection from Boxcar Willie. Instead, it's a a selection of some of the most popular and enduring country standards, performed by the singing hobo. Willie is in good voice throughout and with songs like "In the Jailhouse Now" and "Blue Moon of Kentucky," it's an entertaining listen. —*Stephen Thomas Erlewine*

Rocky Box: Rockabilly / 1993 / K-Tel ✦✦✦
Country music's favorite fake hobo teams up with the Midwest's top roots music combo for a spirited, if at times surreal, outing. The Skeletons, featuring D. Clinton Thompson's excellent fretboard work, provide perfect retro backing on everything, while Boxcar is quite at home on traditional '50s boppers like "Mystery Train" and "Rockin' Bones." But the true candidate for the twilight zone is his version here of "Achy Breaky Heart," complete with his patented train whistle. It doesn't get much weirder than this in any style of music. —*Cub Koda*

King of the Road / Mainstreet ✦✦✦✦
King of the Road is the album that made Boxcar Willie famous. Advertised on English television, the record wound up climbing to No. 5 on the UK charts, setting the stage for his breakthrough success in the United States and Canada. *King of the Road* consists of a number of traditional country songs, including "Wabash Cannonball," "San Antonio Rose," "You Are My Sunshine," "Mule Train," "Rolling in My Sweet Baby's Arms," and three Hank Williams songs, with a couple of cute originals thrown in for good measure. Although it doesn't have his signature song, "Train Medley," it remains his best album. —*Stephen Thomas Erlewine*

Truck Driving Favorites / Madacy ✦✦✦
Featured are such hits as "Phantom 309," "Convoy," "Freightliner Fever," and "Whiteline Fever." —*AMG*

Boy Howdy

Contemporary Country

Boy Howdy, a Los Angeles-based country-rock band reminiscent of Creedence Clearwater Revival and the Eagles, was formed in 1990 by vocalist/bassist Jeffrey Steele. Steele began performing in bands at the age of 17, and was eventually noticed by Dwight Yoakam's producer, Pete Anderson. This led Steele to record the song "Driftin' Man" for the *A Town South of Bakersfield, Vol. 2* compilation. Steele was playing in an L.A. club when he met his future bandmates: drummer Hugh Wright, and Cary and Larry Parks, the talented sons of bluegrass fiddler Ray Parks. (Cary had experience playing guitar and mandolin with ex-Eagles member Randy Meisner, as well as Rick Roberts from the Flying Burrito Brothers.)

The four found an instant rapport and Boy Howdy was born. A popular club band, they finally debuted formally on KZLA Burbank. Their first recorded single, "When Johnny Comes Marchin' Home Again," was released in 1991, just after the Gulf War had begun, and its success led to a deal with Curb Records. That year, they were chosen as Best Vocal Group by the L.A. Chapter of the California Country Music Association. The association also named Steele Best Male Vocalist of the Year and Best Bassist; Wright was also named Best Drummer. In addition, the ACM named Boy Howdy Best Non-Touring Band. Later that year, they released their Chris Farren-produced debut album, *Welcome to Howdywood,* which contained the Top 50 hit "Our Love Was Meant to Be." In 1992, the band appeared in George Strait's film *Pure Country.* One year later, Boy Howdy released their self-titled second album and had more chart success with the single, "A Cowboy's Born with a Broken Heart." They also released a six-track mini album, *She'd Give Anything,* which did very well on the charts during 1994. — *Sandra Brennan*

Welcome to Howdywood / 1992 / Capitol ✦✦✦

● **She'd Give Anything** / Jan. 11, 1994 / Curb ✦✦✦✦

Born That Way / 1995 / Curb ✦✦✦

Bill Boyd

b. Sep. 29, 1910, Fannin County, TX, d. Dec. 7, 1977
Guitar, Vocals / Western Swing, Neo-Traditionalist Country

For true fans of Western swing music, Bill Boyd rates with his contemporary Bob Wills, even though the two utilized very different styles; whereas Wills and His Playboys often used horns and recorded songs from a variety of genres, Boyd remained true to his Western roots, using only a string band, the Cowboy Ramblers.

Born on a ranch near Ladonia, TX, Boyd grew up as a working cowboy, learning the traditional songs from the impromptu campfire jam sessions of the ranch hands. Both he and his younger brother frequently sang with the cowboys, as did their parents. The boys got to be pretty good, and in 1926, made their debut on KFPM in Greenville. The family moved to Dallas in 1929, where Boyd played in a band that included fiddler Art Davis. By this time, Boyd knew he wanted a career in music, first joining a band on WFAA and then the first incarnation of the Cowboy Ramblers in 1932 on WRR. Included in Boyd's new band was his brother Jim on bass, Davis on fiddle, and Walter Kirkes on tenor banjo. When not actually performing, Boyd was out recruiting new sponsors and in this way managed to survive the Depression.

In 1934, he and the band moved to San Antonio to record for Bluebird, cutting hits including the standard "Under the Double Eagle" and "Going Back to My Texas Home." In the late '30s, the band's membership increased to ten; among their better known members were fiddler Carroll Hubbard, piano player Knocky Parker, and steel guitar player Wilson "Lefty" Perkins. During their long association with RCA, Boyd and the Ramblers recorded over 229 singles; in the early 1940s, they appeared in six Hollywood films, including *Raiders of the West* and *Prairie Pals.* However, when the popularity of live radio in Dallas began fading in the 1950s, Boyd was forced to become a deejay. — *Sandra Brennan*

● **Bill Boyd's Cowboy Ramblers** / Aug. 7, 1934-Feb. 7, 1950 / RCA Bluebird ✦✦✦✦

This two-LP set gives one a definitive look at the many versions of Bill Boyd's Cowboy Ramblers, one of the top Western swing groups of the 1930s. Boyd's band was a bit unusual in that it rarely ever traveled, mostly performing in the recording studio and frequently on radio shows. The 32 selections on this two-fer date from 1934-38 (with the exception of three later pieces) and help to define the Western swing sound, emphasizing the jazzier side of Boyd's music; 17 of the performances are instrumentals. Among the sidemen are the fiddles of Jesse Ashlock and Cecil Brower and pianist Knocky Parker. Highlights include "Under the Double Eagle," "Barn Dance Rag," "Goofus," "Fan It," "Beaumont Rag," "New Steel Guitar Rag," "Boyd's Tin Roof Blues," "New Spanish Two Step" and 1950's "Domino Rag." Well worth searching for. — *Scott Yanow*

With His Cowboy Ramblers 1943-1947 / RCA Bluebird ✦✦✦✦

This features "On the Texas Plains," "You're Just About Right," "Boyd's Blues," and more. — *AMG*

BR5-49

Country-Rock, Neo-Traditionalist Country

Blending rock and country with a vigorous energy, BR5—49 became one of the most critically acclaimed country-rock bands of the mid-'90s. For the first half of the decade, the group carved out a dedicated following in Nashville's downtown district on Lower Broadway, playing for a variety of music fans, ranging from honky tonkers to punk rockers. Eventually, the group landed a record contract with Arista Records. Their first release was a live EP, appropriately called *Live at Robert's,* which was released in the spring of 1996. It was followed later that fall with an eponymous full-length record that was greeted with overwhelmingly positive reviews in both the country and rock press. — *Stephen Thomas Erlewine*

Live at Robert's / 1996 / Arista ✦✦✦✦

BR5-49 know where the gems are found when it comes to digging out old material. The band gained its street rep by transforming Nashville's downtown honky tonk scene into a hopping place that draws a blend of punks, hipsters, frat kids, tourists, and drunks; with Live at Robert's, the band makes its first major national move by providing a glimpse of its vibrant, all-night live show. Anyone who has danced through one of the quintet's sets at Robert's Western Wear—where the band has played for tips for five hours a night, four nights a week for the last two years—will recognize the chilling version of the Stanley Brothers' "Knoxville Girl" and the go-for-broke take on Johnny Horton's "Ole Slewfoot." But the live, six-song EP also displays their knack for novel originals, including the rumbling boogie of "18 Wheels and a Crowbar," the soiled innocence of the Bettie Page tribute, "Bettie Bettie," and the crafty wit of the crowd favorite, "Me 'n' Opie (Down by the Duck Pond)," which finds Opie, Goober, Barney, and Otis hitting the homegrown while hiding out from Andy and Aunt Bea. It's the song that explains everything. — *Michael McCall*

● **BR5-49** / Sep. 17, 1996 / Arista ✦✦✦✦

BR5-49 carries through on the promise of their debut EP with their eponymous full-length album. The band slams together a variety of country styles, ranging from traditional ballads to edgy country-rock, and delivers them with a bracing energy that's one part honky tonk grit, one part rock 'n' roll hell-raising. While the energy is impressive, what makes *BR5-49* an album worth returning to is the group's musicality. It's not just that they can play a variety of different styles and play them well, it's that they can fuse them together seamlessly. — *Thom Owens*

Bobby Braddock

Piano, Vocals / Country-Pop, Nashville Sound/Countrypolitan

Bobby Braddock was one of the most successful songwriters in country music. He was born and raised in Florida, and got his professional start in 1964 when he began playing keyboards in Marty Robbins' tour band. In 1966, Robbins had chart success singing Braddock's first song, "While You're Dancing." Later Braddock went to Nashville and replaced Roger Miller at Tree International as a staff writer. He also became a session player during the late '60s.

He began recording in 1967 and had chart success with his second single, "I Know How to Do it," which made it to the Top 75. That year the Oak Ridge Boys reached the Top Ten with his "Would They Love Him Down in Shreveport." He then provided the Statler Brothers with two Top Ten hits, including "You Can't Have Your Kate and Edith Too." Braddock scored his first No. 1 hit when Tammy Wynette sang "D-I-V-O-R-C-E," a song he co-wrote with Curly Putnam. He continued to steadily create hits through early 1978. Some of his biggest songs include "I Believe the South's Gonna Rise Again," which became a big hit for Tanya Tucker; "Come on In" (1976), which provided Sonny James, Jerry Lee Lewis, and later the Oak Ridge Boys with hits; "Something to Brag About" (1978) for Mary Kay Place and Willie Nelson; and "Womanhood," which was a No. 3 hit for Wynette.

In 1979, Braddock signed to Elektra and scored a Top 60 hit with the title track of his 1979 album *Between the Lines*. He continued writing hits for other artists through the early '80s; among them was the song that restored the flagging career of George Jones, "He Stopped Loving Her Today," which he co-wrote with Putnam. In 1980, Braddock again appeared on the charts with a cut from his second Elektra album *Love Bomb*. The following year, he was inducted into the Nashville Songwriters Hall of Fame. His career waned a bit during the mid-'80s, but Braddock continued to write; his "Nashville" appeared on John Anderson's *Solid Ground*. —*Sandra Brennan*

● **Love Bomb** / 1980 / Elektra ✦✦✦
A wry look at social situations circa the late '70s done up southern style. Braddock touches on such topics as drugs, Madison Avenue advertisers, the Klu Klux Klan, failed marriages, and just about anything else that mattered in good ol' Harper Valley, and all done with tongue firmly stuck in cheek. Braddock supplies appropriate melodies for each of these ten tunes and is backed by solid studio pros. A good time for those seeking out a little slice of humor along with a bit of message. —*James Chrispell*

Between the Lines / Elektra ✦✦✦

Owen Bradley

b. Oct. 21, 1915, Westmoreland, TX
Nashville Sound/Countrypolitan
As one of the architects of the Nashville Sound, Owen Bradley was one of the most influential country music producers of the '50s and '60s. Along with his contemporary Chet Atkins, Bradley helped country music move away from its rootsy origins to a more accessible, radio format by blending pop production and songwriting techniques with country. Bradley's country-pop productions relied on non-traditional country instruments like light, easy-listening piano, backup vocals and strings, using steel guitars and fiddles as flourishes instead of a foundation. This smooth production style helped make Patsy Cline and Brenda Lee into stars during the '50s, and its success often overshadowed Bradley's other musical contributions. Owen wasn't just capable of the lush, detailed Nashville Sound—he could also produce bluegrass by Bill Monroe, or hardcore honky tonk by Ernest Tubb and Loretta Lynn. In addition to producing, Bradley was the vice president of Decca Records' Nashville Division, and in that position he was able to produce a huge variety of artists, including Conway Twitty, Kitty Wells, and Webb Pierce. With his work in country-pop, honky tonk, and bluegrass, Bradley left behind a large legacy that proved vastly influential on contemporary country music.

Born outside of Westmoreland, TN, and raised in Nashville, Owen Bradley began playing piano professionally when he was a teenager, playing in local juke joints, clubs, and roadhouses. When he turned 20, he began working at WSM radio, and within five years he had established himself as an integral part of the station. In 1940, he was hired full-time by WSM, working as an arranger and instrumentalist. Two years later, he was made the station's musical director, and started playing regularly on the programs *Noontime Neighbors* and *Sunday Down South*. During this time, Bradley was also leading his own dance band, which

played parties throughout Nashville's high society. The group stayed together until 1964.

Bradley began working for Decca Records in 1947 as an assistant to producer Paul Cohen. By working at Cohen's side, Bradley learned to produce, and assisted in making records by Ernest Tubb and Red Foley, among many others. Eventually, Owen began producing records by himself, whenever his mentor couldn't travel to Nashville from New York.

Owen and his brother Harold opened a film studio in 1951, moving its location to Hillsboro Village within a year. It stayed there for two years, before it was moved again, this time to a house on 16th Avenue South with a Quonset hut attached to the main building. The Quonset Hut was converted into a studio in 1955—it was the first studio on the street that would become known as Music Row. Two years later, RCA built a studio a block away from the Bradley hut; in 1962, the brothers sold the studio to Columbia Records.

Cohen left Decca in 1958, and the label offered Bradley a position as vice president of the label's Nashville Division. At Decca, he began pioneering the Nashville Sound, incorporating orchestration and pop production techniques into country music. Patsy Cline was Bradley's most successful country-pop production. He had worked with her when she was with Four Star, but when she signed with Decca, Cline's music shifted toward country-pop and she began a string of Top Ten hits. Following her success, other artists that he produced in that style, most notably Brenda Lee, became successful as well. During this time, Bradley also produced harder-edged hits by Webb Pierce and Kitty Wells. In addition to his record production, Owen released a handful of records by his instrumental quintet, including the minor 1958 hit "Big Guitar." With his brother Harold, Bradley produced a half-hour television series, *Country Style USA*, during the late '50s.

Bradley bought a farm outside of Nashville in 1961, converting a barn into a demo studio. Within a few years, the barn was upgraded to a first-class recording studio called Bradley's Barn, and over the next two decades, it became one of the most popular and legendary studios in country music. In 1980, it burned down, yet it was rebuilt within a few years in the exact same spot.

Throughout the '60s and '70s, Bradley worked with many of Decca's most famous artists, including Loretta Lynn and Conway Twitty. In 1974, Bradley was inducted into the Country Music Hall of Fame. In the early '80s, he retired from full-time producing, yet he continued to work on the occasional special project. His last major work was k.d. lang's 1988 album, *Shadowland*. —*Stephen Thomas Erlewine*

Paul Brandt

b. Jul. 21, 1972
Vocals / Contemporary Country
Paul Brandt (b. Paul Rennee Belobersycky) was one of the Canadian country singers that was able to take advantage of the massive success of Shania Twain and parlay a successful career for himself in America.

Brandt was born and raised Calgary, Alberta, Canada, where he sang gospel music and learned to play guitar as a child. During high school, he began playing local talent contests, singing his own songs. Most of his original material was directly inspired by neo-traditionalists like Dwight Yoakam and George Strait. Instead of pursuing country music as a full-time career, he decided to attend college and study nursing. For two years, Brandt went to college and practiced as a pediatric nurse at Alberta's Children's Hospital. However, he continued to enter local talent contests and he continued to place well in each event.

The turning point in Brandt's musical career came when he entered a national contest sponsored by the Canadian performance organization SOCAN. At the contest, Brandt won first prize for Best Original Canadian Country Song with "Calm Before the Stone" and placed as the runner-up for Best Performance. The SOCAN competition was monitored by several insiders in the Nashville music community and Warner Bros. expressed interest in signing the singer. A demo tape of Brandt's songs made its way to Reprise's Nashville office. Reprise arranged to see a showcase concert by Brandt and, following the show, the label signed the young singer.

After signing the record contract, Brandt moved to Nashville, where he recorded his debut album with producer Josh Leo, who had previously worked with Kathy Mattea and Alabama. Brandt's debut, *Calm Before the Storm,* was released in June to critical acclaim and strong sales. *—Stephen Thomas Erlewine*

● **Calm Before the Storm** / Jun. 1996 / Reprise ✦✦✦✦

Elton Britt (James Britt Baker)

b. Jun. 27, 1917, Marshall, AR, **d.** Jun. 23, 1972
Vocals / Traditional Country, Honky Tonk
Elton Britt parlayed his Jimmie Rodgers imitation—a yodeling ability and range that surpassed Rodgers'—into country's biggest hit of the World War II era, "There's a Star Spangled Banner Waving Somewhere," which sold four million copies in the early '40s. He was born James Britt Baker in Marshall, AR, on June 27, 1913, and began playing guitar and singing around his hometown while in his mid-teens. Baker's career was made in 1930 when the Beverly Hillbillies returned from California to their Arkansas home to recruit a new vocalist. He won the talent search, and after being re-named Elton Britt, spent three years performing and recording with the Hillbillies. Britt moved to New York in 1933, initially playing in a quartet named Pappy, Zeke, Ezra and Elton. He recorded later in the '30s, as a solo act and also with the Wenatchee Mountaineers, Zeke Manners' Gang, and the Rustic Rhythm Trio.

Britt began his period of fame in 1939, thanks to two factors: his signature on a contract for the discount label RCA Bluebird and—most importantly—his friendship with songwriter/producer Bob Miller. Miller wrote all of Elton Britt's greatest early hits, including "Chime Bells," "Rocky Mountain Lullaby," "Buddy Boy," "Driftwood on the River," and in 1942, "There's a Star Spangled Banner Waving Somewhere." The latter was adopted by patriotic audiences as a symbol of the war effort —much as "Over There" had served World War I sympathizers. President Franklin Roosevelt even invited Britt—billed as "the World's Highest Yodeler"—to the White House in 1942 to perform the hit.

By the time the charts came into existence in 1944, though, Britt had peaked. He did hit the Country Top Ten 11 times during the last half of the '40s, but never topped the charts. "Someday" reached No. 2 in 1946, and six other songs peaked in the Top Five, including the double-sided "Wave to Me, My Lady"/"Blueberry Lane," "Detour," "Gotta Get Together with My Gal," "Candy Kisses" and "Quicksilver." A re-recording of his early hit "Chime Bells" hit No. 6. Britt continued recording with RCA, eventually releasing over 50 albums until 1957, when he moved to ABC/Paramount. He made a brief bid for the presidency in 1960, and recorded the No. 26 "Jimmie Rodgers Blues" eight years later, but retired soon after. *—John Bush*

Yodel Songs / 1955 / Longhorn ✦✦✦

16 Great Country Performances / 1971 / ABC ✦✦✦✦

● **The Best of Elton Britt** / RCA Victor ✦✦✦✦

Lane Brody

b. , Oak Park, IL
Vocals / Country-Pop, Urban Cowboy
Raised in Racine, WI, Lane Brody began singing at the age of five and wrote her first song, "Through the Darkness," at age 12. After founding an all-girl trio while still in high school, at age 18 she went to New York, performed in a couple of groups, and was discovered by Bobby Whiteside. She moved to Chicago and embarked on a lucrative career singing commercial jingles and modeling for print ads and packaging covers.

In 1976 she made her recording debut with the single "You're Gonna Make Love to Me" under the pseudonym Lynn Niles. Brody moved to California in 1978 and began singing at the Palomino club after she won $100 during their talent night. She got her break in 1981 when she signed with Liberty and debuted on the singles charts the next year with the self-penned "He's Taken." Her next release, "More Nights," also made it to the Top 60. Near

the end of the year she had a minor hit duet with Tom Bresh, "When It Comes to Love." In 1981, she made her television acting debut on the series *Taxi* and was nominated for an Emmy the following year for singing "Just a Little More Love" in the TV movie *The Gift of Life.* Her next chart appearance came in 1983 with a song she co-wrote, the Oscar-nominated "Over You," which was featured in the film *Tender Mercies.* She scored a No. 1 hit with her 1984 duet with Johnny Lee, "The Yellow Rose," which she and John Weilder adapted from a Civil War standard for use as the theme song to a short-lived TV series.

Brody's self-titled 1985 debut album contained two hits, including Bobby Lee Springfield's "He Burns Me Up." The next year she and Lee recorded another popular duet, "I Could Get Used to This." She then played a country singer on ABC's TV series *Heart of the City.* Brody continued to tour with Bresh following a joint appearance on a Lee Greenwood special for TNN and their own subsequent special. She also wrote and performed "All the Unsung Heroes" for a documentary on the Vietnam Wall, which still plays at the Smithsonian Institution and Arlington National Cemetery. *—Sandra Brennan*

● **Lane Brody** / 1985 / EMI America ✦✦✦✦

Lisa Brokop

Contemporary Country
Born in the Canadian province of British Columbia, Lisa Brokop made her performing debut at the age of seven, when she joined her accordionist mother and drummer brother in a family group that regularly performed at local churches, hospitals, and charities. By the age of 15, she was singing professionally, fronting her own working band two years later. At 19, Brokop was tapped to appear as a country singer in the motion picture *Harmony Cats,* and in 1993 she released her debut album, *My Love. Every Little Girl's Dream* followed the next year, and in 1995 Brokop issued her self-titled third LP. *—Jason Ankeny*

● **Every Little Girl's Dream** / 1994 / Capitol ✦✦✦✦

Lisa Brokop / 1995 / Patroit ✦✦✦

David Bromberg

b. Sep. 19, 1945, Philadelphia, PA
Dobro, Fiddle, Guitar, Mandolin, Session Musician / Blues, Singer-Songwriter, Contemporary Folk
Often referred to as a musician's musician throughout his career, Bromberg has spent almost as much time being a sideman to people like Bob Dylan and Jerry Jeff Walker as he has fronting his own band. Session credits for albums by Tom Paxton and Jerry Jeff Walker started getting Bromberg attention in the mid-'60s, and he began making the transition from sideman to frontman in the early '70s, when he was signed to record for Columbia Records.

The key to appreciating Bromberg is to realize he has an equal passion for blues, folk, Country & Western, bluegrass, and rock 'n' roll. This diverse range of influences is reflected on all his recordings for Columbia, Fantasy, and Rounder, and in his performances as well. His musical eclecticism over the years may have cost him some fans, but a typical Bromberg concert can be a musical education. *—Richard Skelly*

● **David Bromberg** / 1971 / Columbia ✦✦✦✦
David Bromberg was already a well-known folk instrumentalist before this album proved he was also a top-notch songwriter and an appealing vocalist as well. The styles mix folk, blues, rock, and jug-band music, and the songs alternate from the painfully sensitive ("Sammy's Song") to the rib-tickling "The Holdup," which was co-written by George Harrison. *—William Ruhlmann*

Demon in Disguise / 1972 / Columbia ✦✦✦

Wanted Dead or Alive / 1974 / Columbia ✦✦✦✦
This is a reissue of Bromberg's 1974 album. Backing musicians include several members of the Grateful Dead as well as Andy Statman on mandolin and tenor sax. Some of Bromberg's strongest and best-loved material can be found here, including "The Holdup," "Danger Man," "Send Me to the 'Lectric Chair," "The New Lee Highway Blues," and Bob Dylan's "Wallflower." *—AMG*

Midnight on the Water / 1975 / Columbia ✦✦✦
A big-band blowout album with guest appearances by Bonnie Raitt, Linda Ronstadt, and EmmyLou Harris, it features "The Joke's on Me" and "Don't Put that Thing on Me." —*Richard Meyer*

How Late'll Ya Play 'Til? / 1976 / Fantasy ✦✦✦
Bromberg's band, with two horns and a fiddle player, is capable of playing just about any style of popular music, and most of them are here on a double album, half recorded in the studio and half live. (Fantasy has also issued the two discs separately.) The standout inclusion is Bromberg's "Will Not Be Your Fool," which became his onstage showstopper from here on out. —*William Ruhlmann*

Hillbilly Jazz, Vol. 1 / 1977 / Sonet ✦✦✦

Hillbilly Jazz, Vol. 2 / 1977 / Sonet ✦✦✦

Out of the Blues: Best of David Bromberg / 1977 / Columbia ✦✦✦

Bandit in a Bathing Suit / 1978 / Fantasy ✦✦✦
A lot of hot playing includes Pink Anderson's "Travelin' Man" and "If You Don't Want Me Baby." —*Richard Meyer*

My Own House / 1978 / Fantasy ✦✦✦

You Should See the Rest of the Band / 1980 / Fantasy ✦✦

Sideman Serenade / 1990 / Rounder ✦✦
Bromberg's debut for Rounder includes versions of traditional blues, country, folk and soul/R&B tunes. He sings them earnestly and backs himself tastefully while working with both large groups and small combos. The guest roster includes everyone from Dr. John to Jackson Browne and David Lindley, as well as Chris Daniels and the Kings and some members of what was then Willie Nelson's traveling band. The only problem with this session was that Bromberg, for all his knowledge and zeal, just wasn't that convincing or gripping a vocalist. Still, this is an instructive disc for those interested in hearing faithful recreations of various classic genres. —*Ron Wynn*

Brooks & Dunn

Contemporary Country
Kix Brooks and Ronnie Dunn were the most popular country duo since the Judds and, in the process, became one of the biggest country artists of the '90s. Their music ran from hard-edged honky-tonk to radio-ready contemporary ballads.

Both Brooks (born and raised in Shreveport, LA) and Dunn (born and raised in Coleman, TX) were sons of pipefitters. As a youth, Brooks was influenced by a variety of regional musical styles ranging from Cajun to blues to jazz to country. He was first inspired towards a musical career by his neighbor, Johnny Horton; a friend of Horton's daughter, he would frequently visit their home and be dazzled by all the gold records on the walls. Brooks made his performing debut at the age of 12, singing with Horton's daughter, and continued performing in clubs and at other venues through high school; he also began writing songs frequently.

After working on the Alaskan pipeline, he moved to Maine, where he performed at ski resorts. Eventually he landed in Nashville, where he joined Don Gant's newly established Tree Publishing company. Shortly afterwards artists like the Nitty Gritty Dirt Band, John Conlee, and Highway 101 began finding success with Kix Brooks tunes. In 1983, he launched his own recording career with "Baby, When Your Heart Breaks Down" for Avion. He didn't record again until 1989, when he released his eponymous solo debut.

Ronnie Dunn's journey to Music City was quite different. His father had been a guitarist and sang in a traditional mountain string band as a hobby. While still in high school Dunn learned to play bass. It was his intention to become a Baptist preacher, but he became increasingly infatuated with music, and he spent many evenings performing in honky tonk bars. Dunn and his family later moved to Tulsa, where he began leading the house band at Duke's Country. This led to a record contract with the independent Churchill label, where he had two moderate hits in 1983 and 1984.

Dunn moved to Nashville via a talent contest. At first, he didn't know he had entered—his friend Jimmy Oldecker, who was

drumming for Eric Clapton at the time, submitted one of Dunn's tapes, unbeknownst to the songwriter. He won the regionals in Tulsa with a hastily assembled band, and went to Nashville's Bullpen Lounge for the finals where he won $30,000 and a recording session with producer Scott Hendricks. The two hit it off and for a while, Dunn continued sending his newest material to Hendricks, who saw that some of it got to Tim DuBois, the head of Arista. Eventually Dunn decided to relocate to Nashville.

Upon his arrival in Nashville, Dunn joined Tree Publishing and met Brooks. The two hit it off and soon began not only writing together, but also performing. DuBois was pleased by the new duo and offered them a recording contract. The two started out with a bang in 1990 when their debut single "Brand New Man" shot up to No. 1, as did their follow-up, "My Next Broken Heart." The following year their debut album *Brand New Man* was released and became an immediate success. Later in 1992, they had yet another No. 1 hit with "Neon Moon," but it was the single's flipside, "Boot Scootin' Boogie," that provided them with their biggest hit to date. By 1993, their first album had gone triple platinum; that same year, they also released their second album, *Hard Workin' Man*, and their string of hits continued. In 1996, they released their fourth album, *Borderline*, and had a major hit with their cover of B.W. Stevenson's old pop hit "My Maria" (one of the few hits they did not write). —*Sandra Brennan*

● **Brand New Man** / 1991 / Arista ✦✦✦✦
The title tale of love and redemption was a classic single for all the same reasons that made this would-be modern cowboy duo such a winner: tightly constructed choruses; a perfect balance between romance, macho swagger, and Wild-West imagery; and bracing harmonies that'll clear the trail dust out of your throat quicker than a shot of good whiskey. Four singles from *Brand New Man* topped the country charts: the title tune, "My Next Broken Heart," "Neon Moon," and "Boot Scootin' Boogie." —*Brian Mansfield*

Hard Workin' Man / 1993 / Arista ✦✦✦
As with most second albums, the successful traits started to isolate themselves on *Hard Workin' Man:* Macho stuff like "Hard Workin' Man" and "Rock My World (Little Country Girl)" rock harder than anything on *Brand New Man*, though B&D made sure their women came off as good as they did (catch the "and women too" tag on "Hard Workin' Man"). The slower songs ("That Ain't No Way to Go," "She Used to Be Mine") tend towards the sort of evocative images that run all through the debut. The pair never puts all the elements together they way they did the first time, but they come close enough that few people notice. —*Brian Mansfield*

Waitin' on Sundown / Sep. 27, 1994 / Arista ✦✦✦
Waitin' on Sundown doesn't depart from Brooks & Dunn's formula much, but the fans didn't mind—it sold over three million albums, anyway. By this point, the duo's albums had become a handful of solid singles—this time out, they are "Little Miss Honky Tonk," "She's Not the Cheatin' Kind," and "You're Gonna Miss Me When I'm Gone"—surrounded by filler, but the hits will make the fans forgive the filler. —*Thom Owens*

Borderline / Apr. 1996 / Arista ✦✦
Brooks & Dunn get a lot of mileage out of two potent personalities. Ronnie Dunn's expressive voice, underrated even with the band's huge success, and Kix Brooks' energized stage presence give their otherwise routine material enough of a spin to earn them their status as country music's leading duet team of the 1990s. With *Borderline*, their fourth and weakest album, they have to strain a bit too hard to give their songs weight. The primary exception is an outstanding cover of B.W. Stevenson's 1972 pop hit, "My Maria," which Dunn elevates with an outstanding vocal performance that puts him in a league with the Mavericks' Raul Malo. Other than a powerful ballad or two and an entertaining novelty number about a wife bluntly persuading her man that they are going out on the town that night, too much of *Borderline* relies on country cliches and formulaic arrangements. It's time for these two to make an artistic statement that goes beyond light entertainment. —*Michael McCall*

Garth Brooks

b. Feb. 7, 1962, Tulsa, OK

Guitar, Vocals / Contemporary Country, New Traditionalist

Garth Brooks is a pivotal figure in the history of country music, no matter how much some country purists would like to deny it. With his commercially savvy fusion of post-Merle Haggard country, honky tonk, post-folk-rock sensitive singer-songwriter sensibilities, and '70s arena-rock dramatics, Brooks brought country music to a new audience in the '90s—namely, a mass audience. Before Brooks, it was inconceivable for a country artist to sell a million copies. He shattered that barrier in 1991, when his second album, *No Fences*, began its chart domination and its follow-up, *Ropin' the Wind*, became the first country album to debut at the top of the pop charts; *No Fences* would eventually sell a record-shattering 13 million copies. After Garth, country music had successfully carved a permanent place for itself on the pop charts. In the process, it lost a lot of the traditionalism that had always been its hallmark, but that is precisely why Brooks is important.

Garth Brooks is the son of Troyal and Colleen Carroll Brooks. Colleen was a country singer herself, recording a handful of records for Capitol in the mid-'50s that never experienced any chart success. As a child, Garth was interested in music and frequently sang at family gatherings, but he concentrated on athletics. He received a partial athletic scholarship at Oklahoma State University as a javelin tosser, but he wound up dropping the sport during his collegiate career. While he was at college, Brooks began singing in local Oklahoma clubs, often with lead guitarist Ty England.

After he graduated with an advertising degree in December of 1984, Garth Brooks decided to try to forge out a career as a country singer. In 1985 he moved to Nashville with hopes of being discovered by a record label. Twenty-three hours after moving to Nashville, he returned to Oklahoma, frustrated with the industry, his prospects, and his naive dreams. Brooks continued to perform in Oklahoma clubs, and in 1986, he married his college girlfriend, Sandy Mahl.

The couple moved to Nashville in 1987, this time with a better idea of how the music industry operated. Brooks began making connections with various songwriters and producers, and he sang on a lot of songwriters' demo tapes. Although he had made several connections within the industry and he had a powerful management team, every label in town was refusing to sign him. In 1988, six weeks after Capitol Records passed on his demo, one of the label's executives saw Brooks sing at a local club. Impressed with the performance, the executive convinced the label to sign Brooks.

Brooks recorded his first album with producer Allen Reynolds at the end of 1988; the self-titled debut appeared early in 1989. The album was an instant success, with its first single, "Much Too Young (To Feel This Damn Old)," climbing into the country Top Ten. Brooks' debut was a success, crossing over into the pop album charts, but it was overshadowed by the blockbuster appeal of Clint Black, as well other similar new male vocalists like Travis Tritt and Alan Jackson. Within a year, Brooks would tower above them all with his unexpected widespread success.

Garth Brooks had three other hit singles—the No. 1 "If Tomorrow Never Comes," the No. 2 "Not Counting You," and the No. 1 "The Dance"—but it was his second album, *No Fences*, that established him as a superstar. *No Fences* was released in the fall of 1990, preceded by the massive hit single "Friends in Low Places." *No Fences* spent 23 weeks at the top of the country charts and sold 700,000 copies within the first ten days of its release. Throughout 1990 and 1991, Brooks had a string of No. 1 country hits from the album, including "Unanswered Prayers," "Two of a Kind, Workin' on a Full House," and "The Thunder Rolls." By 1993, *No Fences* would sell over ten million copies.

Not only did his record sales break all the accepted country conventions, but so did Garth Brooks' concerts. By the end of 1990, he was selling out stadiums within minutes and was putting on stadium-sized shows, patterned after '70s rock extravaganzas. Brooks used a cordless, headset microphone so he could run around his large stage. He had an elaborate light show, explo-

sions, and even a harness, so he could swing out above the crowd and sing to them. It was the first time any country artist incorporated such rock'n' roll techniques into their stageshows.

Ropin' the Wind, Brooks' third album, was released in September of 1991 and became the first country record to debut at the top of the pop charts. *Ropin' the Wind* matched the success of *No Fences*, selling over ten million copies within its first two years of release and spawning the No. 1 hit singles "Shameless," "What She's Doing Now," and "The River."

By the end of 1991, Brooks had become a genuine popular music phenomenon—even his 1992 Christmas album, *Beyond the Season*, went multi-platinum—and there were no signs of his momentum slowing down. Naturally, a backlash began to develop in the fall of 1992, beginning with the release of "We Shall Be Free," the first single from his fourth album. Featuring a strong gospel underpinning, the single stalled at No. 12 and many radio stations refused to play it. It was indicative of the eclectic nature of his forthcoming album, *The Chase*, which pushed the boundaries of contemporary country. *The Chase* debuted at No. 1 upon its October 1992 release and by the end of the year, it sold over five million copies. Nevertheless, that number was half the size of the figures for his two previous albums, and there was speculation in the media that Brooks' career had already peaked.

Sensing that he was in danger of losing his core audience, Brooks returned to straight country with 1993's *In Pieces*. The album was critically acclaimed and sold several million copies, though it was clear that Garth would not reach the stratospheric commercial heights of *No Fences* and *Ropin' the Wind* again. Even so, he remains one of the most successful artists in popular music, one of the few that are guaranteed to sell millions of records with each new album, as well as sell out concerts around the world.

The Hits, which was only available for a year, was released in the fall of 1994 and would eventually sell over eight million copies. Garth Brooks released *Fresh Horses*, his first album of new material in two years, in November of 1995; within six months of its release, it had sold over three million copies. —*Stephen Thomas Erlewine*

Garth Brooks / Apr. 12, 1989 / Liberty ✦✦✦

On Garth Brooks' self-titled debut, his fusion of rock 'n' roll and traditional country genres like honky tonk and Western swing was already fully formed, as was his gift for extended metaphors. One listen to his signature song and breakthrough hit, "The Dance," proves that, which is why he broke away from the hat acts that he was initially grouped with. Nevertheless, *Garth Brooks* is the most straightforward of all of his albums—Brooks sticks with neo-traditional country on about half of the tracks. He sings traditional country quite well—"Not Counting You" is a particularly effective honky tonk number, demonstrating a debt to both George Jones and George Strait—but what makes the album an exciting debut are songs like the genre-bending ballads "The Dance" and "If Tomorrow Never Comes," and that is the style that brought him mass success with his next album, *No Fences*. —*Stephen Thomas Erlewine*

☆ **No Fences** / Aug. 27, 1990 / Liberty ✦✦✦✦✦

Essentially, Garth Brooks' second album *No Fences* follows the same pattern as his debut album, but it is a more assured and risky record. Brooks still performs neo-traditional country, such as the honky tonk hit "Friends in Low Places," but now he twists it around with clever pop hooks. Those pop-rock influences are most apparent on the ballads, which alternate between sensitive folk-rock and power-ballad bombast. But what makes *No Fences* such a success is how seamlessly he blends the two seemingly opposing genres, and how he chose a set of material that makes his genre-bending sound subtle and natural. Of course, it doesn't hurt that the songs are consistently entertaining, either. —*Stephen Thomas Erlewine*

Ropin' the Wind / Sep. 1991 / Liberty ✦✦✦✦

With *Ropin' the Wind*, Garth Brooks began to make his '70s rock influences more explicit. Naturally, that was most notable in his reworking of Billy Joel's "Shameless," which he transformed from a rock power ballad into contemporary country. But that influence is also evident on ambitious epics like "The River" and even the honky tonk ravers of "Papa Loved Mama" and "Rodeo." Some might say that those rock influences are what made Brooks a crossover success, but he wouldn't have been nearly as successful if he didn't have a tangible country foundation to his music—even when he comes close to standard arena rock bombast, there are gritty steel guitars or vocal inflections that prove he is trying to expand country's vocabulary, not trying to exploit it. —*Stephen Thomas Erlewine*

Beyond the Season / Aug. 17, 1992 / Liberty ✦✦✦
One of the most succesful Christmas albums ever, *Beyond the Season* is a varied collection for a country star, even one as "progressive" as Brooks. The tunes range from a gospel version of "Go Tell It on the Mountain" to a song-play where Brooks' songwriters take the roles of animals in the manger. It's about half traditional and half original, with Brooks co-writing the hardest rocking tune, "The Old Man's Back in Town." —*Brian Mansfield*

The Chase / Oct. 1992 / Liberty ✦✦✦
The Chase is Garth Brooks' most ambitious and personal album. Not coincidentally, it is one of his least popular releases, selling about half of the previous *Ropin' the Wind*. But in its own way, *The Chase* is more rewarding and deeper than *Ropin' the Wind*. That's partially due to Brooks' naked ambition—not only does he record "We Shall Be Free" with a gospel choir, but he tackles deeper social and personal issues than he has before. However, the true key to the album is Brooks' conviction—even when his musical experiments don't quite work, it's easy to admire and respect his ambition. Although there are light moments like "Night Rider's Lament" and a cover of Little Feat's "Dixie Chicken," *The Chase* is a more somber, reflective record than his previous three albums, but given a bit of a time, it's as satisfying as anything he's ever recorded. —*Stephen Thomas Erlewine*

In Pieces / Aug. 23, 1993 / Liberty ✦✦✦✦
After the relative commercial disappointment of *The Chase*, Garth Brooks toned down his experimental eclecticism on *In Pieces*. Alternating between heavily rock-influenced numbers, dramatic ballads, and revamped honky tonk, *In Pieces* appeals to the audience that found *The Chase* too pretentious and overly serious. That doesn't mean Brooks abandoned his desire to bend the rules—he's just masked his more ambitious material with crowd-pleasing uptempo numbers like "American Honky-Tonk Bar Association" and "Ain't Going Down (Til the Sun Comes Up)." *In Pieces* is an album that was made for the fans and it shows—it is one of Brooks' most energetic and exciting collections. —*Stephen Thomas Erlewine*

★ **The Hits** / 1994 / Liberty ✦✦✦✦✦
The Hits is exactly what it says it is—18 of Garth Brooks' biggest hits, including his first 14 No. 1 singles. Although he has good album tracks on each of his records, this is the essential Garth Brooks album—it gives a good sense of the singer's talents, especially his underappreciated eclecticism. *The Hits* was only in print for a year, but it sold in excess of eight million copies, so it could hardly be called a limited edition. —*Stephen Thomas Erlewine*

Fresh Horses / Nov. 21, 1995 / Capitol Nashville ✦✦✦
Garth Brooks had to move forward in a dramatic way with *Fresh Horses*, his first new album since 1993. Following the massive success of *The Hits*—which effectively recapped why the singer became the single most popular American performer of the '90s—Brooks positioned himself for a new direction with *Fresh Horses*. The problem is, he doesn't know which way he should go. Throughout the album, he swings back and forth between country and rock without any sense of purpose. Brooks tries to rework Aerosmith's "The Fever" into a rowdy rodeo country-rocker, but the end result is forced and half-hearted. The Aerosmith cover illustrates the problems of *Fresh Horses*—Brooks is trying too hard to cover new territory or restore hardcore honky-tonk grit to his slick country-rock. When he lets his guard down—such as on the melancholy ballad "The Beaches of Cheyenne" and the sassy, suggestive "It's Midnight Cinderella"—he can still come up with winners, but those moments don't come frequently on *Fresh Horses*. —*Stephen Thomas Erlewine*

Kix Brooks

b. May 12, 1955, Shreveport, LA
Vocals / Contemporary Country
Before teaming with Ronnie Dunn to form Brooks & Dunn, Shreveport, LA, native Kix Brooks wrote songs in Nashville and cut one unsuccessful album for Capitol Records. The album was reissued by Liberty Records in 1994. —*Brian Mansfield*

Kix Brooks / Oct. 25, 1993 / Capitol ✦✦✦
A worthy addition to the collection of any Brooks & Dunn fan, the album was nevertheless widely ignored upon its release. ("Sacred Ground," the album's only charting single, would become McBride & The Ride's first big hit in 1992.) On his own, Brooks' bayou roots show through, and his music often sounds just as tough as Brooks & Dunn's. —*Brian Mansfield*

Brother Boys

Progressive Bluegrass, Traditional Bluegrass
Led by frontmen Ed Snodderly and Eugene Wolf, the Johnson City, TN, six-piece bluegrass band the Brother Boys followed up their self-titled independent label debut with the 1992 LP *Plow*. *Presley's Grocery* followed in 1995. —*Jason Ankeny*

Plow / 1992 / Sugar Hill ✦✦✦

● **Presley's Grocery** / 1995 / Sugar Hill ✦✦✦✦
The Brother Boys sound like a modern combination of the Everly Brothers with Elvis' rockabilly drive. They offer up a jaunty mixture of old and new tunes distinct enough that any sound-alike comparisons are academic. One low point is an attempt to recast "I Don't Care If the Sun Don't Shine"; the Elvis version is just too epochal to be outshined. The playing is hot, and the album sounds crisp and immediate. *Presley's Grocery* is a good album for fans of country vocals who need a break from bluegrass and the outlaws. —*Richard Meyer*

The Brother Boys / New Hillbilly Music ✦✦✦

Brother Phelps

Contemporary Country
The duo of Brother Phelps consisted of singer-songwriter/bassist Doug and singer-songwriter/guitarist Ricky Lee Phelps, who left the Kentucky Headhunters in 1992 following their *Electric Barnyard* album. The name Brother Phelps, which came about after they held a nationwide contest on TNN's *Crook & Chase*, is a tribute to their father, an Assembly of God preacher nicknamed Brother Phelps by his congregation. The brothers began playing together as teens and developed a style of close harmony singing reminiscent of the Everly Brothers. In 1992, they were signed to the newly formed Asylum Records in Nashville; their debut album, *Let Go*, was in a much more traditional country vein than their work with the Kentucky Headhunters. In mid-1993, the title track hit the Top Ten and stayed there for five months; it was followed up with "Were You Really Livin'." Brother Phelps released their second album, *Any Way the Wind Blows*, early in 1995. In 1996, the duo disbanded, and Doug returned to the Kentucky Headhunters. —*Sandra Brennan*

Let Go / Aug. 3, 1993 / Asylum ✦✦✦
Much more low-key than most people expected, *Let Go* proves that Brother Phelps were the smarts behind the Headhunters. The title cut is a breezy single that recalls Buddy Holly, and elsewhere on the album The Phelps make judicious use of Southern boogie ("Were You Really Livin'") and strings ("What Goes Around"). Not a perfect album, and not as good as the Headhunters at their peak, but *Let Go* still contains some mighty nice listening. —*Brian Mansfield*

● **Any Way the Wind Blows** / Mar. 7, 1995 / Asylum ✦✦✦✦
Any Way the Wind Blows doesn't stray from the laidback, rootsy vibe of the Brother Phelps' debut, but it boasts a more assured performance and a stronger set of songs, making it a more engaging listen. —*Stephen Thomas Erlewine*

Alison Brown

Banjo / Progressive Bluegrass, Traditional Bluegrass
A Harvard graduate who quit a fast-track career as an investment banker to dedicate herself to her music, Brown came to prominence as a standout member of Alison Krauss' Union Station band and later was musical director for Michelle Shocked. Her instrumental albums are melodic and graceful and manage to sound both accessible and adventurous. She wrote all but one song on her first three albums, and her compositions owe more to the influence of David Grisman (who produced her debut) and Bela Fleck than to Earl Scruggs or Alan O'Bryant. —*Michael McCall*

Simple Pleasures / 1990 / Vanguard ◆◆◆◆
Her all-instrumental debut instantly earned respect among progressive acoustic music fans. Produced by David Grisman, and featuring guests Mike Marshall and Alison Krauss, Brown weaves cello, flute, and congas into her hybrid string sound, and she maintains an innate elegance amid the tricky arranging. —*Michael McCall*

★ **Twilight Motel** / 1992 / Vanguard ◆◆◆◆◆
Produced by Mike Marshall, Brown moves in several new directions, showing off the breadth of her talent while keeping the composition at the center of her playing. Jazzier, yet also more relaxed, than her debut. Maura O'Connell provides vocals on a traditional Irish song. —*Michael McCall*

Look Left / 1994 / Vanguard ◆◆◆◆
Brown crisscrosses the globe sonically, taking on Cajun, Celtic, Native American, and Australian Aboriginal music with characteristically relaxed proficiency. —*Michael McCall*

Quartet / 1996 / Vanguard ◆◆◆
Alison Brown scales back her supporting group on *Quartet*, but she doesn't abandon her trademark rootsy eclecticism. Although the songs are based in bluegrass and folk traditions, what stands out more than anything else on the album is how accomplished and jazzy Brown's playing has become—it is the instrumental sections that make the album a rewarding listen. —*Thom Owens*

Hylo Brown & the Timberliners

b. Apr. 20, 1922, River, KY
Vocals / Bluegrass
Bluegrass and country singer Frank Brown earned the nickname "Hylo" thanks to the considerable vocal range that became his trademark. Born in Johnson County, KY—later the birthplace of Loretta Lynn—in 1922, Brown had thoroughly absorbed the music indigenous to his Appalachian home before moving with his family to Ohio, where his career as a performer began to gather steam. There, he played on local radio broadcasts and began writing songs; one composition, a tribute to the Grand Ole Opry, was recorded by Jimmy Martin. In 1950, he sang harmony on a Bradley Kincaid session.
    In 1954, a song titled "Lost to a Stranger" earned Brown a recording contract with Capitol Records; the subsequent single, along with follow-ups like "Lovesick and Sorrow" and "The Wrong Kind of Life," were minor hits. In 1957, Brown joined Lester Flatt and Earl Scruggs, becoming a featured vocalist with the duo's Foggy Mountain Boys. The group's increasing popularity prompted Flatt and Scruggs to form a second Foggy Mountain band, called the Timberliners, with Brown as the unit's frontman; the Timberliners were fleshed out by mandolin player Red Rector, fiddler Clarence "Tater" Tate, Jim Smoak on the banjo, and bassist Joe Phillips.
    At their inception, the Timberliners performed on a circuit of television stations in Tennessee and Mississippi, later swapping schedules with Flatt and Scruggs in order to appear on West Virginia airwaves as well. In 1958, the group released *Hylo Brown and the Timberliners*, an LP that remains a traditional bluegrass classic. However, the advent of syndication and videotape allowed the original Flatt and Scruggs band to appear on any number of TV stations, effectively ending the Timberliners' career soon after although Brown soldiered on for a time with a group including Norman Blake on dobro and Billy Edwards on banjo. After the

Timberliners' demise, Brown rejoined Flatt and Scruggs as a featured singer.
    In the early 1960s, Brown cut a handful of solo records, including 1961's *Bluegrass Balladeer*, 1962's *Bluegrass Goes to College*, and the next year's *Hylo Brown Meets the Lonesome Pine Fiddlers*. Throughout the decade and into the first years of the 1970s, he performed solo in clubs, releasing records infrequently on small labels. However, a gradual diminishment in his vocal range resulted in Brown's eventual retirement around the middle of the decade. —*Jason Ankeny*

Bluegrass Balladeer / 1962 / Starday ◆◆◆
Bluegrass Goes to College / 1962 / Starday ◆◆◆
High Lonesome / Bear Family ◆◆◆◆
This two-fer features bluegrass recorded in the early '30s by the Timberliners and others. —*AMG*

Hylo Brown / Longhorn ◆◆◆◆

Jim Ed Brown (James Edward Brown)

b. Mar. 1, 1934, Sparkman, AR
Vocals / Traditional Country, Honky Tonk, Nashville Sound/ Countrypolitan
Jim Ed Brown came to fame as a member of the '50s vocal group the Browns, where he was the band's lead male vocalist. In 1965, when the group was still together, he embarked on a solo career that would eventually eclipse the success of the Browns.
    Brown and his older sister, Maxine, began performing while he was still in high school. In 1954, the duo signed a contract with the Fabor label, where they released five singles. Later that year, their sister Bonnie joined the duo and they became the Browns. From 1956 until 1967, the Browns were signed to RCA Records, where they had a number of moderately successful hit singles, highlighted by the 1959 No.1 "The Three Bells."
    Brown began his solo career in 1965, two years before the Browns disbanded. Initially, he didn't have much success and just scraped the bottom of the country Top 40. Once the Browns disbanded, Brown began to have more substantial hits, beginning with the No. 18 single "You Can Have Her," which was a cover of the Roy Hamilton hit. That was followed by the beer-drinking anthem "Pop a Top," which climbed to No.3. Although his next single, "Bottle, Bottle," reached No. 13, Brown didn't have any major hits for the rest of the '60s.
    As his chart performance stagnated in 1968, he formed a backing group called the Gems and began a residency at the Sahara Tahoe's Juniper Lounge. In 1969, he hosted the syndicated television show, *The Country Place*, which ran until 1970.
    As *The Country Place* was ending its run, Brown had his first major hit since "Pop a Top," with the No.4 single "Morning." Again, he wasn't able to immediately follow "Morning" with another Top Ten hit, but he began charting more frequently. In 1973, he had two Top Ten hits, "Southern Loving and "Sometime Sunshine," which were followed by the Top Ten "It's That Time of Night" in early 1974.
    Jim Ed Brown had his greatest success in the late '70s, when he regularly dueted with Helen Cornelius. The duo had six Top Ten hits between 1976 and 1980, including their debut single, "I Don't Want to Have to Marry You," which went to No. 1 in 1976. During this time, he had some solo hits, but only two of them broke the Top 40. Brown and Cornelius ended their partnership in 1971, following the No. 13 hit "Don't Bother to Knock."
    After the breakup of his duo with Helen Cornelius, Jim Ed Brown pretty much retired from recording. He made the occasional appearance on the Grand Ole Opry and he sometimes reunited with Cornelius. Brown also hosted TV game shows and talent contests throughout the '80s. Toward the end of the decade, he opened the Jim Ed Brown Theater near Opryland in Nashville, TN, where he performed regularly well into the '90s. —*Stephen Thomas Erlewine*

Greatest Hits / Feb. 1992 / RCA ◆◆◆◆
Greatest Hits collects the biggest hits from Jim Ed Brown's duets with Helen Cornelius, including the Top Ten hits "I Don't Want to Have to Marry You," "Saying Hello, Saying I Love You, Saying

Goodbye," "Lying in Love with You," "If the World Ran Out of Love Tonight," and "Fools," among several others. —*Stephen Thomas Erlewine*

● **Essential Series** / Jan. 30, 1996 / RCA ✦✦✦✦
Essential Series collects all of Jim Ed Brown's solo hits, as well as a selection of his duets with the Browns, ranging from "The Three Bells" and "Scarlet Ribbons (For Her Hair)" to "Pop a Top," "Morning" and "It's That Time of Night." The compilation collects all of the best moments from Brown's long-running, but slightly inconsistent, career, making it the definitive compilation of his hit-making days at RCA Records. —*Stephen Thomas Erlewine*

Junior Brown

Guitar, Vocals / Honky Tonk, Alternative Country, Neo-Traditionalist Country, Americana
A singer and demon guitarist whose raucous blend of country and rock 'n' roll helped make him a successful crossover act, Junior Brown was born in 1953 and raised in the backwoods of Kirksville, IN. He first learned to play the piano from his pianist father, and was exposed to country through radio and TV, becoming a fan of Ernest Tubb's music and television program. He became a professional musician at the tail end of the 1960s, while still in his teens.

After honing his guitar skills in relative anonymity throughout the 1970s, Brown became an instructor at the Hank Thompson School of Country Music, an affiliate of Rogers State College in Oklahoma. There, while teaching under the auspices of steel guitar legend Leon McAuliffe, a onetime member of Bob Wills' Texas Playboys, Brown met "the lovely Miss Tanya Rae," a student whom he would later marry in 1988 and who eventually joined his band as a rhythm guitarist and backing vocalist. At the same time, a dream prompted him to set about creating an instrument fusing a six-string guitar with its steel counterpart. After contacting guitar maker Michael Stevens, in 1985 he developed the "guit-steel," a double-necked guitar combining the standard instrument with the steel. (A decade later, the two men reunited to update the "guit-steel," and Brown's cherry axe "Big Red" was born.)

After moving to Austin, TX, Brown and his group became the house band at the city's Continental Club, where strong word-of-mouth eventually earned them a record deal. He made his long-awaited album debut in 1993 with *12 Shades of Brown*, which featured a tribute to his biggest influence, "My Baby Don't Dance to Nothing but Ernest Tubb." *Guit with It* followed later in the year, and like its predecessor, was met with considerable critical acclaim. After a five-song stopgap EP, 1995's *Junior High*, Brown returned in 1996 with *Semi-Crazy*. —*Jason Ankeny*

12 Shades of Brown / 1989 / Curb ✦✦✦✦
Brown's debut deck shines like gold with standout original material like "They Don't Choose to Live That Way," "My Hillbilly Hula Gal" and "My Baby Don't Dance to Nothing but Ernest Tubb" being particular noteworthy. Possessing a voice that will curl the hair on the back of your neck while picking both single-string picking and slide stylings on his twin neck "guit-steel," this is a mighty talented fella, neo-traditionalist or not. —*Cub Koda*

● **Guit with It** / Aug. 24, 1993 / Curb ✦✦✦✦
Junior Brown's rumbling, strikingly deep voice, tasty electric and steel guitar playing, and splendid honky tonk and Western swing songs have made him a sensation in country circles. There's nothing phony or cliched about Brown's music; this is the genuine, untutored, undiluted article. Brown can sing tunes requiring sincerity, ache or irony with equal flair. The CD's 12 cuts include the nearly 12-minute "Guit-Steel Blues," a sharp cover of Hank Garland's "Sugarfoot Stomp," and the bittersweet "Doin' What Comes Easy to a Fool" and "Holding Pattern." Brown is as vital and refreshing as early John Anderson or Randy Travis. —*Ron Wynn*

Junior High / Jul. 18, 1995 / Curb ✦✦✦
Junior High is an EP that features re-recorded versions of "Highway Patrol," "Sugarfoot Rag," and "My Wife Thinks You're Dead," plus two new songs, "That's Easy for You to Say" and "Lovely Hula Hands." It's a minor entry in Brown's catalog, but it is an enjoyable one, even if it is only necessary for diehard fans. —*Stephen Thomas Erlewine*

Semi-Crazy / May 1996 / Curb ✦✦✦✦
On *Semi-Crazy*, Junior Brown's third full-length album, the suit-and-tied Texas singer's clever lyrics, Ernest Tubb-like voice, and virtuoso guitar playing (on his custom-made, double-necked "guit-steel," which allows him to switch quickly between picking and steel playing) are once again intact and on the mark. *Semi-Crazy* may not bowl Brown fans over immediately—he offers no new twists as either a writer or player. On the other hand, because Brown is one of country music's most stunning guitarists (imagine Ornette Coleman crossed with Speedy West)—not to mention possesses a truly original sound—it's hard not to fall for the classic Brown sound of "I Hung It Up" (a standout for the guitar work), "Gotta Get up Every Morning," and the fun-loving title track (his duet partner, Red Simpson, penned Brown's earlier song "Highway Patrol"). —*Kurt Wolff*

Marty Brown

b. 1965, Maceo, KY
Guitar, Vocals / Contemporary Country, New Traditionalist
Marty Brown, a native of the tobacco-farming community of Maceo, KY, is the kind of guy myths spring up around. He hitchhiked into Nashville with little more than his guitar, a cheap demo tape, and a knowledge of the music industry he'd picked up from TNN. (He's said to have accosted producer Barry Beckett at a music-biz function and said, "I know you! I saw you in a video.") It turned out that was enough. A featured segment on the network news show *48 Hours* and an unannounced visit to performing rights organization BMI led to a scramble to sign Brown to a recording deal.

Brown's pinched voice is a throwback to an earlier time, sort of a Kentucky hill version of Jimmie Rodgers. He recorded three albums for MCA and won a small but strong fan base through a national tour with Jimmie Dale Gilmore and, later, a couple of solo tours playing at Wal-Marts across the country. But while his albums and concerts were critically acclaimed, Brown never had a radio hit, and MCA eventually dropped him. In 1996, however, he was snatched up by the Oakland, CA, indie label HighTone (onetime home to Jimmie Dale Gilmore, Joe Ely, and Robert Cray). He released his first HighTone album, *Here's to the Honky Tonks*, in the fall of that year. —*Brian Mansfield & Kurt Wolff*

● **High & Dry** / 1991 / MCA ✦✦✦✦
If everything here were as pure a hillbilly distillation as the title track or the loopy "Old King Kong," Brown might come off as a simple hick with limited nostalgia appeal. But his range is surprisingly wide. Brown's ballads—"I'll Climb Any Mountain" and "Wildest Dreams"—though simple, build to stunning, emotional climaxes. "Every Now and Then" is the equal of many of The Everly Brothers' best. And "Nobody Knows" is surely one of the most lonesome wails in a long, long time. —*Brian Mansfield*

Wild Kentucky Skies / 1993 / MCA ✦✦✦✦
One of the best things about Marty Brown's music is that it possesses the qualities that people both love and hate about country music. Brown takes a sure-fire hit song, "I Don't Wanna See You," then sings it in a voice that won't let folks forget just how backwoods country music can be. Songs like "It Must Be the Rain" and "Let's Begin Again" have soaring choruses that recall the Everlys at their best. On the other hand, "No Honky Tonkin' Tonight" and "I'd Rather Fish Than Fight" put to shame the lip service some singers pay to Hank Williams, Sr. and Jimmie Rodgers. With the eerie "She's Gone," Brown takes the country death ballad into territory it's never seen before, and he follows it with the sentimental "Kentucky Skies." Brown is pure country without being purist. Flatly put, he's a hillbilly and proud of it. —*Brian Mansfield*

Cryin', Lovin', Leavin' / 1994 / MCA ✦✦✦✦
By his third album, Brown and producer Richard Bennett could be pretty confident they weren't going to get any radio play, so they just cut loose and made as pure an album as Brown had in him. "You Must Be Mistakin' Me" and "Too Blue to Crow" possess a country sound so hard, they make most New Traditionalists sound like Muzak. Brown cuts Moon Mullican's "Cherokee Boogie," sings "Shameless Lies" with Melba Montgomery, shamelessly cops from Buddy Holly's "Crying, Waiting, Hoping" with the

title cut, and finishes with a gorgeous duet with Joy Lynn White on "I Love Only You." — *Brian Mansfield*

Here's to the Honky Tonks / Sep. 17, 1996 / Hightone ✦✦✦
Here's to the Honky Tonks continues Marty Brown's streak of excellent hard country albums. Recording for an independent label, Brown sounds liberated, as if he can freely try out any number of different styles. Divided between driving bluegrass-styled picking and rollicking honky tonk, what makes *Here's to the Honky Tonks* particularly compelling is how Brown's songwriting continues to improve. — *Thom Owens*

Milton Brown

b. Sep. 8, 1903, Stephenville, TX, d. Apr. 13, 1936
Vocals / Western Swing
Milton Brown was one of the fathers of Western swing, a vocalist and bandleader who was one of the first to fuse country, jazz, and pop together into a unique, distinctly American hybrid. Along with Bob Wills—whom he performed with at the beginning of this career—Brown developed the sound and style of Western swing in the early '30s, and for a while he and his band, the Musical Brownies, were just as popular as Wills and His Texas Playboys. Tragically, Milton Brown's career was cut short in 1936 when he died in a car accident, just as he was poised to break into national stardom.

Born in Stephensville, TX, in 1903, Milton Brown moved to Fort Worth, TX, in 1918. After graduating from high school in 1925, he worked as a cigar saleman, but he lost his job when the Great Depression hit in the late '20s. Brown began his musical career in 1930, when he happened to meet Bob Wills at a local Fort Worth dance. The Wills Fiddle Band was performing at the dance and Brown joined the group on a chorus of "St. Louis Blues." Wills was impressed with Brown's voice and immediately asked him and his guitarist brother, Derwood, to join the band.

The Wills Fiddle Band played medicine shows around Texas and landed a regular radio spot on WBAP, where they played a show sponsored by Aladdin Lamp Company, who had the band change their name to the Aladdin Laddies. In early 1991, the group was hired by the Light Crust Flour Company—which was run by Burrus Mill and Elevator Company— to appear daily on the radio station KFJZ. The company, which was managed by W. Lee O'Daniel, who also hosted the radio shows, had the group rename themselves the Light Crust Doughboys.

The Light Crust Doughboys were an instant success, and soon O'Daniel moved them first to another radio station, then syndicated the program statewide. The Doughboys were playing cowboy songs, jazz, blues, and popular songs—a repertoire so diverse that the band's audience continued to expand. In February of 1932, they recorded a single for Victor under the name the Fort Worth Doughboys.

The band was playing dance music and they wanted to play at dances, but O'Daniel was reluctant to let the group play outside of their radio shows. He also was hesitant to pay them much money, which greatly angered Milton Brown. In September of 1932, Brown left the band after he had a argument about money with O'Daniel.

After leaving the Light Crust Doughboys, Brown formed the first Western swing band, the Musical Brownies. The first incarnation of the Brownies featured Brown, guitarist Durwood Brown, bassist Wanna Coffman, Ocie Stockard on tenor banjo, and fiddle player Jesse Ashlock. Shortly afterward, pianist Fred Calhoun and fiddle player Cecil Brower (who replaced Ashlock) joined the group. Like the Light Crust Doughboys, the Musical Brownies played a mixture of country, pop, and jazz, but the Brownies had a harder dance edge than their predecessors.

Almost immediately, Brown and His Musical Brownies were a huge success. The group had a regular spot on the radio station KTAT and drew large crowds at Texas dances. In April of 1934, the band recorded eight songs for Bluebird; they recorded another ten for the label in August.

Toward the end of 1934, the Brownies added an electric steel guitarist named Bob Dunn—the first musician to play an electric instrument in country music. In January of 1935, the band signed with Decca Records and recorded 36 songs for the label. Released as singles over the course of 1935, the songs helped establish the band as the most popular Western swing band in Texas. In March of 1936, the Brownies traveled to New Orleans to record their second set of sessions for Decca. By this time, fiddler Brower had been replaced by Cliff Bruner. At these sessions, the Brownies cut about 50 songs, which were issued throughout 1936 and 1937.

In April of 1936, Brown suffered a major car accident. Although he wasn't killed on impact, he died five days after the crash. Following Milton's death, Durwood Brown kept the Musical Brownies together for two years, recording a dozen sides for Decca in 1937. At the time of his death, Milton Brown rivalled Bob Wills in popularity. Although he never became as famous as Wills, he was equally important in the development of Western swing—without him, the genre as we know it wouldn't exist. — *Stephen Thomas Erlewine*

Country & Western Dance-O-Rama / Western ✦✦✦
Country and Western Dance-O-Rama is an original ten-inch album from Milton Brown that features eight terrific slices of Western swing from one of the genre's founding fathers. At the time this was recorded, the Musical Brownies featured such stellar players as Cecil Brower, Bob Dunn, Cliff Bruner, Fred Calhoun, Durwood Brown, and Ocie Stockard and every musician simply tears into the songs, playing them fast, loose, and with a great deal of fun. Originally released on Decca, the album was later reissued on Western and later appeared as part of the thorough five-disc Milton Brown box. — *Thom Owens*

★ **Pioneer Western Swing Band (1935-1936)** / Jan. 1935+Mar. 1936 / MCA ✦✦✦✦✦
This out-of-print LP from MCA's early '80s *Collectables* series has been superceded by Texas Rose's complete reissuance of all of the recordings of Milton Brown and his Brownies on a five-CD set, but at the time it served as a good sampler of Brown's music. The singer, who led the first important Western swing band on record, heads an impressive octet (which also includes the fiddles of Cliff Bruner and Cecil Brower, the steel guitar of Bob Dunn, and banjoist Ocie Stockard) through a swing-oriented set. Two of the selections are from January 1935 while the other ten are taken from a marathon session in March 1936. Highlights of the spirited program include "The Sheik of Araby," "Yes Suh," "Hesitation Blues," "When I Take My Sugar to Tea" and "Easy Ridin' Papa." — *Scott Yanow*

Taking Off! / 1977 / String ✦✦✦✦
More Decca material, it includes a couple of 1937 cuts recorded without Brown after he died. — *Dan Cooper*

☆ **Complete Recordings of the Father of Western Swing: 1932-1937** / 1996 / Texas Rose ✦✦✦✦✦
Singer Milton Brown led the first Western swing band, beating Bob Wills on record as a bandleader by one year. Milton Brown's Musical Brownies, which consisted of the leader-vocalist, guitarist Derwood Brown, violinist Cecil Brower, pianist Fred Calhoun, bassist Wanna Coffman, banjoist Ocie Stockard and, in its later period, the steel guitar of Bob Dunn and violinist Cliff Bruner, could play swing, sentimental waltzes, country stomps, and novelties with equal skill. Cary Ginell, who wrote a definitive book on Brown, produced this masterful five-CD set, which contains not only all 102 recordings by the Brownies (seven marathon sessions held during 1934-36) but Milton Brown's two numbers with the Fort Worth Doughboys in 1932 (a unit that includes Bob Wills on fiddle), Derwood Brown's 1937 session with the Brownies after his brother Milton's death, and a couple numbers by Roy Lee Brown (one with a reunion band) in 1984 and 1987. Add to that an extensive 40-page booklet, and this is certainly the one Milton Brown set to get! Essential music, available from the small Texas Rose label. — *Scott Yanow*

☆ **With His Musical Brownies 1934** / Texas Rose ✦✦✦✦✦
Containing the complete Bluebird recordings of 1934, it showcases fiddler Cecil Brower and pianist Fred "Papa" Calhoun on a typically wild assortment of blues, pop, jazz, and fiddle tunes. — *Dan Cooper*

T. Graham Brown

b. Oct. 30, 1954, Arabi, GA
Vocals / Country-Rock, Country-Pop, Urban Cowboy

Flashy T. Graham Brown was as much a flamboyant showman as a singer of "Southern beach music," a lively combination of country-rock, soul, and R&B. He was born Anthony Graham Brown in Arabi, GA; while attending the University of Georgia during the early '70s, he would go to school during the day and play beach music as the second half of the locally popular Dirk and Tony at night. Later, Brown went on to become the frontman of the local group Reo Diamond. In keeping with the band's outlaw image, he grew long hair, a beard, pierced an ear, got a tattoo, and wore a ten-gallon hat on stage.

In 1979, Brown changed his look, adopted his stage name, and formed an R&B band, T. Graham Brown and Rack of Spam. In 1982, he and his wife Sheila headed for Nashville, where he got a break when he met Harlan Howard, who helped him find work singing demos. This led him to begin writing and singing commercial jingles for such major companies as McDonald's and Coca-Cola. The following year Brown signed to CBS as a staff writer, later signing to Tree International. His debut single, "Drowning in Memories," made it to the Top 40 in 1985, as did his next single, "I Tell It Like It Used to Be." The following year, Brown scored his first No. 1 hit with "Hell and High Water," and was hired to open for Kenny Rogers.

Brown had an even better year in 1987 when he scored his second No. 1 hit, "Don't Go to Strangers," two more Top Ten hits, and went on a successful promotional tour of Germany and England. Brown also appeared in two feature films, *Greased Lightning* and *Cursed*, that year. In 1988, he had another No. 1 hit, "Darlene." He appeared four more times on the charts and played in his third film, *Heartbreak Hotel*, where he and his band, the Hardtops, portrayed Elvis' band. In 1989 he only had one hit, but made it back to the charts in 1990 with a duet with Tanya Tucker, "Don't Go Out." He also had two more major hits and debuted on the Grand Ole Opry. In addition, he appeared in several Taco Bell commercials. The following year, he only scored two minor hits and was released by his label. — *Sandra Brennan*

I Tell It Like It Used to Be / 1986 / Capitol ✦✦✦✦
With the sessions split between Nashville's Woodland Sound Studio and Muscle Shoals, T. Graham Brown's debut often sounds affectionately like the raw, impassioned work of a garage band. — *Tom Roland*

Brilliant Conversationalist / 1987 / Capitol ✦✦✦
With blaring horns and bluesy growled vocals, this record has more to do with Southside Johnny than any country band one could name. That aside, there are some nice songs on here. Not a great record but if this is your type of thing, you could do worse. — *Jim Worbois*

Bumper to Bumper / 1990 / Capitol ✦✦✦
This contains "I'm Sending One up for You," "If You Could Only See Me Now," and more. — *AMG*

● **The Best of T. Graham Brown** / 1992 / Liberty ✦✦✦✦
It contains "With This Ring," "Never Say Never," and "Moonshadow Road," among other hits. — *AMG*

Jann Browne

b. Mar. 14, 1954, Anderson, IN
Vocals / Contemporary Country

An underrated singer who got lost amid the hat acts of the early '90s, Browne is a past and future member of Asleep at the Wheel who sings honky tonk with daring spirit and ballads with delicate, nicely phrased emotion. — *Michael McCall*

● **Tell Me Why** / 1990 / Curb ✦✦✦✦
This hardcore, rollicking honky tonk includes a duet with Wanda Jackson. — *Michael McCall*

It Only Hurts When I Laugh / 1991 / Capitol ✦✦✦✦
The backbeat rocks as well as swings this time. The song choices are supreme, as she covers everything from a Ray Price shuffle to progressive country by Jim Lauderdale and John Hiatt. — *Michael McCall*

Count Me In / Oct. 1995 / Cross Three ✦✦✦

The Browns

Traditional Country, Nashville Sound/Countrypolitan

During the '50s and '60s, the Browns offered up some of the finest harmonies in country music. The group was originally comprised of brother and sister Jim Ed Brown and Maxine Brown and were later joined by younger sister Bonnie. Both Maxine and Jim were born in Sparkman, AR, where their father owned a sawmill. With the encouragement of their parents, they began singing and developing their close harmonies in childhood.

In 1952, Jim Ed and Maxine began appearing on Little Rock's *Barnyard Frolics* and on other local radio shows, which led to local TV appearances as well. The duo earned national recognition and a guest spot on Ernest Tubb's televison show for their novelty song "Looking Back to See," which hit the Top Ten and stayed on the charts throughout the summer of 1954.

The Browns were joined by recent high school graduate Bonnie and began appearing on *Louisiana Hayride*. By the end of 1955, the trio had another Top Ten hit with "Here Today and Gone Tomorrow," which was given a boost by their national appearances on the *Ozark Jubilee*. The show's producer, Sid Siman, arranged for them to sign with RCA Victor in 1956, and soon afterward they had two major hits, "I Take the Chance" and "I Heard the Bluebirds Sing." When Jim Ed was called to serve in the military, the group continued to record while he was on leave, and sister Norma filled in for him on tours. They scored one of their biggest hits in 1959 with the inspirational, folk-oriented "The Three Bells," which not only spent ten weeks on top of the country charts, but also crossed over and spent four weeks at No. 1 on the pop charts. As a result, the Browns appeared on *Ed Sullivan*, the *Jimmy Dean Show*, and *American Bandstand*.

The Browns remained in the folk mode for their two follow-up hits, "Scarlet Ribbons" and "The Old Lamplighter," both of which did extremely well on the country and pop charts. Their string of hits continued until 1961, when the national folk craze died out. Two years later, the Browns joined the Grand Ole Opry. In late 1967, the Browns disbanded and Maxine and Bonnie went back to Arkansas to concentrate on their families, while Jim Ed focused on the successful solo career he had started in 1965. — *Sandra Brennan*

Jim Edward, Maxine and Bonnie Brown / 1957 / RCA ✦✦✦✦

Sweet Sounds by the Browns / 1959 / RCA ✦✦✦

Town & Country / 1960 / RCA ✦✦✦
Town & Country is an uneven, but highly enjoyable, 1960 album from the Browns, featuring two of their signature hits: "Scarlet Ribbons (For Your Hair)" and "The Old Lamplighter." The 1996 CD reissue includes four bonus tracks: "Love Me Tender," "The Three Bells," "Unchained Melody" and "Oh My Pa-Pa (O Mein Papa)." — *Thom Owens*

Best of the Browns / 1966 / RCA ✦✦✦✦

Rockin' Rollin' Browns / Sep. 1984 / Bear Family ✦✦✦
The Browns didn't really rock or roll, so the title refers to the fact that the album consists of the group's more pop-oriented material, like "The Three Bells," "Buttons and Bows," and "Tobacco Road." Several tracks on the record are previously unreleased and most are album cuts, making the collection necessary only for serious fans that would rather sample from the group's extensive back catalog instead of listening to all of it. Casual fans would be better served with a greatest hits collection. — *Stephen Thomas Erlewine*

● **20 of the Best** / 1985 / RCA ✦✦✦✦
20 of the Best collects the great majority of the Browns' biggest hits. Even though it bypasses early hits like "Looking Back to See," "Here Today and Gone Tomorrow," "I Take the Chance," and "I Heard the Bluebirds Sing"—which were all recorded under the name Jim Edward, Maxine & Bonnie Brown (with the exception of "Looking Back to See," which was recorded without Bonnie)—the compilation is the only recent set to attempt a concise retrospective of the vocal group. — *Stephen Thomas Erlewine*

Looking Back to See / Sep. 1986 / Bear Family ✦✦✦
Looking Back to See collects some of the Browns' big hit singles, including the title track, but it mainly concentrates on obscurities and unreleased tracks from early in their career. Consequently, it's an album that would appeal only to collectors, even though there is some fine music on the record. —*Stephen Thomas Erlewine*

Three Bells / 1993 / Bear Family ✦✦✦✦
It is a lesson in reissue absurdity that the Browns, whose popularity has warranted this attractive but expensive eight-CD box set, have no single-disc compilation available as of mid-1994. But if you know you're a fan, you can do no better than this collection of their complete RCA recordings. —*Dan Cooper*

Ed Bruce

b. Dec. 29, 1939, Keiser, AR
Vocals / Rock & Roll, Traditional Country, Progressive Country, Rockabilly, Outlaw Country
Like so many other artists, singer Ed Bruce got his start as a rockabilly act for Memphis' famed Sun Records; however, he was probably best known for his songwriting acumen. Born William Edwin Bruce, Jr. in Arkansas in 1939, he cut his first sides for Sun at the age of 17. His career as a frenetic rockabilly performer was largely unsuccessful, however, and by 1964 Bruce had moved to Nashville to become a member of the Marijohn Wilkins Singers. He also entered into a lucrative career singing advertising jingles; his best known campaign cast him as a character called "The Tennessean."

In 1966, Bruce signed with RCA, notching his first chart hit with the single "Walker's Woods." More singles and a change of labels followed, but the singer struggled until 1975, when he took his composition "Mamas Don't Let Your Babies Grow Up to Be Cowboys" into the Top 20. The song, Bruce's best-known, was later a monster hit when it was covered by the duo of Waylon Jennings and Willie Nelson in 1977. His songs have also been recorded by the likes of Charlie Louvin, Tex Ritter, Tanya Tucker, and Crystal Gayle.

After a brief tenure at Epic Records between 1977 and 1978, Bruce achieved his greatest commercial success with MCA in the 1980s. "The Last Cowboy Song," featuring guest vocals from Willie Nelson, hit No. 12 in 1980; both "Girls, Women and Ladies" and "(When You Fall in Love) Everything's a Waltz" also fell just short of entering the Top Ten. In 1981, Bruce hit No. 1 with "You're the Best Break This Heart Ever Had"; other Top Five singles included "Ever, Never Lovin' You" (No. 4, 1982), "After All" (No. 4, 1983), "You Turn Me On (Like a Radio)" (No. 3, 1984) and "Nights" (No. 4, 1986). After the 1986 album *Night Things* and a 1988 self-titled follow-up, Bruce made a conscious decision to cut back on his music to focus on his acting career, appearing in several made-for-TV films. —*Jason Ankeny*

Greatest Hits / 1986 / MCA ✦✦✦✦
This album documents the most rewarding period of Ed Bruce's recording career. Easygoing, mid-tempo love songs dominate, particularly with "You're the Best Break This Old Heart Ever Had," "Ever, Never Lovin' You" and "You're Leavin' Here Tonight." The reflective "After All" is permanently haunting. —*Tom Roland*

● **The Best of Ed Bruce** / 1995 / Varèse Sarabande ✦✦✦✦
18 songs from 1975 to 1986, all but two of which were country hits, a half dozen making the Top Ten. Includes the original 1975 version of "Mamas Don't Let Your Babies Grow Up to Be Cowboys," a No. 1 duet for Waylon Jennings and Willie Nelson a few years later; "The Last Cowboy Song," which features a guest vocal by Nelson, and the "Theme from *Bret Maverick*." —*Richie Unterberger*

Puzzles / 1995 / Bear Family ✦✦✦✦
The single-disc, 29-track compilation *Puzzles* collects all of Ed Bruce's RCA recordings from the late '60s, including "Blue Denim Eyes," "By Route of New Orleans," "Walker's Woods," "Last Train to Clarksville," "Painted Girls and Wine," "Memphis Morning," "Why Can't I Come Home," "Ninety Seven More to Go," "Give Me More Than You Can Take," "Something Else to Mess Your Mind" and no less than three versions of the title track. While this material is not among Bruce's best-known, it is among his best.

Though the duplicate versions of some tracks can be tedious—"Puzzles" is presented in three versions, there are two takes of "I'd Be Best Leaving You," there are both dubbed and undubbed versions of "Painted Girls and Wine" and "Blue Bayou"—*Puzzles* nevertheless is an excellent way to become acquainted with a fine, underappreciated talent. —*Thom Owens*

Rockin' and Boppin' Baby / Bear Family ✦✦✦✦

Vin Bruce (Ervin Bruce)

b. Apr. 25, 1932, Cut Off, LA
Guitar, Vocals / Cajun
Known as the "King of Cajun Singers," this native of Cut Off, LA, born Ervin Bruce, first recorded for Columbia in 1951, where he found some success with the ballad "Dans La Louisianne." A decade later this singer/guitarist was recording for Floyd Soileau's Swallow label, where he scored a hit with "Jole Blon" (at least the third go-round for "the Cajun national anthem"). Bruce currently resides in Galliano, LA, and is widely respected in Louisiana for his country-tinged Cajun traditionalism. —*Jeff Hannusch & Mark A. Humphrey*

● **Greatest Hits** / 1979 / Swallow ✦✦✦✦
Recorded by one of the pioneers of Cajun music, these early-'60s sides are a mix of traditional songs and French interpretations of country hits. —*Jeff Hannusch*

Cajun Country / 1979 / Swallow ✦✦✦
A good country-tinged album featuring Doc Guidry on fiddle, Harry Anselm on guitar, and Eldridge "Johnny" Comeaux on steel guitar. —*Chip Renner*

Cliff Bruner

b. Apr. 25, 1915, Houston, TX
Fiddle / Traditional Country, Western Swing, Honky Tonk
A jazz-influenced fiddler who found his greatest success in the 1930s, Cliff Bruner's place in country music history was assured thanks to his 1939 version of Ted Raffan's "Truck Driver's Blues," the first trucker song ever recorded.

Born in Houston, TX, in 1915, by the age of 14 Bruner was performing professionally, and within a few years he had signed on with Dr. Scott's Medicine Show, a traveling caravan hawking a cure-all called Liquidine Tonic. In 1934, Bruner joined the Western swing band Milton Brown and His Musical Brownies, an act that billed itself as "The Greatest String Band on Earth." He cut close to 50 songs with the group before Brown was killed in an auto accident in April 1936.

Shortly thereafter, Bruner returned to Houston, where he formed a group called the Texas Wanderers (sometimes called Cliff Bruner and His Boys) which fused traditional and contemporary roots music with elements of 1920s and '30s pop and jazz. Included among the group's roster were the honky-tonk pianist Aubrey "Moon" Mullican and Bob Dunn, the creator of the amplified steel guitar. In 1938, the band released its biggest hit, a rendition of Floyd Tillman's "It Makes No Difference Now."

While continuing to perform during and after World War II, Bruner's visibility began to slip, and by the early '50s he had left the music industry for a career selling insurance. When Western swing became all the rage in the 1970s, Bruner returned to both the stage and the studio, guesting on Johnny Gimble's 1980 LP *Texas Swing Pioneers*. —*Jason Ankeny*

★ **Cliff Bruner's Texas Wanderers** / 1983 / Texas Rose ✦✦✦✦✦
This is a fine compilation covering the years 1937-44. Beaucoups chops from the aforementioned Bruner, Dunn, and Mullican, as well as Leo Raley, the first Western swinger to "plug in" a mandolin. —*Dan Cooper*

James Bryan

Fiddle / Traditional Bluegrass
Alabama-born traditional bluegrass fiddler James Bryan learned his craft by studying under the legendary Kenny Baker. After gaining fame as a member of Norman Blake's Rising Fawn String Ensemble, Bryan made his solo debut in 1983 with the LP *Lookout Blues*, followed three years later by *The First of May*. After

appearing on a variety of samplers and compilations, in 1995, he teamed with guitarist Carl Jones for the album *Two Pictures*. —*Jason Ankeny*

● **The First of May** / Rounder ✦✦✦✦
This set includes a variety of unusual local tunes and old favorites. —*Charles S. Wolfe*

Lookout Blues / Rounder ✦✦✦✦

Boudleaux Bryant

b. Feb. 13, 1920, Shellman, GA, **d.** Jun. 1987
Rock & Roll, Traditional Country, Nashville Sound/Countrypolitan

He became one of the greatest songwriters in country music history, but Boudleaux Bryant studied classical violin from the age of five and played with the Atlanta Philharmonic during its 1938 season. He joined a country band that same year when a friend needed help and toured with Hank Penny's Radio Cowboys in the early '40s, but had switched his allegiance to jazz music when in 1945 he met Felice Scaduto (b. Aug. 7, 1925, Milwaukee, WI), his future wife and songwriting companion.

They began writing songs together and sent "Country Boy" to Fred Rose, who bought the song and began Acuff-Rose Publishing's long association with the Bryants. Little Jimmy Dickens hit the Country Top Ten with the song in June 1949. Carl Smith recorded the Bryants' "Hey Joe" in 1953 and it also became a hit; Frankie Laine's pop version the same year sold over a million copies. Later in the '50s, Felice and Boudleaux began to move into rock 'n' roll as well, writing a song for Buddy Holly plus most of the Everly Brothers' big hits: "Bye Bye Love," "Problems," "All I Have to Do Is Dream," "Wake Up Little Susie" and "Bird Dog."

Though they had never completely deserted country, the Bryants in the '60s resumed their focus, writing hits for Jim Reeves and Sonny James, among others. In 1967, they left Acuff-Rose and formed their own House of Bryant publishing company. The classics continued to come during the '70s, and in 1979, Boudleaux produced the Bryants' first album as performers, *All I Have to Do Is Dream*—known in the US as *A Touch of Bryant*.

By the late '80s, it was estimated that Boudleaux and Felice's warehouse of 3000 songs had sold over 300 million copies worldwide; the fact made them a shoo-in for the Nashville Songwriters Hall of Fame and even the Country Music Hall of Fame—a rare honor for strict songwriters. Though Boudleaux died in June 1987, Felice Bryant continues to write occasionally. —*John Bush*

● **Boudleaux Bryant's Best Sellers** / 1963 / Monument ✦✦✦✦

Cody Bryant

Cowboy, Western Swing, Bluegrass, Bakersfield Sound
Born Jeff Ruff, Cody Bryant was raised in Whittier, CA. The son of Bob Ruff, a member of the Square Dance Hall of Fame, Cody grew up around the music business since his father also founded Wagon Wheel Records and Windsor Records, two California labels that not only produced square dancers with the calls and tunes they needed, but periodically recorded other artists as well.

Impressed at an early age by Jimmy Bryant, an early mentor rumored to be a relative of the Ruff family, the boy who would grow up to be Cody Bryant took to pickin'. Playing sometimes all through the night in his bedroom, the Ruffs' youngest child soon developed a style of his own. As high school beckoned, so did more and more bluegrass festivals as well as playing in some heavy metal bands. Hitting the road after he finished school, Bryant spent some time in Colorado learning more about playing and songwriting from an old cowboy singer, J.B. Tankersley. Picking up the banjo and eventually the fiddle, Bryant's smooth and clean style of guitar playing became his calling card.

Moving back to California he was befriended by Hank Cochran. Again, Bryant absorbed everything he could. Settling in, he put together two bands, the Caffeine Dream Bluegrass Band and the Cody Bryant Western Band. Playing coffeehouse and acoustic gigs with his bluegrass outfit allowed Cody to delve back into some of the old mountain and hillbilly tunes he was introduced to as youngster. His Western band gave him the format to develop his singing style even further. Often compared to Marty Robbins, Bryant quickly became a known talent on the L.A. scene.

Working with greats Brantley Kearns, Rick Shea, Doug Livingston and Rick Dunham encouraged him along. For a time he hosted a monthly honky tonk showcase in Hollywood that featured the Losin' Brothers, Shea, Kearns, Patty Booker, Barry Holdship, and many other roots, bluegrass, and C&W artists. After putting out several indie cassettes, 1996 was the year Bryant pulled out all the stops and invested in himself and his career and put out a CD. *Big Dose of Country* was launched with a celebration at Jack's Sugar Shack that included friends the Losin' Brothers, Barry Holdship, and the now-defunct Plowboys. Moving beyond Los Angeles, Bryant quickly made a place for himself in Bakersfield after attaining the approval and friendship of Red Simpson. Working at the Golden West Casino in Bakersfield and sitting in with Simpson gave Bryant the courage and the conviction to move forward with his career. —*Jana Pendragon*

Big Dose of Country / 1996 / Wagon Wheel ✦✦✦
Big Dose of Country should have been a reflection of Cody Bryant and not of someone else's idea of what would sell. Somewhere between the two concepts, Cody got lost just enough to make this first CD outing a slight disappointment. While the artist is flawless, and Bryant's guitar and vocals are beyond reproach, there is still something a little too over-produced about *Big Dose* to adequately demonstrate the monster talent that Bryant is. His songs are strictly C&W, yet some of them come off a little too manufactured on this project. Still, the CD shows his strengths. Cuts like "I Don't Want to Go Home Tonight," "Good Ol' Boy" and "Haul Off and Love Me" scintillate. Rick Shea's "Bed of Roses" and Bryant's own "Tell Me I'm Not Losing You" demonstrate the softer side of this Hollywood cowboy. "Too Far Under" establishes Bryant as a romantic balladeer, while his love song to his Cadillac, "Big Iron" (not to be confused with the Marty Robbins' hit), shows how much high speed and power there is in his singing and playing. Neither does the CD reflect his style and charisma with an audience. For serious students of C&W, the Bakersfield Sound and the West Coast country and roots music scene, this is a must. But be forewarned, the real Cody Bryant has yet to be revealed on CD. —*Jana Pendragon*

Felice Bryant

b. Aug. 7, 1925, Milwaukee, WI
Rock & Roll, Traditional Country, Nashville Sound/Countrypolitan

With her husband Boudleaux, Felice Bryant formed one of the most potent songwriting teams in country history, writing many songs that became hits. She had been performing and writing songs since she was a child, but her fame came after she met and married Boudleaux in 1945. They began writing together and sent "Country Boy" to Fred Rose, who bought the song and began Acuff-Rose Publishing's long association with the Bryants. Little Jimmy Dickens hit the Country Top Ten with the song in June 1949. Carl Smith recorded the Bryants' "Hey Joe" in 1953 and it also became a hit; Frankie Laine's pop version the same year sold over a million copies. Later in the '50s, Felice and Boudleaux began to move into rock 'n' roll as well, writing a song for Buddy Holly plus most of the Everly Brothers' big hits: "Bye Bye Love," "Problems," "All I Have to Do Is Dream," "Wake Up Little Susie" and "Bird Dog."

Though they had never deserted country, the Bryants in the '60s resumed their focus, writing hits for Jim Reeves and Sonny James, among others. In 1967, they left Acuff-Rose and formed their own House of Bryant publishing company. The classics continued to come during the '70s, and in 1979, Boudleaux produced the Bryants' first album as performers, *All I Have to Do Is Dream*—known in the US as *A Touch of Bryant*.

By the late '80s, it was estimated that Boudleaux and Felice's warehouse of 3000 songs had sold over 300 million copies worldwide; the fact made them a shoo-in for the Nashville Songwriters Hall of Fame and even the Country Music Hall of Fame—a rare honor for strict songwriters. Though Boudleaux died in June 1987, Felice Bryant continues to write occasionally. —*John Bush*

Jimmy Bryant

b. Mar. 5, 1925, Moultrie, GA, d. Sep. 22, 1980

Guitar / Traditional Country, Instrumental Country

With steel guitar wizard Speedy West, guitarist Jimmy Bryant formed half of the hottest country guitar duo of the 1950s. With lightning speed and jazz-fueled taste for improvisation and adventure, Bryant's boogies, polkas, and country swing—recorded with West and as a solo artist—remain among the most exciting instrumental country recordings of all time. Bryant also waxed major contributions to the early recordings of singers like Tennessee Ernie Ford, Merrill E. Moore, Kay Starr, Billy May, and Ella Mae Morse, and has influenced country guitarists like Buck Owens, James Burton, and Albert Lee. While he enjoyed a career that spanned several decades, it was his sessions with Capitol Records in the early '50s that allowed him the fullest freedom to strut his stuff. —*Richie Unterberger*

Country Cabin Jazz / 1960 / Capitol ✦✦✦✦
Featuring Speedy West on steel guitar and Billy Strange on rhythm, Bryant runs through a dozen swinging instrumentals with panache on this "country jam session." —*Richie Unterberger*

● **Guitar Take-Off** / 1989 / See For Miles ✦✦✦✦
Undisputably the best Bryant compilation. Twenty tracks from 1951 to 1955, many taken from rare singles, and many also featuring Speedy West. Also includes cuts by Ella Mae Morse, Tennessee Ernie Ford, Merrill E. Moore, and Billy May that feature Bryant as a sessionman. "Stratosphere Boogie" and "Catfish Boogie" are breathtaking Bryant/West duels. —*Richie Unterberger*

Richard Buckner

Guitar, Vocals / Singer-Songwriter, Country-Folk, Alternative Country

A husky-voiced country/folk singer-songwriter very much in the mold of the Lubbock, TX, school of mavericks, including Butch Hancock, Terry Allen, and Jimmie Dale Gilmore. Buckner is actually based in San Francisco, but the Lubbock connection is no accident. His debut album *Bloomed* was recorded in Lubbock, for one thing, with producer Lloyd Maines, who has also worked with Hancock, Allen, Joe Ely, and Uncle Tupelo. Maines himself plays several instruments on the record, and Buckner's band is fleshed out with several other Texas musicians, including Hancock (who adds a harmonica cameo) and accordion player Ponty Bon.

Buckner's principal following, however, is not with the country audience, but the alternative rock one. Like Allen and Hancock, the guitarist's work is based in rootsy country traditions, but his lyrics are far too personal and ambitious for those who think of country music as virtually synonymous with Nashville. So, like those Lubbock musicians, he tends to appeal to open-minded rock fans, or adventurous general music fans, more than country ones. The alternative rock thread is strengthened by Buckner's leadership of a San Francisco country-rock band, the Doubters (who do not appear on his album), and a support slot on a Son Volt tour in early 1996. Appearing on a small Texas independent label, his album won good critical notices, and his signing to a major company shortly afterwards probably means that both rock and country listeners will be much more widely exposed to him in the future. —*Richie Unterberger*

Bloomed / 1994 / Dejadics ✦✦✦
Buckner's debut is an accomplished but subdued affair with hardly a trace of rock in sight. The emphasis is on his rich-but-weary vocals and sober tales of romance and restlessness, with dignified Texas prairie backup by such esteemed regionals as Lloyd Maines (who produced) and Ponty Bon. Very much in the vein of Butch Hancock, but much more ordinary at this point, without the eccentricity and boisterousness that characterizes much of Hancock and fellow Lubbockite Terry Allen's work. —*Richie Unterberger*

Buffalo Springfield

Rock & Roll, Country-Rock, Folk-Rock

Few American groups have produced a wealth of talent like that of Buffalo Springfield. The group's formation is the stuff of legend: driving on Sunset Boulevard in Los Angeles, Stephen Stills and Richie Furay spotted a hearse that Stills was sure belonged to Neil Young, a Canadian he had crossed paths with earlier. Indeed it was, and with the addition of fellow hearse passenger and Canadian Bruce Palmer on bass and ex-Dillard Dewey Martin on drums, the cluster of ex-folkies determined, as the Byrds had just done, to become a rock 'n' roll band.

Over a 19-month period, during 1967 and 1968, Buffalo Springfield released three impressive albums. Their debut, including their sole big hit (Stills' "For What It's Worth"), established them as the best folk-rock band in the land bar the Byrds, though the Springfield were a bit more folk and country-oriented. The second album, *Again*, is their masterpiece, as the group expanded their folk-rock base into tough hard rock and psychedelic orchestration. Possessing three strong songwriters with distinctly different yet complementary styles—Stills, Young, and Furay (the last of whom didn't begin writing until the second LP)—they also had strong and often conflicting egos, particularly Stills and Young. The group, which held almost infinite promise, rearranged their lineup several times, Young leaving the group for periods and Palmer fighting deportation, until they disbanded in 1968. Their final album, although it contained some excellent material, clearly shows the group fragmenting into solo directions.

Even more than the Byrds, Buffalo Springfield's sound was undeniably American, drawing from rock, folk, and country. The intense clash of creative energies, however, finally caused the demise of the band in May of 1968. Stephen Stills went on to Crosby, Stills & Nash. Neil Young joined that group briefly for *Déjà Vu*, then went on to pursue an erratic solo career with periods of great success and brilliant music. After Springfield, Jim Messina and Richie Furay founded the country-rock group Poco. After Poco, Messina recorded a string of hits during the '70s with Kenny Loggins, as Loggins & Messina. —*Rick Clark & Richie Unterberger*

Buffalo Springfield / 1967 / Atco ✦✦✦
Their strong debut contains the Stephen Stills classic "For What It's Worth" and Neil Young's "Nowadays Clancy Can't Even Sing." "Sit Down I Think I Love You" and "Go and Say Goodbye" are also highlights. —*Rick Clark*

★ **Buffalo Springfield Again** / 1967 / Atco ✦✦✦✦✦
On what is by far their best effort, Stills, Furay, and Young each contribute some great songs: the hits "Bluebird," "Mr. Soul," and "Rock & Roll Woman," plus standouts like "A Child's Claim to Fame," "Hung Upside Down," "Broken Arrow," "Everydays," and "Expecting to Fly." —*Rick Clark*

Last Time Around / 1968 / Atco ✦✦✦
Their last album showcases a couple of gems in Furay's "Kind Woman" and Young's "On the Way Home." —*Rick Clark*

Best of Buffalo Springfield ... Retrospective / 1969 / Atco ✦✦✦✦
This is a decent sampler for the uninitiated. It contains all their hits and some key album tracks but isn't comprehensive enough to be essential. —*Rick Clark*

● **Buffalo Springfield [Collection]** / 1973 / Atco ✦✦✦✦
Not to be confused with their self-titled debut album, this double LP, which can still be found without too much hassle, is clearly the best Springfield compilation, at least until the overdue day when a box set appears that includes everything recorded by this superb band. It does miss some good songs, especially from the first album, but zeroes in on their very best work, and includes a nine-minute version of "Bluebird" available nowhere else, as well as excellent liner notes. —*Richie Unterberger*

Jimmy Buffett

b. Dec. 25, 1946, Pascogoula, MS

Guitar, Vocals / Country-Rock, Singer-Songwriter, Pop-Rock, Outlaw Country

Singer-songwriter Jimmy Buffett has parlayed his easygoing Gulf Coast persona into more than just a successful recording career—he has expanded into clothing, nightclubs, and literature.

But the basis of the business empire that keeps him on the *Fortune* magazine list of highest-earning entertainers is his music.

Buffett moved to Nashville to try to make it in country music in the late '60s. Signed to Barnaby, he released one album, *Down to Earth* (1970), the single from which, a socially conscious song called "The Christian?" suggested he might be more at home protesting in Greenwich Village. (Barnaby "lost" his second album, *High Cumberland Jubilee*, though they would find it and release it after he became successful.) Instead, Buffett moved to Key West, FL, where he gradually evolved the beach bum character and tropical folk-rock style that would endear him to millions.

Signing to ABC-Dunhill Records (later absorbed by MCA), Buffett achieved notoriety but not much else with his second (released) album, *White Sport Coat and a Pink Crustacean* (1973), which featured a song called, "Why Don't We Get Drunk" ("...and screw?," goes the chorus). Buffett revealed a more thoughtful side on *Living and Dying in 3/4 Time* (1974), with its song of marital separation "Come Monday," his first singles chart entry. But it took the Top Ten song "Margaritaville" and the album in which it was featured, *Changes in Latitudes, Changes in Attitudes* (1977), to capture Buffett's tropical worldview and, for a while, turn him into a pop star.

By the start of the '80s, Buffett's yearly albums had stopped going gold, and he briefly tried the country market again. But by the middle of the decade, it was his yearly summer tours that were filling his bank account, as a steadily growing core of Sun Belt fans he dubbed "Parrotheads" made his concerts into Mardi Gras-like affairs. Buffett launched his Margaritaville line of clothes and opened the first of his Margaritaville clubs in Key West. He also turned to fiction writing, landing on the bestseller lists.

His recording career, meanwhile, languished, though a hits compilation sold millions, a 1990 live album, *Feeding Frenzy*, went gold, and a 1992 boxed set retrospective, *Boats Beaches Bars & Ballads*, became one of the best-selling boxed sets ever. Buffett finally got around to making a new album in 1994, when *Fruitcakes* became one of his fastest-selling records. It was followed in 1995 by *Barometer Soup*. — *William Ruhlmann*

Down to Earth / 1970 / Barnaby ♦♦
On his debut album, Buffett lands squarely in the Kris Kristofferson school of thoughtful Nashville singer-songwriters, notably challenging religious zealots and right-wingers in "The Christian?" One of his earliest story songs, "The Captain and The Kid," is also included. — *William Ruhlmann*

A White Sport Coat & a Pink Crustacean / Jun. 1973 / MCA ♦♦♦
Buffett was beginning to put in place his folk/rock/country sound and his laidback, humorous, hedonistic persona with this album, which features later concert favorites like "Why Don't We Get Drunk [and Screw]" and "Grapefruit—Juicy Fruit." — *William Ruhlmann*

Living & Dying in 3/4 Time / Feb. 1974 / MCA ♦♦♦
Jimmy Buffett was already on the second edition of his Coral Reefer Band by the time his third album rolled around. He had also firmly established his Gulf Coast beach-bum/poet persona, but he hadn't written a classic song until "Come Monday," which put him, and the album, on the map. — *William Ruhlmann*

A-1-A / Dec. 1974 / MCA ♦♦♦
A little hardworking for a beachcomber, Buffett released a second album in 1974. It was his most perfect evocation of noncareerist hedonism yet, even if its most telling song, "A Pirate Looks at Forty," was unusually thoughtful for a party animal. — *William Ruhlmann*

Rancho Deluxe / 1975 / United Artists ♦♦♦
This is the soundtrack to a movie written by Buffett's brother-in-law, novelist Thomas McGuane. Buffett appeared in the movie and sang "Livingston Saturday Night" with slightly more risque lyrics than he would later in his career. — *William Ruhlmann*

High Cumberland Jubilee (1972) / 1976 / Barnaby ♦♦
When Buffett's first album, *Down to Earth*, stiffed, Barnaby let him record this follow-up, then "lost" it. It was finally released

Jimmy Buffett

after his career started to take off in 1976, but is still a minor effort. — *William Ruhlmann*

Havana Daydreamin' / Jan. 1976 / MCA ♦♦♦♦
Buffett's best overall collection of songs yet bears the influence of Steve Goodman, who wrote "This Hotel Room" and co-wrote "Woman Goin' Crazy on Caroline Street." But a personal favorite is Buffett's own "My Head Hurts, My Feet Stink, and I Don't Love Jesus." — *William Ruhlmann*

Changes in Latitudes, Changes in Attitudes / Jan. 1977 / MCA ♦♦♦♦
Buffett's biggest selling regular release contains his biggest hit single, "Margaritaville." It's also a peak in terms of songwriting, both for the artist himself and in his covers of the work of Steve Goodman and Jesse Winchester, among others. Funny, wistful, and celebratory, the album is the definitive statement of Buffett's world view. — *William Ruhlmann*

Son of a Son of a Sailor / Mar. 1978 / MCA ♦♦♦♦
If this album was a slight step down from its predecessor, it was almost equally successful commercially, and it contained its share of terrific material, notably the uptempo hit "Cheeseburger in Paradise" and one of Buffett's older songs, "Livingston Saturday Night." — *William Ruhlmann*

You Had to Be There / Oct. 1978 / MCA ♦♦
Buffett has made most of his considerable fortune out of the following he's developed through his concerts, and this double-record live set recorded before an enthusiastic crowd at the Fox in Atlanta serves notice of what's to come. It also serves as a consistent best-of for the artist, most of whose albums are uneven. — *William Ruhlmann*

Volcano / Aug. 1979 / MCA ♦♦
The album that should have consolidated Buffett's status as a major star after his last two hits instead started him down the road to cult status, largely because songs like "Fins" and the title track, which are entertaining enough in concert, aren't really strong material, and they're the best things here. — *William Ruhlmann*

Coconut Telegraph / Feb. 1981 / MCA ♦♦
More Caribbean rhythms and weak jokes—"The Weather Is Here, Wish You Were Beautiful"—plus, in Mac McAnally's "It's My Job,"

a whiff of the elitism always implied in Buffett's stance. — *William Ruhlmann*

Somewhere over China / Jan. 1982 / MCA ✦✦
Perhaps inevitably, Buffett begins to descend from self-satisfaction to self-pity on tracks like "Where's the Party" and "I Heard I Was in Town." Here and on such tracks as "If I Could Just Get It on Paper," it's apparent that the fast life is losing its charm for the singer. — *William Ruhlmann*

One Particular Harbour / Sep. 1983 / MCA ✦✦
Another collection for the cult, including the humorous "We Are the People Our Parents Warned Us About" and a cover of Van Morrison's "Brown Eyed Girl." — *William Ruhlmann*

Riddles in the Sand / Sep. 1984 / MCA ✦✦
Buffett, who never cared for country music, hires Nashville insider Jimmy Bowen as his producer, goes to Fan Fair, puts on a cowboy hat on his album cover, and scores country hits with cheating songs like "Who's the Blonde Stranger?" Actually, things haven't changed that much; it's just a marketing move. — *William Ruhlmann*

Last Mango in Paris / Jun. 1985 / MCA ✦✦✦
Buffett's rapid recording schedule tended to outrun his muse in the late '70s and early '80s, resulting in some uneven albums with occasional good songs. This time he came up with a far more consistent collection, including three entries on the country charts: "Gypsies in the Palace," "If the Phone Doesn't Ring, It's Me," and "Please Bypass This Heart." — *William Ruhlmann*

● **Songs You Know by Heart** / Oct. 1985 / MCA ✦✦✦✦
If anybody ever needed a compilation, it is Jimmy Buffett, who by this time had put out 14 new studio albums in 15 years but only managed to accumulate a handful of memorable songs among them. And just about all of them are here. Unless you're a Parrothead, this will be all you'll need of Jimmy Buffett. — *William Ruhlmann*

Floridays / Jun. 1986 / MCA ✦✦
If *Mango* suggested a new interest in recording and a new care in songwriting, *Floridays* marked a scuttling of such efforts. The lead-off track, "I Love the Now," was co-written by Buffett and Carrie Fisher, which just goes to show that good novelists don't necessarily write good songs together. — *William Ruhlmann*

Hot Water / Jun. 1988 / MCA ✦✦
The best song is Jesse Winchester's oldie "L'Air De La Louisiane." "Smart Woman (in a Real Short Skirt)" did not restore Buffett to the favor of feminists. And you don't get on the radio by complaining that they don't play your "Homemade Music" because there's something wrong with them. — *William Ruhlmann*

Off to See the Lizard / Jun. 1989 / MCA ✦✦
By this point, record making was starting to become just a small part of Jimmy Buffett, Inc., and this is a piece of musical product, efficiently produced and highly consumable, but not very nourishing. Not surprisingly, Buffett didn't bother to make another studio album for five years. — *William Ruhlmann*

Feeding Frenzy / Oct. 1990 / MCA ✦✦
Buffett's real business is summer touring, and this second live outing was overdue. It also makes a good sampler of his work since his last one, but unfortunately even carefully selected, the later work is inferior to the early work. — *William Ruhlmann*

Boats, Beaches, Bars & Ballads / May 1992 / MCA ✦✦✦✦
This four-disc, 72-track anthology is essential for "Parrotheads" (Buffett fans) who don't miss his concerts but aren't so hardcore that they have to own every single thing Buffett ever released. Each disc revolves around a theme (Boats, Beaches, Bars, Ballads). All of his hits and popular album tracks are here, as well as some previously unreleased material. The box includes the Parrothead Handbook, a 64-page booklet that provides a well-assembled collection of photos, reflections from Buffett, and explanations of his songs. The sound on this set is first-rate. — *Rick Clark*

Before the Beach / May 25, 1993 / MCA ✦✦
Yet another reissue of Buffett's first two Barnaby albums, this time released on his own record label, on one CD, and minus the controversial "The Christian?" — *William Ruhlmann*

Fruitcakes / May 24, 1994 / MCA ✦✦
On his first new studio album in five years, Buffett starts out talking about an investment banker, an appropriate concern for this sun-bleached entrepreneur. Soon enough, the sprung calypso rhythms kick in, and you can imagine the Parrotheads swaying and chuckling along, especially when Buffett indulges in the kind of comic raps common to his stage shows. He also covers the Grateful Dead's "Uncle John's Band," one more appropriation in his careful observation of that band's marketing plan. There's also a cover of The Kinks' "Sunny Afternoon," a wealthy man's lament, which is uncomfortably on target. But even with half a decade to come up with original material, Buffett hasn't gotten much to add to his usual sun-and-sand philosophy, and for all his millions he remains a pleasant, but distinctly minor, singer-songwriter. — *William Ruhlmann*

Barometer Soup / 1995 / Margaritaville ✦✦
Having gotten back the record-making habit with *Fruitcakes*, Jimmy Buffett repaired to the Monroe County Library in Key West during the winter of 1994-95 with cohorts Russ Kunkel, Jay Oliver, Roger Guth, and Peter Mayer, where they read fiction and came up with most of the songs on this album. Hence, we have "Remittance Man," drawn from Mark Twain's *Following the Equator*, and "Diamond as Big as the Ritz," loosely adapted from F. Scott Fitzgerald's short story. Typically, there are also the comedy numbers "Bank of Bad Habits" and "Don't Chu-Know" and an appropriation consistent with Buffett's philosophy, James Taylor's "Mexico." Much of the music is low-key, though there are a couple of uptempo tunes to add to the concert repertoire. As Jimmy Buffett albums go, this is another one. — *William Ruhlmann*

Banana Wind / Jun. 1996 / Margaritaville ✦✦✦
Banana Wind is typical latter-day Jimmy Buffett. Over a laidback, Caribbean-inflected folk-rock, Buffett waxes eloquent over boats, booze, sun, and women. Although the sound of the album certainly is pleasant, there's not a single distinctive song on the record, which means it's good for Parrotheads, but casual fans should let this *Banana Wind* sail on by. — *Stephen Thomas Erlewine*

Christmas Island / Oct. 8, 1996 / Margaritaville ✦✦
Largely comprised of original material, Jimmy Buffett's *Christmas Island* is a holiday album that only Parrotheads will need bother with. Though Buffett is relaxed and entertaining, few of his new Christmas songs are remarkable and his rearrangements of classic carols are rather forced. Still, *Christmas Island* remains a pleasant diversion for his dedicated fans, even if it isn't a particularly memorable one. — *Thom Owens*

Sonny Burgess

b. 1931
Guitar / Rockabilly
Sonny Burgess is one of the wildest rockers to record for the legendary Sun label in Memphis. He and his band the Pacers came out of Newport, AR, with a hard-rocking style that, unlike that of most rockabillies, owed little to nothing in the way of a stylistic debt to country music. With his red-dyed hair, matching stage suit and guitar, and wild stage performances, Burgess and the Pacers made mincemeat of the competition on many of the early '50s rock'n' roll package tours. Though his Sun releases never brought him much in the way of commercial success, Burgess' recordings nonetheless remain landmarks of the early rockabilly style. Currently touring and recording with other Memphis alumni in the Sun Rhythm Section, the rockin' flame that is Sonny Burgess refuses to be snuffed out. — *Cub Koda*

● **We Wanna Boogie** / 1990 / Rounder ✦✦✦✦
If you want a fairly definitive compilation of the Sun material by this minor rockabilly figure, but don't want to go the whole nine yards for the expensive import double CD on Bear Family, this domestic anthology is a recommended alternative. The 13 tracks contain six sides from his '50s singles (including the most noted, "Red Headed Woman" and "My Bucket's Got a Hole in It"), and seven other cuts from the '50s that were unissued at the time. — *Richie Unterberger*

The Classic Recordings 1956-1959 / Jul. 1991 / Bear Family
✦✦✦✦

Burgess' complete output for Sun spread over two CDs. Wild and crazed, featuring Burgess' spitfire guitar and booming vocals, and the relentless drive of the Pacers in support. —*Cub Koda*

Tennessee Border / Feb. 1992 / Hightone ✦✦✦

Sonny Burgess / Rounder ✦✦✦✦

If trying to bring back an old artist from the '50s is an idea that seldom merits results that exceed "you can't go home again" or worse, here is an album that proves it *can* be done and done right. Producer Gary Tallent keeps Burgess focused with the lead vocal and blistering lead guitar duties squarely on his shoulders, gives him a pile of great songs from the likes of Radney Foster, Fred James, Dave Alvin, Steve Forbert, and Springsteen to interpret, then frames it all with a backing band that's the essence of drive and simplicity. The spotlight stays on Burgess throughout, just letting him do what he does best. While it all sounds simple enough, it seldom if ever happens on these kind of affairs, making the achievement of this record all that more astounding. A modern rockabilly classic, this also features a wonderful guest appearance turn by Scotty Moore and the Jordanaires on Henry Gross' "Bigger than Elvis." The tray card on this reads, "Sonny Burgess has still got it." Believe it. —*Cub Koda*

Dorsey Burnette

b. Dec. 28, 1932, Memphis, TN, **d.** Aug. 19, 1979, Canoga Park, CA
Bass, Vocals / Country-Pop, Rockabilly

While his talents were largely eclipsed—both commercially and artistically—by his younger brother Johnny, the pioneering work of singer-songwriter Dorsey Burnette remains pivotal in the evolution of the rockabilly form. Born December 28, 1932 in Memphis, TN, both William Dorsey Burnette, Jr. and his brother John began learning to play the guitar as children. After a brief stab at a boxing career, Dorsey turned exclusively to music in 1951, playing steel guitar in a band featuring Scotty Moore, Bill Black, and Bud Deckleman while accepting a day job at Memphis' Crown Electric. In 1952, at Johnny's urging, the Burnette brothers formed a band with guitarist Paul Burlinson, whom Dorsey had met at a Golden Gloves competition a few years before. Rounding out their sound with pianist Doc McQueen and a saxophonist known only as Frenchy, the Burnette Trio played both traditional country and rockabilly, and in 1953 cut a single for the Von label.

By 1954, the Burnettes' co-worker at the electrical company, Elvis Presley, had signed a contract with Sun Records. After Sun's Sam Phillips turned down the brothers because of their music's similarities to Presley's, they moved to New York City, where they appeared four times on *Ted Mack's Amateur Hour*, taking first prize honors on each show. After naming Mack's orchestra leader Henry Jerome their manager and re-christening the group the Johnny Burnette Rock 'n' Roll Trio, the band traveled as part of a package show featuring Mack alumni; soon after, they were recording in Nashville with Owen Bradley, with Dorsey taking over vocal chores from Johnny on a handful of tracks. Later, the Trio went on tour with Carl Perkins and Gene Vincent, and signed to appear in the feature film *Rock, Rock, Rock;* they also issued their most renowned record, "Train Kept a-Rollin'," later covered by the Yardbirds and by Aerosmith.

By 1956, the commercial failure that met the band's records, combined with the brothers' squabbling, prompted Dorsey to leave the group. After returning to Memphis, he recorded a pair of singles, "Let's Fall in Love" and "At a Distance." In 1957, he rejoined the Trio, but a lack of public interest in their music resulted in another breakup. When Johnny moved to California in late 1957, Dorsey soon followed; after cutting a single, he turned his attentions to songwriting, and here found the success that had so long eluded him. After Ricky Nelson notched hits with a pair of tunes co-written by Johnny and Dorsey, 1957's "Waitin' in School" and 1958's "Believe in What You Say," recording companies were again interested in Dorsey and Johnny. Under the name the Burnette Brothers, they released a 1958 single, "My Honey"; while it didn't fare well, in 1959, Nelson scored another tremendous hit with Dorsey's "It's Late."

With the environmentally conscious 1960 single "Tall Oak Tree," Dorsey finally scored a hit of his own; an LP, *Dorsey Burnette's Tall Oak Tree*, soon followed. In 1961, he released the album *Dorsey Burnette Sings*, on which his long-burgeoning country leanings finally became the predominant element of his music. However, Dorsey's solo work was overshadowed by Johnny's success, as the younger Burnette's singles "You're Sixteen" and "Dreamin'" both achieved hit status. In 1962, Dorsey became the first country artist signed to Reprise Records.

Johnny Burnette died in 1964, the victim of a boating accident; the tragedy left Dorsey shaken, and he recorded and performed infrequently for the next several years. In 1968, Glen Campbell earned a hit with his cover of Dorsey's "Hey Little One," while Burnette himself notched a small success with "The Greatest Love" in 1969, the same year he released the album *Dorsey Burnette's Greatest Hits*. Throughout the late '60s and the decade of the '70s, he moved from label to label, releasing the occasional minor hit in singles like 1972's "In the Spring (The Roses Always Turn Red)," 1973's "Darlin' (Don't Come Back)" and 1975's "Molly (I Ain't Getting Any Younger)." While preparing a retrospective Las Vegas nightclub show, Dorsey Burnette suffered a fatal heart attack on August 19, 1979; a few weeks later, his final hit "Here I Go Again" peaked at No. 77 on the *Billboard* country charts. In the following decade, his son Billy scored a number of country hits before joining the pop group Fleetwood Mac in 1987. —*Jason Ankeny*

Dorsey Burnette / 1963 / Dot ✦✦✦✦

● **Great Shakin' Fever** / Bear Family ✦✦✦✦

Jethro Burns

b. 1920, Conasauga, TN, **d.** Feb. 4, 1989
Instrumental, Mandolin / Traditional Country, Country Humor

As the mandolinist in the classic country comedy duo Homer & Jethro, Kenneth Burns was one of the finest instrumentalists of his generation, yet many people never realized that fact. Behind the country hayseed garb, the hick patter, and the outrageous parodies of popular songs lay expert jazz musicians whose exaggerated hillbilly appearance and zany send-ups of songs belie the cleverness of their comedy and the extraordinarily high quality of their music. From the duo's formation in 1936 to Haynes' death in 1971, "Jethro" Burns and guitarist Henry "Homer" Haynes were immensely popular, selling many records and becoming a fixture at the Grand Ole Opry. After Haynes' death, Burns began a solo career that abandoned comedy in favor of jazzy bluegrass and country. Jethro's music is extremely melodic and graceful, combining elements of jazz, swing, country, folk, and bluegrass, resulting in one of the most distinctive and influential mandolin styles in country music history.

Born in Conasauga, TN, but raised in Knoxville, Jethro Burns (b. Kenneth C. Burns, March 10, 1920; d. February 4, 1989) began playing mandolin when he was a child, picking up his brother Aytchie's instrument. By the age of 11, he had grown into a skilled and accomplished instrumentalist, and he and his brothers frequently entered talent contests across Tennessee. At one of the concerts they lost, the sponsoring station, WNOX, asked the brothers to join a band called the String Dusters with another losing contestant, Henry Haynes. They accepted, and the group quickly earned a following; even at this stage, Jethro's playing demonstrated jazzy influences and inflections.

By 1936, Aytchie had left the group and Burns and Haynes had created the comedic Homer and Jethro characters that brought them to popularity. The duo made a good living from these rubes, winning a Grammy in 1959, starring in Las Vegas, and appearing regularly on TV, including *The Tonight Show*. Although they canned the country corn occasionally (as in *Playing It Straight*, a 1962 album), their onstage wit and parodies of well-known songs ranging from the opera to the Opry made them famous. Regarding his "Jambalaya" being turned into "Jam Bowl Liar," Hank Williams said you know a song's good when it's been given the Homer & Jethro treatment. Other zingers include "She Was Bitten on the Udder by an Adder," "Mama, Get the Hammer (There's a

Fly on Papa's Head)," and "I've Got Tears in My Ears from Lying on My Back in Bed While I Cry over You."

Following the death of Henry Haynes in 1971, Burns continued to perform and teach the mandolin. During that decade, he wrote instructional books on how to play the instrument with Ken Edison, which were published by Mel Bay. During the late '70s, Jethro played with the folk singer Steve Goodman, as well as the great country guitarist Chet Atkins. He also began recording a series of jazz albums during that era, many of which featured his son John on guitar. Jethro Burns continued to perform at string music festivals and concerts until his death in 1989. In the series of swing jazz albums he released during the last decade of his career, Burns demonstrated why he was considered the best mandolin player of a generation and, in the opinion of many, the best who has ever lived. —*David Vinopal*

Old Friends / 1983 / Rebel ✦✦✦

Jethro Live / 1990 / Flying Fish ✦✦✦✦
Some laughs are included, and much "mando-marvelosity." —*Mark A. Humphrey*

● **Tea for One** / Kaleidoscope ✦✦✦✦
Known for cornball comedy as half of Homer & Jethro, Burns was also a deft swing-style mandolinist. This album features Jethro Burns and his mandolin and no one else. —*Mark A. Humphrey*

Back to Back / Kaleidoscope ✦✦✦✦
The two modern giants of mandolin, Jethro Burns and Tiny Moore, are backed by guitar-great Eldon Shamblin of Bob Wills' Texas Playboys. —*David Vinopal*

James Burton

b. Aug. 21, 1939, Shreveport, LA
Guitar / Rock & Roll, Traditional Country, Rockabilly, Bakersfield Sound, Instrumental Country
Revered by rock 'n' roll fans for his lead guitar work with young Ricky Nelson and old Elvis Presley (old on the Pelvis timeline, that is), Shreveport, LA, native James Burton is also one of the most influential country players in history. His "chicken pickin'" Telecaster technique added sting to many of Merle Haggard's already biting hits of the 1960s, as well as Emmylou Harris' landmark early albums. —*Dan Cooper*

Corn Pickin' & Slide Slidin' / 1969 / Capitol ✦✦✦

James Burton / 1971 / A&M ✦✦✦

● **Guitar Sounds of James Burton** / 1971 / A&M ✦✦✦✦

Johnny Bush

b. Feb. 17, 1935, Houston, TX
Vocals / Traditional Country, Honky Tonk
Singer-songwriter/drummer Johnny Bush, born John Bush Shin III in Houston, began his country career as a vocalist and guitar player in 1952 at the Texas Star Inn in San Antonio. Eventually he switched to drums and in the early '60s began working in Willie Nelson's band, the Record Men. A year later, he joined Ray Price's Cherokee Cowboys. During his three years with the band, Bush tried to cut a record deal, but the labels felt he sounded too much like Price to be marketable. Nelson stepped in and paid for Bush to cut his first album, *Sound of a Heartache*. After strong local response, he first hit the charts in 1967 with the minor hit "You Oughta Hear Me Cry." The next year he had three hits, including the Top Ten "Undo the Right."

In 1972, Bush had a Top 20 hit with "I'll Be There," which led to a deal with RCA and a Top Ten hit with his song "Whiskey River," which later became Willie Nelson's signature song. Just as Bush reached the brink of stardom, he started to lose his vocal range. Doctors were not able to diagnose the reason until 1978, when they found he had a rare neurological disorder, spastic dysphonia. This did not prevent his recording, but his career soon took a downturn. Working with "voice builder" Gary Catona in 1985, Bush was able to bring back about 70 percent of his original voice. The following year he and Darrell McCall teamed up to record the successful honky tonk album *Hot Texas Country*. He then assembled a large country band and began performing around San Antonio. In 1994, he and the band released *Time*

Changes Everything and launched a major tour; RCA also released a greatest hits album. —*Sandra Brennan*

● **Greatest Hits 1968-1972** / 1993 / GH ✦✦✦✦

Greatest Hits / 1994 / RCA ✦✦✦✦

Carl Butler

b. Jun. 2, 1927, Knoxville, TN, **d.** Sep. 4, 1992
Guitar, Vocals / Traditional Country, Honky Tonk
Born in Knoxville, TN, on June 2, 1927, Carl Butler blended the popular honky tonk style prevalent in the '50s with the mountain harmony of his Tennessee upbringing. Though his early recordings were as a solo act, most of his popular material was performed with his songwriting wife, Pearl. Carl grew up influenced by the Opry's Roy Acuff as well as the old-timey music and bluegrass prevalent around his home. He began singing at amateur dances at the age of 12, and after service in World War II, he sang with bluegrass bands such as the Bailey Brothers and the Sauceman Brothers.

In 1950, Butler began singing as a solo act at a Knoxville radio station; he signed with Capitol and began recording in his bluegrass style, but later changed to a honky tonk sound inspired by Lefty Frizzell and Hank Williams, who were then tearing up the charts. Though the sides weren't successful, he did meet Pearl Dee Jones at the time; she shared composing credits on his "I Need You So," and the two were married by 1952. Carl moved to Columbia that same year, recording solo and with the Webster Brothers throughout the '50s.

By the end of the '50s, Carl Butler still hadn't produced a charting single, though he had recorded steadily for almost a decade. Finally, in late 1961, his single "Honky Tonkitis" made it to No. 25 on the country charts. The Butlers joined the Grand Ole Opry the following year, and the exposure helped them push "Don't Let Me Cross Over" to No. 1. Their first single as a duet, it spent almost three months at the top of the charts, and led to an appearance in the film *Second Fiddle to a Steel Guitar* in 1963. Carl and Pearl continued to chart as a duo throughout the '60s, hitting the Top Ten with "Too Late to Try Again" and No. 14 with both "Loving Arms" and "I'm Hanging up the Phone." The Butlers had worked with Dolly Parton around Knoxville for quite a while beginning in the late '50s, and they were her biggest initial supporters when she became popular in 1967. They continued to release Columbia albums during the '70s and also recorded for Chart and CMH, but retired in the '80s. Carl Butler attempted something of a comeback in 1990, two years after Pearl's death, but it proved unsuccessful and he died in 1992. —*John Bush*

● **Don't Let Me Cross Over** / 1963 / Columbia ✦✦✦✦
Butler is best remembered for the title track (a country heartbreak style song) but this album is quite versatile and, in one instance, quite innovative (check out the "fuzz" guitar solo on "Wonder Drug"). Butler's wife, Pearl, also joins him on several of the songs including the title track. —*Jim Worbois*

Jerry Byrd

b. 1920, Lima, OH
Instrumental Country
Famed guitarist Jerry Byrd was born on March 9, 1920 in Lima, OH. As a child, he developed a passion for Hawaiian music, although he made his first inroads into performing by playing country on an area radio station between 1935 and 1937. After a stint on Cincinnati's WLW, he joined the *Renfro Valley Barn Dance* in 1941; a year later, he jumped to WJR Detroit, and remained there until he signed on with Ernie Lee's Pleasant Valley Boys in 1944.

Byrd remained with Lee until 1946, when he formed his own group, the Jay-Bird Trio. Two years later, he joined Red Foley's band and became a session staple at King Records. Also in 1948, Byrd cut his first singles, "Mountain Mambo" and, under the name Jerry Robin, "Sun Shadows." Later in the year, he issued his first 78, *Steelin' the Blues*. While at King, Byrd also recorded a handful of Hawaiian songs, and as the years wore on, the music became his primary focus.

Still, Byrd remained an active figure on the country landscape; in 1950 he became a regular on Foley's NBC television program, and from 1954 to 1956 he was featured on the Nashville-based series *Home Folks*. An eight year stint on the program *Country Junction* followed, and in 1964 he became a member of Bobby Lord's TV band. In 1968, Byrd left country for good, moving to Hawaii to focus exclusively on the state's native music. —*Jason Ankeny*

Tracy Byrd

b. Dec. 18, 1966, Vidor, TX
Guitar, Vocals / Contemporary Country, New Traditionalist
Singer-songwriter/guitarist Tracy Byrd was part of a movement of contemporary country performers trying to move away from the trend toward pop/country and back toward the more traditional sounds of the genre; his popularity seemed to show that many fans had similar feelings. He began his career in Beaumont, TX, in a rather odd way—he sang "Your Cheatin' Heart" in a shopping mall "recording studio," and the saleswoman was impressed enough to invite him to perform in a monthly amateur talent show. His success there inspired him to pursue music, working his solo act at night and doing odd jobs during the day. He got a job playing with Mark Chesnutt at a nightclub in Beaumont. After Chesnutt became a success and hit the road, Byrd formed a new group, Only Way to Fly, which became the club's house band. He went to Nashville nearly a year later, but the trip wasn't successful. On his return trip, he was showcased, and did a successful solo audition for MCA executives Bruce Hinton and Tony Brown. The first single from his self-titled debut, "That's the Thing About a Memory," made it to the charts as a minor hit in 1992. The next single, "Someone to Give My Love To," made the Top 50, but the third single, "Holdin' Heaven," climbed all the way to No. 1 in 1993. Byrd released his Jerry Crutchfield-produced second album, *No Ordinary Man*, in 1994, which featured the two collaborating on the title track and "Redneck Roses." The single "Lifestyles of the Not So Rich and Famous" made the Top 20. *Love Lessons*, Byrd's third album, was released in 1995, followed later that year by *Keeper of the Stars*. In 1996, he returned with *Big Love*. —*Sandra Brennan*

Tracy Byrd / Apr. 27, 1993 / MCA ✦✦✦
Tracy Byrd's self-titled debut is an unven but appealing set of new traditionalist country, highlighted by the No. 1 hit, "Holdin' Heaven." On about half of the album's tracks, Byrd sounds confident and skillful, but on the other half, he sounds unsure and timid. Which just means that *Tracy Byrd* is a promising debut album, not a great one. —*Thom Owens*

● **No Ordinary Man** / 1994 / MCA ✦✦✦✦
No Ordinary Man, Tracy Byrd's second album, was his breakthrough record and it's easy to see why. While he was still sorting out the ins and outs of recording on his debut album, Byrd sounds raw, vibrant, and confident throughout *No Ordinary Man*, which is clear from the record's first single, "Lifestyles of the Not So Rich and Famous" and the first-rate weeper "The Keeper of the Stars." Byrd plays ballads and uptempo dance numbers equally well and his set of material on the album is fairly consistent, making the album his best to date. —*Thom Owens*

Love Lessons / 1995 / MCA ✦✦✦
On his third album, *Love Lessons*, Tracy Byrd doesn't come up with quite as winning a collection as he did on *No Ordinary Man*, but he comes close enough to make the record a worthwhile purchase for fans. —*Thom Owens*

Big Love / Oct. 22, 1996 / ✦✦✦✦
Tracy Byrd doesn't change his formula much with *Big Love*. He still works the same new-traditionalist ground that he did with his debut album, only with more confidence—his voice is more assured and, more impressively, his selection of material is stronger and more adventurous. On the whole, *Big Love* is the equal to *No Ordinary Man*. —*Thom Owens*

The Byrds

Country-Rock, Psychedelic, Folk-Rock
Although they only attained the huge success of the Beatles, Rolling Stones, and the Beach Boys for a short time in the mid-'60s, time has judged the Byrds to be nearly as influential as those groups in the long run. They were not solely responsible for devising folk-rock, but they were certainly more responsible than any other single act (Dylan included) for melding the innovations and energy of the British Invasion with the best lyrical and musical elements of contemporary folk music. The jangling, 12-string guitar sound of leader Roger McGuinn's Rickenbacker was permanently absorbed into the vocabulary of rock. They also played a vital role in pioneering psychedelic rock and country-rock, the unifying element being their angelic harmonies and restless eclecticism.

Often described in their early days as a hybrid of Dylan and the Beatles, the Byrds in turn influenced Dylan and the Beatles almost as much as Bob and the Fab Four had influenced the Byrds. The Byrds' innovations have echoed nearly as strongly through subsequent generations, in the work of Tom Petty, R.E.M., and innumerable alternative bands of the post-punk era that feature those jangling guitars and dense harmonies.

Although the Byrds had perfected their blend of folk and rock when their debut single, "Mr. Tambourine Man," topped the charts in mid-1965, it was something of a miracle that the group had managed to coalesce in the first place. Not a single member of the original quintet had extensive experience on electric instruments. Jim McGuinn (he'd change his first name to Roger a few years later), David Crosby, and Gene Clark were all young veterans of both commercial folk-pop troupes and the acoustic coffeehouse scene. They were inspired by the success of the Beatles to mix folk and rock; McGuinn had already been playing Beatle songs acoustically in Los Angeles folk clubs when Clark approached him to form an act, according to subsequent recollections, in the Peter & Gordon style. David Crosby soon joined to make them a trio, and they made a primitive demo as the Jet Set that was nonetheless bursting with promise. With the help of session musicians, they released a single on Elektra as the Beefeaters that, while a flop, showed them getting quite close to the folk-rock sound that would electrify the pop scene in a few months.

The Beefeaters, soon renamed the Byrds, were fleshed out to a quintet with the addition of drummer Michael Clarke and bluegrass mandolinist Chris Hillman, who was enlisted to play electric bass, although he had never played the instrument before. The band were so lacking in equipment in their early stages that Clarke played on cardboard boxes during their first rehearsals, but they determined to master their instruments and become a full-fledged rock band (many demos from this period would later surface for official release). They managed to procure a demo of a new Dylan song, "Mr. Tambourine Man"; by eliminating some verses and adding instantly memorable 12-string guitar leads and Beatlesque harmonies, they came up with the first big folk-rock smash (though the Beau Brummels and others had begun exploring similar territory as well). For the "Mr. Tambourine Man" single, the band's vocals and McGuinn's inimitable Rickenbacker were backed by session musicians, although the band themselves (contrary to some widely circulated rumors) performed on their subsequent recordings.

The first long-haired American group to compete with the British Invasion bands visually as well as musically, the Byrds were soon anointed as the American counterpart to the Beatles by the press, legions of fans, and George Harrison himself. Their 1965 debut LP, *Mr. Tambourine Man*, was a fabulous album that mixed stellar interpretations of Dylan and Pete Seeger tunes with strong, more romantic and pop-based originals, usually written by Gene Clark in the band's early days. A few months later, their version of Seeger's "Turn! Turn! Turn!" became another No. 1 hit and instant classic, featuring more great chiming guitar lines and ethereal, interweaving harmonies. While their second LP (*Turn! Turn! Turn!*) wasn't as strong as their debut full-length, the band continued to move forward at a dizzying pace. In early 1966, the "Eight Miles High" single heralded the birth of psychedelia, with its

The Byrds

drug-like (intentionally or otherwise) lyrical imagery, rumbling bass line, and a frenzied McGuinn guitar solo that took its inspiration from John Coltrane and Indian music.

The Byrds suffered a major loss right after "Eight Miles High" with the departure of Gene Clark, their primary songwriter and, along with McGuinn, chief lead vocalist. The reason for his resignation, ironically, was fear of flying, although other pressures were at work as well. "Eight Miles High," amazingly, would be their last Top 20 single; many radio stations banned the record for its alleged drug references, halting its progress at No. 14. This ended the Byrds' brief period as commercial challengers to the Beatles, but they regrouped impressively in the face of these setbacks. Continuing as a quartet, McGuinn, Crosby, and Hillman would assume a much larger (actually, the entire) chunk of the songwriting responsibilities. The third album, *Fifth Dimension*, contained more ground-breaking folk-rock and psychedelia on tracks like "Fifth Dimension," "I See You," and "John Riley," although it (like several of their classic early albums) mixed sheer brilliance with tracks that were oddly half-baked or carelessly executed.

1967's *Younger than Yesterday*, which included the small hits "So You Want to Be a Rock'n'Roll Star" and "My Back Pages" (another Dylan cover), was another high point, Hillman and Crosby in particular taking their writing to a new level. In 1967, Crosby would assert a much more prominent role in the band, singing and writing some of his best material. He wasn't getting along so well with McGuinn and Hillman, though, and was jettisoned from the Byrds partway into the recording of *The Notorious Byrd Brothers*. Gene Clark, drafted into the band as a replacement, left after only a few weeks, and by the end of 1967, Michael Clarke was also gone. Remarkably, in the midst of this chaos (not to mention diminishing record sales), they continued to sound as good as ever on *Notorious*. This was another effort that mixed electronic experimentation and folk-rock mastery with aplomb, with hints of a growing interest in country music.

As McGuinn and Hillman rebuilt the group one more time in early 1968, McGuinn mused upon the exciting possibility of a double album that would play as nothing less than a history of

contemporary music, evolving from traditional folk and country to jazz and electronic music. Toward this end, he hired Gram Parsons, he has since said, to play keyboards. Under Parsons' influence, however, the Byrds were soon going full blast into country music, with Gram taking a large share of the guitar and vocal chores. In 1968, McGuinn, Hillman, Parsons, and drummer Kevin Kelly recorded *Sweetheart of the Rodeo*, which was probably the first album to be widely labeled as country-rock.

Opinions as to the merits of *Rodeo* remain sharply divided among Byrds fans. Some see it as a natural continuation of the group's innovations; other bewail the loss of the band's trademark crystalline guitar jangle, and the short-circuited potential of McGuinn's most ambitious experiments. However one feels, there's no doubt that it marked the end, or at least a drastic revamping, of the "classic" Byrds sound of the 1965-68 period (bookended by the *Tambourine Man* and *Notorious* albums). Parsons, the main catalyst for the metamorphosis, left the band after about six months, partially in objection to a 1968 Byrds tour of South Africa. It couldn't have helped, though, that McGuinn replaced several of Parsons' lead vocals on *Rodeo* with his own at the last minute, ostensibly due to contractual obstacles that prevented Gram from singing on Columbia releases. (Some tracks with Parsons' lead vocals snuck on anyway, and a few others surfaced in the 1990s on the Byrds box set).

Chris Hillman left the Byrds by the end of 1968 to form the Flying Burrito Brothers with Parsons. Although McGuinn kept the Byrds going for about another five years with other musicians (most notably former country picker Clarence White), essentially the Byrds name was a front for Roger McGuinn and backing band. Opinions, again, remain sharply divided about the merits of latter-day Byrds albums. McGuinn was (and is) such an idiosyncratic and pleasurable talent that fans and critics are inclined to give him some slack; no one else plays the 12-string as well, he's a fine arranger, and his Lennon-meets-Dylan vocals are immediately distinctive. Yet aside from some good echoes of vintage Byrds like "Chestnut Mare," "Jesus Is Just Alright," and "Drug Store Truck Drivin' Man," nothing from the post-1968 Byrds albums resonates with nearly the same effervescent quality and authority as their classic 1965-68 period. This is partly because McGuinn is an erratic (though occasionally fine) songwriter; it's also because the Byrds at their peak were very much a unit of diverse and considerable talents, not just a front for their leader's ideas.

The Byrds' diminishing importance must have stung McGuinn doubly in light of the rising profiles of several Byrds alumni as the '60s turned into the '70s. David Crosby was a superstar with Crosby, Stills, Nash & Young; Hillman, Parsons, and (for a while) Michael Clarke were taking country-rock further with the Flying Burrito Brothers; even Gene Clark, though he'd dropped out of sight commercially, was recording some respected country-rock albums on his own. The original quintet actually got back together for a one-off reunion album in 1973; though it made the Top 20, it was the first, and one of the most flagrant, examples of the futility of a great band reuniting in an attempt to recapture the lightning one last time.

The original Byrds continued to pursue solo careers and outside projects throughout the 1970s and 1980s. McGuinn, Clark, and Hillman had some success at the end of the 1970s with an adult contemporary variation on the Byrds' sound; in the 1980s, Crosby battled drug problems while Hillman enjoyed mainstream country success with the Desert Rose Band. The Byrds' legend was tarnished by squabbles over which members of the original lineup had the rights to use the Byrds name; for quite a while, drummer Michael Clarke even toured with a "Byrds" that featured no other original members. The Byrds were inducted into the Rock & Roll Hall of Fame in 1991; Gene Clark died several months later, and Michael Clarke died in 1993, permanently scotching prospects of a reunion involving the original quintet. —*Richie Unterberger*

★ **The Byrds' Greatest Hits** / 1967 / Columbia ♦♦♦♦♦
Even though this collection only covers the first half of their career, it contains more primo stuff than *20 Essential Tracks* (see below). The mastering here isn't quite as good as that on the boxed set. —*Rick Clark*

The Notorious Byrd Brothers / Jan. 1968 / Columbia ♦♦♦♦
A classic psychedelic opus, it draws from the space-rock of *Younger...* and *Fifth...* while hinting at the country-rock to come with cuts like "Change Is Now" and "Old John Robertson." The 12-string electrics are downplayed. Production techniques like phasing, vari-speeded vocals, sound effects, and baroque string and horn arrangements play a bigger role, while the melodies and vocal execution are much spacier. Highlights include

Carole King's yearning "Goin' Back," "Draft Morning," "Dolphins Smile," and "Wasn't Born to Follow" (featured in the movie *Easy Rider*). —*Rick Clark*

☆ **Sweetheart of the Rodeo** / Aug. 1968 / Columbia ♦♦♦♦♦
The Byrds made this groundbreaking country-rock classic with the songwriting aid of new member Gram Parsons. "One Hundred Years from Now" features some incredibly fine guitar and pedal-steel work from Clarence White and Lloyd Green, respectively. Versions of Dylan's "Nothing Was Delivered" and "You Ain't Going Nowhere" are pure magic, and renditions of The Louvin Brothers' "The Christian Life" and William Bell's "You Don't Miss Your Water" are standouts too. —*Rick Clark*

Dr. Byrd & Mr. Hyde / 1969 / Columbia ♦♦
Not one of their best, this still contains two notable tracks, "This Wheel's on Fire" and "King Apathy III." There is a continued country influence but rock still predominates. —*Rick Clark*

The Ballad of Easy Rider / Feb. 1969 / Columbia ♦♦♦♦
This is another beautiful gem with hardly a weak cut. "Gunga Din," with its delicate arpeggios, is one of the finest moments by a later incarnation of The Byrds. By this time, their characteristic 12-string sound was all but gone. —*Rick Clark*

Untitled / 1970 / Columbia ♦♦♦
Originally a double-record set (one live LP/one studio) and now on single CD, this contains their last hit of any substance, "Chestnut Mare." The studio tracks are uneven, but tracks like the reflective "Just a Season," "Truck Stop Girl," "All the Things" and much of the live stuff make this set worth having, if only for Clarence White's remarkable guitar playing. —*Rick Clark*

☆ **The Byrds [box set]** / 1990 / Columbia ♦♦♦♦♦
This thoughtfully compiled four-disc boxed set features great sound from remastered and remixed tracks. The remixes generally manage to maintain the essential integrity of the original tracks, but there are some that entirely miss the spirit, like "Just a Season" and a toothless "Why" (which, by the way, is *not* the sought-after version found on the B-side of "Eight Miles High"). Regardless, it's a must-own for anyone interested in finding out about one of America's greatest groups. —*Rick Clark*

20 Essential Tracks from the Boxed Set: 1965-90 / 1991 / Columbia ♦♦♦
That may have been the case for the first 16 cuts, but why include the four 1990 reunion tracks, when there's much better material left on the box? An okay choice for the budget-minded; that's about it. —*Rick Clark*

C

Cache Valley Drifters

Traditional Bluegrass, Progressive Country
The Cache Valley Drifters are an eclectic bunch who are comfortable playing boogie, bluegrass, country, Grateful Dead, folk, and old timey music. Cyrus Clarke (guitar, vocals), Bill Griffin (mandolin, vocals), Tom Lee (string bass), and David West (guitar, vocals) are the members. —*Chip Renner*

New Cache Valley Drifters / 1979 / Flying Fish ♦♦♦
Their debut album combines bluegrass with rock for a great sound. —*Chip Renner*

● **Step up to Big Pay** / 1980 / Flying Fish ♦♦♦♦
A great sophomore album. Good vocals and playing, with nice covers of John Prine's "Hello in There" and The Grateful Dead's "Cumberland Blues." —*Chip Renner*

Tools of the Trade / 1983 / Flying Fish ♦♦♦♦
There is a lot of energy on this live album from McCabe's Guitar Shop. Very good! —*Chip Renner*

The Cache Valley Drifters / Flying Fish ♦♦♦

Camp Creek Boys

Traditional Bluegrass, Old-Time
The Camp Creek Boys formed in the 1930s, but didn't become influential in helping preserve and promote old-time string band music until the folk revival of the 1960s. All of the band members hailed from Surrey County in North Carolina's Blue Ridge Mountains. Their leader was banjo picker Kyle Creed, who was accompanied by fiddler Fred Cockerham and guitarist Paul Sutphin. The other members were guitarist Ronald Collins, fiddler Ernest East, mandolin player Verlin Clifton and guitarist Roscoe Russel, making this string band considerably larger than traditional bands, which featured a guitar, a fiddle, and vocalists. The band's name came from the community where Creed was raised. During the 1930s, the Camp Creek Boys started out playing at local social events ranging from dances to corn shuckings. They then began working on the radio and playing at old-time fiddle conventions. Even then the Camp Creek Boys were interested in preserving their musical heritage and the distinctive sound of string band music; after live radio performances became less common, they focused on performing at conventions and in fiddle contests. Eventually Creed became a key figure in the revival of his music. During their career, the Camp Creek Boys recorded four albums for the County and Mountain labels. Their best known songs include "Fortune," "Cider Mill," and the modern bluegrass favorite "Let Me Fall." —*Sandra Brennan*

● **Blue Ridge Square Dance** / Mountain ♦♦♦♦

June Apple / Mountain ♦♦♦

The Camp Creek Boys / County ♦♦♦

Cecil Campbell

b. Mar. 22, 1911, Danbury, NC, **d.** Jun. 18, 1989
Guitar (Steel) / Traditional Country
Cecil Campbell was most famed as a steel guitarist for the Tennessee Ramblers during the 1930s and '40s, although he also played tenor banjo. Born March 22, 1911, in North Carolina, Campbell worked on his father's tobacco farm and played occasionally on WSJS-Winston Salem. While visiting his brother in Pittsburgh in the early '30s, he met Dick Hartman and was asked to join Hartman's Tennessee Ramblers, a large group that played both Western swing and old-time string music. Campbell played on radio broadcasts and Bluebird sessions with the band throughout the '30s, taking over the leadership of the Ramblers' by-then skeleton crew in 1945, when the only original member left was guitarist Harry Blair.

Cecil Campbell and the Tennesse Ramblers gained a contract with RCA Victor in 1946 and recorded throughout the late '40s. Campbell's steel-guitar wizardry was emphasized, and the Ramblers gradually became more Campbell's backing group than an original entity themselves. During his RCA tenure, "Steel Guitar Ramble" became Campbell's only hit when it reached the Country Top Ten in May 1949. Campbell also recorded for Disc and Palmetto Records during the early '50s, but signed with MGM in 1955, mixing some rockabilly material in with his traditional swing. He recorded in the '60s for Starday, and Campbell later founded his own label in North Carolina, occasionally playing shows and recording. He also appeared often at the Western Film Fair (held in Raleigh, NC) until his death in 1989. —*John Bush*

● **Steel Guitar Jamboree** / 1963 / Starday ♦♦♦♦

Greatest Hawaiian Instrumentals / 196 / Winston ♦♦♦

Glen Campbell

b. Apr. 22, 1936, Delight, AR
Banjo, Guitar, Vocals / Country-Pop, Nashville Sound/Country-politan, Urban Cowboy
It isn't accurate to call Glen Campbell "pure country," but his smooth fusion of country mannerisms and pop melodies and production techniques made him one of the most popular country musicians of the late '60s and '70s. Campbell was one of the leading figures of country-pop during that era, racking up a steady stream of Top Ten singles, highlighted by classics like "By the Time I Get to Phoenix," "I Wanna Live," "Wichita Lineman," "Galveston," "Rhinestone Cowboy" and "Southern Nights." Boasting Campbell's smooth vocals and layered arrangements, where steel guitars bounced off sweeping strings, those songs not only became country hits, they crossed over to the pop charts as well, which was appropriate, since that is where he began his musical career. Originally, he was a Los Angeles session musician, playing on hits by the Monkees, Elvis Presley, Frank Sinatra, and Merle Haggard. By the end of the '60s, he had become a successful solo artist, and that success would not abate until the late '80s, when he stopped having radio hits and began concentrating on live performances at his theater in Branson.

Campbell was born and raised in Delight, AR, where he received his first guitar when he was four years old. Learning the instrument from various relatives, he played consistently throughout his childhood, eventually gravitating toward jazz players like Barney Kessel and Django Reinhardt. While he was learning guitar, he also sang in a local church, where he developed his vocal skills. By the time he was 14, he had begun performing with a number of country bands in the Arkansas, Texas, and New Mexico area, including his uncle's group, the Dick Bills Band. When he was 18, he formed his own country band, the Western Wranglers, and began touring the South with the group. Four years later, Campbell moved to Los Angeles, CA, where he became a session musician.

Shortly after arriving in California, Campbell earned the reputation of being an excellent guitarist, playing on records by Bobby Darin and Rick Nelson. In 1960, he briefly joined the instrumental rock 'n' roll group the Champs, who had the hit single "Tequila" two years earlier. The following year, he released his debut single, "Turn Around, Look at Me" on the small Crest label; the single reached No. 62 later in the year. By the summer of 1962, he had released "Too Late to Worry—Too Blue to Cry" on Capitol Records; the single only spent two weeks on the charts, peaking at No. 76. While he was tentatively pursuing a solo career, Campbell continued to play professionally, most notably for Elvis Presley and Dean Martin. Also in 1962, he played guitar and sang on "Kentucky Means Paradise," a single by the one-off group the Green River Boys, who released an album, *Big Bluegrass Special*. "Kentucky Means Paradise" became a hit on the country charts, climbing to No. 20. Instead of pursuing a full-fledged country career after the single's release, Campbell returned to studio work, and over the next two years he played on sessions by Frank Sinatra ("Strangers in the Night"), Merle Haggard ("The Legend of Bonnie and Clyde"), the Monkees ("I'm a Believer"), the Association, and the Mamas & the Papas, among many others.

Following Brian Wilson's breakdown and retirement from the road in 1965, Glen Campbell became a touring member of the Beach Boys for several months. At the end of his tenure as the group's temporary bassist, the Beach Boys offered him a permanent spot in the band, but he turned them down when they wouldn't allow him to have an equal cut of the group's royalties. A few months after rejecting the band's offer, the Beach Boys' record label, Capitol, offered Campbell a full-fledged contract. His first release under his new long-term Capitol contract was a version of Buffy Sainte-Marie's "The Universal Soldier," which peaked at No. 45. For much of 1966, he continued to pursue studio work, but he released "Burning Bridges" toward the end of the year, and it climbed to No. 18 on the country charts early in 1967.

During 1967, Capitol pushed Campbell as a country recording artist, and his breakthrough arrived in the late summer when his folky country-pop rendition of John Hartford's "Gentle on My Mind" became a Top 40 hit on both the country and pop charts. By the end of the year, he had released a cover of Jimmy Webb's "By the Time I Get to Phoenix," which reached No. 2 on the country charts, and No. 26 on the pop charts. Early in 1968, "Gentle on My Mind" won the Grammy Award for Best Country & Western Recording of 1967. Campbell's success continued in 1968, as "I Wanna Live" became his first No. 1 hit and "Dreams of the Everyday Housewife" reached No. 3. The following year, CBS television hired him to host the variety show *The Glen Campbell Good Time Hour*, which became quite popular and helped establish him as not only a country star, but a pop music superstar.

Throughout the late '60s and early '70s, Campbell continued to rack up hit singles, including the No. 1 hits "Wichita Lineman" (1968) and "Galveston" (1969), plus the Top Ten singles "Try a Little Kindness" (1969), "Honey Come Back" (1970), "Everything a Man Could Ever Need" (1970), and "It's Only Make Believe" (1970). In 1968, he began recording duets with Bobbie Gentry, and they had hit singles with their versions of two Everly Brothers songs—"Let It Be Me," which reached No. 14 in 1969, and "All I Have to Do Is Dream," which peaked at No. 6 in 1970. Also in 1969, he began a film career, appearing in the John Wayne movie *True Grit* that year and *Norwood* the following year.

By 1972, Campbell's record sales started slipping. After "Manhattan Kansas" reached No. 6 that year, he had trouble having Top 40 hits for the next two years. Furthermore, his television show was canceled. As his career slowed, he began sinking into drug and alcohol addiction, which continued even through his mid-'70s revival. In 1975, he returned to the Top Ten with "Rhinestone

Cowboy," a huge hit that reached No. 1 on both the country and pop charts. Over the next two years, he had a number of Top Ten country hits, including "Country Boy (You Got Your Feet in L.A.)" and "Don't Pull Your Love" / "Then You Can Tell Me Goodbye," which also reached the pop charts. In 1977, he had his final No. 1 hit with "Southern Nights," which topped both the country and pop charts.

Following the success of "Southern Nights" and its follow-up "Sunflower," Campbell stopped reaching the country Top Ten with regularity, yet he had a string of lesser hits and was an immensely popular performer in concert and television. During the mid-'80s, he experienced a brief commercial revival, as the singles "Faithless Love," "A Lady like You" and "The Hand That Rocks the Cradle" all reached the country Top Ten. By that time, he had begun to clean up his act. Over the course of the mid-'80s, he kicked his addictions to drugs and alcohol and became a born-again Christian. Appropriately, he began recording inspirational albums, yet he didn't abandon country music. As late as 1989, Campbell's smooth, synth-laden contemporary country-pop was reaching the country Top Ten; his last two Top Ten country hits were "I Have You" (1988) and "She's Gone, Gone, Gone" (1989).

Campbell began recording less frequently in the early '90s, especially since he could no longer reach the charts and the radio, since they were dominated by new country artists. Over the course of the decade, he gradually moved into semi-retirement, concentrating on golf and performing at his Goodtime Theater in Branson, MO. In 1994, he published his autobiography, *Rhinestone Cowboy. —Stephen Thomas Erlewine*

Hey, Little One / 1968 / Capitol ✦✦
Campbell seems to be trying to please everyone with this record with covers of recent records from the Union Gap and Bob Dylan to Broadway musicals and country standards. Campbell even redid his 1961 hit "Turn Around and Look at Me" for this record. In his attempt to be all things to all people, nothing really stands out. —*Jim Worbois*

Galveston / 1969 / Capitol ✦✦✦✦
Galveston continued Glen Campbell's strong string of hits supplied to him by Jimmy Webb. Here, though, he includes fine tunes from other writers, such as Buffy Sainte-Marie's "Until It's Time for You to Go" and Randy Sparks' "Today," as well as some of his own compositions. But the big draws on *Galveston* are the Webb tunes "Where's the Playground, Susie?" and the title track, a big hit on both the pop and country charts. —*James Chrispell*

The Glen Campbell Goodtime Album / 1970 / Capitol ✦✦✦
A spin-off of the TV show of the same name, this album is a nice representation of what Campbell was about at the time. In addition to the hit on the album (the cover of Conway Twitty's "It's Only Make Believe"), he dips into the Jimmy Webb songbook for two of the tracks. —*Jim Worbois*

☆ Glen Campbell's Greatest Hits / 1971 / Capitol ✦✦✦✦✦
It covers the most productive period of his recording career, the years in which Al De Lory's soaring string arrangements, Jimmy Webb's snapshot songs, and the identifiable low-tuned guitars vaulted Campbell to the upper strata of both the country and pop charts. You simply weren't alive if you didn't hear "Wichita Lineman," "Galveston," or "Try a Little Kindness." —*Tom Roland*

I Knew Jesus (Before He Was a Star) / 1973 / Capitol ✦✦✦
On this album, Campbell became one of the first (and only) artists to cover, and give exposure to, the talents of Kinky Freidman. Overall, not a great album, but certainly an eclectic batch of songs, including songs that had been recent hits by Charlie Rich, Judy Collins, and Olivia Newton-John. —*Jim Worbois*

I Remember Hank Williams / 1973 / Capitol ✦✦
Good intentions should count for something, but the syrupy strings and background singer will make more than one fan comment, "I don't think Hank done it this way." —*Jim Worbois*

Reunion (The Songs of Jimmy Webb) / 1974 / Capitol ✦✦✦
Glen Campbell has long been a major supporter of the work of Jimmy Webb. In fact, Webb penned several of Campbell's earliest hits. The quality of this material makes one wonder why more artists don't look to Webb for material. —*Jim Worbois*

☆ **Best Of** / 1976 / Capitol ✦✦✦✦✦
This record really does live up to the title. All killer and no filler, covering Campbell's career up through 1976. A nice selection of songs, and it's just right for people who know Campbell for the hits or for someone wanting to get into his music for the first time. —*Jim Worbois*

The Very Best of Glen Campbell / 1987 / Capitol ✦✦✦✦
The 15-track collection *The Very Best of Glen Campbell* contains the great majority of Campbell's biggest hit singles from the late '60s and '70s. Every song on this compilation was a Top 40 country hit, and most of them—including "Wichita Lineman," "Galveston," "By the Time I Get to Phoenix," "Try a Little Kindness," "It's Only Make Believe," "Dream Baby (How Long Must I Dream)," "Rhinestone Cowboy," "Country Boy (You Got Your Feet In L.A.)," "Sunflower," and "Southern Nights"—were Top Ten hits, which makes it an ideal introduction to Campbell's career. —*Stephen Thomas Erlewine*

The Best of the Early Years / 1987 / Curb ✦✦✦✦
Best of the Early Years features Campbell staples like "Gentle on My Mind," "By the Time I Get to Phoenix," "Galveston" and "Wichita Lineman." —*Jason Ankeny*

★ **The Very Best of Glen Campbell** / Mar. 20, 1987 / Liberty ✦✦✦✦✦
The Very Best of Glen Campbell features 15 of his biggest hits, from "Gentle on My Mind" and "Wichita Lineman" to "Rhinestone Cowboy," making it the place to get acquainted with Campbell's career. —*Stephen Thomas Erlewine*

Light Years / 1988 / MCA ✦✦✦
The songs of Jimmy Webb constitute the majority of the material found on *Light Years*. —*Jason Ankeny*

Still within the Sound of My Voice / Aug. 10, 1988 / MCA ✦✦✦
Still within the Sound of My Voice features the chart hits "I Remember You" (a cover of the Frank Ifield hit), "The Hand that Rocks the Cradle" (a duet with Steve Wariner), and the title cut. —*Jason Ankeny*

Greatest Country Hits / 1990 / Curb ✦✦✦
A hodgepodge of material from the mid-'70s through 1989, this displays a variety of Glen Campbell approaches to country. "She's Gone, Gone, Gone" is twangy enough to do originator Lefty Frizzell justice. "Still within the Sound of My Voice" catches Campbell at his most sensitive, and "Southern Nights" is just plain fun. —*Tom Roland*

Classics Collection / May 21, 1990 / Liberty ✦✦✦✦
Classics Collection is a comprehensive anthology of Campbell's biggest chart hits from the 1960s ("Wichita Lineman," "By the Time I Get to Houston," "Galveston," "Gentle on My Mind") and 1970s ("Rhinestone Cowboy," "Southern Nights"). —*Jason Ankeny*

Somebody Like That / 1993 / Capitol ✦✦✦
Hey, for a guy who's been around almost forever, Glen Campbell's *Somebody Like That* cooks nicely. Campbell has always had good taste in songwriters and sidemen and his latest upholds this tradition, recruiting material from Paul Overstreet, Naomi Martin, and Billy Burnette, among others. Only a couple of ballads are given schmaltzy arrangements; for the most part the tracks chug along in mid-tempo, semi-rockabilly fashion. Best bets here are "Swimming Upstream, Ain't It Just Like Love" and (especially) the chorus-kicking title track. For "Love's Old Song," Campbell indulges in some jazzy country-swing. —*Roch Parisien*

Essential, Vol. 2 / 1995 / Capitol ✦✦✦✦
The second installment of *The Essential* series features some of Glen Campbell's biggest hits, including "Rhinestone Cowboy" and "Gentle on My Mind," as well as several live tracks, album cuts, instrumentals, and a couple of previously unreleased songs. All of the material was recorded between 1962 and 1978. —*Stephen Thomas Erlewine*

Essential, Vol. 3 / Oct. 10, 1995 / Capitol ✦✦✦✦
The third installment of Glen Campbell's *Essential* series features his No. 1 hit "Wichita Lineman" among a handful of other hit singles and selected rarities. —*Thom Owens*

★ **Gentle on My Mind: The Collection** / Feb. 18, 1997 / Razor & Tie ✦✦✦✦✦
Gentle on My Mind: The Collection is an excellent double-disc collection that contains all of Glen Campbell's biggest hits, from "By the Time I Get to Phoenix" and "Gentle on My Mind" to "Rhinestone Cowboy" and "Country Boy (You Got Your Feet In L.A.)," making it the definitive retrospective of the extremely popular country-pop vocalist. —*Thom Owens*

Essential, Vol. 1 / Capitol ✦✦✦✦
The first volume of *The Essential Glen Campbell* establishes the pattern of familiar hits and fascinating rarities that make the series a worthwhile purchase for both devoted and casual fans. Although it doesn't follow a strict chronological running order, it offers a good cross-section of his late '60s and '70s hits. —*Thom Owens*

All-Time Greatest Hits / CEMA ✦✦✦
The budget-priced, triple-disc, 35-song set *All-Time Greatest Hits* contains the bulk of Glen Campbell's biggest hits—"Rhinestone Cowboy," "Galveston," "By the Time I Get to Phoenix," "I Wanna Live," "Gentle on My Mind," "Wichita Lineman," "Country Boy "(You Got Your Feet in L.A.)," "Southern Nights"—presented in a nonchronological order and packaged without notes. For a budget-priced collection, *All-Time Greatest Hits* isn't bad—it has most of the hits in their original versions—but it isn't well-thought-out. Razor & Tie's double-disc *The Glen Campbell Collection* remains a better overview of Campbell's career, but *All-Time Greatest Hits* is good on its own terms. —*Stephen Thomas Erlewine*

Stacy Dean Campbell

b. Jul. 27, 1967, Carlsbad, NM
Vocals / Contemporary Country
Singer-songwriter Stacy Dean Campbell was first inspired to become a musician by his father Buddy, a gospel singer. Raised by his grandparents in Carlsbad, NM, he grew up enamored of the music of Marty Robbins, whose smooth crooning influenced Campbell's own vocal style. Encouraged by his brother Spencer, himself a professional musician, Campbell moved to Nashville to pursue a career in country, and soon earned a songwriting contract with Tree Music. In 1992, he released his debut solo record, *Lonesome Wins Again;* the follow-up, the eclectic *Hurt City*, appeared in 1995. —*Jason Ankeny*

● **Lonesome Wins Again** / Feb. 1992 / Columbia ✦✦✦✦
Sexy, low-key rockabilly (like Chris Isaak but not as spooky), this album includes the singles "Rosalee," "Baby Don't You Know," and "Poor Man's Rose." —*Brian Mansfield*

Hurt City / Jul. 25, 1995 / Sony ✦✦✦

Ace Cannon

b. May 5, 1934, Grenada, MS
Instrumental, Saxophone, Session Musician / Soul, R&B, Rock & Roll, Country-Pop, Nashville Sound/Countrypolitan
One of Nashville's premier session men from the late '50s through the early '70s, alto saxophonist Ace Cannon began playing at the age of ten and signed with Sun Records during the early days of rock 'n' roll. He performed with Billy Lee Riley and Brad Suggs but then in 1959 joined the original Bill Black Combo, recording for the Hi label. He stayed with the band until 1961, when he made his solo chart debut with the instrumental "Tuff," which made it to the country Top 20. This in turn was followed by a Top 40 hit, "Blues (Stay Away from Me)," and a minor hit for the Santos label, "Sugar Blues." He had two more hits in the mid-'60s with "Cottonfields" and "Searchin'," both recorded for Hi. A decade later, he became the subject of the 1974 documentary film, *Ace's High*. After moving to Nashville in the mid-'70s, Cannon's version of "Blue Eyes Crying in the Rain" became a minor hit and was nominated for the Best Country Instrumental Performance Grammy that year. Cannon continued to perform into the '90s and frequently toured with such legends of early rock 'n' roll as Carl Perkins. —*Sandra Brennan*

● **Best of Ace Cannon** / Nov. 19, 1996 / Curb ✦✦✦✦

Henson Cargill

b. Feb. 5, 1941, Oklahoma City, OK
Vocals / Traditional Country, Nashville Sound/Countrypolitan
Henson Cargill had tried his hand at being a lawyer, rancher, and
deputy sheriff before settling on country music as a career after
returning to Oklahoma from Colorado State University. He began
playing local bars and was asked to join the Kimberlys by their
leader, Harold Gay. Cargill went to Nashville in the mid-'60s and,
after auditioning for different labels, signed with Fred Foster at
Monument in 1967. Foster teamed Henson with producer Don
Law to record the Jack Moran song "Skip a Rope." The single was
a tremendous success and not only topped the country charts for
five weeks, but also crossed over to the Top 25 on the pop charts.
During 1968-69, Henson went on to have two more Top 20 country hits, including "None of My Business." In 1969, he also began
hosting Avco Broadcasting's syndicated show *Country Hayride*
and recorded steadily for the next few years. In 1971, the single
"The Most Uncomplicated Good-bye I've Ever Heard" hit the Top
20, and two years later he recorded two Top 30 hits, including
"Some Old California Memory." Cargill's next hit, however, was
over six years in coming. Finally in 1979, "Silence on the Line"
made the Top 30. The success proved elusive, though, and Henson
quit recording soon after, returning to his Oklahoma ranch.
— *Sandra Brennan*

● Skip a Rope / 1968 / Monument ✦✦✦✦

This Is Henson Cargill Country / 1974 / Atlantic ✦✦✦✦

Bill Carlisle

b. Dec. 19, 1908, Wakefield, KY
Guitar, Vocals / Traditional Country, Cowboy
Yodeling singer-songwriter/guitarist Bill Carlisle was the younger
brother of popular 1930s country singer Cliff Carlisle. During the
'30s, Bill established himself as a blues singer, but during the '50s
and '60s, he was best known for his novelty songs as he and his
family band, the Carlisles, became regulars on the Grand Ole
Opry.
   Brother Cliff gave young Carlisle his start in 1933 by letting
him audition with the ARC label group. His first single, "Rattlesnake Daddy," became quite popular; during the '40s, it became a
bluegrass favorite. Dubbed "Smilin' Bill" by publicists, he was
noted for his precise and extremely fast runs on the guitar. Eventually Bill became almost as popular as his older brother, with
whom he shared a talent for yodeling and a tendency to sing
songs filled with risqué double entendres, such as "Copper Head
Mama" (1934) and "Jumpin and Jerkin' Blues" (1935). During the
late '30s, Bill signed with Decca and explored different styles, but
still recorded bawdy songs as well.
   During the '30s and '40s, Carlisle worked at different radio stations in Kentucky, the Carolinas, Georgia, and Tennessee, sometimes with Cliff and sometimes solo. In 1946, Bill and Cliff scored
a giant hit with "Rainbow at Midnight." Two years later, Bill had
his own Top 15 hit with "Tramp on the Street." Cliff eventually
retired in 1950, and Bill then organized the Carlisles and went
back to Knoxville to do shows with Don Gibson, Chet Atkins, and
Homer & Jethro, among others. It was during these performances
that he began to leap about on stage and develop his comical
alter-ego "Hot Shot Elmer," a character he created during the
1940s.
   As Elmer, Carlisle would interrupt performances by jumping
over chairs, falling off the stairs, and creating general mayhem on
stage. During the '50s he recorded a series of novelty songs for
Mercury. The first, "Too Old to Cut the Mustard," hit the Top Ten
in 1952. "No Help Wanted" climbed to No. 1 the following year
and stayed there five weeks. That year he had three more hits, all
of which made it to the Top Ten, including the Ira Louvin song
"Taint Nice (To Talk like That)." This string of successes led the
Opry to invite the Carlisles aboard in 1953. Bill's children joined
his band in the 1960s, and he had another hit in 1965 with "What
Kind of Deal Is This." During the '80s and '90s, the fun-loving Bill
was noted for appearing onstage in crazy green wigs and with his

constant theatrical leaps earned the nickname "Jumping" Bill Carlisle. — *Sandra Brennan*

On Stage with the Carlisles / 1958 / Mercury ✦✦✦✦
● The Best of Bill Carlisle / 1966 / Hickory ✦✦✦✦
Jumpin' Bill Carlisle / 1983 / Brylen ✦✦✦
Carlisle Family: Old Time Great Hyms / Old Homestead ✦✦✦

Cliff Carlisle

b. May 6, 1904, Taylorsville, KY, d. Apr. 2, 1983
Guitar, Vocals / Cowboy
During the 1930s, country singer/yodeler/guitarist Cliff Carlisle
rivaled Gene Autry as the era's most prolific recording artist. He
recorded over 300 singles for a variety of labels, including Gennett, Bluebird, ARC, and Decca. In addition to his Jimmie Rodg-
ers-style yodeling, Carlisle was also one of the pioneers of using
the Hawaiian guitar in country music. As a singer, he was known
for his tendency to sing bluesy, double-entendre-filled songs such
as "The Girl in the Blue Velvet Band." At the end of the decade he
branched out into crooning cowboy songs and more sentimental
tunes in addition to his typical bawdy novelty fare. The latter he
occasionally recorded under the alias "Bob Clifford." In the mid-
'30s, he and his brother Bill began recording together. By 1936,
his son Tommy was singing with them and became known as
Sonny Boy Tommy. During the '40s, Cliff and Bill worked
together periodically on radio stations throughout the South and
in recording studios. In 1946, they scored their biggest hit as a
duo with the Top Five "Rainbow at Midnight" on the new King
label. Cliff eventually retired around 1950, but turned to recording albums for independent labels after his music became popular again during the folk revival of the 1960s. — *Sandra Brennan*

● Volume 1-2 / Old Timey ✦✦✦✦
Born in 1904 in Mt. Eden Kentucky, Cliff Carlisle was raised in
tobacco country. He drew on songs he heard growing up and
wrote a number of his own incorporating themes of the Old West.
His style is uptempo with a lot of yodeling and Hawaiian guitar
licks. He performed on the radio in the '30s and with his brother.
These LPs collect his rare original recordings. — *Richard Meyer*

Thumbs Carllile

b. Apr. 2, 1931, St. Louis, MO, d. Jul. 31, 1987
Guitar / Traditional Country
Kenneth Ray "Thumbs" Carllile was an innovative guitar player
and songwriter. The son of an impoverished Illinois tenant
farmer, he began playing music at the age of eight after his sister
Evelyn won a dobro for selling balm. He played the new instrument so much that his irritated sister hid the steel bar, but the
resourceful young man began using his thumbs to practice. When
his father gave him a Silvertone guitar, Carllile's thumbs were too
short and fat to make it around the neck, so he began playing it
on his lap like a dobro. Carllile's family moved to Granite City,
MO, when he was ten. There he made his debut playing "Sweet
Georgia Brown" during a Ferlin Husky performance. He was
tossed out of high school at age 16 for refusing to shave and then
began performing regularly with Husky until he was discovered
by Little Jimmy Dickens during a performance in St. Louis. Dickens was impressed and gave Carllile the nickname "Thumbs," a
moniker Carllile never really liked.
   From 1949 to 1952, Thumbs played with Dickens' Country
Boys. In 1952, he began a two-year stint in the Army's Special Services. He was stationed in Stuttgart, Germany, when he met and
married singer-songwriter Virginia Boyle in 1955. After his discharge, Carllile played with Bill Wimberley's Rhythm Boys and
Red Foley's Troupe. As a soloist, he regularly appeared on the
Ozark Jubilee. He met guitar great Les Paul, who was impressed
by both Boyle's writing and Carllile's skill and took them to his
home recording studio to lay down enough tracks for two albums.
Later that year, Carllile sang a duet with Ginny O'Boyle, "Indian
Girl, Indian Boy." Two years later he joined the Wade Ray Five and
Ray's Las Vegas band. Carllile joined Roger Miller in 1964; later,
Miller helped Carllile sign with Smash Records, where he
released two albums, *Roger Miller Presents Thumbs Carllile* and

All Thumbs, in 1965. During 1966, he released several singles, including "Let It Be Me," "Caravan," "Blue Skies," and "Hold It." In 1968, he made the album *Walking in Guitar Land*. Although no singles were released from it, three songs, "It's a Good Day," "Work Song," and "High Noon," found favor with the public.

In 1986, Carllile, whose daughter Virginia had a minor hit with "Stay Until the Rain Stops" in 1980, underwent surgery for colon cancer. After recovering, he began playing on *Sagebrush Boogie* in Atlanta. In 1987, Carllile was preparing to perform as the opening act for Michael Hedges when he suffered a massive coronary and died. — *Sandra Brennan*

- **Roger Miller Presents Thumbs Carllile** / 1965 / Smash ✦✦✦✦
- **All Thumbs** / 1965 / Smash ✦✦✦
- **Walking in Guitar Land** / 1968 / Capitol ✦✦✦

Paulette Carlson

b. Oct. 11, 1953, Northfield, MN
Guitar, Vocals / Contemporary Country

Singer-songwriter/guitarist Paulette Carlson was best known as a vocalist with the group Highway 101. Born and raised in rural Minnesota, she learned the guitar during her teens and grew up listening to her father's country music. After graduation, Carlson worked in several Minnesota country bands, winning a large local following. Soon, she headed for Nashville, where she made a name for herself as a staff writer with the Oak Ridge Boys' Silverline/Goldmine music publishing companies. Both Gail Davies and Tammy Wynette, among others, recorded her songs. After a few years of successful songwriting, Carlson signed a recording contract in the early 1980s. Although her first singles—"You Gotta Get to My Heart (Before You Lay a Hand on Me)," "I'd Say Yes," and "Can You Fool"—won critical acclaim and some chart success in 1983, they were only minor hits, and the disappointed Carlson went back to Minnesota in 1985, joining the newly formed Highway 101 the next year. She and the band went on to score numerous No. 1 singles and a gold album before Carlson left in 1991 to again promote her solo career. Her first album, 1992's *Love Goes On*, contained the Top 20 hit, "I'll Start with You." — *Sandra Brennan*

- **Love Goes On** / Nov. 11, 1991 / Capitol ✦✦✦
Her best songs continue the feisty, I'm-not-gonna-take-it-anymore attitude she flashed so well in Highway 101. But the collection suffers from overly slick production and a handful of weak songs. — *Michael McCall*

Mary-Chapin Carpenter

b. Feb. 21, 1958, Princeton, NJ
Guitar, Vocals / Contemporary Country, Singer-Songwriter, Country-Folk

Mary-Chapin Carpenter was part of the small movement of folk-influenced, country singer-songwriters of the late '80s. Although many of these performers never achieved commercial success, Carpenter was able to channel her anti-Nashville approach into chart success and industry awards by the early '90s.

Carpenter was born and raised in Princeton, NJ, the daughter of a *Life* magazine executive; she spent two years of her childhood in Japan, when her father was launching the Asian edition of *Life*. During the folk explosion of the early '60s, her mother had begun to play guitar. When Mary-Chapin became interested in music as a child, her mother gave her child her guitar. Carpenter played music during her high school years, but she didn't actively pursue it as a career. In 1974, her family moved to Washington D.C., where she became involved in the city's folk music scene. After graduating from high school in the mid-'70s, she spent a year traveling Europe; when she was finished, she enrolled at Brown University, where she was an American civilization major.

Following her college graduation, she became deeply involved in the Washington-area folk scene, performing a mixture of originals, contemporary singer-songwriter material, and pop covers. Carpenter met guitarist John Jennings during the early '80s and the pair began performing together. Eventually, the duo made a demo tape of their songs, which they sold at their concerts. The tape wound up at Columbia Records, which offered Carpenter an audition. By early 1987, the label had signed her as a recording artist. Her first album, *Hometown Girl*, was released that year.

Hometown Girl and its follow-up—*State of the Heart* (1989)—earned her a dedicated cult following, as well as two Top Ten singles, "Never Had It So Good" and "Quittin' Time." Country radio was hesitant to play her soft, folky, feminist material, but she received good reviews and airplay on more progressive country stations, as well as college radio. *Shooting Straight in the Dark*, released in 1990, managed to break down a lot of the barriers that stood in her way. "Down at the Twist and Shout" became a No. 2 single and the album sold well, setting the stage for her breakthrough album, 1992's *Come on Come On*.

Come on Come On signaled a slight change in direction for Carpenter—although there were still folk songs, she felt freer to loosen up on honky tonk and country-rock songs, which resulted in several hit singles. Two of the singles from the album—"I Feel Lucky" and "Passionate Kisses"—hit No. 4, and "He Thinks He'll Keep Her" became her first No. 1. *Come on Come On* would eventually sell over two million copies. *Stones in the Road*, her fifth album released in 1994, concentrated on the folkier material, but it was still a major success, selling over a million copies within the first six months of release. — *Stephen Thomas Erlewine*

Hometown Girl / Feb. 1987 / Columbia ✦✦✦
Her 1987 debut album contains the title cut, "Heroes and Heroines," "A Lot Like Me," "Other Streets and Other Towns," and more—mostly originals, with her fabulous voice being the reason you just gotta have this. — *Ladyslipper*

State of the Heart / 1989 / Columbia ✦✦✦
Carpenter, a folkie, eventually turned to the country market, especially on her third album, *Shooting Straight in the Dark*. On this, her second album, she's still in transition, which makes her more thoughtful than the average country singer and catchier than the average folkie, especially on her breakthrough country hit, "Never Had It So Good." Also includes "Quittin' Time," "Something of a Dreamer," and "How Do." — *William Ruhlmann*

Shooting Straight in the Dark / 1990 / Columbia ✦✦✦✦
Carpenter's third album expanded on the promise of her breakthrough, with the Searchers-style pop of "Going out Tonight" and a guest spot from Beausoleil on the Cajun-rooted "Down at the Twist and Shout." It also held some of her most penetrating, introspective songs, with payoff lines that would impress Elvis Costello. The album contains the singles "You Win Again" and "Right Now." — *Brian Mansfield*

- **Come on Come On** / 1992 / Columbia ✦✦✦✦
The ultra-serious *Shooting Straight in the Dark* left Carpenter in need of a breather, which she took by covering Dire Straits' "The Bug" and Lucinda Williams' "Passionate Kisses." On "I Feel Lucky," she won the lottery and flirted with Dwight Yoakam and Lyle Lovett in a bar. It's tough to say which she enjoyed more. The line about winning the lottery might have been prescience on Carpenter's part—*Come on Come On* sold more than two million copies and generated six hit singles, including "Not Too Much to Ask" with Joe Diffie, "The Hard Way," and the Geritol-inspired "He Thinks He'll Keep Her," her first No. 1. — *Brian Mansfield*

Stones in the Road / 1994 / Columbia ✦✦✦✦
With *Stones in the Road*, Mary Chapin Carpenter stripped her sound down and returned to the core of her music—namely, her singer-songwriter roots. Although the lyrics are among her best, Carpenter unfortunately cut back the number of hooks and melodies in her songs. Previously, she found a nice balance between the two, but here, she concentrates on the lyrics to the detriment of the actual songs. The sound of *Stones in the Road* is pleasant, but there aren't any songs that stick in your head after the record is finished. — *Thom Owens*

Place in the World / Oct. 22, 1996 / Columbia ✦✦✦
Mary-Chapin Carpenter's breakthrough to stardom occurred with *Stones in the Road*, one of her most introspective collections. In order to consolidate that success with her follow-up, *Place in the World*, Carpenter returned to the looser sounds of *Come on Come*

On, turning in a collection of songs that still touches on reflective folk, but also catchy county-rock. On the whole, *Place in the World* doesn't offer the deeper rewards of *Stones in the Road*, nor is it quite as kinetic as *Come on Come On*. Still, the record is well-crafted and boasts several excellent songs, making it a worthwhile purchase. —*Thom Owens*

Carpetbaggers

Alternative Country-Rock, Alternative Country, Americana
An alternative country trio from, of all places, the affluent Minneapolis suburb of Edina, the Carpetbaggers were formed in 1991 by guitarists Mike Crabtree and John Magnuson, along with upright bassist Rich Copley. Two well-received independent label releases, 1992's *Country Miles Apart* and 1993's *Nowhere to Go but Down*, helped earn the Carpetbaggers a series of high-profile gigs opening for Son Volt. In 1995, the group issued *Sin Now . . . Pray Later*. —*Jason Ankeny*

Country Miles Apart / Sep. 29, 1992 / Twin/Tone ✦✦✦
● **Nowhere to Go but Down** / 1993 / Clean ✦✦✦✦

Fiddlin' John Carson

b. Mar. 23, 1868, Fannin County, GA, d. Dec. 11, 1949, Atlanta, GA
Fiddle / Old-Time
Fiddlin' John Carson was already 55 when in 1923 the Okeh label released "Little Old Log Cabin in the Lane"/"The Old Hen Cackled"—the first recording by a strictly country artist and arguably the beginning of the country music recording industry. Carson was born in the Blue Ridge Mountains of Georgia in 1868, and worked in cotton mills for over 20 years until his fiddling talents won several contests. He began performing on minstrel shows, and came to be quite popular around the Georgia area. So much so that Atlanta furniture salesman Polk Brockman recommended Carson's name to Okeh field-recorder Ralph Peer. Though Peer agreed to record the fiddler, he was disgusted with the results and sent only a few copies to the furniture store—then the only outlet for records. Brockman sold out of several pressings, convincing Peer that there was a market for hillbilly recordings.

Carson was brought to New York late in 1923 to begin recording the first of his over 150 sides for the label. The following year, Carson updated his old-timey sound by recording with a string band called the Virginia Reelers. He also recorded as a comedy duo with his daughter, Rosa Lee (known as Moonshine Kate). Carson's fortunes declined during the Depression, however; his final recordings were for Victor Bluebird in 1934. He later worked as an elevator operator at the Georgia State Capitol, a job he received from governor Eugene Talmadge in return for the popular musician's campaign help. Rounder has released a compilation of the fiddler's recordings with the Virginia Reelers and Moonshine Kate. —*John Bush*

The Old Hen Cackled / 1976 / Rounder ✦✦✦✦

A Fiddlers Convention in Mountain City, Tennessee / County ✦✦✦

Jeff Carson

Vocals / Contemporary Country
Jeff Carson was one of the new country singers that was able to parlay the mass success of country music in the early '90s to a massive hit with his eponymous first album.

Carson was born in Tulsa, OK, but was raised in a small Arkansan town called Gravette. As a child, he sang in church and played harmonica and guitar. While he was in high school, he and his friends formed a band to play their school's talent show, performing the Eagles' "Seven Bridges Road." After the ad-hoc group won second place, Carson decided to pursue a musical career. Following his high school graduation, he entered a talent concert at an entertainment complex called Ozark Mountain Music in Rogers, AR. Although he didn't come in first, the winner asked Carson to play in his house band. For the next four years, he played with the outfit, until they finally disbanded.

Carson moved to Branson, MO, where he played bass in local bands and started writing his own songs. In Branson, he met and

married his wife, Kim Cooper, who encouraged him to move to Nashville. Kim had a friend that played at the Opryland Hotel, and since his group Texana needed a bassist, Carson moved to the Music City in 1989. After some persuasion, he convinced the hotel to book him as a solo act. Around the same time, he signed a songwriting deal with Little Big Town Music and he began singing on demo tapes for a variety of companies. Eventually, publisher/producer Chuck Howard heard Carson's original material and signed a publishing and development deal with him. By 1994, Carson had signed with Curb Records.

Jeff Carson's self-titled debut album was released in early 1995. The first single, "Yeah Buddy," went nowhere, but the second single "Not on Your Love," rocketed to No.1. It was followed by the Top Ten hit, "The Car." —*Stephen Thomas Erlewine*

Jeff Carson / 1995 / MCA/Curb ✦✦✦

Martha Carson (Irene Ambergay)

b. Mar. 19, 1921, Neon, KY
Vocals / Traditional Country, Nashville Sound/Countrypolitan, Country Gospel, Country Boogie
During the 1950s, Martha Carson's rock 'n' roll-flavored gospel tunes had a great influence on her country peers, most notably Elvis Presley. She was also one of the first country artists to seek and find popularity on the pop charts. Most of her early career was spent as one half of the popular Barn Dance Sweethearts.

She was born Irene Amburgey in Neon, KY. With her partner and husband, mandolin player James Carson, she played as the Barn Dance Sweethearts during the '40s. By the time of their divorce in 1950, Martha began pursuing her solo career at WNOX Knoxville. Unfortunately she couldn't record because the Barn Dance Sweethearts' label, Capitol, had them contracted through 1957 and refused to let her go solo. Instead they kept trying to pair her up with other male singers. So she began doing session work and appeared on Bill Carlisle's "Too Old to Cut the Mustard." Things changed after she met Fred Rose in Nashville. He helped convince Capitol to let her record alone and in 1951 made her solo single debut, "Satisfied," a gospel song she had written in response to audience disapproval over her divorce. The song featured backup by Carlisle, Chet Atkins, and her sister, Jean Chapel, and became her biggest hit. By 1954 she had recorded over 24 songs, become a member of the Grand Ole Opry, and done extensive tours with such stars as Jimmy Dickens, Ferlin Huskey, and rising star Elvis Presley. After their performances, she and Presley would sing gospel duets, and later he claimed that she had more influence on his stage style than anyone else.

Around 1954, Carson married Xavier Cosse, a pop promoter who had tried to learn more about the burgeoning phenomenon of country and gospel music by working with Hank Williams and Chet Atkins in Nashville. Carson was exactly what he was looking for so he contacted RCA producer Steve Sholes, who signed her to RCA and whisked her off to Hollywood for a recording session. By 1955, Carson was living and recording all her work in New York. She had a series of minor hits that included "Journey to the Sky," "This Ole House," and "Saints and Chariot," a combination of two old favorites. Elvis later began performing this song at his own concerts. After signing with the William Morris agency in 1957, Carson and Cosse became full-time residents of New York. Another turning point in her career happened when she appeared on *The Steve Allen Show* and gained national exposure. Afterward she moved away from gospel-oriented music toward pure pop music. It was a successful move for a time, but by the late '50s her star began to wane and she returned to the Nashville sound. She continued periodically recording on labels such as Decca, Cadence, and Sims, but had no more chart success. By the 1990s she was living in semi-retirement. —*Sandra Brennan*

Journey to the Sky / 1955 / RCA ✦✦✦
Rock-A My Soul / 1957 / RCA ✦✦✦✦
Satisfied / 1960 / Capitol ✦✦✦
Talk with the Lord / 1962 / Capitol ✦✦✦✦
Martha Carson / 1963 / Sims ✦✦✦
● **Martha Carson's Greatest Gospel Hits** / Starday ✦✦✦✦

The Carter Family

The Carter Family

Fiddle, Guitar, Autoharp, Vocals / Old-Time, Traditional Country, America, Appalachia

The most influential group in country music history, the Carter Family switched the emphasis from hillbilly instrumentals to vocals, made scores of their songs part of the standard country music canon, and made a style of guitar-playing, "Carter-picking," the dominant technique for decades. Along with Jimmie Rodgers, the Carter Family were one of the first country music stars. Comprised of a gaunt, shy gospel quartet member named Alvin P. Carter and two reserved country girls—his wife Sara and their sister-in-law Maybelle—the Carter Family sang a pure, simple harmony that influenced not only the numerous other family groups of the '30s and the '40s, but folk, bluegrass, and rock musicians like Woody Guthrie, Bill Monroe, the Kingston Trio, Doc Watson, Bob Dylan and Emmylou Harris, to mention just a few. It's unlikely that bluegrass music would have existed without the Carter Family. A.P., the family patriarch, collected hundreds of British/Appalachian folk songs and, in arranging these for recording, both enhanced the pure beauty of these "facts-of-life tunes" and at the same time saved them for future generations. Those hundreds of songs the trio found around their Virginia and Tennessee homes, after being sung by A.P., Sara, and Maybelle, became *Carter* songs, even though these were folk songs and in the public domain. Among the more than 300 sides they recorded are "Worried Man Blues," "Wabash Cannonball," "Will the Circle Be Unbroken," "Wildwood Flower," and "Keep on the Sunny Side." The Carter Family's instrumental backup, like their vocals, was unique. On her Gibson L-5 guitar, Maybelle played a bass-strings lead (the guitar being tuned down from the standard pitch) that is the mainstay of bluegrass guitarists to the present. Sara accompanied her on the autoharp or on a second guitar, while A.P. devoted his talent to singing a haunting though idiosyncratic bass or baritone. Although the original Carter Family disbanded in 1943, enough of their recordings remained in the vaults to keep the group current through the '40s. Furthermore, their influence was evident through further generations of musicians, in all forms of popular music, until the end of the century.

Initially, the Carter Family consisted of just A.P. and Sara. Born and raised in the Clinch Mountains of Virginia, A.P. (b. Alvin Pleasant Delaney Carter, April 15, 1891; d. November 7, 1960)

learned to play fiddle as a child, with his mother teaching him several traditional and old-time songs; his father had played violin as a young man, but abandoned the instrument once he married. Once he became an adult, he began singing with two uncles and his older sister in a gospel quartet, but he became restless and soon moved to Indiana, where he worked on the railroad. By 1911, he had returned to Virginia, where he sold fruit trees and wrote songs in his spare time. While he was traveling and selling trees, he met Sara (b. Sara Dougherty, July 21, 1898; d. January 8, 1979). According to legend, she was on her porch playing the autoharp and singing "Engine 143" when he met her. Like A.P., Sara learned how to sing and play through her family. As a child, she learned a variety of instruments, including autoharp, guitar, and banjo, and she played with her friends and cousins. A.P. and Sara fell in love and married on June 18, 1915, settling in Maces Springs, where he worked various jobs while the two of them sang at local parties, socials, and gatherings. For the next 11 years, they played locally. During that time, the duo auditioned for Brunswick Records, but the label was only willing to sign A.P. and only if he recorded fiddle dance songs under the name Fiddlin' Doc; he rejected their offer, believing that it was against his parents' religious beliefs. Eventually, Maybelle Carter (b. Maybelle Addington, May 10, 1909; d. October 23, 1978)—who had married A.P.'s brother Ezra—began singing and playing guitar with Sara and A.P. Following Maybelle's addition to the Carter Family in 1926, the group began auditioning at labels in earnest. In 1927, the group auditioned for Ralph Peer, a New York-based A&R man for Victor Records who was scouting for local talent in Bristol, TN. The Carters recorded six tracks, including "The Wandering Boy" and "Single Girl, Married Girl." Victor released several of the songs as singles, and when the records sold well, the label offered the group a long-range contract.

The Carter Family signed with Victor in 1928 and over the next seven years, the group recorded most of their most famous songs, including "Wabash Cannonball," "I'm Thinking Tonight of My Blue Eyes," "John Hardy Was a Desperate Little Man," "Wildwood Flower," and "Keep on the Sunny Side," which became their signature song. By the end of the '20s, the group had become a well-known national act, but their income was hurt considerably by the Great Depression. Because of the financial crisis, the Carters were unable to play concerts in cities across the US and were stuck playing schoolhouses in Virginia. Eventually, all of the members became so strapped for cash they had to move away from home to find work. In 1929, A.P. moved to Detroit temporarily while Maybelle and her husband relocated to Washington, DC. In addition to the stress of the Great Depression, A.P. and Sara's marriage began to fray, and the couple separated in 1932. For the next few years, the Carters only saw each other at recording sessions, partially because the Depression had cut into the country audience and partially because the women were raising their families. In 1935, the group left Victor for ARC, where they re-recorded their most famous songs. The following year, they signed with Decca. Eventually, the group signed a lucrative radio contract with XERF in Del Rio, TX, which led to contracts at a few other stations along the Mexican and Texas border. Since these stations could broadcast at ranges that far exceeded other American radio stations because of their location, the Carters' radio performances could be heard throughout the nation, either in their live form or as radio transcription. As a result, the band's popularity increased dramatically, and their Decca records became extremely popular.

Just as their career was back in full swing, Sara and A.P.'s marriage fell apart, with the couple divorcing in 1939. Nevertheless, the group continued to perform, remaining in Texas until 1941, when they moved to a radio station in Charlotte, NC. During the early '40s, the band briefly recorded for Columbia before they re-signed with Victor in 1941. Two years later, Sara decided to retire and move out to California with her new husband, Coy Bayes (who was A.P.'s cousin), while A.P. moved back to Virginia, where he ran a country store. Maybelle Carter began recording and touring with her daughters Helen, June, and Anita.

A.P. and Sara re-formed the Carter Family with their grown children in 1952, performing a concert in Maces Spring. Following the successful concert, the Kentucky-based Acme signed A.P., Sara, and their daughter Janette to contract, and over the next four years, they recorded nearly 100 songs that didn't gain much attention at the time. In 1956, the Carter Family disbanded for the second time. Four years later, A.P. died at his Maces Spring home. Following his death, the Carter Family's original recordings began to be reissued. In 1966, Maybelle persuaded Sara to reunite to play a number of folk festivals and record an album for Columbia. The Carter Family became the first group to be inducted into the Country Music Hall of Fame in 1970, which is a fitting tribute to their immense influence and legacy. —*David Vinopal*

☆ **'Mid the Green Fields of Virginia** / 1963 / RCA ✦✦✦✦✦
The Carter Family was the most important group in early country music, and this 16-track album selects some of their most notable initial recordings from the late 1920s and early 30s, among them "My Clinch Mountain Home" and their theme song "Keep on the Sunny Side." —*William Ruhlmann*

Diamonds in the Rough / 1990 / Copper Creek ✦✦✦
Subtitled *Heart Songs, Hymns & Ballads as Featured on Border Radio in 1941*, this radio transcription reissue of the Carter Family's appearances on the legendary Del Rio border radio stations in 1938 is a fine representation of their repertoire of songs about home, hearth, and heartbreak. —*Mark A. Humphrey*

★ **Country Music Hall of Fame** / 1991 / MCA ✦✦✦✦✦
After ending an eight-year association with Victor Records, the Carter Family recorded 60 sides for Decca between 1936 and 1938; 15 of those recordings are collected here. Decca wanted to emphasize new material; this posed no problem for A. P. Carter, who was long accustomed to taking copyright credit for minor rewrites of other people's songs. The Decca songs are less familiar than the recordings for Victor or, later, Okeh, but they're worth hearing. —*Brian Mansfield*

★ **Anchored in Love—Their Complete Victor, 1927** / 1993 / Rounder ✦✦✦✦✦
No American label (except perhaps Arhoolie) deserves a shot at reissuing the treasured Carter Family recordings more than Rounder. The Carter Family's sessions are seminal country music, raw and wonderfully unsophisticated with an emotional directness and honesty that makes a mockery of the slick, overproduced rock/folk now being marketed as country. Charles Wolfe's notes are an ideal combination of insight, historical overview, and musical examination. These are only the first 16 songs in the series, but they get things off to a rousing start. The menu is a sensational mix of originals, mountain and folk tunes, and old-timey hymns. —*Ron Wynn*

☆ **My Clinch Mountain Home—Their Complete Victor Recordings, 1928-1929** / 1993 / Rounder ✦✦✦✦✦
The second volume in the Carter Family reissue series brings things forward to 1928 and 1929. The 16 selections provide family views of their life, home, and background and include a rare topical number, "The Cyclone of Rye Cove," plus prophetic tunes like "The Grave on the Green Hillside" and the reflective selections "The Homestead on the Farm" and the title cut. Rounder plans nine volumes in the line; the first two only make you eager for more. —*Ron Wynn*

☆ **When the Roses Bloom in Dixieland—Their Complete Recordings, Vol. 3** / Oct. 31, 1995 / Rounder ✦✦✦✦✦
The third volume in Rounder's projected eight-disc series of the Carter Family's 1927-1941 recordings for RCA Victor picks up in Atlanta in November 1929, where the family records ten tracks, including "Motherless Children," "Wabash Cannonball," and "Jimmy Brown the Newsboy," among other country classics, then travels to Memphis for six tracks from the Carters' fifth recording session in May 1930. —*William Ruhlmann*

☆ **Worried Man Blues—Their Complete Recordings, Vol. 4 (1930)** / Oct. 31, 1995 / Rounder ✦✦✦✦✦
The fourth volume in Rounder's projected eight-disc series of the Carter Family's 1927-1941 recordings for RCA Victor picks up in Memphis in May 1930 and continues in the same city in November for 16 sides, including the title track and "Lonesome Valley." There are an unusually large number of three-part harmony

vocals in this set, much of which is given over to gospel songs. The only complaints about this brilliant chronological series are that it could be accomplished faster: This disc runs less than 48 minutes, and Rounder seems to be doling out the albums at a rate of two every two years, which means that it could take until the end of 1999 to hear them all. —*William Ruhlmann*

Sunshine in the Shadows: Their Complete Victor Recordings, 1931-32 / 1996 / Rounder ✦✦✦✦
Sixteen tracks from 1931 and 1932, originally recorded for Victor, most penned by A.P. Carter. It displays the Carters' usual unadorned consistency, moving harmonies, and accomplished picking; "Picture on the Wall," "Where We'll Never Grow Old," and "Lonesome for You" are just some of the more striking examples of their skill with material that is both humble and mournfully evocative. Of special interest are a few songs (and a couple corny sketches) on which the clan is joined by Jimmie Rodgers, the most influential country act of the day bar the Carters themselves. —*Richie Unterberger*

Give Me Roses While I Live: Their Complete Recordings, Vol. 6 / Feb. 11, 1997 / Rounder ✦✦✦
Give Me Roses While I Live picks up where *Sunshine in the Shadows* left off, compiling several tracks from the Carter Family's classic early '30s recordings for Victor. This disc features 16 songs the group cut over the course of 1933. —*Thom Owens*

Clinch Mountain Treasures / County ✦✦✦✦
As the title suggests, the songs are treasures, but they're not among the seminal group's best-known songs. Recorded for Okeh Records in Chicago in 1940, it captures the group's instrumentation and vocals at their most incisive. —*Michael McCall*

Early Classics / ACM ✦✦✦✦
Early Classics is a fine collection of highlights from the Carter Family's earliest recordings. Though there are a couple of ringers on the compilation, most of the music here is very fine indeed, and the album functions as an excellent sampler for listeners that don't want to invest in Rounder's comprehensive, multi-disc retrospective series. Completists and purists, however, are recommended to begin with the Rounder set. —*Stephen Thomas Erlewine*

Anita Carter

b. Mar. 31, 1933, Maces Springs, VA
Vocals / Old-Time, Traditional Country
A member of country music's most famous family, Anita Carter found success of her own as a folk solo act during the early '50s and late '60s. The Carter Family had ruled country music during the 1930s, but broke up in 1943 after patriarch A.P. Carter and his ex-wife Sara decided to retire. Sara's cousin Maybelle, the third member of the Carters, re-formed the group the same year—as Mother Maybelle and the Carter Sisters—with her daughters Helen, June, and Anita. The sisters had sung on Carter Family radio broadcasts in 1935, and the new group more than made up for the breakup of the originals. The Carters performed on radio from Virginia, Tennessee, and Missouri during the late '40s, but moved to the Grand Ole Opry in 1950.

In 1951, Anita stormed the charts with a one-off duet with Hank Snow; both "Bluebird Island" and its B-side "Down the Trail of Achin' Hearts" reached the country Top Five. During the mid-'50s, she also performed with the teen trio 'Nita, Rita & Ruby, but spent most of her time with the Carters. The group continued to be popular on the Opry and even opened for Elvis Presley in 1956-57. After A.P. Carter's death in 1960, Mother Maybelle and the Carter Sisters became the Carter Family and performed more contemporary country than gospel.

In 1961, the Carters began a long-running association with Johnny Cash by appearing on his roadshow. They recorded the country Top 15 single "Busted" with Cash in 1963, and after June Carter married him in 1967, the Carters appeared on his ABC-TV show from 1969 to 1971. Though the Carter Family continued to record—usually with Johnny Cash—during the early '70s, they disbanded in 1969. Mother Maybelle became recognized as a major figure in the folk revival that year, appearing with Sara at the

Newport Folk Festival and on the Rounder album, *An Historic Reunion.*

Meanwhile, Anita had begun to record for RCA in 1966, hitting the country charts with "I'm Gonna Leave You." Another single charted in 1967, and her duet with Waylon Jennings on "I Got You" reached No. 4 in March 1968. Later in 1968, Anita moved to United Artists, but several singles proved unsuccessful. She recorded for Capitol in the early '70s and almost hit the Top 40 with "Tulsa County." Her last chart appearance with the Carter Family, "Praise the Lord and Pass the Soup," was released in August 1973. —*John Bush*

Folk Songs Old and New / 1963 / Mercury ✦✦✦✦
● Ring of Fire / Bear Family ✦✦✦✦

Carlene Carter

b. Sep. 26, 1955, Nashville, TN
Guitar, Vocals / Contemporary Country, Roots-Rock, New Wave, Neo-Traditionalist Country

Carlene Carter has always straddled the line between country and rock. Beginning her career as a rock singer in the mid-'70s, she became immersed in the new wave in the late '70s, before emerging as a new country singer in the late '80s, Throughout it all, her music has always infused roots music—whether it's country or rock 'n' roll—with a nervy, edgy energy.

Carlene is the daughter of June Carter and Carl Smith, who divorced when their daughter was just two. June would frequently take her daughter on the Carter Family tours, which meant that Carlene developed a musical interest at an early age. When she was 12, her mother married Johnny Cash. Following the marriage, Carlene and her stepsister Rosanne Cash became backup singers in the Carter/Cash touring show.

At the age of 15 she married Joe Simpkins and had a child; they were divorced within a few years. Carter enrolled in college as a piano major in her late teens, but she never graduated. At 19, she married Jack Routh and had another child; they were divorced within two years.

In 1978, she decided to pursue a musical career, and headed to Los Angeles, where she received a record contract with Warner Bros. Her debut album, *Carlene Carter*, was a rock 'n' roll record recorded in London with Graham Parker's backing band, the Rumour. The following year, she released her second album, *Two Sides to Every Woman*, which featured support from the Doobie Brothers. That same year she married singer-songwriter/producer Nick Lowe, who was currently the co-leader of the new wave rock 'n' roll revival band, Rockpile. Lowe helped Carter shape her musical direction in the early '80s, and her third album—the new wave-inflected country-rock record *Musical Shapes* (1980)—showed the influence of Lowe, Rockpile, and Dave Edmunds. Although the album was critically acclaimed, it was a commercial failure. She followed *Musical Shapes* in 1981 with *Blue Nun*, which continued to pursue a new-wave country direction; like its predecessor, it was ignored.

During the early '80s, Carter was shut off from the country community because she was living in England with Lowe. After *Blue Nun*, she stopped recording, choosing to perform solo shows instead; she also had a starring role in the theatrical production *Pump Boys and Dinettes.* Carter and Lowe's marriage collapsed in the mid-'80s and she returned to the States, where she became part of the touring Carter Family.

In 1989, she began working on a comeback record with Howie Epstein, the bassist for Tom Petty & the Heartbreakers. That same year, she dueted with Southern Comfort on the Top 40 hit, "Time's Up." Reprise signed Carter in 1990 and she released her overdue fifth album, *I Fell in Love*, later that year. *I Fell in Love* still had rock influences, but it was a more straightforward country record than her previous albums, and country radio paid attention. The album became a hit and two singles, "I Fell in Love" and "Come on Back," climbed all the way to No. 3. *Little Love Letters*, her 1993 follow-up (which was released on Giant Records), was equally successful; its first single, "Every Little Thing," was another No. 3 hit. *Little Acts of Treason*, her 1995 album, wasn't as big a hit as its two predecessors, but it still enjoyed moderate

success on the country charts. A hits collection, *Hindsight 20/20*, appeared in the fall of 1996. —*Stephen Thomas Erlewine*

Carlene Carter / 1978 / Warner Brothers ✦✦✦
This album was released in the middle of the new wave movement and is interesting, in part, because of the meeting of the artist with the country music background and new wavers Graham Parker and the Rumour. Somewhat uneven but still worth owning. —*Jim Worbois*

Two Sides to Every Woman / 1979 / Warner Brothers ✦✦✦
This is Carter's second album and not as interesting as the first. Some of the songs are a bit weak and the Rumour have been replaced with studio musicians. It's okay, but not for everyone. —*Jim Worbois*

Musical Shapes / 1980 / F Beat ✦✦✦✦
This is Carter's masterpiece to date. Great songs and production that could easily fit into today's climate of country radio. —*Cub Koda*

Blue Nun / 1981 / F Beat ✦✦✦
Carter's American label passed on this one, and it's too bad. While it's not one of her best albums, when she's on, she's dead on. It's interesting from a historical point because it somewhat chronicles her musical associations with former-husband Nick Lowe and Paul Carrack (ex-Ace, Squeeze, Mike + the Mechanics). —*Jim Worbois*

C'est C Bon / 1983 / Razor & Tie ✦✦
This not particularly interesting album suffers from lack of direction. It was the last album of her early period, before she re-created herself in 1990 as a country singer to be reckoned with. For diehard fans only. —*Jim Worbois*

I Fell in Love / 1990 / Reprise ✦✦✦✦
This comeback album has a perfect mix of old (A.P. Carter's "My Dixie Darlin'") and new (guest spots from Dave Edmunds, David Lindley, and Albert Lee). If Carter hasn't come to terms with her love for rock and her duty to heritage, she's at least learned to balance them. —*Brian Mansfield*

Musical Shapes/Blue Nun / 1992 / Demon ✦✦✦✦
Demon Records reissued Carlene Carter's *Musical Shapes* and *Blue Nun* on one disc in 1992. Neither album is straight country—with their propulsive rhythms and jangling guitars, they exhibit the influence of her then-current husband Nick Lowe—but *Musical Shapes* is one of her best records, and worth getting in any form. —*Stephen Thomas Erlewine*

Little Love Letters / 1993 / Giant ✦✦✦✦
This is the album fans always dreamed she would make. While it shows off her love of, and ability to handle, various styles of music, she never loses her direction. —*Jim Worbois*

Little Acts of Treason / Oct. 1995 / Giant ✦✦✦
Carlene Carter's *Little Acts of Treason* doesn't break much new ground for the singer, but that's not necessarily a bad thing. While she continues in the same vein as *Little Love Letters*, the music is done well, even if the album isn't as infectious and catchy as her previous album. —*Stephen Thomas Erlewine*

★ Hindsight 20/20 / Sep. 9, 1996 / Warner Brothers ✦✦✦✦✦
Hindsight 20/20 is a comprehensive overview of Carlene Carter's career, concentrating on country hits like "Every Little Thing" and "I Fell in Love," but also touching on her earlier recordings like "Never Together but Close Sometimes." The compilation offers an excellent introduction and encapsulation of one of the finest female country singers of the '80s and '90s. —*Stephen Thomas Erlewine*

Deana Carter

b. 1964
Vocals / Contemporary Country, Singer-Songwriter, Country-Folk
Though she didn't begin her musical career until relatively late, Deana Carter managed to defy conventional expectations and unexpectedly shot to the top of the country charts upon the release of her 1996 debut, *Did I Shave My Legs for This?* Carter's success was equally unexpected considering how she didn't quite fit into the mold of a standard female contemporary country

singer. Melding the popular appeal of country chanteuses with folky singer-songwriters like Mary Chapin-Carpenter, Carter racked up both positive reviews and healthy sales with *Did I Shave My Legs for This?*, becoming one of the most pleasant success stories of the post-Garth Brooks generation.

As the daughter of Nashville studio guitarist Fred Carter Jr., Deana Carter grew up in a musical environment, and was exposed to a wide variety of music. Fred played guitar for a wide variety of musicians, including Willie Nelson, Bob Dylan, Waylon Jennings and Simon & Garfunkel. The music of those artists would eventually seep into Deana's own style, which she hadn't yet formed when she initially tried to land a record contract at the age of 17. Despite her efforts and her father's assistance, Carter wasn't able to secure a deal, so she abandoned music to study nursing at the University of Tennessee. While she was a student, she continued to sing for fun, yet she didn't devote much energy to music.

After graduation, Carter worked in a few hospitals before deciding to pursue a musical career at the age of 23. Learning the guitar for the first time, Deana also began to write songs. For several years, she worked odd jobs as she continued to develop her songwriting skills and sing at Nashville nightclubs. Eventually, one of her demo tapes made its way to Willie Nelson, while another wound up in the offices of Capitol Nashville. Nelson, who remembered her from her childhood, was impressed with Carter's songs and asked her to perform at Farm Aid VII in 1994; she was the only female artist on the entire bill. Within a year, Capitol Nashville had signed Deana Carter to a contract.

Boasting six songs co-written by Carter, her debut album *Did I Shave My Legs for This?* was released to strong reviews in late summer of 1996. By the end of the year, the record had climbed to the upper reaches of the country charts and had made inroads on the pop charts, going gold in the process. — *Stephen Thomas Erlewine*

● **Did I Shave My Legs for This?** / 1995 / EMI/Patriot ✦✦✦✦
Deana Carter's *Did I Shave My Legs for This?* is an excellent debut, full of catchy melodies and clever lyrics. While she occasionally strays into new country territory, she shines on folky country ballads, but every song on the album demonstrates she is an artist of enormous potential. — *Thom Owens*

Mother Maybelle Carter (Maybelle Addington Carter)

b. May 10, 1909, Nickelsville, VA, **d.** Oct. 23, 1978, Nashville, TN
Banjo, Guitar, Autoharp / Old-Time, Traditional Country
One-third of the original Carter Family (and the mother of June, Helen, and Anita Carter), Maybelle's guitar and autoharp playing added greatly to the distinctive Carter style. Born May 10, 1909, she joined her brother-in-law A.P. and sister-in-law Sara to form the Carter Family in the late '20s. The group continued to record until 1943, when Maybelle formed the Carter Sisters & Mother Maybelle with her three daughters. The quartet appeared on the Grand Ole Opry beginning in 1948 and joined Johnny Cash in 1961 to play on his tours. The Carters' five chart entries from 1963 to 1973 all featured Cash on vocals; only 1963's "Busted" made the Top 20. Later, Maybelle was sought out by each new musical generation and, as a result, became an integral part of the folk movement of the '60s as well as the Nitty Gritty Dirt Band's 1971 classic album *Will the Circle Be Unbroken.* — *Jim Worbois*

● **Mother Maybelle Carter** / 195 / Ambassador ✦✦✦✦
Queen of the Autoharp / 1964 / Kapp ✦✦✦
Living Legend / 1965 / Columbia ✦✦✦

Sara and Maybelle Carter

Old-Time, Traditional Country
The two female members of the original 1920s lineup of the Carter Family, Sara and Maybelle Carter recorded as a duo only once, at the 1967 Newport Folk Festival. The Carter Family had actually formed in 1915, when Sara Dougherty married A.P. Carter and, along with her sister-in-law, Maybelle (married to A.P.'s brother, Ezra), formed the Carter Family. Though Sara and A.P. divorced in 1936, they continued to record together until

1943, cutting over 250 songs. When Sara and Maybelle were reunited at the 1967 Newport Folk Festival, they released *An Historic Reunion*, their first recording together in 25 years. — *Jim Worbois*

● **Sara & Maybelle Carter** / Bear Family ✦✦✦✦
Bear Family's *Sara & Maybelle Carter* compact disc combines the duo's 1966 album *An Historic Reunion* with Maybelle's solo record, *A Living Legend*, from that same year. *An Historic Reunion* was a moving final album from the duo, divided between gospel and traditional songs. Despite the fact that Sara and Maybelle hadn't sung together in over 20 years, the two sound like they never left; their harmonies, occasionally with Sara and Joe Carter's son A.P. providing a third part, are as spine-chillingly pure as ever. *A Living Legend* isn't quite as thrilling, but there are a handful of fine songs from the record and its inclusion is a nice way to round out the disc. — *Stephen Thomas Erlewine*

Wilf Carter

b. Dec. 18, 1904, Guysboro, NS
Vocals / Traditional Country, Cowboy
Also known as Montana Slim, Wilf Carter was a Canadian cowboy who managed to make inroads in America during the late '30s, setting the stage for a long, prolific career that ran over 60 years. Throughout his career, he never departed from the style that made him famous—traditional cowboy and country music, in the vein of Gene Autry and Jimmie Rodgers. Born and raised in Guysboro, Nova Scotia, Carter became fascinated with music as a child, when he heard a traveling musician named the Yodeling Fool play a local concert. However, it took him several years before he began a musical career. In his late teens, he moved to Boston with the intention of becoming a carpenter, but soon left for Calgary, Alberta, where he became a cowboy.

Carter spent the next several years as a cowboy, before beginning a musical career in 1930, when he landed his own radio show on Calgary's CFCN. Around the same time his show started, Carter began singing on trail rides in the Rockies, which led to him being hired by C.P.R. to sing on their cruise ship, the *Empress of Britain*, on a West Indies voyage in 1933. While on cruise, Carter stopped in Montreal to make his recording debut: a two-song single for Canadian Bluebird. Within a year, he was signed by CBS to do his own show in New York. Upon accepting the offer, Carter began using the nickname "Montana Slim." Shortly after the show began, RCA Victor began releasing his records in America under the stage name; in Canada, they were still credited to his stage name.

Before World War II, Carter recorded nearly 200 songs, with nearly every track seeing an official release. During the war, his recording slowed considerably, due to rationing and health problems due to a car accident. In 1947, he began recording actively for Victor, employing a full band for the first time. Seven years later, he left the label for Decca, where he was produced by Owen Bradley. These singles, which were released on Apex in Canada, were more commercial than his previous recordings, which made Victor interested in Carter again. Since he considered Victor his home, he returned to the label.

Carter's second stint at Victor resulted in records that were primarily released in Canada, although several singles and albums did appear in the US. During the mid-'60s, Carter briefly recorded for Starday, but he essentially spent the rest of his career at Victor, releasing records well into the '80s. Carter's career was always more successful in his native Canada than in the United States, but his legacy of nearly 500 original songs was enough to have him inducted into the Nashville Songwriters Hall of Fame in 1971. Carter continued to tour into the early '90s, when he essentially retired from music. — *Stephen Thomas Erlewine*

● **The Golden Years** / 1996 / CollectorsChoice' ✦✦✦✦
The Golden Years—a collection compiled by the mail-order record catalog, Collector's Choice—contains 24 of Wilf Carter's RCA Victor tracks from the '30s and '40s, capturing the essence of the Canadian singing cowboy on one disc. Included on the set are such classic Western songs as "Goodnight Irene," "Blue Canadian Rockies," and "There's a Love Knot in My Lariat." — *Thom Owens*

A Prairie Legend / 1996 / Bear Family ✦✦✦✦
Bear Family's four-disc Wilf Carter set *A Prairie Legend* contains all of the recordings the singing cowboy made for RCA Victor between 1944 and 1949, as well as a handful of other sessions, including material he cut for Canadian Apex. Covering nearly 100 songs, the box is designed for hardcore collectors—after all, there wasn't quite enough variety in Carter's material to make it consistently compelling for anyone but dedicated listeners. Nevertheless, *A Prairie Legend* is so well-produced that any devoted fan of Carter will find the set to be a worthwhile purchase. —*Thom Owens*

Lionel Cartwright

b. Feb. 10, 1960, Gallipolis, OH
Vocals / Contemporary Country
Lionel Cartwright was a multi-talented performer and songwriter whose career took off in the late '80s. Like his peers Garth Brooks, Travis Tritt, and Alan Jackson, Cartwright favored a contemporary country/pop sound. His love of music began during childhood piano lessons; Cartwright also went on to master the guitar and eight other instruments. At age ten, he began performing at community gatherings in his hometown of Glendale, WV. While in high school, he was a regular on a country radio show in Milton, WV, also appearing on Columbus, OH's *Country Cavalcade*. After joining the *Wheeling Jamboree* in West Virginia as a pianist, he was soon promoted to performer status, and from there became the show's musical director.

Cartwright started working on the Nashville Network music and comedy series *I-40 Paradise* in 1981 and later on the show's spinoff, *Pickin' at the Paradise*. On both shows he served as performer, arranger, and musical director, also writing and performing the theme songs. While working on the show, he met Cindy Stewart, who went on to become his songwriting collaborator and wife. He also met Boudleaux and Felice Bryant, the two composers behind many of the Everly Brothers' greatest hits, who encouraged him to further develop his songwriting skills. While performing live in Knoxville, Cartwright was spotted by MCA producer Tony Brown, who was impressed but felt the young singer needed more experience before he could land a record contract.

In 1986, Cartwright went to Nashville with his best songs and had a formal audition with Brown, who signed him to MCA. In 1988, Cartwright released his debut single "You're Gonna Make Her Mine" and scored a Top 50 hit. He also released a self-titled album in 1989, which contained the aforementioned single and three other Top 20 hits, including "Give Me His Last Chance," which made it to the Top Five. His next album, *I Watched It on the Radio* (1990), contained several hits. He scored his first chart topper, "Leap of Faith," in 1991, from the album *Chasin' the Sun*. —*Sandra Brennan*

● **Lionel Cartwright** / 1989 / MCA ✦✦✦✦
Produced by Tony Brown and Steuart Smith (formerly Rodney Crowell's lead guitarist) Cartwright's debut disc is still his best. It includes the hits "Like Father, Like Son" and "Give Me His Last Chance." —*Dan Cooper*

I Watched It on the Radio / 1990 / MCA ✦✦✦
Featuring "My Heart Is Set on You," "Say It's Not True," "In the Long Run," and other hits. —*AMG*

Chasin' the Sun / 1991 / MCA ✦✦✦
Cartwright's third album features his first chart-topper, "Leap of Faith." —*Jason Ankeny*

Johnny Carver

b. Nov. 24, 1940, Jackson, MS
Vocals / Country-Pop
Johnny Carver is best known for his countrified 1973 cover of "Tie a Yellow Ribbon 'Round the Old Oak Tree." He was born in a rural area near Jackson, MS, and grew up surrounded by country music. As a youth, he sang with his family in a gospel quartet in local churches and on the radio. His first band was the Capital Cowboys, who started out playing at drive-in restaurants. A dairy and an ice cream company became their first sponsors, and soon the Capital Cowboys played everywhere the ice cream was sold. Carver hit the road in 1959 and played at clubs and county fairs all over the US and Canada. In 1965, he and his new wife moved to L.A., where Carver headed the house band at the Palomino club and made regular guest appearances on local television shows.

After Carver wrote "New Lips," which became a Top 20 hit for singer Roy Drusky, Imperial Records' Scotty Turner advised him to try his luck in Nashville. In 1967, Carver made his recording debut with a self-titled album, which contained the Top 30 hit "Your Lily White Hands" and led to a gig as an opening act for George Jones and Connie Smith. Through 1970, Carver scored a series of middle-of-the-road hits, including "I Still Didn't Have the Sense to Go" (1968) and "That's Your Hang Up" (1969). After three more Top 50 hits, he moved to ABC in late 1972 and had a Top Five smash with his version of "Tie a Yellow Ribbon 'Round the Old Oak Tree" while Tony Orlando and Dawn's version of the song was becoming a hit on the pop charts. Carver had a subsequent string of Top 40 hits, including "Don't Tell (That Sweet Old Lady of Mine)" (1974) and a country cover of the pop hit "Afternoon Delight" (1976). Following two Top 40 hits in 1977, "Living Next Door to Alice" and "Down at the Pool," Carver did not have another real hit until 1981, with a cover of the pop group ABBA's "S.O.S.," which made it to the Top 75 and was his last hit. During the early 1990s, Carver played the square and round dance circuit at Branson, MO, with his Nashville All-Star Band. —*Sandra Brennan*

● **The Best of Johnny Carver** / 1977 / ABC/Dot ✦✦✦✦

Johnny Cash

b. Feb. 26, 1932, Kingsland, AR
Guitar, Vocals / Traditional Country, Cowboy, Country-Pop, Rockabilly
Johnny Cash was one of the most imposing and influential figures in post-World War II country music. With his deep, resonant baritone and spare, percussive guitar, he had a basic, distinctive sound. Cash didn't sound like Nashville, nor did he sound like honky tonk or rock 'n' roll. He created his own subgenre, falling halfway between the blunt emotional honesty of folk, the rebelliousness of rock 'n' roll, and the world-weariness of country. Cash's career coincided with the birth of rock 'n' roll, and his rebellious attitude and simple, direct musical attack shared a lot of similarities with rock. However, there was a deep sense of history—as he would later illustrate with his series of historical albums—that kept him forever tied with country. And he was one of country music's biggest stars of the '50s and '60s, scoring well over 100 hit singles.

Johnny Cash was born and raised in Arkansas, moving to Dyess when he was three. By the time he was 12 years old, Cash had begun writing his own songs, inspired by the country songs he had heard on the radio. While he was in high school, he sang on the Arkansas radio station KLCN. Johnny Cash graduated from college in 1950, moving to Detroit to work in an auto factory for a brief while. With the outbreak of the Korean War, he enlisted in the Air Force. While he was in the Air Force, Cash bought his first guitar and taught himself to play. He began writing songs in earnest, including "Folsom Prison Blues." Cash left the Air Force in 1954, married a Texas woman named Vivian Leberto, and moved to Memphis, where he took a radio announcing course at a broadcasting school on the GI Bill. During the evenings, he played country music in a trio that also consisted of guitarist Luther Perkins and bassist Marshall Grant. The trio occasionally played for free on a local radio station, KWEM, and tried to secure gigs and an audition at Sun Records.

Cash finally landed an audition with Sun Records and its founder, Sam Phillips, in 1955. Initially, Cash presented himself as a gospel singer, but Phillips turned him down. Phillips asked him to come back with something more commercial. Cash returned with "Hey Porter," which immediately caught Phillips' ear. Soon, Cash released "Cry Cry Cry" / "Hey Porter" as his debut single for Sun. On the single, Phillips billed Cash as "Johnny," which upset the singer, because he felt it sounded too young; the record producer also dubbed Perkins and Grant the Tennessee Two. "Cry

Cry Cry" became a success upon its release in 1955, entering the country charts at No. 14 and leading to a spot on the *Louisiana Hayride*, where he stayed for nearly a year. A second single, "Folsom Prison Blues," reached the country Top Five in early 1956 and its follow-up, "I Walk the Line," was No.1 for six weeks and crossed over into the pop Top 20.

Johnny Cash had an equally successful year in 1957, scoring several Top Ten country hits. Cash also made his Grand Ole Opry debut that year, appearing all in black where the other performers were decked out in flamboyant, rhinestone-studded outfits. Eventually, he earned the nickname of "The Man in Black." Cash became the first Sun artist to release a long-playing album in November of 1957, when *Johnny Cash with His Hot and Blue Guitar* hit the stores. Cash's success continued throughout 1958, as he earned his biggest hit, "Ballad of a Teenage Queen" (No. 1 for ten weeks), as well another No. 1 single, "Guess Things Happen That Way." For most of 1958, Cash attempted to record a gospel album, but Sun refused to allow him to record one. Sun also was unwilling to increase Cash's record royalties. Both of these were deciding factors in the vocalist's decision to sign with Columbia Records in 1958. By the end of the year, he had released his first single for the label, "All Over Again," which became another Top Five success. Sun continued to release singles and albums of unissued Cash material into the '60s.

"Don't Take Your Guns to Town," Cash's second single for Columbia, was one of his biggest hits, reaching the top of the country charts and crossing over into the pop charts in the beginning of 1959. Throughout that year, Columbia and Sun singles vied for the top of the charts. Generally, the Columbia releases—"Frankie's Man Johnny," "I Got Stripes," and "Five Feet High and Rising"—fared better than the Sun singles, but "Luther Played the Boogie" did climb into the Top Ten. That same year, Cash had the chance to make his gospel record—*Hymns by Johnny Cash*—which kicked off a series of thematic albums that ran into the '70s.

The Tennessee Two became the Tennessee Three in 1960 with the addition of drummer W.S. Holland. Though he was continuing to have hits, the relentless pace of his career was beginning to take its toll on Cash. In 1959, he began taking amphetamines to help him get through his schedule of nearly 300 shows a year. By 1961, his drug intake had increased dramatically and his work was affected, which was reflected by his declining number of hit singles and albums. By 1963, he had moved to New York, leaving his family behind. He was running into trouble with the law, most notably for starting a forest fire out West.

June Carter—who was the wife of one of Cash's drinking buddies, Carl Smith—would provide Cash with his return to the top of the charts with "Ring of Fire," which she co-wrote with Merle Kilgore. "Ring of Fire" spent seven weeks on the top of the charts and was a Top 20 pop hit. Cash continued his success in 1964, as "Understand Your Man" became a No. 1 hit. However, Cash's comeback was shortlived, as he sank further into addiction and his hit singles arrived sporadically. Cash was arrested in El Paso for attempting to smuggle amphetamines into the country through his guitar case in 1965. That same year, the Grand Ole Opry refused to have him perform and he wrecked the establishment's footlights. In 1966, his wife Vivian filed for divorce. After the divorce, Cash moved to Nashville. At first, he was as destructive as he ever had been, but he became close friends with June Carter, who had divorced Carl Smith. With Carter's help, he was able to shake his addictions; she also converted Cash to fundamentalist Christianity. His career began to bounce back as "Jackson" and "Rosanna's Going Wild" became Top Three hits. Early in 1968, Cash proposed marriage to Carter during a concert; the pair were married in the spring of 1968.

In 1968, Johnny Cash recorded and released his most popular album, *Johnny Cash at Folsom Prison*. Recorded during a prison concert, the album spawned the No. 1 country hit "Folsom Prison Blues," which also crossed over into the pop charts. By the end of the year, the record had gone gold. The following year, he released a sequel, *Johnny Cash at San Quentin*, which had his only Top Ten pop single, "A Boy Named Sue," which peaked at No. 3; it also hit No. 1 on the country charts. Johnny Cash then guested on Bob

Johnny Cash

Dylan's 1969 country-rock album, *Nashville Skyline*. Dylan returned the favor by appearing on the first episode of *The Johnny Cash Show*, the singer's television program for ABC. *The Johnny Cash Show* ran for two years, between 1969 and 1971.

Johnny Cash was reaching a second peak of popularity in 1970. In addition to his television show, he performed for President Richard Nixon at the White House, acted with Kirk Douglas in *The Gunfight*, sang with John Willams and the Boston Pops Orchestra, and was the subject of a documentary film. His record sales were equally healthy, as "Sunday Morning Coming Down" and "Flesh and Blood" were No. 1 hits. Throughout 1971, Cash continued to have hits, including the Top Three "Man in Black." Both Cash and Carter became more socially active in the early '70s, campaigning for the civic rights of Native Americans and prisoners, as well as working frequently with Billy Graham.

In the mid-'70s, Cash's presence on the country charts began to decline, but he continued to have a series of minor hits and the occasional chart topper like 1976's "One Piece at a Time," or Top Ten hits like the Waylon Jennings duet "There Ain't No Good Chain Gang" and "(Ghost) Riders in the Sky." *Man in Black*, Johnny Cash's autobiography, was published in 1975. In 1980, Johnny Cash became the youngest inductee to the Country Music Hall of Fame. However, the '80s were a rough time for Cash, as his record sales continued to decline and he ran into trouble with Columbia. Cash, Carl Perkins, and Jerry Lee Lewis teamed up to record *The Survivors* in 1982, which was a mild success. The Highwaymen—a band featuring Cash, Waylon Jennings, Willie Nelson, and Kris Kristofferson—released their first album in 1985, which was also moderately successful. The following year, Cash and Columbia Records ended their relationship and he signed with Mercury Nashville. The new label didn't prove to be a success, as the company and the singer fought over stylistic direction. Furthermore, country radio had begun to favor more contemporary artists, and Cash soon found himself shut out of the charts. Nevertheless, he continued to be a popular concert performer.

The Highwaymen recorded a second album in 1992 and it was more commercially successful than any of Cash's Mercury records. Around that time, his contract with Mercury ended. In 1993, he signed a contract with American Records. His first album for the label, *American Recordings*, was produced by the label's founder, Rick Rubin, and was a stark, acoustic collection of songs. *American Recordings*, while not a blockbuster success, revived his career critically and brought him in touch with a younger, rock-oriented audience. In 1995, the Highwaymen released their third album, *The Road Goes on Forever*. The following year, Johnny Cash released his second album for American Records, *Unchained*, which featured support from Tom Petty & the Heartbreakers. —*Stephen Thomas Erlewine*

Johnny Cash with His Hot & Blue Guitar / 1956 / Sun ✦✦✦✦
More classic Johnny Cash tunes, it includes the original version of "I Walk the Line." In addition to his own compositions, Cash shows his influences by his covers of Hank Williams, Stuart Hamblen, and others. —*Jim Worbois*

The Songs That Made Him Famous / 1958 / Sun ✦✦✦
These early Cash classics provided him with hits and many other artists with some great material. And the sparse sound of the Tennessee Two holds up well. —*Jim Worbois*

The Fabulous Johnny Cash / 1958 / Columbia ✦✦✦✦
The Fabulous Johnny Cash was Cash's first album for Columbia Records and one of his best for the label. Unlike some of his latter-day albums, there wasn't much filler on the record. At the time of its recording, Cash had just been freed from his contract with Sun. Instead of recording these songs for his last Sun sessions, he wound up saving much of his best material for his Columbia album, and that's what makes *The Fabulous* so consistent. The album builds on his basic, spare sound, but it is slightly more polished than his Sun records. But what makes it so entertaining are the songs themselves. From "Don't Take Your Guns to Town" and "Frankie's Man, Johnny," to "Pickin' Time" and "The Troubadour," the album is filled with first-rate songs, with only a handful of mediocre songs like "Supper-Time," that don't distract from the overall quality of the album at all. —*Stephen Thomas Erlewine*

Now, There Was a Song! / 1960 / Columbia ✦✦✦✦
This is an outstanding album of covers of old country songs, from the familiar (Ernest Tubb, Hank Williams, George Jones) to lesser-known gems. —*Michael McCall*

Ride This Train / 1960 / Columbia ✦✦✦✦
Ride This Train was the first explicit Americana concept album that Johnny Cash recorded. As the title implies, the album is about railroads, how they developed and how they changed the land. Apart from a couple of songs, *Ride This Train* isn't comprised of traditional folk ballads—they are songs that tell the history of trains and rails, offering an educational lesson. Cash expounds on the songs with brief spoken narratives. Though it is hard to fault Cash's intentions, the songs aren't very good (although "The Shifting Whispering Sands" is a standout) and the history is a bit simplistic and silly. On the whole, *Ride This Train* sounds as if it is of a piece with the Walt Disney educational features produced at the same time, and like those films, it is more interesting as an historical artifact than a piece of art. —*Stephen Thomas Erlewine*

Blood Sweat & Tears / 1963 / Columbia ✦✦✦
Where *Ride This Train* was about railroads and how they shaped America, *Blood, Sweat and Tears* is not only about the folklore of trains, it's about the fables of the American working man. That means there are classic ballads like "Casey Jones" and "The Legend of John Henry's Hammer," but also relatively recent blues like "Busted," the field song "Pick a Bale of Cotton" and the worker's lament "Tell Him I'm Gone." The delivery is plain, simple and never overly sentimental, but the thing that makes the record really work is the fact that the album consists almost entirely of first-rate material, without much of the unintentionally corny history lessons that weigh down most of Cash's Americana records. —*Stephen Thomas Erlewine*

Ring of Fire / The Best of Johnny Cash / 1963 / Columbia ✦✦✦✦

I Walk the Line / 1964 / Columbia ✦✦✦✦
Despite the title, this is practically a greatest-hits package. Great stuff, it's not to be missed. —*Jim Worbois*

Bitter Tears / 1964 / Columbia ✦✦✦✦
Though on the surface *Bitter Tears* is just another installment in the seemingly endless series of Americana albums that Johnny Cash released in the '60s, it is a more daring collection than any of its predecessors or successors. Where Cash's previous Americana albums had concentrated on cowboys and Western Pioneers,

Bitter Tears is all about Native Americans and their trials and tribulations. It isn't a crass move—it's a sensitive, clear-eyed take on the unfair treatment of the American Indian that uses traditional folk ballads and newly written songs in the same vein. It's stark and moving, perhaps his best Americana album of the '60s. —*Stephen Thomas Erlewine*

Orange Blossom Special / 1965 / Columbia ✦✦✦✦
From the opening notes of the title track to the sparse version of "You Wild Colorado" to the three Dylan tunes and the Carter family classic "Wildwood Flower," this is a fine record full of strong performances by Cash. (Though the sax on "Mama, You Been on My Mind" may have been a bit much.) —*Jim Worbois*

Ballads of the True West / 1965 / Columbia ✦✦✦✦
An effective collection of songs about Western folk legends and cowboys, *Ballads of the True West* is one of Johnny Cash's most effective Americana albums. Taking a cue from Marty Robbins but stripping away the sentiment and over-production that distinguished Robbins' records, Cash creates a simple, direct portrait of the Wild West with traditional songs and newer tunes that expand on the mythology. It's evocative and entertaining, and never preachy, which is what makes it one of Cash's finest albums. —*Stephen Thomas Erlewine*

Mean As Hell / 1965 / Columbia ✦✦✦
Mean As Hell! Ballads from the True West is Johnny Cash's gunslinger album: A collection of songs about cowboys and their myths. That means there are classic Western ballads like "Bury Me Not on the Lone Prairie" and "The Shifting Whispering Sands," fables like "The Blizzard" and the title track, history lessons like "Remember the Alamo," and jokey satires like "25 Minutes to Go." *Mean As Hell* has a handful of good songs—usually the straight ballads, but some of the myths are fun too—but for the most part, there's too much unintentional kitsch on the record to make it necessary. —*Stephen Thomas Erlewine*

From Sea to Shining Sea / 1967 / Columbia ✦✦✦
From Sea to Shining Sea is an ambitious but brief attempt to cross the United States in song. Out of all his concept albums, *From Sea to Shining Sea* relies more on sailing songs than cowboy songs; those tunes that don't involve water are usually about Middle-American events, whether fairs, mines, prisons, or gas stations. Most of the songs rely on their themes, not lyrics or music, and they suffer accordingly: *From Sea to Shining Sea* is enjoyable as a campy snapshot of America, not as an album. —*Stephen Thomas Erlewine*

★ **At Folsom Prison & San Quentin** / 196 / Columbia ✦✦✦✦✦
Originally released in two different double-album sets, these two different albums have been packaged together on CD. There's a certain tension inherent in the concept of playing live to a bunch of convicts, and the tension—as well as Cash's ability to cope with it—is very present. —*Tom Roland*

A Man in Black / 1971 / Columbia ✦✦✦✦
This is the album on which Cash introduces his Man in Black persona and he sounds great. The backing is simple (just the Tennessee Three), which allows the message to come through strong and clear as only Cash can do. —*Jim Worbois*

America / 1973 / Columbia ✦✦
America: A 200-Year Salute in Story and Song is the culmination of all of Johnny Cash's Americana albums: An attempt to tell the entire history of America over the course of a 40-minute album. Of course, America's history is a bit too convoluted to be adequately told with one album, but there's no denying there's a certain kitsch value in hearing songs like "Come Take a Trip on My Airship" and "The Gettysburg Address." Cash doesn't just sing the history, he tells it with narratives that tie the tracks together. On the whole, the album doesn't amount to much more than a curiosity, but it is an entertaining—if campy—one. Just don't expect to learn anything from *America*. —*Stephen Thomas Erlewine*

Any Old Wind That Blows / 1973 / Columbia ✦✦
Several years before Johnny Paycheck told his boss to "Take This Job and Shove It," Cash was getting his revenge in "Oney"; one of several good cuts on this record (and one of the two hits). While it's not great, it's a good-sounding record. —*Jim Worbois*

Junkie & Juicehead / 1974 / Columbia ✦✦✦
Aside from some fine performances from Cash, this album also features solo tracks by two future country music stars: daughter Rosanne and step-daughter Carlene. —*Jim Worbois*

John R Cash / 1974 / Columbia ✦✦✦✦
This album, mostly made up of covers, is one of Johnny Cash's most enjoyable albums of the '70s. Cash has long been recognized for his ability to pick great material by other writers, and this is a prime example of that talent. —*Jim Worbois*

Look at Them Beans / 1975 / Columbia ✦✦
This record has the feeling of a project that never quite got off the ground. Songs like Guy Clark's "Texas-1947" is a song Cash could sink his teeth in and make his own. Yet it sounds as though he's just walking through it. Not a bad record, it still leaves one with the feeling that this record could really have been something. —*Jim Worbois*

Strawberry Cake / 1976 / Columbia ✦✦
This is a live history lesson hosted by Johnny Cash. Between many of the tracks are dialogues that give background on the upcoming song and on what Cash was up to at the time it was recorded. Unlike many live albums, the audience doesn't interfere with the music. Also, the dialogues are separate tracks, so the album can be enjoyed as a whole or, by skipping around, for the music. —*Jim Worbois*

One Piece at a Time / 1976 / Columbia ✦✦
On the heels of 1975's *John R Cash* album, this is a real disappointment. The title track was a big hit and "Let There Be Country" is kind of fun, but added together, they don't add up to a recommendation. —*Jim Worbois*

Last Gunfighter Ballad / 1977 / Columbia ✦✦
This is an OK album with some nice moments, such as the title track and "Silver Haired Daddy," on which Johnny teams up with his brother Tommy. The liner notes, on the other hand, are interesting and funny, and have a real personality. —*Jim Worbois*

The Rambler / 1977 / Columbia ✦✦
Out of all of Johnny Cash's Americana concept albums, *The Rambler* is by far the most forced and stilted. More of a radio play than an album, the record is about Cash's drive across America, where he picks up hitchhikers along the way. Every song on *The Rambler* is tied together by dialogues between Cash and the hitchhikers, which means the record never develops a sense of momentum. Furthermore, the songs themselves are slight, without much musically or lyrically to recommend them. In all, it's an ambitious, overwrought failure that is fascinating for one listen, but nearly impossible to sit through more than once. —*Stephen Thomas Erlewine*

I Would Like to See You Again / 1978 / Columbia ✦✦✦
If there is such a thing as a feel-good album, this could qualify. From the two duets with former roommate Waylon Jennings to the comical "After Taxes" to "I'm Alright Now," this record just plain feels good. —*Jim Worbois*

Silver / 1979 / Columbia ✦✦✦
Producer Brian Ahern gives Cash a different sound on this record that sometimes works to good effect. Singles aside, "The L&N Don't Stop Here," the duet with George Jones (George only provides harmony vocals) on "I'll Say It's True," and "Lately I've Been Leaning" are some of the tracks that benefit from the Ahern touch. —*Jim Worbois*

Greatest Hits, Vol. 3 / 1980 / Columbia ✦✦✦
True, there is no filler on this record. All the songs are hits. But this is not as strong a package as some of the other Johnny Cash hits collections. Good stuff here, but not necessarily a priority. —*Jim Worbois*

Rockabilly Blues / 1980 / Columbia ✦✦✦
Not as earth-shaking as his work with the Tennessee Two, and not really true rockabilly, this is still a convincing album of country-rock songs with more depth than nearly anything else coming from Nashville at the time. —*Michael McCall*

Johnny 99 / 1983 / Columbia ✦✦✦✦
If the Springsteen tunes hadn't been included, this would still have been a good album. But Cash sinks his teeth into "Highway Patrolman" and the title tune and gives them the guts that Springsteen only dreamed of. —*Jim Worbois*

The Sun Years [box set] / 1985 / Charly ✦✦✦✦
Since this five-LP box set was issued, Bear Family has come out with an even more comprehensive box covering the same era (1954-1958) on CD. If you're determined to get a box set of his earliest work, you should probably spring for Bear Family's, but if you want to save some bucks and get Charly's vinyl production (though it may be hard to find these days, used or new), this is hardly an embarrassing substitute. It has virtually everything he did for Sun, including quite a few alternate takes, and versions of previously released recordings that remove the often-distracting additional instruments and voices that were dubbed onto some of his later Sun sides. Some of the alternate takes may be rough going for those whose devotion to Cash is less than fanatical, but otherwise it's surprisingly consistent listening. Almost every track is worth hearing, and much of it is excellent, demonstrating that he had a good deal of fine early material besides the well-known hits. Comes with a full-sized booklet with lots of photos and mountainous liner notes by Hank Davis, Colin Escott, and Martin Hawkins. Incidentally, this is an entirely different release than the 1990 Rhino single-disc CD, *The Sun Years*. —*Richie Unterberger*

Up through the Years, 1955-1957 / 1986 / Bear Family ✦✦✦✦
Up through the Years is the most comprehensive single-disc collection of Johnny Cash's Sun recordings. Featuring a total of 24 songs—including all the big hits, plus interesting minor ones like "Straight A's in Love"—the collection is preferable to Rhino's *The Sun Years* for fans that want to delve a little deeper into the Sun years, but don't want to invest in the massive *The Man in Black* set. —*Stephen Thomas Erlewine*

Classic Cash: Hall of Fame Series / 1987 / Mercury ✦
Johnny Cash's period with Mercury Records was not his finest. It wasn't that he recorded a batch of poor records; it was the fact that those records were barely heard by anyone. However, *Classic Cash* isn't a compilation of those neglected gems—it's a collection of re-recordings of his biggest hits. As re-recordings go, these aren't particularly bad—Cash is in strong voice and his band is tight, professional, and accomplished—but they aren't inspired and hardly are substitutes for the original records. —*Stephen Thomas Erlewine*

☆ **Columbia Records 1958-1986** / 1987 / Columbia ✦✦✦✦✦
Columbia Records 1958-1986 is a terrific single-disc sampler of Cash's lengthy career at Columbia Records, featuring a total of 20 songs, including the classic hits "Ring of Fire," "I Still Miss Someone," "Don't Take Your Guns to Town," "Five Feet High and Rising," "Sunday Mornin' Coming Down," and "A Boy Named Sue." If you just need his latter-day hits, it's the perfect compilation. —*Stephen Thomas Erlewine*

Vintage Years: 1955-1963 / 1987 / Rhino ✦✦✦✦
To a large degree, this compilation of Cash's early work has been superceded by Rhino's own *Sun Years* (which goes into his '50s work in some greater depth), CBS' *Columbia Years 1958-1986* (which goes into his early Columbia work in much greater depth), and the Bear Family *1954-1958* box set (which goes into his early work with as much detail as anyone could ask for). Collectors care about these distinctions a great deal, but the average listener does not. If you just want some early Cash and come across this for a good price, there's no reason to feel ashamed for picking it up. It has all of the big Sun hits (which comprise over two-thirds of the record), a few of his early Columbia smashes ("I Still Miss Someone," "Ring of Fire"), and good liner notes. —*Richie Unterberger*

Is Coming to Town / Apr. 13, 1987 / Mercury ✦✦✦
Johnny Cash doing Elvis Costello? Yes! And it works—as do most of the tracks on this record. Each song is a story and Cash is one of the great storytellers. —*Jim Worbois*

★ **The Sun Years [Rhino]** / 1990 / Rhino ✦✦✦✦✦
Rhino's single-disc compilation *The Sun Years* contains 18 highlights from Johnny Cash's early years, including nearly every one

of his hits for the label (the only ones missing are minor singles or B-sides). During his time at Sun, Cash established his sound and these songs—"Cry! Cry! Cry!," "Folsom Prison Blues," "I Walk the Line"—remained the core of his repertoire throughout his entire career. Hit singles like "There You Go," "Guess Things Happen That Way," "Ballad of a Teenage Queen," and "Luther Played the Boogie" round out *The Sun Years* in an exemplary fashion. There might be more comprehensive collections of Cash's Sun recordings than *The Sun Years*, but this disc contains everything you need to know. —*Stephen Thomas Erlewine*

The Man in Black: 1954-1958 / Sep. 1990 / Bear Family ✦✦✦✦
The Man in Black: 1954-1958 is a five-disc box set that includes everything Johnny Cash recorded for Sun Records, plus the fruits of his first year with Columbia Records. In addition to all of the classic singles—from "Hey Porter" to "Don't Take Your Guns to Town," they're all here—there is a wealth of unreleased material and alternate takes, including a disc that captures an entire recording session from his early days with Columbia. The only problem with the set is its very comprehensiveness—only dedicated fans or historians can listen to this much music, especially with all of the alternate takes mixed in with the official versions. And the disc with the recording session isn't interesting—it's a curiosity that makes for tedious listening. Certainly anyone that is willing to invest in this expensive box will find it rewarding, but only serious listeners should consider purchasing the set. —*Stephen Thomas Erlewine*

Come Along and Ride This Train / 1991 / Bear Family ✦✦✦✦
Bear Family's four-disc box set *Come Along and Ride This Train* collects eight of Johnny Cash's "Americana" albums. On these records, Cash explores different aspects of American history, specializing in a particular theme for each album. On the eight albums included on *Come Along and Ride This Train—Ride This Train, Blood, Sweat and Tears, Mean As Hell! Ballads from the True West, Johnny Cash Sings the Ballads of the True West, America: A 200 Year Salute In Story and Song, Bitter Tears, From Sea to Shining Sea, The Rambler*—Cash covers a wide variety of topics, from cowboys and Native Americans to railroads and highways. Certainly a set this specialized is only for hardcore fans, but it's also a set for listeners that enjoy kitsch—no matter how serious Cash's intentions were, much of this music, with the notable exception of most of *Bitter Tears* and a handful of songs on each record, comes across as unbearably corny and very funny. —*Stephen Thomas Erlewine*

☆ **The Essential Johnny Cash 1955-1983** / 1992 / Columbia/Legacy ✦✦✦✦✦
A three-CD set, this one traces Cash's career from his Sun beginnings with "Hey Porter" and "Cry! Cry! Cry!" through the close of his Columbia association. It includes the obvious highpoints along the way ("Folsom Prison Blues," "Ring of Fire," etc.), but also packs in more obscure hits (like "Blistered" and "Singin' in Vietnam Talkin' Blues"), plus material from some of his later albums, and several appropriate gospel tracks. —*Tom Roland*

American Recordings / 1994 / American ✦✦✦✦
A stark, masterful album featuring Cash and his guitar, it captures the essence of his remarkable, distinctive talent while confirming his stature as one of the most affecting artists of his time. —*Michael McCall*

Wanted Man / 1994 / Mercury ✦✦✦
Wanted Man is an uneven, but useful, sampler of Johnny Cash's brief, scattershot time at Mercury Records. For every strong track like "Wanted Man" or "The Night Hank Williams Came to Town," the ten-song collection has unnecessary items like a remake of "Ballad of a Teenage Queen" (featuring Rosanne Cash and the Everly Brothers) and "Beans for Breakfast." It rescues some songs from obscurity—after all, the Mercury years were Cash's most ignored period—but it doesn't present enough evidence that it was unjustly overlooked. —*Stephen Thomas Erlewine*

The Man in Black: 1963-1969 / Feb. 1996 / Bear Family ✦✦✦✦
The Man in Black: 1963-1969 is Bear Family's fourth box set of Johnny Cash recordings and the third in *The Man in Black* series. *1963-1969* picks up where the previous *Man in Black* box set left

off—in the beginning of the '60s, after Cash established himself as a hitmaker for Columbia. It collects all of the music Cash made for Columbia Records between 1963 and 1969, including outtakes and alternate versions, but not the albums that were issued on the *Come Along and Ride This Train* set. Again, this collection is more for collectors and scholars than fans. There is terrific music here, but the strict chronological order—sequenced by the session date, not release date—makes listening to each disc somewhat tiring. —*Stephen Thomas Erlewine*

Unchained / Nov. 5, 1996 / American ✦✦✦
For all of its critical praise, the all-acoustic Rick Rubin-produced *American Recordings* was slightly listless. For the follow-up, Cash and Rubin wisely decided to ditch the minimalist approach of *American Recordings* and set the Man in Black in front of a full band—namely, Tom Petty & the Heartbreakers. The pairing is surprisingly inspired, as the Heartbreakers prove to be a loose and muscular supporting band, giving Cash the opportunity to invest himself completely in the songs. Cash is more than up to the task, bringing life not only to classic country songs from Jimmie Rodgers and the Louvin Brothers, but also to classic pop by Dean Martin ("Memories Are Made of This"), alternative rockers (Soundgarden's "Rusty Cage," Beck's "Rowboat") and several made-to-order songs from the likes of Petty himself. Occasionally, the pairings are a little forced, but more often than not *Unchained* consists of remarkably vibrant and inspired music that lives up to Cash's status as a legend. —*Stephen Thomas Erlewine*

The Man in Black: 1959-1962 / Bear Family ✦✦✦✦
Picking up where the previous set left off, *The Man in Black: 1959-1962* collects all of the recordings Johnny Cash made for Columbia between '59 and '62; the only music that is left off are his historical albums, which Bear Family had already released on *Come Along and Ride This Train*. Like the other set, it has an abundance of alternate takes and outtakes, plus a disc that captures an actual recording session. Again, it is primarily of interest for historians and dedicated fans willing to take the time to delve deeply into this music—since the songs are presented in chronological order according to their session date, it doesn't make for casual listening. —*Stephen Thomas Erlewine*

Rosanne Cash

b. May 24, 1955, Memphis, TN
Guitar, Vocals / Contemporary Country, Singer-Songwriter, Neo-Traditionalist Country
The history of popular music is littered with the careers of the children of famous artists, performers who manage to carve out some small measure of success based far less on talent than on the recognition that their famous names afford them. Perhaps there is no greater exception to this trend than Rosanne Cash, the daughter of Johnny Cash, whose idiosyncratic and innovative music made her one of the preeminent singer-songwriters of her day.

Born May 24, 1956, to her father and his first wife Vivian Liberto, Rosanne was raised by her mother in Southern California after her parents separated in the early 1960s. She was largely uninfluenced by her father's music until she joined his road show following her graduation from high school; over a three-year period, she was promoted from handling the tour's laundry duties to performing, first as a backup singer and then as an infrequent soloist. Still, Cash remained unsure of choosing a career in music, and took some acting classes; not wishing to succeed solely on the basis of her family's influence, she also worked as a secretary in London and traveled extensively abroad.

After releasing an eponymously titled solo record—later disavowed—in Germany in 1978, Cash signed with Columbia Records, and began performing with Texas singer-songwriter Rodney Crowell, who produced three songs for her American debut, 1979's *Right or Wrong*. The record featured three Top 25 hits, including "No Memories Hangin' Round," a duet with Bobby Bare. The same year, she and Crowell also married. Cash issued her commercial breakthrough, *Seven Year Ache*, in 1981; not only did the album yield three No. 1 singles, the title track even crossed over into the Top 30 on *Billboard's* Pop chart. However, the follow-up, 1982's *Somewhere in the Stars*, was a rush job, recorded during Cash's pregnancy. While failing to repeat *Seven Year Ache*'s success, it did produce two more Top Ten singles, "Ain't No Money" and "I Wonder."

After a three-year hiatus, Cash returned with her most significant artistic statement yet in *Rhythm and Romance*, a deft fusion of country and pop that won wide acclaim from both camps. The record earned her two more No. 1s, "I Don't Know Why You Don't Want Me" (co-written with Crowell) and a cover of Tom Petty's "Never Be You." In 1987, she issued *King's Record Shop*, a meditation on country music traditions that generated four successive No. 1 hits in John Hiatt's "The Way We Make a Broken Heart," "Tennessee Flat Top Box" (a hit for her father in 1961), "If You Change Your Mind," and John Stewart's "Runaway Train." Also hitting No. 1 was "It's Such a Small World," a duet with Crowell from his *Diamonds and Dirt* LP; not surprisingly, she was named *Billboard*'s Top Singles Artist in 1988.

The next year, Cash assembled the retrospective *Hits 1979-1989*; one of the record's few new songs, a cover of the Beatles' "I Don't Want to Spoil the Party," pushed the consecutive No. 1s streak to five. By 1990, her marriage to Crowell was beginning to dissolve; *Interiors*, an essay on the couple's relationship, was released the following year, and while the record was the subject of great critical acclaim, it was a commercial failure that generated only one Top 40 hit, "What We Really Want." In 1991, Cash and Crowell divorced; *The Wheel*, released in 1993, was an unflinchingly confessional examination of the marriage's failure that ranked as her most musically diverse effort to date. After a three-year hiatus, Cash returned with a vengeance in 1996; not only did she publish her first book, a short-story collection titled *Bodies of Water*, but she also issued *10-Song Demo*, an 11-cut collection of stark home recordings released with minimal studio gloss. —*Jason Ankeny*

Right or Wrong / 1979 / Columbia ✦✦✦

Cash's impressive debut features a solid collection of Nashville-meets-California singer-songwriter country-rock, with occasional stylistic nods to folk and light R&B. "No Memories Hangin' 'Round" was a hit duet with Bobby Bare, and "Couldn't Do Nothin' Right" and "Take Me Take Me" also charted. Other highlights include "Man Smart Woman Smarter," "Better Start Turnin' 'Em Down," and the aching ballad "Anybody's Darlin' (Anything but Mine)," one of the finest performances of her career. —*Rick Clark*

★ **Seven Year Ache** / 1981 / Columbia ✦✦✦✦✦

Cash was arguably the most important artist to emerge in country music in the early '80s, and this was her breakthrough album, which introduced a new, assertive, passionate stance for women in country and also helped foster the crossover between folk, rock, and country. Cash's songwriting (the title track and "Blue Moon with a Heartache") is first-rate, and her choices from others, notably Leroy Preston's "My Baby Thinks He's a Train," are equally strong. —*William Ruhlmann*

Somewhere in the Stars / 1982 / Columbia ✦✦✦

A terrific collection, including Rodney Crowell's "Ain't No Money," and Tom T. Hall's "That's How I Got to Memphis." —*William Ruhlmann*

Rhythm & Romance / 1985 / Columbia ✦✦✦

Cash expected criticism for this album, and got it but didn't deserve it. The orange hair and pink fingernails on the cover visually illustrate the musical risks she took in working with Eddie Rabbitt's former producer, David Malloy, and the result is a scorcher. Best cuts: Grammy-winner "I Don't Know Why You Don't Want Me" and "Halfway House." —*Tom Roland*

King's Record Shop / 1988 / Columbia ✦✦✦

After writing most of 1985's *Rhythm & Romance*, Cash returned to largely interpretive work on this powerful collection highlighted by Eliza Gilkyson's feminist anthem "Rosie Strike Back" and her father Johnny Cash's "Tennessee Flat Top Box." —*William Ruhlmann*

Hits 1979-1989 / 1989 / Columbia ✦✦✦

Ten years' worth of hits includes "I Don't Want to Spoil the Party," "Seven Year Ache," "Black and White," and others. —*AMG*

★ **Interiors** / 1990 / Columbia ✦✦✦✦✦

What makes *Interiors* brilliant isn't that Cash produced herself for the first time nor that she wrote all the songs. It's that *Interiors*—the last album Cash made for Columbia's Nashville division—meticulously chronicles the unraveling of a terribly dysfunctional relationship, namely Cash's marriage to Rodney Crowell. Cash gets at the psychology behind country's cheating and drinking themes—the emotional anesthetic of addictions, the desperate grasping for love in affairs. The arrangements are stripped as bare as Cash's soul, but *Interiors* is country at its core. —*Brian Mansfield*

The Wheel / Jan. 19, 1993 / Columbia ✦✦✦✦

Like the dark, cathartic *Interiors*, *The Wheel* is an introspective, soul-searching set of confessional songs revolving around love and relationships. While many of the themes and emotions of *Interiors* are repeated on *The Wheel*, Rosanne Cash hasn't repeated herself, either lyrically or musically. Working from the same combination of folk and country that has fueled her songwriting throughout her career, she has created an album of subtle, melodic grace that helps convey the deep feelings of her lyrics. It's an immaculately produced album, but that never detracts from the emotional core of Cash's music. —*Stephen Thomas Erlewine*

Retrospective / Nov. 7, 1995 / Columbia ✦✦✦

Retrospective is an odd overview of Rosanne Cash's later recordings for Columbia, featuring a combination of hits, album tracks, rarities, and new songs. Which means that while the album does contain hits like the No. 1 "Runaway Train," it concentrates on the lesser-known material, whether it is the minor hit "On the Surface" or Elvis Costello's "Our Little Angel." It's a good compilation, but it's a little unnecessary, since the albums it is culled from—*Interiors*, *The Wheel*—function better as individual albums, and don't lend themselves well to collections. —*Thom Owens*

10-Song Demo / Apr. 2, 1996 / Capitol ✦✦✦✦

Despite its title, *10-Song Demo* isn't really a demo tape, but it is what the title suggests—a stripped-down, direct collection of songs (for the record, there are 11 songs, not ten). Conceptually, it is a brilliant way to signal that Rosanne Cash has severed ties with Nashville, as well as the beginning of her contract with Capitol Records. However, the album doesn't completely work. Essentially, *10-Song Demo* is an official statement from Cash that she is no longer strictly a country singer, but an all-around singer-songwriter. Of course, she has always bent the rules of country music, so this isn't a big departure, as far as songwriting goes. Musically, however, the spare, simple arrangements lack all of the country and pop production flourishes that marked her last two albums. Though it initially sounds fine, there isn't much variation to the music, and her melodies are frequently uncompelling. That can't be said of her lyrics—they are as cutting, emotional, and affecting as they have always been, and they are the main reason for listening to *10-Song Demo*. —*Stephen Thomas Erlewine*

The Cathedrals

Southern Gospel

Formed in 1965, this traditional Southern gospel vocal group (also known as the Cathedral Quartet) appeared regularly on Rex Humbard's *Cathedral of Tomorrow* broadcast in the '60s. The Cathedrals are led by bass George Younce and alto Glen Payne, who are known for their humorous onstage exchanges. Originally, Humbard formed them as a trio, but soon they became a quartet comprised of Payne, Younce, Danny Koker and Bobby Clark. Both Payne and Younce have remained with the group since its inception; the other two spots have been filled by a number of singers. By 1994, the lineup had stabilized with Ernie Haase and Scott Fowler on tenor and baritone vocals, respectively, and Roger Bennett on piano.

The Cathedral Quartet appeared on Humbard's show until 1969 and then set out on their own, traveling from gig to gig in a converted egg truck until they could afford real tour buses. Over the next decade, the group became one of the most popular

Southern gospel groups around. In 1977, they won their first Grammy for Best Gospel Performance, and duplicated the feat in 1978, 1979, and 1982. In 1977, they also won Dove awards for Male Group of the Year and Best Southern Gospel Album (for *Then... And Now*) by the Gospel Music Association. In 1979, Koker and Clark left the group, beginning a long stream of replacements; pianist Roger Bennett also joined up. During the '70s and '80s, the Cathedrals had a long stream of No. 1 gospel hits that included "Step into the Water," "Can He, Could He, Would He," and "I've Just Started Living." From 1986 through 1990, the Cathedrals were featured at Bill Gaither's Praise Gathering for Believers. In 1988, they became the first Southern gospel group to record in England with the London Philharmonic Orchestra for the album *Symphony of Praise.* During the mid- to late '80s, the Cathedrals garnered numerous awards from the GMA. In 1989, the group's 25th anniversary, the *Gospel Music Voice* named them Group of the Year, and *Cash Box* named *Goin' in Style* Southern Gospel Album of the Year. The Cathedrals continue to tour extensively in large churches and concert halls. —*Sandra Brennan*

● **Cathedrals Collection, Vol. 1** / 1988 / Benson ✦✦✦✦
A fine collection of recent hits, styled in the manner of their old hits. —*Bil Carpenter*

Jeff Chance (Jeff Barosh)

Fiddle, Guitar, Vocals / Traditional Country, Contemporary Country
Vocalist, guitarist, and fiddler Jeff Chance was born Jeff Barosh in El Campo, TX. He was the leader of Chance, consisting of himself and his brother, Mick Barosh, on vocals and drums. Chance began his solo career in 1988 with the hits "So Far Not So Good," "Hopelessly Falling," and "Let It Burn." —*AMG*

Picture on the Wall / 1990 / Mercury ✦✦✦
Chance's melancholy debut includes "Talkin' to Your Picture" and "So Far Not So Good." —*Jason Ankeny*

● **Walk Softly on the Bridges** / 1992 / Mercury ✦✦✦✦
A far sunnier record than his solo debut *Picture on the Wall,* Chance's sophomore effort even includes a novelty number, "Alone in San Antone." —*Jason Ankeny*

Beth Nielsen Chapman

b. , Harlington, TX
Vocals / Contemporary Country, Singer-Songwriter, Country-Folk
A Nashville-based singer-songwriter who has written several No. 1 country hits, Chapman's own work leans more toward contemporary adult pop. Her songs are melodic, her themes mostly romantic and obsessed with inner journeys. Comparable to Carole King or the earnest side of Elton John, her range covers insistent pop rock, intimate ballads, sensual soul, and solemn spirituals, all done with an undercurrent of revelation and intelligence. —*Michael McCall*

Hearing It First / 1980 / Capitol ✦✦✦
Produced by Barry Beckett, the album reveals a young, raw talent. —*Michael McCall*

● **Beth Nielsen Chapman** / Sep. 25, 1990 / Reprise ✦✦✦✦
Chapman moved to Nashville in 1985, and the influence of the city's focus on songcraft helped her hone her poetic sensibilities into powerful, personal pop tunes. This includes a strong version of "Down on My Knees," a song covered by country singer Trisha Yearwood. —*Michael McCall*

You Hold the Key / 1993 / Reprise ✦✦✦✦
The arrangements here are peppier, but the subject matter is as intensely internal as on her previous album. —*Michael McCall*

Steven Curtis Chapman

b. Nov. 21, 1962, Paducah, KY
Guitar, Vocals / CCM, Adult Contemporary, Country Gospel
Musically a cross between '70s-style light rock and orchestrated pop, Steven Curtis Chapman has been one of the most prominent performers of contemporary Christian music during the '80s and '90s. Born and raised in Paducah, KY, Chapman learned to play

several instruments while hanging out in his father's music store, excelling at guitar and piano. As a young man, he enrolled as a pre-med student at Anderson College in Indiana. He soon decided to pursue a music career and dropped out to go to Nashville, where he began working in a music show at Opryland USA. When not performing, he was busy writing songs, a skill he learned from his father. One of Chapman's tunes was recorded by the Imperials, a prominent gospel group.

Although several different labels and music publishers were interested in him by 1987, he decided to sign with the major Christian music company, Sparrow. That year he cut his first album, *First Hand.* The first single released from the album, "Weak Days," made it to No. 2 on the contemporary Christian charts. His second album, 1988's *Real Life Conversations,* earned him four more hits, including the No. 1 song "His Eyes." Co-written with James Isaac Elliott, it earned the Contemporary Recorded Song of the Year award from the Gospel Music Association in 1989. That year, he also won a GMA award for Best Songwriter of the Year. Released later that year, his third album, *More to This Life,* contained four No. 1 hits and in 1990 earned him an unprecedented ten nominations at the GMA Awards (he won five). His next album, *For the Sake of the Call,* which contained five No. 1 singles and earned him another slew of GMA awards and his first Grammy in the Best Pop Gospel Album category, only strengthened his position as the king of Christian music.

In 1992, Chapman made a successful bid to attract a more mainstream audience with *The Great Adventure,* which also won a Grammy, and its accompanying title-track video. When Sparrow Records was purchased by EMI/Liberty, they began marketing the album in discount stores and in 1993, it went gold. Also released in 1993 (both as a video and CD), *The Live Adventure* won more GMA awards and also earned Chapman a new award from *American Songwriter* magazine, Songwriter and Artist of the Year. Many of country's brightest stars, including Sandi Patti, Billy Dean, Glen Campbell and Roger Whitaker, have recorded Chapman's songs. He released his seventh album, *Heaven in the Real World,* in 1994 and embarked on a major tour. —*Sandra Brennan*

First Hand / 1987 / Sparrow ✦✦✦
Chapman's freshman debut is infused with country, soft rock, and pop. —*Bil Carpenter*

Real Life Conversations / 1988 / Sparrow ✦✦✦✦
Harder-edged, elaborate, guitar-focused light rock. —*Bil Carpenter*

● **For the Sake of the Call** / 1990 / Sparrow ✦✦✦✦
Chapman's songwriting voice continues to mature, and the stirring title anthem helped make this his most successful album. —*Brian Mansfield*

The Great Adventure / 1992 / Sparrow ✦✦✦
Chapman flirts with country, rap, and Springsteenian rock on his most ambitious project, both musically and lyrically. Includes guest appearances from Ricky Skaggs, DC Talk, and BeBe Winans. —*Brian Mansfield*

The Live Adventure / May 1993 / Sparrow ✦✦✦✦
Heaven in the Real World / 1994 / Sparrow ✦✦✦
Chapman moves into rockier, more electrified territory with his down-home story songs and values. —*Thom Granger*

Sign of Life / Sep. 3, 1996 / Chordant ✦✦✦✦

Chesapeake

Country-Folk, Neo-Traditionalist Country
Chesapeake was a quartet made up of members Mike Auldridge, T. Michael Coleman, Jimmy Giddreau, and Mondi Klein. Their music blended country, folk, and pop sounds. —*Jason Ankeny*

Rising Tide / 1994 / Sugar Hill ✦✦✦
● **Full Sail** / Feb. 1996 / Sugar Hill ✦✦✦✦
On their second record *Full Sail,* Chesapeake combine elements of folk, country, and pop music. Their diverse influences are reflected in their choice of cover material, which includes Little Feat's "Let It Roll," Ricky Skaggs' "One Way Track," Tom Paxton's

"The Last Thing on My Mind" and Steve Gillette's "Sweet Melinda." —*Jason Ankeny*

Mark Chesnutt

b. Sep. 6, 1963, Beaumont, TX
Vocals / Contemporary Country, New Traditionalist
Mark Chesnutt was a major force in the revival of the old-fashioned honky tonk sound made famous by such stars as George Jones and Merle Haggard. Born in Beaumont, TX, Mark, the son of country singer Bob Chesnutt, began learning to play guitar at age five. He made his professional debut around age 16 when he began performing with his father's band. Chesnutt dropped out of high school to become a full-time musician, but later heeded his parents' advice and got his diploma. Chesnutt began playing throughout Texas for the next decade; he and his group, which included future solo star Tracy Byrd, eventually became the house band at Cutters nightclub in Beaumont.

Chesnutt made his recording debut on the AXBAR label in San Antonio, releasing a number of local singles. After signing to MCA, he released "Too Cold at Home," a Top Five hit. The album of the same name was released soon afterward and went gold by 1991. He had his first No. 1 hit with Paul Craft's "Brother Jukebox" in 1991. Over the next two years, the album produced three more Top Ten hits. Chesnutt's second album, *Longnecks and Short Stories*, went gold less than seven months after its 1992 release and contained several hits, including the No. 1 singles "Old Flames Have New Names" and "I'll Think of Something," and had his first crossover hit with "Bubba Shot the Jukebox." His 1993 album, *Almost Goodbye*, went gold four months after its release, and again Chesnutt had a string of hits, including the No. 1 hit "I Just Wanted You to Know." Both 1994's *What a Way to Live* and 1995's *Wings* also proved successful. —*Sandra Brennan*

Too Cold at Home / 1990 / MCA ✦✦✦✦
An impressive traditional country debut that often drew on George Jones and Texas swing, *Too Cold at Home* started Chesnutt off strong with the hits "Too Cold at Home," "Brother Jukebox," "Blame It on Texas," and "Your Love Is a Miracle." It also included a version of "Friends in Low Places" that came out at almost exactly the same time Garth Brooks' did. —*Brian Mansfield*

Longnecks & Short Stories / 1992 / MCA ✦✦✦✦
Longnecks heralded the emergence of a Texas voice that contained both the knack for humor ("Old Flames Have New Names," "Bubba Shot the Jukebox"), and the depth for heartache ("I'll Think of Something"). —*Brian Mansfield*

Almost Goodbye / Jun. 22, 1993 / MCA ✦✦✦
Weak material weighs down Chesnutt's third release, though he still sings like the most romantic Western swinger since George Strait. "Almost Goodbye" is backed by a string arrangement as powerful as the one on "I'll Think of Something," but songs like "Texas Is Bigger" and "My Heart's Too Broke" aren't the attention-grabbers "Old Flames Have New Names" and "Bubba Shot the Jukebox" were. One of Chesnutt's biggest strengths is his casual delivery, but *Almost Goodbye* sounds too easy. "Almost Goodbye" and "It Sure Is Monday" both topped the singles charts. —*Brian Mansfield*

What a Way to Live / 1994 / MCA ✦✦✦
Like its predecessor *Almost Goodbye*, *What a Way to Live* is dogged by inconsistent material, but Chesnutt's fine singing manages to save most of the weaker material from being a bore. —*Stephen Thomas Erlewine*

Wings / Oct. 3, 1995 / MCA ✦✦✦✦
Mark Chesnutt's *Wings* is one of his most impressive efforts, showing the singer expanding his sonic template by stepping away from the commercial leanings of his recent material, yet lending a slight pop and rock influence to his straightforward traditional country. What really makes the album rank among his best is the consistent quality of the songwriting. Featuring songwriters like Jim Lauderdale and Todd Snider, *Wings* is filled with first-rate material that pushes at the borders of contemporary country while preserving its heritage. Ranging from romantic ballads to Bakersfield-type raveups, the record showcases Chesnutt at his finest. —*Stephen Thomas Erlewine*

● Greatest Hits / Nov. 19, 1996 / MCA ✦✦✦✦
Mark Chesnutt's *Greatest Hits* does a fair job of summing up the neo-traditionalist's biggest hits, adding two new songs—"It's a Little Too Late" and "Let It Rain"—to the collection. Though his biggest hits are showcased on the album, many of his proper albums offer a better representation of his talent. —*Thom Owens*

Charlie Chesterman

Roots-Rock, Alternative Country, Americana
Charlie Chesterman first found success as the frontman for the pop-punk outfit Scruffy the Cat; following the group's demise, he began moving in a more roots-oriented direction, as evidenced by his 1994 solo debut *From the Book of Flames*. 1996's *Studebakersfield* continued in a similar vein, tackling rockabilly, blues, and country weepers. —*Jason Ankeny*

● From the Book of Flames / 1994 / Slow River ✦✦✦✦
Studabakersfield / Jan. 30, 1996 / Slow River ✦✦✦

The Chicken Chokers

Progressive Bluegrass, Old-Time, Alternative Country
The Chicken Chokers and Horseflies were two adventurous but short-lived Boston area string bands who played new "old-time" music in the 1980s. The Chicken Chokers were variously inspired by Uncle Dave Macon, reggae, punk, and rap, even though the instruments they played were "old-time" friendly. The Horseflies were more instrumentally adroit and avant-garde in orientation. Appearing as they did in the late Reagan epoch, it's little wonder these two anomalies shone briefly and then sank without a trace. They played with music in a way that was more aligned with the spirit of the Johnson years. *Chokers & Flies* was a Rounder album offering some of each band, while full servings of each eccentric aggregate appear on the Chokers' *Shoot Your Radio* (much fun) and the Flies' darker offering, *Human Fly* (both on Rounder). —*Mark A. Humphrey*

● Shoot Your Radio / 1987 / Rounder ✦✦✦✦
Old-time instrumentation, a pseudo-punk bad attitude, and a hilarious title-track rap from this short-lived but fun band from Boston. —*Mark A. Humphrey*

Old Time Music / Rounder ✦✦✦
On this album, two avant-garde/old-time bands, the Chicken Chokers and the Horseflies, push the envelope of the new/old-time styles. —*Mark A. Humphrey*

Harry Choates

b. Dec. 26, 1922, Rayne, LA, d. Jul. 17, 1951, Austin, TX
Fiddle / Cajun, Western Swing
Cajun fiddle legend Harry Choates lived a troubled life that climaxed with his version of the Cajun standard "Jole Blon" in 1947, but ended just five years later while he was in jail. Choates was born in Rayne, LA, but he grew up in Texas, influenced by the Western swing style of fiddling—a fact that has not endeared him to Cajun purists. Choates joined Leo Soileau's band in the mid-'30s as a guitar player, playing with the band for just over ten years. He went solo in 1946, and his first single, "Jole Blon," hit No. 4 in the country charts in January 1947. (Roy Acuff rode the single into the Top Five later in 1947.)

The quick fame did little good for Choates, who hit the bottle hard as he made the rounds of Texas honky tonks in the late '40s. He had married Helen Daenen in 1945, but was jailed in July 1951 for not supporting her and his children, Edison and Linda. The rest of Harry Choates' life is sketchy, though. His death on July 17, 1951 is a fact, though whether it was a result of delirium, an epileptic fit, police cruelty, or some combination of each is pure conjecture. —*John Bush*

Original Cajun Fiddle of Harry Choates / D ✦✦✦

Jole Blon / 1979 / D ✦✦✦✦
The title cut has become the "Cajun national anthem." Also many other great fiddle-led Cajun tunes. —*Jeff Hannusch*

★ **Fiddle King of Cajun Swing** / 1982 / Arhoolie ✦✦✦✦
Fiddle King of Cajun Swing is a 26-track collection featuring most of Harry Choates' finest recordings. All of the material on this compilation was recorded for Gold Star Records between 1946 and 1950. Though his biggest hit, "Jole Blon," is inexplicably missing, the music on this disc demonstrates Choates' talent for blurring the lines between Western swing and Cajun music. It's an excellent introduction to one of the finest Cajun fiddlers of the '40s and '50s. — *Thom Owens*

Five-Time Lobster / 1990 / Krazy Kat ✦✦✦
A follow-up to "Jole Blon" and 13 other performances, it includes the Hank Williams-inspired "Cat 'n Around." It has a rough sound but great music, blending Cajun, swing, and honky tonk. — *Mark A. Humphrey*

His Original 1946-1949 Recordings / Arhoolie ✦✦✦✦
Sixteen performances by the man dubbed "The Godfather of Cajun Music," include his swingin' takes on such standards as "Allons ... Lafayette" and "Grand Mamou." — *Mark A. Humphrey*

Chris and Carla

Alternative Country-Rock
The duo Chris and Carla was an offshoot of the Seattle folk-punk unit the Walkabouts, featuring the band's singer-songwriters Chris Eckman and Carla Torgerson. An acoustic, folk-based project, Chris and Carla debuted in 1993 with *Shelter for an Evening*, a live collection recorded in Germany. Two years later, they resurfaced with *Life Full of Holes*, a studio LP cut with R.E.M.'s Peter Buck and members of Britain's Tindersticks. *Nights Between Stations*, another live effort—this one recorded in Greece—followed later in 1995. — *Jason Ankeny*

● **Shelter for an Evening** / 1993 / Glitterhouse ✦✦✦✦
The first live effort from Chris and Carla offers acoustic renditions of a number of Walkabouts favorites, including "Jack Candy," "Train to Mercy" and "Glad Nation's Death Song." It also features covers of Neil Young's "On the Beach," Bob Dylan's "Maggie's Farm," and Richard and Linda Thompson's "Down Where the Drunkards Roll." — *Jason Ankeny*

Life Full of Holes / 1995 / Glitterhouse ✦✦✦✦
Chris and Carla's sophomore release is a collection of all-new material written specifically for the project; most of their fellow Walkabouts make guest appearances, as do Peter Buck and members of Tindersticks (with whom Torgerson sang on their eponymous 1995 effort). — *Jason Ankeny*

Nights Between Stations: Live in Thessaloniki 1995 / 1995 / Glitterhouse ✦✦✦
Recorded with the Greek band the Mylos All-Stars, Chris and Carla's second live outing features a number of songs taken from the *Life Full of Holes* LP, along with a few Walkabouts numbers and covers of Townes Van Zandt's "Lungs" and the Carter Family's "Storms Are on the Ocean." — *Jason Ankeny*

Chuck Wagon Gang

Traditional Country, Southern Gospel, Country Gospel
Though the Chuck Wagon Gang has been around since 1936—undergoing many personnel changes over the years—its sound and devotion to old-fashioned gospel has remained much the same. The band's greatest significance is as an important link between country music and the traditional sacred songs of the South.
The original incarnation of the Chuck Wagon Gang was made up of four members of the Carter family—no relation to *the* Carter Family from Virginia. These were Dad Carter (David Parker Carter), his son Jim (born Ernest), daughter Rose (born Rosa Lola), and his daughter Effie. Dad Carter was born in Kentucky, but was raised in Clay County, TX. He was enrolled in a singing school there when he met Carrie Brooks, whom he married in 1909. They bore eight children, and to support them, Carter worked for the Rock Island Railroad in 1927. At other times, he and the family also picked cotton. The band formed around 1935 after one of the children became deathly ill and the family was left destitute. For additional income, Dad Carter talked

the management at station KFYO Lubbock into hiring him as a host for a daily radio program. The original group was called the Carter Quartet, with Dad singing tenor, Jim singing bass and playing guitar, and Rose and Effie singing soprano and alto. They were popular and soon began earning $15 per week. The following year the Carters moved to WBAP and billed themselves as the Chuck Wagon Gang; they were sponsored by Bewley's Best Flour and at this point sang a variety of secular and sometimes sacred songs. Their earliest recording session for ARC produced country singles rather than gospel. As the years passed they gradually became more gospel-oriented and by the early '40s had switched over completely. In 1942 they spent a few months at a Tulsa radio station.
The Chucks broke up for the duration of World War II. Afterward, they reunited and returned to WBAP and Bewley's Flour, remaining primarily a radio band. They began recording again in 1948 for Columbia. Two years later Wally Fowler had them perform at one of his All-Night Singing Conventions in Augusta, GA; they became a full-time touring band after that. In 1953, the band underwent the first of many subsequent membership changes when Jim left and was replaced by Howard Gordon; he remained with the Chucks until he died in 1967. Another brother, Roy, also joined and sang bass in Jim's stead. Dad Carter retired in 1955 and was at first replaced by Eddie Carter. In the late '50s non-family members such as Alynn Billodeau, Patrick McKeehan, Ronnie Page, and Ronnie Crittenden spent time with the Chuck Wagon Gang. Through it all, the band kept touring part-time and making records. By 1975, the Chucks had made 408 masters. After three years of inactivity, the group began recording for the Copperfield label. The Chuck Wagon Gang continued on in a similar vein until 1987 when they once again became a full-time band with new members joining the last of the Carters, Roy and his sister Ruth Ellen Yates. In 1984, Dad Carter (who had died in 1963) was posthumously inducted into the Gospel Music Hall of Fame. By the late '80s, the Chuck Wagon Gang were named Gospel Artist or Group of the Year by *Music City News* for five years in a row. In 1990 Bob Terrell published an authorized history of the group, *The Chuck Wagon Gang: A Legend Lives On*. — *Sandra Brennan*

Family Tradition / 1973 / K-Tel ✦✦✦
This contains "Standing on the Promises" and other performances that show that throughout the many lineup changes this group has experienced, their sound remains a constant. — *AMG*

Looking Away to Heaven / 1976 / Columbia ✦✦✦
This is one of the best of the more recent Columbia sets. — *Charles S. Wolfe*

☆ **Columbia Historic Edition** / 1990 / Columbia ✦✦✦✦✦
Columbia Historic Edition compiles highlights from the Chuck Wagon Gang's Columbia recordings between 1936 and 1960. Many of their greatest songs—including "After the Sunrise," "He Set Me Free," "We Are Climbing," and "I Want to See My Jesus"—are featured on this 16-track collection, making it a terrific introduction to this influential country gospel group. — *Thom Owens*

● **Greatest Hits** / Arrival ✦✦✦✦
Featuring 16 tracks, *Greatest Hits* is a solid compilation of some of the Chuck Wagon Gang's best tracks and offers a good introduction to this contemporary country-gospel vocal group. — *Stephen Thomas Erlewine*

Old Time Hymns, Vol. 2 / Arrival ✦✦✦
The Chuck Wagon Gang's heartfelt renditions of some well-known traditional hymns are somewhat hampered by the sterile production, but their strong performances carry the disc. — *Stephen Thomas Erlewine*

In Harmony / Copperfield ✦✦✦
Featured are "We Are Climbing" and other gospel favorites. — *AMG*

● **Historic Edition** / Columbia ✦✦✦✦

Church Brothers

Traditional Bluegrass
The Church Brothers and their band, the Blue Ridge Gamblers, were early bluegrass musicians. The brothers, Bill, Edwin and Ralph, were all born in Wilkes County, NC. Bill, the eldest, was a guitarist who first worked with Roy Hall and His Blue Ridge Entertainers. While serving in the Army during World War II, his younger brothers, their cousin Ward Eller, and neighbor Drake Walsh began playing music. When Bill returned, he joined their band and, as the Wilkes County Entertainers, began playing on a local radio station with Edwin on fiddle and Ralph on mandolin. Eventually the band underwent a few personnel changes and evolved into the Church Brothers and the Blue Ridge Ramblers.

The group made their recording debut in early 1950. About this time, they enlisted the aid of a young lyricist, Drusilla Adams, to help them develop more original songs. A bit later Noah Adams founded Blue Ridge Records and purchased the group's unreleased masters; he also had the Church Brothers and their Ramblers record a few new singles, all featuring Adams' lyrics. By 1953, the brothers and band members had begun going their separate ways. In 1969, the German label GHP released 12 of the band's masters on an album, and ten years later Rounder released a compilation of 15 Church Brothers songs. *—Sandra Brennan*

The Church Brothers, Traditional Bluegrass / 1969 / GHP ✦✦✦

The Church Brothers / 1978 / Rounder ✦✦✦

● **Early Days of Bluegrass, Vol. 8** / Rounder ✦✦✦✦

Cigar Store Indians

Alternative Country-Rock, Rockabilly Revival
The Atlanta-based rockabilly combo Cigar Store Indians formed in 1993 after the breakup of frontman Ben Friedman's previous band, the alternative rockers IBM. After enlisting Jim "Low Note" Lavender on guitar, Keith Perissi on bass, and Francis "Fast Pedal" Ferran on drums, the band grew quickly from an underground sensation to one of the Atlanta club scene's most popular acts. After releasing a cassette on a local label in 1994, the Cigar Store Indians made their formal bow with a 1995 self-titled LP. *—Jason Ankeny*

Cigar Store Indians / Feb. 1996 / Landslide ✦✦✦✦

Gene Clark

b. Nov. 17, 1946, Tipton, MO, d. May 24, 1991, Sherman Oaks, CA
Guitar, Vocals / Progressive Bluegrass, Country-Rock, Folk-Rock
Very few musicians had as much influence in creating new styles of music as Gene Clark. As co-founder of the Byrds, he helped pioneer what was to become known as folk-rock. Clark and Bob Dylan were the most prolific songwriters of the genre. After leaving the group, he and banjoist Doug Dillard invented newgrass, a progressive blend of traditional bluegrass instrumentation augmented by electronics, drums, piano, and even harpsichord. Clark's first solo album, *Gene Clark with the Gosdin Brothers*, contained country-rock, preceding the Byrds' *Sweetheart of the Rodeo* by nearly two years and the first Flying Burrito Brothers album by three years.

Harold Eugene Clark was the oldest of 12 children. He left college to join the New Christy Minstrels in 1962. Upon hearing the Beatles' "She Loves You," he left the group and moved to California, where he met Roger (then known as Jim) McGuinn and David Crosby. Mandolin player Chris Hillman was given his first electric bass lesson by Clark, and Michael Clarke was recruited from a beach party to play drums. The five became the Jet Set, the Beefeaters, and finally, the Byrds, where their cover of Dylan's "Mr. Tambourine Man" shot to the top of the charts worldwide in May of 1965. Clark left the Byrds in early 1966 to pursue a solo career, releasing *Gene Clark with the Gosdin Brothers* in 1967. The following year *The Fantastic Expedition of Dillard and Clark* heralded the dawning of newgrass. After two years, the ever-restless Clark left the band and recorded the Dylan-esque *White Light*, voted album of the year in Holland in 1971 and praised by *Rolling Stone* as the album he was born to make. The following year *Roadmaster* was released, an 11-song masterpiece that fea-

tured the five original Byrds on two tracks, foreshadowing the reforming of the group in 1973 for *Byrds*, produced by David Crosby. Despite the fact that the record sold millions and went gold, the group quickly disbanded thereafter.

No Other in 1974 and *Two Sides to Every Story* in 1977 reconfirmed Clark as one of the great songwriters of his era. In 1978, Clark joined Roger McGuinn and Chris Hillman for two albums, *McGuinn, Clark and Hillman*, and *City* in 1979. The group toured extensively until Clark departed once again, and it would be five years before Clark would release *Firebyrd*, which includes remakes of "Mr. Tambourine Man" and "Feel a Whole Lot Better." Clark continued to play solo both in the US and Europe before joining up with Carla Olson (Textones) for *So Rebellious a Lover* in 1987. Clark also performed in A Tribute to the Byrds for several years starting in 1985, which included former Byrd Michael Clarke on drums and at various times Rick Danko, Blondie Chaplin, John York, Rick Roberts, Billy Darnell, and Michael Curtis. In addition to his solo efforts, Clark apppeared on albums by the Flying Burrito Brothers, Roger McGuinn, Bob Lind, Cooker, the Textones and Primitive Future. Gene Clark died a few short months after he and the Byrds were inducted into the Rock & Roll Hall of Fame. He left behind hundreds of songs, an indelible mark on folk-rock, bluegrass, and country music, and millions of fans who mourned the loss of one of the greatest songwriters and musical innovators of all time. *—Dan Pavlides*

Gene Clark with the Gosdin Brothers / 1967 / Columbia ✦✦✦
Byrds Michael Clarke and Chris Hillman provide the rhythm section, and future Byrd Clarence White, banjoist Doug Dillard, Glen Campbell, and even Leon Russell help create country-rock and newgrass overtones in addition to Clark's familiar folk-rock stylings. *—Dan Pavlides*

● **Echoes** / 1967 / Columbia ✦✦✦✦
Basically this is a CD reissue of his 1967 debut album, *Gene Clark & The Gosdin Brothers*. The Byrds comparison is really unavoidable: it's both Clark's best solo work, and not coincidentally, the one that resembles the Byrds most strongly. Indeed, this could easily pass for a somewhat less-than-average vintage Byrds album, with actual Byrds Chris Hillman and Michael Clarke forming the rhythm section, and Vern and Rex Gosdin on guitar (hence the LP title). To be brutal, it doesn't measure up to Clark's best songs from his Byrds days, but it's fairly strong, melodic '60s folk-rock nonetheless, perhaps with a bit of a more countrified, laidback, generic feel. "So You Say You Lost Your Baby," "Echoes," and especially "Tried So Hard" are standouts. The CD adds three interesting previously unreleased outtakes from the era, as well as six of his best early Byrds songs graced by Clark's songwriting and vocals. *—Richie Unterberger*

Fantastic Expedition / 1969 / A&M ✦✦✦

Through the Morning / 1969 / A&M ✦✦✦

Gene Clark / 1969 / Together ✦✦✦
Clark's solo debut was recorded with The Gosdin Brothers. *—Kenneth M. Cassidy*

American Flyer / 1971 / MediaArts ✦✦

White Light / 1971 / A&M ✦✦✦
Clark's most Dylanesque album. *—Dan Pavlides*

Roadmaster / 1972 / Edsel ✦✦✦✦
Reunited five Byrds play on two tracks. One of Gene Clark's best ever. *—Dan Pavlides*

No Other / 1974 / Line ✦✦✦
Gene Clark called this album "overdub city" in a 1986 interview, laughing at the glam-rock photo taken of him on the poster insert. It remains a timeless masterpiece from 1974. *—Dan Pavlides*

Kansas City Southern / 1975 / Ariola ✦✦✦

Two Sides to Every Story / 1977 / RSO ✦✦
Byron Berline, Al Perkins, John Hartford, and Emmylou Harris join Gene Clark for this country/folk-rock effort. *—Dan Pavlides*

Firebyrd / 1987 / Takoma ✦✦✦✦
Gene Clark's post-Byrds solo career was as fraught with false starts and unmet promises as his two years with the Byrds were

filled with fame, fulfillment, and recognition. *Firebyrd* was an artistic triumph and a commercial disaster—released to rave reviews and an enthusiastic response, as one of the finest solo projects ever to come from an ex-Byrd, it was killed by poor distribution (demand in Europe, especially Germany and Italy, where fan interest in Clark and the Byrds was very high, resulted in high premiums being paid for used copies). "Rain Song," "Rodeo Rider," and "Something About You" were some of Clark's best songs in years, and his covers of two old Byrds numbers, "Mr. Tambourine Man" and "Feel a Whole Lot Better," are perfectly credible reinterpretations. He even does justice to Gordon Lightfoot's "If You Could Read My Mind." Not a "lost Byrds album" by any means, but a must-own for any serious Byrds fan. —*Bruce Eder*

So Rebellious a Lover / 1987 / Razor & Tie ◆◆◆
Country— and folk-flavored duets include John Fogerty's "Almost Saturday Night" and Clark's haunting motorcycle mantra "Gypsy Rider." —*Dan Pavlides*

Silhouetted in Light / 1992 / Edsel ◆◆◆
A very good 15-track live CD featuring Gene Clark and Carla Olson at their best. The sound is good and the song selection impressive. Pick up this import—highly recommended. —*Chip Renner*

This Byrd Has Flown / Oct. 1995 / Edsel ◆◆◆◆
This Byrd Has Flown is an expanded British import CD of *Firebyrd*, with extra tracks added from later recording sessions. The songs add a considerable amount to the original album: "C'est La Bonne Rue" is a hot little rocker, and "All I Want" is one of Clark's most poignant and impassioned love songs, and by itself is worth the price of the album. The notes by drummer/singer/composer Andy Kandanes add considerably to the information about the circumstances behind the recording of *Firebyrd* and Clark's later career, up until his death in May of 1991. —*Bruce Eder*

Guy Clark

b. Nov. 6, 1941, Rockport, TX
Guitar, Vocals / Progressive Country, Singer-Songwriter, Country-Folk, Outlaw Country, Alternative Country
Guy Clark doesn't just write songs, he crafts them with the kind of hands-on care and respect that a master carpenter (a favorite image of his) would have when faced with a stack of rare hardwood. Clark works slowly and with strict attention to detail—he's only recorded eight albums since he was first signed to RCA in the early '70s—but he has produced an impressive collection of timeless gems, leaving very little waste behind. His albums have never met with much commercial success, but the emotional level of his work consistently transcends sales figures and musical genres. He remains the kind of songwriter who young artists study and seasoned writers (and listeners) admire.

Clark was born in the West Texas town of Monahans, where he was raised mainly by his grandmother (his mother worked and his father was in the Army), who ran the town hotel. One of her residents was an oil well driller who would later end up the subject of one of Clark's most moving and stunningly beautiful songs, "Desperados Waiting for a Train." Many of Clark's songs, in fact, have centered around his days growing up in West Texas, including "Texas 1947" (from his debut album) and the 1992 song "Boats to Build," which harkened back to a summer job he once had as a teenager on the Gulf Coast.

The first songs Clark learned were mostly in Spanish. Later, when he moved to Houston and began working the folk-music circuit, he met fellow songwriter Townes Van Zandt (the two would often tour together) and blues singers Lightnin' Hopkins and Mance Lipscomb. It was here that Clark began playing and writing his sturdy brand of folk- and blues-influenced country music.

In the late '60s, Clark moved to California, living first in San Francisco (where he met and married his wife Susanna, a painter and songwriter) and then in Los Angeles, where he worked in the Dopera Brothers' dobro factory. Tiring quickly of Southern California (sentiments he expressed in another of his classics, "L.A. Freeway"), he and Susanna packed up and headed for Nashville

in 1971, where he picked up work as a writer with publishing companies and, eventually, a recording contract with RCA. Clark's first album, *Old No. 1*, came out in 1975, a few years after Jerry Jeff Walker had turned "L.A. Freeway" into a minor hit. By this time Clark was considered one of the most promising young writers in country music, and while he didn't live in Texas anymore, the state's influence still ran thick in his blood.

Clark recorded one more album for RCA, *Texas Cookin'*, in 1976 before switching to Warner Bros. for his next three albums, released between 1978 and 1983. Three of his songs from these albums cracked the Top 100. By the mid-'80s, however, a number of his songs had been made into hits by country stars such as Johnny Cash, David Allen Coe, Ricky Skaggs (who took "Heartbroke" to No. 1), George Strait, Vince Gill, and the Highwaymen.

Clark continued to work as a writer but didn't record again until 1988's *Old Friends*, released by Sugar Hill. He then switched labels once more, this time to Asylum, which released his 1992 album *Boats to Build* as part of their acclaimed American Explorer series. His eighth album, *Dublin Blues*, came out in 1995, and among its finely crafted moments is a re-reading of one of his most enduring songs, "Randall Knife," about the death of his father. —*Kurt Wolff*

★ **Old No. 1** / 1975 / Sugar Hill ◆◆◆◆◆
Boasting an excellent set of original songs—including the contemporary classics "L.A. Freeway," "She Ain't Goin' Nowhere," and "Desperados Waiting for a Train"—and stripped-back, honest arrangements, Guy Clark's debut album *Old No. 1* set the tone for his career. Though he crafted several fine albums after *Old No. 1*, he never quite matched its consistency, both in terms of songwriting and performance. —*Thom Owens*

Texas Cookin' / 1976 / Sugar Hill ◆◆◆◆
The songs here are more Nashville, hitting many emotions. "Texas Cookin'," "Virginia's Reel," and "Broken Hearted" are all great songs. What a way to finish the album, as Clark and Johnny Cash sing "The Last Gunfighter Ballad." —*Chip Renner*

Fool on the Roof / 1978 / Warner Brothers ◆◆◆◆
This very-overlooked album is more country than Clark's first two RCA albums. Just listen to the vocals (with the Whites, Rodney Crowell, Don Everly, Gordon Payne) and the words. You'll find this album grows on you. —*Chip Renner*

Guy Clark / 1978 / Warner Brothers ◆◆
This is a mediocre album from Guy Clark, in part because of his reliance on material from other sources. He seems to have momentarily lost direction. —*Jim Worbois*

The South Coast of Texas / 1981 / Warner Brothers ◆◆◆◆
A good solid album. Check out Rosanne Cash's vocals on "Cystelle." Vince Gill, Ricky Skaggs, and Rodney Crowell give this album a very polished sound. —*Chip Renner*

Better Days / 1983 / Warner Brothers ◆◆◆◆
Produced by Rodney Crowell, this is a personal favorite containing some of Clark's trademark songs, like "The Carpenter," "Homegrown Tomatoes," and the tear-jerker "The Randall Knife." —*Chip Renner*

Old Friends / 1989 / Sugar Hill ◆◆◆
Clark's finest moment. The production allows Clark to present his songs without any distractions. Sam Bush, Verlon Thompson, Michael Henderson, and Vince Gill blend with Clark perfectly, as do Rosanne Cash and Emmylou Harris. —*Chip Renner*

Boats to Build / 1992 / Elektra/Nonesuch ◆◆◆
As unadorned and uncontrived as ever, Clark's masterful songs get to the heart of the matter and stay there. —*Michael McCall*

Craftsman / 1995 / Philo ◆◆◆◆
Craftsman compiles all three of Clark's Warner Bros. albums—*Guy Clark*, *The South Coast of Texas*, and *Better Days*—on two CDs. A great collection if you already have *Old No. 1* and want to dig deeper. —*Kurt Wolff*

Dublin Blues / Apr. 4, 1995 / Elektra ◆◆◆
Clark's skill as a singer and songwriter has a long way to go before it fades. "Baby Took a Limo to Memphis" is a silly throw-

away, but "Stuff That Works" and the title track are classic Clark. Includes a new version of "The Randall Knife." —*Kurt Wolff*

● **Essential** / Jan. 28, 1997 / RCA ✦✦✦✦
Featuring many of Guy Clark's finest songs, as well as a handful of excellent lesser-known gems, *Essential* is a terrific introduction to one of the best, if underappreciated, songwriters of the '70s. —*Thom Owens*

Roy Clark (Roy Linwood Clark)

b. Apr. 15, 1933, Meherrin, VA
Banjo, Fiddle, Guitar, Vocals / Traditional Country, Country-Pop
In the '70s Roy Clark symbolized country music in the US and abroad. Between guest-hosting for Johnny Carson on *The Tonight Show* and performing to packed houses in the Soviet Union on a tour that sold out all 18 concerts, he used his musical talent and his entertaining personality to bring country music into homes across the world. As one of the hosts of TV's *Hee Haw* (Buck Owens was the other) for more than 20 years Clark picked and sang and offered country corn to 30 million people weekly. He is first and foremost an entertainer, drawing crowds at venues as diverse as Las Vegas, Atlantic City, and the Opry. His middle-of-the-road approach has filled a national void, with Clark offering country that was harder-edged than Kenny Rogers but softer and more accessible than Waylon Jennings. Among his numerous vocal hits are "Yesterday When I Was Young" and "Thank God and Greyhound." Instrumentally he has won awards for both guitar and banjo.

The son of two amateur musicians, Roy Clark began playing banjo, guitar, and mandolin at an early age. By the time he was 14, he was playing guitar behind his father at local dances. Within a few years, he had won two National Banjo Championships, with his second win earning him an appearance at the Grand Ole Opry. Despite his success as a musician, Clark decided to pursue an athletic career, rejecting baseball for boxing. At the age of 17, he won 15 fights in a row before deciding that he would rather be a musician.

Clark found work at local clubs, radio stations, and television shows. By 1955, he was a regular on Jimmy Dean's DC-based television show, *Country Style*. Once Dean left Washington for New York, Clark took over the show, and over the next few years, he earned a reputation as an excellent musician and entertainer. In 1960, he decided to leave the East Coast to pursue his fame and fortune out West. That year, he became the leader of Wanda Jackson's band, playing on her hit singles like "Let's Have a Party," as well as touring with the singer and playing concerts with her in Las Vegas. Once Jackson decided to break up her band, Clark continued to play regularly at the Frontier Hotel in Vegas, and through his new manager, Jackson's ex-manager Jim Halsey, he landed spots on *The Tonight Show* and the sitcom *The Beverly Hillbillies*, where he played both Cousin Roy and Big Mama Halsey.

In 1963, Clark signed to Capitol Records, and his first single for the label, "Tips of My Fingers," became a Top Ten hit. Over the next two years, he had a handful of minor hits before he switched labels, signing to Dot in 1968. At Dot, his career took off again, through covers of pop songs like Charles Aznavour's "Yesterday, When I Was Young" (No. 9, 1969). However, what really turned Clark's career around was not records, but a television show called *Hee Haw*. Conceived as a country version of *Laugh-In*, *Hee Haw* began its run in 1969 on CBS. Roy Clark and Bakersfield country pioneer Buck Owens were picked as co-hosts. Over the next two years, it was one of the most popular shows on television. In 1971, CBS dropped the show because its corny country humor didn't fit the network's new, urban image, but *Hee Haw* quickly moved into syndication, where it continued to thrive throughout the decade.

While *Hee Haw* was at the height of its popularity, Clark had a string of country hits that ranged from Top Ten singles like "I Never Picked Cotton" (1970), "Thank God and Greyhound" (1970), "The Lawrence Welk—Hee Haw Counter-Revolution Polka" (1972), "Come Live with Me" (1973), "Somewhere Between Love and Tomorrow" (1973), "Honeymoon Feelin'" (1974), and "If I Had

It to Do All Over Again" (1976), to a multitude of minor hits. Though he didn't consistently top the country charts, Clark became one of the most recognizable faces in country music, appearing on television commercials, *Hee Haw*, and touring not only the United States, but a number of other countries, including a groundbreaking sojourn to the Soviet Union in 1976. Frequently, he played concerts and recorded albums with a wide variety of musicians from other genres, including the Boston Pops Orchestra and Clarence "Gatemouth" Brown.

In 1979, the momentum of his career began to slow down, as he left his longtime label ABC/Dot for MCA. Over the next two years, he had a number of minor hits before leaving the label. He recorded one inspirational album for Songbird in 1981 before signing to Churchill in 1982. *Hee Haw*'s audience was beginning to decline in the early '80s, but Clark diversified his interests by investing in property, minor-league baseball teams, cattle, publishing, and advertising. None of Clark's recordings for Churchill were big hits, and his brief stays at Silver Dollar in 1986 and Hallmark in 1989 also resulted in no hits. Nevertheless, Clark had become a country icon by the mid-'80s, so his lack of sales didn't matter—he continued to sell out concerts and win awards; he even made the comedy Western *Uphill All the Way* in 1986 with Mel Tillis. In 1987, he was belatedly made a member of the Grand Ole Opry. During the '90s, Clark concentrated on performing at his theater in Branson, MO, sporadically releasing re-recordings of his big hits on a variety of small labels. —*David Vinopal*

The Tips of My Fingers / 1963 / Capitol ✦✦✦
This album features "My Baby's Gone," "Silver Threads & Golden Needles," "Faded Love," and "Take Me As I Am," among others. —*AMG*

● **Greatest Hits** / Sep. 12, 1995 / Varèse Vintage ✦✦✦✦
By concentrating on his biggest straight country hits for Capitol and Dot Records ("Tips of My Fingers," "Yesterday, When I Was Young," "I Never Picked Greyhound," "Thank God and Greyhound," "Come Live with Me") and sidestepping many of the novelty numbers that were associated with *Hee-Haw*, the 14-song *Greatest Hits* makes a case for Roy Clark's talents as songwriter and performer, providing a good introduction to his career. —*Stephen Thomas Erlewine*

Roy Clark & Joe Pass Play Hank Williams / Nov. 1995 / Ranwood ✦✦✦
Play Hank Williams is a charming, understated duet album between Roy Clark and Joe Pass, who effortlessly trade graceful, tasteful licks throughout the entire album. It may not offer any revelations, but the album offers plenty of wonderful music. —*Thom Owens*

Sanford Clark

b. 1935, Tulsa, OK
Vocals / Rock & Roll, Traditional Country
Sanford Clark found fleeting fame with his rendition of the Lee Hazlewood song "The Fool." With a vocal style that blended elements of Johnny Cash with Ricky Nelson, Clark released the song in 1956, and it eventually peaked in the Top Ten of the pop charts and in the Top 15 of the country charts—his first and only hit.

Clark was born in Tulsa, OK, and raised in Phoenix, AZ. A guitar player from childhood, he was influenced by both early rock 'n' roll music and by country music. He got his start in the early '50s playing in Phoenix clubs. While stationed in the South Pacific during his stint in the Air Force, he formed a band and won a talent contest in Hawaii. Eventually, the Air Force stationed him back in Phoenix, where he met his old friend Al Casey, who introduced Clark to Hazlewood, who was still working as a local deejay and hadn't yet made his mark as a songwriter. Soon afterward, Clark recorded "The Fool" with Casey on guitar. The song was released on MCI and went nowhere until a Philadelphia deejay heard it and took the song to Dot Records' Randy Wood, who liked it and had Hazlewood license the song to his label. Afterward, Clark and Casey began a promotional tour opening for such stars as Ray Price and Roy Orbison. In 1957, Clark returned to the studio to record another Hazlewood song, "The Cheat." It only became a minor hit. At this time, Clark was having trouble with

Wood, who wanted him to become a virtual clone of Dot's most popular artist, Pat Boone. The label sent Clark to Hollywood to continue recording, but many of the songs were not released until much later. Those that were released did little or nothing on the charts.

In 1958, Clark signed to Jamie Records. Casey and Hazlewood joined him and began working with Duane Eddy. They also worked with Clark, who recorded "Still as the Night," featuring Eddy on guitar. Nothing happened on the charts, and he began recording on other independent labels. Clark eventually landed in Hollywood, where he hooked up with songwriter/aspiring performer Roger Miller, who was playing the Palomino Club. Miller wanted him to record a few of his songs, but Clark wasn't interested. Clark almost had a hit in 1964, when he recorded Hazlewood's "Houston" for Warner. Unfortunately, Dean Martin also recorded it on Reprise and his version became the hit. The following year, Clark returned to Ramsey's label and created a new version of "The Fool" featuring Waylon Jennings on guitar. By this time Hazlewood had become a prominent producer, and he signed Clark to his LHI label. Clark made an album there, *Return of the Fool*, but it went nowhere and by the early '70s he had finally had enough and joined the construction industry, where he found success at last. Clark continues to record sometimes on his Desert Sun label. —*Sandra Brennan*

The Fool / 1983 / Ace ◆◆◆◆

Rockin' Rollin' / 1986 / Bear Family ◆◆◆◆

Rockin' Rollin' 2 / 1986 / Bear Family ◆◆◆◆

● **Shades** / 1994 / Bear Family ◆◆◆◆
Shades contains all of Sanford Clark's classic early recordings for MCI and Dot, including "The Fool," "(They Call Me) Country," "Pledging My Love," and "Black Jack County Chain." In addition to the studio masters, *Shades* features a handful of rarities and demos, making the compilation both the perfect introduction and the definitive retrospective. —*Thom Owens*

Terri Clark

b. Aug. 5, 1968, Montreal, Canada
Vocals / Contemporary Country
Like her contemporary Shania Twain, Terri Clark came storming out of Canada and captured the attention of America's country music industry in the mid-'90s. Where Twain incorporated more rock 'n' roll into her music, Clark pretty much stayed close to her country roots, even though those roots were more new country than hardcore honky tonk.

Raised in Medicine Hat, Alberta, Canada, Terri Clark was born into a musical family. Her grandparents, Ray and Betty Gauthier, were country stars in Canada, opening shows for stars like George Jones and Little Jimmy Dickens, while her mother sang folk songs in local coffeehouses. As a child, Terri listened to her grandparents' country records and taught herself how to play guitar. Throughout her adolescence, Clark sang, played, and listened to country music; she was particularly inspired by female artists like Reba McEntire, the Judds and Linda Ronstadt. Following her high school graduation in 1987, she moved to Nashville. Upon her arrival, she wandered into Tootsie's Orchid Lounge unannounced and asked if she could sing. Surprisingly, she impressed the management and she landed a job as the club's house singer. Though her initial arrival in Nashville was successful, it took Clark quite a long time to work her way into the actual industry. For the next seven years, she sang at clubs and worked odd jobs, all the while trying to land a record contract. During this time, she met and married a fiddler named Ted Stevenson. In 1994, she landed an audition for Mercury Records. After seeing a live performance from Clark, the label's president signed the singer. Clark's eponymous debut album was released in the summer of 1995.

Terri Clark was a hit upon its release, spawning the Top Ten hits "Better Things to Do," "When Boy Meets Girl" and "If I Were You," as well as going gold. Clark supported the album with a tour opening for George Strait.

In 1996, she was nominated for the Country Music Association's Horizon Award, as well as the Academy of Country Music Awards' Best New Female Vocalist. She won a bevy of Canadian

Country Music awards in 1996, including Album of the Year and Single of the Year; she also was named the Top New Female Country Artist of 1995 by *Billboard* magazine. Her second album, *Just the Same*, was released in the fall of 1996, preceded by the hit single "Poor, Poor Pitiful Me." —*Stephen Thomas Erlewine*

● **Terri Clark** / 1995 / Mercury Nashville ◆◆◆◆
Terri Clark's self-titled debut established the vocalist as a promising singer and songwriter. Working from a basic, traditional country foundation, Clark adds in slight elements of pop and rock, making her music more immediately accessible. Though there are some flaws in the songs—occasionally, the melodies fail to stick—her impassioned, powerful singing make the album consistently entertaining. —*Stephen Thomas Erlewine*

Just the Same / Nov. 5, 1996 / ◆◆◆
Terri Clark's second album, *Just the Same*, exhibits a slightly stronger country-rock influence, as evidenced by the choice of "Poor, Poor Pitiful Me"—a Warren Zevon cover as recorded by Linda Ronstadt—as the first single. Clark has the voice and power to make these rocking updates of traditional country convincing, yet the material is slightly too uneven and the production is slightly too slick to make the album the equal of the debut. Nevertheless, *Just the Same* isn't much of a sophomore slip—in fact, the best moments eclipse the finest parts of *Terri Clark*. You just wish there were more great moments than there are. —*Thom Owens*

Philip Claypool

Contemporary Country, Country-Folk
Memphis-born country-folk performer Philip Claypool began writing songs and leading his first band while in high school. While in college, he became a regular on the university circuit before releasing his debut *A Circus Leaving Town* in 1995. —*Jason Ankeny*

A Circus Leaving Town / Nov. 21, 1995 / Curb ◆◆◆
Phillip Claypool's debut album *Circus Leaving Town* is a diverse collection. Building on a solid contemporary country base, Claypool adds elements of blues, gospel, and folk, making the record a thoroughly Southern affair. Much of the music and production is intriguing, saving even the weakest songs on the record. It has a slightly uneven selection of material, but *Circus Leaving Town* remains a promising debut. —*Stephen Thomas Erlewine*

Lee Clayton

b. Oct. 29, 1942, Russelville, AL
Guitar (Steel), Vocals / Progressive Country, Singer-Songwriter, Outlaw Country
Lee Clayton was one of the original "outlaw" country singer-songwriters and the author of the anthem "Ladies Love Outlaws." He spent his youth in Oak Ridge, TN, and was raised on the songs of Jimmie Rodgers and Red Foley. When Lee turned nine, he received a Hawaiian guitar, and 18 months later debuted on a local radio station playing "Steel Guitar Rag." Soon after his release from the Air Force in 1969, he headed for Nashville. His first success as a songwriter came in 1972 when Waylon Jennings recorded "Ladies Love Outlaws." Clayton recorded his debut album in 1973; it was not successful and the following year, he moved to Joshua Springs, CA, and continued to write songs. His songs soon were in high demand and were performed by the likes of Jerry Jeff Walker, Hoyt Axton, and Willie Nelson.

Inspired by his success, Clayton returned to Nashville and in 1977 signed with Capitol. The following year he released *Border Affair*, and in 1979 recorded *Naked Child*. In 1980, he embarked upon a world tour and then returned home to record the relatively unsuccessful *The Dream Goes On*. Clayton was slated to make a video and release the first single for the album when he suddenly stopped recording, although he did write two autobiographical books and a stage play, *Little Boy Blue*. In 1990, he came back to music and recorded *Another Night*, a live concert in Oslo, Norway. The same year, the Highwaymen recorded his song "Silver Stallion." —*Sandra Brennan*

● **Lee Clayton** / 1973 / MCA ◆◆◆◆

Border Affair / 1978 / Capitol ◆◆◆◆

Naked Child / 1979 / Capitol ✦✦✦
The Dream Goes On / 1981 / Capitol ✦✦✦
Another Night / 1990 / Provogue ✦✦✦

Vassar Clements

b. Apr. 25, 1928, Kinard, SC
Fiddle / Traditional Bluegrass

Combining jazz with country, Vassar Clements became one of the most distinctive, inventive, and popular fiddlers in bluegrass music. Clements first came to prominence as a member of Bill Monroe's band in the early '50s, but he never limited himself to traditional bluegrass. Over the next four decades, he distinguished himself by incorporating a number of different genres into his style. In the process, he became not only one of the most respected fiddlers in bluegrass, he also became a sought-after session musician, playing with artists as diverse as the Monkees, Hank Williams, Paul McCartney, Michelle Shocked, Vince Gill, and Bonnie Raitt.

Clements taught himself to play fiddle at the age of seven. Soon afterward, he formed a band with two of his cousins. By the time he was 21, Clements' skills were impressive enough to attract the attention of Bill Monroe. Monroe hired the young fiddler and Clements appeared on the Grand Ole Opry with the mandolinist in 1949. The following year, the fiddler recorded his first session with Monroe.

For the next six years, Clements stayed with Monroe's band, occasionally leaving for brief periods of time. In 1957, he joined Jim & Jesse's Virginia Boys and stayed with them for the next four years. In the early '60s, Clements was sidelined for a while, as he suffered from alcoholism. By the end of the '60s he had rehabilitated, and he returned to playing in 1967. That year he moved to Nashville and began playing the tenor banjo at a residency at the Dixieland Landing Club. In 1969, he toured with Faron Young and joined John Hartford's Dobrolic Plectorial Society. The band only lasted ten months and after its breakup, Clements joined the Earl Scruggs Revue; he stayed with that band for a year.

Clements began playing sessions in 1971, appearing on albums by Steve Goodman, Gordon Lightfoot, David Bromberg, J.J. Cale, and Mike Audridge over the next two years. In 1972 he was featured on the Nitty Gritty Dirt Band's hit album Will the Circle Be Unbroken, which helped establish him as a country and bluegrass star. Clements capitalized on the record's popularity in 1973, when he released his first solo album, Crossing the Catskills, on Rounder Records and began touring the festival and college circuits. That same year, he appeared on a number of albums, including the Grateful Dead's Wake of the Flood, Jimmy Buffett's A White Sports Coat & A Pink Crustacean, and Mickey Newbury's Heaven Help the Child.

In 1974, Clements signed a record contract with Mercury Records, releasing two albums for the label—Vassar Clements and Superbow—the following year. That same year, he appeared in the bluegrass supergroup Old & In the Way, which also featured Jerry Garcia, David Grisman, Peter Rowan, and John Kahn. He also had a cameo role in Robert Altman's film Nashville in 1975. In 1977, Clements released two albums for two different labels—The Vassar Clements Band on MCA Records and The Bluegrass Session on Flying Fish. It would be four years before he released another solo album. During that time, he toured constantly and appeared on numerous albums. Clements reappeared in 1981 with Hillbilly Rides Again and Vassar, which were both released on Flying Fish.

During the '80s and '90s, Clements continued to record sporadically, but he cut numerous sessions for other artists and played numerous concerts every year. In 1995, Clements reunited with Old & In the Way, who released That High Lonesome Sound in 1996. —Stephen Thomas Erlewine

Crossing the Catskills / 1973 / Rounder ✦✦✦✦
Tasty fiddling from one of the finest. —Mark A. Humphrey

Vassar Clements / Sep. 1975 / Mercury ✦✦✦

● The Bluegrass Sessions / 1977 / Flying Fish ✦✦✦✦
The title tells the truth. —Mark A. Humphrey

Nashville Jam / 1979 / Flying Fish ✦✦✦
As you may guess from the title, this album features a lively jam session with many greats in bluegrass music. —AMG

Vassar / 1980 / Flying Fish ✦✦✦
This album features Clements strutting his stuff on jazz fiddle with sympathetic backing from his band. Clements is one of the very best on his instrument, and the album showcases his talent. —AMG

Westport Drive / 1984 / Mind Dust Music ✦✦✦

Hillbilly Jazz Rides Again / 1987 / Flying Fish ✦✦✦
Hillbilly Jazz Rides Again is a collection of Western swing revival by Vassar Clements, a former sideman for Bill Monroe. With pianist Bob Hoban and guitarists Dave Salyer and Doug Jemigan in tow, the album actually veers closer to swing than Western, which isn't necessarily a bad thing. However, the performances aren't always inspired, which becomes even more noticeable on the numerous mediocre original songs by Hoban. —Stephen Thomas Erlewine

Grass Routes / 1991 / Rounder ✦✦✦
This recent album shows why Clements is one of the greatest fiddlers in modern country music. —Mark A. Humphrey

Once in a While / 1993 / Flying Fish ✦✦✦
Violinist Vassar Clements has demonstrated the improvisational link between bluegrass and jazz, and this was another example of the two styles' affinity. Clements' soaring phrases and adept solos are right at home on such standard jazz tunes as "Perdido," "Cherokee," and "Sonnymoon for Two," but he doesn't stray far from his favorite breakdown riffs or signature country sound. The results are the kind of loose, joyous jam date where labels mean nothing, and musicianship rather than genre rules. —Ron Wynn

Bill Clifton

b. 1931, Riderwood, MD
Guitar, Autoharp, Vocals / Traditional Bluegrass, Traditional Country

Few contributed as much to the preservation and performance of traditional bluegrass music as Bill Clifton. He was born William Marburg to a wealthy family in Riverwood, MD. As a child, he became fascinated by the hillbilly music he heard on the radio. Around 1950, he adopted the stage name Bill Clifton and began performing on the radio and in public. During his college years, he formed a trio called the Dixie Mountain Boys with folk singers Paul Clayton and Dave Sadler. In 1952, the group made their first recordings, which largely went unheard; the trio then added banjoist Johnny Clark and began playing more traditional bluegrass music. After signing with Blue Ridge Records, they appeared on the radio show Wheeling Jamboree. While there, Clifton befriended the Stanley Brothers and A.P. Carter, and after a brief stint in the military, he began recording in the late '50s, releasing five albums over the next seven years.

In 1963, Clifton and his family moved to England. While in Europe, he played many local clubs. In 1967, he was hired by the Peace Corps and spent three years in the Philippines. While there, he visited New Zealand, recording an album with the Hamilton County Bluegrass Band. Clifton occasionally returned to the US to record, and also kept recording in Europe. In 1972, he returned briefly to America to play his first bluegrass festival circuit. Encouraged by the experience, he began visiting the US more frequently and recorded more regularly, signing a contract with County Records. On his third album for the label, he formed the First Generation with mandolinist Red Rector and banjoist Don Stover. After the album's release, the trio toured the bluegrass circuit for the remainder of the 1970s. In the early '80s, Clifton and his family moved to Virginia, where he worked as a businessman. However, Clifton continued to perform at bluegrass festivals and occasional concerts into the '90s. —Sandra Brennan

Getting Folk / 1972 / Bear Family ✦✦✦✦

★ The Early Years (1957-1958) / Jun. 15, 1992 / Rounder ✦✦✦✦✦
Bill Clifton is one of bluegrass' finest guitarists and also an underrated vocalist. He is especially gripping on slow, aching tunes like "Lonely Heart Blues" or gospel numbers like "I'm Living the

Right Life Now" and "When You Kneel at Your Mother's Grave." Clifton's late '50s singles are collected on this CD, featuring him working alongside such musicians as Curley Lambert on mandolin and Johnny Clark on banjo, as well as fiddler Tommy Jackson, Ralph Stanley on banjo, and Gordon Terry on fiddle. These songs are light years away from the polished, intricate newgrass and contemporary bluegrass sounds of the 1980s and '90s. The harmonies, leads, solos, and arrangements reflect simpler, more innocent times, but don't lack intensity or musical quality. —Ron Wynn

Going Back to Dixie / Bear Family ✦✦✦✦

A Bluegrass Session 1952 / Bear Family ✦✦✦✦

Are You from Dixie / Bear Family ✦✦✦✦

Beatle Crazy / Bear Family ✦✦✦✦

Patsy Cline (Virginia Patterson Hensley)
b. Sep. 8, 1932, Gore, VA, **d.** Mar. 5, 1963, Camden, TN
Piano, Vocals / Traditional Country, Rockabilly, Nashville Sound/ Countrypolitan

One of the greatest singers in the history of country music, Patsy Cline also helped blaze a trail for female singers to assert themselves as an integral part of the Nashville-dominated country music industry. She was not alone in this regard; Kitty Wells had become a star several years before Cline's big hits in the early '60s. Brenda Lee, who shared Cline's producer, did just as much to create a country-pop crossover during the same era; Skeeter Davis briefly enjoyed similar success. Cline has the most legendary aura of any female country singer, however, perhaps due to an early death that cut her off just after she had entered her prime.

Cline began recording in the mid-'50s, and although she recorded quite a bit of material between 1955 and 1960 (17 singles in all), only one of them was a hit. That song, "Walkin' After Midnight," was both a classic and a Top 20 pop smash. Those who are accustomed to Cline's famous early '60s hits are in for a bit of a shock when surveying her 1950s sessions (which have been reissued on several Rhino compilations). At times she sang flat-out rockabilly; she also tried some churchy tear-weepers. She couldn't follow up "Walkin' After Midnight," however, in part because of an exploitative deal that limited her to songs from one publishing company.

Circumstances were not wholly to blame for Cline's commercial failures. She would have never made it as a rockabilly singer, lacking the conviction of Wanda Jackson or the spunk of Brenda Lee. In fact, in comparison with her best work, she sounds rather stiff and ill-at-ease on most of her early singles. Things took a radical turn for the better on all fronts in 1960, when her initial contract expired. With the help of producer Owen Bradley (who had worked on her sessions all along), Cline began selecting material that was both more suitable and of a higher quality than her previous outings.

"I Fall to Pieces," cut at the very first session where Cline was at liberty to record what she wanted, was the turning point in her career. Reaching No. 1 in the country charts and No. 12 in the pop charts, it was the first of several country-pop crossovers she was to enjoy over the next couple of years. More important, it set a prototype for commercial Nashville country at its best. Owen Bradley crafted lush orchestral arrangements, with weeping strings and backup vocals by the Jordanaires, that owed more to pop (in the best sense) than country.

The country elements were provided by the cream of Nashville's session musicians, including guitarist Hank Garland, pianist Floyd Cramer, and drummer Buddy Harmon. Patsy's voice sounded richer, more confident, and more mature, with ageless wise and vulnerable qualities that have enabled her records to maintain their appeal with subsequent generations. When k.d. lang recorded her 1988 album *Shadowland* with Owen Bradley, it was this phase of Cline's career that she was specifically attempting to emulate.

It's arguable that too much has been made of Cline's crossover appeal to the pop market. Brenda Lee, whose records were graced with similar Bradley productions, was actually more successful in this area (although her records were likely targeted towards a younger audience). Cline's appeal was undeniably more adult, but she was always more successful with country listeners. Her final four Top Ten country singles, in fact, didn't make the pop Top 40.

Despite a severe auto accident in 1961, Cline remained hot through 1961 and 1962, with "Crazy" and "She's Got You" both becoming big country and pop hits. Much of her achingly romantic material was supplied by fresh talent like Hank Cochran, Harlan Howard, and Willie Nelson (who penned "Crazy"). Although her commercial momentum had faded slightly, she was still at the top of her game when she died in a plane crash in March of 1963, at the age of 30. She was only a big star for a couple of years, but her influence was and remains huge. While the standards of professionalism on her recordings have been emulated ever since, they've rarely been complemented by as much palpable, at times heartbreaking, emotion in the performances. For those who could do without some of the more elaborate arrangements of her later years, many of her relatively unadorned appearances on radio broadcasts have been thankfully preserved and issued. —Richie Unterberger

Patsy Cline Showcase / 1961 / MCA ✦✦✦
Pop and C&W standards are included, plus three of her biggest hits: "I Fall to Pieces," "Crazy," and "Walkin' After Midnight." —George Bedard

Sentimentally Yours / 1962 / MCA ✦✦✦✦
Pop and C&W collection—several Hank Williams songs. Included is the great "She's Got You." —George Bedard

The Patsy Cline Story / 1963 / MCA ✦✦✦
The Patsy Cline Story is a double-record, 24-track collection that Decca released in 1963, shortly after her tragic death. The compilation remains one of the strongest and most thorough retrospectives ever assembled, featuring most of her biggest hits—"Walking After Midnight," "She's Got You," "Crazy," "I Fall to Pieces," "Sweet Dreams"—plus a number of lesser-known gems like "Why Can't He Be You" and "Leavin' on Your Mind." The presence of these relatively unfamiliar tracks means that the album gives a more rounded and complete picture of Cline's career than *12 Greatest Hits*, even if it isn't as thorough as the subsequent four-disc box set *The Patsy Cline Collection*. In short, *The Patsy Cline Story* is the ideal introduction for a listener who wants a little more than the basics, but doesn't want to invest in a box set. —Stephen Thomas Erlewine

A Portrait of Patsy Cline / 1964 / MCA ✦✦✦
Country standards and some lesser-known material are included. Among the highlights: "Faded Love" and "Blue Moon of Kentucky." —George Bedard

That's How a Heartache Begins / 1964 / Decca ✦✦✦
A few pop standards are included, plus some of her best: "There He Goes," "Lovin' in Vain," "He Called Me Baby," "I'm Blue Again." Also a great "Lovesick Blues." —George Bedard

Gotta Lot of Rhythm in My Soul / 1965 / Metro ✦✦✦
How did MGM get ahold of this stuff? A good collection with no pop, it includes stuff from her early Coral years as well as later Decca sides. —George Bedard

Stop the World and Let Me Off / 1966 / Hilltop ✦✦✦
This good collection features stuff from her 1955 Coral sessions—"I Cried All the Way to the Altar," "Honky Tonk Merry Go Round"—through 1960 or so—"There He Goes," "Stop, Look & Listen." —George Bedard

★ **Patsy Cline's Greatest Hits** / 1967 / Decca ✦✦✦✦✦
This is the standard collection of Patsy Cline's most successful singles, containing among its 12 tracks seven of her eight Top Ten country hits, from 1957-1963. Since its release, the album has sold four million copies, and at this writing, it is enjoying its 66th consecutive week at No.1 in *Billboard* magazine's Top Country Catalog Albums chart, a chart that has been in existence for 66 weeks. —William Ruhlmann

Country Great / 1969 / MCA Special Products ✦✦✦
"Three Cigarettes in an Ashtray" and "Then You'll Know" are some highlights of this collection. —George Bedard

★ **12 Greatest Hits** / 1988 / MCA ✦✦✦✦✦

12 Greatest Hits is exactly what it says it is—12 of Patsy Cline's biggest hits, including all of her classic singles: "Walkin' After Midnight," "I Fall to Pieces,' "Sweet Dreams," "Crazy," "She's Got You," "Faded Love," and "Leavin' on Your Mind." There's also a number of lesser-known gems like "Why Can't He Be You," which are as good as the big hits. *12 Greatest Hits* may be brief, but it contains absolutely no filler and leaves no gaps, making it the perfect introduction to one of the greatest singers in country music history. —*Stephen Thomas Erlewine*

Live at the Opry / 1988 / MCA ✦✦✦

As everyone who listened to the Ryman Opry knows, even a good singer can sound pretty bad live over the radio. Cline sounds simply great, with no studio effects and a sometimes pedestrian backup. —*George Bedard*

Live, Vol. 2 / 1989 / MCA ✦✦✦✦

A sequel to *Live at the Opry,* it's not called *Live at the Opry Vol. 2* because it wasn't taken from Opry broadcasts, but from radio shows produced for the US Navy and Armed Forces. The 12 performances date from 1956 to 1962, and are of special interest in that they include five songs that Cline never recorded in the studio for commercial release, including numbers by Roger Miller, Webb Pierce, and Sonny James. Cline's in good form throughout, the fidelity is very good, and the arrangements are on the whole considerably sparer than her studio recordings were wont to employ. The straightahead reading of "Strange," a top-notch 1962 Mel Tillis composition that went on the B-side of "She's Got You," is a particular highlight. This is a good album that will appeal to most country fans, not just Patsy Cline collectors. —*Richie Unterberger*

Walkin' Dreams: Her First Recordings, Vol. 1 / 1989 / Rhino ✦✦✦✦

Although Cline recorded quite a bit during the last half of the 1950s, it was a frustrating period for her, both commercially and artistically. Commercially, there was only one hit; artistically, she had yet to perfect her delivery, and didn't have access to as much first-rate material as she would later on. Rhino's three-part *Her First Recordings* series presents a few dozen sides from this era. While they aren't as impressive as her more widely known '60s recordings, they're worthwhile both for the occasional first-rate performance and the illustration of the various approaches Cline and producer Owen Bradley attempted in her formative days. Vol. 1, focusing on recordings from 1955-57, is variable in both style and quality, as Patsy tries out spirituals, melodramatic ballads, and upbeat country-pop. Includes "Walkin' After Midnight," which is the original pop Top 20 version, not the later re-recording that is featured on many compilations. —*Richie Unterberger*

Her First Recordings, Vol. 2: Hungry for Love / 1989 / Rhino ✦✦✦✦

The second installment of *Her First Recordings*, with 14 tracks from 1957-59, is more pop-oriented than Vol. 1, and perhaps less interesting because of that. It does show Cline and producer Owen Bradley beginning to develop the Nashville Sound that would serve her well in the '60s, with contributions from such regulars as the Anita Kerr Singers, the Jordanaires, Floyd Cramer, Grady Martin, and Hank Garland. With some more work and better material, the prototype would pay big dividends just a year or two down the road. —*Richie Unterberger*

Her First Recordings, Vol. 3: The Rockin' Side / 1989 / Rhino ✦✦✦✦

Patsy Cline—rocker? Well, sort of. At the outset of her recording career in the late '50s, Cline tried a variety of approaches, including rockabilly and uptempo hillbilly. This disc assembles 13 of her rockabilly-flavored recordings from 1956-59. It's not bad, but rockabilly was not Cline's forte—she was much more at ease with ballads and midtempo numbers with a heavier pop/country feel. In comparison with '50s female rockabilly singers like Brenda Lee (who shared Cline's producer), Patsy comes off as rather stiff and inhibited. "Stop, Look, and Listen" (1956) is the clear high-

Patsy Cline

light here, with a natural snare-paced groove absent from the other tracks. —*Richie Unterberger*

☆ **The Patsy Cline Collection** / 1991 / MCA ✦✦✦✦✦

If Hank Williams remains the undisputed King of Country Music, then surely the passage of time has made the Queen of Country Music crown sit just as easy on the head of Patsy Cline's memory. Since her death in 1963, Patsy Cline has always had an audience. Selling 75,000 copies a year, year in and out, 17 years after you're dead is no small achievement; just ask Sid Vicious. But since her movie deification in the '80s, you can take that 75,000 copies a year and multiply it by ten. Patsy Cline is an official growth industry, just like Elvis or poor ol' Hank. So even though MCA has some 20-odd Patsy Cline packages in the catalog already, it makes more than a little sense to release this excellent four-CD box, produced by the Country Music Foundation. The sound, except for the live radio transcription disc stuff, is as cozy, warm, and appealing as you could want. The track lineup, in chronological order, follows Cline's days from hard-line honky tonk belter to the ballad smoothies that made her reputation. There is no place in the four-and-a-half hours of music here that you don't find yourself enjoying what you're hearing, and in the world of box sets, that's saying a lot. In other words, there's not a single level at which this release does not mightily succeed. Because the major reason for Cline's enduring legend and growth-industry status is that the girl just plain sang her ass off, and here's 104 perfect examples of it. —*Cub Koda*

At Her Best / Aug. 29, 1992 / International Marketing Group ✦✦✦

Not strictly a hits collection, *At Her Best* is an excellent but brief nine-track album that features several of Patsy's most familiar songs ("Walkin' After Midnight," "Just out of Reach"), plus many wonderful lesser-known gems, like "Stop the World," "Too Many Secrets," and "Life's Railway to Heaven." —*Stephen Thomas Erlewine*

The Birth of a Star / 1996 / Razor & Tie ✦✦✦

Although Cline only had one hit in the late '50s ("Walking After Midnight"), she managed to appear on Arthur Godfrey's popular network television show several times in 1957-58. This disc presents 17 performances that she delivered on these programs (including two versions of "Walking After Midnight"), accompanied by Godfrey's house band. In truth, this isn't the best context in which to hear Cline. It's far more pop than country in orientation, especially given the mainstream flavor of her accompanists, whose arrangements are far from rootsy and can be downright square, especially with the frequent interjections of brass and clarinet. Cline herself had yet to reach her vocal peak, but she does project with assurance on these songs, which she recorded official versions of in the late '50s. It's not one of the first Cline albums that should be added to your collection, but it's certainly of considerable interest to serious Cline fans, with versions of "Your Cheatin' Heart" and the spirituals "Down by the Riverside" and "The Man Upstairs" rating as the most unusual items. —*Richie Unterberger*

The Four Star Years / 1996 / ✦✦✦✦
The Four Star Years is a double-disc set that contains all 50 recordings that Patsy Cline made for the Four Star record label in the mid-'50s. Recorded before she signed to Decca, these recordings represent Cline at her rawest and roughest—there are none of the string arrangements that graced many of her biggest Decca hits. Since Four Star forced her to sing songs that their company published, the quality of the material is somewhat uneven, but the performances are all first-rate and the set is essential for any serious Patsy Cline fan. —*Stephen Thomas Erlewine*

Jerry Clower

b. Sep. 28, 1926, Liberty, MS
Vocals / Country Humor
If Homer & Jethro are the Abbott & Costello of country humor, then Jerry Clower is certainly country's answer to Bob Hope. As its Crown Prince of comedy, the rotund comic has made many generations laugh with his down-home humor, but he has never crossed over, making him country's best-kept comic secret. A virtual mainstay on any number of shows on The Nashville Network, Clower relates stories dealing with all the issues, but in a G-rated style that's one part Will Rogers, the other part Andy Griffith.

Raised in rural Mississippi, Clower originally planned on a career in agriculture, and during his youth was actively involved in the 4-H Club. After graduating, he joined the Navy, and after that attended Southwest Mississippi Junior College. He received a football scholarship and studied agriculture at Mississippi State University. He then obtained what must be the perfect job for a storyteller: he became a fertilizer salesman. In 1970, following a speaking engagement to a farm group in Lubbock, TX, a local disc jockey encouraged Clower to make a comedy album. The deejay then taped Clower's next talk and sent it to MCA, which called back and offered Clower a contract. His record debut was *Jerry Clower from Yazoo City, Mississippi, Talkin'.* Like the 22 albums to come, this was taped before a live audience—because he thinks laugh tracks are dishonest—and featured songs and stories based on his past and present experiences with Southern country life. He also has a raft of interesting characters such as the lively, fictional "Ledbetter" family, whose members frequently appear in the stories. His debut album was not nationally distributed, yet through word-of-mouth sold 8,000 copies and eventually spent several weeks on the *Billboard* charts. Among his best known routines is "Coon Hunt Story."

In 1987, he deviated a bit from his usual schtick to begin his album *Top Gum* with a rap song. After his 1979 album *Greatest Hits* went gold in 1992, Clower signed a new contract with MCA the following year. When not performing live and recording, Clower hosted the nationally syndicated radio show *Country Crossroads*, plus a syndicated television show. He has also written three bestsellers: *Ain't God Good, Let the Hammer Down* and *Life Everlaughter*. The subject of an award-winning documentary (*Ain't God Good*), Clower himself has received many honors for his good work: in 1976, he was awarded the national "4-H Alumni" award by the Future Farmers of America; his fans and the major trade magazines named him "Country Comic of the Year" ten years in a row; Yazoo City, MS, named a boulevard after him; he earned the "Christian Service Award" from the Southern Baptist Radio and Television Commission; and was awarded an honorary doctorate from Mississippi College. —*Sandra Brennan & Larry Lapka*

● **Jerry Clower's Greatest Hits** / 1994 / MCA ✦✦✦✦

Eddie Cochran

b. Oct. 3, 1938, Oklahoma City, OK, **d.** Apr. 17, 1960, Wiltshire, England
Guitar, Vocals / Rock & Roll, Rockabilly
Somehow, time has not accorded Eddie Cochran quite the same respect as other early rockabilly pioneers like Buddy Holly, or even Ricky Nelson or Gene Vincent. This is partially attributable to his very brief lifespan as a star: he only had a couple of big hits before dying in a car crash during a British tour in 1960. He was in the same league as the best rockabilly stars, though, with a brash, fat guitar sound that helped lay the groundwork for the power chord. He was also a good songwriter and singer, celebrating the joys of teenage life—the parties, the music, the adolescent rebellion—with an economic wit that bore some similarities to Chuck Berry. Cochran was more lighthearted and less ironic than Berry, though, and if his work was less consistent and not as penetrating, it was almost always exuberant.

Cochran's mid-'50s beginnings in the record industry are a bit confusing. His family had moved to Southern California around 1950, and in 1955 he made his first recordings as half of the Cochran Brothers. Here's the confusing part: although the other half of the act was really named Hank Cochran, he was *not* Eddie's brother. (Hank Cochran would become a noted country songwriter in the 1960s.) Eddie was already an accomplished rockabilly guitarist and singer on these early sides, and he started picking up some session work as well, also finding time to make demos and write songs with Jerry Capehart, who became his manager.

Cochran's big break came about in a novel fashion. In mid-1956, while Cochran and Capehart were recording some new music for low-budget films, Boris Petroff asked Eddie if he'd be interested in appearing in a movie that a friend was directing. The film was *The Girl Can't Help It*, and the song he would sing in it was "Twenty-Flight Rock." This is the same song that Paul McCartney would use to impress John Lennon upon their first meeting in 1957 (Paul could not only play it, but knew all of the lyrics).

Cochran had his first Top 20 hit in early 1957, "Sittin' in the Balcony," with an echo-chambered vocal reminiscent of Elvis. That single was written by John D. Loudermilk, but Eddie would write much of his material, including his only Top Ten hit, "Summertime Blues." A definitive teenage anthem with hints of the overt protest that would seep into rock music in the 1960s, it was also a technical tour de force for the time: Cochran overdubbed himself on guitar to create an especially thick sound. One of the classic early rock singles, "Summertime Blues" was revived a decade later by proto-metal group Blue Cheer, and was a concert staple for the Who, who had a small American hit with a cover version. (Let's not mention Alan Jackson's country rendition in the 1990s.)

That, disappointingly, was the extent of Cochran's major commercial success in the US. "C'mon Everybody," a chugging rocker that was almost as good as "Summertime Blues," made the Top 40 in 1959, and also gave Cochran his first British Top Tenner. As is the case with his buddy Gene Vincent, though, you can't judge his importance by mere chart statistics. Cochran was very active in the studio, and while his output wasn't nearly as consistent as Buddy Holly's (another good friend of Eddie's), he laid down a few classic or near-classic cuts that are just as worthy as his hits. "Somethin' Else," "My Way" (which the Who played in concert at the peak of psychedelia), "Weekend" (covered by the Move), and "Nervous Breakdown" are some of the best of these, and belong in the collection of every rockabilly fan. He was also (like Holly) an innovator in the studio, using overdubbing at a time when that practice was barely known on rock recordings.

Cochran is more revered today in Britain than the United States, due in part to the tragic circumstances of his death. In the spring of 1960, he toured the UK with Vincent, to a wild reception, in a country that had rarely had the opportunity to see American rock 'n' roll stars in the flesh. En route to London to fly back to the States for a break, the car Cochran was riding in, with his girlfriend (and songwriter) Sharon Sheeley and Gene Vincent, got into a serious accident. Vincent and Sheeley survived, but Cochran died less than a day later, at the age of 21. —*Richie Unterberger*

Legend in Our Time / 1972 / Union Pacific ◆◆◆
This British release contains some 1956 rockabilly duets with Hank Cochran—check out "Tired and Sleepy" and "Fool's Paradise"—along with live performances on BBC radio from 1960. —*George Bedard*

Eddie Cochran Singles Album / 1979 / United Artists ◆◆◆
Another Brit release has most of the good stuff. —*George Bedard*

Portrait of a Legend / 1985 / Rockstar ◆◆◆
Fine-looking and fine-sounding collection of unreleased stereo versions and alternate takes, this is nonetheless unnecessary for all but Cochran completists. In the spirit of numerous Beatles bootlegs (though this LP is quite official), these are in the main studio recordings with small (sometimes minute) differences in the mixing, or stereo versions that are not easy to come by on official releases, although mono versions of the exact same takes are plentiful. There are plenty of fine songs here ("Weekend," "Summertime Blues," "C'mon Everybody," "Three Steps to Heaven"), but they're better heard both in their more common versions, and in the context of a coherent anthology. And if you need to settle for just one version of "Summertime Blues" or "C'mon Everybody," why spring for the "Summertime Blues" *without* the echoed vocal, or "C'mon Everybody" *missing* a guitar overdub? —*Richie Unterberger*

The Early Years / 1988 / Ace ◆◆◆
Compilation of 16 tracks from the mid-'50s, most or all dating from before Cochran's breakthrough to national recognition with "Twenty Flight Rock." Some were recorded when Eddie was half of the Cochran Brothers, with (the unrelated) Hank Cochran; there are also tracks credited to Jerry Capehart and Albert Stone, which Eddie most likely had a prominent role on, as sessionman or producer (the liner notes are resolutely unhelpful on providing exact details). Most of this is pretty solid rockabilly, not much below the standards of Cochran's best releases. There are also a couple of hot instrumentals, and ballad-type numbers on which Eddie employs a husky, echoed Elvisoid delivery. A decent release, but assembled in a scattershot fashion. If you're interested enough in Cochran to want to track this down, you may well be interested enough in him to spring for a box set, and most or all of these are contained on whatever box set you manage to locate. —*Richie Unterberger*

Box Set / 1988 / Liberty ◆◆◆
This six-LP import—which still, somehow, manages not to include every track Cochran recorded—is excessive for the non-fanatic. Nevertheless, it does include quite a few obscure, interesting prefame performances from the mid-'50s (some as part of the Cochran Brothers). Other bonuses include a live 1960 British TV broadcast, an album's worth of sessions and his work as a producer, and entire sides of instrumentals and stereo versions, as well as a 32-page booklet. —*Richie Unterberger*

★ Legendary Masters / 1990 / EMI America ◆◆◆◆◆
The definitive single-disc collection of Cochran's best: "Summertime Blues," "Cut Across Shorty," "Something Else," "Come on Everybody," and "Twenty Flight Rock." All the hits; all the feeling. —*Cub Koda*

Singin' to My Baby/Never to Be Forgotten / Feb. 23, 1993 / Capitol ◆◆◆◆
Two original albums on one compact disc, with only two hits between the two—"Sittin' in the Balcony" and "Twenty Flight Rock." But for devoted fans of Eddie Cochran, this lovingly packaged CD is worth their time, even if some of the material is slightly weak. *Singin' to My Baby* concentrates on ballad material; the posthumously released *Never to Be Forgotten* has more rockers. —*Stephen Thomas Erlewine*

David Allan Coe
b. Sep. 6, 1939, Akron, OH
Guitar, Vocals / Traditional Country, Outlaw Country
A lifelong renegade, singer-songwriter David Allan Coe was one of the most colorful and unpredictable characters in country music history. One of the pioneering artists of the outlaw country movement of the '70s, he didn't have many big hits—only three of his singles hit the Top Ten—but he was among the biggest cult figures in country music throughout his career.

Born in Akron, OH, Coe first got into trouble with the law at age nine. As a result, he was sent to reform school. For the next 20 years, he never spent more than a handful of months outside of a correctional facility—he spent much of his 20s in the Ohio State Penitentiary. Released from prison in 1967, the wild-haired, earring-wearing, heavily tattooed Coe went straight to Nashville, where he lived in a hearse that he parked in front of the old Ryman Auditorium, the home of the Grand Ole Opry. Although he didn't conform to Nashville's professional standards, he soon gained the attention of an independent label, Plantation Records, which released Coe's debut album *Penitentiary Blues* in 1968. Followed within a year by a second volume, all of the songs on these albums were based on his prison experiences.

Coe then toured with Grand Funk Railroad, a signal that he drew as much from rock's traditions as he did from country. Soon, he began performing in a rhinestone suit given to him by Mel Tillis, as well as a Lone Ranger mask, and began calling himself the "Masked Rhinestone Cowboy." Coe's concerts became notorious for their unpredictability—frequently he would roar up on stage astride his enormous Harley, swearing at the audience. He cultivated a large cult following with his act, but he couldn't break into the mainstream. However, other artists found success with his songs—in 1972, Billie Jo Spears had a minor hit with his "Souvenirs & California Mem'rys," and in 1973, Tanya Tucker had a No. 1 hit with Coe's "Would You Lay with Me (in a Field of Stone)." After Tucker's hit, David Allan Coe suddenly became one of Nashville's hottest songwriters; some of the biggest country artists—including Willie Nelson, George Jones, and Tammy Wynette—recorded his tunes, leading to his own contract with Columbia Records.

Coe's first two singles for Columbia didn't come close to the country Top 40, but his 1975 cover of Steve Goodman's "You Never Even Called Me by My Name" cracked the Top Ten. Although a string of moderate hits followed, he rarely cracked the country Top 40, although in 1977 Johnny Paycheck took Coe's "Take This Job and Shove It" to No.1. During his 13-year association with Columbia, Coe released 26 albums, including the double album set *For the Record . . . The First Ten Years* (1984), 1986's *Son of the South* (featuring Willie, Waylon, Jessi Colter and other "outlaws"), and the highly regarded *Matter of Life . . . .and Death* (1987).

Although Coe had a successful career, it was one plagued with many setbacks. The conservative Nashville music industry frequently snubbed him and he had tax problems with the IRS; at one time, they seized his Key West home, and he went to live in a Tennessee cave until he got back on his feet. Toward the end of the '80s, Coe remarried and began to settle down. Throughout the '90s, he was a popular concert attraction in America and Europe. In addition to his musical career, he also acted in a few movies including *The Last Days of Frank and Jesse James*. He also published a novel, *Psychopath*, and an autobiography. —*Sandra Brennan*

Once upon a Rhyme / 1974 / Columbia ◆◆◆
Whether doing one of his own songs or breathing new life into a tune like "Fraulein," few can touch Coe. This album is full of good songs and strong performances and is well worth looking for. —*Jim Worbois*

Longhaired Redneck / 1976 / Columbia ◆◆◆
This is '70s outlaw country at its most virulent. The tattoos and biker bravado thinly conceal Coe's sentimentality. —*Mark A. Humphrey*

Greatest Hits / 1978 / Columbia ✦✦✦✦
Featuring the hits "You Never Even Called Me by My Name,"
"Longhaired Redneck" and "Willie, Waylon and Me," this ten-track
compilation of mid-'70s material from David Allan Coe is all you
need to know about the ex-con turned country con-man/song-
writer. He was one of country's more intriguing egos from the
'70s. —*Mark A. Humphrey*

Just Divorced / 1984 / Columbia ✦✦✦
It's a theme album (see title). —*Mark A. Humphrey*

17 Greatest Hits / 1985 / Columbia ✦✦✦✦
17 Greatest Hits is the most thorough retrospective assembled of
David Alan Coe's outlaw heyday, containing every one of his biggest hits—including "You Never Even Called Me by My Name,"
"The Ride," "Mona Lisa Lost Her Smile," "Willie, Waylon and Me,"
"Longhaired Redneck," and "She Used to Love Me a Lot"—plus a
wealth of minor hits and lesser-known album tracks. The result is
a comprehensive overview of one of the most respected and
admired, if not necessarily popular, country singers of the late '70s
and early '80s. —*Thom Owens*

● **For the Record: The First 10 Years** / 1985 / Columbia ✦✦✦✦
This is an overview of Coe's Columbia sides. —*Mark A. Humphrey*

Super Hits / Mar. 8, 1993 / Columbia ✦✦✦✦
Yet another repackaging of Coe's handful of successful radio
songs, these hits barely hint at the more outrageous material featured on the albums from which they're drawn. —*Michael McCall*

Best of the Best / 1995 / Federal ✦✦✦✦

Compass Point/I've Got Something to Say / 1995 / Bear Family
✦✦✦✦
Bear Family combined two of David Allan Coe's late '70s/early
'80s albums, *Compass Point* and *I've Got Something to Say,* on
one compact disc. Neither record is among Coe's best—they're
plagued with uneven material ("Take This Job and Shove It Too,"
"Hank Williams Junior-Junior") and occasionally half-hearted performances—but each contains a handful of classic performances,
including "Get a Little Dirt on Your Hands," "Merle and Me,"
"Heads or Tails," "Gone (Like)," "I Could Never Give You Up (For
Someone Else)," and "Take It Easy Rider." —*Thom Owens*

Invictus Means Unconquered/Tennessee Waltz / 1995 / Bear
Family ✦✦✦✦
Bear Family combined two of David Allan Coe's early '80s
albums, *Invictus (Means) Unconquered* and *Tennessee Whiskey,*
on one compact disc. While both records contained some fine
moments—"Stand by Your Man," "Tennessee Whiskey," "Some-
place to Come When It Rains," "If You Ever Think of Me at All,"
"I've Given 'Bout All I Can Take"—they were also marked by an
poor selection of songs ("I Love Robbing Banks," "D-R-U-N-K,"
"Little Orphan Annie," "London Homesick Blues") and disheart-
ingly uneven performances. —*Thom Owens*

Super Hits, Vol. 2 / Mar. 19, 1996 / Columbia ✦✦✦
This ten-song compilation is *Vol. 2* in the sense that it contains
David Allen Coe's less successful "super hits." For "Mona Lisa Lost
Her Smile" and "The Ride," look for *Super Hits.* The biggest hits
here are "Long Haired Redneck" and "She Used to Love Me a
Lot," both of which made the Country Top 40. The rest are minor
chart entries or worse. But that's not to say there isn't some characteristically provocative material here, including the Willie Nelson duet "I've Already Cheated on You" and "Now I Lay Me Down
to Cheat," a song that manages to mix infidelity with prayer. Coe
was always a near-parody of a country singer, and the humor content is high, but so is the fun. And if you want to hear strange,
wait for the duet with Lacy J. Dalton on Bob Dylan's "Gotta Serve
Somebody" that closes the album. —*William Ruhlmann*

Ben Colder

Vocals / Country Humor
Ben Colder, the comic alias of witty singer/actor Sheb Wooley, is
used for parodies of popular country records (similar to the
recordings of Weird Al Yankovic, though Wooley has been at it far
longer). His songs either bear the same name as the song being
parodied (i.e. "Hello Wall No. 2") or have a similar sounding twist

on the original title (i.e. "Fifteen Beers Ago" and "Achy Breaky
Car").
Sheb Wooley had a No. 1 hit in 1962, "That's My Pa," and
decided to branch out with his next single, a parody of Rex Allen's
"Don't Go Near the Indians." Titled "Don't Go Near the Eskimos"
and recorded as Ben Colder, the single hit the country Top 20.
After "Hello Wall No. 2" reached No. 30 a year later, Colder was
silent until 1966, when "Almost Persuaded No. 2" peaked at No. 6
(it was Wooley's second-biggest hit overall). Later recordings—"Harper Valley P.T.A. (Later That Same Day)," "Little Green
Apples No. 2" and "Fifteen Bears Ago"—failed to generate much
chart action. Many Ben Colder albums were released by MGM
throughout the 1960s and early '70s. —*Jim Worbois*

● **Golden Hits** / ✦✦✦✦
Contains such hits as "Easy Lovin'," "Don't Go Near the Eskimos,"
and "Little Green Apples." —*AMG*

Ben Colder & Johnny Bond & Junior Samples / ✦✦✦
This album has such favorites as "Harper Valley P.T.A.," "Ten Little
Bottles," and "Later That Same Day." —*AMG*

B.J. Cole

b. Jun. 17, 1946, London, England
*Guitar (Steel) / Rock & Roll, Traditional Country, Nashville
Sound/Countrypolitan*
B.J. Cole was one of the best and most versatile pedal steel guitarists to come out of Great Britain, playing for such diverse artists
as Elton John, Nazareth, Al Stewart, Ian Matthews & Southern
Comfort, T. Rex, and Garth Brooks. Born Brian John Cole in North
Enfield, Herfordshire, England, he began playing guitar at age 12
after hearing the pop group the Shadows. He eventually mastered
a variety of guitars, but found his favorite was the steel. During
the 1970s, Cole became a popular session man. He founded his
own band, Cochise, in 1970 and over the next two years recorded
three albums, including *Swallow Tales* (1971). When not doing
session work, Cole toured Europe working as a "fixer" (one who
assembles bands for visiting US performers). He was known as
an innovator and experimented with electronically altered versions of steel guitar music. —*Sandra Brennan*

Swallow Tails / 1971 / United Artists ✦✦✦

So Far / 1972 / United Artists ✦✦✦

New Hovering Dog / 1973 / United Artists ✦✦✦

● **Transparent Music** / 1989 / Hannibal ✦✦✦✦
B.J. Cole was the premier session steel guitarist for many English
artists and groups during the late '60s and '70s. Now we have the
first steel guitar space music, and Cole's abilities shine through on
pieces ranging from classics such as "Clair de Lune" and Satie's
"Gnossienne" to original pieces. It's ideal for modern "space cowboys." —*AMG*

Heart of the Moment / 1995 / Resurgence ✦✦✦✦

Mark Collie

b. Jan. 18, 1956, Waynesboro, TN
Guitar, Vocals / Contemporary Country, New Traditionalist
The music of singer-songwriter Mark Collie is a lively blend of
straightahead rock 'n' roll and traditional country. He was born in
Waynesboro, TN, one of six children, and grew up listening to
country music. He was most influenced by the fiery piano playing
of Jerry Lee Lewis, the guitar playing of Carl Perkins, and the
songwriting skills of Willie Nelson and Kris Kristofferson. Collie
learned to play guitar and piano and joined a band when he was
12. In high school, he worked as a part-time deejay at the local
radio station. Following graduation, he joined several bands and
toured the Southwest. In 1982, Collie, encouraged by his wife,
moved to Nashville to become a full-time songwriter at a publishing house. When no one hired him, he began singing his own
songs to live audiences and picked up a following when he began
doing monthly performances at the Douglas Corner Cafe.
A showcase in 1989 led MCA/Nashville to sign him. Collie's
first single, "Something with a Ring to It," made it to the Top 60 in
1990. His next single, "Looks Aren't Everything," made it to the
Top 40; both songs appeared on his first album, *Harden County*

Line (1990). Collie then hit the road and played with Reba McEntire, Conway Twitty, and Charlie Daniels. He made it to the Top 20 for the first time in 1991 and then released his second album, *Born and Raised in Black & White*, which produced two Top 40 hits, including "She's Never Coming Back." The following year, the album produced the Top Five single "Even the Man in the Moon Is Crying." His third album, *Mark Collie*, was released in 1993 and continued to fare well with such popular tunes as "Born to Love You" and "Shame, Shame, Shame, Shame." *Unleashed*, Collie's fourth album, appeared in 1994. After its release, he signed with Warner Records, who issued *Tennessee Plates* in 1995. —*Sandra Brennan*

Born & Raised in Black & White / 1985 / MCA ✦✦✦

The first half of Collie's second album contains some smartly written songs, including "She's Never Coming Back" and "Calloused Hands," but some of the first album's edge has been smoothed off. —*Brian Mansfield*

Hardin County Line / 1990 / MCA ✦✦✦✦

This honky tonk rebel's debut evokes the heart of '50s country, with detailed and compassionate songwriting, wildcat vocals, and guitar by James Burton. One song, "Looks Aren't Everything," hit the Top 40, while two others, "Hardin County Line" and "Something with a Ring to It," didn't fare quite so well. —*John Floyd & Brian Mansfield*

● Mark Collie / 1993 / MCA ✦✦✦✦

At once a move to the mainstream and a return to Collie's West Tennessee rockabilly roots, the album worked fairly well. "Even the Man in the Moon Is Crying" and "Born to Love You" were Collie's first Top Ten hits, and "Shame, Shame, Shame, Shame" rocked as hard as anything he'd done. —*Brian Mansfield*

Unleashed / 1994 / MCA ✦✦✦

In the same vein as *Mark Collie*, this album is more aggressive. "It Is No Secret" followed in Collie's tradition of midtempo romantic singles, while he rocks it up elsewhere. —*Brian Mansfield*

Tennessee Plates / Jul. 18, 1995 / Warner Brothers ✦✦✦

Tennessee Plates delivers the edgy rockabilly punch that fans have come to expect from Mark Collie, but not in quite as consistent a fashion as some of his earlier records. Although it has its share of love songs, the album does continue the stripped-down, direct approach of *Unleashed*—it just doesn't have the same amount of high-quality songs. That said, the best songs on the record are very good indeed, and make the album a fun, entertaining listen. —*Thom Owens*

Collins Kids

Rockabilly

By the time Lawrence (b. 1944) and Lawrencine (b. 1942) Collins were 11 and 13, respectively, they were already tearing it up on country package shows, recording for Columbia Records, and performing on national TV almost weekly. Older sister Lorrie held up the cowgirl fringe-rustling-against-nylons teenage-sensuality department; kid brother Larry was a bundle of hyperkinetic energy, bopping all over the place while laying down exciting, twangy guitar breaks learned firsthand from the "King of Double-necked Mosrite," Joe Maphis. The Collins' recordings as time went on veered from mawkish brother/sister country-style duets to white-hot rockabilly, and they were just reaching their peak when Lorrie eloped, effectively breaking up the act. Revered by rockabilly collectors the world over, their filmed television appearances and recordings are testimony to the fact that the Collins Kids weren't just "good for their age," they were just plain good, period. —*Cub Koda*

● Introducing Larry and Lorrie / 1958 / Columbia ✦✦✦✦

For those who don't want to spring for the lengthy and expensive Bear Family box, this is an excellent distillation of 12 of their best late-'50s rockabilly sides. "Hoy Hoy," "Whistle Bait," "Mercy," "Just Because," and "Party" rank among the most smokin' rockabilly sides ever waxed. —*Richie Unterberger*

Rockin Rollin Collins Kids / 1983 / Bear Family ✦✦✦
Rockin Rollin Collins Kids, Vol. 2 / 1983 / Bear Family ✦✦✦

There's some good stuff on this 16-track anthology, though it's not nearly as good as the domestic Columbia compilation *Introducing Larry and Lorrie*. But with the appearance in 1991 of Bear Family's *Hop Skip & Jump* box set, there's no reason to hunt this (or *Vol. 1*) down anymore. —*Richie Unterberger*

Hop, Skip and Jump / Aug. 1991 / Bear Family ✦✦✦✦

Another excellent CD box set from Bear Family, two discs with booklet in an album-size format. Everything's here; from the great early sides like "Beetle Bug Bop," "The Cuckoo Rock," "I'm in My Teens" and "The Rockaway Rock" to the rockabilly classics "Just Because," "Hoy Hoy," "Mercy," "Sweet Talk," and "Party," through the Maphis/Collins guitar instrumentals to Larry and Lorrie's solo sides from the end of the trail. Joe Maphis' great guitar is sprayed all over the place, and the master tape transfer is as clear as you expect stuff out of the Columbia vaults produced by Don Law to be. A booklet crammed full of great live photos and excellent liners by Colin Escott round out the package. —*Cub Koda*

Rockin' on T.V. / 1993 / Krazy Kat ✦✦✦✦

Thirty-one performances taken from various *Town Hall Party* television performances from 1957 to 1961. The sound is suspect in spots, naturally, but the energy level makes such complaints superfluous. Highlights include "Kokomo," "Chantilly Lace," "Lonesome Road," "Way Down Yonder in New Orleans," and decidedly left-field takes on three Buddy Holly songs. Highly recommended. —*Cub Koda*

Television Party / TV ✦✦✦

Fourteen lo-fi songs from vintage television broadcasts, on a label of questionable legitimacy. There's a 31-song compilation of this stuff on a 1993 Krazy Kat album; hold out for that one instead. —*Richie Unterberger*

Larry Collins

b. 1944, Tulsa, OK

Guitar, Vocals / Traditional Country, Rockabilly

With his sister Lorrie, guitarist and singer Larry Collins was part of the brother-sister duo the Collins Kids, who cut some of the best rockabilly of the 1950s. Playing a doubleneck guitar, Collins was a brilliant guitar prodigy, and took time to cut some hot instrumental duets with mentor Joe Maphis, a country guitarist 20 years his senior. The Collins Kids broke up when Lorrie married, and Larry cut some undistinguished diluted rockabilly-pop before drifting back, like so many early rockabilly singers, to country music. As a songwriter, his most famous credit is co-penning "Delta Dawn." —*Richie Unterberger*

Rockin Rollin / 1983 / Bear Family ✦✦✦

In the mid-'50s, country picker Joe Maphis and early rockabilly guitarist Larry Collins (one-half of the Collins Kids) were both members of the *Town Hall Party*, a barn dance show broadcast from the Los Angeles area. This LP gathers odds and ends from both artists, starting with the four songs the guitarists recorded together on a rare 1957 EP. Both Maphis and Collins (then just 13) smoke on their respective double-necked axes on these instrumentals, which bisect country boogie and rockabilly. Side one closes with four instrumentals Maphis cut on his own between 1955 and 1957; more country-oriented than his sides with Collins, they are respectable country boogie, the standout being "Flying Fingers," which features some of the most blindingly fast guitar work recorded in any genre. The eight songs on side two are entirely given over to solo numbers that Collins cut in the early '60s, a few previously unreleased, a few from rare Columbia singles. Mostly soft rockabilly pop with unexceptional lead vocals (by Collins) and female harmonies, it totally lacks the fire of Larry's '50s work; even the two concluding instrumentals are insubstantial, one a Duane Eddy rip-off, one slightly anticipating the sound of surf music. Side one has some pretty hot country-cum-rockabilly, but the flip weighs this production down into "collectors only" territory. —*Richie Unterberger*

Tommy Collins (Leonard Raymond Sipes)

b. Sep. 28, 1930, Bethany, OK
Guitar, Vocals / Traditional Country, Bakersfield Sound
Along with his contemporary Wynn Stewart, Tommy Collins was one of the first country musicians to establish a distinctive Bakersfield, CA, sound. During the course of the '50s, he released a series of hit singles that lightened up the tone of honky tonk with bouncing back beats, novelty lyrics, and electric guitars. Collins explored a more serious side with his ballads, yet they continued to sound slightly different than his peers—though they weren't as polished as the countrypolitan coming out of Nashville, they didn't have the grit of honky tonk. Legions of West Coast country performers—most notably Buck Owens, who played guitar on several of Tommy's hit singles, and Merle Haggard—built on the sound that Collins established in the early '50s. Collins wasn't able to cash in on the Bakersfield craze of the '60s. By then, he had already quit the music business once, and was mounting a marginally successful comeback. Nevertheless, his influence loomed large, particularly on Haggard, who took Collins' "Carolyn" and "The Roots of My Raising" to the top of the charts in the early '70s.

Collins (b. Leonard Raymond Sipes) was born just outside of Oklahoma City, spending his entire childhood in Oklahoma, where his father worked for the county. As a child, he began to sing and write songs, eventually appearing on local radio shows. Following his high-school graduation in 1948, he attended Edmond State Teachers College while he continued to perform music. During this time, he made a handful of singles for the California-based record label, Morgan. In the early '50s, he was in the Army for a brief time, before he moved to Bakersfield, CA, with his friend Wanda Jackson and her family. Shortly afterward, the Jackson family moved back to Oklahoma, leaving Tommy Collins alone in Bakersfield.

In a short time, Collins had begun to make friends and contacts within the city, eventually becoming friends with Ferlin Husky, and the pair roomed together. After recording a handful of Collins' songs, Husky convinced his record company, Capitol, to offer Collins a record contract, and the fledgling singer-songwriter signed to the label in June of 1953; at the time of signing, he adopted his stage name of Tommy Collins, since it sounded more commercial than Leonard Sipes. Capitol and Collins immediately assembled a backing band, which featured a then-unknown Buck Owens on lead guitar. Following one unsuccessful single, Collins released the jaunty "You Better Not Do That," which became a huge hit in early 1954, spending seven weeks at No. 2 on the country charts. Since the song was a success, Collins continued to pursue a light-hearted, near-novelty direction with his subsequent hits, and the formula initially worked. Between the fall of 1954 and the spring of 1955, he had three Top Ten hits—"Whatcha Gonna Do Now," "Untied," "It Tickles"—and in the fall of 1955, the double A-sided single "I Guess I'm Crazy" and "You Oughta See Pickles Now," which both reached the Top 15. In addition to these hit singles, Faron Young had a huge hit with Collins' "If You Ain't Lovin'," which was one of the many songs that Collins wrote but didn't record that became hits.

Collins was on the fast road to major success, but it stopped just as soon as it began. He had a religious conversion in early 1956, and much of the material he recorded that year was sacred music; occasionally, he recorded duets with his wife, Wanda Lucille Shahan, as well. In 1957, Collins enrolled in the Golden Gate Baptist Seminary with the intention of becoming a minister. Two years later, he became a pastor. During his religious education, Collins continued to record for Capitol, but neither he nor the label were much interested in promoting his records, and he had no hits. When his contract with the label expired in 1960, he stopped recording and enrolled as a student at Sacramento State College. For the next two years, he studied at the university.

In early 1963, Collins decided he was unfulfilled by the ministry, so he left the church and headed back to Bakersfield with the intention of re-entering the music business. Capitol agreed to re-sign him and in 1964, he returned to the lower reaches of the charts with "I Can Do That," a duet with his wife Wanda.

With the help of Johnny Cash, Collins switched labels and signed with Columbia in 1965; the following year, he had a Top Ten hit with "I Can't Bite, Don't Growl." For the next few years, he had a string of minor hit singles, none of which cracked the country Top 40. During this time, he also toured with his proteges, Buck Owens and Merle Haggard, acting as their opening act. By the early '70s, both Collins' professional and personal lives were on the verge of collapse, due to his increasing dependency on drugs and alcohol. In 1971, Wanda filed for a divorce, sending Collins into a deep depression.

Collins began to recover by continuing to write songs, many of which were recorded by Merle Haggard, including the 1972 No. 1 hit single "Carolyn." In 1976, Collins moved to Nashville, where he was able to secure a contract with Starday Records. Later that year, he released *Tommy Collins Callin'*, a collection of his own versions of songs he had provided for other artists. Following the album's release, Collins turned almost entirely to professional songwriting. In 1981, Merle Haggard had a hit single with "Leonard," his tribute to Collins. After the release of "Leonard," the spotlight again turned to Collins, who was now sober. He signed a songwriting contract with Sawgrass Music, where his most notable success was Mel Tillis' Top Ten 1984 hit, "New Patches."

Throughout the '80s, Collins kept a low profile, though his songs continued to be recorded. George Strait recorded no less than two of Collins' compositions during the decade, taking his new version of "If You Ain't Lovin'" to No. 1 on the country charts. European record companies like Bear Family began reissuing his recordings, which led to an appearance at the 1988 Wembley Country Music Festival in England. In 1993, Collins signed a new publishing contract with Ricky Skaggs Music and continued to write songs professionally throughout the mid-'90s. —*Stephen Thomas Erlewine*

Words and Music Country Style / 1957 / Capitol ✦✦✦✦
The Dynamic Tommy Collins / 1966 / Columbia ✦✦✦
Songwriter and country music legend Tommy Collins performs some of his own material. (For more background on Collins, check out Merle Haggard's record, "Leonard.") It's not necessarily some of his best work, but it is fun to hear how the songwriter interprets his own stuff. —*Jim Worbois*

Callin' / 1972 / Starday ✦✦✦✦
Featured are "Cigarette Milnar," "I Could Sing All Night," "You Gotta Have a License," and others. —*AMG*

● **Leonard** / Bear Family ✦✦✦✦
Spanning five discs and well over100 tracks—featuring all of the songs he cut for Capitol in the late '50s and early '60s, including alternate takes and unreleased material—*Leonard* contains too much Tommy Collins for anyone but completists and historians. Nevertheless, it is the only collection of Collins' prime material to appear on CD. Collins was very influential and he deserves this deluxe box set treatment, but a single-disc collection is needed—it would make his music available to country fans that simply can't afford a box set of this magnitude, but still want to hear the singer. If you can afford *Leonard*, it's a worthwhile investment for dedicated country music fans, but there isn't enough first-rate material on the box to justify the expense for listeners that want to explore the roots of the Bakersfield sound. —*Thom Owens*

Jessi Colter (Miriam Johnson Eddy)

b. May 25, 1947, Phoenix, AZ
Piano, Vocals / Traditional Country, Country-Pop, Outlaw Country
Perhaps best known in conjunction with her husband Waylon Jennings, Jessi Colter was the only significant female singer-songwriter to emerge from the mid-'70s "outlaw" movement. Born Miriam Johnson in Phoenix, AZ, Colter in fact affiliated herself with outlaw imagery long before the musical movement blossomed, adopting her stage name in honor of ancestor Jess Colter, a real-life train robber and counterfeiter who rode with Frank and Jesse James.

Raised in a strict Pentecostal home, Colter was just a teenager when she left Phoenix to tour as a vocalist with twang-guitar innovator Duane Eddy, whom she met through her sister Sharon, the wife of producer "Cowboy" Jack Clement. In 1962, she and Eddy married, and after several years of extensive touring (mostly throughout Europe), the couple settled in Los Angeles in 1966. Under the name Miriam Eddy, she wrote songs for Don Gibson, Dottie West, and Nancy Sinatra.

In 1968, she and Eddy divorced, and Colter returned to Phoenix. There she met Waylon Jennings, who was so taken with her voice that he invited her to record a duet with him. After helping secure Colter a record deal with his label, RCA, Jennings co-produced the tracks that would make up her 1970 debut *A Country Star Is Born;* by the time of the record's release, the couple was already married. Under the name Waylon and Jessi, they also issued two Top 40 singles, a 1970 cover of the Elvis Presley hit "Suspicious Minds" and 1971's "Under Your Spell Again." Colter's commercial breakthrough came in 1975 when her composition "I'm Not Lisa," a single from the LP *I'm Jessi Colter,* hit No. 1 on *Billboard's* country charts while also making the Top Five on the pop charts; the album spawned another hit in "What's Happened to Blue Eyes." In 1976, she released two more highly successful albums, *Jessi* and *Diamond in the Rough.*

Also in 1976, Colter teamed with Jennings, Willie Nelson, and Tompall Glaser for the album *Wanted! The Outlaws,* which at the time of its release was the biggest-selling album in country history, and the first country album certified platinum in sales. In between spending much of the remainder of the decade on tour with her husband and Nelson, she also released the albums *Miriam* in 1977 and *That's the Way a Cowboy Rocks and Rolls* in 1978.

Colter and Jennings re-teamed in 1981 for *Leather and Lace,* an album of duets featuring the hits "Storms Never Last" and the medley "Wild Side of Life/It Wasn't God Who Made Honky Tonk Angels." In the same year, she released the solo album *Ridin' Shotgun,* which produced her final chart hit in 1982's "Holdin' On." As the 1980s progressed, Colter's success tapered off; 1985's *Rock 'n' Roll Lullaby,* produced by Chips Moman, was released only on a small label. By the early 1990s, she began directing her energies toward performing children's music, and starred in the home video *Jessi Colter Sings Songs from Around the World Just for Kids,* which featured a guest appearance by Jennings, who recited some of his poetry. — *Jason Ankeny*

A Country Star Is Born / 1970 / RCA ♦♦♦

I'm Jessi Colter / 1975 / Capitol ♦♦♦♦

● **Jessi** / 1976 / Capitol ♦♦♦♦
After the success of "I'm Not Lisa" it's surprising that this record wasn't more popular than it was. Many of these songs are better than her big hit. — *Jim Worbois*

Diamond in the Rough / 1976 / Capitol ♦♦♦♦

Miriam / 1977 / Capitol ♦♦♦

That's the Way a Cowboy Rocks / 1978 / Capitol ♦♦♦

Leather and Lace / 1981 / RCA ♦♦

Ridin' Shotgun / 1981 / Capitol ♦♦♦

Rock n' Roll Lullaby / 1985 / Triad ♦♦

Commander Cody

Rock & Roll, Country-Rock, Western Swing Revival
Commander Cody & His Lost Planet Airmen were equally adept at stripped-down basic rock 'n' roll, R&B, and gritty country-rock. Commander Cody's country-rock rocked harder than the Eagles or Poco—essentially, the group was a bar band. Much like English pub rock bands like Brinsley Schwarz and Ducks Deluxe, Commander Cody resisted the overblown and bombastic trends of early '70s rock, preferring a basic, no-frills approach. Commander Cody & His Lost Planet Airmen never had the impact of the British pub rockers, yet their straightforward energy gave their records a distinguishing drive; they could play country, Western swing, rockabilly, and R&B, and it all sounded convincing.

The group originally formed in 1967 in Ann Arbor, MI; Commander Cody (born George Frayne, IV; piano), John Tichy (lead guitar), Steve Schwartz (guitar), Don Davis (bass), Don Bolton

(aka The West Virginia Creeper; pedal steel guitar), and Ralph Mallory (drums) formed the original lineup. When the group relocated to San Francisco the following year, only Frayne, Bolton, and Tichy made the move; the group's membership included Billy C. Farlowe (vocals, harp), Andy Stein (fiddle, saxophone), guitarist Billy Kirchen, bassist "Buffalo" Bruce Barlow, and drummer Lance Dickerson at the time of their 1971 debut album, *Lost in the Ozone.* The following year the group scored a fluke Top Ten hit with "Hot Rod Lincoln," taken from their second album, *Hot Licks, Cold Steel and Trucker's Favourites.* Commander Cody was never able to capitalize on the single's success, partially because their albums never completely captured their live energy. They continued to release albums until Tichy left the band in 1976. Commander Cody released his first solo album, *Midnight Man,* in 1977, then he re-formed the group as the Commander Cody Band. The group recorded three albums between 1977 and 1980. — *Stephen Thomas Erlewine*

Lost in the Ozone / 1971 / MCA ♦♦♦♦
This is the monumental debut by one of country music's insurgent pioneer bands. Along with the New Riders of the Purple Sage, the Outlaws and .38 Special, the Commander and his boys saved the '70s from the doldrums. Formed in Michigan in 1965 while attending college, they based their music on a theory of Western swing. Playing with electric instruments—including the all important steel and fiddle, and a good dose of irreverence—allowed the band to adhere to their own agenda. Moving to San Francisco, they began to build a following and soon signed on with Paramount. This first release was only a taste of the things to come. A combination of original tunes and some dusty covers, Cody & His Airmen were at the head of a parade that continues on through the '90s. Songs by Billy C. Farlow like "Daddy's Gonna Treat You Right" and the ever popular "Lost in the Ozone" were instant hits with the country-rock and hippy crowds. But, the rednecks loved them too, and this was an amazing social phenomenon. Cody partnered with Farlow on a number of songs from this first collection that still pack a wallop. "Wine Do Yer Stuff" and the tearful "Seeds and Stems (Again)" left no doubt where these boys were coming from. A strong honky tonk album that swings, *Lost in the Ozone* is a viable recording. Cover tunes performed with energy and humor won crowds over everywhere. "Hot Rod Lincoln" is still played on outlaw country radio stations as is "Twenty Flight Rock," a boogie number that lets everything hang out. With not a single cut wasted, this is one of the buried gems of modern country music, displaying guitarman Bill Kirchen at his wildest and Bruce Barlow, Lance Dickerson, Andy Stein, John Tichy, Bobby Black, West Virginia Creeper, Farlow, and Commander Cody comin' out of the chute ready to change the world for the better. — *Jana Pendragon*

Hot Licks, Cold Steel & Truckers' Favorites / 1972 / MCA ♦♦♦
Again, a groundbreaking release from the wildest band in country music during the '70s. This time around they are honoring the American trucker. A part of society few see into, the music that keeps the big rigs running is something else again. With originals and some oldies, the Commander and his band make a big sound that is still reverberating through time. With their own trucker tunes "Truck Stop Rock" and "Semi Truck" leading the way, this LP includes some classics like "Looking' at the World Through a Windshield," "Mama Hated Diesels," and the grandaddy of the bunch, "Truck Drivin' Man," a performance hit for Rick Nelson and the New Riders of the Purple Sage as well. Other high-powered covers include Little Richard's "Tutti Frutti," done up in a way no one will forget. The Cajun "Diggy Liggy Lo" is given a workout, as is "Rip It Up," and the Commander's class-A performance of "It Should've Been Me" leaves no doubt as to the punch this outfit gives to everything they do. From the band comes "Cravin' Your Love," "Watch My .38," and "Kentucky Hills of Tennessee." Again, every cut counts. As with *Lost in the Ozone,* this is top-flight music in every regard that shows another side to this great band. — *Jana Pendragon*

Country Casanova / 1973 / MCA ♦♦♦
A studio effort, this didn't reflect their live prowess but was still a good time. — *Jeff Tamarkin*

● **Live from Deep in the Heart of Texas** / 1974 / MCA ✦✦✦✦
This is Commander Cody & His Lost Planet Airmen at their best, live on stage and out on the road with the New Riders of the Purple Sage. What a bill and what a grand time for a live album. This is how it really was—wild, loud and fun. Again they intersperse their own songs with old favorites. "Armadillo Stomp" was penned for this event, and a woolly version of "Down to Seeds and Stems Again Blues" has the crowd on its feet. Their "Oh Momma Momma" and "Too Much Fun" become legendary during this performance. But it is their reworking of Buck Owens' "Crying Time" that makes them such a wonderful country band. Johnny Horton's "I'm Comin' Home" is also masterful, as is their take on a favorite cowboy tune, "Sunset on the Sage." "Mean Woman Blues" is another highlight. As for the Commander, his wanton style is perfectly at home when he takes the Lieber-Stoller tune "Riot in Cell Block No. 9" and makes it his own vehicle for a musical theatrical performance. Every cut is perfection, every cut is substantial. This 1973 performance, captured here for posterity, is evidence enough to suggest that Commander Cody & His Lost Planet Airmen were one fine honky tonk band, perhaps one of the finest. —*Jana Pendragon*

Commander Cody & His Lost Planet Airmen / 1975 / Warner Brothers ✦✦✦
This was their first recording for Warner Brothers after leaving Paramount. With songs by Hoyt Axton and Lowell George as well as plenty of contributions from Farlow, Tichy, Barlow, and all the rest, this is another good outing for the wild boys. The Tower of Power horn section lends a hand, making their big sound even bigger. Their cover of "Don't Let Go" is outstanding and "House of Blue Lights" never quite rocked or shuffled and twanged the way the Airmen do it. With plenty of hillbilly stuff to go around, "California Okie" stands proud. A tip of the hat to the South is found on "That's What I Like About the South." "Keep on Lovin' Her," "Hawaii Blues" and "Four or Five Times" are also wonders to behold. "Willin'," done up right here, fits the band perfectly. This Lowell George tune is a standard now, and when the Airmen did it their way they gave a whole new meaning to the song. One more time, this band holds all the aces and plays every hand with a poker face that just won't quit. Commander Cody & His Lost Planet Airmen knew exactly what they were doing. —*Jana Pendragon*

Tales from the Ozone / 1975 / Warner Brothers ✦✦✦

We've Got a Live One Here / 1976 / Warner Brothers ✦✦✦✦
This is really the final hurrah for the band, in spite of the fact that there were more recordings to follow. This is a two-record set from their 1976 tour of Europe, with most of the original members still on board. After this tour, George Frayne, aka Commander Cody, broke up the band, which now included Norton Buffalo. While this live recording is just as powerful as the preceding *Live Deep in the Heart of Texas*, it is obvious that some of their fire is burning mighty low. Still, this bunch always did their best work on stage, and they never failed to satisfy. Full of old standards, some new favorites and plenty of wattage to make it all work just right, the standout tunes here are the Commander Cody classics "Seeds and Stems," "Too Much Fun," and "Lost in the Ozone." Other numbers that bring back the good old days include the Airmen's version of "Milkcow Blues" and "San Antonio Rose." Trucker songs, big with the Continental crowd, are "Semi Truck," "Lookin' at the World Through a Windshield" and "18 Wheels." Other numbers of note are "One of Those Nights," written by Farlow, Frayne, and Kirchen, as well as the Commander's sendups of "Smoke! Smoke! Smoke!," "Riot in Cell Block No. 9" and "Hot Rod Lincoln." Always extraordinary, the era of Commander Cody & His Lost Planet Airmen was a special moment in time that created a place for hipsters, cosmic cowboys, rednecks, and the working class to all come together and enjoy some real American music. Never will there be another band like this one or recordings like the ones they made between 1971 and 1976. They ended this project with "Lost in the Ozone," bringing the band and its audience full circle. —*Jana Pendragon*

Midnight Man [Cody Solo] / 1977 / Arista ✦✦

Rock 'n Roll Again / 1977 / Arista ✦✦

Flying Dreams / 1978 / Arista ✦✦

Lose It Tonight / 1980 / Line ✦✦

Let's Rock / 1986 / Blind Pig ✦✦✦
Commander Cody and his boogie-woogie piano are joined by some ex-Lost Planet Airmen, rockin' through originals such as the title track, "Truck Stop at the End of the World," "Angel Got Married," and a couple of covers, including "Your Cash Ain't Nothing but Trash." —*AMG*

Very Best of . . . Plus / 1986 / See For Miles ✦✦✦✦
More tracks than their US best-of and costlier, but this collection provides a grand overview of one of the saving graces of '70s rock. —*Jeff Tamarkin*

Returns from Outer Space / 1987 / Edsel ✦✦✦

Sleazy Roadside Stories / 1988 / Relix ✦✦✦
Cut live in 1973, the Cody septet cooks on this Texas jam. —*Jeff Tamarkin*

Aces High / 1990 / Relix ✦✦✦
The Commander and his current band in various late-'80s recordings. Not as sharp as the original stuff, but still fairly deranged. —*Jeff Tamarkin*

● **Too Much Fun: Best of Commander Cody** / 1990 / MCA ✦✦✦✦
Not only could they play the hell out of their instruments, but C.C. & His Lost Planet Airmen were a virtual melting pot of American music—country, R&B, rockabilly, Western swing. And always too much fun. —*Jeff Tamarkin*

Best Of / Aug. 8, 1995 / Relix ✦✦✦✦

Confederate Railroad

Contemporary Country, Southern Rock
Georgia-based Confederate Railroad was the contemporary cousin to such outlaw Southern rockers as the Allman Brothers, Lynyrd Skynyrd, and Hank Williams, Jr. The group, with their scruffy biker clothes and hard-edged good-time music, got their start as a club band in the late '80s, founded by lead vocalist/guitarist Danny Shirley, who had been playing the club circuit since the early part of the decade. Confederate Railroad—comprised of drummer Mark Dufresne, bassist Wayne Secrest, keyboardist Chris McDaniel, lead guitarist Michael Lamb, and steel guitarist Gates Nichols—released their self-titled debut in 1992. It produced several hits including "Jesus and Mama" (Top Five) and "Queen Memphis" (Top Three), but it was "Trashy Women," the B-side of their "When You Leave That Way You Can Never Go Back," that really gained notoriety. Both the song and the resulting video for "Trashy Women" got considerable media exposure, and made it to the Top Ten on the country charts. In 1994, they released *Notorious* and within less than two months, it went gold. *When and Where* followed a year later. —*Sandra Brennan*

Confederate Railroad / 1992 / Atlantic ✦✦✦
Featured are "Queen of Memphis," "Time Off for Bad Behavior," and "She Took It Like a Man," among other hits. —*AMG*

Notorious / 1994 / Atlantic ✦✦✦✦
Despite its unkempt, biker image, Confederate Railroad is a country band in the tradition of Alabama. Rooted in traditional country sounds and values, both bands also have the breadth to appeal to those outside the genre (in CR's case, Southern rockers). The group rocks hardest on the funny stuff ("Elvis & Andy," "Move over Madonna") but gets serious with some impressive ballads ("Daddy Never Was the Cadillac Kind," "Summer in Dixie," "Three Verses"). —*Brian Mansfield*

When and Where / 1995 / Atlantic ✦✦✦✦
By their third album, Confederate Railroad had established their fusion of Lynyrd Skynyrd and Alabama and knew what worked and what didn't. In other words, *When and Where* offers nothing new from the band, but it is far from a bad record. The group has gotten predictable, but they continue to shine, whether it's on the rowdy rockers or the surprisingly smooth, radio-ready ballads. They do have a problem coming up with a batch of consistent material, but the album is as enjoyable as its predecessor and nearly as solid. —*Thom Owens*

● **Greatest Hits** / Jun. 18, 1996 / Atlantic ✦✦✦✦

Greatest Hits compiles Confederate Railroad's biggest hits, including all of their Top Ten singles, as well as several singles that never made it quite as far up the charts. As an added bonus, the group has added two new songs–which aren't particularly noteworthy–to lure fans that already own all the band's albums to the new collection. Even with the addition of the new songs, *Greatest Hits* remains the province of casual fans–it serves up all the hits in an engaging, concise manner. *–Stephen Thomas Erlewine*

John Conlee

b. Aug. 11, 1946, Versailles, KY

Guitar, Vocals / Country-Pop, Neo-Traditionalist Country

Born and raised on a 200-acre farm in Versailles, KY, John Conlee has continued to till the soil on his own farm in suburban Nashville, even since "hitting it big." Music was–and still is–a hobby as much as a career to him; he didn't even sign his first recording contract until age 30. Instead, he pursued work as a mortician (he still maintains his license) in Kentucky and as a disc jockey at a number of radio stations, including Nashville's WLAC, where he made numerous contacts on Music Row. One of his tapes attracted ABC Records, but Conlee's gruff, down-to-earth delivery wasn't an immediate success. It took a couple of years before "Rose Colored Glasses"–one of the few songs he's written himself–exploded in 1978. The single kicked off nearly ten years of virtually uninterrupted Top Ten country hits, including the No. 1 singles "Lady Lay Down" (1979), "Backside of Thirty" (1979), "Common Man" (1983), "I'm Only in It for the Love" (1983), "In My Eyes" (1983), "As Long as I'm Rockin' with You" (1984), and "Got My Heart Set on You" (1986). By the end of the decade, his sales declined, due to the shifting tastes of the country audience and his own desire to stay at home.

A self-avowed homebody, Conlee was never particularly enamored with touring, and devoted most of his career time to the recording process instead, particularly his song selection. Noted for an astute sense of quality material (he was ably assisted through the bulk of his career by record producer and former Jim Reeves sideman Bud Logan), he made albums that rarely, if ever, contained "fluff." Even when they're not commercial, Conlee's songs are always interesting. *–Tom Roland*

Rose Colored Glasses / 1978 / MCA ✦✦✦

With Love / 1981 / MCA ✦✦✦✦

Nine of the ten cuts in this package came from Tree Publishing, meaning that Conlee and producer Bud Logan limited themselves unnecessarily. But Conlee is extremely convincing on "Only Oklahoma Away" and "What's Forever For," not to mention the mysterious "Miss Emily's Picture." *–Tom Roland*

Busted / 1982 / MCA ✦✦

In My Eyes / 1983 / MCA ✦✦✦

John Conlee's Greatest Hits / 1983 / MCA ✦✦✦✦

With simple, slice-of-life statements about the real world, the songs cover (in)fidelity ("She Can't Say That Anymore," "Baby, You're Something"), relationship issues ("Friday Night Blues"), and personal finance ("Busted," "Common Man"). The asylum piece, "I Don't Remember Loving You," is eternally vivid. *–Tom Roland*

John Conlee's Greatest Hits, Vol. 2 / 1985 / MCA ✦✦✦✦

Songs for the Working Man / 1986 / MCA ✦✦✦

Conley Country / 1986 / MCA ✦✦✦✦

American Faces / 1987 / Columbia ✦✦

Harmony / 1987 / Columbia ✦✦

● **20 Greatest Hits** / 1987 / MCA ✦✦✦✦

20 Greatest Hits combines material from Conlee's *Greatest Hits* and *Greatest Hits, Vol. 2*, leaving off one track from each record ("Baby, You're Something" and "Lifetime Guarantee," respectively). As such, it offers a perfect retrospective of his career. *–Stephen Thomas Erlewine*

Fellow Travelers / 1989 / 16th Avenue ✦✦✦

Earl Thomas Conley

b. Oct. 17, 1941, Portsmouth, OH

Vocals / Country-Pop, Neo-Traditionalist Country, Urban Cowboy

Early in his career, Earl Thomas Conley's music picked up the label "thinking man's country." An accurate description–Conley looks into the heart and soul of his characters, finding the motivations for their actions and beliefs. In the process, the astute listener can find fragments of him/herself in nearly any Conley creation. Born into poverty in Portsmouth, OH, Conley struggled with the limits of his social class. He aspired to be a painter or actor but found that his aspirations for music lingered after the other interests died down. Influenced by everything from Hank Williams to the Eagles, Conley delved into the details of writing, trying to learn the craft by following the rules and regulations of the Music Row songwriting community. Eventually, torn by the limits of the "law," he found his own niche by breaking many of those same rules. His public self-analysis–in both his songs and his interviews–has proven inspirational to some, bothersome to others, but Conley has evolved stylistically, even though the thinking-man label continues to follow him. He's admittedly chased a more commercial sound, with a certain degree of success, but the run for the dollars also put him into a financial bind. He spent part of the late '80s and early '90s overworking himself to pay off his debts. Although he has been a hitmaker for more than a decade, his contributions to country have often gone almost unnoticed.

The son of a railroad man, Conley left his Portsmouth home at the age of 14, once his father lost his job. After living with his older sister in Ohio, he rejected a scholarship to art school, deciding to join the Army instead. While he was in the military, he fell in love with country music. Following his discharge, he worked a number of blue-collar jobs while he played Nashville clubs at night. Conley wasn't making any headway, so he relocated to Huntsville, AL, where he worked in a steel mill. While in Huntsville, he met Nelson Larkin, a producer who helped the fledgling singer sign to the independent label GRT in 1974. Over the next two years, he released four singles on the label–which were all credited to "Earl Conley"– and each one scraped the lower regions of the country charts. While his chart success was respectable for a developing artist, he was soon eclipsed by other artists who were having hits with his songs. Nelson Larkin gave his brother Billy "Leave It Up to Me," which became the first Earl Thomas Conley song to reach the Top 20. It was followed shortly afterward by Mel Street's No. 13 hit "Smokey Mountain Memories" and Conway Twitty's version of "This Time I've Hurt Her More (Than She Loves Me)," which reached No.1 in early 1976. By that time, Conley had moved to Nashville, where he was writing for Nelson Larkin's publishing house.

In 1977, Conley signed with Warner Bros., and in early 1979 he had his first Top 40 hit, "Dreamin's All I Do." By the end of the year, he had begun performing and releasing records under his full name, Earl Thomas Conley. None of his Warner singles became big hits, and he left the label at the end of 1979. After spending six months reassessing his career and musical direction, he signed to Sunbird Records and began working with Nelson Larkin again. Conley's first single for Sunbird, "Silent Treatment," was an immediate Top Ten hit late in 1980, and it was quickly followed by the No. 1 "Fire & Smoke" early in 1981. Following his breakthrough success, RCA signed Conley to a long-term deal. "Tell Me Why," his first single for the label, reached No. 10 in late 1981, followed shortly afterward by the No. 16 "After the Love Slips Away." In the summer of 1982, "Heavenly Bodies" kicked off a string of 21 straight Top Ten hits that ran for seven years. During that time, he had a remarkable 17 No. 1 hits, including the record-setting four No. 1 singles from 1984's *Don't Make It Easy for Me*–it was the first time any artist in any genre had four No. 1 hits from the same albums. Though he had some financial and vocal problems during the mid-'80s, the hits never stopped coming during the entire decade.

By the end of the '80s, he had stopped working with Larkin, preferring to collaborate with Randy Scruggs, which brought his music back to his country and R&B roots. His sales took a dramatic dip during 1990 due to the rise of contemporary country, but he had two new Top Ten hits, "Shadow of a Doubt" and the Keith Whitley duet "Brotherly Love." The singles set the stage for the harder-edged country of his 1991 album *Yours Truly*. Despite receiving some of the best reviews of Conley's career, the record was a commercial failure, and RCA dropped him shortly after its release. For the remainder of the '90s, he was without a record label, yet he continued to give concerts and tour. —*Tom Roland*

Blue Pearl / 1980 / Sunbird ✦✦✦

This is the album that earned Conley the thinking-man label. "Middle-Age Madness" and "Blue and Green" stand out as classically written profiles of people in pain. "Silent Treatment," "Fire and Smoke," and "You Don't Have to Go Too Far" possess a captivating, slick sheen that belies their raw approach. —*Tom Roland*

Fire & Smoke / 1981 / RCA ✦✦✦

Somewhere Between Right & Wrong / 1982 / RCA ✦✦✦

Don't Make It Easy for Me / 1983 / RCA ✦✦✦✦

Conley speaks of "programming" himself to write, and in setting the tone for this album—as well as the follow-up, *Treadin' Water*—he programmed "radio records" into his consciousness. The result: a driving, rock-inflected package that yielded four No. 1 singles—the first time an album did that in any format. The title track and "Your Love's on the Line" are particularly listenable, and there's not a bad cut on it. —*Tom Roland*

Treadin' Water / 1984 / RCA ✦✦

Greatest Hits / 1985 / RCA ✦✦✦✦

Some of his biggest songs are here, including "Angel in Disguise," "Silent Treatment," "Holding Her and Loving You," "Once in a Blue Moon," and others. —*AMG*

● **The Best of Earl Thomas Conley, Vol. 1** / 1988 / RCA ✦✦✦✦

As much as any of his '80s peers, Conley might have benefited from moving his sound toward harder country. The hits he did score ("Fire & Smoke," "Somewhere Between Right and Wrong," among the ones on this album) projected a voice ideally suited to a more Whitley-esque setting. —*Dan Cooper*

The Heart of It All / 1988 / RCA ✦✦✦

This album contains "What I'd Say," "What She Is," "We Believe in Happy Endings," "You Must Not Be Drinking Enough," and other hits. —*AMG*

Greatest Hits, Vol. 2 / 1990 / RCA ✦✦✦✦

Conley was one of the hottest recording artists of the '80s. While this album isn't quite as strong as the first hits package, it shouldn't be ignored. Also features two new tracks. —*Jim Worbois*

Yours Truly / 1991 / RCA ✦✦✦✦

Yours Truly is one of Earl Thomas Conley's finest efforts, boasting a consistently impressive set of songs and wonderful vocals from Conley. —*Thom Owens*

● **Essential** / Apr. 1996 / RCA ✦✦✦✦

Featuring the great majority of his hits plus an intriguing batch of rarities, *Essential* offers the best retrospective of Earl Thomas Conley's career. —*Stephen Thomas Erlewine*

Spade Cooley (Donnell C. Cooley)

b. Feb. 22, 1910, Grand, OK, d. Nov. 23, 1969, Vacaville, CA
Fiddle, Cello / Western Swing

A musician and actor whose often sordid private life tended to overshadow his career as an entertainer, Spade Cooley was the self-proclaimed "King of Western swing," an innovator who at his peak led the largest band ever assembled in the annals of country music. The product of a multi-generational family of fiddle players, Donnell Clyde Cooley was born in Oklahoma in 1910, and at the age of four, his family moved to Oregon. Despite his impoverished background, Cooley was a classically trained fiddler, and by the time he was eight years old, he was performing professionally at square dances with his father John. In 1930, Cooley (who received his nickname thanks to his poker skills) moved to Los Angeles, playing with a number of Western-oriented acts. By the mid-1930s, he was working as an actor, with bit parts in several Westerns; for Republic Studios, he served as Roy Rogers' stand-in.

He also toured with Rogers as a fiddle player, and handled vocal duties with the Riders of the Purple Sage.

Cooley did not begin a recording career until 1941, when he entered the studio while a member of Cal Shrum's band. A year later, he took control of bandleader Jimmy Wakely's group, the house band at Santa Monica, CA's Venice Pier Ballroom, and their Western swing music began attracting thousands of fans each Saturday night. The densely-populated band, home to as many as three vocalists and fiddlers at a time, featured singer Tex Williams and guitarists Joaquin Murphey and John O. Weis. In 1945, Spade Cooley and His Orchestra's first single, "Shame on You," lasted nine weeks atop *Billboard*'s country charts. The first in an unbroken string of six Top Ten singles (including "Detour" and "You Can't Break My Heart"), "Shame on You" would remain Cooley's theme song for years to come. Also in 1945, he married his second wife, Orchestra backup singer Ella Mae Evans. Ultimately, the Orchestra's success led to the dissolution of its most popular lineup; by 1946, Williams, the vocalist on all of the group's hits, was demanding more money, and Cooley refused to pay it. As a result, Williams quit, taking much of the Orchestra with him to form the Western Caravan. In 1947, Cooley began a career in television, hosting a program in Los Angeles titled *The Hoffman Hayride*. The show's popularity grew quickly, and within months an estimated 75 percent of all viewers in the L.A. area tuned into the show each Saturday night. He also resumed his film career, this time with much higher visibility; in addition to significant roles in a number of Westerns, he also starred in two 1949 short subjects, *King of Western Swing* and *Spade Cooley and His Orchestra*.

Throughout the early 1950s, Cooley continued to record, but the group's popularity waned as public tastes changed; after a time, he even fired the Orchestra to replace its members with an all-female band. A heavy drinker, Cooley descended into alcoholism as his career declined, and he suffered a series of minor heart attacks. Furthermore, he was facing financial ruin as a result of problems with a planned water theme park in the Mojave Desert. In 1961, his wife Ella Mae left him; after an argument on April 3, he stomped her to death while the couple's 14-year-old daughter Melody looked on in horror. The resulting trial, a media circus during which Cooley suffered another heart attack, culminated in a sentence of life imprisonment. Throughout his term, he was a model prisoner, and thus was allowed to perform at a sheriff's benefit in Oakland, CA, on November 23, 1969. After playing in front of a crowd of over 3,000, Cooley returned to his dressing room, suffered yet another heart attack, and died. —*Jason Ankeny*

● **Spadella: The Essential** / 1994 / Columbia/Legacy ✦✦✦✦

Spadella: The Essential Spade Cooley collects 20 highlights from Cooley's stint as one of the most popular Western swing bandleaders in America. All of the selections on the album were recorded between 1945 and 1946, when Cooley and his group scored six straight Top Ten singles, all of which are included here ("You Can't Break My Heart" is in an alternate version). This is when the group was at its peak and vocalist Tex Williams was always in stellar form. Though it doesn't cover his entire career, *Spadella* remains the one essential Cooley compilation. —*Stephen Thomas Erlewine*

Coon Creek Girls

Old-Time

One of the most famous all-female string bands in country, the Coon Creek Girls were also among the first female groups to play their own instruments and focus on authentic mountain music, instead of sentimental and cowboy songs.

The founding member of the long-lived group was Lily May Ledford. Born in Pilot, KY, she was the daughter of poor tenant farmers who frequently played string band music; consequently, Lily May learned how to play guitar and fiddle as a child. By the time she was an adolescent, she had formed the Red River Ramblers with her sister Rose and her brother Cayen, and the group began playing local square dances. The Ramblers auditioned for talent scouts in 1935, and Lily May was chosen to appear on WLS Chicago's *Barn Dance*. During her performance, she caught the attention of announcer John Lair, who became her manager; in the process, he landed her a regular spot on the *Barn Dance,* where she became so popular that the station's magazine based a comic strip on her.

Following its success in Chicago, Lair moved the show to Cincinnati and then to Renfro Valley, where he decided to base an all-female string band around Lily May. The original Coon Creek Girls were comprised of Lily May, her sister Rosie, Evelyn "Daisy" Lange, and Esther "Violet" Koehler. On October 9, 1937, they made their live radio debut from Cincinnati Music Hall. Shortly after their debut, the group began appearing on the *Renfro Valley Barn Dance;* they would sing on the program for the next 15 years. In 1938, the Coon Creek Girls cut their first session, although their records, which featured traditional mountain songs, never proved as popular as their radio performances. In 1939, the original group disbanded when Koehler and Lange left to go work with the Callahan Brothers' Blue Ridge Mountain Folk in Dallas. Lily May and Rosie were then joined by their younger sister, Minnie. The Coon Creek Girls kept performing together in various incarnations until 1957.

After the group broke up, Lily May launched her own solo career. In 1980 she published her autobiography, *Coon Creek Girl.* In 1985, Ledford died. Esther Koehler spent time in the Boone County Jamboree and eventually married one of Lily May's brothers. Evelyn Lange married and moved to Indiana, where she sometimes competed in fiddle contests. During the 1980s, John Lair created the New Coon Creek Girls to appear on a revival of his old radio show. The new group later began touring and recording on their own. — *Sandra Brennan*

● **Early Radio Favorites** / Old Homestead ◆◆◆◆
Early Radio Favorites contains all of the music that the Coon Creek Girls recorded during the '30s, including "Banjo Picking Girl" and "How Many Biscuits Can You Eat?" Not only were the Coon Creek Girls one of the last mountain string bands of their era, they were the only female old-timey group, which made them unique. If they were just unique, the band would simply be an historical curiosity, but the girls also made good music, as evidenced by this stellar collection. For fans of string bands, *Early Radio Favorites* is an essential addition to their record collection. — *Stephen Thomas Erlewine*

Lily May, Rosie and Susie / County ◆◆◆

Roger Cooper

Fiddle / Traditional Bluegrass, Old-Time
Roger Cooper is an old-timey country and bluegrass fiddler that began his recording career in the mid-'90s. — *Stephen Thomas Erlewine*

Going Back to Old Kentucky / Oct. 8, 1996 / ◆◆◆◆
Going Back to Old Kentucky is essentially a showcase for the instrumental skills of Roger Cooper, one of the best old-timey fiddlers of the '90s. As a result, there might be a lack of full-fledged songs here—nearly every song is arranged as a vehicle for Cooper's fiddling—but it stands unparalleled as a fiddle record. There is zest and vigor within his playing, which elevates him from the category of a mere technical wonder to that of a fully rounded musician. — *Stephen Thomas Erlewine*

Stoney Cooper

b. Oct. 16, 1918, Harman, WV, d. Mar. 22, 1977
Fiddle, Vocals / Traditional Bluegrass, Traditional Country
Stoney Cooper, with his wife Wilma Lee, became one of the most popular performers on the *Wheeling Jamboree* during the '50s and on the Grand Ole Opry from 1957 until his death in 1977. Born Dale Troy Cooper in Harman, WV, on October 16, 1918, Stoney came from a long line of fiddlers and joined Rusty Hiser's Green Valley Boys while still a teenager. Soon after joining the Singing Learys in the late '30s, he became involved with Wilma Leary (b. Feb. 7, 1921, Valley Head, WV). They married in 1941 and began performing on WWVA's *Wheeling Jamboree.*

Though Wilma Lee and Stoney Cooper moved around during the '40s—performing for stations in Nebraska, Indiana, and Arkansas—they returned to the *Jamboree* by 1947 and stayed for a decade. They had first recorded in 1947 for the Rich-R-Tone

label, but moved to Columbia two years later for an association that lasted five years. The Coopers signed with Acuff-Rose's Hickory label soon after and recorded their first hit, "Cheated Too." The single, backed by the Coopers' Clinch Mountain Clan band, reached the Country Top 15 in September 1956. They moved to the Grand Ole Opry in 1957 and charted three Top Five singles two years after their arrival. "Come Walk with Me" hit No. 4 in January 1959 and featured the Coopers' daughter Carolee—later to gain fame fronting the Carol Lee Singers. May brought "Big Midnight Special"—later a pop hit for Paul Evans—and in October "There's a Big Wheel" reached No. 3.

Wilma Lee and Stoney hit the Top 20 twice in 1960 ("Johnny, My Love" and "This Ole House") and once a year later ("Wreck on the Highway"), but after a 1963 heart attack, Stoney relaxed his schedule. He and his wife continued to perform their popular Opry act and signed to Decca in the mid-'60s. They also recorded for Skylite, Gusto, and Rounder before Stoney died in 1977. Wilma Lee continued to tour and perform on the Opry. — *John Bush*

Sacred Songs / 1960 / Harmony ◆◆◆

Songs of Inspiration / 1963 / Hickory ◆◆◆

● **Sunny Side of the Mountain** / 1966 / Harmony ◆◆◆◆

● **Classic Early Recordings** / County ◆◆◆◆
Originally recorded between 1949 and 1953, the wife-and-husband duo let it fly with passionate zeal on these old-time mountain and gospel songs. Wilma Lee could shake the coal out of the hills with her raw and full-throated voice, and she didn't bother with nuance. — *Michael McCall*

Wilma Lee & Stoney Cooper / 1976 / Starday ◆◆◆◆

Cowboy Copas (Lloyd Copas)

b. Jul. 15, 1913, Adams County, OH, d. Mar. 5, 1963, Camden, TN
Fiddle, Guitar, Vocals / Honky Tonk
A honky tonk singer popular in the late '40s, Cowboy Copas made something of a comeback in the early '60s before he died in the air crash that also killed Patsy Cline and Hawkshaw Hawkins. Born Lloyd Estel Copas on July 15, 1913, he dropped out of school at the age of 14, and began playing fiddle in several string bands around his Ohio home. On a dare, Copas traveled to Cincinnatti to enter a contest and wound up performing on radio shows for Cincinnatti's WLW and later WKRC. By 1940, Copas moved to WNOX-Knoxville with a band called the Gold Star Rangers.

Three years later, Cowboy Copas got his big break: he was tapped to replace Eddy Arnold as the vocalist for Pee Wee King's Golden West Cowboys on WSM-Nashville and the Grand Ole Opry. He signed with King Records in 1946, and his debut single "Filipino Baby" hit No. 4 on the country charts that August. Two years later, Copas was back in the Top Ten with "Signed, Sealed and Delivered" (No. 2), "Tennessee Waltz" (No. 3) and "Tennessee Moon" (No. 7). He also continued to perform with Pee Wee King on the Opry, recording a rival version of "Tennessee Waltz."

After the Top 20 singles "Breeze" and "I'm Waltzing with Tears in My Eyes," Copas hit the Top Ten again in early 1949. "Candy Kisses" peaked at No. 5, "Hangman's Boogie" reached No. 14, and "The Strange Little Girl" hit No. 5. His next single, 1952's "'Tis Sweet to Be Remembered," hit No. 8, but it was his last chart entry for more than eight years. His King contract expired in 1955, and a brief time with the Dot label also failed.

During the late '50s, Copas bided his time on the Opry and finally signed to Starday in 1960. His first single for the label, "Alabama," became the biggest of his career when it captured country's pole position for three months during the last half of 1960. "Flat Top" hit the Top Ten in April 1961, and a remake of his early hit "Signed, Sealed and Delivered" also reached the Top Ten in September. A year and a half later, Copas was returning to Nashville from a benefit show in Kansas City, when his private plane went down, killing him, Patsy Cline, Hawkshaw Hawkins, and Copas' son-in-law, pilot Randy Hughes. Cowboy Copas' last single, "Goodbye Kisses," hit the Top 15 one month after his death. — *John Bush*

Favorite Sacred Songs / 1957 / King ◆◆◆◆

Tragic Tales of Love & Life / 1960 / King ✦✦✦✦
A collection of recordings cut between 1946 and 1955, *Tragic Songs of Love and Life* includes Copas' renditions of "Tragic Romance," "Old Farm for Sale," and the 1949 hit "Hangman's Boogie." —*Jason Ankeny*

Mister Country Music / 1962 / Starday ✦✦✦
In addition to performances of "I Dreamed of a Hillbilly Heaven" and "How Do You Talk to a Baby," *Mister Country Music* offers Copas' take on the 1890s parlor tune "There'll Come a Time Someday." —*Jason Ankeny*

Opry Spotlight / 1962 / Starday ✦✦✦
Opry Star Spotlight includes covers of Porter Wagoner's "A Satisfied Mind," Ferlin Husky's "Wings of a Dove," and Carl Smith's "Loose Talk." —*Jason Ankeny*

● **Legend of Cowboy Copas and Hawkshaw Hawkins** / 1964 / King ✦✦✦✦

Jeff Copley

Vocals / Contemporary Country
Born and raised in West Virginia, vocalist Jeff Copley combines traditional Appalachian music with contemporary '90s country. Copley released his debut album, *Evergreen*, in the fall of 1995. —*Stephen Thomas Erlewine*

Evergreen / Oct. 3, 1995 / Polygram ✦✦✦
Though the album suffers from the occasional awkward song and a bit too much polish, *Evergreen* nevertheless is an impressive debut, showing Jeff Copley's ability to fuse traditional Appalachian music with contemporary country. Copley may not always hit the mark, but his finest moments showcase a vocalist with a unique talent. —*Stephen Thomas Erlewine*

Corbin/Hanner

Contemporary Country
Bob Corbin and David Hanner were a songwriting/singing duo whose music had strong pop overtones, and whose songs usually centered on the lives of working-class city dwellers.

The two teamed up after seeing the Beatles on the *Ed Sullivan Show,* and before even turning 16, they went to New York to record an album. After graduating from different colleges, they went to Pittsburgh together and founded Gravel, which went on to become one of the city's most popular bar bands. Their first break as songwriters came when Bob's wife Edana interviewed Mel Tillis and he came to hear the duo play. Impressed, he signed them to his publishing company. Not long after, they went back to Pittsburgh.

In 1979, Corbin/Hanner recorded "America's Sweetheart," a minor hit. The following year they became the Corbin/Hanner Band with the addition of keyboardist Al Snyder, bass guitarist Kip Paxton, and drummer Dave Freeland. Over the next two years, the band scored four hits, including "Time Has Treated You Well," and recorded two albums, *Son of America* (1980) and *For the Sake of the Song* (1981). They continued touring until 1984, when Corbin and Hanner decided to focus on songwriting separately.

Hanner's song "Can't Keep a Good Man Down" provided Alabama with a No. 1 hit in 1985, while Corbin's 1984 song "Beautiful You" did well for the Oak Ridge Boys. In 1986, Don Williams recorded Corbin's "I'll Never Be in Love Again," also a chart success. Harold Shedd reunited the duo soon after he took over the reins of Mercury Nashville, and helped produce their first Mercury album, *Black and White Photograph* (1991), which contained the popular "Work Song" and the Top 60 single "Concrete Cowboy." They had more chart success in 1992 with *Just Another Hill.* —*Sandra Brennan*

For the Sake of the Song / 1981 / Alfa ✦✦✦

Black & White Photograph / Apr. 1990 / Mercury ✦✦✦✦
Black & White Photograph offers five compositions apiece from the harmony duo of Bob Corbin and Dave Hanner; while Corbin's material leans toward roots-rock, Hanner's work bears the stamp of '60s pop. —*Jason Ankeny*

● **Just Another Hill** / Nov. 1992 / Mercury ✦✦✦✦
Just Another Hill ups the ante on Corbin/Hanner's debut by offering a number of songs—the title cut, "I Could Be the One" and "Any Road" among them—co-written by both vocalists. —*Jason Ankeny*

Helen Cornelius

b. Dec. 6, 1950, Monroe City, MO
Vocals / Country-Pop
Helen Cornelius is known to country music fans as a singer-songwriter, but she also danced, acted, and played several instruments. She was born Helen Lorene Johnson in Monroe City, MO, and grew up on a farm with older brothers who played in bands. She and her sisters Judy and Sharon formed a trio, and their supportive father took the girls to their gigs. Eventually Cornelius left her sisters and began touring with her backup band the Crossroads.

After graduating from high school, Cornelius married and worked as a secretary. She returned to touring during the '60s and became a songwriter, gaining recognition in 1970 when she was signed as a writer to Columbia/Screen Gems Music after submitting a demo tape. After the company folded, Cornelius sent a tape to Jerry Crutchfield and began working for MCA Music; he later helped her sign with Columbia Records. In 1973, she came to Nashville and recorded two unsuccessful singles, later signing to RCA. She released her first single for the label in 1975; neither it nor its follow-up charted.

The key to success proved to be Ferguson's pairing of Cornelius with Jim Ed Brown. The duo debuted in 1976 with "I Don't Want to Have to Marry You," which soon became a major hit. She again tried a solo single, "There's Always a Goodbye," but it did nothing. She had no other hits until she again dueted with Brown on "Saying Hello, Saying I Love You, Saying Goodbye," a Top Three success. Later in 1976, the two began appearing regularly on the TV series *Nashville on the Road;* Cornelius went out on tour with Brown's road show and made her debut on the Grand Ole Opry.

In 1978, she had more chart success with two Top 15 duet singles, "I'll Never Be Free" and "If the World Ran Out of Love Tonight," and scored a solo hit with "What Cha Doin' After Midnight Baby." The Cornelius/Brown hit streak continued until 1981, when Cornelius, feeling as though she was losing her identity as a performer, decided to break up the duo. She then released "Love Never Comes Easy," which made it to the Top 50. Her next hit came in 1983, the year she also worked as a spokesperson for the Cystic Fibrosis Foundation. In 1984, Cornelius changed directions and joined the road revival of *Annie Get Your Gun,* also touring with the Statler Brothers. She released a self-titled album in 1985, and three years later, she joined Brown for the *Reunited Tour '88.* In the 90's, she operated the Helen Cornelius Nashville South dinner theater in Gatlinburg, TN. —*Sandra Brennan*

● **Cornelius, Helen** / 1975 / Dot ✦✦✦✦

The Country Gazette

Progressive Bluegrass
One of the most influential bluegrass acts of the '70s—as well as one of that decade's most popular country artists in Europe—Country Gazette blended bluegrass with country-rock and, in the process, sowed the seeds for the newgrass movement of the '80s. The Los Angeles-based band was originally formed in 1971 by fiddler Byron Berline, bassist Roger Bush, and banjoist Billy Ray Latham, who had all played with Dillard & Clark. The trio added guitarist Herb Pedersen, who was quickly replaced by Alan Munde. Shortly after the band's formation, Berline and Bush played on the Flying Burrito Brothers' *Last of the Red Hot Burritos* album, which turned out to be the last album the group would release before breaking up; they would reunite later in the decade. Berline and Bush convinced guitarist Kenny Wertz to join Country Gazette during the Burrito sessions, and following the Burritos' dissolvement, the trio returned to Country Gazette and finished recording the band's debut, *A Traitor in Our Midst.*

A Traitor in Our Midst was released on United Artists in 1972. During the summer of that year, Country Gazette played gigs at Disneyland and soon landed opening spots for Steve Miller,

Crosby & Nash, and Don McLean, which indicated that the group was aiming for a more rock-oriented audience. Later that year, they recorded and released the *Live in Amsterdam* album. Their second studio album, *Don't Give Up Your Day Job*, appeared in 1973. Following its release, the band switched labels, signing with the European-based Ariola, which released *Bluegrass Special* later in 1973. As the location of their record label indicated, the band was more popular in Europe than America.

In 1975, Byron Berline left the band and formed Sundance; Roger Bush left that same year. The following year, Country Gazette added guitarist/mandolinist/vocalist Roland White to its lineup and released *Live*. After its release, the band added fiddler Dave Ferguson and released *Out to Lunch* on the American independent label Flying Fish; in Europe, the album was called *Sunnyside of the Mountain*. Following the recording of *Out to Lunch*, Wertz left the band. Two albums—1977's *What a Way to Earn a Living*, which was recorded with Berline, not Ferguson, and 1979's *All This and Money Too*—followed on Ridge Runner.

American and Clean and *America's Bluegrass Band* appeared on Flying Fish in 1981 and 1982 respectively. The group disbanded after the release of *America's Bluegrass Band*, but in 1983, they re-formed. The reunited lineup featured Roland White, banjoist Alan Munde, bassist Mike Anderson, and dobroist Gene Wooten. For the next five years, the band toured America and Europe. Country Gazette broke up for a second and final time in 1988. Roland White joined the Nashville Bluegrass Band after the group's split. —*Stephen Thomas Erlewine*

Out to Lunch / 1977 / Flying Fish ✦✦✦
On this album, one of the best of the progressive bands plays some fine newgrass. —*AMG*

Strictly Instrumental / 1981 / Flying Fish ✦✦✦✦
The Country Gazette's impassioned bluegrass goes instrumental on this release, with assistance from fiddler Billy Joe Foster, guitarist David Grier and bassist Kathy Chiavola. Still, the show belongs to Alan Munde's banjo work, which articulately navigates the rest of the group through the dozen traditional tunes contained here. —*Jason Ankeny*

● **Hello Operator . . . This Is Country Gazette** / 1991 / Flying Fish ✦✦✦✦
Hello Operator . . . This Is Country Gazette covers the group's five Flying Fish records, which were made between 1976 and 1987. During that time, a number of excellent musicians made their way through the band, but Country Gazette retained a distinctive progressive bluegrass style, as this compilation demonstrates. Certainly, anyone wanting an idea of what the group achieved during the height of their career should pick up *Hello Operator*, since it sums up their music succinctly and effectively. —*Thom Owens*

Keep on Pushing / 1991 / Flying Fish ✦✦✦
Fourteen great bluegrass cuts with Alan Munde. The Country Gazette's 20th year. —*Chip Renner*

The Country Gentlemen

Progressive Bluegrass, Traditional Bluegrass
The Country Gentlemen expanded the definition of "bluegrass"—they were progressive bluegrass before the term existed. The Gentlemen came along with the first wave of the folk-music revival in the late '50s and quickly made a name for themselves as a band who could not only play traditional material straight but who also brought Bob Dylan and contemporary country material into the genre. Because of their exceptional singing and virtuoso instrumentals, the Gentlemen attracted a broad audience, ranging from traditional country/bluegrass fans to folk and soft-rock lovers.

Formed in Washington, DC, on July 4, 1957, the original lineup of the Country Gentlemen featured guitarist/vocalist Charlie Waller—who has led the band through all of its numerous incarnations—mandolinist/vocalist John Duffey, banjoist Bill Emerson, and bassist Tom Morgan. Waller had spent time with a number of country string bands in the early '50s, most notably Buzz Busby's band the Bayou Boys, which also featured Emerson. After the Bayou Boys suffered a car crash in early 1957, Waller and Emerson put together a group to fulfill the band's regular spot at a Vir-

ginia spot while various members were recovering. That replacement band evolved into the Country Gentlemen.

For the first two years of their existence, the Country Gentlemen went through numerous lineup changes. In 1959, they finally landed on a permanent lineup, with banjoist Eddie Adcock and bassist Tom Gray joining a band that already included Waller and Duffey. This lineup secured a contract with Starday Records and released a handful of singles, as well as one album, *Traveling Dobro Blues*. Following their Starday recordings, the group moved to Folkways, where they released three albums, including their breakthrough *Country Songs Old & New*. After their stint at Folkways, the group moved to Mercury in 1963, where they released *Folk Session Inside*. The following year, they began a long association with Rebel Records.

During the '60s, the Country Gentlemen built up a dedicated fan base in America through constant touring. Although their lineup shifted rapidly—following Gray's 1964 departure, they went through several bassists before settling on Ed McGlothlin—their sound pretty much stayed the same. At the end of the '60s, the core lineup began to splinter as Duffey left in 1969; he was replaced by Jimmy Gaudreau. In the following year, both Adcock and McGlothlin left the group. In 1971, the second classic lineup of the Country Gentlemen—featuring Waller, a rejoined Bill Emerson, mandolinist Doyle Lawson and bassist Bill Yates—fell into place and they stayed together for two years. For the next 20 years, various versions of the Country Gentlemen, which were led by Waller, remained popular on the bluegrass festival circuit. —*Stephen Thomas Erlewine & David Vinopal*

Traveling Dobro Blues / 1959 / Starday ✦✦✦✦

★ **Country Songs Old & New** / 1960 / Smithsonian/Folkways ✦✦✦✦✦
This is a reissue of the 1960 Folkways album that launched their career. Includes "The Little Sparrow," "The Long Black Veil," "Under the Double Eagle," and 13 other classic cuts. A magic album. —*Michael Erlewine*

Return Engagement / 1963 / Rebel ✦✦✦
First issued in 1963, *Return Engagement* features the Gentlemen tackling songs like "Miner's Life," "Lonely Child," and "Lonesome Highway." —*Jason Ankeny*

Award-Winning Country Gentlemen / 1972 / Rebel ✦✦✦✦
Not only does *Award-Winning Country Gentlemen* culminate a major shift in direction for the Country Gentlemen, it is also quite possibly their finest album. Charlie Waller had to reassemble the group in the early '70s, bringing in a new lineup—including mandolinist Doyle Lawson, bassist Bill Yates, and banjoist Bill Emerson—that helped move the Country Gentlemen even further into contemporary music. On *Award-Winning*, the band covers songs by rock and folk songwriters like Bob Dylan and Gordon Lightfoot, bringing a bluegrass attitude and instrumentation to the contemporary numbers. The result is a stunning record, with a great selection of songs and simply excellent musicianship. —*Thom Owens*

Calling My Children Home / 1978 / Rebel ✦✦✦
Thanks to the superb direction of mandolinist Doyle Lawson, *Calling My Children Home* is an excellent bluegrass gospel album, highlighted by a handful of tremendous a cappella quartets. —*Thom Owens*

Live in Japan / 197 / Rebel ✦✦✦✦
Live in Japan captures a strong early '70s concert from the Country Gentlemen, spotlighting much of their best-known material, as well as their excellent harmony and instrumental skills. —*Thom Owens*

One Wide River / 1987 / Rebel ✦✦✦
Nice, but not as energetic or ambitious as other releases. —*Ron Wynn*

Folk Songs & Bluegrass / 1988 / Smithsonian/Folkways ✦✦✦✦
Folk Songs & Bluegrass is one of the Country Gentlemen's best releases, featuring the classic lineup of Eddie Adcock, John Duffey, Tom Gray, and Charlie Waller at the height of their power. Both the songs—which are divided between standards and newer folk numbers—and the performances are first-rate, making *Folk*

Songs & Bluegrass an essential purchase for any bluegrass collection. —*Thom Owens*

☆ **Sit Down Young Stranger** / 1988 / Sugar Hill ✦✦✦✦✦
A tremendous date; brilliant playing by Mike Aulridge. —*Ron Wynn*

Bluegrass at Carnegie Hall / 1988 / Gusto ✦✦✦✦
Originally released on Starday in 1962, *Bluegrass at Carnegie Hall* isn't a live album, even though the title suggests that it is. Instead, it is a collection of excellent studio recordings—made around the same time as their 1961 appearance at Carnegie Hall—that rank among their finest early recordings. —*Thom Owens*

River Bottom / 1989 / Sugar Hill ✦✦✦✦
Great solos and harmonies, excellent compositions. —*Ron Wynn*

The Country Gentlemen Feat. Ricky Skaggs / 198 / Vanguard ✦✦✦
Featuring Ricky Skaggs on Fiddle collects material drawn from Skaggs' early '70s tenure with the band, and features "House of the Rising Sun," "The City of New Orleans," and "Catfish John." —*Jason Ankeny*

Let the Light Shine Down / 1991 / Rebel ✦✦✦
Let the Light Shine Down is a fine compilation of gospel and inspirational songs the Country Gentlemen recorded between 1962 and 1976, including several tracks that have never been available before on compact disc. —*Thom Owens*

Sugar Hill Collection / 1995 / Sugar Hill ✦✦✦✦
As the title suggests, *Sugar Hill Collection* compiles the highlights from the Country Gentlemen's recordings for the independent label Sugar Hill. Although these were made later in their career, the group sounds as good as they ever have. —*Thom Owens*

Classic/Nashville Jail / Copper Creek ✦✦✦
This album contains bluegrass performances from the early '60s. —*AMG*

Sound Off / Rebel ✦✦✦
Good, with a more contemporary sound. —*Ron Wynn*

25 Years / Rebel ✦✦✦✦
25 Years was released in 1980, when the Country Gentlemen were celebrating their 25th anniversary. The compilation covers the group's recordings for Rebel Records, which began in the mid-'60s. Over the course of *25 Years*, various incarnations of the Country Gentlemen are displayed. Each one has its own merits, but the classic lineup of Eddie Adcock, John Duffey, Tom Gray, and Charlie Waller does stand out in particular. Though the other incarnations aren't quite as accomplished as this lineup, the compilation nevertheless remains an excellent purchase and introduction, since it gives a fine overview of the group's career. —*Thom Owens*

The Country Rockers

Roots-Rock, Alternative Country-Rock
The Country Rockers' name alone was a wholly accurate gauge of their sound and aesthetics. A somewhat obscure trio based in Memphis, TN, the group was led by Durand Easley, an accomplished producer and session musician. While drinking in a Mississippi roadhouse in 1986, Easley hooked up with Sam Baird, a singer and guitarist he recognized from the latter's long tenure as a staple of the Memphis club circuit. Though Baird was in his mid-60s at the time, he and the 35-year-old Easley decided to form a band, enlisting Gaius L. "Ringo" Farnham, a then 73-year-old drummer, to fill out their sound.

After developing a repertoire of country standards and eclectic obscurities, the trio cut a demo with Easley's brother Doug, a prominent indie-rock producer. After the session, Easley left for Europe to tour with his old friend Alex Chilton; after shopping the Country Rockers' demo to New Rose Records, Chilton's label, a deal was struck. In 1989, the group issued its debut LP, *Free Range Chicken*, a varied collection of rockabilly, country, and novelty tunes featuring the original demo tracks along with newly recorded material; while the vocal chores were split mainly

between Easley and Baird, Ringo Farnham—just like his namesake in the Beatles—was allowed to sing on one cut. The Country Rockers' second effort, *Cypress Room*, appeared in 1991. —*Jason Ankeny*

● **Free Range Chicken** / 1989 / New Rose ✦✦✦✦
Split between demos and more polished material, *Free Range Chicken* is a wildly eclectic and raucous debut, offering forays into rockabilly ("Rockin' Daddy"), surf ("Wipe Out"), straightforward country ("There Stands the Glass") and the self-explanatory ("Guitar Polka"). —*Jason Ankeny*

Cypress Room / 1991 / New Rose ✦✦✦
Continuing the formula (or lack thereof) established on the Country Rockers' first effort, *Cypress Room* is another diverse affair, this time dabbling in honky tonk, calypso, and lewd R&B. —*Jason Ankeny*

The Cox Family

Progressive Bluegrass, Traditional Bluegrass
The singing Cox Family from Cotton Valley, LA, was comprised of father Willard, son Sidney, and daughters Evelyn and Suzanne, who derived their sound from combining country, bluegrass, and gospel styles. They first began performing together in 1976, and were a popular draw at fairs and festivals, but their career was given a big boost when in the early '90s they met Alison Krauss, who brought them to the attention of Rounder Records. They also gained massive exposure when in 1994 they caught the ear of the multiplatinum-selling Counting Crows' frontman Adam Duritz, who was so impressed with the group he invited them to open for the band during its North American tour. Krauss—who produced all but the family's very first release *Quiet Storm* on Wilcox Records—recorded several of Sidney's songs, which appeared on both of her Grammy-winning albums, including the title track of *I've Got That Old Feeling*. The Cox Family recorded two records of their own on Rounder Records: *Everybody's Reaching Out for Someone* (1993) and *Beyond the City* (1995), which earned them a Grammy nomination for Best Bluegrass Album. They also collaborated with Krauss on an album entitled *I Know Who Holds Tomorrow*, which won a Grammy in 1994 for Best Country/Gospel/Bluegrass Album. The family also shared a Grammy for their participation in the various-artists project *Amazing Grace—A Country Salute to Gospel*. The Cox Family released their major-label debut *Just When We're Thinking It's Over* on Asylum Records in 1996. —*Jack Leaver*

Quiet Storm / Wilcox ✦✦✦

Everybody's Reaching out for Someone / Apr. 1, 1993 / Rounder ✦✦✦

● **Beyond the City** / 1995 / Rounder ✦✦✦✦

Just When You're Thinking It's Over / Jul. 1996 / Asylum ✦✦✦✦
The smooth and effortless vocal blend of the Cox Family make this a pleasurable experience throughout. And although their angelic four-part harmonies are based in bluegrass, to categorize the family in that genre solely would be to pigeonhole them. The performances here also mix in country, gospel, and a touch of blues, with top-notch session players providing a sound foundation that employs electric, as well as acoustic, instruments and includes producer Alison Krauss' fiddle and viola playing on a couple of cuts. All four family members take turns singing lead, and there isn't a weak link in the group or a weak song on the album. Highlights include a great bluegrass reworking of Del Shannon's 1961 hit "Runaway" and the beautiful ballad "Nothing Else I Can Do," penned by Sidney and Suzanne Cox. —*Jack Leaver*

Billy "Crash" Craddock

b. Jun. 16, 1939, Greensboro, NC
Guitar, Vocals / Traditional Country, Rockabilly, Honky Tonk
People often associate the "Crash" nickname with auto racing, but Craddock actually got it as a halfback in high school, crashing into linemen who were twice his size. Growing up in Greensboro, NC, he pantomimed Grand Ole Opry shows in the family's barn with a broomstick as a microphone, alternately pretending he was

Hank Williams, Faron Young, or Carl Smith. But when he signed a recording contract in the late '50s, Columbia tried to mold him as a teen idol, much like Elvis Presley or Fabian. It didn't work in the US, but "Crash" did pick up a trio of hits in Australia. Fifteen years later, he finally got his chance in country music when record producer Ron Chancey signed him to his Cartwheel label. With a knack for making re-makes of pop hits like "Knock Three Times" and "Ruby Baby"—and for adding a certain energy to the country idiom—Craddock picked up the nickname "Mr. Country-rock." —*Tom Roland*

Sings His Greatest Hits / 1978 / MCA ✦✦✦✦

A good summation of his peak years, it includes the ballads "Easy as Pie" and "Broken Down in Tiny Pieces." But Craddock's at his best when he's "in the groove," as in "Ruby Baby," "Still Thinkin' 'Bout You," and his staple, "Rub It In." —*Tom Roland*

Boom Boom Baby / 1992 / Bear Family ✦✦✦✦

● Crash's Smashes / Feb. 20, 1996 / Razor & Tie ✦✦✦✦

Drawing from three different labels—Cartwheel, ABC, and Capitol—*Crash's Smashes: The Hits of Billy "Crash" Craddock* is the definitive compilation of Craddock's career. All of his biggest hits—from "Knock Three Times" and "Dream Lover" through "Rub it In," "Easy as Pie" and "Broken Down in Tiny Pieces" to "If I Could Write a Song as Beautiful as You"—are included on the 19-track single disc, making it both a perfect introduction and retrospective. —*Stephen Thomas Erlewine*

Floyd Cramer

b. Oct. 27, 1933, Samti, LA

Piano, Session Musician / Instrumental Pop, Nashville Sound/ Countrypolitan

A distinctive pianist whose unique, slip-note playing style came to typify the pop-oriented "Nashville Sound" of the late 1950s and early 1960s, session and solo musician Floyd Cramer was born October 27, 1933 in Louisiana. After a childhood spent largely in Arkansas, he returned to his home state in 1951 and began appearing on the radio program *The Louisiana Hayride*, where he performed with the likes of Jim Reeves, Faron Young, Webb Pierce and, in his debut, Elvis Presley.

While Cramer cut a few solo sides in 1953, his most important work in the early 1950s was as a session musician, where he first met Chet Atkins, who encouraged the pianist to move to Nashville. He did in 1955, rejoining Atkins as the house pianist at RCA Records to begin developing what would ultimately be recognized as the Nashville Sound, a style shorn of the elements associated with traditional country and honky tonk that instead favored a more polished, progressive sheen. With Atkins behind the production boards, Cramer began to perfect his unique style of playing, a method not dissimilar to guitar-picking in that he would hit one key and then slide his finger onto the next, creating a blue, lonesome sound. Under Atkins' guidance, Cramer played on hundreds of sessions, including many for Presley, among them "Heartbreak Hotel."

In 1957, Cramer released his own solo debut, *That Honky-Tonk Piano,* and in the next year scored a minor pop hit with the single "Flip, Flop and Bop." As his solo career was largely secondary in relation to his session work, he recorded his own music sporadically, but in 1960 notched a significant country and pop hit with the self-penned instrumental "Last Date." The follow-up, a cover of Bob Wills' "San Antonio Rose," reached the Top Ten of both charts. He also released an LP a year between 1960 and 1962, starting with *Hello Blues* and followed by *Last Date* and *I Remember Hank Williams.*

From 1965 to 1974, Cramer annually released a *Class of...* album, a collection of the year's top hits done in his own inimitable style. In 1971, he also teamed with Atkins and saxophonist Boots Randolph for the album *Chet, Floyd and Boots.* By 1977, Cramer was exploring modern technology, and on the LP *Keyboard Kick Band,* he played a number of instruments, including a synthesizer. In 1980, he released his last significant hit, a recording of the theme from the hit TV drama *Dallas.* Though largely quiet for most of the decade, in 1988 Cramer released three sepa-

rate albums—*Country Gold, Just Me and My Piano!* and *Special Songs of Love.* —*Jason Ankeny*

Hello Blues / 1960 / RCA Victor ✦✦✦✦

Hello Blues is Floyd Cramer's attempt to play the blues in his own distinctive, "slip-note," style. Of course, the laidback tempos and gentle arrangements of all the music on the album mean that it never sounds as gritty or down-home as the best country blues, but that isn't the point of the record—*Hello Blues* is a pleasant collection of bluesy easy listening, not a blues record, and taken on its own terms, it's entertaining. The CD reissue includes four bonus tracks, which are not necessarily "blues": "Sentimental Journey," "Red Roses for a Blue Lady," "Mr. Lonely," and "Love Letters." —*Thom Owens*

Gospel Classics / 1968 / Step One ✦✦✦

Features "The Old Rugged Cross," "Blessed Assurance," and more. —*AMG*

The Best of Floyd Cramer / 1970 / RCA ✦✦✦✦

The Best of Floyd Cramer is a cheap collection and its 12 tracks don't provide a definitive retrospective, but it has enough hits—including "Last Date" and "San Antonio Rose"— to satisfy many fans. —*Stephen Thomas Erlewine*

Special Songs of Love / Mar. 1, 1990 / Step One ✦✦✦

This features "Love Me Tender," "There Goes My Everything," and "Makin' Believe," among others. —*AMG*

Collector's Series / May 23, 1995 / RCA ✦✦✦✦

Collector's Seres is a reasonably thorough overview of Floyd Cramer's career, offering nearly every one of his hits ("Last Date," "Tennessee Waltz," "For the Good Times") in its original version. —*Stephen Thomas Erlewine*

★ Essential Series / Aug. 1, 1995 / RCA ✦✦✦✦✦

Favorite Country Hits / Oct. 1995 / Ranwood ✦✦✦✦

Favorite Country Hits is a condensed, 18-track single disc of Floyd Cramer's mid-'90s double-disc set, which was only sold through television. On the album, Cramer runs through a number of country classics, including his trademark "Last Date." Though Cramer's talent hasn't diminished over the years, *Favorite Country Hits* is best used as easy listening background music, since it rarely hits any peaks or valleys—it's just pleasant, low-key country-pop. —*Thom Owens*

The Piano Magic, Vol. 2 / Apr. 1996 / Ranwood ✦✦

Utterly unmemorable Nashville-muzak versions of standards like "Mona Lisa," "Danny Boy," "Rambling Rose," "Only You," and "You Don't Know Me." —*Richie Unterberger*

Originals / Step One ✦✦

Featured are new recordings of such Cramer favorites as "First Hurt," "On Angel Wings," "Always in My Heart," and "Corn Crib Symphony." —*AMG*

Forever Floyd Cramer / Step One ✦✦

In addition to a number of self-penned originals, Cramer also covers the pop hit "(I've Had The) Time of My Life," taken from the soundtrack of the film *Dirty Dancing.* —*Jason Ankeny*

Dan Crary

Guitar / Progressive Bluegrass, Bluegrass

Crary is among the "sons of Doc" who emerged in the '70s, taking Doc Watson's flatpicked guitar style a step further. The Kansas native was among the founders of the Bluegrass Alliance, and subsequently pursued a solo career while teaching speech communications in California. Recording for Sugar Hill and similar labels, Crary has carved a niche for himself as a distinctive interpreter of traditional material for acoustic 6- and 12-string guitars. He also records original compositions. He may be best known for his work with "Fiddler" Byron Berline and "Banjoist" John Hickman, who combined with Crary in a bluegrass-and-beyond trio that has been active for more than a decade. —*Mark A. Humphrey*

Sweet Southern Girl / 1969 / Sugar Hill ✦✦✦

Bluegrass Guitar / 1970 / Sugar Hill ✦✦✦

Thunderation / 1981 / Pamlico Sound ✦✦✦✦

● **Guitar** / 1983 / Sugar Hill ✦✦✦✦

The title leaves the erroneous impression that this is a solo set. Instead, it's an exciting blowing session featuring the cream of the new generation of bluegrass players who emerged in the '80s—Sam Bush, Mark O'Connor, and Bela Fleck. But on selections ranging from a "Bill Monroe Medley" to a transcribed Mozart piano sonata, Crary and his guitar more than hold their own. — *William Ruhlmann*

Jammed If I Do / May 24, 1994 / Koch ✦✦✦

Take a Step Over / Sugar Hill ✦✦✦

On *Take a Step Over,* Dan Crary once again demonstrates that he is one of the most talented bluegrass acoustic guitarists of his generation. Crary has a knack for interpreting fiddle tunes for the guitar, playing them with a nimble grace and effortless musicality. As long as he sticks to instrumentals, Crary is fine—after all, he has some great duels with Bela Fleck, Sam Bush, John Hickman, and Byron Berline—but when he sings, the album becomes a little tedious; he simply doesn't have the vocal skills to match his instrumental acumen. However, the guitar showcases are strong enough to make the album worthwhile for any fans of bluegrass guitar. — *Stephen Thomas Erlewine*

Rob Crosby

b. Apr. 25, 1954, Sumter, SC

Vocals / Singer-Songwriter, Country-Folk

Rob Crosby was a singer-songwriter noted for his folksy, sensitive lyrics. Born Robert Crosby Hoar in Sumpter, SC, he wrote his first song at age nine and had his first band, the Radiations, while still in fifth grade. Inspired by Kris Kristofferson, Bob Dylan, and Paul Simon, Crosby wrote songs and performed with a three-piece combo in high school. While in college he began playing with the band Savannah in South Carolina nightclubs. He then founded the Rob Crosby Group and toured the Southeast. In 1974, the group broke up and Crosby moved to Nashville with his family; two former band members also moved there, and they and Crosby reteamed to play in local clubs.

A year after getting a job as a staff writer at a small music publishing house, Crosby's 1985 song "She Told Me Yes" was a Top 30 hit for the group Chance. Soon others, including Lee Greenwood, began recording his songs. When not writing, Crosby earned extra money singing commercial jingles for radio and television. A performance at a songwriter's night hosted by the Nashville Entertainment Association led to a record deal, and in 1991, he released his debut album, *Solid Ground,* which contained three Top 20 singles, including "Love Will Bring Her Around." He wrote or co-wrote most of the songs on the album and garnered considerable critical acclaim for his sensitive, female-oriented lyrics. His second album, *Another Time & Place* (1992), did not do as well and Arista dropped him. In 1995, he resurfaced with *Starting Now.* — *Sandra Brennan*

Solid Ground / 1991 / Arista ✦✦✦✦

Solid Ground includes Crosby's first three Top 20 hits, including "Love Will Bring Her Around." — *Jason Ankeny*

● **Another Time & Place** / Jul. 28, 1992 / Arista ✦✦✦✦

Though less commercially successful than his debut *Solid Ground, Another Time & Place* offers some of Crosby's strongest material, including "When Hearts Agree" and "Old News." — *Jason Ankeny*

Starting Now / Oct. 1995 / River North Nashville ✦✦✦

J.D. Crowe

b. Aug. 27, 1937, Lexington, KY

Banjo, Vocals / Progressive Bluegrass

Banjoist J.D. Crowe was one of the most influential progressive bluegrass musicians of the '70s. Initially influenced by Earl Scruggs, as well as rock 'n' roll and the blues, Crowe worked his way through several bands during the '60s, developing a distinctive instrumental style that melded country, bluegrass, rock, and blues. Crowe didn't receive national exposure until the early '70s, when he formed the New South, but after the release of the band's eponymous debut in 1972, he became a fixture on the bluegrass scene for the next 20 years.

Born and raised in Lexington, KY, Crowe picked up the banjo when he was 13 years old, inspired by one of Flatt & Scruggs' performances on the Kentucky Barn Dance. After that show, he regularly attended the duo's performances, sitting down in the front row to study Scruggs' revolutionary picking. Soon, Crowe was playing with various groups in Kentucky, including an outfit that also featured Curley Parker and Pee Wee Lambert. The young banjo player frequently played on local radio stations, and that is where he got his first major break in 1956. Jimmy Martin was driving through Lexington when he heard Crowe on the radio station and was so impressed with what he heard, he drove to the station and asked him to join his band, the Sunny Mountain Boys. Crowe immediately accepted and began touring with Martin. While he was in the Sunny Mountain Boys, J.D. didn't stick to a strict bluegrass set list—he often added rock 'n' roll songs to his repertoire.

After spending six years with Martin, Crowe left the Sunny Mountain Boys in 1962 to pursue a solo career. For a while, he played Lexington bars and hotels, developing a new, progressive direction for bluegrass that incorporated stronger elements of folk, blues, and rock. In the mid-'60s, he formed the Kentucky Mountain Boys with Red Allen and Doyle Lawson, which released their first album, *Bluegrass Holiday,* in 1968 on Lemco Records. The Kentucky Mountain Boys had a varied repertoire, but played solely acoustic instruments. Two other records followed—*Ramblin' Boy* and *The Model Church*—before the group broke up in the early '70s.

Following the breakup of the Kentucky Mountain Boys, J.D. Crowe formed the New South, which was the most revolutionary bluegrass outfit of its time. Originally, the band consisted of guitarist Tony Rice, mandolinist Ricky Skaggs, dobroist Jerry Douglas, and fiddler/bassist Bobby Sloan, and they played a wildly eclectic brand of bluegrass on electric instruments. When they released their debut, *J.D. Crowe & the New South* in 1975 on Rounder Records, it caused an instant sensation—it marked a genuine turning point in the sound of the genre. All of the musicians in the original lineup of the New South were acclaimed and they would later go on to popular solo careers—in fact, most of them had left within a few years of the debut. By the end of the decade, the band featured guitarist/vocalist Keith Whitley, mandolinist Jimmy Gaudreau, fiddler Bobby Slone, and bassist Steve Bryant.

During the '80s, the New South featured an ever-revolving lineup, as former members came back for guest appearances and Crowe discovered fresh, developing talents; the group became known as a source for new musicians that would later go on to individual success. In 1980, Crowe formed the Bluegrass Album Band with Tony Rice, Bobby Hicks, Doyle Lawson, and Todd Phillips. The Bluegrass Album Band toured and recorded sporadically throughout the course of the decade, always to great critical and popular acclaim. J.D. continued with the New South until 1988, when he decided to retire from the road. Following his decision, he appeared at special, one-shot concerts—including a tour with Tony Rice—but he concentrated on studio work, particularly producing records for developing bands. — *Stephen Thomas Erlewine*

Bluegrass Holiday / 1968 / Lemco ✦✦✦

☆ **The Model Church** / 1969 / Rebel ✦✦✦✦✦

Model Church is one of the first gospel albums recorded by a progressive bluegrass band in the late '70s. Both J.D. Crowe and the Kentucky Mountain Boys, whose lineup for this album featured Doyle Lawson, give terrific performances, bringing new life to this material. *Model Church,* in turn, spawned a movement of newgrass bands exploring gospel, yet few of the subsequent albums ever matched the quality of this excellent album. — *Thom Owens*

☆ **J. D. Crowe and the New South** / 1975 / Rounder ✦✦✦✦✦

J.D. Crowe and the New South's eponymous debut album is one of the most influential and pioneering records in the history of bluegrass. For the first edition of the New South, Crowe assembled a stellar group of musicians—including Ricky Skaggs (fiddle, mandolin, vocals), Tony Rice (lead vocals, guitar), and Jerry Douglas (dobro)—and gave them each equal weight. Consequently, this is vibrant collaborative music, not just a leader with some faceless studio hacks. Furthermore, Crowe pushed the music in new directions with his selection of material, taking songs from contemporary singer-songwriters like Gordon Lightfoot, and adding a couple of originals, as well as standards. With such an eclectic selection of songs, plus the band's trailblazing instrumental style, *The New South* did offer a new kind of bluegrass, and its impact could still be felt years after its release. — *Thom Owens*

My Home Ain't in the Hall of Fame / 1978 / Rounder ✦✦✦
Crowe, on banjo and baritone, moves closer to country in the company of Keith Whitley and Doug Jernigan. — *Mark A. Humphrey*

Somewhere Between / 1981 / Rounder ✦✦✦✦
A hard-country album with lovely ballads, it features Lefty Frizzell-style vocals from Keith Whitley. — *Mark A. Humphrey*

Live in Japan / 1982 / Rounder ✦✦✦
Spirited performances with Keith Whitley and the great mandolinist Jimmy Gaudreau. — *Mark A. Humphrey*

Straight Ahead / 1986 / Rounder ✦✦✦
More or less traditional bluegrass, with Sam Bush on mandolin and Jerry Douglas on dobro. — *Mark A. Humphrey*

Blackjack / 1987 / Rebel ✦✦
Blackjack is one of J.D. Crowe and the New South's best albums, featuring a mixture of bluegrass standards and contemporary country-rock and folk songs, like the Flying Burrito Brothers' *Sin City*. It's a stunning display of ambition, progression, and heritage, highlighted by Crowe's excellent instrumental work and Doyle Lawson's wonderful lead vocals. — *Thom Owens*

★ **FlashBack** / 1994 / Rounder ✦✦✦✦✦
FlashBack is a first-rate retrospective of J.D. Crowe's groundbreaking, innovative career and an excellent way to get acquainted with all aspects of his music. — *Thom Owens*

Rodney Crowell

b. Aug. 7, 1950, Houston, TX
Guitar, Vocals / Country-Rock, Contemporary Country, New Traditionalist
While Rodney Crowell first gained widespread recognition as a leader of the "New Traditionalist" movement of the mid-1980s, he in fact was a singer, songwriter, and producer with roots and ambitions extending far beyond the movement's parameters. Born to a musical family on August 7, 1950, in Houston, TX, Crowell formed his first band, the Arbitrators, while in high school, and in 1972 moved to Nashville to become a professional musician. There, he struck up friendships with singer-songwriters Townes Van Zandt and Guy Clark.
    Crowell's first big break came while he was performing as a lounge singer, when one of his acoustic sets was heard by Jerry Reed. Crowell's own "You Can't Keep Me Here in Tennessee" caught the ear of Reed and his manager, and two days later Reed recorded the song after signing Crowell to his publishing company. In 1975, Crowell moved to Los Angeles to join Emmylou Harris' Hot Band as a guitarist, and soon became one of her primary songwriters; among the Crowell compositions Harris first popularized were "Till I Gain Control Again," "Ain't Livin' Long Like This," "Leaving Louisiana in the Broad Daylight," and "Bluebird Wine." In 1977, Crowell exited the Hot Band to form his own group, the Cherry Bombs, and in 1978 released his first album, *Ain't Living Long Like This;* surprisingly, given that he had built his growing reputation as a songwriter, his first two minor hits—"Elvira" and "(Now and Then, There's) A Fool Such As I"—were both covers.
    Also in 1978, Crowell began producing tracks for the album *Right or Wrong*, the American debut from singer-songwriter Rosanne Cash; around the time of the record's 1979 release, he and Cash married. In between recording his own 1980 sophomore record *But What Will the Neighbors Think* and producing Cash's commercial breakthrough *Seven Year Ache*, Crowell's songwriting career took off when "Leavin' Louisiana in the Broad

Daylight" was a No. 1 hit for the Oak Ridge Boys in 1980. Among his other compositions were "Till I Gain Control Again" (a No. 1 for Crystal Gayle in 1983); "Shame on the Moon" (a Top Three pop hit for Bob Seger in 1982); "Long Hard Road (The Sharecropper's Dream)" (a 1984 No. 1 for the Nitty Gritty Dirt Band); and "Somewhere Tonight" (a No. 1 in 1987 for Highway 101).
    In 1980, Crowell issued his own first hit, "Ashes by Now," which was a Top 40 pop crossover success; the follow-up, "Stars on the Water," was popular with both pop and country listeners. In 1981, he issued his third LP, a self-titled effort that was not commercially successful; when a fourth effort was rejected by his label, he turned his energies to writing and producing, most significantly helming Cash's 1985 masterpiece *Rhythm and Romance*. At Cash's urging, Crowell reignited his performing career in 1986 with the acclaimed *Street Language*, an eclectic effort co-produced by Memphis soul legend Booker T. Jones.
    In 1988, Crowell finally broke through commercially with *Diamonds and Dirt*, a record which generated an unbroken string of four No. 1 singles with "It's Such a Small World" (a duet with Cash), "I Couldn't Leave You If I Tried," "She's Crazy for Leavin'" (co-written by Guy Clark), and "After All This Time."
    Keys to the Highway, released in 1989, was also highly successful; the album's first single, "Above and Beyond," was his fifth consecutive chart-topper. Crowell and Cash divorced in 1991, prompting both artists to document their marriage's dissolution with starkly confessional albums; 1992's *Life Is Messy* featured guests Steve Winwood and Linda Ronstadt. He remained a prolific performer throughout the decade, issuing *Let the Picture Paint Itself* in 1994 and both *Jewel of the South* and *Soul Searchin'* the next year. — *Jason Ankeny*

Ain't Living Long Like This / 1978 / Warner Brothers ✦✦✦
Before Rodney Crowell began to have hits of his own, his albums were often raided by other artists for hits. This album features Crowell compositions that became hits for the Oak Ridge Boys, the Nitty Gritty Dirt Band, and Waylon Jennings. It's worth checking out to hear how they were originally done. — *Jim Worbois*

But What Will the Neighbors Think / 1980 / Warner Brothers ✦✦
On his second album, Rodney Crowell demonstrates slight new wave influences, which is evident from his "Here Come the '80s" and a cover of "Queen of Hearts," which demonstrates a debt to Rockpile, as well as his choice of Ramones producer Craig Leon as a collaborator. The problem is, Crowell doesn't quite have the skills or the heart to pull off a country-new wave fusion, as Carlene Carter did successfully around the same time. There are several fine songs on the record, but they are better heard on *The Rodney Crowell Collection*. — *Thom Owens*

Rodney Crowell / 1981 / Warner Brothers ✦✦✦
Crowell plays down his performance on this album. Yes, he's a bit cool toward the material vocally on occasion, but the overall effect is raw, energetic, and natural, in the best garage-band tradition. A good mix of club rock 'n' roll and country-rock, with, incidentally, his own renditions of "Till I Gain Control Again" and "Shame on the Moon." — *Tom Roland*

Street Language / 1986 / Columbia ✦✦
With *Street Language*, Rodney Crowell created an awkward country-soul hybrid. Working with organist Booker T. Jones, Billy Joe Walker, and John Hiatt—whom he also covers—Crowell doesn't quite realize his concept. Although the songs are generally quite good, the sound of the record is forced and hamfisted. At the very least, the album suggests that Crowell is at his best when he is at his most direct. And he became direct on his next album, *Keys to the Highway*. — *Thom Owens*

Keys to the Highway / 1989 / Columbia ✦✦✦✦
This wide-ranging set combines soul, blues, rock, and the country shuffle. Recorded shortly before the May 1989 death of Crowell's father, it's surprisingly upbeat and hopeful in its approach. Still, the two brooding songs most closely linked to James Crowell's passing, "Many a Long and Lonesome Highway" and "Things I Wish I'd Said," stand out most. — *Tom Roland*

● **The Rodney Crowell Collection** / 1989 / Warner Brothers ◆◆◆◆
The best of Crowell's uneven but occasionally brilliant early recordings is condensed into one neat little package. It includes "Shame on the Moon," which Bob Seger rightly turned into a pop hit. This isn't *Diamonds & Dirt*, but it's a good start. —*Brian Mansfield*

Diamonds & Dirt / 1989 / Columbia ◆◆◆◆
Record-producer Tony Brown convinced Crowell to do this one quickly and not second-guess himself; the advice paid off. Leaning hard on the country shuffle, Crowell broke through with this package—live, honest, and unassuming. It yielded five hits, including the Grammy-winning "After All This Time," but the best cut might be the tantalizing "I Know You're Married." —*Tom Roland*

Life Is Messy / May 12, 1992 / Columbia ◆◆◆
Life Is Messy was the first album Rodney Crowell released since his divorce from Rosanne Cash. As the title suggests, Crowell has some trouble coming to terms with the divorce on *Life Is Messy*. Though that might have made for a difficult personal situation, the music on the album is splendid, which is typical for a Crowell release. Alternating between spare, introspective numbers like "It's Not for Me to Judge" and "I Hardly Know How to Be Myself" and rocking country-pop like "Let's Make Trouble," the album is a satisfying blend of musical and lyrical moods, demonstrating Crowell's skills as a songwriter and musician. —*Thom Owens*

● **Greatest Hits** / 1993 / Columbia ◆◆◆◆
The music on *Greatest Hits* is taken from an era when Rodney Crowell actually had hits, including the No. 1s "I Couldn't Leave You If I Tried," "She's Crazy for Leavin'," and "After All This Time." Those songs and several more are collected on *Greatest Hits*, making it a fine introduction to the singer-songwriter. —*Stephen Thomas Erlewine*

Let the Picture Paint Itself / 1994 / MCA ◆◆◆
So much of Crowell's best work has been co-produced by MCA executive Tony Brown, it seemed inevitable he would wind up at MCA himself. This, his first release for his new label, emphasizes Crowell, the thoughtful songwriter, over Crowell the neo-honky tonk band leader. It's a fair trade, but requires repeat listening to fully appreciate. —*Dan Cooper*

Jewel of the South / 1995 / MCA ◆◆◆
Crowell tries to stretch out a bit too much on *Jewel of the South*, but it remains a fine album, nonetheless. Featuring guest performances by the Mavericks' Raul Malo, Bela Fleck, Vince Gill, Kim Richey, and Billy Joe Walker, Jr. among others, the album tries to do too many things, but it does enough of them well enough to make it an entertaining listen. —*Thom Owens*

Bobbie Cryner

b. Sep. 13, 1961, Woodland, CA
Country-Pop, Contemporary Country
Country-pop singer-songwriter Bobbie Cryner issued her honky tonk-flavored self-titled debut LP in 1993 to widespread critical acclaim, but when the record failed commercially, she was dropped by her label. Following a divorce and a battle with alcoholism, she returned in 1996 with *Girl of Your Dreams*, a smoother, more sophisticated effort spotlighting Cryner's gift for singing—and writing—ballads. —*Jason Ankeny*

● **Bobbie Cryner** / 1993 / Epic ◆◆◆◆

Girl of Your Dreams / Feb. 1996 / MCA Nashville ◆◆◆◆
When Bobbie Cryner introduced her sultry voice in 1993, critics lined up to commend her. In a field where most performers come sweet and innocent, whether they are or not, Cryner wasn't afraid to drip an adult sensuality. She doesn't exploit her inherent sexuality, but she doesn't attempt to hide her obvious carnality, either. Unfortunately, her debut proved too distinctive for the conformists who run country radio and never got a fair shake. Hopefully, that will change with *Girl of Your Dreams*, another strong offering by the bold redhead. She opens with Dusty Springfield's "Son of a Preacher Man," a gutsy move that works. No one else in country music would put across the line, "being good ain't always easy," with such believable forwardness; rather than apologizing, she sounds like she's celebrating her lack of virtue. She employs the

same stunning directness when she asks, in another song, "If you want me to stay, just say so." Elsewhere, she confronts her own weaknesses while finding the inner fortitude to overcome them ("I Didn't Know My Own Strength"), and, in the album's most unusual song ("You'd Think He'd Know Me Better"), takes on the role of a mean-spirited spouse who treats her husband with dismissive spite, then wonders why he's cheating on her. Cryner sounds too good to ignore; hopefully, this time radio will accept her rare qualities as the strengths they are. —*Michael McCall*

Dick Curless (Richard Curless)

b. Mar. 17, 1932, Fort Fairfield, ME
Vocals / Bakersfield Sound
Dick Curless was best known for singing truck-drivin' songs such as "Drag 'Em off the Interstate, Sock It to 'Em J.P. Blues." A tall man with an eye patch and rich baritone voice, Curless was often called the "Baron of Country Music," after one of his popular songs, "The Baron."

He was born in Fort Fairfield, ME, and started out professionally in 1948 with the Trail Blazers at a radio station in Ware, MA. While with the group, Curless was billed as the "Tumbleweed Kid." In 1951, he was drafted, and while stationed in the Far East, he frequently appeared on the Armed Forces Network, where he was known as "The Rice Paddy Ranger." He returned to Maine three years later and began singing in Bangor clubs. He got his big break when he won on *Arthur Godfrey Talent Scouts*. Afterward Curless began performing in Las Vegas and Hollywood; a record contract followed, but his budding career was interrupted by an illness.

Curless returned to Maine, and soon was working with such stars as Gene Hooper and Lone Pine and Betty Cody. He reached the country charts in 1965 with the Top Five hit "A Tombstone Every Mile," followed by nine more chart hits, including the successful "Six Times a Day (the Trains Came Down)." In 1970, Curless signed to Capitol and scored a Top 30 hit based on the classic "Wabash Cannonball," titled "Big Wheel Cannonball." The followup "Hard, Hard Traveling Man" (1970) made it to the Top 40.

During his career, Curless had a total of 22 hits. During the '60s, he was a member of the *Wheeling Jamboree*, and from 1966-68 he toured with the Buck Owens show. During the '70s and '80s, Curless recorded infrequently, and eventually became a born-again Christian. He recorded an album in Norway in 1987, and by 1992 was a regular at the Cristy Lane Theater in Branson, MO. Curless died in 1995. —*Sandra Brennan*

● **Tombstone Every Mile** / 1973 / Capitol ◆◆◆◆

Traveling Through / 1995 / Rounder ◆◆◆◆
Traveling Through was the last record Dick Curless ever made, and it's a winner. Recorded in 1994, in Brookfield, MA, the album is a rootsy, stripped-down collection of country, blues, and gospel tunes. Throughout the album, Curless is in fine voice, wrenching out emotion from each of the songs. —*Stephen Thomas Erlewine*

A Tombstone Every Mile [box] / 1996 / Bear Family ◆◆◆◆
A Tombstone Every Mile is a seven-disc, 191-track box set that contains Dick Curless' classic Tower recordings from the '60s, his first sides for Standard, several albums he cut for Tiffany, his duets with guitarist Lenny Breau on Event, and several unreleased, non-commercial Korean war recordings. In short, the set collects everything Curless recorded during the '50s and '60s, stopping when he signed to Capitol in 1970. Curless never had many hits and was always somewhat of a cult artist, which means that a box the size of *A Tombstone Every Mile* plays right into his cult. His dedicated fans will treasure all of the rarities, the excellent biography and the stellar sound on this collection, but the length of the set means that it won't convert neophytes into fans. Nevertheless, any historian or hardcore fan that wants to invest in the box will not be disappointed by the results. —*Thom Owens*

Sonny Curtis

b. May 9, 1937, Meadow, TX
Guitar, Vocals / Traditional Country, Nashville Sound/Country-politan
Sonny Curtis was involved in country music for over 40 years, composing songs recorded by numerous stars, among them the

Everly Brothers, Hank Williams, Jr., and even Bing Crosby. He was born and raised near Lubbock, TX, and began performing as a teen on local radio, playing fiddle on the popular *Buddy and Bob* show, featuring an up-and-coming Buddy Holly. Waylon Jennings was also a deejay at the station, and together they all performed at the town movie theater during intermissions. Curtis joined Holly's band, the Three Tunes, in 1956 as a fiddler, guitar player and backup singer; when the group went to Nashville to record with famed producer Owen Bradley, they recorded one of Curtis' songs, "Rock Around with Ollie Vee." Eventually Curtis amicably left Holly and began touring with Slim Whitman before making his solo debut in 1958 with the single "Wrong Again."

In 1959, after Holly's tragic death, his band, the Crickets, asked Curtis to become their lead guitarist and singer. He was drafted in 1960 and stationed in Fort Ord, where he penned the song "Walk Right Back," a major hit for the Everly Brothers in 1961 and later popularized by Andy Williams, Perry Como, and Anne Murray.

Despite a string of mid-range hits including "My Way of Life," "Atlanta Georgia Stray," and "The Straight Life," Curtis had his greatest success as a songwriter. One of his best known and most recorded songs was "I Fought the Law," which has been done by artists like the Bobby Fuller Four, the Clash, and Lou Reed. He also wrote the theme song for *The Mary Tyler Moore Show*, "Love Is All Around," which became a Top 30 hit on the country charts. In the early '90s, Curtis also wrote the theme song to the TV show *Evening Shade*.

In the early '80s, he and two former Crickets, Joe B. Maudlin and Jerry Allison, reunited and performed with Waylon Jennings' show. He had a Top 15 single with "Good Ole' Girls" for Elektra in 1981, followed by "Married Women," which made it to the Top 40. He made his final chart entry in 1986 with the minor hit "Now I've Got a Heart of Gold." Curtis also made a name for himself as a commercial jingle singer-songwriter, and continued writing country songs for artists such as Keith Whitley, Ricky Skaggs, and John Schneider. In 1991 he was inducted into the Songwriters Hall of Fame by the Nashville Songwriters Association International. — *Sandra Brennan*

Beatle Hits Flamenco Style Guitar / 1964 / Imperial ✦✦

● **The First of Sonny Curtis** / 1968 / Viva ✦✦✦✦

The Sonny Curtis Style / 1969 / Elektra ✦✦✦

Love Is All Around / 1980 / Elektra ✦✦✦

Curtis has been performing since the '50s and writing nearly as long. This album reprises two of the songs he wrote that were hits for someone else. Additionally, the title song was the theme for the *Mary Tyler Moore Show*, which Curtis wrote (he also sang it the first season). But the real gem on this record is Curtis' rebuttal in song to the film *The Buddy Holly Story*. Curtis knew, and played with, Buddy, long before his rise to stardom, and as he says in the song, this is his attempt to set straight some things that weren't right in the film. — *Jim Worbois*

Rollin / 1981 / Elektra ✦✦✦

Spectrum / 1987 / Nightlite ✦✦

Billy Ray Cyrus

b. Aug. 25, 1961, Flatwoods, KY
Guitar, Vocals / Contemporary Country

Billy Ray Cyrus will forever be known for the catchy, lightweight single "Achy, Breaky Heart," which became a line-dancing anthem upon its 1992 release. "Achy, Breaky Heart" made Billy Ray Cyrus famous, but it also proved to be his undoing. No matter how he tried, he could not escape the song, nor could he replicate its success. Cyrus' music was never particularly innovative—it owed as much to the country-rock of the Eagles as it did to the new traditionalism of George Strait, and the new country of Clint Black and Garth Brooks—but his musical worth became irrelevant in the wake of the success of "Achy, Breaky Heart" and its accompanying album, *Some Gave All*. The album became a crossover success after the single became a hit, spending 17 weeks on the top of the album charts. Part of Cyrus' success was due to his handsome, hunky good looks, and part of it was due to the catchiness of "Achy, Breaky Heart." However, both his good looks and the sin-

gle were soon forgotten, and just two years after *Some Gave All* ruled the charts, Cyrus virtually disappeared from both the pop and country charts, and became part of the long history of one-hit-wonders.

Enamored of baseball, Billy Ray Cyrus intended to become another Johnny Bench as he was growing up in Flatlands, KY. While attending Georgetown College on a baseball scholarship, he bought a guitar, and decided that athletics wasn't the proper direction for his life. Instead, he formed a band called Sly Dog with his brother and gave himself a ten-month deadline for finding a place to play. One week prior to that cut-off date, the group went to work as the house band for a club in Ironton, OH, where they remained for two years. When a 1984 fire destroyed the bar— and Cyrus' equipment—he moved to Los Angeles to pursue his career. Eventually, he decided to return to Kentucky and he commuted from there to Nashville in search of a record deal. Grand Ole Opry star Del Reeves got Mercury Records to take a look, and division head Harold Shedd signed him in the summer of 1990. When his first album came out in mid-1992, Cyrus—with his good looks, sculpted body and the infectious "Achy, Breaky Heart"—became an instant groundbreaking sensation. Spending five weeks at the top of the country charts, "Achy, Breaky Heart" made his debut album, *Some Gave All*, a blockbuster success. By the time it fell off the charts, it had sold over nine million copies and spent 17 weeks on the top of the pop charts.

Despite his attempts, Cyrus wasn't able to replicate the success of *Some Gave All*. He quickly followed the album with *It Won't Be the Last* in the summer of 1993. Initially, the album sold well, entering the pop charts at No. 3, but it fell far short of expectations by only reaching platinum status. *Storm in the Heartland*, delivered in the fall of 1994, managed to go gold, even though it was ignored by country radio. However, by the time it finished its chart run, Cyrus had slipped from the public's eye. When he returned with the harder-edged, introspective *Trail of Tears* in 1996, his audience had virtually disappeared—the album only spent four weeks on the charts, and didn't even go gold. — *Tom Roland & Stephen Thomas Erlewine*

● **Some Gave All** / 1992 / Mercury ✦✦✦✦

Some Gave All became the first debut album by a country artist to enter the pop charts at No. 1 (it hit No. 1 on the country charts as well). The album's sales were fueled by the breakout single "Achy, Breaky Heart," which offered Southern-fried Rolling Stones rhythms and a goofy chorus with a hook so big it demanded a reaction. Not one to eschew the obvious, Cyrus pumped his songs full of as much rock 'n' roll as the market would bear, so songs like "Could've Been Me" and "Never Thought I'd Fall in Love with You" appealed to young fans who had just discovered the possibilities (both musical and sexual) of country music. — *Brian Mansfield*

It Won't Be the Last / Jun. 22, 1993 / Mercury ✦✦

Cyrus' follow-up to his smash debut, *Some Gave All*, offers more of the same—country injected with a healthy dose of rock 'n' roll. It won't win him any new fans, but those who loved *Some Gave All* will enjoy *It Won't Be the Last*. — *AMG*

Storm in the Heartland / 1994 / Mercury ✦✦✦

Storm in the Heartland delivers what Billy Ray Cyrus' fans want to hear—good-humored rockers and powerful ballads. In fact, it is a stronger, more assured effort than *It Won't Be the Last*, offering a catchier batch of songs, even though it doesn't have the goofy charm of *Some Gave All*. — *Stephen Thomas Erlewine*

Trail of Tears / 1996 / Mercury ✦✦✦✦

Trail of Tears is the most personal and most accomplished album Billy Ray Cyrus has recorded to date. Cyrus elaborates his pop-oriented country with some rootsy production flourishes—this album sounds edgier and grittier than any of his previous records. Furthermore, Cyrus delivers both his originals and covers with conviction, far more conviction than could have been believed possible from his first two albums. In fact, *Trail of Tears* suggests that he may be able to carve out a successful career for himself, after all. — *Thom Owens*

D

Pappy Daily

b. Feb. 8, 1902, Yoakum, TX

Traditional Country, Honky Tonk, Nashville Sound/Countrypolitan

Pappy Dailey was one of the most important record executives and producers of the post-war era. He didn't have a distinctive production style, nor was he much of a musician, yet he had an ear for talent, and was instrumental in cultivating the careers of George Jones and Gene Pitney, among others. Along with his partner Jack Starnes, Dailey established Starday Records, which was one of the most successful Texas independent labels of the '50s. During the '60s, he founded Musicor with Art Talmage. Throughout both labels, Pappy's fortunes were forever tied to those of George Jones. Dailey's career was strong as long as he had an association with Jones, and when the singer left the producer and Musicor in 1971 for Billy Sherrill and Epic Records, Musicor and Dailey quickly faded from view.

After returning from fighting in the Marine Corps during World War I, Pappy Dailey (b. Harold W. Dailey) was voted the Commander of the American Legion during 1931 and 1932. Following his service in the American Legion, he began working in the country music industry in the early '30s, but he didn't have much of an impact until 1953, when he founded Starday Records with his partner, Jack Starnes. Based in Beaumont, TX, all of Starday's records were originally made at Starnes' house. Early in 1954, the label had its first hit, when its fourth single, Arlie Duff's "You All Come," climbed to No. 7. The following year, Starday signed a young singer named George Jones, whose "Why Baby Why" reached No. 4 in the fall of the year.

Shortly before Jones joined the label, Starnes left Starday and was replaced by Don Pierce. Dailey and Pierce concentrated on cultivating the career of George Jones, and by 1957, Mercury Records was interested in the singer, and the duo's production talents. That year, Jones signed to Mercury and the production team of Dailey and Pierce joined the label; their agreement allowed them to continue to run Starday. For the next four years, they worked with Mercury, producing a respectable string of hits that were mostly by JOnes. During this time, Pappy started a new label called D, which concentrated on releasing music by local Texas artists. Over the next few years, D had a few minor hit singles, including songs by Claude Gray, James O'Gwynn, and Eddie Noack.

In late 1961, Dailey and Pierce ended their relationship and split Starday's assets between the two of them. Pierce took the label itself, while Dailey received the publishing division; both received half of the label's master recordings and catalog. At the end of the year, Dailey moved from Starday and Mercury to United Artists, where he became the label's Country & Western Director. George Jones, who had come to consider Pappy as a father figure and professional advisor, followed him to the label. While at United Artists, Jones continued to have a number of Top Ten hits, but Dailey didn't cultivate the careers of many other artists. A notable exception was Melba Montgomery, whom he signed upon Jones' insistence.

Dailey ended his relationship with United Artists in 1965, the same year he folded D Records. Dailey turned his attention to Musicor, the label he founded with Art Talmadge in 1961. Musicor was a bigger venture than either Starday or D, signing established artists like George Jones, Floyd Tilman, and Gene Pitney. Though Dailey and Talmadge had set their goals high, they weren't equipped to run the label in any sensible fashion, and flooded the market with records, which usually competed with other Musicor releases. Nevertheless, Jones had a number of hits during that time, as did Pitney, but they weren't able to make any of the label's other artists into stars.

By 1971, Gene Pitney was no longer actively recording and George Jones had grown frustrated with his Musicor contract, deciding that he wanted to sign to Epic Records. After some prolonged negotiations, he left the label that year, leaving Musicor without a star. Dailey struggled on with Musicor for the next few years, reissuing a lot of George Jones material, and licensing other Jones tracks to RCA. By the mid-'70s, Dailey quietly retired from the music industry, and Musicor disappeared along with him. — *Stephen Thomas Erlewine*

Vernon Dalhart (Marion Try Slaughter)

b. Apr. 6, 1883, Jefferson, TX, d. Sep. 14, 1948, Bridgeport, CT

Vocals / Old-Time, Traditional Country, Cowboy

Vernon Dalhart was one of the first country performers to gain national recognition, thanks to an ability to make his music palatable to a wider audience. Dalhart was born Marion Try Slaughter in Marion County, TX. His grandfather was a Confederate soldier who became a deputy sheriff and was a member of the Ku Klux Klan; when he was a boy, his father was killed in a knife fight. Dalhart later became a cowboy and sang at community gatherings, where he also played the harmonica and the jew's harp. In the early 1900s, he studied music at the Dallas Conservatory and married. He moved to New York in 1910 and worked in a music store. After studying light opera, he earned extra cash singing for funerals. He appeared in his first opera two years later and in 1913 appeared in *HMS Pinafore* and *Madame Butterfly*.

In 1915, he made his recording debut as a pop singer with "Can't Yo' Hear Me Calling Caroline?" When his version of the "Wreck of the Old '97" became a smash hit, he helped popularize country music, selling over 25 million copies. In 1925, Dalhart had success with a series of topical songs based on current events such as the death of a Kentucky spelunker, the notorious Scopes Trial, and a song about the terrible Santa Barbara Earthquake, selling enough copies to firmly establish the Columbia label's country division. During the '20s and '30s, he used over 135 pseudonyms to record over 5,000 singles; among the names he appeared under are Frank Evans, the Lone Star Ranger, Vernon Dale, Tobe Little, Bob White, Hugh Lattimer, Sid Turner, and Al Carver. He continued on with hits through the late '30s, at which time his rather formal interpretation of hillbilly music fell out of favor as radio stations began airing music from "authentic" country singers such as the Carter Family.

Up through 1942, Dalhart kept trying to convince the labels to record him, but his bids were unsuccessful, and he ended up largely forgotten and working as a night clerk at a hotel in Bridgeport, CT. He died of heart failure in 1948. It wasn't until 1981 that Dalhart's contribution was finally recognized when his few diehard fans successfully lobbied for his election to the Country Music Hall of Fame. —*Sandra Brennan*

Vernon Dalhart (First Recorded Railroad Songs) / 1978 / Mark 56 ✦✦✦✦

● **Ballads & Railroad Songs** / 1980 / ✦✦✦✦

On the Lighter Side / ✦✦✦

That Good Old Country Town, Vol. 4 / ✦✦✦✦
This re-release features Dalhart performing in the '20s with Carson Robison. —*AMG*

Wreck of the Old '97 / ✦✦✦✦
This album contains ballads performed by the first country artist to sell one million records. —*AMG*

Lacy J. Dalton (Jill Byrem)

b. Oct. 13, 1948, Bloomsburg, PA
Vocals / Country-Pop, Contemporary Country, Neo-Traditionalist Country

Lacy J. Dalton, who has a voice one writer described as "honey laced with whiskey," took a circuitous route to Nashville. Born Jill Byrem in Bloomsburg, PA, she attended Brigham Young University but dropped out to become a folk singer. She kicked around Utah, Minnesota, Pennsylvania, and New York before winding up in front of a psychedelic rock band in San Francisco in the late '60s. She married the group's manager, who died as the result of injuries sustained in a swimming pool accident. Dalton kept performing, and a tape of her music eventually reached producer Billy Sherrill, who signed her to Columbia in 1979. The Academy of Country Music named her Best New Female Vocalist in 1979 on the strength of her debut, "Crazy Blue Eyes." Dalton's distinct sound and far-ranging musical interests may have kept her from being the star she could have been, but her records helped open doors for new sounds in country. —*Brian Mansfield*

● **Greatest Hits** / 1983 / Columbia ✦✦✦✦
Dalton's best songs weren't always her hits, but *Greatest Hits* is still a good sampler, including "Crazy Blue Eyes," her first hit; "Hard Times"; remakes of "Tennessee Waltz" and "Dream Baby"; and the music-biz anthem "16th Avenue." —*Brian Mansfield*

Crazy Love / 1991 / Capitol ✦✦✦
The title song is by Van Morrison, and if Dalton is not the vocalist Morrison is, she still may be the best female soul singer country offers, and she's a better one than Michael Bolton, whose "Walk Away" she also covers. *Crazy Love* is an appropriate title because Dalton seems genuinely bewildered by the vagaries of the emotion—why her lover loves her ("Crazy Love"), why he leaves her ("Forever in My Heart"), and why sometimes neither marriage nor divorce makes sense. But she's a great singer, not God. —*Brian Mansfield*

● **The Best of Lacy J. Dalton** / 1993 / Liberty ✦✦✦✦
The Best of Lacy J. Dalton collects many of the highlights from Dalton's late '80s and early '90s albums for Liberty Records. It's a good sampler of Dalton's sound and offers a nice introduction to her work. —*Stephen Thomas Erlewine*

Davis Daniel

b. Mar. 1, 1961, Arlington Heights, IL
Contemporary Country, Singer-Songwriter

Singer-songwriter Davis Daniel was born Robert Andrykowski on March 1, 1961, in Arlington Heights, IL. One of ten children, he and his impoverished family eventually settled in Nebraska, where they lived in a three-room shack without heat. When Daniel was 14, his father died, and the family moved to Denver; a few years later, he won his first regular performing gig at an area pizza parlor. After graduating to the Denver club circuit, he eventually moved to Nashville, where he spent three years honing his skills at songwriter showcases. In 1991, Daniel issued his debut LP, *Fighting Fire with Fire*, which included three Top 40 hits, including "For Crying Out Loud" and "Picture Me." In 1994, he

Charlie Daniels

returned with a self-titled effort, followed two years later by *I Know a Place*. —*Jason Ankeny*

Fighting Fire with Fire / 1991 / Mercury ✦✦✦

Undeniable / 1994 / Mercury ✦✦✦

Davis Daniel / 1994 / Polydor ✦✦✦

● **I Know a Place** / Jun. 18, 1996 / A&M ✦✦✦✦
Daniel Davis' third album, *I Know a Place*, is a breakthrough. For the first time, he's been able to convey the raw energy of his concerts on a recording and that frisky spark gives more dimension to his music. The material on the album remains inconsistent, however. Even though he has written several of the record's songs, Davis hasn't assembled a thoroughly winning collection of songs—he's merely chosen a few enjoyable numbers. Nevertheless, *I Know a Place* is his best album because the quality of the performance makes the weakness of the material less noticeable. And when he does have a good song, the music is simply topdrawer contemporary honky tonk. —*Thom Owens*

The Charlie Daniels Band

b. 1971, Wilmington, NC
Fiddle, Guitar, Violin, Vocals / Country-Rock, Southern Rock, Country Gospel, Urban Cowboy

A talented and showy fiddler, Charlie Daniels and his band fuse hardcore country with a hard-edged Southern rock boogie and blues. The group—which has had a rotating cast of musicians over the years—has always been known for their instrumental dexterity, but they were also notorious for their down-home, good-old boy attitude; in the early '80s they became a virtual symbol of conservative country values. Daniels and his band experienced the height of their popularity at the end of the '70s and early '80s, but they remained a popular concert attraction well into the '90s.

Charlie Daniels was born and raised in North Carolina, playing fiddle and guitar in several bands during his teenage years. At the age of 21, he decided to become a professional musican, assembling an instrumental rock 'n' roll combo called the Jaguars. The group landed a recording session for Epic Records in 1959 with Bob Johnston, who would later become Columbia Records' leading folk and country producer. The record didn't receive much attention, but the band continued to play and Daniels continued to write songs. One of his originals, "It Hurts Me," was recorded by Elvis Presley in 1963. By the late '60s, it had become clear that the Jaguars weren't going to hit the big time, so Johnston recommended to Daniels that he move to Nashville to become a session musician. Daniels followed the advice and he became one of the most popular fiddlers in Nashville. He played on several Bob Dylan albums—*Nashville Skyline, Self Portrait, New Morning,* and *Dylan* as well as Ringo Starr's 1970 record *Beaucoups of Blues.* He also became part of Leonard Cohen's touring band in the late '60s and produced the Youngbloods' *Elephant Memory* album around the same time.

Daniels cut an album for Capitol Records in the early '70s, which was ignored. In 1972, he formed the Charlie Daniels Band, using the Southern rock of the Allman Brothers as a blueprint. The band comprised Daniels (lead guitar, vocals, fiddle), lead guitarist Don Murray, bassist Charlie Hayward, drummer James W. Marshall, and keyboardist Joe DiGregorio. The formula worked and in 1973 they had a minor hit with "Uneasy Rider," which was released on Kama Sutra Records. In 1974, they released *Fire on the Mountain,* which became a gold record within months of its release, thanks to the Top 40 country hit "Texas"; the album would eventually go platinum. *Saddle Tramp,* released in 1976, was nearly as successful, going gold.

Throughout the mid-'70s, the Charlie Daniels Band pursued a Southern rock direction. They were moderately successful, but they never had a breakthrough hit either on the pop or country charts. By the late '70s, Daniels sensed that the audience for Southern rock was evaporating, so he refashioned the band as a more straightforward country band. The change paid off in 1979 when the single "The Devil Went Down to Georgia" became a No. 1 hit, crossing over into the pop charts, where it hit No. 3. The song was named the Country Music Association's Single of the Year and helped its accompanying album, *Million Mile Reflections,* become a multi-platinum success. Daniels wasn't able to follow "The Devil Went Down to Georgia" with another blockbuster single on the country charts, ironically, but he had several rock crossover successes in the years following the success of *Million Mile Reflections*—*Full Moon* (1980) went platinum and 1982's *Windows* went gold.

Although he continued to sell respectably throughout the '80s, he didn't have a big hit until 1989's *Simple Man,* which went gold. In the '90s, his records failed to chart well, although he remained a popular concert draw. —*Stephen Thomas Erlewine*

Charlie Daniels / 1970 / Capitol ✦✦✦
The Charlie Daniels formula was only in its embryonic stages at this point and as such, this record has some enjoyable moments. Still, with the inclusion of songs like "Pope and the Dope," fans of Daniels' later records won't be disappointed either. —*Jim Worbois*

Honey in the Rock / 1973 / Kama Sutra ✦✦✦

☆ **Fire on the Mountain** / 1975 / Epic ✦✦✦✦✦
Fire on the Mountain is the Charlie Daniels Band's finest moment. Daniels finds the perfect middle ground between Southern-rock boogie and hillbilly honky tonk, creating a sound that rocked hard but still had down-home roots. Although he would delve deeper into country, he would never make a stronger, more enjoyable album. —*Thom Owens*

Saddle Tramp / 1976 / Epic ✦✦✦
This record provides more variety in song style, tempo, and subject matter than some of Daniels' other records, making it more of a find. It should be of interest to a wider audience. —*Jim Worbois*

High Lonesome / 1976 / Epic ✦✦✦
This is a little more interesting than many of Daniels' records for the variety alone. Though not divided by sides, this time out Daniels gives us half an album of standard Daniels boogie and half a record of more melodic songs. That alone should make this of interest to more than just his usual fan. —*Jim Worbois*

The Essential Charlie Daniels / 1976 / Kama Sutra ✦✦✦✦

Midnight Wind / 1977 / Epic ✦✦✦
The song "Heaven Can Be Anywhere" and, to a lesser extent "Sugar Hill Saturday Night," save this from being just another Charlie Daniels record. No great shakes but fans won't be disappointed. —*Jim Worbois*

Whiskey / 1977 / Epic ✦✦✦
A whole album of Daniels' brand of Southern boogie may be a bit much for the average listener, but his fans will eat it up. This isn't a bad record but there isn't anything here to recommend it either. —*Jim Worbois*

Volunteers Jam 3 & 4 / 1978 / Epic ✦✦✦
Apart from the third side (featuring Willie Nelson), this record may not appeal to the average country fan. Still, there is some fine music on this record featuring many of the artists who were signed to Capricorn in the '70s. —*Jim Worbois*

Million Mile Reflections / 1979 / Epic ✦✦✦
Despite the inclusion of the hit "The Devil Went Down to Georgia," this is, at best, a mediocre record. Certainly not for everyone, Daniels' fans will still enjoy it. —*Jim Worbois*

Full Moon / 1980 / Epic ✦✦✦

Volunteers Jam 6 / 1980 / Epic ✦✦✦
The Volunteer Jams have always resulted in some of Charlie Daniels' most interesting albums, and this one fits the bill. There is something for everyone—from the country of Crystal Gayle and the blues of Papa John Creach to funk of Rufus and the rock of the "Motor City Madman," Ted Nugent, and others. —*Jim Worbois*

Windows / 1982 / Epic ✦✦✦

● **A Decade of Hits** / 1983 / Epic ✦✦✦✦
At only ten songs, *A Decade of Hits* is awful brief, but it contains the bulk of the Charlie Daniels Band's '70s country and Southern rock hits, including "Uneasy Rider," "The Devil Went Down to Georgia," "Stroker's Theme," "Long Haired Country Boy," "The Legend of Wooley Swamp," "In America" and "Still in Saigon." —*Stephen Thomas Erlewine*

Homesick Heroes / 1988 / Epic ✦✦✦

Simple Man / 1989 / Epic ✦✦✦✦
This album features the title track plus "Play Me Some Fiddle," "Saturday Night Down South," and other hits. —*AMG*

Renegade / 1991 / Epic ✦✦✦✦
This strong collection of Daniels songs rocks harder than usual, despite showing his soft side on "Little Folks" and "Fathers and Sons." Daniels practically gives a cultural history of the violin on "Talk to Me Fiddle," the album's most unusual song, and continues to extol the virtues of country living ("The Twang Factor") and patriotism ("Let Freedom Ring.") —*Brian Mansfield*

● **All-Time Greatest Hits** / 1993 / Epic ✦✦✦✦
This traces his career from early highpoints—"Long Haired Country Boy," "The South's Gonna Do It," "The Devil Went Down to Georgia"—to the desperate attempts to revive his late career with self-referential updates ("Uneasy Rider '88") and jingoistic, red-baiting blather ("Simple Man") that was out of date before he released it. —*Michael McCall*

Super Hits / 1994 / Epic ✦✦✦✦
Super Hits is a budget-priced collection that features a handful of the Charlie Daniels Band's biggest hits, but it doesn't provide a definitive retrospective, nor does it have every hit that a casual fan could want. It's entertaining, but it leaves you wanting more. —*Stephen Thomas Erlewine*

Same Ol' Me / Sep. 12, 1995 / Capitol ✦✦✦
On *Same Ol' Me,* Charlie Daniels returned to the country and rock hybrid that sent him to the top of the charts in the late '70s and early '80s. As always, the album is a bit inconsistent, featuring too much filler, but the best moments on the record are some of the best music he has recorded in the '90s. —*Stephen Thomas Erlewine*

Roots Remain / Oct. 29, 1996 / ✦✦✦✦
Roots Remain is a three-disc box set covering the Charlie Daniels Band's entire career. Over the course of 45 songs, the box touches upon all of his hits—including "The Devil Went Down to Geor-

gia," "Long-Haired Country Boy," and "Uneasy Rider"—plus key album tracks, B-sides, and several unreleased and rare gems, such as his take on Eric Clapton's "Layla." *Roots Remain* is the most comprehensive compilation of Charlie Daniels recordings ever assembled and it misses very few important tracks, making it the one definitive retrospective. —*Stephen Thomas Erlewine*

Darby & Tarlton

Old-Time, Traditional Country

Singer Tom Darby and slide guitarist Jimmie Tarlton were not only legendary bluesmen, but also pioneers of country music. Although they were only together for a brief time during the late '20s and early '30s, they popularized the steel slide guitar in the genre and exerted a heavy influence on the Allen Brothers and the Delmore Brothers..

Tarlton was born in Chesterfield County, SC, the son of share-croppers. His parents taught him traditional songs and the fretless banjo, and by age 12, he was learning to play the slide guitar from the black musicians he encountered in his family's numerous travels. As a young man he became a traveling street musician living off tips. His travels led him across the country, and everywhere he went, he added local songs to his expanding repertoire. On the West Coast in the early '20s, he met Frank Ferrara, who taught him how to use the steel slide to play the more free-flowing Hawaiian guitar.

When Tarlton settled down in Columbus, GA, he met a guitarist and extraordinary blues singer named Tom Darby, a Columbus native who learned his vocal stylings from local black singers. Darby was related to Riley Puckett, star of the Skillet Lickers. A local talent scout convinced the two to team up and landed them an audition with Columbia Records. Their first recorded single made fun of Florida land speculators and was titled "Down in Florida on a Hog." Their next two songs, "Birmingham Jail"—a song Tarlton claimed sprang from his experience there after being incarcerated for moonshining—and "Columbus Stockade Blues," were enormously successful and have since become country standards. Audiences were impressed as well—the record sold close to 200,000 copies. Despite the profits reaped from their records, Darby and Tarlton received only a flat $75 fee.

The duo scored their second major hit in 1928 with "Birmingham Jail No. 2" and "Lonesome Railroad"; among their other hits were the straightahead blues tunes "Travelling Yodel Blues" and "Heavy Hearted Blues." The two experienced contract difficulties with Columbia in late 1929 and finally recorded their last session the following year. They went their separate ways, occasionally reuniting without much success. By 1935, both men gave up and left the music business. They remained largely forgotten until the folk revival of the 1960s, which allowed Tarlton to record an album, appear at folk clubs, and sit for interviews with a number of folklorists. Darby also did a few performances and even reunited briefly with Tarlton, but at their age, neither particularly enjoyed performing. —*Sandra Brennan*

Complete Recordings / 1995 / Bear Family ✦✦✦✦
All of Darby & Tarlton's recordings are showcased on the appropriately titled three-disc box set *Complete Recordings*. Country historians will certainly find the set fascinating—the duo was one of the few white musicians of the '20s, and their music was frequently quite strong—but the curious will find the sheer length of the box, as well as its reliance on rarities like cuts by the Georgia Wildcats and alternate takes, rather intimidating. —*Thom Owens*

Sing the Blues / Old Timey ✦✦✦
● **Darby & Tarlton** / Old Timey ✦✦✦✦

Helen Darling

A former commercial-jingle singer, Helen Darling found open arms in Nashville after her country backup vocals impressed hillbilly heavyweight Garth Brooks. Born in Louisiana and raised in Houston, Darling sang from an early age and first recorded with her University of Texas choir. She moved to Chicago after graduation and sang radio jingles during the early '90s, but moved again to Nashville after a friend encouraged her. After making the

rounds in Music City and getting occasional work, Darling impressed Garth Brooks enough for him to use her vocals on "The Red Strokes" (from *In Pieces*). Signed to a contract herself in 1994, Helen Darling released an eponymous album—with vocal backup from Brooks himself—for Decca in 1995. —*John Bush*

Helen Darling / 1995 / Decca ✦✦✦✦
Helen Darling began her recording career with the encouragement of Garth Brooks and the music on her self-titled debut recalls his rock-inflected country. The first single pulled from the album, "Jenny Come Back," was a straightforward country number, but it was "I Haven't Found It Yet" that brought her to the attention of many country fans. —*Stephen Thomas Erlewine*

Dave & Deke Combo

Alternative Country, Neo-Traditionalist Country

The Dave & Deke Combo, a band of Los Angeles country-rockabillies, consist of three Midwest transplants—leaders Dave Dickerson and Deke Stuckey, plus drummer Lance—and only one West Coast native, bassist Shorty. After releasing several seven-inch singles and an EP, the group's album debut, *Moonshine Melodies*, appeared in 1993 on the British label No Hit Records. After moving to Heyday in 1995, the Dave & Deke Combo released *Hollywood Barn Dance* the following year. —*John Bush*

● **Hollywood Barn Dance** / 1996 / Heyday ✦✦✦✦
Hollywood Barn Dance, the Dave and Deke Combo's second album (their debut was a British release in 1993), is full of sharp harmony singing, Dickerson's excellent guitar leads, and solid rhythms as the combo jumps from one dance-friendly cut to another, most of them (such as "Henpecked Peckerwood" and "Chrome Dome") originals written by Dickerson and Stuckey. These guys aren't just paying tribute to the past, they're having a blast. —*Kurt Wolff*

Gail Davies

b. Sep. 1, 1948, Broken Bow, OK
Guitar, Vocals / Country-Pop, Singer-Songwriter, Country-Folk, Neo-Traditionalist Country

Gail Davies, a member of the first wave of intelligent female country-rock songwriters of the '70s, influenced such artists as Mary-Chapin Carpenter and the Judds. Born Patricia Gail Dickerson in 1948 in Broken Bow, OK, she was the daughter of Tex Dickerson, a former member of the *Louisiana Hayride*. She moved to Seattle as a youngster, though, and was early influenced by rock as well as country. Davies toured with a rock band during the late '60s, but later married a jazz musician and moved to Los Angeles with him. After attempting a career as a jazz singer, she returned to country music. Davies performed for several years around the L.A. area, but turned to songwriting after her doctor cautioned that her voice needed a rest. During the mid-'70s, she gained a songwriting contract with Lawrence Welk's Vogue Music and did some backup vocal work with Hoyt Axton and Roger Miller.

The exposure got her a contract with Lifesong/CBS, which released her self-titled debut album in 1978. The single "No Love Have I" hit No. 26 on the country charts, and the following year "Someone Is Looking for Someone like You" narrowly missed the Top Ten. After signing with Warner Bros. the same year, "Blue Heartache" hit No. 7, and her album *The Game* was applauded by critics. Gail Davies' biggest hit, though, was the title track from her 1980 LP *I'll Be There*. It reached No. 4 in the country charts early in 1981, and was followed by three Top Tens: "It's a Lovely, Lovely World," "Grandma's Song" and "'Round the Clock Lovin'," from *Givin' Herself Away*.

Davies slipped into the Top 20 on three singles from 1983's *What Can I Say*, and moved to RCA the following year. *What's a Woman to Do* also fared poorly on the charts, though Davies still received support from the critics. "Break Away" managed No. 15 on the country charts in 1985. The following year, Gail Davies formed Wild Choir. The band recorded a self-titled album for RCA, and their two singles—"Next Time" and "Heart to Heart"—charted modestly. She returned to solo recording in 1989 with *Pretty Words* for MCA and *The Other Side of Love* released the following year for Capitol. Davies had gradually moved into production during the late '80s, and she accepted a position at Liberty Records as country music's first female staff producer. —*John Bush*

I'll Be There / 1980 / Warner Brothers ✦✦✦✦
Here's another consistently strong album. At a time when Barbara Mandrell and Crystal Gayle were country's biggest female stars, Davies was creating albums as distinctive and progressive as Rosanne Cash. —*Michael McCall*

The Game / 1980 / Warner Brothers ✦✦✦
Her second album was the first in which she displayed her commanding vocals on a blend of folk-influenced ballads and punchy, melodic pop-country. —*Michael McCall*

Giving Herself Away / 1982 / Warner Brothers ✦✦✦✦
Davies brought in such outside-of-Nashville help as guitarist Albert Lee, bassist Leland Sklar, and pianist Bill Payne of Little Feat to create an excellent album that blends Southern California folk-pop with the cutting edge of modern country. Includes the hit "Hold On" as well as a popular version of Joni Mitchell's "You Turn Me On (I'm a Radio)" and "Round the Clock Lovin'," written by a then-unknown K.T. Oslin. —*Michael McCall*

What Can I Say / 1983 / Warner Brothers ✦✦✦
It's lighter-hearted than her others, but even when in a playful mood Davies sounds feisty, as on "Boys like You" and "You're a Hard Dog (To Keep Under the Porch)." Covers come from Rodney Crowell, Harlan Howard, Mark Knopfler, and Ray Charles. —*Michael McCall*

Where Is a Woman to Go / 1984 / RCA ✦✦✦✦
Her fiercest album, as far as emotional content, is her most consistently forceful, as far as musical arrangements. It's an unheralded classic. —*Michael McCall*

Wild Choir / 1986 / RCA ✦✦✦
Billed as a band, Wild Choir's songs and spirit were pure Davies, but the arrangements took on mild new wave/rock tendencies. The record proved to be too progressive at the time, and it still sounds fresher than most Nashville bands of the 1990s. "Walls" and "Never Cross That Line" rank with Davies' best compositions. —*Michael McCall*

Pretty Words / 1989 / MCA ✦✦✦
A touching combination of songs, some seeking spiritual strength, others drenched in melancholy without sinking into bathos. —*Michael McCall*

★ **Best Of** / Jan. 21, 1991 / Liberty ✦✦✦✦✦
A substantial collection of radio hits and crowd favorites, including the poignant "Grandma's Song," "I'll Be There (If You Ever Want Me)," "'Round the Clock Lovin'" and "It's a Lovely, Lovely World." —*Michael McCall*

The Davis Sisters

Country, Traditional Country
Known to country fans mainly as the act in which Skeeter Davis originally rose to fame, the Davis Sisters' career would have surely been much more influential and successful if tragedy hadn't derailed them just after their first hit. Although they only had one big single, ("I Forgot More Than You'll Ever Know," in 1953), their outstanding close dual harmonies helped link the Appalachian harmonies of the Delmore Brothers with the more modern ones of subsequent acts like the Everlys. They were also among the earliest female country singing stars of the post-World War II era, and occasionally went into a boogie mode that foreshadowed the rockabilly movement by a year or two.

The Davis Sisters were in fact not sisters at all. Betty Jack Davis and Mary Frances Penick met in high school in Kentucky in the late 1940s, soon forming a close friendship and musical partnership. Penick changed her name to Skeeter Davis for professional purposes, so that the duo could be billed as a sister combination. By the early '50s they'd performed regularly on radio shows in Cincinnati and Detroit, and made their first studio recordings in Detroit. By 1953 they were recording for RCA, backed by Nashville session players such as Chet Atkins. The mournful "I Forgot More Than You'll Ever Know" was a big hit that made them

immediate stars; just as interesting, in retrospect, was the flip side, "Rock-A-Bye Boogie," which anticipated the rockabilly revolution with its frenetic rhythms and Les Paul-influenced guitar runs.

That first RCA session was to be Betty Jack's last, as the pair were involved in a serious car accident in August 1953; Betty Jack died instantly, though Skeeter would recover. With the support of the Davis family, Skeeter continued the act with Betty Jack's older sister, Georgie. The reconstituted Davis Sisters continued to record through 1956, performing in the same harmony style Skeeter had formulated with Betty Jack. These outings were quite respectable mixes of traditional country ballads with slicker, more uptempo fare, but there were no more hits, and Skeeter couldn't fully re-create the artistic and personal spark she had enjoyed with Betty Jack. While Georgie retired from music, Skeeter would by the 1960s become one of the most successful women singers in the country-pop field. —*Richie Unterberger*

Memories / 1993 / Bear Family ✦✦✦✦
Bear Family does its usual astonishingly thorough job on this double CD compilation, which has no less than 59 tracks recorded by both incarnations of the Davis Sisters between 1952 and 1956 (as well as a brief 1957 Skeeter Davis solo take on "It Wasn't God Who Made Honky Tonk Angels"). The RCA singles are embellished by numerous outtakes, alternates, pre-RCA acetates of radio broadcasts, an unreleased tape of spirituals at a Kentucky Baptist church, and their rare pre-RCA singles for the Fortune label; in fact, half of this collection was previously unreleased. The fidelity isn't always stellar on the non-RCA tracks, but most of the material is strong, and the harmonies always affecting, whether on the sad ballads, spirituals, or the occasional proto-rockabilly outings ("Rock-A-Bye Boogie," "Rag Mop," "Gotta Git A-Goin'"). While Skeeter understandably bemoaned the loss of original partner Betty Jack Davis, the sides with her replacement Georgie Davis (which actually comprise over half the package) are on about the same level as the earlier ones. Chet Atkins' guitar can be heard on most of the tracks. —*Richie Unterberger*

Danny Davis (George Nowlan)

b. Apr. 29, 1925, Randolph, MA
Trumpet, Session Musician / Bakersfield Sound, Nashville Sound / Countrypolitan
Popularizing the use of brass instruments in the string-dominated world of country music, Danny Davis' work with his Nashville Brass inspired Buck Owens to form the Bakersfield Brass and also influenced the music of Ray Pennington, Buddy Emmons, and Merle Haggard. Born George Nowlan in Dorchester, MA, he aspired to be a horn player while in high school. He attended the New England Conservatory of Music and at age 14 became a soloist with the Massachusetts All State Symphony Orchestra. The next year in 1940, he joined jazz drummer Gene Krupa's band and played with some of the greatest musicians of the jazz and swing era, including Bobby Byrne, Bob Crosby, and Art Mooney. After leaving Krupa, he joined Vincent Lopez's band at the Astor Hotel in New York. He remained with Lopez for many years, also working with Blue Barron and Sammy Kay. Davis became a record producer in 1958 for Joy and MGM, producing six No. 1 singles for Connie Francis at the latter. While on a trip to Nashville, Davis met Fred Rose and Chet Atkins; Atkins invited Davis to become a production assistant in Nashville and in 1965, Davis became an executive A&R producer (with Atkins) for several years.

Near the end of the decade, Davis approached Atkins with the idea of adding brass to country music. Atkins gave the go-ahead, and the Nashville Brass was born. Their first album, *The Nashville Brass Featuring Danny Davis Play Nashville Sounds*, came out in 1968 with little fanfare. The following year, they released *More Nashville Sounds*, and people began to take notice. A new Grammy category, Best Country Instrumental Performance, was created to accommodate them, and the CMA voted them Instrumental Group or Band of the Year for five years in a row. Since 1969, they have continued to record steadily. Davis has also collaborated with other country stars; Davis, Atkins, and Floyd

Cramer made *Chet, Floyd and Danny* in 1977, and 1980 witnessed a Nashville Brass/Willie Nelson collaboration album that contained two Top 50 hits, "Night Life" and "Funny How Time Slips Away." Soon afterwards, Davis left RCA and began recording on Wartrace, his own label. The Nashville Brass continues to play in Las Vegas, in Branson, MO, and on television. —*Sandra Brennan*

● **Best of Danny Davis & The Nashville Grass** / 1974 / RCA ✦✦✦✦

Down Home Favorites With / Pair ✦✦✦

The Nashville Sound / RCA ✦✦✦✦

More Nashville Sounds / RCA ✦✦✦✦

Jimmie Davis (James Houston Davis)

b. Sep. 11, 1902, Quitman, LA
Guitar, Vocals / Traditional Country
In a performing career spanning eight decades of the 20th century, Jimmie Davis embraced both risqué country-blues and later traditional gospel, meanwhile maintaining a concurrent public-service career that saw him twice elected governor of Louisiana. In fact, his greatest musical successes came during his two terms as governor, one in the mid-'40s and another in the early '60s.

Born James Houston Davis in Beech Springs, LA, on September 11, 1902, Jimmie Davis was the son of a poor sharecropper, but nevertheless he earned a bachelors degree from Louisiana College Pineville and in 1927 a masters degree from Louisiana State University. The following year, he began teaching history at a small college in Shreveport. Davis began singing occasionally for a local radio station and first recorded in 1928. One year later, he signed with Victor and began recording; these initial releases reflect a style devoted to Jimmie Rodgers, emphasizing Rodgers' penchant for double entendre. Over five years he recorded almost 70 sides for the label, and though none of the singles sold well, Davis was probably less to blame than the Depression-era economy. He moved to Decca in 1934 and gained his first major hit, "Nobody's Darlin' but Mine." Another hit, "It Makes No Difference Now," was bought from Floyd Tillman, but Davis' biggest success came from his own composition, "You Are My Sunshine." First recorded by Davis in 1940, the song quickly entered the first rank of popular and country music standards, covered many times over by artists from both genres.

Meanwhile, Davis had quit teaching and accepted a position at the Criminal Court in Shreveport. He became the chief of police in 1938, and moved to state government four years later by being elected Louisiana Public Service Commissioner. Davis even found time to add another career to his résumé: he appeared in three Western films from 1942-44, and in 1947 starred in the somewhat autobiographical *Louisiana*. Elected governor of Louisiana in 1944, he continued to record and scored five Top Five singles during his first term, including the double-sided hit "Is It Too Late Now"/"There's a Chill on the Hill Tonight" in 1944 and the No. 1 "There's a New Moon over My Shoulder" the following year.

Jimmie Davis moved back to full-time recording in 1948, and after a stint with Capitol, he returned to Decca. Some of his country singles such as "Suppertime" began to please gospel listeners as well, and Davis gradually moved to a more sacred style. He returned to the governorship in 1960 on a segregationist platform, but to his credit prevented much of the unrest apparent in the South through his moderate position. Though he hadn't recorded a hit since his first term, Davis reached the Top 20 in 1962 with "Where the Old River Flows." By 1964, he was back to gospel music, and he recorded heavily throughout the late '60s and early '70s. Decca ended his contract in 1975, but Davis continued to perform and record even into the 1990s. He was elected to the Country Music Hall of Fame in 1971. —*John Bush*

Sounds Like Jimmie Rodgers / 1985 / ACM ✦✦✦✦
Features recordings made by Davis for Victor early in his career. —*AMG*

Barnyard Stomp / 1988 / Bear Family ✦✦✦
This album features performances from the early days of Davis' career of such blues-tinged material as "Alimony Blues," "Shotgun Wedding," "Hum Dum Dinger," and more. —*AMG*

● **Country Music Hall of Fame** / 1991 / MCA ✦✦✦✦
Country Music Hall of Fame contains 16 tracks Jimmie Davis recorded between 1934 and 1954 for Decca Records. The material ranges from country blues and novelties to gospel, Western swing, and honky tonk with a few pop crossovers like his signature hit "You Are My Sunshine" and "Nobody's Darling But Mine" thrown in for good measure. Though some of his biggest hits are missing—including "Is It Too Late Now," "Bang Bang," and "There's a Chill on the Hill Tonight"—the collection nevertheless draws a representative portrait of Davis and his career, making it a nearly definitive retrospective. —*Stephen Thomas Erlewine*

Linda Davis

b. Nov. 26, 1962, Dodson, TX
Vocals / Contemporary Country
Linda Davis made several musical and stylistic changes since her beginnings singing jingles and recording as a duet, Skip and Linda, with Skip Eaton in the early '80s. A talented vocalist, she seemed to lack firm direction until she scored a hit duet with her mentor and co-manager, Reba McEntire, on "Does He Love You?"

A native of Texas, Davis began her singing career at the age of six singing on the local radio show *Gary Jamboree;* later she appeared on the *Louisiana Hayride*. She left Texas in 1982 to move to Nashville. As duets were all the rage, she teamed up with Eaton. In 1982, they scored three minor hits including "If You Could See You Through My Eyes." After splitting up, Davis made her living singing ads for Dr. Pepper and Kentucky Fried Chicken when her solo career stalled.

In 1988, she scored a Top 50 single with "All the Good Ones Are Taken." Two years later she had another minor hit with the title track of her debut album, "In a Different Light." "Some Kinda Woman," also from that album, became a minor hit too. In 1993, her luck changed when she and McEntire recorded their duet; following that No. 1 hit, her music blended torchy country ballads and swamp funk, sounding more than a little like Reba redux on the album *Shoot for the Moon*, which made it to the Top 30 album charts and contained two Top 60 singles. During most of 1994, Davis toured with McEntire. *Some Things Are Meant to Be* was released in 1996. —*Sandra Brennan & Michael McCall*

In a Different Light / 1991 / Liberty ✦✦✦✦
Working with producer Jimmy Bowen, Davis created lush, MOR country rife with emotional drama. —*Michael McCall*

Linda Davis / Apr. 13, 1992 / Liberty ✦✦✦
In the same light. —*Michael McCall*

● **Shoot for the Moon** / Apr. 26, 1994 / Arista ✦✦✦✦
Her post-duet follow-up, the style is steamier and bluesier than her previous work, and it sounds somewhat forced. Her vocals work best on the ballads. The album does not include her duet with McEntire. —*Michael McCall*

Some Things Are Meant to Be / Jan. 30, 1996 / Arista ✦✦✦✦
Linda Davis is another singer who has suffered through struggles to get heard. In her case, however, she tended to release formula-heavy albums devoid of much character or individuality. Always an obvious talent, she bounced between record companies, all of which tried to force her into one ill-fitting trend or another. Davis finally enjoyed some exposure through a hit duet with her co-manager, Reba McEntire. Their song "Does He Love You" won several awards and gained Davis another record contract, this time with Arista Records. Still, her 1994 album with the company had little impact. This time, she attempted to come across as a steamy chanteuse. She danced through several lame swamp-pop songs, a style that proved as unconvincing as her previous guises. However, on each of her albums, she would display her potential when given a chance to sing a grown-up love song. Finally, on her new *Some Things Are Meant to Be*, she doesn't have to try to sing two-steppers or novelties or country-rock or traditional tear-jerkers. Instead, the strong-voiced singer takes on straightahead, middle-of-the-road pop-country songs, and she lives up to her promise. The songs are about women in their 30s and 40s facing up to the problems or the joy in their lives. They're about finding strength through acknowledgement, or how sometimes perseverance is the only reward we have. They're good songs, devoid of

gimmickry. And Davis brings them to life with a subtle, intelligent power. Perseverance, it seems, indeed has its rewards. —*Michael McCall*

Link Davis

Saxophone, Vocals, Session Musician / Cajun, Western Swing, Rockabilly

Multi-instrumentalist Link Davis recorded Western swing, Cajun, and rockabilly over the course of his career. His most notable singles, cut for the Okeh label in the early '50s, were aimed at both the hillbilly and Cajun markets. Few, if any, artists bisected those genres as neatly as Davis. The Cajun influence is most audible in Link's vocals, which have an easygoing slur that often seems on the verge of bursting into chuckles. He recorded sides for the Starday label later in the '50s that were more rock 'n' roll-influenced, and earned a couple footnotes in rock 'n' roll history by playing saxophone on the Big Bopper's "Chantilly Lace" and Johnny Preston's "Running Bear." —*Richie Unterberger*

Cajun Crawdaddy / 1969 / Mercury ✦✦✦
● **Big Mamou** / 1989 / Edsel ✦✦✦✦
Sixteen tracks recorded for Okeh from 1952-54. A standout among these waltzing numbers is "Falling for You," a riveting call-and-response boogie with a great steel guitar solo. —*Richie Unterberger*

Mac Davis

b. Jan. 21, 1942, Lubbock, TX
Guitar, Vocals / Country-Pop, Nashville Sound/Countrypolitan
At his commercial peak in the mid-'70s, Mac Davis was one of America's most popular entertainers, a countrypolitan-styled singer and actor who found considerable success in both fields. Born Scott Davis on January 21, 1942, in Buddy Holly's hometown of Lubbock, TX, he began performing in local rock groups while still in his teens. After moving to Georgia, Davis first broke into the music business in 1962, when he was hired by the Chicago-based record label Vee-Jay as their Atlanta-based regional manager. After joining the Liberty label three years later, in 1967 he moved to Los Angeles to head the company's publishing arm, Metric Music; in addition to running Metric's day-to-day operations, he also began composing his own songs, with Glen Campbell, Bobby Goldsboro, Lou Rawls and Kenny Rogers & the First Edition among the artists recording his work.

In 1968, Elvis Presley recorded Davis' "A Little Less Conversation," and soon after, the King was requesting more of his work. After notching a Top 40 hit with Davis' "Memories," Presley reached the Top Three in 1969 with the songwriter's "In the Ghetto," a single from the landmark *From Elvis in Memphis* LP. Davis also arranged the music for Presley's first television special before signing his own recording contract in 1970. In that year, he released his first chart single, "Whoever Finds This, I Love You," from his debut album *Song Painter*.

In 1972, Davis scored a No. 1 pop hit with "Baby, Don't Get Hooked on Me," which also reached the country Top 20. His crossover success continued throughout the decade, with singles like 1974's "Stop and Smell the Roses," 1975's "Burnin' Thing," and the next year's "Forever Lovers" scoring with listeners in both camps. Between 1974 and 1976, Davis hosted a musical variety show for NBC television, followed by a string of specials; in 1979, he also starred in the film *North Dallas Forty* with Nick Nolte.

Davis' success continued in the early 1980s; "It's Hard to Be Humble," the title track of his 1980 album, was the first of four consecutive Top Ten country hits that culminated with his biggest country single, "Hooked on Music," the next year. In 1980, he also starred in a TV movie, *Cheaper to Keep Her*. However, a co-starring role opposite Jackie Gleason and Karl Malden in 1983's disastrous *The Sting II* effectively ended Davis' career in Hollywood, and by 1985, he had recorded his last Top Ten hit, "I Never Made Love (Till I Made Love with You.)" In 1990, Davis made a comeback as a songwriter, co-authoring Dolly Parton's hit "White Limozeen"; that same year, he also took over the title role in the Broadway hit *The Will Rogers Follies*. *Will Write Songs for Food*, his first LP in nearly a decade, appeared in 1994. —*Jason Ankeny*

I Believe in Music / 1972 / Columbia ✦✦✦
Baby Don't Get Hooked on Me / 1972 / Columbia ✦✦✦
● **Greatest Hits** / 1979 / Columbia ✦✦✦✦
In addition to '70s smashes like "Baby Don't Get Hooked on Me" and "Stop and Smell the Roses," *Greatest Hits* also includes the Davis-styled "In the Ghetto," a major hit for Elvis Presley. —*Jason Ankeny*

Texas in My Rear View Mirror / 1980 / Casablanca ✦✦✦✦
Boasting hits like "Hooked on Music," "Me 'N Fat Boy," and the title track, *Texas in My Rear View Mirror* returned Mac Davis to the top of the charts. Consistently solid songwriting and production help to make this release a worthy effort. —*James Chrispell*

Very Best & More… / 1984 / Casablanca ✦✦✦✦
All of Davis' hits from his 1980-1984 tenure at Casablanca Records are included in the collection *Very Best and More…* In addition to "Hooked on Music," his biggest-seller, the album includes "You're My Bestest Friend," "Texas in My Rear View Mirror," "Let's Keep It That Way," and "It's Hard to Be Humble." —*Jason Ankeny*

Skeeter Davis (Mary Frances Penick)

b. Dec. 30, 1931, Dry Ridge, KY
Vocals / Traditional Country, Country-Rock, Nashville Sound/ Countrypolitan
Skeeter Davis has never gotten a lot of critical attention, but in the '50s and '60s, she recorded some of the most accessible crossover country music, occasionally skirting rock 'n' roll. Born Mary Penick, Davis took her last name after forming a duo with Betty Jack Davis, the Davis Sisters. Their 1953 single "I Forgot More than You'll Ever Know" was a big country hit; its B-side, the remarkable "Rock-A-Bye Boogie," foreshadowed rockabilly. That same year, however, the duo's career was cut short by a tragic car accident in which Betty Jack Davis was killed, and Skeeter was severely injured. Skeeter did attempt to revive the Davis Sisters with Betty Jack's sister, but was soon working as a solo artist.

In the early '60s, Davis followed the heels of Brenda Lee and Patsy Cline to become one of the first big-selling female country crossover acts, although her pop success was pretty short-lived. The weepy ballad "The End of the World," though, was a massive hit, reaching No. 2 in 1963. "I Can't Stay Mad at You," a Top Ten hit the same year, was downright rock 'n' roll; penned by Goffin and King, it sounded like (and was) an authentic Brill Building girl group-styled classic. Goffin and King also wrote another successful girl group knockoff for her, "Let Me Get Close to You," although such efforts were the exception rather than the rule. Usually she sang sentimental, country-oriented tunes with enough pop hooks to catch the ears of a wider audience, such as "I Will."

Davis concentrated on the country market after the early '60s, although she never seemed too comfortable limiting herself to the Nashville crowd. She recorded a Buddy Holly tribute album in 1967, when Holly wasn't a hot ticket with either the country or the rock audience. But she certainly didn't reject country conventions either: she performed on the Grand Ole Opry, and recorded duets with Bobby Bare, Porter Wagoner, and George Hamilton IV. In the 1980s, she had a mild comeback with the rock crowd after recording an album with NRBQ; she also married NRBQ's bass player, Joey Spampinato. —*Richie Unterberger*

Here's the Answer / 1961 / RCA ✦✦
Country's never been afraid to lay on the corn, but even by its own standards, the concept driving this album was hokey. Skeeter sings "answer" songs to hits by Jim Reeves, Hank Locklin, Eddy Arnold, Jim Reeves, and Ray Peterson—"I Really Want You to Know," for instance, in response to Arnold's "I Really Don't Want to Know." As all of those singers happened to be contracted to Skeeter's label, RCA, the original versions were available for inclusion/instant comparison. That means that half of this album isn't Skeeter at all—you'll hear, for instance, Jim Reeves singing "He'll Have to Go," followed immediately by Davis' "He'll Have to Stay"; Ray Peterson's "Tell Laura I Love Her" is countered with Davis' "Tell Tommy I Miss Him"; and so on. It gets really ridicu-

lous when Skeeter sings an answer song ("My Last Date") to Floyd Cramer's *instrumental* hit, "Last Date." Skeeter's songs are OK mainstream country/pop; a couple of them ("(I Can't Help You) I'm Falling Too" and "My Last Date") were even Top 40 pop hits. But alternating her tracks bang-bang with hits by various other male country stars makes for a rather herky-jerky listening experience. A mid-'90s European CD reissue of the album adds four bonus tracks from a 1962 duet single with Porter Wagoner and a 1964 duet single with Bobby Bare (including a cover of "We'll Sing in the Sunshine"), none of which rate among the better performances of either Skeeter or her partners. —*Richie Unterberger*

The End of the World / 1962 / RCA ✦✦✦
Recorded at the peak of Davis' brief stardom, this emphasizes the weepy country-pop that gave her a No. 2 pop hit with the title track. Nothing here measures up to that wonderful smash, but it's tasteful enough period Nashville country, with producers Anita Kerr and Chet Atkins ensuring that the LP measured up to state-of-the-art country-pop production by double-tracking Skeeter's vocals against a background of strings and lazy barroom piano runs. They did let her loose on Little Eva's "Keep Your Hands Off My Baby," which is replete with primitive fuzzy guitar. Though it may sound enticing, the result is actually kind of lousy and ill-fitting. —*Richie Unterberger*

The Best of Skeeter Davis / 1965 / RCA ✦✦✦✦
Skeeter fused country, pop, and even occasional girl-group sounds during her commercial peak in the early '60s, which found her at her most fetching and tuneful. This has 12 of her most successful recordings of the era, including the huge ballad "The End of the World," which hit No. 2 on the pop charts in 1963, and Goffin/King's irresistible girl-group composition "I Can't Stay Mad at You," which reached the Top Ten the same year. —*Richie Unterberger*

My Heart's in the Country / 1966 / RCA ✦✦✦
The cover art, with Skeeter fondling farm animals in front of the barn and extolling the rural life in the liner notes, makes a pretty determined effort at presenting Davis in as much of a pure country light as possible. The actual music, by and large, follows suit. Produced by Felton Jarvis in Nashville, it's plainer and more traditional in mood than her work with Chet Atkins and Anita Kerr. The strings are banished and the guitar picking and fiddles are at the forefront, although the vocals are still double-tracked. It's kind of an average effort, without any particular flaws or standout material. Includes compositions by Dolly Parton and Loretta Lynn, as well as Skeeter's rendition of the traditional "Goin' Down the Road (Feelin' Bad)." —*Richie Unterberger*

Skeeter Davis Sings Buddy Holly / 1967 / RCA ✦✦✦
Twelve Holly covers, produced by Felton Jarvis in Nashville and featuring Waylon Jennings on guitar, at a time when neither Davis nor Holly were exactly in the forefront of pop's collective consciousness. A modest accomplishment, this LP is nevertheless fairly worthwhile, with a much more upbeat sound than Davis' early '60s recordings. The arrangements are pretty straightforward and close to the originals, with solid country-rock backing and occasional light, tasteful strings. —*Richie Unterberger*

Best of Skeeter Davis Vol. 2 / 1973 / RCA ✦✦✦
A ridiculously uneven collection, veering between solid country uptempo numbers and pathetic weepers (which are either effective or embarrassing), a fine girl-group pastiche, a stupid courtroom divorce song, and a couple lousy covers of early-'70s pop hits ("One Tin Soldier"?!). By far the best cut is her girl-group take on Goffin/King's "Let Me Get Close to You," which is in the same class as her similar 1963 Top Ten pop hit "I Can't Stay Mad at You" (also written by Goffin/King). "Sunglasses" is an out-of-character pop number by John Loudermilk, and a couple of the straight country tunes are decent, but this is a very scattershot compilation; surely Skeeter recorded enough decent material to warrant a better selection. —*Richie Unterberger*

She Sings, They Play / 1985 / Rounder ✦✦✦
Skeeter Davis, a prolific country singer since the '50s, teamed up with the versatile NRBQ for this delightful collaboration. Nashville with a kick. —*Jeff Tamarkin*

● **Essential Skeeter Davis** / 1996 / RCA ✦✦✦✦
Featuring 20 tracks, *The Essential Skeeter Davis* collects all of her big hits from both the country and pop charts, making it the one definitive compilation. —*Stephen Thomas Erlewine*

Julian Dawson

Guitar, Vocals / Alternative Country, Americana
Combining British pop and American roots-rock, Julian Dawson first gained prominence in Europe with a single on Rough Trade Records in the mid-'80s. He then released two albums on Polydor Records. He also recorded two albums with Ian Matthews' band, Plainsong. His first domestic release, *Live on the Radio*, appeared in 1990 on Watermelon Records. Dawson then recorded *Fragile as China* the following year for BMG/Ariola. The first single, "How Can I Sleep Without You," reached the charts. 1994 brought a greatest-hits album, *How Human Hearts Behave*, which included a re-recording of "How Can I Sleep Without You" with Lucinda Williams. The next year, *Travel On* was issued, again on Watermelon Records. It featured collaborations with Nicky Hopkins, Jules Shear, and Willie Nile; the Roches and Curtis Stigers contributed vocals. —*John Bush*

Live on the Radio / 1989 / Watermelon ✦✦✦
Dawson—the only Brit on the label, recorded the engaging, thought-provoking *Live on the Radio* before an audience of 500 in a radio station studio in Cologne, Germany. —*Roch Parisien*

● **Travel On** / 1995 / Watermelon ✦✦✦✦

Ronnie Dawson

b. Aug. 11, 1939, Dallas, TX
Guitar, Vocals / Rockabilly
Ronnie Dawson was a late '50s Dallas rockabilly guitarist and singer noted for his shocking white brush cut and high-pitched, boyish vocals, which made him sound even younger than his teenage years. His clutch of rare singles on regional labels are highly valued by rockabilly collectors. Dawson sounded something like a raw, upper-register Gene Vincent, and the connection is not entirely coincidental. He shared Vincent's manager, and his greatest song, the manic "Action Packed" (with its insistent, shouted "Hear me!" refrain), was written by Jack Rhodes, who also wrote a couple of Vincent's best tunes ("Woman Love" and "B-I-Bickey-Bi-Bo-Bo-Go"). Dawson could also sing convincingly on more grinding and bluesy numbers.

After a few singles, Dawson was briefly picked up by Swan Records, which tried to mold him into a teen idol with unsuccessful results (commercially and artistically). After a fine single for Columbia under the name Commonwealth Jones, Ronnie retreated to smaller labels once again for a time. He worked as a session drummer for the semi-legendary Texas producer Major Bill Smith, playing on Bruce Channel's "Hey Baby" and Paul & Paula's "Hey Paula"; like most first-generation rockabilly singers, he tried his hand at country music as well. His rediscovery was hastened by the inclusion of "Action Packed" in Rhino's *Rock this Town* anthology of rockabilly classics, and he has resumed active performing and recording. —*Richie Unterberger*

Still a Lot of Rhythm / 1988 / No Hit ✦✦✦
Dawson's first comeback effort was impressive in that it found him in good (if noticeably lower) voice, though the material was average and the performances a bit restrained. No need to look for the hard-to-find British import; it's been reissued domestically, in its entirety, as bonus material on Crystal Clear's *Monkey Beat!!* CD. —*Richie Unterberger*

Rockinitis / 1989 / Crystal Clear ✦✦✦
Dawson's second LP since his mid-'80s rediscovery is an above-average latter-day rockabilly effort, sensibly avoiding temptations to modernize the sound with too much clutter. Dawson's voice has lowered considerably since his early days, meaning that instead of sounding like a little kid, he sounds like a young man (although

he was about 50 when this was recorded). The American CD reissue adds a bonus cut, "Sloppy Drunk," not on the original British release. —*Richie Unterberger*

● **Rockin' Bones** / 1990 / No Hit ✦✦✦✦
This 20-track CD has all his essential early recordings, with both sides of five singles (the Swan teen idol efforts aren't included). Besides "Action Packed," highlights are the subsequent A-sides "Do Do Do" and "Rockin' Bones," as well as a spooky rendering of "Riders in the Sky." The unreleased tracks include several raw demos he cut prior to his first single, as well as a few outtakes from his Columbia session that feature some harmonica work by Delbert McClinton. —*Richie Unterberger*

Monkey Beat!! / 1994 / Crystal Clear ✦✦✦✦
Monkey Beat!! confirms Dawson's status as the most vital of the middle-aged rockabilly singers still performing and recording in the 1990s. It's actually rawer (in the positive sense of the term) than the two previous comeback albums he recorded for No Hit in the late '80s. He's in fine, spontaneous voice, and the material (including a few originals), as always, avoids overdone standards. As a significant bonus, the CD tacks on the entirety of his 1988 album, *Still a Lot of Rhythm*, originally released on the British No Hit label; it's a respectable but tamer effort than the first half of the program. —*Richie Unterberger*

● **Rockin' Bones: The Legendary Masters** / 1996 / Crystal Clear ✦✦✦✦
Two-CD overview of Dawson's early recordings, spanning 1957 to 1962. Includes most of his singles from the era, and a tall heap of acetates, demos, and alternate takes; in fact, over half of the material was unreleased at the time. The stylistic variety is a little manic, moving from raw home demo rockabilly-blues to straight studio rockabilly (including the classic "Action Packed") to teen idol pop to country arrangements that prominently feature banjo. It's the definitive compilation, though, of the early work of this one-of-a-kind rockabilly singer. It has almost all of the tracks of the previous collection of his early sides (on No Hit), and replaces that disc as the anthology of choice. —*Richie Unterberger*

Just Rockin' & Rollin' / Jun. 1996 / Upstart ✦✦✦
A more easygoing effort than *Monkey Beat!!,* with a decidedly more countrified influence. Echoes of Tex-Mex creep in here and there as well, and a few tracks have a horn section. A lot of Dawson fans will prefer Ronnie's wilder latter-day releases, where he lets go more, and where singing and playing skirt a more reckless, dangerous edge. Rockabilly's a limited form, though, and he should get some credit for playing around with the format mildly, instead of just serving up more of the same. It's still a solid, crisp record of reasonably strong material, though Dawson himself wrote little of it. —*Richie Unterberger*

Curtis Day

b. 1971
Contemporary Country
Born in 1971 near Beaumont, TX, Curtis Day was more interested in football than music while growing up; he earned a scholarship to Lamar University, but when the program folded, he decided to try his hand at country singing. After winning several talent competitions, he formed his own band and toured the area during the early '90s. Inspired by his grandmother, his manager and biggest fan, Day signed to Asylum Records in 1995 and released his eponymous debut album a year later. —*John Bush*

Curtis Day / Jan. 30, 1996 / Elektra ✦✦✦
On his eponymous debut, Curtis Day follows the formula of many country singers of the mid-'90s, turning in line-dance stompers, honky tonk ravers, and tear-jerking ballads. Day is only as strong as his material, and there are only a handful of strong songs on the album. —*Sara Sytsma*

Jimmy Day

b. Jan. 9, 1934, Tuscaloosa, AL
Guitar (Steel) / Western Swing, Honky Tonk
Jimmy Day was one of the greatest steel guitarists in country music, rivaled only by Buddy Emmons and Paul Franklin. He

began playing guitar at age 12, but didn't like it much until he saw Shot Jackson playing steel guitar on television with the Bailes Brothers. He immediately became fascinated with the instrument and decided to master it. In 1951, the 18-year-old was accepted into Webb Pierce's band and began appearing on *Louisiana Hayride.*

In 1952, Day made his recording debut on Pierce's "That Heart Belongs to Me," which hit No. 1. During his stint at *Louisiana Hayride,* Day worked with Red Sovine, which led to a chance to play with Hank Williams, who invited Day to join his band, but died before it could happen. Day began working as a session player for Abbott Recordings in 1952 and played on singles for Jim Reeves. In 1954, he played with Floyd Cramer, Lefty Frizzell, and Elvis Presley, who also wanted to play steel guitar until Day talked him out of it. Day and Cramer were part of the *Louisiana Hayride* house band until 1955, when the former left owing to his dissatisfaction with the program's leanings toward rock 'n' roll. He followed Cramer to Nashville and cut an instrumental single, "Rippin' Out/Blue Wind."

During the mid-'50s, Day toured with Webb Pierce and played with Ray Price's Cherokee Cowboys and Jim Reeves' Blue Boys. He met Willie Nelson, who played briefly in Price's band before forming his own band and taking Day with him. He remained with Nelson for six months and then worked on several George Jones records. After they split up, he bounced back and forth between Ferlin Husky, Buddy Emmons, Price, Nelson, and Little Jimmy Dickens. After leaving Nelson's Record Men in 1973, Day moved to Texas and played for three years before returning to Nashville to perform with Charlie Louvin. He moved back to Texas permanently in 1978. Day was inducted into the International Steel Guitar Hall of Fame in 1982; after more than a decade of semi-retirement, in 1995 he was preparing a series of instructional videos. —*Sandra Brennan*

Golden Steel Guitar Hits / 1962 / Philips ✦✦✦

Steel and Strings / 1963 / Philips ✦✦✦✦

● **Golden Steel Guitar Hits/Steel & Strings** / 1992 / Bear Family ✦✦✦✦
This album, a re-release of two '60s Philips issues, features masterful performances on the steel guitar. —*AMG*

Day with Remington / 1992 / Glad Music ✦✦✦

Jesse Dayton

Raised in Beaumont, TX, near the childhood home of George Jones, Jesse Dayton grew up on the hardcore honky tonk of Jones, Hank Williams, Sr., and Lefty Frizzell, but on also blues artists such as Lightnin' Hopkins and Mance Lipscomb. During the late '80s and early '90s Dayton fronted two rockabilly bands, the Roadkings and the Alamo Jets, playing around the state in honky tonks and dives. After beginning a solo career, he played supporting slots at shows for Willie Nelson, Merle Haggard, and Waylon Jennings, and even appeared as the bandleader in a Pam Tillis video. Signed to Justice Records in 1995, he released *Raisin' Cain* that same year and also appeared on the Willie Nelson tribute record, *Twisted Willie.* Dayton's songs have also appeared in the FOX-TV series *Melrose Place* and in the film *Curse of the Starving Class.* —*John Bush*

Raisin' Cain / Jul. 25, 1995 / Justice ✦✦✦

Billy Dean

b. Apr. 1, 1962, Quincy, FL
Guitar, Vocals / Contemporary Country
Billy Dean received a basketball scholarship to attend East Central Junior College in Decatur, MS, where he majored in physical education, but instead of wearing a whistle around his neck, he opted for a guitar strap. Inspired by Merle Haggard, Marty Robbins, and Dean Martin, he played the club circuit along the Gulf Coast in Florida and used national talent contests as a vehicle for his music. He made the finals of the Wrangler Country *Star Search* in 1982, then won as a Male Vocalist champ on Ed McMahon's *Star Search* program in 1988. Even before the release of his debut album, *Young Man,* he'd already gone on tour as an open-

ing act for Mel Tillis, Gary Morris, and Ronnie Milsap. He's contributed to commercials for Valvoline, McDonald's, and Chevrolet, and had an acting role in the brief Elvis series on ABC-TV in 1990.

His good looks are undeniable, but Dean has the talent to match, as proven when he won the Academy of Country Music's Song of the Year award for the enormously sensitive "Somewhere in My Broken Heart," co-written with Richard Leigh ("Don't It Make My Brown Eyes Blue," "Come from the Heart"). Dean was at the height of his career in the early '90s, when he had a string of seven Top Ten country hits between 1991 and 1992, including the singles "Somewhere in My Broken Heart," "Only Here for a Little While," "Only the Wind," "Billy the Kid," and "If There Hadn't Been You." However, Dean's reign at the top of the charts was short-lived, and by the end of 1994, he had trouble cracking the Top 40. — *Tom Roland*

Young Man / 1990 / Liberty ✦✦✦✦
Nashville launched so many new acts from 1989-1992 that many who deserved a shot were overlooked. Thanks in part to his own songwriting skills, and to signing with SBK Records, which had just one country act to push, he got a good listen and was able to capitalize with a strong debut. His vocals aren't unique, but he sings with strength and conviction, regardless of the style. You can't go wrong with "Somewhere in My Broken Heart." — *Tom Roland*

Billy Dean / 1991 / Liberty ✦✦✦✦
Billy Dean's second album follows the same pattern that made his first so popular: a strong emphasis on the ballads on which his supple baritone thrives. The rollicking "Hammer Down" flies in the face of everything else, but even there the message remains the same: obvious but effective. — *Brian Mansfield*

Fire in the Dark / 1993 / Liberty ✦✦✦
Like *Billy Dean* before it, *Fire in the Dark* doesn't stray from the pattern Dean established on *Young Man*, which might not necessarily be a bad thing. However, there is the problem of diminishing returns—each time he goes back to the well, he's coming back with a lesser number of first-rate songs. There are highlights on *Fire in the Dark*, but nothing on the album represents a progress from his first two albums. — *Thom Owens*

Men'll Be Boys / 1994 / Capitol ✦✦✦
With *Men'll Be Boys*, Billy Dean's formula began to wear thin. Although he was still in good voice and he had a handful of good songs, the calculation behind the album's sound is apparent—the filler isn't as enjoyable as it was on his first three records. — *Thom Owens*

● **Greatest Hits** / Mar. 8, 1994 / Liberty ✦✦✦✦
As the title implies, the ten-track *Greatest Hits* collects Billy Dean's biggest hit singles, which usually happen to be the best parts of his albums. Consequently, *Greatest Hits* is Dean's most consistent and enjoyable album. — *Thom Owens*

It's What I Do / Apr. 1996 / Capitol ✦✦
Billy Dean mixes thoughtful ballads with brisk rockers. But after a couple of memorable early hits, he has settled for songs that carry no distinctive passion or energy. *It's What I Do* follows an extensive lay-off from the road, but the introspective period has done little to improve his work. Mistaking tender sincerity for genuine emotion is an error many acoustic-based artists make. Unfortunately, the more Dean attempts to add tension or drama to his work, the tamer his performances become. With this album, it's hard to delineate exactly what it is that Dean does well. —*Michael McCall*

Eddie Dean

b. Jul. 9, 1907, Posey, TX
Vocals / Cowboy
Singer-songwriter/musician and B-movie cowboy Eddie Dean (born Edgar Dean Glosup) appeared in Hollywood Westerns of the late '30s through the late '40s and also had a modest career in country music. He was born in Posey, TX, to a farmer and a singing school teacher, who taught her son to harmonize. In 1926, Dean moved to Chicago to see if he could make it on the radio,

but was only able to obtain a few guest spots. He shortened his name to Eddie Dean and the following year was hired in Shenandoah, IA.

In 1929, Dean and his older brother Jimmy (not the sausage magnate) began singing together. By late 1933, they were appearing on an early morning Chicago show and the prestigious *National Barn Dance.* Through 1935, they recorded duets for the ARC label under the direction of Art Satherley, plus some gospel tunes for Decca. After the Deans separated, Jimmy moved to a new station and appeared on a network daytime show, *Modern Cinderella.* Dean decided to try his luck in Hollywood in 1936 and began playing minor roles in Westerns. He also appeared regularly on Judy Canova's network radio show and released eight singles between 1941 and 1942, including "On the Banks of the Sunny San Juan." As an actor, Dean got his big break in 1944 when he starred in the musical Western *The Harmony Trail.* After that, he went on to star in 19 more Westerns; at the apex of his film career, Dean was listed among the top ten cowboy stars of the 1940s.

After 1948, Dean retired from films and focused on using his movie fame to promote his singing career. Although a talented vocalist with a remarkably strong, clear voice, Dean never made it big. He did have a few hits and wrote some excellent songs, including "One Has My Name (The Other Has My Heart)," co-written by his wife and recorded by Jimmy Wakely and Jerry Lee Lewis in 1961 and 1969, respectively. As a songwriter, his best-known hit remains 1955's "I Dreamed of a Hillbilly Heaven," a country music classic. Dean continued recording on low-budget labels through the 1970s. Through the 1980s, Dean continued to sing and share anecdotes at Western film fairs, and in 1993 was inducted into the Cowboy Hall of Fame. — *Sandra Brennan*

● **Dean of the West** / WFC ✦✦✦✦
Dean of the West is a ten-track collection featuring songs from Eddie Dean's most popular films, including "Black Hills," "Wagon Wheels," "Tumbleweed Trail," and "Banks of the Sunny San Juan." Neither of his big hits—"One Has My Name (The Other Has My Heart)" and "I Dreamed of a Hillbilly Heaven"—are included on this LP, but it remains a fine collection of cowboy songs, delivered by one of the most theatrical of all the screen cowboys. — *Thom Owens*

Greatest Westerns / 1957 / Sage & Sand ✦✦✦✦

Hi-Country / 1957 / Sage & Sand ✦✦✦

Favorites of Eddie Dean / 1961 / King ✦✦✦

I Dreamed of a Hillbilly Heaven / 1981 / Castle ✦✦✦

Jimmy Dean

b. Aug. 10, 1928, Plainview, TX
Guitar, Piano, Accordion, Vocals / Traditional Country, Country-Pop, Nashville Sound/Countrypolitan
To the general public, singer-songwriter Jimmy Dean was best known as the star of commercials promoting the sausages and processed meats which bore his name. However, he also had a string of country hits in the early '60s; most of his material consisted of narrative songs.

Born in Plainview, TX, Dean spent his early years in dire poverty. He joined the Merchant Marines in his late teens, and two years later entered the Air Force. Dean founded his first band, the Tennessee Haymakers, while stationed at Bolling Air Force Base located near Washington, DC, playing on base and in local clubs. Following his discharge, Dean remained in the area and founded the Texas Wildcats. In 1952 promoter Connie B. Gay arranged for him to tour US military bases in the Caribbean. Later that year, he made his debut single, "Bumming Around," which peaked at No. 5 on the country charts.

Dean's popularity helped win him his own eponymous show on CBS. Unfortunately, it was on at 7 am and fizzled. He signed to Columbia Records in 1957 and though he released ten singles, he didn't have a hit until 1961's "Big Bad John," the story of a courageous ex-con turned miner, which was the first song he'd ever written. The song topped the country and pop charts and even made it to No. 2 in Great Britain. A follow-up, "Dear Ivan," came out in 1962 and was a more moderate crossover success. Later that year, yet another story-song, "P.T. 109," the story of JFK's famous boat, provided a timely hit.

In 1963, Dean launched a new incarnation of his TV show on ABC. It aired daily and was very successful; in 1964, he tried a nighttime version as well, although both shows folded in 1966. In the meantime, he had three more hits, including a cover of Hank Williams' "Mind Your Own Business." Dean continued hitting the charts through the early '70s, and in 1976 had a gold record when his narrative song "I.O.U." became a Top Ten country hit. Beginning in the late '70s, Dean turned his concentration to his business ventures, eventually building the company into a multi-million dollar empire. —*Sandra Brennan*

His Television Favorites / 1957 / Mercury ✦✦✦

Jimmy Dean's Greatest Hits / 1966 / Columbia ✦✦✦✦
This contains "Big Bad John" and "P.T. 109." —*Dan Heilman*

● **American Originals** / 1989 / Columbia ✦✦✦✦
American Originals collects ten of Jimmy Dean's biggest hits from Columbia Records, featuring everything from "Big Bad John" to "The First Thing Ev'ry Morning (And the Last Thing Ev'ry Night)." It only covers five years—between 1961 and 1965—but it offers the best introduction to his sound. —*Stephen Thomas Erlewine*

Country Spotlight / 1991 / Dominion ✦
The cover may lead you to believe that this is a collection of Dean's hits in their original versions, but *Country Spotlight* features ten dreadful re-recordings of Dean's hits. —*Stephen Thomas Erlewine*

Big Bad John / 1993 / Bear Family ✦✦✦✦
This 26-song single-disc collection covers the highlights of Jimmy Dean's 1961-62 recordings for Columbia Records—not everything, but most everything that counts. The sheer diversity of material demonstrates some of the problems that Dean had finding and following up on hits—he was a passable singer and likable personality, but he would follow up a pop-rock piece like "Little Black Book" with a blues piece such as "Gonna Raise a Ruckus Tonight." But apart from the hokiest of these tracks ("A Day That Changed the World"), it all holds up, including the title track; the freewheeling "Smoke, Smoke, Smoke That Cigarette"; the weirdly topical "Dear Ivan"; his cover of Merle Travis' "Sixteen Tons"; the sentimental father-to-daughter soliloquy "To a Sleeping Beauty"; the rough-hewn "Big Bad John" follow-up "The Cajun Queen"; the delightful sequel to both songs, "Little Bitty Big John"; "P.T. 109," a tribute to John Kennedy's World War II exploits written in the same vein as Johnny Horton's "Sink the Bismarck"; the wryly cynical "Walk on Boy"; the workers' anthem "Steel Men"; the pop-rock ballad "Little Black Book"; the old Texas blues "Gonna Raise a Ruckus Tonight"; the strange D day remembrance "A Day That Changed the World"; the breezily folky "Gotta Travel On"; the sad dog (and war) song "Oklahoma Bill"; the effective sub-Elvis "Night Train to Memphis"; and two previously unissued numbers, the slow blues "Lonesome Road" and the swamp ballad "Cajun Joe." —*Bruce Eder*

Larry Dean

Cowboy, Bakersfield Sound, West Coast Country
Larry Dean was one of the chief proponents of the Bakersfield Sound and a strong presence within the West Coast country music scene. Born in Texas and raised in Oklahoma and Idaho, Dean came from a strict religious background that forbade dancing and secular music. As the oldest of two boys, Dean was expected to help out on the family farm, where he spent long hours alone working the fields. It was here that he began writing songs in his head. A self-taught musician, as a teenager he played with various bands in the Middleton, ID, area. In 1980 he packed up and moved to Los Angeles. By 1981 he had formed his own band, Larry Dean and the Shooters. Awarded numerous honors by ASCAP and the California Country Music Association for his skills as a songwriter and a performer, Dean caught the attention of Nashville in 1985. He spent the next two years as a Nashville songwriter honing his craft. In 1989 Dean moved back on the West Coast, but not before accepting an invitation to appear on

Ralph Emery's morning television show on TNN. Working with famed songwriter Wayne Carson, Dean penned tunes for his first CD. This 1989 release, entitled *Outside Chance*, included the title cut, written with Carson, as well as "Old Time Movies." Both singles charted. 1995 saw the release of Dean's second disc, *From a Distance*. This project was critically acclaimed even though country radio failed to take notice.

As a prominent member of the Bakersfield Revolution, Dean garnered the respect and friendship of the legendary Roy Nichols, famed guitar player for Wynn Stewart, Lefty Frizzell, and Merle Haggard. Nichols, who acted as a mentor to Dean, instilled in his student the importance of passing on the heritage of Bakersfield and the West Coast to the next generation. Dean acted as mentor to several young artists, including California native and Merle Haggard disciple Michael Dart. Constantly on the move, Dean performed all across the West, where he was a favorite with the honky tonk crowd as well as with ranchers, rodeo stars, and cowgirls. As a songwriter, he composed in the Bakersfield style as well as paying tribute to the cowboy culture he was so much a part of. As a producer of note, Dean worked both in L.A. and Nashville and was often sought out to help develop younger artists. —*Jana Pendragon*

Outside Chance / 1989 / USA Music Group ✦✦✦✦
This debut from one of the West Coast's finest should have brought Larry Dean the attention someone of his caliber deserves. With as much finesse as George Strait and as much gumption as fellow West Coaster Dwight Yoakam, this release represents Dean's evolution into the ranks of country music's elite. Starting out with his paean to roots rock 'n' roll, "It All Started 30 Years Ago," written with Bill Graham, this cowboy kicks up some dust and never lets up. Even when he is crooning a touching ballad, as he does on the Larry Dean/Rocky Burnette/Ron Coleman tune, "Whispering Wind," this artist is not afraid to expose true emotions. And, as a cowboy singer Dean can stand side by side with Don Edwards and Michael Martin Murphey. Dean's charting hits include "Old Time Cowboy Movies," a slice of Americana pie that documents a time and place long gone. Still, it is his ability to honky tonk that gives Dean his edge and allows him to roam wide and free. "Tramp," "Good Lookin' Liar," and his version of the very classic "There Stands the Glass" all suggest an artist whose talent is elevated above the common and mundane. —*Jana Pendragon*

● **From a Distance** / 1995 / Boulevard ✦✦✦✦
Critically acclaimed, this is Larry Dean's second release. Pure, unadulterated and true to the Bakersfield Sound, Dean shows himself to be a solid country traditionalist with a definite style all his own. A bit of a rebel, Dean has refused to mold himself to the marketing schemes that so often go with a major label deal in Music City. Writing about what he knows allows Dean to tap into the universal appeal that made Country & Western music from decades past so alluring to a wide variety of listeners. Honky tonkin' once again, "I'm Gettin' Known (For All the Wrong Reasons)" sets the stage for this accomplished project. With other outstanding selections such as "Things Are Lookin' Up," "It Must Be Angel Day," and the Kostas song "Brown Paper Bag," this is a lively, provocative release. More thoughtful are Dean's "Sweet Magnolia," which demonstrates his skill with a ballad, and the haunting title track. Musicianship here is quality all the way. Using his own band, the Shooters, as well as some of L.A.'s top players like Taras Prodaniuk, Skip Edwards, and Harry Orlove gives Dean the support his songwriting and vocal skills deserve. *From a Distance* continues to stand as one of 1995's outstanding true country releases and a signpost marking the continuation of an exceptional talent. —*Jana Pendragon*

Tony De La Rosa

Drums / Tex-Mex
Norteno music veteran Tony De La Rosa was one of the first bandleaders to add drums and amplification to the tradition-bound conjunto style. De La Rosa was born in 1931 in Sarita, TX, and began playing a double-row squeezebox accordion at the age of 11. He founded a conjunto band in the mid-'50s, but later

added electric bass, 12-string guitar, and drums. This innovation sparked a new form, called tacuachito. After a long semi-retirement, he has emerged with his no-frills Tex-Mex sound intact, applying his accordion to the ever-popular polkas and rancheras of the Texas border. —*Myles Boisen*

Atotonilco / May 1964 / Arhoolie ✦✦✦✦

★ **Asi Se Baila En Tejas** / Rounder ✦✦✦✦✦
Tony De La Rosa was even more influential in conjunto music than Flaco Jimenez during the late '40s and early '50s. However, the 14 tracks on this anthology are important not for historical reasons, but because they're joyous, rocking examples of De La Rosa's flamboyance as a performer. His charismatic vocals, expert accordion support, and jubilant presence on each cut make them appealing. This is significant music from a conjunto master. —*Ron Wynn*

Delevantes

Country-Rock, Roots-Rock
The Delevantes are the kind of likable, insignificant band that some critics love to praise because they have the right influences and attitudes. That may be casting them in too harsh a light; they play bright and competent country-flavored roots-rock with an extremely strong debt to the Everly Brothers. The Everlys' influence is understandable given that the Delevantes are two brothers, Bob and Mike Delevante, who love to harmonize. Originally from New Jersey, the pair were in a Hoboken band called Who's Your Daddy before relocating to Nashville. There they caught the attention of ex-E Street Band bassist Garry Tallent, who helped produce their 1995 debut and played on the record. —*Richie Unterberger*

Long About That Time / 1995 / Rounder ✦✦✦
The Delevantes are to the Everly Brothers what the Mavericks are to Roy Orbison: a slight modern update of a classic early prototype, with a more prominent country influence. Which means that they aren't terribly original, but their debut is a pleasant enough affair, harmonized and written with care. —*Richie Unterberger*

The Delmore Brothers

Old-Time, Traditional Country, Honky Tonk, Close Harmony
The Delmore Brothers are not nearly as well-known as such early country giants as the Carter Family, Jimmie Rodgers, Bob Wills, and Hank Williams. The reasons for this, upon close inspection of their work, are not readily apparent. They were one of the greatest early country harmonizers, drawing from both gospel and Appalachian folk. They were skilled songwriters, penning literally hundreds of songs, many of which have proven to be durable. Most important, they were among the few early traditional country acts to change with the times, and pioneer some of those changes. Their recordings from the latter half of the 1940s married traditional country to boogie beats and bluesy riffs. In this respect they laid a foundation for rockabilly and early rock 'n' roll, and rate among the most important White progenitors of those forms.

The Delmores were born into poverty in Elkmont, AL, as the sons of tenant farmers. Alton (b. Dec. 25, 1908) would write most of the duo's original material, although his younger brother Rabon (b. Dec. 3, 1916) was also a competent writer. Performing on guitar and vocals from early ages, they were playing as a pair by the time Rabon was ten years old. In the early '30s, they were confident enough to enter professional music, auditioning for Columbia in 1931 and successfully auditioning for Nashville radio station WSM the following year.

Throughout the 1930s, the Delmore Brothers recorded often, as well as performing on several radio stations. They probably gained their most early fame, however, from their long-running stint with the Grand Ole Opry between 1932 and 1938. The music emphasized their beautiful soft harmonies, accomplished guitar picking, and strong original compositions. Unusually for that time (or any other), the Delmores would switch high and low harmony parts from song to song (or even within the same song), although Alton would usually sing lead. Whether performing their own songs, traditional ones, or gospel, they brought a strong bluesy

feeling to both their music and their vocals. It's that element, perhaps, that enables the Delmores, more than many other acts of the time, to speak to listeners of subsequent generations. Not to be underestimated either are their down-to-earth lyrical concerns, which address commonplace struggles and lost love with grace and redeeming, good-natured humor, rarely resorting to cornball tears.

In 1944, the Delmores signed with King, inaugurating an era that found them delving into and innovating more modern forms of country. Although their first sides for the label stuck to a traditional mold, in 1946 they expanded from their acoustic two-piece arrangements into full-band backup, with bass, mandolin, steel guitar, fiddle, harmonica, and additional guitars. Some of those additional guitars were supplied by Merle Travis, who credited Alton Delmore as a key influence.

In retrospect, however, the most important backup musician on these sides was Wayne Raney, who played a "choke" style of harmonica that was heavily influenced by the blues. The Delmores were also leaning increasingly towards uptempo material that reflected the upsurge in Western swing and boogie-woogie. By the end of 1947, they were also using electric guitar and drums. Raney (who also sang) in effect acted as a third member of the Delmores in the late '40s and early '50s, when they plunged full-tilt into hillbilly boogie.

These are the most widely available and, in some ways, best Delmore Brothers sides. They were also the most successful, and in the late '40s the brothers reached their commercial peak, releasing a series of hard-driving boogies with thumping backbeats and bluesy structures. Arguably they milked the cow dry, recording "Hillbilly Boogie," "Steamboat Bill Boogie," "Barnyard Boogie," "Mobile Boogie," "Freight Train Boogie," and even "Pan American Boogie."

These were usually exciting performances though, featuring extended guitar solos that clearly looked forward to the rock era. Listen, for instance, to the lengthy guitar breaks of "Beale Street Boogies" (unreleased at the time)—very few, if any, White or Black artists were riffing so extensively in 1947. And of course "Beale Street" itself was a tribute to the most famous musical street in Memphis, the city that did so much to cross-fertilize Black and White roots music into what became rock 'n' roll.

The Delmores didn't stick entirely to boogies during the King era; they also released some slower bluesy material. One of these, the original "Blues Stay Away from Me," became their biggest hit, and indeed the most famous Delmore Brothers song of all, often covered by subsequent country and pop artists. Interestingly, the Delmores continued to record gospel on the side, as part of the Brown's Ferry Four, a quartet that also included (at various points) Grandpa Jones, Merle Travis, and Red Foley.

As influential as the Delmores' King sides may have been on the future of American pop, the Delmores themselves would not be able to capitalize on that future. By the early '50s, their commercial success was fading. After the death of his young daughter, Alton drank heavily; worse, Rabon died of lung cancer on December 4, 1952. Alton (like longtime accompanist Wayne Raney) did record some material as a solo act, in both the gospel and rockabilly fields. Alton was way too old to begin a new career as a rockabilly singer though, and he didn't record much for the last decade of his life. He wrote the hard-to-find autobiography *Truth Is Stranger than Fiction* (published posthumously in 1977 by CMF) before dying on June 9, 1964. By that time the Delmore Brothers' work had already proven extremely influential, particularly on the harmonies of fellow sibling acts the Louvin Brothers and the Everly Brothers. They left behind an extraordinarily lengthy and consistent body of recorded work—virtually none of their sides are lousy, at least the ones that have been reissued. Much of the Delmores' early material, unfortunately, can be hard to locate, although many of the King sides have recently been reissued on CD. —*Richie Unterberger*

The Best Of / 1970 / Starday ✦✦✦✦
Terrific nasal vocal harmonies, their brisk, bubblin' tenor, and six-string guitars and Wayne Raney's wailin' locomotive harmonica make the Delmores' late-'40s King label hits the most accessible

of their early brother-duo material. Sounding a mite like the amiable smalltown uncles of Elvis and the Everly Brothers, the chooglin' "hillbilly boogie" of the Delmores was just a hairpin curve away from rockabilly. —*Mark A. Humphrey*

Weary Lonesome Blues / 1983 / Old Homestead ✦✦✦✦
Unfortunately, there's no documentation on this 18-song set, but it's a safe guess that the tracks date from the 1930s and early 1940s. It's another strong and varied set of blues, ballads, and spirituals, duplicating virtually nothing from the other Delmore Brothers reissues that have been compiled. —*Richie Unterberger*

Singing My Troubles Away / 1984 / ✦✦✦
The Delmores recorded over 200 sides, many of which have been reissued by Old Homestead. The quality is so consistently high and the material so similar in focus, that there's really little to differentiate them; if you like their sound, you'll like any given album. This one focuses mostly on their early days in the '30s, reaching back as far as 1933 (a couple of previously unissued cuts in a much more boogie-oriented style from 1946 and 1947 are also included). Perhaps more traditional in focus than some of their other compilations, it includes a fair number of blues-derived tunes. The harmonies and guitar playing are consistently fine. —*Richie Unterberger*

When They Let the Hammer Fall / 1984 / Bear Family ✦✦✦✦
Contains 18 of the "boogie" sides this great country duo cut (with harmonica player Wayne Raney) between 1945 and 1952, though it inexplicably fails to include their biggest hit from this time, "Blues Stay Away from Me" (later recorded by Johnny Burnette and Gene Vincent). This is the bluesiest and most raucous material cut by the harmonizing siblings. These tunes sound about as close to rock 'n' roll as any other music recorded by White musicians prior to the 1950s, and still makes fine party music today, with its thumping shuffle beats, bluesy solos, and loose abandon. The great "Beale Street Boogie," cut in 1947 (and unissued at the time), is one of the dozens of songs that could make a strong case for being the first rock 'n' roll record. There's a classic opening bluesy call-and-response riff, a long electric guitar solo duel, and an appropriate homage to Memphis' famed Beale Street, certainly one of the locales most responsible for brewing together the basic ingredients of rock 'n' roll—"the Beale Street Boogie is eight beats to the bar," they sing in unison, just in case you don't get the point. Compared to their early recordings, the Delmores seem less pious and devout on these sessions and more concerned with celebration than lamentation. —*Richie Unterberger*

Lonesome Yodel Blues / 1985 / Old Homestead ✦✦✦✦
Eighteen of their early sides, recorded between 1933 and 1940, focusing on the more traditional elements of their repertoire. As the title implies, the brothers do often actually yodel throughout the proceedings, although in a more restrained fashioned than many of their peers. Remastered nicely from original copies of these rare singles, though some unavoidable surface noise is evident. —*Richie Unterberger*

Early Sacred Songs / 1985 / Old Homestead ✦✦✦✦
Fourteen of their more spiritually inclined tracks, mostly cut between 1935 and 1940. Those who favor secular material over gospel or traditional spirituals shouldn't be wary of this release because of its lyrical content. If you enjoy early country harmonizing, or any of the other material the Delmores cut in their early days, you'll like this as well. Aside from the nominally different lyrical concerns (presented here with humility and without preaching), the basic strengths of the pair remain intact: peerless close harmonizing, fine acoustic guitar playing, and strong songs that can be enjoyed regardless of what your faith (or lack thereof) may be. —*Richie Unterberger*

Sand Mountain Blues / 1986 / County ✦✦✦✦
The Delmores' recordings for King in the mid-'40s found them shifting away from traditional sounds into more energetic boogies that foreshadowed—however faintly—the blend of R&B and country that would give birth to rock 'n' roll. This has 14 sides from 1944-49, some of which feature stellar sidemen as guitarist Merle Travis, mandolinist Jethro Burns, and harmonica player Wayne Raney. —*Richie Unterberger*

★ **Freight Train Boogie** / 1993 / Ace ✦✦✦✦✦
It's kind of a toss-up as to whether this or the German *When They Let the Hammer Fall* is the best compilation of the Delmores' best work from the late '40s and early '50s. *When They Let the Hammer Fall* is more raucous and uptempo; the 20-track *Freight Train Boogie*, though, has more variety. *Freight Train Boogie* is much easier to locate in the US than *When They Let the Hammer Fall*. In addition, there's a fair amount of duplication between the anthologies, though each includes several noteworthy songs not on the other. In any case, you won't be disappointed by *Freight Train Boogie*, whether it's your first exposure to the Delmores or not. Featuring King material from 1946-1951, it has plenty of high-spirited country boogies, balanced by more traditionally folk-oriented material ("Sand Mountain Blues," "Weary Day") and bluesy, slower numbers, including their biggest hit (and one of their best), "Blues Stay Away from Me." These sides were not only some of the finest country music of the era, but important building blocks of rockabilly and early rock 'n' roll. —*Richie Unterberger*

Brown's Ferry Blues / County ✦✦✦
The Delmores recorded a wealth of material in the 1930s and early 1940s, encompassing both country and sacred songs; many of these sides have been reissued on the County label. All of them are good. *Brown's Ferry Blues* may be recommended as an introductory volume because of its range of material (ranging from 1933 to 1941), much of which is bluesy in nature. —*Richie Unterberger*

Iris Dement

b. Jan. 5, 1961, Paragould, AR
Guitar, Vocals / Singer-Songwriter, Country-Folk, Alternative Country, Neo-Traditionalist Country
One of the most celebrated country-folk performers of her day, singer-songwriter Iris Dement was born on January 5, 1961, in rural Paragould, AR, the youngest of 14 children. At the age of three, her devoutly religious family moved to California, where she grew up singing gospel music; during her teenage years, however, she was first exposed to country, folk, and R&B, drawing influence from Loretta Lynn, Johnny Cash, Bob Dylan, and Joni Mitchell. Upon graduating high school, she relocated to Kansas City to attend college.

After a series of jobs waitressing and typing, Dement first began composing songs at the age of 25. Honing her skills at open-mike nights, in 1988 she moved to Nashville, where she contacted producer Jim Rooney, who helped her land a record contract. Dement did not make her recording debut until 1992, when her independent label offering *Infamous Angel* won almost universal acclaim thanks to her pure, evocative vocal style and spare, heartfelt songcraft. Despite a complete lack of support from country radio, the record's word-of-mouth praise earned her a deal with Warner Bros., which reissued *Infamous Angel* in 1993 as well as its follow-up, 1994's stunning *My Life*. Her third LP, 1996's eclectic *The Way I Should*, marked a dramatic change not only in its more rock-influenced sound but also in its subject matter; where Dement's prior work was introspective and deeply personal, *The Way I Should* was fiercely political, tackling topics like sexual abuse, religion, government policy, and Vietnam. —*Jason Ankeny*

● **Infamous Angel** / 1992 / Philo ✦✦✦✦
Dement emerges as a wonderfully gifted performer with this debut, a loose concept record about family, innocence, and maturity. Though largely a country/folk outing, the bluesy "Sweet Forgiveness" hints at the eclecticism of her later work; already firmly ensconced is her remarkable voice, which evokes the emotional upheaval of her songs with stunning clarity. —*Jason Ankeny*

My Life / 1993 / Warner Brothers ✦✦✦✦
Since her beautiful debut record on Philo, Iris Dement has graduated to the majors with her style intact. She has a confessional spirit and maintains her perspective as a free thinker all the while. The album is dedicated to her father and it is lovely throughout. These are songs that sound like they've always been around. —*Richard Meyer*

The Way I Should Be / Oct. 8, 1996 / ✦✦✦

Derailers
....
Honky Tonk, Bakersfield Sound, Alternative Country
A honky-tonk band in the tradition of Buck Owens and the Buck-aroos, Austin, TX's Derailers were led by vocalist/rhythm guitarist Tony Villanueva and lead guitarist Brian Hofeldt, longtime friends who grew up together in Oregon. After playing in various Portland-area rockabilly outfits, Villanueva relocated to Texas at the age of 19, and Hofeldt soon tagged along; after settling in Aus-tin, the duo joined forces with Vic Gerard Ziolkowski, the bassist in a band called Two Hoots and a Holler, and began focusing on playing straightforward honky tonk music. In 1995, the Derailers issued their first LP, *Live Tracks;* following their second release, 1996's *Jackpot,* Terry Kirkendall became the group's permanent drummer. —*Jason Ankeny*

Jackpot / Feb. 27, 1996 / WTR ✦✦✦

Desert Rose Band
....
Country-Rock
The Desert Rose Band formed in 1985. One of the founders was Chris Hillman, a former member of the Byrds and the Flying Burrito Brothers, who sang lead vocals, played guitar and mando-lin and functioned as the group's primary songwriter. The original lineup included banjoist/guitarist Herb Pedersen, guitarist John Jorgenson, pedal steel guitarist Jay Dee Maness, bassist Bill Bry-son, and drummer Steve Duncan. Nearly all of the members were professional studio musicians before joining the group.

In 1986, the Desert Rose Band released a cover of Johnnie and Jack's hit "Ashes of Love." The song hit the Top 30 the following year, as did their self-titled debut album, which also produced three Top Ten singles, including the No. 1 "He's Back and I'm Blue." In 1988, the group released their second album, *Running;* among their subsequent hits were "Summer Wind" and the chart topper "I Still Believe in You." The band's 1989 album *Pages of Life* spawned three more major hits including the Top Ten "Story of Love," which would prove to be their last major hit. In 1992, the group's lineup underwent a few changes when Duncan was replaced by Tim Grogan, Maness was replaced by Tom Brumley, and Jeff Ross replaced Jorgenson. The new lineup of the Desert Rose Band recorded three more albums, *True Love* (1992), *Tradi-tional,* and *Life Goes On* (both 1993), before breaking up in 1994. —*Sandra Brennan*

The Desert Rose Band / 1987 / Curb ✦✦✦✦
For those concerned that California country might have disap-peared, the mid-'80s emergence of the Desert Rose Band, South-ern Pacific, and Dwight Yoakam put those fears to rest. While S-Pac leaned toward country-rock, and Yoakam hits hard on the honky tonk sound, TDRB offers just a tinge of bluegrass, lots of energy, and intriguing harmonies. The cuts "One Step Forward," "Love Reunited," and "Leave This Town" are simply stunning. —*Tom Roland*

★ **Running** / 1988 / Curb ✦✦✦✦✦
This is certainly a good representation of the work the Desert Rose Band did in their prime and a project that remains a favor-ite. With some solid songwriting by Chris Hillman and a cover of Buck Owens' " Hello Trouble," this second release is a definitive work. With hits like "I Still Believe in You," "Summer Wind" and John Hiatt's "She Don't Love Nobody," there is nothing lacking in either performance, production, or material. Like their first release, 1987's *Desert Rose Band, Running* was based upon the experience of the bandmembers as musicians, songwriters, and singers who were (and continue to be) an important part of the Bakersfield-Los Angeles music community. Both Hillman and Herb Pedersen have impressive resumes that include working with the Byrds, Gram Parsons, Buck Owens, and Emmylou Har-ris. As for Steve Duncan, Bill Bryson, Jay Dee Maness, and John Jorgenson, each had equally brilliant backgrounds as California musicians and were recognized as such. Be it Bakersfield honky tonk, love songs or bluegrass, the Desert Rose Band delivered. This release was followed by *Pages of Love* in 1989 and a great-est-hits package in 1990, *A Dozen Roses/Greatest Hits.* By 1992

members started leaving the band and the last American release was issued in 1993 on Curb, *Life Goes On.* Still, *Running* is the work that listeners will remember with the most affection and longing. —*Jana Pendragon*

She Don't Love Nobody / 1989 / Curb ✦✦✦

Pages of Life / 1990 / Curb ✦✦✦
This contains "In Another Lifetime," "Time Passes Me By," "Start All Over Again," and other favorites. —*AMG*

● **A Dozen Roses: Greatest Hits** / 1991 / Curb ✦✦✦✦
A showcase for Hillman's pop-country vocals and the consider-able chops of bandmembers such as Herb Pedersen. Together they made some of the best country singles of the late '80s, all col-lected here. —*William Ruhlmann*

True Love / 1991 / Curb ✦✦✦
True Love proves that the Desert Rose Band has a knack for mix-ing a country-pop attack with pure bluegrass harmonies, making music that is accessible to both mainstream country fans and hardcore bluegrass fanatics. Though *True Love* has too much mediocre material to make it rank among their best, it is never-theless a very good collection, featuring a wonderful version of Peter Rowan's "Undying Love" that features gorgeous duet vocals between Chris Hillman and Alison Krauss. —*Stephen Thomas Erlewine*

Traditional / 1993 / Curb ✦✦

Life Goes On / Sep. 21, 1993 / Curb ✦✦✦✦

Al Dexter (Albert Poindexter)
....
b. May 4, 1902, Jacksonville, TX, d. Jan. 28, 1984, Lewisville, TX
Guitar, Violin, Vocals / Traditional Country, Cowboy, Honky Tonk, Nashville Sound/Countrypolitan
Al Dexter earned a spot in the popular music canon when he wrote "Pistol Packin' Mama" in 1942. Recorded by him a year later, the single sold three million copies—not counting sheet music—in less than two years, and was ranked the third most popular song of the war years. Both Bing Crosby (with the Andrew Sisters) and Frank Sinatra recorded "Pistol Packin' Mama" for hits, and the song influenced country's pop-influenced Nashville Sound of the '50s. It's difficult to believe, but Dexter also managed to influence the honky tonk style that later proved a vivid counterpoint to the Nashville Sound. He owned a bar for a time during the '30s, and popularized the term honky tonk—slang for both rowdy bars and later the music that emerged from their jukeboxes—on his 1937 recording "Honky Tonk Blues." However, the popular theory that Dexter actually coined the term is full of holes; he had never heard of honky tonk before his songwriting partner James B. Paris suggested it as a title in 1936.

Al Dexter began playing square dances around oil-rich eastern Texas during the 1920s. The Depression forced him to work as a house painter, but Dexter began moonlighting after he formed the Texas Troopers in the early '30s. The group recorded for Okeh and Vocalion during the rest of the '30s and into the '40s. In 1944—the first year the charts could be accurately pre-dicted—Dexter scored four No. 1s on the Country charts. "Pistol Packin' Mama" was re-released on the B-side of "Rosalita," and both songs hit No. 1 in January 1944. His biggest hit of the year came in March, though, when "So Long Pal" spent 13 weeks at No. 1 on the country charts—its B-side "Too Late to Worry, Too Blue to Cry" stayed at the top for two weeks.

The last of the war years was also successful for Al Dexter: "I'm Losing My Mind over You" / "I'll Wait for You Dear," hit No. 1 and No. 2 respectively in January 1945, with the former spending seven weeks at No. 1. His second double-sided hit of the year, "Tri-flin' Gal" / "I'm Lost Without You," both hit the Top Five in August. In February 1946, Dexter's "Guitar Polka" spent almost four months at No. 1; it was his biggest country hit and managed the Top 20 on the pop charts (also producing the No. 2 B-side "Honey Do You Think It's Wrong"). After "Wine, Women and Song" also hit No. 1 later in 1946, Dexter recorded three more Top Five singles during 1946-47, "It's Up to You," "Kokomo Island" and

"Down at the Roadside Inn." His final chart singles were the 1948 Top 15's "Rock and Rye Rag" and "Calico Rag."

All told, Al Dexter received 12 gold records for million-sellers in the five-year period from 1943 to 1948. He won an Oscar for "Guitar Polka" and was voted the Leading Artist of 1946 by the Jukebox Operators Association. In the late '40s, Al Dexter opened his own club in Dallas; he performed there until his retirement. Dexter was inducted into the Nashville Songwriters Hall of Fame in 1971. —*John Bush*

● **Pistol Packin' Mama** / 1961 / Harmony ✦✦✦✦

Diamond Rio

Progressive Bluegrass, Contemporary Country

Diamond Rio is a '90s country band with bluegrass sensibilities noted for its exceptional musicianship. Each of the four members—lead vocalist/guitarist Marty Roe, lead guitarist/banjo player Jimmy Olander, mandolin player/singer Gene Johnson, keyboardist Dan Truman, bassist Dana Williams, and drummer Brian Prout—were involved in music long before the band's formation: Roe began performing professionally and touring at age 12 with Windsong, while Jimmy Olander was a veteran of the Nitty Gritty Dirt Band and Foster & Lloyd. Johnson, meanwhile, had worked with David Bromberg and J.D. Crowe; Williams' uncles were the famed Osborne Brothers, and Truman, a classically trained pianist, got his start playing with Brigham Young University's Young Ambassadors.

In time, each future member of Diamond Rio ended up playing at Nashville's Opryland as the Tennessee River Boys. After performing bluegrass there for seven years, the band managed to snag a contract with Arista, taking their current band name from a passing truck. Diamond Rio released their self-titled debut album in 1991. "Meet Me in the Middle," the first single, went to No.1 ; both follow-up singles, "Mirror Mirror" and "Mama Don't Forget to Pray for Me," were also substantial hits. Later that year, their second album, *Close to the Edge*, came out and their string of successes continued. *Love a Little Stronger* appeared in 1994, followed by *IV* in 1996. —*Sandra Brennan*

● **Diamond Rio** / 1991 / Arista ✦✦✦✦

One of the most successful debut albums in country music, *Diamond Rio* sparked plenty of hits—"Meet Me in the Middle," "Mama Don't Forget to Pray for Me," "Nowhere Bound," "Norma Jean Riley"—by combining bluegrass harmonies, old-fashioned country virtues, and just enough rock to keep things moving. —*Brian Mansfield*

Close to the Edge / 1992 / Arista ✦✦✦

On *Close to the Edge*, Diamond Rio took the cue of the debut's best songs and created an entire album cut from the same cloth. Diamond Rio's strongest material emphasizes the virtues of God, family, and honest living—traditional stuff, no doubt influenced by the members' bluegrass background. But while most folks who'd claim divine intervention in their relationship sound sappy at best, Marty Roe comes off as earnest and convincing. Unfortunately, amid hits like "In a Week or Two" and "Oh Me, Oh My, Sweet Baby," *Close to the Edge* reveals such weaknesses as a penchant for bad puns ("This Romeo ain't got Julie yet"—ouch!). —*Brian Mansfield*

Love a Little Stronger / 1994 / Arista ✦✦✦

Spurred by the relatively lackluster performance of *Close to the Edge* (it barely went gold compared to the debut's platinum), Diamond Rio explored the musical possibilities of their talents rather than going for easy commercial success. The instrumentalists, particularly Jimmy Olander and mandolinist Gene Johnson, assume larger roles on songs like "Love a Little Stronger" and the instrumental "Appalachian Dream," but they rarely show off. The band members even tap into an acoustic jazz-rock mode for "Kentucky Mine," one of the best songs they've ever recorded. —*Brian Mansfield*

IV / Feb. 27, 1996 / Arista ✦✦✦✦

Though the group wasn't able to regain its commercial status with *Love a Little Stronger,* Diamond Rio decided not to play things safe with *IV.* Taking its cue from its predecessor, *IV*

explores a number of different country subgenres, thereby demonstrating the versatility and depth of its musicians. However, there's a problem when musicians are this talented—the music is impressive on the surface, but it rarely gels together into something memorable. —*Thom Owens*

Hazel Dickens

b. Jun. 1, 1935, Mercer County, WV
Vocals / Folk, Old-Time, Traditional Country

Protest and folk singer Hazel Dickens grew up the eighth of 11 children in a large, poor mining family in West Virginia, and she has since used elements of country and bluegrass to speak about two causes close to her heart: the plight of non-unionized mineworkers and feminism, the latter born not of the '60s movement but out of traditional values. Dickens learned about music from her father, an occasional banjo player and Baptist minister who drove trucks for a mining company to make a living. She was influenced early by country traditionalists such as Uncle Dave Macon, the Monroe Brothers, and the Carter Family. Her family's dire poverty forced Dickens to move to Baltimore when she was 19, where she worked in factories with her sister and two brothers.

The four displaced siblings often attended old-timey festivals and gatherings, watching others and performing themselves. At one of these festivals, Hazel Dickens met Mike Seeger (younger brother of folk legend Pete Seeger), and the two formed a band with her brothers. Over the ensuing decade, Dickens became active in the folk/bluegrass movement around the Baltimore/Washington, D.C. area, playing bass and singing with several bands, including the Greenbriar Boys, who toured with Joan Baez in the '60s.

Around this time she met Mike Seeger's wife, Alice Gerrard, a classically trained singer also interested in old-time music. At the nearby Library of Congress, the two began researching early feminist songs and then incorporated them into their repertoire. The duo performed throughout the country—particularly the South—and recorded two albums for Folkways, *Who's That Knocking (And Other Bluegrass Country Music)* (1965) and *Won't You Come & Sing for Me* (1973).

The two separated in 1973—two later albums were compiled from previous recordings—and Hazel Dickens began her solo career with a flourish. She recorded four songs for the soundtrack to the Academy Award-winning documentary about coal-mining, *Harlan Country, USA.* Three years later, she contributed to the soundtrack for *With Babies and Banners,* and began a solo career five years later. Her three solo albums for Rounder, *Hard Hitting Songs for Hard Hit People* (1981), *By the Sweat of My Brow* (1983), and *It's Hard to Tell the Singer from the Song* (1987), include old-timey country alongside protest songs and songs in a more contemporary country style. Rounder's *A Few Old Memories* distills the best of the three albums onto one disc. —*John Bush*

Hard Hitting Songs / 1980 / Rounder ✦✦✦

Hard Hitting Songs for Hard Hit People is a very good record that deals with the out-of-work, down-on-his-luck, average American. It features Nancy & Norman Blake, Tony Trischka, Ross Barenberg, James Bryan, Matt Glaser, Barry Mitterhoff, and Buddy Spicher. —*Chip Renner*

★ **By the Sweat of My Brow** / 1983 / Rounder ✦✦✦✦✦

A great record, which features "By the Sweat of My Brow," "Old & in the Way," "The Ballad of Ira Hayes," and "Your Greedy Heart." —*Chip Renner*

Hard to Tell the Singer from the Song / 1987 / Rounder ✦✦✦✦

Dickens covers Dylan's "Only a Hobo" and Dallas Frazier's "California Cottonfields." Jerry Douglas, Pat Enright, Roy Husky, Ross Barenberg, and Mike Compton back her up. —*Chip Renner*

Hazel & Alice / 1995 / Rounder ✦✦✦✦

A Few Old Memories / Rounder ✦✦✦

A Few Old Memories collects highlights from Hazel Dickens' early '80s albums for Rounder Records. Like the original studio albums, the compilation balances excellent renditions of standards with new songs written in the same vein. Consequently, *Few Old Mem-*

ories is a terrific overview of Dickens' old timey revival and a good introduction to her surprisingly influential career. —*Thom Owens*

Won't You Come & Sing for Me / Smithsonian/Folkways ✦✦✦✦

Little Jimmy Dickens

b. Dec. 19, 1925, Bolt, WV
Guitar, Vocals / Novelty, Traditional Country, Nashville Sound/ Countrypolitan

Little Jimmy Dickens is the master of the country novelty songs, as well as a renowned ballad singer. He is also known for his diminutive stature—he's less than five feet tall—and his affection for flamboyant, rhinestone-studded outfits and country humor. Although he never had a consistent presence on the charts, he managed to have hits in every decade between the 1940s and the 1970s, and he became one of the Grand Ole Opry's most popular performers.

Dickens was the 13th child of a West Virginian farmer. During his childhood, he fell in love with music and had a dream of performing on the Grand Ole Opry. He began performing professionally while he was a student at the University of West Virginia in the late '30s, singing on a local radio station. Dickens left school shortly after he received his regular radio job. He began traveling around the country, singing on radio shows in Indiana, Ohio, and Michigan under the name Jimmy the Kid. Roy Acuff heard Dickens sing on a radio show in Saginaw, MI, and invited him to sing on the Grand Ole Opry.

In 1949, Dickens—who was now using the name Little Jimmy Dickens—became a permanent member of the Grand Ole Opry. That year, he also signed a record contract with Columbia Records, releasing his first single, "Take an Old Cold Tater (And Wait)," in the spring of 1949. The song became a Top Ten hit and launched a string of hit novelty, ballad, and honky tonk singles that lasted for a year, which included "Country Boy," "A-Sleeping at the Foot of the Bed," "Hillbilly Fever," and "My Heart's Bouquet." Early in the '50s, he formed a band called the Country Boys, which featured a steel guitar, two lead guitars, and drums. With their spirited, traditional country approach and vague rockabilly inflections, the band didn't sound like their Nashville contemporaries. Perhaps that's why Dickens only had one hit between 1950 and 1962—1954's "Out Behind the Barn."

Dickens bounced back to the Top Ten with the ballad "The Violet and the Rose" in 1962. Three years later, he had his biggest hit, "May the Bird of Paradise Fly Up Your Nose." The single topped the country charts and crossed over to No. 15 on the pop charts. Although his next single, "When the Ship Hit the Sand," was moderately successful, Dickens wasn't able to replicate the success of "May the Bird of Paradise Fly Up Your Nose." In 1968, he stopped recording for Columbia, signing with Decca Records, where he had three minor hits in the late '60s and early '70s. In 1971, he moved to United Artists, which resulted in two more small hits, but by that time he had begun to concentrate on performing as his main creative outlet. Dickens continued to tour and perform at the Grand Ole Opry into the '90s, becoming one of the most beloved characters in country music. —*Stephen Thomas Erlewine*

Raisin' the Dickens / 1957 / Columbia ✦✦✦
Aside from the fact that this contains a couple of Dickens' hits, the album is just OK. It relies a little too much on his gimmick of being the little guy with a lot of energy and not enough in the songs. —*Jim Worbois*

Little Jimmy Dickens Sings Out Behind the Barn / 1962 / Columbia ✦✦✦

Out Behind the Barn / 1962 / Columbia ✦✦

May the Bird of Paradise Fly Up Your Nose / 1965 / Columbia ✦✦✦

Big Man in Country Music / 1968 / Columbia ✦✦✦

● **I'm Little but I'm Loud: The Little Jimmy Dickens Collection** / May 1996 / Razor & Tie ✦✦✦✦
I'm Little but I'm Loud: The Little Jimmy Dickens Collection is a thorough retrospective of Dickens' prime years, running from the 1949 Top Ten hit "Take an Old Cold Tater (And Wait)" to the 1967

Top 40 hit "Country Music Lover." In between those two songs are no less than 20 tracks, including all of his Top Ten hits ("Country Boy," "My Heart's Bouquet," "A-Sleeping at the Foot of the Bed," "Hillbilly Fever," "Out Behind the Barn," "The Violet and a Rose," and the No. 1 "May the Bird of Paradise Fly Up Your Nose"). In short, *I'm Little but I'm Loud* is the only comprehensive retrospective ever assembled on Jimmy Dickens. —*Stephen Thomas Erlewine*

Joe Diffie

b. 1958, Tulsa, OK
Vocals / Progressive Country, Contemporary Country, New Traditionalist

Joe Diffie was among the generation of artists who blended traditional country sounds with '90s sensibilities. Born to a musical family in Tulsa, Diffie was a member of his high school's gospel group Genesis II, local rockers Blitz, and the bluegrass band the Special Edition. After college, the Special Edition began to gain an audience and appeared in several festivals. Diffie then began playing country music with his aunt Dawn Anita and his sister Monica. Soon, one of his early songs, "Love on the Rocks," was recorded by Hank Thompson. Diffie moved to Nashville and began working for Gibson Guitars while continuing to write songs. Holly Dunn recorded one of his collaborations, "There Goes My Heart Again," in 1989.

Diffie's debut single, "Home," climbed to No.1 in 1990; that year he also debuted at the Grand Ole Opry. This was followed by three Top Five hits, all of which he co-wrote, as well as a 1990 debut album, *A Thousand Winding Roads*. Diffie's second album, *Regular Joe*, contained several hits, including "Is It Cold in Here." In 1993, he released his third album, *Honky Tonk Attitude*. *Third Rock from the Sun* appeared in 1994 and both *Life's So Funny* and *Mr. Christmas* were released the following year. —*Sandra Brennan*

A Thousand Winding Roads / 1990 / Epic ✦✦✦✦
This likeable new country voice from Oklahoma praises home and hearth. —*Mark A. Humphrey*

● **Regular Joe** / 1992 / Epic ✦✦✦✦
Diffie's second album has all the cliches of country music, and all the good stuff too. If "Ain't That Bad Enough" is a run-of-the-mill song, Diffie rescues it by tearing the melody loose from its mooring. He's also willing to push the line: of all Diffie's country heroes—and you'll be able to name them after one listen—maybe only Merle Haggard would rock out as hard as Diffie does on the title track. —*Brian Mansfield*

Honky Tonk Attitude / Apr. 20, 1993 / Epic ✦✦✦
Taking a cue from some of his peers, balladeer Diffie makes a point to get rowdy on this, his most commercially successful album to date. Besides the title track, it includes the hits "Prop Me up Beside the Jukebox (If I Die)" and "John Deere Green." —*Dan Cooper*

Third Rock from the Sun / 1994 / Epic ✦✦✦✦
Third Rock from the Sun represents a bit of a musical departure for Joe Diffie. Though he keeps his basic honky tonk roots, he experiments more, adding more rock flourishes to his sound. Not all of his attempts are successful, and his ballads are frequently compelling. Nevertheless, it's a little distressing that he has only written one song on the album—there's no reason for his well to dry up by only his fourth record. —*Thom Owens*

Mr. Christmas / 1995 / Epic ✦✦✦
Joe Diffie's holiday album is a collection of standards and newly written Christmas material, all performed in the singer's trademark style. Most of his fans will enjoy the record, although the record lacks genuine inspiration; it's pleasant, but it's not particularly distinguished. —*Stephen Thomas Erlewine*

Life's So Funny / 1995 / Epic ✦✦✦
Led by the tongue-in-cheek single "Bigger Than the Beatles," Joe Diffie's fifth album *Life's So Funny* delivers the relaxed, funny contemporary country that fans have come to expect from the singer. *Life's So Funny* isn't as consistently engaging as his previous *Third Rock from the Sun*, yet its warm sense of humor and

Joe Diffie

varied collection of ballads and mid-tempo rockers makes it a worthy follow-up to the most popular record Diffie ever released. —*Thom Owens*

Dillard & Clark

Progressive Bluegrass, Traditional Bluegrass, Country-Rock

Dillard & Clark, a duo featuring former Byrd Gene Clark and Doug Dillard of the Dillards, was one of the first country-rock groups to form in the late '60s. The group formed in 1968 and became one of pioneers of country-rock, but dissolved after releasing only two albums.

In 1969, Doug Dillard recorded his first solo album, *The Banjo Album*, which featured such rock musicians as Gene Clark and Bernie Leadon. In the spring of 1968, Dillard toured England as a member of the Byrds, which led to the duo of Dillard & Clark, which officially formed later that summer. The duo secured a record contract with A&M and released their debut album, *The Fantastic Expedition of Dillard and Clark*, late in 1968. The record was recorded with Bernie Leadon (guitar), Don Beck (dobro, mandolin), and David Jackson (bass). Dillard & Clark toured following the release of the album; their supporting band featured former Byrd Michael Clarke on drums.

Dillard & Clark began recording a second album early in 1969 with a new supporting band. The new lineup featured Leadon, fiddler Byron Berline, drummer Jon Corneal, and guitarist Donna Washburn; steel guitarist Sneaky Pete Kleinow and Chris Hillman, who were both members of the Flying Burrito Brothers, also guested on the album. The resulting record, *Through the Morning, Through the Night*, appeared later in the year. After its release, Leadon left the duo; he would join the Eagles soon after his departure. Clark decided to pursue a solo career in early 1970. Dillard continued his solo career, using the remaining members of the duo's backing band as the core of his new outfit, the Expedition.

Dillard and Clark continued to pursue solo careers throughout the '80s and '90s, with Dillard garnering more success and critical acclaim than Clark. Gene Clark died in 1991 at the age of 49. —*Stephen Thomas Erlewine*

★ **The Fantastic Expedition/Through the Morning** / 1968 / Mobile Fidelity ✦✦✦✦✦

There's good writing, singing, and playing on this single-disc containing Dillard & Clark's two albums, *Fantastic Expedition* and *Through the Morning, Through the Night*. Songs on these two albums have been covered by Linda Ronstadt, the Eagles, and others. —*Kenneth M. Cassidy*

Grass Roots (Half LP + Half Burritoes) / 1972 / Mayfair ✦✦✦

Gene Clark & Doug Dillard / 1975 / Ariola ✦✦✦✦

Kansas City Southern / 1975 / Ariola ✦✦✦

Take Me Along for the Ride / 1992 / Vanguard ✦✦
This latter-day effort from the Dillards features new material molded in the band's late-'60s electric bluegrass sound. —*Jason Ankeny*

Doug Dillard

b. Mar. 6, 1937, Salem, MO
Banjo, Guitar, Vocals / Progressive Bluegrass, Traditional Bluegrass, Country-Rock

Doug Dillard's music blended bluegrass, country-rock, and pop. Throughout his long and varied career, he was one of the leading banjoists in country and bluegrass music, pioneering a distinctive instrumental style. Dillard was raised in Salem, MO, where he and his younger brother Rodney began playing bluegrass music together in grade school. After playing together in a series of bands, they formed the Dillards in 1962, issuing the first in a series of successful LPs a year later.

In addition to working with the side project the Folkswingers, in 1966 Doug played with ex-Byrd Gene Clark and the Gosdin Brothers on their self-titled collaboration, and in 1967, he and Rodney played on the soundtrack for *Bonnie & Clyde*. Also in 1967, Doug left the Dillards to form a duo with Gene Clark. Dillard & Clark released their debut album, *Fantastic Expedition*, in 1968, supported by a band that included guitarist Bernie Leadon, bassist David Jackson, and dobro/mandolin player Don Beck. Ex-Byrd drummer Michael Clarke joined Dillard & Clark on their first tour and second album, 1969's *Through the Morning, Through the Night*. Clark left the band in 1970. Dillard continued with the group, renaming them Dillard and the Expedition. However, he left the band in 1971; the remaining members became Country Gazette.

In 1971, Dillard formed a new band, Dillard & the Country Coalition, but he went solo by the end of the year. His first solo effort was the soundtrack for *Vanishing Point*. In 1973 and 1974, Dillard released two albums, *Dueling Banjos* and *Douglas Flint Dillard—You Don't Need a Reason to Sing*. During this time, he also did session work. In 1977, he recorded *Glitter-Grass from the Nashwood Hollyville Strings* with his brother Rodney and John Hartford.. The following year, Doug released his third solo album, *Heaven*, which was produced by Rodney. Following its release, he formed the Doug Dillard Band, which featured fiddler Byron Berline. In 1979, Doug, Rodney, and Berline appeared in the film *The Rose*. In 1980, he returned to Salem to record a reunion album with the Dillards. That year Dillard also worked on the soundtrack of *Popeye*. During the '80s and '90s, Doug Dillard continued to record and play live concerts; occasionally, he reunited with his brother Rodney. —*Sandra Brennan*

The Banjo Album / 1969 / Together ✦✦✦✦
Recorded following Gene Clark's exit from the Dillard and Clark Expedition, Doug Dillard cut *The Banjo Album* with the group's remaining members. Byron Berline also makes a cameo. —*Jason Ankeny*

Duelin' Banjos / 1973 / 20th Century ✦✦✦✦

Douglas Flint Dillard / 1974 / 20th Century ✦✦✦

You Don't Need a Reason to Sing / 1974 / 20th Century ✦✦

Heaven / 1979 / Flying Fish ✦✦✦
A gospel album featuring Dan Crary, Byron Berline, John Hartford, and Herb Pedersen. It includes an excellent cover of "Turn Your Radio On." —*Chip Renner*

● **Jackrabbit** / 1980 / Flying Fish ✦✦✦✦
A live album from the Telluride Bluegrass Festival, with guests Sam Bush and Byron Berline. —*Chip Renner*

What's That? / 1986 / Flying Fish ✦✦✦
A solid album. —*Chip Renner*

Heartbreak Hotel / 1989 / Flying Fish ✦✦

The Dillards

Progressive Bluegrass, Traditional Bluegrass, Country-Rock

During the '60s, the Dillards helped bring bluegrass to a wider audience, both through their records and their appearances on television and film. For the next three decades, the band continued to perform in various incarnations, all the while remaining one of the most popular bluegrass bands in America.

Brothers Doug and Rodney Dillard formed the core of the original lineup of the Dillards. The brothers were born and raised in Salem, MO; while attending grade school, they began playing bluegrass together—Doug played the banjo, while Rodney played the guitar. From the mid- to late '50s, the brothers appeared on the Ozark Mountain Boys' radio program, the *Ozark Jubilee*. In 1958, Doug and Rodney recorded two singles—"Doug's Breakdown" and "Mama Don't 'Low"—for K-Ark Records. Between 1958 and 1960, the duo played with three bluegrass bands—the Hawthorn Brothers, the Lewis Brothers, and Joe Noel & the Dixie Ramblers—before forming the first incarnation of the Dillards with Mitch Jayne and Dean Webb.

The Dillards headed to California in 1962. Less than a week after their arrival, Jim Dickson saw them jamming with the Greenbriar Boys and he signed the group to Elektra. After the Dillards inked their deal, they were also hired to appear on the *Andy Griffith Show* as the slightly demented hayseeds the Darling Family.

In 1963, the Dillards released their first album, *Back Porch Bluegrass*. That same year, Doug and Rodney joined with Dean Webb, Glen Campbell, and Tut Taylor to form the Folkswingers, a side project that released two albums of string-band music for the World Pacific label during the mid-'60s.

In 1964, the Dillards released *Live....Almost!* By the time the album was released, the group had amplified their instruments, angering the purists that formed the core of the American bluegrass audience. Nevertheless, they developed a strong fan base. In 1965, they released the album *Pickin' and Fiddlin'*, which featured fiddler Byron Berline. Two years later, Doug and Rodney played on the soundtrack to *Bonnie and Clyde;* soon after, Doug left the band to form the Dillard & Clark Expedition with former Byrd Gene Clark.

He was replaced by banjo player Herb Pedersen and the group recorded their fourth album, *Wheatstraw Suite;* released in 1968, it featured an increasingly adventurous musical approach, as did its follow-up, 1970's *Copperfields*. On these two albums, the Dillards added drums and steel guitar to their sound and began covering rock and folk songwriters like Bob Dylan, Lennon & McCartney, Gordon Lightfoot, John Prine, and Tim Hardin. Although neither record was a commercial success, they opened the doors for progressive bluegrass bands in the '70s.

In 1971, the Dillards had a minor pop hit with "It's About Time" and opened for Elton John on his first American tour. The following year, they released *Tribute to the American Duck*, but didn't release another album for a number of years, at which time the lineup had changed drastically to include Rodney Dillard, banjoist Billy Ray Lathum, bassist Jeff Gilkinson, drummer Paul York, and steel guitarist Buddy Emmons. In 1977, the Dillards released two albums, *The Dillards vs. the Incredible L.A. Time Machine* and *Glitter-Grass from the Nashwood Hollyville Strings;* the latter featured John Hartford and a reunion between Rodney and Doug. Three years later, they released *Homecoming and Reunion*, a document of the band's reunion in Salem on the town's "Dillard Day" celebration on August 8, 1980.

Later that same year, the group released *Mountain Rock*. Following the completion of the album, York retired from performing and the Dillards restructured their lineup; by the end of the year, the group consisted of Rodney Dillard, Joe Villegas, Eddie Ponder, and Peter Grant. For the next year, the band played a handful of concerts, but soon Rodney turned his attention to his new group, the Rodney Dillard Band.

Throughout the '80s, the Dillards were inactive, but the original lineup occasionally reunited. In the '90s, the Rodney Dillard Band regularly played at Silver Dollar City in Branson, and the Doug Dillard Band was a popular attraction on the bluegrass and folk circuit. —*Sandra Brennan*

Wheatstraw Suite / 1968 / Elektra ✦✦✦✦
A country-rock landmark of sorts, this album sounds sort of like a missing link between the Byrds and the Eagles, but with more of a country-bluegrass flavor than either of those groups ever had. The rock feel comes courtesy of an electric rhythm section, but the harmonies are very much country. Features mostly strong original material, along with imaginative covers of the Beatles' "I've Just Seen a Face" and Tim Hardin's "Reason to Believe." Another highlight is the overlooked "She Sang Hymns out of Tune," a great song that was obviously beloved on the late '60s L.A. scene, as at least four acts (Nilsson, the Dillards, Hearts & Flowers, and co-songwriter Jesse Lee Kincaid) tried to record it without hit success. —*Richie Unterberger*

Decade Waltz / 1979 / Flying Fish ✦✦✦
On this album one of the most important bands in the development of country-rock returns to its beginnings. —*AMG*

Homecoming & Family Reunion / 1979 / Flying Fish ✦✦✦
This is a pleasant album of several Dillard generations live at a picnic. —*Mark A. Humphrey*

★ **There Is a Time (1963-70)** / 1991 / Vanguard ✦✦✦✦✦
This is a 29-track retrospective of their influential 1963-1970 Elektra recordings of urban bluegrass. —*Mark A. Humphrey*

Let It Fly / 1991 / Vanguard ✦✦✦
Produced by Herb Pedersen of the Desert Rose Band, *Let It Fly* is a strong collection of traditional bluegrass with an electric twist. The album is one of the best records from the late '80s and '90s incarnation of the Dillards. —*Thom Owens*

Take Me Along for the Ride / 1992 / Vanguard ✦✦✦✦
Rodney Dillard leads the band's latter-day lineup through songs including "In My Life" and "Like a Hurricane" on this strong LP. —*Jason Ankeny*

Dean Dillon

b. Mar. 26, 1955, Lake City, TN

Vocals / Contemporary Country, Neo-Traditionalist Country

Dean Dillon was one of a wave of country performers in the early '90s trying to return the music to its traditional roots—in the process, he became one of the most successful songwriters of his day. Born in Lake City, TN, and raised in Detroit, Dillon learned to play guitar by watching his stepfather and two years later debuted in public singing Merle Haggard songs. He wrote his first songs at the age of 11 and began appearing on the Kathy Hill television show in Knoxville when he was 15.

Following high school, Dillon headed for Nashville, where he was eventually taken under the wing of songwriter Frank Dycus and had the opportunity to meet and play for his idol, Merle Haggard. Dillon traveled around North America for the next three years, pausing only to make a single, "Las Vegas Girl," as "Dean Dalton." In 1976, he landed the role of Hank Williams in the Country Music Show at Opryland USA in Knoxville. While there, a friend introduced him to songwriter John Schweers, who became Dillon's mentor. Three weeks later, Barbara Mandrell recorded three of Dillon's songs. In 1979, Jim Ed Brown and Helen Cornelius had a No. 1 hit with his "Lying Here in Love with You."

Dillon made his recording debut with "I'm into the Bottle (To Get You Out of My Mind)," a Top 30 hit. His next two singles also did well, and that year, he and Dycus penned George Strait's first hit, "Unwound"; several years later, Strait covered one of Dillon's early singles, "Nobody in His Right Mind (Would Have Left Her)," and had a No. 1 hit, further establishing Dillon's reputation as a songwriter. However, as Dillon's career developed, so did his problem with drugs and alcohol. In 1982, Jerry Bradley, who had signed him to RCA, paired the young songwriter—who had just been released from a rehabilitation center—with "King of the Honky Tonkers" Gary Stewart. The pairing worked, and their album *Brotherly Love* did well on the international markets.

When Dillon took a five-year hiatus from recording to concentrate on songwriting (and get his personal life in order), more artists covered his originals and collaborations, including Johnny

Rodriguez, Hank Williams, Jr., George Jones, David Allan Coe, Vern Gosdin, Steve Wariner, and Keith Whitley. In 1988, he released *Slick Nickel*, which contained the Top 40 hit "I Go to Pieces," written by Del Shannon. His 1989 album *I've Learned to Live* featured a duet with Tanya Tucker and three songs penned with Dycus. Dillon signed with Atlantic Records in 1991 and released *Out of Your Ever-Lovin' Mind*, his most successful album to date. — *Sandra Brennan*

I've Learned to Live / 1989 / Capitol ✦✦✦

Hot, Country, & Single / 1991 / Atlantic ✦✦✦✦
Dillon's second album features "Holed Up in Some Honky Tonk," recut from his *Out of Your Ever-Lovin Mind* LP. More serious fare can be found in "Everybody Knows," the latest in a long line of country portraits of hard-drinking loners. — *Jason Ankeny*

● **Out of Your Ever-Lovin' Mind** / 1991 / Atlantic ✦✦✦✦
Dillon's most commercially successful effort, *Out of Your Ever-Lovin' Mind* features such well-crafted compositions as "Holding My Own" and "Friday Night's Woman." — *Jason Ankeny*

Dixiana

Contemporary Country
Dixiana is a country band formed in 1986 by brothers Mark (bass/vocals) and Phil Lister (string instruments/vocals), along with keyboardist Randall Griffith and drummer Colonel Shuford. The group was scheduled to appear on *Nashville Now* when they suddenly lost their original lead singer; fortunately, the Listers' childhood friend Cindy Murphy, formerly a member of the bluegrass Wooden Nickel Band, agreed to be their primary vocalist. The group signed to Epic in 1992 and released their first self-titled album, which contained two Top 40 singles, "Waitin' for the Deal to Go Down" and "That's What I'm Working on Tonight." — *Sandra Brennan*

● **Dixiana** / Aug. 1991 / Epic ✦✦✦
This album contains "Are You over Her?," "Waitin' for the Deal to Go Down," and "A Little in Love," among other favorites. — *AMG*

Dixie Chicks

Progressive Bluegrass, Contemporary Folk
A charming acoustic group that combines Texas swing, upbeat bluegrass and Lennon Sister-style pop harmonies, the Dixie Chicks started as sidewalk singers in Dallas and grew to become favorites in folk clubs across the United States and Europe. Originally a quartet, singer-guitarist Robin Lacy left after the second album. Singer-bassist Laura Lynch, fiddler Martie Erwin, and banjo player Emily Erwin continued as a trio, augmented by two non-chick instrumentalists on drums and guitar. — *Michael McCall*

Thank Heavens for Dale Evans / 1992 / Crystal Clear ✦✦✦
Their first album captures their charm and eclectic tastes in its early, amateurish stages. Ragged in spots, but gloriously enthusiastic. — *Michael McCall*

● **Shouldn't a Told You That** / 1993 / Crystal Clear ✦✦✦✦
Down to a trio, the sound is more focused now, but only slightly less varied. With Laura Lynch taking lead vocals, and with help from producer Steve Fishell, the band sounds more professional and as delightful as ever. — *Michael McCall*

Little Ol' Cowgirl / Crystal Clear ✦✦✦
Their non-stop performance schedule quickly tightened the Dixie Chicks' sound, and their musical ability leaps forward in confidence and flair. They're still willing to try anything, at least once, which results in a collection that's uneven but entertaining. — *Michael McCall*

Dixie Gentlemen

Progressive Bluegrass, Traditional Bluegrass
During the folk revival of the early '60s, the Dixie Gentlemen were one of the most original bluegrass bands performing. The Alabama-based band was formed in the mid-'50s by mandolinist/vocalist Herschel Sizemore and banjoist/vocalist Rual Yarbrough, who met while playing in the Alabamians. When their guitarist

friend Jake Landers was discharged from the military, the three formed the Dixie Gentlemen.

During the late '50s, the group played in clubs throughout the South and appeared on local television shows. Fiddler Vassar Clements played with the Gentlemen for a time, as did fiddler Al Lester and a number of bassists. In 1959, the Dixie Gentlemen released their first singles—the gospel songs "Pray for Me" and "Three Steps." Later that year, the group recorded two albums of classic bluegrass songs, *Hootenanny N' Blue Grass* and *Blue Grass Down Home*, under the name the Blue Ridge Mountain Boys. Also in 1959, the group recorded an album with Tommy Jackson.

In 1963, the group released *The Country Style of the Dixie Gentlemen*, a record consisting of original songs, primarily writtten by Jake Landers. In 1966, the Dixie Gentlemen made their final album, *Blues and Bluegrass*, which featured Vassar Clements on fiddle and Tut Taylor on dobro. Following its release, the members pursued careers as sidemen for popular artists like Jimmy Martin. In 1971, Landers and Sizemore reunited as the Dixiemen and recorded four albums. The original Dixie Gentlemen and Vassar Clements reunited in 1972 to record *Together Once More*. Close to 20 years later, they again took time out from their solo careers to make *Take Me Back to Dixie*. — *Sandra Brennan*

● **Country Style of the Dixie Gentlemen** / 1963 / United Artists ✦✦✦✦

Deryl Dodd

Contemporary Country
Honky-tonker Deryl Dodd grew up in Dallas, TX, where he favored football over music throughout his formative years. When an injury permanently derailed his athletic career, his fellow students at Baylor University encouraged him to begin performing his music in public, and soon, he was one of the biggest attractions on the Waco club circuit. After graduating in 1987, he pursued music full-time, moving in 1991 to Nashville to form a band with his friend Brett Beavers. After supporting Martina McBride during her 1992 tour opening for Garth Brooks, Dodd sang backing vocals on McBride's second LP before embarking on a solo career. He also played in Tracy Lawrence's band and sang harmony on records by Radney Foster and George Ducas. After a 1994 demo deal fell through, Dodd issued his debut album *One Ride in Vegas* in 1996. — *Jason Ankeny*

One Ride in Vegas / Oct. 8, 1996 / ✦✦✦✦

John Doe

b. 1954, Decatur, IL
Bass, Vocals / Roots-Rock, Alternative Country-Rock
As one of the founding members of the Los Angeles punk band X, John Doe was one of the most influential figures in American alternative rock during the early '80s, but when he launched a solo career in the early '90s, he decided to pursue a rootsy, country-rock direction instead of continue with punk. X's latter-day albums exhibited a rockabilly and country influence, but it wasn't until Doe's 1990 debut, *Meet John Doe*, that he recorded a pure country album.

Meet John Doe was recorded during a hiatus in X's career. Following the release of the 1988 live album *Live at the Whiskey A Go-Go* the band went on hiatus. Initially, Doe concentrated on the acting career he began in 1986 with Oliver Stone's *Salvador*, appearing in *Road House* and the Jerry Lee Lewis biopic *Great Balls of Fire* in 1989. The following year, *Meet John Doe* was released on DGC to positive reviews, yet it didn't appeal to an audience outside of X's cult, peaking at 193 on the pop charts. Later in 1990, X began playing live again and Doe's solo musical career went on hiatus, although he continued to act in movies like *Pure Country, Liquid Dreams, Roadside Prophets, Wyatt Earp,* and *Georgia*.

Following X's 1993 reunion album *Hey Zeus!*, Doe signed a solo contract with Rhino/Forward. In the summer of 1995, Doe released *Kissingsohard*, a punkier album than his debut. A few months after its release, X released the live *Unclogged*, which would turn out to be its final album. In early 1996, X broke up, with John Doe turning his attention to his musical and acting career. — *Stephen Thomas Erlewine*

● **Meet John Doe** / 1990 / Geffen ✦✦✦✦
From the rock-out sound, slashing guitars, and near-howl of the unison singing, not to mention the temper of the lyrics, the lead-off track, "Let's Be Mad," could be by X, Doe's former band. Elsewhere on his debut solo album he takes a less punky approach, but this is still a charged, rocking record. — *William Ruhlmann*

Kissingsohard / 1995 / Forward/Rhino ✦✦✦
On John Doe's second solo album, *Kissingsohard*, he adds a bit more of a punk edge to his stark, country-based songs. While his songwriting isn't consistent, there's enough solid material here to make the album an engaging listen. — *Stephen Thomas Erlewine*

Johnny Dollar

b. Mar. 8, 1933, Kilgore, TX, d. Apr. 13, 1986
Vocals / Traditional Country, Nashville Sound/Countrypolitan
Vocalist Johnny Dollar (born John Washington Dollar, Jr. in Kilgore, TX) began his recording career in 1952 on Shelby Singleton's D Records, but these songs went nowhere. He then became a deejay in Louisiana and New Mexico while also leading the Texas Sons, who played regularly on *Louisiana Hayride*. By 1955, he left the Sons to join Martin McCullough's Light Crust Doughboys. Dollar signed with Columbia in 1964 but did not have a hit until two years later with the Top 50 song "Tear-Talk." His next song, "Stop the Start (Of Tears in My Heart)," reached the Top 15 and stayed there for months. That year and the following year he won Best New Artist awards from *Billboard* and *Record World* magazines, respectively. Dollar signed with Dot in 1967 and scored a minor hit before moving on to the Date label. There he scored two Top 40 hits with "The Wheels Fell Off the Wagon Again" (1967) and "Everybody's Got to Be Somewhere" (1968), billing himself as Johnny $ Dollar on the latter. After that, he moved to Chart and had two minor hits with "Big Rig Rollin' Man" (1968) and "Big Wheels Sing for Me" (1969). In 1970, he returned to Johnny Dollar and scored his final hit for Chart with "Truck Driver's Lament." When not involved in the music business, Dollar worked as a trucker, in the oil fields, in lumber yards, on a cattle ranch, and in life insurance. He died in 1986. — *Sandra Brennan*

Johnny Dollar / 1967 / Date ✦✦✦
● **Big Rig Rollin' Man** / 1969 / Chart ✦✦✦✦
Counry Hit Parade / 1969 / Chart ✦✦✦
My Soul Is Blue / 1980 / Isabel ✦✦✦

Jerry Douglas

b. 1955, Columbus, OH
Dobro / Progressive Bluegrass
As one of the premiere dobro players in bluegrass, new-acoustic, and country music, Jerry "Flux" Douglas toured and recorded with everyone from Emmylou Harris, Ricky Skaggs, and the Nitty Gritty Dirt Band to mandolin sensation David Grisman and banjo innovator Bela Fleck. Douglas' albums as a leader fully exploited the dobro's resonant guitar sound, his aggressive touch, incredibly fast finger picking, and deft use of the steel bar giving the instrument a bright, cutting tone-quality.

Born in Columbus, OH, Douglas was eight years old when his father, a bluegrass musician, introduced him to the dobro. He became further fascinated with the instrument upon hearing Josh Graves play it at a 1963 Flatt & Scruggs concert. By the time he was 16, Douglas had been playing in his father's band for a number of years; when the group played at a festival alongside the Country Gentlemen, the Gentlemen were impressed with the youth's playing and invited him to join them for the rest of the summer. Later Douglas worked with J.D. Crowe and the New South as well as David Grisman, and Boone Creek with Ricky Skaggs.

In 1978, Douglas made his solo debut with *Fluxology*. His next album, *Tennessee Fluxedo*, came out three years later. He began playing and recording with the Whites in 1983, and eventually left to focus on his solo career and much sought-after session

work. He recorded three albums for MCA in the late 1980s, most notably 1989's *Plant Early*, which marked a change toward a calmer, more textured direction. In the early '90s, Douglas and guitarists Albert Lee and Tal Farlow embarked upon a European tour for the National Council of Traditional Arts; he also began producing other artists and making regular appearances on the TNN show *American Music Shop*. In 1993, Douglas, guitarist Russ Barenberg, and bassist Edgar Meyer released the Sugar Hill album *Skip, Hop & Wobble*. — *Sandra Brennan & Linda Kohanov*

Fluxology / 1978 / Rounder ✦✦✦✦
A good bluegrass album with Tony Rice, Darol Anger, Todd Phillips, and Ricky Skaggs. — *Chip Renner*

Tennessee Fluxedo / 1981 / Rounder ✦✦✦
A smoother sound, which has become his trademark with Strength in Numbers. Featuring Sam Bush, Bela Fleck, the Whites, Mark Shatz, and Russ Barenberg. — *Chip Renner*

Under the Wire / 1986 / MCA ✦✦✦
Though all of his releases are dobro tour-de-forces, this is a highly sophisticated ensemble album with some of the best players in the new-acoustic realm, including Mark O'Connor, Russ Barenberg, Bela Fleck, and Sam Bush. With seven of the ten tracks written by Douglas, the album is also a tribute to his inventive compositional style. — *Linda Kohanov*

Changing Channels / 1987 / MCA ✦✦✦
Everything Is Gonna Work out Fine / 1987 / Rounder ✦✦✦✦
Everything Is Gonna Work Out features Jerry Douglas' first two albums—*Fluxology* and *Fluxedo*—on one compact disc. The two records showcase the dobroist at his rootiest, and contain some wonderful traditionatl bluegrass, which is occasionally spiked by jazzy flourishes. — *Thom Owens*

Plant Early / 1989 / MCA ✦✦
Douglas explores jazz-country fusion on *Plant Early*. — *Jason Ankeny*

● **Slide Rule** / 1992 / Sugar Hill ✦✦✦✦
On *Slide Rule*, Jerry Douglas moves away from the jazz experiments of *Plant Early*, returning to the straightforward bluegrass of his early work. The result is a stunner, featuring not only a remarkable performance from Douglas, but also an impressive list of guest musicians, including Alison Krauss, Sam Bush, Maura O'Connell, Stuart Duncan, and Tim O'Brien. — *Thom Owens*

Skip Hop & Wobble / 1993 / Sugar Hill ✦✦

Ronnie Dove

b. Sep. 7, 1940, Herndon, VA
Vocals / Nashville Sound/Countrypolitan
Best-known as a mid-'60s pop star, Ronnie Dove also notched several country hits during the early '70s. He was raised in Baltimore and grew up influenced by the music of Hank Williams, Webb Pierce, and Elvis Presley. As a nine-year-old, Dove was deeply impressed when he had the chance to meet country giant Ernest Tubb during a concert sponsored by his father's police department. In high school, however, Dove sang with a rock group and joined the Coast Guard after graduation. When not working, he entertained his crewmates with songs, and they encouraged him to sing at a waterfront cafe in Baltimore. He did so and was offered five dollars a night to sing there on his nights off. In 1964, Dove signed with the independent Diamond label and recorded a pop song, "Say You." The single made the Top 20, beginning a series of major pop hits. In 1965, he scored five hits, all but one making it to the Top 20 or higher, and the next year he had five more. In 1967, he only had three hits, and his white-hot but short-lived star began to wane. In 1971, Dove signed with Decca and scored two minor hits on the country charts with "Kiss the Hurt Away" (1972) and "Lilacs in Winter" (1973). He signed to Melodyland Records in 1975 and had two hits that year. Dove re-signed with Diamond in 1987 and had one final entry on the charts, "Rise and Shine." — *Sandra Brennan*

For Collectors Only / Feb. 1996 / Collectables ✦✦✦
For Collectors Only is an extensive three-disc set that contains all of Dove's biggest hits, as well as a wealth of rarities. As the title

suggests, it is only for dedicated fans and collectors, and even they may be dismayed by the haphazard packaging and production on the set. Nevertheless, they'll find a number of hidden gems among the numerous cuts on the collection, making its purchase worthwhile. — *Thom Owens*

● **The Best of Ronnie Dove** / Diamond ✦✦✦✦

Big Al Downing

b. 1940, Centralia, OK
Vocals / R&B, Rock & Roll, Traditional Country, Rockabilly
An unsung figure of early Black rock 'n' roll, Downing had a series of enjoyable if derivative singles in the late '50s and early '60s for several small labels that didn't achieve anything other than regional success. Downing was an eclectic pianist/singer who did not owe his allegiance to just pure R&B, but also to rockabilly and Country & Western, with occasional hints of New Orleans music, hewing closer to White rock 'n' roll than most African-American performers of his era. On some of his early sides, in fact, Downing sounds like a Black Jerry Lee Lewis, with impressively hyper piano runs and slicing electric guitar breaks; at other points, he lands closer to Little Richard or Fats Domino territory. His material and production wasn't strong enough to place him in the major leagues, but his early work has an engaging looseness (sometimes verging on sloppiness). Still active today, he started to focus on Country & Western in the late '70s, although he still plays some rock 'n' roll in his live shows. — *Richie Unterberger*

● **Rockin' 'N Rollin'** / Mar. 19, 1996 / Schoolkids ✦✦✦✦
Two of the greatest rock 'n' roll records ever have to be "Down on the Farm" and "Georgia Slop" by Big Al Downing. For icepick-in-the-ear rockabilly lead guitar, you have to go some to burn "Down on the Farm," and "Georgia Slop" is one of those absolutely perfect, not-a-wasted-note-on-it-anywhere records that come along once in a very blue moon. To have both discs on this collection is the main incentive for purchasing it. This 18-tracker collects just about everything you'll ever need on this underrated performer. Downing was versatile; he could do voices from Fats Domino to Little Richard and pound one very cool piano into the bargain. All the essentials are here plus some very hip bonuses, including his Little Richard entrance with a chorus of "Good Golly Miss Molly" mid-song on Poe's white-white-white-refrigerator-white "Rock 'N Roll Record Girl." — *Cub Koda*

Roy Drusky

b. Jun. 22, 1930, Atlanta, GA
Guitar, Vocals / Nashville Sound/Countrypolitan
A singer-songwriter often called "the Perry Como of country music," Roy Drusky enjoyed success throughout the 1960s as a performer in the Nashville Sound vein. Drusky's mother, a church organist, tried for years to interest her son in music, but throughout his childhood he focused the majority of his energies on sports. It was not until a two-year stint in the US Navy that he bought his first guitar, and soon after began performing for his fellow crew members.

After leaving the Navy, Drusky returned to college, and unsuccessfully tried out for baseball's Cleveland Indians. In 1951, he started his first band, the Southern Ranch Boys; the group's success on a Decatur, GA, radio talent show landed Drusky work as a deejay, where he attracted a substantial following among listeners. He also continued to perform in local clubs after the Southern Ranch Boys called it quits, and on the strength of a 1953 single, "Such a Fool," he was signed to Columbia Records in 1955.

After moving to Minneapolis to continue his work in radio, Drusky began headlining at the Twin Cities' prestigious Flame Club, where word of his talents began spreading to Nashville. As a result, Faron Young recorded Drusky's "Alone with You" in 1958; the single was the biggest of Young's career, topping the charts for 13 weeks. Soon after, Drusky moved to Nashville, and in 1960 released back-to-back Top Three hits, the honky tonk ballads "Another" and "Anymore," which led to an invitation to join the Grand Ole Opry. In the same year, he also released a hit duet with Kitty Wells, "I Can't Tell My Heart That."

In 1961, Drusky released the double-sided hit "I'd Rather Loan You Out"/"Three Hearts in a Tangle," and also issued his first LP, *Anymore With Roy Drusky*. The next year, he reached the Top Ten again with "Second Hand Rose," from the album *It's My Way*. Throughout the first half of the decade, he continued to release chart hits, peaking in 1965 with his lone No. 1, "Yes, Mr. Peters." He also issued two separate albums in 1964, *Songs of the Cities* and *Yesterday's Gone*. In 1965, Drusky appeared in his first film, *White Lightnin' Express*, and also sang the feature's title song; he later appeared in two other films, *The Golden Guitar* and *Forty-Acre Feud*. In the middle of the decade, he also began recording with singer Priscilla Mitchell, and with her released two albums of duets, 1965's *Love's Eternal Triangle* and *Together Again* in 1966. In addition, Drusky began a career as a producer for acts like Pete Sayers and Brenda Byers.

As a recording artist, Drusky's success tapered off after 1965; although he released 11 chart hits between 1966 and 1969, only two, "Where the Blue and Lonely Go" and "Such a Fool," reached the Top Ten. However, in the early years of the next decade he made a comeback: 1970's "Long Long Texas Road," from the album *All My Hard Times*, was his first Top Five hit in six years. It was also his last, however, and as Drusky's brand of country fell victim to changing tastes, his singles and albums were less and less successful; after releasing two LPs in 1976, *This Life of Mine* and *Night Flying*, he returned to writing and producing. After remaining silent throughout the 1980s, he began a new sideline as a country-influenced gospel balladeer in the early 1990s. — *Jason Ankeny*

Songs of the Cities / 1964 / Mercury ✦✦✦✦

● **The Pick of the Country** / 1964 / Mercury ✦✦✦✦

Love's Eternal Triangle / 1965 / Mercury ✦✦✦

Roy Drusky / 1965 / Buckboard ✦✦✦

Roy Drusky's Greatest Hits, Vol. 2 / 1968 / Mercury ✦✦✦

Country Special / 1970 / Vocalion ✦✦✦

New Lips / Hilltop ✦✦✦

Songs of Love and Life / 1995 / Mercury Nashville ✦✦✦
Songs of Love and Life features Roy Drusky's versions of country classics like "Tip of My Fingers" and "Make the World Go Away," but the album doesn't contain enough songs to make it a bargain. — *Stephen Thomas Erlewine*

Dry Branch Fire Squad

Traditional Bluegrass
The Dry Branch Fire Squad was a modern bluegrass band committed to keeping the old-time Appalachian traditional music alive. This southern Ohio bluegrass group was fronted by Ron Thomason, a mandolinist and comedian who grew up in Russell County, VA. While working as a high school English teacher and administrator in the Springfield area, Thomason also played in a local bluegrass band with Frank Wakefield and later went on to spend a year touring with Ralph Stanley's Clinch Mountain Boys.

Thomason formed the Dry Branch Fire Squad in 1976, after he spent time with Lee Allen's Dew Mountain Boys. The earliest incarnation of the band included guitarist John Baker, banjo player Robert Leach, and bass player John Carpenter. Two years later, Mary Jo Leet became the group's vocalist. During the late 1970s, the Fire Squad recorded a series of independent records, and were later joined by bassist Dick Erwin and banjoist John Hisey, who would remain with the band for the next ten years. During that time, the Dry Branch Fire Squad became favorites on the festival circuit. Over the years the band underwent many subsequent personnel changes, but remained dedicated to preserving the old mountain sounds. — *Sandra Brennan and David Vinopal*

Antiques & Inventions / 1966 / Rounder ✦✦
Kenny Baker and Hazel Dickens give this a nice flavor. — *Chip Renner*

Long Journey / 1972 / Rounder ✦✦✦✦
Old timey—in a modern way. Very good. — *Chip Renner*

Spiritual Songs from Dry Branch / 1977 / RT ✦✦✦

Born to Be Lonesome / 1978 / Rounder ✦✦✦
Good. Featuring Kenny Baker, Bobby Osborne. A nice cover of "Brand New Tennessee Waltz." —*Chip Renner*

Dry Branch Fire Squad / 1978 / RT ✦✦✦

Dry Branch Fire Squad on Tour / 1979 / Gordo ✦✦✦

Fannin' the Flames / 1982 / Rounder ✦✦✦
Very nice album. —*Chip Renner*

Fertile Ground / 1983 / Rounder ✦✦✦✦
Very good. "Devil Take the Farmer" and "Bonaparte Crossing the Rhine." —*Chip Renner*

● **Good Neighbours & Friends** / 1985 / Rounder ✦✦✦✦
Tight mountain harmonies on 14 cuts. A must-have. —*Chip Renner*

Golgotha / 1986 / Rounder ✦✦✦
A nice gospel album. —*Chip Renner*

Tried & True / 1988 / Rounder ✦✦

Just for the Record / 1993 / Rounder ✦✦✦

Live at Last / Oct. 8, 1996 / Rounder ✦✦✦✦
Live at Last captures the mid-'90s incarnation of the Dry Branch Fire Squad in concert, running through most of their favorites. Thanks to the group's buoyant, joyous performance, this isn't just a rote concert affair—it's a testament to the band's talent and taste, and arguably one of their best albums ever. —*Thom Owens*

George Ducas

b. Aug. 1, 1966, Texas City, TX
Contemporary Country
Singer-songwriter George Ducas was born on August 1, 1966, in Texas City, TX, but was raised in San Diego, where he received his first guitar at the age of ten. Growing up on a steady diet of Willie Nelson records, Ducas spent much of his high school years privately writing songs for his girlfriends, and did not perform professionally until he attended college at Nashville's Vanderbilt University. After graduation, he accepted a banking job in Atlanta, but returned to Nashville in 1990 to pursue music on a full-time basis. There a mutual friend introduced him to Radney Foster, and a songwriting partnership was forged; Ducas eventually co-wrote Foster's first solo hit, "Just Call Me Lonesome." A growing reputation as a live performer helped earn Ducas his own recording contract, and in 1994 he issued his self-titled debut LP, which generated the Top Ten hit "Lipstick Promises." In 1997, he released his second effort, *Where I Stand.* —*Jason Ankeny*

George Ducas / 1995 / Liberty ✦✦✦

● **Where I Stand** / Jan. 14, 1997 / Liberty ✦✦✦✦

Dave Dudley (Dave Pedruska)

b. May 3, 1928, Spencer, WI
Guitar, Vocals / Traditional Country, Honky Tonk, Bakersfield Sound
Dave Dudley is the father of truck-driving country music. With his 1963 song "Six Days on the Road," he founded a new genre of country music—a variation of honky tonk and rock-inflected country that concentrated lyrically on the lifestyles of truck drivers. Dudley had a string of Top 15 singles that ran through the '60s, while he continued to have Top 40 hits well into the '70s, establishing himself as one of the most popular singers of his era.

At the age of 11, Dudley's father gave him a guitar, but he had his heart set on being a baseball player. Throughout his teenage years he played ball, becoming a member of the Gainesville, TX, Owls as a young adult. However, his career was cut short by an arm injury. Following his retirement from baseball, he became a DJ at a local Texas station, where he would sometimes play along with the songs on the air. The station owner encouraged him to become a performer and Dudley followed the advice.

Dudley moved to Idaho in the early '50s, where he formed the Dave Dudley Trio, which didn't have much success in its seven years together. In 1960, following the breakup of the trio, he moved to Minneapolis, where he formed a group called the Country Gentlemen, which quickly built up a dedicated following. His career was thrown off track in December of 1960, when he was struck by a hit-and-run driver as he was packing his guitar into his car. After several months, he recovered and managed to secure a record deal with Vee Records. His first single, "Maybe I Do," was a minor hit in the fall of 1961 and it was followed by another minor hit, "Under Cover of the Night," the following year on Jubilee Records.

In the summer of 1963, he had his breakthrough hit, "Six Days on the Road," which was released on Golden Wing. The song became a massive success, peaking at No. 2 on the country charts and making the pop Top 40. That same year, he signed with Mercury Records, releasing his first single for the label, "Last Day in the Mines," by the end of the year. Throughout the '60s, he had a long string of truck-driving singles, including "Truck Drivin' Son-of-a-Gun," "Trucker's Prayer," "Anything Leaving Town Today," "There Ain't No Easy Run," and "Two Six Packs Away." By the end of the decade, he was also making conservative, good-old-boy anthems.

During the early '70s, Dudley had several hits—notably the 1971 Top Ten singles "Comin' Down" and "Fly Away Again"—but by the beginning of the '80s, he was no longer a presence on the charts. His last hit single was 1980's "Rolaids, Doan's Pills and Preparation H." During the '80s and '90s, Dudley didn't record much, but he remained a popular concert draw. And truck drivers still loved him—the Teamsters Union awarded him an honorary, solid gold membership card. —*Stephen Thomas Erlewine*

● **20 Great Truck Hits: Dave Dudley** / 1983 / EMI ✦✦✦✦
This Swedish import collection includes a smattering of Dudley's hits like "Six Days on the Road," "Counterfeit Cowboy," and "Me and Ole C.B." —*Rick Clark*

Johnny Duncan

b. Oct. 5, 1938, Dublin, TX
Guitar, Vocals / Country, Skiffle
Singer-songwriter Johnny Duncan was one of the most popular country stars of the mid-'70s and early '80s. He was born to a family of noted musicians in Dublin, TX; among his relatives were Jimmy and Dan Seals. His mother taught him to play guitar, and he was influenced by Merle Travis and Chet Atkins. While still young, he, his mother, the Seals brothers, and his uncle, fiddler Ben Moroney, formed a dance band and played at local gatherings.

After moving to Clovis, NM, in 1959, he joined Norman Petty's group for three years. Producer Petty tried to make him into a pop star, but Duncan wasn't interested and eventually moved to Nashville. He held several odd jobs before appearing on Ralph Emery's television show in 1966. There Duncan was seen by Columbia Records producer Don Law, who signed him to work with producer Frank Jones. His first single, "Hard Luck Joe," made it to the Top 60 in 1967. The following year, his single "To My Sorrow" hit the Top 50. Later in 1968, he had his first Top 20 hit with "Jackson Ain't a Very Big Town," a duet with June Stearns.

His popularity leveled off through 1970 until producer Billy Sherrill took over. In 1971, Duncan's "There's Something About a Lady" made the Top 20, and his third single of the year, "Baby's Smile, Woman's Kiss," hit the Top 15. He had his first Top Ten hit with "Sweet Country Woman" in 1973. After 1974, his career stalled, and he asked Columbia to free him from his contract, but the label wanted one more single. He recorded the Gatlin Brothers' "Jo and the Cowboy" with the then-unknown Janie Fricke and had a Top 30 hit. In 1976, Duncan's straightahead country singing began to catch fire, giving him two smash hits with Kris Kristofferson's "Stranger" and "Thinkin' of a Rendezvous," his first No. 1 hit. The following year, he had three more Top Five hits, including the No. 1 "It Couldn't Have Been Any Better."

Both 1978 and 1979 saw Duncan's hot streak continue with such hits as "She Can Put Her Shoes under My Bed (Anytime)" and "Hello Mexico (And Adios Baby to You)." In 1980, his career began to wane a bit, and although he had four hits, none made it past the Top Ten. In 1981, he only had one Top 40 hit, "All Night Long." Duncan all but disappeared until 1986, when he made a minor comeback with "The Look of a Lady in Love" and "Texas Moon." —*Sandra Brennan*

The Best of Johnny Duncan / 1976 / Columbia ✦✦✦✦
Come a Little Bit Closer / 1977 / Columbia ✦✦✦
See You When the Sun Goes Down / 1979 / Columbia ✦✦✦
● Greatest Hits / 1989 / Columbia ✦✦✦✦

Steve Duncan

Alternative Country, California Country
Steve Duncan was the product of a musical background. Born in Knoxville, TN, he started playing guitar at the age of seven. His father, known as Roy Snede, had a television show that came out of Visalia and was broadcast up and down the central valley. A favorite in Bakersfield, Snede was a member of the Grand Ole Opry and the *Louisiana Hayride*. At the age of 14 Duncan began playing the drums and expanding his horizons while working with his father's Western swing band. A lifelong player, he evolved into a top-flight performer and stick man. In 1975 Rick Nelson asked Duncan to move to Los Angeles and become the drummer for his Stone Canyon Band. For three-and-a-half years Steve Duncan kept Nelson on track. Noted for his ability to play a wide variety of styles, Duncan never limited himself, and worked with the Byrds, the Flying Burrito Brothers, the Palomino Riders, Roger Miller, Carl Perkins, the Desert Rose Band, former Stray Cat Lee Rocker, and Ronnie Mack's Barn Dance Band, and was an official member of the Hellecasters. Duncan also played with the Desert Rose Band, and as a studio musician his credits included Rose Maddox, Emmylou Harris, Freddy Fender, John Denver, Steve Wariner and many more. Duncan also served as a member of the on-air backing band for the ACM award shows, and was the drummer for the house band on Dick Clark's *Hot Country Nights* television show. *—Jana Pendragon*

Tommy Duncan

b. Jan. 11, 1911, Hillsboro, TX, d. Jul. 25, 1967
Vocals / Traditional Country, Western Swing
As the lead singer for the classic lineup of Bob Wills' Texas Playboys, Tommy Duncan was the definitive Western swing vocalist. Crossing the smooth croon of Bing Crosby with the twang of Jimmie Rodgers and the bluesy inclinations of Emmett Miller, Duncan had a warm, distinctive, and welcoming voice that helped the Playboys cross over to a wider audience. Not only was he a wonderful, trend-setting vocalist, Duncan also wrote many of the Texas Playboys' biggest hits, including "Time Changes Everything," "Stay a Little Longer," "Take Me Back to Tulsa," "New Spanish Two Step," and "Bubbles in My Beer." Throughout the '30s and '40s, he remained with Wills, leaving in 1948 when tensions between the two musicians became too great. Following his departure, Duncan launched a solo career that resulted in one major hit single, "Gamblin' Polka Dot Blues." Throughout the '50s, he sang both as a solo artist and a member of the Miller Brothers Band. In 1960, he and Wills patched up their differences and recorded several albums. Following his reunion with Wills, he began touring as a solo artist, and he remained on the road until his death in 1967.

Tommy Duncan was hired by Bob Wills in 1933 to fill the vacant spot left in the Light Crust Doughboys by vocalist/pianist Milton Brown, who had left the band when W. Lee O'Daniel, sponsor of the group's radio show, refused to let the band play dances. Wills auditioned a total of 67 singers before hiring Duncan. Later that year, Wills was fired from the radio station by O'Daniel for showing up drunk, and Duncan chose to join Bob's new band, the Texas Playboys, instead of staying with the Light Crust Doughboys.

Once the Texas Playboys settled in Tulsa in 1934, Duncan moved to permanent lead vocalist, leaving the piano to Alton Stricklin. Over the next eight years, the group had a regular show on Tulsa's KVOO and recorded a number of hit singles for the American Recording Company, including "Right or Wrong" and "New San Antonio Rose." In 1942, Duncan left the band to join the Army and fight in World War II. Duncan's departure began a wave of defections from the Playboys, as many of the members enlisted in the service. The Playboys' popularity crumbled with the absence of so many key musicians, yet they bounced back up

the charts once Duncan and several other members rejoined following the end of the war.

Duncan stayed with Wills until 1948, when the fiddler fired the singer, believing that Tommy was commanding too much attention. Upon leaving the Playboys, Duncan formed a Western swing band with several former members of the Texas Playboys and signed to Capitol Records. "Gamblin' Polka Dot Blues," his debut single, was a hit upon its summer release in 1949, peaking at No. 8 on the charts. After touring with the band from '1948–49, Duncan joined the Miller Brothers Band in the early '50s, recording with them on Intro Records as well as doing a solo album for Coral. During the latter half of the decade, Tommy recorded for a variety of small labels, including Cheyenne, Fire, and Award. Despite his constant touring and recording, Duncan failed to have much success, primarily because Western swing had fallen out of favor with many contemporary country fans.

Wills and Duncan reunited in 1960, recording a number of sessions that were released as albums and singles over the next two years. One single, "The Image of Me," became a minor Top 40 country hit in early 1961. Following his brief reunion with Wills, Tommy continued to tour as a solo artist throughout the rest of the decade, usually employing a house band as his supporting group. In 1966, Duncan released his last single, "I Brought It on Myself" / "Let Me Take You Out," on Smash Records. The following year, he suffered a major heart attack and died in July, leaving behind a legacy of classic recordings and songs. *—Stephen Thomas Erlewine*

● Texas Moon / 1996 / Bear Family ✦✦✦✦
The 24-track compilation *Texas Moon* contains every song that Tommy Duncan recorded for Capitol Records in 1959, including the Top Ten hit "Gambling Polka Dot Blues," as well as his lone single on Natural, his first two sessions for Intro, and two singles that his brother Glynn recorded with Tommy's band, the Western All-Stars. Much of this material is in the vein of Duncan's classic work with Bob Wills, though the quality of the music is slightly inconsistent. Nevertheless, *Texas Moon* and its companion volume, *Beneath a Neon Star in a Honky Tonk*, are necessary for hardcore collectors of Western swing in general and Duncan in particular. *—Thom Owens*

Beneath a Neon Star in a Honky Tonk / 1996 / Bear Family ✦✦✦✦
The 27-track compilation *Beneath a Neon Star in a Honky Tonk* contains every song Tommy Duncan recorded for Intro Records between 1951 and 1953, as well as his lone single for Fire Records, which featured Buck Owens on guitar. The music on this disc is slightly more straightforward than conventional Western swing, yet it should appeal to fans of Duncan's classic recordings with Bob Wills, even with the slightly inconsistent musical quality. Nevertheless, *Beneath a Neon Star in a Honky Tonk* and its companion volume, *Texas Moon*, are necessary for hardcore collectors of Western swing. *—Thom Owens*

Holly Dunn

b. Aug. 22, 1957, San Antonio, TX
Vocals / Contemporary Country
Singer-songwriter Holly Dunn, the sister of Nashville songwriter Chris Waters, had barely graduated from college when she found herself soaring to success. Dunn led her first group, the Freedom Folk, in high school; in 1976, the band was selected to represent Texas at the bicentennial celebrations at the White House, and went on to tour the South and appear on television. She later became a member of the Abilene Christian University USO touring choir the Hilltop Singers.

In 1978, a song she had co-written with her brother, "Out of Sight, Not Out of Mind," was recorded by Christy Lane. She moved to Nashville to join her brother after obtaining her degree. At first she worked odd jobs and sang demos for music publishers before signing with CBS Songs, where her brother also worked. In 1984, Dunn was hired as a songwriter for MTM, and several top female singers recorded her songs, including Louise Mandrell, who took "I'm Not Through Loving You Yet" to the country Top Ten.

In 1985, Dunn signed with MTM records and released three singles which became minor hits. Her eponymous debut appeared in 1986, around the same time "Daddy's Hands," her breakthrough hit, was released. Her next album, 1987's *Cornerstone*, contained two Top Five hits. She made her debut as a producer with her next album, 1988's *Across the Rio Grande*.

MTM went out of business in 1988 and Dunn signed with Warner Bros. Her initial Warner album, *The Blue Rose of Texas*, produced her first No. 1 hit, "Are You Gonna Love Me." In 1991, following a chart slump, her label released *Milestones: Greatest Hits*. A small controversy erupted over one of the songs, "Maybe I Mean Yes"; some listeners felt it encouraged women to blame themselves for date rape, and Dunn had the song pulled from the album. During the '90s, her popularity declined, resulting in Dunn's departure from Warner in 1993. In 1995, she released *Life and Love and All the Stages*. —Sandra Brennan

Holly Dunn / 1986 / MTM ✦✦✦

Cornerstone / 1987 / MTM ✦✦✦
Dunn's second effort includes the hits "Love Someone like Me" and "Only When I Love." —Jason Ankeny

Across the Rio Grande / 1988 / MTM ✦✦✦✦
Dunn took over the production reins for her third album, which features the hits "That's What Your Love Does to Me" and "(It's Always Gonna Be) Someday." —Jason Ankeny

The Blue Rose of Texas / 1989 / Warner Brothers ✦✦✦
This "nu-country/pop" belter has an occasional rock punch and a Western swing and sway. —Mark A. Humphrey

Heart Full of Love / 1990 / Warner Brothers ✦✦✦
Here are more of Dunn's radio-friendly songs. —Mark A. Humphrey

● **Milestones: Greatest Hits** / 1991 / Warner Brothers ✦✦✦✦
Milestones: Greatest Hits contains 11 of Holly Dunn's biggest hits from the late '80s, including "Daddy's Hands," "Love Someone Like Me," "Only When I Love," "Are You Ever Gonna Love Me," "You Really Had Me Going" and "Maybe I Mean Yes." Dunn was one of the finest female country singers of her era, and this collection contains the absolute best of her output, making it an essential addition to a contemporary country library. —Thom Owens

Getting It Dunn / 1992 / Warner Brothers ✦✦✦✦
It contains the hits "You Say You Will," "A Simple I Love You," "No Love Have," and others. —AMG

Life and Love and All the Stages / Apr. 18, 1995 / River North Nashville ✦✦✦

Bobby Durham

Vocals / Traditional Country, Bakersfield Sound
Bakersfield, CA, has become legendary as one of the alternatives to Nashville in country music, and Durham is one of the journeyman singers who has worked the bars there for three decades. He never attained the fame of Bakersfield's best-known sons, Buck Owens and Merle Haggard, but he did make a few good singles for Capitol in the '60s and, in the late '80s, a fine album for Hightone. —Mark A. Humphrey

Where I Grew Up / 1987 / Hightone ✦✦✦✦
Bakersfield in the late '80s is still kickin'! —Mark A. Humphrey

Slim Dusty (David Gordon Kilpatrick)

b. Jun. 1927, Kempsey, New Wales
Guitar, Vocals / Traditional Country
One of the giants of Australian country music, Slim Dusty recorded over 80 albums, all of which are still in print in Australia. He was born David Gordon Kilpatrick and raised on a dairy farm at Nulla Nulla Creek in New South Wales. Among those that influenced his music were Jimmie Rodgers, Gene Autry, Vernon Dalhart, and Carson Robison. After adopting the name Slim Dusty at age 11, he wrote his first song a year later and made his first radio broadcast at the age of 14. He took his demo 300 miles south to Sydney several times before receiving a letter from Columbia in 1946 offering him a chance to record. He was paid $15 for the session and forfeited all rights to his royalties. These songs were released on Regal-Zonophone (now EMI), the label he stayed with until the end of his career. Dusty moved to Sydney and began appearing regularly on Tim McNamara's 2SM country music sessions in 1950. The next year he married singer-songwriter Joy McKean, who wrote much of his material. In 1953, he quit his job as a plasterer to become a full-time performer and was soon being hailed the "King of Country Music."

Dusty recorded numerous singles between 1954 and 1957. Although he was popular, he didn't become truly famous until he recorded "A Pub with No Beer" in 1957. This monster hit became the first and last gold disc ever awarded to a 78-rpm record and was a No. 3 hit in Great Britain. Dusty released his first album, *Slim Dusty Sings*, in 1960. In 1964 he began what would become an annual trans-Australian ten-month tour. He received the MBE (Member of the Order of the British Empire) recognition from Queen Elizabeth II in 1970. In 1972, he received his first Eddy Award (akin to the Grammys) from the Federation of Australian Broadcasters. He also won numerous Gold Guitar awards at the Australasian Country Music Awards over the years. In 1974, Dusty began suffering from throat problems, but this did not stop him from singing to a full house in the Concert Hall of the Sydney Opera House in April 1975. In 1979, a brass plaque imprinted with his likeness was mounted on a granite boulder outside Radio 2TM and he became the fourth person to join the CMAA's Roll of Renown. In 1980, Dusty published his autobiography, *Walk a Country Mile*, and simultaneously released a special album of the same name. Dusty made his first US and European tour in 1989. —Sandra Brennan

Australia Is His Name / Philo ✦✦✦✦

Bob Dylan

b. May 24, 1941, Duluth, MN
Guitar, Harmonica, Piano, Keyboards, Vocals / Rock & Roll, Country-Rock, Singer Songwriter, Folk-Rock
The greatest songwriter of his generation and a figure of incalculable influence on popular music from the '60s on, Bob Dylan is also, with the possible exception of Elvis Presley, the most important individual in rock music ever.

Dylan came from Minnesota to New York City in 1961, at the age of 19, as an acolyte of folksinger Woody Guthrie, although he had played rock music in the late '50s. He met Guthrie (who was slowly dying in a hospital) and was quickly taken up by the New York folk community. He signed to Columbia Records and, in March 1962, released his first album, *Bob Dylan*, consisting largely of folk-blues covers. By this time, however, he had begun to write original songs, many in the philosophical/political style of his Greenwich Village compatriots (though far superior in quality), the best early example being "Blowin' in the Wind." Many of these songs were on Dylan's second album, *The Freewheelin' Bob Dylan*, released in May 1963. That summer, the popular folk group Peter, Paul & Mary took "Blowin' in the Wind" to the Top Ten in the national charts. Thereafter, Bob Dylan songs became favorites among many pop and folk performers. As the result of such exposure, *Freewheelin'* became a chart hit in September 1963.

Dylan followed with two albums in 1964, the heavily protest-oriented *The Times They Are A-Changin'* and the more introspective *Another Side of Bob Dylan*. In 1965, he began recording and playing concerts with rock musicians, which vastly increased his following but also led to controversy within the folk community. His singles "Like a Rolling Stone" and "Positively 4th Street" were Top Ten hits, as were the albums *Bringing It All Back Home* and *Highway 61 Revisited*, and the "folk-rock" sound of his music could be heard on any number of other artists' records, many of them written by Dylan himself. Dylan undertook a world tour in 1966 to promote the double album *Blonde on Blonde*, which featured the Top Ten single "Rainy Day Women No. 12 & 35." That summer he was in a motorcycle accident and he withdrew from public view for a year and a half, meanwhile recording the informal material later released as *The Basement Tapes*.

When Dylan returned to action in late 1967, it was with the quieter *John Wesley Harding* album, followed in 1969 by the country-flavored *Nashville Skyline* and its Top Ten single "Lay Lady Lay." Critics expecting Dylan's more complex work were disappointed and they savaged his two-disc *Self-Portrait* in 1970, though most saw *New Morning*, released only a few months later, as a return to form.

Dylan was not much heard from in the early '70s (he played at George Harrison's Bangladesh benefit concert in 1971, and in 1973 he appeared in the film *Pat Garrett and Billy the Kid* and wrote its score), but he returned in 1974 with a national concert tour and the No. 1 album *Planet Waves*. This was followed in 1975 by *Blood on the Tracks*, regarded by many as his best collection of the decade. The same year, Dylan organized a roving band of musicians as the Rolling Thunder Revue and toured the Northeast, later appearing in other parts of the country in 1976.

A film crew was part of the entourage, and Dylan put together a sprawling film, *Renaldo & Clara*, which was released in 1978. With that done, he went on an international tour and released a new album, *Street Legal*. In 1979, Dylan converted to Christianity and released the first of three overtly religious albums, *Slow Train Coming*.

The religious fervor became less apparent by the time of *Infidels* in 1983, and Dylan has released several excellent albums since, while touring more or less continually. The '80s and early '90s have also seen the welcome legitimate release of much previously unissued vintage Dylan material (some of it widely available on bootlegs). *— William Ruhlmann*

★ **Bob Dylan's Greatest Hits** / Mar. 27, 1967 / Columbia ♦♦♦♦♦
A ten-song retrospective of the work of the most impressive—and most protean—singer-songwriter of the period 1963 to 1966. Please note that, while this album is listed as the "pick" of this period of Dylan's career due to its general accessibility, a full understanding of the popular music of the '60s is impossible unless the listener is familiar with its three predecessors. *Greatest Hits* combines folk-protest standards like "Blowin' in the Wind" and "The Times They Are A-Changin'" with his folk/rock hits "Like a Rolling Stone" and "Rainy Day Women No. 12 & 35."
— William Ruhlmann

☆ **John Wesley Harding** / Dec. 27, 1967 / Columbia ♦♦♦♦♦
A quieter, simpler album than those Dylan had made in the mid-'60s, this "comeback" record nevertheless contained open-ended, parable-like songs, the most memorable of which has turned out to be "All Along the Watchtower." *— William Ruhlmann*

☆ **Nashville Skyline** / Apr. 9, 1969 / Columbia ♦♦♦♦♦
Dylan reached a sales peak with this album of simple, country-inflected songs (including "Lay Lady Lay"). *— William Ruhlmann*

New Morning / Oct. 21, 1970 / Columbia ♦♦♦♦
While retaining some of the bucolic, sunny outlook of his recent work, Dylan partially turned back to a grittier rock sound (Al Kooper again in the mix) and the more ironic, poetic lyrics of his mid-'60s songs. *— William Ruhlmann*

★ **Bob Dylan's Greatest Hits, Vol. 2** / Nov. 17, 1971 / Columbia ♦♦♦♦♦
A grab bag of material dating back to 1963, this sprawling two-

disc set is notable for its rarities, especially the 1971 single "Watching the River Flow" and the 1963 live performance of "Tomorrow Is a Long Time." *— William Ruhlmann*

☆ **The Basement Tapes** / Jun. 26, 1975 / Columbia ♦♦♦♦♦
A two-disc set of ad hoc performances from 1967, albeit refurbished slightly for this release, *The Basement Tapes* provides the missing link between Dylan's long, poetic songs of the mid-'60s and the shorter, more direct songs of the late '60s. Some of the songs had already become well known: "Too Much of Nothing," "Tears of Rage," "This Wheel's on Fire," and "You Ain't Goin' Nowhere." *— William Ruhlmann*

☆ **Biograph** / Oct. 28, 1985 / Columbia ♦♦♦♦♦
A five-LP, three-CD retrospective of Dylan's first 20 years of recording, with an emphasis on presenting some of the mountain of unreleased songs that began leaking out unofficially in the late '60s. The only reason this massive, brilliantly executed album is not listed as an essential pick is its expense—in fact, it's not a bad place to start in trying to appreciate the whole of Dylan's achievement. *— William Ruhlmann*

Bootleg Series / Mar. 26, 1991 / Columbia ♦♦♦♦
The floodgates opened with the release of this 58-song collection of outtakes and unreleased songs from throughout Dylan's career, an outpouring that demonstrated what all the bootleggers and their customers had known all along: that Dylan's throwaways were better than everyone else's keepers. It's amazing to think that, while turning out some of the most impressive albums of his time, Dylan was holding back material often equally good. *— William Ruhlmann*

The Dylan/Cash Sessions / Spank ♦♦♦
During the *Nashville Skyline* sessions in February 1969, Dylan teamed up with Johnny Cash to record over a dozen songs. Only one of these made it onto *Nashville Skyline* ("Girl from the North Country"). Most of the rest are here, in perfect fidelity. If you were to judge this as a proper studio album, the notices wouldn't be too positive, due to the ragged and tentative performances. Judged as a loose, informal meeting of two giants, it's very pleasurable listening, though more for Cash's contributions than Dylan's. With full band backing (including Carl Perkins on electric guitar), the pair run through easygoing, rockabilly-tinged versions of Dylan songs, Cash songs, old Sun rockabilly chestnuts ("That's All Right Mama" and "Matchbox"), and a bit of country gospel. Cash, in fact, dominates the proceedings: he sings lead more often, and the mere two Dylan tunes ("Girl from the North Country" and "One Too Many Mornings") are outweighed by a larger heaping of Cash classics ("Big River," "I Walk the Line," "I Still Miss Someone," "Ring of Fire," "Guess Things Happen That Way"). The CD might even appeal more to Cash fans than Dylan ones, especially as Dylan's singing is not up to scratch: his timing is off, he often sings on one note, and he even needs to be occasionally cued by Johnny for the right words. The disc also includes three interesting Dylan performances from a TV broadcast on *The Johnny Cash Show* in May 1969, as well as five less essential quadrophonic mixes of *Nashville Skyline* tracks. *— Richie Unterberger*

E

The Eagles

Country-Rock, Soft Rock, Pop-Rock

The Eagles were among the most successful rock groups of the '70s, and their blend of country, folk, and rock continues to sell well in catalog. The group's four original members were Los Angeles session men and group veterans assembled by producer John Boylan in 1970 as backup musicians for Linda Ronstadt on her *Silk Purse* album. They then served as her backup band for two years. The four were Glenn Frey (b. Nov 6, 1948) on guitar; Bernie Leadon (b. Jul 19, 1947) on banjo and mandolin; Randy Meisner (b. Mar 8, 1948) on bass; and Don Henley (b. Jul 22, 1947) on drums. All four sang, though Henley and Frey took most leads. Signed to Ronstadt's label, Asylum, they issued their first album, *Eagles*, in June 1972. It was a moderate hit (going gold a year and a half later) and produced the Top 40 hits "Take It Easy" (written by Frey and Jackson Browne), "Witchy Woman," and "Peaceful Easy Feeling."

The second Eagles LP, a semi-concept album called *Desperado* (1973) that emphasized an "outlaw" image, was somewhat less successful. For their third album, *On the Border* (1974), the group added guitarist Don Felder. This was a breakthrough record, going gold in three months and producing the No. 1 hit "Best of My Love," which didn't top the charts until almost a year after the album's release, just in time to set up their fourth album. *One of These Nights* (1975), the first of four straight albums to top the charts, featured the title track, "Lyin' Eyes," and "Take It to the Limit," all Top Ten hits.

The Eagles released a greatest-hits album in 1976 (it now stands at 14 million sales, the best-selling hits record of all time) and suffered the loss of Leadon, who was replaced by former James Gang leader Joe Walsh (b. Nov 20, 1947). At the end of the year, they released *Hotel California*, which has now sold nine million copies. Its hits included the ominous title track, "New Kid in Town," and "Life in the Fast Lane."

In 1977, Meisner left the band and was replaced by former Poco member Timothy B. Schmit (b. Oct 30, 1947). It took the Eagles until the fall of 1979 to complete *The Long Run*, another million-seller, featuring the chart-topper "Heartache Tonight" and Top Ten successes in the title track and "I Can't Tell You Why." The next year saw the release of a live album, but by 1981 the Eagles had split up. All five members have since released solo albums, the most successful of which have been by Henley and Frey.

In 1994, the Eagles reunited for a summer stadium tour and recorded an album as part of an appearance on the TV show *MTV Unplugged* that featured several new songs. The resulting album, *Hell Freezes Over* was released in November of 1994; it debuted at No. 1 and sold over five million copies by June of 1995. — *William Ruhlmann*

The Eagles / Jun. 1972 / Asylum ✦✦✦
The Eagles' tentative debut album is notable for its single hits, "Take It Easy," "Witchy Woman," and "Peaceful Easy Feeling." (It also contains a rare Jackson Browne composition, "Nightingale.") The album has more of a bluegrass tone (courtesy of Bernie Leadon) than the band would later pursue. — *William Ruhlmann*

Desperado / Apr. 1973 / Asylum ✦✦✦
A concept album equating rock 'n' roll musicians with Old West outlaws, the Eagles' second album contains the hit "Tequila Sunrise," the song "Desperado," which has become a standard, and the recurring "Doolin-Dalton," co-written with J.D. Souther and Jackson Browne. — *William Ruhlmann*

On the Border / Mar. 1974 / Asylum ✦✦✦
A transitional Eagles album (and their commercial breakthrough), this contained songs like "Already Gone" and "James Dean" (co-written by Jackson Browne) that hark back to their earlier uptempo rock style, but also "Best of My Love" and Tom Waits' "Ol' 55," ballads that showed off their harmonies and won them a whole new audience. — *William Ruhlmann*

One of These Nights / Jun. 1975 / Asylum ✦✦✦
The Eagles' breakthrough album, a convincing mix of heady rockers and lush ballads, featuring the Top Ten hits "One of These Nights," "Lyin' Eyes," and "Take It to the Limit." — *William Ruhlmann*

★ **Their Greatest Hits (1971-1975)** / Feb. 1976 / Asylum ✦✦✦✦✦
The reason this is such a great greatest-hits album is that it includes almost all the best tracks from the Eagles' first four albums, eight Top 40 hits including the No. 1s "Best of My Love" and "One of These Nights," plus the favorites "Tequila Sunrise" and "Desperado." This is the essential Eagles for the period. (As of mid-1995, *Their Greatest Hits [1971-1975]* was the second-best-selling album of all time in the US, with certified sales of 22 million copies.) — *William Ruhlmann*

☆ **Hotel California** / Dec. 1976 / Asylum ✦✦✦✦
A concept album about the dissipated life of Southern California rock stars, from being the "New Kid in Town" to living "Life in the Fast Lane" to holing up in the "Hotel California" fearing it's all been "Wasted Time" and turning to "The Last Resort." This album and Pink Floyd's *The Wall* are aural versions of *A Star Is Born* for the rock generation. — *William Ruhlmann*

The Long Run / Sep. 1979 / Asylum ✦✦✦
The long-awaited follow-up to *Hotel California* and the Eagles' last studio album proved a considerable disappointment, although it sold in the expected multimillions and included the hits "Heartache Tonight," "The Long Run," and "I Can't Tell You Why." — *William Ruhlmann*

Eagles Live / Nov. 1980 / Asylum ✦✦
The Eagles were always a yawn in concert, and this profit-taking re-creation of their hits demonstrates the lifelessness they brought to live work. Today's fans should listen before forking over all those bucks to sit in the stadiums and experience it themselves. — *William Ruhlmann*

Eagles Greatest Hits, Vol. 2 / Oct. 1982 / Asylum ✦✦✦
This will save you from having to buy *The Long Run*, an inconsistent album best remembered for its hit songs, all of which are here, along with the ones from *Hotel California*. — *William Ruhlmann*

Hell Freezes Over / Nov. 8, 1994 / Geffen ✦✦
The Eagles were never a great live band, which makes the process of reinventing their hits slightly harder. But they are smart busi-

nessmen, so they realized that they didn't need to reinvent themselves; if they reunited, the public would only care about seeing the band again and just hearing the hits. When the Eagles finally reunited in 1994 for a mammoth tour, they began their tour with an *MTV Unplugged* set. The result is *Hell Freezes Over*. The band accentuates their country leanings, but everything winds up sounding much duller than their original recordings because they accentuate their relaxed vibe, not their rootsiness. Although the album sold well, it's not nearly as captivating as the original versions. — *Stephen Thomas Erlewine*

Fred J. Eaglesmith

Singer-Songwriter, Country-Folk, Americana
Country-folk singer-songwriter Fred J. Eaglesmith was one of nine children born to a farming family in rural southern Ontario. Often employing his difficult upbringing as raw material for his heartland narratives, he issued his self-titled debut LP in 1980. He recorded infrequently throughout the remainder of the decade, releasing only two more albums, *The Boy That Just Went Wrong* and *Indiana Road*. However, Eaglesmith gradually became an underground favorite in his native Canada, thanks largely to a relentless touring schedule in tandem with bassist Ralph Schipper and mandolinist Willie P. Bennett. In 1991, he released the double live collection *There Ain't No Easy Road*, followed two years later by *Things Is Changin'.* Another live set, *Paradise Motel*, appeared in 1994, and in 1995 Eaglesmith returned with *Drive-In Movie*. — *Jason Ankeny*

From the Paradise Motel / Oct. 1995 / Barbed Wire ✦✦✦
● **Drive-In Movie** / 1996 / Vertical ✦✦✦✦
Fred Eaglesmith comes across as a friendly, but slightly twisted, guy-next-door. After years of writing boldly perceptive songs about the plight of farmers and the fate of those who grow up in harsh rural surroundings, the Canadian got his first US record deal in 1995, receiving the honor of being the first artist released on a highly touted Nashville independent, Vertical Records. Eaglesmith's *Drive-In Movie* proves worthy of the position. His heartland songs roll to a rough-and-tumble acoustic sound, with the hammer coming down hard on several arrangements. He reflects small-town life in a style that can be as brutally funny as it is painfully introspective, which is fitting for his characters, who turn to rowdiness to hide how much they hurt. — *Michael McCall*

Jim Eanes

b. Dec. 6, 1923, Mountain Valley, VA
Guitar, Vocals / Traditional Bluegrass
Though never considered a major star, Smilin' Jim Eanes was an influential figure in both bluegrass and country music for over five decades. He was born Homer Robert Eanes, Jr. in Mountain Valley, VA, and received his first guitar at age nine from his banjo-picking father. While young, Eanes suffered an injury to his left hand; despite the difficulty and pain, he still managed to master rhythm guitar. He spent his early teen years playing square dances with his father's informal string band, and at age 16 joined Roy Hall's Blue Ridge Entertainers at a Roanoke radio station, and remained with the band until Hall died in 1943. Following World War II, Eanes joined Uncle Joe and the Blue Mountain Boys. He also worked briefly with Bill Monroe in 1948.

Eanes made his recording debut in 1949 under his given name, backed by fiddler Homer Sherrill and banjo player Snuffy Jenkins. Eanes organized the Shenandoah Valley Boys in 1951 after getting a radio gig in Virginia; the band cut a few singles on the tiny Blue Ridge label before signing with Decca. Until then, Eanes' music was heavily slanted towards bluegrass, but Decca groomed him to play country music. The singles he released sold well enough, but they didn't make the charts. His contract with Decca expired in 1955 and Eanes, now billing the band as Smilin' Jim and His Boys, began recording with Starday. His debut single, "Your Old Standby," became one of his signature songs. Over the next five years, he and the Shenandoah Valley Boys recorded albums on both Starday and Blue Ridge. Eanes wrote many of his own songs, and one of his best from this period was "I Wouldn't

Change You If I Could," which became a No. 1 hit for Ricky Skaggs in 1982.

During the 1960s, Eanes worked as a deejay on different Virginia radio stations; he also occasionally performed, and recorded songs on small independent labels. Eanes recorded his first bluegrass album, *Your Old Standby*, in 1967. His next two albums, *Jim Eanes* and *Rural Rhythms Present Jim Eanes*, featured backing by Red Smiley's Bluegrass Cut-Ups. Smiley and his band appeared regularly on WWVA's *Wheeling Jamboree* and when Red decided to retire, Eanes took over the band, and renamed it the Shenandoah Cutups. The band cut an album in 1970 and shortly after broke up.

Eanes began hosting festivals and recording bluegrass albums for smaller labels; among them was the excellent *Cool Waters Flow*. His heavy touring schedule was interrupted in 1978 when he suffered a heart attack. He recovered by the next year and launched a tour of Western Europe, which he repeated in 1980 and 1982; while visiting Belgium, he cut an album with a local band, Smoketown Strut. During the rest of the 1980s, Eanes cut back on his touring, but continued recording. In 1990, he celebrated his five decades in the industry with the album *50th Anniversary*. — *Sandra Brennan*

Early Days of Bluegrass, Vol. 4 / 1979 / Rounder ✦✦✦
50th Anniversary Celebration / 1990 / Rebel ✦✦
Heart of the South / 1991 / Rural Rhythm ✦✦✦
● **Classic Bluegrass** / Rebel ✦✦✦✦

Steve Earle

b. Jan. 17, 1955, Fort Monroe, VA
Guitar, Vocals / Country-Rock, Singer-Songwriter, Roots-Rock, New Traditionalist
In the strictest sense, Steve Earle isn't a country artist—he's a roots rocker. Earle emerged in the mid-'80s, after Bruce Springsteen had popularized populist rock 'n' roll and Dwight Yoakam had kick-started the neo-traditionalist movement in country music. At first, Earle appeared to be more toward the rock side than the country. He played a stripped-down neo-rockabilly that occasionally verged on outlaw country. His unwillingness to conform to the rules of Nashville or to rock 'n' roll meant that he never broke through into the mainstream. Instead, he cultivated a dedicated cult following, drawing from both the country and rock audiences. Toward the early '90s, his career was thrown off track by personal problems and substance abuse, but in the mid-'90s he re-emerged stronger and healthier, producing two of his most critically acclaimed albums ever.

Born in Fort Monroe, VA, but raised near San Antonio, TX, Steve Earle is the son of an air traffic controller. At the age of 11, he received his first guitar and by the time he was 13, he had become proficient enough to win a talent contest at his school. Though he showed a talent for music, he was a wild child, often getting in trouble with local authorities. Furthermore, his rebellious, long-haired appearance and anti-Vietnam war stance was scorned by local country fans. After completing the eighth grade, Earle dropped out of school and at the age of 16 he left home with his uncle, Nick Fain, and began traveling across the state. Eventually, he settled in Houston at the age of 18, where he married his first wife, Sandie, and began working odd jobs. While he was in Houston, he met singer-songwriter Townes Van Zandt and Jerry Jeff Walker, who would become Earle's foremost role model and inspiration. A year later, Earle moved to Nashville.

While he was in Nashville, Earle worked blue-collar jobs during the day; during the night, he wrote songs and played bass in Guy Clark's backing band, appearing on a cut on Clark's 1975 album *Old No. 1*. Steve stayed in Nashville for several years, making connections within the industry and eventually landing a job as a staff writer for the publisher Sunbury Dunbar. Patty Loveless and Johnny Lee recorded Earle's songs and Elvis Presley was scheduled to cut one of Earle's songs, but he never showed up at the session; Earle also appeared in Robert Altman's 1975 film, *Nashville*. After staying in Nashville for a few years, he grew tired of the city and returned to Texas.

Back in Texas, he assembled a backing band called the Dukes and began playing local clubs. A year later, he returned to Nashville, where he married his second wife, a local cocaine dealer named Cynthia. The marriage to Cynthia was short-lived and he quickly married Carol, who gave birth to Earle's first child, a son named Justin Townes. Carol helped straighten Earle out, at least temporarily; for a while, he cut back on drugs and concentrated on music.

Publishers Roy Dea and Pat Clark signed Earle as a songwriter in the early '80s. Dea and Clark brought "When You Fall in Love" to Johnny Lee, who took the song to No. 14 on the country charts in 1982; shortly before the success of "When You Fall in Love," Carl Perkins cut Earle's "Mustang Wine" and Zella Lehr recorded two of his songs. With his reputation as a songwriter growing, Earle wanted to become a recording artist in his own right. Dea and Clark had recently formed an independent record label called LSI and the pair signed Earle.

Earle's first release was an EP called *Pink and Black* in 1982. The record featured a formative version of the Dukes and earned good reviews. One writer, John Lomax, sent the EP to Epic Records, which was impressed enough to sign Earle in 1983. Shortly before the signing of the contract, Lomax became Earle's manager. Although the prospect of being signed to a major label seemed promising, relationships between Epic and Earle quickly soured. After releasing the *Pink and Black* track "Nothin' but You" as a single, Epic sat on the song, refusing to promote the record; instead, they concentrated on their new signing. Earle entered the studio and cut an album of neo-rockabilly songs that the label was reluctant to send to radio and therefore, they refused to release the record. Epic suggested Earle re-enter the studio with a new, more commercially oriented producer, Emory Gordy, Jr. The pair cut four more songs, which were released as two singles, but the records failed.

With his recording career going nowhere, Earle lost his publishing contract with Dea and Carter. He moved over to Silverline Goldline, where he met Tony Brown, a producer at MCA Records. At the end of 1984, Epic dropped Earle from their roster. In early 1985, Brown persuaded MCA to sign Earle and Lomax was fired as Earle's manager. In 1986, Steve Earle's debut album, *Guitar Town*, was released. Upon its appearance, Earle was grouped into the new traditionalist movement begun by Dwight Yoakam and Randy Travis, but he also gained the attention of rock critics and fans who saw similarities between Earle's populist sentiments and the heartland rock of Bruce Springsteen and John Mellencamp. *Guitar Town* became a hit, with its title track becoming a Top Ten single in the summer of 1986 and "Goodbye's All We've Got Left" reaching the Top Ten in early 1987. Following the album's success, Epic quickly assembled a compilation of Earle tracks they never released, entitling it *The Early Tracks* and releasing it in early 1987. Later that year, Earle released his second album, *Exit O*, which bore a shared credit for his backing band the Dukes, which signaled the more rock-oriented direction on the album. Like the debut, *Exit O* was critically acclaimed and it sold well, even if it didn't match the levels of the debut.

Though his career was taking off, Earle's personal life was becoming a wreck. He had divorced his third wife, married a fourth named Lou, whom he quickly divorced, and then he married a sixth wife, Teresa Ensenat, who worked for MCA. He was also delving deeper and deeper into drugs and alcohol. With his third album, 1988's *Copperhead Road*, Earle's rock 'n' roll flirtations came to the forefront and country radio responded in kind—none of the songs from the album charted or received much airplay. However, album-rock radio embraced him, sending the album's title track into the album rock Top Ten, which helped make the album his highest charting effort, peaking at No. 56. Not only had *Copperhead Road* been accepted by AOR, but it established him as a star in Europe; the duet with the Irish punk-folk group the Pogues on *Copperhead Road* signaled he had an affection for the area. In the late '80s, Earle frequently toured England and Europe and even produced the alternative rock band the Bible.

Earle's acceptance by the rock community didn't please the country establishment in Nashville. Although it seemed for a time that Earle wouldn't need Nashville anymore, his newfound success quickly began to collapse. Uni, a division of MCA Records, had released *Copperhead Road* instead of MCA proper and just before the album went gold, Uni went bankrupt, taking *Copperhead Road* along with it. Meanwhile, Earle's addictions and fondness for breaking rules began spinning out of control. On New Years' Eve, he was arrested in Dallas for assaulting a security guard at his own concert; he was charged with aggravated assault, fined $500, and given a year's unsupervised probation. Sandie, his first wife, sued for more alimony and he was served with a paternity suit by a woman in Tennessee. The title of his 1990 album, *The Hard Way*, reflected his problems, as did the record's tough, dark sound. Though the record was critically acclaimed and spawned a minor AOR hit with "The Other Kind," it received no support from the country market and quickly fell off the charts.

The commercial failure of *The Hard Way* was just the beginning of a round of serious setbacks for Earle. Later in 1990, he recorded an album of material that MCA refused to release. Instead, the label decided to release the live album *Shut Up and Die Like an Aviator* in 1991. At the end of the year, MCA decided not to renew Earle's record contract. For the next several years, Earle was severely addicted to cocaine and heroin and had several run-ins with the law. In 1994, he was arrested in Nashville for possession of heroin and was sentenced to a year in jail. He served in a rehab center instead of jail. This time, the treatment worked.

Late in 1994, he was released from the rehab center and he started working again. In 1995, he signed to Winter Harvest and released the acoustic *Train A Comin'*, his first studio album in five years. *Train A Comin'* received terrific reviews and strong sales, despite Earle's claim that the label botched the album's song sequence. The attention led to a new record contract with Warner Bros., which released *I Feel Alright* in early 1996, again to strong reviews and respectable sales. Steve Earle had returned from the brink and re-established himself as a vital artist. In the process, he won back the country audience he had abandoned in the late '80s.
—Stephen Thomas Erlewine

● **Guitar Town** / 1986 / MCA ✦✦✦✦
Steve Earle rode a suspiciously rocking band into Nashville and up to the top of the country charts with this album, after which it was decided he was just a little too extreme for the country market, which means this record is "on the edge" in more ways than one. *— William Ruhlmann*

Early Tracks / 1987 / Epic ✦✦✦
In the wake of *Guitar Town's* success, Epic rushed out this collection of early Earle tracks recorded from 1982 to 1985, including songs from 1982's *Pink & Black* EP. While much of this is by-the-book rockabilly fare, it provides a good look at his formative years. *—Chris Woodstra*

Exit O / 1987 / MCA ✦✦✦
Exit O essentially follows the same formula as *Guitar Town*, and while it isn't as uniformly excellent as his debut, Steve Earle has come up with a couple of his best songs, including the yearning "I Ain't Ever Satisfied." The major difference between the two albums is the fact that Earle insisted on working with his road band the Dukes, which gives *Exit O* a tougher sound. If the material had matched the sound of the album, the record would have surpassed *Guitar Town*, but since the songs are uneven, it's just a respectable follow-up. *— Thom Owens*

Copperhead Road / 1988 / MCA ✦✦✦
Earle finally got around to re-recording his early classic, "The Devil's Right Hand," on an album that was heavily influenced by a hillbilly attitude and old Rolling Stones records. It was a potent combination. Irish punk-folksters the Pogues pitch in on some of the proceedings. The title track became Earle's first FM rock hit. *— William Ruhlmann & Rick Clark*

The Hard Way / 1990 / MCA ✦✦✦
Some of Earle's best songwriting is on this album. The anthemic "The Other Kind" is a classic. On "Country Girl," Earle and his band (the Dukes) do their best NRBQ grooves. "Billy Austin" is a compassionate character sketch of a Native American on death row. Former Lone Justice lead singer Maria McKee offers vocal

support on this album. On the downside, the subtleties of these songs are occasionally buried under a sea of cinematic production. Earle sometimes sounds too tired to emote anything, and the heavily compressed mix doesn't help matters. Regardless, fans of rock that contains well-written lyrics might enjoy this. —*Rick Clark*

Shut up and Die Like an Aviator (Live) / 1991 / MCA ✦✦

● **Essential Steve Earle** / 1993 / MCA ✦✦✦✦
Steve Earle lives up to the title billing here. While some of Earle's recent work (and live shows) have been inclined to excess, this disc collects lean, mean, and vital material from Earle's first three outings—the country-rock masterpiece *Guitar Town*, the inward-looking *Exit O*, and the angry lashing out of *Copperhead Road*. *Essential* is topped off by "Continental Trailways Blues," previously available only on a 1987 compilation. Thirteen tracks is a little skimpy; some rarities from the vaults would have been a nice touch. —*Roch Parisien*

Train A Comin' / 1995 / Winter Harvest ✦✦✦✦
Supported by Norman Blake, Roy Husky, and Peter Rowan, Earle has made a comeback record of sorts. It's a greasy, homey, soulful country-folk album that sounds great and keeps asking to be played again. This is an album full of stories of men with hard hearts and broken lives. Earle sings with a believable voice, which is all too rare these days. He turns in a breezy "I'm Looking Through You" to top it all off, reminiscent of the mid-'60s *Beatle Country* album by The Charles River Valley Boys. —*Richard Meyer*

I Feel Alright / Mar. 5, 1996 / Warner Brothers ✦✦✦✦
"Be careful what you wish for friends, I've been to hell and now I'm back again," Earle sings on the title track of *I Feel Alright*, immediately drawing us into one of the finest albums of his career. This is the Steve Earle we've been waiting for, as unadorned, unashamed, and plain-faced honest about his roots, dreams, and dirty past lives as any of country music's most heralded singers. From the drifting, hard-loving woman in "Now She's Gone" to the withdrawn junkie in the ghostly "CCKMP" ("cocaine cannot kill my pain") to the teenage outlaw in "Billy and Bonnie," Earle's characters are a string of loners, often down and out but at the same time loyal, self-aware, and romantics right to the bitter end. Few artists can give us a picture of life's other side with such electrifying clarity. But despite its subject matter, "I Feel Alright" is imbued with true moments of hope. The closing duet with Lucinda Williams, "You're Still Standin' There," for example, is as strong a statement of faith as any Earle has written. —*Kurt Wolff*

Ain't Ever Satisfied / Jul. 1996 / HIPP ✦✦✦✦
Although his personal life was plagued with troubles during the late '80s, Steve Earle wrote a ton of first-rate songs during that time and the majority of those tunes are collected on this double-disc set. Spanning his career from 1985's *Guitar Town* to 1991's *The Hard Way, Ain't Ever Satisfied* hits nearly every high point from his studio albums and throws in a handful of rarities, including live covers of the Rolling Stones and Bruce Springsteen, for good measure. It's an excellent retrospective, illustrating exactly why Earle was one of the most acclaimed country singer-songwriters of the latter half of the '80s. —*Thom Owens*

Jack Earls

Vocals / Rock & Roll, Rockabilly
One of the more obscure names in the annals of Sun Records, Jack Earls' lone original single, "Slow Down" (covered by rock group The Paladins), is one of the shining crude examples of rockabilly. Never comfortable as a full-time musician, Earls moved from Memphis to Detroit to work full-time at the Chrysler plant, a job he maintains to this day. Occasionally playing and recording for small collector-oriented labels, Earls has a cracked-mountain tenor that is still intact and capable of scraping the paint off walls any time he feels like it. —*Cub Koda*

Remember Me Baby / 1963 / Collectables ✦✦✦

● **Let's Bop** / 1990 / Bear Family ✦✦✦✦
Complete collection of Earls' Sun recordings, raw rockabilly at its finest. —*Cub Koda*

Don Edwards

b. Mar. 30, 1939, Boonton, NJ
Vocals / Cowboy
Singer-songwriter Don Edwards dedicated his musical career to recapturing and preserving the spirit of the Old West by recording old and new cowboy songs. Edwards was born and raised in Boonton, a New Jersey farming community, and was inspired by the books of cowboy author Will James (i.e., *The Lone Cowboy*). A guitar player since age ten, he learned his first Western songs from the films of cowboy crooners Gene Autry and Tex Ritter, later discovering Jimmie Rodgers. At age 16, Edwards left home to work in the oil fields and ranches of Texas and New Mexico in order to experience cowboy life firsthand.

He made his professional debut in 1961 after he was hired as a singer, actor, and stuntman at the newly opened amusement park Six Flags Over Texas. He worked there for five years before moving to Nashville to seek a recording contract. Although the folk revival was all the rage, no one was interested in Western music. Edwards eventually recorded an album comprised of old songs and his own compositions on the independent Stop label. Some of the songs were played on the radio, but they never hit the charts, and Edwards returned to Texas and settled in the Fort Worth area.

In 1980, Larry Scott, an L.A. deejay, helped Edwards record the *Happy Cowboy* album, which featured backup musicians from Gene Autry's band and the Sons of the Pioneers. Edwards released the album on his own Sevenshoux label. A visit to the Cowboy Poetry Gathering in Elko, NV, in the early '80s inspired him to create a 24-song tribute to Jack Thorpe, the cowboy musician who first began collecting the old songs, on a cassette packaged with a book entitled *Songs of the Cowboy*. He then released a second book/cassette anthology, *Guitars and Saddle Songs*, and in 1990 released the album *Desert Nights and Cowtown Blues*. His 1993 album *Going Back to Texas* contained new Western songs by some of the best writers in Nashville. —*Sandra Brennan*

Happy Cowboy / 1980 / Sevenshoux ✦✦✦

Desert Nights and Cowtown Blues / 1990 / Sevenshoux ✦✦✦✦

● **Songs of the Trail** / Jan. 1992 / Warner Brothers ✦✦✦✦
Texas rancher Don Edwards spent several years researching and compiling the songs that comprise the excellent *Songs of the Trail*. Each tune on the album is an old cowboy song that was well-known at the turn of the century. Edwards' delivery is spare, emotional, and powerful—these songs don't sound like artifacts, they sound alive. It's one of those rare historical releases that is as entertaining as it is educational. —*Thom Owens*

Goin' Back to Texas / Feb. 1993 / Warner Brothers ✦✦✦✦

West Of Yesterday / Mar. 19, 1996 / Warner Western ✦✦✦

Jonathan Edwards

b. Jul. 28, 1946, Aitkin, MN
Guitar, Harmonica, Vocals / Progressive Bluegrass, Singer-Songwriter, Folk-Rock
Best remembered for his crossover hit "Sunshine," country and folk singer-songwriter Jonathan Edwards was born July 28, 1946 in Aitkin, MN, and grew up in Virginia. While attending military school, he began playing guitar and composing his own songs. After moving to Ohio to study art, he became a fixture on local club stages, playing with a variety of rock, folk, and blues outfits, often in tandem with fellow students Malcolm McKinney and Joe Dolce.

In 1967, Edwards and his bandmates relocated to Boston, where they permanently changed their name to Sugar Creek and became a full-time blues act, issuing the 1969 LP *Please Tell a Friend*. Wanting to return to acoustic performing, Edwards left the group to record a solo album. Near the end of the 1970 sessions, one of the finished tracks, "Please Find Me," was accidentally erased, forcing Edwards to record a brand new composition instead. The song was "Sunshine," and when it was released as a single the following year, it quickly became a Top Five pop hit.

With the release of 1972's *Honky-Tonk Stardust Cowboy*, Edwards' music began gravitating towards straightahead country; his label was at a loss as to how to market the record, however, and over the course of two more albums, 1973's *Have a Good Time for Me* and the following year's live *Lucky Day*, his sales sharply declined. Soon, Edwards dropped out of music, buying a farm in Nova Scotia.

In 1976, Edwards' friend Emmylou Harris enlisted him to sing backup on her sophomore record *Elite Hotel;* the cameo resulted in a new record deal and the LP *Rockin' Chair*, recorded with Harris' Hot Band. *Sail Boat*, cut with most of the same personnel, appeared a year later. Another layoff followed, however, and when Edwards resurfaced—with an eponymous 1982 live record—it was on his own label, Chronic.

After touring the nation with a production of the musical *Pumping Boys and Dinettes*, Edwards joined the bluegrass group the Seldom Scene, issuing the 1983 LP *Blue Ridge*. After a 1987 solo children's record, *Little Hands*, Edwards moved to Nashville; his 1989 album *The Natural Thing* generated his biggest country hit, "We Need to Be Locked Away." A follow-up, *One Day Closer*, appeared in 1994.

● **Jonathan Edwards** / 1971 / Atco ✦✦✦✦
This album is best known for Edwards' hit, "Sunshine" and the song "Shanty," which radio stations around the country call "The Friday Song." If either of these songs is as far as you've gotten with this album, you are missing a great deal. Edwards has a great sense of melody, which means there is not a weak track on this record. Aside from the previously mentioned numbers, one or two of the songs on the record have taken on a life of their own. "Don't Cry Blue," for instance, has been knocking around bluegrass circles for some years. One listen and you'll know why this album has never gone out of print. —*Jim Worbois*

Honky-Tonk Stardust Cowboy / 1972 / Atco ✦✦✦✦
Edwards continues where the first record left off and continues to grow as an artist. In addition to some fine songs, Edwards chose to include a few covers like Jesse Colin Young's "Sugar Babe," the Mills Brothers' "Paper Doll" (complete with faux "trombone" solo), and the title track. The title track did receive some airplay on country radio in 1972 but was never the hit it should have been. If you find a copy of this one, grab it. —*Jim Worbois*

Have a Good Time for Me / 1973 / Atco ✦✦✦
While this album has no Edwards originals, there is no shortage of tasty tunes. Edwards has mainly covered songs by three writers—Joe Dolce, Malcom McKinney, and the Orphans' Eric Lillyequist (who has appeared on each of Edwards' records to this point)—each of whom has captured the style and essence of Jonathan Edwards. Highly enjoyable. —*Jim Worbois*

Lucky Day / 1974 / Atco ✦✦✦
Unlike many live albums where you get to hear the artist rehash their hits and not much else, Edwards not only gives us a look at his musical roots (Merle Haggard, Jimmy Martin, and Gov. Jimmie Davis), but some surprises as well. One of the most surprising things is a highly irreverent version of the Chi-Lites' hit, "Have You Seen Her?" with Edwards' seemingly improvised recitation. This is also the first of Edwards' records on which his band Orphan is credited by name. (Their records are also well worth checking out.) Recommended. —*Jim Worbois*

Rockin' Chair / 1976 / Reprise ✦✦
1976 found Edwards with a new label, new backing musicians, and a new producer, the then *very* hot Brian Ahern. Unfortunately, change is not always a good thing. The songs and the band are both very good, but the intimate feel of the early albums is missing here and that was one of the things that always made Edwards' records so appealing. That lack of intimacy seems to fall on the producer's shoulders and should not be held against the artist. Despite the flaws in production, this is still a fine collection of songs and performances from a regrettably overlooked artist. —*Jim Worbois*

Sailboat / 1977 / Reprise ✦✦
This just doesn't have the feel of a Jonathan Edwards album. It could be blamed on the relatively few Edwards originals, which leave the feeling that the creation of this record was more or less removed from the artist's hands. It's a pleasant enough collection, especially if you ever wondered what Jonathan Edwards would sound like singing other songwriters' songs. (His version of "Never Together" predates Carlene Carter's near hit by a year.) Still, if this is your first exposure to this artist, you may be tempted to skip the rest of his work and that would be a major mistake. —*Jim Worbois*

Live / 1980 / Chronic ✦✦✦

Blue Ridge / 1985 / Sugar Hill ✦✦✦

Stoney Edwards

b. Dec. 24, 1937, Seminole, OK
Vocals / Traditional Country, Honky Tonk
Stoney Edwards never made it to the big time, yet he and his soulful honky tonk sound had a devoted following, and he was one of the few African-American performers to try his hand in the genre. He was born Frenchy Edwards in rural Oklahoma, one of seven children. Even as a boy, Edwards dreamed of playing on the Grand Ole Opry like his hero, Bob Wills. By the time he was 13, he had mastered several instruments and frequently jammed with his uncles. After leaving home as a teen, in 1954 he married and moved to San Francisco to settle down for the next 15 years. When not working, he played music. After breaking his back in a job-related mishap, Edwards was ordered by his doctors to avoid heavy work. Left without an income, Edwards seriously considered leaving his family so they could receive welfare, but just as he was about to go his daughter presented him with a wind-up toy as a gift. Deeply moved, the gesture inspired Edwards to write his first song, "A Two-Dollar Toy," and begin to focus his energy on a music career.

In 1970, he was invited to play at a benefit for Bob Wills in Oakland, and his performance led to a contract with Capitol Records. The following year, he released his first album, *Stoney Edwards, A Country Singer*, and made his single debut with "A Two-Dollar Toy," which made the Top 70. In 1972, Edwards released his second album, *Down Home in the Country*, and began to attract a following. "He's My Rock" came out in 1973 and stayed in the Top 20 for almost four months. Although his subsequent releases were generally minor hits, some have are regarded as country classics, such as his version of the Frazier & Owens song "Hank and Lefty Raised My Country Soul." He continued recording and appearing on the charts through the early '80s, when his career and his health began to wane. Eventually he had part of his right leg amputated due to problems with diabetes. In 1986, Edwards returned to make an album with Johnny Gimble, Ray Benson, Floyd Domino, Jimmy Day, Leon Rausch, and Ralph Mooney. —*Sandra Brennan*

Stoney Edwards / 1971 / Capitol ✦✦✦✦

She's My Rock / 1973 / Capitol ✦✦✦

● **Mississippi, You're on My Mind** / 1975 / Capitol ✦✦✦✦

Blackbird / 1976 / Capitol ✦✦✦✦

No Way to Back Down a Memory / 1981 / MCA ✦✦

Joe Ely

b. Feb. 9, 1947, Amarillo, TX
Guitar, Vocals / Progressive Country, Country-Rock, Outlaw Country, Americana
In the '70s, C&W was full of artists referred to as "outlaws," mavericks who bucked the stodgy Nashville music establishment by writing their own songs, recording with their road bands, and producing their own records. The genre produced a slew of acts, but Lubbock, TX, native Joe Ely epitomized the form. Unlike most of that era's big names, Ely remains a viable artist. He got his start back in the early '70s, working with Butch Hancock and Jimmie Dale Gilmore in a group called the Flatlanders. Their only album didn't go far, and the group broke up. (Rounder reissued the album in 1990.) Around the mid-'70s, Ely formed an eclectic

group that was able to swing from Cajun and Western to honky tonk stomps and rockabilly; it was signed to MCA in 1977. Ely released an eponymous debut that year, using songs written by ex-Flatlanders Gilmore and Butch Hancock and throwing in some of his own road-worn, oddly poetic originals. The next year brought *Honky Tonk Masquerade*, the cornerstone of Ely's legacy and one of modern country's most ambitious albums. Further albums (especially *Live Shots*, recorded during his European tour with the Clash) brought Ely to the attention of rock fans and netted ecstatic reviews in country and pop magazines (but, mysteriously, produced no hits). MCA dropped Ely in 1983, and he woodshedded until 1987, when the independent Hightone label signed him and released *Lord of the Highway*. Another Hightone album followed before Ely (whose influence was being felt by the new breed of country neo-traditionalists) re-signed with MCA, releasing another live set and the album *Love and Danger*. He's yet to top his late '70s achievements, but Ely remains an energetic and passionate live performer and an occasionally inspired songwriter, with much potential for the future. —*John Floyd*

Joe Ely / 1977 / MCA ✦✦✦✦

Ely's first album came out while country's outlaw movement was in full swing, but *Joe Ely* took it one better. This is a roots-rocking country album with tunes by Jimmie Dale Gilmore ("Treat Me Like a Saturday Night") and Butch Hancock ("She Never Spoke Spanish to Me," "If You Were a Bluebird") that deserve the near-classic status their cult of fans has bestowed on them. —*Brian Mansfield*

● **Honky Tonk Masquerade** / 1978 / MCA ✦✦✦✦

Ely's best album, *Honky Tonk Masquerade* contains everything from Texas weepers ("Because of the Wind") to roadhouse rockers ("Fingernails"). Among the best tunes are Jimmie Dale Gilmore's "Tonight I Think I'm Gonna Go Downtown" and Butch Hancock's "West Texas Waltz." Nobody made country records like this in 1978. Come to think of it, they still don't. —*Brian Mansfield*

Down in the Drag / 1979 / MCA ✦✦✦

Simply another set of decent country songs. Ely's momentum was gone: His band, for the first time, sounded like tired and bored pros. —*John Floyd*

Live Shots / 1980 / MCA ✦✦✦✦

Ely partakes of the musical diversity of his hometown, Lubbock, TX, freely mixing country, rock, Tex-Mex, and hard honky-tonk music in excellent songs he writes himself or borrows from his friend Butch Hancock. This is a live best-of covering his first three albums, recorded on tour in England. — *William Ruhlmann*

Musta Notta Gotta Lotta / 1981 / MCA ✦✦✦

If you're making a tape of Ely's greatest hits, "Musta Notta Gotta Lotta" is a must—"Dallas" and "Wishin' for You" ensure its necessity. But anyone who has shed tears (and danced them away) to *Honky Tonk Masquerade* will feel cheated by such obvious covers as Roy Brown's "Good Rockin' Tonight" and Buddy Holly's "Rock Me My Baby." —*John Floyd*

Hi-Res / 1984 / MCA ✦✦

The only one of Ely's MCA albums the label hasn't issued on CD, *Hi-Res* is a synthesizer-heavy record that came after Ely learned about Apple computers. Preferable versions of "Cool Rockin' Loretta" and "She Gotta Get the Gettin'" appear on *Live at Liberty Lunch*. —*Brian Mansfield*

Lord of the Highway / 1987 / Hightone ✦✦✦

After a long recording layoff, Ely picked up where he'd left off in 1984 with this typical collection, whose best songs—"Me and Billy the Kid" and "Are You Listenin' Lucky?"—were Ely originals. —*William Ruhlmann*

Dig All Night / 1988 / Hightone ✦✦✦

Milkshakes & Malts / 1988 / Sunstorm ✦✦✦

Live at Liberty Lunch / 1990 / MCA ✦✦✦

This album was recorded over two days at Liberty Lunch in Austin, TX. Ely's band has evolved from a country band with Tejano roots to a hard-rocking Texas ensemble highlighted by guitarist David Grissom, who later defected to John Cougar Mellencamp. —*Brian Mansfield*

Love & Danger / 1992 / MCA ✦✦✦✦

Ely is stark and restless.... His muse still roams the highways in search of whatever, his romance doomed by a twist of fate. He's a more objective observer; a storyteller who captures the tragic side to the well-defined characters of "The Road Goes on Forever" and "Every Night About This Time." Ely conveys much—if not most—of a song's emotion through his inspired electric guitar playing. The string-bending is at high-pressure intensity for "Love Is the Beating of Hearts," then drops deep, sonorous and echoing for "Slow You Down." —*Roch Parisien*

No Bad Talk or Loud Talk 1977-'81 / 1995 / Edsel ✦✦✦✦

Letter to Laredo / Aug. 29, 1995 / MCA ✦✦✦✦

Flamenco guitarist Teye is the dominant instrumentalist on a Joe Ely album that fits the "unplugged" tag—drums, electric bass, various, mostly acoustic guitars, and occasional accordion and harmonica—and that could be played without complaint in any cantina along the Rio Grande. Ely is joined in his story songs about Southwest life and romantic devotion by Raul Malo, Jimmie Dale Gilmore, and Bruce Springsteen, while Butch Hancock and Tom Russell contribute the strongest material—Hancock's sequel, "She Finally Spoke Spanish to Me," and Russell's tragic tale of a man who bets his future on a cockfight. *Letter to Laredo* is a mood piece with less of the raw energy of many of Ely's albums, but the singer is in his element and his mastery of the form is obvious. —*William Ruhlmann*

Bill Emerson

b. Jan. 22, 1938, Washington, D.C.

Organ, Guitar, Piano, Vocals / R&B, Rock & Roll, Gospel, Electric Memphis Blues

Slashing blues, infectious R&B, formulaic rock 'n' roll, moving gospel—keyboardist Billy "The Kid" Emerson played all those interrelated styles during a lengthy career that began in Florida and later transported him up to Memphis and Chicago.

Emerson had already learned his way around a piano when he entered the Navy in 1943. After the war, he began playing around Tarpon Springs, attending Florida A&M during the late '40s and early '50s. He picked up his nickname while playing a joint in St. Petersburg; the club owner dressed the band up in cowboy duds that begged comparison with a certain murderous outlaw.

A 1952-53 stint in the Air Force found Emerson stationed in Greenville, MS. That's where he met young bandleader Ike Turner, who whipped Emerson into shape as an entertainer while he sang with Turner's Kings of Rhythm. Turner also got Emerson through the door at Sun Records in 1954, playing guitar on the Kid's debut waxing "No Teasing Around."

Emerson's songwriting skills made him a valuable commodity around Sun—but more as a source for other performers' material later on. His bluesy 1955 outing "When It Rains It Pours" elicited a cover from Elvis a few years later at RCA, while Emerson's "Red Hot" (a takeoff on an old cheerleaders chant from Emerson's school days) became a savage rockabilly anthem revived by Billy Lee Riley for Sun and Bob Luman for Imperial.

After his "Little Fine Healthy Thing" failed to sell, Emerson exited Sun to sign with Chicago's Vee-Jay Records in late 1955. Despite first-rate offerings such as the jumping "Every Woman I Know (Crazy 'Bout Automobiles)" and a sophisticated "Don't Start Me to Lying," national recognition eluded Emerson at Vee-Jay too.

It was on to Chess in 1958, recording "Holy Mackerel Baby" and the unusual novelty "Woodchuck" (a remake of an earlier Sun single) during his year or so there. 45s for Mad, USA, M-Pac! (where he waxed the dance workout "The Whip"), and Constellation preceded the formation of Emerson's own logo, Tarpon, in 1966. In addition to Emerson's own stuff, Tarpon issued Denise LaSalle's debut single.

A prolific writer, Emerson penned songs for Junior Wells, Willie Mabon, Wynonie Harris, and Buddy Guy during the early '60s, often in conjunction with Willie Dixon. When recording opportunities slowed, Emerson played jazzy R&B in lounges and supper clubs (guitarist Lacy Gibson was a member of his trio for a while). Emerson took Europe by surprise with a dynamic segment on the American Blues Legends 1979 tour. More recently, he's rumored to have reverted to playing gospel in his native state of Florida. —*Bill Dahl*

● **Little Healthy Thing** / 1980 / Charly ✦✦✦✦
Since no CD reissues are easily accessible by this important Florida-born R&B pianist, this vinyl compendium of his 1954-55 Sun catalog will have to suffice for now. Emerson's jumping proto-rock style at Sun supplied notable rockabillies with killer material—"Red Hot," as first cut by Emerson, was later done full justice by Billy Lee Riley, while Elvis found the hip-grinding "When It Rains It Pours" to his liking. Emerson's bluesy "No Teasing Around" (with Ike Turner on guitar) and the upbeat "Something for Nothing" and the title cut are among the many highlights of this enjoyable LP. —*Bill Dahl*

Crazy 'bout Automobiles / 1982 / Charly ✦✦✦✦
Another vinyl-only collection, this one a ten-incher with only ten songs, covering Emerson's 1955-57 stay at Chicago's Vee-Jay label. Emerson bonded well with Vee-Jay's house bands, especially on the romping "Every Woman I Know (Crazy 'Bout Automobiles)" and a sophisticated "Don't Start Me to Lying." As with his Sun stuff, the big-voiced Emerson was a captivating performer. —*Bill Dahl*

Reunion / Sep. 1991 / ✦✦✦✦

Banjo Man / 1996 / Webco/Pinecastle ✦✦✦

Home of the Red Fox / Rebel ✦✦✦
It features such guest artists on the banjo as Jerry Douglas and Tony Rice. —*AMG*

Gold Plated Banjo / Rebel ✦✦

Emilio

Latin Pop, Contemporary Country, Tejano
While Emilio first attracted mainstream attention with his 1995 country hit "It's Not the End of the World," he came to Nashville only after establishing himself as a massively popular Tejano artist. Born Emilio Navaira in San Antonio, TX, he left college to become a professional musician, and spent several years touring with David Lee Garza before founding his own group, Rio. After honing a sound that fused traditional country with Latin-influenced rock, Emilio became one of Tejano's biggest stars, debuting in 1991 with the album *Unsung Highways*. A series of successful records followed, including 1993's *Emilio Live*, 1993's *Southern Exposure*, and 1994's *Soundlife*. In 1995, he released the contemporary country LP *Life Is Good*. —*Jason Ankeny*

Soundlife / Nov. 29, 1994 / EMI Latin ✦✦✦
● **Life Is Good** / Sep. 26, 1995 / Capitol Nashville ✦✦✦✦

Buddy Emmons

b. Jan. 27, 1937, Mishawaka, IN
Bass, Piano, Guitar (Steel), Vocals / Instrumental, Traditional Country
Buddy Emmons is among Nashville's elite as one of the finest steel guitar players in the business. Born in Mishawaka, IN, he first fell in love with the instrument at age 11 when he received a six-string lap steel guitar as a gift. As a teen, he enrolled at the Hawaiian Conservatory of Music in South Bend, IN, and began playing professionally in Calumet City and Chicago at age 16. In 1956, Emmons went to Detroit to fill in for Walter Haynes in a performance with Little Jimmy Dickens and soon afterward he was invited to join Dickens' Country Boys. He appeared with them a few times on the Grand Ole Opry and recorded a few singles, including "Buddy's Boogie" (1957). He also recorded a pair of solo singles for Columbia, "Cold Rolled Steel" (1956) and "Silver Bells" (1957).
In the late '50s, Emmons began playing occasionally with Ernest Tubb's band on *Midnight Jamboree*. In 1963, he began a five-year stint with Ray Price and His Cherokee Cowboys, and in 1965 teamed up with fellow steel player Shot Jackson to record the LP *Steel Guitar & Dobro Sound*. This led the two to create the Sho-Bud Company, which sold an innovative steel guitar that used push-rod pedals. In 1969, Emmons joined Roger Miller's Los Angeles-based band as a bass player. When not touring with

Miller, he did session work for a variety of artists. He quit Miller's band in 1973 and signed a solo contract, releasing several albums in the late '70s. After 1978, Emmons began playing on a number of small labels, where he and Ray Pennington occasionally collaborated with some of Nashville's finest side men as the Swing Shift Band. In 1993, Emmons began touring with the Everly Brothers. Throughout the '90s, he continued to do session work. —*Sandra Brennan*

● **Steel Guitar Jazz** / Sep. 1963 / Mercury ✦✦✦✦

Singing Strings of Steel and Dobro / 1965 / Starday ✦✦✦✦

Best of Western Swing / 196 / Cumberland ✦✦✦✦

Sings Bob Wills / 1976 / Flying Fish ✦✦✦✦
This album features some of the best pickers in Nashville, with Pig Robbins and Johnny Gimble. —*AMG*

Buddies / 1977 / Flying Fish ✦✦✦
Two of the best session players in Nashville play some fine country jazz. —*AMG*

Live from Austin City Limits / 1979 / Flying Fish ✦✦✦

Minors Aloud / 1979 / Flying Fish ✦✦✦
Here, jazz-guitar great Lenny Breau teams with steel master Emmons for an album of lively music. —*AMG*

Emmons Live, Vol. 1 / Midland Int. ✦✦

Emmons Live, Vol. 2 / Midland Int. ✦✦

Swingin' by Request / 1992 / Step One ✦✦✦

Buddy & Lenny / Flying Fish ✦✦✦✦
Country meets jazz as two super-pickers, Buddy Emmons and Lenny Breau (pedal steel and electric guitar), collide on this very creative and innovative album. —*Hank Davis*

Ty England

Guitar, Vocals, Session Musician / Contemporary Country
Ty England may have struck out on a solo career in 1995 to some success, but to most new country fans he was most recognizable as Garth Brooks' touring guitarist during the height of Brooks' stardom. Raised in Oklahoma, England began playing guitar as a child, teaching himself the instrument on his grandfather's guitar. Over the course of his childhood and adolescence, he delved deeply into country, learning the work of classic singers like Roy Acuff and Hank Williams, as well as contemporary stylists like Don Williams and Keith Whitley. While he was in high school, England sang with a number of bands in addition to the school choir. Following graduation, he attended college at Oklahoma State, singing at a campus coffeeshop at night. One night, he met a fellow student by the name of Garth Brooks. The two became roommates and began playing music together. Eventually, England's grades began to slip, so his parents took him out of school and got him a job back home. Working at night, he finished his marketing degree, but instead of pursuing that degree, he got a job as an auto plant representative.
While he was working at the auto plant, he received a call from Garth Brooks, who had just signed a record contract in Nashville. England immediately moved to Nashville and became Brooks' guitarist, backup vocalist, and onstage comedic foil. After six years, he sought out his own record contract with the assistance of Garth Fundis, a record producer for RCA. Fundis helped England sign a solo deal and the guitarist released his eponymous debut album in the summer of 1995. The first single from the record, "Should've Asked Her Faster," peaked at No. 3, while the second single, "Smoke in Her Eyes," became a lesser hit. —*Stephen Thomas Erlewine*

● **Ty England** / 1995 / RCA ✦✦✦✦
While his voice hearkens back to classic honky tonk singers like Lefty Frizzell, Ty England's music falls halfway between Garth Brooks and Randy Travis, ranging from uptempo stomps to heartfelt ballads. —*Stephen Thomas Erlewine*

Two Ways to Fall / Sep. 17, 1996 / RCA ✦✦✦✦
Ty England's second album, *Two Ways to Fall*, is nearly as strong as his debut album, boasting an excellent selection of ballads and

honky tonk ravers that establish him as one of the finest main-stream country singers of the mid-'90s. —*Thom Owens*

Bill Engvall

Born in Galveston, TX, Bill Engvall was working as a nightclub DJ in Dallas when he decided to attempt stand-up comedy. After startling amateur-night audiences at several local clubs, he moved to Los Angeles in 1990. He hosted the *Pair of Jokers* cable special with Rosie O'Donnell and also appeared on *Evening at the Improv* and *The Tonight Show with Jay Leno*. In 1992, he was awarded Best Male Stand-Up at the American Comedy Awards, and moved into sitcom TV with an appearance on *Designing Women* and a regular role on the short-lived *Delta*. Signed to Warner Bros. in 1996, Engvall released his countrified debut album *Here's Your Sign*—also the title of his most famed bit. —*John Bush*

Here's Your Sign / 1996 / Warner Brothers ◆◆◆

Alejandro Escovedo

Guitar, Vocals / Progressive Country, Roots-Rock, Alternative Country-Rock, Americana
Alejandro Escovedo's family tree includes former Santana percussionist Pete Escovedo and Pete's daughter, pop star Sheila E (Prince's former drummer). He began his music career with the Nuns, a mid-'70s punk band based in San Francisco. He co-founded the cowpunk band Rank and File in 1979, which moved to Austin, TX, in 1981 after a stint in New York City. The band released *Sundown* on Slash Records; shortly after, Escovedo left to form the True Believers with brother Javier. The band recorded two albums for EMI (the second of which was never released, causing the band to break up in 1988) and toured the country, often as an opening act for Los Lobos. Escovedo released a solo album in 1992 on Watermelon Records, *Gravity*, uniting his wide variety of styles; the album was produced by Stephen Bruton of Bonnie Raitt's band. —*John Bush*

● Gravity / 1992 / Watermelon ◆◆◆◆
Escovedo's got a sandpaper quality to his voice that gives credibility to these songs, many of which have an edge of danger or desperation. This is guitar-based music enhanced by dramatic arrangements that make use of orchestral touches and a rockin' band. "Broken Bottle" is like a beautiful chamber work. —*Richard Meyer*

Thirteen Years / 1994 / Watermelon ◆◆◆◆
The Austin singer-songwriter reaches deep once again, adding triple violins, harp, and cello to his palette of movingly introspective material. Overall, the expanded lineup provides for plenty of tonal space. Before the mood ever gets maudlin, Escovedo cranks up the volume with guest guitarist Charlie Sexton on "Losing Your Touch," a playful rocker that could have come from the Replacements/Paul Westerberg camp. With the exception of this track, "Mountain of Mud," and the John Cougar-ish "The End," *Thirteen Years* keeps to fragile, graceful interiors. —*Roch Parisien*

The End/Losing Your Touch / 1994 / Watermelon ◆◆◆

With These Hands / Jun. 18, 1996 / Rykodisc ◆◆◆◆
Alejandro Escovedo's fourth solo album, *With These Hands*, is his most direct, straightforward collection to date. Stripping away some of the ambitious musical eclecticism that characterized his earlier records, Escovedo sticks to rock 'n' roll and country-rock, and the results are frequently bracing. The songs feature his trademark cutting lyricism, brought to the fore by the lean attack of his band. Both Escovedo's incisive songwriting and his passionate performing make *With These Hands* a roots-rock record that matters. —*Stephen Thomas Erlewine*

Evangeline

b. 1988
Contemporary Country
This New Orleans-based band blends good-time, Bayou country tunes with sweetly sensitive balladry. Their first album features a quintet led by the smooth vocals of guitarist Kathleen Stieffel and the rowdier vocals of bassist and washboard specialist Sharon

Leger. Austin keyboard vet Beth McKee also adds vocals, with lead guitarist Rhonda Lohmeyer contributing the bulk of the original songs, and Nancy Buchan filling out the sound on fiddle and mandolin. Buchan left before the recording of the second album. —*Michael McCall*

Evangeline / 1992 / Margaritaville ◆◆◆
The Louisiana influence is subdued, except when highlighted on an obvious track like "Bayou Boy," but it does give this band a sound that separates it from most Nashville pop-country groups. —*Michael McCall*

● French Quarter Moon / 1993 / Margaritaville ◆◆◆◆
More spirited and more country than their debut, this album is aided by a better selection of songs. Evangeline's version of "The Wild One" kicks harder than Faith Hill's better-known hit. —*Michael McCall*

Leon Everette

b. Jun. 21, 1948, Aiken, SC
Vocals / Country-Pop, Urban Cowboy
Singer-songwriter Leon Everette achieved his greatest popularity from the late '70s to the mid-'80s. Born Leon Everette Baughman in South Carolina, he was raised in Queens, NY. Following his high school graduation, Everette joined the Navy and served on an aircraft carrier in the South Pacific. While on leave in the Philippines, he bought a guitar and taught himself to play, and soon won a Navy talent contest. After his discharge, Everette married and returned to South Carolina, issuing a series of singles that went nowhere. Eventually, he got a job in True Records' Nashville mail room. He later signed with the label, and was assigned to do a tribute to Elvis, *Goodbye King of Rock and Roll*, in 1977. Everette was less than thrilled at the prospect, and ripped up his contract. Later that year, True released Everette's single "I Love That Woman (Like the Devil Loves Sin)," which became a minor hit.

Meanwhile, Everette continued to play in Augusta, GA, where he was seen by Orlando Records founder Carroll Fulmer. Fulmer signed Everette to his label and hired Jerry Foster and Bill Rice to write songs for him. In 1979, Orlando released four of Everette's singles, including "Don't Feel Like the Lone Ranger," and all became minor hits. Everette's success allowed him to sign with RCA the following year, where he had several major hits, among them the label's reissue of the single "Giving Up Easy." His string of Top 20 hits continued with "Just Give Me What You Think Is Fair" and "Soul Searching," both from 1982. In 1984, Everette became unhappy with RCA's promotion and switched to Mercury Records, where he had three minor hits in 1985, including "Till a Tear Becomes a Rose." By the end of the year, he had moved back to Orlando and in 1986 hit the charts with three singles, including "Still in the Picture." In 1988, he left country music to open an imported wicker shop in Ward, SC. —*Sandra Brennan*

Goodbye King of Rock n' Roll / 1977 / True ◆◆◆

I Don't Want to Lose / 1980 / Orlando ◆◆◆

Hurricane / 1981 / RCA ◆◆◆◆

Maverick / 1982 / RCA ◆◆◆◆

Doin' What I Feel / 1984 / RCA ◆◆◆

Where's the Fire / 1985 / Mercury ◆◆◆

● Best of Leon Everette / 1985 / RCA ◆◆◆◆

The Everly Brothers

Rock & Roll, Country-Rock, Pop-Rock, Close Harmony
The Everly Brothers were not only among the most important and best early rock 'n' roll stars, but also among the most influential rockers of any era. They set unmatched standards for close, two-part harmonies, and infused early rock 'n' roll with some of the best elements of country and pop music. Their legacy was and is felt enormously in all rock acts that employ harmonies as prime features, from the Beatles, Simon & Garfunkel, and legions of country-rockers to modern-day roots rockers like Dave Edmunds and Nick Lowe (who once recorded an EP of Everlys songs together).

Don (born February 1, 1937) and Phil (born January 19, 1939) were professionals way before their teens, schooled by their accomplished guitarist father Ike, and singing with their family on radio broadcasts in Iowa. In the mid-'50s, they made a brief stab at conventional Nashville country with Columbia. When their single flopped, they were cast adrift for quite a while until they latched onto Cadence. Don invested their first single for the label, "Bye Bye Love," with a Bo Diddley beat that helped lift the song to No. 2 in 1957.

"Bye Bye Love" began a phenomenal three-year string of classic hit singles for Cadence, including "Wake Up Little Susie," "All I Have to Do Is Dream," "Bird Dog," "(Til) I Kissed You," and "When Will I Be Loved." The Everlys sang of young love with a heartrending yearning and compelling melodies. The harmonies owed audible debts to Appalachian country music, but were imbued with a keen modern pop sensibility that made them more accessible without sacrificing any power or beauty. The Everlys were not as raw as the wild rockabilly men from Sun Records, but they could rock hard when they wanted. Even their mid-tempo numbers and ballads were executed with a force missing in the straight country and pop tunes of the era. The duo enjoyed top-notch support, with producer Archie Bleyer, great Nashville session players like Chet Atkins, and the brilliant songwriting team of Boudleaux and Felice Bryant. Don and (occasionally) Phil wrote excellent songs of their own as well.

In 1960, the Everlys left Cadence for a lucrative contract with the then-young Warner Bros. label (though it's not often noted, the Everlys would do a lot to establish Warners as a major force in the record business). It's sometimes been written that the duo never recaptured the magic of their Cadence recordings, but actually Phil and Don peaked both commercially and artistically with their first Warners releases. "Cathy's Clown," their first Warners single, was one of their greatest songs and a No. 1 hit. Their first two Warners LPs, employing a fuller and brasher production than their Cadence work, were not just among their best work, but two of the best rock albums of the early '60s. The hits kept coming for a couple of years, some great ("Walk Right Back," "Temptation"), others displaying a distressing, increasing tendency towards soft pop and maudlin sentiments ("Ebony Eyes," "That's Old Fashioned").

Don and Phil's personal lives came under a lot of stress in the early '60s: they were drafted into the Army (together), and studied acting for six months, but never made a motion picture. More seriously, Don developed an addiction to speed and almost died of an overdose in late 1962. By that time, their career as chart titans in the US had ended; "That's Old Fashioned" (1962) was their last Top Ten hit. Their albums became careless, erratic affairs, which was all the more frustrating because many of their flop singles of the time were fine, even near-classic efforts that demonstrated they could still deliver the goods.

Virtually alone among first-generation rock 'n' roll superstars, the Everlys stuck with no-nonsense rock 'n' roll and remained determined to keep their sound contemporary, rather than drifting toward soft pop or country like so many others. Although their mid-'60s recordings were largely ignored in America, they contained some of their finest work, including a ferocious Top 40 single in 1964 ("Gone, Gone, Gone"). They remained big stars overseas—in 1965, "Price of Love" went to No. 2 in the UK at the height of the British Invasion. They incorporated jangling Beatle/ Byrdesque guitars into some of their songs, and recorded a fine album with the Hollies (who were probably more blatantly influenced by the Everlys than any other British band of the time). In the late '60s, the Everlys helped pioneer country-rock with the 1968 album Roots, their most sophisticated and unified full-length statement. None of this revived their career as hitmakers, though they could always command huge audiences on international tours, and hosted a network TV variety show in 1970.

The decades of enforced professional togetherness finally took their toll on the pair in the early '70s, which saw a few dispirited albums and, finally, an acrimonious breakup in 1973. The Everlys spent the next decade performing solo, which only proved—as is so often the case in close-knit artistic partnerships—how much each brother needed the other to sound his best. In 1983, enough

The Everly Brothers

water had flowed under the bridge for the two to resume performing and recording together. The tours, with a backup band led by guitarist Albert Lee, proved they could still sing well. The records (both live and studio) were fair efforts that, in the final estimation, were not in nearly the same league as their '50s and '60s classics, although Paul McCartney penned a small hit single for them ("On the Wings of a Nightingale"). Although it was one of the most successful and dignified reunions in rock annals, this too could not last; as of this writing, the Everlys have not performed or recorded together since the early '90s. —Richie Unterberger

The Everly Brothers / 1958 / Cadence ✦✦✦✦
Although the Everlys hadn't quite fully matured as artists, their debut is a fine, consistent effort divided between original material and respectably energetic covers of early rockers by Little Richard, Gene Vincent, and Ray Charles. Besides their first few hits, it includes some superb, underappreciated tracks that are nearly as good, like "Should We Tell Him" and "I Wonder If I Care As Much." —Richie Unterberger

Songs Our Daddy Taught Us / 1959 / Rhino ✦✦✦
The Everlys had reached their commercial peak when they made this album of sparsely arranged traditional songs, a concept which was quite a surprise from a top rock 'n' roll act, and considerably ahead of its time. It's actually not as enduring as their early rockers and pop ballads, but the singing is superb on their interpretations of standards like "Barbara Allen" and "Kentucky." —Richie Unterberger

The Fabulous Style of the Everly Brothers / 1960 / Rhino ✦✦✦✦
The best of their original Cadence albums, packed with hits ("Bird Dog," "All I Have To Do Is Dream," "When Will I Be Loved," "Til I Kissed You") and other classic tracks ("Devoted to You," "Let It Be Me," "Since You Broke My Heart," "Like Strangers"). Almost all of the songs show up on their greatest hits collections, so it might be a superfluous purchase for all but serious fans, despite its top-drawer quality. —Richie Unterberger

It's Everly Time / 1960 / Warner Brothers ✦✦✦✦
While the Everlys' sound was diluted by more elaborate production in the '60s, that's not at all true on this LP, which is one of

their very best. Not a stiff among the 12 tracks, most of which are barely known outside of serious Everly fans. Includes six stellar contributions by Boudleaux and Felice Bryant, one of Don Everly's best compositions ("So Sad"), and incredible harmony singing throughout. —*Richie Unterberger*

A Date with the Everly Brothers / 1961 / Warner Brothers ✦✦✦✦
Although the material is not on the killer level of *Everly Time*, there are some very fine songs on their second Warner LP. Includes "Cathy's Clown," their raucous cover of Little Richard's "Lucille," "Love Hurts" (which preceded Roy Orbison's hit version), and "So How Come" (covered by the Beatles in 1963 on the BBC). —*Richie Unterberger*

Roots / 1968 / Warner Brothers ✦✦✦✦
Considered one of the finest early country-rock albums, this showed the Everlys, unlike virtually every other top rock 'n' roll act of the '50s, keeping abreast of contemporary rock and pop trends. In the manner of their 1958 LP *Songs Our Daddy Taught Us*, the concept was to cover songs by performers and composers that had been influential on the duo, including Jimmie Rodgers, Merle Haggard, traditional standards, and a couple of numbers by Ron Elliott of the Beau Brummels. Although this laidback, tasteful, acoustic-oriented recording isn't as outstanding as their classic early hits, the vocals are superb, conveying qualities of innocence tempered by experience. —*Richie Unterberger*

All They Had to Do Was Dream / 1985 / Rhino ✦✦✦
Alternate takes of much of their strongest material from the Cadence era, cut between 1957 and 1960. A bit more tentative than the familiar renditions, these aren't as good as the versions that ended up on official releases, but are enjoyable and fascinating glimpses at works in progress, and the singing is excellent throughout. Includes different versions of hits like "Wake Up Little Susie," "All I Have to Do Is Dream," "Till I Kissed You," and "When Will I Be Loved." —*Richie Unterberger*

★ **Cadence Classics: Their 20 Greatest Hits** / 1986 / Rhino ✦✦✦✦✦
The single-disc collection *Cadence Classics: Their 20 Greatest Hits* compiles all of the Everly Brothers' hits, plus many terrific album tracks, from the duo's recordings for Cadence Records in the late '50s. Every one of the Everlys' biggest hits, including "Bye Bye Love," "I Wonder If I Care As Much," "Wake Up, Little Susie," "This Little Girl of Mine," "All I Have to Do Is Dream," "Claudette," "Bird Dog," "Devoted to You," "Problems," "Message to Mary," "('Til) I Kissed You," "Let It Be Me," and "When Will I Be Loved." *Cadence Classics* misses no essential track, making it a definitive collection and the perfect introduction to the duo's sound. —*Stephen Thomas Erlewine*

Hidden Gems from the Warner Years / 1989 / Ace ✦✦✦✦
This collects 14 songs that originally appeared on non-hit singles between 1962 and 1965; many of them had never been on LP. This material strongly counters the view that the Everlys faded artistically after "Cathy's Clown." The writing credits for these strong compositions read a bit like a Who's Who of early '60s pop-rock, with contributions from Gerry Goffin, Mann/Weill, Doc Pomus & Mort Shuman, Sonny Curtis, Boudleaux and Felice Bryant, and the Everlys themselves. The singing is fabulous, and the arrangements are strong, rock-oriented, and tastefully produced. Tracks like "Nancy's Minuet" (1963), a great Don Everly original and one of their best paeans to lovelorn melancholia, and "You're the One I Love" (1964), a fine brooding mid-tempo rocker, stand with their very best work. Only three of these appear on the '60s Everlys anthology *Walk Right Back*, making this a necessary purchase for Everlys fans. —*Richie Unterberger*

Classic Everly Brothers / 1992 / Bear Family ✦✦✦✦
The three-disc box set *Classic Everly Brothers* collects all of their Cadence recordings, including alternate takes, as well as several early radio shows and the four tracks the duo recorded for Columbia in 1955. While this music is the most essential the brothers ever made, the disc of rarities is only of interest to devoted fans. Nevertheless, the sound on the box is stellar, the liner notes are excellent, and the whole package is wonderful; for hardcore fans, the set is worth the money. —*Stephen Thomas Erlewine*

☆ **Walk Right Back: The Everly Brothers on Warner Bros.** / 1993 / Warner Archive ✦✦✦✦✦
This two-CD, 50-track compilation assembles the Everly Brothers' most memorable recordings of the 1960s. Although their work from this period has sometimes been criticized for being inferior to their classic '50s recordings for Cadence, the best of these songs are a match for anything the duo recorded. As it happens, the strongest of these tunes are drawn from their first two albums for Warners in the 1960s, including the hits "Cathy's Clown" and "So Sad." In the following years, their material suffered from increasing inconsistency and ill-suited production. Yet the Brothers continued to intermittently hit the mark squarely—not only with early '60s hits like "Crying in the Rain" and "Temptation," but neglected flop singles like "Nancy's Minuet" and "You're the One I Love," as well as the hard-rocking minor 1964 hit "Gone, Gone, Gone" (their last Top 40 single). They also showed a willingness to incorporate the hard-rocking beat of the British Invasion into their work, which was not shared by any of the other major stars of the '50s. This compilation misses a number of fine B-sides and non-hit singles from the early and mid-'60s (check the Ace import collection *Hidden Gems* for those), and perhaps leans too heavily on their tepid late '60s country-rock. But it's a good overview of a body of work that is often unfairly overlooked. —*Richie Unterberger*

☆ **Heartaches & Harmonies [Box Set]** / 1994 / Rhino ✦✦✦✦✦
This four-CD, 102-song set includes all of the Everlys' key performances, as well as many overlooked ones, dating from a previously unreleased 1951 radio performance of "Don't Let Our Love Die" to a 1990 live rendition of the very same tune. Opening with a disc's worth of classic Cadence performances, most of the next three CDs are given over to the Everlys' largely overlooked Warner Bros. '60s output, including many interesting flop singles and album tracks, as well as top-notch rarities like an alternate version of the supremely moody "Nancy's Minuet" and the mid-'60s outtake "And I'll Go." The set contains fine liner notes with detailed comments from the Everlys themselves, but it still manages to miss some great tunes (like the 1964 single "You're the One I Love" and various tracks from their late '50s and early '60s LPs), and shouldn't be considered a definitive collection of all their great performances. And the hard fact is, a lot of their post-1966 material (which comprises some of disc three and all of disc four) is kind of boring. —*Richie Unterberger*

Skip Ewing

b. Mar. 6, 1964, Redlands, CA
Vocals / Contemporary Country

Skip Ewing was more famous for his songwriting than his performing. Born the son of a naval lieutenant commander in Redlands, CA, Donald Ralph Ewing—"Skip," short for "Little Skipper"—was a nickname he received in childhood—spent much of his childhood traveling around the country. At a young age he heard Merle Haggard and Lefty Frizzell on the radio and was inspired to become a country musician himself. Ewing was playing guitar before he was literate and began writing his first songs as a teen. During high school, Ewing also participated in plays and played his banjo at local bluegrass festivals.

Ewing was performing in the Old Country show at Busch Gardens in Virginia when someone asked him if he were interested in performing at Opryland. Though only 19, he moved to Nashville and spent two-and-a-half years imitating famous country stars at the Music City theme park, earning extra cash singing commercial jingles. He also continued to develop his songwriting skills. Eventually Ewing signed to Acuff-Rose Music as a staff writer. While there, his songs were recorded by such stars as George Jones, George Strait, and Charley Pride.

In 1987, he signed to MCA, where he co-produced his debut album, *The Coast of Colorado* with Jimmy Bowen. The following year he hit the Top 20 with his single "Your Memory Wins Again." His next two singles, "Don't Have Far to Fall" and "Burnin' a Hole in My Heart," made it to the Top Ten and the Top Three respectively. He remained with MCA through 1991 and made one more album there before moving to Capitol, where Jimmy Bowen was now in charge. Two albums, *Naturally* and *Homegrown Love*, followed. Ewing continued to write and co-write songs, and has been further recorded by Kenny Rogers, Willie Nelson, Randy Travis, and Lorrie Morgan. —*Sandra Brennan*

Dad / 1986 / MCA ✦✦✦✦

Coast of Colorado / Apr. 4, 1988 / MCA ✦✦✦✦
Coast of Colorado stands as Ewing's most consistently strong collection of songs; the highlights include the Top Ten hits "Burnin' a Hole in My Heart" and "I Don't Have Far to Fall." —*Jason Ankeny*

● **Greatest Hits** / 1991 / MCA ✦✦✦✦
This collection of Ewing's hits includes "Your Memory Wins Again," "If a Man Could Live on Love Alone" and "Burnin' a Hole in My Heart." —*Jason Ankeny*

Naturally / Jun. 10, 1991 / Capitol ✦✦✦
Naturally features a pair of minor chart entries, "I Get the Picture" and the title song. —*Jason Ankeny*

Homegrown Love / 1993 / Capitol ✦✦✦

Healin' Fire / MCA ✦✦✦
Here are such Ewing favorites as "I'm OK (And Gettin' Better)," "The Dotted Line," and "I'm Your Man." —*AMG*

The Will to Love / MCA ✦✦✦
The Top Five hit "It's You Again" is the centerpiece of Ewing's third LP. —*Jason Ankeny*

Exile

Country-Rock, Country-Pop
Although the Kentucky-based group Exile's first hit "Kiss You All Over" was a major pop smash, they experienced their greatest success as a country band in the latter half of the '80s. Exile was co-founded by J.P. Pennington, the son of former Coon Creek Girl Lily May Ledford, in 1963. Originally known as the Exiles, they got their start touring with Dick Clark in 1965. In 1973, they changed their name to Exile and had their first minor chart success with "Try It On." They followed it up with "Kiss You All Over," which hit No. 1 on the US pop charts in 1978. After delivering several unsuccessful follow-ups to their hit single, Exile returned to Kentucky to retool their sound by working in local clubs.

They soon gained a popular following, and several of their songs from the period were covered by major artists such as Janie Fricke ("It Ain't Easy Being Easy") and Alabama ("The Closer You Get"). By the time they finally re-emerged onto the country music scene in the 1980s, the band had gone from mellow pop band to a high voltage five-piece band of Southern rockers consisting of Pennington, Les Taylor, Sonny Lemaire, Marlon Hargis, and Steve Goetzman. The group signed to Epic Records in 1983 and their

first country single, "High Cost of Leaving," reached No. 27. An eponymous album followed and it produced two chart-toppers, "Woke Up in Love" and "I Don't Wanna Be a Memory." In 1984, Exile's second country album, *Kentucky Hearts*, provided three more No. 1 hits, including "Crazy for Your Love." Released in 1985, *Hang on to Your Heart* was even more successful, producing four No. 1 singles, including the title track and "I Could Get Used to You."

During 1986, Exile took an extended break, returning with *Shelter from the Night* in 1987. Although it contained the No. 1 hit "I Can't Get Close Enough," the album wasn't as successful as its predecessors. The band then underwent personnel changes over the next two years. First Hargis was replaced by keyboardist Lee Carroll, then Taylor left the group in 1989, with Mark Jones replacing him. Finally, after nearly three decades, founder Pennington left and guitar player Paul Martin took his place. Exile signed to Arista in 1990 and later released *Still Standing*. The album produced two Top Ten hits, "Nobody's Talking" and "Yet." They released one more album, 1991's *Justice*, which contained the hit "Even Now." Arista dropped the group in 1993; left without a record label, Exile decided to disband. —*Sandra Brennan*

Exile / 1973 / Wooden Nickel ✦✦✦✦

Kentucky Hearts / 1984 / Epic ✦✦✦

● **Greatest Hits** / 1986 / Epic ✦✦✦✦
Exile—Greatest Hits offers a good cross-section of the band's late-'70s and early-80s country-rock hits, including "Kiss You All Over" and "Woke Up in Love." —*Stephen Thomas Erlewine*

Shelter from the Night / 1987 / Epic ✦✦✦
Almost a decade removed from "Kiss You All Over," the band leans closer to Top 40 rock than country—don't read that as a complaint. The band commuted to Connecticut on off-days during a summer-long tour to record in Stamford with Bruce Hornsby-producer Elliot Scheiner, and their effort is surprisingly inspired. If you can't dance to "I Can't Get Close Enough," "Just One Kiss," or "She's Already Gone," you can't dance. —*Tom Roland*

Still Standing / 1990 / Arista ✦✦✦✦
A fun, peppy country album, this is their best. —*Bil Carpenter*

The Complete Collection / 1991 / Curb ✦✦✦✦
The Complete Collection is a good summation of Exile's '80s career, concentrating on lesser-known tracks, not chart-toppers. For the big hits, stick with *Greatest Hits*, but if you want to dig a little deeper, start with *The Complete Collection*. —*Stephen Thomas Erlewine*

Super Hits / Mar. 9, 1993 / Epic ✦✦✦✦

F

Barbara Fairchild

b. Nov. 12, 1950, Knobel, AR
Vocals / Traditional Country, Country-Pop
Singer-songwriter Barbara Fairchild began her performing career at the age of five, when she won a grade-school talent contest. When she was 13, her family moved from her native Knobel, AR, to St. Louis. Two years later, Fairchild cut her first single, "Brand New Bed of Roses," for Norman; she also began making TV appearances. After high school, she went to Nashville with a friend to try to sell her songs and get a recording contract. She was encouraged by a meeting with MCA record executive Jerry Crutchfield, who liked her songs and suggested she return home and write seven more of equal quality. Two months later, Fairchild returned with 15 songs, and Crutchfield signed her to his writing staff. He then sent a demo of her singing her song "Love Is a Gentle Thing" to Billy Sherrill, Vice President of Columbia Nashville's A&R. Fairchild soon had a recording contract with Columbia, which released her demo in 1969 as a single. Both it and a follow-up became Top 70 hits. The following year, her third single "A Girl Who'll Satisfy Her Man," hit the Top 30. After releasing two moderately successful songs in 1971, she scored a Top 40 hit the following year with her cover of Petula Clark's earlier hit "Color My World." At the end of the year she had the biggest hit of her career with "Teddy Bear Song," which was No. 1 for two weeks and even crossed over to the pop charts. This resulted in a Grammy nomination and appearances on national TV shows. Fairchild also went to England to do a special for BBC-TV. Her next hit, "Kid Stuff," also crossed over to the pop charts in 1973 and hit No. 3 on the country charts. Between 1975 and 1978, she appeared on the singles charts ten times, hitting the Top 15 with "Cheatin Is."

Fairchild's star began to wane by the turn of the decade, and none of her subsequent singles made it past the Top 40. She left the music industry in 1979 and moved to San Antonio to be with her children. One year later, she and Billy Walker recorded a few duets on the Paid label. In 1982 she married evangelical singer-songwriter Milton Carol (her third marriage), and in 1984 went back to Nashville to attempt a comeback. She failed as a solo artist, but in 1989 was asked to join the gospel group Heirloom. In 1991, she released her first solo gospel album, *The Light*, which contained a great deal of self-penned material and produced the hits "Turn Right and Then Go Straight" and "Mary Washed His Feet." When not recording gospel songs, Fairchild performs in Branson, MO. —*Sandra Brennan*

● It Takes Two / 1979 / Paid ✦✦✦✦

The Light / Benson ✦✦✦

The Son in My Eyes / Benson ✦✦✦

Donna Fargo (Yvonne Vaughn)

b. Nov. 10, 1949, Mount Airy, NC
Guitar, Vocals / Country-Pop
In the early '70s, Donna Fargo was an unusual country star for a couple of reasons. She was one of the few female country singers to write her own material, and one of the few country singers of any sort to cross over to the pop charts in a big way, which she did

in 1972 with "The Happiest Girl in the Whole USA." (No. 11) and "Funny Face" (No. 5). She never made the pop Top 40 again, but placed over a dozen more singles in the country Top Ten in the '70s, most self-penned. As an artist, she was squarely in the mainstream, her slightly lisping voice delivering upbeat, sweetly produced homilies to romance, home, and America. She faded after developing multiple sclerosis in 1979, although she continued writing and performing. —*Richie Unterberger*

The Best of Donna Fargo / 1977 / MCA ✦✦✦✦
Contains the hits "Funny Face" and "The Happiest Girl in the Whole USA," but has since been superceded by the collection on Varèse Vintage.—*Dan Heilman*

● Best of Donna Fargo / 1995 / Varèse Vintage ✦✦✦✦
Eighteen songs, all but one dating from her 1972-75 prime, when she recorded for Dot. Contains ten Top Ten country hits, including, of course, "Funny Face" and "The Happiest Girl in the Whole USA." —*Richie Unterberger*

Country Spotlight / Dominion ✦
Fargo's hits are here, but not in the original versions; instead, they're in new stereo rerecordings, which pale next to the originals. Leave this one on the shelf. —*Stephen Thomas Erlewine*

Encore / Bear Family ✦✦✦✦
This features "Great Balls of Fire," "Y'All Come Back Soon," and "I Know a Heartache," among other songs. —*AMG*

Farm Dogs

Blues, Folk
Assembled and led by Bernie Taupin, best known for being the lyrical half of an extremely successful and long-running songwriting collaboration with Elton John, Farm Dogs is a labor of love for the storyteller, who has always been infatuated with American roots music. It was Taupin's intention to make a record that captured that simple, uncluttered sound; therefore the idea behind the Farm Dogs' project was to use only acoustic instruments, which the band stuck to save for the use of percussion and some sparse electric guitar for effect. The album was recorded at Taupin's home studio in the Santa Ynez Valley, where he runs a ranch with his wife. Since his childhood, Taupin has been fascinated by American culture and the wild, wild West, so it's not surprising that the Elton John album *Tumbleweed Connection* was Taupin's vision and that the Farm Dogs project brings him full circle. For Taupin, *Last Stand in Open Country* picks up where *Tumbleweed Connection* left off, with the new songs bringing to life a string of colorful characters that include fast women, drunkards, misfits, and movie stars. Along with Taupin, Farm Dogs is comprised of guitarist Jim Cregan and guitarist/dobro player Robin Le Mesurier, both of whom have served long tenures as sidemen for Rod Stewart. Rounding out the group is Dennis Tufano, former lead singer for the '60s group the Buckinghams. Tufanoalso worked on Taupin's second solo album, *He Who Rides the Tiger*. Taupin's other efforts include an early-'70s, self-titled spoken word album, as well as his third solo project, *Tribe*. —*Jack Leaver*

● **Last Stand in Open Country** / 1996 / Discovery ✦✦✦
Best known for his work as a lyricist with Elton John, Farm Dogs
is the dream band Bernie Taupin has always wanted to form. Collaborating with veteran musicians Jim Cregan, Dennis Tufano,
and Robin Le Mesurier, Taupin has made a fine acoustic-oriented
record that combines rootsy country, blues, and folk music with
his immense talent as a storyteller. Much of this record recalls
some of the early and more countrified work with Elton during
the *Tumbleweed Connection* period, and lyrically it stands up to
his best efforts. The songs are steeped with Americana and come
alive with colorful and humorously twisted wordplay, while the
folky instrumental backing and three—and four-part harmonies
give the record a homey, front porch quality. While there might
not be anything as awe-inspiring as "Your Song," or "Goodbye
Yellow Brick Road," *Last Stand in Open Country* has plenty of
highlights. Taupin and company pull out the stops on songs such
as the clever talking blues of "The Ballad of Dennis Hopper and
Harry Dean," and the vivid imagery of "Burn This Bed" and "Barstool." —*Jack Leaver*

Hugh & Karl Farr

Cowboy, Western Swing
Hugh and Karl Farr were the most important fiddle-and-guitar
duo in the history of country or western music, a team of brother
virtuosos who brought the vocabulary and dexterity of the best
jazz into the confines of country and cowboy songs for more than
25 years. That they aren't better known as a duo stems from the
fact that their work from the mid-1930s onward was largely confined to membership in the Sons of the Pioneers.

Hugh Farr was born in Llano, TX, on December 6, 1903. Karl
was born April 25, 1909, in Rochele, TX. Their father and mother
were both part-time musicians; when he wasn't working as a
building contractor and she wasn't raising a family, they played
local dances as a fiddle and guitar duo. Hugh took up the guitar
at age seven, mastered it quickly, and within a year was playing
local dances as part of a duet with his father, playing songs like
"Texas Crapshooter," "The Arkansas Traveler," and "Fire in the
Mountain." His father wanted a fiddle player, however, and by age
nine Hugh had not only learned the instrument but also knew
how to play every song in their repertory. Hugh's fiddle style, as it
developed in the late 1910s and early 1920s, was influenced
heavily by the jazz of the era, especially the work of the Kansas
City Nite Hawks. By 1916 Karl was playing with Hugh and their
brother Glen on the mandolin. He later picked up the banjo and
finally the guitar.

The three Farr brothers continued to play together after their
father moved the family to California in early 1925. Hugh had
landed a gig with a local combo at a place called Mammy's Shack,
and by 1928, when the group broke up, he was ready to pursue
music as a permanent career. Karl later followed suit, after he and
his brothers made their first appearance on radio in Los Angeles.
Hugh and Karl joined Len Nash and His Country Boys, a Los
Angeles country music group that hosted the program *Len Nash
and His Country Boys' Barn Dance.* The program lasted from
1929 until 1933, during which Hugh appeared on several Len
Nash records, among them "On the Road to California," "Going
Down to Town," and "Kelly Waltz." In 1933, the group moved to a
new dance hall in Anaheim, which was unsuccessful, and they
broke up. Hugh and Karl then formed a group, the Haywire Trio,
with fellow bandmember Ira McCullough.

Hugh joined Jack LeFevre and His Texas Outlaws, while Karl
worked as a staff musician at radio station KFOX. It was while
playing with LeFevre's group on Los Angeles radio station KFWB
that Hugh made the acquaintance of a group of musicians called
the Pioneer Trio. Sometime in late 1933 or early 1934, Hugh was
asked by Pioneers Leonard Slye, Bob Nolan, and Tim Spencer to
join, and the quartet was renamed the Sons of the Pioneers. In
addition to playing the fiddle, Hugh also sang the bass parts on
their records. Meanwhile, Karl continued playing with different
groups around Los Angeles. The Pioneers, however, knew that
they needed a proper guitar player who could handle lead parts;
Hugh proposed his brother, and in 1935 Karl Farr joined the
group. While Nolan and Spencer were brilliant songwriters and

Slye was a great performing talent with a comedy, the Farrs
brought an instrumental dexterity that was extraordinary. The
brothers were also quite capable improvisers, able to come up
with material to fill time on radio shows at a moment's notice.

The Farr brothers remained with the Pioneers for more than 20
years, sacrificing some of the recognition that they might've
received on behalf of the group. Karl Farr could easily have been
another Merle Travis or Chet Atkins—he was that good—and was
sufficiently well known within professional music circles to have
been given one of Fender's very first Telecasters in 1949. For
Hugh Farr, however, the lack of recognition created considerable
tension, particularly as the band's membership went through
massive lineup changes during the mid-1950s, and he left the
group late in 1957. Karl remained with the Sons of the Pioneers
until his death, when at a show in Massachusetts on September
20, 1961, a string broke on his guitar in the middle of a solo and,
struggling to change it, he collapsed and died of a heart attack.

After leaving the Pioneers, Hugh Farr tried for a time to lead
his own version of the Sons of the Pioneers, claiming ownership
of the name as the last active member of the original quartet.
Farr's group failed to find an audience, however, and disbanded
soon after it was organized. He played with singing cowboy star
Jimmy Wakely, and later co-founded the Country Gentlemen with
Pat Patterson, Kenny Baker, and Jimmie Widener, who broke up
after a short but successful performing career and one album.
Farr spent the 1960s playing with different groups, and passed
away on April 17, 1980. —*Bruce Eder*

Texas Crapshooter / 1978 / J.E.M.F. ✦✦✦

● **Texas Stomp 1934-1944** / 1993 / Country Routes ✦✦✦✦
Two dozen radio transcriptions of songs by Hugh and Karl Farr
from the mid-1930s, showing the duo in top form before they
became a permanent part of the Sons of the Pioneers. Karl's playing here anticipates the best work of Merle Travis and Chet
Atkins, which was still a decade or two away, and Hugh's playing
on the fiddle would humble fans of such players as Byron Berline
and other modern country fiddlers, not to mention a jazzman or
two. Their playing is even more striking for the good-natured ease
with which they present it—they were the best at what they did,
incorporating jazz and classical influences into country and cowboy songs as easily as most of us breathe, and they even made it
seem easy. —*Bruce Eder*

Charlie Feathers

b. Jun. 12, 1932, Holly Springs, MS
Guitar, Vocals / Traditional Country, Rockabilly
Charlie Feathers is many things to many fans of rock and country
music. To some, he's a superb country stylist who can take almost
any piece of material and stamp it with the full force of his personality. To others, he's one of the great rockabilly pioneers and
still fully functioning practitioners, there at the dawn of Sun
Records. And Feathers' stubborn insistence on combining elements of country, raw blues, and bluegrass to make his own version of the rockabilly experience has shown him to be one of the
genre's most original and enduring artists.

He was born in Holly Springs, MS, with music all around the
sharecropping community he grew up in. After day jobs in Illinois
and Texas, Feathers moved to Memphis in 1950, working for a
box manufacturer until a bout with spinal meningitis left him
hospitalized. Listening to the radio there on a daily basis, he
emerged from his stay determined to become a professional
singer. By 1954, Feathers was working his way into the confines
of Sam Phillips' Memphis Recording Service, with an eye toward
getting something released on Sun Records. He filled in whenever
and wherever he could, helping with arrangement ideas, even
playing spoons on a Miller Sisters session. Demoing songs for
steel guitarist Stan Kesler found him getting half credit on the
Elvis Sun side, "I Forgot to Remember to Forget." Phillips decided
to start a local non-union label called Flip to test out new artists
and, after pairing Feathers with country session songwriter-musi-
cians Bill Cantrell and Quinton Claunch, released the first Feathers single on that label, the classic "Peepin' Eyes" coupled with
"I've Been Deceived." The record kicked enough noise locally to

get Feathers transferred to Sun for a second single, but the artist had bigger visions. Although Phillips saw him "as a superb country stylist," Feathers wanted to rock, and cut many Sun demo sessions in that style. When Phillips turned a deaf ear to it all, Feathers' impatience led him to Memphis rival Meteor Records, where he waxed the double-sided rockabilly classic "Tongue Tied Jill" and "Get with It." This single garnered enough Memphis airplay to cement him a deal with King Records, and it is here that the Charlie Feathers as rockabilly legend story begins in earnest. The dozen or so sides he cut as singles for King are the greatest '50s rockabilly tracks to escape the hegemony of the Sun studios with "One Hand Loose," "Bottle to the Baby," "Everybody's Lovin' My Baby" and "I Can't Hardly Stand It" all becoming classics of the genre. Their territorial success got Feathers on numerous package tours and multiple appearances on Dallas' Big D Jamboree. When the King contract ran out, Feathers continued to record one-off singles for a variety of Memphis labels, all of them of a very high musical quality, while stubbornly playing his music for whatever local audience cared to listen.

When the rockabilly revival started up in Europe in the early '70s, Charlie Feathers became the first living artist up for deification by collectors. His old 45s suddenly became worth hundreds of dollars and every interviewer wanted to know why Feathers never really made it big and what his true involvement with Sun consisted of. Feathers embroidered the story with his own skewed view of rock 'n' roll history with each retelling, to be sure, but once he picked up his guitar and sang to reinforce his point, the truth came out in his music. Never mind why he didn't make it back in the '50s; he could still deliver the goods now.

Although health problems plague him from his diabetes and one lung was surgically removed, Feathers continues on his own irascible course, recording his first album for a major label in 1991 (Elektra's American Masters series) and continuing to perform and record for his wide European fan base. Charlie Feathers is truly an American music original. —Cub Koda

Tip Top Daddy / Norton ✦✦✦

Call this one "Charlie Feathers Unplugged" if you want to, but what we have here is a bushelbasket of unissued acoustic demos from 1958 to 1973 from the King of Rockabilly. It doesn't much matter when Feathers cut something as long as he was into it when the tape was rollin', and here's 23 tracks that bear that simple fact out. It also doesn't seem to matter much if Feathers wrote the tune or not, because everything he puts his pipes to—along with his consummate arranging talents—stamps it with the crazed redneck mark of his own personality. Electric guitar fleshes out a couple of tracks here and there, but in the main it's pure, unvarnished Charlie Feathers, and that's worth more than the next dozen hat hunk albums that come down the pike. —Cub Koda

Live in Memphis / 1979 / Barrelhouse ✦✦✦

Loose early-'70s recordings. Great, but unfortunately out of print. —Cub Koda

● Jungle Fever / 1987 / Kay ✦✦✦✦

Boasting a generous 20 tracks, Jungle Fever is the best available compilation of Charlie Feathers' original rockabilly recordings; all of his best-known songs are collected here, including "Get with It" and "Tongue-Tied Jill." —Stephen Thomas Erlewine

Charlie Feathers / 1991 / Elektra/Nonesuch ✦✦✦

This disc feels more like a musicologist's preservation project than the kind of whiplash rockabilly it's meant to epitomize.... On his first major-label recording, Feathers comes across more like a crotchety holdout than the maverick genius he thinks he is. —John Floyd

Rock-A-Billy / May 1991 / Zu-Zazz ✦✦✦✦

Superb collection of rare and unissued sides from 1954-1973, showcasing Feathers' mastery of rockabilly and country material. —Cub Koda

Dick Feller

b. Jan. 2, 1943, Bronaugh, MO
Vocals / Novelty, Country-Pop, Country Humor
Dick Feller wrote several offbeat but popular country songs during the 1970s, such as the narrative "Biff, the Friendly Purple Bear" and "The Credit Card Song." The Missouri born and raised Feller started his career in Nashville and then moved to L.A. to play in a band and hone his songwriting skills. He made a few demos of his songs and sent them to publishers, but didn't have much success, so he went back home to play in local bands until1966, when he returned to Nashville.

There he eked out a living as a demo player and performer in Mel Tillis' touring band, the Statesiders. In the early '70s, he signed as a staff writer with Johnny Cash's House of Cash and penned the singer's 1972 hit "Any Old Wind That Blows." Later Tex Ritter recorded Feller's song "The Night Ms. Nancy Ann's Hotel for Single Girls Burned Down." The following year he penned "Lord Mr. Ford," which he'd intended for Jimmy Dean but gave to Jerry Reed, who made the song a No. 1 hit. Reed and Feller became co-writers for a while and some of their songs can be heard on the soundtracks of films such as Smokey and the Bandit and its first sequel.

Feller made his own recording debut in 1973 with "Biff, the Friendly Purple Bear," which made it to the Top 25 and crossed over to become a minor pop hit as well. His next single, "Makin' the Best of a Bad Situation," made it to the Top 15 and again crept into the pop charts. "The Credit Card Song" remains one of his best-known tunes. It came out in 1974 and reached the Top Ten. Not all of Feller's songs were in the novelty category; in 1981, John Denver recorded Feller's lovely "Some Days Are Diamonds (Some Days Are Stone)," and scored a major country-pop hit. As a performer, Feller's last chart entry came in 1975 with "Uncle Hiram and the Homemade Beer," which made it to the Top 50. In 1984, Feller recorded a self-titled album. —Sandra Brennan

Dick Feller Wrote / 1973 / United Artists ✦✦✦

● No Words on Me / 1975 / Asylum ✦✦✦✦

Some Days Are Diamonds / 1975 / Asylum ✦✦✦

Then I Wrote / 1976 / United Artists ✦✦✦

Narvel Felts

b. Nov. 11, 1938, Bernie, MO
Guitar, Vocals / Traditional Country, Rockabilly
Singer-songwriter Narvel Felts has been in the country music business for over 30 years. Born in Bernie, MO, he was a self-taught guitar player inspired by the country music of such performers as Ernest Tubb and Floyd Tillman. Felts started out in 1956 when he won his high school talent contest with a rousing rendition of "Blue Suede Shoes." A deejay from Dexter, MO, was in the audience, and was so impressed that the next day he announced over the air that his station, KDEX, wanted to get in touch with Narvel Felts. The excited teen and his father drove eight miles to the nearest phone, and soon Felts was appearing at the station for his own Saturday afternoon show.

Felts got his real break when he asked Jerry Mercer if he could jam with the latter's band during a performance. Soon Felts was a member and when Mercer left in 1956, 17-year-old Felts became the new frontman for the Rockets. His first manager was a record shop owner who arranged for the group to audition for Sun Records in Nashville. Felts and one band member attended the first tryout in front of Jack Clement, who suggested they return home, write a few more songs, and return with the whole band; they did, but these first sessions were not released until much later. The Rockets returned to performing, and while opening for the film Rock, Pretty Baby at a theater in St. Louis, a regional promoter from Mercury heard them and eventually signed them to his label.They cut five singles with Mercury but were released in 1959.

Felts continued recording some of the band's songs on independent labels and in 1960 had minor chart success with a cover of the Drifters' "Honey Love." This success led him to sign with MGM; he remained with them for two years but released nothing.

Through the '60s, Felts continued performing and recording, but concentrated much of his energy on his wife and kids. In 1973, he finally got a big break in music when he signed to the Cinnamon label. His second single, "Drift Away," provided Felts with his first Top Ten record. He followed it with a string of hits including "All in the Name of Love" (1973) and "I Want to Stay" (1974). The label folded in 1975 and Felts then signed with ABC/Dot, where he continued having chart success. It was about this time that Felts scored his biggest hit, "Reconsider Me." The song made it to No. 3 and received accolades from industry magazines. Again, a string of hits, including "Lonely Teardrops," followed. Another smash was the 1978 song "Run for the Roses."

Felts lost his contract with ABC when the label was purchased by MCA. His road manager fired the Rockets in the mid-'70s and began booking Felts as a solo act backed by the band Wild Country. After a while Felts and the band went their separate ways, and the band went on to become the supergroup Alabama. Later Felts formed a new band, the Driftaways, and in the late '70s became a favorite performer at England's Wembley Festival. In the '80s, he found religion and turned toward gospel music, recording the albums *On the Wings of a Song* and *Seasons Greetings*, a Christmas record. —*Sandra Brennan*

Memphis Days / Bear Family ✦✦✦✦
This is a re-release of music originally recorded in the '60s by Roland Janes. —*AMG*

Reconsider Me / 1975 / Dot ✦✦✦

This Time / 1976 / Hi ✦✦✦
Another pleasant record from Felts that doesn't quite deliver the goods. There are some nice interpretations here but this isn't "The Record" he was meant to make. —*Jim Worbois*

Narvel the Marvel / 1976 / Dot ✦✦✦
Felts has an incredible voice (comparable to the late Jackie Wilson) and is able to handle most any style of music. The problem is, not many of these songs are up to his voice. Not a bad record, but something is missing that keeps it from being really good. —*Jim Worbois*

Narvel Felts' Greatest Hits, Vol. 1 / 1976 / Dot ✦✦✦✦

Touch of Felts / 1977 / Dot ✦✦

● **Drift Away** / 1996 / Bear Family ✦✦✦✦
Drift Away is a 28-track compilation of all of Narvel Felts' '70s country hits for ABC/Dot and Cinnamon, including "Lonely Teardrops," "Funny How Time Slips Away," "Reconsider Me," and "Drift Away." The single-disc compilation is the most complete collection ever assembled on Felts, and it stands as the defintiive retrospective of this underrated roots musican. —*Thom Owens*

Freddy Fender (Baldemar Huerta)

b. Jun. 4, 1937, San Benito, TX
Guitar, Vocals / Rock & Roll, Traditional Country, Cajun, Country-Pop, Tex-Mex
Freddy Fender was one of the few Hispanic stars in country music, a singer and songwriter whose work was defined largely by its strong Latin sensibility. Born Baldemar Huerta to a family of migrant laborers in San Benito, TX, on June 4, 1937, Fender began playing guitar early in his childhood. After dropping out of school at the age of 16 to join the Marine Corps, he released his first Spanish-language recordings under his given name in 1958.

While his initial sides were successful with listeners in Texas and Mexico, in 1959 he decided to adopt his stage name, along with a stronger rockabilly feel, in order to attract "gringo" audiences. The following year, he released the self-penned "Wasted Days and Wasted Nights," his most successful single yet. But in May of 1960, Fender was convicted of marijuana possession, and was sentenced to five years in Louisiana's notorious Angola State Prison (the same correctional facility that once held blues legend Leadbelly). After serving three years, he was paroled thanks to the efforts of Louisiana governor Jimmie Davis, on the condition that upon Fender's release he stay away from the corruptive influences of the music scene. After his parole ended, Fender tried to reignite his career, but with the exception of a few scattered night-

club gigs in the New Orleans area, he found little success, and ultimately returned to San Benito.

In Texas, he spent several years working as an auto mechanic, and even returned to school to pursue a degree in sociology. In 1974, he met Huey P. Meaux, the owner of the Houston-based Crazy Cajun label; after agreeing on a recording deal, Meaux suggested Fender move in the direction of Country & Western while maintaining his music's Hispanic roots. After Fender's first Meaux-produced single, " Before the Next Teardrop Falls," failed to attract the attention of a major label, it was released on Crazy Cajun; in the first weeks of 1975, the song hit the top of both the country and pop charts, and Fender became an overnight star. For the follow-up, he re-recorded his early single "Wasted Days and Wasted Nights," and notched his second straight No. 1 country hit. Before the year ended, he had released yet another chart-topper, "Secret Love," and also issued two LPs, *Since I Met You Baby* and a self-titled effort.

Throughout the remainder of the '70s, Fender's success continued, most notably with the No. 2 single "Living It Down" in 1976. That same year, he released two more albums, *Your Cheatin' Heart* and *Rock 'N' Country*. In 1977, he also issued a holiday record, *Merry Christmas—Feliz Navidad*. As the 1980s dawned, however, his popularity began slipping; after his final chart hit, 1983's "Chokin' Kind," he focused on an acting career, highlighted by an appearance in the 1988 Robert Redford film *The Milagro Beanfield War*. He remained largely silent as a musician until 1990, when he formed the Tex-Mex supergroup Texas Tornados with Doug Sahm, Flaco Jimenez, and Augie Meyers. After three albums, the group disbanded, and Fender again resumed his solo career. —*Jason Ankeny*

Canciones De Mi Barrio: The Roots of Tejano Rock / 1959 / Arhoolie ✦✦✦
Fender's earliest Tejano rock recordings are compiled on *Canciones de Mi Barrio*, a fine collection of singles first issued between 1959 and 1964 on the tiny San Benito, TX, label Ideal. Sung mostly in Spanish, these "canciones" bear a large debt to Elvis Presley's hits—there's even a cover of "Devil in Disguise"—although Fender's clear, sweet voice and the music's strong Latin roots combine to give his formative efforts their own distinct identity. —*Jason Ankeny*

Before the Next Teardrop Falls / 1975 / Collectables ✦✦✦
Textbook blend of Tex-Mex and country, spiced by Fender's immortal hit. —*Ron Wynn*

Swamp Gold / 1978 / ABC ✦✦✦✦
Certainly not a country record. More like a roots record. These are the songs that Fender, the struggling performer, used to do; a little Tex-Mex, a little New Orleans, a little soul, a little.... It's obvious from the performance that these songs mean a lot to Fender. —*Jim Worbois*

Early Years: 1959-1963 / 1986 / Krazy Kat ✦✦✦
These 16 sides are taken from rare regional singles that were cut for tiny labels in the days when Fender was only known in Texas and Louisiana. While Fender's earliest recordings were in Spanish, he only sings in English on these cuts of decent, though not thrilling, early swamp-pop. Freddy takes his inspiration from rockabilly, doo-wop, Tex-Mex, and smoldering R&B ballads on these singles, which include his first (and possibly best) version of "Wasted Days and Wasted Nights." One of the relatively few early rock performers to flavor his sound with Texas border music, these sides were most likely influential on Doug Sahm, although they were unheard by a national audience. —*Richie Unterberger*

● **Collection** / 1991 / Reprise ✦✦✦✦
The Freddy Fender Collection is a ten-track compilation that contains his biggest hits, from the country-pop crossovers "Wasted Days and Wasted Nights" and "Before the Next Teardrop Falls" to country chart-toppers "Secret Love" and "You'll Lose a Good Thing." It's a brief but consistent collection, featuring nearly every one of his best singles from the mid-'70s, making it an excellent introduction to his long, prolific career, even if isn't as comprehensive as it could have been. —*Stephen Thomas Erlewine*

Best of Freddy Fender / Jul. 15, 1996 / MCA ✦✦✦✦
The Best of Freddy Fender contains the bulk of Fender's '70s hits, including the Top Ten hits "Wasted Days and Wasted Nights" and "Until the Next Teardrop Falls." Although it is missing a couple of key tracks, this single-disc collection remains a good introduction—in fact, it's nearly a definitive retrospective. —*Thom Owens*

Cathy Fink

b. Aug. 9, 1953, Baltimore, MD
Dulcimer, Banjo, Guitar, Vocals / Folk, Children's
Cathy Fink may be best-known for the many children's albums she has recorded over the years, but she is also a key figure in feminist-oriented folk and country music. Born and raised in Baltimore, she got her professional start in 1973 at the Yellow Door coffeehouse in Montreal, at the height of the folk revival. There she became well-known for her excellent banjo and guitar playing, as well as her yodeling. The following year she debuted on CBC Canada and has since played in every major North American folk festival. She and Duck Donald teamed up that year and stayed together until the end of the decade. Fink made her recording debut in 1975 with *Kissing Is a Crime* for Likeable Records. Three years later, she and Duck released a self-titled album on Flying Fish; the two released their first children's album, *I'm Gonna Tell*, in 1980. Following the breakup with Duck, she moved to Takoma Park, MD, and has immersed herself in the folk, bluegrass, and old-time music scene, playing over 5,000 concerts. In 1983, she teamed up with Marcie Marxer. In 1985, she recorded *The Leading Role* for Rounder (her first "adult" album in several years) and began producing other artists a year later. In 1988, she moved to Sugar Hill and recorded *Blue Rose;* the next year, Fink and Marxer released a self-titled album. She also produced an album for Great Dreams and, along with Marxer and Si Kahn, released cassette tapes of the best-selling children's books *The Runaway Bunny/Goodnight Moon* for Harper & Row. In 1991, she released a solo album on Sugar Hill and then put together 80 songs to contribute to the Macmillan/McGraw-Hill reading curriculum, a project entitled *A New View* (1992). In 1993 she produced Si Kahn's children's album *Goodtimes and Bedtimes.* —*Sandra Brennan*

Grandma Slid Down the Mountain / 1984 / Rounder ✦✦✦✦
Fink sings, plays, and produces up a storm. Imaginative songs impart good, generally positive, values. For ages four to seven. —*Bob Hinkle*

When the Rain Comes Down / 1987 / Rounder ✦✦✦✦
A definitively outstanding children's production by a woman who has been a leader in providing excellent material for kids....First-rate youngsters deserve first-rate music like this. —*Ladyslipper*

Help Yourself / 1990 / Rounder ✦✦✦
A how-to-take-care-of-yourself recording, with Marcy Marxer. Usually, such albums are a bit preachy, but this one is much less so. For ages four to seven. —*Bob Hinkle*

Banjo Haiku / Community Music ✦✦✦✦
This 1992 release is a terrific collection of 26 clawhammer banjo tunes, played by an award-winning, expert instrumentalist. Diverse enough for the banjo connoisseur and tasteful enough for all acoustic instrumental fans to enjoy, Fink covers a wide variety of tunings, tempos, and timbres, demonstrating the versatility of the old-time banjo. —*Ladyslipper*

● **The Leading Role** / Rounder ✦✦✦✦

Cathy Fink & Duck Donald / Flying Fish ✦✦✦
This album features skillful performances of old-timey and hillbilly music, some of it comic, all of it sprightly. —*AMG*

Cathy Fink & Marcy Marxer / Sugar Hill ✦✦✦

Firefall

Country-Rock, Adult Contemporary, Soft Rock, Pop-Rock
The mellow, easy country-rock sounds of Firefall, coupled with the group's penchant for pop melodies and high-pitched harmonies, produced a series of successful LPs in the late '70s and a series of chart singles, including the Top Ten hit "You Are the

Woman." The group was formed by former Flying Burrito Brother Rick Roberts, who handled vocals, guitar, and most of the songwriting duties; he was joined by fellow ex-Burrito and Byrd Michael Clarke on drums, ex-Spirit and Jo Jo Gunne bassist Mark Andes, guitarist/vocalist Jock Bartley, guitarist/vocalist/songwriter Larry Burnett, and keyboardist/woodwind player David Muse, who joined in 1977. The group recorded its self-titled debut in 1976; it and its follow-up, *Luna Sea*, both went gold, and their third album, *Elan*, went platinum. However, the group's commercial fortunes began to decline, and even though Muse experimented with adding different instruments to the overall sound, Firefall's relaxed, toned-down approach simply wore out its welcome as pop trends moved elsewhere. Jock Bartley reformed the group in 1994 for the album *Messenger.* —*Steve Huey*

Firefall / 1976 / Atlantic ✦✦✦✦
This debut effort, their best album, includes the hits "You Are the Woman" and "Cinderella." —*Rick Clark*

● **Greatest Hits** / Rhino ✦✦✦✦
A greatest-hits collection, it includes almost all the essential tracks. —*Rick Clark*

5 Chinese Brothers

Contemporary Folk
The 5 Chinese Brothers are not Chinese or brothers. What they are is a five-piece band that plays a combination of folk, rock, and country. The New York-based band is made up of Tom Meltzer (lead vocals, acoustic guitar), Paul Foglino (bass), Charlie Shaw (drums), Neil Thomas (accordion, piano, vocals), and Kevin Trainor (lead guitar, vocals). —*Chip Renner*

● **Singer, Songwriter, Beggarman, Thief** / 1992 / 1-800-Prime CD ✦✦✦✦
After some remixing of their indie cassette and the addition of a few tracks, 5 Chinese Brothers have released their first album after ten years of the New York scene. Tom Meltzer and Paul Foglino handle the writing separately, though their styles complement each other so well you'd think they were a team. These songs have open-hearted humor and the performances are tight but animated with a very live feeling. This is a great record that captures the fun of the band live but with the precision of a studio. Not a bad cut on this record; it's a must have. —*Richard Meyer*

Shiney Brite/Santa Claustrophibia / 1994 / 1-800-Prime CD ✦✦✦
The 5CBs weigh in here with a Christmas EP containing three new songs and selections from their great debut *Singer-Songwriter-Beggarman Thief.* "The Avalanche Song" and "Chrismas on 'Interstate 80' " are as good as anything else they have done. This limited-release disc is worth finding for the tracks that didn't make it onto their second full-length album, *Stone Soup.* —*Richard Meyer*

Stone Soup / Aug. 1, 1995 / 1-800-Prime CD ✦✦✦
This, the second 5 Chinese Brothers CD, doesn't have quite the irrepressible drive and bite of their first disc, but this one is still so good that it's not a fair comparison. The standout song is "Mole in the Ground." Tom Meltzer's elastic voice adds the right amount of energy and edge to the 5CBs' sound. Like *Singer, Songwriter, Beggarman, Thief*, you ought to play this until it is part of you. —*Richard Meyer*

Flatlanders

Alternative Country
The Flatlanders became legends long after they broke up, because the band's three primary members—Jimmie Dale Gilmore, Joe Ely, and Butch Hancock—each attracted a large, loyal cult following as solo performers. In 1972, when their lone album was recorded, they were part-time musicians who hooked up after each had returned to their native Texas after exploring a different region of the world. The record wasn't released, and they went their separate ways, each abandoning music briefly. Their careers continued to intertwine in the ensuing decades with great results. —*Michael McCall*

One More Road (1972 Recording) / 1980 / Charly ✦✦✦
One More Road (1972 Recording) is a vinyl collection of the Flat-landers' only recording session, which has since been supplanted by several CD issues of the same material. —*Thom Owens*

● **More a Legend Than a Band** / 1990 / Rounder ✦✦✦✦
The title refers to the status these "lost" tapes acquired as time passed and the reputations of Ely, Gilmore, and Hancock grew. The music itself is odd and effective, a blend of old-time acoustic music (including a musical saw) matched with lyrics that look at the world as only modern Texas mystics could. Gilmore takes most of the lead vocals. It features the first recorded versions of two of his classics, "Dallas" and "Tonight I'm Gonna Go Down-town." —*Michael McCall*

Flatt & Scruggs

Traditional Bluegrass
Probably the most famous bluegrass band of all time was Flatt & Scruggs and the Foggy Mountain Boys. They made the genre famous in ways that not even Bill Monroe, who pretty much invented the sound, ever could. Because of a guitar player and vocalist from Tennessee named Lester Flatt and an extraordinary banjo player from North Carolina named Earl Scruggs, bluegrass music has become popular the world over and has entered the mainstream in the world of music.

Like so many other bluegrass legends, Flatt & Scruggs were graduates of Bill Monroe's Blue Grass Boys. Because of the unique sound they added ("overdrive," one critic called it), Monroe felt let down after Flatt's quality vocals and Scruggs' banjo leads left in 1948. Quickly the two assembled a band that in the opinion of many was among the best ever, with Chubby Wise on fiddle and Cedric Rainwater on bass; a later band, with Paul Warren on fiddle and Josh Graves on dobro, was equally superb. With so many extraordinary musicians and the solid, controlled vocals of Flatt, it's no wonder the Foggy Mountain Boys was the band that brought bluegrass to international prominence. From 1948 until 1969, when Flatt & Scruggs split up to pursue different musical directions, they were *the* bluegrass band, due to their Martha White Flour segment at the Opry and, especially, their tremen-dous exposure from TV and movies.

Lester Flatt and Earl Scruggs were originally brought together by Bill Monroe in 1945, when they joined a band that also fea-tured fiddler Chubby Wise and bassist Cedric Rainwater. This quintet created the sound of bluegrass and helped bring it to national recognition through radio shows, records, and concerts. After three years with Monroe, Flatt left the mandolinist behind in 1948 and Scruggs followed his lead shortly afterward. The duo formed their own band, the Foggy Mountain Boys, and within a few months, they recruited ex-Blue Grass Boy Rainwater, fiddler Jim Shumate, and guitarist/vocalist Mac Wiseman. Initially, the band played on radio stations across the South, landing a record contract with Mercury Records in late 1948. Over the next two years, they toured the US constantly, played many radio shows, and recorded several sessions on Mercury. One of the sessions produced the original version of "Foggy Mountain Breakdown," which would become a bluegrass standard.

In 1951, Flatt & Scruggs switched record labels, signing with Columbia Records. By this point, the band now featured mando-linist/vocalist Curly Seckler, fiddler Paul Warren, and bassist Jake Tullock. Where the careers of other bluegrass and hard country acts stalled in the early and mid-'50s, the Foggy Mountain Boys flourished. One of their first singles for Columbia, "'Tis Sweet to Be Remembered," reached the Top Ten in 1952, and in 1953, the Martha White Flour Company sponsored a regular radio show for the group on WSM in Nashville. In 1955, the band joined the Grand Ole Opry. The following year, they added a dobro player named Buck Graves to the lineup.

Flatt & Scruggs reached a new audience in the late '50s, when the folk music revival sparked the interest of a younger genera-tion of listeners. The duo played a number of festivals targeted at the new breed of bluegrass and folk fans. At the same time, coun-try music television programs went into syndication and the duo became regulars on these shows. In the summer of 1959, Flatt &

Scruggs began a streak of Top 40 country singles that ran into 1968—their chart performance was directly tied to their increased exposure. The duo's popularity peaked in 1962, when they recorded the theme song to the television sitcom *The Beverly Hill-billies*. The theme, called "The Ballad of Jed Clampett," became the first No. 1 bluegrass single in early 1963 and the duo made a number of cameos on the show.

The Beverly Hillbillies began a streak of cameo appearances and soundtrack work for Flatt & Scruggs in television and film, most notably with the appearance of "Foggy Mountain Break-down" in Arthur Penn's 1968 film *Bonnie and Clyde*. With all of their TV, film, and festival appearances, Flatt & Scruggs popular-ized bluegrass music more than any artist, even Bill Monroe. Iron-ically, that popularity helped drive the duo apart. Scruggs wanted to expand their sound, and pushed Flatt to cover Bob Dylan's "Like a Rolling Stone" in 1968, as well as booked concert appear-ances in venues that normally booked rock 'n' roll acts. Flatt wanted to continue in a traditional bluegrass vein. Inevitably, the opposing forces came to a head and the duo parted ways in 1969. Appropriately, Flatt formed a traditional bluegrass band, the Nashville Grass, while Scruggs assembled a more progressive outfit, the Earl Scruggs Revue.

Throughout the '70s, both Flatt and Scruggs enjoyed successful solo careers. In 1979, the duo began ironing out the details of a proposed reunion album, but they were scrapped upon Flatt's death on May 11, 1979. Scruggs retired in the '80s. In 1985, Flatt & Scruggs were inducted into the Country Music Hall of Fame. —*Stephen Thomas Erlewine & David Vinopal*

Songs of the Famous Carter Family / 1961 / Columbia/Legacy ✦✦✦
Depression-era country/folk performed bluegrass style. —*Mark A. Humphrey*

☆ **Foggy Mountain Banjo** / 1961 / Columbia ✦✦✦✦✦
The album that secured their standing among folk music enthusi-asts in the 1960s, it focuses on Scruggs' instrumental prowess as well as his sharp interplay with dobroist Josh Graves, fiddler Paul Warren, and Flatt's flat-picking guitar. The album also features drummer Buddy Harmon, whose appearance shocked purists. —*Michael McCall*

Flatt and Scruggs at Carnegie Hall! / 1962 / Columbia ✦✦✦
This is a highly influential "folk-boom" concert album. —*Mark A. Humphrey*

Live at Vanderbilt University / 1964 / Columbia ✦✦✦
Featured a performance from the early '60s. —*AMG*

Greatest Hits / 1966 / Columbia ✦✦✦
A concise sampler for those who don't want their *20 All-Time Great Recordings* album. —*Mark A. Humphrey*

Strictly Instrumental / 1967 / Columbia ✦✦✦✦
Strictly Instrumental is a delightful duet album between Flatt & Scruggs and Doc Watson, giving the three musicians an opportu-nity to flaunt their exceptional instrumental talents. Sticking to a selection of songs that are traditional in approach, but that are not played frequently ("John Hardy Was a Desperate Little Man," "Pick Along," "Spanish Two-Step"), Flatt & Scruggs and Watson play with a startling fluidity—these instrumentals are so rich and skillful that vocals would have been superfluous. For lovers of instrumental bluegrass, this album is a must-hear. —*Thom Owens*

The Golden Era 1950-55 / 1977 / Rounder ✦✦✦
Golden Era: 1950-55 contains a selection of highlights from Flatt & Scruggs' early days at Columbia. —*Thom Owens*

Blue Ridge Cabin Home / 1979 / Rebel ✦✦✦✦
Blue Ridge Cabin Home contains a selection of Flatt & Scruggs' finest recordings from the '50s, material that demonstrates why they had to leave Bill Monroe's band. Where Monroe wanted to keep the music pure, Flatt & Scruggs were constantly pushing the boundaries of what bluegrass could do, bringing in heavy ele-ments of country, folk, gospel, and even pop. The recordings on this compilation helped popularize bluegrass, and while it is available on more comprehensive collections, *Blue Ridge Cabin Home* remains a terrific single-disc sampler of their sound. —*Thom Owens*

Columbia Historic Edition / 1982 / Columbia ✦✦✦
Wonderful '50s recordings, including some rarities. —*Mark A. Humphrey*

☆ **20 All Time Great Recordings** / 1983 / Columbia ✦✦✦✦✦
Three-part gospel-style harmonies, breakneck banjo, flinty Americana, and "a bubblin' crude" are in this cornerstone collection of bluegrass at its best. —*Mark A. Humphrey*

Mercury Sessions, Vol. 1 / 1987 / Rounder ✦✦✦✦
Mercury Sessions, Vol. 1 collects the first 14 tracks that Flatt & Scruggs recorded for Mercury Records between 1948 and 1950. The duo made these recordings after they broke away from Bill Monroe, and the adventurous quality of the music demonstrates why they had to split from the father of bluegrass—they were expanding the boundaries of the music. Consequently, these songs are rightly regarded as Flatt & Scruggs' best and most influential recordings, and the duo's instrumental skills and harmonies are still breathtaking several decades after they were recorded. Any serious bluegrass collection isn't complete without Flatt & Scruggs' Mercury recordings, either in this format or in Mercury's single-disc *The Complete Mercury Sessions*. —*Thom Owens*

Mercury Sessions, Vol. 2 / 1987 / Rounder ✦✦✦✦
Mercury Sessions, Vol. 2 collects the remaining 14 tracks that Flatt & Scruggs recorded for Mercury Records between 1948 and 1950, including the original version of their classic song, "Foggy Mountain Breakdown." This music is generally considered the finest that the duo ever recorded, and a cursory listen will reveal why—the duo's harmonies and instrumental interplay are simply astounding. Any serious bluegrass collection needs Flatt & Scruggs' Mercury Recordings, either in this format or in Mercury's single-disc *The Complete Mercury Sessions*. —*Thom Owens*

You Can Feel It in Your Soul / 1988 / County ✦✦✦✦
You Can Feel It in Your Soul contains 13 gospel songs that Flatt & Scruggs recorded during the '50s. Though it is brief, the compilation is a nice complement to the numerous collections of the duo's secular material, and the group sounds fantastic on each track here. Several cuts also benefit from the appearance of guitarist Chet Atkins. —*Thom Owens*

☆ **1949-1959** / 1992 / Bear Family ✦✦✦✦✦
1949-1959 is a four-disc box set filled with the very best Flatt & Scruggs tunes recorded during their peak years at Decca. A Bear Family import with superb liner notes, and music beyond compare. —*Michael Erlewine*

Don't Get Above Your Raisin' / 1992 / Rounder ✦✦✦
Flatt's song became a back-to-basics anthem when Ricky Skaggs waxed it ca. 1981. The original is here, along with other greats from the '50s, on this 15-track compilation of material that was originally released on Columbia Records. —*Mark A. Humphrey*

☆ **1959-1963** / 1992 / Bear Family ✦✦✦✦✦
Although the material covered on the five-disc box set *1959-1963* isn't as innovative as the music on Bear Family's first Flatt & Scruggs box, *1949-1959*, it's nearly as good. During these five years, the duo brought bluegrass into the mainstream, and this collection shows why. Over the set's 129 tracks—which include a wealth of unreleased material and alternate takes, most notably the complete Carnegie Hall concert from December of 1962—Flatt & Scruggs run through a selection of originals and standards, including some re-recorded versions of their earlier Mercury hits. They might not sound quite as lively as they did a decade earlier, but this remains classic bluegrass. —*Thom Owens*

★ **The Complete Mercury Sessions** / Aug. 4, 1992 / Mercury ✦✦✦✦✦
The integral early recordings of this seminal bluegrass band. Included is their classic "Foggy Mountain Breakdown," "Roll in My Sweet Baby's Arms," "Old Salty Dog Blues," and others. It's indispensable for bluegrass fans. —*Michael McCall*

1964-1969, Plus / Feb. 1996 / Bear Family ✦✦✦✦
Bear Family's third box set of Flatt & Scruggs material is necessary for completists and historians, but it doesn't have the revelatory spark of the first box, nor the crossover appeal of the second. There is plenty of enjoyable music on the set, but the completist

approach—all of the released studio recordings are included, plus alternate takes and unreleased tracks—makes listening to the box somewhat difficult. Nevertheless, for diehard Flatt & Scruggs fans, *1964-1969, Plus* is as essential a purchase as the first two Bear Family boxes. —*Thom Owens*

★ **'Tis Sweet to Be Remembered: The Essential** / Jan. 28, 1997 / Legacy/Columbia ✦✦✦✦✦
'Tis Sweet to Be Remembered: The Essential Flatt & Scruggs is a double-disc set that covers all of the essential items that the ground-breaking bluegrass duo recorded for Columbia Records, including the hit singles "'Tis Sweet to Be Remembered," "Cabin in the Hills," "Go Home," "The Ballad of Jed Clampett," "Pearl Pearl Pearl," and "Foggy Mountain Breakdown." Though the compilation is a little too extensive for casual listeners, for dedicated bluegrass fans it's an essential purchase—it may not be as thorough as the Bear Family box sets, but it is considerably more digestible, which means it gives a better sense of Flatt & Scruggs' career and their considerable accomplishments. —*Thom Owens*

Lester Flatt (Lester Raymond Flatt)

b. Jun. 19, 1914, Overton County, TN, **d.** May 11, 1979, Nashville, TN

Guitar, Mandolin, Vocals / Traditional Bluegrass

After Lester Flatt and Earl Scruggs parted ways in 1969, Flatt reassembled many of the Foggy Mountain Boys, renamed the group Nashville Grass, and toured very successfully until his death in 1979. Unlike Scruggs, who with his sons moved on to music that was only marginally country, Flatt and the Grass stuck to traditional bluegrass material. Even without Scruggs, the band shone, and Flatt's vocals, musical direction, and taste received the credit they had so long deserved. —*David Vinopal*

Live at the Bluegrass Festival / 1986 / RCA ✦✦✦
A bluegrass veteran in concert in the '70s. —*Mark A. Humphrey*

Don't Get Above Your Raisin' / 1988 / Rounder ✦✦✦✦

The Golden Era / 1988 / Rounder ✦✦✦✦

Lester Flatt's Greatest Performance / 1989 / CMH ✦✦✦✦

Lester Raymond Flatt / 1989 / Flying Fish ✦✦✦
Here this bluegrass legend turns to more basic music. —*AMG*

Nashville Grass: Fantastic Pickin' / CMH ✦✦✦

● **Greatest Bluegrass Hits, Vol. 1** / CMH ✦✦✦✦
This is a good overview of Flatt's post-Scruggs recordings with Nashville Grass, a band that included a young Marty Stuart on mandolin. —*Mark A. Humphrey*

Bela Fleck

b. 1958, New York City, NY

Banjo / Progressive Bluegrass

Premiere banjo player Bela Fleck is considered one of the most innovative pickers in the world and has done much to demonstrate the versatility of his instrument, which he uses to play everything from traditional bluegrass to progressive jazz. Named after composer Béla Bartók, Fleck was born in New York City. Around age 15, he became fascinated with the banjo after hearing Flatt & Scruggs' "Ballad of Jed Clampett" and Weissberg & Mandell's "Dueling Banjos," and his grandfather soon gave him one. While attending the High School of Music and Art in New York, Fleck worked on adapting bebop music for the banjo. Fleck always had diverse musical interests, and his own style was influenced by Tony Trischka, Earl Scruggs, Chick Corea, Charlie Parker, John Coltrane, the Allman Brothers, Aretha Franklin, the Byrds, and Little Feat. After graduation, he joined the Tasty Licks, a group from Boston. They recorded two albums and dissolved in 1979. Afterwards, Fleck joined the Kentucky band Spectrum. That year, only five years after he took up the instrument, he made his solo recording debut with *Crossing the Tracks*, which the Readers' Poll in *Frets* magazine named Best Overall Album. In 1982, he joined New Grass Revival and stayed with them until the end of the decade. During this time, his reputation continued to grow and in 1990, *Frets* magazine added his name to their Hall of Greats. In 1988, one of his compositions, "Drive" (from the album

New Grass Revival), was nominated for a Grammy. Fleck, mandolin player Sam Bush, fiddler Mark O'Connor, bassist Edgar Meyer, and dobro player Jerry Douglas teamed up in 1989 to form Strength In Numbers and record *The Telluride Sessions*. Later that year, Fleck was asked by PBS television to play on the upcoming *Lonesome Pine Special;* in response he gathered together a veritable "dream team" of musicians to form the Flecktones. The original members included Howard Levy, who played piano, harmonica and ocarina, among other instruments; bass guitarist Victor Lemonte Wooten; and Lemonte's brother Roy "Futureman" Wooten on the drumitar, an electronic drum shaped like a guitar. Though the special wasn't aired until 1992, the Flecktones recorded their eponymous debut album in 1990 and followed it up with *Flight of the Cosmic Hippo* (1991). In 1993 they released their fourth album, *UFO Tofu*, which featured music blending different genres ranging from bluegrass to R&B to worldbeat. In 1995, they released *Tales from an Acoustic Planet*. *—Sandra Brennan*

Crossing the Tracks / 1979 / Rounder ✦✦✦

Natural Bridge / 1982 / Rounder ✦✦✦

Double Time / 1984 / Rounder ✦✦✦

Inroads / 1986 / Rounder ✦✦✦
Now available for the first time on compact disc, this 1986 release features banjoist Bela Fleck performing an all-instrumental group of original compositions. Fleck is well-known for expanding the horizons of bluegrass, and he creates lots of new sounds here, ably assisted by other talented musicians such as mandolinist Sam Bush, dobroist Jerry Douglas, and violinist Mark O'Connor. Tracks include "Ireland," "Four Wheel Drive," "Perplexed," and "The Old Country." *—AMG*

Daybreak / 1988 / Rounder ✦✦✦✦

Drive / 1988 / Rounder ✦✦✦

Bela Fleck & the Flecktones / 1990 / Warner Brothers ✦✦✦✦
After disbanding New Grass Revival, Bela Fleck began re-creating the role of the banjo in the same way Charlie Parker redefined the role of the saxophone. But Fleck may be the least innovative member of this quartet: Howard Levy gets chromatics from his blues harp, Victor Wooten picks banjo rolls on his bass, and Roy "Future Man" Wooten plays a Frankenstein-monster drum-machine/guitar synthesizer. For all the flash, there's little pretense; the group's astonishing musicianship keeps an "aw-shucks" accessibility that lets everybody follow the melody while they marvel. *—Brian Mansfield*

★ **Flight of the Cosmic Hippo** / 1991 / Warner Brothers ✦✦✦✦✦
The Flecktones owe more to bebop than bluegrass, and here the group finally names its style "blu-bop." That's why *Cosmic Hippo* topped the jazz, not the country, chart. The Flecktones continue to make it look easy, adding banjo power chords to "Turtle Rock" and reworking Lennon/McCartney's "Michelle." *—Brian Mansfield*

UFO Tofu / 1992 / Warner Brothers ✦✦✦
Though the Flecktones don't change their formula with their third album, *UFO Tofu*, they do manage to craft one of their more consistent and impressive efforts. The band's fusion of jazz, bluegrass, and funk gels quite well on *UFO Tofu*–not only does Bela Fleck turn in a rich, eclectic performance, but pianist Howard Levy's deft lines and inventive phrasing dominates the album. Occasionally, the material is lightweight, functioning only as a vehicle for the group's solos. Then again, the whole point of Fleck's music *is* the solos, so that shouldn't upset his fans too much. Of course, it doesn't help him win new ones, either. *—Thom Owens*

Three Flew over the Cuckoo's Nest / 1993 / Warner Brothers ✦✦✦

Tales from the Acoustic Planet / 1995 / Warner Brothers ✦✦✦✦

Live Art / Sep. 9, 1996 / Warner Brothers ✦✦✦
Live Art is a double-disc, 20-track anthology of live performances by Bela Fleck & the Flecktones, spanning four years in the mid-'90s. The song selections cover the group's entire career, ranging from new arrangements of several classics to covers and seven previously unrecorded originals. There are a couple of vocals on the record, but the core of the album is Fleck & the Flecktones' dynamite instrumental improvisations, where they can demonstrate the true range of their eclecticism and talent. Of special note are the songs that feature jams with Branford Marsalis, Chick Corea, and Bruce Hornsby, who help spur the Flecktones to new heights. *—Thom Owens*

Rosie Flores

b. Sep. 10, 1950, San Antonio, TX
Guitar, Vocals / Rockabilly, Alternative Country, Neo-Traditionalist Country, Americana
Since the late '70s, guitarist, singer, and songwriter Rosie Flores has been a steady figure on the alternative country scene in both Austin, TX, and Los Angeles. She's a hard-working, independently minded artist who's well-respected for her gritty, energetic vocals and fiery guitar solos.

Flores' first band was Rosie and the Screamers—based in Southern California during the punk-rock era of the late 1970s—who played hard country and rockabilly material, much of it written by Flores. A few years later she began working as a solo acoustic artist, but eventually formed an all-female band, the Screaming Sirens, who recorded the album *Fiesta* in 1984.

In 1987 Flores recorded her first solo album, *Rosie Flores*, produced by Pete Anderson (Dwight Yoakam's producer and guitarist) and released by Warner Bros. Flores eventually parted ways with Warner Bros. and signed to the indie label Hightone. In 1992 she released her second solo album, *After the Farm*, followed by *Once More with Feeling* a year later. Flores then spent the better part of 1994 playing lead guitar in Butch Hancock's band.

In 1995 Flores recorded *Rockabilly Filly*, a spirited tribute to the music she grew up with. The album featured duets with her longtime idols Wanda Jackson and Janis Martin, both of whom Flores brought out of retirement for the project. The album led to a cross-country tour with Jackson, who hadn't played in nightclubs in over 20 years. *—Kurt Wolff*

● **Rosie Flores** / 1987 / Reprise ✦✦✦✦
Produced by Pete Anderson, Rosie Flores' debut made her out to be the female answer to Dwight Yoakam. Flores probably felt like that image straitjacketed her, but from a musical standpoint, it worked beautifully, incorporating Flores' San Antonio roots into Anderson's California country vision. Includes "Crying over You," "Somebody Loses, Somebody Wins," and "Blue Side of Town," which Patty Loveless wouldn't do nearly as well the following year. *—Brian Mansfield*

After the Farm / 1992 / Hightone ✦✦✦✦
From start to finish, there is something special about this CD. Flores is a great guitarist, backed by Greg Liesz, David Lindley, Duane "DJ" Jarvis, and Dusty Wakeman. They rock, with some real killer slide-guitar work. If you like your country hard, you'll love it. *—Chip Renner*

Once More with Feeling / 1993 / Hightone ✦✦✦
Closer to modern commercial country than *After the Farm*, *Once More with Feeling* doesn't have the sleekly professional touch of *Rosie Flores*, but it's not without its charms. It includes a duet with Joe Ely ("Love and Danger," which Flores wrote with Jason & the Scorchers' Jason Ringenberg). Other songs were contributed by Wendy Waldman ("Ruin This Romance") and Katy Moffatt ("Real Man"). *—Brian Mansfield*

Rockabilly Filly / Oct. 1995 / Hightone ✦✦✦
As the title indicates, *Rockabilly Filly* is Rosie Flores' first album that consists entirely of rockabilly tunes. Of course, she has always flirted with the genre, but it is refreshing to hear her take a full-fledged plunge. It's all the more impressive when you consider that it was recorded after she recovered from an accident that shattered her wrist—she plays with the vitality of a wild, young rockabilly cat throughout the album. *—Sara Sytsma*

A Little Bit of Heartache / Jan. 21, 1997 / Watermelon ✦✦✦✦

The Flying Burrito Brothers

Country-Rock

The Flying Burrito Brothers helped forge the connection between rock and country, and with their 1969 debut album, *The Gilded Palace of Sin*, they virtually invented the blueprint for country-rock. Though the band's glory days were brief, they left behind a small body of work that proved vastly influential both in rock and country. The Flying Burrito Brothers reunited later in the '70s, albeit without their founding members Gram Parsons and Chris Hillman, and continued performing and recording in a variety of incarnations into the '80s.

Originally, the Flying Burrito Brothers were a group of Los Angeles musicians who gathered together to jam. Gram Parsons and Chris Hillman took the band's name when they were forming their own band after leaving the Byrds. Parsons had helped steer the Byrds in a country direction during his brief stint with the band, as captured on the 1968 album *Sweetheart of the Rodeo*. Following the release of *Sweetheart*, he left the Byrds, followed shortly afterward by Hillman. The duo added pedal steel guitarist "Sneaky" Pete Kleinow and bassist Chris Ethridge to the band and set about recording their debut album with a variety of session drummers.

The Gilded Palace of Sin, the Flying Burrito Brothers' debut album, was released in the spring of 1969. Although the album only sold 40,000 copies, the band developed a devoted following, which happened to include many prominent musicians in Los Angeles, Bob Dylan, and the Rolling Stones. Around this time, Parsons and Stones guitarist Keith Richards became good friends, which led to Parsons losing interest in the Burritos. Before the band recorded their second album, Ethridge left the band and was replaced by Bernie Leadon, and the group hired ex-Byrd Michael Clarke as their permanent drummer.

Burrito DeLuxe, the group's second album, was released in the spring of 1970. After its release, Gram Parsons left the group and was replaced by Rick Roberts, a local Californian songwriter. Roberts' first album with the band, *The Flying Burrito Brothers*, was released in 1971. After its release, Kleinow left the band to become a session musician and Leadon departed to join the Eagles. The Burritos hired pedal steel guitarist Al Perkins and bassist Roger Bush to replace them, as well as adding guitarist Kenny Wertz and fiddler Byron Berline to the lineup. This new version of the group recorded the live album *The Last of the Red Hot Burritos*, which was released in 1972. Before its release, the band splintered apart. Berline, Bush, and Wertz all left to form Country Gazette, while Hillman and Perkins joined Manassas. Roberts assembled a new band to tour Europe in 1973 and then dissolved the group, choosing to pursue a solo career. Roberts would later form Firefall with Michael Clarke.

Close Up the Honky Tonks, a double-album Flying Burrito Brothers compilation, was released in 1974 because of the burgeoning interest in Gram Parsons. Capitalizing on the collection and the cult forming around Parsons, Kleinow and Ethridge formed a new version of the Flying Burrito Brothers in 1975. The duo recruited Floyd "Gib" Gilbeau (vocals, guitar, fiddle), bassist Joel Scott Hill, and drummer Gene Parsons and recorded *Flying Again*, which was released on Columbia Records in 1975.

Ethridge left the band after the release of *Flying Again;* he was replaced by Skip Battin, who appeared on the 1976 album *Airborne*. Also in 1976, a collection of Gram Parsons-era outtakes entitled *Sleepless Nights* was released on A&M Records.

For the two decades following their 1975 reunion, the Flying Burrito Brothers performed and recorded sporadically, undergoing the occasional lineup change. In 1979, the group released *Live from Tokyo* on Regency Records; the album spawned their first country hit, a cover of Merle Haggard's "White Line Fever," which hit the charts in 1980. Also in 1980, the group abbreviated its name to the Burrito Brothers when they signed a contract with Curb Records. The Burrito Brothers' *Hearts on the Line* spawned three minor country chart hits in 1981. *Sunset Sundown*, the Brothers second Curb album, appeared in 1982 and like its predecessor, it produced three minor hits. Following the release of *Sunset Sundown*, Kleinow left the band to become an animator and

special-effects creator in Hollywood. The group carried on without him, led by Gib Gilbeau and John Beland. That incarnation of the band fell apart in 1985, the same year that Kleinow assembled yet another version of the band. For the next three years, this incarnation of the Flying Burrito Brothers toured America and Europe. In 1988, the group split apart again, although it did occasionally reunite for further tours and recordings in the '90s. *—Stephen Thomas Erlewine*

☆ **The Gilded Palace of Sin** / Feb. 1969 / A&M ✦✦✦✦✦
The birth of country-rock. Gram Parsons and Chris Hillman, aided by Sneaky Pete Kleinow and Chris Ethridge, create a hybrid by combining rock attitude with country sentiments, and change the course of popular music. Really. *—William Ruhlmann*

Burrito Deluxe / Apr. 1970 / A&M ✦✦✦✦
The follow-up to the brilliant *Guilded Palace of Sin* finds the band somewhat directionless, with Gram Parsons losing interest and playing a less active role. While the Parsons/Hillman-penned "Cody Cody" and a touching rendition of the Rolling Stones' "Wild Horses" capture some of the previous album's magic, *Burrito Deluxe* is somewhat of a letdown. Parsons left for a solo career shortly after. *—Chris Woodstra*

The Flying Burrito Brothers / May 1971 / A&M ✦✦✦
On their first post-Parsons album, the Burritos (now led by Hillman and Rick Roberts, and with future Eagle Bernie Leadon replacing Ethridge) make an honest step forward in country-rock. Includes the Roberts song "Colorado." *—William Ruhlmann*

The Last of the Red Hot Burritos / Apr. 1972 / A&M ✦✦
The Last of the Red Hot Burritos, the fourth Flying Burrito Brothers album, was a live recording by the current lineup, led by sole original member Chris Hillman. It was billed as the group's swan song and released after their breakup. By now, the Burritos had evolved into a competent country-rock band with a repertoire of country standards such as "Orange Blossom Special" (featuring Byron Berline on fiddle), but few of the originals by Gram Parsons and Hillman. *Last of the Red Hot Burritos* would have been a respectable, if unexceptional, way to go out, if in fact this had been the end of the group. But three years later, Kleinow and original bass player Chris Ethridge would resurrect the name, and there would be editions of the Burritos performing and recording, with legal, if not moral, legitimacy, long into the future. *—William Ruhlmann*

Close up the Honky-Tonks / Jun. 1974 / A&M ✦✦✦✦
A&M Records seemed to close the book on the Flying Burrito Brothers with *Close Up the Honky-Tonks*, a 23-track, double-LP compilation. A combination best-of and odds-and-sods career wrap-up, the album contains one LP given over to tracks from the Burritos' first two records, *The Gilded Palace of Sin* and *Burrito Deluxe*, plus the non-LP single "The Train Song." The second disc presents 11 previously unreleased tracks, most of them cover songs, ranging from the Bee Gees' "To Love Somebody" to the Everly Brothers' "Wake Up, Little Susie." Co-founder Gram Parsons is featured on five songs on side three, while side four comes from the Rick Roberts era of the band. The Burritos would lack a one-disc best-of until A&M came up with the CD/cassette release *Farther Along* in 1988. So, for more than a decade, *Close Up the Honky-Tonks* was the definitive Burritos compilation, and even now, when it is out of print, it contains some excellent performances available nowhere else. *—William Ruhlmann*

Flying Again / Sep. 1975 / Columbia ✦✦
The last that had been heard of the Flying Burrito Brothers was a 1973 European tour organized by Rick Roberts, the replacement for founding member Gram Parsons, with a few hired guns. But with Parsons' growing posthumous legend, the band's name retained currency, and former bassist Chris Ethridge and former pedal steel guitarist "Sneaky" Pete Kleinow retained legal rights to that name. They brought in guitarist/fiddle player Floyd "Gib" Gilbeau, guitarist Joel Scott Hill, and former Byrds drummer Gene Parsons, and relaunched the Burritos with this album of competently played country-rock. Words like "travesty" and "insult" have been used to describe it, on the grounds that Ethridge and Kleinow were trading on Parsons' reputation, but on

its own, the album is an adequate, if unremarkable, set. Just don't pick it up looking for the old glory. (Out of print.) — *William Ruhlmann*

Sleepless Nights / Apr. 1976 / A&M ✦✦✦
A&M Records seemed to have exhausted its stock of Flying Burrito Brothers outtakes on *Close Up the Honky-Tonks* in 1974, but the continuing posthumous regard for Gram Parsons caused the company to unearth another seven tracks, six covers of country classics like "Tonight the Bottle Let Me Down" and "Green, Green Grass of Home," plus a version of the Rolling Stones' "Honky Tonk Women," all originally intended for what annotator Bud Scoppa called "a pure, honest country album" that the Burritos apparently never finished. To this half-of-an-album, A&M added two tracks from *Close Up the Honky-Tonks* and three Parsons solo outtakes (with Emmylou Harris on backup vocals) licensed from Reprise Records. The result, credited to "Gram Parsons/The Flying Burrito Brothers," is a tribute to Parsons' heartbreaking tenor, especially because the tracks are little more than underproduced demos. It's not on par with *The Gilded Palace of Sin, Burrito Deluxe*, or *G.P.*, but should be of interest to fans. — *William Ruhlmann*

Live from Tokyo / 1978 / Regency ✦✦
The second edition of the Flying Burrito Brothers, launched by "Sneaky" Pete Kleinow in 1975, turned out to have as many personnel shifts as the first edition put together by Gram Parsons in 1968. This lineup played familiar Burrito songs such as "Hot Burrito No. 2" and "Colorado," as well as a selection of honky-tonk country standards. Far from the greatest of Burrito Brothers bands, this one nevertheless was superior to later versions, and the music was efficiently played before an enthusiastic audience. As the group's live albums go, however, the one to get is still *Last of the Red Hot Burritos*. (*Live from Tokyo* was reissued by Relix Records in 1991 under the title *Close Encounters to the West Coast*.) — *William Ruhlmann*

Cabin Fever / 1985 / Relix ✦
This 1985 live album chronicles a Burritos lineup anchored by original member "Sneaky" Pete Kleinow and singer/guitarist Skip Battin, who first joined the band in 1976. It is in essence a Gram Parsons/Burritos/Byrds tribute album on which the band tries unsuccessfully to address Parsons classics like "Wheels" and "Hickory Wind" as well as the Byrds' "Mr. Spaceman." The sound quality is low and the performances substandard. Skimpy packaging fails to tell you where it was recorded or even who the other members of the band are. — *William Ruhlmann*

Live from Europe / 1986 / Relix ✦✦
Relix Records, which has curious ideas about marketing, released a second Flying Burrito Brothers live album in 1986, the year after it released the live *Cabin Fever*. The same lineup of original member "Sneaky" Pete Kleinow, guitarist Skip Battin, and the previously uncredited rhythm section of bassist Greg Harris and Jim Goodall once again come off as a Burritos/Gram Parsons/Byrds tribute band, with a few of their own new originals thrown in. It was a reasonable enough concept for a live show, but back home on the record player versions of songs like "Christine's Tune (Devil in Disguise)" and "Citizen Kane" don't hold a candle to the original recordings. Maybe to Relix and its Dead Head fans, who hew to the notion that all live shows should be taped and disseminated, this sort of release made sense, but not to average fans. — *William Ruhlmann*

Dim Lights, Thick Smoke & Loud, Loud Music / Mar. 1987 / Edsel ✦✦✦
The British Edsel label's *Dim Lights, Thick Smoke & Loud, Loud Music*, their first try at a Flying Burrito Brothers-compilation in a decade, is not a best-of. Because the label had recently reissued the Burritos' first two albums, *The Gilded Palace of Sin* and *Burrito Deluxe*, this 13-song collection is drawn from the rarities and outtakes first released on the A&M albums *Close Up the Honky-Tonks* and *Sleepless Nights* after the original group's (and Gram Parsons') demise. Specifically, as the album notes report, " . . . [I]t brings together for the first time on one record all the Burritos' material that features Gram Parsons and that wasn't on those first two LPs." The songs are for the most part covers of country

music standards presented as demos or working versions that probably never would have been released if it were not for Parsons' death. Parsons, of course, is the reason the Burritos continue to interest fans, and he sings well here, but this half-finished material does not compare to the first two albums. — *William Ruhlmann*

★ **Farther Along: Best Of** / 1988 / A&M ✦✦✦✦✦
Farther Along: The Best of the Flying Burrito Brothers is a nearly flawless compilation, containing a full 21 tracks of the pioneering group's best material. All but two of the songs from *The Gilded Palace of Sin* are included on the collection, as are all of the highlights from *Burrito Deluxe* and a handful of rarities and outtakes. In short, it's a definitive collection containing all of the Burrito Brothers' finest moments. It's indispensable to any rock or country collection. — *Stephen Thomas Erlewine*

Close Encounters to the West Coast / 1991 / Relix ✦✦
The second edition of the Flying Burrito Brothers, launched by "Sneaky" Pete Kleinow in 1975, turned out to have as many personnel shifts as the first edition put together by Gram Parsons in 1968. This lineup played familiar Burrito songs such as "Hot Burrito No. 2" and "Colorado," as well as a selection of honky-tonk country standards. Far from the greatest of Burrito Brothers bands, this one nevertheless was superior to later versions, and the music was efficiently played before an enthusiastic audience. As the group's live albums go, however, the one to get is still *Last of the Red Hot Burritos*. (*Close Encounters to the West Coast* is a 1991 reissue of the 1978 Regency Records album *Live from Tokyo*.) — *William Ruhlmann*

Red Foley (Clyde Julian Foley)

b. Jun. 17, 1910, Blue Lick, KY, d. Sep. 19, 1968, Fort Wayne, IN
Guitar, Vocals / Bluegrass, Traditional Country, Honky Tonk, Country Gospel

Red Foley was one of the biggest stars in country during the postwar era, a silky-voiced singer who sold some 25 million records between 1944 and 1965 and whose popularity went far in making country music a viable mainstream commodity. Born Clyde Julian Foley on June 17, 1910, in Blue Lick, KY, he began playing guitar and harmonica at a young age, and by the time he was 17 had taken first prize in a statewide talent competition. While attending college in 1930, he was spotted by a talent scout from Chicago's WLS radio and was tapped to sing with producer John Lair's Cumberland Ridge Runners, the house band on the program *National Barn Dance*.

After seven years with the Ridge Runners, Lair created a new show, *Renfro Valley Barn Dance*, especially to showcase Foley's talents. The singer remained with the program until late 1939, performing everything from ballads to boogie to blues. At the same time, he became the first country artist to host his own network radio program, *Avalon Time* (co-hosted by comedian Red Skelton), and performed extensively in theaters and clubs and at fairs. After exiting the *Renfro Valley Barn Dance*, Foley returned for another seven-year stint at the *National Barn Dance* show. In 1941, the same year he made his film debut with Tex Ritter in the Western *The Pioneers*, he signed a lifetime contract with Decca Records. His first chart single, 1944's "Smoke on the Water," topped the charts for 13 consecutive weeks; in 1945, he was the first major performer to record in Nashville.

In 1946, Foley signed on to emcee and perform on *The Prince Albert Show*, a segment of the Grand Ole Opry program broadcast on NBC; his popularity with listeners is often credited with establishing the Opry as country's pre-eminent radio show. Beginning in 1947, he began recording with his backing band, the Cumberland Valley Boys, earning another No. 1 single with "New Jolie Blonde (New Pretty Blonde)." With the group, he recorded seven Top Five hits between 1947 and 1949, including "Tennessee Saturday Night," a chart-topper in 1948. Again recording solo in 1950, he issued the song that would become his trademark tune, "Chattanoogie Shoe Shine Boy," which stayed in the No. 1 position for 13 weeks.

In 1951, Foley's second wife, Eva Overstake, committed suicide, reportedly over the singer's affair with another woman. In order

Tennessee Ernie Ford

to devote the majority of his time to raising a family, he cut back considerably on his performing commitments, although he continued to release hit after hit in a variety of musical styles, including rockabilly and R&B; "(There'll Be) Peace in the Valley (For Me)," a 1951 smash, was the first record ever to sell one million copies on the gospel charts. In the same year, he also released his first LP, *Red Foley Souvenir Album*. After several years spent in virtual retirement, in 1954 Foley was named to host *The Ozark Jubilee*, a country showcase for ABC television; the show was a hit, and ran through 1960. Also in 1954, he recorded the chart-topping "One by One," the first of many duets with Kitty Wells.

After *The Ozark Jubilee* went off the air, he spent one season co-starring with Fess Parker in the program *Mr. Smith Goes to Washington*. Although Foley continued recording throughout most of the 1960s, his hit-making days were largely behind him. In 1967, he was elected to the Country Music Hall of Fame. After a performance in Fort Wayne, IN, on September 19, 1968, Foley died of a heart attack. Among the survivors were his daughter Betty, a popular country vocalist in her own right, and another daughter Shirley, the wife of pop crooner Pat Boone. —*Jason Ankeny*

Red and Ernie / 1956 / Decca ✦✦✦✦
Foley recorded four albums with his good friend Ernest Tubb, whose good humor always managed to bring out the best in his partner. —*Michael McCall*

Souvenir Album / 1958 / Decca ✦✦✦✦

Beyond the Sunset / 1958 / Decca ✦✦✦✦
Foley's gospel albums ranked with Tennessee Ernie Ford's as the most popular of the era among country fans. This is his best. —*Michael McCall*

He Walks with Thee / 1958 / Decca ✦✦✦

Let's All Sing with Red Foley / 1959 / Decca ✦✦✦

Red Foley's Golden Favorites / 1961 / Decca ✦✦✦✦

Dear Hearts and Gentle People / 1962 / Decca ✦✦✦✦
Dear Hearts and Gentle People is a laidback, pleasant album highlighted by "Down Yonder," "The Happy Song," and "River, Stay 'Way from My Door." —*Thom Owens*

Songs Everybody Knows / 1965 / Decca ✦✦

Songs for the Soul / 1967 / Decca ✦✦✦

★ **Country Music Hall of Fame** / 1991 / MCA ✦✦✦✦✦
Country Music Hall of Fame contains a good cross-section of Red Foley's heyday in the late '40s and early '50s. All of the selections

of this 16-track, single-disc compilation were recorded for Decca Records. While not all of his hits are present—even some of his biggest singles, including "Smoke on the Water," are missing—most of the essential items ("Chattanoogie Shoe Shine Boy," "Tennessee Saturday Night," "Peace in the Valley") are here, making it an essential introduction to one of country's biggest stars. —*Stephen Thomas Erlewine*

1937-39, Vol. 1 / Document ✦✦✦✦

Tennessee Saturday Night / Charly ✦✦✦
Another strong compilation, its emphasis is on Foley's boogie and uptempo material. —*Richard Lieberson*

Allen Fontenot

b. 1932, Grand Prairie, LA
Fiddle, Vocals / Cajun
Allen Fontenot is one of the best-known fiddlers in Cajun music. Fontenot always loved the fiddle and made his own on several occasions out of such materials as a ukulele, cigar boxes, bow and arrow sets, and wire. At age 15, his grandfather, also a fiddler, bought him his first real one. After working for several years as a bill collector, Fontenot founded the five-piece Country Cajuns in the early '70s. The first members—concertina player Leroy Veilloa, guitarist Hudson Dauzat, drummer Darrel Brasseaux, and bass player John Scott—recorded a few singles and played at the Jazz and Heritage Festival. The Country Cajuns also appeared regularly on a Sunday morning radio show and made their feature film debut in 1975 in Charles Bronson's *Hard Times*. They also appeared on the television shows *Good Morning America* and *Austin City Limits*. When not playing with the band, Fontenot worked as a popular deejay in Slidell, LA. In the late '70s, he opened the Cajun Bandstand in Kenner, LA, which served authentic Cajun cuisine and showcased authentic Cajun music; he and his band frequently played there until he sold the club in 1982. Fontenot's work can be found on the Great Southern, Antilles, and Delta labels. —*Sandra Brennan*

Jole Blon & Other Cajun Honky Tonk Songs / Jan. 1980 / Great Southern ✦✦✦✦

Brownie Ford

Vocals / Cowboy
Ford was an Oklahoma-born cowboy who learned the old songs as a lad, spun a few of his own, told a few ribald tales, and offered to the world his wry take on life in a 1990 Flying Fish album, part field recording (Ford and guitar) and part recording session with an acoustic country band. Ford's wizened vocals and open spirit merited an unlikely nod from *People*, which said kind words over the sole recorded testament of an 80-something individualist. —*Mark A. Humphrey*

Stories from Mountains, Swamps & Honky-Tonks / 1990 / Flying Fish ✦✦✦✦
A delightful geezer, he recalls skinny-dippin' in Oklahoma. He wails wizened folk and country to the guitar accompaniment of Dave Doucet and D. L. Menard. —*Mark A. Humphrey*

Tennessee Ernie Ford

b. Feb. 13, 1919, Bristol, TN, **d.** Oct. 17, 1991, Los Angeles, CA
Vocals / Traditional Country, Country-Folk, Nashville Sound/ Countrypolitan, Country Gospel, Country Boogie
Tennessee Ernie Ford was a beloved personality and performer during the '50s and '60s whose best known song was his version of Merle Travis' "Sixteen Tons." During his long career, Ford recorded over 100 albums and earned numerous honors and awards, including the distinguished Medal of Freedom. A native of Bristol, TN, he began his career as deejay on a local radio station. In the late '30s, he left to study classical music and voice at the Cincinnati Conservatory of Music. After serving in World War II, he moved his family to San Bernardino, CA, to work at a local radio station. It is there that he first took on the name "Tennessee Ernie."

Ford later moved to a Pasadena station, where his potential as a singer was recognized by Cliffie Stone, who hired Ford as a featured act on two of his radio shows. From there, he signed to Capitol Records in 1949. Five singles were released that year, including "Tennessee Border" and "Smokey Mountain Boogie" (both Top Ten) and his first No. 1 single, "Mule Train." Early in 1951, "The Shot Gun Boogie" became his second No. 1, spending 14 weeks at the top of the country charts. By the beginning of 1953, Ford wasn't having as many hits, but he remained popular not only in America, but also in England; he was the first country singer to star at the London Palladium. He became a television quizmaster in 1954, hosting NBC's *College of Musical Knowledge*. He also had his own daily show and continued recording.

Ford had two Top Ten country hits in 1955 with "Ballad of Davy Crockett" and his biggest success, "Sixteen Tons," which spent ten weeks at No. 1 on the country charts and eight weeks at No. 1 on the pop charts. Between 1956 and 1961 he helmed his own primetime NBC show, which popularized the catch-phrase "Bless your little pea-pickin' hearts." As a recording artist, he had great success with his first gospel album, *Hymns* (1956), which became the first religious album to go gold. Ford's second gospel album, *Great Gospel Songs*, earned him a Grammy. In 1965, he had his last chart entry with the Top Ten single "Hicktown." Ford joined the ranks of the Country Music Hall of Fame in 1990, a year before he died of liver failure. — *Sandra Brennan*

Tennesse Ernie Ford Deluxe Set / 1968 / Capitol ✦✦✦✦

★ **16 Tons of Boogie: the Best of . . .** / 1990 / Rhino ✦✦✦✦✦
In his later years, Ford's little pea-pickin' heart was closely associated with gospel and patriotic music, but in earlier years he knew how to—as the album title says—boogie. This includes all the essential material from that period: "Sixteen Tons," "The Shot Gun Boogie," "Mule Train," and "Blackberry Boogie," for starters. — *Tom Roland*

All-Time Greatest Hymns / 1990 / Curb ✦✦✦✦
Ford uses his superb baritone on traditional hymns. — *Bil Carpenter*

Country Gospel Classics, Vol. 1 & 2 / 1991 / Capitol ✦✦✦✦
The '60s follow-up to the previous decade's *All-Time Greatest Hymns* wasn't as overwhelmingly successful, but it holds up better. The interplay between Ford's baritone and the Jordanaires' harmony support is beautiful. — *Michael McCall*

Sings Songs of the Civil War / Feb. 4, 1991 / Capitol ✦✦✦
The 1991 release combines two evocative albums of Civil War-era songs Ford recorded for that conflict's centennial remembrance in 1961. His somber style perfectly fits the subject matter. — *Michael McCall*

Country Gospel Classics, Vol. 2 / Jun. 10, 1991 / Capitol ✦✦✦✦
The Jordanaires join Ford on many of these spiritual songs, including "How Great Thou Art," "Just a Closer Walk with Thee," and the standard "Peace in the Valley." — *Jason Ankeny*

Red, White & Blue / Jun. 24, 1991 / Capitol ✦✦✦
This gathers together his patriotic songs, including the complete *America the Beautiful* LP from 1970. — *Michael McCall*

Capitol Collector's Series / Jul. 8, 1991 / Capitol ✦✦✦✦
Tennessee Ernie Ford's *Capitol Collector's Series* contains 29 of his biggest hits and best-known songs, including "Sixteen Tons," "The Shot Gun Boogie," "Mule Train," "The Cry of the Wild Goose," and "I'll Never Be Free," as well as a handful of lesser-known gems, making it the perfect single-disc introduction to one of the most popular country singers of the early '50s. — *Stephen Thomas Erlewine*

☆ **Sixteen Tons** / Oct. 10, 1995 / Capitol ✦✦✦✦✦
Though named after Tennessee Ernie Ford's biggest hit, *Sixteen Tons* was released five years after the single was a hit. The large gap of time between the release of the single and album is inconsequential—in essence, the album is a compilation of Ford's greatest hits of the '50s, containing not only the title track, but also "Mule Train," "The Cry of the Wild Goose," and "The Shot Gun Boogie." Though more comprehensive compilations of Ford's work were later released, *Sixteen Tons* remains an entertaining listen from start to finish; in fact, in terms of sheer listenability, it rivals any of the latter-day collections. — *Stephen Thomas Erlewine*

The Forester Sisters

● **The Tennessee Ernie Ford Collection (1949-1965)** / Mar. 18, 1997 / Razor & Tie ✦✦✦✦
Razor & Tie's *The Tennessee Ernie Ford Collection (1949-1965)* contains all of Ford's biggest hits, from "Tennessee Border" and "Mule Train" through "The Shot Gun Boogie" to "Sixteen Tons" and "Hicktown." The song selection on *Collection* is nearly identical to Rhino's *16 Tons of Boogie*, and both are definitive overviews of Tennessee's career, but the Razor & Tie disc has a slight edge, since it contains more songs and it has a tighter, more listenable sequencing. — *Thom Owens*

Favorite Hymns / Vanguard ✦✦✦✦
This collection of Ford's spiritual recordings includes "What a Friend We Have in Jesus," "His Eye Is on the Sparrow," and "Nearer My God to Thee." — *Jason Ankeny*

The Forester Sisters

Progressive Country, Contemporary Country, Neo-Traditionalist Country

The four Forester Sisters—Kathy, June, Kim, and Christy—began performing together professionally in 1982 and had numerous hits. All of the sisters were born and raised in Lookout Mountain, GA, where they later maintained their base of operations. Elder sisters Kathy and June first began singing in the choir of the local United Methodist Church. Both worked as schoolteachers after college, and at night played with a local band at parties and clubs. The band frequently changed male personnel, and soon after Kim joined in 1978, the sisters decided to form an all-female group. After Kim and Christy finished college, the older sisters quit teaching and the foursome began to pursue a music career in earnest.

While performing at an arts festival, the Forester Sisters were spotted by songwriters Bobby Keel and Billy Stone, who gave them a song that would eventually appear on their debut album, "Yankee Go Home." The group cut a demo at Muscle Shoals and signed to Warner Brothers in 1984. The Foresters then toured as the opening act for the Gatlin Brothers. In early 1985, their debut single, "(That's What You Do) When You're in Love," hit the Top Ten; their self-titled debut album soon followed and produced three more hits, including "Just in Case." That year, the Bellamy Brothers asked them to sing on "Too Much Is Not Enough." The two acts then toured together in 1986. The Sisters' second album, *Perfume, Ribbons & Pearls*, didn't do as well, producing only the hit "Lonely Again," but their third album, *You Again*, proved a solid rebound. They continued to appear on the charts at least once or twice a year through 1991. The Forester Sisters continued to tour and occasionally perform throughout the '90s, releasing the LP *More Than I Am* in 1996. — *Sandra Brennan*

The Forester Sisters / 1985 / Warner Brothers ✦✦✦✦
Rock music had the Go-Gos, Motown had the Supremes, and the standard pop era had the Andrews Sisters and the McGuire Sisters. Country music finally got an all-girl vocal group with the advent of the Foresters, and their debut is surprisingly uptempo and energetic. This is a debut album that should have received more attention. — *Tom Roland*

I'd Choose You Again / 1987 / Warner Brothers ✦✦✦

You Again / 1987 / Warner Brothers ✦✦✦

Sincerely / 1988 / Warner Brothers ✦✦✦✦
Already the possessors of a wonderful vocal harmony style, the Foresters hit a peak when they hooked up with writer/producer Wendy Waldman for this album, cutting her "Letter Home" and other strong material (note especially the shoulda-been-a-single "You Love Me," co-written by Matraca Berg). — *William Ruhlmann*

All I Need / 1989 / Warner Brothers ✦✦✦✦
All I Need is a collection of gospel staples and latter-day Christian songs. — *Jason Ankeny*

● **Greatest Hits** / 1989 / Warner Brothers ✦✦✦✦
A good selection of Forester singles presents the various stylistic approaches they've taken with country material, which range from good to terrific. — *William Ruhlmann*

Talkin' 'Bout Men / 1991 / Warner Brothers ✦✦✦
Love songs, love-gone-wrong songs, a little bit of swing, a little bit of reggae and, oh yeah, some country, too, are included. The novelty hit "Men" (with lines like "You can't beat 'em up, 'cause they're bigger than you/You can't live with 'em and you just can't shoot 'em") was written by two guys. — *Brian Mansfield*

I Got a Date / 1992 / Warner Brothers ✦✦✦✦
Somewhere along the line, some executive got the idea that this Lookout Mountain group should concentrate primarily on ballads. As a result, their non-ballad material could've been better, but that's rectified in this collection, an excellent portrayal of the humor and heartaches faced by women in modern relationships. It's wide-ranging stylistically, with a strong dose of wit, particularly in the title track and "Redneck Romeo." — *Tom Roland*

More Than I Am / Aug. 27, 1996 / Warner Brothers ✦✦✦
More Than I Am is a diverse blend of adult pop and country styles, giving the Forester Sisters a wider array of sounds than they have ever previously displayed before on record. It's not wildly eclectic—all of the styles are fused into one sound. Unfortunately, it's not all entirely successful either. Roughly half the tracks are worthwhile, while the others rank as failed experiments. — *Thom Owens*

Peggy Forman

b. Centerville, LA
Vocals / Country-Pop
Peggy Forman was a well-known Nashville songwriter. The daughter of an oilfield worker and a homemaker, she hailed from Centerville, LA. A music lover and singer since childhood, young Peggy met her husband Wayne Forman while still in high school. After their marriage, they began performing together in a band with Wayne singing leads and playing guitar and Peggy on harmonies. Later, she became the lead singer. At the time, she was also writing songs, and one of them was recorded by Joe Lewis. Not long after, her "Out of My Head and Back in My Bed" became a chart topping hit for Loretta Lynn. In 1978, Conway Twitty, an early supporter, recorded her "Yours to Hurt Tomorrow," and helped Forman sign a recording contract with MCA in the mid-'70s. He and Snuffy Miller then became the producers of her debut single "The Danger Zone," which became a minor hit. She recorded several other singles, but they never made it to the charts. Around 1980, she signed to Dimension Records and had a small string of hits beginning with "There Ain't Nothing like a Rainy Night" and ending in 1982 with "That's What Your Lovin' Does to Me." Forman has had considerably more success as a writer; many prominent artists such as Bill Anderson, Jean Shepard, and George Strait recorded her songs. — *Sandra Brennan*

● **Presenting Peggy Forman** / Dimension ✦✦✦✦

Foster & Lloyd

Country-Rock, Contemporary Country, New Traditionalist
During the mid- to late 1980s, Foster & Lloyd were a popular songwriting and singing duo. As singers, they were known for their close harmonies and lively country-rock sound, which is reminiscent of Poco or the Eagles. A lawyer's son from Del Rio, TX, Radney Foster attended the University of Sewanee, TN, performing in local clubs on weekends. Based on the encouragement he got at the club, Foster took a year off of college to try his luck in Nashville. He was successful and signed with MTM Music Group as a songwriter. Bill Lloyd, born in Bowling Green, KY, was a military "brat" who saw much of the world during childhood due to his father's frequent relocations. He began writing songs as a teenager, and went on to study communications at Western Kentucky University; however, he, like Foster, he eventually dropped out to enter the country music business. He came to Nashville in 1982 to pursue a solo career, but it was a long time before he got any real breaks. Around 1986, Lloyd was teamed up with Foster and the two began writing such successful songs as "Since I Found You," which became a hit for the Sweethearts of the Rodeo. The two turned to singing the following year and signed with RCA. Foster and Lloyd were given free rein with their eponymous first album; their debut single, "Crazy Over You," made it to the Top Five, where it stayed for over four months. That fall, the duo debuted on the Grand Ole Opry, and later they performed on the annual CMA awards show. In 1988, their second single, "Sure Thing" made it to the Top Ten, and its follow-up made it to the Top 20. Their third single, "What Do You Want from Me This Time," was a Top Ten hit for several months. They released their second album *Faster and Llouder* (a take-off on their names) in 1989. The album produced a Top Five and a Top 50 hit. Foster and Lloyd released *Version of the Truth*, their final album, in 1990. They amicably split to pursue solo careers after that. In 1992, Foster released his solo debut *Del Rio, TX, 1959* for Arista. It was more acoustic and country oriented than his earlier works, and Foster wrote or co-wrote all ten tracks. Several of these songs, including "Just Call Me Lonesome," have become hits. Lloyd continues song writing and working as a session guitarist. — *Sandra Brennan*

Foster & Lloyd / 1987 / RCA ✦✦✦
This self-titled debut effort contains the duo's most recognizable radio tracks, particularly "Crazy over You," a Top Five hit. Other hits included here are "Sure Thing," "What Do You Want from Me This Time?," and "Texas in 1880." — *Rick Clark*

Faster & Llouder / 1989 / RCA ✦✦✦✦
Foster & Lloyd's sophomore effort presents a harder, edgier collection of songs, which are even stronger than the ones found on their first album. Highlights include "Happy for Awhile," the roots-rocker "Fat Lady Sings," and the title track. Power-pop artist Marshall Crenshaw guests on "She Knows What She Wants." — *Rick Clark*

Version of the Truth / 1990 / RCA ✦✦✦
Foster & Lloyd's third album synthesizes the energy of *Faster and Llouder* with the radio accessibility of their first album. Two versions of the album exist, featuring different mixes. An instrumental, "Whoa," was nominated for a Grammy in 1990 and featured the guest artists Duane Eddy, Albert Lee, Felix Cavaliere (of The Rascals), and Rusty Young (of Poco). — *Rick Clark*

● **Essential Foster & Lloyd** / Apr. 1996 / RCA ✦✦✦✦
The Essential Foster & Lloyd groups together 19 tracks by this influential duo who scored several hits in the 1980s. The two merged Lloyd's melodic pop smarts with Foster's Texas literary soul, giving them catchiness and substance in the same package. They also could rock out, leaning toward a rockabilly energy that didn't carry a trace of the redneck swagger of Southern rock. Instead, this was solid, clean-rocking fun with brains. The duo split in 1990 after three albums, but this collection is a good reminder that they anticipated the country youth movement that followed them. — *Michael McCall*

Radney Foster

b. 1959, Del Rio, TX

Guitar, Vocals / Contemporary Country, New Traditionalist

Radney Foster first gained attention as half of the duo Foster & Lloyd in the late '80s, but he established himself as a solo artist in his own right in the early '90s with a pair of successful solo albums. Born and raised in Del Rio, TX, Foster began playing guitar at the age of 12. He attended the University of South in Sewanee, TN, after graduating from high school. While he was in college, he began performing at local clubs during weekends. During one of these shows, a fan who happened to know a few people in Nashville suggested that Foster travel to the Music City to become a professional. Foster declined the fan's offer but he later decided to take a year off of college and move to Nashville to seek out contacts on his own. After a little searching, he was hired by MTM Music Publishing in 1985.

Two months after he joined MTM, Bill Lloyd also became a staff writer for the company. During the course of the summer, the pair became friends and writing partners. The following year, they had their first hit single when Sweethearts of the Rodeo took their "Since I Found You" to the Top Ten. Later in 1986, RCA heard a demo tape of Foster & Lloyd's songs and signed the duo as recording artists. In 1987, the pair released their eponymous debut, which became a hit thanks to the No. 4 single "Crazy Over You." For the next two years, they had a string of Top Ten singles ("Crazy Over You," "Sure Thing," "What Do You Want From Me This Time," "Fair Shake") and two hit albums (*Foster and Lloyd, Faster and Llouder*). However, their third album, 1990's *Version of the Truth*, stiffed, producing only one minor Top 40 hit in "Can't Have Nothin.'"

In 1991, Foster & Lloyd seperated and the following year Radney Foster released his debut solo album, *Del Rio, Texas, 1959*, on Arista Records. *Del Rio, Texas, 1959*, produced four Top 40 hits, including the No. 10 hit "Just Call Me Lonesome" and the No. 2 single "Nobody Wins." *Labor of Love*, Foster's second solo album, was released in early 1995. Although the record received good reviews, none of its singles cracked the Top 40. *—Stephen Thomas Erlewine*

● **Del Rio, Texas, 1959** / 1992 / Arista ✦✦✦✦

Radney Foster's first album since dissolving the much-missed Foster & Lloyd duo is a tribute to the songwriter's coming of age in small-town Texas and all the musical baggage that stowed aboard for the ride. On many of the tracks, Foster seems a little too conscious of wanting to deliver a pure country effort. The songs are solid, but there's a slight archival feel to the result. I admit that personal biases may be at work here, having been a Foster & Lloyd fan, but it's the more contemporary hybrids that strike me as the disc's best moments. The gutsy "A Fine Line," the infectious "Nobody Wins" (with Mary Chapin Carpenter on background vocals), and the gospelly country-rocker "Hammer and Nails" are worth the price of admission alone. *—Roch Parisien*

Labor of Love / 1995 / Arista ✦✦✦

4 Runner

Contemporary Country

The country vocal group 4 Runner toured with Tim McGraw, Blackhawk and Kenny Rogers during the 1980s and '90s, and moved to the big leagues themselves with an album in 1995. Lead Craig Morris had appeared with Marie Osmond and Ronnie McDowell before he met baritone Billy Simon in Nashville, where both were working as staff writers. Working around Music City led them to the doors of bass vocalist Jim Chapman and tenor Lee Hilliard, who had sung with Higher Ground. The foursome united as 4 Runner, and worked the country live circuit for several years before recording *4 Runner* for Polydor's Nashville division in 1995. *—John Bush*

4 Runner / 1995 / Polydor Nashville ✦✦✦

Curley Fox

b. Nov. 9, 1910, Graysville, TN

Fiddle / Traditional Country

During the '40s and '50s, Curly Fox and Texas Ruby were the pre-eminent husband and wife team in country music. Fox remains one of the great hillbilly fiddlers, while Ruby was one of the first female singers to become a major star.

Curly was born Arnim LeRoy Fox in Graysville, TN. His father, a barber, taught him to play the fiddle, with help from James McCarroll of the Roane Country Ramblers. He began his professional career playing and traveling with Chief White Owl's "Indian" medicine show. Fox soon began working with Claude Davis and the Carolina Tar Heels in Atlanta and founded the Tennessee Firecrackers. He played and recorded with the Shelton Brothers in New Orleans from 1934 to 1936, also recording three singles himself. In 1937, Fox met Texas Ruby (born Ruby Agnes Owens in Wise County, TX) at the Texas centennial celebration. Ruby, a true cowgirl and sister of radio cowboy Tex Owens, had sung several times on the Grand Ole Opry and various radio stations with Zeke Clements and His Bronco Busters. Soon after meeting Fox, the two married and began appearing on the Opry from 1937-39 and again from 1944-48. In between, they worked in Cincinnati and at other major stations as well.

The duo did make some recordings, but according to Fox, Ruby's throaty contralto didn't sound as good on records as it did on the radio. Her best recordings were made for King in 1947. In 1948 the couple moved to Houston, where they lived and worked for ten years bringing country music to local television. In 1960, they returned to the Grand Ole Opry. Unfortunately, Ruby's health was failing, so Fox often played alone. They did manage to record an album for Starday in 1963, but shortly thereafter, Ruby burned to death in a mobile home fire while her husband was playing on the Opry. Fox continued his solo career for a while after her death, but then left for Chicago to live with one of his daughters. Though he too suffered ill health, he made some albums and occasionally appeared live. He returned to his hometown in the mid-'70s and worked with a local bluegrass band before retiring to live with an older sister. *—Sandra Brennan*

Curley Fox & Texas Ruby / 1962 / Starday ✦✦✦

● **Champion Fiddler Curly Fox, Vol. 1** / 1972 / Rural Rhythm ✦✦✦✦

Champion Fiddler Curly Fox, Vol. 2 / 1972 / Rural Rhythm ✦✦✦✦

George Fox

b. Cochrane, Alberta, Canada

Vocals / Contemporary Country

Although he was raised on an Alberta cattle ranch, Canadian singer-songwriter George Fox cared little about country music until he was 21 years old and preparing to stay in Sweden. His host family requested that he bring some American country albums with him on his visit; Fox began listening to them and was hooked. Upon his return, he began playing music in public on weekends and decided to make an album, which he paid for himself out of money set aside to buy a new tractor. He sent tapes of his music to various stations and went back to the ranch until he got a call from Warner Bros. in Toronto, who released the eponymous album in 1988.

With a style similar to that of John Prine, his second single, "Long Distance," made the Top 20 on the Canadian charts. That year he also signed with Anne Murray's manager, Leonard Rambeau, who hadn't accepted a new client since the late '70s. The following year was even better for Fox when three of his singles hit the Canadian Top 20. On his second album, 1990's *With All My Might*, Fox wrote all but one of the songs, and before the year ended, the album had gone gold in Canada. In 1990 he starred in his own TV special for the CBC and guested on three others, including Anne Murray's *Family Christmas*. His next two albums, *Spice of Life* (1991) and *Mustang Heart* (1993), continued Fox's hit streak. *—Sandra Brennan*

Spice of Life / 1980 / Warner Brothers ✦✦✦
Fox had a hand in writing less than half of the songs that make up *Spice of Life*, resulting in more faceless fare than his earlier work; still, the inclusion of material like Buck Owens' "There Goes My Love" is always welcome. —*Jason Ankeny*

George Fox / 1988 / Warner Brothers ✦✦✦

● **With All My Might** / 1990 / Warner Brothers ✦✦✦✦
Produced by Brian Ahern (Emmylou Harris), this album contains an affecting version of Dylan's "I Threw It All Away." There are good but unexceptional originals, the best being "Lonesome Avenue Goodbye" and "Angelina." —*Rick Clark*

Mustang Heart / Warner Brothers ✦✦✦
Recorded in Nashville, with material co-written and produced by Bob Gaudio (Four Seasons, Neil Diamond), *Mustang Heart* is a well-rounded effort from Alberta's George Fox. This fourth outing features warm, expansive sound that perfectly suits Fox's vocals on a diverse collection of songs ranging from the patriotic "Clearly Canadian" to the poignant "Breakfast Alone." Sinewy fiddle provides the musical muscle on the best tracks, while purists will cringe at the overuse of keyboards on others, especially the gooey, synth-laden "Better Love Next Time." —*Roch Parisien*

Jeff Foxworthy

Contemporary Country, Country Humor
The biggest-selling comedian in recording history, Jeff Foxworthy rode his famous routine—"You might be a redneck if . . ."—into over ten best-selling books, a TV show (for ABC and later NBC), and a series of platinum albums that contained his countrified Southern humor. The first, *You Might Be a Redneck If . . .*, was released in 1993 on Laughing Hyena. It sold the most copies of any comedy album in history, with totals of almost four million units. Warner Bros. purchased Foxworthy's contract a year later, and released his second proper album, *Games Rednecks Play*, in 1995. It went double-platinum, and earned the comedian a Grammy nomination. The first non-spoken work, *Crank It Up—The Music Album*, was released in September 1996 and enjoyed a gold certification. —*John Bush*

● **You Might Be a Redneck If . . .** / 1994 / Warner Brothers ✦✦✦✦
You Might Be a Redneck If . . . encapsulates the humor of Jeff Foxworthy on a single disc. Essentially variations on the title phrase "You Might Be a Redneck," Foxworthy's jokes are simple but never crude. Like any comedy album, it appeals to a specific taste. If you find Foxworthy's repetitive jokes hilarious, you might be a fan. If you don't find him funny, you might be better off leaving the album in the store. —*Sara Sytsma*

Redneck Test, Vol. 11 / Aug. 26, 1994 / Laughing Hyena ✦✦
Jeff Foxworthy's line of *Redneck Test* collections contains some good comedy, but by and large the records are poorly packaged and produced; stick with his Warner records. —*Stephen Thomas Erlewine*

Redneck Test , Vol. 43 / 1995 / Laughing Hyena ✦✦

The Original / 1995 / Laughing Hyena ✦✦✦
The Original is a collection of early Jeff Foxworthy performances. While his humor is often as good as his better-known albums, the album isn't as consistent as his two major label albums. —*Sara Sytsma*

Sold Out / 1995 / Laughing Hyena ✦✦✦
Sold Out is a live concert featuring Jeff Foxworthy's trademark "redneck" humor. The crowd interacts well with the comedian and his performance is consistently funny, even if it isn't particularly special. —*Sara Sytsma*

Games Rednecks Play / Jul. 18, 1995 / Warner Brothers ✦✦✦✦
Games Rednecks Play was Jeff Foxworthy's follow-up to his breakthrough major-label debut, *You Might Be a Redneck If . . .* Like its predecessor, the album is basically variations on his down-home humor, which does show a genuine affection for the "rednecks" he jokes about. *Games Rednecks Play* is as funny as *You Might Be a Redneck*, but if you don't like that kind of humor, it's certainly not going to convince you that you were wrong. —*Sara Sytsma*

Crank It Up: Music Album / Aug. 27, 1996 / Warner Brothers ✦✦✦
Jeff Foxworthy attempted to expand his recorded repertoire with *Crank It Up: Music Album*. The record was the first time he tried to make an album that didn't rely on redneck jokes. Don't worry, though—there's still plenty of humor here. It's just mixed in with competent neo-traditional honky tonk and slick new country. Though there's nothing particularly promising about the music, it isn't bad and *Crank It Up: Music Album* is far from the disaster it could have been. —*Thom Owens*

Cleve Francis

b. Apr. 22, 1945, Jennings, LA
Vocals / Contemporary Country
Cleve Francis is a promising 1990s singer-songwriter. Born Cleveland Francis, Jr. in Jennings, LA, he began playing music at age eight with a simple homemade guitar comprised of a cigar box and window screen wire. A year later, his mother brought him a real guitar. Francis obtained his medical degree in cardiology from the Medical College of Virginia in Richmond in 1973, and performed during summer vacations from college. He focused on medicine after getting his practitioner's license, but still managed to record three albums on his own label, Cleve Francis Productions.

Francis returned to his music through heart attack patient Olaf Hall, whose brother was "Big John" Garfield Hall, a member of the R&B band the Heartbeats. Big John helped Francis get an audition with Playback Records, who signed him and released an album; while it didn't sell well, his debut single and video "Love Light," released in 1990, both won critical acclaim. When the head of Liberty Records, Jimmy Bowen, saw the video, he offered Francis a contract. His first Liberty album, *Tourist in Paradise* (1991), featured a new recording and video of "Love Light" and two other songs, which all became minor chart hits. The title cut from his second album, *Walkin'* (1993), also became a minor hit. In 1994, he followed with *You've Got Me Now.* —*Sandra Brennan*

● **Tourist in Paradise** / Mar. 16, 1992 / Liberty ✦✦✦✦
Tourist in Paradise highlights Francis' engaging tenor on songs like "You Do My Heart Good" and "Love Light." —*Jason Ankeny*

Walkin' / May 10, 1993 / Capitol ✦✦✦✦
Francis' second effort is a more wide-ranging affair featuring the ballads "I Won't Let You Walk Away" and "Your Love Stays with Me." —*Jason Ankeny*

You've Got Me Now / 1994 / Liberty ✦✦✦

Dallas Frazier

b. Oct. 27, 1939, Spiro, OK
Vocals / Rock & Roll, Traditional Country, Honky Tonk, Bakersfield Sound, Nashville Sound/Countrypolitan
One of country's most enduring songwriters, Dallas Frazier was born on October 27, 1939 in Spiro, OK. Raised in Bakersfield, CA, he was skilled on a number of musical instruments by the age of 12; while still in his teens, he became a featured member of Ferlin Husky's band, cutting his first solo single, "Space Command," in 1954. Soon after, he was named a regular on the *Hometown Jamboree* program, where he was often paired with fellow teen star Molly Bee.

In 1957, Frazier scored a hit with a cover of the Hollywood Argyles' "Alley Oop." When *Hometown Jamboree* was canceled at the end of the decade, he moved to Nashville to work as a songwriter, composing Husky's 1964 hit "Timber I'm Falling." Two years later, his career caught fire; in addition to releasing his own debut album, *Elvira*, he penned three huge hits—Jack Greene's "There Goes My Everything," Connie Smith's "Ain't Had No Lovin'," and George Jones' "I'm a People." In 1967, Frazier released *Tell It Like It Is*, although his biggest success came on the pop charts, via Engelbert Humperdinck's rendition of "There Goes My Everything."

As the decade drew to a close, Frazier's songs remained popular fodder for other artists; in addition to supplying more hits for Jones, Greene, and Smith, his compositions were recorded by the likes of Willie Nelson, Brenda Lee, Charley Pride, and Merle Haggard, who included three Frazier songs on his 1968 LP *The Legend of Bonnie and Clyde*. Frazier's success only increased in the 1970s; in addition to generating a pair of solo records—1970's *Singing My Songs* and the following year's *My Baby Packed Up My Mind and Left Me*—Frazier became one of Nashville's most sought-after writers, composing hits for Elvis Presley, Moe Bandy, Roy Head, Rodney Crowell, and Ronnie Hawkins, as well as frequent collaborators like Husky, Pride, and Greene. In 1972, he joined Connie Smith for three cuts on her LP *If It Ain't Love (& Other Great Dallas Frazier Songs)*.

Frazier's songs continued to hit the charts well into the 1980s; his "Elvira" was a tremendous crossover smash for the Oak Ridge Boys, while Emmylou Harris topped the charts with "Beneath Still Waters." Even younger artists like George Strait, Randy Travis, and Patty Loveless found success with his compositions. In 1988, however, Frazier retired from songwriting, leaving Nashville to pursue a career in the ministry. —*Jason Ankeny*

● **Elvira** / 1966 / Capitol ✦✦✦✦
After penning hits for both R&B and country artists, Frazier decided to take a stab at performing his own songs for this album in 1966. The material chosen focuses on his more playful novelty numbers like "Alley Oop," "She's a Yum Yum," and "Whoop It on 'Um" and includes other hits such as the title track and "Mohair Sam." The arrangements are by-the-numbers pop R&B and while he's clearly a capable singer, Frazier's voice lacks the grit to make these songs as bluesy as he'd obviously like them to be. —*Chris Woodstra*

Freakwater

Alternative Country-Rock
An acoustic side project of the Eleventh Dream Day family tree, featuring Dream Day drummer/singer Janet Bean (who plays guitar in Freakwater) and her friend Catherine Ann Irwin, with contributions from various other musicians. This is only "alternative rock" in the marketing sense; the Kentucky-bred singers largely stick to acoustic folk/country with close harmonies and strong Appalachian overtones, sometimes employing fiddle, pedal steel, mandolin, and dobro. Mixing strong original material (mostly written by Irwin) with traditional numbers and songs by the likes of Bill Monroe, Freakwater's albums stand as some of the finest maverick, progressive acoustic records of recent years. —*Richie Unterberger*

Freakwater / 1989 / Amoeba ✦✦✦
Their debut, a short LP or a long EP, depending on how you look at it, presents plaintive, raw country-folk in a modern context without sounding forced. —*Richie Unterberger*

● **Dancing under Water** / 1991 / Amoeba ✦✦✦✦
A bit more polished than their debut, but hardly slick, with harmonies and the sobbing lead vocals of Irwin at the fore. This is recommended above the debut for a simple reason: the CD includes all of the songs from *Freakwater* as bonus tracks, eliminating the need to look for the first album. —*Richie Unterberger*

Old Paint / Oct. 10, 1995 / Thrill Jockey ✦✦✦✦
After a four-year gap since their second album, Freakwater returned with another solid effort that's not as bare-bones as their debut, but a little earthier than *Dancing under Water*. Not a lot of new ground is broken, yet it somehow doesn't sound at all tiresome. All of their strengths remain in place: fine, mournful harmonies, good original songs, some well-chosen covers (Loudon Wainwright's "Out of this World" is a particular highlight), and nice unobtrusive touches of pedal steel and fiddle embellishing the acoustic guitars. This is modern country-folk at its best, and in fact would really be more suitable for the roots country audience, except that the execution is too direct, the production too basic, and the songwriting too heartfelt for the contemporary country marketplace. Thus it is that the group's primary listenership is the alternative rock community, which is country's loss: few performers today are performing roots music so convincingly, without sounding forced or dated. —*Richie Unterberger*

Janie Fricke

b. Dec. 19, 1952, South Whitney, IN
Guitar, Vocals / Country-Pop
Vocalist Janie Fricke was studying to be a teacher in the mid-'60s when the work of Joan Baez, Judy Collins, and Neil Diamond inspired her to try music herself. Fricke had always been musically inclined, as both of her parents played instruments and taught her to play piano and guitar as a child. She began singing jingles at a Memphis radio station while in college, and even after receiving her teaching certificate in 1972 continued to work in advertising. Fricke came to Nashville in 1975 to sing backup vocals, appearing on albums by artists like Ronnie Milsap, Charley Pride, Loretta Lynn, and England Dan & John Ford Coley. In total, she sang on over 1,200 albums.

Fricke got her big break from producer Billy Sherrill, who paired her with Johnny Duncan. During 1977, the duo had three successful singles, "Stranger" (on which Fricke sang uncredited), "Thinkin' of a Rainbow," and "It Couldn't Have Been Better." The latter two singles hit No. 1, and their success convinced Sherrill to sign Fricke as a solo artist. She released her first solo single, "What're You Doin' Tonight," in 1977, and it made the Top 30. The following year she released another duet with Duncan, which made the Top Five. Under Sherrill's direction, Fricke made three successful albums during the late 1970s and had several hits, including a No. 1 duet with Charlie Rich, "On My Knees" (1978). In 1979 she and Duncan recorded the album *Nice 'n' Easy*.

Fricke had trouble finding a clear direction with her singing style on her first albums, so Sherrill advised her to choose a style and stick with it. Her next two albums were considerably more unified as she began to focus on country ballads. As a result, her popularity began to rise, and in 1981, she had three hits from her album *Sleeping with Your Memory*. In 1982, she had a No. 1 hit with "Don't Worry 'Bout Me Baby." That year she moved away from soft songs to show another, more hard-driving, side of her talent on the album *It Ain't Easy*. It too was successful, and she continued to rack up hits through the 1980s, periodically changing styles.

Fricke returned to ballad singing in 1989 with her album *Labor of Love*. She then left Columbia and did not sign with another label until 1990, when she released a self-titled album on the independent Intersound. She signed with Branson Entertainment in 1992 and released two albums with the label, *Crossroads* (1992) and *Now & Then* (1993). —*Sandra Brennan*

Singer of Songs / 1978 / Columbia ✦✦✦
Fricke has a big voice and gives the impression she can do a lot with it. She just never gets around to it on this record. Maybe it's the songs or maybe the arrangements, but she never seems to get into these songs or come close to putting any emotion in her performances. —*Jim Worbois*

Greatest Hits / 1982 / Columbia ✦✦✦✦
While by no means a comprehensive collection of Fricke's hits, this anthology does offer the chart-topping "Don't Worry 'bout Me Baby" along with "Pass Me By (If You're Only Passing Through)," "Down to My Last Broken Heart," and "Please Help Me, I'm Falling (In Love with You)." —*Jason Ankeny*

It Ain't Easy / 1982 / Columbia ✦✦✦
The versatility that made Fricke a jingles success might have been a liability as a solo performer. She's so adaptable that her voice might not have been distinctive enough. Here she sounds like a strong woman who's very familiar with heartache, and producer Bob Montgomery gives her some rockin' material to shout on. —*Tom Roland*

Somebody Else's Fire / 1985 / Columbia ✦✦✦
Somebody Else's Fire is a typically fine collection of tunes from one of the finest contemporary country singers of the '80s. The upbeat "Party Shoes," "Single Again," "Somebody Else's Fire," and the great tearjerker "Easy to Please" are among the album's highlights. —*James Chrispell*

The Very Best of Janie Fricke / 1986 / Columbia ✦✦✦✦
The Very Best of Janie Fricke offers many of the singer's biggest hits, including "He's a Heartache (Looking for a Place to Happen),"

"Tell Me a Lie," "Your Heart's Not in It" and "It Ain't Easy Bein' Easy"; while not all-encompassing, it's one of the best anthologies of her work to date. —*Jason Ankeny*

● **17 Greatest Hits** / 1986 / Columbia ✦✦✦✦
Just like the title says—17 of Fricke's biggest hits from the early '80s, including the No. 1s "He's a Heartache (Looking for a Place to Happen)," "It Ain't Easy Bein' Easy," "Don' Worry 'Bout Me Baby," and "Your Heart's Not in It." —*Thom Owens*

Saddle the Wind / 1988 / Columbia ✦✦✦
Saddle the Wind includes the minor hits "Where Does Love Go (When It's Gone)," "I'll Walk Before I'll Crawl" and "Heart." —*Jason Ankeny*

Labor of Love / 1989 / Columbia ✦✦✦
Fricke tackles songs by Steve Earle ("My Old Friend the Blues") and Katy Moffatt and Tom Russell ("Walking on the Moon") on *Labor of Love.* —*Jason Ankeny*

Kinky Friedman (Richard Friedman)

b. Oct. 31, 1944, Rio Duckworth, Palestine, TX
Vocals / Country-Rock, Country Humor, Outlaw Country
Outrageous and irreverent but nearly always thought-provoking, Kinky Friedman wrote and performed satirical country songs during the 1970s and has been hailed the Frank Zappa of country music. He was born Richard F. Friedman, the son of a University of Texas professor who raised his children on the family ranch, Rio Duckworth. Friedman studied psychology at Texas and founded his first band (King Arthur & the Carrots) while there. However, King Arthur & the Carrots—a group that poked fun at surf music—recorded only one 1966 single. After graduation, Friedman served three years in the Peace Corps and was stationed in Borneo, where he worked as an agricultural extension worker.

By 1971 he had founded his second band, Kinky Friedman & His Texas Jewboys. In keeping with the group's satirical nature, each member had deliberately un-PC names such as Little Jewford, Big Nig, Panama Red, Rainbow Colors, and Snakebite Jacobs. Friedman got his break in 1973 thanks to Commander Cody, who contacted Vanguard Music on behalf of the acerbic young performer. That was the year Friedman and his group made their debut album, *Sold American*, featuring John Hartford and Tompall Glaser. The title track barely made it onto the charts, but Friedman did attract enough attention to be invited to the Grand Old Opry. In 1974, he recorded a self-titled album for ABC Records. It was produced by Willie Nelson and Nelson, Waylon Jennings, and Glaser performed along with Friedman. Among the album's best-known tracks is Friedman's response to anti-Semitism, "They Ain't Making Jews like Jesus Anymore." In the mid-'70s, Friedman and his band began touring with Bob Dylan's Rolling Thunder Revue. In 1976 Friedman made his third album, *Lasso from El Paso*, featuring Dylan and Eric Clapton. The Texas Jewboys disbanded three years later and Friedman moved to New York, where he played at the Lone Star Cafe. In 1983, he released *Under the Double Ego* for Sunrise Records. It was his last recording to date and since then Friedman has turned toward writing. He has not only been a critic for *Rolling Stone* magazine, but a mystery writer of tales such as *Greenwich Killing Time, A Case of Lone Star,* and *Frequent Flyer,* all of which feature "The Kinkster," a Jewish country-singer turned Greenwich Village private eye. —*Sandra Brennan*

Sold American / 1973 / Vanguard ✦✦✦✦
A renegade figure who often stresses the outrageous. The title song is a gem. Part of the '70s country/folk/rock wave. —*Hank Davis*

Kinky Friedman / 1974 / Varèse Sarabande ✦✦✦

● **Lasso from El Paso** / 1976 / Epic ✦✦✦✦
Of the many albums that grew out of Bob Dylan's Rolling Thunder Revue, this must be the strangest. Friedman has a husky voice and an off-kilter sense of humor best captured on the live-from-

the-revue track, "Sold American." Also notable for a version of the Bob Dylan outtake, "Catfish." —*William Ruhlmann*

Under the Double Ego / 1983 / Sunrise ✦✦✦

Old Testaments & New Revelations / 1992 / Fruit of the Tune ✦✦✦
Kinky Friedman, backed by his faithful combo the Texas Jewboys, brings old-time swing to Hollywood with plenty of satire on *Old Testaments & New Revelations*. Social satire from a Jewish perspective is Friedman's forte, and this generous live recording blends classics like "We Refuse the Right to Refuse Service to You" with a whole new set of barbed hooks. —*Roch Parisien*

From One Good American to Another / Oct. 1995 / Fruit of the Tune ✦✦✦

David Frizzell

b. Sep. 26, 1941, El Dorado, AR
Vocals / Traditional Country, Honky Tonk
Though he's standing in the shadows of a very famous man, David Frizzell became a country star in his own right during the '80s. The younger brother of country legend Lefty Frizzell, David was born September 26, 1941, in El Dorado, AR. At the age of 12, he hitchhiked to California to join Lefty, who added the youth to his show and persuaded Columbia to sign him in 1958. Nothing came of the deal, however, and David spent the '60s touring with his brother, recording for several minor labels, and spending time in the Air Force. He returned to Columbia in 1970 and placed two singles on the country charts, including the Top 40 entry "I Just Can't Help Believing." (B.J. Thomas took it to the pop Top Ten the same year.)

David Frizzell moved to Nashville a year later and recorded for the Cartwheel label. Just after he joined Buck Owens' *All American TV Show* in 1973, Frizzell signed a contract with Capitol and recorded two modest hits, "Words Don't Come Easy" and "Take Me One More Ride." After some mid-'70s recordings for RSO and MCA, he joined his younger brother Allen and Allen's wife Shelly West on a tour around the Southwest.

David and West recorded some material, and their single "You're the Reason God Made Oklahoma," was included on Clint Eastwood's 1981 film *Any Which Way You Can;* it topped the country charts early that year. "A Texas State of Mind" hit No. 9 in June, and the duo closed out 1981 with "Husbands and Wives," a Top 20 hit. The following year, Frizzell and West hit the Top Ten again on the strength of "Another Honky-Tonk Night on Broadway" and "I Just Came Here to Dance." They won numerous Duo of the Year awards beginning that year.

Jump-started by his duet success, David Frizzell hit No. 1 as a solo act in 1982 with "I'm Gonna Hire a Wino to Decorate Our Home," from *Family's Fine, but This One's All Mine*. His next two singles, "Lost My Baby Blues" and "Where Are You Spending Your Nights These Days," hit the Top Ten during 1982-83. He recorded only one more Top 40 single, "A Million Light Beers Ago," but Frizzell and West had back-to-back hits in 1984: "Silent Partners" and "It's a Be Together Night." Frizzell continued to record during the '80s for Nashville America, Compleat, and BFE. —*John Bush*

Carryin' on the Family Name / 1981 / Warner Brothers ✦✦✦

Family's Fine, but This One's All Mine / 1982 / Warner Brothers ✦✦✦
Featured is "I'm Gonna Hire a Wino to Decorate Our Home," a No. 1 country novelty that's made an even bigger splash in oldies rotation. —*Dan Cooper*

Our Best to You / 1982 / Viva ✦✦✦

On My Own Again / 1983 / Viva ✦✦✦✦

In Session / 1983 / Viva ✦✦✦

● **Golden Duets (w/Shelly West)** / 1984 / Viva ✦✦✦✦
"You're the Reason God Made Oklahoma" (the most majestic component of the Clint Eastwood movie *Any Which Way You Can*) spawned a run of duet hits by Frizzell and West. The significant ones, including "You're the Reason . . . ," are all here. —*Dan Cooper*

Lefty Frizzell (William Orville Frizzell)

b. Mar. 31, 1928, Corsicana, TX, **d.** Jul. 19, 1975, Nashville, TN

Guitar, Vocals / Traditional Country, Honky Tonk

Lefty Frizzell was the definitive honky tonk singer, the vocalist that set the style for generations of vocalists that followed him. Frizzell smoothed out the rough edges of honky tonk by singing longer, flowing phrases—essentially, he made honky tonk more acceptable for the mainstream without losing its gritty, bar-room roots. In the process, he changed the way country vocalists sang forever. From George Jones, Merle Haggard, and Willie Nelson to George Strait, John Anderson, Randy Travis, and Keith Whitley, hundreds of artists have emulated and expanded Lefty's innovations. Frizzell's singing became the foundation of how hard country should be sung.

Despite his influence, there was a time when Lefty Frizzell wasn't regarded as one of country's definitive artists. Unlike Hank Williams—the only contemporary of Lefty that had greater influence—he didn't die young, leaving behind a romantic legend. After his popularity peaked in the early and mid-'50s, Frizzell continued to record, without having much success. However, his recordings continued to reach new listeners and his reputation was restored by the new traditionalists of the '80s, nearly ten years after Lefty's death.

Lefty Frizzell (born William Orville Frizzell) was born in Corsicana, TX, in 1928, a son of an oiler; he was the first of eight children. During his childhood, his family moved to El Dorado, AR. As a child he was called Sonny, but his nickname changed to Lefty when he was 14, because he won a schoolyard fight; it was later suggested that he earned his nickname after winning a Golden Gloves boxing match, but that was eventually proven to be a hatched publicity stunt by his record company. Initially, Lefty was attracted to music through his parents' Jimmie Rodgers records. He began singing professionally before he was a teenager, landing a regular spot on KELD El Dorado.

Frizzell spent his teenage years playing throughout the region, singing on radio shows, in nightclubs, for dances, and in talent contests. He traveled throughout the south, playing in Arkansas, Texas, New Mexico, and even Las Vegas. During this time, he was refining his style, drawing from influences like Jimmie Rodgers, Ernest Tubb, and Ted Daffan. Lefty's career was going fine until he was arrested in the mid-'40s, serving a jail sentence for statutory rape.

Frizzell's run-in with the law led him away from music, as he temporarily worked in the oil fields with his father. However, his time as an oiler was brief and he was soon performing in clubs again. By 1950, he had landed a regular job at the Texas club Ace of Clubs, where he developed a dedicated following of fans. At one of his concerts at the Ace of Clubs he caught the attention of Jim Beck, the owner of a local recording studio. Beck recorded music for several major record labels, and he also had connections within the publishing industry. Impressed with Lefty's performance, he invited the singer to make some demos at the studio. In April of 1950, Frizzell cut several demos of his original songs, including a new song called "If You've Got the Money, I've Got the Time," which Beck took to Nashville. Beck intended to pitch the song to Little Jimmy Dickens, but Dickens disliked the song. However, Columbia record producer Don Law heard the tape and liked Frizzell's voice. After hearing Lefty live in concert, Law signed the singer to Columbia; within a few months, he had his first recording session.

"If You've Got the Money, I've Got the Time," Lefty's first single, climbed to No. 1 upon its release. It was a huge hit—its B-side, "I Love You a Thousand Ways," even hit No. 1—with other artists hurrying into the studio to cut their own versions; over 40 performers wound up recording the song. Within 17 days of the single's release, Columbia had Frizzell record another single. The result, "Look What Thoughts Will Do"/"Shine, Shave, Shower (It's Saturday)," wasn't as big a hit, but it did reach the Top Ten.

By now, the Lefty Frizzell sound was being perfected by the vocalist and Don Law. Frizzell was working with a core group of Dallas-based studio musicians, highlighted by pianist Madge Sutee. In the beginning of 1951, he formed the Western Chero-

kees, which was led by Blackie Crawford. Soon, the Western Cherokees became his primary band for both live and recording situations. Lefty was frequently in the studio, recording singles. His third single, "I Want to Be with You Always," was No. 1 for 11 weeks and its follow-up, "Always Late (With Your Kisses)," spent 12 weeks at No. 1. At one point in early 1951, Frizzell had a total of four songs in the country Top Ten, setting a record that was never broken. Frizzell was a popular concert attraction, playing shows with the Louisiana Hayride and the Grand Ole Opry. He had three more Top Ten hits in 1951—"Mom and Dad's Waltz," "Travelin' Blues," and the No.1 "Give Me More, More, More (Of Your Kisses)."

The hits continued throughout 1952, as "How Long Will It Take (To Stop Loving You)," "Don't Stay Away (Till Love Grows Cold)," "Forever (And Always)," "I'm An Old, Old Man (Tryin' to Live While I Can)" all went to the Top Ten. Even though he was at the peak of his popularity, things began to unravel for Lefty behind the scenes. Frizzell fired both his manager and his band. He joined the Grand Ole Opry, but he decided he didn't like it and left almost immediately. Lefty was earning a lot of money but he was spending nearly all of it. He worked with Wayne Raney, but the sessions were a failure. In early 1953, he moved from Texas to Los Angeles, where he got a regular job on Town Hall Party. That year, he had only one hit—the Top Ten "(Honey, Baby, Hurry!) Bring Your Sweet Self Back to Me)."

Early in 1954, Lefty reached the Top Ten with "Run 'Em Off," but it would be his last Top Ten record for five years. During the mid-'50s, Frizzell felt burned out and he didn't have the energy to invest in his career. He only had a total of two hits between 1954 and 1959—"I Love You Mostly" in 1955, and "Cigarettes and Coffee Blues"—because he decided to stop recording. Lefty was frustrated that Columbia wasn't releasing what he believed to be his best material, so he simply stopped writing and recording songs. However, he did tour sporadically, occasionally with his brother, David Frizzell.

Deciding it was time for a change, Lefty began working with Jim Denny's Nashville-based Cedarwood publishing company in 1959. Cedarwood gave him "The Long Black Veil," a song written by Danny Dill and Marijohn Wilkin that had overt folk music influences. Lefty recorded the song and it became a surprise Top Ten hit in the summer of 1959. Encouraged by its success, Frizzell moved to Nashville in 1961, after Town Hall Party closed in 1960. He began touring and recording at a more rapid rate, although this only resulted in a couple of minor hits. Lefty's last big hit arrived early in 1964, when "Saginaw, Michigan" climbed to No. 1 and spent four weeks on the top of the charts. After that, he came close to the Top Ten with 1965's "She's Gone, Gone, Gone," but he usually struggled to have any of his songs break the Top 20 for the next decade.

Frizzell didn't stop recording, but he did develop a debilitating problem with alcohol that plagued him throughout the late '60s and '70s. However, alcohol wasn't the only thing holding his career back—Columbia was only releasing handfuls of his albums and singles, though Lefty was recording an abundance of material. Since his records weren't as successful, he drastically cut back the number of concerts he performed. In 1968, he cut some songs with June Stearns under the name Agnes and Orville, but none of the tracks became hits. The lack of success helped him sink deeper into alcoholism.

In 1972, Lefty left Columbia, signing with ABC Records. Though the change in labels helped revitalize him artistically, he didn't sell many more records. However, he did regain the enthusiasm to record albums, as well as play concerts and television shows. Yet Frizzell's alcohol addiction worsened and he developed high blood pressure; he wouldn't take his medication because he thought it would interfere with his drinking. As a result, he looked older than his 47 years when he died of a stroke in 1975.

Years of mediocre and poorly marketed records had diminished Lefty Frizzell's reputation, but after his death, a new generation of artists hailed him as an influence and an idol. Merle Haggard, Willie Nelson, and George Jones had all sung his praises before, but in the mid-'80s, the kind words of George Strait and Randy Travis were supported by a series of Frizzell reissues, beginning with Bear Family's 14-LP set, *His Life—His Music* (later replaced by the 12-CD *Life's Like Poetry*). In 1982, Frizzell was inducted into the Country Music Hall of Fame, but the greatest testament to his music remains the fact that his voice can be heard in every hard country singer that has followed. —*Stephen Thomas Erlewine*

Lefty Frizzell's Greatest Hits / 1966 / Columbia ✦✦
Lefty Frizzell's Greatest Hits presents a selection of Frizzell's best-known songs in re-recorded or overdubbed versions, which are decidedly inferior to the originals. Stick with Rhino's *The Best of Lefty Frizzell*. —*Stephen Thomas Erlewine*

☆ **Treasures Untold** / 1980 / Rounder ✦✦✦✦✦
A wonderful selection of early performances, it's rugged Texas honky tonk delivered in a melifluous drawl that Merle Haggard and others emulated. An archetype. —*Mark A. Humphrey*

★ **The Best of Lefty Frizzell** / 1991 / Rhino ✦✦✦✦✦
These 18 tracks cover 15 years (1950-65) in the career of a singer whom Merle Haggard once called "the most unique thing that ever happened to country music." Included are such timeless Frizzell gems as "If You've Got the Money, I've Got the Time," "I Love You a Thousand Ways," "I Want to Be with You Always," "Always Late (With Your Kisses)," and "The Long Black Veil." This is a must-hear for anyone interested in the origins of a vocal style so influential it rules country radio to this very day. —*Dan Cooper*

That's the Way Love Goes: Final Recordings Of / Oct. 22, 1996 / ✦✦✦✦
That's the Way Love Goes: Final Recordings of Lefty Frizzell collects the highlights from Lefty's latter-day recordings for ABC Records, including the minor hit singles "Life's like Poetry," "Lucky Arms" and "I Never Go Around Mirrors." Though his material for ABC wasn't as consistently compelling as his early recordings, *That's the Way Love Goes* salvages his finest moments from this era, making a convincing argument that Frizzell's vocal abilities had not deteriorated much at all. In fact, the best moments on this compilation stand with Lefty's best work ever. It just happens that not every song on the collection is terrific, but enough songs are brilliant to make it a worthwhile purchase. —*Stephen Thomas Erlewine*

★ **Look What Thoughts Will Do: The Essential, 1950-1963** / Jan. 28, 1997 / Legacy/Columbia ✦✦✦✦✦
Look What Thoughts Will Do: The Essential Lefty Frizzell, 1950-1963 is a double-disc set covering all of Lefty's biggest hits ("If You've Got the Money I've Got the Time," "I Love You a Thousand Ways," "I Want to Be with You Always," "Always Late (With Your Kisses)," "Give Me More, More More (Of Your Kisses)," "Run 'Em Off," "The Long Black Veil," "Saginaw, Michigan"), plus several lesser-known singles, B-sides, and album tracks. Essentially, the compilation is an expanded version of Rhino's excellent single-disc *The Best of Lefty Frizzell*, featuring all of that disc's 18 tracks. What makes *Look What Thoughts Will Do* exciting for fans that already have the older compilation is the wealth of gems that haven't made it to compact disc in the past. For neophytes, the double-disc is an excellent introduction, since it draws a full portrait of one of the greatest honky tonk singers to ever live. Casual listeners will want to stick with the Rhino compilation, but *Look What Thoughts Will Do* is the definitive overview of Frizzell's heyday, making it an essential addition to any serious country collection. —*Stephen Thomas Erlewine*

American Originals / Columbia ✦✦✦✦
American Originals collects most of Frizzell's biggest hits, but all of those are available in a more cohesive fashion on Rhino's *The Best of Lefty Frizzell*. Nevertheless, there are some songs on *American Originals* that aren't on *The Best of Lefty Frizzell*, and it does offer a good ten-song sampling of some of his best work, even if the presentation is decidedly haphazard. —*Stephen Thomas Erlewine*

Life's Like Poetry / Bear Family ✦✦✦✦
Life's Like Poetry is a gigantic, 12-disc box set that includes all of Lefty Frizzell's recordings for Columbia and ABC, plus early demos, a session with Jay Miller, and several radio transcriptions—everything he recorded between 1950 and 1975. Certainly,

the box is designed for collectors—no one but the most devoted fan could listen to all 330 tracks. Though all of his classic material is included, there is also a fair share of mediocre material, including some ill-advised attempts at country-pop. Nevertheless, there are gems sprinkled throughout the collection and it offers proof of his far-reaching talents and influence, as well as demonstrating that several of Lefty's later recordings were as worthwhile as his early singles. For any serious fan, it is an indispensable collection. —*Stephen Thomas Erlewine*

Robbie Fulks

Alternative Country
After spending his childhood years in living in Pennsylvania, Virginia, and Creedmoor, NC, Robbie Fulks attended Columbia University in New York City, before relocating to Chicago in 1983. He sang and played guitar with the Special Consensus Bluegrass Band and appeared on their 1989 Grammy-nominated album *Hole in My Heart*, before becoming a cast member in the award-winning *Woody Guthrie's American Song*. Forming the Trailer Trash Revue, a four-piece rock band complete with go-go dancers, Fulks independently released a 45-rpm single with two country-flavored originals, "Little King" and "Jean Arthur," which garnered some regional radio airplay. When Bloodshot Records released its 1994 *For a Life of Sin: A Compilation of Insurgent Chicago Country* a Fulks original, "Cigarette State," which was recorded by Steve Albini, was included. When the label released its 1995 follow-up compilation *Hell Bent: Insurgent Country Volume 2*, they used another Albini-recorded Fulks original, entitled "She Took a Lot of Pills (And Died)." Fulks subsequently signed with the label and in 1996, working again with Albini at the recording console, he released his first album, *Country Love Songs*. Featuring 13 Fulks originals, the album featured musical backing by the Skeletons along with legendary pedal steel guitarist Tom Brumley, a former Buck Owens sideman. —*Jack Leaver*

● **Country Love Songs** / 1996 / Bloodshot ✦✦✦✦
Fulks is cleverly twisted, deliciously irreverent, and one of the best of the new country singer-songwriters. Musically, *Country Love Songs* supplies plenty of hardcore, bottle-tippin,' honky tonk country, with a '50s production that sounds like it's supposed to be there. Fulks writes and sings country music that bears little or no resemblance to what dominates the airwaves; rather his material harkens back to an era when humor and dark subject matter shared the same page of a writer's composition book. Paying homage to the classic Bakersfield sound, with former Buckeroo Tom Brumley shining on pedal steel, Fulks delivers "The Buck Starts Here," which just might be the best country song since "He Stopped Loving Her Today." Lyrically, Fulks can travel some pretty spooky highway, like in the descriptive ballad "Barely Human," a drinking song, that's as tortured as they get, with the song's character "barely human from twilight 'til dawn." Other strong tracks include the saga of an aging movie starlet who loses it in "She Took a Lot of Pills (And Died)"— which first appeared on the second volume of the label's Insurgent Country compilations—and the swingin' "Every Kind of Music but Country." —*Jack Leaver*

Tony Furtado

Banjo / Progressive Bluegrass, Traditional Bluegrass
Tony Furtado is a highly regarded banjo player who hits all styles of banjo music: bluegrass, old-time, swing, and jazz style. —*Chip Renner*

Swamped / Feb. 1989 / Rounder ✦✦✦✦
A very good album, featuring Laurie Lewis, Darol Anger, and Todd Phillips. —*Chip Renner*

● **Within Reach** / 1992 / Rounder ✦✦✦✦
Tony Furtado's banjo shines throughout *Within Reach*, yet uneven material prevents the album from being truly captivating. Of special interest is Alison Krauss' gorgeous vocals on a version of the Beatles' "I Will." —*Thom Owens*

Full Circle / 1994 / Rounder ✦✦✦

G

Chris Gaffney

Guitar, Accordion, Vocals / Progressive Country, Tex-Mex, Conjunto, Americana

Austrian-born Gaffney has been playing music for two decades, based in the American Southwest. A talented songwriter with the ability to make his songs' characters and locales come alive, Gaffney handles vocals, guitar, and accordion, with the five-piece Cold Hard Facts backing him up. Gaffney seamlessly blends country, conjunto, rockabilly, zydeco, and more. Ex-Blasters guitarist Dave Alvin adds a few guitar licks to Gaffney's two releases and co-writes two songs with Gaffney on *Mi Vida Loca. —Dennis MacDonald*

Road to India / 1986 / Cactus Club ✦✦✦✦
Chris Gaffney's *Road to India* is an excellent fusion of '50s rock 'n' roll, Bakersfield country, and careening Tex-Mex. With the assistance of a top-flight backing band, Gaffney has made a rocking, rootsy record that effortlessly recreates not only the sound, but the ambience, of '60s roadhouse country and rock. —*Thom Owens*

Chris Gaffney & Cold Hard Facts / 1989 / ROM ✦✦✦
Los Angeles dock-worker, singer, songwriter, and accordionist reflects Hispanic influences and working-class themes in songs of steely poetry. —*Mark A. Humphrey*

● **Mi Vida Loca** / 1992 / Hightone ✦✦✦✦
Gaffney infuses hard country with elements of Tex-Mex and pure rock 'n' roll, coming off like a cross between Merle Haggard and the Blasters. Gaffney has a dusty voice with perfect country phrasing for ballads like "Quiet Desperation" and "Waltz for Minnie," but he's at his peak with rockers like "'68," a powerful song about a man who lost his best friend in Vietnam, and "Silent Partner," which sounds like a souped-up George Jones. —*Brian Mansfield*

Loser's Paradise / 1995 / Hightone ✦✦✦✦
Although not quite the standout album that *Mi Vida Loca* is, *Loser's Paradise* is another consistent effort, serving up the same winning mix of country, roots-rock, soul, and Norteno. This time around friend Dave Alvin handles the production, as well as providing some inspired six-string work, and contributing a couple of gems with the Cajun-flavored "East of Houston, West of Baton Rouge," and the honky-tonkin' "Help You Dream." As with his other records, Gaffney's songwriting is superb, bringing hard-luck tales and characters to life with his weathered voice and keen roots sensibility. For instance, check out his George Jones-like ballad, "Glasshouse," the melancholy "My Baby's Got a Dead Man's Number," and the lovely Norteno number "Azulito." His cover choices are also excellent: Lucinda Williams duets on a wonderful version of the Intruders' 1968 soul chestnut "Cowboys to Girls," and Gaffney thoughtfully rediscovers the Ed Bruce-penned, 1964 Charlie Louvin hit "See The Big Man Cry." Gaffney plays guitar, accordion, and piano, while enlisting instrumental backing from a standout band that includes longtime Rod Stewart sideman Ian McLagan on Hammond organ, and pedal steel guitarist Scott Wells. And the vocal backup reads like an alternative country who's who, featuring Rosie Flores, Jim Lauderdale, Dale Watson, and Tony Villanueva (lead singer of the Derailers). A must-have

for Gaffney fans, and a good introduction for new ones as well. —*Jack Leaver*

Jerry Garcia

b. Aug. 1, 1942, San Francisco, CA, **d.** Aug. 9, 1995, San Francisco, CA

Guitar, Vocals / Rock & Roll, Country-Rock, Folk-Rock

Jerry Garcia was the lead guitarist, vocalist, and spokesman for the seminal '60s rock 'n' roll band the Grateful Dead. Throughout his career, he led the Dead through numerous changes, becoming one of the most famous figures in the history of rock 'n' roll. Simultaneously, Garcia pursued an eclectic array of side projects, ranging from the bluegrass group Old & In the Way to his folky solo recordings. Garcia stayed active as a member of the Grateful Dead and as a solo performer until his death in 1995.

Garcia learned to play guitar when he was 15 years old, originally playing folk and rock 'n' roll. In 1959, when he was 17 years old, he spent a brief time in the Army. When he left the military after a matter of months, he moved to Palo Alto, CA, where he met and became friends with Robert Hunter, who would later become his lyricist. Garcia bought a banjo in 1962 and began playing in local bluegrass bands. Within a few years, he was a member of Mother McCree's Uptown Jug Champions, a popular local bluegrass and folk band whose membership also included Bob Weir and Pigpen. In 1965, this group evolved into the Warlocks, which would in turn become the Greatful Dead in 1966.

Over the course of the next five years, the Grateful Dead began building a reputation as a mesmerizing live act. During this time, Garcia guested with a number of bands, both in concert and in the studio; among the artists he appeared with are the New Riders of the Purple Sage (a band which he helped form), Jefferson Starship, and Crosby, Stills, Nash & Young. In 1970, the Grateful Dead began to shift their music back toward their folk, country, and bluegrass roots with the albums *Workingman's Dead* and *American Beauty.* The following year, Garcia began a solo career with *Hooteroll?,* which was released on Douglas Records. For the next few years, Garcia recorded solo albums frequently, often with keyboardist Merl Saunders. In 1973, he was one of the founding members of the bluegrass supergroup Old & In the Way, which also featured David Grisman, Vassar Clements, and John Kahn.

Garcia's solo efforts slowed in the early '80s, as he battled heroin addiction and diabetes. After the Grateful Dead scored their first hit album in 1987 with *In the Dark,* Garcia pursued a number of solo projects, including several acoustic duet records with David Grisman and a handful of live tours and albums with the Jerry Garcia acoustic band. For the first half of the '90s, Garcia concentrated on Grateful Dead tours and albums, as the band confirmed their status as one of the most popular concert acts in America. However, the guitarist slowly sank back into heroin addiction. Late in the summer of 1995, he entered Serenity Knolls, a drug rehabilitation facility in Forest Knolls, CA. While he was attempting to recover, Garcia died in his sleep of a heart attack on August 9, 1995. Several months after his death, the Grateful Dead announced their disbandment. —*Stephen Thomas Erlewine*

Hooteroll? / 1971 / Grateful Dead ✦✦✦
Howard Wales, who is co-credited on this album, is a keyboard player, and Jerry Garcia's first non-Grateful Dead album release finds the two, along with such Garcia band stalwarts as drummer Bill Vitt and bassist John Kahn, playing exploratory instrumental music that touches on jazz and rock. Originally released in 1971 on Douglas Records, the album was reissued on CD on Grateful Dead Records in 1987 with two added tracks. *— William Ruhlmann*

● **Garcia** / Jan. 1972 / Grateful Dead ✦✦✦✦
In essence, this is a Grateful Dead record, featuring as it does the band's leader/singer/guitarist, its drummer, and its lyricist. Except for the few instrumental/experimental cuts, the material has been incorporated into the Dead's concert repertoire. In fact, this is a perfect follow-up to the folk-rock song albums the Dead produced in 1970, *Workingman's Dead* and *American Beauty*—albums the band itself has never really followed up. *— William Ruhlmann*

Live at the Keystone / 1973 / Fantasy ✦✦
A live double album recorded in July 1973 by a band featuring Garcia with keyboardist Merl Saunders, bassist John Kahn, and drummer Bill Vitt. The set indicates Garcia's eclectic taste: the band covers Bob Dylan, Jimmy Cliff, Rodgers and Hart, and Arthur Crudup, among others. Somehow, though, it all has the same loosely structured, unhurried style familiar from Garcia's work with the Grateful Dead and dominated by his dense, considered, single-note guitar solos and calmly trembling tenor voice. *— William Ruhlmann*

Reflections / Jan. 1976 / Grateful Dead ✦✦✦
Again, a Dead album in everything but name, with several tracks featuring the Grateful Dead, perhaps most memorably on "It Must Have Been the Roses." *— William Ruhlmann*

Cats under the Stars / 1978 / Arista ✦✦✦
The first real "Garcia Band" album is paced by songs that would not sound out of place at a Dead concert. As a matter of fact, the album has garnered increased interest in the '90s as the Dead added the leadoff track "Rubin and Cherise" to its repertoire. *— William Ruhlmann*

Run for the Roses / 1982 / Arista ✦✦✦
One of the last Dead-related albums released before the band's hiatus from recording in the mid-'80s, this is a typical effort, with covers of the Beatles and Bob Dylan, plus a couple of minor Garcia-Hunter compositions. *— William Ruhlmann*

Almost Acoustic / Dec. 1988 / Grateful Dead ✦✦✦
Garcia got his start in bluegrass, and here he assembles the Jerry Garcia Acoustic Band (some of whom he started playing with) to handle a live set full of Jimmie Rodgers, Mississippi John Hurt, and traditional mountain music. *— William Ruhlmann*

Compliments of Garcia / 1989 / Grateful Dead ✦✦
On his second solo album, Garcia adopts an approach more typical of his solo live shows than the Grateful Dead, writing none of the material himself and tackling everything from Irving Berlin's "Russian Lullaby" to Smokey Robinson's "The Hunter Gets Captured by the Game." The songs are at slightly sluggish tempos compared to the originals, especially ones that used to be frantic rockers. Most of this material is beyond Garcia's limited vocal range, but he gets points for trying. (Since Garcia unimaginatively gave this album the same title as his first solo album, Deadheads differentiated between the two by referring to the *Compliments of Garcia* legend written on promotional copies of this album. (In reissuing the album on CD in 1989, Grateful Dead Records adopted their title.) *— William Ruhlmann*

Jerry Garcia Band / 1991 / Arista ✦✦✦
A double live album recorded in 1990 and featuring extended versions of songs by Bruce Cockburn, Bob Dylan, Smokey Robinson, the Beatles, the Band, Los Lobos, and others. The Garcia Band serves a kind of songbook function for its listeners (as, indeed, does the Dead), which may mean that the album's chief virtue is as instruction: if you're familiar with the originals, you don't really need to hear Garcia's covers, but if, like many Deadheads, you don't hear much music outside the band's orbit, this may help lead you to other good music. *— William Ruhlmann*

Jerry Garcia & David Grisman / 1991 / Acoustic Disc ✦✦✦✦
A guitar-and-mandolin duet album, exquisitely produced, with this pair trying a variety of styles from Garcia's "Friend of the Devil" to the ambitious instrumental "Arabia." *— William Ruhlmann*

Not for Kids Only / Oct. 1993 / Acoustic Disc ✦✦✦
On their second duo album, Jerry Garcia and David Grisman play songs either written for or applicable to children, among them Elizabeth Cotten's "Freight Train" and "Teddy Bears' Picnic." It's a delightful record that lives up to its title, and also marks the development of Garcia/Grisman as a full partnership, with Grisman contributing as many vocals as Garcia and the two trading off on guitar and mandolin. *— William Ruhlmann*

Shady Grove / 1996 / Acoustic Disc ✦✦✦

Hank Garland (Walter Louis Garland)

b. Nov. 11, 1930, Cowpens, SC
Guitar, Session Musician / Traditional Country, Nashville Sound/ Countrypolitan
Garland grew up outside Spartanburg, SC, listening to Arthur "Guitar Boogie" Smith and Mother Maybelle Carter on the radio as early inspirations. By his teens he had his own radio show, and his immense prowess on his instrument brought him to Nashville, where he signed as a solo artist in 1949 (as competition for the already established Merle Travis and Chet Atkins). But it was as a session player that Garland truly made his mark, playing on countless hits by Patsy Cline, Elvis Presley, the Everly Brothers, Brenda Lee, and others. Along with Ernest Tubb's guitarist, Jimmy Byrd, he co-designed the still-popular Byrdland model for Gibson guitars in the early '50s. Garland's incredible talent was moving in a more jazz-oriented direction when an automobile accident in 1961 left his memory and coordination skills impaired, sadly putting his playing days to an end. *— Cub Koda*

Jazz Winds from a New Direction / 1960 / Columbia Special Products ✦✦✦✦
This isn't the prolific pianist, but the guitarist better known for his country sessions. Garland's '60s album was a breath of fresh air and a big surprise to both jazz and country fans. It also featured Gary Burton and Joe Morello, and has been reissued on CD. *— Ron Wynn*

★ **And His Sugar Footers** / 1992 / Bear Family ✦✦✦✦✦
The best of Garland's solo sides from the early '50s, featuring his signature tune, "Sugarfoot Rag," and 19 others equally abounding with hot guitar passages. Some of country's best guitar work is right here for the listening. *— Cub Koda*

Gathering Field

Roots-Rock, Alternative Country-Rock
Roots-rockers the Gathering Field formed in Pittsburgh, PA, in 1994. Led by singer/guitarist Bill Deasy, the band, which also included guitarist Dave Brown, bassist Eric Riebling, and drummer Ray DeFade, released their debut LP *Lost in America* on their own independent label Mudpuppy. The title track became a smash on local radio, and in 1996 a remastered edition of the album was released on Atlantic Records. *— Jason Ankeny*

Lost in America / Aug. 20, 1996 / Atlantic ✦✦✦

Gatlin Brothers

Country-Pop, Neo-Traditionalist Country, Urban Cowboy
Led by Larry Gatlin, the Gatlin Brothers are one of the most popular country groups in the music's history. Adapting the close harmony vocal techniques of the Louvins and the Everlys to the highly polished country-pop era, Larry and the Gatlin Brothers scored a number of hits during the '70s and '80s. Often, the group walked the line between intricate, inventive country and pure commercial material, which resulted in strong sales but occasionally poor reviews. Nevertheless, they remained near the top of the charts until the late '80s, when the new-traditionalists began to gain popularity. Following their decline in popularity, Gatlin and the Gatlin Brothers went into semi-retirement during the early

'90s, which resulted in the group relocating to Branson, MO, where they ran their own theater.

The Gatlin Brothers didn't officially form until 1979, when Larry Gatlin began crediting them as a supporting band on his solo singles, but the three brothers—Larry, Steve, and Rudy—had been performing together since childhood, when they sang in church and on several local Texas television shows. While they were still in their teens, they recorded a religious album for the independent Sword & Shield label. Following high school graduation, Larry, who was the eldest of the brothers, headed off to the University of Houston, where he briefly joined the gospel group the Imperials. Larry performed with the Imperials in Las Vegas, where he met Dottie West, who was impressed enough by his songwriting talents to record two of his songs, "You're the Other Half of Me" and "Once You Were Mine," and pay for him to move to Nashville. Once he arrived in Nashville, he found that West had been circulating his demo tapes, which led to Kris Kristofferson playing Larry's demo for Monument Records executive Fred Foster. Impressed by the tape, Foster offered Gatlin a contract in 1973. By that time, Larry had already invited his brothers to Nashville to form a backing group, and they wound up singing on his debut album, *The Pilgrim*, which featured his first country hit, "Sweet Becky Walker."

Gatlin's second album, *Rain Rainbow*, also featured support from his brothers and contained "Delta Dirt," which climbed to No. 14. The third Larry Gatlin album was officially credited to Gatlin with Family and Friends, and contained his first Top Ten hit, "Broken Lady," which peaked at No. 5 in early 1976. Later that year, the Gatlin Brothers were made members of the Grand Ole Opry. In 1977, Gatlin's fourth album, *High Time*, was credited to Larry with Brothers and Friends and it contained his first No. 1 hit, "I Just Wish You Were Someone I Love." After releasing one more solo album, the Gatlin Brothers were officially credited as Larry's backing band as of 1979, just as he signed to Columbia Records. The first hit single to bear this name was the No. 1 "All the Gold in California."

Throughout the '80s, the Gatlin Brothers ran up a string of 15 Top 40 hits, including "Houston (Means I'm One Day Closer to You)," "Denver," "The Lady Takes the Cowboy Everytime," and "She Used to Be Somebody's Baby." All of their recordings during this time were released under a variety of names, including Larry & the Gatlin Brothers Band, Larry & the Gatlin Brothers, and Larry, Steve, Rudy: The Gatlin Brothers. By the end of the decade, the group's popularity began to decline, due to the popularity of new traditionalist performers. In 1991, the group decided to retire after a farewell tour. Larry appeared in the lead role in the Broadway musical *The Will Rogers Follies* two years later, while Steve recorded an inspirational album, and Rudy opened two Gatlin Brothers Music City Grilles. In 1991, the group opened their own theater in Branson, MO, where they began performing regularly; they also sang frequently in Las Vegas. That same year, the group signed to the small label, Branson Entertainment, and released *Moments to Remember*, which was followed by *Cool Water* the next year. —*Stephen Thomas Erlewine*

Night Time Magic / 1978 / Bear Family ✦✦✦
This features "Statues Without Hearts," "I Just Wish You Were Someone I Love," and more. —*AMG*

Greatest Hits / 1978 / Columbia ✦✦✦✦
The first volume of the Gatlin Brothers' *Greatest Hits* concentrates on Larry Gatlin's solo hits. —*AMG*

Straight Ahead / 1979 / Columbia ✦✦✦✦
Occasionally overstated but predominantly satisfying, this album contains a little jazz, a little gospel, a little pop, and a little country. Every country fan knows "All the Gold in California," but the best cuts are the controversial "Midnight Choir (Mogen David)" and a sweet little piece of ear candy: "Taking Somebody with Me When I Fall." —*Tom Roland*

Help Yourself / 1980 / Columbia ✦✦✦
Heavy on ballads that effectively show off the Gatlins' trademark genetic harmony. As always, all ten cuts are written by Larry; "Daytime Heroes," a nod to Prince Valium and the soaps, is most inspired. The Gatlin Brothers recorded "Songwriter's Trilogy"

live—whether insightful or self-indulgent depends on the listener's viewpoint. —*Tom Roland*

Sure Feels Like Love / 1982 / Columbia ✦✦✦

Greatest Hits, Vol. 2 / 1983 / Columbia ✦✦✦✦
Greatest Hits, Vol. 2 features the best of the Gatlin Brothers' late '70s hits. —*AMG*

17 Greatest Hits / 1985 / Columbia ✦✦✦
Despite the omission of a couple of Larry Gatlin's best-known songs, like "I've Done Enough Dyin' Today," *17 Greatest Hits* rounds up the majority of Gatlin and the Gatlin Brothers biggest hits from the '70s and early '80s, including "Broken Lady," "Statues Without Hearts," "I Don't Wanna Cry," "I Just Wish You Were Someone I Love," "Sure Feels Like Love," "What Are We Doin' Lonesome," "Denver," and "Houston (Means I'm One Day Closer to You)." *17 Greatest Hits* balances Gatlin's best songs with his most popular (and often more commercial) hits, making it an excellent retrospective and introduction. —*Stephen Thomas Erlewine*

Biggest Hits / 1988 / Columbia ✦✦✦
The Gatlins' *Biggest Hits* these aren't; while songs like "She Used to Be Somebody's Baby," "The Lady Takes the Cowboy Everytime" and "Denver" achieved significant chart success, neither of the trio's number one singles, "All the Gold in California" and "Houston (Means I'm One Day Closer to You)," are included. —*Jason Ankeny*

Adios / 1991 / Liberty ✦✦✦
This album features such Gatlin favorites as "Half Moon Hotel," "Pretty Woman Have Mercy," and "Already on Fire," among others. —*AMG*

● **Best of the Gatlins: All the Gold in California** / 1996 / Columbia/Legacy ✦✦✦✦
This 18-track compilation traces the work of Larry Gatlin, his brothers, family, and friends (as the various billings on the records had it) from 1975 to 1988. A greatest-hits collection, it slightly favors Gatlin's early work, including "Sweet Becky Walker" and "Delta Dirt," which were among his first chart singles, while skipping "Night Time Magic" and "Nothing but Your Love Matters," which were bigger hits. Otherwise, it's all country Top Ten singles, including the No. 1s "I've Done Enough Dyin' Today," "All the Gold in California," and "Houston (Means I'm One Day Closer to You)." Gatlin, who wrote all the songs and sings all the lead vocals, has a traditionalist bent; though the productions are not as lush as the '60s Nashville sound, the romantic lyrics are more erotic (it was the '70s, after all), and the best songs, such as "All the Gold In California," are unique efforts thematically and musically. (The unnecessarily brief 55-minute CD running time probably is due to song publishing royalties: all the albums in Columbia/Legacy's Country Classics series have only 18 tracks.) —*William Ruhlmann*

Larry Gatlin (Larry Wayne Gatlin)

b. May 28, 1948, Seminole, TX
Guitar, Vocals / Country-Pop, Neo-Traditionalist Country, Urban Cowboy

Larry Gatlin was the founder of the Gatlin Brothers, but before starting the popular 1980s trio, he had a successful career of his own.

Gatlin was raised listening to and performing gospel music. As a child, he teamed with his brothers to sing on a local radio station. After college, he joined the gospel-oriented Imperials as part of Jimmy Dean's Las Vegas show in the 1960s. While there he met Dottie West, and she became his friend and mentor. Later he sent her a demo of his songs. She was so impressed that she sent him plane tickets to Nashville in her reply. After West recorded two of those songs, "Once You Are Mine," and "You're the Other Half of Me," Gatlin moved to Music City and began singing with West's newly formed First Generation Music Company. Soon afterward, he began singing backup for Kris Kristofferson, who helped Gatlin get a contract with Monument Records in 1973.

Gatlin's first single, "Sweet Becky Walker," reached the country Top 40 and his third single, "Delta Dirt," made it to the Top 15 in

1974. In late 1975, he gathered his brothers and a few others to form Larry Gatlin with Family and Friends. In 1978, he recorded a few solo singles, and two of them—"Night Time Magic" and "I've Done Enough Dyin' Today"—reached the Top Ten. In 1979, he created the Gatlin Brothers Band, and for the next five years had great success with them.

The Gatlin Brothers continued recording and touring regularly until 1991, when they opened a theater in Branson, MO. For the rest of the decade, the Gatlins regularly performed at the venue. In 1993, Larry played the part of Will Rogers in the *Will Rogers Follies* on Broadway. Later that year, he and his brothers returned to the recording studio to record a tribute to their favorite musicians, entitled *Moments to Remember*. —*Sandra Brennan*

● **Larry Gatlin's Greatest Hits** / Columbia ♦♦♦♦
As the title suggests, *Larry Gatlin's Greatest Hits* features the biggest hits from both his pre-Gatlin Brothers solo career, as well as his late '70s solo hits. —*Thom Owens*

Danny Gatton

d. Oct. 20, 1994
Guitar / Rock & Roll, Country-Rock, Bop, Neo-Traditionalist Country, Rockabilly Revival
Guitar virtuoso Danny Gatton was known for the incredibly wide stylistic range of his playing; based in rockabilly, Gatton's musical vocabulary included R&B, pop, country, rock, and jazz, all of which he could play effectively. Gatton began playing at age nine, joining his first band, the Lancers, three years later. In 1960, Gatton pursued a jazz direction when he joined the Offbeats, where pianist/organist Dick Heintze proved to be one of Gatton's biggest influences. The band broke up four years later, and Gatton moved to Nashville to get into session work; there he met Roy Buchanan, who briefly became his roommate and taught him more about his instrument of choice. Eventually, Gatton built a reputation as a top-notch guitarist around his native Washington, DC, area through his club performances. He recorded an album with his backing band the Fat Boys titled *American Music* in 1975 and followed it with *Redneck Jazz* in 1978. The band on the latter featured steel guitarist Buddy Emmons, drummer Dave Elliott, and eventual longtime cohorts Evan Johns on vocals and rhythm guitar and John Previti on bass.

Gatton's albums led to offers from other musicians to join their bands. Lowell George extended an invitation after leaving Little Feat, but was found dead two days later. Gatton wound up touring with country singer Roger Miller and rockabilly artist Robert Gordon, giving him national exposure and a growing cult among guitar fans, who traded bootlegs of Gatton concerts. Gatton returned to Washington, DC, to be near his friends and family while playing up and down the East Coast with several bands and doing session work. When Gatton purchased an old farmhouse in need of expensive renovations in 1988, he decided to pursue his music career more seriously. He released his first solo album since 1978, *Unfinished Business*, the next year, which drew notices from several guitar-oriented magazines, as well as *Rolling Stone*. Elektra Records signed him during the summer, and he made his major-label debut in 1991 with the tremendously varied instrumental album *88 Elmira St*. 1992 saw Gatton's first straightahead jazz album, *New York Stories*, recorded for none other than Blue Note. Gatton toured the nation solo for the first time in 1993 in support of *Cruisin' Deuces*, but its lack of success, coupled with the departure of A&R man Howard Thompson from Elektra, spelled the end of Gatton's association with the label. Gatton returned to session work to pay the bills, but sustained a further blow when rhythm guitarist Billy Windsor died of a heart attack early in 1994. Gatton collaborated with organ virtuoso Joey DeFrancesco on *Relentless* in May and toured Europe during the summer. Sadly, on October 4, 1994, Gatton locked himself in his garage and shot himself. He left behind no explanation. —*Steve Huey*

Unfinished Business / 1987 / NRG ♦♦♦♦
Perhaps the most underrated guitarist there is. Gatton does it all, and dazzles at every turn. —*Jeff Tamarkin*

● **88 Elmira Street** / 1991 / Elektra ♦♦♦♦
After years of knocking around the Washington, DC-area circuit, local guitar legend Danny Gatton finally got to cut his first album for a major label, and it was indeed worth the wait. Spot-welding blinding speed and immaculate chops that go in a million different directions (jazz, country, rockabilly, blues, you name it) to a musical sensibility that makes this all-instrumental album a whole lot more than just yer average fretboard wanking jam-fest, Gatton's Telecaster really shines on material as diverse as Martin Denny's "Quiet Village," the roadhouse shuffle "Funky Mama," and the off-the-wall rendition of "The Simpsons' Theme." Kudos to Elektra for having the corporate balls to put this out; short, chunky and middle-aged, Danny Gatton was a bona-fide guitar hero for the '90s, putting the lie to the hard canard that only the speedburner metal mega-hair dudes can make the front covers of the guitar mags. —*Cub Koda*

Redneck Jazz / 1991 / NRG ♦♦♦
Just like the title says. The music on this album is required listening for those who think they've heard it all. —*Jeff Tamarkin*

Danny Gatton / 1993 / Asylum ♦♦♦♦

Cruisin' Deuces / May 18, 1993 / Elektra ♦♦
Following the brief jazz departure of *New York Stories*, Danny Gatton returned to his blues and rock 'n' roll roots with 1993's *Cruisin' Deuces*, which is essentially the follow-up to 1991's *88 Elmira St*. Like that album, *Cruisin' Deuces* is peppered with stinging rockabilly leads and amazing country and blues licks. Gatton's skill is tasteful and lightning fast—he can sound like two guitars playing simultaneously, but he never sounds cluttered or heavy-handed. And his guitar playing is the reason why you listen to a Danny Gatton album—the occasional appearance of guest vocalists like Delbert McClinton and Rodney Crowell is just an annoyance. With its reliance on country-oriented material, *Cruisin' Deuces* isn't as diverse as his previous efforts, but it is no less impressive than its predecessors. —*Thom Owens*

Relentless / 1994 / Big Mo ♦♦♦♦
This was a logical match up. Danny Gatton was a high-powered and very versatile guitarist who could play virtually any modern style. His tonal distortions and use of feedback were impressive but he could also swing as hard as anyone around. The same could be said of organist Joey DeFrancesco and, together with bassist John Previti and drummer Timm Biery, the lead voices romp on a variety of fairly basic material with lots of blues and a few standards. Although no new revelations are offered, the joyful chancetaking of Danny Gatton keeps the music from ever becoming predictable or too relaxed; he certainly challenges DeFrancesco throughout this set. —*Scott Yanow*

Blazing Telecasters / Powerhouse ♦♦♦
Guitar freaks beware—when axe-killer Gatton and blues-whiz Tom Principato get cookin' in this live set, sparks fly. —*Jeff Tamarkin*

Crystal Gayle (Brenda Gail Webb)

b. Jan. 9, 1951, Paintsville, KY
Vocals / Country-Pop, Urban Cowboy
With her rich voice and trademark long hair, Crystal Gayle was a popular performer of mainstream country ballads during the '70s and '80s. Born Brenda Gail Webb in Paintsville, KY, she was the younger sister of country legend Loretta Lynn, a relationship that both boosted and hindered her career. Though they shared the same biological father, Gayle and Lynn had very different upbringings. After 1955 Gayle was raised in Wabash, IN; when she was 16, she began touring with Lynn's show. Her sibling's connections helped Gayle get a contract with Decca Records in 1970.

Her first single was a cover of her sister's song "I've Cried the Blue Right Out of My Eyes," which peaked at No. 23 on the country charts. While it was a promising start to her career, Gayle was troubled by the belief that most of her success came from her lineage, not her talent. She sang Lynn's songs and was encouraged to utilize her big sister's style. Matters were not helped by the fact that Lynn and Gayle shared the same manager, Lynn's husband Moony, and that Loretta nicknamed her sister Crystal as a joke—as a child, Gayle had a fondness for Krystal hamburgers. Gayle struggled to move out from her bigger sister's shadow. She began appearing regularly on Jim Ed Brown's *The Country Place* television show in 1972 and later signed to United Artists, where she began working with producer Allen Reynolds, who helped her develop a gentler style.

Gayle released her eponymous debut album in 1975 and it provided her with three hits. One of them, "Wrong Road Again," climbed to No. 6 on the country charts. Later in 1975, she released her second album, *Somebody Loves You,* and by the year's end, she had begun to develop her own fan base. In 1976, Gayle had her first No. 1 country hit with "I'll Get Over You." The tune also marked the first of several forays onto the pop charts. At the end of the year, she released "You Never Miss a Real Good Thing (Till He Says Goodbye)," which became her second No. 1 single.

In the summer of 1977, Gayle had her biggest hit with "Don't It Make My Brown Eyes Blue." Written by Richard Leigh, the song was designed as Gayle's pop breakthrough and the strategy worked—not only did the song spend four weeks on the top of the country charts, it reached No. 2 on the pop charts. *We Must Believe in Magic,* the album that contained "Don't It Make My Brown Eyes Blue," went platinum within a year of its 1977 release. Gayle had three other No. 1 hits—"Ready for the Times to Get Better," "Talking in Your Sleep," and "Why Have You Left the One You Left Me For." In 1979, she became the first country artist to visit China when she participated in a Bob Hope television special.

During the early '80s, Gayle continued to rack up No. 1 and Top Ten hits. In 1980, she signed with Columbia and her first album for the label, *Miss the Mississippi,* went gold. Gayle continued to have extraordinary chart success through the spring of 1987, after which her popularity gradually declined. In the early '90s, her contract with Warners expired and she signed with Branson, where she recorded new versions of her old hits. During the '90s, she recorded infrequently, preferring to concentrate on touring America and Europe. —*Sandra Brennan*

Miss the Mississippi / 1979 / Capitol ✦✦✦
Gayle's first LP for Columbia, *Miss the Mississippi* contains the hits "It's Like We Never Said Goodbye," "The Blue Side" and "Half the Way." —*Jason Ankeny*

● **Classic Crystal** / 1979 / EMI America ✦✦✦✦
Of Gayle's many overlapping hits collections, this one's the best. Given her crossover success ("Don't It Make My Brown Eyes Blue," included here, hit No. 2 on the pop charts) it's interesting to note that all of these tracks were produced by Allen Reynolds, known these days for his work with Garth Brooks. —*Dan Cooper*

These Days / 1980 / Columbia ✦✦✦
These Days earned Gayle two more No.1 hits, "Too Many Lovers" and "If You Ever Change Your Mind." —*Jason Ankeny*

Hollywood, Tennessee / 1981 / Capitol ✦✦✦
Hollywood, Tennessee features the Top Ten hits "You Never Gave Up on Me," "Livin' in These Troubled Times" and "The Woman in Me," as well as a cover of the Bill Withers classic "Ain't No Sunshine." —*Jason Ankeny*

True Love / 1982 / Elektra ✦✦✦✦
When Gayle delivered the album to then Elektra division head Jimmy Bowen, he complained that it rocked too much. Producer Allen Reynolds refused to make changes, so Bowen produced three new tracks that seem out of place. Yeah, the Reynolds tracks do rock. So what? Gayle gives some of her best performances ever on "Our Love Is on the Faultline" and "Deeper in the Fire." —*Tom Roland*

Crystal Gayle's Greatest Hits / 1983 / Columbia ✦✦✦✦
Always greatly influenced by pop sounds, Gayle embraced that aspect of her musical heritage more in the late '70s and early '80s than any other period. This set covers it well ("Half the Way" is classic), and provides a nice cover photo too. —*Tom Roland*

What If We Fall in Love / 1987 / Warner Brothers ✦✦✦✦
Easy-listening and pop, with Gary Morris. —*Bil Carpenter*

I Love Country / 1987 / CBS [UK] ✦✦✦

Nobody's Angel / 1988 / Warner Brothers ✦✦
Nobody's Angel, Gayle's final album for Warner Bros., features the title cut and the minor hit "Tennessee Nights." —*Jason Ankeny*

All-Time Greatest Hits / 1990 / Curb ✦✦✦
Besides covering many of the hits that appear on *Classic Crystal* ("Don't It Make My Brown Eyes Blue," "You Never Miss a Real Good Thing [Till He Says Goodbye]," "Talkin' in Your Sleep," "Why Have You Left the One You Left Me For"), the 12-track *All-Time Greatest Hits* also has Gayle's debut single, "I've Cried (The Blue Right out of My Eyes)," which was written by her sister, Loretta Lynn. —*Dan Cooper*

The Geezinslaws

Country Humor, Nashville Sound/Countrypolitan
The Geezinslaws were a musical country comedy duo known for their boozy bar-room humor and parodies of standard songs. The "brothers" were mandolin player/singer Sam Allred and guitarist/singer Raymond "Son" Smith. Both were natives of Austin, TX, and met in high school; they chose the name "Geezinslaw" for its humorous ring. They began appearing locally and got their big break in 1961, when they were discovered by Arthur Godfrey, who brought them to New York to appear on his show. They remained in New York through the 1970s and during that time played in several clubs and occasionally on television.

They cut their first album, *The Kooky World of the Geezinslaw Brothers,* for Columbia in 1963. From 1966 to 1969, they made four more albums for Capitol and scored three minor hits on the country charts, including 1967's "Chubby (Please Take Your Love to Town)." When not playing in New York, they toured the US, playing in numerous clubs and appearing on such television programs as *The Tonight Show, Ed Sullivan,* and *The Jackie Gleason Show.* During the late 1960s, the Geezinslaws were frequent visitors on Ralph Emery's *Pop Goes the Country* radio show in Nashville.

In the 1970s, the brothers disappeared for quite some time, making only occasional appearances. In 1986, they appeared on Emery's TV show *Nashville Now,* then began recording albums again in 1989. Their first two, *The Geezinslaws* and *World Tour* (1990), were a mixture of comedy and straight country music. They had their first hit in 25 years in 1992 with the single "Help, I'm White and I Can't Get Down," which made the Top 60. The Geezinslaws began to appear more frequently on the country scene and even made their first video in 1993. In 1994, they released a straight comedy album, *I Wish I Had a Job to Shove.* —*Sandra Brennan*

The Geezinslaws / 1989 / Step One ✦✦✦✦
In addition to a frenetic take on "Over the Rainbow" and the tongue-in-cheek "Hank Williams Led a Happy Life," the Geezinslaws offer more straightforward covers of ace songwriters John Prine ("Fryin' Pan") and Robert Earl Keen, Jr. ("Swervin' in My Lane"). —*Jason Ankeny*

● **World Tour** / 1990 / Step One ✦✦✦✦
Though the best of the Geezinslaws' earlier tracks have yet to be anthologized, this album comes the closest to capturing their peculiar brand of country mayhem. —*Cub Koda*

Feelin' Good, Gittin' Up, Gittin' Down / 1992 / Step One ✦✦
While *Feelin' Good* is made up of the usual Geezinslaws fare (the original "Help . . . I'm White and I Can't Get Down," a cover of Shel Silverstein's "Diet Song"), for some inexplicable reason the duo decided to add canned laughter between cuts, which makes their humor seem forced and uninspired. —*Jason Ankeny*

Bobbie Gentry (Roberta Streeter)

b. Jul. 27, 1944, Chickasaw County, MS
Guitar, Vocals / Country-Pop
Bobbie Gentry was best-known for the late-'60s hit "Ode to Billy Joe." Born Roberta Streeter, she was raised in Mississippi by her grandparents, and taught herself to play piano by listening to the church accompanist. Her family moved to Palm Springs, CA, when she was 13 and during her early teens she taught herself the banjo, guitar, bass, and vibes. She began her performing

career in a local country club while still in high school. To help pay for college, she sometimes sang in night clubs, and eventually transferred to the Los Angeles Conservatory of Music. Following school, she performed in local theater and was a dancer in Las Vegas, taking her stage name from the movie *Ruby Gentry*.

In 1967, she signed to Capitol, where she recorded her debut single "Ode to Billy Joe." It was a tremendous hit and stayed at the top of the pop charts for a month and then crossed over to become a Top 20 hit on the country charts. The follow-up, "I Saw an Angel Die," was a flop but "Okolona River Bottom Band" made it to the Top 60. By late 1968, it looked as if the suspicions that Gentry was only a "one-hit wonder" were true until "Mornin' Glory"—a duet with Glen Campbell—reached the Top 75 on the pop charts, while the B-side of the single, "Less of Me," nearly reached the Top 40 on the country charts. It set the stage for Gentry and Campbell's hit cover of the Everly Brothers' "Let It Be Me," which reached No. 14 on the country charts in 1969; a year later, the duo took "All I Have to Do Is Dream" to No. 6 on the country charts. Gentry and Campbell continued recording together until 1979.

Gentry had a No. 1 hit in the United Kingdom in 1970 with her cover of Burt Bacharach's "I'll Never Fall in Love Again." While her popularity was declining in America, her star in Great Britain was on the rise. She began appearing on numerous TV shows there, including an appearance on the *Tom Jones Show* which led to her own self-titled British variety show. Later Gentry began appearing on Armed Forces Radio, where she was a popular emcee. After a brief marriage to Jim Stafford in the late '70s, she basically retired from the music industry and became involved in television production. —*Sandra Brennan*

● **Greatest Hits** / 1990 / Curb ✦✦✦✦
Bobbie Gentry's biggest hits from the late '60s including "Ode to Billie Joe," "Louisiana Man," "Fancy," plus her hit duets with Glen Campbell, "Let It Be Me" and "All I Have to Do Is Dream." —*Thom Owens*

Mark Germino

Vocals / Country-Rock, Singer-Songwriter, Americana
Originally a poet, Mark Germino eventually became a folk-rock artist as a means of furthering his literary aspirations. Born in North Carolina, he moved to Nashville in 1974; although he never intended to become a musician, he bought a guitar a few months later after reasoning that performing songs would be easier than reciting poetry. A trucker by day, Germino began performing in area clubs at night, and signed a music publishing deal in 1981. After working as a songwriter for much of the decade, in the late '80s and early '90s Germino issued three major-label albums in a vein of heartland rock much like the work of Steve Earle, including 1990's *Radartown* (recorded with a backing band called the Sluggers) and *London Moon and Barnyard Remedies*. In 1995, he issued the folkier *Rank & File*. —*Jason Ankeny*

Radartown (Mark Germino & The Sluggers) / 1990 / Zoo ✦✦✦✦
Germino's melodic skills may be fairly pedestrian (B-grade Steve Earle/Springsteen with Irish influences), but he does deliver some nice story songs in a hard-hitting Heartland rock fashion. Lyrically, Germino is quite a good storyteller. "Rex Bob Lowenstein" is a modern folk song about a DJ bucking the highly formatted world of pro radio. —*Rick Clark*

● **Rank & File** / May 15, 1995 / Passport ✦✦✦✦
More proof that there are still plenty of decent writers in Nashville—ones who can write songs that tell a story and have some meat to them. Germino's cleverly written songs have popped up on other artists' records, including Confederate Railroad. But Germino is a poet at heart, and this record is far from a commercial country album. Rather, *Rank & File* is a folk-oriented record, giving Germino the room to stretch with literary detail. Armed with a gravelly voice and working within an acoustic setting, Germino falls somewhere between the music of John Prine and Steve Earle. Germino's songs are also similar to both of these artists in the way he can weave a yarn, bringing characters to life through his biting wit and uncompromising sincerity. "Rex Bob Lowen-

stein" tells the saga of a popular disc jockey, who has the freedom to play "Madonna next to George Jones," only to be axed, when a radio consultant sells the station on the promise of better ratings if they play Top 40. There's plenty of humor, but by no means is it all lighter fare. There are serious songs, and they cut deep, such as "Poet's Lament," which deals with the responsibility of a writer. —*Jack Leaver*

London Moon and Barnyard Remedies / RCA ✦✦✦

Terri Gibbs

b. Jun. 15, 1954, Augusta, GA
Vocals / Country-Pop, Adult Contemporary, Urban Cowboy
Singer-songwriter/keyboardist Terri Gibbs was raised on gospel music, and most of her country hits have been gospel-oriented. Born Teresa Fay Gibbs in Augusta, GA, she was blind from birth. She began learning the piano at age three and even then was a talented musician. Her early influences were the Everly Brothers, Patti Page, Elvis Presley, Pat Boone, and Ray Charles; she also listened frequently to the Grand Ole Opry. As a child and young teen she won several talent contests and sang in various choirs. Chet Atkins helped her launch her career after meeting her backstage at the Bell Auditorium in Augusta. At his request, she sent him a demo tape. He called her on her 18th birthday and suggested she go to Nashville, but the trip was unsuccessful, and she returned to Miami to become the keyboardist for Sound Dimension. In 1973, she left the group to attend college for two semesters, but dropped out to focus on songwriting. She founded her own band in 1975 and began playing at a restaurant in Augusta. In 1980, producer/songwriter Ed Penney, who had received two of her demos in 1979, came to Augusta to hear her and signed her to MCA. Her debut album, *Somebody's Knockin'*, and the title single were well received, the latter becoming a major hit on both pop and country charts in 1981. In 1980, Gibbs was named Best New Female Vocalist by both the ACM and *Cash Box* magazine. *Record World* also named her Most Promising Female Vocalist of Contemporary Music. In 1981, she had two medium hits and debuted on the Grand Ole Opry. That year she was honored with the CMA's first Horizon Award and was nominated for a Grammy. She released two more albums in 1981 and 1982 and began an extensive tour with George Jones, with whom she sang duets. She continued to make regular chart appearances through 1984. In 1986, Gibbs switched to gospel music and signed with Word Records. The title track of 1987's *Turn Around* became a minor hit on the country charts. In 1988, Gibbs appeared three times on the contemporary Christian charts with the Top Five hits "Promise Land," "Comfort the People" and "Unconditional Love." In 1990, Gibbs released *Great Day* for Morning Gate. She has since temporarily retired from music to concentrate on raising her son, but plans to return. —*Sandra Brennan*

Somebody's Knockin' / 1981 / MCA ✦✦✦✦

● **The Best of Terri Gibbs** / 1996 / Varèse Vintage ✦✦✦✦
All of Terri Gibbs' biggest hits from the early '80s—including "Somebody's Knockin'," "Rich Man," "Mis'ry River," "Ashes to Ashes," and "Anybody Else's Heart but Mine"—are included on this comprehensive, definitive collection. —*Thom Owens*

Don Gibson

b. Apr. 3, 1928, Shelby, NC
Guitar, Vocals / Traditional Country, Country-Pop, Nashville Sound/Countrypolitan
Singer-songwriter Don Gibson was one of the most popular and influential forces in '50s and '60s country, scoring numerous hit singles as a performer and a songwriter. Gibson's music touched on both traditional country and highly produced country-pop, which is part of the reason he had such a broad audience. For nearly a decade after his first hit single "Sweet Dreams" in 1956, he was a reliable hitmaker, and his songs have become country classics—they have been covered by a wide range of artists, including Patsy Cline, Ray Charles, Kitty Wells, Emmylou Harris, Neil Young, and Ronnie Milsap.

Gibson began playing guitar while he was a high school student in North Carolina, playing local radio stations and dances. In

1946, he became a regular with the Tennessee Barn Dance in Knoxville. Around the same time, he began recording Western songs with the Sons of the Soil, both on Mercury and RCA Victor Records. In 1950, Gibson assumed control of the band, renaming them Don Gibson and His King Cotton Kinfolks and switching their musical direction to honky tonk. Although their sound was more focused, they remained unsuccessful. Gibson continued to perform on the radio, as well as at Esslinger's Club in Tennessee. At the nightclub, Wesley Rose saw Gibson perform and offered him a writing contract. Don would only accept the deal if he was allowed to record. Rose managed to get Gibson a contract with Columbia, which proved unsuccessful. Rose secured him another contract, this time with MGM. Gibson's first single for the label, "Sweet Dreams," became a Top Ten hit and was covered by Faron Young, who took it to No. 3.

Following the success of "Sweet Dreams," Gibson was signed to RCA in 1957 by Chet Atkins, who would become his producer for the next seven years. Released early in 1958, Gibson's first RCA single, "Oh Lonesome Me," was a blockbuster, spending eight weeks at the top of the country charts and crossing over into the pop Top Ten. Gibson and Atkins developed a pop-friendly style that featured rock 'n' roll flourishes, which brought him to a larger audience. In the course of 1958-1961, Gibson had a total of 11 Top Ten singles, including "I Can't Stop Lovin' You, "Blue Blue Day," "Who Cares," "Don't Tell Me Your Troubles," "Just One Time," "Sea of Heartbreak," and "Lonesome Number One."

Although his career wasn't as successful in the latter half of the '60s, he still had the occasional Top Ten single, including "(Yes) I'm Hurting" (1966), "Funny, Familiar, Forgotten, Feelings" (1966), "Rings of Gold" (1969), and "There's a Story (Goin' Round)" (1969). During the late '60s, he suffered from alcoholism and drug addiction, but he cleaned up in the early '70s, which led to a comeback in 1971. Switching record labels from RCA to Hickory, Gibson had a Top Ten hit with "Country Green" in 1972. The following summer, he had his last No. 1 single, "Woman (Sensuous Woman)." He also had a series of duets with Sue Thompson between 1971 and 1976, which were all moderately successful. After two Top Ten hits in 1974—"One Day at a Time" and "Bring Back Your Love to Me"—he settled into a string of minor hits that ran until 1980's "Love Fires." During the '80s and '90s, he continued to tour and perform at the Grand Ole Opry. —*Stephen Thomas Erlewine*

Oh Lonesome Me / 1958 / Intersound ✦✦✦✦
This record contains some of Gibson's best-known compositions. And, while his performance on songs like "I Can't Stop Loving You" doesn't have the flash of Conway Twitty or Ray Charles versions, it's still worth tracking down to hear how the writer did his own material. —*Jim Worbois*

No One Stands Alone / 1959 / RCA Victor ✦✦✦
No One Stands Alone was recorded shortly after Don Gibson established himself as a popular recording artist as well as a successful songwriter. It was his first gospel album and it balances traditional songs with a handful of original cuts. Gibson is in good voice throughout the record and the production is typical of late '50s country-pop records, featuring choirs and strings. Though it isn't a major album for Gibson, it is enjoyable and the best gospel record he recorded. The CD reissue includes four bonus tracks. —*Stephen Thomas Erlewine*

That Gibson Boy / 1959 / RCA Victor ✦✦✦✦
Gibson covers tunes from some of the best country songwriters of the period (himself included) to make this record, one of the finest examples of Gibson as an artist. Atkins' production, the Jordanaires' background vocals, and Gibson's performances are all right on. —*Jim Worbois*

Sweet Dreams / 1960 / RCA Victor ✦✦✦
This is a nice collection of some of Gibson's classic compositions and some fine covers. In addition to the title track, which was a hit for Patsy Cline, several of these songs became hits by other artists. —*Jim Worbois*

Girls, Guitars and Gibson / 1961 / RCA Victor ✦✦✦
This record features some odd song selections that yield mixed results. While standards like "Born to Lose" and "Beautiful

Dreamer" sound as if they were written for Gibson, the inclusion of "Camptown Races" and a throwaway version of "Above and Beyond" leave the listener asking why. —*Jim Worbois*

Some Favorites of Mine / 1962 / RCA Victor ✦✦✦
Gibson covers songs from four of country music's greatest songwriters. An interesting album, it doesn't work quite as well as one would hope. —*Jim Worbois*

The Fabulous Don Gibson / 1965 / Harmony ✦✦✦
The Fabulous Don Gibson is an LP released on Columbia's subsidiary Harmony. While it contains several good songs, like "Ice Cold Heart," it also has its share of filler, making it just an average piece of product for the country audience of the mid-'60s. —*Thom Owens*

Great Country Songs / 1966 / RCA Victor ✦✦✦✦
This record focuses more on Gibson the performer and less on his work as a songwriter. Gibson certainly has a way with a song, even one he didn't write. Just listen to how much he gets out of Jeannie Seely's 1966 hit, "Don't Touch Me," as he bends and weaves his way through the melody. —*Jim Worbois*

★ **A Legend in His Time** / 1988 / Bear Family ✦✦✦✦✦
A Legend in His Time contains 26 tracks from Don Gibson's peak years of 1957-1965, including all of his country Top Ten hits ("Oh Lonesome Me," "I Can't Stop Lovin' You," "Blue Blue Day," "Sweet Dreams," and several others), as well as a selection of lesser-known material that is all first-rate. It's the definitive retrospective. Although hardcore fans will want Bear Family's box sets and casual fans might want a collection that's a little more concise, *A Legend in His Time* has every essential item from the classic singer-songwriter. —*Stephen Thomas Erlewine*

★ **All-Time Greatest Hits** / 1990 / RCA ✦✦✦✦✦
All-Time Greatest Hits lives up to its title. The album contains 20 of Don Gibson's RCA singles, including all of his big hits—"Oh Lonesome Me," "Sweet Dreams," "I Can't Stop Loving You," and many more. It's a definitive compilation—it has all the necessary songs and illustrates Gibson's songwriting genius quite effectively. —*Stephen Thomas Erlewine*

18 Greatest Hits / 1991 / Curb ✦✦✦
Gibson's best-known hits were recorded in the late '50s and early '60s for RCA with Chet Atkins producing. These recordings are drawn from his work for Hickory Records in the early '70s. They include "Woman, Sensuous Woman," "Country Green," and several remakes of his earlier hits. —*Michael McCall*

The Singer, the Songwriter (1949-1960) / 1991 / Bear Family ✦✦✦✦
Although it contains way too much material for most listeners, completists and historians will find the multidisc box *The Singer, The Songwriter (1949-1960)* invaluable. Containing everything that Gibson cut for MGM and RCA during that period—including several demos—the set offers plenty of brilliant music, but it's mixed in with mediocre material that is all too indicative of its era. The best of Gibson's songs transcends their time quite effortlessly, and all of those songs are here, but they're more effectively heard on other compilations. However, this set is fascinating for the diehard fan, even if the sheer extensiveness of the set is a little intimidating. —*Stephen Thomas Erlewine*

Country Spotlight / 1992 / Dominion ✦
Don't let the cover fool you—*Country Spotlight* features new, stereo rerecordings of ten of Gibson's greatest hits. Gibson is in good voice, but the new recordings can't touch the originals. —*Stephen Thomas Erlewine*

Gibson/Miller Band

Country-Rock, Contemporary Country, New Traditionalist
The hard-driving Gibson/Miller Band was one of many country-rock groups to spring up in the wake of the honky tonk revival of the early 1990s. Frontmen Dave Gibson and Bill "Blue" Miller were guitarists from very different backgrounds. Gibson was born and raised in Arkansas surrounded by the music of Eddy Arnold, Hank Williams, and Elvis Presley. As a young man, he worked with John Prine and Steve Goodman before becoming a well-known songwriter in Nashville. Miller hailed from Detroit and

played on recordings by Bob Seger and the Silver Bullet Band; he also sang jingles, traveled with Isaac Hayes, and even won an Emmy for providing the theme of an ABC documentary. After living in various cities, he eventually settled in Nashville, despite having never before played country music.

Gibson and Miller were introduced by Epic Records Vice President Doug Johnson, who thought they might make a good writing team. They put together a band, made a demo and sent it back to Johnson, who was impressed enough to sign them. The other band members were bassist Bryan Grassmeyer, who had previously played with Vince Gill and Suzy Bogguss; drummer Steve Grossman, who had worked closely with Grassmeyer; and steel guitarist Mike Daly, who had worked with Gibson for several years and played on all of his demos. The Gibson/Miller Band debuted in 1992 with the single "Big Heart," which, along with its video, was well-received and landed them in the Top 40 the following year. Their second single, "High Rollin'," made the Top 20, and their third, "Texas Tattoo," created quite a stir with its provocative video. This led to their first album, *Where There's Smoke* (1993). In 1994, their single "Stone Cold Country" reached the Top 40, followed by the album *Red, White & Blue Collar*. —*Sandra Brennan*

● **Where There's Smoke** / 1993 / Epic ✦✦✦✦
Gibson/Miller's Southern boogie debut features the hits "Big Heart," "Texas Tattoo," and "Stone Cold Country." —*Jason Ankeny*

Red, White & Blue Collar / 1994 / Epic ✦✦✦

Vince Gill

b. Apr. 12, 1957, Norman, OK
Guitar, Vocals / Progressive Bluegrass, Contemporary Country, New Traditionalist

Vince Gill was one of the most popular mainstream country performers of the early '90s. He grew up in Oklahoma playing banjo and guitar with local bluegrass musicians. At age 18 he joined the Bluegrass Alliance in Louisville, KY and played alongside band members Sam Bush and Dan Crary. After one year, he went to L.A. to play with Byron Berline and his band Sundance.

Two years later he accompanied a friend to an audition for Pure Prairie League. The band members remembered Gill because his high school band Mountain Smoke had opened for them years before, and immediately offered him a job. In 1979, he became the band's lead singer. During his three years with them, the band had a Top 40 pop hit with his song, "I'm Almost Ready" (1980). He left Pure Prairie League soon after the single's success to spend time with his then-pregnant wife Janis Oliver, a well-known bluegrass singer on the West Coast. After the birth of the child, Gill contacted Rodney Crowell to see if his band the Cherry Bombs needed a guitarist. He joined Crowell's group and, shortly afterward, former Cherry Bomb keyboard player Tony Brown signed Gill to a solo contract at RCA.

In 1984, Gill moved his family to Nashville and cut his debut EP, *Turn Me Loose*. His second single, "Victim of Life's Circumstances," cracked the country Top 40, beginning a string of hit singles that ran well into the '90s. In 1985, Gill had two Top Ten hits including "If It Weren't for Him," which featured harmonies from Rosanne Cash. In addition to his hit singles, Gill sang harmonies and played guitar on over 120 records, wrote and co-wrote songs with artists like Rosanne Cash, and toured with Emmylou Harris' band during the latter half of the '80s. In 1989, his career fired up again after he signed with MCA. His first album with the label, *When I Call Your Name*, produced the Top 25 hit "Never Alone," a song co-written with Cash. Following "Oklahoma Swing," a hit duet with Reba McEntire in 1990, Gill released "Never Knew Lonely," a No. 3 hit in the fall of 1990 that began a string of Top Ten hits that ran for five straight years.

Gill's 1991 album *Pocket Full of Gold* went platinum a year after its release, and more hits and accolades followed.

By the time he was asked to join the Grand Ole Opry in 1992, Gill had become a bonafide superstar—his '92 album *I Still Believe in You* went platinum within two months of its release. He had three Top Three hits in 1993, including "One More Chance." In 1993, Gill's RCA best-of album went gold, as did his

Christmas album *Let There Be Peace on Earth*. In 1994, he released *When Love Finds You*, which hit the Top Three on the country album charts and crossed over to land on the Top Ten pop album chart. In June of 1996, Gill released *High Lonesome Sound*. —*Sandra Brennan*

Turn Me Loose / 1983 / RCA ✦✦✦
This is one of the mini-LPs RCA, and several other labels, experimented with in the '80s. While Gill had been on the musical scene for several years, including a stint with Pure Prairie League, this is a nice sampler to display Gill's skills as both a performer and a writer. —*Jim Worbois*

The Way Back Home / 1987 / RCA ✦✦
For the most part this record doesn't sound much different than Gill's work with Pure Prairie League or, for that matter, the average Eagles album. Which isn't to say it's bad. Just that, except for the title song, nothing really stands out here. —*Jim Worbois*

When I Call Your Name / 1989 / MCA ✦✦✦✦
"Oklahoma Swing," Gill's duet with Reba McEntire, announced his return to a rootsier sound after leaving RCA. But it was the title cut, with Patty Loveless providing the harmonies, that soared highest from car radios and announced the arrival of a major star. —*Dan Cooper*

Pocket Full of Gold / 1991 / MCA ✦✦✦✦
A hit album with high bluegrass vocals, traditional country arrangement, and contemporary production. —*Mark A. Humphrey*

I Still Believe in You / 1992 / MCA ✦✦✦✦
Lots of folks inject a shot of R&B cliches into their honky tonk and call it country soul. Vince Gill is country's real soul man, and not because of a familiarity with black artists' catalogues (though "Nothin' Like a Woman" comes close to sounding what lovers imagine Percy Sledge's "When a Man Loves a Woman" to be). It's because Gill's voice captures pain and promise, love and loneliness—all in a distillation so smooth that you don't even notice it sneaking up to blindside you. With his high tenor harmonies on songs like "Tryin' to Get Over You" and "No Future in the Past," you might even call this bluegrass soul—and you know that's gotta be lonesome. —*Brian Mansfield*

I Never Knew Lonely / Mar. 1992 / RCA ✦✦✦
One of Gill's more pop-oriented efforts, *I Never Knew Lonely* features the title tune, "Everybody's Sweetheart" and "True Love." —*Jason Ankeny*

Let There Be Peace on Earth / 1993 / MCA ✦✦✦✦
Christmas music releases have become a country music tradition, but the result is often generic mushy background instrumentation on the same moldy standards. Vince Gill is guilty of this— *Let There Be Peace on Earth* is as cliche-ridden as they come. —*Roch Parisien*

When Love Finds You / 1994 / MCA ✦✦✦
That Vince Gill—he sure is a nice guy. But at this point, we sure would welcome some serious nastiness from him to keep us awake. —*Dan Cooper*

● **The Essential Vince Gill** / 1995 / RCA ✦✦✦✦
The Essential Vince Gill collects highlights from the singer's pop-inflected material for RCA in the early '80s. While Gill didn't have as many hits during this era, the best songs stand up well next to his better-known songs. —*Thom Owens*

● **Souvenirs** / Nov. 21, 1995 / MCA Nashville ✦✦✦✦
Souvenirs collects the greatest hits from Vince Gill's most popular period—his recordings for MCA in the late '80s and early '90s. As such, it contains a wealth of first-rate songs and hits—including the number ones "I Still Believe in You" and "Don't Let Our Love Start Slippin' Away"—and functions as a good introduction to his music. —*Thom Owens*

High Lonesome Sound / Jun. 1996 / MCA ✦✦✦
Vince Gill takes off on a tour of American music on *High Lonesome Sound*. The title cut steps back to a time he hasn't visited in a while, drawing on his days as a bluegrass singer and guitarist to create a soaring, harmony-driven sound that applies Appalachian drive to modern country rhythms. Most of the rest of the album

moves in new directions. The aggressive guitar riff that opens "One Dance with You" is straight Chicago blues, while the jaunty feel that enlivens "Down to New Orleans" draws on that city's funky polyrhythms with a deft touch worthy of Little Feat. "Tell Me Lover," also bearing the footprint of Little Feat, dances through a swampy groove. The problem isn't with the arrangements; Gill and producer Tony Brown give traditional sounds a modern shine while maintaining a distinct regional flavor. Gill gets much more room to show off his impressive guitar prowess than on past albums. But the lyrics too often deaden the excitement; Gill over-sweetens the blues with a corny chorus, then drags every Cajun cliche imaginable into his Louisiana homage. The album works best when he's not straining for authenticity: "Worlds Apart," "Given More Time," and "Pretty Little Adriana" leaven Gill's tried-and-true formula into arrangements that are more progressively atmospheric than his past hits. Gill has too many strengths to transform himself into Lowell George or Bonnie Raitt at this point in his career. —*Michael McCall*

Super Hits / Oct. 15, 1996 / ✦✦✦
Super Hits is a budget-priced compilation that features ten of Vince Gill's biggest hits for RCA Records, including "I Never Knew Lonely," "The Radio," and "Oklahoma Borderline." Though the album isn't comprehensive, it is nevertheless is an excellent collection by budget-line standards. —*Stephen Thomas Erlewine*

Steve Gillette (and Cindy Mangsen)

Contemporary Country
Steve Gillette is a singer-songwriter whose songs have been covered by Gordon Lightfoot, Garth Brooks, John Denver, Waylon Jennings, Tony Rice, Kenny Rogers, and others. His song "Darcy Farrow" is a classic. Cindy Mangsen plays guitar, banjo, English concertina, and mountain dulcimer. Her vocals are rich and beautiful. She has recorded with Anne Hills and Priscilla Herdman. —*Chip Renner*

Steve Gillette / 1967 / Vanguard ✦✦✦✦

A Little Warmth / 1979 / Regency ✦✦✦
A Little Warmth is exactly what this pleasant-sounding record exudes. Producer Graham Nash selects the best of Los Angeles' country musicians to back Gillette on a collection of minor, if interesting, songs. The album seems to fit more into the '90s country market than it did back in the late '70s, and should be sought out for a pleasing listening experience that is different from the usual cowboy hat performers. —*James Chrispell*

Alone / 1980 / Sierra ✦✦✦✦

● **Live in Concert** / 1991 / Compass Rose ✦✦✦✦
This live recording was captured on DAT, giving it a nice sound quality. Over 60 minutes and 19 songs—quantity and quality! Their vocals blend nicely and Gillette's guitar work is impressive. "Grapes on the Vine" is well done. Gillette and Mangsen do a great cover of "Shake Sugaree." This album also has a stunning cover of "Annachie Gordon." This one is highly recommended. —*Chip Renner*

Mickey Gilley

b. Mar. 9, 1937, Ferriday, LA
Piano, Vocals / Traditional Country, Country-Pop, Honky Tonk, Urban Cowboy
For most of his career, pianist/vocalist Mickey Gilley lived in the shadow of his cousin, Jerry Lee Lewis, playing a similar fusion of country, rock, blues, and R&B. In the early '70s, he managed to break through into country stardom, but it wasn't until the late '70s, when he became associated with the Urban Cowboy movement, that he became a superstar.

Gilley, like Lewis, was raised in Ferriday, LA. It wasn't until Jerry Lee had a hit with his first Sun single, "Crazy Arms," that Mickey decided he wanted to pursue a musical career. Gilley began recording for a number of independent Texas labels without much success in the late '50s. In the early '60s, he became a local favorite by playing a never-ending series of bars and clubs. A few of the singles became Texas hits, but he didn't have a

national hit until 1968 with the minor hit "Now I Can Live Again" on Paula Records.

In 1970, he opened Gilley's Club in Pasadena; the honky tonk had previously been known as Sherry's Club and its owner, Sherwood Cryer, asked Mickey to re-open the bar with him. In 1974, he had another local hit with "Room Full of Roses," which was released on Astro Records. Playboy Records, which was distributed by Epic, heard the record and acquired national distribution for the single. It became a No. 1 country hit, crossing over to No. 50 on the pop charts. "Room Full of Roses" launched a string of updated, countrypolitan-inflected honky tonk hits for Gilly that ran for just over a decade. Gilley racked up 16 No. 1 hits besides "Room Full of Roses," including "I Overlooked an Orchid," "City Lights," "She's Pulling Me Back Again," "True Love Ways," "Stand by Me," "That's All That Matters," and "A Headache Tomorrow (Or a Heartache Tonight)."

Gilley signed with Epic Records after Playboy folded in 1978. The following year, the film *Urban Cowboy*—which was based on Gilley's Club and featured a cameo by Mickey, as well as several of his songs—brought him to national attention, which resulted in a string of six straight No. 1 singles. He continued to have Top Ten hits until 1986, when his career began to slip. The late '80s were filled with problems for Gilley. Not only had a new generation of country singers replaced him on the charts, but he had financial problems, which culminated in the closing of Gilley's Club. Mickey turned his career around in the early '90s, when he became one of the first country stars to open a permanent theater in Branson, MO. Although he recorded some albums in the '90s—which were primarily available through television advertisements—he focused his career on the theater. —*Stephen Thomas Erlewine*

Lonely Wine / 1964 / Astro ✦✦✦

Gilley's Smokin' / 1976 / Playboy ✦✦✦✦
The barrelhouse-barroom piano style of Mickey Gilley is highlighted here on *Gilley's Smokin'*. On the record, Mickey covers such tunes as Lloyd Price's "Lawdy Miss Clawdy" and Sam Cooke's "Bring It on Home to Me" as well as punching up the old spiritual "I'll Fly Away." The big hit "Don't the Girls All Get Prettier at Closing Time" is also a great recommendation for seeking out this hot-rockin' record. —*James Chrispell*

Greatest Hits, Vol. 1 / 1976 / Epic ✦✦✦✦
Early Gilley hits like "Faded Love," "Window Up Above," "Bouquet of Roses" and the chart-topping "Room Full Oof Roses" are all here alongside many others. —*James Chrispell*

Live at Gilley's / 1978 / Epic ✦✦✦
This is a rough and rowdy roadhouse honky tonk performance. —*Mark A. Humphrey*

Mickey Gilley / 1978 / Paula ✦✦✦
Alternating between country tearjerker ballads and more mainstream pop tunes, *Mickey Gilley* shows off the pianist's flair for both genres. Although somewhat of a transitional album, nothing here is out of place in Gilley's vast catalogue of music. It's good listening, but not the best way to enjoy the talents of Mickey Gilley. —*James Chrispell*

Songs We Made Love To / 1979 / Epic ✦✦✦
Songs We Made Love To is more smooth honky tonk from the piano and voice of Mickey Gilley, featuring the highlights "Tonight I'll Help You Say Goodbye Again," "Even the Good Can Go Bad" and the title track. —*James Chrispell*

Down the Line / 1980 / Charly ✦✦✦

That's All That Matters to Me / 1980 / Epic ✦✦✦✦
This is the album that benefited most from Gilley's *Urban Cowboy* associations, and there's a perfunctory back-cover shot of some cowboy riding a mechanical bull at Gilley's night club. Though Gilley the Balladeer became pretty formulaic during the progression of the '80s, it was a new wrinkle with this album, and he delivers it convincingly. Gilley says the title track is his best performance ever. —*Tom Roland*

You Don't Know Me / 1981 / Epic ✦✦✦

Biggest Hits / 1982 / Epic ✦✦✦✦
This is a concise sampling of his '70s and '80s honky tonk hits.
—*Mark A. Humphrey*

You've Really Got a Hold on Me / 1983 / Epic ✦✦✦

Too Good to Stop Now / 1984 / Epic ✦✦✦✦

● **Ten Years of Hits** / 1984 / Epic ✦✦✦✦
It's a shame people have such a hard time dissociating Mickey Gilley from Stepford bulls. At his best, Jerry Lee Lewis' cousin has proven himself a legitimately soulful country singer, as evidenced here on No. 1 hits like "That's All That Matters to Me" and "A Headache Tomorrow (Or a Heartache Tonight)." —*Dan Cooper*

Greatest Hits, Vol. 2 / Playboy ✦✦✦✦
Collecting Mickey Gilley's hits of the mid-'70s, including "Don't the Grils All Get Prettier at Closing Time" and "She's Pulling Me Back Again," *Greatest Hits, Vol. 2* lives up to its title. While Gilley was never an original songwriter of much note, he could interpret most any style of music into his own niche. Perhaps that is why he appeals to such a diverse audience. This great sampler of his hits is an excellent way to become acquainted with his best mid-'70s work. —*James Chrispell*

Jimmie Dale Gilmore

b. May 6, 1945, Tulia, TX
Guitar, Vocals / Progressive Country, Contemporary Country, Singer-Songwriter, Country-Folk, Alternative Country
With his warm, warbling tenor voice and folksy, friendly approach to both his music and his audiences, Jimmie Dale Gilmore is an easy guy to like. His music is a rich blend of traditional country, folk, blues, and rock styles, and his lyrics reflect both his philosophical interests and his inherent downhome nature. Since moving to Austin, TX, and reviving his career in the 1980s, Gilmore has in many ways come to represent the current Austin music scene—its rootsy mix of country, rock, and folk music—the way Willie Nelson once reigned as king of the town's cosmic cowboys in the 1970s.

Gilmore's roots go back to Tulia, a small West Texas town where his father played lead guitar in a country band. When Gilmore was in grade school the family moved to Lubbock, a Panhandle town known for being the starting point for a surprising number of musicians (including Buddy Holly, Waylon Jennings, Terry Allen, and Gilmore's onetime singing partners Butch Hancock and Joe Ely). Growing up in Lubbock, Gilmore met Butch Hancock when they were both 12, and they've remained friends and frequent musical collaborators ever since. Gilmore later met Terry Allen, who he says inspired him to write his own songs. One of the first songs Gilmore wrote, in fact—when he was around 20—was "Treat Me Like a Saturday Night," which is today one of his most enduring pieces. Later, another casual friend of Gilmore's, Joe Ely, turned him on to the music of Townes Van Zandt, which Gilmore says was a revelation for the way Van Zandt integrated the worlds of folk and country music.

Gilmore and Ely began playing music together around Lubbock as the T. Nickel House Band. Later, after a brief stint in Austin, Gilmore hooked up again back in Lubbock with Ely and Hancock and formed the Flatlanders, a now-legendary band that also included Steve Wesson, Tony Pearson, and several peripheral members. The group recorded an album in Nashville in 1972, but it was only ever released on the time on 8-track tape. (Long a collector's item, it was finally re-released by Rounder Records in 1990 under the title *More a Legend than a Band.*) A mix of acoustic folk, string-band country, and country blues, the album included another of Gilmore's best-known songs, "Dallas," which was actually released as a promo single at the time but generated little interest. By the end of the year the band had split up.

Gilmore moved to Denver, playing music only as a hobby. Ely, meanwhile, had gotten a record contract, and had recorded some of Gilmore's songs. In 1980, Gilmore moved back to Austin, where he began playing regular gigs in local clubs. Finally, in 1988, Gilmore released his debut solo album, *Fair and Square,* on Hightone, Ely's label at the time. This and his 1989 follow-up, *Jimmie Dale Gilmore,* featured songs by Gilmore as well as Hancock and Ely played in a more straightforward honky tonk style than

anything Gilmore has done previously or since. These two albums gained Gilmore newfound acclaim just as Austin itself was becoming a musical hot spot again. In 1990, the Flatlanders album was re-released and Virgin Australia put out *Two Roads,* a duet album with Hancock that was recorded live during the pair's Australian tour. Gilmore was soon signed to Elektra, which released *After Awhile* in 1991 as part of the label's American Explorer series. The album retained a country feeling, but was less honky tonk in nature, and it attracted Gilmore even more acclaim. Nashville showed little interest in Gilmore's brand of country music, but he earned the praise of many critics. His next album, *Spinning Around the Sun,* came out in 1993 and again featured a mix of contemporary and traditional country-flavored songs and a fuller instrumental sound fronted by Gilmore's rich, warm voice. In 1996 he released *Braver Newer World,* produced by T-Bone Burnett. —*Kurt Wolff*

Fair and Square / 1988 / Hightone ✦✦✦
Jimmie Dale's debut solo album is straightahead honky tonk, featuring two Gilmore originals along with songs by Hancock, Ely, David Halley, and Townes Van Zandt ("White Freight Liner Blues"). Gilmore's sweet, warbling, nasal-inflected tenor voice takes center stage, where it belongs. —*Kurt Wolff*

Jimmie Dale Gilmore / 1989 / Hightone ✦✦✦✦
This follow-up album is sharper and tighter than Gilmore's debut, with a traditional honky-tonk sound that's as raw and visceral as anything in his repertoire. It contains a new version of "Dallas" and an excellent Hancock song, "When the Nights Are Cold." This album helped gain Gilmore national attention and place him firmly at the forefront of a new generation of alternative country artists. —*Kurt Wolff*

● **After Awhile** / 1991 / Elektra/Nonesuch ✦✦✦✦
While traditionalism is still a driving force, Gilmore's hardcore honky tonk is toned down. The album is somewhat quieter and more introspective in tone. The songs shift between the playful and the spiritual, Gilmore's vocals enhanced by a rich assortment of acoustic and electric instruments. The album contains a new version of the Gilmore classics "Tonight I Think I'm Gonna Go Downtown," from the Flatlanders album, and "Treat Me Like a Saturday Night," formerly covered by Ely. —*Kurt Wolff*

Spinning Around the Sun / 1993 / Elektra ✦✦✦
Recorded in Nashville instead of Austin, this album continues where "After Awhile" left off in terms of instrumental depth and refined, contemporary feeling. The production is shinier, but thankfully no one can take the earthiness out of Jimmie Dale's voice. The album contains another version of Hancock's "Just a Wave" and a beautiful duet with Lucinda Williams ("Reunion"). —*Kurt Wolff*

Braver Newer World / Jun. 25, 1996 / Elektra ✦✦✦
T-Bone Burnett produced this album, which spins Gilmore's music even further away from his honky tonk roots. This is a sophisticated album, full of sensual, textural beauty and with a heavier emphasis on rhythm and percussion. The mysticism is more prominent, but Gilmore's warbling twang keeps the experience grounded. —*Kurt Wolff*

Johnny Gimble

b. May 30, 1926, Tyler, TX
Fiddle / Traditional Bluegrass, Instrumental, Western Swing
One of the most impressive fiddle players in country music's history, Johnny Gimble confounds most of his rivals by using a five-string fiddle. He gained most of his early success with Bob Wills' Texas Playboys, but Gimble has also recorded over ten albums of his own and picked up awards as Instrumentalist of the Year (CMA) and Best Fiddle Player (ACM).

John Paul Gimble was born on May 30, 1926, in Tyler, TX. At the age of 12, he played in a band with his four brothers, and in the early '30s formed the Rose City Swingsters with brothers Gene and Jerry. The band played on local radio, but Gimble soon moved to Louisiana to play with Jimmie Davis. In the late '40s he joined Bob Wills, playing fiddle and electric mandolin with the

Texas Playboys. From 1951-53, Gimble led his own group, which played as house band at Wills' club. He then returned to the Playboys, but the decline of Western swing in the late '50s and early '60s forced him out of the business.

Johnny Gimble worked as a barber and a hospital worker during the '60s, but returned to record with Bob Wills in 1969. The experience primed him for heavy session work during the early '70s, including Merle Haggard's 1970 Wills tribute album and Wills' final appearance on LP, *The Last Time* (1974). That same year, he recorded the first of his many solo albums, *Fiddlin' Around*.

Johnny Gimble gained the first of his five Best Instrumentalist and eight Best Fiddle Player awards in the late '70s, and performed with Willie Nelson's touring band from 1979-81. Gimble finally hit the charts in 1983 with his Texas Swing group and the added attraction of Ray Price on vocals. The single, "One Fiddle, Two Fiddle," was taken from the Clint Eastwood film *Honkytonk Man*, and it reached No. 70. The B-side, Bob Wills' famous standard "San Antonio Rose," also charted. The sidemen credits also continued to add up, and in 1993, Gimble was nominated for a Grammy award in the Best Country Instrumental Performance category for his work on Mark O'Connor's fiddler tribute album, *Heroes*. Gimble is often seen playing on *Austin City Limits* and Garrison Keillor's TV programs. —*John Bush*

Fiddlin' Around / 1974 / Capitol ✦✦✦

Johnny Gimble, Texas Dance Party / 1975 / Lone Star ✦✦✦✦

Johnny Gimble's Texas Dance Party / 1975 / Columbia/Lone Star ✦✦✦

Recorded live in Austin in 1975, *Johnny Gimble's Texas Dance Party* is a reunion of Gimble and several of his colleagues and former bandmates, including pianist Curly Hollingsworth. It's an affectionate, fun tribute to the golden age of Western swing , even though none of the genre's standards are included on the album. Instead, the album does something more important—it captures the spirit of the genre. —*Thom Owens*

Still Swingin': Johnny Gimble and the Texas Swing Pioneers / 1976 / CMH ✦✦✦✦

Western style, that is. —*Mark A. Humphrey*

● **Texas Fiddle Collection** / 1981 / CMH ✦✦✦✦

Texas Fiddle Collection is a 28-song collection assembled from mid-'70s recordings with other former Texas Playboys, which means it offers a respresentative portrait of the fiddler's swinging Western style. —*Thom Owens*

Still Fiddlin' Around / Jun. 13, 1988 / MCA ✦✦✦

Although the production on *Still Fiddlin' Around* is a little too slick for most Western swing aficionados, Gimble and his band play very well and it is recommended for any serious fan of the genre. —*Thom Owens*

Texas Honky-Tonk Hits / CMH ✦✦✦

Johnny Gimble recorded *Texas Honky-Tonk Hits* with a stable of guest artists, including Mac Wiseman and Merle Travis. The combination never quite gels, but Gimble plays well throughout the album. —*Stephen Thomas Erlewine*

Jim Glaser

b. Dec. 16, 1937, Spalding, NE
Vocals / Traditional Country, Country-Pop, Urban Cowboy
Singer-songwriter Jim Glaser spent most of his professional career with Tompall & the Glaser Brothers, a group that began its existence in the 1950s. In 1961, Glaser attempted to launch a solo career on Starday. He scored a few mid-range hits after signing with RCA, including "Please Take Me Back" and "Molly." During this time, Glaser worked on his songwriting; his "Sittin' in an All Nite Cafe" was a major hit for Warner Mack in 1965. Three years later, "Woman Woman," a song he co-wrote with Jimmy Payne, became a huge hit for Gary Puckett and the Union Gap. In 1973, following the breakup of the Glaser Brothers, he signed to MGM, the group's old label, and again had a few medium-level hits, like "Forgettin' 'Bout You" (1974). The following year, he released his own version of "Woman Woman." Glaser was most successful in 1982 when he scored a Top 20 hit with "When You're Not a Lady."

He had a Top 30 hit with "You Got Me Running" and reached the Top 20 with the title cut from his album *The Man in the Mirror* in 1983. Glaser finally hit the Top Ten in 1984 with "If I Could Only Dance with You." This was followed by his biggest hit "You're Gettin' to Me Again," which went all the way to the top of the charts. Unfortunately, by the end of 1985, Glaser's winning streak was over, and his next two albums only produced one Top 30 hit, "In Another Minute," which resulted in his release from MCA. During the '90s, Glaser put his energy into a stage show that includes a tribute to Marty Robbins. —*Sandra Brennan*

● **The Very Best of Jim Glaser** / 1985 / Country Store [UK] ✦✦✦✦

Everybody Knows I'm Yours / Noble Vision ✦✦

Man in the Mirror / Noble Vision ✦✦✦

Past the Point of No Return / Noble Vision ✦✦✦

Tompall Glaser

b. Sep. 3, 1933, Spalding, NE
Vocals / Traditional Country, Outlaw Country
Of all the "outlaw" singers of the mid-'70s, Tompall Glaser was the one who most exploited his newfound moniker. He even titled one album *The Great Tompall and His Outlaw Band*, which brazenly featured a huge picture of him, shirt unbuttoned halfway down his chest, on the cover. It's ironic, then, that even though he had numerous chart records alone and with his brothers, Chuck and Jim, into the 1980s, he's the least remembered of the four artists—Willie Nelson, Waylon Jennings, Jessi Colter, and Tompall—who were packaged together on the immensely popular 1976 album *Wanted! The Outlaws*.

Tompall, however, deserves far more recognition for his achievements. Over the past four decades he's written and recorded a wealth of excellent folk- and rock-influenced country songs, and his rich, husky-sweet tenor voice is immediately distinct. He's as at home with a tender love ballad or a playful novelty number as he is with a bottomed-out cowboy lament like the Kinky Friedman classic "Sold American."

Tompall and his brothers, Chuck and Jim, hailed from Spaulding, NE, and started singing together as the folk trio Tompall and the Glaser Brothers in the late '50s. Their tight harmony singing impressed Marty Robbins, who signed them to his label. Their debut single was "Five Penny Nickel." They then moved to Nashville in 1958 and signed with Decca in 1959, worked also as session players, toured with Johnny Cash, and then joined the Grand Ole Opry in 1962. In 1965 they hooked up with producer Jack Clement, and a year later signed with MGM, which released several excellent albums. Songs like "Gone, On the Other Hand," "Through the Eyes of Love," and "California Girl (and the Tennessee Square)" made the charts, and the brothers remained a popular group throughout the decade. Tompall's "Streets of Baltimore" (co-written with Harlan Howard) also became a hit for Bobby Bare in 1966.

In 1969 the brothers opened their own recording studio in Nashville, which soon became known as Hillbilly Central and a focal point of the burgeoning outlaw movement. By this time they also had their own group of music publishing companies; Nashville's old boy network was shaken up when one of their discoveries, John Hartford's "Gentle on My Mind"—which had been turned down by nearly every publishing house in town—became a smash hit for Glen Campbell.

In 1973 the group split up, Tompall began recording as a solo artist, and outlaw became his badge of honor. But his intentions were true, and his 1973 album, *Charlie*, stands as one of the finest of that genre. It includes a stunning version of "Sold American" as well as the Tompall originals "Big Jim Colson" (about an unwed mother) and the excellent title track. The novelty song "Put Another Log on the Fire," from his 1975 album *Tompall (Sings the Songs of Shel Silverstein)*, became a chart hit, and it was one of two Tompall songs included on *Wanted! The Outlaws* a year later. Further Tompall hits from that decade include "T for Texas" and "Drinking Them Beers," though these are by no means his best material. Tompall had also become a close friend and business associate of Waylon Jennings, but the two eventually had a major falling out.

The brothers reunited and signed with Elektra Records in 1980, and again they met success, especially with the Kris Kristofferson song "Lovin' Her Was Easier (Than Anything I'll Ever Do Again)." The group split again in 1983, and Tompall returned to his Nashville recording studio. He released the solo album *Nights on the Borderline* for MCA Dot in 1986. —*Kurt Wolff*

This Land-Folk Songs / 1960 / Decca ◆◆◆

Just Looking for a Home / 1961 / Starday ◆◆◆

The Ballad of Namu the Killer Whale / 1966 / United Artists ◆◆◆

Charlie / 1973 / MGM ◆◆◆◆
By far Tompall's best release as a solo artist or otherwise, *Charlie* is one of the true classics of outlaw country. "Gideon Bible," the title track, and a knockout version of Kinky Friedman's "Sold American" are just the highlights. Tompall sings about loneliness and staring at closed doors like a true pro. —*Kurt Wolff*

Tompall / 1974 / MGM ◆◆◆◆
On this collection of songs written by Shel Silverstein, the arrangements are outlaw sparse, the players are top-notch, and there's some great material among the typical (and often annoying) Silverstein novelty numbers. "Put Another Log on the Fire" turned into a hit for Tompall (and was later included on the compilation *Wanted! The Outlaws*). —*Kurt Wolff*

Great Tompall and His Outlaw Band / 1976 / MGM ◆◆◆◆
The first of two albums to feature Tompall's hot new band that included acclaimed guitarist Mel Brown. Blues, soul, barroom country, and Western swing are among the subtle but solid moods on this well-crafted and superbly arranged collection. —*Kurt Wolff*

The Outlaw / 1977 / Bear Family ◆◆◆◆

Nights on the Borderline / 1986 / Dot ◆◆◆

● **The Rogue** / Bear Family ◆◆◆◆
This album, recorded in the early '70s, has 22 cuts. —*AMG*

Golden Smog

Alternative Country-Rock
A boozy, side-project covers band that gradually evolved into a kind of roots-rock supergroup, Golden Smog was a loosely affiliated unit comprised, at various times, of members of Soul Asylum, the Replacements, Wilco, the Jayhawks, Run Westy Run, and the Honeydogs. The group first came together in the Minneapolis area in the late 1980s as a country-rock reaction to the punk and hardcore sounds that dominated the Twin Cities' musical scene at the time; eventually Golden Smog became something of a fixture at local clubs, where they played a handful of shows annually. From the onset, the lineup was mercurial, although Run Westy Run vocalist Kraig Johnson as well as guitarists Dan Murphy (Soul Asylum) and Gary Louris (the Jayhawks) were relative constants. Smog shows were usually thematically based, in keeping with the tongue-in-cheek nature of the project; one performance was devoted exclusively to Eagles covers, while another paid homage to the Rolling Stones, and was billed "Her Satanic Majesty's Paycheck."

Somewhat unexpectedly, a five-cut covers EP, *On Golden Smog*, appeared in 1992. While the closing track, a rendition of Thin Lizzy's "Cowboy Song" sung by Soul Asylum roadie Bill Sullivan, followed in the project's original devil-may-care spirit, the remainder of the record was considerably more focused, keeping in line with the primary musical work of the band members—who, this time out, were essentially Johnson, Murphy, Louris, Jayhawks bassist Marc Perlman and ex-Replacements drummer Chris Mars, along with Soul Asylum vocalist Dave Pirner (on a cover of Bad Company's "Shooting Star"). Even more unexpectedly, the next Golden Smog effort—1996's full-length *Down by the Old Mainstream*—was made up largely of original material composed strictly for the project. With a lineup that included Johnson, Murphy, Louris, Perlman, Wilco frontman Jeff Tweedy, and Honeydogs drummer Noah Levy (all of whom recorded under pseudonyms as a result of contractual obligations), the record bore few reminders of the Smog's beer-soaked

origins, instead revealing a more mature and thoughtful band breaking free of the restraints of their day jobs and having some serious fun in the process. —*Jason Ankeny*

On Golden Smog / 1992 / Crackpot ◆◆◆
After a few years of haphazard shows in and about their native Minneapolis, the members of Golden Smog were approached by a small local label to put out a record; many, many beers later, *On Golden Smog* appeared. Complete with sleeve art by then-drummer Chris Mars, the five-song EP is comprised entirely of covers, including *Hair*'s "Easy to Be Hard," the obscure '60s band Michelangelo's "Son," Bad Company's "Shooting Star" (sung by Soul Asylum's Dave Pirner), and Thin Lizzy's "Cowboy Song," fronted by Soul Asylum roadie Bill Sullivan. —*Jason Ankeny*

● **Down by the Old Mainstream** / 1995 / Rykodisc ◆◆◆◆
Like most supergroup projects, Golden Smog's *Down by the Old Mainstream* is a loose, relaxed affair that sounds like it was a lot of fun to record. Unlike most supergroups, the members of Golden Smog improve on their regular bands. Comprised of a number of alternative country-rock stars—including Wilco's Jeff Tweedy, the Jayhawks' Gary Louris, and Soul Asylum's Dan Murphy—the musicians are relaxed and loose, giving the songs a raw, rootsy kick. Since the album wasn't carefully considered, it has an offhand, relaxed charm that is sometimes lacking from Jayhawks and Soul Asylum albums. Not all of the songs are first-rate—"Pecan Pie" and "Red Headed Stepchild" are a bit too cute to be effective—but the performances are full of grit and fire, which is what makes *Down by the Old Mainstream* such an engaging listen. —*Stephen Thomas Erlewine*

William Lee Golden

b. Jan. 12, 1939, Brewton, AL
Vocals / Country-Pop, Urban Cowboy
After more than two decades with the Oak Ridge Boys, baritone vocalist William Lee Golden was fired in 1986 when the other members wished to change the country band's image. He had joined the group in 1964, when the Oaks were a gospel/folk group, and he accompanied their rise through the country charts during the '70s. In 1985, Golden recorded the solo album *American Vagabond* for MCA with help from Booker T. Jones and Joe Walsh. Two singles, "Love Is the Only Way Out" and "You Can't Take It with You," appeared on the country charts, but then the Oak Ridge Boys let him go. He filed a $40 million lawsuit, which was settled out of court, and then began to record with his sons Rusty and Chris. They moved to Mercury in 1990, and recorded the single "Louisiana Red Dirt Highway." Four years later, Golden released an album for North/South, a division of Atlantic. —*John Bush*

American Vagabond / MCA ◆◆◆

The Goldens

Country, Country-Pop, Contemporary Country, Country Gospel
The Golden brothers, Rusty and Chris, literally grew up surrounded by country music; their father was William Lee Golden, a member of the Oak Ridge Boys. The brothers grew up listening to the harmonies of Southern gospel music. Both were born in Brewton, AL, and in the summers worked on their grandparents' farm and sang in church. Chris played drums, keyboards, acoustic guitar, and mandolin. He began playing piano with the Telestials, a gospel group, when he was 15. Three years later, he joined Cedar Creek, a band that found some success in Canada and the US. When he was 19, he debuted as a lead vocalist on the TV show *Hee Haw*. His brother Rusty was inspired to learn the piano at age 12 after seeing Elton John in concert, using John's music to teach himself to play. Before learning piano, he played drums for the Oak Ridge Boys on weekends, starting at age eight. By the time he was 15, Rusty was proficient on both instruments and began playing occasional professional gigs with his father's band. Three years later, he joined Larry Gatlin's band in the studio and on tour for several years. He founded a pop band, the Boys Band, with B. James Lowry and Greg Gorden, in the early 1980s. They signed with Elektra/Asylum and had a minor chart single, "Please Don't Stop Me Baby (I'm on Fire)," in 1982. Just before graduating

from high school, Chris played with the Boys Band. Rusty began writing songs and signed with EMI/Combine as a writer in 1987. That year, the brothers teamed up to become the Goldens and released two minor hits on CBS/Epic, "Put Us Together Again" and "Sorry Girls." They released their first album in 1991; *Rush for Gold* only produced one minor hit, "Keep the Faith." The lineup included Chris on lead vocals, Rusty on keyboards, bassist Don Breland, guitarist Skip Mitchell, fiddler and steel guitar player Bobby Randall, and drummer Buster Phillips. —*Sandra Brennan*

● **Rush for Gold** / Sep. 10, 1990 / Capitol ✦✦✦✦

The Goldens / Epic ✦✦✦

Gosdin Brothers

Progressive Bluegrass, Neo-Traditionalist Country

Vern and Rex Gosdin were always on the cutting edge of bluegrass and country-rock, yet they never quite broke through to the mainstream audience they deserved. In 1961, the Alabama natives moved out to California, where they began playing in the bluegrass band, the Golden State Boys. The Gosdins' time in the Golden State Boys earned the attention of Chris Hillman, who asked them to join his group, the Hillmen. Within a few years, Hillman had joined the Byrds, while Vern found work as a session musician and continued to play duos with Rex.

In 1966, the Gosdin Brothers supported former Byrd Gene Clark on the record *Gene Clark with the Gosdin Brothers*. The following year, the duo had a minor hit with "Hangin' On," but they were not able to deliver another hit single. Following this lack of success, Vern grew frustrated with the music business and retired from performing for several years. He made a comeback in 1976 with a new version of "Hangin' On" and once again hit the road with Rex. While Vern at last found some success, charting more than 27 records over 12 years, Rex was not as lucky. Of the three chart records he had before his death in 1983, the biggest hit was a duet with Waylon Jennings' brother Tommy. Following Rex's death, Vern continued to tour and perform well into the '90s. —*Jim Worbois*

Sounds of Goodbye / 1968 / Capitol ✦✦✦✦

Too Far Gone / 1984 / RCA ✦✦✦

Chiseled in Stone / 1988 / Columbia ✦✦✦✦

Chiseled in Stone is Vern Gosdin's late '80s comeback album, a record that confirms his vocal talents and, arguably, delivers more than any of his other records. Gosdin's voice is gorgeously worn, and the material is stellar, divided between classics and new songs that sound as old as the hills. Even though it was recorded late in his career, few albums explain the appeal of Vern Gosdin as much as *Chiseled in Stone*. —*Thom Owens*

Rough Around the Edges / 1989 / RCA ✦✦✦

Rough Around the Edges is a brief, eight-song collection of songs Vern Gosdin recorded in the early '80s for A.M.I. that concentrates on ballads like "When Love Was All We Had" and "Lovin' You Is Music to My Mind." Since it only contains eight songs, the album can't be anything more than a sampler, yet it showcases his vocal skills quite effectively. —*Thom Owens*

Alone / 1989 / Columbia ✦✦✦

Written and released immediately after a painful divorce, *Alone* is a moving set of honky tonk that works better in theory than it does in practice. Though Vern Gosdin's performance is frequently sublime, his songs aren't always strong. However, when he has a good song at his disposal—such as "Right in the Wrong Direction," "I'm Only Going Crazy," "That Just About Does It," and "I'm Still Crazy"—his heartfelt delivery and tortured lyrics makes for some truly memorable music. —*Thom Owens*

10 Years of Greatest Hits Newly Recorded / 1990 / Columbia ✦✦✦✦

Gosdin has George Jones' keening desperation in his vocals and an ironic wit in his writing. A fine overview of a great artist. —*Mark A. Humphrey*

Vern Gosdin

Out of My Heart / 1991 / Columbia ✦✦✦✦

Out of My Heart is a typically excellent album from Vern Gosdin, yet the power of his vocals—he's singing his heart out throughout the record—and the quiet grace of the music make this one to treasure. —*Thom Owens*

Gene Clarke with the Gosdin Brothers / Columbia ✦✦✦

● **Best of Vern Gosdin** / Warner Brothers ✦✦✦✦

The Best of Vern Gosdin contains ten of his late '70s hits, which were originally released in the '70s. Although they bear all the hallmarks of the era—these are slick, string-laden productions—they remain pure, impressive country. Gosdin sounds especially good when Emmylou Harris or Janie Fricke provide harmonies. —*Thom Owens*

Vern Gosdin

b. Aug. 5, 1934, Woodland, AL

Guitar, Vocals / Progressive Bluegrass, Traditional Bluegrass, Traditional Country

Vern Gosdin was one of the best and most subtle traditional vocalists in country music. Born in Woodland, AL, Gosdin first learned to sing in church. His appreciation of country music came from listening to his idols the Louvin Brothers on the Grand Ole Opry. It was an older brother who taught him to play guitar at age 13. When he was in his late teens, his family moved to Birmingham to host the *Gosdin Family Gospel Show* on a local radio station. Gosdin and his brother Rex moved to Long Beach, CA, in 1961. Both had day jobs, but at night played with the Golden State Boys, a bluegrass group that included Don Parmley. Later Chris Hillman joined the group and they changed their name to the Hillmen. In the mid-'60s, Hillman left to become the bassist for the Byrds. Vern and Rex teamed up to sing country music as the Gosdin Brothers, and had a Top 40 country hit in 1967 with "Hangin On."

By 1968, the Gosdins had broken up and Vern had moved to Atlanta to open a glass and mirror shop. Though he focused on raising his family and building his business, he occasionally performed at local clubs. He decided to retry music as a career in 1976 and went to Nashville to re-record "Hangin On" for Elektra. The single reached the country Top 20. However, its B-side, "Yesterday's Gone"—which featured harmonies from Emmylou Harris—reached the Top Ten, and Gosdin's career took off. The following year he had seven major hits including "Till the End," "Never My Love," and "Mother Country Music."

In 1980, Elektra shut down its country division and Gosdin signed to Ovation. The following year, he had Top Ten success with "Dream of Me" and in 1982 again made it to the Top Ten with "Today My World Slipped Away" for AMI. In 1983, Gosdin had two Top Five hits—"If You're Gonna Do Me Wrong (Do It Right)" and "Way Down Deep." The following year he had a No. 1 hit with "I Can Tell by the Way You Dance (You're Gonna Love Me Tonight)" and two additional Top Ten hits. His career hit a lull in the mid-'80s, but he bounced back into the Top Ten in 1987, when "Do You Believe Me Now" became a No. 4 hit and was followed in 1988 by the No. 1 "Set 'Em Up Joe" and the Top Ten hit "Chiseled in Stone." In the early '90s, Gosdin's popularity declined —after 1990's "Is It Raining at Your House," he wasn't able to crack the Top 40—but he continued recording and performing. —*Sandra Brennan*

Till the End / 1977 / Elektra ✦✦✦✦
This is probably one of Gosdin's strongest records overall. Additionally, it netted him four hits. —*Jim Worbois*

There Is a Season / 1984 / Compleat ✦✦✦✦
Throughout the album, Emmylou Harris provides nice harmonies reminiscent of Rex Gosdin's style. Additionally, Roger McGuinn adds vocals (background and accompanying) and the 12-string instrumental break to "Turn Turn Turn"; very different from the break on the Byrds' version. —*Jim Worbois*

If Jesus Comes Tomorrow / 1984 / Compleat ✦✦✦
If Jesus Comes Tomorrow (What Then) is part gospel standards, part complementary originals, all sung by a honky tonk voice hoping for heaven. —*Brian Mansfield*

The Best of Vern Gosdin / 1989 / Warner Brothers ✦✦✦✦
Some fine performances from the early and mid-'80s, they are a mite over-produced. Get his Columbia work first. —*Mark A. Humphrey*

10 Years of Hits—Newly Recorded / 1990 / Columbia ✦✦✦
As the title says, *10 Years of Hits—Newly Recorded* has seven of Gosdin's Compleat hits—like "I Can Tell by the Way You Dance (You're Gonna Love Me Tonight)"—from the early '80s re-recorded for his new label, Columbia, as well as four new tracks. Although they aren't the originals, Gosdin is in good voice and the new versions are nearly equal to the hit singles. —*Stephen Thomas Erlewine*

Nickels & Dimes & Love / Mar. 9, 1993 / Columbia ✦✦✦
Nickels & Dimes & Love features Gosdin's final chart hit, "Back When." —*Jason Ankeny*

● **Super Hits** / 1994 / Columbia ✦✦✦✦
Super Hits collects all of the biggest hits Vern Gosdin had on Columbia Records in the late '80s, including all of his Top Ten hits and the No. 1s "I'm Still Crazy" and "Set 'Em Up Joe." —*Thom Owens*

Billy Grammer

b. Sep. 28, 1925, Benton, IL
Guitar, Vocals / Traditional Country, Nashville Sound/Country-politan
Longtime Grand Ole Opry member Billy Grammer was one of the great guitar players of country music; he even had a flat top guitar named after him and installed in the Country Music Hall of Fame in 1969. One of 13 children born to a coal mining family in Franklin County, IL, during childhood he often played fiddle, guitar, or mandolin at local gatherings. Following service in World War II, Grammer decided to become a professional musician. He got his first opportunity on Connie Gay's *Radio Ranch* in Arlington, VA. Two years later, he made his recording debut. In 1955, Gay suggested to Jimmy Dean that Grammer join his television show. During his years on *The Jimmy Dean Show*, Grammer was a sideman in several bands, including those of Clyde Moody, Grandpa Jones, and Hawkshaw Hawkins. He founded his own band in 1958 and also began recording as a solo act. In 1959, he had his first hit with "Gotta Travel On," which peaked in the Top

Five on the country charts and did well on the pop charts. In 1962 he had chart success with "I Wanna Go Home." He occasionally appeared on the charts in the '60s with such songs as "I'll Leave the Porch Lights a-Burning" and "Bottles." In the '70s, Grammer recorded two final solo albums and continued to do session work. He later retired from studio work, but continued to perform regularly on the Opry. —*Sandra Brennan*

The Grateful Dead

Rock & Roll, Country-Rock, Psychedelic, Folk-Rock
The Grateful Dead are the longest-lived of the San Francisco "acid rock" groups of the '60s. In the '90s, after more than 25 years in action, the Dead were still playing to enough satisfied customers on the road (most of them "Deadheads") to make them one of the top-grossing concert acts in the music business.

The group was formed in 1965 by bluegrass enthusiast Jerry Garcia (b. Aug 1, 1942—d. Aug 9, 1995) on guitar and vocals, Ron "Pigpen" McKernan (b. Sep 8, 1945—d. Mar 8, 1973) on vocals and organ, Bob Weir (b. Oct 16, 1947) on guitar and vocals, classical music student Phil Lesh (b. Mar, 15, 1945) on bass and vocals, and Bill Kreutzmann (b. Apr 7, 1946) on drums. From the beginning, they brought together a variety of influences, from Garcia's country background to Pigpen's feeling for blues (his father was an R&B radio DJ) and Lesh's education in contemporary "serious" music. Add to that the experimentation encouraged at some of the group's first performances at novelist Ken Kesey's "acid test" parties—multimedia events intended to replicate (or accompany) the experience of taking the then-legal drug LSD—and you had a musical mixture of styles often played with extended improvisational sections that could go off in nearly any direction.

The band signed to Warner Bros. in 1967, experiencing some difficulties early on with the restrictions of standard recording practices and the company's interest in producing a conventionally commercial product. As a result, the group's first few albums were somewhat tentative but showed promise for the future, especially with the key additions of Mickey Hart as a second drummer in 1967 and Garcia's old friend Robert Hunter as the band's lyricist.

The Dead finally hit their stride with the release of *Live/Dead*, a double album, in 1969. (They were always more comfortable on stage than in the studio.) Two studio albums in 1970, *Workingman's Dead* and *American Beauty*, found them exploring folk-rock and more tightly constructed song forms and, along with extensive touring, won them a much larger audience.

In the second half of the '70s, the Dead recorded a series of commercially-oriented albums for Arista, then concentrated on road work for the better part of the '80s. *In the Dark*, released in 1987, was their first studio album in seven years. It sold a million copies and produced the band's first Top Ten hit in "Touch of Grey." The Dead continued to tour, notably doing shows with Bob Dylan, and at the start of the '90s, they began to release vintage material on their own Grateful Dead Merchandising label.

Garcia died of heart failure on August 9, 1995. A few months after his death, the surviving members of the Grateful Dead disbanded. —*William Ruhlmann*

☆ **Workingman's Dead** / May 1970 / Warner Brothers ✦✦✦✦✦
A folk-rock, tightly arranged Dead, singing (in harmony!) some of their best songs, from "Uncle John's Band" to "Casey Jones." —*William Ruhlmann*

★ **American Beauty** / Nov. 1970 / Warner Brothers ✦✦✦✦✦
Workingman's Dead, part two—more of the songs that have served as the band's basic repertoire ever since these albums were released. Includes "Box of Rain," "Friend of the Devil," "Sugar Magnolia," "Ripple," and, of course, "Truckin'." —*William Ruhlmann*

Grateful Dead / Oct. 1971 / Warner Brothers ✦✦✦
The Dead's second double live album (now on a single CD) introduces a couple of excellent Garcia/Hunter compositions, "Bertha" and "Wharf Rat," and allows Bob Weir to indulge his taste for what Deadheads would come to call "cowboy songs": Merle Haggard's "Mama Tried" and Kris Kristofferson's "Me & Bobby McGee." The album became the Dead's first gold record, probably

on the momentum of *Workingman's Dead* and *American Beauty*. It also failed to match *Live/Dead* as a concert album, so that, coming off the band's recent peaks, it seemed less effective than it was. Now, it seems like one of the Dead's better, more coherent records. (Not to be confused with *The Grateful Dead*, the band's debut album. They resorted to *Grateful Dead* as a title when Warner wouldn't let them call the album *Skull Fuck*). — *William Ruhlmann*

Europe '72 / Nov. 1972 / Warner Brothers ◆◆◆◆
Released as a three-record set, *Europe '72* is now a double CD. But it's still a long album, notable for introducing more Garcia-Hunter songs, especially "Brown-Eyed Woman," and for incorporating onto one album the variety of musical styles to be heard at a Dead concert, as well as the sheer duration necessary to appreciate the experience. Which means that, while this may not be the place a new fan wants to start, it's a Deadhead favorite. — *William Ruhlmann*

History of the Grateful Dead, Vol. 1 (Bear's Choice) / Jul. 13, 1973 / Warner Brothers ◆◆◆
This is a contractual obligation album, a record given to Warner Bros. to complete the Dead's commitment to the label. It was recorded in February 1970 and is something of a tribute to the late keyboardist/vocalist Ron "Pigpen" McKernan, who is heard frequently. Pigpen highlights an 18-minute version of Howlin' Wolf's "Smokestack Lightnin'." But this is a nonessential Dead album. "Bear" is the band's friend/soundman/drug manufacturer Owsley Stanley. The album is misnamed: it does not provide a "history" and there was never any Volume 2. — *William Ruhlmann*

Wake of the Flood / Nov. 15, 1973 / Grateful Dead ◆◆◆◆
The Grateful Dead's first studio album in three years was also their first for their own record label. It's a strong collection, featuring such Garcia-Hunter songs as "Mississippi Half-Step Uptown Toodleoo," "Row Jimmy," and "Stella Blue," songs that would become concert staples, as well as Bob Weir's "Weather Report Suite." — *William Ruhlmann*

Skeletons from the Closet: The Best of the Grateful Dead / 1974 / Warner Brothers ◆◆◆
This is an 11-song compilation, five of whose songs come from *Workingman's Dead* or *American Beauty*. It presents a sampling of the Dead's 1967-1972 period, focusing on their more accessible material. In that sense, it is recommended to the uninitiated who want to get a feel for the group; not surprisingly, it is a perennial seller, turning up week after week on *Billboard* magazine's Top Pop Catalog chart. The initiated, however, despise it: In a survey of Deadheads conducted by *DeadBase*, it was rated above only *Dylan & the Dead* as the worst Grateful Dead album. — *William Ruhlmann*

Grateful Dead from the Mars Hotel / Jun. 27, 1974 / Grateful Dead ◆◆◆
The Grateful Dead's second independent album was an uneven one, containing favorites like "Scarlet Begonians," "US Blues," and "China Doll," but also a fair amount of filler. — *William Ruhlmann*

Blues for Allah / Sep. 1, 1975 / Grateful Dead ◆◆◆◆
Opening with the suite that has become a concert favorite, "Help on the Way"/"Slip Knot!"/"Franklin's Tower," and also containing the anthemic "The Music Never Stopped," *Blues for Allah* is another Grateful Dead album containing a few band classics and a lot of filler. Note, however, that some fans seem to like the filler. In its survey of Deadheads, *DeadBase* found *Blues for Allah* to be the band's most popular studio album after *Workingman's Dead* and *American Beauty*. — *William Ruhlmann*

Steal Your Face / Jun. 26, 1976 / Grateful Dead ◆◆
A double live album recorded in October 1974 just before the start of a hiatus in performing by the Dead and not released until 20 months later, to coincide with the feature film *The Grateful Dead Movie*, shot at the same shows. It is universally hated by Deadheads, and why would anyone else want to listen to it? Primary evidence that the Dead needed to take a break from touring in 1974. — *William Ruhlmann*

● **What a Long Strange Trip It's Been** / 1977 / Warner Brothers ◆◆◆◆
This is a two-disc compilation of The Grateful Dead, covering its tenure at Warner Bros., 1967-1972, and as such the most extensive sampler of their work in existence. Well-chosen, it contains many of their best songs from the period and is notable for giving album release to the studio-recorded single version of "Dark Star," the Dead's most requested song. Relative newcomers to the band (those who bought *Skeletons from the Closet* and liked it) can get a stronger dose here, and then perhaps go on to the individual albums. Of course, Deadheads hate this record. — *William Ruhlmann*

Terrapin Station / Jul. 27, 1977 / Arista ◆◆◆
The best of the early Arista albums, containing the extended "Terrapin Station" suite. — *William Ruhlmann*

Shakedown Street / Nov. 15, 1978 / Arista ◆◆
Using Little Feat leader Lowell George as producer should have been a great idea, but somehow it didn't work out. The Dead have salvaged "Fire on the Mountain" and "I Need a Miracle" for live work from this collection, but it's one of their least satisfactory studio ventures. — *William Ruhlmann*

Reckoning / Apr. 1, 1981 / Arista ◆◆◆
Having given up on studio work after the disaster of *Go to Heaven*, the Dead recorded a series of concerts in New York and San Francisco in October 1980 for two live albums. This is the first, a set of acoustic material that will remind many listeners of the rustic feel of the classic *Workingman's Dead* and *American Beauty* albums, although much of it consists of traditional and bluegrass material favored by Jerry Garcia. (The original two-LP set was fit onto one CD in 1987 by eliminating the Dead's cover of Elizabeth Cotten's "Oh Babe It Ain't No Lie"). — *William Ruhlmann*

In the Dark / Jul. 6, 1987 / Arista ◆◆◆◆
The comeback, with "Touch of Grey," "West L.A. Fadeaway," and "Black Muddy River." For anyone who wondered how these old hippies could have such a following 20 years after the hippies disappeared, here's the answer. — *William Ruhlmann*

Built to Last / Oct. 31, 1989 / Arista ◆◆
Supposedly, the Dead had broken their studio jinx with *In the Dark* and finally learned how to make good albums without an audience in front of them. So why was this follow-up such a letdown? Perhaps because they hadn't taken seven years to write and perfect new material as they had with the previous album. The dominant songwriter here was keyboard player Brent Mydland (who died the following year), while the crucial songwriting team of Garcia and Hunter contributed only minor efforts. Chastened, the Dead once again retreated from studio work. — *William Ruhlmann*

Josh Graves

b. Tellico Springs, TN

Dobro / Traditional Bluegrass

For over five decades, the legendary Josh Graves (born Burkett Graves) remained one of the major forces keeping the unique sounds of the dobro alive in both country and bluegrass music. Born and raised in Tellico Springs, TN, he was only nine when he heard Cliff Carlisle of the Carlisle Brothers performing a few Jimmie Rodgers tunes on the dobro. Graves loved the sound and later became close friends with Carlisle; still, he spent much of his early career as a bass player.

In 1942, Graves joined the Pierce Brothers. Later he played with Esco Hankins and Mac Wiseman before becoming a member of the Wheeling Jamboree with Wilma Lee and Stoney Cooper, where he remained through the mid-'50s. During a performance with the Coopers at the Grand Ole Opry, Graves made a big impression upon Lester Flatt and Earl Scruggs, who invited him to join their Foggy Mountain Boys. In the late '50s, acoustic instruments were out of favor, due to the popularity of rock 'n' roll; the survival of the dobro as an important instrument in country can largely be attributed to Graves, who electrified audiences with a red-hot picking style and then cooled them down with bluesy, sweet mellowness.

He remained a primary member of the Foggy Mountain Boys until the group disbanded in 1969. Afterward, he joined Flatt's Nashville Grass and did session work on the side. In 1971, he began playing with the Earl Scruggs Review; three years later, he went solo with the LP *Alone at Last*. He also continued session work, playing with artists like Charlie McCoy, J.J. Cale, Steve Young, and Kris Kristofferson, and collaborating with other musicians, such as on his 1975 duet album with Jake Tullock, *Just Joshing*. Graves continued in a similar vein through the 1980s and '90s, teaming with such greats as Kenny Baker, Eddie Adcock, and Jesse McReynolds in 1989 to form the Masters. —*Sandra Brennan*

Alone at Last / 1974 / Epic ✦✦✦✦

Sweet Sunny South / 1976 / CMH ✦✦✦

Same Old Blues / 1979 / CMH ✦✦✦

Josh Graves and Friends / 1979 / Cowboy Carl ✦✦

● **King of the Dobro** / 1982 / CMH ✦✦✦✦
This is the man who created bluegrass-style dobro with his bluesy hound-dog slide playing. —*Mark A. Humphrey*

The Puritan Sessions / Rebel ✦✦✦✦
Longtime fiddler Kenny Baker appears in an uncharacteristic role as a fingerstyle guitarist in a delightfully low-key set of tunes and songs with dobroist (and sometime-singer) Graves. —*Mark A. Humphrey*

Dad of the Dobro Man / CMH ✦✦✦

Billy Gray

b. Dec. 29, 1924, Paris, TX, d. Mar. 27, 1975
Guitar, Vocals / Western Swing
Singer-songwriter/guitarist Billy Gray only had one chart hit, but headed a popular Western swing band for years. He was born near Paris, TX, to a poor family. The 15-year-old Gray picked cotton to earn money for his first guitar, which he purchased from a pawn shop; the following year, he debuted on a local radio station. He organized his first band when he was 19 and had his own radio show in Paris in 1943, which was popular for the next three years. After teaming with ex-Louisiana Governor James E. Knoe to tour the state, he and his band also toured the Southwest before he settled in Dallas to spend two years leading Hank Thompson's Brazos Valley Boys. He and Thompson eventually founded the Texoma Music Publishing Company and the Brazos Valley Publishing Company, and the two co-wrote some of Thompson's greatest hits, including "Waiting in the Lobby of Your Heart," "The New Wears Off Too Fast" and "A Fool, a Faker."

In 1954, Gray had his lone hit, "You Can't Have My Love," a duet with Wanda Jackson. The following year, he and his band the Western Oakies released *Dance-O-Rama*, but had no hits. His large band eventually became too expensive to tour with, so he returned to Hank Thompson and the Brazos Valley Boys. Gray went on to work as a sideman for other bands, including the Nuggets and the Cowtowners, also appearing on the syndicated TV show *Music Country Style*. He recorded one more album in 1965 on Longhorn Records, but it produced no hits. Gray died in 1975 while undergoing heart surgery. —*Sandra Brennan*

Dance-O-Rama #7 / 1955 / Decca ✦✦✦

● **Billy Gray** / 1965 / Longhorn ✦✦✦✦

Mark Gray

b. 1952, Vicksburg, MS
Vocals / Country-Pop, Urban Cowboy
Over his career, singer-songwriter Mark Gray endured many ups and downs. He was born in Vicksburg, MS, the youngest of seven children. His mother died when he was two, and he was raised on Lookout Mountain, GA, by his aunt and uncle. It was there that he began singing gospel music and learned to play piano. He returned to his father's 250-acre Mississippi farm when he was 15 and later became a finalist on the *Ted Mack Amateur Hour*. He also began singing commercial jingles.

In 1972, Gray was selling spots for an R&B radio station while singing with the Revelations, a gospel group he founded, on weekends. The Revelations were performing in Meridian, MS, when they were spotted by the Oak Ridge Boys, who asked Gray to join their publishing company and appear on their tours. Gray moved to Nashville, but took a substantial cut in income and spent several impoverished years. He eventually left the Oaks to join another gospel group, the Downings. He became so popular that the group fired him, and he returned to Vicksburg, where he performed in Jackson nightclubs.

In 1979, his luck began to change and he was invited to join Exile. Gray honed his songwriting skills when not performing with the group, and two songs co-written with J.P. Pennington, "Take Me Down" (1982) and "The Closer You Get" (1983), became major hits for Alabama. Gray recorded two albums with Exile and remained with them until 1981, when he left to pursue a solo career and sell songs. After Janie Fricke recorded his "Losing Ain't Nothing Like Losing a Friend," he signed to Columbia Records. His first solo single, "If It Ain't Real (It Ain't You)," made it to the Top 30 in early 1983; his second effort, "Wounded Hearts," made it to the Top 20. In addition, performers such as Engelbert Humperdinck and Melissa Manchester continued to record his songs. In 1984, Gray scored four Top Ten hits, including "Diamond in the Dust," from his second album, *This Ol' Piano*. In 1985, he had two more Top Ten hits, but within a year his solo career had ground to a halt. Gray asked Columbia to release him from his contract, and continued to record for independent labels. —*Sandra Brennan*

Magic / Columbia ✦✦✦

● **That Feeling Inside** / Columbia ✦✦✦✦

This Ol' Piano / Columbia ✦✦✦

Grayson & Whitter

Old-Time, Traditional Country
G.B. Grayson and Henry Whitter sang together for only three years during the late '20s and early '30s, but they had a tremendous effect on country music; even contemporary performers continue to cover their songs, which include "Handsome Molly" (recorded by Bob Dylan and Mick Jagger), "Cluck Old Hen," "Tom Dooley," "Rose Conley" and "Lee Highway Blues (Going Down the Lee Highway)."

Fiddler/singer Gilliam Banmon Grayson was born in Ashe Country, NC. As a young man, he made his living as a minstrel, traveling through mountain towns playing at fairs and dances. He eventually settled near the Tennessee-Virginia border, where he played with such noted musicians as Clarence Tom Ashley and Doc Walsh. An excellent fiddler, Grayson was also an exceptional singer, and after teaming up with Whitter frequently sang lead vocals on their recordings.

Guitarist/singer Henry Whitter was born in Fries, VA; while not an exceptional musician or singer, he was devoted to promoting old-time music and was able to arrange many recording sessions. Whitter and Grayson met at a fiddlers' convention in Mountain City, TN, in 1927. They teamed up, and by autumn of that year, Whitter had gotten them two record deals. They recorded eight songs for the Gennet label and six for Victor, among them the classic "Handsome Molly," which sold over 50,000 copies. In total, the two recorded 40 songs in three years. Grayson was killed in an auto accident in August, 1930, while hitchhiking; Whitter was devastated, but continued performing and occasionally recording until his 1941 death from diabetes. —*Sandra Brennan*

Early Recordings 1928-1930 / Old Homestead ✦✦✦✦

● **Grayson and Whitter, Complete Works** / Old Homestead ✦✦✦✦

Great Plains

Country-Rock, Contemporary Country
The Eagles-influenced country-rock band Great Plains was formed in 1991. Its members included lead guitarist/pedal steel guitarist Russ Pahl, drummer/percussionist Michael Young, lead vocalist/acoustic guitarist Jack Sundrud, and bassist/vocalist Denny Dadmun-Bixby. Great Plains got their break through producer Brent Maher, who asked Young, also an expert in restoring

old cars, to work on one of his vintage models; while on the job, Young convinced Maher that Great Plains would be a valuable asset to his publishing company. In 1991, Great Plains released their self-titled debut album; their first chart hit was "A Picture of You," and their popularity was given a push when they began opening for Garth Brooks. In 1992, they had two mid-level hits, "Faster Gun" and "Iola." In 1993, Pahl and Young left the band to pursue their own interests. —*Sandra Brennan*

● **Great Plains** / Apr. 1991 / Columbia ✦✦✦✦
Great Plains' country-rock debut includes the hits "Iola" (a nod to the struggles of farmers) and the outlaw ode "Faster Gun." —*Jason Ankeny*

Lloyd Green

b. Oct. 4, 1937, Mobile, AL
Dobro, Guitar, Guitar (Steel), Session Musician / Country-Pop, Honky Tonk, Nashville Sound/Countrypolitan
Steel guitar and dobro player Lloyd Green was one of the busiest studio musicians in country music during the '60s and '70s. His work with such artists as Johnny Gimble and Charlie McCoy was particularly appreciated by British audiences and he was a popular musician at the annual Wembley Festival. Green made his professional debut at age ten, and as an adolescent, he played local clubs and bars on the weekends. In 1956, he decided to take a year off from college to try his hand in Nashville.

Once in Music City, he roomed with another great steel guitarist, Jimmy Day. Green got one of his first breaks on New Year's Day, 1957, when he was hired to play with Faron Young. He stayed with Young's band for 18 months and then left to be with his new wife in Mobile. During those months, he appeared on one George Jones side, "Too Much Water Runs under the Bridge" (1957). While in Mobile, Green played in numerous clubs and managed to save enough money to return to Nashville nine months later. He only occasionally received session work; after a month spent touring with Ferlin Husky, he swore never to tour again and gave up playing to become a shoe salesman. When the legendary Fred Rose's wife learned of his decison, she paid his musician's union dues, giving Green the chance to play with Carl and Pearl Butler and Curly Fox.

In 1964 he began working as a part-time assistant at the SESAC office for Roy Drusky. Although the pay was low, the job did give Green the opportunity to make demos and do session work. He remained with SESAC for three years, and soon was earning $50,000 a year from session work. Green worked with pop musicians as well, including Dame Vera Lynn, Paul McCartney, and Ringo Starr, as well as on the Byrds' seminal *Sweetheart of the Rodeo*. He had just a handful of solo chart hits, including instrumental versions of the pop tunes "I Can See Clearly Now" and "Here Comes the Sun" in the early '70s. He also made the charts singing "You and Me." During the 1980s, an ear infection forced him to stop working, but Green eventually returned to session work as a dobro player. —*Sandra Brennan*

Big Steel Guitar / 1964 / Time ✦✦✦✦

Day for Decision / 1966 / Little Darlin' ✦✦✦✦

Mr. Nashville Sound / 1968 / Chart ✦✦✦✦

● **Green Country** / 1969 / Little Darlin' ✦✦✦✦

Shades of Steel / 1973 / Monument ✦✦✦

Steel Rides / 1976 / Monument ✦✦✦

California Dreamin' / Flying Fish ✦✦✦

Jack Greene

b. Jan. 7, 1930, Maryville, TN
Guitar, Drums, Vocals / Traditional Country, Nashville Sound/Countrypolitan
Hailing from Maryville, TN, Greene got his start in the record business as a vocalist in Ernest Tubb's band, but he hardly had the same almost-on-key "twang" as his boss. In fact, Greene's smooth, pleasant sound contrasted a great deal with Tubb's blue-collar intonation. Nicknamed "the Jolly Green Giant," Greene learned guitar and drums but mined his vocal chords for a solid

string of hit records from 1966-1969, including one with Jeannie Seely, who joined his road show and recorded duets with him for several years.

A bit of trivia: In 1967, Greene became the first country artist ever to appear in the Macy's Thanksgiving Day Parade. —*Tom Roland*

● **Greatest Hits** / 1986 / Gusto ✦✦✦✦
This basically sums up his peak years and includes all the classics: "All the Time," "There Goes My Everything," and "Statue of a Fool." —*Tom Roland*

Richard Greene

b. 1945, Beverly Hills, CA
Fiddle, Session Musician / Traditional Bluegrass, Country-Rock, Country-Pop
A session fiddler with hundreds of credits—who has performed with dozens of bands—Richard Greene's most famous period was the 1960s, when he played with both Bill Monroe's Blue Grass Boys and Seatrain. He was born November 9, 1945, in Los Angeles, where he studied classical violin beginning at the age of five. By the time he entered high school, though, Greene switched his focus to folk music. He entered the University of California-Berkeley in 1960, and began playing in the Coast Mountain Ramblers and later the Dry City Scat Band. After college, Greene took a job in real estate, but also played with the Pine Valley Boys in San Francisco. On a trip to New York in 1964, he met Bill Keith of the Blue Grass Boys, and the association influenced Bill Monroe's decision to hire the youngster two years later. Greene played at the Grand Ole Opry with Monroe, and appeared on Monroe's Decca album *Bluegrass Time*.

After only one year with the Blue Grass Boys, Richard Greene joined the Jim Kweskin Jug Band—which also included Bill Keith plus Geoff and Maria Muldaur—and played on that band's 1968 album *Garden of Joy*. Not content to stay in one place, he split for California after one year and joined the Blues Project, which then evolved into Seatrain. Greene stayed for over three years, playing on the band's self-titled 1969 album for A&M, another self-titled LP for Capitol two years later, and 1972's *Marblehead Messenger*. He then formed the Blue Velvet Band with Eric Weissberg, Jim Rooney and his old friend Bill Keith, which recorded only one album, *Sweet Moments*. Greene spent the rest of the '70s playing with James Taylor, Emmylou Harris, Rod Stewart, Muleskinner, Taj Mahal, David Grisman, and Loggins & Messina, in addition to recording three albums as a solo act with his backing band, the Zone. The first two, *Duets* (1977) and *Ramblin'* (1979), appeared on Rounder, while 1980's *Blue Rondo* was released on the Sierra label. An early-'80s tour of Japan with Tony Trischka and Peter Rowan was documented on the Japanese Nippon label by *Bluegrass Album* and *Hiroshima Mon-Amour* (both 1980). —*John Bush*

Marblehead Messenger / 1971 / Capitol ✦✦✦

● **Muleskinner** / 1973 / Warner Brothers ✦✦✦✦

Duets / 1978 / Rounder ✦✦✦✦

Ramblin' / 1980 / Rounder ✦✦✦

Bluegrass Album / 1980 / Nippon Columbia [Japan] ✦✦✦

Somebody's Gonna Love You / 1983 / MCA ✦✦✦

Lee Greenwood

b. Oct. 17, 1942, Los Angeles, CA
Banjo, Bass, Guitar, Piano, Saxophone, Vocals / Country-Pop, Adult Contemporary, Urban Cowboy
Born with a good voice and a wide range, Lee Greenwood turned it into a unique voice accidentally, by over-working it in a less-than-healthy setting. Hailing from Sacramento, he used his musical training on the casino circuit, working in the green-felt jungles of Reno and Las Vegas, where he dealt cards by day and sang in dark lounges by night. The physical toll of two jobs, the vocal strain of performing six nights a week, and the damaging endeavor of singing in smoky nightclubs before the advent of smoking ordinances gave Greenwood a permanent hoarseness. He's used it to his advantage, becoming one of country music's

premier balladeers. Discovered by Mel Tillis' road manager, Larry McFaden, Greenwood paid for his own ticket to fly to Nashville and cut a few demos, and it took more than a year for that effort to pay off. When it finally did, Greenwood broke through in late 1981 with "It Turns Me Inside Out," in which his exaggerated vibrato brought frequent comparisons to Kenny Rogers. In short order, Greenwood disposed of the "Kenny clone" image, but he continued to mine romantic material for the bulk of his hits. Occasional exceptions include "Touch and Go Crazy" and "Mornin' Ride," but the biggest exception is also his signature song, the self-written "God Bless the USA," which earned Song of the Year honors from the Country Music Association.

Growing up on a Sacramento farm, Lee Greenwood was musical at a very early age, teaching himself how to play saxophone when he was nine years old. In his preadolescence, he played in a Western dance band called My Moondreams. At the age of 13, he moved with his recently remarried mother to Anaheim, CA, but three years later he returned to Sacramento to live with his grandparents. Between the two moves, he played in a variety of country and Dixieland bands. Upon his return to Sacramento, Greenwood joined Chester Smith's band, which raised his profile within California. Soon, Del Reeves hired Greenwood to play saxophone, and while he was with the singer, Greenwood learned how to become a showman. In 1962, he formed his own band, a pop combo named Apollo, and the group moved to Las Vegas. Within five years, the group was renamed the Lee Greenwood Affair, and relocated to Los Angeles, where they made a handful of records for Paramount. Once the record label went out of business, Greenwood was asked to join the fledgling Rascals by Felix Cavaliere and Dino Danelli, but he declined. Instead, he moved back to Las Vegas, where he worked as an arranger, backup vocalist, and a lounge pianist, as well as accompanying strippers by playing organ. By 1973, he became the lead singer and bassist in the *Bare Touch of Vegas* revue, while he continued to work as a blackjack dealer at the Tropicana. He held down both jobs for much of the mid-'70s.

By the end of the '70s, he was singing in lounges in Reno, which is where he met Larry McFaden, who was then leading Mel Tillis' touring band. Greenwood was initially reluctant to record, but he eventually traveled to Nashville, where he recorded a set of demos. Shortly afterward, McFaden became his manager and helped the singer sign a deal with MCA Records in June of 1981. Four months later, his first single, "It Turns Me Inside Out," climbed into the country Top 20. Greenwood's initial success was helped enormously by the similarity between his husky voice—toughened up by years of working in smoky casinos—and that of Kenny Rogers. In March of 1982, his second single "Ring on Her Finger, Time on Her Hands" climbed into the Top Ten, beginning a streak of 19 Top Ten singles that ran virtually uninterrupted for the next six years. During that time, he racked up no less than seven No. 1 hits: "Somebody's Gonna Love You" (1983), "Going, Going, Gone" (1984), "Dixie Road" (1985), "I Don't Mind the Thorns (If You're the Rose)" (1985), "Don't Underestimate My Love for You" (1986), "Hearts Aren't Made to Break (They're Made to Love)" (1986), and "Mornin' Ride" (1986). In addition to his solo hits, Lee had a number of hit duets with Barbara Mandrell, including the No. 3 hit "To Me" (1984). None of Greenwood's music was close to pure country—it was adult contemporary country-pop, in the vein of Kenny Rogers. Unlike Rogers, however, Greenwood rarely crossed over into the pop charts and when he did, it was only in 1983, when slickly produced country-pop could make inroads on adult contemporary radio. His popularity was at its peak during the mid-'80s, when his conservative music and neo-conservative lyrics managed to capture the imagination of the nation; though "God Bless the USA" only peaked at No. 7 on the country charts in 1984, it became a recurring theme song for several Republican political campaigns during the Reagan and Bush administrations. Furthermore, Greenwood won many popularity polls and awards from various country music magazines and associations.

Greenwood switched labels in 1990, signing to Capitol Records. His initial singles for the label, "Holdin' a Good Hand" and "We've Got It Made," were successful, but his audience steadily declined during the first half of the decade. Though he tried to retain his audience through patriotic work during the 1991 Gulf War—even earning the Congressional Medal of Honor Society's Patriot Award and a Points of Light Foundation Award—he couldn't successfully battle the onslaught of harder-edged, contemporary country artists that overtook country radio in the early '90s. By the middle of the decade, he was no longer charting singles, and he had begun re-recording his biggest hits for a variety of labels; he also continued to tour and give concerts. —*Tom Roland*

Inside Out / 1982 / MCA ✦✦✦✦
Inside Out features "It Turns Me Inside Out," the confessional hit that made Greenwood a star, as well as the Top Ten singles "Ring on Her Finger, Time on Her Hands," "She's Lying" and "Ain't No Trick (It Takes Magic)." —*Jason Ankeny*

If There's Any Justice / 1983 / MCA ✦✦✦✦

The Wind Beneath My Wings / 1984 / MCA ✦✦✦

Somebody's Gonna Love You / 1985 / MCA ✦✦✦
Greenwood's sophomore effort includes the back-to-back chart-toppers "Somebody's Gonna Love You" and "Going, Going, Gone." —*Jason Ankeny*

You've Got a Good Love Comin' / 1985 / MCA ✦✦✦

● **Greatest Hits** / 1985 / MCA ✦✦✦✦
The extent to which Greenwood relies on ballads is fully evident here, although his departures—"Dixie Road" and "Ain't No Trick"—are most memorable. "God Bless the USA" is the last track; if you're not inclined to ultra-patriotism, you can simply lift the needle or push "Stop." —*Tom Roland*

Greatest Hits, Vol. 2 / 1989 / MCA ✦✦✦

Holdin' a Good Hand / 1991 / Capitol ✦✦✦
Here you'll find performances of such songs as "Just like Me," "Enough Already," "The Moment You Were Mine," and others. —*AMG*

When You're in Love / 1991 / Capitol ✦✦✦
This album includes "Between a Rock and a Heartache," "If You'll Let This Fool Back In," and other hits. —*AMG*

American Patriot / 1992 / Liberty ✦✦✦
Contains such patriotic selections as "America the Beautiful," "The Pledge of Allegiance," and "The Battle Hymn of the Republic." —*AMG*

Super Hits / Mar. 19, 1996 / Epic ✦✦
Consumer advisory: In small print on the back of this record are the words: "All songs recorded 1994." This ten-track album contains Lee Greenwood's re-recordings of some of his biggest MCA Records hits of the 1980s, such as "Dixie Road" and "Hearts Aren't Made to Break (They're Made to Love)," along with several gospel tunes. —*William Ruhlmann*

God Bless the USA / MCA ✦✦✦
God Bless the USA is a budget-line collection that alternates between Lee Greenwood's slick country-pop hits and his inspirational works. Several of his biggest country hits—including the title track, "Ring on Her Finger, Time on Her Hands," "Dixie Road," "Somebody's Gonna Love You," and "Hearts Aren't Made to Break (They're Made to Love)"—are included on the collection, as well as recent recordings of standards like "Amazing Grace" and "O Holy Night." It's not a perfect collection, but Greenwood's biggest hits are present and accounted for and the album gives a good idea of his sound, making it a nice introduction for the budget-conscious. —*Rodney Batdorf*

Clinton Gregory

b. Mar. 1, 1966, Martinsville, VA
Fiddle, Vocals / Contemporary Country
Clinton Gregory was living proof that a musician need not be signed to a major record company to find success. He was born in Martinsville, VA, and came from a long line of fiddle players. He began playing at age three and made his performing debut at bluegrass festivals within a year. He went to Nashville at age 12, where his father was playing at the Grand Ole Opry after winning a fiddling contest. While there, young Gregory met stars like Marty Robbins, Roy Acuff, and Lester Flatt, who inspired him to

become a professional musician. Gregory returned to Nashville in 1987 to play fiddle with Suzy Bogguss' band. Eighteen months later, he joined the McCarters, a sister trio with whom he occasionally sang. His first single for independent label Step One, the title track of his 1990 debut album, *Music 'N Me*, went nowhere; however, the next single, "Couldn't Love Have Picked a Better Place to Die," made it to the Top 70. Gregory's second album produced his first Top 30 hit, "If It Weren't for Country Music (I'd Go Crazy)," and two other medium-level hits. His 1992 album *Freeborn Man* did even better and produced two Top 30 hits, including "Who Needs It." In 1994, Gregory left Step One and signed with Polydor Nashville after his 1993 singles did moderately well on the charts. A self-titled LP appeared in 1995. — *Sandra Brennan*

Music 'n Me / 1990 / Step One ♦♦♦
Gregory reveals his influences by tapping them for material, recording Merle Haggard's "I Can't Be Myself," Mel Street's "Loving on Backstreets," and Jimmie Davis' 1935 hit, "Nobody's Darlin." He also includes "Made for Loving You," later a hit for Doug Stone. — *Michael McCall*

● **I'd Go Crazy If It Weren't for Country Music** / 1991 / Step One ♦♦♦♦
His commercial breakthrough came with "If It Weren't for Country Music (I'd Go Crazy)." His confidence and vocal range shows growth, and the album features "One Shot at a Time," a memorable song about the devastation drinking can cause. — *Michael McCall*

Freeborn Man / Dec. 1991 / Step One ♦♦♦
Gregory kicks a bit harder, as displayed on the hit "Play Ruby Play," but he still leans more on honky tonk than country-rock. — *Michael McCall*

Clinton Gregory / 1995 / Polydor Nashville ♦♦♦

Grievous Angels

Progressive Bluegrass, Country-Folk
A Canadian band featuring Chuck Angus (guitar, vocals), Michelle Rumball (lead vocals, triangle), Peter Jellard (accordion, fiddle, saxophone, harmonica, vocals), Tim Hadley (string bass), and Peter Duffin (drums, vocals). They have a country-folk sound with songs that often deal with social injustices. — *Chip Renner*

One Job Town / Stony Plain ♦♦♦
Grievous Angels has a talent for blending honky tonk, rock 'n' roll, and contemporary folk, creating a unique sound that has the musical muscle of the purest country, but the narrative force of the finest folk character sketches. Occasionally, their ambitions get the best of them, resulting in wordy songs with weak melodies, but most of *One Job Town* is powerfully direct, with haunting vocals and stories as well as excellent musicianship. Most noteworthy are "The Ballad of Leonard and Cecile," "Crossing the Causeway" and "Death's Dark Stream." — *Thom Owens*

Rex Griffin

b. Aug. 12, 1912, Gasden, AL, **d.** Oct. 11, 1959
Vocals / Traditional Country, Honky Tonk
For many country fans, Rex Griffin is an unknown, yet there is no denying the significant role he played in the music's history. Griffin began his career in the '30s singing traditional music in the vein of Jimmie Rodgers, but his music quickly metamorphosed into a prototype for honky tonk, complete with rougher vocals and instrumentation. Although he never had any hits, Griffin was influential on a number of musicians in the '40s, most notably Hank Williams, who learned Emmett Miller's "Lovesick Blues" from Griffin. Furthermore, many of his songs—including "Just Call Me Lonesome," "The Last Letter" and "Everybody's Trying to Be My Baby"—became country and pop standards, and he was elected to the Nashville Songwriter's Hall of Fame.

Griffin began his career in the early '30s, making appearances at radio stations across the country, including Atlanta, Chicago, Memphis, Dallas, Nashville, and Birmingham, where he was given his nickname Rex. At the start of his career, he sounded remarkably similar to Jimmie Rodgers, and this is the sound on

Griffin's first recordings. Griffin signed to Decca in March of 1935 and over the next four years he recorded 38 songs for the label. None of the singles became major hits, but the songs themselves—"Over the River," "The Last Letter," "Everybody's Trying to Be My Baby"—grew to be standards. At the end of his stint at Decca, he recorded Emmett Miller's "Lovesick Blues." The song became a minor hit for Griffin, but it was more important in providing the basis for Hank Williams' 1949 version, which became his breakthrough hit single. Williams learned the song from Griffin, and then used the recorded version as the template for his own single.

During the '40s, Griffin retired from recording, concentrating on radio performances. He remained close friends with Ernest Tubb throughout the decade, yet he couldn't use his connections to restart his recording career. Furthermore, his health was declining rapidly, as he suffered from both diabetes and alcoholism. Griffin finally succumbed to his illnesses on October 11, 1959. After his death, he was inducted into the Nashville Songwriter's Hall of Fame, and his songs continued to be performed and recorded by several generations of country musicians. — *Stephen Thomas Erlewine*

Last Letter / 1996 / Bear Family ♦♦♦♦
Rex Griffin is one of the great unsung heroes of country music. Griffin began recording in the '30s and was instrumental in country's transition from the old-time, traditional music of Jimmy Rodgers to the honky tonk of the '40s, even though he never had a major hit. Despite his lack of commercial success, he left behind a legacy of songs and recordings that proved enormously influential, especially on Hank Williams, who learned Emmett Miller's "Lovesick Blues" from Griffin. Griffin's own version of "Lovesick Blues," as well as his original versions of country classics like "Just Call Me Lonesome," "The Last Letter," "Everybody's Trying to Be My Baby," and "Over the River," are included on *The Last Letter*, a three-disc box set that compiles every song he ever recorded. Over the course of the set, every one of Griffin's classic Decca recordings are showcased, as well as his latter-day sessions for King and his radio transcriptions for World, plus a handful of tracks by his brother Buddy. Though *The Last Letter* is a little too scholarly in its approach to make for easy listening, it is nevertheless an important historical document, and any serious country fan needs to hear the recordings and songs of Rex Griffin. — *Thom Owens*

Nanci Griffith

b. Jul. 6, 1953, Austin, TX
Guitar, Vocals / Progressive Country, Singer-Songwriter, Country-Folk
Riding the fine line between folk and country music, Nanci Griffith has become as well-known for her brilliant confessional songwriting as her beautiful voice. A self-styled "folkabilly" singer, Griffith started out as a kindergarten teacher and occasional folksinger. The country scene took her to heart in the mid-'80s, and she gained a reputation as a quality songwriter through hit covers of Griffith's songs by Kathy Mattea and Suzy Bogguss. Finding no luck with commercial country radio however, Nanci Griffith recorded several pop-oriented albums and had returned to her folk roots by the mid-'90s.

Griffith was the daughter of musical parents, and she spent her childhood involved with theater and literature as well as music. She began playing clubs around Austin at the tender age of 14, and continued to perform during her college years at the University of Texas as well as teaching kindergarten in the mid-'70s. Griffith finally decided to make music her full-time ambition in 1977.

Her songwriting won an award at the Kerrville Folk Festival, prompting the local label BF Deal to record Griffith for a compilation and later for her debut album, *There's a Light Beyond These Woods* (1978). Griffith's hectic touring schedule took her all over North America, playing festivals and TV shows in addition to the small clubs in which she had begun. Meanwhile, she recorded albums in 1982 (*Poet in My Window*) and 1985 (*Once in a Very Blue Moon*).

Finally, in 1986, Nanci Griffith got her big break after moving to Nashville. The title song from *Once in a Very Blue Moon* placed modestly on the country charts, she released the acclaimed *Last of the True Believers* on Philo (the label that later reissued her first three albums), and—most importantly—Kathy Mattea's cover of "Love at the Five & Dime" reached No. 3 on the country charts. Though *Last of the True Believers* was nominated for a Grammy as Best Contemporary Folk Recording, perhaps because of that fact, commercial country radio still found it difficult to accept Griffith. She signed with MCA, and abandoned Nashville to begin recording in Los Angeles.

Nanci Griffith's major-label debut, *Lone Star State of Mind,* popularized the Julie Gold song "From a Distance"—later covered by Bette Midler—but also gave Griffith her first country Top 40 hit, the title song. Two other singles from the album, "Trouble in the Fields" and "Cold Hearts/Closed Minds," also grazed the country charts. *Little Love Affairs* and the live album *One Fair Summer Evening* (both 1988) were slight disappointments, though "I Knew Love" became Griffith's second country Top 40 hit. MCA paired her with noted rock producer Glyn Johns for 1989's *Storms;* the album included guest stars Phil Everly, Albert Lee, and former Eagle Bernie Leadon, and became her best-seller, though it featured no successful singles. A move from rock to pop—helped by producers Rod Argent and Peter Van Hook—characterized *Late Night Grande Hotel* (1991); it was clear by then that Griffith's move away from Nashville was also compromising her folk and country roots.

A move to Elektra in 1992 marked a return to form for Griffith; her 1993 LP *Other Voices, Other Rooms* was a tribute to her influences, and several of them—including Emmylou Harris, Chet Atkins, and John Prine—made appearances. A compilation release of her best from the MCA years also appeared in 1993. The following year, Griffith's tenth studio album, *Flyer,* continued her dedication to folk. —*John Bush*

There's a Light Beyond These Woods / 1978 / Philo ✦✦
There's a Light Beyond These Woods is an uneven, but promising, debut album from Nanci Griffith, highlighted by the moving title track, which is a tribute to her childhood best friend. —*Thom Owens*

Poet in My Window / 1982 / Philo ✦✦
On her second album, Nanci Griffith begins to delve deeper into country music, as far as the music is concerned. Lyrically, she retains the folky narrative eye for detail that she demonstrated on her debut, yet songs like "Heart of a Miner" and "Julie Anne" also prove that her talent has begun to deepen. Even with a handful of highlights, the album remains somewhat uneven, and is primarily of interest to dedicated Griffith fans. —*Thom Owens*

Once in a Very Blue Moon / 1985 / Philo ✦✦✦✦
After two promising albums, Nanci Griffith finally perfected her mixture of singer-songwriter folk and Texas-based country on this lovely collection, which features her own story-songs such as "Mary & Omie" and well-chosen covers such as the Pat Alger/Eugene Levine title tune. —*William Ruhlmann*

★ **The Last of the True Believers** / 1986 / Philo ✦✦✦✦✦
Griffith hit her peak as a songwriter here with classics such as "Love at the Five & Dime" and "Banks of the Pontchartrain," while singing over an always-appropriate backup provided by the '80s new bluegrass specialists Bela Fleck, Mark O'Connor, and others. The album earned her a major-label contract with MCA and provided the basis of country singer Kathy Mattea's entire career, but it is also a pivotal '80s folk album. —*William Ruhlmann*

Lone Star State of Mind / 1987 / MCA ✦✦✦
Lone Star State of Mind was Nanci Griffith's commercial breakthrough, largely because it was her first step directly toward mainstream contemporary country. Instead of diluting her introspective folk songs, the full-fledged production actually enhances her music, as the steel guitars and dobros add body to her songs. Griffith responds in kind, delivering the most textured and nuanced vocal performance of her career, as evidenced by her version of "From a Distance." Of course, her songwriting is as good as it ever was; "Ford Econoline," "Sing One for Sister," "Bea-

con Street," and a revamped version of "Mary Margaret" called "There's a Light Beyond These Woods" are all terrific, ranking among her best songs. *Lone Star State of Mind* is one of the rare commercial moves that actually improves an artist's music instead of compromising it. —*Thom Owens*

One Fair Summer Evening / 1988 / MCA ✦✦✦
Recorded in Houston, *One Fair Summer Evening* captures a live 1988 performance of Nanci Griffith, as she runs through solo arrangements of several of her best songs, including "Love at the Five & Dime" and "From a Distance." Griffith's performance is subtle and her voice is frequently beautiful, making it a worth-while momento for dedicated fans. —*Stephen Thomas Erlewine*

Little Love Affairs / 1988 / MCA ✦✦✦✦
All of Griffith's albums have songs to recommend them; of her country-folk albums, this one has the most written by her, as well as good tunes by Harlan Howard and fellow Texan Robert Earl Keen, Jr. The first half's prime Griffith, and the second suggests that, if she'd stuck with country, she might have started outselling her press—Suzy Bogguss later turned "Outbound Plane" into a hit, and there's probably at least one more hit tucked away here. —*Brian Mansfield*

Storms / 1989 / MCA ✦✦✦
Though it suffers somewhat from inconsistent material, *Storms* is a gorgeous collection of ballads and gentle observational country-rockers, highlighted by "It's a Hard Life Wherever You Go" and "Drive-In Movies and Dashboard Lights." —*Thom Owen*

Late Night Grande Hotel / 1991 / MCA ✦✦✦
Two albums out of Nashville and Griffith no longer fits in the new-country/folkie role in which she was once cast. Britishers Rod Argent and Peter Van Hooke insulate Griffith with strings and moody atmospheres that complement her wallflower fantasies. She's likely partial to "Power Lines" and "Down 'n' Outer," both tales of folks who fall through society's cracks. Probably, come to think of it, because she identifies with them. —*Brian Mansfield*

Other Voices, Other Rooms / 1993 / Elektra ✦✦✦✦
Griffith pays homage to a wide cut of folk music heroes, from Woody Guthrie to Townes Van Zandt, from Bob Dylan to Kate Wolf, from Malvina Reynolds to John Prine. She sounds looser and more spirited than usual, and her earnest adoration for the songs shines through in these compelling remakes. —*Michael McCall*

● **The MCA Years: A Retrospective** / 1993 / MCA ✦✦✦✦

Flyer / 1994 / Elektra ✦✦✦

David Grisman

b. 1945, Hackensack, NJ
Mandolin / Progressive Bluegrass, Swing
One of the finest mandolin players in bluegrass history, David Grisman was credited with creating the "new acoustic" sound, a hybrid of jazz, folk, and bluegrass that he dubbed "dawg music."

Grisman was born and raised in Hackensack, NJ. By the time he was a teen, he could play a variety of instruments, including the mandolin, the piano, and the saxophone. He later attended New York University and began playing in different folk groups, among them the Even Dozen Jug Band. Grisman graduated in the mid-'60s and moved to San Francisco, where he began moving away from his bluegrass roots toward rock 'n' roll, joining Peter Rowan's Earth Opera in time for their 1968 debut album. The group disbanded by the end of the year and Grisman became a session player and sideman until 1973, when he joined Rowan and Jerry Garcia in Old & In the Way along with fiddler Vassar Clements and bassist John Kahn. Grisman and Rowan also belonged to Muleskinner, a bluegrass band, in 1973.

In 1974, Grisman founded the Great American Music Band, featuring Richard Greene and bassist Taj Mahal. He recorded his first solo effort, *The David Grisman Rounder Album,* in 1976 and shortly afterward founded the David Grisman Quintet. The group recorded a self-titled album in 1976 and then came out with *Hot Dawg* in 1979. The Quintet frequently appeared at jazz clubs and also opened for several major rock bands, and even backed

Stephane Grappelli when he toured America. A revamped lineup of Grisman, guitarist/fiddler Mark O'Connor, bassist Rob Wasserman, violin and string player Darol Anger, and mandolinist Mike Marshall released *Quintet '80.*

In 1982, Grisman, Herb Pedersen and Jim Buchanan teamed to create "supergrass," a new kind of bluegrass music which can be heard on their album *Here Today.* Afterward the trio broke up. When not playing with his own group, Grisman appeared with the likes of Judy Collins, John Sebastian, James Taylor, Dolly Parton, Bela Fleck, and Alison Brown. In 1983 he released *Dawg Jazz/Dawg Grass,* and followed it up with a holiday album, *Acoustic Christmas.* In 1985, he began recording for Zebra Acoustic, debuting with the album *Acousticity.* Among his other endeavors were 1987's *Svingin' with Svend* (with Svend Asmussen), *Dawg '90,* and *Garcia/Grisman* (1991). In 1992, he appeared with Herb Pedersen, Jim Buchanan, Jim Kerwin, Red Allen, and Garcia on the album *Bluegrass Reunion.* In 1996, he appeared with the reunited Old & In the Way and released his own *DGQ-20.* *—Sandra Brennan*

★ **The David Grisman Quintet** / 1977 / Rhino ✦✦✦✦✦
This is a creative and adventurous session by this jazz/bluegrass group. *—Hank Davis*

Hot Dawg / 1979 / A&M ✦✦✦✦
With Stephane Grappelli and a Django-esque sound. *—Hank Davis*

Early Dawg / 1980 / Sugar Hill ✦✦✦
Bluegrass meets jazz. *—Hank Davis*

Quintet: '80 / 1980 / Warner Brothers ✦✦
Although not a jazz musician, David Grisman's "Dawg" music reflects his awareness of and respect for that tradition. An accomplished acoustic guitarist, mandolin player, composer, and bandleader, Grisman created a fresh, vital sound that had jazz, folk, rock, country, and blues elements. This album was one in an extensive string that attracted diverse audiences and critical attention. *—Ron Wynn*

Mondo Mando / Jul. 7, 1981-Jul. 16, 1981 / Zebra ✦✦✦✦
An '81 date that finds Grisman's "dawg music" synthesis at its peak. This has acoustic bluegrass compositions, but the band members venture into other areas as well. They play with improvisational elan, yet also have a loose, relaxed country/folk attitude. *—Ron Wynn*

Here Today / 1982 / Rounder ✦✦

Dawg Grass / Dawg Jazz / 1983 / Warner Brothers ✦✦✦✦

Mandolin Abstractions / 1983 / Rounder ✦✦✦
Modern mandolin playing in a variety of acoustic settings, this album is hot and driving at times, but also melodic and haunting, and occasionally abstract and eerie. This is challenging yet pleasant music with guest Andy Statman. *—Hank Davis*

Acousticity / 1985 / Zebra ✦✦

Home Is Where the Heart Is / 1988 / Rounder ✦✦✦
A more traditional country and bluegrass album than his "dawg" sessions, Rounder issued this Grisman session in 1988. He's playing with J.D. Crowe, Ricky Skaggs, and Doc Watson, among others. There's little jazz here, but there are some superb bluegrass, country, and folk selections, plus marvelous playing. *—Ron Wynn*

Svingin' with Svend / 1987 / Zebra ✦✦
Included is the David Grisman Quintet featuring Svend Asmussen. *—AMG*

Dawg '90 / 1990 / Acoustic Disc ✦✦✦✦

Dawgwood / 1993 / Acoustic Disc ✦✦✦

David Grisman Rounder Album / 1993 / Rounder ✦✦✦

Tone Poems / 1994 / Acoustic Disc ✦✦✦

Dawganova / 1995 / Acoustic Disc ✦✦✦
On *Dawganova,* Grisman and his quintet add Latin and bossa nova rhythms and melodies to their distinctive blend of bluegrass, folk, and jazz; the results are energetic, and generally quite successful. *—Stephen Thomas Erlewine*

Tone Poems 2 / Oct. 31, 1995 / Acoustic Disc ✦✦✦
Tone Poems-2 is one of David Grisman's jazziest efforts, falling between the boundaries of progressive bluegrass and the ethereal qualities of new age. Grisman and his collaborator, jazz guitarist Martin Taylor, perform on no less than 41 different vintage acoustic instruments, giving the music both a timeless and modern quality; the acoustics root the music in tradition, but the music floats in a jazzy, new age territory, combining a number of different genres and textures. For fans of Grisman's dawg music, it isn't particularly satisfying, yet for those fans who like to hear him stretch the boundaries of his talents, it's a worthwhile listen. *—Thom Owens*

DGQ-20 / Jul. 1996 / AD ✦✦✦
On *DGQ-20,* David Grisman celebrates the 20th anniversary of his Quintet with a record that reiterates why their music has been so important and influential. But *DGQ-20* isn't merely nostalgia-mongering. It illustrates the reason why Grisman has remained at the top of the new acoustic game: he is willing to change with the times, creating new hybrids without abandoning faith in the sweet purity of traditional bluegrass. So, while *DGQ-20* demonstrates exactly how much he has accomplished, the performances also suggest that he has a lot left to do. *—Thom Owens*

Hardrock Gunter

b. Feb. 27, 1925, Birmingham, AL
Vocals / Rock & Roll, Rockabilly, Country Boogie
Hardrock Gunter was a key figure in the development of rockabilly, and is best remembered as the composer of standards like "Baby Let's Play House," "Birmingham Bounce," and "Jukebox Help Me Find My Baby."

He was born Sidney Louis Gunter, Jr., in Birmingham, AL, and earned his nickname "Hardrock" when a car hood fell on his head and left him without a scratch. As a youth, Gunter was influenced by Hank Penny, and had his first band, the Hoot Owl Ramblers, as a teen. Later he joined Happy Wilson's popular Golden River Boys, and in time came to manage the band. In 1949, Gunter began appearing on a local television show, and later in the year made his recording debut. One of his earliest hits was "Dad Gave My Hog Away," a spoof of the T. Texas Tyler story *Dad Gave My Dog Away.* He also recorded "Birmingham Bounce," but it didn't become a major hit until Red Foley recorded it for Decca, with which Gunter signed in 1951 and began singing boogie-style country. That year he and Roberta Lee teamed to become one of the first country acts to record an R&B hit, "Sixty Minute Man."

After serving in the Army, Gunter returned to record on Sun and MGM, but had no chart success on either label. During the early '50s, he spent time as a deejay at WJLD Birmingham and at WWVA Wheeling, WV on the *Wheeling Jamboree.* In 1955, he recorded his own version of "Jukebox Help Me Find My Baby;" it seemed to have all the makings of a hit, but Sam Phillips leased it for Sun and re-edited it, and the song went nowhere. Gunter continued recording on different labels through 1964 without success. He soon quit music to run his own insurance agency. *—Sandra Brennan*

Boogie Woogie on a Saturday Night / 1984 / Charly ✦✦✦✦

Jack Guthrie

b. Nov. 13, 1915, Olive, OK, d. Jan. 15, 1948
Vocals / Traditional Country
During the late '40s, singer-songwriter Jack Guthrie was briefly among the most influential and popular singers in country music. He was born Leon Jerry Guthrie in Olive, OK, the son of a blacksmith. His father was a fiddler, and legend has it that Guthrie learned a few guitar chords from Gene Autry. His family moved to Sacramento, CA during the Dust Bowl era, where young Guthrie rode in rodeos and worked in the forests for the WPA. In 1934, he married and with his wife formed an act where he would use his bullwhip to snap lit cigarettes out of her mouth. Later in the decade, he and his cousin Woody Guthrie, who had just moved out from Oklahoma, formed a duet and began starring on *The Oklahoman and Woody Show* on station KFVD Hollywood in 1937. However, Jack had children to feed, so he soon quit to

become a construction worker. Meanwhile, Woody had written a song for Jack before he moved to New York; Jack added "Oklahoma Hills" to his act and it became quite popular.

He cut a demo in 1944 and signed to Capitol; with a pickup band, he recorded Woody's song and "When the Cactus Is in Bloom." Guthrie was drafted before the single was released, and was stationed at Iwo Jima when he learned that his single had been at the top of the country charts for over six weeks. Later he was stationed in Tacoma, Washington in 1946 and began playing with Buck Ritchey and his K-6 Wranglers. He also continued recording and had another major hit in 1947 with "Oakie Boogie." However, Guthrie began feeling poorly, and a check-up revealed that he had tuberculosis, resulting in his discharge from the service. He did make one appearance in a film, 1947's *Hollywood Barn Dance*, but soon after, weighing only 95 pounds, he checked into a veterans hospital with little hope of recovery.

Despite his illness, Guthrie managed to record a total of 33 songs and many radio transcriptions. He cut his final record in the summer of 1947 and was so sick that he had to be driven to the session in an ambulance. He died on January 15 of the following year. Guthrie's music lived on in the hands of Woody's son Arlo, who recorded many of his uncle's best songs. —*Sandra Brennan*

Jack Guthrie's Greatest Songs / 1966 / Capitol ✦✦✦✦

● **Oklahoma Hills** / Bear Family ✦✦✦✦
Oklahoma Hills contains all 29 recordings that Jack Guthrie made between 1944 and 1947 for Capitol Records, including his signature songs "Oakie Boogie" and "Oklahoma Hills." —*Stephen Thomas Erlewine*

Woody Guthrie
....

b. Jul. 14, 1912, Okemah, OK, **d.** Oct. 3, 1967, Queens, New York City, NY
Harmonica, Vocals / Traditional Folk
Woody Guthrie was the most important American folk music artist of the first half of the 20th century. Coming out of Oklahoma, Guthrie had firsthand knowledge of the dustbowl diaspora chronicled in John Steinbeck's novel, *The Grapes of Wrath.* In fact, Guthrie wrote his own version of the story in a song called "Tom Joad." By the time he gained recognition in the '40s, Guthrie had written hundreds of songs, many of which remain folk standards to this day. When he was interviewed by Alan Lomax for the Library of Congress in March 1940, Guthrie punctuated his reminiscences by singing "So Long, It's Been Good to Know You," "Dust Bowl Blues," "Do-Re-Mi," "Pretty Boy Floyd," "I Ain't Got No Home," and other songs. He later wrote "Pastures of Plenty," "The Grand Coulee Dam," and his masterpiece, "This Land Is Your Land." He was also an author (*Bound for Glory*) and a newspaper columnist.

Guthrie made some recordings for RCA in 1940, but much of his work was issued on the small Folkways label. Meanwhile, in the late '40s and early '50s, versions of his songs became hits for such artists as the Weavers. By then, Guthrie himself was in physical decline, suffering from Huntington's chorea, a hereditary neurological disorder. But during his long illness, Guthrie's influence spread to the next generation, fostering the folk boom of the late '50s and early '60s. Not only is Bob Dylan unimaginable without him, but large segments of popular music are permanently affected by Guthrie's concerns as a songwriter and his approach to the form. Guthrie also composed a body of children's music toward the end of his performing career in the early '50s, when he was raising a family with his wife Marjorie. The songs, many sung from a child's point of view, have been covered and performed extensively since. —*William Ruhlmann*

Sings Folk Songs / 1962 / Smithsonian/Folkways ✦✦✦✦
Guthrie sings traditional material here, with Leadbelly and others. —*William Ruhlmann*

☆ **Library of Congress Recordings, Vols. 1-3** / 1964 / Rounder ✦✦✦✦✦
A multi-disc set of songs and conversations from 1940. —*William Ruhlmann*

★ **Dust Bowl Ballads** / 1964 / Rounder ✦✦✦✦✦
Woody Guthrie's powerful, evocative, insightful narratives about the life and trials of Southwestern migrant workers battling the Dust Bowl were initially issued on two six-song albums in 1940. Later, the entire 14-song session was released on a 1964 album. This LP was reissued on CD in 1988. It includes some of Guthrie's finest, most memorable prose, coupled with poignant vocals and sparse, effective harmonica accompaniment. The resiliency, spirit, and memories of both his early life and people he'd known are presented on such cuts as "I Ain't Got No Home," "Dust Pneumonia Blues" and "Dust Bowl Blues." Guthrie was a master storyteller, and his semi-autobiographical accounts remain among American music's most striking some 54 years after their original issue. —*Ron Wynn*

☆ **This Land Is Your Land** / 1967 / Smithsonian/Folkways ✦✦✦✦✦
The title track and some of the Columbia River songs. —*William Ruhlmann*

★ **The Greatest Songs of Woody Guthrie** / 1972 / Vanguard ✦✦✦✦✦

Struggle / 1976 / Smithsonian/Folkways ✦✦✦✦
This album features Woody Guthrie, Cisco Houston, and Pete Seeger playing political songs including "The Dying Miner," "Ludlow Massacre," and "Union Burying Ground." It's an energetic album. —*Richard Meyer*

Columbia River Collection / 1988 / Rounder ✦✦✦
An intelligent reconstruction of Guthrie's Columbia River songs, including "Grand Coulee Dam" and "Pastures of Plenty." —*William Ruhlmann*

H

Hackberry Ramblers

Cajun, String Band

The most important Cajun band of the 1930s, the Hackberry Ramblers—also known as the Riverside Ramblers—were formed in 1933 by fiddler Luderin Darbone (b. Jan. 14, 1913, Evangeline, LA). Darbone spent much of his early life in Texas, listening to—and becoming influenced by—Western swing as well as Cajun music. He studied at a business college in the early '30s, but formed the Hackberry Ramblers soon after and found work at KFDM-Lake Charles, LA.

The Ramblers soon became the best-known band around the area, and they began recording for RCA Bluebird in 1935 with a lineup including Darbone, vocalist Lennis Sonnier, guitarists Glen Croker, Lonnie Rainwater, Floyd Shreve and Joe Werner, bassist Johnnie Parket, and occasional accordion player Edwin Duhon. The initial sides were recorded in French, but a partnership with Montgomery Ward to perform on KVOL-Lafayette prompted the Ramblers to record in English as the Riverside Ramblers—after Ward's brand of tires. Joe Werner provided most of the English vocals, and 1936's "Wondering" became a modest hit, sparking his brief solo contract with Decca.

The band broke up early in the World War II years, but reformed in 1946, recording for Deluxe and establishing a Saturday-night residency at a Lake Charles club that lasted ten years. The part-time band recorded an album for Arhoolie in 1963 and a few titles for Old Gold, and is still together, playing the occasional festival or event. In 1988, the Old Timey label released the best of the Bluebird and Deluxe material as *Early Recordings 1935-1948.* —*John Bush*

Jolie Blonde / 1963 / Arhoolie ✦✦✦✦

Early Recordings: 1935-1948 / 1988 / Old Timey ✦✦✦✦

The Hackberry Ramblers were arguably the most influential Cajun string band from Louisana, creating a raw fusion of Western swing, old timey string bands, and Cajun. The Ramblers never used accordions—they were a pure string band, creating a distinctly New Orleans brand of country music. *Early Recordings, 1935-1948* collects highlights from the group's Bluebird and Deluxe material and offers a perfect distillation of why the Ramblers were important. —*Thom Owens*

● **Cajun Boogie** / Jun. 1992 / Flying Fish ✦✦✦✦

As they sing on the theme song that opens this CD, the Hackberry Ramblers "play you some music and try to make you smile" with their infectious brand of hoedown music. By and large the Hackberry, LA, band succeeds on this album, which features original members Glen Croker (guitar) and Luderin Darbone (fiddle). Since 1933, they've been blending Cajun, country, and Western swing music with touches of blues and pop. Croker and Darbone are now in their eighties, but haven't lost their manic energy and taste for get-down party sounds. Besides presenting several of their own compositions, they cover tunes by Bob Wills, Ray Price, and Howlin' Wolf. This CD features guest fiddle by zydeco star Michael Doucet on four tracks, as well as a guest vocal by country star Rodney Crowell on "Old Pipeliner." —*Richie Unterberger*

Hagers

Country-Pop, Country Humor

The Hagers were the only identical twins to make it big in country music, and were best known for their work on the television series *Hee Haw* as singers, musicians, and cornball comics. Jon and Jim were adopted by Rev. John Hager and his wife Fran as infants. The boys learned to love music from their parents; in high school, they often performed locally and appeared on a Saturday morning music TV show for teens. They went to college and served a stint in the Army, where they were sent to Vietnam to perform in USO tours and in officer and NCO clubs. They later returned to their hometown of Park Ridge, IL, and performed in Chicago lounges for 18 months.

The Hagers then went to California, where they were discovered by New Christy Minstrel Randy Sparks and hired to appear at his Los Angeles club, Ledbetters. During a stint at Disneyland they were seen by Buck Owens, who took over their management and put them in his All-American Show for the next two years. In 1969, they released their first single, "Gotta Get to Oklahoma ('Cause California's Gettin' to Me)." The next year, they released their debut album and joined *Hee Haw;* they were originally contracted to perform two songs, but remained with the program for 18 years. During 1970, they had three minor hits, including "Silver Wings"; their last chart entry was "I'm Miles Away" (1971). When not in the studio or on *Hee Haw* the brothers appeared frequently as actors; in 1976, they appeared in the TV-movie *Twin Detectives* starring Lillian Gish. They also made many commercials and hosted *Country Kitchen* with Florence Henderson on TNN in 1987. During the mid-'70s, the Hagers tried their hand at stand-up country comedy. They left *Hee Haw* in 1987 and prepared a sitcom/variety show, *Doubles,* but it never got off the ground. In 1990, the brothers made their first video for the single "I'm Wishin' I Could Go Fishin' Forever." —*Sandra Brennan*

● **The Hagers** / 1970 / Capitol ✦✦✦✦

Two Hagers Are Better Than One / 1970 / Capitol ✦✦✦

Motherhood, Apple Pie and the Flag / 1971 / Capitol ✦✦✦

Countryside / 1972 / Barnaby ✦✦✦

The Hagers / 1974 / Elektra ✦✦✦

Merle Haggard

b. Apr. 6, 1937, Bakersfield, CA
Fiddle, Guitar, Vocals / Traditional Country, Bakersfield Sound, Western Swing Revival

As a performer and a songwriter, Merle Haggard was the most important country artist to emerge in the 1960s. Haggard became one of the leading figures of the Bakersfield country scene in the '60s. While his music remained hardcore country, he pushed the boundaries of the music quite far. Like his idol Bob Wills, his music was a melting pot that drew from all forms of traditional American music—country, jazz, blues, and folk—and in the process, developed a distinctive style of its own. As a performer, singer, and musician, Haggard was one of the best, influencing countless other artists. Not coincidentally, he was the best singer-songwriter in country music since Hank Williams, writing a body of songs that became classics. Throughout his career, Haggard has been a champion of the working man, largely due to his rough and tumble history.

It's impossible to separate Haggard's music from his life. Haggard was born to James and Flossie Haggard on April 6, 1937. His parents moved from Oklahoma to California during the Great Depression, converting an old boxcar into a home. Before their marriage, James played fiddle in local honky tonk bars. Flossie was a member of The Church of Christ, which led to her forcing her husband to stop playing the honky tonks. James died from a brain tumor when Merle was nine years old. After his father's death, Merle became rebellious. In an attempt to straighten her son out, his mother put him in several juvenile detention centers, but it had little effect on Merle's behavior. As a teenager, he fell in love with country music, particularly Bob Wills, Lefty Frizzell, and Hank Williams. When he was 12 years old, Haggard was given his first guitar by his older brother; he taught himself how to play by listening to records that were lying around the house.

Even though he had begun to pursue music, Haggard continued to rebel, running away with his friend Bob Teague to Texas when he was 14 years old. A few months later, the pair returned to California, where they were arrested as robbery suspects. After the real thieves were caught, Haggard was sent back to juvenile hall, but he and Teague took off to Modesto, CA. For a brief time, he did manual labor, was a short order cook, drove a truck, and committed a series of small crimes. Soon after he moved to Modesto, Haggard made his performing debut with Teague at a bar named the Fun Center; the two were paid five dollars and given all the beer that they could drink.

By the end of 1951, Haggard had returned home and he was again arrested for truancy, as well as petty larceny. In the beginning of 1952, he was sent to Fred C. Nelles School for Boys in Whittier, CA; again, he ran away. This time, the courts decided he was incorrigible and sent him to the high-security Preston School of Industry; he was released after 15 months. Shortly after his release, he and a boy he met at PSI beat up a local boy during an attempted robbery, and Haggard was sent back to PSI.

After getting out of PSI for the second time, Merle Haggard had the first major event in his musical career. Haggard went with Teague to see Lefty Frizzell in concert in Bakersfield. Before the show, he went backstage with several friends and he sang a couple songs for Frizzell. Lefty was so impressed he refused to go on stage until Haggard was allowed to sing a song. Merle went out and sang a few songs to an enthusiastic response from the audience.

The reception persuaded Haggard to actively pursue a musical career. Working during the day in oilfields and farms, he performed in local Bakersfield clubs at night. His performances led to a spot on a local television show, *Chuck Wagon*. In 1956, he married Leona Hobbs; the couple moved into his family's old converted boxcar. Throughout 1957, Haggard was plagued by financial problems, which made him turn to robbery. At the end of the year, he attempted to rob a restaurant along with two other burglars; the three were drunk at the time. Believing it was 3 o'clock in the morning, the trio tried to open up the back door of the restaurant. However, it was 10:30 and the establishment was open. Although the trio fled the scene, Haggard was arrested that day. The following day, he escaped from prison in order to make peace with his wife and family; later that day, he was recaptured. Haggard was sentenced to a 15-year term and sent to San Quentin prison.

Prison didn't immediately rehabilitate Haggard. He was fired from a series of prison jobs and planned an escape from the jail, but was talked out of it by fellow inmates. Nearly two years into his sentence, Haggard discovered that his wife was pregnant with another man's child. The news sent Haggard over the edge. Soon, he and his cellmate began running a gambling racket and brewing beer in their cell. Before long, Haggard was caught drunk and was placed in isolation for a week. During his time in isolation, he had several conversations with Caryl Chessman, an author and a member of death row. The conversations and the time in isolation convinced Haggard to turn his life around. After he left isolation, he began working in the prison's textile plant and took some

high school equivalency courses; he was also allowed to play in the prison's country band. At his second parole hearing in 1960, Haggard was given a five-year sentence—two years and nine months in jail, two years and three months on parole; he left prison 90 days later.

Merle moved back in with Leona and returned to manual labor. In the meantime, he sang at local clubs at night. After taking second place at a local talent contest, Haggard was asked to become a relief singer for a band led by Johnny Barnett at one of the most popular Bakersfield clubs, Lucky Spot. Soon, Merle was making enough money playing music to quit his ditch-digging job. While singing with Barnett, he gained the attention of Fuzzy Owen, who owned the small record label Tally Records. Owen and his cousin Lewis Talley were instrumental in establishing Haggard's musical career. Owen made the first recording of Haggard, cutting a demo version of one of the singer's first songs, "Skid Row." Shortly after the recording, Haggard called Talley, who had praised him earlier in his career. Talley was able to land Haggard a job at Paul's Cocktail Lounge, which led to a slot on a local music television show.

During this time, Bakersfield country was beginning to become a national scene, largely due to the hit singles of Buck Owens. At a time when mainstream country was dominated by the lush, smooth countrypolitan sound of Nashville, Bakersfield country grew out of hardcore honky tonk, adding elements of Western swing. Bakersfield country also relied on electric instruments and amplification more than other subgenres of country, giving the music a hard, driving, edgy flavor. During the late '50s, Tommy Collins and Wynn Stewart were two of the Bakersfield artists to have hits, and both were influential on Merle Haggard's career, musically as well as professionally. Haggard had admired Stewart's vocal style, and it helped shape his phrasing.

Early in 1962, Haggard traveled to Las Vegas to see Wynn Stewart's club show. Stewart was not at the club, having left to find a replacement bass player. During the show, one of Stewart's guitarists remembered Haggard and invited him to sing a couple of songs on stage. Stewart walked in while Haggard was singing and was impressed, asking him to join his band as a bassist. For six months in 1962 and 1963, Merle played with Stewart's band. During this time, Haggard heard Wynn's song "Sing a Sad Song" and asked the star if he could record it. Stewart gave him the song and Merle recorded it for Tally Records in 1963. Although Tally had minimal distribution, the record became a national hit, climbing to No. 19 on the country charts early in 1964.

"Sam Hill," Haggard's second single, wasn't as successful, but a duet with Bonnie Owens, the former wife of Buck Owens, called "Just between the Two of Us," broke into the Top 30. The next year, Haggard's version of Liz Anderson's "(My Friends Are Gonna Be) Strangers" broke him into the Top Ten and established him as a budding star. Capitol Records bought out his contract with Tally and Merle released "I'm Gonna Break Every Heart I Can," his first single for Capitol, in the fall of 1965. The single wasn't a success, scratching into the Top 50, but his next single, "Swinging Doors," was a smash hit, rocketing to No. 5 in the spring of 1966. Late in 1965, Haggard began recruiting a backing band and named them the Strangers.

Merle Haggard became a genuine country superstar in 1966, with three Top Ten hits, including "Swinging Doors." "The Bottle Let Me Down" climbed to No. 3 and "The Fugitive" (later retitled "I'm a Lonesome Fugitive") hit No. 1. He was voted the "Top Male Vocalist" by the Academy of Country Music Awards, while he and Bonnie were named the "Top Vocal Group" for the second year in a row.

Haggard's songwriting was beginning to blossom and audiences embraced his music, sending his "I Threw Away the Rose" to No. 3 early in 1937, beginning a remarkable streak of 37 straight Top Ten hits, including 23 No. 1 singles.

"I Threw Away the Rose" was followed by four straight No. 1 hits—"Branded Man," "Sing Me Back Home," "The Legend of Bonnie and Clyde," and "Mama Tried," which was heard in *Killers Three*, a movie that featured Haggard's debut as an actor. With the exception of "Bonnie and Clyde," the songs represented a change in Haggard's songwriting, as he began to directly address his troubled history. By 1970, he was talking about his time in San Quentin in the press, yet these songs represented the first time he had mentioned his past directly. Each single was a bigger hit than the previous song, which encouraged Haggard to continue writing in a more personal style.

Throughout 1968, Haggard's star continued to rise, with two No. 1 hits ("Bonnie and Clyde," "Mama Tried") and the No. 3 "I Take a Lot of Pride in What I Am," as well as four albums. Later that year, he recorded his first conceptual album, *Same Train, Different Train: A Tribute to Jimmie Rodgers*. Released in early 1969, the record was not only an affectionate salute to one of Haggard's heroes, it reflected a fascination with American history and a desire to expand his music by adding stronger elements of Western swing, jazz, and blues.

Merle released three singles in 1969—"Hungry Eyes," "Workin' Man Blues," and "Okie from Muskogee"—and all three reached No. 1. In particular, "Okie from Muskogee" sparked a tremendous amount of attention. An attack on the liberal hippies that represented American pop culture in the late '60s, the song struck a chord in audiences across the country, just missing the pop Top 40. Because of the song, Haggard was asked to endorse George Wallace, but he refused. "Okie from Muskogee" cemented the singer's stardom, and he won a large amount of awards in 1969 and 1970. In both years, he was named the "Top Male Vocalist" by the ACM, and the Strangers were voted the best band, while the new Country Music Association voted him "Entertainer of the Year" and "Top Male Vocalist" in 1970.

Haggard released a sequel to "Okie" called "The Fightin' Side of Me" at the beginning of 1970, and it also shot to No. 1. That year, he released *A Tribute to the Best Damn Fiddle Player in the World (Or My Salute to Bob Wills)*, which helped spark a revival of Western swing in the '70s. Throughout 1971 and 1972, the hits kept coming, including "Soldier's Last Letter," "Someday We'll Look Back," "Daddy Frank (The Guitar Man)," "Carolyn," "Grandma Harp," "It's Not Love (But It's Not Bad)," and "I Wonder If They Ever Think of Me." In 1972, the governor of California, Ronald Reagan, granted Haggard a full pardon. The following year, his hit streak continued, and he scored his biggest hit, "If We Make It Through December," which peaked at No. 28 on the pop charts. As his reign on the top of the country charts continued in 1974, he played on Bob Wills' last album, *For the Last Time*. Wills died in 1975, leaving Merle his fiddle.

Haggard stayed with Capitol Records until 1977, and never once did his grip on the American audience slip during his tenure there. During his time on MCA, he continued to have a number of hits, but his work was becoming slightly inconsistent. His first two singles for the record label, "If We're Not Back in Love by Monday" and "Ramblin' Fever," hit No. 2 and he continued to have hits with the label throughout the end of the decade and the first part of the '80s. "I'm Always on a Mountain When I Fall" and "It's Been a Great Afternoon" were No. 2 hits in 1978. In 1979, he only had two hits, while in 1980 two selections from the Clint Eastwood movie *Bronco Billy* reached the Top Three, "The Way I Am" and "Misery and Gin"; Haggard also appeared in the film. The two hits paved the way for his two biggest singles with MCA, the No. 1 duet with Eastwood, "Bar Room Buddies," and the No. 1 "I Think I'll Just Stay Here and Drink." Early in 1981, Haggard had a Top Ten hit with "Leonard," a tribute to his old friend Tommy Collins.

Later that year, Haggard published his autobiography, *Sing Me Back Home;* he also left MCA and signed with Epic Records. Once he began recording for Epic, he began producing his own records, which gave the music a leaner sound. His first two singles for the label, "My Favorite Memory" and "Big City," were No. 1 hits. The following year, he released a duet album with George Jones, called *A Taste of Yesterday's Wine*, which featured the No. 1 single "Yesterday's Wine" and the Top Ten "C.C. Waterback." From 1983 until the beginning of 1985, Haggard continued to score No. 1 hits, including the No. 1 duet with Willie Nelson, "Pancho and Lefty."

Merle's chart fortunes began to change in 1985, as a new breed of singers began to dominate the charts. Nearly every one of the artists, from George Strait to Randy Travis, was greatly influenced by Haggard, but their idol's new singles now had a tough time reaching the top of the charts. He had two Top Ten hits in 1986,

Merle Haggard

and 1987's *Chill Factor* was a success, spawning the Top Ten title track and "Twinkle, Twinkle Lucky Star," which would prove to be his last No.1 hit. In 1990, he signed with Curb Records, but he continued to have trouble reaching the charts; *1994* spawned his last Top 60 hit, "In My Next Life."

Even when success eluded him, Merle Haggard's music remained some of the most consistently interesting and inventive in country music. Not only have his recordings stayed fresh, but each subsequent generation of country singers owes a great debt to his work. That fact stands as a testament to his great talent even more than his induction into the Country Music Hall of Fame. —*Stephen Thomas Erlewine*

Strangers / 1965 / Capitol ◆◆◆
Merle Haggard's first album is an impressive debut. Apart from the classic singles "(My Friends Are Gonna Be) Strangers," "Sam Hill," "Sing a Sad Song," and "I'm Gonna Break Every Heart I Can," there's a number of fine album cuts, including "I'd Trade All of My Tomorrows," "If I Had Left It up to You," and "You Don't Even Try." Granted, there is some filler on *Strangers*, but that was the case for nearly every country album recorded in the '60s. What counts is the good stuff, and the best songs on the record richly illustrate Haggard's talent and his potential. —*Stephen Thomas Erlewine*

Just Between the Two of Us / 1966 / Capitol ◆◆◆
For his second album, Merle Haggard released a duet with Bonnie Owens. Named after their hit single, *Just Between the Two of Us* is more or less a straight ahead honky tonk record, filled with barroom weepers. Though the material is slightly uneven, the strongest songs on the album—the title track, "Stranger in My Arms," "Slowly but Surely" and "Forever and Ever"—are first-rate honky tonk. Still, the material is a bit too undistinguished and uneven to make it an essential purchase. —*Stephen Thomas Erlewine*

☆ **Swinging Doors/The Bottle Let Me Down** / 1966 / Capitol ◆◆◆◆◆
Merle Haggard's third album, *Swinging Doors / The Bottle Let Me Down*, was assembled from a variety of singles and sessions like its two predecessors, but it contains a stronger overall selection of material than either album. In addition to the two masterpieces from which the album took its name, the record includes a terrific version of Tommy Collins' "High on a Hilltop," plus excellent songs like "The Girl Turned Ripe," "If I Could Be Him," and "Someone Else You've Known." There are a few weak tracks, but Haggard and his band are in fine form, making the filler enjoyable. —*Stephen Thomas Erlewine*

I'm a Lonesome Fugitive / 1967 / Capitol ✦✦✦
This early Capitol album contains the haunting "House of Memories." Haggard begins to really let his roots show on this one—see "Rough and Rowdy Ways," the Jimmie Rodgers classic. In this great early period Haggard, while seeming entirely contemporary, could evoke the Ghosts of Country Past in an absolutely convincing way without nostalgia or imitation. —George Bedard

Branded Man/I Threw Away the Rose / 1967 / Koch ✦✦✦✦
Like *Swinging Doors* before it, *Branded Man / I Threw Away the Rose* is merely a collection of songs pieced together to cash in on a couple of hit singles. Nevertheless, the intent of an album such as this doesn't really matter when the songs are this fine. In addition to the two title tracks, Haggard co-writes "You Don't Have Very Far to Go" and "Somewhere Between" (with Red Simpson and Bonnie Owens, respectively). While the latter isn't as good as his three other original songs ("Branded Man," "I Threw Away the Rose," "You Don't Have Very Far to Go"), the remainder of the album is comprised of outside material that ranks among some of Merle's finest performances ("Go Home," "Long Black Limousine," "I Made the Prison Band," "Don't Get Married," "Loneliness Is Eating Me Alive"). —Stephen Thomas Erlewine

Sing Me Back Home / 1968 / Capitol ✦✦✦✦
Sing Me Back Home follows the blueprint of Merle Haggard's first three albums, balancing a hit single with album tracks and a couple of covers, but there is a difference. Where the previous album *Branded Man* was a transitional album, hinting that Haggard's talents were deepening substantially, *Sing Me Back Home* is the result of the flowering of his talent. Like any '60s country album, there are a couple of throwaways (like "The Bottle Let Me Down," a rewrite of "I'll Leave the Bottle on the Bar") , but the majority of the album is full of rich material, like "The Son of Hickory Holler's Tramp," "Good Times," and "Wine Take Me Away." —Stephen Thomas Erlewine

Legend of Bonnie & Clyde / 1968 / Capitol ✦✦✦✦
Though the title suggests that the LP is a concept album, *The Legend of Bonnie & Clyde* doesn't differ drastically from other Merle Haggard records of the late '60s—it is simply a collection of strong, often remarkable songs. If anything, the title *Bonnie & Clyde* is misleading, since it suggests that Haggard is resorting to gimmickry in his songwriting, but the rolling epic of the title track illustrates that isn't the case. Furthermore, he continues to have excellent taste in outside material, bringing Dallas Frazier's "The Train Never Stops" and Leon Payne's "You Still Have a Place in My Heart" to life, but the true standout on the record is Hag's own "(Today) I Started Loving You Again." —Stephen Thomas Erlewine

Best of Merle Haggard / 1968 / Capitol ✦✦✦✦
As the first Haggard greatest hits collection ever released, *The Best of Merle Haggard* is quite good, hitting all the major points ("I'm a Lonesome Fugitive," "I Threw Away the Rose," "Swinging Doors," "[My Friends Are Gonna Be] Strangers," "Sing Me Back Home," "Branded Man," "The Bottle Let Me Down," "Sam Hill"), but it does leave off a few hits for album cuts like "House of Memories," "Shade Tree (Fix-It Man)," and "High on a Hilltop," which are all good but not quite as strong as the singles. Nevertheless, the LP functions as a fine introduction to Hag's early career. However, it has been replaced by better, more thorough compilations. —Stephen Thomas Erlewine

Mama Tried / 1968 / Capitol ✦✦✦✦
Mama Tried is a typically fine late-'60s LP from Merle Haggard, comprised of a number of strong originals and several excellent covers. While "Mama Tried" stands out among Haggard's original material, "I'll Always Know" and "You'll Never Love Me Now" are both solid songs. Still, those two tracks pale next to the best covers on the record. Merle delivers "Little Ole Wine Drinker Me," "In the Good Old Days (When Times Were Bad)," "Teach Me to Forget," "Run 'Em Off" and "Too Many Bridges to Cross Over" with grit and an open, affecting honesty that makes *Mama Tried* one of Hag's best records. —Stephen Thomas Erlewine

☆ **Same Train, Different Time** / 1969 / Bear Family ✦✦✦✦✦
Same Train, Different Time is Merle Haggard's affectionate tribute to Jimmie Rodgers. Haggard provides narration between the

songs, offering tales of Rodgers' life and music. While the album is rooted in the past, the key to its success is how Haggard updates these traditional songs without losing sight of their roots. There are contemporary folk, country, and blues influences scattered throughout the record, adding depth to the music and proving that Rodgers' music is indeed timeless. —Stephen Thomas Erlewine

Introducing My Friends, the Strangers / 1970 / Capitol ✦✦✦
The second all-instrumental effort by Merle Haggard and the Strangers is as enjoyable as the first, featuring a selection of Western swing, honky tonk, and Bakersfield instruments that both swing and rock with ease. Though lead guitarist Roy Nichols and steel guitarist Norm Hamlet remain from the classic incarnation of the Strangers, the rhythm section has been reworked; it now features drummer Biff Adam, bassist Dennis Hromek, and rhythm guitarist Bobby Wayner, all excellent musicians in their own right. Most of the album is comprised of Nichols and Hamlet collaborations, but the songs that truly stand out are Nichols' jaunty instrumental "Street Singer" and Haggard's "Workin' Man Blues," which also happens to be the only vocal on the LP. —Stephen Thomas Erlewine

Okie from Muskogee / 1970 / Pair ✦✦✦
Okie from Muskogee was recorded to cash in on the success of the title song, which became a pop music sensation upon its release in the fall of 1969. Haggard and the Strangers went to Muskogee, OK, where they ran through a number of their hits and working class anthems. The first side is devoted to classics like "Mama Tried," "Swinging Doors," "Sing Me Back Home," and "Workin' Man Blues," while the first part of the second side has songs about the mythological "Hobo Bill," before it concludes with rousing versions of "White Line Fever" and "Okie from Muskogee." While record isn't necessary, it is a hell of a lot of fun and not bad evidence of why Hag was the most popular figure in country music at the end of the '60s. —Stephen Thomas Erlewine

The Fightin' Side of Me / 1970 / Capitol ✦✦✦✦
Like its predecessor, *Okie from Muskogee*, *The Fightin' Side of Me* was a rush-released live album designed to cash in on the success of Haggard's ultra-patriotic hit single of the same name. *The Fightin' Side of Me* was recorded live in Philadelphia, in front of a capacity crowd. The songs are a good representation of a typical Haggard concert from the early '70s: a classic hit opens the record ("I Take a Lot of Pride in What I Am"), followed by some selections from his recent records, a couple of songs from Bonnie Owens and the Strangers, a medley of other singers performed as imitations and, finally, three recent hits—including "Okie from Muskogee" and "The Fightin' Side of Me"—to close the show. It's a fun record, and one that gives a better indication of what a typical Haggard concert was like in the early '70s, but it's ultimately a minor entry in his catalog. —Stephen Thomas Erlewine

☆ **Tribute to the Best Damn Fiddle Player** / 1970 / Koch ✦✦✦✦✦
After releasing his tribute to Jimmie Rodgers, Merle Haggard immediately set about working on a tribute to his other major musical idol, Bob Wills. Haggard learned how to play fiddle and, within a month, he had recruited many of the original Playboys to augment the Strangers and began recording the album that became *A Tribute to the Best Damn Fiddle Player: My Salute to Bob Wills*. Where *Same Train, Different Time* was a measured, heartfelt tribute, *Best Damn Fiddle Player* is a ragged, enthusiastic good time. Haggard, the Strangers, and the Playboys play their hearts out, breathing life into Wills' warhorses like "Right or Wrong," "Stay a Little Longer," "Time Changes Everything," and "San Antonio Rose," while bringing attention to lesser-known songs like "Brain Cloudy Blues," "I Knew the Moment I Lost You," and "Old-Fashioned Love." The fact that Western swing re-established itself as a viable country genre after the release of *A Tribute to the Best Damn Fiddle Player* is a testament to the power and charm of this record. —Stephen Thomas Erlewine

Hag / 1971 / Capitol ✦✦✦
Highlighted by no less than four hit singles ("Soldier's Last Letter," "Jesus, Take a Hold," "I Can't Be Myself," "Sidewalks of Chicago"), *Hag* is an excellent collection of short songs that alternate between folky country, western swing, and country ballads. *Hag* has a higher concentration of original material than many of his

'60s albums—there are only three covers on the ten-song LP—and very few of the cuts function as filler. There aren't many major statements on *Hag*, but it's a record of simple, quiet grace and beauty. —*Stephen Thomas Erlewine*

Someday We'll Look Back / 1971 / Capitol ✦✦✦✦

Someday We'll Look Back is a terrific early-'70s LP from Merle Haggard, one that showcases not only his exceptional songwriting skills, but also his rich, subtle eclecticism. Much of the album is given over to ballads, including both lush, string-laden country-pop crossovers and simple, folky tunes, but there are also hints of twangy Bakersfield honky tonk and blues, as well as Western swing. But what really makes the record so distinctive is the quality of the material. Haggard's original songs—including "Someday We'll Look Back," "Tulare Dust," "I'd Rather Be Gone," and "One Sweet Hello"—are uniformly excellent, while he invests considerable emotion into covers of Tommy Collins' "Carolyn," Dallas Frazier and Elizabeth Montgomery's "California Cottonfields," and Roger Miller's "Train of Life." The result is one of the finest albums he ever recorded. —*Stephen Thomas Erlewine*

Let Me Tell You About a Song / 1972 / Capitol ✦✦✦

In a way, *Let Me Tell You About a Song* is a children's album from Merle Haggard, filled with folky story songs that have an innocent, charming quality. Two hit singles, "Daddy Frank (The Guitar Man)" and "Grandma Harp," illustrate the tenor of the album. The first is about a blind father and a deaf mother who lead a family across the country, singing wherever they go; the second is an affectionate tribute to Haggard's departed grandmother. Both are simple and direct, with a universal appeal, and the rest of the album follows in that vein. There are a few detours toward Western swing (Bob Wills' "Bring It Down to My House, Honey") and gritty Bakersfield country (Tommy Collins' "The Funeral"), but the LP is an endearingly straightforward and old-fashioned record, full of life and fun. —*Stephen Thomas Erlewine*

The Best of the Best of Merle Haggard / 1972 / Capitol ✦✦✦✦

Included is "Today I Started Loving You Again," "No Reason to Quit," "Every Fool Has a Rainbow," "Hungry Eyes"—some of his best ballads—plus the jingoistic faves "Okie from Muskogee" and "Fightin' Side of Me." There are a few duds, though—some of the early Capitol albums are more consistent. —*George Bedard*

It's Not Love (But It's Not Bad) / 1972 / Capitol ✦✦✦

Despite the excellent title track, *It's Not Love (But It's Not Bad)* is only a fitfully entertaining album, equally divided between the excellent and the mediocre. A few of the throwaways are entertaining, particularly the rolling "New York City Blues," but songs like "Dad's Old Fiddle" and "My Woman Keeps Lovin' Her Man" fail to make an impression. There are a handful of hidden gems ("I Wonder Where I'll Find You at Tonight," "I Wonder What She'll Think About Me Leaving," "Goodbye Comes Hard for Me"), but the record remains a frustrating listen. —*Stephen Thomas Erlewine*

I Love Dixie Blues ... So I Recorded "Live" in New Orleans / 1973 / Capitol ✦✦✦

I Love Dixie Blues was recorded live in New Orleans, not only with the Strangers but with a brass section to give the music the feel of authentic Dixieland jazz. Haggard's gamble works quite well, since the brass section never feels like it's grafted onto the core band—they sound integrated, unlike his previous experiments with Dixieland horns. Of course, it helps that Hag has picked a selection of songs that emphasizes these strengths, such as his own anthem "Everybody's Had the Blues," "Way Down Yonder in New Orleans," "Lovesick Blues," and "The Emptiest Arms in the World." The only thing that slows the album's momentum is Merle's insistence on providing narration between the songs in an attempt to tell the history of Dixie blues. He should have known that the music itself tells the story well enough. —*Stephen Thomas Erlewine*

Totally Instrumental ... With One Exception / 1973 / Capitol ✦✦✦

Designed as a showcase for Haggard's backing band the Strangers, *Totally Instrumental ... With One Exception* is a thoroughly enjoyable set of relaxed, jazzy Western swing and honky tonk that illustrates the depths of instrumental talent in the group. In this incarnation, the Strangers feature lead guitarist Roy Nichols,

rhythm guitarists Bobby Wayne and Marcia Nichols, steel guitarist Norm Hamlet, bassist Dennis Hromek, and drummer Biff Adam. While this isn't the classic '60s incarnation of the Strangers, it is still a tight, exceptional group, and they make this set of short instrumentals (only "Cotton Picker" features Merle's vocals) into a fun record. —*Stephen Thomas Erlewine*

If We Make It through December / 1974 / Capitol ✦✦✦

Usually, Merle Haggard's musical eclecticism is a virtue, but on *If We Make It through December*, it hurts the overall impact of the album. Many of the individual tracks—particularly the gentle, yearning title track and good versions of Lefty Frizzell's "I'm an Old, Old Man (Tryin' to Live While I Can)" and the country standard "To Each His Own"—work well on their own, but often the straight-up country, Western swing, Dixieland experiments, and pop-tinged ballads seem at odds with each other. As a result, the LP never quite gels, yet there are enough fine moments to make it a worthwhile purchase. —*Stephen Thomas Erlewine*

Merle Haggard Presents His 30th Album / 1974 / Capitol ✦✦✦

The fact that Merle Haggard released 30 albums in less than ten years says as much about the country music industry's insatiable need for product as it does about Hag's own prolific creativity. Unfortunately, *His 30th Album* leans more to the industry side of the equation than Merle's artistic side, yet it still remains an enjoyable listen. There is a fair share of filler on the record, including a song sung by the Strangers' rhythm guitarist Ronnie Reno ("Travelin'"), but "Old Man from the Mountain," "White Man Singin' the Blues," "Holding Things Together" and "It Don't Bother Me" make the LP worthwhile for fans. —*Stephen Thomas Erlewine*

☆ Songs I'll Always Sing / 1976 / Capitol ✦✦✦✦✦

Though many compilations have followed it since it was first released in 1976, *Songs I'll Always Sing* remains one of the definitive Merle Haggard compilations. Relying not only on hit singles, the 20-track double-album set features a number of album tracks and obscurities—such as "Love and Honor," "Silver Wings," "Honky Tonk Night Time Man," "Things Aren't Funny Anymore," and "I Forget You Every Day"—that give a more rounded and accurate picture of Hag's classic Capitol recordings. After all, there were always a handful of killer songs on his individual albums that rivaled his hit singles in terms of quality. In terms of comprehensiveness, both the four-disc box *Down Every Road* and the double-disc *The Lonesome Fugitive* have superseded *Songs I'll Always Sing*, but the double album set will always remain an excellent summation of his heyday. —*Stephen Thomas Erlewine*

My Farewell to Elvis / 1977 / MCA ✦✦

Like much of America, Haggard was touched by the death of Elvis. And Haggard, like many of us, enjoys singing Elvis' tunes. Fortunately, most of us don't record and release those impressions. Sadly, Merle did. —*Jim Worbois*

I'm Always on a Mountain When I Fall / 1978 / MCA ✦✦✦

Country Boy / 1978 / Pair ✦✦✦

Haggard's early years on Capitol are recalled on *Country Boy*, which includes "Everybody's Had the Blues," "Carolyn," and "Things Aren't Funny Anymore." —*Jason Ankeny*

Serving 190 Proof / 1979 / MCA ✦✦✦

Haggard appears here in the midst of what he admitted was a mid-life crisis. That's no reason to dismiss this record, however, as crisis introspection served him well. Possibly the best of his MCA albums, it includes "Red Bandana," "My Own Kind of a Hat," and a brooding meditation on the emptiness of stardom called "Footlights." —*Dan Cooper*

Back to the Barrooms / 1980 / MCA ✦✦✦

Haggard bucked conventional wisdom by releasing this straightforward honky tonk outing at the peak of the *Urban Cowboy* craze; the result was another strong effort and another hit, highlighted by the chart-topping "I Think I'll Just Stay Here and Drink" and "Leonard," his tribute to mentor Tommy Collins. —*Jason Ankeny*

Rainbow Stew: Live at Anaheim Stadium / 1981 / MCA ✦✦✦

Rainbow Stew: Live at Anaheim boasts an augmented Strangers, with former Texas Playboys Eldon Shamblin, Tiny Moore, and Gordon Terry, and a horn section filling out the band's sound. The result is a wonderful, swinging album that brings a new spin not only to classics like "I'm a Lonesome Fugitive" and "Sing Me Back Home," but also to Hag's newer songs, "Misery and Gin," "I Think I'll Just Stay Here and Drink," and the title track. —*Stephen Thomas Erlewine*

Big City / 1981 / Epic ♦♦♦
Coming on the heels of a short-lived semiretirement, Haggard's Epic debut is an appropriate group of songs that celebrates relaxation and expresses discontent with the situation forced on blue-collar America. Ironically, he puts plenty of energy into his work here. —*Tom Roland*

Going Where the Lonely Go / 1982 / Epic ♦♦♦
This dark, brooding package includes some leftovers from the *Big City* sessions. Occasionally uplifting musically, it's certainly a study in pain. Besides the title track, check out "Someday You're Gonna Need Your Friends Again," "Shopping for Dresses," and the Willie Nelson-penned "Half a Man." —*Tom Roland*

A Taste of Yesterday's Wine / 1982 / Epic ♦♦♦
Merle Haggard and George Jones, the two most influential country stylists of the modern country era, hook up together. It's occasionally disappointing in that respect, but a case study in music to down Jack Daniels by. They take a self-deprecating poke at George Jones' former reliability problem in "No Show Jones." —*Tom Roland*

Epic Collection [Recorded Live] / 1983 / Epic ♦
The Epic Collection (Recorded Live) is an intimate live set, swinging gently with jazzy, bluesy inflections. Much of the material comes from Haggard's recent Epic albums, but he also digs deep into his catalog, reviving "Sing a Sad Song," "Trouble in Mind," "(My Friends Are Gonna Be) Strangers," and "Blue Yodel No. 2." The result is a warm, engaging live set that illustrates the depth and diversity of Hag's music. —*Stephen Thomas Erlewine*

Pancho & Lefty / 1983 / Epic ♦♦♦
This album, with Willie Nelson, is for those curious as to why younger artists try to imitate Haggard rather than Nelson. Funny thing that, though it's a duet album, they very rarely sing in harmony. Some versions spell Pancho as Poncho and are supposedly collector's items. The title track is one of the best-produced country cuts in history. —*Tom Roland*

His Epic Hits: First Eleven to Be Continued / 1984 / Epic ♦♦♦
As the title implies, *His Epic Hits: First Eleven* covers the first 11 hits Merle Haggard had on Epic Records, including "Are the Good Times Really Over (I Wish a Buck Was Still Silver)," "Pancho & Lefty," "Reasons to Quit," "That's the Way Love Goes," "My Favorite Memory," "What Am I Gonna Do (With the Rest of My LIfe)," and "You Take Me for Granted." Since most of his early Epic albums were uneven, *His Epic Hits* is especially useful, gathering his best material onto one disc. It should be supplemented by *Greatest Hits of the '80s*, which covers his mid-'80s hits for Epic, as well as a few fine cuts that didn't make this collection. —*Stephen Thomas Erlewine*

His Greatest & His Best / 1985 / MCA ♦♦♦♦
Haggard's tenure on MCA was brief but productive. Highlights, all included here, are "If We're Not Back in Love by Monday," "Leonard" (a tribute to songwriter Tommy Collins), and "Misery and Gin." —*Dan Cooper*

Chill Factor / 1988 / Epic ♦♦♦

5:01 Blues / 1989 / Epic ♦♦♦
Though it is a bit uneven, *5:01 Blues* is a mature, subtle, and often engaging latter-day release from Merle Haggard. Hag's voice has become jazzier and more nuanced with age, which helps give weight to the lesser material on the album. When he's matched with a terrific song, such as "Sea of Heartbreak," the results are magnificent. —*Stephen Thomas Erlewine*

Greatest Hits of the '80s / 1990 / Epic ♦♦♦
Greatest Hits of the '80s is a nice ten-track collection that covers many of Merle Haggard's biggest hits for Epic Records, including "Chill Factor," "Natural High," "Twinkle, Twinkle Lucky Star," "Let's Chase Each Other Around the Room," and "I Had a Beautiful Time." The rest of the songs are album tracks and concert

favorites like "Yesterday's Wine." Though it isn't a comprehensive retrospective of his Epic work, *Greatest Hits of the '80s* remains a good overview and introduction to his latter-day career. —*Stephen Thomas Erlewine*

Blue Jungle / 1990 / Curb ♦♦♦

The Best of Country Blues / 1990 / Curb ♦♦♦
A worthwhile, ten-track budget-line collection, *The Best of Country Blues* includes his treatments of Bob Wills and Jimmie Rodgers, plus original material, all taken from his heyday at Capitol Records. —*Richard Lieberson*

☆ **Capitol Collectors Series** / Jan. 29, 1990 / Capitol ♦♦♦♦♦
Like any *Capitol Collectors Series*, Merle Haggard's compilation contains an odd mix of classic and lesser-known hits, with a couple of obscurities thrown in for good measure. Though many of his very best songs—"Swinging Doors," "The Bottle Let Me Down," "Sing Me Back Home," "Hungry Eyes," "Okie from Muskogee"—are featured, classics like "Mama Tried," "Sing a Sad Song," "Branded Man," "Carolyn," "If We Make It through December," and "Kentucky Gambler" aren't included. Which means that *Capitol Collectors Series* is a good sampler of Haggard's classic work and therefore a good introduction to his sound, even if it isn't a definitive retrospective. At the time of its release, some of the gaps *Capitol Collectors Series* left were filled by *More of the Best*. Both discs have since been superseded by the comprehensive double-disc *The Lonesome Fugitive*. —*Stephen Thomas Erlewine*

☆ **More of the Best** / Feb. 1990 / Rhino ♦♦♦♦♦
Rhino's *More of the Best* was designed to complement the hits compilation *Capitol Collectors Series* that was released concurrently, and the single-disc collection certainly does cover many of the songs that failed to make Capitol's cut. Not only does it have hits like "Sing a Sad Song," "Branded Man," "Mama Tried," "Someday We'll Look Back," and "If We Make It through December," it also has a couple of terrific Capitol-era album tracks ("Silver Wings," "White Line Fever") and MCA hits like "If We're Not Back in Love by Monday," "Ramblin' Fever," "Red Bandana," "I Think I'll Just Stay Here and Drink" and "Rainbow Stew." The MCA hits makes *More of the Best* valuable not only as a supplement to *Capitol Collectors Series*, but as a portrait of his late '70s work. Of course, the four-disc box set *Down Every Road* has superseded *Capitol Collectors Series* and *More of the Best* in terms of comprehensiveness, but the pair of discs are useful for beginners looking for a broad overview of Hag's career, not just the Capitol hits covered by the double-disc *The Lonesome Fugitive*. —*Stephen Thomas Erlewine*

18 Rare Classics / 1991 / Curb ♦♦♦
18 Rare Classics haphazardly compiles No. 1 hits like "Kentucky Gambler" and "Grandma Harp" alongside obscure material like "Silver Wings" and "Here in Frisco." —*Jason Ankeny*

Best of the Early Years / 1991 / Curb ♦♦♦
The Best of the Early Years is a fine budget-priced collection of 12 songs Merle Haggard recorded in the late '60s and early '70s, including "Mama Tried," "Today, I Started Loving You Again," "(My Friends Are Gonna Be) Strangers" and "Sam Hill." Though it isn't a comprehensive overview, and it is missing several key tracks, it is a fine mid-line compilation. —*Stephen Thomas Erlewine*

Super Hits / Mar. 8, 1993 / Epic ♦♦♦
Super Hits offers an overview of Haggard's early-'80s tenure at Epic, and includes the hits "That's the Way Love Goes," "Are the Good Times Really Over (I Wish a Buck Was Still Silver)," and "Going Where the Lonely Go." —*Jason Ankeny*

1994 / Mar. 22, 1994 / Curb ♦♦♦
After a four-year recording silence, Haggard returns with his strongest record since 1981's *Big City*. The first single, "In My Next Life" (written by Max D. Barnes), is the latest entry in Haggard's incomparable registry of the unfulfilled dreams of the salt of the bitter earth. —*Dan Cooper*

★ **Lonesome Fugitive: The Merle Haggard Anthology (1963-1977)** / 1995 / Razor & Tie ♦♦♦♦♦
Lonesome Fugitive: The Merle Haggard Anthology is an excellent double-disc retrospective of Hag's Capitol recordings. Over the

course of the 40-track set, every hit country single Haggard had between 1963 and 1972 is included, as is the majority of his hits between 1973 and 1976. While not every great performance and song Merle recorded during this era is included—he was so prolific it would have been impossible to condense *everything* onto a double-disc set—*Lonesome Fugitive* remains a definitive collection. It has all of the hits, most of his greatest songs, and illustrates the depth of his music in the most concise manner possible. Furthermore, *Lonesome Fugitive* is the only place all of Haggard's classic hits are available on one collection, which means it is both the perfect introduction and career-defining retrospective. —*Stephen Thomas Erlewine*

☆ **Untamed Hawk [box]** / 1995 / Bear Family ♦♦♦♦♦
In typical Bear Family fashion, the German record company compiled all of Haggard's early Capitol recordings (1962-1968)—including unreleased tracks and alternate takes—over the course of a five-disc box set called *Untamed Hawk*. Like any Bear Family set, *Untamed Hawk* is too exhausting to listen to in a single sitting. In fact, the company's insistence on presenting all the music in session order instead of how it was actually released makes listening to any of the individual discs rather difficult—the box plays like a history lesson, not like an album. Nevertheless, there is a wealth of wonderful, timeless music on *Untamed Hawk*, and no Haggard completist should be without it, even if it is essentially a library piece. However, casual fans—even those who enjoy the original '60s albums like *Sing Me Back Home*—should leave *Untamed Hawk* on the shelf. —*Stephen Thomas Erlewine*

I'm a Lonesome Fugitive / Mama Tried / 1996 / Capitol ♦♦♦♦
I'm a Lonesome Fugitive and *Mama Tried*, two of Merle Haggard's classic late '60s albums for Capitol Records, are included on this single disc. Though there is a handful of filler on each of the albums, the overall quality of the music on both records is very high—not only are classic singles like "Mama Tried," "I'm a Lonesome Fugitive," and "Someone Told My Story" present, but so are excellent album tracks like "Little Ole Wine Drinker Me," "In the Good Old Days (When Times Were Bad)," "Run 'Em Off," "Skid Row," and "Mary's Mine." —*Stephen Thomas Erlewine*

1996 / Jan. 23, 1996 / Curb ♦♦♦♦
In late 1995, Merle Haggard stood on the stage of the Grand Ole Opry House acknowledging the music industry's ovation as he accepted his induction into the Country Music Hall of Fame. A few months later, however, his next album came out with no fanfare at all. His record company didn't send promotional copies to reviewers until the album had been out for nearly a month, and there was no advertising or promotion on behalf of the music. The album artwork and cover reflect this lack of care: The title, *1996*, is boxed on the cover like a tomb, exactly like Hag's last set, *1994*. What's inside deserves more attention. Recorded in Bakersfield, Haggard's latest takes a jaunty yet melancholy look at a middle-aged man's concerns. Not everything works—"Kids Get Lonesome Too" has a grandfatherly sentimentality, but it's not very substantial. The rest carries plenty of meat: "Sin City Blues" bemoans the temptations of New Orleans with Dixieland verve, "Beer Can Hill" is a humorous reminiscence about honky tonkin' in Bakersfield, and "Untanglin' My Mind" (a hit for co-writer Clint Black) is a textbook example of the difference between the stiff perfection of Nashville over-production and the loose, life-affirming musicianship that Haggard prefers. The album's standout is a cover of Iris Dement's great "No Time to Cry," which Merle fills with aged, tired wisdom. —*Michael McCall*

Vintage Collection Series / Jan. 23, 1996 / Capitol ♦♦♦♦
Vintage features a good cross-section of Merle Haggard's biggest hits, including "Mama Tried" and "Hungry Eyes," as well as a handful of rarities that should please both collectors and neophytes. Razor & Tie's *The Lonesome Fugitive* offers a more thorough overview and *Capitol Collector's Series* has more diversity, but *Vintage* offers a fine introduction to one of country's greatest singer-songwriters. —*Stephen Thomas Erlewine*

☆ **Down Every Road** / Apr. 1996 / Capitol ♦♦♦♦♦
Merle Haggard has been served by a countless number of compilations, but *Down Every Road* is the first multi-disc box set to attempt to give an overview of his career. Spanning from his first

singles for Tally through his glory days on Capitol to his scattershot later career, *Down Every Road* features every one of Haggard's necessary songs, as well as a couple of more obscure gems, including a handful of unreleased songs. Though most casual fans will be better served by *The Lonesome Fugitive*, a lean double-disc set that contains all of his essential songs, *Down Every Road* is ideal for listeners that want to dig a little deeper. It gives an excellent picture of the full scope of Haggard's talents as a songwriter and musician. —*Stephen Thomas Erlewine*

It's All in the Movies / Capitol ♦♦♦
While the title track is a gentle, affecting ballad, *It's All in the Movies* doesn't contain enough similarly engaging material to make the record successful. The album is at its best when Haggard delves into Western swing, such as on "Living with the Shades Pulled Down," or when he delivers straightforward ballads like "Nothin's Worse Than Losing" and "I Know an Ending When It Comes," but too many of the songs on the LP are pleasant, but inconsequential, filler. —*Stephen Thomas Erlewine*

Bill Haley (William John Clifton Haley)

b. Jul. 6, 1925, Highland Park, MI, **d.** Feb. 9, 1981, Harlingen, TX
Guitar, Vocals / Rock & Roll, Western Swing, Rockabilly
The Bill Haley & the Comets recording of "Rock Around the Clock," which topped the charts for eight weeks in 1955, is remembered as the beginning of the rock era. Though it also represented Haley's peak as a performer, his career had begun some time before and would continue for a long time after. Born in Michigan, Haley began leading Western swing bands under various names in the late '40s, slowly starting to incorporate elements of R&B. Soon after he began recording for Essex in the early '50s, his backup band was named the Comets.

Because of his somewhat square image and his undeniably White sound, Haley, it could be argued, has been short changed by latter-day rock historians. He was among the first performers—perhaps he was even the very first—of any color to combine R&B and C&W in a way that can readily be identified by listeners of any era as bona fide rock 'n' roll. Although their initial impact was regional, his early '50s sides rank among his most exciting, steering Country & Western and big band forms into uncharted regions that were more frenetic and reckless. Haley also wrote much of his own material, and one of his compositions, "Crazy, Man, Crazy," became one of the first Top 20 rock 'n' roll hits in 1953. In 1954, he moved to the major label Decca, where his sides became increasingly formulaic, though for a time very successful, after "Rock Around the Clock."

It is his Decca sides, however, that are his most famous. In 1954, he went to No. 12 with "Shake, Rattle and Roll," and in 1955 he hit with "Dim, Dim the Lights," "Mambo Rock," and "Birth of the Boogie." But it was "Rock Around the Clock," previously recorded and released as a B-side in 1954 and reissued as the theme song for the movie *Blackboard Jungle*, that became his biggest hit. At that time the band consisted of Haley on guitar and vocals, Danny Cedrone on lead guitar, Joey D'Ambrose on sax, Billy Williamson on steel guitar, Johnny Grande on piano, Marshall Lytle on bass, and Dick Richards on drums.

Following the success of "Rock Around the Clock," Haley & the Comets placed nine more records in the Top 40 over the next three years, among them the Top Tens "Burn that Candle" and "See You Later, Alligator." Haley was largely eclipsed as the king of rock 'n' roll by Elvis Presley and the other more flamboyant performers who followed him from 1956 on. Nevertheless, Haley continued to perform overseas and in oldies shows in the United States, and "Rock Around the Clock" even got back into the Top 40 in 1974. —*William Ruhlmann & Richie Unterberger*

Greatest Hits / 1985 / MCA ♦♦♦
The mini-skirted go-go dancers pictured on the cover reveal the year of release, a considerable distance from Haley's classic period, and it is amazing that Decca didn't have a hits compilation out earlier. The songs speak for themselves, and loudly, however—apart from "Rock Around the Clock" and "Shake Rattle and Roll," the highlights include "Thirteen Women," a delightfully surreal end-of-the-world rockabilly fantasy about a man on a post-

nuclear world who finds himself the only male to service 13 fertile female survivors. —*Bruce Eder*

★ **From the Original Master Tapes** / 1985 / MCA ✦✦✦✦✦
This is it—the Bill Haley record to own! Compiled by producer Steve Hoffman from the original session masters (you even get studio chatter ahead of "Rock Around the Clock"), this 20-song collection is the definitive Haley hits collection, with every song of consequence that he recorded for Decca Records during the years 1954-56. The sound is extraordinary—you haven't really heard Haley's music till you've heard this disc—and the sessionography adds a great deal to our knowledge of the players. From "Rock Around the Clock" and "Thirteen Women" to "Don't Knock the Rock," this is the best representation of Haley's peak years. —*Bruce Eder*

Rock the Joint! / 1995 / Schoolkids ✦✦✦✦
This 22-track collection that collects sides from 1951-53. Those who haven't heard this material before will be astonished to discover bona fide rock 'n' roll dating from three to four years earlier than the era ('54-55) more commonly associated with the music's birth. Haley's sound is similar to the country-boogie of the late '40s, retaining the steel guitar prominent in much of the era's country music, but it's clearly more driving and forward-looking. The songs owe a lot to jump R&B, but are transformed into the basic model of rock 'n' roll with slapping bass, ricky-tick drums, and extended electric guitar riffing. Listen to Haley's version of Jackie Brenston's "Rocket 88" (which has itself been pegged as one of the first rock 'n' roll records) and you'll be astounded to note the basics of rockabilly already in place—in 1951. The low-buzzing, distorted guitar on "Green Tree Boogie" (also from 1951) is also a revelation, as is the guitar solo on 1952's "Rock the Joint," which is almost identical to the much more famous one on "Rock Around the Clock" a couple of years later. The later sides introduce a honking sax, which would become such a prominent feature in '50s rock 'n' roll. Includes "Crazy Man Crazy," the first rock 'n' roll song to make the Top 20. —*Richie Unterberger*

American Legends #20 / Apr. 1996 / LaserLight ✦✦
Leaving Decca Records, where he had recorded his hits, at the start of the 1960s, Bill Haley & the Comets landed a deal with then-fledgling Warner Bros. Records, for which they naturally re-recorded their hits. (The 1960 release was called *Bill Haley & His Comets*, Warner Bros. 1378.) Thirty-six years later, here they are again, on a budget label and of course without any indication on the cover that these are not the original versions. In 27 minutes, the group revives "Rock Around the Clock, "Crazy Man, Crazy" and such contemporaneous hits as "Blue Suede Shoes" and "Blueberry Hill." If you aren't expecting the hit versions and pay no more than the budget price, this album is a minor curiosity; otherwise, it's a rip-off. —*William Ruhlmann*

Connie Hall

b. Jun. 24, 1929, Walden, KY
Vocals / Traditional Country, Nashville Sound/Countrypolitan
Singer-songwriter Connie Hall had a brief country music career during the 1960s. She was born in Kentucky, but raised in Cincinnati, OH, and began performing in her teens. After high school she worked at the Jimmie Skinner Music Center in Ohio and then became a regular singer on radio WZIP in Covington, KY. In 1954, Skinner hired her to sing on his radio show at WNOP Newport, KY. She appeared on his show and others for several years and even worked as a weather girl on an area television station.
Hall's recording debut was a 1957 duet with Skinner, "We've Got Things in Common." She released her first solo effort in 1958, "I'm the Girl in the USA," and had her first hit the following year with "The Bottle or Me," which peaked near the Top 20. She moved to Decca in 1960, where producer Harry Silverstein helped her make it to the Top 25 with "Poison in Your Hand" and the Top 20 with its B-side "It's Not Wrong," a response to Warner Mack's 1958 hit "Is It Wrong (for Loving You)." She remained with Decca for three years and produced seven more respectable hits including "Sleep, Baby, Sleep" and "Fool Me Once." She also appeared on the Grand Ole Opry, *Louisiana Hayride*, and *Midwestern Hayride*. —*Sandra Brennan*

● **Connie Hall** / 1962 / Decca ✦✦✦✦

Country Songs / 1965 / Vocalion ✦✦✦
Country Style / 1965 / Vocalion ✦✦✦

Tom T. Hall

b. May 25, 1936, Olive Hill, KY
Guitar, Vocals / Progressive Country, Country-Pop, Singer-Songwriter, Country-Folk
Tom T. Hall is known as a storyteller, a songwriter with a keen eye for detail and a knack for narrative. Many musicians have covered his songs—most notably Jeannie C. Riley's 1968 hit, "Harper Valley P.T.A."—and he also has racked up a number of solo hits, including seven No.1 singles.
Hall is the son of a brick-laying minister, who gave his child a guitar at the age of eight. Hall had already begun to write poetry, so it was a natural progression for him to begin writing songs. Hall began learning music and performing techniques from a local musician called Clayton Delaney. At the age of 11, his mother died. Four years later, his father was shot in a fishing accident, which prevented him from working. In order to support himself and his father, Hall quit school and took a job in a local garment factory. While he was working in the factory, he formed his first band, the Kentucky Travelers. The group played bluegrass and gigged at local schools, as well as a radio station in Morehead, KY. The station was sponsored by the Polar Bear Flour Company; Hall wrote a jingle for the company. After the Kentucky Travelers broke up, Hall became a DJ at the radio station.
In 1957, Hall enlisted in the Army and was stationed in Germany. While in Germany, he perfomed at local NCO clubs on the Armed Forces Radio Network, where he sang mostly original material, which usually had a comic bent to it. After four years of service, he was discharged in 1961. Once he returned to the States, he enrolled in Roanoke College as a journalism student; he supported himself by DJing at a radio station in Salem, VA.
One day a Nashville songwriter was visiting the Salem radio station and he heard Hall's songs. Impressed, the songwriter sent the songs to a publisher named Jimmy Key, who ran New Key Publishing. Key signed Hall as a songwriter, bringing the songs to a variety of recording artists. The first singer to have a hit with one of Tom's songs was Jimmy Newman, who brought "DJ for a Day" to No. 1 on the country charts in 1963. In early 1964, Dave Dudley took "Mad" to the Top Ten. The back-to-back success convinced Hall to move to Nashville, where he was going to continue his career as a professional songwriter.
After Johnny Wright had a No. 1 hit with Hall's "Hello Vietnam," the music industry was pressuring Tom to become a performer. He decided to take the plunge in 1967, signing a contract with Mercury Records. His first single, "I Washed My Face in the Morning Dew," was released in the summer of 1967 and became a minor hit. Hall followed the single with two other singles in 1968 that failed to crack the Top 40. Then, in the late summer of 1968, Jeannie C. Riley had a major hit with Hall's "Harper Valley P.T.A.," which spent three weeks at the top of the charts and was voted the Single of the Year by the Country Music Association. Its success brought attention to Hall's own recording career, which was evident from the performance of "Ballad of Forty Dollars." The song became his first Top Ten hit, climbing all the way to No. 4.
Throughout 1969, Hall had a string of hit singles, culminating in the release of the No. 1 single "A Week in a Country Jail" at the end of the year. The following year was just as successful, as "Shoeshine Man" and "Salute to a Switchblade" both hit the Top Ten. In 1971, he had his second No. 1 single and his biggest hit, "The Year That Clayton Delaney Died," which was based on his childhood hero.
For most of the early '70s, Hall was a consistent hit-maker as well as a popular concert attraction. Between 1971 and 1976, he had five No. 1 hits besides "The Year That Clayton Delaney Died": "(Old Dogs-Children And) Watermelon Wine," "I Love," "Country Is," "I Care," and "Faster Horses (The Cowboy and the Poet)." Hall was appearing on television shows with regularity during this time, particularly *Hee Haw*. He also wrote a book on songwriting, which led to his authorship of a pair of books in the late '70s and early '80s—the semi-autobiography *The Storyteller's Nashville*

(1979) and the novel *The Laughing Man of Woodmont* (1982). Although he continued to have the occasional Top Ten hit in the late '70s—most notably the No. 4 "You Man Loves You, Honey" (1977)—Hall didn't deliver hit singles as consistently as he did the first half of the decade. That pattern continued in the early '80s, when he began having trouble cracking the Top 40; only 1984's "P.S. I Love You," a cover of a 1934 Rudy Vallee hit, made it into the Top Ten. After 1986, Hall retired from recording, although artists continued to record his songs. In 1996, he delivered *Songs from Sopchoppy*, his first album in ten years. —*Stephen Thomas Erlewine*

Ballad of Forty Dollars / 1969 / Mercury ✦✦✦✦
Ballad of Forty Dollars and *Homecoming*, two of Tom T. Hall's excellent late '60s albums, are combined on this single compact disc. Although many of the best songs were featured on *Greatest Hits* and *Storyteller, Poet Philosopher,* these albums work well as individual records and they're well worth acquiring for any Hall fan. —*Thom Owens*

☆ In Search of a Song / 1971 / Mercury ✦✦✦✦✦
Hall gathered this material while driving solo through rural America, and his songs are literal and compassionate—but not romantic or sentimental. Instead, he fills his heartland stories with extraordinary realism and humanity. —*Michael McCall*

Greatest Hits, Vol. 1 / 1972 / Mercury ✦✦✦✦
Greatest Hits contains the bulk of Tom T. Hall's biggest hits from the late '60s and early '70s, including all his Top Ten hits from that era—"Ballad of Forty Dollars," "Homecoming," "A Week in a Country Jail," "Shoeshine Man,' "Salute to a Switchblade," "The Year That Clayton Delaney Died," and "Me and Jesus"—but the record only hints at his talent as a songwriter. Many of his best songs are on *Greatest Hits* and the collection does avoid his tendency for cuteness (with only a couple of exceptions), making *Greatest Hits* a good introduction, even though it does bypass plenty of fine songs. —*Thom Owens*

Tom T. Hall . . . The Storyteller / 1972 / Mercury ✦✦✦✦
It seemed like Hall could do no wrong in the early '70s, and this album adds more fuel to that idea. Another fine album of Hall originals (plus one by Billy Joe Shaver); including one of Hall's finest in "Old Dogs, Children and Watermelon Wine." —*Jim Worbois*

We All Got Together And . . . / 1972 / Mercury ✦✦✦✦
More great songs from Hall including "Pamela Brown," which was later covered by Leo Kottke, and the political satire of "Monkey That Became President"; a song that is still as potent today. Not to be missed. —*Jim Worbois*

The Rhymer and Other Five and Dimers / 1973 / Mercury ✦✦✦✦
More great songs from the man called "The Storyteller"; including one from Billy Joe Shaver. This record picked up a little negative publicity when the folks in Spokane took exception to "Spokane Motel Blues." Still, no one else will find anything to complain about. —*Jim Worbois*

Greatest Hits, Vol. 2 / 1975 / Mercury ✦✦✦
Where *Greatest Hits* had the bulk of Tom T. Hall's greatest story songs, *Greatest Hits, Vol. 2* concentrates on his silly, cutesy songs, like "Sneaky Snake," "I Like Beer," "I Love," and "Old Dogs, Children and Watermelon Wine," among seven others. For fans of his detailed narratives, these songs can be quite grating, but for listeners that want all of these hits in one package, *Greatest Hits, Vol. 2* functions quite nicely. —*Thom Owens*

The Magnificent Music Machine / 1976 / Mercury ✦✦✦

Greatest Hits, Vol. 3 / 1978 / Mercury ✦✦✦
Beginning with 1976's "Faster Horses" and running through 1977's "Your Man Love You, Honey" and "It's All in the Game," *Greatest Hits, Vol. 3* collects the remainder of Tom T. Hall's '70s hit singles for Mercury Records. It does feature his biggest hit singles from the mid-'70s, as well as some less interesting, lesser-known songs, but the material on *Greatest Hits, Vol. 3* isn't quite as strong as Hall's two previous hit collections. The album does pick up some highlights from a number of weaker albums, but casual fans will be better served by the first two *Greatest Hits* collections or, better yet, the box set *Storyteller, Poet Philosopher*. —*Thom Owens*

★ Essential Tom T. Hall / 1988 / Mercury ✦✦✦✦✦
Tom T.s songs are stories filled with interesting characters. And, some of his most interesting characters are gathered on this record,. which celebrates the first 20 years of Hall's career as a performer. (Hall was a writer first, with his most famous pre-performer song being "Harper Valley PTA.") Whether you're looking for a hits package (which this isn't, strictly speaking) or just want to learn more about Hall, this is a fine place to start. —*Jim Worbois*

Greatest Hits, Vols. 1 & 2 / 1993 / Mercury ✦✦✦✦
Greatest Hits, Vols. 1 & 2 combines Tom T. Hall's first two greatest hits albums on one CD. Although it is a good bargain, the two albums don't necessarily fit well together—the earlier story songs are considerably more heartfelt and substantial than the psuedo-novelties that comprise the latter songs. Nevertheless, the two-fer CD works as the best single-disc retrospective of Tom T. Hall's career, although it still misses a couple of key tracks. —*Stephen Thomas Erlewine*

Great Country Hits / 1994 / Special Music ✦✦✦
Featured are "The Year That Clayton Delaney Died" and "Old Dogs, Children and Watermelon Wine," among others. —*AMG*

★ Storyteller, Poet, Philosopher / Nov. 14, 1995 / Mercury ✦✦✦✦
The double-disc box set *Storyteller, Poet, Philosopher* concentrates on Tom T. Hall's talents as a narrative songwriter, eschewing some of his better-known novelties for lesser-known, but better-written, serious songs. That doesn't mean the box is devoid of hits—all of the important ones are here. What it does mean is that *Storyteller, Poet, Philosopher* is the first Tom T. Hall compilation to accurately convey the scope of his talents, as well as his achievements. —*Thom Owens*

Songs from Sopchoppy / 1996 / Mercury ✦✦
Tom T. Hall's two-disc box set—the outstanding *Storyteller, Poet, Philosopher*—revived interest in the one-of-a-kind performer. So Mercury Records, the label that Hall worked for from 1967 to 1986, agreed to release *Songs from Sopchoppy*, his first album of original tunes in ten years (not counting a children's project). Unfortunately, the collection is not up to Hall's usual standards. Part of the problem comes from production. Tom Collins once guided hits for Ronnie Milsap and Barbara Mandrell, but he hasn't been active in record production since the mid-1980s. That's where his sound seems stuck, as he saddles Hall with a decidedly old-fashioned, stilted sound. Hall's observations are still witty, but rarely as incisive as on such classics as "Homecoming" and "Ballad of Forty Dollars." Still, the best song on the new album, a ballad titled "Shoes and Dress That Alice Wore," is a devastating and artful piece of work. It suggests Hall still has it, if someone is willing to push him to dig a little deeper. —*Michael McCall*

Ballad of Forty Dollars/Homecoming / Bear Family ✦✦✦✦

I Witness Life/100 Children / Bear Family ✦✦✦✦
I Witness Life and *100 Children*, two of Tom T. Hall's excellent late '60s albums, are combined on this single compact disc. Although many of the best songs were featured on *Greatest Hits* and *Storyteller, Poet Philosopher,* these albums work well as individual records and they're well worth acquiring for any Hall fan. —*Thom Owens*

George Hamilton IV

b. Jul. 19, 1937, Winston-Salem, NC
Guitar, Vocals / Traditional Country, Country-Pop, Country-Folk, Nashville Sound/Countrypolitan

Proclaimed the International Ambassador of Country Music thanks to his performances around the world during the 1970s, George Hamilton IV began his career in the late '50s not as a country artist but as a teen-oriented pop star. After his first hit, "A Rose and a Baby Ruth," hit No. 6 on the pop charts in 1956, he toured with Buddy Holly and the Everly Brothers but cracked the pop Top Ten only once more time. Instead, Hamilton moved to the country charts by 1959, where nine of his hits spent time in the Top Ten, including his only No. 1, "Abilene."

Though he began in pop, Hamilton's primary interest in country music stretched back all the way to his hometown of Winston-

Salem, NC. Born July 19, 1937, George Hamilton IV was raised on the Westerns of Gene Autry and began playing guitar at the age of 12. He formed a country band in high school and while still a freshman at the University of South Carolina, he met John D. Loudermilk, then a struggling songwriter. With a contract in hand from the Colonial label, Hamilton recorded "A Rose and a Baby Ruth," Loudermilk's attempt at approximating rockabilly music. The single did well regionally during 1956, and was picked up by ABC-Paramount later that year. After it hit No. 6 on the pop charts, ABC signed Hamilton to a regular contract.

Somewhat uncomfortable on the pop charts, George Hamilton IV never equalled the success of "A Rose and a Baby Ruth." The 1957 single "Why Don't They Understand" barely made the Top Ten, and his 1958 inspirational record "The Teen Commandments"—recorded with Paul Anka and Johnny Nash—stalled at No. 29. After appearing on *The Jimmy Dean Show* during 1957-58, Hamilton was given his own show by ABC-TV in 1959; it ended before the year was out.

After the failure of his own show, Hamilton joined the Grand Ole Opry in 1959, making his claim to country audiences more sincere by not affecting the Western trappings of most country artists. His first entry on the country charts ("Before This Day Ends") made No. 4 in late 1960. One year later, Hamilton was signed to RCA Victor by Chet Atkins. After Top Ten entries in 1961 ("Three Steps to the Phone [Millions of Miles]") and 1962 ("If You Don't Know I Ain't Gonna Tell You"), George Hamilton IV hit it big in 1963 with "Abilene." The single, his second to be written by John D. Loudermilk, topped the country charts for four weeks in June and crossed over to No. 15 on the pop charts. During 1964, Hamilton charted three singles and returned to the Top Ten with "Fort Worth, Dallas or Houston."

Increasingly inspired by folk music during 1965, Hamilton began recording the songs of Gordon Lightfoot; both "Steel Rail Blues" and "Early Morning Rain" hit the country Top 15 during 1966, and Hamilton went on to record more Gordon Lightfoot songs than any other artist. "Urge for Going" (written by another folkie, Joni Mitchell) hit No. 7 in 1967 and "Break My Mind" did the single one better later in the year. He continued to record for RCA until 1974, but chart success largely eluded him—except for the No. 3 hit "She's a Little Bit Country" in 1970.

Undaunted by his lack of domestic success, George Hamilton IV took country music around the world during the '70s. Besides more than ten tours of Great Britain and several BBC-TV productions, he hosted the Gospel Celebration and the International Country Festival, both of which were held in England. In 1973, he organized the longest international tour ever by a country artist, doing 73 shows over a period of three months. One year later, Hamilton became the first country artist to perform behind the Iron Curtain, where he lectured about country music as well as playing shows (one Czechoslovakian concert even featured a Czech country group backing him). Besides Europe, he toured Africa, the Orient, New Zealand, Australia, and even the Middle East during the late '70s.

Signed to ABC-Dot in 1976, George Hamilton IV just barely made the country charts several times during 1977-78. Since then, he has concentrated on gospel recordings, for both Word and Lion & Lamb. His son, George Hamilton V, toured with his father's backup band and charted a single during 1988. — *John Bush*

● **The ABC Collection: George Hamilton IV** / 1977 / ABC ✦✦✦✦

● **The Very Best of George Hamilton IV** / 1986 / Country Store [UK] ✦✦✦✦

1954-65 / 1995 / Bear Family ✦✦✦✦

1954-65 is a six-disc box set containing all of George Hamilton IV's most popular recordings, including all of his records for ABC/Paramount and the bulk of his RCA recordings. Hamilton's pop hits often obscured his talents as a country singer, but this set demonstrates that he was a talented and versatile singer. Nevertheless, it's the kind of set that is designed for hardcore fans—there may be several gems buried in this weighty box set, but its sheer bulk makes *1954-65* intimidating to anyone else. — *Thom Owens*

Hancock & Gilmore

Progressive Country, Country-Rock, Singer-Songwriter, Alternative Country

Butch Hancock and Jimmie Dale Gilmore are Texas-based singer-songwriters. Along with Joe Ely, they were members of the Flatlanders in the early '70s and since then have maintained solo careers, though they reunited to make the album *Two Roads* in 1990. — *William Ruhlmann*

Two Roads / 1990 / Caroline ✦✦✦

Gilmore and Hancock take turns singing and accompanying each other on this live album recorded during an Australian tour. — *Kurt Wolff*

Butch Hancock

b. Jul. 12, 1945, Lubbock, TX

Guitar, Vocals / Progressive Country, Singer-Songwriter, Country-Folk, Alternative Country, Americana

An obscure, legendary Texas songwriter whose work has been covered by Jerry Jeff Walker and Joe Ely, Hancock has a gift for wordplay and nuance. His songs become gradually more accessible, as the tentative voice-and-guitar approach is replaced by surprisingly full folk-rock settings and assured singing. — *William Ruhlmann*

West Texas Waltees / 1978 / Rainlight ✦✦✦✦

The Wind's Domimou / 1979 / Rainlight ✦✦✦

Diamond Hill / 1980 / Rainlight ✦✦✦✦

1981: A Spare Odyssey / 1981 / Rainlight ✦✦

Firewater / 1981 / Rainlight ✦✦✦✦

Off-the-cuff versions of Hancock's classics are here, including "The Wind's Dominion," and "If You Were a Bluebird." The band includes Jimmy Dale Gilmore. — *Richard Meyer*

Yella Rose with Marce Lacoutre / 1985 / Rainlight ✦✦✦

This album has a rather big band with occasional horns, congas, and accordion. A good one. — *Richard Meyer*

Split & Slide / 1986 / Rainlight ✦✦✦

● **Own & Own** / 1989 / Sugar Hill ✦✦✦✦

This compilation is culled from Hancock's many albums on his own Rainlight label from 1978 to 1987 (plus four tracks from 1989). — *William Ruhlmann*

Live in Australia / 1990 / Virgin ✦✦✦

An energetic live album of duets by Hancock and Gilmore, it was recorded in Sydney in 1990. The Flatlander "hit" "Dallas" is here and other ragged but right cuts from these musical pals. — *Richard Meyer*

Cause of the Cactus / 1991 / Rainlight ✦✦✦✦

Two Roads / Jul. 3, 1992 / Caroline ✦✦✦

Own the Way over Here / 1993 / Sugar Hill ✦✦✦

Eats Away the Night / 1995 / Sugar Hill ✦✦✦✦

After about 20 years, Butch Hancock has released his first produced studio album for a national label not compiled from his previously released Rainlight Records LPs. In many ways, Hancock set his style down with his very first self-produced album, *West Texas Waltz*. All the elements from that period remain—the Dylanesque vocal sound, his love of wordplay, and a deep feeling for the stories that make up an individual's life. The warm sound of this album makes it easier for newcomers to get past his dry voice, and the inclusion of his hit "If You Were a Bluebird" will help a new audience locate him properly in the contemporary Texas songwriting scene. The band is tight and steps back enough to let Hancock's stories and personality shine through. — *Richard Meyer*

No Two Alike / Rainlight ✦✦✦✦

This 14-tape series (available by subscription only) is a document of six nights at the Cactus Cafe, where Hancock performed with a host of great guests and never repeated a single one of his songs. — *Richard Meyer*

Wayne Hancock

Vocals / Alternative Country, Neo-Traditionalist Country, Americana

Wayne Hancock is something of a throwback in modern country: an unrepentant hillbilly who appropriates the elder Hank Williams' aversion to the Nashville machine, as well as bits of his style. Hancock's music is hardcore country, a mix of honky tonk, swing, and rockabilly that seems retro but has actually never been thrown together in quite such a way. Hancock's first album, *Thunderstorms and Neon Signs*, was released by Dejadisc in 1995. —*Steve Huey*

Thunderstorms and Neon Signs / Oct. 1995 / Dejadisc ✦✦✦✦
Hancock has a voice that swings like Hank Williams' "Move It on Over," but he's a modern guy with all the complexities that brings. Still he's working the same street as Williams—lonesome nights and the many sides of love. These tunes have spunk and heart and you can tell the band loves what they are playing; it's loose, warm, playful and witty. This is such a refreshing album, it reminds you what you were listening through all the other dreck to find. It is hard to pick out individual tracks; this record is all of a piece. —*Richard Meyer*

Hank Flamingo

Contemporary Country, New Traditionalist

This six-man band (with no Hank Flamingo) formed in Tennessee in the late '80s and recorded a self-titled debut for Giant Records in 1993. The band has a contemporary take on traditional country music, and consists of Eddie Grigg (guitar, vocals), Ben Northern (bass, vocals), Stuart E. Stuart (fiddle, vocals), Trent Summar (vocals), Philip Wallace (guitar), and Roy Watts (drums). —*John Bush*

Hank Flamingo / Giant ✦✦✦✦

The Happy Goodman Family

Southern Gospel, Country Gospel

For nearly four decades, the Happy Goodman Family brightened the world with their gospel songs. Founded in Alabama in the 1940s by Howard and Gussie Goodman, over the years, the Happy Goodman Family expanded and changed membership until it finally became a quartet composed of Ruth, Sam, Rusty, and Bob Goodman. The group was later joined by Vestal Goodman and the only non-Goodman, tenor Johnny Cook. The family was most successful during the 1960s and '70s. In 1968, their album *The Happy Gospel of the Happy Goodmans* won a Grammy for Best Gospel Album. The following year, Vestal received a Dove Award for Female Vocalist of the Year. The Happy Goodmans were some of the first members of the TV show *The Gospel Singing Jubilee*, which has won numerous Dove awards. —*Sandra Brennan*

● **Greatest Hits** / 1985 / Canaan ✦✦✦✦
A live recording of The Goodman Family's country gospel. —*Bil Carpenter*

Harden Trio

Country-Pop, Nashville Sound/Countrypolitan

Sibling act the Harden Trio was basically a one hit wonder, but they spent many years at the Grand Ole Opry. Robbie, Arleen, and Bobby Harden were all born in England, AR, an area of the Ozarks noted for its rich musical heritage. They teamed as teens and performed locally, first gaining professional notice when they joined *Barnyard Frolics* in Little Rock. They became popular and joined the *Ozark Mountain Jubilee* in Springfield, MO, as well as the *Louisiana Hayride*. Their success led them to Nashville, where they appeared on WSM's *Opry Almanac*.

In 1965, they made their recording debut with "Poor Boy," which did nothing on the charts. Their second single, "Tippy Toeing," was their biggest; it hit No. 3 on the country charts, crossed over to the pop Top 50, and earned the group a spot on the Opry. In 1967, Arleen and Robbie left the group to go solo. Bobby tried to keep the band going with Karen Wheeler and Shirley Michaels, but the trio broke up in 1968, and Bobby went solo as well.

Arleen, who changed her name to Arlene, did have some success as a singer, making the charts 16 times over the six years she spent with Columbia. In 1968, she and Bobby had success with a duet, "Who Loves You." In 1974, she changed her name back and scored one minor hit, her version of Helen Reddy's "Leave Me Alone (Little Ruby Red Dress)." Meanwhile, Bobby found his calling as a successful songwriter. —*Sandra Brennan*

Tippy Toeing / 1966 / Columbia ✦✦✦

Sing Me Back Home / 1968 / Columbia ✦✦✦

Nashville Sensation / 1969 / Starday ✦✦✦✦

● **Great Country Hits** / 1970 / Harmony ✦✦✦✦

Linda Hargrove

b. Feb. 3, 1951, Tallahassee, FL

Vocals / Country-Rock, Country-Pop, Urban Cowboy

Linda Hargrove was a singer, songwriter, and multi-instrumentalist who forever seemed to be in the wrong place at the wrong time. In the mid-'70s, she was one of the first Nashville artists to coat country sounds with a modern pop-rock sheen; by the time that hybrid came to dominate the charts a decade later, however, Hargrove was largely out of the music industry.

Born in Tallahassee, FL, on February 3, 1951, Hargrove began playing piano and guitar while still a pre-teen. Throughout her formative years, she was largely unresponsive to country music, preferring instead pop and R&B, and by the tail end of the 1960s was performing in a local blue-eyed soul band. It was not until the release of Bob Dylan's *Nashville Skyline* album that she became fascinated by the possibilities that country music offered; when another Florida group, After All, decided to record seven of Hargrove's songs, she followed the band to Nashville in 1970. A year later, Sandy Posey recorded Hargrove's "Saw Someone Else before Me," which brought her to the attention of producers Billy Sherrill and Pete Drake, who helped the fledgling performer find work as a session guitarist and songwriter.

In 1973, Leon Russell recorded a pair of Hargrove tunes for his country album *Hank Wilson Is Back*. In the same year, Drake introduced her to ex-Monkee Michael Nesmith; together with James Miner, Hargrove and Nesmith co-wrote the song "Winonah," which the latter recorded for his *Pretty Much Your Standard Ranch Stash* album. Nesmith also signed Hargrove to his short-lived experimental C&W label Countryside; she recorded an LP for the label, but it never saw the light of day after Countryside was dropped by its parent company, Elektra/Asylum. Elektra did, however, release her 1973 album *Music Is Your Mistress*, as well as its follow-up, the next year's *Blue Jean Country Queen*.

In 1975, Hargrove moved to Capitol Records, for which she released her only Top 40 hit, "Love Was (Once Around the Dance Floor)," from the LP *Love, You're the Teacher*. In the same year, Johnny Rodriguez took her composition "Just Get up and Close the Door" to the top of the charts. She released two more country albums, 1976's *Just Like You* and 1977's *Impressions*, but found little commercial success. Shortly thereafter, she began to focus exclusively on inspirational music, and under her married name of Linda Bartholomew released the Christian album *A New Song* in 1981. She was largely out of music for the next several years until another inspirational record, *Greater Works*, was issued in 1987. Following its release, she again left the industry due to health problems; after recovering from leukemia, in the mid-'90s she began making tentative steps towards resuming her career as a country performer. —*Jason Ankeny*

Music Is Your Mistress / 1973 / Elektra ✦✦✦
Hargrove is an excellent songwriter, which is borne out by the fact that several of these songs have been covered other places. She's also a fine performer. But something in the production keeps this from being the killer record it could have been. In some places it sounds thin and in others the mix works against the voice. Still, the songs make this record worth having. —*Jim Worbois*

Blue Jean Country Queen / 1974 / Elektra ✦✦✦

● **Love, You're the Teacher** / 1975 / Capitol ✦✦✦✦
More good stuff from Hargrove, including her original version of
the Johnny Rodriguez hit "Just Get up and Close the Door." Everything is in place (songs, performance, production) making this,
easily, one of her best. —*Jim Worbois*

Just Like You / 1976 / Capitol ✦✦✦
Good songs. Some of the best players and singers around. Mike
Nesmith is a writing partner on one song. Why didn't this catch
on in a big way? . . . one of life's great mysteries. This is a good
album. —*Jim Worbois*

Impressions / 1977 / Capitol ✦✦✦

Bill Harrell

b. Sep. 14, 1934, Marion, VA
Vocals / Traditional Bluegrass
A player who favored a subtle, traditional approach to his music,
singer and multi-instrumentalist Bill Harrell remained one of
bluegrass' most popular figures for several decades. Born in Marion, VA, on September 14, 1934, Harrell's passion for music began
during his childhood, when he started playing guitar and taking
piano lessons. While attending college in Maryland, he first
became enamored of bluegrass, and began playing mandolin in a
trio. Tenures in other Washington, DC-area groups, including the
Rocky Mountain Boys, followed as he played with musicians like
Eddie Adcock, Donny Bryant, Smiley Hobbs, Smitty Irvin, Carl
Nelson, and Roy Self.
While serving in the armed forces, Harrell was injured in an
auto accident, and spent close to a year recovering in a military
hospital. Upon his release, he returned to Washington and cut his
first recordings. In 1960, he formed the Virginians with Irvin on
banjo, Buck Ryan on fiddle, and Stoney Edwards on bass. The
group released the album *The Wonderful World of Bluegrass
Music* in 1963 and followed it two years later with *Ballads and
Bluegrass*. In addition to hosting a weekly television program from
Harrisonburg, VA, the group played dates up and down the East
Coast and guested frequently on Jimmy Dean's network series.
Irvin left the band in 1965, and was replaced by Don Stover.
Harrell soon departed to join Don Reno and the Tennessee Cut-
Ups, remaining with Reno for over a decade; their partnership
coincided with a resurgence in the public's interest in bluegrass as
a result of a growing festival circuit. Soon after Harrell joined the
group, his Virginians bandmate Buck Ryan signed on as well, and
in 1966 Reno and Harrell released the LP *The Most Requested
Songs*. Around the time of 1969's *I'm Using My Bible for a Road-
map*, Reno's former partner Red Smiley came out of retirement,
and began performing with the group onstage and in the studio.
After several more records with Reno, Harrell and bassist Ed
Ferris amicably left the group to reform the Virginians with Har-
rell's old friend Carl Nelson on fiddle and newcomer Darrell
Sanders on banjo. The band released the record *Bluegrass and
Ballads* in 1978, followed by the back-to-back *Bluegrass Gospel,
Pure and Simple* and *I Can Hear Virginia Calling Me* in 1980.
Despite a revolving-door lineup, Harrell continued to steer the
Virginians well into the 1990s, issuing records like 1983's *Walk-
ing in the Early Morning Dew*, 1986's *Blue Virginia Blue*, and
1990's *After Sunrise*. —*Jason Ankeny*

Ballads & Bluegrass / Adelphi ✦✦✦
● **Classic Bluegrass** / Rebel ✦✦✦✦

Emmylou Harris

b. Apr. 2, 1947, Birmingham, AL
*Guitar, Vocals / Traditional Country, Progressive Country, Coun-
try-Rock, Contemporary Country, Folk-Rock*
Though other performers sold more records and earned greater
fame, few left as profound an impact on contemporary music as
Emmylou Harris. Blessed with a crystalline voice, a remarkable gift
for phrasing, and a restless creative spirit, she traveled a singular
artistic path, proudly carrying the torch of "Cosmic American
music" passed down by her mentor, Gram Parsons. With the sole
exception of Neil Young—not surprisingly an occasional collaborator—no other mainstream star established a similarly large body of

work as consistently iconoclastic, eclectic, or daring; even more
than three decades into her career, Harris' latter-day music
remained as heartfelt, visionary, and vital as her earliest recordings.
Harris was born on April 2, 1947, to a military family stationed
in Birmingham, AL. After spending much of her childhood in
North Carolina, she moved to Woodbridge, VA, while in her teens,
and graduated high school there as her class valedictorian. After
winning a dramatic scholarship at the University of North Carolina, she began to seriously study music, learning to play songs by
Bob Dylan and Joan Baez. Soon, Harris was performing in a duo
with fellow UNC student Mike Williams, eventually quitting
school to move to New York, only to find the city's folk music
community dying out in the wake of the psychedelic era.
Still, Harris remained in New York, traveling the Greenwich Village club circuit before becoming a regular at Gerdes Folk City,
where she struck up friendships with folkies Jerry Jeff Walker,
David Bromberg, and Paul Siebel. After marrying songwriter Tom
Slocum in 1969, she recorded her debut LP, 1970's *Gliding Bird*.
Shortly after the record's release, however, Harris' label declared
bankruptcy, and while pregnant with her first child, her marriage
began to fall apart. After moving to Nashville, she and Slocum
divorced, leaving Harris to raise daughter Hallie on her own. After
several months of struggle and poverty, she moved back in with her
parents, who had since bought a farm outside of Washington, DC.
There she returned to performing, starting a trio with local
musicians Gerry Mule and Tom Guidera. One evening in 1971,
while playing at an area club called Clyde's, the trio performed to
a crowd that included members of the country-rock pioneers the
Flying Burrito Brothers. In the wake of the departure of Gram
Parsons, the band's founder, the Burritos were then led by ex-Byrd
Chris Hillman, who was so impressed by Harris' talents that he
considered inviting her to join the group. Instead, Hillman himself
quit to join Stephen Stills' Manassas, but he recommended her to
Parsons, who wanted a female vocalist to flesh out the sound of
his solo work, a trailblazing fusion of country and rock 'n' roll he
dubbed "Cosmic American music." Their connection was instant,
and soon Harris was learning about country music and singing
harmony on Parsons' solo debut, 1972's *GP*. A tour with Parsons'
backup unit the Fallen Angels followed, and in 1973 they
returned to the studio to cut his landmark LP *Grievous Angel*.
On September 19, just weeks after the album sessions ended,
Parsons' fondness for drugs and alcohol finally caught up with
him, and he was found dead in a hotel room outside of the Joshua
Tree National Monument in California. At the time, Harris was
back in Washington, collecting her daughter for a planned move to
the West Coast. Instead, she remained in DC, reuniting with Tom
Guidera to form the Angel Band. The group signed to Reprise and
relocated to Los Angeles to begin work on Harris' solo major label
debut, 1975's acclaimed *Pieces of the Sky*, an impeccable collection
made up largely of diverse covers ranging in origin from Merle
Haggard to the Beatles. Produced by Brian Ahern, who would go
on to helm Harris' next ten records—as well as becoming her second husband—*Pieces of the Sky's* second single, a rendition of the
Louvin Brothers' "If I Could Only Win Your Love," became her first
Top Five hit. "Light of the Stable," a Christmas single complete
with backing vocals from Dolly Parton, Linda Ronstadt, and Neil
Young, soon followed; Harris then repaid the favor by singing on
Ronstadt's "The Sweetest Gift" and Young's "Star of Bethlehem."
For her second LP, 1976's *Elite Hotel*, Harris established a new
backing unit, the Hot Band, which featured legendary Elvis Pres-
ley sidemen James Burton and Glen D. Hardin as well as a young
songwriter named Rodney Crowell on backup vocals and rhythm
guitar. The resulting album proved to be a smash, with covers of
Buck Owens' "Together Again" and the Patsy Cline perennial
"Sweet Dreams" both topping the charts. Before beginning ses-
sions for her third effort, 1977's *Luxury Liner*, Harris guested on
Bob Dylan's *Desire* and appeared in Martin Scorsese's filmed doc-
ument of the Band's legendary final performance, *The Last Waltz*.
Quarter Moon in a Ten Cent Town followed in 1978, led by the
single "Two More Bottles of Wine," her third No. 1. The record was
Crowell's last with the Hot Band; one of the tracks, "Green Rolling
Hills," included backing from Ricky Skaggs, soon to become
Crowell's replacement as Harris' vocal partner.

1979's *Blue Kentucky Girl* was her most country-oriented work to date, an indication of what was to come a year later with *Roses in the Snow*, a full-fledged excursion into acoustic bluegrass. In the summer of 1980, a duet with Roy Orbison, "That Lovin' You Feelin' Again," hit the Top Ten; a yuletide LP, *Light of the Stable: The Christmas Album*, followed at the end of the year, at a time during which Harris had quit touring to focus on raising her second daughter, Meghann. *Evangeline*, a patchwork of songs left off of previous albums, appeared in 1981. Shortly after, Skaggs left the Hot Band to embark on a solo career; his replacement was Barry Tashian, a singer-songwriter best known for fronting the 1960s rock band the Remains.

In 1982, drummer John Ware, the final holdover from the first Hot Band lineup, left the group; at the same time, Harris' marriage to Ahern was also beginning to disintegrate. After 1981's *Cimarron*, Harris and the Hot Band cut a live album, *Last Date*, named in honor of the album's chart-topping single "(Lost His Love) On Our Last Date," a vocal version of the Floyd Cramer instrumental. Quickly, they returned to the studio to record *White Shoes*, Harris' final LP with Ahern at the helm. Her most far-ranging affair yet, it included covers of Donna Summer's "On the Radio," Johnny Ace's "Pledging My Love," and Sandy Denny's "Old-Fashioned Waltz."

After leaving Ahern, Harris and her children moved back to Nashville. There, Harris joined forces with singer-songwriter Paul Kennerley, on whose 1980 concept album *The Legend of Jesse James* she had sung backup. Together, they began formulating a record called *The Ballad of Sally Rose*, employing the pseudonym Harris often used on the road to veil what was otherwise a clearly autobiographical portrait of her own life. Though a commercial failure, the 1985 record proved pivotal in Harris' continued evolution as an artist and a risk-taker; it also marked another chapter in her personal life when she and Kennerley wed shortly after concluding their tour. *Angel Band*, a subtle, acoustic collection of traditional country spirituals, followed, although the record was not issued until 1987, after the release of its immediate follow-up, *Thirteen*.

Harris, Dolly Parton, and Linda Ronstadt had first toyed with the idea of recording an album together as far back as 1977, only to watch the project falter in light of touring commitments and other red tape. Finally, in 1987, they issued *Trio*, a collection that proved to be Harris' best-selling album to date, generating the hits "To Know Him Is to Love Him" (a cover of the Phil Spector classic), "Telling Me Lies," and "Those Memories of You." The record's success spurred the 1990 release of *Duets*, a compilation of her earlier hits in conjunction with George Jones, Willie Nelson, Gram Parsons, and others. Fronting a new band, the Nash Ramblers, in 1992 Harris issued *At the Ryman*, a live set recorded at Nashville's legendary Ryman Auditorium, the former home of the Grand Ole Opry. At the time of the record's release, Harris was also serving a term as President of the Country Music Foundation.

In 1993, she ended her long association with Warner Bros./Reprise to move to Asylum Records, where she released *Cowgirl's Prayer* shortly after her separation from Paul Kennerley. Two years later, at a stage in her career at which most performers retreat to the safety of rehashing their greatest hits again and again, Harris issued *Wrecking Ball*, perhaps her most adventuresome record to date. Produced by Daniel Lanois, the New Orleans-based artist best known for his atmospheric work with U2, Peter Gabriel, and Bob Dylan, *Wrecking Ball* was a hypnotic, staggeringly beautiful work comprised of songs ranging from the Neil Young-penned title track (which featured its writer on backing vocals) to Jimi Hendrix's "May This Be Love" and the talented newcomer Gillian Welch's "Orphan Girl." A three-disc retrospective of her years with Warner Bros., *Portraits*, appeared in 1996. —*Jason Ankeny*

Gliding Bird / 1970 / Amos ♦♦

Harris typically omits *Gliding Bird* from her discography; her first record, it was issued on the folk label Jubilee, which filed for bankruptcy within weeks of the LP's release. Cut before her tenure with Gram Parsons, it's a straightforward folk effort, owing more to Joni Mitchell than anything else; although most of the songs were composed by Tom Slocum, Harris' first husband, there are also a number of ill-suited covers, including Hank Williams' "I

Saw the Light" and the Burt Bacharach/Hal David composition "I'll Never Fall in Love Again." —*Jason Ankeny*

★ **Pieces of the Sky** / 1975 / Reprise ♦♦♦♦♦

Harris' major-label solo debut quickly establishes the pattern that the vast majority of her subsequent work would follow: *Pieces of the Sky* is bravely eclectic, impeccably performed, and achingly beautiful. Amidst a collection of songs that rank among her most well-chosen—ranging from the catalogs of the Beatles ("For No One") to Boudleaux & Felice Bryant ("Sleepless Nights") and the Louvin Brothers (the hit "If I Could Only Win Your Love")—the record's centerpiece is one of Harris' rare original compositions, "Boulder to Birmingham," her stirring tribute to fallen mentor Gram Parsons. —*Jason Ankeny*

Elite Hotel / 1976 / Reprise ♦♦♦♦

While much of Harris' career has been spent carrying on the legacy of Gram Parsons, *Elite Hotel* ranks among her most overt tributes to his genius, thanks to its covers of the Flying Burrito Brothers' "Sin City" and "Wheels," along with "Ooh Las Vegas" from the *Grievous Angel* album. In addition to the usual eclectic mix of covers—which includes the Beatles' "Here, There and Everywhere" and Hank Williams' "Jambalaya" this time out—*Elite Hotel* offers renditions of the country perennials "Together Again" and "Sweet Dreams," which were, respectively, Harris' first two No. 1 chart hits. —*Jason Ankeny*

Luxury Liner / 1977 / Reprise ♦♦♦♦

Luxury Liner ranks as Harris' best-selling solo record to date, and it's one of her most engaging efforts as well; her Hot Band is in peak form, and the songs are even more far afield than usual, including Chuck Berry's "(You Never Can Tell) C'est La Vie" and Townes Van Zandt's painterly tale of aging outlaws, "Pancho & Lefty." —*Jason Ankeny*

☆ **Profile (The Best of Emmylou Harris)** / 1978 / Reprise ♦♦♦♦♦

Profile (The Best of Emmylou Harris) collects 12 of Harris' biggest hits from the mid-'70s, including the No. 1 hits "Together Again," "Sweet Dreams," "Two More Bottles of Wine," and the Top Ten hits "One of These Days," "If I Could Only Win Your Love," "You Never Can Tell," "Making Believe," and "To Daddy." —*Stephen Thomas Erlewine*

A Quarter Moon in a Ten Cent Town / 1978 / Reprise ♦♦♦♦

Quarter Moon in a Ten Cent Town is a transitional effort that bridges the curveballs of Harris' earliest solo work with the more traditional country albums that comprise the bulk of the second phase of her career. For the first time, she doesn't cover Gram Parsons tunes or pop music chestnuts, relying instead on newly exited Hot Band member Rodney Crowell for two songs ("Leaving Louisiana in the Broad Daylight" and "I Ain't Living Long like This") and Dolly Parton for another (the devastating "To Daddy"); the highlight is a gorgeous cover of Jesse Winchester's "Defying Gravity." —*Jason Ankeny*

Blue Kentucky Girl / 1979 / Reprise ♦♦♦

In response to criticism that her records weren't "country" enough, Harris recorded *Blue Kentucky Girl*, one of her most traditional outings. Relying on a more acoustic sound, the album largely forsakes contemporary pop songs in favor of standard country fare, including the Louvin Brothers' "Everytime You Leave" and Leon Payne's "They'll Never Take His Love from Me." The cover of Dallas Frazier's "Beneath Still Waters" earned Harris her fourth No. 1 single. —*Jason Ankeny*

Christmas Album (Light in the Stable) / 1980 / Reprise ♦♦♦♦

Taking her cue from the title track, a Christmas single first issued in 1975 (complete with backing vocals by Neil Young, Dolly Parton, and Linda Ronstadt), Harris compiled this collection of holiday music, originally issued in 1980. Along with "Angel Eyes (Angel Eyes)," a Rodney Crowell song composed specifically for the project, the album includes traditional fare like "O Little Town of Bethlehem," "Little Drummer Boy," and "Silent Night," rendered in much the same acoustic style as her previous studio effort *Roses in the Snow*. —*Jason Ankeny*

Roses in the Snow / 1980 / Reprise ♦♦♦♦

Combining acoustic bluegrass with traditional Appalachian melodies (and tossing one contemporary tune, Paul Simon's "The

Boxer," into the mix), *Roses in the Snow* ranks among Harris' riskiest—and most satisfying—gambits. —*Jason Ankeny*

Evangeline / 1981 / Reprise ♦♦
Comprised largely of leftovers from earlier sessions, *Evangeline* is a scattershot affair encompassing rock, folk, and bluegrass, which stands among Harris' few disappointing efforts. —*Jason Ankeny*

Cimarron / Mar. 1981 / Reprise ♦♦♦
Harris' marriage to producer Brian Ahern was beginning to unravel by the beginning of the 1980s, and the seams in their relationship are clearly coming apart throughout *Cimarron*. While the record never explicitly acknowledges the couple's impending breakup, their troubles are evident in the uneven and uninspired performances. —*Jason Ankeny*

Last Date / 1982 / Reprise ♦♦♦
Last Date offers a good indication of Harris' live sets with the Hot Band during the early '80s. Taking its title from her hit vocal version of the Floyd Cramer country standard, the record leans heavily on Harris favorites, in addition to covers of Buck Owens' "Buckaroo," Hank Snow's "I'm Movin' On," Neil Young's "Long May You Run," and Gram Parsons' "Return of the Grievous Angel." —*Jason Ankeny*

White Shoes / 1983 / Reprise ♦♦♦
Harris' final album with longtime producer (and husband) Brian Ahern is among her most surprising and diverse, perhaps the closest she's ever come to a straightahead rock LP. Among the unusual cover choices: Johnny Ace's "Pledging My Love" and Donna Summer's "On the Radio." —*Jason Ankeny*

Profile II: The Best of Emmylou Harris / 1984 / Reprise ♦♦♦♦
Harris' second hits collection is highlighted by a pair of chart-toppers, "Beneath Still Waters" and "(Lost His Love) On Our Last Date." It also includes the Top Five smashes "Born to Run," "I'm Movin' On" and "Save the Last Dance for Me." —*Jason Ankeny*

The Ballad of Sally Rose / 1985 / Reprise ♦♦♦♦
Harris switched gears on this album, co-writing with Paul Kennerley a semi-autobiographical song cycle that makes you wonder why she had spent so much time interpreting the work of others. The album is unique in her catalog, but it's a successful attempt to try something different. —*William Ruhlmann*

Thirteen / 1986 / Reprise ♦♦
Thirteen takes its title from the number of solo efforts Harris had recorded to date; her numbering didn't take into account hits collections or her true debut, *Gliding Bird*, an album she later disowned. For that matter, *Thirteen* is no great shakes either—with the exception of a lovely cover of Bruce Springsteen's "My Father's House," both the material and the performances are lackluster. —*Jason Ankeny*

Angel Band / 1987 / Reprise ♦♦♦♦
Angel Band is yet another fascinating left turn, an acoustic record comprised of country-gospel songs like "We Shall Rise," "If I Be Lifted Up," and "Someday My Ship Will Sail," performed with great subtlety and nuance. —*Jason Ankeny*

Bluebird / 1988 / Reprise ♦♦♦
Like most of Emmylou Harris' albums, *Bluebird* is an expertly performed album, featuring some truly startling and affecting tour-de-forces by Harris. However, the material—while featuring a handful of truly great songs, like John Hiatt's "Icy Blue Heart" and her original "A River for Him"—is too uneven to rank among her finest efforts. —*Thom Owens*

Brand New Dance / 1990 / Reprise ♦♦♦
Though a pleasant enough record, *Brand New Dance* is nonetheless a disappointment; the material is merely so-so, and while the performances are up to par, the collection lacks the kinetic excitement of Harris' finest work. —*Jason Ankeny*

Duets / Jul. 24, 1990 / Reprise ♦♦♦
On the heels of *Trio*, Harris' smash studio collaboration with Dolly Parton and Linda Ronstadt, comes the compilation *Duets*, which collects previously released performances recorded in conjunction with Neil Young, Willie Nelson, and others. Obviously intended to cash in on the success of *Trio*, the record is by no means an essential addition to the Harris oeuvre: virtually every-

thing included is readily available on other albums, and the selections are erratic at best—by and large, Harris' finest material is her solo work, although the power of "Love Hurts," recorded during her all-too-brief period with Gram Parsons, remains undeniable. —*Jason Ankeny*

At the Ryman / 1992 / Reprise ♦♦♦♦
This is the album debut of the Nashville Ramblers, her acoustic backing band featuring Sam Bush and Roy Huskey, Jr., recorded over three nights in the former home of the Grand Ole Opry. Harris' choice of songs strikes a balance between hillbilly classics and folk-influenced rock, with Bill Monroe receiving heaviest tribute but sharing space with Tex Owens, Bruce Springsteen, and John Fogerty. —*Brian Mansfield*

Cowgirl's Prayer / 1993 / Asylum ♦♦♦♦
This is a collection of reflective, wholly adult songs set to exquisitely austere arrangements. —*Michael McCall*

Songs of the West / 1994 / Warner Brothers ♦♦
Following Harris' departure from Warner Bros., the label saw fit to compile *Songs of the West*, a collection of previously released performances linked thematically by their connection, however tenuous, to Western music, life, and mythology. Stripped of their original album context, the individual tracks fail to happily co-exist; the record's lone selling point is that a pair of cuts—one culled from her autobiographical song cycle *The Ballad of Sally Rose*, the other a cover of Poco's "Rose of Cimarron"—make their domestic CD bow herein. —*Jason Ankeny*

☆ **Wrecking Ball** / Sep. 26, 1995 / Grapevine ♦♦♦♦♦
Wrecking Ball is a left-field masterpiece, the most wide-ranging, innovative, and daring record in a career built on such notions. Rich in atmosphere and haunting in its dark complexity, much of the due credit belongs to producer Daniel Lanois; best known for his work with pop superstars like U2 and Peter Gabriel, on *Wrecking Ball* Lanois taps into the very essence of what makes Harris tick—the gossamer vocals, the flawless phrasing—while also opening up innumerable new avenues for her talents to explore. The songs shimmer and swirl, given life through Lanois' trademark ringing guitar textures and the almost primal drumming of U2's Larry Mullen, Jr. The fixed point remains Harris' voice, which leaps into each and every one of these diverse compositions—culled from the pens of Neil Young, Bob Dylan, Jimi Hendrix, Steve Earle, and others—with utter fearlessness, as if this were the album she'd been waiting her entire life to make. Maybe it is. —*Jason Ankeny*

Portraits / Oct. 8, 1996 / Warner Brothers ♦♦♦♦
Portraits is a three-disc, 61-track box set covering Emmylou Harris' career for Reprise and Warner Records, which spans from 1974 to 1992. Not only does the box select highlights from classic albums like *Luxury Liner, Roses in the Snow*, and *Blue Kentucky Girl*, but it also features her early duets with Gram Parsons and selections from the *Trio* album she recorded with Dolly Parton and Linda Ronstadt. *Portraits* doesn't dwell too long on unreleased material—there are only five unearthed tracks on the entire set—preferring to sketch out a full overview of her career. While there might be a few favorite tracks missing, the box nevertheless fulfills its goals quite nicely—anyone looking for a comprehensive compilation of Emmylou's career will not be disappointed. —*Thom Owens*

Freddie Hart

b. Dec. 21, 1933, Lochapoka, AL
Guitar, Vocals / Traditional Country, Country-Pop, Honky Tonk
Freddie Hart, a popular singer-songwriter during the 1970s, began life as one of 15 sharecropper's children. He was only five when his grandfather fashioned him a "guitar" out of a cigar box and wire from a Model T Ford. Hart first ran away from home at age seven. At age 12, his parents sent him to a Civilian Conservation Corps camp. When he was 16, Hart lied about his age and joined the Marines, and was sent to Iwo Jima and Okinawa. When not in battle, he entertained at the non-commissioned officer's clubs. Following the military, Hart began working odd jobs all over the country.
In 1949, he moved to Nashville to work as a roadie for Hank Williams, who helped Hart learn to write songs. Later that year, he cut his first single, "Every Little Thing Rolled into One," a song

written by George Morgan. Hart moved to Phoenix, AZ, in 1950 to work in a cotton-seed mill; there he met Lefty Frizzell and tried to sell him one of his songs. Instead, Frizzell ended up signing him to tour. Hart also signed with Capitol at this time, but had no chart success with his songs. In 1953, Hart left Frizzell's show to work as a regular on *Town Hall Party* in Southern California. Three years later he became a black-belt karate instructor for the L.A. Police Academy.

In 1955, he penned "Loose Talk," and it was recorded by Carl Smith. The song has since become a country standard recorded by numerous artists. Hart signed to Columbia in 1959 and finally began to gain popularity with two respectable hits, "The Wall" and the "Chain Gang." Through 1961, he appeared on the charts three more times and later that year debuted on the Grand Ole Opry. He didn't chart again until 1965, when he and his band the Heartbeats released "Togetherness" and "Born a Fool." He went back to Capitol in 1970 and had a hit with "The Whole World Holding Hands." 1971 was a banner year, starting with his No. 1 hit "Easy Lovin'," which also crossed over to become a Top 20 pop hit. It was followed by four more No. 1 hits through 1973, among them "Bless Your Heart." Hart's star waned through the rest of the decade, however, and though he continued to appear on the charts it was with decreasing frequency. He began label-hopping during the '80s and in 1987 had one of his last hits with "Best Love I Never Had." He continued to tour and write songs, and appeared frequently in Branson, MO. —*Sandra Brennan*

Spirited Freddie Hart / 1962 / Columbia ✦✦✦
Folks who are only familiar with Hart's string of hits from the '70s may be surprised by this record. A little honky tonk, a little early-'60s rock, and a ballad or two. Overall, quite a nice record. —*Jim Worbois*

Freddie Hart's Greatest Hits / 1969 / Kapp ✦✦✦✦

World Of / 1972 / Columbia ✦✦✦
While it appears that this record was released to cash in on Hart's 1970s success, it's still a fine collection of his work on Columbia (and includes both of his hits on that label). If you only know Hart's work from the '70s, this record may be a surprise. Still, there are some fine performances that should not be missed. —*Jim Worbois*

● **Best of Freddie Hart** / 1975 / MCA ✦✦✦✦

John Hartford

b. Dec. 30, 1937, New York City, NY
Banjo, Fiddle, Guitar, Vocals / Old-Time, Traditional Country, Progressive Country, Country-Rock
John Hartford is one of country music's true eccentrics. Best-known for the pop standard "Gentle on My Mind," he is a multi-talented musician who plays a variety of stringed instruments. As a songwriter he is known for a sharp, offbeat wit and music wavering between folk, modern country, and old-timey string music.

The son of a doctor and a painter, John Hartford was born in New York City. When he was an infant, his family moved to St. Louis. It was there that Hartford developed his lifelong passion for the Mississippi and its riverboats. By age 13, he was an accomplished fiddler and five-string banjo player whose main influences were Stringbean and Earl Scruggs. He founded his first bluegrass band in high school and went on to work various odd jobs ranging from deejaying to working as a deckhand on a riverboat. In the early '60s, Hartford cut a few singles, but they went nowhere. He moved to Nashville and began working as a deejay and a session man. There he got involved with songwriters Kris Kristofferson and Mickey Newbury and attempted to sell his songs to record labels and publishing companies.

In 1966, Hartford released his debut album, *John Hartford Looks at Life*, which was produced by Chet Atkins. The following year, he released *Earthwords & Music*, which featured his first hit single, "Gentle on My Mind." In 1967, Glen Campbell's cover of the song became a Top 40 country and pop hit in the US; following Campbell's example, a number of other artists—including Frank Sinatra, Dean Martin, and Aretha Franklin—recorded the song, providing Hartford with enough money to turn his back on pop stardom and record his own music. Still, he became a star of sorts, appearing regularly on CBS' *Smothers Brothers Comedy Hour* and later on

the *Glen Campbell Goodtime Hour*. He also played on the Byrds' 1968 album *Sweetheart of the Rodeo* and Doug Dillard's *The Banjo Album*. By the end of the decade, Hartford also earned his riverboat pilot's license, and frequently worked aboard the *Julia Belle Swain*.

In 1971, Hartford left California and founded a bluegrass band featuring guitarist Norman Blake, dobro player Tut Taylor, and master fiddler Vassar Clements. In the course of the next year, he also cut two solo albums, *Aero Plain* and *Morning Bugle*, and made guest appearances on albums by James Taylor, Seals & Croft, Hoyt Axton, and the Dillards. Hartford recorded *Tennessee Jubilee* in 1975 with the assistance of Benny Martin and Lester Flatt. In 1976, he released one of his best albums, *Mark Twang*, and continued recording steadily through the '70s and '80s. Among his most notable albums were his 1980 rock 'n' roll-meets-bluegrass reunion with the Dillards, *Permanent Wave*, and Shel Silverstein's *The Great Conch Train Robbery*. He began performing with his son Jamie in the late '80s and also became involved with Opryland, where he helped launch an old-fashioned steamboat ride. He also recorded and reissued his earlier work on his own Small Dog A-Barkin' label. —*Sandra Brennan*

Earthwords and Music / 1967 / RCA ✦✦✦
Aside from the obvious bonus of containing Hartford's own version of his classic "Gentle on My Mind," this record also contains other gems such as "Washing Machine," on which he imitates the difference in the sounds made by both the old and new machines (using only his voice) and his "rap" about the many uses of baking soda. Also contains some fine straight songs. Good stuff. —*Jim Worbois*

The Love Album / 1968 / RCA ✦✦✦
Too many instances where good songs get buried behind unnecessary strings and things. There is some good material here, so the record shouldn't be overlooked . . . just what was added to the tracks. —*Jim Worbois*

Iron Mountain Depot / 1970 / RCA ✦✦✦
Someone at RCA must have decided Hartford would benefit from more production, so strings and background singers have been added this time out. The songs are still good, but the added production values keep this from being the record it could have been. —*Jim Worbois*

Aereo-Plain / 1971 / Warner Brothers ✦✦✦
This record comes as close to explaining Hartford as both an artist and a writer as one is likely to get. While some of the songs may seem offensive ("Holding" or "Boogie" for instance), the album is filled with humor, good songs, and fine picking. Good stuff! —*Jim Worbois*

Morning Bugle / 1972 / Rounder ✦✦✦✦
One of Hartford's finest records. Recorded mostly live in the studio with virtually no overdubs, this is a fine collection of songs covering a variety of subjects. Two of the most poignant are "Howard Hughes Blues" and "Nobody Eats at Linebaugh's," which addresses country music's abandonment of the Ryman and downtown Nashville in favor of "the park." —*Jim Worbois*

Down on the River / 1972 / Flying Fish ✦✦✦
John Hartford's *Down on the River* is an old-timey tribute to the Mississippi River and its steamboats, casinos, and saloons, filled with campy salutes to a forgotten lifestyle, as well as surprisingly affectionate paeans to a lost era. Hartford's approach may be too kitschy for some—after all, there are several songs driven by a calliope—yet it's a thoroughly entertaining album for listeners that share his obsessions, or at least his fondness for fine, old-timey banjo. —*Thom Owens*

Nobody Knows What You Do / 1976 / Flying Fish ✦✦
On this album Hartford performs with such major artists as Buddy Emmons, Curly Sechler, Sam Bush, and Benny Martin, among others. —*AMG*

Mark Twang / 1976 / Flying Fish ✦✦✦✦
This record is the antithesis of *Iron Mountain*. Here you find just the man and his instruments. Not only did Hartford make up every one of these songs, but on each track he shows his versatility and expertise on a variety of instruments as well as his ability to clog dance while he plays the fiddle. (If you've ever seen him in concert, you know it's not a studio trick.) —*Jim Worbois*

Tennessee Jubilee / 1976 / Flying Fish ✦✦✦

● **Me Oh My, How the Time Does Fly** / 1982 / Flying Fish ✦✦✦✦
Me Oh My, How the Time Doed Fly is an 18-song compilation that culls from Hartford's nine Flying Fish albums, which were recorded between 1976-1987. The collection gives a good sense of his depth as a songwriter and instrumentalist. *—Thom Owens*

Catalogue / 1985 / Flying Fish ✦✦✦
This re-recording includes some hits from Hartford's days on RCA. *—Charles S. Wolfe*

Gum Tree Canoe / 1987 / Flying Fish ✦✦✦✦
The most well-rounded of all the Flying Fish albums, it has everything from bluegrass to Civil War songs. *—Charles S. Wolfe*

Hartford & Hartford / 1991 / Flying Fish ✦✦✦
Hartford's son Jamie is a fine mandolin player, and he joins his father for this album. *—Charles S. Wolfe*

Cadillac Rag / Small Dog A-Barkin'✦✦✦✦
As a musician, John Hartford vacillates between writing modern folk singer-songwriter tunes and being an academic revivalist, researching and recording traditional country and folk songs in their original arrangements. *Cadillac Rag* is one of his academic albums—ten traditional tunes, played simply and directly by Hartford (banjo), fiddler Ted Masden, Buddy Spicher, and John Yudkin. Occasionally the sleek professional production and studied performances make these traditional songs sound lifeless, which prevents *Cadillac Rag* from being a truly engaging listen. However, it is an interesting one, particularly if you're interested in studying traditional country from an academic standpoint. *—Thom Owens*

Dale Hawkins

b. Aug. 30, 1938
Guitar, Vocals / Rock & Roll, Rockabilly
This Louisiana guitarist's 1957 hit "Suzy Q," with its crackling, bluesy guitar and insistent cowbell, was one of the most exciting early rockabilly singles. Recording for Chess (as one of its few White artists) between 1956 and 1961, Hawkins never quite duplicated its success, either commercially or artistically, but came close enough on a number of occasions to warrant respect as one of the better rockabilly singers. His drawling delivery, sense of humor, affinity for blues, and sharp guitar work (which was actually provided by such ace players as Roy Buchanan, Scotty Moore, and James Burton) are heard to good effect on his 1958 album and a number of non-hit singles. Hawkins went on to become a producer of some note in the 1960s, working with the Five Americans and Bruce Channel. *—Richie Unterberger*

Susie Q / 1958 / Chess ✦✦✦✦
A way-above-average '50s rock 'n' roll album, including both sides of Dale's first four singles. Highlights are "Suzie Q," its killer B-side ("Don't Treat Me This Way"), and the goofy "See You Soon Baboon" and "Mrs. Mergitory's Daughter." *—Richie Unterberger*

My Babe / 1987 / Argo ✦✦✦
Rare singles and other interesting material that Hawkins cut, mostly for Chess, between 1958 and 1962. Includes his sole Top 40 hit besides "Suzie Q" ("La-Do-Dada") and some fine rockabilly interpretations of blues hits. *—Richie Unterberger*

● **Oh Suzy Q** / Oct. 24, 1995 / Chess ✦✦✦✦
Eighteen tracks from Hawkins' Chess prime, all but one from the late '50s. Includes "Susie Q" and some obscure rockabilly cuts that are nearly as good, such as "Don't Treat Me This Way," "Liza Jane," and "Ain't That Lovin' You Babe." James Burton, Roy Buchanan, and Scotty Moore are the most prominent of the excellent guitarists to be heard on these sides. One could quibble over the absence of "Mrs. Mergitory's Daughter," "Yea Yea (Class Cutter)," and the post-Chess single "Stay at Home Lulu," but this is definitely the best Hawkins compilation ever assembled. *—Richie Unterberger*

Hawkshaw Hawkins (Harold Hawkins)

b. Dec. 22, 1921, Huntington, WV, d. Mar. 5, 1963, Camden, TN
Guitar, Vocals / Country, Traditional Country, Honky Tonk
Born Harold F. Hawkins, Hawkshaw is a country singer, guitarist, songwriter, and entertainer. A large man (6 ft., 6 in.) with a deep singing voice, Hawkins was an immensely popular performer in country music for many years without the benefit of big record success. He started on radio, becoming a regular on WWVA's *Wheeling Jamboree* by 1946 and making his first records for the King label around that time. By 1953 he had signed with RCA Victor and had become a regular member of the Grand Ole Opry by 1955. Described as "the man with eleven-and-a-half yards of personality," Hawkins was a warm and engaging performer both on stage and on records, able to pull off a wide variety of material from maudlin weepers to uptempo novelties. His label-jumping from Columbia by the late '50s and back to King by the early '60s moved his material closer to commercial mainstream country, but his time in the spotlight ran out when he perished in the same plane crash as Cowboy Copas and Patsy Cline.

Hawkshaw Hawkins was born and raised in Huntington, WV. His first foray into performing came at the age of 15, when he won a talent contest at a local radio station, WSAZ. After this, he began working at the station, eventually moving to WCHS in Charleston by the end of the '30s; at WCHS, he frequently sang with Clarence "Sherlock" Jack. During 1941, he traveled the United States with a revue. The following year, he joined the military, where he was stationed in the Philippines; in Manila, he sang on the local Army radio.

Following his discharge from the Army, Hawkins signed with King Records, releasing the minor hit—and the song that would eventually become his signature tune—"The Sunny Side of the Mountain." In addition to recording for King, he was a regular on WWVA's *Wheeling Jamboree* betwen 1946 and 1954. In 1948, he had his first hit single with "Pan American," which climbed into the country Top Ten. Over the next three years, he had four other Top Ten singles—"Dog House Boogie" (1948), "I Love You a Thousand Ways" (1951), "I'm Waiting Just for You" (1951), and "Slow Poke" (1951). In 1953, he left King and signed with RCA, but he had no hits for the label. In 1955, Hawkins became a member of the Grand Ole Opry.

Hawkins joined Columbia's roster in 1959, releasing the No. 15 single "Soldier's Joy" later that year. The following year, he married fellow country singer Jean Shepard, and they made their home on a farm outside of Nashville, where he bred horses. Hawkins re-signed to King in 1963, releasing "Lonesome 7-7203" as a comeback single early that spring. Though it became a No. 1 hit, Hawkins didn't live to see it reach the top of the charts—he tragically died in the same airplane crash that killed Patsy Cline and Cowboy Copas on March 5, 1963. Shepard was pregnant with their child at the time of the crash; the boy was named after his father. Hawkins' recorded legacy was treated haphazardly in the three decades after his death, but in 1991, Bear Family released a comprehensive, multi-disc overview of his RCA and Columbia records called *Hawk*. *—Cub Koda*

● **Hawkshaw Hawkins, Vol. 1** / 1958 / King ✦✦✦✦
Hawkshaw Hawkins, Vol. 1 has a cross-section of his King recordings, which were made between 1946 and 1953. Not all of his hits are included, but the collection does have "Sunny Side of the Mountain," "I Am Slowly Dying of a Broken Heart," and "Rattlesnakin' Daddy," which makes it an effective introduction. *—Stephen Thomas Erlewine*

Taken from Our Vaults, Vol. 1 / 1963 / King ✦✦✦✦

Taken from Our Vaults, Vol. 2 / 1963 / King ✦✦✦✦

Taken from Our Vaults, Vol. 3 / 1964 / King ✦✦✦✦

Hawk 1953-61 / 1991 / Bear Family ✦✦✦✦
An excellent 3-CD boxed set. All the RCA-Victor and Columbia recordings, with superlative sound and liner notes. *—Cub Koda*

Ronnie Hawkins

b. Jan. 10, 1935, Huntsville, AL
Guitar, Vocals / Rock & Roll, Rockabilly
Hawkins is a rockabilly singer who formed his original backing band, the Hawks, while attending the University of Arkansas. After auditioning unsuccessfully for Sun in 1957, he started working regularly in Canada the following year, eventually taking up permanent residence there. After one release on the Canadian

Quality label, he signed with Roulette in New York in 1959, having hits with "Forty Days" and "Mary Lou." The live fervor of Hawkins (known as Mr. Dynamo) & the Hawks' show continued in Canada after all the original members except Levon Helm headed back to the US. Hawkins quickly hired Canadian players Robbie Robertson, Garth Hudson, Rick Danko, and Richard Manuel as the new Hawks. They stayed with him until 1963, but later became Bob Dylan's backing group and went on to a career of their own as the Band. Hawkins has remained a legend in Canada, recording unrepentant rockabilly sides and gigging constantly. He's still the original Mr. Dynamo, capable of shaking the walls down any old time he feels like it. — *Cub Koda*

● **The Best of Ronnie Hawkins & His Band** / 1990 / Rhino ✦✦✦✦
In the late 1950s and early 1960s, Ronnie Hawkins was one of the few rock 'n' rollers committed to performing and recording unapologetic rockabilly while others were returning to their country roots or going the teen idol route. This 18-song compilation focuses mostly on his initial burst of activity for Roulette in 1959 and 1960, with a few later odds and ends thrown in. While Hawkins deserves respect for keeping the torch of rock 'n' roll's roots burning during some of its leaner years, he didn't match the greatness of rockabilly's kingpins. His vocals and performance were energetic but not brilliant; his material was a bit pedestrian. The best of these tunes are "Mary Lou" (his sole Top 30 hit), "Forty Days" (an update of Chuck Berry's "Thirty Days"), and "One of These Days" (later covered by the Searchers). What he's really known for, of course, is giving a bunch of mostly Canadian kids their start as his backing band, the Hawks. A later edition of the Hawks eventually toured with Bob Dylan and evolved into the Band. Only two of these songs, though, feature that lineup (the 1963 single "Bo Diddley"/"Who Do You Love"). On "Who Do You Love" especially, Robbie Robertson lets rip with a roaring solo that's a good few years ahead of its time in its manic distorted intensity. It's by far the most exciting track on this compilation of a respectable but minor performer from rock's early days. — *Richie Unterberger*

Wade Hayes

Guitar, Vocals / Contemporary Country
Raised in Bethel Acres, OK, Wade Hayes grew up around country music. His father Don was a professional musician who played bars and honky tonks across Oklahoma. Through the influence of his father, he began playing music as a child. Initially, he played mandolin for a while, but he switched to guitar at the age of 11. Inspired by honky tonk, outlaw country, and bluegrass, Hayes developed a distinctive style at an early age.

When Hayes was a pre-teen, his father signed a contract with a Nashville-based independent record label and moved the family to the Music City. Within a year, the label had folded, leaving the Hayes family broke. They struggled back to Oklahoma, where Wade began playing guitar and singing backup in his father's band, Country Heritage. Following his graduation from high school, Hayes went to three different colleges, but he decided to drop out of school to pursue music after seeing Ricky Skaggs on the 1991 Country Music Awards show. He moved to Nashville and began playing on demo tapes, all the while working on his own material. Shortly after he settled down in Nashville, Hayes began writing songs with Chick Rains, who arranged an audition for the vocalist with record producer Don Cook (the Mavericks, Brooks & Dunn). Cook was impressed and began working with the singer, eventually getting him in contact with executives at Columbia Records.

Old Enough to Know Better, Hayes' debut album, was released in 1995. The record was an immediate hit, with its title track becoming a No. 1 single. The Academy of Country Music nominated him for Top New Male Vocalist of the Year for 1995. Hayes' second album, *On a Good Night,* was released in the summer of 1996. Although it wasn't as big a hit as his debut, it still sold respectably. — *Stephen Thomas Erlewine*

● **Old Enough to Know Better** / 1995 / Columbia ✦✦✦✦

On a Good Night / Jun. 25, 1996 / Columbia ✦✦✦
Wade Hayes' eagerly awaited second album, *On a Good Night,* doesn't have the front-to-back consistency of his debut album, but there are enough first-rate songs—particularly the first single "On a Good Night"—to make it a successful album. — *Thom Owens*

Lee Hazlewood

Vocals / Country-Rock, Country-Pop
Lee Hazlewood has had his hand in so many pies it's hard to know where to start in describing his long and varied music career. He's recorded an impressive number of pop and country albums himself—immediately distinguished by his deep, dark vocal style and playfully existential lyrics—but he's best known for two accomplishments: Discovering Duane Eddy (he created Eddy's trademark twangy guitar sound), and producing and writing the song "These Boots Are Made for Walking" and other hits for Nancy Sinatra, which turned her into a 1960s icon of sassy miniskirt pop.

Born in Oklahoma, Hazlewood was raised in Port Arthur, TX, attended Southern Methodist University, and was eventually drafted to fight in Korea. Later he settled in Phoenix, where he worked as a DJ in the 1950s. As a songwriter, his first hit was "The Fool," recorded by Sanford Clark, which also featured Al Casey on guitar, who would become a longtime Hazlewood collaborator. The song hit the charts in 1956, and its success enabled Hazlewood to form the record company Jamie with Dick Clark, host of *American Bandstand.* The label became the launching pad for Eddy's career, and Hazlewood wrote, co-wrote, produced, and "supervised" most of the guitarist's major hits.

In the 1960s Hazlewood, now an established producer and songwriter, formed another record company, Lee Hazlewood Industries (LHI), and released an album by the International Submarine Band, *Safe at Home,* which featured Gram Parsons. When Parsons left LHI to join the Byrds for the album *Sweetheart of the Rodeo,* Hazlewood declared that he owned the rights to Parsons' vocal performances; Parsons' voice was subsequently stripped from *Sweetheart* by Columbia Records.

Hazlewood also worked as a producer for Reprise, where he eventually hooked up with Nancy Sinatra and turned her career into a goldmine with songs like "Boots" and "Sugar Town." The pair also recorded several singles together, including "Summer Wine," "Some Velvet Morning," and "Jackson," all of which charted and eventually were released on the album *Nancy & Lee.* The pair recorded a follow-up, *Nancy & Lee Again,* in 1972.

Hazlewood's own solo singles and albums are some of the era's most unique pop and country creations. His voice is deeper than Johnny Cash's, and his material walks the line between dark, philosophical introspection and wry, playful humor, often on the same song. He's released albums on several different labels throughout the 1960s and into the '70s, including *Trouble Is a Lonesome Town, The N.S.V.I.P (Not So Very Important People), Friday's Child* (re-released as *Houston,* a song of his that had been a hit for Dean Martin), *The Very Special World of Lee Hazlewood* (featuring his own rendition of *Boots), Hazlewoodism—Its Cause and Cure, Love and Other Crimes, The Cowboy and the Lady* (a duet album with Ann-Margret), *Forty,* and *Poet, Fool & Bum.*

Hazlewood retreated into obscurity in the 1970s. He moved to Sweden, where he continued recording. Occasionally he played shows in Europe, but he was tired of the music business by this time, and preferred to stay out of the spotlight. He briefly resurfaced in 1995, touring the US with Nancy Sinatra after her comeback album, *One More Time.* He also contributed two vocal tracks to the Al Casey album *Sidewinder,* recorded in Phoenix and released in 1995 by the German label Bear Family. — *Kurt Wolff*

Trouble Is a Lonesome Town / 1963 / LHI ✦✦✦
The songs center around the people of a fictional Western town called Trouble. Re-released in 1969 on LHI. — *Kurt Wolff*

N.S.V.I.P. (Not So Very Important People) / 1965 / Reprise ✦✦✦
Kooky, funny, but surprisingly insightful songs and stories about small-town weirdos—a companion album to *Trouble.* A quirky anomaly, this album is easily one of the seven wonders of the pop music world. — *Kurt Wolff*

Lee Hazlewood Sings Friday's Child / 1966 / Reprise ✦✦✦✦
Re-released in 1968 on Columbia as "Houston." —*Kurt Wolff*

Very Special World of Lee Hazlewood / 1966 / MGM ✦✦✦✦
Contains his own hilarious reading of "These Boots Are Made for Walking," the sad "My Autumn's Done Come," and an earlier version of "Sand" with Suze Jane Hokum. —*Kurt Wolff*

Lee Hazlewoodism: Its Cause and Cure / 1966 / MGM ✦✦✦✦

Love and Other Crimes / 1968 / Reprise ✦✦
If you're looking for evidence of Lee Hazlewood the weirdo, this album will not disappoint. As pure music it's another story. Hazlewood usually sounds like Johnny Cash gone pop, after gargling with razor blades; sometimes he sounds like a drunk taking over the cocktail piano, with soused accompaniment by such estimable session greats as guitarist James Burton and drummer Hal Blaine. Check out "She's Funny That Way," which suddenly fades into a silly excerpt of Ray Charles' "Drown in My Own Tears"; there's also "Pour Man" (sic), a jaunty ballad sung by a convicted murderer on his last night of life. "Forget Marie" is reasonably solid country-pop in the style of the material he fashioned for Nancy Sinatra, but overall this has the ambience of a tax write-off or a vanity project, knocked off with a bit of extra studio time. —*Richie Unterberger*

Nancy & Lee / 1968 / Reprise ✦✦✦✦
Lee's first duet album with Nancy Sinatra is a classic of '60s pop. He plays the leering, deep-throated, trail-worn cowboy to her bright-eyed girl-child, and the match on songs like "Summer Wine," "Sand," "Jackson," and "Some Velvet Morning" is a smart, sexy, lip-smacking bowl of mind candy. —*Kurt Wolff*

The Cowboy and the Lady (with Ann-Margret) / 1971 / LHI ✦✦✦
This doesn't come close to his duet work with Nancy Sinatra, and it lacks even a single Hazlewood composition, but "No Regrets" and "Greyhound Bus Depot" are standouts, and the inside cover art is well worth the price of admission. —*Kurt Wolff*

Forty / 1971 / LHI ✦✦✦
Another dearth of Hazlewood originals in lieu of mediocre showtunes ("It Was a Very Good Year," "September Song"); nonetheless the hardcore downer "The Bed" and his dark, turgid, but almost saucy take on Randy Newman's "Let's Burn Down the Cornfield" are stellar. —*Kurt Wolff*

Nancy & Lee Again / 1972 / RCA ✦✦✦✦
Not as charmingly succinct a package as the pair's debut, their reunion album "Again" has a more "adult" feel. Nonetheless it contains some excellent work that alternates between the serious ("Down from Dover," a Dolly Parton song, where Lee's voice dips deeper than any man has gone before) and the silly ("Did You Ever"). "Got It Together" is a cute and personable conversation-style song. —*Kurt Wolff*

Poet, Fool & Bum / 1973 / Capitol ✦✦✦✦
The title track mixes black humor, clever rhymes, and cowboy existentialism; "The Performer" is a stark and somewhat autobiographical picture of a singer who's sick of the game; and the epic "Nancy and Me" is some sort of fantasy-ramble that likely never happened, but stands among the best songs Lee ever wrote. Includes a drawling version of Tom Waits' "Those Were Days of Roses (Martha)." —*Kurt Wolff*

Fairy Tales and Fantasies / 1989 / Rhino ✦✦✦✦
This CD compilation includes the entire *Nancy & Lee* album and four songs from their follow-up: "Did You Ever," "Down from Dover," "Paris Summer," and "Arkansas Coal (Suite)." —*Kurt Wolff*

● **The Many Sides of Lee** / 1991 / Request ✦✦✦✦
Twenty-five-song import compilation of rare Hazlewood tracks, most or all dating from the 1960s, including solo numbers and collaborations with Suzi Jane Hokom, the Shacklefords, and Mark Robinson. The most countryish cuts are like a debauched Johnny Cash; the bullfighter narrative "Jose" is Hazlewood at his most compellingly cheesy and melodramatic; and there are shades of his Duane Eddy roots in the more rock-oriented cuts, like the grungy "Della" and the rockabilly-tinged "Pretty Jane." There are also solo renditions of several songs that he produced for Nancy

Sinatra, although Sinatra's versions are uniformly better. You could justifiably call this the work of an idiot-savant, or (at its worst) just a plain idiot, but it is, like much of Hazlewood's stuff, intriguing in its blend of banal '60s pop/country and eccentric production, lyrics, and vocals. It would have been nice to have even a shred of documentation as far as dates and sources, and there's no question that his collaborations with Nancy Sinatra offer a much better context for his work as a songwriter and producer. But this is the best available distillation of the man's erratic and large solo output into one place, if you can find it. —*Richie Unterberger*

Roy Head

b. Jan. 9, 1943, Three Rivers, TX
Vocals / R&B, Rock & Roll, Traditional Country
Actually a country and rock vocalist rather than an R&B star, Roy Head nevertheless cut one of the great pieces of uptempo soul in the mid-'60s. "Treat Her Right" on Back Beat made it to No. 2 on the R&B charts and No. 2 on the pop charts, and the fact that Head was White was soft-pedaled in R&B circles while the song made its way up the charts. That performance alone was enough to qualify Head as one of the finest blue-eyed soul singers of the 1960s. But in fact, Head was one of the most versatile stylists of the era, capable of hard R&B/rock tunes (even cutting material with a pre-fame Johnny Winter on backup guitar), mournful, soul-tinged country, and straight R&B and blues covers. Head was also an excellent entertainer, and his live shows of the period even included some fancy footwork clearly under the influence of James Brown. The Texan singer is remembered as a one-shot artist, but he actually cut many records (some under the auspices of noted producer Huey Meaux) throughout the 1960s on a confusing variety of labels. A few of these were tiny hits in the wake of "Treat Her Right," only a couple ("Just a Little Bit" and "Apple of My Eye") sneaking into the Top 40. Quite a few of his records were dynamic, sleek hybrids (in varying degrees) of soul, rock, and country, all featuring Head's cocky, confident vocals. In a sense, though, he was damned by his versatility, not fitting comfortably into any niche or marketing plan; the tiny labels he recorded for lacked national promotional muscle in any case. In the 1970s, after several years without success in the rock or R&B fields, Head returned to country, and landed quite a few chart hits in the arena between 1974 and 1985. —*Ron Wynn & Richie Unterberger*

Treat Me Right / 1965 / Bear Family ✦✦✦✦
Read the title carefully; it's not "Treat Her Right," the title of Head's 1965 megasmash, but *Treat Me Right*, an entirely different song. Yes indeed, this is an exploitation release of material Head cut for a different label than the one that issued "Treat Her Right," repackaged after the hit to capitalize on its unexpected success. The final punchline is that, as exploitative as this LP is, it's quite good. The ten songs—mostly revved-up R&B, with a bit of country soul thrown in—are solid evidence of Head's stature as one of the finest White soul singers of the '60s. The small combo R&B arrangements are spare and tight, investing even overdone standards like "Money" with excitement. Long out of print, it still shows up in the used bins from time to time and is worth picking up. —*Richie Unterberger*

Slip Away: His Best Recordings / 1993 / Collectables ✦✦✦
Not only are these *not* his best recordings by a long shot, but this package also matches the shoddiest standards of the Collectables label, a company often (justly) criticized for a variety of inadequacies. The documentation on these 14 tracks is totally nonexistent—not a clue as to when they were first released or recorded. A good many came out in the mid-'60s (though "Treat Her Right" and most of the other best Back Beat singles are absent); others have a heavier soul/blues feel that sounds as though they might date from a few years later, or even much later. What's more, a few tracks that appear (in better fidelity) on the Varese Sarabande compilation are presented here with different track titles, although you might mistakenly think at a glance that it doesn't duplicate anything from that anthology. There *are* a few very good cuts here that aren't on *The Best of Roy Head*, such as the

talking soul rap "Slip Away," the deep soul ballad "The Feeling Is Gone," and the zany psychedelic/jazz-flavored "Easy Loving Girl" (written by Johnny Winter, who plays fuzz guitar on the song). Just be warned that this is a carelessly assembled package, much inferior to the Varèse Sarabande compilation, if you only want one disc. —*Richie Unterberger*

● **Treat Her Right: Best of Roy Head** / 1995 / Varèse Vintage ✦✦✦✦

A long overdue anthology of Head's best sides, mostly recorded for the Back Beat label in the mid-'60s. Besides "Treat Her Right," it has all five of his other singles that dented the charts at the time. These aren't necessarily the highlights of these 18 tracks; "Pain" is country-soul moan at its best (although it's a thinly veiled rewrite of Lonnie Mack's "Why"), "To Make a Big Man Cry" is his best foray into country-pop from the period, and "You're (Almost) Tuff" is one of his toughest rockers, with a sound that almost verges on Texas garage. This collection is the most solid evidence of Head's superb talents, which were never rewarded with the consistent material or national recognition he deserved. —*Richie Unterberger*

Health & Happiness Show

Alternative Country-Rock

James Mastro, a music veteran who played with a post-Television Richard Lloyd as a teenager, and St. Vincent DeNunzio (former Feelies and Richard Hell drummer) first began jamming in their kitchen. Gradually adding bassist Tony Shanahan, guitarist Kerryn Tolhurst, fiddlers Todd Reynolds and Eileen Ivers, the power-country sextet signed with Bar/None and released their 1993 debut, *Tonic. —John Bush*

● **Tonic** / Bar/None ✦✦✦✦

Instant Living / 1995 / Bar/None ✦✦✦✦

Jimmy Heap

b. Mar. 3, 1922, Taylor, TX, d. Dec. 4, 1977
Guitar, Vocals / Western Swing, Honky Tonk

Western swing bandleader Jimmy Heap led the Melody Masters for over three decades and contributed one country classic to the genre, "The Wild Side of Life," covered by Hank Thompson, Burl Ives & Grady Martin, Freddy Fender, and most recently, Waylon Jennings & Jessi Colter. Heap's "Release Me" also provided Esther Phillips and Englebert Humperdinck with their first Top Ten popular hits, in 1962 and 1967 respectively.

James Arthur Heap formed the Melody Masters just after his service in World War II, with sidemen Arlie Carter, Louis Renson, Bill Glendining, and Horace Barnett. A continuing spot on local radio gave the Melody Masters a bit of renown around central Texas, and Imperial Records signed the band in 1949. Some time before the initial recordings, Heap—who played only lead guitar—hired Houston "Perk" Williams (b. 1926) to provide vocals along with his fiddling duties. Though Williams had never sung before, his excellent performance on their debut release "Today, Tonight, and Tomorrow" guaranteed him the spot ever after. Another song, "Haunted Hungry Heart," was covered by Slim Whitman, but it was "The Wild Side of Life" that provided Jimmy Heap & the Melody Masters with their big break. Hank Thompson & the Brazos Valley Boys took it to No. 1 in March 1952, and the single spent 15 weeks there.

But even before Thompson had borrowed the biggest hit of his career, the country star had advised Capitol Records to sign Heap. Over five years the Melody Makers recorded 32 sides for Capitol, including their big hit "Release Me," which charted in the Top Five in January 1954. No other Capitol singles charted, and Heap left the label in the mid-'50s to form Fame Records. The Melody Masters recorded for Fame throughout the 1950s and '60s, and even integrated rock 'n' roll inspirations. Heap disbanded the group in July 1977, and drowned in a boating accident before the year was over. —*John Bush*

● **Release Me** / 1992 / Bear Family ✦✦✦✦

A great 30-track, single-disc compilation of Heap's earliest and best sides. Includes the title track, "Let's Do It Just Once," "It Takes

a Heap of Lovin'," and "Ethyl in My Gas Tank (No Gal in My Arms)." This is great Western swing-style material in transition. —*Cub Koda*

Hearts & Flowers

Country-Rock, Folk-Rock

Of the many folk-rock groups in southern California in the 1960s, Hearts & Flowers were one of the relatively few that were closer to "folk" than "rock." Founding guitarist Larry Murray was a member of the Scottsville Squirrel Barkers bluegrass group in the late '50s and early '60s; Chris Hillman and Bernie Leadon were also members of that group for a time. Murray teamed up with David Dawson and Rick Cunha to form Hearts & Flowers, a self-described "Georgia country-folk meets Hawaiian ukelele folk-rock" group, in the mid-'60s. They released a couple albums of pleasant but inessential country-folk-rock in the late '60s. —*Richie Unterberger*

Now Is the Time for Hearts & Flowers / 1967 / Capitol ✦✦✦✦

This debut album is an overlooked precursor to country-rock, echoing the late-'60s Byrds, Stone Poneys, Gene Clark, and most especially, as Brian Hogg points out in his lengthy liner notes, the Dillards. There are earnest vocals and conscientious harmonies on this subdued, acoustic, and countrified take on folk-rock, with mild Eastern/psychedelic dabs of autoharp. The songs mix original tunes with covers of Donovan, Tim Hardin, Hoyt Axton, Kaleidoscope, and Carole King. There's little to criticize, but it lacks the innovative spark that characterizes the best folk-rock of the time. —*Richie Unterberger*

Of Horses, Kids and Forgotten Women / 1968 / Capitol ✦✦✦✦

Future Flying Burrito Brother/Eagle Bernie Leadon replaced Rick Cunha for the group's second and final album, which is actually a considerably more L.A. pop-flavored production than their debut. Country-seasoned folk-rock remains at the core of the group's sound, but producer Nik Venet provides occasional tasteful, psychedelic-tinged orchestral arrangements. The material—about half original—is fairly strong, especially their covers of Arlo Guthrie's "Highway in the Wind" and Jesse Lee Kincaid's "She Sang Hymns out of Tune" (also covered by Harry Nilsson on his first album). The unquestioned highlight is Larry Murray's "Ode to a Tin Angel"; by far the group's most psychedelic slice of folk-rock, with its swimming strings, tripped-out lyrics, and sweet harmonies, it's also their most atypical track. A slicker, but better, album than their first effort. —*Richie Unterberger*

● **Now Is the Time for Hearts & Flowers/Of Horses, Kids and Forgotten Women** / Oct. 1995 / Edsel ✦✦✦✦

Edsel does '60s collectors a favor by combining both of Hearts & Flowers' hard-to-find LPs onto one compact disc, which puts the group's entire repertoire in one place. —*Richie Unterberger*

Bobby Helms

b. Aug. 15, 1933, Bloomington, IN
Guitar, Vocals / Rock & Roll, Traditional Country, Country-Pop, Nashville Sound/Countrypolitan

Though his name is unfamiliar to most, Bobby Helms rules the airwaves every year around December 25th. His single "Jingle Bell Rock" first became a hit in 1957, and it re-appeared on the charts four of the following five years to become an all-time Christmas classic. Before he was pigeonholed, though, Helms had a successful country career with two No. 1 hits to his credit.

Born on August 15, 1933, in Bloomington, IN, Helms first performed on his father Fred's *Monroe County Jamboree*, singing while brother Freddie played guitar. The Helms Brothers, as they were billed, became a regional attraction. Bobby later cut a single called "Tennessee Rock and Roll," but then returned to Bloomington to appear on the *Hayloft Frolic* radio show. While on the program, he was encouraged to go to Nashville to sing background vocals on an Ernest Tubb session. Tubb recommended him to Decca Records, and the label signed him in 1956. His debut single "Fraulein" initially flopped in January 1957, but then hit No. 1 on the country charts in April. (The song also hit the Pop Top 40 in July of 1957.) In October, Helms released another No. 1, "My Special Angel," which stayed four weeks at the top and crossed over to No. 7 on the pop charts.

Bobby Helms' next recording was "Jingle Bell Rock"; though Decca released it only two days before Christmas 1957, the single still peaked at No. 6 on the pop charts. Two 1958 singles—"Just a Little Lonesome" and "Jacqueline"—hit the country Top Ten but flopped elsewhere, though a reissue of "Jingle Bell Rock" made the Pop Top 40. The country single "Lonely River Rhine" hit the Top 20 in 1960, but subsequent new material from Helms had little success. (Decca reissued his Christmas hit each year from 1960 to 1962 with diminishing returns.)

Bobby Helms toured throughout the '60s, and recorded two albums for Kapp in 1966, *I'm the Man* and *Sorry My Name Isn't Fred*—a nod either to brother Freddie or father Fred. Two years later, he released *All for You* on the Little Darlin' label. Several singles placed modestly on the country charts during 1967-68, including "He Thought He'd Die Laughing" and "So Long." The 1970 Certron single "Mary Goes 'Round" was his last hit, but Helms recorded *Pop-A-Billy* for MCA as late as 1983. —*John Bush*

To My Special Angel / 1957 / Decca ✦✦✦✦

● **The Best of Bobby Helms** / 1963 / Columbia ✦✦✦✦

Bobby Helms Sings Fraulein / 1967 / Harmony ✦✦✦

All New Just for You / 1968 / Little Darlin'✦✦✦

Pop-A-Billy / 1983 / MCA ✦✦✦

Fraulein: The Classic Years / 1994 / Bear Family ✦✦✦✦
Fraulein: The Classic Years is a double-disc collection that contains all of Bobby Helms' Decca recordings, including "Fraulein," "My Special Angel," "Jingle Bell Rock," "Just a Little Lonesome," "Jacqueline," "New River Train" and "Lonely River Rhine." In addition to the well-known songs, *Fraulein* also includes several unreleased songs, alternate takes, and failed attempts at crossover hits. While the packaging and sound is superb, the set is simply too extensive for anyone but dedicated fans. Casual fans will find cuts like "Captain Santa Claus" and "I Guess I'll Miss the Prom" extraneous, and they'd be right—it's the kind of material that only appeals to hardcore collectors, and *Fraulein* is designed for them. —*Stephen Thomas Erlewine*

Michael Henderson

b. Jul. 7, 1951, Yazoo City, MS
Guitar (Bass), Guitar (Electric) / Contemporary Country
A behind the scenes star-of-all-trades for years, Henderson had done everything but put out a solo album prior to joining RCA. A Missouri native, he once led a club band, the Bel-Airs, based in Columbia. After moving to Nashville, he became an in-demand session guitarist and mandolinist, a road musician who backed Kevin Welch and Tracy Nelson (among others), and leader of a couple of the toughest bar bands in Music City (the Bluebloods, the Snakes). He also enjoyed success as a songwriter—his hits include "Powerful Stuff" by the Fabulous Thunderbirds. —*Michael McCall*

● **Country Music Made Me Do It** / Mar. 15, 1994 / RCA ✦✦✦✦
This is pure roadhouse honky tonk, stoked with bent notes, twisted humor, and a couple of tough, bittersweet ballads. —*Michael McCall*

Don Henry

Guitar / Contemporary Country
Don Henry came to prominence when Kathy Mattea's version of "Where've You Been" (co-written with Mattea's husband Jon Vezner) won every award in sight in 1990 and 1991. Henry grew up in suburban San Jose, CA, and moved to Nashville in 1979, where he spent four years copying tapes for publisher Tree International (now Sony/Tree) and then became a staff songwriter there. He wrote tunes for Mattea, John Conlee, T.G. Sheppard, and Conway Twitty and won Tree's Writer of the Year award in 1990 before recording his first album. —*Brian Mansfield*

Wild in the Backyard / 1991 / Epic ✦✦✦✦
Henry's debut album can only be classifed country because of its high moral sense (which it actually gets from folk) and from the

styles of the session players. With its malls and Mercedes, *Wild in the Backyard* isn't country—it's suburban. Henry's a singer-songwriter capable of drama and humor within the same song. But his real strength is his ability to create honest humanity, a trait equally present in "Harley," about a boy named after a chopper, and "Half a Heart," a touching tale of unfulfilled promise. —*Brian Mansfield*

Ty Herndon

Vocals / Contemporary Country, New Traditionalist
Like many new country singers of the mid-'90s, Ty Herndon fused neo-traditionalist country with a slick, rock-oriented sense of style and production. Like many of his contemporaries, his blend of genres proved commercially successful, as his first album became one of the biggest hits of 1995. Herndon was a little wilder, at least off the stage, than many of his peers, but his records had a down-to-earth sense of sentimentality that initially gave him a broad fan base.

Born and raised in Butler, AL, Ty Herndon became involved in music as he was growing up. He sang gospel music and learned how to play piano. After he graduated from high school, he moved to Nashville. Initially, he had a difficult time gaining a foothold in the music industry, spending ten years without making any real headway. Herndon left the Music City and headed to Texas, where he began slogging it out in local honky tonks, developing a dedicated following of fans. In 1993, he won the Texas Entertainer of the Year. Later that year, he signed to Epic Records.

Ty Herndon's first single "What Mattered Most" hit No. 1 in the spring of 1995. An album of the same name was released in April and it became a Top Ten country hit. The second single, "I Want My Goodbye Back," became a No. 7 hit. Seemingly, the world was in his hands, but his first year of stardom was a difficult one, as he was arrested for drug possession on June 13, 1995, in Fort Worth, TX. Nevertheless, the arrest didn't halt his career. The third single, "Heart Half Empty" was a hit and Herndon's second album, *Living in a Moment*, debuted at No. 6 upon its summer 1996 release. —*Stephen Thomas Erlewine*

● **What Mattered Most** / Apr. 18, 1995 / Epic ✦✦✦✦

Living in a Moment / Aug. 13, 1996 / Epic ✦✦✦
Although he is in fine voice throughout the album, Ty Herndon's *Living in a Moment* is bogged down by mediocre material that fails to give him a proper showcase for his talents. Herndon doesn't write his own material, which might not necessarily be a bad thing—after all, hundreds of country singers don't write their own songs—but he doesn't have the best ear for selecting songs. When he does have a strong song—like the title track or "Don't Tell Mama"—he sounds terrific, but otherwise Herndon simply sounds adequate. Furthermore, on the undistinguished numbers, the production sounds generic and canned, which also hurts the record. Although Herndon still shows promise, it's hard to avoid that *Living in a Moment* sounds like a sophomore slump. —*Thom Owens*

John Hiatt

b. 1952, Indianapolis, IN
Guitar, Piano, Vocals / Rock & Roll, Country-Rock, Singer-Songwriter, Americana
John Hiatt's sales never quite matched his reputation. Hiatt's songs were covered successfully by everyone from Bonnie Raitt, Ronnie Milsap, and Dr. Feelgood to Iggy Pop, Three Dog Night, and the Neville Brothers, yet it took him 13 years to reach the charts himself. Of course, it nearly took him that long to find his own style. Hiatt began his solo career in 1974, and over the next decade, he ran through a number of different styles from rock 'n' roll to new wave pop before he finally settled on a rootsy fusion of rock 'n' roll, country, blues, and folk with his 1987 album *Bring the Family*. Though the album didn't set the charts on fire, it became his first album to reach the charts, and several of the songs on the record became hits for other artists, including Raitt and Milsap. Following its success, Hiatt became a reliable hit songwriter for other artists, and he developed a strong cult following that continued to gain strength into the mid-'90s.

While he was growing up in his hometown of Indianapolis, IN, John Hiatt played in a number of garage bands. Initially, he was inspired by the Rolling Stones and Bob Dylan, and the music of those two artists would echo strongly throughout his work. Out of all the bar bands he played with in the late '60s, a group called the White Ducks was the one that received the most attention. Following his high school graduation, he moved to Nashville at the age of 18, where he landed a job as a songwriter for Tree Publishing. For the next several years, he wrote and performed at local clubs and hotels. Within a few years, his songs were being recorded by several different artists, including Conway Twitty, Tracy Nelson, and Three Dog Night, who took Hiatt's "Sure as I'm Sittin' Here" to No. 16 in the summer of 1974. Eventually, his manager secured him an audition at Epic Records, and the label signed him in 1974, releasing his debut album *Hangin' Around the Observatory* later that year. Despite their critical acclaim, neither *Hangin' Around the Observatory* nor its 1975 follow-up *Overcoats* sold many copies, and he was dropped by the label. By the end of the year, Tree Publishing had let him go as well.

Following his failure in Nashville, Hiatt moved out to California. By the summer of 1978 he had settled in Los Angeles, where he began playing in clubs and opening for folk musicians like Leo Kottke. With Kottke's assistence, Hiatt hired a new manager, Denny Bruce, who helped him secure a record contract with MCA Records. *Slug Line*, his first record for MCA, was released in the summer of 1979. Where his first two records were straightahead rock 'n' roll and folk-rock, *Slug Line* was in the new wave vein of angry English singer-songwriters like Elvis Costello, Graham Parker, and Joe Jackson, as if Hiatt was vying for the role of the American angry young man. The new approach earned some strong reviews, yet it failed to generate any sales. *Two Bit Monsters*, his second MCA album, faced the same situation. Although it was well-received critically upon its 1980 release, it made no impression on the charts, and the label dropped him.

Apart from working on *Two Bit Monsters*, Hiatt spent most of 1980 as a member of Ry Cooder's backing band, playing rhythm guitar on the *Borderline* album and touring with the guitarist. Hiatt stayed with Cooder throughout 1981, signing a new contract with Geffen Records by the end of the year. Produced by Tony Visconti (David Bowie, T. Rex), his Geffen debut *All of a Sudden* was released in 1982, followed by the Nick Lowe/Scott Matthews & Ron Nagel-produced *Riding with the King* in 1983. As with his previous records for Epic and MCA, neither of his first two Geffen releases sold well. By this time, Hiatt's personal life was beginning to spin out of control as he was sinking deep into alcoholism. Around the time he completed 1985's *Warming up to the Ice Age*, his first wife committed suicide. Following the release of *Warming up to the Ice Age*, Hiatt was dropped by Geffen. By the end of 1985, he had entered a rehabilitation program. During 1986, he remarried and signed a new deal with A&M Records.

For his A&M debut, Hiatt assembled a small band comprised of his former associates Ry Cooder (guitar), Nick Lowe (bass), and Jim Keltner (drums). Recorded over the course of a handful of days, the resulting album *Bring the Family* had a direct, stripped-down, rootsy sound that differed greatly from his earlier albums. Upon its summer 1987 release, *Bring the Family* received the best reviews of his career and, for once, the reviews began to pay off, as the album turned into a cult hit, peaking at 107 on the US charts; it was his first charting album. Hiatt attempted to record a follow-up with Cooder, Lowe, and Keltner, but the musicians failed to agree on the financial terms for the sessions. Undaunted, he recorded an album with John Doe, David Lindley, and Dave Mattacks, but he scrapped the completed project, deciding that the result was too forced. Hiatt's final attempt at recording the follow-up to *Bring the Family* was orchestrated by veteran producer Glyn Johns, who had him record with his touring band, the Goners. Despite all of the behind-the-scenes troubles behind its recording, the follow-up album, *Slow Turning*, actually appeared rather quickly, in the summer of 1988.

Slow Turning, like *Bring the Family* before it, received nearly unanimous positive reviews and it was fairly well-received commercially, spending 31 weeks on the US charts and peaking at 98. Within the next year, Hiatt successfully toured throughout Amer-

John Hiatt

ica and Europe, strengthening his fan base along the way. Inspired by the success of Hiatt's two A&M albums, Geffen released the compilation *Y'All Caught? The Ones That Got Away 1979-85* in 1989. That same year, other artists began digging through Hiatt's catalog of songs, most notably Bonnie Raitt, who covered "Thing Called Love" for her multi-platinum comeback album, *Nick of Time*.

In 1990, Hiatt returned with *Stolen Moments*, which was nearly as successful as *Slow Turning*, both critically and commercially. "Bring Back Your Love to Me," an album track from *Stolen Moments* that was also recorded by Earl Thomas Conley, won BMI's 1991 Country Music Award. By the time "Bring Back Your Love to Me" won that award, it had become a standard practice for artists to cover Hiatt's songs, as artists as diverse as Bob Dylan, Ronnie Milsap, Suzy Bogguss, and Iggy Pop all covered his songs in the early '90s. In 1993, Rhino Records released *Love Gets Strange: The Songs of John Hiatt*, which collected many of the cover versions that were recorded during the '80s and '90s.

During 1991, the group that recorded *Bring the Family*—Hiatt, Cooder, Lowe, and Keltner—re-formed as a band called Little Village, releasing their eponymous debut in early 1992. Based on the success of *Bring the Family* and Hiatt's A&M albums, expectations for Little Village were quite high, yet the record and its supporting tour were considered a major disappointment. Later, the individual members would agree that the band was a failure, mainly due to conflicting egos.

Hiatt decided to back away from the superstar nature of Little Village for his next album, 1993's *Perfectly Good Guitar*. Recorded in just two weeks with a backing band comprised of members of alternative rock bands School of Fish and Wire Train, the album was looser than any record since *Bring the Family*, but it didn't quite have the staying power of its two predecessors, spending only 11 weeks on the charts and peaking at No. 47. The following year, he released his first live album, *Hiatt Comes Alive at Budokan?*. Hiatt left A&M Records after the release of the record, signing with Capitol Records the following year.

Walk On, Hiatt's first Capitol album, was recorded during his supporting tour for *Perfectly Good Guitar* and featured guest appearances by the Jayhawks and Bonnie Raitt. *Walk On* entered the charts at 48, but slipped off the charts in nine weeks, indicating that his audience had settled into a dedicated cult following. —*Stephen Thomas Erlewine*

Hangin' Around the Observatory / 1974 / Epic ✦✦✦

John Hiatt mixed pop, folk, rock, R&B, country, and gospel on his debut album, immediately becoming an uncategorizable (and thus uncommercial) entity. Although this album was cut in Nashville, it owes more to Van Morrison than it does to Conway Twitty, and like the Belfast bluesman, Indianian Hiatt came to his influences somewhat secondhand, however sincerely he evoked them. What he really was, of course, was a singer-songwriter, albeit not in a style easily recognizable in 1974. The title indicates his position: Hiatt's songs show him to be an acute observer. But the performances require him to dig in, and although he does so with alacrity, the result is too diffuse. Nevertheless, Hiatt earned critical kudos for this album, and Three Dog Night (who knew good songwriting when they heard it) covered "Sure as I'm Sittin' Here," getting a Top 40 single out of it. — *William Ruhlmann*

Overcoats / 1975 / Epic ♦♦
John Hiatt is better at imitating Howlin' Wolf than he is James Taylor, and that he tries both here as well as Bob Dylan and Ben E. King is some indication of his ambition, if not his accomplishment. Conversely, he begins to become more himself on this, his second album, at least on such songs as "I'm Tired of Your Stuff" and "I Killed an Ant with My Guitar," if not on the more lugubrious numbers, such as "Distance" or on the ones that sound like publishing demos for a more popular singer, such as "Down Home." — *William Ruhlmann*

Slug Line / 1979 / MCA ♦♦♦
Conventional wisdom at the time was that MCA Records had signed John Hiatt (who had languished without a record contract for four years) with the idea that he would be their Elvis Costello—a singer-songwriter in the fashionable punk/new wave style. Certainly, Hiatt has stripped down and roughed up the sound from his Epic records here, fronting a straightahead guitar rock band (that was capable, of course, of playing the obligatory reggae number), eschewing the stylistic diversity he reveled in before, and throwing out snappy, aphoristic lyrics in a highly processed voice. None of this quite turns him into Elvis Costello, although the mean streak he reveals would serve him well later. — *William Ruhlmann*

Two Bit Monsters / 1980 / MCA ♦♦♦
At the time of its release, *Two Bit Monsters* was perceived by critics who had caught up with John Hiatt on *Slug Line* as a less impressive follow-up to that record. In retrospect, it may be the better of the two albums, boasting an even more simplified musical approach and such notable songs (and future Rosanne Cash covers) as "Pink Bedroom" and "It Hasn't Happened Yet." Hiatt here was starting to emerge from the "new Elvis Costello" tag that had been affixed to him with *Slug Line*, but his reviewers, however well-meaning, seemed determined to keep him in that category. (In any case, record buyers were paying little attention—*Slug Line* was Hiatt's fourth straight album to miss the charts, and MCA dropped him as Epic had before.) — *William Ruhlmann*

All of a Sudden / 1982 / Geffen ♦♦♦
Hiatt's fifth album and his first for Geffen, his third record label, was given a somewhat inappropriate big-gloss production (all shimmering keyboards and filtered vocals) by Tony Visconti, known for his work with David Bowie. What counts with Hiatt, though, is the songs, and this album contains "I Look for Love," as knowing a dissection of the dating scene as anyone has yet attempted. — *William Ruhlmann*

Riding with the King / 1983 / Geffen ♦♦♦♦
One half of Hiatt's best Geffen album is played by him and Scott Matthews, while the other half features a band including Paul Carrack and Nick Lowe. But what matters is the songs: Hiatt's trenchant observations on life and love, especially the perceptive and painfully funny "She Loves the Jerk." — *William Ruhlmann*

Warming up to the Ice Age / Jan. 1985 / Geffen ♦♦♦
Hiatt turned to veteran country producer Norbert Putnam here, but the result still rocked hard, with the occasional soul touch (notably those obnoxious thumb-struck bass lines that are so prevalent in '80s music). Highlights here are "The Usual," later covered by Bob Dylan, and "She Said the Same Things to Me." There is also an odd duet with Elvis Costello on the old Spinners hit "Living a Little, Laughing a Little" (try and tell them apart).

Critics' darling or not, when this album went into the tank, Geffen became the third label to drop Hiatt. — *William Ruhlmann*

★ **Bring the Family** / May 1987 / A&M ♦♦♦♦♦
Not only is the small-band playing impeccable, but this is Hiatt's best collection of songs, which is saying a lot for so talented a writer. "Memphis in the Meantime" is a knowledgeable look at the fame game, "Your Dad Did" perfectly skewers domestic life, and "Have a Little Faith in Me" is a touching evocation of persistent love. And that's just three of them. — *William Ruhlmann*

Slow Turning / 1988 / A&M ♦♦♦♦
Only a notch below *Bring the Family*, with such strong songs as "Drive South" and the wild criminals-on-the-loose song "Tennessee Plates." — *William Ruhlmann*

Y' All Caught? The Ones That Got Away 1979-1985 / 1989 / Geffen ♦♦♦♦
Though John Hiatt's three records for Geffen were all quite strong, none of them received much attention other than a handful of good reviews at the time of release. After *Bring the Family* brought Hiatt to a wider audience, Geffen compiled *Y'All Caught? The Ones That Got Away*, a collection of the highlights from his three Geffen records that attempted to win over his new fans. Though the new wave overtones of the production won't appeal to some of his roots rock fans, *Y'All Caught?* still features an abundance of first-rate songs, including "Radio Girl," "Riding with the King," "She Said the Same Things to Me," "It Hasn't Happened Yet," "Slug Line," and "She Loves the Jerk," making it an excellent sampler for fans of Hiatt's latter-day work. — *Stephen Thomas Erlewine*

Stolen Moments / Jun. 1990 / A&M ♦♦♦
John Hiatt's highest charting album yet is a step down from the dizzy heights of *Bring the Family* and *Slow Turning*, as he abandons his more acid commentaries and turns in a self-deprecating set full of promises of reformation and celebrations of marriage and family life. But the observations remain acute, and Hiatt's singing (so much camouflaged in his early days) is becoming his secret weapon. — *William Ruhlmann*

Perfectly Good Guitar / 1993 / A&M ♦♦
Perfectly Good Guitar is clearly a John Hiatt rock album, harking back to his mid-period *Riding with the King* days. It might disappoint some ardent admirers of the more subtle roots approach that defined Hiatt's peak "highway" twin-pack *Bring the Family* and *Slow Turning*, but most listeners should not be deterred by this perfectly good release. — *Roch Parisien*

Hiatt Comes Alive at Budokan? / Nov. 22, 1994 / A&M ♦♦♦
John Hiatt's first live album was recorded during a 1994 winter-spring tour of the US (the title is a joke) and finds the singer-songwriter backed by the Guilty Dogs, a guitar-bass-drums trio. He doesn't need any more ammunition than that, not when he's got a set of 15 songs drawn from his last four critically acclaimed albums, including "Thing Called Love" and "Tennessee Plates." Hiatt gives his songs a rougher treatment than some of those who have covered them, his throaty voice giving even love songs like "Angel Eyes" an unsentimental force. In the absence of an A&M best-of, *Hiatt Comes Alive at Budokan?* makes a good sampler of his work, 1987-1993. — *William Ruhlmann*

Walk On / Oct. 24, 1995 / Capitol ♦♦♦
Walk On is a classic "road" album in the sense that its songs largely seem written to or about people who are not present, either because the singer is away from them, he is singing about the past, or they are dead. John Hiatt exploits the resulting feelings of longing, anger, and mourning inherent in that premise, sometimes, as in "I Can't Wait," singing about wanting to be back home, sometimes, as in the odd love song "Ethylene," wishing for a departed lover, sometimes, as in "Dust Down a Country Road," reflecting as in a dream on the past. He employs rustic nature imagery, but frequently for ominous effects rather than gentle ones, and he is supported by spare, guitar-dominated backup that is alternately soothing and disturbing. Hiatt's label debut for Capitol (though they didn't do much to promote it), *Walk On* is not among Hiatt's more consistent or more accessible works, but he remains a highly imaginative and craftsmanlike writer who can

startle you. The raucous "Shredding the Document" is among the half dozen best songs of the year, if not the decade. —*William Ruhlmann*

Living a Little, Laughing a Little / Raven ✦✦✦✦
Living a Little, Laughing a Little does a good job as an early-career summary, drawing material from each of Hiatt's albums released from 1974 to 1985—*Hangin' Around the Observatory, Overcoats, Slug Line, Two Bit Monster, All of a Sudden, Riding with the King,* and *Warming up to the Ice Age.* For those who are only familiar with his critically acclaimed work from the late '80s on, this provides an introduction to his formative years and a fascinating look at a man finding his voice—from an average '70s-style singer-songwriter to a rocker a la Elvis Costello to the first hints of his better known, later rootsy incarnation. A 1985 interview and a track Hiatt contributed to the *Cruisin'* soundtrack have been added as a bonus to those who already have the albums. —*Chris Woodstra*

Sara Hickman

b. Mar. 1, 1963, Jacksonville, NC

Vocals / Singer-Songwriter, Country-Folk, Alternative Country, Contemporary Folk

A Texas singer-songwriter, Hickman takes perceptive lyrics that find the wondrous and inexplicable in daily life, and wraps her observations in whimsical, intricate acoustic pop arrangements. When Elektra Records refused to release her third album, she started a fund drive among fans, raising enough to buy the tapes and release them. She also occasionally performs in the band Domestic Science Club with ex-Dixie Chick Robin Macy and bluegrass instrumentalist Patty Lege. —*Michael McCall*

Equal Scary People / 1989 / Discoveries ✦✦✦
Hickman's clever debut, this reveals her unusual slant on life—and the fact that she has more musical smarts than most Texas singer-songwriters. —*Michael McCall*

● Shortstop / 1990 / Elektra ✦✦✦✦
She's clearly enjoying herself, and so will the listener, though the cuteness sometimes becomes a crutch. —*Michael McCall*

Sara Hickman / 1993 / Asylum ✦✦✦

Necessary Angels / 1994 / Discovery ✦✦✦✦
An album worth fighting to get out, it's her boldest, most mature, and most musically sophisticated offering to date. —*Michael McCall*

Dan Hicks

b. Dec. 9, 1941

Vocals / Rock & Roll, Progressive Country, Country-Rock

Throughout his decades-long career, Dan Hicks has stood as one of contemporary music's true eccentrics. While steeped in folk, his acoustic sound knew few musical boundaries, drawing on country, call-and-response vocals, jazz phrasing, and no small amount of humor to create a distinctive, albeit sporadic, body of work that earned him a devoted cult following.

Hicks was born December 9, 1941 to a military family then living in Arkansas, and grew up in California, where he was a drummer in a number of high school bands. He attended college in San Francisco, where he switched to guitar and began playing folk music. He returned to the drums, however, when he joined the Charlatans, one of the Bay City's first psychedelic bands. Although the Charlatans were short-lived—they issued only one single during their existence—they proved influential throughout the San Francisco musical community, and were one of the first acts to play the legendary Family Dog.

Hicks had formed the acoustic group Dan Hicks and His Hot Licks in 1968 as an opener for the Charlatans, but soon the new band became his primary project. After adding a pair of female backing vocalists—"the Lickettes"—the group issued its debut LP *Original Recordings* in 1969. After a pair of 1971 records, *Where's the Money?* and *Striking It Rich,* they issued 1973's *Last Train to Hicksville,* which proved to be the Hot Licks' most successful album yet. At the peak of the group's popularity, however, Hicks dissolved the band, and did not resurface until 1978, releasing the

solo LP *It Happened One Bite,* the soundtrack to an uncompleted feature by animator Ralph Bakshi. He then phased in and out of the music industry for more than a decade, and did not issue another major recording until 1994's *Shootin' Straight,* a live recording cut with a new band, the Acoustic Warriors. —*Jason Ankeny*

Original Recordings / 1969 / Epic ✦✦✦

Where's the Money / 1971 / MCA ✦✦✦✦
This strong live outing showcases Hicks' dry tongue-in-cheek delivery and his band's chemistry to good effect. —*Rick Clark*

Striking It Rich / 1972 / MCA ✦✦✦✦
This is Hicks' most solid studio outing. —*Rick Clark*

Last Train to Hicksville / 1973 / MCA ✦✦✦
Almost as good as *Striking It Rich,* this features some exceptional playing, but the songs aren't quite up to snuff. —*Rick Clark*

Hey Good Lookin' / 1975 / Warner Brothers ✦✦

● It Happened One Bite / 1978 / Warner Brothers ✦✦✦✦

Rich & Happy in Hicksville / 1986 / See For Miles ✦✦✦

Shootin' Straight / 1994 / Private Music ✦✦✦

Dan Hicks & His Hot Licks / Columbia Special Products ✦✦✦

Moody Richard / MCA ✦✦

Highway 101

Country-Rock, Contemporary Country

The country-rock band Highway 101 formed in 1986 when Nitty Gritty Dirt Band manager Chuck Morris decided to create a showcase for his newest discovery, Paulette Carlson, a talented singer and guitarist from Minnesota. Morris brought together guitarist/vocalist Jack Daniels, drummer/vocalist Cactus Moser, and bassist/guitarist/mandolin player Curtis Stone, all of whom enjoyed successful music careers before joining the band; Daniels and Stone first worked together in the late '70s, when they toured with Burton Cummings, and later formed a duo, the Lizards. Carlson wrote Highway 101's debut single, "The Bed You Made for Me," which became a No. 4 hit in early 1987. The band's eponymous debut album, also released in 1987, produced two more hits—the No. 3 "Whiskey, If You Were a Woman" and "Somewhere Tonight," which became their first No. 1 hit.

Highway 101 went on to score numerous Top Ten singles, including three other no. 1 hits, in the latter half of the '80s. In 1990, Carlson left the band to pursue a solo career, and Nikki Nelson was brought in to replace her. Their first single with Nelson was the title cut from *Bing Bang Boom* (1991), which became a Top 15 single. However, the group wasn't as popular following the departure of Paulette Carlson—by the end of 1992, they could no longer crack the Top 40. Jack Daniels left the group in 1993, reducing it to a trio. The group signed with Liberty Records and released *The New Frontier,* a major commercial disappointment. In 1995, Carlson rejoined Highway 101 to celebrate their ten-year anniversary; the following year they released the aptly titled *Reunion.* —*Sandra Brennan*

Highway 101 / 1987 / Warner Brothers ✦✦✦✦
The main thing that this country-rock quartet had going for it was lead singer Paulette Carlson, who approximated the throaty, torn vocal style of Stevie Nicks, but with a Southern accent. The group was heard best on its debut album, which included such characteristic hits as "Whiskey, If You Were a Woman" and "The Bed You Made for Me." —*William Ruhlmann*

Highway 101 2 / 1988 / Warner Brothers ✦✦✦
Highway 101's second album followed the same rocking country formula that made their debut a success, but its best songs—"Setting Me Up" and "Honky Tonk Heart"—are as good as anything on the first album. —*Thom Owens*

Paint the Town / 1989 / Warner Brothers ✦✦✦
Highway 101 was beginning to show signs of stagnation on *Paint the Town.* Although there were still some good songs on it—particularly the No. 1 single "Who's Lonely Now"—the quality of material wasn't as strong as on their first two albums,w and the

group was sounding tired, verging on the formulaic. *—Thom Owens*

● **Greatest Hits** / Sep. 11, 1990 / Warner Brothers ✦✦✦✦
Greatest Hits collects all of the hits from Highway 101's late '80s highwater mark, including the No. 1s "Somewhere Tonight" and "(Do You Love Me) Just Say Yes," plus the classic "Whiskey, If You Were a Woman." *—Thom Owens*

Bing Bang Boom / 1991 / Warner Brothers ✦✦
Bing Bang Boom is the first album Highway 101 recorded with vocalist Nikki Nelson. Although Nelson has an attractive voice, she couldn't fill Carlson's shoes. Furthermore, the band had trouble coming up with consistently compelling material, apart from the hit title track, making *Bing Bang Boom* one of the weakest entries in the group's catalog. *—Thom Owens*

The New Frontier / Sep. 13, 1993 / Liberty ✦✦
On *New Frontier,* Highway 101 sounds like they're floundering. Not only did new vocalist Nikki Nelson not fit into the group particularly well, Jack Daniels left the band—as a result, the group sounds like half a band. Although "You Baby You" isn't bad, Highway 101 is clearly lacking inspiration throughout the album. *—Thom Owens*

Reunited / Feb. 27, 1996 / WillowTree ✦✦✦
Reunited was recorded around Highway 101's tenth anniversary. To celebrate, Paulette Carlson joined the band again and the difference is apparent. The band and Carlson need each other—they are more energetic and dynamic together than they are apart. Unfortunately, Highway 101 didn't create an album of all-new material—out of the 12 tracks, four are re-recordings of their biggest hits. These are fine, but they don't have the spark of the originals, nor do they have the charm of the new songs. Though it isn't as good as their first two albums, it is better than either of their Liberty albums. *—Thom Owens*

Highwaymen

Traditional Country
The Highwaymen is a country supergroup featuring Johnny Cash, Willie Nelson, Waylon Jennings, and Kris Kristofferson. The group formed in 1985, the same year they released their eponymous debut. *The Highwaymen* went to No. 1 on the country charts, spawned the hit single "Desperados Waiting for a Train" and went gold within a year of its release. In the years immediately following the release of the record, the group was quiet, choosing to reconvene in 1990 to record and release their second album. *Highwaymen 2* wasn't quite as successful, yet it still launched the Top 30 hit, "Silver Stallion." Another five years later, the group reunited to record their third album, *The Road Goes on Forever.* The album was their least successful effort to date, failing to yield any hit singles. *—Stephen Thomas Erlewine*

● **The Highwaymen** / 1985 / Columbia ✦✦✦✦
These old friends have appeared together in various combinations, but never as effectively as on the epic title song here, written by Jimmy Webb. And the rest of the record, including Guy Clark's "Desperados Waiting for a Train" and Woody Guthrie's "Deportee," lives up to the leadoff hit. *—William Ruhlmann*

Highwaymen 2 / 1990 / Columbia ✦✦✦

The Road Goes on Forever / 1995 / Liberty ✦✦✦
For their third album *The Road Goes on Forever,* the Highwaymen hired Don Was to produce. Was had previously worked with every member of the group but Johnny Cash, so he was theoretically a natural choice and, on the surface, *The Road Goes on Forever* has all the trappings of being *the* classic Highwaymen album. It has great material, from standards like Dallas Frazier's "True Love Travels on a Gravel Road" to contemporary favorites by Steve Earle ("The Devil's Right Hand") and Billy Joe Shaver ("Live Forever") to new cuts from all four members. It has a crisp sound and a focused production, with fine performances from everyone involved. The problem is, the whole thing sounds too damn serious—Was and the Highwaymen may have all the right cards, but they don't know how to play them. Instead of capturing a kinetic energy or intense introspection, *The Road Goes on Forever* just sounds studious and overlabored, as if the group wanted

to produce music that lived up to their mythological legacy, not the music itself. *—Stephen Thomas Erlewine*

Faith Hill

b. Sep. 21, 1967, Jackson, MS
Vocals / Contemporary Country
Faith Hill was one of the '90s' most popular female singers. Raised in Star, MS, she grew up idolizing Reba McEntire, and sang anywhere she could. When Hill was 19, she left Jackson and headed for Nashville, where she got a job selling T-shirts at Fan Fair. Eventually, she landed a job at Gary Morris' Nashville company, and worked there one year before making her professional debut with songwriter/musician Gary Burr, who went on to become her co-producer. Hill released her debut single, "Wild One," in the fall of 1993; the song became a major hit, spending four weeks at No. 1 on the country charts. Hill released her debut album, *Take Me as I Am,* in 1994. The record reached the Top Ten on the country charts and went gold within a year of its release. Also in 1994, her second single, "Piece of My Heart," also became a No. 1 hit. *It Matters to Me,* Hill's second album, was released in 1995. The following year, she married fellow Nashville star Tim McGraw. *—Sandra Brennan & Brian Mansfield*

Take Me as I Am / 1994 / Warner Brothers ✦✦✦
Whether she's singing songs associated with Janis Joplin ("Piece of My Heart") or Maura O'Connell ("I Would Be Stronger Than That"), Faith Hill sounds every bit the new-generation Reba McEntire heir her press makes her out to be. Hill sings with a natural tear in her voice that recalls McEntire without ever mimicking her. Hill sounds like a star on all ten cuts, whether she's fronting minimal acoustic accompaniment on "Just Around the Eyes" or rocking out on "Wild One." *—Brian Mansfield*

● **It Matters to Me** / 1995 / Warner Brothers ✦✦✦✦
On her second album, Faith Hill confirmed that *Take Me as I Am* was no fluke. Like her debut album, *It Matters to Me* is an ambitious, diverse set of contemporary country that proves Hill can tackle virtually every subgenre of country, singing rockers, ballads, socially aware stories, and love songs with an equal amount of grace. The singles "Let's Go to Vegas" and "It Matters to Me" aren't the only strong songs here—the entire album is rich with first-rate songs, as well as superb singing from Hill, one of the most promising female vocalists of the mid-'90s. *—Stephen Thomas Erlewine*

Goldie Hill

b. Jan. 11, 1933, Karnes County, TX
Vocals / Traditional Country, Honky Tonk
During the 1950s, Goldie Hill was known as the "Golden Hillbilly," and at one time was considered the successor to the "Queen of Country," Kitty Wells. Born Angolda Voncile Hill in Karnes County, TX, she got her professional start on Shreveport's *Louisiana Hayride* in 1952 and by early 1953 had signed to Decca. Her first single debuted without fanfare, but her second single, "I Let the Stars Get in My Eyes," a reply to Skeets McDonald and Slim Willet's 1952 hit "Don't Let the Stars Get in Your Eyes," hit the top of the charts for three weeks in 1953, the same year she debuted on the Grand Ole Opry. The following year she reached the Top Five with "Looking Back to See," a duet with Justin Tubb. A second duet with Tubb, "Sure Fire Kisses," made the Top 15. In 1955, Hill scored yet another hit duet, this time with Red Sovine on "Are You Mine." Following her marriage to honky tonk star Carl Smith and subsequent retirement, Decca continued to release her songs, and in 1959 she found herself with a Top 20 hit, "Yankee, Go Home." Hill staged a brief comeback in 1968 billed as Goldie Hill Smith, and recorded two albums. A lone single, "Lovable," was only a minor hit, so Hill returned to the home front. *—Sandra Brennan*

● **Goldie Hill** / 1960 / Decca ✦✦✦✦

Chris Hillman

b. Dec. 4, 1944, Los Angeles, CA

Bass, Mandolin / Progressive Bluegrass, Progressive Country, Country-Rock

Along with frequent collaborator Gram Parsons, Chris Hillman was the key figure in the development of country-rock, virtually defining the genre through his seminal work with the Byrds and the Flying Burrito Brothers. Hillman was born on December 4, 1944 in Los Angeles, where he grew up listening to Spade Cooley and Cliffie Stone and teaching himself to play guitar. In 1961, he and a pair of high school friends formed the Scottsville Squirrel Barkers, and cut an album; a year later, he joined the Golden Gate Boys, a bluegrass band featuring Vern Gosdin. In honor of their new vocalist's prowess on the mandolin, the group renamed itself the Hillmen; after recording a self-titled LP with producer Jim Dickson, they broke up in 1963.

In 1964, the Beefeaters, an L.A. folk trio comprised of guitarists Jim (later Roger) McGuinn, David Crosby, and Gene Clark, released a single, "Please Let Me Love You;" after its commercial failure, they decided to add a bassist and drummer to their lineup. Their producer, Dickson, suggested Hillman for the bass position; although he had never picked up the instrument before, thanks to his bluegrass background he was able to quickly develop his own unique, melodic performance style. After the addition of drummer Michael Clarke, the quintet renamed itself the Byrds. At their label's insistence, they cut their first record with session men, which meant that Hillman and Clarke sat on the sidelines during production; the resulting single, a jangly cover of Bob Dylan's "Mr. Tambourine Man," was a tremendous hit that marked the birth of the folk-rock form.

During the mid-1960s, the Byrds ranked as one of the most successful and influential American pop groups, issuing a string of massive hits like "Turn! Turn! Turn!," "Eight Miles High," and "So You Want to Be a Rock 'N' Roll Star" along with acclaimed albums like 1967's *Younger Than Yesterday* and 1968's brilliant *The Notorious Byrd Brothers*. Internal strife dogged the band, however, and by late 1967 only Hillman and McGuinn remained from the original roster. At about the same time, Gram Parsons entered the picture, and in December 1967 McGuinn invited him to join the group as a jazz pianist for a planned project embracing the history of American popular music. However, Parsons' mastery of country soon became the sessions' dominant focus, much to Hillman's delight, and the album the Byrds ultimately recorded, 1968's *Sweetheart of the Rodeo*, became the blueprint for all country-rock efforts released in its wake.

A tour followed, and so did disaster; Parsons did not agree with the group's decision to play apartheid-torn South Africa, and subsequently quit the Byrds in July 1968. Three months later, Hillman followed suit, and joined Parsons as a vocalist and guitarist in the reformed Flying Burrito Brothers along with bassist Chris Ethridge, pedal steel player "Sneaky" Pete Kleinow, and drummer Jon Corneal. Further honing their hybrid sound by combining the energy and instrumentation of rock with the issues and themes of country, the Burritos recorded the landmark *Gilded Palace of Sin*, followed in 1970 by *Burrito Deluxe*. After Parsons left the group in 1971, Hillman stayed on for two less successful records, a self-titled 1971 effort and the following year's *Last of the Red Hot Burritos*. After they disbanded, Hillman joined Stephen Stills' Manassas, where he remained until 1973, when he briefly rejoined the Byrds.

In 1974, Hillman teamed with singer-songwriters John David Souther and Richie Furay to form Souther, Hillman & Furay; after recording two LPs with the trio, Hillman issued a pair of solo albums, 1976's *Slippin' Away* and 1977's *Clear Sailin'.* By 1978, he had rejoined Roger McGuinn and Gene Clark to record a 1979 album under the name McGuinn, Clark & Hillman, producing the Top 40 pop hit "Don't You Write Her Off." The album *City* followed a year later, this time as Roger McGuinn and Chris Hillman Featuring Gene Clark. They soon went their separate ways, and in 1982 Hillman issued a straightforward country record, *Morning Sky.* Two years later, he released *Desert Rose*, which contained the minor country hits "Somebody's Back in Town" and

"Running the Roadblocks"; the album's title proved indicative of things to come, and in 1986 he formed the Desert Rose Band, a country-rock outfit featuring Nashville session aces Herb Pedersen, John Jorgenson, Jay Dee Maness, Steve Duncan, and Bill Bryson.

The Desert Rose Band proved to be Hillman's most commercially successful post-Byrds project; their first LP, an eponymously titled 1987 outing, generated a pair of Top Ten country hits, "Love Reunited" and "One Step Forward," which peaked at No. 2. 1988's "He's Back and I'm Blue" topped the country charts, as did "I Still Believe in You," from the album *Running.* Two other singles from the record, "Summer Wind" and a cover of John Hiatt's "She Don't Love Nobody," reached the Top Three. The follow-up, 1989's *Pages of Love,* was also highly successful, with two more Top Ten hits, "Start All Over Again" and "Story of Love." Subsequent releases like 1991's *True Love* and 1993's *Traditional* failed to achieve the same degree of popularity, however, and after one final LP, *Life Goes On,* the group called it quits in 1994.

At the peak of the Desert Rose Band's success, Hillman had also begun appearing infrequently with McGuinn, releasing the Top Ten country duet "You Ain't Going Nowhere" in 1989. Soon, the pair joined Crosby in a reformed Byrds, playing a handful of club dates. In 1990, they appeared at a tribute to the late Roy Orbison, performing "Mr. Tambourine Man" along with the song's composer, Bob Dylan. The same year, the Byrds cut four new songs for inclusion in a career-spanning box set, and in 1991 were inducted into the Rock & Roll Hall of Fame. In 1996, Hillman reunited with Desert Rose alumnus Herb Pedersen in *Bakersfield Bound. —Jason Ankeny*

● **Chris Hillman** / 1971 / Together ✦✦✦✦
This album does as much to explain Hillman's background as the Byrds' *Sweetheart of the Rodeo* album. This fine bluegrass band also featured the Gosdin brothers, who not only had country hits during the '70s and '80s, but also made a fine record with Gene Clark. Worth looking for, not only for these reasons but also for some fine music. *—Jim Worbois*

Slippin' Away / 1976 / Asylum ✦✦✦
Having recently departed Souther, Hillman, & Furay, this album more heavily reflects Hillman's association with Manassas than anything he did with SH&F. A nice batch of songs overall but the high point is the killer version of the bluegrass standard, "Take Me in Your Lifeboat," that closes the album. *—Jim Worbois*

Clear Sailin' / 1977 / Asylum ✦✦
This is not one of those records that transcends the period in which it was made. It could easily be confused with Fools Gold, Firefall, or any one of a number of bands from the late '70s. *—Jim Worbois*

Ever Call Ready / 1978 / A&M ✦✦✦

● **Morning Sky** / 1982 / Sugar Hill ✦✦✦✦
A back-to-the-roots album (of sorts), Hillman has given up the bass in favor of the mandolin and acoustic guitar for this mostly acoustic album of other people's tunes. The band is made up of people with whom Hillman has worked over the years and it's obvious they are comfortable together. Listening to this album is almost like eavesdropping on a group of friends making music in their living room. *—Jim Worbois*

Desert Rose / 1984 / Sugar Hill ✦✦✦✦
Bluegrass, country, and country-rock, Hillman played mandolin on this album, but his main instrument (with the Byrds and Desert Rose Band) is bass. *—Mark A. Humphrey*

Sixteen Roses: Greatest Hits / 1995 / Curb ✦✦✦

Bakersfield Bound / May 21, 1996 / Sugar Hill ✦✦✦✦
Hillman and former Desert Rose Band mate Herb Pedersen reunited to cut this collection of straightforward covers, cast in the mold of prime Bakersfield Sound country-rock. Backed by another Desert Rose alum, pedal steel guitarist Jay Dee Maness, Hillman and Pedersen join forces to tackle duets drawn from the catalogs of some of music's premiere brother acts, including the Louvins, the Everlys, and the Wilburns. *—Jason Ankeny*

THE HILLMEN

ALL MUSIC GUIDE TO COUNTRY

The Hillmen

Progressive Bluegrass
An early '60s, West Coast bluegrass band with Chris Hillman, Vern and Rex Gosdin, and Dan Parmley (later a Bluegrass Cardinal), which evolved from the Scottsville Squirrel Barkers. —*Mark A. Humphrey*

● **The Hillmen** / 1970 / Sugar Hill ✦✦✦✦
Traditional bluegrass, it also has Dylan covers. —*Mark A. Humphrey*

Tish Hinojosa

b. Dec. 6, 1955, San Antonio, TX
Guitar, Piano, Vocals / Folk, Tex-Mex, Singer-Songwriter, Contemporary Folk
In the liner notes to her album *Homeland,* Tish Hinojosa writes of a dilemma she faced as she began to emerge as a singer-songwriter. She writes of " . . . wondering how my love for my parents' humble Mexican heritage and language would mix with idealistic images of a musical future." With four albums and one EP now behind her, Hinojosa has fashioned her blend of cultures into a compelling voice in American music. Typically a Tish Hinojosa album or concert moves effortlessly from songs of loves forgotten and family struggles remembered to eloquent cries against injustice and playful evocations of sawdust dance floors to the rolling endless highways of the Southwest to the lonely struggles of the disenfranchised.

Hinojosa was born Leticia Hinojosa in San Antonio to a large blended family, went to parochial school, listened to the songs of her parents as well as the Beatles and Woodstock, and began her musical career doing jingles and recording for a small Tejano label before leaving Texas for Taos. In the spectacular beauty of northern New Mexico, she further honed her art and recorded an EP featuring three original songs. Nashville was her next stop.

Although she worked steadily—touring, doing demo work, even recording a successful single, "I'll Pull You Through," for Curb Records—she never felt that she could find her niche in Music City. She says, "Nashville requires a delicate balance. I began to see that incorporating aspects of my ethnic heritage into my music was a problem, at least at that time (early '80s)."

In 1985 Hinojosa returned to New Mexico, where she recorded an independent cassette, *Taos to Tennessee.* The recording features some of her compositions which would later appear on *Homeland,* her 1989 A&M/Americana major label debut. Finding the opportunity for work limited as a Taos-based artist, she moved to Austin in the summer of 1988. She rapidly became an integral part of the vibrant Austin musical scene by making many club appearances but also standing up for her social concerns by being a willing participant in benefits for migrant farmworkers. Her concern for the dangers of picking pesticide-laced crops was also evident in her song "Something in the Rain," a moving account of the tragedy of unsafe crop spraying practices told through the eyes of a small boy. Hinojosa also has a loyal following overseas, and her touring itinerary often includes stops in Amsterdam and Scandinavia as well as the more familiar confines of clubs in Houston, Cambridge, and Taos.

The highpoint of her recording career so far is the 1990 album *Culture Swing* on Rounder Records. This is an essential album in the classic folk tradition of Baez and Dylan. With all of the songs written by Hinojosa, *Culture Swing* is a singer-songwriter tour-de-force that bridges the folk and country idioms. The 1994 album *Destiny's Gate* carries on the Hinojosa tradition in the vein of *Culture Swing.*

Recently, Hinojosa has produced a couple of theme albums on the Rounder label: a collection of border songs, *Frontejas* (1995) and a bilingual album designed for kids, *Cada Nino (Every Child)* (1996). —*Alonso Jasso & Michael Erlewine*

Taos to Tennessee / 1987 / Watermelon ✦✦✦✦
Recorded in 1987, *Taos to Tennessee* predates the more successful *Culture Swing,* but shows the same kind of style and clarity. Hinojosa wrote six of the 12 songs on this album and most are outstanding, including the gorgeous "Prairie Moon," "Taos to Tennes-

see," "Amanecer," "Who Showed You the Way to My Heart," and "Let Me Remember." The Peter Rowan song "Midnight Moonlight" is also very fine. Singer-songwriter Hinojosa is a treasure very rare. —*Michael Erlewine*

Homeland / 1989 / A&M ✦✦✦✦
This is Hinojosa's first album and a clear harbinger of what is to come. With most songs written by Hinojosa herself, already she has her own sound and style. Good songwriters are rare. Outstanding songs are "The Border Trilogy," "Voice of the Big Guitar," "Who Showed You the Way to My Heart," "Let Me Remember," and "Amanecer." —*Michael Erlewine*

★ **Culture Swing** / Aug. 27, 1990 / A&M ✦✦✦✦✦
With a voice that rivals Joan Baez in quality and a sense of humor all her own, Tish Hinojosa is proof that really great singer-songwriters still appear from time to time. Each generation has but a few perfect folk albums and *Culture Swing* (all songs are written by Hinojosa) is one of these—an instant classic. —*Michael Erlewine*

Memorabilia Navidena / 1991 / Watermelon ✦✦✦
Memorabilia Navidena is a pleasing Christmas collection that alternates between English and Spanish renditions of old and new seasonal songs. —*Roch Parisien*

Aquella Noche / 1991 / Watermelon ✦✦✦
A largely Spanish album, this balances traditional Mexican songs with Hinojosa's own romantic, clear-eyed originals. This was recorded live at Austin's Waterloo Icehouse the week of Cinco de Mayo 1991. —*Michael McCall*

Destiny's Gate / 1994 / Warner Brothers ✦✦✦
Hinojosa continues to move into the mainstream with *Destiny's Gate* without losing the magic of *Culture Swing.* With a beautiful voice reminiscent of Joan Baez and Emmylou Harris, she seems to have perfected her unique blend of Mexican folk and country music. "I Want to See You Again" stands out as one of her finest songs. —*Chris Woodstra*

Frontejas / 1995 / Rounder ✦✦✦
Not your standard album release, but a theme recording. This is a collection of border songs sung in Spanish, some written by Hinojosa, some by others. The inspiration for this collection was her apprenticeship with Don Americo Paredes, the anthropologist, border historian, and professor emeritus at the University of Texas at Austin. Hinojosa writes, ". . . a series of sessions in which I listened and enriched my soul with 'corridos' (ballads that tell stories, news or history), love songs, and anecdotes of the borderland where he was raised and where my family's roots lie deeply embedded. These sessions continue still and the knowledge I receive is a precious resource from which I'll always draw." A number of these songs involve assistance from the likes of Flaco Jimenez, Ray Benson, Peter Rowan, and others. This makes for enjoyable listening but is not the creative and fiery Hinojosa on an album like *Culture Swing.* —*Michael Erlewine*

Cada Nino (Every Child) / 1996 / Rounder ✦✦
A theme album. Not for us old folks, but 11 bilingual songs (English/Spanish) for kids. With titles like "Barnyard Dance," "Music Scale," and "Always Grandma," these really are for children. Although sung in Hinojosa's clear and vibrant voice, they are too cutesy for most of us. Kids will like this. —*Michael Erlewine*

Dreaming from the Labyrinth / May 1996 / Warner Brothers ✦✦✦
Tish Hinojosa's new album, *Dreaming from the Labyrinth* (her second for Warner Bros.), is more what comes to mind with the word "traditional." Hinojosa was born in Texas to Mexican immigrants, and her multicultural upbringing is a defining characteristic of her acoustic folk music (she sings in both Spanish and English, for example), as is her association with the current folk and country scene in Austin. Hinojosa's music, however, is often so sweet and nice around the edges that it becomes a turn-off. The songs on *Labyrinth* are as pretty as Hinojosa's voice, but there's no dirt under the fingernails, which is exactly what makes the music of Lucinda Williams, for instance (another Austin-based artist), so vibrant and alive. —*Kurt Wolff*

214

Becky Hobbs

b. Jan. 24, 1950, Bartlesville, OK
Piano, Vocals / Honky Tonk, Neo-Traditionalist Country
Piano-pounding honky tonker Becky Hobbs is an Oklahoma native and violinist's daughter who began playing and making up tunes at age nine. When she was 14, Hobbs began writing Bob Dylan-influenced protest songs and singing in a folk duo with her pal Beth Morrison. The following year she started the Four Faces of Eve, an all-girl band. While attending Tulsa University, she played in Sir Prize Package. In 1971 she was performing with Swampfox. Three years later she moved to Los Angeles, where she had some success as a songwriter for Helen Reddy and Jane Oliver before eventually moving to Nashville. In 1974, Hobbs released her self-titled debut album. The following year, she released *From the Heartland,* followed two years later by *Everyday.* In 1978, Hobbs recorded "The More I Get the More I Want," her first minor hit. Her next single, "I Can't Say Goodbye to You," made it to the Top 50, and led to three more minor hits. Meanwhile, she continued writing; during the '80s, performers including Lacy J. Dalton and the Tennessee Valley Boys had success with her songs.

In 1983, Hobbs scored a Top Ten hit for Columbia with "Let's Get Over Them Together," a duet with Moe Bandy. Over the next two years, she had four hits for Liberty/EMI-America, among them "Hottest 'Ex' in Texas," and her songs were recorded by George Jones and Loretta Lynn ("We Sure Made Good Love"), Alabama ("I Want to Know You Before We Make Love," "Christmas Memories"), Moe Bandy and Joe Stampley ("Still on a Roll"), and Shelly West ("I'll Dance the Two Step," "How It All Went Wrong"). Hobbs debuted on the Grand Ole Opry in 1985. Two years later she had hit songs recorded by Conway Twitty, Glen Campbell, and Emmylou Harris. In 1988 Hobbs released the album *All Keyed Up,* which produced three successful singles including "Jones on the Jukebox." In 1992 she and her band the Heartthrobs toured Africa as part of the US Government agency Arts America.
—Sandra Brennan & Michael McCall

Becky Hobbs / 1974 / MCA ✦✦✦✦

From the Heartland / 1975 / Tattoo ✦✦✦

Everyday / 1977 / Tattoo ✦✦✦

● **All Keyed Up** / 1988 / RCA ✦✦✦✦
Originally released on MTM Records, Hobbs' contract and album were picked up by RCA after MTM's demise. It was her sixth label in a decade, and getting a second chance with this worthy album didn't help much. She deserves better. *—Michael McCall*

Adolph Hofner

b. Jun. 8, 1916, Moulton, TX
Vocals / Western Swing
Adolph Hofner played Western swing music for over 50 years. He was born in Moulton, TX, and raised on a farm in Lavaca County to parents from Germany and Czechoslovakia. While growing up, Hofner learned a lot about Bohemian music and later recorded some of it on ethnic albums. He and his family moved to San Antonio in 1928, where, four years later, Adolph and Emil began performing in local clubs. At first Adolph aspired to emulate Bing Crosby, but after hearing the music of Milton Brown and Bob Wills, he became a Western swing artist. Hofner worked during the day as a mechanic and at night he performed with different San Antonio bands. He also recorded with Jimmie Revard's Oklahoma Playboys and Tom Dickey's Showboys; his vocal work on the latter's single "Makes No Difference Now" won favorable response and led Hofner to form his own band in 1939. At first the band was known as Adolph Hofner and His Texans, but when they began recording for Okeh and Columbia in the early '40s, they were called the San Antonians. Among their best known tunes were "Maria Elena" and the "Alamo Rag."

The band spent the early '40s working in Southern California. During World War II, Adolph adopted the nickname "Dub" because his first name had become so unpopular. After the war he began using his own name again and returned to Texas where, in addition to Western swing, he also began recording Czech and

Tish Hinojosa

German polka music. In 1949, in honor of new sponsor Pearl Beer, his band became the Pearl Wranglers for radio, but remained the San Antonians on record. Although they changed labels a few times over the years, the group continued performing in the San Antonio area through the 1980s. *—Sandra Brennan*

Dance-O-Rama / 1955 / Decca ✦✦✦

● **South Texas Swing** / 1980 / Arhoolie ✦✦✦✦
This music from the mid-'30s includes the title track, "Why Should I Cry over You?" and more. *—AMG*

Buddy Holly (Charles Hardin Holley)

b. Sep. 7, 1936, Lubbock, TX, d. Feb. 3, 1959, Mason City, IA
Guitar, Vocals / Rock & Roll, Rockabilly, Pop-Rock
An enormously important and influential performer, Buddy Holly started in his native Texas playing country music with boyhood friend Bob Montgomery, eventually adding R&B numbers to the set list after meeting Elvis Presley. He recorded early rockabilly sides in Nashville, resulting in the Decca singles "Blue Days, Black Nights" (April 1956) and "Modern Don Juan" (December 1956). But success didn't come until he formed the Crickets and recorded in Norman Petty's New Mexico studio, producing the No. 1 hit "That'll Be the Day" (May 1957). Holly and Petty experimented in the studio, utilizing double-tracking ("Words of Love" [June 1957]), different forms of echo ("Peggy Sue" [September 1957], a second gold-selling Top Ten hit), and close-miking techniques, now commonplace in the industry. Holly recorded under his own name and the name of the Crickets interchangeably ("That'll Be the Day" was credited to the group, "Peggy Sue" to him alone). With the Crickets, he had the further chart hits "Oh, Boy!" (October 1957) (another Top Ten), "Maybe Baby" (February 1958), and "Think It Over"/"Fool's Paradise" (May 1958), while "Rave On" (April 1958) was a Holly "solo" hit.

Holly went solo for real during 1958, however, marrying and relocating to New York. He charted with "Early in the Morning" (July 1958) and "Heartbeat" (November 1958), and released "It Doesn't Matter Anymore"/"Raining in My Heart" (January 1959) before embarking on the Winter Dance Party package tour, during which, on February 3, along with the Big Bopper and Ritchie Valens, he was killed in an airplane crash.

After Holly's death, much of his earlier pre-Crickets music was overdubbed by Petty, using the Fireballs, to keep up with fan demand for more product. In England, where "It Doesn't Matter Anymore" went to No. 1 in the wake of his death, Holly continued to score hits through the mid-'60s, and he exerted tremendous influence on the developing beat groups both for his music and for his self-contained approach to his work—writing his own songs, playing them with his own group. As late as 1978, Holly could still top the UK charts with a hits collection, *20 Golden Greats*.

Buddy Holly's moment in the spotlight lasted barely 18 months, and the movie version of his life story only got it about half right, but his music still sounds fresh and continues to influence musicians to this day. —*Cub Koda & William Ruhlmann*

☆ **The Chirping Crickets** / 1957 / MCA ✦✦✦✦✦
The debut album by the Crickets and the only one featuring Buddy Holly released during his lifetime, *The "Chirping" Crickets* contains the group's No. 1 single "That'll Be the Day" and its Top Ten hit "Oh, Boy!" Other Crickets classics include "Not Fade Away," "Maybe Baby," and "I'm Looking for Someone to Love." The rest of the 12 tracks are not up to the standard set by those five, but those five are among the best rock 'n' roll songs of the 1950s or ever, making this one of the most significant album debuts in rock 'n' roll history, ranking with *Elvis Presley* and *Meet the Beatles*. —*William Ruhlmann*

That'll Be the Day / 1958 / Decca ✦✦
This album consists of material Buddy Holly recorded prior to his breakthrough with "That'll Be the Day" in 1957. On songs like "Blue Days—Black Nights," he adopts a distinctly rockabilly feel, though "Rock Around with Ollie Vee" is a lost classic. The album also includes the earlier, more country-oriented version of "That'll Be the Day." There is practically no Holly that is without merit, but this skimpy album is largely of historical interest. (Originally released on LP by Decca Records [as Decca 8707] in April 1958, *That'll Be the Day* was reissued, with the song "Ting-A-Ling" deleted, under the title *The Great Buddy Holly* on the Decca subsidiary Vocalion [as Vocalion 73811] in October 1967. It was reissued on CD under its second title on MCA [as MCA 31037] in June 1988. —*William Ruhlmann*

Buddy Holly / 1958 / Coral Records ✦✦✦✦
When Buddy Holly and the Crickets broke through nationally in 1957, they were marketed by Decca Records as two different acts whose records were released on two different Decca subsidiaries—Brunswick for Crickets records, Coral for Holly records. But there was no real musical distinction between the two, except perhaps that the "Crickets" sides had more prominent backup vocals. Nevertheless, coming three months after *The "Chirping" Crickets*, this was the debut album credited to Buddy Holly. It featured Holly's Top Ten single "Peggy Sue" plus several songs that have turned out to be standards—"I'm Gonna Love You Too," "Listen to Me," "Everyday," "Words of Love," and "Rave On." The rest of the 12 tracks weren't as distinctive, though Holly's takes on such rock 'n' roll hits as "Ready Teddy" and "You're So Square (Baby, I Don't Care)" provide an interesting contrast with the more familiar versions by Elvis Presley. This was the final new album featuring Holly to be released during his lifetime. Every subsequent album was an archival or posthumous collection. (Originally released on LP by Coral Records [as Coral 57210] on February 20, 1958, *Buddy Holly* was reissued on CD by MCA Records in 1988.) —*William Ruhlmann*

Reminiscing / 1963 / Pair ✦✦
With the release of *The Buddy Holly Story, Volume 2* in 1960, Decca Records (of which Coral was a subsidiary) had exhausted its stock of Buddy Holly and the Crickets finished master recordings. But with demand remaining strong, especially in England, the label made a deal with Holly's former producer, Norman Petty, to turn unfinished Holly recordings into releasable product by overdubbing new tracks. These were provided by the Fireballs, the band known for "Sugar Shack" and "Bottle of Wine," and *Reminiscing* was the first result, a "new" Buddy Holly album released four years after his death. It was predictably mediocre, consisting

of run-throughs of rock 'n' roll hits, the overdubbed music sounding jarringly different from Holly's vocals. —*William Ruhlmann*

Showcase / 1964 / Coral ✦✦✦
The second of the posthumously overdubbed albums, *Showcase* presented a number of rock 'n' roll cover songs performed by Buddy Holly, most of them recorded during his sessions in Nashville in 1956. It was not Holly at his best, though the performances were often spirited. —*William Ruhlmann*

Holly in the Hills / 1965 / Coral ✦✦
The third album of Buddy Holly recordings augmented with posthumous overdubbing, *Holly in the Hills* presented Holly and Bob Montgomery's country-tinged tracks from 1954-1955. It had some historical interest, but was a far cry from the Buddy Holly music of 1957-1958. —*William Ruhlmann*

Western & Bop / 1978 / MCA ✦✦
This is an album made up of the "Buddy & Bob" demos of 1954-1955, country music recorded by Buddy Holly and Bob Montgomery before Holly turned to rock 'n' roll and became a star. —*William Ruhlmann*

☆ **The Complete Buddy Holly** / 1979 / MCA ✦✦✦✦✦
In the wake of the No. 1 British ranking for *20 Golden Greats* in 1978 and the release of the feature film *The Buddy Holly Story*, MCA UK assembled this six-LP box set (which finally was released in the US in February 1981). It traces Buddy Holly's career from his Country & Western duo with Bob Montgomery in 1954/1955 to his 1956 Nashville sessions for Decca Records; the Clovis, NM, recordings with the Crickets and producer Norman Petty that launched his career in 1957; the New York sessions of 1958; the final 1958 demo recordings; the various posthumously overdubbed versions of the demos; and other assorted rarities. In other words, all the material that Decca/MCA previously had spread across seven LPs—*The "Chirping" Crickets, Buddy Holly, That'll Be the Day, Reminiscing, Showcase, Holly in the Hills*, and *Giant*—between 1957 and 1969 (not counting the many compilations) was here, plus more. The box also contained an extensive scrapbook, lots of liner notes, and a detailed discography. It was thus the state of the art in box sets just prior to the CD era, and given Holly's importance in the history of rock 'n' roll, an essential album for any serious collector. With the passing of the LP era, it is out of print, and MCA claims to be gathering more unreleased material for a comparable box set, though years go by without its appearing. Meanwhile, if you needed one record album to demonstrate what the most popular music of the second half of the 20th century sounded like, this would be it. —*William Ruhlmann*

For the First Time Anywhere / 1983 / MCA ✦✦✦✦
Powerful undubbed rockabilly sides. —*Cub Koda*

★ **From the Original Master Tapes** / 1985 / MCA ✦✦✦✦✦
From the Original Master Tapes is the best single-disc collection of Buddy Holly, featuring 20 of his biggest hits. Although the songs aren't presented in chronological order, the disc flows well, running through every one of his hits and all of his best-known songs—"That'll Be the Day," "Peggy Sue," "Oh, Boy!," "Maybe Baby," "Rave On," "Think It Over," "Heartbeat," "It Doesn't Matter Anymore," "Raining in My Heart," "Everyday," "Not Fade Away," "Well . . . All Right," and many others. A few terrific songs are missing, but *From the Original Master Tapes* remains a first-rate introduction and a nearly definitive retrospective of Holly's brief career. —*Stephen Thomas Erlewine*

The Great Buddy Holly / 1988 / MCA ✦✦
This ten-song, 22-minute album consists of material Buddy Holly recorded prior to his breakthrough with "That'll Be the Day" in 1957. On songs like "Blue Days—Black Nights," he adopts a distinctly rockabilly feel, though "Rock Around with Ollie Vee" is a lost classic. The album also includes the earlier, more country-oriented version of "That'll Be the Day." There is practically no Holly that is without merit, but this skimpy album is largely of historical interest. (Originally released as an 11-track LP under the title *That'll Be the Day* by Decca Records [as Decca 8707] in April 1958, *The Great Buddy Holly* was reissued, with the song "Ting-A-Ling" deleted, on the Decca subsidiary Vocalion [as Vocalion 73811] in October 1967. It was reissued on CD under its second

title on MCA [as MCA 31037] in June 1988.) —*William Ruhlmann*

☆ **The Buddy Holly Collection** / 1993 / MCA ✦✦✦✦✦
The first comprehensive, remastered CD retrospective of Holly's work, including early tracks recorded in the Holly family garage, the Owen Bradley-produced singles, all the rockin' hits, orchestrated ballads, and tracks overdubbed with instrumentation after Holly's tragic death. Two discs, solid liner notes. —*Roch Parisien*

David Holt

b. Oct. 15, 1946, Gatesville, TX
Banjo, Vocals / Folk, Old-Time, Traditional Country, Traditional Folk, String Bands
Contemporary banjo player and storyteller David Holt is devoted to keeping old-time music and stories alive. Best-known as the host of TNN's *Fire on the Mountain* and *The American Music Shop*, he also records children's albums. He was born into an established Texas family and began playing the family's traditional instruments, the spoons and bones, at age ten. When he was a teen, the family moved to California, where he began playing the drums and gained experience in several rock 'n' roll and jazz bands. His budding interest in traditional music bloomed after hearing an inspiring 78-rpm single by cowboy singer Carl T. Sprague, whom he traveled to Bryan, TX, to see. Sprague taught Holt to play harmonica and encouraged his interest in old songs.
In 1969, Holt and his college buddy, banjo player Steve Keith, visited the southern Appalachians, where they immersed themselves in the local musical traditions; Holt learned the clawhammer banjo style straight from the sources. Soon after receiving his teaching certificate and degrees in biology and art from the University of California, Holt moved to Asheville, NC, to learn more about mountain music. For many years he interviewed and taped traditional musicians and convinced them to play at local festivals. (Much of the research and recordings have been placed in the Library of Congress.) Moffatt also founded and helmed the Appalachian Music program at Warren Wilson College in Swannanoa, NC, in 1975.
Holt began his own recording career on the June Appal label, and decided to become a full-time performer in 1980. With his trademark white fedora, Holt soon became a major figure in traditional music and won the Best Old-Time Banjoist in *Frets* magazine's Readers' Poll three times. He founded his own label, High Windy, and has released many albums. He also developed shows such as *Banjo Reb and the Blue Ghost* to bring the music to wider audiences. He continues to tour and has appeared on *Hee Haw*, *Nashville Now* and the Grand Ole Opry, where he has the distinction of being the first performer to play a paper sack on stage. In addition to hosting TNN shows, Holt has produced the seven-part series *Folkways for PBS* radio. He also hosted and starred in American Public Radio's *Riverwalk: Live from the Landing*, which was broadcast from San Antonio. In 1992, Holt released the Grammy-nominated *Grandfather's Greatest Hits*, featuring Chet Atkins and Duane Eddy. Two years later, he issued an album called *I Got a Bullfrog: Folksongs for the Fun of It.* —*Sandra Brennan*

Doodle Daddle Day: Old Time Sing-alongs for Everyone / High Windy ✦✦✦✦

● **Grandfather's Greatest Hits** / High Windy ✦✦✦✦
David Holt was one of the main old timey revivalists of the '80s and *Grandfather's Greatest Hits* is his finest achievement. With *Grandfather's Greatest Hits*, Holt constructed a set list of classic country songs—from "John Henry" and "Fire on the Mountain" to "Wabash Cannonball," "Pretty Polly," and "Wreck of the Old '97"—drafted in a handful of superstar guests (Mark O'Connor, Doc Watson, Duane Eddy, Jerry Douglas, Chet Atkins), and turned in a convincing, good-humored performance that revived traditional country without embalming it. It's a wonderful, fun album that establishes Holt as one of the leading traditional revivalists of the latter half of the 20th century. —*Thom Owens*

Hairyman—Southern Folktales / High Windy ✦✦✦
Hairyman contains Southern folk tales including "The First Motorcycle in Black Mountain," a story about the problems encountered when an isolated mountain town first experiences a roaring motorcycle. "Barney McCabe" is a folk tale from the Black tradition of St. John's Island, SC, that tells how a brother, sister, and three dogs outsmart an evil witch. . . . Listeners will hear both traditional and original tales with banjo, harmonica, guitar, and fiddle. —*MusD*

Reel & Rock / 1986 / Flying Fish ✦✦✦✦
Holt plays some great banjo. This album is all music, featuring Doc and Merle Watson and Jerry Douglas. —*Chip Renner*

Homer & Jethro

Traditional Country, Country Humor
Known as "the thinking man's hillbillies," Homer Haynes and Jethro Burns got a lot of mileage out of an act that shouldn't have lasted or gone as far as it did, at least on the surface of things. Certainly there were other, far more established duos mining similar turf on the country music circuit, with Lonzo and Oscar leading the way. But Homer & Jethro were far more than just two hayseeds doing cornball sendups of pop tunes. Underneath the cornpone facade were two top-flight musicians with a decidedly perverse sense of humor and a keen sense of satire.
Homer D. Haynes was the older of the two men, born in Knoxville, TN, on July 27, 1918. Jethro was born with the decidedly non-show biz moniker of Kenneth D. Burns, also in Knoxville, on March 10, 1923. The duo met in their early teens and started playing music together almost immediately, with Haynes on guitar and Burns alternating between mandolin and banjo. In the mid-'30s, they worked at local radio station WNOX as part of a larger group, the String Dusters. One night, the boys heard a radio broadcast of a pop singer doing a broad—and fairly denigrating—takeoff of a hillbilly singer singing a country tune. Using exaggerated vowel and consonant stressing (trademarks of bluegrass singing) and deliberately going off key as much as possible, the singer's performance irked the duo to no end. They decided right then and there that payback was the only logical solution to this kind of insult. From here on out, they would take current popular songs and send them up as hillbilly renditions, performed in deadpan earnest by Haynes and Burns, who now took the stage name of Jethro. They started working in the act while the rest of the group took a break during the broadcast. The new duo's "intermission" turn proved to be immensely popular and within four years' time, their characters and their timing were honed to a razor edge.
By 1938, they had broken off from the String Dusters and moved up to the more prestigious *Renfro Valley Barn Dance*, later broadcasting on the Chicago-based *Plantation Party*. World War II split the duo up, with Homer serving in Europe and "Jethro" serving in the Pacific theater. Getting back together after their respective discharges, they started up their radio appearances again, this time working on the Cincinnati based *Midwestern Hayride*. Their recording careers also began during this time period, signing with King Records out of Cincinnati and issuing several 78s between 1946 and 1948. By the end of the year, country producer legend Steve Sholes had signed them to RCA Victor, where they would spend the rest of their recording careers, cutting records—especially in the '60s—as if nothing could contain them. The duo joined up briefly with Spike Jones & His City Slickers, appearing in his stage show for a while, recording at least one session with him in 1950 ("Pal-Yat-Chee"), and letting Jones' agency handle all their bookings.
It was from the late '40s into the 1950s, basing themselves out of the Windy City, that the duo hit their true stride. Their first big hit was a takeoff on "Baby, It's Cold Outside" with a quite young June Carter contributing on vocals. The success of this single brought them to the attention of powerful radio station WLS, thus securing Homer & Jethro a regular spot on the *National Barn Dance*. Joining in 1949, the duo would stay faithful to the original version of the Grand Ole Opry, staying with the show until 1958. The national hookup did wonders for their career, which got an added boost when they started working double duty as regulars on *Don McNeil's Breakfast Club*, one of the top-rated morning-radio chat shows of its time, also based out of Chicago. The 1950s found them scoring big with numerous guest shots on television.

The beauty of Homer & Jethro (as opposed to other country novelty acts) was that they could work *anywhere* and be understood. They could be on the bill with Roy Rogers or trading cornball put-downs with Jimmy Dean or slickly one-upping Johnny Carson and they always held their own. As time went on, their act became more deadpan and if anything, even more polished, as if to distance themselves from everything else that had existed before them in their little corner of the country world. State-fair work was replaced with the glitzier surroundings of Las Vegas and the like. RCA Victor Living Stereo album covers aside, Homer & Jethro never had to dress up in bib overalls and play hicks to get their act over. If anything, the straighter they dressed, the straighter they acted, the funnier they were.

They were still singing with broad accents, but the satires were getting more acerbic with each release, giving rise to their lasting sobriquet as "the thinking man's hillbillies." Their satire of Patti Page's "How Much Is That Doggie in the Window?" (Homer and Jethro'd into "How Much Is That Hound Dog in the Winder?") became their first crossover hit in 1953. In 1959, the duo won their first—and only—Grammy award for "The Battle of Kooka-monga," their hilarious spoof of Johnny Horton's "The Battle of New Orleans," a country crossover record that cut a wide swath on the charts that year.

When Southern country humor became a small phenomenon of the 1960s with the success of television shows like *The Beverly Hillbillies*, *Petticoat Junction*, and *Green Acres*, Homer & Jethro's career went into overdrive. They (and RCA Victor) released an avalanche of records like there was no tomorrow, issuing eight albums of new material between 1966 and 1967 alone. Their studio efforts were produced by Chet Atkins with the cream of Nashville sidemen and one album, *Playing It Straight*, found them in an all-instrumental setting, showing there were chops a-plenty behind the cornball vocals and broad satires. The duo also participated in a wildly successful advertising campaign in the mid-'60s for Kellogg's Corn Flakes, even issuing an album based on the ad's catch phrase, *Ooh, That's Corny!*, to brisk sales.

The duo continued until Homer's death in 1971. Jethro Burns went into semi-retirement for a few years, until he was coaxed back into show business by folk singer Steve Goodman, who brought him out on tour, spotlighting him to much recognition as a fine jazz-influenced mandolinist. Homer & Jethro were inducted into the Country Music Hall of Fame in 1985. —*Cub Koda*

The Worst of Homer & Jethro / 1957 / RCA Victor ✦✦✦✦
Their best early parodies include the hilarious "How Much Is That Hound Dog in the Winder?" and "Jam Bowl Liar," a recasting of Hank Williams' "Jambalaya." —*Michael McCall*

Playing It Straight / 1962 / RCA Victor ✦✦✦✦
This shows off their instrumental talents. —*Michael McCall*

Assault the Rock & Roll Era / 1989 / Bear Family ✦✦✦
This album features "Hart Brake Motel" and others. —*AMG*

The Best Of / 1992 / RCA ✦✦✦✦
Their latter favorites include their version of the Beatles' "I Want to Hold Your Hand" and "The Battle of Kookamonga," based on Johnny Horton's "The Battle of New Orleans." —*Michael McCall*

★ **America's Favorite Song Butchers: The Weird World of Homer & Jethro** / Feb. 18, 1997 / Razor & Tie ✦✦✦✦✦
America's Favorite Song Butchers: The Weird World of Homer and Jethro is the first comprehensive single-disc overview of the country comedy duo's career, featuring all of their biggest hits and best-known songs. In the process, it showcases not only the duo's sense of humor, but also their amazing instrumental virtuosity. Their dual talents meant that Homer & Jethro were never just another run-of-the-mill cornball comedy team—they were the definitive comedic country duo, with instrumental talents that could run rings around their competitors. While some of the songs and jokes on *America's Favorite Song Butchers* have dated, the sheer musicality of the album remains awe-inspiring. —*Thom Owens*

Hoosier Hot Shots

Novelty, Old-Time, Traditional Country, Country Humor
In the 1930s, at the height of the Depression, rural Americans desperate for a laugh tuned in their radios to enjoy the cornball musical antics of the Hoosier Hot Shots. Their odd-sounding blend of a slide whistle and clarinet as the two lead instruments, the solid rhythm of the washboard, and their bizarre song lyrics made them the top novelty act of their day and the true precursor to the latter-day success of Spike Jones and His City Slickers. In the passage of some 50 to 60 years since their heyday and in the current climate of digital samplers, it becomes hard to imagine just how weird this four-piece combo sounded to the average listener. As clarinetist band leader Gabe Ward put it, "People started to laugh as soon as we started playing. We had a funny sound with the whistle and the clarinet. The way Hezzie played it, it was funny." The Hezzie that Ward refers to was one Paul "Hezzie" Trietsch, the washboard-playing, slide-whistle-blowing heart of the group. Ward had met him and his older brother Ken in their teenage years. All three had music in their blood, and by the late 1920s, they were playing together in an outfit called Ezra Buzzington's Rube Band. Buzzington's outfit worked the vaudeville circuit, its main claim to fame being its huge assortment of freak musical instruments. It was here that the trio stared honing their chops, with Ken becoming equally adept on guitar and banjo, Gabe's clarinet style veering from swing to sweet to silly, and Hezzie coming into his own playing washboard, slide whistle, and a wild assortment of whistles, bells, and horns.

The three stayed with Buzzington until he disbanded the group in 1929. Vowing to stay in touch, they played together in various on and off situations. In 1932, the Trietsch Brothers and Ward—their stage moniker at the time—were broadcasting over WOWO in Fort Wayne, IN. Doing a charity broadcast to help Ohio River Valley flood victims, they quickly found and developed their style doing novelty renditions of good-time songs, playing one after another during the course of the radiothon. They picked up a 15-minute sustaining program on the station for no pay, but with the chance to promote their own live appearances over the airwaves. They soon came to even wider prominence via their radio appearances on the *National Barn Dance*, broadcast over the powerful station WLS in Chicago. The show was the first of its type to be broadcast to a wide audience, predating the subsequent success of Nashville's Grand Ole Opry, and counting a young Gene Autry, Lulubelle and Scotty, and Red Foley among its many stars.

The show became a radio staple, broadcasting every Saturday night across the country for over 35 years. The trio—under their new name, the Hoosier Hot Shots—were an immediate hit, considering it an honor to be hooked up with the most prestigious show in country music. But the group just as quickly moved over to a regular guest spot on the Uncle Ezra Pinex Cough Syrup program, and when Uncle Ezra secured a national spot with NBC, he took the Hot Shots with him, and the group's national success was quickly assured.

The Hot Shots started making records around this time and they couldn't have asked for a more sympathetic producer on their sessions than Art Satherly. Satherly, a distinguished Englishman, was in charge of Columbia Records' (at that time, ARC) country and blues A&R division. As Gabe Ward put it, "What Art Satherly wanted on record was out visualness; he was trying to get that through. And he succeeded with us, because we were about the only people who could make people laugh after only four bars of music!" Satherly, for his part, would strip down to his shirt, put a bath towel around his neck, and go into the studio and dance to illustrate the tempo he wanted the Hot Shots to record at. The formula—with Gabe calling out, "Are you ready, Hezzie?" at the start of each tune—was a wildly successful one, with the band's records fitting comfortably on jukeboxes around the country in the "novelty dance" category. Among their hits were "I Like Bananas (Because They Have No Bones)," "The Coat and Pants Do All the Work," and "From the Indies to the Andies in His Undies," exactly the type of tunes that fitted the group like a glove. "We were tops in the novelty field," Ward would later reminisce, "all because of Art Satherly. He had the nerve to put them on the jukeboxes, even though they weren't always the top tunes. We'd do it for Art Satherly, with a beat for the jukeboxes." What Ward also fails to mention, however, is the group's tireless promotion of those records, making in-store appearances at all the Sears and Roebuck outlets nationwide when their 78s started appearing on the company's budget label, Perfect.

By the late 1930s the Hot Shots started making movie appearances, debuting in *In Old Monterey* in 1939. The success of this and a couple of other movies led the group to give up their sustaining radio spot with Uncle Ezra, relocating to the West Coast after World War II. Signing a movie deal with Columbia Pictures, the Hot Shots would go on to appear in 22 films into the early '50s.

With the public's changing tastes and the rise of television, the boys' star started to fall somewhat, although they found steady work on the Nevada gambling casino circuit. The group soldiered on into the '70s, when Paul "Hezzie" Trietsch's death broke up the original group. Although nowhere near as wild as Spike Jones, and lacking the "thinking man's hillbillies" personas of Homer & Jethro, it is impossible to think of either of those two acts existing—much less prospering and finding an audience—without the groundbreaking efforts of the Hoosier Hot Shots. — *Cub Koda*

● **Rural Rhythm** / Aug. 18, 1992 / Columbia/Legacy ✦✦✦✦
A 20-track lunatic collection of sides from the hokey side of country music. Titles include "I Like Bananas (Because They Have No Bones)," "Connie's Got Connections in Connecticut," "From the Indies to the Andies in His Undies," "The Coat and the Pants Do All the Work," and "Moving Day in Jungletown." Corny beyond belief, and great fun every step of the way, there's never been anything in country music that remotely sounds like this. — *Cub Koda*

Johnny Horton

b. Apr. 3, 1929, Tyler, TX, d. Nov. 5, 1960
Vocals / Traditional Country, Rockabilly, Honky Tonk, Nashville Sound/Countrypolitan, Country Boogie
Although he is better remembered for hit historical songs, Johnny Horton was one of the best and most popular honky tonk singers of the late '50s. Horton managed to infuse honky tonk with an urgent rockabilly sensibility. His career may have been cut short by a fatal car crash in 1960, but his music reverberated through the next three decades.

Horton was born in Los Angeles in 1925, the son of sharecropping parents. During his childhood, his family continually moved between California and Texas in an attempt to find work. His mother taught him how to play guitar at the age of 11. Horton graduated from high school in 1944 and attended a Methodist seminary intending to join a ministry. After a short while, he left the seminary and began traveling across the country, eventually moving to Alaska in 1949, where he became a fisherman. While he was in Alaska, he began writing songs in earnest.

The following year, Horton moved back to east Texas, where he entered a talent contest hosted by Jim Reeves, then an unknown vocalist. He won the contest, which encouraged him to pursue a career as a performer. Horton began playing talent contests throughout Texas, soon gaining the attention of Fabor Robison, a music manager notorious for his incompetence and scams. In early 1951, Robison became Horton's manager and secured him a recording contract with Corman Records. However, shortly after he was signed, the label folded. Robison then founded his own label, Abbott Records, with the specific intent of recording Horton. Yet none of these records had any chart success. During 1951, Horton began performing on various Los Angeles TV shows and hosted a radio show in Pasadena, performing under the name "the Singing Fisherman." By early 1952, Robison had moved Horton to Mercury Records.

At the end of 1951, Horton relocated from California to Shreveport, LA, where he became a regular on the *Louisiana Hayride*. However, Horton's time in Lousiana was filled with pitfalls—his first wife left him shortly after the move and Robison severed all ties with Horton when the latter became Jim Reeves' manager. During 1952, Hank Williams rejoined the cast of the *Hayride* and became a kind of mentor for Horton. After Hank died on New Year's eve in 1952, Horton became close with his widow, Billie Jean; the couple married in September of 1953.

Although he had a regular job on the *Hayride*, Horton's recording career was going nowhere—none of his Mercury records were selling and rock 'n' roll was beginning to overtake country's share of the marketplace. Horton's fortunes changed in the latter half of 1955, however, when he hired Webb Pierce's manager Tillman Franks to manage him and quit Mercury Records. Tillman had Pierce help him secure a contract for Horton with Columbia Records by the end of 1955. The change in record labels breathed life into Horton's career. At his first Columbia session, he cut "Honky Tonk Man," his first single for the label, which would eventually become a honky tonk classic. By the spring of 1956, the song had reached the country Top Ten and Horton was well on his way to becoming a star.

"Honky Tonk Man" was edgy enough to have Horton grouped in with the more country-oriented side of rockabilly. Wearing a large cowboy hat to hide his receding hairline, he became a popular concert attraction and racked up three more hit singles—"I'm a One-Woman Man" (No. 7), "I'm Coming Home" (No. 11), "The Woman I Need" (No. 9)—in the next year. However, the hits dried up soon after; for the latter half of 1957 and 1958, Horton didn't hit the charts at all. Instead he cut some rockabilly, which was beginning to fall out of favor by the time his singles were released.

In the fall of 1958, Horton bounced back with the Top Ten "All Grown Up," but it wasn't until the ballad "When It's Springtime in Alaska (It's Forty Below)" hit the charts in early 1959 that he made a comeback. The song fit neatly into the folk-based story songs that were becoming popular in the late '50s, and it climbed all the way to No. 1. Its success inspired his next single, "The Battle of New Orleans." Taken from a 1958 Jimmie Driftwood album, the song was a historical saga song like "When It's Springtime in Alaska," but it was far more humorous. It was also far more successful, topping the country charts for ten weeks and crossing over into the pop charts, where it was No. 1 for six weeks. After the back-to-back No. 1 successes of "When It's Springtime in Alaska" and "The Battle of New Orleans," Horton concentrated solely on folky saga songs. "Johnny Reb" became a Top Ten hit in the fall of 1959 and "Sink the Bismarck" was a Top Ten hit in the spring of 1960, followed by the No. 1 hit "North to Alaska" in the fall of 1960.

Around the time of "North to Alaska"'s November release, Horton claimed that he was getting premonitions of an early death. Sadly, his premonitions came true. On November 4, 1960, he got into a car accident driving home to Shreveport after a concert in Austin, TX. Horton was still alive after the wreck, but he died on the way to the hospital; the other passengers in his car had severe injuries, but they survived.

Although he died young, Johnny Horton left behind a recorded legacy that proved to be quite influential. Artists like George Jones and Dwight Yoakam have covered his songs, and echoes of Horton's music can still be heard in honky tonk and country-rock music well into the '90s. — *Stephen Thomas Erlewine*

Honky-Tonk Man / 1957 / Columbia ✦✦✦✦
Honky-Tonk Man contains 12 of Johnny Horton's hardest honky tonk material, including "I'm a One-Woman Man," "The Wild One," "I'm Coming Home" and the title track. It's a brief, but excellent, summation of Horton's often-forgotten talent for pure country and rocking honky tonk. — *Stephen Thomas Erlewine*

Johnny Horton's Greatest Hits / 1961 / Columbia ✦✦✦
Johnny Horton's Greatest Hits concentrates on the singer's historical story songs, throwing in a handful of ballads and honky tonk numbers. It's not a bad listen—most of these songs were hits—but it doesn't accurately represent Horton's career, especially his hard country roots and his way with a ballad. — *Stephen Thomas Erlewine*

Rockin' Rollin' Johnny Horton / 1981 / Bear Family ✦✦✦✦
Although several of his hits are featured—including "Honky Tonk Man," "The Woman I Need," and "All Grown Up"—most of *Rockin' Rollin' Johnny Horton* is comprised of obscurities, culled from his early career. The album veers between his rockabilly experiments and honky tonk, and the entire CD is a highly enjoyable compila-

tion for fans of his harder-edged music, even though a handful of tracks haven't aged particularly well. — *Stephen Thomas Erlewine*

American Originals / 1989 / Columbia ◆◆◆◆
American Originals is a brief, ten-track collection that captures Horton's biggest hits. Though it gives a more balanced overview than *Greatest Hits*, it doesn't have the breadth of the double-disc set *Honky Tonk Man: The Essential Johnny Horton 1956-1960*, which is the definitive collection. — *Stephen Thomas Erlewine*

The Early Years / 1991 / Bear Family ◆◆◆
Johnny Horton: The Early Years was the first extensive Johnny Horton collection that Bear Family assembled. Spanning seven LPs, the set includes all of Horton's recordings for the Cormac, Abbott and Mercury labels, as well as two albums' worth of demos and two albums' worth of overdubbed Abbott recordings issued on the Briar and Dot labels. Though these early recordings aren't quite as accomplished as his later, better-known work for Columbia, there's a lot of exciting material here—from proto-rockabilly and off-center honky tonk like "On the Banks of the Beautiful Nile," to "I'm a Fishin' Man" and "The Train with the Rhumba Beat"—especially for dedicated fans. Of course, the sheer size of the set means that only dedicated fans will ever pick up the box, but it is worth the investment for those fans, since these obscurities are often more interesting than the more polished recordings that followed later in his career. — *Stephen Thomas Erlewine*

1956-1960 / 1991 / Bear Family ◆◆◆◆
Johnny Horton's complete recorded works for Columbia Records, as well as all of his demos, are collected on this four-disc box set. Although it is certainly designed for collectors and diehards, there is enough first-rate music on the set to make it a worthwhile investment for serious honky tonk fans. — *Stephen Thomas Erlewine*

★ **Honky Tonk Man: The Essential Johnny Horton 1956-1960** / 1996 / Columbia/Legacy ◆◆◆◆◆
This 36-track double-CD set, running just under an hour and a half, effectively chronicles Johnny Horton's Columbia Records career. The first disc, which is in mono, traces Horton's honkytonk work of 1956-1957, starting with "Honky Tonk Man." Though lacking the crossover appeal of his later work at the time, this is the material on which his reputation stands today, with people like Dwight Yoakam resurrecting it. The end of the first disc and the beginning of the second (which is in stereo) present the stylistic fishing expedition of Horton's commercially unsuccessful middle period, as he goes looking for a hit. He finds it, of course, with the martial rhythms and historical theme of "The Battle of New Orleans," a chart-topping novelty that leads to a string of similar productions. By the end, in songs like "The Mansion You Stole," Horton seems headed toward the lush, string-filled Nashville Sound, though he died before it gained dominance. Along the way, all of Horton's country chart singles and most of his pop chart singles are included, along with two tracks previously unreleased in the US. Of course, the set could have been considerably longer (or, better yet, shaved by a few tracks and fit onto a single disc), but nothing essential is missing. — *William Ruhlmann*

Somebody's Rockin' / 1996 / Bear Family ◆◆◆◆
Supplementing Bear Family's *Rockin' Rollin' Johnny Horton*, the 31-track *Somebody's Rockin'* contains a selection of good, if obscure, rock 'n' roll and honky tonk Horton recorded in the mid-'50s, including "Devlish Lovelight," "Mean Mean Son of a Gun," "Happy Millionaire," "Coal Smoke, Valve Oil and Steel," "Talk Gobbler Talk," "Bawlin' Baby," and "Tennessee Jive." Much of this material is fun, but it's only for hardcore fans, since the primary appeal of the music is its very obscurity; on the whole, it does not rank among his finest works. — *Thom Owens*

Hot Rize

Progressive Bluegrass, Traditional Bluegrass
The eclectic Colorado progressive bluegrass band Hot Rize also played traditional bluegrass, jazz, and rock. They came together in 1976 and were named after the secret ingredient of Martha White Self-Rising Flour, the product Flatt & Scruggs promoted early in their careers. The band members were Tim O'Brien on lead and

harmony vocals, mandolin and fiddle; Pete Wernick on banjo and harmony vocals; and Charles Sawtelle on bass guitar, guitar, harmonies and lead vocals. Mike Scap departed in 1976 and was replaced by bass player, guitarist and vocalist Nick Forster, who also became the group's emcee. Hot Rize recorded its self-titled debut album, a blend of traditional and new material, in 1979. Their second album, *Radio Boogie*, came out in 1981. A year later, their alter ego Red Knuckles and the Trail Blazers, a parody of hardcore '50s country music, recorded their own album, *Hot Rize Presents Red Knuckles and the Trail Blazers*. In 1984, Hot Rize released a concert album largely comprised of traditional hits, and in 1985 released *Traditional Ties*, followed. In 1991 another Red Knuckles album, *Shades of the Past*, followed. Their final album, *Take It Home*, came out in 1992; O'Brien and Wernick subsequently went on to pursue solo careers. — *Sandra Brennan*

Hot Rize / 1979 / Flying Fish ◆◆◆◆
Hot Rize's debut album demonstrated that traditional bluegrass bands could bring the music into the modern era without turning totally progressive or losing the music's roots. Over the album's 14 tracks, Hot Rize turns in consistently engaging and exciting performances, particularly from vocalist/fiddler/mandolinist Tim O'Brien and banjoist Pete Wernick. It's a terrific debut. — *Thom Owens*

Radio Boogie / 1981 / Flying Fish ◆◆◆◆
No sophomore highjinks on this release. Solid album, highly recommended. — *Chip Renner*

Red Knuckles & Hot Rize: Live / 1982 / Flying Fish ◆◆◆

In Concert / 1984 / Flying Fish ◆◆◆
Good live presentation. — *Chip Renner*

Traditional Ties / 1986 / Sugar Hill ◆◆◆◆
Traditional Ties is the first album Hot Rize recorded for Sugar Hill, and it is arguably their best effort ever, capturing their skill for both traditional material, originals (Tim O'Brien's "Walk the Way the Wind Blows," which became a Top ten hit for Kathy Mattea), and progressive bluegrass (Keith Whitley's "You Don't Have to Move the Mountain"). — *Thom Owens*

Shades of the Past / 1989 / Sugar Hill ◆◆◆
In addition to comic material, the Hot Rize, alias Red Knuckles & the Trailblazers, run through honky tonk favorites like "The Window Up Above" and "Always Late." — *Jason Ankeny*

● **Untold Stories** / 1989 / Sugar Hill ◆◆◆◆
It all comes together on this CD, Tim O'Brien's swan song. — *Chip Renner*

Take It Home / 1992 / Sugar Hill ◆◆◆◆
Take It Home, Hot Rize's final album, demonstrates that the group continued to improve the longer they stayed together. The group's instrumental interplay is astonishing and their harmonies are quite beautiful—their performances are effortlessly graceful, making it a farewell album to treasure. — *Thom Owens*

David Houston

b. Dec. 9, 1938, Bossier City, LA, **d.** Nov. 30, 1993
Guitar, Vocals / Traditional Country, Country-Pop, Honky Tonk, Nashville Sound/Countrypolitan
Houston apparently came from good stock: his lineage includes Sam Houston and Gen. Robert E. Lee. Born and raised in Bossier City, LA, Houston became a regular on the *Louisiana Hayride* as a teenager. Apparently his soaring tenor voice wasn't totally appreciated; he found trouble getting work in the music business, and ended up as an insurance underwriter. But record producer Billy Sherrill brought Houston into the fold when Epic Records was still a young label (the early '60s), and Houston brought the company its first real hit with "Mountain of Love." In 1966 he broke through to major status with "Almost Persuaded," which netted a pair of Grammy awards and brought pop recognition as well. A member of the Grand Ole Opry since 1971, he racked up 28 hit records over a decade, including duets with Tammy Wynette and Barbara Mandrell. — *Tom Roland*

Greatest Hits / 1969 / Epic ◆◆◆◆

David Houston's Greatest Hits, Vol. 2 / 1972 / Epic ◆◆◆◆

● **American Originals** / 1989 / Epic ✦✦✦✦

Houston's soaring falsetto is well represented in this greatest hits collection on CD. "Almost Persuaded," "Baby Baby (I Know You're a Lady)," "Mountain of Love," and "My Elusive Dreams" (duet with Tammy Wynette) are all here, though, sad to say, "Livin' in a House Full of Love" is missing. —*Tom Roland*

Jan Howard (Lula Grace Johnson)

b. Mar. 13, 1932, West Plains, MO
Vocals / Country-Pop, Nashville Sound/Countrypolitan

During the '60s, Jan Howard was one of the hottest female vocalists in country music. Born Lula Grace Johnson in West Plains, MO, she moved to L.A. in 1953 and became involved with songwriter Harlan Howard, whom she married a month after they first met. Howard helped her break into country music, sending her demos to various companies. As a result she began singing demos for Tex Ritter and Johnny Bond. In 1959, using the pseudonym "Jan Howard," she recorded "Yankee Go Home."

In 1960, the Howards went to Nashville; there, Jan appeared on the *Prince Albert Show* segment of the Grand Ole Opry. Later that year, the Howards moved to Nashville permanently, where Jan's successful duet with Wynn Stewart resulted in her first solo single, "The One You Slip Around With," which made the Top 15; her next song, another duet with Stewart, reached the Top 30. In 1962, she charted with "I Wish I Was a Single Girl Again" and issued an eponymous album. Although she didn't do well on the charts, she continued to tour extensively.

Two years later her career finally caught fire. Her songs of the period reflected her troubled marriage; in 1965, she reached the Top 30 with "What Makes a Man Wander?" Later that year, Howard joined Bill Anderson's touring and television shows. In 1966, she and Anderson scored two hits with "I Know You're Married (But I Love You Still)" and "Time Out." She then scored a Top Five hit with her solo "Evil on Your Mind." Her next hit was "Bad Seed," and towards the end of the year, she had her only No. 1 hit with "For Loving You," a duet with Anderson.

In October 1968, Howard dreamed that her eldest son had been killed in Vietnam, which turned out to be true; shortly thereafter, she released the Top 15 single "My Son." In 1971, Howard became a member of the Grand Ole Opry; two years later, her youngest son committed suicide. She joined the *Johnny Cash Show* and in 1977 had three minor hits, including "To Love a Rolling Stone." In 1979, she and Tammy Wynette embarked on a tour of the US and Great Britain. In 1984, Howard released the album *Tainted Love*, followed by *Life of a Country Girl Singer* in 1987. The same year, she published her best-selling autobiography *Sunshine and Shadow*. Howard remarried in 1990 and continued to appear on the Opry. —*Sandra Brennan*

Jan Howard / 1962 / Dot ✦✦✦✦

Ray Wylie Hubbard

b. Nov. 13, 1946, Soper, OK
Vocals / Progressive Country, Singer-Songwriter

Singer-songwriter Ray Wylie Hubbard was an underground hero best known for penning the song "Up Against the Wall, Redneck Mother," popularized by Jerry Jeff Walker. Hubbard was born and raised in Soper, OK and Oak Cliff, TX. He attended Adamson High School, also the alma mater for contemporaries like Larry Gross and Michael Martin Murphey, with whom Hubbard played in a folk group at local coffeehouses. Influenced by the Kingston Trio and Woody Guthrie, he formed the Coachmen after graduating, and following college, Hubbard and the band moved to Red River, NM, where they bought and played in their own club, the Outpost. When the band split, Hubbard played coffeehouses throughout the major cities of Texas.

He eventually went back to Red River and founded Ray Wylie Hubbard & the Cowboy Twinkies. After befriending Walker, who sold him a vintage guitar, the two began working and writing songs together, including "Redneck Mother." Hubbard's band signed to Atlantic, but wasn't successful as they fit neither the rock nor the country genre. In 1975, Warner signed the band, and they recorded their eponymous debut in Nashville. Again, it failed

to find an audience, and the band disintegrated. Hubbard recorded a solo album, *Off the Wall*, in 1978, which contained his own version of "Up Against the Wall, Redneck Mother," plus a mix of originals and covers. The next year, he took over Walker's old backup group, the Lost Gonzo Band, and renamed it the Ray Wylie Hubbard Band. They recorded a live album, *Caught in the Act*, at the Soap Creek Saloon in Texas. His next album, *Something About the Night*, featured Walker. In 1992, he released *Lost Train of Thought* on the Misery Loves Company label, followed in 1995 by *Loco Gringo's Lament*. —*Sandra Brennan*

Off the Wall / 1978 / Lone Star ✦✦✦✦

● **Loco Gringo's Lament** / 1994 / Dejadisc ✦✦✦✦

With *Loco Gringo's Lament* this Texas troubadour plants himself firmly in the thick of life and love, delivering a deeply introspective and honest album that rivals his best work. Poignant songs chronicling the self-discovery that comes as a result of living hard and surviving are presented with solid instrumental backing that adds to their power and emotional impact. "After the Fall" is a masterpiece of song; a journey of struggle and enlightenment, sung over a prominent choppy guitar vamp, while "Wanna Rock and Roll," rocks hard, underneath Hubbard's brilliant telling of a dark and murderous tale. "I've Seen That Old Highway" is a spirited observation in Texas country style, and the title track is a song for musicians, outlaws, and people of the road—a mournful saga of the life. —*Jack Leaver*

● **Lost Train of Thought** / 1995 / Dejadisc ✦✦✦✦

Hubbard's 1992 release *Lost Train of Thought* has been given a new life via Dejadisc's reissue program. It was the artist's own independent release, available only at performances. He is backed up by a ragged-but-right band that can easily switch musical gears for more sedate tunes. "Sweet Lips Goodbye" is one classic of the mysterious power of woman brand, while "These Eyes" performed with Willie Nelson is, as it happens, a perfect Willie Nelson-style ballad. The energy is directed and clean. Hubbard has produced himself without excess and finds the right balance to keep his style hopping and songwriting cohesive. —*Richard Meyer*

Ray Wylie Hubbard & The Cowboy Twinkies / Warner Brothers ✦✦✦

Marcus Hummon

Contemporary Country, Singer-Songwriter, Alternative Country

The son of a career diplomat, singer-songwriter Marcus Hummon spent his formative years traveling the globe; at various times, he lived in areas as far-ranging as Italy, Africa, and the Philippines. After settling in Washington, DC, as a teen, he began performing with his three sisters in a group named Harmony; following college, in 1984 he moved to Los Angeles to seek a record deal. After months of frustration, he relocated to Nashville in 1986. While quickly finding success on the city's club circuit, a recording contract consistently eluded Hummon and his band Red Wing for years; his first taste of success came as a songwriter, when Wynonna notched a Top Three hit in 1993 with his "Only Love." The following year, Alabama scored with his "Cheap Seats," and after his songs were also covered by the likes of Hal Ketchum, Patty Loveless, and the Nitty Gritty Dirt Band, Hummon finally debuted with the LP *All in Good Time* in 1995. —*Jason Ankeny*

All in Good Time / Sep. 5, 1995 / Epic ✦✦✦✦

Michael Hurley

b. Dec. 20, 1941
Drums / Folk, Progressive Bluegrass, Progressive Country, Country-Rock

A singer-songwriter in the subversive Greenwich Village folk scene of the late '60s and '70s, who gave several songs to the Holy Modal Rounders, Michael Hurley maintained an infrequent solo career into the '90s but was more famed for his writing credits. Born on December 20, 1941, in Pennsylvania, he migrated to Greenwich Village by the early '60s and was ready to sign a major record deal when he contracted mononucleosis; after spending several years in the hospital, Hurley returned to music and released a Folkways album in 1964 titled *First Songs*. Though he was inactive through the rest of the '60s, several songs from his first LP were borrowed by both the Holy Modal Rounders and the Youngbloods, who signed Hurley to their Raccoon label in 1970. He delivered two albums for Raccoon, *Armchair Boogie* and *Hi-Fi Shock Uptown*, but was inactive again by 1972.

Four years later, Holy Modal Rounders' leader Peter Stampfel recruited Hurley for a 1976 project, Have Moicy. The group's self-titled album was critically praised, landing recommendations for Album of the Year by the *Village Voice* and Top 20 LPs of the '70s by *Rolling Stone*. Hurley's prominent place on the album—guitar, fiddle, several lead vocals—gave notice that he was ready to resume his solo career, and he signed to the folk label Rounder in 1977. Hurley released only two LPs for the label (*Long Journey* and *Snockgrass*), spending most of his time on his farm in Vermont or playing sideman on several albums. He resurfaced occasionally, recording LPs in 1984, 1988 and 1995. —*John Bush*

First Songs / 1964 / Folk Era ✦✦✦

Armchairboogie / 1970 / Warner Brothers ✦✦✦

Hi Fi Shock Uptown / 1972 / Racoon ✦✦✦✦

● **Long Journey** / 1977 / Rounder ✦✦✦✦

Snockgrass / 1980 / Rounder ✦✦✦✦

Watertower / 1988 / Fundamental ✦✦✦

Wolfways / Oct. 1995 / Koch ✦✦✦

Michael Hurley / Rounder ✦✦✦

Ferlin Husky

b. Dec. 3, 1927, Flat River, MO

Guitar, Vocals / Traditional Country, Country-Pop, Country Humor, Honky Tonk, Bakersfield Sound, Nashville Sound/ Countrypolitan

Ferlin Husky had three separate careers. Out of the three, the best-known is his country-pop career, which brought him to the top of the charts in the late '50s, but he was also known as a honky tonk singer called Terry Preston and a country comic named Simon Crum. Of course, Preston and Crum are just footnotes to Husky's very popular career, even though Crum nearly became a household name as well. During the late '50s and early '60s, he had a string of Top 40 country hits, highlighted by two No. 1 hits—"Gone" and "Wings of a Dove"—which each spent ten weeks at the top of the charts. Husky wasn't able to sustain that momentum, but both of the songs became country classics.

Born and raised on a Missouri farm, Ferlin Husky became infatuated with music and began to play guitar as a child. During World War II, he enlisted in the Merchant Marines, where he occasionally entertained the troops on board his ship. Following the war, he became a DJ in Missouri, then in Bakersfield, CA.

While he was in California, Ferlin began using the name Terry Preston, because he believed his given name sounded too rural. He also began singing in honky tonks, using the Preston name. At one of his gigs, Tennessee Ernie Ford's manager Cliffie Stone heard Husky and took him under his wing. Stone helped Husky secure a record contract at Capitol Records in 1953. As soon as he signed with Capitol, he reverted to using Ferlin Husky as his performing name.

Husky's first records were generally ignored. It wasn't until he sang on Jean Shepard's "A Dear John Letter" that he had a hit. "A Dear John Letter" became a No. 1 hit, but Husky wasn't able to follow it immediately with a solo hit, although the duo had a sequel, "Forgive Me John," later that year. Husky didn't have a solo hit until 1955, when "I Feel Better All Over (More Than Anywhere's Else)" and its flipside, "Little Tom," climbed into the country Top Ten. Around the same time, he developed his comic alter-ego, Simon Crum. Husky signed to a separate record contract with Capitol under the Crum alias and began releasing records under that name.

Husky racked up a consistent string of hits during the late '50s, reaching his peak in 1957, when "Gone" spent ten weeks at No. 1; the song crossed over into the pop charts, climbing to No. 4. That same year, he began an acting career, starting with a spot on the *Kraft TV Theatre* television program and the film *Mr. Rock & Roll*. In 1958, Simon Crum had a No. 2 hit with "Country Music Is Here to Stay." Though he had several hits in 1959, none of his songs broke the Top Ten. In 1960, he had his biggest hit, the gospel song "Wings of a Dove," which was No. 1 for a total of ten weeks and reached No. 12 on the pop charts.

Despite the massive success of "Wings of a Dove," Husky wasn't able to sustain a presence on the country charts during the '60s. He remained a popular concert attraction, but he had no Top Ten hits between "Wings of a Dove" and "Once," which hit No. 4 in 1966. A year after "Once," Ferlin had his final Top Ten hit with "Just for You." In the late '60s, Husky managed to incorporate the slicker, heavily produced sounds of contemporary country-pop into his music, which resulted in a brief revitalization of his career. Husky kept racking up minor hits until 1975. In 1977, he had heart surgery and briefly retired from performing. During the '80s and '90s, he performed regularly at the Grand Ole Opry, as well as Christy Lane's Theater in Branson, MO. —*Stephen Thomas Erlewine*

Capitol Collector's Series / 1989 / Capitol ✦✦✦✦

Although *Capitol Collector's Series* is a fairly comprehensive overview of Ferlin Husky's hit-making peak, it's missing a couple of essential items, most notably his first hit, "A Dear John Letter." It concentrates on his country-pop hits, picking up the great majority of his hits, including "Wings of a Dove," "Gone," "A Fallen Star," "Just for You," and 16 other songs. —*Stephen Thomas Erlewine*

Greatest Hits / 1990 / Curb ✦✦✦✦

Although it's brief and cheaply produced, *Greatest Hits* contains many of the essential Husky tracks, including "A Dear John Letter," which isn't on *Capitol Collector's Series*, "Gone," and "Wings of a Dove." For the budget-conscious it isn't a bad purchase, although *Capitol Collector's Series* offers a greater selection for an equivalent price. —*Stephen Thomas Erlewine*

With Feelin' / 1991 / Pair ✦✦✦

On *With Feelin'*, Husky tackles some of country's most revered songs, including "I'm So Lonesome I Could Cry," "I Fall to Pieces," and "She Thinks I Still Care." —*Jason Ankeny*

Country Music Is Here to Stay / 1993 / Laserlight ✦✦

Country Music Is Here to Stay includes a remake of "Wings of a Dove," Husky's biggest hit. —*Jason Ankeny*

● **Vintage** / 1996 / Capitol ✦✦✦✦

Vintage contains nearly all of the essential items from Ferlin Husky's peak years at Capitol Records. Featuring almost 20 tracks—including the hits "Wings of a Dove," "A Dear John Letter," "Once," "Stormy Weather" and "Gone," which is included in both its hit single version and the original version released under the name "Terry Preston"— it's the closest thing to a definitive retrospective yet assembled. —*Thom Owens*

Walter Hyatt

Guitar, Vocals / Progressive Country, Singer-Songwriter, Alternative Country, Americana

Walter Hyatt is a Texas singer, songwriter, and guitar player. He is the first vocalist to be included in the MCA Master Series. His music is unique, with original ideas built into a foundation of classic jazz and blues to create a tasteful, moving, highly individual sound. —*Chip Renner*

Music Town / 1993 / Sugar Hill ✦✦✦

● **King Tears** / MCA ✦✦✦✦

This cocktail country is a must for Lyle Lovett fans. —*Robert Gordon*

I

Frank Ifield

b. Nov. 30, 1937, Coventry, England
Vocals / Traditional Country, Country-Pop

Australian singer-songwriter/yodeler Frank Ifield was one of the more original country artists to come from overseas. He was born in England, and moved to Australia in 1948. His father was an inventor and engineer famed for creating the Ifield pump, a device used in fuel systems for jet aircraft. While still in his teens, he became a regular on *Bonnington's Bunkhouse,* a popular radio program, and dropped out of school to pursue a music career full-time. He appeared on other radio shows as well, finally landing on the traveling *Ted Quigg Show,* where he stayed for many years.

Ifield signed with EMI Australia in 1953 and released two successful singles including "There's a Loveknot in My Lariat." Soon he was hosting his weekly television show *Campfire Favourites.* By 1959, Ifield was appearing on all three of the Sydney TV channels. Later that year, he went to London, and had his first British hit in 1960 with "Lucky Devil." He remained in England and in 1962 became a star with his yodeling classic "I Remember You." The song stayed at the top of the British charts for over two months, and when released in the States it hit the Top Five on the pop charts. His most successful year was 1963, when he scored two British No. 1 hits; one of the chart toppers, "Confessin'," a cover of a Rudy Vallee hit, made it to the middle reaches of the US pop charts as well.

He continued having chart success through 1964, but after that his career in Britain began to wane. He came to Nashville in 1966 and was made an Honorary Tennessean by the state's governor, Frank Clement. Ifield recorded two albums in Nashville and debuted on the Grand Ole Opry, where he was a great success. Over the next two years, he had several mid-range hits. He again found popularity in Europe during the '70s, particularly in Belgium, Holland, and Luxembourg, and continued to tour and perform at country music festivals and cabarets. *— Sandra Brennan*

I Remember You / 1963 / Vee-Jay ✦✦✦

The Best of Frank Ifield / Curb ✦✦✦✦

This combines a hillbilly yodel with slick pop stylings. *— Hank Davis*

I'm Confessin' / 196 / Capitol ✦✦✦✦

This album, half made up of standards and half of country music classics, is done as only Frank Ifield could do them. There's nothing about these songs that makes them stand out on this record; they are background music at best. Best remembered for "I Remember You" in the US; nothing on this record comes close. *— Jim Worbois*

Portrait of Frank Ifield / 1983 / PRT [UK] ✦✦✦✦

● **The EMI Years** / Capitol ✦✦✦✦

A generous 20-track sampler of Ifield's biggest hits (circa 1960), it includes "I Remember You." *— Hank Davis*

Jack Ingram

Vocals / Contemporary Country, New Traditionalist

The Texas-based modern-day honky tonker Jack Ingram first carved out a niche for himself in the bars and roadhouses of Texas. By the mid-'90s, he had released two well-received independent albums and had opened for artists like Merle Haggard and Mark Chesnutt. By the end of 1996, he had signed with Warner, who reissued his first two indie albums, and had begun work on his major-label debut with producer Steve Earle. *— Stephen Thomas Erlewine*

● **Live at Adair's** / Nov. 21, 1995 / Warner Brothers ✦✦✦✦

Jack Ingram's independent debut album *Live at Adair's* captures the roadhouse energy of the traditionalist honky tonker. Running through a selection of his original material, Ingram is energetic and convincing, making modern country sound more alive, gritty, and vibrant than it usually does. Largely, that's due to his stellar backing band, who drive the songs home for all they're worth; but don't discount Ingram's talent for leading the band, as well as his knack for writing tight, memorable weepers and honky tonk ravers. Those are the things that make *Live at Adair's* such an invigorating, promising debut. *— Thom Owens*

Lonesome Question / Dec. 1995 / Crystal Clear Sound ✦✦✦

International Submarine Band

Country-Rock

The International Submarine Band is best remembered as country-rock pioneer Gram Parsons' first band, which isn't surprising since the group received almost no publicity when they were active in the late '60s. Though the band never quite realized their potential, their sole album, 1968's *Safe at Home,* suggests the path Parsons would later follow.

Parsons formed the International Submarine band with guitarist John Nuese, bassist Ian Dunlop, and drummer Mickey Gauvin while he was studying theology at Harvard in the mid-'60s. Parsons dropped out of college in 1966 and had the band move its operations to New York, where they began to develop their synthesis of country and rock. By the end of the year, they had recorded two singles for Goldstar which were ignored. The group also recorded an album, which went unreleased; the tapes were later lost.

Early in 1967, the band moved out to Los Angeles on the advice of former child actor Brandon deWilde, who told the band he could get them into the movies. The International Submarine Band did indeed appear in a movie—Roger Corman's *The Trip,* which starred Peter Fonda. However, the group's music was erased, with the psychedelic blues of the Electric Flag overdubbed on the ISB's performance. Still, the band benefited from its performance in *The Trip,* since it increased their profile in the L.A. underground; Fonda even recorded Parsons' original song "November Nights."

However, relations between the band members were beginning to fray, and Dunlop and Guavin left the group in the spring of 1967. A few months later, Parsons' childhood friend Jon Corneal joined as a drummer, and they hired a temporary bassist in order to audition for Lee Hazelwood's LHI Records. On the basis of the audition, the group landed a contract. LHI's in-house producer Suzi Jane Hokum was hired as the group's producer and Chris Ethridge was hired as the group's bassist. By the end of 1967, the International Submarine Band had completed their debut album, *Safe at Home*.

Although the group's fortunes were beginning to improve, Gram Parsons left the band in February of 1968 to join the Byrds. However, he hadn't told LHI that he intended to leave the Submarine Band before he became a Byrd, and he had to sell his rights to the ISB name to Lee Hazelwood in order to avoid a lawsuit; Hazelwood was also able to prevent Parsons' vocals from appearing on his first album with the Byrds, 1968's *Sweetheart of the Rodeo*. Following Parsons' departure, the International Submarine Band attempted to replace the vocalist, but they couldn't find any appropriate candidates. By the time the ISB's debut album, *Safe at Home*, was released in the spring of 1968, the group had broken up. — *Stephen Thomas Erlewine*

● **Safe at Home** / 1968 / Shiloh ✦✦✦✦
While the International Submarine Band's lone album *Safe at Home* is slightly inconsistent, it contains enough brilliant moments to make it necessary for hardcore Gram Parsons fans and serious country-rock fans. Arguably the first country-rock album ever recorded, the fusions on *Safe at Home* sometimes sound tentative—the group doesn't quite have a handle on some of their covers, including "I Still Miss Someone" and "Millers Cave"—but at its best, the record is stunning in its rural beauty. "Luxury Liner" is Parsons' first masterpiece, while "Do You Know How It Feels to Be Lonesome" and "Blue Eyes" are nearly as good. Furthermore, the band invests Merle Haggard's "I Must Be Somebody Else You've Known," "Folsom Prison Blues/That's All Right," and "A Satisfied Mind" with passion and soul. There may be a few weak spots, but the best cuts on *Safe at Home* make it a country-rock landmark. — *Stephen Thomas Erlewine*

James Intveld

Roots-Rock, Neo-Traditionalist Country, California Country
James Intveld was a native of Los Angeles who started his career at an early age listening and singing along to his parents' recordings of Hank Williams, Sr., Dean Martin, Lefty Frizzell, and Elvis. During the cowpunk movement of the '80s, Intveld was working the same clubs as Dwight Yoakam and Rosie Flores, playing his own brand of rockabilly, and so impressed *A Town South of Bakersfield* producers Pete Anderson and Dusty Wakeman that he was included on the second volume of the compilation series.

Initially, Intveld worked with his younger brother Ricky and friend Pat Woodward in a band known as the Rockin' Shadows. The group dissolved when Ricky and Woodward left to work with Rick Nelson's Stone Canyon Band; both later died in the same airplane accident that took Nelson's life, a tragedy that cut deeply

into Intveld's heart and soul. On his own, he worked as a singer-songwriter and concentrated on acting. Continuously cast in movies, TV and videos, he was the singing voice of Johnny Depp's character in the John Waters film *Cry Baby* and served as a prominent player and character in videos by such artists as Kathy Mattea.

Still, his music remained the centerpiece of his creative life. As a writer, Intveld wrote the Rosie Flores hit "Cryin' Over You" as well as all the material on his own 1996 effort *James Intveld*. Named the best studio recording project and the best country or roots CD of 1996 by *California's Music Connection* magazine, Intveld successfully produced, arranged, sang, and played all the parts on this magnificent release, dedicated to his brother and best friend, Ricky. Continuing to write and perform on a continual basis, Intveld also remained in demand for his skills as a player; as adept at the slap bass, slide, steel, and drums as on guitar, he sat in with the Blasters periodically and often held down percussion duties for bluesman Lester Butler. A regular player around L.A., Intveld was also involved in recording projects with Kathy Robertson and the tribute CD *Turning the World Blue*, honoring Gene Vincent. — *Jana Pendragon*

● **James Intveld** / 1996 / Bear Family ✦✦✦✦
This self-titled release is far and away the closest to perfection of any studio project in a very long time. With every aspect of the production, performance, and choice of material handled by the artist himself, there is a continuity and purity about it that is missing in even the top-selling discs that chart and receive platinum recognition.

Vocally, no one can come close to Intveld's irreproachable style. His ability to evoke emotion from a song, even those he did not write, is dumbfounding; his version of Don Gibson's "Blue Blue Day" is evidence of this. As a writer, Intveld is stunning in his clarity and storytelling ability; listen carefully to the earthy tale of "Kermit Vale." While he does not consider himself a country writer per se, he is quite capable of concocting a mean shuffle and accentuating it with the optimal amount of twang, as exhibited on "Your Lovin'" and "Barely Hangin' On." His own rendition of his classic hit, "Cryin' Over You," made famous by Rosie Flores, also demonstrates Intveld's obvious understanding of traditional country music.

A noteworthy balladeer, James Intveld takes this art form to the highest level. His own "You Say Goodnight, I'll Say Goodbye" is not only emotionally evocative, but also intelligent. The entire affair is dedicated to his late brother, Ricky Intveld, which makes this, his first Bear Family CD, all the more meaningful for James and his many fans the world over. As they say, nobody does it better than James Intveld; in a perfect world where music and musicians are rewarded for talent, ability, and original creativity, the enticing Mr. Intveld would be continually sitting at No. 1 on all the music charts and this CD would be double or triple platinum at least. — *Jana Pendragon*

J

Alan Jackson

b. Oct. 17, 1958, Newnan, GA
Guitar, Vocals / Contemporary Country, New Traditionalist
Through the '80s and '90s, Alan Jackson quietly worked to become one of the most popular modern honky tonkers of his era. Born in Newman, GA, as a youth he sang gospel music in church and at home. As a teen, he sang at parties and choirs in a country duo. Jackson left school to sell cars and later work in construction. Starting at the age of 20, he only gradually began to perform music professionally, first by sitting in with other musicians and then by starting his own band, Dixie Steel, with whom he played the local club circuit.

Still, music was just a hobby for Jackson—he wrote songs only in his spare time. His wife Denise, a flight attendant, played a major part in getting Jackson on the road to Nashville. Around 1985, she encountered Glen Campbell in an airport and asked the singer for some advice for her husband. Campbell gave her the address and phone number of his publishing company. Jackson decided to sell his home and move to Nashville, bringing along a demo tape of some of his songs. Campbell's company was impressed by Jackson's singing ability, but suggested he hone his songwriting a bit. To support himself and his family, Jackson took odd jobs, including working in the mailroom of the Nashville Network and doing some session and demo work. The following year, he joined the staff of Glen Campbell Music.

When not writing, he performed in local clubs. After a while, he recorded a new demo tape with fellow songwriter Keith Stegall. The tape caught the attention of Arista Records, which was in the process of setting up a Nashville division, and he became the first artist on the label. Jackson released his debut album, *Here in the Real World*, in 1990; a year later it went platinum. It produced three chart toppers including "I'd Love You All Over Again" and "Someday." 1991 was even better: his second album *Don't Rock the Jukebox* went double-platinum within its first year of release. That same year, he became a member of the Grand Ole Opry.

In the fall of 1992, Jackson released *A Lot About Livin' (& a Little 'Bout Love)*, his most successful release to date, spawning no less than five Top Five singles, including the No. 1s "Love's Got a Hold on You," "She's Got the Rhythm (And I Got the Blues)," and "Chattahoochee." Jackson released a holiday album, *Honky Tonk Christmas*, in 1993. The following year, he delivered his follow-up to *A Lot About Livin', Who I Am*, which went double platinum within a year of its release. *Who I Am* spawned the No. 1 hit singles "Summertime Blues," "Gone Country," "Livin' on Love," and "I Don't Even Know Your Name." In 1995, Jackson released *The Greatest Hits Collection*, which went triple platinum within a year of its release. *Everything I Love* surfaced in 1996. —*Sandra Brennan*

Here in the Real World / 1990 / Arista ✦✦✦✦
"I'd Love You All Over Again" was Jackson's fifth single but his first No. 1. But any country fan of the time would also recognize the title track and "Chasin' That Neon Rainbow." —*Brian Mansfield*

Don't Rock the Jukebox / 1991 / Arista ✦✦✦
The album art is really ugly, but the music isn't—"Don't Rock the Jukebox," "Someday," "Love's Got a Hold on You," and "Dallas" all

hit the top of the singles charts. And "Midnight in Montgomery," which details a ghostly encounter with Hank Williams' spirit, became a video classic. —*Brian Mansfield*

☆ **A Lot About Livin' (& a Little 'Bout Love)** / 1992 / Arista ✦✦✦✦✦
By this third album—when many artists start to run out of ideas—Jackson sounds like he's just starting to hit his stride with songs like "Tonight I Climbed the Wall," "She's Got the Rhythm (And I Got the Blues)" (co-written with Randy Travis), and "Chattahoochee," one of country's great summer singles. He also continues a proud tradition of country artists covering blues tunes by singing "Mercury Blues," a song by a minor Bay Area bluesman named K.C. Douglas. —*Brian Mansfield*

Honky Tonk Christmas / Oct. 12, 1993 / Arista ✦✦✦✦
One of the best country Christmas albums, this smart blend of old and new songs doesn't have a traditional carol in the bunch. Jackson starts off strong with the rocking "Honky Tonk Christmas" and then sings a gorgeous duet with Alison Krauss. He adds his voice to a previously taped track by the late Keith Whitley on "There's a New Kid in Town" and does a credible job with Merle Haggard's "If We Make It Through December." Save for a silly duet with the cartoon Chipmunks, this is a fabulous album. —*Brian Mansfield*

Who I Am / 1994 / Arista ✦✦✦✦
The huge singles aren't as readily apparent here, but Jackson begins to reveal more of himself with his album. "Gone Country" is a subtly brilliant jab at people who discover country music only when there's money to be made. The joke is that Jackson leads the album with Eddie Cochran's teenage-angst anthem "Summertime Blues." Jackson pulls out chestnuts from the catalogues of Con Hunley and the Kendalls, and writes "Job Description" to explain to his daughter why daddy's never home. In a time when even artists had trouble telling all the young hat acts apart, a personal statement like *Who I Am* was possibly the smartest move Jackson could have made. —*Brian Mansfield*

★ **Greatest Hits Collection** / Nov. 21, 1995 / Arista ✦✦✦✦✦
As the title indicates, all of Alan Jackson's greatest hits—including the No. 1 singles "Chattahoochee," "She's Got the Rhythm (And I Got the Blues)," "I'd Love You All Over Again," and "Don't Rock the Jukebox"—are collected on this single disc, making it the perfect introduction to the singer. —*Stephen Thomas Erlewine*

Everything I Love / Oct. 29, 1996 / ✦✦✦✦
Everything I Love is further proof that Alan Jackson is one of the finest country singers of the '90s. Jackson continues to mine traditional country and honky tonk for source material, yet he isn't afraid to update the sound with electronic instruments. That fearless experimentation is kept in check by his ability to keep his music simple and straightforward—there is no question that Jackson deals only in pure honky tonk. Of course, his musical experimentation wouldn't be quite so effective if he didn't have a fine set of songs to back him up, and on *Everything I Love*, he has some of his finest ever, including "Little Bitty," "A House with No Curtains" and "Must've Had a Ball." —*Thom Owens*

Alan Jackson

Aunt Molly Jackson (Mary Magdalene Garland)

b. 1880, Clay County, KY, **d.** Sep. 1, 1960
Vocals / Old-Time

Aunt Molly Jackson was not only an old-time country singer-songwriter who spent much of her career trying to preserve the traditional mountain folksongs of her native Kentucky, she was also influential in the struggle for miners' rights during the '20s and '30s. She was born Mary Magdalene Garland in Clay County, KY. When she was only six, her mother starved to death; she married at 14 and then watched as the coal mines killed her brother, husband, and son. Shortly thereafter, Jackson began to express her grief and anger by writing songs such as "Poor Miner's Farewell" and "Dishonest Miller." Through the 1920s, Jackson continued to work for miners' rights; in 1931, she went to New York and recorded the single "Kentucky Miner's Wife."

She relocated to New York to continue her fight, befriending other musicians on the New York folk scene including Woody Guthrie. In 1935, folklorists Alan Lomax and Mary Barnicle convinced Jackson to record 150 songs for the Library of Congress, which took her four years. After appearing with Leadbelly and Josh White in the *Cavalcade of American Song* in 1940, Jackson eventually settled in California, where she lived until the folk revival of the late '50s. Her music was an important part of that revival, although Aunt Molly never received a single dime in royalties for the protest songs she had written. In 1960, impoverished and nearly forgotten, Jackson was working on an autobiographical LP with John Greenway when she died suddenly. During the 1970s, some of the songs she recorded for the Library of Congress were released on a Rounder anthology. —*Sandra Brennan*

The Songs & Stories of Aunt Molly Jackson / Smithsonian/Folkways ✦✦✦✦

Library of Congress Recordings / Rounder ✦✦✦✦

Carl Jackson

b. Sep. 18, 1953, Louisville, KY
Banjo / Traditional Bluegrass

Carl Jackson, an accomplished bluegrass instrumentalist and songwriter, was born September 18, 1953, in Louisville, KY. While

playing in his father's bluegrass band at the age of 14, he was approached by Jim & Jesse to join their backing group, the Virginia Boys. He accepted and spent most of his teenage years playing banjo for Jim & Jesse and other groups at the Grand Ole Opry. Jackson's talents earned him a contract with the independent Prize label, where he recorded the album *Bluegrass Festival* in the late '60s.

In 1971, Jackson left to play with the Sullivan Family, but after less than a year, he moved to Ohio to form the Country Store with Keith Whitley and Jimmy Gaudreau. A short time later, he jumped at the chance to join Glen Campbell's backing band. He spent 12 years with Campbell, but during that time he also recorded the albums *Banjo Player* and *Old Friend* for Capitol. In 1981, Jackson signed with Sugar Hill and released his tribute to Earl Scruggs, *Banjo Man*. The following year brought *Song of the South*, and in 1983 he joined with old friends Jim & Jesse for *Banjo Hits*.

After signing with Columbia in 1984, Carl Jackson left Glen Campbell and began to hit the charts. His Lefty Frizzell cover "She's Gone, Gone, Gone" reached No. 44 in 1984, though three later singles never matched its relative success. (Jackson did write the hit "(Love Always) Letter to Home" which peaked in the Top 15 for Campbell in May 1984.) During the late '80s, his rich harmony vocals brightened recordings by Emmylou Harris, Ricky Skaggs, Vince Gill, Garth Brooks, Roger Miller, and many other acts. In the '90s, Carl Jackson began to be rewarded for his years of work. He earned the International Bluegrass Association's "Song of the Year" award in 1990 for "Little Mountain Church Home," recorded by Ricky Skaggs & the Nitty Gritty Dirt Band on *Will the Circle Be Unbroken, Vol. 2*, and won a "Best Bluegrass Album" Grammy the following year with John Starling and the Nash Ramblers for *Spring Training*. —*John Bush*

Song of the South / 1970 / Sugar Hill ✦✦✦
Banjo Player / 1973 / Capitol ✦✦✦✦
Banjo Man: A Tribute to Earl Scruggs / Sugar Hill ✦✦✦
Spring Training / Sugar Hill ✦✦✦
● **Banjo Hits** / Sugar Hill ✦✦✦✦

Shot Jackson

b. Sep. 4, 1920, Wilmington, NC, **d.** Jan. 24, 1991
Dobro, Guitar (Steel), Session Musician / Traditional Country, Instrumental Country

One of the premiere steel guitar and dobro players of the postwar generation, Shot Jackson was a solo and session artist who also gained fame as a designer and manufacturer of musical instruments. Born Harold B. Jackson on September 4, 1920 in Wilmington, NC, he earned the nickname "Buckshot"—later abbreviated to simply "Shot"—while still a child. His interest in music also began at an early age, and he became a devoted fan of the Grand Ole Opry, in particular of Roy Acuff's Smoky Mountain Boys and their dobro player Bashful Brother Oswald. In 1941, Jackson joined the house band on a local country radio station, and in 1944, he moved to Nashville to sign on with the Opry as a sideman for Cousin Wilbur Westbrooks.

After a year in the Navy, Jackson began playing electric steel guitar with the Bailes Brothers, and continued performing with the group throughout their tenure on the Shreveport, LA, station KWKH's *Louisiana Hayride* program. After the Bailes Brothers left the show, Jackson remained at KWKH, where he performed and recorded with the likes of Webb Pierce, Jimmie Osborne, and Red Sovine. In 1951, he joined Johnnie & Jack's Tennessee Mountain Boys, and over the next half-dozen years, he played dobro on virtually all of the group's live dates and studio sessions. He also played on many of Kitty Wells' first hits, in addition to recording a few solo sides.

In 1957, Jackson fulfilled a personal dream by becoming the electric steel player for Acuff's Smoky Mountain Boys, and remained with the group for five years. During his affiliation with Acuff, Jackson and Buddy Emmons designed an electric pedal steel guitar; to market it, they founded their own company, Sho-Bud. Gradually, the company's success began to absorb more and more of Jackson's time, and he left the Smoky Mountain Boys, although he did remain an active musician, particularly as a steel player for Melba Montgomery, who had also left Acuff to go solo some time before. In addition to working with Montgomery (on both her solo work and her duets with George Jones), he recorded with many other artists, and even cut his own solo LP, *Singing Strings of Steel Guitar and Dobro*, in 1962.

Jackson rejoined Acuff full-time in 1964, but his tenure abruptly ended in July of 1965 when he, Acuff, and singer June Stearns were all sidelined by a near-fatal car crash. After a long recovery period, he began performing with his wife Donna Darlene, a former vocalist on the *Jamboree* program; in 1965, he also issued the solo record *Bluegrass Dobro*. His latest creation, a seven-string resonator guitar called the Sho-Bro, hit the market not long after, and again, Jackson distanced himself from music to focus on business. Still, he continued to play on occasion, rejoining the Bailes Brothers for a number of reunion concerts and recordings. He also hooked up with the Roy Clark Family Band for a pair of albums and appearances on the TV program *Hee Haw*. In 1980, Baldwin-Gretsch purchased Sho-Bud, and three years later, Jackson sold his instrument repair business as well. Soon after retirement, he suffered a stroke, which left him unable to speak and play music. In 1986, he was inducted into the Steel Guitar Hall of Fame; shortly after suffering another stroke several years later, Shot Jackson died on January 24, 1991. —*Jason Ankeny*

● **Singing Strings of Steel Guitar and Dobro** / 1962 / Starday ✦✦✦✦

Bluegrass Dobro / 1965 / Cumberland ✦✦✦

20 Beautiful Waltzes / ✦✦✦

Stonewall Jackson

b. Nov. 6, 1932, Tabor City, NC
Guitar, Vocals / Traditional Country, Honky Tonk, Nashville Sound/Countrypolitan

A descendant of the famed Confederate general, Stonewall Jackson was one of the more popular country music stars of the early '60s, scoring a handful of Top Ten country hits and becoming a fixture at the Grand Ole Opry.

Jackson began singing professionally in the mid-'50s, moving to Nashville in 1956. Once in Nashville, he made a couple of demos for Acuff-Rose. Wesley Rose heard the demo and set up an audition for Jackson at the Grand Ole Opry, and he soon became the first entertainer to join the Opry without a recording contract. After the audition, he was assigned to perform on the Friday Night Frolic before his official Opry debut. Backed by Ernest Tubb's Texas Troubadours, he proved so popular that the audience demanded four encores.

Eventually Jackson hit the road with Tubb. By the beginning of 1957, Stonewall signed a recording contract with Columbia Records, and cut his first record, "Don't Be Angry," in early 1957. The follow-up, Jackson's cover of George Jones' "Life to Go," became the singer's first major hit, peaking at No. 2 in early 1959. It was followed by "Waterloo," which became his first No. 1 hit, spending five weeks at the top of the country charts and hitting No. 4 on the pop charts. Jackson then had a string of Top 40 hits that was highlighted by "Why I'm Walkin'" (No. 6, 1960), "A Wound Time Can't Erase" (No. 3, 1962), and "Leona" (No. 9, 1962). Jackson's second No. 1 hit, "B.J. the D.J.," charted in early 1964.

During the latter half of the '60s, he reached the upper reaches of the Top 40 less frequently, scoring only one Top Ten hit—1967's "Stamp Out Loneliness"—during the last five years of the decade. By 1970, he wasn't even hitting the Top 40. He bounced back briefly in 1971, when he covered Lobo's "Me and You and a Dog Named Boo." In 1973, he had his last hit with "Herman Schwartz," which reached No. 41. After that, Jackson quietly entered semi-retirement. He continued to record occasionally, releasing albums like the inspirational *Make Me Like a Child Again*. He also re-recorded versions of his old hits, and privately published his autobiography, *From the Bottom Up*, in 1991. —*Sandra Brennan*

Wanda Jackson

The Dynamite Stonewall Jackson / 1959 / Columbia ✦✦✦
This collection of early hits—"Waterloo," "George Jones," "Life to Go," "Smoke Along the Track," "Why I'm Walking"—are almost all good songs, delivered in his powerful, homely but engaging voice. —*George Bedard*

● **American Originals** / 1989 / Columbia ✦✦✦✦
A re-packaging of many of Jackson's best-known songs includes the great "Don't Be Angry," "A Wound Time Can't Erase," and "Smoke Along the Tracks," the latter revived by Dwight Yoakam. For some unfathomable reason, "I Washed My Hands in Muddy Water" is missing. These kinds of omissions were standard in this half-hearted oldies series. —*Michael McCall*

Waterloo / 1993 / Laserlight ✦
Waterloo offers inferior remakes of some of Jackson's hits, including the title cut. —*Jason Ankeny*

Wanda Jackson

b. Oct. 20, 1937, Maud, OK
Vocals / Traditional Country, Rockabilly, CCM, Country Gospel
Wanda Jackson was only halfway through high school when, in 1954, country singer Hank Thompson heard her on an Oklahoma City radio show and asked her to record with his band, the Brazos Valley Boys. By the end of the decade, Jackson had become one of America's first major female country and rockabilly singers.

Jackson was born in Oklahoma, but her father Tom—himself a country singer who quit because of the Depression—moved the family to California in 1941. He bought Wanda her first guitar two years later, gave her lessons, and encouraged her to play piano as well. In addition, he took her to see such acts as Tex Williams, Spade Cooley, and Bob Wills, which left a lasting impression on her young mind. Tom moved the family back to Oklahoma City when his daughter was 12 years old. In 1952, she won a local talent contest and was given a 15-minute daily show on KLPR. The program, soon upped to 30 minutes, lasted throughout Jackson's high school years. It's here that Thompson heard her sing. Jackson recorded several songs with the Brazos Valley Boys, including "You Can't Have My Love," a duet with Thompson's bandleader, Billy Gray. The song, on the Decca label, became a national hit, and Jackson's career was off and running. She had wanted to sign with Capitol, Thompson's label, but was turned down, so she signed with Decca instead.

Jackson insisted on finishing high school before hitting the road. When she did, her father came with her. Her mother made and helped design Wanda's stage outfits. "I was the first one to put some glamour in the country music—fringe dresses, high heels, long earrings," Jackson says of these outfits. When Jackson first toured in 1955 and 1956, she was placed on a bill with none other than Elvis Presley. The two hit it off almost immediately. Jackson says it was Presley, along with her father, who encouraged her to sing rockabilly.

In 1956, Jackson finally signed with Capitol, a relationship that lasted until the early '70s. Her recording career bounced back and forth between country and rockabilly; she did this by often putting one song in each style on either side of a single. Jackson cut the rockabilly hit "Fujiyama Mama" in 1958, which became a major success in Japan. Her version of "Let's Have a Party," which Elvis had cut earlier, was a US Top 40 pop hit for her in 1960, after which she began calling her band the Party Timers. A year later, she was back in the country Top Ten with "Right or Wrong" and "In the Middle of a Heartache." In 1965, she topped the German charts with "Santa Domingo," sung in Dutch. In 1966, she hit the US Top 20 with "The Box It Came In" and "Tears Will Be the Chaser for the Wine." Jackson's popularity continued through the end of the decade.

Jackson toured regularly, was twice nominated for a Grammy, and was a big attraction in Las Vegas from the mid-'50s into the '70s. She married IBM programmer Wendell Goodman in 1961, and instead of quitting the business—as many women singers had done at the time—Goodman gave up his job in order to manage his wife's career. He also packaged Jackson's syndicated TV show, *Music Village*. In 1971, Jackson and her husband discovered Christianity, which she says saved their marriage. She released one gospel album on Capitol in 1972, *Praise the Lord*, before shifting to the Myrrh label for three more gospel albums. In 1977, she switched again, this time to Word Records, and released another two.

In the early 1980s, Jackson was invited to Europe to play rockabilly and country festivals and to record. She's since been back numerous times. More recently, American country artists Pam Tillis, Jann Browne, and Rosie Flores have acknowledged Jackson as a major influence. In 1995, Flores released a rockabilly album, *Rockabilly Filly*, and invited Jackson, her longtime idol, to sing two duets on it with her. Jackson embarked on a major US tour with Flores later that year. It was her first secular tour in this country since the '70s not to mention, her first time back in a nightclub atmosphere. —*Kurt Wolff*

There's a Party Goin' On / 1959 / Capitol ◆◆◆
While this doesn't have most of Wanda's best rockabilly sides (check the compilation *Rockin' with Wanda* for those), it's a pretty solid and energetic set. About half of it is taken up with retreads of the "Let's Have a Party" theme and covers of early rock hits like "Tweedlee Dee" and "Kansas City," which are, admittedly, well done. "Fallin'" and, especially, "Hard Headed Woman" are really fine cuts that rank among her best rock 'n' roll performances. The real surprise of this album is the lightning-speed rockabilly riffing by Roy Clark; his playing on "Hard Headed Woman" is downright savage, almost enough to redeem all those horrible *Hee Haw* programs. —*Richie Unterberger*

Rockin' with Wanda / 1960 / Capitol ◆◆◆◆
Absolutely the best collection of her rockabilly recordings, including her key 1956-60 singles—"Fujiyama Mama," "Mean Mean Man," "Hot Dog! That Made Him Mad," and others. A leading candidate for the best female rock 'n' roll album of the 1950s. The British reissue adds four worthwhile bonus cuts, including the essential "Let's Have a Party." —*Richie Unterberger*

● **Rockin' in the Country: Best of Wanda Jackson** / 1990 / Rhino ◆◆◆◆
Perhaps the greatest of the rockabilly women, Wanda Jackson later turned to pure country. Rhino's *Best of Wanda Jackson—Rockin' in the Country* presents the best of both eras here on this 18-track collection. —*Jeff Tamarkin*

Ultimate Compilation / 1996 / ◆◆◆
The *Ultimate Compilation* is a single-disc collection from Belgium that contains most of Jackson's biggest hits and best-known songs, including "Let's Have a Party," "Right or Wrong," "Stupid Cupid," "There's a Party Goin' On," and "Fujiyama Mama," among

several other songs. Although the disc is good, there are plenty of better, more thorough collections available, and they're all easier to find. —*Thom Owens*

Hits & Rarities / 1996 / ◆◆◆
Since *Hits & Rarities* is a single-disc compilation that contains both well-known numbers like "Right and Wrong" and "Let's Have a Party," as well as several obscurities, the result is an entertaining collection, but one that's unsuited for both neophytes, who won't appreciate the rarities, and serious fans, who will find the inclusion of the familiar cuts extraneous. —*Thom Owens*

Vintage Collection Series / Jan. 23, 1996 / Capitol ◆◆◆◆
This 20-track anthology of Jackson's early work is roughly equal to Rhino's *Rockin' in the Country* in value. *Rockin' in the Country* offers a considerably wider range, chronologically speaking. *Vintage Collections*, on the other hand, focuses on 1956-61 recordings, affording greater depth for what is acknowledged as her most fertile period. Although it's issued on Capitol Nashville, it mixes rockabilly and straight country, including her biggest hits in each style ("Let's Have a Party," "Fujiyama Mama," "Right or Wrong") and some worthy obscurities. Those with an appetite for both rock 'n' roll and country will find this the best compilation of her work; those who want just the rock 'n' roll should look for the harder-to-find *Rockin' with Wanda* instead. —*Richie Unterberger*

Sonny James (Jimmy Loden)

b. May 1, 1929, Hackleburg, AL
Guitar, Vocals / Country-Pop, Nashville Sound/Countrypolitan

Sonny James, the Southern Gentleman, used the popular Nashville sound of the '60s to countrify pop hits of the past into a form accessible to many, broadening country music's appeal across the nation. James even moved over to the pop charts for a time in the late '50s, but found the secret of his success by the time he returned to the country. During the late '60s, he scored an incredible five-year run of No. 1 singles, which locked up the top spot for a combined 45 weeks during the late '60s.

Born James Loden on May 1, 1929, he began performing with his show-business family at the age of three and played with his four sisters as the Loden Family while in his teens. The group appeared around the South and on radio shows like the *Louisiana Hayride* and *Saturday Night Shindig*. After spending time overseas during the Korean War, Loden took Sonny James as his stage name—after his teenage nickname—and joined the local bar circuit. He met and played with Chet Atkins, who later got him a tryout with Capitol Records. The label liked what it heard and offered James a contract.

His first single, "That's Me Without You," hit the Country Top Ten in early 1953, but it was three years before "For Rent (One Empty Heart)" became his second big hit. James, who played guitar on virtually all of his records, followed up with two 1956 Top Ten near-misses, "Twenty Feet of Muddy Water" and "The Cat Came Back." His next single became his biggest hit: "Young Love" spent nine weeks at No. 1 during 1956-57, and crossed over to top the pop charts also.

Beginning in 1957, Sonny James began to focus his attention on the popular charts. "First Date, First Kiss, First Love" made the Top 25, but no follow-up placed as high. Several of his failures had still managed to go Top Ten on the country charts, so James returned to country with a vengeance in 1964. "You're the Only World I Know" hit No. 1 on the country charts late that year, and spent four weeks there.

That began one of the greatest runs country music has ever known: 21 of his next 25 singles hit No. 1 (and the other four were near-misses either 2 or 3). Sonny James completely dominated the charts from 1964 to 1972, though only a few singles crossed over for modest placements on the popular charts. That fact is somewhat surprising, since three-quarters of James' No. 1 songs had previously been pop hits, including "Take Good Care of Her" for Adam Wade, "I'll Never Find Another You" and "A World of Our Own" for the Seekers, "Born to Be with You" for the Chordettes and Roy Orbison's "Only the Lonely." Backed by his Southern Gentlemen band, James toured the country and overseas, appeared on *The Ed Sullivan Show, Hee Haw*, and *The Bob Hope*

Show, and made several movies, including *Las Vegas Hillbillies* (1966), *Second Fiddle to a Steel Guitar,* (1967) and *Nashville Rebel* (1967). *Billboard* named him the Number One Artist of 1969.

Even after Sonny James' No. 1 streak ended in January 1972, he continued to place high on the charts. The No. 2 "Only Love Can Break a Heart" (a pop hit for Gene Pitney ten years earlier) was followed by the No. 1s "That's Why I Love You like I Do" and—after moving to Columbia in mid-1972—"When the Snow Is on the Roses." James' next chart-topping single, "Is It Wrong (For Loving You)," was released in March 1974, and it began his last major run. He followed with four consecutive Top Ten hits, "A Mi Esposa con Amor (To My Wife with Love)," "A Little Bit South of Saskatoon," "Little Band of Gold," and "What in the World's Come over You."

By the early '70s, James had moved into producing and music publishing also; he oversaw three of Marie Osmond's albums, and still managed occasional Top Tens himself. He picked up the prestigious Country Music's Male Artist of the Decade award from *Record World* in 1977, and moved to the Monument label in 1979, then to Dimension two years later. He retired in 1983, and now raises cattle in Alabama. —*John Bush*

Young Love / 1962 / Pair ✦✦✦✦
Young Love includes hits like the title track and "Here Comes Honey Again." —*Jason Ankeny*

American Originals / 1989 / Columbia ✦✦✦
American Originals is a cross-section of Sonny James' later hits from Columbia, beginning with the 1974 No. 1 "Is It Wrong (For Loving You)" and running through a selection of '70s hits. James was still popular during this period, even if he was showing signs of age. Although it is brief, *American Originals* provides a good summation of his later career. —*Stephen Thomas Erlewine*

● **Capitol Collector's Series** / 1990 / Capitol ✦✦✦✦
Capitol Collector's Series has 20 of Sonny James' chart-topping hits for Capitol Records, ranging from 1956's breakthrough "Young Love" to 1972's "When the Snow Is on the Roses." Although it's missing a handful of No. 1 hits, it remains a thorough, entertaining, and definitive compilation. —*Stephen Thomas Erlewine*

Greatest Hits / 1992 / Columbia ✦✦✦
While by no means comprehensive, *Greatest Hits* is among the best collections of James' chart smashes; it includes the No. 1 hits "Young Love," "You're the Only World I Know," "Behind the Tear" and "Take Good Care of Her." —*Jason Ankeny*

Jason

Guitar, Vocals / Roots-Rock, Alternative Country, Americana
Jason is Jason Ringenberg, one-time leader of Jason & the (Nashville) Scorchers, a group that were influenced as much by punk music as by Hank Williams. After the band broke up, Jason decided to ignore the punk and explore country music more fully. —*Jim Worbois*

One Foot in the Honky Tonk / 1992 / Liberty ✦✦✦
One Foot in the Honky Tonk is the first solo album from Jason Ringenberg, the leader of Jason & the Scorchers. On his own, Jason sticks closer to country than he does to rock 'n' roll, delving deep into honky tonk and the twang of Bakersfield, turning out a tough but poignant set of stomping, rocking country. A couple of cuts miss the mark, but the best songs on *One Foot in the Honky Tonk* equal his work with Jason & the Scorchers. —*Stephen Thomas Erlewine*

Jason & the Scorchers

Rock & Roll, Country-Rock, Roots-Rock
A country/hard rock band formed by Illinois native Jason Ringenberg in 1981, Jason & the Scorchers came careening onto the indie-rock scene seemingly out of nowhere (truth was, it was Nashville) with a debut EP whose most killer track (among a slew of killer tracks) was a fire breathing cover of Bob Dylan's "Absolutely Sweet Marie." This amalgam of speedy hard rock fused with Ringenberg's decidedly country twang, along with the band's abil-

ity to deftly negotiate between Rolling Stones-style stomps and quieter, more melodic acoustic country music, led to Jason & the Scorchers becoming a critically lauded and fairly popular '80s band. Capitalizing quickly on the notoriety brought by their debut EP, the Scorchers kicked out two fine LPs (*Lost & Found* and *Still Standing*) that sounded perfect for radio, but not so slick as to sound manufactured. With Ringenberg's yowling voice pushed way up front, the band's sonic power came from the synchronous playing of Nashville rock veterans Warner Hodges (guitar), Jeff Johnson (bass), and Perry Baggs (drums). Sharing similar musical backgrounds that valued the music of Hank Williams and Johnny Cash as much as the Stones or Beatles, these guys could crank out mega-amped hard rock one minute and sound like the Flying Burrito Brothers the next, all of it done with great skill and excitement.

Despite their obvious talent, by the release of 1986's *Still Standing,* it seemed as though the band wasn't going anywhere. They had achieved a modicum of success, but weren't able to break through to mass acclaim, partly because they came along just before the explosion of country radio in the late '80s/early '90s. Hence, rock radio was reluctant to play them because they sounded too country, and country radio thought they were too rock; it's an old story that usually spells doom for the band in question. After a three-year break that saw Johnson's departure, the Scorchers released a desultory third album (*Thunder and Fire*) that sounded like a desperate attempt at hard-rock credibility. They broke up soon after. Ringenberg went on to record country-oriented solo work, re-formed the original Scorchers in 1994, and released a modest reunion record (*A Blazing Grace*) that sounded like the Scorchers of old. —*John Dougan*

Fervor / 1983 / EMI America ✦✦✦✦
Their debut EP has "Absolutely Sweet Marie" (which you'll play over and over and over), as well as some wonderful country-rock like "Hot Nights in Georgia." Ringenberg's twangy voice is a hoot to listen to, and Warner Hodges plays some great guitar. A wonderful, if too brief, record and a harbinger of some great rock 'n' roll to come. R.E.M.'s Michael Stipe contributes a song ("Both Sides Of The Line") and some backup vocals. —*John Dougan*

Lost & Found / 1985 / EMI America ✦✦✦✦
Of The Scorchers' three full-length LPs, this is by far the best. There is so much pent-up energy and excitement on this record, it sounds as if it will fly off your turntable (assuming you still have a turntable) at any moment. With Hodges (as usual) driving this machine, Ringenberg's wild-eyed country-punk persona is here in full fury, and the good times never let up. This should have been the album that made them stars, but it did solidify their audience and place them in larger concert venues, where they tore it up. —*John Dougan*

Still Standing / 1986 / EMI Australia ✦✦✦
Produced by veteran hard rock producer Tom Werman, *Still Standing* is a fine record, but also shows subtle signs of the band in decline: the hard rock is stiffer and Hodges' guitar is smoother and more akin to the anonymous hard rock/heavy metal guitar sound that defined AOR radio in the '80s. That notwithstanding, there are still songs like "Golden Ball and Chain," which sounds like an outtake from *Exile on Main Street* and, continuing with the Rolling Stones motif, a ripsnortin' cover of "19th Nervous Breakdown." A teensy bit disappointing in comparison to *Lost & Found,* but by no means a bad record or one to ignore. If you've liked the Scorchers up to this point, you'll want *Still Standing.* —*John Dougan*

Thunder & Fire / 1989 / A&M ✦✦✦
With the release of *Thunder & Fire,* Jason & the Scorchers should have shot to the top. Unfortunately, that didn't happen. They broke up instead. But the record they left behind does have its moments. Hard-hitting rockers like "Now That You're Mine" and "6 Feet Underground" fit snugly alongside "Close up the Road," a country-tinged weeper, and "Bible & a Gun," which recalls the best things about the roots-rock movement of the late '80s. —*James Chrispell*

● **Essential, Vol. 1 (Are You Ready for the Country)** / 1992 / Capitol ✦✦✦✦

A Blazing Grace / 1995 / Mammoth ✦✦✦
Jason & the Scorchers came "blazing" back with this rockin' barrelhouse of a release. Containing sure-fire rockers in "Where Bridges Never Burn" and "Cry by Night Operator," the Scorchers never sounded better. But also check out their hard-drivin' covers of both John Denver's "Take Me Home, Country Road" and George Jones' "Why Baby Why." They're great! Coming back with just the original four members, Jason & the Scorchers prove that there is life after punk . . . or were they roots-rock, or maybe cowpunk, or. . . . Ah, you get the picture. A Blazing Grace is superb!
—*James Chrispell*

Both Sides of the Line / Sep. 1996 / EMI ✦✦✦✦
This CD reissue combines the *Fervor* EP and *Lost & Found* album onto one disc, and thus offers the best way to collect their early material. —*Richie Unterberger*

Clear Impetuous Morning / Oct. 1996 / Mammoth ✦✦✦
Here comes yet another steam-rolling, country-rock release from Jason & the Scorchers. Pushin' the pedal to the metal, *Clear Impetuous Morning* sounds a lot like a band that has just found an open stretch of highway and is jammin' in high gear. Just about everything here rocks out in fine form, including a cover of the Byrds' "Drug Store Truck Drivin' Man." Emmylou Harris even drops by to guest on "Everything Has a Cost" to great effect. You won't be disappointed if you choose to get a hold of this disc.
—*James Chrispell*

Jayhawks

Alternative Country-Rock
Led by the gifted songwriting, impeccable playing, and honeyed harmonies of vocalists/guitarists Mark Olson and Gary Louris, the Jayhawks' shimmering blend of country, folk, and bar-band rock made them one of the most widely acclaimed artists to emerge from the alternative country scene. The group sprung up in 1985 out of the fertile Minneapolis musical community, where Olson had been playing stand-up bass in a rockabilly band called Stagger Lee until his desire to write and perform his own country-folk material prompted him to begin a solo career. He enlisted Marc Perlman, the guitarist for a local band called the Neglecters, whom Olson then convinced to take up the bass; after the addition of drummer Norm Rogers, the group first played in front of a crowd of less than a dozen people. One of those patrons, however, was Gary Louris, a veteran of the local bands Safety Last and Schnauzer; after the show, he and Olson began talking, and by the end of the evening Louris, a guitarist famed locally for his innovative, pedal steel-like sound, had become a member of the group, eventually named the Jayhawks.

Drawing on influences like Gram Parsons, the Louvin Brothers, Tim Hardin, and *Nashville Skyline*-era Bob Dylan, the Jayhawks quickly became a local favorite, honing their sound in Twin Cities clubs before releasing their eponymous debut in 1986. Issued in a pressing of just a few thousand copies, the album was well-received by those who heard it; a major recording deal did not follow, however, so the band continued to polish their craft live, with more and more of their songs bearing writing credits belonging to both Olson and Louris. In October 1988, after a lineup change that saw the departure of Rogers (who joined the Cows) followed by the addition of drummer Thad Spencer, Louris was nearly killed in an auto accident, and the Jayhawks went on hiatus. At much the same time, however, executives at the Minneapolis independent label Twin/Tone decided to issue the demos the group had been stockpiling over the past few years, and after some overdubbing and remixing, *The Blue Earth* appeared in 1989. Richer in sound and more complex in its themes and concerns, the record's release brought the group considerable attention, and also brought Louris back into the fold. After another drummer switch (Spencer for Ken Callahan), the band hit the road for a national tour.

The Jayhawks were signed to major label (Def) American Records after producer George Drakoulias heard *The Blue Earth* playing in the background during a phone call to Twin/Tone's

offices. With Drakoulias in the producer's seat, the band recorded their breakthrough album *Hollywood Town Hall* in 1991; a mainstay of critics' annual "best of" lists, the album generated the alternative radio hits "Waiting for the Sun," "Take Me with You (When You Go)," and "Settled Down Like Rain." After a tour that saw the permanent addition of Minneapolis pianist Karen Grotberg, the individual band members guested on albums from Counting Crows, Soul Asylum, Maria McKee, Joe Henry, and others. Before recording the fourth Jayhawks album, Callahan departed, and was replaced by session drummer Don Heffington. The resulting record, 1995's *Tomorrow the Green Grass*, was the group's finest, a beautiful collection of songs led off by the elegiac single "Blue," the recipient of significant airplay. A tour followed, but after some months on the road, Olson announced he was quitting the band. In 1997 the Jayhawks—now consisting of Louris, Perlman, Grotberg, and drummer Tim O'Reagan—released the album *Sound of Lies*. —*Jason Ankeny*

The Jayhawks / 1986 / Bunkhouse ✦✦✦
Though lacking the almost telepathic interplay later developed by frontmen Mark Olson and Gary Louris, the Jayhawks' self-titled debut—issued in a tiny pressing of just a few thousand copies—is a fair indication of the remarkable things still to come from the band. Complete with song titles that could have been cribbed from old Replacements records—"Six Pack on the Dashboard," "The Liquor Store Came First," "I'm Not in Prison," and so forth—the record owes a clear debt to the group's Minneapolis stomping grounds, but evidence of the Jayhawks' own distinct identity can be found in the fluid guitar work as well as in Olson and Louris' harmonies, which even this early in the game are graceful and rich. —*Jason Ankeny*

Blue Earth / 1989 / Twin/Tone ✦✦✦
The songs which make up *Blue Earth* originated as demos, and save for some minor studio tinkering, are presented here in their original embryonic state. As a consequence, the record lacks punch; spare and economical, the songs are simply too primitive to come to life in this setting. Nonetheless, the growth of the band's songwriting skills over their debut is substantial; while many of the themes—drifting, drinking, and lost love—remain the same, they're handled with greater insight and clarity than before, with a keen eye for detail and nuance. —*Jason Ankeny*

Hollywood Town Hall / 1992 / Def American ✦✦✦✦
Hollywood Town Hall is the Jayhawks' breakthrough record, a uniformly strong collection heralding a dramatic leap in maturity and depth over the band's earlier work. Benefiting greatly from the increased production values afforded by their newfound major label status, the group's songs—a handful of them redone from the earlier *Blue Earth*—shimmer like never before; the guitars crackle with energy, and Mark Olson and Gary Louris' harmonies lock together so organically that at times it's impossible to distinguish where one voice ends and the other begins. —*Jason Ankeny*

● **Tomorrow the Green Grass** / 1995 / American ✦✦✦✦
The Jayhawks' final record with singer-songwriter Mark Olson, *Tomorrow the Green Grass* is also the group's finest. While the band's earlier efforts perfected a more traditonal brand of country-rock, their fourth record is marvelously eclectic, both musically and emotionally; never before had they rocked as hard as on "Real Light," dug as painfully deep as on "Two Hearts," or hit quite the same peaks of exuberance as on "Miss Williams' Guitar," a tribute to Olson's new wife, neo-folkie Victoria Williams. The addition of keyboardist Karen Grotberg brings rich new layers to the Jayhawks' sound, as does the inclusion of a string section on cuts like "Blue" and "I'd Run Away," a soaring pop song that's quite possibly the best thing the group ever recorded. A fitting legacy, indeed. —*Jason Ankeny*

Paul Jefferson

Contemporary Country, Singer-Songwriter
Combining elements of country, bluegrass, and folk music, this singer-songwriter writes songs that concentrate on positive examinations of love, whether it be romantic or spiritual. Jefferson's first taste of success was as a songwriter, co-writing Aaron Tip-

pin's chart-topper "That's as Close as I'll Get to Loving You." Hailing from the hills and ranches of Woodside, CA, in the Santa Cruz Mountains above Palo Alto, Jefferson began listening to country music as a child. While attending college for engineering, Jefferson—who is also a pilot—developed a large regional following playing in a country band, eventually striking out on his own and marketing a tape of his original songs. After signing a publishing deal in L.A., the company took him to Nashville, where he linked up with the newly formed Almo Sounds record label, started by music veterans Herb Alpert and Jerry Moss. The company released Jefferson's debut in 1996 and the album's first single, "Check Please," was a Top 40 hit. —*Jack Leaver*

Paul Jefferson / Jul. 15, 1996 / Almo ◆◆◆
Before the release of his eponymous debut album, Paul Jefferson had spent some time in Nashville writing songs professionally. In fact, he cowrote Aaron Tippin's No. 1 hit "That's As Close As I'll Get To Loving You," which gives an idea of what kind of music Jefferson plays on his debut. Jefferson sounds like a mainstream new country singer, with polished production and anthemic choruses. However, the actual songs boast more lyrical detail and narrative thrust than the standard Nashville song. That's what makes *Paul Jefferson* an intriguing, promising debut. —*Thom Owens*

Waylon Jennings (Waylon Arnold Jennings)

b. Jun. 15, 1937, Littlefield, TX
Guitar, Vocals / Traditional Country, Progressive Country, Outlaw Country
If any one performer personified the outlaw country movement of the '70s, it was Waylon Jennings. Though he had been a professional musician since the late '50s, it wasn't until the '70s that Waylon, with his imposing baritone and stripped-down, updated honky tonk, became a superstar. Jennings rejected the conventions of Nashville, refusing to record with the industry's legions of studio musicians and insisting that his music never resemble the string-laden, pop-inflected sounds that were coming out of Nashville in the '60s and '70s. Many artists, including Willie Nelson and Kris Kristofferson, followed Waylon's anti-Nashville stance, and eventually the whole "outlaw" movement—so-named because of the artists' ragged, maverick image and their independence from Nashville—became one of the most significant country forces of the '70s, helping the genre adhere to its hardcore honky tonk roots. Jennings didn't write many songs, but his music—which combined the grittiest aspects of honky tonk with a rock 'n' roll rhythm and attitude, making the music spare, direct and edgy—defined hardcore country, and it influenced countless musicians, including members of the new-traditionalist and alternative country subgenres of the '80s.

Jennings was born and raised in Littlefield, TX, where he learned how to play guitar by the time he was eight. When he was 12 years old, he was a DJ for a local radio station and, shortly afterward, he formed his first band. Two years later he left school and spent the next few years picking cotton, eventually moving to Lubbock, TX, in 1954. Once he was in Lubbock, he got a job at the radio station KLLL, where he befriended Buddy Holly during one of the station's shows. Holly became Jennings' mentor, teaching him guitar licks, collaborating on songs, and producing Jennings' first single, "Jole Blon," which was released on Brunswick in 1958. Later that year, Waylon became the temporary bass player for Buddy's band the Crickets, playing with the rock 'n' roller on his final tour. Jennings was also scheduled to fly on the plane ride that ended in Holly's tragic death in early 1959, but he gave up his seat at the last minute to the Big Bopper, who was suffering from a cold.

Following Buddy's death, Jennings returned to Lubbock, where he spent two years mourning the loss of his friend and working as a DJ. In late 1960, he moved to Phoenix where he founded a rockabilly band called the Waylors. Jennings and the Waylors began to earn a local following through their performances at the local club JD's, eventually signing to the independent label Trend in 1961. None of the group's singles made any impact and Jennings began working for Audio Recorders as a record producer. In

1963, Waylon moved to Los Angeles, where he landed a contract with Herb Alpert's A&M Records. By this point, Waylon's music was pure country, and Alpert wanted to move him toward the pop market; Jennings didn't cave in to the demands and his sole single, "Sing the Girl a Song, Bill," and album for A&M flopped.

Following the A&M debacle, Jennings landed a contract with RCA with help from Chet Atkins and Bobby Bare, and he moved to Nashville in 1965. After arriving in Nashville, he moved in with Johnny Cash, and the two musicians began a long-lasting friendship, which eventually resulted in a collaboration in the form of the Highwaymen in the '80s. Waylon released his first single for RCA, "That's the Chance I'll Have to Take," late in the summer of 1965 and it became a minor hit. With his second single, "Stop the World (And Let Me Off)," he had his first Top 40 country hit and it began a string of moderate hits that eventually developed into several Top Ten singles—"Walk on Out of My Mind," "I Got You," "Only Daddy That'll Walk the Line," "Yours Love"—in 1968. At this point, he was working with Nashville session men and developing a sound that was halfway between honky tonk and folk. As the next decade began, he started to move his music toward hardcore country.

In 1970, Jennings recorded several songs by a struggling but promising songwriter called Kris Kristofferson, which led to a pair of ambitious albums—*Singer of Sad Songs* and *Ladies Love Outlaws*—the following year. On these two records, he developed the roots of outlaw country, creating a harder, tougher, muscular sound with a selection of songs by writers like Alex Harvey and Hoyt Axton. During the following year, Waylon began collaborating with Willie Nelson, recording and writing several songs with the songwriter. Just as importantly, he also renegotiated his contract with RCA in 1972, demanding that he assume the production and artistic control of his records. *Honky Tonk Heroes*, released in 1973, was the first album released under this new contract. Comprised almost entirely of songs by the then-unknown songwriter Billy Joe Shaver and recorded with Jennings' road band, the album was an edgy, bass-driven, and surly variation on stripped-down honky tonk. Jennings and his new sound slowly began to gain more fans, and in 1974 he had his first No. 1, "This Time," followed by yet another No. 1 single, "I'm a Ramblin' Man," and the No. 2 "Rainy Day Woman."

Waylon's success continued throughout 1975, as *Dreaming My Dreams*—featuring one of his signature songs, the No. 1 "Are You Sure Hank Done It This Way"—reached No. 49 on the pop charts; he was also voted the Country Music Association's Male Vocalist of the Year. Jennings truly crossed over into the mainstream in 1976, when *Wanted! The Outlaws*—a various-artists compilation of previously-released material that concentrated on Waylon, but also featured songs from his wife Jessi Colter, Willie Nelson, and Tompall Glaser—peaked at No. 1 on the pop charts. Following the success of *Wanted!*, Waylon became a superstar, as well known to the mainstream pop audience as he was to the country audience. For the next six years, Jennings' albums consistently charted in the pop Top 50 and went gold. During this time, he recorded a number of duets with Nelson, including the multi-platinum *Waylon & Willie* (1978) which featured the No. 1 single "Mammas Don't Let Your Babies Grow Up to Be Cowboys." Over the course of the late '70s and early '80s, Jennings scored ten No. 1 hits, including "Luckenbach, Texas (Back to the Basics of Love)" (which hit No. 25 on the pop charts and spent six weeks at the top of the country charts), "The Wurlitzer Prize (I Don't Want to Get Over You)," "I've Always Been Crazy," "Amanda," "Theme from 'The Dukes of Hazzard' (Good Ol' Boys)" and three duets with Nelson.

By the mid-'80s, the momentum of Waylon's career began to slow somewhat, due to his drug abuse and the decline of the entire outlaw country movement. Jennings kicked his substance habits cold turkey in the mid-'80s and formed the supergroup the Highwaymen with Willie Nelson, Kris Kristofferson, and Johnny Cash in 1985; over the next decade, the band released three albums, yet none of them were more successful than their debut, which spawned the No. 1 single, "Highwayman." Also in 1985, Jennings parted ways with RCA, signing with MCA Records the following year. At first, he had several hit singles for the label, including the No. 1 "Rose in Paradise," but by the end of the '80s, he was no longer able to crack the Top 40. In 1990, Waylon switched labels again, signing with Epic. "Wrong," his first single for the label, reached the Top ten in 1990 and "The Eagle" reached the Top 40 the following year, but after that minor hit, none of his singles were charting.

Despite his decreased sales—which were largely due to the shifting tastes in country music—Waylon Jennings remained a superstar throughout the '90s, and drew large crowds whenever he performed a concert, and continued to receive positive reviews for many of his records. In 1996, he signed to Justice Records, where he released the acclaimed *Right for the Time*. —*Stephen Thomas Erlewine*

Love of the Common People / 1967 / RCA ✦✦✦✦
Jennings proves he can handle all types of music from a Beatles track to Marty Robbins-style Western songs ("Taos, NM"). Songs like "Money Cannot Make the Man" seem to point in the direction of the sound he adopted in the '70s. Overall, a good-sounding record. —*Jim Worbois*

A Man Called Hoss / 1967 / MCA ✦✦✦✦
A Man Called Hoss features the hits "My Rough and Rowdy Days" and "If Ole Hank Could Only See Us Now (Chapter Five . . . Nashville)." —*Jason Ankeny*

Hangin' On / 1968 / RCA ✦✦✦
Somewhat uneven album but one with some nice moments, including "Hangin' On" and "Let Me Talk to You." Jennings also proves he has the vocal range to take on Roy Orbison. —*Jim Worbois*

Collector's Series / 1968 / RCA ✦✦✦
The budget-priced *Collector's Series* only features eight tracks, and a handful of hits, but each song on the album is prime Waylon, including the signature songs "Are You Sure Hank Done It This Way?" and "Lonesome, On'ry and Mean." —*Thom Owens*

Just to Satisfy You / 1969 / RCA ✦✦✦
The title track on this album is the strongest track here. Co-written by Jennings and country music funny-man/songwriter Don Bowman, it's been covered several times (including by Glen Campbell), but never done better than Jennings. He sounds good, but overall, not one of his best. —*Jim Worbois*

Waylon Jennings / 1969 / Vocalion ✦✦✦
Jennings has often been quoted as saying he couldn't go pop with a mouthful of firecrackers. Once you hear him rip through Barrett Strong's "Money," you'll understand just what he means. That aside, this album serves as a nice sample of his early work by filling in the gap between the tracks produced by Buddy Holly and his signing with A&M. —*Jim Worbois*

☆ **The Taker/Tulsa** / 1971 / Mobile Fidelity ✦✦✦✦✦
The Taker/Tulsa essentially began the progressive country and outlaw movements of the early '70s. The record represents the discovery of Kris Kristofferson by Waylon Jennings; though it isn't entirely a repertoire album, most of the songs on the album were written by Kristofferson, who worked outside of the conventions of Nashville. The result is one of Jennings' first major statements. Although there are a couple of weak spots on the record, there's no denying that it helped spark a movement that revolutionized the country music industry. —*Thom Owens*

Ladies Love Outlaws / 1972 / RCA ✦✦✦
Jennings was frustrated with this record because he felt that RCA had too much control over making it. That aside, there are some fine moments on this album, including the title track, his cover of a tune written by the man playing steel for him at the time ("Crazy Arms"), and a nice duet with his wife Jessi Colter on the Buck Owens classic, "Under Your Spell Again." —*Jim Worbois*

Nashville Rebel [O.S.T.] / 1973 / RCA ✦✦✦
Not only did Jennings provide the music for the film (the whole first side of the album and one track on the second side), but he starred in the title role of the film. While the songs are better than those found on many soundtrack albums, it's not one of his best. From a distance, the title seems prophetic. —*Jim Worbois*

Lonesome, On'ry and Mean / 1973 / RCA ✦✦✦
With this album, Jennings began producing his own records and going after the type of sound he wanted to create. He also used his road band in the studio, a luxury most artists weren't permitted. Suddenly, he had a new look (a beard), a new sound, and the outlaw movement was about to begin. —*Jim Worbois*

☆ **Honky Tonk Heroes** / 1973 / Pair ✦✦✦✦✦
As he himself once noted, the "outlaw bit" got out of hand pretty fast. It's no accident that this, his defining outlaw-era album, hit the streets before the term ever did. Nine of the ten songs are from the pen of then-unknown Billy Joe Shaver, a gritty Texas songwriter from whom more would definitely be heard. —*Dan Cooper*

This Time / 1974 / RCA ✦✦✦✦
Waylon & Willie were as thick as thieves, so it's no surprise to see Nelson's name as co-producer on this one. Another classic Jennings album. A note of interest: the four Willie Nelson tracks also appeared on his classic *Phases & Stages*, which also came out in 1974. —*Jim Worbois*

Ramblin' Man / 1974 / RCA ✦✦✦✦
Jennings was hot through most of the '70s, and this album is a fine example of why. Filled with great songs, "Rainy Day Woman" stands out as one of the best things he's ever done! —*Jim Worbois*

Dreaming My Dreams / 1975 / RCA ✦✦✦✦
As a spokesperson (though not by choice) for the "outlaw" movement, Jennings comments on changes taking place in country music in 1975 ("Are You Sure Hank Done It This Way") and the move to Texas by so many artists. In the title track, he provides one of his finest love songs. —*Jim Worbois*

Are You Ready for the Country / 1976 / RCA ✦✦
This is about one-half of a good album. There's one-half (roughly) made up of pointless covers (including a song where Jennings covers himself) and a few other fairly uninteresting songs. Then there's the half where he turns in fine performances on his own compositions ("I'll Go Back to Her" and "Old Friend") as well as a cover of a former Dr. Hook hit. —*Jim Worbois*

Live / 1976 / RCA ✦✦✦
This nice-sounding record provides all the evidence anyone would need to show why Jennings insisted on using his road band in the studio; they're good. Additionally, this is not just a recycling of the hits in a live format. If you've never seen Waylon in concert, this could be just what it takes to correct that situation. —*Jim Worbois*

Ol' Waylon / 1977 / RCA ✦✦
This is a mixed album, some of which is really, really good. Among the best cuts are "Brand New Goodbye Song," "Satin Sheets" by the often-overlooked Willis Alan Ramsey, and a fine cover of Jimmy Webb's "If You See Me Getting Smaller." Unfortunately, some of it's not very good. —*Jim Worbois*

Waylon & Willie / 1978 / RCA ✦✦✦
This is an album aimed at the audience that bought *Outlaws*. It's a somewhat uneven album, but there are a few moments on here, including the chance to hear Willie & Waylon duet on a song each had done on their own: "Pick up the Tempo." —*Jim Worbois*

I've Always Been Crazy / 1978 / RCA ✦✦✦
On this album, Jennings had become tired of the "outlaw" movement and he expresses not only those feelings but addresses those who are constantly looking over his shoulder and questioning his actions ("I've Always Been Crazy"). At the same time, he explores his roots as a friend and bandmate of Buddy Holly (not a member of The Crickets, as so often stated), as well as the music of some of his musical influences. Not one of his best, but still a good album. —*Jim Worbois*

Early Years / 1979 / RCA ✦✦✦
This is pre-outlaw Jennings, though "Only Daddy That'll Walk the Line" is as tough as any of his '70s work. —*Dan Cooper*

★ **Greatest Hits** / 1979 / RCA ✦✦✦✦✦
Jennings' career dates back to his days working with Buddy Holly in the '50s, but it wasn't until the '70s that he began to define a particular hard-edged subgenre of country music with his rock shuffles and his deep, sardonic voice on songs like "Lonesome,

On'ry and Mean" and "Luckenbach, Texas," the best of which are included here. (A second volume, released in 1984, is also recommended.) —*William Ruhlmann*

What Goes Around / 1979 / RCA ✦✦
Another of those records that amounts to half a good album, the first side is made up of the familiar Jennings groove that, by this time, was somewhat stale. On the second side, he opens up and concentrates more on the melody than the groove. —*Jim Worbois*

Music Man / 1980 / RCA ✦✦
It almost seems that Jennings was so busy doing *The Dukes of Hazzard* that he didn't really have the time to put much thought into making a record. This is definitely one of the least interesting of all his records. —*Jim Worbois*

Black on Black / 1982 / RCA ✦✦
This is another album where one-half (roughly) is made up of pointless covers; including an occasion where Jennings covers himself. Then there's the half with good songs by Paul Kennerley (who wrote the *White Mansions* project on which Jennings worked), Emmons & Moman, and Rodney Crowell. —*Jim Worbois*

Waylon & Company / 1983 / RCA ✦✦
This is a duets album with some guests you would expect (Hank Williams, Jr., Jessi Colter, and Willie Nelson) and some surprises (Ernest Tubb, Mel Tillis, and actor James Garner). Fun for what it is. —*Jim Worbois*

Will the Wolf Survive / 1985 / MCA ✦✦✦
Moving to MCA after a long stay at RCA brought Jennings a new producer in Jimmy Bowen and a fresh approach, resulting in one of his better albums, typified by his version of The Los Lobos title track and a cover of Steve Earle's tailor-made "The Devil's Right Hand." —*William Ruhlmann*

Greatest Hits, Vol. 2 / 1985 / RCA ✦✦✦✦
Greatest Hits, Vol. 2 contains ten of Waylon Jennings' biggest hits from the late '70s and early '80s, including "America," "I Ain't Living Long Like This," "Come With Me," "Women Do Know How to Carry On," "Don't You Think This Outlaw Bit's Done Got Out of Hand," and "Dukes of Hazzard." —*Stephen Thomas Erlewine*

Waylon: Best of Waylon Jennings / 1985 / RCA ✦✦✦
Waylon: The Best of Waylon Jennings is an adequate nine-song budget-line compilation of some of his Top ten hits from the early '80s, including "Lucille," "Drinkin' and Dreamin'," "I May Be Used (But Baby I Ain't Used Up)," and "Breakin' Down." —*Thom Owens*

New Classic Waylon / 1989 / MCA ✦✦✦
New Classic Waylon compiles the highlights from Jennings' first four albums on MCA, and includes "Fallin' Out," "My Rough and Rowdy Days" and his cover of Los Lobos' "Will the Wolf Survive." —*Jason Ankeny*

The Eagle / Feb. 1990 / Epic ✦✦
The Eagle includes the Top Five hit "Wrong" as well as "Where Corn Don't Grow," "What Bothers Me Most" and the title track. —*Jason Ankeny*

Clean Shirt / Feb. 1991 / Epic ✦✦✦
Two aging outlaws swap reminisces and argue good-naturedly about who's caused the most trouble. Every once in a while they work themselves up to doing more damage. Small flashes of tossed-off brilliance appear in nearly every song, but sometimes it's hard to tell what's part of the pair's casual charm and what's just laziness: when the clever "Old Age and Treachery" (always overcome youth and skill) falls apart at the end, it's infuriating. Like much of either singer's output, *Clean Shirt* sounds a bit wrinkled at first, but most of the album holds up to repeated listening. —*Brian Mansfield*

★ **Only Daddy That'll Walk the Line: The RCA Years** / 1993 / RCA ✦✦✦✦✦
You wouldn't think that two CDs with 40 cuts could adequately summarize a career as important as Jennings', but quite the opposite is true. If anything, this box set highlights more than we might want to know of his creative rise, peak, and artistic decline. The first disc, covering the years 1965-74, will be a revelation to anyone unfamiliar with Jennings' luminous early work. On cuts like "Stop the World (And Let Me Off)" and "Just to Satisfy You"

Waylon Jennings

his struggle to free himself from the suffocating Nashville Sound is palpable. On "Lonesome, On'ry and Mean" and "I'm a Ramblin' Man," Jennings success at doing the same is vicariously liberating. Disc two picks up in the midst of the revolution ("Are You Sure Hank Done It This Way?," "Bob Wills Is Still the King") and carries on through the Napoleonic expansion ("Luckenbach, Texas," a Top 40 pop hit). But the last quarter of the set is really quite depressing, as the performances become more and more self-consciously outlaw. Call "Theme from the Dukes of Hazzard" Jennings' Waterloo, if you will. The one gem from the 1980s, Jessi Colter's lovely "Storms Never Last," can be taken more than one way. —*Dan Cooper*

Right for the Time / May 21, 1996 / Justice ✦✦✦
Waylon Jennings' later albums have consistently been more interesting than those of most others from his aging generation, and his new album, *Right for the Time*—his first for his new label, Justice Records—is one of his strongest of the '80s and '90s. His voice is rich and beautiful, his arrangements spare and casual, and his songs explore life, love, and dreams with honesty and wisdom. He waxes nostalgic for small-town life on "Cactus Texas," and mixes bitter sentiments with a snap-crackle wit on "Kissing You Goodbye." Never shy about his feelings, Waylon again comments (as he has on recent albums) on the "new hats" in country music, doing so with good-natured sarcasm on the spoken-word acoustic song "Living Legends Pt. II." —*Kurt Wolff*

Essential Waylon Jennings / Jun. 18, 1996 / RCA ✦✦✦✦
The Essential Waylon Jennings may not contain every hit Jennings ever recorded or every fine album track he cut, but—as the title implies—it does have the bare-bone essentials ("Only Daddy That'll Walk the Line," "Are You Sure Hank Done It This Way?," and several others), making it the best single-disc retrospective assembled on the groundbreaking country singer. —*Thom Owens*

Are You Sure Hank Done It This Way? / RCA ✦✦✦✦
Finding Jennings coming to terms with the entire outlaw country phenomenon, *Are You Sure Hank Done It This Way?* is one of Jennings' finest albums, featuring the classic title track and "Don't You Think This Outlaw Bit's Done Got out of Hand." —*Thom Owens*

White Lightning / Laserlight ♦♦

White Lightning collects some of Jennings' earliest material, including his first single "Jole Blon" (produced by Buddy Holly) and cuts from his first LP *Waylon Jennings at J.D.'s.* —*Jason Ankeny*

Leavin' Town / Sings Ol' Harlan / RCA ♦♦♦

Two of Jennings' early records are combined on this single disc, *Leavin' Town* and *Waylon Jennings Sings Ol' Harlan.* Though they didn't enjoy the crossover success of his '70s records, both albums were considerable country hits. *Leavin' Town* shows Jennings' development of a distinctive blend of country and folk while *Sings Ol' Harlan* is an affectionate and enjoyable tribute to Harlan Howard, one of Jennings' idols. —*Stephen Thomas Erlewine*

Jim & Jesse (Jim and Jesse McReynolds)

Traditional Bluegrass, Close Harmony
One of the greatest bluegrass bands in history, brothers Jim (b. 1927) and Jesse (b. 1929) McReynolds and their Virginia Boys remained at the top by changing with the times. Starting as a traditional brothers duet, Jim on guitar and Jesse on mandolin showed their versatility by following country's changing tastes, moving to country/folk when necessary to keep a road band going. Whatever style they played (including *Berry Pickin' in the Country,* an album of bluegrass versions of Chuck Berry tunes), they retained a pure country core, due in no small part to Jim's pure, high tenor and Jesse's virtuoso, cross-picking mandolin playing.

Raised in Virginia, Jim & Jesse were born into a musical family. Their grandfather, Charles McReynolds, was a fiddler who had recorded a single for Victor in 1927 with the Bull Mountain Moonshiners. The brothers learned to play a number of stringed instruments while they were children, occasionally playing local dances and events as teenagers. However, the duo didn't begin playing professionally until they were in their 20s and Jim had left the Army. At this point, Jim played guitar and Jesse played mandolin. In 1947, they landed a daily 15-minute spot on a local Norton radio station. For the next few years, they played on a variety of southern radio stations, eventually securing a regular spot on Augusta, GA's WGAC in 1949. After staying with the station for a year, they moved to the Midwest where they played stations in Iowa and Kansas without gathering much of a following. In 1951, they relocated to Middletown, OH, where they had a regular spot at WPFB. While they were at WPFB they cut ten songs with vocalist Larry Roll under the name the Virginian Trio; the records didn't receive much attention.

For the remainder of 1951 and much of 1952, Jim & Jesse played at a variety of radio stations throughout the country. Finally, in 1952, the group secured a major label deal with Capitol Records. However, their career was interrupted when Jesse was drafted into the Army to serve in the Korean War. After he was discharged in 1954, he rejoined Jim, who was still playing the Tennessee Barn Dance in Knoxville, TN. For the rest of the decade, they played radio and television stations across the country—including stations in Alabama, Georgia, and Florida—building up a fan base. During this time, their band the Virginia Boys, included such musicians as fiddler Vassar Clements and banjoist Bobby Thompson. In 1958, they recorded a handful of sides for Starday Records.

Martha White Mills flour company became Jim & Jesse's sponsors in 1959; the duo was the company's second major sponsorship, following Flatt & Scruggs. In 1961, they debuted at the Grand Ole Opry; three years later, they became members of the Opry. Jim & Jesse switched record labels in 1962, signing with Epic Records. The change in labels resulted in success for the duo, as "Cotton Mill Man" became their first charting country single in the summer of 1964. For the next few years, they continued in a straight bluegrass direction, scoring the occasional hit. In the late '60s, Jim & Jesse adopted a more country-oriented direction, which resulted in their biggest hit singles, including the No. 18 "Diesel on My Tail."

In 1970, Jim & Jesse re-signed with Capitol Records and the first album they released under their new contract featured electric instruments. However, the duo quickly returned to a traditional bluegrass sound, since a bluegrass revival had gripped the attention of many country fans and college students across the United States. For the next two decades, the duo was a staple on the bluegrass festival scene, and they recorded for a variety of independent labels, including CMH, Rounder, and their own Old Dominion and Double J labels. In 1982, they had a minor hit single with "North Wind," which was recorded with Charlie Louvin. —*Stephen Thomas Erlewine & David Vinopal*

☆ Bluegrass Special / 1963 / Epic ♦♦♦♦♦

Bluegrass Special / Bluegrass Classics is a double-LP set containing 24 tracks Jim & Jesse cut for Epic Records. These songs were recorded in the early '60s, during the era when folk and bluegrass were experiencing a revival in popularity. The bluegrass boom happened to coincide with the time that Jim & Jesse were reaching their musical peak, at least according to many observers. These Epic songs—which contain many of their popular favorites ("Drifting and Dreaming of You," "Stoney Creek") but none of their hits from that era—feature an accomplished, streamlined band that effortlessly play dazzling instrumental leads. It's a fine introduction to one of bluegrass' best duos; even though it is missing some hits, it captures Jim & Jesse at their best. —*Thom Owens*

Jim & Jesse Saluting the Louvin Brothers / 1969 / Epic ♦♦♦

Here is the best of the duo's recordings with electric country, rather than bluegrass, accompaniment. —*Richard Lieberson*

Jim & Jesse Story: 24 Greatest / 1980 / CMH ♦♦♦♦

The Jim & Jesse Story: 24 Greatest Hits contains the majority of the duo's biggest hits and most familiar numbers, including "Diesel on My Tail," "Paradise," "Cotton Mill Man," "Better Times A-Coming," and "Are You Missing Me." However, the disc does *not* contain original recordings—it is all re-recordings from the early '90s. Nevertheless, the album does boast a number of excellent performances, since the duo is supported by several of the finest former Virginia Boys, and Jim & Jesse sound energetic and surprisingly lively, making *The Jim & Jesse Story* a fine introduction to the duo's sound. —*Thom Owens*

In the Tradition / 1987 / Rounder ♦♦♦

In the Traditon features new Jim & Jesse material as well as re-recorded versions of their hits. —*Jason Ankeny*

Music among Friends / 1991 / Rounder ♦♦♦♦

A celebration of this bluegrass duo's 25 years on the Grand Ole Opry includes guest appearances by Bill Monroe, Emmylou Harris, Porter Wagoner, and others. —*Mark A. Humphrey*

★ Jim & Jesse: 1952-1955 / 1992 / Bear Family ♦♦♦♦♦

Twenty stunning performances for the Capitol label (their first label) feature hand-in-glove harmonies and Jesse's unique banjo-influenced mandolin. —*Mark A. Humphrey*

Bluegrass & More / Bear Family ♦♦♦♦

Bluegrass & More is a comprehensive multi-disc box set that includes all of the material, including alternate takes and unreleased tracks, from Jim & Jesse's prime years for Epic Records in the '50s. There's plenty of fine music on the set, but it is primarily of interest for completists and historians—casual fans should stick with the single-disc *Jim & Jesse: 1952-1955.* —*Thom Owens*

Flaco Jimenez

b. Mar. 11, 1939, San Antonio, TX

Accordion / Zydeco, Tex-Mex, Norteño
Flaco Jimenez is the best known of the talented Jimenez family of Tex-Mex accordionists. He has always been popular in the border region, and came to the attention of the wider pop-music-buying public with the help of roots-music enthusiast Ry Cooder. Since then Jimenez has toured internationally, made guest appearances on a number of recordings, teamed up with Doug Sahm and Freddy Fender in the Texas Tornados, and continued to record on small labels for the Texas Norteno community. —*Myles Boisen*

Flaco Jimenez & His Conjunto / 1978 / Arhoolie ✦✦✦
Flaco, son of El Flaco, is the second generation of accordion players in his family (his son is now an up-and-comer). There was a time when the fringes of the rock world flirted with him. But here he plays the righteous border sound, with some fancier flourishes and more Anglo touches than the men of his father's era. These are classic polkas, rancheras, and corridos (including one on Hurricane Beulah and his father's great *Mojado sin Licensia*). —*John Storm Roberts*

Sonido de San Antonio / 1980 / Arhoolie ✦✦✦

★ **Ay Te Dejo en San Antonio** / 1986 / Arhoolie ✦✦✦✦✦
With two Arhoolie albums in one, it's a generous helping of 22 Tex-Mex winners with lots of rancheras and polkas. —*Myles Boisen*

Arriba El Norte / 1988 / Rounder ✦✦✦✦
Another in a series of Rounder anthologies featuring Flaco Jimenez. These were all done for the DBL label in San Antonio, and are short, predominantly polka and ranchero tunes. They're mostly rousing, celebratory party songs, sung with passion and played exuberantly by Jimenez. Unlike some other performers, Jimenez's approach and appeal are quite insular; he doesn't attempt to do anything flamboyant, unusual or non-traditional, opting to sing and play the material in vintage conjunto style. As a result, while it's often quite delightful, the differences in song structure over the 14 numbers will seem minimal to those who aren't fans of the idiom. —*Ron Wynn*

Flaco's Amigos / 1988 / Arhoolie ✦✦✦
His most eclectic album features Ry Cooder and others. Some songs are in English to enhance his crossover appeal. —*Myles Boisen*

Entre Humo y Botellas / 1989 / Rounder ✦✦✦
Flaco Jimenez has been the most popular accordionist to perform, compose, and record conjunto music, not only cutting numerous singles and albums for regional labels but also serving as a sideman for well-known rockers like Doug Sahm and Ry Cooder. This anthology was pulled from singles he recorded between 1982 and 1987 and features the major styles preferred by conjunto performers; these include the swaying, arresting polkas, rancheras, and boleros, all done in Spanish, with Jimenez's accordion and vocals prominently in the upper register. Despite the absence of thematic or musical variety, this is a good opportunity to hear one of the masters and popularizers of a folk idiom at his best. —*Ron Wynn*

San Antonio Soul / 1991 / Rounder ✦✦✦
Flaco Jimenez has recorded dozens of conjunto songs and albums and done material for both the American and Latino markets. This 14-cut Rounder anthology features material recorded for the Mexican-American audience, and includes tunes that address such issues as immigration and the lifestyle of the border community. There are three rollicking instrumentals that showcase Jimenez's ability and flashy style on accordion. Other songs include romantic fare and traditional polkas and rancheros. His vocals and instrumental abilities are quite impressive, and provide solid examples of classic ethnic music seldom heard outside its target area. —*Ron Wynn*

Partners / 1992 / Warner Brothers ✦✦✦

Un Mojado Sin Licencia / 1993 / Arhoolie ✦✦✦✦
These legend-making songs were recorded between 1955 and 1967 in San Antonio before Norteno music was big anywhere else and feature the title cut ("A Wetback Without a Green Card") written by Flaco's father Santiago, as well as songs about Vietnam, Hurricane Beulah, and truck drivers. The work that has made Flaco famous is his flashy accordion playing (with Ry Cooder et al), yet the plain man performances here are even more engaging. About half the CD appeared as an LP—Arhoolie 3007 —*Carl Hoyt*

☆ **Flaco's First!** / 1995 / Arhoolie ✦✦✦✦✦
Containing material recorded between 1955 and 1956, *Flaco's First!* contains the first recordings that Flaco Jimenez ever made. Throughout this compilation, he is supported by bajo sexto player

Henry Zimmerle, and the duo stand out among the rest of the band. —*Thom Owens*

Buena Suerte Senorita / Jun. 1996 / Arista ✦✦✦

Santiago Jimenez, Jr.

b. Jun. 22, 1984
Accordion, Vocals / Zydeco, Tex-Mex, Norteño
The namesake of one of the pioneers of Norteno music, this singer and accordionist takes a more traditional approach than that of his more celebrated brother, Flaco. Santiago favors the two-row button accordion, and many of his recordings offer the basic two voices, accordion, and guitar presentation of Tex-Mex music. In addition to recording extensively for local San Antonio labels, Santiago has recorded for Arhoolie and Rounder and has appeared in the documentary film, *Chulas Fronteras*. —*Mark A. Humphrey*

Familia y Tradicion / 1989 / Rounder ✦✦✦
The songs on Jimenez's 1988 session for Rounder are mostly rigid, but spirited, they emphasize the polka and mid-tempo beats and are sung in Spanish. Jimenez plays the two-row button accordion, and his riffs and solos are fluidly expressed and superbly played, while his singing is intense and earnest. Only on "You Are My Sunshine" does Jimenez veer away from strict ethnic traditions to do a fun/throwaway piece. Otherwise, these are topical and/or vintage numbers that celebrate the conjunto sound with vigor and love. —*Ron Wynn*

El Gato Negro / 1990 / Rounder ✦✦✦
Santiago Jimenez, Jr.'s trademarks are the two-row button accordion and passionate, fiery singing in the classic conjunto mode. This session features 14 tracks, with Jimenez doing polkas, rancheros and boleros, but no pop or rock covers. The short numbers (none longer than four-and-a-half minutes) are structured to give Jimenez's vocals and accordion bursts maximum space, while the backing players fill in tightly underneath him. This is contemporary conjunto with an authentic and vintage sensibility, performed by one of the idiom's major stars. —*Ron Wynn*

● **El Mero Mero de San Antonio** / Nov. 1990 / Arhoolie ✦✦✦✦
More traditional than his hermano Flaco, singer and accordionist Santiago plays Norte͂o music much the same as his celebrated father did in the '40s. —*Mark A. Humphrey*

Corazon de Piedra / 1992 / Watermelon ✦✦✦
Santiago Jimenez, Jr. has long labored in the obscuring shadow cast by his famous father Dom Santiago, Sr. and elder brother Flaco. *Corazon de Piedra* doesn't try to compete, but quietly and assuredly offers an intimate, backporch glimpse of one of Austin's masters of old-time traditional Tex-Mex conjunto music. This vintage working class form originated historically from a mingling of German and Czech settlers' waltzes and polkas with Mexican corrido song stories. The perfect disc for fans of Los Lobos who would enjoy exploring those roots somewhat deeper. —*Roch Parisien*

His First & Last Recordings / 1994 / Arhoolie ✦✦✦✦

Canciones de Mi Padre / 1994 / Watermelon ✦✦✦

Musica De Tiempos Pasados, Del Presente, Y Futuro / 1995 / Watermelon ✦✦✦✦
What a beautiful, moving, and great-sounding album this is. Jimenez (his friends call him Chief, according to the liner notes) plays great accordion and sings the border songs that he has revitalized, learned from his father in the old-time tradition. It is so great to hear the loose, interdependent textures of this music. One can really get a sense of small-town celebrations untouched by the pervasive influence of contemporary American pop. The recording is so wonderfully full that the shifting dynamics through these tracks convey the immediacy of the playing even more. Some terrific tracks are "La Nopalera" (a polka) and "Prisonero en Tus Brazos" (a ranchero). —*Richard Meyer*

Santiago Jimenez / Arhoolie ✦✦✦

Santiago Strikes Again / Arhoolie ✦✦✦

Johnnie & Jack

Traditional Bluegrass, Traditional Country, Close Harmony

Johnnie & Jack mined the familiar turf of singing brother duos in the late '40s through the late '50s with a few distinct twists. For openers, they weren't blood brothers, just brothers in law. Secondly, they brought a new rhythmic strain to country music, both in their use of Latin beats and the unfettered drive of their combo, the Tennessee Mountain Boys. And of all the singing duos, they were the most inclined to stretch the boundaries of their sound, from bluegrass to sacred to amazing covers of R&B tunes, with none of their country soul diluted in the bargain. But for all their melding of outside influences, few artists—even in the mid-'50s—were as wholly committed to sounding as "country" as they were. Whatever they played, sang, or wrote, it *always* sounded like Johnnie & Jack.

Johnnie Wright and Jack Anglin started playing together in 1938, forming a loose-knit country string band featuring Johnnie's new wife Muriel Deason, whom he would later rename Kitty Wells. Their sound in the early days was heavily influenced by both the Delmore Brothers and the Monroe Brothers, Charlie and Bill. As Johnnie plainly put it, "We were so green we didn't know you needed to develop your own style. We just out and out copied their sound in the beginning." An important member of the unit was Jack's brother, Jim Anglin, who contributed a high, lonesome tenor harmony both live and on records and contributed mightily as a songwriter during the duo's 25-year partnership.

Johnnie & Jack's band, now named the Tennessee Hillbillies, were just starting up the country food chain with sustaining radio broadcasts on local stations when World War II temporarily put the project on hold as Jack joined the Army. Reunited after the war, Johnnie & Jack—with Kitty now a permanent fixture of the band—picked up where they left off, adding an emcee/bass player named Smilin' Eddie Hill and a young guitarist named Chet Atkins to the fold. By 1947, they were filling in for Roy Acuff on the Grand Ole Opry, under the edict that they change their billing (Opry officials were loath to associate with any acts that used the word "hillbilly" in their name) to the Tennessee Mountain Boys and that Kitty sit out the radio performances as the Opry was topheavy with female singers at the time.

At year's end, they had finally made their first records for the R&B-based Apollo Records out of New York City. After the nonsuccess of those early 78s (the company refused to send promotional copies to radio stations to promote sales and airplay) and a quick side project with Ray Atkins and Clyde Moody as the King Sacred Quartette for the King label, the duo started recording for RCA Victor—their longest-lasting label affiliation—in 1949. But even with Kitty recording solo and supplying high baritone harmonies on the duo's records, success proved elusive for the next few years. The troupe moved from one radio station to another, logging in time with the *Louisiana Hayride* and stations as far afield as Georgia and North Carolina. All of that changed with the release of their first hit, "Poison Love," in 1951, which made the Top Ten on all three *Billboard* country charts at the time. What Johnnie & Jack had done to crack the charts was to take their straight bluegrass harmonies and wed them to a distinct rhumba beat, principally supplied by studio bassist Ernie Newton, playing a maraca and wire brush simultaneously while handling the bass part. In the dark days of country music, where drums were outlawed on the stage of the Grand Ole Opry and electric instruments were only grudgingly accepted, this new approach was novel and influential. The combination proved a winner, one that the duo would return to on several recordings, complete with cha-cha-cha endings, which would become a Johnnie & Jack trademark. With Kitty's success assured after the mega-success of "It Wasn't God Who Made Honky Tonk Angels," the duo combined with her to become one of the most in-demand road shows in country music. Within a couple of years, their sound would change again, adding bass singer Culley Holt from the Jordanaires to countrify a batch of rhythm and blues recordings including the Moonglows' "Sincerely," the Four Knights' "(Oh Baby Mine) I Get So Lonely," the Delta Rhythm Boys' "Kiss Crazy Baby," and the

Spaniels' "Goodnight, Sweetheart, Goodnight," all hits in the country field for the duo. This helped them handle the onslaught of rock 'n' roll better than most country artists of the day while keeping the roots of their sound intact. Johnnie & Jack made the *Billboard* country charts a total of 15 times and probably would have had more entries if the mid-'50s charts weren't limited to only mirroring the Top Ten songs of the day.

But by the late '50s, Johnnie & Jack's records were being mainstreamed into the Nashville Sound, with the Jordanaires, the Anita Kerr Singers, saxophones, and full rhythm sections burying their plaintive vocals beneath layers of reverb and pop sugar coating. Dissatisfied, the duo let their contract run out and signed with Decca Records in 1961. Their new company changed the spelling of their name to "Johnny & Jack," but at last the duo and Kitty Wells were all on the same label again and with label mates like Patsy Cline, Ernest Tubb, Webb Pierce, Red Foley, and Bill Monroe, they couldn't have been in better company. The contract produced no more hits than the tail end of their tenure with RCA, but with Kitty racking up hit after hit, the troupe had all the road work it could handle. It was coming back from one of these road trips that they were to learn of the deaths of Patsy Cline, Cline's manager, Randy Hughes, Hawkshaw Hawkins, and Cowboy Copas in a plane crash. On his way to the funeral parlor to attend memorial services for his fellow performers, Jack Anglin's car spun out of control, killing him instantly, thus ending the duo of Johnnie & Jack on an especially sad note.

As of this writing, Johnnie Wright and Kitty Wells continue to tour together, with Johnnie still reprising some of the old Johnnie & Jack hits in their show with Wright's son Bobby filling in for Jack. The duo that set country music on fire with rhythm is no more, but in the finest country tradition, the family that plays together, stays together. *—Cub Koda*

All the Best of Johnnie & Jack / 1970 / RCA Victor ✦✦✦✦
All the Best of Johnnie & Jack is a double-LP that contains 24 of Johnnie & Jack's biggest hits for RCA Records, which were all recorded during the '50s and early '60s. The hit singles "(Oh Baby Mine) I Get So Lonely," "Poison Love," "Cryin' Heart Blues," "Three Ways of Knowing," "Goodnight, Sweetheart, Goodnight," and "Stop the World (And Let Me Off)" are all included, as are several other, lesser-known gems, making it an excellent, concise retrospective. It's the perfect introduction to one of the finest, and most underappreciated, groups in all of bluegrass and it is a shame that it isn't available on compact disc. *— Thom Owens*

At KWKH / 1994 / Bear Family ✦✦✦✦
At KWKH presents an excellent, vibrant radio concert by Johnnie & Jack and Kitty Wells. For the entire show, Johnnie & Jack provide the instrumental backing, and they trade lead vocals with Wells and Paul Warren. The duo sing "It's Raining on the Mountain," "Orange Blossom Special," "My Bucket's Got a Hole In It," and "Cheatam County Breakdown," among several others; Kitty takes lead on "The Singing Waterfall," "Death of Little Kathy Fiscus," and "Love or Hate," while Warren sings "Wake Up, Susan," "Mississippi Sawyer," and "Cotton-Eyed Joe." While the disc will primarily be of interest to hardcore fans of the three primary artists, those listeners will find much to treasure on *At KWKH*. *—Thom Owens*

● **Early Country Love** / ACM ✦✦✦✦

And the Tennessee Mountain Boys / Bear Family ✦✦✦✦
Multi-disc box set of everything this country duo ever recorded. From their early bluegrass and gospel sides (some featuring Kitty Wells) to their rhumba beat hits of the '50s, it's all here. With heartfelt singing and playing, great songwriting and much good humor, all box set retrospectives should be this much fun to listen to. Highly recommended. *— Cub Koda*

The Johnson Mountain Boys

Traditional Bluegrass

During the 1980s, the Johnson Mountain Boys were contemporary masters of traditional bluegrass music who remained faithful to the old styles while keeping the songs fresh and original. The band was founded in the suburbs of Washington, DC, by vocalist/banjoist/guitarist Dudley Connell, banjoist Richie Underwood, mandolinist David McLaughlin, fiddler Eddie Stubbs, and Larry Robbins bassist. The personnel changed over the years, but the group's sound remained consistent. The Johnson Mountain Boys made their recording debut with a single in late 1978; an EP soon followed and helped build a loyal audience in the DC area. They became festival favorites after the release of their self-titled debut. Their second album, *Walls of Time*, came out in 1982 and featured Connell, McLaughlin, Stubbs and vocalist/banjoist/mandolinist Tom Adams. The same lineup recorded four more albums during the early '80s. In 1988, the Johnson Mountain Boys announced that they planned to retire after a farewell concert in Lucketts, VA. Two years later, the Boys reunited briefly to play two festivals. In the early '90s, the band began actively performing again and released a new album, *Blue Diamond*, in 1993. —*Sandra Brennan*

☆ **Working Close** / 1983 / Rounder ♦♦♦♦♦
Dudley Connell's chilling, high-lonesome lead vocals were only one of the delights of this militantly traditional, young bluegrass band. Any of their albums are among the best bluegrass of recent decades. —*Mark A. Humphrey*

● **Favorites** / 1987 / Rounder ♦♦♦♦
Favorites features a terrific cross-section of highlights from the Johnson Mountain Boys' early-'80s Rounder albums and is the perfect introduction to their traditionalist bluegrass. —*Thom Owens*

Let the Whole World Talk / 1987 / Rounder ♦♦♦
One of the finest records the Johnson Mountain Boys ever recorded, *Let the Whole World Talk* is an audaciously accomplished set of modernized bluegrass. The group slips a couple of excellent contemporary folk songs onto the record, but it is mainly notable for the way they make traditional songs into vibrant, vital and undeniably contemporary music. For its instrumentals, harmonies, and arrangements, *Let the Whole World Talk* is one of the finest contemporary bluegrass albums of the late '80s. —*Thom Owens*

Requests / 1988 / Rounder ♦♦♦
This is an eclectic album by the short-lived but brilliant quintet. —*Mark A. Humphrey*

At the Old Schoolhouse / 1989 / Rounder ♦♦♦♦
At the Old Schoolhouse was recorded on the Johnson Mountain Boys' intended "farewell tour" of the late '80s. The group later decided to stick together, perhaps because they knew they were giving performances as good as this. Throughout *At the Old Schoolhouse*, the group gives lively, invigorating performances that prove traditional bluegrass isn't boring. It's a terrific live album, and one of the Johnson Mountain Boys' finest moments. —*Thom Owens*

Blue Diamond / 1993 / Rounder ♦♦♦
Blue Diamond is an excellent newgrass album that juxtaposes contemporary folk songs by Bob Dylan with standards by Carter Stanley and country songs by Buck Owens. It proves that the Johnson Mountain Boys remain one of the best progressive bluegrass combos of the '70s and '80s. —*Thom Owens*

Michael Johnson

b. Aug. 8, 1944, Alamosa, CO
Guitar, Vocals / Progressive Country
It's difficult to pinpoint Michael Johnson's musical style . As a teenage guitar player, he took notes from seminal rocker Chuck Berry and jazzman Charlie Byrd. At age 21, he spent a year in Barcelona, studying under classical guitarist Graciano Tarrago; once he'd returned to the US, he signed up for a one-year folk tour as a member of the Mitchell Trio, which included John Denver. To complicate matters, when he first made inroads in the record business, he did it in pop, racking up hits with "Bluer Than Blue," "Almost Like Being in Love," and "This Night Won't Last Forever." He hadn't yet covered polka music, or country, but he tackled the latter style after signing with RCA Records in the winter of 1985. His pleasant intonation, relaxed phrasing, and unusual pronunciations blend well with his usual acoustic

arrangements, although Johnson has never quite earned the level of recognition his talents deserve. —*Tom Roland*

Wings / 1987 / RCA ♦♦♦♦
Johnson's first country album didn't stray far from the formula that gave him pop hits. The band on *Wings* is essentially the same as on "Bluer Than Blue," but Johnson leaned toward songs by Nashville writers. And what songs they were. *Wings* yielded two No. 1 singles, "Give Me Wings" and the ultra-romantic "The Moon Is Still over Her Shoulder." Those are the hits, but the quality songwriting runs as deep as any country album of the time. —*Brian Mansfield*

That's That / 1988 / RCA ♦♦♦
Dobro great Jerry Douglas guests on *That's That*, which features Johnson's chart-topping "The Moon Is Still Over Her Shoulder." —*Jason Ankeny*

● **The Best of Michael Johnson** / 1990 / RCA ♦♦♦♦
A pair of No. 1 hits—"Give Me Wings" and "The Moon Is Still Over Her Shoulder"—highlight *The Best of Michael Johnson*. —*Jason Ankeny*

Freedy Johnston

Guitar, Vocals / Singer-Songwriter, Folk-Rock, Adult Alternative Pop-Rock, Americana
Pitting acute, evocative portraits of outsiders and beautiful losers against fragile, shimmering country-pop melodies, the acclaimed work of Freedy Johnston earned him a reputation as one of the brightest singer-songwriters to emerge in the 1990s. Born and raised on his family's farm in the small town of Kinsley, KS, Johnston bought his first guitar at the age of 16; because there was no local music store, he was forced to order the instrument through a mail order service. After entering college in nearby Lawrence, he began composing his first songs, and was soon focusing all of his energies on becoming a musician. In 1985, he moved to New York, where one of his demos earned him a recording contract.

In 1990, Johnston issued his debut LP, *The Trouble Tree*. The album attracted a cult following domestically, and became a sizable hit abroad, especially in the Netherlands, where it made him a star. However, Johnston remained a struggling musician at home, and in order to complete his 1992 sophomore effort *Can You Fly?*, he was forced to sell the family farm, which he had inherited from his grandfather. The resulting recording, however, was a critical smash that ended up on a number of prominent year-end lists, and after another EP, *Unlucky*, he was signed to Elektra Records. His 1994 major-label debut, the Butch Vig-produced *This Perfect World*, proved to be Johnston's most satisfying release to date; its first single, "Bad Reputation," even earned him significant airplay on alternative radio formats. In 1996, he composed the score for the film comedy *Kingpin;* the full-length LP *Never Home* surfaced in early 1997. —*Jason Ankeny*

Trouble Tree / 1990 / Bar/None ♦♦♦♦
Johnston's debut, though not without its rough edges, firmly established him as a talent to be reckoned with—even his earliest songs are marked by great maturity and insight. —*Jason Ankeny*

Can You Fly / Apr. 14, 1992 / Bar/None ♦♦♦♦
"Well I sold the dirt to feed the band" goes the opening line of Johnston's sophomore effort, a reference to the sale of his family farm, a measure necessary to pay for the record's completion. The move was a risky one, but *Can You Fly* was worth it; this is a uniformly excellent collection of songs, highlighted by the lilting "Tearing Down This Place" and "Down in Love," a beautiful duet with Syd Straw. —*Jason Ankeny*

Unlucky / 1993 / Restless ♦♦♦
The six-song EP *Unlucky* features *Can You Fly*'s tale of Las Vegas woe, "The Lucky One," in both its completed and demo forms. In addition to three new Johnston originals, it also contains a terrific cover of Jimmy Webb's "Wichita Lineman." —*Jason Ankeny*

● **This Perfect World** / 1994 / Elektra ♦♦♦♦
The songwriting gifts of Freedy Johnston grow in depth and resonance with each effort, and with *This Perfect World*, he makes his biggest leap yet. Richly produced by Butch Vig, the record is a col-

lection of poignant character studies, finely etched portraits of alienation, loneliness, and rejection. —*Jason Ankeny*

Buddy Jones (Burgher William Jones)

b. Feb. 17, 1924, Hope, AR, **d.** 1950
Bass, Vocals / Traditional Country, Honky Tonk
Buddy Jones is one of the most interesting, but sadly overlooked, figures of early honky tonk. A police officer from Shreveport, LA, Jones recorded several singles for Decca Records during the late '30s and early '40s before abandoning his musical career. Jones began singing with Jimmie Davis, a Louisiana politician, in 1935, recording a number of duets for Decca over the course of the next year and a half. Buddy went solo in 1937, recording with his brother Buster on steel guitar. After releasing a series of singles, which were nearly all risque honky tonk, Bob Dunn, a former steel guitarist for Cliff Bruner, replaced Buster in Buddy's band.

Jones continued to record for Decca until 1945, when he essentially retired from the music business. He died in 1950. —*Stephen Thomas Erlewine*

● **Louisiana Honky Tonk Man** / Texas Rose ◆◆◆◆
Louisiana Honky Tonk Man covers the highlights of Buddy Jones' recordings for Decca Records. Jones was one of the forgotten pioneers of honky tonk, and these recordings—which were made between 1935 and 1941—are among the most risque honky tonk of the era. There are prototypical honky tonk blues like "Shreveport County Jail Blues" and "Ease My Troubled Mind," but much of Jones' material grew out of the dirty blues, as evidenced by "She's a Hum-Dum Dinger," "Butcher Man Blues," "I'm Going to Get Me a Honky Tonky Baby," and "She's Sellin' What She Used to Give Away." *Louisiana Honky Tonk Man* has 16 of his best cuts, functioning as the finest retrospective—indeed, the *only* retrospective—of his unappreciated career to date. —*Stephen Thomas Erlewine*

David Lynn Jones

b. Jan. 15, 1950, Bexar, AR
Guitar, Vocals / Progressive Country, Contemporary Country, New Traditionalist
David Lynn Jones burst on the country music scene in 1987 with a string of hits that included "Bonnie Jean," "High Ridin' Heroes," "The Rogue," and "Tonite in America." Although he never was able to equal the success of that string of hits, he remained popular throughout the early '90s.

Born in Bexar, AR, Jones began performing in local clubs while still a teenager. For a while during the late '60s, he worked as a car salesman, quitting in 1970 to become the bass player for Freddy Morrison and the Bandana Blues Band and to hone his songwriting skills. Jones tried to sell his songs in Music City, but he wasn't successful; by 1975, he was barely making a living as a Houston session musician. Matters improved in 1976 when he provided Randy Corner with "Heart Don't Fail Me Now," which became a Top 40 hit. Later, with the help of producer Richie Albright, Jones made a demo tape for Mercury Records. He played every instrument but the saxophone on the tape, which eventually made its way to Willie Nelson, who recorded Jones' song "Living in the Promiseland" in 1986. The song became a No. 1 hit.

The following year, Jones released his successful debut album *Hard Times on Easy Street*. Albright produced the album as well as its successor, *Wood Wind and Stone* (1989). Jones moved to Liberty Records in 1992 and recorded *Mixed Emotions* in his private studio. In 1994, he released *Play by Ear*. —*Sandra Brennan*

Hard Times on Easy Street / 1980 / Mercury ◆◆◆
David Lynn Jones' debut album *Hard Times on Easy Street* showcases a talent that arrived fully formed. Though Jones doesn't push any musical boundaries, his ear for straightforward, rock-inflected, rootsy country is impeccable, as is his talent for Dylanesque lyrics and Springsteenesque narratives. Jones would later push out into more adventurous musical directions, but the straightforward country and heartland rock on *Hard Times on Easy Street* remains his most rewarding outing. —*Thom Owens*

Wood, Wind & Stone / 1989 / Mercury ◆◆
Jones' label considered employing *Wood, Wind & Stone* as a means of breaking the singer into the pop market; while the plan fell through, the record still feels slick and overproduced, its glossy sheen at odds with Jones' soul-searching lyrics. —*Jason Ankeny*

● **Mixed Emotions** / 1992 / Liberty ◆◆◆◆
After two albums for Mercury that left his promise unfulfilled, David Lynn Jones switched labels and recorded an album in his home studio in Bexar, AR. Like a saved man flirting with sin, Jones forsakes Nashville wisdom and takes his cues from renegade American rockers like Leon Russell and Robbie Robertson. In his heart he's still country, but he revs the tempos, cranks the guitars, and lays on the horns as he takes off screaming into the Arkansas Delta. —*Brian Mansfield*

Play by Ear / Apr. 5, 1994 / Liberty ◆◆◆

George Jones

b. Sep. 12, 1931, Saratoga, TX
Guitar, Vocals / Traditional Country, Country-Pop, Honky Tonk, Nashville Sound/Countrypolitan
By most accounts, George Jones is the finest vocalist in the recorded history of country music. Initially, he was a hardcore honky tonker in the tradition of Hank Williams, but over the course of his career he developed an affecting, nuanced ballad style. In the course of his career, he never left the top of the country charts, even as he suffered innumerable personal and professional difficulties. Only Eddy Arnold had more Top Ten hits than Jones, and George always stayed closer to the roots of hardcore country.

George Jones was born and raised in East Texas, near the city of Beaumont. At an early age, he displayed an affection for music. He enjoyed the gospel he heard in church and on the family's Carter Family records, but he truly became fascinated with country music when his family bought a radio when he was seven. When he was nine, his father bought him his first guitar. Soon, his father had George playing and singing on the streets on Beaumont, earning spare change. At 16, he ran away to Jasper, TX, where he sang at a local radio station. Jones married Dorothy, his first wife, in 1950 when he was 19 years old. The marriage collapsed within a year and he enlisted in the Marines at the end of 1951. Though the US was at war with Korea, Jones never served overseas—he was stationed at a military camp in California, where he kept singing in bars. After he was discharged, Jones immediately began performing again.

In 1953, Jones was discovered by record producer Pappy Daily, who was also the co-owner of Starday Records, a local Texas label. Impressed with Jones' potential, Daily signed the singer to Starday. "No Money in This Deal," Jones' first single, was released in early 1954, but it received no attention. Starday released three more singles that year, which were all ignored. Jones released "Why, Baby, Why" late in the summer of 1955 and the single became his first hit, peaking at No. 4. However, its momentum was halted by a cover version by Webb Pierce and Red Sovine that hit number one on the country charts.

Nonetheless, George Jones was on the road to success and Pappy Daily secured the singer a spot on the *Louisiana Hayride*, where Jones co-billed with Elvis Presley. Jones reached the Top Ten with regularity in 1956 with such singles as "What Am I Worth" and "Just One More." That same year, he recorded some rockabilly singles under the name Thumper Jones that were unsuccessful, both commercially and artistically. In August, he joined the cast of the Grand Ole Opry and his first album appeared by the end of the year. In 1957, Starday Records signed a distribution deal with Mercury Records and George Jones' records began appearing under the Mercury label. Pappy Daily began recording Jones in Nashville and his first single for the new label, "Don't Stop the Music," was another Top Ten hit. Throughout 1958, his songs were landing near the top of the charts, culminating with "White Lightning," which spent five weeks at No. 1 in the spring of 1959. His next big hit arrived two years later, when the ballad "Tender Years" spent seven weeks at No. 1. "Tender Years" displayed a smoother production and larger arrangement than his previous hits, and it pointed the way toward Jones' later success as a balladeer.

In early 1962, Jones reached No. 5 with "Aching, Breaking Heart," which would turn out to be his last hit for Mercury Records. Pappy Daily became a staff producer for United Artists Records in 1962 and Jones followed him to the label. His first single for UA, "She Thinks I Still Care," was his third No. 1 hit. In 1963, Jones began performing and recording with Melba Montgomery. During the early '60s, mainstream country music was getting increasingly slick, but Jones and Montgomery's harmonies were raw and laden with bluegrass influences.

Their first duet, "We Must Have Been Out of Our Minds" (spring 1963), was their biggest hit, peaking at No. 3. The pair continued to record together throughout 1963 and 1964, although they never again had a Top Ten hit; they also reunited in 1966 and 1967, recording a couple of albums and singles for Musicor. Jones had a number of solo hits in 1963 and 1964 as well, peaking with the No. 3 "The Race Is On" in the fall of 1964.

Under the direction of Pappy Daily, George Jones moved to the new record label Musicor in 1965. Jones' first single for Musicor, "Things Have Gone to Pieces," was a Top Ten hit in the spring of 1965. Between 1965 and 1970, he had 17 Top Ten hits for Musicor. While at Musicor, Jones recorded almost 300 songs in five years. During that time, he cut a number of first-rate songs, including country classics like "Love Bug," "Walk Through This World with Me," and "A Good Year for the Roses." He also recorded a fair share of mediocre material and given the sheer amount of songs he sang, that isn't surprising. Although Jones made a couple of records that were genuine tributes or experiments, he also tried to fit into contemporary country styles, such as the Bakersfield Sound. Not all of the attempts resulted in hits, but he consistently charted in the Top Ten with his singles, if not with his albums. Musicor wound up flooding the market with George Jones records for the rest of the '60s. Jones' albums for Musicor tended to be arranged thematically and only two, his 1965 duet *George Jones & Gene Pitney* and 1969's *I'll Share My World with You*, charted. That meant that while Jones was one of the most popular and acclaimed singers in country music, there was still a surplus of material.

Like his discography, George Jones' personal life was spinning out of control. He was drinking heavily and began missing concerts. His second wife Shirley filed for divorce in 1968, and Jones moved to Nashville, where he met Tammy Wynette, the most popular new female singer in country music. Soon, Jones and Wynette fell in love; they married on February 16, 1969.

At the same time Jones married Wynette, tensions that had been building between Jones and his longtime producer Pappy Daily erupted. Jones was unhappy with the sound of his Musicor records, and he placed most of the blame on Dally. After his marriage, Jones wanted to record with Wynette, but Musicor wouldn't allow him to appear on her label, Epic, and Epic wouldn't let her sing on a Musicor album. Furthermore, Epic wanted to lure Jones away from Musicor. Jones was more than willing to leave, but he had to fulfill his contract before the company would let him go.

While he continued recording material for Musicor, Epic entered contract negotiations with their rivals and halfway through 1971, Jones severed ties with Musicor and Pappy Daily. He signed away all the rights to his Musicor recordings in the process. The label continued to release Jones albums for a couple of years and they also licensed recordings to RCA, who released two singles and a series of budget-priced albums in the early '70s.

Jones signed with Epic Records in October of 1971. It was the culmination of a busy year for Jones and Wynette, they had become the biggest stars in country music, they racked up a number of Top Ten hits separately, and they sold out concerts across the country as a duo. Jones had successfully remade his image from a short-haired, crazed honky tonker to more relaxed, sensitive balladeer. At the end of the year, he cut his first records for Epic.

George Jones' new record producer was Billy Sherrill, who had been responsible for Tammy Wynette's hit albums. Sherrill was known for his lush, string-laden productions and his precise,

aggressive approach in the studio. Under his direction, musicians were there to obey his orders and that included the singers as well. Jones had been accustomed to the relaxed style of Pappy Daily, who was the polar opposite of Sherrill. As a result, the singer and producer were tense at first, but soon the pair developed a fruitful working relationship. With Sherrill, Jones became a full-fledged balladeer, sanding away the rough edges of his hardcore honky tonk roots.

"We Can Make It," his first solo single for Epic, was a celebration of Jones' marriage to Wynette written by Sherrill and Glenn Sutton. The song was a No. 2 hit early in 1972, kicking off a successful career at Epic. "The Ceremony," Jones and Wynette's second duet, followed. "We Can Make It," and also became a Top Ten hit. "Loving You Could Never Be Better," followed its predecessors into the Top Ten at the end of 1972. By now, the couple's marriage was becoming a public soap opera, with their audience following each single as if they were news reports. Even though they were proclaiming their love through their music, the couple had begun to fight frequently. Jones was sinking deep into alcoholism and drug abuse, which escalated as the couple continued to tour together.

Though every single he released in 1973 went into the Top Ten, George Jones' personal life was becoming increasingly difficult. Tammy Wynette filed for divorce in August, 1973. Shortly after she filed the papers, the couple decided to reconcile and her petition was withdrawn. Following her withdrawal, the duo had a No. 1 single with the appropriately titled "We're Gonna Hold On." In the summer of 1974, Jones had his first No. 1 hit since "Walk Through This World with Me" with "The Grand Tour," a song that drew a deft portrait of a broken marriage. He followed it with another No. 1 hit, "The Door." Not long after its release, he recorded "These Days (I Barely Get By)," which featured lyrics co-written by Wynette. Two days after he recorded the song, Wynette left Jones; they divorced within a year.

The late '70s were plagued with trouble for George Jones. Between 1975 and the beginning of 1980, he had only two Top Ten solo hits—"These Days (I Barely Get By)" (1975) and "Her Name Is" (1976). Though they divorced, Jones and Wynette continued to record and tour together, and that is where he racked up the hits, beginning with the back-to-back 1976 No. 1s, "Golden Ring" and "Near You." The decrease in hits accurately reflects the downward spiral in Jones' health in the late '70s, when he became addicted not only to alcohol, but to cocaine as well. Jones became notorious for his drunken, intoxicated rampages, often involving both drugs and shotguns. Jones would disappear for days at a time. He began missing a substantial amount of concerts—in 1979 alone, he missed 54 shows—which earned him the nickname "No-Show Jones."

Jones' career began to pick up in 1978, when he began flirting with rock 'n' roll, covering Chuck Berry's "Maybellene" with Johnny Paycheck and recording a duet with James Taylor called "Bartender's Blues." The success of the singles—both went Top Ten—led to an album of duets, *My Very Special Guests*, in 1979. Though it was poised to be a return to the top of the charts for Jones, he neglected to appear at the scheduled recording sessions and had to overdub his vocals after his partners recorded theirs. That same year, doctors told the singer he had to quit drinking, otherwise his life was in jeopardy. Jones checked into a rehab clinic, but left after a month, uncured. Due to his cocaine addiction, his weight had fallen from 150 pounds to a mere 100. Despite his declining health, Jones managed a comeback in 1980. It began with a Top Ten duet with Tammy Wynette, "Two Story House," early in the year, but the song that pushed him back to the top of the charts was the dramatic ballad "He Stopped Loving Her Today." The single hit No. 1 in the spring of the year, beginning a new series of Top Ten hits and No. 1 singles that ran through 1986. The string of hits was so successful, it rivaled the peak of his popularity in the '60s. "He Stopped Loving Her Today" was followed by the Top Ten "I'm Not Ready Yet" and an album, *I Am What I Am*, in the fall of 1980. *I Am What I Am* became his most successful album, going platinum.

Throughout 1981 and 1983, Jones had eight Top Ten hits. Although he was having hits again, Jones hadn't kicked his addictions. He was still going on crazed, intoxicated rampages; these culminated in a televised police chase of Jones driving drunk through the streets of Nashville.

Following his arrest, Jones managed to shake his drug and alcohol addictions with the support of his fourth wife, Nancy Sepulvada. Jones and Sepulvada married in March of 1983. Soon after their marriage, he began to detox and by the end of 1983, he had completed his rehabilitation.

Jones continued to have Top Ten hits regularly until 1987, when country radio became dominated by newer artists; ironically, the artists that kept him off the charts—singers like Randy Travis, Keith Whitley, and Dwight Yoakam—were heavily influenced by Jones himself. Jones and Sepulvada moved back to Nashville in 1987. In 1988, he recorded his final album with Billy Sherrill, *One Woman Man*. The title song, which was a hit for Johnny Horton in 1956, was Jones' final Top Ten hit. *One Woman Man* was his last record for Epic Records.

After its release, Jones moved to MCA, releasing his first record for the label, *And Along Came Jones*, in the fall of 1991. Between *One Woman Man* and the release of *And Along Came Jones*, he recorded a duet with Randy Travis, "A Few Ole Country Boys," which was a Top Ten hit in the fall of 1990. Jones' records for MCA didn't sell nearly as well as his Epic albums, but his albums usually were critically acclaimed. In 1995, he reunited with Tammy Wynette to record *One*. In April of 1996, Jones published his autobiography, *I Lived to Tell It All. —Stephen Thomas Erlewine*

George Jones Salutes Hank Williams / 1960 / Mercury ✦✦✦✦
George Jones Salutes Hank Williams was recorded at Mercury Records, toward the beginning of Jones' career. At this stage, George still sounded similar to Hank Williams, but he had begun to incorporate much of Williams' vocal techniques into a distinctive vocal style of his own. If Jones had recorded these songs while still at Starday, they wouldn't be as exciting as they are now—since he had moved beyond mimicking into his own style, he's able to invest Williams' songs with grit and passion, instead of just copying Hank. It's an affectionate, entertaining tribute, featuring some of the greatest songs ("Cold Cold Heart," "Hey Good Lookin'," "Half As Much," "Jambalaya," "Why Don't You Love Me," "Honky Tonkin'," "Settin' the Woods on Fire") in country music. (The 1984 reissue is slightly shorter than the original issue and features liner notes by Elvis Costello.) —*Stephen Thomas Erlewine*

George Jones Sings Bob Wills / 1962 / Razor & Tie ✦✦✦
Rather than try to ape the Wills arrangements, producer Pappy Daily sets Jones up in front of a honky tonk combo and lets the Ol' Possum rip. The combo rips, too, on a couple of instrumentals. —*Dan Cooper*

Sings the Hits of His Country Cousins / 1962 / Razor & Tie ✦✦✦
A compilation of various performances George Jones recorded at United Artists, including album tracks, singles, and new performances, *Sings the Hits of His Country Cousins* is an entertaining hodge-podge of Jones' versions of classic country songs. There's a wide variety of styles on the album, from the Western swing of Bob Wills' "Silver Dew on the Blue Grass" and the honky tonk of Hank Williams' "I Could Never Be Ashamed" and Webb Pierce's "The Same Sweet Girl," to the pop leanings of Hank Cochran's "A Little Bitty Tear," the traditional country of Roy Acuff's "The Precious Jewel" and the country gospel of "Peace in the Valley" and "Wings of a Dove." Despite the fact that the album features songs recorded at different sessions and music that is stylistically opposed, every cut is first-rate, which makes *Sings the Hits of the Country Cousins* one of his most enjoyable, if not one of his most consequential, United Artists albums. —*Stephen Thomas Erlewine*

Homecoming in Heaven / 1962 / Razor & Tie ✦✦
Boasting a more lavish production than his secular albums, *Homecoming in Heaven* is George Jones' second collection of gospel songs. The majority of the songs on the album are newly written, including selections from Willie Nelson, J.P. Richardson (the Big Bopper), and George himself. Pappy Daily has assembled a choir to support Jones, which places the music somewhere between traditional, stripped-down country gospel and polished,

Nashville country-pop. George is in good voice throughout, but there are only two genuine classics on the album, "Wings of a Dove" and "Peace in the Valley," which are both available on Liberty's more consistent collection *All-Time Greatest Hits. —Stephen Thomas Erlewine*

My Favorites of Hank Williams / 1962 / United Artists ✦✦✦
George Jones' second tribute to Hank Williams in a matter of years, *My Favorites of Hank Williams* was originally released on United Artists in the early '60s. None of the songs on *My Favorites* were featured on George's Hank tribute on Mercury Records, but given Williams' extensive catalog, that isn't surprising. *My Favorites* does differ from the previous Mercury recordings in terms of production—the UA release is slightly smoother, yet it is still firmly in the honky tonk tradition. George doesn't put a new spin on any of these songs—which include "You Win Again," "Your Cheatin' Heart," "I Could Never Be Ashamed of You," "You're Gonna Change (Or I'm Gonna Leave)," "Mansion on the Hill"—but he delivers them with affection and grit, making the record a thoroughly enjoyable listen. —*Stephen Thomas Erlewine*

The New Favorites of George Jones / 1962 / United Artists ✦✦✦
The New Favorites of George Jones, the Possum's first album for United Artists, is a mixed bag that is highly indicative of the crossroads country music faced in the early '60s. Stylistically, *New Favorites* is all over the place, as it tries to appeal to not only Jones' hardcore honky tonk audience, but also to country-pop fans and those listeners who had been seduced by the burgeoning rock 'n' roll audience. So, honky tonk weepers like "She Once Lived Here" and "She Thinks I Still Care" sit next to uptempo country-pop cuts like "What Am I Worth" and "Imitation of Love," and that only scratches the surface of what's here. There are also folk ballads ("Open Pit Mine"), crossover attempts ("Poor Little Rich Boy," "Running Bear"), the requisite novelties ("Best Guitar Picker"), and the ridiculous "White Lightnin'" rewrite, "Root Beer." Even the dated material like the novelties and crossovers are enjoyable, but Jones is at his best when he's singing honky tonk or country-pop. Still, the wide range of material on *New Favorites* does prove that neither artists, producers, nor labels knew how to retain the splintering country audience of the '50s. —*Stephen Thomas Erlewine*

The Ballad Side of George Jones / 1963 / Mercury ✦✦✦✦
A good portrait of the later Mercury-era Jones, the title is something of a misnomer, as there are several uptempo songs. It includes several of his own compositions (notably "Glad to Let Her Go" and "The First One") and the incredible "Mr. Fool." —*George Bedard*

George Jones Sings Like the Dickens! / 1964 / United Artists ✦✦✦
Given George Jones' love for novelty songs, it isn't surprising that he recorded a tribute album to the king of country novelties, Little Jimmy Dickens. What is surprising is his approach. On *George Jones Sings Like the Dickens!* Jones bypasses all of Dickens' biggest hits, choosing to concentrate on personal favorites, which happen to be songs that Dickens interpreted, not ones that he wrote (only two of the 12 songs were co-written by Dickens). Jones realizes that although Dickens was famous for his novelties, he was a first-rate balladeer and he patterns his own album according to his idol's strengths. Jones gives a fine performance, but it's a bit too laidback to make a lasting impression. There are a handful of gems (particularly "We Could," "It Scares Me Half to Death," "Making the Rounds," and "I've Just Got to See You Once More") scattered throughout *Sings Like the Dickens!* and the album is never anything less than enjoyable, even though nothing on the record approaches the transcendent. ["It Scares Me Half to Death" and "Take Me As I Am (Or Let Me Go)" also appear on *The Race Is On.*] —*Stephen Thomas Erlewine*

Country & Western #1 Male Singer / 1964 / Mercury ✦✦✦
A fine collection of Mercury stuff with the emphasis on honky tonk, it includes "Out of Control (What Goes Wrong with the Mind of a Man in a Bar?)" and the classic "You're Still on My Mind." —*George Bedard*

Old Brush Arbors / 1965 / Musicor ✦✦✦
Old Brush Arbors features 12 country gospel songs and is notable not only for Jones' particularly strong performances but also for being one of the rare times that Jones is credited with writing more than half of the songs himself. —*Chris Woodstra*

Mr. Country & Western Music / 1965 / Musicor ✦✦✦
This early Musicor offering features "Don't You Ever Get Tired" (a great version of the Hank Cochran song) and a couple of gems written by Joe Poovey, "How Proud I Would Have Been" and the good-sport "Worst of Luck." It may be maudlin, but it'll get ya. —*George Bedard*

New Country Hits / 1965 / Musicor ✦✦✦
It includes the early Musicor hits "Love Bug" and "Things Have Gone to Pieces" plus some little-known gems like "Till I Hear from You" and "Memory Is," both co-written by Jones. The cover features the 1965 version of the Jones Boys featuring Johnny Paycheck (Donny Young) on bass and harmony vocals. —*George Bedard*

The Race Is On / 1965 / Razor & Tie ✦✦✦
The title track to *The Race Is On* is one of George Jones' biggest hits. With its galloping beat and clever, funny lyrics, the single gives the impression that the rest of the record is a return to Jones' honky tonk roots. Although there are several uptempo numbers, *The Race Is On* is dominated by ballads, like the majority of his UA albums. But *The Race Is On* boasts a stronger, more varied set of songs than most of his '60s albums, ranging from ballads like "They'll Never Take Her Love from Me," to the Western swing of "Time Changes Everything," and the skittering honky tonk of "Don't Let the Stars Get in Your Eyes." There's a couple of weak moments—ironically, one is "She's Mine," which was co-written by Jones—but the album remains one of his strongest from the mid-'60s. "It Scares Me Half to Death" and "Take Me As I Am (Or Let Me Go)" also appear on *Sings Like the Dickens!* and "Time Changes Everything" appears on *Sings Bob Wills*. —*Stephen Thomas Erlewine*

Trouble in Mind / 1965 / United Artists ✦✦✦✦
One of his best albums, there are sappy vocal choruses on some of the tunes, but they can't diminish George Jones. A few that don't—"You Done Me Wrong" (written by him) and "It's a Sin"—are among the best things he's ever recorded. Also included on this essential release are great versions of a couple of Hank Williams songs and a couple of truly definitive songs: "My Tears Are Overdue" and "Sometimes You Just Can't Win." —*George Bedard*

We Found Heaven Right Here on Earth at "4033" / 1966 / Musicor ✦✦✦
We Found Heaven Right Here on Earth at "4033" includes the haunting "From Here to the Door" and "Developing My Pictures." —*George Bedard*

I'm a People / 1966 / Musicor ✦✦✦
One of the more consistent Musicor offerings, it features a good mix of uptempo honky tonk and novelty ("I'm a People," "Ship of Love," and "Blindfold of Love"), ballads (the eerie "The Lonely Know My Secret"), and sacred songs ("If You Believe" and "Old Brush Arbors"). —*George Bedard*

Love Bug / 1966 / Musicor ✦✦✦✦
A couple of Jones' hits—the title song and "Things Have Gone to Pieces"—are included, plus Jones' versions of hits by other artists—"Six Days on the Road" (Dave Dudley), "Strangers" (Merle Haggard), and more. Highlights include "Blue Side of Lonesome" and "Unfaithful Man." —*George Bedard*

Walk through This World with Me / 1967 / Musicor ✦✦✦
Included is the hit title song, plus Jones' versions of hits by others, "Almost Persuaded" and a great version of "Lonely Street." —*George Bedard*

The Young George Jones / 1967 / United Artists ✦✦✦
Included are re-recordings of some of his old Starday tunes, a couple of great Hank Williams covers, and a great version of Ted Daffan's "Worried Mind." —*George Bedard*

George Jones

George Jones & Melba Montgomery / 1968 / Deluxe ✦✦✦
These are great duets with Tennessee beauty Melba Montgomery—her voice suits Jones' better than Wynette's. It includes the eerie "Long as We're Dreaming" and "Long Walk off a Tall Rock." Lots of dobro; it's not for the countrypolitan. —*George Bedard*

If My Heart Had Windows / 1968 / Musicor ✦✦✦
After some experimentation (both failed and successful) at Musicor, George returned for a more-or-less straight honky tonk album with *If My Heart Had Windows*. Though the record boasts his typical overblown late 60s production, it's kept in check for the most part. Two Top Ten hits—the title track and "Say It's Not You"—are included on the record, as well as the classic "Your Angel Steps Out of Heaven" and the quirky album closer "Poor Chinee." —*Chris Woodstra*

Sings the Songs of Dallas Frazier / 1968 / Musicor ✦✦✦✦
Since his beginnings at Musicor, George Jones covered countless songs by Dallas Frazier—Frazier's songs would frequently occupy more than half of an album—so an entire album devoted to his songwriting comes as no surprise. And while the big production numbers, complete with backup by the Jordanaires, may put off some country purists, the album serves as a true testament to both the singer and the songwriter. In light of the label's constant recycling and repackaging of material, the most surprising thing about this record is that none of the songs have appeared on any previous albums. —*Chris Woodstra*

I'll Share My World with You / 1969 / Musicor ✦✦✦
A couple of Jones' best mid-'60s honky tonk songs are included: "Heartaches & Hangovers" and "Do What You Think's Best." Tammy Wynette is on the cover. —*George Bedard*

Where Grass Won't Grow / 1969 / Musicor ✦✦✦
The title song is a big production number about the wretchedness of unsuccessful dirt farming. Other depressing highlights include "Old Blue Tomorrow" about approaching death, and "For Better or for Worse (But Not for Long)" (self-explanatory). —*George Bedard*

Book of Memories / United Artists ✦✦✦
The haunting title tune is included, plus "There's No Justice" and one of Jones' best drinking laments, "Warm Red Wine." —*George Bedard*

Will You Visit Me on Sunday? / 1970 / Musicor ✦✦
When people criticize Jones' Musicor recordings for over-the-top arrangements and intrusive, sappy, vocal choruses, they're probably thinking of albums like this one. Released during Jones' last year at Musicor, *Will You Visit Me on Sunday* doesn't sound like a country album. In fact it doesn't even *look* like a country

album—the cover shows a seductive model and spells out the title in neo-psychedelic, wavy orange print. While *Will You Visit Me on Sunday* lacked hits and its sound may have represented a new peak in slick production for Jones, the songs on the album (many of which were written by Dallas Frazier) are all top-notch. Jones' voice has never sounded this confident and his overall approach on this album serves as a blueprint for his '70s work on Epic. —*Chris Woodstra*

Best of [Musicor] / 1970 / Musicor ✦✦✦

This fine package features George Jones tracks from his Musicor output. The only complaint about this record is that it's too short. One standout on this record is "Your Angel Steps Out," which Gram Parsons later covered. —*Jim Worbois*

The Great Songs of Leon Payne / 1971 / Musicor ✦✦✦✦

One of many songbook albums that George Jones recorded while at Musicor Records, *The Great Songs of Leon Payne* is one of the finest minor gems in the Possum's catalog. Though Payne's reputation as a terrific honky tonk songwriter was well-known among country music fans, he only had a handful of hits, which were often recorded by other artists. Granted, the biggest of those were Hank Williams' versions of "Lost Highway" and "They'll Never Take Her Love from Me" as well as Payne's own "I Love You Because," but the depth of his songwriting is not well-known to many casual country fans. George Jones' tribute album remedies that fact. Apart from "They'll Never Take Her Love from Me" and Jones' hit single "Things Have Gone to Pieces," these songs are all rather obscure and there's not a bad one in the bunch. From ballads like "Blue Side of Lonesome" to uptempo honky tonkers like "Brothers of a Bottle," all of the cuts on *The Great Songs of Leon Payne* are first-rate and Jones brings each of them to life. It's a forgotten album in Jones' catalog—and Leon Payne's reputation has faded somewhat in the decades following his death—but that doesn't change the fact that *The Great Songs of Leon Payne* is one of Jones' best records of the '60s. —*Stephen Thomas Erlewine*

☆ **George Jones with Love** / 1971 / Musicor ✦✦✦✦✦

By 1970, George Jones' stay at Musicor had been marked by a glut of sloppy releases that continually repackaged and repeated his material into different thematically based "concept" albums. Initially it seemed that *George Jones with Love*, with its all-love-based-songs lineup, would fall into this disposable category. One listen, however, shows this to be an exception to the rule. Beginning with the wonderful "A Good Year for the Roses" (one of Jones' all-time greatest performances) he tackles affairs of the heart from all directions—from the joy and excitement of newfound love to the warmth of a settled relationship to the pain and despair of separation and its aftermath. He's clearly focused on each song, pouring the proper emotion and passion into each performance. It still may not be a "concept album" by rock 'n' roll standards, but it does serve as a high point for Jones' Musicor period and as one of his greatest, most consistent albums. —*Chris Woodstra*

The Best of Sacred Music / 1971 / Musicor ✦✦✦✦

Country-gospel classics like "I'll Fly Away" are included, plus a great song co-written by Jones, "Small Time Laboring Man." Highly recommended, it also includes "Family Bible." —*George Bedard*

We Go Together / 1971 / Epic ✦✦✦

Jones made his debut for Epic with *We Go Together*, his first duet album with his wife Tammy Wynette. Recorded only three years into their marriage, the album focuses on the joys of their love and has an optimistic eye toward the future—chapter one of the soap opera the two would commit to vinyl over the next several years. The two redo three songs from Jones' catalog—"Take Me" (a Top Ten hit both times), "Never Grow Cold," and "A Girl I Used to Know" (retitled as "Someone I Used to Know"). —*Chris Woodstra*

George Jones (We Can Make It) / 1972 / Epic ✦✦✦

Jones' first solo outing for Epic in 1972 is a rough concept album built around his optimism and joy about his marriage to Tammy Wynette, even though cracks were beginning to show in their relationship. Jones' voice sounds mature, settled and smooth—a

perfect combination with Billy Sherrill's decidedly non-country, slick production style. —*Chris Woodstra*

Me and the First Lady / 1972 / Epic ✦✦✦

The second chapter in the George and Tammy saga still finds the couple pretty happy, settling into a mostly imaginary domestic life. Not all is well though, as told in "A Lovely Place to Cry" and "The Great Divide," which contemplate fading love and the possibility of divorce. The two continue to hold on, still in love, and even go as far as to re-create their wedding ceremony in the album closer, "The Ceremony," seemingly to reaffirm their vows. —*Chris Woodstra*

We Love to Sing about Jesus / 1972 / Razor & Tie ✦✦

George Jones and Tammy Wynette had both made fine gospel records as solo artists, but when it came time to record their first gospel record together, they failed to come up with something memorable. Overproduced, overwrought and underwritten, *We Love to Sing about Jesus* is largely comprised of songs by Elizabeth Montgomery, with the rest of the album devoted to contemporary country gospel by the likes of Dallas Frazier and Tom T. Hall. Billy Sherrill's trademark grandiose productions are made even bigger by the presence of the Jordanaires and the Nashville Edition on backing vocals. Though the production is overbearing, it would be forgivable if more than a handful of songs—namely, the single "Old Fashioned Singing," the sing-along title track, and Hall's "Me and Jesus"—were memorable. Instead, the songs are almost entirely mediocre and forgettable, making the production the only noticeable thing about the album. Though the album is short, the bombastic production becomes a little nerve-wracking about halfway through the album, and by the end of the record, the music hasn't provided much inspiration. In all, a wasted opportunity. —*Stephen Thomas Erlewine*

Nothing Ever Hurt Me / 1973 / Epic ✦✦✦

Aside from the title track (which was a hit), this album is full of songs that could be hits. Jones' version of "Mom and Dad's Waltz" is easily as good as Lefty's. —*Jim Worbois*

We're Gonna Hold On / 1973 / Epic ✦✦

Only the album cover—two separate, non-smiling photos of George and Tammy partially overlapping each other—and a handful of the tracks attempt to directly tell the story of their dissolving marriage on this, their fourth duet album. Far more telling is the inclusion of rather disjointed crowd pleasers like "Roll in My Sweet Baby's Arms" and the semi-novelty hit "(We're Not) The Jet Set." By this point, the two had become a part of the touring machine and the album seems to be built around a stage show. The songs, outside of the title track (a No. 1 hit), aren't particularly memorable. —*Chris Woodstra*

The Grand Tour / 1974 / Epic ✦✦✦

The Grand Tour is arguably the peak achievement of George Jones and Billy Sherrill in the early '70s. By the time the album was recorded, Sherrill had moved Jones' distinctive ballad styles into a more commercial setting, complete with strings, layered guitars and pianos, and even sound effects. Though the pair had recorded several classic singles in the two years preceding *The Grand Tour*, the album was the culmination of this lavish production style. There are very few weak spots on the record, and the best material—the epic title track, the heart-tugging "Once You've Had the Best," and the wonderful "She Told Me So"—are genuine showstoppers, demonstrating not only Jones' rich voice, but also Sherrill's grandly textured production. And it's not just the ballads that cut deep; novelties like "The Weatherman" and the blazing anti-gossip tirade "Our Private Life" also make a lasting impression. *The Grand Tour* is a consistently engaging, always entertaining album and one of Jones' best records of the '70s. —*Stephen Thomas Erlewine*

Battle / 1976 / Epic ✦✦✦

This is a good solid country album as only George Jones can do it. So often liner notes are more hype than fact, but the notes Emmylou Harris provides accurately sum up this record and much of the magic of George Jones. —*Jim Worbois*

Alone Again / 1976 / Epic ✦✦✦

The classic cover—a picture of George alone in a diner, staring forlornly at his milkshake—pretty much sums up the feeling of this *Alone Again*, a low-key, morning-after look at regret and loneliness. As always, Jones sings from the heart and from his own real-life experiences dealing with the aftermath of his failed marriage. Despite a generally depressive mood, Jones pulls off one of his greatest novelty songs, "Her Name Is . . . ," one of only a handful of hits he managed during his mid-'70s slump. —*Chris Woodstra*

Greatest Hits [George Jones & Tammy Wynette] / 1977 / Epic ✦✦✦✦

The President and First Lady take one of country music's great tabloid love affairs into the studio. Included is "Golden Ring," "Take Me," and "(We're Not) The Jet Set" ("we're the . . . Jones and Wynette set"). —*Dan Cooper*

Bartender's Blues / 1978 / Epic ✦✦

Recorded at the height of the rock 'n' roll establishment's infatuation with George Jones in the late '70s, *Bartender's Blues* is one of the most uneven and misdirected albums in his catalog. Though the production is dated, leaning too close to soft-rock with its electric pianos, the main flaw of the album is the material. Apart from the excellent weeper "I'll Just Take It out in Love," the strongest song is the forced title track, which is essentially James Taylor's impression of what life in a honky tonk must be. The remaining songs don't deal in such hackneyed cliches, but they don't have the same melodic force, either. That means that the album becomes just a wash of songs, despite Jones' fine performance. —*Stephen Thomas Erlewine*

The Best of George Jones [Epic] / 1978 / Epic ✦✦✦✦

Most of the best mid-'70s production numbers—"The Door," "The Grand Tour," and "These Days I Barely Got By" are included, plus the all-time great performance, "A Picture of Me without You." —*George Bedard*

My Very Special Guests / 1979 / Epic ✦✦✦

Jones duets with some expected country contemporaries (Tammy Wynette, Johnny Paycheck), some outlaws (Waylon Jennings, Willie Nelson), and, most interestingly, some up-and-coming and pop-oriented guests (Emmylou Harris, Linda Ronstadt, Elvis Costello), often to beneficial effect. —*William Ruhlmann*

Greatest Hits, Vol. 2 [Epic] / 197 / Epic ✦✦✦

Some of the most popular duets from this former husband-and-wife team: "The World Needs Melody," "We Go Together," "Two Story House," and more. —*AMG*

I Am What I Am / 1980 / Epic ✦✦✦✦

I Am What I Am announced that George Jones had officially returned to form artistically, and it became his biggest hit album ever. It's easy to see why—the production is commercial without being slick, the songs are balanced between aching ballads and restrained honky tonk numbers, and Jones gives a nuanced, moving performance. "He Stopped Loving Her Today," "I'm Not Ready Yet," and "If Drinkin' Don't Kill Me (Her Memory Will)" are the hits, but the remaining seven album tracks are exceptionally strong, without a weak track in the bunch. It's mature country, both in the laidback approach and subject matter, but that doesn't mean it's dull—like the best country music, these are lived-in songs that are simple, direct, and emotionally powerful, even with the smooth production. *I Am What I Am* is the sound of George Jones at his peak and is the highlight of his later years. —*Stephen Thomas Erlewine*

Together Again / 1980 / Razor & Tie ✦✦✦

Recorded just as George Jones was beginning his remarkable early '80s comeback, the George and Tammy reunion album *Together Again* doesn't have the spark of some of their earlier duets, but it has its share of fine moments. Both of the singers sound terrific, particularly on the hit singles "Two Story House" and "A Pair of Old Sneakers." Even when the material isn't up to their talents, the duo sounds recharged, which makes *Together Again* a thoroughly enjoyable, if inconsistent, listen. —*Stephen Thomas Erlewine*

Double Trouble / 1980 / Razor & Tie ✦

At the time *Double Trouble* was recorded, George Jones was enjoying the attention of hip rock 'n' rollers, thanks to a glowing article in *Rolling Stone*. Jones and Billy Sherrill decided to make the most of his new rock audience, as evidenced by the presence of James Taylor on the previous year's *Bartender's Blues*. But their attempts to court the rock audience came to fruition with *Double Trouble*, recorded as a duet album with Johnny Paycheck. Primarily consisting of '50s rock 'n' roll covers—"Maybelline," "Along Came Jones," "Roll over Beethoven," etc.—the arrangements are flat, lifeless, and overproduced, featuring an overbearing chorus of female supporting vocalists. That's not to say that Jones and Paycheck are mellow. The pair sound as if they were on one of their notorious drinking and drugging binges, making jokes with each other throughout every song (except the closing "You Better Move On") and singing without regard to key. There is a bizarre fascination in hearing the duo so completely out of their heads, but it is an embarrassing record, particularly since it illustrates that Jones and Sherrill had no idea why a rock audience would be attracted to Jones' music. It's easily the worst album Jones ever recorded. —*Stephen Thomas Erlewine*

Still the Same Ole Me / 1981 / Epic ✦✦✦

Recorded at the peak of his popularity, this album is sometimes restrained, and sometimes finds Jones at his uncontrollable best. Though predominantly honky tonk ballads, the best cuts (besides the obvious hits) include: "Good Ones and Bad Ones," "Together Alone," and the raucous "You Can't Get the Hell out of Texas." —*Tom Roland*

Encore: George Jones & Tammy Wynette / 1981 / Epic ✦✦✦✦

One album in an entire series of greatest-hits releases for CBS artists, this package documents the very best singles by George Jones and Tammy Wynette, an act that was once country music's top running soap opera. The sad hitch in Wynette's voice, and the greasy slides in the Possum's make for an interesting contrast. They sound just as good after their 1975 breakup ("Golden Ring," "Two Story House") as before ("We're Gonna Hold On," "Near You"). —*Tom Roland*

★ **Anniversary: Ten Years of Hits** / 1982 / Epic ✦✦✦✦✦

This covers the first ten years of Jones' two-decade association with Epic Records and, more importantly, record producer Billy Sherrill. Owing much to Sherrill's knack for locating quality material, the hits range from amusing ("Nothing Ever Hurt Me," "Her Name Is . . . ") to morbid ("He Stopped Loving Her Today") to classic ("The Grand Tour," "A Picture of Me without You"). Best cuts include "Bartender's Blues," "The Door," and "Still Doin' Time." —*Tom Roland*

Ladies' Choice / 1984 / Epic ✦✦

Conceptually linked to *My Special Guests, Ladies' Choice* is a collection of duets with country music's biggest female stars of the time, including Janie Fricke, Barbara Mandrell, Lacy J. Dalton, Deborah Allen, and Emmylou Harris. Though the liner notes claim that Jones personally selected his partners for these recordings, more than likely this was a marketing decision to pair the old-school singer with the up-and-coming country ladies of the '80s. The album did have two moderate hits ("Hallelujah, I Love You So" and "Size Seven Round [Made of Gold]") but rarely does this album hit anything above average. —*Chris Woodstra*

White Lightning [ACE] / 1984 / Ace ✦✦✦✦

Uptempo material from the Starday and Mercury eras, it includes the rockabilly experiments from Starday. —*George Bedard*

The Lone Star Legend / 1985 / Ace ✦✦✦✦

Mostly Mercury material, this also includes a couple of Starday cuts. Emphasis is on the ballads, including previously unissued songs. The great "Hearts in My Dreams" is included, and the incredible "Mr. Fool" is one of the most masterful pieces of country singing ever recorded. Along with *White Lightnin',* this is a good portrait of the '50s Jones. —*George Bedard*

Burn the Honky-Tonk Down / 1986 / Rounder ✦✦✦✦

A good collection of songs from the Musicor era are included, such as the beautiful and hard-to-find "Beneath Still Waters." The liner notes go to great length to carp about the overproduction of

Jones' records over the years. Ironically, some of the more elaborate Musicor productions such as "Good Year for the Roses" are included here. A bit too much is made of this—fans of '60s mainstream country learn how to tune out sappy vocal choruses and such. In any case, this and the other Rounder selection, *Heartaches & Hangovers*, have the great advantage of including stuff from Jones' peak period that may actually be available for purchase. —*George Bedard*

Live at Dancetown U.S.A. / 1987 / Ace ✦✦✦✦
There have been very few live recordings of George Jones, particularly of his early years, which makes *Live at Dance Town USA* so valuable. Recorded in June of 1965, the compact disc features 26 tracks—including nine songs performed by Jones' supporting vocalist Don Adams—that capture Jones running through his biggest hits, plus a couple of left-field covers like "Bony Moronie" and "Jole Blon." Jones is wired and energetic, breathing fire into the songs; one of the biggest joys of the entire disc is his between-song patter, such as when he tells the audience that he's taking a "liquor-mission" halfway through the set. Not only is the music superb—on this date, the Jones Boys featured steel guitarist Buddy Emmons and Cajun fiddler Rufus Thibideaux—but it illustrates exactly what a honky tonk concert was like in the '60s. For hardcore George Jones fans, it's an essential addition, one that's revelatory and highly entertaining. —*Stephen Thomas Erlewine*

Super Hits / 1987 / Epic ✦✦✦
George Jones and Tammy Wynette's *Super Hits* contains the bulk of the duo's biggest hits, including "The Ceremony," "We're Gonna Hold On," "Golden Ring," "Southern California," "Two Story House," and "(We're Not) The Jet Set." It's not a thorough retropective, but it's a nice ten-track sampler that is only missing a couple necessary items, namely "Take Me," "We Loved It Away," "Near You" and "A Pair of Old Sneakers." —*Stephen Thomas Erlewine*

Don't Stop the Music / 1987 / Ace ✦✦✦✦
The most extensive look at Jones' early Starday and Mercury recordings available, *Don't Stop the Music* is a perfect complement to Rhino's collection. The disc's 22 tracks document the formative years (1954-61) where Jones grew from a Hank Williams soundalike to one of the most distinctive voices in country music. Essential listening worth seeking out. Import only. —*Chris Woodstra*

One Woman Man / Feb. 1989 / Epic ✦✦✦
One of Jones' best Epic albums, this succeeds despite two previously released songs being tagged on to fill it out. One of those is "Radio Lover," a bizarre tale of adultery. Things get even stranger with "Ya Ba Da Ba Do (So Are You)," in which Jones gets drunk and talks to a Fred Flintstone glass and an Elvis Presley wine decanter (it also sparked legal action by Hanna-Barbera). Beyond that, it's quality Jones honky tonk and weepers, including a first-rate remake of "Just out of Reach (Of My Two Empty Arms)." —*Brian Mansfield*

Heartaches & Hangovers / Rounder ✦✦✦✦
An excellent collection of some of Jones' best Musicor sides, this features some of the best country singing ever recorded by anyone. The liner notes do an excellent job of describing Jones' style and importance. —*George Bedard*

Mr. Country Music / 198 / Classic Country ✦✦
Mr. Country Music offers a basic 18-track collection of Jones' Musicor recordings. While the occasional re-recording creeps onto the disc, the real downfall of this compilation is the muffled sound and tape dropouts throughout the disc. The three non-hits included ("I'm Wasting Good Paper," "Say It's Not You," "My Favorite Lies") are a nice change, but that's not enough to recommend the disc to anyone but Musicor-starved fans. —*Chris Woodstra*

Greatest Country Hits / 1990 / Curb ✦✦
Greatest Country Hits is a budget-line, 11-track CD covering Jones' biggest hits for United Artists, all presented in their original recordings. While this collection does a fair job, subsequent reissues have made this largely unnecessary. It is notable for the inclusion of "You Comb Her Hair," a No. 5 hit in 1963 that is unavailable on the other UA collections. —*Chris Woodstra*

Friends in High Places / 1991 / Epic ✦✦✦
This album features duets with some of country's biggest stars, including Buck Owens, Emmylou Harris, Vern Gosdin, Randy Travis, Charlie Daniels, Ricky Van Shelton, and others. —*AMG*

☆ **The Best of George Jones, Vol. 1: Hardcore Honky Tonk** / 1991 / Mercury ✦✦✦✦✦
The Best of George Jones, Vol. 1: Hardcore Honky Tonk collects 20 tracks from his early recordings for Mercury, including classics like "Why Baby Why," "Color of the Blues," "The Window up Above," "Aching, Breaking Heart," "Just One More," and "Tall Tall Trees." As the title implies, the music here *is* hardcore honky tonk, capturing Jones at the peak of his powers as a gritty juke joint vocalist. On a few songs, it's possible to hear the beginnings of his signature ballad style, but there are no strings apart from fiddles, no legatos outside of the steel guitar. *The Best of George Jones, Vol. 1: Hardcore Honky Tonk* is the best-single disc collection of Jones' breakthrough singles and the best introduction to the first part of Jones' long career. —*Stephen Thomas Erlewine*

★ **The Best of 1955-1967** / 1991 / Rhino ✦✦✦✦✦
The 18-track *The Best of 1955-1967* is a good overview of George Jones' early career, containing most of the necessary hits from his first decade or so of hits. It's skewed toward his Mercury hits, featuring everything from "Why Baby Why" to "Aching Breaking Heart," picking up "Just One More," "The Window up Above," and "Tender Years" along the way. Five wisely chosen United Artists tracks are featured, as are four Musicor tracks. It doesn't have every hit from '55-'67, but *The Best Of* does contain every truly necessary song Jones recorded during that time. —*Stephen Thomas Erlewine*

And Along Came Jones / 1991 / MCA ✦✦
Jones ended a long association with Epic and producer Billy Sherrill in 1990 when he jumped ship to MCA and producer Kyle Lehning. His MCA debut wasn't a masterpiece, but it was stronger than almost everything he'd done in the '80s. The abandoned house in "Where the Tall Grass Grows" is yet another symbol for Jones' unchecked memories, and the Post-it Notes in "You Couldn't Get the Picture" are the kind of trivial detail he loves. The Cajun remake of "You Done Me Wrong" (co-written in 1960 with Ray Price) works, and the only moment of true silliness is "Heckel and Jeckel." —*Brian Mansfield*

Walls Can Fall / 1992 / MCA ✦✦✦
"Wrong's What I Do Best," Jones sings in one song from *Walls Can Fall*, and listening to the album you almost believe he's telling the truth. Jones makes the same albums he's always made; two producers (this time Emory Gordy, Jr.) since Billy Sherrill have failed to do more than decrease the number of novelty songs and tune up Jones' sound, which is still defined by low piano melodies and sawing fiddle. Jones continues to play off his legend: Songs like "I Don't Need Your Rockin' Chair," "Drive Me to Drink," and a cover of Merle Haggard's "The Bottle Let Me Down" sound scarier because of Jones' past. The thing is, wrong isn't what Jones does best. What Jones does best is consequences, which is why "There's the Door" sounds more emotionally devastating than anything else here. —*Brian Mansfield*

High-Tech Redneck / 1993 / MCA ✦✦
George Jones' third MCA album is a ten-track, pure country outing. Despite the digital sound and short running time (less than 32 minutes), it is produced in classic fiddle/steel instrumental glory. Jones sounds steely on the title cut, and such songs as "I've Still Got Some Hurtin' Left to Do" and "Tear Me Out of the Picture" are the type of earnest, unsophisticated heartache songs that define country. He concludes things with a tribute to the departed Conway Twitty, an urgent "Hello Darlin'" that rivals any version Twitty ever issued. —*Ron Wynn*

The Bradley Barn Sessions / 1994 / MCA ✦✦
The concept behind *The Bradley Barn Sessions* was an intriguing one: Place George Jones in the hands of traditionalist country producer Brian Ahern, record at Owen Bradley's legendary studios, compile a selection of Jones' greatest hits and have him sing duets with contemporary vocalists (and Tammy Wynette) that have cited him as an influence. In theory, it should have worked, but in

practice, it's a stilted, nearly lifeless album. The production is too clean and polished, lacking any of the grit of true honky tonk records. Furthermore, songs like "A Good Year for the Roses" suffer from the stringless, stripped-down arrangements. And although all of Jones' duet partners—including Marty Stuart, Alan Jackson, Vince Gill, Ricky Skaggs, Trisha Yearwood, and Travis Tritt—are respectful, only Keith Richards captures the spirit of a roadside honky tonk. —*Stephen Thomas Erlewine*

☆ **Cup of Loneliness: The Mercury Years** / 1994 / Mercury ✦✦✦✦✦
Jones was still developing his style on the earliest tracks of *Cup of Loneliness*, but this is the music that established him as one of the great vocalists of the 20th century, country or otherwise. *Cup of Loneliness* gathers together most of his Mercury recordings, as well as several highlights from his time at Starday. These recordings feature Jones at his purest—no strings, no backing vocals, only pure honky tonk. At the beginning of the double-disc set, traces of Hank Williams can be detected in Jones' vocals, but by the end of the first disc, Jones had become one of the most distinctive and popular country vocalists. His classic ballad style doesn't begin to develop until the end of the second disc. Mercury released two different versions of *Cup of Loneliness*—a standard two-disc set in a jewel box and a collector's edition that features extra songs; naturally, most fans will want the songs on the collector's edition, simply because they were recorded at a peak in Jones' career. —*Stephen Thomas Erlewine*

★ **The Spirit of Country: The Essential George Jones** / 1994 / Epic/Legacy ✦✦✦✦✦
As the only collection that draws from all the labels George Jones recorded for—only his later recordings for MCA are missing—the double-disc set *The Spirit of Country: The Essential George Jones* is clearly a fine introduction to his prolific careeer. Since it was released on Epic/Legacy, it does favor the Billy Sherrill-produced '70s and '80s recordings. However, it also contains a majority of the truly essential items from Starday, Mercury, United Artists, and Musicor. From "Why Baby Why" to "A Good Year for the Roses," most of his classic '50s and '60s songs are on the first disc, as are his first classic Epic recordings, "We Can Make It," "A Picture of Me (Without You)," and "The Grand Tour." The second disc is devoted to his '70s and '80s hits, adding greater detail to the ground *Anniversary* already covered. Although the set doesn't give his early, hardcore honky tonk recordings the proper showcase, *The Spirit of Country* is a necessary purchase—there is simply no better way to get acquainted with Jones' catalog and all of the twists and turns of his career. —*Stephen Thomas Erlewine*

All-Time Greatest Hits [UA] / 1994 / Liberty ✦✦✦
All-Time Greatest Hits is culled from George Jones' United Artists recordings. During these years, he had two of his definitive hits—"She Thinks I Still Care" and "The Race Is On"—but it was largely a transition period for Jones, as this entertaining but scatter-shot collection shows. Not all of his hits from his UA recordings are included—particularly the No. 3 "A Girl I Used to Know" and the No. 5 "You Comb Her Hair," which are featured on Rhino's *The Best of 1955-1967*—and several of the songs here weren't hits and don't deserve to be included, particularly his version of "Running Bear." Still, the album gives a good sense of his time at the label and contains the great majority of his hits of the early '60s. —*Stephen Thomas Erlewine*

White Lightning / 1994 / Drive Archive ✦
Based on the track listing, it would seem that *White Lightning*, which boasts 14 tracks mainly from now woefully scarce Musicor years, would be an essential collection. Unfortunately, this disc is marred by horrible sound and inferior re-recordings best exemplified by "A Good Year for the Roses," one of the many remakes/alternate takes that sound like Jones is singing under water. A handful of the songs are indeed original versions but it's not enough to make up for the low points. —*Chris Woodstra*

One / 1995 / MCA ✦✦
More of a trip down memory lane than an album, *One* is the long-awaited reunion album by George Jones and Tammy Wynette, their first in 15 years. It's a pleasant listen, with both George and Tammy in fine voice. The problem is that much of the material is often indifferent—there are a few fine songs, particu-

larly the title track and a lament about modern country radio called "They're Playing Our Song," but many of the songs fail to make an impression either way. The main pleasure of the record is hearing George and Tammy together again, after all these years, but if *One* is judged by their previous efforts, it looks rather thin. —*Stephen Thomas Erlewine*

George Jones & Gene Pitney / 1995 / Bear Family ✦✦✦✦
When George Jones left United Artists to join Musicor in 1965, it was decided that he would start off with a duet recording session with teen idol (and labelmate) Gene Pitney. The session resulted in two duet albums—*George Jones & Gene Pitney* and *It's Country Time Again*—as well as a solo country album by Pitney, *The Country Side of Gene Pitney*. Bear Family's *George Jones & Gene Pitney* collects the 31 songs recorded during these sessions. For a seemingly unlikely pairing, the two complemented each other well, with Pitney proving himself not only a fan of the genre but also a competent country singer as well. Though only two hits came from the albums ("Love Bug" and the brilliant "Thing Have Gone to Pieces"—the latter absent from this collection for some reason), this disc captures some truly inspired moments by both artists. In light of the scarcity of good CD collections of George Jones' Musicor recordings, this disc is essential to anyone who wants a complete picture of Jones' career. —*Chris Woodstra*

Vintage Collection Series / Jan. 23, 1996 / Capitol ✦✦✦✦
Vintage collects nearly all of George Jones and Melba Montgomery's duets for United Artists. These songs, originally released on *What's in Our Hearts* and *Bluegrass Hootenanny*, illustrate how well-suited the pair was for each other—there may be a couple of weak songs, but there are no weak performances. In fact, *Vintage* makes a good argument that Montgomery was Jones' best duet partner. —*Stephen Thomas Erlewine*

I Lived to Tell It All / Aug. 13, 1996 / MCA ✦✦✦
A companion piece to his best-selling autobiography of the same name, *I Lived to Tell It All* is a surprising return to form by George Jones. Where *The Bradley Barn Sessions* tried to be an authentic release in the vein of a Hightone record and where *High-Tech Redneck* was clueless in its calculation, *I Lived to Tell It All* is an effortless encapsulation of Jones' gifts. There are honky tonk raveups, heart-tugging barroom weepers, and, best of all, several novelty songs that rank among the most clever and self-deprecating that Jones has ever recorded. Those that were seeking the pseudo-gritty production of *The Bradley Barn Sessions* may be discouraged by the slicker sound of *I Lived to Tell It All*, but there's no denying that Jones sounds recharged and energetic—he's getting a genuine kick singing these songs, which are all loosely auto-biographical. In terms of content and performance, it's his best record since *I Am What I Am*. —*Stephen Thomas Erlewine*

White Lightnin' [Classic Sound] / Classic Sound ✦✦
Not to be confused with the Drive Archive release or the classic hit of the same name, *White Lightning* collects 15 Musicor recordings. Most of the tracks are original takes, yet they sound muddy at times. A few of the songs are anemic re-recordings but overall, this collection stands out due to its interesting selection of songs. The back cover may get the sequencing wrong, but the non-hit material included on *White Lighning* makes it a disc to own for obsessive Jones collectors biding their time until his Musicor catalog is handled properly. —*Chris Woodstra*

20 Great Country Hits / Woodford Music ✦✦
Combining a couple of United Artist re-recordings (probably done after signing to Musicor) and a basic selection of Musicor hits, *20 Great Country Hits* continues the trend of using bad tape sources, inferior takes, lifeless re-recordings, and odd mixes. While some of the songs are originals or at least close versions, two of his finest songs—"Things Have Gone to Pieces" and "Once a Day"—are completely slaughtered by the poor re-recordings. —*Chris Woodstra*

20 Greatest Hits / Deluxe ✦✦✦
Jones' Musicor recordings have been criminally mistreated through the years with a flood of rip-off collections filled with muddy re-recordings. The budget-priced *20 Greatest* isn't a per-

fect collection, but there are a lot worse. The disc consists mainly of re-recordings, but at least they seem to come from the same time period as the originals, and the sound isn't too bad. In addition to the Musicor material, his early hit "Why Baby Why" is included in its original form, although the sound is bad. —Chris Woodstra

Golden Hits / Hollywood ♦♦

Hollywood's shoddy packaging of George Jones is notorious, but Golden Hits is one of the company's better efforts. The quality of the recordings is fairly good, though a close listen reveals a few instances of vinyl sources, and the re-recordings are not bad ("I'll Follow You on up to Our Cloud" and "Walk through This World with Me" seem to be the only originals). Golden Hits only features ten tracks, but there are much worse Jones budget-line collections on the market. —Chris Woodstra

Grandpa Jones (Louis Marshall Jones)

b. Oct. 20, 1913, Niagra, KY

Banjo, Guitar, Vocals / Old-Time, Traditional Country, Country Humor

Louis Marshall "Grandpa" Jones was one person who aged right into his makeup. Like his appearance, however, his actual background and role in country music were deceptive, and more complex than they seemed. Beginning in the 1920s, he started attracting attention with his boisterous performing style, old-time banjo playing, and powerful singing, and by the 1940s, with hits like "Rattler" and "Mountain Dew," he began receiving national attention. He joined the Grand Ole Opry in 1946, and remained there throughout his career; in the 1960s, with hits like "T for Texas," he continued making a place for himself on the country charts, and as a regular on Hee Haw since its inception in 1969, he became a television celebrity. But Jones' influence went much further than that chain of successes would indicate—he was almost single-handedly responsible for keeping the banjo alive as a country music instrument during the 1930s and 1940s, and in addition to his own work and songs, he was an important associate and collaborator of Merle Travis.

Jones was born in Niagra, KY, and grew up not in the mountains or the countryside, as one would gather from his music, but in industrial Ohio and Kentucky, living in factory towns. His father was a fiddle player, and his mother was a ballad singer. He listened to a lot of radio growing up, especially the National Barn Dance out of Chicago, and his strongest influences included old-time country music and gospel songs, as well as the music of Jimmie Rodgers, which led him to begin yodeling. In 1929 at the age of 18 he received radio play as "The Young Singer of Old Songs." Later on he moved to Chicago teamed with "Bashful Harmonica Joe," and appeared on the Lum and Abner show. During the mid-1930s, he started working with Bradley Kincaid, the man who gave Jones the "Grandpa" moniker, a result of his grouchy moods during their early morning radio broadcasts—Jones thought the name worked, and adopted makeup to match. Coupled with his skills as a comedian and raconteur, the image was a natural. Jones moved to Boston along with Kincaid, where their brand of country music proved extremely popular among rural New Englanders.

As a solo act later in the 1930s, Jones had radio shows on numerous stations from West Virginia and Connecticut to Cincinnati, where he sang folk ballads and more old-time country ballads, as well as gospel songs. He also learned to play the banjo, and made it an integral part of his act at a time when the instrument had all but vanished from country music; it was the combination of Jones' old-time repertory and humor that helped to keep the banjo alive as a viable, popular country instrument. Jones later hooked up with Alton and Rabon Delmore and Merle Travis, and played with them throughout World War II as Brown's Ferry Four. He and Travis also became the first artists to record for the newly founded King label, under the name of the Shepherd Brothers. Jones' own earliest solo records were also done for King during this period, among them "It's Raining Here This Morning," "Eight More Miles to Louisville," "Rattler," and "Mountain Dew."

Those singles brought Grandpa Jones to national attention, and he was poised for the next step in his career, a move to Nashville. Before relocating, however, he married Ramona Riggins, who became not only his wife but his accompanist on fiddle and mandolin. In 1946, he began playing on the Grand Ole Opry and touring with acts such as Lonzo and Oscar and Cowboy Copas. He didn't stay in Nashville too long at first, moving to Lorton, VA, and a radio show in Arlington, and later on the Old Dominion Barn Dance in Richmond. Finally, he returned to Nashville as a regular member of the Opry. Jones recorded with King Records from 1945 until 1952, when he moved to RCA-Victor, where he remained for four years, recording both traditional-sounding country and topical songs ("I'm No Communist").

In 1956, he began a six-year stint on Decca Records, recording a total of 16 songs including the talking blues country hit "The All-American Boy" in 1959. Jones moved to Fred Foster's Monument Records in 1962, and had a Top Five country hit the following year with "T for Texas." His career during the 1960s continued uninterrupted, and in 1969 he joined the cast of the new country music/comedy showcase Hee Haw, which gave him unprecedented national exposure for the next two decades. By 1978, he'd been elected to the Country Music Hall of Fame, and by that time was taking on the real-life role of elder statesman within the community. He continued recording into the 1980s, although his music is somewhat underrepresented today on compact disc, apart from the Monument and Decca sides. In 1984, Jones published his autobiography, Everybody's Grandpa. —Bruce Eder

Grandpa Jones-Live / 1969 / Sony ♦♦♦♦

Grandpa Jones had been signed to Fred Foster's Monument label for seven years when producer Ray Pennington recorded this concert at the Black Stallion in Cincinnati on December 29, 1969. The result is a priceless document of Jones' stage act, and the only one of his albums currently available on compact disc—ironically, Jones himself regards this as the least favorite of his Monument records because he doesn't feel he was prepared or that his voice sounds very good. None of that is very obvious, for the performance is excellent and his singing seems just fine. Surprisingly, he covers none of his Monument hits such as "T for Texas" or "Mountain Dew," choosing new material instead. The songs range from the rollicking "Dooley" and "Rocky Top" to eloquent gospel such as "The Air, the Sunshine, and the Rain" (a great showcase for Jones' wife Ramona's fiddle playing, as is "I Don't Love Nobody") to traditional folk tunes like a banjo-driven version of "John Henry" and "My Bonnie Lies over the Ocean" played on cowbells. The band includes Joe Edwards on guitar, and Ramona sings harmony. The tunes are spiced by Jones' vaudeville patter, including his ribald retelling of the story of the three bears as "The Three Old Maids." Nothing on this recording is less than first-rate, including the sound, which captures the mix of instruments and voices with wonderful fidelity. —Bruce Eder

Grandpa Jones Story / 1976 / CMH ♦♦♦♦

The Hee Haw banjo comic in a pleasant folksy setting with Ramona. —Mark A. Humphrey

Family Album / 1979 / CMH ♦♦♦

This album features 25 classic old-time songs. —AMG

Good Ole Mountain Dew / Dec. 1, 1995 / Sony Special Products ♦♦♦♦

This ten-song, 22-minute budget-priced release includes the hits "T for Texas" and "Mountain Dew" (a 1960s re-recording) as well as such familiar fare as the classic dog songs "Old Rattler" and "Old Blue," the rip-roaring banjo workout "Are You from Dixie," and relatively reflective songs such as the idyllic Tennessee paean "Nashville on My Mind." The most interesting number here is Jones' own topical "King of the Cannon County Hills," sort of his answer to "Okie from Muskogee," with digs at hippies ("let the hippie have his LSD and pills") and college students amid his description of rural southern life. Anyone who's heard "T for Texas" as done by the Everly Bros. or anyone else since Jimmie Rodgers hasn't really heard the song until they've heard Grandpa Jones' version here, which has the richness of a page out of a William Faulkner novel. The sound is crisp if unexceptional, with nice stereo separation, and there are no notes, but until a proper

Monument collection is released domestically this $7 job will have to suffice. —*Bruce Eder*

A Pickin' and A Grinnin' / Dec. 1, 1995 / Sony Special Products ✦✦✦✦

Essentially a cut-down version of Grandpa Jones' 1963 album *Yodeling Hits*, basically a Jimmie Rodgers tribute, containing ten songs. A fine and valuable recording, despite slight overlap with the other current studio release. —*Bruce Eder*

Everybody's Grandpa / 1996 / Bear Family ✦✦✦✦

Everybody's Grandpa is a comprehensive five-disc box set, containing all of the recordings Jones made between 1960 and 1973, including several unreleased tracks, many rarities, and all of his hits ("T for Texas"). Most of the box draws from his Monument recordings, but there are also a few cuts he made for smaller labels. Though the music here isn't quite as thrilling as his earliest recordings for King, it does form the bulk of his popular legacy, and any dedicated fan should invest in this weighty package. —*Thom Owens*

Hall of Fame Series / MCA ✦✦✦✦

Hall of Fame Series contains all of the material Grandpa Jones recorded for Decca Records during the mid-'50s, including the Top 40 hit "The All-American Boy." Though this music is neither Jones' most accomplished nor his most representative, it is a well-produced collection that gives a good indication of his prodigious skills on the banjo, as well as his cornball sense of humor. —*Thom Owens*

Poems & Songs / ✦✦✦

This album features "The Christmas Guest" and other Jones favorites. —*AMG*

● **16 Greatest Hits** / Hollywood ✦✦✦✦

16 Greatest Hits on Hollywood Records compiles a number of highlights from Grandpa Jones' original '40s recordings for King Records, including "Eight More Miles to Louisville," "Mountain Dew," "Old Rattler," and "It's Raining Here This Morning." During this era, Jones helped pioneer the fusion of old-time string music with modern electric instruments, such as the pedal steel and electric guitar. His band featured such luminaries as guitarist Merle Travis—who dazzles on the handful of tracks included here—and backup vocalist Cowboy Copas. These are the songs that earned Grandpa Jones a national reputation and were among the hits that helped established King Records as the most successful country indie label of its era. Unfortunately, *16 Greatest Hits* isn't the best possible representation of these songs—not only did Hollywood include "Old Rattler" twice, the disc's packaging is shoddy and the sound is below average. Still, these are important recordings and are the best music Grandpa Jones ever made, so *16 Greatest Hits* currently stands as his best available disc until something better replaces it. —*Stephen Thomas Erlewine*

Esteban Steve Jordan

Accordion / Mexico, Norteño

Esteban Jordan bears the moniker "El Parche" for his trademark eye patch, and admirers have also called him "the Jimi Hendrix of the accordion" for his aggressive rock attack and use of such effects as phase shifters. His music, however, is firmly rooted in the Norteño tradition and his influences are reflected in his traditional core repertoire. His wonderful '60s rock-meets-Norteño singles for regional labels have been reissued on Arhoolie, while more recent recordings have appeared on sundry Texas labels, Rounder, and RCA. Jordan appeared in David Byrne's 1986 film *True Stories* and was featured in the soundtrack of *Born in East LA*. —*Mark A. Humphrey*

Corrido de Johnny el Pachuco / Rounder ✦✦✦

Las Coronelas / Arhoolie ✦✦✦✦

Jordan has been called the Jimi Hendrix of the accordion—a dumb analogy, but it gives you an idea of his rep. He combines a blisteringly brilliant instrumental style with a typically tejano ability to play both polka and classic rock 'n' roll. But Jordan fuses, confuses, and infuses these styles till they roll over and become his own. And then he launches into squeezebox salsa. —*John Storm Roberts*

Many Sounds of Steve Jordan / 1985 / Arhoolie ✦✦✦

Some of his earliest and greatest traditional Norteño accordion music, it doesn't include much of his trademark lunacy. —*Myles Boisen*

★ **Return of El Parche** / 1986 / Rounder ✦✦✦✦✦

Steve Jordan's facility with uptempo or ballad material, polkas, waltzes, traditional Mexican and reworked American rock, pop and country helped establish his base, as did a number of regional singles and albums. The 12 tunes on this anthology were recorded between 1976 and 1984 for the Freddie and Joe labels in Corpus Christi and San Antonio, including salsa/Afro-Latin jazz cuts, blues, and country-tinged numbers. Jordan's vocals were soulful and exuberant, while his accordion playing was fast, dashing, and enticing. Jordan also utilized an Echoplex and phase-shifter, creating some intriguing sounds. The songs were mostly short, catchy, and diversified, expertly showing Jordan's total range and stylistic adaptability. —*Ron Wynn*

El Hurracane / 1987 / Rounder ✦✦✦✦

For many, Steve Jordan is probably a novelty item—his first LP on Arhoolie (now on CD as well) was so good that, paradoxically, people didn't feel the overpowering need for more. Jordan is the very essence of an American almost gone, and his legend will be less interesting when he's gone. He plays the most amazing Tex-Mex accordion ever heard—these songs were recorded in the late '70s and mid-'80s for the Hacienda label. —*John Storm Roberts*

The Jordanaires

Country-Pop, Pop, Nashville Sound/Countrypolitan

For over 40 years, the Jordanaires remained one of the premier backup vocal groups in country music, working with such greats as Jim Reeves, Patsy Cline, George Jones, and, of course, Elvis Presley. The quartet began in Springfield, MO, during the late '40s, singing barbershop and spirituals and featuring original members Bob Hubbard, Bill Matthews, Monty Matthews, and Culley Holt. They debuted on the Grand Ole Opry in 1949. The group changed members during the early '50s with Gordon Stoker and Hoyt Hawkins replacing Hubbard, who was drafted, and Bill Matthews, who became seriously ill. In 1953, Monty Matthews had to leave the group and was replaced by Neal Matthews.

By 1954, the Jordanaires were singing behind artists such as Elton Britt, Red Foley, and Jimmy Wakely. That year they appeared on Eddy Arnold's television show, but didn't get their big break until Elvis Presley, a longtime fan, invited the group to back him after he received a major recording contract from RCA Victor. When Elvis became a star, he honored his promise to keep them as his backup singers, and they worked with him until 1970, appearing in most of his films and on his gospel recordings. In 1958, Culley Holt became ill and was replaced by Hugh Jarrett; he left before the end of the year and was replaced by Ray Walker.

When not backing Elvis, the Jordanaires were busy making their own mark in country music. Neal Matthews was a talented arranger and was responsible for Jim Reeves' "Four Walls" (1957). In 1959, the Jordanaires began working with Patsy Cline, and also devised the Nashville number system of chords that is still widely used in recording studios and performances. The quartet also recorded their own gospel and country albums. It was the Jordanaires who provided the main impetus for the formation of the American Federation of Television/Radio Artists-Screen Actors' Guild in Nashville. They also established Nashville's commercial jingle market, which helped singers like Janie Fricke and Judy Rodman get their start. —*Sandra Brennan*

Big Country Hits / 1966 / Columbia ✦✦✦

Not what one would necessarily look for from this group, but with some worthwhile moments for those who appreciate their sound. —*Bruce Eder*

● **Monster Makers** / 197 / Stop ✦✦✦✦

The grotesque cover, intended as a joke, hides some superb music-making. The hauntingly beautiful rendition of the country-gospel number "Skip-a-Rope" is possibly their best record ever. —*Bruce Eder*

Sing Gospel / 1992 / K-Tel ✦✦✦
After all these years, the Jordanaires are still in good form, and their gospel album is a fine collection, offering ten pleasant readings of mostly traditional material. It's only slightly hampered by rather sterile production and the occasional intrusive synthesizer. —*Stephen Thomas Erlewine*

Will the Circle Be Unbroken / 1992 / CEMA ✦✦✦
Features "Rock of Ages," "How Great Thou Art," and other gospel standards. —*AMG*

Tribute to Elvis / Step One ✦✦✦✦
They sang on his originals; now they sing without him. —*Hank Davis*

John Jorgenson

b. Jul. 6, 1956, Madison, WI

Progressive Bluegrass, Country-Rock, Bluegrass, Instrumental Country

Southern California native John Jorgenson, a three-time winner of the Academy of Country Music award for "Guitarist of the Year," was destined to be a part of the music business from an early age. Classically trained as a child, his father conducted for Benny Goodman. Jorgenson, who idolized Goodman, played with Goodman while his father was conducting. Later, he went on to work for eight years as a member of the Jazz and Bluegrass group at Disneyland. While employed at the "happiest place on earth," Jorgenson contributed his skills on a number of instruments including mandolin, saxophone, guitar, and clarinet. Later in his career he was the featured bassoonist for the L.A. Camerata. Still, it was Jorgenson's expertise as a guitarist that brought him fame and respect; he recorded with the groundbreaking Byrds as well as Rose Maddox, Roy Orbison, Bob Dylan, John Prine, Bonnie Raitt, Dan Fogelberg, and even Michael Nesmith.

In 1986 Jorgenson hooked up with some of the most influential musicians on the West Coast in order to form a traditional country-rock outfit called the Desert Rose Band. Comprised of former Byrd Chris Hillman, Herb Pedersen, Bill Bryson, Steve Duncan, and steel player Jay Dee Maness, Jorgenson's power-driven 12-string was an essential component of the band's sound. Their first single was a remake of the classic Johnny & Jack hit, "Ashes of Love," from their self-titled debut album. With the release of their second project in 1988, *Running*, they were named the Academy of Country Music's "Touring Band of the Year." This honor was repeated in 1989 and 1990. Also, in 1989 and 1990 the band was nominated for the Country Music Association's "Best Vocal Group" award.

In spite of the No. 1 hits, the classic covers they brought back to life and all the Top Ten singles, by 1992 the Desert Rose Band began to crumble. Jorgenson left to pursue other interests, including his guitar work with the Hellecasters, a band that came together after a one-time-only gig in 1991. Comprised of Jorgenson and fellow Telecaster disciples Will Ray and Jerry Donahue, the Hellecasters were made up of three lead players, none of whom sang. *The Return of the Hellecasters*, their debut recording, was voted both "Album of the Year" and "Country Album of the Year" in 1993 by the *Guitar Player* magazine Reader's Poll. A second Hellecasters project in 1995, *Escape from Hollywood*, continued to refine and redefine guitar techniques. In 1996 John recorded a bluegrass project with the legendary Rose Maddox at Mad Dog Studios. Released that same year, *The Moon Is Rising* was also produced by Jorgenson. —*Jana Pendragon*

After You've Gone / 1988 / Curb ✦✦

Scott Joss

Western Swing, Bakersfield Sound, Neo-Traditionalist Country, Americana, West Coast Country

Scott Joss was often praised as the "heir to the Bakersfield throne" because of his early association with Tiny Moore and Merle Haggard and his later affiliation with Buck Owens and Dwight Yoakam. Born in Long Beach and raised in Redding, Joss learned to play fiddle from Jana Jae, the former wife of Buck Owens and fiddle player for his band Buck Owens and the Buckaroos. Befriended by one of Bob Wills' surviving Playboys, Tiny Moore,

Joss was encouraged to develop his talent on a professional level after winning numerous California State Fiddle Championships. In 1980, at the age of 18, hewas invited to join Merle Haggard's band. His first show as one of the Strangers was at Carnegie Hall. Still a little green, Joss returned to Redding to continue working on his performance skills before he joined up with Merle and the band on the road. While with the Strangers, Joss spent time with Bakersfield guitarman Roy Nichols, who saw great promise in the young fiddle player.

Leaving the road and Merle was a hard decision, but Joss wanted to begin work on a band of his own. After moving to Sacramento, he hooked up with Dennis Barney, another California player from the early days. Barney, who became mentor and friend to the fledgling frontman, showed Joss the ropes and became a member of his band. After playing around California for a while, Joss was spotted by Pete Anderson, who produced, arranged, and played guitar for Dwight Yoakam, also acting as bandleader. Bringing Joss into the fold in 1988 allowed Anderson to keep an eye on him and his career growth. Commuting between Sacramento and Los Angeles became a way of life for Yoakam's fiddle player and harmony vocalist. On the road and in the studio, Joss had a full-time job as a member of the Babylonian Cowboys. Still, whenever he was in Sacramento he would pull together Barney, brother-in-law Don Weeks., and some other players and work on his solo venture. Eight years after signing on with Yoakam, Anderson and respected L.A. producer/engineer/ bassman Dusty Wakeman (Rosie Flores, Dwight Yoakam, Lonesome Strangers, Reach Around) took Joss into the all new Mad Dog Studios to start work on his first solo project.

Souvenirs was released in 1996 and hit Gavin's Americana chart with all the force of a fast-moving train, landing at No 7. Top cuts included two Jim Lauderdale songs, "Stay Out of My Arms," a traditional shuffle, and the anthemic "Doin' Time in Bakersfield." Also included was one Joss original, "I Never Got Anywhere with You," which proved that Scott Joss was indeed a worthy successor to Buck, Merle, and all the rest who created the Bakersfield Sound. —*Jana Pendragon*

● **Souvenirs** / 1996 / Little Dog ✦✦✦✦
An award-winning fiddle player, whose musical résumé includes playing behind Dwight Yoakam and legends Merle Haggard and Buck Owens, Scott Joss' debut is an impressive nod to the classic California country sound, while also offering up a contemporary feel. Possessing a deep, rich, and well-oiled voice, Joss especially shines on the traditional-sounding cuts—particularly two cool Jim Lauderdale-penned tunes, "Doin' Time in Bakersfield" and "Stay out of My Arms." And although most of the 11 cuts come from such notable writers as Kostas, Kevin Welch, and Tom Russell, among others, Joss proves himself a more than capable songwriter with the standout ballad "I Never Got Anywhere with You." His fiddle playing is good, but the spotlight here is on his vocals. The rest of the musical muscle is provided by producer Pete Anderson's signature lead guitar, as well as the inspired and memorable performances of the rest of the band. —*Jack Leaver*

Cledus T. Judd

Vocals / Contemporary Country, Country Humor

Reprising the long history of country "novelty records," which had lost their appeal in the 1980s, Cledus T. Judd lampooned hits by Shania Twain, the Charlie Daniels Band, and Alan Jackson by rearranging lyrics for humorous impact, Weird Al Yankovic style. In Judd's hands, Shania Twain's "If You're Not in It for Love" became "I'm Not in Here for Love (Just Yer Beer)" and "The Devil Went Down to Georgia" was transformed into a Jeff Foxworthy parody called "Cledus Went Down to Florida." The country humorist released a self-titled album for Razor & Tie in 1995, and followed with *I Stoled This Record* one year later. —*John Bush*

Cledus T. Judd (No Relation) / 1995 / Razor & Tie ✦✦✦✦
The parenthetical comment in the title gives you an indication of what you're in for if you listen to Cledus T. Judd's debut album. Cledus' jokes are rarely more clever than his observation that he is "no relation" to the famous singing duo of Naomi and Wynonna

Judd—however, that simple-minded humor is part of his appeal. The fact of the matter is, if you don't like corny country humor, you will not find *Cledus T. Judd (No Relation)* amusing. But if you do find Jeff Foxworthy and *Hee Haw* funny, *(No Relation)* is a laugh riot—though he doesn't have a distinctive routine like Foxworthy, Judd is more consistently funny and his music, on its own terms, is pretty enjoyable. —*Leo Stanley*

● **I Stoled This Record** / May 21, 1996 / Razor & Tie ✦✦✦✦
Cledus T. Judd's debut album indicated that he was a first-rate country comic for the '90s, but his second effort, *I Stoled This Record*, is where his talents truly blossom. Judd's humor is simple and direct—witness how he lusts after superstar country vocalist Shania Twain on "If Shania Was Mine" or the Charlie Daniels parody "Cledus Went Down to Florida" or the obvious Elmo & Patsy sendup "Grandpa Got Runned Over by a John Deere." It doesn't take a comic genius to come up with these endearingly sophomoric and corny jokes, but it does take some guts to actually follow them through, and that's what makes *I Stoled This Record* surprisingly engaging and fun. Besides, the music is better than you would imagine (Joe Diffie and Shania herself guest on "[She's Got A Butt] Bigger Than the Beatles"). —*Thom Owens*

Wynonna Judd (Christina Ciminella)

b. May 30, 1964, Ashland, KY
Guitar, Vocals / Contemporary Country
Wynonna Judd launched a solo career after the Judds disbanded in 1992. On her own, Wynonna has been more eclectic—drawing not only from country, but rock, pop, and folk—than she was as part of the duo that made her famous.

Born in 1964, Wynonna was the first child of Michael and Diana Ciminella. When she was four years old, the family moved to Los Angeles. Shortly after the move, her parents divorced and she went to live with her mother. The pair changed their names to Naomi and Wynonna shortly after her mother's divorce. The duo began performing together after they moved back to Kentucky in the early '80s. They went to Nashville, where they landed a recording contract in 1984. The Judds became the most popular duo in country music history during the '80s. In 1991, Naomi was forced to retire after she was diagnosed with a chronic liver disease.

Instead of retiring with her mother, Wynonna launched a solo career in 1992 with her eponymous solo album. *Wynonna* featured three consecutive No. 1 singles—"She Is His Only Need," "I Saw the Light," "No One Else on Earth"—and went triple platinum. The following year, she delivered her second album, *Tell Me Why*, which went platinum and spawned four Top Ten songs—"Tell Me Why," "A Bad Goodbye" (a duet with Clint Black), "Girls with Guitars," and "Rock Bottom." In early 1996, she released her third album, *Revelations*. It went platinum within four months of its release. —*Stephen Thomas Erlewine*

Wynonna / 1992 / MCA/Curb ✦✦✦
Daughter Judd stakes out her own territory. It's probably safe to say that she had more in her than most people guessed. From the tender "She Is His Only Need" to the Southern rock 'n' soul of "No One Else on Earth," Wynonna sings with the same smoldering sensuality that pulsed beneath the surface of the duo's best records—even "Live with Jesus" sounds sexy. After a few more albums like this, folks may not even remember the Judds. It also includes "I Saw the Light" and "My Strongest Weakness." —*Brian Mansfield*

● **Tell Me Why** / May 11, 1993 / MCA/Curb ✦✦✦✦
Wynonna's second album, *Tell Me Why*, is a more confident and diverse collection than her debut. Drawing from sources as varied as gospel, folk, and blues-rock, Wynonna doesn't necessarily deliver a pure country album, but her blend of roots genres does qualify as a cleverly constructed contemporary country record. The selection of material is first-rate, but what makes *Tell Me Why* her best solo effort is how she ties all of the songs together with her assured—and surprisingly subtle—vocals. —*Thom Owens*

The Judds

Revelations / 1996 / MCA/Curb ✦✦✦✦
Wynonna has no problem with the spotlight—or, as the tabloids regularly reveal, with opening up her private life for all to poke through and ponder. For all of her cultivating of celebrity, her albums continue to turn down the lights and focus on the softer glow of the emotional verities of her albums. *Revelations* is another worthy solo effort by the younger member of the Judds, the mother-daughter duo through which she first found massive fame. Often somber, and just as often right on the money, her songs examine spirituality (without sermons) and the quiet discoveries that come with mature relationships. Ballads like "Don't Look Back," "Love by Grace" and "My Angel Is Here"—all album highlights—prove how sympathetic her rich, expressive voice can be when applied to a well-written, sensitive lyric. As in the past, she's equally convincing on uptempo, R&B-infused strutters, such as Delbert McClinton's "Somebody to Love You" or the gospel rave-up, "Dance! Shout!" It's a mystery as to why she would include her version of "Freebird," which previously was released as part of a Lynyrd Skynyrd tribute album. (Maybe someone should tell her that those people who yelled it out during encores were kidding.) Otherwise, *Revelations* is just that—a revealing next step by a country music star who understands the power of subtlety in an age that tends to prefer overstatement. —*Michael McCall*

● **Greatest Hits** / Mar. 25, 1997 / MCA/Curb ✦✦✦✦
Greatest Hits contains all of the highlights and big hits from Wynonna's three albums (*Wynonna, Tell Me Why, Revelations*), including the hits "Tell Me Why," "Rock Bottom," "Girls With Guitars," and the No. 1 singles "She Is His Only Need," "I Saw the Light," and "No One Else on Earth." —*Thom Owens*

The Judds

Contemporary Country
Naomi Judd and her daughter Wynonna were one of the most popular country acts of the 1980s, eventually becoming the most successful duo in the genre's history. With Wynonna's strong, bluesy style and Naomi's exquisite harmonies, the Judds presented an arresting image that was both home-spun and city slick. During the eight years they performed together, they had many hits, including 14 No. 1 singles.

Born Dianna Ellen Judd in Ashland, KY, Naomi was 18 when she gave birth to Wynonna (born Christina Ciminella Judd). When Wynonna was four, Naomi—who had since given birth to Ashley and divorced the girls' father—decided to take her children to Los Angeles. Struggling to support her family over the next seven years, Naomi held a variety of jobs that ranged from modeling to working as the personal secretary for the Fifth Dimension. She was also in a relationship at that time, but when it turned abusive, she decided to return to Kentucky in 1976, where the family lived in a rural area with few modern conveniences until Wynonna was 12. As Naomi would not buy a television, or a phone, they entertained themselves at night by listening to local musicians and the Grand Ole Opry on radio. Then a local singer named Songbird Yancy and her mother Minnie inspired the Judds to begin singing together. About a year later, when Wynonna was in her early teens, Naomi moved the family to Northern California, where she intended to complete her nursing studies. By this time, she realized that her oldest daughter had real talent and decided to move to Nashville to see if they could build a music career.

The Judds arrived in Nashville in 1979 and while Naomi worked as a nurse, Wynonna finished high school. As they continued to hone their singing skills, they began performing occasionally on the early-morning *Ralph Emery* show. Frequently, the Judds' idea of networking was to simply sit down and sing to whoever would listen. It was through such a live audition that the two came to be managed by Woody Bowles and Ken Stilts. Their managers brought a crudely recorded demo containing songs Naomi had written to noted producer Brent Maher. Impressed by the potential in Wynonna's still-developing voice, and by the intelligence of Naomi's songs, Maher helped the duo get an audition with Dick Whitehouse at Curb Records. In turn, Whitehouse sent a demo to RCA, who requested a live demo with the group in Los Angeles. The Judds had no idea that the seven men they sang for were the label's upper-level executives. With only Wynonna's guitar to accompany them, the women sang for 30 minutes and were immediately offered a contract. In late 1983, they released their first single, "Had a Dream (For the Heart)," and reached the country Top 20. A mini-album, *The Judds: Wynonna and Naomi,* followed and a hastily assembled tour came after that.

With "Mama He's Crazy" in early 1984, the Judds began a streak of eight consecutive No. 1 hits. "Why Not Me," their second No. 1 hit, won the Country Music Association's Single of the Year award for 1984. Between 1985 and 1990, the duo issued hit after hit; their albums proved equally successful, with *Rockin' with the Rhythm* (1985), *Heartland* (1987), *Greatest Hits* (1988) and *Love Can Build a Bridge* (1990) all reaching platinum-selling status. By the turn of the decade, however, Naomi had contracted chronic, acute hepatitis, an incurable, life-threatening disease. The constant touring had seriously weakened her health and it began to show in 1990. For most of that year, she spent much of her time offstage bedridden and too weak to move.

Naomi's poor health led to the duo's to disbandment in 1991. Before Naomi retired, the Judds embarked upon a 124-date farewell tour, called "Love Can Build a Bridge." It was grueling for Naomi and emotionally wrenching for Wynonna, who, though encouraged by her mother and her managers to continue singing, was unsure about whether she wanted to go solo. Yet by the end of 1991, Wynonna had decided to continue performing and signed a contract with MCA Records. Early in 1992, she released her eponymous debut album, which became a multi-platinum success. Naomi published her autobiography, *Love Can Build a Bridge,* in 1993. Her younger daughter, Ashley, became an acclaimed actress in the mid-'90s, appearing in the films *Heat* and *A Time to Kill.* —*Sandra Brennan*

Why Not Me? / 1984 / RCA ✦✦✦✦
On their second album, Wynonna establishes herself as a formidable and sultry belter. The production is built around an essentially acoustic base. —*Mark A. Humphrey*

The Judds / 1984 / RCA ✦✦✦
Though it lacks a strong set of songs, the Judds' eponymous debut album established that the vocals of Wynonna and Naomi played off of each other beautifully, and songs like the hit "Had a Dream (For the Heart)" provide the foundation for their later hit singles. The best moments on *The Judds* are also included on their hit compilations. —*Thom Owens*

Rockin' with the Rhythm / 1985 / RCA ✦✦✦
On the duo's third album, "Have Mercy" and the title track (among others) kick with a funky glee that makes this the most plainly joyous Judds album. —*Mark A. Humphrey*

Heartland / 1987 / RCA ✦✦

★ **The Greatest Hits** / 1988 / RCA ✦✦✦✦✦
These singles document the rise of Naomi and Wynonna Judd, a mother-daughter team that seemed, at times, to be singing for every bank teller, teacher, and struggling single mama in every small town in America. Songs like "Why Not Me," "Mama He's Crazy," and "Girl's Night Out" were more than country hits; they were validation for every woman brave enough to believe in innocence even when her faith was challenged. —*Dan Cooper*

River of Time / 1989 / RCA ✦✦✦
River of Time earned the Judds two more No. 1 singles, "Young Love" and "Let Me Tell You About Love." —*Jason Ankeny*

Love Can Build a Bridge / 1990 / RCA ✦✦✦
The Judds' last album, *Love Can Build a Bridge,* suffers from a selection of songs that sound too similiar to several earlier, better compositions, but there are a couple of highlights—namely the hit title song, "Born to Be Blue," "One Hundred and Two," and a re-recording of their 1984 song, "John Deere Tractor"—that made it a nice farewell for dedicated fans. —*Thom Owens*

Greatest Hits, Vol. 2 / 1991 / RCA ✦✦✦✦
While songs like "Young Love" and "Love Can Build a Bridge" continue to emphasize the Judds' warm and fuzzy middle-American sensibilities, several other hits—"Let Me Tell You About Love," for instance—showcase the side of Wynonna influenced by Bonnie Raitt. —*Dan Cooper*

The Judds Collection 1983-1990 / 1992 / RCA ✦✦✦✦
The three-disc box set *The Judds Collection 1983-1990* is an example of a wasted opportunity. Instead of providing a thorough, exhaustive overview of the duo's immensely popular career, the set simply combines their first two *Greatest Hits* albums with a disc of demos, which are only of interest to hardcore fans, who will already have all of the music on the first two discs. This makes the set useful to no one—casual fans are better served by the individual collections, while dedicated fans would be forced to purchase two discs they already have if they want to get the rarities, which aren't that revelatory in the first place. —*Thom Owens*

Collector's Series / Feb. 1993 / RCA ✦✦✦
This contains "Have Mercy," "Love Is Alive," "Cry Myself to Sleep," and more. —*AMG*

★ **The Essential Judds** / Oct. 1995 / RCA ✦✦✦✦✦
The Essential Judds contains a great majority of the duo's biggest hits, as well as a wisely chosen selection of rarities, making it a definitive compilation. —*Stephen Thomas Erlewine*

K

Kieran Kane

b. Oct. 7, 1949, Queens, New York City, NY
Country-Folk
Formerly one-half of the O'Kanes, this New York native returned to a solo career after a four-year break. His solo work continues the sparse, casual, evocative style of the O'Kanes. If anything, Kane is more austere on his own, supplementing insistent but unobtrusive rhythms with fragmentary lyrics that are seductively idealistic and occasionally haunting. —*Michael McCall*

● **Find My Way Home** / Atlantic ◆◆◆◆
Kane quietly and effectively examines his relationships and decisions in songs that are as acutely accurate as they are minimally drawn. —*Michael McCall*

Dead Reckoning / Oct. 1995 / Dead Rekoning ◆◆◆

Buell Kazee

b. Aug. 29, 1900, Burton Fork, KY, **d.** Aug. 1976
Banjo, Vocals / Traditional Bluegrass, Traditional Folk
Buell Kazee was a minister who played banjo and sang the ancient songs of his beloved Kentucky mountains during the 1920s. Considered one of the very best folk singers in US history, he was a master of the high, "lonesome" singing style of the Appalachian balladeer. Kazee was born in the foothill town of Burton Fork, KY, and learned most of his songs from his family. He began picking banjo at age five and often played during local gatherings. He prepared for the clergy as a teen, and after high school began studying English, Greek, and Latin at Georgetown College, KY. It was there that he began to understand the significance of his family and friends' traditional songs. Kazee formally studied singing and music in order to transcribe the old songs and make them more contemporary. Following his graduation in 1925, he gave a "folk music" concert at the University of Kentucky. He wore a tie and tails while playing the banjo and piano, sang in his specially trained "formal" voice, and gave lectures about the history of the songs. The show was a great success, so he repeated it several times over the following years.

In 1927, he was asked to record the songs for Brunswick in New York, and he was signed to the label on the condition that he sing using his high, tight "mountain" voice and forgoing his formal vocal training. Over the next two years, he recorded over 50 songs backed by New York musicians. Many were religious, but others ranged from traditional to popular ballads, including "Lady Gay," "The Sporting Bachelors," and "The Orphan Girl." His biggest hit was a version of "On Top of Old Smoky" called "Little Mohee," which sold over 15,000 copies. In the early '30s, the recently married Kazee lost interest in pursuing a music career and stopped touring to become the minister of a church in Morehead, KY. For the next 22 years, he only sang publicly at revival meetings. Much later, he began using folk themes to compose formal music, such as a cantata based on the old Sacred Harp piece "The White Pilgrim." During the folk revival of the early 1960s, he made a comeback and was one of the first to appear at the Newport festivals. In addition to preaching and singing, Kazee also wrote three religious books and a book on banjo playing. He died in 1976. —*Sandra Brennan*

● **Buell Kazee Sings & Plays** / Smithsonian/Folkways ◆◆◆◆

Brantley Kearns

Progressive Bluegrass, Western Swing, Bakersfield Sound
Born in the Southeast and educated on the East Coast, Brantley Kearns was a Renaissance man. A trained stage actor as well as a musician, he first came to the attention of the masses and the industry when he started playing with Dwight Yoakam in the mid-'80s. It was Kearns' fiddle playing that kept Yoakam's debut release, *Guitars, Cadillacs, Etc., Etc.* so traditional. The video of the title track also focused on Kearns' magnificent playing style. He was a featured player and background vocalist on *Hillbilly Deluxe* and *Just Lookin' for a Hit*, and his background vocals were prominent on *Buenas Noches from a Lonely Room.* As a player he mastered many instruments; mandolin and guitar were also part of his arsenal. Revered as one of the best fiddle players in the business, Kearns was a favorite around L.A., where he was often a guest on recording sessions and live performances. A close friend of Rick Shea, the two often performed as an acoustic duo; as a soloist, Kearns not only performed Western swing tunes a la Bob Wills but also ancient mountain and hillbilly songs. Kearns also joined Billy Joe and Eddy Shaver and their band for a tour in support of *Highway of Life,* and continued to play, perform, and record with numerous members of the Los Angeles country and roots music community as well as select others from around the country. He occasionally did theater, combining his music and acting skills. —*Jana Pendragon*

Robert Earl Keen, Jr.

Guitar, Vocals / Progressive Country, Singer-Songwriter, Country-Folk, Alternative Country, Contemporary Folk
Singer-songwriter Robert Earl Keen, a native of Bandera, TX, began playing the guitar as a diversion from journalism classes at Texas A&M. To fend off boredom, he and neighbor Lyle Lovett jammed together and, on Sunday mornings, serenaded churchgoers across the street from Keen's house sitting on the front porch in their underwear. As Keen's songwriting talent blossomed and he began to make a name for himself in Austin, Lovett recorded one of his songs, as did Nanci Griffith, Joe Ely, and Kelly Willis. This provided a springboard for a solo career, which culminated in the simultaneous release of Keen's fifth and most accomplished album, 1994's *Gringo Honeymoon,* and the birth of his daughter. Keen's sixth album, *Number 2 Live Dinner,* was released in March of 1996. —*Steve Huey*

● **No Kinda Dancer** / 1984 / Philo ◆◆◆◆
A well-crafted debut; not one bad song. "Armadillo Jackal & This Old Porch," co-written by Lyle Lovett, features Lovett and Nanci Griffith singing harmony. —*Chip Renner*

The Live Album / 1988 / Sugar Hill ◆◆◆◆
Good sound, new material, good stories, plus audience interaction make this worthwhile. Featuring great mandolin and fiddle by

Johnathan Yadkin and a nice cut of "I Would Change My Life."
—*Chip Renner*

West Textures / 1989 / Sugar Hill ✦✦✦
Solid and well-produced, with Jerry Douglas on dobro and a cover of the Koller/Silverstein song "Jennifer Johnson & Me." —*Chip Renner*

A Bigger Piece of Sky / 1993 / Sugar Hill ✦✦✦
This album contains the radio hit "Tangled up in Blue," sound-alike song "Jesse with the Long Hair," as well as more of Keen's rough and tumble story-songs. —*Richard Meyer*

Gringo Honeymoon / 1994 / Sugar Hill ✦✦✦✦

Merry Christmas from the Family / Nov. 21, 1995 / Sugar Hill ✦✦✦
After Keen's mordant yuletide song "Merry Christmas from the Family" was tapped by the country-themed syndicated radio program *The John Boy & Billy Big Show* for heavy airplay during the 1994 holiday season, the singer decided to re-cut the song live for release the following year. The single was packaged with its original source album *Gringo Honeymoon* for release during 1995. —*Jason Ankeny*

Number 2 Live Dinner / Mar. 19, 1996 / Sugar Hill ✦✦✦
Robert Earl Keen Jr. is a Texan who did not take the express lane to the radio airwaves. Instead, he spent more than a decade seasoning his talent while entertaining folks in the—yep, you guessed it—friendly honky tonks of Texas, where music fans tend to like individualists with plenty of personality. *No. 2 Live Dinner* finished off a consistently powerful string of albums recorded for Sugar Hill Records. Taped in front of rowdy, beer-swilling crowds in two Texas towns, Keen delivers his good-natured raspiness on songs of desperation, danger, and raucous humor. A contemporary of Steve Earle, Lyle Lovett, and Nanci Griffith, Keen's work has been as consistent and occasionally as strong as that of his friends. It's taken him longer to gain a national profile, but it's coming at a deserving time. For those unfamiliar with him, this live album will convey how well he's loved in his home state. Listen closely, and the songs will explain why, too. —*Michael McCall*

Bill Keith

b. Dec. 20, 1939, Boston, MA
Banjo / Progressive Bluegrass, Instrumental
Bill Keith had a great impact on modern banjo playing, particularly in the direction of "newgrass." He even had a picking style informally named after him.

　Born in Boston, MA, Keith began taking banjo lessons at a young age, and also learned to play piano and ukulele. During his adolescence, he played in a few Dixieland bands, but by the late '50s, he became interested in folk music after listening to such inspirational artists as Pete Seeger and Earl Scruggs. Using instruction books, the Amherst college student began learning their two different styles. Eventually, Keith began developing his own unique style, which became known as the melodic, chromatic or "Keith" picking style. This distinct technique was borne of his desire to play fiddle melodies on his instruments. In 1958, he teamed up with fellow Amherst student Jim Rooney and began playing at local coffeehouses and on campus. Eventually they hooked up with promoter Manny Greenhill; with his assistance they founded the Connecticut Folklore Society, which sponsored a series of traveling campus concerts throughout New England.

　Following graduation and a brief stint in the US Air Force Reserve, Keith began learning to make banjos with Tom Morgan. Later he, Rooney, mandolin player Frank Wakefield, and guitarist Red Allen formed the Kentuckians. In 1963, Earl Scruggs contacted Keith to lay out the tablature for the instructional book *Earl Scruggs and the 5-String Banjo*. Later that year, Keith and his former Amherst classmate Dan Bump developed a new kind of tuning peg that was adopted by Scruggs, who provided a name for the resulting company in 1964. In the mid-'60s, Keith joined Bill Monroe's Blue Grass Boys, where he was listed as Brad Keith. He left the band after only eight months to do more session work and by the year's end had joined Jim Kweskin's Jug Band, where

he would stay for four years. After that he played with the Blue Velvet Band. He abandoned the banjo for a while in 1968 to become a pedal steel guitarist. In 1970, Keith moved to Woodstock, NY, and spent a year with Jonathan Edwards. He then went on to work with Judy Collins. He and longtime cohort Rooney also toured together in both the US and in Europe during the '70s and '80s, with Keith developing a particularly large following in France. When back home in Woodstock, Keith began playing banjo for the Woodstock Mountain Review. In 1977, he worked briefly as a columnist for *Frets* magazine. Later, in 1989, Keith, Rooney, Eric Weissberg, and Kenny Koseck re-formed their old group, calling it the New Blue Velvet Band. —*Sandra Brennan*

Livin' on the Mountain / 1963 / Prestige Folklore ✦✦✦✦

● **Something Auld, Something Newgrass, Something Borrowed** / 1976 / Rounder ✦✦✦✦
Catch Tony Rice, David Grisman, Jim Rooney, Tom Grey, Vassar Clements, Ken Kasek, and Al Jones on this album. The bluegrass is top-notch, and Bill Keith struts his stuff. —*Chip Renner*

Banjoistics / 1984 / Rounder ✦✦✦

Fiddle Tunes for Banjo / Rounder ✦✦✦

Beating Around the Bush / Green Linnet ✦✦✦

Toby Keith

b. Jul. 8, 1961, Oklahoma City, OK
Vocals / Contemporary Country, New Traditionalist
Toby Keith was one of many new traditionalist honky tonk singers that had a string of hit singles in the early '90s. Born in Oklahoma City, his interest in country music was sparked in childhood by the musicians who played at his grandmother's dinner club. Keith did not choose music as his career he lost his job in the oil industry. With nothing to do, he began playing in country-rock garage bands. Eventually he and some of the musicians he worked with teamed up to form Keith's Easy Money Band, which began playing at honky tonks in South Oklahoma City and neighboring Norman. He returned to the oil fields and later played football in the short-lived USFL while continuing to play music. By 1988, Keith was recording for independent labels and decided to try his luck in Nashville. He got his big break when former Alabama producer Harold Shedd, who worked for Mercury Records, heard Keith's demo and flew to Oklahoma to meet and listen to the band. He was impressed and offered Keith a record deal. Toby Keith's eponymous debut album was released in 1993. The first single from the album, "Should've Been a Cowboy," became a No. 1 single, and his next two singles—"He Ain't Worth Missing" and "A Little Less Talk and a Lot More Action"—made the Top ten. In 1995, he released the seasonal album, *Christmas to Christmas*. In 1996, he delivered his second album, *Blue Moon*. —*Sandra Brennan*

Toby Keith / 1993 / Polygram ✦✦
Keith's hit "Should've Been a Cowboy" is the featured cut on this self-titled debut. —*Jason Ankeny*

Boomtown / 1995 / Polygram ✦✦✦

Christmas to Christmas / Oct. 17, 1995 / Polygram ✦✦✦
All the songs on *Christmas to Christmas* are new compositions, several by Keith himself. They range from playful ("Blame It on the Mistletoe") and thoughtful ("Jesus Gets Jealous of Santa Claus") to devastatingly sad ("Santa I'm Right Here"). The playing is casual, back-porch rootsy. It is first and foremost a collection of good songs, well-performed, that just happen to be about Christmas. —*Roch Parisien*

● **Blue Moon** / Apr. 1996 / A&M ✦✦✦✦

The Kendalls

Traditional Country, Country-Pop
The Kendalls were a successful father-daughter vocal team. Father Royce Kendall was born in St. Louis, MO. He began playing guitar as a Merchant Marine. During the late '50s he and his brother Floyce, a mandolin player, formed the Austin Brothers and went to Los Angeles to appear on the television show *Town Hall Party* with Cal Smith and Hank Cochran. Two years later, Kendall went

back to St. Louis to be with his wife and attend barber school. Eventually they started up a barber shop/beauty salon. Jeannie, Kendall's daughter, was also born in St. Louis. As a child, she developed an interest in folk and country music. She and her father formed a duo when she was 15.

Following a visit to the Grand Ole Opry, the Kendall family decided to pay for a recording session. Afterward, they sold their record through mail order, and it sold very well. The Kendalls also began performing in St. Louis. A local deejay brought them to the attention of Stop Records in 1970. The label signed the duo and released their cover of John Denver's "Leavin' on a Jet Plane." After the song became a minor hit, the family moved to Nashville. Although they had a promising start, the Kendalls didn't really find success until 1977, when "Heaven's Just a Sin Away" climbed to No. 1 on the country charts and crossed over to become a minor pop hit. For the next eight years the duo had a string of Top 40 singles, including the No. 1 hits "Sweet Desire" (1978) and "Thank God for the Radio" (1984). During the latter half of the '80s, the duo continued recording, but had no Top 40 hits. During the '90s, the Kendalls continued to tour and occasionally record. —Sandra Brennan & David Vinopal

Meet the Kendalls / 1970 / Stop ✦✦✦

Two Divided by Love / 1972 / Dot ✦✦✦

1978 Grammy Award Winner-Best Country Duo / 1978 / Gusto ✦✦

Movin' Train / 1983 / Mercury ✦✦✦

Two Heart Harmony / 1985 / Mercury ✦✦✦

Fire at First Sight / 1986 / MCA/Curb ✦✦✦

Break the Routine / 1987 / Step One ✦✦✦✦
Break the Routine offers the minor chart hits "Dancin' with Myself Tonight," "Routine," "Still Pickin' up After You" and "The Rhythm of Romance." —*Jason Ankeny*

16 Greatest Hits / 1988 / Deluxe ✦✦✦✦
This represents the bulk of their best work, with those cut-to-the-quick harmonies fully present. One sad note: Royce and Jeannie claim they don't receive a dime for this stuff, thanks to (il)legal wranglings when the original label, Ovation, went under. —*Tom Roland*

Best of the Kendalls / Apr. 5, 1994 / Curb ✦✦✦✦

● **20 Favorites** / Epic ✦✦✦✦
Jeannie Kendall has a winsome hillbilly soprano. Daddy Royce sings hand-in-glove harmony. Daddy and daughter delivered some of the best cheatin' anthems of the late '70s and early '80s and *20 Favorites* collects the bulk of them, including the Top ten hits "Heaven's Just a Sin Away," "It Don't Feel Like Sinnin' to Me," "Pittsburgh Stealers," "Sweet Desire," "I Had a Lovely Time," "You'd Make an Angel Wanna Cheat," "I'm Already Blue," and "Thank God for the Radio." —*Mark A. Humphrey*

Kennedy Rose

Country-Rock, Contemporary Country
Pam Rose and Mary Ann Kennedy, otherwise known as Kennedy Rose, have provided backup singing support for artists like Emmylou Harris, Dan Fogelberg, and Sting. Their songs have been covered by Reba McEntire, Art Garfunkel, and Restless Heart. As artists, this Nashville-based duo has fashioned a distinctive hard acoustic pop-rock sound that has showcased their fine vocal sound to great effect. —*Rick Clark*

● **Hai Ku** / 1989 / IRS ✦✦✦✦
Kennedy and Rose's decision to turn to performing resulted in this debut, which reprises familiar songs of theirs, such as "Love Like This" and "The Only Chain." The production is deep and echoey, with sharply recorded acoustic instruments, and the swinging is as forceful as the writing. —*William Ruhlmann*

Walk the Line / Feb. 8, 1994 / IRS ✦✦✦
Working with co-producer Ray Kennedy, an unrelated country singer with a few offbeat hits, Kennedy Rose created a tighter, leaner sound for *Walk the Line*. The duo's spacious music resonates with possibilities, and guest appearances by Emmylou Har-

ris and David Lanz suggest that Kennedy Rose is in the process of creating a New Age alternative to country. —*Brian Mansfield*

Ray Kennedy

b. May 13, 1954, Buffalo, NY
Bass, Guitar, Drums, Keyboards, Vocals / Progressive Country, Neo-Traditionalist Country
In the country music business, multitalented Ray Kennedy did it all. He was the master of several instruments, wrote and arranged songs, and was a producer and a recording engineer.

He was born in New York to Ray Kennedy, Sr., the National Vice President for Sears and the man behind the Discover credit card. His father's work kept young Kennedy and his family on the move. As a teen, his parents refused to get him a guitar, so Kennedy built his own. He briefly attended college, where he majored in business, but at that time he found himself drawn to music and dropped out to play in Midwestern clubs. He spent some time in Oregon and in 1980 moved to Nashville, where he built his own studio and learned engineering when he began recording his own demos. He got his start as an engineer and was responsible for producing most of Tree Publishing's pop demos. Pop singer Stevie Nicks recorded one of his songs, "Battle of the Dragon," and Kennedy became a staff writer at Tree, where his tunes were occasionally recorded by John Anderson, Charley Pride, David Allan Coe, and others. Because his songs weren't selling well enough to suit him, Kennedy decided to become a recording artist and cover them himself.

In 1990, he signed to Atlantic Records and debuted with *What a Way to Go*. Kennedy not only produced the album in his own studio, he also played all of the instruments but the dobro, steel guitar, and Wessenborn. He also penned or co-penned all of the songs on it. Kennedy made his single debut with the album's title track, which peaked on the Top Ten, with the album making it to the Top 60. He released two more singles from the album, but they only became minor hits. In 1991, he produced and engineered an album for songwriter Don Henry, *Wild in the Backyard*. In 1992, Kennedy teamed up with producer/songwriter Monty Powell and made *Guitar Man*. —*Sandra Brennan*

Ray Kennedy / 1980 / Columbia ✦✦
First off, there is no way anyone would mistake this for a country album. Secondly, Kennedy's claim to fame is that he co-wrote "Sail on Sailor" with Brian Wilson for the Beach Boys' *Holland* album. Aside from an excuse to hear Kennedy's version of that song, there really isn't a lot of reason to get this album. —*Jim Worbois*

● **What a Way to Go** / 1990 / Atlantic ✦✦✦✦
Recorded entirely in his home studio, Kennedy's debut LP includes the title track, his first Top Ten hit. —*Jason Ankeny*

Guitar Man / 1992 / Atlantic ✦✦✦
Kennedy's second album features the minor novelty hit "No Way Jose." —*Jason Ankeny*

The Kentucky Colonels

Progressive Bluegrass
Progressive bluegrass band the Kentucky Colonels had a short but legendary career during the folk revival of the late '50s and early '60s. The band was formed in Los Angeles in the early '50s by brothers Roland, Eric and Clarence White, and their sister Joann. When Joann dropped out, the three brothers began billing themselves as the Three Little Country Boys and appeared on local television after winning first prize in a talent contest. In 1958, Arkansas native Billy Ray Lathum became their banjo player, and dobro player Le Roy Mack joined the band the next year. Lathum's arrival allowed Roland White to switch to mandolin, his instrument of choice.

As the Country Boys, the group recorded their first single, "I'm Head over Heels in Love with You." They began appearing on *Town Hall Party* and *Hometown Jamboree* and recording on Gene Autry's label. Bassist and banjoist Roger Bush joined the band in 1961 after Eric dropped out to get married. The Boys then recorded *Songs, Themes & Laughs from the Andy Griffith Show* for Capitol. Before the year was out, Roland was drafted and left the band for two years, leaving them without a mandolinist. The group cut its first album on Briar, which disliked the band's moniker and suggested a series of names, the best of which was the Kentucky Colonels. In 1963, fiddler Bobby Sloane joined the Colonels and Roland returned as well. By this time, the Colonels had begun to gather a following through their US tours, and appeared at both the UCLA and Newport Folk festivals in 1964. The band recorded several albums and appeared in the movie *The Farmer's Other Daughter*. They really took off musically when fiddler Scott Stoneman replaced Sloane, but broke up shortly thereafter in 1965. Tragically, Clarence White was killed on July 14, 1973, when he was hit by a car while loading equipment after a show. —*Sandra Brennan*

New Sound of Bluegrass / 1963 / Briar ✦✦✦✦

★ **Long Journey Home** / 1964 / Vanguard ✦✦✦✦✦
These great recordings from a 1964 live performance at the Newport Folk Festival feature Clarence White and many others, including duets with Doc Watson. —*Richard Lieberson & Mark A. Humphrey*

☆ **Appalachian Swing!** / 1964 / Rounder ✦✦✦✦✦
Appalachian Swing is one of the most influential albums in the whole of bluegrass music, primarily because of the stunning playing of Clarence White. With his vibrant, innovative flatpicking, White helped pioneer a new style in bluegrass—namely, redefining the acoustic guitar as a solo instrument instead of confining it to just background status. The sound was revolutionary upon its release in 1964 and the music still sounds alive, even timeless, because of the strength of White's vision and talent. He was one of the greatest musicians in bluegrass history, and the fact that *Appalachian Swing* still sounds fresh makes his tragic death all the more painful. —*Thom Owens*

Kentucky Colonels / 1974 / Shiloh ✦✦✦

The Kentucky Colonels 1965-1966 / 1979 / Rounder ✦✦✦✦

The White Brothers Live in Sweden / 1979 / Rounder ✦✦✦

Clarence White & the Kentucky Colonels / 1980 / Rounder ✦✦✦✦

On Stage / 1984 / Rounder ✦✦✦

Kentucky Headhunters

Country-Rock, Contemporary Country, Southern Rock
The Kentucky Headhunters marked a change of pace from the new traditionalists and country-pop that dominated the country charts at the end of the '80s. Instead of conforming to Nashville traditions, the Headhunters created a hybrid of honky tonk, blues, and southern rock that appealed to both rock and country artists as well as music critics. The group only stayed together for a few albums, but during their time together, they were one of the most popular fringe country acts of the era.

Consisting of members from two different southern families, the Kentucky Headhunters formed in 1968, when Fred and Richard Young began playing together with their cousins Greg Martin and Anthony Kenney at the Youngs' grandmother's home. Mark Orr joined them a little later. The first incarnation of the band was called the Itchy Brothers, and the group played together informally for over a decade. After about 13 years, the band members began launching separate careers: Richard Young went off to write songs for Acuff-Rose while Fred Young began touring with Sylvia. Martin became a member of Ronnie McDowell's band, while Kenney dropped out of music. While playing with McDowell, Martin met Doug Phelps. In 1985, Martin decided to reassemble the Itchy Brothers, but Kenney declined to join again, so they invited Phelps and later his brother Ricky Lee to join, and the band became the Kentucky Headhunters.

They got their start playing twice monthly on the *Chitlin' Show*, a radio program on WLOC in Munfordville, KY. From these 90-minute performances, the Headhunters built up a following. They sent an eight-song demo to Mercury and the label signed the group. The original demo tape was remixed and became the basis of their first album, 1989's *Pickin' on Nashville*, which upon its release received overwhelmingly positive reviews and quickly became a hit. "Dumas Walker" reached No. 15 in the spring of

1990, followed by the group's biggest hit, the No. 6 "Oh, Lonesome Me." In 1991, the Kentucky Headhunters released their second album, *Electric Barnyard*. The album received mixed reviews and weak sales, and none of its songs became hits. In the summer of 1992, the Phelps brothers left the group to form Brothers Phelps, a more traditional country group. The remaining Headhunters brought former Itchy Brothers Anthony Kenney and Mark Orr to the group. The new lineup released *Rave On* in 1993. WIth *Rave On*, the Kentucky Headhunters began refashioning themselves as a bluesy southern rock act and followed that direction on their subsequent album, *That'll Work*. In 1996, Doug Phelps returned to the group to take over lead vocal duties; in 1997, the band issued *Stompin' Grounds*. —*Sandra Brennan*

Pickin' on Nashville / 1989 / Mercury ✦✦✦✦
As their album title suggests, the Headhunters aren't entirely comfortable with the country tag, which is appropriate when you hear their guitar-heavy, rambunctious music. The vocals have that twang, but these good old boys are often closer to Lynyrd Skynyrd than they are to Merle Haggard, and all the better for it. —*William Ruhlmann*

Electric Barnyard / 1991 / Mercury ✦✦✦
The Kentucky Headhunters aren't a remarkable country mutation, just a top-notch Southern rock band with a sense of humor. "The Ballad of Davy Crockett" is the kind of clever novelty that won't work twice; "Big Mexican Dinner" is a novelty that doesn't even work the first time. Once again, the country and bluegrass covers—"Only Daddy That'll Walk the Line," "With Body and Soul"—are the highlights, and most of the originals (the Beatlesque shuffle "Always Makin' Love" aside) are offbeat, adequate filler. —*Brian Mansfield*

Rave On! / 1993 / Mercury ✦✦
It's hard to tell if it was the new guys or just the direction the band was headed, but most of the novelty had worn off The Kentucky HeadHunters by the group's third album. New lead singer Mark Orr replaced Richard Phelps' backwoods country voice with a Southern-rock wail; Anthony Kenney (cousin to drummer Fred Young and guitarist Richard Young) took Doug Phelps' place on bass. The original songs aren't as idiosyncratic as the ones on *Pickin' on Nashville* or *Electric Barnyard*, and the Headhunters continue to cover Bill Monroe, this time with "Blue Moon of Kentucky." Covers of Carl Perkins ("Dixiefried") and the Lovin' Spoonful ("My Gal") are less obvious. The Headhunters started as a hard-rock country band, a novel idea; here, they've devolved into a redneck boogie group. —*Brian Mansfield*

● **Best of the Kentucky Headhunters: Still Pickin'** / 1994 / Mercury ✦✦✦✦
The Best of the Kentucky Headhunters is a first-rate compilation of the highlights from the group's first three albums. Although their debut remains a worthwhile purchase, this collection salvages the good songs from the band's two uneven follow-ups to their exciting breakthrough first album. —*Thom Owens*

That'll Work / Elektra/Nonesuch ✦✦
With *That'll Work*, the Kentucky Headhunters made their bluesrock roots explicit, which is both for better and worse. They certainly can work a heavy, bluesy groove with dexterity, but they lack the gonzo charm they had on their debut, *Pickin' on Nashville*—there simply isn't the sense of careening fun, nor is there the reckless fusions that resulted in such an invigorating listen. What's left is enjoyable and competent, but not particularly special. —*Thom Owens*

Anita Kerr

b. Oct. 31, 1927, Memphis, TN
Piano, Vocals / Pop, Nashville Sound/Countrypolitan
Anita Kerr was the vocal embodiment of the "Nashville Sound" that dominated country music throughout the mid-1950s and 1960s. Along with the Jordanaires, her group, the Anita Kerr Singers, was the seminal backing vocal unit of the era, and it is estimated that at their early-'60s peak, they graced the cover of fully one quarter of all of the records coming out of Nashville's studios.

Kerr was born Anita Jean Grilli on Halloween, 1927, in Memphis, TN; her mother hosted a local radio program there, and by the age of four, Anita herself was taking piano lessons. In her early teens, she formed her own girl group, the Grilli Sisters, which soon became a fixture on her mother's radio show. At age 14, she was hired as the station's staff pianist. In 1948, Kerr left Memphis, and began playing piano on the club circuit. The following year, she formed the Anita Kerr Singers, which also featured alto Dottie Dillard, tenor Gil Wright, and baritone Louis Nunley. After gaining some fame on regional radio, NBC hired the Singers for the program *Sunday Down South*, with Kerr brought aboard as Chorus Director.

In 1951, the group signed to Decca Records, and began their career as a studio backing unit. Five years later, the Singers made their first appearance on the New York-based *Arthur Godfrey Talent Scouts* television program, and quickly became featured players, splitting their time between the broadcast and their session work. In the mid-1950s, Anita Kerr joined forces with Chet Atkins, then the head of RCA Records' country division and the creator of the pop-centric "Nashville Sound," which employed vocal choruses as a means of smoothing over country music's rougher edges. The Anita Kerr Singers appeared on literally hundreds of the era's most prominent recordings, including releases from Jim Reeves, Roy Orbison, Floyd Cramer, Dottie West, Hank Snow, Eddy Arnold, and Lorne Greene; even pop singers like Perry Como and Brook Benton enlisted Kerr's talents. She also produced Skeeter Davis' *End of the World* album, making her one of the very first women to oversee a Nashville recording.

After touring Europe in 1964, she moved to California the next year to focus her energies on freelance production and songwriting, even as two of the Singers' LPs, *We Dig Mancini* and *Southland Favorites*, were winning Grammy awards (in the Vocal Group and Gospel categories, respectively). In the later years of the decade, Kerr teamed with poet Rod McKuen for a series of mood-music records, titled *The Sea, The Earth* and *The Sky*, for which the Singers were renamed the San Sebastian Strings and Singers. At the same time, the group was featured weekly on the Smothers Brothers' sketch comedy program. By the 1970s, Kerr produced a number of easy listening records before moving to her second husband Alex Grob's native Switzerland to compose music for films. Eventually, she returned to Memphis. — *Jason Ankeny*

● **Anita Kerr Singers Reflect on the Hits of Burt Bacharach & Hal David** / 1969 / Dot ✦✦✦✦

Velvet Voices and Bold Brass / 1969 / Dot ✦✦✦

Simon & Garfunkel Songbook / 1971 / Bainbridge ✦✦

Anita Kerr & The French Connection / 1977 / RCA ✦✦

Music Is Her Name / 1992 / Columbia ✦✦✦✦

In the Soul / Gaia ✦✦
In the Soul bears little resemblance to Kerr's work during the Nashville Sound era; performed almost entirely on synthesizers, the album alternates between spare electronic accompaniment and lush symphonic passages, while maintaining its focus on Kerr's readings of Walt Whitman poetry and new age doctrine. — *Jason Ankeny*

David Kersh

Vocals / Contemporary Country
Born and raised in Humble, Tx, contemporary country singer David Kersh spent his early 20s working the local Texas dance hall circuit, eventually landing a major label record contract. Kersh's debut album, *Goodnight Sweetheart*, was released in the fall of 1996. — *Stephen Thomas Erlewine*

Goodnight Sweetheart / Oct. 1, 1996 / Curb ✦✦✦
David Kersh's debut album *Goodnight Sweetheart* is a pleasant set of contemporary country that emphasizes slick, uptempo, line-dancing country-rock and polished ballads. Kersh has a winning voice and personality, yet he lacks strong material. For every strong number, there's one that doesn't quite catch hold. Despite this, *Goodnight Sweetheart* is a promising debut, simply because it introduces an engaging vocal talent. — *Thom Owens*

Doug Kershaw (Douglas James Kershaw)

b. Jan. 24, 1936, Tiel Ridge, LA
Fiddle, Vocals / Cajun
Doug Kershaw has combined a pioneering style of Cajun fiddling with exciting live performances, which often include his Cajun standard "Louisiana Man"—covered by other artists over 800 times. Born January 24, 1936, in Tiel Ridge, LA, Kershaw played in his first band at the age of nine, but began performing with brothers Pee Wee and Rusty in the group Pee Wee Kershaw & the Continental Playboys at the age of 12. Though the group initially sang only in French, a meeting with J.D. Miller—who owned the Feature label—convinced them to begin writing songs in English. As a duo, Rusty & Doug recorded "So Lovely, Baby" in 1955; Miller shopped the single around Nashville, and came up with a contract for Hickory Records. The single reached the Country Top 15 in August 1955.

With pianist Wiley Barkdull and guitarist Hank Garland, Rusty & Doug's Music Makers played on both the *Louisiana Hayride* and the *Wheeling Jamboree* during the late '50s and continued to chart: "Love Me to Pieces" also hit the Top 15 in late 1957, and "Hey Sheriff" almost reached the Top 20. Doug and Rusty entered the Army in 1959, and spent one year in the service. Doug wrote "Louisiana Man" soon after he returned home; the song became one of the most performed in Cajun music, and reached the Country Top Ten in February 1961. "Diggy Liggy Lo" made the Top 15 later in 1961, but after a short stint on RCA Victor, the brothers split in 1963.

Doug Kershaw began recording for Mercury and MGM, and though his live performances kept him quite popular with fans, chart success didn't necessarily follow. Things began to look up in 1968 when he signed with Warner Brothers and appeared on *The Johnny Cash Show* with Bob Dylan. He scraped the nether reaches of the country charts in 1969 with a re-recording—though with a slightly modified title—called "Diggy Diggy Lo." Kershaw averaged more than one album per year for Warner Bros. throughout the 1970s, but charted only three times; he moved to Scotti Bros. in 1981. That same year, "Hello Woman" became his biggest solo hit, reaching No. 29. Kershaw was unable to follow up, however, as he battled drug and alcohol dependency until 1984. A contract with BGM in 1988 yielded the intriguing "Cajun Baby," a duet with Hank Williams, Jr., which made the Top 50. — *John Bush*

The Cajun Way / 1969 / Warner Brothers ✦✦✦
Kershaw's first calling card is very good. — *Jeff Hannusch*

Louisiana Man / 1971 / Warner Brothers ✦✦✦
This contains the infamous title-track hit and several other goodies. — *Jeff Hannusch*

Cajun Country Rockers / 1979 / Bear Family ✦✦✦✦

More Cajun Country Rock / 1984 / Bear Family ✦✦✦✦

★ **The Best of Doug Kershaw** / Aug. 8, 1989 / Warner Brothers ✦✦✦✦✦
This compilation of Kershaw's '60s/'70s Warner Bros. sides features "Everly-Brothers-on-the-bayou" vocal harmonies, Doug Kershaw's fiddle, and crisp Nashville production. — *Mark A. Humphrey*

The Best of Doug & Rusty Kershaw / 1991 / Curb ✦✦✦✦
The Best of Doug & Rusty Kershaw collects 12 of the Kershaw brothers' recordings for Hickory Records in the late '50s, including the hit singles "Louisiana Man" and "Diggy, Diggy Lo." During this time, the group sounded like a cross between a Cajun string band and the Everly Brothers, which resulted in one of the most unique sounds of the late '50s. They might not have had many hits, and some of their material now sounds dated, but Doug and Rusty's musical interplay still sounds fresh. *The Best of* isn't a perfect collection—it's missing the hits "So Lovely, Baby," "Love Me to Pieces," and "Hey Sheriff"—but what is here is very good, making it an adequate retrospective. — *Thom Owens*

That Rockin' Cajun Country / Bear Family ✦✦✦✦

Sammy Kershaw

b. Feb. 24, 1958, Kaplan, LA

Vocals / Contemporary Country, New Traditionalist

Sammy Kershaw's blend of honky tonk and Southern-rock made him a popular recording artist in the early '90s. The third cousin of legendary Cajun fiddler Doug Kershaw, Sammy was born in Kaplan, LA, the eldest of five children. He grew up listening to Hank Williams, Conway Twitty, Buck Owens, and his idol, George Jones. When Kershaw was 11, his grandfather gave him an electric guitar for Christmas; he debuted professionally at age 12 with J.B. Perry, a popular local musician. With Perry, Kershaw toured the South, playing clubs and opening for several major acts; the repertoire included songs by Jones, Charlie Rich, Ray Charles, and the Allman Brothers. After overcoming financial difficulties that forced him to take day jobs, Kershaw joined Blackwater, which played the club circuit in the South and West. He also cut some independent solo singles. By the late '80s, tired of the constant touring and to save his crumbling second marriage, he left music to work for Wal-Mart for two years. Eventually, songwriter Barry Jackson suggested that Kershaw send a demo and picture to Nashville. In 1991, he did a showcase there and was signed to Mercury Records.

His first album, *Don't Go Near the Water*, contained the song "Cadillac Style," which peaked at No. 1 and spent five months on the charts. Kershaw's next two singles—"Don't Go Near the Water" and "Yard Sale"—reached the Top 20, and the fourth single, "Anywhere but Here," peaked at No. 10. *Haunted Heart*, his second album, was released in 1993. The first single, "She Don't Know She's Beautiful," became his first number one hit and produced three more Top 10 singles—"Haunted Heart," "Double Wide Trailer," and "I Can't Reach Her Anymore." In 1994, he released his third album, *Feelin' Good Train;* he also released the holiday album, *Christmas Time's A Comin',* in 1994. The retrospective *Hits: Chapter 1* was released in 1995. In 1996, Kershaw released his fourth studio album, *Politics, Religion and Her.* —*Sandra Brennan*

Don't Go Near the Water / 1991 / Mercury ✦✦✦

"Cadillac Style," Kershaw's first single, started him off strong. This album, which made his Jones influence explicit with a cover of "What Am I Worth," also produced the hits "Don't Go Near the Water," "Yard Sale," and "Anywhere but Here." —*Brian Mansfield*

Haunted Heart / 1993 / Mercury ✦✦✦✦

The more you know about Sammy Kershaw, the more there is to like about his albums. Though Kershaw doesn't write his songs, he makes some of the most autobiographical albums to come from Music Row. If you know that Kershaw quit performing for a year and a half when it threatened his marriage, "Still Lovin' You" assumes greater significance. Even a song as strange as "Queen of My Double Wide Trailer" makes more sense when you learn that Kershaw still owns a trailer in Louisiana, "in case things don't work out." Sure, he still sounds a lot like George Jones with a South Louisiana accent. But *Haunted Heart* shows that Kershaw was coming into his own as a vocalist. Just as important, he was choosing songs that set him apart from the pack. If some of those were as offbeat as "Double Wide" and "Neon Leon," well, that's just part of what made him distinctive. —*Brian Mansfield*

Feelin' Good Train / 1994 / Mercury ✦✦✦

"National Working Woman's Holiday" was a perfect example of Kershaw's strengths and weaknesses: few people, if any, had sung about the psychological toll the economic reality of the two-income family took on Southern men whose mothers had probably stayed at home to raise them. Unfortunately, Kershaw addresses it with a song whose chorus sounds like it belongs on a T-shirt. He still sounds too much like Jones to be a great singer (just try to tell the two apart on the duet "Never Bit a Bullet Like This"), but he gets in a couple of strong ballads with "If You Ever Come This Way Again" and "Southbound." It also contains a cover of the Amazing Rhythm Aces' 1975 hit "Third Rate Romance." —*Brian Mansfield*

● Hits: Chapter 1 / Sep. 12, 1995 / Mercury Nashville ✦✦✦✦

Sammy Kershaw had only been recording for four years when he released *The Hits, Chapter 1*, but its appearance didn't seem premature. During that time, he had racked up a considerable number of Top Ten country hits, including the No. 1s "National Working Woman's Holiday" and "She Don't Know She's Beautiful." Both of those songs are included, as well as eight others that prove why he was one of the most popular country singers in the early '90s. —*Stephen Thomas Erlewine*

Politics, Religion and Her / 1996 / Mercury Nashville ✦✦

Sammy Kershaw knows the sights and smells of true honky tonks, but he keeps moving further away from the soulful slur and fun-loving style that made him sound so promising a few years ago. After too many novelty songs and misdirected pop-country moves, Kershaw tries to focus himself and get serious on *Politics, Religion and Her.* Unfortunately, his material fails him. A couple of powerful, soul-baring ballads only serve to show how superficial the rest of the song choices are. And his stiff version of Chuck Berry's "Memphis, Tennessee" would get the vote for worst cover of the year, except it gets topped by his pale take on Sammy Johns' ludicrous '70s hit, "Chevy Van." —*Michael McCall*

Clark Kessinger

b. Jul. 27, 1896, Kanawha County, WV, **d.** Jun. 4, 1975

Fiddle / Progressive Bluegrass, Traditional Bluegrass, Instrumental

One of the greatest of old-time fiddlers, Kessinger and his nephew, Luches, were billed as the Kessinger Brothers and recorded for the Brunswick company in the late '20s, producing records that greatly influenced other fiddle players around the South. When Kessinger was "rediscovered" during the folk revival of 1960, he appeared on the Opry, giving two encores because of audience demand. He entered many of the better-known fiddle contests, winning first place and the title as World's Champion Fiddler at the 47th Annual Union Grove, when he was in his mid-80s. —*David Vinopal*

★ Clark Kessinger: Fiddler / 1966 / Smithsonian/Folkways ✦✦✦✦✦

These tunes are played with incredible drive. (Like all Folkways albums, it's now available on tape from Smithsonian/Folkways.) —*Charles S. Wolfe*

Live at Union Grove / 1984 / Smithsonian/Folkways ✦✦✦✦

Clark Kessinger (Old-Time Music w/ Fiddle & Guitar) / 1984 / Rounder ✦✦✦✦

A West Virginian who began recording in 1928, Kessinger was rediscovered in the '60s and made several "comeback" albums, of which this is one of the best. —*Charles S. Wolfe*

Hal Ketchum

b. Apr. 9, 1953, Greenwich, NY

Drums, Vocals / Contemporary Country

Singer-songwriter/drummer Hal Ketchum was raised in the Adirondack Mountains in upstate New York. He began drumming at age 15 and soon joined an R&B trio. At age 17, Ketchum moved to Florida and then to Texas, where he quickly got involved playing at a local dance hall and began to hone his songwriting skills. He went to Nashville in 1986 to write songs, and three years later released his debut album, *Threadbare Alibis;* soon after, Ketchum signed with Forerunner Music, which eventually led to a record contract with Curb. He released his first Curb album, *Past the Point of Rescue,* in 1991. "Small Town Saturday Night," the first single, reached No. 2 and the second single, "I Know Where Love Lies," reached No. 13. In 1992, he scored two more hits and released his third album, *Sure Love,* which produced three Top 20 hits, including the No. 2 "Hearts Are Gonna Roll." The following year, Ketchum joined the *Grand Ole Opry.* In 1994, he released his fourth album, *Every Little Word,* which, while not quite as successful as its predecessors, still produced two Top 40 hits. In 1995, he released *Greatest Hits.* —*Sandra Brennan*

Threadbare Alibis / 1988 / Watermelon ✦✦✦
Recorded as Hal Michael Ketchum in Austin before he moved to Nashville, this is folkier and less musically focused than his country recordings. But the thoughtfulness that informs Ketchum's best work is in place, as is the willingness to take chances with his songwriting. —*Michael McCall*

Past the Point of Rescue / 1991 / Curb ✦✦✦✦
Hal Ketchum writes simple, sometimes moving songs about relationships and life's dilemmas, and communicates them in an attractive, unadorned package. But although many of these numbers espouse country themes, Ketchum's delivery, as well as the arrangements and sensibility, leans toward easy-listening pop and light folk. Certainly every country artist isn't a honky-tonking, tough-talking drinker whining about lost love, but Ketchum comes perilously close on "Past the Point of Rescue" or his cover of The Vogues' "Five O'Clock World" to the super-smooth "Nashville Sound" of days past. —*Ron Wynn*

Sure Love / 1992 / Curb ✦✦✦
Ketchum was surprised by the success of his major-label debut, and he followed up with a slicker, peppier album. The melodies are stout, and he's at his best on the working class tributes "Mama Knows the Highway" and "Daddy's Oldsmobile." —*Michael McCall*

Every Little Word / 1994 / Curb ✦✦✦✦
Ketchum reconciles the thoughtfulness of his folkie heart with the verve of modern country, tapping into the directness and earthiness that ties them together. His most country album, it's also his most consistent. —*Michael McCall*

● **Greatest Hits** / Mar. 26, 1996 / Curb ✦✦✦✦
Although it doesn't collect every worthwhile cut Ketchum recorded, *Greatest Hits* has the great majority of his big hits, making it a good introduction to the vocalist. —*Stephen Thomas Erlewine*

Royal Wade Kimes

Vocals / Contemporary Country, New Traditionalist
Royal Wade Kimes spent a decade as a professional songwriter in Nashville before he released his debut album, *Another Man's Sky*, in 1996. Before he launched his music career, Kimes—a descendent of Ozark Mountain bankrobbers—worked as a ranch hand for Loretta Lynn. A chance meeting with Eddy Arnold helped him land a job as a songwriter in Nashville. After writing hits for several artists, Kimes decided to launch a career as a new traditionalist vocalist in the mid-'90s. —*Stephen Thomas Erlewine*

Another Man's Sky / Oct. 29, 1996 / ✦✦✦
Though Royal Wade Kimes had earned quite a reputation as a professional songwriter before he became a recording artist, he wasn't able to come up with a set of winning material for his debut album, *Another Man's Sky*. Kimes does show some spark and vigor over the course of the album, but the record is bogged down by uneven material. Furthermore, he sounds more like a songwriter than a performer—he may deliver these songs with a gravelly conviction, but he doesn't quite know how to turn these songs into great performances. *Another Man's Sky* shows promise—and the best of his songs are very good—but Kimes needs to distinguish himself more as a performer before he can be truly memorable. —*Stephen Thomas Erlewine*

Claude King

b. Feb. 5, 1933, Shreveport, LA, **d.** 1983
Vocals / Traditional Country, Country-Pop, Nashville Sound/ Countrypolitan
Singer-songwriter and actor Claude King will best be remembered for his one big crossover hit, "Wolverton Mountain," the song that attracted international attention and made him a bona fide country star. The Shreveport, LA, native was a natural athlete as a child. When he was 12, he learned how to play guitar. After attending college on a baseball scholarship, he spent the '50s working as a construction engineer and performing music in local clubs and on TV and radio. King recorded his first singles in 1952,

but none of them were released. In 1961, King signed to Columbia and released his first single, "Big River, Big Man." The song became a Top Ten country hit, as well as a minor pop hit. The follow-up "The Comancheros," also made it to the Top Ten in 1962. After "The Comancheros," King released "Wolverton Mountain," which spent nine weeks at the top of the country charts and peaked at No. 6 on the pop charts. Two more hits—the Top Ten "The Burning of Atlanta" and the No. 11 "I've Got the World by the Tail"—followed that year, and he and his band, the Nashville Knights, became hot tickets. Through 1964, King continued his string of successes with singles like "Hey Lucille!," "Sam Hill," and "Building a Bridge," but his hits became more sporadic in the latter half of the '60s. King left Columbia in 1971 and began recording without success on independent labels. "Cotton Dan," which barely scraped the bottom of the charts, became his last hit in 1977. During his career, King also appeared in two feature films, *Swamp Girl* and *Year of the Wahoo*. He also appeared in the 1982 television mini-series *The Blue and the Gray*. —*Sandra Brennan*

Claude King's Greatest Hits / 1977 / True ✦✦✦✦

● **American Originals** / 1990 / Columbia ✦✦✦✦
Though he had been recording since the late '40s, Claude King didn't rise to national attention until the early '60s, when Columbia Records positioned the vocalist as the heir to the departed Johnny Horton's legacy of story-songs. *American Originals* contains all of King's country-pop hits, including "Wolverton Mountain," "Big River, Big Man," "The Comancheros," "The Burning of Atlanta," and "All for the Love of a Girl," among many others, making it the perfect retrospective of his hit-making heyday. —*Thom Owens*

More Than Climbing That Mountain / 1994 / Bear Family ✦✦✦✦
Wolverton Mountain is a five-disc box set containing all of Claude King's recordings for Columbia Records, from 1961's "Big River, Big Man" to 1972's "He Ain't Country." In addition to all of the released masters and hit singles, the box also features a number of unreleased songs, rarities, alternate takes and King's early recordings for Gotham Records. Certainly, a box set of this size is only of interest to historians and hardcore fans—there is simply too much marginal material for casual fans—but for those devoted listeners, *Wolverton Mountain* is the definitive retrospective. —*Thom Owens*

Pee Wee King (Julius Frank Kuczynski)

b. Feb. 18, 1914, Milwaukee, WI
Violin, Accordion / Traditional Country, Cowboy
As an instrumentalist, bandleader, actor, songwriter, and businessman, Pee Wee King has had a long and varied career. Born Julius Frank Kuczynski in 1914 in Wisconsin, he learned concertina, fiddle, and accordion while playing in his father's polka band. After graduation, while fronting his own band, he met Gene Autry; the future cowboy star was hosting his own program on Chicago's WLS and offered King an opportunity to back him. By 1934, Autry and King had moved to WHAS Louisville, but after less than a year, Autry departed for Hollywood.

After a year spent playing with Frankie More's Log Cabin Boys, Pee Wee King formed his own Golden West Cowboys with vocalist Texas Daisy, fiddler Abner Sims and guitarist Curly Rhodes. King ran a tight ship, organizing arrangements and intricate stage shows that promoted the band around the Louisville area. By 1937, the Golden West Cowboys had accepted a spot on the *Grand Ole Opry*.

During the early-to-mid-'40s, King's band proved an important breeding ground for vocalists; in the span of just five years, Eddy Arnold, Milton Estes, Cowboy Copas, and Tommy Sosebee all spent time with the Golden West Cowboys. Redd Stewart, who had joined in 1937 and outlasted them all, became the star of the show on King's charting hits, beginning with the No. 3 hit "Tennessee Waltz" in 1948. During the next six years, the Golden West Cowboys hit the Top 15 ten times in succession. King's only No. 1, "Slow Poke," was a giant hit in 1951—it spent 15 weeks at No. 1 and crossed over to number one pop as well (for three weeks).

Though the band failed to chart after 1954, King continued to lead the Golden West Cowboys until 1969, when he retired to work on the business side of country music. A past director of the Country Music Foundation, Pee Wee King was inducted into both the Nashville Songwriters Hall of Fame and, in 1974, the Country Music Hall of Fame. —*Jim Worbois*

The Best of Pee Wee King & Redd Stewart / 1975 / Starday ✦✦✦✦

Rompin', Stompin', Singin', Swingin' / 1983 / Bear Family ✦✦✦✦

Hog Wild Too! / 1990 / ✦✦✦
Featured are 16 cuts of Western swing and boogie-woogie music. —*AMG*

● **Pee Wee King and His Golden West Cowboys** / 1995 / Bear Family ✦✦✦✦

Sid King

Western Swing, Rockabilly, Country Boogie
One of the first White rock 'n' rollers to record for a major label (Columbia), Sid King was also one of the first young Southern musicians to go from Western swing to rockabilly in the mid-'50s. He never quite jumped into rock head over his heels, though; nor did he ever break through to a national audience. The only vintage King available on CD domestically is an interesting, but not wholly representative, set of radio broadcasts from the mid-'50s that are closer to hillbilly than rockabilly; his Columbia recordings have been reissued in Germany on Bear Family's *Gonna Shake This Shack Tonight*. —*Richie Unterberger*

Rockin' on the Radio / Mar. 19, 1996 / Schoolkids'✦✦✦
Sixteen tracks broadcast live on Texas radio stations in 1954 and 1955. With muffled (though listenable) fidelity, this is more of a historical document than a sampling of King at his best; it also finds him and his group much more grounded in hot Western swing (complete with steel guitar) than rock 'n' roll. As an archival glimpse of the first stirrings of hillbilly turning into rockabilly, though, it's not bad. The group runs through the country boogies and ballads with zesty, unpolished flair, and edge close to rockabilly with their covers of "That's All Right," "Maybellene," and "Flip, Flop & Fly." —*Richie Unterberger*

● **Gonna Shake This Shack Tonight** / Bear Family ✦✦✦✦
Sid King and the Five Strings were one of the weirdest and most enjoyable of the pre-rock 'n' roll hillbilly country bands. Not only did King and the Five Strings play country boogie and nervy honky tonk, they tore their way through R&B and blues, performing all their songs with a wild, backwoods humor. *Gonna Shake This Shack Tonight* contains all 29 songs the group recorded between 1953 and 1959. Primarily, this is music for collectors—though there is a lot of really weird, wonderful proto-rock 'n' roll here, you have to have a taste for the obscure to truly appreciate it. For those that do have a taste for the obscure, the music on *Gonna Shake This Shack Tonight* is a true treasure. —*Thom Owens*

Bill Kirchen

b. Jan. 29, 1948, Ann Arbor, MI
Guitar, Vocals / Country-Rock, Alternative Country, Americana
Bill Kirchen is best known for his work in the '70s with the rebel band Commander Cody & His Lost Planet Airmen. This gang of rock 'n' roll honky tonkers cut a wide swath through country and rock, creating an intersection where both could meet and meld together seamlessly.
Bill Kirchen was a dominating force behind the success of the Airmen. Meeting up with George Frayne, later known as Commander Cody, in his hometown of Ann Arbor, Michigan set the wheels of Kirchen's musical career into motion.
Born and raised in Ann Arbor, the future guitar god first learned to play the trombone. While in high school he meet folk singer David Siglin and proceeded to place himself in the middle of the local folk scene. This was a training ground for Kirchen's prospective endeavors. He learned to play banjo and guitar, and his fascination with folk eventually segued into an interest in the blues and string bands. While still in college, Kirchen started his

own band, an outfit best described as "psycho folk-rock." It was around this same time that Detroit-based Frayne and future airman John Tichy decided to put a country band together. Having gone to the University of Michigan, Ann Arbor, Kirchen, Frayne and some of the other Airmen knew each other: thus Commander Cody & His Lost Planet Airmen were born.
By 1969 Kirchen knew something had to be done or the band would idle away in obscurity. Aware of the music coming out of San Francisco, he convinced the rest of the band to move to the West Coast, where they took off and became legendary outlaws, lauded by Waylon Jennings and Willie Nelson as well as the Allman Brothers and the Grateful Dead. Bill Kirchen's power as a vocalist, player, performer, and songwriter began to solidify, and became known for his vocals and hot guitar licks on "Mama Hated Diesels" and the ever popular "Down to Seeds and Stems Again Blues" from two of their preeminent releases, *Hot Licks, Cold Steel & Truckers Favorites* and *Lost in the Ozone*, respectively. As a performer Kirchen came into his own while onstage in Austin for the live recording of the critically acclaimed *Live from Deep in the Heart of Texas*, recorded in November of 1973 at the Armadillo World Headquarters. Kirchen's work during this phase in the all-too-short career of Commander Cody & His Lost Planet Airmen is still remembered with awe.
The 1976 breakup of the band lead Kirchen to form the Moonlighters, a swing orchestra. British star Nick Lowe, who'd become interested in Kirchen's work while he was still with the Airmen, sought him out. The two formed a bond that is still intact. As the producer of the first Moonlighters' album, Lowe found a soulmate in the talented American. Kirchen toured internationally with his friend and even joined him in the studio. While in England Kirchen's style was a hot property, as is evidenced by his participation on recording projects for Elvis Costello, rockabilly king Gene Vincent, and Link Wray.
By 1986 Kirchen had moved to the Washington, DC area, establishing himself as a leader on the music scene. Prior to his signing on with Black Top Records in 1994, Kirchen recorded *Tombstone Every Mile*. This high-powered project was initially released on Costello's label, Demon Records, in England. Available in the States on Black Top, this was just the beginning of Bill Kirchen's recording renaissance.
1996 was the year Kirchen saw the release of *Have Love, Will Travel*. Critically acclaimed, it is an eclectic disc that displays the various aspects of Bill Kirchen's artistry and talent. Praised as one of the pioneers who marked territory for a new radio format, Americana, this still-wild guitar slinger is also noted as a forefather of the Twangcore Movement, which encompasses everyone from the king of California, Dave Alvin, to rockabilly bands and roots-rock outfits like Big Sandy & His Fly-rite Boys and Wilco. It is also believed that fellow madman Junior Brown was given a career boost thanks to Kirchen's dominating spirit, which has served as a point of light for rebels of every stripe and color.
Married for over 25 years to the same woman, and a proud father, Bill Kirchen has been instrumental in keeping the work of many musical pioneers alive. Using his 1950s Telecaster and his chameleon-like voice, he has told the tale of Bakersfield's top bard, Red Simpson, and maverick songwriter Blackie Farrell. Ernest Tubb's former man of pedal steel, Buddy Charleton, whose infallible twang and moan can be heard throughout *Have Love, Will Travel*, is a featured player in Kirchen's world. Always ahead of his time, Kirchen remains a man of distinction who looks at music not as something to be categorized, but as an art form that has no boundaries. —*Jana Pendragon*

Tombstone Every Mile / 1994 / Edsel ✦✦✦✦
This first Black Top release by honky tonker Bill Kirchen is an Americana roots music vault of valuables. With plenty of traditional C&W riffs underscored by the brilliant pedal steel of onetime Ernest Tubb steel player Buddy Charlton and the powerful piano of Mitch Collins, this project is more than mere buried treasure that contemporary radio overlooked. Kirchen, a living legend of sorts, takes a very broad stance and combines the best elements of C&W, hillbilly, blues, rockabilly, and honky tonk

music to come up with cuts like "Bottle Baby Boogie," a rip-it-up rockabilly tune that shows off Kirchen's guitar master skills, and "All Tore Up," another rocker. The Farrell-Preston song, "Fool on a Stool," is given an outstanding retooling with plenty of steel that is true to the tenets of C&W music. Covering Johnny Horton's hit, "One Woman Man," is a brave move that comes off convincingly and sounding as honest as the original. In "Secrets of Love," he teams up with bassman Jeff Sari and wife Louise Kirchen; this triple threat not only displays Bill Kirchen's songwriting skills, but a spectacular piece of music. Also noteworthy is "Think It Over," a Donley-Meaux tune that is haunting in the hands of a master. With a nod to friend Nick Lowe, Kirchen adds Louise's beautiful harmony vocals to his own multifaceted vocal style on Lowe's "Without Love" to come up with a moment that leaves time standing still. A mighty accomplishment in musical terms. This disc is only an indication of what the future holds for one of the few solid survivors of the country-rock phenomenon of the 1970s. With all his talent on display here, it is easy to understand why Kirchen has survived, even in the face of the '90s pop-bubblegum-country cookie-cutter mentality. —*Jana Pendragon*

● **Have Love, Will Travel** / Mar. 19, 1996 / Black Top ✦✦✦✦
This is one of the top releases of 1996 and it is a real mystery why it did not go platinum. The talent, the licks, and the tunes are all here. The production is right on target and Kirchen's vocals are strong and meaningful. What makes this all the more sweet is that Kirchen is one of country music's heroes from the dreadful '70s. He is one reason why so many could endure the overproduction of Nashville and rock's ridiculous disco fever that never seemed to break. As a member of Commander Cody & His Lost Planet Airmen, Kirchen and his bright and lively guitar brought tradition back in style. He is as adept at such rockers as "Don't Be True" as he is with Western Swing tunes such as his rendition of de Lone and Johnson's "Swingin' Teardrops." Cooler still is the inclusion of a few trucker songs. "Womb to the Womb," "I Heard the Highway" and the always popular, "Nitro Express" are joyful and fun. Blues, a touch of surf, some hoochie coochie music, and the very hip stylistic title cut, "Have Love, Will Travel" all demonstrate what a huge talent Bill Kirchen continues to be. With plenty of steel by Buddy Charleston and a crack core band made up of bassman Johnny Castle and percussionist Jack O'Dell, this is one hot disc that covers plenty of country and roots territory with a whole lot of class. Ending with a sweet, almost Southern gospel honeysuckle-scented refrain that is presented in pure simplicity, "I Don't Like to Work" makes this release a solid gem of brilliant dimensions. Like good whiskey or true love, Kirchen just gets better with time. —*Jana Pendragon*

Sneaky Pete Kleinow

b. Aug. 20, 1934, South Bend, IN
Traditional Country, Country-Rock
One of the unsung heroes of the country-rock movement, steel guitarist and songwriter Sneaky Pete Kleinow was born August 20, 1934 in South Bend, IN. Influenced by the music of Jerry Byrd, he took up the steel guitar at the age of 17, and after graduating high school, spent over a decade as a road maintenance worker for the Michigan State Highway Department. In 1963, Kleinow relocated to Los Angeles, where he became a regular performer on the city's club circuit; he also found work composing jingles, and even wrote the theme music for the children's series *Gumby*. In addition, he began working in Hollywood developing special effects for films.

In 1965, Kleinow played on his first record, backing the Ventures on their song "Blue Star." While performing in an area club, he met Gram Parsons and Chris Hillman, who approached Kleinow about joining the band they were organizing apart from their current venture, the folk-rock pioneer band the Byrds. Kleinow agreed, and after a brief tenure as a Byrds sideman he joined Parsons and Hillman in the Flying Burrito Brothers; the band's 1969 debut, *The Gilded Palace of Sin*, established the blueprint for the country-rock genre.

Kleinow remained with the Burritos through April 1971, appearing on the 1970 LP *Burrito Deluxe* and its eponymously titled follow-up. At the same time, he became a sought-after session musician who played on records by Joe Cocker, Delaney & Bonnie, and Little Feat. After departing the Burritos, he focused all of his energies on session work, appearing with John Lennon, Frank Zappa, Stevie Wonder, Jackson Browne, Linda Ronstadt, and the Steve Miller Band. In 1974, Kleinow briefly joined the band Cold Steel; the following year, he signed on with a reformed Flying Burrito Brothers for the album *Flying Again*.

After two more Burritos LPs—1976's *Airborne* and 1978's *Live in Tokyo*—Kleinow cut his first solo record, *Sneaky Pete*, in 1978. Following one final Burritos album, 1981's *Hearts on the Line*, he gradually withdrew from the music industry to focus on creating special effects; the films he worked on included *The Empire Strikes Back*, *The Right Stuff*, *Gremlins*, and both *Terminator* features. Nevertheless, he occasionally returned to music, performing with diverse artists like Leonard Cohen, Medicine, and the Golden Palominos. In 1994, he released the solo effort *The Legend and the Legacy*, and led a new Burritos lineup on a tour of Europe. —*Jason Ankeny*

Cold Steel / 1974 / Ariola ✦✦✦
Sneaky Pete / 1979 / Rhino ✦✦✦
● **Legend & The Legacy** / 1994 / Shiloh ✦✦✦✦

Cheri Knight

Alternative Country-Rock, Americana
Cheri Knight made her initial foray into music as the bassist for the alternative bluegrass unit the Blood Oranges. After the band's break-up, she moved from Massachusetts to New York, where she met up with musicians Eric Ambel and Will Rigby, who aided her in recording her 1996 solo debut *The Knitter*. —*Jason Ankeny*

The Knitter / Mar. 19, 1996 / East Side Digital ✦✦✦✦
Mandolinist Jimmy Ryan may have been the driving force behind the Blood Oranges, but bassist Cheri Knight's strong, earthy voice and beautifully melancholic songs marked many of that band's finest moments. On "The Knitter," she takes a confident and much-deserved step into the foreground (she even plays guitar this time around). The songs are an organic mix of strong-willed power chords, country-driven rhythms, and rural acoustic ballads, and the lyrics ring with vivid images of loneliness, anger, emotional confusion, and moments of undeniable love. Cheri Knight is the real deal, and *The Knitter* is a solid and promising debut. —*Kurt Wolff*

Jeff Knight

Vocals / Contemporary Country
Jeff Knight was born in El Paso but raised in the Allegheny Mountains region of Central Pennsylvania. Influenced by Johnny Cash, Kris Kristofferson, John Prine, and Paul Simon, Knight began performing around his hometown and later joined a touring band. He honed his music while working as a truck driver and signed a contract with the Music of the World Publishing Company. After Jeff Knight's songs were performed by Johnny Cash, Vince Gill, and Pirates of the Mississippi, Mercury Records signed him and released his debut album, *Easy Street* (1993). —*John Bush*

● **They've Been Talkin' about Me** / 1992 / Mercury ✦✦✦✦
Knight's debut spotlights his soulful readings of ballads. —*Jason Ankeny*

Easy Street / Dec. 1992 / Mercury ✦✦✦

The Knitters

Roots-Rock, Alternative Country-Rock
The Knitters was a one-off country side project of the famed Los Angeles punk band X featuring the group's vocalist Exene Cervenka, singer/bassist John Doe, and drummer D.J. Bonebrake, as well as the Blasters' guitarist Dave Alvin. (Ironically, when original X guitar player Billy Zoom left the band in 1986, it was Alvin who replaced him, albeit briefly.) The Knitters' lone LP, 1985's

Poor Little Critter on the Road, was a collection of originals, covers, and acoustic revampings of earlier X material, redone in a variety of country-based styles running from swing to traditional. —*Jason Ankeny*

Poor Little Critters on the Road / 1985 / Warner Brothers ✦✦✦
The lone recording from this X side project is a heartfelt tribute to country and folk. In addition to renditions of Leadbelly and Merle Haggard tunes, there are a handful of covers of the band's own songs, including "The New World" and "Love Shack," presaging the acoustic *Unclogged* overview the band would cut a decade later. —*Jason Ankeny*

Buddy Knox (Wayne Knox)

b. Jul. 20, 1933, Happy, TX
Guitar, Vocals / Rock & Roll, Rockabilly, Pop
The brand of Texas rockabilly that Buddy Knox cooked up around 1957 wasn't quite as raw as that of his Memphis cohorts at Sun, but it was just as commercially potent. Knox sported a light, almost gentle vocal style, and his band, the Rhythm Orchids, obliged with upbeat backing that suited him well. Formed at West Texas State University, the Rhythm Orchids also included Jimmy Bowen on upright bass, and it was Bowen's equally lighthearted vocal on "I'm Stickin' with You" that originally graced the flip side of Knox's first smash, "Party Doll." Roulette Records astutely picked up the master from the tiny Triple-D logo, separated the sides, and the fledgling firm enjoyed two giant hits for the price of one.

"Party Doll" soared to the very top of the pops, and Knox encored with the equally tuneful "Rock Your Little Baby to Sleep" and "Hula Love," which he performed in the 1957 rock flick *Jamboree*. Knox waxed the fine rockabilly-based "Swingin' Daddy," "Devil Woman," and a cover of Ruth Brown's "Somebody Touched Me" for Roulette before moving to Liberty and hitting with a pop-flavored rendition of the Clovers' song "Lovey Dovey" in 1960. Over three decades later, the Texas rocker remains a popular act on the oldies front. —*Bill Dahl*

● **The Best of Buddy Knox** / 1990 / Rhino ✦✦✦✦
This gentle, catchy Texas rockabilly has a pop slant. —*Bill Dahl*

The Complete Roulette Recordings / 1996 / Sequel ✦✦✦
Knox only has one-half of this double CD; the second disc is devoted to tracks by his friend and contemporary, Jimmy Bowen. The approach isn't as odd as it seems: when Knox and Bowen began their recording careers, they were both part of the Rhythm Orchids, and a similar lineup of Orchids backs each solo singer on their respective recordings. Most listeners will be much better off with Rhino's briefer, more selective Knox best-of. Completists, however, will find all 30 of Knox's 1956-60 Roulette tracks on disc one of this two-pack. Including five previously unreleased songs, it's pleasant Tex-Mex rockabilly, tamer than Buddy Holly, but far gutsier than the Jimmy Bowen solo cuts that take up all of disc two. —*Richie Unterberger*

Liberty Takes / Charly ✦✦✦

Fred Koller

Vocals / Progressive Country, Contemporary Country, Singer-Songwriter, Contemporary Folk
Fred Koller is a Nashville songwriter whose songs have been covered by Kathy Mattea (three No. 1 hits), the Jeff Healey Band, Nanci Griffith, Peter Rowan, New Grass Revival, the Forester Sisters, and Lacy J. Dalton. Koller has collaborated with such artists as John Prine, Tom Paxton, John Hiatt, Shel Silverstein, John Gorka, Bill Staines, and others. He is the author of a book on songwriting, *How to Pitch and Promote Your Songs*. Koller has developed a cult following that appreciates his deep, rough-edged vocals and powerful, often humorous songwriting. —*Chip Renner*

● **Songs from the Night Before** / 1989 / Alcazar ✦✦✦✦
Koller's first solo album, this portrays the eclectic character of Koller's colorful insights and his balance of troubling observations, hard-eyed irony, and sentimental yearnings. "Life as We Knew It" recalls a friendlier, slower America, while "This Hell We Created"

and "Showbizness" wonderfully spoofs modern relationships and entertainment. —*Michael McCall*

Night of the Living Fred / 1989 / Alcazar ✦✦✦
Accentuating his broad humor and biting irony, instead of lingering in the shadows, here his wit hogs the spotlight. —*Michael McCall*

Where the Fast Lane Ends / 1990 / Alcazar ✦✦✦✦
Koller's versions of his songs "Goin' Gone" and "Lone Star State of Mind" are here, but he has a deep, bluesy voice that puts a very different spin on these familiar tunes. —*William Ruhlmann*

Alison Krauss

b. Jul. 23, 1971, Decatur, IL
Fiddle / Progressive Bluegrass, Traditional Bluegrass, Contemporary Country
Alison Krauss helped bring bluegrass to a new audience in the '90s. Blending bluegrass with folk, Krauss was instantly acclaimed from the start of her career, but it wasn't until her platinum-selling 1995 compilation, *Now That I've Found You*, that she became a mainstream star. Between her 1987 debut *Too Late to Cry* and *Now That I've Found You*, she matured from a child prodigy into a versatile, ambitious, and diverse musician and, in the process, made some of the freshest bluegrass of the late '80s and early '90s.

When she was five years old, Krauss began playing the violin, taking classical lessons. She soon tired of the regiments of classical playing and began performing country and bluegrass licks. At the age of eight, she began entering talent contests in and around her native Champaign, IL. Two years later, she had her own band. In 1983, when she was 12 years old, she won the Illinois State Fiddle Championship and the Society for the Preservation of Bluegrass in America named her the Most Promising Fiddler in the Midwest. In 1985, Krauss made her recording debut on an album, playing on a record made by her brother Viktor, Jim Hoiles, and Bruce Weiss. The album was called *Different Strokes* and appeared on the independent Fiddle Tunes label. Later that year, she signed to Rounder Records. She was 14 years old at the time.

Too Late to Cry, Alison's debut album, appeared in 1987 to very positive reviews. The album was recorded with Krauss' backup band, the Union Station, which featured guitarist Jeff White, banjoist Alison Brown, and bassist Viktor Krauss; the following year, the group won the Society for the Preservation of Bluegrass in America's National Band Championship contest. In 1989, Krauss and Union Station released *Two Highways*, which was nominated for a Grammy Award for Best Bluegrass Recording. Although the album didn't win the award, her next album, 1990's *I've Got That Old Feeling*, did. The success of *I've Got That Old Feeling* was unprecedented for bluegrass acts in the '80s and it laid the groundwork for Krauss' breakthrough in the '90s. By this time, the Union Station's lineup had more or less settled—it now featured mandolinist Adam Steffey, banjoist/guitarist Ron Block, bassist Barry Bales, and guitarist Tim Stafford; Stafford later left the group and was replaced by Dan Tyminski.

In 1992, Alison Krauss and Union Station released *Every Time You Say Goodbye*, which featured a typically eclectic array of material—everything from "Orange Blossom Special" to the Beatles' "I Will" and Shawn Colvin's "I Don't Know Why" were covered. The album appeared in the country charts and Krauss' videos were shown on Country Music Television. *I Know Who Holds Tomorrow* was released in 1994 and was even more successful. But it was the 1995 compilation, *Now That I've Found You: A Collection*, that made Krauss a star. The album reached No. 2 on the country charts and—even more remarkably—went into the pop Top Ten and sold over a million copies. Its success confirmed her status as bluegrass' leading light in the '90s. —*Stephen Thomas Erlewine*

Different Strokes / 1985 / Fiddle Tunes ✦✦✦
Different Strokes is the first album to feature an appearance by Alison Krauss. Released on the very small independent record label Fiddle Tunes when Krauss was only 14, the record is a col-

lection fo bluegrass and traditional folk material performed by Alison, her brother Viktor, Bruce Weiss, and Jim Hoiles. —*Thom Owens*

Too Late to Cry / 1987 / Rounder ✦✦✦
Alison Krauss may have recorded *Too Late to Cry* when she was only 14 years old, but her sound was already well-developed and astonishingly accomplished. Throughout the album, she demonstrates a mastery of bluegrass, singing and playing with a distinctive grace. It's an impressive debut, but it would pale in comparison to the albums that followed. —*Thom Owens*

Two Highways / 1989 / Rounder ✦✦✦✦
Two Highways is the first album Alison Krauss recorded with her excellent backing band, Union Station, and, appropriately, it demonstrates that she could lead a band through a number of bluegrass standards, as well as several more contemporary numbers. Of course, her instrumental solos continue to be the most impressive thing about her music on *Two Highways*, but her duets with guitarists Jeff White demonstrate that her vocals are beginning to come into their own. —*Thom Owens*

I've Got That Old Feeling / 1990 / Rounder ✦✦✦✦
There's a sweet voice, fine fiddling, and a tight plaintive band on this breakthrough bluegrass/country/pop album that produced the first music video for bluegrass. —*Mark A. Humphrey*

Every Time You Say Goodbye / 1992 / Rounder ✦✦✦✦
On *Every Time You Say Goodbye*, Alison Krauss continues to expand the boundaries of bluegrass without ever abandoning its roots. Krauss combines contemporary folk covers (such as Shawn Colvin's "I Don't Know Why") with more traditional material, interpreting both in fresh, inventive ways. She plays and sings beautifully throughout the album, proving that she is the most progressive, exciting bluegrass musician of the '90s. —*Thom Owens*

I Know Who Holds Tomorrow / 1994 / Rounder ✦✦✦
I Know Who Holds Tomorrow isn't as consistently engaging as *Every Time You Say Goodbye*, but that's only a relative term—from any other artist, this would be a masterpiece. From Krauss, it's another reliably wonderful collection of jaw-dropping fiddling and breathtaking singing. —*Thom Owens*

★ **Now That I've Found You: A Collection** / Feb. 7, 1995 / Rounder ✦✦✦✦✦
Alison Krauss had been recording a decade before she gained stardom, but she became a star in a big way. *Now That I've Found You: A Collection*, a retrospective of her ten-year recording career for Rounder, became the surprise hit of 1995, rocketing to No. 2 on the country charts and into the Top 15 on the *pop* charts, which is remarkable for a musician that had never captured the attention of a mass audience. It may have been a surprising success, but it also was deserved. Krauss was arguably the leading bluegrass musician of the late '80s and early '90s, pushing the music into new directions without losing sight of its roots. *Now That I've Found You* does a splendid job of chronicling her career, hitting all of the highlights and encouraging new listeners to seek out her albums. —*Stephen Thomas Erlewine*

Kris Kristofferson

b. Jun. 22, 1936, Brownsville, TX
Guitar, Vocals / Traditional Country, Progressive Country, Singer-Songwriter, Outlaw Country
The '70s was a decade ripe and waiting for rebels. The Nashville establishment, though, which had sold a lot of records with the bland "Nashville Sound," wasn't quite ready for this former soldier, West Point instructor, and Rhodes Scholar who, with long beard and dressed in jeans, in 1970 walked onstage at the Country Music Association Awards and got his songwriting award for "Sunday Mornin' Comin' Down," which his friend Johnny Cash had turned into a No. 1 hit. When in the next year Janis Joplin sold a million records with "Me and Bobby McGee" (one of several Kristofferson songs previously covered by Roger Miller), he was on his way, anti-establishment or not. Then Sammi Smith's version of "Help Me Make It through the Night" was a hit on both the country and pop charts, also in 1971; suddenly Kristofferson's

Alison Krauss

creative lyrics and memorable music made the establishment forget about his image.

In 1973, the year he and singer Rita Coolidge married, two of his albums, *The Silver Tongued Devil and I* and *Jesus Was a Capricorn* (which contained his first No. 1 hit as a singer, "Why Me?"), went gold. Meanwhile his duets with Coolidge sold well and produced two Grammys for them.

Kristofferson's acting career also took off in the early 1970s, beginning with Dennis Hopper's *The Last Movie*. Film roles have cropped up regularly for him ever since, among them *Cisco Pike*, Sam Peckinpah's *Pat Garrett and Billy the Kid* (with James Coburn and Bob Dylan), Martin Scorsese's *Alice Doesn't Live Here Anymore*, *The Sailor Who Fell from Grace with the Sea*, *A Star Is Born* (with Barbra Streisand; his shirtless image on the album cover may have done his career more harm than good in the long run), *Convoy, Heaven's Gate, Songwriter*, and John Sayles' 1996 film *Lone Star*. He also contributed songs to the soundtracks of a number of these and other films. Kristofferson's last big chart success as a solo performer, in fact, was "Watch Closely Now" from the multiplatinum soundtrack to *A Star Is Born*. He continued to have minor chart hits into the 1980s, but nothing like his phenomenal sales of the previous decade.

In the mid-1980s Kristofferson teamed up with pals Johnny Cash, Waylon Jennings, and Willie Nelson under the name the Highwaymen, which released their first album in 1985. They've since recorded two more albums, *Highwaymen II* (1990) and *The Road Goes on Forever* (1995); the latter's title song seriously boosted the career of its author, Robert Earl Keen. Also in 1995, Kristofferson was signed onto the roster of the growing Texas label Justice, which released his first new solo album in almost a decade, *A Moment of Forever*. —*David Vinopal & Kurt Wolff*

Kristofferson / 1970 / Monument ✦✦✦✦
This classic first album from Kristofferson showcases his versions of songs made famous by others. While he sometimes went to

extremes to get these songs heard in the first place (landing a helicopter in Johnny Cash's yard in an effort to get the singer to hear his songs), this album should not be missed by anyone who's ever liked any of these songs. Once Monument realized what a talent they had, they reissued this record as *Me & Bobby McGee*. —*Jim Worbois*

The Silver Tongued Devil and I / 1971 / Monument ✦✦✦✦
This second album from Kristofferson continues where the first one left off: with more great songs that were readily snapped up and made into hits by other artists. In addition to original versions of songs that were hits by Bobby Bare and Ray Price, this album also features the first appearance of Rita Coolidge on one of Kristofferson's albums (billed as The Lady). —*Jim Worbois*

☆ **Me & Bobby McGee** / 1971 / Monument ✦✦✦✦✦
In the late '60s and early '70s, Kris Kristofferson's adult, reality-based songs were the most shocking thing to hit Nashville in a long time, and what's more, they were hits. This album contains his own versions of some of the best, including the title song, "Help Make It through the Night," and "Sunday Mornin' Comin' Down." —*William Ruhlmann*

Border Lord / 1972 / One Way ✦✦✦✦
While the quality of the songwriting remains high on this album, the overall feel of the record is more "down." Monument seemed to be showing some faith in Kristofferson as an artist by releasing "Josie" as a single. Unfortunately, it wasn't a hit. Still, this album should not be missed. —*Jim Worbois*

Jesus Was a Capricorn / 1972 / Monument ✦✦✦
After a visit to the church of Jimmy Snow, Kristofferson was inspired to write the song that was his first hit as a performer: "Why Me?" This is also the first time Kristofferson covered a song by another writer. Another strong album worth looking for. —*Jim Worbois*

Full Moon / 1973 / A&M ✦✦
The Nelson Eddy-Jeanette McDonald of country-rock, Kris Kristofferson and Rita Coolidge come across as true lovers trying hard to convey their affections to their audience. Since Kris seems to be sleepwalking through his parts and Rita sounds as if she's only half-trying, the result is an uneven record full of flashes of greatness ("Tennessee Blues") and touches of care ("Loving Arms"), as well as cliched awkwardness ("From the Bottle to the Bottom"). Worthy as a document of two star-crossed lovers giddy from the initial rush of passion and little else. —*James Chrispell*

Spooky Lady's Sideshow / 1974 / One Way ✦✦✦
Kris Kristofferson continued on a downhill slide with the release of this record, although it did get a lot of attention. With his twisted look at his life and times, tracks such as "Star Spangled Bummer" and "Stairway to the Bottom" evoke the mood of his record. Most of the songs are poor, but the record has a certain sad appeal. —*James Chrispell*

Breakaway / 1974 / Monument ✦✦
Cut with then-wife Rita Coolidge, *Breakaway* includes the minor hit "Rain." —*Jason Ankeny*

Who's to Bless and Who's to Blame / 1975 / Monument ✦✦
Sounding like leftovers from a Kris and Rita duo project, there is not much here to bless, but you sure know who to blame. Kristofferson doesn't seem to care about what he's doing at this time—he's just going through the motions, hoping something that he's throwing at his audience will stick. Not much here does, unfortunately, and it's a shame. —*James Chrispell*

★ **The Songs of Kristofferson** / 1977 / Monument ✦✦✦✦✦
This greatest-hits collection features most of the songs he wrote but that others turned into hits, including "Sunday Morning Coming Down," "The Pilgrim Number 33," "For the Good Times," "Help Me Make It through the Night," and "Why Me?" His idiosyncratic versions aren't pretty, but they're intimate and often powerful. —*Michael McCall*

A Star Is Born / 1977 / Monument ✦✦

Shake Hands with the Devil / 1979 / One Way ✦✦
Using cover shots taken from Kris Kristofferson's starring role in the motion picture, *A Star Is Born*, this collection of tracks could be anything. What they aren't is a good Kristofferson album. The album is just Kris going through the motions. While the title track does have something to recommend it, not much else can be said for the remainder of the album. —*James Chrispell*

Music from Songwriter / 1984 / Monument ✦✦✦
With Willie Nelson. The title song was nominated for an Oscar. —*Kurt Wolff*

Repossessed / 1986 / Mercury ✦✦
Includes Kristofferson's version of the Bob Dylan song "They Killed Him." —*Kurt Wolf*

Singer/Songwriter / 1991 / Monument ✦✦✦✦
An interesting concept: a two-disc set, one featuring Kristofferson's version of 17 of his songs, the other featuring covers of the same songs by Ray Price, Janis Joplin, Bob Dylan, Johnny Cash, and others. —*Michael McCall*

Live at the Philharmonic / 1992 / Monument ✦✦✦✦
Recorded in New York City on December 2, 1972, but not released until two decades later, this live concert showcases Kristofferson during his most musically creative period. The impressive set list includes John Prine's "Late John Garfield Blues," the soul classic "Rainbow Road," the overlooked "Billy Dee," and an update on "Okie from Muskogee." Willie Nelson, Rita Coolidge, and Larry Gatlin help him out, as does an excellent band that includes Donnie Fritts and Stephen Bruton. —*Kurt Wolff*

A Moment of Forever / 1995 / Justice ✦✦✦✦
An impressive batch of new songs, from "Shipwrecked in the Eighties" to "New Mister Me," fills what's easily Kristofferson's best album in years. His voice is even rougher around the edges than it was 25 years ago, but the production (by Don Was) and Kristofferson's soul (dustier but wiser) are both honest and easy. The stellar band of L.A. session players includes Jim Keltner, Benmont Tench, Waddy Wachtel, and Danny Timms. —*Kurt Wolff*

The Best of Kris Kristofferson / Dec. 1, 1995 / Sony Special Products ✦✦✦✦

L

Sleepy La Beef (Thomas Paulsley La Beff)

b. Jul. 11, 1935, Smackover, AR

Guitar, Vocals / Traditional Country, Rockabilly

Sleepy La Beef was one of the best rockabilly musicians around. He was born Thomas Paulsley La Beff in Smackover, AR. The 6'7" singer has heavily lidded eyes which make him appear half-asleep, hence his nickname. He was raised on a melon farm and was influenced by both country and blues music. La Beef moved to Houson at age 18 where he worked at several odd jobs before beginning to sing gospel music on local radio shows. Eventually, he formed his own band and began playing rockabilly and straight rock 'n' roll during the 1950s. He made his first recordings in 1957 on Starday. He subsequently recorded on many different labels, where he used his own name or sometimes appeared as Tommy LaBeff. He moved to Nashville in 1964 and one year later signed to Columbia. His sixth single for the label, "Every Day," provided La Beef with his lower chart debut in 1968. He moved to Shelby Singleton's Plantation label in 1969 and finally began having more success. His third single, "Blackland Farmer," penned by Frankie Miller, hit the Top 70 and became his biggest chart single. He moved with Singleton to Sun Records in the mid-'70s and continued releasing rockabilly singles such as "Thunder Road," "There Ain't Much After Taxes," and "Boogie Woogie Country Girl." La Beef is more popular in Europe than in the US and has appeared at England's Wembley Festival twice. He signed to Rounder in 1981 and released *It Ain't What You Eat (It's the Way You Chew It)* in the US and in Europe. The towering baritone La Beef made his movie debut as a swamp monster in *The Exotic Ones.* —*Sandra Brennan*

● **Nothin' but the Truth** / 1985 / Rounder ✦✦✦✦

There aren't many legitimate characters left in popular music; the rotund Sleepy La Beef isn't a media concoction or collection of outrageous cliches exploiting a carefully built image. He's a simple, hard-rocking vocalist with a manic performance style and musical approach that seamlessly blends rockabilly, classic rock 'n' roll, gospel, and country boogie into a non-stop, attacking mode. This 12-track live set from 1985 includes La Beef renditions of "Milk Cow Blues," "Ring of Fire," "Tore up over You," "My Toot Toot" and a rousing concluding medley that includes "Jambalaya" and "Folsom Prison Blues." No-frills, unsophisticated, joyous roots music without reverence or pomp. —*Ron Wynn*

Strange Things Happening / Mar. 30, 1994 / Rounder ✦✦✦

Sleepy La Beef is a bawdy, exuberant performer whose musical skills are slightly above average, but whose heart and energy are king-sized. He rips through Western swing, rockabilly, R&B, and rock on this 14-track set, doing originals and vintage pieces with equal ferocity. La Beef doesn't coast through any songs; he sings "Standing in the Need of Prayer" and "Strange Things Happening" with the same aggressiveness as "Sittin' on Top of the World" and "Stagger Lee." His slashing guitar riffs and authoritative vocals setting the pace, Sleepy La Beef makes music for those who feel the spirit, no matter what the song. —*Ron Wynn*

Larger Than Life / 1996 / Bear Family ✦✦✦✦

All of Sleepy La Beef's most important records—from his early singles for Starday to his latter-day sides for Sun—are included on the mammoth, six-disc box set *Larger Than Life.* La Beef recorded for a number of different labels during his career, and during that time, he explored a variety of roots music, from rockabilly and country to blues and soul. Spanning three full decades, *Larger Than Life* contains 158 tracks, including all of his recordings for Starday, Dixie, Columbia, and Sun. The box begins in the '50s and ends in the '70s, hitting all of La Beef's best moments in the interim. A set of this size is designed for hardcore fans, and they are the ones that will treasure it—for less dedicated listeners, the music may become rather monotonous, since the sheer length of the box is overwhelming. However, *Larger Than Life* is a treasure for devoted followers, since it collects many rare items—La Beef's records have never been very easy to track down—adding an excellent booklet and many demos and outtakes. For those fans, it's a necessary addition to their collection. —*Thom Owens*

I'll Never Lay My Guitar Down / Jun. 1996 / Rounder ✦✦✦✦

Original rockabilly basso profundo Sleepy La Beef is back with a new album and the great news is that it's even better than the last one he put out on the Rounder imprint, the truly involved *Strange Things Happening.* Like the last one, this new biscuit is produced by Jake Guralnick (who guests on lap steel and guitar), and features Duke Levine on guitar, Paul Bryan on bass, Dave Keyes on piano, and the right-in-the-pocket Lisa Pankratz on drums. For his part, Mister La Beef tears through 11 country, rockabilly, rock 'n' roll, and bluesy favorites, giving each of 'em the flattening stamp of his whole personality. When Sleepy's into it, he's just the best, and this time it's evident by his screams and yelps that the pilot light was lit full blast. If your idea of rockabilly is some guy with a pompadour hiccuping himself into an early grave, do yourself a favor and pick up Sleepy's latest. He may be 60 years old, but he knows how to rock; after all, he was there when they invented it. —*Cub Koda*

Jimmy LaFave

Vocals / Singer-Songwriter, Alternative Country, Americana

A local favorite specifically around the Austin area and generally throughout Texas, Jimmy LaFave released his national debut, *Austin Skyline,* on Bohemia Beat Records. The live album features backing by Night Tribe (Larry Wilson on lead guitar, bassist Randy Glines, keyboardist David Webb, and drummer Mark Patterson). *Highway Trance* (1994) and *Buffalo Return to the Plains* (1995) have both followed. —*John Bush*

● **Austin Skyline** / 1992 / Bohemia Beat ✦✦✦✦

Highway Trance / 1994 / Bohemia Beat ✦✦✦✦

His plaintive voice embraces his lyrics with the feelings of his heart. His singing and songwriting (he wrote all the songs except "Early Summer Rain") evoke the wide open sky of Texas, with the great spaces between people as evident as the stars in the wide open sky. His tight band keeps the sound moving behind him. He deftly varies the rhythms and song styles so that the album never lets you fall into that "Highway Trance" which he sings of. His lyrics are sharp on the variety of subjects he addresses. Maybe a notch below *Austin Skyline*, but it's a small step down, and a big step forward. —*Bob Gottlieb*

Buffalo Return to the Plains / 1995 / Bohemia Beat ✦✦✦✦
Jimmy LaFave's dry, rootsy songs are full of details of life, which is what makes *Buffalo Return to the Plains* another winning addition to his catalog. —*David Jehnzen*

Lambchop

Indie Rock, Alternative Country-Rock
One of the hands-down weirdest groups to appear on the alternative scene in the mid-'90s (although they had been active for some years before that), it's hard to tell whether Lambchop play alternative rock with a heavy Nashville country influence, straight country music with a heavy alternative rock influence, or whether the whole thing is just an ironic joke. The group are actually from Nashville, and numbers about ten members (although the lineup fluctuates). The chief of this zany crew, however, is singer-songwriter/guitarist Kurt Wagner, whose stream-of-consciousness laments are distinctly at odds with the (usually) comfortably normal-sounding country-pop arrangements.

Musically, Lambchop can (and often does) offer a reasonable facsimile of the MOR Nashville country devised by producers such as Billy Sherrill (who handled Charlie Rich's most popular work, and worked with Tammy Wynette and Tanya Tucker in the '70s). It is doubtful, however, that any release on the Merge label (also home to acts like Magnetic Fields and Superchunk) is aimed at the mainstream country music audience. Lambchop subverts the clichés of Nashville country with lyrics about suicide, bowling, and Theodore Dreiser-ish narratives about mundane everyday activities. There are also occasional interjections of post-punk guitar, thrash, clarinets, organ, and recorders that will not find a home in many trailer parks. Nor will Wagner's uneasy mumbling vocal style, which has more in common with Morrissey than Garth Brooks.

This is not the solace that most listeners turn to country-pop for as a respite from their day-to-day activities; it *is* their day-to-day activities, rendered too unflinchingly for comfort. Nor is it, despite considerable critical acclaim, the art statement some make it out to be, with plenty of what's-the-point lyrics and a nagging suspicion that the whole thing is a tongue-in-cheek art-school project that's gotten out of hand. Of their two albums, the debut is by far the more rock-influenced; 1995's *How I Quit Smoking* embraces mushy country production values much more wholeheartedly, without much alteration to the off-kilter, unsettling (and occasionally profane) tone of the lyrics. —*Richie Unterberger*

I Hope You're Sitting Down [aka Jack's Tulips] / 1994 / Merge ✦✦✦
A mix of post-modernism and straight (not roots) country music. The spooky organ fills, saxes, clarinets, and cello make this sound at times like the Art Ensemble of Chicago-as-country-band. Kurt Wagner's morose, resigned lyrics and dry, almost spoken delivery can get hard to take over the course of the hour-plus disc. "Soaker in the Pooper," a song about suicide in the bathroom, gave Wagner almost instant notoriety, and many of the other songs deal with similarly downbeat matters, although usually not as directly. —*Richie Unterberger*

● **How I Quit Smoking** / Jan. 30, 1996 / Merge ✦✦✦✦
Bona fide string arrangements give Lambchop's second album a much more "authentic" Nashville country feel than the first—meaning, ironically, that it sometimes sounds as gloppy, sentimental, and superficial as "real" Nashville country records. The arrangements are more inventive as well, mixing conventional country instruments like steel and acoustic guitars with saxes, clarinet, cornet, banjo, and tin whistle, along with the same kind of off-center organ featured on the first album. Wagner continues to mine the same offbeat lyrical territory, though unlike other audio verité talents like (say) Lou Reed, he doesn't bring much passion to his inner monologues. —*Richie Unterberger*

Cristy Lane (Eleanor Johnston)

b. Jan. 8, 1940, Peoria, IL
Vocals / Country-Pop, CCM, Inspirational
Best remembered for 1979's "One Day at a Time," one of the biggest-selling gospel songs of all time, Cristy Lane was born Eleanor Johnston to a family of 12 in Peoria, IL. After marrying Lee Stoller at the age of 17, she made a demo tape which her husband used to convince a nightclub owner of her talents. After Lane made another demo tape and began sending it to radio stations, the *National Barn Dance* eventually hired her for $87 an appearance. She took her stage name from a local deejay, "Chris Lane."

In 1966, Stoller directed his wife toward Nashville. He had her dye her naturally dark hair blonde, and once in Music City, paid to have her record two songs she had written, "Stop Fooling with Me" and "Heart in the Sand." Stoller then began taking the demo directly to record companies, but had no luck until he decided to market her himself through K-Ark record distributors. They manufactured 800 records for the Stollers, who sent 300 of them to national radio stations. Again, nothing happened and Lane went back to performing at the club they owned together. In 1969, Stoller took her on an ill-advised tour of Vietnam, on which she performed 120 shows for the troops and was involved in a helicopter crash that left her stranded in the midst of a battle.

Upon her return to the States, Lane returned to the club circuits and military bases. In 1972, they moved to a Nashville suburb and Stoller continued his attempts to get Lane's career off the ground. Stoller formed LS Records in the mid-'70s and finally found success when Lane's debut single, "Tryin' to Forget About You," and its follow-up, "Sweet Deceiver," appeared on the charts in 1977. That year she also made it to the Top Ten and the Top 20 with "Let Me Down Easy" and "Shake Me I Rattle," respectively. She scored three more hits the following year and in 1979 was named the ACM's New Vocalist of the Year. During the ceremony, Lane sang "I Just Can't Stay Married to You," which later became a Top Five hit. In late 1979, Lane signed to United Artists Records and had three more hits before persuading the label to release "One Day at a Time." After it hit No. 1 on the country charts, she released "Sweet Sexy Eyes," her final Top Ten hit. Lane marketed her 1986 album *One Day at a Time* on television, which helped it become a big seller. During the '90s, Lane has spent most of her time performing at her theater in Branson, MO. —*Sandra Brennan*

One Day at a Time / 1978 / Arrival ✦✦✦✦
A simplistic, soft-pop style of gospel from her gentle voice. —*Bil Carpenter*

● **Footprints in the Sand** / 1983 / Liberty ✦✦✦✦
Because of the strong selection of songs and consistent performances, this compilation is the one to get out of the several Lane discs available from Arrival. —*Stephen Thomas Erlewine*

Amazing Grace, Vol. 2 / 1986 / Arrival ✦✦✦
A solid, if unspectacular, set of popular gospel tunes that are nicely performed by Lane, even if she is occasionally dominated by an intrusive synthesizer. —*Stephen Thomas Erlewine*

All in His Hands / 1989 / Heartwarming ✦✦✦
Lane's pristine sounds come through best on the '50s-style "He Loves Me Still." —*Bil Carpenter*

My Best to You / 1992 / Arrival ✦✦✦
A good compilation of some of Lane's most popular gospel material, which is somewhat undermined by the number of tracks duplicated from *Footprints in the Sand.* —*Stephen Thomas Erlewine*

k.d. lang

b. Nov. 2, 1961, Consort, Alberta, Canada
Vocals / Adult Alternative Pop-Rock, Alternative Country
When k.d. lang released her first major label album in 1987, she caused considerable controversy within the traditional world of country music. With her vaguely campy approach, androgynous appearance, and edgy, rock-inflected music, very few observers

knew what to make of her or her music, although no one questioned her considerable vocal talents. That confusion never quite dissipated over the course of her career, even when she abandoned country music for torchy adult contemporary pop in 1992, with her fourth album, *Ingenue*.

Born in Alberta, Canada, lang was first drawn toward music while she was in college. In particular, she was attracted to the music of Patsy Cline. She became acquainted with Cline's music while she was preparing to star in a collegiate theatrical production based on the vocalist's life. Soon, lang immersed herself in studying Cline's life and music and decided that she would pursue a career as a professional singer. With the help of guitarist/co-songwriter Ben Mink, she formed a band (named the re-clines in tribute to Patsy Cline) in 1983 and they recorded a debut album, *Friday Dance Promenade*, which received some positive notices in independent papers. A follow-up album, *A Truly Western Experience*, was released in 1984, received even better reviews, and led to national attention. In 1985, lang was named the Most Promising Female Vocalist by the Juno Awards.

All of the Canadian attention led to the interest of a number of American record labels. Sire signed lang in early 1986 and she recorded her first record for the label later that year. The result, *Angel with a Lariat*, was produced by Dave Edmunds and appeared in the fall of 1986. The mix of '50s-styled ballads, kitschy rockabilly and honky tonk numbers on *Angel with a Lariat* received good reviews, especially from rock critics. The album had heavy support from college radio, as well as cutting-edge country stations. Though it was a mainstream hit in Canada and an underground smash in the US, Nashville resisted lang, especially her tongue-in-cheek concert appearances. As she was recording her second Nashville album in 1987, lang duetted with Roy Orbison on his old hit "Crying," which was recorded for the film *Hiding Out*. The single was released at the end of the year and it was a hit, marking her first appearance on the country charts.

Shadowland, her second Sire album, made her debt to Patsy Cline explicit. Recorded with Cline's producer, Owen Bradley, the album lacked the campy humor of *Angel with a Lariat*, which helped it succeed in traditional country circles—"I'm Down to My Last Cigarette," the first single from the record, was her first to break the country Top 40. *Shadowland* became a sizable word-of-mouth hit, both in modern country and alternative music circles, which led to it going gold. The following year lang released the harder-edged *Absolute Torch and Twang*, which increased her mainstream American country audience, in addition to being a college radio and Canadian hit. lang won a Grammy—Best Country Vocal Performance, Female—for the album in 1989 and "Full Moon of Love" became a Top 25 hit in the summer of 1989. The attention made lang a minor celebrity, which meant that when she launched a protest against meat eating in 1990, it became a media sensation.

Before the release of her fourth album, lang declared that she was a lesbian in an interview in *The Advocate*, which could have been a risky proposition, since Nashville's industry was notorious for not accepting people that fell outside of the margins of the mainstream. However, the new album was not a country album. *Ingenue* was a set of adult contemporary pop that owed very little to country. Its first single, "Constant Craving," became a Top 40 American hit and won the Grammy Award for Best Pop Vocal Performance, Female, leading the album to platinum status in America, Britain, and Australia; it went double platinum in Canada.

Ingenue won lang a new audience, but she didn't immediately produce a follow-up to the album. Instead, her next recorded work was the largely instrumental soundtrack for Gus Van Zant's film adaptation of Tom Robbins' *Even Cowgirls Get the Blues* in 1993; the soundtrack was actually released several months before the film. It wasn't until 1995 that lang delivered *All You Can Eat*, her full-fledged follow-up to *Ingenue*. *All You Can Eat* continued the pop direction of its predecessor, showing no traces of country. The album didn't enjoy the mass commercial acceptance of *Ingenue*, but it was a moderate success, proving that she had a dedicated cult following. —*Stephen Thomas Erlewine*

A Truly Western Experience / 1984 / Bumstead ✦✦✦
k.d. lang's first independent album is an uneven but exciting revamp of '50s country. She alternates between rocking honky tonk numbers and Patsy Cline-influenced weepers, sometimes assuming an ironic distance. It may be flawed, but *A Truly Western Experience* has an almost punky kick and illustrates why lang would soon be considered as the freshest female vocalist in country music in the late '80s. —*Stephen Thomas Erlewine*

Angel with a Lariat / 1987 / Sire ✦✦✦
On her debut album, big-voiced k. d. lang took a rockabilly approach, with Dave Edmunds as her perfect producer choice. Edmunds brought out the sharp, rhythmic aspects of her band the Reclines, and long wailed over them. The record, which was underappreciated at the time of its release, was an amazingly confident first effort. —*William Ruhlmann*

★ **Shadowland** / 1988 / Sire ✦✦✦✦✦
Rebuffed commercially, lang turned to veteran Nashville producer Owen Bradley for this genre exercise, which recreates the kind of country diva style of Patsy Cline. It was an accomplished, if puzzling, effort that broke lang through to the country market, at least temporarily. —*William Ruhlmann*

Absolute Torch and Twang / 1989 / Sire ✦✦✦✦
As the title suggests, lang's third (and last country) album combines the best qualities of the first two—the affected-but-original country songwriting of *Angel with a Lariat* and the soaring, Patsy Cline-influenced vocals of *Shadowland*. —*Brian Mansfield*

Ingenue / 1992 / Sire ✦✦✦✦
Canada's angel with a lariat has chucked the spurs for *Ingenue* in favor of a classic, Tin-Pan-Alley pop approach. lang's turnaround is a great success. *Ingenue* is an achingly beautiful work, all melancholy longing and heartbreak that strikes a perfect balance between the pain and pleasure of love. To stake out her own individual territory somewhere between Patsy Cline and Billie Holliday without relying on pop standards is a feat in itself. The ten original compositions give full rein to lang's spectacularly expressive voice. One misses the sense of humor and playful spirit that has infused lang's music in the past, but that can wait until next time 'round when she's recovered from whatever major personal crisis served as inspiration for *Ingenue*. For now, listen and weep. —*Roch Parisien*

All You Can Eat / Oct. 10, 1995 / Sire ✦✦✦
k.d. lang followed through on the promise of her adult contemporary changeover *Ingenue* with *All You Can Eat*. A more experimental and realized record than its predecessor, there are more daring production touches on *All You Can Eat*—it's clear that she has been listening to contemporary pop, not just torch songs. This isn't immediately accessible—the production is low-key, the melodies are gentle and subtle (although her cutesy, tongue-in-cheek song titles suggest otherwise), and lang gives a nuanced, sophisticated performance. Though it lacks a standout song like the aching "Constant Craving," *All You Can Eat* has a more consistent set of songs and, given time, is a more rewarding listen. —*Stephen Thomas Erlewine*

Nicolette Larson

b. Jul. 17, 1952, Helena, MT
Vocals / Country-Rock, Country-Pop, Soft Rock, Pop-Rock, Urban Cowboy

After working as a backup vocalist for several country-rock acts and serving as a member of Commander Cody's Lost Planet Airmen for several years during the mid'-70s, vocalist Nicolette Larson launched a solo career in the late '70s. Initially, Larson followed the sound of laidback Californian country-rock, which resulted in a Top Ten pop hit in 1979 with "Lotta Love." In the years following the success of "Lotta Love," Larson continued to mine the soft-rock California sound, eventually leaving it behind for country music in the mid-'80s. During the course of the '80s, she racked up a number of country hits, before moving into semi-retirement.

Born in Montana, Nicolette Larson and her family eventually settled in Kansas City. Following her high-school graduation, she moved out to San Francisco, where she began working on the Golden Gate Country/Bluegrass Festival. While she was working the festival, she met a number of musicians, who were all impressed by her voice and encouraged her to pursue a professional musical career. Larson followed their advice, joining David Nichtern and the Nocturnes, playing clubs around the Bay Area. Eventually, she came to the attention of Commander Cody & His Lost Planet Airmen, who invited her to sing on their 1975 album, *Tales from the Ozone*. Following its release, Larson toured with the band, and over the next three years, she sang on two of the group's albums—*Rock 'n' Roll Again* and *Flying Dreams*—in addition to touring with the band.

Around the same time that she began singing with Commander Cody, Nicolette Larson moved to Los Angeles, where she began singing as a studio musician. Over the next four years, she appeared on numerous albums by country and rock musicians, including records by Neil Young, Linda Ronstadt, Hoyt Axton, Guy Clark, Jesse Winchester, Emmylou Harris, Jesse Colin Young, John Stewart, the Doobie Brothers, Rodney Crowell, and Graham Nash. In 1978, she signed a record contract with Warner Brothers, releasing her first single, a cover of Young's "Lotta Love," at the end of the year. "Lotta Love" became a huge hit, reaching No. 8 on the pop charts, helping to send her debut album *Nicolette* into gold status. Though *Nicolette* and "Lotta Love" were hits right out of the box, she wasn't able to replicate her success, as "Rhumba Girl" stalled at No. 47, which also happened to be the peak chart position of her second album, *In the Nick of Time*. The album did spawn a hit with the Top 40 "Let Me Go, Love," a duet with Michael McDonald, but her third album, *Radioland* (1980), was largely ignored.

Following one other attempt at pop success with 1982's *All Dressed up and No Place to Go* and the single "I Only Want to Be with You," Larson retreated from the mainstream and starred in the country musical *Pump Boys and Dinettes*. Larson received positive reviews for her performance, which led to a record contract with MCA in 1983. On the basis of her performance, the Academy of Country Music named her the Best New Female Vocalist in 1984, even though she had yet to have any country hits. Larson finally released a country album in 1985 with ... Say When, but the record didn't live up to its hype. Though it was critically acclaimed, the album was far from a commercial success, with only one single—"Only Love Will Make It Right"—reaching the Top 50; yet the record was strong enough for *Cash Box* to name Larson the Best New Female Vocalist of the year.

Larson finally broke into the country charts in 1986 when "That's How You Know When Love's Right," a duet with Steve Wariner, climbed into the Top ten and stayed in the charts for five months. "That's How You Know When Love's Right" was drawn from *Rose of My Heart*, which performed respectably. However, Larson didn't choose to follow the album up with another country record. In 1987, she recorded an album, *Shadows of Love*, in Italy and in the next year, she began pursuing an acting career. In 1988, she appeared on *Family Reunion*, a black gospel television show and the Arnold Schwarzenegger/Danny DeVito comedy *Twins*, as well as the television series *Throb*. During the early '90s, she began touring with singers Valerie Carter and Lauren Wood, and the trio went on a USO tour. In 1994, she released a children's album titled *Sleep Baby Sleep*. —*Stephen Thomas Erlewine*

● **Nicolette** / 1978 / Warner Brothers ◆◆◆◆

In the Nick of Time / 1979 / Warner Brothers ◆◆◆

Live at the Roxy / 1979 / Warner Brothers ◆◆

Radioland / 1980 / Warner Brothers ◆◆

All Dressed up & No Place to Go / 1982 / Warner Brothers ◆◆◆

Jim Lauderdale

b. Apr. 11, 1957, Statesville, NC

Contemporary Country, Singer-Songwriter, Neo-Traditionalist Country

North Carolina-born Jim Lauderdale is a Nashville-based songwriter whose big influences were Gram Parsons, George Jones,

Buck Owens, Hank Williams, and Merle Haggard. He considers himself a country artist with rock, soul, and blues influences thrown in. —*Chip Renner*

● **Pretty Close to the Truth** / Atlantic ◆◆◆◆
Lauderdale's outstanding debut received little support from the country establishment, so he transferred to the New York office of Atlantic and created another compelling, authoritative album that more freely roams through his various roots influences. —*Michael McCall*

Planet of Love / 1991 / Reprise ◆◆◆◆
Jim Leventhal and Rodney Crowell produced and helped out on this release, and Shawn Colvin and Emmylou Harris provide great vocal support. It is a great debut—an example of the new singer-songwriter "traditionalist" coming out in country music today. —*Chip Renner*

Every Second Counts / Sep. 5, 1995 / Atlantic ◆◆◆
Jim Lauderdale has had success writing songs others have had hits with. Jim Lauderdale has been favorably compared to the late Gram Parsons. Jim Lauderdale sounds an awful lot like a tame Rodney Crowell. Jim Lauderdale is playing it safe when he releases albums such as *Every Second Counts*. Jim Lauderdale should be more famous than he is. Either all, some, or none of the above are true. If you want to find out which statement is which, seek out a copy of *Every Second Counts* and find out for yourself. It's as simple as that. You will not be disappointed. —*James Chrispell*

Persimmons / Sep. 3, 1996 / ◆◆◆◆
Persimmons continues Jim Lauderdale's string of excellent albums. Though it isn't any different than his previous solo albums—it still is a down-to-earth fusion of roots music from soul to blues, all tied together by a basic country songwriting template—what impresses is Lauderdale's consistency and imaginative songwriting. Though he uses the same ingredients every time, he puts enough of an original spin on his rockers and ballads, giving them slight melodic or lyrical twists, which make, *Persimmons* more rewarding with each listen. —*Thom Owens*

Tracy Lawrence

b. Jan. 27, 1968, Atlanta, TX

Vocals / Contemporary Country, New Traditionalist

Tracy Lawrence was a new traditionalist honky tonk singer of the mid-'90s, producing a string of hit singles and critically acclaimed albums. Born in Texas but raised in Foreman, AR, Lawrence played in his first band at age 16. In 1990, he went to Nashville, where he worked as a telemarketer and ironworker. While looking for his big break, he began participating in talent contests, and made enough from his winnings—he always took first or second place—to live on. One of those contests led to a spot on *Live at Libby's*, a local TV show. In 1991, he had a showcase at the Bluebird Cafe, and there met Wayne Edwards, who would soon become his manager. Later that year, Lawrence signed with Atlantic Records and released his debut album, *Sticks and Stones*.

On May 31, 1991, he was celebrating the album's release with his former girlfriend. As he walked her to her hotel door, three gun-toting youths robbed them and tried to force the two into the woman's room. Lawrence, fearing that his friend would be raped, resisted and was shot four times while she escaped. Two of the shots nicked him, but a third had to be surgically removed from his knee and the fourth remained deeply embedded in his pelvis, dangerously close to a major artery. Fortunately, he recovered quickly and performed benefit shows to help with his tremendous medical bills and ensuing physical therapy. His debut single, "Sticks and Stones," made it to No. 1 on the strength of the publicity surrounding the shooting, and began a streak of Top ten singles. His second album, *Alibis*, went gold 17 days after its release and soon went platinum. The record spawned three straight No. 1 singles—"Alibis," "Can't Break It to My Heart," and "My Second Home." Lawrence's third album, *I See It Now*, was released in 1994; like its predecessors, it was a platinum success. *Live and Unplugged* was released in

1995 and was followed by *Time Marches On* in 1996. *—Sandra Brennan*

Sticks and Stones / 1991 / Atlantic ✦✦✦

Lawrence's first two chart-toppers, "Sticks and Stones" and "Today's Lonely Fool," are included on this debut outing. *—Jason Ankeny*

Alibis / 1993 / Atlantic ✦✦✦✦

While not as consistent as his debut *Sticks and Stones*, Lawrence's strong baritone is still well-served on *Alibis*. *—Jason Ankeny*

● **I See It Now** / Sep. 20, 1994 / Atlantic ✦✦✦✦

Live and Unplugged / Sep. 19, 1995 / Atlantic ✦✦✦

Time Marches On / Jan. 23, 1996 / Atlantic ✦✦✦

Tracy Lawrence's *Time Marches On*, the singer's fourth album, is another crowd-pleasing set of contemporary country. Like his previous albums, the song selection is a hit-or-miss affair, with about half of the songs failing to make much of an impression. The remainder, however, prove why Lawrence is one of the most popular singers in Nashville. *—Stephen Thomas Erlewine*

Doyle Lawson

b. Apr. 20, 1944, Kingsport, TN

Traditional Bluegrass, Country Gospel

Doyle Lawson was considered one of the premiere bluegrass mandolin players by his peers; his bluegrass-gospel band Quicksilver was equally respected. Lawson was born in Kingsport, TN, and became interested in bluegrass when he was five. During his youth, he listened to such greats as the Stanley Brothers, Flatt & Scruggs, and Bill Monroe. It was the latter who inspired young Lawson to learn the mandolin. He borrowed his first one at age 11 from a member of his father's gospel quartet, and eventually taught himself the five-string banjo and guitar as well. In 1963, Lawson began playing banjo with Martin's Sunny Mountain Boys. Seven months later, he moved to Louisville to play with different groups. He became a part-time guitarist with J.D. Crowe in 1966 and eventually joined his Kentucky Mountain Boys as a mandolin player. Lawson made his recording debut with Red Allen and bassist Bobby Slone on *Bluegrass Holiday* and subsequently recorded two albums with Crowe.

In 1971, Lawson joined the Country Gentlemen and toured Japan with them the following year. He remained with the band for several years and recorded ten albums with them. Lawson also recorded an album of mandolin instrumentals, *Tennessee Dream*, in 1977; the album also featured Crowe, Jerry Douglas, and Kenny Baker. In 1979, he put his band Quicksilver together with banjo player Terry Baucom, guitarist Jimmy Haley, and electric bass player Lou Reid. In 1980, Quicksilver released its self-titled debut album and followed it up with *Rock My Soul*. In 1981, *Quicksilver Rides Again*, featuring Douglas, Mike Auldridge, and Sam Bush, came out. They also released a gospel album, *Heavenly Treasures*, which proved an even bigger seller. Quicksilver's next album appeared in 1985 and featured both bluegrass and gospel tunes. In 1986, Lawson recorded *Beyond the Shadows* with new players Scott Vestal on banjo, Curtis Vestal on electric bass, and Russell Moore on guitar. In 1987, Lawson and the band released an a cappella gospel album, *Heaven's Joy Awaits*. Between 1987 and 1991, Lawson and Quicksilver, which continually changed personnel, released seven more albums. *—Sandra Brennan*

Tennessee Dream / 1977 / County ✦✦✦

Doyle Lawson & Quicksilver / 1980 / Sugar Hill ✦✦✦✦

● **Rock My Soul** / 1981 / Sugar Hill ✦✦✦✦

Rock My Soul is the first gospel album that Doyle Lawson recorded and it's a wonderful record of simple, graceful beauty. The key to the success of *Rock My Soul* is that Lawson has opened up bluegrass gospel by incorporating elements of country and southern gospel, which made it accessible to a wider audience. *—Thom Owens*

I'll Wander Back Someday / 1988 / Sugar Hill ✦✦✦

Relying primarily on traditional songs and standards, *I'll Wander Back Someday* is another excellent effort from Doyle Lawson and

Quicksilver, highlighting the group's innovative vocal arrangements and acumen for driving, straight-edged instrumental support. *—Thom Owens*

Hymn Time in the Country / 1988 / Sugar Hill ✦✦✦

Doyle Lawson & Quicksilver's *Hymn Time in the Country* is an excellent contemporary bluegrass gospel album. Though there's a couple of weak tracks—it would have been nice to hear "John the Revelator" with a full instrumental accompaniment—the album has enough terrific harmonies and spirit to satisfy both traditional bluegrass fans and contemporary Christian fans. *—Rodney Batdorf*

I Heard the Angels Singing / 1989 / Sugar Hill ✦✦✦

Lawson returns to gospel on *I Heard the Angels Singing*, which features his rendition of Carl Jackson's "The Little Mountain Church House." *—Jason Ankeny*

The Gospel Collection 1 / 1990 / Sugar Hill ✦✦✦✦

Gospel Collection, Vol. 1 contains 13 tracks that Doyle Lawson and Quicksilver released on their earliest albums, as well as two previously unreleased songs, all of which demonstrate that Lawson's talent for modernizing bluegrass gospel was unparalleled in his era. *—Thom Owens*

My Heart Is Yours / 1990 / Sugar Hill ✦✦✦✦

As good as *Rock My Soul*. First-class bluegrass. *—Chip Renner*

Pressing on Regardless / 1992 / Brentwood ✦✦✦

Pressing on Regardless is one of Lawson and Quicksilver's occasional secular recordings, released in tandem with the gospel record *Treasures Money Can't Buy*. *—Jason Ankeny*

Treasures Money Can't Buy / 1992 / Brentwood ✦✦✦

The all-gospel *Treasures Money Can't Buy* features "Just a Little Talk with Jesus" and "Buckle of the Bible Belt." *—Jason Ankeny*

Never Walk Away / 1995 / Sugar Hill ✦✦✦

This album is crystal clear from the first notes of the Buck Owens tune "Rosie Jones" to the end of "Ancient History." It is a tight ensemble album where the instrumental playing is all the more impressive for being excellent but not showy. Strong songs include "Jealous," "In the Gravel Yard" and "Your Crazy Heart." There's nothing groundbreaking here, just a solid rootsy bluegrass band album, and that's not bad. *—Richard Meyer*

There's a Light Guiding Me / Feb. 20, 1996 / Sugar Hill ✦✦✦✦

Doyle Lawson and Quicksilver are among bluegrass music's most heavenly harmonizers, as they prove once again on the timeless music featured in *There's a Light Guiding Me*. Largely a cappella, and completely focused on spirituals, these songs will fill the soul with warmth. No matter what one believes, this music—just like that of spiritual singers from Tibet, Hungary, Pakistan, or Cambodia—strikes a resonant chord deep within. *—Michael McCall*

Ledford String Band

Old-Time, String Band

The Ledford String Band was led by master fiddler Steve Ledford, who first found success as one of the most popular players of the 1930s. Ledford was born and raised in Bakersville, NC, and won his first fiddling contest at age nine. He and his family began performing as a string band at local one-room school houses in the Roan Mountain region. Eventually, they became known as the Carolina Ramblers Stringband and moved to New York in 1931, where they began playing on area radio. In 1932, they recorded 20 songs for the American Record Company, eight of which were released on labels such as Perfect and Romeo. Ledford later returned to his home to marry and farm. A few years later, he teamed with Wade Mainer; while with Mainer's band, Ledford recorded his signature fiddle tune "Little Maggie." Through the early '40s, Ledford appeared regularly on a Roanoake radio station with Jay Hall and his brother Roy. He returned to farming in 1942; a few more years passed and Ledford formed a new incarnation of the Carolina Ramblers with his little brother Wayne and their relative James Gardner. They eventually called themselves the Ledford String Band, and in 1971 cut an album for Rounder. They also released a couple singles on the Roan Mountain label. *—Sandra Brennan*

Ledford String Band / Rounder ✦✦✦✦

Chris LeDoux

b. Oct. 2, 1948, Biloxi, MS
Guitar, Vocals / Cowboy, Contemporary Country, Neo-Traditionalist Country
Chris LeDoux was not only a successful country singer and songwriter, but also a champion rodeo rider. Born in Biloxi, MS, he and his family moved to Austin, TX, when he was 12. LeDoux won the Wyoming State Rodeo Championship, subsequently became Intercollegiate National Bareback Riding Champion, and reached the pinnacle of his rodeo career in 1976 when he became World Champion Bareback Rider. While riding and traveling, he began writing rodeo songs such as "Rodeo Life," "Bareback Jack," and "Bull Rider."

In 1980, he left the cowboy circuit to focus on a music career. He first recorded in a basement studio in Sheridan, and his father arranged a Nashville recording session with some of the city's best session players. His debut album was released on Lucky Man, a subsidiary of his family's music business American Cowboy Songs. For the next two decades, LeDoux recorded 22 albums on independent labels which contained a blend of originals and traditional cowboy songs. Many of the albums were sold on the rodeo circuit, and over the years he developed a loyal following. Between 1979 and 1980, he had three minor hits with "Lean, Mean and Hungry," "Ten Seconds in the Saddle," and "Caballo Diablo."

By 1990, LeDoux had become popular enough to sign with Liberty Records. In addition to releasing his new albums, the label arranged to reissue his earlier work. His first new album for Liberty was *Western Underground*, which produced the minor hit "This Cowboy Hat." The song made it to the Top 70, as did the follow-up "Working Man's Dollar." In 1992 LeDoux teamed up with longtime friend Garth Brooks—who helped popularize LeDoux by mentioning his name in his 1989 hit "Much Too Young (To Feel This Damn Old)"—to sing the title track of *Watcha Gonna Do with a Cowboy*. The song became LeDoux's only Top ten hit; following its success, he and Brooks toured together. In 1993, LeDoux had a Top 20 hit with "Cadillac Ranch," from *Under This Old Hat*, which also produced three more moderate hits. —*Sandra Brennan*

Songs of Rodeo Life / Oct. 28, 1971 / Liberty ✦✦✦

Rodeo Songs "Old & New" / 1973 / Liberty ✦✦✦✦
The title tells the tale. —*Mark A. Humphrey*

Rodeo & Living Free / 1974 / Liberty ✦✦✦
Rodeo & Living Free, first issued in 1974, contains the bronc-riding tributes "Bucking Machine" and "Fourth of July Rodeos." —*Jason Ankeny*

Songs of Rodeo & Country / 1974 / Liberty ✦✦✦✦

Sing Me a Song Mr. Rodeo Man / 1977 / Liberty ✦✦
Tributes to "Billy the Kid" and a "Bad Brahma Bull" flesh out the 1977 release *Sing Me a Song Mr. Rodeo Man*. —*Jason Ankeny*

Old Cowboy Heroes / 1980 / Liberty ✦✦✦
The 1981 LP *Old Cowboy Heroes* includes the character studies "Little Joe the Wrangler" and "Old Jake." —*Jason Ankeny*

Western Tunesmith / 1980 / Liberty ✦✦✦✦
1980's *Western Tunesmith* features LeDoux's rendition of "My Heroes Have Always Been Cowboys" and the hit "Ten Seconds in the Saddle." —*Jason Ankeny*

Used to Want to Be a Cowboy / 1982 / Liberty ✦✦✦
1982's *Used to Want to Be a Cowboy* includes the minor hit "This Cowboy Hat." —*Jason Ankeny*

Old Cowboy Classics / 1983 / Liberty ✦✦✦
Old Cowboy Classics, which first appeared in 1983, collects LeDoux favorites like "Old Paint," "Ballad of Will Rogers," and "Tennessee Stud." —*Jason Ankeny*

Thirty Dollar Cowboy / 1983 / Liberty ✦✦
1983's *Thirty Dollar Cowboy* offers "It Ain't the Years, It's the Miles" and "They Couldn't Understand My Cowboy Songs." —*Jason Ankeny*

Wild & Wooly / 1986 / Liberty ✦✦
"Little Long-Haired Outlaw" and "Foggy Mountain Breakdown" are two of the highlights of 1986's *Wild and Wooly*. —*Jason Ankeny*

Western Underground / Jul. 22, 1991 / Liberty ✦✦✦
After nearly 20 years and as many self-produced albums, LeDoux found himself attracting attention as the rodeo singer mentioned in Garth Brooks' first hit, "Much Too Young (To Feel This Damn Old)." Brooks' company soon offered the cowboy his first major-label contract. Here, his producers try to turn him into a conventional Nashville hat act. —*Michael McCall*

Whatcha Gonna Do with a Cowboy / Jul. 20, 1992 / Liberty ✦✦✦✦
Brooks helps out his new friend again by joining him for a duet on the title cut, and LeDoux flashes more of his own personality and gritty charm. —*Michael McCall*

Under This Old Hat / Jul. 5, 1993 / Liberty ✦✦✦
LeDoux learns to rock, taking to the punched-up sound like he's been riding the horse all his life. Included is his wild 'n' woolly version of Joe Ely's "For Your Love." —*Michael McCall*

● **Best of Chris Le Doux** / Mar. 8, 1994 / Liberty ✦✦✦✦
Twelve tracks from the genuine rodeo cowboy and former bareback bronc-riding champion of country music. *The Best Of* collects the strongest tracks from *Western Underground*, *Whatcha Gonna Do with a Cowboy*, and *Under This Old Hat*, serving up an almost perfect blend of earthy honesty and commercial tunefulness. —*Roch Parisien*

Rodeo Rock and Roll Collection / Aug. 15, 1995 / Liberty ✦✦
An entertaining live compilation, featuring many of Chris LeDoux's biggest hits, including "Cadillac Ranch," "Call of the Wild," and a version of "Copenhagen," recorded with Toby Keith. —*Stephen Thomas Erlewine*

Albert Lee

b. Dec. 21, 1943, Leominster, England
Guitar, Session Musician / Country-Rock, Neo-Traditionalist Country, Rockabilly Revival
Lee is an English guitarist, highly proficient in a multitude of styles but primarily gifted in country and rockabilly picking. The ultimate sideman on countless sessions over the last two decades, his Telecaster twangings have graced the recordings of Eric Clapton, Jerry Lee Lewis, and Emmylou Harris, to name just a few. Also notable as the music director when the Everly Brothers reunited a few years back, Lee has released a few solo albums of his own in the last few years, all of them informed by his clean, articulate picking. —*Cub Koda*

Hiding / 1979 / A&M ✦✦✦
Standard country-rock album. —*Jeff Tamarkin*

Albert Lee / 1982 / Polydor ✦✦
Disappointing rock effort still features brilliant guitar. —*Jeff Tamarkin*

Country Guitar Man / Nov. 1986 / Magnum ✦✦✦✦
This collection of Lee's early-'70s work with Head, Hands, & Feet is fairly remarkable, particularly Lee's guitar work. —*Jeff Tamarkin*

Speechless / Feb. 1987 / MCA ✦✦✦✦
One of the guitar world's best-kept secrets, the former Everly Brothers and Emmylou Harris sideman explores his roots in this instrumental jewel. Albert Lee co-produced this album. Included is a very clean sound on a very good cover of "Arkansas Traveler" featuring Lee on guitar, mandolin and piano, Jim Cox, Greg Humphrey, Sterling Biff Ball, and Chad Wackerman. —*Jeff Tamarkin & Chip Renner*

● **Gagged but Not Bound** / Mar. 1988 / MCA ✦✦✦✦
The master musician plays unworldly guitar on this acoustic/electric country-, rock-, and traditional-oriented masterpiece. Exquisitely recorded. —*Jeff Tamarkin*

Black Claw & Country Fever / Oct. 1991 / Line ✦✦✦✦
This collection of late-'60s material is raw yet engaging; the musicianship is stunning. —*Jeff Tamarkin*

Brenda Lee (Brenda Mae Tarpley)

b. Dec. 11, 1944, Lithonia, GA

Vocals / Rock & Roll, Country-Pop, Pop, Nashville Sound/Countrypolitan

One of the biggest pop stars of the early '60s, Brenda Lee hasn't attracted as much critical respect as she deserves. She is sometimes inaccurately characterized as one of the few female teen idols. More crucially, the credit for achieving success with pop-country crossovers usually goes to Patsy Cline, although Lee's efforts in this era were arguably of equal importance. While she made few recordings of note after the mid-'60s, the best of her first decade is fine indeed, encompassing not just the pop ballads that were her biggest hits, but straight country and some surprisingly fierce rockabilly.

Lee was a child prodigy, appearing on national television by the age of ten, and making her first recordings for Decca the following year (1956). Her first few Decca singles, in fact, make a pretty fair bid for the best pre-teen rock 'n' roll performances this side of Michael Jackson. "BIGELOW 6-200," "Dyamite," and "Little Jonah" are all exceptionally powerful rockabilly performances, with robust vocals and white-hot backing from the cream of Nashville's session musicians (including Owen Bradley, Grady Martin, Hank Garland, and Floyd Cramer). Lee would not have her first big hits until 1960, when she tempered the rockabilly with teen idol pop on "Sweet Nothin's," which went to the Top Five.

The comparison between Lee and Cline is to be expected, given that both singers were produced by Owen Bradley in the early '60s. Naturally, many of the same session musicians and backup vocalists were employed. Brenda, however, had a bigger in with the pop audience, not just because she was still a teenager, but because her material was more pop than Cline's, and not as country. Between 1960 and 1962, she had a stunning series of huge hits—"I'm Sorry," "I Want to Be Wanted," "Emotions," "You Can Depend on Me," "Dum Dum," "Fool No. 1," "Break It to Me Gently," and "All Alone Am I" all made the Top Ten. Their crossover appeal is no mystery. While these were ballads, they were delivered with enough lovesick yearning to appeal to adolescents, and enough maturity for the adults. The first-class melodic songwriting and professional, orchestral production guaranteed that they would not be ghettoized in the country market.

Lee's last Top Ten pop hit was in 1963, with "Losing You." While she still had hits through the mid-'60s, these became smaller and less frequent with the rise of the British Invasion (although she remained very popular overseas). The best of her later hits, "Is It True?," was a surprisingly hard-rocking performance, recorded in 1964 in London with Jimmy Page on guitar. 1966's "Coming on Strong," however, would prove to be her last Top 20 entry.

In the early '70s, Lee reunited with Owen Bradley and, like so many early White rock 'n' roll stars, returned to country music. For a time she was fairly successful in this field, making the country Top Ten half a dozen times in 1973-74. Although she remained active as a recording and touring artist, for the last couple of decades she's been little more than a living legend, directing her intermittent artistic efforts to the country audience. —*Richie Unterberger*

Brenda Lee / 1960 / Decca ✦✦✦✦

Brenda Lee's nickname at 15 was "Miss Dynamite" and it's no lie. Some of her early hits are included—"Sweet Nothin's," "That's All You Gotta Do," plus "I'm Sorry," a great rocking reworking of "Weep No More My Lady," the bluesy "Be My Love Again," and "Just Let Me Dream." —*George Bedard*

Miss Dynamite / 1961 / Brunswick ✦✦✦✦

Brenda Sings Songs Everybody Knows / 1964 / Decca ✦✦✦

The Brenda Lee Story (Her Greatest Hits) / 1974 / MCA ✦✦✦✦

This 22-song, two-LP set included the bulk of her biggest hits, although it misses somes some significant singles (like "Is It True?"). The two-volume *Anthology* CD, with nearly twice as much material, is a much better investment. —*Richie Unterberger*

★ Anthology, Vols. 1 & 2 (1956-1980) / 1991 / MCA ✦✦✦✦✦

A 40-song, two-CD collection, this proves Lee was the best White female rock singer of the pre-Beatles '60s. By the time she turned 18, Lee had hit the pop Top Ten 11 times. All of those cuts are here, from the innocently salacious "Sweet Nothin's" to the string-laden "I'm Sorry" and her remake of Earl "Fatha" Hines' "You Can Depend on Me." Her best country singles, "Johnny One Time" and "Big Four Poster Bed," are also included. The compilers wisely passed over some minor hits in favor of obscure sides like the odd rockabilly "Let's Jump the Broomstick," a cover of Edith Piaf's "If You Love Me (Really Love Me)," and "Is It True?," a middling hit from 1964, which features guitarist Jimmy Page (who is 11 months older than Lee). *Anthology* thoroughly traces Lee's development as a vocalist, from early-childish exuberance to mature, graceful phrasing. —*Brian Mansfield*

Dickey Lee (Dickey Lipscomb)

b. Sep. 21, 1940, Memphis, TN

Vocals / Country-Pop, Rockabilly, Pop, Brill Building pop

Country songwriter Dickey Lee began his career recording for the Sun label. He was born Dickey Lipscomb on September 21, 1940, in Memphis, and began playing in a band while in high school. The group won several talent shows, earning them a spot on a local radio station. Deejay Dewey Phillips convinced Sun Records to sign Dickey Lee, so the singer recorded two singles in 1957, "Good Lovin'" and "Fool, Fool, Fool." Neither did especially well, so he moved to Texas and continued to play. Dickey Lee finally hit the bigtime in early 1962 when George Jones took his song "She Thinks I Still Care" to the top of the country charts, where it stayed for six weeks. The record became one of Jones' biggest hits, and also hit No. 1 when Anne Murray recorded it in 1974.

On the wings of Jones, Dickey Lee's "Patches" hit No. 6 on the pop charts in August 1962; "I Saw Linda Yesterday" entered the same year and ended up at No. 14 early in 1963. Lee recorded one other pop hit, 1965's "Laurie (Strange Things Happen)," but then focused strictly on production and songwriting during the late '60s. Persuaded to return to Nashville in 1969, he signed to RCA and in 1971 recorded a modest hit called "The Mahogany Pulpit." Dickey Lee's next single, "Never Ending Song of Love," crashed the country Top Ten in late 1971 and eventually reached No. 8. He continued to record over the course of the '70s, usually peaking in the 30s and 40s except for two massive hits—"Rocky," which topped the charts in 1975, and its No. 3 follow-up, "9,999,999 Tears."

Dickey Lee stayed with RCA until 1978 and re-emerged on Mercury a year later. His two highlights during the Mercury years were Top 30 singles from 1980, "Workin' My Way to Your Heart" and "Lost in Love." The latter, a duet with Kathy Burdick, became a pop hit for Air Supply the same year. After his contract expired, Dickey Lee continued to write songs and perform on occasional package shows. —*John Bush*

● Tale of Patches / 1962 / Smash ✦✦✦✦

Sings Laurie / 1965 / TCF Hall ✦✦✦

Laurie and the Girl from Peyton Place / 1965 / TCF Hall ✦✦✦

Peyton Place / 1965 / TCF Hall ✦✦✦

Never Ending Song of Love / 1972 / RCA ✦✦✦

Ashes of Love / 1976 / RCA ✦✦

Everybody Loves a Winner / 1981 / Mercury ✦✦✦

Johnny Lee (John Lee Harn)

b. Jul. 3, 1946, Texas City, TX

Guitar, Vocals / Country-Pop, Adult Contemporary, Urban Cowboy

Like many his age, Johnny Lee grew up on the music of Chuck Berry, Elvis Presley, and Jerry Lee Lewis. Raised on a dairy farm in Alta Loma, TX, he formed his first band, Johnny Lee & the Road Runners, during high school. He tricked his way into playing onstage with Mickey Gilley at a Houston club called the Nesadel, and that shot brought him a long-term run at Gilley's clubs. When *Urban Cowboy* was shot at Gilley's, record executive

Irving Azoff offered Lee an opportunity to sing in the picture, and he ended up with a song that more than 20 artists had previously rejected. In his hands, that song—"Lookin' for Love"—became a million-seller and the musical centerpiece of the movie. Stardom occurred practically overnight for Lee, but it was a mixed bag. He and Gilley toured steadily; Lee got a substantial string of hits for about three years and ended up marrying Dallas starlet Charlene Tilton. But the marriage soured, he found his name constantly in the tabloids, and he was forced to record a large amount of same-sounding material. Nevertheless, Johnny Lee had an important role in a huge era for country music, and his easygoing vocal style still makes him very listenable.

Following the demise of his high school band, the Road Runners, Johnny Lee enlisted in the Navy, serving in Southeast Asia (including Vietnam) during the mid-'60s. After his discharge, he floated between California and Texas before settling near Houston. Lee convinced Mickey Gilley into lettting him join his band as a backup singer and trumpeter in 1968, telling the pianist that they had previously met in Galveston, when in fact they hadn't. For the next ten years, Johnny worked closely with Gilley, becoming an integral party of the pianist's Pasadena club, Gilley's. When Mickey was on tour, Johnny acted as the headliner at the club. Lee decided to go solo in 1973, but his records for the independent label Astro were unsuccessful, so he returned to the club within a year.

By the end of 1975, he signed a contract with ABC/Dot and his first single for the label, "Sometimes," became a minor hit. The following year, he moved to GRT, where he released several minor hits in the next two years, highlighted by the No. 15 placing of "Country Party" in 1977; the song was a reworking of Rick Nelson's hit "Garden Party." In 1979, he appeared in a made-for-television film, *The Girls in the Office*, which paved the way for his appearance in the 1980 film, *Urban Cowboy*. Starring John Travolta, *Urban Cowboy* glamorized the sound and style of modern honky tonks like Gilley's, and the movie and its soundtrack became huge hits. Lee contributed "Lookin' for Love" to the soundtrack, and the single became a gigantic crossover success, spending three weeks at the top of the country charts in the summer of 1980 while peaking at No. 5 on the pop charts. Johnny Lee became a star thanks to *Urban Cowboy*, and his records for his new label Full Moon began appearing in the country Top Ten with regularity. "One in a Million" became another No. 1 hit late in 1980, followed by "Pickin' Up Strangers" early the next year.

In the wake of the success of "Lookin' for Love" and *Urban Cowboy*, Lee officially left Gilley's band in 1981, forming not only his own group, the Western Union Band, but also his own rival nightclub, Johnny Lee's, which was located just down the road from Gilley's. Throughout 1981 and 1982, Lee's star burned bright, as the Academy of Country Music named him the Best New Artist of 1980, and he had Top Ten hits like "Prisoner of Hope" (1981), the No. 1 "Bet Your Heart on Me" (1981), and "Be There for Me Baby" (1982). In 1982, he married actress Charlene Tilton, one of the stars of the nighttime soap opera *Dallas*. Lee's success continued in 1983 and 1984 with Top Ten singles like "Sounds like Love" (1983), "Hey Bartender" (1983), and the No. 1 singles "The Yellow Rose" (1984) and "You Could've Heard a Heart Break" (1984).

Johnny Lee's career cooled down as quickly as it heated up. Though he had one Top Ten single, "Rollin' Lonely," in 1985, by the beginning of 1986, he had trouble reaching the Top 40. Warner, who inherited his Full Moon contract in 1984, dropped him from their roster in 1986 and his marriage to Tilton collapsed in 1987. Over the next two years, he struggled to find a contract, as he came to the realization his management took most of his earnings from his hit-making days. During this time, he released a single and three EPs on his own Lee record label, as well as an independent record on JMS. In 1989, he signed to Curb Records, but none of his records for the label were hits. By the end of the decade, he published his autobiography, *Lookin' for Love*.

During the '90s, Johnny Lee continued to tour across the country, playing clubs and honky tonks. He lacked a record con-

tract, and he had long been estranged from his mentor Mickey Gilley due to his management problems and his rival club, but he continued to draw sizable crowds at his concerts. *—Tom Roland*

For Lovers Only / 1977 / JMS ✦✦✦✦

Lookin' for Love / 1980 / Asylum ✦✦✦✦

Bet Your Heart on Me / 1981 / Full Moon ✦✦✦

● **Greatest Hits** / 1983 / Full Moon ✦✦✦✦
Lots of mid-tempo love songs are here, much in the vein of "Lookin' for Love." Too bad Lee couldn't break out of that mold a little sooner—"Sounds like Love" and "Hey Bartender" show some real teeth. *—Tom Roland*

Hey Bartender / 1983 / Full Moon ✦✦

Johnny Lee / 1984 / Audio Fidelity ✦✦

Johnny Lee & Willie Nelson / 1984 / Astan ✦✦✦

'Til the Bars Burn Down / 1984 / Full Moon ✦✦✦

New Directions / 1989 / Curb ✦✦
The songs that comprise *New Directions* fail to live up to the standard enjoyed by Johnny Lee at his early-'80s peak. *—Jason Ankeny*

Robin Lee (Robin Irwin)

b. Nov. 7, 1953, Nashville, TN
Vocals / Contemporary Country, Urban Cowboy
Singer-songwriter Robin Lee was born and raised in Nashville. She began her career in music while attending high school, performing at school dances and talent shows. She later made demo recordings for local publishing companies. In 1982, Lee debuted on the charts with the minor hit "Turning Back the Covers"; "Heart for a Heart" came the following year. In 1984, four songs became low-level hits, including "Angel in Your Arms"; "Paint the Town Blue" and "Safe in the Arms of Love" both hit the Top 50 the next year. In 1988 she had three Top 50 hits, including "This Old Flame." Lee did not appear on the charts again until 1990 with the title cut of *Black Velvet*, which made the Top 15 and became her biggest hit to date. The album hit the Top 25, and two other cuts from it reached the Top 70. She had one hit in 1991, "Nothin' but You." *—Sandra Brennan*

This Old Flame / 1984 / Atlantic ✦✦

Black Velvet / 1990 / Atlantic ✦✦✦
In keeping with the title song, a cover of the Alannah Myles pop hit, *Black Velvet* offers renditions of rock material recast in the Nashville mold. *—Jason Ankeny*

● **Heart on a Chain** / 1990 / Atlantic ✦✦✦✦
A significant improvement over Lee's debut, *Heart on a Chain* focuses on more straightahead country material, performed by a crack session band. *—Jason Ankeny*

Lewis & Kallick

Progressive Bluegrass, Traditional Bluegrass
Both early members of Good Ol' Persons, Laurie Lewis has recorded with Blue Rose and produced two well-received solo albums. Kathy Kallick is a highly respected guitarist and has played on many projects. *—Chip Renner*

Together: Lewis & Kallick / 1990 / Kaleidoscope ✦✦✦✦
Laurie Lewis and Kathy Kallick perform some really fine duets on this long-awaited collaboration. Lewis' violin playing is first-rate and her vocals are always a joy to listen to. Kallick's songwriting is spotlighted, along with her strong rhythm guitar work. *—Chip Renner*

The Lewis Family

Traditional Bluegrass, Country Gospel
Take the best of bluegrass, add the best of traditional Appalachian gospel, and you have the Lewis Family. In the mid-'50s they gained recognition through their TV show in Augusta, GA, their hometown. Starting in the early '70s they became regulars at bluegrass festivals across the country, touring widely with at least seven members of the family, led by "Pop" Wallace and featuring

Little Roy Lewis (a great talent) on banjo. Along with Carl Story, the Lewises have specialized in bluegrass gospel and, with their tight harmonies, female leads, and quality instrumentals, are at the top of their genre. —*David Vinopal*

● **16 Greatest Hits** / Starday ✦✦✦✦

20 Country Bluegrass Hymns / Benson ✦✦✦✦

Golden Gospel Greats / Starday ✦✦✦

20 Bluegrass Favorites, Vol. 3 / Benson ✦✦✦

Jerry Lee Lewis

b. Sep. 29, 1935, Ferriday, LA
Piano, Vocals / Rock & Roll, Traditional Country, Honky Tonk

Is there an early rock 'n' roller that has a crazier reputation than the Killer, Jerry Lee Lewis? His exploits as a piano-thumping ego-centric wild man with an unquenched thirst for living have become the fodder for numerous biographies, film documentaries, and a full-length Hollywood movie. Certainly few other artists came to the party with more ego and talent than he and lived to tell the tale. And certainly even fewer could successfully channel that energy into their music and prosper doing it as well as Jerry Lee. When he broke on the national scene in 1957 with his classic "Whole Lot of Shakin' Going On," he was every parents' worst nightmare perfectly realized: a long, blonde-haired Southerner who played the piano and sang with uncontrolled fury and abandon, while simultaneously reveling in his own sexuality. He was rock 'n' roll's first great wild man and also rock 'n' roll's first great eclectic. Ignoring all manner of musical boundaries is something that has not only allowed his music to have wide variety but to survive the fads and fashions as well. Whether singing a melancholy country ballad, a lowdown blues or a blazing rocker, Lewis' wholesale commitment to the moment brings forth performances that are totally grounded in his personality and all singularly of one piece. Like the recordings of Hank Williams, Louis Armstrong and few others, Jerry Lee's early recorded work is one of the most amazing collections of American music in existence.

He was born to Elmo and Mamie Lewis on September 29, 1935. Though the family was dirt poor, there was enough money to be had to purchase a third-hand upright piano for the family's country shack in Ferriday, LA. Sharing piano lessons with his two cousins, Mickey Gilley and Jimmy Lee Swaggart, a ten-year-old Jerry Lee showed remarkable aptitude toward the instrument. A visit from piano-playing older cousin Carl McVoy unlocked the secrets to the boogie-woogie styles he was hearing on the radio and across the tracks at Haney's Big House, owned by his uncle, Lee Calhoun and catering to Blacks exclusively. Lewis mixed that up with gospel and country and started coming up with his own style. He even mixed genres in the way he syncopated his rhythms on the piano; his left hand generally played a rock-solid boogie pattern while his right played the high keys with much flamboyant filigree and showiness, equal parts gospel fervor and Liberace showmanship. By the time he was 14, by all family accounts, he was as good as he was ever going to get. Jerry Lee was already ready for prime time.

But his Mother Mamie had other plans for the young family prodigy. Not wanting to squander Jerry Lee's gifts on the sordid world of show business, she enrolled him in a bible college in Waxahatchie, TX, secure in the knowledge that her son would now be exclusively singing his songs to the Lord. But legend has it that the Killer tore into a boogie-woogie rendition of "My God Is Real" at a church assembly that sent him packing the same night. The split personality of Jerry Lee, torn between the sacred and the profane (rock 'n' roll music) is something that has eaten away at him most of his adult life, causing untold aberrant personality changes over the years with no clear-cut answers to the problem. What is certain is that by the time a 21-year-old Jerry Lee showed up in Memphis on the doorstep of the Sun studios, he had been thrown out of bible college, been a complete failure as a swing-machine salesman, been turned down by most Nashville-based record companies and the *Louisiana Hayride*, been married twice, jailed once, and burned with the passion that he truly was the next big thing.

Jerry Lee Lewis

Sam Phillips was on vacation when he arrived, but his assistant Jack Clement put Roland Janes on guitar and J.M. Van Eaton on drums behind Jerry Lee, whose fluid left hand made a bass player superfluous. This little unit would become the core of Jerry Lee's recording band for almost the entire seven years he recorded at Sun. The first single, a hopped-up rendition of Ray Price's "Crazy Arms," sold in respectable enough quantities that Phillips kept bringing Lewis back in for more sessions, astounded by his prodigious memory for old songs and his penchant for rocking them up. A few days after his first single was released, Jerry Lee was in the Sun studios earning some Christmas money, playing backup piano on a Carl Perkins session that yielded the classics "Matchbox" and "Your True Love." At the tail end of the recording, Elvis Presley showed up, Clement turned on the tape machine, and the impromptu *Million Dollar Quartet* jam session ensued, with Perkins, Presley, and Lewis all having the time of their lives.

With the release of his first single, the road beckoned and it was here that Jerry Lee's lasting stage persona was developed. Discouraged because he couldn't dance around the stage strumming a guitar like Carl Perkins, he stood up in midsong, kicked back the piano stool and, as Carl has so saliently pointed out, "a new Jerry Lee Lewis was born." This new-found stage confidence was not lost on Sam Phillips. While he loved the music of Carl Perkins and Johnny Cash, he saw neither artist as a true contender to Elvis' throne; with Jerry Lee he thought he had a real shot. For the first time in his very parsimonious life, Sam Phillips threw every dime of promotional capital he had into Jerry Lee's next single, and the gamble paid off a million times over. "Whole Lot of Shakin' Going On" went to No. 1 on the country and the R&B charts, and was only held out of the top spot on the pop charts by Debbie Reynolds' "Tammy." Suddenly Jerry Lee was the hottest, newest, most exciting rock 'n' roller out there. His television appearances and stage shows were legendary for their manic energy, and his competitive need to outdo anyone else on the bill led to the story about how he once set his piano on fire at the set's end to make it impossible for Chuck Berry to follow his act. Nobody messed with the Killer.

Jerry Lee's follow-up to "Shakin'" was another defining moment for his career, as well as the music's. "Great Balls of Fire" featured only piano and drums, but sounded huge with Phillips' production behind it. It got him into a rock 'n' roll movie (*Jamboree*) and his fame was spreading to such a degree that Johnny Cash and Carl Perkins left Sun to go to Columbia Records. His next single, "Breathless," had a promotional tie-in with Dick Clark's Saturday night *Bandstand* show, making it three hits in a row for the newcomer.

But Jerry Lee was sowing the seeds of his own destruction in record time.

He sneaked off and married his 13-year-old cousin, Myra Gale Brown, the daughter of his bass-playing uncle, J.W. Brown. With the Killer insisting that she accompany him on a debut tour of England, the British press got wind of the marriage and proceeded to crucify him in the press. The tour was canceled and Jerry Lee arrived back in the US to find his career in absolute disarray. His records were banned nationwide by radio stations and his booking price went from $10,000 a night to $250 bucks in any honky tonk that would still have him. Undeterred, he kept right on doing what he had been doing, head unbowed and determined to make it back to the bigs, Jerry Lee Lewis style. It took him almost a dozen years to pull it off, but finally, with a sympathetic producer and a new record company willing to exact a truce with country disc jockeys, the Killer found a new groove, cutting one hit after another for Smash Records throughout the late '60s into the '70s. Still playing rock 'n' roll onstage whenever the mood struck him (which was often) while keeping all his releases pure country struck a creative bargain that suited Lewis well into the mid-'70s.

But while his career was soaring again, his personal life was falling apart. The next decade and a half saw several marriages fall apart (starting with his 13-year-long union with Myra), the deaths of his parents and oldest son, battles with the I.R.S. and bouts with alcohol and pills that frequently left him hospitalized. Suddenly the Ferriday Fireball was nearing middle age and the raging fire seemed to be burned out.

But the mid-'80s saw another jumpstart to his career. A movie entitled Great Balls of Fire was about to be made of his life and Lewis was called in to sing the songs for the soundtrack. Showing everyone who was the real Killer, Jerry Lee sounded energetic enough to make you believe it was 1957 all over again with the pilot light of inspiration still burning bright. He also got a boost back to major-label land with a one-song appearance on the soundtrack for Dick Tracy.

With box sets and compilations, documentaries, a bioflick and his induction to the Rock & Roll Hall of Fame all celebrating his legacy, Jerry Lee still continues to record and tour, delivering work that vacillates from tepid to absolutely inspired. While his influence will continue to loom large until there's no one left to play rock 'n' roll piano anymore, the plain truth is that there's only one Jerry Lee Lewis and American music will never see another one like him. —Cub Koda

Jerry Lee Lewis / 1957 / Rhino ✦✦✦✦
Jerry Lee Lewis' debut album was a virtual greatest hits album, featuring "Whole Lotta Shakin' Goin' On." —AMG

Jerry Lee's Greatest / 1961 / Rhino ✦✦✦
Jerry Lee's second record followed the same formula as the first, mixing singles—including "Great Balls of Fire"—with album tracks that were nearly as good as the hits. —AMG

The Greatest Live Show on Earth / 1964 / Bear Family ✦✦✦✦
Combining two live albums originally issued in the '60s, Lewis proves that the onslaught of the British Invasion hadn't lowered his rocking quotient one single bit. Blazing performances. —Cub Koda

☆ **Live at the Star Club** / 1965 / Rhino ✦✦✦✦✦
The Killer at his storming best, dragging his backup group, the Nashville Teens, by the scruff of the neck through a blazing set that earmarks this recording as one of the finest live albums ever made. —Cub Koda

★ **18 Original Sun Greatest Hits** / 1984 / Rhino ✦✦✦✦
Solid single-disc collection of the records that got Lewis into the Rock & Roll Hall of Fame on the first ballot; "Whole Lotta Shakin' Goin' On," "Great Balls of Fire," "High School Confidential," and "Breathless" being merely the tip of the iceberg. —Cub Koda

Milestones / 1985 / Rhino ✦✦✦✦
There are so many Jerry Lee Lewis compilations out, ranging from single-disc Sun retrospectives to mammoth German imports documenting a few years in particular, that it's easy to lose track of what the best ones are. All you need to know about this double

LP is that it's a good selection of his most famous material, properly emphasizing the late-'50s classics, with excellent liner notes. It also throws on enough of his most notable post-Sun cuts ("What's Made Milwaukee Famous," "Me and Bobby McGee") to make rock-oriented listeners feel that they have a sense of his post-rockabilly career without boring them to death. Those looking for one Jerry Lee album should get Rhino's All Killer, No Filler anthology instead. Those who are satisfied with Milestones as supplying all the Jerry Lee they want have no need to replace it. —Richie Unterberger

☆ **Classic** / 1989 / Bear Family ✦✦✦✦✦
Eight-disc boxed set of Lewis' complete output for Sun Records. Along with Muddy Waters' Chess recordings, Louis Armstrong's Hot Fives & Sevens, and Hank Williams' undubbed MGM sides, this box comprises one of the finest bodies of American music ever recorded. —Cub Koda

Killer: The Mercury Years, Vol. 1 (1963-1968) / 1989 / Mercury ✦✦✦✦
This three-volume set takes you through the best of the Mercury years, country, rock and gospel styles. —Hank Davis

Killer: The Mercury Years, Vol. 2 (1969-1972) / 1989 / Mercury ✦✦✦✦

Killer: The Mercury Years, Vol. 3 (1973-1977) / 1989 / Mercury ✦✦✦✦

★ **All Killer, No Filler: The Anthology** / May 18, 1993 / Rhino ✦✦✦✦✦
Out of all of the Jerry Lee Lewis compilations available on the market, only All Killer, No Filler contains material from all of the different labels he recorded for. Although there are twelve Sun tracks (including all of the major hits), the set doesn't draw enough from those early years; but then again, that's the intent. All Killer, No Filler is out to prove to an audience only familiar with his Sun singles that his country material is as brilliant as his rock 'n' roll, and it succeeds. Stick with the 18 Original Sun Greatest Hits if you only want rock 'n' roll. If you want an idea of the scope of Lewis' talents and how consistently rich his music was throughout his career, you can't go wrong here. —Stephen Thomas Erlewine

Locust Years . . . and the Return to the Promised Land / 1994 / Bear Family ✦✦✦✦
Picking up where the eight-CD set Classic left off, this eight-CD box Locust Years . . . and the Return to the Promised Land rivals its predecessor in musical quality. Tracing Jerry Lee Lewis' '60s career at Smash Records, the first two discs find the pianist trying to replicate his rock 'n' roll success; while the performances were good, it was clear he was out of touch with the times. On the third disc, he begins to concentrate on country music. The fourth, fifth, and sixth discs match his Sun recordings for consistently brilliant performances; several of the songs became big hits on the country charts, establishing him as a country star. The seventh disc chronicles an exciting unreleased show, while the eighth disc is an unexceptional interview. For dedicated Jerry Lee Lewis fans, The Locust Years is every bit as essential as Classic. —Stephen Thomas Erlewine

● **Killer Country** / 1995 / Mercury ✦✦✦✦
Killer Country is a well-chosen selection of Jerry Lee Lewis' biggest and best country hits between 1963 and 1977, which feature some of his finest performances, including "Another Place, Another Time," "What's Made Milwaukee Famous," "She Still Comes Around (To Love What's Left of Me)," and "She Even Woke Me Up to Say Goodbye." —Stephen Thomas Erlewine

Young Blood / 1995 / Sire ✦✦
Jerry Lee Lewis made a comeback effort in 1995 with Young Blood. Although the Killer's performance is impressive—his voice continues to weather well with age and he hasn't lost much of his instrumental prowess—the selection of material is fairly uninspired and predictable. This wouldn't have been a problem if Jerry Lee was allowed to work with a top-notch backing band, which would have elevated the pedestrian material to a higher level. Instead, Young Blood was made like most albums in the mid-'90s—each song was constructed track-by-track, with the musi-

cians laying down their parts at different times. Consequently, the record is stripped of most of its potential power, leaving behind a well-produced but thoroughly unengaging album. — *Stephen Thomas Erlewine*

Laurie Lewis

b. 1950, Berkeley, CA
Violin, Vocals / Progressive Bluegrass, Traditional Bluegrass
Playing a unique blend of old-time country, bluegrass, Western Swing, Cajun, and Tejano, Laurie Lewis and her Grant Street String Band were not easy to pigeonhole. Lewis, a key figure in helping female musicians break into the traditionally male-dominated genre, was an exceptional, versatile fiddler and a singer blessed with a smooth, musical voice. She also wrote well crafted, thought provoking songs, some of which were recorded by singers like Patsy Montana and Kathy Mattea.

Born and raised in the San Francisco Bay Area, Lewis mastered the violin at an early age. While growing up during the '60s, she was greatly influenced by the folk movement and frequently attended the Berkeley Folk festivals, where she was exposed to a variety of classic bluegrass acts including Doc Watson, the Greenbriar Boys, and Mississippi John Hurt. By the early '70s, Lewis began entering fiddle contests and was a two-time winner of the California State Women's Championship. She also began performing both bluegrass and Western swing while touring with different bands.

She and friend Kathy Kallick, a veteran of the Phantoms of the Opry and Arkansas Sheiks, teamed up to form the all-woman band Good Ol' Persons, soon developed a large West Coast following. Lewis left the group in 1979 to found her Grant Street String Band, which released their critically acclaimed eponymous debut album in the early '80s. Lewis also made her solo debut, *Restless Rambling Heart*, in 1986, and continued dividing her time between her solo and group work for the next several years. The popularity of Grant Street got a boost when mandolin player Tom Rozum joined in 1987, and in 1991, Lewis reteamed with former Good Ol' Persons bandmate Kathy Kallick to record *Together*. After the 1994 Grant Street release *True Stories*, she and the band were involved in a terrible automobile wreck and they spent much of the year in recovery. Fortunately, in 1995, she, Rozum and the band recorded *Oak and the Laurel*, featuring special guest appearances by artists like Mike Marshall and Craig Smith. — *Sandra Brennan*

● **Restless Rambling Heart** / 1986 / Flying Fish ✦✦✦✦
The first solo album from this Bay Area singer and fiddler is sweet but not saccharine, a mix of old-time, bluegrass, and rootsy contemporary folk. — *Mark A. Humphrey*

Love Chooses You / 1989 / Flying Fish ✦✦✦
A follow-up in the spirit of the first, it has a good choice of material. — *Mark A. Humphrey*

Singin' My Troubles Away / 1990 / Flying Fish ✦✦✦✦
With *Singin' My Troubles Away*, Laurie Lewis balances her music between folk-tinged country and progressive bluegrass. Though Lewis' fiddle certainly takes the center stage, she has assembled a first-class backing band—featuring guitarist Scott Nygaard, banjoist Tony Furtado, bassist Tammy Fassaert, and mandolinist Tom Rozum—that keeps the music vibrant and alive. — *Thom Owens*

Together / 1991 / Kaleidoscope ✦✦✦
Together is a fine, understated duet album between Laurie Lewis and Kathy Kallick, her former partner in the Good Ol' Persons. — *Thom Owens*

True Stories / 1993 / Rounder ✦✦✦

The Oak and the Laurel / 1995 / Rounder ✦✦✦

The Light Crust Doughboys

Western Swing
Originated in 1931 as a trio consisting of Bob Wills, Milton Brown, and Herman Arnspiger, the Light Crust Doughboys were just as famous for their association with announcer "Pappy" W. Lee O'Daniel, later a hugely controversial Texas politico and a man to whom Wills did not particularly cotton. — *Dan Cooper*

The Lightcrust Doughboys / 1959 / Audio Lab ✦✦✦

String Band Swing / 1981 / Longhorn ✦✦✦✦

● **Light Crust Doughboys 1936-39** / 1982 / Texas Rose ✦✦✦✦
These 16 sides catch the band long after Wills and Brown left, but still laying down solid, bluesy licks. "Pussy, Pussy, Pussy" is simply not to be believed. — *Dan Cooper*

The Lilly Brothers

Traditional Bluegrass
The Lilly Brothers, Everett and B., played old-time/bluegrass music together for over three decades. They may best be remembered in New England, where they were a fixture in the downtown Boston music scene from the early '60s through 1980.

Charles Everett and older sibling Michel Burt Lilly were born three years apart in Clear Creek, WV. Everett played the mandolin, banjo and fiddle while B. played guitar; both brothers sang; early influences included the Delmore Brothers, the Callahan Brothers, and the Monroes. The Lillys debuted in 1938 singing old-time country on a West Virginia radio station. They initially billed themselves as the Lonesome Holler Boys. Later they added a banjo and became a bluegrass group. In 1939, they began performing regularly at the newly established WKLS Beckley, where they performed together and with other musicians. After that they spent a few years at various southern stations playing in such groups as the Smiling Mountain Boys and Red Belcher's Kentucky Ridge Runners.

They made their recording debut in 1948 while working with the latter group at WWVA. They remained at the station through 1950, whereupon they returned home after a heated fight with Belcher over money. From there the Lillys split up for a time; Everett became a mandolin player and tenor with Flatt & Scruggs' Foggy Mountain Boys, and remained with them through early 1952, when he left to join his brother, fiddler Tex Logan, and banjo picker Don Stover in Boston. They got their first job playing on WCOP's *Hayloft Jamboree* and from there hit the local club circuit.

The Lilly Brothers recorded fairly frequently during the 1950s. Between 1958 and 1959, Everett spent another year with Flatt & Scruggs while Stover did a bit of touring with other bands. But for that, the Lilly Brothers remained intact through 1970. In addition to playing downtown Boston, they also played the local festival circuit and were instrumental in the development of urban bluegrass. In the early '70s, Everett's son was killed in a car crash, causing him and his wife Joann to leave Beantown and return to West Virginia. B. Lilly came down a while later to help Everett host a local television show, but eventually returned to the city. After 1971, Everett infrequently joined the band to perform at festivals during the summers and to occasionally record with them. The Lilly Brothers' career was later chronicled in a 1979 documentary *True Facts in a Country Song*. — *Sandra Brennan*

Folk Songs from Southern Mountains / 1961 / Folkways ✦✦✦

Bluegrass Breakdown / 1963 / Rounder ✦✦✦✦
Great 1964 performances. — *Mark A. Humphrey*

Country Songs / 1964 / Rounder ✦✦✦

★ **Early Recordings** / 1971 / Rebel ✦✦✦✦✦
These driving, late-'50s performances have breathtaking banjo from Don Stover and hand-in-glove vocal harmonies. It is one of the best bluegrass albums ever. — *Mark A. Humphrey*

What Will I Leave Behind / 1973 / Country ✦✦✦

Little Texas

Country-Rock, Contemporary Country
Drawing from country and rock 'n' roll, Little Texas was one of the more popular country bands of the early '90s. The origins of the group began in 1984, when vocalist Tim Rushlow teamed up with vocalist/acoustic guitarist Dwayne O'Brien in Arlington, TX. After two years of working together, Rushlow left for Nashville while O'Brien finished up his chemistry degree. The following year, he followed Rushlow to Music City. They were subsequently joined by lead guitarist Porter Howell and bass guitarist Duane

Propes, and the group began touring. While performing in Massachusetts, they hooked up with keyboardist Brady Seals and drummer Del Gray. In 1988, future manager Christy DiNapoli convinced Doug Grau from Warner Brothers to come listen to one of the band's performances in Birmingham, and he signed them to the label.

Upon signing the contract, the group named themselves Little Texas—after their old rehearsal spot on Little Texas Road—and began touring the country in a beat-up van and a homemade trailer. By the end of 1990, they had enough material to record their debut album, *First Time for Everything*. The album was released in the summer of 1991, after the band's debut single, "Some Guys Have All the Love," became a Top Ten hit. The band really began to take off in 1994 with the release of their second album, *Big Time*. The album produced the No. 2 country hit "What Might Have Been," which also became a minor pop hit. This was followed by "God Blessed Texas," a line-dancing favorite that reached the Top Five. In early 1994, Little Texas scored its first No. 1 hit with "My Love," and *Big Time* went platinum. Later in 1994, the group released their third album, *Kick a Little*, which went platinum and produced two Top ten singles in the title track and "Amy's Back in Austin." In 1995, Little Texas released *Greatest Hits*, which featured two new songs, including the No. 5 hit "Life Goes On." —*Sandra Brennan*

First Time for Everything / Mar. 3, 1992 / Warner Brothers ♦♦
First Time for Everything bears the strong influence of mellow '70s pop, especially on hits like "You and Forever and Me." —*Jason Ankeny*

Little Texas / Mar. 3, 1992 / Warner Brothers ♦♦♦

Big Time / 1993 / Warner Brothers ♦♦♦
Little Texas hit chart paydirt with the aptly titled *Big Time*, which features the No. 1 smash "My Love" along with "What Might Have Been" and "God Blessed Texas." —*Jason Ankeny*

Kick a Little / 1994 / Warner Brothers ♦♦♦♦

● **Greatest Hits** / Oct. 1995 / Warner Brothers ♦♦♦♦
Collecting all of Little Texas' best numbers, *Greatest Hits* is the perfect introduction to the country-pop band, as well as being their most consistent and enjoyable album. —*Stephen Thomas Erlewine*

Hank Locklin

b. Feb. 15, 1918, McLellan, FL
Guitar, Vocals / Traditional Country, Honky Tonk, Nashville Sound/Countrypolitan
Hank Locklin (b. Lawrence Hankins Locklin), one of country music's great tenors, was born February 15, 1918 in the small town of McLellan located in the lumbering district of the Florida Panhandle. The youngest son of four children, he went to a one-room schoolhouse and was musical even as a young child. Hank was injured at the age of eight in an accident and it was during the long recovery process that he first began to learn music. Although interested in the guitar early on, it was not until his mid-teens that he really began to master the instrument. Locklin was active in music in high school (which he never finished), and at 18 won first prize in a talent show. He went on to do spots on the local radio station as he became more and more interested in entertaining. By the mid-1940s he was playing on the radio and doing in-person performances in Florida and nearby states. For the next ten years or so, Locklin worked many jobs (musical and otherwise), played with a variety of groups, and, through a variety of trials, gradually worked his way up the country music ladder to recognition. (A good account of these years can be found in the Bear Family box liner notes, written by Otto Kissinger.)

His career did not really take off until he joined the RCA Victor label in the spring of 1955. Locklin's work with RCA has the added advantage that almost all of it was produced by Chet Atkins, often with Atkins himself on rhythm or lead guitar and with the added trills and fill-ins of Floyd Cramer on piano. The extreme simplicity of his early works makes this combination of his clear voice and these particular sidemen very effective. Every-

one knows Hank's big hits—"Send Me the Pillow that You Dream On", "Geisha Girl," and "Please Help Me I'm Falling"—but real Locklin fans are in love with his very simple, heartfelt tunes like "Who Am I to Cast the First Stone," "A Good Woman's Love," "Seven or Eleven," "I'm Tired of Bummin' Around," "Golden Wristwatch," "Sitting Alone at a Table for Two," and many others. These early songs are characterized by Locklin's crystal clear tenor, the ultra-simplicity of the songs themselves, and their straight-to-the heart emotional plea. Kitty Wells has this same kind of gift. The result is a group of incredible songs that, first released as singles, later became available on Camden, RCA's budget label. Now, after many years of neglect, many of these songs are now available on the Bear family box *Hank Locklin, Please Help Me I'm Falling*. Locklin stayed with the RCA label until the mid-1960s.

Locklin helped pioneer the idea of concept albums; *Foreign Love* and *Irish Songs, Country Style* are examples. He also recorded an album tribute to Roy Acuff, *A Tribute to Roy Acuff, King of Country Music*. His Irish songs are pretty near definitive. On later albums, the vocal chorus begins to creep in a little more than purists might like, but his crystal clear tenor never deserts him.

Hank hit the top ten charts again in 1968 with "The Country Hall of Fame." In the 1970s he toured overseas often, was very popular in Ireland and Great Britian, and made at least one tour with Chet Atkins to the Far East (Japan). After leaving RCA, he went on to record for a number of labels including MGM and Plantation. He is retired now and lives in Brewton, AL, only some 20 miles from his birth place. —*Michael Erlewine*

Foreign Love / 1958 / RCA Victor ♦♦♦

Please Help Me I'm Falling / 1960 / RCA Victor ♦♦♦♦

Encores / 1961 / RCA Victor ♦♦♦♦

A Tribute to Roy Acuff, King of Country Music / 1962 / RCA Victor ♦♦♦

Irish Songs, Country Style / 1964 / RCA Victor ♦♦

Sings Hank Williams / 1964 / RCA Victor ♦♦♦♦

My Kind of Country Music / 1965 / RCA Camden ♦♦♦♦
Released on RCA's subsidary Camden Records, *My Kind of Country* may only contain only one hit ("Wooden Soldier") but the LP demonstrates Hank Locklin's gift for tear-jerking ballads and pure traditional country. —*Thom Owens*

The Best of Hank Locklin / 1966 / RCA Victor ♦♦♦♦

The Girls Get Prettier / 1966 / RCA Victor ♦♦♦

Nashville Women / 1967 / RCA Victor ♦♦♦♦
Although it has a couple of slow spots, *Nashville Women* is a highly enjoyable LP, boasting a number of engaging country-pop songs like "Nashville Women," "After the Hurt Is Gone," "Hasta Luego (See You Later)," "The Best Part of Loving You," "Release Me," and "I Feel a Cry Coming On." —*Thom Owens*

Country Hall of Fame / 1968 / RCA Victor ♦♦♦♦
Country Hall of Fame is a terrifically entertaining tribute to not only the institution of the Country Music Hall of Fame (the hit title song is a corny but strong tribute to the foundation) but the performers that grace its halls. Over the course of the LP, Hank Locklin sings standards like "High Noon (Do Not Forsake Me)," "Four Walls," "Walking the Floor over You," "Lovesick Blues," "Blue Yodel ('T for Texas)," and "Peace in the Valley," giving them each his patented high, lonesome tenor. It's a very entertaining and even moving record, and it ranks as one of his best albums of the late '60s. —*Thom Owens*

My Love Song for You / 1968 / RCA Victor ♦♦♦♦
My Love Song for You is an excellent collection of country ballads highlighted by "Danny Boy," "Longing to Hold You Again," "I Came So Close to Living Alone," and the hit single "Lovin' You (The Way I Do)." —*Thom Owens*

Lookin' Back / 1969 / RCA Victor ♦♦
Though Hank Locklin is in fine voice throughout *Lookin' Back*, the LP is burdened by too many average songs and an overblown production that makes the record a frustrating listen. —*Thom Owens*

Hank Locklin & Danny Davis & The Nashville Brass / 1970 / RCA Victor ✦✦

Hank Locklin & Danny Davis & the Nashville Brass is an awkward fusion of Locklin's pure country with brass bands. A few of the tracks—namely "Blue Moon of Kentucky," "Laura (What's He Got That I Ain't Got)," "Once a Day," and the hit single "Flying South"—work, but many of the songs, particularly "Please Help Me, I'm Falling," sound overburdened with horns. —*Thom Owens*

★ **Please Help Me I'm Falling [Box]** / Dec. 1995 / Bear Family ✦✦✦✦✦

This is a four-disc retrospective of Locklin's years with RCA Victor from 1955 through the mid 1960s. Of course Hank's big popular hits "Send Me the Pillow that You Dream On,", "Geisha Girl," and "Please Help Me I'm Falling" are there. While a great many important early Locklin songs are missing from this collection ("I'm Tired of Bummin' Around," "Sitting Alone at a Table for Two," and "Golden Wristwatch"), many fine songs are included that have been unavailable for many years; songs like "Who Am I to Cast the First Stone," "A Good Woman's Love," "Seven or Eleven." Most were produced by Chet Atkins, often with Atkins on guitar, and almost all with the excellent piano accompaniment of Floyd Cramer. Also included are a number of Locklin's concept albums: *Foreign Love, Irish Songs, Country Style,* plus his album tribute to Roy Acuff, *A Tribute to Roy Acuff, King of Country Music.* Of course his early material on Four Star Records (pre-RCA) and his later material on MGM and Plantation are not here. Most of these songs in this box set are taken from albums that appeared on Camden and RCA. They are *My Kind of Country Blues* (Camden CAL 912), *Hank Locklin* (Camden CAL 905), *Please Help Me I'm Falling* (RCA LPM 2291), *Foreign Love* (RCA LPM 1673), *This Song Is Just For You* (Camden CAL 765), *Happy Journey* (RCA LSP 2464), *A Tribute to Roy Acuff, King of Country Music* (RCA LSP 2597), *The Ways of Life* (RCA LSP 2680), and *Irish Songs, Country Style* (RCA LSP 2801). Unless RCA decides to release all the early Camden material, this fine box set from Bear Family is what we have for now. —*Michael Erlewine*

★ **Send Me the Pillow that You Dream On** / 1997 / Bear Family ✦✦✦✦✦

Send Me the Pillow that You Dream On is a three-disc box set that contains all of the recordings Hank Locklin made between 1948 and 1955, including all of his seminal waxings for Four Star Records. It's an essential compilation, containing many of his very best performances. —*Thom Owens*

☆ **Hank Locklin** / Wrangler ✦✦✦✦✦

One of the most perfect early country albums ever recorded; heart-wrenching songs sung in Locklin's perfect tenor—before the hits. It does not get any better than this. A hard-to-find album, but quintessential. —*Michael Erlewine*

Jimmie Logsdon

b. Apr. 1, 1922, Panther, KY

Vocals / Traditional Country, Nashville Sound/Countrypolitan

During the 1950s, Jimmie Logsdon was an extremely popular singer and a top country deejay. He was born in Panther, KY, to a Methodist minister, and began performing at age 12 in the church choir with his sister Martha Jean. He later played clarinet in his high school band, and also learned to play guitar. He was married in 1940, and entered the Air Force and World War II in 1944, where he sang songs he had written to his comrades. Upon his return, Logsdon opened a record and radio shop in LeGrange, KY, and continued to perform professionally. He began his radio career in 1950 on WGN Chicago, and later got his own 15-minute show in Louisville, KY. In 1952, he toured with his friend Hank Williams; following Williams' death, Logsdon honored his friend and mentor with the double-sided single "The Death of Hank Williams/Hank Williams Sings the Blues No More." Logsdon's career was boosted in 1953 when he became the host of the live *Country & Music Show* on WHAS-TV, which also featured his backup group, the Golden Harvest Boys. Although he released singles and albums through 1962, Logsdon never appeared on the charts. During the '60s, he returned to his career

as a deejay and penned songs for such stars as Johnny Horton, Carl Perkins, and even jazz artist Woody Herman. He augmented his income by working in his brother-in-law's swimming pool business, while also making commercials and singing in nightclubs. —*Sandra Brennan*

Howdy Neighbors / 1963 / King ✦✦✦

Doing It Hank's Way / 1980 / Castle ✦✦✦✦

● **I Got a Rocket in My** / 1993 / Bear Family ✦✦✦✦

The complete '50s output of this second-line country artist who also recorded rockabilly under the name Jimmy Lloyd. Includes the title track, one of rockabilly's finest moments, as well as traditional country material like "The Death of Hank Williams" and "That's When I'll Love You the Best." Fans of '50s-style country will love this one. —*Cub Koda*

Lone Justice

Country-Rock, Roots-Rock

The roots-rock band Lone Justice was formed in Los Angeles by guitarist Ryan Hedgecock and singer Maria McKee. The half-sister of Bryan MacLean, a member of the seminal psychedelic outfit Love, McKee's involvement in the L.A. club scene dated back to her infancy; at the age of three, she joined MacLean at a performance at the famed Whisky-a-Go-Go and was befriended by Frank Zappa and members of the Doors. As a teen, she studied musical theater, and briefly performed in duos with MacLean and local blues singer Top Jimmy. McKee and Hedgecock first met while dabbling in the L.A. rockabilly scene, and their mutual affection for country music inspired them to found Lone Justice in 1982.

Initially, the group was strictly a cover band, but the additions of veteran bassist Marvin Etzioni and Don Heffington, a former drummer in Emmylou Harris' Hot Band, prompted McKee to begin composing original material inspired by Dust Bowl-era balladry. Gradually, elements of rock began creeping into the Lone Justice sound, and soon the band became a local favorite. At the urging of Linda Ronstadt, they were awarded a contract with Geffen Records; their self-titled debut appeared in 1985, followed by a tour in support of U2. Still, despite good press and media hype, *Lone Justice* failed to sell; slickly produced by the band's manager Jimmy Iovine, it failed to connect with either country or rock audiences. In the record's wake, Hedgecock, Etzioni and Heffington all exited the band, leaving McKee to lead Lone Justice alone. After enlisting guitarist Shayne Fontayne, bassist Greg Sutton, drummer Rudy Richardson and keyboardist Bruce Brody, Lone Justice recorded its second LP, *Shelter*. Shortly after the record's release, McKee broke up the band for good and went on to a solo career. Heffington became a successful session drummer, while Etzioni recorded under the guise Marvin the Mandolin Man. After a decade removed from the music industry, Hedgecock returned in 1996 as half of the duo Parlor James. —*Jason Ankeny*

● **Lone Justice** / 1985 / Geffen ✦✦✦✦

Maria McKee has one of those aching, little-girl voices (not unlike Stevie Nicks'), and it's heard to great effect on these country-rock tunes, especially Tom Petty and Mike Campbell's "Ways to Be Wicked." —*William Ruhlmann*

Shelter / 1986 / Geffen ✦✦✦

Lonesome Pine Fiddlers

Traditional Bluegrass

The Lonesome Pine Fiddlers were an enduring force in the development of bluegrass music for over three decades. Over the years, the band underwent many personnel changes and played a variety of styles, ranging from old-time string music to bluegrass to country.

The group was founded in 1938 by Ray Cline in Baisden, WV. Originally it consisted of Cline and his adolescent cousins. The Lonesome Pine Fiddlers started out playing at WHIS Bluefield, and soon after, Gordon Jennings joined them. The Fiddlers temporarily broke up during World War II. After the war they reunited back on WHIS, joined by Charlie Cline, who sang duets with Ray. In 1949, the Cline Brothers were replaced by fiddler Ray Morgan, Bob Osborne, and Larry Richardson. By 1950, they had become a full-fledged bluegrass band. Bob and Larry left the following year and were replaced by Jimmy and Paul Williams. More personnel changes ensued and in 1953, the band began playing at WJR in Detroit. There they cut six sides for Victor in Chicago, among them their best-known song, "Dirty Dishes Blues."

The Lonesome Pine Fiddlers then moved to WLSI Pikeville, KY, and stayed there the rest of their career. They recorded eight singles in 1954, including two bluegrass classics, "Windy Mountain" and "No Curb Service." The band had a golden opportunity that year to perform on the Martha White-sponsored program at WSM, but they refused and Flatt & Scruggs took it instead. This refusal limited the band's exposure to the Appalachian area, where they remained popular on radio and television shows while recording and performing full-time through 1964, when they decreased the pace of their schedule. By 1966, the members of the Lonesome Pine Fiddlers had gone their separate ways. In 1988, some of the founding members reunited for a reunion album. Charlie Cline still uses the band's name for his own country music group. —*Sandra Brennan*

Early Bluegrass, Vol. 1 / 1979 / Old Homestead ✦✦✦✦

Early Bluegrass, Vol. 2 / 1983 / Old Homestead ✦✦✦✦

● **Windy Mountain** / 1992 / Bear Family ✦✦✦✦

Windy Mountain contains all of the material the Lonesome Pine Fiddlers recorded for Cozy and RCA Records during the early '50s. Though the 26-track collection is exhaustive, it is also exhausting—no matter how good these tracks are as individual songs, the relentless chronological sequencing of the material on this compact disc makes the record more of a history lesson than a casual listen. Nevertheless, *Windy Mountain* functions as the definitive retrospective of one of the finest and most important bluegrass bands of the '50s and features great performances by Bobby Osborne, Charline Cline, Paul Williams, and Curly Ray Cline. For bluegrass historians, it's essential. —*Stephen Thomas Erlewine*

Early Days of Bluegrass, Vol. 3 (New Sounds Ramblin from Coast to Coast) / Rounder ✦✦✦

Lonesome River Band

Bluegrass

Featuring some of the major bluegrass talents of the '90s, the members of the Lonesome River Band have recorded solo albums and won many instrumentalist awards, but each have made their best music as a unit. Vocalist Ronnie Bowman, banjo player Sammy Shelor, guitarist Kenny Smith, and mandolin player Don Rigsby form the main lineup, but they often receive help from players Aubrey Haymie and Randy Howard on fiddle, and Jerry Douglas on dobro guitar. The Lonesome River Band released two albums on Rebel Records during the early '90s, and signed to Sugar Hill in 1994 for *Old Country Town*. After the album's release and several months of touring, Bowman recorded *Cold Virginia Night* (for which he won the 1995 Album of the Year at the IBMA Awards); Rigsby as well has recorded on his own, including *A Tribute to Hank Williams* and *Music*. Even Shelor—honored as Banjo Player of the Year at the same IBMA Awards ceremony—got into the act by releasing *ACUTAB Transcriptions, Vol. 1*. The group's second album for Sugar Hill, *One Step Forward*, appeared in 1996. —*John Bush*

● **Old Country Town** / 1994 / Sugar Hill ✦✦✦✦

High-speed playing and high lonesome vocals characterize this quartet's smooth bluegrass album. —*Richard Meyer*

One Step Forward / Mar. 19, 1996 / Koch ✦✦✦

Carrying the Tradition / Rebel ✦✦✦

Looking for Yourself / Rebel ✦✦✦

Lonesome Strangers

Alternative Pop-Rock, Roots-Rock, Alternative Country-Rock, Alternative Country, Americana, California Country

This unique Los Angeles outfit was formed in the 1980s during the cowpunk explosion that brought to light such stars as Dwight Yoakam, Rosie Flores, James Intveld, and the Coal Porters. The core of the Lonesome Strangers consisted of founders Randy Weeks and Jeff Rymes. Known for their fraternal harmonies, Weeks and Rymes stayed true to their vision in spite of the many ups and downs that the music business and life threw their way. A constant presence on the L.A. country and roots music scene, the Lonesome Strangers were hometown favorites and often opened for Yoakam, at his request.

Weeks, a native of Minnesota, and Rymes, from Colorado, first came together in 1984 when they played "Fugitive's Lament," a Delmore Brothers' song. Blending together effortlessly, both knew they had stumbled upon something very special, forming a band that began to play around town. Attracting the attention of producer Pete Anderson, the Lonesome Strangers joined Yoakam, Intveld, Flores, Albert Lee, Kathy Robertson and a list of other Los Angeles/Bakersfield-inspired artists on the 1985 compilation, *A Town South of Bakersfield*. This lead to their first full-length project in 1986: *Lonesome Pines*, produced by Anderson, was a critic's delight.

To fill out the band Weeks and Rymes brought in drummer Mike McLean and on bass, Lorne Rall, touring extensively during 1986 and 1987 and gaining the respect of their peers. Giving tour support to both Yoakam and Dave Alvin allowed them to move forward. Weeks and Rymes showed up on Yoakam's *Buenas Noches from a Lonely Room* displaying their scintillating harmonies. In 1988, Hightone Records signed the band and in January 1989 released their self-titled LP. Produced by Hightone executive Bruce Bromberg and California country music professional Wyman Reese, guests on the project included Alvin, Greg Leisz, and former Long Ryder Stephen McCarthy. Hitting the charts with their own version of Johnny Horton's "Hello Baby Doll" and supporting it with the Delmores' "Lay Down My Old Guitar," "Another Fool Like Me," and "Daddy's Gone Gray," this release caused a sensation as well as landing their video on CMT. Riding the crest of their popularity, the Lonesome Strangers generated not only industry interest, but also a strong following that continued to support them.

As things died down, McClean and Rall left the band. Weeks and Rymes continued on and eventually began working in the studio with producer and Lonesome Strangers' supporter Dusty Wakeman. With Wakeman providing a steady, guiding hand as well as the expertise of his bass playing, *Land of Opportunity* was created. All the cuts, with the exception of the well-known Nashville Teens' hit "Tobacco Road," were penned by Weeks and Rymes. Released in 1997 after much anticipation, *Land of Opportunity* marked the Lonesome Strangers' musical marriage between traditional hillbilly harmonies with roots rock beats and California's country heritage. New members of the band included former Plowboy Kenny Griffin on drums for a time, later replaced by Greg Perry, and Jeff Roberts, another experienced member of the California country coalition, playing bass. —*Jana Pendragon*

● **Lonesome Strangers** / 1989 / Hightone ✦✦✦✦

This sophomore effort by one of California's most influential bands not only brought them fame, if not fortune, but also helped them build a strong following that continues to support their efforts. Fronted by the brotherly harmonies of Randy Weeks and Jeff Rymes, the Lonesome Strangers borrowed from such great brother duos as the Stanley Brothers, the Delmores, and the Everlys while bringing a fresh and harder-edged perspective to their rock 'n' roll hillbilly style. Their remake of Johnny Horton's "Goodbye Lonesome, Hello Baby Doll" brought the country music industry to attention. Adding a Buddy Holly twist, the very hillbilly "Daddy's Gone Gray" takes things to a whole new level. "We Used to Fuss" recalls the humor that old-time country music and Buck Owens made so pleasing. As for ballads, "Clementine" and "Oh My Train" are bittersweet and executed with genuine feeling. Also good is their crack cover of a Delmore Brothers standard,

"Lay Down My Old Guitar," "Don't Back Down" and the almost morose "Another Fool like Me." Simply put, every cut counts. With production credits going to friend and some-time Lonesome Stranger Wyman Reese and Hightone mogul Bruce Bromberg and the mixing handled by another intimate and major California player, Dusty Wakeman, this second Lonesome Strangers project is ground breaking. —*Jana Pendragon*

Land of Opportunity / 1997 / Little Dog ✦✦✦✦
From the jaunty opening track "And It Hurts" to the Norteno rendering of the Louvin Brothers' gem "I Don't Believe You've Met My Baby" that closes the set, the Lonesome Strangers demonstrate that they just might be the closest country music will ever get to a reincarnation of the Delmore Brothers. Capturing the same fun and wild abandon of that early hillbilly boogie, Jeff Rhymes and Randy Weeks could easily be mistaken as one of the great brother duos, melding their nasal voices seamlessly. Just listen to the backwoods treatment and vitality they inject into the winded, but still spooky, classic "Tobacco Road." Rhymes and Weeks' style is based in country and roots-rock, but they also have a great pop sense, writing songs with a Holly-esque flair such as "Sharon," which sounds like something Buddy might have thrown the Everly Brothers' way. Other highlights include the swampy, tremolo drenched "Ton of Shame," and the cheerful, dance-inspiring "Ramblin' Around." Guitar ace and Little Dog founder/president Pete Anderson produced this ten-song collection, and his band backs the duo solidly, with musical touches that include some tasty Hammond B-3. —*Jack Leaver*

Lonesome Val

Bass, Vocals / Singer-Songwriter, Country-Folk, Americana
Manhattanite Lonesome Val first came to national and critical attention in 1988, when her country- and folk-tinged tunes got her named *Musician* magazine's Best Unsigned Artist of the Year. But Val went through a difficult breakup, which left her musical career in a shambles until she met Roches member Suzzy Roche. The two started playing together, and Roche helped Val make a demo tape. The Bar/None record label was impressed enough to ask for an entire album from Val, which Roche produced and played guitar on. The results, *NYC*, were released in the summer of 1994. —*Steve Huey*

● **Lonesome Val** / 1990 / Restless ✦✦✦✦
Here is a fun, rockin', slightly country, guitar-driven album with songs and vocals by Lonesome Val. She sets up the mood with the leadoff track "To Be Young." The album features electric guitars by Stuart Lerman, drums by Howie Wyeth, and vocals by Greg Trouper. —*Richard Meyer*

NYC / 1994 / Bar/None ✦✦✦

Lonestar

Country-Rock, Contemporary Country
Though their name might lead you to believe that Lonestar was formed in Texas, the quintet actually hails from Tennessee. Originally called Texassee, the band features Richie McDonald (lead vocals, guitar), John Rich (lead vocals, bass), Michael Britt (lead guitar, background vocals), Dean Sams (keyboard, background vocals) and Keech Rainwater (drums). All the members are in fact Texas natives—they just formed in Tennessee in 1992.

In 1993, Lonestar played their first concert at Backstage Pass in Nashville in January of 1993. A booking agent happened to hear the show. Impressed, he added the group to his roster and the group headed out on the road. Over the next two years, they played nearly 500 shows. In 1994, the group landed a record contract with BNA Records. The following year they released their eponymous debut, which spawned the Top ten hit "Tequila Talkin'." —*Stephen Thomas Erlewine*

Lonestar / Oct. 10, 1995 / BNA ✦✦✦✦
The Texan group Lonestar's self-titled debut is accomplished and impassioned hardcore honky tonk, drawing from such influences as Lefty Frizzell, George Jones, and Merle Haggard. —*Stephen Thomas Erlewine*

Long Ryders

Country-Rock, Roots-Rock
Although they played the same clubs as most of Los Angeles' "paisley underground" bands (i.e., Dream Syndicate, Rain Parade) and even featured Dream Syndicate leader Steve Wynn in an early lineup, the Long Ryders were actually more a roots-rock group influenced strongly by Gram Parsons. The group was founded by Kentucky native Sid Griffin—a Parsons devotee who moved to Los Angeles after hearing about that city's punk scene—guitarist Stephen McCarthy, the only two members to remain throughout the group's tenure. Its first rhythm section featured bassist Barry Shank and drummer Matt Roberts; they, along with Griffin, had previously been members of the Unclaimed. The band's 1983 debut EP, *10-5-60*, was a blend of punk attitude, '60s rock, and traditional country (Griffin played steel guitar, autoharp, and mandolin). Their first full-length album, the following year's *Native Sons*, was also arguably their best, and featured guest vocals from former Byrd Gene Clark. Subsequent albums failed to find an audience, and unhappy with their label's promotional efforts but unable to secure a release from their contract, the Long Ryders called it quits in 1987. McCarthy formed Gutterball and, along with Griffin, contributed to the 1993 Gram Parsons tribute album *Commemorativo*. Griffin, meanwhile, moved to London and formed the Coal Porters; today he works as a music critic and writer, foreshadowed by his definitive 1985 biography of (who else?) Gram Parsons. —*Steve Huey*

10 5 60 / 1983 / PVC ✦✦✦

Native Sons / 1984 / Frontier ✦✦✦✦
This updates the Byrds and Gram Parsons. —*Robert Gordon*

● **State of Our Union** / 1985 / Island ✦✦✦✦
American country-tinged rock 'n' roll. —*Robert Gordon*

Two Fisted Tales / 1987 / Island ✦✦✦
This, *Two Fisted Tales*, the last album by the Long Ryders, pulls together all the various elements that had distinguished them from the rest of the jangly, '60s revisionist rock bands of the mid-'80s. the Long Ryders' sound was a unique blending of McGuinn-esque guitar figures with well-defined parameters that encompassed Gram Parsons' country-rock sensibilities and the various tenets of traditional roots-rock. Highlights include the kickoff track "Gunslinger Man," a powerful guitar assault that displays the band's ability to rock hard. In contrast, "I Want You Bad," a Terry Adams-penned tune, also covered by Dave Edmunds, is a melodic song of long distance desire. Here the vocal quality is particularly expressive and appropriate to the song's message. On the other hand, formative years in the South are reflected on Sid Griffin's "Harriet Tubman's Gonna Carry Me Home." The overall instrumentation, which includes mandolin, autoharp, lap steel, and a guest accordion by David Hidalgo from Los Lobos, reflects their allegiance to traditional Americana music. Unfortunately *Two Fisted Tales* was to be the Long Ryders swan song. However, in the '90s there are still those who recall the pioneering spirit of the Long Ryders. —*Jack Leaver*

Metallic B.O. / 1989 / Long Ryders Fan Club ✦✦✦

BBC Radio 1 Live in Concert / 1995 / Windsong ✦✦✦

Lost & Found

Psychedelic
Everybody's Here / 1968 / International Artist ✦✦✦
"Okay, nothing special" seems to be a weird phrase to describe an album as avowedly psychedelic as this one, in its music, lyrics, and sleeve art. But that's really what it is—very much like the 13th Floor Elevators, but not as distinctive. —*Richie Unterberger*

Lost & Found No 2 / 1973 / Tempo ✦✦✦

The Lost & Found

Progressive Bluegrass
Formed in 1973, the original lineup of the Lost & Found bluegrass band consisted of bass fiddler Allen Mills, banjo player Gene Parker, mandolin player Dempsey Young, and guitarist Roger Handy. The band became quite popular playing bluegrass

festivals, with Mills' exceptional songwriting contributing much to the group's fame; "Love of the Mountains," recorded by the original lineup, has become a contemporary bluegrass standard. In addition to contemporary songs, the band also recorded more traditional fare, such as "The Man Who Wrote 'Home Sweet Home' Never Was a Married Man." Most of their albums feature similar material, and the band continues to be a strong positive force in contemporary bluegrass music. By the mid-'90s, only Mills and Young had stayed, recruiting guitarist Ray Berrier and banjo player Lynwood Lunsford as replacements. —*Sandra Brennan*

● **The Best of Lost and Found** / 1984 / Rebel ✦✦✦✦
Hymn Time / 1988 / Rebel ✦✦✦
The Lost and Found / 1991 / Rebel ✦✦✦
Bluegrass Classics / 1991 / Rebel ✦✦✦✦
January Rain / 1992 / Rebel ✦✦✦
Classic Bluegrass / Rebel ✦✦✦✦
● **New Day** / Rebel ✦✦✦✦

New Day features a new lead vocalist/guitarist in Ronnie Bowman, plus new banjoist Jody King. The addition of the two new members has reinvigorated Lost & Found, giving them a new kick which is evident both on the covers (particularly a tough version of Buck Owens' "Trouble"), and on their original numbers. *New Day* does indeed represent a new beginning for Lost & Found. —*Thom Owens*

John D. Loudermilk

b. Mar. 31, 1934, Durham, NC
Trombone, Trumpet, Drums (Bass), Saxophone, Vocals / Rock & Roll, Traditional Country, Pop-Rock
Although his music isn't exactly weird, John D. Loudermilk is one of the weirdest figures of early rock 'n' roll. Much more famous as a songwriter than a performer (although he made plenty of records), his material was incredibly erratic. His songs could range from the most mindless, sappy pop to hard-bitten, bluesy tunes that rang with as much authentic grit as a Mississippi Delta blues classic. One such tune was "Tobacco Road," and if he'd written nothing else, Loudermilk would have been worth a footnote in any history of popular music for that song alone.

Loudermilk wrote plenty of other songs, though, in a lengthy career that saw him straddling the fields of rock, pop, and country. Originally striving to be a performer in a very mild pop-rockabilly style, he found his first success as a songwriter, when George Hamilton IV took "A Rose and a Baby Ruth" into the Top Ten in 1956. Recording as Johnny Dee, Loudermilk made a few singles for the small Colonial label in North Carolina. The best and most successful of these was "Sittin' in the Balcony," which made the Top 40 in 1957. Eddie Cochran's cover, based closely on Loudermilk's version (though performed with more force and style), stole most of John's thunder when it outsold the original by a wide margin, making the Top 20.

Johnny Dee changed his name back to John Loudermilk when he signed with Columbia in 1958, and also decided to concentrate on songwriting when he relocated to Nashville, eventually working for Chet Atkins at RCA. Although Loudermilk had a pleasantly passable voice, his early records aren't worth much, often purveying material that was mindlessly lightweight or, worse, idiotically humorous ("Asiatic Flu"). "Tobacco Road" was a different story—a stark, stomping tale of hard-bitten Southern poverty, it has a strong blues flavor that is virtually absent from most of his material. It took a one-shot British Invasion group, the Nashville Teens, to fully realize the song's menace in their magnificent, hard-rocking 1964 cover, which made the US Top 20. The song was also covered by Lou Rawls, the Jefferson Airplane, Edgar Winter, and others.

"Tobacco Road" was far from Loudermilk's only success. In the late '50s and early '60s, he supplied material for country stars, teen idols, and pop-rock singers, including "Waterloo" (Stonewall Jackson), "Angela Jones" (Johnny Ferguson), "Ebony Eyes" (the Everly Brothers), "Norman" (Sue Thompson), and "Abilene" (George Hamilton IV). In the mid-'60s, he was briefly in vogue in

Britain: the Nashville Teens did both "Tobacco Road" and "Google Eyes" (the latter of which was a hit in the UK, though a flop stateside), and Marianne Faithfull had a British hit with the moody "This Little Bird."

Loudermilk continued to record on his own, though more as an afterthought than a specialty, reserving most of his focus for writing songs for other performers. Much of his material followed a faint-hearted, goofy pop/novelty thread, which made his somber efforts seem all the more incongruous. His last big songwriting success was another of his serious-minded tunes, "Indian Reservation," which topped the charts for Paul Revere & the Raiders in 1971 (it had previously been a hit for British singer Don Fardon). He withdrew from professional activities to spend most of the last two decades studying ethnomusicology. —*Richie Unterberger*

12 Sides Of / 1962 / RCA Victor ✦✦
Although this contains some of Loudermilk's own versions of some of his most famous songs, it's a surprisingly disposable effort. The production is period Nashville pop-lite, Loudermilk's voice is almost devoid of character, and the songs themselves are usually downright dippy in their slightness. Much of this is Loudermilk at his worst—chipper, mindless romantic trifles, or trivial tunes about characters who are, one would guess, supposed to be laughably eccentric, though the results are about as funny as your average prime-time sitcom. Includes versions of "Angela Jones," "Google Eyes," and "This Little Bird" (here titled, for some reason, "The Little Bird"), all of which were big hits in the hands of others. Beware, though—the version of "Tobacco Road" here is not the original, basic thumper on Loudermilk's 1960 Columbia single, but a vastly inferior remake with an inappropriately jaunty arrangement. —*Richie Unterberger*

Sings a Bizarre Collection / 1965 / RCA Victor ✦✦✦
Suburban Attitudes / 1967 / RCA Victor ✦✦✦
Country Love Songs / 1968 / RCA Victor ✦✦✦
The Open Mind of J. D. Loudermilk / 1969 / RCA Victor ✦✦✦
Blue Train / 1989 / Bear Family ✦✦✦✦
It's My Time / 1989 / Bear Family ✦✦✦✦
● **Sittin' in the Balcony** / 1995 / Bear Family ✦✦✦✦
23-song collection of his earliest material from 1957-60. Includes both sides of all five singles he recorded for Colonial (when he was known as Johnny Dee), and early Columbia singles, as well as three previously unreleased songs from the early Columbia era. "Sittin' in the Balcony" and the original, stark version of "Tobacco Road" are the clear highlights here. Most of the rest is timid rockabilly/pop, with songwriting that's riddled with goody-goody teen cliches; the novelty "Asiatic Flu" and "The Happy Wanderer (Val-De-Ri Val-De-Ra)" are downright unbearable. Still, it's probably Loudermilk's best work, considering that from 1960 on he principally worked as a songwriter, recording his own work only as a sideline. The previously unissued "The Angel of Flight 509" stirs mild interest, as it's a prototype of sorts for "Ebony Eyes," minus the tragic elements. —*Richie Unterberger*

The Louvin Brothers

Traditional Country, Close Harmony
From the close-harmony brother acts of the '30s evolved Charlie and Ira Louvin, ranking among the top duos in country music history. With Ira's incredibly high, pure tenor and Charlie's emotional and smooth melody tenor, they influenced by the Bolick Brothers (the Blue Sky Boys), the Monroe Brothers, the Delmore Brothers and other major family duos of the previous generation, preserving the old-time flavor while bringing this genre into the '50s, when country music moved to a newer sound. Whatever type of songs they recorded—gospel, folk, hillbilly, or '50s pop—those songs became the Louvins. Add to the list the many Louvin compositions (for example, "If I Could Only Win Your Love," Emmylou Harris' first hit), and you have an act that is outstanding in country music history. Their career took a while to get going, partly because of interruptions from WW II and the Korean War. In the early '50s, after developing a reputation for unexcelled gospel singing, the Louvins broadened their repertoire, recording "The Get Acquainted Waltz" (with Chet Atkins adding another

guitar to Charlie's and to Ira's mandolin), a fair hit that showed success was reachable with non-religious music. The electric guitar, with the duo's unique harmony and Ira's exceptional tenor, created a sound that fans asked for in increasing numbers. In 1955, after ten unsuccessful auditions, they finally joined the Opry, where they performed to great acclaim until 1963, when they broke up. They had a number of hits, including the much-covered "When I Stop Dreaming" and "Cash on the Barrel Head." Following the duo's breakup, Ira and Charlie both pursued solo careers.

Born and raised in the Appalachian mountains in Alabama, both Charlie (born Charlie Elzer Loudermilk, July 7, 1927) and Ira (born Lonnie Ira Loudermilk, April 21, 1924; d. June 20, 1965) were attracted to the close-harmony country brother duets of the Blue Sky Boys, the Delmore Brothers, the Callahan Brothers and the Monroe Brothers when they reached their adolescence. Previously, they had sung gospel songs in church and their parents encouraged their sons to play music, despite the family's poverty. Ira began playing mandolin while Charlie picked up the guitar, and the two began harmonizing. After a while, they began performing at a small, local radio station in Chattanooga, where they frequently played on an early-morning show.

The brothers' career was interrupted in the early '40s when Charlie joined the Army for a short while. While his brother was in the service, Ira played with Charlie Monroe. Once Charlie returned from the Army, the duo moved to Knoxville, TN, where they received a regular spot on a WROL radio show; they later moved to WNOX. Around this time, they decided to abandon their given name for Louvin, which appeared to be a better stage name. (Their cousin John D. Loudermilk retained the family name.) Following their stint in Knoxville, they moved to Memphis, where they broadcast on WMPS and cut one single for Apollo Records. After their brief stay in Memphis, they returned to Knoxville.

In 1949, the Louvin Brothers recorded a single for Decca Records, which failed to make much of an impact. Two years later, they signed with MGM Records and over the next year, they recorded 12 songs. Shortly after their MGM sessions were finished, Charlie and Ira moved back to Memphis, where they worked as postal clerks while playing concerts and radio shows at night. Eventually, they got the attention of Acuff-Rose, who signed the duo to a publishing contract. Fred Rose, the owner of the publishing house, helped the duo sign a contract with Capitol Records. The Louvins' debut single for the label, "The Family Who Prays," was a moderate success (it would later become a gospel standard), yet they were unable to capitalize on its success because Charlie was recalled by the Army to serve in the Korean War.

Upon Charlie's discharge from the Army, the Louvins relocated to Birmingham, where they planned to restart their career through appearances on the radio station WOVK. However, a duo called Rebe and Rabe had already carved out a close-harmony niche in the area, using several of the Louvins' own songs. When Charlie and Ira were reaching a point of desperation, Capitol's Ken Nelson was able to convince the Grand Ole Opry to hire the duo. Prior to joining the Opry, the duo had been marketed as gospel artists, but they began singing secular material as soon as they landed a slot on the show, primarily because a tobacco company sponsoring its broadcast told the Opry and the Louvins "you can't sell tobacco with gospel music." While they didn't abandon gospel, the brothers began writing and performing secular material again, starting with "When I Stop Dreaming." The single became a Top Ten hit upon its release in the fall of 1955 and would eventually become a country standard. It was followed shortly afterward by "I Don't Believe You've Met My Baby," which spent two weeks at No. 1 early in 1956. No less than three of the duo's other singles—"Hoping That You're Hoping," "You're Running Wild," "Cash on the Barrel Head"—reached the Top Ten that year, and they also released the albums *Tragic Songs of Life* and *Nearer My God to Thee*. The Louvins' success in 1956 was particularly impressive considering that rock 'n' roll was breaking big that year, sapping the sales of many established country artists.

However, the Louvins weren't able to escape being hurt by rock 'n' roll. They had two relatively big hits in 1957, "Don't Laugh" and "Plenty of Everything but You," "My Baby's Gone" reached the Top Ten in late 1958, and their classic version of the traditional ballad "Knoxville Girl" was a moderate hit in early 1959, but those four hit singles arrived in the space of three years; they charted four songs in 1956 alone. Soon, the Louvins were receiving pressure from Capitol to update their sound. They tried to cut a couple of rockabilly numbers, but they were quite unsuccessful. Eventually, Ken Nelson suggested that the duo abandon the mandolin in order to appeal to the same audience as the Everly Brothers. The Louvins didn't accept his advice, but the remark did considerable damage to Ira's ego and he began to sink into alcoholism.

The Louvin Brothers continued to record during the early '60s, turning out a number of theme albums—including tributes to the Delmore Brothers and Roy Acuff, as well as gospel records like *Satan Is Real*—as well as singles. "I Love You Best of All" and "How's the World Treating You" reached Nos. 12 and 26 respectively in 1961, the first year they had two hit singles since 1957. However, the duo began fighting frequently, and Ira's alcoholism worsened. Following one last hit single, "Must You Throw Dirt in My Face," in the fall of 1962, the duo decided to disband in the summer of 1963.

Charlie and Ira both launched solo careers on Capitol Records shortly after the breakup. Charlie was the more successful of the two, with his debut single "I Don't Love You Anymore" reaching No. 4 upon its summer release in 1964. For the next decade, he racked up a total of 30 hit singles, though most of the records didn't make the Top 40. Ira's luck wasn't as good as his brother's. Shortly after the Louvins disbanded, he had a raging, alcohol-fueled argument with his third wife Faye that resulted in a shooting that nearly killed him. He continued to perform afterward, singing with his fourth wife Anne Young. The duo were performing a week of concerts in Kansas City in June of 1965 when they were both killed in a car crash in Williamsburg, MO. After his death, his single "Yodel, Sweet Molly" became a moderate hit.

The Louvin Brothers' reputation continued to grow in the decades following their breakup, as their harmonies and hard-driving take on traditional country provided the blueprint for many generations of country and rock musicians. The Everly Brothers were clearly influenced by the duo, while country-rock pioneer Gram Parsons drew heavily from the Louvins' deep catalog of classic songs, recording "The Christian Life" with the Byrds and "Cash on the Barrelhead" as a solo artist. Though they haven't been inducted into the Country Music of Hall of Fame, the Louvin Brothers and their music is truly legendary. —*David Vinopal*

Tragic Songs of Life / 1956 / Rounder ✦✦✦✦
A reissue of their first Capitol album, it's a sort of tribute album to the country duos that preceded them; it's the Louvins at their best. —*George Bedard*

Louvin Brothers [JS] / 1957 / JS ✦✦✦✦
The best of their later non-sacred recordings are included: "When I Stop Dreaming" and "My Baby's Gone." Probably the ultimate expression of country music's brother-duet tradition, it was previously released on Capitol. —*George Bedard*

Ira and Charlie / 1958 / Stetson ✦✦✦
Issued in Capitol in 1958 (and reissued on LP in England), this is a fairly traditional outing, with only one song penned by the Louvins. It's solid enough, but some of their other Capitol work (such as the 1960 LP *My Baby's Gone*) is more imaginative, and places a greater weight on original material. —*Richie Unterberger*

☆ The Family Who Prays / 1958 / Capitol ✦✦✦✦✦
This all-sacred album was completely written by the brothers themselves, with one exception ("Swing Low Sweet Chariot"). Country duos just don't come any better. —*George Bedard*

My Baby's Gone / 1960 / Stetson ✦✦✦✦
The Louvins' Capitol output was extremely consistent, and this 1960 LP (reissued on LP in England by Stetson) is no exception. Working under producer Ken Nelson, the traditional core of their

harmonies and guitar remained intact, updated only very slightly with some fuller arrangements and mild pop touches. Most of the material is love laments, with "I Wish It Had Been a Dream" and "She Didn't Even Know I Was Gone" (mournfully heart-breaking even by country standards) being standouts. *—Richie Unterberger*

Satan Is Real / 1960 / Capitol ✦✦✦

Much of *Satan Is Real's* reputation stems from its cover, a bizarre photo depicting the Louvins—awkwardly posed and in gleaming white suits—standing amidst the flames of hellfire, a 12-foot-tall plywood Lucifer looming behind them. The jacket is so notorious, in fact, that it merited inclusion in the second volume of the *Incredibly Strange Music* book series. It's a shame the album has acquired such a high kitsch quotient, because in reality *Satan Is Real* is one of the Louvins' finest and most impassioned record-ings. The duo's second all-gospel LP, its songs—most of them orig-inals—explore the brothers' deeply held beliefs without pulling any punches. The title track, in which Ira preaches that any acknowledgment of a higher power demands a similar nod to the reality of darker forces, sets a haunting tone that carries through-out the course of the set; from "The Christian Life" (later covered by the Byrds on their country-rock landmark *Sweetheart of the Rodeo*) to the stinging "Are You Afraid to Die," these tales of death, sin, and despair resonate with raw power and stark beauty. *—Jason Ankeny*

Weapon of Prayer / 1962 / Capitol ✦✦✦

Included is a re-recording for Capitol of the title song and "The Great Atomic Power," plus "Searching for a Soldier's Grave" and other mostly sacred "songs of those who serve God and country." *—George Bedard*

Songs That Tell a Story / 1981 / Rounder ✦✦✦✦

Arguably the greatest duet and brother act in country history, Ira and Charlie Louvin made remarkably moving, simply performed songs about their faith and lives with only guitar and mandolin backing, and reflected the values of country with more sincerity and genuine feeling than hundreds of elaborately produced and packaged albums have since. Rounder issued these numbers on LP in the late '70s, and reissued them on CD in 1991. The digital backdrop doesn't drain the authority from their voices; instead, it simply reaffirms the glory and splendor of the Louvins on 15 short, but brilliant gospel numbers. *—Ron Wynn*

Radio Favorites 1951-57 / 1987 / Country Music Foundation ✦✦✦✦

Radio Favorites 1951-57 contains a selection of radio perfor-mances from the Louvin Brothers, largely drawn from appear-ances at the Grand Ole Opry. Over the course of the compilation, several of the Louvins' best-known songs are featured, including both gospel numbers and secular songs. Though the perfor-mances and sound quality aren't quite as strong as the original studio versions, *Radio Favorites* remains of considerable interest for dedicated fans, since the brothers occasionally offer a new, unexpected turn in both their harmonies and instrumentals. *—Thom Owens*

Live at New River Ranch / 1989 / Copper Creek ✦✦✦

Recorded in Maryland in 1956, *Live at New River Ranch* perfectly captures the Louvin Brothers' live show of the late '50s, present-ing not only their stunningly affecting music, but also their sur-prisingly goofy onstage banter. For dedicated fans, this mix of great music and corny schtick is an invaluable find. *—Thom Owens*

☆ **Close Harmony** / 1992 / Bear Family ✦✦✦✦✦

A gargantuan, eight-disc box set, *Close Harmony* is essential for serious country fans and scholars. Collecting everything the Louvin Brothers recorded for Capitol, Apollo, Decca, and MGM, the set may have too much music for casual fans, but those will-ing to delve deeply into these 219 tracks will learn much not only about the duo, but also about the evolution of country music in the '50s—many of the roots of contemporary country and rock 'n' roll are apparent throughout the set. *—Stephen Tho-mas Erlewine*

★ **When I Stop Dreaming: The Best of the Louvin Brothers** / 1995

/ Razor & Tie ✦✦✦✦✦

Razor & Tie's single-disc collection *When I Stop Dreaming: The Best of the Louvin Brothers* contains all of the absolute essentials from the groundbreaking country duo, including all of their big-gest hits from the '50s. For most casual fans, it's not only the per-fect introduction, it's the definitive compilation. *—Stephen Tho-mas Erlewine*

Early MGM Recordings / Rounder ✦✦✦✦

Louvin Brothers [Rounder] / Rounder ✦✦✦

Included are mostly sacred songs from three MGM recording ses-sions. This features the original recording of "Weapon of Prayer," their first successful record. It's a fine example of their early work. *—George Bedard*

Best of the Early Louvins / Rebel ✦✦✦✦

The Best of the Early Louvin Brothers contains a good, if brief, selection of 12 songs from the Louvin Brothers' mid-'50s record-ings for Capitol Records, including the hits "When I Stop Dream-ing," "I Don't Believe You've Met My Baby," "Hoping That You're Hoping," "You're Running Wild," "My Baby's Gone," and "Cash on the Barrelhead." It's an excellent introduction, but it has been sup-planted by Razor & Tie's comprehensive single-disc *When I Stop Dreaming: The Best of the Louvin Brothers*. *—Stephen Thomas Erlewine*

Charlie Louvin (Charles Loudermilk)

b. Jul. 7, 1927, Rainesville, AL
Vocals / Traditional Country, Close Harmony

As half of the Louvin Brothers, Charlie Louvin (born Charlie Elzer Loudermilk, July 7, 1927) was one of the most influential musi-cians of the '40s and '50s; the Louvins defined close harmony duet singing for several generations of country fans. After the Louvins disbanded in 1963, Charlie began a solo career, recording for Capitol Records until 1972. During that time, he had two Top Ten hits—"I Don't Love You Anymore" (No. 4, 1964) and "See the Big Man Cry (No. 7, 1965)—as well as a series of minor hits. Lou-vin continued to perform and record for a variety of labels well into the '90s. *—Stephen Thomas Erlewine*

● **50 Years of Makin' Music** / 1991 / Playback ✦✦✦✦

Hoping That You're Hoping / 1992 / Copper Creek ✦✦✦

Longest Train / Sep. 24, 1996 / Watermelon ✦✦✦

Longest Train is an album designed for fans who became inter-ested in Charlie Louvin and the Louvin Brothers through the music of Gram Parsons and the Byrds. The album features latter-day recordings of signature Louvin songs like "The Christian Life" and "In the Pines," all songs that country-rockers and rockers have covered. Consequently, it's not a bad way to learn about the Louvins, but it really isn't as compelling as the original Louvin Brothers recordings and those do provide a better introduction than *Longest Train*. *—Thom Owens*

And That's the Gospel / Playback ✦✦✦

Patty Loveless

b. Jan. 4, 1957, Pikeville, KY
Vocals / Country-Rock, Contemporary Country

Patty Loveless (born Patricia Ramey, Pikeville, KY) was one of the most popular female country vocalists of the late '80s and early '90s. Her music drew from country's honky tonk tradition, while also adding a slight rock 'n' roll edge.

Loveless began writing and singing songs with her older brother Roger before she was 12 years old. By the age of 14 she had an impressive repertoire of self-penned songs, and her brother took her to Nashville. There she met Porter Wagoner, who became her close friend and mentor. Loveless got her first break upon meeting Doyle and Teddy Wilburn, who were searching for a singer to replace Loretta Lynn in the Wilburn Brothers. She became their featured singer for three years and signed to their publishing company, Surefire Music, as a songwriter after she graduated from high school. She also married ex-Wilburn drum-mer Terry Loveless. The newlyweds moved to his home at Kings Mountain near Charlotte, where they played in several local bands.

In 1985, Loveless went back to Nashville and recorded a demo tape, which attracted the attention of several record companies; two months later she signed with MCA and divorced her husband. Between 1985 and 1987, she appeared on the Top 50 charts four times with songs such as "Wicked Ways" and "After All." Later in 1987, she broke into the Top Ten and Top Five respectively with "If My Heart Had Windows" and "A Little Bit of Love." In 1988, Loveless' career rose meteorically when she released the album *Honky Tonk Angel*, which produced five tremendously successful singles, including the No. 1 hits "Timber I'm Falling in Love" and "Chains." Her 1990 album *On Down the Line* was also successful, as was 1991's *Up against My Heart*, her final album for MCA. In 1993, the label released Loveless' *Greatest Hits* album. Later that year, she released *Only What I Feel*, her first album for Epic Records. Within a year, the album went gold and produced several hits, including the No. 1 "Blame It on Your Heart." In 1994, she released *When Fallen Angels Fly*, which also went gold and yielded several Top ten hits. *Trouble with the Truth*, Loveless' eighth album, was released in 1996. —*Sandra Brennan*

Patty Loveless / Feb. 1987 / MCA ✦✦

If My Heart Had Windows / 1988 / MCA ✦✦✦✦
Included are fine songs by Steve Earle, Dallas Frazier, and others. —*Dan Heilman*

Honky Tonk Angel / 1988 / MCA ✦✦✦
The song subjects hardly classify Loveless as a honky tonk angel, at least by Hank Thompson's definition. But this was the album that established Loveless as a major presence, and it includes two of her biggest singles—"Chains," "Timber I'm Falling in Love"—and two of her best—"Blue Side of Town" and "Don't Toss Us Away," a duet with Rodney Crowell. —*Brian Mansfield*

On Down the Line / May 15, 1990 / MCA ✦✦✦
Featured are the hits "The Night's Too Long," "I've Got to Stop Loving You (And Start Living Again)," and "Blue Memories," among others. —*AMG*

Up against My Heart / 1991 / MCA ✦✦✦
Loveless gets a little more adventurous with each album, though she never forgets to include sure-fire hits like "Hurt Me Bad (In a Real Good Way)" and "Jealous Bone." This time she invites comparisons to Patsy Cline with "Can't Stop Myself from Loving You" and implies that God is female by switching the pronouns in Lyle Lovett's "God Will." —*Brian Mansfield*

Only What I Feel / Apr. 20, 1993 / Epic ✦✦✦✦
Loveless underwent throat surgery and switched labels before creating this album, and both helped. She sounds stronger and more impassioned than she has in years, and her artistic drive seems more confident and determined. "Nothin' but the Wheel" ranks with her best ballads. —*Michael McCall*

● **Greatest Hits** / May 11, 1993 / MCA ✦✦✦✦
The inevitable hits compilation chronicling Patty Loveless' five years and five albums at MCA is, in the Nashville tradition, not exactly generous: It contains only ten tracks and runs 31 1/2 minutes. In that space, though, you get most of Loveless' big hits between 1988 and 1992, from "If My Heart Had Windows" to "Jealous Bone," and including the chart toppers "Timber I'm Falling in Love" and "Chains." Oddly, "A Little Bit in Love," which just missed hitting No. 1, is not included. The set traces Loveless' rise as part of the neo-traditionalist movement of the 1980s, a movement that had faded, and that Loveless was ready to move beyond, by the time she ended her tenure at MCA. The music included here is fine, bedrock country, but a little faceless for all its authenticity. This is one artist whose second hits collection is likely to be more interesting than her first. —*William Ruhlmann*

When Fallen Angels Fly / 1994 / Epic ✦✦✦✦
Patty Loveless expanded on the success of her comeback album, *Only What I Feel*, with its successor, *When Fallen Angels Fly*, which made the country Top Ten, went gold, spawned four Top Ten singles, and was named the Country Music Association's Album of the Year. Songs like the feisty hit "Halfway Down" had a bouncy rockabilly feel, and Loveless rode the rhythms well,

Patty Loveless

while on the ballad "Here I Am," another hit, she sounded like a country Stevie Nicks. And then there was "I Try to Think About Elvis," a comic rocker that was one of the best pieces of material to turn up in Nashville that year, and which Loveless performed with just enough tongue in her cheek. Of course, there were a couple of those hopelessly hokey Gretchen Peters ballads, but even one of those, "You Don't Even Know Who I Am," was a hit. —*William Ruhlmann*

Trouble with the Truth / Jan. 23, 1996 / Epic ✦✦✦✦
On stage, Patty Loveless may be the antithesis of modern music stars. She can come across as shy, awkward, unsure of herself. On record, however, those traits help define the complexities she's capable of instilling in a good lyric. On *Trouble with the Truth*, she again crystallizes emotions to their core. When playing the part of a spurned lover, she can sound tough and direct without losing her vulnerability. When facing her own faults, as she does on the outstanding title song, she can sound contemplative and regretful without drowning in self-pity. When looking for a good time, she can sound rowdy and spirited without relying on silly novelty themes that overrun country radio. Loveless long ago established that she can be relied upon to dig up good material and elevate it with sensitivity and style. But, in recent years, one of country music's most consistently solid singers seems to be raising her own stakes. *Trouble with the Truth* continues her streak of excellence. —*Michael McCall*

Lyle Lovett

b. Nov. 1, 1957, Klein, TX
Guitar, Vocals / Singer-Songwriter, Alternative Country
Lyle Lovett was one of the most distinctive and original singer-songwriters to emerge during the '80s. Though he was initially labeled as a country singer, the tag never quite fit him. Lovett had more in common with '70s singer-songwriters like Guy Clark, Jesse Winchester, Randy Newman, and Townes Van Zandt, combining a talent for incisive, witty lyrical detail with an eclectic array of music, ranging from country and folk to big-band swing and traditional pop. Lovett's literate, multi-layered songs stood out among the formulaic Nashville hit singles of the late '80s, as well as the new traditionalists that were beginning to take over country music. Drawing from alternative country and rock fans, Lovett

quickly built up a cult following, which began to spill over into the mainstream with his second album, 1988's *Pontiac*. Following *Pontiac*, his country audience declined but his reputation as a songwriter and musician continued to grow, and he sustained a dedicated cult following well into the '90s.

Born in Klein, TX—a small town named after his great-grandfather, a Bavarian weaver named Adam Klein, that later became a Houston suburb—Lyle Lovett was raised on his family horse ranch. Lovett didn't begin his musical career until he began writing songs while attending Texas A&M University in the late '70s, where he studied journalism and German. While he was a student, he performed covers and original songs at local folk festivals and clubs. As a graduate student, he traveled to Germany to study and continued to write and play while he was in Europe. However, he didn't begin to pursue a musical career in earnest until he returned to America in the early '80s.

Upon his return to the States, Lovett played clubs throughout Texas, eventually landing a spot in the 1983 Mickey Rooney TV movie, *Bill: On His Own*. The following year Nanci Griffith, whom Lovett had interviewed for a school paper while he was in college, recorded his "If I Were the Woman You Wanted" on her *Once in a Very Blue Moon* album. Lovett also sang on the album, as well as on her 1985 record, *Last of the True Believers*. Guy Clark heard a demo tape of Lovett's songs in 1984 and directed it to Tony Brown of MCA Records. Over the next year, MCA worked out the details of a record contract with Lyle. In the meantime, he made his first recorded appearance on *Fast Folk Musical Magazine, Vol. 2: No. 8.* later in the year.

Lovett signed with MCA/Curb in 1986, releasing his eponymous debut later in the year. *Lyle Lovett* received excellent reviews and five of its singles—"Farther Down the Line," the Top Ten "Cowboy Man," "God Will," "Why I Don't Know" and "Give Back My Heart"—reached the country Top 40. Despite his strong showing on the country charts, it was clear from the outset that Lovett's musical tastes didn't rely on country, though the genre provided the foundation of his sound. Instead, he incorporated jazz, folk, and pop into a country framework, pushing the musical boundaries of each genre. *Pontiac*, his second album, revealed exactly how eclectic and literate Lovett was. Greeted with overwhelmingly positive reviews from both country and mainstream publications upon its early 1988 release, *Pontiac* expanded his audience in the pop and rock markets. The album charted in the lower reaches of the pop charts and slowly worked its way toward gold status. While his pop audience grew, his country fanbase began to shrink—"She's No Lady" and "I Loved You Yesterday" both made the Top 30, but after those two songs, none of his other singles cracked the country Top 40.

It didn't matter that Lovett's country audience was disappearing—*Pontiac* had gained enough new fans in the pop mainstream to guarantee him a strong cult following. To support *Pontiac*, he assembled His Large Band, which was a modified big band complete with guitars, a cellist, a pianist, horns, and a gospel-trained backup singer named Francine Reed. Lovett recorded his third album, *Lyle Lovett & His Large Band*, with his touring band. Like its two predecessors, the album was well-received critically upon its early 1989 release and it performed well commercially, peaking at No. 62 and eventually going gold. Perhaps because of the album's eclectic, jazzy sound, the album produced only one minor country hit in "I Married Her Just Because She Looks like You," but his straight rendition of Tammy Wynette's "Stand by Your Man" received a great deal of attention in the media.

Following the release of *His Large Band*, Lovett settled in California, which signaled that he was abandoning country. After settling in Los Angeles, he spent the next two years collaborating and working on his fourth album. In 1990, he produced Walter Hyatt's *King Tears* album; the following year, he sang on Leo Kottke's *Great Big Boy* and donated a cover of "Friend of the Devil" to the Grateful Dead tribute album, *Deadicated*. Also in 1991, he made his acting debut in Robert Altman's *The Player*, which was released in the spring of 1992. A few months after *The Player* hit the theaters, Lovett's fourth album, *Joshua Judges Ruth*, was released. Boasting a heavy gospel and R&B influence,

Joshua Judges Ruth was his most successful album to date, peaking at No. 57 and going gold. On the whole, the album was ignored by country radio, but pop audiences embraced the record and Lovett became a staple on adult alternative radio and VH-1.

Despite the success of *Joshua Judges Ruth*, Lyle Lovett became a near-superstar for a completely different reason in 1993—his surprise marriage to actress Julia Roberts. Upon the announcement of their marriage, Lovett became the subject of many gossip segments and tabloid stories, elevating him to a level of fame he had not experienced before. Lyle's first project after his marriage was a role in Altman's 1993 film *Short Cuts*. He didn't release another album until the fall of 1994, when *I Love Everybody* hit the stores. A collection of songs Lovett wrote in the late '70s and early '80s, *I Love Everybody* continued his move away from country, and it was the first record he had released that didn't expand his audience in some way. After it entered the charts at No. 26, it disappeared 13 weeks later, failing to go gold.

Lovett and Roberts divorced in the spring of 1995 and Lyle began to retreat from the spotlight somewhat, spending the remainder of the year touring and writing. Lovett re-emerged with *The Road to Enseñada*, the first album since *Pontiac* to be dominated by country songs, in the summer of 1996. In addition to performing well on the pop charts, where it entered at a career peak of No. 24, *The Road to Enseñada* performed strongly on the country charts, entering at No. 4. —*Stephen Thomas Erlewine*

Lyle Lovett / 1986 / Curb ✦✦✦✦

Lyle Lovett has an ironic overview of the world, expressed in songs he sings with the dead seriousness of the true comic. But he also has a finely defined sense of romantic troubles that sometimes isn't funny at all. Songs like "God Will" and "If I Were the Man You Wanted" mark him as one of the best new writers of the decade. —*William Ruhlmann*

★ Pontiac / 1987 / Curb ✦✦✦✦✦

Lovett's best overall collection of songs includes the gently absurd "If I Had a Boat," the subtly murderous "L.A. County," and the Henny Youngman-style "She's No Lady," among other gems. —*William Ruhlmann*

Lyle Lovett & His Large Band / 1989 / Curb ✦✦✦✦

On his third album, Lovett continues to explore a synthesis of country and big band. Included is his version of Tammy Wynette's country classic on "Stand by Your Man" and the bittersweet "I Married Her Just Because She Looks like You." —*Rick Clark*

Joshua Judges Ruth / 1992 / Curb ✦✦✦

Lyle Lovett goes folk-gospel. To be fair, the country tag was never a comfortable fit for Lovett's eclectic musings. *Joshua Judges Ruth* distances him from the category without firmly boxing him into any new ones. There is a Southern-fried gospel feel throughout much of the album, even if it's sometimes irreverent. "Church" best displays Lovett's surreal, dry wit, recounting a hunger-driven church rebellion complete with full gospel backing vocals. "She's Leaving Me," featuring guest vocals from Emmylou Harris, is the one sop offered to traditional country. Overall, though, the mood is sombre bordering on bleak. Like the album cover and insert photos, *Joshua* deals in shades of grey and themes of loneliness and death. What one misses the most on this release is the infrequent surfacing of Lovett's weird, playful sense of humor. —*Roch Parisien*

I Love Everybody / 1994 / Curb ✦✦✦

A collection of odds and ends that Lyle Lovett has written over the years (some of the tunes date back to the late '70s), *I Love Everybody* doesn't have the self-conscious artistic importance of *Joshua Judges Ruth*, and it's all the better for it. Instead, Lovett offers a set of relaxed, casual songs, accentuating his infamous, off-kilter sense of humor ("Skinny Legs," "Penguins"). At the same time, the songs offer hints of Lovett's sly, subtle sense of menace, particularly "Creeps Like Me." —*Stephen Thomas Erlewine*

Road to Ensenada / Jun. 18, 1996 / Curb ✦✦✦✦
Since *Pontiac*, Lyle Lovett has been experimenting with different sounds, whether it was the big band posturing of *And His Large Band*, the gospel overtones of *Joshua Judges Ruth*, or the '70s singer-songwriter flourishes of *I Love Everybody*. With *The Road to Ensenada*, he hunkers down and produces his most straightforward album since *Pontiac*. As it happens, it is also his best record since that breakthrough album. Lovett strips the sound of the album down to the bare country essentials, allowing it to drift into Western swing, country-rock, folk, and honky tonk when necessary. He also decides to balance his weightier material ("Private Conversation," "Who Loves You Better," "It Ought to Be Easier," "I Can't Love You Anymore," "Christmas Morning") with fun, lighthearted numbers like "Don't Touch My Hat," "Fiona," and "That's Right (You're Not from Texas)," which are funny without being silly. In fact, *The Road to Ensenada* is the lightest album Lyle Lovett has ever made—the darkness that hung around the fringes of *Pontiac, Joshua Judges Ruth,* and *I Love Everybody* has drifted away, leaving his wry sense of humor and a newly found empathetic sentimentality. The combination of straightforward instrumentation and lean, catchy, and incisive songwriting results in one of the best albums of his career—he's just as eclectic and offhandedly brilliant as he always been, but on *The Road to Ensenada* he's more focused and less flashy about his own talent than he's ever been. —*Stephen Thomas Erlewine*

Lulu Belle (Myrtle Eleanor Cooper)

b. Dec. 24, 1913, Boone, NC
Vocals / Traditional Country
Lulu Belle and husband Scotty were a popular duo during the 1930s credited with helping make country music more popular and accessible to mainstream audiences. Scotty Wiseman also penned songs such as "Remember Me" and "Have I Told You Lately That I Love You" which went on to become country standards. In addition to headlining WLS Chicago's *National Barn Dance* for close to two decades, the duo appeared in seven motion pictures, including *Shine on Harvest Moon*.

Lulu was born Myrtle Eleanor Cooper in Boone, NC, and got her start on the *National Barn Dance* when she was 19. There she worked as a cornball comedian à la Minnie Pearl with Red Foley. Later the station teamed her up with Skyland Scotty Wiseman, another North Carolina native, when Foley's wife began getting jealous of Lulu. It was a good move, as she and Scotty clicked both professionally and personally, and they married in 1934.

Though Lulu Belle and Scotty did record periodically, they were never as popular on wax as they were on the air. The couple left the *Barn Dance* in 1958, at which point Scotty returned to college and obtained a Master's degree. He then became a teacher, a farmer, and a bank director. Lulu Belle was active in community activities and eventually went on to serve two terms in the legislature of North Carolina as the Democratic representative for three counties. They also occasionally recorded during these years, and made three albums for Starday during the '60s and one in 1974 for Old Homestead. Scotty died in 1981 and two years later Lulu Belle married an old family friend. In 1986, she recorded a solo album for Homestead. —*Sandra Brennan*

● **The Sweethearts of Country Music** / 1963 / Starday ✦✦✦✦

Down Memory Lane / 1964 / Starday ✦✦✦✦

Lulu Belle & Scotty / 1965 / Starday ✦✦✦

Just a Closer Walk with Thee / 1974 / Birch ✦✦✦

Have I Told You Lately? / 1974 / ✦✦

Lulu Belle and Scotty / 1980 / Castle ✦✦✦

Early & Great, Vol. 1 / 1985 / ✦✦✦✦

Bob Luman

b. Apr. 15, 1937, Nacogdoches, TX, **d.** Dec. 27, 1978, Nashville, TN
Guitar, Vocals / Traditional Country, Country-Rock, Rockabilly
Bob Luman started out as a rockabilly performer, switched to country and then in the late '50s nearly ditched the music industry altogether; were it not for the interference of the Everly Brothers, Nashville would have lost a popular and talented performer to major-league baseball.

Lyle Lovett

Luman was born in Nacogdoches, TX, and grew up loving both sports and music. As a teen, Luman was a high school baseball star, and was so good that he caught the eye of several major league baseball scouts. Through his teens, Luman was primarily interested in singing country music like his idol Lefty Frizzell, but then he saw Elvis perform at a country music show. This inspired him to try his hand at the rockabilly sound and found his own band, which soon began performing at school activities and for area clubs. Soon after graduating, Luman won a talent contest, leading to his debut on the *Louisiana Hayride*. He was well received and became a regular in the mid-'50s. He was handsome, young and talented to boot, so it was only natural that Luman begin appearing on television. In 1957, he had a small role in a Hollywood film, *Carnival Rock*. He also appeared in Las Vegas along with Tex Ritter and Johnny Cash. Still, his singles did nothing on the charts.

In 1959, the Pittsburgh Pirates offered young Luman a lucrative contract. Fed up with his lack of success, he decided to go for it and announced this during a concert one night. The Everly Brothers happened to be in the audience and after the show, they talked him into giving country music one more try. They suggested he record the Boudleaux Bryant song "Let's Think About Living," and sure enough, it was a Top Ten hit on both the country and pop charts. His follow-up, "The Great Snowman," was also a hit and Luman began organizing a promotional tour. Unfortunately he was drafted and spent the next two years in the military. He was discharged in 1964 and began recording for Hickory Records.

His debut single, "The File," made it to the Top 25. The following year, he became a member of the Grand Ole Opry. Luman eventually signed with Epic Records and soon had a string of major hits on his hands beginning with the Top 20 "Ain't Got Time to Be Happy." Over the next ten years, Luman issued many more singles that made it into the Top 25 or better, including the Top Five hit "Lonely Women Make Good Lovers" in 1972. During these years, Luman toured extensively and frequently. The first country performer to perform in Puerto Rico, he also appeared on national and international television shows and remained a regular on the Opry, where his lively performances raised the eyebrows of the old timers who thought his music veered dangerously close to rock 'n' roll at times. Luman had a major heart attack in 1975, and it took him nearly five months to recover. (Afterwards, he joked about his enormous medical bills during his Opry performances.) His final chart appearance came in 1977 with the Top 15 hit "The Pay Phone." The following year he contracted pneumonia and died at the age of 41. —Sandra Brennan

● **American Originals** / 1984 / Columbia ✦✦✦✦
American Originals offers most of Luman's hits, including "Lonely Women Make Good Lovers," "Still Loving You," "Let's Think About Living" and "Ain't Got Time to Be Unhappy." —*Jason Ankeny*

Loretta Lynn (Loretta Webb)
b. Apr. 14, 1934, Butcher's Hollow, KY
Guitar, Vocals / Traditional Country, Honky Tonk, Nashville Sound/Countrypolitan

Loretta Lynn is one of the classic country singers. During the '60s and '70s, she ruled the charts, racking up over 70 hits as a solo artist and a duet partner. Lynn helped forge the way for strong, independent women in country music.

As her song (and movie and book) says, Loretta Lynn is a coal miner's daughter, born in Butcher's Hollow, KY, in 1934. As a child, she sang in church and a variety of local concerts. In January 1948, she married Oliver "Mooney" Lynn. She was 13 years old at the time. Following their marriage, the couple moved to Custer, WA, where they raised four children.

After a decade of motherhood, Lynn began performing her own songs in local clubs, backed by a band led by her brother, Jay Lee Webb. It took her a decade of gigging before she was noticed by a record label. In 1959, she signed a contract with Zero Records, which released her debut single, "I'm a Honky Tonk Girl," in 1960. The honky tonk ballad became a hit thanks to the insistent, independent promotion of Lynn and her husband. The pair would drive from one radio station to the next, getting the DJs to play her single, and sent out thousands of copies to stations. All of the effort paid off—the single reached No. 14 on the charts and attracted the attention of the Wilburn Brothers. The Wilburns hired Lynn to tour with them in 1960 and advised her to relocate to Nashville. She followed their advice and moved to the city in late 1960. After she arrived in Nashville, she signed with Decca Records. At Decca, she would work with Owen Bradley, who had produced Patsy Cline.

Lynn released her first Decca single, "Success," in 1962 and it went straight to No. 6, beginning a string of Top Ten singles that would run through the rest of the decade and throughout the next. She was a hard honky tonk singer for the first half of the '60s and rarely strayed from the genre. Although she still worked within the confines of honky tonk in the latter half of the decade, her sound became more personal, varied and ambitious, particularly lyrically. Beginning with 1966's No. 2 hit "You Ain't Woman Enough," Lynn began writing songs that had a feminist viewpoint, which was unheard of in country music. Her lyrical stance became more autobiographical and realistic as time wore on, highlighted by such hits as "Don't Come Home A-Drinkin' (With Lovin' on Your Mind)" (1966), "Your Squaw Is on the Warpath" (1968), "Woman of the World (Leave My World Alone)" (1969), and a tune about birth control called "The Pill" (1974).

Between 1966 and 1970, Loretta Lynn racked up 13 Top Ten hits, including four No. 1 hits—"Don't Come Home A' Drinkin'," "Fist City" (1968), "Woman of the World," and the autobiographical "Coal Miner's Daughter." In 1971, she began a professional partnership with Conway Twitty. As a duo, Lynn and Twitty had five consecutive No. 1 hits between 1971 and 1975—"After the Fire Is Gone" (1971), "Lead Me On" (1971), "Louisiana Woman, Mississippi Man" (1973), "As Soon As I Hang up the Phone" (1974), and "Feelin's" (1974). The hit-streak kick-started what would become one of the most successful duos of country history. For four consecutive years (1972-1975), Lynn and Twitty were named the Vocal Duo of the Year by the Country Music Association. In addition to

their five No. 1 singles, they had seven other Top Ten hits between 1976 and 1981.

Loretta Lynn published her autobiography, *Coal Miner's Daughter*, in the mid-'70s. In 1980, the book was adapted for the screen, with Sissy Spacek as Lynn. The film was one of the most critically acclaimed and successful films of the year and Spacek would win the Academy Award for her performance. All of the attention surrounding the movie made Loretta Lynn a household name with the American mainstream. Although she continued to be a popular concert attraction throughout the '80s, she wasn't able to continue her domination of the country charts. "I Lie," her last Top Ten single, arrived in early 1982, while her last Top 40 single, "Heart Don't Do This to Me," was in 1985. In light of her declining record sales, Lynn backed away from recording frequently during the late '80s and '90s, concentrating on performing instead. In 1993, she recorded the *Honky Tonk Angels* album with Tammy Wynette and Dolly Parton. —*Stephen Thomas Erlewine*

Hymns / 1965 / MCA ✦✦✦
This features such gospel hits as "The Third Man," "I'd Rather Have Jesus," and "Everybody Wants to Go to Heaven." —*AMG*

You Ain't Woman Enough / 1966 / MCA ✦✦✦✦
Don't Come Home a Drinkin' / 1967 / MCA ✦✦✦✦
☆ **Greatest Hits** / 1968 / MCA ✦✦✦✦✦
Lynn had a big hand in raising Nashville's perception of women as capable and competent (although the city still has a way to go). "Don't Come Home A-Drinkin'" and "You Ain't Woman Enough" are particularly representative: sassy, honest, and aggressive. —*Tom Roland*

Fist City / 1968 / Decca ✦✦✦✦
Here's Loretta Lynn / 1968 / Columbia ✦✦✦✦
A collection of her earliest recordings, it was made for the Zero label (unfortunately not including "Honky Tonk Girl," her first hit). Good, bluesy honky tonk, it features Lynn already in top form and a very swinging band. —*George Bedard*

Your Squaw Is on the Warpath / 1969 / Decca ✦✦✦✦
Boasting one of the classic politically incorrect album covers—which depicts Loretta as a sexy, tomahawk-wielding Native American—*Your Squaw Is on the Warpath* takes its title from the equally inappropriate track that begins the album. And while it may seem that this album's real value comes from its now kitschy artifact status, the rest of the album stands as a good collection, showcasing Lynn's talents as singer and interpreter of others' songs. —*Chris Woodstra*

Coal Miner's Daughter / 1971 / MCA ✦✦✦✦
Unlike the song, autobiography, and film of the same name, the album *Coal Miner's Daughter* isn't a reflection on Loretta Lynn's upbringing. Instead, it's merely a standard, early-'70s collection of originals and covers, all performed with gusto by Lynn. *Coal Miner's Daughter* boasts a stronger, more consistent selection of material than most of her other albums from the period, and contains a number of her classics, like the title song and "I'm a Honky Tonk Girl," plus a handful of lesser-known gems. —*Thom Owens*

Greatest Hits, Vol. 2 / 1974 / MCA ✦✦✦✦
In the liner notes, Pete Axthelm cites "the range of her personality," and that range is in evidence here: reflective ("Coal Miner's Daughter"), feisty ("Fist City"), humorous ("One's on the Way"), and sentimental ("Love Is the Foundation"). —*Tom Roland*

Greatest Hits Live / 1978 / K-Tel ✦✦
Lynn shines throughout this live performance from 1978, which features some of her best-known material; the supporting musicians could have been a little better, but they don't hurt the disc in the slightest. —*Stephen Thomas Erlewine*

20 Greatest Hits / 1987 / MCA ✦✦✦✦
20 Greatest Hits contains every one of Loretta Lynn and Conway Twitty's hits from the '70s, including the No. 1 singles "After the Fire Is Gone," "Lead Me On," "Louisiana Woman, Mississippi Man," "As Soon As I Hang up the Phone," and "Feelins." In addition to the obvious hit singles, there are a number of lesser-

known album tracks which are, with only a few exceptions, the equal of the hits. In short, *20 Greatest Hits* presents the very best perhaps of the greatest country duet teams of the '70s and is a necessary addition to any country record collection. —*Stephen Thomas Erlewine*

The Very Best Of / 1988 / MCA ✦✦✦
The Very Best of Loretta Lynn and Conway Twitty contains the duo's 14 biggest hits, including the No. 1 singles "After the Fire Is Gone," "Lead Me On," "Louisiana Woman, Mississippi Man," "As Soon As I Hang up the Phone," "Feelins'," and "The Letter" among several other hits. The record is definitive proof that Loretta and Conway were one of the greatest—if not *the* greatest—vocal duos in country music history. —*Stephen Thomas Erlewine*

Who Was That Stranger / 1989 / MCA ✦✦✦
Who Was That Stranger is a mildly successful attempt at updating Lynn's sound to fit with the hard-country sound in vogue at the tail end of the 1980s. —*Jason Ankeny*

★ **Country Music Hall of Fame** / 1991 / MCA ✦✦✦✦✦
Few greatest-hits packages pack the wallop of these 16 performances, which were all recorded for Decca Records between 1961-1976. This album includes duets with Ernest Tubb and Conway Twitty, men who knew to stand clear when Lynn wailed "Your Squaw Is on the Warpath" or "Fist City." —*Mark A. Humphrey*

☆ **Honky Tonk Girl: Collection** / 1994 / MCA ✦✦✦✦✦
Loretta Lynn's three-disc box set *Honky Tonk Girl* has the requisite rarities, but the real strength of the collection is that it offers all of her essential tracks—from 1960's "I'm a Honky Tonk Girl" to 1988's "Who Was That Stranger"—in one place. Not only are her classic hits like "Fist City" and "Coal Miner's Daughter" included, but so are most of her hit duets with Conway Twitty, such as "After the Fire Are Gone" and "As Soon As I Hang Up the Phone." A few hits are missing—notably "Louisiana Woman, Mississippi Man"—but *Honky Tonk Girl* remains the one comprehensive and essential Loretta Lynn collection. —*Stephen Thomas Erlewine*

Shelby Lynne

b. Oct. 22, 1968, Alabama
Fiddle, Vocals / Contemporary Country, Western Swing Revival
Tipped as a hot country newcomer in the early '90s, Shelby Lynne has yet to become a commercial force, though her five albums have shown a unique progression from contemporary country to incorporating elements of the blues and even big-band jazz. She was born October 22, 1968, to a very musical family. Lynne's father was a local singer, and her mother taught

vocal harmony to Shelby and her sister Allison. A promising mother-daughter duo career was cut short in the mid-'80s when Lynne's father shot his wife during an argument and turned the gun on himself also.

Shelby Lynne was forced to raise her sister alone, and raised money around their southern Alabama home by performing in clubs and singing contests. She recorded a few demos in 1987, that were heard by the Nashville Network. After one performance on TNN's *Nashville Now,* four major labels showed interest and no less a figure than George Jones asked her to sing a duet with him, "If I Could Bottle This Up." The single scratched the Country Top 50 in September 1988, and Lynne signed with Epic.

Though her debut single as a solo act, "Under Your Spell Again," barely hit the Top 100 in 1989, critics praised Lynne's *Sunrise* album. The singer toured as a support act for Jones, Willie Nelson, and Randy Travis, and two singles from her second album *Tough All Over* hit the Top 30, "Things Are Tough All Over" and "What About the Love We Made." *Tough All Over* made the best-of lists of many critics, who likened her emotional power to the Queen of Country, Patsy Cline.

Shelby Lynne became frustrated with Epic after 1991's *Soft Talk,* and moved to Morgan Creek two years later for *Temptation,* an album that first included Lynne's affection for big band and jazz. Two years later, another label change—this time to Magnatone—resulted in *Restless,* and the single "Slow Me Down" made the Top 60. —*John Bush*

Sunrise / Jan. 1976 / Epic ✦✦✦
Lynne's debut album, released when she was barely out of her teens, contains a duet with George Jones called "If I Could Bottle This Up." —*Brian Mansfield*

● **Tough All Over** / 1989 / Epic ✦✦✦✦
This contains "Things Are Tough All Over," her most successful single, as well as covers of Johnny Cash's "I Walk the Line" and Duke Ellington's "Don't Get Around Much Anymore." —*Brian Mansfield*

Soft Talk / 1991 / Epic ✦✦✦
Defiant, emotionally drenched country. Contains "The Very First Lasting Love," a duet with former Exile member Les Taylor. —*Bil Carpenter*

Temptation / Jul. 6, 1993 / Morgan Creek ✦✦✦
An album of big-band country swing, this was produced by Brent Maher (the Judds). "Feelin' Kind of Lonely Tonight" had limited success as a single. —*Brian Mansfield*

Restless / Jul. 18, 1995 / Magnatone ✦✦✦

M

Ronnie Mack

Rockabilly, Roots-Rock, Americana, California Country

Ronnie Mack made a name for himself as a savior of sorts on the Los Angeles country and roots music circuit. A native of Baltimore, he was born April 18, 1954. From an early age he was impressed by the guitar. Both of his grandfathers were musical and influenced him greatly. His paternal grandfather, Bill Mack, gave the youngster toy instruments upon which he played and began to learn chords.

The radio also was an important tool in Mack's development as a musician. This is where he first heard Elvis, the Everly Brothers, Eddie Cochran, and his hero, Ricky Nelson. Almost as a preview of his future loyalty to Nelson, Mack's first performance consisted of "Hello Mary Lou" when he was in second grade. The budding performer knew only three of the six chords in the song but still pulled off a somewhat exemplary performance. As a teenager he was surrounded by the psychedelic world that followed the British Invasion of the early 1960s. Convinced that this was not the way to go, Ronnie Mack devoted himself more and more to the ideals of "Blue Suede Shoes." But he still needed to play and did so with some reservations. While he had to learn the latest Cream or Hendrix single, he also began to write his own rockabilly songs.

After high school he began to think about moving to Los Angeles. Nelson's Stone Canyon Band was doing well; and the Flying Burrito Brothers, Poco, the New Riders of the Purple Sage, and Commander Cody and His Lost Planet Airmen were all twangin' away, a much closer cousin to the rockabilly he loved so much more than what was happening in Baltimore. Packing up and moving to the West Coast, Mack broke into the diverse L.A. music scene with a fury. The punk rock aspect of the scene was open to anything, even rockabilly. Putting together a band, Ronnie Mack and the Black Slacks, Mack followed the punker circuit, the same one that allowed Dwight Yoakam to play his music. He also played showcases with the Blasters and other roots rock acts and made a bid for his share of the audience with his rockabilly sound. The payoff came around 1979, when roots music took off. For the first time since the 1950s, rockabilly had garnered some respect. Signing with the roots rock label Rollin' Rock, Mack recorded a series of singles; "You Make Me Wanna Rock" and "I Wanna Dance With You" were two of the most memorable, both co-writes with partner Greg Loeb. He later went on to record a country track for volume three of the *Town South of Bakersfield* compilation, and worked with Dwight Yoakam, Ray Campi, Rosie Flores, Buck Owens, James Intveld, Cliffie Stone, Marty Stuart, the Jordanaires, and D.J. Fontana.

In 1988 James Intveld began the Barn Dance, a weekly showcase for big names as well as newer artists living and working around Los Angeles. But with a career that was taking off in several directions at once, Intveld soon found he could not keep up with the demands, so he turned the Barn Dance over to Mack. Moving from the Little Nashville Club to the world-renowned Club Palomino in North Hollywood, Ronnie Mack's Barn Dance continued to promote California roots music until shortly before the Pal closed for good in 1995. Moving to a new venue at the corner of Hollywood and Vine gave new life to Mack, the show,and the entire scene. Located at Jack's Sugar Shack, every Tuesday night was a celebration as well as a meeting place for local musicians and those from out of town seeking some companionship and a cold one. Visitors like Connie Smith, Robert Reynolds, Bruce Springsteen, and Bob Woodruff were not uncommon in the audience or on the stage.

Another aspect of Ronnie Mack's good standing in the community was his work with and for various charities. As the host of the annual Elvis Birthday Bash, another event that was the brainchild of Intveld, Mack worked alongside local industry insider Art Fein to pull off the big show that featured a wide variety of acts, all doing Elvis songs. Besides Mack, Yoakam, Flores, and Intveld, the Elvis tribute attracted Dave Alvin, Wanda Jackson, Johnny Rivers, Lee Rocker, Big Sandy, and roots rock royalty Barry Holdship and Florida Slim. The money raised from this event always went to a charity for the homeless. While his own success was fleeting, he never faltered from his chosen path. In 1996 the Swedish SunJay label released a 28-cut compilation built around the many singles he recorded for Rollin' Rock, Lonesome Town, and SunJay Records between June 1981 and a live recording from the Palomino in 1994, including Mack's 1986 cover of the James Intveld hit "My Heart is Achin' for You." *—Jana Pendragon*

● **Ronnie Mack Is Born to Rock** / 1996 / SunJay ✦✦✦✦
This is a compilation project that spans the period from 1981 through 1990, an important time for Ronnie Mack professionally. With an emphasis on rockabilly, Mack's largess to that genre has kept rockabilly alive for many fans around the world. Like many American artists who are overlooked at home, Mack is a star in Europe, where his singles are hits that still merit air play. His devotion to country and roots music is reflected via Mack's covers of John Hiatt's "Doll Hospital," the Merle Travis tune "Kentucky Means Paradise" and the Bryant & Bryant-penned "Brand New Heartache," a duet with Rosie Flores. As a chronicle of a vibrant career that has benefited many, this CD defines Mack's genius. *—Jana Pendragon*

Warner Mack (Warner McPherson)

b. Apr. 2, 1938, Nashville, TN
Vocals / Traditional Country, Nashville Sound/Countrypolitan
Warner Mack was a popular performer for Decca Records during the 1960s. He was born Warner MacPherson, the son of a Presbyterian minister, and raised in Vicksburg, MS, where he taught himself to play guitar as a youth. A talented athlete, he had offers to play both college baseball and football; he was also offered a spot on the St. Louis Cardinals, but Mack really wanted to be a musician. He got his start on the KWKH *Louisiana Hayride* and then appeared on Red Foley's *Ozark Jamboree*, gaining an even greater following. He still kept a day job at a tire company and worked as an announcer on a Vicksburg radio station.

Mack moved to Nashville in the late '50s; in 1957 he began his profitable association with Decca, becoming "Mack" thanks to an inattentive secretary. He wrote his debut single "Is It Wrong (For Loving You)" and scored a Top Ten hit that remained on the country charts for more than nine months and crossed over to become a minor pop hit. He later signed with Kapp Records and produced several albums for them. After performing on the *Grand Ole Opry*, he re-signed to Decca, where "Sittin' in an All Nite Cafe" made it to the Top Five. Unfortunately, he had a serious auto accident in 1964 and spent several months recovering. In 1965 he scored his career hit with "Bridge Washed Out," which topped the charts for months. This was followed by a series of hits that stretched until 1973; among his most popular songs were ""Sittin' on a Rock (Crying in a Creek)," "Talkin' to the Wall," and "Leave My Dreams Alone." Mack left Decca in 1973. Four years later he signed to Pageboy Records and had one minor hit, "These Crazy Thoughts (Run Through My Mind)," his final chart entry.—*Sandra Brennan*

● **Golden Country Hits** / 1961 / London ✦✦✦

Kate MacKenzie

Vocals / Progressive Bluegrass, Contemporary Folk
Kate MacKenzie is probably best known for her regular performances on Garrison Keillor's *Prairie Home Companion* radio broadcasts as a member of the Hopeful Gospel Quartet, which also features Keillor and Robin and Linda Williams. MacKenzie's duties on the program have required her to sing in numerous genres of music, and her listening tastes range from the Elvis Presley and Patsy Cline records she grew up with to Motown, Irish folk, classical, pop, bluegrass, blues, and country. The latter three styles are most prevalent on her solo debut album *Let Them Talk*, which was released in 1994. She became interested in folk and bluegrass music while at the University of Minnesota and taught herself to play the guitar, but it took awhile to overcome her shyness about singing—until she was 28, in fact. Her first singing gig was with the bluegrass band Stoney Lonesome, and from there, MacKenzie went on to *A Prairie Home Companion* and finally recorded her first album, *Age of Innocence*, 15 years later. —*Steve Huey*

Age of Innocence / Oct. 15, 1996 / ✦✦✦✦
Kate MacKenzie's solo debut album *Age of Innocence* is a shining demonstration of her talents. MacKenzie is able to push bluegrass music into new directions without diluting its purity. The key to the success of *Age of Innocence* is how MacKenzie delivers folk and country as gracefully as bluegrass. There's depth and beauty to this music, but most of all there's a gentle, subtle charm that makes it a rewarding musical experience. —*Stephen Thomas Erlewine*

Uncle Dave Macon

b. Oct. 7, 1870, Smart Station, TN, **d.** Mar. 22, 1952, Readyville, TN
Banjo, Vocals / Old-Time, Traditional Country
David Harrison Macon, born in Smart Station, TN, didn't perform professionally until he was past 50, but he became one of the first superstars of country music. A talented banjoist and comic (and sometimes preacher and farmer), Uncle Dave Macon was the Grand Ole Opry's first major star and an audience favorite from 1925 until his death in 1952. He derived much of his repertoire and stage patter from vaudeville and minstrel shows, but his songs reflected a wide variety of subjects from political corruption to current events like the advent of the automobile. His presence affected country music like none before it; even today a three-day festival, Uncle Dave Macon Days, is held in Murfreesboro, TN, the site of the National Old-Time Banjo Championship. —*Brian Mansfield*

At Home / 1976 / Bear Family ✦✦✦
Featuring "Banjo Solo," "Rabbit in the Pea Patch," "Mountain Dew," and others, these were his last recordings, made in 1950. —*AMG*

Laugh Your Blue / 1979 / Rounder ✦✦✦

Keep My Skillet Good & Greasy / 1979 / ✦✦✦✦
This features "All in Down & Out Blues," "I'll Tickle Nancy," "Cumberland Mountain Deer Race," and others. —*AMG*

★ **Country Music Hall of Fame Series** / 1992 / MCA ✦✦✦✦✦
"Shout if you are happy!" Uncle Dave Macon exclaims during "Tom and Jerry" as Mazy Todd saws away at her fiddle. "Kill

yo'self!" That's the kind of enthusiasm Macon brings to these 16 fine examples of string-band music, recorded between 1926 and 1934 for the Vocalion, Brunswick, and Champion labels. Macon, who was 55 at the first of these recording sessions, frequently starts the songs with a spoken anecdote (including a plug for his Macon Midway Mule and Wagon Transportation Company). This collection is essentially an expanded version of *Uncle Dave Macon: First Featured Star of the Grand Ole Opry*, a retrospective issued in 1966 after his posthumous election to the Country Music Hall of Fame. —*Brian Mansfield*

Travelin' Down the Road / 1995 / Country/BMG ✦✦✦✦
This CD is a reissue containing many of Uncle Dave Macon's best sides. All these tunes were transfers from original 78s recorded in 1935. The sound is still quite clear and enjoyable. There is a good selection of religious and secular tunes, all performed with vitality. You can really hear what draws people to old-timey music. —*Richard Meyer*

The Maddox Brothers

Traditional Country
The Maddox Brothers (Cliff, Cal, Fred, Don, and "friendly Henry, the working girl's friend") and their sister Rose called themselves "America's Most Colorful Hillbilly Band." They weren't kidding. It wasn't just a matter of hillbilly couture—though with their matching Turk suits and spangles the family had style, in spades. But colorful described their sound, as well. On the air in Modesto, CA, by 1937, the group made their first records, for the 4-Star label, in 1946. From 1951 'til 1956 they recorded for Columbia. At that point the family act broke up, though Rose maintained a successful solo career for many years. But throughout the 1940s and '50s, the Maddox Brothers and Sister Rose tore down the honky-tonks from the Pacific Northwest to the Gulf Coast with slap-bass boogie and an iconoclastic attitude toward the stiffer mores of conventional country. In other words, they rocked the house.

It all started in 1933, when the Maddox family—Charlie and Lula and five of their seven children—hitchhiked and rode the rails from Boaz, AL, to California, where they worked in the migrant labor camps of the San Joaquin Valley. Fred Maddox quickly tired of picking fruit and wrangled a radio spot on KTRB Modesto for his intensely musical family (which featured 11-year-old Rose on decidedly raw lead vocals). In addition to playing on KTRB, the group performed at local barns and festivals, and in 1939 they were named the best band at the California State Fair. Early the next year they began playing at KFBK in Sacramento, and their show was syndicated throughout the West Coast.

Though the future was bright for the Maddox Brothers and Rose, their career was interrupted by the advent of World War II. Fred, Cal, and Don were drafted into the military (Cliff was too ill and Henry was too young to serve), leaving the remaining members to play with different bands during the course of the war. Rose sang with Arky Stark and Dave Stogner; she also was turned away from the Texas Playboys. Meanwhile, Cliff headed his own band, the Rhythm Ramblers. After the war, the Maddox Brothers and Rose re-formed, settling at KGDM in Stockton, CA. Over the next decade their fan base grew steadily, as their blend of music and comedy played well not only in concert, but on the radio. During the '40s and early '50s, they cut a number of records for 4-Star. ·

In 1951 the Maddoxes switched labels and signed with Columbia Records. Over the next six years they recorded more than 40 singles for the label. During the '50s the group appeared on both the *Louisiana Hayride* and the Grand Ole Opry, often performing with an augmented lineup that featured steel guitarist Bud Duncan and either Roy Nichols, Jimmy Winkle, or Gene Breeden on lead guitar. At the end of their stint with Columbia, Rose began to pursue a solo career, leading toward the band's breakup in the summer of 1956. Rose began a solo career with the assistance of Cal, while the remaining members operated as a new band. Despite the breakup, the Maddox Brothers and Rose recorded a final session for Columbia in the summer of 1957.

After the disbandment of the Maddox Brothers, Rose had a successful solo career on Capitol Records, while the band comprised of the remaining members quickly fell apart. Fred opened a night club, the Fred Maddox Playhouse, which was quite successful during the late '50s and early '60s. Henry went on to accompany Rose on her recordings for Capitol. Over the course of the '70s and '80s, all of the members of the Maddox Brothers—with the notable exception of Rose, who continued to perform into the late '80s—quietly retired from music. —*Dan Cooper*

★ **Maddox Brothers & Rose, 1946-1951, Vol. 1** / 1961 / Arhoolie ✦✦✦✦✦

Consisting of 27 cuts from 1946-51, this disc is indispensable to anyone seeking a dose of vintage country music at its most hedonistically raucous. Though the archaic sound quality may make an audiophile cringe, the musical vitality of these boogie, blues, and ballad recordings is absolutely astonishing. So is the degree of nerve they show with their winking versions of "Whoa Sailor" and "Sally Let Your Bangs Hang Down." —*Dan Cooper*

The Maddox Brothers & Rose / 1962 / Forum Circle ✦✦✦

Bluehonkabilly madness from this raucous and irrepressible combo. Highlights include "That'll Learn Ya, Durn Ya" and their amazing version of "Honky Tonkin'." —*George Bedard*

Rose Maddox Sings Bluegrass / 1962 / Capitol ✦✦✦✦

Of the many fine (and now rare) LPs she cut for Capitol, this humdinger is the best one to break your neck trying to find. On this bluegrass sung with honky tonk fire, sparks do fly. —*Dan Cooper*

Go Honky Tonkin' / 1965 / Hilltop ✦✦✦

More of the same—"Mama Says It's Naughty," "Water Baby Blues," "Shimmy Shakin' Daddy." —*George Bedard*

On the Air, Vol. 1 / 1983 / Arhoolie ✦✦✦

America's Most Colorful Hillbilly Band / 1993 / Arhoolie ✦✦✦

America's Most Colorful Hillbilly Band is a compilation of music that the Maddox Brothers and Rose recorded at the height of their career. Several of their most famous songs are included, including "Step It Up and Go," "Reno Blues," and "I Wish I Was a Single Girl Again." These aren't the versions that became hits, which were on Columbia, but a selection of their early recordings for 4-Star. For traditional country fans, *America's Most Colorful Hillbilly Band* is a valuable collection, since these early recordings prove that the group was fully formed at the outset of their career. —*Thom Owens*

Rockin' & Rollin' / Bear Family ✦✦✦✦

This German import contains a fair cross-section of their bizarre bluegrass/honky tonk/rockabilly madness. It includes "Ugly and Sloughy (That's the Way I Like 'Em)" and "The Death of Rock & Roll." —*George Bedard*

Columbia Historic Edition / Columbia ✦✦✦✦

A too-short-lived (and, at only 13 songs, too brief) LP, this sampler from their Columbia years—1951 through 1957—further showcases their relentless chops and outrageous sense of humor. Though the Bear Family LPs draw from the same source, a full CD collection of the Maddoxes' Columbia work is desperately needed. —*Dan Cooper*

Maddox Brothers & Rose on the Air, Vol. 1 & 2 / Arhoolie ✦✦✦✦

A fascinating document, this double-length cassette (formerly the Arhoolie LPs 5028 and 5033) includes radio broadcasts from as early as 1940 (six years before the Maddoxes cut their first record) and on into the early '50s. It's not the place to find out if you're a Maddox family fan, but if you are one already, this collection (which includes their only appearance on the Grand Ole Opry) will give you a sense of what it must have been like to hear Rose wreak havoc with '50s gender roles by taking the lead on a cover of Hank Snow's "The Gold Rush Is Over." —*Dan Cooper*

☆ **Maddox Brothers & Rose: "Their Original Hits"** / Arhoolie ✦✦✦✦✦

Featured is the same material as above, except more of it. Available only on cassette, it combines the out-of-print Arhoolie LPs 5016 and 5017. —*Dan Cooper*

Rose Maddox

b. Aug. 15, 1925, Boaz, AL

Vocals / Traditional Bluegrass, Traditional Country, Western Swing, Honky Tonk

Rose Maddox exerted a heavy influence on honky tonk females through her recordings with the Maddox Brothers, but later turned to traditional bluegrass forms to inspire folk revivalists of the 1960s and '70s. Born Roselea Brogdon on August 15, 1925, she moved from Alabama to Modesto, CA, with her family to make a better living as farm laborers. After several years of hard work and occasional amateur musical appearances, Fred Maddox lobbied KTRB-Modesto to give a time slot to him and his brothers Cliff, Cal, Don, and Henry. The radio station agreed, but on the condition that the Maddoxes include a female singer. Rose was recruited—as an 11-year-old—and the group soon appeared in bars as well as on the radio show. They won a contest at the California State Fair in 1939 and began to broadcast at KFBK-Sacramento, which included several stations in nearby states as part of its coverage.

World War II interrupted the career of the Maddox Brothers and Rose, with Cal, Fred, and Don entering the services. The group re-formed in the late '40s and became more popular than ever. They recorded for 4-Star and Columbia, making annual trips east to appear on the *Louisiana Hayride* and Grand Ole Opry. The Maddoxes' popularity was biggest on the West Coast, however; they performed on several radio shows with good music and comic hillbilly routines that appealed to the masses of dispossessed Southerners in California.

The Maddox Brothers last recorded in 1957, and Rose decided to go solo a year later with help from brothers Cal and Henry. She signed to Capitol but didn't have much success until 1961, in which she accounted for five Top 20 hits. Both "Kissing My Pillow" and its B-side "I Want to Live Again" hit the country Top 15 early in the year. "Mental Cruelty" made it to number eight in May, and her duet with Buck Owens called "Loose Talk" hit number four the same month. She ended the year with another Top 15 single, "Conscience, I'm Guilty." Her biggest hit, "Sing a Little Song of Heartache," came the following year, reaching number three in late 1962. More Top 20 singles followed in 1963, including "Lonely Teardrops," "Down to the River," "We're the Talk of the Town," "Somebody Told Somebody" and another duet with Owens, "Sweethearts in Heaven."

In 1962, Bill Monroe suggested that her voice would be perfect for bluegrass recordings, and the resulting *Rose Maddox Sings Bluegrass* (with Monroe, Don Reno, and Red Smiley) became a big hit with folk revivalists of the mid-'60s. Maddox' Capitol contract ended in 1965, and after recording with several smaller labels, she began to concentrate on tours, with brothers Cal and Henry in addition to her son, Donnie. During the '80s Rose suffered several heart attacks but continued to perform at folk and bluegrass festivals and record for Arhoolie, Varrick, and Takoma. —*John Bush*

● **The Moon Is Rising** / 1996 / Country Town Music ✦✦✦✦

This bluegrass project was started in 1987 and finally finished at Mad Dog Studios in 1996. Between the time Maddox and guitarist John Jorgenson began this album and the time they finished it, their lives had taken drastic twists and turns. Still, California country and western legend Maddox is without a doubt one of the consummate performers to come out of the central valley and make a contribution to the Bakersfield Sound. Known for her solo work as well as her time as a member of the Modesto-based Maddox Brothers and Sister Rose, her joining with the younger Jorgenson provides an interesting look at how two generations can come together for the sake of the music. Both are outstanding, and Rose has a feel for Western bluegrass that has inspired Laurie Lewis and her band, Front Range. Their cover of Buck Owens' "Down to the River" is most entertaining. Another California legend, Bill Bryson, who adds his skills as a bluegrass bassman and background vocalist to the mix with good results, contributes his song "Love Me or Leave Me Alone," an outstanding composition made better because of the talent involved. Making their presence known on this recording are L.A. players Jay Dee Maness on pedal steel and dobro and percussion master and background vocalist Steve Duncan. Overall, Jorgenson's production works nicely with Rose's vast experience. The material is steeped in tradition, as are the players, making for a pleasant and uplifting experience. —*Jana Pendragon*

J.E. Mainer

b. Jul. 20, 1898, Weaversville, NC, **d.** Jun. 12, 1971
Old-Time, String Band

Fiddler J.E. Mainer and his Mountaineers were one of the most popular string bands of the early '30s, an important link in the transition from old-time string music to bluegrass. Mainer was born in Buncombe County, NC, and was raised in the mountains. He left home at age 12 to work in a cotton mill; he married in 1922 and settled down in Concord. He started out playing banjo with his fiddle-playing brother-in-law Roscoe Banks at local gatherings, but soon took up the fiddle himself. When Mainer's younger brother Wade moved to the area, the two siblings began playing together; joined by guitarist/singer "Daddy" John Love and Lester and Howard Lay, they eventually formed the first incarnation of the Mountaineers. After winning several talent contests, the band played on radio stations in Gastonia, Charlotte, New Orleans, and Ashville; upon returning to Charlotte, Love and Zeke Morris replaced the Lay brothers.

The Mountaineers made their recording debut with Bluebird in 1935, cutting 14 songs; the most popular was "Maple on the Hill," an old Victorian standard featuring J.E. on the fiddle. In 1936 Wade and Zeke left to form the Sons of the Mountaineers, while J.E. and his new lineup, consisting of Snuffy Jenkins, George Morris, and Leonard Stokes, spent more than a year playing with radio stations in Spartanburg and Columbia. Mainer left the band and in 1939 recorded again for Bluebird with Clyde Moody and Jay Hugh Hall. He assembled a new band the next year that worked on various radio stations. During the 1940s Mainer returned to Concord and stayed for nearly 20 years, playing throughout the Carolinas and neighboring states. He recorded for the last time for 15 years in 1946 with a band featuring his sons Curly and Glenn.

The Mountaineers were rediscovered during the folk revival in 1962 by Chris Strachwitz of the California-based Arhoolie label. At that time, Mainer and his Mountaineers recorded *The Legendary Family from the Blue Ridge Mountains*, which introduced his music to a whole new generation. Five years later Mainer recorded several more albums and made appearances on the radio and at festivals, and he continued to play until his death in 1971. —*Sandra Brennan*

● **A Legendary Family from the Blue Ridge Mountains** / 1963 / Arhoolie ✦✦✦✦

Wade Mainer

b. Apr. 21, 1907, Weaversville, NC
Banjo, Vocals / Traditional Bluegrass, Traditional Country

For more than six decades, Wade Mainer was an influential figure in the development of modern bluegrass music. Among his innovations was a distinctive two-finger banjo picking style crossing the traditional clawhammer with the modern three-finger picking style used by performers such as Earl Scruggs.

Mainer grew up on a tiny mountain farm near Weaverville, NC. He was raised listening to old mountain songs and was greatly influenced by the fiddling of Roscoe Banks, his brother-in-law. As a young man, he moved to Concord to work in a cotton mill. Later he joined his brother J.E.'s Mainer Mountaineers, and began performing on radio. He remained with the band through 1936, when he and fellow bandmate Zeke Morris left to work as a duet. They split up when Morris' younger brother Wiley joined to form the Morris Brothers.

Mainer's new band was named the Sons of the Mountaineers; its first members included guitarists Jay Hugh Hall and Clyde Moody and fiddler Steve Ledford. They performed on the radio and recorded many songs for Bluebird. The band underwent several personnel changes over the years; members included Jack and Curly Shelton, Tiny Dodson, Red Rector, and Fred Smith. In

1939 they had a good-sized hit with "Sparkling Blue Eyes." Mainer briefly stopped appearing on the radio during WW II because he couldn't afford to squander valuable gasoline on long trips to the radio station, and so settled down to work his farm. He and another version of the Mountaineers did make it to Washington, D.C., to play a 1942 concert at the White House, though. They also appeared in a British production of *The Chisholm Trail* in New York. Following the war, he reorganized his band and began playing at various North Carolina radio stations. He recorded only sporadically over the next few years, as old-time music was slowly fading from vogue.

In 1953 Mainer found God and retired from the entertainment industry; he did spend some time singing at gospel revivals in Flint, MI, where he eventually settled to work at a General Motors plant. He spent a few years singing at religious functions but renounced his banjo playing for a long time until Molly O'Day convinced him that the instrument could be used in gospel music. He recorded again in 1961 with his wife, Julia, and continued recording mountain gospel music infrequently through the '60s. He retired from GM in 1973, ultimately recording some new material and even touring a bit. In 1987 his contribution to American music was recognized with a "National Heritage Award," bestowed upon him by President Reagan. —*Sandra Brennan*

Soulful Sacred Songs / 1961 / King ✦✦✦✦

Sacred Songs of Mother and Home / 1971 / Old Homestead ✦✦✦✦

The Songs of Wade Mainer / 1973 / County ✦✦✦

★ **In the Land of Melody** / June Appal ✦✦✦✦✦

In the Land of Melody is a latter-day recording (and first compact disc) by Wade Mainer, one of the most prolific and influential country stars of the '30s. When Mainer re-emerged in the '70s, he began performing with his wife, Julia, and the pair recorded *In the Land of Melody* in the late '80s. The record is divided between standards, originals, instrumentals, and novelties, with none of Wade's obvious hits making an appearance. Instead, the record is a carefully assembled collection that intends to revive the feeling of '30s traditional country, not just Mainer's career. Though the sound is too clean and Wade and Judy occasionally show signs of wear and tear, *In the Land of Melody* is a joyous celebration that hints at the accomplishments of Mainer's career. —*Thom Owens*

Charlie Major

b. Dec. 31, 1954, Aylmer, Quebec, Canada
Vocals / Contemporary Country, Singer-Songwriter

A major star in his native Canada, Charlie Major had a string of No. 1 hits and numerous awards, including winning the Juno Award for Country Male Vocalist of the Year three years running, beginning in 1994. Deciding he wanted to be a musician in 1974, Major became a traveling troubadour and for the next 15 years sharpened his writing and playing skills on the road. At one point he lived in Spain, where he played for tourists and put together a few country bands. Back in Canada, he won a songwriting contest in 1986, part of the prize entitling him to record and release a single. Soon his songs were being recorded by the likes of Canadian stars Matt Minglewood and Patricia Conroy. On a visit to Nashville in 1989 he did some recording, and one of the songs, "Backroads," ended up being a No. 1 hit for Ricky Van Shelton three years later. Then in 1993 Major released his first album *The Other Side* in Canada, and it sold double-platinum there, yielding six number one hits and winning numerous awards, including the Canadian Country Music Association 1994 Album of the Year and Single of the Year ("I'm Gonna Drive You Out of My Mind"). He moved to Nashville in 1994 and was briefly signed to Arista Records before Imprint Records bought his contract and issued his second album and US debut, *Here and Now*, in 1996. —*Jack Leaver*

Here & Now / Oct. 8, 1996 / Imprint ✦✦✦

An award-winning singer-songwriter in his native Canada, Major shines on his sophomore album and first American release. Major's record will appeal to country fans who like the rootsy, rock side of the genre. The vocals, as well as the music, bear a strong resemblance to Lee Roy Parnell, in the way they combine

Barbara Mandrell

blues-based country with infectious upbeat melodies. Strong cuts include the memorable "(I Do It) For the Money," and the slide guitar-driven "I Can See Forever in Your Eyes." Some might remember Major's song "Backroads," which was a number one hit for Ricky Van Shelton. —*Jack Leaver*

Tim Malchak

b. Jun. 25, 1957, Binghamton, NY
Vocals / Country-Pop, Contemporary Country, Urban Cowboy
Singer-songwriter Tim Malchak was best known for his musical partnership with Dwight Rucker; they were the first black/white duo in country music history to have a chart single. Malchak was born in Binghamton, NY, and joined his first band in the fifth grade. He began singing folk songs in college and moved to Southern California in the late '70s, where he found work as an opening act for Commander Cody and Spyro Gyra. He returned to New York in 1982, where he met health-food restaurant owner Rucker, who had played jazz fusion during the early 1970s and also tried his luck as a pop singer. Soon after teaming up, the duo received an opening slot for Michael Martin Murphey. In 1983 they went to Nashville and signed with Revolver Records, where they had two minor hits, "Just Like That" and "Why Didn't I Think of That." That year they moved to Alpine Records, the label established by their co-producer, Johnny Ruten Schroer. Their Alpine debut, "I Could Love You in a Heartbeat," made the Top 70, and the ensuing video spawned considerable interest. The duo scored two more minor hits the next year but then broke up.

Malchak remained with Alpine, and his self-penned solo debut single "Easy Does It" made the Top 70 in 1987. The following year, he hit the Top 40 twice with the original "Colorado Moon" (the title cut of his first album) and "Restless Angel." Malchak had two Top 50 hits in 1988 before switching to Universal just after releasing his second album, *American Man.* The next year he released a very similar album, *Different Circles,* and had two minor hits with "Not Like This" and "If You Had a Heart." —*Sandra Brennan*

● **Colorado Moon** / 1987 / Alpine ◆◆◆◆

Different Circles / Universal ◆◆◆◆

Barbara Mandrell

b. Dec. 25, 1948, Houston, TX
Guitar (Steel), Vocals / Country-Pop, Urban Cowboy
Thanks to a string of hit singles and a popular television variety series, vocalist Barbara Mandrell was arguably the biggest female star in country music in the late 1970s and early 1980s. Born the oldest daughter in a musical family in Houston, TX, on Christmas Day 1948, Mandrell was reading music and playing accordion by the age of five. Just six years later she was so adept at playing the steel guitar that her father escorted her to a music trade convention in Chicago, where her talents caught the attention of Chet Atkins and Joe Maphis. Soon after, she was a featured performer in Maphis' Las Vegas nightclub show, followed by television performances and tours with Red Foley, Johnny Cash, and Tex Ritter.

When Mandrell was 14, her family formed its own group, with her father, Irby, on vocals and guitar, her mother, Mary Ellen, on bass, and Barbara handling pedal steel and saxophone. The band included drummer Ken Dudley, whom Mandrell would eventually marry. The Mandrells toured the US and Asia before Barbara made her first recordings in 1963, among them the minor hit "Queen for a Day." After a few more years of touring, Mandrell briefly retired in order to become a housewife, but she soon grew restless and returned to the music business. After signing with Columbia in 1969, she notched her first chart hit, a cover of the Otis Redding classic "I've Been Loving You Too Long." In 1970 Mandrell scored the first of many Top 40 hits with "Playin' Around With Love." In the same year, she began performing with singer David Houston, and their partnership also generated considerable chart success .

In 1975 Mandrell jumped to the ABC/Dot label, and under the guidance of producer Tom Collins reached the Top Five for the first time with the single "Standing Room Only." After a series of successive hits, she earned her first No. 1 with 1978's "Sleeping Single in a Double Bed," which was immediately followed by another chart-topper, "(If Loving You Is Wrong) I Don't Want to Be Right," in early 1979. Later in the year, "Years" also reached No. 1, as did three more singles—"I Was Country When Country Wasn't Cool," "'Til You're Gone," and "One of a Kind Pair of Fools"—between 1981 and 1983, a period during which Mandrell also received numerous industry awards and accolades.

In 1980 the TV program *Barbara Mandrell and the Mandrell Sisters* premiered on NBC. In addition to hosts Barbara, Louise, and Irlene Mandrell, the show featured musical guests and comedy sketches. Each broadcast closed with a gospel song, and in 1982 Mandrell released her own inspirational album, *He Set My Life to Music.* As a result of her busy schedule she began suffering from vocal strain, and on doctor's orders pulled the plug on her television program in 1982. In 1983 she premiered *The Lady Is a Champ,* a Las Vegas stage show, and released two LPs, *Black and White* and *Spun Gold.*

A collection of duets with Lee Greenwood, *Clean Cut,* followed in 1984. Tragedy struck later in the year, when Mandrell and two of her children were involved in a head-on car crash that left the other driver dead. Though Mandrell and her kids survived, all three faced a long period of recovery. When she finally returned to performing a year later, the country music landscape had changed dramatically, with the "New Traditionalist" movement gaining dominance while the glitzier, more pop-influenced music Mandrell favored began falling out of favor. As the 1980s became the 1990s, she began focusing almost exclusively on live performing, where she remained a significant draw; she also published her autobiography, *Get to the Heart: My Story.* —*Jason Ankeny*

● **The Best of Barbara Mandrell** / 1979 / MCA ◆◆◆◆
The Best of Barbara Mandrell collects her biggest hits from the late '70s, including "After the Lovin'," "Married But Not to Each Other," "Tonight," "Woman to Woman," and "Sleeping Single in a Double Bed." —*Stephen Thomas Erlewine*

Greatest Hits / 1985 / MCA ◆◆◆◆
Hank Williams definitely didn't do it this way. Nevertheless, "I Was Country When Country Wasn't Cool" summed up a lot of folks' feelings as the Travolta crowd tried to claim him as their own. Also included are the number ones "Sleeping Single in a Double Bed," "(If Loving You Is Wrong) I Don't Want to Be Right," and "Years." —*Dan Cooper*

Greatest Country Hits / 1987 / Curb ✦✦✦

While *Greatest Country Hits* does, as advertised, contain some of Mandrell's most popular recordings, many of these 11 songs were minor hits, and others never reached the charts at all. However, it does offer three of her chart-toppers—"Years," "One of a Kind Pair of Fools," and "I Was Country When Country Wasn't Cool." —*Jason Ankeny*

Best of Barbara Mandrell / 1992 / Liberty ✦✦✦

This features "I'll Be Your Jukebox Tonight," "Tall Drink of Water," "Feed the Fire," and more. —*AMG*

Best of Barbara Mandrell / ABC ✦✦✦✦

ABC's 10-track *The Best of Barbara Mandrell* collects all of Mandrell's sweet, sometimes syrupy, country hits through 1979, including such highlights as "Sleeping Single In A Double Bed," "Woman To Woman," and "That's What Friends Are For." —*James Chrispell*

Joe Maphis

b. May 12, 1921, Suffolk, VA, **d.** Jun. 27, 1986

Guitar, Session Musician / Traditional Bluegrass, Instrumental, Traditional Country, Bakersfield Sound

Joe and Rose Maphis were a popular husband-and-wife act in the late '40s and early '50s, singing traditional material backed by the amazing instrumental talent of Joe, who played everything with strings on it, especially the twin-neck guitar. The honky-tonk anthem "Dim Lights, Thick Smoke (And Loud, Loud Music)" was their big hit. Until his death in 1986, Joe was a sessions instrumentalist, backing such stars as Rick Nelson, Tex Ritter, and Wanda Jackson. —*David Vinopal*

● **Flat-Picking Spectacular** / 1982 / CMH ✦✦✦✦

These are later recordings made by this '40s-era sessionman and singer. —*Charles S. Wolfe*

Rose Lee Maphis

b. Dec. 29, 1922, Baltimore, MD

Vocals / Traditional Bluegrass, Traditional Country, Honky Tonk

During the 1950s and 1960s, Joe and Rose Lee Maphis—"Mr. and Mrs. Country Music"—ranked as one of show business' most successful husband-and-wife duos, thanks largely to Joe's distinctive, highly influential brand of guitar picking. Otis Wilson Maphis was born May 12, 1921, in Suffolk, VA; Rose Lee Schetrompf was born December 29, 1922, in Baltimore, MD. Both became active in music at a young age. After playing guitar with his family's group, the Railsplitters, at local square dances, in 1938 Joe became a full-time musician and not long after joined Sunshine Sue (Workman)'s backing outfit, the Rangers, in Cincinnati, OH. He began to perfect his unique approach to playing, which favored hyperkinetic finger-picked melody lines over more basic chord accompaniment. Rose Lee, meanwhile, began singing on local radio in Hagerstown, VA, at the age of 15 as a member of the girl group the Saddle Sweethearts, and soon graduated to appearances in large markets like Baltimore and St. Louis.

After serving in World War II, Joe returned to Virginia, where he briefly joined Sunshine Sue's radio jamboree, *The Old Dominion Barn Dance*, which also featured young singer Rose Lee Schetrompf. However Maphis soon departed for Chicago; when he came back to Virginia in 1947, he took up the electric guitar and rejoined the radio program. He and Rose Lee soon began performing together on the air and on the road; however, in 1951 Merle Travis convinced Joe to move to California to work in television, and only after Rose followed a year later did the couple finally wed. In 1953 the duo cut their first sides, among them the self-penned "Dim Lights, Thick Smoke (and Loud, Loud Music)," which has since become a honky-tonk standard.

Throughout the decade, "Mr. and Mrs. Country Music" (as they were dubbed) remained staples of the West Coast scene, and even as Rose turned her attentions to raising a family, Joe continued performing both as a solo instrumentalist and a highly regarded session musician. In 1954 he became one of the very first performers to play a double-necked guitar by adopting the Mos-Rite Special, an instrument he helped design. Through his work on solo records like 1957's *Fire on the Strings* and on sessions for

other country stars as well as rockers like Ricky Nelson and vocal groups such as the Four Preps, Maphis earned another nickname, "The King of Strings." In addition to a number of duets with his young protege Larry Collins (of the Collins Kids), Joe released a tenor banjo record, *Hi-Fi Holiday for Banjo*, in 1959. Two years later, Rose Lee followed with a self-titled solo collection of country standards.

In 1962 the couple joined the Blue Ridge Mountain Boys for *Rose Lee & Joe Maphis*, an album of bluegrass duets; later in the year Joe released another solo effort, *King of the Strings*. Two years later he and Merle Travis teamed for a record of guitar duets, followed shortly by another collaboration with Rose titled *Mr. and Mrs. Country* and a solo outing, *Hootenanny Star*. In addition to a lucrative side career composing theme music for television programs, Joe released the solo offerings *Golden Gospel* in 1966 and *New Sound of Joe Maphis* a year later.

The Maphis family moved to Nashville in 1968 and largely dropped out of music for a few years until Joe and the couple's eldest son, Jody, released the LP *Guitaration Gap* in 1971. Six years later Joe released the solo *Grass 'n' Jazz*, and was joined by Rose in 1978 for *Dim Lights, Thick Smoke*. Two more albums—1979's *Boogie Woogie Flattop Guitar Pickin' Man* and *Honky Tonk Cowboy*, from 1980—followed. In 1986 Joe Maphis succumbed to lung cancer. Rose Lee left performing to work as a costumer at Opryland. —*Jason Ankeny*

Rose Lee Maphis / 1961 / Columbia ✦✦✦✦

The Marshall Tucker Band

Country-Rock, Southern Rock

One of the major Southern-rock bands of the '70s, the Marshall Tucker Band was formed in Spartanburg, SC, in 1971 by singer Doug Gray; guitarist Toy Caldwell (b.1948); his brother, bassist Tommy Caldwell (b.1950–d.Apr 4, 1980); guitarist George McCorkle; drummer Paul Riddle; and reed player Jerry Eubanks. The group's style combined rock, country, and jazz, and featured extended instrumental passages on which lead guitarist Toy Caldwell shone. The band was signed to Capricorn Records and released its debut album, *The Marshall Tucker Band*, in March 1973. They gained recognition through a tour with the Allman Brothers Band and found significant success during the course of the '70s, with most of their albums going gold. Their peak came with the million-selling album *Carolina Dreams* and its Top 15 single "Heard It in a Love Song" in 1977. The band was slowed down by the death of Tommy Caldwell in a car accident in 1980, and it faded from the album charts after 1982. Toy Caldwell left for a solo career, and by the early '90s, Marshall Tucker consisted of Doug Gray, Jerry Eubanks, guitarist Rusty Milner, bassist Tim Lawter, drummer Ace Allen, and pianist Don Cameron. —*William Ruhlmann*

The Marshall Tucker Band / 1973 / AJK ✦✦✦✦

With flute and the occasional blast of horns, the Marshall Tucker Band was one of the most laidback Southern country-rock outfits of the late '70s. Their first album easily demonstrates this, and it still holds up well, with "Take the Highway," "Can't You See," and "Ramblin'" sounding particularly strong. —*Stephen Thomas Erlewine*

A New Life / 1974 / AJK ✦✦✦✦

On their second release, the Marshall Tucker Band becomes slightly rootsier and bluesier without sacrificing any of the relaxed charm of their first record. Overall it is a stronger, more consistent album, highlighted by "Southern Woman," "Blue Ridge Mountain Sky," and "Too Stubborn." —*Stephen Thomas Erlewine*

Where We All Belong / 1974 / AJK ✦✦✦✦

Although it runs a little long, *Where We All Belong* captures the sound of the Marshall Tucker Band coming into its own. Half the tracks are new studio recordings, which are more focused than their previous releases; the other half is a harder-edged, jam-oriented live set. Taken together, they show that the band was progressing musically. —*Stephen Thomas Erlewine*

Searchin' for a Rainbow / 1975 / AJK ✦✦✦✦
With *Searchin' for a Rainbow*, the Marshall Tucker Band retreats somewhat from the grittier sounds of *Where We All Belong* without abandoning their country and blues roots. —*Stephen Thomas Erlewine*

Long Hard Ride / 1976 / AJK ✦✦✦
On *Long Hard Ride*, the Marshall Tucker Band's country influences come to the fore, resulting in a strong record that failed to gain many hits. Still, the final product is well worth listening to—it's one of their better releases. Be sure to listen for Charlie Daniels' guest appearance. —*Stephen Thomas Erlewine*

Carolina Dreams / 1977 / AJK ✦✦✦
Carolina Dreams marks a retreat from the more pronounced country leanings of *Long Hard Ride* to the more successful country-tinged pop-rock of "Heard It In a Love Song" and "Fly Like An Eagle." They gathered more hits with this approach, and although the hits hold up well, the rest of the album doesn't live up to their quality. —*Stephen Thomas Erlewine*

● **Greatest Hits** / 1978 / AJK ✦✦✦✦
If you are looking for a place to start with this band, *Greatest Hits* covers all the main bases. Included are "Can't You See," "Heard It in a Love Song," "Fire on the Mountain," and "This Ol' Cowboy." —*Rick Clark*

Together Forever / 1978 / AJK ✦✦✦
Together Forever boasts a more mainstream rock approach than any of its predecessors, halfway between the country-tinged *Long Hard Ride* and the pop-oriented *Carolina Dreams*. Although the band sounds good, the songs don't match the strength of their performances. —*Stephen Thomas Erlewine*

Best Of...The Capricorn Years / 1995 / ERA ✦✦✦✦
Country Tucker / Aug. 1996 / K-Tel ✦✦✦✦
Country Tucker compiles tracks from the Marshall Tucker Band's mid-'70s heyday. As the title implies, all of the songs included on this collection lean toward the group's country roots; many of them, including "Heard It In A Love Song," were minor country hits. In fact, *Country Tucker* works as a greatest hits collection, since it does feature pop hits like "Fire on the Mountain" (presented in its original single version) and "Can't You See" that nevertheless demonstrate strong country leanings. In short, it's a useful introduction and a nearly definitive compilation that should satiate the desires of most casual fans. —*Stephen Thomas Erlewine*

Asa Martin

b. Jun. 28, 1900, Winchester, KY, **d.** Aug. 15, 1979
Guitar, Vocals / Old-Time, Traditional Country
Old-time Kentucky singer Asa Martin made many records during the '20s and '30s and was closely associated with the famed fiddler Doc Roberts, for whom he played rhythm guitar. In turn, Roberts frequently played mandolin on Martin's recordings; Roberts' son James even sang duets with Martin under the name Martin and Roberts.

Martin was born in Clark County, KY, and grew up listening to the traditional music presented in minstrel shows and vaudeville productions. Inspired to become a performer, he joined a traveling show or two and learned to play guitar. It was during this time that he met Doc Roberts, who had him sit in on a recording session in Richmond, IN. His first solo songs were mostly parodies, such as "The Virginia Bootlegger" and "There's No Place like Home (For a Married Man)." Martin moved to more traditional ballads after he teamed up with James Roberts in the late 1920s, including "Knoxville Girl," "Lilly Dale," and "Give My Love to Nell." Occasionally the two also sang contemporary old-time style songs, such as "The Little Box of Pine on the 7:29." They continued to record together until 1934, when Martin became the host of the *Morning Roundup* in Lexington. He returned to recording in 1938, again focusing on comedy songs with the occasional ballad, like the haunting "Harlan Town Tragedy."

Martin quit music after the outbreak of World War II, initially working for a munitions factory in Middletown, OH. He retired in 1965 and moved to Kentucky, where he founded the Cumberland

Rangers. In 1968 his early contributions were unearthed by music scholars Archie Green and Norm Cohen, who helped arrange a reunion concert between Martin and Roberts. In 1974 Martin and the Cumberland Rangers recorded an old-time music album, *Dr. Ginger Blue*. —*Sandra Brennan*

● **Asa Martin** / Rounder ✦✦✦✦
Dr. Ginger Blue / Rounder ✦✦✦

Jimmy Martin (James Henry Martin)

b. 1927, Sneedville, TN
Guitar, Vocals / Traditional Bluegrass
Blessed with a great tenor voice, this traditional bluegrass singer and guitarist mastered his craft as lead vocalist for Bill Monroe's Blue Grass Boys for much of 1949-1951 and again in 1952-1953. Martin's vocals and his dynamic guitar playing complemented Monroe perfectly, and in the opinion of many, he was the finest lead singer and guitarist Bill Monroe ever had. In 1951, between stints with Monroe's band, Martin joined the Osborne Brothers, forming the Sunny Mountain Boys. Though this association lasted only until 1955, Martin has used this band name up to the present. In keeping up such high standards over the years, Martin has hired numerous major-league musicians, including banjo players J. D. Crowe, Bill Emerson, Vic Jordan, and Alan Munde, and mandolin player Paul Williams, all of whom subsequently made it big in bluegrass. Jimmy Martin is required listening for anyone with more than a passing interest in bluegrass.

Jimmy Martin was born and raised in the Cumberland Mountains of East Tennessee. As a teenager, he fell in love with Bill Monroe's music, which inspired him to pursue a career as a singer. He began working at radio stations around Morristown, TN, to gain experience; he also worked as a housepainter to make ends meet. At the age of 22, he auditioned successfully in Nashville for Monroe's band to replace Mac Wiseman. For the next four years Martin stayed with Monroe, recording 46 sides for Decca Records. In 1951 Martin briefly sang with Bob Osborne, which was captured on a series of singles for King Records. At the same time, he was a member of the Monroe side project the Shenandoah Valley Trio, which cut several songs for Columbia.

Martin split from Monroe for good in 1954, joining Bobby and Sonny Osborne's duo as a lead singer. He stayed with the Osbornes for about a year, recording several sessions for RCA-Victor. He left the brothers the following year, taking the band name Sunny Mountain Boys—which had previously been used by the Osborne Brothers—with him. In the spring of 1956 Martin signed with Decca Records and made his first solo recordings. Through his solo records and performances on the Grand Ole Opry and the "Louisiana Hayride," Martin helped bring bluegrass into the mainstream. This was primarily because he concentrated on bluegrass that focused on the vocals, not the instruments. Within two years he began charting in the country Top 40, beginning with the No. 14 single "Rock Hearts." Throughout the '60s he had the occasional hit single and became a staple of the bluegrass festival circuit.

Over the years, Martin's Sunny Mountain Boys hosted a wealth of new musical talents, including Doyle Lawson, Bill Emerson, Clarence "Tater" Tate, Paul Williams, Alan Munde, and J.D. Crowe. Although the lineup of the band changed constantly, the quality of the musicians remained high throughout his career.

In 1971 Jimmy Martin sang "I Saw the Light" and "Sunny Side of the Mountain" on the Nitty Gritty Dirt Band's *Will the Circle Be Unbroken*, which helped increase his audience. Martin parted from Decca Records in 1974, signing with Starday/Gusto Records shortly afterward. He stayed at Gusto for nearly a decade, releasing six albums during his tenure at the label. After Gusto went out of business in the '80s, Martin began his own record label, King of Bluegrass, which reissued his classic Decca recordings. Martin continued to perform concerts and bluegrass festivals into the '90s. —*Stephen Thomas Erlewine & David Vinopal*

★ **You Don't Know My Mind (1956-1966)** / 1990 / Rounder ✦✦✦✦✦
This is a Monroe band veteran with astonishing high pipes and a penchant for blending bluegrass and honky tonk. *You Don't*

Know My Mind (1956-1966) is a 14-track collection that boasts many highlights from his ten-year stint at Decca Records. These are great bands, great songs, and classic sides. *—Mark A. Humphrey*

Jimmy Martin and the Sunny Mountain Boys / 1994 / Bear Family ✦✦✦✦

The six-disc set *Jimmy Martin & the Sunny Mountain Boys* contains all of the classic recordings the group made for Decca Records in the late '50s and '60s. For the collector, it's an ideal investment, but most fans will find that the set is simply too exhaustive for their tastes. *—Thom Owens*

20 Greatest Hits / Deluxe ✦✦

20 Greatest Hits contains re-recorded versions of Martin favorites done in the mid-'70s. *Jason Ankeny*

Greatest Bluegrass Hits / Hollywood ✦✦✦

Seventies-era rerecordings of Martin's bluegrass classics are compiled on *Greatest Bluegrass Hits*. *—Jason Ankeny*

Mason Dixon

Country-Rock, Urban Cowboy

Mason Dixon was a popular 1980s country band that took its name from its mixed lineup of Southerners and Yankees. The group had its beginnings in a duo made up of New Yorker Frank Gilligan and Texas native Rick Henderson, who attended college together during the mid-'70s. They performed throughout southern Texas until 1979, when they were joined by Jerry Dengler, a solo performer from Odessa, TX. The trio hired a drummer and decided to tour; they hired three more musicians but retained only one, as they were unable to generate enough bookings.

Their first single, "Armadillo Country," was recorded on their own label. Manager, promoter, and producer Don Schafer heard the song and invited Mason Dixon to perform on his yearly *Texas Music and Talent Showcase;* he also signed them to his Texas Records. They scored a minor hit with a cover of the Police' "Every Breath You Take" in late 1983. The next year, Mason Dixon scored two modest hits with "I Never Had a Chance with You" and "Gettin' Over You." In 1985 the band released their debut album, *The Spirit of Texas*, in celebration of their state's sesquicentennial, donating proceeds to the Salesmanship Club's Youth Camps.

Mason Dixon switched to a new independent label, Premier Once Records, in 1986. With new producer Dan Mitchell the band achieved greater chart success and through 1987 scored three mid-range hits, including "3935 West End Avenue." They signed with Capitol in early 1988 and released *Exception to the Rule*, which produced two more medium hits, "Dangerous Road" and "When Karen Comes Around." They scored two more hits the following year, when Henderson left and was replaced by Terry Casburn. In 1990 the group performed to benefit the Cowboy Crisis Relief Fund Drive and released their second Capitol album *Reach for It*. *—Sandra Brennan*

Our Thing / 1969 / Tower ✦✦✦

● **Exception to the Rule** / Capitol ✦✦✦✦

Reach for It / Capitol ✦✦✦

Mila Mason

Vocals / Contemporary Country

Born and raised near Dawson Springs, KY, modern country singer Mila Mason secured a record contract with Atlantic Nashville by the mid-'90s, releasing her debut album *That's Enough of That* in the fall of 1996. *—Stephen Thomas Erlewine*

That's Enough of That / Sep. 17, 1996 / Atlantic ✦✦✦✦

Mila Mason's debut album *That's Enough of That* is a competent but undistinguished set of modern country. The album boasts a number of songs written by professional Nashville songwriters, as well as a clean commercial production, and Mason has a fine voice, but nothing on *That's Enough of That* demonstrates much originality or spark. It's simply pleasant background music. *— Thom Owens*

Country Johnny Mathis

b. Sep. 28, 1933, Maude, TX

Vocals / Traditional Country, Nashville Sound/Countrypolitan

During the '50s and '60s, Country Johnny Mathis— who added the "Country" before his name so as not to be confused with his more popular and enduring contemporary of the same name—was a well known country singer. He was born John Wesley Mathis in Maude, TX, and as a child played guitar and sang in the Church of Christ his father headed. Mathis spent three years in a Dallas hospital recovering from the bone disease osteomyelitis, and eased his boredom by writing songs. He got his professional break singing on the "Big D Jamboree" in Dallas and then performed on "Louisiana Hayride" until 1960. He recorded on several labels and scored a Top Three hit in 1954 with a self-penned duet with Jimmy Lee Fautheree, "If You Don't Somebody Else Will." In 1957 he teamed up with Johnny Horton on "You're My Baby." In 1960 Mathis had two more hits, "I've Been Known to Cry" and "Carl Chessman"; a year later, he and Fautheree collaborated again on "Let Me Be the One." In 1963 Mathis had a big solo hit with "Please Talk to My Heart," which hit the Top 15. He began singing gospel songs in 1965 and recorded *Country Johnny Mathis* for Hilltop Records. He made his last albums in 1967 for Little Darlin' Records. *—Sandra Brennan*

● **Country Johnny Mathis** / 1965 / Hilltop ✦✦✦✦

Kathy Mattea

b. 1959, Cross Lane, WV

Guitar, Vocals / Country-Pop, Contemporary Country, Country-Folk

Singer-songwriter Kathy Mattea worked primarily in a country tradition, but her songs were tinged with the confessional folk of songwriters like Joni Mitchell, Buffy Sainte-Marie, and James Taylor. Mattea began playing guitar in junior high school; she also received operatic voice training during this time. She became interested in bluegrass music while attending college in the mid-'70s. In 1976 she joined the bluegrass group Pennsboro, and two years later, she dropped out of school to try her luck in Nashville. She spent a few years working as a waitress and tour guide before landing a job as a demo and jingle singer.

In 1984 she released her eponymous debut album. Her first two singles, "Street Talk" and "Someone Is Falling in Love," both reached the Top 30, and "You've Got a Soft Place to Fall" and "That's Easy for You to Say" both made the Top 50.

The 1985 album *From My Heart* produced three more hits, with "He Won't Give In" making it to the Top 25. Her third album, 1986's *Walk the Way the Wind Blows*, provided her with her first Top Ten country hits, "Love At the Five and Dime," "Walk the Way the Wind Blows," "You're the Power," and "Train of Memories."

Untasted Honey, released in 1987, elevated Mattea to the status of a genuine star, producing the back-to-back No. 1 hits "Goin' Gone" and "Eighteen Wheels and a Dozen Roses." She married songwriter Jon Vezner in 1988 and subsequently released *Willow in the Wind*, which continued her successful streak. Mattea continued to have Top 10 hits into the early '90s, highlighted by 1989's "Where've You Been," which became a crossover hit on the adult contemporary charts. During the early '90s, Mattea's commercial standing declined somewhat; she was no longer able to reach the Top Ten with regularity, but she continued to have Top 40 hits throughout the decade. *—Sandra Brennan*

Kathy Mattea / 1984 / Mercury ✦✦

From My Heart / 1985 / Mercury ✦✦✦

Walk the Way the Wind Blows / 1986 / Mercury ✦✦✦✦

An injection of brash, bluegrass-style energy gave her music a needed lift. This is her strongest collection, matching her folkie sensitivity with an innocent verve that is truly catchy. It includes her hit version of Nanci Griffith's "Love at the Five and Dime." *—Michael McCall*

Untasted Honey / Sep. 28, 1987 / Mercury ✦✦✦

Featured is one of her best uptempo tunes, "Untold Stories," and one of her most wistful ballads, "Life as We Knew It." *—Michael McCall*

Willow in the Wind / 1989 / Mercury ✦✦✦

Willow in the Wind captured a maturing Kathy Mattea, as she added stronger folk elements to her country-pop. The result was the beautiful and understated elegance of *Willow in the Wind*, as demonstrated on the hit singles "Burnin' Old Memories," "Where've You Been," and "Come from the Heart." —*Stephen Thomas Erlewine*

● **A Collection of Hits** / 1990 / Mercury ✦✦✦✦

Kathy Mattea has risen to near the top of the Nashville ranks because of a haunting, soulful voice, well-produced recordings that have a simple, folkie directness, and, most especially, an amazing talent for picking the best songs being written for the country market, among them "Eighteen Wheels and a Dozen Roses," "Goin' Gone," and the heartbreaking "Where've You Been." —*William Ruhlmann*

Time Passes By / 1991 / Mercury ✦✦✦✦

On her most ambitious album, Mattea gets impeccably chosen songs (as usual) and strong supporting performances (from Emmylou Harris, Dougie MacLean, and the Roches). She doesn't write her own stuff, so she may not be the romantic dreamer of "Asking Us to Dance," but she sure sounds like it. Songs like "Time Passes By," co-written by husband Jon Vezner, suggest there's more honesty here than image. She can even make the half-baked "From a Distance" convincing. —*Brian Mansfield*

Lonesome Standard Time / 1992 / Mercury ✦✦✦✦

Mattea had vocal-cord surgery that threatened to end her career before she made *Lonesome Standard Time*, but you couldn't prove it by listening: her voice hasn't lost a bit of its deep alto warmth. *Lonesome Standard Time* isn't as ambitious as *Time Passes By*, but it's filled with lovely performances from Mattea's favorite sources: bluegrass ("Lonesome Standard Time"), gospel-influenced country ("Standing Knee Deep in a River (Dying of Thirst)") and Nanci Griffith ("Listen to the Radio"). —*Brian Mansfield*

Good News / 1993 / Mercury ✦✦✦

Mattea's outing is delightfully true to her folk-country style: ten moving, original pieces scoring a big zero on the saccharine and hackneyed front. A gorgeous voice, pristine production, and a true highlight of the season. —*Roch Parisien*

Walking Away a Winner / Oct. 1993 / Mercury ✦✦✦✦

Tired of having critics rave while radio programmers yawned, Mattea enlisted contempo-country producer Josh Leo to help brighten her sound for commercial consumption. It worked. The title cut was a hit right out of the box. —*Dan Cooper*

Love Travels / Feb. 4, 1997 / Mercury ✦✦✦

Matthews, Wright & King

Country-Rock, Contemporary Country

Matthews, Wright & King were a country-rock band whose brief career lasted only three years before lack of chart success caused their break-up. The band was the brainchild of Columbia producer Larry Strickland, who was looking for a sound similar to that of the recently disbanded Shenandoah. For the new group, the company chose vocalist/guitarist Raymond Matthews (who was already contracted with Columbia to do a solo album), bassist/vocalist Woody Wright, and guitarist/vocalist Tony King. Their voices matched beautifully, and they became Matthews, Wright & King. The trio had their first chart success in 1992 with the title cut from *The Power of Love*, which made the Top 50 and became their biggest hit. The group had two more medium-level hits with "Mother's Eyes" and "House Huntin'." Matthews wrote four songs, including the title cut, on their second album, *Dream Seekers*. The band broke up in 1994. —*Sandra Brennan*

● **Power of Love** / Dec. 1991 / Columbia ✦✦✦✦

The debut from this country-rock trio contains the hits "Mothers Eyes" and "House Huntin'." —*Jason Ankeny*

Dream Seekers / Columbia ✦✦✦

The Mavericks

Country-Rock, Contemporary Country, New Traditionalist, Americana

Fusing traditional country with traditional rock 'n' roll, the Mavericks became one of the most critically acclaimed and commercially successful groups of the early '90s. Led by singer-songwriter Raul Malo (b. August 7, 1965, Miami, FL), the band was formed in Florida in the late '80s. Malo had played in several bands while he was in high school, as did bassist Robert Reynolds (born Robert Earl Reynolds, April 30, 1962, Kansas City, MO). The pair met at school and discovered they had similar musical tastes—they both enjoyed the music of Roy Orbison, Patsy Cline, Elvis Presley, Hank Williams, and Johnny Cash—and decided to form a band. Reynolds persuaded his best friend, Paul Deakin (born Paul Wylie Deakin, September 2, 1959, Miami, FL)—who had been a drummer in progresssive rock bands and had done some session work—to join the fledgling country band.

Taking the name the Mavericks, the band began playing rock clubs around the Miami area and built up a solid local following. The group chose to play rock clubs because the country bars wanted to book only bands that played covers, and the Mavericks preferred to concentrate on original material. In the fall of 1990 the band released an eponymous independent album. The record worked its way onto playlists across Florida and made its way to Nashville, where it gained the attention of nearly every major record label.

In May 1991 the group went to Nashville to play a showcase gig. Scouts from all of the town's major labels were in attendance, but the band decided to sign with MCA Records. Later that year the Mavericks set about recording their first major label album; before the sessions began, they added lead guitarist David Lee Holt, who had played with Joe Ely, Rosie Flores, and Carlene Carter. Titled *From Hell to Paradise*, the record consisted primarily of Malo's original songs and was released in 1992. Although it was critically acclaimed, the album wasn't a commercial success; only a cover of Hank Williams' standard "Hey Good Lookin'" made the charts, and that peaked at No. 74.

The Mavericks' commercial fortunes turned around with their second major label album, *What a Crying Shame*. Produced by Don Cook (Brooks & Dunn, Mark Collie), the album was more streamlined and focused. It became a hit upon its release early in 1994, with the title track becoming a Top 40 hit. Shortly after the release of *What a Crying Shame*, the group replaced Holt with Nick Kane (born Nicholas James Kane, August 21, 1954, Jerusalem, GA).

Throughout 1994 the band racked up Top 40 hit singles. "O What a Thrill" went to No. 18 in the summer, with "There Goes My Heart" reaching No. 20 in the fall. By the spring of 1995, *What a Crying Shame* had gone platinum. During the first half of 1995 the Mavericks recorded their fourth album, *Music for All Occasions*. Like its predecessor, it was critically acclaimed and a commercial success. By the spring of 1996 the album had gone gold. —*Stephen Thomas Erlewine*

Mavericks / 1990 / Y&T ✦✦✦

The group's first indie release, this album includes early versions of four songs recut for *From Hell to Paradise:* "The End of the Line," "This Broken Heart," "A Better Way," and "Mr. Jones." —*Brian Mansfield*

From Hell to Paradise / 1992 / MCA ✦✦✦✦

In spite of Malo's Cuban heritage and the band's Miami roots—*because* of them, in fact—the Mavericks understand outsiders like Buck Owens and Hank Williams (both of whom the group covers) better than most of country's recent comers. And originals like "I Got You," "This Broken Heart," and the scathing title track about Malo's aunt's escape from Cuban oppression are so good that the covers don't really matter. —*Brian Mansfield*

● **What a Crying Shame** / 1994 / MCA ✦✦✦✦

Superb, highly accessible follow-up to *From Hell to Paradise* included songs that made overt comparisons between Raul Malo and Roy Orbison ("I Should Have Been True," Jesse Winchester's "O What a Thrill"). Those who didn't realize the power of Malo's

The Mavericks

voice knew after those, when he didn't come off looking like a fool. Plenty of hot rockabilly shuffles are included, and the title track, with its Byrdsian guitar hook and bittersweet melody, became the first single by an "alternative" country act since Dwight Yoakam to break radio's Top 30. —*Brian Mansfield*

Music for All Occasions / Oct. 1995 / MCA ✦✦✦

With their fourth album, the Mavericks added slick country-pop to their arsenal of retro-country styles. The result straddles the line between affectation and camp, since the band never goes completely overboard by drenching their songs with strings, and Raul Malo retains his aching Orbisonesque voice. However, that doesn't mean their songwriting has slipped, as all 11 originals are first-rate updated honky-tonk ravers or countrypolitan numbers. And the closing cover of "Somethin' Stupid," recorded with Trisha Yearwood, is a fun, kitschy delight. —*Stephen Thomas Erlewine*

Mac McAnally

b. Jul. 1, 1959, Belmont, MS
Guitar, Vocals / Country-Pop, Singer-Songwriter, Country-Folk
Born in rural Mississippi and based in Muscle Shoals, AL, McAnally scored a huge radio hit, "It's a Crazy World," as a 19-year-old in 1977. Since then he's recorded primarily what he refers to as "unintentional collector's items." They all feature his distinctively optimistic slant on James Taylor-style acoustic pop, and they've all slipped through the cracks for one reason or another. He's been enjoying greater success as a country songwriter as of late. —*Michael McCall*

Mac McAnally / 1977 / Ariola ✦✦✦✦

McAnally's debut revealed uncommon wisdom and spiritual reflection for such a young singer-songwriter. It features the favorite, "It's a Crazy World." —*Michael McCall*

Finish Lines / 1980 / Geffen ✦✦✦

Nothin' But the Truth / 1989 / Geffen ✦✦✦

Simple Life / Feb. 13, 1990 / Warner Brothers ✦✦✦

McAnally has an ability to inject exceptional compassion into mannered, country-pop songs. The album features well-crafted lyrics, fastidious acoustic-pop arrangements, and his unremarkable voice. —*Michael McCall*

● **Live & Learn** / 1992 / MCA ✦✦✦✦

Writing songs packed with gentle emotions and hard-earned life lessons seems to come easy for McAnally. However, hits don't—at least not when he's singing. —*Michael McCall*

Leon McAuliffe (William Leon McAuliffe)

b. Mar. 1, 1917, Houston, TX, **d.** Sep. 20, 1988
Guitar (Steel) / Western Swing
During the heyday of Western swing, the immortal words "Take it away, Leon" nearly became a household phrase in the South. Spoken by Bob Wills, they referred to Leon McAuliffe, one of the best and most famous steel guitarists in the world; though most associated with Wills' Texas Playboys, he also had a respectable solo career. A native of Houston, TX, McAuliffe began playing both Hawaiian and standard guitar at age 14. He began appearing on a local radio station as part of the Waikiki Strummers in 1931. Two years later he joined Lee O'Daniel's Light Crust Doughboys, with whom he recorded on ARC in Chicago. He learned to electronically amplify his National resonator guitar from Houston's Bob Dunn, a member of Milton Brown's Brownies.

Jesse Ashlock invited the 18-year-old McAuliffe to join the Texas Playboys in 1935. He remained with the band for a number of years, recording many classic songs before moving to California, where he appeared in a few motion pictures. His signature song was "Steel Guitar Rag," a tune he adapted from Sylvester Weaver. During World War II McAuliffe was a flight instructor. After the war he founded a big band, the Cimarron Boys. By this time Western swing was all the rage, so he combined the styles to create something new and unique. After working on a Tulsa radio station, he and his band began recording; one of his most famous tunes, "Panhandle Guitar," became a Top Ten hit in 1949. By the 1960s, Western swing had fallen out of vogue and McAuliffe began playing only locally. He also recorded a couple of albums, and later in the decade he purchased radio station KAMO in Rogers, AR. Western swing music was rediscovered in the early '70s, and in 1971 he and Wills made a reunion recording. After Wills died a few years later, McAuliffe occasionally staged reunions of the Texas Playboys. He also recorded a few solo albums.—*Sandra Brennan*

● **Columbia Historic Edition** / Columbia ✦✦✦✦

Leon McAuliffe came to prominence as a member of Bob Wills' Texas Playboys. He had to leave the group to serve in World War

II, and after he returned from the army, he chose to form his own band. After recording a couple of tracks for Majestic Records, McAuliffe signed to Columbia Records, who were looking for a Western swing star to replace Wills. *Columbia Historic Edition* collects the highlights from McAuliffe's time at Columbia, including the Top Ten hit "Panhandle Rag" and "The Steel Guitar Polka." The compilation is a good testament to McAuliffe's prodigious instrumental skill and features some of his best playing. It may be a little brief, but it nevertheless borders on a definitive overview of his Columbia recordings. —*Thom Owens*

McBride & the Ride

Country-Rock, Contemporary Country
In the tradition of Alabama came McBride & the Ride, a country trio noted for their close harmonies and contemporary honky-tonk sounds. The group was the creation of Tony Brown, MCA Nashville's Executive Vice President, who introduced songwriter Terry McBride to session players Ray Herndon and Billy Thomas. The three clicked, and their harmonies blended perfectly.

McBride, the son of vocalist Dale McBride, was born and raised in Texas. He played guitar since childhood and had a longtime interest in traditional and Texas music. After high school he auditioned to join his father's band and worked with him for three years before joining Delbert McClinton and touring with John Fogerty. He then moved to Nashville to work on his songwriting. Herndon and his siblings started out as child stars on the Phoenix-based TV show *Lew King Rangers*, where the three-year-old played accordion and guitar and sang and tap-danced. At age four Herndon cut the novelty single "Christmas Eve." Later he teamed with Lyle Lovett, singing a duet on his debut album and joining Lovett's Large Band. Like the others, drummer Billy Thomas began playing as a child. He started out in rock 'n' roll and in 1973 moved to L.A. to work with Rick Nelson, Mac Davis, and the Hudson Brothers. Two years later he was doing session work in Nashville, and he worked with numerous stars including Emmylou Harris, Vince Gill, Dan Seals, and Jann Brown.

McBride & the Ride debuted in Detroit and soon launched an extensive cross-country tour. Their debut album, 1991's *Burnin' Up the Road*, featured nine songs written or co-written by McBride and won them a gig as the Judds' opening act. By the end of the year viewers discovered the video of their single "Can I Count on You," which saved the group from losing their contract with MCA, as the single soon made the Top 15. Their next single, "Same Old Star," made it to the Top 30. In 1992 the Ride scored their first Top Five hit with the title cut from their album *Sacred Ground*, which also produced two more Top Ten hits. Their 1993 album *Hurry Sundown* contained four popular singles, including "No More Cryin'," which appeared on the soundtrack of the film *8 Seconds*. In early 1994 Herndon and Thomas left and were replaced by Kenny Vaughn, Randy Frazier, and Keith Edwards. The band was then renamed Terry McBride & the Ride. —*Sandra Brennan*

Burnin' up the Road / 1990 / MCA ✦✦✦
Terry McBride had a hand in writing all but one of the 10 cuts on this debut effort, which features the hit "Can I Count on You." —*Jason Ankeny*

● **Sacred Ground** / 1992 / MCA ✦✦✦✦
The title cut was the biggest hit from *Sacred Ground*, a more confident and thoughtful record than the band's debut *Burnin' Up the Road.* —*Jason Ankeny*

Hurry Sundown / 1993 / MCA ✦✦✦✦
The third record from McBride & the Ride continues to hone the group's close harmony style. —*Jason Ankeny*

Terry McBride & The Ride / Sep. 13, 1994 / MCA ✦✦✦

Martina McBride

b. Jul. 29, 1966, Sharon, KS
Vocals / Contemporary Country, New Traditionalist
A Kansas native who sang with power and tenderness, Martina McBride started out in a more traditional country vein in the early '90s, then kicked up the beat and the tempo as her career

progressed. Born Martina Mariea Schiff in Sharon, KS, she grew up in Texas, where she became infatuated with traditional country music. She began singing and playing keyboards at local clubs and barn dances with her father's band, the Schifters. After graduating from high school, she began touring Kansas with a variety of country bands. She later married soundman John McBride and in 1990 moved with him to Nashville, where he worked for such stars as Charlie Daniels and Ricky Van Shelton while she waited tables and sang demos. John then produced a demo tape of her work and they tried sell it to several record labels. This led to a contract with RCA at the end of 1991. Around the same time John became Garth Brooks' production manager, and Martina became the singer's opening act. She released her debut album, *The Time Has Come*, in 1992. It spent six months in the country album Top 50. The title track was released as her first single and it stayed on the charts for five months, while her next two, "That's Me" and "Cheap Whiskey," nearly cracked the Top 40. *The Way That I Am*, McBride's second album, was released in 1993 and became her breakthrough. The record's first single, "My Baby Loves Me," reached No. 2, and "Life No. 9" also became a Top Ten hit. Her third album, *Wild Angels*, was released in the fall of 1995; the title track later became her first No. 1 hit. —*Sandra Brennan*

The Time Has Come / 1992 / RCA ✦✦✦
Her bold debut blends traditional country ("Cheap Whiskey," "That's Me") with acoustic rave-ups, as in the title song. —*Michael McCall*

● **The Way That I Am** / 1993 / RCA ✦✦✦✦
McBride revamps her image, flashing a new haircut and a more forceful, uptempo style. She matches the music with a feisty, daring collection of distinguished songs, including the hit "My Baby Loves Me" and the remarkable "Independence Day," about an abused wife who takes justice into her own hands. —*Michael McCall*

Wild Angels / Sep. 26, 1995 / RCA ✦✦✦
On *Wild Angels* country singer Martina McBride continued to improve her skills, offering another selection of songs that showcase her incisive, emotional voice. —*David Jehnzen*

Don McCalister, Jr.

Vocals / Progressive Bluegrass, Neo-Traditionalist Country, Texas Country, Western Swing Revival
From the musical hotbed of Austin, TX, sprang Don McCalister, Jr., a singer-songwriter with a revolving group of friends and musicians that made up his Cowboy Jazz Revue. Intelligent songwriting and McCalister's smooth tenor, backed by a Western swing and jazz-tinged country sound, drew comparisons to other Texas mainstays, including Ray Benson ("Asleep at the Wheel"), Lyle Lovett, Hal Ketchum, and the music of Bob Wills and His Texas Playboys. On any given night the Revue could appear as just a trio, with McCalister and Boomer Norman on guitar and Carl Keesee on bass, or expand to a full orchestra with as many as 14 musicians on stage. Some of the notable musicians that occasionally played with McCalister included the Grammy award-winning Floyd Domino on piano, Champ Hood on fiddle, Lynn Frazier on pedal steel, Stan Smith on clarinet, and Maryann Price on vocals.

The son of a college professor, McCalister was raised in California, Arkansas, Tennessee, North Carolina, Maine, Alabama, and New Orleans. As a result, he cites a variety of musical influences, such as Muddy Waters, Flatts and Scruggs, Norman Blake, and Duane Allman. Moving to Austin in 1981, McCalister formed his first band, the short-lived Bluegrass Demons, in 1986 before helping found the Flakey Biscuit Boys, which became a popular Central Texas bluegrass band that performed regularly at the renowned Kerrville Folk Festival. After that group dissolved, McCalister independently released a cassette in 1990 entitled *Silver Moon* that moved in a folk music direction and concentrated on his songwriting. Shortly thereafter, he assembled the Cowboy Jazz Revue. McCalister was signed to Dejadisc in 1993, and his debut album, *Brand New Ways*, garnered McCalister rave reviews in and around Austin, plus airplay on regional radio stations. —*Jack Leaver*

● **Brand New Ways** / 1993 / Dejadisc ✦✦✦✦
A solid 12-song debut ensconced in the tradition of Western swing, and flavored with jazz, with a sprinkling of blues for good measure. McCalister's smooth tenor has a light and relaxed feel that's inviting and is reminiscent of the late Walter Hyatt and Ray Benson of Asleep at the Wheel. The playing is first rate, provided by the core of the Cowboy Jazz Revue, with help from stellar Austin musicians that include Johnny Gimble, Floyd Domino, Maryann Price, and Champ Hood. This record swings, and highlights include the romantic "Silver Moon," co-written by McCalister, which could easily be mistaken for a standard, and a swingin' cover of the Louvin Brothers' classic "Cash on the Barrelhead."
—*Jack Leaver*

C.W. McCall (William Fries)

b. Nov. 15, 1928, Audubon, IA
Vocals / Country, Country-Pop, Bakersfield Sound, Urban Cowboy
Essentially a character created by advertising executive William Fries, C.W. McCall was the instrumental figure behind the truck-driving craze that swept America in the mid-'70s. Fries was born November 15, 1928, in Audubon, IA, and while he displayed musical promise as a child, he was more interested in graphic design. While attending the University of Iowa, Fries studied music and played in the school's concert band, but his major was in fine arts, and after graduation he began handling the art chores at an Omaha, NE, television station. After five years there, he was hosting his own program, on which he drew caricatures of celebrities.

Fries signed on as the art director for an Omaha advertising agency in the early 1960s, and it was there that he created the character C.W. McCall as a selling tool for an area bakery. A trucker for the fictional Old Home Bread Company who spent much of his time in a diner called "The Old Home Filler-Up-an'-Keep-On-a-Truckin' Cafe," the McCall character was a huge hit with viewers, and the radio campaign won Fries the advertising industry's prestigious Clio Award. In 1974 Fries decided to cut a record under the McCall moniker, and the single, a monologue with country backing titled after the aforementioned cafe, was a Top 20 hit. A follow-up, "Wolf Creek Pass," was even more successful.

In 1975, McCall released the album *Black Bear Road;* the single "Convoy" hit number one on both the pop and country charts, and a national craze was born. The song proved so successful that it influenced the famed filmmaker Sam Peckinpah to direct the 1978 film *Convoy*, starring Kris Kristofferson. By the time of the film's release, however, McCall's career was largely over. He released two more LPs, 1975's *Wolf Creek Pass* and 1977's *Roses for Mama*, which did spawn a major hit in its title track. But shortly after the latter album's release, McCall turned his back on the music industry to focus on the burgeoning environmental movement and moved to the small town of Ouray, CO, of which he was elected mayor in 1982. An attempt at a comeback in 1990 proved unsuccessful. —*Jason Ankeny*

● **Greatest Hits** / 1990 / Polygram ✦✦✦✦
Virtually all of the novelty hits charted by William Fries' "C.W. McCall" character are included in this collection, which features "Roses for Mama," "Wolf Creek Pass," "Old Home Filler-Up an' Keep-On-a-Truckin' Cafe," and the smash "Convoy." —*Jason Ankeny*

Darrell McCall

b. Apr. 30, 1940, New Jasper, OH
Vocals / Traditional Country, Honky Tonk
Though his initial singles were pop, Darrell McCall was a hard-core country vocalist to the core, singing tough honky tonk during the majority of his career, without caring for trends and fashions. After coming to prominence as a member of the Little Dippers in 1960, McCall broke away from the group the next year, and by 1963 his sound had evolved into pure country. He sang both traditional country and honky tonk during the '60s, but he eventually became devoted to roadhouse country. As a result, his sales suffered somewhat. Darrell had a few hits over the course of his career, sliding into the charts every few years, when-

ever hardcore country crossed over into the mainstream, but for the bulk of his career he remained essentially a semi-popular artist with a diehard cult following.

Born in and raised in New Jasper, OH, McCall began his musical career by landing a slot as a Saturday morning DJ on a local radio station when he was 15 years old. Around the same time, he was playing local dances and events as a musician. After his high school graduation, he joined the Army, where he was stationed in Kentucky. After his tour of duty was completed, he and his childhood friend Johnny Paycheck moved to Nashville in 1958. McCall and Paycheck attempted to record as a duo, but they were unsuccessful. Eventually, McCall became a studio harmony vocalist, singing on records by Faron Young, George Jones, and Ray Price, among others. In a short time, the studio work metamorphosized into road work, as he played bass and sang harmony for several different touring bands, including those of Young, Price, and Hank Williams, Jr.

During a recording session in 1959 McCall met Buddy Killen, a famous Nashville producer and publisher. Impressed with McCall's abilities, Killen asked him to join a group he was assembling called the Little Dippers, which also featured Hurshel Wigintin, Delores Dinning, and Emily Gilmore. McCall agreed, and the Little Dippers had one major pop hit, the Top Ten single "Forever," in 1960. The next year he signed a solo contract with Capitol. During 1961 he released two pop singles for the label, "My Kind of Lovin'" and "Call the Zoo," but both failed miserably, and the label dropped him. In light of his unsuccessful forays into the pop marketplace, McCall returned to country in 1962 and signed a contract with Phillips. In January 1963 "A Stranger Was Here," his first—and, as it would turn out, his biggest—country hit appeared. Peaking at No. 17, the single spent eight weeks on the charts and seemed to be a positive beginning to his country career, but he wasn't able to deliver a hit followup, even though he sang the theme to the Paul Newman film *Hud* that same year.

McCall abandoned music for a short while in the mid-'60s, launching an acting career in 1965. That year he appeared in the film *Nashville Rebel* and the next year he was in *Road to Nashville* and *What Am I Bid*. During that time, Darrell also worked as a cowboy in the Southwest and appeared in several minor rodeos. He didn't return to recording until 1968, when he joined the roster of the independent label Wayside Records. Over the next two years he had four minor hits for the label—"I'd Love to Live with You Again," "Wall of Pictures," "Hurry Up," "The Arms of My Weakness"—and released one album, 1970's *Meet Darrell McCall*, which was distributed by Mercury. The contract with Wayside expired in 1971, and McCall didn't immediately sign another recording contract. However, Hank Williams Jr. took McCall's "Eleven Roses" (which he co-wrote with Lamar Morris) to number one, which led to Tree International's signing him as a professional songwriter.

Darrell McCall didn't reactivate his recording career until 1974, when he signed with Atlantic. His debut single for the label, "There's Still a Lot of Love in San Antone," nearly reached the country Top 50 that year. In 1975 he left Atlantic for Columbia, where he had his greatest period of chart success since the early '60s. Although his first single for the label, "Pins and Needles (in My Heart)," didn't do much better than "There's Still a Lot of Love in San Antone," his second single, "Lily Dale," was a duet with Willie Nelson that cracked the country Top 40. McCall's new success was due partially to the popularity of outlaw country, and he neatly fit into its rough and ready musical style. "Lily Dale" was named Best Duet of 1977 by *Cash Box* magazine, and it was followed by "Dreams of a Dreamer," Darrell's first solo Top 40 hit since 1963. The brief McCall renaissance began to lose its luster in 1978, as outlaw country began to lose its stronghold on the country charts. His singles "Down the Roads of Daddy's Dreams" and "The Weeds Outlived the Roses" failed to make the Top 40, and he was soon dropped by Columbia.

In 1980 he signed with Hillside Records, where he had only one hit single—a duet on "San Antonio Medley" with Curtis Potter. After that reached the lower levels of the country charts in the spring, he switched to RCA, where he nearly reached the Top 40 in the fall with "Long Line of Empties." At that time the tastes of country radio and the genre's audience had shifted from outlaw country and settled on the smooth, rock-influenced textures of Urban Cowboy. Consequently, McCall's recording career suffered. Over the next four years he recorded only sporadically, most notably as the uncredited "friend" on Connie Hanson and Friend's minor 1982 hit, "There's Still a Lot of Love in San Antone." Two years later he had his final charting hit with "Memphis in May," which was released on Indigo Records. In 1986 McCall cut two albums: a record with his old backing group the Tennessee Volunteers called *Reunion* (released on BGM), and *Hot Texas Country*, a duet record with Johnny Bush.

After 1986 McCall essentially retired from recording, though he continued to play the occasional concert and worked constantly for the Muscular Dystrophy Association. McCall spent the remainder of the '80s and most of the '90s at his Texas home with his wife, Mona Vary, who used to play in Audrey Williams' band. —*Stephen Thomas Erlewine*

The Real McCall / 1996 / Bear Family ◆◆◆◆
Darrell McCall was a hardcore traditional country singer, keeping the flame of pure, gritty honky tonk alive during the country-pop crazes of '60s and '70s. Though he never had many hits—only his debut single, "A Stranger Was Here," broke the Top 20—he gained a dedicated cult following among fans of traditional country, which translated into a string of moderate hits that ran from the early '60s until 1980. The five-disc box set *The Real McCall* collects all of the recordings he made during that time, including every song he cut for Starday, Wayside, Atlantic, American Heritage, Columbia, and RCA. In addition to the released recordings, *The Real McCall* features a handful of demos (including some he made for Jimmy Reed), radio transcriptions, and radio commercials—everything a dedicated fan could ever want from McCall. Of course such an exhaustive approach means that listening to the box is a daunting task for anyone but the most devoted fan, but it will satisfy all of his hardcore followers with its excellent sound and lavish, detailed packaging. —*Thom Owens*

The McCarters

Contemporary Country, New Traditionalist
The McCarters were a sister act with a classic country sound who enjoyed brief popularity during the late 1980s. Jennifer McCarter and twins Lisa and Teresa were all born in Knoxville, TN, and raised in Sevierville, Dolly Parton's birthplace. They got their start as clog dancers at their county's bicentennial celebration, which led to four years' dancing on a Knoxville television show. Their father told the girls that the first to learn to play guitar could have his 1969 Martin; Jennifer won it at age 14, and her younger sisters sang high harmonies while she played and sang lead. The trio became well known in their hometown, where they sang for tips on the steps of the county courthouse. They moved to Music City in 1987 and signed with Warner Brothers, who were seeking an act like their successful Forrester Sisters. Later that year the McCarters embarked on a worldwide USO tour with Randy Travis. They made their chart debut in early 1988 with "Timeless and True Love," which hit the Top Five, and later they appeared on the *Dolly Show* at the invitation of Parton herself. The title track of their debut album, *The Gift*, was an even bigger hit, but their third single, "I Give You Music," made only the Top 30. Over the next two years the McCarters made one more album, *Better Be Home Soon*, and scored a few low-level hits. In 1990 they were released from Warner, later focusing on live performances while also breaking into modeling and selling commercial products. —*Sandra Brennan*

● **The Gift** / Jun. 21, 1988 / Warner Brothers ◆◆◆◆
The Gift is an exceptional debut album from the McCarters, three sisters that hail from Tennessee. Throughout the record, the trio demonstrates their remarkable vocal talents, as their beautiful harmonies grace a set of traditional country tunes. —*Thom Owens*

Better Be Home Soon / 1990 / Warner Brothers ◆◆◆
While the McCarters' debut focused on the trio's harmonies, *Better Be Home Soon* focuses the spotlight almost exclusively on sister Jennifer, pushing twins Lisa and Teresa into the background. —*Jason Ankeny*

Mary McCaslin

b. Dec. 22, 1946, Indianapolis, IN
Banjo, Guitar, Vocals / Singer-Songwriter, Country-Folk, Contemporary Folk
As a singer-songwriter who wrote story-songs combining elements of country, folk, and pop, Mary McCaslin was one of the most appealing contemporary folk performers of the 1970s. As a country-folk singer working totally outside of the Nashville sphere, she sang of prairies and Old West images in almost mythic terms. Her audience was confined to the folk circuit (though within that boundary, it was very wide). Yet her ability to appeal to rock and pop listeners helped pave the way for country-folk-pop stars like Nanci Griffith and Mary-Chapin Carpenter, although her influence in this area has remained relatively unacknowledged.

Born in Indiana, McCaslin moved to Southern California with her family at a young age. Inspired both by country narrators like Marty Robbins and singer-songwriters like Joni Mitchell, she recorded her first album, *Goodnight, Everybody,* for Barnaby in 1969. At this point her repertoire consisted entirely of covers; she didn't begin writing until her 20s, coming up with one of her signature tunes, "Way Out West," on her second try. That composition would be the title track of her first Philo album (1973), recorded after a brief liaison with Capitol (which produced one single).

Way Out West was the first of three albums she made for Philo in the 1970s, featuring her finely wrought songs, strong upper-register vocals, and sympathetic, fully arranged accompaniment. Two of the tracks that attracted widest notice were her acoustic interpretations of two Beatles' songs ("Things We Said Today" and "Blackbird"), which were not only among the few truly fine folk renditions of Lennon-McCartney tunes, but among the best Beatles covers ever attempted. Her Philo era is recognized as her artistic peak, although she maintained her presence on the folk scene with albums for Mercury (*Sunny California,* 1979) and Flying Fish (*A Life and a Time,* 1981). She also did a duo album with her husband, guitarist and songwriter Jim Ringer (who also played on Mary's albums), in the late '70s.

Surprisingly little was heard from McCaslin in the 1980s. Ringer (from whom she separated in 1989) became very ill, and her family problems put her songwriting on hold; she once estimated that she wrote only three songs between 1981 and 1989. *Broken Promises* in 1994 was her first album in 13 years. —*Richie Unterberger*

Goodnight Everybody / 1969 / Barnaby ◆◆◆

Way Out West / 1974 / Philo ◆◆◆◆
This was the album that established McCaslin as a major folk performer. Her interpretive skills are in evidence on covers of "Let It Be" and Randy Newman's "Living Without You," but most of the set was devoted to original material, showing her to be an impressive songwriter (if not quite as impressive a singer). The title track and "San Bernardino Waltz" are standouts, the latter being probably her most famous song. —*Richie Unterberger*

Prairie in the Sky / 1976 / Philo ◆◆◆

Old Friends / 1977 / Philo ◆◆◆
Who'd ever think anyone could send chills up your spine by singing the Supremes' song "My World Is Empty Without You Babe" or the Beatles' "Things We Said Today?" Mary has done it on this record, with an unusual minor guitar tuning and exquisite harmonies in her arrangements. These two songs, plus her original title cut, make this album one of our favorites. —*Ladyslipper*

● **The Best of Mary McCaslin** / 1990 / Philo ◆◆◆◆
The best of her 1970s material, taken from her first three solo albums. Many strong originals, and two excellent Beatle covers ("Things We Said Today" and "Blackbird") that remain among the best folk interpretations of Lennon/McCartney compositions. —*Richie Unterberger*

Things We Said Today (Best of Mary McCaslin) / Philo ++++
This collection features the dusty vocals and wide-open country/
folk sound of Mary McCaslin. Her fascination with the West
comes through on a number of songs, specifically on her own
"Prairie in the Sky" and a version of "Ghost Riders in the Sky."
She also covers "My World Is Empty Without You" and the Beatles' "Blackbird" and "Things We Said Today," but the bulk of the
tunes are originals. Culled from four previous Philo releases, it
includes some of her best-loved compositions, such as "The Bramble and the Rose" and "Way Out West." McCaslin is backed by her
own guitar and banjo as well as a number of other musicians.
—Roundup newsletter

Charly McClain (Charlotte Denise McClain)

h Mar 26, 1956, Memphis, TN
Vocals / Country-Pop, Urban Cowboy
Originally named Charlotte, Charly McClain was given her mas-
culine moniker by neighborhood friends in Memphis, and she
used it when she started playing hotel lounges. Epic Records
decided it was more "catchy" than Charlotte, and it became a permanent professional banner. Her father had tuberculosis when
she was eight, and since she was under age for visitation rights at
the hospital, she had to communicate with him through a tape
recorder. That inspired her interest in recording, and by age 17
she was a regular on the club circuit. Signed to her first recording
contract in 1976, McClain's distinct vocal sound provided an edge
in recognizability—as did her appearance. She hit country's Top
Ten fairly regularly from 1978-1985, both as a solo artist and in
duets with Mickey Gilley and former soap star Wayne Massey,
whom she married in 1984. *— Tom Roland*

Greatest Hits / 1982 / Epic ++++
McClain's Southern heritage is very much in evidence in her
vocal style. No other woman sounds as simultaneously tough and
feminine as she does; this is simply McClain at her best—"Men,"
"Sleepin' with the Radio On," "Who's Cheatin' Who," and "The
Very Best Is You." *— Tom Roland*

Paradise / 1983 / Epic +++
Charly McCalin is a pleasant-sounding female vocalist who came
to fame by opening for such artists as Mickey Gilley and George
Jones. In fact, Gilley even duets with Charly on the track "Paradise
Tonight." While it doesn't break any new ground, *Paradise* is a
strong collection of easy-listening honky tonk for the discerning
country fan. *—James Chrispell*

● **Biggest Hits** / 1985 / Epic ++++
Covering the ground since 1982's *Greatest Hits*, *Biggest Hits* does
indeed contain Charly McClain's most popular songs. From the
number one "Paradise Tonight" to her biggest hit, "Radio Heart,"
the collection is not only a good representation of her mid-'80s
peak, it's an excellent introduction to her music. *— Thom Owens*

Delbert McClinton

b. Nov. 4, 1940, Lubbock, TX
*Harmonica, Vocals / Modern Electric Blues, Blues-Rock, Country-
Rock*
A Texas music institution, McClinton honed his musical chops to
razor sharpness as a teenage harmonica man learning firsthand
from blues legends traveling through the area. His harp work on
Bruce Channel's hit, "Hey Baby," got him on the big-time circuit,
making it over to tour England and eventually giving harmonica
lessons to a young John Lennon. Much behind the scenes work
throughout the '60s ensued, with McClinton fronting the Rondells,
who hit the Hot 100 with "If You Really Want Me To, I'll Go." He
hit the charts again in the '70s with Glen Clark as Delbert & Glen.
Around this period, McClinton's songs started getting covered by
country acts, Waylon Jennings and Emmylou Harris both having
hits with his material. The Blues Brothers used his "B-Movie Box
Car Blues" on their first album and their hit movie. McClinton
has released idiosyncratic solo efforts and guested on albums
with everyone from Roy Buchanan to Bonnie Raitt. *—Cub Koda*

Delbert & Glen / 1972 / Clean +++
Subject to Change / 1973 / Clean +++

Victim of Life's Circumstances / 1975 / ABC +++
This album contains a few strong originals and successfully cap-
tures McClinton's aggressive blend of country and R&B. *—Rick
Clark*

Love Rustler / 1977 / ABC +++

Second Wind / 1978 / Mercury ++++
McClinton lays on the grease with two great originals, "'B' Movie"
and "Maybe Someday Baby" (featuring a wailing support vocal by
Clydie King). Also included is a decent collection of covers
("Spoonful" and "Big River"). *—Rick Clark*

Keeper of the Flame / 1979 / Mercury +++

The Jealous Kind / 1980 / Capitol +++

Plain from the Heart / 1981 / Capitol +++

● **The Best of Delbert McClinton** / 1989 / Curb ++++
It's only 11 tracks, but *The Best of Delbert McClinton* contains
nearly everything you need to know about how the eclectic blues/
country/soul performer sounds, even if it doesn't have every good
song he recorded. Nevertheless, it has the best moments from his
early '70s records—including "Two More Bottles of Wine" and "Let
Love Come Between Us"—and is a terrific introduction to his
work. *— Thom Owens*

Honky Tonkin' [Alligator] / 1989 / Alligator +++

Live from Austin / 1989 / Alligator ++++
This rock-solid, gritty roadhouse R&B is performed with a no-nonsense spirit. *—Rick Clark*

I'm with You / 1990 / Curb +++

Never Been Rocked Enough / 1992 / Curb +++
One of those influential "musician's musician" types, vocalist/
harp-player Delbert McClinton was able to call on the likes of
Bonnie Raitt, Tom Petty, and Melissa Etheridge for support on
Never Been Rocked Enough. The results cover the whole checker-
board while remaining vintage McClinton: his harp wails on
"Everytime I Roll the Dice"; "Can I Change My Mind" flirts with
Motown soul; "Blues as Blues Can Get" defines the confessional
blues ballad; "I Used to Worry" and the title track chug into Band/
Little Feat territory. The disc also includes the performer's
Grammy-winning duet with Bonnie Raitt, "Good Man, Good
Woman." *—Roch Parisien*

Delbert McClinton / Jul. 13, 1993 / Curb ++++

● **Classics, Vol. 1: The Jealous Kind** / Apr. 5, 1994 / Curb ++++

Great Songs: Come Together / 1995 / Curb ++

Classics, Vol. 2: Plain from the Heart / Curb ++++

Honky Tonk 'n Blues / MCA +++

The McCoury Brothers

Traditional Bluegrass, Close Harmony
Del and Jerry McCoury pursued individual careers in bluegrass
before the Pennsylvania-born siblings teamed up for the 1987
Rounder album *The McCoury Brothers*. Older brother Del had
played banjo before switching to guitar and singing lead with Bill
Monroe's Blue Grass Boys in 1963-1964. He subsequently led his
Dixie Pals and recorded for both Rounder and Rebel. Jerry sang
and played bass with Red Allen and the Kentuckians, as well as
with Don Reno and Bill Harrell. The McCoury Brothers' sole
album together to date is a wonderful close-harmony exposition
of bluegrass, rooted in the "brother duo" tradition. *—Mark A.
Humphrey*

The McCoury Brothers / 1995 / Rounder ++++
Jerry and Del McCoury fit together like hand-in-glove on these
fine performances. *—Mark A. Humphrey*

Del McCoury

b. Feb. 1, 1930, Bakersville, NC
Guitar, Vocals / Traditional Bluegrass
The voice of Del McCourty, among the most distinguished practi-
tioners of traditional bluegrass, was for more than three decades
the epitome of the "high lonesome sound." Born Delano Floyd
McCoury, he was raised in Bakersville, NC. In 1941 he and his

family moved to Glen Rock, PA, where he got his start as a five-string banjo picker with Keith Daniels and the Blue Ridge Ramblers. Later he played with Jack Cooke's Virginia Mountain Boys in Baltimore. McCoury got his first big break in 1963, when Bill Monroe hired the Virginia Mountain Boys to play a few New York gigs. Monroe was impressed by the young banjo player and invited him to join his Blue Grass Boys. Shortly after accepting Monroe's offer, McCoury became the group's lead vocalist and took up rhythm guitar. In early 1964 he recorded one single with Monroe, but a month later returned home to marry.

After his marriage, he and fiddler Billy Baker spent three months in California, playing with the Golden State Boys. Upon his return back East, McCoury began playing and recording with the Shady Valley Boys. He left the group in 1967 and founded the Dixie Pals with Bill Emerson, Wayne Yates, and Billy Baker. McCoury and his Dixie Pals, which underwent several membership changes, played together for more than 20 years and recorded on such labels as Rounder, Revonah, Leather, and Rebel. In 1987 the unit was renamed the Del McCoury Band, after the additions of his sons Ronnie on mandolin and Robbie on banjo, along with fiddler Tad Marks and bass player Mike Brantley. —*Sandra Brennan*

I Wonder Where You Are Tonight / 1968 / Arhoolie ♦♦

McCoury's first album (the CD reissue includes a number of previously unreleased cuts). A favorite of purists, McCoury still hadn't developed the vocal style that would make him great in the '90s. —*Brian Mansfield*

Del McCoury Sings Bluegrass / 1968 / Arhoolie ♦♦♦

Livin' on the Mountain / 1971 / Rebel ♦♦♦

Recorded in 1971 with a band that doesn't meet McCoury's usual standards, it wasn't released for five years. —*Brian Mansfield*

Collector's Special / 1971 / Grassound ♦♦

High on a Mountain / 1972 / Rounder ♦♦♦

More grand bluegrass. —*Mark A. Humphrey*

Del McCoury and the Dixie Pals / 1975 / Revonah ♦♦♦

Live in Japan / 1980 / Copper Creek ♦♦♦

A live concert with excellent performances and strong material, the recording nevertheless leaves something to be desired. —*Brian Mansfield*

Don't Stop the Music / 1988 / Rounder ♦♦♦♦

Don't Stop the Music is a typically entertaining and surprisingly bluesy release from the Del McCoury Band, featuring a selection of originals and covers, including a version of the George Jones title track. —*Thom Owens*

★ **Classic Bluegrass** / 1991 / Rebel ♦♦♦♦♦

Rebel label recordings from the '70s by the man who sometimes sounds more like Bill Monroe than Monroe himself. Stunning, pure, high-lonesome pipes and mountain bluesy songs. Beautiful. —*Mark A. Humphrey*

Blue Side of Town / May 15, 1992 / Rounder ♦♦♦♦

Named for his version of the Patty Loveless hit "The Blue Side of Town," McCoury covers Steve Earle's "If You Need a Fool" and Arthur "Big Boy" Crudup's "That's Alright Mama." When it comes to song choice, he may be the most well-rounded man in bluegrass. —*Brian Mansfield*

☆ **Deeper Shade of Blue** / 1993 / Rounder ♦♦♦♦♦

A classic from the word go, McCoury's love affair with blues is never more explicit than here, where songs with the titles like "Cheek to Cheek with the Blues," "A Deeper Shade of Blue," and "The Bluest Man in Town" are the order of the day. Never a purist when it comes to songs, McCoury covers Kevin Welch's "True Love Never Dies," Willie Nelson's "Man with the Blues," and the Jerry Lee Lewis hit "What Made Milwaukee Famous." His version of Lefty Frizzell's "If You've Got the Money Honey" is downright piercing. —*Brian Mansfield*

Cold Hard Facts / Sep. 17, 1996 / Rounder ♦♦♦

Charlie McCoy

b. Mar. 28, 1941, West Virginia
Guitar, Mandolin, Vocals / Traditional Country, Country-Rock, Country-Pop, Nashville Sound/Countrypolitan

Charlie McCoy was perhaps the definitive Nashville session musician, a multi-talented performer best known for his harmonica playing. His mastery of the instrument virtually defined its role in the context of modern country music. Though born in West Virginia on March 28, 1941, Charles Ray McCoy was raised in Miami, FL, where he first picked up the harmonica at the age of eight. By his mid-teens, he was playing harmonica and guitar in an area rock 'n' roll band, and a few years later graduated to traveling the Florida rock and country circuits as a backup performer. At one local gig, he met Mel Tillis, who instructed McCoy to move to Nashville, which he did in 1959. After finding little work as a session player, he journeyed back to Florida, where he began studying music theory and taking vocal lessons in addition to working as an arranger and conductor.

In 1960 McCoy auditioned as a guitarist for singer Johnny Ferguson, only to learn that the opening had been filled. Ferguson was still looking for a drummer, however, so McCoy bought a kit, learned to play, and won the job. After contacting Tillis, he was introduced to agent Jim Denny, who helped the upstart musician find some work in Nashville. McCoy's first session was Roy Orbison's 1961 "Candy Man," and within months he was one of the most sought-after players on the scene. He also toured extensively as a drummer in Stonewall Jackson's band throughout the early 1960s, and released a handful of solo singles.

By the mid-1960s McCoy was a fixture on Elvis Presley's Nashville and Los Angeles sessions, and in 1965 he began working with Bob Dylan, appearing on a string of legendary LPs that included *Highway 61 Revisited, Blonde on Blonde, John Wesley Harding,* and *Nashville Skyline.* As a result, McCoy became as much in demand among rock and folk artists as he was within the Nashville community, and he began performing with the likes of Ringo Starr, Al Kooper, Gordon Lightfoot, and John Stewart. At his peak, he was performing on more than 400 sessions annually.

In 1969 McCoy joined the country-rock band Area Code 615, with whom he recorded a self-titled LP, followed by *A Trip in the Country* in 1970. Also in 1969, he released a solo effort, *The Real McCoy;* while the album garnered little notice at the time of its release; in 1971 a Florida deejay began playing the track "I Started Loving Her Again" to massive listener response. A single was soon available, and the song reached the Top 20 in 1972. Even as his solo career began taking off, McCoy remained a constant in Nashville studios, and in the early 1970s alone he worked with Paul Simon, Joan Baez, Kris Kristofferson, Leon Russell, and Steve Young.

When the remnants of Area Code 615 reformed as Barefoot Jerry, McCoy signed on, and with the group issued three albums—1975's *You Can't Get Off With Your Shoes On,* the following year's *Keys to the Country,* and 1977's *Barefootin'.* At the same time, he played on records for Waylon Jennings, Tanya Tucker, and Wanda Jackson and began a tenure as the musical director for the country comedy program *Hee Haw,* where he remained for many years. In 1978 he played England's Wembley Festival with Lloyd Green, and his popularity across the Atlantic soared. In the 1980s he toured Europe frequently and began recording extensively there, as well. By the early 1990s McCoy had cut back considerably on his studio work, although he continued to play with many prestigious artists. In 1996 he led a number of Nashville studio luminaries like the Jordanaires, Russ Hicks, Hargus "Pig" Robbins, and Bobby Ogdin during the sessions for the cult duo Ween's *12 Golden Country Greats* —*Jason Ankeny*

The World of Charlie McCoy / 1968 / Monument ♦♦♦

Real McCoy / 1969 / Monument ♦♦♦

Fastest Harp in the South / 1973 / Monument ♦♦♦♦

Harpin' the Blues / 1975 / Monument ✦✦✦✦
One of McCoy's strongest solo efforts, *Harpin' the Blues* is an homage to his hero, Chicago blues master Little Walter. —*Jason Ankeny*

● **Greatest Hits** / Monument ✦✦✦✦

Charlie McCoy's Thirteenth / 1988 / Step One ✦✦✦✦
McCoy focuses on country standards for album number 13, including Hank Williams' "I'm So Lonesome I Could Cry" and Merle Haggard and Buck Owens' "I Started Loving You Again." He also makes an excursion into jazz to take on Count Basie's "One O'Clock Jump." —*Jason Ankeny*

Beam Me Up Charlie / 1989 / Step One ✦✦✦
McCoy recut a pair of old Area Code 615 numbers, "Southern Comfort" and "Katy Hill," for this release recorded in Denmark. He also covers Hank Williams' "Cold, Cold Heart" and fellow session ace Russ Hicks' "Funky Country Music." —*Jason Ankeny*

Out on a Limb / Dec. 1991 / Step One ✦✦✦
For *Out on a Limb*, McCoy enlisted the diverse talents of the well-regarded European touring unit the United, the Jordanaires, and Nashville session kings like Bobby Ogdin, Russ Hicks and Pig Robbins to tackle chestnuts like "You Don't Know Me" and Leon Payne's "You've Still Got a Place in My Heart." —*Jason Ankeny*

Neal McCoy

b. Jul. 30, 1963, Jacksonville, TX
Vocals / Contemporary Country
Neal McCoy had a string of hit singles in the early '90s with his brand of revivalist honky tonk. McCoy was born and raised in Jacksonville, TX,to Irish-Filipino parents who enjoyed a wide assortment of music. After graduating from high school, he began playing the Texas honky-tonk circuit and won a nightclub talent contest, where he was seen by Janie Fricke, who later arranged for McCoy to replace her as Charlie Pride's opening act when she left to pursue a full-fledged solo career in the early '80s. McCoy remained with Pride for seven years before releasing his 1988 debut single, the minor hit "That's How Much I Love You," as "Neal McCoy." In 1991 he released his debut album, *At This Moment;* it produced two Top 50 singles—"If I Built a Fire" and "This Time I Hurt Her More (Than She Loves Me)." McCoy released his second album, *Where Forever Begins*, in 1992, but he didn't have a genuine hit until 1994's *No Doubt About It*, which produced the number one singles "No Doubt About It" and "Wink." His success continued with 1995's *You Gotta Love That!*, which went platinum within a year of its release, and 1996's eponymous album. —*Sandra Brennan*

At This Moment / 1990 / Atlantic ✦✦✦
This debut's most notable song is its title track, a country version of the Billy Vera prom-night pop hit. —*Brian Mansfield*

Where Forever Begins / 1992 / Atlantic ✦✦✦
It includes the singles "Where Forever Begins," "There Ain't Nothin' I Don't Like About You," and "Now I Pray for Rain." —*Brian Mansfield*

● **No Doubt About It** / 1994 / Atlantic ✦✦✦✦
This Barry Beckett-produced disc was the first to capture the rock-influenced sound of McCoy's stage show (which usually included a rap version of *the Beverly Hillbillies* theme). Though McCoy had never had a single chart above No.21, the album gave the singer his first two No. 1 hits: "No Doubt About It" and "Wink." —*Brian Mansfield*

You Gotta Love That / 1995 / Atlantic ✦✦✦✦

Neal McCoy / Jun. 1996 / Atlantic ✦✦✦
Neal McCoy's eponymous album is another set of immaculately crafted contemporary country music. From McCoy's polished but heartfelt performance to the slick, seamless selection of songs, there isn't an obvious flaw on the album. Some may complain that McCoy's approach is getting a bit too pat and predictable, but the highlights—including the longtime stage favorite "Hillbilly Rap," which features segments of "Day-O," "The Ballad of Jed Clampett," and "Rapper's Delight"—are well worth the time of any fun. —*Thom Owens*

Mindy McCready

Vocals / Contemporary Country
Mindy McCready's debut album *Ten Thousand Angels* elevated her into Nashville's music spotlight and established her as a promising singer.

Born and raised in southern Florida, Mindy McCready (b. Malinda Gayle McCready) graduated from high school at the age of 16 with the intention of beginning her musical career early. She took a part-time job in her mother's ambulance company and began concentrating on performing her music. When she was 18 years old, she moved to Nashville. She had promised her mother that she would go to college if she failed to break into the music industry within a year. After a few months in Nashville she met producer/songwriter Norro Wilson, who directed her demo tapes to producer David Malloy. Impressed with her tapes, Malloy agreed to work with McCready. For the next year McCready and Malloy refined the singer's style and crafted a high-class demo tape. Eventually, Malloy took the tape to RLG Records, who signed McCready after seeing her perform a live concert; she completed the deal exactly 51 weeks after she moved to Nashville.

McCready released her debut album, *Ten Thousand Angels*, in April 1996 to positive reviews. Within six months of its release, it had gone gold. —*Stephen Thomas Erlewine*

● **Ten Thousand Angels** / Apr. 1996 / BNA ✦✦✦✦

Mel McDaniel

b. Sep. 6, 1942, Checotah, OK
Guitar, Trumpet, Vocals / Country-Pop, Urban Cowboy
McDaniel collects tools for a hobby and collects hits for a living. Born in Checotah, OK, he decided at age 14, inspired by seeing Elvis Presley on TV, that he had to pursue music. After establishing himself on the Tulsa club circuit, he moved briefly to Nashville, then headed off to Anchorage, AK, where he refined his stage skills. When he returned to Music City, he signed his first recording deal in 1976 with Capitol Records, but it took five years for him to first hit the Top Ten. He had sporadic success thereafter, but his signature song, "Baby's Got Her Blue Jeans On," invited a bevy of recognitions, including multiple nominations for Grammy and Country Music Association awards. —*Tom Roland*

● **Greatest Hits** / 1987 / Capitol ✦✦✦✦
He is gravelly voiced and has a limited range, but McDaniel gets the most out of his talents by concentrating on songs with the proper "groove." "Louisiana Saturday Night" and "Baby's Got Her Blue Jeans On" are staples; "Stand Up" and "Big Ole Brew" are pretty damn good. —*Tom Roland*

Skeets McDonald

b. Oct. 1, 1915, Greenway, AR, **d.** Mar. 31, 1968
Vocals / Traditional Country, Honky Tonk
Best known for his self-penned chart-topper "Don't Let the Stars Get in Your Eyes," Skeets McDonald was a honky tonk singer and songwriter whose work helped serve to bridge the gap between country and rock 'n' roll. The youngest of seven children, Enos William McDonald was born October 1, 1915, in Greenway, AR, and earned his nickname after an incident involving a swarm of mosquitoes. He became interested in music at a young age, and according to McDonald family legend, even traded his hound dog for a guitar and six dollars. When his older brother moved to Michigan several years later, McDonald followed, and joined his first band, the Lonesome Cowboys, in Detroit in 1935. He continued to perform on local radio stations until he was drafted in 1943 to serve in World War II.

After returning from battle, McDonald began performing on a Detroit-area television program, and in 1950 he cut his first records with fiddler Johnnie White and His Rough Riders. In 1951 Skeets and his family moved to Los Angeles, where he was signed to perform on Cliffie Stone's TV program "Hometown Jamboree." Soon after, McDonald joined Capitol Records, and in 1952 he released "Don't Let the Stars Get in Your Eyes," which was by far his biggest hit. McDonald remained with the label until 1959, the year he released the LP *The Country's Best*, and while he scored few chart successes, his music's evolution from honky tonk to straightforward rockabilly proved to be influential with other musicians.

In 1959 McDonald signed with Columbia, which mandated that he return to country music. In the early '60s he notched a handful of hits, including "Call Me Mr. Brown," which reached the Top Ten in 1963. A year later he issued the album *Call Me Skeets!* As the decade wore on, he began branching out from the West Coast music scene, recording in Nashville and appearing on the Grand Ole Opry. Despite the country industry's shift towards slicker, more pop-oriented productions, McDonald remained a purist throughout his career; he died March 31, 1968, after suffering a massive heart attack. —*Jason Ankeny*

Goin' Steady with the Blues / 1958 / Capitol ♦♦

● **Skeets McDonald's Tattooed . . .** / 1959 / Fortune ♦♦♦♦
McDonald checks in here with the risque title track and "Birthday Cake Boogie," while the rest of the album features equally naughty fare by the York Brothers, Tommy Odim, Johnny Bucket, Roy Hall, and Rufus Shoffner. Great fun all. —*Cub Koda*

The Country's Best / 1959 / Capitol ♦♦♦♦

Call Me Skeets! / 1964 / Columbia ♦♦♦

Skeets / 1966 / Sears ♦♦♦♦

Ronnie McDowell

b. Mar. 26, 1950, Fountain Head, TN
Guitar, Vocals / Country-Pop, Urban Cowboy
Raised in rural Portland, TN, north of Nashville, McDowell didn't take performing seriously until he was stationed in the Philippines with the navy. The first song he performed in public: "It's Now or Never," appropriate since Elvis Presley has had a huge impact on his career. McDowell wrote his first hit, "The King Is Gone," the day that Elvis died. Enough people shared his grief that a reported three million copies were sold. McDowell did all the Elvis vocal imitations for a 1979 Elvis TV movie starring Kurt Russell, and he began to take on the image of an Elvis imitator. McDowell consciously distanced himself from those comparisons, which became easier when record producer Buddy Killen took over the reins of his career, bringing in solid uptempo material that consistently showcased McDowell's strong (though a bit nondescript) vocal talents. Now comfortable with his reputation, he's returned on occasion to more "Elvis" work, providing the vocal parts for the short-lived ABC series *Elvis* in 1990. —*Tom Roland*

Country Boy's Heart / 1983 / Epic ♦♦♦

Personally / 1983 / Epic ♦♦♦

In a New York Minute / 1985 / Epic ♦♦♦

● **Older Women and Other Greatest Hits** / 1987 / Epic ♦♦♦♦
McDowell fell into this "clone" thing for a couple of years where he remade his own hits; and all three soundalikes ("Older Women," "Wandering Eyes," "Watchin' Girls Go By") are curiously placed back-to-back. His later material is the most emotive, especially "I Dream of Women like You," "In a New York Minute," and "Love Talks," recorded with Exile. —*Tom Roland*

American Music / 1989 / Curb ♦♦♦♦
On *American Music*, McDowell is backed by musicians Doug Phelps and Greg Martin, who went on to form the Kentucky Headhunters. —*Jason Ankeny*

The Best of / 1990 / Curb ♦♦♦♦
Along with "The King Is Gone," the song which forever established McDowell's remarkable vocal similarities to Elvis Presley, this hits collection includes "I Love You, I Love You, I Love You," "All Tied Up" and "It's Only Make Believe." It does not, however, feature either of his chart-topping hits, "Older Women" and "You're Gonna Ruin My Bad Reputation." —*Jason Ankeny*

Your Precious Love / 1991 / Curb ♦♦♦
On *Your Precious Love*, McDowell covers a number of soul classics, including "Lover's Question" and, of course, "For Your Precious Love." —*Jason Ankeny*

Unchained Melody / 1991 / Curb ♦♦♦
Duets with Jerry Lee Lewis, Wayne Newton, Jack Scott, and Bobby Vinton highlight *Unchained Melody.* —*Jason Ankeny*

Reba McEntire

b. Mar. 28, 1954, Chockie, OK
Guitar, Vocals / Contemporary Country, Neo-Traditionalist Country
Reba McEntire was one of the most successful new country vocalists to emerge in the early '80s. The only problem was, she began her recording career in the mid-'70s. It may have taken her several years to reach the top of the country charts, but once she got there she stayed there. McEntire was the single most successful female country vocalist of the '80s and '90s, scoring a consistent stream of Top Ten singles and a grand total of 18 No. 1 singles.

McEntire is the daughter of Clark McEntire, a professional rodeo rider. As a child, Reba was a rodeo rider, as were her sisters Alice and Susie and her brother Pake. While their father taught them how to ride, their mother Jackie taught them music. As young adults, the four siblings formed a vocal group that landed a local hit in 1971 with "The Ballad of John McEntire," a song dedicated to their grandfather.

The McEntire children intended to become a professional singing group, but those plans were thrown for a loop when Reba sang the national anthem at the National Rodeo Finals in Oklahoma City in 1974. Red Steagall had heard her sing the anthem and immediately suggested that she go to Nashville and record a demo. McEntire was initially hesitant to pursue a solo career, but the family eventually decided it was better for her to take the chance while it was there.

With some help from Steagall, McEntire signed with Mercury Records in 1975, releasing her first record that same year. Initially, she was a traditional hard country singer at a time when the radio wasn't receptive to that sound—her first singles didn't come close to cracking the Top 40. Around the time of the release of her first album, she married Charlie Battles, a professional steer wrestler and bulldogger, and completed her teaching degree, in case her musical career floundered.

In 1978 McEntire began to make some headway on the charts, as the double A-sided "Three Sheets in the Wind" / "I'd Really Love to See You Tonight" reached No. 20. However, she didn't have any significant hits until the summer of 1980, when "(You Lift Me) Up to Heaven" made it to No. 8. By this time, she had begun to cut more ballad-oriented material, and the slight shift in musical direction paid off. McEntire stayed with Mercury Records for three more years. In that time her audience dramatically expanded—at the end of 1982, she had her first No. 1 single, "Can't Even Get the Blues."

Reba McEntire switched labels in 1984, abandoning Mercury for MCA Records. At MCA she established herself as one of the decade's most popular artists, selling more than 20 million albums and winning four Female Vocalist of the Year awards from the Country Music Association. Between 1985 and 1992 she had 24 straight Top Ten hits, including 14 No. 1 singles. McEntire began toying with rock and pop influences, both in her music and in her image.

She divorced Charlie Battles in 1987. Two years after the divorce she married Narvel Blackstock, her road manager and steel guitarist; the pair assumed complete control of all aspects of her career, from recording to merchandising and marketing. In the '90s Reba stayed as popular as she was in the previous decade, as both her albums and her singles consistently charted in the Top Ten, frequently at No. 1. McEntire also begun an acting career in the early '90s, appearing in TV movies and feature films, most notably the cult horror film *Tremors.* —*Stephen Thomas Erlewine*

Heart to Heart / 1981 / Mercury ♦♦

Behind the Scene / 1983 / Mercury ♦♦♦

The Best of Reba McEntire / 1985 / Mercury ♦♦♦♦
The Best of Reba McEntire contains 10 of her biggest hits from the early '80s, which were all recorded for Mercury Records. These hit singles—including "(You Lift Me) Up to Heaven," "Today

All Over Again," "I'm Not That Lonely Yet," "Can't Even Get the Blues," "You're the First Time I've Thought About Leaving," and "Why Do We Want (What We Know We Can't Have)"—represent the first songs where McEntire truly found a voice of her own. Occasionally Jerry Buckler's productions are a little too sanitary, but McEntire overcomes any overly-commercial flourishes with her gritty, gutsy vocals, and the best of these songs are as good as her finest moments for MCA. *—Thom Owens*

My Kind of Country / 1986 / MCA ✦✦✦✦
McEntire's celebration of the back-to-basics movement in country has many country shuffles. These are her purest country performances and most straightforward production. *—Mark A. Humphrey*

Whoever's in New England / 1986 / MCA ✦✦✦✦
This is the album that elevated McEntire from pretty good country singer to megastar. A number of the melodies have pop sensibilities, but the production is decidedly country. *—Tom Roland*

What Am I Gonna Do About You / 1986 / MCA ✦✦✦✦
The chart-topping title cut highlights *What Am I Gonna Do About You*, which also features the No. 1 hit "One Promise Too Late." *—Jason Ankeny*

The Last One to Know / 1987 / MCA ✦✦✦
Recorded as McEntire went through the process of divorce from first husband Charlie Battles, it's understandably heavy on songs about breakups and the uncertainty of the future. "The Stairs"—about domestic violence—is particularly moving. Despite her personal pain, she still holds out hope in "Love Will Find Its Way to You." *—Tom Roland*

★ **Greatest Hits** / 1987 / MCA ✦✦✦✦✦
Reba McEntire's first collection of hits on MCA Records draws entirely from the beginning of her string of Top Ten hits in the mid-'80s. *Greatest Hits* covers her singles from 1984, 1985, and 1986 and features nearly every Top Ten hit she had, including the No. 1 hits "How Blue," "Somebody Should Leave," "Whoever's in New England," "Little Rock," "What Am I Gonna Do About You," and "One Promise Too Late." *—Stephen Thomas Erlewine*

Reba / Apr. 18, 1988 / MCA ✦✦✦
This contains the hits "I Know How He Feels," "Sunday Kind of Love," and others. *—AMG*

Sweet Sixteen / 1989 / MCA ✦✦✦
It features "Somebody up There Likes Me," "Cathy's Clown," and "Walk On," among other hits. *—AMG*

Reba Live / 1989 / MCA ✦✦✦
Live is a predictable but enjoyable live set featuring 19 of Reba McEntire's biggest hits and best-known songs, plus a selection of covers ("Mama Tried," "San Antonio Rose," "Night Life," "Sweet Dreams," "Respect"). For fans, it's a fun but ultimately unnecessary set, since it offers no revelations and very little kinetic energy. *—Thom Owens*

Rumor Has It / 1990 / MCA ✦✦✦
It features "Fallin' Out of Love," "You Lie," "Climb that Mountain High," and other hits. *—AMG*

☆ **For My Broken Heart** / 1991 / MCA ✦✦✦✦✦
Only the quietly moving "If I Had Only Known" might be considered a tribute to the members of McEntire's band who died in a 1990 plane crash, but the tragedy creeps into McEntire's voice and her song selection. Throughout the album, McEntire dwells on regrets, unvoiced feelings, and missed chances. The best songs aren't the hits "For My Broken Heart" and "Is There Life Out There" but a group of evocative story-songs which unfold slowly, leaving loose threads and developing complex emotional undercurrents. *For My Broken Heart* may be the strongest album of McEntire's career; it's certainly her most heartbreaking. *—Brian Mansfield*

It's Your Call / 1992 / MCA ✦✦✦
McEntire possesses one of the most undeniably emotional voices in country music—one well chosen phrase in her Oklahoma accent can start hearts breaking. The overwhelming number of ballads on *It's Your Call* take maximum advantage of that talent, especially on "Straight from You" and "The Heart Won't Lie," a duet with label mate Vince Gill. While *It's Your Call* may have the

Reba McEntire

same intensity of emotion as the double-platinum *For My Broken Heart*, it lacks similar depth—taken as a whole, these songs make McEntire sound like a victim, a role she no longer plays well. The ballads leave few places for McEntire's strength of character, and the bluesy "Take It Back" and "Go Down Easy" serve only as breaks in the despair. McEntire showed her best on *For My Broken Heart;* while she's not holding back here, only casual or partial listeners will be moved as much. *—Brian Mansfield*

Forever in Your Eyes / Apr. 15, 1993 / Spm ✦✦

☆ **Greatest Hits, Vol. 2** / Oct. 1993 / MCA ✦✦✦✦✦
Greatest Hits, Vol. 2 collects Reba McEntire's biggest hits of the late '80s, including the No. 1 singles "You Lie," "For My Broken Heart," and her biggest hit, "Is There Life Out There," and seven other songs. *—Stephen Thomas Erlewine*

Read My Mind / Apr. 26, 1994 / MCA ✦✦✦

Starting Over / Oct. 3, 1995 / MCA ✦✦✦
Starting Over isn't quite a rebirth for Reba McEntire; rather, it's a tribute to her formative influences. Consisting of nothing but covers of a selection of her favorite songs from the '50s, '60s, and '70s, the album is an engaging listen. Some of the tracks demonstrate her roots, while others are nothing more than entertainment. McEntire doesn't reimagine these songs, but she delivers strong, confident performances that make them sound fresh. *—Stephen Thomas Erlewine*

What If It's You / Nov. 5, 1996 / MCA ✦✦✦
What If It's You doesn't offer any new tricks from Reba McEntire, but it is nevertheless an excellent reminder of her deep talents as a vocalist. The album is slightly uneven, but at its best—such as on the singles "The Fear of Being Alone," "She's Calling it Love" and "I'd Rather Ride Around with You"—it is as good as anything McEntire has ever done. *—Thom Owens*

John McEuen

b. Dec. 19, 1945, Garden Grove, CA
Guitar, Violin, Vocals / Progressive Bluegrass, Progressive Country
Best known for his long tenure as a key member of the venerable Nitty Gritty Dirt Band, John "the String Wizard" McEuen was one of the most influential figures in contemporary American country, bluegrass and even pop music. Credited with introducing both the banjo and the mandolin to pop, he was a master string player who developed a devoted fan base on the festival circuit. Born and raised in Garden Grove, CA, McEuen began learning to play the banjo when he was 18. At that time he was attending college and

earning extra money by working at nearby Disneyland; comedian Steve Martin was a co-worker, and McEuen taught him how to play banjo. (Much later Martin and the NGBD would frequently appear together in concert.) McEuen decided to become a professional musician in 1964 after seeing the Dillards perform live; inspired by their energy and musicianship, he began to study the banjo in earnest. In 1965 he hooked up with Michael Martin Murphey for a year and subsequently performed on all five of Murphey's albums.

In 1966, he was visiting a guitar shop in Long Beach when he met the Illegitimate Jug Band, who had just lost member Jackson Browne and were deciding to regroup. McEuen joined and the group became the Nitty Gritty Dirt Band. He remained with them for more than two decades, singing and playing banjo, mandolin, fiddle, and other stringed instruments through the watershed period that produced such classic albums as *Uncle Charlie and His Dog Teddy* (1970) and the landmark compilation *Will the Circle Be Unbroken* (1972). McEuen was also there during the band's subsequent dry spells, as they struggled to reshape their style before again finding success in the mid-'80s. For reasons that remain unclear, McEuen abruptly left the Dirt Band in 1987.

During his years with the group, McEuen had played solos at every show and occasionally appeared as a solo act. He also made guest appearances on other albums and did session work for such artists as Bill Wyman, Marshall Tucker, and Hoyt Axton. McEuen also composed music for film and television soundtracks, including the scores for *Paint Your Wagon* (1969) and *Samuel Beckett Is Coming Soon* (1993). In 1989 he briefly rejoined the Dirt Band to perform on their *Will the Circle Be Unbroken II* album. The next year he directed a concert video and produced an album for the Dillards. In 1992 he released the album *String Wizards*, an all-star venture featuring such illustrious artists as Earl Scruggs, Vassar Clements, and Byron Berline. A follow-up, *String Wizards II*, appeared in 1994, at about the same time McEuen founded his own label—named, appropriately enough, String Wizard. *Acoustic Traveller* was released in 1996. —*Sandra Brennan*

John McEuen / Apr. 1985 / Warner Brothers ✦✦✦✦
String Wizards / 1991 / Vanguard ✦✦✦
String Wizards 2 / Sep. 1993 / Vanguard ✦✦✦
● **Acoustic Traveller** / 1996 / Vanguard ✦✦✦✦
John McEuen plays a variety of stringed instruments, including mandolin, guitar, banjo, dulcimer, lap steel guitar, and even a Japanese koto on this accomplished album of folk-, country-, bluegrass-, and Western-flavored traditional-sounding original instrumentals, with one vocal track, "I Am a Pilgrim." There are many familiar sounds from McEuen's long career, including "Mr. Bojangles (suite)." —*William Ruhlmann*

Sam McGee

b. 1894, Franklin, TN, **d.** Aug. 21, 1975
Guitar / Old-Time

Flat-top guitar picker Sam McGee and his fiddling brother Kirk were among the earliest fraternal duets in country music, and were also extraordinary sidemen for such legendary performers as Uncle Dave Macon and Fiddling Arthur Smith. The McGee brothers were born just south of Nashville in Williamson County, TN, and were influenced by their old-time fiddle-playing father and other members of their family. Sam got his professional start playing at a square dance in the early 1900s. He began as a banjo player, as guitars were very rare in Tennessee during that era, but became intrigued with the instrument and the blues songs sung by black railroad laborers congregating outside his father's store. Meanwhile, Kirk followed his father and learned to play the fiddle while also practicing his singing. He enjoyed more traditional, sentimental songs, while Sam was drawn to comic material. Kirk also found the blues interesting and learned songs from the records of such performers as Papa Charlie Jackson and Kokomo Arnold.

In 1925 Sam began a longtime affiliation with Uncle Dave Macon, who would become his mentor and occasional rival. It was with Macon that Sam made his recording debut on guitar instrumentals like "Buck Dancer's Choice" and "Knoxville Blues." Two years later, Kirk also joined Macon's band, the Fruit Jar Drinkers, and recorded with them in New York. Around this time,

the brothers also began recording their own songs; in 1928, Kirk and his cousin Blythe Poteet cut a few singles for Gennett, including the popular "Kicking Mule," and performed on the Grand Ole Opry with Macon. In 1931 the brothers began working with fiddler Arthur Smith as the Dixieliners, becoming one of the most popular string bands during the 1930s. Although they played during most of Smith's live performances, the McGees never recorded with him.

The brothers abandoned country music during the 1940s for a time. Later Kirk began his decade-long intermittent association with Bill Monroe. By 1955 the McGees were in danger of losing their tenure at the Opry and were told to resume touring. The next year they staged a comeback, entertaining a new generation of folk music lovers. The brothers reunited with Smith in 1957 and recorded two albums for Folkways, also playing Northern folk festivals. The McGees began to specialize in old-time music during the 1960s. They recorded together and separately on a variety of independent labels before forming their own record company, MBA, in the early 1970s. They played their final engagement at the old Ryman Auditorium, the original home of the Opry, in 1974; by that time they were the senior members of the show and were honored by being the first act to play at the new Opry house. One year later, Sam was killed in a farming accident. Kirk kept on playing alone and with the Fruit Jar Drinkers. —*Sandra Brennan*

Sam & Kirk McGee & The Crook Brothers / 1962 / Starday ✦✦✦
● **Grand Dad of the Country Guitar Pickers** / 1963 / Arhoolie ✦✦✦✦

Tim McGraw

b. May 1, 1967, Delhi, LA
Vocals / Contemporary Country

Tim McGraw was best-known for his hit single, "Indian Outlaw," a controversial single that made him a star in the mid-'90s. The son of baseball player Tug McGraw, Tim was raised in Start, LA, where he listened to country, Motown, rock 'n' roll and R&B. Like his father, he was a natural athlete and attended college on sports scholarships. McGraw didn't become interested in performing music until he bought a pawn shop guitar while attending school. He moved to Nashville in 1989 and later played gigs in the Deep South. In 1992 he released his first single, "Welcome to the Club," which reached the country Top 50. In 1993 he released his eponymous debut, which produced two more minor hits. In 1994 McGraw released his second album, *Not a Moment Too Soon*, which contained "Indian Outlaw." The song reached No. 8 on the country charts and No. 15 on the pop charts amidst controversy over the Native American stereotypes presented in the lyrics. Nevertheless, *Not a Moment Too Soon* became a crossover hit—the album hit No. 2 on the pop charts and went triple-platinum within months of its release. "Don't Take the Girl," the follow-up single, was another crossover success, reaching No. 17 on the pop charts and No. 1 on the country charts. In 1995 McGraw released his third album, *All I Want*, which became another multi-platinum hit. —*Sandra Brennan*

Tim McGraw / 1993 / Capitol ✦✦✦
Three songs—"Welcome to the Club," "Memory Lane," and "Two Steppin' Mind"—appeared on the bottom half of the *Billboard* singles chart, which suggested McGraw had some talent but wasn't anything special. During a year that introduced Clay Walker and Doug Supernaw, hardly anybody noticed this young hat act. —*Brian Mansfield*

● **Not a Moment Too Soon** / Mar. 22, 1994 / Curb ✦✦✦✦
"Indian Outlaw," with its controversy and its resemblance to the Raiders' "Indian Reservation," made McGraw a star, and the ballad "Don't Take the Girl" reinforced the image. *Not a Moment Too Soon* contained better hooks than its predecessor, but it also belabored the obvious with songs like "It Don't Get Any Countrier than This" and "Give It to Me Straight." —*Brian Mansfield*

All I Want / Sep. 19, 1995 / Curb ✦✦✦

Tim McGraw's albums suffer from uneven material, but *All I Want* is a surprisingly consistent record that consolidates his strengths while expanding into new territory. He hasn't abandoned the honky tonk and jokey country-rock that made him famous, but he's made it harder and more believable. Similarly, his ballads are heartfelt, delivered with convincing sincerity. In other words, he has grown musically and developed into a thoroughly entertaining vocalist. And that growth is what makes *All I Want* his best record. It is still fairly uneven, with several weak songs, but McGraw now knows how to disguise the flaws in the material with his singing. —*Stephen Thomas Erlewine*

McGuinn, Clark & Hillman

Country Rock, Folk-Rock

The trio of Roger McGuinn, Gene Clark, and Chris Hillman first joined forces in the mid-1960s, when—along with David Crosby and Michael Clarke—they made up the first and most successful incarnation of the folk-rock avatars the Byrds. Despite a series of commercially and critically acclaimed recordings, beginning with 1965's landmark single "Mr. Tambourine Man," the group was plagued by internal conflict, and by the end of 1968 frontman McGuinn was the only founding Byrd still in the lineup, continuing to steer the band until its dissolution in 1973.

At the end of 1977, singer/guitarist McGuinn, vocalist Clark, and bassist Hillman reunited to record a self-titled LP far removed from the folk-rock and country sounds that had initially earned the three men their reputations. Produced by Ron and Howard Albert, 1979's *McGuinn, Clark and Hillman* was a product of its era, a slick, glossy album that earned the trio a Top 40 pop single, "Don't You Write Her Off." After a tour, the group reunited for the 1980 record *Home;* in the middle of recording, however, Clark exited, and so the album was released under the name Roger McGuinn and Chris Hillman Featuring Gene Clark. The remaining duo released one final record in 1981, *McGuinn/Hillman,* before an ugly confrontation between Hillman and a label executive prompted McGuinn to dissolve their partnership. The two did rejoin fellow Byrds alum David Crosby for a series of club dates in 1989, followed a year later by a handful of recordings projected for a Byrds retrospective. —*Jason Ankeny*

● **McGuinn, Clark & Hillman** / 1979 / Capitol ✦✦✦✦

City / 1979 / Capitol ✦✦✦

Three-fifths of the original Byrds. The self-titled first album contained the hit "Don't You Write Her Off." Clark, as always, provides the best songs of the group. —*Dan Pavlides*

McGuinn, Hillman / 1981 / Capitol ✦✦

Return Flight / Edsel ✦✦✦

Roger McGuinn

b. Jul. 13, 1942, Chicago, IL

Guitar, Vocals / Rock & Roll, Country-Rock, Folk-Rock, Pop-Rock

As the frontman of the Byrds, Roger McGuinn and his trademark 12-string Rickenbacker guitar pioneered folk-rock and, by extension, country-rock, influencing everyone from contemporaries like the Beatles to acolytes like Tom Petty and R.E.M. in the process. James Joseph McGuinn was born on July 13, 1942, in Chicago, where by his teenage years he was already something of a folk music prodigy. After touring with the Limeliters, in 1960 he signed on as an accompanist with the Chad Mitchell Trio, appearing on the LPs *Mighty Day on Campus* and *Live at the Bitter End;* frustrated with his limited role in the group, he soon joined Bobby Darin's group when the singer moved from pop to folk.

After appearing on sessions for Hoyt Axton, Judy Collins, and Tom & Jerry (soon to be known as Simon and Garfunkel), McGuinn began playing solo dates around the Los Angeles area, where he soon formed the Jet Set with area musicians David Crosby and Gene Clark. After a failed single under the name the Beefeaters, the group recruited bassist Chris Hillman and drummer Michael Clarke, changed their name to the Byrds, and set about crystallizing McGuinn's vision of merging the poetic folk music of Bob Dylan with the miraculous pop sounds heard via the British Invasion. McGuinn was the only member of the Byrds to play on their landmark debut single "Mr. Tambourine Man," but his jangly guitar work quickly became the very definition of the burgeoning folk-rock form; still, despite the Byrds' immediate success, the group was plagued by internal strife, and after the release of their 1968 country-rock breakthrough *Sweetheart of the Rodeo,* McGuinn was the only founding member still in the band.

Under the direction of McGuinn—who had changed his first name to Roger after a flirtation with the Subud religion—the Byrds soldiered on, delving further and further into country and roots music before finally dissolving in February 1973. That same year, McGuinn issued his self-titled solo debut, an ambitious, eclectic affair which explored not only folk and country but surf and even space rock. *Peace on You* in 1974 and 1975's *Roger McGuinn and Band* preceded a stint with Bob Dylan's Rolling Thunder Revue which helped revitalize his standing within the musical community. *Cardiff Rose* in 1976 was regarded as his best solo effort to date, but the next year's *Thunderbyrd,* which featured a cover of Tom Petty's "American Girl," failed to connect with audiences. In late 1977 McGuinn reunited with Byrds mates Chris Hillman and Gene Clark; the resulting LP, 1979's *McGuinn, Clark & Hillman,* notched a Top 40 pop hit with the McGuinn-penned "Don't You Write Her Off." Midway through recording the follow-up, 1980's *Home,* Clark departed, and the album was released under the name Roger McGuinn and Chris Hillman Featuring Gene Clark. After another effort, 1981's *McGuinn/Hillman,* they went their separate ways. After undergoing another religious conversion, this time becoming a born-again Christian, McGuinn spent the remainder of the 1980s without a recording contract and performing solo dates.

The appearance of a faux-Byrds led by Michael Clarke prompted McGuinn to reform the group with Hillman and David Crosby in 1989, resulting in a series of club performances, an appearance at a Roy Orbison tribute, and a handful of new recordings for inclusion on a box set retrospective. In 1991—the same year the Byrds were inducted into the Rock and Roll Hall of Fame—McGuinn issued his first new solo recordings in over a decade, *Back to Rio,* which was met with great public and critical acclaim. *Live From Mars,* a retrospective of songs and stories, appeared in 1996. —*Jason Ankeny*

Roger McGuinn / 1973 / Columbia ✦✦✦

Peace on You / 1974 / Columbia ✦✦✦

Roger McGuinn & His Band / 1975 / Columbia ✦✦✦

Cardiff Rose / 1976 / Columbia ✦✦✦✦

Thunderbyrd / 1977 / Columbia ✦✦✦

Back from Rio / 1990 / Arista ✦✦✦✦

This comeback effort put McGuinn together with Tom Petty & the Heartbreakers, former Byrds Chris Hillman and David Crosby, and other guest artists eager to pay tribute, like Michael Penn and Timothy B. Schmit. "King of the Hill" was a substantial FM rock hit. Other highlights include Elvis Costello's "You Bowed Down" and a fine version of Jules Shear's "If We Never Meet Again." The mainstream AOR production values make McGuinn sound like he's guesting on a Tom Petty record—which is not a bad thing, just an observation. —*Rick Clark*

● **Born to Rock & Roll** / Mar. 1992 / Columbia ✦✦✦✦

A well-chosen overview of McGuinn's post-Byrds solo work, it includes "American Girl," "I'm So Restless," "Lover of the Bayou," "My New Woman," and "Peace on You." —*Rick Clark*

Live from Mars / Nov. 19, 1996 / Hollywood ✦✦✦

Taking his cue from Ray Davies' "Storyteller" tour to support his autobiography *X-Ray,* Roger McGuinn constructed his live performances of the mid-'90s as a series of greatest hits, new songs, neglected gems and witty, affectionate anecdotes of his life in the music industry. *Live from Mars* replicates one of these concerts, featuring classics like "Mr. Tambourine Man," "Turn, Turn, Turn," and "So You Want to Be a Rock N Roll Star" intercut with humorous stories and two new songs, "May the Road Rise to Meet You" and "Fireworks." For fans, *Live from Mars* is a small treasure, since it is one of McGuinn's friendliest and most relaxed recordings. —*Stephen Thomas Erlewine*

Maria McKee

b. Aug. 17, 1964, Los Angeles, CA

Guitar, Vocals / Rock 'n' Roll, Country-Rock, Alternative Pop-Rock
While she was with Lone Justice, Maria McKee always showed promise; her gritty, soulful mix of R&B, rock, and country helped distinguish the band from the multitude of '80s roots rockers. When she released her first solo album in the late '80s, it suffered from the same problem as Lone Justice—lots of potential, but no delivery. However, 1993's *You Gotta Sin to Get Saved* showed McKee making good on her promise, with an album of impassioned rockers and ballads. Three years later, McKee released her third solo album, *Life Is Sweet*, an album that marked a departure from her roots-rock roots and a movement toward alternative and art-rock. — *Stephen Thomas Erlewine*

Maria McKee / 1989 / Geffen ♦♦♦
Three years after Lone Justice's last album, Maria McKee released her self-titled debut, which showed that her skills as a songwriter had grown considerably since her first band. Not only were her songs better, but McKee's singing had improved; while it was still a little thin, her voice had grown grittier and more soulful, which made her songs all the more convincing. Unfortunately, most of McKee's musical growth was obscured by Mitchell Froom's mushy overproduction. — *Stephen Thomas Erlewine*

● **You Gotta Sin to Get Saved** / Jun. 22, 1993 / Geffen ♦♦♦♦
A few years after an underappreciated solo album, former Lone Justice leader Maria McKee returns with *You Gotta Sin to Get Saved*, her best album yet. With Black Crowes and Jayhawks producer George Drakoulias at the helm, *You Gotta Sin to Get Saved* evokes the country-rock vibe of the early '70s (much like the aforementioned groups) without sounding like a studied replica. McKee sings a dynamic mix of originals and covers with genuine conviction, making *You Gotta Sin to Get Saved* an album that demands repeated plays. — *Stephen Thomas Erlewine*

Life Is Sweet / Mar. 26, 1996 / Geffen ♦♦♦
For most of her career, Maria McKee has not deviated from country-rock, but *Life Is Sweet* is a bold departure from her trademark sound, taking her into new sonic territories. Although the loud, distorted guitars are the first noticeable change, it soon becomes apparent that the thing that makes the album sound so different is its latent progressive-rock influences. Throughout the album, McKee weaves complex, layered arrangements that interweave strings, guitars, and keyboards. Appropriately, her melodies are more convoluted than ever before, yet they never become too obtuse. Lyrically, she has become more cryptic and angry, but that is all part of the plan—*Life Is Sweet* is McKee's bid to be taken seriously as an artist. For some reason, that means she has constructed a hybrid of the prog-rock arrangements that dominate the first half of the album and the confessional songwriting that is prominent on the second. Fortunately, the results sound better than they read, primarily because beneath all of the bombastic arrangements, McKee has retained her keen sense of songcraft. Still, with its art-rock tendencies and naked ambition, *Life Is Sweet* may not appeal to fans who have become attached to McKee's country-rock. For those willing to accept her pretensions, it is a frustrating but rewarding album. — *Stephen Thomas Erlewine*

Larry McNeely

b. Jan. 3, 1948, Lafayette, IN

Banjo, Guitar, Harmonica, Vocals / Traditional Bluegrass
Larry McNeely was a talented session musician best known for his work with Roy Acuff and Glen Campbell. A native of Lafayette, IN, he was born into a musical family, but didn't begin learning to play piano until he was 13. He then learned guitar and banjo. He got his start at 17 with the Pinnacle Mountain Boys. In 1965 he moved to Nashville to work for the Sho-Bud Guitar Company. There he met Acuff and joined his Smoky Mountain Boys. He remained with them through the decade's end and then moved to California, where he joined Glen Campbell's band after John Hartford left. He recorded his first solo album, *Glen Campbell Presents Larry McNeely*, in 1971. He remained with Campbell

through 1974, and then left the touring circuit to work as a session man. McNeely played on numerous albums, movie soundtracks, and commercials. In 1977 he recorded two albums for different labels. He went back to Nashville in 1984 to try the bluegrass scene but soon returned to work with Acuff, with whom he played until Acuff's death in 1992. After that McNeely began working with Russ and Becky Jeffers and Smoky Mountain Sunshine. — *Sandra Brennan*

● **Rhapsody for Banjo** / 1979 / Flying Fish ♦♦♦♦
This album features lightning-fast, skillful banjo picking by one of the instrument's most original players. — *AMG*

Randy Meisner

b. Mar. 8, 1946, Scottsbluff, NE

Vocals / Country-Rock, Adult Contemporary, Pop-Rock
Meisner is probably best known as the bassist of the Eagles. His career began in the early '60s with obscure bands such as the Dynamics and the Poor. He became a founding member of the country-rock band Poco, but disagreements led him to leave for Rick Nelson's Stone Canyon Band. In 1971 he joined the Linda Ronstadt backing band that eventually became the Eagles, leaving in 1977 to pursue a solo career. He had several Top 40 singles before taking some time off. Meisner joined a reunited Poco in 1989, but friction resurfaced, and he joined a group called Black Tie, which then had a country hit with Buddy Holly's "Learning the Game." — *Steve Huey*

● **One More Song** / 1980 / Epic ♦♦♦♦
Randy Meisner / 1982 / Asylum ♦♦♦

Ken Mellons

b. Jul. 10, 1965
A resident of Nashville since the age of three, Ken Mellons found a Music City contract with Epic in 1994, after several appearances on the Grand Ole Opry spread the word about his talents. Born in Kingsport, TN, on July 10, 1965, Mellons soon moved to Nashville with his family, where he grew up on the standard honky tonk heroes: Merle Haggard, George Jones, and Lefty Frizzell. He played guitar, sang at school talent shows, and moved on to the clubs after high-school graduation. Impressed by one performance, the general manager of the Grand Ole Opry invited Mellons to make a guest appearance. He was invited back several times and earned many songwriting credits during the early '90s. Signed to Epic in 1993, Mellons' self-titled debut album was released one year later. The follow-up, *Where Forever Begins*, appeared in 1995. — *John Bush*

● **Ken Mellons** / 1994 / Epic ♦♦♦♦
Where Forever Begins / 1995 / Epic ♦♦♦
On his second album, Ken Mellons constructs a balanced mix of tearjerking ballads, honky tonk rockers, and plaintive, straightforward traditional country. Mellons performs the songs convincingly, but he is occasionally hurt by a lack of quality songwriting, as evidenced by the single "Rub-A-Dubbin." Although he might not be a powerful enough vocalist to pull off lightweight material, he can deliver good songs forcefully, which is what makes the majority of *Where Forever Begins* an entertaining listen. — *Stephen Thomas Erlewine*

Jo Dee Messina

Vocals / Contemporary Country
Jo Dee Messina's eponymous 1996 album established the vocalist as one of the most popular new female country singers of the year.

During her teens she sang in country bands around her New England homebase. At the age of 19, she left for Nashville. For several years, Messina played local talent contests. By chance, she met a Curb Records executive at a Fan Fair and joked that she would be a good addition to the label. Producer James Stroud persuaded Curb that her demo tape was worth listening to, and by the end of 1994 she had signed to the record label.

Messina recorded her first album with producers Tim McGraw and Byron Gallimore over the course of 1995. The resulting record, *Jo Dee Messina*, was released in the spring of 1996 and was a hit upon its release. —*Stephen Thomas Erlewine*

Jo Dee Messina / Mar. 26, 1996 / Curb ✦✦✦

Buddy Miller

Progressive Country, Country-Rock, Singer-Songwriter, Alternative Country, Americana

A well traveled guitarist, songwriter, singer, and producer, Buddy Miller began playing music in the late '60's, first as an upright bass player in bluegrass bands while in high school. Later he switched to acoustic guitar and began logging miles, playing in San Francisco, Austin, Los Angeles, and New York, where he started the Buddy Miller Band, which included singer-songwriter Shawn Colvin on vocals and guitar. He later developed what became a lasting partnership with country singer and songwriter Jim Lauderdale and eventually wound up in Nashville. Miller was a fine lead guitar player and singer and appeared on albums by Victoria Williams, Jim Lauderdale, and Heather Myles. He produced and recorded his solo debut, *Your Love and Other Lies* himself. It was released on HighTone Records in 1995. —*Jack Leaver*

● **Your Love and Other Lies** / 1995 / Hightone ✦✦✦✦
A talented guitarist/singer-songwriter and producer, Buddy Miller merges a love for classic country with a rock 'n' roll sense of urgency and do-it-yourself ethic. Witness the fact that a good share of this record was recorded in Miller's living room. The results, however, are memorable—not low-budget. Miller enlists some great vocal support from longtime duo partner Jim Lauderdale, Lucinda Williams, Emmylou Harris, and Dan Penn. His wife, Julie Miller, also provides moving harmonies, particularly on a stunning cover of the Louvin Brothers' classic "You're Running Wild," as well as sharing writing credits with her husband on a good share of the songs. She authored two of the album's strongest tracks, the haunting "Don't Listen to the Wind" and the tender ballad "Through the Eyes of a Broken Heart." And although it's been largely overlooked, Buddy Miller arguably turns in the finest version of Tom T. Hall's lonesome "That's How I Got to Memphis" since the original. —*Jack Leaver*

Emmett Miller

Vocals / Old-Time

Although his vocal delivery influenced several major country singers, Emmett Miller was basically a vaudeville singer, with far stronger aural links to Al Jolson than Merle Haggard. Performing in Blackface, Miller was an exponent of the minstrel school of performance, touring widely with minstrel shows for several decades. The most influential aspect of his recordings was his yodeling trill, and there can be no doubt that it heavily influenced country singers such as Jimmie Rodgers, Lefty Frizzell, and Hank Williams (who learned "Lovesick Blues" from a Miller record). Bob Wills asked his early lead singer to copy Miller's style, and a bit of Miller's easygoing ragtime sensibility can be heard in Leon Redbone.

But Miller, to quote Donald Sutherland's description of John Milton in *Animal House*, does not speak well to our generation. That's not just because the vaudeville arrangements of his 1920s recordings will strike most modern-day listeners as quaint. It's also because the blackface minstrel tradition—which was just part of the scene in Miller's heyday—strikes us as somewhat distasteful in the post-segregation era in its perpetuation of some disagreeable Black stereotypes.

Miller began recording for OKeh in the mid-1920s and made his most important singles for the label at the end of the decade with accompaniment by the Georgia Crackers, which included both Tommy and Jimmy Dorsey. The minstrel tradition faded drastically in popularity after 1930, although Miller did record for Bluebird in 1936 and continued to perform in minstrel shows to dwindling crowds through the early '50s. —*Richie Unterberger*

● **Minstrel Man from Georgia** / Feb. 6, 1996 / Columbia/Legacy ✦✦✦✦
God knows what this is doing in Legacy's Roots 'n' Blues series; it's a long way from Blind Willie McTell and Bukka White to this. Anyway, this has 20 of his OKeh sides from the late '20s, includ-

ing a "Lovesick Blues" that served as the model for Hank Williams' hit with the same song in 1949. The Georgia Crackers accompany Miller on every cut, with a cast including Tommy and Jimmy Dorsey (present on every track), Jack Teagarden, and Gene Krupa. It is more of historical interest and musical significance than anything else, with a thorough sleeve note from country music authority Charles Wolfe. —*Richie Unterberger*

Frankie Miller

b. Dec. 17, 1931, Victoria, TX

Vocals / Traditional Country, Country-Rock, Honky Tonk

Frankie Miller recorded several dozen sides for Starday during the late '50s and '60s including two country hits in 1959. Born in Victoria, TX, on December 17, 1931, Miller earned a football scholarship to a local junior college, at which time he formed the Drifting Texans and began broadcasting on the area station KNAL. He also worked in Houston, where he gained a contract with the 4 Star subsidiary Guilt Edge. Though he recorded several numbers in 1951, Miller soon left to serve in the Korean War. He returned two years later with a Bronze Star, and signed to Columbia in 1954. None of the dozen sides he recorded in the subsequent year placed on the charts, though. Miller appeared around Texas (including on Fort Worth's "Cowtown Hoedown") during the late '50s and recorded occasional one-off singles for local labels.

Don Pierce, owner of the Starday label, had been of the few who appreciated Miller's Guilt Edge recordings, so he signed the young singer in 1959. Miller rewarded the label-owner's confidence that same year when "Black Land Farmer" hit the country Top Five and became one of Starday's most popular recordings. "Family Man" reached No. 7 in October 1959, and Miller was tapped as *Cashbox*'s Most Promising Country Artist for 1960. He joined the Louisiana Hayride and appeared on the Grand Ole Opry several times.

Unfortunately, Miller had already reached the pinnacle of his success—he hit the charts only three more times. "Baby Rocked Her Dolly" entered the Top 15 in 1960, and "A Little South of Memphis" hit No. 34 in 1964, while a re-release of "Black Land Farmer" hit No. 16 in 1961. Frankie Miller recorded for United Artists in 1965, but retired from music to work at a Chrysler dealership in Arlington, TX. The German label Bear Family re-released three of his albums during the '80s. —*John Bush*

● **Rockin' Rollin'** / 1983 / Bear Family ✦✦✦✦
This stunning 18-track selection of tracks, cut for the Nashville Starday label between 1959 and 1963, makes for distinctive and haunting music. —*Hank Davis*

Hey! Where You Going? / 1984 / Bear Family ✦✦✦✦
It's the complete collection of this country "groaner's" early 1954-1956 Columbia sides. —*Hank Davis*

● **The Very Best of Frankie Miller** / May 4, 1993 / Capitol ✦✦✦✦

Sugar Coated Baby / 1996 / Bear Family ✦✦✦✦
Though it doesn't contain any of his '50s hits ("Black Land Farmer," "Family Man"), the single-disc, 29-track *Sugar Coated Baby* contains all of Frankie Miller's mid-'60s recordings. While none of these songs ("Living Doll," "I'm Only Wishin'," "I'm So Blue I Don't Know What to Do," "Baby We're Really in Love") is as well-known as his '50s cuts, they are nevertheless enjoyable, and most Miller fans will find the compilation quite entertaining. —*Thom Owens*

Jody Miller

b. Nov. 29, 1941, Phoenix, AZ

Vocals / Traditional Country, Country-Folk

Although she became famous for "Queen of the House," her response to Roger Miller's "King of the Road," Jody Miller pioneered a fusion of folk, country, and pop that set the stage for the folky country-pop of the '70s. Raised in Oklahoma, she was born Myrna Joy Miller, and, inspired by the music of Joan Baez, learned to play guitar at the age of 14. Soon after, Miller joined a folk trio and began performing at a local coffeehouse. Lou Gotlieb, a member of folk group the Limelighters, heard her sing and was impressed enough to offer to help her get a recording contract, provided she move to Los Angeles. Miller initially declined, as she had recently married; but eventually she and her husband went to California to test the waters. A friend of the family arranged an audition with Capitol Records, which signed Miller and suggested that she change her name from Myrna to the folkier "Jody."

In 1963 Miller recorded her debut album *Wednesday's Child Is Full of Woe*, which did fairly well and led to appearances on Tom Paxton's folk music television show. In 1964 she had a minor pop hit with "He Walks like a Man," but her breakthrough arrived in 1965, when "Queen of the House" reached No. 5 on the country charts and No. 12 on the pop charts. Despite her success on the country charts, Miller continued to have more hits as a pop act; "Silver Threads and Golden Needles," her follow-up to "Queen of the House," was a minor hit in the summer of 1965, as was the protest song "Home of the Brave." During the latter half of the '60s, she released a handful of albums and singles, none of which gained much attention.

At the end of the '60s, Miller left the West Coast and returned to her Oklahoma ranch to spend more time with her family. After a few years of semi-retirement, she began recording with Billy Sherrill in Nashville in late 1970; the result, *Look at Mine*, was released in 1971 and featured a mixture of country-pop songs and a few traditional tunes. The album produced her first string of country hits, as "He's So Fine" and "Baby I'm Yours" reached the Top Ten, and several other songs from the record reached the Top 40. Throughout 1972 and 1973, Miller hit the Top Ten with regularity. Her comeback, however, ended as quickly as it had begun—as of 1974, she no longer was able to crack the Top 40, although she did have a string of minor hits. She managed to bounce back into the Top 40 in 1977 with "Darling, You Can Always Come Back Home," but by and large, her career had stalled. In 1979 her contract with Epic expired and she chose to retire to her ranch with her family.

Miller returned in 1987 with the independently released *My Country*, which consisted entirely of patriotic songs; it caught the attention of President-elect George Bush, who invited her to perform at his 1988 inaugural ball. Afterward, Miller's now-grown daughter Robin encouraged her to return to country music, and the two formed a duo. In 1990 they tried to secure a record contract in Nashville but were unsuccessful. —*Sandra Brennan*

Queen of the House / 1965 / Capitol ✦✦✦✦

● **The Best of Jody Miller** / Capitol ✦✦✦✦

Ned Miller

b. Apr. 12, 1925, Raines, UT

Vocals / Traditional Country, Nashville Sound/Countrypolitan

While Ned Miller was best known for his international 1962 hit "From a Jack to a King," during the 1960s he had 11 chart hits and made it to the pop charts three times. Miller was born in Raines, UT, and started writing songs and singing at local parties and on the radio when he was only 16. After his discharge from the Marines, Miller worked at several jobs before moving to California in 1956 to become a full-time songwriter. The next year, singer Gale Storm scored a Top Five hit with his song "Dark Moon"; Bonnie Guitar also had a hit with the composition, and both continued to record Miller's songs. He began his own recording career in 1957; his first single was an early version of "From a Jack to a King." Later that year, he released "Roll O Rollin' Stone" without much notice. In 1962 he recorded a new version of "From a Jack to a King," which soared to the Top Three on the country charts, the Top Ten on the pop charts, and even made it to No. 2 on the British pop charts. The next year Miller scored two Top 30 hits, "One Among the Many" and "Another Fool like Me." In 1965 he had another Top Ten hit, "Do What You Do Do Well," which later provided success for Ernest Tubb; Miller's version also crossed over to the Top 60 on the pop charts. Later that year he signed to Capitol. Songs he wrote or co-wrote with his wife Susan also found chart success for other artists, among them Gale Storm's "Love by the Juke Box Light," Faron Young's "Safely in Love Again," Porter Wagoner's "Your Kind of People," and Hank Snow's "The Man Behind the Gun." Miller faded into obscurity

after the 1960s, but decades later Ricky Van Shelton recorded "From a Jack to a King" and had a No. 1 hit. —*Sandra Brennan*

From a Jack to a King / 1963 / Fabor ✦✦✦

Ned Miller Sings the Songs of Ned Miller / 1965 / Capitol ✦✦✦✦

● **The Best of Ned Miller** / 1966 / Capitol ✦✦✦✦

Teardrop Lane / 1967 / Capitol ✦✦✦

In the Name of Love / 1968 / Capitol ✦✦✦

Ned Miller's Back / 1970 / Republic ✦✦

Roger Miller

b. Jan. 2, 1936, Fort Worth, TX, d. Oct. 25, 1992

Guitar, Vocals / Traditional Country, Honky Tonk, Nashville Sound/Countrypolitan

Roger Miller is best known for his humorous novelty songs, which overshadow his considerable songwriting talents, as well as his hardcore honky tonk roots. After writing hits for a number of artists in the '50s, Miller racked up a number of hits during the '60s that became not only country classics, but popular classics, as well.

Miller was born in Fort Worth, TX, but raised in the small town of Erick, OK, by his aunt and uncle, after the death of his father and his mother's debilitating sickness. Initially he was attracted to music by hearing country radio and by his brother-in-law, Sheb Wooley. By the time Miller was ten, he had earned enough money picking cotton to buy himself a guitar. When Miller was 11, Wooley gave him a fiddle and encouraged him to pursue a performing career. Miller completed the eighth grade and left school to become a ranch-hand and rodeo rider. Throughout his adolescence, he played music in addition to working the ranch. Soon, he was able to play not only guitar and fiddle, but also piano, banjo, and drums.

In 1956 he joined the Army during the Korean War. Miller was stationed in South Carolina, where he met the brother of Jethro Burns, who arranged an audition for him at RCA Nashville. Early in 1957 Miller left the army and auditioned for Chet Atkins at RCA. The session was unsuccessful, and he spent a year as a bellhop at a Nashville hotel. While in Nashville, Miller met George Jones and Pappy Dailey, who introduced him to Don Pierce, an executive at Mercury Records. Pierce signed Miller and had him cut three songs. Miller's first single, "Poor Little John," disappeared without a trace. He continued to work at the hotel and tour with other musicians—he played fiddle with Minnie Pearl for a short time and then became the drummer for Faron Young. After a few months he was signed as a songwriter for Tree Music Publishing and stopped performing as a supporting musician. Instead of playing music, he became a fireman in Amarillo, TX. The abandonment of performing was short-lived, however—within a few months, he became the drummer for Ray Price's Cherokee Cowboys.

In 1958 Price recorded Miller's "Invitation to the Blues," and it went to No. 3. It was soon followed by three other successful versions of his songs—Faron Young's "That's the Way I Feel" and Ernest Tubb's "Half A Mind" both went Top Ten, while Jim Reeves had a No. 1 hit with "Billy Bayou." That same year, George Jones recorded "Tall Tall Trees" and "Nothing Can Stop My Love," which he had written with Miller; neither of the songs was a hit. The next year Reeves had a hit with another one of Miller's songs, "Home."

Since his songwriting career was flourishing, Miller decided it was again time to try to become a performing artist. He recorded a few tracks for Decca that weren't successful, and then he signed to RCA Records. "You Don't Want My Love," one of his first singles for the label, reached No. 14 in early 1961, followed by the Top Ten "When Two Worlds Collide" later that summer. Miller wasn't able to immediately follow the songs with another hit single. Two years later "Lock, Stock and Teardrops" scraped the charts, and he left the record label.

Around that time, Roger moved to Hollywood and began appearing regularly on "The Jimmy Dean Show" and "The Merv Griffin Show," two of the most popular television programs in the country. His guest spots showcased his new style; instead of concentrating on hardcore country, he had developed a willfully goofy persona, singing silly novelty songs. He signed a record contract with Smash Records and released his first single for the label, "Dang Me," in the summer of 1964. It was an immediate smash, vaulting to No. 1 and spending six weeks at the top of the charts; it also crossed over into the pop charts, peaking at No. 7. "Chug-a-Lug" followed a few months later, reaching No. 3 on the country charts and 9 on the pop charts. At the end of the year, "Do-Wacka-Do" was released, becoming a No. 15 hit.

Roger began 1965 with his best-known song, "King of the Road." The single spent five weeks at the top of the country charts and became his biggest pop hit, peaking at No. 4. Its accompanying album, *The Return of Roger Miller*, was another crossover success, also peaking at No. 4 on the pop album charts and going gold. Miller was at his peak in 1965. Every song he released that year—"Engine Engine No.9," "One Dyin' and a Buryin'," "Kansas City Star," "England Swings"—reached the country Top Ten, and at the end of the year his *Golden Hits* album went Top Ten; it would eventually go gold. In the summer of 1965 he released *The Third Time Around*, a record that leaned toward his honky tonk roots; it peaked at No. 13.

After the watershed year of 1965, Roger Miller's career dipped slightly. Although other artists were still having hits with his songs—Eddy Arnold took "The Last Word in Lonesome Is Me" to number two—Miller had trouble breaking the Top 40 following the number five hit "Husbands and Wives" in early 1966. He continued to record throughout the late '60s, but fewer and fewer of the songs were becoming hits. Occasionally he would record the songs of emerging songwriters, whether it was Bobby Russell's "Little Green Apples" (No. 6, 1968) or Kris Kristofferson's "Me and Bobby McGee" (No. 12, 1969). Toward the end of the decade and beginning of the '70s, he began to concentrate on honky tonk, although he still made his trademark novelties.

During the '70s he recorded sporadically, preferring to concentrate on his hotel chain, appropriately called King of the Road. "Tomorrow Night in Baltimore," released in the spring of 1971, was his biggest hit of the decade, climbing to No. 11. Early in the decade he wrote songs for Walt Disney's animated adaptation of *Robin Hood*—he also provided a voice for the rooster in the film—and for the movie *Waterhole Three*. In 1973 he left Smash/Mercury for Columbia Records. He spent four years at Columbia, and only his debut single for the label, "Open Up Your Heart," was a hit, peaking at No. 14.

Miller didn't record much during the '80s—his biggest hit was "Old Friends," recorded with Willie Nelson and Ray Price. In the mid-'80s he wrote the music for *Big River*, a Broadway adaptation of Mark Twain's works. Both the play and Roger's music were critically acclaimed and enormously popular. *Big River* won seven Tony Awards, and two of those went to Miller, for Best Musical and Outstanding Score.

Big River would be the last major work of Roger Miller's career. In 1991 he was diagnosed with throat cancer, and he died a year later. After his death, his legacy remained strong, as each new generation of country singers found songs in his catalog to cover and reinterpret. — *Stephen Thomas Erlewine*

☆ **Golden Hits** / 1965 / Smash ✦✦✦✦✦
Years before Waylon Jennings and Willie Nelson grew their hair long, Miller took country to the counterculture with these hipster twists on the Nashville sound. No tunesmith in Music City had ever tossed off songs like "Dang Me," "King of the Road," "Chug-a-Lug," and "Engine Engine No. 9." No one has since. — *Dan Cooper*

★ **Best of Roger Miller, Vol. 1: Country Tunesmith** / 1991 / Polygram ✦✦✦✦✦
Downplaying his humorous muse in favor of showing off his skill as a straightahead country writer, these 21 tracks (including some strongly Ray Price-influenced fare from 1957) were either written or co-written by Miller. It's well worth the money to hear his own versions of such standards as "Invitation to the Blues," "Half a Mind," and "Don't We All Have the Right." — *Dan Cooper*

★ **The Best of Roger Miller, Vol. 2: King of the Road** / Aug. 4, 1992 / Mercury ✦✦✦✦✦
Where *The Best of Roger Miller, Vol. 1: Country Tunesmith* concentrated on Miller's lesser-known honky tonk numbers and hits

he wrote for other artists, *Best of Roger Miller, Vol. 2: King of the Road* is strictly Miller's biggest hits. From the novelties of "Dang Me," "Chug-A-Lug," "Do-Wacka-Do," and "Kansas City Star" to the relatively straightforward "King of the Road" and "Engine Engine No. 9," all of Miller's big hits from the mid-'60s are included, as are selected lesser hits from the late '60s like "Little Green Apples" and "Me and Bobby McGee." Combined, *Country Tunesmith* and *King of the Road* offer a definitive overview of Roger Miller's career that eclipses even the subsequently released box set, *King of the Road*. — *Stephen Thomas Erlewine*

☆ **King of the Road [Box]** / 1995 / Mercury Nashville ✦✦✦✦✦
Over the course of three discs, the box set *King of the Road* contains every essential item Roger Miller ever recorded. Unfortunately, the compilation isn't consistent; although there are more great songs than weak ones, there are still too many lesser numbers to make the set a truly essential purchase. All of the necessary items are available on Mercury's two-volume *Best of Roger Miller* collection (*Country Tunesmith* and *King of the Road*), which are leaner, more consistent collections that are preferable to this slightly padded three-disc box. — *Thom Owens*

Super Hits / Mar. 19, 1996 / Epic ✦✦
Consumer advisory: Although this album does contain a small-print statement on the back reading, "This compact disc was previously released as 'Roger Miller King of the Road,'" it does not explain that that album contained '70s re-recordings of Roger Miller's '60s hits. Here, then, are ten selections running 22 minutes and 19 seconds, among them such popular songs as "Dang Me," "King of the Road," "Chug-a-Lug," and "England Swings," redone. The originals were on Smash, a division of Mercury that is owned by PolyGram. — *William Ruhlmann*

Ronnie Milsap

b. Jan. 16, 1944, Robbinsville, NC
Piano, Vocals / Country-Pop, Urban Cowboy
Ronnie Milsap was one of the major figures of country music in the 1970s, developing a hybrid of country and pop that brought him a large audience. Milsap was born in Robbinsville, NC, and was raised by his father and grandparents after his parents' divorce. He was born blind from congenital glaucoma, and when he was five began attending the Governor Moorhead School for the Blind. When he was seven, his instructors noticed his extraordinary musical talents, and he began to study classical music formally. A single year after he began learning the violin, Milsap was declared a virtuoso; he also mastered piano, guitar, and a variety of other stringed instruments, as well as various woodwinds. Eventually he became interested in rock 'n' roll music and while still in school formed his first rock band, the Apparitions. He briefly attended college in Atlanta, where he studied pre-law; though he was awarded a comprehensive scholarship, Milsap decided to become a full-time musician instead. His first professional gig was as a member of J.J. Cale's band in the early '60s.

In 1965 Milsap started his own band, and four years later, after having an R&B hit with "Never Had It So Good," he moved to Memphis where he frequently worked for Chips Moman and can be heard playing keyboards on Elvis' "Kentucky Rain" and singing harmony on "Don't Cry Daddy." When not doing session work, Milsap and his backing group were the house band at TJ's Club. In 1970 he had a pop hit with "Loving You Is a Natural Thing." In 1971 he released his eponymous debut. Two years later Milsap moved to Nashville in hopes of jump-starting his flagging career, and he became a client of Charley Pride's manager, Jack D. Johnson. Within a year he signed to RCA Victor, where he would remain for the bulk of his career. "I Hate You," his first single for RCA, reached the country Top Ten in the summer of 1973. The next year he had three No. 1 hits in a row—"Pure Love," "Please Don't Tell Me How the Story Ends," and "(I'd Be) A Legend in My Time," a cover of Don Gibson's classic.

Milsap had a handful of Top Ten hits in 1975, and in late 1976 he became a genuine star, with a string of six No. 1 hits in a row. That string of hits began a remarkable run where Milsap didn't leave the Top Ten for 15 straight years. During that time he had a number of pop crossover hits, beginning with 1977's "It Was Almost like a Song." Between 1980 and 1982 Milsap had ten more consecutive No. 1 hits, including the crossover smashes "Smoky Mountain Rain," "No Gettin' Over Me," and "Any Day Now." Milsap had yet another string of uninterrupted No. 1 hits between 1985 and 1987, racking up eight consecutive chart toppers. He had his last No. 1 hit in 1989, when "A Woman in Love" spent two weeks on the top of the charts. In total, he had 35 No. 1 singles.

In the early '90s Milsap's commercial appeal began to decline—after 1992, he wasn't able to break into the country Top Ten. Nevertheless, he continued to record. In 1992,he left RCA and signed to Liberty, where he recorded *True Believer,* which failed to yield any major hits. Despite his decline in popularity, Milsap continued to record and perform successfully throughout the '90s. —*Sandra Brennan*

It Was Almost like a Song / 1977 / RCA ✦✦✦
This album features such Milsap favorites as "Here in Love," "What a Difference You've Made in My Life," and "Long-Distance Memory." —*AMG*

● **Greatest Hits** / 1980 / RCA ✦✦✦✦
This is a solid, albeit random assessment of Milsap's first seven years in country music. Mainstream country is featured, with "Pure Love" and "(I'm A) Stand by My Woman Man," but Milsap really shines on the elaborate and challenging arrangements of "(I'd Be) A Legend in My Time," "It Was Almost like a Song," and "Let's Take the Long Way Around the World." One previously unreleased track is here: "Smoky Mountain Rain." —*Tom Roland*

Keyed Up / 1983 / RCA ✦✦✦
The eclectic *Keyed Up* features a pair of No. 1 singles, "Show Her" and "Don't You Know How Much I Love You," as well as the Top Five hit "Stranger in My House." —*Jason Ankeny*

One More Try for Love / 1984 / RCA ✦✦✦
In his effort to expand the boundaries of country, Milsap pushes the edge harder here than in any other album. The electronically altered vocals in the tracks "She Loves My Car" and "Suburbia" have a winning effect—tasteful, not overdone. —*Tom Roland*

Greatest Hits, Vol. 2 / 1985 / RCA ✦✦✦✦
Juxtaposed to the first *Greatest Hits* package, this one nicely displays the evolution of a motivated risk-taker. Milsap redefines the outer limits of the commercial country format with his soul—and/or rock-inflected singles "(There's) No Gettin' Over Me," "Lost in the Fifties Tonight," and (most dramatically) "Stranger in My House." —*Tom Roland*

Heart and Soul / 1987 / RCA ✦✦✦
One of Milsap's more diverse efforts, *Heart and Soul* includes the chart-topping "Snap Your Fingers," "Make No Mistake, She's Mine" (a duet with Kenny Rogers), and "Where Do the Nights Go." —*Jason Ankeny*

Greatest Hits, Vol. 3 / 1991 / RCA ✦✦✦
Greatest Hits, Vol. 3 collects the bulk of Ronnie Milsap's late '80s hits, including "Happy, Happy Birthday Baby," "How Do I Turn You On?," "Snap Your Fingers," "Where Do the Nights Go," "Button off My Shirt," "A Woman in Love," and "Stranger Things Have Happened." Although it bypasses some of his hits ("In Love," "Houston Solution," "Are You Lovin' Me Like I'm Lovin' You") at the expense of lesser-known material ("L.A. to the Moon"), the collection remains a good sampling of Milsap's final round of Top Ten hits. —*Thom Owens*

Back to the Grindstone / 1991 / RCA ✦✦✦
Back to the Grindstone was an excellent return to form from Ronnie Milsap and, not coincidentally, it was his last great record, as well as his last hit album. Throughout *Back to the Grindstone,* Milsap displays his talent for eclectic, soul-inflected R&B, tearing through a gritty duet with Patti LaBelle on "Love Certified," covering "Since I Don't Have You" with heart, and then slipping into hard country with "Turn That Radio On." Not one of the ten songs on the record is weak, and Milsap responds with a gutsy, powerful performance, easily making *Back to the Grindstone* one of his best albums. —*Thom Owens*

True Believer / Jun. 7, 1993 / Liberty ✦✦✦
If only the whole album had the energy of the John Hiatt title track (not to mention the wit of the Hoss Allen intro), Milsap's Liberty debut would have been a record to reckon with. —*Dan Cooper*

● **Essential Ronnie Milsap** / 1995 / RCA ✦✦✦✦
The Essential Ronnie Milsap isn't necessarily a definitive collection—Milsap simply had too many big hits to fit on a single-disc compilation, for starters—but it does come close. Many of his biggest hits are included on *Essential,* as well as a handful of obscurities, including album tracks and lesser-known hits. Consequently, the compilation is a nice cross-section that offers a good representation of Milsap's sound, even if it doesn't come close to being a definitive retrospective. —*Thom Owens*

Sings His Best Hits For Capitol Records / Sep. 17, 1996 / Capitol ✦✦
As the title suggests, Ronnie Milsap's *Sings His Best Hits for Capitol Records* consists of re-recorded versions of ten of his biggest hits—including "Lost in the Fifties Tonight," "Snap Your Fingers," "(I'm A) Stand by Your Woman Man" and "(There's) No Gettin' Over Me"—which were all originally recorded for RCA Records. Though these new versions aren't particularly bad, they are neither as good nor as familiar as the originals, making it a collection to avoid, especially if you're looking for a strong hits collection. —*Thom Owens*

Waddie Mitchell

b. 1950, Elko, NV
Vocals / Cowboy
Waddie Mitchell was a real cowboy who became a world-renowned cowboy storyteller and poet, enchanting contemporary audiences with tales of life in the rugged West. He was born Bruce Douglas Mitchell on the enormous Horseshoe Ranch, located more than 30 miles south of Elko, NV. Young Bruce, nicknamed "Waddie" (a synonym for "cowboy") by his father, spent most of his time with real cowboys and at night listened to their stories and memorized their poems. He dropped out of school at 16 to become a full-time wrangler and chuck wagon driver. He was drafted into the Army and was stationed at Fort Carson, CO, on a 24,000-acre ranch where he broke and trained horses for the US Cavalry. While working as the foreman of a ranch, Mitchell appeared in an early-'80s PBS documentary about the last real cowboys in America, "The Vanishing Breed." The documentary featured some of Mitchell's own poetry, and Johnny Carson invited him to visit "The Tonight Show." Mitchell didn't even know who Carson was, but he was a big hit on the show after reciting Wallace McCray's famous poem "Reincarnation," and he later returned several times. He also appeared on several other programs, including Larry King's radio show and a *National Geographic* special.

In 1984 he and pal Hal Cannon organized the first Elko Cowboy Poetry Gathering. Two thousand people attended the first year, and by 1994 the attendance soared to nearly 14,000. Later in 1984 Mitchell recorded his first album of poetry at Cannon's house in Idaho. His second album sold More than 10,000 copies. In 1992 Mitchell was one of the first artists to record on Warner Brothers' newly established Warner Western label with *Lone Driftin' Rider.* He and colleague Don Edwards embarked upon an extensive promotional tour of festivals, concert halls, schools, and universities to sell the album and to educate audiences about their nearly extinct way of life. Mitchell released his second Warner album, *Buckaroo Poet,* in 1994. He next appeared as a guest host on the cable-TV channel VH1's "Country Country" show. He also won numerous honors for his poetry and storytelling, and was inducted into the Cowboy Poets and Singers' Hall of Fame. —*Sandra Brennan*

● **Lone Driftin' Rider** / Jan. 1992 / Warner Brothers ✦✦✦✦
Waddie Mitchell revives the tradition of storytelling cowboy songs with the intimate, entertaining "Lone Driftin' Rider," which is equally divided between standards and poetic originals. —*Thom Owens*

Buckaroo Poet / Aug. 3, 1993 / Warner Brothers ✦✦✦✦

Moby Grape

Rock 'n' Roll, Country-Rock, Psychedelic, Folk-Rock

One of the best '60s San Francisco bands, Moby Grape was also one of the most versatile. Although they are most often identified with the psychedelic scene, their specialty was combining all sorts of roots music—folk, blues, country, and classic rock 'n' roll—with some Summer of Love vibes and multilayered, triple-guitar arrangements. All of those elements truly coalesced, however, only for their 1967 debut LP. Although subsequent albums had more good moments than many listeners are aware of, a combination of personal problems and bad management effectively killed off the group by the end of the 1960s.

Many San Francisco bands of the era were assembled by recent immigrants to the area, but Moby Grape had even more tenuous roots in the region than most. Matthew Katz, who managed the Jefferson Airplane in their early days, helped put together Moby Grape around Skip Spence. Spence, a legendarily colorful Canadian native whose first instrument was the guitar, had played drums in the Airplane's first lineup at the instigation of Marty Balin. Spence left the Airplane after their first album and reverted to his natural guitarist and songwriting role for the Grape. (The Airplane had already recorded some of his compositions.) Guitarist Jerry Miller and drummer Don Stevenson were recruited from the Northwest bar band the Frantics; guitarist Peter Lewis had played in Southern California surf bands like the Cornells; and bassist Bob Moseley had also played with outfits from Southern California.

The group's relative unfamiliarity with each other may have sown seeds for their future problems, but they jelled surprisingly quickly, with all five members contributing more or less equally to the songwriting on their self-titled debut (1967). *Moby Grape* remains their signature statement, though the folk-rock and country-rock worked better than the boogies; "Omaha," "Sittin' by the Window," "Changes," and "Lazy Me" are some of their best songs. Columbia Records, though, damaged the band's credibility with over-hype, releasing no less than five singles from the LP simultaneously. Worse, three members of the group were caught consorting with underage girls. Though charges were eventually dropped, the legal hassles, combined with an increasingly strained relationship with manager Katz, sapped the band's drive.

Moby Grape's follow-up, the double LP *Wow*, was one of the most disappointing records of the '60s, in light of the high expectations fostered by the debut. The studio half of the package had much more erratic songwriting than the first recording, and the group members didn't blend their instrumental and vocal skills nearly as well. The "bonus" disc was almost a total waste, consisting of bad jams. Spence departed while the album was being recorded in New York in 1968, as a result of a famous incident in which he entered the studio with a fire axe, apparently intending to use it on Stevenson. Committed to New York's Bellevue Hospital, he did re-emerge to record a wonderful acid-folk solo album at the end of 1968, but that would be his only notable post-Grape project; he struggles with mental illness to this day.

Another unexpected blow was dealt when Moseley, despite his membership in a band that emerged from the Haight-Ashbury psychedelic scene, joined the Marine Corps at the beginning of 1969. The band did struggle on and release a couple more albums during that year, and the best tracks from these (particularly the earlier one, *Moby Grape '69*) proved they could still deliver the goods, though usually in a more subdued, countrified fashion than their earliest material. The group broke up at the end of the '60s, although they would periodically reunite for nearly unheard albums over the next two decades, in lineups featuring varying original members. Their problems were exacerbated by Matthew Katz, who owned the Moby Grape name and sometimes prevented the oritignal members from using the name when they worked together. —*Richie Unterberger*

Moby Grape / Jun. 1967 / San Francisco Sound ✦✦✦✦
Some consider this 1967 debut to be the most impressive of the San Francisco rock revolution. Not a wasted moment, and the Grape do jam. —*Jeff Tamarkin*

Wow/Grape Jam / 1968 / San Francisco Sound ✦✦✦
Could Moby Grape live up to the hype following the release of their first album? The answer was "No." That fact alone nearly broke up the band. They went back into the studio and recorded a flawed, but essential, gem, which they titled *Wow*. Great R&B and blues workouts co-existed alongside hallucinogenic raveups and introspective ballads. Production gimmicks did marr such near-classic cuts such as "The Place and the Time" and "Bitter Wind," but on the whole, this album is well worth the time. *Grape Jam* is just that, a jam between Moby Grape members and famous friends such as Mike Bloomfield and Al Kooper essentially making things up as they went along. For historical purposes only. —*James Chrispell*

Moby Grape '69 / 1969 / Columbia ✦✦✦

Truly Fine Citizen / 1969 / Columbia ✦✦
Recorded in just three days in Nashville, *Truly Fine Citizen* was little more than a contractual obligation, with the Grape pared down to a trio. Augmented by sessionmen, it does have its moments. "Right Before My Eyes" has a relaxed country feel to it, and the title track rocks out like the old days, if only briefly. The end of Moby Grape came about just as the "country-rock" sound was about to become the Next Big Thing. —*James Chrispell*

20 Granite Creek / 1971 / Reprise ✦✦✦✦
Re-grouping with all the original members, Moby Grape attempted a comeback that fell just short of its mark. The move to the country was highlighted in several tracks but couldn't mask their R&B/rock roots. Although uneven, this set has flashes of the ol' Grape electricity interwoven with short country ditties. Sort of a poor man's "Workingman's Dead." —*James Chrispell*

Moby Grape '84 / 1984 / San Francisco Sound ✦✦✦
The Grape go country-rock and pull it off. —*Jeff Tamarkin*

● **Vintage: The Very Best of Moby Grape** / May 11, 1993 / Columbia/Legacy ✦✦✦✦
It's hard to imagine a better-produced package of Moby Grape's work than this two-disc, 48-track condensation of their best late-'60s recordings. The first disc of this set centers on their entire 1967 self-titled debut LP (included in its entirety), which mixed blues, country, and folk influences with hard-charging psychedelic rock 'n' roll. The result was one of the Summer of Love's more enduring works. The second disc boils down their wildly inconsistent 1968-69 material to a fairly strong and coherent selection. While it doesn't match the peak of the group's initial burst, it features some strong folk and country-rock originals that wear much better in the absence of the bloated jams and half-baked hard rock that could make their albums a chore to sit through. Each disc includes interesting demos, outtakes, and live performances that round out the legacy of this prodigiously talented but ill-fated band, which was overcome by internal strife and label/management difficulties after their promising debut. —*Richie Unterberger*

Hugh Moffatt

b. Nov. 10, 1948, Fort Worth, TX

Guitar, Vocals / Progressive Country, Singer-Songwriter, Country-Folk

Singer-songwriter Hugh Moffatt was born in Fort Worth, TX, and learned to play piano and trumpet as a boy. Influenced by the Sons of the Pioneers, Moffatt performed in a high school group specializing in big-band swing music. During the late '60s he moved to Houston, where he listened to blues, learned to play guitar, and joined the pop band Rollin' Wood. After a brief move to Austin, Moffatt headed for Washington, D.C., in 1973 but paused in Nashville; after seeing Stringbean and Marty Robbins perform at the Grand Ole Opry, he decided to stay and try writing songs.

As a songwriter, Hugh Moffatt was heavily influenced by Kris Kristofferson and later Ed Penney, who became his mentor. In 1974 Ronnie Milsap recorded Moffatt's "Just in Case" and scored a Top Five hit. In 1977 Moffatt signed a recording contract with Mercury and had a minor hit with his debut single "The Gambler," but his second single went nowhere and he was dropped. In 1978 Joe Sun recorded Moffatt's "Old Flames (Can't Hold a Candle to You)," his most famous song. In 1980 Dolly Parton recorded it and had a No. 1 hit. Several artists had success with Moffatt's songs during the early '80s, including Lacy J. Dalton with "Wild Turkey," Alabama with "Words at Twenty Paces," and Johnny Rodriguez with "How Could I Love Her So Much." Around that time, Moffatt founded the four-piece band Ratz, who recorded the five-song EP *Puttin' on the Ratz* in 1984. He cut some solo tracks in 1986 and signed to Philo/Rounder the next year; using some of his unreleased tracks, he completed *Loving You.* In 1989 he released another album, *Troubadour,* and then cut *Dance Me Outside* (1991) with his sister Kate. His songs have also been covered by Bobby Bare and Jerry Lee Lewis. — *Sandra Brennan*

Loving You / 1987 / Philo ◆◆◆◆
A very good debut album with solid songwriting. Russ Barrenberg and Jerry Douglas back up Moffatt. — *Chip Renner*

● **Troubadour** / 1989 / Philo ◆◆◆◆
Highly recommended. Moffatt's songwriting is at its best. — *Chip Renner*

Dance Me Outside / 1992 / Philo ◆◆◆
Siblings Hugh and Katy Moffatt have pursued different musical roads over the years. Hugh has established himself in Nashville as songwriter and folk-influenced singer, while Katy has leaned in a more overt country direction. This is their first full collaboration, and it showcases Hugh's troubadour-like rich baritone and poetic lyrics and Katy's dynamic country vocals and passionate songs. The top-notch backing musicians include Buddy Emmons (steel guitar, dobro), Tim O'Brien (mandolin), Stuart Duncan (fiddle), and Albert Lee (lead guitar on two songs). — *Roundup Newsletter*

Katy Moffatt

b. Nov. 19, 1950, Fort Worth, TX
Guitar, Vocals / Progressive Country, Country-Rock, Contemporary Country, Country-Folk, Americana
Though mainstream success has eluded Katy Moffatt, her blend of country, rock, blues, and folk has gathered a devoted following of fans and colleagues just the same. Born in Fort Worth, TX, (her brother is country songwriter Hugh Moffatt), Moffatt started out singing Leonard Cohen's "Dress Rehearsal Rag" in a local coffeehouse. In 1969 while studying at St. John's College in Santa Fe, she sang in the movie *Black Jack.* After making the film, she dropped out of school and moved to Corpus Christi, TX, to work at a local TV station and sing with a local blues band. After the station was destroyed by a hurricane, she moved first to Austin and later to Colorado. While singing on a Denver radio station beginning in 1973, she became locally popular and signed to Columbia by 1975. Columbia released her rock-oriented debut *Katy* as a country album, but one of the singles, "I Can Almost See Houston from Here," still became a low-level country hit. Changing its promotional direction yet again, Columbia released her second LP *Kissin' in the California Sun* (1977) as a pop album, while Moffatt opened for such performers as Charlie Daniels, Warren Zevon, Muddy Waters, and Steve Martin and toured with guitarist Leo Kottke. During the rest of the '70s, she worked with Willie Nelson and Andrew Gold, appeared with Poco and John Prine, and toured with Jerry Jeff Walker, J.D. Souther, and the Allman Brothers.

Continuing her backup career during the early '80s, Moffatt sang with Tanya Tucker, Lynn Anderson, and Hoyt Axton until she gained a contract with Permian Records in 1983. Label president Chuck Robinson valued her distinctive style and set her up with producer Jerry Crutchfield, a partnership that spawned three impressive singles, including "This Ain't Tennessee and He Ain't You" (1984). Even though none of them charted above the Top 70, she was nominated as the ACM's Female Vocalist of the Year in 1985. In the mid-'80s the Permian label folded and she moved to Philo/Rounder, where her albums gained wider exposure. With her brother Hugh, she recorded the 1991 duet album, *Dance Me Outside,* and has also done duet work with Tom Russell, Mary Flower, and Rosie Flores. Moffatt debuted at the Wembley Festival in England in 1990. Two years later, she snagged roles in the films *Honeymoon in Vegas* and *The Thing Called Love.* — *Sandra Brennan*

Walkin' on the Moon / 1976 / Philo ◆◆◆◆
Katy Moffatt's *Walkin' on the Moon* is not overproduced. It features her on vocals and acoustic guitar and Andrew Harden on vocals and guitar. Moffatt co-wrote with Tom Russell and covers three of her brother Hugh Moffatt's songs. Nice job on "Walkin' on the Moon." — *Chip Renner*

Katy Moffatt / 1976 / Columbia ◆◆◆◆
A nice album. Features Dickie Betts, Chuck Leavell (Sea Level), the Allman Brothers rhythm section, and the Muscle Shoals horn section. — *Chip Renner*

Kissin' in the California Sun / 1978 / Columbia ◆◆◆

Child Bride / 1990 / Philo ◆◆◆
. . . a startling departure from last year's introspective and acoustic *Walkin' on the Moon.* — *Mark A. Humphrey, Rock & Roll Disc*

Indoor Fireworks / 1992 / Red Moon ◆◆◆
This release is closer in style to *Childe Bride* than other recent Moffatt albums. She takes on ballads and rockers such as Dave Alvin's "Rich Man's Town" and "Words at Twenty Paces." Recorded live in Switzerland in 1991 with a country band, this CD has a loose country-rock sound. As always, Katy Moffatt's captivating voice pulls it all together. — *Richard Meyer*

★ **The Evangeline Hotel** / 1993 / Philo ◆◆◆◆◆
The first thing to be aware of is that this album was briefly released with a different cover and title — *The Greatest Show on Earth.* Be assured, it is the same album, and a great one it is, too. Many of the tracks were co-written with Tom Russell, who produced the CD. Andy Hardin plays great parts, as usual, and it's all held together by some of the most open and honest-sounding vocals among contemporary songwriters. — *Richard Meyer*

Hearts Gone Wild / 1994 / Watermelon ◆◆
Hearts Gone Wild is Katy Moffatt's seventh album. This one most closely resembles *Walkin' on the Moon* in that the arrangements are primarily acoustic and the songs are mostly personal and romantic. Many of the songs were co-written with Tom Russell, but the emphasis is not on stories as much as it was on her CD *The Greatest Show on Earth.* Her voice, as always, is a wonder, heartbreaking and reassuring. — *Richard Meyer*

Midnight Radio / 1996 / Watermelon ◆◆◆

Bill Monroe (William Smith Monroe)

b. Sep. 13, 1911, Rosine, KY, d. Sep. 9, 1996
Fiddle, Guitar, Mandolin, Vocals / Traditional Bluegrass
Bill Monroe is the father of bluegrass. He invented the style, invented the name, and, for the great majority of the 20th century, embodied the art form. Beginning with his Blue Grass Boys in the '40s, Monroe defined a hard-edged style of country that emphasized instrumental virtuosity, close vocal harmonies, and a fast, driving tempo. The musical genre took its name from the Blue Grass Boys, and Monroe's music forever has defined the sound of classical bluegrass — a five-piece acoustic string band, playing precisely and rapidly, switching solos and singing in a plaintive, high lonesome voice. Not only did he invent the very sound of the music, Bill Monroe was the mentor for several generations of musicians. Over the years Monroe's band hosted all of the major bluegrass artists of the '50s and '60s, including Flatt and Scruggs, Reno and Smiley, Vassar Clements, Carter Stanley, and Mac Wiseman. Though the lineup of the Blue Grass Boys changed over the years, Monroe always remained devoted to bluegrass in its purest form.

Monroe was born into a musical family. His father had been known around their hometown of Rosine, KY, as a step-dancer, while his mother played a variety of instruments and sang. His uncle, Pendleton Vanderver, was a locally renowned fiddler. Both of his older brothers, Harry and Birch, played fiddle, while his brother Charlie and sister Bertha played guitar. Bill himself became involved with music as a child, learning the mandolin at the age of ten. After the death of his parents when he was a pre-adolescent, Bill Monroe went to live with his Uncle Pen. Soon Monroe was playing in his uncle's band at local dances, playing guitar instead of mandolin. During this time Monroe met local blues guitarist Arnold Shultz, who became a major influence on the budding musician.

Bill Monroe

When Bill Monroe turned 18, he moved to East Chicago, IN, where his brothers Birch and Charlie were working at an oil refinery. Bill also got a job at the Sinclair oil refinery and began playing with his brothers in a country string band at night. Within a few years, they performed on the "Barn Dance" on WLS Chicago, which led to the brothers' appearance in a square dance revue called the "WLS Jamboree" in 1932. The Monroes continued to perform at night, but Birch left the band in 1934. Ironically, it was just before the group landed the sponsorship of the Texas Crystals Company, who made laxatives. Charlie and Bill decided to continue performing as the Monroe Brothers.

The Monroe Brothers began playing in other states, including radio shows in Nebraska, Iowa, and both North and South Carolina. Such exposure led to record label interest, but the Monroe Brothers were initially reluctant to sign a recording contract. After some persuasion, they inked a deal with RCA-Victor's Bluebird division and recorded their first session in February 1936. One of the songs from the sessions, "What Would You Give in Exchange," became a minor hit, and the duo recorded another 60 tracks for Bluebird over the next two years.

In the beginning of 1938, Bill and Charlie parted ways, with Charlie forming the Kentucky Pardners. Bill assembled his own band with the intention of creating a new form of country that melded old-time string bands with blues and challenged the instrumental abilities of the musicians. He moved to Little Rock, where he formed the Kentuckians, but that band was short-lived. He then relocated to Atlanta, where he formed the Blue Grass Boys and began appearing on the Crossroad Rollies radio program. Monroe debuted on the Grand Ole Opry in October 1939, singing "New Muleskinner Blues." It was a performance that made Monroe's career, as well as establishing the new genre of bluegrass.

In the early '40s Monroe and the Blue Grass Boys spent some time developing their style, often sounding similar to other contemporary string bands. The most notable element of the band's sound was Monroe's high, piercing tenor voice and his driving mandolin. The Blue Grass Boys toured with the Grand Ole Opry's road shows and appeared weekly on the radio. Between 1940 and 1941 he cut a number of songs for RCA-Victor, but war-time restrictions prevented his recording for several years. The classic lineup of the Blue Grass Boys fell into place in 1944, when guitarist/vocalist Lester Flatt and banjoist Earl Scruggs joined a lineup that already included Monroe, fiddler Chubby Wise, and bassist Howard Watts. This is the group that supported Monroe when he returned to the studio in 1945, recording a number of songs for Columbia. Early in 1946 he had his first charting hit with "Ken-

tucky Waltz," which climbed to No. 3; it was followed by the No. 5 hit "Footprints in the Snow."

Throughout 1946 the Blue Grass Boys were one of the most popular acts in country music, scoring hits and touring to large crowds across America. At each town they played, the band would perform in a large circus tent they set up themselves; the tent would also host a variety of other attractions, including Monroe's baseball team, which would play local teams before the concert began. During the late '40s the Blue Grass Boys remained popular, landing five additional Top 20 singles. Numerous other acts began imitating Monroe's sound, most notably the Stanley Brothers.

Flatt and Scruggs left the Blue Grass Boys in 1948 to form their own band. Their departure ushered in an era of stagnation for Bill Monroe. Monroe left Columbia Records in 1949, because they had signed the Stanley Brothers, who he felt were simply imitating his style. The next year he signed with Decca Records, who tried to persuade Monroe to attempt some mainstream-oriented productions. He went as far as cutting a few songs with an electric guitar, but he soon returned to his pure bluegrass sound. At these sessions he did meet Jimmy Martin, who became his supporting vocalist in the early '50s.

Throughout the '50s—indeed, throughout the rest of his career—Monroe toured relentlessly, performing hundreds of shows a year. In 1951 Monroe opened a country music park at Bean Blossom, IN; over the years, the venue featured performances from a number of bluegrass acts. Monroe had a serious car accident in January 1953 that sidelined his career for several months. The next year, Elvis Presley performed Monroe's "Blue Moon of Kentucky" at his one and only Grand Ole Opry appearance, radically reworking the arrangement; Presley apologized for his adaptation, but Monroe would later perform the same arrangement at his concerts.

Bill Monroe released his first album, *Knee Deep in Bluegrass*, in 1958, the same year he appeared on the country singles chart with "Scotland"; the No. 27 single was his first hit in more than a decade. By the late '50s, however, his stardom was eclipsed by Flatt and Scruggs. Monroe was not helped by his legendary stubbornness. Numerous musicians passed through his band because of his temperament and his quest for detail. He rarely granted press interviews, and he would rarely perform on television; he even cancelled a concert at Carnegie Hall because he believed the promoter, Alan Lomax, was a communist. In the '60s Monroe received a great career boost from the folk music revival, which made him popular with a new generation of listeners. Thanks to his new manager, ex-Greenbriar Boys member Ralph Rinzler,

Monroe played bluegrass festivals across the US, frequently on college campuses. In 1967 he founded his own bluegrass festival, the Bill Monroe Bean Blossom Festival, which continued to run into the '90s at his country music park.

In 1970 he was inducted into the Country Music Hall of Fame; the next year, the Nashville Songwriters Association International Hall of Fame. Throughout the '70s he toured constantly. In 1981 Monroe was diagnosed with cancer and underwent succesful treatment. After his recovery, he resumed his busy touring schedule, which he kept into the '90s. In 1991 he had a double coronary bypass, but he quickly recovered and continued performing and hosting weekly at the Grand Ole Opry. In 1993 the Grammys gave Monroe a Lifetime Achievement Award. After suffering a stroke in early 1995, Bill Monroe died on September 9, 1995, four days short of his 85th birthday. — *Stephen Thomas Erlewine*

The High Lonesome Sound of Bill Monroe / 1966 / Decca
◆◆◆◆

Live at the Opry: Celebrating 50 Years on the Grand Ole Opry / 1989 / MCA ◆◆◆
Recorded live in 1989, Monroe had by this time turned over a majority of lead vocal turns to guitarist Tom Ewing. But the music proves how vibrant and aggressive Monroe's mandolin skills remained. It also features one fantastic cut from a 1948 Opry date. —*Michael McCall*

Columbia Historic Edition / 1989 / Columbia ◆◆◆◆
Columbia Historic Edition has a nice selection of ten songs that Bill Monroe cut for Columbia in the early '40s, including "Kentucky Waltz," "Blue Yodel No. 4 (California Blues)," and "Bluegrass Special." Several hits are missing, and several compilations released in the '90s cover the same ground more thoroughly, but this record remains an enjoyable listen. —*Thom Owens*

☆ **Bluegrass 1950-1958** / 1990 / Bear Family ◆◆◆◆◆
This superb four-CD boxed set from Bear Family (import) offers the most comprehensive collection of Bill Monroe ever assembled. The liner notes are beautifully done—pictures, discography, the works. A second box covering the period from 1959 on is also available. —*Michael Erlewine*

Cryin' Holy Unto the Lord / 1991 / MCA ◆◆◆
An all-gospel album propped up with some stellar guests, it includes Ricky Skaggs, Ralph Stanley, the Osborne Brothers, Jim & Jesse McReynolds, and Mac Wiseman. —*Michael McCall*

Mule Skinner Blues / 1991 / RCA ◆◆◆
Mule Skinner Blues contains the first recordings that Bill Monroe made with the Blue Grass Boys in 1940 and 1941 for RCA. On these recordings of the earliest and loosest bluegrass band, Monroe is wearing his blues, old-time, and even swing influences on his sleeve. —*Mark A. Humphrey*

★ **Country Music Hall of Fame** / 1991 / MCA ◆◆◆◆◆
Bill Monroe made his most famous and popular—and arguably his best—recordings after he signed to Decca Records in 1950. For the next 40 years he cut a number of classics, and 16 of his finest tracks are collected on *Country Music Hall of Fame*. The original versions of many of Monroe's best-known songs, including "New Mule Skinner Blues" and "Uncle Pen," are included, as well as his popular remake of his standard "Blue Moon of Kentucky." Of course with a career as long and varied as Monroe's, it's hard to boil it down to just 16 tracks, and inevitably some of the latter-day cuts won't please some dedicated fans. Nevertheless, it's hard to beat *Country Music Hall of Fame* as a single-disc introduction to one of the greatest musicians in country music history. —*Stephen Thomas Erlewine*

☆ **Bluegrass 1959-1969** / 1991 / Bear Family ◆◆◆◆◆
This, the companion set to the above, comprises over 100 tracks on four CDs, including such hits as "The Long Black Veil," "Midnight on the Stormy Deep," "Big River," "Dusty Miller," and many other Monroe favorites, and also several recordings released here for the first time. —*AMG*

☆ **The Essential Bill Monroe (1945-1949)** / 1992 / Columbia/Legacy ◆◆◆◆◆
On the surface, *The Essential Bill Monroe: 1945-49* seems like the perfect compilation, containing 40 tracks of Monroe and the Blue

Grass Boys' Columbia recordings. However, the set wasn't executed with care—no less than 16 of these songs are represented with alternate takes, not the original versions. Though these alternates are interesting, they don't have a place in a set like this, which purports to be an extensive *introduction*, not an exhaustive compilation of Monroe's complete recordings; the alternates would have been more acceptable if they were placed in conjuction with the master takes. Still, *The Essential Bill Monroe* is a necessary set for bluegrass historians, since it does contain the bulk of his groundbreaking '40s recordings, including versions of "Blue Moon of Kentucky," "Kentucky Waltz," and "Rocky Road Blues." It's just not quite as good as it could have been. (The 16 master takes that were not included on this box were later issued by Columbia as the single-disc *16 Gems* collection.) —*Stephen Thomas Erlewine*

Live Recordings 1956-1959 / 1993 / Smithsonian/Folkways
◆◆◆
The 27 numbers presented here offer Monroe in more intimate settings, including workshops, jam sessions, and live performances where he's casually swapping yarns, offering anecdotes, and displaying the blistering, yet folksy and down-home style that's made him a musical legend. His group included a number of marvelous players and future stars such as Del McCoury, Peter Rowan, Bill Keith, and Tex Logan. Monroe was also playing with brothers Charlie and Birch. This is 75 minutes of breakdowns, folk tunes, railroad and work songs, such classics as "Blue Grass Stomp" and "Blue Moon of Kentucky," and many others performed in a loose, next-door neighbor atmosphere. —*Ron Wynn*

Live Duet Recordings 1963-1980 / 1993 / Smithsonian/Folkways ◆◆◆
Live Duet Recordings 1963-1980 contains a good cross-section of live performances from a variety of different settings and years. What's remarkable is how consistent the quality of the disc is—no matter where he is or who he's playing with, Bill Monroe sounds energetic and lively. —*Thom Owens*

☆ **The Music of Bill Monroe** / 1994 / MCA ◆◆◆◆◆
A four-disc set covering his entire career from 1936 to 1994, this is a meticulously re-mastered and researched four hours and 20 minutes of music and features important recordings from seven decades of recordings for RCA, Columbia, Decca, and MCA. It's an exceptional box set, put together with great care and knowledge, and it's essential for any fan of bluegrass or traditional country music. —*Michael McCall*

Bluegrass (1970-1979) / 1995 / Bear Family ◆◆◆◆
Bluegrass (1970-1979) is a four-disc box set containing all of Monroe's '70s recordings for Decca, including several unreleased cuts and a live album featuring Jim & Jesse, James Monroe, Jimmy Martin, Lester Flatt, and Carl Jackson. By the time he made these recordings, Monroe was no longer making any innovations with his music. Instead he just demonstrated his skill and artistry—the music on *Bluegrass (1970-1979)* is for aficionados, the kinds of listeners who can discern subtle differences between supporting bands and solos. Overall, the material on the box isn't as strong as the previous two box sets, but no Monroe completist will be disappointed by the set. —*Stephen Thomas Erlewine*

☆ **16 Gems** / 1996 / Columbia/Legacy ◆◆◆◆◆
Sony's decision to use 16 alternate takes for the double-CD *Essential* collection was disagreeable to some completists. That omission is rectified by *16 Gems*, which makes all 16 of the official versions of those tunes available on CD and creates a useful adjunct to the *Essential* set for collectors. On its own merits, it's hardly dismissable, with an appeal not limited to Monroe obsessives. Spanning 1945-49, it includes such notable cuts as "Kentucky Waltz" and "Blue Grass Special." —*Richie Unterberger*

Patsy Montana (Ruby Blevins)

b. Oct. 30, 1914, Hot Springs, AR, d. 1996
Vocals / Traditional Country, Cowboy
One of the true pioneers of country music was Patsy Montana, the original yodeling cowgirl. She was the first woman in country music to have a million-selling single—1935's "I Want to Be a

Cowboy's Sweetheart"—and was a mainstay on WLS Chicago's "National Barn Dance" for more than 25 years. In the '30s and '40s she was the sweetheart of many a movie cowpoke, appearing in numerous Western films, and her success encouraged the traditionally male-oriented country music business to welcome and respect the scores of female performers who followed her.

Patsy Montana was born Ruby Blevins in Hot Springs, AR, the eleventh child and first daughter of a farmer. She was influenced early on by the music of Jimmie Rodgers, and as a child learned to yodel and play organ, guitar, and violin. In 1930 she moved to California with her older brother and his wife. Montana won a talent contest there and began appearing on a local radio station as "Ruby Blevins, the Yodeling Cowgirl from San Antone." She continued in radio with country-western star Stuart Hamblen as part of the Montana Cowgirls. Two years later she returned to Arkansas for a visit and wound up in a recording session at Victor with Jimmie Davis. She recorded four of her own songs under the name "Patsy Montana"—Hamblen called her Patsy because he liked Irish names, and her signature song was "Montana Plains."

In 1933 she began singing with the Prairie Ramblers, who became her backup band, at WLS Chicago and then became a regular on the "National Barn Dance." She also cut many records; 1935's "I Want to Be a Cowboy's Sweetheart" became her signature song, but it was not her only hit; others included "Rodeo Sweetheart," "I Wanna Be a Western Cowgirl," "Back on the Montana Plains," and "I Want to Be a Cowboy's Dream." In 1939 she made her full-length feature film debut with Gene Autry in *Colorado Sunset*.

Montana moved to Decca in 1941 and released only 12 songs over the next four years. After World War II, audience tastes shifted towards honky tonk, so Montana's yodeling cowgirl style was not as popular as it had been in the '30s. In 1948 she returned to Arkansas to live on a farm with her husband and two children, appearing on the radio daily in Hot Springs and on many Saturdays on the "Louisiana Hayride." Later she and her husband moved back to California. Over the years Montana remained active in the music industry, appearing on many country music shows. In 1964 she cut a live album at the Matador room in Safford, AZ; among her bandmates was young guitarist Waylon Jennings. In the '80s and '90s she recorded albums for a number of independent labels. She died May 3, 1996. —*Sandra Brennan*

The New Sound of Patsy Montana / 1964 / Sims ✦✦✦

Precious Memories / 1977 / Burch ✦✦✦
Featured are "O Lord I Am Not Worthy," "When It's Prayer-Meetin' Time in the Hollow," and other gospel songs. —*AMG*

Original Hits from the West / 1980 / Cattle [Germany] ✦✦✦✦

Early Country Favorites / 1983 / Old Homestead ✦✦✦

The Cowboy's Sweetheart / 1988 / Flying Fish ✦✦✦✦
These are late recordings by the Western radio star. The title track, from 1935, was the first million-selling female country vocal performance. —*Mark A. Humphrey*

● **Columbia Historic Edition** / Columbia ✦✦✦✦

John Michael Montgomery

b. Jan. 20, 1965, Danville, KY
Vocals / Contemporary Country, New Traditionalist
Even though his music leaned closer to pop music than most honky tonkers, John Michael Montgomery was at the forefront of the new traditionalists' movement in the early '90s. Montgomery was born in Danville, KY, to a guitar-playing father and a mother who played the drums. He made his debut at age five during one of his parents' concerts. He began playing in local bands at 15, and when his parents divorced two years later, he began playing in a group with his father and brother. He first gained notice while playing at the Austin City Saloon in Lexington, KY. By 1991 he had signed with Atlantic Records. Montgomery's debut, *Life's a Dance*, was released in 1992 to positive reviews and strong sales, climbing into the Top Five on the country album charts and the Top 30 on the pop album charts. It produced several hits, including the title cut and "I Love the Way You Love Me," which became

a No. 1 country and a moderate pop hit as well. His second album, *Kickin' It Up*, came out in 1994 and contained the chart-topper "I Swear," which remained No. 1 for more than a month. The album reached No. 1 within a month of its release; it quickly went multiplatinum as well. In the spring of 1995, he released his eponymous third album. —*Sandra Brennan*

Life's a Dance / 1992 / Atlantic ✦✦
Montgomery's baritone lends itself well to the romantic songs, ensuring his success in the heartthrob-heavy country field of the early '90s. That he also does some competent Oklahoma swing counts in his favor. —*Brian Mansfield*

● **Kickin' It Up** / Jan. 25, 1994 / Atlantic ✦✦✦✦
As the title suggests, Montgomery kicks up the tempos and reveals a stronger country-rock bent. He still leans heavily on contemporary ballads ("I Swear," "Rope the Moon") but proves just as capable on the brawnier songs. It became a No. 1 album on the pop charts shortly after its release. —*Michael McCall*

John Michael Montgomery / Mar. 28, 1995 / Atlantic ✦✦✦✦
It doesn't really matter that *John Michael Montgomery* replicates the formula of its hit predecessor, *Kickin' it Up*. Even though it has the same country-pop ballads and slick country-rock and honky tonk numbers that made *Kickin' It Up* a monster commercial success, the record doesn't sound dull or repetitive. Most of the album's success is due to the clean, commercial production, which makes even the weak material entertaining. —*Stephen Thomas Erlewine*

What I Do the Best / Sep. 24, 1996 / Atlantic ✦✦✦
John Michael Montgomery's fourth album, *What I Do the Best*, doesn't tamper with his hitmaking blueprint at all. Essentially it follows the same pattern as its three predecessors, relying equally on heart-tugging ballads and clean, uptempo, neo-honky tonk, and country-rock. Occasionally the material is below par, and Montgomery's delivery doesn't quite save the weaker songs; yet the best moments of *What I Do the Best* are among his best, blending well written songs with crisp production and assured singing. —*Stephen Thomas Erlewine*

Melba Montgomery

b. Oct. 14, 1938, Iron City, TN
Vocals / Traditional Bluegrass, Traditional Country
While a successful singer in her own right, Melba Montgomery is perhaps best remembered for her string of duet recordings with the likes of George Jones, Charlie Louvin, and Gene Pitney. Born October 14, 1938, in Iron City, TN, and raised in Florence, AL, Montgomery gained her first exposure to music through her father, a fiddler and guitarist who gave vocal lessons at the town's Methodist church. At the age of ten, she was given her own guitar, and a decade later, she and her brother won an amateur talent contest held at Nashville radio station WSM's Studio C, which then housed the Grand Ole Opry. Montgomery's performance so impressed contest judge Roy Acuff that he asked the young singer to replace his departing lead vocalist June Webb; she accepted, and toured with Acuff for the next four years.

After going solo in 1962, Montgomery released a self-titled LP, and then teamed for a series of duets with George Jones. Their first joint effort, a rendition of Montgomery's self-penned "We Must Have Been Out of Our Minds," reached the Top Three in 1963, and the follow-up, "What's in Our Heart"/"Let's Invite Them Over," was a two-sided Top 20 hit. Between 1963 and 1967 the Jones-Montgomery team generated a total of five Top 40 hits and two LPs (1966's *Close Together* and 1967's *Let's Get Together*), and while Montgomery maintained a successful solo career during the same period, she remained best known as a duet singer, and so recorded an album of collaborations with Gene Pitney titled *Being Together* in 1966.

After a few minor solo hits in the late 1960s, in 1970 Montgomery found new partners in Charlie Louvin and producer Pete Drake. The duo's first hit, "Something to Brag About," was also their biggest, and after a string of singles and a 1971 album—also titled *Something to Brag About*—she and Louvin parted ways, although Montgomery did continue with Drake. In 1974 he produced her lone No. 1 hit, a rendition of Harlan Howard's "No

Charge," culled from the LP *Melba Montgomery—No Charge*. While she continued to record throughout the decade, subsequent albums like *Don't Let the Good Times Fool You* and *Aching Breaking Heart* found little commercial success, and by the 1980s Montgomery focused largely on touring and appearing at festivals. In 1988 she published a cookbook of family recipes. —*Jason Ankeny*

Down Home / 1964 / United Artists ✦✦✦

America's Number One Country and Western Girl Singer / 1964 / United Artists ✦✦✦

Blue Grass Hootenanny / 1964 / United Artists ✦✦✦

I Can't Get Used to Being Lonely / 1965 / United Artists ✦✦✦

The Hallelujah Road / 1966 / Musicor ✦✦✦

Being Together / 1966 / Musicor ✦✦✦✦

Country Girl / 1966 / Musicor ✦✦✦

Melba Toast / 1967 / Musicor ✦✦✦✦

Don't Keep Me Lonely Too Long / 1967 / Musicor ✦✦✦

I'm Just Living / 1967 / Musicor ✦✦✦

The Mood I'm In / 1967 / Unart ✦✦✦

● **Something to Brag About** / 1971 / Capitol ✦✦✦✦

Clyde Moody (Hillbilly Waltz King)

b. Sep. 19, 1915, Cherokee, NC, **d.** Apr. 7, 1989
Guitar, Vocals / Traditional Bluegrass
Best remembered as one of Bill Monroe's original Blue Grass Boys, singer-songwriter/string player Clyde Moody also played in almost every other subgenre of country music during his more than 50-year career, and even performed as a solo artist. During the '40s he was known as the "Hillbilly Waltz King" after his song "Shenandoah Waltz" became a certified gold hit.

Moody was born and raised in Cherokee, NC, and was greatly influenced by the traditional mountain music he heard there. During the mid-'30s, he and Jay Hugh, the brother of Roy Hall, teamed up to appear as the Happy-Go-Lucky Boys on the radio in Spartanburg, NC. They then joined Wade Mainer, and with fiddler Steve Ledford they became the Sons of the Mountaineers. Moody joined Monroe in 1940 and performed with the Blue Grass Boys at WSM and at the Grand Ole Opry. About this time Monroe and his Boys were becoming a bluegrass band, and the changes can clearly be heard in Moody's mandolin playing on the classic "Six White Horses." A year later, Moody spent a few months in Burlington, NC, playing radio duets with Lester Flatt. He later returned to the Blue Grass Boys and remained with them until again attempting a solo career in 1945.

He joined the Opry as a featured artist for a few weeks and then recorded for Columbia. He had his biggest hit, the sentimental "Shenandoah Waltz," in 1947, and followed it up with a series of similar tunes such as "Cherokee Waltz" and "I Waltz Alone." He had a few more hits through the end of the decade and then moved to Washington, D.C., to work for Connie B. Gay. In 1952 Moody signed with Decca, but he had only a few singles up through the mid-'50s, when his health began to fail. He left music to become a mobile home salesman, but returned in 1962 with a solo album. He then tried a modern country album. During the folk revival, he played at bluegrass festivals and moved back to Nashville in 1972, where he performed both bluegrass and country music until his death in 1989. —*Sandra Brennan*

● **The Best of Clyde Moody** / 1964 / King ✦✦✦✦

Ralph Mooney

b. Sep. 16, 1928, Duncan, OK
Traditional Country, Bakersfield Sound
For more than 40 years, talented session man/songwriter Ralph Mooney played his steel guitar behind some of country music's biggest stars, including Buck Owens and Waylon Jennings; among the songs he wrote were the standards "Crazy Arms" and "Falling for You."

Mooney's brother-in-law taught him to play the guitar, mandolin, and fiddle. After hearing steel guitarist Leon McAuliffe play,

he imitated the sound by using an old knife to fret his guitar. He was living in Bell Gardens, a Los Angeles neighborhood comprised of other Oklahomans, when he met his neighbor Merle Lindsey, a bandleader, who hired young Mooney for a one-night gig with his Oklahoma Nightriders. This led to weekend gigs and then to session work with players such as Skeets McDonald. For the early years of his career, he played a homemade steel guitar he had fashioned out of birch planks, coat hangers, and steel rods. He appeared regularly on Squeakin' Deacon's radio show in the 1950s and afterwards went to live and work in Las Vegas. Soon after his return, Mooney began working with singer Wynn Stewart, whom he greatly admired.

By the end of the decade, Mooney, with his distinctive rolling chord sound, had become known as one of the premiere steel guitar players on the West Coast and was playing behind numerous country stars. In 1961 he and Stewart opened the Nashville Nevada Club in Las Vegas. In 1963 he recorded behind Merle Haggard, who had joined Stewart's band the previous year. In the late '60s, Mooney joined Waylon Jennings' band and stayed on for 20 years. During his retirement he appeared infrequently at guitar shows and conventions, where he discussed his career and demonstrated new steel guitar techniques. —*Sandra Brennan*

● **Corn Pickin' and Slick Slidin'** / 1968 / Capitol ✦✦✦✦
This reissue of a 1968 instrumental album features steel guitar hero Ralph Mooney. —*Dan Cooper*

Charlie Moore

b. Feb. 13, 1935, Piedmont, SC
Vocals / Traditional Bluegrass
Raised in Piedmont, SC, Charlie Moore grew up surrounded by the radio stars of neighboring towns such as Charlotte and Greenville. He became a well known bluegrass singer, but rather than the "high lonesome sound" favored by such artists as Bill Monroe, Moore developed a smooth singing style like that of Red Smiley or Clyde Moody. Moore started out performing on local radio and television shows during the early '50s. In 1958 he made his recording debut for Starday, performing simple songs accompanied only by string instruments. Two years later he began recording for the American label. About this time Moore and Bill Napier (formerly with the Stanley Brothers) teamed up to form the Dixie Partners. The group signed to King Records and recorded nine albums during the '60s. Although the band was never tremendously popular, critics frequently praised Moore's singing. Of the 108 songs they recorded on King, "Truck Driver's Queen" became the best known, thanks to cover versions by both Jimmy Martin and the Willis Brothers. After the band broke up in 1969, Moore staged a comeback in the early '70s with a new edition of the Dixie Partners. The band cut one album for the Country Jubilee label, and recorded for other independent labels during the next two years. During this time, Moore became a member of the popular Wheeling Jamboree USA and made frequent appearances on the festival circuit and in clubs. After 1973 Moore recorded mostly for the Old Homestead label. One of his biggest hits was a reworking of an earlier song he'd written, "The Legend of the Rebel Soldier," which was later placed in the Smithsonian Collection of Classic Country Music. During the '70s Moore endured several personal tragedies, and his drinking habits led to liver difficulties and poor health. Although he attempted to keep performing and touring, Moore died in 1979 after falling into a coma. —*Sandra Brennan*

● **The Best of Charlie Moore & Bill Napier** / 1975 / Starday ✦✦✦✦

Merrill Moore

b. Sep. 26, 1923, Algona, IA
Piano, Vocals / R&B, Boogie-Woogie, Traditional Country
Merrill Moore spent the bulk of his career as a lounge act in various hotels and nightclubs, where he played his distinctive mixture of Western swing, boogie-woogie, and R&B. A native of Algona, IA, and a formally trained pianist from the age of six, Moore began his career on a Des Moines radio station when he was only 12. Deciding to be a full-time musician after serving in World War II and moving to San Diego with his wife, he founded the Saddle

Rhythm Boys in 1950 and played at clubs owned by Jimmy Kennedy. Kennedy helped Moore and his band get a contract with Capitol Records, where their debut release was "Big Bug Boogie." The Saddles couldn't do much promotion or follow-up for the singles, because Kennedy forced them to keep playing at his clubs six and a half days a week. Moore released his best-known song, "House of Blue Lights," in 1953. He moved to L.A. in 1955 and played with Cliffie Stone on *Hometown Jamboree;* he also did session work for about three years and can be heard on such rockabilly tunes as Tommy Sands' "Teenage Crush." Moore eventually returned to San Diego to play clubs. —*Sandra Brennan*

● **Boogie My Blues Away** / Bear Family ♦♦♦♦

Tiny Moore

b. 1920, Hamilton County, TX, d. Dec. 15, 1987
Mandolin / Progressive Bluegrass, Traditional Bluegrass, Instrumental, Traditional Country, Western Swing
Three of the greatest mandolin players of all time (and probably the greatest) only obliquely played country music, devoting their time instead to swing and jazz. Dave Apollon and Jethro Burns are covered elsewhere in this book, and Tiny Moore is the third. Tiny played lead mandolin with Bob Wills' Texas Playboys in the '40s. In the '50s he invented a five-string electric mandolin that he has played while touring with Merle Haggard's band, the Strangers, a group famed for its instrumental excellence. Moore's virtuosity is a joy to listen to. —*David Vinopal*

Tiny Moore Music / 1972 / Kaleidoscope ♦♦♦♦
Tiny Moore's electric mandolin carries you through some great jazz-swing music. Merle Haggard, David Grisman, and Jethro Burns guest on the album. —*Chip Renner*

★ **Back to Back** / Kaleidoscope ♦♦♦♦♦
Tiny Moore, Jethro Burns, and Eldon Shamblin play country-jazz magnificently. —*David Vinopal*

George Morgan

b. Jun. 28, 1925, Waverly, TN, d. Jul. 7, 1975
Guitar, Vocals / Traditional Country, Nashville Sound/Country-politan
The Candy Kid—as George Morgan was known after his first hit "Candy Kisses" spent three weeks at the top of the country chart—was a grand country crooner in the tradition of Eddy Arnold, whom he replaced on the Grand Old Opry in 1948. Born in Waverly, TN, on June 28, 1924, Morgan moved to Ohio with his family not long after. He grew up listening to the Opry and formed his first band in the mid-'40s. Occasional spots on local radio did little for Morgan's career, but after he wrote "Candy Kisses," WWVA-Wheeling (WV) hired him for the "Wheelin Jamboree." The Grand Old Opry called soon after, and Columbia Records contracted Morgan in 1948.

"Candy Kisses" was finally released early the next year, and it hit No. 1 in April; though it proved George Morgan's only chart-topper, he placed six of his next seven singles in the country Top Ten. "Please Don't Let Me Love You," the B-side of "Candy Kisses," reached the Top Five soon after, and another double-sided hit, "Rainbow in My Heart"/"All I Need Is Some More Lovin'" continued the success. Three Top Ten singles (plus the near-miss "All I Need") in the span of a month was simply astonishing for a debut artist, and Morgan proved he was no fluke by closing out 1949 with three more Top Five hits: "Room Full of Roses," "Cry-Baby Heart," and "I Love Everything About You."

It was almost inevitable that Morgan's chart success would taper somewhat, though the three-year gap between hits from late 1949 to 1952 was surprising. "Almost" reached No. 2 in April 1952, however, and Morgan's performances on the Grand Old Opry sustained his reputation. He left the show in 1956 to host a TV program in Nashville, but returned to the Opry three years later. He christened his return in 1959 with "I'm in Love Again," which hit No. 3. Early the next year, "You're the Only Good Thing (That's Happened to You)" hit No. 4, but it was Morgan's last Top 20 entry.

From 1965 to 1975 George Morgan remained with the Opry and recorded frequently, hitting the nether reaches of the country charts consistently. Morgan witnessed his daughter Lorrie's debut on the Opry but didn't live to see her musical success in the late '80s; he passed away in July 1975 after a heart attack. The posthumous father-daughter duet, "I'm Completely Satisfied with You," hit the charts in 1979. —*John Bush*

Morgan, By George / 1957 / Columbia ♦♦♦♦
Golden Memories / 1961 / Columbia ♦♦♦
Red Roses for a Blue Lady / 1965 / Columbia ♦♦♦♦
American Originals / 1977 / Columbia ♦♦♦♦
All of his famous hits, including "Candy Kisses" and "Room Full of Roses," are featured, although not necessarily in their original form. Contrary to the album title, a few of these songs are 1959 remakes of earlier hits. —*Michael McCall*

● **Room Full of Roses: The Best of George Morgan** / 1996 / Razor & Tie ♦♦♦♦
Room Full of Roses contains a generous selection of George Morgan's hits from the late '40s and '50s, including "Candy Kisses," "Please Don't Let Me Love You," "Almost," "I'm In Love Again," and the title track. Every cut is presented in its original hit version, making the compilation the definitive single disc retrospective of his hit-making peak at Columbia Records. —*Stephen Thomas Erlewine*

Candy Kisses / 1996 / Bear Family ♦♦♦♦
Candy Kisses contains George Morgan's complete recordings for Columbia between 1949 and 1966. Spanning eight discs and 200 songs, all of Morgan's major hits—"Candy Kisses," "Almost," "I'm In Love Again," "Room Full of Roses," "Please Don't Let Me Love You," and "You're the Only Good Thing (That's Happened to Me)"—are included on this extensive compilation, which is designed for hardcore fans. The consistency of Morgan's material is somewhat uneven, which makes the set a little tedious for any listener who isn't a fanatic or a historian; yet the box—with its excellent biography, sound, and sessionography—is worthwhile for anyone willing to invest the time and money. —*Stephen Thomas Erlewine*

Lorrie Morgan

b. 1960, Nashville, TN
Vocals / Contemporary Country, Neo-Traditionalist Country
Although she spent most of her life singing, Lorrie Morgan didn't become a star until the early '90s, when she scored a string of Top Ten country hits. Born Loretta Lynn Morgan, she was the daughter of Grand Ole Opry star George Morgan, and made her professional debut at age 13 on the Opry, where her rendition of "Paper Roses" received a standing ovation. When her father died in 1975, she took over his band and began leading the group through various club gigs. Within a few years, she disbanded the group, and in 1977 she went on to play with the Little Roy Wiggins band. She then became a receptionist and demo singer at Acuff-Rose, where she also wrote songs. In 1978 she had one minor hit single; the next year another minor hit with "I'm Completely Satisfied," an electronically dubbed duet with her late father. She began touring Nashville nightclubs and opened for a number of acts, including Jack Greene, Billy Thunderkloud, and Jeanie Seely. She also toured as a duet partner with George Jones and spent two years as part of the Opryland USA bluegrass show and as a guest singer on TNN's "Nashville Now."

In 1984 Morgan scored a minor hit with "Don't Go Changing." That year she became the youngest singer ever to join the Grand Ole Opry. She married Keith Whitley in 1986 and two years later had a Top 20 hit, "Trainwreck of Emotion." Morgan's popularity was blossoming, and she had just scored a major hit with "Dear Me" when Whitley died suddenly in 1989. Though devastated, she continued to work, and that year her album *Leave the Light On* went gold. In 1990 she had her first Number 1 single, "Five Minutes," along with several other Top 10 hits. *Something in Red*, her second album, was released in 1991; it went platinum and spawned the No. 1 single "What Part of No." Morgan's third album, *Watch Me*, was released in 1992; *Merry Christmas from London* (1993) and *War Paint* (1994) followed before she issued her *Greatest Hits* in 1995. She released her fifth studio album, *Greater Need*, in 1996. —*Sandra Brennan*

Leave the Light On / 1989 / RCA ✦✦✦✦
Lorrie Morgan's debut album for RCA Records, *Leave the Light On*, is a skilled and assured blend of traditional country, honky tonk, country-rock and modern pop sensibilities that pointed the direction toward the sound, style and musical eclecticism of '90s contemporary country. Boasting a clean production and uncluttered arrangements, the record shifts between straightforward country-rockers and ballads, to soul-inflected numbers, all of which help showcase Morgan's exceptional voice. —*Thom Owens*

Something in Red / 1991 / RCA ✦✦✦
Morgan backs off the sad songs for her second album—a wise move. (She went through the first part of her life known as George Morgan's daughter; she wouldn't want to spend the rest of it as Keith Whitley's widow.) Instead she concentrates on laidback country and ballads like the title track, which is about the dress colors during different stages of a woman's life. Dolly Parton duets on "Best Woman Wins." —*Brian Mansfield*

● **Watch Me** / Oct. 1992 / RCA ✦✦✦✦
Morgan's second and third albums each improved on the last. *Watch Me* contains more good songs than the first two combined, including "I Guess You Had to Be There" and "From Our House to Yours" but not "What Part of No" or the remake of Bonnie Tyler's 1978 hit "It's a Heartache." —*Brian Mansfield*

Trainwreck of Emotion / 1993 / BNA ✦✦✦

War Paint / May 10, 1994 / BNA ✦✦

● **Greatest Hits** / Oct. 1995 / BNA ✦✦✦✦
As the title implies, *Greatest Hits* contains all of Lorrie Morgan's biggest hits. Morgan's albums tend to be slightly inconsistent; yet her singles have been quite strong. Consequently, *Greatest Hits* is useful both for the casual and the dedicated fan. By featuring nothing but singles, it is her most entertaining album. —*Stephen Thomas Erlewine*

Greater Need / Jun. 1996 / BNA ✦✦✦

Morris Brothers

Traditional Country
The Morris Brothers were a popular duo during the late 1930s, best known for their song "Let Me Be Your Salty Dog," which later became the bluegrass standard "Salty Dog Blues." Zeke and Wiley Morris were born three years apart in Old Fort, NC. Their eldest brother, George, was the first to get into music, working with J.E. Mainer and his brother Wade. Mainer's fiddler, John Love, tried to convince George to join the band, but Love instead ended up with 17-year-old Zeke, who remained with the Mainers for three years and participated in the band's first recording session for Bluebird in 1935. Wade Mainer and Zeke soon left to form their own group, adding fiddler Homer Sherrill. They continued recording for Bluebird and worked at a Raleigh radio station. After Mainer left, Morris, Sherrill, and the rest of the group stayed together to appear on a Danville station. By 1938 Wiley Morris had joined them, and Wiley, Zeke, and Homer recorded several singles for Bluebird, changing their name to the Morris Brothers a few months later for a nine-song session that included the first version of "Salty Dog Blues." The Brothers continued appearing on local radio stations, occasionally joined by George.

The Morris Brothers usually worked as a duo and didn't always have a backing band; sometimes they led separate groups. The two split up in Knoxville in the early 1940s; Wiley joined the Dixie Pardners, while Zeke joined a band at Johnson City radio. The Morris Brothers recorded together for the last time in 1945 for RCA Victor. Among the songs was a new version of their signature tune, plus "Tragic Romance" and "Somebody Loves You Darling." They went into semi-retirement, eventually moving to Black Mountain, NC, and opening an auto body shop. They did perform infrequently through the '60s and '70s at various festivals, and in 1972 recorded an album featuring the fiddle playing of Homer Sherrill. They also joined Earl Scruggs and appeared on a PBS-TV special on which they recorded yet another version of "Salty Dog Blues." In 1985 the Morris Brothers appeared at a

Charlotte radio old-timers reunion for their final performance. Five years later, Wiley died; Zeke remained at his body shop and expressed no further interest in performing. —*Sandra Brennan*

Wiley Zeke & Homer / Rounder ✦✦✦

Gary Morris

b. Dec. 7, 1948, Fort Worth, TX
Vocals / Progressive Country, Country-Folk
An artist who refuses to be categorized, Morris has explored a variety of country sounds—acoustic folk, rock-edged commercial songs, romantic ballads—but also accepted a couple of roles on Broadway, including the physically demanding part of Jean Valjean in *Les Miserables*. Born and raised in Texas, Morris got his "break" by working on Jimmy Carter's 1976 election campaign. For his efforts, he got a chance to play for some influential members of the Country Music Association at a Presidential function, and when his demo tape crossed the desk of Warner's executive Norro Wilson, Wilson remembered him immediately and signed him to a recording deal. Frustrated by the restrictions inherent in the marketing of modern music, Morris refuses to compromise his musical integrity, and some of his work has thus fallen between the cracks. But few country artists—if any—have been able to match Morris for his vocal strength and clarity. —*Tom Roland*

Gary Morris / 1982 / Warner Brothers ✦✦✦

Why Lady Why / 1983 / Warner Brothers ✦✦✦
Morris' second LP contains his first significant hits, including "Velvet Chains," "The Love She Found in Me," "The Wind Beneath My Wings" and the title cut, all of which reached the Top Ten. —*Jason Ankeny*

Faded Blue / 1984 / Warner Brothers ✦✦✦

Anything Goes / 1985 / Warner Brothers ✦✦

Plain Brown Wrapper / 1986 / Warner Brothers ✦✦
Plain Brown Wrapper features "Leave Me Lonely," Morris' fourth No. 1 hit, as well as the title cut, which reached the Top Ten. —*Jason Ankeny*

Second Hand Heart / 1986 / Warner Brothers ✦✦✦

● **Hits** / 1987 / Warner Brothers ✦✦✦✦
Morris may have the best "pipes" in country music, but he works so hard at showcasing them that most of his studio albums are bogged down by ballads. This collection includes the best of those ballads ("The Love She Found in Me," "100% Chance of Rain"), plus his best overall material ("I'll Never Stop Loving You," "Baby Bye Bye," "Velvet Chains"), which he seemingly undervalues. For those who appreciate such things, it also includes a sampling of his Broadway work, with a song from *La Boheme*. —*Tom Roland*

What If We Fell in Love / 1987 / Warner Brothers ✦✦✦

Stones / 1989 / Liberty ✦✦

Greatest Hits, Vol. 2 / 1990 / Warner Brothers ✦✦✦✦
Greatest Hits, Vol. 2 contains most of Gary Morris' biggest hits from the mid-'80s that didn't make his first compilation, including "Why Lady Why," "Between Two Fires," "Second Hand Heart," and the duet with Lynn Anderson, "You're Welcome to Tonight." —*Thom Owens*

These Days / 1990 / Liberty ✦✦✦
Contains the hit "Miles Across the Bedroom" and other Morris favorites. —*AMG*

Full Moon, Empty Heart / 1991 / Liberty ✦✦

Lynn Morris

Traditional Bluegrass
Lynn Morris is a well-respected vocalist and guitar player. Her band consists of Tom Adams (banjo), David McLaughlin (mandolin), Stuart Duncan (fiddle), and Marshall Wilborn (bass and vocals). They play a blend of bluegrass, folk, and country music. —*Chip Renner*

● **The Lynn Morris Band** / 1990 / Rounder ✦✦✦✦
Great sound, great vocals, and outstanding bluegrass. It includes "Enjoy Black Pony" and "Come Early Morning." —*Chip Renner*

The Bramble and the Rose / 1992 / Rounder ✦✦✦
A solid release, with great vocals and a good cover of "Blue Skies and Teardrops." Another fine effort. Lynn Morris and Marshall Wilborn's harmonies are very good. Stuart Duncan stands out on fiddle. —*Chip Renner*

Mama's Hand / Oct. 1995 / Rounder ✦✦✦

Moon Mullican

b. Mar. 29, 1909, Corrigan, Polk County, TX, **d.** Jan. 1, 1967, Beaumont, TX
Piano, Vocals / Instrumental, Traditional Country, Western Swing, Honky Tonk
A piano-pounding honky tonk man, born and raised deep in the heart of East Texas, Aubrey "Moon" Mullican is said to have had a significant musical influence on Jerry Lee Lewis, among others. Throughout the Depression and war years, he cut his ivory teeth on Western swing, most notably as vocalist and piano player in Cliff Bruner's Texas Wanderers. In 1946 he signed with the emerging independent powerhouse King Records. A performer of wide-ranging tastes, Mullican was comfortable singing straight country, treacly pop, or White boy boogie. Indeed, many of his King sides, cut with Black producer Henry Glover, jumped to the beat of hardcore R&B. —*Dan Cooper*

Seven Nights to Rock / Sep. 1946-Jan. 26, 1956 / Western ✦✦✦✦
An important but somewhat forgotten country music pioneer, Moon Mullican was one of the music's first singing pianists (inspiring Jerry Lee Lewis indirectly) and was quite popular during the period covered by this Western LP. The opening number, a spirited "Seven Nights to Rock," is worthy of Bill Haley, while other selections feature hard-driving country swing with occasional ballads. Although it would have been preferable for Western to reissue Mullican's music in chronological order (so one could easily experience his musical evolution), the 16 selections on this album (which can be called late-period Western swing or early rockabilly) give one a strong sampling of Moon Mullican's music. —*Scott Yanow*

Sings His All-Time Greatest Hits / 1958 / King ✦✦✦✦
Originally released in 1958, *Sings His All-Time Greatest Hits* is Moon Mullican's first album and, essentially, it *is* a greatest hits collection, featuring 12 of his hit singles from the late '40s and '50s. Drawn entirely from his King Recordings, this collection contains the bulk of his signature songs: "I'll Sail My Ship Alone," "Cherokee Boogie," "Mona Lisa," "You Don't Have to Be a Baby to Cry," "Pipeliner's Blues," and "I Was Sorta Wondering." It's a fine introduction and retrospective. There is one slight problem: The compact disc reissue is cheaply packaged and contains poor sound, but the music is good enough to make those flaws forgivable. —*Stephen Thomas Erlewine*

★ **Moonshine Jamboree** / 1993 / Ace ✦✦✦✦✦
The best available compilation, this import CD includes "I'll Sail My Ship Alone," the one bona fide smash hit of Mullican's under-appreciated career, and 22 lesser successes or hits that never were. —*Dan Cooper*

Moon's Rock / Bear Family ✦✦✦✦
This draws from Mullican's later years, after his career had gone into commercial decline. —*Dan Cooper*

Seven Years to Rock: The King Years, 1946-56 / Western ✦✦✦✦
Not a hits compilation, it's still a good sampling of Moon in his boogie phase. His take on Tiny Bradshaw's "Well, Oh Well" is required listening for anyone who thinks Elvis invented the hillbilly/R&B cover. —*Dan Cooper*

Michael Martin Murphey

b. Mar. 13, 1945, Dallas, TX
Guitar, Vocals / Cowboy, Progressive Country, Neo-Traditionalist Country
Michael Martin Murphey has merged successful country and pop careers as both a songwriter and singer, all the while remaining true to his Western cowboy roots, as exemplified by his three volumes of *Cowboy Songs* released in the early '90s. Murphey spent much of his early life working on family ranches. While still in

Michael Martin Murphey

high school, he played in a country/folk band that toured clubs around Texas. Murphey studied for a time at North Texas State College, but moved to California to attend UCLA. Sparrow Music offered a songwriting contract soon after he got there, and he joined the Trinity River Boys with future Monkee Michael Nesmith. In 1967 Murphey formed the Lewis & Clark Expedition with Owen "Boomer" Castleman. The band recorded one album, and the title track "I Feel Good (I Feel Bad)" reached No. 64 on the pop charts later that year.

Unsatisfied with his early success, Murphey moved from Los Angeles into the Mojave Desert and began to write a great many songs that were recorded by Flatt & Scruggs, Roger Miller, and Bobbie Gentry. Michael Nesmith also asked him to write a song for the Monkees, and Murphey obliged with "What Am I Doing Hangin' Around."

Michael Murphey moved back home in 1971 and became involved with the outlaw movement in Texas; he played with Willie Nelson and Jerry Jeff Walker, and signed a contract with A&M that same year. The title track from his debut album, *Geronimo's Cadillac*, hit the popular Top 40 in 1972 and became an anthem for Native American activists. After 1973's *Cosmic Cowboy Souvenir*, Murphey signed with Epic and released *Blue Sky—Night Thunder* in 1975. The album included the No. 3 hit "Wildfire" and "Carolina in the Pines," which barely missed the Top 20.

Up to this point, Murphey had been marketed purely as a pop artist, somewhat in the singer-songwriter vein, though his interchangeable style soon proved amenable to country music. Epic changed its focus on a second 1975 album, *Swans Against the Sun*. The singer's first entry on the country charts, "A Mansion on the Hill," reached No. 36—the ever-industrious Murphey even slipped a pop Top 40 hit ("Renegade") on the B-side. He returned to the country charts in 1977 with "Cherokee Fiddle," from *Flowing Free Forever*. (The song was a hit five years later for Johnny Lee with Murphey and Charlie Daniels on backing vocals.) Murphey finished his Epic contract by 1979 with two albums, *Lone Wolf* and *Peaks, Valleys, Honky Tonks and Alleys*. Two singles from the era grazed the country Top 100.

The next three years saw Michael Murphey disappear from the recording industry. He married Mary Maciukas (his second wife), moved to New Mexico, and studied the culture of the American West, but he continued to write songs and even a screenplay for the film *Hard Country*. He also appeared in that film and in *Take This Job and Shove It* (1981). Because of the latter role, Murphey added his middle name to differentiate himself from the actor Michael Murphy.

Michael Martin Murphey returned to recording in 1982 with a contract from Liberty Records. He released a self-titled album that same year, scoring his first No. 1 on the country charts with "What's Forever For." (The single hit the Top 20 on the popular charts.) He hit the country Top Ten four times in the next two years, including the No. 3 "Still Taking Chances," which was also a pop hit.

The Country Music Association gave Murphey the extremely belated honor of Best New Artist in 1984—though almost ten years had passed since his Top Five pop hit "Wildfire." His last Liberty album, *The Best of Michael Martin Murphey*, compiled his best '70s pop singles with country hits from the early '80s, and an updated version of "Carolina in the Pines"—with Ricky Skaggs on mandolin—invaded the country Top Ten in May 1985. That same year Murphey signed to Warner Brothers, though his first three singles were disappointing. By 1987 he was back in gear. "A Face in the Crowd" (with Holly Dunn) began a streak of four straight country Top Five hits, including "A Long Line of Love," which became Murphey's second No. 1. November spawned the No. 3 "I'm Gonna Miss You, Girl," and April 1988 brought a performance with his son Ryan titled "Talkin' to the Wrong Man." After one comparative miss stalled in the Top 30, Murphey's last two Top Ten hits—"From the Word Go" and "Never Givin' Up on Love" (from *Pink Cadillac*)—provided a coda to his commercial career.

Though Michael Martin Murphey wasn't a guaranteed hitmaker after 1989, his artistic career was the better for it. He launched WestFest, an annual festival of music and culture held in the Southwest, and recorded his first album of *Cowboy Songs* in 1990. Critics praised him, the album outsold each of his previous Warner Bros. albums—with no Top 40 hits—and its success convinced the label to begin the Warner Western label specifically for Western music. The next year brought *Cowboy Christmas*, and 1993's *Cowboy Songs III* featured a duet with Hal Ketchum and a re-recording of Marty Robbins' "Big Iron" with Robbins' original vocals. —*John Bush*

Geronimo's Cadillac / 1972 / A&M ✦✦✦✦
Often lumped in with the "Outlaws," this album is partially made up of songs Murphey wrote for the First Edition's album *Ballad of Calico*. Good songs, well done. Other songs were covered by the Monkees and Jerry Jeff Walker. —*Jim Worbois*

Cosmic Cowboy Souvenir / 1973 / A&M ✦✦✦
For his second A&M album, Murphey continued to celebrate the Texas music scene. The band on this record includes a couple members of Jerry Jeff Walker's Lost Gonzo Band. With songs like "Promethius Bound," Murphey shows he is deeper than the Cosmic Cowboy thing would indicate. All in all, a good record. —*Jim Worbois*

Michael Murphey / 1973 / Epic ✦✦✦
Despite titles that still promote the Texas movement, this record was done in Nashville with Nashville Cats. Songs like "Nobody's Gonna Tell Me How . . ." and "You Can Only Say So Much" seem to indicate this has worn thin for Murphey. Still, there is some good stuff on here. —*Jim Worbois*

● **Blue Sky—Night Thunder** / 1975 / Epic ✦✦✦✦
The change in musical direction hinted at on *Michael Murphey* has come to pass on this record. The Western feel of this record could qualify it as the follow-up to the *Ballad of Calico* songs he wrote for The First Edition. Also, with this album, the commercial success which had eluded him over the course of his previous albums was finally his. —*Jim Worbois*

Swans Against the Sun / 1976 / Epic ✦✦✦
With guest stars aplenty sharing vocals and filling out instrumental roles, this album feels more like a novelty item than a real record. One of the oddest items is John Denver singing Hank Williams, though it sort of works. —*Jim Worbois*

Peaks, Valleys, Honky Tonks and Alleys / 1979 / Epic ✦✦✦
This live album showcases Murphey's early work with some interesting twists. His "Cosmic Cowboy" turns into a breakdown, while his song "Another Cheap Western" is coupled with the Olympics' 1958 hit, "Western Movies." Not a particularly memorable album, it's still kind of fun. —*Jim Worbois*

The Best of Michael Martin Murphey / 1982 / EMI America ✦✦✦
This collection features his best from the early '80s. —*Kenneth M. Cassidy*

The Heart Never Lies / 1983 / Liberty ✦✦

Tonight We Ride / 1986 / Warner Brothers ✦✦✦

Americana / 1987 / Warner Brothers ✦✦

River of Time / 1988 / Warner Brothers ✦✦✦✦
Murphey's best includes "From the Word Go," "I'm Gonna Miss You Girl," "Talking to the Wrong Man," and "What Am I Doing Hanging Around," a song Murphey originally wrote for The Monkees. —*Kenneth M. Cassidy*

Cowboy Songs / 1990 / Warner Brothers ✦✦✦
A collection of mostly cowboy standards, it includes "Tumbling Tumbleweeds" and "Happy Trails," with some new tunes. Murphey shines throughout. —*Kenneth M. Cassidy*

Cowboy Christmas / May 1991 / Warner Brothers ✦✦
Michael Martin Murphey, in his typical tradition, is able to pull off the unexpected with *Cowboy Christmas*. As on his other records, Murphey balances traditional songs with originals that manage to capture not just the style, but the very feel, of classic cowboy songs; it has a down-home warmth and honesty lacking on most Christmas albums, including most country Christmas albums. —*Thom Owens*

Cowboy Songs 3 / Oct. 12, 1993 / Warner Western ✦✦✦
Murphey's third album of songs devoted to cowboy folklore and true tales of the West (the second was a Christmas album of Western songs) focuses on real-life outlaws, from Jesse James to Billy the Kid to Belle Starr, and related topics, such as "Birmingham Jail" and "Prisoner's Song." All are performed with a scholar's eye and a fan's heart. —*Michael McCall*

Sagebrush Symphony / Sep. 12, 1995 / Warner Brothers ✦✦
Recorded live with the San Antonio Symphony Orchestra, *Sagebrush Symphony* contains a selection of Michael Martin Murphey's most popular songs, as well as several cowboy standards. Although the combination of orchestra and cowboy songs initially seems forced, it works quite well, particularly because Murphey turns in an impassioned performance. In addition, the presence of guest artists Sons of the San Joaquin, Ric Orozco, Herb Jeffries, and Robert Mirabal adds to the musical diversity and richness of the album. —*Stephen Thomas Erlewine*

David Lee Murphy

Vocals / Contemporary Country, New Traditionalist
David Lee Murphy's polished blend of neo-traditional country and mainstream rock flourishes made the vocalist a star in the mid-'90s. Murphy moved to Nashville with hopes of become a star in 1983. For ten years he struggled in the Music City, honing his craft but never catching the attention of the music industry. By the early '90s, he had gained a reputation in Nashville and in 1992, he signed with MCA Records. Murphy's first recording was a contribution to the soundtrack of the Luke Perry rodeo movie *Eight Seconds*.

Out with a Bang, his first album, was released in early 1995. "Party Crowd" became the most-played song on country radio in 1995 and the record's second single, "Dust on the Bottle," spent two weeks at No. 1. *Out with a Bang* would go platinum and become the best-selling debut album by a male country singer for the entire year of 1995. The Academy of Country Music nominated him for Top New Male Vocalist at the end of the year.

Released in the summer of 1996, his second album, *Gettin' Out the Good Stuff*, wasn't quite as successful, although the single "The Road You Leave Behind" reached No. 14. —*Stephen Thomas Erlewine*

Out with a Bang / 1995 / MCA ✦✦✦

● **Gettin' Out the Good Stuff** / May 21, 1996 / MCA ✦✦✦✦

Anne Murray

b. Jun. 20, 1946, Springhill, Nova Scotia, Canada

Ukulele, Vocals / Country-Pop, Soft Rock

As a child in Nova Scotia, music was always one of Anne Murray's hobbies. While she was enrolled at the University of New Brunswick studying physical eduation, she auditioned for a spot on the Halifax-based weekly CBC television series "Singalong Jubilee," but she wasn't hired because they already had an alto singer. After the rejection, Murray graduated from college and began teaching physical education at the high school level. Two years after the initial "Singalong Jubilee" audition, the show's producer, Bill Langstroth, called her with the information that a new television show, "Let's Go," needed an alto. After some persuasion, Murray agreed to join the program, although she did not give up her teaching job. For the next four years, she sang on "Let's Go," eventually striking up a professional relationship with the program's musical director, Brian Ahern.

Anne Murray began her career as a recording artist in 1968. Early that year, she was still teaching when she received a call from Ahern, asking her to record for the independent label, Arc. Accepting the offer, Murray recorded and released her debut album, *What About Me*, that year. The record was well received and popular for an independent album, thereby earning the attnetion of Capitol Records, whose Canadian division signed her to a long-term contract in 1969. The next year, her debut single for the label, "Snowbird," became an international hit, reaching the Top Ten on both the country and pop charts in America, while reaching the British Top 40. After the success of "Snowbird," Murray moved to Los Angeles, where she began to appear regularly on Glen Campbell's syndicated television show. She didn't like the California lifestyle, however, and she quickly returned to Canada.

Over the course of 1971, it looked as if "Snowbird" would be Anne Murray's only big hit, since none of her followup singles gained much attention; only "A Stranger in My Place" cracked the Top 40. A cover of Gordon Lightfoot's "Cotton Jenny" in early 1972 returned her to the higher regions of the country Top 40, peaking at No. 11, while its follow-up, "Danny's Song," became a Top Ten hit on both the pop and country charts in early 1973. After two minor country hits, she returned to the Top Ten early in 1974 with "Love Song." The single was followed by two Top Ten country hits—the No. 1 "He Thinks I Still Care" and "Son of a Rotten Gambler." After those two successes, Murray spent a number of years struggling to crack either the pop or country Top 40; during this time, she concentrated on raising a family (she married Bill Langstroth and had a son) more than her musical career.

Murray entered her period of greatest commercial success in 1978, as a cover of "Walk Right Back" climbed to No. 4 on the country charts, followed shortly afterward by "You Need Me," her biggest hit since "Snowbird"; the single reached No. 4 on the country charts and topped the pop charts, going gold by the end of the year. For the next eight years, she had a virtually uninterrupted string of Top Ten country hits, highlighted by nine No. 1 hits: "I Just Fall in Love Again" (1979), "Shadows in the Moonlight" (1979), "Broken Hearted Me" (1979), "Could I Have This Dance" (1980), "Blessed Are the Believers" (1981), "A Little Good News" (1983), "Just Another Woman in Love" (1984), "Nobody Loves Me Like You Do" (1984), and "Now and Forever (You and Me)" (1986). Murray prospered during the era of *Urban Cowboy*, since her music drew as much from pop and easy listening as it did from country.

Murray's sales began to decline in the latter half of the '80s, primarily due to the shifting tastes of the country audience, who were beginning to seek out harder-edged, new traditionalist performers. Nevertheless, she maintained a dedicated following during the late '80s and '90s through her occasional recordings

("Feed This Fire" became a surprise Top Ten hit in the summer of 1990) and her concerts. —*Tom Roland*

● **Greatest Hits** / 1980 / Liberty ✦✦✦✦

This covers Murray's first decade in the international limelight, beginning with "Snowbird" and concluding with "Could I Have This Dance?," a track from the 1980 movie *Urban Cowboy*. It ranges from the folky "Danny's Song" to her cover of the Beatles' "You Won't See Me," but the middle-of-the-road approach is quite obvious. —*Tom Roland*

Little Good News / 1983 / Liberty ✦✦✦

A Little Good News features the title song, anotther in Murray's long list of No. 1 hits. —*Jason Ankeny*

Country Hits / 1987 / Liberty ✦✦✦

Ann Murray's Country Hits contains a good 15-track cross-section of Murray's pop-country hits from the '70s and early '80s, including "Cotton Jenny," "Walk Right Back," "He Thinks I Still Care," "Son of A Rotten Gambler," "I Don't Think I'm Ready for You," and "A Little Good News." Though *Country Hits* doesn't have hits like "Snowbird," "I Just Fall in Love Again," and "Could I Have This Dance," *Country Hits* has a good sampling of her best country-leaning material. —*Stephen Thomas Erlewine*

As I Am / 1988 / Capitol ✦✦

As I Am features the minor hits "Flying on Your Own," "Slow Passin' Time," and "Who But You." —*Jason Ankeny*

Greatest Hits, Vol. 2 / 1989 / Liberty ✦✦✦✦

With her country base firmly established, Murray grew restless in the early and mid-'80s, very much desirous of conquering the pop market. It never quite happened, though she made a nice stab at it in her duet with Dave Loggins, "Nobody Loves Me like You Do." She may not be country in the classic sense, but good music is good music and it's hard not to like "Time Don't Run Out on Me" or "Now and Forever (You and Me)." —*Tom Roland*

You Will / 1990 / Liberty ✦✦✦

The Top Five hit "Feed the Fire" and "Bluebird" are the highlights of *You Will.* —*Jason Ankeny*

Yes I Do / 1991 / Liberty ✦✦

Yes I Do includes Murray's final chart hit, "Everyday." —*Jason Ankeny*

15 of the Best / Apr. 27, 1992 / Liberty ✦✦✦✦

15 of the Best contains the majority of Anne Murray's best-known songs, including "Snowbird," "Danny's Song," "I Just Fall in Love Again," "Broken Hearted Me," "Shadows in the Moonlight," and "You Need Me," making it an excellent introduction to her smooth country-pop style. —*Thom Owens*

Now & Forever / 1994 / EMI ✦✦✦✦

This three-disc box contains an excellent booklet and 64 freshly remastered tracks, with a generous helping of alternate mixes, live recordings, and previously unreleased material, including several early, pre-fame nuggets. —*Roch Parisien*

The Best ... So Far / 1994 / EMI ✦✦✦✦

A serviceable 20-song distillation of the biggest hits from the box set. However, here's the kicker: the single disc includes "Over You," a new-old track from the vaults (released as a single) which is not included in the box set. So if you want to have it all ... —*Roch Parisien*

Anne Murray / Aug. 7, 1996 / Capitol ✦✦✦

Anne Murray is the vocalist's 30th album and, unlike some of the ones that immediately preceded it, this record is carefully assembled and produced. Murray always straddled the line between country-pop and adult contemporary pop and, with this album, she abandons country for smooth, easy listening pop, designed for adults. For the most part, the results are successful. Producer Ed Cherney has crafted some meticulous arrangements that are easy on the ears and the duet with Aaron Neville on "That's What My Love Is For" is a nice touch. Of course, that means the music is never ear-grabbing, but as pleasant background music *Anne Murray* works. —*Rodney Batdorf*

N

The Nashville Bluegrass Band

Progressive Bluegrass, Traditional Bluegrass
The Nashville Bluegrass Band was made up of several excellent musicians more interested in preserving their group sound than showing off their individual expertise. The band favored a traditional, earthy sound that led one critic to call them the band that "put the blues back in bluegrass."

The Nashville Bluegrass Band was founded by guitarist Pat Enright, banjo picker Alan O'Bryant, mandolin player Mike Compton, and acoustic bassist Mark Hembree. North Carolina native O'Bryant came to Nashville in the mid-'70s, where he did session work with such artists as Bill Monroe, Doc Watson, and John Starling. He was also a songwriter whose tunes, including "Those Memories of You," were recorded by several major artists. An Indiana native, Enright began playing with the popular bluegrass band Phantoms of the Opry while living in San Francisco in the early 1970s. He too went to Nashville in 1974 and there met O'Bryant, and they teamed up and were soon playing clubs. In 1978, Enright moved to Boston and joined Tasty Licks. The following year he returned to Music City and recorded with the Dreadful Snakes and Bela Fleck. Compton hailed from Mississippi and moved to Nashville in 1976, where he teamed up with banjo picker Hubert Davis. Compton's style was influenced by Bill Monroe and blues player Robert Johnson. Hembree came from Wisconsin and first gained experience with the Monroe Doctrine, whom he joined in 1977. He came to Nashville in 1979 to work with Bill Monroe, spending five years as a Blue Grass Boy. He met Compton as he and the Dreadful Snakes were recording *Snakes Alive.*

The Nashville Bluegrass Band came together in 1985 and released *My Native Home*, which featured fiddle player Blaine Sprouse and production by Bela Fleck. Before the year's end fiddler Stuart Duncan, a session player and sideman from California, joined the band. In 1987, they released another Fleck-produced album, *Idle Time*, and before the end of the year released a bluegrass/gospel album, *To Be His Child.* In 1988, they were involved in a terrible bus accident near Roanoke, Virginia; Hembree was so badly hurt that he had to leave the band, and Compton, whose mandolin was also broken in the accident, soon left the group as well. They were eventually replaced by bassist Gene Libbea and mandolin player Roland White. In 1990, the Nashville Bluegrass Band released *The Boys Are Back in Town.* Two more albums followed, including 1993's *Waiting for the Hard Time to Go. —Sandra Brennan*

My Native Home / 1985 / Rounder ✦✦✦✦
A flawless album. One of their best. *—Chip Renner*

The Nashville Bluegrass Band / 1987 / Rounder ✦✦✦✦
The Nashville Bluegrass Band selects highlights from the group's first two albums for Rounder Records. Though the band's music would improve with time, this is a terrific overview of the group's origins. *—Thom Owens*

Idletime / 1987 / Rounder ✦✦✦
This hits on all cylinders with 12 tight songs. Has the classic "The Train Carryin' Jimmie Rodgers Home." *—Chip Renner*

To Be His Child / 1987 / Rounder ✦✦✦✦
To Be His Child is an affecting sampling of the Nashville Bluegrass Band's gospel material, featuring both their string work and several tracks that feature an a cappella quartet. *—Thom Owens*

The Boys Are Back in Town / 1990 / Sugar Hill ✦✦✦✦
The Boys Are Back in Town is one of the most exciting releases from the Nashville Bluegrass Band, demonstrating their dazzling vocal arrangements and excellent taste in material, as they perform both driving, uptempo cuts and soulful ballads. *—Thom Owens*

New Moon Rising / 1991 / Sugar Hill ✦✦✦

Home of the Blues / 1991 / Sugar Hill ✦✦✦
Home of the Blues is one of the Nashville Bluegrass Band's finest albums, boasting a handful of excellent originals like "Blue Train," interpretations of standards like "Old Daingerfield," and, as a bonus, a live cut with the black gospel group the Fairfield Four. *—Thom Owens*

★ **Waitin' for the Hard Times to Go** / 1993 / Sugar Hill ✦✦✦✦✦
Waitin' for the Hard Times to Go is an excellent collection from a stellar bluegrass band. Instead of choosing to follow either a traditional or progressive direction, the Nashville Bluegrass Band decided to alternate between the two approaches, which makes it a considerably richer and eclectic record than most contemporary bluegrass albums. *Waitin' for the Hard Times to Go* won the 1993 Grammy Award for Best Bluegrass Album. *—Thom Owens*

Still Unplugged / Oct. 1995 / Sugar Hill ✦✦

Unleashed / Oct. 1995 / Sugar Hill ✦✦✦
The new CD from the all-star Nashville Bluegrass Band is a jaunty, highly musical collection of contemporary tunes with a few trads. thrown in for good measure. The bluegrass and light gospel singing is very agreeable, unforced, and as always with this band, it seems completely natural. Too often this style of country singing is adopted but not lived in. Not the case here. This is a very strong album. Instrumentalists trade licks with casual authority. Some of the highlights are "I Got a Date," "Tear My Stillhouse Down," and "The Doorstep of Trouble." *—Richard Meyer*

Nashville Guitars

Country-Pop, Contemporary Country
Nashville Guitars is a conglomeration of several Nashville session musicians who record instrumental versions of contemporary country hits. *—Stephen Thomas Erlewine*

Pickin' the Hits / Oct. 3, 1995 / Dominion ✦✦✦
Nashville Guitars' *Pickin' the Hits* is comprised of pleasant instrumental versions of 12 Top Ten country hits by the likes of Garth Brooks, John Michael Montgomery, and Brooks & Dunn, as performed by several professional Nashville studio musicians. The results are entertaining and lively. In fact, with the galloping guitars, they might even be more country than the original versions—but only guitar fanatics and fans of accomplished Nashville playing will find this totally enthralling. *—Thom Owens*

Rick Nelson (Eric Hilliard Nelson)

b. May 8, 1940, Teaneck, NJ, **d.** Dec. 31, 1985, Dallas, TX
Guitar, Vocals / Rock 'n' Roll, Country-Rock, Pop-Rock, Teen Idol

Rick Nelson was one of the very biggest of the '50s teen idols, so it took a while for him to attain the same level of critical respectability as other early rock greats. Yet now the consensus is that he made some of the finest pop-rock recordings of his era. Sure, he had more promotional push than any other rock musician of the '50s; no, he wasn't the greatest singer; and yes, Elvis, Gene Vincent, Carl Perkins, and others rocked harder. But Nelson was extraordinarily consistent during the first five years of his recording career, crafting pleasant pop-rockabilly hybrids with ace session players, and projecting an archetype of the sensitive, reticent young adult with his accomplished vocals. He also played a somewhat underestimated role in rock 'n' roll's absorption into mainstream America—how bad could rock be if it was featured on one of America's favorite family situation comedies on a weekly basis?

Nelson entered professional entertainment before his tenth birthday, when he appeared with father Ozzie (once a jazz musician), mother Harriet, and brother David on a radio comedy series based around the family. By the early '50s, the series was on television, and Ricky grew into a teenager in public. He was just the right age to have his life turned around by rock 'n' roll in 1956, and he started his recording career almost accidentally the following year. The story's sometimes been told that he had no professional singing ambitions until he recorded his debut single to impress a girlfriend. The single, a cover of Fats Domino's "I'm Walkin'," that went to No. 4, was helped immensely (as all of his early singles would be) by plugs on the "Ozzie and Harriet" TV show.

So far the script was adhering to the Pat Boone teen idol prototype—a whitewash of an R&B hit stealing the thunder from the pop audience, sung by a young, good-looking fella with barely any musical experience to speak of. What happened next was easy to predict commercially, but surprisingly satisfying musically as well. Nelson was a fairly hip kid who preferred the rockabilly of Carl Perkins and Elvis Presley to the fodder dished out for teen idols, and over the next five years he would offer his own brand of rockabilly music, albeit one with some smooth Hollywood production touches and occasional pure pop ballads. Nelson recruited one of the greatest early rock guitarists, James Burton, to supply authentic licks (another great guitarist, Joe Maphis, played on some early sides). Some of his best and toughest songs ("Believe What You Say," "It's Late") were written by Johnny and/or Dorsey Burnette, who had previously been in one of the best rockabilly combos, the Johnny Burnette Rock 'n' Roll Trio. Nelson could rock pretty hard when he wanted to, as on "Be-Bop Baby" and "Stood Up," though in a polished fashion that wasn't quite as wild and threatening as rockabilly's Southern originators'.

Nelson really hit his stride, though, with midtempo numbers and ballads that provided a more secure niche for his calm vocals and narrow range. From 1957 to 1962, he was about the highest-selling singer in the US except for Elvis, making the Top 40 about 30 times. "Poor Little Fool" and "Lonesome Town" (1958) were early indications of his ballad style; in the early '60s, "Travelin' Man," "Young World," "Teen Age Idol," and other hits pointed to a more countrified, mature style as he honed in on his 21st birthday (by which time he would shorten his billing from "Ricky" to "Rick"). He could still play rockabilly from time to time, the most memorable example being "Hello, Mary Lou" (co-written by Gene Pitney), with its electrifying James Burton solos.

Nelson was lured away from the Imperial label by a mammoth 20-year contract with Decca in 1963 (which would be terminated prematurely in the mid-'70s), and for a year or so the hits continued, at a less frenetic pace. Early 1964's "For You," however, would be his last big smash of the '60s. The fault wasn't all the Beatles' and changing music trends—on both singles and albums, much of the material was either substandard pop or dusty Tin Pan Alley standards, although isolated tracks still generated some sparks. He wasn't exactly starving, as he continued to appear on "Ozzie

and Harriet." But by the mid-'60s even that institution was declining in popularity, leading to its cancellation in 1966.

Nelson had a strong country feel to much of his material from the beginning, and by the late '60s it was becoming dominant. He covered straight country material by the likes of Willie Nelson and Doug Kershaw, and formed one of the earliest country-rock groups, the Stone Canyon Band, with musicians who had played (or would play) with Poco, Buck Owens, Little Feat, and Roger McGuinn. A cover of Bob Dylan's "She Belongs to Me" made the Top 40 in 1970, but his country-rock outings attracted more critical acclaim than commercial success until 1972's "Garden Party." A rare self-composed number, based around the frosty reception granted his contemporary material at a rock 'n' roll oldies show, it became his last Top Ten hit.

Nelson would continue to record off and on for the next dozen years and he toured constantly, but he was unable to capitalize on his assets. A big part of the problem was that although Nelson wanted to play contemporary music, he didn't write much of his own material, which was a basic precept of self-respecting rock acts after the advent of the Beatles. Nor did he tap into good outside compositions, and there's little of interest on the albums he recorded over the last decade or so of his life. He died (along with his fiancee) in a private plane crash on December 31, 1985, on his way to a New Year's Eve gig in Dallas, at the age of 45. *—Richie Unterberger*

Ricky / 1957 / United Artists ◆◆◆
This debut is filled with bopping covers and Joe Maphis on lead guitar. *—Bill Dahl*

Ricky Nelson / 1958 / Imperial ◆◆◆◆
His second Imperial album is a classic, introducing the brilliant guitar of James Burton. *—Bill Dahl*

Songs by Ricky / 1959 / Imperial ◆◆◆◆
More first-class rockers by Ricky, and James Burton is amazing. *—Bill Dahl*

Rick Is 21 / 1961 / Imperial ◆◆◆◆
. . . and he celebrates with some fine rock 'n' roll, including "Hello Mary Lou." *—Bill Dahl*

Album Seven / 1962 / Imperial ◆◆◆
This underrated set contains several exceptional rockers. *—Bill Dahl*

Rick Nelson Sings for You / 1963 / MCA ◆◆◆
Still rocking, it includes James Burton's ringing lead guitar. *—Bill Dahl*

For Your Sweet Love / 1963 / Decca ◆◆◆
His first Decca album is also his best, with a searing cover of "I've Got a Woman." *—Bill Dahl*

Ricky Nelson / 1971 / United Artists ◆◆◆◆
If vinyl's your preference, this two-album, 26-track compilation is a fine overview of his prime, although it misses some minor hits. Otherwise, it makes much more sense to pick up EMI's two lengthy CD retrospectives of the same era. *—Richie Unterberger*

Garden Party / 1972 / MCA ◆◆◆◆
This comeback introduced Nelson to a new generation. *—Bill Dahl*

Hey Pretty Baby / 1986 / Rockstar ◆◆◆
If you're looking for Imperial-era material that's not on the EMI best-of compilation CDs, this 16-track British import offers a good selection. Much of this is not present on those domestic CDs, and the collection emphasizes his more rocking side, with James Burton frequently contributing his tasty licks. But it doesn't compare with the best of his vintage material, though it's pleasant enough (and quite innocuous); most listeners will be content to pick up the greatest-hits comps and leave it at that. *—Richie Unterberger*

★ **Legendary Masters** / 1990 / EMI America ◆◆◆◆◆
Legendary Masters compiles all of the hits Ricky Nelson released for Imperial Records in the late '50s, including "Be-Bop Baby," "Stood Up," "Lonesome Town," "It's Late," "Poor Little Fool," "Sweeter than You," "Just a Little Too Much," "Never Be Anyone Else But You," and "Believe What You Say." A few essential items are missing—such as the Verve sides "A Teenager's Romance" and

"I'm Walking"—and it would have been nice if the disc had extended into the early '60s, so songs like "Travelin' Man" and "Mary Lou" could have been included, but *Legendary Masters* remains a vital collection from one of the most undervalued early rock 'n' rollers. —*Stephen Thomas Erlewine*

Best of 1963-1975 / 1990 / MCA ✦✦✦
No longer Rockin' Ricky, but Responsible Rick, his Decca output was wildly inconsistent. The early efforts like "Fools Rush In" and "String Along" still feature guitarist James Burton prominently. —*Bill Dahl*

Best of Rick Nelson, Vol. 2 / 1991 / Capitol ✦✦✦✦
Focusing primarily on Rick's early-'60s material for Imperial, this 27-cut disc is not quite as rocking as Vol. 1, but it still offers plenty of worthy moments. It includes all of his massive, midtempo teen idol ballad hits of the era: "Young World," "A Wonder like You," "Teenage Idol," "It's Up to You," and the No. 1 hit "Travelin' Man." Teen ballads they might have been, but James Burton's masterful guitar licks and Nelson's assured, committed delivery placed them leagues above other teen-idol hits of the period. Of more interest to serious fans is the inclusion of several minor hit singles and covers of R&B tunes. And of course, there's the first-class rockabilly hit "Hello Mary Lou" (penned by Gene Pitney), perhaps his best recording of the decade. His surprisingly raucous cover of "Summertime" features, amazingly, the same bass line used as a hook on the Blues Magoos' psych-pop-garage hit "We Ain't Got Anything Yet" years later. The pleasures of this CD are modest but consistent. —*Richie Unterberger*

Rockin' with Ricky / 1996 / Ace ✦✦✦✦
Originally released as an LP in 1984, the CD version of this collection of Nelson's hardest-rocking early material doubles in length to include a whopping 32 tracks (on one disc) from the late '50s and early '60s. This has most of his uptempo smashes, a la "Be-Bop Baby," "Waitin' in School," and "Believe What You Say," with a host of LP tracks, many of them covers of songs made famous by Elvis, Carl Perkins, Roy Orbison, and the like. The two volumes of greatest hits on EMI are more well-rounded, and on the whole better, retrospectives of his classic era. This is pretty good proof that he could rock respectably, though, with some good cuts that are hard to find on reissues, like "You're So Fine" and "Poor Loser." —*Richie Unterberger*

Stay Young: The Epic Recordings / Epic ✦✦✦
Stay Young is an entertaining overview of Rick Nelson's country-tinged years at Epic, proving that he recorded plenty of worthwhile material in the '70s. —*Stephen Thomas Erlewine*

Willie Nelson (Willie Hugh Nelson)

b. Apr. 30, 1933, Fort Worth, TX
Bass, Guitar, Vocals / Traditional Country, Progressive Country, Country-Pop, Nashville Sound/Countrypolitan, Outlaw Country

As a songwriter and a performer, Willie Nelson played a vital role in post-rock 'n' roll country music. Although he didn't become a star until the mid-'70s, Nelson spent the '60s writing songs that became hits for stars like Ray Price ("Nite Life"), Patsy Cline ("Crazy"), Faron Young ("Hello Walls"), and Billy Walker ("Funny How Time Slips Away"), as well as releasing a series of records on Liberty and RCA that earned him a small, but devoted, cult following. During the early '70s, Nelson aligned himself with Waylon Jennings and the burgeoning outlaw country movement that made him a star in 1975. After the crossover success of that year's *The Red Headed Stranger* and "Blue Eyes Crying in the Rain," Nelson was a genuine star, as recognizable in pop circles as he was to the country audience; in addition to recording, he launched an acting career in the early '80s. Even when he was a star, Nelson never played it safe musically. Instead, he borrowed from a wide variety of styles, including traditional pop, Western swing, jazz, traditional country, cowboy songs, honky tonk, rock 'n' roll, folk, and the blues, creating a distinctive, elastic hybrid. Nelson remained at the top of the country charts until the mid-'80s, when his lifestyle—which had always been close to the outlaw cliches his music flirted with—began to spiral out of control, culminating in an infamous battle with the IRS in the late '80s. During the

'90s, Nelson's sales never reached the heights that he had experienced a decade earlier, but he remained vital in country music, having greatly influenced the new country, new traditionalist, and alternative country movements of the '80s and '90s, as well as leaving a legacy of classic songs and recordings.

Willie Nelson began performing music as a child growing up in Abbott, TX. After his father died and his mother ran away, Nelson and his sister Bobbie were raised by their grandparents, who encouraged both children to play instruments. Willie picked up the guitar, and by the time he was 7, he was writing songs. Bobbie learned to play piano, eventually meeting—and later marrying—fiddler Bud Fletcher, who invited both siblings to join his band. Nelson had already played with with Raychecks' Polka Band, but with Fletcher he acted as the group's frontman. Nelson stayed with Fletcher throughout high school. Upon his graduation, he joined the Air Force but had to leave shortly afterward, when he became plagued by back problems. He began looking for full-time work. After he worked several part-time jobs, he landed a job as a country DJ at Fort Worth's KCNC in 1954. Nelson continued to sing in honky tonks as he worked as a DJ, deciding to make a stab at recording career by 1956. That year he headed to Vancouver, WA, where he recorded Leon Payne's "Lumberjack." At that time Payne was a DJ and he plugged "Lumberjack" on the air, which eventually resulted in sales of 3,000—a respectable figure for an independent single, but not enough to gain much attention. For the next few years Nelson continued to DJ and sing in clubs. During this time, he sold "Family Bible" to a guitar instructor for $50; when the song became a hit for Claude Gray in 1960, Nelson decided to move to Nashville to try his luck. Though his nasal voice and jazzy, off-center phrasing didn't win him many friends—several demos were made and then rejected by various labels—his songwriting ability didn't go unnoticed, and soon Hank Cochran helped him land a publishing contract at Pamper Music. Ray Price, who co-owned Pamper Music, recorded Nelson's "Night Life" and invited him to join his touring band, the Cherokee Cowboys, as a bassist.

Arriving at the beginning of 1961, Price's invitation began a watershed year for Nelson. Not only did he play with Price—eventually taking members of the Cherokee Cowboys to form his own touring band—but his songs provided major hits for several other artists. Faron Young took "Hello Walls" to No. 1 for nine weeks, Billy Walker made "Funny How Time Slips Away" into a Top 40 country smash, and Patsy Cline made "Crazy" into a Top Ten pop crossover hit. Earlier in the year, Nelson had signed a contract with Liberty Records and began releasing a series of singles that were usually drenched in strings. "Willingly," a duet with his then-wife Shirley Collie, became a Top Ten hit for Nelson early in 1962, and it was followed by another Top Ten single, "Touch Me," later that year. Both singles made it seem that Nelson was primed to become a star, but his career stalled just as quickly as it had taken off and he was soon charting in the lower regions of the Top 40. Liberty closed its country division in 1964, the same year Roy Orbison had a hit with "Pretty Paper."

When the Monument recordings failed to become hits, Nelson moved to RCA Records in 1965, the same year he became a member of the Grand Ole Opry. Over the next seven years, Nelson had a steady stream of minor hits, highlighted by the No. 13 hit "Bring Me Sunshine" in 1969. Toward the end of his stint with RCA, he had grown frustrated with the label, who had continually tried to shoehorn him into the heavily produced Nashville sound. By 1972 he wasn't even able to reach the country Top 40. Discouraged by his lack of success, Nelson decided to retire from country music, moving back to Austin, TX, after a brief and disastrous sojourn into pig farming. Once he arrived in Austin, Nelson realized that many young rock fans were listening to country music along with the traditional honky tonk audience. Spotting an opportunity, Nelson began performing again, scrapping his pop-oriented Nashville sound and image for a rock- and folk-influenced redneck outlaw image. Soon he had earned a contract with Atlantic Records.

Shotgun Willie (1973), Nelson's first album for Atlantic, was evidence of the shift of his musical style, and although it initially didn't sell well, it earned good reviews and cultivated a dedicated cult following. By the fall of 1973, his version of Bob Wills' "Stay

All Night (Stay a Little Longer)" had cracked the country Top 40. The next year he delivered the concept album *Phases and Stages*, which increased his following even more with the hit singles "Bloody Mary Morning" and "After the Fire Is Gone." But the real commercial breakthrough didn't arrive until 1975, when he severed ties with Atlantic and signed to Columbia Records, who gave him complete creative control of his records. Nelson's first album for Columbia, *The Red Headed Stranger*, was a spare concept album about a preacher, featuring only his guitar and his sister's piano. The label was reluctant to release it with such stark arrangements, but they relented and it became a huge hit, thanks to Nelson's understated cover of Roy Acuff's "Blue Eyes Crying in the Rain."

After the breakthrough success of *The Red Headed Stranger*, as well as Waylon Jennings' simultaneous success, outlaw country—so named because it worked outside of the confines of the Nashville industry—became a sensation, and RCA compiled the various artists album *Wanted: The Outlaws*, using material Nelson, Jennings, Tompall Glaser, and Jessi Colter had previously recorded for the label. The compilation boasted a No. 1 single in the form of the newly recorded Jennings and Nelson duet "Good Hearted Woman," which was also named the Country Music Association's single of the year. For the next five years Nelson consistently charted on both the country and pop charts, with "Remember Me," "If You've Got the Money I've Got the Time," and "Uncloudy Day" becoming Top Ten country singles in 1976; "I Love You a Thousand Ways" and the Mary Kay Place duet "Something to Brag About" were Top Ten country singles the next year.

In 1978 he charted with two very dissimilar albums. *Waylon and Willie*, his first duet album with Jennings, was a major success early in the year, spawning the signature song "Mammas Don't Let Your Babies Grow Up to Be Cowboys." Later in the year he released *Stardust*, a string-augmented collection of pop standards produced by Booker T. Jones. Most observers believed that the unconventional album would derail Nelson's career, but it unexpectedly became one of the most successful records in his catalog, spending almost ten years in the country charts and eventually selling over four million copies. After the success of *Stardust*, Nelson branched out into film, appearing in the Robert Redford movie *The Electric Horseman* in 1979 and starring in *Honeysuckle Rose* the next year. The latter spawned the hit "On the Road Again," which became another one of Nelson's signature songs.

Nelson continued to have hits throughout the early '80s, when he had a major crossover success in 1982 with a cover of Elvis Presley's hit "Always on My Mind." The single spent two weeks at No. 1 and crossed over to No. 5 on the pop charts, sending the album of the same name to No. 2 on the pop charts, as well as quadruple-platinum status. Over the next two years he had hit duet albums with Merle Haggard (1983's *Poncho and Lefty*) and Waylon Jennings (1982's *WWII* and 1983's *Take It to the Limit*), while "To All the Girls I've Loved Before," a duet with Latin pop star Julio Iglesias, became another major crossover success in 1984, peaking at No. 5 on the pop charts and No. 1 on the singles chart.

After a string of No. 1 singles in early 1985, including "Highwayman," the first single from the Highwaymen, a supergroup he formed with Waylon Jennings, Johnny Cash, and Kris Kristofferson, Nelson's popularity began to erode. A new generation of artists had captured the attention of the country audience. For the remainder of the decade, he recorded less frequently and remained on the road; he also continued to do charity work, most notably Farm Aid, an annual concert he founded in 1985 to provide aid to farmers. While he career was declining, an old demon began to creep up on Nelson—the IRS. In November 1990 he was given a bill for $16.7 million in back taxes. During the next year almost all of his assets—including several houses, studios, farms, and other property—were taken away. To help pay his bill, he released the double-album *The IRS Tapes: Who'll Buy My Memories*. Originally released as two separate albums, the records were marketed through television commercials, and all the profits were directed to the IRS. By 1993—the year he turned 60—his debts had been paid off, and he relaunched his recording career with

Willie Nelson

Across the Borderline, an ambitious album produced by Don Was and featuring cameos by Bob Dylan, Bonnie Raitt, Paul Simon, Sinead O'Connor, David Crosby, and Kris Kristofferson. The record received strong reviews and became his first solo album to appear in the pop charts since 1985.

After the release of *Across the Borderline*, Nelson continued to work steadily, releasing at least one album a year and constantly touring. In 1993 he was inducted into the Country Music Hall of Fame, but by that time, he had already become a legend for all country music fans across the world. —*Stephen Thomas Erlewine*

Country Willie: His Own Songs / 1965 / RCA ✦✦✦✦
The back of this record says, "Willie writes the songs . . . You make them into hits" and proceeds to talk about some of the artists who have had hits from the pen of Willie Nelson. While some of these tunes showed up in their original versions on the United Artist album *Best of Willie Nelson*, this is still worth tracking down. —*Jim Worbois*

Live Country Music Concert / 1966 / RCA ✦✦✦
This is an interesting album chronicling an early show by Nelson. From time to time, the audience will shout song titles, and he actually talks between songs. While many people don't like live albums, this is more fun than some of his later live records. —*Jim Worbois*

The Party's Over / 1967 / RCA ✦✦✦
The title track sums up this album perfectly. This is one of those records that sounds incredible at 2 o'clock in the morning when one is feeling reflective after a busy night. Included are 12 Willie Nelson originals and 12 strong performances. —*Jim Worbois*

Texas in My Soul / 1968 / RCA ✦✦✦
Five years before heading to Texas was the popular thing to do, Nelson celebrated his home state in song. Despite the fact that there's not a Nelson original on this record (though there are three by fellow Texan Ernest Tubb), there's not a weak track here. —*Jim Worbois*

Good Times / 1968 / RCA ✦✦✦
This is kind of an odd record. One side is very sparse instrumentally, while the other has three different people providing arrangements. The songs are okay (maybe subpar for Nelson), with one of the most interesting being his cover of Mickey Newbury's "Sweet Memories." —*Jim Worbois*

My Own Peculiar Way / 1969 / RCA ✦✦✦
When Nelson gets into a song, he has a way of playing with the sounds and rhythm of words to get everything possible. Nearly every song on this record is like that, whether it's one he penned or a cover like John Hartford's "Natural to Be Gone." The only song on this record that doesn't work is "That's All." But don't let that stop you. —*Jim Worbois*

Both Sides Now / 1970 / RCA ✦✦

The title track aside, this is a pretty good album. While there aren't as many originals as on some of his other albums released around this time, he manages to get something new out of several of his covers. Listening to "Everybody's Talkin'," you don't find yourself longing for Harry Nilsson's version. Similarly, after Jerry Lee ripped up "One Has My Name," Nelson still makes it sound fresh. —*Jim Worbois*

Laying My Burdens Down / 1970 / RCA ✦✦✦

This is what can best be described as a pleasant album. There are some nice things on here, but too many are buried under the Nashville Sound and don't seem to be able to stand on their own. Not great, but you could do worse. —*Jim Worbois*

Columbus Stockade / 1970 / RCA ✦✦

For this record, RCA raided their vaults for vintage tracks of Nelson doing favorites made hits by other artists. Included are songs by his former boss, Ray Price ("Don't You Ever Get Tired . . . ," "Heartaches by the Number"), George Jones ("Season of My Heart"), Bob Wills ("San Antonio Rose"), and Leon Payne. Not a bad album. —*Jim Worbois*

Yesterday's Wine / 1971 / RCA ✦✦✦✦

This early concept album tracks the life of one man from birth to death. Nelson wrote all the tracks, and this is easily one of his best all-around records. —*Jim Worbois*

Willie Nelson and Family / 1971 / RCA ✦✦✦

Over the years, Nelson has shown that he sometimes looks at relationships differently than the average songwriter (such as "Crazy"), with a little more thought and from new perspectives. After all, not everyone's life is moon, June, and honeymoon. Two of the finest examples of the Willie way are on this album: "I'm A Memory" and, especially, "What Can You Do to Me Now?" By his standards, this isn't good enough to be called a classic album, but it would still blow many other artists out of the water. —*Jim Worbois*

The Willie Way / 1972 / RCA ✦✦✦

Classic Willie Nelson songwriting fills this album (except for two covers) with performances as only he knows how. "You Left Me a Long, Long Time Ago" alone is worth the price of this record. And Nelson's version of "Undo the Right" is easily as good as Johnny Bush's 1968 hit. —*Jim Worbois*

The Words Don't Fit the Picture / 1972 / RCA ✦✦✦

Another fine album of Nelson originals, it's not quite as strong as some of his other albums released about this time, but it's still good. —*Jim Worbois*

Shotgun Willie / 1973 / Atlantic ✦✦✦✦

This album marks a reunion of sorts. When Nelson and Leon Russell began to work on this record, Russell told Nelson that he had played keyboards on some of Nelson's Liberty sessions. With this album, they began a loose partnership that lasted over the next several years. Nelson is in good form as a songwriter on this disc, with some of his best-ever songs. "The Devil," by the way, is Nelson's longtime drummer Paul English. —*Jim Worbois*

Best of Willie Nelson / 1973 / United Artists ✦✦✦✦

By the time this record was made, Nelson already had quite a reputation as a songwriter. Here he does many of the songs he had written for other artists. While many of these songs would be rerecorded when he switched to RCA, these are still the ultimate Nelson versions. —*Jim Worbois*

☆ **Shotgun Willie/Phases and Stages** / 1974 / Mobile Fidelity ✦✦✦✦✦

Although Willie Nelson's two albums for Atlantic Records—*Shotgun Willie* and *Phases and Stages*—were among his most unsuccessful records commercially, they were groundbreaking, pivotal releases that rank among his finest and most introspective works. The albums straddle the lines between outlaw country, folk, and traditional pop—they are innovative and introspective, unlike his previous work. Additionally, both are concept albums, with the songs intertwining to tell a story. *Shotgun Willie* is about a legendary outlaw; *Phases and Stages* is about a divorce, with the first side taking the perspective of the male, the second taking the female viewpoint. Neither album produced big hits, but they are some of the strongest efforts Willie Nelson ever made, making this single-disc collection an excellent bargain. —*Stephen Thomas Erlewine*

Phases and Stages / 1974 / Atlantic ✦✦✦✦

Country Willie Nelson and R&B producer Jerry Wexler might seem like an unlikely combo, but they work magic together on the likes of "Bloody Mary Morning" and "Heaven and Hell." —*Dan Cooper*

☆ **Red Headed Stranger/Sound in Your Mind** / 1975 / Columbia ✦✦✦✦✦

Recorded in Texas, Nelson's sparsely produced concept album about the old West subverted the old ways in Nashville and made country converts of hippies everywhere. In fact, it did more than that, as "Blue Eyes Crying in the Rain" became one of the unlikeliest Top 40 hits in pop music history. —*Dan Cooper*

The Sound in Your Mind / 1976 / Columbia ✦✦

The Sound in Your Mind includes Nelson's second No. 1, "If You've Got the Money I've Got the Time," as well as his perennial "Crazy." —*Jason Ankeny*

The Troublemaker / 1976 / Columbia ✦✦✦✦

An interesting biblical allegory. —*Dan Heilman*

To Lefty from Willie / 1977 / Columbia ✦✦✦

To Lefty from Willie is an affectionate and thoroughly enjoyable salute to Lefty Frizzell, featuring stellar versions of a number of Lefty's best-known songs—including "Always Late (With Your Kisses)," "She's Gone, Gone, Gone," "I Never Go Around Mirrors" and "That's the Way Love Goes"—plus revealing takes on a number of obscurities from the influential vocalist's catalog. Nelson is respectful without being reverential, giving his own spin to each song without abandoning its honky tonk roots. —*Stephen Thomas Erlewine*

Before His Time / 1977 / RCA ✦✦

This album is interesting because Waylon Jennings and his drummer/producer Richie Albright took some old Nelson tapes, remixed them, added one previously unreleased track, and created this album. This doesn't necessarily make it good. In fact, "I'm a Memory" actually sounds as if the mix wasn't completed. That aside, there are some good performances here that are not easily found elsewhere. Not great, but don't overlook this one. —*Jim Worbois*

☆ **Stardust** / 1978 / Columbia ✦✦✦✦✦

The record label didn't want Nelson to do this project, inspired partially by the death of pop crooner Bing Crosby. Standard material—"Moonlight in Vermont," "All of Me," "Don't Get Around Much Anymore"—is arranged by Booker T. Jones (of "Green Onions" fame) and recorded in Nelson's inimitable style in Emmylou Harris' house. —*Tom Roland*

Waylon & Willie / 1978 / RCA ✦✦✦

Waylon & Willie, the first duet album by two of country music's favorite performers, has a little bit of something for everybody, particularly the hit single "Mamas Don't Let Your Babies Grow Up to Be Cowboys," which solidified this record in fans' hearts. While only five of the tracks are by Jennings and Nelson together, the rest are not without recommendation. The record is not up to their high standards, to be sure, but it's enjoyable listening, nonetheless. —*James Chrispell*

Face of Fighter / 1978 / Lone Star ✦✦✦✦

This is vintage Nelson, originally recorded in 1961 and finally released when he got his own label in 1978. There are ten originals played by some of Nashville's best. —*Jim Worbois*

Willie and Family Live / 1978 / Columbia ✦✦

This exceptionally long two-record set seems to prove two things: the family can jam (sometimes to the extent that you ask yourself what the point is), and Nelson seems to be bored with some of his own material. Instead of singing, he talks his way through the songs. If you need this to fill out the collection, that's one thing. If you want to hear him do these songs, look for the studio albums. —*Jim Worbois*

Sings Kris Kristofferson / 1979 / Columbia ✦✦✦
Sings Kris Kristofferson is one of Willie Nelson's finest albums of the late '70s. Kristofferson was never blessed with the terrific vocals of Nelson, who performs some of the very best versions of these songs ever recorded. As this record shows, Kristofferson never had a better interpreter than Nelson. —*Thom Owens*

San Antonio Rose / 1980 / Columbia ✦✦✦
Nelson is joined by his former bandstand boss, Ray Price, for remakes of "Crazy Arms," "Night Life," and a gorgeous version of "Faded Love." —*Dan Cooper*

One for the Road / 1980 / Columbia ✦✦
Nelson and Leon Russell continue the relationship begun on *Shotgun Willie* with this two-record live set. Anyone familiar with Russell's *Hank Wilson's Back* LP and the fact that he had been doing Willie Nelson songs in concert for years shouldn't be surprised by this friendship. While this can't really be termed a country record, there is a wide mix of styles here and everyone is obviously having a lot of fun. It can be recommended for that alone. —*Jim Worbois*

Somewhere over the Rainbow / 1981 / Columbia ✦✦✦
Somewhere over the Rainbow is a collection of more '40s pop standards, as arranged by Willie Nelson. While it isn't quite a continuation of what he did on *Stardust* and *Always on My Mind*, the record is a safe resting spot and something all the grandmas can enjoy. —*James Chrispell*

★ **Greatest Hits (& Some That Will Be)** / 1981 / Columbia ✦✦✦✦✦
This capsulizes Nelson's first five years in the spotlight, with lots of classics: "On the Road Again," "Blue Eyes Crying in the Rain," "Heartbreak Hotel" (a duet with Leon Russell), as well as the smartly produced "My Heroes Have Always Been Cowboys." —*Tom Roland*

Always on My Mind / 1982 / Columbia ✦✦✦
Willie Nelson's smooth interpretation of "Always on My Mind" became an unexpected pop crossover hit, climbing into the Top 10 and spending two weeks at the top of the country charts. The accompanying album of the same name contains a handful of songs that match the casual grace of "Always on My Mind," including fine versions of "Do Right Woman, Do Right Man," "Let It Be Me,"and "Bridge over Troubled Water," plus lesser-known songs and originals like "Old Fords and a Natural Stone" and "Party's Over." There's a handful of mediocre songs, including an awkward "Whiter Shade of Pale," but *Always on My Mind* is a laidback, nearly pop album that is one of his best contemporary crossover efforts. —*Thom Owens*

Poncho & Lefty / 1982 / Columbia ✦✦✦
Nelson teamed up with Merle Haggard for this album and, for my money, theirs is the definitive version of "Pancho & Lefty." At first they might seem to be an odd couple, but they do sound good together. Not all the tracks are as strong as "Pancho & Lefty", but it's still a nice album. —*Jim Worbois*

Tougher Than Leather / 1983 / Columbia ✦✦
Tougher Than Leather is a stark, plaintive rumination on life and death, written shortly after Willie Nelson survived a collapsed lung. Nelson dealt with his near-death experience with this moving song cycle, which focused on a gunfighter's brush with mortality. It's an odd album, particularly since it followed the extremely popular crossover hit "Always oOn My Mind," but it is one of Nelson's most distinctive and moving efforts. For the dedicated fan who wants to meet Nelson halfway, *Tougher Than Leather* is a rewarding, challenging listen. —*Thom Owens*

Without a Song / 1983 / Columbia ✦✦
The title track, a cover of the 1930 Paul Whiteman hit, was the lone chart entry from *Without a Song*. —*Jason Ankeny*

Take It to the Limit / 1983 / Columbia ✦
Billed as "with Waylon Jennings," *Take It to the Limit* is not a return of the Outlaws from just a few years back. In fact, it sounds as if these two hombres are just plain tired and saddle-sore from all the high-riding days of the past. Most of the tunes are covers of previous hits by other artists and have little in association with what Nelson (or Jennings) are about except for their take on

George Jones' "Why Baby Why." By this time, fans were beginning to say the same thing. —*James Chrispell*

Angel Eyes / 1984 / Columbia ✦✦
Angel Eyes boasts only eight songs and is billed as "featuring the guitar of Jackie King." By this time, Nelson seemed to be releasing an album every three months or so, and this record certainly sounds as if he was spreading himself too thin. —*James Chrispell*

City of New Orleans / 1984 / Columbia ✦✦
The Arlo Guthrie-penned title cut of *City of New Orleans* was Nelson's umpteenth No. 1 hit; other highlights include his renditions of "Please Come to Boston" and "Wind Beneath My Wings." —*Jason Ankeny*

Half Nelson / 1985 / Columbia ✦✦✦
This is an appropriate collection, since Nelson has recorded more duets with more fellow performers than any other country singer in history. This runs the gamut, from traditional country singers Merle Haggard and George Jones, to soulman Ray Charles, to Latin-lover Julio Iglesias, and the rock band Santana. It even has a duet with the late Hank Williams, arranged through modern studio recording technology. —*Tom Roland*

What a Wonderful / Mar. 1988 / Columbia ✦✦✦
Nelson makes one of his occasional dips into the Great American Songbook for *What a Wonderful World*, which features his renditions of "Moon River," "Twilight Time," and "Spanish Eyes," another successful duet with Julio Iglesias. —*Jason Ankeny*

A Horse Called Music / 1989 / Columbia ✦✦✦
In addition to "Nothing I Can Do About It Now," Nelson's final NO. 1 single, *A Horse Called Music* includes the minor hit "The Highway." —*Jason Ankeny*

★ **Nite Life: Greatest Hits and Rare Tracks, 1959-1971** / 1989 / Rhino ✦✦✦✦✦
Nite Life: Greatest Hits and Rare Tracks collects material Willie Nelson wrote and recorded while he was trying to launch a career as a professional songwriter during the '60s. At this time, he also made two albums and several singles for Liberty, and many recordings for RCA. These songs, including some rarities, are compiled for this flawless single-disc collection. *Nite Life* runs through all of the songs other performers had hits with and made standards, including the title tracks, "Crazy," "Funny How Time Slips Away," and "Hello, Walls." Not only does it have the songs that established Nelson's reputation, the disc shows that even early in his career, he was creating an eclectic, far-reaching music that never stayed within the boundaries of traditional country. —*Stephen Thomas Erlewine*

Born for Trouble / 1990 / Columbia ✦✦
Born for Trouble includes the chart hits "Ain't Necessarily So," "The Piper Came Today," and "Ten with a Two." —*Jason Ankeny*

Who'll Buy My Memories . . . / 1992 / Columbia ✦✦✦✦
Commonly known as *The IRS Tapes* because it was made to help pay Willie Nelson's IRS debts, *Who'll Buy My Memories* is a double-disc, 25-track collection of demos, outtakes, and stripped-down recordings that feature only Nelson and his guitar. Over the course of the set, Nelson plays a handful of unusual tracks, several new tunes, and a few of his most familiar songs. The result is one of Nelson's most direct and affecting albums, featuring several of his finest vocal performances. —*Thom Owens*

Across the Borderline / 1993 / Columbia ✦✦✦
Nelson took a bold move by going into the studio with a hot rock producer, Don Was, and it resulted in a strikingly artistic album, the equal of *Stardust* and *Red Headed Stranger*. It includes duets with Sinead O'Connor, Bonnie Raitt, and Paul Simon. —*Michael McCall*

Moonlight Becomes You / Feb. 15, 1994 / Justice ✦✦✦
It's an indication of how out of whack the country boom has gotten at major labels when a proven giant like Willie Nelson must cut tremendous records for tiny independents. There are wonderful originals and sympathetic, engaging covers; Nelson approaches his *Stardust* peak vocally; and a great cast plays these songs with consummate skill and ease, blending country, Western swing, jazz, and pop elements. Those with rigid definitions of

country may wonder how a CD with "Sentimental Journey" and the title track fits into the genre; anyone with open ears knows the answer. —*Ron Wynn*

The Early Years / Feb. 15, 1994 / Scotti Bros. ✦✦✦
Those who enjoyed Willie Nelson at his most unadorned on the *IRS Tapes* might also enjoy hearing the bare-bones arrangements of *The Early Years*. The 14 tracks on *The Early Years* were recorded by Nelson as songwriter demos in the early '60s, just before he signed with Liberty. At this point, Nelson was considered more of a songwriter than a performer. Accordingly, there is a sparse feel to most of these performances, which sometimes feature nothing more than his voice or guitar. Not that there's anything especially wrong with that. Willie re-recorded several of these tunes for Liberty and RCA, and one could argue that the arrangements were sometimes less sympathetic than the minimal backing on these tapes. While the demo ambience could be said to add warmth and character, one should also be aware that these aren't the most polished performances; perfunctory arrangements, flat production, and the occasional bum vocal phrase are also found. But fans of Nashville country without the syrup should find something to like here. It includes an early version of "I Hope So," a country hit for Nelson in 1969, and "Undo The Right," which would be a Top Ten country hit for Johnny Bush in 1968. —*Richie Unterberger*

☆ **The Early Years: The Complete Liberty Recordings Plus More** / May 3, 1994 / Liberty ✦✦✦✦✦
Not only a fine compilation, it was a gutsy move. Nelson's 1962-64 sessions for Liberty Records, the first label to sign him as an artist, have never been held in high regard by his fans. On many cuts, the strings were poured on so thick even Eddy Arnold would have protested. But if one dispenses with prejudice and gives this two-CD box set an open-minded listen, there's a wealth of fine work to appreciate among the 61 singles, album cuts, and alternate takes. And no matter the production—lush or spare—his songwriting is a joy. Besides the familiar (including a riveting, pre-Liberty version of "Night Life" that opens the set) are any number of near-forgotten songs that would have been another writer's best work. Excellent liner notes are provided by Joseph F. Laredo, who deserves credit for not pretending the strings aren't there. —*Dan Cooper*

A Classic and Unreleased Collection / 1995 / Rhino ✦✦✦
Originally a mail-order-only release through the Home Shopping Network, the three-disc *A Classic and Unreleased Collection* compiles a selection of unreleased and rare material recorded between 1957 and the mid-'80s. Considering that all of the set is composed of rarities, the "classic" in the title is a little dubious. Nevertheless, the music throughout the box is fine and occasionally excellent. Opening with Nelson's first independently released single, the set runs through a number of music-publishing demos he made for Pamper Music, unreleased Atlantic recordings, a complete unreleased live album (*Live at the Texas Opry House*) from 1974, the unreleased *Sugar Moon* from the mid-'80s, a handful of tracks from the scrapped record *Willie Alone* and, finally, *Willie Sings Hank Williams*, another unreleased album from the '80s. Since it covers such a large time-frame, it isn't surprising that the set features a bit of everything that made Nelson famous—his Western swing and honky tonk roots, as well as his fondness for pop standards, jazz, country-pop, and folk. Even though there is music on the box that would please the casual fan, *A Classic and Unreleased Collection* remains a treasure chest for collectors, who will find plenty of rough gems within the set. —*Stephen Thomas Erlewine*

☆ **Revolutions of Time: The Journey 1975-1993** / 1995 / Columbia/Legacy ✦✦✦✦✦
Compiling material from Willie Nelson's later career, the box set *Revolutions of Time: The Journey 1975-1993* provides a through overview of the singer's most popular recordings, as well as some of his most obscure. Divided into three thematic discs—*Pilgrimage, Sojourns, Exodus*—the box contains most of his hits from the era, including selections from *The Red Headed Stranger* and *Stardust*. These songs are on *Pilgrimage*. *Sojourns* concentrates on his duets, while *Exodus* is filled with songs from the late '80s and

early '90s. It doesn't round up all of his best songs of the era—there are still several gems hidden away on the original albums—but it does provide an effective and throughly entertaining portrait of Nelson's later career. *Revolutions of Time* could be all that the casual fan needs to hear from Nelson's later career, and every country fan should be familiar with most of these songs. —*Stephen Thomas Erlewine*

The Essential Willie Nelson / Aug. 1, 1995 / RCA ✦✦✦✦
Willie Nelson didn't have many hits while he was on RCA Records, but the majority of them, including some selected rarities, are collected on *The Essential Willie Nelson*. —*Stephen Thomas Erlewine*

Spirit / Jun. 1996 / Island ✦✦✦
Spirit is a stripped-down, laid-back acoustic collection that recalls Willie Nelson's pre-Atlantic recordings in terms of sound, but not in terms of impact. Nelson turns in a few first-rate songs, but the sound makes the tracks blend, leaving *Spirit* as a pleasant wash of sound, not a set of distinctive individual songs. —*Thom Owens*

How Great Thou Art / Jul. 1996 / Fine Arts ✦✦✦
How Great Thou Art is a stripped-down collection of gospel standards, performed on guitar, piano and, occasionally, upright bass. Apart from two new songs from Willie Nelson, the album consists entirely of traditional gospel material, such as "Swing Low, Sweet Chariot." Nelson offers no revelations over the course of *How Great Thou Art*, but it is a pleasing, idiosyncratic country gospel record. —*Stephen Thomas Erlewine*

All-Time Hits, Vol. 1 / RCA ✦✦✦✦
All-Time Greatest Hits, Vol. 1 covers Nelson's mid–to late-'60s tenure on RCA; among the selections are "The Party's Over," "Blackjack County Chain," "San Antonio," and "Funny How Time Slips Away." —*Jason Ankeny*

Michael Nesmith

b. Dec. 30, 1943, Houston, TX
Guitar, Vocals / Country-Rock, Singer-Songwriter, Folk-Rock
Even when he was a member of the '60s teen-idol sensation the Monkees, Michael Nesmith was a respected songwriter and musician. Before he joined the group in 1966, he had written and recorded several singles, and two of his songs—"Different Drum" and "Mary Mary"—were recorded, respectively, by the Stone Poneys and Paul Butterfield. In the Monkees, Nesmith was the only member to consistently write songs and he was the only one who knew how to play an instrument proficiently. So it isn't surprising that after he left the Monkees in 1969, he was the only member to sustain a solo career. What is surprising is that his late-'60s and early-'70s works were among the groundbreaking country-rock recordings of the era. Throughout the 1970s, '80s, and '90s, Nesmith continued to record sporadically, in addition to pioneering the concept of music video with his communications company, Pacific Arts.

Michael Nesmith was born December 30, 1943, in Houston, TX. He listened to the blues and played saxophone while growing up, but after spending two years in the Air Force, Nesmith became fascinated with folk and learned to play the guitar. He played back-up guitar in Memphis on recordings for the Stax-Volt label. Nesmith moved to Los Angeles in the mid-'60s and formed the folk-rock duo Mike and John with John London. He also recorded several singles as a solo act before auditioning to join the Monkees in 1965.

"The Monkees" TV show ran from 1966 to 1968. During its first few years the show was a big hit in America, especially with teenagers. The group's popularity with teenagers and its fabricated origins didn't earn respect within much of the rock 'n' roll intelligentsia, nor did the fact that the members did not play any instruments on their first three records. Nesmith led the fight to have the Monkees play on their own records, as well as contribute some songs to each release. Colgems, the band's record label, acquiesced, and the first album to feature the Monkees playing their own instruments was 1967's *Headquarters*. In 1968 Nesmith recorded a solo album called *Wichita Train Whistle Songs* for Dot Records; he left the band—then only a trio—one year later.

Nesmith's first act independent of the Monkees was the formation of the First National Band, with old friend John London on bass, John Ware on drums, and one of country music's best steel guitarists, Red Rhodes. The group signed to RCA Victor and released two albums in 1970, *Magnetic South* and *Loose Salute*. The single "Joanne" hit the pop Top 25, and "Silver Moon" charted later in the year. Nesmith added several members for 1971's *Nevada Fighter* and credited it to the Second National Band. The title track skirted the bottom of the charts for several weeks, but Nesmith provided the Nitty Gritty Dirt Band with their hit "Some of Shelly's Blues." The next year the National Band released *Tantamount to Treason*.

Michael Nesmith dropped the group credit later that year, recording *And the Hits Keep Comin'* as a solo artist—though Red Rhodes continued to play with him, Nesmith's 1973 album *Pretty Much Your Standard Ranch Stash* was his last for RCA Victor, as he formed the music/communications label Pacific Arts in 1974. The next year he released *The Prison* and co-wrote Olivia Newton-John's hit "Let It Shine." Nesmith re-entered the charts with 1977's *From a Radio Engine to a Photon Wing;* the single "Rio" was a hit in the UK, and a filmed version of the song helped develop the concept of music video.

In 1977 Nesmith furthered his efforts in the field of music video by creating a TV chart show called "Popclips"; Warner bought the idea from him and later developed it into MTV. A stop-gap live album (*Live at Palais*) appeared in 1978; *Infinite Rider on the Big Dogma* (Nesmith's last solo album for 13 years) was released the next year. During the '80s Pacific Arts became the most important video publishing company in America. Nesmith moved into film and TV production, winning the first Video Grammy award in 1981 for *Elephant Parts*. He returned to the music business in 1989, appearing with the Monkees once on stage during their reunion tour. Nesmith also released a compilation of rare solo tracks called *The Newer Stuff* for England's Awareness Records. Rhino Records followed two years later with a recording of the best of his early-'70s material called *The Older Stuff*. In 1992 Nesmith released his first album of new material in 13 years, *Tropical Campfires*. Four years later he reunited with the Monkees to record *Justus*, the first Monkees album since 1968 to feature all four original members. —*John Bush*

Mike Nesmith Presents the Wichita Train Whistle Sings / 1968 / Dot ♦♦
Nesmith stepped away from the Monkees for this instrumental rendering of many of the songs he'd written for them. Looking back on the record's experimentation with musical styles, it seems to point to some of the music Nesmith would make on Pacific Arts. For that reason, the album is somewhat interesting, though it's certainly not a necessity for your Nesmith collection. —*Jim Worbois*

Magnetic South / 1970 / Pacific Arts ♦♦♦♦
This fine collection features not only Nesmith originals (and his first solo hit) but one of the most interesting versions of "Beyond the Blue Horizon" ever committed to vinyl. For nearly six minutes we follow a day-in-the-life of the singer, from the minute he wakes in the morning and goes off to work on his tractor, 'til the time he returns at day's end. At least two of the Nesmith originals were songs from his Monkee days, but the Monkee versions of these songs would not be heard until the issue of the *Missing Links* series nearly 20 years later. —*Jim Worbois*

Loose Salute / 1970 / Pacific Arts ♦♦♦
With this record, Nesmith's momentum builds, as this album is even better than the first. While the single from this album didn't do as well as his previous hit, it was a better song and kicks off the album nicely. Steel player extraordinaire "Red" Rhodes is beginning to take a more dominant role in the sound of the band. Of special interest are Nesmith's third go at recording "Listen to the Band," a fine cover of Patsy Cline's "I Fall to Pieces," and his renewed interest in Latin rhythms. —*Jim Worbois*

Nevada Fighter / 1971 / Pacific Arts ♦♦♦
This album stands in contrast to the previous two, in part because of the use of several members of Elvis' band, which gives the album a slightly different sound. Also notable is the fact that

Nesmith wrote only half the tracks. Still, the songs he wrote were as strong as anything he'd written to this point, and the covers he chose fit well with the feel and spirit of his own material. —*Jim Worbois*

Tantamount to Treason / 1972 / Pacific Arts ♦♦♦
Tantamount to Treason has a lazy feel to it, perhaps inspired by the beer recipe Papa Nes includes in the album's liner notes. That laziness is the reason the album is not as listenable as the previous three records, since you almost need to be "in the mood" to put this one on. That said, it's still quite a nice album and is worth tracking down. —*Jim Worbois*

And the Hits Just Keep on Comin' / 1972 / Pacific Arts ♦♦♦♦
If you don't own this record, there is a huge hole in your collection. Nesmith's own version of "Different Drum" (a song that introduced Linda Ronstadt to many of us back in 1968 and that most of us had heard only as a speeded up, mumbled "audition" on an old Monkees episode) may be the lure, but every song is a gem. This is easily some of Nesmith's finest work as both a songwriter and an artist. Between Nesmith and Red Rhodes, the sound is so full that it's easy to forget that a full band wasn't used in creating this record. —*Jim Worbois*

Pretty Much Your Standard Ranch Stash / 1973 / Pacific Arts ♦♦♦♦
Despite the comment inside the cover that "After two or three months this album may lose potency, although some of the aroma may linger" this record holds up some 20 years later as one of Nesmith's finest. He continues to mix originals and a nice selection of covers as before, but somehow this record feels more "comfortable" than his previous efforts. This seems to be due in part to the strong musical bond between Nesmith and steel player Red Rhodes. If the "Buy This Record" inducement on the front cover doesn't make this a must for your collection, one listen to the music inside will! —*Jim Worbois*

The Prison / 1974 / Pacific Arts ♦♦
If Nesmith's albums are listened to in chronological order, this record is startling in how different it is to his previous work, especially the previous two records. It may even be a little off-putting. Accepted on its own, its actually a nice album. That said, it's not one of those records one feels compelled to listen to more than a few times. —*Jim Worbois*

From a Radio Engine to the Photon Wing / 1977 / Pacific Arts ♦♦
"Rio" is probably the best-known song on this album, as well as the most memorable. Most of the tracks seem to be meant to evoke a mood more than to be actual songs and, for that reason, tend to be a bit more interesting on their own rather than as a collection. —*Jim Worbois*

Live at Palais / 1978 / Pacific Arts ♦♦
On this album, recorded on tour in Australia in 1977, Nesmith reintroduces some of the music from his years on RCA. These are not mere copies, though, as each song is performed differently, and, in each case, is presented as a longer version of the original. These songs obviously still mean something to their writer. —*Jim Worbois*

Infinite Rider on the Big Dogma / 1979 / Pacific Arts ♦♦♦
This is easily Nesmith's most interesting record from the '70s Pacific Arts material, and the one that calls for repeated listenings. By this time he was getting heavily into video, so a number of these tracks were also turned into music videos (check out the Grammy-winning *Elephant Parts*). While not a must, it's still a record worth searching out. —*Jim Worbois*

Newer Stuff / 1989 / Rhino ♦♦♦
This compilation of later solo material is often glossy and overreaching but still quite impressive. —*Jeff Tamarkin*

● **The Older Stuff: Best of Michael Nesmith (1970-1973)** / 1991 / Rhino ♦♦♦♦
Post-Monkees country-oriented material is proof that at least one member of the "pre-fab four" possessed genuine musical talent. —*Jeff Tamarkin*

Tropical Campfires / 1992 / Pacific Arts ✦✦✦

Nesmith plays desert music—quiet, contemplative, digni-fied—embellished, as the album title suggests, with splashes of lush tropical rhythms. His yearning vocals are ably supported by a cast of crack sessioneers, including the legendary Red Rhodes on pedal steel. Nesmith penned nine of the disc's 12 tracks, the others being covers of the samba chestnut "Brazil" and two Cole Porter tunes. Somehow, *Tropical Campfires* makes exceedingly pleasant (if mellow) listening overall. The disc's highlight is Nesmith's weepy "Moon over the Rio Grande"; close your eyes and hear the campfire crackle and the coyotes wail. —*Roch Parisien*

● **Complete** / 1993 / Pacific Arts ✦✦✦✦

All of Michael Nesmith and the First National Band's three albums are collected on this superb two-disc set, proving what a surprisingly inventive musician the former Monkee is. —*Stephen Thomas Erlewine*

Garden / 1994 / Rio Royal ✦✦

New Coon Creek Girls

Traditional Bluegrass, Traditional Folk

The New Coon Creek Girls carried on the bluegrass traditions that made the original Coon Creek Girls a popular act between the late '30s and early '50s. The band was the brainchild of pro-ducer John Lair, who was trying to recreate the magic of the orig-inal group. The New Coon Creek Girls remained on Lair's show through 1983 and then moved out on their own; during the '80s and '90s, they were a popular concert attraction on the bluegrass and folk festival circuit. In addition to performing, the group occa-sionally recorded, releasing *The L&N Don't Stop Here Anymore* in 1994. A year later, a lineup including guitarist Vicki Simmons, lead singer/rhythm guitarist Dale Ann Bradley, mandolinist/vocalist Pam Perry, and banjoist Ramona Church Taylor issued *Ain't Love a Good Thing*. In 1996 they released *Everything You Do*. —*Sandra Brennan*

● **So I'll Ride** / 1991 / Turquoise ✦✦✦✦

This well-crafted album features a high energy level. Jesse McRey-nolds, Dempsey Young, Mike Stevens, Edgar Meyer, and Ray-mond McLain were guests. —*Chip Renner*

L & N Don't Stop Here Anymore / 1994 / Pinecastle ✦✦✦

Ain't Love a Good Thing / 1995 / Pinecastle ✦✦✦

Everything You Do / 1996 / Pinecastle ✦✦✦✦

Playing Our Respect / Turquoise ✦✦✦

Pictures / Turquoise ✦✦✦

The New Grass Revival

Progressive Bluegrass

The New Grass Revival, formed in 1972 by four former members of the Bluegrass Alliance, flourished in a decade when numerous groups took traditional bluegrass and changed it to varying degrees. The group was successful enough to have the group's name become a generic label: "newgrass." The band's image, with long hair and occasionally electrified instruments, as well as its musical material, contrasted greatly with standard (traditional) bluegrass like that played by Bill Monroe, Ralph Stanley, the Lilly Brothers, and Lester Flatt's band. In terms of longevity, popularity, and exposure, the Revival, with its hip reputation, was perhaps the most successful in competition against II Generation, Seldom Scene, the Country Gentlemen, and others.

The origins of the New Grass Revival lay in the Bluegrass Alli-ance, which Sam Bush (vocals, fiddle, guitar, mandolin) and Courtney Johnson (banjo, vocals) joined in 1970. At the time the Alliance also featured bassist Ebo Walker and fiddler Lonnie Peerce. Within a year of Bush and Johnson's arrival, Curtis Burch (dobro, guitar, vocals) joined the band. In 1972 Peerce left, and the remaining members decided to continue under a new name—the New Grass Revival. The band released their eponymous debut, *Arrival of the New Grass Revival*, later that year on Starday Records.

After the release of their debut, Walker parted ways with the band and the group replaced him with Butch Robbins, who was with the band for only a short time. He was replaced by John Cowan, an Evansville, IN, native. This lineup was stable through-out the '70s, recording a number of albums for Flying Fish Records. As their name suggested, the New Grass Revival never played traditional bluegrass—all of the members brought ele-ments of rock 'n' roll, jazz, and blues to the group's sound. Conse-quently, certain portions of the bluegrass community scorned them, but they also gained a devoted following of listeners who believed they were moving the genre in a new, fresh direction.

In 1981 Johnson and Burch left the band, claiming they were tired of touring. Bush and Cowan continued the group, replacing them with banjoist Bela Fleck and mandolinist/guitarist Pat Flynn. The New Grass Revival moved to Sugar Hill Records in 1984 and released their first album featuring the new lineup, *On the Boulevard*. Two years later, the band signed with EMI Records and released an eponymous album, which proved to be their breakthrough into the mainstream. Two of the singles from the album—"What You Do to Me" and "Ain't That Peculiar"—were minor hits on the country charts, and Fleck's showcase "Seven by Seven" was nominated for a Grammy for Best Country Instru-mental. *Hold On to a Dream,* released in 1987, was just as success-ful as its predecessor, featuring the hits "Unconditional Love" and "Can't Stop Now," which both nearly made the Top 40.

In 1989 the New Grass Revival released their third major label album, *Friday Night In America,* which was yet another commeri-cal success. "Callin' Baton Rouge" became their first Top 40 sin-gle, followed by the No. 58 hit "You Plant Your Fields." Even though the band was more popular than ever, Sam Bush decided to pull the plug on the group after the release of *Friday Night in America*. Bush became a session musician and Fleck went on to a very successful and respected solo career. —*Stephen Thomas Erlewine & David Vinopal*

Arrival of the New Grass Revival / 1972 / Starday ✦✦✦

Fly Through the Country / 1975 / Flying Fish ✦✦✦✦

This first version of New Grass was not so polished as their sec-ond era, but they had good chemistry. You've gotta love "These Days," "Skippin'," "All Night Train," and "Fly Through the Coun-try." —*Chip Renner*

Too Late to Turn Back Now / 1977 / Flying Fish ✦✦✦

Recorded live at Telluride, CO, with guests J. Hartford and Peter Rowan, this one has a good-time feel. —*Chip Renner*

When the Storm Is Over / 1977 / Flying Fish ✦✦✦

New Grass Revival's *When the Storm is Over* is one of the group's earliest albums and, as the record demonstrates, the group had developed a distinctive sound even at this formative stage. *When the Storm is Over* is combined on one compact disc with *Fly Through the Country*. —*Thom Owens*

Barren County / 1979 / Flying Fish ✦✦✦✦

The first incarnation of this band was never better than on this one. Strong songs and vocals. —*Chip Renner*

Commonwealth / 1981 / Flying Fish ✦✦✦✦

The best of their newer era, with guests Leon Russell, Sharon White, and Kenny Malone. The cover of Hartford's "Steam Pow-ered Aereo Plane" is great. —*Chip Renner*

Live / 1984 / Sugar Hill ✦✦

Live captures a boisterous, lively performance from the New Grass Revival, as they tear through their best material. The new additions to the band—banjoist Bela Fleck and guitarist Pat Flynn—have energized the band, and vocalist John Cowan helps spur the band on to truly remarkable performances. —*Thom Owens*

On the Boulevard / 1984 / Sugar Hill ✦✦✦✦

An overlooked CD with a couple of standout tracks. Played begin-ning to end, this one will leave you fulfilled. —*Chip Renner*

New Grass Revival / 1986 / EMI America ✦✦✦✦

A solid release, and a great cover of Peter Rowan's "Revival." Pat Flynn shows some good songwriting on "In the Middle of the Night," "Lonely Rider," "Sweet Release," and "How Many Hearts."

Sam Busit and John Cowan come together well on T. Moore's "Saw You Runnin'." —*Chip Renner*

Hold to a Dream / 1987 / Capitol ✦✦✦
A good use of drums on this one. It worked. Standout tracks include "Looking Past You," "Unconditional Love," "Metric Lips," and the title track. —*Chip Renner*

Friday Night in America / 1989 / Capitol ✦✦✦
Their last album covers John Hiatt's "Angel Eyes," Jesse Winchester's "Let's Make a Baby King," and Bela Fleck's "Big Foot." Hot! These guys will be missed. —*Chip Renner*

New Grass Anthology / Aug. 27, 1990 / Capitol ✦✦✦✦

● **Best of New Grass Revival** / Mar. 8, 1994 / Liberty ✦✦✦✦
Best of New Grass Revival is a first-rate, 18-track collection of the band's biggest hits of the late '80s, plus a number of significant album tracks. It's the perfect way to get acquainted with the group. —*Thom Owens*

The New Lost City Ramblers

Old-Time, Traditional Folk, String Band
During the folk boom of the late '50s and early '60s, the NLCR introduced the authentic string-band sound of the 1920s and 1930s, in the process educating a generation that had never heard this uniquely American sound of old-time music. While maintaining music with a social conscience, they added guts and reality to the folk movement, performing with humor and obvious reverence for the music.

Mike Seeger, John Cohen, and Tom Paley in 1958 modeled their band after groups like the Skillet Lickers, the Fruit Jar Drinkers, and the Aristocratic Pigs, choosing a name in keeping with the past. When Tracy Schwarz replaced Paley in 1962, tThe Ramblers added solo songs from the Appalachian folk repertoire, religious and secular, educating a large segment of the American population about traditional music. Folkways recorded the NLCR on five albums in the early '60s, making the Ramblers famous and leading to TV appearances, successful tours, and appearances at the Newport Folk Festival. A songbook with 125 of their songs came out in 1964 and sold well.

The NLCR served at least three important purposes: They brought real folk music to a huge audience, they entertained us well, and they led us to rediscover the original music on which they had based their band. In the early 70s the group broke up. Tracy Schwarz went on the road with his wife and then his son, gradually leaning toward Cajun squeezebox music; Mike Seeger toured with his wife, Alice, and did many solo spots; and John Cohen continued playing in a string band, while making award-winning documentaries about the old music. —*David Vinopal*

20th Anniversary Concert: Live at Carnegie Hall / 1987 / Flying Fish ✦✦✦
This is a nicely spirited celebration of a band that was longer-lived than many of its old-time role models. —*Mark A. Humphrey*

★ **Early Years (1958-1962)** / 1991 / Smithsonian/Folkways ✦✦✦✦✦
These influential revivalists of old-time string-band music played it straight, but with spirit and a keen ear for the music's inherent humor. —*Mark A. Humphrey*

The New Riders of the Purple Sage

Country-Rock
Founded in 1969 as an offshoot of the Grateful Dead, the New Riders of the Purple Sage documented the Dead's change in musical direction from straight acid-rock to a more country-oriented style. It all started during a jam session when Jerry Garcia got hold of a steel guitar and wanted to play around; John "Marmaduke" Dawson suggested that they form a band. With an original lineup including Garcia on steel guitar, Dawson as chief songwriter and rhythm guitarist, drummer Mickey Hart, and bassist Phil Lesh, the band released their self-titled debut album in 1971 after signing with Columbia.

By this time, the New Riders featured ex-Jefferson Airplane drummer Spencer Dryden and bassist Dave Torbert. Soon the band's musical direction split away from the Dead, and Garcia

found it increasingly difficult to play in two bands at once. He was replaced by steel guitarist Buddy Cage, who had once played with Ian & Sylvia and Anne Murray. (Over the years, however, Garcia occasionally returned for guest appearances on their albums.) In 1972 the New Riders released *Powerglide* and featured Nicky Hopkins on keyboards and Garcia on guitar. Their first chart entry was "I Don't Need No Doctor," which became a minor hit. The next year, their membership stabilized and they released *Gypsy Cowboy*, featuring fiddler Richard Green. After the release of the 1973 breakthrough album *The Adventures of Panama Red*, several albums followed for Columbia during 1974-75, but the band seemed to lose its direction after moving to MCA in 1975. A number of rather tepid albums followed; the band underwent more personnel changes and pretty much disappeared until 1981, when they signed to A&M. Their first album, *Feelin' All Right*, again failed to measure up to earlier efforts. The lineup changed again in 1983, with only Dawson remaining from the original group. In 1990, they had another new lineup for the album *Keep on Keepin' On*. As of the mid-'90s, the New Riders of the Purple Sage continued to tour. —*Sandra Brennan*

New Riders of the Purple Sage / 1971 / Columbia ✦✦✦✦
An album for anyone who liked the sagebrush country-rock of the Grateful Dead's *Workingman's Dead* and *American Beauty* albums, dominated by John Dawson's songs and Jerry Garcia-like voice. —*William Ruhlmann*

Powerglide / 1972 / Columbia ✦✦✦
The New Riders' debut album was fueled by the group's close connection to the Grateful Dead and the songs of John Dawson. On *Powerglide*, their second release, the Dead are nowhere in evidence, Buddy Cage having replaced Jerry Garcia as the band's steel guitar player. And Dawson's songs aren't as strong or as many; Dave Torbert contributed songs as well, and there are covers of country-rock staples like "Hello, Mary Lou (Goodbye Heart)." (The single was a countrified version of Ashford and Simpson's "I Don't Need No Doctor" that charted briefly.) As a result, *Powerglide* is not as effective an album as the debut, though the New Riders remain a charming, if lightweight, band. —*William Ruhlmann*

The Adventures of Panama Red / 1973 / Columbia ✦✦✦✦
The Adventures of Panama Red was the New Riders of the Purple Sage's most popular album (their only one to go gold), primarily because of the Peter Rowan-penned title track, which made the connection between their dual identifications with cowboys and hippies—"Panama Red" was both the name of a (fictional) legendary outlaw and an (actual) legendary type of marijuana. But the album was the New Riders' best since their debut for other reasons: they brought in country producer Norbert Putnam; they employed a more democratic approach to songwriting and singing (leader John Dawson contributed only two songs); and they renewed their association with the Grateful Dead, with Dead lyricist Robert Hunter contributing "Kick in the Head," one of the album's better songs, and Dead singer Donna Godchaux singing backup vocals. Still, it was the doper/Old West persona that put them across, especially on the title song and Rowan's other contribution, the even more explicitly drug-laden "Lonesome L.A. Cowboy." —*William Ruhlmann*

Oh, What a Mighty Time / 1975 / Columbia ✦✦
By the time of this, their sixth album, the New Riders of the Purple Sage had deteriorated to the point of recording novelty songs like "I Heard You've Been Layin' My Old Lady" and aging standards like "La Bamba." They managed to talk old friend Jerry Garcia into sitting in on a few songs, but that was no indication that they were back at the level of their first album. Rather, *Oh, What a Mighty Time* sounded like the work of a competent Marin County bar band, which is pretty much what the New Riders were by this time. The album, their worst seller so far, was their last for Columbia Records. —*William Ruhlmann*

Before Time Began / 1976 / Relix ✦✦
Before Time Began is an album of archival material assembled for Relix Records by New Rider Dave Nelson. It contains two songs recorded by New Rider John Dawson on July 31, 1968; the New Riders' (Nelson, Dawson, Jerry Garcia, Phil Lesh, and Mickey

Hart) four-song demo tape of November 1969; and an entire LP side of experimental tapes made by Nelson, recording tracks backwards. The first side will be of interest to New Riders fans interested in hearing the elements that went into making the group's 1971 debut album. The second side may interest members of Nelson's family. — *William Ruhlmann*

● **The Best of the New Riders of the Purple Sage** / 1976 / Columbia ✦✦✦✦

A good selection from the group's Columbia catalog, featuring "Glendale Train," "Panama Red," and other favorites. — *William Ruhlmann*

Take a Red / MCA ✦✦

Between 1976 and 1978 the New Riders of the Purple Sage made three albums for MCA Records, *New Riders*, *Who Are These Guys?*, and *Marin County Line*. *Take a Red* is an eight-track compilation album culled from those releases and issued by the discount-priced MCA Special Products division. The late-'70s edition of the band was a tighter, more country-oriented unit than the bunch of hippies who made the Columbia Records albums in the early '70s, but it was also much less fun. The early New Riders were funny and fey, even if you sometimes wondered whether they'd make it to the chorus. There's no such suspense here, nor is there anything to distinguish the new New Riders from other country bands. — *William Ruhlmann*

Vintage / Relix ✦✦

Vintage collects unreleased material from the New Riders' prime, when the band's lineup included guitarists David Nelson and John Dawson and featured the Grateful Dead's Jerry Garcia on steel guitar. While the opening cuts represent some fairly strong country music, as the album progresses the playing begins to grow increasingly lifeless and mediocre; for the most part, the music on *Vintage* went unreleased for a reason. — *Jason Ankeny*

Mickey Newbury

b. May 19, 1940, Houston, TX

Guitar, Vocals / Traditional Country, Progressive Country, Honky Tonk, Outlaw Country

Along with fellow songwriters Kris Kristofferson, Willie Nelson, and Tom T. Hall, Mickey Newbury helped revolutionize country music in the 1960s and '70s by bringing new, broader musical influences as well as a frank, emotional depth to the music—while at the same time never losing respect for tradition. Newbury infused his country music with haunting beauty and spiritual melancholy, creating an impressive collection of introspective, emotionally complex songs that are more spiritual cousins of the work of Leonard Cohen than that of Roy Acuff. (Newbury, in fact, calls himself a folksinger, and has never toured with a band, preferring the ambience of a quiet coffeehouse.) The fact that many of his songs became hits for singers from Don Gibson to Elvis Presley was proof that the industry and the public were hungry for a change.

Like many of his generation, however—such as his friend Townes Van Zandt—Newbury is better known as a songwriter than as a singer. Newbury has recorded 15 albums over a nearly 30-year period—right up to 1996's "Lulled by the Moonlight," a limited-edition release sold by mail order—but his soft, beautiful tenor voice has rarely reached the charts.

Newbury spent his teens in Houston absorbing a wide range of music, learning to play guitar, and writing poetry, which he began reading in local coffeehouses. Folk music was on the rise at the time, and he soon turned to writing songs. He sang in a vocal group called the Embers during this time (they were briefly on Mercury), and played and hung out in Houston's black R&B and blues clubs, where he was nicknamed "The Little White Wolf" by Gatemouth Brown.

Newbury joined the Air Force and was stationed in England. After his discharge, he turned back to music. In 1963 a friend landed him a writing job with Acuff Rose, and Newbury moved to Nashville. During the next several years, he became friends with such singers as Roy Orbison, Roger Miller, Kris Kristofferson, and Townes Van Zandt. He was also instrumental in getting both

Kristofferson and Van Zandt—among others—noticed in Nashville.

In 1966 Don Gibson had a Top Ten hit with Newbury's "Funny Familiar Forgotten Feelings," and Newbury's writing career was off and running. A long string of hit songs followed, recorded by such artists as Kenny Rogers and the First Edition ("Just Dropped In"), Eddy Arnold ("Here Comes the Rain, Baby"), and Andy Williams ("Sweet Memories").

Newbury's first album of his own was *Harlequin Melodies* for RCA in 1968, recorded in RCA's big Nashville studio (it's an album he now detests). He quickly got out of his RCA contract and turned to a small four-track studio run by engineer Wayne Moss in a converted garage (becoming, before the word "outlaw" ever became fashionable, one of the first Nashville artists to work outside the studio system). It was here that he recorded some of his best solo albums, starting with *Looks Like Rain* for Mercury; this contained initial versions of two of his most enduring songs, "San Francisco Mabel Joy" (which he's recorded several more times) and "33rd of August."

But Mercury didn't support the album, and Newbury switched to Elektra in 1970. With this label he released a string of superb albums, including *Frisco Mabel Joy*, *Heaven Help the Child*, and the acoustic *Live at Montezuma Hall;* the latter was paired with a re-release of *Looks Like Rain*. These contained such songs as "Cortelia Clark" (about a blind street singer), the almost painfully lonely "Frisco Depot," and "Heaven Help the Child," a sweeping mini-epic of a song that makes references to Fitzgerald and Paris in the 1920s. In 1972 Newbury had a Top 30 hit with "American Trilogy," a suite-like arrangement of "Dixie," "Battle Hymn of the Republic," and "All My Trials." The song later became a major hit for Elvis Presley and a standard in his repertoire.

Newbury recorded three albums for ABC/Hickory in the late 1970s, and was inducted into the Nashville Songwriter's Hall of Fame in 1980, but he was more and more becoming something of a recluse. He had given up concert touring some years before and had moved to Oregon. In the 1980s, he released only two albums. In 1994 he resurfaced with *Nights When I Am Sane*, an acoustic album recorded live with guitarist Jack Williams. As of the mid-1990s, he still lives in Oregon, performs occasionally at festivals, and writes plenty of new songs. Since he's been out of the spotlight for more than a decade, though, and his catalog is largely out of print, he's little known in contemporary country circles. People familiar with his work, however, recognize Newbury as one of country music's most inspired and moving artists. —*Kurt Wolff*

Harlequinn Melodies / 1968 / RCA Victor ✦✦✦✦

Sings His Own / 1968 / RCA ✦✦✦✦

Looks Like Rain / 1969 / Mercury ✦✦✦✦

The first to employ the thunderstorm sound effects (courtesy of a Mystic Moods Orchestra record) that, along with train sounds, have become a Newbury trademark. Contains his first recordings of the classics "33rd of August," "She Even Woke Me Up to Say Goodbye," and "San Francisco Mabel Joy." This album, *Frisco Mabel Joy*, and *Heaven Help the Child* make an excellent trilogy. —*Kurt Wolff*

Frisco Mabel Joy / 1971 / Elektra ✦✦✦✦

Contains his only near-hit song, "An American Trilogy," and mixes revved-up bluesy rock songs such as "Mobile Blue" with the ultra-quiet, deeply sad "Frisco Depot" and the almost disturbingly melancholic "The Future's Not What It Used to Be." —*Kurt Wolff*

● **Heaven Help the Child** / 1973 / Elektra ✦✦✦✦

"Why You Been Gone So Long?" is one of Newbury's best roots-rock songs, "Heaven Help the Child" and "Cortelia Clark" are mini-epic character studies, and "San Francisco Mabel Joy" (his second reading of the song) is a career-topping masterpiece. —*Kurt Wolff*

Live at Montezuma / 1973 / Elektra ✦✦✦✦

A double album that packages an excellent solo acoustic concert with the sought-after 1969 album *Looks Like Rain*. The humorous concert banter shows Newbury's personality to be much brighter than his moody songs might indicate. —*Kurt Wolff*

In a New Age / 1988 / Airborne ✦✦

Newbury is accompanied only by his own guitar, violinist "Arizona St. Marie" Rhines, and bassist Edgar Meyer. The versions of "Cortelia Clark," "Frisco Depot," "Poison Red Berries," "San Francisco Mabel Joy," and other Newbury regulars are sweeter and less emotionally piercing than his Elektra recordings. —*Kurt Wolff*

The Best of Mickey Newbury / 1991 / Curb ✦✦

Curb's *The Best of Mickey Newbury* has a misleading title. Not only are many of his best known songs not included, neither are his best known versions. Instead, it has a handful of his famous songs—including "She Even Woke Me Up to Say Goodbye" and "An American Trilogy"—in slick, overly polished versions that give only a hint of his talents. —*Thom Owens*

Jimmy C. Newman

b. Aug. 27, 1927, Big Mamou, LA
Vocals / Traditional Country, Cajun

The 'C' stands for Cajun, and though much of Jimmy C. Newman's early country material has little swamp styling, he developed a fusion on several 1960s albums that established him as a forerunner in Cajun-country music. Newman was born August 27, 1927, in High Point, LA; as a child, he listened more to Gene Autry than the Cajun music of the area, but he still included several Cajun songs in his repertoire with Chuck Guillory's Rhythm Boys, which he joined while still a teenager. Newman recorded several unsuccessful sides in the late '40s for J.D. Miller's Feature label, but Miller later convinced Nashville legend Fred Rose to give the budding singer a shot. After recording four songs in 1953, Newman signed to Dot Records and scored a hit the next year, when "Cry, Cry, Darling" reached No. 4 in the country charts.

Newman's chart success prompted the "Louisiana Hayride" to hire him as a regular performer. His next four hits all made Top Ten, including 1955's "Daydreamin'," "Blue Darlin'," and "God Was So Good." Newman moved up to the Grand Ole Opry—a position he still has—in 1956 and released "A Fallen Star" the next year. The single, his biggest hit, spent two weeks at No. 2 and entered the Pop Top 25. The singer was unhappy with his Dot contract, though, and moved to MGM in 1958.

By November of that year, Jimmy C. Newman charted another Top Ten hit, "You're Makin' a Fool out of Me"; he closed out the decade with three Top 30 singles and the Top Ten "Grin and Bear It" in July 1959. Newman began the '60s with success also, bringing "A Lovely Work of Art" to No. 6 and "Wanting You to Be with Me" to No. 11. Not content with his popularity at MGM, he switched labels again, signing with Decca in 1961.

Now that he was an established artist, Newman began to integrate Cajun influences in such Top 25 singles as "Alligator Man" and "Bayou Talk." His 1963 album *Folk Songs of the Bayou Country* was a milestone in the popularization of Cajun music and included great work by accordionist Shorty LeBlanc and Newman regular Rufus Thibodeaux on fiddle. He hit the country Top Ten at the end of the year with "D.J. for a Day," and his recordings soon moved back to the Nashville sound, with occasional Cajun influences. (One notable exception is 1967's *Louisiana Saturday Night*.)

Jimmy C. Newman reached the Top Ten twice within six months in 1965-66 with "Artificial Rose" and "Back Pocket Money," but they proved to be his final hits. The next three years saw occasional placements in the Top 30, and his last chart entry was 1970's "I'm Holding Your Memory (But He's Holding You)." After his commercial decline, Newman moved back to Cajun music, recording for the La Louisianne, Swallow, and Rounder labels. His performances continue to excite many in Europe as well as America, and his Grand Ole Opry slot also keeps him busy. —*John Bush*

Folk Songs of the Bayou Country / 1963 / Decca ✦✦✦✦

Jimmy Newman Sings Country Songs / 1966 / Decca ✦✦✦✦

Country Crossroads / 1966 / Dot ✦✦✦

Cajun Cowboy / 1978 / Plantation ✦✦✦

Jimmy C. Newman and Cajun Country / 1986 / Dot ✦✦✦✦

This is a collection of Newman's country/Cajun hits. —*Jeff Hannusch*

● Bob a Hula-Diggy Liggy Lo / 1990 / Bear Family ✦✦✦✦

This two-fer contains all the material recorded by Newman for Dot Records, 47 tracks in all. —*AMG*

The Alligator Man / 1991 / Rounder ✦✦✦✦

Jimmy C. Newman has artfully integrated a country sensibility into his Cajun roots and crafted a style with a foot in both camps. This session emphasized the Cajun side, although it still contained numbers that were thoroughly country, from arrangements to Newman's earnest vocals. But he displayed his Cajun side quite forcefully, whether paying tribute to such greats as Johnnie Allen and D.L. Menard with crackling versions of their songs or doing his own arrangements of traditional Cajun music backed by a quality band. —*Ron Wynn*

Louisiana Saturday Night / Charly ✦✦✦

Louisiana Saturday Night is divided between new songs and re-recorded versions of Newman's '50s and '60s hits. The re-recordings are far from an embarrassment—if anything, they help give the album some weight. The old songs mesh with a handful of excellent new tracks, resulting in a thoroughly engaging and entertaining record. —*Thom Owens*

Juice Newton

b. Feb. 18, 1952, Lakehurst, NJ
Guitar, Vocals / Country-Rock, Country-Pop, Adult Contemporary, Urban Cowboy

Juice Newton (born Judy Kay Newton, February 18, 1952, Lakehurst, NJ) was part of the first wave of country singers raised on rock, folk-rock, and singer-songwriters, which is evident from her hit singles. "Angel of the Morning" and "Queen of Hearts," her two crossover hits, have country-pop arrangements, but their roots are in '60s pop and new wave roots rock, respectively. That's why she managed pop crossover hits in the early '80s and also why she was able to sustain country success throughout the decade.

Although Newton was born in New Jersey, she was reared in Virginia. As she entered high school, her mother gave her a guitar, prompting her infatuation with folk music. After graduating from high school, she attended Foothills College in Los Altos Hills, CA, where she continued to play folk in coffeehouses. During this time she met Otha Young, a fellow guitarist and songwriter. The two formed a folk-rock band called Dixie Peach and began playing bars around northern California.

Dixie Peach lasted only a year, but they did gain a local following. After the band broke up, Newton and Young formed Juice Newton and Silver Spur, which had more country leanings than Dixie Peach. They were also more successful. Their fan base was large enough to convice the band to go to Los Angeles and try to land a record contract. In 1975 Juice Newton and Silver Spur signed to RCA Records and released an eponymous debut, which spawned the minor hit single "Love is a Word" in early 1976. Later that year, the group released *After the Dust Settles*, which didn't attract much attention, and RCA dropped them after its release. The band signed with Capitol Records, releasing *Come to Me* in 1978. Like its predecessor, the album was more or less ignored, causing the Silver Spur to disband.

Though Silver Spur had broken up, Juice Newton and Otha Young continued to work together. Newton still had a contract with Capitol, and the pair immediately began working on her solo debut. The result, *Juice*, was released in early 1981 and it quickly became a crossover hit. The first single from the record, "Angel of the Morning," reached No. 4 on the pop charts; on the country charts, it peaked at 22. "Queen of Hearts" was a bigger hit, reaching No. 2 on the pop charts and No. 14 on the country charts. "The Sweetest Thing (I've Ever Known)," the third single taken from *Juice*, was her biggest country hit, peaking at No. 1; on the pop charts, it hit No. 7. *Juice* would eventually go platinum.

Newton's follow-up album to *Juice*, *Quiet Lies*, was released in the spring of 1982. It was also hit, spawning the pop Top Ten

"Love's Been A Little Bit Hard on Me" and the No. 2 country hit "Break It to Me Gently." The album won a Grammy for Best Country Vocal Performance, Female; it also went gold by the end of the year. *Dirty Looks*, her third solo album, was released in 1983. The record marked the first time Newton failed to crack either the pop or country Top 40.

In 1984 she switched labels, signing with RCA. Juice's first album for the label, *Can't Wait All Night*, was a transitionary album, moving away from pop and beginning to concentrate on country. *Old Flame*, released in 1985, was her country break-through, spawning the hits "You Make Me Want to Make You Mine," "Hurt," and the duet with Eddie Rabbitt "Both to Each Other (Friends and Lovers)," which all went to No. 1; the album had three additional Top Ten hits—"Old Flame," "Cheap Love," and "What Can I Do with My Heart."

Old Flame happened to be Newton's only major country hit. Its follow-up, 1987's *Emotion*, yielded only one Top Ten hit, "Tell Me True." In 1989 she released *Ain't Gonna Cry*, which featured the single "When Love Comes Around the Bend," which barely scraped the Top 40.

Ain't Gonna Cry turned out be Juice Newton's last album. She abandoned country and began performing showy mainstream pop in nightclubs. Throughout the '90s she continued to perform live concerts without recording any new material. —*Stephen Thomas Erlewine*

Juice Newton and Silver Spur / 1975 / RCA ✦✦
While on many of the albums Silver Spur acts more as a backup band than a real group, this record works more as a group effort. Juice still handles most of the vocals, but Silver Spur checks in with "Roll On, Trucker," which sounds very much like mid-period Pure Prairie League. —*Jim Worbois*

After the Dust Settles / 1977 / RCA ✦✦

Come to Me / 1977 / Capitol ✦✦
Otha Young's writing style has always seemed to suit Newton's vocal style the best, and that continues to be the case with this record. Of the two tracks written by her labelmate Bob Seger, "Fire Down Below" works the best, though Newton's soaring voice doesn't quite equal Seger's growl. —*Jim Worbois*

Well Kept Secret / 1978 / Capitol ✦✦
The title of this album seems to apply to her career as much as anything. She was still a couple years away from any substantial success. Newton seems to be without direction on this record and, as such, is trying some harder-edged material. While she doesn't do a bad job, there are so many others who do it better. —*Jim Worbois*

Take Heart / 1979 / Capitol ✦✦
This is not the place to start if you are just getting into Newton's music. It features less original music than many of her albums, and the covers she chooses to do don't really stand out. An average album at best. —*Jim Worbois*

Juice / 1981 / Capitol ✦✦✦✦
Juice was Juice Newton's breakthrough album, sending her not only into the country Top Ten, but to the top of the pop charts. The key to her success was how her country-pop drew not only from country roots, but also '60s AM pop, folk-rock, and roots rock. For instance, the country production on "Angel of the Morning" can't disguise its soft-rock roots. Similarly, "Queen of Hearts" simply replicates Dave Edmunds' version from *Repeat When Necessary*, down to the vocal inflections and guitar breaks. But Newton's version is slicker, which appealed both to country and pop radio. Throughout *Juice*, Newton straddles the line between country and pop, playing to both sides of the market. As it happened, she appealed to both. As an album, *Juice* has its weak moments, but she sings well throughout the record, and when she has the right material—as on the hit singles—the results are highly entertaining. —*Stephen Thomas Erlewine*

Quiet Lies / 1982 / Capitol ✦✦✦✦
This album assured Newton three country hits (the first three tracks) as she found her way back to the country-rock sound she seems to do best. Her choice of covers works better this time as

well. Her Brenda Lee netted her a hit, and her Gene Pitney cover wasn't bad either. —*Jim Worbois*

Can't Wait All Night / 1984 / RCA ✦✦
A largely uninteresting album. Newton seems to have lost not only her direction but her drive. —*Jim Worbois*

● Greatest Hits / 1984 / Capitol ✦✦✦✦
All of Juice Newton's big hits from the early '80s, including "Angel of the Morning," "Queen of Hearts," and "Love's Been a Little Bit Hard on Me," are collected on the single-disc set. —*Thom Owens*

Ain't Gonna Cry / 1985 / RCA ✦✦✦

Old Flame / 1986 / RCA ✦✦✦✦
Out of all of Juice Newton's albums, *Old Flame* has the strongest country roots and influences. Newton is still equally informed by rock and pop—after all, she doesn't sing hardcore honky tonk on the album, she sings somewhat roots country-pop. However, *Old Flame* proves that she can perform this material with conviction. Most of the production on the record is too slick and indicative of its time, but the singles—as well as Newton's singing—remain effective. —*Thom Owens*

Emotion / 1987 / RCA ✦✦✦

Greatest Country Hits / 1990 / Curb ✦✦✦

Greatest Hits [Cema] / 1992 / Capitol ✦✦✦

Olivia Newton-John

b. Sep. 26, 1948, Cambridge, England
Vocals / Pop-Rock

Olivia Newton-John skillfully made the transition from popular country-pop singer to popular mainstream soft-rock singer, becoming one of the most successful vocalists of the '70s in the process. The transition itself wasn't much of a stretch—her early '70s hits "I Honestly Love You" and "Have You Never Been Mellow" were country only in the loosest sense—yet the extent of her success in both fields was remarkable. As a country singer, her first five charting singles all went Top Ten in the US; as a pop singer, she had no less than 15 Top Ten hits, including five No. 1 singles, highlighted by "Physical," which spent ten weeks at No. 1 in 1981-82. Newton-John's sweet voice suited both country-pop and soft-rock perfectly, which is what kept her at the top of the charts until the mid-'80s. After 1984 she was no longer able to reach the Top 40, partly because of shifting musical tastes and partly because she was unable to successfully record sexy dance-pop, no matter how hard she tried. Nevertheless, her '70s and '80s hits remained soft-rock and adult contemporary staples into the '90s, when she was no longer recording frequently

Although she was born in Cambridge, England, Olivia Newton-John was raised in Melbourne, Australia, where her father was the headmaster of Ormond College. (Her grandfather, Max Born, won the Nobel Prize for physics.) She tentatively entered show business at the age of 12, when she won a local Haley Mills-look-alike contest. A few years later, she formed an all-female vocal group called the Sol Four with three school friends. Once the Sol Four disbanded, Newton-John entered a television talent contest, winning the grand prize of a trip to London. There she formed a duo with Pat Carroll, another Australian-based vocalist, and tried to work her way into the music industry. Though her partnership with Carroll was short-lived—Pat was sent back to Australia when her visa expired—Olivia was making inroads in the business. After Carrol's departure, Newton-John recorded and released her first single, a version of Jackie DeShannon's "Till You Say You'll Be Mine." Shortly afterward she became a member of Toomorrow, a bubblegum group assembled by Don Kirshner in hopes of creating a British version of the Monkees.

Toomorrow appeared in a science-fiction movie of the same name and had one minor British hit single, "I Could Never Live Without Your Love," in early 1970 before the group disbanded. After the failure of Toomorrow, Newton-John became part of Cliff Richard's touring show, appearing both as an opening act at his concerts and on his British television series, "It's Cliff!." The exposure as a singer and comedienne on the show helped

Newton-John's career immersurably, and her first single for Uni Records, a version of Bob Dylan's "If Not for You" became a Top Ten hit in the UK in the spring of 1971; in America, it was surprisingly successful, spending three weeks at the top of the Adult Contemporary charts and peaking at No. 25 on the pop charts. For the next two years Newton-John's success was primarily in Britain, where she had a string of lesser hits with covers of George Harrison's "What Is Life" and John Denver's "Take Me Home Country Roads." In America her career was stalled—her followup single, "Banks of the Ohio," barely scraped the lower reaches of the Top 100. On the other hand, she didn't release a full-length album in the US until 1973, when *Let Me Be There* appeared. The title track from the record became a huge hit, going gold in early 1974 and peaking in the Top Ten country and pop charts. "Let Me Be There" won the Grammy for Best Country Vocal Performance, Female, to the consternation of many members of Nashville's music industry.

"Let Me Be There" was followed by four other Top Ten hits—"If You Love Me (Let Me Know)" (No. 2 country, No. 5 pop, 1974), "I Honestly Love You" (No. 6 country, No. 1 pop, 1974), "Have You Never Been Mellow" (No. 3 country, No. 1 pop, 1975), and "Please Mr. Please" (No. 5 country, No. 3 pop, 1975). Newton-John moved to Los Angeles late in 1974, and early the next year, she won the Female Vocalist of the Year award from the Country Music Association. As a protest, several members of the CMA quit the organization. Ironically, Olivia Newton-John was already planning to move away from country. During 1976 and 1977 she had a number of minor hits with soft-rock songs. Though none of these was a big pop success, they began to establish her as a pop singer, not a country-pop singer.

Olivia Newton-John's transformation into a mildly sexy pop singer was complete in 1978, when she starred in the movie version of the popular Broadway musical *Grease*. Also starring John Travolta, *Grease* was an international hit, and it spawned three huge hit singles—"Hopelessly Devoted to You," "Summer Nights" and "You're the One That I Want"; the latter two were duets between Newton-John and Travolta. "You're the One That I Want," in particular, was a massive success, reaching No. 1 in both America and Britain; in the UK, it spent a staggering nine weeks at No. 1. During 1979 Olivia released the *Totally Hot* album, which boasted a mixture of soft rock and light disco. The record was another hit, with the first single "A Little More Love" peaking at No. 3 on the US pop charts and going gold. Early in 1980 Newton-John starred in the roller-disco fantasy film *Xanadu*. While the movie was an unqualified bomb, the soundtrack was a huge hit. "Magic" spent four weeks at the top of the US pop charts, while the ELO duet "Xanadu" reached No. 8, and her duet with Cliff Richard, "Suddenly," peaked at No. 20.

With her next album, *Physical*, Newton-John continued to rework her image, reinventing herself as a sexy aerobics fanatic. The first single from the record, the suggestive "Physical," was a huge hit, spending 10 weeks at No. 1 during the fall and winter of 1981-82. *Physical* spawned two other Top Ten hits—"Make a Move on Me" and "Heart Attack"—and became her most successful record. After the album's success, she was awarded the Order of the British Empire. In 1983 Newton-John again starred with Travolta, this time in the comedy *Two of a Kind*. The movie was a bomb, but a song she recorded for the soundtrack, "Twist of Fate," became a Top Ten hit in early 1984.

By the end of 1984 Newton-John had married actor Matt Lattanzi. The next year, she released the *Physical* clone *Soul Kiss*, which produced only one minor hit with its title track. In 1986 she had a daughter, Chloe, and opened a clothing store chain called Koala Blue. Newton-John attempted to launch a comeback in 1988 with *The Rumour*, but the album was ignored. She signed with Geffen the next year, releasing the children's album *Warm and Tender*. During the late '80s and '90s, she devoted herself to her family and business, as well as several environmental activist organizations. In 1992 Koala Blue folded, and Newton-John was diagnosed with breast cancer. Over the next year, she successfully underwent treatment for the disease. In 1994 she returned to recording with the independently released and self-produced album *Gaia*. —*Stephen Thomas Erlewine*

● **Back to Basics** / 1992 / Geffen ◆◆◆◆
An artist well-defined by her hit singles, Olivia Newton-John has had a stylistically varied career, as is illustrated on *Back to Basics: The Essential Collection 1971-1992*, a set that ranges from her teary ballad "I Honestly Love You" to that bouncy paean to getting horizontal, "Physical." Fans may quibble that such hits as "Let Me Be There" and "Make a Move on Me" are not included, but Newton-John's two greatest-hits albums are out of print, and this is the only collection to combine both her good-girl and bad-girl personae. —*William Ruhlmann*

Roy Nichols

Traditional Country, Bakersfield Sound, California Country
Roy Nichols made his way to Bakersfield from Fresno in the days when Bakersfield was just starting to boom. Distinctive in his style throughout his career, he made a name for himself through supporting Lefty Frizzell, Wynn Stewart, and Merle Haggard. Born in 1932 to parents who owned a migrant farm-worker camp in Fresno, the youngster spent his early years running free on the acreage that held the camp. Nichols first got interested in music after spending many nights sitting outside the gypsy camp that set up at the back of his parents' property. Night after night the boy would sit in the shadows beyond the fire and listen to the gypsies play and sing. This experience struck a chord and led him to pick up a guitar.

Leaving Fresno in search of gigs, Nichols landed right in the middle of a revolution. Teeming with life and plenty of talent, the San Joaquin Valley town attracted quality players from all across the West. Working the circuit and playing on recording sessions kept Nichols busy. After joining up with Merle Haggard, he proceeded to perfect his licks and became so proficient that it was not uncommon for future pickers to sit around listening to Haggard cuts and picking out Roy's distinctive riffs. An inspiration to the next generation, Nichols made a significant contribution to the careers of Scott Joss, Larry Dean, and other California country and Western artists. Although a stroke left him weakened and unable to play, he still supported the music and the many he mentored, remaining an important element to the Bakersfield Sound and one of the founding fathers of the West Coast sound. —*Jana Pendragon*

The Nitty Gritty Dirt Band

Progressive Bluegrass, Progressive Country, Country-Rock
Founded in California in 1965, the Nitty Gritty Dirt Band has lasted longer than virtually any other country-based rock group of their era. Younger contemporaries of the Byrds, they played an almost equally important role in the transformation from folk-rock into country-rock, and have been an influence on such bands as the Eagles and Alabama. The Nitty Gritty Dirt Band's beginnings lay with the New Coast Two, a folk duo consisting of Jeff Hanna (guitar, vocals) and Bruce Kunkel (guitar, washtub bass), formed while both were in high school in the early '60s. By the time they were college students, they were having informal jams at a Long Beach, CA, guitar shop called McCabe's. It was there that they met Ralph Barr (guitar, washtub bass), Les Thompson (vocals, mandolin, bass, guitar, banjo, percussion), Jimmie Fadden (harmonica, vocals, drums, percussion), and Jackson Browne (guitar, vocals).

This lineup became the Nitty Gritty Dirt Band in late 1965, and began playing jug band music at local clubs. At that time, Southern California was undergoing a musical renaissance, courtesy of the folk-rock movement, and the Nitty Gritty Dirt Band fit in with these other folkies-turned-rockers. Browne left after a few months to pursue a solo career, and was replaced by John McEuen (banjo, fiddle, mandolin, steel guitar, vocals), the younger brother of the group's new manager, Bill McEuen. With the elder McEuen's guidance, the group landed a recording contract with Liberty Records and released their debut album, *The Nitty Gritty Dirt Band*, in April 1967. Their first single, "Buy for Me the Rain," became a modest hit and got the band some television appearances.

A second album, *Ricochet*, released seven months later, was a critical success but a commercial failure. The group now found itself at an impasse over the issue of whether to go electric. During the dispute, Kunkel, who wanted to add an electric guitar to their sound, exited the lineup. He was replaced by Chris Darrow (guitar, fiddle). Ironically, by mid-1968 the group had gone electric and added drums to their sound. Their first electric album, *Rare Junk*, released in June 1968, was also a commercial failure. The band was barely working, a far cry from their success of a year earlier. The band persevered, however, and released *Alive!* in May 1969. The album was another commercial disaster, and the Nitty Gritty Dirt Band closed up shop soon after.

The members scattered, but six months later the group was back for another try; the new lineup included McEuen, Hanna, Fadden, Thompson, and Jim Ibbotson (guitars, accordion, drums, percussion, piano, vocals). They returned to their record company with a demand for control over their recordings, and the record company agreed. Bill McEuen became the group's producer as well as its manager. The first result of this new era in the Nitty Gritty Dirt Band's history was *Uncle Charlie and His Dog Teddy*, issued in 1970. Rooted tightly in their jugband sound, the album had a country feel but no trace of the vaudeville and novelty numbers that had appeared on their earlier records. The album yielded what is the group's best-known single, their cover of Jerry Jeff Walker's "Mr. Bojangles." Suddenly, the band had a following bigger than anything they'd known during their brief bout of success in 1967. Their next album, *All the Good Times*, released in early 1972, had an even more countrified feel.

By 1972 several rock bands, most notably the Byrds and the Beau Brummels, had gone to Nashville seeking credibility from the country music community there, only to be received poorly and to have their resulting work ignored by the press and public. At the suggestion of manager Bill McEuen, however, the Nitty Gritty Dirt Band went to Nashville in 1972 and recorded a selection of traditional country numbers with the likes of Roy Acuff, Earl Scruggs, Mother Maybelle Carter, and other members of country and bluegrass music's veteran elite. Some of the veteran Nashville stars were skeptical and suspicious at first of the band-members and their amplified instruments, but the ice was broken when they saw how respectful the band was toward them, their work, and their music, as well as how serious they were about their own music.

The resulting triple album, *Will the Circle Be Unbroken*, released in January 1973, became a million-seller and elicited positive reviews from both the rock and country music press. The band had by now eclipsed the competition as a "crossover" act, reaching country and bluegrass audiences even as their rock listeners acquired a new appreciation for musicians such as Acuff and Carter. The Nitty Gritty Dirt Band succeeded with *Will the Circle Be Unbroken* because they were willing to meet country and bluegrass music on the terms of those two branches of traditional music, rather than as rock musicians.

During the year and a half that followed the success of *Will the Circle Be Unbroken*, Les Thompson left the group, reducing the Dirt Band to a quartet. Their next album, *Stars and Stripes Forever*, issued in the summer of 1974, was a peculiar live album, mixing concert performances and dialogue. After one more original album, *Dream* (1975), the group received its first retrospective treatment, a triple-LP compilation entitled *Dirt, Silver and Gold*, issued late in 1976. Jim Ibbotson left the lineup around this time and was replaced initially by session player Bob Carpenter. The remaining trio of Jeff Hanna, John McEuen, and Jimmie Fadden shortened the band's official name to the Dirt Band. In this incarnation, the group became a much more mainstream, pop-rock outfit with a smoother sound, with Jeff Hanna guiding them as producer. Their records were far less eccentric, although they continued to be popular.

The band's next albums were decidedly more laidback than previous records and didn't attract nearly as much attention. *An American Dream*, released in 1980, did relatively well, as did *Make a Little Magic* (1981). By 1982, however, they were back to their country roots, renamed the Nitty Gritty Dirt Band, and Jim Ibbotson was playing with them again. *Let's Go*, released in the middle of 1983, heralded their return to country music, as a largely acoustic band. In 1984, after 17 years with Liberty/UA/Capitol, they switched to Warner Bros., and that same year made some headlines as the first American rock band to tour the Soviet Union. Their Warner albums sold well, but by the end of the 1980s the group was moving between labels.

In 1989, both as a reflection of the changing times and as though to make sure that everyone got the point that the band was once again mining its country roots, they made *Will the Circle Be Unbroken 2* for MCA/Universal Records, reuniting with country and bluegrass veterans from the original album and adding a whole roster of new players, including Johnny Cash, Chris Hillman, and Ricky Skaggs. This album won the Grammy for Best Country Vocal Performance (duo or group) and the Country Music Association's Album of the Year Award in 1989. By this time, the Dirt Band was working alongside any number of country/bluegrass crossover artists whose career paths were made easier by that first record, including John Hiatt, Mary Chapin Carpenter, and Rosanne Cash. Their next several albums saw them never veering very far from their country/bluegrass roots. The group continues to record a new album every year or so, most recently a new concert album, *Live Two-Five*, celebrating their 25th anniversary as a band, and the self-explanatory *Acoustic*. —*Bruce Eder*

The Nitty Gritty Dirt Band / 1967 / Liberty ◆◆◆

A strong debut album by one of the most offbeat folk/country-rock bands of the 1960's. Apart from the one unabashed classic, "Buy for Me the Rain," which was a modest hit and the group's biggest claim to musical fame for the next three years, the album also contained the delightful banjo-dominated McEuen/McEuen instrumental "Dismal Swamp" (which was anything but dismal), the Jackson Browne ballad "Holding," the rousing "You're Gonna Get It in the End," and Bruce Kunkel's haunting, ethereal "Song to Jutta" (as fine a song as anything the Byrds were doing at the time, and better played). In those days, the band wasn't too far removed from the sound of the early Grateful Dead or the Charlatans, but as this album reveals, drugs played less of a role in their music-making than humor, and some of the material was a little too comedic—the Rev. Gary Davis' "Candy Man," for example, comes off more upbeat than blues covers were supposed to be in those days, and may have *seemed* a little too much like a minstrel show interpretation (though one suspects Davis would have loved it), in a time when White versions of such songs were supposed to be either heavily electrified or reverent to the point of being somber. —*Bruce Eder*

Ricochet / 1967 / BGO ◆◆◆◆

The Nitty Gritty Dirt Band's second album is a masterpiece. From the opening bars of Jackson Browne's "Shadow Dream Song," the high spirits overflow the grooves (or ones and zeros, on the CD) of the record. The singing and playing are more confident, and some of the songs, including the bluesy "Ooh Po Pe Do Girl" and the hook-laden "I'll Search the Sky" by Jeff Hanna, and Copeland and Noonan's (the "Buy for Me the Rain" team) "Tide of Love," is as solid as anything coming out of California. Even the kazoo-dominated "Coney Island Washboard" and "Happy Fat Annie," and the nostalgic 20's-styled Jackson Browne-written "It's Raining Here in Long Beach" (which sounds a lot like Michael Nesmith's "Magnolia Sims," except the NGDB cut this months before Nesmith's song was out), fit well into the mix, reflecting the full range of the band's influences. As to why this record never caught on, it could be the timing—released late in 1967, in the wake of *Sergeant Pepper* (which had its own music hall influences, albeit of the English variety, and covered with lots of psychedelic overdubbing) and the Summer of Love, it just wasn't what college kids starting their search for the Lost Chord were looking for. Maybe a kazoo or two less would've helped, and a real drug song or two wouldn't have hurt, but these guys would play a jugband number ahead of a drug anthem any time. Their cover of Brewer and Shipley's "Truly Right" is pretty spacy in its production, but "The Teddy Bear's Picnic"—an adaptation of an old children's song—was probably beyond the pale for most listeners. Beyond NGDB completists, anyone looking for a companion to *Notorious*

Byrd Bros. or the Monkees' *Aquarius, Capricorn Pisces and Jones Ltd.*, or a precursor to Crazy Horse's *At Crooked Lake* need look no further. (British import) — *Bruce Eder*

Rare Junk / 1968 / Liberty ◆◆◆◆
This, the group's third album release, was actually an odds-and-sods type compilation of leftover tracks and singles that formed a respectable 10-song 30-minute-plus LP. As a sign of just how strong the band was, it still represented a step forward from their second album, and is one of the great unknown albums of 1968. — *Bruce Eder*

Pure Dirt / 1968 / BGO ◆◆◆◆
The group's first compilation album, made up of six songs from the first album and eight from *Ricochet*, assembled and released by Liberty Records in England (where neither of the original albums had appeared). A fair representation of the original Nitty Gritty Dirt Band, though serious fans would be more advised to pick up the complete albums. "Buy for Me the Rain" is here, along with some of the more rousing cuts off the first LP. (British import) — *Bruce Eder*

Alive / 1969 / Liberty ◆◆◆◆
How many live albums—forget decent ones—were left behind by bands in 1967/68? This is one, and it's better than decent, and almost a gift from heaven, capturing an early incarnation of the group (circa 1967) on a good night at the L.A. Troubadour. Someone has earned a place in musical heaven recording the show. — *Bruce Eder*

Uncle Charlie and His Dog Teddy / 1970 / Liberty ◆◆◆◆
This is the album that gave them a career. Their laidback mix of country and California folk gave a breezy feel to well-selected songs, including their million-selling version of Jerry Jeff Walker's "Mr. Bojangles." — *Michael McCall*

★ **Will the Circle Be Unbroken** / 1972 / EMI America ◆◆◆◆◆
The influence of this two-disc set, which brought the previously pop-oriented Dirt Band together with some of the seminal names in country music, is incalculable. Mother Maybelle Carter, Earl Scruggs, Doc Watson, Roy Acuff, and others sat down with a bunch of longhairs, found common ground on the best of old-time country music, and changed the direction of popular music. Two decades on, it still sounds great. — *William Ruhlmann*

Stars and Stripes Forever / 1974 / Beat Goes On ◆◆◆
Whatever your preconceptions of the Dirt Band, this record will blow them away. One minute they are doing one of their early hits, the next reminiscing about the '50s and covering the Jive 5. They mix Hank Williams, Buddy Holly, and the "Sheik of Araby." This is an incredibly fun live album. — *Jim Worbois*

Dream / 1975 / United Artists ◆◆◆
Most of the songs work on this eclectic mix of tunes and arrangements. One of the standouts on this album is the J.D. Souther tune, which Souther did not release until 1979. — *Jim Worbois*

Dirt, Silver and Gold / 1976 / One Way ◆◆◆◆
The 37 songs here were originally on three LPs (now two CDs), and this remains the biggest anthology ever done on the NGDB. As is usual with such collections, the group's early history is represented by only five songs, one of which is (of course) "Buy for Me the Rain." A lot of the rest will be familiar to people who came in after *Uncle Charlie and His Dog Teddy*, but in lieu of owning all of those subsequent albums (though why anyone would want to pass up owning *Will the Circle Be Unbroken* is beyond this writer's ability to understand), this is a handy assembly of songs, covering their output up through 1976 and the album *Dream. The Best of the Nitty Gritty Dirt Band* from EMI has fewer songs, but it does have notes, which this was (and is still) sorely lacking, despite the presence of a list showing some of the different line-ups of the NGDB. — *Bruce Eder*

Dirt Band / 1978 / United Artists ◆◆
In the late '70s, several key members of the Nitty Gritty Dirt Band left the group, and the remaining members truncated their name to "The Dirt Band." The new lineup debuted on *The Dirt Band*, and the record is a bit less intriguing than previous efforts, partly due to the change in band personnel, and partly due to poorer song selection. Where they used to have their own distinct sound,

Nitty Gritty Dirt Band

the group now sounds like just another L.A. country-rock band. In other words, this is the Dirt Band's transitional phase, and it makes for decidedly mediocre listening. — *James Chrispell*

American Dream (Dirt Band) / 1979 / United Artists ◆◆
The Dirt Band's *An American Dream* showed signs of the group's getting tired of the good-time music tag they'd been labeled with. That said, much of the music here—such as a hit cover of Rodney Crowell's "An American Dream" and a version of Claude King's "Wolverton Mountain"—has some of the old good-time charm, while other tracks seemed to mirror the L.A. slickness of their previous eponymous effort. *An American Dream* is a hodge-podge, but its best moments still make for worthwhile listening. — *James Chrispell*

Plain Dirt Fashion / 1984 / Warner Brothers ◆◆
While this is a nice-sounding album, there is really nothing here to distinguish it from Poco, the Eagles, or any of the other country-rock bands making records throughout the late '70s and early '80s. — *Jim Worbois*

20 Years of Dirt... / 1986 / Warner Brothers ◆◆◆◆
20 Years of Dirt: The Best of the Nitty Gritty Dirt Band traces the development of the Nitty Gritty Dirt Band from a pop outfit with folk and country edges into a contemporary country band. Their version of "Mr. Bojangles" remains memorable, as does "American Dream"; other tracks are sturdy, middle-of-the-road, '80s Nashville. — *William Ruhlmann*

Workin' Band / Aug. 9, 1988 / Warner Brothers ◆◆◆
Much of the magic of the Nitty Gritty Dirt Band returned on *Workin' Band*. Switching labels and signing to Warner Brothers, the group put a lot of effort into this disc and it shows. Perhaps the assistance of former Eagle Bernie Leadon helped gel their ideas, but by now, they had embraced country music, and the result was a fine effort from a veteran band. — *James Chrispell*

More Great Dirt (Best, Vol. 2) / 1989 / Warner Brothers ◆◆◆◆
Tight harmonies and infectious arrangements are the staple of this compilation. "I've Been Lookin'," "Fishin' in the Dark," and "Baby's Got a Hold on Me" are the musical equivalent of a good book—you can't put 'em down. — *Tom Roland*

Will the Circle Be Unbroken, Vol. 2 / 1989 / Universal ◆◆◆
This easily won the Country Music Association's Album of the Year Award, thanks to a stellar cast that includes John Denver, Johnny Cash, the Carter Family, Bruce Hornsby, Ricky Skaggs, Chris Hillman, Roger McGuinn, Rosanne Cash, Steve Wariner, Roy Acuff, Chet Atkins... you get the message. Tracks were all

recorded in one "take," with no overdubs, making the outstanding musicianship particularly noteworthy. Atheists beware: there's a lot of gospel. —*Tom Roland*

The Rest of the Dream / Jun. 26, 1991 / MCA ✦✦✦
This features "Wishing Well," "Hillbilly Hollywood," "Waitin' on a Dark-Eyed Gal," "From Small Things (Big Things One Day Come)," and other hits. —*AMG*

Acoustic / May 31, 1994 / Liberty ✦✦✦
Mighty professional sounding when compared to Uncle Charlie, but after more than 25 years as music pros, they still sound best when at their most casual, as they are here. —*Michael McCall*

Alive/Rare Junk / 1995 / BGO ✦✦✦✦
Two superb albums on one CD equals one must-own CD. The studio sides on Rare Junk include covers of the jazz standard "Willie the Weeper" (with its familiar "Hi de hi dee ho" chorus), "Collegiana" (done jug band style), "Cornbread and 'Lasses," Tim Hardin's "Reason to Believe" and Jackson Browne's "These Days" in one of its better (and surprisingly upbeat) versions. Some of this stuff is so self-conconscious in its humor—"Sadie Green the Vamp of New Orleans" and "Dr. Heckle and Mr. Jibe" come to mind—that it's hard to believe that it was recorded with much confidence of success, but it works musically, capturing the vaudeville side of the band's orientation better than anything on their first two LPs. One also gets the feeling that these guys, if they hadn't been around during the late 1960s, might've been equally suited to providing the musical scores to Max Fleischer's Betty Boop cartoons. *Alive*, recorded at the L.A. Troubadour circa 1967, is one of the great live albums of its decade, capturing the early group in top form, clowning around in a loosely structured show that has them covering "Buy for Me the Rain" (which was already a hit) as well as B.B. King's "Rock Me Baby," the Reverend Gary Davis' "Candy Man" (in a version superior to the first album's studio cover), and Earl Scruggs' "Foggy Mountain Breakdown." That this recording was held back for over a year, and then released only during the period in which the group had ceased to exist, is understandable—Liberty probably didn't have a clue as to what to do with an opening number featuring a kazoo solo. But it is a great set. The guitars, mandolins, and banjos glitter in the clarity of the recording; and it is an honest, fully representative show, complete with wrong notes, false starts, and jokes that usually (but don't always) work. The ten tracks are a vital addition to any folk-rock, country-rock, or even a partly serious NGDB fan's collection. —*Bruce Eder*

Norma Jean (Norma Jean Beaser)

b. Jan. 30, 1938, Wellston, OK
Vocals / Traditional Country, Honky Tonk
Singer Norma Jean remains best remembered as Porter Wagoner's partner before he was paired with Dolly Parton; she was also known for her many songs about the joys and tribulations of being a blue-collar worker. Norma Jean Beasler was no stranger to poverty herself, born into a hard-working but poor family on a farm near Wellston, OK. As a child, she wanted to be a country star like Kitty Wells, whom she tried to emulate. She made her professional debut singing "If Teardrops Were Pennies" at age 12 on the radio in Oklahoma City. In high school she toured with a few Western swing bands, including those of Billy Gray and Merle Lindsay.

Her big break came in 1958, when she became a cast member of the Springfield, MO-based ABC-TV show "Ozark Jubilee," where Red Foley suggested shortening her name to "Norma Jean." The young singer hit Nashville in 1960, where she became a backup vocalist for Porter Wagoner's touring and television shows, leading to a contract with RCA Victor. She had her first chart single, "Let's Go All the Way," in 1964; the song made the

Top 15 and was followed by the Top 25 hit "I'm a Walkin' Advertisement (For the Blues)." That year she had her first Top 10 single, "Go Cat Go," which stayed on the country charts for four months and became a minor pop hit as well. Her chart success continued through the mid-'60s with songs such as "I Wouldn't Buy a Used Car from Him" and "The Game of Triangles" (both 1965).

On television Norma Jean presented a wholesome image at odds with her hurtin' and cheatin' songs; yet in her personal life, both images were accurate. Around the mid-'60s, she became romantically involved with her mentor Wagoner, who was separated from his wife at the time. The affair led her to leave Wagoner's organization, although she continued to appear on the Grand Ole Opry and recorded more singles for RCA. In 1967 she had two Top 30 hits, "Don't Let that Doorknob Hit You" and "Heaven Help the Working Girl," an early feminist song. In the late '60s Norma Jean returned to Oklahoma after marrying Jody Taylor; she had her last chart hit in 1971 with "The Kind of Needin' I Need." She continued to record occasionally on independent labels, and in 1982 she and Claude Gray teamed for a minor hit with a remake of "Let's Go All the Way." —*Sandra Brennan*

Let's Go All the Way / 1964 / RCA Victor ✦✦✦✦

Pretty Miss Norma Jean / 1965 / RCA Victor ✦✦✦

Please Don't Hurt Me / 1966 / RCA Victor ✦✦✦✦

Tribute to Kitty Wells / 1966 / RCA Victor ✦✦✦

● **Norma Jean Sings Porter Wagoner** / 1967 / RCA Victor ✦✦✦✦

Jackson Ain't a Very Big Town / 1967 / RCA Victor ✦✦✦

Heaven's Just a Prayer Away / 1968 / RCA Victor ✦✦✦

Norma Jean / 1971 / Bearsville ✦✦✦

The Notting Hillbillies

Country-Rock, Americana
After the mega-platinum success of Dire Straits' 1984 *Brothers in Arms* LP, the group's frontman, guitarist extraordinaire Mark Knopfler, opted to temporarily shift gears by forming the Notting Hillbillies, a one-off country side-project. Among the band's first recruits was Steve Phillips, a fellow guitar player whom Knopfler had first met in Yorkshire in 1968 when both men interviewed a local country and blues musician (also named, curiously enough, Steve Phillips). Soon the two aspiring journalists formed the two-man Duolian String Pickers, and they continued performing together until Knopfler entered college in 1970; after graduating three years later, he moved to London to start Dire Straits.

Phillips, in the meantime, formed a rockabilly outfit, the Steve Phillips Juke Band. In 1976 he met Brendan Croker, a onetime member of the Juke Band, and the pair began performing as Nev and Norris. By 1980 Phillips had left the music scene to focus on an art career, leaving Croker to form the 5 O'Clock Shadows. In 1986, Knopfler came calling, and in May of that year the Notting Hillbillies played their first gig at a tiny Leeds club with a lineup featuring Knopfler, Phillips, and Croker as well as drummer Ed Bicknell (moonlighting from his day job as Dire Straits' manager), guitarist Guy Fletcher, pedal steel guitarist Paul Franklin, and Croker's fellow 5 O'Clock Shadow Marcus Cliff on bass. A tour followed, although the group's lone album, *Missing...Presumed Having a Good Time*, did not appear until 1990, at which point the members of the Notting Hillbillies had already returned to their main projects. —*Jason Ankeny*

Missing...Presumed Having a Good Time / 1990 / Warner Brothers ✦✦✦✦
Missing...Presumed Having a Good Time is a superb collection with strong country leanings, melodic and memorable. —*Hank Davis*

O

The Oak Ridge Boys

Country-Pop, Country Gospel
Over the course of their long career, the Oak Ridge Boys became a country music institution. The vocal group went through a number of personnel changes over the years, but their sound remained the same, as they never strayed from their gospel-inflected country-pop.

The Oak Ridge Boys began as a gospel group named the Oak Ridge Quartet in 1945. In 1949 Bob Weber purchased the rights to the group's name from lead singer Wally Fowler and ascribed it to his group, the Cavalry Quartet. The Oak Ridge Quartet remained together through the mid-'50s, becoming one of the top gospel groups in America. Smitty Gatlin later created a new Oak Ridge Quartet after purchasing the name from Weber. Gatlin decided to steer the group towards secular success and changed their name to the Oak Ridge Boys in 1961. Although they were concentrating on commercial material, the group continued to sing gospel music. In the late '60s, the Oak Ridge Boys underwent an image makeover, growing their hair long and singing almost nothing but pop-oriented material. In the early '70s, they gradually incorporated more gospel in their repertoire.

By 1973 the group's core lineup—Duane Allen (lead vocals), Joe Bonsall (tenor), William Lee Golden (baritone), and Richard Sterban (bass)—had fallen into place, and they made their first entry in the country charts with a cover of Johnny Cash's "Praise the Lord and Pass the Soup." The next year they signed to Columbia, although they nearly disbanded due to financial difficulties. In 1977 the group decided to switch over completely to secular music, beginning with the hit singles "Y'All Come Back Saloon" and "You're the One." Almost immediately the Oak Ridge Boys became a fixture in the country Top Ten; for the next eight years, they had a string of 25 Top Ten singles, including 13 No. 1 hits. In 1978 they had their first No. 1 single with "I'll Be True to You." In 1981 the Oaks had their biggest hit with the crossover smash "Elvira."

By the late '80s the group's momentum began to slow down. They still had Top 40 hits, but they no longer dominated the Top Ten as they had in the early '80s. In 1987 Golden, who had been with the group since 1964, was fired by the rest of the group, who believed that his burly appearance and long beard no longer fit their image. The Oaks' backup guitarist and singer Steve Sanders replaced him, and the group quickly returned to the Top Ten. Over the next three years they had four No. 1 hits, including "It Takes a Little Rain (To Make Love Grow)," "Gonna Take a Lot of River," and "No Matter How High." In 1990, their comeback slowed down. One more Top Ten hit, "Lucky Moon," followed in 1991, but the group had all but disappeared from the country charts by the end of 1992. The Oak Ridge Boys continued to tour and record throughout the '90s. *—Sandra Brennan*

Together / 1966 / MCA ◆◆◆
The Top Three hits "Heart of Mine" and "Beautiful You" are featured on *Together. —Jason Ankeny*

Y'All Come Back Saloon / 1977 / MCA ◆◆◆◆
"You're the One" and the title cut are the featured selections on *Y'All Come Back Saloon. —Jason Ankeny*

Room Service / 1978 / MCA ◆◆◆◆
Room Service includes the Oaks' first No. 1 single, "I'll Be True to You," as well as the Top Three hits "Come On In" and "Cryin' Again." *—Jason Ankeny*

Greatest Hits, Vol. 1 / 1980 / MCA ◆◆◆◆
Earliest package of hits, with gospel roots showing on material like "Y'All Come Back Saloon." *—Cub Koda*

Fancy Free / 1981 / MCA ◆◆◆◆
This is their best-selling album, thanks to the presence of "Elvira." Each of the Oaks gets a turn at the lead part, although Duane Allen is easily best suited to that role. Includes some quasi-folk and straightahead country, but the best track is the obligatory gospel tune "I Would Crawl All the Way (To the River)." *—Tom Roland*

● **Greatest Hits, Vol. 2** / 1984 / MCA ◆◆◆◆
This covers the Oaks at their peak, with repetitive, singalong choruses predominating in "American Made," "Love Song," and "Everyday." The delicate "I Guess It Never Hurts to Hurt Sometimes" is a nice change of pace, but why did MCA hold out "Bobbie Sue" until *Greatest Hits 3? —Tom Roland*

Monongahela / 1987 / MCA ◆◆◆◆
Though *Heartbeat* was recorded after the dismissal of William Lee Golden, this is the first album in which replacement Steve Sanders was involved from beginning to end in the recording process. Harmonies are understandably more soulful—and more in tune—and the project is generally more uplifting. It includes "Gonna Take a Lot of River." *—Tom Roland*

Sensational Oak Ridge Boys / 1987 / Starday ◆◆◆◆
Solid collection of their early gospel recordings. Interesting to compare to their secular success. *—Cub Koda*

American Dreams / 1989 / MCA ◆◆◆
It features such hits as "An American Family," "Cajun Girl," "Bed of Roses," and others. *—AMG*

Greatest Hits, Vol. 3 / 1989 / MCA ◆◆◆◆
This contains "Gonna Take a Lot of River," "Take Pride in America," "This Crazy Love," and other hits from the mid—and late '80s. *—AMG*

The Long Haul / 1992 / RCA ◆◆◆
While the title proved wholly inappropriate—this LP was the group's last with longtime label MCA—*The Long Haul* is one of the Oaks' more consistent efforts and contains the minor hit "Fall." *—Jason Ankeny*

The Oak Ridge Boys/J.D. Sumner and the Stamps / 1992 / Arrival ◆◆◆
If you don't remember when the Oaks were a gospel group or have never heard the Stamps except in their role as background singers for Elvis, here is a disc that will introduce you to each group as they perform the type of music they were first known for. Among the five tracks by the Oaks are "Less of Me," "At Last," and "I Wouldn't Take Nothing for My Journey," while the Stamps do "My Savior Knows," "The Old Rugged Cross," and "Amazing Grace." *—Jim Worbois*

The Oak Ridge Boys

The Collection / Apr. 21, 1992 / MCA ✦✦✦
Featured are "Fancy Free," "Trying to Love Two Women," "Thank God for Kids," "American Made," and other hits. —*AMG*

The Best of the Oakridge Boys / Columbia ✦✦✦✦
Best of the Oak Ridge Boys collects the group's early, gospel-styled recordings. —*Jason Ankeny*

Mollie O'Brien

Traditional Bluegrass, Progressive Country
The older sister of Hot Rize member Tim, bluegrass performer Mollie O'Brien grew up in Wheeling, WV, where during high school she and her brother teamed as a folk duo. After studying voice in college, O'Brien moved to New York City, where she worked as a buyer for the garment industry. In 1980 inspired by Tim's success in Hot Rize, she joined him in Colorado, where she became a fixture on the R&B and jazz club circuits. In 1984 the O'Brien siblings reunited for a Mother's Day concert, and four years later they recorded a duets album, *Take Me Back.* Concurrently, O'Brien continued her solo career, issuing her debut LP *I Never Move Too Soon* in 1987. She also joined the Mother Folkers for 1989's *Live at the Arvada Center.* In the decade that followed, O'Brien continued to divide her time between solo and duo work, releasing her *Every Night in the Week* in 1990 and rejoining Tim two years later for *Remember Me.* Another duet collection, *Away Out on the Mountain*, appeared in 1994, and in 1996 O'Brien issued the solo effort *Time to Talk.* —*Jason Ankeny*

I Never Move Too Soon / 1987 / Resounding ✦✦✦
● **Tell It True** / Mar. 19, 1996 / Sugar Hill ✦✦✦✦
Every Night in the Week / Resounding ✦✦✦

Maura O'Connell

Vocals / Progressive Bluegrass, Celtic, Singer-Songwriter, Contemporary Folk
Maura O'Connell embodies many paradoxes: lead singer for De Dannon, she was not a traditional Celtic singer; resident of Nashville, she is not American; collaborator with New Grass Revival, she is not a bluegrass performer. Nevertheless, O'Connell has made a name for herself on two continents as a superb singer.

O'Connell was born and raised in County Clare, Ireland, where she began singing at an early age. Involvement in the folk club scene led to an invitation from celtic traditionalists De Dannon to join their ranks. Her involvement with De Dannon resulted in the recording of *Star Spangled Mollie*, a clear indication of interest in trans-Atlantic culture. O'Connell then began to collaborate with members of New Grass Revival, and in particular with Bela Fleck, who produced several of her tracks. Together with Fleck and others, she recorded *Just in Time* and made the decision to settle in

Nashville. Since then she has released *Helpless Heart, Blue Is the Colour of Hope*, and *Real Life Story*, each album registering a move toward a pop synthesis. —*Leon Jackson*

Just in Time / 1988 / Philo ✦✦✦
This album, produced by Bela Fleck with string arrangements by Edgar Meyer, is one of O'Connell's cleanest and most uncluttered. Her voice sounds beautifully free; while some of her recordings sound forced, this one is relaxed and natural. This album demonstrates why she is often compared to Mary Black. The album's band is an all-star affair with Jerry Douglas, Bela Fleck, Mark O'Conner, and Nanci Griffith contributing. Maura O'Connell can be given credit here for picking up Paul McCartney's "I Will" seven years before Alison Krauss. —*Richard Meyer*

● **Helpless Heart** / 1989 / Warner Brothers ✦✦✦✦
Irish interpretive singer O'Connell has suffered from the inability of her record company to figure out whether she's a folkie, a country singer, or a pop artist. Meanwhile, she keeps singing her heart out, cherrypicking the work of such writers as Paul Brady, Nanci Griffith, Linda Thompson, and others. If you already own the albums those writers have made, maybe she's redundant. However, great songs still benefit greatly from being performed by great singers, and if you're looking for a sympathetic sampler of the best of today's songwriters, here it is. — *William Ruhlmann*

A Real Life Story / 1991 / Warner Brothers ✦✦✦
Moving into a more slick production and electric sound can't hide the fact that Maura's lovely voice is deepening into a seasoned richness as rare as it is enjoyable—joined on one cut ("A Family Tie," about alcoholism) by her three sisters. Other highlights include Shawn Colvin's "I Don't Know Why," Janis Ian's "Unwinding," and Lennon/McCartney's "For No One," with only dobro and acoustic guitar accompaniment—gorgeous. —*Ladyslipper*

Blue Is the Colour of Hope / 1992 / Warner Brothers ✦✦✦
This charmingly eclectic album may be O'Connell's best. Working with producer Jerry Douglas, O'Connell finds sympathetic accompaniment on all these songs, whether it' the piano and arco bass on the gently painful "So Soft Your Goodbye," the small-combo swing on "Love to Learn," or the full-band acoustic pop on "Still Hurts Sometimes." Though O'Connell records songs by Nashville stalwarts like Pat McLaughlin and Tom Kimmel, her ear for a wider range of material makes *Blue Is the Color of Hope* such a joy. "Bad News at the Best of Times," by rockers Paul Carrack and John Wesley Harding, is a real find, and O'Connell's cover of Mary-Chapin Carpenter's "It Don't Bring You" is simply gorgeous. —*Brian Mansfield*

Stories / Oct. 1995 / Hannibal ✦✦✦

Mark O'Connor

b. Aug. 5, 1961, Seattle, WA
Fiddle, Session Musician / Progressive Bluegrass, Instrumental, Progressive Country
Born and raised in Seattle, O'Connor was always a bit out of sync with his teenage peers. Understandably so, since he was winning fiddle contests and had even mapped out a sketchy career path. O'Connor moved to Nashville in 1983, already a former sideman for jazz violinist Stephane Grappelli, a job that allowed him to play the stage at Carnegie Hall. At the time O'Connor arrived in Music City (the post-*Urban Cowboy* era), fiddle was hardly in vogue, and it took a couple of years for him to make his mark. Finally, in 1985 the Nitty Gritty Dirt Band used him in its single "High Horse." Thanks to that work, O'Connor's phone number became a popular one with country record producers. Over the next five years he played on 450 albums, including such stellar projects as *Trio* by Dolly Parton, Linda Ronstadt, and Emmylou Harris; *Always and Forever* by Randy Travis; *Killin' Time* by Clint Black; and *Loving Proof* by Ricky Van Shelton. Despite his success, O'Connor gave up session work to concentrate on his own solo career, in the process providing a new focus on Nashville's studio players while simultaneously building a reputation for himself with the general public. —*Tom Roland*

Markology / 1980 / Rounder ✦✦✦
An acoustic guitar album. —*Chip Renner*

On the Rampage / 1980 / Rounder ✦✦✦

Soppin' the Gravy / 1981 / Rounder ✦✦✦✦
This is a good collection of mainly traditional Texas fiddle music.
—*Brian Mansfield*

Meanings Of / 1986 / Warner Brothers ✦✦✦

Elysian Forest / 1988 / Warner Brothers ✦✦✦
More in the new age frontier. Mark O'Connor's fiddle turns into a
violin right in front of your ears, if you know what I mean. —*Chip
Renner*

Stone from Which the Arch Was Made / 1990 / Warner Brothers
✦✦✦
R&B featuring Bela Fleck, Jerry Douglas, John McCutheon, and
Maura O'Connell. Very nice; more rock and electric. —*Chip Ren-
ner*

On the Mark / 1989 / Warner Brothers ✦✦✦
Featuring James Taylor, Jerry Douglas, and Michael Brecker (one
of my favorites). Great sax on "Get Set, Go." A must-have for
O'Connor fans. —*Chip Renner*

Championship Years / 1990 / Country Music Foundation ✦✦✦✦
O'Connor at his earliest and most traditional. These recordings
were made during his National Fiddling Championships competitions between 1975 and 1984. —*Brian Mansfield*

The New Nashville Cats / 1991 / Warner Brothers ✦✦✦✦
With an incredible lineup of Nashville's very best musicians, this
package covers a wide range of musical territory, from bluegrass
to the blues, with plenty of stellar pickin'. Ironically, this mostly
instrumental album won a vocal Grammy when Vince Gill, Ricky
Skaggs, and Steve Wariner teamed with O'Connor on "Restless."
—*Tom Roland*

Heroes / 1993 / Warner Brothers ✦✦✦✦
O'Connor performs with his favorite fiddlers from a variety of
styles, including Jean-Luc Ponty, Johnny Gimble, Vassar Clements,
Pinchas Zukerman, and L. Shankar. The set features "The Devil
Comes Back to Georgia," a sequel to Charlie Daniels' 1979 hit
"The Devil Went Down to Georgia." —*Brian Mansfield*

The Fiddle Concerto / 1995 / Warner Brothers ✦✦✦

Markology / Rounder ✦✦✦✦

False Dawn / Rounder ✦✦✦
New age acoustic music. A turning-point album in which O'Connor comes of age. —*Chip Renner*

Mark O'Connor / Rounder ✦✦✦
An early album. Raw. —*Chip Renner*

● **Retrospective** / Rounder ✦✦✦✦
This is a chronological overview of O'Connor's first six Rounder
albums. —*Brian Mansfield*

Fiddle / Rounder ✦✦✦✦

Molly O'Day (LaVerne Williamson)

b. Jul. 9, 1923, Pike County, KY, **d.** Dec. 5, 1987
Vocals / Traditional Country, Honky Tonk
A pioneering vocalist whose soulful, gut-wrenching performances
helped redefine the role of the female country solo artist, Molly
O'Day's career was relatively brief, but her lasting influence has
proven massive. Born Lois LaVerne Williamson on July 9, 1923, to
a coal-mining family living in a remote Appalachian community
in eastern Kentucky, she spent her childhood enamored of cowgirl
singers like Patsy Montana, Lulu Belle Wiseman, Texas Ruby
Owens, and Lily May Ledford, and eventually began singing and
playing guitar in a string band with her brothers Cecil ("Skeets")
on fiddle and Joe ("Duke") on banjo. In 1939 Skeets began playing on a radio station in Charleston, WV, and his sister soon followed, adopting the stage name "Mountain Fern." A year later,
now under the name "Dixie Lee Williamson," she joined guitarist
Lynn Davis' band the Forty-Niners, and in 1941 she and Davis
married.

Over the next five years, the Forty-Niners toured the South
extensively, building a substantial fan base along the way. By the

time the group settled in for an extended stay in Louisville, KY, in
1946, the name "Molly O'Day" was firmly entrenched. While
Davis and O'Day's duets were popular with audiences, it was her
deeply felt solo performances of inspirational songs that had the
biggest impact and that led writer/publisher Fred Rose to sign the
singer to Columbia Records. There O'Day performed a number of
songs written by a young Hank Williams, whom she knew from
their days on the radio circuit; in fact, it was Williams who taught
O'Day her best-loved song, "Tramp on the Street," one of eight
tunes she cut during her first studio session in late 1946. Backed
by Davis, her brother Skeets, bassist Mac Wiseman, and George
"Speedy" Krise on the dobro, the recordings gave a further boost
to O'Day's surging popularity but already she was having trouble
coping with her success.

O'Day and Davis spent much of 1947 out of music, but in
December of that year she returned to the studio, where she
recorded her crowd-pleaser "Matthew Twenty-Four." She and
Davis spent much of the next several years on the road, where she
began performing religious material almost exclusively. In mid-
1949 she cut another session, recording songs like "Teardrops
Falling in the Snow," "Poor Ellen Smith," and Williams' "On the
Evening Train." In the latter half of the year, O'Day suffered a nervous breakdown and was hospitalized; although she did record
again in 1950 and 1951, she largely turned her back on show
business afterwards, focusing on performing in churches. In 1954
Davis became an ordained minister, and in the following decades
the couple preached throughout the coal-mining communities of
West Virginia. O'Day did record for a few small gospel labels in
the 1960s, and in 1973 she and Davis began hosting a daily gospel program on a West Virginia radio station. She died of cancer
December 5, 1987. —*Jason Ankeny*

Hymns for the Country Folks / 1960 / Audio Lab ✦✦✦

The Living Legend of Country Music / 1966 / Starday ✦✦✦✦

★ **And the Cumberland Mountain Folks** / 1992 / Bear Family
✦✦✦✦✦
Molly O'Day and the Cumberland Mountain Folks is a double-
disc, 36-track collection that compiles all of the recordings O'Day
made for Columbia Records between 1946 and 1951. Though her
music presages the upcoming honky tonk era, O'Day was more
closely tied to the mountain music that dominated country music
in the first half of the 20th Century. As such, her music can be a
little difficult for contemporary ears—her thick nasal twang is
something that modern listeners will have to accommodate. For
country historians, however, *Molly O'Day and the Cumberland
Mountain Folks* is worthwhile. Not only did she bridge the gap
between string bands and honky tonk with her old-timey banjo
playing and twang, but she was one of the first country artists to
record a Hank Williams song. As such, this double-disc set is
worth investigation for serious musicologists. —*Stephen Thomas
Erlewine*

With Lynn Davis, Vol. 1 / Old Homestead ✦✦✦✦
It features "I Have But One Goal," "I'm Going Home on the Morning Train," and "I'm Going to Walk Right In." —*AMG*

In Memory / Old Homestead ✦✦✦✦
It features O'Day performing with husband Lynn Davis and the
Cumberland Mountain Folk during the early days of her career.
—*AMG*

James O'Gwynn

b. Jan. 26, 1928, Winchester, MS
Vocals / Traditional Country, Nashville Sound/Countrypolitan
"The Smilin' Irishman of Country Music," James O'Gwynn was
briefly popular in the late '50s and early '60s. He was born a Mississippi farmboy and raised near Hattiesburg, the son of a
mechanic and a talented musician. He learned the guitar as a
child from his mother, and his earliest influences were Jimmie
Rodgers and Hank Williams. He dropped out of grade school to
help out at his father's business and later served as a US Marine
for four years. During his tour of duty, he decided to become a
country singer. While on leave he made his debut appearance
during a campaign rally for a gubernatorial candidate. The candi-

date suggested O'Gwynn contact Houston deejay Hal Harris, who in turn introduced the young soldier to Biff Collie, the producer and host of "Houston Jamboree." O'Gwynn joined the show in 1954, as did George Jones. Eventually he hooked up with renowned producer Pappy Dailey and in 1956 recorded "Losing Game." O'Gwynn joined the "Louisiana Hayride" and released two more singles the next year. In 1958 he signed with Dailey's D label, where he finally found chart success with such songs as the Top Ten "Talk to Me Lonesome Heart" and "Blue Memories," which peaked in the Top 30. In 1959 O'Gwynn released two more hit singles, and, with the help of Jim Reeves, debuted on the Grand Ole Opry. He moved to Nashville in 1961 and appeared on the Opry for the next two years. He scored two more minor hits, including "My Name Is Mud," his last chart appearance. During the 1960s O'Gwynn worked with different major and independent labels, but to no avail; by the end of the decade, he had moved to Arkansas and gone into semi-retirement. In 1971 O'Gwynn tried a comeback, with no success. —*Sandra Brennan*

● **Best of James O'Gwynn** / 1962 / Mercury ✦✦✦✦

Heartaches and Memories / 1964 / Mercury Wing ✦✦✦✦

Greatest Hits / 1976 / Plantation ✦✦✦

Country Dance Time / 1978 / Plantation ✦✦✦

Jamie O'Hara

b. Aug. 8, 1950, Toledo, OH
Vocals / Contemporary Country, Neo-Traditionalist Country
Former member of the O'Kanes, and one-time college football star, Jamie O'Hara was a hit songwriter before gaining a short blast of acclaim in his partnership with Kieran Kane. On his own, he creates rugged, sparse, country music that is simple, literate, and effective. —*Michael McCall*

Rise Above It / Apr. 1994 / RCA ✦✦✦✦
O'Hara wrote all ten songs himself, a rare and commendable thing in Nashville. The songs are primal and direct, with a slight but chugging rhythm and bluesy underpinning lending a swagger to his lean, seductive lyricism. "Cold, Hard Truth" is a great hard-country ballad about a man coming face-to-face with his deceitful ways. —*Michael McCall*

The O'Kanes

Country, Country-Rock, Contemporary Country, Neo-Traditionalist Country
During their relatively brief time together, Kieran Kane and Jamie O'Hara, otherwise known as the O'Kanes, produced three albums of absolutely superb country music. The self-titled, first, and arguably strongest effort contains everything that is best about the O'Kanes' sound. It is rich in country music's finest traditions, yet it is by no means a nostalgia album. It is sparse in instrumentation, yet richly textured. Most of all, the album contains direct, honest music whose emotional intensity stays with the listener long after the sound waves have stopped vibrating. The O'Kanes' vocals recall the best of country harmony. Some critics liken them to the Louvin Brothers. Others, because of the more driving sound of their backing, compare them to the Everlys. The instrumental sound ranges from bluegrass (prominent mandolin) to the tense drive of Sun rockabilly (their hit "O Darlin'" is evidence of this). The addition of an accordion adds both Tex-Mex and unmistakably bluesy feels to the proceedings. This is truly hybrid music.

Out of the core members of the O'Kanes, Kieran Kane was always the more musically inclined. At the age of nine Kane began playing drums in his older brother's rock 'n' roll band. By the time he was in his teens, he was also playing bluegrass and folk, performing at festivals across the Northeast. Eventually his reputation had grown enough that he was opening for rock 'n'roll groups like Country Joe and the Fish and the Steve Miller Band. When he was 21 he moved to Los Angeles, where he worked as a session guitarist and a professional songwriter. Eight years later, he relocated to Nashville, where he also worked as a session musician and songwriter. Within two years he had landed a contract with Elektra, and over the next three years he had a string of minor hits for both Elektra and later Warner. For his part, Jamie

O'Hara didn't begin playing guitar until he was 22 years old, after a knee injury that prevented his pursuing a career as a professional football player. After writing several original songs, he began to play clubs across the Midwest, while working odd jobs. In 1975 he arrived in Nashville, landing a contract with Tree Publishing. By the early '80s artists had begun to cover his songs, with Ronnie McDowell taking "Wandering Eyes" and "Older Women" to the Top Ten in 1981.

Kane and O'Hara began collaborating in 1985, when the two songwriters worked on "Bluegrass Blues" for Tree. Southern Pacific and the Judds would both later record the song. Throughout 1985 the pair wrote songs and recorded demos together, deciding to become a performing duo in 1986. Columbia signed them, and their eponymous debut consisted entirely of their demo tapes. "Oh Darlin'," the first single from the record, became a hit, climbing into the Top Ten; the album also reached the country Top Ten. In 1987 the group had three Top Ten hits—including the No. 1 "Can't Stop My Heart from Loving You," "Daddies Need to Grow Up Too," and "Just Loving You"—all taken from *The O'Kanes.* The next year they released their second album, *Tired of the Runnin',* which produced an additional two Top Ten singles in "One True Love" and "Blue Love." The third single from the record, "Rocky Road," didn't even make the Top 40.

After recording their third album, Kane and O'Hara parted ways in 1989; the third record, *Imagine That,* was released to little attention in 1990. After the group's breakup, both members continued to work as professional songwriters. In 1993 Kane released his eponymous solo debut on Atlantic Records; O'Hara released his first solo album, *Rise Above It,* the next year on RCA. —*Hank Davis*

The O'Kanes / 1987 / Columbia ✦✦✦
Introspective lyrics and occasional guitar/mandolin jams make an interesting concept from Music City before the "hat" proliferation of 1990. —*Mark A. Humphrey*

● **Tired of the Runnin'** / 1988 / Columbia ✦✦✦✦
A strong title song, austerely folkish, represented this short-lived duo at its best. —*Mark A. Humphrey*

Old and in the Way

Traditional Bluegrass
Old and in the Way was a one-shot bluegrass band whose legacy lasted far longer than the band. Led by Grateful Dead member Jerry Garcia (banjo, vocals), the band also featured David Grisman (mandolin, vocals), Vassar Clements (fiddle), Peter Rowan (guitar, vocals), and John Kahn (bass). Garcia formed the band in 1973 as a way to revisit his bluegrass roots and demonstrate his affection for the music. To round out the lineup, he recruited Clements and Kahn, as well as Grisman and Rowan, who were both West Coast session musicians who had played together in the band Muleskinner. Taking their name from an old bluegrass standard, Old and in the Way played a handful of gigs, most of them at the Boarding House in San Francisco in October. An album, also called *Old and in the Way,* was culled from these shows and released later in 1973 on the Grateful Dead's own record label, Round. The record combined standards and Rowan originals, which later became standards. Although the album was the only one the lineup recorded, the members continued to play together in various permutations over the next two decades, and the record continued to sell steadily. The group reunited after Garcia's death in 1995, releasing a second album, *That High Lonesome Sound,* in early 1996. —*Stephen Thomas Erlewine*

★ **Old and in the Way** / Oct. 1973 / Grateful Dead ✦✦✦✦✦
This release was one of the greatest things to happen to bluegrass music, in that it exposed a whole new audience to bluegrass music and acoustic music. —*Chip Renner*

That High Lonesome Sound / Feb. 20, 1996 / Acoustic Disc ✦✦✦✦
Twenty-one years after the first album, *Old and in the Way,* came the second, an amazing development for a group that existed for only nine months and about 30 gigs in 1973. *That High Lonesome Sound,* like its predecessor, was drawn from the group's stand at the Boarding House in San Francisco in October 1973. And like

that release, it combined traditional bluegrass material, in this case standards like "Orange Blossom Special" and "Uncle Pen," with interpolations from the world of rock 'n' roll ("The Great Pretender") and new originals that touched on contemporary issues (Peter Rowan's "Lonesome L.A. Cowboy," a comment on the Southern California country-rock scene of the time). *Old and in the Way* was a great crossover album, largely because the bandmembers had enjoyed careers in rock, especially banjo player and singer Jerry Garcia, moonlighting from his day job with the Grateful Dead. What was less well known was that the group had real roots in the music, as Neil V. Rosenberg pointed out in the second album's liner notes. Four of the five members had experience in bluegrass, and two had been members of Bill Monroe's Blue Grass Boys. Old and in the Way was a hybrid, but it was far more bluegrass than rock. — *William Ruhlmann*

Old 97s

Progressive Bluegrass, Alternative Country-Rock, Americana
The Dallas, TX, electric bluegrass quartet the Old 97s formed in 1993, led by singer and guitarist Rhett Miller. Along with bassist Murry Hammond and second guitarist Ken Bethea, the group cut their initial demos at Austin's famed Cedar Creek Recording. After the addition of drummer Philip Peeples, the Old 97s issued their debut LP, *Wreck Your Life*, in 1995. — *Jason Ankeny*

Wreck Your Life / Oct. 3, 1995 / Bloodshot ✦✦✦✦
Wreck Your Life is full of smart lyrics and catchy, rocked-up country melodies, easily putting these guys on a path toward wider recognition. Rhett Miller is a superb vocalist, and songs like "The Other Shoe" and "Dressing Room Walls" give him plenty of room. "You Belong to My Heart" has an attractive Norteno flavor, and "My Sweet Blue-Eyed Darlin'" is a stoked-up Bill Monroe cover. (Bloodshot Records, 912 Addison, Chicago, Ill., 60613) — *Kurt Wolf*

Carla Olson

Vocals / Country-Rock, Roots-Rock, Pop-Rock, Americana
Along with Kathy Valentine (a future member of the Go-Gos), Carla Olson formed the Textones in the early '80s for a few singles on IRS. (Most of these tracks appear on *Through the Canyon* [Rhino] and *Back in Time* [Demon UK].) The band's major-label debut, *Midnight Mission* (A&M), included help from Don Henley, Ry Cooder, Barry Goldberg, and Gene Clark. *Cedar Creek*, the band's second album, appeared in 1987 on Enigma Records. Olson then worked on many projects, including ones by John Fogerty, Henley, Eric Johnson, and a duet album with Clark. In 1988 she recorded a self-titled solo album (for Amigo Musik) in Sweden, backed by Wilmer X. After another duet project, this time with former Stones guitarist Mick Taylor, Olson's second solo LP (*Within an Ace*) was released in 1993 on Watermelon Records. — *John Bush*

Too Hot for Snakes / 1977 / Razor & Tie ✦✦✦✦

Midnight Mission / 1984 / Varèse Vintage ✦✦✦✦
Carla Olson recorded *Midnight Mission* with a number of country-rock guest stars—including Don Henley, Ry Cooder, and Gene Clark—but the presence of such big-name musicians doesn't dilute the impact of the album at all. In fact, Olson and her backing band, the Textones, flourish in the setting, creating a tough, energetic, and melodic fusion of country-rock and roots rock. The Varese reissue includes the bonus track "It's Okay." — *Thom Owens*

So Rebellious a Lover / 1986 / Razor & Tie ✦✦✦✦

Within an Ace / 1993 / Watermelon ✦✦✦

Reap the Whirlwind / 1994 / Watermelon ✦✦✦

● **Wave of the Hand: Best of Carla Olson** / Oct. 17, 1995 / Watermelon ✦✦✦✦
It continues to amaze me that people keep snapping up Bonnie Raitt's recent snoozeramas while Carla Olson continues to go relatively unnoticed. A "female Tom Petty" is the easy comparison, but Olson is definitely her own roots-rockin' woman. *Wave of the Hand* gathers choice material from her former band the Textones, the excellent *So Rebellious a Lover* collaboration with ex-Byrds Gene Clark, several solo albums, and three newly recorded tracks.

Roy Orbison

Guests and sidemen who know a good thing when they hear it include Mick Taylor, Ry Cooder, Ian McLagan, Percy Sledge, and Don Henley. — *Roch Parisien*

Roy Orbison

b. Apr. 23, 1936, Vernon, TX, d. Dec. 6, 1988, Madison, TN
Guitar, Vocals / Rock 'n' Roll, Rockabilly, Pop-Rock
Although he shared the same rockabilly roots as Carl Perkins, Johnny Cash, and Elvis Presley, Roy Orbison went on to pioneer an entirely different brand of country/pop-based rock 'n' roll in the early '60s. What he lacked in charisma and photogenic looks, Orbison made up for in spades with his quavering operatic voice and melodramatic narratives of unrequited love and yearning. In the process, he established rock 'n' roll archetypes of the underdog and the hopelessly romantic loser. These were not only amplified by peers such as Del Shannon and Gene Pitney, but influenced future generations of roots rockers such as Bruce Springsteen and Chris Isaak and current country stars the Mavericks.

Orbison made his first widely distributed recordings for Sun Records in 1956. He was a capable rockabilly singer and had a small national hit with his first Sun single, "Ooby Dooby." But even then, he was far more comfortable as a ballad singer than as a hepped-up rockabilly jive cat. Other Sun singles met with no success, and by the late '50s he was concentrating on building a career as a songwriter, his biggest early success being "Claudette" (recorded by the Everly Brothers).

After a brief, unsuccessful stint with RCA, Orbison finally found his voice with Monument Records, scoring a No. 2 hit in 1960 with "Only the Lonely." This established the Roy Orbison persona for good: a brooding rockaballad of failed love with a sweet, haunting melody, enhanced by his Caruso-like vocal trills at the song's emotional climax. These and his subsequent Monument hits also boasted innovative, quasi-symphonic production, with Orbison's voice and guitar backed by surging strings, ominous drum rolls, and heavenly choirs of backup vocalists.

Between 1960 and 1965, Orbison would have 15 Top 40 hits for Monument, including such nail-biting mini-dramas as "Running Scared," "Crying," "In Dreams," and "It's Over." Not just a singer of tear-jerking ballads, he was also capable of effecting a tough, bluesy swagger on "Dream Baby," "Candy Man," and "Mean

Woman Blues." In fact, his biggest and best hit was also his hardest-rocking: "Oh, Pretty Woman" soared to No. 1 in late 1964, at the peak of the British Invasion.

It seemed at that time that Orbison was well equipped to survive the British onslaught of the mid-'60s. He had even toured with the Beatles in Britain in 1963, and John Lennon has admitted trying to emulate Orbison when writing the Beatles' first British chart-topper, "Please Please Me." But Orbison's fortunes declined rapidly after he left Monument for MGM in 1965. It would be easy to say that the major label couldn't replicate the unique production values of the classic Monument singles, but that's only part of the story. Orbison, after all, was still writing most of his material, and his early MGM records were produced in a style that closely approximated the Monument era. The harder truth to face was that his songs were starting to sound like lesser variations of themselves, and that contemporary trends in rock and soul were making him sound outdated.

Orbison, like many early rock greats, could always depend on large overseas audiences to pay the bills. The two decades between the mid-'60s and mid-'80s were undeniably tough ones for him, though, both personally and professionally. A late-'60s stab at acting failed miserably. In 1966 his wife died in a motorcycle accident; a couple of years later, his house burned down and two of his sons perished in the flames. Periodic comeback attempts with desultory albums in the 1970s came to naught.

Orbison's return to the public eye came about through unexpected circumstances. In the mid-'80s, David Lynch's film *Blue Velvet* prominently featured "In Dreams" on its soundtrack. That led to the singer's making an entire album of re-recordings of hits, with T-Bone Burnett acting as producer. The record was no substitute for the originals, but it did help restore him to prominence within the industry. Shortly afterwards, he joined George Harrison, Bob Dylan, Tom Petty, and Jeff Lynne in the Traveling Wilburys. Their successful album set the stage for Orbison's best album in more than 20 years, *Mystery Girl*, which emulated the sound of his classic 1960s work without sounding hackneyed. By the time it reached the charts in early 1989, however, Orbison was dead, claimed by a heart attack in December 1988. —*Richie Unterberger*

Crying / 1962 / Columbia ✦✦

Roy Orbison's second album was above average by the standards of the time, but was a fairly slight effort nonetheless. In its favor, the album features nearly all original material by Orbison and some of the writers who frequently tailored songs for him, such as Boudleaux and Felice Bryant and Joe Melson. The trademark early Orbison production flourishes, with swooping strings and full vocal choruses, are also present. What's missing is truly first-rate songwriting. With the exception of "Love Hurts," the title track, and the epic hit "Running Scared," most of the cuts lean toward the Big O's more sentimental side and are pleasantly forgettable. Of the obscure cuts here, the best are the uptempo "Nite Life" and "Let's Make a Memory," with its bouncing string arrangement, but neither could be classified among his best early work. —*Richie Unterberger*

There Is Only One / 1965 / Polygram ✦✦

Orbison explains in the liner notes that MGM will allow him "a new climate of freedom" as an artist, but the results of his first album for the label were unimpressive. He forsakes much of the rock 'n' roll foundation of his classic early-'60s hits for Nashville country and western on most of the LP, complete with barroom piano. The material (mostly written by Orbison with various collaborators) doesn't approach the magnificence of his best work, and his version of his composition "Claudette" isn't nearly as good as the Everly Brothers' hit rendition from 1958. The highlight is the strange, almost rambling minor hit single, "Ride Away." —*Richie Unterberger*

Fastest Guitar Alive / 1968 / Columbia Special Products ✦✦

Orbison's one bid for film stardom, *The Fastest Guitar Alive*, was an unqualified flop. The soundtrack fares slightly better, but only slightly. With ten songs clocking in at a mere 27 minutes, most of the tunes—which Roy composed with longtime collaborator Bill Dees—borrow from the cheesiest elements of cowboy music, with

quasi-Mexican guitar riffs, silly Indian chants, and uneasy spaghetti-Western pathos. For all its ill-conceived failure, it includes what may be his best obscure tune, the little-anthologized "Whirlwind." With its galloping rhythm, emotive operatic vocals, swirling strings, and ghostly backing vocals, it recalls the best uptempo ballads that he recorded during his early-'60s heyday at the Monument label. In 1968, of course, few listeners were interested. —*Richie Unterberger*

All-Time Greatest Hits of Roy Orbison / 1976 / Monument ✦✦✦✦

The All-Time Greatest Hits of Roy Orbison is an essential collection. It rounds up 20 of the Big O's best '60s recordings, with some fine album tracks thrown in. —*John Floyd*

All-Time Greatest Hits of Roy Orbison, Vols. 1 & 2 / 1985 / Monument ✦✦✦

Although it's missing his early Sun hit "Ooby Dooby," the 20-track *All-Time Greatest Hits of Roy Orbison* contains every one of his big hits for Monument Records, including "Up Town," "Only the Lonely," "Blue Angel," "I'm Hurtin'," "Running Scared," "Crying," "Dream Baby," "Leah," "Working for the Man," "Candy Man," "In Dreams," "Falling," "Mean Woman Blues," "Blue Bayou," "Pretty Paper," "It's Over," and "Oh, Pretty Woman." In other words, it is nearly as complete as Rhino's 18-track *For the Lonely*. The main difference between the two collections is the fact that the Rhino disc contains some Sun material, which makes it the preferable retrospective. Nevertheless, *All-Time Greatest Hits* remains a first-rate collection, especially if you're just looking for hits. —*Stephen Thomas Erlewine*

★ **For the Lonely: 18 Greatest Hits** / 1988 / Rhino ✦✦✦✦✦

For the Lonely: Roy Orbison Anthology (1956-1965) offers the usual Monument hits along with a few Sun tunes—18 in all. Buyers beware: the vinyl version contains more cuts than the CD. —*John Floyd*

The Legendary Roy Orbison / 1988 / Sony ✦✦✦✦

While the Rhino set *For the Lonely: Roy Orbison Anthology (1956-1965)* is the essential single-disc release of Orbison's work, *The Legendary Roy Orbison* tries to flesh out the picture considerably with a four-disc, 75-track box set. It may be overkill for some, and certain tracks feel like pointless inclusions, but fans who want more than just a hits collection should like this set. The enclosed booklet contains a wealth of photos, and the annotation is passionate and informative. —*Rick Clark*

Sun Years / 1989 / Rhino ✦✦✦✦

This 20-track compilation of Orbison's Sun sides includes both sides of all four of his official Sun 45s and a dozen tracks he recorded for the label that remained unissued at the time. Orbison at this point was a decent but somewhat also-ran rockabilly singer and not nearly as suited for the style as fellow Sun artists Elvis Presley, Jerry Lee Lewis, and Carl Perkins. He had yet to find his songwriting or singing voice with balladeering pop-rock material, so this collection may disappoint those who expect something along the lines of Orbison's famous Monument hits. It's not at all bad, with standout cuts such as "Ooby Dooby," "Rock House," and "Devil Doll"; it's just not Orbison at his best or most comfortable. —*Richie Unterberger*

The Classic Roy Orbison (1965-1968) / 1989 / Rhino ✦✦✦

The hits dried up when Orbison left the Monument label for MGM in 1965. The 14 recordings here, taken from singles and LP tracks, feature arrangements and production not far removed from his classic Monument era. The singing is wonderful, but stacked up against his classic hits, a lot is missing. Lacking the ace songwriting of his best work, there's lots of midtempo, melodramatic rock balladry here, but somehow nothing nearly as gripping as his best compositions. —*Richie Unterberger*

Our Love Song / 1989 / Monument ✦✦✦

Skimpily assembled package of a dozen obscurities, most from the early—and mid-'60s Monument era. "(I Get So Sentimental)" and "Born on the Wind" count as some of his better unknown tunes from that time, but on the whole it's a poor and haphazard collection. —*Richie Unterberger*

Mystery Girl / 1989 / Virgin ✦✦✦✦
Orbison's comeback is remarkable in that every song, from "You Got It" and "She's a Mystery to Me" to "The Only One," proves that the formula of his '60s stuff is still vital 30 years later. This album really deserved a follow-up. —*John Floyd*

Singles Collection / 1989 / Polygram ✦✦✦
Overlooked at the time of its issue, as it was released almost simultaneously with Rhino's *The Classic Roy Orbison (1965-1968)*, this offers a more comprehensive look at his post-Monument recordings. That doesn't mean that it's better. Most of the 1965-68 cuts on this album are also on the Rhino one, though "She" and "Heartache," which are only on *Singles Collection*, are a couple of his better late-'60s songs. The post-1968 tracks that take up the rest of the anthology are a waste, an embarrassment at worst, as Orbison failed to either successfully incorporate contemporary influences or offer quality variations on his tested formula. Stick with the cheaper, more succinct, and easier-to-find *The Classic Roy Orbison* for an overview of this era. —*Richie Unterberger*

The Sun Years 1956-58 / Apr. 1989 / Bear Family ✦✦✦✦
It contains Orbison's complete Sun output, featuring many undubbed recordings and the pile-driving "Domino." —*John Floyd*

Rock Legends / 1990 / RCA ✦✦✦
A compilation of rare and early works by Roy Orbison and Little Richard that makes odd bedfellows of two extremely dissimilar performers, borne out of the necessity of cleaning out old vault material to capitalize on the CD reissue explosion. The first eight tracks belong to Little Richard, who won a recording contract with RCA after winning a talent contest in Atlanta. These sides, cut in 1951 and 1952, show barely a hint of his later wildness, owing far more to the jump blues R&B of Roy Brown and others. Orbison's seven songs were cut in the late '50s, between his rockabilly days at Sun and his ascent to stardom on Monument. You can hear tentative explorations of the soaring romanticism with which he'd find his niche in 1960, but the material is basic, weak, typical late-'50s teen fodder, courtesy of Roy himself and noted songwriters John Loudermilk, Boudleaux Bryant, and Felice Bryant. The yearning "Seems to Me" (written by Boudleaux, who would write many fine hits for Orbison and the Everly Brothers) is the only track that even begins to approximate his future glory. This cheese 'n' chalk compilation is recommended only to those wishing to glean historical insight into these giants' beginnings, though it may well be that the Little Richard fanatic isn't necessarily a Roy Orbison devotee (and vice versa). —*Richie Unterberger*

King of Hearts / 1992 / Virgin ✦✦✦
The posthumously released *King of Hearts* collects a handful of Orbison's final vocal tracks, along with a few demos and non-LP singles, including the Jeff Lynne-produced "Heartbreak Radio." The highlight, however, is an amazing duet of "Crying" recorded with k.d. lang. —*Jason Ankeny*

Gold Collection / Dec. 3, 1996 / Tristar ✦✦✦
The Gold Collection is a 15-track hits compilation that contains most of Orbison's biggest hits, including "Only the Lonely," "Pretty Woman," "It's Over," "Blue Bayou," "Crying," and "Candy Man." While it hits most of the high points, it leaves out a handful of necessary tracks and isn't as strong as Rhino's *For the Lonely* or Monument's *All-Time Greatest Hits*. The reason to pick up *The Gold Collection* is that it is a gold-disc, and while the sound is good on the disc, it isn't a dramatic improvement over the other discs on the market. —*Stephen Thomas Erlewine*

Osborne Brothers

Progressive Bluegrass, Traditional Bluegrass, Close Harmony
The Osborne Brothers were one of the most popular and innovative bluegrass groups of the post-war era, taking the music in new directions and gaining a large audience. Among their most notable achievements are their pioneering, inventive use of amplification, twin harmony banjos, steel guitars, and drums. They were the first bluegrass group to expand the genre's sonic palette in such a fashion.

Bobby and Sonny Osborne were born in Hyden, KY, but reared in Dayton, OH. When they were children, their father instilled a love for traditional music. Bobby picked up the electic guitar as a teenager, playing in various local bands. A few years later Sonny picked up the banjo. In 1949 Bobby formed a duo with banjoist Larry Richardson. The pair was hired by a West Virginian radio station and stayed in the state for a while, eventually hooking up with the Lonesome Pine Fiddlers. During their stay with the Fiddlers, they helped change the group's sound to bluegrass and made four singles for Cozy Records. Bobby Osborne left the band in the summer of 1951, forming a band with Jimmy Martin that fell apart shortly after its inception. After making a one-shot single, "New Freedom Bell," with his siblings Louise and Sonny, he joined the Stanley Brothers for a short while before being drafted into the army.

Sonny spent some time with Bill Monroe's Blue Grass Boys in the early '50s, appearing on several sides on Decca Records. He also cut some covers of popular Monroe and Flatt and Scruggs songs for the budget label Gateway. After Bobby returned from the Army, he and Sonny formed a band. Initially they supported Jimmy Martin on his RCA session while they had their own spot on a Knoxville radio station. In 1956 they joined the "Wheeling Jamboree"; they would stay with the radio program for four years. In March of that year, Red Allen joined the brothers. Four months after his arrival, they recorded their first session for MGM records. For the next year they toured and recorded, steadily gaining a large audience. In the spring of 1958 "Once More" became a No. 13 hit on the country charts. Its success helped push the band into the mainstream.

Shortly after the success of "Once More," Allen left the band and the Osbornes filled his vacancy with a string of musicians and vocalists, including Johnny Dacus and Benny Birchfield. The duo stayed with the "Wheeling Jamboree" and MGM Records into the early '60s. The Osbornes became the first bluegrass act to play a college campus in 1960, when they played Antioch College in Yellow Springs, OH. That appearance ushered in a new era for bluegrass, creating a new, younger audience for the music.

The Osbornes left MGM in 1963, signing with Decca Records. On their mid-'60s records for Decca, the duo began experimenting more with their music, adding piano, steel guitar, and electric instruments. Their adventurousness made them more accessible to a mass audience, as their string of late-'60s and early-'70s hit singles proves. Although their experimentation angered many bluegrass traditionalists, the Osbornes were the only bluegrass group to consistently have country hits during this time, even if their singles were only minor hits.

In 1975 the Osbornes left Decca but continued to play the Grand Ole Opry and bluegrass festivals across America. Later in the '70s the duo returned to a more traditional sound. Throughout the '80s and '90s they stuck to this sound, playing concerts and festivals frequently and recording albums for CMH, RCA, Sugar Hill, and Pinecastle. Forty years after their formation, the Osborne Brothers remained an active act in the mid-'90s. —*Stephen Thomas Erlewine*

Country Pickin' and Hillside Singin / 1959 / MGM ✦✦✦

☆ **The Osborne Brothers** / 1971 / Rounder ✦✦✦✦✦
Great vocal harmonies and tightly woven banjo-mandolin conversations come together on this, the best early material from 1959-1963. —*Mark A. Humphrey*

Early Recordings of Sonny Osborne, Vol. 1-3 / 1973 / Gateway ✦✦✦

★ **Best of the Osborne Brothers** / 1975 / MCA ✦✦✦✦✦
Their 1963-1967 Decca hits blend smooth bluegrass with then-contemporary country production. A unique sound, it's radical for its time. —*Mark A. Humphrey*

From Rocky Top to Muddy Bottom / 1977 / CMH ✦✦✦
This album contains such cuts as "We Could," "Love Hurts," "Rocky Top," and more. —*AMG*

The Bluegrass Collection / 1978 / CMH ✦✦✦✦
Recorded in 1978, *Bluegrass Collection* is the Osborne Brothers' tribute to the fathers of bluegrass—Bill Monroe, Flatt & Scruggs,

and the Stanley Brothers. The duo throws in nice, but unremarkable, remakes of their older hits as well, making the album a pleasant exercise in nostalgia. — *Thom Owens*

Bobby and His Mandolin / 1981 / CMH ✦✦✦
This nice album features sprightly mandolin renditions of traditional fiddle tunes. — *Mark A. Humphrey*

Singing Shouting Praises / 1988 / Sugar Hill ✦✦✦
Nice bluegrass gospel. — *Mark A. Humphrey*

Once More, Vols. 1 and 2 / 1991 / Sugar Hill ✦✦✦✦
Once More, Vols. 1 and 2 combines two original vinyl albums that originated from the same sessions onto one compact disc. The *Once More* albums were recorded in the mid-'80s for Sugar Hill. At these sessions, the Osborne Brothers tackled a large chunk of their earlier repertoire, including songs that were originally recorded for Decca and MGM. These versions are harder and purer than the originals, which frequently featured electric instruments, and — unlike many re-recordings — these cuts don't sound labored or tired. If anything, *Once More, Vols. 1 and 2* contains music that is even more alive and vital than the originals and, since it contains a diverse selection of material, it functions as an excellent primer on one of the finest bluegrass bands ever. However, if you're looking for hits, go elsewhere — *Once More, Vols. 1 and 2* concentrates on pure bluegrass, so the Osbornes have excised their hits in favor of high, lonesome obscurities. — *Thom Owens*

Hillbilly Fever / 1991 / CMH ✦✦✦
Recorded in 1991, *Hillbilly Fever* might not live up to the standards of the Osborne Brothers' earliest and best recordings, but it's a fun listen that shows the duo still has life in them, nearly 40 years after their formation. — *Thom Owens*

1968-74 / 1995 / Bear Family ✦✦✦✦
Picking up where Bear Family's previous box set left off, the four-disc *1968-1974* contains all of the recordings the Osborne Brothers made for Decca Records during the late '60s and early '70s. Though the Osbornes were past their creative peak, they were experiencing a commercial revival during this era. Much of this music ranks among the duo's most enjoyable, and any serious Osborne Brothers fan will want to invest in this excellent set. — *Thom Owens*

Bluegrass 1956-68 [box] / 1995 / Bear Family ✦✦✦✦
Bluegrass 1956-68 is a multi-disc box set that contains everything the Osborne Brothers recorded between those years. During that time they recorded for two major labels, MGM and Decca Records. All the songs the duo released on those two labels, plus alternate takes and unreleased tracks, are included on the box. With all of that material, the set is simply too large for any but historians and completists to enjoy. Nevertheless, there's lots of wonderful music on the collection, and no one with the patience (and the funds) to invest in the box will be disappointed. — *Thom Owens*

Greatest Bluegrass Hits / CMH ✦✦✦
This is a good "favorites" collection. — *Mark A. Humphrey*

The MGM Days of the Osborne Brothers / Polydor ✦✦✦✦
MGM Days of the Osborne Brothers is an extensive, three-disc set that covers 60 tracks the group cut for MGM Records between 1956 and 1963. Over the course of this set, it's possible to hear the group develop from Bill Monroe imitators to distinctive, progressive musicians in their own right; their introduction of electric instruments, varied tempos, and complex vocal harmonies still sounds stunning when placed in this chronological context. Despite the wealth of fine music included on *MGM Days of the Osborne Brothers*, it is an album designed only for historians, musicologists, and dedicated fans — there is simply too much material for casual fans to digest. — *Thom Owens*

K.T. Oslin

b. 1942, Crossett, AR
Vocals / Country-Pop, Contemporary Country
During the late '80s, K.T. Oslin had a string of hit singles with her pop-inflected modern country. Most of Oslin's material was directed at — in the words of her breakthrough single — "'80s

Ladies," which meant her songs were about modern women and were recorded with modern equipment, including synthesizers. For a brief time she was one of the most popular singers in country music, earning four No. 1 singles and two platinum albums. However, her fall from the top was as quick as her rise — by the mid-'90s, she still had a large cult following but was no longer able to have a Top 40 single.

An Arkansas native, she was born Kay Toinette Oslin, the daughter of a singer and a paper-mill foreman. Her father died when she was five, forcing her mother to abandon her singing career and begin working as a medical lab technician. After moving around the South for a while, Oslin and her mother settled in Houston. Later she studied drama before forming a folk trio with Guy Clark and David Jones in the '60s. She later paired up with Frank Davis and began recording an album in Los Angeles; it was never released, and she returned to Houston alone. Oslin began appearing in musical productions, including Carol Channing's National Touring Company's production of *Hello Dolly!*, after she returned to Texas, and went on to appear in the Betty Grable Broadway company version of the play in New York. She remained in the Big Apple for a while, appearing in other shows, singing commercial jingles, and doing session work.

In 1974 Oslin began writing songs, recording a minor hit debut single, "Clean Your Own Tables," in 1981. Meanwhile, country singers Gail Davis and Dottie West had chart success with two of Oslin's songs. In 1984 she appeared on a public radio broadcast with several established stars, and her song "Come Next Monday" was recorded by Judy Rodman. Two years later, Oslin felt ready to make her own bid for stardom; after borrowing $7,000, she showcased herself in Nashville. Harold Shedd, Alabama's producer, was in the audience, and helped get her signed to RCA. Oslin's first album, *'80s Ladies*, debuted in the country Top 15 in 1987, becoming the highest-charting debut album for a female since Loretta Lynn's in 1964. The album's title track reached the Top Ten, and Oslin hit No. 1 with its follow-up single, "Do Ya." Her successful streak lasted through 1989; in those two years, she recorded three albums and had four other Top Ten hits. Both her first and second album, *This Woman*, went platinum, and her third album, *Love in a Small Town*, went gold. Oslin released the compilation *Greatest Hits: Songs from an Aging Sex Bomb* in 1993. Three years later she released the covers album *My Roots Are Showing*. — *Sandra Brennan*

80's Ladies / 1987 / RCA ✦✦✦✦
With her breakthrough album *'80's Ladies*, K.T. Oslin established a new voice in country music — that of an upscale, middle-aged divorcee trying to cope with the turmoil of life. The subject matter basically remained the same, but it was given a new viewpoint. *'80's Ladies* suffered from a few weak tracks, but on the whole, it was an exciting, fresh change. — *Rodney Batdorf*

This Woman / 1988 / RCA ✦✦✦
This album features the hits "Didn't Expect It to Go Down This Way," "Hold Me," and "This Woman," among others. — *AMG*

New Way Home / 1990 / RCA ✦✦✦

Love in a Small Town / 1990 / RCA ✦✦✦✦
Oslin built this loosely defined concept album from ten years of song, including the first one she wrote. Oslin sings of the guises romance wears in the small-town South: Nelda Jean Prudie waxes nostalgic about weekend dances of her Texas youth; a young girl enthuses about a pick-up-driving Romeo named Cornell Crawford; and people searching for the perfect partner wind up lonely. *Love in a Small Town* also contains a low-key version of the 1946 standard "You Call Everybody Darling" and a cover of Mickey and Sylvia's "Love Is Strange." Oslin's coyness isn't always appealing, and the arrangements sometimes border on a new countrypolitan, but those moments are rare. On most of *Small Town*, Oslin displays her best assets: her worldly sensibility and complex maturity. — *Brian Mansfield*

● **Greatest Hits: Songs From an Aging Sex Bomb ...** / Apr. 27, 1993 / RCA ✦✦✦✦
Greatest Hits: Songs From an Aging Sex Bomb collects all of K.T. Oslin's biggest hits from the late '80s, featuring the No. 1 singles "Do Ya," "I'll Always Come Back," "Hold Me," and "Come Next

Monday," as well as seven other songs, including her three other Top Ten hits, "'80's Ladies," "Hey Bobby" and "This Woman." — *Thom Owens*

My Roots Are Showing / Oct. 1, 1996 / RCA ✦✦✦
My Roots Are Showing is K.T. Oslin's first studio album since 1990, and she decided to return to recording with a tribute album. Selecting songs that span 1845 to 1972, Oslin updates all of the songs to make them sound as if they were written in the '90s. Occasionally this results in imaginative rearrangements and inspired performances, but more often the end results are ill-conceived and puzzling. Oslin's voice remains strong; yet the album isn't a convincing return to form for one of the strongest female vocalists of the '80s. — *Thom Owens*

Marie Osmond

b. Oct. 13, 1959, Ogden, UT
Vocals / Country-Pop, Soft Rock, Pop-Rock
Marie Osmond found popularity as a country singer when she was barely 14, when her cover of "Paper Roses" became a No. 1 country hit and reached the Top Five on the pop charts. She was raised in a deeply religious Mormon family in Provo, UT, with eight brothers. In the early '60s, four of the elder Osmond boys appeared regularly on "The Andy Williams Show," where Marie made her debut when she was only three. When she was 13, Osmond Brothers producer Mike Curb, who had helped popularize Donny and his younger brother Jimmy, wondered if he could get their only sister into the act. Marie was more interested in country than mainstream pop, so Curb teamed her up with veteran songwriter-turned-producer Sonny James, who helped her record "Paper Roses." This led her to begin touring with her brothers, most frequently Donny, on the nightclub circuit. She also appeared regularly on the charts with songs such as "In My Little Corner of the World" and "Who's Sorry Now." In 1975 Donny and Marie began hosting their own variety show; produced at the state-of-the-art Osmond Studios in Provo, it ran for four years. She and Donny made their feature film debut in 1978 with *Goin' Coconuts*, and the next year, she appeared by herself in *The Gift of Love*. In 1981 she signed to Curb's new label but had only one modest hit, "Back to Believing Again." Three years later she found success again on a duet with Dan Seals, "Meet Me in Montana," which hit No. 1, as did her solo follow-up "There's No Stopping Your Heart." Between 1986 and 1989, Osmond had a string of successful hits both as a solo artist and a duet partner, including the Top Five hit "Read My Lips." In 1990, billed only as Marie, she had her final chart hit, "Like a Hurricane." — *Sandra Brennan*

25 Hits Special Collection / Nov. 7, 1995 / Curb ✦✦✦
A good budget-priced compilation of Marie Osmond's biggest hits, *25 Hits Special Collection* spans from 1973's "Paper Roses" to 1990's "Like a Hurricane." It's a thorough overview of her solo career, hitting all of her best-known songs, including her hit duets with Dan Seals and Paul Davis ("Meet Me in Montana" and "You're Still New to Me," respectively). It's not just for the budget-minded—it's a complete retrospective that offers an excellent encapsulation of Osmond's solo career. — *Thom Owens*

Paul Overstreet

b. 1929, Newton, MO
Vocals / Country-Pop, Contemporary Country, Country Gospel
Paul Overstreet was one of the most successful songwriters in contemporary country music, penning hits for artists like George Jones, Randy Travis, Tanya Tucker, and Marie Osmond, as well as scoring hits on his own. He wrote his first songs as a boy in Newton, MO. In 1973 he graduated from high school and headed for Nashville, where he played in country bands at night and worked blue-collar jobs during the day. Despite his efforts, Overstreet couldn't break into the industry.

Eventually, his songs were being recorded by other, more established artists. In 1982 his "Same Ole Me" was recorded by George Jones, who took the song to No. 5. That same year, Overstreet had his first charting single when "Beautiful Baby" climbed to No. 76. Three years later the Forrester Sisters took his "I Fell in Love Again Last Night"—which he co-wrote with Thom Schuyler—to

No. 1. Later in 1985 Randy Travis had hits with two Overstreet compositions—"On the Other Hand" (which was co-written with Don Schlitz) and "Diggin' Up Bones," the singer's first No. 1 hit. Tanya Tucker, Marie Osmond, and Paul Davis also had success with Overstreet songs that year.

Overstreet became a full-fledged recording artist in 1986 when he teamed up with Schuyler and Fred Knobloch to form SKO, which scored a No. 1 hit with "Baby's Got a New Baby." In 1987 Overstreet scored one of his biggest songwriting hits when he provided Randy Travis with "Forever and Ever, Amen." As his string of hits for other artists continued, Overstreet released his 1989 debut album, *Sowin' Love*, which made it to the Top 40 and produced a few hits. His second album, *Heroes*, came out in 1991 and stayed on the charts for nearly a year. When his third album, 1992's *Love Is Strong*, was a commercial disappointment, Overstreet shifted his focus to writing more religious material and began recording with Susie Luchsinger, the sister of Reba McEntire. — *Sandra Brennan*

Sowin' Love / 1989 / RCA ✦✦✦✦
In addition to the popular title cut, *Sowin Love* offers the hits "Seein' My Father in Me," "All the Fun," "Love Helps Those" and "Richest Man on Earth." — *Jason Ankeny*

Heroes / 1991 / RCA ✦✦✦
Heroes is highlighted by Overstreet's first solo No. 1 hit, "Daddy's Come Around"; both the title track and "Ball and Chain" reached the Top Five. — *Jason Ankeny*

Love Is Strong / 1992 / RCA ✦✦✦
Love Is Strong represents Overstreet at his most eclectic, exploring pop ("Me and My Baby"), country-rock ("Take Another Run"), and swing ("Still Out There Swinging"). — *Jason Ankeny*

● **The Best of Paul Overstreet** / Feb. 1994 / RCA ✦✦✦✦
The ultimate New Traditionalist factory songwriter, Overstreet's best work is the series of hits he wrote (usually with Don Shlitz) for Randy Travis in the 1980s. On his own, as evidenced by this collection, he's a bit too obsessed with convincing everybody that he's a good Christian man who just can't wait to get home to his wife. There's more to life—and music—than family values, no matter how you define them. — *Dan Cooper*

Tommy Overstreet

b. Sep. 10, 1937, Oklahoma City, OK
Vocals / Country-Pop, Nashville Sound/Countrypolitan
Tommy Overstreet was a countrypolitan-styled singer who achieved his greatest success in the early '70s, although he probably gained his most significant exposure as a frequent guest on the program "Hee Haw." He was born September 10, 1937, in Oklahoma City, and an early interest in music was encouraged by his cousin Gene Austin, a singer who had garnered some fame in the 1920s with records like "My Blue Heaven" and "Ramona." In his teens, Overstreet began performing pop music on radio stations in the Houston, TX, area, and appeared in a musical titled *Hit the Road*. While studying broadcasting at the University of Texas, he began playing in local clubs under the name "Tommy Dean from Abilene," and toured frequently with Austin.

After a stint in the Army, Overstreet moved to Los Angeles in the early 1960s to begin a songwriting career, contributing material to pop crooner Pat Boone. He also signed a recording deal, although none of his studio work from the period was ever issued. After returning to Texas, he began appearing on the TV program "The Slim Willet Show," and formed his own group to play club dates. In 1967 he moved to Nashville, where he became the regional professional manager of Dot Records in addition to signing with the label as a recording artist. His debut single, 1969's "Rocking a Memory (That Won't Go to Sleep)," was a minor hit, and his next record, "If You're Looking for a Fool," did even better. In 1971 he scored his first smash with "Gwen (Congratulations)," the title track from his debut LP, followed by "I Don't Know You (Anymore)."

In 1972 Overstreet scored his biggest hit, "Ann (Don't Go Runnin')," which reached No. 2 on the charts. A series of Top Ten hits followed, among them the same year's "Heaven Is My Woman's Love," 1974's "(Jeannie Marie) You Were a Lady," and 1975's

"That's When My Woman Begins." Although he continued to chart throughout the 1970s, he failed to reach the same heights he did in the first half of the decade. Overstreet's hit-making days were largely over by the 1980s, but he remained a popular concert draw and continued touring with his group the Nashville Express. —*Jason Ankeny*

Gwen, Congratulations / 1971 / MCA ✦✦✦

● **Greatest Hits** / Hollywood ✦✦✦✦
This album features such hits as "Send Me No Roses" and "Heaven Is My Woman's Love." —*AMG*

Bonnie Owens

b. Oct. 1, 1932, Blanchard, OK
Traditional Country, Bakersfield Sound, West Coast Country
Born Bonnie Campbell in Blanchard, OK, on October 1, 1932, Bonnie Owens met and married a then-unknown singer by the name of Buck Owens when she was 16. Known even as a teenager for her ability to yodel, she hooked up with her new husband on the "Buck and Britt Show" on Mesa, AZ, radio station KTLY. Both were eventually members of Mac's Skillet Lickers and toured the country. After having two sons, Buddy and Mike, they moved to Bakersfield in 1951, where Bonnie worked as a cocktail waitress for a time. The marriage ended and Bonnie decided to have a career of her own. Remaining on friendly terms, Bonnie and Buck made separate contributions to the growing Bakersfield sound.

With several charting hits in the '60s, Bonnie recorded for Marvel and Tally Records. In 1964 her duet with Merle Haggard, "Just Between the Two of Us," won praise and attention from the industry and fans alike. In 1965 Bonnie and Merle married, and both moved on to Capitol Records. Her role as a major player in Bakersfield and L.A., as well as a featured performer in Haggard's band, elevated her to superstar status. In 1966 she and Merle were named Best Vocal Group by the Academy of Country Music, and Bonnie was singled out as Top Female Vocalist. Touring with Merle she had no time to follow her own career path. Tired of the road, by 1975 she was running the business from home while Merle and the Strangers played. She also filed for a legal separation and eventually divorced Merle in 1978. Just as she had with Buck, who generously made sure the mother of his children was financially secure, Bonnie remained close to Merle. She continued to work with him and remained a trusted confidant to Buck. She also continued writing songs and leading the way for women in the country music industry. —*Jana Pendragon*

Buck Owens (Alvis Edgar Owens)

b. Aug. 12, 1929, Sherman, TX
Guitar, Trumpet, Saxophone, Vocals / Traditional Country, Honky Tonk, Bakersfield Sound
Buck Owens, along with Merle Haggard, was the leader of the Bakersfield Sound, a twangy, electrified, rock-influenced interpretation of hardcore honky tonk that emerged in the '60s. Owens was the first bona fide country star to emerge from Bakersfield, scoring a total of 15 consecutive No. 1 hits in the mid-'60s. In the process, he provided an edgy alternative to the string-laden country-pop that was being produced during the '60s. Later in his career, his musical impact was forgotten by some as he became a television personality through the country comedy show "Hee Haw." Nevertheless, several generations of musicians—from Gram Parsons in the late '60s to Dwight Yoakam in the '80s—were influenced by his music, which wound up being one of the blueprints for modern country music.

Buck Owens was born in Texas, but his family moved to Mesa, AZ, when he was a child, seeking work during the Great Depression. Owens developed a fervent interest in music as a child, learning to play guitar in his early teens. He dropped out of high school in ninth grade, working on the farm to help his family but also spending a significant amount of time learning how to play the guitar. By his late teens, he had an occasional spot on a local radio station, KTYL Mesa, and was playing gigs in honky tonks and clubs around Phoenix with his friend Theryl Ray Britten.

When he was 19 years old, he married Bonnie Campbell, also a country singer. By 1950 the couple had two sons.

Buck and Bonnie Owens decided to leave Arizona in 1951, moving to Bakersfield, CA. In Bakersfield, he became a regular performer in a number of clubs, particularly the Blackboard, where he was the lead singer and played rhythm guitar for Bill Woods and the Orange Blossom Playboys. Soon, he formed his own band, the Schoolhouse Playboys, which also played the Blackboard. Buck's exposure in Bakersfield led to some session work for Capitol Records, beginning with Tommy Collins' 1954 hit, "You Better Not Do That." During all of this, Buck and Bonnie grew apart and divorced in 1953. They remained friends and shared custody of their children.

Between 1954 and 1958, Owens played guitar on a number of Capitol country records produced by Ken Nelson, including some by Faron Young, Tommy Sands, and Wanda Jackson. Occasionally he was a session musician at the local Bakersfield studio Lu-Tal, run by Lewis Talley. Owens made his first solo recordings at Talley's studio in 1956, cutting ten songs for an independent label called Pep. The singles—which included the often-covered "Down on the Corner of Love" and "Sweethearts in Heaven," as well as two rockabilly sides released under the name Corky Jones—were unsuccessful, but they attracted the attention of many country music business insiders. Around this time, Owens met Harlan Howard, a struggling country singer-songwriter. The pair became friends and collaboraters, with Buck writing the music and Harlan writing the lyrics. Owens and Howard formed Blue Book Music that year to publish their songs.

Buck Owens continued to play regularly in Bakersfield clubs. At these concerts he attracted the attention of Johnny Bond and Joe Maphis, who were performers on "Town Hall Party" and signed to Columbia Records. Impressed with Owens' music, the pair sent a demo to their record label, who immediately became interested in signing Buck. Several people at Capitol were trying to persuade Ken Nelson, the label's country A&R head, to sign Owens as a recording artist, but he wasn't convinced that Buck was a capable lead singer or songwriter. It wasn't until a Capitol recording artist, the Farmer Boys, picked Owens' songs to record instead of Nelson's that the A&R head decided to sign the guitarist in February 1957.

Initially, Buck Owens' singles for Capitol Records were ignored. They were country-pop numbers, complete with a choral group singing backing vocals. Such a big production didn't fit comfortably with Owens' unvarnished honky tonk roots, and both singles sank without a trace when they were released in 1957. Hurting financially from the lack of sales, Owens moved to a suburb of Tacoma, WA, to work at radio station KAYE in January 1958. In addition to DJing and selling ads for the station, he played clubs around the area. By the summer, Owens was convinced that his recording career was over, but Ken Nelson refused to let him out of his contract. In the fall of 1958 Owens had another session for Capitol Records, but this time he was allowed to use a steel guitar and a fiddle. One of the songs from the session, "Second Fiddle," was released as a single and became a surprise hit, climbing to No. 24 on the country charts. Even though he had his first taste of success, Buck remained skeptical about his future as a recording artist, so he remained in Tacoma, hosting his own live show on KTNT. On the show, he featured a new local singer named Loretta Lynn. More importantly for Owens he met Don Rich (born Donald Eugene Ulrich) on the radio show. Rich would become Owens' partner in the next decade and would have an immense influence over his music.

"Under Your Spell Again," the fall 1959 follow-up to "Second Fiddle," broke the doors open for Owens. Climbing to No. 4, the single began a streak of Top Ten singles that ran more or less uninterrupted into the '70s. After "Under Your Spell Again" became a success, Owens moved back to Bakersfield. That winter Don Rich also moved to Bakersfield, joining Owens' band as a fiddler and guitarist. Early in 1960 Owens took over Harlan Howard's share of Blue Book Music, leaving him in total control of the publishing of all of his songs. "Above and Beyond" became a No. 3 hit in the spring.

Owens had his next hit, "Excuse Me (I Think I've Got a Heartache)," in the fall of 1960. It was followed in January 1961 with *Buck Owens*, his first album, as well as the single "Foolin' Around," which spent eight weeks at No. 2. That spring he had a hit single, "Mental Cruelty"/"Loose Talk," recorded with Rose Maddox. Owens and Rich began touring the country together, playing with pickup bands in each honky tonk they visited. Soon, the pair stopped playing acoustic guitars and began playing Fender Telecasters, electric guitars with a bright, punchy twang. Rich would eventually become the lead guitarist. This change was evident in Buck's two Top Ten hits in 1962, "Kickin' Our Hearts Around" and "You're for Me." Instead of the shuffling honky tonk numbers that had been Owens' signature, the songs were bright, driving tracks in 2/4 that showed a hint of rock 'n' roll influence. By the beginning of 1963, Owens had begun to assemble his own band, featuring a drummer, bassist, and a pedal steel guitarist. One of the first bassists for the band was Merle Haggard, who named the group the Buckaroos.

Buck Owens' first No. 1 single, "Act Naturally," arrived in the spring of 1963. "Act Naturally" elevated Buck from a successful singer into stardom, starting a streak of 15 consecutive No. 1 singles. Its follow-up single, "Love's Gonna Live Here," became his biggest hit, spending 16 weeks at No. 1. "My Heart Skips a Beat," released in the spring of 1964, was nearly as successful, spending seven weeks at the top of the charts. It was replaced at the top by its B-side, "Together Again"; later that year, "I Don't Care (Just as Long as You Love Me)" spent six weeks at No. 1.

In 1965 his No. 1 hits included "I've Got a Tiger by the Tail," "Before You Go," "Only You (Can Break My Heart)," and the instrumental showcase "Buckaroo." That spring, Buck took out an advertisement in the Nashville-based publication *Music City News* claiming: "I Shall Make No Record That Is Not a Country Record." He then released his ninth album, *I've Got a Tiger by the Tail*, which featured a version of Chuck Berry's "Memphis." Owens explained that "Memphis" was a rockabilly song, a genre he believed to be part of country music. Also in 1965 he demonstrated his knack for business by forming Buck Owens Enterprises (which was managed by his sister Dorothy) and the booking agency OMAC Artists Corporation. Blue Book Music was also becoming quite successful, with the songs of both Buck and Merle Haggard earning the company significant amounts of money. The following year, Owens began purchasing radio stations; by the end of the decade, he owned four.

Buck Owens' success had spearheaded the national acceptance of the Bakersfield Sound. In addition to Owens, Merle Haggard, Wynn Stewart, and Tommy Collins were all grouped under this heading. The Bakersfield artists updated honky tonk, standing in direct contrast to the smooth country-pop of Nashville. Consequently, Owens was one of the biggest stars in popular music in the mid-'60s. He was playing hundreds of shows a year, selling thousands of records, and selling out concerts across the country. He continued to build his streak of No. 1 hits with "Waitin' in Your Welfare Line," "Think of Me," and "Open Up Your Heart" in 1966. That year Owens launched his first television series with "Buck Owens' Ranch." The program was a half-hour music show that ran throughout the year and was syndicated to 100 markets at the peak of its popularity. Buck's string of No. 1 hits continued throughout 1967, as "Where Does the Good Times Go," "Sam's Place," and "Your Tender Loving Care" all hit the top of the charts. His streak ended at the end of the year, when "It Takes People like You (To Make People like Me)" peaked at No. 2.

Owens began to branch out musically in 1968, adding more textures, tempos, and stylistic flourishes to his music. Though he only had one No. 1 hit that year with "How Long Will My Baby Be Gone," all of his singles from 1968—"How Long Will My Baby Be Gone," "Sweet Rosie Jones," "Let the World Keep On a Turnin'," "I've Got You on My Mind Again"—charted in the Top Ten, and all but one reached the Top Five. The next year Owens opened a state-of-the-art, 16-track recording studio in downtown Bakersfield, appropriately called Buck Owens Studios. Capitol allowed him to record himself and several other artists—including Susan Raye, Tony Booth, and Buddy Alan—at the studio; the label would merely press and package the records.

Buck Owens and the Buckaroos

While Buck Owens had a dedicated country following, he also had picked up a number of pop and rock fans as well. Not only did the Beatles cover "Act Naturally" on their 1965 *Help!* album, but in the fall of 1968, Owens headlined and sold out two concerts at the legendary rock 'n' roll venue Fillmore West. Owens continued to experiment musically, as evidenced by the two 1969 No. 1 singles, "Who's Gonna Mow Your Grass" and "Tall Dark Stranger." In the summer of 1969, Buck Owens' second television show, "Hee Haw," premiered. "Hee Haw" was the concept of two Canadian TV producers, who envisioned it as a down-home, country version of the popular "Laugh-In." Owens was hired as its host, and he brought on singer/guitarist Roy Clark as co-host. Owens had to tape the show only twice a year—once in June and once in October—and his segments were spread throughout the season's shows. Initially, the show was just a summer replacement for "The Smothers Brothers Comedy Hour," but its summer run was so successful that CBS scheduled it for the fall. As "Hee Haw" became more popular, so did Buck Owens. In the span of just over a year—December 1969 to February 1971— Capitol released no less than nine Buck albums, including reissues and three new studio records. During that time, he continued to chart in the Top Ten with regularity, as "The Kansas City Song" peaked at No. 2 in the summer of 1970 and "I Wouldn't Live in New York City (If They Gave Me the Whole Dang Town)" reached the Top Ten at the end of the year.

At the beginning of 1971, Owens signed what would turn out to be his last contract with Capitol. He would record for the label for another four years, and after his contract expired, he would gain ownership of all of his Capitol recordings from 1957 to 1975; Capitol could continue to manufacture Buck Owens records until 1980, when the masters would all return to Owens. Throughout 1971 he continued to have Top Ten hits, including a version of Simon and Garfunkel's "Bridge over Troubled Water," "Ruby (Are You Mad)," and "Rollin' in My Sweet Baby's Arms." In 1971 CBS cancelled "Hee Haw," and the show moved into syndication, where it became even more popular. By 1973 it had been so successful that it forced "Buck Owens' Ranch" off the air, simply because Owens' first program couldn't compete with the high ratings of his second show. In the spring of 1972 he had his final No.1 single as a solo artist, the ballad "Made in Japan." However, his career began to slide after that. It took him more than a year to reach the Top Ten again with "Big Game Hunter" at the end of 1973. Two other Top Ten hits followed in the spring and summer of 1974, though both songs—a rewrite of Dr. Hook's "On the Cover of the Rolling Stone" called "On the Cover of the Music City News" and "(It's A) Monsters' Holiday"—were novelty numbers.

In July 1974 Don Rich, Owens' longtime partner and guitarist, died in a motorcycle crash, which sent Owens into a deep depression. Though he had one more Top Ten hit that fall with "Great Expectations," he had trouble breaking the Top 40 in the years after Rich's death. Owens' contract with Capitol expired in 1975 and he moved to Warner Brothers, where he began recording in Nashville. Appropriately, his music began to sound more like country-pop than the hard-edged Bakersfield sound he had become famous for, but that's because he relinquished creative control of his records to the producers. Owens' record sales had significantly declined, but "Hee Haw" remained popular. Ironically, its success had an unwanted side effect—for many listeners in the general audience, Buck Owens became the cornball country comedian he was in the show, not the hardcore honky tonker he was at heart. That perception remained throughout the end of the '70s and even a hit duet with Emmylou Harris, "Play Together Again Again," in 1979 couldn't erase it. In 1980 Owens decided he didn't want to continue with the grind of constant performing and recording. He ended his contract with Warner and drastically cut back his performances. Even though he was semi-retired, he continued to tape "Hee Haw" until 1986.

Buck Owens was out of public view for the early and mid-'80s, when a new generation of country singers was developing. Like Owens in the '60s, they stood in opposition to the pop-inflected country of Nashville, building their sound on the Bakersfield country of Owens and Merle Haggard. One of the leading performers of the new traditionalists, Dwight Yoakam, persuaded Owens to join him on a re-recording of Buck's 1972 song "Streets of Bakersfield." After they performed it on a CBS television special, the duo recorded the song, releasing it in the summer of 1988. "Streets of Bakersfield" became a major hit, reaching No. 1; it was the first time since 1972 that Owens had a No.1 hit. Its success spurred him back into the recording studio, where he made an album called *Hot Dog*. It was a moderate success and it re-energized Owens. He assembled a new version of the Buckaroos and continued to perform and record, including a duet of "Act Naturally" with Ringo Starr.

Buck Owens didn't record or perform frequently in the '90s, but his classic Capitol recordings began to appear on compact disc; they hadn't been in print since 1980, when he gained control of the tapes from Capitol. Furthermore, Owens' influence continued to reverberate throughout country music, as well as some quarters of rock 'n' roll. —*Stephen Thomas Erlewine*

Buck Owens / Jan. 30, 1961 / Sundazed ✦✦✦

Buck Owens Sings Harlan Howard / Aug. 28, 1961 / Capitol ✦✦✦✦

Harlan Howard wrote many of Buck Owens' biggest hits and best songs, including "I've Got a Tiger by the Tail," "Above and Beyond," "Excuse Me (I Think I've Got a Heartache)," and "Under the Influence of Love," so it's only natural that Owens recorded an entire album of Howard's material. Nor is it surprising that it's a stunner. Owens sang Howard better than nearly anybody, and *Buck Owens Sings Harlan Howard* is full of wonderful songs and performances. Only "Foolin' Around" is regularly featured on Owens' hit compilations, which means there's a wealth of lesser-known gems ——including "Heartaches by the Number," "Pick Me Up on Your Way Down," "Keys in the Mailbox" and "Let's Agree to Disagree"—that form the core of this record, one of Owens' most enjoyable LPs of the '60s. —*Stephen Thomas Erlewine*

On the Bandstand / Apr. 29, 1963 / Sundazed ✦✦✦

One of Owens' rootsier '60s Capitol albums, including only one hit ("Kickin' Our Hearts") and giving plenty of instrumental and vocal space to the rest of the band. It's not as heavy on original material as some of his other Capitol LPs, including numbers by Wanda Jackson, Willie Nelson, Leadbelly, and John D. Loudermilk, as well as an arrangment of "Orange Blossom Special." The CD reissue adds two cuts from a 1963 Top 20 duet single he recorded with Rose Maddox. —*Richie Unterberger*

Country Hit Maker #1 / 1964 / Starday ✦✦✦

Pre-Capitol material, half of this album consists of Owens' very early recordings like "Sweethearts in Heaven" and "There Goes My Love" (covered later by Highway 101), which show his developing vocal style. It's a little more down-home than his later stuff. The other half consists of covers of Owens' later material by other artists. —*George Bedard*

The Best of Buck Owens / Jun. 1, 1964 / Capitol ✦✦✦

This classic collection of late-'50s and early-'60s hits includes "Above and Beyond," "Love's Gonna Live Here," "Act Naturally," and "Under Your Spell Again"—mostly written by Owens. —*George Bedard*

Together Again/My Heart Skips a Beat / Jul. 20, 1964 / Sundazed ✦✦✦

Named after his double-sided No. 1 hit single of early 1964, *Together Again/My Heart Skips a Beat* is one of Buck Owens' strongest albums of the '60s, as well as one of his few records to stick firmly in the honky tonk camp. Despite the rolling drums of "My Heart Skips a Beat," the jumpy "Truck Drivin' Man," the jokey "Ain't It Amazin' Gracie," and a Bakersfield overhaul of "Save the Last Dance for Me," the majority of the album is straightahead honky tonk. Whether it's Owens' excellent weepers "I Don't Hear You" and "Getting Used to Losing You," or terrific versions of classics like "Close Up the Honky Tonks" and "A-11," the record is filled with superb, pure honky tonk. Sundazed's CD reissue adds the singles "Love's Gonna Live Here" and "Act Naturally," which don't follow in the honky tonk theme of the album; but since both are classics, it's not worth complaining. —*Stephen Thomas Erlewine*

I Don't Care / Nov. 2, 1964 / Capitol ✦✦✦

This is the studio-album version of Owens and the Buckaroos' mid-'60s stage show—Owens plays "Buck's Polka." Doyle Holly and Don Rich are featured—also "Loose Talk," a duet with Owens and Rose Maddox. —*George Bedard*

I've Got a Tiger by the Tail / Mar. 1, 1965 / Capitol ✦✦✦✦

The title track is included, plus some great ballads, such as "Cryin' Time." These '60s Capitol albums are not just mish-mashes, like many C&W albums of the period; they're well thought out, usually including a vocal or two by Don Rich (one of C&W's unsung heroes) or the deep-voiced bass player Doyle Holly and a fiddle or steel-guitar instrumental by Don or Tom Brumley, respectively. —*George Bedard*

Before You Go/No One But You / Jul. 26, 1965 / Sundazed ✦✦✦

When it comes to Owens' mid-'60s Capitol LPs, there really isn't much to choose between. If you like his Bakersfield sound, you'll like all of them; if you're trying to zero in on just one or two collections, you'd be better off with greatest-hits surveys, because the individual albums sound rather interchangeable to the non-enthusiast. This has the usual competent original material and accomplished guitar picking, paced by the No. 1 title track, with occasional instrumentals thrown in for a change of pace. The CD reissue adds a couple of instrumental bonus cuts from his 1966 album, *The Buck Owens Songbook*. —*Richie Unterberger*

Roll Out the Red Carpet / Feb. 7, 1966 / Sundazed ✦✦✦✦

Mostly written or co-written by Owens, this is Owens and the boys at their peak. —*George Bedard*

The Best of Buck Owens, Vol. 2 / Apr. 1, 1968 / Capitol ✦✦✦✦

"I've Got a Tiger by the Tail," "Together Again," "My Heart Skips a Beat"—all these are classic Owens from his mid-'60s peak. It features the Fabulous Buckaroos, including Don Rich on lead guitar and harmonies and Tom Brumley on steel. It's a must for any serious country and western fan. —*George Bedard*

Act Naturally / Oct. 4, 1989 / Capitol ✦✦✦

On *Act Naturally*, Buck Owens runs through his back catalog, remaking several of his classic hits and a handful of obscurities, as well as recording three unremarkable new songs. Though Owens is in fine voice and his backing band can replicate the twangy Bakersfield sound, the record's production is a little too thick, sterile, and unaffecting to make the album consistently enjoyable. — *Thom Owens*

☆ **Live at Carnegie Hall** / Dec. 1989 / Country Music Foundation ✦✦✦✦✦

Buck Owens and the Buckaroos' 1966 concert at Carnegie Hall was a landmark not only for the band, but for country music. It signalled that it had firmly integrated itself not only into America's popular music mainstream, but also into urban centers like New York. Buck and the Buckaroos had to deliver a stellar performance, and they did—the group sounded like dynamite, tearing through a selection of their classic hits with vigor. Several decades removed from the performance itself, what really comes through is how musical and gifted the Buckaroos were, particularly Don Rich. For dedicated fans, it's a necessary addition to the colleciton. — *Stephen Thomas Erlewine*

All-Time Greatest Hits, Vol. 1 / Aug. 13, 1990 / Curb ✦✦✦✦

Curb's *All-Time Greatest Hits* was released two years before Buck Owens allowed Rhino Records to release his catalog in the form of a box set and two compilations. Consequently, the compilation isn't much more than a place-holder—12 songs that contain a few of his biggest hits ("Act Naturally," "Streets of Bakersfield," "I've Got a Tiger by the Tail") plus several lesser-known singles ("Think of Me," "Big in Vegas"). It's an adequate collection, but it doesn't have the comprehensiveness, or the listenability, of any of the Rhino collections, which are all better introductions and retrospectives. — *Stephen Thomas Erlewine*

☆ **The Buck Owens Collection (1959-1990)** / 1992 / Rhino ✦✦✦✦✦

Spanning three discs, *The Buck Owens Collection* is the most comprehensive compilation ever assembled on one of the founders of the Bakersfield sound. Although his earliest recordings aren't included, all of his greatest Capitol hits are present, as is his 1988 duet on "Streets of Bakersfield" with Dwight Yoakam and its follow-up single, "Hot Dog." The box is a necessary purchase, simply because it presents all of Owens' biggest hits in one place. There might not be many rarities on *The Buck Owens Collection*, but with an artist as consistent as Buck, all you need is the good stuff and that is all on this essential set. — *Stephen Thomas Erlewine*

★ **Very Best of Buck Owens, Vol. 1** / 1994 / Rhino ✦✦✦✦✦

The Very Best of Buck Owens, Vol. 1 contains a great deal of Owens' most essential songs, including "Under Your Spell Again," "Act Naturally," "I've Got a Tiger by the Tail," and "Waitin' in Your Welfare Line." The set runs from 1959 to 1971, picking up a good cross-section of his biggest hits along the way. The compilation is a perfect introduction, and what songs it doesn't cover are readily available on *The Very Best of Buck Owens, Vol. 2*. Of course, listeners who want the most comprehensive set available should invest in the triple-disc box set, *The Buck Owens Collection*. — *Stephen Thomas Erlewine*

☆ **Very Best of Buck Owens, Vol. 2** / 1994 / Rhino ✦✦✦✦✦

The Very Best of Buck Owens, Vol. 2 contains all the essential Owens songs the first volume didn't cover, including "Above and Beyond," "Love's Gonna Live Here," "My Heart Skips a Beat," "Cryin' Time," "Buckaroo," and "Big in Vegas." Like its predecessor, the collection spans 1959 to 1971 and features an excellent cross-section of his biggest hits along the way. Not only is it a perfect supplement to *The Very Best of Buck Owens, Vol. 1*, the compilation works as a good introduction, even though the first collection is a better choice for a new fan. Of course listeners who want the most comprehensive set available should invest in the triple-disc box set, *The Buck Owens Collection*. — *Stephen Thomas Erlewine*

Duets: Half a Buck / Mar. 19, 1996 / K-Tel ✦✦✦

Buck Owens' Greatest Duets: Half a Buck is a 10-track compilation of Owens' personal favorite duets, including cuts he recorded with Rose Maddox, Susan Raye, Buddy Allan, and Ringo Starr. Of course the hit duets with Maddox—"Loose Talk" and "Mental Cruelty"—are the particular standouts, but the remaining cuts are all very good and, as in the case of Allan's "Let the World Keep on Turning," occasionally excellent. *Half a Buck* may be a budget-line release, but the overall quality of the material is so strong that it is worthwhile. — *Stephen Thomas Erlewine*

Tex Owens

b. Jun. 15, 1892, Kileen, TX, **d.** Sep. 9, 1962

Vocals / Traditional Country, Cowboy

An original cowboy who sang on broadcasts with his Texas Cowboys, Tex Owens is known to country fans as the writer of Eddy Arnold's 1955 hit, "The Cattle Call." He was born on June 15, 1892, in Kileen, TX, the youngest of 12 children. Before beginning his performance life, Owens worked as a deputy sheriff and mechanic in addition to riding the range. With his Texas Rangers, he broadcast on KMBC-Kansas City during the 1930s and made additional appearances singing with the Beverly Hill Billies. Owens also appeared in several films, including John Wayne's 1948 vehicle *Red River*. He had written "The Cattle Call" in 1934 while in Kansas City, and less than 20 years later, Eddy Arnold took the song to No. 1 on the country charts. Tex Owens died in 1962 of a heart attack. — *John Bush*

● **Cattle Call** / 1995 / Bear Family ✦✦✦✦

Vernon Oxford

b. Jun. 8, 1941, Rogers, AR

Vocals / Country, Traditional Country, Honky Tonk

Vernon Oxford was a country artist with a traditional sound who found himself more successful in Europe than his native United States. He was born and raised the son of an old-time fiddler in Arkansas, and after his family moved to Wichita, KS, young Oxford learned to play fiddle and guitar and sing honky tonk music. He made his professional debut in 1960 in a club in Utah, then returned to Kansas to play in clubs and at square dances. In 1964 he decided to try his luck in Nashville, but pop-country was all the rage and the labels weren't interested in such a traditional singer. Still, thanks to Harlan Howard, Oxford managed to land a contract with RCA Victor and made his recording debut in 1965. He recorded and released seven singles and an album over the next two years. Traditional country music fans loved his work, but nothing he released appeared on the charts. Eventually RCA dropped him and Oxford moved to Stop, again with no success until his old-fashioned sound was discovered in Great Britain. In 1974 RCA released a double album of his work, sent him on a tour of England, and offered to sign him up again. In the mid-'70s, he had his first US chart entry with "Shadows of My Mind." He didn't score a major hit until later in the year, when he released "Redneck (The Redneck National Anthem)." He had three more mid-range hits in the US. Meanwhile, his songs continued to sell well in the UK, where he had such hits as "I've Got to Get Peter off Your Mind" and "Field of Flowers." After 1977 Oxford vanished from the charts until 1981, where he reappeared as a "born-again" gospel singer. He continued to record and even preach around the country, and remained popular in Britain. — *Sandra Brennan*

● **Twenty of the Best** / 1984 / RCA [UK] ✦✦✦✦

Keeper of the Flame / 1995 / Bear Family ✦✦✦✦

Keeper of the Flame is a five-disc box set containing all of Vernon Oxford's recordings for RCA Records, including all of his minor hit singles from the mid-'70s and a wealth of album tracks and rarities. Though Oxford was a talented hard country singer, his talent was limited, which means that a set of this size is of interest only to hardcore fans. Casual listeners will find the sheer bulk of the set rather tedious, even though there are a number of forgotten treasures buried in the comprehensive box. — *Thom Owens*

Ozark Mountain Daredevils

Country-Rock, Southern Rock

One of the pre-eminent country-rock bands of the 1970s, the Ozark Mountain Daredevils were formed in 1971 by vocalist and harmonica player Steve Cash, multi-instrumentalists John Dillon and Larry Lee, and vocalist/bassist Mike "Supe" Granda. The individual members first met while playing in and around their hometown of Springfield, MO; initially, they performed under the name of the Emergency Band and consisted of Cash, Lee, and Dillon, as well as the latter's wife. After a series of name changes (including the Buffalo Chips, the Burlap Socks, and the Family Tree), they settled on the Ozark Mountain Daredevils after the addition of Granda cemented their line-up.

After the group's manager, Steve Plesser, sent their demo to the famed rock producer Glyn Johns, they were offered a contract by A&M Records' David Anderle, who joined Johns to produce the Daredevils' self-titled 1973 LP, recorded with recent band additions Randle Chowning (vocals, guitar, and harmonica) and Buddy Brayfield (keyboards, oboe, and vocals). The single "If You Wanna Get to Heaven" was a pop hit in 1974, and later in the year the band issued their sophomore release, *It'll Shine When It Shines*, featuring the pop smash "Jackie Blue."

A year later the Daredevils' third LP *The Car Over the Lake Album*, featured the minor pop hit "If I Only Knew." Shortly after its release, the group welcomed drummer and guitarist Steve Canady, who had played on their original demo. In 1976 Brayfield left the band and was replaced by former deejay Jerry Mills. Later in the year the album *Men from Earth* was released; its single "You Made It Right" was the Daredevils' lone country chart hit. After the 1977 record *Don't Look Now*, they released 1978's double concert album *It's Alive*, which proved to be Larry Lee's final work with the group before exiting for a solo career. (Under the name Larry Michael Lee, he became a successful Nashville producer.)

After moving to Columbia in 1980, the Ozark Mountain Daredevils released another self-titled effort, after which the group seemingly vanished. It was not until 1989 that the Daredevils reappeared, sporting the five-piece roster of Cash, Dillon, Granda, Canady, and guitarist D. Clinton Thompson; after issuing the album *Modern History*, they again dropped out of sight. —*Jason Ankeny*

● **The Best of Ozark Mountain Daredevils** / 1983 / A&M ✦✦✦✦
This solid selection of their best features "If You Want to Get to Heaven" and "Jackie Blue." —*Dan Heilman*

P

Patti Page (Clara Ann Fowler)

b. Nov. 8, 1927, Muskogee, OK

Vocals / Country-Pop, Nashville Sound/Countrypolitan, Traditional Pop

Patti Page was one of pop music's leading singers during the early '50s. Her double-tracked vocals, highly innovative at the time, translated into gigantic commercial success. By the age of 19, Page was working as a singer at a Tulsa radio station, and she signed with Mercury in 1948. Page's use of multi-tracked vocals gave her a unique, full sound, and in 1950 her renditions of "All My Love" and "Tennessee Waltz" were pop chart-toppers, the latter for a good three months. "Mockin' Bird Hill" (1951), "I Went to Your Wedding" (1952), and "Doggie in the Window" (1953) were only a few of her gold records for Mercury, and she persevered through the early rock era with "Allegheny Moon" in 1956 and "Old Cape Cod" the next year. Her last major pop smash in 1965, "Hush, Hush, Sweet Charlotte," was the theme song to a popular movie. *—Bill Dahl*

★ **The Mercury Years, Vol. 1** / Jan. 1991 / Mercury ✦✦✦✦✦
These original hits from 1948-1952 include "Tennessee Waltz" in an excellent package. *—Hank Davis*

The Mercury Years, Vol. 2 / Feb. 1991 / Mercury ✦✦✦✦
Twenty hits from 1952-1962, including "Old Cape Cod" and "Allegheny Moon." Informative packaging. *—Hank Davis*

Palace

Guitar, Vocals / Indie Rock, Alternative Country-Rock, Alternative Country

Will Oldham, the brains and brawn behind releases such as Palace Brothers, Palace Songs, Palace Music, and just plain Palace, is loosely grouped with the '90s anti-folk movement that includes Bill Callahan of Smog, a labelmate of Oldham's on Chicago's Drag City Records. Often mistaken for an old man because of his cracking vocals, sparse guitar pickings and Biblical dialect, Oldham has recorded since 1992 with a variety of sidemen—basically, any friends or acquaintances who can play an instrument.

Raised in Louisville, KY, Will Oldham first became involved in acting; he starred in John Sayles' 1987 mining film *Matewan*, playing—with considerable ease—an elderly miner who relates the action over a series of flashbacks. Two years later, he moved to TV for "Everybody's Baby: The Rescue of Jessica McClure" and returned to the cinema in 1991 for *Thousand Pieces of Gold*, another mining film. At the same time, Oldham was involved in the fertile indie-rock scene in Louisville, picking up his first musical credit with Slint, for the photograph on the cover of the band's 1991 album, *Spiderland*.

Will Oldham the musical artist debuted in 1992, with the single "Ohio River Boat Song" on Drag City Records. Though he's credited as Palace Songs on the single, Oldham's debut album the following year was filed under Palace Brothers—in part to denote the work of Todd Brashear. *There Is No-One What Will Take Care of You* introduced several of Oldham's continuing themes: drunkenness, sin in general, and the varied results of each.

Recording regularly during 1993-94, Oldham released several singles and an EP (*An Arrow Through the Bitch*) before his second album—self-titled but also listed as *Days in the Wake*—was issued by Drag City in 1994. Again, Oldham followed with a string of limited-release singles and one EP, but mixed things up for late 1995's *Viva Last Blues* (as Palace Music); Oldham recruited a band, with guitarist Bryan Rich, organist Liam Hayes, and bassist Jason Loewenstein (from Sebadoh). The next year's *Arise, Therefore* found Oldham back in a largely solitary setting. *—John Bush*

There Is No One What Will Take Care of You / Jun. 14, 1993 / Drag City ✦✦✦
The name says it all. Dramatic, desperate country-indie rock that focuses on the dark side of life. *—Heather Phares*

● **Palace Brothers [EP]** / 1994 / Drag City ✦✦✦✦
Oldham's second EP is even more spartan and gaunt-sounding than Palace's debut. Strumming away on an acoustic guitar, his feeble voice barely topping a whisper, Oldham croaks out tunes of quiet despair like "Pushkin" and "I Am a Cinematographer." *—Heather Phares*

Viva Last Blues / 1995 / Drag City ✦✦✦
Viva Last Blues continues Oldham and company's trend of spare acoustic tunes with sad, world-weary themes. Palace seems to be refining and honing both their playing and songwriting skills with each album. *—Heather Phares*

Arise Therefore / Apr. 1996 / Drag City ✦✦✦✦
Once again Will Oldham emerges from the murky, Midwestern haze with another helping of lovely, low-key musings on his fourth full-length album, *Arise Therefore*, this time recorded under the name Palace Music (previously Palace Brothers, Palace Songs, or just plain Palace). Much quieter than last year's *Viva Last Blues*, and less Appalachian in its folk-spirit than Palace's earlier music, the songs on *Arise Therefore* shift and moan with breathy cracks and shivers, Oldham's meandering, poet-speak vocals, and guitar accompanied by his brother Ned's bass, David Grubbs' piano, and (surprise!) a Maya Tone drum machine. The lyrics (included for the first time) are as beautiful in their stark, pale honesty as they are indecipherable. "I watch things painted on public walls, now but I see other things as well, behind but right fuck in front of my spirit is how the real road's laid out in a line" he sings on "Kid of Harith." Don't ask for an interpretation. It will come with time, or it won't. *—Kurt Wolff*

Brave New World / Atlantic ✦✦✦

Billy Parker

b. Jul. 19, 1939, Okemah, OK

Vocals / Traditional Country, Honky Tonk

While Billy Parker was a mainstay on country radio. His claim to fame was as an influential disc jockey, not as a performer, ironically, for of all the Top 40 hits he spun over the course of his decades on the air, not one was his own. Born July 19, 1939, in Okemah, OK, he began playing guitar as a child, and by the age of 14 had made his professional debut on the Tulsa radio program

353

"Big Red Jamboree." A few years later he began performing in clubs, and in 1959, landed his first deejay work.

By 1963 Parker was the regular daytime disc jockey on Wichita, KS, KFDI, and also hosted a Tulsa television program. In the same year, he cut his first single, "The Line Between Love and Hate," and was named "Mr. DJ USA." in a nationwide poll, which helped land him at Nashville's WSM. After releasing another record, "I'm Drinking All the Time," in 1966, Parker began playing with Ernest Tubb's Troubadors in 1968; he stayed with the group for three years and then joined Tulsa's KVOO.

In 1975 Parker was named "Disc Jockey of the Year" by the Academy of Country and Western Music; he won the award again in 1977, 1978, and 1984. In 1976 he scored his first chart hit with "It's Bad When You're Caught (With the Goods)," from the album *Average Man.* A series of singles followed, including a tribute to Ernest Tubb titled "Thanks E.T. Thanks a Lot"; while most charted, none came in higher than No. 50. In 1982 he scored his biggest success with the title track from the LP *(Who's Gonna Sing) The Last Country Song,* an album of collaborations with the likes of Darrell McCall and Vassar Clements.

After a record of duets, 1983's *Something Old, Something New,* he retreated from performing to focus on his work as KVOO's program director, but he returned in 1988 with the album *Always Country.* In 1990 he released a gospel record, *I'll Speak Out for You, Jesus;* two years later, he was inducted by the Country Music Disc Jockey Hall of Fame. At about the same time, he was appointed KVOO's executive director. *—Jason Ankeny*

Billy Parker and Friends / Bear Family ✦✦✦
Some of Parker's friends (Webb Pierce, Jack Greene, and Ernest Tubb) join him on this re-release of material originally recorded during the '80s for the Soundwaves label. An informative booklet accompanies this release. *—AMG*

● **Average Man** / Sunshine Country ✦✦✦✦

Parlor James

Alternative Country-Rock
The Brooklyn-based duo Parlor James pitted the crystalline tenor of Ryan Hedgecock (the founder of roots-rockers Lone Justice) against the rootsy twang of Amy Allison (daughter of jazz great Mose Allison) to create a gothic sound steeped in the traditions of country vocal harmony. The pair first teamed in 1994, after Hedgecock returned from a long, self-imposed exile from the music industry after the dissolution of Lone Justice. He met Allison, the onetime frontwoman for the country-rock band the Maudlins, at a New York songwriters' showcase, and soon they were writing and performing as a duo. In 1996 Parlor James issued their debut EP, the six-song collection *Dreadful Sorry.* *—Jason Ankeny*

● **Dreadful Sorry** / Jul. 29, 1996 / Discovery ✦✦✦✦
Sometimes described as an American version of Fairport Convention, the duo Parlor James—comprised of Ryan Hedgecock and Amy Allison, augmented by a flexible group of musicians—deliver a rustic, yet thoroughly compelling six-song (seven counting the hidden track) EP. Steeped in traditional music styling, Allison's nasal twang and Hedgecock's lonesome tenor at times resemble an Appalacian-sounding Emmylou Harris and Gram Parsons, as in Allison's forlorn ballad "Cheater's World." Mixing haunting originals like Hedgecock's dark and powerfully driven "Devil's Door" with affecting readings of traditional numbers such as "Snow Dove" and the hidden track "Cowboy Song," *Dreadful Sorry* leaves you wanting more. *—Jack Leaver*

Lee Roy Parnell

b. Dec. 21, 1957, Abilene, TX
Guitar, Vocals / Contemporary Country, New Traditionalist, Western Swing Revival
Singer-songwriter and slide guitarist Lee Roy Parnell sang with a Texas-style Western swing enlivened with just a hint of blues. In addition to having a string of Top Ten singles of his own, Parnell wrote songs for artists as diverse as Sweethearts of the Rodeo, Jo-El Sonnier, and David Wills and Johnny Lee. The son of a travelling medicine show musician, Parnell was influenced early on by

Bob Wills. Raised on his parents' ranch, Parnell made his debut singing "San Antonio Rose" on Wills' radio show in Fort Worth. As a teenager, he drummed in a local band but soon switched to guitar. After high school, Parnell moved to Austin and set about touring for the next dozen years. Eventually he settled down, married, and got a job selling ads at a local radio station. In the early '70s, Parnell visited Nashville, but he returned to Austin without signing with a record company. However, he soon signed a publishing contract with Welk Music. While playing in a local cafe, he was heard by Tim Dubois, the head of Arista Records, who signed the aspiring singer to the label. Parnell released his eponymous debut album in 1990, and the record yielded three minor hits. Released in 1992, his second album, *Love Without Mercy,* produced the No. 2 smash "What Kind of Fool Do You Think I Am." After its success, he had four consecutive Top Ten hits—"Love Without Mercy," "Tender Moment," "On the Road," and "I'm Holding My Own." The latter two were taken from his third album, *On the Road,* released in the fall of 1993. In 1995 he returned back to the Top Ten with "A Little Bit of You," taken from his fourth album, *We All Get Lucky Sometimes. —Sandra Brennan*

Lee Roy Parnell / 1990 / Arista ✦✦✦✦
Hard-rocking country soul, complete with horn section, this album was produced by Barry Beckett, whose experiences at Muscle Shoals mean he knows how to make this kind of record. *—Brian Mansfield*

● **Love Without Mercy** / 1992 / Arista ✦✦✦✦
For his second album, Parnell dropped the horns and gave his slide guitar a bigger role. He was still a Texas rocker disguised by a pedal steel, but the album produced three Top Ten hits—"Love Without Mercy," "What Kind of Fool Do You Think I Am," and "Tender Moment." *—Brian Mansfield*

On the Road / Oct. 26, 1993 / Arista ✦✦✦
More roots-rocking road music, though not as perfectly realized as *Love Without Mercy.* The title track and "I'm Holding My Own" were hits, and Parnell sang with Brooks and Dunn's Ronnie Dunn on the Hank Williams standard "Take These Chains from My Heart." *—Brian Mansfield*

We All Get Lucky Sometimes / 1995 / Career ✦✦✦
On *We All Get Lucky Sometimes,* Lee Roy Parnell tempers his mixture of country, R&B, blues, and rock 'n' roll somewhat with a subdued production, designed to attract the attention of country radio. Even when his music is slightly tamed, Parnell turns in a fine effort, filled with enough true grit to satisfy his fans. *—Stephen Thomas Erlewine*

Gene Parsons

b. Sep. 4, 1944, Los Angeles, CA
Bass, Guitar, Drums, Vocals / Country-Rock, Folk-Rock
Country-rock pioneer Gene Parsons was born September 4, 1944, in Los Angeles. In 1963 he and friend Gib Gilbeau formed the Castaways, followed four years later by their partnership as Cajun Gib and Gene. In 1968 the duo signed on with Clarence White and Wayne Moore's Nashville West for the group's self-titled debut LP.

Later that year, Parsons and White joined the Byrds. Parsons remained their drummer through 1972, when he depart for a solo career. His debut album, *Kindling,* was released the next year. Also in 1973 he reunited with Gilbeau and played on sessions for Arlo Guthrie and Elliott Murphy. In 1974 Parsons joined the Flying Burrito Brothers and appeared on two of the group's final LPs, 1975's *Flying Again* and 1976's *Airborne.*

A recurring wrist injury kept him from performing live for several years, but in 1980 he joined Sierra Records both as an A&R executive and as a performer, issuing the solo effort *Melodies.* Shortly thereafter, he formed the Gene Parsons Trio with bassist Peter Oliba and drummer Richie Rosenbaum. In 1985 Parsons joined forces with singer/guitarist Meridian Green, the daughter of folk singer Bob Gibson. The couple, who married in 1986, initially performed as a duo before forming the group Parsons Green in 1991. The band's debut, *Birds of a Feather,* appeared in 1992. *—Jason Ankeny*

● **Kindling** / 1973 / Warner Brothers ✦✦✦✦
This exquisite album contains the finest cover of "Willin'." "Drunk-ards Dream" and "Do Not Disturb" also stand out. Backed by Clarence White, Vassar Clements, Roger Bush, Gib Guilbeau, and Bill Payne. Out of print—check those used-record stores! —*Chip Renner*

Melodies / 1979 / Sierra ✦✦✦
A nice record featuring Albert Lee, Herb Pedersen, Greg Harris, and Roger Bush. Gene covers Phil Ochs' "My Kingdom for a Car." "Hot Burrito No. 1" stands out. —*Chip Renner*

Birds of a Feather / 1987 / Sierra ✦✦✦✦
Gene teams up with Meridian Green to produce a nice album fea turing good harmonies. "Catch the Wind" and "Wind and Rain" are great. Gene has taken a different path. How about a second album? —*Chip Renner*

Kindling Collection / 1995 / Sierra ✦✦✦

Gram Parsons (Cecil Ingram Connor)

b. Nov. 5, 1946, Winterhaven, FL, **d.** Sep. 19, 1973, Joshua Tree, CA
Guitar, Vocals / Country-Rock
Gram Parsons is the father of country-rock. With the International Submarine Band, the Byrds, and the Flying Burrito Brothers, Par-sons pioneered the concept of a rock band playing country music, and as a solo artist he moved even further into country music, blending the two genres to the point that they became indistin-guishable. Parsons never sold many records, but he influenced countless fellow musicians, from the Rolling Stones to the Byrds. In the years since his death, his stature has grown, as numerous rock and country artists build on his small, but enormously influ-ential, body of work.

Gram Parsons was born Cecil Ingram Connor on November 5, 1946. Parsons was the grandson of John Snivley, who owned about one-third of all the citrus fields in Florida. Snivley's daugh-ter married Coon Dog Connor. Gram learned to play the piano at the age of nine, the same year he saw Elvis Presley perform at his school; after that performance, Parsons decided to become a musician. When Gram was 12, his father committed suicide. After Connor's death, Gram and his mother moved in with her parents in Winter Haven, FL; a year after the move, his mother married Robert Parsons, who adopted Gram and legally changed his name to Gram Parsons.

At the age of 14, Parsons began playing in the local rock 'n' roll band the Pacers, which evolved into the Legends. During its time together, the Legends featured Jim Stafford and Kent Lavoie, who would later come to fame under the name Lobo. In 1963 Parsons formed a folk group called the Shilos, who performed throughout Florida and cut two singles for Columbia Records. In 1965 Par-sons graduated from high school; on the same day he graduated, his mother died of alcohol poisoning.

After his graduation, Gram Parsons enrolled at Harvard, where he studied theology. Parsons spent only one semester at Harvard, and while he was there, he spent more time playing music than attending classes. During this time he formed the International Submarine Band with guitarist John Nuese, bassist Ian Dunlop, and drummer Mickey Gauvin. After he dropped out of college, he moved to New York with the International Submarine Band in 1966. The group spent a year in New York, developing a heavily country-influenced rock 'n' roll sound and cutting two unsuccess-ful singles for Columbia. The band relocated to Los Angeles in 1967, where they secured a record contract with Lee Hazlewood's LHI record label. The group's debut album, *Safe at Home*, was released in early 1968, but by the time it appeared in the stores, the group had disbanded.

Around the time the International Submarine Band dissolved, Parsons met Chris Hillman, the bassist for the Byrds. The Byrds were rebuilding their lineup, and Hillman recommended to the band's leader, Roger McGuinn, that Parsons join the band. By the spring of 1968 Parsons had become a member of the Byrds, and he was largely responsible for the group's shift toward country music with their album *Sweetheart of the Rodeo*. Originally the album was going to feature Parsons' lead vocals, but he was still

Gram Parsons

contractually obligated to LHI, so his voice had to be stripped from the record.

Gram Parsons spent only a few months with the Byrds, leaving the band in the fall of 1968 because he refused to accompany them on a tour of South Africa, allegedly because he opposed apartheid. Chris Hillman left the band shortly after that, and the duo formed the Flying Burrito Brothers in late 1968. Parsons and Hillman enlisted pedal steel guitarist "Sneaky" Pete Kleinow and bassist Chris Ethridge to complete the band's lineup and recorded their debut album with a series of session drummers. *The Gilded Palace of Sin*, the Flying Burrito Brothers' debut album, was released in 1969. Although the album sold only a few thousand copies, the group gathered a dedicated cult following composed mainly of musicians, including the Rolling Stones. In fact by the time the album was released, Parsons had begun hanging around the Rolling Stones frequently and became close friends with Keith Richards. Before his time with the Stones, Parsons had experi-mented with drugs and alcohol, but in 1969 he dove deep into sub-stance abuse, which he supported with his huge trust fund.

Parsons recorded a second album with the Flying Burrito Brothers, but by the time the record—titled *Burrito Deluxe*—appeared in the spring of 1970, he had left the band. Shortly after leaving the group, he recorded a handful of songs with producer Terry Melcher, but he never completed the album. After these sessions, Parsons entered a holding pattern where he acted the role of being a rock star instead of actually playing music. He spent much of his time either hanging out with the Stones or ingesting large amounts of drugs and alcohol; fre-quently, he did a combination of the two. In 1971 he toured with the Rolling Stones in England and attended the recording of the band's *Exile on Main Street;* it appeared that he would sign with the band's record label. Instead, he headed back to Los Angeles late in 1971, spending the rest of the year and the first half of 1972 writing material for an impending solo album. In 1972 he met Emmylou Harris through Chris Hillman, and Parsons asked her to join his backing band; she accepted.

By the summer of 1972, he was prepared to enter the studio to record his first solo album. Parsons had assembled a band—which included Harris, guitarist James Burton, bassist Rick Grech, Barry Tashain, Glen D. Hardin, and Ronnie Tutt—and had asked Merle Haggard to produce the album. After meeting Parsons, Haggard turned the offer down, and Parsons chose Haggard's engineer, Hugh Davis, as the album's producer. The resulting album, *G.P.,* was released late in 1972 to good reviews but poor sales.

After the release of *G.P.,* Parsons embarked on a small tour with his backing band, the Fallen Angels. After the tour was completed, they entered the studio to record his second album, *Grievous Angel*. The album was completed toward the end of the summer. A few weeks after the sessions, Parsons went on vacation near Joshua Tree National Monument in Arizona. He spent most of his time there consuming drugs and alcohol. On September 19, 1973, he overdosed on morphine and tequila and was rushed to the Yucca Valley Hospital, where he was pronounced dead on arrival. According to the funeral plans, his body was to be flown back to New Orleans for burial. However, Parsons' road manager stole the body after the funeral and carried it back out to the Joshua Tree desert, where he cremated the body. Phil Kaufman revealed that the cremation had been Parsons' wish. Kaufman could not be convicted for stealing the body, but he was arrested for stealing and burning the coffin.

In the two decades after Gram Parsons' death, his legacy continued to grow, as both country and rock musicians built on the music he left behind. Everyone from Emmylou Harris to Elvis Costello has covered his songs, and his influence could still be heard well into the '90s. — *Stephen Thomas Erlewine*

Gram Parsons Int Sub Band (Safe at Home) / 1967 / Shiloh ✦✦✦

Safe at Home represents some of Gram Parsons' earliest recordings as a part of the International Submarine Band. Arguably the first country-rock album, this more than hints at Parsons' greatness to come. This charming document is essential listening. — *Chris Woodstra*

★ G.P./Grievous Angel / 1973 / Reprise ✦✦✦✦✦

Parsons' two best albums appear on one compact disc. Seeking to synthesize his ideas with those of classic country and rock, Parsons hired Merle Haggard's recording engineer (he had approached Haggard himself about producing) and members of Elvis Presley's band, including pianist Glen D. Hardin and guitarist James Burton. The result had its roots in everything but sounded like nothing else. Parsons' songs were the musings of a wounded soul, and his taste in others' material ran from Harlan Howard to the J. Geils Band. On *Grievous Angel*, Emmylou Harris emerges from the background to provide an angelic foil for Parsons' lost folkie voice. — *Brian Mansfield*

Sleepless Nights / 1976 / A&M ✦✦✦

Sleepless Nights is a collection of unreleased Gram Parsons material recorded while he was in the Flying Burrito Brothers. Most of the material is covers, yet the selection demonstrates how Parsons closed the gap between rock and country. — *Stephen Thomas Erlewine*

Gram Parsons and the Fallen Angels / 1981 / Sierra ✦✦✦✦

A good live document of Parsons' last tour, it was recorded at radio station WLIR in New York. — *Kenneth M. Cassidy*

Warm Evenings, Pale Mornings, Bottled Blues / 1992 / Raven ✦✦✦✦

Although all of Parsons' albums are essential, this import-only collection provides an excellent sampling of his entire career, including his stints with the Shilos, the International Submarine Band, the Byrds (complete with Parsons' vocals restored), the Flying Burrito Brothers, and the solo years. — *Chris Woodstra*

Cosmic American Music / Jul. 18, 1995 / Sundown ✦✦

Cosmic American is a collection of demos made in various homes and hotel rooms in 1972. In an informal, sing-along environment, Parsons works through embryonic versions of songs and old favorites with friends Emmylou Harris, Barry Tashian, and Ric Grech (among others). Several songs never made it to the studio. Though the quality of the recordings can be off-putting to the casual fan, those who count themselves among GP's ever-growing cult will find this a compulsive listen. — *Chris Woodstra*

Dolly Parton (Dolly Rebecca Parton)

b. Jan. 19, 1946, Locust Ridge, TN

Banjo, Guitar, Vocals / Progressive Country, Country-Pop, Contemporary Country, Country-Folk, Urban Cowboy

It's difficult to find a country performer who has moved from country roots to international fame more successfully than Dolly Parton. Her autobiographical single "Coat of Many Colors" shows the poverty of growing up one of 12 children on a run-down farm in Locust Ridge, TN. At 12 she was appearing on Knoxville television; at 13 she was recording on a small label and appearing on the Grand Ole Opry. Her 1967 hit "Dumb Blonde" (and she's not) caught Porter Wagoner's ear, and he hired Parton to appear on his television show, where their duet numbers became famous. By the time her "Joshua" reached No. 1 in 1970, Parton's fame had overshadowed the boss', and she had struck out on her own, though she still recorded duets with him. During the mid-'70s, she established herself as a country superstar, crossing over into the pop mainstream in the early '80s, when she smoothed out the rough edges in her music and began singing pop as well as country. In the early '80s, she also began appearing in movies, most notably the hit *9 to 5*. Though her savvy marketing, image manipulation—her big, dumb blonde stage persona is an *act*—extracurricular forays into film, and her flirtations with country-pop have occasionally overshadowed her music, at her core Dolly Parton is a country gal and a tremendously gifted singer-songwriter. Among her classics are "Coat of Many Colors," "Jolene," "Kentucky Gambler," "I Will Always Love You," "But You Known I Love You," and "Tennessee Homesick Blues"; they give a hint to why her contribution to bringing country music to a wide audience, not only in America but throughout the world, cannot be underestimated.

Throughout Dolly's childhood Parton's family struggled to survive. Often she was ridiculed for her poverty, yet often music soothed her worries. Though her farming father did not play, her half-Cherokee mother played guitar, and her grandfather, the Rev. Jake Owens, was a fiddler and songwriter. (His "Singing His Praise" was recorded by Kitty Wells.) When Dolly was seven, her uncle, Bill Owens, gave her a guitar; within three years she was a regular on WIVK Knoxville's "The Cas Walker Farm and Home Hour." Over the next two years, her career built steadily, and in 1959 she made her debut on the Grand Ole Opry; the next year, she recorded her first single, "Puppy Love," for Goldband.

When she was 14 years old, Parton signed to Mercury Records, but her 1962 debut for the label, "It's Sure Gonna Hurt," was a bomb, and the label immediately dropped her. Over the next five years, she shopped for a new contract and did indeed record a number of songs, which were later reissued through budget-line records. She continued to attend high school, playing snare drum in the marching band. After she graduated, she moved to Nashville, where she stayed with Bill Owens. Both songwriters pitched songs across Nashville to no success, and Parton began singing on demos. Early in 1965 both Parton and Owens finally found work when Fred Foster signed him to his publishing house, Combine Music; Foster subsequently signed her to Monument Records. Parton's first records for Monument were marketed to pop audiences, and her second record, "Happy, Happy Birthday Baby," nearly made the charts. In 1966, Bill Phillips took two of Parton's and Owens' songs—"Put It Off Until Tomorrow" and "The Company You Keep"—to the Top Ten, setting the stage for Parton's breakthrough single, "Dumb Blonde." Released early in 1967, the record climbed to No. 24, followed shortly afterward by the No. 17 "Something Fishy."

The two hit Monument singles attracted the attention of country star Porter Wagoner, who was looking for a new female singer for his syndicated television show. Parton accepted the offer and began appearing on the show on September 5, 1967. Initially, his audience rejected Parton and chanted for Norma Jean, the singer she replaced; but with Wagoner's assistance, she was accepted. Wagoner convinced his label, RCA, to sign Parton. Since female performers were not particularly popular in the late '60s, the label decided to protect their investment by releasing her first single as a duet with Wagoner. The duo's first single, "The Last Thing on My Mind," reached the country Top Ten early in 1968, launching a six-year streak of virtually uninterrupted Top Ten singles. Parton's first solo single, "Just Because I'm a Woman," was released in the summer of 1968 and it was a moderate hit, reaching No. 17. For the remainder of the decade, none of her solo efforts—even "In the Good Old Days (When Times Were Bad)," which would later become a standard—were as successful as her duets. The duo was named Vocal Group of the Year in 1968 by the Country Music

Association, but Parton's solo records were continually ignored. Wagoner and Dolly were both frustrated by her lack of solo success, because he had a significant financial stake in her future—as of 1969, he was her co-producer and owned nearly half of the publishing company, Owepar.

By 1970 both Parton and Wagoner had grown frustrated by her lack of solo success, and he had her sing Jimmie Rodgers' "Mule Skinner Blues (Blue Yodel No. 8)," a gimmick that worked. The record shot to No. 3 on the charts, followed closely by her first No. 1 single, "Joshua." For the next two years she had a number of solo hits—including her signature song "Coat of Many Colors" (No. 4, 1971)—in addition to her duets. Though she had successful singles, none of them was a blockbuster until "Jolene" reached No. 1 in early 1974. Parton stopped travelling with Wagoner after its release, but she continued to appear on television and sing duets with him until 1976.

Once she left Wagoner, Parton's records became more eclectic and diverse, ranging from the ballad "I Will Always Love You" (No. 1, 1974) and the racy "The Bargain Store" (No. 1, 1975) to the crossover pop of "Here You Come Again" (No. 1, 1977) and the disco experiments of "Baby I'm Burning" (No. 25 pop, 1978). From 1974 to 1980 she consistently charted in the country Top Ten, with no less than eight singles reaching No. 1. Parton had her own syndicated television show, "Dolly," in 1976, and by the next year she had gained the right to produce her own albums, which immediately resulted in diverse efforts like 1977's *New Harvest, First Gathering*. In addition to having her own hits during the late '70s, many artists, from Rose Maddox and Kitty Wells to Olivia Newton-John, Emmylou Harris, and Linda Ronstadt, covered her songs; her siblings Randy and Stella received recording contracts of their own.

Though she was quite popular, Dolly Parton became a genuine superstar in 1977, when the Barry Mann/Cynthia Weill song "Here You Come Again" became a huge crossover hit, reaching No. 3 on the pop charts, spending five weeks at the top of the country charts, and going gold. Its accompanying album went platinum and the followup, *Heartbreaker*, went gold. Soon she was on the cover of country and mainstream publications alike. With the new financial windfall, a lawsuit against Porter Wagoner—who had received a significant portion of her royalties—ensued. When it was settled, she regained her copyrights, while Wagoner was given a nominal fee and the studio the duo shared. In the wake of the lawsuit, a delayed duet album, *Making Plans*, appeared in 1980; its title track hit No. 2 on the country charts.

Parton's commercial success continued to grow during 1980, as she had three No. 1 hits in a row: the Donna Summer-written "Starting Over Again," "Old Flames Can't Hold a Candle to You," and "9 to 5." The latter was the theme song to Parton's acting debut, *9 to 5*. Also starring Jane Fonda and Lily Tomlin, the movie became a huge success, establishing Parton as a movie star. The song became her first No. 1 pop single, as well. *9 to 5* gave Parton's career momentum that lasted throughout the early '80s. She began appearing in more films, including the Burt Reynolds musical *The Best Little Whorehouse in Texas* (1982) and the Sylvester Stallone comedy *Rhinestone* (1984). Parton's singles continued to appear consistently in the country Top Ten: between 1981 and 1985, she had 12 Top Ten hits and half of those were No. 1 singles. Parton continued to make inroads on the pop charts, as well, with a re-recorded version of "I Will Always Love You" from *The Best Little Whorehouse in Texas* scraping the Top 50 and her Kenny Rogers duet "Islands in the Stream" (which was written by the Bee Gees and produced by Barry Gibb) spending two weeks at No. 1.

However, by 1985 many old-time fans had felt that Dolly was spending too much time courting the mainstream. Most of her albums were dominated by the adult-contemporary pop of songs like "Islands in the Stream," and it had been years since she had sung straightforward country. She also continued to explore new business and entertainment ventures, such as her Dollywood theme park, which opened in 1985. Despite these misgivings, she had continued to chart well until 1986, when none of her singles reached the Top Ten. RCA Records didn't renew her contract that year, and she signed with Columbia in 1987. Before she released

Dolly Parton

her Columbia debut, Parton joined forces with Linda Ronstadt and Emmylou Harris to record the rootsy *Trio* album. *Trio* became a huge hit, earning both critical and popular acclaim, selling over a million copies, and peaking at No. 6 on the pop charts; it also spawned three Top Ten country singles: "To Know Him Is to Love Him," "Telling Me Lies," and "Those Memories of You." After the success of the album, she had a weekly variety television show, "Dolly," on ABC which lasted only one season. *Trio* also provided a perfect launching pad for her first Columbia album, 1989's *White Limozeen*, which produced two No. 1 hits in "Why'd You Come in Here Lookin' like That" and "Yellow Roses."

Though it looked as if Dolly Parton's career had been revived, it was actually just a brief revival before contemporary country came along in the early '90s and pushed all veteran artists out of the charts. Parton had a No. 1 duet with Ricky Van Shelton, "Rockin' Years," in 1991, but after that single, she slowly crept out of the Top Ten and later the Top 40. Parton was one of the most outspoken critics of radio's treatment of older stars. While her sales had declined, she didn't disappear. Despite her lack of sales, Parton remained an iconic figure in country music, appearing in films (the 1991 TV-movie *Wild Texas Wind*, 1992's *Straight Talk*), selling out concerts, and releasing a series of acclaimed albums—including 1993's *Honky Tonk Angels*, a collaboration with Tammy Wynette and Loretta Lynn—that all sold respectably. Furthermore, "I Will Always Love You" was covered in 1992 by Whitney Houston, who took it to No. 1 on the pop charts; the single spent 14 weeks at No. 1, becoming the biggest pop hit of the rock 'n' roll era (it was unseated four years later by Mariah Carey and Boyz II Men's "One Sweet Day"). In 1994 she published her autobiography *My Life and Other Unfinished Business*. *Treasures*, her 1996 album, was a praised collection of unusual covers, ranging from Merle Haggard to Neil Young. —*David Vinopal*

Just Because I'm a Woman / 1968 / RCA ✦✦✦✦
It's a measure of how impressed producer Bob Ferguson must have been with Parton that he (and possibly Porter Wagoner in the background) made no attempt to crowd her with strings or choruses on her first RCA album. In fact, it's almost frightening to hear how fully realized her talent was in 1968. —*Dan Cooper*

My Tennessee Mountain Home / 1975 / RCA ✦✦✦
My Tennessee Mountain Home is one of the rootsiest records of Dolly Parton's career. With its affectionate homages and salutes to her childhood in Tennessee, the record is a direct and moving slice of mountain music that isn't dressed up in cosmpolitan pro-

duction. Parton wrote every song on the record, creating a loose, musical autobiography with 11 songs. Though the sound of the record isn't particularly rowdy, it is heartfelt and rootsy, and Parton's songs—"Old Black Kettle," "The Letter," "The Good Old Days When Times Were Bad," and "The Better Part of Life"—are among her best and most affecting. — *Stephen Thomas Erlewine*

The Best of Dolly Parton / 1975 / RCA ♦♦♦♦
She projects an admirable child-like sense of hope and positivism, which is matched to some degree by her thin, girlish vocal quality. It translates well in her pre-Hollywood, unencumbered productions, notably "Coat of Many Colors," "Love Is like a Butterfly," and "The Bargain Store." — *Tom Roland*

9 to 5 and Odd Jobs / 1980 / RCA ♦♦♦♦
Dolly Parton has never been an albums artist, and RCA has always been adept at shoving poorly organized products onto the market (look how they've treated Elvis Presley). Hence, though she is an important country figure, most of Parton's albums are hard to recommend. This one contains the title hit, plus a few other Parton originals and a version of Woody Guthrie's "Deportee" among its eight tracks. But that's enough to put it a notch above most of Parton's RCA catalog. — *William Ruhlmann*

Greatest Hits / 1982 / RCA ♦♦♦♦
This is a good sampling of Parton's work in the first few years that she deliberately chased a crossover career in Hollywood. The country-pop stuff might offend purists, but it still gets the toe tappin'. "Hard Candy Christmas" and her updated version of "I Will Always Love You" (both from *The Best Little Whorehouse in Texas*) show her growth as an interpreter. — *Tom Roland*

The Great Pretender / 1984 / RCA ♦♦
The Great Pretender includes Parton's hit remake of the Drifters' "Save the Last Dance for Me," along with a rendition of Petula Clark's "Downtown." — *Jason Ankeny*

Collector's Series / 1985 / RCA ♦♦♦
This is a well-programmed selection of Parton's RCA hits, among them "Jolene," "Coat of Many Colors," and "Me and Little Andy." — *William Ruhlmann*

Real Love / 1985 / RCA ♦♦♦
A lot of critics would push this one aside, perhaps with good reason since she turned over much of the creative control on the project to David Malloy. But Malloy set out to highlight the bright, bubbly facet of her personality, and he succeeded. — *Tom Roland*

The World of Dolly Parton, Vol. 1 / 1988 / Monument ♦♦♦♦
This captures young Parton on Monument Records circa 1967, just before she hooked up with Porter. — *Dan Cooper*

The World of Dolly Parton, Vol. 2 / 1988 / Monument ♦♦♦♦
World of Dolly Parton, Vol. 2 contains the remaining 12 songs from Parton's days at Monument Records, including "Daddy Won't Be Home Anymore," "This Boy Has Been Hurt," and "I'm Not Worth the Tears." Though they didn't storm the charts like her RCA material, Parton's Monument recordings are among her rootsiest and hardest country recordings, and they should be heard by any of her fans. — *Thom Owens*

White Limozeen / 1989 / Columbia ♦♦♦♦
Parton moved to Columbia in the late '80s and started paying more attention to her recordings, the best of which is this album. It's produced by Ricky Skaggs, who brought in such fast-picking cronies as Bela Fleck and Jerry Douglas and used more of Parton's own songs than usual. The result is an unusual consistency and a musical revitalization for the singer. — *William Ruhlmann*

Eagle When She Flies / 1991 / Columbia ♦♦♦
She confirms that she's fully returned to the country fold, and is rewarded with her first million-selling album that wasn't a great-est-hits package. The title song is a powerful female anthem. —*Michael McCall*

Slow Dancing with the Moon / 1993 / Columbia ♦♦♦
Slow Dancing with the Moon features a who's who of country music circa 1993; guests Tanya Tucker, Vince Gill, Mary-Chapin Carpenter, Chet Atkins, Kathy Mattea, and Billy Ray Cyrus are just a handful of the singers and players joining Parton on this outing. Ironically, it's the simpler, sparer songs that work best here;

stripped of all the gloss and star power that sink the guest-dominated tracks, they allow Parton's emotional vocals to really shine through. —*Jason Ankeny*

★ **The RCA Years 1967-1986** / May 25, 1993 / RCA ♦♦♦♦♦
The long-overdue box set turns out to be a cursory two-CD set that cheats on her better early years in favor of latter-day hits. Still, it's the best retrospective available, and it emphasizes her stature as a truly significant songwriter, which is easy to forget in the shadow of her "Daisy Mae in Hollywood" image. —*Michael McCall*

Something Special / 1995 / Columbia ♦♦♦
Something Special is something of a mixed bag from Dolly Parton, featuring a selection of new songs and re-recorded old material. While the newer songs are fine, they pale in comparison with classics like "Jolene" and "I Will Always Love You," recorded as a duet with Vince Gill. If the new songs had been included on an album that featured only new material, they would have formed a strong record; but they take a back seat to Parton's older songs, which are more inspired and better-written. Nevertheless, the album provides several fine moments, even though it doesn't rank among her best works. —*Stephen Thomas Erlewine*

The Essential Dolly Parton / Mar. 28, 1995 / RCA ♦♦♦♦
The Essential Dolly Parton has a good cross-section of her early hits and her latter-day countrypolitan numbers. It isn't as thorough as the double-disc RCA years, but it provides a good introduction to the most popular portion of her career. —*Thom Owens*

Treasures / Sep. 24, 1996 / RCA ♦♦♦
Treasures is an ambitious album from Dolly Parton, an attempt to pay tribute to some of the finest singer-songwriters of the '60s and '70s. Not only does she honor country songwriters like Merle Haggard and Kris Kristofferson, she also tackles Neil Young and Cat Stevens. For her own versions, she teams with a number of guest artists such as Alison Krauss, John Sebastian, Los Lobos' David Hidalgo, Blues Traveler's John Popper, Ladysmith Black Mambazo, and Raul Malo from the Mavericks. There's too much starpower on board to make *Treasures* completely successful. Simply by being present, the extra musicians draw attention to themselves, not to the songs. As a consequence, *Treasures* is a jumble, veering from the excellent (her duet with Alison Krauss on "Just When I Need You Most" is terrific) to the merely middling. Unfortunately, that just makes it one of Dolly's many failed experiments of the '80s and '90s. —*Thom Owens*

Johnny Paycheck (Don Eugene Lytle)

b. May 31, 1938, Greenfield, OH
Bass, Guitar, Guitar (Steel), Vocals / Traditional Country, Country-Rock, Outlaw Country

The first that many people ever heard of Johnny Paycheck was in 1977, when his "Take This Job and Shove It" inspired one-man wildcat strikes all over America. The next time was in 1985, when he was arrested for shooting a man at a bar in Hillsboro, OH. That Paycheck is remembered for a novelty song and a violent crime (for which he spent two years in prison) is a shame, for he is one of the mightiest honky tonkers of his time. Born and raised in Greenfield, OH, Paycheck was performing in talent contests by the age of nine and riding the rails as a drifter by the time he turned 15. After a Navy stint landed him in the brig for two years, he arrived in Nashville, where he performed in the bands of Porter Wagoner, Faron Young, Ray Price, and George Jones. He recorded several singles under the name Donny Young. In 1965 he cut his first sides as Johnny Paycheck for the Hilltop label. A year later, he and gadfly producer Aubrey Mayhew started the Little Darlin' label, for which Paycheck recorded his greatest work. Marked by Lloyd Green's knockout steel guitar and Paycheck's broad, resonant vocals (not to mention his rounder's sense of humor), his Little Darlin' records of the 1960s have since become cult favorites. After splitting with Mayhew (and after running his life into the gutter), Paycheck made a celebrated comeback on Epic in the 1970s. "Take This Job and Shove It" was the most famous result, though ballads like "She's All I Got" and "Someone to Give My Love To" are far more indicative of his stylistic range.

Born Donald Lytle, Paycheck began playing guitar when he was six, and within three years, he was performing talent contests across the state. When he was 15, he ran away from home, hitch-hiking and hoboing his away across the country, singing in honky tonks and clubs along the way. By his late teens, he had joined the Navy; but while he was serving, he assaulted a superior officer and was convicted of court martial. As a result, he spent two years in the brig. Upon his release, he moved to Nashville, where he made the acquaintence of Buddy Killen at Decca Records, who offered him a contract. At Decca, Paycheck released two rockabilly singles under the name Donny Young; neither was a hit. Shortly afterward he moved to Mercury, where he released two country singles that were also failures. By that time, he had begun supporting other musicians, playing bass and occasionally steel guitar with Porter Wagoner, Faron Young, and Ray Price. He frequently moved between employers because of his short-fused temper. Paycheck finally found his match in George Jones. He stayed with Jones for four years, fronting the Jones Boys between 1962 and 1966, and singing backup on Jones' hits "I'm a People," "The Race Is On," and "Love Bug."

Toward the end of his stint with Jones, Donald Lytle refashioned himself as Johnny Paycheck, taking his name from a Chicago heavyweight boxer. Late in 1965 he relaunched his solo career with the assistence of producer Aubrey Mayhew, who produced a pair of singles—"A-11" and "Heartbreak Tennessee"—for Hilltop Records. Though it charted only at No. 26, "A-11" caused a sensation within the country community, earning several Grammy nominations as well as reviews that compared Paycheck to his mentor, George Jones. In 1966 he and Mayhew formed Little Darlin' Records, primarily to promote Paycheck, but also recording Jeannie C. Riley, Bobby Helms, and Lloyd Green. That summer "The Lovin' Machine" became Paycheck's first Top Ten hit. Also that year he wrote Tammy Wynette's first hit, "Apartment No. 9," with Bobby Austin and Fuzzy Owen; Paycheck also wrote Ray Price's No. 3 hit "Touch My Heart."

All of Paycheck's recordings for Little Darlin' Records rank among his grittiest, hardest country, but they weren't necessarily big hits. Between 1967 and 1969, Paycheck had eight more hit singles, with each record charting at a lower position than its predecessor—"Motel Time Again" reached No. 13 in early 1967, while "If I'm Gonna Sink" climbed to No. 73 in late 1968. Though "Wherever You Are" showed signs of a comeback in the summer of 1969, peaking at No. 31, the label went bankrupt shortly after its release, partially becuause of Paycheck's declining commercial performance and partially because of his heavy drinking and erratic behavior. Over the course of the next year he moved to California and sank deeply into substance abuse. Meanwhile, Billy Sherrill at Epic Records had been searching for Paycheck with the hopes of producing his records. The label finally tracked him down in 1971 and offered him a contract, provided that he clean himself up. Paycheck accepted the offer and, with Sherrill's assistence, kicked his addictions.

Like many of Sherrill's records of the early '70s, his Johnny Paycheck recordings were heavily produced and often layered with strings. Though this was a shift from the hardcore country that Paycheck made on Little Darlin', the new approach was a hit—his debut single for the label, "She's All I Got," became a No. 2 hit upon its fall 1971 release. It was quickly followed by another Top Ten hit, "Someone to Give My Love To," and Paycheck was finally becoming a star. During the next four years, he had 12 additional hit singles—including 1973's Top Ten singles "Something About You I Love" and "Mr. Lovemaker," and 1974's "For a Minute There"—that the more accessible, pop-oriented Sherrill crafted for him, but Paycheck's wild ways hadn't changed all that much. In 1972 he was convicted of check forgery, and in 1976 he was saddled with a paternity suit, tax problems, and bankruptcy. Accordingly, he shifted his musical style in the mid-'70s to put him in step with the renegade outlaw country movement.

Johnny Paycheck's first outlaw album, 1976's *11 Months and 29 Days* (which happened to be the length of his suspended sentence for passing a bad check), featured a photo of him in a jail cell on the cover, signalling his change of direction. Initially, his outlaw records weren't hits, but early in 1977 he returned to the Top Ten

with a pair of Top Ten singles, "Slide Off of Your Satin Sheets" and "I'm the Only Hell (Mama Ever Raised)." Later that year, he released his cover of David Allan Coe's "Take This Job and Shove It," which became his biggest hit, spending two weeks at No. 1; its B-side, "Colorado Kool-Aid," charted at No. 50. Soon Paycheck's records were becoming near-parodies of his lifestyle, as the title "Me and the I.R.S." and "D.O.A. (Drunk on Arrival) indicated. Nevertheless, he stayed at the top of the charts, with "Friend, Lover, Wife" and "Mabellene" both reaching No. 7 in late 1978 and early 1979.

Shortly after the twin success of those singles, his career began to crumble due to his excessive, violent behavior. In 1979 his former manager Glenn Ferguson began a prolonged and difficult legal battle. In 1981 a flight attendant for Frontier Airlines sued him for slander after he began a fight on a plane. The next year, he was arrested for alleged rape. The charges were later reduced and he was fined, but by that point, Epic had had enough and dropped him. Paycheck moved over to AMI, where he had a number of small hit singles between 1984 and 1985. Later in 1985 he had a barroom brawl with a stranger in Hillsboro, OH, that ended with Paycheck's shooting and injuring his opponent. The singer was arrested for aggravated assault and spent the next four years appealing the sentence, while he recorded for Mercury Records. None of his singles for the label reached the Top 40, and he was dropped in 1987. He spent 1988 at Desperado Records before signing with Damascus the next year, after his conversion to Christianity.

In 1989 Paycheck's appeals had expired, and he was sentenced to the Chillicothe Correctional Institute. He spent two years at the prison, even performing a concert with Merle Haggard during his stint, before being released on parole in January 1991. After his release, Paycheck kept a low profile, playing shows in Branson, MO, and recording for the small label Playback Records.—*Dan Cooper*

Johnny Paycheck at Carnegie Hall / 1966 / Little Darlin' ✦✦✦✦
Despite the title and the photo of Paycheck in black-tie garb, his debut album is actually a Nashville studio product. But what a hopped-up product it is, making most mid-'60s honky tonk sound like Jim Nabors with steel guitar. —*Dan Cooper*

The Lovin' Machine / 1966 / Little Darlin' ✦✦✦✦
Recorded during his mid-'60s peak, *Lovin' Machine* features a few of Johnny Paycheck's most famous songs, as well as some wonderful obscure gems, including no less than three murder ballads. —*Thom Owens*

Jukebox Charlie / 1967 / Little Darlin' ✦✦✦✦
One of the all-time great honky tonk singers before his bad habits got the better of him, he included two of the greatest country songs ever—"Apartment No. 9" and "Touch My Heart," both written by Paycheck. —*George Bedard*

Again / 1970 / Certron ✦✦✦
Post-Little Darlin', but still Mayhew-produced, he keeps right on kicking. Included is "Living the Life of a Dog," a hilarious romp that probably had multiple meanings for Paycheck. —*Dan Cooper*

Take This Job and Shove It / 1978 / Epic ✦✦✦
His big '70s novelty hit and an uneven selection of tunes are included, but it's worth having for "Colorado Kool-Aid"—a sort of Red Sovine-from-hell recitation on the subject of barroom etiquette. —*George Bedard*

Bars, Booze and Blondes / 1979 / Little Darlin' ✦✦✦
More repackaged '60s classics are here, such as the memorable "I Drop More than I Drink" and "The Pint of No Return." —*Michael McCall*

Mr. Hag Told My Story / 1981 / Epic ✦✦

Extra Special / 1982 / Accord ✦✦✦✦
A budget-line release, it features a handful of characteristically bizzare honky tonk songs recorded in the 1960s around the time he was recording for Little Darlin'. —*Michael McCall*

● **Biggest Hits** / 1983 / Epic ✦✦✦✦
Heavy on the late-'70s outlaw sound, this is where to find the original "Take This Job and Shove It" on CD. —*Dan Cooper*

● **The Real Mr. Heartache** / 1996 / Country Music Foundation ✦✦✦✦

For the casual country fan who knows Johnny Paycheck only from his late '70s outlaw period ("Take This Job and Shove It," a hit song so huge that its title was made into a major film), these 24 sides from the mid-'60s will come as a major revelation. Paycheck has always come by his outlaw image honestly; and he had been knocking around Nashville since 1958, cutting rockabilly country singles under the name Donny Young, when he came to the attention of producer-record executive Aubrey Mayhew in 1962. Forming a partnership, they produced a spate of hard country singles for Hilltop before starting up their own label, Little Darlin'. Figuring the easiest way to get noticed was to be as wild as possible, they uncorked a rash of singles (and a couple of albums) that pushed the darkest side of honky tonk lyrics to their limits, while simultaneously widening the limits of 45-rpm reproduction with stinging, high-end mixes perfect for AM country radio stations and truck-stop jukeboxes. These weren't merely honky tonk records bucking the tide of the '60s Nashville Sound; this was country music with an unrepentant redneck attitude. This is reflected in many of the titles, from "If I'm Gonna Sink (I Might as Well Go to the Bottom)," to "He's in a Hurry (To Get Home to My Wife)," to the absolutely scary "(Pardon Me) I've Got Someone to Kill," the mood getting blacker and blacker with each keening wail of Lloyd Green's steel guitar. Paycheck may have had bigger (much bigger) hits than the 24 tracks collected here, but he never made any greater music than this. —*Cub Koda*

Leon Payne

b. Jun. 15, 1917, Alba, TX, **d.** Sep. 11, 1969
Vocals / Traditional Country, Honky Tonk, Nashville Sound/ Countrypolitan
A popular singer and multi-instrumentalist of the postwar era, Leon Payne achieved his lasting fame as a songwriter whose most successful works—among them "Lost Highway" and "I Love You Because"—remain among the country music canon's most enduring compositions. Payne was born blind on June 15, 1917, in Alba, TX, and until the age of 18 he attended the Texas School for the Blind in Austin. There, he was encouraged by teachers to begin learning music as a method of supporting himself, and he became adept on guitar, piano, organ, drums, and trombone. In the mid-1930s he began performing with a number of area groups, and he began playing on radio in 1935.

Payne joined Bob Wills' Texas Playboys in 1938, and he remained affiliated with the group to some degree for the majority of his career. At about the same time, he began writing the first of the several thousand songs he would compose over the course of his lifetime. In 1939 he cut his first solo recordings, including "You Don't Love Me but I'll Always Care" and "Down Where the Violets Grow," which evidenced his smooth, subtle vocal technique. After spending a large part of the next decade drifting through Texas performing under the moniker "The Texas Blind Hitchhiker," he hooked up with Jack Rhodes and the Rhythm Boys in 1948. He also played frequently with Wills.

In 1949 Payne formed his own band, the Lone Star Buddies, which guested on programs like the Grand Ole Opry, "The Lousiana Hayride," and "The Big D Jamboree." Two of his songs reached the charts in cover versions: George Morgan scored a big hit with "Cry-Baby Heart," and more significantly, Hank Williams cut "Lost Highway," one of his most popular efforts. Payne's own recording of his "I Love You Because," penned for his wife Myrtle, became his biggest hit in 1950; in the same year, both Ernest Tubb and Clyde Moody cut their own versions of the song. Williams had another hit with Payne's "They'll Never Take Her Love from Me." As the decade wore on, his songs grew even more popular among his contemporaries; among the most successful were Hank Snow's 1953 "For Now and Always" and a pair of hits for Carl Smith, 1954's "More than Anything Else in the World" and 1956's "Doorstep to Heaven."

Payne continued to record through 1964; in 1963, he issued two LPs, *Leon Payne: A Living Legend of Country Music* and *Americana*, and at one point he even cut a rockabilly single, "That

Ain't It," under the alias "Rock Rogers." Still, he never repeated the success of "I Love You Because," which was resurrected by Johnny Cash in 1960 and was a huge 1963 pop hit for Al Martino. A year later it was also covered by Jim Reeves, who earned success with Payne's "Blue Side of Lonesome" in 1966 and "I Heard a Heart Break Last Night" in 1968. Also charting with renditions of "I Love You Because" were Carl Smith in 1969, Don Gibson in 1978, and Roger Whittaker in 1983; most importantly, it was one of the songs recorded by Elvis Presley during his legendary Sun Records sessions of 1954.

In 1965 Payne suffered a heart attack that forced him to curtail his touring; that same year, his "Things Have Gone to Pieces" was a hit for George Jones. In 1967 Gibson covered "Lost Highway," and Johnny Darrell was successful with "They'll Never Take Her Love from Me." On September 11, 1969, Payne died after another heart attack. —*Jason Ankeny*

● **Leon Payne** / 1963 / Starday ✦✦✦✦
Americana / 1963 / Starday ✦✦✦

Minnie Pearl (Sarah Ophelia Colley)

b. Oct. 25, 1912, Centerville, TN
Traditional Country, Country Humor
Among the Grand Ole Opry's most beloved longterm members, comedienne Minnie Pearl got her first Opry laughs in 1940. She was born Sarah Ophelia Colley in the middle Tennessee town of Centerville. The actress daughter of a sawmill owner, she was in real life by no means the cornpone hillbilly—price tag hanging from her straw hat—that she played on stage. Rather, it's a credit to her comedic skill that plain folks not only bought her manhungry, downhome sister act, but ultimately took her closer to their hearts than any other Opry star except Roy Acuff. After a prolonged period of poor health in the early '90s, Minnie passed away in 1996. —*Dan Cooper*

● **The Best of Minnie Pearl** / Nashville ✦✦✦✦
Featured are "Gossip from Grinder's Switch," "The Party Kissing Game," and others. —*AMG*

Herb Pedersen

b. Apr. 27, 1944, Berkeley, CA
Progressive Bluegrass, Traditional Bluegrass
A longtime staple of the bluegrass scene, singer and multi-instrumentalist Herb Pedersen was born April 27, 1944, in Berkeley, CA. The child of a policeman, he was introduced to country music at numerous Bay Area folk festivals, finding kindred spirits in other aspiring musicians like Jerry Garcia (who went on to form the Grateful Dead) and David Nelson (later of New Riders of the Purple Sage). In his mid-teens Pedersen formed his first bluegrass band, the Pine Valley Boys, with a young mandolinist named Chris Hillman.

In 1961 Pedersen moved to Nashville, where within a few months he was performing on "Carl Tipton's Bluegrass TV Show." After a 1963 stint with David Grisman's Smokey Valley Boys, he joined the veteran bluegrass performers Vern and Ray as a singer and five-string banjo player. His work with the duo brought him to the attention of Lester Flatt, who in 1967 tapped Pedersen to fill in for Earl Scruggs during his recovery from a hip operation. A year later, he replaced Doug Dillard in the Dillards for 1968's *Wheatstraw Suite* and 1970's *Copperfields*.

After leaving the Dillards, Pedersen remained in Los Angeles, where he became a highly regarded session player, working with the likes of Gram Parsons, Emmylou Harris, Linda Ronstadt, Kris Kristofferson, and John Prine. After spending the first half of the decade in the studio, in 1975 Pedersen joined Jackson Browne's tour, and the next year released his first solo LP, *Southwest*. After 1976's *Sandman*, he joined John Denver's band from 1977 to 1980, and he continued his extensive session and production work well into the next decade before cutting a third solo effort, *Lonesome Feeling*, in 1984. He also ventured into scoring television programs, composing the music for series including "The Rockford Files," "Kojak," "The Dukes of Hazzard," and "The A-Team."

Throughout the years, Pedersen had occasionally reunited with his old friend Chris Hillman, who had made his mark as a member of the Byrds and the Flying Burrito Brothers. In 1986 the two musicians again joined forces to form the Desert Rose Band, a highly successful country-rock act that scored a series of major hits. A year after the group disbanded in 1993, Pedersen founded the bluegrass outfit the Laurel Canyon Ramblers, which released the LP *Rambler's Blues* in 1995. The group's second effort, *Blue Rambler No. 2,* followed in 1996, as did *Bakersfield Bound,* another reunion between Pedersen and Hillman. —*Jason Ankeny*

Hank Penny

b. Aug. 18, 1918, Birmingham, AL, **d.** Apr. 17, 1992, California

Vocals / Traditional Country, Western Swing

While he never achieved the kind of success enjoyed by fellow bandleaders Bob Wills or Spade Cooley, during the late '40s and early '50s, Hank Penny ranked as one of the foremost practitioners of the Western swing sound. He was born Herbert Clayton Penny on August 18, 1918, in Birmingham, AL. His father was a disabled coal miner who inspired young Hank with his skills as a guitarist, poet, and magician before his death in 1928. By the age of 15, Penny was performing professionally on local radio; in 1936, he moved to New Orleans, where he first fell under the sway of Western swing pioneers like Wills and Milton Brown. A friendship with steel virtuoso Noel Boggs to furthered his enthusiasm for the swing form.

After a few years with New Orleans' WWL as a solo performer, Penny returned to Birmingham, where he formed the Radio Cowboys, which featured guitarist Julian Akins, steel guitarist Sammy Forsmark, tenor banjo player Louis Damont, bassist Carl Stewart, and vocalist, guitarist, and fiddler Sheldon Bennett. In 1938 the group (minus Akins) first entered the studio under the guidance of legendary producer Art Satherly to record numbers like "When I Take My Sugar to Tea" and Penny's own "Flamin' Mamie." After the Radio Cowboys joined the cast of the Atlanta-based program "Crossroad Follies," Forsmark left the group, to be replaced by Noel Boggs; at the same time, they welcomed a new fiddle player, Boudleaux Bryant.

After turning down offers to take over vocal chores for both Pee Wee King's Golden West Cowboys and the Light Crust Doughboys, Penny moved the group to Nashville in 1939, where they again recorded with Satherley. Shortly after, Boggs left the group to join Jimmy Wakely, and was replaced by Eddie Duncan. After recording songs like "Tobacco State Swing" and "Peach Tree Shuffle" in Chicago in mid-1940, the band was forced to dissolve after most of its members were drafted. Penny remained in Chicago working as a disc jockey before assembling a new group for a 1941 session in North Carolina, which generated the songs "Why Did I Cry" and "Lonesome Train Blues."

After signing with the Cincinnati station WLW's programs "Boone Country Jamboree" and "The Midwestern Hayride," Penny formed a new band called the Plantation Boys, which included Radio Cowboy Carl Stewart on fiddle along with guitarist/bassist Louis Innis, fiddler Zed Tennis, and lead guitarist Roy Langham. In addition to work with the Delmore Brothers, Merle Travis, Bradley Kincaid, and Grandpa Jones, they backed WLW's pop singer Doris Day. After the departure of Langham, in 1944 the band toured with the USO before Penny traveled to California at the urging of Merle Travis. There he became enamored with the music of Spade Cooley, and met Cooley's onetime manager, Foreman Phillips, who offered Penny work as a bandleader. After a brief return to Cincinnati that led to a recording date, Penny returned to California to assemble another band, which included Noel Boggs; however, when Phillips began telling Penny how to play, the bandleader balked and the group disbanded.

Soon he was fronting an all-girl band at a Los Angeles club, but he was approached by Bobbie Bennett, Cooley's then-manager, to lead one of several groups formed to play at the bookings Cooley and his orchestra were too busy to fill. While Tex Ritter led one band and Travis led another, Penny fronted the Painted Post Rangers, which scored a pair of significant chart hits with "Steel Guitar Stomp" and "Get Yourself a Redhead." When the Painted

Minnie Pearl

Post Club went bankrupt, he moved to lead the large house band at the Riverside Rancho. In 1946 he joined Slim Duncan's ABC network show "Roundup Time" as a comedian. After moving to Cincinnati and then to Arlington, VA, he returned to California and took a deejay position. He also formed yet another new band, the Penny Serenaders, which included guitarist Speedy West, accordion player Bud Sievert, fiddler Billy Hill, and bassist Hank Caldwell. With club owner Amand Gautier, Penny also opened his own dance hall, which featured Bob Wills on its opening night.

In June 1948 Penny joined Cooley's massively popular television program, where he performed as a comedian best known for his backwoods character "That Plain Ol' Country Boy." A year later he recorded a number of songs, among them "Hillbilly Bebop," the first known bop effort cut by a country act, and the 1950 hit "Bloodshot Eyes." After he and Gautier opened another club, the legendary Palomino, he re-formed the Penny Serenaders, which included singer Mary Morgan, later known as Jaye P. Morgan. The group issued "Remington Ride" and "Wham Bam! Thank You, Ma'am" before calling it quits and then re-forming again, this time with guitarist Billy Strange and steel guitar whiz Joaquin Murphy. In 1952 Penny left Cooley to join Dude Martin's program; after first stealing Martin's wife, singer Sue Thompson, he began hosting his own series, "The Hank Penny Show," which was cancelled after only seven weeks.

By 1954 Penny had moved to Las Vegas, where he began a seven-year run as a performer at the Golden Nugget Casino, fronting a band that included the likes of Roy Clark. He also continued to record, even cutting a jazz record in 1961. After divorcing Thompson, he also recorded a comedy album before moving to Carson City, NV, in 1970 to begin performing with his protege, Thom Bresh, the son of Merle Travis. After leaving his band to Bresh, Penny moved to Nashville, where he was in the running for a slot hosting "Hee Haw" but lost out, ironically enough, to Roy Clark. After a tenure on radio in Wichita, KS, and his fifth wife Shari returned to California in the mid-1970s, and for the most part he retired. Hank Penny died of a heart attack on April 17, 1992. —*Jason Ankeny*

Hank Penny Sings / 195 / Audio Lab ✦✦✦✦

Tobacco State Swing / 1981 / Rambler ✦✦✦✦

On this LP, Hank Penny's early career as a Western swing bandleader with his Alabama-based Radio Cowboys is explored. The 14 selections (which include four instrumentals) feature Penny, fiddlers Sheldon Bennett and Boudleaux Bryant, banjoist Louis

Dumont, and steel guitarists Noel Boggs and Eddie Duncan. An enjoyable and often hard-driving set. —*Scott Yanow*

● **Rompin', Stompin'** / 1983 / Bear Family ✦✦✦✦

Perfect Stranger

Contemporary Country, Neo-Traditionalist Country
The Texan group Perfect Stranger became an indie-level sensation in the mid-'90s with their rowdy, rocking, neo-traditionalist honky tonk. Eventually the band garnered a strong following, which translated into a major label contract and national success in 1995.

Featuring Andy Ginn (drums), Shayne Morrison (bass), Steve Murray (lead vocals), and Richard Raines (lead guitar), Perfect Stranger formed in Carthage, TX, in the early '90s. During the first few years of their existence, Perfect Stranger developed a strong regional fan base through constant touring.

After completing the video for "Ridin' the Rodeo," the band was told that the song would be added to the Country Music Television playlist. Shortly afterward, "Ridin' the Rodeo" became the No. 1 independent country song in America. "You Have the Right to Remain Silent," the group's second single, hit the airwaves in the spring of 1995. Shortly afterward, the band signed a deal with Curb Records. Curb reissued "You Have the Right to Remain Silent," which eventually worked its way to No. 4. —*Stephen Thomas Erlewine*

You Have the Right to Remain Silent / Jun. 13, 1995 / Curb ✦✦✦

Carl Perkins (Carl Lee Perkins)

b. Apr. 9, 1932, Tiptonville, TN
Guitar, Vocals / Rock 'n' Roll, Traditional Country, Rockabilly
While some ill-informed revisionist writers of rock history would like to dismiss Carl Perkins as a rockabilly artist who became a one-hit wonder at the dawn of rock 'n' roll, a deeper look at his music and career reveals much more. His songwriting portfolio includes"Daddy Sang Bass" for Johnny Cash, "I Was So Wrong" for Patsy Cline, and "Let Me Tell You About Love" for the Judds, big hits and classics all. The quintessential rockabilly artist has played a big part in the development of every generation of rocker from the Beatles' George Harrison to the Stray Cats' Brian Setzer to a myriad of others in the country field. His guitar style is the other twin peak—along with that of Elvis' lead man Scotty Moore—of rockabilly's instrumental center, so pervasive that modern-day players automatically gravitate toward it when called upon to deliver the style, not even realizing that they're playing Carl Perkins licks, sometimes note for note. As a singer, his interpretation of country ballads is every bit as fine as that of better known rockers. And within the framework of the best of his music is a strong sense of family and roots.

He was born to sharecroppers Buck and Louise Perkins (misspelled on his birth certificate as "Perkings") and was soon out in the fields picking cotton and living in a country shack with his parents, older brother Jay and younger brother Clayton. When Carl was given a second-hand guitar, he went to a local sharecropper for lessons, learning first-hand the boogie rhythm on which he would later build a career. By his teens, Carl was playing electric guitar and had recruited his brothers Jay (rhythm guitar) and Clayton (string bass) for his first band. The Perkins Brothers Band, featuring both Carl and Jay on lead vocals, quickly established itself as the hottest band in the Jackson, TN, honky tonk circuit. It was here that Carl started composing his first songs. Watching the dance floor for a reaction, Perkins kept reshaping these loosely structured songs until he had a completed composition, which would then be put to paper. Carl was already sending demos to New York record companies, who kept rejecting him, sometimes explaining that this strange new hybrid of country with a Black rhythm fit no current commercial trend. But once Perkins heard Elvis on the radio, he not only knew what to call it but knew that there was a record company person who finally understood it and was willing to gamble in promoting it. The man was Sam Phillips; the record company was Sun Records. That's where Perkins headed in 1954 for an audition.

At his first Sun audition, the structure of the Perkins Brothers Band changed forever. Phillips didn't show the least bit of interest in Jay's Ernest Tubb-styled vocals, but he flipped over Carl's singing and guitar playing. Four months later he had issued the first Carl Perkins record, "Movie Magg" and "Turn Around," both sides written by the artist. By his second session, he had added W.S. Holland—a friend of Clayton's—to the band playing drums, relatively new to country music at the time. Phillips was still channeling Perkins in a strictly hillbilly vein, feeling that two artists doing the same type of music (in this case, Elvis and rockabilly) would cancel each other out. But after Elvis' contract was sold to RCA Victor in December, Perkins was encouraged to let his rocking soul come up for air. And rock he did, with a double-whammy blast that proved to be his ticket to the bigs. The chance overhearing of a conversation between two teenagers at a dance one night, coupled with a song idea suggestion from label mate Johnny Cash, led Perkins to approach Sam with a song he had written called "Blue Suede Shoes." After cutting two sides that Phillips planned to release as a single by the Perkins Brothers Band, Carl laid down three takes each of "Blue Suede Shoes" and another rocker, "Honey Don't." A month later, Sam decided to shelve the two country sides and go with the rockers as Carl's next single. Three months later, "Blue Suede Shoes," a tune that borrowed stylistically from pop, country, and R&B, was at the top of all charts, the first record to accomplish such a feat and Sun's first million seller.

Ready to cash in on a national basis, Carl and the boys headed up to New York for the first time to appear on the "Perry Como Show." While en route their car rammed the back of a poultry truck, putting Carl and his brother Jay in the hospital with a cracked skull and broken neck, respectively. While in traction, Perkins saw Presley performing his song on the "Dorsey Brothers Stage Show," his moment of fame and recognition snatched away from him. Carl shrugged and went back to the road and the Sun studios, to pick up where he left off.

The follow-ups to "Shoes" were, in many ways, superior to his initial hit, but each succeeding Sun single had diminishing sales; it wasn't until the British Invasion and the subsequent rockabilly revival of the early '70s that the general public got to truly savor classics like "Boppin' the Blues," "Matchbox," "Everybody's Trying to Be My Baby," "Your True Love," "Dixie Fried," "Put Your Cat Clothes On," and "All Mama's Children." While labelmates Johnny Cash and Jerry Lee Lewis (who played piano on "Matchbox") were scoring hit after hit, Carl was becoming disillusioned with his fate, fueled by his increasing dependence on alcohol and the death of brother Jay to cancer. He kept plugging along, and when Johnny Cash left Sun to go to Columbia in 1958, Perkins followed. The royalty rate was better, and Carl had no shortage of great songs to record, but Columbia's Nashville watch-the-clock production methods killed the spontaneity that was the charm of the Sun records. By the early '60s, after being dropped by Columbia and moving to Decca with little success, Carl was back playing the honky tonks and contemplating getting out of the business altogether.

A call from a booking agent in 1964 offering a tour of England changed all that. Temporarily swearing off the bottle, Perkins was greeted in Britain as a conquering hero, playing to sold-out audiences and being particularly lauded by a young beat group on the top of the charts named the Beatles. George Harrison had cut his musical teeth on Perkins' Sun recordings (as had most British guitarists) and the Fab Four ended up recording more tunes by him than any other artist except themselves. The British tour not only rejuvenated his outlook but made him realize that he had gone—through no maneuvering of his own—from has-been to legend in a country he had never played in before. Upon his return to the States, he hooked up with old friend and former labelmate Johnny Cash and was a regular fixture of his road show for the next ten years, bringing his battle with alcohol to an end. The '80s dawned with Perkins going on his own with a new band consisting of his sons. His election to the Rock and Roll Hall of Fame in the mid-'80s was no less than his due. While battles with throat cancer and other ailments have curtailed his work in the '90s, Carl Perkins continues to write, record, and perform, still grateful to be a part of the music business and assured of a place in the history books. —*Cub Koda*

Up Through the Years, 1954-1957 / 1986 / Bear Family ✦✦✦✦
An import collection of Perkins' groundbreaking Sun singles, *Up Through the Years* offers eight more tracks than Rhino's *Original Sun Greatest Hits;* both discs are definitive collections. —*Stephen Thomas Erlewine*

★ **Original Sun Greatest Hits** / 1986 / Rhino ✦✦✦✦✦
Original Sun Greatest Hits is exactly what it says it is—16 tracks of Carl Perkins' best sides for Sun, including all of the hits ("Blue Suede Shoes," "Boppin' the Blues," "Your True Love") and all of his most legendary songs ("Honey Don't," "Everybody's Trying to Be My Baby," "Movie Magg," "All Mama's Children," "Matchbox," "Dixie Fried," "Lend Me Your Comb," "Glad All Over"). It's the essential collection, providing everything you need to know about Carl Perkins and offering no filler. —*Stephen Thomas Erlewine*

Honky Tonk Gal / Apr. 1989 / Rounder ✦✦✦
Quirky, obscure, and offbeat, this is a much deeper look into Perkins' Sun period, with emphasis on hillbilly roots. —*Hank Davis*

The Jive After Five: Best of Carl Perkins (1958-1978) / 1990 / Rhino ✦✦✦✦
His later CBS work, much of it excellent. —*Hank Davis*

The Classic / Feb. 1990 / Bear Family ✦✦✦✦
Simply the most comprehensive collection imaginable, including all of his essential Sun tracks and alternate takes on five discs. All the 1958-1962 CBS sides are here, plus his 1963-1964 Decca sessions. It is indispensable for the serious fan and completist. —*Hank Davis*

Restless: The Columbia Recordings / May 12, 1992 / Columbia ✦✦✦
A strong collection of Perkins' singles for Columbia, concentrating on the late '50s and early '60s; some of his finest songs, including "Pink Pedal Pushers" and "Jive After Five," are included. —*Stephen Thomas Erlewine*

Country Boy's Dream: The Dollie Masters / 1994 / Bear Family ✦✦✦
Upon signing to Dollie records in 1966, Carl Perkins decided to concentrate on country music. The result was two minor country hits, "Country Boy's Dream" and "Shine, Shine, Shine," that marked the first time he had been on the charts since the late '50s. Though the Dollie recordings weren't blockbusters, they were solid, straightahead country and paved the way for Perkins' major label deal with Columbia, as well as a slot in Johnny Cash's band. *Country Boy's Dream: The Dollie Masters* contains all of Perkins' recordings for Dollie, including a handful of rare and unreleased tracks. Fans of Perkins' harder-edged, rocking sound won't find much to like on the compilation, but it demonstrates that he was equally adept at country. Nevertheless, even fans of Perkins' country records will find *Country Boy's Dream* a little tedious, since many of the songs on the album are unremarkable. —*Stephen Thomas Erlewine*

Go Cat Go / Oct. 15, 1996 / BMG ✦✦✦
This album is a curious mixture. It isn't really a Carl Perkins album as much as it is an all-star tribute with some of the big-name guests actually getting to interface with their hero. Both John Lennon and Jimi Hendrix appear via the tape vaults, contributing their versions of "Blue Suede Shoes" to the proceedings. And Perkins works with live guests Tom Petty, Johnny Cash, Bono, Ringo Starr, George Harrison, Paul McCartney, John Fogerty, and Paul Simon in fine fashion. But the bottom line is that the real star of the show is Perkins himself, just playing and singing in a most masterful and rockin' way. —*Cub Koda*

Gretchen Peters

Contemporary Country, Singer-Songwriter, Country-Folk
Known as a writer of intelligent and introspective songs in the country/folk/pop vein, Gretchen Peters achieved notoriety through country stars' covering her material. Among the artists to have hits with her songs were Trisha Yearwood, Pam Tillis,

George Strait, Martina McBride, and Patty Loveless. Peters was born in Westchester County, NY, and lived there until her parents divorced when she was eight. She moved with her mother to Boulder, CO, where as a teenager she was writing songs and performing in the town's thriving live music scene. She moved to Nashville in 1988 and signed several writing deals before moving to Sony Tree in 1992. Having written a string of critically acclaimed hits, Peters received her first Grammy nomination for Song of the Year in 1995 for "Independence Day" (recorded by Martina McBride), her powerful anthem about a woman who fights back against an abusive husband. In the Country Music Awards that year, the song took home the same award, as well as a CMA Video of the Year in 1994. She was nominated again for a Song of the Year Grammy in 1996 with the Patty Loveless charttopper "You Don't Even Know Who I Am." Peters' scope isn't limited to the country music arena, as she demonstrated by co-writing "Rock Steady" with rock artist Bryan Adams—a song that appeared on Bonnie Raitt's *Road Tested.* Peters released her debut album, *The Secret of Life,* on Imprint Records in 1996. —*Jack Leaver*

The Secret of Life / 1996 / Imprint ✦✦✦
Although this record is stylistically more folk and pop than country, Peters' songs are similar to Mary-Chapin Carpenter's work in that they contain thoughtful and intelligent lyrics that are at times highly introspective. Ten of the 11 tracks were written or co-written by Peters, and she turns in a credible cover of Steve Earle's "I Ain't Ever Satisfied," with Earle and Harris providing harmony vocals. Other guests include Raul Malo singing background on the beautiful "Border Town" and James House on "A Room with a View," a song written from the perspective of a cab driver. Another highlight is the opening track, "Waiting for the Light to Turn Green," co-written with Suzy Bogguss. Overall an impressive first outing for this talented singer-songwriter. —*Jack Leaver*

Pierce Pettis

Guitar, Vocals / Singer-Songwriter, Country-Folk, Contemporary Folk
An excellent songwriter who was probably first heard by most people when Joan Baez covered his "Song at the End of the Movie" on her *Blowin' Away* album in 1979. Pierce Pettis put out his independent album, *Moments,* in 1984 and has since been releasing albums on Windham Hill, the most recent of which is *Tinseltown.* —*William Ruhlmann*

Moments / 1987 / Small World ✦✦✦✦
Containing the title cut, "Grandmother's Song," and "St. Paul's Song," this is his first album, and his best. —*Richard Meyer*

Tinseltown / 1991 / High Street ✦✦✦

● **While the Serpent Lies Sleeping** / Jan. 15, 1992 / Windham Hill ✦✦✦✦
The keen observations in Pettis' songwriting gain force from the caught-in-the-throat emotionalism of his singing. As befits this record label, the instrumental settings are somewhat busy in a new age way. But where the drum and keyboard programming leave off, a strong contemporary folk album remains, especially on "Legacy," in which Pettis confronts the conflicts of his Southern heritage. —*William Ruhlmann*

Chase the Buffalo / 1993 / High Street ✦✦✦
Pierce Pettis' fourth album, *Chase the Buffalo,* shows a great deal of growth as a writer and studio performer. Pettis' other releases have had some high points, but on this CD, Pettis' politics and Southern gothic folk style are better integrated. His writing is more consistent and stands up to his mature and controlled vocals. The production by David Miner is also more focused on Pettis' style than before. This album is worth tracking down. —*Richard Meyer*

Making Light / Oct. 8, 1996 / High Street ✦✦✦✦
Produced by David Miner, *Making Light* has a somewhat more polished surface than Pierce Pettis' previous albums, but that doesn't diminish the quiet power of his songs. —*Thom Owens*

Picketts

Contemporary Country, Alternative Country-Rock
From Seattle, the five-member Picketts play Stones-influenced honky tonk on a 1995 album for Rounder, *Wicked Picketts.* Vocalist Christy McWilson leads the band through a cover of Yoko Ono's "Walking on Thin Ice" and "If You Love Me." —*John Bush*

Paper Doll / 1992 / Pop Llama ✦✦✦
The Picketts are a country-rock group that is heavily in debt to classic '50s honky tonk and '60s Bakersfield country, as well as punk, rockabilly, and rock 'n' roll. *Paper Doll* is an energetic, rollicking record, full of stomping rockers and terrific ballads. The Picketts might be just a revival band, but performed as well as *Paper Doll* is, a lack of originality is excusable. —*Thom Owens*

● **The Wicked Picketts** / 1995 / Rounder ✦✦✦✦
The Picketts draw equally from country and rock 'n' roll, including punk rock, which makes their stripped-down, Bakersfield-influenced honky tonk quite exciting. Their second album, *The Wicked Picketts,* has a bit more studio gloss than *Paper Doll,* but it remains a tough, enjoyable listen. —*Stephen Thomas Erlewine*

Jo Carol Pierce

b. Jul. 20, 1944, Wellington, TX
Vocals / Progressive Country, Singer-Songwriter, Country-Folk, Alternative Country
An unconventional singer-songwriter from the musical wellspring of Lubbock, TX—home to the likes of Buddy Holly, Joe Ely, Jimmie Dale Gilmore, and Butch Hancock—Jo Carol Pierce is as much a monologuist and performance artist as a musician. Her songs, a blend of country and postmodern folk sung in a shaky, conversational style, are steeped more in theater than in any traditional musical idiom; nonetheless, her work proved so popular with other performers that a tribute LP was recorded.

Pierce was born July 20, 1944, near old Route 66 in Wellington, TX. After her father was killed in Korea, she and her mother moved to Lubbock, where she attended school with the likes of Ely and Hancock. In 1963 she married her high school sweetheart, Gilmore; after having a child, Elyse, the couple divorced in 1967. Pierce moved to Austin in the early 1970s, where she found employment as a social worker. After hours, she also began writing a novel and composing the occasional song. By the next decade she had become a playwright and screenwriter, authoring such works as *Falling, Papergirls, New World Tango* (a musical scored by Joe Ely), *Bad Girls Upset by the Truth,* and *In the West,* a drama performed at the Kennedy Center in 1991.

Pierce did not begin to take songwriting seriously until the middle of the 1980s, when Ely and fellow Lubbock alum David Halley started encouraging her to become a performer. After enlisting backing vocalist Robert Jacks and accordionist Mike Maddux, she quickly became a popular fixture on the Austin club circuit. Friends and fans Michael Hall (formerly of the Wild Seeds) and Troy Campbell (of the Loose Diamonds, named after a Pierce song) began organizing the 1993 album *Across the Great Divide: Songs of Jo Carol Pierce,* a tribute LP compiling renditions of Pierce songs performed by musicians like Ely, Gilmore, Terry Allen, Darden Smith, and Kathy McCarty and Gretchen Phillips. A group tour in support of the record followed; and in 1996, at the age of 51, Pierce finally made her own recording debut with *Bad Girls Upset by the Truth,* a semi-autobiographical performance piece drawn from her absurdist musical comedy. —*Jason Ankeny*

● **Bad Girls Upset by the Truth** / Jan. 23, 1996 / MH ✦✦✦✦
Pierce's debut, while for all practical purposes a country record, is virtually unprecedented stuff: based on the singer's autobiographical absurdist satire of the same name, *Bad Girls Upset by the Truth* is essentially a performance piece, grounded more in theater than in music. A comic tale masking bitter themes including mental illness and victimization, the narrative kicks off with the suicide of the central character (also named Jo Carol) and culminates with the birth of the baby girl Jesus inside a supermarket. Stuffed in between are meditations on sex, monogamy, and spirituality, sung in Pierce's conversational style and set against country, folk, rock, and even Cajun backdrops. —*Jason Ankeny*

Webb Pierce

b. Aug. 8, 1926, West Monroe, LA, **d.** Feb. 24, 1991, Nashville, TN
Guitar, Vocals / Traditional Country, Honky Tonk
Webb Pierce was one of the most popular honky tonk vocalists of the '50s, racking up more No. 1 hits than similar artists like Hank Williams, Eddy Arnold, Lefty Frizzell, and Ernest Tubb. For most of the general public, Pierce—with his lavish, flamboyant Nudie suits—became the most recognizable face of country music and of its excesses; after all, he boasted about his pair of convertibles lined with silver dollars and his guitar-shaped swimming pool. For all of his success, Pierce never amassed the reputation of his contemporaries, even though he continued to chart regularly well into the '70s. His weakness for gaudy ornaments and his reluctance to break away from hardcore honky tonk meant that he had neither supporters in the industry nor the ability to sustain the ever-changing tastes of a popular audience. Nevertheless, he remains one of the cornerstone figures of honky tonk.

As a child in West Monroe, LA, Webb Pierce became infatuated with Gene Autry films and his mother's hillbilly records, particularly those of Jimmie Rodgers and various Western swing and Cajun groups. He began to play guitar before he was a teenager. At the age of 15 he was hired as a singer by Monroe's KMLB. During World War II, Pierce served in the Army. While he was in the service, he married Betty Jane Lewis in June of 1942. After he was discharged, Pierce and his wife went back to Monroe, but by 1944 they had moved to Shreveport. Pierce got a job at Sears Roebuck and began singing with Betty Jane at radio stations, night clubs, and dances. At first they were featured on an early morning radio show on KTBS and performed in the evening at clubs. It took five years before they were noticed by the industry. In 1949 the California-based 4 Star Records signed the duo under separate recording contracts. Webb signed under his own name, while his wife was signed for duets with her husband under the name Betty Jane and Her Boyfriends. However, success didn't come to the duo—it came only for Webb. In the summer of 1950, the couple divorced.

In late 1949 Pierce accepted a spot on the "Louisiana Hayride," a radio program on KWKH that was instrumental in launching the careers of many country artists. He began to assemble a band of local Shreveport musicians, recruiting pianist Floyd Cramer, guitarist/vocalist Faron Young, bassist Tillman Franks, and vocalists Teddy and Doyl Wilburn. The Wilburns and Franks all wrote songs, which provided the basis for the set list. Pierce also founded a record label called Pacemaker, and Ark-La-Tex Music, a publishing company, with Horace Logan, the director of the Lousiana Hayride. On Pacemaker, Pierce made several records between 1950 and 1951. They weren't designed to be big sellers—they were created with the intent of attracting radio play around Louisiana. In 1951 he was able to get out of his 4-Star contract, and Decca Records signed him immediately. Pierce's second single, "Wondering," became his breakthrough hit, climbing to No. 1 early in 1952. After the single became a hit, Pierce left Louisiana for Nashville, where he met and married Audrey Grisham. In June of 1952 he had his second No. 1 single with "That Heart Belongs to Me." The following September, the Grand Ole Opry needed to fill the vacancy left by the firing of Hank Williams, so they invited Pierce to join the cast. After Williams' death, Pierce became the most popular singer in country music. For the next four years, every single he released hit the Top Ten, with a total of ten reaching No. 1, including "There Stands the Glass" (1953), "Slowly" (1954), "More and More" (1954), and "In the Jailhouse Now" (1955).

Pierce and Opry manager Jim Denny formed Cedarwood Music, a publishing company, in 1953; later, the pair would invest in radio stations together. Their business ventures were not looked upon kindly by the Opry superiors, who began pressuring the duo to cease any outside interests. At the same time, Pierce was growing tired of being confined to the Grand Ole Opry—he thought wasn't being treated with the respect a star of his stature deserved, and he wanted the financial rewards that came with touring. Pierce left the Opry in 1955 and began appearing on "Ozark Jubilee," a television program on ABC. After the show completed its run in 1956, he returned to the Opry, but he left for good the next year.

Pierce continued to have hits until the end of the '50s, but his popularity did take a significant dip after rock 'n' roll's arrival in the late '50s. Nevertheless, he stayed on the charts, primarily because he kept in close touch with DJs across the country, which meant that he was able to keep his streak of 34 consecutive Top Ten hits running into 1957. For a while, Pierce tried to keep up with rock 'n' roll, covering the Everly Brothers and recording pseudo-rockabilly numbers. When those proved unsuccessful, he stuck with honky tonk and continued to rack up Top Ten hits right through 1964.

By 1965 the country-pop leanings of the Nashville Sound had pushed honky tonk from the top of the country charts. Pierce remained a star, but he simply didn't have many big hits in the latter half of the '60s—the most notable was "Fool Fool Fool" in 1967. Since his music had faded from the spotlight, he became known for his excessive lifestyle. Instead of indulging in intoxicants, Pierce indulged in material items. Pierce had Nudie Cohen, a Hollywood tailor famous for his flamboyant custom-made clothing, line two Pontiac convertibles with silver dollars. He built a guitar-shaped swimming pool at his Nashville home. The swimming pool became a popular tourist attraction—nearly 3,000 people visited it each week—causing his neighbors, led by Ray Stevens, to file suit to prevent visitors from coming into their neighborhood.

Throughout the '70s Pierce continued to record, but most of his income came from his highly lucrative financial investments. Webb left Decca Records in 1975, making a handful of records for Plantation Records that didn't experience much chart success. His last hit came in 1982, when his duet on "In the Jailhouse Now" with Willie Nelson scraped the bottom of the country charts.

Despite all of his success, Webb Pierce was never inducted into the Country Music Hall of Fame. It's likely that the members never forgave him for his rejection of the Grand Ole Opry and the Nashville industry. Webb Pierce died of pancreatic cancer on February 24, 1991. Just months before his death, he failed to receive enough votes to be inducted to the Hall of Fame. Nevertheless, his career stands as one of the most successful in the history of country music. —*Stephen Thomas Erlewine*

That Wondering Boy / 1956 / Decca ◆◆◆◆
That Wondering Boy is an original 10-inch album released on Decca Records in the mid-'50s. Though all of this material has been reissued in various forms, this original track sequence is dynamite, featuring Pierce classics like "There Stands the Glass," "Back Street Affair," and "Slowly," and is one of his best albums of the '50s. —*Stephen Thomas Erlewine*

Walking the Streets / 1960 / Decca ◆◆◆
Good weepers are included, such as "Drinkin' My Blues Away."
—*George Bedard*

Webb with a Beat! / 1960 / Decca ◆◆◆◆
Included is "I Ain't Never" (co-written by Mel Tillis) and "In the Jailhouse Now." The title is a bit misleading, but "I Ain't Never" definitely rocks. —*George Bedard*

In the Jailhouse Now / 1982 / Intersound ◆◆◆
Intersound's 12-track *In the Jailhouse Now* offers a representative selection of Webb Pierce's biggest hits—including "I Ain't Never," "There Stands the Glass," "Back Street Affair," and "I'm Tired"—but the album doesn't have particularly good sound or packaging. The Country Music Foundation's *King of the Honky Tonk* is a better, more thorough retrospective, but *In the Jailhouse Now* is an acceptable budget-line issue. —*Stephen Thomas Erlewine*

☆ **The Wondering Boy (1951-1958)** / 1990 / Bear Family ◆◆◆◆◆
For the devout, Germany's Bear Family offers a four-CD box set of Pierce's primal honky tonk, a total of 113 songs by one of the seminal post-war country artists, including duets with Kitty Wells, Red Sovine, and the Wilburn Brothers. This is the best sound quality and presentation available of this influential music.
—*Mark A. Humphrey*

Sands of Gold/Sweet Memories / 1993 / Mobile Fidelity ◆◆◆◆
Oo-ooh, what a little remastering can do. Two Nashville Sound LPs from the downside of Pierce's career feature Pierce singing more of other people's hits than his own. But reissued Mofi-style, Pierce and the echo chamber sound great. —*Dan Cooper*

★ **Webb Pierce: King of the Honky-Tonk: From the Original Master Tapes** / 1994 / Country Music Foundation ◆◆◆◆◆
No one ever accused Pierce of being a singer's singer; nevertheless, his classic country oeuvre is totally individualistic, which is really more important. Any fan of '50s fiddle-and-steel honky tonk will want this collection, which features such Pierce immortals as "There Stands the Glass," "Slowly," a rollicking 1954 remake of Jimmie Rodgers' "In the Jailhouse Now," and the to-the-point "Honky Tonk Song." The latter is one of several cuts from the pen of a young Mel Tillis. —*Dan Cooper*

Hayride Boogie, 1950-1951 / Krazy Kat ◆◆◆◆
The 16-track album *Hayride Boogie, 1950-1951* contains nearly all the material Webb Pierce recorded for the local Shreveport, LA, record label Pacemaker. Though some of this material does capture Pierce at a rough, developmental stage, much of it is downright terrific; it is all fascinating listening for dedicated fans or country music historians. —*Stephen Thomas Erlewine*

Ray Pillow

b. Jul. 4, 1937, Lynchburg, VA
Vocals / Country-Pop, Nashville Sound/Countrypolitan
Ray Pillow is a singer and songwriter best known as a prominent publisher with a rare gift of matching performers with high-quality songs right for their style. Pillow was born in Lynchburg, VA, and learned to play the guitar while bedridden as a teen. He graduated from high school in 1954 and joined the Navy. After his discharge, Pillow earned a bachelor's degree in business and made his professional and personal singing debut playing with his uncle's band, the Stardusters. Later he became their leader and remained with the band for several years. In 1961 Pillow won second place at the regional National Pet Milk talent contest in Nashville. Though he needed to go back to Lynchburg, he accepted an invitation to appear on the Grand Ole Opry. He soon returned to Nashville and looked up Joe Taylor, the head of promotion with the Martha White Company, who had promised to help Pillow after hearing him perform. Taylor was true to his word, and Pillow signed a personal management contract with the company. In 1963 he released his first two singles, but he didn't really have chart success until 1965, with the Top 50 "Take Your Hands Off My Heart" and his first Top 20 hit, "Thank You Ma'am." In 1966 he had two Top 40 hits and a Top Ten duet with Jean Shepherd, "I'll Take the Dog." He later joined the Opry and remained there for more than two decades. He continued with a steady stream of hits through 1970 but fell off the charts until 1972 with the minor hits "Since Then" and "She's Doing It to Me Again." Pillow's involvement in the administrative end of the business began in the mid-'60s, when he paired up with Taylor in Joe Taylor Artist Management, Shoji Music Publications, and Ming Music, Inc. In the early '80s Pillow teamed with Larry McFaden to begin Sycamore. In the late '80s he began working with the A&R team at Capitol Records and later became an independent record consultant. —*Sandra Brennan*

● **Presenting Ray Pillow** / 1965 / Capitol ◆◆◆◆
Even When It's Bad, It's Good / 1967 / Capitol ◆◆◆◆
Ray Pillow Sings / 1969 / ABC ◆◆◆
Slippin' Around with Ray Pillow / 1972 / Mega ◆◆◆
One Too Many Memories / Allegiance ◆◆

Pinkard & Bowden

Traditional Country, Country Humor
In the tradition of Homer and Jethro came the riotous barnyard humor and song parodies of Sandy Pinkard and Richard Bowden. Unlike their forebears, Pinkard and Bowden's humor was often coarse, and their language was sometimes rough enough to warrant explicit language warnings on their records; in fact, they

were the first country comedy artists to have such an advisory posted on their music.

Both Pinkard and Bowden were successful singers and songwriters before teaming up. Pinkard began his music career with Ramblin' Jack Elliott in California. He made one unsuccessful bid to get signed in Nashville and entered the professional rodeo in Fort Worth, TX. In 1975 he met John Anderson, who listened to Pinkard's demos and encouraged him to try Nashville again, even giving him a round-trip ticket. This time he succeeded, and such artists as Tanya Tucker, Ray Charles, and Brenda Lee recorded his songs; in 1979, Mel Tillis had a No. 1 hit with Pinkard's "Coca Cola Cowboy." Other singers scoring top hits with his songs included David Frizzell and Shelly West ("You're the Reason God Made Oklahoma"), Anne Murray ("Blessed Are the Believers"), and Vern Gosdin ("I Can Tell by the Way You Dance").

Bowden got his start working in the Texas band Shiloh alongside future Eagle Don Henley. After the group disbanded, the two joined Linda Ronstadt's band, which included another future Eagle, Glenn Frey. When Frey and Henley left to form the Eagles, Bowden briefly teamed with former Flying Burrito Brother Sneaky Pete Kleinow. He then hit the road and played with different performers, including Roger McGuinn. During the early '80s, he and his band Blue Steel opened for the Eagles.

Pinkard and Bowden were introduced through their mutual friend, record producer Jim Ed Norman. They began writing songs together; although they tried to write seriously, they found that everything they penned was funny, so they took their act onto the national comedy club circuit and built a following. Their debut album, *Writers in Disguise*, featured such musical parodies as "Blue Hairs Drivin' in My Lane." The two had their first chart success with "Adventures in Parodies," a montage of clips. Among their other favorites: "Elvis Was a Narc," "She Thinks I Steal Cars," and "Libyans on a Jet Plane." In 1992 they released *Cousins, Cattle, and Other Love Stories*, which featured takeoffs on pop songs like Eric Clapton's "Cocaine" ("Propane"). By the early '90s Pinkard and Bowden were more involved in performing at comedy clubs than with country music; they also began appearing on rock radio station morning shows to promote their evening gigs. After making the switch, their comedy has became a little bluer and definitely blacker, as seen in their song "Friends in Crawl Spaces," inspired by serial killer/cannibal Jeffrey Dahmer. *—Sandra Brennan*

Writers in Disguise / 1984 / Warner Brothers ✦✦✦

● **Live in Front of a Bunch of Dickheads** / 1990 / Warner Brothers ✦✦✦✦
On this concert LP, Pinkard and Bowden offer up crowd-pleasers like "Elvis Was a Narc," "Driving Others to Christ Through Barnyard Innuendo," and "She Dances with Meat." Their families must be very proud. *—Jason Ankeny*

Cousins, Cattle and Other Love Stories / 1992 / Warner Brothers ✦✦✦
Unlike the homespun country comedy of a bygone era, the music of Pinkard and Bowden is proudly and defiantly raunchy; the opening cut even taunts their label to "Censor Us." (The album does indeed bear a parental advisory sticker, by the way.) Also featured: "Trailer Park Woman" and "Since My Baby Turned Gay." *—Jason Ankeny*

Pirates of the Mississippi

Contemporary Country
A group of five session musicians who formed in 1987 to have a little fun, the Pirates of the Mississippi were one of a handful of country bands who emerged in the wake of the Kentucky Headhunters' success in the early '90s. The Pirates of the Mississippi didn't blend genres or joke around like the Kentucky Headhunters, nor were they smooth country-rock like Alabama. Instead, they were a straightforward country band, with hints of ragged enthusiasm and exceptional instrumental and vocal skills. Though the band wasn't able to capitalize on the success of their one big hit single, 1991's No. 15 "Feed Jake," the group continued to record through the mid-'90s.

All five members of the Pirates of the Mississippi—Bill McCorvey (lead vocals, guitar), Rich Alves (guitar), Dean Townson (bass), Jimmy Lowe (drums), and Pat Severs (steel guitar)—were Nashville session musicians during the '80s. In 1987 they began playing together regularly, usually in clubs around Nashville. Eventually, an A&R representative at Capitol Nashville signed the group. In the summer of 1990 their eponymous debut was released, as was their cover of Hank Williams' "Honky Tonk Blues." The single reached No. 30, but the followup, "Rollin' Home," stiffed.

Walk the Plank, the band's second album, appeared in 1991, and it proved to be their breakthrough release, thanks to the single "Feed Jake." A sentimental song about the death of a childhood friend, "Feed Jake" and its video became a big hit, leading to the band's being named the Top New Vocal Group by the Academy of Country Music. Though they had two other singles from the album—"Speak of the Devil" and "Fighting for You"—nothing else from the record was a hit. *A Street Man Named Desire*, the band's third album, also suffered poor sales upon its 1992 release, as did its fourth record, 1993's *Dream You*.

After the poor sales of *Dream You*, the compilation *Best of the Pirates of the Mississippi* appeared in 1994, and the band was dropped from Liberty and Capitol Nashville. Later that year Pat Severs left the group and was replaced by Greg Trostle. In 1995 the Pirates of the Mississippi signed with Giant Records and released *Sure Sign.* *—Stephen Thomas Erlewine*

Pirates of the Mississippi / Jun. 18, 1990 / Capitol ✦✦✦✦
The Pirates made their name with their third single, "Feed Jake," which had a video that became country music's version of *Old Yeller*. The rest of the debut is a cross between Alabama country and Southern rock. (The album starts with a speeded-up version of "Honky Tonk Blues," if that's a hint of what's to come.) There are a few twists, though, namely a Guy Clark song ("I Take My Comfort in You") and a surf-country instrumental. *—Brian Mansfield*

Walk the Plank / Sep. 30, 1991 / Capitol ✦✦✦
As country, the Pirates' Allman Brothers cops are more exciting than their stone-country material, although that's certainly competent enough. The white-country-soul "Till I'm Holding You Again"—which tries to rock out when you're not looking—is probably the best of all. *—Brian Mansfield*

A Street Man Named Desire / Sep. 28, 1992 / Liberty ✦✦✦
"Street Man Named Desire" may not be the most clear-cut metaphor given the phrase's origins, but if you're going to make literary allusions, you can do worse than Tennessee Williams. While that's the title tune, the Allman and Doobie Brothers influences in the instrumental "Mystery Ship" tell more about the band—namely, that they're a tamed biker band. The Pirates are good-natured renegades, but they never take the image too far. So "Mississippi Homegrown" is about music, not marijuana (and contains another Williams reference), "The Hard Side of Love" only hints at the Southern boogie the guys might have in them, and "All Your Eyes Can See" is a tender love song for the ladies. Powerful in spots, the album is pedestrian in others. *—Brian Mansfield*

Dream You / Oct. 11, 1993 / Liberty ✦✦✦
Basically a party album, it contains songs like "Save the Wild Life," "Pop from the Top," "The Night They Rocked the Grand Ole Opry," and a full-tilt cover of Hank Thompson's "The Wild Side of Life." *—Brian Mansfield*

● **Best of the Pirates of the Mississippi** / Mar. 8, 1994 / Liberty ✦✦✦✦
Beyond the video for "Feed Jake," the Pirates of the Mississippi never found great success (five Top 40 hits in four years, none making the Top Ten). Even so, they were a pretty decent singles band, as this collection shows, especially when they nail the fast stuff (like "Rollin' Home" and "Speak of the Devil"). *Best Of* also includes dance mixes of two tunes from *Dream You:* "Dream You" and "Pop from the Top." *—Brian Mansfield*

Paradise / 1995 / Giant ✦✦✦

Poco

Country-Rock, Soft Rock

Founded by Jim Messina and Richie Furay during the dying days of Buffalo Springfield, with Randy Meisner (who dropped out shortly before the recording of their first album), Rusty Young, and George Grantham, the band built a solid reputation in Los Angeles as an innovative country-rock ensemble. Their first album, *Pickin' Up the Pieces*, was one of the strongest debut records of its era, a blend of country and Western influences, Beatlesque harmonies, and mainstream rock, all within one cover. They began developing a major national reputation with the release of their second album, *Poco*, at the same time that the group's membership entered what proved to be a virtually constant state of flux. By the mid-'70s, the band had become an established fixture in the middle reaches of the national charts, but Messina and Furay were long gone. The band continued recording into the late '70s on MCA after leaving Epic, and their following was strong enough to justify a live album from Epic at the same time. The original quintet, which never did get to record, finally went into the studio under the auspices of RCA in the late '80s. —*Bruce Eder*

Pickin' Up the Pieces / 1969 / Epic ✦✦✦✦
Their debut album, which is as accomplished as anything by Buffalo Springfield, also recalls the Beatles and the Byrds in its musical orientation. —*Bruce Eder*

Poco / May 6, 1970 / Epic ✦✦✦
The second Epic album has a slightly harder sound than the debut. It reflects the results of an additional eight months of work, plus a fresh membership change. —*Bruce Eder*

From the Inside / 1971 / Epic ✦✦
A most unusual record, produced by Memphis guitarist Steve Cropper. Much harder-edged than the rest of the group's output, this album is much more a solid rock album and relies less on the harmony sound than their other records. —*Bruce Eder*

Deliverin' / Jan. 13, 1971 / Epic ✦✦✦✦
The first of two live albums, *Deliverin'* consists of mostly new material and is a major country-rock success, capturing not only the lyricism and upbeat approach of the band, but also the infectiously positive attitude of its fans. —*Bruce Eder*

A Good Feelin' to Know / Oct. 25, 1972 / Epic ✦✦✦
The title track is a failed attempt at a hit single, but the record as a whole is much more pure rock than they were known for. —*Bruce Eder*

Crazy Eyes / 1973 / Epic ✦✦✦
Richie Furay's final album with Poco is a mixed effort, containing Gram Parsons' "Brass Buttons" and Furay's title track, a song about Parsons, who died shortly after the album's release. —*William Ruhlmann*

Seven / 1974 / Epic ✦✦
Poco's first album as the quartet of Rusty Young, George Grantham, Timothy Schmit, and Paul Cotton finds them expanding as songwriters, with even Young contributing "Rocky Mountain Breakdown." —*William Ruhlmann*

Cantamos / Dec. 1974 / Epic ✦✦✦
This album marks the emergence of Rusty Young as a composer of merit. Side one rocks out hard and fresh, while the second side deals with lost love and broken-hearted romance. Much of the magic of their earlier albums has been recaptured. —*Jim Chrispell*

Head over Heels / Jul. 1975 / MCA ✦✦✦✦
Keeping the songs short and to the point, Poco lets loose with a fine batch of material. This time out, they even cover the Becker-Fagen song "Dallas" with great verve. There's less country and a lot more pop. —*Jim Chrispell*

The Very Best of Poco / Sep. 1975 / Epic ✦✦✦✦
A well-chosen double LP compilation (now on one CD) chronicling Poco's Epic Records period, 1969-1974. —*William Ruhlmann*

Rose of Cimarron / 1976 / One Way ✦✦✦
Lushly produced pop-rock, *Rose of Cimmaron* hosts an array of sidemen, most notably Al Garth, formerly of Loggin and Messina, and keyboardist Steve Ferguson. The country influence is nearly abandoned except for the Rusty Young tune "Company's Comin'/Slow Poke." There are great tunes with great arrangements throughout. —*Jim Chrispell*

Live / Apr. 1976 / Epic ✦✦✦
Epic Records released this live album, recorded in November 1974, in 1976, long after the band had left the label. It's not bad, but it isn't a patch on Poco's previous live effort, *Deliverin'*. —*William Ruhlmann*

Indian Summer / 1977 / MCA ✦✦✦
Although highly listenable, this album marks the slow descent of a band once at the forefront of the country-rock movement. High points include the title track and the mini-suite entitled "The Dance." Donald Fagen of Steely Dan adds synths here and there. —*Jim Chrispell*

Legend / Nov. 1978 / MCA ✦✦✦
The departure of Timothy B. Schmitt to the Eagles should have signalled the end for Poco. They turned in a surprisingly tight set, however, and got their first Top 40 hit with "Crazy Love." —*Jim Chrispell*

Under the Gun / 1980 / MCA ✦✦
A deliberate followup to *Legend*, *Under The Gun* was a workmanlike but unremarkable effort. —*William Ruhlmann*

Blue and Gray / 1981 / MCA ✦✦
A concept album about the Civil War, not well executed. —*William Ruhlmann*

Cowboys and Englishmen / 1982 / One Way ✦
Poco's contractual obligation album to get off MCA Records (which had taken over ABC Records) was a throwaway effort at a time when their career needed rejuvenation, not another wound. (Originally released on LP by MCA Records, *Cowboys and Englishmen* was licensed to One Way Records for CD reissue.) —*William Ruhlmann*

Backtracks / 1982 / MCA ✦✦✦✦
A nine-song compilation of Poco's tenure at ABC (later MCA) Records, 1975-1982, judiciously chosen. Later expanded for CD release and retitled *Crazy Loving: The Best Of Poco 1975-1982*. —*William Ruhlmann*

Ghost Town / 1982 / Atlantic ✦✦✦
Surprise! Just when they had been written off by even the most loyal fans, Poco rebounds nicely here. "Shoot for the Moon," "When Hearts Collide," and the title track are pleasant reminders of a band that once was. —*Jim Chrispell*

Inamorata / 1984 / Atlantic ✦✦
Poco was down to the duo of Rusty Young and Paul Cotton by this point, which may be why, having been visited in the studio by former members Richie Furay, Timothy Schmit, and George Grantham, they structured the credits in such a way that you might think the old group had re-formed. Not so. Rather, this was a mediocre (and final) effort by an act long past its prime. —*William Ruhlmann*

Crazy Loving: Best of Poco 1975-1982 / 1989 / MCA ✦✦✦✦
In the wake of Poco's success with *Legacy*, MCA Records resurrected their 1982 best-of, *Backtracks*, added tracks to fill it out to respectable CD length, threw in some liner notes, and reissued it under a new title. It's not Poco's best period, but this is a good selection that will satisfy most casual listeners. —*William Ruhlmann*

Legacy / Aug. 1989 / RCA ✦✦
A reunion of the "Original Poco" could not stand up to the hype that surrounded its release. Jim Messina does his best on the hit "Call It Love," and Randy Meisner covers Richard Marx's tune "Nothin' to Hide." Other selections fall short of the mark. —*Jim Chrispell*

● **The Forgotten Trail (1969-1974)** / 1990 / Epic ✦✦✦✦
This definitive two-CD collection is full of wonderful moments and great songs, so it is the obvious starting point. —*Bruce Eder*

Charlie Poole

b. Mar. 22, 1892, Randolph County, NC, d. May 1931
Banjo / Old-Time, String Band
Charlie Poole and his North Carolina Ramblers were one of the most popular string bands of the 1920s and had a great influence on the development of bluegrass music. Poole is largely responsible for popularizing the banjo and created a unique playing style involving his thumb and two fingers.

He was born in Randolph County, NC, and spent much of his adult life working in textile mills. He learned banjo as a youth and also played baseball. (It is believed that his playing style stemmed from a baseball accident involving his thumb.) When not working in mills, he would travel from town to town across the country to play banjo and work. He ended up settling in Spry, NC, in 1918 and married two years later. He and his brother-in-law, fiddler Posey Rorer, would often play with other local musicians, and they became the North Carolina Ramblers. Poole and Rorer teamed up with guitarist Norm Woodlief in 1925 and began recording careers in New York for Columbia Records. There they cut four songs; all were successful, including the bluesy "Don't Let Your Deal Go Down," a country standard and Poole's signature song. The Ramblers were suddenly a popular string band. Though the personnel changed frequently over the years, the band's unusual sound remained consistent. Poole sang with a plain, uninflected style that complemented his complex banjo picking. The songs were a mixture of minstrel songs, Victorian ballads, and humorous burlesques, all delivered with Poole's straight-faced dry wit. Through the rest of the decade, the Ramblers released close to 60 singles for Columbia. Like many country performers to follow, Poole lived a fast life; he was a hard-drinking man, rowdy and reckless.

When the Depression hit in 1930, Poole's career had peaked and his popularity began waning—as did his self-confidence. As a result, he began drinking even more heavily. Scheduled to appear in a film in 1931, he unfortunately went on a bender and died of heart failure before he could get to Hollywood. After his death, Rorer (who had left the band in 1929) and guitarist Roy Harvey (who'd replaced Woodlief about the same time) began leading the North Carolina Ramblers. (The group continued to record and perform for a quite a few years afterward.) Poole's music enjoyed renewed popularity during the folk revival of the '60s, and in 1993 a CD of his best songs was released. Kenny Rorer wrote and published a biography of the great banjo player. —*Sandra Brennan*

Old-Time Songs / County ✦✦✦
Old-Time Songs contains 16 songs Charlie Poole recorded for Columbia Records between 1925 and 1930. This sampling features nearly every one of his best songs—including the hits "Don't Let Your Deal Go Down Blues" and "Can I Sleep in Your Barn Tonight, Mister"—and provides the definitive retrospective of Poole, as well as a good glimpse into the style and sound of old-timey country music in the first half of the 20th Century. —*Thom Owens*

★ **Charlie Poole and the North Carolina Ramblers 1926-30** / Historical ✦✦✦✦✦

Sandy Posey

b. Jun. 18, 1947, Jasper, AL
Vocals / Country-Pop, Nashville Sound/Countrypolitan
Despite having several moderate hits in both the country and pop charts, Sandy Posey was never fully embraced by either audience and is far from being a household name.

Sandy Posey was born in Jasper, AL, in 1947. She relocated to Memphis in her teens, where she secured a job as a receptionist in a local studio. Eventually she was given a chance to sing back-up during recording sessions, which led to work at several other studios in Memphis and Nashville. Her clear voice was perfectly suited for the ultra-slick Nashville "countrypolitan" sound of the day. MGM records signed her at age 18 to a solo deal on the strength of her demo recording of "Born a Woman," and despite her country roots and the country feel of her material, MGM mar-

keted her as a pop singer—in retrospect, a wise decision. "Born a Woman" and "Single Girl" became her first hits (both reached No. 12 in the pop charts in 1966). Since both songs were written by Martha Sharp, it was mistakenly reported during this time that Sandy Posey was a pseudonym assumed by Sharp for recording purposes. Posey had two more pop hits with the Top 40 "What a Woman in Love Won't Do" and the No. 12 "I Take It Back." By 1968 Posey's woman-as-a-helpless-victim themes were decidedly out of touch with the times, and the hits stopped coming. She went into semi-retirement.

She returned in 1970 for phase two of her career—"the country years." She signed to Columbia Records, where she had another string of hits—this time in the country charts—including the Top 20 Vietnam War-inspired "Bring Him Home Safely to Me," the slightly risque "Why Don't We Go Somewhere and Love" (a minor hit in 1975), "Happy Birthday Baby," and "Don't" (both Top 40). She moved to Monument Records in 1976 and later to Warner Brothers, where she hit again with a series of oldies revivals—the Chordettes' "Born to Be with You" and a medley of "Love, Love, Love" and "Chapel of Love." Her last hit was in 1979 with "Love Is Sometimes Easy." In 1983 she signed to the independent label Audiograph and released her final solo album. Since then she has stayed busy as a session singer and tours infrequently with her husband, Wade Cummings, an Elvis impersonator. —*Chris Woodstra*

Born a Woman / 1966 / MGM ✦✦✦✦
Sandy Posey's debut record starts off with her signature hit song, "Born A Woman," and the rest of the songs, which are mostly laments on lost love and loneliness, set the blueprint she would follow for her pop phase with MGM. The ultra-slick Nashville pop gloss of the arrangements helped secure a pop audience, but Posey clearly demonstrated that she had the soul of a country singer. —*Chris Woodstra*

I Take It Back / 1967 / MGM ✦✦✦
Posey's third album features a mix of originals and covers, including songs that had been hits for Miss Toni Fisher ("The Big Hurt"), Tony Orlando ("Halfway to Paradise"), and the Fleetwoods ("Come Softly to Me"). —*Jim Worbois*

Single Girl / 1967 / MGM ✦✦✦
Posey's defiant stance on the cover and the title are slightly deceptive—this isn't a testament to the independence and joy of being a "single girl" but rather another case of Sandy mourning her life without "her man." The title track preaches, "A single girl needs a good-hearted man to lean on." Aside from outdated anti-feminist statements, the album's real strengths lie in the haunting, slightly skewed arrangements, which cross "countrypolitan" with pure '60s pop, best exemplified in the overlooked classic "Hey Mister." —*Chris Woodstra*

Looking at You / 1968 / MGM ✦✦
While there is really nothing outstanding about this record, it is pleasant to listen to and doesn't get in the way while one is doing something else. One song of some interest is her version of "Shades of Gray," which was issued by the Monkees as a single about this time. —*Jim Worbois*

Sandy Posey / 1970 / MGM ✦✦✦

Why Don't We Go Somewhere and Love / 1972 / Columbia ✦✦✦
Producer Billy Sherrill stripped away the double-tracked vocals and gave her records the same type of feel he applied to the records of Tammy Wynette. This resulted in a modest hit on the title track. The record is also interesting because it includes one track co-written by future game-show host Chuck Woolery and another by future country music star Eddie Rabbitt. —*Jim Worbois*

Tennessee Rose / 1983 / 51 West ✦✦

● **Best of Sandy Posey** / 1996 / Collectables ✦✦✦✦
The Best of Sandy Posey is a 14-track collection covering Posey's first recording period for MGM, including the classic forgotten hits "Born a Woman," "Single Girl," and "I Take It Back"; oddly, all three peaked at No. 12. Posey's mid-'60s songs, almost all depicting a woman helpless without—or alternately, trapped with—"her

man," were slightly out-of-touch at the time and are artifacts now, but the slick pop-country arrangements have a timeless charm. Posey would have later success in the country charts in the '70s, but unfortunately those hits are not represented here. Though the album appears to be a straight reissue of the MGM's *The Best of Sandy Posey*, this package actually expands on it by three tracks. —*Chris Woodstra*

Prairie Oyster

Western Swing Revival

The Canadian Western swing group Prairie Oyster made a brief splash on the US charts in the early 1990s but began playing together in 1975, when they were a trio consisting of lead singer/ bassist Russell de Carle, guitarist Keith Glass, and steel guitar player Denis Delorme. Initially they toured and appeared on television but did not record; they disbanded in 1978, but in 1982 reunited, along with new member John P. Allen, to do some gigs. They also took on keyboardist/songwriter Joan Besen and finally, in 1986, drummer Bruce Moffett. As the new Prairie Oyster, they recorded their debut, *Oyster Tracks*. Eventually some of their demos, recorded by Steve Berlin, made it to RCA executive Joe Galante in Nashville, who signed them after seeing the group perform. For RCA, Oyster recorded *Different Kind of Fire*, with guest appearances by Berlin; the first single, "Goodbye, So Long, Hello," made it to the Top 70 on the US country charts in 1990. In 1991 they again won numerous kudos for their second album, *Everybody Knows*, and its resulting singles. They did not appeared on the US charts beyond 1991, but they continued to work and record in their native Canada. —*Sandra Brennan*

Different Kind of Fire / 1991 / RCA ✦✦✦
The first US release from this Canadian sextet puts a modern spin on traditional country sounds. —*Jason Ankeny*

● **Everybody Knows** / Sep. 1991 / RCA ✦✦✦✦
On *Everybody Knows*, Prairie Oyster shed their other influences to fully embrace honky tonk. —*Jason Ankeny*

Goodbye, So Long, Hello / RCA ✦✦✦

Elvis Presley (Elvis Aron Presley)

b. Jan. 8, 1935, Tupelo, MS, **d.** Aug. 16, 1977, Memphis, TN
Guitar, Vocals / Rock 'n' Roll, Rockabilly, Pop-Rock

Elvis Presley may be the single most important figure in American 20th century popular music. Not necessarily the *best*, and certainly not the most consistent. But no one could argue that he was not the musician most responsible for popularizing rock 'n' roll on an international level. Viewed in cold sales figures, his impact was phenomenal. Dozens upon dozens of international smashes from the mid-'50s to the mid-'70s, as well as the steady sales of his catalog and reissues since his death in 1977, may make him the single highest-selling performer in history.

More important from a music lover's perspective, however, are his remarkable artistic achievements. Presley was not the very first White man to sing rhythm and blues; Bill Haley predated him in that regard, and there may have been others, as well. Elvis was certainly the first, however, to assertively fuse country and blues music into the style known as rockabilly. While rockabilly arrangements were the foundations of his first (and possibly best) recordings, Presley could not have become a mainstream superstar without a much more varied palette that incorporated pop, gospel, and even some bits of bluegrass and operatic schmaltz here and there. His 1950s recordings established the basic language of rock 'n' roll; his explosive and sexual stage presence set standards for the music's visual image; his vocals were incredibly powerful and versatile.

Unfortunately, to much of the public, Elvis is more icon than artist. Innumerable bad Hollywood movies, increasingly caricatured records and mannerisms, and a personal life that became steadily more sheltered from real-world concerns (and steadily more bizarre) gave his story a somewhat mythic status. By the time of his death, he'd become more a symbol of gross Americana than of cultural innovation. The continued speculation about his incredible career has sustained interest in his life and supported a large tourist/entertainment industry that may last indefinitely,

Elvis Presley

even if the fascination is fueled more by his celebrity than his music.

Born to a poor Mississippi family in the heart of Depression, Elvis had moved to Memphis by his teens, where he absorbed the vibrant melting pot of Southern popular music in the form of blues, country, bluegrass, and gospel. After graduating from high school, he became a truck driver, rarely if ever singing in public. Some 1953 and 1954 demos, recorded at the emerging Sun label in Memphis primarily for Elvis' own pleasure, helped stir interest on the part of Sun owner Sam Phillips. In mid-1954 Phillips, looking for a White singer with a Black feel, teamed Presley with guitarist Scotty Moore and bassist Bill Black. Almost by accident, apparently, the trio hit upon a version of an Arthur Crudup blues tune, "That's All Right Mama," that became Elvis' first single.

Elvis' five Sun singles pioneered the blend of R&B and C&W that would characterize rockabilly music. For quite a few scholars, they remain not only Elvis' best singles, but the best rock 'n' roll ever recorded. Claiming that Elvis made blues acceptable for the White market is not the whole picture; the singles usually teamed blues covers with country and pop, all made into rock 'n' roll (at this point a term that barely existed) with the pulsing beat, slapback echo, and Elvis' soaring, frenetic vocals. "That's All Right Mama," "Blue Moon of Kentucky," "Good Rockin' Tonight," "Baby Let's Play House," and "Mystery Train" remain core early rock classics.

The singles sold well in the Memphis area immediately, and by 1955 they were starting to sell well to country audiences throughout the South. Presley, Moore, and Black hit the road with a stage show that grew ever wilder and more provocative, Elvis' swiveling hips causing enormous controversy. The move to all-out rock was hastened by the addition of drums. The last Sun single, "I Forgot to Remember to Forget"/"Mystery Train," hit No. 1 on the national country charts in late 1955. Presley was obviously a performer with superstar potential, attracting the interest of bigger labels and Colonel Tom Parker, who became Elvis' manager. In need of capital to expand the Sun label, Sam Phillips sold Presley's contract to RCA in late 1955 for $35,000—a bargain in hindsight, but an astronomical sum at the time.

This is the point where musical historians start to diverge in opinion. For many, the whole of his subsequent work for RCA—encompassing more than 20 years—was a steady letdown, never recapturing the pure, primal energy harnessed so effectively on the handful of Sun singles. Elvis, however, was not a purist. What he wanted was to be successful. To do that, his material needed more of a pop feel; in any case, he'd never exactly been one to disparage the mainstream, naming Dean Martin as one of his heroes from the get-go. At RCA his rockabilly was leavened with enough pop flavor to make all of the charts, not just the country ones.

At the beginning, at least, the results were hardly any tamer than the Sun sessions. "Heartbreak Hotel," his first single, rose to No. 1 and, aided by some national television appearances, helped make Elvis an instant superstar. "I Want You, I Need You, I Love You" was a No. 1 follow-up; the double-sided monster "Hound Dog"/"Don't Be Cruel" was one of the bigest-selling singles the industry had experienced. Albums and EPs were also chart-toppers, not just in the US but throughout the world. The 1956 RCA recordings, while a bit more sophisticated in production and a bit less rootsy in orientation than his previous work, were still often magnificent, among the best and most influential recordings of early rock 'n' roll.

Elvis' (and Colonel Parker's) aspirations were too big to be limited to records and live appearances. By late 1956 his first Hollywood movie, *Love Me Tender,* had been released; other screen vehicles would follow in the next few years, *Jailhouse Rock* being the best. The hits continued unabated, several of them ("Jailhouse Rock," "All Shook Up," "Too Much") excellent, and often benefiting from the efforts of top early rock songwriter Otis Blackwell, as well as the emerging team of Jerry Leiber-Mike Stoller. The Jordanaires added both pop and gospel elements with their smooth backup vocals.

Yet worrisome signs were creeping in. The Dean Martin influence began rearing its head in smoky, sentimental ballads such as "Loving You"; the vocal swoops became more exaggerated and stereotypical, although the overall quality of output remained high. And although Moore and Black continued to back Elvis on his early RCA recordings, within a few years they had gone their own ways.

Presley's recording and movie careers were interrupted by his induction by the Army in early 1958. There was enough material in the can to flood the charts throughout his two-year absence (during which he served largely in Germany). When he re-entered civilian life in 1960, his popularity, remarkably, was just as great as when he left.

One couldn't, unfortunately, say the same for the quality of his music, which was not only becoming more sedate, but was starting to either repeat itself or opt for operatic ballads that didn't have a whole lot to do with rock. Elvis' rebellious, wild image had been tamed as well, as he and Parker began designing a career built around Hollywood films. Shortly after leaving the Army, in fact, Presley gave up live performing altogether for nearly a decade to concentrate on movie-making. The films, in turn, would serve as vehicles to both promote his records and to generate maximum revenue with minimal effort. For the rest of the '60s, Presley ground out two or three movies a year that, while mostly profitable, had little going for them in the way of story, acting, or social value.

While there were some quality efforts on Presley's early '60s albums, his discography was soon dominated by forgettable soundtracks, mostly featuring material that was dispensable or downright ridiculous. He became largely disinterested in devoting much time to his craft in the studio. The soundtrack LPs themselves were sometimes filled out with outtakes that had been in the can for years (and these, sadly, were often the highlights of the albums). There were some good singles in the early '60s, like "Return to Sender"; once in a while there was even a flash of superb, tough rock, like "Little Sister," or "(Marie's the Name) His Latest Flame." But by 1963 or so there was little to get excited about, although he continued to sell in large quantities.

The 1962-67 era has generated a school of Elvis apologists. They point out that Presley was assigned poor material, and assert that Colonel Parker was largely responsible for Presley's emasculation. True to a point, but on the other hand it could be claimed, with some validity, that Presley was doing little to rouse

himself from his artistic stupor, letting Parker destroy his artistic credibility without much apparent protest, and holing up in his mansion with a retinue of yes-men who protected him from much day-to-day contact with a fast-changing world.

The Beatles, all big Elvis fans, displaced Presley as the biggest rock act in the world in 1964. What's more, they did so by writing their own material and playing their own instruments—something Elvis had never been capable of, or particularly aspired to. They, and the British and American groups the Beatles influenced, were not shy about expressing their opinions, experimenting musically, and taking the reins of artistic direction into their own hands. The net effect was to make Elvis Presley, still churning out movies in Hollywood as psychedelia and soul music became the rage, seem irrelevant, even as he managed to squeeze out an obscure Dylan cover ("Tomorrow Is a Long Time") on a 1966 soundtrack album.

By 1967 and 1968 there were stirrings of an artistic reawakening by Elvis. Singles like "Guitar Man," "Big Boss Man," and "US Male," though hardly classics, were at least genuine rock 'n' roll that sounded better than much of what he'd been turning out for years. A 1968 television special gave Presley the opportunity he needed to reinvent himself as an all-out leather-coated rocker, still capable of magnetizing an audience, and eager to revisit his blues and country roots.

The 1968 album *Elvis in Memphis* was the first LP in nearly a decade in which Presley seemed cognizant of current trends, as he updated his sounds with contemporary compositions and touches of soul to create some reasonably gutsy late-'60s pop-rock. This material, and 1969 hits like "Suspicious Minds" and "In the Ghetto," returned him to the top of the charts. Arguably, it's been overrated by critics, who were so glad to have him singing rock again that they weren't about to carp about the slickness of some of the production, or the mediocrity of some of the songwriting.

But Elvis' voice *did* sound good, and he returned to live performing in 1969, breaking in with weeks of shows in Las Vegas. This was followed by national tours that proved him still to be an excellent live entertainer, even if the exercises often reeked of show-biz extravaganza. (Elvis never did play outside of North America and Hawaii, possibly because Colonel Parker, it was later revealed, was an illegal alien who could have faced serious problems if he traveled abroad.) Hollywood was history, but studio and live albums were generated at a rapid pace, usually selling reasonably well, although Presley never had a Top Ten hit after 1972's "Burning Love."

Presley's 1970s recordings, like most of his '60s work, are the focus of divergent critical opinion. Some declare them to be, when Elvis was on, the equal of anything he did, especially in terms of artistic diversity. It's true that the material was pretty eclectic, running from country to blues to all-out rock to gospel. (Presley periodically recorded gospel-only releases, going all the way back to 1957.) At the same time, his vocal mannerisms were often stilted, and the material—though not nearly as awful as that '60s soundtrack filler—sometimes substandard. Those who are not serious Elvis fans will usually find this late-period material to hold only a fraction of the interest of his '50s classics.

Elvis' final years have been the subject of a cottage industry of celebrity bios, tell-alls, and gossip screeds from those who knew him well, or (more likely) purported to know him well. Those activities are really beyond the scope of a mini-bio such as this, but it's enough to note that his behavior was becoming increasingly unstable. His weight fluctuated wildly; his marriage broke up; he became dependent upon a variety of prescription drugs. Worst of all, he became isolated from the outside world except for professional purposes (he continued to tour until the end), rarely venturing outside of his Graceland mansion in Memphis. Colonel Parker's financial decisions on behalf of his client have also come in for much criticism.

On August 16, 1977, Presley was found dead in Graceland. The cause of death remains a subject of widespread speculation, although it seems likely that drugs played a part. An immediate cult (if cult is the way to describe millions of people) sprang up; every year hundreds of thousands of visitors make the pilgrimage to Graceland. Elvis memorabilia, much of it kitsch, is an industry in its own right. Dozens if not hundreds make a comfortable living by impersonating the King in live performance. And then there are all those Elvis sightings, reported in tabloids on a seemingly weekly basis.

Although Presley had recorded a mammoth quantity of both released and unreleased material for RCA, the label didn't show much interest in repackaging it with the respect due such a pioneer. Haphazard collections of outtakes and live performances were far rarer than budget reissues and countless repackagings of the big hits. In the CD age, RCA finally began to treat the catalog with some of the reverence it deserved, at long last assembling a box set containing nearly all of the 1950s recordings. Similar, although less exciting, box sets were documenting the 1960s, the 1970s, and his soundtrack recordings. And exploitative reissues of Elvis' material continue to appear constantly, often baited with one or two rare outtakes or alternates to entice the completists (of which there are many). In death, as in life, Presley continues to be one of RCA's most consistent earners. Fortunately, with a little discretion, a good Elvis library can be built with little duplication, sticking largely to the most highly recommended selections. —*Richie Unterberger*

☆ **Elvis Presley** / Mar. 1956 / RCA ✦✦✦✦✦
While RCA had the material, they opted to play it safe and combine five Sun outtakes with seven new recordings and release the Hillbilly Cat's first album. This is a great way to begin a career! The best material here is on a par with the Sun singles. While "Blue Suede Shoes" is a cultural cornerstone of sorts, hearing Elvis' version of Clyde McPhatter's "Money Honey" is still, after four decades, revelatory. —*Neal Umphred*

☆ **Elvis** / Nov. 1956 / RCA ✦✦✦✦✦
Almost any rocker of the '50s could have claimed this as their best album. While there are some excellent rhythm numbers ("Rip It Up," "Paralyzed," and the too-country "When My Blue Moon Turns to Gold Again"), the album's standout is the panting "Love Me." —*Neal Umphred*

Elvis' Golden Records, Vol. 1 / Mar. 1958 / RCA ✦✦✦✦
This is the greatest-hits album by which all greatest-hits albums need be measured. Fourteen sides had sold umpteen bejillion records in the previous two years. The only discrepancy is the inclusion of "That's When Your Heartaches Begin," which failed to reached the Top 40 as the flip of "All Shook Up," at the expense of "I Was the One," "My Baby Left Me," and "Playing for Keeps," each a much bigger hit. —*Neal Umphred*

50,000,000 Elvis Fans Can't Be Wrong: Elvis' Golden Records, Vol. 2 / 1960 / RCA ✦✦✦✦
The beginner is pointed toward the first two gold record sets, which contain the obvious hits that make up oldies fare, and the not so well known, such as—in the case of this second volume—the smoldering "One Night" and the rousing "I Need Your Love Tonight." —*Neal Umphred*

Elvis Is Back! / Apr. 1960 / RCA ✦✦✦
The first album after the Army, *Elvis Is Back!* captures him at his secular best, which is nonetheless moved by gospel undertones. The sheer intensity of the performances from Elvis on vocals and rhythm guitar and from the all-star band (which, aside from the regulars, includes Floyd Cramer, Hank Garland, and Boots Randolph) overcomes any shortcomings the material might offer. "Make Me Know It," "Fever," and "The Girl of My Best Friend" (a hit for sound-alike Ral Donner here and for Elvis abroad) could have been chart-toppers. "Dirty, Dirty Feeling," "Reconsider Baby," and "Such a Night" are among the very best—and "dirtiest"—numbers Elvis ever cut. —*Neal Umphred*

Elvis' Golden Records, Vol. 3 / Sep. 1964 / RCA ✦✦✦✦
This third package of gold captures most of the hits from 1960-1962 and is a marvelous album, a model in selection and programming. The songs are all excellent; Elvis was in a period that is always overlooked by fans, critics and biographers; the band often cooked; and the production and engineering were flawless. Much of what Elvis achieved here on songs like "(Marie's the Name) His Latest Flame" and "Little Sister" has not been dupli-

cated, although the influences are sprouting up in contemporary country. —*Neal Umphred*

Elvis' Gold Records, Vol. 4 / Feb. 1968 / RCA ✦✦✦
This is one of Elvis' most misunderstood albums. At the time of release, the reviews almost without exception discussed how Elvis' gold was drained and he was reduced to filling up the fourth volume with B-sides. Actually there was more than enough gold for the set; "Wooden Heart," "Can't Help Falling in Love," and "Return to Sender" are the most obvious. "A Mess of Blues," "Witchcraft," and "Please Don't Drag That String Around" are fine uptempo numbers, while "Love Letters" and "It Hurts Me" are among the best ballads Elvis—or anyone else—recorded during the decade. —*Neal Umphred*

☆ **NBC TV Special** / Dec. 1968 / RCA ✦✦✦✦✦
After years of making abysmal movies, Presley appeared before a live audience, scared to death. That he more than rose to the challenge is evidenced here, a masterly performance highlighted by the jam-session segment with DJ Fontana and Scotty Moore, where Presley plays electric guitar and knocks out drop-dead versions of "Baby, What You Want Me to Do" and "Tiger Man." —*Cub Koda*

☆ **From Elvis in Memphis** / May 1969 / RCA ✦✦✦✦✦
Presley returned to Memphis, recording 30-odd songs in Chips Moman's American Sound Studios in 1969, leading to his artistic and commercial resurgence ("In the Ghetto" and "Suspicious Minds") and what may be his single greatest album, *From Elvis in Memphis*. The first track opens with Elvis' hoarsely shouting "I had to leave town for a little while . . . " and then announces—in no uncertain terms—that he's back. Elvis sings a brilliant selection of material as if his life depended on it. (It didn't; his career did.) The musicians (all regulars from Chips Moman's American Sound Studios) cook, and the overdubbed horns and background vocals are among the most appropriate ever used on a White singer's record. —*Neal Umphred*

From Memphis to Vegas / From Vegas to Memphis / Nov. 1969 / RCA ✦✦✦✦
One half of the imponderably titled *From Memphis to Vegas / From Vegas to Memphis* (later issued as a separate album, *Elvis in Person at the International Hotel*) captures Elvis in the summer of 1969, while the exhilaration of conquest was still evident. It's a nice compromise between mere entertainment and the revelatory. The first few songs are old hits to pull you in; the second side opens with a roaring medley of "Mystery Train" and Rufus Thomas' "Tiger Man" and leads to a staggering seven-minute "Suspicious Minds." The studio album, ten tracks from the previous Memphis sessions, is a letdown; even at the time of release, the two-fer concept seemed ill conceived. Had the best of the rest of the Memphis material been collected on a single album and titled *Suspicious Minds*, it's possible this album could have leapt to No. 1 and outsold the first. —*Neal Umphred*

That's the Way It Is / Dec. 1970 / RCA ✦✦✦✦
Returning to the more familiar haunts of Nashville in 1970, Elvis & Co. recorded three dozen tracks, the best of which are on a par with the Memphis recordings from the preceding year. From these, two albums emerged, both flawed, both excellent. *That's the Way It Is*, purporting to be the soundtrack from the documentary of the same name, contains eight of those sides, with Elvis at his most delicious ease. The live recordings are negligible and sink the album's basic level *except* for Elvis' magnificent "I Just Can't Help Believin'." —*Neal Umphred*

Elvis Country / Jan. 1971 / RCA ✦✦✦✦
Elvis Country was the second album from the June 1970 sessions. It is Elvis' best single album from the '70s and one of his very best ever. Every performance has something to offer, from the pleading of "I Really Don't Want to Know" to the raving "(I Washed My Hands in) Muddy Water." Even "Snowbird" is sung with passion! —*Neal Umphred*

Elvis Today / May 1975 / RCA ✦✦✦
Elvis Today is often cited by writers as Elvis' uncertain return to his Sun origins. There really isn't that much difference from the trio that resulted from 1973's Stax sessions, with the lesser tracks

being a bit more substantial. The sound is better, but the packaging had become offensive; one color close-up after another, almost all from the *Aloha from Hawaii* special (or that pre-bloated period), back covers with no noted or technical data, just ads for other Presley Product. Still, an album with "Susan When She Tried," "T-R-O-U-B-L-E," and a hilariously appropriate reading of "I Can Help" is worth listening to any time. *—Neal Umphred*

From Elvis Presley Boulevard, Memphis, Tennessee / May 1976 / RCA ✦✦✦

By 1976 Elvis was recording at home in Graceland, cutting what would be the final recordings of his career. Filled with bathos and showing little rock 'n' roll vitality, these remain interesting nonetheless, as they implied his accepting his age somewhat and attempting to combine old-fashioned, melodramatic soul with contemporary country-pop. While the pain and decay are evident—especially in hindsight—Elvis could still sing: "Hurt" is excellent, one of his best, and, on "Danny Boy," Elvis reaches with an aching falsetto that closes the song appropriately. Still, this is hardly the album to begin your collection. *—Neal Umphred*

Moody Blue / Jul. 1977 / RCA ✦✦

For some reason this album sold briskly on release, heading for the most respectable sales an Elvis album had had in years. Then, nothing. This is not one of his best, combining a few recently recorded tracks (October, back in his home studios) with leftovers from the February sessions and a couple of live tracks, one of which had previously been released on the already deleted *Recorded Live on Stage in Memphis. —Neal Umphred*

Elvis' Golden Records, Vol. 5 / 1984 / RCA ✦✦✦✦

The last volume in the Elvis Presley *Gold Records* compilation series had been released in February 1968, but Presley reissue producer Joan Deary (on her final project before turning over the reins to Gregg Geller) had the idea to revive it with a fifth volume in November 1984. It would have been a good idea in, say, 1978, since Presley had scored 14 gold or platinum singles since the last volume. It still wasn't that bad an idea in 1984 (leaving aside the redundancy factor), though the ten-track selection was skimpy, leaving out "Don't Cry Daddy," "The Wonder of You," "I've Lost You," "You Don't Have to Say You Love Me," "I Really Don't Want to Know," "Separate Ways," and "My Way." It was also idiosyncratic, including "If You Talk in Your Sleep" and "Moody Blue," which made the Top 40, but did not go gold, as well as "For the Heart," the B-side of the Top 40 hit "Hurt," an inclusion that is justifiable on aesthetic grounds (it's terrific) and for its influence (under the title "Had a Dream," it had been the Judds' first country hit earlier in the year). But the rest, from 1968's "If I Can Dream" to 1977's "Way Down," were Presley's most successful records of his final eight years and, in tunes like "Suspicious Minds" and "Burning Love," among his best recordings. *—William Ruhlmann*

☆ Reconsider Baby / 1985 / RCA ✦✦✦✦✦

A 12-song, budget-priced compilation of Elvis' most notable blues sides for the label. A good place to start digging Elvis' commitment to the music—always returning to it right up through the '70s like an old friend, whenever he needed a quick fix of the *real* thing—as he takes on everything from R&B slices like Tommy Tucker's "High Heel Sneakers" to Percy Mayfield's "Stranger in My Own Home Town." Major highlights on this collection are Elvis playing acoustic rhythm guitar and driving the band through a take of the Lowell Fulson title track, blistering versions of two Arthur Crudup songs, an unreleased Sun recording of Lonnie Johnson's "Tomorrow Night," and the R-rated take of Smiley Lewis' "One Night (of Sin)." *—Cub Koda*

Return of the Rocker / Mar. 1986 / RCA ✦✦✦

A companion to the *Rocker* compilation, *Return of the Rocker* presented harder-edged material recorded by Elvis Presley in the early '60s. Presley was moderating his sound in this period, so even the rockier stuff wasn't as hard as what he had recorded in the 1950s. But songs like "Little Sister," "A Mess of Blues," and "Return to Sender" still maintained his standard for uptempo rock 'n' roll, and this is some of the best material Presley recorded in the decade. *—William Ruhlmann*

★ Top Ten Hits / 1987 / RCA ✦✦✦✦✦

The Top Ten Hits is exactly what it says it is—every Top Ten hit that Elvis Presley ever had during the course of his career, from "Heartbreak Hotel" in 1956 to "Burning Love" in 1972. Even though this double-disc set covers a lot of ground, there's a huge amount of terrific material that *isn't* included. There's none of his Sun recordings, none of his gritty blues, none of his gospel, precious little of his country recordings; many great singles for RCA aren't included. Still, the 38 songs on *The Top Ten Hits* are absolutely first-rate—there's no arguing with "I Want You, I Need You, I Love You," "Don't Be Cruel," "Hound Dog," "Love Me Tender," "Love Me," "All Shook Up," "Jailhouse Rock," "One Night," "A Fool Such as I," "(Marie's the Name) His Latest Flame," "Can't Help Falling in Love," "Little Sister," "Return to Sender," "Suspicious Minds," and many, many others. It's the perfect way to start an Elvis collection and, for many casual fans, the only set to own. *—Stephen Thomas Erlewine*

The Number One Hits / 1987 / RCA ✦✦✦✦

Number One Hits contains 18 No. 1 records from the charts of *Billboard*, who somehow didn't rank "Crying in the Chapel," "In the Ghetto," "Burning Love," and "Way Down" as chart-toppers, although other national surveys did. In fact, according to RCA, every copy of "Way Down" was sold out within days after Presley's death, not just here but all over the planet, and somehow, amazingly, it didn't even make the magazine's Top Ten! *—Neal Umphred*

☆ The Memphis Record / 1987 / RCA ✦✦✦✦✦

Hot on the heels of his breakthrough NBC special in 1968, Presley returned to Memphis to record for the first time in 12 years and laid down 20 tracks in four days. He was hot, he was inspired, and it's all here. *—Cub Koda*

★ The Complete Sun Sessions / 1987 / RCA ✦✦✦✦✦

This is it, your perfect starting point to understanding how Elvis—as Howlin' Wolf so aptly put it—"made his *pull* from the blues." All the source points are there for the hearing; Arthur Crudup's "That's All Right (Mama)," Roy Brown's "Good Rockin' Tonight," Kokomo Arnold's "Milkcow Blues Boogie," Arthur Gunter's "Baby, Let's Play House," and Junior Parker's "Mystery Train." Modern-day listeners coming to these recordings for the first time will want to reclassify this music into a million sub-genres, with all the hyphens firmly in place. But what we have here is a young Elvis Presley mixing elements of blues, gospel, and hillbilly music and getting ready to unleash its end result—rock 'n' roll—on an unsuspecting world. *—Cub Koda*

Essential Elvis: The First Movies / 1988 / RCA ✦✦✦✦

A great collection of movie-soundtrack alternates, it includes great, eye-opening versions of "Jailhouse Rock" and "Got a Lot of Livin' to Do." *—Hank Davis & Cub Koda*

Hits Like Never Before: Essential Elvis, Vol. 3 / 1990 / RCA ✦✦✦

A whopping 24 alternate takes from his 1958 sessions. This has some substantially different versions of most of his big late-'50s hits—"I Got Stung," "A Fool Such as I," "I Need Your Love Tonight," "Wear My Ring Around Your Neck," and "A Big Hunk o' Love"—as well as alternates of songs from the *King Creole* film. Not exactly essential, but decent stuff. *—Richie Unterberger*

☆ Million Dollar Quartet / 1990 / RCA ✦✦✦✦✦

For years available only as a poor-fidelity bootleg, this is Elvis jamming in the Sun studios with Carl Perkins, Jerry Lee Lewis, and others on a set of primarily gospel and hillbilly material. Loose as a goose, with a true jam-session spirit, it offers a fascinating glimpse of one of the few times Presley let his true musical soul come up for air with somebody (Sam Phillips) there to record it. *—Cub Koda*

The Lost Album / 1991 / RCA ✦✦✦

The Lost Album consists of tracks recorded in May 1963 and January 1964 in Nashville. The initial sessions provided RCA with enough material to issue Elvis' fifth studio album of the '60s, a likely successor to the preceding pair, *Something for Everybody* and *Pot Luck*. That is, a rather modest collection of rockers, ballads, and a lil' ol' country. There are some strong numbers, especially the ones that ended up on singles: "(You're the) Devil in Disguise," "Please Don't Drag That String Around," and "Witchcraft." The January session produced what many consider one of Elvis' finest moments as a ballad singer, "It Hurts Me," which was, all too typically by then, relegated to the B-side of an abysmal soundtrack song as a summer single. *The Lost Album* collects them all in one place with fine sound and is a lot of fun, if of little significance. —*Neal Umphred*

☆ **The King of Rock 'n' Roll: The Complete '50s Masters** / 1992 / RCA ✦✦✦✦✦
A casual Elvis fan wanting to assemble a decent overview of the King's '50s sides could probably sweat it down to the *Sun Sessions* CD and Volume 1 of the *Top Ten Hits* compilation. But for those of you who take your '50s Presley seriously, *The King of Rock 'n' Roll: The Complete '50s Masters* is absolutely essential. For the hardcore Elvis fan, the booklet and CD graphics for this five-disc set provide incentive enough to justify its purchase. The liner notes by Presley expert Peter Guralnick are passionate, contagious in their enthusiasm, and filled with a real sense of history, time, and place. The treasure-trove of unpublished photos, session information, and Elvis memorabilia accompanying the booklet text is no less inspiring. But it's the music (140 tracks in all) that's the real meat and potatoes. Every studio track cut during the '50s—the seminal Sun sides, the early RCA hits, movie soundtracks, alternates, live performances, rarities (including both sides of the long-lost acetate he cut for his mother in 1953)—they're all here in one gorgeous package. Soundwise, this box makes any of the previous issues of this material pale by comparison, the proper (non-reverbed) inclusion of the Sun masters being a particular treat. This is no mere rehash of what's been around a dozen times before—there's a lot of thought and care behind this package, and no serious fan of American rock 'n' roll should consider a collection complete without it. —*Cub Koda*

☆ **From Nashville to Memphis: The Essential '60s Masters** / 1993 / RCA ✦✦✦✦✦
Continues the tradition of first-quality sound remastering and packaging. Much of Elvis' '60s work is arguably not as essential as the '50s stuff, but this meticulous five-disc/130-track set makes an impressive case for the defense. A thick booklet contains riveting liner notes, full-color photos, complete discography, and session listings; a sheet of RCA album cover stamps tops off the set. —*Roch Parisien*

Amazing Grace: His Greatest Sacred Songs / 1994 / RCA ✦✦✦
Elvis recorded quite a bit of gospel over the course of his career, and this two-CD, 55-song has the bulk of it. Most of this is drawn from his three gospel LPs (*His Hand in Mine*, 1960; *How Great Thou Art*, 1967; *He Touched Me*, 1972), as well as a 1957 EP. Presley was undoubtedly heavily influenced by gospel (at times he indicated regret at not having chosen to become a gospel singer), and this material has played pretty well with critics. Elvis sings with skill and reasonable commitment, and the backing musicians include such Elvis/Nashville standbys as Scotty Moore, Hank Garland, Floyd Cramer, Charlie McCoy, Pete Drake, the Jordanaires, and James Burton. At the same time, let's have a reality check here. Rock— and pop-oriented fans are going to find this two-and-a-half hour set tough going, unless they have a taste for spirituals as well. Things get a little more accessible when the tempos brighten, but often it's on the sedate side. For both collectors and listeners, highlights of the collection are five previously unreleased tracks from 1972. Recorded with only Charlie Hodges on piano and J.D. Sumner and the Stamps on backing vocals, they present Presley's gospel at its sparsest and most spontaneous. —*Richie Unterberger*

Command Performances: The Essential '60s Masters II / 1995 / RCA ✦✦✦
Elvis Presley's 1960s film soundtracks are renowned as the repository of his most frivolous (many would say ridiculous) material. This 62-song, double CD draws from no less than 26 of these screen vehicles to present the "best" of these performances; the idea is to complement the first volume of *Essential '60s Masters*, which focused on his non-soundtrack recordings from the decade, and doesn't include any of the cuts from this collection. The goal

of this package may have been to boil away the dross (as big as this is, there's a LOT of stuff they left off). But if anything, it perhaps inadvertently demonstrates just how lousy most of those recordings were; even this selective, chronologically programmed set feels way too long, and could probably have been cut to a single CD without too much loss. That's not to say that what's here is entirely negligible. There are some classic singles ("Return to Sender," "Can't Help Falling in Love"), fair rockers ("What'd I Say," "Little Egypt"), and more than a few cuts that are transcendentally great/awful in their mindless silliness ("Rock-a-Hula Baby," "Viva Las Vegas," "Do the Clam"), songs that are archetypes, for better or worse, of the kitschiest facet of Presley's myth. But much of the rest is just unremarkable, or even bad: stupid novelties ("Poison Ivy League"), drab ballads, and many mediocre rock tunes. This doesn't include such legendarily idiotic tunes as "No Room to Rhumba in a Sports Car," "Yoga Is as Yoga Does," and "Fort Lauderdale Chamber of Commerce"; you can find those on the original soundtracks, or a famous out-of-print bootleg, the aptly-titled *Elvis' Greatest Shit*. —*Richie Unterberger*

Heart and Soul / Jan. 24, 1995 / RCA ✦✦
The concept that seems to be guiding this, one of the latest in a long line of rehash packages, is a focus on romantic ballads. You get well-worn hits like "Love Me Tender," "Can't Help Falling in Love," and "Suspicious Minds," not-so-well-worn hits like "She's Not You," the original version of "The Girl of My Best Friend" (covered by Ral Donner for a big hit), and other odds and ends on this 22-track compilation. Not appealing for either the novice or serious fan, the rarities, if you could call them that, are a stereo version of "I've Lost You" and a version of "Bridge over Troubled Water" with the dubbed applause removed. Only regular pilgrims to Graceland need get in line. —*Richie Unterberger*

☆ **Walk a Mile in My Shoes: The Essential '70s Masters** / Oct. 10, 1995 / RCA ✦✦✦✦✦
In most conventional rock criticism, Elvis Presley's '70s records are considered his weakest, as they were recorded while he was falling deeper into drug addiction. However, as Dave Marsh argues in the liner notes, the music on the five-CD box set is among the most personal and adventurous of Elvis' career, even if the individual albums don't always reflect that diversity. By cutting away all of the dross that accumulated over the decade and sequencing the songs in a logical, entertaining manner, *Walk a Mile in My Shoes* supports the argument. On the first two discs, all of the singles Presley released during the '70s are presented. —*Stephen Thomas Erlewine*

Elvis Presley '56 / Mar. 5, 1996 / RCA ✦✦✦✦
Sure the music on here's great. How could it not be? It has 22 of the hottest tracks from his first year at RCA, including not only the hits "Heartbreak Hotel," "Hound Dog," "Don't Be Cruel," and "Too Much," but such noted early rockers as "My Baby Left Me," "Blue Suede Shoes," "Money Honey," and "So Glad You're Mine." From a collector's viewpoint, though, you have to wonder whether it was really necessary. The only previously unreleased item is a sparser earlier take of "Heartbreak Hotel." Everything else has been widely available (even on CD) for years, and it's a good bet that many of the Elvis fans who buy this already have virtually all of the contents on the *King of Rock 'n' Roll* box set. —*Richie Unterberger*

Essential Elvis, Vol. 4: 100 Years from Now / Jul. 1996 / RCA ✦✦✦✦
100 Years from Now is the fourth installment in RCA's *The Essential Elvis* series. The previous three volumes were all comprehensive box sets, but *100 Years From Now* is a single-disc collection that focuses on a very specific time frame—namely, the sessions Elvis cut in Nashville during 1970 and 1971. With the addition of some between-song narration, the music from these sessions would later become the *Elvis: Country* album. All of the *Elvis: Country* record is presented on *100 Years from Now* in its original form—sans narration, without overdubs, and in full running time. There are also the standard rarities and previously unreleased songs, like a version of "The Lord's Prayer." Even with the newly discovered material, what is special about this set is the original *Elvis: Country* album, which represents his last great album and

sounds even better in its original, uncut version. —*Stephen Thomas Erlewine*

Ray Price (Ray Noble Price)

b. Jan. 12, 1926, Perryville, TX
Guitar, Vocals / Traditional Country, Country-Pop, Honky Tonk, Nashville Sound/Countrypolitan

Ray Price has covered—and kicked up—as much musical turf as any country singer of the postwar era. He's been lionized as the man who saved hard country when Nashville went pop, and vilified as the man who went pop when hard country was starting to call its own name with pride. Actually, he was—and still is—no more than a musically ambitious singer, always looking for the next challenge for a voice that could bring down roadhouse walls. Circa 1949, Price cut his first record for Bullet at the Famous Jim Beck in Dallas. In 1951 he was picked up by Columbia, the label for which he would record for more than 20 years. After knocking around in Lefty Frizzell's camp for six months or so (his first Columbia single was a Frizzell composition), Price befriended Hank Williams. The connection brought him to the Opry and profoundly affected his singing style. After Williams died, Price starting stretching out more as a singer and arranger. His experimentation culminated in the 4/4 bass-driven "Crazy Arms," the country song of the year for 1956. The intensely rhythmic sound he discovered with "Crazy Arms" would dominate his—and much of country in general's—music for the next six years. To this day, people in Nashville refer to a 4/4 country shuffle as the "Ray Price beat." Heavy on fiddle, steel, and high tenor harmony, his country work from the late '50s is as lively as the rock 'n' roll of the same era. Price tired of that sound, however, and started messing around with strings. His lush 1967 version of "Danny Boy" and his 1970 take on Kris Kristofferson's "For the Good Times" were, in their crossover way, landmark records. But few of his old fans appreciated the fact. In the three decades after "For the Good Times," Price's career was often an awkward balancing act in which twin Texas fiddles were weighed against orchestras.

Born in tiny Perryville, TX, Price spent most of his youth in Dallas. It was there that he learned to play guitar and sing. After his high-school graduation, he studied veterinary medicine at North Texas Agricultural College in Abilene before joining the Marines in 1942. Price stayed in the service throughout World War II, returing to Texas and to college in 1946. He began to perform at local clubs and honky tonks, as well as on the local radio station KRBC, where he was dubbed the Cherokee Cowboy. Three years later he was invited to join the Dallas-based "The Big D Jamboree," which convinced him to make music his full-time career. Shortly after he joined "The Big D Jamboree," the show began to be televised by CBS, which helped him release a single, "Your Wedding Corsage" / "Jealous Lies," on the independent Dallas label Bullet.

Price moved to Nashville to pursue a major-label record contract in 1951. After auditioning and failing several times, he signed to Columbia Records after A&R representative Troy Martin convinced the label's chief executive, Don Law, that Decca was prepared to give the singer a contract. Previously, Law had been uninterested in Price—he turned him down 20 times and ordered Martin never to mention his name again—but he was unprepared to give a rival company a chance at the vocalist. Just before "Talk to Your Heart" became a No. 3 hit for Price in the spring of 1952, he met his idol, Hank Williams, who immediately became a close friend. Over the the next year, Williams performed a number of favors for Price, including giving him "Weary Blues" to record and helping him join the Grand Ole Opry. Price also became the permanent substitute for Williams whenever he was missing or too drunk to perform. After Williams' death in 1953, Price inherited the Drifting Cowboys.

After the success of "Don't Let the Stars Get in Your Eyes" in the fall of 1952, Price was quiet for much of 1953. It wasn't until 1954 that he returned to the charts with "I'll Be There (If You Ever Want Me)," a No. 2 hit that kicked off a successful year for Price that also included the Top Ten singles "Release Me" and "If You Don't, Somebody Else Will." Instead of capitalizing on that success, he disappeared from the charts during 1955, as he spent the

year forming the Cherokee Cowboys. Over the course of the previous two years, he had realized that performing with the Drifting Cowboys had made him sound too similar to Hank Williams, so he decided to form his own group. Originally, most of the members were lifted from Lefty Frizzell's Western Cherokees, but over the years a number of gifted musicians began their careers in this band, including Roger Miller, Johnny Paycheck, Buddy Emmons, Johnny Bush, and Willie Nelson.

Ray returned to the charts in 1956, first with "Run Boy" and then with "Crazy Arms," a driving honky tonk number that immediately became a country classic. The song was one of the first country records to be recorded with a drum kit, which gave it a relentless, pulsating rhythm. Until Price, most country artists had been reluctant to use drums, and the instrument was even banned from the stage of the Grand Ole Opry. The blockbuster status of the single helped change that situation. Spending an astonishing 20 weeks at the top of the country charts, "Crazy Arms" not only crossed over into the lower reaches of the pop charts, but it established Price as a star. After the success of the single, he remained at or near the top of the charts for the next ten years, racking up 23 Top Ten singles between 1956 and 1966. During this time he recorded a remarkable number of country classics, including "I've Got a New Heartache" (No. 2, 1956), "My Shoes Keep Walking Back to You" (No. 1, 1957), "Make the World Go Away" (No. 2, 1963) and "City Lights," which spent 13 weeks at the top of the charts in 1958.

The momentum of Price's career had slowed somewhat by the mid-'60s; though he was still having hits, they weren't as frequent or as big. His musical inclinations were also shifting, bringing him closer to the crooning styles of traditional pop singers. Price abandoned the cowboy suits and brought in strings to accompany him, making him one of the first to explore the smooth, orchestrated sounds of late '60s and early '70s country-pop. While it alienated some hardcore honky tonk fans, the change in approach resulted in another round of Top Ten hits. However, it took a little while for the country audience to warm to this new sound—it wasn't until 1970, when his cover of Kris Kristofferson's "For the Good Times" hit No. 1, that he returned to the top of the charts. Over the next three years he scored an additional three No. 1 singles ("I Won't Mention It Again," "She's Got to Be a Saint," "You're the Best Thing That Ever Happened to Me").

By the mid-'70s, the appeal of his string-laden country-pop hits had diminished, and he spent the rest of the decade struggling to get into the charts. In 1974 he left his longtime home of Columbia Records to sign to Myrrh, where he had two Top Ten hits over the next year. By the end of 1975 he had left the label, signing to ABC/Dot. Though he hadn't changed his style, his records became less popular about the same time he signed to ABC/Dot; only 1977's "Mansion on the Hill" gained much attention. In 1978 he switched labels again, signing with Monument, which proved to be another unsuccessful venture. In 1980 Price reunited with bassist Willie Nelson, recording the duet album *San Antonio Rose*, which was a major success, spawning the No. 3 hit "Faded Love." *San Antonio Rose* reignited Price's career, and in 1981 he had two Top Ten singles—"It Don't Hurt Me Half as Bad," "Diamonds in the Stars"—for his new label, Dimension. Price left Dimension in 1983, signing with Warner Records. He remained at the label for one year, and by that time his new spell of popularity had cooled considerably; now he was having trouble reaching the Top 40. That situation didn't remedy itself for the remainder of the decade, even though he signed with two new labels: Viva (1983-1984) and Step One (1985-1989).

By the late '80s, Ray Price had stopped concentrating on recording and had turned his efforts toward a theater he owned in Branson, MO. For most of the '90s he sang and performed at his theater in Branson, occasionally stopping to record. Of all of his '90s records, the most notable was the 1992 album *Sometimes a Rose*, which was produced by Norro Wilson. —*Dan Cooper*

Talk to Your Heart / 1958 / Columbia ✦✦✦✦

A great collection of "weepers," honky tonk, and Western swingy numbers from the '50s, it includes several songs by Floyd Tillman. Featured is "I'll Keep on Loving You," "Deep Water," and "I

Gotta Have My Baby Back," and "I'm Tired." This is a real "Texas-flavored" record by a honky tonk master. — *George Bedard*

San Antonio Rose / 1962 / Columbia ✦✦✦✦
Fans of Ray Price or Bob Wills won't want to miss Price's 1961 album *San Antonio Rose: A Tribute to the Great Bob Wills.* Price, who acknowledged Wills as a primary influence, became the first of many to devote an album to covering the songs of the renowned master of Southwestern dance music. Price recorded the album in a nine-hour period, using many of Nashville's best musicians, including guitarist Grady Martin, fiddler Tommy Jackson, pedal steel specialist Jimmy Day, and pianist Pig Robbins (in one of his first Nashville sessions). Also sitting in on acoustic guitar was a new Music City arrival, a little-known songwriter named Willie Nelson, who had just been hired to crank out songs for Price's publishing company. The record finds Price crooning with smooth, easy richness while the band lets it fly. — *Michael McCall*

Night Life / 1963 / Columbia ✦✦✦
Probably the first country and western "concept" album. Willie Nelson penned the title track and three other AM classics—tied together by the masterful steel guitar of Buddy Emmons. — *George Bedard*

Another Bridge to Burn / 1966 / Columbia ✦✦✦

The Best of Ray Price / 1976 / Columbia ✦✦✦✦
This compilation presents the highlights of Price's string-laden years. "For the Good Times" is simply one of the most mature singles ever recorded. "She's Got to Be a Saint" has somehow gotten lost over the years. — *Tom Roland*

Happens to Be the Best / 1983 / Pair ✦✦✦
Happens to Be the Best collects 16 of Ray Price's latter-day hits, including "For the Good Times," "I'd Rather Be Sorry," and "You're the Best Thing That Ever Happened to Me." While the collection does overlook several big hits from the late '60s and '70s, replacing them with lesser-known singles and album tracks, it nevertheless is a good, if incomplete, supplement to the excellent *The Essential Ray Price.* — *Thom Owens*

American Originals / 1989 / Columbia ✦✦✦✦
The brief, ten-track collection *American Originals* contains several of Ray Price's biggest hits—including "Crazy Arms," "Under Your Spell Again," "Faded Love," "For the Good Times," and "Funny How Time Slips Away"—dividing the album between his '50s honky tonk hits and his '60s countrypolitan singles. *American Originals* misses many of Price's most famous songs, such as "My Shoes Keep Walking Back to You" and "City Lights," usually at the expense of covers of songs made famous by other vocalists ("Crazy"). And that means *American Originals* isn't an ideal collection. It is of use only to budget-minded, casual fans and those who want a handful of his latter-day singles. *The Essential Ray Price: 1951-1962* is a preferable compilation. — *Stephen Thomas Erlewine*

★ **The Essential Ray Price (1951-1962)** / 1991 / Columbia ✦✦✦✦✦
A not completely accurate title. This 20-track compilation excludes a few later necessities like "Night Life" and "For the Good Times." The important stuff from Price's hard-country heyday is all here, however, from the teetering rise and fall of "Crazy Arms" (the first of a thousand country songs to employ a walking bassline and modified swing beat, which became known as the "Ray Price shuffle") to Harlan Howard's "Heartaches by the Number." The fake stereo that marred earlier reissues of his '50s material is happily absent here. This is essential country music. — *Brian Mansfield & Mark A. Humphrey*

The Honky Tonk Years (1950-1966) / 1996 / Bear Family ✦✦✦✦
The Honky Tonk Years (1950-1966) is an accurate title for this mammoth ten-disc set. Tracing Ray Price's career through his heyday in the '50s and stopping in the late '60s, just as he abandoned honky tonk for country-pop, the set documents one of the finest singers and bandleaders in country music. During this era, Price had a long, impressive string of Top ten singles—including "Don't Let the Stars Get in Your Eyes," "I'll Be There (If You Ever Want Me)," "My Shoes Keep Walking Back to You," "City Lights," and the massive hit "Crazy Arms"—and led a band that featured, at

various times, such musicians as Willie Nelson, Johnny Paycheck, and Roger Miller. Price and his band were talented enough to make weak material, which helps make this exhaustive set interesting; after all, there's bound to be a few lesser cuts in a box that runs more than 260 tracks. Though the strict chronological session order is occasionally tedious, the quality of the music far outweighs the flaws in presentation. For serious listeners and musicologists, *The Honky Tonk Years* is an essential purchase, since it offers a complete picture of one of the biggest figures in country music. Neophytes and casual listeners, however, are advised to stick with the single-disc collection, *The Essential Ray Price*, simply because it is far easier to digest. — *Stephen Thomas Erlewine*

Night Life / Koch ✦✦✦✦
Depending upon which lens of the historical perspective you view this through, this 12-song collection is the last gasp of true honky tonk, the first stab at mainstreaming it into the Nashville sound of the 1960s, or country music's first concept album. In 1962 Ray Price was at the peak of his form as a honky tonker of major repute. His regular touring band, the Cherokee Cowboys, were the finest of their kind, and Ray's voice was an instrument of wonder, full of reflection with every lyrical reading. As a traveling musician, Price knew well of the "night life" depicted in Willie Nelson's title track, a life of hotels, bar rooms, one-night stands, heartache, and regrets. This album, full of well written songs paying homage to that sinful life and its road to nowhere, evokes the sound, feel, and ambience of classic honky tonk music as few others do. As the decade wore on, Price would go on to major superstardom as a mellow balladeer, working with full string sections, reaching audiences that never heard this music or the other honky tonk classics that preceded it. More's the pity, for this album just may be Price's defining moment as an artist. — *Cub Koda*

Charley Pride

b. Mar. 18, 1938, Sledge, MS
Guitar, Vocals / Traditional Country, Country-Pop
With 36 No. 1 hits under his belt, Charley Pride, who is Black, has helped prove how little race matters to the majority of country music fans. It's taken a long time to understand that, though. His first single, "Snakes Crawl at Night," was released without publicity photos, as some in the industry feared listeners would automatically reject a Black country singer. Since then, Pride's 12 gold albums in the United States, combined with 30 gold and four platinum internationally, place him in the top 15 all-time country record sellers. His easygoing singing style and easy-to-listen-to voice show why these honors have come his way. From picking cotton in his native Mississippi, Pride ended up working in a smelting plant in Montana, after a stint as a semi-pro baseball player. At the suggestion of Red Sovine, Pride moved to Nashville, where he was signed by Chet Atkins of RCA. In 1966 "Just Between You and Me" brought Pride a Grammy nomination and national fame. At the end of the '60s and the early part of the '70s, he had five No. 1 singles in a row, including "All I Have to Offer Is Me" and "Is Anybody Goin' to San Antone?" Numerous awards came in 1971 and 1972, with many more hits following, among them "She's Too Good to Be True," "Kiss an Angel Good Mornin'," and "Night Games." Pride's warm baritone voice and relaxed style made him the best-selling act for RCA since Elvis Presley.

Charley Pride was born on a cotton farm in Sledge, MS. His father was a sharecropper on the farm. When he was 14 years old, Charley bought a guitar from Sears & Roebuck and proceeded to learn how to play by listening to country music on the radio. Two years later he turned his attention to baseball. He joined the Negro American league, playing with the Detroit Eagles and the Memphis Red Sox. After playing ball for two years, Pride joined the US Army, where he served for two years. Upon his discharge, he intended to return to baseball, but he sustained injuries that affected his throwing arm. Discouraged that he couldn't qualify for the major leagues, Pride began working construction in Helena, MT, while he still played in the minors. He earned a tryout for the California Angels in 1961, but they turned him down; the next year, the New York Mets rejected him, as well.

Charley Pride

Pride turned his attention to music, and in 1963 he sang "Lovesick Blues" for Red Foley and Red Sovine backstage at one of Sovine's concerts. The veteran musicians were impressed and told Charley to go to Nashville. Heeding their advice, he travelled to Music City, but he couldn't break into the industry. However, both the Reds and Webb Pierce kept recommending the fledgling singer to their associates, and eventually they helped him secure a management deal with Jack Johnson.

Through Johnson, Pride met Jack Clement, who sent a demo tape to Chet Atkins at RCA, who signed the vocalist in 1966. Later that year Pride's debut single, "The Snakes Crawl at Night," was released without a publicity photograph, since the label was afraid that radio programmers would be reluctant to lend support to a Black country singer. Both "The Snakes Crawl at Night" and his second song, "Before I Met You," gained a small audience," but it wasn't until "Just Between You and Me" that Pride became a star. Released at the end of 1966, "Just Between You and Me" climbed to No. 9 and began a virtually uninterrupted streak of Top Ten singles that ran until 1984.

However, Charley Pride's success didn't arrive as easily as it may seem. Though he was praised upon the release of "Just Between You and Me" and won a Grammy for the single, there remained resistence in certain quarters of the country audience to a Black performer. Nevertheless, the consistent quality of Pride's music and the support from his fellow musicians helped break down doors. And the doors began to open very quickly—on January 7, 1967, he became the first Black artist to perform on the Grand Ole Opry since DeFord Bailey in 1925.

Over the next two years his star steadily rose, and between 1969 and 1971 he had six straight No. 1 singles: "All I Have to Offer You (Is Me)," "I'm So Afraid of Losing You Again," "Is Anyboy Goin' to San Antone," "Wonder Could I Live There Anymore" "I Can't Believe That You've Stopped Loving Me," and "I'd Rather Live You." All of those singles also charted in the lower regions of the pop charts, giving evidence of his smooth, country-pop crossover appeal. "Let Me Live," taken from his gospel album *Did You Think to Pray?*, temporarily broke his streak of No. 1

singles in the spring of 1971, but it won a Grammy for Best Gospel Performance. Directly after "Let Me Live," two of his biggest hits—"I'm Just Me" and "Kiss an Angel Good Mornin'"—arrived, earning him his greatest success on both the country and pop charts.

Throughout the '70s he continued to chart in the upper regions of the country charts, earning No. 1 singles like "It's Gonna Take a Little Bit Longer" (1972), "She's Too Good to Be True" (1972), "A Shoulder to Cry On" (1973), "Then Who Am I" (1975), "She's Just an Old Love Turned Memory" (1977), and "Where Do I Put Her Memory." During this entire time, he never changed his country-pop style, though he promoted new performers and songwriters like Ronnie Milsap, Gary Stewart, and Kris Kristofferson. Pride's success continued during the first half of the '80s, as he continued to have No. 1 hits like "Honky Tonk Blues" (1980), "Mountain of Love" (1982), "You're So Good When You're Bad" (1982), and "Night Games" (1983). During 1984 and 1985, however, he grew frustrated with RCA Records, who began to promote newer artists at the expense of veteran performers. He left the label at the end of 1986, signing with Opryland's 16th Avenue label, where he returned to working with his old producer Jerry Bradley. Pride had a number of minor hits for the label, highlighted by 1988's No. 5 "Shouldn't It Be Easier than This," before it collapsed.

Pride moved on to Honest Entertainment in the early '90s and released *My 6 Latest and 6 Greatest*, where he dueted with the likes of Marty Stuart and Travis Tritt. Pride didn't record much after that album, but he continued to be a popular concert attraction. On each of his shows he was supported by his son, Dion, who played lead guitar. In 1994 Charley Pride was given the Academy of Country Music's Pioneer Award.—*David Vinopal*

● **The Best of Charley Pride** / 1969 / Curb ✦✦✦✦
Pride sang in a Hank Williams-influenced voice that yielded some of the best country performances of the late '60s and early '70s. —*Mark A. Humphrey*

The Best of Charley Pride, Vol. 2 / 1972 / RCA ✦✦✦✦
Perhaps because RCA wanted to leave no doubts about Pride's country heritage, his early career mined the standard three-chord structure almost exclusively. As with the first volume, this set does that, but in "Kiss an Angel Good Mornin'" and "Is Anybody Goin' to San Antone?," his performance is a notch or two above the previous package. —*Tom Roland*

The Best of Charley Pride, Vol. 3 / 1977 / RCA ✦✦✦✦
To be honest, Pride sounds a bit bored with some of this material. But "Mississippi Cotton Pickin' Delta Town" is practically a page out of his life. By the way, the cover art, with its rope script and blue-jeans-and-patches sports suit, is so '70s it's camp. —*Tom Roland*

There's a Little Bit of Hank (Williams) in Me / 1980 / RCA Victor ✦✦✦
Charley Pride salutes Hank Williams on this fine collection by covering Williams' "I Can't Help It (If I'm Still in Love with You)," "Honky Tonk Blues," and "I'm So Lonesome I Could Cry." There's also an original tribute, "There's A Little Bit of Hank in Me." —*James Chrispell*

Greatest Hits / 1981 / RCA ✦✦✦✦
Greatest Hits is a brief eight-track collection, but it does contain many of Charlie Pride's biggest RCA hits from the '70s, including "Burgers and Fries," "She's Just an Old Love Turned Memory," "When I Stop Leaving (I'll Be Gone)," "A Whole Lotta Things to Sing About," and "You're My Jamaica." Several of his biggest hits, including "Kiss an Angel Good Mornin'," "I'm Just Me," "It's Gonna Take a Little Bit Longer," and "She's Too Good to Be True" are missing, so this *Greatest Hits* can't be called definitive, but it remains a good sampler. —*Stephen Thomas Erlewine*

Charley Sings Everybody's Choice / 1982 / RCA ✦✦✦✦
Dumb title, but it's an excellent album. Producer Norro Wilson revitalized Pride's career by bringing out the Memphis soul that rests in the shadows of his country veneer. —*Tom Roland*

36 All-Time Greatest Hits / 1996 / ✦✦✦✦
Available only through mail order, the three-disc *36 All-Time Greatest Hits* contains the majority of Charley Pride's greatest hits, including "I Can't Believe That You've Stopped Loving Me," "Just Between You and Me," and "Kiss an Angel Good Mornin'." Though the packaging is somewhat haphazard—there are only 12 songs on each disc, and there is a lack of liner notes—no other compilation contains as many hits in one place. — *Thom Owens*

Super Hits / Oct. 15, 1996 / RCA ✦✦✦✦
Super Hits is a budget-priced compilation that features ten of Charley Pride's biggest hits for RCA Records, including "Is Anybody Goin' to San Antone," "I'm So Afraid of Losing You Again," and "Where Do I Put Her Memory." Though the album isn't comprehensive, it nevertheless is an excellent collection by budget line standards. — *Stephen Thomas Erlewine*

Jeanne Pruett (Norma Jean Bowman)

b. Jan. 30, 1937, Pell City, AL
Vocals / Traditional Country, Country-Pop
Jeanne Pruett frequently appeared on the Grand Ole Opry, which she joined in 1973. She was born Norma Jean Bowman and raised on a farm in Alabama. She sang every chance she got during high school and went to Nashville in 1956, where she married Jack Pruett, Marty Robbins' guitar player. She became a songwriter for Robbins Enterprises in the mid-1960s, staying through the early '70s. Among the songs she penned for Robbins were "Count Me Out," "Waiting in Reno," and "Christmas Is for the Kids." She also did a little session work. In 1971 Pruett debuted with the single "Hold On to My Unchanging Love," which became a minor hit. In 1973 she had her first Top Ten hit with "I'm Your Woman." Several popular records followed, including "You Don't Need to Move a Mountain" and "Please Sing Satin Sheets for Me." Her best years was 1980; she had three Top Ten hits, including "Temporarily Yours," but didn't appear on the charts again until 1983, dubbing a duet with the recently deceased Marty Robbins. She spent much of her subsequent time promoting her *Feedin' Friends Cookbook.* — *Sandra Brennan*

● **Love Me** / 1972 / Decca ✦✦✦✦

Satin Sheets / 1973 / MCA ✦✦✦

Encore / 1979 / IBC ✦✦✦

Star Studded Nights / 1982 / Audiograph ✦✦✦

Stand by Your Man / 1984 / Allegiance ✦✦

Jeanne Pruett / 1985 / MCA ✦✦✦✦

Riley Puckett

b. May 7, 1884, Alpharetta, GA, d. Jul. 14, 1946, East Point, GA
Banjo, Guitar, Vocals / Old-Time, String Bands
Riley Puckett was one of the pioneers of country music, a singer whose output both as a solo performer and as a member of the supergroup the Skillet Lickers left an indelible mark on the work produced in his wake. He was born George Riley Puckett on May 7, 1884, in Alpharetta, GA. Though at birth he had the ability to see, a medical mishap during his infancy left him blind. He attended the Macon School for the Blind, where he learned to read Braille and began playing the banjo, followed by the guitar, developing a unique, arhythmic style of playing bass-note runs to bridge chord changes. He also attracted attention at regional fiddling contests.

Puckett made his radio debut with Clayton McMichen's Hometown Band on WSB Atlanta in 1922. He soon became one of the station's most popular performers and began appearing as a soloist. The next year, he joined mandolinist Ted Hawkins and fiddler Lowe Stokes to form the Hometown Boys, where his smooth vocal style and yodeling abilities earned the group a devoted following among WSB listeners, who began calling the singer "the Ball Mountain Caruso." In 1924 Puckett accompanied James "Gideon" Tanner to Columbia Records' New York City studios, where he cut his first sides, including a cover of Fiddlin' John Carson's "The Little Old Log Cabin," "Steamboat Bill," and "Rock All Our Babies to Sleep," believed to contain the first-ever appearance of yodeling on a country record. The results proved highly

successful, and later in the year a second session followed. Accompanying himself on banjo, Puckett recorded "Oh Susannah" and "You'll Never Miss Your Mother Till She's Gone."

In 1925 Columbia introduced their 15000-D Hillbilly Series, and Puckett quickly became one of the imprint's most successful acts; only Vernon Dalhart sold more records. A year later, he joined the Skillet Lickers, which also featured Gid Tanner and Clayton McMichen, and remained with the group through 1931. In 1927 he joined high tenor Hugh Cross for the very first recording of "Red River Valley." The duo cut two more sessions together, generating songs like "Gonna Raise a Ruckus Tonight" (released under the name Alabama Barn Stormers), "Call Me Back Pal o' Mine," and "My Wild Irish Rose."

While the onset of the Depression did not crush Puckett's career as it did so many of his contemporaries', it did force him to curtail his prolific recording schedule. The records he cut appeared under a variety of group names and aliases, the most successful being 1931's "My Carolina Home," issued as McMichen's Melody Men. After the demise of the Skillet Lickers, Puckett performed with McMichen's Georgia Wildcats. In 1932 the Skillet Lickers began anew, and Puckett also signed on with Bert Layne's Mountaineers. In addition, he recorded a number of duets with Red Jones, including "I Only Want a Buddy, Not a Sweetheart" and "St. Louis Blues."

By 1936 he was touring with former Mainer Mountaineer "Daddy" John Love, and also performed again with Bert Layne. After organizing his own tent show to tour throughout the South, he returned to New York to record with Red Jones, duetting on "Altoona Train Wreck," "Take Me Back to My Carolina Home," and "The Broken Engagement." Puckett did not record again until 1940, when he cut the pop-oriented "Oh, Johnny, Oh," "Little Sir Echo," and "South of the Border." In 1941 he entered the studio one last time, performing "How Come You Do Me Like You Do," "Railroad Blues," and "Peach Picking Time in Georgia." Puckett continued performing on radio with the Stone Mountain Boys until he died July 14, 1946, from blood poisoning that resulted from an untreated boil on his neck. — *Jason Ankeny*

Old Time Greats / 1978 / ✦✦✦✦

Old Time Greats, Vol. 2 / 1978 / ✦✦✦✦

● **Red Sails in the Sunset** / 1988 / Bear Family ✦✦✦✦
These are '30s performances of old-timey music. — *AMG*

Pure Prairie League

Country-Rock
For a short time, Pure Prairie League was one of America's best country-rock bands, but personnel shifts destroyed its early promise. The group was formed in 1971 by vocalists/guitarists Craig Lee Fuller (the band's main songwriter) and George Powell, steel guitarist John Call, bassist Jim Lanham, and drummer Jim Caughlin. They recorded their self-titled debut album just a year later. Its fusion of laid-back singer-songwriter-styled rock and country earned critical praise, but much of the group departed, leaving only Fuller, Powell, and several session musicians. Even so, *Bustin' Out* proved to be an unqualified success, featuring the innovative addition of string arrangements by David Bowie guitarist Mick Ronson. Unfortunately, Fuller left in 1975, leaving the group without a strong songwriter or leader. Powell carried on with guitarist Larry Goshorn, bassist Mike Reilly, and pianist Michael Connor for several albums, none of which was as commercially or artistically successful as *Bustin' Out.* The group did enjoy a brief resurgence in 1980 with the Top Ten single "Let Me Love You Tonight," featuring future country star Vince Gill on lead vocals, but they called it quits in 1983. Fuller has since joined Little Feat. — *Steve Huey*

Let Me Love You Tonight and Other Hits / 1971 / Polygram ✦✦✦

● **Bustin' Out** / 1972 / RCA ✦✦✦✦
Bustin' Out was this band's most distinctive album, featuring very bright, thin-sounding acoustic guitars and dramatic string arrangements, courtesy of David Bowie's lead player Mick Ronson. "Amie" became a standard of sorts for the college coffeehouse crowd. Other highlights include "Jazzman," "Early Morning Riser,"

"Boulder Skies," "Call Me Tell Me," and "Angel," a song originally recorded on J. D. Blackfoot's *The Ultimate Prophecy.* —*Rick Clark*

Pure Prairie League / 1972 / RCA ✦✦✦✦

Those who think the Eagles are the be all and end all of country-rock owe it to themselves to search out this album. Any track here (or on the followup, *Bustin' Out*) holds up as well as, if not better than, anything by the Eagles. This album also proves that Craig Fuller is a grossly underrated songwriter. A country-rock must! —*Jim Worbois*

Two Lane Highway / 1975 / RCA ✦✦✦

With the departure of Fuller, the face (and sound) of Prairie League changed considerably. Larry Goshorn (ex-Sacred Mushroom) has replaced Fuller as the main songwriter in the band. And while the overall album isn't up to its predecessors, there are still some nice moments, including the title track, "Runner," and a humorous tribute to country music legend Merle Haggard. —*Jim Worbois*

If the Shoe Fits / 1976 / RCA ✦✦✦

PPL continues in the same vein as the last LP, with only a couple of George Powell tunes bearing any resemblance to the sound of the first two records. Not a bad record, but it's becoming harder to find any traces of what made this band so special. —*Jim Worbois*

Dance / 1976 / RCA ✦✦

It's getting more difficult to find positive things to say about the band's records by this time. Aside from some fine playing by Andy Stein (ex-Lost Planet Airman), JD Call's superb pedal steel work, and the track "All the Way," there isn't much to recommend this album. —*Jim Worbois*

Live Takin' the Stage / 1977 / RCA ✦✦

Live, PPL fairly accurately re-created their studio sound. Which makes one wonder, why buy this record if you have all the previous albums? The band doesn't seem to feel they have anything to prove, so they walk through these tracks adding nothing. If you already like these songs, stick with the studio versions, since nothing is added on this one. —*Jim Worbois*

Just Fly / 1978 / RCA ✦✦

Can't Hold Back / 1979 / RCA ✦✦

Another shake-up finds Goshorn and longtime steel player JD Call gone. Goshorn has been replaced by future modern-country star Vince Gill, as both main writer and leader of the group. By this time they are PPL in name only, as there is no resemblance between this and the original band. In fact, if you play "Rude Rude Awakening" next to the Eagles' "One of These Nights," it would be difficult to distinguish between the two bands. —*Jim Worbois*

Firin' Up / 1980 / Casablanca ✦

This last gasp effort provided the band with their highest charting single, "Let Me Love You Tonight." By now, the band's sound was nearly indistinguishable from Firefall and many other bands of the period. A sad end to a band that had begun with such promise. Single aside, there is no reason to look for this album. —*Jim Worbois*

Amie and Other Hits / 1981 / RCA ✦✦✦✦

This best-of collection contains all the hits and most of the essential album cuts, including a healthy sampling from *Bustin' Out.* —*Rick Clark*

Home on the Range / 1983 / Pair ✦✦

Mementos 1971-1987 / 1987 / Rushmore ✦✦✦

● **Best of Pure Prairie League** / 1995 / Mercury Nashville ✦✦✦✦

Containing most of their hits and key album tracks, *Best of Pure Prairie League* provides an effective introduction to the country-rock group. —*Sara Sytsma*

R

Eddie Rabbitt (Edward Thomas)

b. Nov. 27, 1941, Brooklyn, NY

Guitar, Vocals / Country-Pop, Urban Cowboy

One of country music's most innovative artists during the late '70s and early '80s, Eddie Rabbitt has made contributions to the format that have often gone overlooked. Especially in songs like the R&B-inflected "Suspicions" and the rockin' "Someone Could Lose a Heart Tonight," Rabbitt challenged the commonly recognized creative boundaries of the idiom.

Hailing from Brooklyn and New Jersey, Rabbitt moved to Nashville in 1968. Though it took a few years to get his recording career off the ground, he paid the rent through songwriting, authoring Elvis Presley's "Kentucky Rain" and Ronnie Milsap's "Pure Love." Eddie continued to write professionally until 1975, when he signed with Elektra Records' newly established country division. Initially, Rabbitt made recordings that were decidedly country—mostly uptempo material, like "Two Dollars in the Jukebox" and "Drinkin' My Baby (Off My Mind)"—with thick, inimitable harmonies, most of them overdubbed by Rabbitt himself. However, with the assistance of his then-associates David Malloy and Even Stevens, Rabbitt's records became "progressively progressive." In 1976, he started a string of Top Ten hits that ran uninterrupted until 1989. During that time, he had 16 No. 1 singles, including "Drinkin' My Baby (Off My Mind)" (1976), "You Don't Love Me Anymore" (1978), "Every Which Way but Loose" (1979), "Drivin' My Life Away" (1980), "I Love a Rainy Night" (1980), "Step by Step" (1980), and "You and I," a 1982 duet with Crystal Gayle.

In the late '80s he returned to more traditional sounds, as his country shuffle "On Second Thought" demonstrates. However, it was too late for Rabbitt to return to the top of the country charts, since he had already been supplanted by a newer generation of artists. He continued to record and perform sporadically throughout the '90s. *—Tom Roland*

The Best of Eddie Rabbitt / 1979 / Elektra ✦✦✦✦
Strong melodies are enhanced by Rabbitt's searing harmonies. The instruments are "hotter" in the final mix than in other productions from the same period, so even the mainstream country fare is a little different from that of his mid-'70s contemporaries. *—Tom Roland*

Loveline / 1979 / Elektra ✦✦✦
Fellow reviewers will cringe at this choice, but it displays Rabbitt at his most daring. Lots of R&B influence—even a bit of a "disco" feel on a couple of tracks—inspired melodies and unusual chord progressions throughout. Lyrically lightweight, but hey, this is music, not poetry. *—Tom Roland*

Horizon / 1980 / Elektra ✦✦✦✦
This is Rabbitt's rockabilly release. "I Love a Rainy Night" and "Drivin' My Life Away" set the pace for side one: Sun-inspired, guitar-based productions, heavy on the echo. Side two is a bit ballad-heavy, though most of the tracks stand up well individually. "That's Just the Way It Is" is something of a forerunner for "Someone Could Lose a Heart Tonight." *—Tom Roland*

Greatest Country Hits / 1991 / Curb ✦✦✦
Greatest Country Hits offers a few of Rabbitt's bigger hits, including "Drinkin' My Baby (Off My Mind)," "You Don't Love Me Anymore" and "I Just Want to Love You." However, much of the remaining material is filler, and Rabbitt's top sellers—"Every Which Way But Loose" and "I Love a Rainy Night," to name just two—are nowhere to be found. *—Jason Ankeny*

★ **All Time Greatest Hits** / Mar. 12, 1991 / Warner Brothers ✦✦✦✦✦
The ten-track *All Time Greatest Hits* covers Eddie Rabbitt's most commercially productive period—the late '70s and early '80s. "Drivin' My Life Away," "I Love a Rainy Night," and "Step by Step" were all Top Ten pop hits, in addition to hitting No. 1 country. "Drivin'" and "Rainy," in fact, were million-sellers. *—Dan Cooper*

Radio Flyer

Progressive Bluegrass

Filling the void left by the breakup of New Grass Revival, Radio Flyer combines solid musicianship with a newgrass sound. The band includes guitarist Dudly Murphy, fiddler and mandolinist David Wilson, bassist Steve Duede, and banjoist Roger Matthews. *—Chip Renner*

● **Old Strings New Strings** / 1991 / Turquoise ✦✦✦✦
This CD has the kind of bluegrass sound that makes you want to hear more. Their contemporary-sounding vocals help fill the void left by the New Grass Revival and Hot Rize. *—Chip Renner*

Radio Flyer / Turquoise ✦✦✦
Good album. If you are looking for an unknown bluegrass band to watch mature, this is it. Great potential. *—Chip Renner*

Marvin Rainwater

b. Jul. 2, 1925, Wichita, KS

Vocals / Traditional Country, Rockabilly, Nashville Sound/Countrypolitan

In the current climate of political correctness, it's amazing to think that a scant 40 years ago, a quarter-Cherokee country singer named Marvin Rainwater would shamelessly trade on his Indian pedigree to make himself a name on the country music circuit. But backing up this ridiculous charade was some very solid music from an artist who could work and create in a multiplicity of styles. Few artists in country music ever made music as quirky and just plain weird as that of Marvin Rainwater. His recorded cannonade—featuring his strong, rumbling baritone—showed that he was equally adept at Western ballads and pop confections with breathtaking go- for-broke forays into rockabilly.

He was born Marvin Percy Rainwater in 1925. After serving as a pharmacist's mate in the Navy during World War II, he turned to music full time. He had originally been a classically trained pianist, but after an accident removed part of his right thumb, he turned to country music and soon learned to strum a guitar proficiently enough to accompany his singing and compose songs on it. After putting down roots in Virginia, Rainwater quickly became a fixture on the Washington D.C. area honky tonk circuit, putting together his first band featuring a young Roy Clark on lead guitar and himself decked out in buckskin jacket and Indian headband. His first recordings came through the auspices of Bill McCall at 4-Star Records. Picturing himself as a songwriter first and performer second, Rainwater was hooked up through McCall with Ben Adleman, a songwriter with a small studio. Marvin recorded several song demos to be pitched to other artists through Adleman's and McCall's publishing concerns, only to see the demos poorly overdubbed and released at the height of his later fame on a myriad of dimestore budget labels like Crown and others too microscopic to mention.

But McCall also took three completed masters from other sessions ("I Gotta Go Get My Baby," "Hearts' Hall of Fame," and "Albino Stallion"), had them pressed on a custom promotional 45, and sold the masters to Coral Records. Rainwater's recording of "I Gotta Go Get My Baby" was handed over to Teresa Brewer, who had a hit with it in the pop market. But what propelled Rainwater up the show business ladder was a successful television performance on "Arthur Godfrey's Talent Scouts," the early-'50s equivalent of today's "Star Search." Godfrey had a top-rated morning show as well, and after his win, Rainwater made frequent guest spots on it, reaching a national audience for the first time. Rainwater recorded a composition in Godfrey's honor, "Tea Bag Romeo," a reference to the show's sponsor, Lipton Tea. By late 1955 he was a full-time member of Red Foley's Ozark Jubilee television and touring show, relocating to Springfield, MO. On one package show, he was introduced backstage to a precocious little girl who wanted to sing that night on the show. After hearing the moppet belt out part of a tune, Rainwater was convinced and introduced young Brenda Lee Tarpley to Red Foley and the rest is both country and rock 'n' roll history.

Shortly after signing with Foley, Rainwater started recording for M-G-M Records, his longest lasting label affiliation. The recordings are as scatter-gun an approach to commercial recording as you can possibly imagine. Solemn Americana recitations ("Pink Eyed Stallion") sat alongside novelty fluff like "Tennessee Hound Dog Yodel," which were B-sided by straightahead country weepers rife with down-home sentiments. At his next recording session in March 1956, Rainwater shifted gears again, deciding to cast his lot with the emerging rockabilly sound. The result was a two-sided blast of tonal mayhem, coupling the out-of-control "Hot and Cold" with the slightly less frenetic "Mr. Blues." Though both sides kicked up sufficient noise, it cost him big-time with country fans, who were confused when the former folk balladeer became an apostle for the big beat.

But rockabilly was a way for country artists to achieve pop stardom, and with the first successful attempts at crossover appeal already in place, Rainwater didn't have to wait long to find his song. That tune was "Gonna Find Me a Bluebird," a tune that went to No. 3 on the country charts while simultaneously climbing to No. 18 on the pop charts. Suddenly flush with success, Rainwater quit the Ozark Jubilee and moved his base of operations to New York City, ready to take on the world. But the follow-ups to "Gonna Find Me a Bluebird" were as diverse and quirky as his pre-hit output (one included a duet with Connie Francis); and his slide from the charts, coupled with one bad business deal after another, was swift and sure. In order to keep his slippery footing on any kind of chart, Rainwater had taken on a personal appearance schedule that would reduce lesser individuals to babbling protoplasm. By 1961, with his days on the pop charts largely behind him, he showed up for several recording sessions with his voice so burned out from show dates that he was unrecordable. His final M-G-M sessions not only remained unissued, but most of them appear to have been either lost or destroyed. In Rainwater's own words, "I had no voice and no money."

After a nine-month layoff, he signed with Warwick Records; with Link Wray and the Raymen backing him, he put out a pair of singles that were as fine as anything he had recorded in his heyday. But the marketplace in both pop and country had changed a lot since 1957, and the sides fell stillborn at the presses. Going for it one more time, Rainwater and new partner Bill Guess built a studio in Chicago and started up Brave Records, devoting its catalog to new songs from the singer. Aside from a brief stay with United Artists in 1964 and a one-off session for Warner Brothers

in 1969, the Brave singles document Rainwater's last commercial sides. Since the '70s—aside from an occasional appearance on a European rockabilly revival—Rainwater first has been living in a house trailer in Northern Minnesota on an undeveloped tract of land, spending most of his time ruminating on what might have been. He may not have become a big name, but he left behind a great number of sides that showed real musical depth and originality. —Cub Koda

With a Heart with a Beat / 1958 / MGM ✦✦✦✦

Gonna Find Me a Bluebird / 1962 / MGM ✦✦✦✦

Rockin' Rollin' Rainwater / 1982 / Bear Family ✦✦✦✦

Classic Recordings / 1992 / Bear Family ✦✦✦✦
A massive four-CD set of just about everything Marvin ever put down on tape and then some. All the M-G-M sides are here, his early demos (later overdubbed and released on a brace of budget labels), duets with Connie Francis and his sister Patty, as well as his later singles for Brave, United Artists, and Warner Brothers. The biggest bonus comes on the final disc, with a chaotic live radio performance from the Wheeling, WV, Jamboree, recorded in 1962. If you can't get enough Marvin, this box should do it. —Cub Koda

● **Whole Lotta Woman** / 1994 / Bear Family ✦✦✦✦
A superb single disc of Rainwater's most rocking sides, 26 in all, although inexplicably leaving off his biggest hit, "Gonna Find Me a Bluebird." But there's much here to love, including the chugging "Mr. Blues" and "Hot and Cold", featuring explosive guitar from Roy Clark; and "Boo Hoo," "Tough Top Cat," and "There's a Honky Tonk in Your Heart," which features backing from Link Wray and the Raymen. This is Marvin at his quirkiest. If you can live without his big hit, this is the package to grab. —Cub Koda

Bonnie Raitt

b. Nov. 8, 1949, Cleveland, OH
Guitar, Vocals / Blues-Rock, Singer-Songwriter, Adult Contemporary, Pop-Rock
While some blues critics like to act as if *all* White practitioners of the music—especially those who achieve any kind of mainstream success—are little more than modern-day carpetbaggers, few artists on the modern-day charts have earned their success more honestly than Bonnie Raitt. Purists and naysayers will point out that she's never made an album of just straight blues, but it took Eric Clapton 30-plus years to get around to doing one, It's almost a certainty that the prolific redhead won't make blues lovers wait *quite* that long. As a vocalist she's never been any less than soulful, and as a guitarist—especially on slide, her specialty— she reduces the old macho saw of "she plays pretty for a girl" into the same antiquated thought processes as expecting all women to look and act like June Cleaver.

Born in 1949 into a show business family (her Dad is bigvoiced Broadway star John Raitt) Bonnie started on guitar early on but really got the blues bug when she attended college in Cambridge, MA, in the '60s. Learning the ropes first-hand from blues legends Son House, Mississippi Fred McDowell (her twin inspirators on slide), and classic blues vocalist Sippie Wallace, she started doing the local coffeehouse circuit (usually opening for John Hammond, Jr.). She caught the eye of Dick Waterman, who managed all three artists and was soon managing her as well. She soon was appearing with the three performers, appearing on every folk and blues festival in existence and establishing herself as the little hippie girl who was undoubtedly the real deal. A recording contract with Warner Brothers soon followed, and her eponymously titled debut opus featured the talents of Chicago blues legends Junior Wells and A.C. Reed. But with eclectic tastes in abundance, Raitt was soon flexing her interpretive muscles on future outings, showing her love for the work of great modern songwriters of all genres.

Dividing her time equally with more pop-oriented albums while playing smaller venues as a solo act, the years of trying to party hearty with the older bluesmen finally caught up with her. The mid-'80s found her overweight and with an alcohol and drug problem. To make matters even worse, Warner Brothers—her label of 15 years—dumped her. But her turnaround—both personally and professionally— couldn't have more dramatic. With her booze and drug problems clearly behind her, she became the comeback kid with the 1989 Grammy-winning success of the aptly titled *Nick of Time*. She continued the run for the gold (or in this case, platinum) with the follow-ups *Luck of the Draw* and *Longing in Their Hearts*. Her contributions to John Lee Hooker's 1990 album *The Healer* and her tireless efforts on behalf of the Rhythm and Blues Foundation clearly illustrated that she hadn't left her blues roots in the trunk of the limo. —*Cub Koda*

Bonnie Raitt / 1971 / Warner Brothers ✦✦✦
By the time Raitt recorded this impressive self-titled debut, she had developed quite a set of blues chops playing with artists like Mississippi Fred McDowell, Howlin' Wolf, and other blues greats In fact, she enlisted Chicago bluesmen Junior Wells and A.C. Reed to aid in the proceedings, which are relaxed and earthy. —*Rick Clark*

● **Give It Up** / Sep. 1972 / Warner Brothers ✦✦✦✦
Raitt's sophomore release is a classic. Of all the albums from her days with Warner, this is the one that put together her folky singer-songwriter sensitivities with her love for country-blues. *Give It Up*, which took 13 years to go gold, showcased an intelligent song selection, with tracks by Jackson Browne ("Under the Falling Sky"), Eric Kaz ("Love Has No Pride"), and Joel Zoss ("Been Too Long at the Fair"). Her self-penned "Love Me like a Man" highlighted her impressive guitar technique. —*Rick Clark*

Takin' My Time / 1973 / Warner Brothers ✦✦✦✦
Raitt continued her streak of quality albums with *Takin' My Time*. As on her previous efforts, Raitt drew from the cream of the songwriting crop. Randy Newman's "Guilty" and Jackson Browne's "I Thought I Was a Child" are highlights. —*Rick Clark*

Streetlights / 1974 / Warner Brothers ✦✦✦
This album was undermined by slick production and unnecessary orchestration. Raitt seems to be fighting the production by Jerry Ragovoy. Versions of Joni Mitchell's "That Song About the Midway" and Allen Toussaint's "What Is Success?" are the highlights. —*Rick Clark*

Homeplate / 1975 / Warner Brothers ✦✦✦
On this return to form, Raitt shines with some great songs, particularly "Good Enough," "Your Sweet and Shiny Eyes," and "Run like a Thief." —*Rick Clark*

Sweet Forgiveness / Apr. 1977 / Warner Brothers ✦✦
One of Raitt's lesser efforts, it includes her version of Del Shannon's "Runaway," a minor hit despite being pretty lifeless-sounding. Even though the production isn't quite as slick as *Streetlights*, the relatively weak selection of material is this album's failing. —*Rick Clark*

The Glow / 1979 / Warner Brothers ✦✦✦
With the success of "Runaway," Warner felt it was time to take Raitt all the way by pairing her up with hit producer Peter Asher (Linda Ronstadt, James Taylor). Gone is the natural earthiness Raitt possessed on her first albums. In its place was an airbrushed slickness—from the cover photo all the way down to the grooves. A rendition of Isaac Hayes and David Porter's "Your Good Thing" and an original, "Standing by the Same Old Love," are among *The Glow*'s few highlights. The single from this album was a Robert Palmer song, "You're Gonna Get What's Coming." —*Rick Clark*

Green Light / 1982 / Warner Brothers ✦✦✦✦
Raitt dumps the slick stuff and goes for the grit with this energetic set featuring her band, which included keyboardist Ian MacLagan, whose credits included the Stones and Faces. Raitt's sensitive electric slide-guitar work was finally up front in the mix. It's one of her very best albums. Raitt does spirited versions of NRBQ's "Green Light" and "Me and the Boys." Other standouts include the rockers "Willya Wontcha" and "I Can't Help Myself." "River of Tears" is a powerful track that Raitt has dedicated to the memory of Little Feat's Lowell George in shows over the years. —*Rick Clark*

Nine Lives / 1986 / Warner Brothers ✦✦✦
Bonnie Raitt's ninth and final album for Warner Bros. Records was a star-crossed affair that began in 1983 in a session with producer Rob Fraboni that was a typical Raitt mixture of genres and songwriters, from Jerry Williams ("Excited") and Eric Kaz ("Angel") to reggae star Toots Hibbert ("True Love Is Hard to Find"), in a style similar to her 1982 LP *Green Light*. The record seems to have been rejected by Warner, but three years later Raitt returned to the studio with Bill Payne (Little Feat) and George Massenburgh and cut a group of commercial-sounding songs by the likes of Bryan Adams and Tom Snow. *Nine Lives* splits the difference between the two sessions, with four tracks rescued from '83, and five added from '86, plus the theme from a forgotten Farrah Fawcett movie ("Stand Up to the Night" from *Extremities*). The result is predictably scattered and strained, and it was Raitt's lowest-charting album since her debut. Not surprisingly, it was also the last straw in her relationship with Warner. —*William Ruhlmann*

● **Nick of Time** / Mar. 1989 / Capitol ✦✦✦✦
Few comebacks have been as celebrated as Raitt's multi-platinum hit *Nick of Time*, an album that included some of her strongest performances as a musician and singer. The determined "I Will Not Be Denied" seemed to say it all. Her poignant self-penned title cut revealed Raitt as a mature songwriter, on the level of the best writers whose work she had covered. She dug deep with some solid roadhouse R&B in "Love Letter," "Road's My Middle Name," and "Real Man." Her playful version of John Hiatt's "Thing Called Love" was another highlight. This is a seamless album. Highly recommended. —*Rick Clark*

The Bonnie Raitt Collection / 1990 / Warner Brothers ✦✦✦✦
A good (not great) sampler of Raitt's years at Warner, it's also a good starting place. —*Rick Clark*

Luck of the Draw / Jun. 1991 / Capitol ✦✦✦✦
Raitt followed *Nick of Time* with *Luck of the Draw*, another great album. Among the album's many highlights are "I Can't Make You Love Me" and a duet with Delbert McClinton on "Good Man, Good Woman." —*Rick Clark*

Longing in Their Hearts / Mar. 14, 1994 / Capitol ✦✦✦✦
On the followup to the followup (and another million-selling No. 1 hit), Bonnie Raitt contributes more than her usual share of original songs, writing four songs herself and setting a lyric of her husband's to music for a fifth. Elsewhere, she draws on such strong writers as Richard Thompson and Paul Brady, all for a collection devoted to devotion. Song after song expresses passion, usually with happy results—this is not the album of a woman with the blues. Even when she's dressing down a parent in her own "Circle Dance," Raitt offers forgiveness and understanding. There and in other songs the object of her emotion rarely seems to be perfect, but she takes that in and loves him, anyway. Co-producer Don Was provides a detailed production in which single elements—an accordion, a harmony vocal by Levon Helm or David Crosby—effectively color arrangements and complement Raitt's always soulful singing. —*William Ruhlmann*

Road Tested / Nov. 7, 1995 / Capitol ✦✦✦✦
In a 24-year recording career, Bonnie Raitt had not previously released a live album, so this concert set was overdue. Coming off three multiplatinum studio albums, Raitt and Capitol pulled out all the stops, compiling a 22-track double-disc package from dates recorded in July 1995 in Portland and Oakland. Raitt ranged over her career, reaching back to her early folk-blues days and forward to the pop-rock songs that finally made her a big star in the late '80s and early '90s. She also shared the spotlight with such guests as Bruce Hornsby, Ruth Brown, Charles Brown, Kim Wilson of the Fabulous Thunderbirds, Bryan Adams, and Jackson Browne. But that didn't keep an artist who has spent the bulk of her career pleasing live audiences rather than cutting hits from displaying her personal warmth along with her singing and playing skills. She also introduced half a dozen songs new to her repertoire, including a surprising cover of Talking Heads' "Burning Down the House" and a few that had potential to help promote the album as singles, including "Never Make Your Move Too Soon" and "Shake a Little." Inexplicably, Capitol (which probably wished the album had been a more reasonably priced single-disc) failed to bring the record home to consumers. The company's choice for a single was the anonymous Adams rocker "Rock Steady," done

as a duet with him—apparently, they were confusing Raitt with Tina Turner. As a result, the album stopped at gold, spending less than six months in the charts. Despite that commercial disappointment, it will be for many Bonnie Raitt fans an example of her best that effectively bridges the two parts of her career, and it's a good sampler for first-time listeners. —*William Ruhlmann*

Ranch Romance

Alternative Country, Western Swing Revival
Taking their name from a Western pulp magazine published in the 1930s, the genre-hopping swing band Ranch Romance formed in the late 1980s. In the Seattle-based group's initial incarnation, Ranch Romance was an all-female quartet featuring singer/guitarist Jo Miller, bassist Nancy Katz, fiddler Barbara Lamb, and mandolinist Lisa Theo. In 1989 they issued their debut LP, *Western Dream.* After touring in support of k.d. lang, Theo left the band in 1991 and was replaced by accordionist Nova Karina Devonie and David Keenen on guitar, mandolin, and banjo. Lamb departed to attempt a solo career before release of the second Ranch Romance effort, *Blue Blazes; Flip City* followed in 1993. —*Jason Ankeny*

● **Western Dream** / 1990 / Sugar Hill ✦✦✦✦
Ranch Romance's debut album *Western Dream* is a promising fusion of post-punk attitude and traditional country. It's an energetic, danceable record that gets by on its audacious conceptual fusion. —*Thom Owens*

Blue Blazes / 1991 / Sugar Hill ✦✦✦✦
Ranch Romance is a post-modern mix of Western swing, rockabilly, honky tonk, and rock 'n' roll, fusing excellent traditional country music with contemporary lyrics. Though a few of the songs fall flat, the group has enough energy to pull off their concept. —*Thom Owens*

Flip City / 1993 / Sugar Hill ✦✦✦
The four women/one guy who comprise Seattle's Ranch Romance stir up an unconventional but tasty cocktail with *Flip City.* Guitar, accordion, fiddle, mandolin, and upright bass breed an infectious cross of jazzy swing, bluegrass, Tex-Mex, lonesome prairie ballads, and funky zydeco. —*Roch Parisien*

Boots Randolph (Homer Louis Randolph III)

b. 1925, Paducah, KY
Trombone, Saxophone / Instrumental, Country-Pop, Pop-Rock, Nashville Sound/Countrypolitan
Tenor saxophonist Randolph has been a very influential instrumentalist within the country field, with his peak years in the '60s. Randolph switched from trombone to tenor sax in high school and played in local combos in Evansville in the '40s and '50s. He scored with "Yakety Sax," a novelty work co-written by James Rich, and was signed to RCA by Chet Atkins. His playing was and is quite simple; pleasant melodies, catchy themes, and occasional use of vocal effects have made up his signature style. He became a featured session musician and did many "countrypolitan" dates, placing 13 albums on the charts in the '60s and '70s. —*Ron Wynn*

Boots Randolph's Yakety Sax / 1963 / Monument ✦✦✦✦
Nashville session tenor saxman doing what he does best on a rocking set. —*Bill Dahl*

The Yakin' Sax Man / 1964 / Camden ✦✦✦
This album contains such hits as "So Rare," "Teach Me Tonight," "Bongo Band," and "Sleep Walk." —*AMG*

Sunday Sax / 1968 / Monument ✦✦✦
Tasty, fun, and more country than jazz. —*Ron Wynn*

Country Boots / 1972 / Monument ✦✦✦
Randolph is a fine country saxist. —*Ron Wynn*

Sentimental Journey / 1973 / Monument ✦✦✦✦
Nice stuff. More jazz-influenced country than country-tinged jazz. —*Ron Wynn*

● **Greatest Hits** / 1976 / Monument ✦✦✦✦
This country saxman shows his versatility. —*Bill Dahl*

Wayne Raney

b. Aug. 17, 1921, Wolf Bayou, AR, d. Jan. 23, 1993
Harmonica, Vocals / Traditional Country
Although he was a well known country singer from the '40s through the early '50s, Wayne Raney is best remembered for his extraordinary harmonica playing. He was born on a farm near Wolf Bayou, AR, but his crippled foot prevented him from doing heavy farm work, so he spent many hours loafing around town. There he heard a local busker "choke" a harmonica and was inspired to learn the instrument himself. In 1932 he met harmonica player Lonnie Glosson, with whom Raney teamed up in 1938 to play on a radio station in Little Rock. They spent a year working together, and even after they split up they would occasionally reunite to play together. Raney became famous for his mail-order harmonica business, which sold one million harmonicas a year. In 1948 he hit the charts with two Top 15 singles, "Lost John Boogie" and "Jack and Jill Boogie." In 1949 he had his first No. 1 hit, "Why Don't You Haul Off and Love," which he recorded with Glosson. The song crossed over to the pop Top 25 and was his biggest hit. Raney also did a few boogie and novelty songs, such as "Pardon My Whiskers" and "Undertakin' Daddy." He was with the Grand Ole Opry for one year and then spent a few months touring with Lefty Frizzell in 1953. Afterwards he returned to radio as a deejay and transcription artist. He recorded a few singles in the late '50s and continued to sell harmonicas through 1960, when the craze passed. Raney then returned to Arkansas and recorded a gospel album, *Don't Try to Be What You Ain't.* He also ran a chicken farm and founded Rimrock Records, whose best-known artists included Red Smiley, the Stanley Brothers, and Glosson. Eventually his health began to fail; his voicebox was removed in the late '80s. In 1990 he published a brief autobiography, *Life Has Not Been a Bed of Roses.* —*Sandra Brennan*

● **Songs from the Hills** / 1958 / King ✦✦✦✦
One of the great country harmonica players, Raney also qualifies as as one of the most important in the history of American pop, as he was one of the first musicians of any sort to fuse country and blues. This 16-cut collection functions as a best-of, including the big hits "Why Don't You Haul Off and Love Me," "Lost John Boogie," and "Jack and Jill Boogie." Despite what the title might lead you to believe, it's not exactly rural country-folk—it's hard-driving early country boogie with a decidedly urban influence. With the Delmore Brothers on backup, "Jack and Jill Boogie" in particular sounds like proto-rockabilly, with lengthy back-and-forth guitar exchanges that are about as close to White rock 'n' roll as anyone got in 1948. Despite the no-frills package (even a bit of historical information and liner notes would have been nice), it's the best available anthology of this somewhat overlooked country and pop pioneer. —*Richie Unterberger*

Wayne Raney and the Raney Family / 1960 / Starday ✦✦✦✦
Don't Try to Be What You Ain't / 1964 / Starday ✦✦✦
Real Hot Boogie / Charly ✦✦✦
More Hot Boogie / Charly ✦✦✦

The Rankin Family

Celtic, Contemporary Folk
The Rankin Family, from Cape Breton, Canada, began performing at family parties. John Morris Rankin (piano, fiddle) and vocalists Cookie, Heather, Jimmy, and Raylene Rankin began playing various folk festivals in 1989. The group released two independent cassettes, a self-titled debut album in 1989 and *Fare Thee Well Love* the next year. EMI signed the Rankin Family in 1992, re-released their first two albums, and issued *North Country* in 1993. —*John Bush*

Fare Thee Well Love / 1992 / Capitol ✦✦✦
North Country / 1994 / EMI ✦✦✦✦
North Country solidifies the group's wholesome reputation. You can always count on the Rankins for at least one exquisite, standout pop melody per recording; the one here is the title track's tribute to Canadian wilderness. The voices of Cookie, Heather, and Raylene Rankin blend effectively with an intuitive sense of har-

mony. These are pure, attractive voices, but with a certain lack of emotional depth that parallels Jimmy and John Morris Rankin's sometimes over-sweetened, keyboard-dominated instrumentation. Three tracks rendered in Gaelic are pleasant, while Lisa Brown overdoses on the group's sugary, "golly-gee" side. For those who prefer eating the icing off the cake. —*Roch Parisien*

● **Rankin Family Collection** / 1996 / EMI Canada ✦✦✦✦
The album finds Cape Breton's leading "Celtic Lite" siblings the Rankin Family compiling 13 favorite samples of traditional-inspired Maritimes music delivered in a cozy, multi-harmony pop setting—heavy on folksy, down-home charm. Includes new recordings "Down by the Sally Gardens" and the Celtic "Fail-il E." An average quality multimedia component allows computer/CD-ROM-equipped fans to view biography and discography informa-tion, video clips, and live footage. —*Roch Parisien*

Endless Seasons / Feb. 1996 / EMI ✦✦✦

Rarely Herd

Progressive Bluegrass, Traditional Bluegrass
The Rarely Herd were among the finest contemporary bluegrass bands to come out of Ohio and became quite popular on the festi-val circuit. Playing a wide variety of progressive and traditional bluegrass along with their own unique compositions and adapta-tions from other genres, the Rarely Herd were especially noted for their close vocal harmonies and energetic performances. Their lineup included guitarist and lead singer Jim Stack; his brother, fiddler/mandolinist/vocalist Alan, a former child prodigy; and bassist Jim Weaver. —*Sandra Brennan*

Heartbreak City / 1994 / Pinecastle ✦✦✦

● **Pure Homemade Love** / 1995 / Pinecastle ✦✦✦✦

Midnight Loneliness / Pinecastle ✦✦✦

Rattlesnake Annie (Annie McGowan)

Guitar, Vocals / Progressive Country, Outlaw Country
Rattlesnake Annie was born Rosan Gallimore and raised on her family's cotton and tobacco farm near Puryear, TN. Her father was a renowned blues and country singer, and in her spare time Annie began writing poetry and learning to play the guitar. When she was about 12, she and two cousins formed the Gallimore Sis-ters and performed professionally at local churches and political rallies, as well as funerals. In 1953 the Gallimores appeared on TV in Paris, TN, and won a statewide talent contest. After high school, the girls went their separate ways.

At age 16, Annie set out alone for Memphis and then to Hunts-ville, AL, where she regularly performed at the Carriage House. She moved to Texas near the end of the '60s and married the man who would become her manager, Max McGowan. She met Willie Nelson in 1969 and they became friends, sometimes trading songs. She earned the nickname "Rattlesnake" from her refusal to allow the killing of snakes on her ranch as per her Cherokee descent, where the rattler is a healing symbol. She released her first single, "Texas Lullabye," in 1974. Her critically acclaimed debut *Rattlesnakes and Rusty Water* did nothing in the US but enjoyed popularity in Europe. She recorded with Nelson in 1982 and subsequently toured the US with Floyd Tillman.

In the mid-'80s Annie returned from a stay in England and recorded *Country Livin'.* She returned to Europe and became the first female country singer to play the Eastern Bloc countries. While in East Germany, she appeared on television, and in Czech-oslovakia she made an album with Czech country singer Michael Teny, *Rattlesnake Annie and the Last Cowboy.* In 1987 she finally won recognition in the US when she and Rick Blackmon pro-duced her self-titled album. One of the cuts, "Goodbye to a River," became the anthem of the West German chapter of Greenpeace, while two other cuts became minor chart hits in the US. In 1991 Rattlesnake Annie became the first American country performer to sign to Sony Music Japan and recorded several albums for the label, including *Painted Bird* (1993). —*Sandra Brennan*

Rattlesnakes and Rusty Water / 1980 / Rattlesnake ✦✦✦✦

Country Livin' / 1986 / Rattlesnake ✦✦✦

Rattlesnake Annie

● **Rattlesnake Annie** / 1987 / Columbia ✦✦✦✦

Rattlesnake Annie and the Last Cowboy / 1987 / Supraphone ✦✦✦

Indian Dreams / 1991 / Sony ✦✦✦

Eddy Raven

b. Aug. 19, 1945, Lafayette, LA
Vocals / Cajun, Country-Pop, Urban Cowboy
Born Edward Garvin Futch, it's no wonder that his name was changed by a record executive to Eddy Raven on his very first sin-gle, released on tiny Cosmos Records in the the late '60s. Numer-ous influences have made his music almost indescribable: the Cajun sounds of his native Louisiana, the blues influence from working with Johnny Winter, the rock 'n' roll of his idol Elvis Pres-ley, and the pure country of the Grand Ole Opry. Befriended by Jimmy C. Newman, Raven made the first of many trips to Nash-ville in 1970, though he didn't move permanently for a couple of years. Signed to a publishing deal with Acuff-Rose, he wrote songs for Don Gibson and Roy Acuff, among others, and started making records himself in 1974. Despite the acclaim of his peers, Raven didn't actually earn a hit record as a recording artist until 1981, with the release of his *Desperate Dreams* album. After he lost his recording contract in a 1983 consolidation involving Elek-tra and Warner, Raven took the next year to realign his business. The Oak Ridge Boys earned a hit at that time with his song "Thank God for Kids," and Raven came out of his forced vacation strong, signing with RCA and gaining his first No. 1 single with "I Got Mexico." For the next half-dozen years, Raven remained a consistent staple of country radio. He was frequently adventurous and always listenable.

Eddy Raven began playing music when he was a child in Lafayette, LA, joining a garage rock band when he was 13 years old. Three years later, his family moved to Georgia, where Eddy landed a job working in a radio station. He also managed to cut his own song, "Once a Fool," for the local independent label, Cosmo. The record was released under the name "Eddy Raven," and Edward Futch used that moniker as his stage name from that day forward. In 1963 the family moved back to Lafayette, and

Raven began working in a record shop called La Louisianne. The store's owner had a label of the same name, and Raven cut several records for the label, including his 1969 debut album *That Crazy Cajun Sound*.

Jimmy C. Newman happened to hear *That Crazy Cajun Sound* and was impressed enough to land Raven a publishing deal with Acuff-Rose. After the record's release, Raven began singing for Jimmie Davis' band. By 1971 other artists had begun recording Raven's songs, with Don Gibson taking "Country Green" into the Top Five; Gibson also recorded "Touch the Morning," while Jeannie C. Riley covered "Good Morning, Country Rain" and Roy Acuff sang "Back in the Country." Soon, Raven had gained a reputation within Nashville as a songwriter and a performer; and once Don Gant of Acuff-Rose became an A&R man for ABC Records, Raven had a record deal of his own in 1974. For the next two years, he had a series of minor hits for the label, highlighted by the No. 27 "Good News, Bad News" in 1975. He left the label in 1978, staying with Monument for one year before signing with Dimension the next year. None of his singles for either label was a big hit, and he left Dimension in 1981.

Later in 1981 he signed with Elektra, where he had his first big hit with the No. 13 "I Should've Called." Over the next two years Raven had three Top 20 singles for Elektra, setting the stage for his breakthrough into the Top Ten in 1984. After spending 1983 resolving legal and managerial problems, Raven signed with RCA Records, releasing "I Got Mexico" in the spring. The single was a big hit, becoming not only his first Top Ten single, but his first No. 1 hit. For the remainder of the decade, he had a string of Top Ten hits for the label, including the No. 1 singles "Shine, Shine, Shine" (1987), "I'm Gonna Get You" (1988), and "Joe Knows How to Live" (1988). He left RCA for Universal in 1989, and he had two No. 1 singles for the label—"In a Letter to You" and "Bayou Boys." Once Universal collapsed in 1989, he moved to their parent company, Capitol, but his records for the label were largely ignored because radio was beginning to program newer artists instead of veterans like Raven. During the '90s Eddy Raven lacked a record label, but he continued to tour and perform. —*Tom Roland*

Desperate Dreams / 1981 / Elektra ✦✦✦
Raven had more creative control than in previous efforts and developed a tough-sounding album. It's heavy on rhythm guitar, long on bravado. —*Tom Roland*

● **The Best of Eddy Raven** / 1988 / RCA ✦✦✦✦
After his 1983 layoff, Raven put together a string of some of the best "in-the-groove" records Nashville had to offer. Many of them—"I Got Mexico," "Shine, Shine, Shine," and "Sometimes a Lady"—are here, plus his refried Cajun effort, "I'm Gonna Get You." —*Tom Roland*

Temporary Sanity / 1989 / Liberty ✦✦✦✦
Temporary Sanity is a mixed bag highlighting Raven at his best (the moody ballad "Island") and worst (the ham-fisted Cajun stylings of "Bayou Boys"). —*Jason Ankeny*

Greatest Country Hits / 1990 / Curb ✦✦✦✦
Greatest Country Hits is the most comprehensive collection of Raven's hits; it features three of his chart-toppers—"I Got Mexico," "Shine, Shine, Shine," and "I'm Gonna Get You." —*Jason Ankeny*

Greatest Hits / 1990 / Warner Brothers ✦✦✦
Greatest Hits these aren't; only one cut, "She's Playing Hard to Forget," even made the country Top Ten. —*Jason Ankeny*

● **Best of Eddy Raven** / 1992 / Liberty ✦✦✦✦

Wade Ray

b. Apr. 13, 1913, Evansville, IN
Fiddle, Vocals / Western Swing
Wade Ray was a popular fiddler who performed in concert and on radio and television for more than three decades; unfortunately, despite his long career, he cut only a few singles in the 1950s and two old-time revival albums during the '60s. He was born in 1916 in Evansville, IN, but raised in Boynton, AR. When he was four, his parents gave him a homemade violin made out of a cigar box; the next year he was playing a real one on stage, billed as "The Youngest Violin Player in the World." Ray learned to play the

tenor banjo before joining the Orpheum Vaudeville Circuit and touring Indiana until 1931, when he turned 18. He next joined Pappy Cheshire's National Champion Hillbillies on a St. Louis radio station, and remained there as a musician and musical director until he was inducted by the Army in 1943. He then joined the Prairie Ramblers on the WLS Chicago "National Barn Dance," where he recorded and performed with Patsy Montana. In 1949 he left the show to record with the Ozark Mountain Boys. Ray next appeared on the "Rex Allen Show" on CBS-TV in Los Angeles; he made his feature film debut in *Hollywood*. During the '50s and '60s, he made guest appearances on the Grand Ole Opry and the "Ernest Tubb Show." Between 1951 and 1957 Ray released 23 singles for RCA, but none of them appeared on the charts. In 1966 he cut the album *A Ray of Country Sun;* his second album, *Down Yonder—The Country Fiddlers*, featured a number of former country stars. In 1979 he moved to join the KSD-AM St. Louis roadshow, but poor health forced him to leave. Eventually Ray moved to Florida to retire. —*Sandra Brennan*

A Ray of Country Sun / 1966 / ABC/Paramount ✦✦✦
A Ray of Country Sun may be slightly uneven, but it has enough strong moments—"Within Your Crowd," "A Penny for Your Thoughts," "Any Old Arms Won't Do" and "Too Many Rivers" among them—to make it an enjoyable LP. —*Thom Owens*

● **Walk Softly (And Other Country Songs)** / 1966 / RCA Camden ✦✦✦✦

Down Yonder: The Country Fiddlers / 1967 / RCA Victor ✦✦✦

Collin Raye

b. Aug. 22, 1959, DeQueen, AR
Vocals / Contemporary Country, New Traditionalist
Singer-songwriter Collin Raye's blend of Western swing, rockabilly, country-rock, and sentimental ballads brought him a string of hit singles in the early '90s. Floyd Collin Wray's mother was a well known local country singer who performed with such stars as Johnny Cash, Carl Perkins, and Elvis Presley, and she sometimes brought Collin and his brother Scott up on stage to sing harmony. Collin, billing himself as "Bubba," and Scott founded the country-rock Wray Brothers Band in the late '70s and moved West to perform. The brothers made their recording debut in 1983 and had some chart success with their first single, "Reason to Believe." Over the next four years the Wrays released a number of singles on different record labels, but they had no real success until 1987, when they had a Top 50 hit with "You Lay a Lotta Love on Me." After the single's success, the band broke up, and Collin began performing on his own in Nevada clubs. In 1991 he signed to Epic and released his solo debut, *All I Can Be*. Raye's first single, "All I Can Be (Is a Sweet Memory)," reached the country Top 40 but it was his second single, "Love, Me," that made him a star when it climbed to No. 1 in early 1992 and stayed at the top of the charts for three weeks, kick-starting a string of Top Ten hits that ran for a number of years. Raye's second album, *In This Life* (1992), went gold and produced three hits, including "Somebody Else's Moon." His third album, *Extremes*, went gold by the end of 1994, spawning the Top Ten hits "Little Rock," "Man of My Word," and "My Kind of Girl." In 1995 Raye released his fourth solo album, *I Think About You*. —*Sandra Brennan*

All I Can Be / Dec. 1990 / Epic ✦✦
Many people compared Raye to Vince Gill, especially since Gill sang harmony on the album's lead track and first single, "All I Can Be (Is a Sweet Memory)." Raye hit the top of the charts with the three-hankie "Love, Me," which his fans sometimes play at funerals. —*Brian Mansfield*

In This Life / Aug. 25, 1992 / Epic ✦✦✦
The soft-focus, yet rugged, album art helps establish Raye as the heartthrob his silky smooth tenor makes him out to be. Inside, it's an even smoother mix than *All I Can Be*, with Raye indulging his tendencies at every turn, including a revival of the Everly Brothers' make-out classic "Let It Be Me." The hit "I Want You Bad (And That Ain't Good)" put some sweat and muscle into Raye's image, but even the trucker song, "Latter Day Cowboy," sounds as if it was written for the women back home. The album also includes

"In This Life," a No. 1 hit; "Somebody Else's Moon;" and "That Was a River." —*Brian Mansfield*

● **Extremes** / 1994 / Epic ✦✦✦✦
Tired of the balladeer image "Love, Me" and "In This Life" had tagged him with, Raye set out to show that he was made of stronger material. The first single, the rollicking "That's My Story," was a Lee Roy Parnell tune that Raye roared through. *Extremes*, as its title suggested, caromed recklessly from that type of song to, of course, ballads—but "Little Rock," about a recovering alcoholic, and "Dreaming My Dreams with You," earlier cut by Waylon Jennings, were two of the most powerful recordings of Raye's career. —*Brian Mansfield*

I Think About You / 1995 / Epic ✦✦✦✦
After attempting a somewhat rougher approach with *Extremes*, Collin Raye returned to his smooth ballad stylings on *I Think About You*. Though he still sings the occasional honky tonk raver, the high points on his fourth album come when he slows the pace down. *I Think About You* does suffer from a few bland tracks, but the album demonstrates why Raye was one of the most popular country singers of the mid-'90s. —*Stephen Thomas Erlewine*

Christmas: Gift / Oct. 29, 1996 / Epic ✦✦✦
Collin Raye's holiday album *Christmas: Gift* contains his versions of Christmas classics like "The First Noel," "Silent Night," "Away in a Manger," and "The Christmas Song." Raye delivers all the songs competently and the music is pleasant, yet there is no spark to the album. Only dedicated fans need pick up this *Gift*. —*Thom Owens*

● **Best of Collin Raye** / Mar. 11, 1997 / Epic ✦✦✦✦
The Best of Collin Raye contains all of the contemporary country singer's biggest hits and best-known songs—including "Every Second," "That Was A River," "Little Rock," "One Boy, One Girl," "Not That Different," and the No. 1 singles "Love, Me," "In This Life," and "My Kind of Girl"—making it an excellent introduction to the popular vocalist. —*Thom Owens*

Susan Raye

b. Oct. 8, 1944, Eugene, OR
Vocals / Traditional Country, Country-Pop, Bakersfield Sound
Best known for her work in conjunction with mentor Buck Owens, singer Susan Raye was born October 8, 1944, in Eugene, OR. She first began singing with a high school rock group, but after the band called it quits, she auditioned for a local country station. Not only did she begin performing on the radio, she also landed work as a deejay, eventually becoming the host of a Portland TV program called "Hoedown."

At one of Raye's performances at an area nightclub she met Jack McFadden, Buck Owens' manager. McFadden was so impressed with her vocal talents that he persuaded Owens to fly her to his home in Bakersfield, CA, for an audition. Owens offered Raye a slot on an upcoming tour, and in 1969 she cut her first record, "Maybe if I Close My Eyes (It'll Go Away)." Her next record, a cover of Jackie DeShannon's pop smash "Put a Little Love in Your Heart," was also her first Top 30 hit. At about the same time, she began a nine-year stint as a featured performer on the program "Hee Haw."

Raye issued her first solo LP, *One Night Stand*, in 1970; the single "Willy Jones" became her first Top Ten hit, lending its name to the title of her follow-up album the next year. Also in 1970 she released two duet records with Owens, *We're Gonna Get Together* and *The Great White Horse*. Her biggest year as a solo artist came in 1971, when she issued three consecutive Top Ten hits—"L.A. International Airport," "Pitty, Pitty, Patter," and "(I've Got a) Happy Heart." The title track of 1972's *My Heart Has a Mind of Its Own* also reached the Top Ten.

After hitting No.9 in 1974 with "Whatcha Gonna Do With a Dog Like That" and scoring a success with Owens on a cover of the Mickey and Sylvia classic "Love Is Strange," Raye's hit-making days were largely over; after issuing the 1976 LP *Honey, Toast and Sunshine*, she left Buck Owens' tutelage to release a self-titled album in 1977. A year later, she retired in order to raise her six kids and returned to college to pursue a degree in psychology. In 1985, she came out of exile to release the album *Susan Raye:*

There and Back, which generated the minor hit single "I Just Can't Take the Leaving Anymore." —*Jason Ankeny*

We're Gonna Get Together / 1970 / Capitol ✦✦✦
One Night Stand / 1970 / Capitol ✦✦✦
● **L.A. International Airport: 25 Great Hits** / 1971 / Capitol ✦✦✦✦
Cheating Game / 1973 / EMI ✦✦✦✦

The Red Clay Ramblers

Old-Time, String Band
One of the most authentic of the string-band revival groups, the Red Clay Ramblers perform traditional Appalachian folk music and contemporary compositions; they mix genres with such talent and authority that for years they were considered among the best of the modern revivalists of string-band music. The Chapel Hill, NC-based quintet includes Tommy Thompson (banjo, vocals), Jim Watson (guitar, mandolin, vocals), Mike Craver (piano, harmonium, vocals), Jack Herrick (bouzouki, guitar, harmonica, bass, cello, flute, harmonium, vocals) and Clay Buckner (fiddle, harmonica, vocals). The Ramblers reached their widest audience through scoring and performing in off-Broadway productions; one of their most highly acclaimed albums was their score from Sam Shepard's *A Lie of the Mind*. —*David Vinopal and Sandra Brennan*

The Red Clay Ramblers / 1972 / Smithsonian/Folkways ✦✦✦✦
Stolen Love / 1976 / Flying Fish ✦✦✦
The Ramblers hit on all cylinders: old-timey, jazz, country, fiddle tunes, and blues. —*Chip Renner*

Twisted Laurel / 1977 / Flying Fish ✦✦✦✦
Twisted Laurel is an excellent distillation of the group's desire to preserve the traditions of string band music while moving beyond the boundaries of old-timey music. Not all of their fusions and experimentations work, but their wish to create ambitious string music rings through loud and clear. Though it is occasionally awkward, it is an interesting and worthwhile release for dedicated fans. —*Thom Owens*

Chuckin' the Frizz / 1979 / Flying Fish ✦✦✦
Good music from this innovative old-time group is featured. —*AMG*

Hard Times / 1981 / Flying Fish ✦✦✦
A good collection of music: 13 songs. Guest Triona Ni Dhomhnaill. —*Chip Renner*

It Ain't Right / 1986 / Flying Fish ✦✦✦
It Ain't Right is an ambitious record, demonstrating the Red Clay Ramblers' ability to meld all sorts of string-band music, from Celtic to folk, adding elements of folk and pop to the mixture. The album is augmented by cameos from trombonist Chris Frank and an occasional rhythm section. —*Thom Owens*

A Lie of the Mind / 1986 / Rykodisc ✦✦✦
The soundtrack for Sam Shepard's screenplay. Very clean sound. —*Chip Renner*

Far North / 1989 / Sugar Hill ✦✦✦
From Sam Shepard's film *Far North*, this is a very good soundtrack album. —*Chip Renner*

● **Twisted Laurel/Merchants Lunch** / 1991 / Flying Fish ✦✦✦✦
Two of the Red Clay Ramblers' best albums—*Twisted Laurel* (1976) and *Merchant's Lunch* (1977)—are collected on this outstanding two-fer CD. This is the sound of the band coming into its own. —*Thom Owens*

Rambler / 1992 / Sugar Hill ✦✦
Rambler is a latter-day recording by the Red Clay Ramblers, made more than 20 years after their formation, but the group shows very few signs of wear and tear. The Ramblers run through a number of classic songs—not only bluegrass, but Celtic, gospel, folk, and pop classics, as well. The diversity of the material and the effortlessness of the group's performance prove that the Red Clay Ramblers are getting better and more assured with age. —*Thom Owens*

Merchant's Lunch / Flying Fish ✦✦✦✦
One of their top three albums. Flying Fish features *Merchant's Lunch* and *Twisted Laurel* on one CD. —*Chip Renner*

Blind Alfred Reed

b. 1880, Floyd, VA, **d.** Jan. 17, 1956
Fiddle, Vocals / Old-Time, Traditional Country, Traditional Folk
This West Virginia singer-songwriter and fiddler was one of Ralph Peer's discoveries on the legendary 1927 Bristol field trip that unearthed the Carter Family and Jimmie Rodgers. Reed was one of those uniquely Southern contradictions, both reactionary and progressive in his songs. "How Can a Poor Man Stand Such Times and Live?" echoed the sentiments of the rural poor, who tasted none of the Roaring Twenties' prosperity (a myth for all but a privileged few). "Why Do You Bob Your Hair, Girls?" invoked Biblical sanctions against flappers. Topical commentary of this sort was rare in early hillbilly recordings: Reed's contemporaries usually pruned a branch from the folk tree or swiped a page from Mom's Victorian songbook. Incongruously, Reed was a protest singer-songwriter out of time and place. Ry Cooder revived a couple of his songs in the '70s, the decade of Rounder's reissue of several Reed performances, *How Can a Poor Man Stand Such Times and Live?* —*Mark A. Humphrey*

● **How Can a Poor Man ...** / 1920 / Rounder ✦✦✦✦
How Can a Poor Man Stand Such Times and Live is '20s hillbilly social commentary, both reactionary ("Why Do You Bob Your Hair, Girls?") and progressive ("How Can a Poor Man Stand Such Times and Live") from this West Virginia singer and fiddler. It's austere and engaging. —*Mark A. Humphrey*

Jerry Reed (Jerry Reed Hubbard)

b. Mar. 20, 1937, Atlanta, GA
Guitar, Vocals, Session Musician / Instrumental, Traditional Country, Progressive Country, Country-Pop, Rockabilly
Known throughout country music as "The Guitar Man," singer-songwriter Jerry Reed gained recognition not only for a successful solo career but also as an actor and ace session player. Jerry Reed Hubbard was born in Atlanta, GA, on March 20, 1937. After picking up the guitar as a child, he was signed by publisher and producer Bill Lowery to cut his first record, "If the Good Lord's Willing and the Creeks Don't Rise," at the age of 18. He continued releasing both country and rockabilly singles to little notice until rocker Gene Vincent covered his "Crazy Legs" in 1958.

After a two-year tenure in the military, Reed moved to Nashville in 1961 to continue his songwriting career, which had continued to gather steam even while he was in the armed forces, thanks to Brenda Lee's 1960 cover of his "That's All You Got to Do." He also became a popular session and tour guitarist. In 1962 he scored some success with the singles "Goodnight Irene" and "Hully Gully Guitar," which found their way to Chet Atkins, who produced Reed's 1965 "If I Don't Live Up to It." In 1967 he notched his first chart hit with "Guitar Man," which Elvis Presley soon covered. After Presley recorded another of Reed's songs, "US Male," the songwriter recorded an Elvis tribute, "Tupelo Mississippi Flash," which proved to be his first Top 20 hit.

After releasing the 1970 crossover hit "Amos Moses," a hybrid of rock, country, and cajun styles, Reed teamed with Atkins for the duet LP *Me and Jerry*. During the 1970 television season, he was a regular on the "Glen Campbell Goodtime Hour," and in 1971 he issued his biggest hit, the chart-topper "When You're Hot, You're Hot," which was also the title track of his first solo album. A second collaboration with Atkins, *Me and Chet*, followed in 1972, as did a series of Top 40 singles, which alternated between frenetic, straightforward country offerings and more pop-flavored, countrypolitan material. A year later, he scored his second No. 1, "Lord, Mr. Ford," from the album *The Uptown Poker Club*.

In the mid-1970s Reed's recording career began to take a backseat to his acting aspirations, and in 1974 he co-starred with his close friend Burt Reynolds in the film *W.W. and the Dixie Dancekings*. While he continued to record throughout the decade, his greatest visibility was as a motion picture star, almost always in tandem with headliner Reynolds; after 1976's *Gator*, Reed

appeared in 1978's *High Ballin'* and 1979's *Hot Stuff*. He also co-starred in all three of the *Smokey and the Bandit* films; the first, which premiered in 1977, landed Reed a No. 2 hit with the soundtrack's "East Bound and Down."

In 1979 he released a record comprised of both vocal and instrumental selections titled, appropriately enough, *Half & Half*. It was followed two years later by *Jerry Reed Sings Jim Croce*, a tribute to the late singer-songwriter. In 1982 Reed's career as a singles artist was revitalized by the chart-topping novelty hit "She Got the Goldmine (I Got the Shaft)," followed by "The Bird," which peaked at No. 2. His last chart hit, "I'm a Slave," appeared in 1983. After an unsuccessful 1986 LP, *Lookin' at You*, Reed focused on touring until 1992, when he and Atkins reunited for the album *Sneakin' Around* before he again returned to the road. —*Jason Ankeny*

Me and Jerry / 1971 / RCA ✦✦✦✦
Me and Jerry is the first of Reed's many collaborations with mentor Chet Atkins. —*Jason Ankeny*

When You're Hot, You're Hot / 1971 / RCA ✦✦✦✦
Reed's best-selling LP. The title track was his biggest chart hit; the album also includes "Ko-Ko Joe" and a cover of Bob Dylan's "Don't Think Twice (It's All Right)." —*Jason Ankeny*

Best of Jerry Reed / 1972 / RCA ✦✦✦✦
It features several key hits ("Amos Moses," "Guitar Man," "When You're Hot, You're Hot") and some crackling instrumentals. Alimony-payers looking for "She Got the Goldmine (I Got the Shaft" will be disappointed, however. It's not here. —*Dan Cooper*

Half & Half / 1974 / RCA ✦✦✦
Half & Half is split evenly between Reed's vocal performances and his instrumental guitar workouts. —*Jason Ankeny*

Me and Chet / 1976 / RCA ✦✦✦
Me and Chet is a sequel to a 1970 collection of duets with mentor Chet Atkins, *Me and Jerry*. —*Jason Ankeny*

East Bound and Down / 1977 / RCA ✦✦✦
The title song was Reed's last sizable hit. —*Dan Heilman*

● **The Essential Jerry Reed** / Aug. 1, 1995 / RCA ✦✦✦✦
The Essential Jerry Reed contains more than 20 of the singer-songwriter's greatest htis, from "Amos Moses" to "East Bound and Down," hitting the No. 1s "When You're Hot, You're Hot," "Lord, Mr. Ford," and "She Got the Goldmine (I Got the Shaft)." In addition to the hits, there's a handful of obscurities, but it remains the best single overview of Reed's career. —*Thom Owens*

Del Reeves

b. Jul. 14, 1934, Sparta, NC
Guitar, Vocals / Traditional Country, Nashville Sound/Country-politan
Singer-songwriter Del Reeves was born Franklin Delano Reeves in Sparta, NC; the youngest of 11 children, he learned to play the guitar as a boy by using his brothers' six-strings while they were serving in World War II. By the time Reeves was 12, he was hosting his own radio show. While stationed at Travis Air Force Base in California, he appeared on television's "Chester Smith Show," and he made his recording debut with Smith in 1958 with "Love Love Love." He remained in California after his discharge and eventually hosted his own "Del Reeves' Country Carnival." Four years later, he and his new wife became a successful songwriting team whose tunes were recorded by such artists as Carl Smith, Rose Maddox, and Roy Drusky. In 1961 Reeves scored his first Top Ten hit with "Be Quiet Mind." A year later he had his second hit, "He Stands Real Tall," which reached the Top 15. He moved to Columbia the following year, but scored only one mid-level hit. In 1965 he scored his first chart-topper with "Girl on the Billboard," plus two more major hits that year. The next year none of his three hits made it past the Top 30, but in 1967 Reeves again made the Top 20 with "A Dime at a Time." He had even bigger hits with "Looking at the World Through a Windshield" and "Good Time Charlies;" the latter became his signature song. He continued with a string of hits through the end of the decade and appeared in six feature films, including 1969's Burt Reynolds vehicle *Sam Whiskey*. For Reeves the 1970s brought a few major hits such as

"A Lover's Question" and "Land Mark Tavern," but he had mostly medium-level hits.In 1980 he again had a string of low- to mid-range hits. Reeves remained a regular performer at the Grand Ole Opry, of which he had been a member since 1966. —*Sandra Brennan*

Del Reeves Sings Jim Reeves / 1966 / United Artists ◆◆◆

Santa's Boy / 1966 / United Artists ◆◆

Gettin' Any Feed for Your Chickens? / 1966 / United Artists ◆◆◆

Struttin' My Stuff / 1967 / United Artists ◆◆◆

Six of One, Half-a-Dozen of the Other / 1967 / United Artists ◆◆◆

The Little Church in the Dell / 1967 / United Artists ◆◆

The Best of Del Reeves / 1967 / United Artists ◆◆◆◆

Best of Del Reeves, Vol. 2 / 1969 / United Artists ◆◆◆◆

Baby I Love You / Bear Family ◆◆◆◆

● **The Best of** / Capitol ◆◆◆◆
This features "Wild Blood," "Goodtime Charlies," "The Best Is Yet to Come," and other hits. —*AMG*

Goebel Reeves

b. Oct. 9, 1899, Sherman, TX, **d.** 1959, California
Vocals / Traditional Country, Traditional Folk
Goebel Reeves was a singer-songwriter who eschewed his middle-class upbringing to become a hobo known as "the Texas Drifter" and sometimes as "George Riley, the Yodeling Rustler." He penned one of Woody Guthrie's signature tunes, "Hobo's Lullaby," and according to legend, he taught Jimmie Rodgers to yodel. Reeves was born the son of a Texas state legislator in Sherman, TX. In 1917 he joined the US Army and was shot while fighting overseas on the front lines. He was discharged in 1921 and chose to become a vagabond, earning a meager living as a singer. He did a stint with the Merchant Marines before making his recording debut in 1929, and he began using the above-mentioned monikers the next year. His last recordings were made in 1938 for a transcription company in Hollywood; they were mostly recitations and poems. Occasionally Reeves appeared on radio stations in both the US and Canada. Later in the '30s, he rejoined the Merchant Marines and spent time in Japan. During World War II, he entertained US troops and then, because he spoke some Japanese, worked for the US government to help out in Japanese-American relocation camps. Reeves died in a veterans' hospital in Long Beach, CA, in 1969. —*Sandra Brennan*

● **The Legendary Texas Drifter, Vol. 1** / 1972 / CMH ◆◆◆◆

The Legendary Texas Drifter, Vol. 2 / 1973 / CMH ◆◆◆◆

Hobo's Lullaby / 1994 / Bear Family ◆◆◆◆
Hobo's Lullaby contains all the studio recordings Goebel Reeves made during his lifetime, including "The Drifter," "The Tramp's Mother," "The Wayward Son," "The Drifter's Buddy (The Drifter's Prayer)," and "When the Clock Struck Seventeen," among 21 other tracks. —*Thom Owens*

Jim Reeves (James Travis Reeves)

b. Aug. 20, 1924, Galloway, Panola County, TX, **d.** Jul. 31, 1964, Nashville, TN
Guitar, Vocals / Country-Pop, Nashville Sound/Countrypolitan
Gentleman Jim Reeves was perhaps the biggest male star to emerge from the Nashville Sound. His mellow baritone voice and muted velvet orchestration combined to create a sound that echoed around his world and has lasted to this day. Detractors will call the sound country-pop (or plain pop), but none can argue against the large audience that loves this music. Reeves was capable of singing hard country ("Mexican Joe" went to No. 1 in 1953), but he made his greatest impact as a country-pop crooner. From 1955 through 1969, Reeves was consistently in the country and pop charts—an amazing fact in light of his death in an airplane accident in 1964. Not only was he a presence in the American charts, but he became country music's foremost international ambassador; he was even more popular in Europe and Britain

Jim Reeves

than he was in his native America. After his death, his fan base didn't diminish at all, and several of his posthumous hits actually outsold his earlier singles; no less than six No. 1 singles arrived in the three years after his burial. In fact during the '70s and '80s, he continued to have hits with both unreleased material and electronic duets like "Take Me in Your Arms and Hold Me" with Deborah Allen and "Have You Ever Been Lonely?" with his smooth-singing female counterpart of the plush Nashville Sound, Patsy Cline, who also perished in an airplane crash, in 1963. But Reeves' legacy remains with lush country-pop singles like "Four Walls" (1957) and "He'll Have to Go" (1959), which defined both his style and an entire era of country music.

Jim Reeves was born and raised in Galloway, TX, where he was one of nine children. His father died when Jim was only ten months old, forcing his mother to farm to raise her family. At the age of five, he was given an old guitar, and shortly afterward, he heard a Jimmie Rodgers record. From that moment on, Reeves was entranced by country music and Rodgers in particular. By the time he was 12 years old, he had already appeared on a radio show in Shreveport, LA. Though he was fascinated with music, Reeves was also a talented athlete; and during his teens he decided he was going to pursue a career as a baseball player. Winning an athletic scholarship to the University of Texas, Reeves enrolled to study speech and drama, but he dropped out after six weeks to work at the shipyards in Houston. Soon he had returned to baseball, playing in the semi-professional leagues before signing with the St. Louis Cardinals in 1944. He stayed with the team for three years before seriously injuring his ankle, ruining his chances of an athletic career.

For the next few years Reeves went through a number of blue-collar jobs while trying to decide on a profession. He began singing as an amateur, appearing both as a solo artist and as the frontman for Moon Mullican's band. In 1949 Reeves cut a number of songs for the small independent Macy label, none of which was particularly successful. In the early '50s Reeves decided that he would make broadcasting his vocation, initially working for KSIG in Gladewater, TX, before establishing himself at KGRI in Henderson. Over the next few years, Reeves was a disc jockey and newscaster at KGRI, moving to KWKH in Shreveport, LA, in November 1952, becoming host of the popular "Louisiana Hayride." Late in 1952 Hank Williams failed to make an appearance on the show, and Reeves sang in his place. His performance was enthusiastically received, and Abbott Records signed him to a record contract.

"Mexican Joe" was Reeves' debut single for Abbott, and it quickly climbed to No. 1 in the spring of 1953, spending nine weeks at the top of the charts. It was followed by another No. 1 hit, "Bimbo," later in 1953; later that same year, he was made a full-time member of the "Louisiana Hayride." During 1954 and 1955, he had four other hit singles for Abbott and its parent company, Fabor, before RCA signed him to a long-term deal in 1955;

that same year, he joined the Grand Ole Opry. At RCA Reeves began to develop the distinctively smooth, lush, and pop-oriented style of country that made him a superstar and earned him the nickname Gentleman Jim. Peaking at No. 4, "Yonder Comes a Sucker" was his first Top Ten hit for RCA in the summer of 1955. It kicked off a remarkable streak of 40 hit singles, most of which charted in the Top Ten. Many of his singles also became pop crossovers, which indicates exactly how much a pop influence there was on Reeves' music. Indeed, his vocal style was derived from the crooning of Frank Sinatra and Bing Crosby, and early in his career he abandoned cowboy outfits for upscale suits. In the process, he brought country music to a new, urban audience.

Throughout the '50s and early '60s, Reeves' racked up a number of major hits and country classics like "Four Walls" (No. 1 for eight weeks, 1957), "Anna Marie" (1958), "Blue Boy" (No. 2, 1958), "Billy Bayou" (No. 1 for five weeks, 1959), "He'll Have to Go" (No. 1 for 14 weeks, 1960), "Adios Amigo" (No. 2, 1962), "Welcome to My World" (No. 2, 1964), and "I Guess I'm Crazy" (No. 1 for seven weeks, 1964). "Four Walls" was the turning point in his career, proving to both Reeves and his producer, Chet Atkins, that his main source of success would come from ballads. As a result, Reeves became an even bigger star, not only in America but throughout the world. He toured Europe and South Africa, building a strong following in countries that rarely had been open to country music in the past.

Jim Reeves was at the height of his career when his private plane crashed outside of Nashville on July 31, 1964. The bodies of Reeves and his manager, Dean Manuel, were found two days later; Reeves was buried in his homestate of Texas. His popularity did not vanish—in fact, his sales increased after his death. Throughout the late '60s, RCA released a series of posthumous singles, many of which—including "This Is It" (1965), "Is It Really Over?" (1965), "Distant Drums" (1966), and "I Won't Come in While He's There" (1967)—hit No. 1. The previously unissued songs were frequently mixed with previously released material on album releases, making his catalog confusing, but profitable for RCA. The flow of unreleased Reeves material did not cease during the '70s or '80s—in fact, there wasn't a year between 1970 and 1984 without a Jim Reeves single in the charts. Reeves was inducted by the Country Music Hall of Fame in 1967; two years later, the Academy of Country Music instituted the Jim Reeves Memorial Award. Though the flood of unreleased material ceased in the mid-'80s, the cult surrounding Jim Reeves never declined, and in the '90s, Bear Family released Welcome to My World, a 16-disc box set containing his entire recorded works. —David Vinopal

☆ **He'll Have to Go and Other Hits** / 1960 / RCA ♦♦♦♦♦
There may have been other country crooners as smooth, but no one else in his era had the hand-in-glove marriage of great songs and appropriate "countrypolitan" production. This brief collection doesn't contain all of his biggest hits, but the most essential singles—"He'll Have to Go," "Four Walls," "Billy Bayou," and "Anna Marie"—are included. —Mark A. Humphrey

The Intimate Jim Reeves / 1960 / RCA Victor ♦♦♦
As the title indicates, The Intimate Jim Reeves emphasizes the ballad stylings of the countrypolitan singer, highlighted by the hit single "I'm Gettin' Better." Like most of Reeves' studio albums, it suffers from an uneven selection of material, but his performance is smooth and convincing, as is the stylish production. Together, they make the album an enjoyable listen, even if its appeal is limited to dedicated Reeves fans. The CD reissue includes four bonus tracks, including the hits "I Missed Me" and "Am I Losing You." —Stephen Thomas Erlewine

The Country Side of Jim Reeves / 1962 / Pair ♦♦
It features "My Lips Are Sealed," "A Railroad Bum," and other hits. —AMG

Collector's Series / 1985 / RCA ♦♦♦
This is a fine overview of RCA hits by Reeves. —Mark A. Humphrey

Live at the Grand Ole Opry / 1987 / Country Music Foundation ♦♦♦
While it may seem strange that a live album offers a nearly complete introduction to an artist as important as Jim Reeves, Live At the Opry fits that bill. A compilation of radio performances recorded at the Grand Ole Opry between 1953 and 1960, the music on Live At the Opry is uniformly excellent, demonstrating Reeves' talent for country-pop as well as his command of a live audience. Most of his biggest hits are here, as well as a handful of unfamiliar numbers, and all are delivered with style by eithe his backing band Blue Boys or an Opry pickup band. For both dedicated fans and neophytes, there's plenty to treasure on Live At the Opry. —Thom Owens

★ **Four Walls—The Legend Begins** / Aug. 1991 / RCA ♦♦♦♦♦
Four Walls—The Legend Begins collects 20 songs Jim Reeves recorded between 1953 and 1957, including his earliest hits, "Mexican Joe," "Bimbo," "According to My Heart," and "My Lips Are Sealed." —Stephen Thomas Erlewine

★ **Welcome to My World: The Essential Jim Reeves Collection** / 1993 / RCA ♦♦♦♦♦
Welcome to My World: The Essential Jim Reeves Collection is a double disc box set that offers an overview of his entire career, even if its balance is a bit uneven. Beginning with his early '50s hit, the box runs through most of his biggest hits, concentrating on his smooth countrypolitan '60s hits. Though fans of his early honky tonk material will feel that side of Reeves is overlooked, Welcome to My World is the best overall Reeves retrospective available. —Stephen Thomas Erlewine

The Essential Jim Reeves / Aug. 1, 1995 / RCA ♦♦♦♦
The Essential Jim Reeves runs through 20 of Reeves' biggest hits, throwing in a couple of rarities along the way. It's by no means definitive, but it offers a good introduction to his countrypolitan sound. —Stephen Thomas Erlewine

We Thank Thee / 1996 / RCA ♦♦♦
We Thank Thee is an inspirational album Jim Reeves released in 1962. Though it is pleasant—Reeves' voice is in good shape and the country-pop productions sound nice—nothing on the album particularly stands out. The compact disc reissue includes four bonus tracks: "An Evening Prayer," "Teach Me How to Pray," "How Long Has It Been," and "The Padre of Old San Antone." —Thom Owens

Welcome to My World / 1996 / Bear Family ♦♦♦♦
The sheer size of Welcome to My World is intimidating. Spanning a full 16 discs and 446 tracks, the box set covers every recording Jim Reeves ever made—certainly it's a set designed for the fanatic, not the neophyte. All of Reeves' classic hits for RCA are present, as are his recordings for Macy's, Fabor, Abbott, several demos, and undubbed singles, and they're all presented in chronological order, according to when they were recorded. For fanatics, the set is essential, since it comes with a detailed biography and sessionography, as well as first-rate sound, but the very size of the compilation makes it difficult to digest, even for the serious fan. —Thom Owens

Gentleman Jim 1955-1959 / Bear Family ♦♦♦♦
This four-disc set, which contains 110 tracks, has Reeves' first ventures into pop as well as some of his best country performances of favorites such as "Am I Losing You?," "Just Call Me Lonesome," and "According to My Heart." A discography accompanies the set. —AMG

Ronna Reeves

b. Sep. 21, 1958, Big Spring, TX
Vocals / Contemporary Country

Singer-songwriter Ronna Reeves spent most of her life in the music industry and was one of the more promising female singers to emerge in the 1990s. She was raised in Big Spring, TX, and began singing along with the radio and phonograph at age six. She won the Little Miss Big Spring competition at age eight; the judges' enthusiastic reaction to her singing in the show's talent segment inspired her parents to take her to a local guitar/fiddle teacher to evaluate her abilities, and he ended up adding Reeves to his band. By age 11, she had her own group, which played in Fort Worth night clubs. There she met Ron and Joy Cotton, promoters working out of Waco. When she was 17, the Cottons invited her to open for George Strait, a gig she performed for the next 18 months. She went on to open for Ronnie Milsap, Randy Travis, Garth Brooks, the Judds, and Reba McEntire. Her 1991 debut album *Only the Heart* was released with little notice. Her second album *The More I Learn* produced three minor hits, including "The More I Learn (The Less I Understand About Love)." *What Comes Naturally* (1993), although receiving critical praise, failed to produce any chart hits. — *Sandra Brennan*

Only the Heart / 1963 / Mercury ✦✦✦
Only the Heart includes Reeves' cover of Ernie Ashworth's "Talk Back Trembling Lips," as well as contributions from noted Nashville songwriters like Dickey Lee and Bob McDill. — *Jason Ankeny*

● **The More I Learn** / 1992 / Mercury ✦✦✦✦
Reeves' second effort features "There's Love on the Line," her duet with Sammy Kershaw. — *Jason Ankeny*

What Comes Naturally / Dec. 1992 / Mercury ✦✦✦

Ronna Reeves / Nov. 7, 1995 / River North Nashville ✦✦✦
Rednex became an international sensation with their campy country-disco stomp "Cotton Eye Joe," a stupid, silly European view of American white trash culture. It was certainly a fun, guilty pleasure, but that can't be said for the rest of the album. *Sex & Violins* is filled with songs that sound like "Cotton Eye Joe" but not as infectious, funny, or catchy. For fans of the manic Euro-dance sound, it might provide some thrills, but most listeners will find the record tedious. — *Stephen Thomas Erlewine*

After the Dance / Nov. 7, 1995 / Polygram ✦✦✦✦
Like its predecessors, *After the Dance* is a well-crafted and rootsy album of modern country that displays just a bit too much grit for contemporary country radio and too much polish for fans of alternative-country. *After the Dance* never found the audience it deserves. It may suffer from a couple of undistinguished songs, but Reeves' voice is powerful and graceful throughout the album, giving weight even to the weaker material. *After the Dance* is not a perfect album, but it demonstrates that Ronna Reeves should have a bigger audience than she does. — *Thom Owens*

Mike Reid

b. May 24, 1947, Altoona, PA
Keyboards, Vocals / Contemporary Country
A former defensive tackle for the NFL's Cincinnati Bengals, Mike Reid was one of the most sensitive writers of romantic songs in contemporary country music. He was born in Altoona, PA, the son of a railroad worker. Although he was a piano player from age six, Reid's real passion was sports; in 1969 he won the Outland Trophy as the best collegiate defensive lineman in the country. Reid also began to develop his musical talents, playing with local bands and graduating with a degree in music. He was drafted in the first round and became the league's Defensive Rookie of the Year in 1970.

In addition to playing football, Reid played music with local bands. While recovering from an injury, he met Larry Gatlin, who encouraged Reid's music and admired his song "Time Runs Away." In the off-season, Reid performed as a classical pianist with symphony orchestras in Dallas, Cincinnati, and Utah. In 1975, after undergoing knee surgery, Reid left football, joined the Apple Butter Band, and began playing Colorado ski resorts. As a songwriter, he was inspired by Leonard Cohen and Randy Newman. One of his songs was recorded by Jerry Jeff Walker in 1978, spurring him to pursue a solo career. He signed to ATV Publishing in 1980 and remained there for a year and a half. After meeting the head of Milsap Music, Rob Galbraith, Reid moved to the label and penned a few songs that appeared on Ronnie Milsap's 1982 album *Inside*, providing Milsap with a No. 1 single, "Stranger in My House." Sylvia also scored a major hit with one of Reid's songs. He continued as a successful songwriter for other artists as well, including Mark Gray, Marie Osmond, Tanya Tucker, and Conway Twitty, who had a major hit with "Fallin' for You for Years."

Through the '80s, Reid penned 11 No. 1 hits. In 1990 he began his recording career, signing to Columbia and releasing *Turning for Home*, which contained the No. 1 hit "Walk on Faith." Reid appeared on the charts three more times in 1991 with songs such as "As Simple as That." His most successful year was 1992, when he wrote several No. 1 hits for others, including Collin Raye's "In This Life." — *Sandra Brennan*

● **Turning for Home** / 1991 / Columbia ✦✦✦✦
Turning for Home is Mike Reid's most consistent release, demonstrating not only his talent for crafting a fine contemporary country song, but also his ability to deliver it. Reid had long been known for writing terrific commercial songs, but with *Turning for Home*, he showed that he could sing them with emotion as well as anyone. Though there are a couple of mediocre songs scattered throughout the record, the best moments—such as the surging hit single "Walk on Faith"—make a convincing argument for Reid's talents as a vocalist. — *Thom Owens*

Twilight Town / 1992 / Columbia ✦✦✦
While *Twilight Town* was not a commercial success, it does feature Reid's gem "I Can't Make You Love Me," later covered by the likes of Bonnie Raitt, Prince, and George Michael. — *Jason Ankeny*

Reno & Smiley

Traditional Bluegrass
Don Reno, Red Smiley, and the Tennessee Cutups were a bluegrass band of such high quality that the group gave serious competition to Flatt and Scruggs in the '50s. Don Reno, an unsurpassed master of the banjo, played for Bill Monroe in 1948, replacing Earl Scruggs. With a smooth and mellow baritone, Red Smiley made a perfect partner for Reno, singing lead to his high harmony part. Reno's incredible talent carried over to guitar playing and songwriting. Among his compositions are the exquisite "Emotions," as well as "Feuding Banjos," the unforgettable song in the film *Deliverance*, co-written with Arthur "Guitar Boogie" Smith. You don't know the five-string banjo if you haven't heard Don Reno.

Reno and Smiley grew up in different, rural sections of North Carolina and played with the Morris Brothers at different times in their formative years. Both served in the Army during World War II, and after they were discharged they played in a variety of country bands before they met in December 1949. Both were recruited by fiddler Tommy Magness to play in his band the Tennessee Buddies. In the summer of 1950, the pair began playing duets. After cutting a few singles with Magness for King Records (which were eventually released on Federal) in the spring of 1951, they left the fiddler and began working with Toby Stroud's Blue Mountain Boys in Roanoke, VA. In the fall of that year, the pair finally formed their own band, the Tennessee Cut-Ups.

Initially, Reno and Smiley found it difficult to land jobs in Virginia and South Carolina. Nevertheless, they cut several sides for King early in 1952. Before those singles were issued, the duo had split, because they couldn't find work. When the records appeared, they sold fairly well; King's owner, Syd Nathan, convinced the duo to continue recording, even if they weren't actively performing. For the next three years, they made assorted records for King while Reno played with Arthur "Guitar Boogie" Smith and Smiley worked as a mechanic. On the first batch of recordings, they were supported by musicians Jimmy Lunsford and Tommy Faile. By November 1954, they were allowed to use their longtime backing musicians, fiddler Mack Magaha and bassist John Palmer.

In the spring of 1955, Reno and Smiley reunited as a performing duo and soon landed a regular gig on WRVA's "Old Dominion Barn Dance." Within a year, they secured a daily morning television show in Roanoke, as well as various shows for a station in Harrisonburg, VA. The pair made a handful of recordings for Dot in 1957, but they continued their relationship with King until 1964, recording a wealth of material.

At the end of 1964, Reno and Smiley parted ways. Red Smiley was suffering from diabetes and no longer wanted to travel; he continued to do the television show in Roanoke but toured only occasionally. By the spring 1968, he had retired. Don Reno played with a few bands before teaming up with Bill Harrell in 1966. For nearly two decades, Reno remained active in the bluegrass community, cutting numerous records and playing with a variety of collaborators. —*Stephen Thomas Erlewine & David Vinopal*

Good Old Country Ballads / 1959 / King ✦✦✦✦

Good Old Country Ballads is an original King album from 1959 that collects several singles that the bluegrass Reno and Smiley recorded during the '50s. There are no any weak tracks, and several songs, including "Country Boy Rock 'n' Roll," rank among their very best. It would have been nice to see the compact disc reissue fleshed out with bonus tracks, liner notes, or even credits, but it's good to have the music in any form. —*Thom Owens*

A Variety of Country Songs / 1959 / King ✦✦✦✦

Like *Good Old Country Ballads*, *A Variety of Country Songs* is an original King album from 1959 that contains several singles Reno and Smiley recorded during the '50s. Where the predecessor concentrated on mid-tempo numbers, the songs on *A Variety* are generally speedier and more infectious, whether it is straightforward bluegrass or country gospel. Taken with *Good Old Country Ballads*, *A Variety of Country Songs* gives a good idea of the depth of Reno and Smiley's talents. —*Stephen Thomas Erlewine*

● Early Years 1951-59 / 1994 / King ✦✦✦✦

Early Years: 1951-1959 is a four-disc box set that presents all of Reno and Smiley and the Tennessee Cutups' recordings for King Records in chronological order, as well as four sides they recorded for Federal as supporting musicians for Tommy Magness. The set contains many of Reno and Smiley's finest and most influential moments, most of which feature the support of bassist John Palmer and fiddler Mack MaGaha. As a historical recording, *Early Years: 1951-59* is invaluable, since it documents the greatest recordings from one of the best bluegrass groups in history. However, it is a difficult listen—this is educational listening, not entertainment. For musicologists and dedicated fans, it's a necessary purchase, but country and bluegrass fans intending to build a basic bluegrass collection don't need this set. —*Thom Owens*

Reno Brothers

Traditional Bluegrass

The Reno Brothers—Ronnie, Dale and Don Wayne—were the sons of legendary banjo picker Don Reno; like their father, they focused on string-band and bluegrass music. Ronnie entered the music business around 1956, playing mandolin with his dad and Red Smiley on Roanoke, VA's, "*Top o' the Mornin'*" TV show. Ronnie and his father kept hosting the show after Smiley left. During the late 1960s, he began playing bass with the Osborne Brothers. He remained with the Osbornes through the early '70s and then became the frontman for Merle Haggard's Strangers. Reno made his first solo entry on the charts in 1983 with "Homemade Love," three years after making his feature film debut in the Clint Eastwood film *Bronco Billy*. While Ronnie was forging his own career, his brothers joined their dad's Tennessee Cut-Ups and played with them long after he and his partner Bill Harrell split in the mid-'70s. After their father died in 1984, the brothers got together to play music that was a cross between bluegrass and country. Their first recordings included a cover of "Yonder Comes a Freight Train" and "Love Will Never Be the Same." The trio also began hosting a regular TV show for the Americana cable network in 1993, then the only nationally broadcast program to focus on bluegrass music. —*Sandra Brennan*

● Good Old Country Ballads / King ✦✦✦✦

Restless Heart

Contemporary Country, Adult Contemporary

John Dittrich (b. April 7, 1951), Dave Innis (b. April 9, 1959), Greg Jennings (b. October 2, 1954), and Paul Gregg (b. December 3, 1954). The origins of Restless Heart are a bit unusual. Songwriter Tim DuBois couldn't find an outlet for some of his material—"too pop" for many Nashville acts, "too country" for Los Angeles—and he sought five of his friends to help work up the songs for demo tapes.

The combination worked better than anyone expected. The group pursued a recording deal and signed with RCA Records in 1983. Just as they started to work on the first album, lead vocalist Verlon Thompson had second thoughts, and Larry Stewart was brought in as his replacement.

Often compared to the Eagles in their early days, Restless Heart displayed a strong reliance on tenor harmonies, working country-rock territory. Despite a resurgence in traditional country, the band was able to consistently place its hybrid sound on country radio. In 1986 they began a streak of ten Top Ten singles in a row, highlighted by the No. 1 hits "That Rock Won't Roll" (1986), "I'll Still Be Loving You" (1987), "Why Does It Have to Be (Wrong or Right)" (1987), "Wheels" (1987), "Bluest Eyes in Texas" (1988), and "A Tender Lie" (1989). At the end of 1991 Stewart left for a solo career. By that time, the hits weren't coming as frequently for the band. Restless Heart continued as a quartet, releasing *Big Iron Horses* in 1992. It was followed in 1994 by *Matters of the Heart*. —*Tom Roland*

Restless Heart / 1985 / RCA ✦✦✦

The band's debut includes the hits "Let the Heartache Ride," "I Want Everyone to Cry," and "(Back to the) Heartbreak Kid." —*Jason Ankeny*

Wheels / 1986 / RCA ✦✦✦✦

The guys found their niche with this project. Big, overpowering sound, heavy backbeats, and very tight harmonies are here. In contrast, the ballads "I'll Still Be Loving You" and "New York (Hold Her Tight)" are incredibly sensitive. —*Tom Roland*

Big Dreams in a Small Town / 1988 / RCA ✦✦✦

It contains the hits "A Tender Lie" and "The Bluest Eyes in Texas," among others. —*AMG*

Fast Movin' Train / 1989 / RCA ✦✦✦

This album has "Long Lost Friend," "Dancy's Dream," and other hits. —*AMG*

● The Best of Restless Heart / Oct. 1991 / RCA ✦✦✦✦

Restless Heart's biggest hits are compiled on the appropriatelyb titled *The Best of Restless Heart*, including the No. 1 singles "That Rock Won't Roll," "I'll Still Be Loving You," "Why Does It Have to Be (Wrong or Right)," "Wheels," "Bluest Eyes in Texas," and "A Tender Lie," plus four other songs. —*Stephen Thomas Erlewine*

Big Iron Horses / 1992 / RCA ✦✦✦

Down to a quartet, the guys in Restless Heart still have the highest Eagles rating in country music—they get the vocals right almost every time, and "Blame It on Love" evokes memories of "Witchy Woman." Musically, not much changed for the members of the band; they still like a good train song, and they're more likely to show the influence of Bruce Hornsby ("Meet Me on the Other Side") and Creedence Clearwater Revival ("Born in a High Wind") than any of country's honky-tonk heroes. Another song, "When She Cries," became one of the biggest crossover hits of 1992. Paul Gregg, John Dittrich, and Dave Innis (who left the group after the album's release, reducing Restless Heart to a trio) trade lead vocals; they blend well from song to song, though Dittrich sounds the most like Don Henley, but it's definitely those harmonies that make *Big Iron Horses* run smooth. —*Brian Mansfield*

Matters of the Heart / May 24, 1994 / RCA ✦✦

Kimmie Rhodes

Progressive Country, Singer-Songwriter, Alternative Country, Americana

The singing career of Lubbock, TX, native Kimmie Rhodes kicked off at the age of six, when she first performed with her family gospel trio. During her teens she began learning guitar and writing songs, and in 1979 she moved to Austin, where she met her future husband and producer, Joe Gracey. Two years later Rhodes released her debut LP, *Kimmie Rhodes and the Jackalope Brothers*, followed in 1985 by *Man in the Moon*. She recorded her third album, 1989's *Angels Get the Blues*, at Sun Studios in Memphis.

While commercial success eluded Rhodes, her music proved popular with other performers; her song "I Just Drove By" was covered by Wynonna on the *Tell Me Why* album, and the duet pairing of Trisha Yearwood and Willie Nelson recorded "Hard Promises to Keep" for Yearwood's *The Song Remembers When*. Rhodes herself cut a pair of duets with Nelson for his *Just One Love* LP; Nelson returned the favor for Rhodes' 1996 effort *West Texas Heaven*, on which she also teamed with Waylon Jennings and Townes Van Zandt. —*Jason Ankeny*

Angels Get the Blues / 1989 / Heartland UK ◆◆◆

● **West Texas Heaven** / Apr. 1996 / Justice ◆◆◆◆
Kimmie Rhodes may not be well known outside of her home state, but she has been recording for the last 15 years, getting attention from European audiences and writing songs that have been recorded by stars like Willie Nelson, Wynonna Judd, and Trisha Yearwood. Rhodes' new album, *West Texas Heaven*, is a melodic and dreamy, sweet and sad work of dryland, lonesome road beauty. Her voice is folksinger pretty and brings to mind Nanci Griffith and Iris Dement, but she tastefully avoids the cute and quaint in her writing and subtle arrangements. Highlights are a series of duets with Nelson, Waylon Jennings, and Townes Van Zandt (who delivers one of his best vocal performances in years). —*Kurt Wolff*

Red Rhodes

b. Dec. 30, 1930, Alton, IL
Guitar (Steel) / Traditional Country, Country-Pop
Born Orville J. Rhodes in East Alston, IL, Red Rhodes was one of the most versatile steel guitarists in country music. His mother taught him to play the dobro when he was only five; at 15, he switched to the lap steel guitar, using a homemade stand. He played his first professional gig alongside his stepfather before moving to L.A. in 1960 to do session work. Eight years later, he was one of the most in-demand session men on the West Coast and played with artists like the Byrds. Rhodes and his band played at the Palomino in L.A. during the late '60s and even worked on several Monkees sessions, which led to work as a steel player for Michael Nesmith's First National Band in 1969. He remained with Nesmith through both incarnations of the group and continued his session work throughout the '70s, appearing with James Taylor, John Phillips, the Carpenters, Carole King, Chilli Willi and the Red Hot Peppers, and Seals and Crofts. Rhodes also occasionally held guitar workshops for beginners. —*Sandra Brennan*

Once a Day / 1961 / Crown ◆◆◆

Blue Blue Day / 1962 / Crown ◆◆◆

● **Steel Guitar Rag** / 1963 / Crown ◆◆◆◆

Velvet Hammer in a Cowboy Band / 1973 / Countryside ◆◆◆

Fantastic Steel Guitar / 1980 / Exact ◆◆◆

Live at the Palomino / 198 / Happy Tiger ◆◆

Larry Rice

Mandolin / Traditional Bluegrass
Larry Rice, a renowned mandolin player, began his bluegrass career by playing in his father's band, the Golden State Boys. He later formed his own band, (the Haphazards,) with brothers Tony and Ronnie. In the '70s he co-founded the New South with J.D. Crowe, Doyle Lawson, Red Allen, and Bobby Slone. After leaving the band in 1976 (Ricky Skaggs replaced him), Rice toured with Dickey Betts. His first solo album, *Hurricanes and Daydreams* (1985), was followed by *Time Machine*. Both albums are on Rebel Records. —*John Bush*

Hurricanes and Daydreams / 1986 / Rebel ◆◆◆

● **Artesia** / Rebel ◆◆◆◆

Tony Rice

b. Jun. 8, 1951, Danville, VA
Guitar / Progressive Bluegrass, Traditional Bluegrass
Innovative guitarist Tony Rice was a master flat-picker who combined elements of bluegrass, jazz, and classical music to create a unique acoustic sound. The Virginia-born Rice was raised in California and started out playing bluegrass with his father and brothers Larry and Wayne. In 1970 he began playing with the Ken-

tucky-based Bluegrass Alliance and then with the progressive Crowe's New South. He stayed with the latter band through the mid-'70s and then joined the David Grisman Quintet, which played string music with a classical and jazz twist. Rice began his solo career in 1977 and released an eponymous debut album on which he not only played guitar but sang with a surprisingly soulful voice that was a mixture of traditional, pop, and folk inflections. He released two more solo albums, *Acoustics* and *Manzanita*, and then formed the Bluegrass Album Band with Bobby Hicks, Doyle Lawson, and Todd Phillips. The band recorded five albums in the early '80s. In 1980 he also formed the Tony Rice Unit, with whom he played his innovative "spacegrass" jazz interpretations of modern folksongs by such artists as Ian Tyson, Joni Mitchell, and Gordon Lightfoot. This music can be heard on such critically acclaimed albums as 1984's *Cold on the Shoulder*. Later Rice cut two albums with Norman Blake and had a reunion album with his brothers. In 1993 he cut a traditional bluegrass album titled *Tony Rice Plays and Sings Bluegrass* that featured covers of Bill Monroe classics as well as those of Flatt and Scruggs, the Stanley Brothers, and Bob Dylan. —*Sandra Brennan*

California Autumn / 1975 / Rebel ◆◆◆
Rice splits the material on *California Autumn* between vocal numbers and instrumentals while resurrecting old-time songs including "Billy in the Lowground," "Beaumont Rag," and "Red Haired Boy." —*Jason Ankeny*

Tony Rice / 1977 / Rounder ◆◆◆
On his eponymous 1977 album, Tony Rice finds a middle ground between traditional acoustic bluegrass music and newgrass. Of course, he had been working on a hybrid of the two bluegrass genres for a number of years, as a member of the Bluegrass Alliance, the New South and the David Grisman Quartet, but *Tony Rice* was one of his first solo albums to match the richness of his work with his previous bands. —*Thom Owens*

Manzanita / 1979 / Rounder ◆◆◆◆
Comprised of both traditional songs and contemporary numbers, *Manzanita* was the third record in a row to demonstrate Tony Rice's considerable instrumental talent. On this album he is backed by a band featuring Sam Bush, Ricky Skaggs, and Jerry Douglas, who give him incredibly sympathetic and nuanced support. —*Thom Owens*

Guitar / 197 / Rebel ◆◆◆
On *Guitar*, Rice focuses on instrumental renditions of songs like "Lonesome Reuben" and "Faded Love." Among the guests are J.D. Crowe and Bobby Slone. —*Jason Ankeny*

Bluegrass Album / 1981 / Rounder ◆◆◆◆

Backwaters / 1982 / Rounder ◆◆◆◆

Bluegrass Album, Vol. 2 / 1982 / Rounder ◆◆◆◆

Church Street Blues / 1983 / Sugar Hill ◆◆◆◆
Church Street Blues is essentially a solo album by Tony Rice, demonstrating his musical eclecticism—the record features everything from contemporary folk to traditional country and blues—as well as his nimble instrumental grace. —*Thom Owens*

Bluegrass Album, Vol. 3: California Connection / 1983 / Rounder ◆◆◆◆

Cold on the Shoulder / 1984 / Rounder ◆◆◆◆
Bela Fleck, Vassar Clements, and Jerry Douglas are just a few of the guests on *Cold on the Shoulder*, on which Rice performs songs by Bob Dylan, Randy Newman, and Rodney Crowell. —*Jason Ankeny*

The Bluegrass Album, Vol. 4 / 1985 / Rounder ◆◆◆

Me and My Guitar / 1986 / Rounder ◆◆
Me and My Guitar sports several Gordon Lightfoot compositions, including "Fine as Fine Can Be" and "Early Morning Rain." —*Jason Ankeny*

Native American / 1988 / Rounder ◆◆
Like its predecessor *Me and My Guitar*, *Native American* features a song about the assassination of Abraham Lincoln; this time out, it's "John Wilkes Booth," penned by Mary-Chapin Carpenter. —*Jason Ankeny*

Bluegrass Album, Vol. 5: Sweet Sunny South / 1989 / Rounder
◆◆◆

Tony Rice Sings Gordon Lightfoot / May 28, 1996 / Rounder
◆◆◆◆
Bluegrass singer/guitarist Tony Rice has been recording songs
written by Gordon Lightfoot throughout his career, and this 17-
track compilation brings them together, adding a previously unreleased version of "Whispers of the North" that was cut for Rice's
Me and My Guitar album. Included are tracks Rice recorded as
part of J.D. Crowe and the New South, the Tony Rice Unit, the Rice
Brothers, in a duo with Norman Blake, and as a solo artist. That
means that on the various tracks he's joined by a newgrass who's
who that includes Jerry Douglas, Ricky Skaggs, Sam Bush, Vassar
Clements, and Bela Fleck, among others. The selections include
"Wreck of the Edmund Fitzgerald" and "Early Morning Rain," but
for the most part Rice eschewed Lightfoot's better known compositions, and the collection serves to illustrate the overall quality of
the songwriter's catalog. Rice did not just use the songs as platforms for picking sessions, either. His singing clearly influenced
by Lightfoot's, he brought a strong interpretive ability to the lyrics.
Of course, the picking is pretty hot, too. — William Ruhlmann

● **Devlin** / Rounder ◆◆◆◆
Devlin collects a selection of material from his Rounder albums
of the '70s and '80s, making it a perfect introduction to his music.
—Thom Owens

Wyatt Rice

Guitar / Progressive Bluegrass, Traditional Bluegrass
The brother of Tony Rice, guitarist Wyatt Rice played in his
brother's bluegrass band before forming his own group in the late
'80s. The Wyatt Rice band has since recorded two albums in two
different incarnations. The first version of the group was a sextet
featuring violinist Richie Simpkins and mandolinist Ray Legere;
they released New Market Gap in 1989. By the mid-'90s, the
group had become a quintet, and this lineup released Picture in a
Tear in 1996. —Stephen Thomas Erlewine

New Market Gap / Feb. 1989 / Rounder ◆◆◆◆
On a leave of absence from his brother's Tony Rice Unit, Wyatt's
put together a sextet featuring the talents of violinist Richie Simpkins and mandolinist Ray Legere. Most of their material is made
up of traditional compositions or Bill Monroe songs, but the
record has a surprisingly modern sound that's as much folk as it
is traditional bluegrass. —Jason Ankeny

● **Picture in a Tear** / Oct. 8, 1996 / Rounder ◆◆◆◆
Wyatt Rice's progressive bluegrass quintet shines on Picture in a
Tear. Relying primarily on original material, Rice and his band
pull energetic, vibrant performances out of each song, even the
weaker material. Fortunately, there isn't too much weak material
here—the Wyatt Rice combo sounds as if they've been playing
together for years. —Thom Owens

Charlie Rich

b. Dec. 14, 1932, Colt, AR, d. Jul. 24, 1995
*Piano, Vocals / Traditional Country, Progressive Country, Coun-
try-Pop, Rockabilly, Nashville Sound/Countrypolitan*
Charlie Rich was simultaneously one of the most critically
acclaimed and most erratic country singers of post-World War II
era. Rich had all the elements of being one of the great country
stars of the '60s and '70s, but his popularity never matched his
critical notices. What made him a critical favorite also kept him
from mass success. Throughout his career, Rich willfully blended
genres, fusing country, jazz, blues, gospel, rockabilly, and soul.
Though he had 45 country hits in a career that spanned nearly
four decades, he became best known for his lush, Billy Sherrill-
produced countrypolitan records of the early '70s. Instead of
embracing the stardom those records brought him, Rich shunned
it, retreating into semi-retirement by the '80s.
Charlie Rich began his professional musical career while in
the US Air Force in the early '50s. While stationed in Oklahoma,
he formed a group called the Velvetones that played jazz and
blues and featured his fiancee, Margaret Ann, on lead vocals.

Rich left the military in 1956 and began performing in clubs
around Memphis, playing both jazz and R&B; he also began
writing his own material. Rich managed to land a job as a session musician for Judd Records, which was owned by Judd Phillips, the brother of Sun Records' founder Sam Phillips. About
this time, saxophonist and Sun recording artist Bill Justis heard
Rich play at the Sharecropper Club and asked him to write
arrangements for Justis. Sam Phillips saw Rich perform with
Justis at a club gig and asked him to record some demos at Sun
Studios. Phillips rejected the resulting demos, claiming they
were too jazzy. After absorbing some Jerry Lee Lewis records
Justis gave him, Rich returned to Sun and became a regular session musician for the label in 1958, playing and/or singing on
records by Lewis, Johnny Cash, Justis, Warren Smith, Billy Lee
Riley, Carl Mann, and Ray Smith. He was also writing songs,
including "Break Up" for Jerry Lee Lewis, "The Ways of a
Woman in Love" for Johnny Cash, and "I'm Comin' Home" for
Carl Mann, which was later cut by Elvis Presley.
In August 1958, Rich released his first single, "Whirlwind," for
the Sun subsidiary Phillips International. Throughout 1959 he
recorded a number of songs at Sun, though only a handful were
actually released. Rich didn't have a hit until 1960, when his third
Phillips International single, "Lonely Weekends," became a Top 30
pop hit. However, none of its seven follow-up singles was a success, though several of the songs would become staples in his set,
including "Who Will the Next Fool Be?," "Sittin' and Thinkin'," and
"Midnight Blues." In the early '60s, Rich's career remained stalled.
He left Sun Records in 1964, signing with Groove, a newly-estab-
lished subsidiary of RCA. His first single, "Big Boss Man," was an
underground, word-of-mouth hit, but its Chet Atkins-produced
follow-ups all stiffed. On Groove, he jazzily interpreted standards,
but he also performed a handful of originals, including "Tomorrow Night" and "I Don't See Me in Your Eyes Anymore." Groove
went out of business by the beginning of 1965, leaving Rich without a record contract.
Under the direction of Shelby Singleton, Smash Records signed
Charlie Rich early in 1965. Singleton and Rich's producer, Jerry
Kennedy, encouraged the pianist to emphasize his country and
rock 'n' roll leanings. The first single for Smash was "Mohair
Sam," an R&B-inflected novelty number written by Dallas Frazier.
"Mohair Sam" became a Top 30 pop hit, but none of its follow-ups
was successful. Again Rich changed labels, moving to Hi Records,
where he recorded straight country; but none of his singles for the
label made any impression on the country charts.
Despite his lack of consistent commercial success, Epic Records
signed Charlie Rich in 1967, mainly on the recommendation of
producer Billy Sherrill. Sherrill helped Rich refashion himself as a
Nashville-based, smooth, middle-of-the-road balladeer. At first the
singles were only moderately successful—"Set Me Free" and "Rag-
gedy Ann" charted in the mid-40s in 1968—but persistence paid
off in the summer of 1972, when "I Take It On Home" rocketed to
No. 6. "I Take It On Home" set the stage for Rich's big breakthrough into the mainstream, 1973's Behind Closed Doors. The
title track became a No. 1 hit early in 1973, crossing over into the
Top 20 on the pop charts. After the success of "Behind Closed
Doors," RCA re-released "Tomorrow Night," and it reached the
Top 30; but it was "The Most Beautiful Girl," the proper follow-up
to his first No. 1 single, that established him as a star. "The Most
Beautiful Girl" spent three weeks at the top of the country charts
and two weeks at the top of the pop charts. Behind Closed Doors
won three awards from the Country Music Association that year:
Best Male Vocalist, Album of the Year, and Single of the Year for
the title track. The album was also certified Gold. Rich won a
Grammy for Best Country Vocal Performance, Male, and took
home four ACM awards.
After "The Most Beautiful Girl," No. 1 hits came
quickly—"There Won't Be Anymore" (re-released from his RCA
sessions), "A Very Special Love Song," "I Don't See Me in Your
Eyes Anymore" (also from RCA), "I Love My Friend," and "She
Called Me Baby" (RCA) all topped the country charts, and several
of the songs crossed over into the pop charts. Mercury began rereleasing his Smash recordings and two of them—"A Field of Yellow Daisies" and "Something Just Came Over Me"—became

minor hits. All of this success led the CMA to name him Entertainer of the Year in 1974.

Rich didn't dominate the charts in 1975 as he had the previous year, but he did have three Top Five hits: "My Elusive Dreams," "Every Time You Touch Me (I Get High)," and "All Over Me," plus the Top Ten "Since I Fell for You." Even though he was at the peak of his popularity, Rich had begun to drink heavily, causing considerable problems offstage. His destructive behavior culminated at the CMA ceremony for 1975, when he presented the award for that year's Entertainer of the Year. Instead of reading the name of the winner, he set fire to the certificate that named the new winner, who happened to be John Denver. Fans and industry insiders were outraged, and Rich had trouble having hits throughout 1976—none of his singles cracked the Top 20.

The slump in his career couldn't be attributed entirely to Rich's behavior. His records had begun to sound increasingly similar, as he and Sherrill were working over the same territory they had begun exploring in 1968. There were exceptions—such as 1976's acclaimed gospel record *Silver Linings*—but it took Rich until 1977 to break back into the Top Ten with the No. 1 "Rollin' with the Flow." Early in 1978 he signed with United Artists, and throughout that year he had hits on both Epic and UA. Rich worked with Larry Butler at United Artists, a producer with a style similar style to Sherrill's. Epic continued to have hits, as "Beautiful Woman" reached the Top Ten in the summer, and a duet with Janie Fricke, "On My Knees," became his last No. 1 hit that fall. "I'll Wake You Up When I Get Home," taken from the Clint Eastwood movie *Every Which Way but Loose*, was a No. 3 hit early in 1979; it would be his last Top Ten single.

Rich struggled throughout 1979, but none of his singles was anything more than a minor success. In 1980 he switched to Elektra, resulting in the No. 12 single "A Man Just Don't Know What a Woman Goes Through" in the fall of that year. One more Top 40 hit followed—"Are We Dreamin' the Same Dream" early in 1981—but Charlie Rich decided to remove himself from the spotlight. For more than a decade Rich was silent, living in semi-retirement and playing only the occasional concert. He returned in 1992 with *Pictures and Paintings*, a jazzy record produced by journalist Peter Guralnick and released on Sire.

Pictures and Paintings received positive reviews and restored Rich's reputation, but it would be his last record. Charlie Rich died from a blood clot in his lung in the summer of 1995, as he was traveling to Florida with his wife, Margaret Ann. *—Stephen Thomas Erlewine*

Charlie Rich Sings Country and Western / 1967 / Hi ✦✦✦

Rich interpreted 12 songs written by or associated with Hank Williams for this middling 1967 album, including "Hey Good Lookin'," "Cold Cold Heart," "I'm So Lonesome I Could Cry," and less celebrated tunes. It's been reissued with 13 blue-eyed soul cuts that Rich recorded for Hi around the same time on the British import CD *Charlie Rich Sings the Songs of Hank Williams Plus the R&B Sessions*, which is the recommended alternative to searching for the out-of-print vinyl release. *—Richie Unterberger*

Set Me Free / 1968 / Koch ✦✦✦✦

Set Me Free was Charlie Rich's first album for Epic Records and the first record he ever cut with Nashville producer Billy Sherrill. Previously, Rich's producers hadn't known what to do with his eclectic style, although his sessions for Smash came close to capturing all sides of his personality. With Sherrill, Rich had a producer whose musical tastes were nearly as eclectic as his own, and that is captured on the freewheeling, diverse sounds of *Set Me Free*. Purists may be uncomfortable with Sherrill's lush production—he sets Rich's voice in a bed of strings, keyboards, horns, and backing vocals. Consequently, the sound of *Set Me Free* is laidback and relaxed; occasionally, Rich sounds *too* relaxed, as if he didn't connect with the material. Although there are a handful of poor songs and half-hearted performances on the record, *Set Me Free* has an overall tone lacking on Rich's previous records that makes up for its assorted weaknesses. The songs come from a variety of sources, ranging from country and blues to jazz and pop, but they're all given a cohesive Nashville production by Sher-

Charlie Rich

rill, which is what makes *Set Me Free* one of Rich's best, most consistent albums. *—Stephen Thomas Erlewine*

☆ Fabulous Charlie Rich / 1969 / Koch ✦✦✦✦

The Fabulous Charlie Rich follows the same formula as its predecessor, *Set Me Free*, but with more successful results. For starters, the record has a more consistent set of material—these are songs that Rich can really sink his teeth into, as evidenced by the beautiful, melancholy "Life Has Its Little Ups and Downs" (written by his wife, Margaret Ann) and his own "Sittin' and Thinkin'." Furthermore, the core of each song—from the bluesy "July 12, 1939" and "Bright Lights, Big City" (which is done essentially as a Jimmy Reed medley, performed in the style of Ray Charles) to the soulful "I Almost Lost My Mind" and the country-pop stylings of "San Francisco Is A Lonely Town" and "Love Waits for Me"—are more apparent, thanks to Sherrill's relatively trimmed-down production. There are still strings, vocal choruses, and horns throughout the album, but Sherrill has incorporated them into Rich's style more effectively. Occasionally, there is a fairly uninspired number, but *The Fabulous Charlie Rich* does capture the eclectic nature of Rich's music better than the great majority of his albums, even if the sumptuous production will make it less palatable for country purists. *—Stephen Thomas Erlewine*

Boss Man / Aug. 1970 / Koch ✦✦✦✦

Charlie Rich and Billy Sherrill reached a peak with *The Fabulous Charlie Rich*, creating a perfect middle ground between Rich's rootsier tendencies and Sherrill's country-pop leanings. Like many of Rich's records, it didn't sell, and that might have been one of the reasons its followup, *Boss Man*, was their weakest effort to date. Although there are quite a few high spots, and the album essentially follows the same formula as their previous efforts, the material isn't consistent, alternating between bluesy shuffles and country weepers; both range from the brilliant to the boring. What's even worse is the fact that Rich sounds uninspired, giving competent but unenthusiastic performances. There's enough prime material to make *Boss Man* an enjoyable listen, particularly for Rich fans who know that he rarely comes up with consistent albums. However, it didn't have the spark of *The Fabulous Charlie Rich*, nor did it have the immaculate sheen of *Behind Closed Doors*, the country-pop masterpiece that followed *Boss Man*. Nevertheless, *Boss Man* had enough fine songs to make it an essential purchase for true Rich fans. *—Stephen Thomas Erlewine*

The Best of Charlie Rich / 1972 / Epic ✦✦✦
This album was released before Rich actually had any hits on this label. Fans will recognize some of the titles from earlier releases on other labels ("Big Boss Man," "Sittin' and Thinkin'") but none of these versions could be considered a hit. That aside, there are still some good songs here. Don't be put off just because the title isn't accurate. —*Jim Worbois*

☆ **Behind Closed Doors** / 1973 / Epic ✦✦✦✦✦
Charlie Rich had been heading toward full-blown country-pop on his previous Epic records, but *Behind Closed Doors* is where Billy Sherrill pulled out all of the stops and created a heavily orchestrated, pop-oriented album. It's to Rich's credit that he never sounds as if he's drowning admist the grand production and layers of instruments—in an odd way, he thrives. While *Behind Closed Doors* doesn't have the casual eclecticism that distinguished all of Rich's past recordings, it is an expertly crafted album; it's easy to see why it made the Silver Fox a superstar. All of the material, from the hit singles ("Behind Closed Doors," "The Most Beautiful Girl," "I Take It On Home") to the album tracks, is classy, designed to appeal to a maturing country audience. Furthermore, the arrangements expertly walk the line between pop and schmaltz—the sound of *Behind Closed Doors* is *the* sound of early '70s countrypolitan, and numerous artists used the record as a template for their own style. Rich made better, grittier records, but the combined collaborative effort of the vocalist and Sherrill resulted in a seamless, influential work—even if it is one that earned the scorn of hardcore country purists. —*Stephen Thomas Erlewine*

There Won't Be Anymore / 1974 / RCA ✦✦✦
Even though this record was issued to cash in on his success on another label, it did yield a couple of hits. One track that makes this album worth almost any price is "Turn Around and Face Me," which was written by Rich's wife. Not only is it a good song, it sounds as if it could or should be a big Gene Pitney hit. —*Jim Worbois*

The Silver Fox / 1974 / Epic ✦✦✦✦
If you ever wondered what it would be like to have Charlie Rich in your own living room, playing music and talking about his life, this should be the answer to your dreams. If the talking isn't to your liking, a little diligence will unearth a couple of real gems, especially "Feel Like Going Home," which the Notting Hillbillies later faithfully covered. —*Jim Worbois*

Greatest Hits / 1976 / Epic ✦✦✦✦
This focuses on his biggest hits ("Behind Close Doors," "The Most Beautiful Girl") though not necessarily the most representative work. Ignore the cheesy production, however, and you'll hear his vocals as utterly sublime. —*Dan Cooper*

American Originals / 1989 / Columbia ✦✦✦✦
Essentially the same material as the Epic *Greatest Hits*, it adds the almost claustrophobically intimate version of "Since I Fell For You." —*Dan Cooper*

Pictures and Paintings / 1992 / Sire ✦✦✦✦
Charlie Rich's comeback album *Pictures and Paintings*—which would turn out to be his final recording—is one of his most rewarding. It is a stripped-down, relaxed album that captures Rich running through a mixture of covers, originals, and new versions of classics like "Don't Put No Headstone on My Grave." It's one of the few albums he made that captures all facets of his talent, featuring jazzy playing, bluesy singing, and simple, straightforward country. —*Stephen Thomas Erlewine*

☆ **The Complete Smash Sessions** / Aug. 4, 1992 / Mercury ✦✦✦✦✦
The Complete Smash Sessions contains everything that Charlie Rich recorded and released for Smash during the mid-'60s. Many of these songs forshadow the music Elvis Presley would make during his comeback in 1968, as well as the country-pop of the early '70s. Skillfully mixing rock, blues, R&B, country, and soul, Rich was at the top of his form when he made this. He may have had only one hit during this period—"Mohair Sam" reached No. 21 in 1965—but his tenure at Smash remained one of his most fruitful and creative periods. —*Stephen Thomas Erlewine*

Charlie Rich Sings the Songs of Hank Williams Plus the R&B Sessions / 1994 / Diabolo/Demon ✦✦✦
Why the tongue-twisting title? Because this British import CD reissues his 1967 Hi LP *Sings Country and Western*, which consisted entirely of songs written by or associated with Hank Williams, adding 13 R&B/soul-oriented tunes he cut for the Hi label (some unreleased at the time) around the same era. The Hank Williams numbers are about what you would expect, or a little less. Rich offers competent updates of a dozen of Hank's tunes, and while the singing is good, the arrangements are pretty conservative, in a sort of take-no-risks crossover fashion. Far more interesting are the R&B sides, which bolster Rich's strong case as one of the great White soul singers. The backing is suitably funk/bluesy, and Rich's vocals are great. Some of the material may have been too jazzy or offbeat to stand much of a chance for commercial success at the time, but there's some notable buried treasure here, including a couple of Hayes-Porter covers. The Rich original "I'll Shed No Tears" is as close as soul and country come to mating, and "Pass On By" (written by Charlie's wife Margaret Ann) is blue-eyed soul at its jazziest and most sophisticated. —*Richie Unterberger*

☆ **Lonely Weekends: Best of the Sun Years** / Mar. 19, 1996 / AVI ✦✦✦✦✦
If you want to get in on the ground floor and experience some of the wide variety and depth of the Rich's prodigious talents, here's where you go to get straight. Sam Phillips pretty much let Rich do whatever he wanted to do at 706 Union, making a "Complete Sun Sessions" a real unlikely vote-getter on the reissue horizon simply because Rich had so much talent in so many different directions (jazz vs. country, blues vs. crass banality) that putting it all out makes almost no sense at all. That's why this compilation is so refreshing; no filler, no dumb stuff, just the hits and the best tracks from a five—or six-year period when Rich was one of the last glimmers of hope for the label. All the early hits like "Lonely Weekends," "Sittin' and Thinkin'," and "Who Will the Next Fool Be" are aboard, along with several stereo tracks remixed from the original multi-track masters for the first time ever, with sparkling sound. Charlie Rich was one talented man, and here's where you find some of his best. —*Cub Koda*

Sun Sessions / Mar. 26, 1996 / Varèse Vintage ✦✦✦✦
Concise collection of the best material that Rich recorded for Sun in the late '50s and early '60s for those who want only a single disc's worth, rather than the lengthier Sun retrospectives that have been available on import. This has all of his key singles from the era ("Lonely Weekends," "Who Will the Next Fool Be," "Midnite Blues," "Philadelphia Baby"), as well as some choice B-sides and other hard-to-find tracks. The harder-rocking tracks show that Rich could be a convincing rockabilly singer, while the bluesier and more contemplative sides offer evidence of his versatility and sensitivity. —*Richie Unterberger*

★ **Feel Like Going Home: The Essential** / Jan. 28, 1997 / Legacy/ Columbia ✦✦✦✦✦
Though it bypasses his late-'70s and early-'80s records for United Artists and Elektra, the double-disc, 36-track set *Feel Like Going Home: The Essential Charlie Rich* covers Rich's best (and best-known) work for Sun/Phillips, Groove, Smash, and Epic, making it the first cross-licensed compilation ever assembled on the idiosyncratic vocalist and pianist. The multi-label approach works wonders in illustrating the depths of Rich's talents, since the compilation showcases all of his stylistic detours and his rich musical eclecticism. The song selection also helps showcase his versatility. While *Feel Like Going Home* contains all of his best-known songs in their original hit versions ("Lonely Weekends," "Who Will the Next Fool Be," "Sittin' and Thinkin'," "Big Boss Man," "Mohair Sam," "I Washed My Hands in Muddy Waters," "Set Me Free," "Don't Put No Headstone on My Grave," "Life's Little Ups and Downs," "Behind Closed Doors," "The Most Beautiful Girl"), it overlooks several big country hits from the mid-'70s in favor of lesser-known '60s and early '70s recordings that are stronger performances. As a consequence, *Feel Like Going Home* is the only compilation that truly shows the scope of Rich's talent, and it

works both as an introduction and as a definitive retrospective. —*Stephen Thomas Erlewine*

Ricochet

Contemporary Country

Ricochet emerged in the spring of 1996 to become one of the most successful new country groups of the year, spending the better part of the year in the Top 40 of the country charts.

Ricochet formed in 1993, when drummer Jeff Bryant asked guitarist Heath Wright to join his band Lariat, which also featured Bryant's brother Junior (fiddle/mandolin). After Wright joined Lariat, the group quickly disbanded, but the Bryants and Heath decided to give it another try under the name of Ricochet. The trio held auditions to complete the band, and several members floated through in the ensuing months. By the beginning of 1994, the final lineup had fallen into place. In addition to Heath Wright (lead singer/lead guitarist), Jeff Bryant (drums), and Junior Bryant (fiddle, mandolin, backing vocals), the group featured Greg Cook (bass, backing vocals), Teddy Carr (steel guitar), and Eddie Kilgallon (keyboards, rhythm guitar, saxophone, backing vocals). For the next two years, Ricochet toured the South and the West Coast, building up a fan base and developing its energetic, edgy neo-traditional sound. They would often spend their down time rehearsing and writing songs.

The group's original manager was friends with record producer Ron Chancey, who was known for his work with the Oak Ridge Boys. Chancey heard the group and arranged for the band to cut a demo. Chancey directed the tape to his son Blake, who was the A&R director for Columbia Records in Nashville. After hearing the group live, Blake and a handful of other Columbia executives decided to sign Ricochet to a development deal under the direction of producer Ed Seay (Martina McBride, Colin Raye). In early 1995 the deal turned into a full-fledged record contract. During the spring, the group recorded their debut album. For the rest of the year, they toured the country as a supporting act for Merle Haggard, Doug Stone, and Charlie Daniels.

Produced by Ron Chancey and Ed Seay, Ricochet's eponymous debut album was released in early 1996. Preceded by the No. 3 hit single "What Do I Know," the album was a hit and stayed on the charts for most of the rest of 1996. —*Stephen Thomas Erlewine*

Ricochet / Jun. 1996 / Columbia ◆◆◆

Riders in the Sky

Cowboy

Beginning each performance with their trademark greeting "Mighty fine and a great big Western 'Howdy,'" all you buckaroos and buckarettes," Riders in the Sky simultaneously paid tribute to and poked gentle fun at classic B-movie cowboy songs from the '40s and '50s, particularly the work of Roy Rogers and Gene Autry. During the '70s and '80s, the group built a strong cult following in America, especially on college campuses. The Riders were comprised of lead singer Ranger Doug (born Douglas B. Green), Woody Paul (born Paul Chrisman) on fiddle and vocals, and Too Slim (string bass/guitar/accordion). Before forming the band, the Michigan-born Ranger Doug was a member of Bill Monroe's Bluegrass Boys and a country music journalist, editing the *Country Music Foundation Press* and the *Journal of Country Music*. Before joining the Rangers, Woody Paul played fiddle with Loggins and Messina, and Too Slim was a member of Dickey Lee's band in addition to being a songwriter. The trio formed in the mid-'70s, playing a weekly gig at a Nashville nightclub, which led to a job with TNN's *Tumbleweed Theater*. In the early '80s they released five albums, and in 1985 the Riders in the Sky appeared in *Sweet Dreams*, the film biography of Patsy Cline. The group signed to MCA in 1987, releasing their first album for the label—*Riders Radio Theater*—a year later. The record was a success, which led to the program "Riders Radio Theater" on National Public Radio. They recorded two more albums with MCA and in 1991 moved to Columbia, where they recorded the children's album *Harmony Ranch*, which led to a short-lived CBS TV Saturday-morning television show. The Riders in the Sky con-

tinued recording and touring through the mid-'90s. —*Sandra Brennan*

Three on the Trail / 1979 / Rounder ◆◆◆◆
Three on the Trail, Riders in the Sky's debut album, established their tongue-in-cheek tribute to cowboys and Western music. Though the humor is piled on a little thicker here than on their later releases, the music is often quite good, and they never deviated from this formula—slightly ironic covers, affectionate jokes, and made-to-order originals—on any of their subsequent records. They also rarely did it any better. —*Thom Owens*

The Best of the West / 1988 / Rounder ◆◆◆◆
Best of the West contains 25 highlights from the Riders in the Sky's first five albums for Rounder Records, including such Western standards as "Tumbling Tumbleweeds," "Here Comes the Santa Fe," "Don't Fence Me In," "Blue Montana Skies," and the group's namesake, "Ghost Riders in the Sky." —*Thom Owens*

Radio Theatre / Jun. 27, 1988 / MCA ◆◆◆
This contains 18 digitally recorded selections such as "Trail Traffic Report" and "Bio Feedbag." Known for their odd outlooks, these three cowboys are some of America's favorites. —*AMG*

Saturday Morning with Riders / 1992 / MCA ◆◆
Saturday Morning with Riders in the Sky collects favorites like "Back in the Saddle Again," "That's How the Yodel Was Born," and the group's eponymous theme song. —*Jason Ankeny*

Live / Mar. 15, 1992 / Rounder ◆◆◆
This square-but-hip comedy has songs crooned in lush Sons of the Pioneers-style Western harmony. —*Mark A. Humphrey*

Cowboys in Love / 1994 / Epic ◆◆◆◆
Putting the skits aside for the time being, the Riders focus largely on their underrated musical ability. Ranger Doug shows off his sublime baritone on several Western-style love songs, including an exquisite duet with Emmylou Harris on "One Has My Name, the Other Has My Heart." The instrumentals, especially Woody Paul's expert fiddling, are superb, as is the spirited take with guests Asleep at the Wheel on "I'm a Ding Dong Daddy from Dumas." —*Michael McCall*

Always Drink Upstream from the Herd / Oct. 31, 1995 / Rounder ◆◆◆◆
As they get older, Riders in the Sky sound more accomplished and, more importantly, they sound more sincere. Like any of the group's albums, *Always Drink Upstream from the Herd* combines standards with original material, but what makes it noteworthy is that sincerity—they still make jokes, but they can deliver the material more gracefully and skillfully than ever before, making it one of their most enjoyable efforts. —*Thom Owens*

Public Cowboy / Oct. 22, 1996 / Rounder ◆◆◆◆
The Riders in the Sky cut this record in the wake of their performing a Gene Autry medley in a television appearance with Autry himself in the audience. The songs are done reverently but with a real sense of fun, essentially the same balancing act that has made them a success on stage and television. Their main innovations are the harmony singing, which works well throughout, and a jazzy approach to Jimmie Rodgers' "Can't Shake the Sands of Texas from My Shoes." Autry's versions have held up magnificently well, but this loving tribute album is a necessary addition to any fan's collection. —*Bruce Eder*

● **Best of the West Rides Again** / Rounder ◆◆◆◆
Best of the West Rides Again contains 25 tracks, all selected from the Riders in the Sky's first five albums for Rounder. Among the highlights are versions of "Back in the Saddle," "Cool Water," "Pecos Bill," and "Streets of Laredo." —*Thom Owens*

Billy Lee Riley

b. 1933
Bass, Guitar, Harmonica, Drums, Vocals / Rockabilly
Billy Lee Riley is a rockabilly singer and multi-instrumentalist. An alumnus of Sun Records, he was one of the most crazed, unabashed rockers that label had to offer; in the company of Jerry Lee Lewis, Carl Perkins, and Sonny Burgess, that's saying a lot. Proficient at harmonica, guitar, bass, and drums, Riley contributed

as a sideman to many a classic Sun session, and his combo the Little Green Men (most notably guitarist Roland Janes and drummer J.M. Van Eaton) in time became the Sun house band. Riley recorded for a number of labels in a variety of styles; he was especially effective with blues. Though never commercially successful, Riley's Sun recordings of "Flying Saucer Rock 'n' Roll" and "Red Hot" (both covered in wooden renditions by Robert Gordon) remain landmarks of the genre. — *Cub Koda*

● **Classic Recordings, 1956-1960** / Jul. 1990 / Bear Family ✦✦✦✦
All the classic Sun sides, plus later Memphis recordings in a brilliant two-CD set. Raw rockin' at its finest. — *Cub Koda*

Blue Collar Blues / 1992 / Hightone ✦✦✦✦

Jeannie C. Riley (Jeanne Stephenson)

b. Sep. 19, 1945, Anson, TX
Vocals / Gospel, Country-Pop, CCM
Best known for her international crossover hit "Harper Valley P.T.A.," Jeannie C. Riley was born Jeanne Carolyn Stephenson in Anson, TX, where she developed a love of country music as a girl. When she was a teenager, she made her first public performance, appearing on her uncle's jamboree show. Soon after high school graduation, she married Mickey Riley; she wanted to become a professional musician, so she and her husband moved to Nashville, where she performed secretarial work at Passkey Music. She also made a few demos that led to her recording "What About Them" as Jean Riley; the single wasn't successful. Her manager, Paul Perry, hooked Riley up with producer Shelby Singleton, with whom she recorded "Harper Valley P.T.A." The song became an instant hit, reaching No. 1 on both the pop and country charts. Later in 1968, Riley debuted on the Grand Ole Opry and released "The Girl Most Likely," which reached No. 6 on the country charts. During the early '70s, she had a string of minor hits and five other Top Ten singles, including "Country Girl," "Oh, Singer," and "Good Enough to Be Your Wife." Around 1974 Riley became a born-again Christian and formed a new band, Red River Symphony, which had a minor hit in 1976, "The Best I've Ever Had." After its release, Riley founded and began recording on the God's Country label. In 1981 she recorded the gospel album *From Harper Valley to the Mountain Top.* Throughout the '80s and '90s, she continued to be a popular contemporary Christian recording and performing artist. — *Sandra Brennan*

● **Best of Jeannie C. Riley** / Oct. 22, 1996 / Varese Sarabande ✦✦✦✦
Fifteen-song compilation concentrating on her late-'60s/early-'70s prime; everything's from 1968-71, except for a couple of nonessential '80s cuts tacked onto the end. Sometimes thought of as a one-shot artist, Riley was one of the better country singers of her era, with a far saucier delivery than was the norm. The material, much of it penned by the songwriting team of Myra Smith and Margaret Lewis, is almost schizophrenic in its reach. "The Rib" could be heard as an early, dignified plea for women's rights; "The Generation Gap" had some muted anti-establishment undertones; and of course Tom Hall's "Harper Valley P.T.A." poked fun at small-town hypocrisy. At the same time, she released bathetic ballads like "Things Go Better with Love"; "There Never Was a Time" is as corny an ode to family, God, and honest struggle as you can find in the country field. At any rate, the anthology as a whole is above average, including the hits "Oh, Singer," "Good Enough to Be Your Wife," "Country Girl," and "The Girl Most Likely." — *Richie Unterberger*

LeAnn Rimes

b. Aug. 28, 1982, Jackson, MS
Vocals / Contemporary Country
In 1996 LeAnn Rimes burst out of nowhere with her debut single "Blue," which immediately captured the attention of country fans across America. It wasn't just the fact that her rich, powerful vocals were remarkably similar to Patsy Cline's—it was the fact that LeAnn Rimes was only 13 years old. Like Tanya Tucker and Brenda Lee, she had a hit with her debut single; and she was barely a teenager at the time. It was quite an auspicious way to begin a career.

Born in Jackson, MS, but raised in Garland, TX, LeAnn Rimes began singing as a child, performing at local talent contests. At the age of 11, she released her first album on an independent record label called Nor Va Jak. That same year Bill Mack, a Dallas disc jockey and record promoter, met Rimes and, impressed by her talents, took her under his wing and began cultivating a plan to break her into the mainstream. The cornerstone of Mack's plan was a song called "Blue," which he had written in the '60s. Mack claimed that he had written the tune for Patsy Cline but that she had died before she was able to record the song.

Throughout 1995 Rimes' career continued to gain momentum, as she performed more than 100 concerts and appeared on television shows across Texas.

After Mack arranged a record contract for Rimes with Curb Records, the label sent out a release with the single of "Blue" that claimed the DJ had been waiting more than 30 years to find the right vocalist to sing "Blue." The story was an exaggeration; "Blue" had been recorded by no less than three artists, including Bill Mack and Kenny Roberts, who both released versions on Starday in the '60s, and Kathryn Pitt, who released the record as a single in 1993 in her native Australia. Nevertheless, the story was repeated throughout the country and mainstream music press, adding to the growing myth that Rimes was the successor to Cline's tradition. "Blue" and its accompanying album of the same name became a major hit in the summer of 1996.

Blue debuted at No. 3 on the pop charts, selling more than 123,000 copies within a week of its release—the largest figure in the history of the SoundScan tracking system. Rimes was nominated for the Country Music Association Horizon award and the CMA Best Country Singer, becoming the youngest singer in the history of the CMA awards to receive a nomination; she won neither award. — *Stephen Thomas Erlewine*

● **Blue** / 1996 / Curb ✦✦✦✦
With her debut single "Blue," the 13 year-old Leann Rimes made a major impression on Nashville. Although her age made her a novelty, what made a lasting impression was the depth and richness of her voice, which sounded for all the world like that of a young Patsy Cline. Stylistically, "Blue" is the closest Rimes gets to Cline on her debut album, which is also titled *Blue.* Though Cline's twangy countrypolitan is an undercurrent throughout *Blue,* Rimes' music is designed for mid-'90s listeners, so there are flourishes of commercially oriented new country, new traditionalism, and country-pop. Naturally, the quality of the songs is somewhat uneven, but Rimes' vibrant voice sounds exquisite throughout the album and suggests that she'll be able to develop her talent into something truly unique. — *Thom Owens*

Jim Ringer

b. Feb. 29, 1936, Yell County, AR, d. Mar. 17, 1992
Vocals / Progressive Bluegrass, Progressive Country, Contemporary Folk
At one time, it appeared that singer-songwriter Jim Ringer would be a major star; instead, he wound up as a cult figure with a small but devoted following. He was born in Yell County in the Arkansas Ozarks; during the Dust Bowl years of the 1930s, his family migrated to California's Central Valley. It was a rough life, and by 18 Ringer was serving a three-year prison sentence. For a few years afterward, he was a transient, hopping freight trains from job to job until 1969, when he became a professional musician. Two years later he was a hippie in Berkeley, where he and 12 friends bought a 1948 Chevy school bus and formed the Portable Folk Festival; the group spent 1971 touring the country and performing. Near the end of the year, Ringer began performing with Kenny Hall and the Sweet's Mill String Band; he cut an album with them in 1972. That year he also cut his first solo album, *Waitin' for the Hard Times to Go,* for Folk-Legacy Records. After meeting singer Mary McCaslin in 1972, Ringer teamed up with her professionally and personally, but he continued to play individually, too. In 1973 Ringer signed to Philo and released *Good to Get Home.* Two more albums followed in the next three years. After he and McCaslin were married, they recorded a duet for Philo called *The Bramble and the Rose.* Ringer signed to Flying

Fish in 1981 and recorded *Endangered Species*, which produced the highly touted "Whiskey and Cocaine" and featured performances by the Dillards, the Burrito Brothers, and the Hot Band. He and McCaslin split up in 1989, and three years later, Jim Ringer died on St. Patrick's Day. —*Sandra Brennan*

Waitin' for the Hard Times to Go / 1972 / Folk Legacy ✦✦✦

● **Good to Get Home** / 1973 / Philo ✦✦✦✦

Any Old Wind That Blows / 1975 / Philo ✦✦✦

Tramps and Hawkers / 1977 / Philo ✦✦✦✦

Bramble and the Rose / 1978 / Philo ✦✦✦

Endangered Species / 1981 / Flying Fish ✦✦✦✦

Tex Ritter (Woodward Maurice Ritter)

b Jan. 12, 1907, Murval, TX, d. Jan. 2, 1973, Nashville, TN
Guitar, Vocals / Traditional Country, Cowboy
Singing cowboy Tex Ritter stood as one of the biggest names in country music throughout the postwar era, thanks to a diverse career that led him from the Broadway stage to the political arena. He was born Maurice Woodward Ritter in Marvaul, TX, on January 12, 1907, and grew up on a ranch in Beaumont. After graduating at the top of his high school class, he majored in law at the University of Texas. During college, however, he was bitten by the acting bug, and moved to New York in 1928 to join a theatrical troupe. After a few years of struggle, he briefly returned to school, only to leave again to pursue stardom.

Ritter was playing cowboy songs on the radio when he returned to New York in 1931 to act in the Broadway production *Green Grow the Lilacs;* during scene changes, he also performed on his guitar. Thanks to his success on the stage, he began hosting radio programs like "Tex Ritter's Campfire" and "Cowboy Tom's Roundup" before entering the studio with producer Art Satherly in 1933, where his deep, lived-in voice graced songs like "Rye Whiskey." He caught the attention of Hollywood producer Edward Finney, who was searching for a cowboy singer in the mold of the highly successful Gene Autry, and was tapped to star in the 1936 Western *Song of the Gringo*. Over the next two years Ritter starred in a dozen films, including 1937's *Trouble in Texas* (costarring a young Rita Hayworth), before Finney's studio Grand National Pictures folded. Ritter then switched to Monogram Studios, for whom he made some 20 Westerns, including 1940's *Take Me Back to Oklahoma* with co-star Bob Wills. Work at Columbia and Universal followed, and by the time of his movie swan song, 1945's *The Texas Rangers*, he had appeared in 85 films.

As Ritter's Hollywood career went into decline, his music career began to blossom, and in 1942 he became the first country artist signed to Capitol Records, where he recorded everything from traditional folk tunes to patriotic material to sentimental songs. In 1944 Tex Ritter and His Texans topped the charts with the single "I'm Wastin' My Tears on You." The record's flip side, "There's a New Moon Over My Shoulder," peaked at No. 2, as did the follow-up, "Jealous Heart." 1945's "You Two-Timed Me One Time Too Often" proved to be Ritter's greatest success, holding at No. 1 for 11 consecutive weeks. Among his other successes in the 1940s were 1945's No. 1 "You Will Have to Pay," 1948's "Rock and Rye," and 1950's "Daddy's Last Letter (Private First Class John H. McCormick)," based on the actual correspondence of a soldier slain during the Korean War.

Ritter recorded the theme to the Fred Zinneman classic *High Noon* in 1953, and the resulting single proved extremely successful with pop audiences, helping win him the job as the emcee of the television program "Town Hall Party," which he hosted between 1953 and 1960. In 1958 he issued his first full-length LP, *Songs from the Western Screen*, followed the next year by *Psalms*. After leaving "Town Hall Party," he released the LP *Blood on the Saddle*, a dark collection of cowboy narrative songs, and in 1961 he returned to the country charts after an 11-year absence with the Top Five hit "I Dreamed of a Hill-Billy Heaven." In 1963 Ritter began a two-year tenure as president of the Country Music Association, and in 1965 he moved to Nashville to join the Grand Ole Opry. After an unsuccessful bid for the US Senate in 1970, Ritter died of a heart attack on January 2, 1974; his son John Ritter car-

ried on the family name as a popular actor in TV sitcoms like "Three's Company" and "Hooperman." —*Jason Ankeny*

Blood on the Saddle / 1960 / Capitol ✦✦✦✦
Inspired by the success of Marty Robbins and Johnnie Horton, Ritter set about recording an LP of folk-based narrative material; taking its cue from the title track, *Blood on the Saddle* is a collection of dark, even grisly, cowboy tales. —*Jason Ankeny*

Greatest Hits / 1990 / Curb ✦✦✦✦
Virtually all of Ritter's hits from his years with Capitol Records are included in this 12-cut collection, including "I'm Wastin' My Tears on You," his first chart-topper. Also featured: "You Two-Timed Me One Time Too Often," "Jealous Heart," and "You Will Have to Pay." —*Jason Ankeny*

Country Music Hall of Fame / 1991 / MCA ✦✦✦✦
Pure Texan, Ritter was grittier than most of Hollywood's singing cowboys and nearer the roots of Western song. His 1935-1939 sides are here. —*Mark A. Humphrey*

● **Capitol Collectors Series** / Feb. 17, 1992 / Capitol ✦✦✦✦
Ritter spent more than three decades with Capitol, and the 25 songs (including the great "Rye Whiskey" and "Blood on the Saddle") on this well-annotated set feature Ritter's yelping theatricality at its best. —*Michael McCall*

High Noon / Bear Family ✦✦✦✦
High Noon is an excellent compilation of 28 of Tex Ritter's finest recordings for Capitol Records. All of the material on the single-disc collection was recorded between 1942 and 1957, and the album charts Ritter's move from simple Western folk songs to Hollywood cowboy tunes such as "(I Got Spurs That) Jingle, Jangle, Jingle," "Gunsmoke," "Remember the Alamo," and the title track. Along the way, *High Noon* adds some obscurities—such as the weird "Buffalo Dream"—but the collection functions primarily as a retrospective, and it succeeds in being a comprehensive overview of Tex Ritter's most popular era. —*Thom Owens*

Dennis Robbins

b. , Hazelwood, NC
Vocals, Slide Guitar / Contemporary Country
A slide guitarist and former member of the Detroit blues-rock band the Rockets, Dennis Robbins also performed with the country-songwriter supergroup Billy Hill; among the songs he wrote were Garth Brooks' "Two of a Kind, Workin' on a Full House" and Shenandoah's "Church on Cumberland Road." Robbins was born in Hazelwood, NC, and grew up listening to traditional bluegrass music as well as rock 'n' roll. He began playing different styles of guitar music as a teen. After high school, Robbins was a US Marine. He eventually moved to Detroit, where he played in different bands before joining up with the Rockets as a slide guitar player. The band was quite popular and opened for the likes of ZZ Top, Kiss, and Bob Seger. Tiring of touring, Robbins returned to North Carolina and then moved to Nashville, where in 1986 he released his debut solo album *The First of Me*. His lack of success spurred Robbins to form Billy Hill, which broke up in 1990 after only one album. Soon afterward he became the first country artist to sign to Giant's new country division. His first single for the label, "Home Sweet Home," became a minor hit and later appeared on the album *Man with the Plan* (1992). —*Sandra Brennan & Brian Mansfield*

The First of Me / 1986 / MCA ✦✦✦

I Am Just a Rebel / 1989 / Warner Brothers ✦✦✦✦

● **Man with a Plan** / Jun. 16, 1992 / Giant ✦✦✦✦
Redneck rock that lives and dies by the slide guitar. (Think of Hank Williams Jr. with a sneakier sense of humor.) Tracy Lawrence found "Paris, Tennessee" here, and Confederate Railroad got "I Am Just a Rebel" (which Robbins had earlier recorded with Billy Hill). Robbins broke the Top 40 with the slice-of-life "Home Sweet Home." —*Brian Mansfield*

Hargus Robbins

b. Jan. 18, 1938, Spring City, TN
Keyboards, Session Musician / Traditional Country, Western Swing, Nashville Sound/Countrypolitan

For more than three decades, Hargus "Pig" Robbins remained one of the top session keyboardists in Nashville, and he played with some of country music's most illustrious stars. While a child in Spring City, TN, Robbins accidentally put out his eye while playing with his father's knife; he was totally blind by age four. He began learning classical piano at age seven while attending the Tennessee School for the Blind in Nashville and was influenced by the music of Tex Ritter, his idol. Robbins learned country music by listening to records and the radio, and after leaving the school, he began playing in various Nashville clubs. After playing on a friend's demo, he became a session man, and in 1959 he played on George Jones' "White Lightning." In 1963 Robbins recorded a solo album, *A Bit of Country Piano.* He also played on non-country albums; a 1966 appearance on Bob Dylan's *Blonde on Blonde* left him in great demand with pop, folk, and country artists. In 1978 Robbins released *Pig in a Poke,* his second album for Elektra. Even though younger keyboardists appeared continually in Nashville, Robbins remained the first choice of many artists, and he played with Merle Haggard, Loretta Lynn, Kenny Rogers, Tanya Tucker, Ronnie Milsap, Tom T. Hall, Alan Jackson, Mark Chesnutt, George Jones, and Travis Tritt. — *Sandra Brennan*

Hargus Robbins / 1969 / Chart ✦✦✦

● Country Instrumentalist of the Year / 1977 / Elektra ✦✦✦✦

A Pig in a Poke / 1978 / Elektra ✦✦✦

Alive from Austin City Limits / 1979 / Flying Fish ✦✦✦

Unbreakable Hearts / 1979 / Elektra ✦✦✦

Marty Robbins (Martin David Robertson)

b. Sep. 26, 1925, Glendale, AZ, **d.** Dec. 8, 1982, Nashville, TN
Guitar, Vocals / Traditional Country, Cowboy, Country-Pop, Rockabilly, Nashville Sound/Countrypolitan

No artist in the history of country music has had a more stylistically diverse career than Marty Robbins. Never content to remain just a country singer, Robbins performed successfully in a dazzling array of styles during more than 30 years in the business. To his credit, Robbins rarely followed trends, but he often took off in directions that stunned both his peers and fans. Plainly Robbins was not hemmed in by anyone's definition of country music. Although his earliest recordings were unremarkable weepers, by the mid-'50s Robbins was making forays into rock music, adding fiddles to the works of Chuck Berry and Little Richard. By the late '50s, Robbins had pop hits of his own with teen fare like "A White Sport Coat (and a Pink Carnation)." Almost simultaneously, he completed work on *Hawaiian Songs of the Islands.* In 1959 Robbins stretched even further with the hit single "El Paso," thus heralding a pattern of "gunfighter ballads" that lasted the balance of his career. Robbins also enjoyed bluesy hits like "Don't Worry," which introduced a pop audience to fuzztone guitar in 1961. Barely a year later Robbins scored a calypso hit with "Devil Woman." Marty Robbins also left a legacy of gospel music and a string of sentimental ballads, showing that he could croon with nary a touch of hillbilly twang.

Born and raised in Glendale, AZ, Marty Robbins was exposed to music at an early age. His mother's father was "Texas" Bob Heckle, a former medicine show man who told his grandson cowboy stories and tales of the traveling show. Marty became enraptured by the cowboy tales; when he became a teenager, he worked on his older brother's ranch outside of Phoenix, concentrating more on his cowboy duties than his studies. Indeed, he never graduated from high school, and by his late teens, he had started turning petty crimes while living as a hobo. In 1943 he joined the US Navy to fight in World War II, and while he was in the service, he learned how to play guitar and developed a taste for Hawaiian music. Robbins left the Navy in 1947, returning to Glendale, where he began to sing in local clubs and radio stations. Often he performed under the name "Jack Robinson" in an attempt to disguise his endeavors from his disapproving mother.

Within three years he had developed a strong reputation throughout Arizona and was appearing regularly on a Mesa radio station and had his own television show, "Western Caravan," in Phoenix. By that time, he had settled on the stage name of Marty Robbins.

Robbins landed a recording contract with Columbia in 1951 with the assistance of Little Jimmy Dickens, who had been a fan ever since appearing on "Western Caravan." Early in 1952, Robbins released his first single, "Love Me or Leave Me Alone." It wasn't a success, and neither was its follow-up, "Crying 'Cause I Love You"; but "I'll Go On Alone" soared to No. 1 in January 1953. After its blockbuster success, Robbins signed a publishing deal with Acuff-Rose and joined the Grand Ole Opry. "I Couldn't Keep From Crying" kept him in the Top Ten in the spring of 1953, but his two 1954 singles—"Pretty Words" and "Call Me Up (and I'll Come Calling On You)"—stalled on the charts. A couple of rock 'n' roll covers, "That's All Right" and "Maybellene," returned him to the country Top Ten in 1955, but it wasn't until "Singing the Blues" shot to No. 1 in the fall of 1956 that his career was truly launched. Staying at No. 1 for a remarkable 13 weeks, "Singing the Blues" established Robbins as a star, but its progress on the pop charts was impeded by Guy Mitchell's cover, which was released shortly after Robbins' original and quickly leapfrogged to No. 1. The process repeated itself on "Knee Deep in the Blues," which went to No. 3 on the country charts but didn't even appear on the pop charts because of Mitchell's hastily released cover. To head off such competition, Robbins decided to record with easy-listening conductor Ray Conniff for his next singles. It was a crafty move and one that kept him commercially viable during the peak of rock 'n' roll. The first of these collaborations, "A White Sport Coat (and a Pink Carnation)," became a huge hit, spending five weeks at the top of the country charts in the spring of 1957 and peaking at No. 2 on the pop charts, giving him his long-awaited breakthrough record.

After "A White Sport Coat (and a Pink Carnation)," Marty Robbins was a fixture on the pop and country charts until the mid-'60s. The Burt Bacharach and Hal David composition "The Story of My Life" returned Robbins to the No. 1 country slot in early 1957 (No. 15 pop), while "Just Married," "Stairway of Love," and "She Was Only Seventeen (He Was One Year More)" kept him in teen-pop territory, as well as the upper reaches of the charts, throughout 1958. In addition to his pop records, Robbins recorded rockabilly singles and Hawaiian albums that earned their own audience. During that time, he began a couple of business ventures, including a booking agency and a record label called Robbins. He also ventured into movies, appearing in the Westerns *Raiders of Old California* (1957) and *Badge of Marshal Brennan* (1958), where he played a Mexican named Felipe. The films not only demonstrated his love for Western myths and legends, but they signalled the shift in musical direction he was about to take. Over the course of 1958 and 1959, he recorded a number of cowboy and Western songs, and the first of these—"The Hanging Tree," the theme to the Gary Cooper film of the same name—became a hit in the spring of 1959. However, the song just set the stage for Robbins' signature song and biggest Western hit, "El Paso." Released in the summer, the single spent six months on the country charts, including seven weeks at No. 1, while hitting the top of the pop charts. A full album of Western songs, *Gunfighter Ballads and Trail Songs,* became equally successful, reaching No. 6 on the pop charts; by the mid-'60s, it had gone platinum.

"El Paso" began a very successful decade for Marty Robbins. "Big Iron," another Western song, followed its predecessor to the Top Ten of the country charts in 1960, but it wasn't until 1961 that he had another huge hit in the form of "Don't Worry." Fueled by a fuzz-toned guitar (the first country record to feature such an effect), "Don't Worry" spent ten weeks at No. 1 and crossed over to No. 3 on the pop charts. The next year, "Devil Woman" became nearly as successful, spending eight weeks at No. 1; it was followed by another No. 1, "Ruby Ann." Between "Don't Worry" and "Devil Woman," he had a number of smaller hits, most notably the Top Ten "It's Your World." For the rest of the decade, his biggest hits alternated with more moderate successes. With his career sailing along, Robbins began exploring race-car driving in 1962, initially driving in dirt-track racing competitions before competing in a NASCAR race. However, car racing was just a hobby, and he continued to have hits in 1963, including the No. 1 "Begging to You." The next year he starred in the film *Ballad of a Gunfighter*, which was based on songs from his classic album.

Robbins' chart success continued throughout 1964, before suddenly dipping after he took Gordon Lightfoot's "Ribbon of Darkness" to No. 1 in the spring of 1965. For the remainder of the year and much of the next, his singles failed to crack the Top Ten, and he concentrated on filming a television series called "The Drifter," based on a character he had created. He also acted frequently, including the Nashville exploitation films *Country Music Caravan, The Nashville Story,* and *Tennessee Jamboree,* and the stock-car drama *Hell on Wheels.* Though "The Shoe Goes on the Other Foot Tonight" reached No. 3 in 1966, it wasn't until "Tonight Car men" reached No. 1 on the country charts in 1967 that his career picked up considerably. During the next two years, he regularly hit the Top Ten with country-pop songs like "I Walk Alone" and "It's a Sin." Robbins suffered a heart attack while on tour in August 1969, which lead to a bypass operation in 1970. Despite his brush with death, he continued to record, tour, and act. Early in 1970 "My Woman My Woman, My Wife" became his last major crossover hit, reaching No. 1 on the country charts and 42 on the pop charts, and eventually earning a Grammy award.

Robbins left Columbia Records in 1972, spending the next three years at Decca/MCA. Though "Walking Piece of Heaven," "Love Me," and "Twentieth Century Drifter" all reached the Top Ten, most of his singles were unenthusiastically received. Nevertheless, he sustained his popularity through concerts and film appearances, including the Lee Marvin movie *A Man and a Train* and *Guns of a Stranger.* In March 1974 Robbins became the last performer to play at the Ryman Auditorium, the original location of the Grand Ole Opry; a week later, he was the first to play at the new Grand Ole Opry House. The honors and tributes to Robbins continued to roll out during the mid-'70s, as he was inducted into the Nashville Songwriters International Hall of Fame in 1975. That same year he returned to Columbia Records, and over 1976 and 1977 he had his last sustained string of Top Ten hits, with "El Paso City" and "Among My Souvenirs" reaching No. 1. After this two-year burst of success, Robbins settled into a series of minor hits for the next four years. In October 1982 he was inducted into the Country Music Hall of Fame. Two months later he suffered his third major heart attack (his second arrived in early 1981), and although he had surgery, he died December 8. In the wake of his death, his theme song to Clint Eastwood's movie *Honky Tonk Man* was released and climbed to No. 10. Robbins left an immense legacy, including no less than 94 charting country hits and a body of recorded work that proved how eclectic country music can be. *—Hank Davis*

Rock 'n' Rollin' Robbins / Koch ✦✦✦✦

When rockabilly reared its ugly head in country music circles in the mid-'50s, hillbilly artists generally took one of two approaches: ignore it or take a stab at it. One country singer who decided to test these uncharted waters was Marty Robbins and, as this 12-song package clearly shows, he was well equipped to take on the new sound. This compilation combines the original cover and the half-dozen songs that comprised a ten-inch vinyl album issued in the 1950s, with six more tracks (five of which were Columbia singles) released during the same period. While the accent is on the "billy" side of the rockabilly equation along with Music City's attempt to tame the style down for an audience more accustomed to Grandpa Jones than Gene Vincent, this is very credible music indeed. Rather than just covering the hits of the day (Robbins was the first to cover Elvis' "That's All Right," included here), he also contributed solid self-penned ditties like "Tennessee Toddy," "Respectfully Miss Brooks," and "Mean Mama Blues," although his best known rocking effort—"Sugaree"—is curiously missing from this collection. That a ballad singer whose sobriquet was "Mister Teardrop" could jump into this music so wholeheartedly is one of the more interesting footnotes to this confusing period in country music's history. *—Cub Koda*

Marty Robbins

Gunfighter Ballads and Trail Songs / 1959 / Columbia ✦✦✦✦

Gunfighter Ballads and Trail Songs was Marty Robbins' first album to consist entirely of Western and cowboy music. Containing the hit single "El Paso," the album was divided between originals, traditional cowboy songs, and contemporary Western songs. The result was a successful and thoroughly entertaining celebration of cowboy songs and Western movies, particularly since the songs are alternately idealistic and adventurous. Sure, *Gunfighter Ballads and Trail Songs* doesn't deal in reality, but it is grounded in myth. It just happens to be one of the most effective and romantic statements of the cowboy mythology recorded in the late '50s and early '60s. *—Stephen Thomas Erlewine*

More Gunfighter Ballads and Trail Songs / 1960 / Columbia ✦✦✦✦

Marty Robbins' sequel to *Gunfighter Ballads and Trail Songs* followed the same formula as its predecessor, including traditional cowboy songs and original numbers by Robbins. Though the album didn't feature any hit singles, it was the equal to its predecessor; "San Angelo" is one of Robbins' best cowboy songs, while his version of "Streets of Laredo" boasts one of his finest vocals. *—Stephen Thomas Erlewine*

Hawaii's Calling Me / 1963 / Bear Family ✦✦✦

Take a complete look at Robbins' Hawaiian period on these 28 tracks. *—Hank Davis*

The Drifter / 1966 / Columbia ✦✦✦✦

Based of Marty Robbins' syndicated television series of the same name, *The Drifter* was one of the purest cowboy albums Robbins ever made. Though Robbins had made several cowboy albums before—indeed, his love of Western music informed much of his music—the instrumentation and song selection on *The Drifter* was stripped-down and direct, concentrating almost entirely on epic Western narrative sagas. The lack of concise songs resulted in a less successful album by commercial standards—only "Mr. Shorty" was a hit, while the "El Paso" sequel "Feleena" ran more than eight minutes—but *The Drifter* was one of Robbins' most artistically ambitious albums, as well as one of his most accomplished. *—Stephen Thomas Erlewine*

★ All-Time Greatest Hits / 1972 / Columbia/Legacy ✦✦✦✦✦

Released in 1972, the double-album/single-CD *All-Time Greatest Hits* remains one of the best compilations ever assembled on Marty Robbins. Featuring 20 tracks—including most of his big hits—very few essential tracks are missing from the collection. As an introduction, this relatively concise compilation is a bit more manageable than the double-disc *Essential Marty Robbins* and therefore more attractive to neophytes. *—Stephen Thomas Erlewine*

All Around Cowboy / 1979 / Columbia ✦✦✦
All Around Cowboy is the final cowboy album Marty Robbins recorded, and it stands out as one of the best of his latter-day records. Though many of his latter-day recordings were hampered by mediocre material and indifferent performances, Robbins sounds lively on *All Around Cowboy*, breathing life into the songs and assembling a collection of terrfic Western tunes. Though the production relies a little too heavily on contemporary late-'70s trends, Robbins' convincing performances make those flaws easy to ignore. *All Around Cowboy* may pale slightly in comparison to his early cowboy classics like *Gunfighter Ballads and Trail Songs*, but it's heart-warming to hear him this committed. *—Stephen Thomas Erlewine*

Biggest Hits / 1982 / Columbia ✦✦✦✦
Biggest Hits covers Robbins' early years as a recording artist and includes hits like "El Paso," "A White Sport Coat (and a Pink Carnation)," "Singing the Blues," and "The Story of My Life," as well as many lesser-known efforts. *—Jason Ankeny*

☆ **Rockin' Rollin' Robbins** / 1985 / Bear Family ✦✦✦✦✦
The jewel of Bear Family's exhaustive Robbins reissue project, the title does not lie. He shakes and rattles in fine style on "That's Allright," "Maybelline," "Singing the Blues," and 14 other good rockin' numbers. Much of this material appeared on a 1956 album of the same name, which is many country LP collectors' Holy Grail. *—Dan Cooper*

American Originals / 1989 / Columbia ✦✦✦
American Originals is one of many Robbins collections split between hits (here, "Singing the Blues," "Ruby Ann," "Tonight Carmen") and much less popular recordings. *—Jason Ankeny*

★ **The Essential Marty Robbins: 1951-1982** / 1991 / Columbia ✦✦✦✦✦
The double-disc set *The Essential Marty Robbins: 1951-1982* effectively presents an overview of Robbins' long, prolific career, taking in nearly every style he tried out during that time. There are honky tonk and hillbilly numbers and cowboy songs, country-pop, rockabilly, and Hawaiian tunes; in all, there are 50 songs, including the great majority of his big hit singles. In short, it's the perfect place to begin exploring his varied career, and it's a necessary addition to any country music library. *—Stephen Thomas Erlewine*

Country 1951-1958 / 1991 / Bear Family ✦✦✦✦
Listeners charmed by his pre-*El Paso* country have a motherlode to explore in this five-disc box set filled with dewy-eyed weepers (his earliest recordings), rockabilly (he cut the first cover of "Maybellene"), ancient country-folk accompanied solely by acoustic guitar ("The Dream of the Miner's Chill"), Hawaiiana ("Aloha Oe"), and a handful of his country-pop outings arranged by Ray Conniff. *—Mark A. Humphrey*

Lost and Found / 1994 / Columbia ✦✦✦
Included is previously unreleased material and a studio-manufactured duet with Michael Martin Murphey on "Big Iron." *—Dan Cooper*

Musical Journey to the Caribbean and Mexico / 1994 / Bear Family ✦✦✦✦
Bear Family's *A Musical Journey to the Carribean and Mexico* contains all of Marty Robbins' calypso, Jamaican, and Latin experiments, from "Calypso Vacation" and "Calypso Girl" to "Bahama Mama," "Tahitian Boy," "La Borrachita," and "Adios Marquita Linda." Robbins did have a flair for this material—indeed, the very best songs here are quite enjoyable—but he often is saddled with mediocre material. Furthermore, Bear Family's quest for completeness means there are three versions of "Girl from Spanish Two" and two versions of "Kingston Girl" on the single disc, which makes it rather tedious listening for anyone but dedicated fans. Nevertheless, those dedicated fans will be delighted with the collection, since this music has rarely been in print since its original release. *—Stephen Thomas Erlewine*

Ruby Ann: Rockin' Rollin' Robbins, Vol. 3 / 1996 / Bear Family ✦✦✦✦
These are the best of his bluesy rockers from the early '60s. *—Hank Davis*

★ **The Story of My Life: The Best of Marty Robbins** / 1996 / Columbia/Legacy ✦✦✦✦✦
This 18-track compilation covering the first half of Marty Robbins' recording career is almost an exact duplication of a chronological list of Robbins' biggest country hit singles of the period, the only exception being "I Can't Quit Her (I've Gone Too Far)," which, while a Top Ten entry, was not as big a hit as "She Was Only Seventeen (He Was One Year More)," which has been left out. (No one seems to have told annotator Rick Kienzle, who mentions the missing track and not the included one.) That means Robbins' 11 chart toppers are here, from "I'll Go On Alone" to "Ribbon of Darkness," with such massive hits as "Singing the Blues," "El Paso," "Don't Worry," and "Devil Woman" in between. The songs, 11 of which were written by Robbins himself, are amazingly diverse, covering country, western, pop, and folk styles, but the set is held together by Robbins' warm, country-tinged voice. The only objection to this set is that, at only 49+ minutes, it could have been longer by half. *—William Ruhlmann*

Gunfighter Ballads and Trail Songs/More Gunfighter Ballads / 1996 / CollectorsChoice'✦✦✦✦
Two of Marty Robbins' very finest albums, *Gunfighter Ballads and Trail Songs* and *More Gunfighter Ballads and Trail Songs*, are combined on this excellent single disc. With his cowboy albums, Robbins helped keep Western music alive during the late '50s and early '60s, and the warm, affectionate spirit of this music illustrates why. The disc contains such hits as "El Paso," "Big Iron," and "Five Brothers," as well as classic versions of "Streets of Laredo," "Strawberry Roan," and other Western standards. *—Stephen Thomas Erlewine*

Country (1960-1966) / 1996 / Bear Family ✦✦✦✦
Cutting away all of Marty Robbins' rock 'n' roll, Hawaiian, and cowboy recordings, Bear Family's four-disc box set *Country (1960-1966)* contains nothing but his straight country and country-pop recordings of the early '60s. During that era, Robbins was one of the most popular performers in country music, scoring an impressive series of Top Ten hits and pop crossovers like "Don't Worry" and "Devil Woman," which are included on this set. Where many Bear Family sets are so thorough and complete they wind up being exhausting, *Country (1960-1966)* is entertaining from start to finish, since it is sequenced in a logical, listenable order and doesn't dwell on the rarities. Any serious fan of Robbins will find the set essential, and it is arguably the finest Robbins box Bear Family has released. *—Stephen Thomas Erlewine*

Under Western Skies / Feb. 1996 / Bear Family ✦✦✦✦
Bear Family's four-disc set *Under Western Skies* collects all of Marty Robbins' Western and cowboy-themed albums from the '50s and '60s. For the hardcore collector, there's plenty of interest here, but the material is too specialized to appeal to anyone but diehard fans. *—Stephen Thomas Erlewine*

Kenny Roberts

Vocals / Traditional Country, Cowboy
Best-known for his 1949 hit "I Never See Maggie Alone," Kenny Roberts was one of the last country singers to specialize in the legendary vocal technique of the blue yodel. Inspired by Yodelin' Slim Clark, Jimmie Rodgers, and several singing cowboys, Roberts first came to prominence in the late '40s. Over the next five years he built a fan base through his recording, frequent tours, and appearances at yodeling concerts. Though he never had many hits—he only charted four times, between 1949 and 1950—he nevertheless remained a popular concert attraction well into the '80s.

Roberts was born in Lenoir City, TN, but he was reared on a farm outside of Greenfield, MA. As a child, he became fascinated by the music of Yodelin' Slim Clark and began singing, making his first radio appearance when he was 15. Soon he became part of the Down Homers, a local group who had a regular gig at WKNE, a New Hampshire radio station. Eventually the group made their way toward the Midwest, playing at radio stations in Iowa and later settling in Fort Wayne, IN, where they regularly played a show called "The Hoosier Hop." In a short time, Roberts had developed a reputation as a first-rate singer and yodeler.

The Down Homers—who also featured Bob Mason, Guy Campbell, Shorty Cook, and Lloyd Cornell—cut a record released as a Vogue Picture Disc. Roberts enlisted in the US Navy in early 1945. When the war was over, he returned to Fort Wayne, where he began a solo career. After a few months he moved to St. Louis, where he appeared regularly on several shows on KMOX, as well as the CBS Saturday morning show "Barnyard Frolics." Roberts released one single on Vitacoustic before signing to Coral Records in 1948.

Kenny Roberts' career took off in 1949, as his single "I Never See Maggie Alone" reached No. 4 on the country charts in the summer. The flip-side, "Wedding Bells," also was a hit, reaching No. 15, while his second single, "Jealous Heart," reached No. 14. In the spring of 1950, "Choc'late Ice Cream Cone" became his second Top Ten single; it would also prove to be his last charting single.

Roberts moved to Cincinnati, where he had a show on WLW Cincinnati and appeared regularly on "The Midwestern Hayride." For the remainder of the decade, he concentrated his efforts on the Midwest, becoming a big regional star through his television shows in Dayton, OH (which became his home in 1952), Indianapolis, and Saginaw, MI. He continued to appear regularly on daytime Midwestern television—and, as of 1962, WWVA's "Wheeling Jamboree"— until the mid-'60s. Around that time, he released an EP on the independent label Essgee, which led to a contract with Starday Records in 1965. Over the next five years, he released four albums for the label. Once his deal with Starday expired, he recorded briefly in the early '70s for Nashville Records.

In the early '70s, Roberts moved back to Dayton and concentrated on working in the Midwest and Canda. During the mid-'70s, he made a pair of albums for the Canadian label Point. By the end of the decade, he had moved back to his home state of Massachusetts, where he began playing concerts across the East. Roberts released one album for Palomino around 1980, which was followed by Longhorn's Then and Now, which combined historical cuts with new recordings. A few years later, Kenny Roberts moved to a farm near his childhood home in Greenfield. Though he was essentially retired, he continued to give concerts around the Northeast throughout the decade. —Stephen Thomas Erlewine

● Jumpin' and Yodelin' / 1996 / Bear Family ◆◆◆◆
Jumpin' and Yodelin' contains 31 of Kenny Roberts' best recordings for Coral and Decca, including all four of his charting hits—"I Never See Maggie Alone," "Wedding Bells," "Jealous Heart," and "Choc'late Ice Cream Cone"—making it the best single-disc retrospective assembled on the country singer. —Thom Owens

Kathy Robertson

Tex-Mex, Bakersfield Sound, Western Swing Revival
Kathy Robertson was born in Texas and reared in California. A singer most of her life, she graduated with a master's degree and taught kindergarten during the day in order to support her music. Refusing to bend to Nashville or allow someone to tell her how to sing or dress or what material to chose, she produced and marketed her own recordings. With as much luck as talent, Robertson managed to get the attention of a great many fans and industry people the world over.

Another featured artist from the A Town South of Bakersfield compilation, Robertson got her music business education while working on the road with Bakersfield legend and songwriter Red Simpson. Singing with Simpson, the man responsible for 30-some hits for Buck Owens, gave Robertson the knowledge she needed to make her own way. Supported by the friendship and advice of Bakersfield's queen, Bonnie Owens, Kathy Robertson carried on the Bakersfield tradition with gusto. Always playing with a full honky tonk band, Robertson worked not only with Simpson, Owens, and many other Bakersfield notables, but wrote and sang with Rosie Flores, Chris Gaffney, Katy Moffatt, Paul Marshall, and Mel Harker. The release of a cassette in the 1980s that included the Lawton Jiles' hit "Let the Teardrops Fall" eventually lead to her 1996 record At the Cantina. After its release, Robertson hit the trail in earnest and played Nashville as well as some other spots around the Southwest and California between recording sessions and teaching. —Jana Pendragon

● At the Cantina / 1996 / Kitty LA Tour Music ◆◆◆◆
This 14-cut CD was produced by Robertson with Hellecaster Jerry Donohue and David Vaught. The material is classic and displays Robertson's voice well. Guests include Bonnie Owens, Rosie Flores, Katy Moffatt, Big Sandy and Abe Manuel, Jr., and Don Markham from Merle Haggard's band. With every cut a potential hit, tunes like the Bonnie Owens-Leona Williams collaboration "Leona" have special meaning. A cover of the Tennessee Ernie Ford-Kay Starr hit "I'll Never Be Free" is as good as the original. For fun, Robertson includes a song she wrote with L.A. talent Mel Harker. Written for a mutual friend, "Queen of the Honky Tonks" depicts a slice of that world with humor and affection. A cover of Jean Shepard's "Twice the Lovin'" is a fast ride, as is the Flores-Julian Dawson number "It Came from Memphis." But the highlight of this collection is the Owens tune, "Startin' Today." Owens, Flores, and Moffatt join in on this song of independence, and nothing can compare with the emotion and conviction that Queen Bonnie poured into every word and note. A joyful assortment of musical treats, At the Cantina deserves to be heard. —Jana Pendragon

Carson Robison

b. Aug. 4, 1890, Oswego, Labette County, KS, d. Mar. 24, 1957, Pleasant Valley, NY
Guitar, Vocals / Novelty, Cowboy, Hillbilly, Country Humor
Carson Robison, known in some circles as "the granddaddy of the hillbillies," has mysteriously missed the recognition that has come the way of such contemporaries as Vernon Dalhart, not to mention successors such as Gene Autry and Merle Travis. A singer, guitarist, whistler, and actor, the sheer diversity of his talent, coupled with the relatively early beginning of his recording career, may have harmed him in terms of posterity.

Robison's father was a champion fiddler; his mother was a singer and pianist. By the time he was 14 years old, he was already playing guitar professionally. A year later he was playing in bands and singing, and by his 20s he was proficient on a range of instruments and was an accomplished whistler. It was in the latter capacity that Robison first came into the recording studio, as part of backing groups behind Vernon Dalhart and Wendell Hall. Ultimately he teamed with Dalhart, and the two recorded and toured together from 1924 until 1928. Robison also worked with the Crowe Brothers and co-wrote songs with Frank Luther Crowe ("My Blue Ridge Mountain Home," "Barnacle Bill the Sailor"). Other artists with whom Robison performed and recorded included singers Gene Austin and Frank Crumit and guitarist Roy Smeck.

In 1931 Robison formed his own group, the Pioneers, later rechristened the Buckaroos, which included John and Bill Mitchell, Frank Novak, and Pearl Pickens. The first country-and-Western group to tour England, they had a considerable recording and broadcast career abroad as well as in America before World War II. Robison had a hit in 1942 with the old standard "Turkey in the Straw" and wrote songs on behalf of the war effort, including "We're Gonna Have to Slap That Dirty Little Jap." As late as 1948, he had a chart entry with "Life Gits Tee-Jus, Don't It?" and the year before his death, he recorded the novelty rock 'n' roll number "Rockin' and Rollin' with Grandmaw."

A fine technician as well as a good judge of songs, Carson Robison was perhaps too sophisticated to be grouped with hillbilly singers, cowboy singers, or country music in general. His music had a veneer of pop sophistication that, in some ways, made it at times closer in spirit to Bing Crosby or even Eddie Cantor (check out "Everybody's Goin' but Me") than to Gene Autry, while also lacking the honest directness (as well as the extraordinary harmonies) of the Sons of the Pioneers. Under other circumstances, he might've made a name in movies, providing musical backgrounds, but media exposure beyond the radio eluded him. —Bruce Eder

Life Gets Tee-Jus, Don't It / 1958 / MGM ◆◆◆◆
Just a Melody / 1981 / Old Homestead ◆◆◆

The Kansas Jayhawk / 1987 / Cattle [Germany] ✦✦✦

A Hillbilly Mixture / 1988 / Axis ✦✦

● Home Sweet Home on the Prairie / 1996 / ASV ✦✦✦✦
Home Sweet Home on the Prairie contains 25 of Carson Robison's original RCA Victor recordings, including his versions of "I'm an Old Cowhand," "Oh, Susanna!," "When Your Hair Has Turned to Silver," "Sweet Virginia," and "Tree-Top Serenade." Though some of his classic songs are missing, the disc nevertheless remains an excellent introduction to one of the most famous hillbilly cowboys of the '20s. — *Thom Owens*

Ted Roddy

Singer-Songwriter, Roots-Rock, Alternative Country, Americana
A staple of the Austin, TX, club scene, singer-songwriter/harmonica wizard Ted Roddy paid his dues alongside the likes of Dale Watson, the Reverend Horton Heat, and the Bad Livers. Born in Corpus Christi, Roddy played his first live shows in the late 1970s, eventually moving to Dallas to form the Midnighters wth blues guitarist Mark Pollack. After the group disbanded, he turned to rockabilly, and in 1983 he started a new outfit, Ted Roddy and the Talltops, with Jim Heath (later known as Horton Heat) and Danny Barnes (who went on to join the Bad Livers). After relocating to Austin, the Talltops began to build a strong fan base, not only locally but abroad, releasing several records in Europe. After going solo, Roddy played on LPs by Watson and Chris Smither before releasing his 1995 debut *Full Circle*. — *Jason Ankeny*

Full Circle / Oct. 1995 / Hightone ✦✦✦✦

Jimmie Rodgers (James Charles Rodgers)

b. Sep. 8, 1897, Meridan, MS, **d.** May 26, 1933, New York City, NY
Banjo, Guitar, Vocals / Traditional Country
His brass plaque in the Country Music Hall of Fame reads, "Jimmie Rodgers' name stands foremost in the country music field as *the man who started it all.*" This is a fair assessment. The "Singing Brakeman" and the "Mississippi Blue Yodeler," whose six-year career was cut short by tuberculosis, became the first nationally known star of country music and the direct influence of many later performers from Hank Snow, Ernest Tubb, and Hank Williams to Lefty Frizzell and Merle Haggard. Rodgers sang about rounders and gamblers, bounders and ramblers—and he knew what he sang about. At age 14 he went to work as a railroad brakeman, and on the rails he stayed until a pulmonary hemorrhage sidetracked him to the medicine show circuit in 1925. The years with the trains harmed his health but helped his music. In an era when Rodgers' contemporaries were singing only mountain and mountain/folk music, he fused hillbilly country, gospel, jazz, blues, pop, cowboy, and folk. Many of his best songs were his compositions, including "TB Blues," "Waiting for a Train," "Travelin' Blues," "Train Whistle Blues," and his 13 blue yodels. Although Rodgers wasn't the first to yodel on records, his style was distinct from all the others. His yodel wasn't merely sugarcoating on the song, it was as important as the lyric, mournful and plaintive or happy and carefree, depending on a song's emotional content. His instrumental accompaniment consisted sometimes of his guitar only, while at other times a full jazz band (horns and all) backed him up. Country fans could have asked for no better hero/star—someone who thought what they thought, felt what they felt, and sang about the common person honestly and beautifully. In his last recording session, Rodgers was so racked and ravaged by tuberculosis that a cot had to be set up in the studio, so he could rest before attempting that one song more.

The youngest son of a railroad man, Jimmie Rodgers was born and reared in Meridian, MS. After his mother's death in 1904, he and his older brother went to live with their mother's sister, where he first became interested in music. Jimmie's aunt was a former teacher who held degrees in music and English, and she exposed him to a number of different styles of music, including vaudeville, pop, and dance hall. Though he was attracted to music, he was a mischievous boy and often got into trouble. When he returned to his father's care in 1911, Jimmie ran wild, hanging out in pool halls and dives; but he never got into any serious trouble. When he was 12, he experienced his first taste of fame when he sang

"Steamboat Bill" at a local talent contest. Rodgers won the concert and, inspired by his success, he decided to head out on the road in his own traveling tent show. His father tracked him down and brought him back home, but he ran away again, this time joining a medicine show. The romance of performing with the show wore off by the time his father hunted him down. Given the choice of school or the railroad, Jimmie chose to join his father on the tracks.

For the next ten years, Rodgers worked on the railroad, performing a variety of jobs along the south and west coasts. In May 1917 he married Sandra Kelly after knowing her for only a handful of weeks; by the fall, they had separated, even though she was pregnant (their daughter died in 1938). Two years later they officially divorced, and around the same time, he met Carrie Williamson, a preacher's daughter. Rodgers married Carrie in April 1920, while she was still in high school. Shortly after their marriage, Jimmie was laid off by the New Orleans & Northeastern Railroad, and he began performing various blue-collar jobs, looking for opportunities to sing. Over the next three years, the couple was plagued with problems ranging from financial to health—the second of their two daughters died of diphtheria six months after her birth in 1923. By that time, Rodgers had begun to play regularly in traveling shows, and he was on the road at the time of her death. Though these years were difficult, they were important in the development of his musical style, as he began to develop his distinctive blue yodel and worked on his guitar skills.

In 1924 Jimmie Rodgers was diagnosed with tuberculosis, but instead of heeding the doctor's warning about the seriousness of the disease, he discharged himself from the hospital to form a trio with fiddler Slim Rozell and Elsie McWilliams. Rodgers continued to work on the railroad and perform Blackface comedy with medicine shows while he sang. Two years after being diagnosed with TB, he moved his family to Tucson, AZ, believing the change in location would improve his health. In Tucson he continued to sing at local clubs and events. The railroad believed these extracurricular activities interfered with his work and fired him. Moving back to Meridian, Jimmie and Carrie lived with her parents, before he moved to Asheville, NC in 1927. Rodgers was going to work on the railroad, but his health was so poor he couldn't handle the labor; he would never work the rails again. Instead, he began working as a janitor and cab driver, singing on a local radio station and at events as well. Soon he moved to Johnson City, TN, where he began singing with the string band the Teneva Ramblers. The group had been a trio, but he persuaded the members to become his backing band because he had a regular show in Asheville. The Ramblers relented, and the group's name took second billing to Rodgers. They began playing various concerts in addition to the radio show. Eventually Rodgers heard that Ralph Peer, an RCA talent scout, was recording hillbilly and string bands in Bristol, TN. Rodgers convinced the band to travel to Bristol, but on the eve of the audition, they had a huge argument about the way they should be billed, resulting in the Teneva Ramblers' breaking away from Rodgers. He went to the audition as a solo artist, and Peer recorded two songs—the old standards "The Soldier's Sweetheart" and "Sleep, Baby, Sleep"—after rejecting Rodgers' signature song, "T for Texas."

Released in October 1927, the record was not a hit, but Victor did agree to record Rodgers again, this time as a solo artist. In November 1927, he cut four songs, including "T for Texas." Retitled "Blue Yodel" upon its release, the song became a huge hit and one of only a handful of early country records to sell a million copies. Shortly after its release, Jimmie and Carrie moved to Washington, where he began appearing on a weekly local radio show billed as the Singing Brakeman. Though "Blue Yodel" was a success, its sales grew steadily throughout early 1928, which meant that the couple weren't able to reap the financial benefits until the end of the year. By that time, Rodgers had recorded several more singles, including the hits "Way Out on the Mountain," "Blue Yodel No. 4," "Waiting for a Train," and "In the Jailhouse Now." On various sessions Peer experimented with Rodgers' backing band, occasionally recording him with two other string instrumentalists and recording him solo, as well. Over the next two years, Peer and Rodgers tried out a number of different backing bands, including a jazz group featuring Louis Armstrong, orchestras, and a Hawaiian combo.

By 1929 Jimmie Rodgers had become an official star, as his concerts became major attractions and his records consistently sold well. During 1929 he made a small film called *The Singing Brakeman*, recorded many songs, and toured throughout the country. Though his activity kept his star shining and the money rolling in, his health began to decline under all the stress. Nevertheless, he continued to plow forward, recording numerous songs and building a large home in Kerrville, TX, as well as working with Will Rogers on several fund-raising tours for the Red Cross that were designed to help those suffering during the Depression. By the middle of 1931 the Depression was beginning to affect Rodgers as well, as his concert bookings decreased dramatically and his records stopped selling. Despite the financial hardships, Jimmie continued to record.

Not only did the Great Depression cut into Jimmie's career, but so did his poor health. He had to decrease the number of concerts he performed in both 1931 and 1932, and by 1933, his health affected his recording and forced him to cancel plans for several films. Despite his condition, he refused to stop performing, telling his wife that "I want to die with my shoes on." By early 1933 the family was running short on money, and he had to perform anywhere he could—including vaudeville shows and nickelodeons—to make ends meet. For a while he performed on a radio show in San Antonio, but in February he collapsed and was sent to the hospital. Realizing that he was close to death, he convinced Peer to schedule a recording session in May. Rodgers used that session to provide needed financial support for his family. At that session, he was accompanied by a nurse and rested on a cot in between songs. He died of a lung hemorrhage on May 26, 1933, two days after the sessions were completed. His body was taken to Meridian by train, in a converted baggage car. Hundreds of country fans awaited the body's arrival in Meridian, and the train blew its whistle throughout the journey. For several days after the body arrived in Rodgers' hometown, it lay in state as hundreds, if not thousands, of people paid tribute to the departed musician.

The massive display of affection at Jimmie Rodgers' funeral services indicated what a popular and beloved star he was. His influence wasn't limited to the '30s, however. Throughout country music's history, echoes of Jimmie Rodgers can be heard, from Hank Williams to Merle Haggard. In 1961 Rodgers became the first artist inducted into the Country Music Hall of Fame; 25 years later, he was inducted as a founding father at the Rock and Roll Hall of Fame. Though both honors are impressive, they give only a small indication of what Rodgers accomplished—and how he affected the history of country music by making it a viable, commercially popular medium—during his lifetime. —*David Vinopal*

My Old Pal / 1989 / ASV ✦✦✦✦
This album contains rich and varied material in its 18 tracks, including three blue yodels, Rodgers' wife's tribute to her husband recorded three years after his death, and a duet with Sara Carter. —*AMG*

☆ **First Sessions** / Jan. 1991 / Rounder ✦✦✦✦✦
The opening volume in Rounder's mammoth eight-disc Jimmie Rodgers reissue series presents his earliest, and in some cases most tentatively performed, material from 1927 and 1928. Rodgers quickly makes the leap from raw, if engaging singer to emphatic, distinctive artist. Midway through he has established a singular sound and riveting delivery, with his trademark yodel and mastery of blues inflection and sensibility in place. These cuts include the signature track "Blue Yodel," plus other classics such as "In the Jailhouse Now," "Treasures Untold," and "Memphis Yodel," as well as "The Brakemen's Blues." Things would never be the same for Rodgers, and these were the songs that helped make him an institution. —*Ron Wynn*

☆ **The Early Years 1928-29** / Feb. 1991 / Rounder ✦✦✦✦✦
The second disc in the Jimmie Rodgers series covers 1928 and 1929, the years in which Rodgers solidified his stature as a premier performer. These 16 tracks saw him doing both his brilliant solo yodeling blues and working with bands on some cuts. "Desert Blues" featured Rodgers backed by a group with cornet,

clarinet, tuba, and piano among the instrumentation. Steel guitarist John Westbrook provided tingling accompaniment on "I'm Lonely and Blue," "My Carolina Sunshine Girl," and "Blue Yodel No. 4." But once more, it's such cuts as "Daddy and Home," "You and My Old Guitar," and "Never No Mo' Blues" that are the triumphs, with Rodgers simply wailing, singing, and yodeling, displaying the emotional clout and memorable style that turned these numbers into anthems. —*Ron Wynn*

☆ **On the Way Up 1929** / Mar. 1991 / Rounder ✦✦✦✦
This third Jimmie Rodgers disc in the eight-CD line covers arguably his greatest year, 1929. Rodgers scored huge hits doing popular novelty cuts like "Frankie and Johnny" and railroad numbers like "Train Whistle Blues" and continued cutting yodeling tunes, as well as cowboy songs and bawdy blues. The 17 cuts include the marvelous "Everybody Does It in Hawaii," with Weldon Burkes on ukulele and Joe Kapo on steel, and the memorable "Hobo Bill's Last Rides." The session also contains alternate takes of "The Land of My Boyhood Dreams" and "Frankie and Johnny." Rodgers was now ably mixing identities and personas, alternating between yodeling blues singer, railroad narrator, and carefree cowboy. —*Ron Wynn*

★ **Riding High 1929-1930** / Apr. 1991 / Rounder ✦✦✦✦✦
Jimmie Rodgers was enjoying the fruits of his labors in 1929 and 1930, the years covered on this fourth CD in Rounder's historic eight-disc retrospective series. The 17 numbers highlighted here were done either during his final 1929 session or in Hollywood the next year. They're primarily yodeling blues tunes, with Rodgers backed by guitarist Billy Burkes. There are two versions of "Anniversary Blue Yodel (Blue Yodel No. 7)," "Mississippi River Blues," and "Why Did You Give Me Your Love?," as well as stark, marvelous numbers like "She Was Happy Till She Met You," "A Drunkard's Child," and "Why Should I Be Lonely." This set includes Rodgers' working with Lani McIntire's Hawaiians on two tunes and with Bob Sawyer's Jazz Band on the finale, "My Blue-Eyed Jane." —*Ron Wynn*

☆ **America's Blue Yodeler 1930-31** / May 1991 / Rounder ✦✦✦✦
This fifth set of vintage Jimmie Rodgers performances included some spectacular collaborations. While neither sounded fully comfortable, the meeting of Rodgers and Louis Armstrong on "Blue Yodel No. 9" is a landmark in music annals, two immortals finding a way to make seemingly disparate styles mesh on a short tune. Armstrong's wife at the time, Lil Hardin, accompanied the pair on piano. Rodgers also teamed frequently with Lani McIntire's Hawaiians on this set, often on throwaway tunes that Rodgers' vocals made enjoyable. There's another collaboration with a blues artist, this time Clifford Gibson on "Let Me Be Your Side Track," a great bawdy/innuendo number. Rodgers was paired with the Carter Family on two wonderful classic country numbers, the heartbreak tune "Why There's a Tear in My Eye" and the gospel song "The Wonderful City." —*Ron Wynn*

☆ **Down the Old Road 1931-32** / Jun. 1991 / Rounder ✦✦✦✦
This CD features Jimmie Rodgers working in fresh formats as producer Ralph Peer attempted to break a sales slump. Rodgers recorded with the Louisville Jug Band on "My Good Gal's Gone Blues" and teamed with the Carter Family again in both Kentucky and Texas in 1931. They made four songs together, but three were unissued until after Rodgers' death. They're pleasant and often nicely sung, but not among either artist's finest. Rodgers teamed with steel guitarist Cliff Carlisle and guitarist Wilber Ball on three songs, with Rodgers adding ukulele backing. The final four cuts saw Rodgers return to his trademark railroad numbers and yodeling blues in 1932. For the most part these weren't great tunes, as they show Rodgers experimenting and finally opting to do comfortable, familiar material rather than try new things. —*Ron Wynn*

☆ **No Hard Times, 1932** / Jul. 1991 / Rounder ✦✦✦✦✦
Although he was nearing the end, Jimmie Rodgers kept going in 1932, turning out several sterling numbers. Among them were the dynamic "Blue Yodel No. 10" and riveting "No Hard Times" and "Long Tall Mama Blues," with Oddie McWinders on banjo. Rodgers also displayed his affection for his mother on "Mother, the Queen of My Heart" and the interesting confessional number

"I've Only Loved Three Women." Rodgers teamed effectively with guitarist Slim Bryant on "Prairie Lullaby," "Miss the Mississippi and You" and "In the Hills of Tennessee," and once more sang frankly and movingly about his illness on "Whippin' That Old T.B.," although it wasn't as triumphant as "The T.B. Blues." —Ron Wynn

☆ Last Sessions, 1933 / Aug. 1991 / Rounder ✦✦✦✦✦
Illness ravaged Jimmie Rodgers during his final days, as he attempted to record as much as possible. There's an eerie quality to such tunes as "The Yodeling Ranger," "Years Ago," and "Somewhere Down The Line," as it's evident that Rodgers was far from top vocal form. But despite the shortness of breath, lack of range, and weak quality, he could still deliver emotionally gripping performances. The earlier cuts on the disc, "Blue Yodel No. 13," "Dreaming With Tears In My Eyes," and "I'm Free (From the Chain Gang Now)" have a hypnotic finality and edge, even when his vocals falter. Rodgers died 48 hours after he finished his final song, not turning in a particularly great performance, as might be expected. But his accomplishments had long ago established him as one of the most memorable performers in American music annals. —Ron Wynn

American Legends #16 / Apr. 1996 / LaserLight ✦✦✦
With Jimmie Rodgers' Victor Records catalog now issued on eight Rounder Records CDs in the US and on a six-CD box set from Bear Family in Germany, there has been a need for a good single-disc compilation. (Hint: RCA could do worse than reissuing its 12-track 1965 The Best of the Legendary Jimmie Rodgers at a discount price or its 18-track 1973 This Is Jimmie Rodgers at full price.) This low-priced sampler, containing 12 tracks licensed from RCA by Stanyan Records and in turn licensed to LaserLight, is not the compilation we've been waiting for. At 35 minutes, it's short for an LP, never mind a CD. And the selections, while enjoyable, are not Rodgers' best; in fact, they just appear to be 12 random songs. But the digital transfer and remastering have resulted in good sound, and for a complete neophyte who just wants to hear what Rodgers sounded like, this makes an inexpensive introduction. (Don't expect to learn anything about Rodgers beyond the music, though, as there is no annotation to speak of.) —William Ruhlmann

The Singing Brakeman / Bear Family ✦✦✦✦
The Singing Brakeman is a six-disc set that compiles every song Jimmie Rodgers ever recorded. It covers the same ground as Rounder's eight-disc set, but Bear Family's set condenses the material into six CDs and adds a large booklet that features a thorough discography and biography. Although it essentially has the same material, adding a few alternate takes that weren't on the Rounder series, The Singing Brakeman has a more scholarly approach. The discs are designed for intense, concentrated listening, not casual listening. In the end, however, it's neither superior or inferior to Rounder's series. No matter how they are presented, Rodgers' recordings constitute essential listening. —Stephen Thomas Erlewine

Johnny Rodriguez

b. Dec. 10, 1952, Sabinal, TX
Guitar, Vocals / Traditional Country, Progressive Country, Country-Pop, Tex-Mex, Outlaw Country
Johnny Rodriguez was a singing stagecoach driver at the Alamo Village when Bobby Bare and Tom T. Hall heard him, brought him to Nashville, and made him one of Hall's Storytellers. He was born in Sabinal, TX, 90 miles north of the Mexican border. His country music-loving older brother Andres bought the seven-year-old Rodriguez his first guitar; as a teen, he was an altar boy and a letterman and captain of the football team. His father died of cancer when Johnny was 16, and Rodriguez began getting into trouble. By the time he was 18, he had been jailed four times. While he was in prison, a Texas Ranger named Joaquin Jackson heard the young man sing. Impressed, Jackson directed the attention of promoter Happy Shahan to the vocalist, and Shahan booked shows for the 19-year-old Rodriguez at the Alamo Village Amusement Park in Bracketville upon his release. During the summers of 1970 and 1971, he worked as a stagecoach driver.

Soon after Rodriguez joined the Storytellers, Hall helped him sign a solo contract with Mercury Records. His first single, "Pass Me By (if You're Only Passing Through)," reached the Top Ten in early 1973, beginning a string of 15 consecutive Top Ten hits that ran into 1977. When he signed with Epic in 1979, his career was entering a period of decline; but Rodriguez continued to have Top 40 hits into the mid-'80s, highlighted by the 1983 Top Ten singles "Foolin'" and "How Could I Love Her So Much." In 1987 the single "I Didn't (Every Chance I Had)," reached No. 12, but none of his subsequent singles made the Top 40. In 1993 he released Run for the Border. You Can Say That Again appeared in 1996. —Sandra Brennan & David Vinopal

Introducing / 1973 / Mercury ✦✦✦✦
Stunning mid-'70s debut. —Ron Wynn

● Greatest Hits / 1976 / Polygram ✦✦✦✦
Greatest Hits contains 14 of Johnny Rodriguez' biggest hits from the early '70s, including the No. 1 hits "You Always Come Back (to Hurting Me)," "Ridin' My Thumb to Mexico," "That's the Way Love Goes," "I Just Can't Get Her Out of My Mind," "Just Get Up and Close the Door," and "Love Put a Song in My Heart." —Stephen Thomas Erlewine

Rodriguez / 1979 / Epic ✦✦✦✦
Through My Eyes / 1980 / Epic ✦✦✦
Biggest Hits / 1982 / Epic ✦✦✦✦
Foolin' with Fire / 1984 / Epic ✦✦✦
Full Circle / 1986 / Epic ✦✦✦
Gracias / 1988 / Capitol ✦✦✦
Run for the Border / 1993 / Intersound ✦✦✦
Super Hits / Sep. 5, 1995 / Epic ✦✦✦
You Can Say That Again / Jul. 1996 / Hightone ✦✦✦✦
Quite possibly the strongest release Johnny Rodriguez has offered since his heyday of the late '70s and early '80s, You Can Say That Again captures his honky tonk roots perfectly. Rodriguez alternates between honky tonk standards and new tunes written in the tradition. Not all of the new songs are fit to stand in comparison to the classics, but Rodriguez' sweaty energy and gritty, soulful vigor make You Can Say That Again a joy. —Thom Owens

Kenny Rogers (Kenneth Donald Rogers)

b. Aug. 21, 1938, Houston, TX
Bass, Guitar, Vocals / Country-Pop, Adult Contemporary, Soft Rock, Urban Cowboy
It took several tries before Kenny Rogers became a star. As a member of the First Edition (and the New Christy Minstrels before that), he shared in some million-sellers, among them "Reuben James" and "Ruby, Don't Take Your Love to Town," an excellent Mel Tillis song about a disabled veteran. But superstardom lay ahead for this Texan, and it arrived in the late '70s. His experience with the two previous pop groups had prepared him well. He knew the easy-listening audience was out there, and he supplied them with middle-of-the-road songs with a country flavor. Having gone solo, in 1976 Rogers charted with "Love Lifted Me." But it was with an outstanding song by writer Don Schlitz, "Lucille," that his star shot upward. The rest is history: award-winning duets with Dottie West and Dolly Parton, 12 TV specials, another song-of-the-year with "The Gambler," "Daytime Friends," "Coward of the County," "We've Got Tonight," "Crazy," "Lady" (his first pop No. 1), etc. And that's just the musical side of Kenny Rogers. In 1980 the made-for-TV movie The Gambler blasted the competition, followed quickly by Coward of the County and enough sequels to The Gambler to get him to Roman numeral IV. Throughout the '80s, Rogers remained a celebrity, even when his sales were declining. Even in the '90s, when he rarely charted, his name, face, and music were recognizable in a series of concerts, television specials, films, and even fast food restaurants.

Like many country superstars, Kenny Rogers came from humble roots. Born in Houston, TX, Rogers and his seven siblings were reared in one of the poorest sections of town. Nevertheless, Kenny progressed through high school, all the while learning how to play guitar and fiddle. When he was a senior, he played in a rockabilly band called the Scholars, who released three singles, including "Kangewah," which was written by Louella Parsons. After his graduation, he released two singles, "We'll Always Fall in Love Again" and "For You Alone," on the local independent label Carlton. The B-side of the first single, "That Crazy Feeling," was popular enough to earn him a slot on "American Bandstand." In 1959 he briefly attended the University of Texas, but he soon dropped out to play bass in the jazz combo the Bobby Doyle Three. While he was with the group, Rogers continued to explore other musical venues, and he played bass on Mickey Gilley's 1960 single, "Is It Wrong." The Bobby Doyle Three released one album, *In a Most Unusual Way,* before Rogers left to play with the Kirby Stone Four. He didn't stay long with Stone, and he soon landed a solo record contract with Mercury.

Rogers released a handful of singles on Mercury, all of which failed. When Mercury dropped the singer, he joined the New Christy Minstrels in 1966. He stayed with the folk group for year, leaving with several other band members—Mike Settle, Terry Williams, and Thelma Lou Camacho—in 1967 to form the First Edition. Adding drummer Terry Jones, the First Edition signed with Reprise and recorded the pop-psychedelic single "Just Dropped In (to See What Condition My Condition Was In)." The single became a hit early in 1968, climbing to No. five. Within a year the group was billed as Kenny Rogers and the First Edition, and in the summer of 1969 they had their second and final Top Ten hit, "Ruby, Don't Take Your Love to Town." The country overtones of the single hinted at the direction Rogers was taking, as did the minor hit follow-up, "Reuben James." For the next two years the First Edition bounced between country, pop, and mild psychedelia, scoring their last big hit with Mac Davis' "Something's Burning" in early 1970. By the end of 1972, the group had their own syndicated television show, but their sales were drying up. They left Reprise the next year, signing to Rogers' new label, Jolly Rogers. None of their singles became major hits, though a version of Merle Haggard's "Today I Started Loving You Again" reached the lower regions of the country charts late in 1973. Rogers left the group in 1974, and the band broke up the next year.

At the time the band broke up, Kenny Rogers was severely in debt, and Jolly Rogers was out of business. In order to jump-start his career, he signed to United Artists in 1975, and with the help of producer Larry Butler, he devised an accessible, radio-ready and immaculately crafted take on country-pop that leaned toward adult contemporary pop. "Love Lifted Me," his debut single for the label, was a minor hit early in 1976, but it took a full year for Rogers to have a genuine breakthrough hit with "Lucille." Climbing to No. 1 early in 1977, "Lucille" was not only a major country hit, earning the Country Music Association's single of the year award, but it was a huge crossover success, peaking at No. 5 on the pop charts. For the next six years Rogers had a steady string of Top Ten hits on both the country and pop charts. His crossover success is important—his lush, easy-listening productions and smooth croons showed that country stars could conquer the pop audience, if produced and marketed correctly. During the late '70s and early '80s, much of country radio was dominated by either urban cowboy or country-pop in the vein of Rogers' own singles. Between 1978 and 1980, he had five straight No. 1 country singles—"Love or Something like It," "The Gambler," "She Believes in Me," "You Decorated My Life," "Coward of the County"—most of which also reached the pop Top Ten. In addition to his solo hits, he had a series of Top Ten duets with Dottie West, including the No. 1 hits "Every Time Two Fools Collide" (1978), "All I Ever Need Is You" (1979) and "What Are We Doin' in Love" (1981). Not only did his singles sell well, but so did his albums, with every record he released between 1976's *Kenny Rogers* and 1984's *Once upon a Christmas* going gold or platinum.

By the beginning of the '80s, Rogers' audience was as much pop as it was country, and singles like his cover of Lionel Richie's "Lady" confirmed that fact, spending six weeks at the top of the pop charts. Rogers also began singing duets with pop singers like Kim Carnes ("Don't Fall in Love with a Dreamer," No. 3 country, No. 4 pop, 1980) and Sheena Easton ("We've Got Tonight," No. 1 country, No. 6 pop, 1983). Rogers also began making inroads into television and film, appearing in a number of TV specials and

Kenny Rogers

made-for-TV movies, including 1982's *Six Pack* and two movies based on his songs "The Gambler" and "Coward of the County." Late in 1983 he left United Artists/Liberty for RCA Records, releasing a duet with Dolly Parton called "Islands in the Stream" as his first single for the label. Written by the Bee Gees and produced by Barry Gibb, the record became one of his biggest hits, spending two weeks on the top of both the country and pop charts. Rogers stayed at RCA for five years, during which time he alternated between MOR, adult contemporary pop, and slick country-pop. The hits didn't come as often as they used to, and they were frequently competing with releases from Liberty's vaults, but he managed to log five No. 1 singles for the label, in addition to "Islands in the Stream": "Crazy" (1984), "Real Love" (1985), "Morning Desire" (1985), "Tomb of the Unknown Love" (1986), and the Ronnie Milsap duet "Make No Mistake, She's Mine" (1987). Despite his country successes, he no longer had pop crossover hits. Nevertheless, Rogers' concerts continued to be popular, as did his made-for-television movies. Still, the lack of blockbuster records meant that RCA failed to renew his contract when it expired in 1988. Rogers returned to his first label, Reprise, where he had one major hit—1989's Top Ten "The Vows Go Unbroken (Always True to You)," taken from the gold album *Something Inside So Strong*—before his singles started charting in the lower half of the Top 40.

Throughout the late '80s and '90s, Rogers kept busy with charity work, concerts, his fast-food chain Kenny Rogers' Roasters, television specials, movies, and photography, publishing two books, *Kenny Rogers' America* and *Kenny Rogers: Your Friends and Mine,* of his photos. Rogers continued to record, releasing albums nearly every year, but they failed to break beyond his large, devoted fanbase and made only a slight impact on the charts. —*David Vinopal and Stephen Thomas Erlewine*

The First Edition / 1967 / Reprise ✦✦✦

The Second Edition / 1969 / Reprise ✦✦

Ruby Don't Take Your Love to Town / 1969 / Reprise ✦✦✦

Something's Burning / 1970 / Reprise ✦✦

There's not much to recommend this record. The title track was a hit but is on the *Greatest Hits* LP. The rest of the tracks aren't really that interesting. By the way, "Elvira" is the same song the Oak Ridge Boys had a hit with 11 years later. —*Jim Worbois*

Kenny Rogers and the First Edition Greatest Hits / 1971 / Reprise ✦✦✦✦

Ballad of Calico / 1972 / Reprise ✦✦✦
Years before Michael Murphey began singing songs about cowboys as a recording artist, he wrote the material on this album as a tribute to a ghost town in the Mojave Desert called New Vegas. Though not all of the songs work, the concept and packaging (including the enclosed booklet with notes and lyrics) make this one worth having. —*Jim Worbois*

Kenny Rogers / 1976 / Liberty ✦✦✦✦
Kenny Rogers got a new lease on his career with this record, as its first single, "Lucille," topped both the country and pop charts. In addition to "Lucille," the album includes such other fine tunes as the hit single "Lay Down Beside Me" and "The Son of Hickory Holler's Tramp." —*James Chrispell*

Daytime Friends / 1977 / EMI America ✦✦✦

Every Time Two Fools Collide / 1978 / United Artists ✦✦✦
Country-pop with Dottie West. —*Bil Carpenter*

The Gambler / 1978 / EMI America ✦✦✦✦
Kenny Rogers took a bit of a chance in releasing this loosely based concept album at the time, but boy, did it pay off! Sales for the album went through the roof, as the title track and "She Believes in Me" became pop crossover hits, with the latter reaching the pop Top Ten. Later, "The Gambler" was turned into a string of made-for-television movies. —*James Chrispell*

Kenny / 1979 / United Artists ✦✦✦✦
Kenny took a more romantic approach with *Kenny*. Though it contained the hit character sketch "Coward of the County," the album was comprised mainly of love songs like "You Decorated My Life" and "She's a Mystery." With such strong singles, the album actually became a bigger hit than its predecessor, *The Gambler*. —*James Chrispell*

Ten Years of Gold / 1979 / EMI America ✦✦✦✦
Ten Years of Gold is a fine starting point for anyone looking for an overview of Kenny Rogers' early career, spanning his early hits with the First Edition like "Just Dropped In (to See What Condition My Condition Was In)" to later solo hits like "Lucille" and "Love Lifted Me." —*James Chrispell*

Classics / 1979 / United Artists ✦✦✦✦
Kenny and Dottie team up to perform such great tunes as "Just the Way You Are," "You Needed Me," Buck Owens' "Together Again," the Righteous Brothers' "You've Lost That Lovin' Feelin,'" as well as the chart topping "All I Ever Need Is You." Produced by Larry Butler, the album boasts the highly professional sound that came out of Nashville in the late '70s, but there is some fine listening here. —*James Chrispell*

● **Greatest Hits** / 1980 / EMI America ✦✦✦✦
This shows off both Rogers the storyteller ("Lucille," "The Gambler," "Coward of the County") and Rogers the hero of easy listeners ("She Believes in Me," "Lady"). —*Dan Cooper*

Share Your Love / 1981 / Liberty ✦✦✦
Share Your Love began a downturn in Kenny Rogers' popularity. Comprised almost entirely of Lionel Richie songs, the album was pleasant, but its adult contemporary pop direction was quite a departure at the time and was not greeted well by Rogers' country fans. A miss after a long string of hits. —*James Chrispell*

Love Will Turn You Around / Sep. 1, 1982 / EMI America ✦✦✦

Eyes That See in the Dark / 1983 / RCA ✦✦✦
Contemporary pop, with Bee Gees production. —*Bil Carpenter*

Duets / 1984 / Capitol ✦✦✦
Includes duets with Kim Carnes, Sheena Easton, and others. —*Bil Carpenter*

25 Greatest Hits / 1987 / EMI America ✦✦✦✦
This two-CD set includes much the same material as *Greatest Hits*, but also has "Daytime Friends," "Love or Something like It," and "Love Will Turn You Around." —*Dan Cooper*

All-Time Greatest Hits / 1996 / CEMA ✦✦✦✦
A budget-line, triple-disc set containing 36 tracks, *All-Time Greatest Hits* isn't necessarily a definitive Kenny Rogers collection. It doesn't contain the First Edition's "Just Dropped In (to See What Condition My Condition Was In)" or "Islands in the Stream"; it

isn't presented in chronological order; it doesn't have any liner notes; and it all could have fit on two discs. But it does contain the bulk of his biggest hits, including "Lucille," "She Believes in Me," "You Decorated My Life," "Ruby, Don't Take Your Love to Town," "Lady," "Don't Fall in Love with A Dreamer," "Every Time Two Fools Collide," "Coward of the County," "We've Got Tonight," and "The Gambler." As a result, it is an excellent bargain, even if there are more thoughtfully assembled packages on the market. —*Stephen Thomas Erlewine*

● **Greatest Hits** / Sep. 24, 1996 / HIPP ✦✦✦✦
Kenny Rogers and the First Edition's *Greatest Hits* contains all of the group's greatest hits, including "Ruby, Don't Take Your Love to Town" and "Just Dropped In (to See What Condition My Condition Is In)," plus a number of lesser-known singles. Though the group didn't have enough strong material to make the compilation consistently entertaining, this single-disc collection is nevertheless the definitive retrospective of Rogers' early years. —*Stephen Thomas Erlewine*

Roy Rogers (Leonard Slye)

b. Nov. 5, 1911, Cincinnati, OH
Guitar, Vocals / Traditional Country, Cowboy, Country Gospel
When Cincinnati-born Leonard Franklin Slye headed west in the spring of 1931, he was a would-be musician, working jobs ranging from driving a gravel truck to picking fruit in California's Central Valley. In less than two years, he'd co-founded the greatest Western singing group of all time, the Sons of the Pioneers, and barely four years after that, he'd started a career as a movie star under the new name Roy Rogers. Ultimately he found great fame as a movie and TV cowboy, and even founded a very successful chain of restaurants.

He was born in Cincinnati, OH, the son of Andrew and Mattie Womack Slye. The entire household was musical, and by the time he was a teenager Len could play the guitar and the mandolin. Although he later took on the role of a cowboy before the public, the closest he got to riding the range was working the family farm in a small town outside of Cincinnati. By age 19, he'd headed to California, where chance led him to enter an amateur singing contest on the radio, resulting in an offer to join the Rocky Mountaineers. There he made the acquaintance of Bob Nolan. They developed a harmonious friendship that worked well within the group for several months, until Nolan exited in frustration over their lack of success. His replacement was Tim Spencer, and eventually Slye, Spencer, and a singer named Slumber Nichols quit the Rocky Mountaineers in the spring of 1932 to form a trio of their own, which never quite came off. Slye decided to push on, joining Jack LeFevre and His Texas Outlaws.

In early 1933 he got Spencer and Nolan together to form what was then known as the Pioneer Trio. Their mix of singing and yodeling, coupled with their good spirits, won them a job on radio. Within a few weeks, they were developing a large following on Lefevre's show, with their harmony singing eliciting lots of mail. A fourth member, fiddle player Hugh Farr, was added to firm up their sound early in 1934. The group's name was altered by accident—on one broadcast the station's announcer introduced them as "The Sons of the Pioneers." The group sold large numbers of records from the very beginning, with the classic Nolan original "Tumbling Tumbleweeds" cut at their very first session. Two more new members, Lloyd Perryman and Hugh Farr's guitarist brother Karl, were added; and by the mid-1930s the sextet was one of the top-selling country acts, performing to sell-out audiences and sought by radio stations and sponsors eager to back them on the air.

During this period, Slye did occasional work as a movie extra and bit player in B-westerns under the name Dick Weston at Republic Pictures, where the reigning king of Western movies was another singer, Gene Autry, whose records outsold even the Pioneers'. In 1938 Autry entered a contractual dispute with Republic that resulted in his failure to report for his next movie. Republic, anticipating the dispute, had put out the word—apparently more as a ploy than a real attempt to replace their top male star—that they were looking for a new leading actor for their

Westerns. Slye tried sneaking onto the lot with a group of extras and was caught, but a sympathetic director permitted him to take a screen test. He tested extremely well and got the part. At the time, the Pioneers had just signed a contract with Columbia Pictures to appear in and play musical support to Charles Starrett in a series of B-Westerns, and he was forced to leave the group to sign his own contract at Republic.

A new name was required, and "Roy Rogers" was selected, the Rogers coming from Will Rogers and Roy coming off a list. He made his debut in *Under Western Stars;* not only did it introduce Roy Rogers as a new star, but also his horse, Trigger. A long-term contract followed, and for the next 13 years, he was one of the studio's mainstays, rivaling and later surpassing Autry at the box office. By 1940 Roy Rogers was successful enough to approach Republic with a request for a salary increase. The studio was notoriously reticent on such matters, and he was denied any raise. But in lieu of the request, he extracted a much more valuable concession—the rights to the name Roy Rogers and all merchandising that went with it. The early 1940s saw Rogers turn into a national institution. His Westerns became even more popular and accessible once they were taken out of the "historic" West of the 19th century, and moved into the modern West, which allowed for more freedom in plotting and dialogue. With director Joseph Kane helming his movies, Rogers became the undisputed "King of the Cowboys" after Gene Autry joined the US Army Air Force in 1942. By 1944, however, the movies and records represented only a small part of the success that Rogers had achieved. The merchandising of Roy Rogers memorabilia and other items—not just toys, but cereals, and electric ranges—coupled with a syndicated radio show, made him one of the most familiar figures in popular culture throughout the war years.

In 1944, with his first teaming with featured actress Dale Evans, the next major element in his screen success was in place. Their relationship was, at first, purely professional, but their chemistry on screen was undeniable, and Republic was soon pairing them up regularly. With the return of master action director William Witney from service in the war in 1945, Rogers' film career was poised for success for years to come, as Witney toughened up the Rogers movies and elevated their action sequences. All of this success, and the whirlwind of activity surrounding it, was negated by the death of Rogers' wife Arline from an embolism after the birth of their son Roy Jr. on November 3, 1946. Rogers continued making movies and recording, along with his personal appearances and radio broadcasts. In the course of their work together in pictures, he and Dale Evans (who had already been designated "The Queen of the West" by Republic's publicity office) became ever closer. Finally, on December 31, 1947, the two were married. They made movies together for the remainder of the 1940s, and when the market for B-Westerns began to disappear with the advent of television, Rogers followed the lead of Western star William ("Hopalong Cassidy") Boyd and devised a television series of his own. "The Roy Rogers Show," starring Rogers and Evans and co-starring Roy's Pioneers replacement Pat Brady, went on the air on NBC in December 1951, beginning a seven-year network run that introduced his work to yet another generation of fans.

His first solo recordings featured backup by Hugh and Karl Farr and Bob Nolan, and the complete Pioneers supported him in most of his recording sessions for the remainder of 1937 and 1938. Later on, however, Rogers was backed by Spade Cooley and his Buckle-Busters as well as various anonymous studio orchestras, although Karl Farr would turn up on his sessions into the 1940's. On record as a solo artist, Rogers was never as successful as the Pioneers or Gene Autry, although he did have one promising early hit in 1938 with "Hi-Yo Silver," which reached No. 13 on the charts. Even Rogers' sessions on his own recordings with the Sons of the Pioneers, however, little resembled his earlier work as a member of the Pioneers, for his was now the lead voice. And where Bob Nolan and Tim Spencer (the principal songwriters within the group) never strayed too far from some contact with the reality of the West, Rogers' music quickly took on the aura of more typical Hollywood Western songs, pleasant but not gener-

ally profound. His covers of songs such as "Don't Fence Me In" are probably the best remembered versions, thanks to his movies, and as songs like "San Fernando Valley" or "Home in Oklahoma" reveal, he had an extremely appealing tenor voice, not as memorable as Gene Autry's, but very pleasing to the ear, nonetheless. Perhaps the most well known of all Rogers' songs was one written by Evans and (originally) recorded by them together, "Happy Trails," which became the theme of the "Roy Rogers Show." From the 1950s onward, his repertory included country music as well as Western songs and spirituals, the latter often recorded with Evans.

Rogers continued to record into the 1970s, and he scored a hit in 1972 with "Candy Kisses." Roy and Dale continued making personal appearances, often in the context of religious broadcasts and gatherings, as well as television broadcasts, into the early 1990's. Rogers' main influence was in keeping the image of the singing cowboy alive. Along with Autry, who retired from personal appearances at the end of the 1950s, he was one of the most popular Western stars ever to record, and he was an influence on an entire generation of country and Western singers that followed. In 1988 Roy Rogers was elected to the Country Music Hall of Fame, giving him a second spot (the first having come as a member of the Sons of the Pioneers, who had been elected some years earlier). Two years later, the next generation of country musicians, including Emmylou Harris and Randy Travis, participated in a most unusual record, *The Roy Rogers Tribute,* covering Rogers' best known songs with him, including an all-star rendition of "Happy Trails." Two years later, Rogers, his wife, and eldest son recorded a new album of spiritual songs. *—Bruce Eder*

The Bible Tells Me So / 1962 / Capitol ✦✦✦
This album features "Amazing Grace," "How Great Thou Art," "It Is No Secret," "Peace in the Valley," "Take My Hand," and other gospel standards. *—AMG*

16 Great Songs of the Old West / 1963 / Golden ✦✦✦✦

Roll on Texas Moon / 1986 / Bear Family ✦✦✦✦
This picture disc features 16 cuts recorded from 1945 to 1952. *—AMG*

The Best of Roy Rogers / 1990 / Curb ✦✦✦✦
The singing cowboy croons 12 of his hits here, including "Money Can't Buy Love" and more. *—Mark A. Humphrey*

Tribute / 1991 / RCA ✦✦✦
At 79, Rogers' voice wasn't as sure as it was in his heyday. But Richard Landis gave him sympathetic production, and none of his guests sound like paid hands or hired guns. Everyone involved—from Rogers' son Dusty to The Kentucky HeadHunters—sounds more committed to making a good record than to adding star power. The material has been chosen accordingly, a good blend of old and new. The tribute's best when young singers repay an obvious debt (the duets with Ricky Van Shelton, Clint Black and Randy Travis), but even when K.T. Oslin and Restless Heart join in The Sons of the Pioneers' theme, "Tumbling Tumbleweeds," they bring new life to an old workhorse. And Rogers' yodel is still in great shape. *—Brian Mansfield*

● Country Music Hall of Fame Series / 1992 / MCA ✦✦✦✦
When Gene Autry got into a contract dispute with Republic Pictures in 1937, the studio replaced him with Sons of the Pioneers member Len Slye, whose name they changed to Roy Rogers. These Decca tracks, which range from 1934 to 1942, cover Rogers' output just before he became "King of the Cowboys" with the release of *Ridin' Down the Canyon.* Two of these cuts were recorded with The Sons of the Pioneers; the rest are solo. *—Brian Mansfield*

Peace in the Valley / 1996 / Pair ✦✦✦✦
Peace in the Valley is a good collection of Roy Rogers and Dale Evans' most popular gospel recordings, including versions of "There'll Be Peace in the Valley," "Cowboy Heaven," "Love Lifted Me," and "Sweet Hour of Prayer." Most of this material dates from the duo's heyday, and it makes a fine complement to any of their hits collections. *—Thom Owens*

Columbia Historic Edition / Columbia ✦✦✦✦

Tammy Rogers

Progressive Bluegrass, Progressive Country, Contemporary Country

Fiddler Tammy Rogers was born in Tennessee in 1966 and reared in Irving, TX. As an adolescent, she was taught classical music but also performed regularly with her family at bluegrass festivals. After graduating from college, she joined Patty Loveless' backing band, which she followed with a stint backing Trisha Yearwood. After leaving Yearwood, Rogers became a prominent session musician, supporting Kieran Kane on both his final record for Atlantic Records and on his subsequent tour. When Kane was dropped by Atlantic, he formed his own label, Dead Reckoning, and Rogers soon became one of the company's first signings. Her 1995 debut, *In the Red*, was a collaborative instrumental effort with noted session drummer Don Heffington; her next effort, an eponymously titled 1996 effort, featured both her songwriting and vocal skills. — *Jason Ankeny*

● **In the Red** / 1995 / Dead Reckoning ✦✦✦✦

Tammy Rogers / Jun. 1996 / Dead Reckoning ✦✦✦

Linda Ronstadt

b. Jul. 15, 1946, Tucson, AZ

Vocals / Country-Rock, Adult Contemporary, Soft Rock, Folk-Rock, Pop-Rock

With roots in the Los Angeles country and folk-rock scenes, Linda Ronstadt became one of the most popular interpretive singers of the '70s, earning a string of platinum-selling albums and Top 40 singles. Throughout the '70s, her laidback pop never lost sight of her folky roots. As she moved into the '80s, she began to change her sound with the times, adding new wave influences. After a brief flirtation with pre-rock pop, Ronstadt settled into a pattern of adult contemporary pop and Latin albums, sustaining her popularity in both fields.

While Ronstadt was a student at Arizona State University, she met guitarist Bob Kimmel. The duo moved to Los Angeles, where guitarist/songwriter Kenny Edwards joined them. Calling themselves the Stone Poneys, the group became a leading attraction on California's folk circuit, recording their first album in 1967. The band's second album, *Evergreen, Vol. 2*, featured the Top 20 hit "Different Drum," written by Michael Nesmith. After recording one more album with the group, Ronstadt left for a solo career at the end of 1968.

Ronstadt's first two solo albums—*Hand Sown, Home Grown* (1969) and *Silk Purse* (1970)—accentuated her country roots, featuring several honky tonk numbers. Released in 1971, her self-titled third album was pivotal in her career. Featuring a group of session musicians that would later form the Eagles, the album was a softer, more laidback variation of the country-rock she had been recording. With the inclusion of songs from singer-songwriters like Jackson Browne, Neil Young, and Eric Anderson, *Linda Ronstadt* had folk-rock connections as well. *Don't Cry Now*, released in 1973, followed the same formula to greater success, but it was 1974's *Heart like a Wheel* that perfected the sound, making Ronstadt a star. Featuring the hit covers "You're No Good," "When Will I Be Loved," and "It Doesn't Matter Anymore," *Heart like a Wheel* reached No. 1 and sold more than two million copies.

Released in the fall of 1975, *Prisoner in Disguise* followed the same pattern as *Heart like a Wheel* and was nearly as successful. *Hasten Down the Wind*, released in 1976, suggested a holding pattern, even if it charted higher than *Prisoner in Disguise*. *Simple Dreams* (1977) expanded the formula by adding a more rock-oriented supporting band, which breathed life into the Rolling Stones' "Tumbling Dice" and Warren Zevon's "Poor Poor Pitiful Me." The record became the singer's biggest hit, staying on the top of the charts for five weeks and selling more than three million copies. With *Living in the USA* (1978) Ronstadt began experimenting with new wave, recording Elvis Costello's "Alison"; the album was another No. 1 hit. On 1980's *Mad Love*, she made a full-fledged new wave record, recording three Costello songs and adopting a synth-laden sound. While the album was a commercial success, it signalled that her patented formula was beginning to run out of steam. That suspicion was confirmed with 1982's *Get Closer*, her first album since *Heart like a Wheel* to fail to go platinum.

Sensing it was time to change direction, Ronstadt starred in the Broadway production of Gilbert and Sullivan's *Pirates of Penzance*, as well as the accompanying movie. *Pirates of Penzance* led the singer to a collaboration with Nelson Riddle, who arranged and conducted her 1983 collection of pop standards, *What's New*. While it received lukewarm reviews, it was a considerable hit, reaching No 3 on the charts and selling more than two million copies. Ronstadt's next two albums—*Lush Life* (1984) and *For Sentimental Reasons* (1986)—were also albums of pre-rock standards recorded with Riddle.

At the end of 1986 Ronstadt returned to contemporary pop, recording "Somewhere Out There," the theme to the animated *An American Tail*, with James Ingram; the single became a No. 2 hit. She also returned to her country roots in 1987, recording the *Trio* album with Dolly Parton and Emmylou Harris. That same year, Ronstadt recorded *Canciones de mi Padre*, a set of traditional Mexican songs, which became a surprise hit. Two years later she recorded *Cry like a Rainstorm—Howl like the Wind*—her first contemporary pop album since 1982's *Get Closer*. Featuring four duets with Aaron Neville, including the No. 2 hit "Don't Know Much," the album sold more than two million copies. Ronstadt returned to traditional Mexican and Spanish material with *Mas Canciones* (1991) and *Frenesí* (1992). She returned to pop with 1994's *Winter Light*, which failed to generate a hit single, as did 1995's *Feels like Home*. — *Stephen Thomas Erlewine*

Hand Sown Home Grown / 1969 / Capitol ✦✦

Linda Ronstadt's debut album is a transitional effort, as the vocalist began to abandon the folk leanings of the Stone Poneys for a relaxed country-rock approach. Several of the songs are well performed; but the majority of the music is unfocused, and Ronstadt occasionally sounds unsure of herself. — *Stephen Thomas Erlewine*

Silk Purse / 1970 / Capitol ✦✦✦

While it followed the same musical approach as the debut, *Silk Purse* was an improvement on *Hand Sown Home Grown*, featuring more confident vocals from Linda Ronstadt and a stronger selection of songs, including "Lovesick Blues" and "Long Long Time." — *Stephen Thomas Erlewine*

Linda Ronstadt / 1971 / Capitol ✦✦✦

Linda Ronstadt's self-titled third album captured the singer moving away from the rootsier charms of her first two albums, toward a more polished take on country-rock. Supported by the Eagles throughout the record, Ronstadt turns in a strong performance, aided by a fine selection of material, including "Rock Me on the Water," "Crazy Arms," "I Still Miss Someone," and "I Fall to Pieces." — *Stephen Thomas Erlewine*

Don't Cry Now / 1973 / Asylum ✦✦✦

Don't Cry Now expanded the pop-rock concessions of *Linda Ronstadt*, and the result was the singer's first genuine hit record, peaking at No. 45 on the charts. — *Stephen Thomas Erlewine*

Different Drum / 1974 / Capitol ✦✦✦✦

Different Drum collects the highlights of Linda Ronstadt's first three solo albums, adding five Stone Poneys tracks, including the hit "Different Drum," for good measure. It misses some fine tracks from her solo records, but the album remains a fine introduction to her early years. — *Stephen Thomas Erlewine*

☆ **Heart like a Wheel** / 1974 / Capitol ✦✦✦✦✦

Ronstadt's breakthrough album, and her most perfectly realized. Solid from top to bottom, featuring the title track, "When Will I Be Loved?," "Desperado," and "You're No Good." Essential. — *Cub Koda*

Prisoner in Disguise / 1975 / Asylum ✦✦✦✦

Linda Ronstadt followed the commercial and critical breakthrough success of *Heart like a Wheel* with *Prisoner in Disguise*, a record that essentially repeated the formula of its predecessor. While it lacked the consistency of *Heart like a Wheel*, it was thoroughly enjoyable, highlighted by sturdy remakes of the Motown classics "Tracks of My Tears" and "Heat Wave." —*Stephen Thomas Erlewine*

● **Greatest Hits, Vol. 1** / 1976 / Asylum ✦✦✦✦
A concise collection of her chart successes. —*Dan Heilman*

Hasten Down the Wind / 1976 / Asylum ✦✦✦
Again, Linda Ronstadt repeats her slick, California pop/country-rock formula on *Hasten Down the Wind*. When the material is first-rate—such as "That'll Be the Day" or "Crazy"—Ronstadt's performances are terrific, but on the sub-par songs—such as the three Karla Bonoff numbers—she's dragged down by her material. —*Stephen Thomas Erlewine*

Retrospective / 1977 / Capitol ✦✦✦✦
A nice compilation of primarily country-influenced, pre-hit material. —*Cub Koda*

Simple Dreams / 1977 / Asylum ✦✦✦✦
Featuring a broader array of styles than any previous Linda Ronstadt record, *Simple Dreams* reconfirms her substantial talents as an interpretive singer. Ronstadt sings Dolly Parton ("I Never Will Marry") with the same conviction as the Rolling Stones ("Tumbling Dice"), and she manages to update Roy Orbison ("Blue Bayou") and direct attention to the caustic, fledgling singer-songwriter Warren Zevon ("Poor Poor Pitiful Me" and "Carmelita"). The consistently adventurous material and Ronstadt's powerful performance make the record rival *Heart like a Wheel* in quality. —*Stephen Thomas Erlewine*

Living in the U.S.A. / 1978 / Asylum ✦✦✦
On *Living in the USA.*, Linda Ronstadt made the ill-advised move to incorporate some current musical trends, such as new wave, into her successful formula. While some of the record sounds good, the majority of the album is poorly executed, particularly her take on Elvis Costello's "Alison." —*Stephen Thomas Erlewine*

Greatest Hits, Vol. 2 / 1980 / Asylum ✦✦✦✦
Her next dozen hits, more formulaic in content, but bigger on the charts. —*Cub Koda*

Mad Love / 1980 / Asylum ✦✦
Linda Ronstadt made a full-fledged, new wave-influenced pop album with *Mad Love*. It's an unfocused, stilted effort that suggested her career at the top of the charts was coming to a close. —*Stephen Thomas Erlewine*

Round Midnight with Nelson Riddle and his Orchestra / 1981 / Asylum ✦✦✦

Get Closer / 1982 / Asylum ✦✦
Get Closer was another successful album for Ronstadt, even though it didn't perform up to her platinum standards. Part of the reason for the relative lack of success was the lackluster material, which again signals that Ronstadt had lost touch with the mainstream pop scene. —*Stephen Thomas Erlewine*

What's New / 1983 / Asylum ✦✦✦
Instead of trying to compete with a newer, fashion-conscious pop marketplace, Linda Ronstadt removed herself from the rat race, recording an album of traditional-pop standards with Nelson Riddle. Ronstadt's voice isn't always showcased to full effect on these songs, but the record is an interesting change of pace. And it would have been more interesting if she hadn't repeated its formula on her next two records. —*Stephen Thomas Erlewine*

Lush Life / 1984 / Asylum ✦✦

For Sentimental Reasons / Feb. 1986 / Asylum ✦✦

Canciones de mi Padre / 1987 / Asylum ✦✦✦
Rondstadt's first all-Spanish album is a heartfelt tribute to her heritage. It also contains some of her finest performances of the '80s. —*AMG*

The Trio / 1987 / Warner Brothers ✦✦✦✦

Cry like a Rainstorm—Howl like the Wind / 1989 / Asylum ✦✦✦
On the strength of the hit duet with Aaron Neville, "Don't Know Much," *Cry like a Rainstorm—Howl like the Wind* returned Linda Ronstadt to the top of the charts. The album was a collection of well constructed adult contemporary pop, which suits her voice better than the traditional pop she recorded during the mid-'80s.

Musically, *Cry Like A Rainstorm* isn't as adventurous as *Canciones de mi Padre*, nor is it as consistent as *Trio*, the album she recorded with Emmylou Harris and Dolly Parton, but it is the most satisfying mainstream pop album she has made since the late '70s. —*Stephen Thomas Erlewine*

Mas Canciones / 1990 / Asylum ✦✦✦

Frenesi / 1992 / Asylum ✦✦
Frenesi is Linda Ronstadt's third in a series of Spanish language releases. This one—inspired by her work on the soundtrack to the film *Mambo Kings*—tackles Afro-Cuban pop and jazz. While some tracks, especially "Entre Abismos," swing mightily, there's little that sounds street level or rootsy about these sessions. I can't help picturing a wind up lounge band holding court at some tourist-trap Holiday Inn in Acapulco. —*Roch Parisien*

Winter Light / 1994 / Asylum ✦✦✦

Feels Like Home / 1995 / Asylum ✦✦

Dedicated to the One I Love / Jun. 1996 / Elektra ✦✦✦
Throughout her career, Linda Ronstadt has interpreted rock and pop classics, but *Dedicated to the One I Love* is different from the rest of her albums. This time around, she reinterprets the oldies as children's lullabies. All of the songs are given lush, sweet, and soft arrangements, even when that approach is ludicrous; it might be a cute idea to deliver Queen's "We Will Rock You" as a rock-a-bye chant, but in practice it is simply ridiculous. Fortunately, most of the album relies on songs—"Be My Baby," "In My Room"—that can be sung as lullabies and she sings them very well. Of course the appeal of *Dedicated to the One I Love* is limited—only baby boomer parents will really find this interesting—but fans who find the concept intriguing won't be disappointed. —*Stephen Thomas Erlewine*

Peter Rowan

b. Jul. 4, 1942, Boston, MA
Guitar, Vocals / Progressive Bluegrass, Contemporary Folk
Peter Rowan was one of the major cult bluegrass artists of the '80s, winning a devoted, international fan base through his independent records and constant touring. A skilled singer-songwriter, Rowan also yodeled and played numerous stringed instruments and the saxophone. He was born in Boston; his parents and many of his relatives were musicians, and it seemed only natural that Rowan, too, would become one. When he was a teenager, he frequently hung out at the Hillbilly Ranch, where he heard such bluegrass and old-time bands as the Lilly Brothers. He also enjoyed listening to the blues.

Rowan formed the Tex-Mex band the Cupids while he was in high school. The group became a popular New England attraction and independently released a single. After college he decided to become a professional musician, and in 1963 he joined the Cambridge-based Mother Bay State Entertainers as a mandolin player and singer, appearing on their LP *The String Band Project*. In 1964, after performing with Jim Rooney and Bill Keith, Rowan became a rhythm guitarist and lead singer with Bill Monroe and his Blue Grass Boys. He remained with them through 1967, leaving to join mandolinist David Grisman in the folk-rock band Earth Opera. The group recorded a couple of albums and toured (frequently opening for the Doors) until the early '70s. One of their albums, *The Great Eagle Tragedy* (1969) produced a minor hit single, "Home to You."

While with Monroe and Earth Opera, Rowan had begun to write and co-write songs, some of which were used in both bands. After leaving Earth Opera, he became a part of Sea Train, a rock-fusion unit whose records were produced by George Martin. Rowan left the band in 1972 to form the Rowan Brothers with siblings Chris and Lorin; they recorded one eponymous album. After the group disbanded Rowan recorded *Old and in the Way* with Grisman, Jerry Garcia, Vassar Clements, and John Kahn. In 1974 Rowan, Grisman, Clarence White, and Richard Greene formed Muleskinner, a bluegrass band. Muleskinner released one album and then disbanded. He then reunited the Rowan Brothers, who this time played together until the early '80s. Meanwhile, Rowan also began playing rock and bluegrass with Mexican Airforce, which featured accordion player Flaco Jimenez. In the mid-'80s, he and Jimenez again reteamed to record *Flaco Jimenez and Peter Rowan: Live Rockin' Tex-Mex*. He founded the Nashville-based Wild Stallions in 1983, and throughout the '80s and '90s he continued to work with a variety of musicians and tour as a solo act. —*Sandra Brennan*

Peter Rowan / 1978 / Flying Fish ✦✦✦
The solo debut album of this bluegrass vocalist features an original mixture of styles and backing from Flaco Jimenez, Richard Greene, and Tex Logan. —*AMG*

Medicine Trail / 1980 / Flying Fish ✦✦✦
Tex-Mex bluegrass and contemporary styling come from this virtuoso original. —*AMG*

The Walls of Time / 1981 / Sugar Hill ✦✦✦
This release is hard to put a finger on. The music takes on a feel like that of Old and in the Way, but it's missing the "something special" that project had. —*Chip Renner*

Texican Badman / 1981 / Appaloosa ✦✦✦✦

Red Hot Pickers / 1984 / Sugar Hill ✦✦✦
Joining Rowan on this 1995 release are the Red Hot Pickers, a group comprised of Richard Greene, Roger Mason, Andy Statman, and Tony Trischka. The record marks a reunion for Rowan and Greene, both of whom were Blue Grass Boys with Bill Monroe before joining forces in Earth Opera, Sea Train, and Muleskinner. —*Jason Ankeny*

The First Whippoorwill / 1985 / Sugar Hill ✦✦✦
The First Whippoorwill is a tribute album by Peter Rowan to his mentor, Bill Monroe, and it is one of the most moving salutes ever recorded in country music. What makes the record so successful is how Rowan affectionately demonstrates his debt to Monroe with invigorating, lively performances instead of treating the music as a museum piece. Rowan assembled a crackerjack backing band—featuring Buddy Spicher, Sam Bush, Roy Huskey Jr., Bill Keith, and Richard Greene—which helps him make one of the best, most focused records of his career. —*Thom Owens*

● **New Moon Rising** / 1988 / Sugar Hill ✦✦✦✦
Tight album. Rowan is backed by Tte Nashville Bluegrass Band. Maura O'Connell sings harmony vocals on "Meadow Green," and Jerry Douglas is featured on dobro. —*Chip Renner*

Dust Bowl Children / 1990 / Sugar Hill ✦✦✦
A very good album. It is all acoustic, featuring Peter Rowan alone on guitar, mandola, and vocals. This grows on you. —*Chip Renner*

All on a Rising Day / 1991 / Sugar Hill ✦✦✦✦
An all-around fine release. Rowan picks up where he left off on *Dust Bowl* but improves on the idea with some great backup musicians—Stuart Duncan, Sam Bush, Jerry Douglas, Alison Krauss, Roy Husky Jr, Alan O'Bryant, and Edgar Meyer. The result is a highly recommended album, boasting 12 solid songs. —*Chip Renner*

Tree on a Hill / 1994 / Sugar Hill ✦✦✦

Yonder / Apr. 1996 / Sugar Hill ✦✦

The Rowans

Progressive Bluegrass
Formed in the mid-'70s, the group consists of brothers Peter, Chris, and Lorin Rowan. The Rowans produced three albums of original songs and rich harmonies. This was a turning point for Peter Rowan, away from his rock efforts. —*Chip Renner*

● **The Rowans** / 1975 / Asylum ✦✦✦✦
The Rowans put out a strong album featuring killer songs of Peter's—"Midnight Moonlight," "Thunder on the Mountain," and "Beggar in Bluejeans." The album also features Lorin's "On the Ground" and Chris' "Here Today and Gone Tomorrow." First-class album. —*Chip Renner*

Jubilations / 1977 / Asylum ✦✦✦
The final Rowans album. Peter steps back, producing only three songs. —*Chip Renner*

Sibling Rivalry / 1978 / Asylum ✦✦✦
Not as good as their debut album. Includes Peter and Lorin's "Tired Hands" and "Mongolian Swamp/Kings Men." —*Chip Renner*

The Walls of Time / 1981 / Sugar Hill ✦✦✦
Walls of Time is a fine slice of traditional bluegrass and country, performed by several of the finest newgrass musicians, including Sam Bush, Ricky Skaggs, and the Rowan siblings. Though the album focuses on vocal material, not instrumental, it remains an enjoyable, heartfelt evocation of classic bluegrass by some of the very best progressive bluegrass performers of the '70s and '80s. —*Thom Owens*

Dave & Sugar Rowland

Country-Pop
Dave and Sugar were one of the most popular vocal groups in country music from the mid-'70s through the early '80s. Lead singer Dave Rowland was the group's one constant, while the two females comprising Sugar were subject to frequent change. Rowland was the son of a minister. He began his career singing with a dance band. He was drafted in the mid-'60s and became a trumpet player with an Army band; he formed his own group while stationed at Fort Belvoir, VA. In 1970 Rowland graduated from the Stamps Music School in Texas and headed for Nashville, where he joined the Stamps Quartet. In 1974 he left the Stamps to join the more country-oriented Four Guys, singing behind Charley Pride and appearing on the Grand Ole Opry. After leaving the group, he worked as a singing waiter at Papa Leone's in Nashville, later forming a country-rock band, Wild Oates. When Rowland learned that Pride and Tammy Wynette were looking for backup groups, he formed the first incarnation of Sugar with Jackie Frantz and Vicki Hackeman. It was Pride who helped Dave and Sugar sign to RCA in 1975; that year the trio released their first single, the Shel Silverstein-penned "Queen of the Silver Dollar," and had a Top 25 hit.

Over the next few years, the threesome had many hits, including "I'm Gonna Love You," "That's the Way Love Should Be," and "I'm Knee Deep in Loving You." In 1977 Frantz tired of touring and was replaced by Sue Powell; the next year Hackeman was replaced by Melissa Dean, and Dave and Sugar had their first No. 1 hit, "Tear Time." They had their second No. 1 with Kenny Rogers in 1979. After touring with Kenny Rogers in 1980, a regular succession of personnel turnovers began. Dave and Sugar's last shot at chart success came in 1981 with two Top 40 hits, including "It's a Heartache," and the Top Ten hit "Fool by Your Side." Later, Rowland's label Elektra talked him into recording the solo album *Sugar Free*, which produced two unsuccessful singles. He then reunited with Dean and Powell without much success, so he created a new Sugar with Cindy Smith and Lisa Alvey. The latest Sugar lineup included Regina Leigh and Lori Mason. —*Sandra Brennan*

New York Wine, Tennessee Shine / 1980 / RCA ✦✦✦

Pleasure / 1981 / Elektra ✦✦✦

Sugar Free / 1982 / Elektra ✦✦✦

Golden Tears / Stay with Me / RCA ✦✦✦

Billy Joe Royal

b. 1945, Valdosta, GA
Vocals / Country-Pop, Pop-Rock
Best-known for his pop-rock hit "Down in the Boondocks," Billy Joe Royal had a long career that saw him shifting his attentions toward country music in the '80s. Although he never had another hit as large as "Down in the Boondocks," he racked up a number of successful country singles over the course of the 1980s.

Royal was born into a family of musical entertainers in Valdosta, GA, and debuted on his uncle's radio show at the age of 11. The next year he learned to play steel guitar and joined the *Atlanta Jubilee* at age 14, performing with Joe South, Jerry Reed, and Ray Stevens. Royal had his own rock band during high school and was regularly singing around Atlanta by the age of 16. In 1962 he recorded an independent single that went unnoticed.

Three years later South contacted him with a song he wanted Royal to sing as a demo, in the hope that Gene Pitney would record it. Royal flew to Atlanta and recorded "Down in the Boondocks" inside the studio's septic tank, which had been converted into an echo chamber.

The demo ended up at Columbia, and they signed Royal to a six-year deal. The song became his breakthrough single, reaching No. 9 on the pop charts and making the vocalist into a teen idol. After its success, Royal had a string of lesser hits, including the Top 40 pop singles "I Knew You When," "I've Got to Be Somebody" and "Cherry Hill Park." By the end of the decade, Royal's star waned, and he became a regular performer in Las Vegas and Lake Tahoe. He also did a bit of acting on television, in feature films, and commercials. In 1978 he recorded a cover of "Under the Boardwalk" and scored a minor hit.

During the early 1980s Royal worked on establishing himself as a country artist, but he had trouble finding a label. In 1984 he finally got a break when he recorded Gary Burr's "Burned like a Rocket." It was picked up by Atlantic Records, who signed Royal. The single became a hit and reached the country Top Ten in early 1986. For the next two years, he had a string of Top 40 hits, breaking into the Top Ten in late 1987 with "I'll Pin a Note on Your Pillow." In 1989 he released the album *Tell It like It Is;* the title cut became his biggest hit, peaking at No. 2, while the album itself stayed in the Top 15 for over a year. By 1990 Royal's style of pop-inflected country had been replaced by neo-traditional honky-tonk at the top of the charts, and his popularity declined. He continued to have minor hits into 1992 and toured throughout the decade. —*Sandra Brennan*

Down in the Boondocks / 1965 / Columbia ✦✦✦✦
Albums in the early '60s were often put out only after an artist had a couple of hits that could be packaged with other tunes. This is what appears to have been the case with *Down in the Boondocks*, with the album containing the title hit, as well as "I Knew You When." Some of the other songs here showed promise, as well. Produced by Joe South, the record is well worth seeking out. —*James Chrispell*

Cherry Hill Park / 1969 / Columbia ✦✦✦

The Royal Treatment / 1987 / Atlantic ✦✦✦

Looking Ahead / 1987 / Atlantic ✦✦✦
A very dated, sometimes rather slick, production of many good tunes is what awaits you on *Looking Ahead*. Billy Joe Royal did have hits with some of these tunes, too, and rightly so. While not his best, the record kept his name before the audience at a time when other long-established artists were falling by the wayside. —*James Chrispell*

● **Greatest Hits [Columbia]** / 1989 / Columbia ✦✦✦✦
Can't go wrong with this one, featuring his two biggies, "Down in the Boondocks" and "Cherry Hill Park." —*Cub Koda*

Tell It like It Is / 1989 / Atlantic ✦✦✦
Features include "He Don't Know," "'Till I Can't Take It Anymore," "Are We There Yet?" and others. —*AMG*

Greatest Hits [Atlantic] / 1991 / Atlantic ✦✦✦
Billy Joe Royal's *Greatest Hits* on Atlantic contains the biggest country-pop hits from the '80s, including his debut country hit, "Burned like a Rocket." —*Thom Owens*

Billy Joe Royal / 1992 / Atlantic ✦✦
Featured are "Funny How Time Slips Away," "Are We There Yet?" and "Familiar Pain," among others. —*AMG*

● **The Best of Billy Joe Royal** / Dec. 1, 1995 / Sony Special Products ✦✦✦✦

Run C & W

Progressive Bluegrass, Contemporary Country, Country Humor
Former Eagle Bernie Leadon, former Amazing Rhythm Ace Russell Smith, and Nashville songwriters Vince Melamed and Jim Photoglo formed this novelty act in Nashville clubs, playing soul music "the way it ought to be played—bluegrass style." —*Brian Mansfield*

● **Into the Twangy-first Century** / 1993 / MCA ✦✦✦
If you don't believe a bluegrass version of a soul classic is an inspired gag, listen to the beginning of Run C&W's "Stop in the Name of Love" and imagine the possibilities. The quartet also rewrote Arthur Conley's "Sweet Soul Music" to poke fun at Lee Greenwood and Tanya Tucker, among others, and parodied Billy Ray Cyrus' "Achy Breaky Heart" with "Itchy Twitchy Spot." —*Brian Mansfield*

Row vs Wade / 1995 / MCA ✦✦✦
As the name suggests, Run C&W is a parody of rap and soul, taking standard hip-hop lingo and forcing it into a country format. Like most comedy records, it's vaguely amusing at first and runs thin near the end of the disc. Fortunately, the group's instrumental acumen saves the record from being tedious, even when the jokes are sophomoric. —*Thom Owens*

Bobby Russell

b. Apr. 19, 1941, Nashville, TN, **d.** Nov. 19, 1992
Vocals / Country Pop
Although Bobby Russell had a successful recording career, he is best remembered as the songwriter who penned the 1960s hits "Honey" and "Little Green Apples." Born and raised in Nashville, Russell first attracted notice with "The Joker Went Wild," which provided Brian Hyland with a Top 20 pop hit. Two years later he penned "Little Green Apples" for Roger Miller; it became a Top Ten country hit and crossed over to the pop Top 40. Later in 1968, Bobby Goldsboro earned a No. 1 hit and a gold record for his rendition of "Honey;" O.C. Smith also recorded "Little Green Apples," and had a No. 3 hit. Russell made his own recording debut with "1432 Franklin Pike Circle Hero," which hit the Top 40 on the pop charts. The following year, he cut two more minor hits, including "Better Homes and Gardens." Two years later Russell had a major crossover hit with "Saturday Morning Confusion," which reached the Top 25 on the country charts and the Top 30 on the pop charts. In 1973 he penned "The Night the Lights Went Out in Georgia," and it became a No. 1 hit for his wife Vicki Lawrence; it was also her only hit. Later that year, Russell had a minor hit with "Mid American Manufacturing Tycoon," his final chart appearance. He died of coronary disease in 1992, and two years later was inducted into the Nashville Songwriters Hall of Fame. —*Sandra Brennan*

Words, Music, Laughter and Tears / 1968 / Elf ✦✦✦

● **Dial-a-Hit** / 1969 / Bell ✦✦✦✦

Saturday Morning Confusion / United Artists ✦✦✦

Johnny Russell (John W. Russell)

b. Jun. 4, 1909, Charlotte, NC
Sax (Tenor), Vocals / Traditional Country, Country-Pop
Johnny Russell was a successful country songwriter and performer whose songs were recorded by some of the biggest names in country music, including Jim Reeves, Buck Owens, Loretta Lynn, Dolly Parton, and even the Beatles. He was born and raised in Roundway, MS, and was first influenced by the music of Ernest Tubb, Lefty Frizzell, Roy Acuff, and the Grand Ole Opry. His family moved to Fresno, CA, when Russell was 11. In high school, he entered and won various talent contests and even became a character actor on television.

A longtime songwriter, he recorded his first song, "In a Mansion Stands My Love," in 1958. Soon after its release, he appeared on "Ralph Emery's Late Night Show," where he met Chet Atkins, Eddy Arnold, Hank Locklin, and Archie Campbell. Later that year he moved to Nashville, where Jim Reeves recorded a cover of "In a Mansion Stands My Love" and helped establish Russell's reputation as a songwriter. His performing career went nowhere, though, and later that year he went back to California to hone his writing skills. In 1963 Buck Owens recorded Russell's "Act Naturally" and had a No. 1 hit. Two years later the Beatles had success with a cover of the tune, and a remake by Owens and Ringo Starr became a hit as well.

In 1971 Russell, trying again to become a recording star, returned to Nashville, where Atkins signed him to RCA. His debut

"Mr. and Mrs. Untrue" and its follow-up, "What a Price," both became mid-level hits. Russell had his first Top 20 hit in 1973 with "Catfish John," and later that year had his biggest hit, "Rednecks, White Socks and Blue Ribbon Beer," which peaked in the Top Five. He had six more hits through 1975, including "Hello I Love You." In 1977 he finished his stint at RCA with six more mid-range hits, including "The Son of Hickory Holler's Tramp." He then switched to Mercury and had a Top 30 hit with "How Deep in Love Am I?" He had several more hits with the label, including "Here's to the Horses," but none of them made it past the Top 50.

Through the 1980s Russell continued to find success as a songwriter. In the mid-'80s, he joined the Grand Ole Opry as a comedy and singing act. He went on to appear on various country music variety shows, including "Hee Haw." Russell teamed up with Little David Wilkins in 1987 to record the minor hit "Butterbeans." Before the year was out, Russell had a mild stroke, and the next year he underwent surgery to remove a blockage from his chest. Still, he continued to perform and tour as before. — *Sandra Brennan*

Mr and Mrs Untrue / 1972 / RCA ✦✦✦

Catfish John / 1972 / RCA ✦✦✦

● **Rednecks, White Socks and Blue Ribbon Beer** / 1973 / RCA ✦✦✦✦

Russell is probably better known for the songs he's written or his appearances on country music television programs than as an artist. But this record is fun. From the liner notes that parody his most famous composition ("Act Naturally") and his girth, to the title track that just invites you to sing along. Not a landmark record, but fun to listen to. — *Jim Worbois*

She's in Love with a Rodeo Man / 1974 / RCA ✦✦✦

Here Comes Johnny Russell / 1975 / RCA ✦✦✦✦

Greatest Hits / Dominion ✦✦✦

Russell sounds good on these ten new stereo recordings, but overall, they are no match for the original versions. — *Stephen Thomas Erlewine*

Tom Russell

b. California

Vocals / Contemporary Country, Singer-Songwriter, Contemporary Folk, Americana

Tom Russell is a New York-based singer-songwriter who has co-written songs with Nanci Griffith, Peter Case, Ian Tyson, Sylvia Tyson, Katy Moffatt, and Dave Alvin. His band features Andrew Hardin (guitar), Fats Kaplin (pedal steel, fiddle, and accordion), Billy Troiani (bass), and Charles Caldarola (percussion). The sound varies from country to Tex-Mex to rock. — *Chip Renner*

Road to Bayamon / 1988 / Philo ✦✦✦✦

A great CD, with songs full of images. Songwriters do not get much better. This contains a great cover of Tom Waits' "Downtown Train." — *Chip Renner*

Poor Man's Dream / 1990 / Philo ✦✦✦✦

This CD is as good as *Road to Bayamon*. The songs might even be more polished. "Blue Wing," "Veterans Day," and "Navajo Rag" are all classics. Russell co-writes with Nanci Griffith, Kathy Moffatt, and Ian Tyson. — *Chip Renner*

Hurricane Season / 1991 / Philo ✦✦✦

A solid performance, and the band clicks. Features a great song about Bill Haley's demise, plus Russell co-writes with Peter Case, Bob Neuwirth, Sylvia Tyson, and Dave Alvin. — *Chip Renner*

Cowboy Real / 1992 / Philo ✦✦✦

A real nice cowboy/Western release featuring new and old Tom Russell favorites. Russell scales down the production on "Navajo Rug," "Gallo Del Cielo," and an old Hardin and Russell song, "Zane Grey." — *Chip Renner*

Box of Visions / Dec. 1992 / Philo ✦✦✦

Box of Visions is a latter-day album from Tom Russell, and like many of his efforts, it is an understated and engaging release that

demands your attention; if you don't actively listen to the record, much of it blends together in the background, since his songs rarely depart from his country-tinged folk foundation. There are a couple of mediocre cuts on *Box of Visions*, but the album, by and large, finds Russell at the top of his form. — *Thom Owens*

● **The Rose of the San Joaquin** / Oct. 1995 / Hightone ✦✦✦✦

Tom Russell has grown consistently in the course of his many albums into one of the most articulate singer-songwriters on the country side of the tracks. His efforts with Barrence Whitfield and earlier incarnations of the Tom Russell Band have the guitar work of Tom's longtime partner Andrew Hardin. On this record, however, Russell, along with producers Dave Alvin and Greg Leisz, has chosen to create a more linear feel to the album, with each song feeling as if it takes place in the border town Russell has been so good at describing. Each song is a miniature film soundtrack, with characters clearly drawn. "The Sky Above and the Mud Below" is one of the key tracks that, with its slow tempo and plain-spoken telling, truly brings the listener a sense of despair in the middle of nowhere. It is ominous in the way it builds to the inevitable conclusion, as potent after repeated listening as the tragic ending in Russell's earlier *Gallo Del Ciello*. On the other hand, "Out in California" celebrates lust and longing for that girl with the red dress, driven home by some high-octane playing. "Somebody's Husband, Somebody's Son" (with Peter Case and Dave Alvin) is a hobo's waltz. The album has some soft lovers' ballads, "Hand Carved Heart" and "Strawberry Moon." The liner notes include Russell's reminiscence about the appearance and subsequent disappearance about a long-lost relative that is perfectly in keeping with the tone of the album's songs. He has carved out a place for himself as a compelling storyteller, and this is one of his strongest albums of the '90s. — *Richard Meyer*

Heart on a Sleeve / Bear Family ✦✦✦✦

John Wesley Ryles

b. Dec. 2, 1950, Bastrop, LA

Guitar, Vocals / Country-Pop

Although singer-songwriter John Wesley Ryles had more than 30 chart singles between 1968 and 1988, he never reached the heights of some of his contemporaries. He was raised in rural Louisiana and Texas in a family who entertained themselves in the evening by singing. A guitar player from age six, he made his radio debut the next year. His family formed the Ryles Family Singers and entertained on various local radio stations until accepting an invitation to become regulars on Fort Worth's "Cowtown Hoedown," which led to joining the "Big D Jamboree" in Dallas. The whole family moved to Nashville in 1965, and Ryles decided to go solo. He began singing demos, gained experience working as a studio engineer, and frequently appeared with various local club bands. In 1968 he released the single "Kay," which gave the 18-year-old Ryles, billing himself as John Wesley I, a Top Ten country and crossover pop hit. He recorded two follow-ups in 1969 that made it to only to the middle of the charts, but made it to the Top 20 in 1970 with "I've Just Been Wasting My Time." The next year he had a Top 40 hit with "Reconsider Me." By this time, however, young Ryles had become disillusioned and discouraged, and he left Music City to begin performing at various clubs. In 1976 he made another bid for stardom with two minor hit singles. In 1977 he recorded "Fool'" at first it did nothing, but four months after its release it became a Top 20 hit. He followed with his biggest hit, "Lifetime Thing," which reached the Top Five. After that, he had several mid-range hits through the end of the '80s before becoming a session musician and demo singer. — *Sandra Brennan*

Kay / 1969 / Columbia ✦✦✦✦

● **John Wesley Ryles** / 1977 / ABC/Dot ✦✦✦✦

Shine on Me / 1978 / MCA ✦✦✦

Let the Night Begin / 1979 / MCA ✦✦✦

Reconsider Me / Plantation ✦✦✦

S

Doug Sahm

b. Nov. 6, 1941, San Antonio, TX
Guitar, Vocals / Rock & Roll, Blues-Rock, Progressive Country, Country-Rock, Tex-Mex, Roots-Rock, Americana

Guitarist, composer, arranger, and songwriter Doug Sahm hasn't exactly carved a niche for himself as a straightahead blues player over the years. But one of his recent albums, *The Last Real Texas Blues Band,* was nominated for a Grammy award. It's a firecracker of an album, perhaps the best thing he's ever recorded.

Sahm, born November 6, 1941, in San Antonio, TX, is a knowledgeable music historian and veteran performer who's equally comfortable in a range of styles, including Texas blues, country, rock 'n' roll, Western swing and Cajun. He began his performing career at age nine when he was featured on a San Antonio area radio station, playing steel guitar. Sahm began recording for a procession of small labels (Harlem, Warrior, Renner, and Personality) in 1955 with "A Real American Joe" under the name Little Doug Sahm. Three years later he was leading a group called the Pharoahs. Sahm recorded a series of singles for Texas-based record companies including "Crazy Daisy" (1959), "Sapphire" (1961), and "If You Ever Need Me" (1964). After being prompted in 1965 to assemble a group by producer Huey Meaux, Sahm asked his friends Augie Meyers (keyboards), Frank Morin (saxophone), Harvey Kagan (bass), and Johnny Perez (drums) if they would join him. Meaux gave the group the name the Sir Douglas Quintet. The group had some success on the radio with "The Rains Came," but Sahm later moved to California after the group broke up, where he formed the Honkey Blues Band. He reformed his quintet in California and recorded a now-classic single, "Mendocino." The resulting album was a groundbreaking record in the then emerging country-rock scene. The Sir Douglas Quintet followed *Mendocino* with *Together After Five,* an album that led them to a larger fan base.

But it was Atlantic Records producer Jerry Wexler who realized that country-rock sounds were coming into vogue (and there was no place in Nashville for people like Sahm), so he signed both Sahm and Willie Nelson. One of his greatest albums, *Doug Sahm and Band* (1973, Atlantic), was recorded in New York City with Bob Dylan, Dr. John, and accordionist Flaco Jimenez, and a resulting single, "Is Anybody Going to San Antone?" had some radio success. The Sir Douglas Quintet got back together to record two more albums, *Wanted Very Much Alive* and *Back to the 'Dillo.*

Among Sahm's most essential blues records are *Hell of a Spell,* (1980, Takoma) a blues album dedicated to Guitar Slim, and his Grammy-nominated studio album for Antone's, *The Last Real Texas Blues Band.*

For his other material, there are several good compilations, including *The Best of Doug Sahm* and *The Sir Douglas Quintet* (Rhino). —*Richard Skelly*

Honky Blues (Sir Douglas) / 1968 / Smash ✦✦✦

Mendocino / 1969 / Smash ✦✦✦✦

Together After Five / 1970 / Smash ✦✦✦✦

Rough Edges / 1973 / Mercury ✦✦

Doug Sahm and the Band / Jan. 1973 / Atlantic ✦✦✦
Since major label Atlantic signed Doug Sahm as a solo artist and put him in a New York studio with top-flight producers Jerry Wexler and Arif Mardin and star sidemen like Bob Dylan, Dr. John, and David Bromberg (not to mention old stalwarts like Augie Meyers, Flaco Jimenez, and Martin Fierro), you might expect that the resulting album would be Sahm's big career move, a swing toward professionalism and the mainstream, and that's how it was perceived when it was released. Maybe that's why it also was dismissed when it didn't become a big hit. Trouble is, the record isn't slick at all—it sounds as loose as any of the Sir Douglas Quintet albums, if a little more country-oriented. But the album remains a Bob Dylan curio; Dylan's otherwise unavailable composition "Wallflower" is included, and he sings it and "Blues Stay Away From Me" with Sahm. —*William Ruhlmann*

Return of the Formerly Bros. / 1988 / Rykodisc ✦✦✦✦
Texan folk hero Sir Doug Sahm meets underrated guitarist Amos Garrett and ex-Blasters keyboardist Gene Taylor, and they cook like an Austin barbecue. (Originally released on Stony Plain Records in Canada in 1988, *The Return of the Formerly Brothers* was released in the US by Rykodisc in 1989.) —*Jeff Tamarkin*

● **Juke Box Music** / 1989 / Antones'✦✦✦✦
Sahm shimmies and strolls through this set of doo wop and R&B covers, a gorgeous slow-dancing gem. —*John Floyd*

● **The Best of Doug Sahm (1968-1975)** / 1991 / Rhino ✦✦✦✦
This is not as thorough as *Sir Doug's Recording Trip,* but it's easier to find and gives you 22 essential tracks in sterling digital fidelity. —*John Floyd*

Best of Doug's Sahm's Atlantic Sessions / 1995 / Sequel ✦✦✦✦

Buffy Sainte-Marie

b. Feb. 20, 1941, Saskatchewan, Canada
Guitar, Vocals / Country-Pop, Singer-Songwriter, Folk-Rock, Pop-Rock, Contemporary Folk

Buffy Sainte-Marie has enjoyed a long career that has seen her rise to stardom on the folk circuit and try her hand at country, rock, soundtrack themes, acting, activism, and children's television. For most listeners, she remains identified with the material she wrote and sang for Vanguard in the mid-'60s. Her songs that addressed the plight of the Native American, particularly "Now That the Buffalo's Gone" and "My Country 'tis of Thy People You're Dying," were the ones that generated the most controversy. Yet she was also skilled at addressing broader themes of war and justice ("Universal Soldier") and romance ("Until It's Time for You to Go"). She was also a capable interpreter of outside material, although her idiosyncratic vibrato made large-scale commercial success out of the question.

Sainte-Marie was born to Cree Indian parents and adopted by a White family. Signed to Vanguard, she was one of the folk scene's more prominent rising stars in the '60s, and certainly the only widely heard performer articulating Native American viewpoints in song. Much of her best material from this era, however, gained its greatest commercial inroads via cover versions. "Universal Soldier" was one of Donovan's first hits. "Until It's Time for You to

Go," perhaps her best composition, was covered by numerous pop singers and became a big British hit for Elvis Presley in the early '70s. "Cod'ine," one of the few '60s songs to explicitly address the dangers of drugs, was covered by Californian rock bands Quicksilver Messenger Service and the Charlatans.

Sainte-Marie didn't pigeonhole herself as a folkie, though, recording in Nashville in the late '60s in attempts to break into the country market. In the 1970s, she would make some rock records, including one (1971's *She Used to Wanna Be a Ballerina*) with contributions from Ry Cooder and Crazy Horse. These country and rock outings were far less successful, both commercially and artistically, than her early folk efforts.

But Sainte-Marie was never as reliant on selling units as most musicians. She kept busy with a long-running stint on *Sesame Street*, performing benefits for and organizing on behalf of Native Americans, and composing for movies. (She won an Oscar for the theme to *An Officer and a Gentleman*, co-written with her husband, producer Jack Nitzsche.) She hadn't made an album for 15 years before issuing *Coincidence and Likely Stories* in 1992. —*Richie Unterberger*

☆ **It's My Way!** / 1964 / Vanguard ♦♦♦♦♦
This is one of the most scathing topical folk albums ever made. Sainte-Marie sings in an emotional, vibrato-laden voice of war ("The Universal Soldier," later a hit for Donovan), drugs ("Cod'ine"), sex ("The Incest Song"), and most telling, the mistreatment of Native Americans, of which Sainte-Marie is one ("Now That the Buffalo's Gone"). Even decades later, the album's power is moving and disturbing. —*William Ruhlmann*

Many a Mile / 1965 / Fontana ♦♦♦

Little Wheel Spin / 1966 / Vanguard ♦♦♦♦
Recorded in 1966, this classic album reveals the roots of Buffy's musical career, the folk and protest songs that revolutionized the '60s. Drawing on a repertoire of traditional European ballads with more than a hint of irony, she also introduces "My Country 'Tis of Thy People You're Dying," probably the first recording to confront White America on its racism towards Native Americans. It includes acoustic and electric guitar accompaniment, plus mouthbow. —*Ladyslipper*

Fire and Fleet and Candlelight / 1967 / Vanguard ♦♦♦

I'm Gonna Be a Country Girl Again / 1968 / Vanguard ♦♦
And, one hopes, she'll *never* be a country girl again. Sainte-Marie went to Nashville to record this album, with help from such session vets as Grady Martin, Floyd Cramer, and the Jordanaires. As expected, it doesn't jell that well, although it's not as poor as you might fear. Sainte-Marie's strengths, though, are best amplified by folk material; her vibrato isn't suited for Nashville country. Predictably, the best songs are the ones which most recall her early folkie work. "Now That the Buffalo's Gone," like several of her better songs, touches upon Native American issues, and the stark, somber "Tall Trees in Georgia," a solo acoustic guitar piece, seems like a refugee from an earlier album. —*Richie Unterberger*

Illuminations / 1970 / Vanguard ♦♦

● **The Best of Buffy Sainte Marie [Double]** / 1970 / Vanguard ♦♦♦♦
Sainte-Marie pursued a variety of musical styles, from folk to country to experimental rock, and all are represented on this wide-ranging double-record compilation. It doesn't all work, but there are some terrific songs, among them the Native American lament "My Country 'Tis of Thy People You're Dying," the romantic "Until It's Time for You to Go," and a musical adaptation of a passage from a Leonard Cohen novel, "God Is Alive, Magic Is Afoot." (Beware of the abbreviated version, Vanguard 73113.) —*William Ruhlmann*

She Used to Wanna Be a Ballerina / 1971 / Vanguard ♦♦♦
This reissue of Sainte-Marie's 1971 classic is welcomed most gratefully and enthusiastically. If you've never heard it, treat yourself and thank the heavens you didn't miss it; if you're familiar with it, set aside that battered LP, put this on, and savor the trip back. It includes "Soldier Blue," Neil Young's "Helpless," the hypnotic "The Surfer" (also recorded by Gaurdabarranco), and Leonard Cohen's "Bells." —*Ladyslipper*

The Best of, Vol. 2 / 1971 / Vanguard ♦♦♦♦

Moon Shot / 1972 / Vanguard ♦

Quiet Places / 1973 / Vanguard ♦♦
You know you're in trouble when the first track roars in like a Tina Turner tune, as Sainte-Marie unsuccessfully plays her hand at ballsy bar-band rock 'n' boogie. Actually, most of the rest of the album eschews that approach in favor of more expected singer-songwriter territory, but this still makes for an unimpressive effort, with unsuitably mainstream rock production values hovering over much of the content. Sainte-Marie mixes her own compositions with covers of songs by Joni Mitchell, Randy Newman, and Carole King, but the only real highlight of the record is the final tune, the reflective and haunting ballad "The Jewels of Hanalei." —*Richie Unterberger*

Native North American Child: An Odyssey / 1974 / Vanguard ♦♦♦

Coincidence and Likely Stories / 1992 / Chrysalis ♦♦♦
Back after a hiatus of many years, she returns with the distinctive voice and strong mix of pointed political and personal songs that endeared her to, and perhaps woke up, an entire generation. Almost all original and mostly new material on this 1992 release, though songs like "Starwalker" will sound welcome and familiar to some of us. Unfortunately, her indictments of the US government in its dealings with Native-American communities and other disenfranchised populations are as relevant as they were 30 years ago, and her commentaries on money and power junkies have become even more scathing. Included are "Bury My Heart at Wounded Knee," "Disinformation," "The Priests of the Golden Bull," and "Emma Lee." —*Ladyslipper*

Up Where We Belong / Feb. 1996 / EMI Premier ♦♦♦

Junior Samples (Alvin Junior Samples)

b. 1927, Cumming, GA, d. Nov. 13, 1983, Cumming, GA
Harmonica, Vocals / Traditional Country, Country-Pop, Country Humor
Cornball comic/country singer/harmonica player Junior Samples was a beloved performer on the long-running country variety show "Hee-Haw," where he was best known for his ability to spin yarns with his authentic, almost incomprehensible Georgia drawl, old-fashioned manner, and bizarre usage of common words. Born Alvin Samples in Cumming, GA, he dropped out of school in the sixth grade and didn't find fame until he was well past 40, when his son found a huge fish head which Samples told friends came from a 22-pound, nine-ounce bass he had caught. The state Fish and Game Commission sent an interviewer to get the story, so Samples told his tale over the radio in 1966. The tape got to Chart Records, which added background music and released it as a single titled "World's Biggest Whopper." The novelty single made the Top 60 on the country charts and led to several radio and television appearances for Samples, who soon found himself a full-fledged comedian. He signed to CBS' "Hee Haw" soon after its debut in 1969 and became one of the show's biggest hits, not only for his stories but for his inadvertent misreadings of cue cards. He stayed with the show until his death in 1983. —*Sandra Brennan*

The World of Junior Samples / 1967 / Chart ♦♦♦♦

Bull Session at Bull's Gap / 1968 / Chart ♦♦♦

That's a Hee Haw / 1970 / Chart ♦♦♦

● **The Best of** / Nashville ♦♦♦♦
This features "The Disorderly Horse," "Moonshining," "Tobe the Mule," and more. —*AMG*

Ray Sanders

b. Oct. 1, 1935, St. John, KY
Vocals / Traditional Country
Singer-songwriter Ray Sanders had more than 14 chart hits during his 20-year career, but he was most popular on the club circuit. The Kentucky native started out as a deejay in Elizabethtown in 1950. In addition to the seven years he spent there, he also appeared on the "Lincoln Jamboree" and the "Renfro Valley Barn Dance" through most of the 1950s. After graduating from college

in 1957, he made his recording debut, without chart success. He debuted on the Grand Ole Opry in 1959, which led to his big break in 1960 when he signed with Liberty and debuted with "World So Full of Love," which made the Top 20. The next year "Lonelyville" also made it to the Top 20. Sanders didn't have another hit until the end of the decade, but in 1969, he appeared again on the country charts with "Beer Drinkin' Music." The next year he had a Top 20 hit with "All I Ever Need Is You." In 1977 he became the house act at the White Sands in Riverside, CA. —*Sandra Brennan*

Feeling Good Is Easy / 1969 / Imperial ◆◆◆

● **Ray Sanders** / 1972 / United Artists ◆◆◆◆

Texas Dance Hall Music / 1980 / Hillside ◆◆◆

Art Satherly

Traditional Country, Cowboy

One of the most important pioneers in the field of country music production, "Uncle" Art Satherly was also the only British citizen to be inducted by the Country Music Hall of Fame. He was born in the English West Country on a Somerset farm, the son of a minister. Satherly visited Wisconsin in 1913 and began working for the Wisconsin Chair Company, which made cabinets to house Edison's early phonographs. Eventually Satherly began working for one of the newly founded record labels, Paramount, where he promoted blues artists such as Blind Lemon Jefferson. He stayed there until 1928, when he became recording manager at QS Records. In 1929 he joined the American Record Corporation and signed various artists; among them was a young Gene Autry, who was signed for his similarity to Jimmie Rodgers. Satherly produced many of Autry's singles, helped launch the cowboy crooner's career, and got him involved in movies. When Columbia took over ARC, Satherly began working as an A&R man. He recorded Roy Acuff and Hank Penny on Columbia's Okeh label before retiring in 1952. Among the artists he signed were Lefty Frizzell, Little Jimmy Dickens, Marty Robbins, and Carl Smith. He was also influential in the careers of Bob Wills, Red Foley, Al Dexter, and Tex Ritter. Satherly died in 1986. —*Sandra Brennan*

● **Uncle Art Satherley: Country Music's Father** / 1991 / Columbia ◆◆◆◆

Sawyer Brown

Contemporary Country

Country-rockers Sawyer Brown got their big break with a victory on the nationally syndicated talent show "Star Search." They originated in 1979, when lead guitarist Bobby Randall came to Nashville with the intention of starting a band. While working with Don King, he met drummer Joe Smyth; a year later, they teamed up with bass guitarist Jim Scholten, lead vocalist/rhythm guitarist Mark Miller, and keyboardist Hobie Hubbard. After King stopped touring in 1981, the band members decided to continue performing, naming themselves Sawyer Brown in tribute to the Nashville street where they used to rehearse.

Sawyer Brown toured the country for two years before their agent asked them to make a video in Nashville, which turned out to be an audition for the televised television contest "Star Search." The band performed on the show and wound up earning $100,000. The subsequent publicity helped them land a contract with Capitol/Curb in 1984. Later that year they released their self-titled debut album and had a Top 20 hit with their debut single, "Leona." The next year, the band had its first No. 1 hit with their second single, "Step That Step."

Despite their initial success, Sawyer Brown experienced a backlash from many country radio stations, which found their music a bit too slickly produced. By 1987 their singles had plummeted to the bottom half of the charts, until "This Missin' You Heart of Mine" became a No. 2 hit in early 1988. Their next major hit came in 1989 with "The Race Is On." The album it was pulled from, *The Boys Are Back*, did equally well on the charts. During the low spots, Sawyer Brown honed their live act with plenty of touring. In late 1991 they burst back onto the country music scene with *The Dirt Road*, which produced two Top Five hits.

After its release, the group enjoyed their greatest period of success, as they produced a string of Top 10 hits and successful albums like 1993's *Outskirts of Town* and 1995's *This Thing Called Wantin' and Havin' It All*. —*Sandra Brennan*

Sawyer Brown / 1985 / Capitol ◆◆◆

Sawyer Brown / Feb. 26, 1987 / Liberty ◆◆◆

The Boys Are Back / Jun. 1989 / Liberty ◆◆◆

Greatest Hits / Aug. 27, 1990 / Liberty ◆◆◆◆

Buick / Jan. 7, 1991 / Liberty ◆◆◆
More songs about girls and cars—or, better yet, girls in cars. "The Walk" did so well as a single, the group included it on the next album, too. —*Brian Mansfield*

Cafe on the Corner / 1992 / Capitol ◆◆◆◆
By *Cafe on the Corner*, the members of Sawyer Brown had essentially (i.e., for recording purposes at least) given up on being rock 'n' rollers and revealed themselves to be a pretty decent country band. "Cafe on the Corner" paints a graphic picture of small-town desolation, but these guys are smart enough to avoid preaching: most of the album reflects the marvels of love. The rock 'n' roll sneaks back in on the last two cuts, but by then it's too late to matter. A album filled with good songs, it also includes a great one (Mac McAnally's "All These Years"). —*Brian Mansfield*

The Dirt Road / Jan. 6, 1992 / Liberty ◆◆◆
The band's robust work ethic makes it into these songs about simple life and small-town values, and Mark Miller controls a tendency to over-sing them, maybe because he believes them. Miller's heart is still filled with cliches like "Burning Bridges (On a Rocky Road)," but the sleaze in his voice is convincing on "Ruby Red Shoes," which has to be a song of lust for Judy Garland. —*Brian Mansfield*

● **Greatest Hits 1990-1995** / 1995 / Curb ◆◆◆◆
Greatest Hits 1990-1995 is a solid retrospective of Sawyer Brown's career highlights, featuring nearly all of their biggest hits. —*David Jehnzen*

Don Schlitz

b. Aug. 29, 1952, Durham, NC
Contemporary Country, Urban Cowboy

A 1993 inductee into the Nashville Songwriters Hall of Fame, Don Schlitz was one of Nashville's preeminent songwriters and the author of numerous chart-topping hits. He was a native of Durham, NC, and after a short stint at Duke University in the early '70s, he moved to Nashville to seek his fortune, working as a swing-shift computer operator for five years while honing his songwriting skills. Schlitz got his big break in 1978 when Kenny Rogers had a monster hit with his "The Gambler." The No. 1 smash not only became one of Rogers' signature songs, but spawned a series of TV-movies; later, Schlitz recorded and released his own version of the hit on his debut album, *Dreamers Matinee*. During the '80s, many other prominent artists recorded his songs, including John Conlee, Alabama, Randy Travis, Tanya Tucker, and Keith Whitley. Schlitz frequently co-wrote songs with Paul Overstreet; one of their most distinguished collaborations was "Forever and Ever Amen," which became an enormous hit for Randy Travis. In 1987 Schlitz wrote or co-wrote five No. 1 singles, including "On the Other Hand," another hit for Travis. He continued steadily churning out hit songs and was even commissioned by President George Bush to compose a theme for his "Points of Light" campaign in the early '90s. —*Sandra Brennan*

● **Dreamers Matinee** / 1980 / Capitol ◆◆◆◆

Timothy B. Schmit

b. Oct. 30, 1947, Sacramento, CA
Bass, Vocals / Country-Rock, Pop-Rock

Although he delivered a number of solo records, Timothy B. Schmit earned his greatest fame as a vocalist with the Eagles and Poco, two of the era's most successful mainstream country rock outfits. Born October 30, 1947, in Sacramento, CA, Schmit joined Poco before recording the band's 1971 LP *Deliverin',* and remained with the group for nine more albums. After the release of the band's 1977 *Indian Summer,* he was invited to join the Eagles, signing on, ironically enough, as a replacement for another former Poco member, Randy Meisner. Schmit's arrival coincided with the sessions for the Eagles' final LP, 1979's *The Long Run;* his contribution, "I Can't Tell You Why," proved to be a tremendous hit.

After internal dissent triggered the Eagles' break-up in 1982, Schmit began a solo career, issuing three LPs—1984's *Playin' It Cool,* 1987's *Timothy B,* and 1990's *Tell Me the Truth.* He rejoined Poco for 1984's *Inomorata* and was also a popular guest musician, appearing on dozens of records, including solo projects from onetime bandmates like Don Henley, Don Felder, and Richie Furay as well as LPs from Crosby, Stills and Nash, Jimmy Buffett, and Bob Seger. In 1989 Poco again reunited for the album *Legacy,* and in 1992 Schmit joined Ringo Starr's All-Starr Band, performing his showcase number "I Can't Tell You Why" on a live LP recorded in Montreux. Shortly after, the Eagles ended months of speculation by announcing a reunion of the band's *Long Run-era lineup; the subsequent tour and live LP, both dubbed Hell Freezes Over,* were incredibly successful, reaffirming the Eagles' status as one of the world's most popular artists. *—Jason Ankeny*

● **Tell Me the Truth** / 1983 / MCA ✦✦✦✦

Playing It Cool / 1984 / Asylum ✦✦✦

Timothy B. / 1987 / MCA ✦✦✦

Schramms

Alternative Country-Rock
The country-folk group Schramms drew their name from singer/guitarist Dave Schramm, a New York musician and veteran of critics' darlings like the Human Switchboard and Yo La Tengo. After playing on the latter's debut LP *Ride the Tiger,* he left the band to form his own unit, originally called the Walking Wounded. After learning of a Los Angeles band performing under the same name, they jokingly became the Schramms for a handful of performances, only to see the name stick permanently.

In addition to frontman Schramm, the outfit's original lineup featured ex-Human Switchboard drummer Ron Metz and bassist Terry Karydes, who switched over to the organ after her original instrument was stolen. The group soon swelled to include new bassist Mike Lewis, also a Yo La Tengo alum, as well as guitarist Todd Novak and saxophonist Pete Linzell. After recording their 1990 debut *Walk to Delphi,* the three new additions left the group, followed shortly thereafter by Karydes. Stepping in were bassist Al Greller, formerly of the Tall Lonesome Pines and Peter Stampfel and the Bottlecaps, and organist George Usher, late of the Bongos and Beat Rodeo. With their lineup firmly in place, the Schramms issued their second record, *Rock, Paper, Scissors, Dynamite,* in 1992. *Little Apocalypse* appeared in 1994, followed two years later by *Dizzy Spell. —Jason Ankeny*

● **Walk to Delphi** / 1990 / Okra ✦✦✦✦

Rock, Paper, Scissors, Dynamite / Oct. 3, 1995 / East Side Digital ✦✦✦✦

Schuyler Knobloch & Bickhardt

Contemporary Country, Country-Folk
Thom Schuyler, J. Fred Knobloch, and Craig Bickhardt were three prominent Nashville songwriters who briefly got together to form a rather eclectic band that played a blend of country, folk, and pop. Originally formed in 1986 as Schuyler, Knobloch and Overstreet (with songwriter Paul Overstreet), the trio signed with MTM Records. Their debut single, "You Can't Stop Love," made it to the country Top Ten and remained on the charts more than six months. The band changed its name to the more manageable S-K-O in 1987. Overstreet left to pursue his own songwriting career, and Craig Bickhardt replaced him. The title track of S-K-B's *No Easy Horses* hit the Top 20, and the trio's next cut, "This Old House," made it to the Top 25. When MTM folded, they found themselves without a contract and disbanded soon after. Schuyler has since become the vice president of RCA's country division, while Knobloch and Bickhardt have continued to write excellent songs. *—Sandra Brennan*

● **No Easy Horses** / MTM ✦✦✦✦

Tracy Schwarz

b. Nov. 13, 1938, New York City, NY
Fiddle, Session Musician / Traditional Bluegrass, Cajun
Tracy Schwarz is one of the greatest traditional fiddlers in America. His credits run from the New Lost City Ramblers and the Strange Creek Singers to recordings with other traditional musicians, his family, and in more recent years with many Cajun greats.

New York City-born and raised, Schwarz first came to love country music from radio broadcasts of the late '40s. The music he heard inspired him to learn the banjo and guitar. While in college, Schwarz also mastered the mandolin and the bass fiddle. He soon began playing in assorted bluegrass bands around Washington, DC. During the early '60s, Schwarz enlisted in the Army for two years and during that time learned to play the fiddle. He began working with the New Lost City Ramblers as a replacement for Tom Paley in 1962, and eventually became a full-time member for ten years; his involvement in the band later tapered off as he became more interested in spending time on his Pennsylvania farm. He continued to appear with other bands, most notably the Strange Creek Singers, through the 1970s. He continues to perform and explore new areas of traditional music. *—Sandra Brennan & Don Stevens*

● **Home Among the Hills** / Bear Family ✦✦✦✦

Jack Scott (Jack Scafone Jr)

b. Jan. 24, 1936, Windsor, Ontario, Canada
Guitar, Vocals / Rock & Roll, Traditional Country, Rockabilly
Jack Scott sounded tough, like someone you wouldn't want to meet in a dark alley unless he had a guitar in his hands. When he growled "The Way I Walk," wise men (and women) stepped aside. Despite his snarling rockabilly attitude, Scott hailed from Ontario, Canada, and grew up near Detroit, developing a love for hillbilly music along the way. His first sides for ABC-Paramount in 1957 exhibited a profound country-rock synthesis, and after moving to the Carlton label, Scott hit the charts the next year with the tremulous ballad "My True Love," backed by his vocal group, the Chantones. Flip it over, however, and you have the hauling rocker "Leroy," all about some wacked-out tough guy who's content to remain behind the bars of his local jail. Scott's pronounced emphasis on acoustic guitar distinguishes atmospheric rockers like "Goodbye Baby," "Go Wild Little Sadie," "Midgie," and "Geraldine." But his principal pop success came with tears-in-your-beer country-based ballads—"What in the World's Come Over You" and "Burning Bridges" were massive smashes on Top Rank in 1960, and he recorded an entire album's worth of Hank Williams covers for the firm the same year.

Scott moved to a town on the outskirts of Detroit when he was ten years old. At the age of 18, he formed the Southern Drifters, and after leading the band for three years, he signed to ABC as a solo artist in 1957. Over the next year, he released a handful of singles for the label, before moving to Carlton Records the following year. His double-A-sided debut for Carlton, "My True Love" / "Leroy," was a huge hit, with the first song peaking at No. 3 and thaelatter at No. 11; it also became a Top Ten hit in England. During the next two years, Scott had a number of minor hits for Carlton, highlighted by the No. 8 hit "Goodbye Baby" (fall 1958). On most of these tracks, the Chantones provided vocal support.

Late in 1959 he switched labels, signing with Top Rank. His first single for the label, "What in the World's Come Over You," became a No. 5 hit early in 1960. It was followed a few months later by another Top Ten hit, the No. 3 single "Burning Bridges." The singles were his last major hits, and over the next two years his singles charted at progressively lower positions. Early in 1961 he signed with Capitol Records, but none of his three singles made the Top 40.

Scott continued to vacillate between cowboy crooner and rough-edged rocker throughout the remainder of the '60s and '70s, recording for a variety of labels, including Groove and Dot. In 1974 he managed to have a minor country hit with his Dot single "You're Just Gettin' Better." During the '80s and '90s, Scott occasionally turned up on the oldies circuit, still looking and sounding like a man you didn't want to mess with. *—Bill Dahl*

Scott on Groove / 1989 / Bear Family ✦✦✦✦
The music on *Scott on Groove* was recorded after Jack Scott's hit-making era on Capitol was finished. Scott recorded for Groove in the early '60s. During this time, he was trying to refashion his sound in a rock 'n' roll/rockabilly direction. Not all of the attempts were successful. The set is interesting for dedicated fans, but they would probably rather acquire this material on the more comprehensive box set, *Classic Scott. —Stephen Thomas Erlewine*

Capitol Collectors Series / Oct. 8, 1990 / Capitol ✦✦✦✦

Classic Scott / Bear Family ✦✦✦✦
Bear Family's *Classic Scott* in a four-disc, 158-track box set that contains all of Jack Scott's recordings for Capitol from the '50s, as well as a selection of material he recorded for smaller, independent labels like Groove in the early '60s. While the set is far too comprehensive for casual fans, it is ideal for collectors and worth their investment. *—Stephen Thomas Erlewine*

● **Greatest Hits** / Curb ✦✦✦✦
Curb's *Greatest Hits* was the only American Jack Scott compilation available in the mid-'90s, after Capitol pulled its *Collector's Series* from the market. Although *Greatest Hits* has only 11 tracks—including a recently recorded version of "Running Scared"—it has the essential big hits ("My True Love," "Goodbye Baby," "Burning Bridges," "Leroy," "The Way I Walk," "What in the World's Come Over You") and is a serviceable collection, even if it is frustratingly brief. *—Stephen Thomas Erlewine*

Scratch Band

Country-Pop
The Scratch Band was best remembered as Don Williams' backing unit, but in 1982 the quartet stepped into the limelight to record their own album, *The Scratch Band Featuring Danny Flowers*. Lead guitarist and frontman Flowers, a native of North Carolina, arrived in Nashville around 1971, where he worked as a session guitarist; he met Williams during one of these sessions. Flowers was also a songwriter; in 1973, Emmylou Harris recorded his "Before Believing."

Flowers joined Williams' band in 1974. Four years later, he wrote "Tulsa Time" while stranded in that city during a snow storm, and it became a No. 1 hit for Williams; Eric Clapton later recorded the song, as well. Keyboard player and guitarist Biff Watson was born and raised in Virginia and he, too, came to Nashville in 1971, where he joined Tennessee Pulleybone and went on to work with Tracy Nelson and Crystal Gayle's band Peace and Quiet. He joined Williams in 1979. Bass guitarist Dave Pomeroy was raised in Alexandria, VA, and briefly studied history in college before dropping out to become a full-time musician. After playing with other bands, he toured with Sleepy LaBeef and came to Music City in 1978. He joined Williams in 1980 after working with Guy Clark and Billy Joe Shaver. Drummer Pat McInerney was born and raised in England. He earned a college degree in sociology and in 1974 became a full-time musician, playing with Jimmy James and the Vagabonds, a popular soul band. By 1976 he was playing in a rock band, Limey, and later subbed for Williams' drummer during a European tour in 1977. He ended up joining Williams' band the next year. After releasing their only album, Scratch went back to working with Williams until he stopped touring. *—Sandra Brennan*

The Scratch Band / 1977 / Big Sound ✦✦✦
● **The Scratch Band Featuring Danny Flowers** / 1982 / MCA ✦✦✦✦

Earl Scruggs (Earl Eugene Scruggs)

b. Jan. 6, 1924, Flint Hill, NC
Banjo / Traditional Bluegrass
Earl Scruggs is to the five-string banjo what Paganini was to the violin. After more than 20 years with the Foggy Mountain Boys, forming the most famous band in bluegrass history, Scruggs and

Scudd Mountain Boys

Lester Flatt parted company in 1969 because of artistic differences, with Flatt pursuing more traditional sounds and Scruggs forming the Earl Scruggs Revue with his two sons. The Revue appealed more to a young and urban audience and, with dobro player Josh Graves, played rock and other non-country music. Scruggs has made many albums since his parting with Flatt (including *The Storyteller and the Banjoman* with Tom T. Hall in 1982) and is seen on TV, often for reunion appearances. *—David Vinopal*

● **Dueling Banjos** / 1973 / Columbia ✦✦✦✦
A classic album. Scruggs shines on this one. *—Chip Renner*

Scud Mountain Boys

Indie Rock, Alternative Country-Rock
The cult popularity of Uncle Tupelo and its spinoff groups Wilco and Son Volt has opened the doors for what's become an entire new generation of musicians who grew up in the punk-rock generation but have found genuine connection with traditional country music—especially as interpreted through Gram Parsons, who's more or less the granddaddy of country-rock. The Scud Mountain Boys—Joe Pernice, Stephen Desaulniers, Bruce Tull, and Tom Shea—clearly fit into this camp.

The band originally played electric rock 'n' roll under the name the Scuds. Pernice, Desaulniers, and Tull formed the group in Northampton, MA, in 1991, and they gained a respectable local following. But the band members soon tired of hauling equipment around and found they much more enjoyed the after-show get-togethers playing acoustic country songs around the kitchen table at home. Finally they decided to haul the kitchen table to a club. Finding the response positive, they've kept with the new format.

The band's debut album, "Pine Box" (originally just a cassette release), features slow, intensely quiet originals alongside covers of '70s pop-country songs such as "Gypsies, Tramps and Thieves" and "Please, Mister, Please." It was literally recorded live around the kitchen table. Their second album, *Dance the Night Away*—which added a couple of rock songs from their Scuds days into the mix again—came out on Chunk Records in 1995, and national interest in the band grew quickly. In early 1996 they were signed to Sub Pop, and the label released the band's third album in less than two years, *Massachusetts. —Kurt Wolff*

Dance the Night Away / 1995 / Chunk ✦✦✦✦
Dance the Night Away, one of two albums the Scud Mountain Boys released in 1995 (*Pine Box* was the other), is a quiet but immediately compelling collection of 13 original songs plus two covers—one being the Jimmy Webb pop classic "Where's the Playground, Susie," which is likely the most reverent version of the song this side of Glen Campbell's. (Chunk Records, Box 244, Easthampton, Mass., 01027) *—Kurt Wolf*

Pine Box / 1995 / Chunk ✦✦✦✦

Originally released only on cassette, the Massachusetts label Chunk made this album available on vinyl as well. Contains beautiful, delicate original acoustic songs as well as covers of "Gypsies, Tramps and Thieves," "Please, Mister, Please," and "Wichita Lineman" that are as fun in spirit as they are moving. Recorded with a single mike in guitarist Bruce Tull's kitchen in Northampton, MA. —*Kurt Wolff*

● **Massachusetts** / Apr. 1996 / Sub Pop ✦✦✦✦

In just a short time, the Scud Mountain Boys have risen from relative obscurity (two 1995 albums for indie label Chunk) to a well-earned spot on the Sub Pop roster. The Boys' new album, *Massachusetts*, is once again a quiet, mostly acoustic collection of soft-spoken songs based on spare country rhythms and laidback, whisper-light melodies. *Massachusetts* is more down-to-earth than the faux-hillbilly ramble poems of Palace Music, but also far less Americana-ized than Son Volt or any of the No Depression hangers-on. The sudden national attention seems not to have spooked the Scuds, and so while *Massachusetts* feels better-crafted than the band's previous two albums—more mature in terms of songwriting—it retains the easy-going, kitchen-table spirit that marked the band's earlier work. This is music that moves slowly but grows on you quickly. —*Kurt Wolff*

Dan Seals

b. 1948, McCamey, TX

Guitar, Vocals / Country-Pop, Adult Contemporary, Soft Rock

One of the most popular members of the musical Seals family, singer-songwriter Dan Seals had a string of hit singles in the '70s as part of the duo England Dan and John Ford Coley and as a solo performer in the '80s with his country-inflected soft rock. Seals was born in McCamey, TX. At the age of four, he learned to play string bass and began playing with the Seals Family band. Eventually Dan's parents divorced and he remained with his mother. For the next few years, they moved throughout the state before settling in Dallas in 1958. During high school, Seals played in a variety of garage rock bands, which is how he met John Ford Coley. In 1965 Seals, Coley, and Shane Keister recorded some demos in Nashville under the name the Shimmerers, but their producer died before he could secure a record contract for the group. In 1967 the trio switched their name to the Southwest F.O.B. and released their debut single, "The Smell of Incense," which reached the national pop charts. Despite the promising success of the record, however, the group's next three singles all stiffed.

In 1969 Seals and Coley left the group to form a soft-rock duo. After failing to land a record contract in California, the duo returned to Texas, where, performing under the name England Dan and John Ford Coley, they were signed to A&M. Their first singles for the label didn't sell well, and the label dropped the duo in 1973. For the next few years they played clubs. In 1976 they recorded a demo of a song called "I'd Really Love to See You Tonight" and began shopping the tape to various record labels. The single became England Dan and John Ford Coley's breakthrough hit in the summer of 1976, peaking at No. 2 on the US pop charts. The duo's follow-up, "Nights Are Forever Without You," reached the Top Ten and the group's album, also titled *Nights Are Forever Without You*, went gold by the end of 1976. Throughout the late '70s, the group had a string of pop and adult contemporary hits.

In 1980 Seals left the duo and pursued a solo career, signing with Atlantic Records; he was still billed as England Dan. His first solo single became a moderate pop hit in the fall of 1980. In 1981 Seals went through a devastating battle with the IRS. By the end of the year, he had lost virtually everything he had, leaving him almost destitute. In 1983 he began to focus on breaking the country market. The shift in style worked—he had three Top 40 hits that year, including "Everybody's Dream Girl." He had three Top Ten hits in 1984, and in 1985 began a streak of nine straight No. 1 hits with "Meet Me in Montana," a duet with Marie Osmond. Seals continually charted in the Top Ten until the end of 1990,

when mainstream country shifted away from his pop-inflected soft country. In 1991 Seals signed a contract with Warner Brothers Records, releasing *Walking the Wire* the next year. Neither the album or its singles were hits, and the vocalist effectively retired from recording in the mid-'90s, choosing to concentrate on touring instead. —*Sandra Brennan*

San Antone / 1984 / Capitol ✦✦✦

I Won't Be Blue Anymore / 1985 / EMI America ✦✦✦

● **The Best of Dan Seals** / 1987 / Liberty ✦✦✦✦

The Best of Dan Seals contains 11 of Seals' smooth contemporary country hits from the mid— and late '80s, including the No. 1 singles "Three Time Loser," "You Still Move Me," "Bop," "Everything That Glitters (Is Not Gold)," "Meet Me in Montana," "I Will Be There," and "One Friend." A couple of hits are missing, but every truly essential item is here, making it the best retrospective of Seals' hit-making peak. —*Thom Owens*

Classics Collection, Vol. 1 / 1988 / Liberty ✦✦✦

Featured are "Meet Me in Montana," "God Must Be a Cowboy," "My Baby's Got Good Timing," and more. —*AMG*

Rage On / 1988 / Liberty ✦✦✦✦

On *Rage On*, Seals tells stories woven around traditional country themes while rarely resorting to country cliches. "Addicted," "They Rage On," "Five Generations of Rock County Wilsons"—these are tales of quiet desperation, and the empathy in Seals' voice makes their impact devastating. Almost as good as his *Best*. —*Brian Mansfield*

On Arrival / Nov. 1990 / Liberty ✦✦✦

This is the product of a man very much in touch with his emotions. In "Bordertown," "A Heart in Search of Love" and "Wood," he works the listener's heart with the skill of a surgeon. At the same time, "Good Times" and "Love on Arrival" are incredibly celebratory. —*Tom Roland*

Greatest Hits / 1991 / Liberty ✦✦✦

Greatest Hits contains Dan Seals' biggest contemporary country hits from the late '80s, including the No. 1 singles "Addicted," "Big Wheels in the Moonlight," "Bop," and "Everything That Glitters (Is Not Gold)," among other hits. Though it is a good collection, *The Best of Dan Seals* edges *Greatest Hits* out slightly, due to its larger concentration of big hits. —*Thom Owens*

Early Dan Seals / 1991 / Liberty ✦✦✦✦

As the title indicates, this anthology draws from Seals' first several years as a country artist; although a few songs were hits, including "Three Time Loser," "My Baby's Got Good Timing" and "My Old Yellow Car," most never cracked the charts. —*Jason Ankeny*

Walking the Wire / 1991 / Warner Brothers ✦✦✦

It features "A Good Rain," "We Are One," and "Mason Dixon Line," among others. —*AMG*

The Songwriter / Apr. 27, 1992 / Liberty ✦✦✦✦

Ths album contains such hits as "One Friend," "Wood," "Love on Arrival," "Three-Time Loser," and others. —*AMG*

In a Quiet Room / Oct. 1995 / Intersound ✦✦

In a Quiet Room is an acoustic album featuring Dan Seals running through a number of his biggest hits, as well as two new songs, one of which—"The Healing Kind"—boasts a guest appearance by Alison Krauss. It's a pleasant album, yet it doesn't offer any new revelations or great performances, which means it's a record only hardcore fans need to pick up. —*Thom Owens*

Dawn Sears

Vocals / Contemporary Country, Alternative Country, Americana

Dawn Sears owns a brash, emotionally convincing voice that grabs a song with impressive authority—she's sort of a modern Wanda Jackson with just a touch of polish, or Brenda Lee with more honky tonk feeling. Her excellent debut didn't receive much a chance from her record company, but she recently signed with Decca Records after a couple of years of singing harmony in Vince Gill's band. —*Michael McCall*

● **What a Woman Wants to Hear** / Oct. 15, 1991 / Warner Brothers ✦✦✦✦

Her powerful debut, produced by Barry Beckett, reveals her ability with a forceful country-rocker ("Good Goodbye") as well as a touching ballad ("'Til You Come Back to Me."). —*Michael McCall*

Jeannie Seely

b. Jul. 16, 1940, Titusville, PA
Vocals / Traditional Country, Country-Pop
A Pennsylvanian who started performing on the radio at age 11, Jeannie Seely is associated almost as strongly with her duet partners—Porter Wagoner, Ernest Tubb, and Jack Greene—as she is with her own music. Her first single, "Don't Touch Me," won her a Grammy in 1967, and she continued to have charting hits for the next 11 years. Most of her material came from fellow country songwriter (and eventual husband) Hank Cochran. She has been a cast member of the Grand Ole Opry since 1967. —*Brian Mansfield*

Seely Style / 1966 / Monument ✦✦✦

Thanks Hank / 1967 / Monument ✦✦✦

● **Greatest Hits on Monument** / 1993 / Monument ✦✦✦✦
Seely recorded her hits for four labels—Decca, MCA, Columbia, and Monument—and much of that material is currently out of print. These Monument recordings document only about the first three years of her career, but they include some great records, especially "Don't Touch Me," "'I'll Love You More (Than You Need)," and the brutally fatalistic "It's Only Love." —*Brian Mansfield*

Seldom Scene

Progressive Bluegrass
"Old-fashioned" was never a word used to describe Seldom Scene's take on bluegrass. Since their inception in 1971, the Washington DC-based group remained a driving force in "newgrass" and was considered among the finest modern bands around.

The Seldom Scene began as a one-off jam session but quickly grew into something much more permanent. The band's founder, John Duffey, had spent 12 years as a charter member of the Country Gentlemen. A rather flamboyant character onstage, he was noted for playing amazing solos on the mandolin, dobro, and guitar, and for his powerful, exceptionally flexible voice. Banjoist Ben Eldridge was a veteran of Cliff Waldron's New Shades of Grass, as was Mike Auldridge, considered among the top dobro players in the world. These three distinguished musicians formed the band's core and remained together through the mid-'90s. Other charter members included former Country Gentleman Tom Gray and John Starling, a former army surgeon. By the summer of 1971 the group was touring on the bluegrass festival circuit and soon found themselves quite popular on the East Coast.

The original lineup of the Seldom Scene recorded seven albums for independent Rebel Records in the first half of the '70s. In 1977 Starling left and was replaced by Phil Rosenthal; in 1986, Rosenthal was replaced by Lou Reid, and Gray was replaced with electric bassist T. Michael Coleman. Starling returned to the Seldom Scene in 1993, replacing Reid in the band's lineup. By 1995 Starling had left again; he was replaced by Moondi Klein. In 1996 the Seldom Scene's lineup fractured, as half the group left the band to form Chesapeake. The remaining members released *Dream Scene;* on December 10, 1996, John Duffey died after suffering a heart attack. —*Sandra Brennan*

Act One / 1972 / Rebel ✦✦✦
Seldom Scene's debut album *Act One* established the band as a trailblazing bluegrass outfit, one that kept the sound of traditional bluegrass intact but infused it with a contemporary sensibility. Out of all of their albums, *Act One* is the most vibrant—it's teeming with life and possibility, as well as skillful, graceful musicianship. —*Thom Owens*

Act Two / 1973 / Rebel ✦✦✦✦
They cover some good songs by Gene Clark and B. Lead on "Train Leaves Here," Norman Blake's "Last Train," and Hank Williams' "House of Gold." —*Chip Renner*

Act Three / 1973 / Rebel ✦✦✦
Seldom Scene's *Act Three* is a low-key but entertaining progressive bluegrass album, capturing several of the genre's best musicians—including John Duffey, Ricky Skaggs, Mike Auldridge, John Starling, Ben Eldridge, and Tom Gray—at the very beginning of their career. None of the musicians over-emphasizes his skills, even on the jam "Rider," and the result is a subtly impressive set of excellent harmonies and brief, enticing instrumental leads. —*Thom Owens*

Old Train / 1974 / Rebel ✦✦✦
Catch this album featuring Duffy, Starling, Eldridge, Auldridge, and Gray, plus Linda Ronstadt, Ricky Skaggs, Paul Craft, and Bob Williams. Includes a good cover of "Pan American." —*Chip Renner*

Live at the Cellar Door / 1975 / Rebel ✦✦✦
A two-record set of a very good live show from the mid-'70s, with covers of "City of New Orleans," "Raw Hide," and "If I Were a Carpenter." —*Chip Renner*

New Seldom Scene Album / 1976 / Rebel ✦✦✦✦
Duffey, Starling, Auldridge, Eldridge, and Gray put out one of the best bluegrass albums ever. Linda Ronstadt sings with them on one song. It doesn't get much better than this. —*Chip Renner*

Act Four / 1978 / Sugar Hill ✦✦✦
Features a good cover of Bob Wills' "San Antonio Rose." —*Chip Renner*

Baptizing / 1978 / Rebel ✦✦✦
An enjoyable gospel album, with guest Ricky Skaggs. —*Chip Renner*

After Midnight / 1981 / Sugar Hill ✦✦✦
Good vocals, with covers of Eric Clapton's "Lay Down Sally" and J. J. Cale's "After Midnight." —*Chip Renner*

15th Anniversary Celebration / Feb. 1981 / Sugar Hill ✦✦✦✦
A 20-song live CD with Duffey, Auldridge, Mike Reid, Eldridge, and Gray. A must for fans, with special guests galore—Emmylou Harris, Ricky Skaggs, Linda Ronstadt, John Starling, Tony Rice, Jonathan Edwards, and others. —*Chip Renner*

At the Scene / 1983 / Sugar Hill ✦✦✦
Highlighted by a cover of Jackson Browne's "Jamaica, Say You Will" and two original inspirational numbers, *At the Scene* is a typically impressive effort by the Seldom Scene that emphasizes their considerable instrumental and vocal skills. —*Thom Owens*

Blue Ridge / 1985 / Sugar Hill ✦✦✦✦
Songwriter and vocalist Jonathan Edwards ("Sunshine") teams with the Seldom Scene's flawless playing. Featuring Edwards, John Duffey, Mike Auldridge, Phil Rosenthal, Ben Eldridge, Tom Gray, Robbie Magruder, and Kenny White. —*Chip Renner*

● **Best of Seldom Scene, Vol. 1** / 1987 / Rebel ✦✦✦✦
The Best of Seldom Scene, Vol. 1 contains a sampling of the band's best songs from their first four albums and gives a good sense of what the band is about. —*Thom Owens*

Change of Scenery / 1988 / Sugar Hill ✦✦✦
Their vocal sound is changed here, but this is a first-class CD. Check out "West Texas Wind." —*Chip Renner*

Scenic Roots / 1990 / Sugar Hill ✦✦✦
With *Scenic Roots*, Seldom Scene returned to their traditional bluegrass roots. Although the music occasionally sounds forced, much of it is lively and wonderful, making the disc a worthwhile purchase for longtime fans, even if it isn't the place to start with this perennial bluegrass favorite. —*Thom Owens*

Scene 20: 20th Anniversary Concert / 1991 / Sugar Hill ✦✦✦
For their 20th anniversary, Seldom Scene held a concert and invited all of the former members of the group to join them onstage. Everyone turned up, and the results are captured on the splendidly entertaining *Scene 20: 20th Anniversary Concert.* Seldom Scene runs through a wide variety of material, playing everything from traditional bluegrass numbers to Wilson Pickett's "In the Midnight Hour." For fans of the group, this album is an unexpected and totally delightful treat. —*Thom Owens*

Shady Grove Band

Progressive Bluegrass, Traditional Bluegrass
The Shady Grove Band was a bluegrass quartet that played both traditional and newgrass. They were founded in the early '80s by singer/guitarist Jerry Brown in Chapel Hill, NC. Other band members included singer-songwriter/bassist Adael Shinn, who was born and raised in Kannapolis, NC, and got her start playing bass with such artists as Earl Scruggs and John Hartford; Charles Pettee, who played mandolin and wrote many of the songs; and banjo picker Jason Shore. Between 1985 and 1994, Shady Grove recorded four albums, including *The Chapel Hillbilly Way*. — *Sandra Brennan*

● **On the Line** / 198 / Flying Fish ◆◆◆◆
A good, solid bluegrass album. — *Chip Renner*

Mulberry Moon / 1990 / Flying Fish ◆◆◆◆
Same level as *On the Line*. — *Chip Renner*

Chapel Hillbilly Way / 1995 / Flying Fish ◆◆◆

Kevin Sharp

Vocals / Contemporary Country
Though Kevin Sharp has come to light in the country field, his music is heavily commercial and could easily fit in several different genres, considering his dance-inspired production, heavy emphasis on ballads, and his cover of the Tony Rich Project's "Nobody Knows."

Born in 1970 in rural northern California, Sharp first hit the stage at age three, performing at church with his musical parents and seven siblings. At age seven, he and his family moved to Weiser, ID—the home of the National Fiddle Festival—to begin a restaurant. Learning much about music from the fiddlers who packed Weiser every year for the festival, Sharp sang in local musicals and choral groups while in high school. The family moved back to California in 1985, but he stayed active in music, singing in choral groups and a Sacramento light-opera company while excelling at sports as well. He dreamed of a college football scholarship but began to experience periods of fatigue and dizziness in 1989. Doctors later diagnosed bone cancer and gave Sharp little chance to recover. After intensive radiation treatments permanently balded him, his prospects began to look even worse. Encouraged by the Make-a-Wish Foundation, Sharp asked to meet Los Angeles producer/songwriter David Foster, long an idol of his. The two became fast friends.

After years of treatment, Kevin Sharp finally beat cancer by 1993. He began working at the Great America theme park in Santa Clara, pitching a demo tape to various talent shows in the meantime. With David Foster's name still in his Rolodex, he called the producer and sent him a tape. Foster was at first hesitant but changed his mind after one song. Sharp was introduced to several country A&R representatives, made another demo, and was signed by Elektra/Asylum in 1995. His debut solo album *Measure of a Man* was released in November 1996 and hit the Top 20 country charts. — *John Bush*

● **Kevin Sharp** / Sep. 24, 1996 / Elektra/Asylum ◆◆◆◆
Kevin Sharp's eponymous debut album is essentially a countrified take on middle-of-the-road adult conemporary pop. Under the direction of producer David Foster, Sharp runs through a number of power ballads—including a cover of the Tony Rich Project's "Nobody Knows"—and tame dance-oriented uptempo numbers. Sharp is a fine, if rather faceless, singer—he sounds good, but he brings no spark to these expertly crafted backing tracks. In other words, it's pleasant background music, but it never grabs your attention. — *Thom Owens*

Billy Joe Shaver

b. Sep. 15, 1941, Corsicana, TX
Guitar, Vocals / Progressive Country, Country-Rock, Singer-Songwriter, Outlaw Country, Americana
Billy Joe Shaver never became a household name, but his songs—including "Good Christian Soldier," "Willie the Wandering Gypsy and Me," and "I Been to Georgia on a Fast Train"—became

country standards during the '70s, and his reputation among musicians and critics didn't diminish during the next two decades.

One of the best synopses of Billy Joe Shaver's upbringing is his own song, "I Been to Georgia on a Fast Train." When he sings that "my grandma's old-age pension is the reason that I'm standing here today," he ain't kidding. The "good Christian raising" and "eighth grade education"—not to mention being abandoned by his parents shortly after being born, working on his uncles' farms instead of going to high school, and losing part of his fingers during a job at a sawmill—are all part of his life story. "I got all my country learning," he sings, "picking cotton, raising hell, and bailing hay."

Shaver did a quick turn in the Navy and worked a series of nowhere jobs (including the one in the sawmill) before trying his luck in Nashville. After several back and forth trips between Texas and Tennessee that gained him no response, he appeared one day in 1968 in Bobby Bare's Nashville office, where he convinced Bare to listen to him play. Bare ended up giving him a writing job.

Shaver recorded one song for Mercury, "Chicken on the Ground," which went nowhere, but soon his songs began to see the light thanks to Kris Kristofferson ("Good Christian Soldier"), Tom T. Hall ("Willie the Wandering Gypsy and Me"), Bare ("Ride Me Down Easy"), and, later, the Allman Brothers ("Sweet Mama") and Elvis Presley ("You Asked Me To"). Shaver's real breakthrough, though, came in 1973 when Jennings recorded an album composed almost entirely of Shaver's songs, *Honky Tonk Heroes*—largely considered the first true "outlaw" album.

Shaver's debut album was *Old Five and Dimers Like Me*, produced by Kristofferson and released by Monument (Kristofferson's label) in 1973. Along with the title track, it contained the now-classic Shaver songs "Willie the Wandering Gypsy and Me" and the aforementioned "Georgia on a Fast Train." Shaver switched to MGM a year later, but no album materialized. "Raising hell" as he had sung, part of his lifestyle at the time, and it kept him out of sight for a couple years. In 1976 Shaver resurfaced with *When I Get My Wings* on Capricorn, and followed it up a year later with *Gypsy Boy*. Johnny Cash recorded Shaver's "I'm Just an Old Lump of Coal (But I'm Gonna Be a Diamond Some Day)" in 1978, a song Shaver wrote just after he chose to give up drugs and booze and turned to God for help. Religious references do crop up in his songs (including "Chunk of Coal"), but they never dominate the emotions or get in the way of the earthy rhythms and melodies.

Shaver switched labels again, this time to Columbia, in 1980, and recorded three more albums during the next decade: *I'm Just an Old Lump of Coal (But I'm Gonna Be a Diamond Some Day)*, *Billy Joe Shaver*, and *Salt of the Earth*. The latter was produced by Shaver with his son, Eddy, who has played on every Billy Joe record since *Old Chunk of Coal* (he also toured in Dwight Yoakam's band in the 1980s). After a few more years out of the spotlight, Billy Joe returned in 1993, this time recording under the name Shaver. *Tramp on Your Street*, released on Zoo/Praxis, featured Eddy on lead guitar and Billy Joe's own raspy but loveable voice, and coming out during a time when hunky hat acts were the new flavor in Nashville, it was quickly recognized as one of the strongest and hardest country records to hit the shelves in many years. Shaver toured regularly over the next couple of years and recorded a live album for Zoo, *Unshaven*, in 1995, but he was dropped by the label a year later. He's currently signed to Justice Records. — *Kurt Wolff*

Old Five and Dimers Like Me / 1973 / Monument ◆◆◆◆
Billy Joe Shaver's debut *Old Five and Dimers Like Me* is full of songs that Shaver wrote and that artists like Waylon Jennings, Tom T. Hall, and Johnny Cash scrambled to record. Though his readings of these songs weren't quite commercial enough to be hits, these were important songs that affected the way country music developed in the '70s. It's a must for anyone interested in good songwriting, as well as the development of outlaw country. — *Jim Worbois*

When I Get My Wings / 1976 / Capricorn ✦✦✦✦
Here's proof that his blend of sawdust-floor honkers and spiritually endowed ballads were in place from the start. — *Michael McCall*

I'm Just an Old Chunk of Coal / 1981 / Columbia ✦✦✦✦
Again, he combines straight-from-the-soul spirituals like the title cut with some of the most colorful honky tonk ever written, including "Fit to Kill and Going Out in Style" and "Saturday Night," as well as an astounding "Ragged Old Truck," in which he begins by contemplating suicide before deciding all he needs is a good, hard night on the town. — *Michael McCall*

Billy Joe Shaver / 1982 / Columbia ✦✦✦
As with the title, this is his most straightforward collection of Texas soul music. It includes a few remakes of earlier classics. — *Michael McCall*

Salt of the Earth / 1987 / Columbia ✦✦✦
A steady, blue-collar rock 'n' roll beat dominates most of the material here, with a few acoustic tunes mixed in. "Manual Labor" is one standout on an otherwise mediocre release. — *Kurt Wolff*

Tramp on Your Street / Aug. 10, 1993 / Zoo ✦✦✦✦
His rawest, rockingest setting comes courtesy of his guitar-slinging son, Eddie Shaver, who gooses his old man in all the right places. Then, on the more introspective tunes, the father dispenses his hard-earned wisdom in unforgettable fashion. It's a true classic. — *Michael McCall*

Unshaven: Live at Smith's Olde Bar / Jun. 27, 1995 / Zoo ✦✦✦✦
As anyone knows, seeing Billy Joe Shaver live is a religious experience. Add to that the firebrand guitar of son Eddy Shaver and you have a powderkeg of talent ready to explode. This, Billy Joe's only live recording, is proof that you can't keep a talent such as his out of the spotlight. Coming off the success of *Tramp on Your Street*, his first recording in many years and the first with Eddy and his own band, this disc is an historical event that captures not only the power of the performance, but the subtle, gentle spirit that is the man. Kicking off with the sizzling "The Hottest Thing in Town," which shows off the tight band that supports Billy Joe, the stage is set. Working through some old and some new compositions, every song is a Shaver orignal. "Georgia on a Fast Train" and "Old Chunk of Coal," longtime favorites that were covered by other less capable artists, come across as fresh. The Waylon Jennings hit that set off the explosion known as the Outlaw Movement during the 1970s, "Honky Tonk Heroes," is more heartfelt than ever. As sensuous and sexy as any performer who ever set foot on a stage, Billy Joe's writing and vocal delivery on "Love You 'Til the Cows Come Home" and the almost raunchy "Sweet Mama" evoke erotic longing from the listener. Heartfelt and tender, the man who has been compared to Hank Sr. in terms of talent and skill makes even the coldest heart feel again as he sings "Live Forever," joined by Eddy, and the definitive love song, "Because You Asked Me To." As with most artists who have attained spirituality, Billy Joe Shaver is not only far ahead of his time, but also outdistances 'most everyone else when he gets in front of a crowd. Obviously the centerpiece of the band, he is also gracious and humble, giving all the players their due and glowing in the success of the son he loves so well. This is one live recording that not only works, it is an important document commemorating a moment in the life of one of the world's most exalted artists. — *Jana Pendragon*

● **Restless Wind: The Legendary Billy Joe Shaver 1973-1987** / Oct. 1995 / Razor & Tie ✦✦✦✦
Restless Wind: The Legendary Billy Joe Shaver 1973-1987 covers the highlights of Shaver's acclaimed career effectively, providing a fine introduction to a distinctive, idiosyncratic singer-songwriter. — *Thom Owens*

Highway of Life / Justice ✦✦✦✦
This first disc on the prominent Texas label Justice Records is a thoughtful, more sensitive acoustic version of Billy Joe and Eddy. With a new lineup that includes California country fiddle phenomenon Brantley Kearns, *Highway of Life* is a poetic look back on the rough and tumble life that has been the fodder for Billy

Joe's artistry. A poet as well as bard and philosopher, Billy Joe is once again at the center of Shaver's performance and style. Starting off with "Yesterday Tomorrow Was Today," a wordsmith's delight, and ending with a love song, "The First and the Last Time," written especially for his loving wife Brenda Joyce Shaver, this release is revealing. The upbeat "West Texas Waltz" is moving in that it transports the listener back in time with its infectious and swaying rhythms, creating a romantic picture about dancing arm in arm with a lover beneath a clear and star-studded west Texas sky. Never at a loss to find humor in even his most introspective moments, "You're Only as Young as the Woman You Feel" is outstanding and makes a clear statement about growing older from a man's perspective. A different side of Billy Joe, Eddy and their band of merry men, but still a noteworthy project that adds new depth and scope to the legend of Billy Joe Shaver. — *Jana Pendragon*

George Beverly Shea

b. Feb. 1, 1909, Winchester, Ontario, Canada
Vocals / Country Gospel
Gospel vocalist George Beverly Shea spent most of his 45-year career closely associated with evangelist Billy Graham. His best-known song is "How Great Thou Art," which was written by Rev. Stuart K. Hine in the 1920s. Shea is also a distinguished writer of popular hymns such as "The Wonder of It All." Born the son of a Wesleyan Methodist minister in Winchester, Ontario, he was raised in the New York area and spent much time as a youth singing in church choirs. He briefly attended Houghton College in New York, dropping out when his family's financial difficulties necessitated it. Shea began working as a clerk, but he received voice lessons and sang in churches and on local religious radio stations. The latter led to an audition for the Lynn Murray Singers, but he declined their invitation because they sang secular music. He married his high-school sweetheart in 1934 and moved to Chicago. After ten years in the Windy City, Shea got national exposure when he was hired to appear on "Club Time," a show he sang with for the next eight years. During this time Shea also became prominent in the Youth for Christ movement of the 1940s and '50s. He hooked up with Graham in 1947 and signed to RCA Victor in 1951. *Southland Favorites* received a 1965 Grammy for Best Gospel or Other Religious Recording (Musical). Shea was inducted by the Gospel Music Association Hall of Fame in 1978. — *Sandra Brennan*

Christmas with George Beverly Shea / Aug. 26, 1992 / Essex ✦✦✦

Moments, Vol. 1 / 1996 / Starsong ✦✦✦

Christmas Hymns / Special Music ✦✦

Bev Shea and Friends / Word ✦✦✦

Collector's Series / RCA ✦✦✦✦

Early in the Morning / Word ✦✦✦

● **My Favorite Songs (Best of George Beverly Shea)** / Word ✦✦✦✦

The Old Rugged Cross / Word ✦✦✦

Rick Shea

Bakersfield Sound, California Country
The son of a career Air Force officer, Rick Shea was born in 1953 when the family was stationed at Annapolis. As a child, Shea and his family traveled wherever the Air Force sent them. The elder Shea retired to San Bernardino, CA, when Rick was in junior high. This was the starting point for Shea's association with California's country music and the Bakersfield sound.
Shea is an alumnus of volume three of the *A Town South of Bakersfield* project, and his song "Foot in the Fire" continues to be popular. However, before there was even an inkling of a project like the *TSOB* compilation series, Shea had to discover the guitar. He began to play in bands and gig from the time he was in seventh or eighth grade. By high school he had discovered Merle Haggard. After high school he did acoustic solo dates wherever he could. He also began learning the basics of recording. Hanging

out in studios owned by friends and other players gave him the education he would need.

In 1989 Rick Shea released his first project, which featured a striking duet with another California country singer who also scored with the *TSOB* project, Patty Booker. *Outside of Nashville*, produced with Wyman Reese and John Lee White III, was a good record of Shea's career progress. A popular player around Los Angeles, he was often featured with Chris Gaffney and Brantley Kearns, and he recorded with Heather Miles.

A steel player as well as a guitarist, his songs were often scooped up by other performers, as is the case with his "Bed of Roses," which was included on Cody Bryant's debut disc. A 1995 CD, *Buffalo Show,* caught the attention of Americana radio, and included story songs like "The Rattlesnake Daddy's Daughter," "Georgia Pines," and several Tex-Mex numbers sung in Spanish. In 1997 Shea went into the studio to record his next project. He was also a member of the band $1000 Wedding, joining old friend Wyman Reese as well as former Plowboy Tracy Huffman. As a sideline, he was known to do a little journalism. His review of the George Jones bio was published in the *L.A. Times* during the summer of 1996. *—Jana Pendragon*

Outside of Nashville / 1989 / Independent ✦✦✦✦
This first effort by Rick Shea, available only on cassette, establishes him firmly in the California country tradition. A follower of Merle Haggard, Shea's work here reflects that preference. Outstanding even in 1989, Shea makes a stunning debut, and his Bonnie Owens-Merle Haggard-esque duet with Patty Booker on "A House Divided" speaks volumes about the potency of the duet as an art form. Also good are Shea's "Against My Better Judgement," "Guns That Blaze Like Thunder," and the Shea-Gary Brandlin tune "Every Rose." *—Jana Pendragon*

● **The Buffalo Show** / 1995 / Major Label ✦✦✦✦
In the years since Shea's first release, *Outside of Nashville,* he has developed into a songwriter of uncommon talent. This sophomore release takes the listener on one sweet ride. Reflecting the culture of Southern California as much as the honky tonk culture of which he is a part, Shea's work here is dark and moody as well as picturesque. "Georgia Pines" is a mountain tale that enchants the listener with its imagery, as does "Sycamore Grove." "Border Town Girl" reveals the clash that takes place when two cultures meet. Another song that stands out is "One More Night," a joint venture between Shea and Wyman Reese. With good production, again Shea is assisted by Reese, John Lee White III, and Gary Mandell. The musicianship is exceptional, with artists like Brantley Kearns, Chris Gaffney, Skip Edwards, Keith Rosier, and Reese filling up the band. Background and harmony vocals are handled by Jann Browne, Heather Miles, Lonesome Stranger Randy Weeks, Gaffney, and Reese. An all-star lineup that results in a project that will remain solid and a sparkling representation of the artistry involved. *—Jana Pendragon*

Shenandoah

Contemporary Country
Most country groups of the '80s favored a commercial pop-oriented approach that alienated many traditional listeners but captured the ear of the mainstream. Shenandoah was one of the first groups to rebel against the urban cowboy image of the '80s and lead the way to the roots-country of the '90s. The group was initially formed in 1985 as a house band in Muscle Shoals, AL, and was comprised of vocalist Marty Raybon, guitarist Jim Seales, keyboard player Stan Thorn, bassist Ralph Ezell, and drummer Mike McGuire. One night McGuire invited his friend, songwriter Robert Byrne, to hear the MGM band. He was impressed enough to record the band and offer the tapes to CBS, who christened and signed Shenandoah.

The group's self-titled album, released in 1987, leaned a little close to the pop-schmaltz they later rebelled against, though they reached the country Top 30 early in 1988 with "Stop the Rain." The next year, *Road Not Taken* outlined the group's approach to traditional country and became their most successful album; six singles reached the country Top Ten, led by the number ones "The Church on Cumberland Road," "Sunday in the South," and "Two

Dozen Roses." *Road Not Taken* reached Gold status by 1991 and earned Shenandoah the Favorite Newcomer award from *Music City News.*

The first single from third album *Extra Mile* (1990) continued—and even topped—Shenandoah's success. "Next to You, Next to Me" became Shenandoah's biggest hit, topping the country charts for three weeks. It was followed into the Top Ten during 1990-91 by "Ghost in This House," "I Got You," and "The Moon over Georgia." The group's streak of hit singles ended with the mere Top 40 "When You Were Mine" in September 1991.

Despite the success, trouble was brewing. Three other bands came forward in 1991 claiming the Shenandoah name, and the resulting court costs and legal fees bankrupted the group by the end of the year. To make it even worse, CBS—who had named Shenandoah in the first place—dropped the group from its roster. The band settled the differences by 1992 and returned to country music with a contract from RCA and the No. 2 hit "Rock My Baby" in April of that year. Shenandoah's fourth album, *Long Time Comin',* also featured the Top 15 "Leavin's Been a Long Time Comin'."

Their fifth album, *Under the Kudzu* (1993), continued Shenandoah's popularity, with the Top Five single "I Want to Be Loved like That" and the group's fifth Country chart-topper in early 1994, "If Bubba Can Dance (I Can Too)." Shenandoah moved to Liberty-Capitol in late 1994 for their sixth album, *In the Vicinity of the Heart.* The album was released in January 1995, and featured the Top Tens "Somewhere in the Vicinity of the Heart" (with Alison Krauss) and "Darned If I Don't (Danged If I Do)." Shenandoah returned to its roots in 1996 for *Now and Then,* which combined re-recorded versions of CBS singles with four new songs. *—John Bush*

Shenandoah / 1987 / Columbia ✦✦✦
It contains "What She Wants," "She Doesn't Cry Anymore," "She's Still Here," and other songs. *—AMG*

The Road Not Taken / 1989 / Columbia ✦✦✦✦
The songs mix the day-to-day struggles of everyday-Joe with a steady respect for love, personal roots, and family. It doesn't hurt to have six bona fide hits on it, either. *—Tom Roland*

Extra Mile / 1990 / Columbia ✦✦✦
Features "She's a Natural," "Puttin' New Roots Down," and other hits. *—AMG*

Long Time Comin' / 1992 / RCA ✦✦✦
This album contains such hits as "Same Old Heart," "Rattle the Windows," and "Rock My Baby." *—AMG*

● **Greatest Hits** / Mar. 31, 1992 / Columbia ✦✦✦✦
This album features some of their most popular music, songs like "Two Dozen Roses," "The Moon over Georgia," "Any Ole Stretch of Blacktop," and "Ghost in This House." *—AMG*

Under the Kudzu / 1993 / RCA ✦✦✦

Super Hits / May 31, 1994 / Columbia ✦✦✦✦

In the Vicinity of the Heart / 1995 / Liberty ✦✦✦

Now and Then / Apr. 1996 / Capitol ✦✦
Uh-oh. It is always a mistake when recording artists allow a new record company to talk them into re-recording their old hits. Not only is it a consumer rip-off, but it also sends the message that the artists are spent as a contemporary force. One would not have thought that Shenandoah, coming off the Top Ten, Grammy-winning hit "In the Vicinity of the Heart," was in such dire straits, but the departure of 40% of the band before the release of this album indicates otherwise. And the decision to put only five new songs on the record, along with nine re-recordings and a repeat of "In the Vicinity of the Heart" from last time give the impression that a stop-gap was thought necessary. One can only hope that the remaining trio rebounds from this misstep. *—William Ruhlmann*

Shenandoah Christmas / Sep. 17, 1996 / Capitol ✦✦✦
Shenandoah Christmas is an enjoyable collection of holiday classics as performed by the popular modern country band. Though none of the versions of these classic carols—including "Rudolph the Red-Nosed Reindeer," "Santa Claus Is Coming to Town," "White Christmas," and "Winter Wonderland"—are particularly

noteworthy, the album is enjoyable for fans of the group. —*Thom Owens*

Jean Shepard

Bass, Vocals / Traditional Country, Honky Tonk

Few country singers—let alone female country singers—working since the 1950s have produced a large body of work as enduring as Jean Shepard's. Her voice is pure country—accent on both words. Born in Oklahoma, she grew up in Southern California, where Hank Thompson discovered her. She had her first Top Ten hit in 1953, and her last almost exactly 20 years later. In between, she cut one great record after another, mostly on Capitol Records. Nearly all of them crackle, no matter the topic, with honky tonk angel spunk.

Born in Oklahoma, Shepard grew up in the area surrounding Bakersfield, CA. As a teenager she began her musical career by playing bass in the Melody Ranch Girls, an all-female band formed in 1948. Hank Thompson discovered Shepard a few years after the group formed. Impressed by her talents, he helped her set up a record deal at Capitol Records, where she worked with Thompson's producer Ken Nelson.

Shepard's first chart appearance was in 1943 as a duet partner with Ferlin Husky, with "A Dear John Letter" and its sequel, "Forgive Me John." Jean and Ferlin toured the country after their hit singles. In 1955 she had her first solo Top Ten single, "A Satisfied Mind," which was backed by the No. 13 hit "Take Possession." Later in the year she had another Top Ten hit with "Beautiful Lies" / "I Thought of You." Her streak of hit singles led to an invitation to join the Grand Ole Opry in 1956. That same year she joined Red Foley's Ozark Jubilee and recorded *Songs of a Love Affair*, arguably the first concept album in country music history. Its 12 songs—which were all written by Shepard—depict a marriage torn apart by a love affair.

For nearly ten years after the release of "Beautiful Lies," Shepard wasn't able to get a song into the Top Ten. In fact, she had only two Top 40 hits during that period—"I Want to Go Where No One Knows Me" (No. 18, 1958) and "Have Heart, Will Love" (No. 30, 1959). She continued to record and tour—she was even named the Top Female Singer of 1959 by *Cash Box*—but nothing was breaking through to the public. This was primarily because she was a hardcore honky tonk singer at a time that country-pop was ruling the charts. In 1963 her husband Hawkshaw Hawkins died in the same plane crash that killed Patsy Cline. The next year Shepard returned to the Top Ten with "Second Fiddle (To an Old Guitar)." The song began a string of hits. Although many of them failed to chart in the Top 20, she racked up 15 Top 40 hits between 1965 and 1970, including the Top Ten hits "Ill Take the Dog" (a duet with Ray Pillow, 1966), "If Teardrops Were Silver" (1966), and "Then He Touched Me" (1970).

Shepard's hits continued throughout the '70s, though as the decade wore on she hit the Top 40 with less and less frequency. Her last hit single was 1978's "The Real Thing," which peaked at No. 85.

During the '80s and '90s Jean Shepard didn't record, but she continued to perform at the Grand Ole Opry and to tour, particularly in the UK, where she had a strong fan base.—*Dan Cooper & Stephen Thomas Erlewine*

Songs of a Love Affair / 1956 / Capitol ✦✦✦✦

This Is Jean Shepard / 1959 / Capitol ✦✦✦✦

One of her earlier LPs is strong on her voice and steel-friendly West Coast production. It includes her spry, proto-feminist "Two Whoops and a Holler." —*Dan Cooper*

Lonesome Love / 1959 / Capitol ✦✦✦✦

Best Of / 1963 / Capitol ✦✦✦✦

A good compilation of her first wave of hits ("A Dear John Letter," "A Satisfied Mind"), this is also the LP that shows up most often in used record bins. —*Dan Cooper*

I'll Take the Dog / 1966 / Capitol ✦✦✦

Declassified Jean Shepard / 1971 / Mercury ✦✦✦

● **Honky Tonk Heroine** / Dec. 1995 / Country Music Foundation ✦✦✦✦

At a time when most of her contemporaries were heading down the country-pop route, Jean Shepard was one of the few female honky tonk singers to stay true to the genre in the '50s and '60s. The definitive *Honky Tonk Heroine: Classic Capitol Recordings, 1952-1962* is a terrific anthology of her peak years. Most of her biggest hits are included, as are a handful of rarities that should delight casual fans as much as dedicated fans. —*Stephen Thomas Erlewine*

The Melody Ranch Girl / 1996 / Bear Family ✦✦✦✦

The five-disc box set *The Melody Ranch Girl* collects all 151 tracks that Jean Shepard recorded for Capitol Records between 1952 and 1964. Shepard's recordings for Capitol were undeniably her best—by and large, this is fiery, passionate honky tonk. All of her hits from this era, from "A Dear John Letter" and "A Satisfied Mind" to "Beautiful Lies" and "Second Fiddle (To An Old Guitar)," are included, as are several rarities, outtakes, and complete albums, including *Songs of a Love Affair*, one of the first country concept albums. The set also includes a thorough discography and biography, as well as many rare photos. For casual fans, *The Melody Ranch Girl* is far too lengthy and detailed to be pleasurable listening, but for dedicated followers, it's essential. —*Thom Owens*

T.G. Sheppard (William Neal Browder)

b. Jul. 20, 1942, Humboldt, TN

Guitar, Vocals / Country-Pop, Urban Cowboy

After working his way through the record industry, T.G. Sheppard emerged in the mid-'70s as one of the leading country-pop singers, bringing the music closer to the rock-influenced, cosmopolitan sounds of urban cowboy. As the nephew of the Grand Ole Opry comedian Rod Brasfield, T.G. Sheppard was exposed to music at a young age; throughout his childhood, his mother gave him piano lessons. At the age of 16 he ran away from home, arriving in Memphis where he became a backup vocalist and guitarist in the Travis Wammack Band. During this time, he was billing himself as Brian Stacy, and that was the credit on his first singles for Sonic Records. The label dropped him after all of his records failed, and he moved to Atlantic's Atco divison, where he released the rock 'n' roll single "High School Days" in 1966. Though it didn't break nationally, it was a hit in the South, and soon he was opening for the likes of the Beach Boys and the Animals, while befriending Elvis Presley.

Instead of leading him toward a performing career, the minor success of "High School Days" made Sheppard decide to work behind the scenes in the record industry, and later in 1966 he became a record promoter for Hot Line Distibutors. Initially, he worked for Stax, but he quickly became the Southern regional promoter for RCA, where he helped push records by his friend Presley, as well as John Denver. While he was working for RCA, he also founded his own production and promotion company, Umbrella Productions. While working at promotion for Umbrella in 1972, he discovered a song by Bobby David called "Devil in a Bottle." Every record company he directed it to over the next year and a half turned the song down, so he decided to record a version himself. Eventually, he convinced Motown's developing country subsidiary Melodyland to license the record. Deciding to use T.G. Sheppard as his performing name, the vocalist released the record in the fall of 1974. "Devil in the Bottle" unexpectedly climbed to No. 1 early in 1975, followed shortly by another No. 1 single, "Tryin' to Beat the Morning Home." Later in the year, "Another Woman" reached No. 14 and "Motels and Memories" peaked at No. 7, establishing Sheppard as a promising artist. Shortly after the release of "Motels and Memories," Motown was sued by a Los Angeles church over the right to use the name "Melodyland," and the label had to change its name to Hitsville. Sheppard had four other hit singles on Hitsville—including a cover of Neil Diamond's "Solitary Man" and the No. 8 "Show Me a Man" (1976)—before Motown finally decided to shut the label down.

By the time Hitsville collapsed, Sheppard was on his way to becoming a star—*Cash Box* magazine named him Best New Male

Artist of 1976—so he was immediately snapped up by Warner. T.G. became a genuine country star at Warner, partially because the label promoted him correctly and partially because his sound—a smooth fusion of R&B rhythms, pop production, and country songwriting—became the blueprint for the urban cowboy movement that became country's most popular genre of the late '70s. After having two No. 13 singles ("Mister D.J.," "Don't Ever Say Good-Bye" early in 1978, Sheppard released "When Can We Do This Again" in the summer. The single started a streak of 15 straight Top Ten hits that ran for the next five years. During that time he had no less than ten No. 1 singles: "Last Cheater's Waltz" (1979), "I'll Be Coming Back for More" (1979), "Do You Wanna Go to Heaven" (1980), "I Feel like Loving You Again" (1980), "I Loved 'Em Every One" (1981), "Party Time" (1981), "Only One You" (1981), "Finally" (1982), "War Is Hell (On the Homefront Too)" (1982), and the Karen Brooks duet "Faking Love" (1982). Over those five years, his style rarely changed—every record was well-crafted, highly produced country-pop highlighted by Sheppard's smooth croon.

T.G. Sheppard continued to chart well throughout the latter half of the '80s, and between 1986 and 1987 he had a No. 1 single and three No. 2 records in a row ("Strong Heart," "Half Past Forever ('Til I'm Blue in the Heart)," "You're My First Lady," and "One for the Money)" after he switched labels and signed to Columbia. However, his audience dipped dramatically in 1988, when his radio-ready sound became usurped by a number of new traditionalist performers like Dwight Yoakam, Randy Travis, and George Strait. Between 1989 and 1990 he didn't record at all, and he was dropped by Columbia. In 1991 he returned to the charts with the Curb/Capitol single "Born in a High Wind," but he didn't remain with the label long. For the remainder of the '90s, he continued to tour and play concerts across the country, all the time lacking a new record contract. — *Tom Roland*

Slow Burn / 1983 / Warner Brothers ✦✦✦
This album has its weak moments, but Sheppard's performance is stronger than in previous albums. He's more confident, probably understands the craft of singing a little better, and—this being his first outing with record producer Jim Ed Norman—the arrangements don't bury him. — *Tom Roland*

Biggest Hits / 1988 / Columbia ✦✦✦
While *Biggest Hits* contains nothing from Sheppard's remarkable 1979-1983 string of 11 No. 1 hits, it does feature the high points from his late-'80s comeback on Columbia, including the chart-topping "Strong Heart" as well as "Half Past Forever ('Til I'm Blue in the Heart)," "You're My First Lady," and "One for the Money," all three of which peaked at No. 2. — *Jason Ankeny*

● **The Best Of** / 1992 / Curb ✦✦✦✦
You'll have to look for this one at used-record stores. A sampler released only to radio, it covers the half-dozen years up to and including "I Loved 'Em Every One." Some of the performances are a little stiff but it lends appreciation for his improved, later work. — *Tom Roland*

Billy Sherrill

b. Nov. 5, 1936, Phil Campbell, AL
Country-Pop, Nashville Sound/Countrypolitan
As a producer, songwriter and an A&R man, Billy Sherrill was one of the most influential non-performing figures in country music of the '60s and '70s. Sherrill was responsible for shaping the lush countrypolitan sound that helped changed the production styles of country music during the '70s. Instead of relying on standard country instruments like steel guitars and fiddles, he recorded with string sections and vocal choruses, often overdubbing parts to give the music a grandiose, epic sound; in essence, it was the country version of pop producer Phil Spector's famous "Wall of Sound." Some critics complained that his style wasn't pure country, but there is no denying that he helped bring country music to a pop audience with the recordings he made with George Jones, Tammy Wynette, Charlie Rich, and Johnny Paycheck, as well as many, many others. Sherrill also helped build up the Epic artist roster during the '60s, making it into a formidable country label. Furthermore, he wrote and co-wrote many songs

that have since become country classics, including "Stand by Your Man," "Your Good Girl's Gonna Go Bad," "I Don't Wanna Play House," "We Can Make It," and "The Most Beautiful Girl."

For someone with such an important place in country music history, Billy Sherrill ironically wasn't interested in the music at all as a child—initially, he was attracted to blues, R&B, and jazz. Born and raised in Alabama, Sherrill was the son of an evangelical preacher. Billy learned how to play piano when he was a child, and he often played at revival meetings and funerals his father held. When he was a teenager, Sherrill learned how to play saxophone and led a jump-blues band that played R&B and jazz. Soon he was touring the South, playing in R&B and rock 'n' roll combos. Eventually he was signed as a solo artist by a small independent label in the late '50s, but none of his singles made any impact.

In 1962 Sherrill discovered, when a royalty check arrived in the mail, that an unknown Nashville country artist had cut one of his songs. Encouraged by the royalties, he moved to Nashville to pursue a career in the country music industry. Upon his arrival in Nashville, Sherrill was hired by Sam Phillips to oversee Sun Records' Nashville studios. After Sun and Phillips went bankrupt the next year, Epic Records' Nashville hired him as an in-house producer, and he was assigned to record any artist that all of the label's other producers had already rejected.

Before he moved to Nashville, Sherrill paid no attention to country music, and when he was hired by Epic, he was still unfamiliar with many of its production techniques and musical conventions. Instead of heeding the advice of the studio musicians he was working with, Sherrill forged ahead and created his own style, telling the professional musicians what to play. Basing his sound on the work of Phil Spector, Don Law, and Chet Atkins, he began pushing the boundaries of the Nashville Sound of the '50s by making the productions bigger and more sweeping. Sherrill also decided to select the songs that his artists would record, often co-writing the songs to suit the singer's style and his own production.

Sherrill's first major hit arrived in 1965, when he overhauled the sound and career of David Houston, who had had a hit two years earlier with "Mountain of Love." Houston hadn't had another big hit since that single, but Billy gave him "Livin' in a House Full of Love," which reached No. 3 late in 1965. The next year Houston recorded the Sherrill/Glenn Sutton song "Almost Persuaded," which spent nine weeks at No. 1. "Almost Persuaded" quickly became a standard, winning the Grammy for Best Country and Western Song and becoming the subject of cover versions by artists as diverse as Louis Armstrong, Louis Prima, and Etta James.

Throughout 1966 Sherrill continued working with David Houston, and later in the year he discovered Tammy Wynette, an Alabama hairdresser and waitress who entered his office unannounced. Wynette had previously approached several other record labels but had been rejected. Sherrill signed her, co-writing "Your Good Girl's Gonna Go Bad" with Sutton with her specifically in mind. The single became a hit upon its early 1967 release, launching a very successful career for Wynette. Over the course of 1967 Sherrill turned out several No. 1 singles by both Houston ("With One Exception," "You Mean the World to Me," which both were No. 1 hits) and Wynette ("I Don't Wanna Play House"), plus "My Elusive Dream," a duet between the two vocalists. Also in 1967 Sherrill released the instrumental *Classical Country* under the name the Billy Sherrill Quintet.

The next year, Sherrill continued to work on recordings by Houston and Wynette, and he signed Charlie Rich, with whom he had worked at Sun, to Epic. Though the first few records Sherrill made with Rich were unsuccessful, the pair would have some major hits during the early '70s. Billy's most successful artists for 1968 remained Houston and Wynette, as David's "Have a Little Faith" and "Already It's Heaven," and Tammy's "Take Me to Your World," "D-I-V-O-R-C-E," and "Stand by Your Man" all reached No. 1. Not only did he produce those tracks, he wrote or co-wrote the majority of the songs. Sherrill's success with Houston and Wynette continued through 1969 and 1970, with both artists racking up several more No. 1 hits.

Billy signed Barbara Mandrell to Columbia in 1969, and the next year he wrote and produced her first Top 40 single, "Playin' Around with Love." Mandrell's career continued to build momentum for the next four years, before she left Columbia, and Sherrill had a hand in producing or writing most of her hits for the label. Though Mandrell would later emerge as a star, the most significant addition to Sherrill's roster of vocalists was George Jones, who left Musicor for Epic in 1971. At first the producer and signer didn't hit it off—Jones was accustomed to Pappy Dailey's loose, nearly lazy, production technique and it took some time for him to feel comfortable with Sherrill's painstaking, demanding style—but the relationship would prove to be the most fruitful collaboration either artist would have. Sherrill expanded Jones' classic ballad style, bringing an epic sweep to his ballads while remaining close to Jones' honky tonk roots. Their first single, "We Can Make It," arrived in early 1972, a year after George and Tammy's "Take Me" became a Top Ten hit. For the next five years, Jones not only recorded solo singles with Sherrill but made a series of duets with Wynette, and their hits often reflected the turbulent nature of their romance.

George Jones wasn't the only artist to occupy Billy Sherrill's time in 1972. In addition to Jones, Wynette, Houston, and Mandrell, Sherrill worked with a wide variety of singers, including Jody Miller, Sandy Posey, Freddy Weller, and the teenaged Tanya Tucker. Billy's career continued to gain momentum over the next two years, as his regular stable of artists continued to have hits, and Charlie Rich finally began to chart with singles from the album *Behind Closed Doors*. Rich's title track and "The Most Beautiful Girl" became huge hits, reaching not only the top of the country charts, but also the pop charts; the latter also became a NO. 1 hit in England. Also that year he began to write songs for Joe Stampley, who would sign to Epic within two years.

By the time Stampley joined the Epic roster in 1975, Sherrill had become the most reliable hitmaker in Nashville, and both established and developing artists clamored to work with him. Over the latter half of the decade, he not only worked with his old favorites like Wynette, Jones, Rich, Mandrell, and Stampley, he produced or wrote songs for Johnny Paycheck, Marty Robbins, Ronnie Milsap, Janie Fricke, Ray Charles, David Allan Coe, Johnny Duncan, Bob Luman, David Wills, and Kenny Rogers and Dottie West. As the '80s arrived, Sherrill's hitmaking skills began to slip somewhat. Though he was invaluable in George Jones' early-'80s comeback—producing and/or writing hits like "He Stopped Loving Her Today," "I'm Not Ready Yet," "If Drinkin' Don't Kill Me (Her Memory Will)," and "Same Ole Me," among others—Sherrill's songwriting wasn't being covered quite as frequently. Nevertheless, his songs continued to reach the charts, as Moe Bandy, Johnny Cash, Johnny Rodriguez, and Lacy J. Dalton made his songs into hits. In addition to his Nashville connections, Sherrill produced Elvis Costello's country album, *Almost Blue*, in 1981.

By 1980 Billy Sherrill had been named vice president/executive producer of CBS in Nashville, and he stayed in that position for the first half of the decade. In the middle of the decade, he left CBS to become an independent producer, working on Ray Charles' country duets album, *Friendship*, but he returned to the label in 1986. Though he was signed to CBS, he worked infrequently, and his productions didn't hit the charts as frequently as they had during the previous two decades; he soon slipped into retirement. Still, Sherrill didn't need any new hits to confirm his status as one of country music's premier producers and songwriters—his endless string of hits stands as a testament to his talents. —*Stephen Thomas Erlewine*

Shivers

Alternative Country-Rock, Alternative Country, Americana

A trio comprised of singer/guitarist Carey Kemper; his wife, singer/bassist Kelly Bell; and drummer Barry Haney, the Shivers delivered a low-key melding of folk, roots-rock, and country described as "Gothic Country." Their arrangements were stark, usually acoustic or electric guitars and bass, embellished occasionally with lap steel, dobro, fiddle, cello, and mandolin. The

band at different times hailed from Austin, TX; Portland, OR; the Twin Cities; and Chattanooga, TN. —*Jack Leaver*

Shivers / 1994 / Restless ♦♦♦

● **Buried Life** / Jan. 16, 1996 / Restless ♦♦♦♦
An earthy collection of rootsy country and folk delivered with an unpracticed energy and raw emotion. Some of the songs are upbeat and pushed along by drummer Barry Haney, while others are presented in stark fashion, with just acoustic guitar and voice, or the added textures of accordion, dobro, fiddle, and lap steel. The lyrical content evokes dark imagery, as in Carey Kemper's "Cult 45," while the music is hauntingly beautiful, particularly in songs like Kelly Bell's "House of the Spirits," with guest musician Jacqueline Ferrier-Ulton adding the lone and sad cello part over a strumming acoustic guitar. Kemper and Bell are especially compelling when they're singing together, sometimes recalling the dual-octave vocal style of X, and there's a sensual quality to songs like "No Love Lost." Bell gives a wistfully unforgettable performance on her "Make a Wish," and Kemper sounds a little reminiscent of a young Johnny Cash on "Cannonball." —*Jack Leaver*

Steve Sholes

b. Feb. 12, 1911, Washington, D.C., d. Apr. 22, 1968, Nashville, TN
Nashville Sound/Countrypolitan
Steve Sholes was one of the most influential producers in postwar music; he was responsible not only for the birth of the Nashville Sound, but also for signing Chet Atkins and Elvis Presley to RCA. Sholes was born in Washington, DC in 1911, but his family moved to New Jersey in the 1920s, and it was while attending high school in 1929 that he first took a part-time job in sales with RCA-Victor Records. In 1935, after college, he returned to RCA, joining the jazz artists and repertory department. During World War II, while serving in the army, he was responsible for producing "V-Discs"—records made for distribution specifically to servicemen overseas as part of the war effort—by Fats Waller.

In 1945, upon his release from the military, Sholes returned to RCA and became manager of the company's country and Western and rhythm and blues A&R. Among his first signings were the Sons of the Pioneers, who became the linchpin of the company's burgeoning country and Western lineup. In 1949 Sholes signed guitarist Chet Atkins to provide RCA with a competitor to Merle Travis on Capitol. He ended up getting far more than a guitar virtuoso—Atkins proved to be a master arranger and producer as well. Although cowboy groups like the Pioneers hit hard times in the early 1950s, country music was undergoing a boom, and Sholes was prepared to expand the company's roster. He brought such artists as Elton Britt, Eddie Arnold, the Browns, Homer & Jethro, Hank Snow, Hank Locklin, Jim Reeves, Pee Wee King, and Elvis Presley to RCA. By the end of the 1950s, RCA was a country music powerhouse, with one of the strongest rosters in the business, much of it Sholes' doing.

In 1957 Sholes promoted Chet Atkins to production manager in Nashville, and he became one of the most successful producers in the history of country music. In the 1960s RCA became the home to such artists as Porter Wagoner, Dolly Parton, and Waylon Jennings, even as its best 1950s artists continued to fare well in the marketplace. This was the decade that the so-called "Nashville Sound" nurtured by Sholes and Atkins came into its own as the dominant commercial force in country music, and RCA was the label that best exemplified that sound. Sholes was also a key player in organizing and raising money for the Country Music Hall of Fame, which opened in 1967. By that time, Sholes was nearing the uppermost echelon of RCA management, having been promoted to vice president in charge of pop artists and repertory that same year. He was elected to the Country Music Hall of Fame in 1967, the year that it opened. He died of a heart attack in Nashville at the age of 57. —*Bruce Eder*

Sidesaddle

Progressive Bluegrass
Sidesaddle is a bluegrass band that has country, Western, Irish, and folk influences. The band features Kim Elking (mandolin),

Lee Anne Caswell (fiddle), Sheila McCormick (guitar), Jackie Miller (guitar), and Sonia Shell (banjo). —*Chip Renner*

● **Daylight Train** / 1991 / Turquoise ✦✦✦✦
Sidesaddle's unique sound sets it apart from other bluegrass bands. The vocals blend nicely, with an Irish feel at times. These are also first-class musicians. An exciting album. —*Chip Renner*

The Girl from the Red Rose Saloon / Turquoise ✦✦✦
A very good record—nominated for Best Bluegrass Album (NAIRD). —*Chip Renner*

Blueberry Gossip / Turquoise ✦✦✦✦

Paul Siebel

Vocals / Singer-Songwriter, Country-Folk, Contemporary Folk
Despite the undeniably high quality of his songs—which have been covered by the likes of Linda Ronstadt, Bonnie Raitt, Ian Matthews, and Waylon Jennings—Paul Siebel is far from being a household name. Within folk circles and among songwriters, however, his two albums—1969's *Woodsmoke and Oranges* and 1971's *Jack-Knife Gypsy*—are legendary.

Paul Siebel was born in 1937 in Buffalo, NY. Inspired by Hank Williams and Hank Snow, he taught himself to play guitar while in his teens. By the early '60s, after serving in the military, he began playing playing folk clubs, eventually moving to Greenwich Village, where he found support on the coffeehouse circuit. In 1969 a collection of demos he made with David Bromberg caught the attention of Elektra Records owner Jac Holzman, who offered a him a modest recording deal. (Reportedly he was given only enough money to finance four three-hour recording sessions). The resulting album, *Woodsmoke and Oranges*, was met with critical praise from the media, including *Rolling Stone* magazine. Despite the attention, the album and its equally praised follow-up, *Jack-Knife Gypsy*, sold disappointingly little. Aside from a live album released in 1981, *Live at McCabes*, Siebel hasn't released an album since. —*Chris Woodstra*

☆ **Wood Smoke and Oranges** / 1970 / Elektra ✦✦✦✦✦
Fans of Linda Ronstadt, Bonnie Raitt, or Ian Matthews records from the '70s will know some of these tunes already. Let their interpretations stand only as your introduction to this fine songwriter. While his style may not be as polished or commercial as that of any of the people who covered him, this is a fine batch of songs and deserves to be heard. —*Jim Worbois*

Jack Knife Gypsy / 1971 / Elektra ✦✦✦
The first record may have drawn listeners for the opportunity to hear Siebel originals of songs they knew from elsewhere. This record does not have that same kind of pull but is every bit as good. His strong sense of melody and storytelling style paved the way for such current songwriters as Butch Hancock and Robert Earl Keen. —*Jim Worbois*

Live at McCabes / 1981 / Rag Baby ✦✦✦✦
Recorded in an intimate concert setting, it includes some of his signature tunes such as "Louise," along with perennials like "I'm So Lonesome I Could Cry" and "In the Jailhouse Now." —*Richard Meyer*

★ **Paul Siebel** / Oct. 31, 1995 / Philo ✦✦✦✦✦
Though known mainly through others' interpretations of his songs (Ian Matthews, Linda Ronstadt, Bonnie Raitt), Paul Siebel's first two albums for Elektra are prime examples of the New York folk scene of the early '70s and easily among the scene's finest moments. While these albums were sadly overlooked at the time by all but his singer-songwriter peers and critics, they have since reached near-legendary status. *Paul Siebel* is a long-overdue collection of the high points of both albums, featuring *Woodsmoke and Oranges* in its entirety and five tracks from the follow-up, *Jack-Knife Gypsy*. —*Chris Woodstra*

Red Simpson

b. Mar. 6, 1934, Higley, AZ
Vocals / Traditional Country, Bakersfield Sound
Best known for his string of trucking songs, Red Simpson was raised in Bakersfield, CA, the youngest of a dozen children. At age 14 he wrote his first song—about chickens—and sang it to his

family's fowl. During the Korean War, he served aboard a naval hospital ship, the *Repose*, where he found relief by forming the Repose Ramblers, who played any instruments they could scrounge up. He bought better ones in Japan and began to practice in earnest, and he became a professional musician in California after his discharge.

Simpson was working at the Wagon Wheel in Lamont when Fuzzy Owens saw him and arranged for Simpson to work at his Clover Club as a piano player. He then got a job replacing Buck Owens at the Blackboard Club on weekends. Simpson was influenced by Owens, Merle Haggard, and Bill Woods, who asked Red if he would write a song about driving trucks. (By the time Simpson handed him four truck songs, however, Woods had stopped recording.) Simpson began writing songs with Buck Owens in 1962, including the Top Ten hit "Gonna Have Love."

In 1965 Capitol's Ken Nelson was looking for someone to record some songs about trucking. His first choice was Haggard, who wasn't interested, but Simpson readily agreed. His first, Tommy Collins' "Roll, Truck, Roll," became a Top 40 country hit, and Simpson recorded an album of the same name. That year he offered up two more trucking songs, both of which made it to the Top 50 or beyond. As a songwriter, he scored his first No. 1 hit with "Sam's Place," recorded by Buck Owens. After that, Simpson decided to become a full-time writer. He returned to performing in 1971 with his Top Five hit "I'm a Truck," which had been written by postman Bob Staunton.

In 1972 he debuted on the Grand Ole Opry and had two more "truck" hits for Capitol. In 1976 Simpson signed to Warner Brothers and released "Truck Driver's Heaven." The next year he teamed up with Lorraine Walden for a series of duets that included "Truck Driver Man and Wife." In 1979 Simpson appeared for the last time on the charts with "The Flying Saucer Man and the Truck Driver." Haggard recorded his song "Lucky Old Colorado" in 1988; later that year Simpson was diagnosed with skin cancer and underwent surgery; he recovered fully and continued his writing and performing career. —*Sandra Brennan*

Roll Truck Roll / 1960 / Capitol ✦✦✦

The Man Behind the Badge / 1966 / Capitol ✦✦✦

Truck Drivin' Fool / 1967 / Capitol ✦✦✦✦

Red Simpson Sings a Bakersfield Dozen / 1967 / Capitol ✦✦✦✦

I'm a Truck / 1971 / Capitol ✦✦✦

The Very Real Red Simpson / 1972 / Capitol ✦✦✦

● **Best of Red Simpson** / 1995 / King ✦✦✦✦

Daryle Singletary

Vocals / Contemporary Country
Born and raised just outside of Whigham, GA, modern country singer Daryle Singletary worked the same new-traditionalist territory as many of his mid-'90s contemporaries. Released on Giant Records in the spring of 1995, his eponymous debut was a success, spawning the hit country singles "I'm Living Up to Her Low Expectations" (number 39), "I Let Her Lie" (number two), and "Too Much Fun" (number four). Singletary released his second album, *All Because of You*, in the fall of 1996. —*Stephen Thomas Erlewine*

Daryle Singletary / 1995 / Giant ✦✦✦

● **All Because of You** / Oct. 8, 1996 / ✦✦✦✦
Daryle Singletary's debut album was a fine slice of neo-traditional country, but his followup, *All Because of You*, is even better, boasting a stronger set of songs—such as the single "Amen Kinda Love"—and a more confident performance by Singletary. There are still a couple of weak tracks, which suffer from underdeveloped songs or slick production, but *All Because of You* remains a solid neo-traditional modern country record. —*Thom Owens*

Ricky Skaggs

b. Jul. 18, 1954, Cordell, KY
Banjo, Fiddle, Guitar, Mandolin, Vocals / Progressive Bluegrass, Traditional Bluegrass, Progressive Country, New Traditionalist.
By the time he was in his mid-30s, Kentuckian Ricky Skaggs had produced a career's worth of music. At age seven he appeared on

TV with Flatt and Scruggs; at 15 he was a member of legendary Ralph Stanley's bluegrass band (with fellow teenager, the late Keith Whitley). None of his '80s peers, male or female, had better musical credentials than Ricky. The term "multi-talented" lacks the power to characterize this extraordinary singer and instrumentalist. Not only can he sing and pick with the best in progressive country, his broad and deep experience in traditional music separates him from the crowd. In the estimation of many, he is without peer as a combination vocalist and instrumentalist (guitar, mandolin, fiddle, banjo). After playing with Ralph Stanley for three years, Ricky moved on to progressive bluegrass bands the Country Gentlemen and J.D. Crowe and the New South. With his own band, Boone Creek, he mixed the old and the new, adding Django Rheinhardt. Skaggs took Rodney Crowell's place in Emmylou Harris' Hot Band in 1977 and the band's excellent *Roses in the Snow* album showcased Ricky's versatility. Two No. 1 hits came out of his 1981 album *Waiting for the Sun to Shine*, and the awards started arriving. Skaggs is largely responsible for a back-to-basics movement in country music. He showed many that a bluegrass tenor with impeccable taste and enormous talent could sell traditional country in the '80s, a time when pop music had invaded the land of rural rhythm.

Ricky Skaggs began playing music at a very early age, having been given a mandolin from his father at the age of five. Before his father had the time to teach Ricky how to play, the child had learned the instrument himself; and by the end of 1959, he had performed onstage during a Bill Monroe concert, playing "Ruby Are You Mad at Your Man" to great acclaim. Two years later, when Skaggs was seven, he appeared on Flatt and Scruggs' television show, again to positive response. Shortly afterward, he learned how to play both fiddle and guitar and began playing with his parents in a group called the Skaggs Family. In addition to traditional bluegrass, Skaggs began absorbing the honky tonk of George Jones and Ray Price and the British Invasion rock 'n' roll of the Beatles and the Rolling Stones. In his adolescence, he briefly played in rock 'n' roll bands, but he never truly abandoned traditional and roots music.

During a talent concert in his mid-teens, he met Keith Whitley, a fellow fiddler. The two adolescents became friends and began playing together, with Keith's brother Dwight on banjo, at various radio shows. By 1970, they earned a spot opening for Ralph Stanley. Following their performance, Stanley invited the duo to join his supporting band, the Clinch Mountain Boys, and they accepted. Over the next two years, they played many concerts with the bluegrass legend and appeared on his record *Cry from the Cross*. Skaggs also appeared on Whitley's solo album, *2nd Generation Bluegrass*, in 1972.

Though he had made his way into the bluegrass circuit and was actively recording, Skaggs had grown tired of the hard work and low pay in the Clinch Mountain Boys and left the group at the end of 1972. For a short while he abandoned music and worked in a boiler room for the Virginia Electric Power Company in Washington, DC, but he returned to performing when the Country Gentlemen invited him to join in 1973. Skaggs spent the next two years with the group, primarily playing fiddle, before joining the progressive bluegrass band J.D. Crowe and the New South in 1974. The next year, he recorded another duet album with Keith Whitley, *That's It*, and then formed his own newgrass band, Boone Creek, in 1976. In addition to bluegrass, the outfit played honky tonk and Western swing. Boone Creek earned the attention of Emmylou Harris, who invited Skaggs to join her supporting band. After declining several times, he finally became a member of her Hot Band when Rodney Crowell left in 1977.

Between 1977 and 1980, Skaggs helped push Harris toward traditional country and bluegrass, often to great acclaim. He also pursued a number of other musical venues while he was with Emmylou, recording a final album with Boone Creek (1978's *One Way Track*), two duet albums with Tony Rice (1978's *Take Me Home Tonight in a Song*, 1980's *Skaggs and Rice*) and, finally, his first solo album, *Sweet Temptation*, which was released on Sugar Hill. *Sweet Temptation* was a major bluegrass hit, earning the attention of the major label Epic Records. The label offered him a contract in 1981, releasing *Waitin' for the Sun to Shine* later that

Ricky Skaggs

year. The album was a big hit, earning acclaim not only in country circles, but also in rock 'n' roll publications. By the end of the year Ricky Skaggs had become a star, and in the process, he brought rootsy, traditional country back into the consciousness of the country audience.

During 1982 and early 1983, he had five straight No. 1 singles—"Crying My Heart Out Over You," "I Don't Care," "Heartbroke," "I Wouldn't Change You If I Could," "Highway 40 Blues"—as well as earning numerous awards. Later in 1982 he was made the youngest member of the Grand Ole Opry. For the next four years, he was a major artistic and commercial force within country music, raking up a string of Top Ten hits and Grammy award-winning albums. His success helped spark the entire new traditionalist movement, opening the doors for performers like George Strait and Randy Travis. Toward the end of the decade, Skaggs wasn't charting as frequently as he had in the past, but he had established himself as an icon. Each of his records sold well, and he collaborated with a number of musicians, including Rodney Crowell, the Bellamy Brothers, Johnny Cash, Jesse Winchester, and Dolly Parton.

During the early '90s, Skaggs' traditional music was hit hard by the slick sounds of contemporary country; his records ceased to sell as consistently as they had ten years earlier. Columbia Records dropped him in 1992. However, Skaggs continued to perform concerts and festivals frequently, as well as hosting his own syndicated radio program, "The Simple Life," which hit the airwaves in 1994. The next year, Ricky Skaggs returned to recording with *Solid Ground*, his first album for Atlantic Records. *—David Vinopal*

Sweet Temptation / 1979 / Sugar Hill ✦✦✦✦

With guest vocals by then-boss Emmylou Harris, Skaggs' first solo effort (not counting the Boone Creek project) is equal parts bluegrass and Harris-styled new traditionalism. *—Dan Cooper*

Skaggs and Rice / 1980 / Sugar Hill ✦✦✦✦

Skaggs & Rice is a lovely duet album between Ricky Skaggs and Tony Rice. The two musicians run through a number of bluegrass classics, performing them in a spare, simple old-timey style, backed only by their guitar and mandolin. Not only are the performances breathtaking, but the song selection is first-rate. It features Bill Monroe classics like "Mansions for Me" and "Tennessee

Blues," as well as other standards like "Talk About Suffering" and "Have You Someone in Heaven Awaiting." —*Thom Owens*

Waitin' for the Sun to Shine / 1981 / Epic ✦✦✦
His first album after signing with Epic Records, this one took Skaggs into the mainstream, in effect beginning the new-traditionalist movement. It has a simple, mountain approach, with lots of remakes and Skaggs' mournful vocal tones. The best cut is the plaintive title track. —*Tom Roland*

Highways and Heartaches / 1982 / Epic ✦✦✦✦
Long a sideman or supporting vocalist in previous situations, Skaggs wasn't totally comfortable with his role as a lead vocalist when he signed with Epic Records. Thanks to a year of touring and greater support from his record label (when Epic signed him, the company honestly didn't think he'd sell more than 100,000 copies of his debut for the company), he had greater confidence vocally the second time around. And the material's more upbeat. —*Tom Roland*

Family and Friends / 1982 / Rounder ✦✦✦
Skaggs' last breath of pure bluegrass was recorded with help from the Whites, guitarist Peter Rowan, dobroist Jerry Douglas, and others. Included are two songs by Carter Stanley, one by Bill Monroe, and some fine examples of Appalachian gospel, including a stunning a cappella trio vocal on "Talk About Sufferin'." —*Brian Mansfield*

Don't Cheat in Our Hometown / 1983 / Epic ✦✦✦
Dedicated to the Stanley Brothers, *Don't Cheat in Our Hometown* spotlights both bluegrass and honky tonk material. Songs include the chart-topping title track, "Honey (Open That Door)," and a cover of Bill Monroe's "Uncle Pen." —*Jason Ankeny*

Country Boy / 1984 / Epic ✦✦✦✦
Every one of Ricky Skaggs' albums is a pickin' festival and a country delight. Not only is this one no exception, but it includes Bill Monroe's "Wheel Hoss" with Monroe himself picking along on mandolin, which earns it a listing here. If you like this album, you'll probably like every one Skaggs has made. —*William Ruhlmann*

● **Live in London** / 1985 / Epic ✦✦✦✦
This is the one Skaggs album to own if you can have only one. Because it's a live recording, the picking is just that much more exciting, and the album serves as an unofficial best-of, its highlights including "Heartbroke," "Uncle Pen," and a version of "Don't Get Above Your Raising" that features noted country fan Elvis Costello. —*William Ruhlmann*

Love's Gonna Get Ya / 1986 / Epic ✦✦✦
Skaggs continued to inch closer to modern mainstream country on *Love's Gonna Get Ya*, which features the hit "Love's Gonna Get You Someday." —*Jason Ankeny*

Comin' Home to Stay / 1988 / Epic ✦✦✦
Comin' Home to Stay marks Skaggs' return to traditional country and includes "I'm Tired," "Thanks Again," and "(Angel on My Mind) That's Why I'm Walkin'." —*Jason Ankeny*

Kentucky Thunder / 1989 / Epic ✦✦✦
This contains such Skaggs favorites as "Let It Be You," "Heartbreak Hurricane," and more. —*AMG*

My Father's Son / 1991 / Epic ✦✦✦
A concept album about families, *My Father's Son* is the Skaggs album that owes the least to bluegrass. Skaggs is concerned with the legacies fathers leave their sons, both the wisdom ("Father Knows Best") and the limitations ("My Father's Son"). He also sees materialism for the distracting, destructive force it is. His duet with Waylon Jennings on "Only Daddy That'll Walk the Line" fits neatly, though perhaps not the way the writer intended. And because Skaggs' background is bluegrass rather than honky tonk, every father image is inextricably bound to God. —*Brian Mansfield*

Super Hits / Aug. 24, 1993 / Epic ✦✦✦✦

Solid Ground / Nov. 7, 1995 / Atlantic ✦✦✦
Country's most amicable music maker made a comeback with *Solid Ground*, his first release for Atlantic, a label not known for its country artists. From the cover of Harry Chapin's "Cat's in the

Cradle" to the title track's wry drive, the album is put together well. These tunes are all pretty fair and comforting, and there is no ground more solid for an album to built upon. —*James Chrispell*

Skillet Lickers

Old-Time, String Band
The Skillet Lickers were one of the most important and influential string bands of the '20s and '30s. Led by fiddler Gid Tanner, the band combined old-timey country music with a wacky sense of humor and showmanship that made the group one of the most popular country bands in America. The original lineup of the band featured the dexterous and stunning interplay of Tanner, guitarist Riley Puckett, fiddler Clayton McMichen, and banjoist Fate Norris. From 1926 to 1931, the Skillet Lickers were the most popular country band in the country. After the dissolution of the original band, Puckett and latter-day fiddler Bert Layne led various bands called the Skillet Lickers, but the group wasn't relaunched until 1934, when Tanner formed a new lineup that recorded one final session that yielded their biggest hit, "Down Yonder."

Gid Tanner did have the right to the Skillet Lickers name—after all, he was the musician who sparked Columbia Records A&R representative Frank Walker to assemble the band in 1925. Prior to the formation of the Skillet Lickers, Tanner had worked his way up through the conventional circuit of festivals and traveling shows that fiddlers frequented. His first great success arrived when he began to regularly win fiddling conventions in Atlanta. In addition to playing, Tanner was an accomplished comedian, which meant he was an all-around entertainer, capable of winning audiences easily. Eventually Columbia Records asked him to record for their label, and in early 1924 he traveled to New York with his longtime friend and accompanist Riley Puckett, where they made a handful of singles.

The next year, Columbia's Frank Walker traveled to Atlanta with the intention of forming a string supergroup. Remembering Tanner and his records, he asked the fiddler and Puckett to be the core of this group, adding Clayton McMichen and Fate Norris to the lineup. Choosing the name the Skillet Lickers (a tribute to the Lickskillet Band, a string band that used to play fiddler contests), the band recorded and released their first singles in 1926. The Skillet Lickers were an immediate hit, shooting to the top of the charts with the double A-sided single "Bully of the Town"/"Pass Around the Bottle and We'll All Take a Drink." The single was followed quickly by "Watermelon Hanging on the Vine"/"You," which confirmed their status as hillbilly stars.

For their third single, the Skillet Lickers released a comedy record, "A Corn Licker Still in Georgia," which alternated music with comic dialogue about backwoods moonshiners. The record was their biggest single yet, equalled by their second comedy hit, "A Fiddler's Convention in Georgia." Not only did the comedy records sell better than the straight instrumental records; any single featuring Puckett singing became a huge hit.

Along with the success came tension within the band. All of their records were credited to "Gid Tanner and His Skillet Lickers," which became a source of irritation to Puckett and McMichen, both of whom felt that they were more integral to the sound of the band than Tanner. A compromise was reached, and the records bore the convoluted credit "Gid Tanner and His Skillet Lickers with Clayton McMichen and Riley Puckett." However, that didn't put an end to friction within the group, which by then included several new, younger members like fiddlers Lowe Stokes and Bert Layne. The new members wanted to move the Skillet Lickers toward Western swing music. McMichen sided with the newer members, but the remaining trio wanted to stay true to their folk roots. By 1930 the members had stopped touring regularly. In addition to working with the Skillet Lickers, McMichen became a studio musician for Columbia Records and played with Jimmie Rodgers. Finally, he formed a new stringband called the Georgia Wildcats. McMichen nevertheless participated in all of the studio sessions for the Skillet Lickers, which came to a halt in 1931.

Following the disbanding of the Skillet Lickers in 1931, Puckett and Layne toured and recorded with groups called "the Skillet Lickers," but the name was officially reclaimed by Gid Tanner in 1934, when he signed to Victor's Bluebird label. Tanner assembled a new group of Skillet Lickers—including Puckett, mandolinist Ted Hawkins, guitarist Mike Whitten, guitarist Hoke Rice, guitarist Hugh Cross, and his sons Arthur and Gordon, on banjo and fiddle respectively—and recorded over 30 songs in San Antonio. It was the last time Tanner ever entered a studio. The sessions produced "Down Yonder," which became Tanner and the Skillet Lickers' last big hit.

After the 1934 session, the Skillet Licker name was retired, and not long after that, Tanner himself retired. Puckett, McMichen, and Layne pursued solo careers. After Gid Tanner's death in 1960, his son Gordon continued fiddling, preserving the tradition of his father and the Skillet Lickers. —Stephen Thomas Erlewine

● Skillet Lickers / 1996 / County ◆◆◆◆
The single-disc compilation Skillet Lickers contains 16 tracks that the hillbilly musical comedy group recorded between 1926 and 1931, including "Ride Old Buck to the Water," "Dixie," and "Leather Breeches." The Skillet Lickers were one of the most popular groups of their time, and although their music and humor have become dated considerably in the decades since, the musical talents of fiddler Gid Tanner remain impressive, and this compilation is the best way to hear him and his group. —Thom Owens

Skyline

Progressive Bluegrass
Featuring banjoist Tony Trischka, Skyline helped pioneer the newgrass sound in the '80s, combining a bluegrass/country blend with strong songs and tight harmonies. —Chip Renner

Skyline Drive / 1977 / Flying Fish ◆◆◆
A strong project with great harmonies. —Chip Renner

Before the Dawn / 1979 / Accord ◆◆

Late to Work / Jan. 1979 / Flying Fish ◆◆◆
Skyline's debut album. Strong songs. Trischka's band blends vocals to perfection. —Chip Renner

Fire of Grace / Feb. 1979 / Flying Fish ◆◆◆
Rachel Kalen replaced DeDe Wyland on this record. —Chip Renner

● **Stranded in the Moonlight** / 1980 / Flying Fish ◆◆◆◆
The band hits its stride on this very rich album. Tight harmonies and great original compositions. —Chip Renner

The Smith Brothers

Traditional Country, Cowboy, Country Gospel
The Smith Brothers were active in both gospel and country music for more than 25 years, and they appeared in a few Westerns during the '40s. John Onvia Smith and Aubrey Lee Smith were born in the mountains of East Tennessee. They formed their first string band when they were children. In 1938 they got a job at a Cincinnati radio station, where they met Milton "Ace" Richman. The three men teamed up and moved to Columbus, where they worked with Hank Newman's Georgia Crackers. In 1940 they went to Charleston, SC, and sang Western music as the Red River Rangers. They finally settled in Atlanta and were joined by Eddie Wallace. They billed themselves as the Sunshine Boys Quartet and sang a wide variety of songs ranging from gospel to Western swing to barbershop at assorted Atlanta radio stations. During the mid-'40s, they went to Hollywood periodically to appear in movies featuring cowboy stars like Lash LaRue, Charles Starrett, and Eddie Dean. They also recorded a single as the Sunshine Boys.

The Smith Brothers worked primarily as a duo after 1948 and appeared on a daily 75-minute program in Atlanta for nine years; they also had a 15-minute gospel show called "Camp Meeting." As a duo, they made their recording debut in 1951 with the tearjerker "Happy Birthday in Heaven." Two years later they signed to Capitol as a gospel duo. Among their best-known songs were "I Have But One Goal," "Working in God's Factory," and "God's Rocket Ship." The Smiths later moved to Pittsburgh, appearing on WWVA's "Wheeling Jamboree" on Saturday nights. They continued at other stations and made one album for the Sing label before retiring from music in 1965. —Sandra Brennan

That's My Jesus / 1964 / Sing ◆◆◆

● **The Grass Section** / Red Clay ◆◆◆◆

Arthur Smith (Arthur 'Guitar Boogie' Smith)

b. Apr. 1, 1921, Clinton, SC, **d.** 1973
Banjo, Guitar, Mandolin / Traditional Country, Nashville Sound/ Countrypolitan, Country Boogie
Best remembered for the instrumental hit that gave him his nickname, Arthur "Guitar Boogie" Smith was considered one of the finest guitarists in country music during the '50s and '60s. He was born and raised in South Carolina and worked in the state's textile mills, founding a Dixieland band and performing during his spare time. Eventually the group became a country band called Smith's Carolina Crackerjacks. It was around this time that Smith began to experiment with electric guitar and incorporate a jazzy feel in his music. In 1943 he moved to Charlotte and worked as a replacement guitarist in two bands. With one, the Tennessee Ramblers, he recorded his first version of "Guitar Boogie" in 1945. He and the Crackerjacks continued to work on radio and television, and Smith had three instrumental hits in 1948, including "Banjo Boogie" and "Boomerang." He spent much of the '50s and '60s hosting a weekly local television show. In 1955 he wrote and performed the song "Feudin' Banjos" with Don Reno; in 1972, the song was retitled "Duelin' Banjos" and featured in the movie *Deliverance*. In 1959 the Virtues recorded his "Guitar Boogie," retitled it "Guitar Boogie Shuffle," and scored a Top Five pop hit. Throughout the 1970s, Smith cut many albums in his own Charlotte Studio. Later, he used the studio to record commercial jingles and subsequently retired from performing. —Sandra Brennan

● **Original Guitar Boogie** / 1964 / Dot ◆◆◆◆

Cal Smith (Calvin Grant Shofner)

b. Jul. 4, 1932, Gans, OK
Guitar, Vocals / Traditional Country, Country-Pop, Honky Tonk
Singer Cal Smith was a former member of Ernest Tubb's band who enjoyed popularity between the late '60s and mid-'70s. He was born in Oklahoma, but raised in Oakland, CA. A guitar player since childhood, he got his start in various talent contests and began playing professionally in his early teens in local clubs in San Jose. During the 1950s, he continued playing music and supplementing his income by doing various odd jobs ranging from truck driver to bronco buster. He was briefly married, but when his wife made him choose between music and her, Smith chose the former.

He began appearing on "California Hayride" in 1954. Two years later he joined the military, and after his discharge he worked as a deejay and began playing in a group in San Jose. Tubb heard him play and hired him as a Texas Troubador in 1961. Five years later, Tubb helped Smith land his first solo recording contract with Kapp Records, where he released his first single, "I'll Just Go Home." He made his first chart entry with his second effort, "The Only Thing I Want," which made it to the Top 60. During his long association with Kapp he had eight more midrange to minor hits, including "Drinking Champagne" (1968) and "Heaven Is Just a Touch Away."

In late 1970 he signed with Decca and in 1972 made it to the Top Five with "I've Found Someone of My Own." A few months later he scored his first No. 1 hit, "The Lord Knows I'm Drinking," which crossed over to become a minor pop hit. His next few singles did not do as well, but in 1974 his luck began to change and he scored his second No. 1 hit with "Country Bumpkin," a Don Wayne-penned tune that became Smith's signature song. Later that year he had his third No. 1, "It's Time to Pay the Fiddler." He continued appearing on the charts through 1979. —Sandra Brennan

I've Found Someone of My Own / 1972 / Decca ◆◆◆
I've Found Someone of My Own is arguably the finest album from one of the most neglected vocalists of the late '60s and '70s,

Cal Smith. On this record, he tackles classic honky tonk tunes, new country cuts, pop songs, R&B, and soul numbers, which are all given a contemporary, early-'70s gloss. But Smith, with his haunting, pure voice, gives each cut country grit, bringing each song down to earth. It's a record that convinces you Smith, in a perfect world, would have been a star. —*Thom Owens*

● **The Best of Cal Smith** / 1973 / MCA ✦✦✦✦

Country Bumpkin / 1974 / MCA ✦✦✦

It's Time to Play the Fiddler / 1975 / MCA ✦✦✦

Carl Smith

b. Mar. 15, 1927, Maynardsville, TN
Guitar, Vocals / Traditional Country, Honky Tonk, Western Swing Revival

Known as "Mr. Country," Carl Smith was one of the most popular honky tonkers of the '50s, racking up more than 30 Top Ten hits over the course of the decade. Smith was also able to sustain that popularity into the late '70s, when he had a charting single for every year except one. Smith had a talent for singing smooth ballads that polished the rough edges of hardcore country. Nevertheless, he could sing pure honky tonk with the best of them, and his hardest country was made tougher by the addition of a drum kit. Smith was one of the very first country artists to perform regularly with a drummer, and though it earned him criticism at the time, the hard-driving sound of those uptempo numbers proved to be influential. Smith also occasionally dabbled in Western swing, and as he continued to record, he delved deeper into the genre. Since he specialized in honky tonk ballads and Western swing, Smith rarely crossed over into the pop audience. Still, he was one of the most popular and best-known country singers of his era, recording several classics—including "Let's Live a Little," "Let Old Mother Nature Have Her Way," "This Orchard Means Goodbye," "Cut Across Shorty," "Loose Talk," "(When You Feel like You're in Love) Don't Just Stand There" and "Hey Joe!"—appearing in a handful of movies, and hosting his own television show. By the time he retired in the early '80s, he had hit the country charts nearly 100 times.

Carl Smith was born and raised in Maynardsville, TN, which was also the hometown of Roy Acuff. As a child, Smith idolized Acuff, Ernest Tubb, and Bill Monroe. When he was a teenager, he taught himself how to play guitar. According to legend, he bought his first guitar with money he earned by selling flower seeds. At the age of 15, he was singing in the San Francisco-based country band Kitty Dibble and Her Dude Ranch Ranglers. Two years later he learned to play string bass and spent his summer vacation working at WROL, a radio station in Knoxville. After Smith finished high school, he briefly served in the US Navy. When he returned to Tennessee, he continued to perform at WROL, usually playing bass for Skeets Williamson and Molly O'Day. Eventually he began singing as well, and one of his colleagues at the station sent an acetate of Smith's singing to WSM in Nashville. WSM signed Smith, and he began working for the station and singing at the Grand Ole Opry. By 1950 Columbia Records signed Smith. His first hit, "Let's Live a Little," arrived in 1951, climbing to No. 2. Over the course of the year, he racked up no less than three other hits, including the classic "If Teardrops Were Pennies" and his first No. 1 single, "Let Old Mother Nature Have Her Way." Also that year he married June Carter, the daughter of Maybelle Carter; the two would later divorce, but they had a daughter, Carlene, who would become a musician in her own right during the '70s.

Throughout the '50s, Carl Smith was a consistent presence in the country charts, racking up no less than 31 Top Ten singles during the course of the decade. In addition to recording, he began appearing in Western movies, like 1957's *The Badge of Marshal Brennan.* In 1956 he resigned from the Grand Ole Opry and joined a package tour organized by Phillip Morris. In 1957 he married country singer Goldie Hill, best-known for the No. 1 hit "I Let the Stars Get in My Eyes."

As the '50s ended, Smith was no longer as dominant in the upper reaches of the country charts as he had been earlier in the decade, but he never stopped having hits. During the '60s he consistently charted in the Top 40, which was indicative of his status

as a country music statesman. In 1961 he appeared on ABC's country television series "Four Star Jubilee," and a few years later he began hosting "Carl Smith's Country Music Hall" for Canadian television; the series also was syndicated in America. Throughout the '60s and early '70s, he began to incorporate more Western swing into his repertoire, especially on his albums. Smith continued to release albums and singles on Columbia Records until 1975, when he signed with Hickory. After having a handful of minor hits for the label—including several that were released on ABC/Hickory—he decided to retire in the late '70s.

Though he recorded an album of his greatest hits in the early '80s, Carl Smith retreated from the spotlight after his 1979 retirement. He and his wife lived on their horse farm outside of Franklin, TN, and the two began to show horses professionally. —*Stephen Thomas Erlewine*

Old Lonesome Times / 1988 / Rounder ✦✦✦
This album features such guest artists as Ray Price and Lefty Frizzell in recordings made in the early '50s. Included are such favorites as "Loose Talk" and "Hey Joe." —*AMG*

★ **The Essential Carl Smith (1950-1956)** / 1991 / Columbia/Legacy ✦✦✦✦✦
The Essential Carl Smith (1950-1956) collects 20 tracks from the height of Smith's career, including classics like "Are You Teasing Me," "If Teardrops Were Pennies," "(When You Feel Like You're In Love) Don't Just Stand There," "Hey, Joe," "Back Up Buddy," and "Loose Talk." Smith bridged the gap between raw honky tonk and smoother Nashville pop, and these sides capture him at his very best. —*Stephen Thomas Erlewine*

Satisfaction Guaranteed / 1996 / Bear Family ✦✦✦✦
Every song that Carl Smith recorded during the '50s is included on *Satisfaction Guaranteed,* a five-disc, 143-track box set that stands as the most comprehensive retrospective of the honky tonk star's peak period. During the era that *Satisfaction Guaranteed* covers, Smith scored more Top Ten hits than either Hank Williams or Lefty Frizzell, and many of his best songs—"Loose Talk," "Let Old Mother Nature Have Her Way," "Hey Joe!," "Are You Teasing Me," and "(When You Feel Like You're In Love) Don't Just Stand There," among them—are stone-cold honky tonk classics. For serious Smith and honky tonk fans, the set is essential, but the sheer length of the box—not to mention its strict chronological sequence—is tedious for anyone who isn't willing to dedicate the time to plow through the abundance of material here. —*Stephen Thomas Erlewine*

Connie Smith

b. Aug. 14, 1941, Elkhart, IN
Guitar, Vocals / Country-Pop, Country Gospel

In less than a year, Connie Smith moved from small-town Ohio housewife to country star, with a No. 1 single to her credit. Perhaps overly compared to and identified with Patsy Cline, Smith is still considered by many to be one of the best, most underrated, vocalists in country history. Her lonely desperation came straight from the heart; her father was abusive when she was a child, causing Smith to suffer a mental breakdown while she was in her teens.

Connie Smith was born Constance Meadows on August 14, 1941, in Elkhart, IN, but spent her early life first in West Virginia and later in Ohio. She married and became a housewife in the early '60s, singing occasionally on local TV shows around her home in Marietta, OH. She was singing near Columbus in August 1963 when country star Bill Anderson heard her and offered his help in getting a contract. She signed to RCA after a few months and recorded several selections in July 1964 with Chet Atkins at the helm. "Once a Day"—written especially for her by Anderson—was released as a single in September, and it hit the top of the country charts, reigning as No. 1 for eight weeks.

Connie Smith's follow-up "Then and Only Then" hit No. 4 (even the flip side reached the Top 25) and her Top Ten streak continued unabated until late 1968, including the big hits "If I Talk to Him," "Ain't Had No Lovin'," and "The Hurtin' All Over." Meanwhile, her success began to take a toll; constant appearances on the road, in films, and on "The Lawrence Welk Show" pushed Smith to the brink of suicide in 1968. She credits her Christian faith with saving her.

After Smith recovered from the pressure of being a fawned-over female country star, she began to balance chart success with a lighter schedule. Though her country hits were rarer than in her mid-'60s heyday, she was a better performer—and person—for it. Smith still managed the Top Tens "You and Your Sweet Love" in 1969, "I Never Once Stopped Loving You" the next year, and "Just One Time" in 1971. Her most successful year during the '70s was 1972. She recorded three big hits: the No. 5 "Just What I Am," the No. 7 "If It Ain't Love (Let's Leave It Alone)," and "Love Is the Look You're Looking For," which hit No. 8.

By 1972 Connie Smith began to incorporate more gospel into her act. With the help of her third husband, evangelist Marshall Haynes, she turned her live show into a travelling gospel roadshow and signed with Columbia, which permitted her to record more straight gospel songs. Though the material didn't score as well on the charts as her secular singles had, she managed to stay in the Top 20 during much of the '70s. After she signed with Monument in 1977, most of her singles dropped out of the Top 40. Though she has not been a commercial force since the '70s, Connie Smith continues to perform with the Grand Ole Opry. —*John Bush*

☆ **Connie Smith** / 1965 / RCA ♦♦♦♦♦
Cut in Music City, Smith's first LP (which includes "Once a Day") features her blowing through the Nashville sound production like a down-home Streisand fronting the Lennon Sisters. —*Dan Cooper*

Miss Smith Goes to Nashville / 1966 / RCA ♦♦♦♦

Sings Great Sacred Songs / 1966 / RCA ♦♦♦♦

Connie Smith Sings Bill Anderson / 1967 / RCA ♦♦♦

Soul of Country Music / 1968 / RCA ♦♦♦
More of the same unearthly sound, but this has Smith covering—at times burying—other singers' hits. Her version of Rex Griffin's "The Last Letter" is almost literally to die for. —*Dan Cooper*

Back in Baby's Arms / 1969 / RCA ♦♦♦♦
If any Thomas ever doubted Smith's religious convictions (which are as much a part of her story as her voice is) one listen to this LP's "How Great Thou Art" should take care of that mistrust. —*Dan Cooper*

The Best of Connie Smith / Jan. 1992 / RCA ♦♦♦
The Best of Connie Smith is a much-too-brief sampling of Connie Smith's biggest hits. Though there are some classic performances here—"Once A Day," "Then and Only Then," "If I Talk to Him," "Ain't Had No Lovin'," "The Hurtin's All Over," and "I'll Come Runnin'"—there is no reason why this stops short at eight tracks. Furthermore, there is even less reason why *The Best of Connie Smith* was the only collection of Smith's material in print during the '90s. As this proves, she was an excellent vocalist, one of the best country music had to offer in the '60s. —*Thom Owens*

★ **The Essential Connie Smith** / Apr. 1996 / RCA ♦♦♦♦♦
The Essential Connie Smith is the only thorough compilation of her '60s hits for RCA, featuring all of her Top Ten hits—including the No. 1 "Once A Day," "If I Talk to Him," "Ain't Had No Lovin'," "Then and Only Then," "Burning a Hole in My Mind," "Just One Time," and "Nobody But a Fool (Would Love You)"—and a selection of her lesser-known material. —*Thom Owens*

Greatest Hits on Monument / Sony ♦♦♦♦
Smith in the '70s has too much syrupy production. —*Dan Cooper*

Darden Smith

b. Mar. 11, 1962, Blenham, TX
Guitar, Vocals / Blues-Rock, Contemporary Country, Americana
Named for a local rodeo rider, Darden Smith grew up in Austin, TX, and placed two singles, "Little Maggie" and "Day After Tomorrow," on the country charts in 1988. His untitled major-label debut was released in 1988 on Epic. In 1989 he teamed up with British songwriter Boo Hewerdine of the Bible rock band to

record *Evidence*, which expanded his following beyond the country market. Smith's second solo album, *Trouble No More*, appeared in 1990. —*William Ruhlmann*

Native Soul / 1986 / Watermelon ♦♦♦
A fine debut album. Nanci Griffith sings harmony vocal on "Two Dollar Novels." Lyle Lovett sings harmony on five songs. This one's a gem. Smith is just breaking out and developing his style. —*Chip Renner*

● **Darden Smith** / 1988 / Epic ♦♦♦♦
Darden's big-label debut features three cuts off his *Native Soul* album. This time the production is better, with strings and extra vocals. Nanci Griffith and Lyle Lovett back him, along with Roland Denney and Paul Pearcy. All of his songs are strong, and the playing is dead-on. It's a keeper. —*Chip Renner*

Trouble No More / 1990 / Columbia ♦♦♦
A strong album, not as diverse as *Darden Smith*, but as good. Contains "Midnight Train," "Frankie and Sue," "Trouble No More," "Fall Apart at the Seams," and the list goes on. With two songs co-written with buddy Boo Hewerdine. —*Chip Renner*

Little Victories / Apr. 27, 1993 / Chaos ♦♦♦♦
Little Victories was recorded with pop producer Richard Gottehrer; while far removed from country music, it stands among Smith's most mature and ambitious work. —*Jason Ankeny*

Sammi Smith

b. Aug. 5, 1943, Orange, CA
Vocals / Progressive Country, Country-Pop, Outlaw Country
In the tradition of Waylon Jennings and Willie Nelson, singer-songwriter Sammi Smith was considered a country music outlaw, unafraid to sing songs that reflected the sometimes gritty realities of modern life. She first came to fame singing Kris Kristofferson's "Help Me Make It Through the Night" and was noted for her husky voice, the result of spending many years singing in smoke-filled clubs.

She was born Jewel Fay Smith in California, but she spent her childhood living in different Southwestern states. At age 11 Smith dropped out of school and the next year began singing professionally in clubs. She married at age 15 and produced four children. At songwriter Gene Sullivan's urging, a newly divorced Smith moved to Nashville in 1967. A year later she had her first minor hit, "So Long, Charlie Brown, Don't Look for Me Around." In 1970 she had another minor hit, but it was not until the end of the year that she had her first major smash with "Help Me Make It Through the Night," which made it to the top of the country charts and became a Top Ten pop hit. Later that year she wrote "Cedartown, Georgia," which became a major hit for Waylon Jennings.

In 1973 Smith moved to Dallas to join Jennings and Willie Nelson and became an "outlaw." Through 1975 she had several hits, including "Then You Walk In" and "Today I Started Loving You Again." She moved to Elektra in 1975 and remained with them for three years. During that time, she had several chart entries with such songs as "Loving Arms," "Days That End in 'Y'" (both 1977), and "Norma Jean" (1978), a tribute to Marilyn Monroe. In 1979 she signed to the independent label Cyclone and had a Top 20 hit with "What a Lie." In 1980 she moved to Sound Factory and had one Top 40 and two Top 20 hits, including "I Cry When I'm Alone." Her last hit came in 1986 with "Love Me All Over." —*Sandra Brennan*

Lonesome / 1971 / Mega ♦♦♦♦
Hot early-'60s album; Matt Murphy contributes sizzling guitar. —*Bill Dahl*

Today I Started Loving You Again / 1975 / Mega ♦♦♦

Help Me Make It Through the Night / 1976 / Mega ♦♦♦

Mixed Emotions / 1977 / Elektra ♦♦♦♦
Sammi sounds great on this album. In addition to her 1977 hit on Tom Jan's "Loving Arms," she takes songs like "A Woman Left Lonely" and "I've Seen Better Days" and makes them so thoroughly her own, you can't imagine anyone else ever trying to tackle them. —*Jim Worbois*

New Winds-All Quadrants / 1978 / Elektra ✦✦✦
More pop than country but there are a couple nice moments. The standout is the song "You Were Gone Before You Had a Chance to Say Goodbye." —*Jim Worbois*

Girl Hero / 1979 / Cyclone ✦✦
This is a rather disappointing record, with at least half the songs featuring what might pass as a disco beat. Sammi is the kind of singer who could have really done nice things with some of these tracks, especially the Amazing Rhythm Aces' "Dancing the Night Away." —*Jim Worbois*

● **Best of Sammi Smith** / Oct. 22, 1996 / ✦✦✦✦
The 16-track *The Best of Sammi Smith: Help Me Make It Through the Night* is the most comprehensive retrospective of Smith's prime hit-making years of the early '70s, featuring all of her biggest hits, including "Help Me Make It Through the Night" and "Then You Walk In." —*Stephen Thomas Erlewine*

Warren Smith

b. Feb. 7, 1933, **d.** Jan. 31, 1980
Vocals / Traditional Country, Rockabilly
For sheer, heartfelt vocalizing abilities, of all the folks who stood in front of the microphone at Sun studio, Warren Smith may have been the most talented. Equally adept at storming rockabilly and the most gut-wrenching of country ballads, Smith always sang from the heart, without giving in to phony rasping or histrionics. Though typecast as strictly a rocker, Smith left Sun and achieved minor success in the '60s in country music, his first love. —*Cub Koda*

The Classic Recordings 1956-59 / 1992 / Bear Family ✦✦✦✦
Smith's entire output (31 tracks in all) for Sun Records. Includes the rockabilly classics "Rock & Roll Ruby," "Ubangi Stomp," and "Miss Froggie," as well as heartfelt country performances on "The Darkest Cloud," "I'd Rather Be Safe than Sorry," and "Goodbye Mr. Love." No Sun collection can be considered complete without this one. —*Cub Koda*

● **Uranium Rock: Best Of** / 1995 / AVI ✦✦✦✦

Smokin' Armadillos

Country-Rock, Country-Rock, Bakersfield Sound
An energetic and wildly spirited country-rock sextet hailing from Bakersfield, the Smokin' Armadillos amazed the record industry by selling an astounding 150,000 copies of their independently released EP before they ever laid eyes on a recording contract. Comprised of Scott Meek (guitar, vocals), Rick Russell (lead vocals), Darrin Kirkindoll (drums), Aaron Casida (bass, vocals), and fiddle champion Jason Theiste, the band formed during the summer of 1992, with four of the group's six members knowing each other from high school. They developed a huge following regionally, and on the advice of a friend who worked for a major label, began to release singles and send them to radio stations. Even with stiff competition for airplay slots, some reporting stations began playing the singles, and soon a demand was created for their music. The band released a five-song EP and shipped copies from an office in Bakersfield, as well as selling units at their popular live shows. The Smokin' Armadillos released three singles, "My Girlfriend Might," "I'm a Cowboy," and "Red Rock," which took them to the top of the independent charts, before signing with MCG/Curb in 1994. They released their debut album in 1995, along with a reissued version of the EP. —*Jack Leaver*

● **Smokin' Armadillos** / Mar. 12, 1996 / MCA/Curb ✦✦✦✦
The Smokin' Armadillos' debut is pumped up country music with a heavy lean to power rock influences. This sextet from Bakersfield—ranging in age from 19 to 26—play with an unbridled enthusiasm that serves the material well. Nine of the 12 tracks were written by the band, and most of them are driven by the burning championship fiddle playing of the youngest Armadillo, Jason Theiste. Although none of the tracks here is likely to change the world, original songs like "Thump Factor" and "Too Hot to Handle" exude a youthful charm and show some songwriting potential. Southern rock king Charlie Daniels makes an appearance on a cover of his spooky '70s hit "The Legend of Wooley

Swamp," and the boys include reworked versions of a couple of their independent singles—the ones that started all the commotion. "My Girlfriend Might" is a catchy, lighthearted tune; but the country rap and probable live favorite "I'm a Cowboy" borders on the ridiculous. —*Jack Leaver*

● **Out of the Burrow** / Gramac ✦✦✦

Todd Snider

Singer-Songwriter, Roots-Rock, Alternative Country
Todd Snider is a sharp-witted, street-wise singer-songwriter whose songs address greed, shallowness, child abuse, and Christianity, among other subjects, and are delivered over a rootsy musical framework that combines rock, outlaw country, folk, and blues. A native of Portland, OR, Snider wound up in Austin, TX, at age 19, and started writing songs. His first taste of performing was playing his own songs at an open mic night. In 1992 Snider came to the attention of Capitol, and he was signed to a development deal that never panned out. While playing at the famed Bluebird in Nashville, he was heard by people from Margaritaville/MCA and he subsequently signed with the label. Snider's songs have been recorded by country artists Mark Chesnutt ("Trouble") and Rick Trevino ("She Just Left Me Lounge"). —*Jack Leaver*

Songs for the Daily Planet / 1994 / MCA ✦✦✦✦
It's ironic that Todd Snider's first radio exposure would come from a song included on his debut as an afterthought and a "hidden" track. "Talking Seattle Grunge-Rock Blues" is reminiscent of early Dylan, hilarious in its satire as a clever dose of good-natured pokes at the industry hype surrounding the Seattle music scene (including references to Eddie Vedder and Nirvana). Although he is a very talented songwriter with a keen wit, at times Snider is just a little too consciously contrived for his own good, threatening to reduce his art to novelty. For instance, the extremely countrified "My Generation (Part 2)" and the Mellencamp-esque "Alright Guy" are very humorous observations, but they're dangerously close to sounding trite, especially when compared to the seriousness of the chilling "You Think You Know Somebody," which deals with the ramifications of child abuse. A rootsy record that combines country and folk elements with a genuine rock 'n' roll sensibility, *Songs for the Daily Planet* also features some cutting fretwork by one of Nashville's finest young guitarists, Eddie Shaver, the son of country outlaw Billy Joe Shaver, one of Snider's heroes. Overall a fine introduction to a remarkable voice. —*Jack Leaver*

● **Step Right Up** / Apr. 1996 / MCA ✦✦✦✦
Picking up where he left off with his exceptional debut *Songs for the Daily Planet*, Todd Snider continues his ragged-but-right blend of folk, country, and rootsy rock 'n' roll on this 14-song release. At times brilliant, Snider's songwriting talent is still intact, as are his passionate voice and the superb instrumental backing by his band the Nervous Wrecks. The first single, "I Believe You," is a hopeful testament to the singer's faith in human nature. Keen observations of social and political issues are honestly presented, using wit and humor, as in "Side Show Blues," "Tension," and with kick-in-the-gut seriousness—"T.V. Guide," "24 Hours a Day." It's not all weighty stuff though; the swampy "Moon Dawg's Tavern" and the Chuck Berry-esque rocker "Late Last Night" are just plain fun. Hear him out; he's got a lot to say. —*Jack Leaver*

Hank Snow (Clarence Eugene Snow)

b. May 9, 1914, Liverpool, Nova Scotia, Canada
Guitar, Vocals / Traditional Country, Cowboy, Honky Tonk, Country Boogie
Canada's greatest contribution to country music, Hank Snow was famous for his "traveling" songs. It's no wonder. At age 12 he ran away from his Nova Scotia home and joined the Merchant Marines, working as a cabin boy and laborer for four years. Once back on shore, he listened to Jimmie Rodgers records and started playing in public, building up a following in Halifax. His original nickname, the Yodelling Ranger, was modified to the Singing Ranger when his high voice changed to the great baritone that graced his hit records. In 1950, the year he became an Opry regu-

lar, his self-penned "I'm Moving On" (the first of his many great traveling songs) became a smash hit, reaching No. 1 and remaining there for 21 weeks. "Golden Rocket" (also 1950) and "I've Been Everywhere" (1962), two other hits, show his lifelong love of trains and travel. But he was as much at home with two other styles, the ballad and the rhumba/boogie. Among his many great ballads are "Bluebird Island" (with Anita Carter, of the Carter Family), "Fool Such as I," and "Hello, Love," a hit when Snow was 60 years old. Snow appeared regularly on the Opry into the '90s, proving that his incredible voice suffered no loss of quality over the last half century, as well as what a tasteful, understated guitar stylist he is. With small stature and huge voice, Snow is a country traditionalist who has given much more to the business than he's taken.

Born and raised in Nova Scotia, Hank Snow (born Clarence Eugene Snow) moved in with his grandmother when he was eight years old, after the divorce of his parents. Four years later, he re-joined his mother when she re-married, but his stepfather was an abusive, violent man who frequently beat Hank. Tired of the abuse, Snow ran away from home when he was 12 years old, joining the Merchant Marine. For the next four years he served as a cabin boy, often singing for the sailors onboard. When he was 16, he returned home, where he began working odd jobs and trying to launch a performing career. His mother had given him a stack of Jimmie Rodgers records that inspired him greatly. Within a few weeks of hearing Rodgers, Snow ordered a cheap, mail-order guitar and tried to learn his idol's trademark blue yodel. For the next few years he sang around Nova Scotia before finally mustering the courage to travel to Halifax in 1933. Snow landed a weekly unpaid appearance on CHNS' "Down on the Farm," where he was billed as both the cowboy Blue Yodeller and Clarence Snow and His Guitar. The next year, CHNS' chief announcer Cecil Landry suggested to Snow that he should change his name to Hank, since it sounded more Western.

Hank continued to perform in Halifax for the next three years, often struggling to get by. The severity of the financial situation was compounded when he married Minnie Aaiders in 1936, but he landed a regular paid program on the network Canadian Farm Hour, billed as Hank the Yodelling Ranger. By the end of the year, Snow had signed a deal with RCA-Victor's Montreal branch and recorded two original songs: "The Prisoned Cowboy" and "Lonesome Blue Yodel." The songs were hits, beginning a string of Canadian-only hit singles that ran for the next ten years; during that time, he recorded nearly 90 songs. In the early '40s, he had a regular show on CBC, based in Montreal and New Brunswick. In 1944 he switched to CKCW in New Brunswick. Around that time he switched his stage name to Hank the Singing Ranger, since his voice had deepened and he could no longer yodel.

Though he had become a star in Canada, the American market remained untapped. Snow tried to break into the US several times, playing "The Wheeling Jamboree" in West Virginia and briefly moving to Hollywood and performing concerts with his trick pony Shawnee, but he was having no luck finding fans. He was trying to find an audience that wasn't there, since most citizens were concentrating on World War II. Another stumbling block was RCA Records, who refused to let Snow release records in the US until he was well known in the country. By 1948 Snow was singing on "The Big D Jamboree" in Dallas, where he befriended the honky tonk legend Ernest Tubb. ET pulled enough weight at the Grand Ole Opry to get Snow a slot in early 1950, and by that time, RCA had agreed to record Snow for the American audience.

Hank Snow's American debut single "Marriage Vow" became a minor hit at the end of 1949, but it fell off the charts after a week. Similarly, his debut appearance at the Grand Ole Opry in January was not well received, prompting him to consider moving back to Canada. However, those ideas were abandoned when his breakthrough arrived in the summer of 1950. That July, "I'm Moving On" began its remarkable ascent up the charts, eventually landing at No. 1 and staying there for a full 21 weeks. In the year after the release of "I'm Moving On," "The Golden Rocket" and "The Rhumba Boogie" both hit No. 1 (the latter staying there for eight weeks), establishing Hank Snow as a genuine star. Between 1951

and the 'end of 1955, Snow had a remarkable 24 Top Ten hits, including the massive hit single "I Don't Hurt Anymore," which spent 20 weeks at No. 1 in 1954. Snow not only played his trademark traveling songs, but country-boogie, Hawaiian music, rhumbas, and cowboys songs. By the middle of the decade, he was a star not only in the United States and Canada, but throughout the world, gaining a particularly strong following over the years in the United Kingdom.

Around 1954 Snow formed a booking agency with Colonel Tom Parker, who would later become infamous as Elvis Presley's manager. Indeed, Snow played a formative role in Presley's early career, convincing the Grand Ole Opry to give the singer a chance in 1954. Though Elvis' appearance at the Opry was ill-received, Snow continued to push Presley to move toward country, and Hank was quite upset when Parker took complete control of Elvis' management around 1955. Still, Snow found a way to combat rock 'n' roll—he recorded some light rockabilly singles himself. "Hula Rock" and "Rockin', Rollin' Ocean" were attempts to capture the beat of rock 'n' roll, but they were diluted by the rhumbas and boogie that made his singles hits during the early '50s. Though he was experimenting with the new genre, he hadn't abandoned country and he continued to regularly chart in the country Top Ten until 1965 with hits like "Big Wheels" (No. 7, 1958), "Miller's Cave" (No. 9, 1960), "Beggar to a King (No. 5, 1961), "I've Been Everywhere" (No. 1, 1962), and "Ninety Miles an Hour (Down a Dead End Street)" (No. 2, 1963).

During the latter half of the '60s, Snow's career slowed considerably, as he wasn't able to make the transition to the new, heavily orchestrated country-pop sounds, nor was he able to keep pace with the twangy roll of Bakersfield. Instead, his singles placed in the lower reaches of the charts, while his concerts and Grand Ole Opry appearances continued to be quite popular. It wasn't until 1974 that another monster hit arrived in the form of "Hello Love," which unexpectedly climbed to No. 1. Instead of sparking a revival, "Hello Love" proved to be a last gasp; between its release in 1974 and 1980, Hank had only two other Top 40 hits, which both arrived the same year as "Hello Love." Despite his declining record sales, his profile remained high through his concerts and several lifetime-achievement awards, including his induction by the Nashville Songwriters International Hall of Fame in 1978 and the Country Music Hall of Fame in 1979.

In 1981 Hank Snow's recording career ended when RCA dropped him after a 45-year relationship. Snow was very upset with the label's treatment of him, as well as the direction that country music was taking, claiming that "80% of today's country music is a joke and not fit to listen to." He was equally angry that country's roots were being diluted by pop and rock production values. Though he never recorded again, Snow remained active in the Grand Ole Opry into the '90s, and he spent a lot of time working for his Foundation for Child Abuse. In the late '80s, Bear Family began a lengthy retrospective of several multi-disc box sets that chronicled his entire recording career. In 1994 Snow published his autobiography, The Hank Snow Story. Late the following year, he was stricken with a respiratory illness, but he recovered in 1996, returning to the Grand Ole Opry in August of that year. —David Vinopal

Hank Snow Sings Jimmie Rodgers Songs / 1960 / RCA ✦✦✦✦

Jimmie Rodgers was one of Snow's greatest influences, and this record is a work of pure love. Snow doesn't just "sing" these songs, as the title suggests. He gets inside them, lives them, and makes them his. —Jim Worbois

The Singing Ranger: 1949-1953 / 1989 / Bear Family ✦✦✦✦

Bear Family's The Singing Ranger: 1949-1953 contains every song Hank Snow recorded for RCA in the beginning of his career. Not only are career-making songs like "I'm Movin' On," "Marriage Vow," and "The Rhumba Boogie" included, but so are a wealth of unreleased songs and alternate takes. For diehard Hank Snow fans, this first volume of The Singing Ranger series is essential. —Stephen Thomas Erlewine

★ I'm Movin' On and Other Country Hits / 1990 / RCA ✦✦✦✦✦

I'm Movin' On and Other Hits doesn't have all the hits Hank Snow had over the course of his career, but it has 20 essential tracks from the early '50s, including "The Rhumba Boogie," "Silver Bell," "The Wreck of the Old '97," "Marriage Vow," and the title track. These are the songs that made his career, and while he had decades worth of other hits, this disc gives an accurate sense of what Snow accomplished. —*Stephen Thomas Erlewine*

The Singing Ranger, Vol. 2 / 1990 / Bear Family ◆◆◆◆
Running from 1953 to 1958, the four-disc box set *The Singing Ranger, Vol. 2* contains everything Hank Snow recorded during those five years, including all the hits and a bevy of outtakes. Again, the set is not for the fair-weather fan—there's plenty of brilliant music here, but its very scope makes it appealing only to completists, who will find much to treasure. —*Stephen Thomas Erlewine*

The Thesaurus Transcriptions / 1991 / Bear Family ◆◆◆◆
Bear Family's five-disc box set *The Thesaurus Transcriptions* contains 138 radio transcriptions that Hank Snow cut during the early '50s, when he was one of the biggest stars in country. Many of these songs were never recorded in the studio, and Snow is in superb voice throughout. It's not a set for neophytes or casual fans, but those diehard fans and historians willing to invest in such a mammoth box will find it fascinating. —*Stephen Thomas Erlewine*

The Singing Ranger, Vol. 3 / 1994 / Bear Family ◆◆◆◆
Singing Ranger, Vol. 3 picks up where the second box set left off and presents the final recordings Hank Snow made. The box is extremely lengthy, running a total of 12 discs and spanning all of his '60s material. It contains less first-rate material than Bear Family's other three box sets, but it remains necessary for completists. —*Stephen Thomas Erlewine*

Yodelling Ranger (1936-1947) [Box] / 1994 / Bear Family ◆◆◆◆
The Yodelling Ranger (1936-1947) is a five-disc box set containing all of Hank Snow's early recordings, including all of his material for RCA Canada and several unreleased songs, alternate takes, and rarities. This material is primarily of interest to hardcore Snow fans; there aren't many well known hits on the collection, but there are good versions of contemporary hits, as well as several answer records. For dedicated listeners, the set's comprehensiveness and loving liner notes are a worthwhile investment. Consumer warning: the fifth disc contains just four tracks—a two-part "Life Story" and two demos. —*Thom Owens*

My Early Country Favorites / 1996 / RCA Camden ◆◆
The material on this compilation isn't bad at all, featuring Snow on some of his more traditional performances. The problem is in the packaging—there are only ten tracks, there's absolutely no annotation, and the sound quality is substandard, with noticeable surface noise throughout. The music is all right, but there are better ways to get it. —*Richie Unterberger*

Collector's Series / RCA ◆◆◆
Collector's Series is a haphazard collection. Out of the eight tracks, four of the selections weren't hits for Snow, and one track, "(Now and Then There's) A Fool Such As I," is Snow reciting portions of his autobiography over a string-laden instrumental. —*Stephen Thomas Erlewine*

Son Volt

Alternative Country-Rock
After the acrimonious dissolution of the influential alternative country trio Uncle Tupelo, the group's singer/guitarist Jay Farrar formed the roots-rock unit Son Volt. Joined by onetime Tupelo drummer Mike Heidorn and brothers Jim (bass, vocals) and Dave Boquist (guitar, banjo, fiddle, lap steel), Farrar set about authoring the group's 1995 debut record, *Trace*, an edgy, stark affair that earned virtually unanimous praise from the critical community and scored a minor hit with its first single, "Drown." Son Volt rerturned in the spring of 1997 with the album *Straightaway*.—*Jason Ankeny*

● **Trace** / Sep. 19, 1995 / Warner Brothers ◆◆◆◆
Jay Farrar always provided the darkest, grittiest moments in Uncle Tupelo, so it comes as no surprise that this is a rawer record

than *A.M.*, the first album by Wilco, a band led by his former partner Jeff Tweedy. Throughout Son Volt's debut *Trace*, the group reworks classic honky tonk and rock 'n' roll, adding a desperate, determined edge to their performances. Even when they rock out, there is a palpable sense of melancholy to Farrar's voice, which lends a poignancy to the music. *Trace* isn't a great step forward from Tupelo's last album, the lovely *Anodyne*, but it is a fine continuation of the ideas Farrar has pursued over the course of his career. —*Stephen Thomas Erlewine*

Jo-El Sonnier

b. 1946, Rayne, LA
Guitar, Accordion, Vocals / *Progressive Country, Cajun, Americana*

In the late '80s, when Nashville realized that country consisted of more than the Tennessee-Texas axis, they started looking for new sounds. One of the best was that of Cajun accordionist Jo-El Sonnier, who had kicked around for a number of years, gaining a reputation as a "musician's musician." Sonnier initially caused a major fuss in Nashville and a minor one elsewhere, though his songs—a blend of Cajun music, twangy guitars, and New Orleans R&B—briefly added a touch of spice to country radio.

Sonnier was born the son of French-speaking sharecroppers near Rayne, LA. He was raised in extreme poverty, often working in the cotton fields with his parents. Sonnier began playing his much-older brother's battered accordion at age three and first performed on the radio when he was six. He then began playing Cajun music in local clubs, making his recording debut at age 13. He remained a local sensation through his mid-20s, occasionally recording for regional labels. He moved to California to try for a solo career, but ended up a session man. After a second move, to Nashville in the mid-'70s, Sonnier continued writing songs and playing backup. After six years, he returned to Louisiana so bitterly disappointed that he almost stopped playing. At a low point in his career, Sonnier got a badly needed break when Merle Haggard hired him to work as his opening act on a few road shows.

In 1982 Sonnier and his wife went back to California where, thanks to the help of a few notable friends, including guitarist Albert Lee, he began putting on solo shows in Los Angeles. He recorded *Cajun Life* for Rounder in 1984 and garnered his first Grammy nomination. In 1987 he signed to RCA and, though encouraged to continue recording pure Cajun material, began exploring country-, rock-, and pop-influenced music. The result was *Come On Joe* (1988), an acclaimed album with several country Top 20 hits, including "Tear Stained Letter." He signed to Capitol-Nashville in the early '90s and though few would dispute his expertise and versatility on the accordion, Sonnier's career did not take off. —*Brian Mansfield and Sandra Brennan*

Cajun Life / 1975 / Rounder ◆◆◆
Jo-El Sonnier, like Jimmy C. Newman, has found a comfortable middle ground between traditional Cajun and contemporary country music, working both styles and achieving a measure of commercial and aesthetic success in each. This session accented the Cajun side, although it included competent pop/country material as well. Besides the autobiographical title track, Sonnier demonstrated his roots facilty on "Yes Yeux Bleu," "Jolie Blon," and "Les Grands Bois." Sonnier has gone on to become a bigger name in country, but this earlier date will appeal both to lovers of vintage material and those unaware of his solid Cajun skills and background. —*Ron Wynn*

Cajun Valentine / 1979 / Goldband ◆◆◆

Hurricane Avory / 1979 / Goldband ◆◆

Scene Today in Cajun Music / 1979 / Goldband ◆◆

● **Come on Joe** / 1987 / RCA ◆◆◆◆
Sonnier's French-Cajun accent brings new life to songs by Randy Newman, Richard Thompson, Moon Martin, and Dave Alvin. Steve Winwood takes an organ solo on a cover of Slim Harpo's "Raining in My Heart." Cajun-tinged contemporary country with a rock edge and intelligent songs, it is the best of Sonnier's Nashville work. —*Brian Mansfield & Mark A. Humphrey*

Have a Little Faith / 1990 / RCA ✦✦✦
The emphasis here lies more heavily on ballads, as Sonnier discovers John Hiatt and delivers penetrating versions of his "Have a Little Faith" and "I'll Never Get Over You." The album also includes a remake of Iry LeJeune's 1945 "Evangeline Special" and a straight-country single in "If Your Heart Should Ever Roll This Way Again." —*Brian Mansfield*

Tears of Joy / 1991 / Liberty ✦✦✦
It's in the Cajun/pop/country mold of his RCA albums. —*Mark A. Humphrey*

The Complete Mercury Sessions / 1992 / Mercury ✦✦✦✦
Fifteen fine '70s country songs are here, including the aching "Blue Is Not a Word." —*Mark A. Humphrey*

Hello Happiness Again / Sep. 28, 1992 / Liberty ✦✦✦

Cajun Roots / May 28, 1994 / Rounder ✦✦✦✦

The Sons of the Pioneers

Traditional Country, Cowboy
The Sons of the Pioneers were the foremost vocal and instrumental group in Western music, and the definitive group specializing in cowboy songs, setting the standard for every group since. They were also one of the longest surviving country music vocal groups, going into their seventh decade. More important than their longevity, however, was the sheer quality of their work. Their superb harmonies and brilliant arrangements delighted three generations of listeners and inspired numerous performers.

The group's roots lay in the depths of the Great Depression. Cincinnati-born Leonard Franklin Slye (b. Nov. 5, 1911—see separate entry under Roy Rogers) had headed out to California in the spring of 1931 from his native Ohio, working jobs ranging from driving a gravel truck to picking fruit for the DelMonte company in California's Central Valley. By sheer chance, he entered an amateur singing contest on a Los Angeles radio show called "Midnight Frolics," and a few days later got an invitation to join a group called the Rocky Mountaineers.

Slye played guitar, sang, and yodeled with the group, and before long they wanted an additional singer so they could extend their range. The man who answered the ad was Bob Nolan (born Robert Clarence Nobles, Apr. 1, 1908, New Brunswick, Canada), from Tucson, AZ. Nolan had lived the life of an itinerant singer for a few years before settling down in Los Angeles, where he'd worked as a lifeguard as well as trying to make a living singing. Nolan joined the Rocky Mountaineers, and he and Slye developed a harmonious relationship that worked for several months, until he exited in frustration over the group's lack of success. Nolan was, in turn, replaced by Tim Spencer (born Vernon Spencer, July 13, 1908, Webb City, MO), who'd been earning his keep working in a Safeway Stores warehouse.

Slye, Spencer, and another singer named Slumber Nichols quit the Rocky Mountaineers in the spring of 1932 to form a trio of their own, which never quite came off. Instead, Slye and Spencer spent a year moving in and out of the lineups of short-lived groups like the International Cowboys and the O-Bar-O Cowboys. The latter group broke up after a disastrous tour, and Spencer left music for a time. Slye decided to push on with an attempt at a career, joining yet another group, Jack LeFevre and His Texas Outlaws, who were fixtures on a local Los Angeles radio station.

In early 1933, things began looking up. He convinced Spencer to give up the security of a steady job once more, and recruited Bob Nolan, who was working as a caddy at a golf course in Bel Air. Weeks of rehearsals followed as they honed their singing hour after hour, while Slye continued to work with his radio singing group and Spencer and Nolan wrote songs.

The group was called the Pioneer Trio, and made its debut on KFWB radio, after an audition that included the Nolan song "Way Out There." Their mix of singing and yodeling, coupled with their good spirits, won them a job. Within a few weeks, they were developing a large following on Lefevre's show, with their harmony singing eliciting lots of mail, and soon they were featured on the station's morning and evening lineups.

The group in its earliest form consisted of Slye, Nolan, and Spencer on vocals, with Nolan playing string bass and Slye on

rhythm guitar. A fourth member was needed to firm up their sound, and he arrived in the form of fiddle player Hugh Farr (b. Plano, TX, Dec. 6, 1906), early in 1934, who also added a bass voice to the group, and occasionally served as lead singer.

The group's name was altered by accident on the eve of their going national. On one broadcast the station's announcer introduced them as "The Sons of the Pioneers." Asked why he'd done this, the announcer gave the excuse that they were too young to have been pioneers, but that they could be sons of pioneers. The name stuck.

The Sons of the Pioneers' fame quickly spread well beyond the confines of Los Angeles, as a result of an informal syndication project undertaken by their station, which recorded the group in 15- and 30-minute segments for rebroadcast all over the country. It wasn't long before a recording contract with the newly founded Decca label (now part of MCA) was signed, and on August 8, 1934, (the same day that Bing Crosby made his debut for the label), the Sons of the Pioneers made their first commercial recording. The group would cut 32 songs with Decca over the next two years.

One of the songs cut at the first session was a Bob Nolan original called "Tumbling Tumbleweeds," which he'd originally written on a rainy day in 1932 as "Tumbling Leaves." The group had introduced it on the radio as "Tumbling Leaves," but later changed it to "tumbleweeds" as more in keeping with their Western image. It became their theme song and was quickly picked up by singers and bands all over the country. In 1935 the song was also licensed for use as the title of a Gene Autry Western, the first —but not the last—time that the paths of Autry and the Pioneers would cross.

In 1935 a fifth member, Hugh Farr's brother Karl (b. Rochelle, TX, Apr. 25, 1909), who had played with Hugh on the radio during the 1930s, was added to the group on lead guitar, bringing the Pioneers' instrumental capabilities up to a par with their singing. Early that same year, they began appearing in movies, initially in short films, and providing the music for an Oswald the Rabbit cartoon, before making their first appearance in a full-length movie, *The Old Homestead.* Later that year they appeared in *The Gallant Defender.* They followed this with *Song of the Saddle* (1936), starring singer-turned-cowboy star Dick Foran, then with *The Mysterious Avenger* (1936), and in the Bing Crosby vehicle *Rhythm of the Range.* That same year, they appeared in a Gene Autry movie, *The Big Show.*

Tim Spencer left the group in September 1936 and was replaced by Lloyd Perryman (b. Ruth, AR, Jan. 29, 1917), who was a fan of the Pioneers as well as a veteran of several singing groups, and who had already served as a "fill-in" Pioneer on occasion. Perryman was later to become a key member of the group, doing most of their vocal arrangements, serving as their onstage spokesman, and handling the group's business affairs as well, and would remain with them longer than anyone else, 41 years. Their broadcasts, concerts, and film appearances continued, with work in the Foran-starring *California Mail* at Warner Bros., and in Autry's *The Old Corral* at Republic. In late 1937 the group was signed by Columbia to work in Charles Starrett's Western films on a steady basis, beginning with *The Old Wyoming Trail.*

It was the movies that led to the next major change in the Pioneers' line-up. Leonard Slye had previously played bit acting parts in a handful of B-Westerns, including an appearance in a small role in a Gene Autry film, under the name Dick Weston. But in 1938 Autry and the studio found themselves in a contractual dispute that they were unable to resolve, and the cowboy star failed to report for his next movie. Autry was placed on suspension, and the studio began looking for a replacement that they could put into the picture.

Slye auditioned and won the part; in the process he was given a new name for his first starring film: Roy Rogers. *Under Western Stars,* as the film was eventually titled, was a hit, and Leonard Slye/Roy Rogers had a whole new career. In order to do the movie, however, he was forced to leave the Sons of the Pioneers, who were under exclusive contract with Columbia Pictures. To replace Slye, the group chose a friend of his, a singer and comic named Pat Brady, who played bass and handled much of the comedy within the group, although vocally he was weaker than the others, which forced the Pioneers to expand their lineup once more in 1938, with Tim Spencer returning to fill out the harmony parts. The group continued to make movies with Charles Starrett, appearing in 28 movies with him between 1937 and 1941.

The Sons of the Pioneers' recording career kept pace with their movie and radio work. They left Decca Records in 1936 to sign with the American Record Company (later part of Columbia Records), and appeared on that label's Okeh and Vocalion imprints on 32 songs in two sessions in late 1937. Although he'd officially left the group to pursue his film career, Roy Rogers returned to sing with the Sons of the Pioneers on those sessions. The 1938-1942 version of the group, consisting of Nolan, Spencer, Perryman, the Farrs, and Brady, became the "classic" Pioneers line-up, the version of the group most familiar to audiences, largely because of their screen appearances.

In 1941 the group's contract with Columbia was up and, after years of Rogers' entreaties, Republic Pictures signed the Pioneers to appear in his movies, beginning with *Red River Valley* (1941), in which they were billed as "Bob Nolan and the Sons of the Pioneers." The same year that they signed their contract with Republic, the group also signed with Decca Records.

The American entry into World War II brought about the next change in the Pioneers' lineup. Perryman and Brady were both called up for the draft. Perryman was replaced by Ken Carson while he was with the American forces in Burma, while Brady became a soldier in Patton's Third Army and was replaced by musician and comic (George) Shug Fisher.

In 1944 the Sons of the Pioneers moved to RCA-Victor, signed up by the head of the company's country music division, Steve Sholes (who was also later responsible for bringing Elvis Presley to the label). They would be associated with RCA longer than any other label, 24 years broken by a brief one-year stint elsewhere.

The change in labels resulted in the first major alteration in the Pioneers' sound since their founding. Previously, they'd been a self-contained outfit, providing virtually all of the sounds, vocal and instrumental, needed on their records. RCA, however, saw fit to provide the group's music with additional backup in the form of fuller instrumentation, including small-scale orchestration. At first it worked reasonably well, as the Pioneers re-recorded several of their standards (including "Cool Water" and "Tumbling Tumbleweeds") with new arrangements that proved popular, and many fans regard their mid-1940's versions of their classic songs as the best of the many renditions that they recorded. They also recorded more gospel material, as well as many pop-oriented and novelty songs. The Pioneers also provided backup for other performers throughout their time at RCA, including Roy Rogers and Dale Evans, and Vaughn Monroe.

Amid all of this varied activity, which yielded hundreds of songs, they recorded a number of new Western classics during their stay on the label, most notably Stan Jones' "(Ghost) Riders in the Sky" in 1949. Originally, Bob Nolan had declined the song, but after it became a hit for Vaughn Monroe, the Pioneers covered it themselves. The group had ceased appearing in movies with the end of Rogers' B-Westerns at Republic in 1948, but two years later a new career opened up for them in movies courtesy of John Ford, who used their singing in three of his most acclaimed Westerns, *Wagon Master* (1950)—in which they had four songs, including "Wagons West"—*Rio Grande* (1950), and *The Searchers* (1956).

Perryman was back in the lineup in 1946, although his interim replacement, Ken Carson (who later became a well known singer in his own right on "The Garry Moore Show"), continued to record with the group for another year. During this era, the group made some magnificent recordings; Spencer contributed more than his share of important songs, Fisher contributed as a songwriter, and Perryman took the lead vocals on some numbers. Pat Brady returned to the lineup later in 1946, and the group continued working in Roy Rogers' Western movies through 1948.

These were golden years for the Sons of the Pioneers. Their hits on the country singles chart included "Stars and Stripes on Iwo Jima" (1945), "No One to Cry To" (1946), "Baby Doll," "Cool Water," and "Tear Drops in My Heart" (all Top Five in 1947), "Tumbling Tumbleweeds" and "Cool Water" (both 1948), "My Best to You" and "Room Full of Roses" (both 1949). It wasn't to last, however, as time and changing public tastes were to take their toll on the group.

Spencer, who had written many of the group's more important originals, left the group in 1949, after several years of worsening problems with his voice. He was replaced by Ken Curtis (b. Lamar, CO, July 2, 1916), a former singer with Tommy Dorsey and a sometime actor, who later became immortalized on television as Festus, Marshal Matt Dillon's grizzled backwoods deputy, on "Gunsmoke." As a parting gesture, Spencer gave the group one of his best songs, "Room Full of Roses," which became Curtis' first lead vocal with the group. Soon after, Roy Rogers began shooting his television series and recruited Brady as his comic relief sidekick. He was replaced by his wartime fill-in, Fisher.

But it was the retirement of Bob Nolan in 1949 that caused the biggest change in the group's lineup. Essentially, his exit came about purely for personal reasons. He was a very private individual to begin with, and 16 years with the Pioneers, although rewarding musically and financially, had begun to wear on him. He wanted more time to himself, and more time to write songs. But the gap he left was huge—apart from having written many of the Pioneers' best-known songs, Nolan had been the lead singer on many of their hits. He did continue to provide them with songs after his retirement, and even rejoined them in the studio.

Lloyd Perryman stepped into the breech opened by Nolan's exit. He had been taking a leadership role in the group over the previous few years and now took over leadership, recruiting a new sixth member, Tommy Doss (b. Weiser, ID, Sept. 26, 1920). Doss was an excellent singer, and his voice meshed beautifully with Perryman and Curtis, but within a year of his joining—through no fault of his—the group's record sales began to decline. There was an overall drop of interest in cowboy songs and Western music, which resulted in RCA's attempts to push the Pioneers into the pop vocal market. These efforts failed, and simultaneously lost them part of their country audience.

Ironically, in 1952, the same year that the Pioneers got their first LP releases, the 10-inch discs *Cowboy Hymns and Spirituals* (made up of recordings from 1947), and *Cowboy Classics* (made up of material from 1945 and 1946), the group left RCA, in the wake of their declining sales figures. They didn't record at all in 1953, but at the end of the year the group signed once again to Coral Records. Simultaneously with the move, Curtis and Fisher both exited the lineup, to go into television and film work. They co-starred on one television series, and Curtis would later serve as co-producer on a pair of low-budget horror films at the end of the 1950s, one of which, *The Giant Gila Monster* (1958), would feature Fisher.

They were replaced by Dale Warren (b. Summerville, KY, June 1, 1925), a veteran of Foy Willing and the Riders of the Purple Sage, and Deuce Spriggens (born George R. Braunsdorf), a former member of Spade Cooley's band. The group's one-year stay at Coral proved no more successful than the last few years at RCA, however.

By 1955 they were back with RCA, where they stayed for another 14 years. In a major change of strategy, RCA now wanted the old Bob Nolan/Tim Spencer sound. Nolan agreed to return to record with the group in the studio, but Spencer was no longer in good enough health or voice to be part of the group, so Ken Curtis was asked to return as part of the studio version of the Pioneers. Pat Brady also came back as bassist in the studio. The Sons of the Pioneers, in effect, became two groups—Nolan, Perryman, and Curtis were the studio vocal trio, backed by Brady and Hugh and Karl Farr, recreating the group's classic sound on record; Perryman, Doss, Warren, the Farrs, and Spriggens (who left soon after this arrangement began) played the concerts. It wasn't until 1958 that the touring version of the Pioneers began making their records as well.

By that time, more changes had overtaken the lineup. Nolan retired as a singer once and for all, and Hugh Farr, who felt that his fiddle playing wasn't appreciated by the other members, quit as well in 1958. Karl Farr continued as a member, but on September 20, 1961, in the middle of a concert performance, he became agitated over a guitar string that had broken, and suddenly collapsed and died of heart failure. The same month, Roy Lanham (b. Corbin, KY, Jan. 16, 1923), one of the busiest session guitarists on the West Coast, joined the group as Karl Farr's successor. Pat Brady was also back in the lineup by then, having rejoined to replace Shug Fisher, who retired in 1959. Brady remained with the group until 1967.

The next major change in the lineup came in 1963, when Tommy Doss retired from touring with the group, although he recorded with them until 1967. In 1968 Luther Nallie joined the group as lead singer, and he remained with the Pioneers until 1974. They were still very much a going concern, not only on the concert stage but in the recording studio; over a 12-year period from 1957 until 1969, RCA released 21 albums by the group.

Bob Nolan and Tim Spencer were both elected to the Nashville Songwriter Hall of Fame in 1971. A 1972 gathering at the Ambassador Hotel in Los Angeles brought together most of the surviving members of the Sons of the Pioneers except for Ken Curtis, including a reunion of the original Pioneer Trio of Roy Rogers, Bob Nolan, and Tim Spencer. And in 1976, the Sons of the Pioneers were inducted by the Country Music Hall of Fame.

This was a last hurrah for the original and early group members. Tim Spencer died on April 26, 1976, and Lloyd Perryman, who had been with the group since 1936, died on May 31, 1977. Hugh Farr, who had retired from the group in 1958, passed away on April 17, 1980, and Bob Nolan died almost exactly two months later, on June 16, 1980.

After Perryman passed away, the leadership of the Sons of the Pioneers was taken over by Dale Warren, who had joined in 1952. He carried the group into the 1990s. They continued to perform in concert, and recorded as well, with a lineup that featured Rusty Richards (vocals), Doye O'Dell (guitar, vocals), Billy Armstrong (fiddle), Billy Liebert (accordion), and Rome Johnson (vocals). These Pioneers, along with younger country music groups such as the Riders in the Sky, were a constant reminder of the legacy of this much-loved Western group. —Bruce Eder

Cowboy Classics / 1952 / RCA Victor ♦♦♦
"Cool Water" and "Tumbling Tumbleweeds," in their 1945 and 1946 versions—often considered the best—with "Blue Prairie," "The Timber Trail," "Trees," and "Cowboy Camp Meetin'." These songs have been compiled elsewhere since, but this is a collectable disc as one of their first two LPs. —Bruce Eder

Cowboy Hymns and Spirituals / 1952 / RCA Victor ♦♦♦
The classic postwar Sons of the Pioneers, featuring Bob Nolan, Tim Spencer, Lloyd Perryman, Hugh and Karl Farr, and Pat Brady, doing gospel and spiritual songs. The material, cut in 1947, captures the devotional side of the Pioneers, which was an important alternate to their songs of the trail. Since supplanted by 12-inch collections containing more songs, but a collectable disc. —Bruce Eder

Western Classics / 1953 / RCA Victor ♦♦♦
A second volume of Western songs, including "Riders in the Sky," "Red River Valley," "Outlaws," and "Wind." The material covers 1946 through 1951, and the lineups range from Bob Nolan, Tim Spencer, Lloyd Perryman, Ken Carson, Hugh and Karl Farr, and Pat Brady ("Have I Told You Lately That I Love You") through Nolan, Spencer, Perryman, the Farrs, and Pat Brady ("The Last Round-Up"), and Nolan, Perryman, Ken Curtis, the Farrs, and Brady ("Riders in the Sky"), up through Perryman, Tommy Doss, Curtis, the Farrs, and Shug Fisher ("Wind"). The different lineups are confusing, but this record is a good chance to compare the different postwar versions of the group at their respective bests. —Bruce Eder

How Great Thou Art / 1957 / RCA Victor ♦♦♦
The Pioneers' second gospel collection, essentially an expanded version of Cowboy Hymns and Spirituals, comprised of recordings done in 1947 up through 1956, with Bob Nolan the common thread through most of it. —Bruce Eder

One Man's Songs / 1957 / RCA Victor ♦♦♦
The last new recording by the mid-1950s studio version of the Pioneers, led by Bob Nolan. —Bruce Eder

Wagons West / 1958 / RCA Special Music ♦♦♦♦
Wonderful sounding CD transfer of a 1958 compilation of some of the group's previously unanthologized (in 1958) songs, ranging from the 1950 vintage title track (which appeared on the soundtrack of John Ford's Wagon Master—the premiere of the network TV series "Wagon Train," based on the Ford movie, facilitated this release) to 1947's "The Whiffenpoof Song." The Nolan/Perryman/Spencer/Carson version of the group is featured (on "Cowboy Camp Meetin'"), as is the Perryman/Curtis/Doss lineup ("Wagons West"). The singing is impeccable throughout, the sound glowing and crisp, and the songs comprise a solid representation of material beyond the Pioneers' best known hits. The only flaw is a funny one involving the art work—on the 1996 CD reissue, someone at Special Music's art department accidentally had "Wagons East" (the name of John Candy's final film) printed on the jewelbox spine. —Bruce Eder

Cool Water / 1959 / RCA ♦♦
The title and cover art of the 1959 Cool Water LP were reused for this very unfortunate CD reissue, on which only half of the original's songs were included, without any notes. The compact disc is something of an insult to the intelligence of the modern listener. What is there sounds good, but the compact disc of Cool Water is still an abomination. —Bruce Eder

Cool Water (and 17 Timeless Favorites) / 1959 / RCA ♦♦♦♦
The LP version of this album—the Pioneers' first in stereo—was generally regarded as the best of the modern group's RCA albums. The first recording of the late-1950s touring lineup of the Pioneers (Lloyd Perryman, Tommy Doss, Dale Warren, and Karl Farr) was chock full of superb harmonies and exquisite arrangements, and became the bestselling album in the Pioneers' history. —Bruce Eder

Room Full of Roses / 1960 / RCA ♦♦♦
A ten-song budget reissue of some of the Pioneers' 1940s and mid-1950s songs, all in a romantic vein. —Bruce Eder

Westwood Ho! / 1961 / RCA ♦♦♦
Collection of earlier material by the group, covering the 1940s and early 1950s, through an entire side from 1957. —Bruce Eder

Lure of the West / 1961 / RCA ♦♦♦
More Western material, recorded in November and December of 1960 by Perryman, Doss, Warren, and Karl Farr. Highlights include "Ragtime Cowboy Joe" and "Cimarron." This is rightfully considered one of the modern group's best harmony showcases. —Bruce Eder

Tumbleweed Trails / 1962 / RCA ♦♦♦♦
The last recordings of the group with Karl Farr, from April 1961, with the group in excellent voice, especially on the title track. —Bruce Eder

Good Old Country Music / 1963 / RCA ♦♦
A shorter, budget-priced version of 1957's One Man's Songs. —Bruce Eder

Hymns of the Cowboy / 1963 / RCA ♦♦♦
The modern group's only pure gospel album, recorded in November and December of 1962. —Bruce Eder

Our Men Out West / 1963 / RCA ♦♦♦
Solid harmony singing as usual, and some excellent songs, including modern covers of "South of the Border." Recorded in August 1962, this album featured the first appearance of guitarist Roy Lanham as a member of the Pioneers, and Wade Ray appears on backup fiddle. By this time, the group's arrangements were very slick and modern, and far more sophisticated than the original trio or their 1950s successors. Some of the material on this album later appeared on the compilation San Antonio Rose. —Bruce Eder

Trail Dust / 1963 / RCA ♦♦♦
The modern Pioneers—Perryman, Tommy Doss, Dale Warren, and Roy Lanham—cover Tim Spencer's songs. —Bruce Eder

Sons of the Pioneers Best / 1964 / Columbia-Harmony ✦✦✦
A collection derived from the original Pioneers' short stay at the American Record Company in 1937. Not the best work of the group, but a necessary addition for any completist. —*Bruce Eder*

Tumbleweed Trails [1964] / 1964 / Vocalion ✦✦✦
A collection of the group's Coral Records material, including their cover of the title song from the Marilyn Monroe movie *River of No Return* from 1954, and a lot of early 1940s recordings ("Home in San Antone" etc.). Better collections than this could be done, unifying the Coral, Vocalion, and early Decca sides. —*Bruce Eder*

Down Memory Trail / 1964 / RCA ✦✦✦
Another nostalgic journey through the West, featuring "Bonaparte's Retreat," "Gone," "Left My Gal in the Mountains," and "Born to Lose," among others, performed by the then-current group. —*Bruce Eder*

Country Fare / 1964 / RCA ✦✦✦✦
A country album by the Pioneers, and one unusually strong on the instrumental side, featuring the most impressive guitar array in their history, Roy Lanham joining guest musicians Neil Levang and Glen Campbell. It's difficult to imagine that anyone could do an engaging version of a chestnut like "Listen to the Mockingbird," but these guys pull it off, despite the slickness of their arrangements. Some of this material appears on the budget compilation *San Antonio Rose.* —*Bruce Eder*

Legends of the West / 1965 / RCA ✦✦✦
Old songs about the West, and about the West's outlaws, including "Jesse James" and "Billy the Kid," "The Strawberry Roan," "O Bury Me Not on the Lone Prairie," etc. A powerful retro album by this most retro of Western groups. —*Bruce Eder*

Best of the Sons of the Pioneers / 1966 / RCA ✦✦✦
Part of RCA's same series with *The Best of Sam Cooke Vol. 2* etc. This release features the middle/late 1940s version of the group in their classic original recordings, including "Tumbling Tumbleweeds," "Cool Water," "Riders in the Sky," "The Last Round-Up," and "San Antonio Rose." —*Bruce Eder*

The Songs of Bob Nolan / 1966 / RCA ✦✦✦✦
A collection of Bob Nolan songs that are far less well known, but only slightly less compelling, than "Tumbling Tumbleweeds" or his other standards. Any real fan will want it, and RCA or Special Music should reissue it. —*Bruce Eder*

Campfire Favorites / 1967 / RCA ✦✦✦✦
More romance of the range ("Don't Fence Me In"), straight romantic ballads ("I Love You Truly"), and country songs, as well as re-recordings of old standards. —*Bruce Eder*

San Antonio Rose and Other Country Favorites / 1968 / RCA Special Music ✦✦✦✦
Excellent sounding CD reissue of the above LP. —*Bruce Eder*

South of the Border / 1968 / RCA ✦✦✦
The modern group's December 1967 recordings of more standards, this time in a Spanish/Mexican vein. These sessions also marked the end of Tommy Doss' and Pat Brady's recording careers with the group. —*Bruce Eder*

San Antonio Rose [LP] / 1968 / RCA Camden ✦✦✦✦
A ten-song budget compilation of early 1960s sides, mostly drawn from *Our Men Out West* and *Country Fare.* —*Bruce Eder*

The Sons of the Pioneers Visit the South Seas / 1969 / RCA ✦✦✦
The final RCA lineup of the group—Perryman, Warren, Nallie, and Lanham—apply their considerable harmony skills to songs associated with Hawaii and other points in the Pacific ("Hawaiian Lullaby," "Tiny Bubbles," etc.) and do surprisingly well with this repertory. —*Bruce Eder*

Riders in the Sky / 1973 / RCA ✦✦
Like the rest of the albums in this RCA mid-priced reissue series, this was a nice idea badly executed. A paltry 18 songs spread over two long-playing discs, and featuring "Cool Water" and "Riders in the Sky" from the 1940s, but no "Tumbling Tumbleweeds." Also included are "Cigareets, Whisky and Wild Women," "High Noon," "The Ballad of Davy Crockett," "Home on

the Range," and "Blue Prairie," but none of this is done with much sense (modern stereo sides are juxtaposed with mid-1940s mono) of order or purpose, other than slapping a collection together. —*Bruce Eder*

☆ **Columbia Historic Edition** / 1982 / Columbia ✦✦✦✦✦
This group wrote the book on dreamy, close-harmony crooning to panoramic vistas. Leader Bob Nolan supplies poetic lyrics, and Hugh and Karl Farr provide the Django Reinhardt/Stephane Grappelli-inspired accompaniment. Archetypal sounds from the '30s. —*Mark A. Humphrey*

Tumbling Tumbleweeds / 1986 / MCA ✦✦✦✦
This budget-priced ten-song CD is fairly enjoyable and doesn't overlap with MCA's *Country Music Hall of Fame.* "I'm an Old Cowhand (From the Rio Grande)" is a great showcase for the guitar skills of Karl Farr and the fiddle virtuosity of Hugh Farr, and "Song of the Pioneers" is a great vehicle for Karl Farr, one of his best performances on guitar. Other songs include the late 1936 re-recording of "Tumbling Tumbleweeds" by the six-man Pioneers, which is otherwise unavailable on CD, "Cool Water," "Blue Bonnet Girl," "Empty Saddles," and "Blue Prairie." The singing, as always, is impeccable. —*Bruce Eder*

Tumbling Tumbleweeds / 1989 / RCA ✦✦✦
A mixed bag, combining the new Pioneers—Lloyd Perryman, Dale Warren, Luther Nallie, and Roy Lanham—and their re-recording of the title track, "Song of the Land I Love," and "King of the Fools" from late 1968, with early 1960s recordings by the previous lineup, including "Ramona," "Chant of the Wanderer," "He Walks with the Wild and the Lonely." —*Bruce Eder*

★ **Country Music Hall of Fame** / 1991 / MCA ✦✦✦✦✦
The nearest-perfect collection of the Sons of the Pioneers' early work—which is their best work—currently available, 16 songs, half of which were recorded during the early and mid-1930s by the original group of Bob Nolan, Tim Spencer, and Roy Rogers (then known as Leonard Slye), and Lloyd Perryman, and Hugh and Karl Farr. No collection of theirs could open with anything stronger than the first two songs the Pioneers ever cut, "Way Out There" and the original, never-to-be-duplicated version of "Tumbling Tumbleweeds." They and the original version of "Cool Water" all rely on the Pioneers' three-part harmonies and their own instruments (acoustic guitars, fiddle, upright bass) and sound like musical gold pouring out of a portal from another age. Some of the songs are topical and, in their way, rather poignant reminders of the Great Depression, such as "When Our Old Age Pension Check Comes to Our Door." Other highlights include "There's a Round-Up in the Sky," "Ride Ranger Ride," "Private Buckaroo" (a topical song about World War II), "When the Moon Comes over Sun Valley," and one previously unreleased gospel gem from their 1954 stay at Coral Records, "Somebody Bigger than You and I." —*Bruce Eder*

Wagons West / 1996 / Bear Family ✦✦✦✦
Wagons West is a thorough four-disc box set containing 115 songs the Sons of the Pioneers recorded for RCA/Victor during the '40s, when the group was at the height of their popularity. Containing all of their best-known songs and hits like "Cool Water," "Stars and Stripes on Iwo Jima," and "Tumbling Tumbleweeds," plus several unreleased tracks and alternate takes, the set is the most complete portrait of the group's peak that has ever been drawn. Of course the sheer length and weight of the set means that only musicologists and diehard fans will find *Wagons West* consistently compelling, but it still stands as one of the most essential—and comprehensive—Western and cowboy box sets ever assembled. —*Thom Owens*

The Sons of the Pioneers / JEM ✦✦✦
This album features '40s transcriptions of such songs as "I Wonder if She Waits for Me Tonight," "When Payday Rolls Around," "The Howlin' Pup," and others. —*AMG*

Empty Saddles / MCA ✦✦✦✦
All of the Pioneers' '30s-era compilations are fine, but this includes Bob Nolan's darkest and most beautiful song, "Blue Prairie." —*Mark A. Humphrey*

Sons of the San Joaquin

Cowboy

Sons of the San Joaquin is a '90s group that revives the sounds and styles of Western and cowboy music. —*Stephen Thomas Erlewine*

● **A Cowboy Has to Sing** / Jan. 1992 / Warner Brothers ✦✦✦✦

With *The Cowboy Has to Sing,* the Sons of the San Joaquin effortlessly re-create the classic Western and cowboy sounds of the Sons of the Pioneers, which results in a thoroughly entertaining listen. —*Thom Owens*

From Whence Came the Cowboy / Oct. 31, 1995 / Warner Brothers ✦✦✦✦

On their third album, *From Whence Came the Cowboy,* the Sons of the San Joaquin rely almost entirely on original songs, which are all written in the cowboy and Western tradition. If the group weren't able to write convincingly, the album would be a stilted paean to forgotten ways, but the group effortlessly captures the spirit of the West, making it an evocative and intriguing listen, and their best album to date. —*Thom Owens*

The Sons of the West

Western Swing

The Sons of the West were a Western swing band established in 1936 by Son Lansford, a cousin of Western swing pioneer Bob Wills and onetime member of Wills' Texas Playboys. The Sons of the West were together for only a short time and mainly played at the Rainbow Gardens dance hall in Amarillo. They had an incredibly high turnover rate and went through 11 members, including innovative steel guitarist Billy Briggs, who added a seventh string to his guitar to play three-string syncopated chords. In 1938 the Sons recorded an eponymous album for Decca that contained a mixture of pop and Tin Pan Alley songs. Their most popular cut was "Sally's Got a Wooden Leg," which they released in 1941. Though never a nationally known band, they might have continued through the '40s had not many of the members been called to arms during World War II. —*Sandra Brennan*

Sons of the West / Texas Rose ✦✦✦

● **1938-1941** / Texas Rose ✦✦✦✦

This features "There's Evil in You Chillun," "Prairie Queen," "Am I Blue," "Spanish Cavalier," and more. —*AMG*

Souther Hillman Furay Band

Country-Rock

Formed in 1973 at the urging of Asylum Records' president David Geffen, Souther-Hillman-Furay was the offspring of just about every notable country-rock band. Richie Furay was a founding member of both Buffalo Springfield and Poco; Chris Hillman had been with the Byrds, the Flying Burrito Brothers, and Stephen Stills' Manassas; and J.D. Souther formed Longbranch Pennywhistle with Eagle Glenn Frey, as well as recording a solo record for Asylum and penning tunes for artists like Linda Ronstadt, Bonnie Raitt, and the Eagles. S-H-F's supporting cast also came with impressive credentials, including studio stalwart Paul Harris on piano, Al Perkins (Flying Burrito Brothers, Manassas) on pedal steel guitar, and former Derek and the Dominos drummer Jim Gordon, who also wrote the piano piece that concludes "Layla."

Although the band, which was meant to be a sort of country-rock version of Crosby, Stills and Nash, received a great deal of hype and promotion, things never really gelled. Their debut sold reasonably well, but the aptly titled *Trouble in Paradise* was poorly received. S-H-F broke up shortly thereafter, with each member going on to a solo career. Souther released a couple of solo efforts, achieving a minor success with "You're Only Lonely"; Hillman recorded unsuccessfully for Asylum before teaming with former Byrd-mates Roger McGuinn and Gene Clark in McGuinn, Clark, and Hillman, and then forming the popular country-rock Desert Rose Band; and Furay, who became a minister in Colorado, made three Christian-influenced albums, as well as rejoining Poco for their 20th-anniversary recording. —*Brett Hartenbach*

● **The Souther, Hillman, Furay Band** / 1974 / Asylum ✦✦✦

An occassionally pleasant, but for the most part disappointing, debut. The chemistry is never really there among the three, but Furay probably comes closest to living up to his past accomplishments with the Poco-like rocker, "Fallin' in Love," and the ballad "Believe Me." *Souther-Hillman-Furay Band* is a relatively lightweight country-rock, singer-songwriter affair that may appeal to fans. —*Brett Hartenbach*

Trouble in Paradise / 1975 / Asylum ✦✦✦

With producer Tom Dowd, known for his work at Atlantic Records, at the helm, S-H-F seems to be going for a funkier, less country-rock feel. Weaker than the first record, although the title cut and "Prisoner in Disguises," both written by J.D. Douther, stand out. —*Brett Hartenbach*

Southern Pacific

Country-Rock, Contemporary Country, Roots-Rock

Stu Cook, John McFee, Tim Goodman, David Jenkins, and Kurt Howell formed this group in mid-1983. Southern Pacific's rock 'n' roll past constantly dogged the group's reputation. Keith Knudsen and John McFee were former members of the Doobie Brothers. (McFee had also played alongside Huey Lewis in a band called Clover); original lead vocalist Tim Goodman had recorded a solo album; and Stu Cook performed in Creedence Clearwater Revival. When Goodman left the band, they replaced him with another ex-rocker, former Pablo Cruise vocalist David Jenkins. They did have one member with strong country roots: Kurt Howell played keyboards for Crystal Gayle.

Southern Pacific signed with Warner and released a strong debut album in 1985, though the media continually questioned the band's commitment to country. The group plied a very danceable brand of country, and hit a high point with their 1988 album *Zuma,* which included their biggest single, "New Shade of Blue."

Eventually Southern Pacific left country music, intending to pursue a pop career. —*Tom Roland*

Southern Pacific / 1985 / Warner Brothers ✦✦✦

Southern Pacific tried to cross country and rock, sometimes with mixed results. Born from the ashes of the Doobie Brothers and Emmylou Harris' Hot Band, Southern Pacific's eponymous debut doesn't have a bad cut on it. Rock songs like Tom Petty's "Thing About You" and "Luann," which was written by Lou Gramm and Mick Jones of Foreigner, dove-tail nicely with original cuts and more standard country fare from the likes of Rodney Crowell ("Bluebird Wine") and Chuck Pyle ("Jaded Lover"). In all, the album is a very promising first effort. —*James Chrispell*

Killbilly Hill / 1986 / Warner Brothers ✦✦✦✦

Instead of being weakened by changes in the band's membership, Southern Pacific actually grew stronger with the new lineup, as their second album, *Killbilly Hill,* demonstrates. Highlights on the record include the title cut and a cover of Bruce Springsteen's "Pink Cadillac," which was a sizable hit. The record is more country than their debut, which makes *Killbilly Hill* all the more highly recommended. —*James Chrispell*

Zuma / Jun. 21, 1988 / Warner Brothers ✦✦✦✦

Zuma features the country-rock unit's biggest hit, "New Shade of Blue." —*Jason Ankeny*

County Line / 1989 / Warner Brothers ✦✦✦

After the exit of vocalist/guitarist David Jenkins, *County Line* marked Southern Pacific's shift towards a more eclectic sound, as evidenced by guest appearances by Carlene Carter and the Beach Boys. —*Jason Ankeny*

● **Greatest Hits** / 1991 / Warner Brothers ✦✦✦✦

Why this group never quite made "the big time" remains a mystery. The material's sometimes two-step-able, sometimes kick-ass, and in "New Shade of Blue," they out-Eagled the Eagles. —*Tom Roland*

Southern Rail

Traditional Bluegrass

Southern Rail was a Boston-based bluegrass quartet noted for their fine harmonies and excellent musicianship. The husband-

and-wife team of Jim Muller and Sharon Horovitch founded the group around 1989. Muller, who hailed from Richmond, VA, was the band's lead singer/rhythm guitarist, while Horovitch, a native of Montreal, Quebec, played bass and sang harmony. Bass singer and dobro player Roger Williams hailed from Danville, NH, and was a noted sideman before joining Southern Rail, while Dave Dick of Waterbury, CT, rounded out the group with his banjo picking. Between 1989 and 1996, the band recorded five albums, including 1993's acclaimed *Carolina Lightning.* —*Sandra Brennan*

● **Drive by Night** / 1991 / Turquoise ✦✦✦✦
Good solid bluegrass. Clean, with rich vocals and first-class playing. —*Chip Renner*

Roadwork / 1992 / Turquoise ✦✦✦

Carolina Lightning / 1993 / Turquoise ✦✦✦

Glory Train / 1995 / Pinecastle ✦✦✦

Red Sovine (Woodrow Wilson Sovine)

b. Jul. 17, 1918, Charleston, WV, d. Apr. 4, 1980, Nashville, TN
Guitar, Vocals / Traditional Country, Honky Tonk
Though he had a long, distinguished career in country music, singer-songwriter and guitarist Red Sovine is best remembered for his earnest, funny and, at times, highly sentimental odes to the life of the American trucker. Born to an impoverished family in Charleston, WV, he was inspired as a child by WCHS radio musicians Buddy Starcher and Frank Welling. Sovine and his childhood friend Johnnie Bailes joined Jim Pike's Carolina Tar Heels and performed as "the Singing Sailors." It was not a particularly successful venture, and Sovine later became a factory worker. He also continued to put on a local radio show, while his friend Johnnie went on to form the Bailes Brothers.

Bailes continued to encourage Sovine to return to music, and in the late '40s, he finally began pursuing a radio career again. He landed a job at KWKH, Shreveport, but they gave him an early morning spot and his performances went unnoticed. Frustrated, he was ready to quit the business when Hank Williams helped him get a better position at WFSA in Montgomery, AL, where he soon developed a large following. With Williams' help, Sovine landed a contract with MGM Records in 1949, and over the next four years he recorded 28 singles, mostly honky tonk, that didn't make much of a dent on the charts but did establish him as a solid performer. When not recording, Sovine starred on Shreveport's "Louisiana Hayride."

In the early '50s Webb Pierce, one of his fellow "Hayride" performers, began a string of Top Ten country hits. Pierce convinced Sovine to lead his Wondering Boys band and helped Red sign to Decca in 1954. He continued recording but had no hits until cutting a duet with Goldie Hill, "Are You Mine?," which peaked in the Top 15 in 1955. The next year, he had his first No. 1 when he duetted with Webb Pierce on George Jones' "Why Baby Why." Also in 1956 Sovine had two other Top Five singles and started a brief stint on the Grand Ole Opry. After producing close to 50 sides with Decca by 1959, Sovine signed to Starday and began touring the club circuit as a solo act. It took him five years to produce a hit for the label with "Dream House for Sale," which reached No. 22 in 1964, nearly eight years after his last hit.

In 1966 Sovine at last found his niche when he recorded "Giddyup Go," his very first spoken-word truck driver song. The single spent six weeks atop the country charts and even crossed over to become a minor pop hit. Subsequent truck-driving hits included the ghost story "Phantom 309" and the tearjerking tale of a crippled child's CB-radio relationship with caring truckers, "Teddy Bear." The latter was his biggest hit since "Giddyup Go," spending three weeks at the top of the country charts in 1976 and reaching No. 40 on the pop charts. He followed "Teddy Bear" with "Little Joe," the tale of a blinded trucker and his devoted canine friend, which became his last big hit. Sovine died in 1980, suffering a heart attack while driving his van. —*Sandra Brennan*

One and Only Red Sovine / 1961 / Starday ✦✦✦✦
While *The One and Only Red Sovine* features honky tonk classics like "Why Baby Why," the sound quality is dismal, rendering this

otherwise comprehensive collection a disappointment. —*Jason Ankeny*

Giddy Up Go / 1966 / Hollywood ✦✦✦
The *Giddy-Up-Go* title cut was Sovine's biggest hit; unfortunately, it's also the only hit on this collection, which is otherwise made up of filler. —*Jason Ankeny*

Phantom 309 / 1967 / Deluxe ✦✦✦
Besides the title track, *Phantom 309* offers none of Sovine's chart hits. It is for completists only. —*Jason Ankeny*

Teddy Bear / 1976 / Deluxe ✦✦✦
Teddy Bear collects a few of Sovine's mid-'70s hits, including the title track, "Little Joe," and "Woman Behind the Man Behind the Wheel." —*Jason Ankeny*

Best of Red Sovine [TeeVee] / 1995 / TeeVee ✦✦✦

Famous Duets / Hollywood ✦✦✦
Famous Duets is a misnomer; while these songs are duets, they're hardly famous. None of them even charted, and only those with Jean Shepard show any signs of life. —*Jason Ankeny*

Golden Hits / Hollywood ✦✦✦✦
Golden Hits contains a handful of Sovine's biggest successes, including "Teddy Bear" and "Little Rosa." However, the rest of the songs—"Daddy's Girl," "Lay Down Sally," "Last Goodbye," and so forth—were minor hits if they charted at all. —*Jason Ankeny*

Sings Hank Williams / Deluxe ✦✦✦✦
This album includes such songs as "The Funeral," "Everything's OK," "Just Waitin'," and "Men with Broken Hearts." —*AMG*

Red Sovine and Del Reeves / Exact ✦✦✦✦

● **The Best of Red Sovine** / Starday ✦✦✦✦
Although it doesn't have many tracks, *The Best of Red Sovine* contains all his big hits and is an excellent introduction to one of the kings of truck-driving songs. —*Thom Owens*

Larry Sparks

b. Sep. 15, 1947, Lebanon, OH
Vocals / Progressive Bluegrass, Traditional Bluegrass
One of the finer lead singers in contemporary bluegrass, Larry Sparks filled in with Ralph Stanley's band after the death of the great Carter Stanley and later went on to head the traditional bluegrass group the Lonesome Ramblers. Sparks was born and raised in Lebanon, OH, and began learning to play guitar as a child. In his teens he played in bluegrass, country, and rock bands. In 1966 he cut his first bluegrass single and began his association with the Stanley Brothers' Clinch Mountain Boys. He recorded five albums with the band and stayed through 1969. After that he formed the Lonesome Ramblers. After the mid-'80s, he began recording less frequently and eventually moved to Richmond, IN, where he continued to perform on the bluegrass circuit; earning a reputation as one of the premiere bluegrass players, he remained dedicated to preserving the traditional styles of the Stanley Brothers. —*Sandra Brennan & David Vinopal*

Ramblin' Guitar / 1970 / Pine Tree ✦✦✦✦

New Gospel Songs / 1971 / Pine Tree ✦✦✦

Ramblin' Bluegrass / 1972 / Starday ✦✦✦✦

Bluegrass Old and New / 1972 / Old Homestead ✦✦✦✦

Larry Sparks Sings Hank Williams / 1977 / Rebel ✦✦✦✦
Larry Sparks expertly recasts several of Hank Williams' finest songs as bluegrass numbers in *Sings Hank Williams*, one of the finest records he ever released. Of special interest is the supporting band, which features a terrific performance from a young mandolinist named Ricky Skaggs. —*Thom Owens*

The Best of Larry Sparks / 1983 / Rebel ✦✦✦✦
Best of Larry Sparks is an adequate collection for this fine traditional bluegrass singer. —*Mark A. Humphrey*

★ **Classic Bluegrass** / 1989 / Rebel ✦✦✦✦✦
Classic Bluegrass collects the highlights of Larry Sparks '70s and '80s albums, which were recorded for a variety of different labels. The compilation hits all the high points of the records, providing a definitive retrospective of his career, as well as an excellent, concise introduction to one of bluegrass' best singers. —*Thom Owens*

Silver Reflections / 1991 / Rebel ✦✦✦

Sparks updates his bluegrass sound for the 1990s on *Silver Reflections. —Jason Ankeny*

Billie Jo Spears

b. Jan. 14, 1937, Beaumont, TX

Vocals / Traditional Country, Progressive Country

Sultry-voiced, blues-influenced singer-songwriter Billie Jo Spears had a career filled with ups and downs in the US, but she remained a popular performer in the United Kingdom and Europe. Born in Beaumont, TX, she made her professional debut at age 13 at an all-star country show in Houston featuring George Jones, Jean Shepard, Sonny Burns, and Blackie Crawford and the Western Cherokees. With a little help from a family friend, songwriter Jack Rhodes, she signed to Abbott Records in 1953 and released "Too Old for Toys, Too Young for Boys," which appeared on the B-side of Mel Blanc's "I Dess I Dotta Doe." On the single she appeared as Billie Jo Moore, and later sang the song on "Louisiana Hayride."

After high school she became a nightclub singer; accompanied by Rhodes, who wrote her songs, she made several attempts to find a label in Nashville but had little success until renowned producer Pete Drake asked her to record a few demos. She moved to Music City in 1964 to sign with United Artists. Her first singles, produced by Kelso Herston, went nowhere. She moved with Herston to Capitol and recorded "Harper Valley P.T.A.," again without success. She finally scored a mid-range hit with her follow-up single, "He's Got More Love in His Little Finger." "Mr. Walker, It's All Over" hit the Top Five and crossed over to become a minor pop hit. She had a string of minor hits through 1970; "Stepchild" inspired the name of her backing band, the Stepchildren, which she later renamed Owlkatraz after her passion for collecting owls.

Unfortunately, Spears had to curtail her budding career when a nodule was discovered on one of her vocal cords. She spent six months unable to speak, and it took a full year for her to recover. Upon her return, Spears recorded on different independent labels. In 1974, polyps were discovered growing in her larynx, and doctors feared she would lose her voice for good; she spent another half year in silence. She returned to United Artists at the end of the year and recorded "See the Funny Little Clown," but it was only a minor hit. However, she had her first No. 1 hit with the follow-up, "Blanket on the Ground," in 1975. The next year was Spears' most successful, beginning with a major trans-Atlantic hit, "What I've Got in Mind." She finished 1976 with five hits, including "Sing Me an Old Fashioned Song."

Spears remained associated with United Artists through 1981 and in between had many more hits on both sides of the ocean. In 1977 she appeared at England's Wembley Festival and then spent much of the year touring with the Dillards as part of the Nashville Cavalcade. In 1983 she recorded *B.J.—Billie Joe Spears Today* on the Irish Ritz label. She also had two mid-range hits on the Parliament label in 1984. After again stopping her career—this time for triple bypass surgery—she resumed performing. *—Sandra Brennan*

The Voice of Billie Joe Spears / 1968 / Capitol ✦✦✦✦

Country Girl / 1970 / Capitol ✦✦✦✦

Blanket on the Ground / 1975 / United Artists ✦✦✦

Billie Jo Singles Album / 1979 / United Artists ✦✦✦✦

● **Best of Billie Jo Spears** / 1992 / CEMA ✦✦✦✦

Billie Jo / United Artists ✦✦✦✦

Billy Jo is another fine effort from Spears and her producer, Larry Butler, who penned several of the songs on the record, including the hit "(Hey Won't You Play) Another Somebody Done Somebody Wrong Song." Billie Jo's big hit this time around, however, was "Silver Wings and Golden Rings," which topped country charts and made *Billie Jo* such a delight for easy-listening country music fans to enjoy. *—James Chrispell*

The Speer Family

Southern Gospel, Country Gospel

An important reference point in the appreciation of traditional Southern gospel quartet singing, the Speer Family emerged when there were countless Southern gospel quartets, but they continued to perform into the 1990s. Though the Speer lineup had changed over the years, their music in the '90s was still true to the music they were making when the group was formed by patriarch G.T. in 1921.

G.T. Speer was born in a rural community near Fayetteville, GA, and worked as a teacher at the Stamps-Baxter School of Music in Dallas. He also taught at the Vaughan School of Music, Lawrenceburg, TN. The first incarnation of the Speers was formed in 1921 with his wife Lena, his sister, and her husband. Until then, virtually every gospel group was made up of males only. G.T. persisted with his original lineup and, much to the surprise of gospel "purists," became popular. He also strayed from the norm by having the Speers sing only gospel music. Soon other groups followed suit.

In 1925 his sister and brother-in-law left, so G.T. and Lena added their children Rosa Nell and Mary Tom to the lineup. They eventually left to raise their own children, but returned to become permanent members a few years later. Over the years, the Speer Family often contained other musicians, most notably Harold Lane, who spent two decades with them.

Through the 1950s and '60s, the Speers were frequent guests on radio station WLAC Nashville. In 1966 G.T. suddenly died and became the first person inducted into the "deceased" category of the Gospel Music Hall of Fame. His wife Lena died the next year and in 1972 became the second so honored. During its long career, the group has won numerous awards and honors, but one of the highest came in 1981 on the group's 60th anniversary; the Speers were entered into the Congressional Record and received a plaque that contained their first commercial record. To celebrate these events, the Benson Company distributed a commemorative anniversary album and packaged a multimedia presentation chronicling the distinguished family's history. In 1993 they released a new album, *A Beautiful Day. —Sandra Brennan & Bill Carpenter*

Hallelujah Time / 1990 / HB ✦✦✦

● **He's Still in the Fire** / 1990 / HB ✦✦✦✦

All Night Singing / 1991 / Starday ✦✦✦

Buddy Spicher

Fiddle, Session Musician / Progressive Bluegrass, Instrumental

Since playing with the progressive country band Area Code 615 in the late '60s, Buddy has been a much-in-demand session fiddler. He has recorded with the Pointer Sisters and Henry Mancini, along with making albums of his own. *—David Vinopal*

Buddies / 1977 / Sonet ✦✦✦

Platinum Fiddle / 1980 / President ✦✦✦

American Sampler / 1988 / Flying Fish ✦✦✦✦

Varied dates with fine playing by Spicher. *—Ron Wynn*

● **Fiddle Classics** / 1988 / Flying Fish ✦✦✦✦

A high-caliber acoustic session by Spicher, showcasing country, folk, and blues influences. *—Ron Wynn*

Great American Fiddle Collection / 1988 / CMH ✦✦✦✦

Me and My Heroes / 1990 / Flying Fish ✦✦✦

A nice folk/jazz/country mixture. *—Ron Wynn*

Carl T. Sprague

b. 1895, Houston, TX, d. 1978

Vocals / Cowboy

Carl T. Sprague was one of the first cowboys on record, paving the way for such fine rangeland singers as Jules Allen, the Cartwright Brothers, and Harry McClintock. He was born in Houston and spent time as a youth involved in ranching and farming; the cowboy songs he performed were authentic, learned around late night campfires. After graduating from college in 1922, he began occasionally playing on radio, and was inspired to record after hearing Vernon Dalhart's "The Prisoner's Song." Sprague went to Camden, NJ, in 1925 and cut his debut recordings "When the Work's All Done This Fall" and "Bad Companions." Both of the cowboy tunes became quite successful, and he continued recording for Victor through 1929. In the '30s he worked several different jobs after settling down permanently in Bryan, TX, but he did return to performing during the folk revival years, and in the early '70s, he recorded for Bear Family. — *Sandra Brennan*

The First Popular Singing Cowboy / 1973 / Bear Family ✦✦✦✦

Cowboy Songs from Texas / 1975 / Bear Family ✦✦✦✦

● **Classic Cowboy Songs** / Bear Family ✦✦✦✦

Jim Stafford

b. Jan. 16, 1944, Eloise, FL
Banjo, Guitar, Keyboards, Vocals / Country-Pop, Country Humor
Multi-talented entertainer Jim Stafford remains best remembered for the novelty songs he released in the 1970s, particularly the single "Spiders and Snakes," which made him an international star. Born to a musical family in Eloise, FL, he was playing guitar in his first band at age 14. As soon as he graduated from high school, Stafford went to Nashville, where he was a backup musician for Jumpin' Bill Carlisle.

Stafford began his famous one-man-band act during a session when his drummer suddenly quit. He also continued to hone his songwriting skills, focusing on novelty songs because he felt his singing voice wasn't very good. He started out playing dance clubs, where he offered humorous running commentaries on the skills of the go-go dancers. He was performing in Clearwater, FL, when he reunited with Nashville friend Lobo; Stafford asked him to perform his song "Swamp Witch," but Lobo convinced Stafford to perform it himself. The song eventually made its way to Mike Curb, who signed Stafford to MGM Records. The single was released in 1973 and became a Top 40 pop hit. Stafford then released "Spiders and Snakes," which was a smash hit on both the pop and country charts and went gold in 1974. His next hit was the playful "My Girl Bill," which did better on the pop charts than the country charts. He had two more hits, "Wildwood Weed" (co-written with Don Bowman) and "Your Bulldog Drinks Champagne."

In 1975 he hosted the summer replacement series "The Jim Stafford Show," which featured Mel Blanc and others. Although Stafford's quirky songs brought him fame, the show gave him a chance to showcase his exceptional ability as a guitar player. In late 1975 he had another pop hit for MGM, "I Got Stoned and I Missed It." He had two more minor pop hits in the '70s. In 1980, after a divorce from singer Bobbie Gentry, he appeared in Clint Eastwood's *Any Which Way You Can* and penned the song "Cow Patti," which made the Top 70 on the country charts in 1981. The next year he hosted "Nashville on the Road" with Rex Allen, Jr. and Sue Powell, and composed three songs for Disney's animated feature *The Fox and the Hound.* In subsequent years, Stafford performed in Las Vegas and at small concerts and county fairs. — *Sandra Brennan*

Spiders and Snakes / 1974 / Polygram ✦✦✦

● **Jim Stafford** / 1974 / Polygram ✦✦✦✦

Not Just Another Pretty Foot / 1975 / MGM ✦✦

Terry Stafford

b. Hollis, OK
Vocals / Country-Pop, Pop-Rock
Terry Stafford is best-known for his lone Top Ten 1964 hit single, "Suspicion." Stafford's voice uncannily resembled Elvis Presley's, espcially on "Suspicion," which was originally recorded by Presley on his 1962 album *Pot Luck.* After "Suspicion" peaked at No. 3 early in 1964, he had another Top 40 hit with "I'll Touch a Star," which reached No. 23 in the summer of that year. AFter "I'll Touch a Star," none of Stafford's singles made the charts. In the late '60s he turned to professional songwriting, and he continued writing songs into the '80s. Two of his best-known songs are Buck Owens' "Big in Vegas" and George Strait's "Amarillo by Morning." — *Stephen Thomas Erlewine*

● **Best of Terry Stafford** / Oct. 15, 1996 / Curb ✦✦✦✦
The Best of Terry Stafford, of course, contains his big hit single "Suspicion," but it also contains a number of other lesser-known singles, including his only other Top 40 hit, "I'll Touch a Star." Although the rest of the material on the compilation isn't the equal of "Suspicion," it is frequently entertaining. Stafford's voice is excellent and the '60s mainstream pop arrangements are usually engaging, even when the material is less than first-rate. — *Stephen Thomas Erlewine*

Joe Stampley

b. Jun. 6, 1943, Springhill, LA
Vocals / Traditional Country, Country-Pop, Honky Tonk
As the leader of the Uniques in the 1960s, Stampley played the sort of hybrid of rock, pop, soul, and country performed by many Southern rock groups of the time. In the early '70s, he went solo and started a straight country career, rolling off a lengthy series of hit singles throughout the decade, including several that got to No. 1: "All These Things" (1976), "Soul Song" (1972), "Roll On, Big Mama" (1975), and "Just Good Ol' Boys" (1979). The material from his prime (including a version of "The Most Beautiful Girl" that pre-dates Charlie Rich's hit rendition) is generally typical of Nashville's commercial sound during the '70s, with occasional hints of his R&B and rock influences. He continues to write and perform, and it's been speculated that he was an influence on Travis Tritt. — *Richie Unterberger*

● **The Best of Joe Stampley** / 1995 / Varèse Sarabande ✦✦✦✦
Eighteen songs from the '70s, most of them big country hits, drawing primarily from his recordings for Dot in the early part of the decade (including his version of "The Most Beautiful Girl"). Also includes the No. 1 hits he cut after leaving Dot for Epic, "Roll On, Big Mama" and "Just Good Ol' Boys." — *Richie Unterberger*

Good Ol' Boy / 1995 / Razor & Tie ✦✦✦✦
While Varèse's *The Best of Joe Stampley* covers his ABC/Dot recordings, Razor & Tie's *Good Old Boy: The Greatest Hits* concentrates on the singer's big hits for Epic Records during the latter half of the '70s. Though his Dot and ABC records were harder country and bigger hits, the Epic singles were often just as good, as this collection demonstrates. Boasting such hits as "Red Wine and Blue Memories," "If You've Got Ten Minutes (Let's Fall in Love)," "Do You Ever Fool Around," "Put Your Clothes Back On," and the Moe Bandy duet "Just Good Ol' Boys," *Good Old Boy* is an excellent overview of the latter half of Stampley's career. — *Stephen Thomas Erlewine*

Greatest Hits / Epic ✦✦✦✦
This has his 1975 No. 1, "Roll On Big Mama," and a well-intentioned but weak cover of Arthur Alexander's "Every Day I Have to Cry Some." — *Dan Cooper*

And the Uniques: Gold / Paula/Flyright ✦✦✦
Before his country career, Louisianan Stampley fronted the Uniques, a '60s roots-rock band that probably needed its roots sunk a little deeper than they were. — *Dan Cooper*

The Stanley Brothers

Traditional Bluegrass
If you even *think* you know bluegrass, you have to know Ralph (b. 1927) and Carter Stanley (b. 1925), the Stanley Brothers. Parallel to Flatt and Scruggs and Bill Monroe's Blue Grass Boys, though not with their renown, were Virginians Ralph and Carter, mountain boys who took those mountains and their traditions and their songs and wove them into a traditional bluegrass sound of utter purity, simplicity, and astonishing beauty. Their first band, formed around 1947, played more of a mountain/folk music reminiscent of the old string bands, changing to their style of ultra-traditional bluegrass when Bill Monroe's band became popular. Even on their recordings in the early '50s, the Stanleys' unmistakable sound is there, with guitarist Carter singing lead and banjo player Ralph singing tenor harmony. In the opinion of many, Carter possessed the best lead voice in bluegrass history–rich, emotional, and (in the best sense of the word) lonely. He took a happy song and sang it sad; he took a sad song and sang it sadder. And

Ralph's unworldly mountain tenor matched his brother's voice perfectly, soaring above and often lightening the emotional load of the lyrics, creating a duet unsurpassed in country history.

Ralph and Carter were born into a musical family—their father sang and their mother played banjo. As teenagers, the brothers began performing around their hometown. After graduating from high school, the siblings both served in the army during World War II. Carter was discharged before Ralph. When he returned to the States he got a job singing in Roy Sykes' Blue Ridge Mountain Boys. He quit the group as soon as Ralph returned from the Army in October 1946, and the brothers formed a band, the Clinch Mountain Boys.

The Stanley Brothers had a regular gig at WNVA Norton for a few months. Then they moved to the Bristol, TN-based WCYB, where they appeared regularly on the "Farm and Fun Time" program. They gained quite a following, and they soon signed a contract with the Rich-R-Tone label. The Stanleys made their first records early in 1947, the same year they began playing various radio stations in the South, including ones in North Carolina, Lousiana, and Kentucky. The brothers and their five-piece Clinch Mountain Boys were developing their style, moving from traditional string band sounds to a Bill Monroe-inspired bluegrass style. During the late '40s and early '50s, several well-respected musicians passed through the band, including Curly Lambert, Pee Wee Lambert, Chubby Anthony, and Bill Napier.

After recording ten songs for Rich-R-Tone, the Stanley Brothers were signed to Columbia in 1948. For the next three years, they stayed with Columbia, producing 22 songs that would become bluegrass classics. For a brief time in 1951, the Stanley Brothers broke up. Carter sang with Bill Monroe and made a handful of records with the father of bluegrass. Ralph was sidelined for several months after a car crash. The break was brief, and the band was back together before the end of the year.

In the summer of 1953 they left Columbia for Mercury Records. During the mid-'50s, they made a series of recordings that expanded their boundaries, as they played gospel, honky tonk, instrumentals, and a number of original songs.

At the end of the decade, the Brothers left Mercury and signed to both Starday and King, moved to Live Oak, FL, and began playing the Swannee River Jamboree. In the early '60s, they played a number of television shows and concerts throughout the South and made numerous records. The duo began to suffer financial problems in 1961, which meant they couldn't afford to retain a whole band. Nevertheless, the Stanley Brothers continued to tour, playing clubs and various bluegrass festivals. However, they rarely left the South, and their career suffered because of this. They recorded for a number of smaller labels after leaving King, though none of the records sold much. In 1966 Carter Stanley became seriously ill. On December 1 of that year, he passed away; he was only 41 years old.

Ralph Stanley continued performing with a new lineup of the Clinch Mountain Boys. For the next three decades he performed with various new lineups of the band, playing festivals and clubs and making numerous records. —*Stephen Thomas Erlewine & David Vinopal*

Hymns and Sacred Songs / 1959 / King ◆◆◆
Hymns and Sacred Songs is an original album that the Stanley Brothers recorded for King Records in 1959. Comprised entirely of classic country gospel numbers, the music on the album is completely beautiful and haunting, thanks to the brothers' extraordinary harmonies. —*Thom Owens*

Everybody's Country Favorites / 1959 / King ◆◆◆
Features "Sweeter than the Flowers," "Shenandoah," "I'm a Man of Constant Sorrow," and other hits. —*AMG*

Long Journey Home / 1961 / Rebel ◆◆◆
Long Journey Home features 16 songs that the Stanley Brothers recorded in the early '60s for the Wango record label. Originally released under the name of John's Country Quartet, the album consists entirely of classic old-timey songs, all of which are delivered with gusto by the brothers and a supporting duo. —*Thom Owens*

Columbia Sessions #2 / 1982 / Rounder ◆◆◆
More wonderful early performances. —*Mark A. Humphrey*

Stanley Series, Vol. 1 #1 / Copper Creek ◆◆◆
Each of the 11 albums in this series contains live performances by the Stanley Brothers and the Clinch Mountain Boys in concerts recorded during the golden years of bluegrass. This member of the series was recorded on May 21, 1961, at the New River Ranch, Rising Sun, MD. —*AMG*

Stanley Series, Vol. 1 #2 / Copper Creek ◆◆◆
The Stanley Series is a multi-volume series of live concerts from the Stanley Brothers. The 16-song *Vol. 1: No. 2* captures a 1960 show performed with mandolinist Curley Lambert, bassist Lindy Clear, and fiddler Ralph Mayo. Over the course of the show, the group's energy rarely fails, and they perform fine versions of "Turkey in the Straw" and "How Far to Little Rock." —*Thom Owens*

Stanley Series, Vol. 1 #3 / Copper Creek ◆◆◆
The 18-song *Vol. 1: No.3* captures a 1955 show—which happens to be the earliest in this entire series—that was performed with bassist Doug Morris and mandolinist Jim Williams. One of the highlights is "Rabbit in the Log," which is performed solo by Ralph and Carter. —*Thom Owens*

Stanley Series, Vol. 1 #4 / Copper Creek ◆◆◆
The 15-song *Vol. 1: No.4* captures a 1966 show where the brothers were supported by bassist Melvin Goins, guitarist George Shuffler, and fiddler Birch Monroe. The concert happened to be one of the last Carter played with Ralph, and the music is appropriately poignant, particularly the fine versions of "Searching for a Soldier's Grave" and Carter's "I Know What It Means to Be Lonesome." —*Thom Owens*

Stanley Series, Vol. 2 #1 / 1989 / Copper Creek ◆◆◆
The 17-song *Vol. 2: No.1* captures a 1956 show where the brothers were supported by fiddler Chubby Anthony, mandolinist Curley Lambert, and bassist Doug Morris, who all shine on this cross-section of originals and standards. Of special note is Chubby's powerful fiddle, plus the group's excellent versions of Bill Monroe's "A Voice from on High" and the Stanleys' "Little Glass of Wine." —*Thom Owens*

Stanley Series, Vol. 2 #2 / Copper Creek ◆◆◆
It was recorded at a concert in Oak Leaf Park in Luray, VA, on May 28, 1961. —*AMG*

Stanley Series, Vol. 2 #3 / Copper Creek ◆◆◆
The 14-song *Vol. 2: No.3* captures a 1961 show that was performed with fiddler Chubby Anthony, mandolinist Curley Lambert, and bassist Doug Morris. One of the highlights is the brothers' harmonies on Hank Williams' "I Saw the Light." —*Thom Owens*

Stanley Series, Vol. 2 #4 / Copper Creek ◆◆◆
The 12-song *Vol. 2: No.4* captures a 1962 show that was performed with mandolinist Curley Lambert, bassist Roger Bush, and fiddler Vernon Derrick. What makes this volume of *The Stanley Series* particularly noteworthy is the fact that the bluegrass duo is performing in front of a folk crowd, which means they run through most of their best-known material, including "Salty Dog Blues" and "The Little Girl and the Dreadful Blues." And that means, for most casual fans, this edition of *The Stanley Series* is the one to get. —*Thom Owens*

Stanley Series, Vol. 3 #1 / Copper Creek ◆◆◆
The 14-song *Vol. 3: No.1* captures a 1956 show that was rained out, but the duo was able to squeeze out some wonderful music before it was canceled, and those performances are what's captured here, including a terrific "Going to Georgia." —*Stephen Thomas Erlewine*

Stanley Series, Vol. 3 #2 / Copper Creek ◆◆◆
The 14-song *Vol. 3: No.2* captures a 1962 show performed in Ash Grove, which was typically exciting. Of special note is their revamped version of the honky tonk standard, "The Wild Side of Life." —*Thom Owens*

Stanley Series, Vol. 3 #3 / 1989 / Copper Creek ◆◆◆
The 27-song *Vol. 3: No.3* captures a 1958 show recorded with mandolinist Bill Napier, fiddler Ralph Mayo, and bassist Jack

Cooke. One of the highlights of the disc is "Going to the Races," which the duo never recorded commercially; another is "No School Bus in Heaven," a contemporary folk song about a Kentucky school-bus crash. — *Thom Owens*

Stanley Series, Vol. 3 #4 / Copper Creek ◆◆◆
Stanley Series, Vol. 3: No.4 contains highlights from an afternoon of concerts given in Rising Sun, MD, on September 7, 1958. During the show, the Stanley Brothers ran through familiar numbers and several songs they knew only partially, which means that some of the songs suffer from forgotten lines. Despite the mistakes, it is an exciting and vibrant live show, demonstrating the duo's vocal and instrumental skills. For dedicated fans, it is a necessary purchase. — *Thom Owens*

☆ 1953-59 / 1994 / Bear Family ◆◆◆◆◆
The Stanley Brothers and the Clinch Mountain Boys, 1953-1958 & 1959 is a double-disc containing everything the group recorded during the latter half of the '50s for Mercury, Starday, and King Records. These recordings are generally considered to be among their best work, and this set is the only one to make complete sense of the recordings. All of the group's best moments, plus many forgotten but equally fine gems, are included on the collection, making it a comprehensive retrospective. Nevertheless, it also functions as a good, if rather lengthy, introduction to the Stanley Brothers, since it showcases the richness and depth of their music. In short, it's an essential addition to any serious bluegrass collection. — *Thom Owens*

Early Years 1958-61 / 1994 / King ◆◆◆◆
The Early Starday-King Years: 1958-1961 is a 109-track, four-disc box set that compiles every track the Stanley Brothers cut for Starday and King during that era. At the time, the group was releasing albums both on Starday and King, so there was an immense amount of confusion between the releases; the box set helps clarify matters, by gathering all of the music and presenting it in chronological order. This way, it's possible to hear their progression, as well as the differences between the recordings for the two labels; on the King recordings, the Stanley Brothers tended to be more experimental, working in electric instrumentation. Though there is plenty of fine music on the set, *The Early Starday-King Years* is, overall, too thorough and extensive for any but bluegrass historians. — *Thom Owens*

★ Angel Band: The Classic Mercury Recordings / 1995 / Mercury Nashville ◆◆◆◆◆
Angel Band collects the bulk of the Stanley Brothers' mid-'50s recordings, when they were expanding their sound slightly. Although it isn't always straight bluegrass, it shows how versatile and talented the Stanleys were. It's an essential purchase for a bluegrass collection. — *Thom Owens*

★ Complete Columbia Recordings / Mar. 1996 / Columbia/Legacy ◆◆◆◆
While this doesn't have the two alternate takes that surfaced on the nearly identical Bear Family collection *(1949-1952)*, this does have all 22 of the sides they officially released on Columbia, and it will be much easier to find in the US. It's classic bluegrass of great historical importance, featuring mostly original compositions. — *Richie Unterberger*

☆ Columbia Sessions 1949-1950 #1 / Rounder ◆◆◆◆◆
These beautiful vocal harmonies and piquant songs are bluegrass poetry at its purest. — *Mark A. Humphrey*

☆ The Stanley Brothers (1949-1952) / Bear Family ◆◆◆◆◆
All 22 of their Columbia recordings are here, superbly remastered, including the issued and alternate takes of two classics, "The Fields Have Turned Brown" and "Little Glass of Wine." Carter Stanley's dramatic story songs are underpinned by chilling vocal harmonies and an ensemble sound that bore their unique signature. — *Mark A. Humphrey*

Ralph Stanley (Ralph Edmond Stanley)

b. Feb. 25, 1927, Stratton, VA
Banjo, Vocals / Traditional Bluegrass
Born in Stratton, VA, in 1927, Ralph Stanley and his older brother Carter formed the Stanley Brothers and the Clinch Mountain

Boys. In 1946 Ralph and Carter were being broadcast from radio station WCYB in Bristol, VA. The music, which was inspired by their Virginia mountain home, was encouraged by their mother, who taught Ralph the claw-hammer style of banjo picking for which he and Carter became famous. They recorded for such companies as the small Rich-R-Tone label and later Columbia, a relationship that lasted from 1949 until 1952. These classic sessions defined the Stanleys' own approach to bluegrass and made them as important as Bill Monroe. After leaving Columbia, the Stanleys were with Mercury, Starday, and King. Leaning toward more gospel at times, Carter and Ralph made a place for themselves in the music industry. In December 1966, Carter Stanley died in a Virginia hospital after a steady decline in health. He was just 41 years old. After much consideration and grief, Ralph carried on without Carter. Already their haunting mountain melodies made them stand apart from other bluegrass bands, but Ralph expanded upon this foundation and took his own "high lonesome" vocals to a new plane.

Popular at bluegrass festivals, Ralph and each edition of the Clinch Mountain Boys grew to be one of the most respected outfits in bluegrass. As far as west as California and even up in the hollars of Kentucky, people were drawn to the poignant, mournful sound of Ralph Stanley's style. Different from all the rest, Ralph's ability to hit the right notes and chords made him a singer of trailblazing proportions. Ralph continued to record for a wide variety of labels, including Jalyn, Rebel, King Bluegrass, Blue Jay, Jessup, Stanleytone, his own label, and Freeland. A devoted family man, his constant touring took its toll on his first marriage, a union that produced daughters Lisa Joy and Tonya and son Timothy. His second wife, Jimmie, also a singer, gave him another son late in life; Ralph II followed in his father's and uncle's footsteps and played in the Clinch Mountain Boys. A Bluegrass Hall of Fame member along with Carter, Ralph Stanley was an inspiration to Dwight Yoakam, Emmylou Harris, the late Keith Whitley, and even Monroe acolyte Ricky Skaggs. With his raw emotions and Mother Stanley's three-fingered banjo technique, he helped bring the mountain style of bluegrass music to mainstream audiences. — *Jana Pendragon*

● Saturday Night and Sunday / 1992 / Freeland ◆◆◆◆
This 31-cut, two-disc project is a masterpiece that reflects both the secular and spiritual sides of Ralph Stanley's artistry. It is also a concept he mulled over in his mind for some time before executing it. The idea was to include performers from both the country and bluegrass worlds doing songs that somehow fit into the Stanley Brothers' tradition. With the inclusion of some Stanley originals as well as tunes written by Bill Monroe, Dwight Yoakam, Tom T. Hall, and Roy McMillan, this is not only a diverse compilation of material, but also one that never fails to interest the listener. Certainly the start-off number, McMillan's "Mountain Folks," which is done up just right by Stanley and the Clinch Mountain Boys, sets the tone. Followed by a duet between Ralph and Yoakam on the infectious "Down Where the River Bends," it quickly moves through to the final secular duet between Stanley and fellow bluegrasser Bill Monroe. Their teamwork on "Letter from My Darling" is monumental. The spiritual numbers include Ralph and Tom T. Hall on the well known gospel number "Rank Stranger" and Carter Stanley's sadly descriptive "The Fields Have All Turned Brown." But the most beguiling track is the fervent version of Yoakam's tribute song to his coal-mining grandfather, Luther Tibbs. "Miner's Prayer" is given a gospel overhaul that actually makes what was already a brilliant creation into an even more ageless tune that will be played, loved, and remembered for many generations to come. Ralph Stanley's High Lonesome sound fits in perfectly here and is endlessly effective. Outstanding performances in both categories come from diva Patty Loveless, Allison Krauss, George Jones, Jimmy Martin, and Emmylou Harris, to name just a few. A concept that works well for Stanley and his many friends, this is certainly a project that belongs in every bluegrass or gospel collection. — *Jana Pendragon*

Back to the Cross / Aug. 15, 1992 / Freeland ◆◆◆
Like Bill Monroe, Ralph Stanley maintained his skills and spirit into the 1990s, still singing and picking classic bluegrass. He

joined Freeland in 1992, and appropriately made his label debut a gospel session with the Clinch Mountain Boys. You wouldn't expect any surprises, and there weren't any; nor were there low points. The CD contained 12 wonderful renditions of traditional hymns and praise songs performed with the humility, grace, and down-home artistry that have always characterized Ralph Stanley's music. —*Ron Wynn*

Almost Home / Rebel ✦✦✦
Almost Home is a collection of gospel hymns and "White spirituals" sung a cappella by Stanley and his Clinch Mountain Boys. —*Jason Ankeny*

Classic Bluegrass / Rebel ✦✦✦
Classic Bluegrass contains a cross-section of Ralph Stanley's recordings during the '70s, providing a good introduction to the trailblazing bluegrass artist. —*Thom Owens*

☆ **Bound to Ride** / Rebel ✦✦✦✦✦
This legendary singer and banjoist's most atavistic performances include claw-hammer banjo and terrific wailing Baptist banshee vocals on old-time songs. —*Mark A. Humphrey*

John Starling

b. Mar. 26, 1940, Durham, NC
Guitar, Vocals / Progressive Bluegrass
A US Army surgeon, guitarist, and singer, Starling played with The Seldom Scene progressive bluegrass band from 1971 until 1977. After playing with various other groups in the 80s, he rejoined Seldom Scene in the early '90s. —*David Vinopal*

● **Long Time Gone** / Sugar Hill ✦✦✦✦
This is the kind of album you play over and over again. Featuring Lowell George, Emmylou Harris, Tony Rice, and Ricky Skaggs. Highly recommended. —*Chip Renner*

Waitin' on a Southern Train / Sugar Hill ✦✦✦
Another strong effort. Mike Auldridge, Sam Bush, and John Cowan back up John. Good selection of songs; "New Delhi Freight Train" stands out. —*Chip Renner*

Lucille Starr

b. St. Boniface, Canada
Vocals / Traditional Country, Country-Pop
Canadian singer-songwriter and yodeler Lucille Starr (born Lucille Marie Raymonde Savoie) was one of Canada's most popular country performers. She started her career singing with a British Columbia choir, Les Hirondelles, and then became the female lead with the Keray Regan Band. Eventually she and band member Bob Regan left to tour the country as Lucille and Bob. The duo had several successful singles in both the US and Canada, including "No Help Wanted." With her powerful voice and vibrant performances, Starr soon attracted notice from several label executives, one of whom dubbed the act the Canadian Sweethearts. While in California, the two frequently appeared on local country music shows and on ABC's *Country America* show, where they appeared regularly for two years. They also appeared on the Grand Ole Opry, and toured North America with Hank Snow, Wilf Carter and Little Jimmy Dickens. Both Starr and the Canadian Sweethearts signed to A&M Records in 1963, the latter reaching the Top 50 with "Hootenanny Express." They also had two top-rated hits in Canada, including "Looking Back to See." Starr went solo with *The French Cut*, which was produced by Herb Alpert and featured his Tijuana Brass. The title cut became a chart-topper, and the album produced five more hits. In 1967, the Canadian Sweethearts recorded in Nashville with producer Billy Sherrill. She appeared regularly on the charts through the mid-'70s. In 1977, she put an end to the Sweethearts partnership and cut another solo album, *The Sun Shines Again*, and it did quite well. Her subsequent album, *Back to You*, did very well in Canada and produced three hits, including a number one. —*Sandra Brennan*

Lucille Starr / A&M ✦✦✦
Lonely Street / Columbia ✦✦✦
Back to You / Quality Canada ✦✦✦

The Statler Brothers

Side by Side / Columbia ✦✦✦✦
● **Mississippi** / Koch International ✦✦✦✦

The Statler Brothers

Traditional Country, Country-Pop, Country Gospel
Named after a brand of tissues, the four members of the Statler Brothers did not, in fact, share a fraternal bond; what they did share was the distinction of being one of the most successful vocal harmony groups in the history of country music. Formed in the group's homebase of Staunton, VA, in 1955, the Statlers were originally a church trio comprised of bass vocalist Harold Reid (born August 21, 1939), baritone Phil Balsley (August 8, 1939), and tenor Lew DeWitt (March 8, 1938). In 1960, Reid's younger brother Don (born June 5, 1945) signed on to take the lead vocal reins, and the quartet performed gospel music under the name the Kingsmen.

After arranging a meeting with the promotional department for a local Johnny Cash concert, the Kingsmen were asked to open the performance. Cash was so impressed that he invited the group to join the tour, and after changing their name to the Statler Brothers, they remained on the road with Cash from 1963 to 1971. The Statlers signed to Columbia Records in 1964 and a year later scored a huge country and pop hit with DeWitt's "Flowers on the Wall," which also lent its name to their 1966 debut album. 1967's *The Statler Brothers Sing the Big Hits* held true to its title's promise, generating a pair of Top Ten singles in "Ruthless" and "You Can't Have Your Kate and Edith, Too."

In 1969 the quartet moved to Mercury Records, where they remained for more than two decades; their first single for the label, 1970's "Bed of Rose's," was a Top Ten hit. In the same year they held their first Fourth of July picnic; for decades, the celebration remained an annual holiday staple, drawing tens of thousands of fans each summer. Throughout the first half of the 1970s, the Statlers remained fixtures on the Top 40 charts, thanks to a string of nostalgic singles like 1972's "Do You Remember These" and "The Class of '57," 1973's "Carry Me Back," and 1974's "Whatever Happened to Randolph Scott." Their LPs of the period were often concept records: 1972's *The Statler Brothers Sing Country Symphonies in E Major* was whimsically formatted like an orchestral performance (complete with side-break "intermission"), while 1975's joint release *Holy Bible/Old Testament* and *Holy Bible/New Testament* fulfilled a long-standing dream to record a gospel project. *Alive at the Johnny Mack Brown High School*, on the other hand, was a tongue-in-cheek effort recorded in 1973 under the group's comic alias Lester "Roadhog" Moran and the Cadillac Cowboys.

The sentimental "I'll Go to My Grave Loving You" was a Top Five hit in 1975, and was included on the Statlers' first *Best of* compilation, released later the same year. After a series of Top Ten hits that included 1977's "The Movies" (another recurring Statler theme) and "I Was There," they earned their first chart-topper in 1978 with "Do You Know You Are My Sunshine," from the album *Entertainers... On and Off the Record*. In 1980 the Statler Brothers celebrated their first decade on Mercury with *10th Anniversary*, which featured the smash "Charlotte's Web," taken from the film *Smokey and the Bandit Part 2*, in which the group also co-starred.

After 1982's *The Legend Lives On*, Lew DeWitt was forced to leave the group as a result of Crohn's disease; the illness ultimately killed him on August 15, 1990. The remaining Statlers tapped Jimmy Fortune as his successor, and immediately Fortune earned the group its second No. 1 with his "Elizabeth" (an homage to actress Elizabeth Taylor), from the album *Today*. Their next two LPs, 1984's *Atlanta Blue* and 1985's *Pardners in Crime*, were credited simply to the Statlers; each record generated a No. 1 hit—"My Only Love" and "Too Much on My Heart," respectively—again composed by Fortune. They returned as the Statler Brothers for the 1986 inspirational release *Radio Gospel Favorites*, followed later in the year by *Four for the Show. Maple Street Memories* in 1987 produced the Top Ten single "Forever;" 1989's "More than a Name on the Wall," which peaked at No. 6, was their last significant hit. They continued releasing albums, however, and in addition to remaining a popular touring act in the 1990s, the Statler Brothers hosted a long-running variety show on TNN. —*Jason Ankeny*

Oh Happy Day / 1969 / Columbia ✦✦✦✦
Another "roots" effort, this one from the '60s. —*Ron Wynn*

Bed of Roses / 1971 / Mercury ✦✦✦✦
Their first Mercury album. —*Ron Wynn*

The World of the Statler Brothers / 1972 / Columbia ✦✦✦
An overview of mid-'60s; duplication with earlier albums. —*Ron Wynn*

Country Music Then and Now / 1972 / Mercury ✦✦✦✦
From the early '70s. A bit rougher and less slick than some '80s dates. —*Ron Wynn*

Sing Country Symphonies in E Major / 1972 / Mercury ✦✦✦
The Statler Brothers Sing Country Symphonies in E Major is a concept album of sorts, formatted like an orchestral performance (there's even an "intermission" instead of a side break); with the exception of the occasional string performance, however, this is an otherwise straightforward Statlers effort, featuring the minor hits "Monday Morning Secretary" and "Woman Without a Home." —*Jason Ankeny*

Alive at the Johnny Mack Brown High School / 1974 / Mercury ✦✦✦
Alive at the Johnny Mack Brown High School is a tongue-in-cheek effort from the Statlers' alias, Lester "Roadhog" Moran and the Cadillac Cowboys. —*Jason Ankeny*

Holy Bible: Old Testament / 1975 / Mercury ✦✦✦✦
The Statlers realized a long-held dream with this collection of country gospel songs, the first of two records celebrating the band's Christian upbringing. —*Jason Ankeny*

★ **The Best of the Statler Brothers** / 1975 / Mercury ✦✦✦✦✦
The Statlers' first decade of recording is recalled in their initial *Best Of* collection. The compilation includes all of the quartet's biggest Mercury hits from the first half of the 1970s, including "Do You Remember These," "I'll Go to My Grave Loving You," and "Bed of Rose's." However, only one song from their late-'60s tenure at Columbia—the classic "Flowers on the Wall"—makes the cut. —*Jason Ankeny*

Holy Bible: New Testament / 1975 / Mercury ✦✦✦✦
Released in tandem with its companion piece *Holy Bible: The Old Testament*, the Statlers spent more than eight years in preparation for this collection of country gospel. —*Jason Ankeny*

Entertainers On and Off / 1978 / Mercury ✦✦✦
Entertainers... On and Off the Record was one of the Statlers' most successful efforts from the 1970s, courtesy of their first No. 1 hit, "Do You Know You Are My Sunshine" as well as "Who Am I to Say" and "The Official Historian on Shirley Jean Berrell." —*Jason Ankeny*

The Best of the Statler Brothers, Vol. 2 / 1980 / Mercury ✦✦✦✦
Released just four years after their first hits collection, *The Best of the Statler Bros. Rides Again Volume II* collects their biggest singles from the bottom half of the 1970s. In addition to "Do You Know You Are My Sunshine," the group's first number one, the collection features "Who Am I to Say," "How to Be a Country Star," and "The Official Historian on Shirley Jean Berrell." —*Jason Ankeny*

10th Anniversary / 1980 / Mercury ✦✦✦✦
The Statlers celebrated their first decade as members of the Mercury Records roster with this collection, which includes the hit "Don't Forget Yourself" as well as "Charlotte's Web," taken from the motion picture *Smokey and the Bandit II. —Jason Ankeny*

Years Ago / 1981 / Mercury ✦✦✦
Before recording *Years Ago*, the Statlers purchased their old grammar school in their hometown of Staunton, VA, renovating the building to serve as their offices. (On the album cover, the group is photographed on the auditorium's stage.) Perhaps as a result, the record is even more nostalgic and sentimental than most of the Statlers' efforts, as evidenced by the song titles alone, including "Memories Are Made of This" and "Today I Went Back." Among the record's hits were "Don't Wait on Me" and "You'll Be Back (Every Night in My Dreams)." —*Jason Ankeny*

Today / 1983 / Mercury ✦✦✦✦
After the departure of Lew DeWitt, who left the group because of health problems, *Today* marked the addition of new tenor vocalist Jimmy Fortune, who immediately proved his worth by penning the Statlers' second chart-topper, "Elizabeth." Among the other hits: a cover of the Four Knights' "Oh Baby Mine (I Get So Lonely)" and "Guilty." —*Jason Ankeny*

Atlanta Blue / 1984 / Mercury ✦✦✦✦
After replacing founding member Lew DeWitt with Jimmy Fortune in the early '80s, the Statler Brothers made a considerable commercial comeback, which culminated with the *Atlanta Blue* album. What makes *Atlanta Blue* noticeably stronger than its predecessor or successor is the uniform excellence of the material—including the hit singles "Atlanta Blue," "One Takes the Blame," and the No. 1 "My Only Love"—and the gorgeous harmonies of the Statler Brothers. —*Thom Owens*

Pardners in Rhyme / 1985 / Mercury ✦✦✦✦
The Statlers notched three consecutive Top Ten hits from *Pardners in Rhyme*, including the chart-topping "Too Much on My Heart," "Sweeter and Sweeter," and a cover of Ricky Nelson's "Hello Mary Lou." —*Jason Ankeny*

Radio Gospel Favorites / 1986 / Mercury ✦✦✦
Radio Gospel Favorites is a mixed bag of covers and original spirituals recorded directly for the project, rounded out with other similarly themed songs ("One Size Fits All," "Sweet By and By," and "Amazing Grace") culled from previous LPs. —*Jason Ankeny*

Maple Street Memories / 1987 / Mercury ✦✦✦✦
Nice autobiographical touches. —*Ron Wynn*

The Greatest Hits / 1988 / Mercury ✦✦✦
A recycled greatest/best-of, including such Statler favorites as "Elizabeth," "Atlanta Blue," and "Guilty." —*Ron Wynn*

Live and Sold Out / Jun. 1989 / Mercury ✦✦✦
Live and Sold out is a satisfying live show from 1989 that features the Statler Brothers running through 11 of their biggest hits and most familiar songs, including "I'll Go to My Grave Loving You," "Walking Heartache in Disguise," and "This Ole House." Though many favorites are missing—there's no "Flowers on the Wall" or "The Class of '57," for instance—the group sounds very good, and the record is an enjoyable, if inconsequential, listen. —*Thom Owens*

Music, Memories and You / 1990 / Mercury ✦✦
Music, Memories and You features the Statlers' last chart single to date, "Small Small World." *—Jason Ankeny*

All American Country / 1991 / Mercury ✦✦
Released on the downslope of the Statlers' popularity as recording artists, *All American Country* generated no chart singles, ending the group's run of 25 consecutive years with Top 100 hits. *—Jason Ankeny*

Home / 1993 / Mercury ✦✦
As the title indicates, *Home* is another of the Statlers' periodic reminiscences about their lives in small-town Virginia. There's also another of the group's occasional tributes to Chet Atkins, "Chet, You're the Reason." *—Jason Ankeny*

Today's Gospel Favorites / Jun. 22, 1993 / Mercury ✦✦✦
Today's Gospel Favorites is a collection of contemporary inspirational material, capably performed by the Statler Brothers. While the music is impeccably produced and the group is in fine voice, the disc doesn't provide many distinguished moments, even though the entire album is pleasant. *— Stephen Thomas Erlewine*

30th Anniversary Celebration / Nov. 21, 1995 / Mercury ✦✦✦✦
A 30th Anniversary Celebration is a three-disc compilation covering the Statler Brothers' entire career, from their early days at Columbia to their hit-making peak at Mercury. Over the course of 62 tracks, all 27 of their Top Ten hits—including "Flowers on the Wall," "Do You Remember These," "The Class of '57," "Do You Know You Are My Sunshine," "Who Am I to Say," "Oh Baby Mine (I Get So Lonely)," "Elizabeth," "My Only Love," and "Too Much on My Heart"—are featured, as are a handful of lesser-known gems. For any fan of the group, this is an essential purchase, since it is a lovingly produced, definitive retrospective of the Statlers' best-known material. In fact, it may be all the Statlers most listeners will ever need to own. *— Thom Owens*

★ **Flowers on the Wall: The Essential Statler Brothers** / Mar. 1996 / Columbia/Legacy ✦✦✦✦✦
The Statler Brothers started their recording career at Columbia Records and cut eight albums for the label in five years, scoring eight country singles chart entries, including the Top Ten hits "Ruthless," "You Can't Have Your Kate and Edith, Too," and the pop Top Ten crossover "Flowers on the Wall." This 18-track compilation includes all those hits, along with standards like "The Wreck of the Old '97," "Green Grass," and the gospel pop song "Oh Happy Day." It also includes one previously unreleased track, "Half a Man," which, despite having been recorded two years later, sounds like the logical follow-up to "Flowers on the Wall." The influence of the Statlers' employer, Johnny Cash, is apparent, especially on "Hammer and Nails," on which he appears. At this early stage, without losing the sound of the classic country quartet, the Statlers also sang pop, folk, and gospel well. The only complaint to be made about this set is that, in the CD age, a running time of 42:15 is short for a compilation (if typical of country music). But nothing essential is missing. *— William Ruhlmann*

Red Steagall (Russell Steagall)

b. 1937, Gainesville, TX
Guitar, Mandolin / Traditional Country, Country-Pop
In 1991 Western singer-songwriter Red Steagall was named Cowboy Poet of Texas by the state's legislature for his efforts in keeping the traditional artform vital while preserving its rich past. He was raised in the ranching community of Sanford, TX, surrounded by working cowboys and rodeos. He was a teenage bullrider when, at age 15, he contracted polio. During his recovery, he learned the guitar and mandolin to help him regain the use of his left arm and hand. Steagall founded his first country band to help cover his collegiate expenses; after graduation, he sold agro-chemicals by day and played music at night. He moved to the Los Angeles area in the mid-'60s, where he began performing in assorted folk clubs and writing songs. In 1967 Ray Charles recorded Steagall's "Here We Go Again" and had a hit, as did Nancy Sinatra sometime later. Steagall also worked as a writer at United Artists Music before quitting to found his own company.

He had his first hit in 1972 with "Party Dolls and Wine," which hit the Top 30; his follow-up, "Somewhere My Love," climbed ten notches higher. Steagall moved to Nashville the next year and appeared on the charts with songs such as "True Love." He discovered Reba McEntire at the National Rodeo Finals in Oklahoma City and took her to Nashville, where he helped her make a demo and sign with Mercury. Meanwhile, he continued to enjoy chart success with his own singles, scoring his biggest hit in 1976 with "Lone Star Beer and Bob Wills Music," which reached the Top 15. Steagall was also a respected songwriter; more than 200 of his songs have been recorded by stars ranging from Dean Martin to Del Reeves to George Strait. Steagall had his last run of country hits in 1979, among them "Goodtime Charlie's Got the Blues." His career began to wind down in the early '80s, and eventually he returned to his ranch near Fort Worth, TX. He continued to tour and was a draw at fairs and rodeos with his brand of cowboy poetry. Steagall also helmed the annual Cowboy Gathering and Western Swing Festival in Fort Worth. *—Sandra Brennan*

Party Dolls and Wine / 1972 / Capitol ✦✦✦✦
● **Somewhere My Love** / 1973 / Capitol ✦✦✦✦
If You've Got the Time / 1973 / Capitol ✦✦✦
The Finer Things in Life / 1974 / Capitol ✦✦✦
Lone Star Beer and Bob Wills Music / 1976 / MCA ✦✦✦✦
From the opening track to the closing note on side two, this is one fine example of Texas swing/honky tonk music, created at a time when America was rediscovering Bob Wills and this type of music. Even old chestnuts like "Someday You'll Want Me" or "Truck Drivin' Man," with Johnny Gimble's smoking fiddle break, are hot. *—Jim Worbois*

Texas Red / 1976 / ABC ✦✦✦
For All Our Cowboy Friends / 1977 / MCA ✦✦✦
Hang on Feelin' / 1978 / ABC/Dot ✦✦✦
Born to This Land / Jan. 1993 / Warner Western ✦✦✦✦
Faith and Values / Aug. 8, 1995 / Warner Brothers ✦✦✦

Keith Stegall

b. 1955, Wichita Falls, TX
Guitar, Vocals / Country-Pop, Urban Cowboy
Singer-songwriter Keith Stegall began playing piano when he was only four and began performing at age eight. By age 12, he was a guitarist and had founded his first country band, the Pacesetters. As a teen, he developed an appreciation for Aretha Franklin and R&B music; he later learned the drums and joined a rock group. At age 15 he became an acoustic guitarist for the Cheerful Givers, a folk outfit, and eventually moved to Shreveport, LA, where he worked as a lounge singer on Saturday nights and as the musical director of a Methodist church on Sundays. He met Kris Kristofferson, who encouraged him to keep up with his songwriting and try his luck in Nashville, which is just what Stegall did in 1978. He hit the Top 60 with his debut single, "The Fool Who Fooled Around," in 1980; he also scored with a lesser hit, "Won't You Be My Baby." In 1983 he had a Top 25 hit with "I Want to Go Somewhere" and then a Top 20 hit with "Whatever Turns You On." In 1985 he had his biggest hit with the Top Ten "Pretty Lady." A noted songwriter, he also provided material for a wide variety of artists ranging from Mickey Gilley to Al Jarreau to Helen Reddy. In the 1990s he worked more as a music publisher and record producer for the likes of Alan Jackson. *—Sandra Brennan*

● **Passages** / Feb. 27, 1996 / Polygram ✦✦✦✦
Keith Stegall / Epic ✦✦✦✦

Jeff Steven

Country-Pop, Contemporary Country
Jeff Stevens and the Bullets were a family vocal trio formed in Alum Creek, WV, in 1975 consisting of brothers Jeff and Warren Stevens and cousin Terry Dotson. Jeff was born in Alum Creek and was influenced as a child by the music of Johnny Cash. He and Warren entered their first talent contest when Jeff was nine.

They won first prize, and Jeff knew he wanted to be a country performer. Early in their career, the band opened for such big-name acts as George Jones, Tammy Wynette, Johnny Cash, and Conway Twitty. In the early '80s, Jeff and Dotson became a songwriting team and provided Atlanta with two major hits,"Atlanta Burned Again Last Night" and "Sweet Country Music." In 1986 Stevens and the Bullets released a cover of Bruce Springsteen's "Darlington County" as their debut single. It made the Top 70, and their debut album followed. They released their second album in 1987 and had their biggest hit with a cover of Michael Martin Murphey's "Geronimo's Cadillac." The trio disbanded in 1990, and Jeff tried to forge a solo career. In 1991 he made an album for Atlantic, but it was never released. With producer Keith Stegall's help, he began working with such established writers as Roger Murrah and Jim McBride. In 1993 Stevens co-authored "I Fell in the Water" with Jerry Salley and provided John Anderson with a Top Ten hit; working with Michael Clark, he later wrote Alabama's No. 1 hit "Reckless." —*Sandra Brennan*

● **Jeff Stevens and the Bullets** / 1975 / Atlantic ◆◆◆◆

Bolt out of the Blue / Atlantic ◆◆◆

Ray Stevens

b. Jan. 24, 1939, Clarksdale, GA
Piano, Vocals / Comedy, Country-Pop, Country Humor
Singer-songwriter/multi-instrumentalist Ray Stevens found fame as a performer of novelty and parody songs. Born Harry Ray Ragsdale in Clarksdale, GA, Stevens was a trained classical pianist who founded an R&B band, the Barons, in high school. In the mid-'50s he attended Georgia State University to study music theory, composition, and classical piano. In 1957 he signed with Capitol and attempted a recording career on their Prep label, but the resulting two singles went nowhere; however, he did find work arranging and producing for Patti Page, Brook Benton, and Brenda Lee.

Stevens hooked up with Mercury in 1961 and had his first chart success with the advertising parody "Jeremiah Peabody's Poly Unsaturated Quick Dissolving Fast Acting Pleasant Tasting Green and Purple Pills," which climbed to the Top 40 on the pop charts. His next release, "Ahab the Arab" (1962), made Stevens a bona fide star and was a Top Five pop hit. He then moved to Nashville, had two more hits, including "Santa Claus is Watching You," and did session work. His career really didn't take off until 1969 with the Top Ten pop parody "Gitarzan," which became his first gold record and was followed by the Top 30 hit "Along Came Jones." That year he debuted on the country charts with a cover of Kris Kristofferson's "Sunday Mornin' Comin' Down."

In the early '70s Stevens had an international chart-topper with "Everything Is Beautiful," which became his second gold record and made the pop and country charts. In 1971 he had a major country hit with a more serious tune, "Turn Your Radio On." His novelty number "Bridget the Midget" was also successful. In 1973 and 1974 Stevens appeared regularly on the "Music Country" television show; in 1974, he also had a No. 1 pop and No. 3 country hit with "The Streak." The next year he had major success with a bluegrass-influenced cover of "Misty." In 1977, billing himself as the Henhouse Five Plus Too, he recorded a version of the swing standard "In the Mood" on which all vocal parts were clucked like a chicken. His final pop hit was "I Need Your Help, Barry Manilow" (1979).

In 1980 he began to concentrate on country novelty songs and had a big hit with "Shriner's Convention." Other major hits from the '80s included "Mississippi Squirrel Revival" and "It's Me Again Margaret." He founded his own label, Clyde Records, in 1988. A frequent performer in Las Vegas, he also built the 2,000-seat Ray Stevens Theatre in Branson, MO. Through the '90s he continued recording and began making videos such as *Ray Stevens: Comedy Video Classics*. —*Sandra Brennan*

Gitarzan / 1969 / Varèse Sarabande ◆◆◆
Stevens plies his stock-in-trade pop novelties on this 1969 album, replete with hayseed monologues, skilled mimicry of various voices (spoken and sung), and Vegas-soul female backup singers. It sounds hokey now—and probably sounded hokey then—but

not to everyone, as the title track made the Top Ten, and the remake of the Coasters' "Along Came Jones" made the Top Thirty. The rest of the album's divided between Stevenized covers of vintage rock novelties ("Yakety Yak," "Alley Oop") and satirical originals that ensured his stature as the Top 40's answer to *Hee Haw*. The CD reissue adds three bonus tracks, including "Bridget the Midget," a small hit from 1970, and "The Streak," his No.1 single from 1974. Better than anything else on the disc, though, is his 1974 single "The Moonlight Special" (included here). This satire of DJ Wolfman Jack's TV show is actually genuinely funny in places, complete with spot-on send-ups of Jerry Lee Lewis and a Gladys Knight-type soul group. —*Richie Unterberger*

Greatest Hits / 1983 / RCA ◆◆◆◆
Greatest Hits collects Stevens' novelty songs like "The Streak," "Ahab the Arab," and "Everything Is Beautiful." —*Jason Ankeny*

Greatest Hits, Vol. 2 / Sep. 7, 1987 / MCA ◆◆◆◆

His All-Time Greatest Comic Hits / 1990 / Capitol ◆◆◆
His All-Time Greatest Comic Hits contains ten of Ray Stevens' most popular novelty numbers from the '70s and '80s, including "The Streak," "Shriner's Convention," "Gitarzan," "In the Mood," "It's Me Again, Margaret," "Ahab the Arab," and "Would Jesus Wear A Rolex." Though it doesn't have country-pop hits like "Everything Is Beautiful" and "Misty," the record nevertheless remains a definitive collection. After all, nearly every listener identifies Stevens with his novelties and for those listeners who want more funny stuff than what is on *Greatest Hits, His All-Time Greatest Comic Hits* is the place to go. —*Thom Owens*

● **Collection** / Feb. 2, 1993 / MCA ◆◆◆◆

The Gospel Side of Ray Stevens / K-Tel ◆◆◆◆
A solid collection of Stevens' inspirational work, featuring both original numbers like "Everything Is Beautiful" and "Yes, Jesus Loves Me" with traditional numbers like "Love Lifted Me" and "All My Trials." —*Stephen Thomas Erlewine*

Gary Stewart

b. May 28, 1945, Letcher County, KY
Bass, Guitar, Piano / Traditional Country, Progressive Country, Country-Rock, Honky Tonk
While much of what passes for contemporary country music these days sounds like reheated Eagles and Lynyrd Skynyrd, what's really annoying is what a youth-driven market it has become, leaving many great country performers of the '60s and '70s out in the cold. This is especially irritating when considering the career of Gary Stewart, one of the greatest of the hardcore honky tonk school who, at his peak in the mid- to late '70s, could write and sing circles around just about any contemporary country star you can mention. A native of Florida, Stewart escaped a lifetime of working in an airplane factory in the late '60s by pitching some songs he'd written to soon-to-be RCA country label honcho Jerry Bradley. At the time, Stewart (who was composing with his friend Bill Eldridge) didn't aspire to more than being an in-demand Nashville songwriter, but after a couple of years writing with some success, and through Bradley's continued intercession, he was given the opportunity to record on his own. With his huge, vibrato-laden tenor voice (which sounds a bit like Jerry Lee Lewis'), Stewart, with the inestimable help of songwriter Wayne Carson, released 1975's *Out of Hand*, one of the finest honky tonk records of all time. Paced by the hit "She's Actin' Single (I'm Drinkin' Doubles)," Gary Stewart was quickly becoming a country music star.

Although he composed songs for traditional Grand Ole Opry stars (Cal Smith, Hank Snow), Stewart himself never emulated the traditional values espoused by the Nashville establishment; as one of his song titles stated, he was more of a "flat natural-born good-timin' man." He hung out (and caroused plenty) with Southern rock musicians, using them on his albums at a time when this was still considered radical. He was a renegade, unwilling to play the Nashville game, and his increasing success provided him with the autonomy he needed to do his own thing. However, this generally meant conspicuous excess, especially when it came to substance abuse. Still, from 1975 through 1980, Stewart's recorded work is mostly excellent, with a conspicuous high point coming in 1977 with the release of *Your Place or Mine*. A hard-driving slice of aggressive honky tonk, it was a rollickingly good piece of work, not the equal of *Out of Hand*, but as important an assertion of Stewart's independence from the machinations of country music's starmaking machinery. There were problems, however; Stewart was too country for rock audiences and too rock for country audiences, and that limited any stab at broader appeal.

In 1980 he released *Cactus and a Rose*, with considerable help from Southern rock vets Gregg Allman, Dickey Betts, Mike Lawler, and Bonnie Bramlett. It was a fine record but attracted only Stewart's core audience, and at this point in his career, that simply wasn't enough. Suddenly it seemed as if his desire and creativity vanished. He hooked up with Dean Dillon and made a couple of terrible two-good-ol'boy records that made the redneck rowdiness of Hank Williams, Jr. sound philosophical by comparison. Not long afterwards, Stewart returned to Florida and stopped recording. After his alcoholism and drug use pretty much canceled out a large part of the '80s, Stewart returned, clean and sober, with a strong comeback record, *Brand New*, in 1988. It wasn't the Gary Stewart of old, but it was a respectable record, and it was enough to propel a comeback that continues with his recent *I'm a Texan*. Considering that most folks had given him up for dead, this was a remarkable turn of events. His heyday was in the '70s, but Gary Stewart deserves to be celebrated for his considerable talent, tenacity, and influence. —*John Dougan*

You're Not the Woman You Used to Be / 1973 / MCA ✦✦✦
MCA put this album out in an attempt to capitalize on Gary's RCA success. Except for two tracks, all this material had been released while he'd been signed with Kapp and, in most cases, shows that Stewart hadn't yet found his voice or his style. The title track, though, is nearly as good as anything he did at RCA. —*Jim Worbois*

☆ **Out of Hand** / 1975 / Hightone ✦✦✦✦✦
Stewart's best album and one of the greatest honky tonk records ever recorded, *Out of Hand* has "Drinkin' Thing," "She's Actin' Single (I'm Drinkin' Doubles)," and "I See the Want To in Your Eyes," as strong a grouping of songs as on any Stewart record. Few, if any, country performers have made a better hard honky tonk record (although Joe Ely came the closest). If you get tired of the songs about drinking and want something a little less self-pitying and uplifting, this won't be for you, but a true fan of country music better own this. —*John Dougan*

Steppin' Out / 1976 / RCA ✦✦✦
Not one of Stewart's strongest efforts but worth the price of admission just to hear him cover Willie Nelson's "I Still Can't Believe You're Gone." The original album came with an iron-on patch (or in the case of my copy, two) featuring Stewart playing his guitar. —*Jim Worbois*

Your Place or Mine / 1977 / RCA ✦✦✦✦
If anything has hurt this record since its release, it's that some of the tracks ("Rachel" and "Broken Hearted People") sound a bit pro forma, and the drinking songs sound a little tired. But the best tracks (the title cut and "Ten Years of This") are as good as anything on *Out of Hand*. The record's diamond is Stewart's version of Rodney Crowell's "Ain't Living Long Like This," which he sings as if his life depended on it. It's a truly transcendent moment, perhaps Stewart's best single moment on record (although his vocal on the title track comes pretty close). One of the great hard country records of all time, *Your Place or Mine* (though few will admit it) is one of the records from which contemporary country artists borrow shamelessly. —*John Dougan*

Cactus and Rose / 1980 / RCA ✦✦✦
This is not the kind of record most people would associate with Gary Stewart, one of the finest honky tonk singers ever. For this effort, he has teamed up with people like Allman Brother members Gregg Allman and Dickey Betts as well as Bonnie Bramlett (ex-Delaney, Bonnie and Friends) and Randy Scruggs. And what do we learn? That Stewart could easily have fronted the Allman Brothers or Marshall Tucker or vocally kicked Charlie Daniels'

Southern rock butt from here to Pascagoula as a great honky tonk singer. —*Jim Worbois*

☆ **Greatest Hits** / 1981 / RCA ✦✦✦✦✦
A little on the short side (ten tracks), but with 50% of them coming from either *Out of Hand* or *Your Place or Mine*, this is a filler-free and succinct career summation of this great artist. Ironically, much of this sounds similar to what has made Garth Brooks and his ilk millionaires many times over, and Stewart (who was truly ahead of his time) was nearly forgotten. No one ever said life (especially in the music business) was fair, but a few spins of this and you will soon understand that nearly 20 years later, Stewart still stands taller than virtually all of the country performers making a mint from imitating his style. A perfect place to start. —*John Dougan*

Brand New / 1988 / Hightone ✦✦✦
Stewart ends a lengthy recording hiatus, showing a newfound maturity while tackling songs that are still rife with tortured self-revelation. His voice has lost little of its edge. —*Michael McCall*

Battleground / 1990 / Hightone ✦✦✦
Battleground focuses on Stewart's Southern rock leanings on tracks like "Nothin' but a Woman" and "Let's Go Jukin'." —*Jason Ankeny*

★ **Gary's Greatest** / 1992 / Hightone ✦✦✦✦✦
Featuring material recorded from 1973 to 1990—including songs from both his RCA and HighTone days—*Gary's Greatest* has 17 of Stewart's best songs and is an excellent introduction to the under-appreciated singer-songwriter. —*Thom Owens*

I'm a Texan / Oct. 15, 1993 / Hightone ✦✦✦
More impassioned than ever, Stewart continues to excel at raw-boned honky tonk and revved-up country-rock. The songs don't all live up to his treatment, but when they do, as on "Honky Tonk Hardwood Floor" or the inviting "Come On In," he reveals the timidity that undercuts the new traditionalists of the modern country era. —*Michael McCall*

Essential / Jan. 28, 1997 / RCA ✦✦✦✦
Gary Stewart's *Essential* is an excellent cross-section of hit singles, rarities, and album tracks that demonstrates his talents as a songwriter and as a gritty honky tonk performer. *Gary's Greatest* remains a better way to become acquainted with Stewart's entire catalog, but *Essential* is still a fine sampler. —*Thom Owens*

John Stewart

b. Sep. 5, 1939, San Diego, CA
Guitar, Vocals / Singer-Songwriter, Adult Contemporary, Soft Rock, Contemporary Folk
John Stewart first gained recognition as a songwriter when his songs were recorded by the Kingston Trio. In 1960 he formed the Cumberland Three, which recorded three albums for Roulette. The next year, he joined the Kingston Trio, replacing Dave Guard, and stayed with them until 1967. His song "Daydream Believer" was a No. 1 hit for the Monkees at the end of that year. Stewart traveled with Senator Robert Kennedy on his 1968 Presidential campaign, an experience that affected him deeply. In 1969 he released his classic album *California Bloodlines*, the first of seven solo albums to reach the charts through 1980. Stewart found his biggest commercial success with the Top Ten album *Bombs Away Dream Babies* and its single "Gold" in 1979. He released several of his albums and albums by others on his own Homecoming label starting in the 1980s. —*William Ruhlmann*

● **California Bloodline/Willard (Minus 2)** / 1969-1970 / Bear Family ✦✦✦✦
This German import contains some of Stewart's most powerful work. *California Bloodlines* offers 12 original tunes backed by Nashville's finest studio musicians. *Willard Minus 2*, though not so powerful as *Bloodlines*, still features many great songs (two tracks missing from the original) and a good cast of musicians. Highly recommended. —*Chip Renner*

Lonesome Picker Rides Again / 1971 / Warner Brothers ✦✦✦
Good collection of music, with more energy than his first two records. —*Chip Renner*

Sunstorm Live 1972 / 1972 / Bear Family ✦✦✦
Featuring Russ Kunkel, James Burton, Buddy Emmons, and brother Michael Stewart. Contains the song "Kansas Rain." A good, solid release. —*Chip Renner*

Cannons in the Rain/Wingless Angel / 1973-1975 / Bear Family ✦✦✦✦
In this two-fer (*Cannons in the Rain/Wingless Angels*) the *Wingless Angels* release is the stronger collection of music, featuring Robert "Waddy" Wachtel on guitar and a guest appearance by John Denver. *Cannons*... is a nice collection of ballads and folkrock. —*Chip Renner*

Complete Phoenix Concerts / 1974 / Bear Family ✦✦✦✦
A great collection of live music covering Stewart's first five albums. —*Chip Renner*

Trancas / 1984 / Affordable Dreams ✦✦✦
Stewart's electric guitar is nicely backed by touches of strings, drums, keyboards, and synthesized sounds. This album is positive in content and easy listening. —*Chip Renner*

The Last Campaign / 1985 / Homecoming ✦✦✦
Influenced by Robert Kennedy's campaign for president, the songs paint a tapestry of America. Very good. —*Chip Renner*

Secret Tapes '86 / 1986 / Homecoming ✦✦✦
An 80-minute tape featuring songs recorded in Stewart's studio. Includes "California Bloodlines," "Chilly Winds," "Cheyenne," "The River." A must for any serious collector. —*Chip Renner*

Secret Tapes II / 1986 / Homecoming ✦✦✦
Another collection, featuring "A Grace of Rain," "Seven Angels," "Tears of the Sun," "Quarter Moon on the Golden Gate," and "Irresistible Targets." Another must-have for the serious collector. —*Chip Renner*

Punch the Big Guy / 1987 / Cypress ✦✦✦✦
An exceptional release. Stewart stands out on his electric guitar with minimal backup. Bela Fleck, Sam Bush, and Pat Flynn (New Grass Revival), along with Rosanne Cash, Edgar Meyers, Brent Rowan, and others add just enough, but do not take away from Stewart's sound. Great job on "Runaway Trains." A classic. —*Chip Renner*

Neon Beach / 1991 / Line ✦✦✦
Over 60 minutes of great live music, featuring some old and new favorites: "Angels with Guns," "Lady Came from Baltimore," "Seven Angels," "Gold Medley," and "Bad Rats," to name a few. Stewart's talking between songs is insightful. —*Chip Renner*

Deep in the Neon: Live at McCabe's / Jun. 1991 / Homecoming ✦✦✦
Deep in the Neon—Live at McCabe's features just Stewart and Dave Batti and 16 well-performed songs. The audience is into the show, and Stewart plays an easy and relaxed, quiet set. —*Chip Renner*

● **Turning Love into Gold: The Best Of** / 1995 / Polydor ✦✦✦✦

Larry Stewart

b. Mar. 2, 1959, Paducah, KY
Vocals / Contemporary Country
Best known as the frontman for the vocal group Restless Heart, singer Larry Stewart first came to Nashville with hopes of a career in baseball, not music; the recipient of an athletic scholarship to Nashville's Belmont College, he quickly found himself drawn to the music business instead, and decided to pursue a career as a performer. After working a series of menial industry jobs, his vocals on a series of demo recordings helped win him the lead spot with Restless Heart. After leaving the group, in 1993 Stewart issued his solo debut, *Down the Road. Heart like a Hurricane* followed a year later, and in 1996 he returned with *Why Can't You*. —*Jason Ankeny*

● **Down the Road** / Apr. 27, 1993 / RCA ✦✦✦✦
Yeah, Restless Heart had its biggest success after he left. Judging from *Down the Road*, though, the split was one of those situations where the parts are greater than the sum. Just when "Alright Already" and "I'll Cry Tomorrow" convince you Stewart has made a country record, he tosses off a pop gem like "We Can Love." He

also cut Kevin Welch's "I Came Straight to You," a definite plus. —*Brian Mansfield*

Heart Like a Hurricane / 1994 / Columbia ✦✦✦

Why Can't You / Sep. 3, 1996 / Sony ✦✦✦
Larry Stewart's third album suffers from an uneven selection of material and production that plays it too close to the vest, but the singer manages to salvage about half the songs with a convincing, powerful performance, making *Why Can't You* a marginal improvement over its predecessor, *Heart Like A Hurricane*. —*Thom Owens*

Wynn Stewart

b. Jun. 7, 1934, Morrisville, MO, d. Jul. 17, 1985, Hendersonville, TN
Vocals / Traditional Country, Bakersfield Sound
Wynn Stewart was one of the leading figures of West Coast country music, developing in the early '50s the style that would later become known as the Bakersfield sound. Along with Tommy Collins and Buck Owens, Stewart stripped down the sound of honky tonk, taking away the steel guitars and relying on electric instruments, a driving beat, and loud, energetic performances. For most of the late '50s and early '60s, Wynn released a series of independent singles that performed respectably but failed to break into the mainstream. By the end of the '60s, he had modified his sound slightly, bringing himself closer to country-pop territory. The shift in style was successful, resulting in his lone No. 1 hit single, "It's Such a Pretty World Today," but Stewart wasn't able to become a genuine country star, despite his steady stream of records during the '70s and '80s. At the time of his sudden death in 1985, he was preparing for another comeback, which might have resulted in some long-overdue critical and popular acclaim. Even though he never received those accolades while he was alive, his early singles like "Wishful Thinking" and "Big, Big Love" clearly inspired contemporaries like Owens and Haggard, as well as '80s neo-traditionalists and alternative country musicians like Dwight Yoakam and k.d. lang, which guarantees him a place in the history of contemporary country music.

Stewart was born in Morrisville, MO, and spent most of his childhood moving around the country with his sharecropping family. After World War II, he spent a year working for KWTO in Springfield, MO, before moving to California in 1948 with his family. Originally, Wynn wanted to become a professional baseball player, but he suffered from a hand disease and was too short to play ball professionally, so he concentrated on a musical career. While he was still in high school, he formed a band and began playing clubs around California. Eventually, he met steel guitarist Ralph Mooney, who joined Wynn's band; rounding out the group's lineup were guitarist Roy Nichols and bassist Bobby Austin. In 1954 Stewart signed a contract with the independent label Intro, where he released "I've Waited a Lifetime" and "Strolling." The second single drew the attention of Wynn's idol, Skeets McDonald, who arranged an audition at Capitol Records for Stewart. By the summer of 1956, he had signed with Capitol and released his first single for the label, "Waltz of the Angels," which spent one week at No. 14 on the country chart; the song was later a hit for George Jones and Margie Singleton. Subsequent singles were released on Capitol, but none of the records made any impact, and Stewart left the label.

With the help of Harlan Howard, Wynn signed with Jackpot, a subsidiary of Challenge Records, in early 1958. Occasionally employing Mooney on steel guitar, Stewart made a series of singles that explored a number of different styles, from rockabilly and pop to pure honky tonk. In late 1959 he finally had a hit with "Wishful Thinking," which climbed to No. 5 early in 1960. Shortly after the success of "Wishful Thinking," he moved to Las Vegas, where he hosted a local television show and opened the Nashville Nevada Club. By the early '60s, Stewart's reputation was considerable, and he continued to have a string of moderate hit singles, including the Jan Howard duet "Wrong Company," "Big, Big Love," and "Another Day, Another Dollar." In 1962 Merle Haggard joined Stewart's band as a bassist, and Wynn eventually gave him "Sing a Sad Song" for his debut single.

After his Vegas ventures went bankrupt, Stewart headed back to California in 1965, re-signing with Capitol Records. Early in 1967 he had his first significant hit for the label, "It's Such a Pretty World Today," which spent two weeks at No. 1. After its success, Stewart concentrated on softer, more commercially acceptable material, and the result was a string of hit singles that ran into the early '70s. By 1972 his sales were beginning to decrease, and Wynn switched record labels, signing with RCA. Over the next three years he released a number of singles, none of which cracked the Top 40. In 1975 he signed with Playboy Records, scoring a comeback single with the Top Ten "After the Storm" the next year. He stayed with Playboy for two more years, which resulted in only one other hit single: his own version of "Sing a Sad Song."

Stewart launched his own independent label, WIN, in 1978; his first single, "Eyes Big as Dallas," scraped the bottom of the Top 40. Though the musical climate of the '70s was changing rapidly, leaving Wynn behind, he his developing alcoholism was also keeping him from achieving more success. Eventually, he decided to step back from performing in the early '80s, using the time away from the spotlight. During the mid-'80s, Stewart decided to launch a comeback with an extensive tour and a new album on his Pretty World record label, but he died suddenly of a heart attack on the eve of the tour. After his death, the posthumous "Wait 'Til I Get My Hands on You" became a minor hit. —Stephen Thomas Erlewine

★ California Country: The Best of the Challenge Masters / 1995 / AVI ✦✦✦✦✦

This masterful collection is the best of Wynn Stewart, the early years. Twenty-nine cuts that range from the hits to some of the more obscure numbers he recorded in California while signed to both Jackpot and Challenge are included here: "Come On" (a rockabilly tune), "Wishful Thinkin'," and two of the three big Challenge hits, "Big, Big Love" and "Another Day, Another Dollar." As good as anything recorded since. Wynn Stewart's voice was always notable. Best described as having a "rolling chord style," Stewart continues to be praised as one of the outstanding vocalists of the genre. His contribution to the West Coast country scene and to the Bakersfield sound makes him one of the founding fathers of that musical ilk. Tunes that demonstrate this include "Playboy," "Falling for You" (a Ralph Mooney tune), and "Heartaches for a Dime." His duets with Jan Howard, then married to Harlan Howard, convinced the young woman to pursue a singing career. "How the Other Half Lives," "Wrong Company," and "We'll Never Love Again" continue to set a standard for couple's duets. Ending with the bleak "The Black Limousine" seems fitting, since Stewart's career was cut short in 1985 when he died of a heart attack just as he was about to make another bid for success. Underappreciated, especially in the States, Wynn Stewart and the songs he wrote and recorded continue to draw attention to a talent and a career that never quite took off, yet are more remarkable than those of most of the artists who find themselves sitting at the top of the charts with their pockets full of gold. This is an exceptional introduction to Wynn Stewart, as well as a remarkable collection for Wynn Stewart fans to savor. —Jana Pendragon

Cliffie Stone (Clifford Gilpin Snyder)

b. Mar. 1, 1917, Burbank, CA

Bass / Traditional Country

A native of California, Cliffie Stone was born Clifford Gilpin Snyder in Burbank on March 1, 1917. The son of entertainer, comedy star, and banjo picker Herman the Hermit, Stone was known for his struggle to bring California's country and Western music into favor in post-World War II America. He began playing bass in big bands with Freddie Slack and Anson Weeks as well as with other bands around Hollywood and Pasadena, but it was his work on radio stations KFUD and KFWB that brought him respect. Shows such as "Covered Wagon Jubilee" and "Lucky Stars," broadcast out of Los Angeles, allowed him to show off his numerous skills. Working as a DJ, comedian, performer, and host, Stone won fame doing 28 radio shows a week between 1943 and 1947. As a featured performer on the "Hollywood Barn Dance," he made a place for himself in country music history. In 1946 he accepted a position with Capitol Records, which was gearing up for the still as yet undefined Bakersfield movement. An A&R executive with Capitol for 20 years, Stone discovered Tennessee Ernie Ford, whom he managed from 1947 to 1957, Molly Bee, Hank Thompson, and others who were flocking to Los Angeles to record.

In spite of his success at Capitol, Stone was best remembered for his radio work. His show on Pasadena radio station KXLA, "Dinner Bell Roundup," was a daily variety presentation that brought large numbers of country and Western entertainers into the homes of his listeners. In 1944 the show moved to El Monte. The new location brought with it a new name, "Hometown Jamboree." Recording six albums of his own, he earned co-writing credits on hits "Divorce Me C.O.D.," "So Round, So Firm, So Fully Packed," and in 1947, "Silver Stars, Purple Sage, Eyes of Blue." He recorded with various versions of his own band, including Cliffie Stone and His Orchestra, Cliffie Stone and His Barn Dance Band, and Cliffie Stone's Country Hombres.

Concentrating on the business side of things, the 1960s saw Stone's publishing company, Central Songs, flourish. He even headed up a label, Granite, for a time. The father of Curtis Stone, one of the founding members of Highway 101, Stone wrote several books including Everything You Always Wanted to Know About Songwriting But Didn't Know Who to Ask, published in 1991. —Jana Pendragon

Doug Stone

b. Jun. 19, 1956, Newnan, GA

Vocals / Contemporary Country, New Traditionalist

Doug Stone's sensitive Deep South baritone has made him one of country's premier romantic balladeers. This Georgian can sing hard traditional country and easy country with equal ease. For years diesel mechanics was his day job, and he hated it. This dissatisfaction carries over into his music and his stage presence, which presents him as distant and alone; he knows what he's singing about. With the release of his first album, his record company announced the dawning of a new "Stone Age." They weren't far off, as acceptance from country's female-dominated audience was almost immediate; his second album, 1991's I Thought It Was You, overdid the self-pity but yielded a couple of hits, including the title cut. "I'd Be Better Off (In a Pine Box)" was his breakthrough song. Shortly before the release of his third album, From the Heart, in 1992, 35 years of Southern-fried food sent Stone under the surgeon's knife for quadruple bypass surgery. —Brian Mansfield & David Vinopal

More Love / 1983 / Epic ✦✦✦

With "Addicted to a Dollar," balladeer Stone stakes his claim for "hot country" status alongside all his Nashville peers. —Dan Cooper

Doug Stone / 1990 / Epic ✦✦✦✦

"I'd Be Better Off (In a Pine Box)" is a towering expression of self-pity that most singers could spend a career trying to top. If Stone never bested his performance on his debut, he came close with ballads like "In a Different Light" and "My Hat's off to Him," becoming a genuine heartthrob in the process. —Brian Mansfield

I Thought It Was You / 1991 / Epic ✦✦✦

Self-pity has always played an integral role in country music, but it's more effective a song at a time, not spread over an entire album. Unlike some harder-voiced honky tonkers who funnel their emotions into cathartic country blues, Stone seems to wallow in sorrow. His ex is showing him up; his kid's growing up too fast; his new wife's walking out on him and telling him to shut up. This guy's favorite honky tonk even gets turned into a fern bar. —Brian Mansfield

From the Heart / 1992 / Epic ✦✦✦

Song for song, Stone's third album is his strongest, lacking the peak-and-valley terrain of his debut and the incessant self-pity of I Thought It Was You. Stone's voice is at its pain-wracked best with "Warning Labels" and "This Empty House," and if you think he pulls the heartstrings with the sad songs, wait'll you hear what he does with "Made for Loving You" and "Too Busy Being in Love." The heart references take on a special meaning given the openheart surgery that preceded this album; in "Warning Labels,"

Stone gives a first-hand account of the serious damage those country tearjerkers can do. —*Brian Mansfield*

The First Christmas / Apr. 1992 / Epic ✦✦✦
Given the number of songwriters in Nashville, it's surprising the town hasn't produced more Christmas songs. *The First Christmas* gets a bunch of them, though. Songs like "An Angel like You" play off Stone's romantic-balladeer image, and "When December Comes Around" would sound great any time of year. "Sailing Home for Christmas" depicts the irony of soldiers celebrating the coming of "peace on earth" while stationed on a battleship. —*Brian Mansfield*

● **Greatest Hits, Vol. 1** / 1995 / Epic ✦✦✦✦
Greatest Hits, Vol. 1 does an effective job of chronicling all of Stone's biggest hits from the early '90s. Most of his Top Ten hits are featured, including the No. 1 singles "In a Different Light," "A Jukebox with a Country Song," "Too Busy Being in Love," and "Why Didn't I Think of That." —*Thom Owens*

Faith in Me Faith in You / 1995 / Columbia ✦✦✦

● **Super Hits** / Mar. 4, 1997 / Columbia ✦✦✦✦
Super Hits contains the bulk of Doug Stone's best songs, including the No. 1 singles "In a Different Light" and "A Jukebox with a Country Song," plus several other hits, making the brief compilation a good, concise introduction to the modern country vocalist. —*Thom Owens*

The Stoneman Family

Old-Time, Traditional Country
The Stonemans are literally the first family of country music. Patriarch E.V. "Pop" Stoneman recorded "The Sinking of the Titanic" in 1925 and watched it become one of the biggest-selling country records of the decade. With fiddler Hattie Stoneman, his wife, he toured widely until the Depression cut into recording and personal appearances. In the '50s, when the 13 kids had taught themselves the family music, the Stonemans became a popular act, appearing on the Opry in 1962 and at numerous folk festivals. The spots on national TV, combined with their albums for Starday and Folkways, gave them coast-to-coast exposure. When "Pop" died in 1966, the family kept going, making them the longest continuous act in country music. —*David Vinopal*

● **Old Time Tunes from the South** / 1957 / Smithsonian/Folkways ✦✦✦✦

First Family of Country Music / 1981 / CMH ✦✦✦✦
These are new recordings by members of the classic group, whose patriarch began recording in 1924. —*Charles S. Wolfe*

Ernest V. Stoneman

b. May 25, 1893, Monorat, VA, **d.** Jun. 14, 1968
Vocals / Traditional Country
Ernest "Pop" Stoneman was one of the first, and most popular, early country artists. He was born in Carroll Country, VA, and raised by his father and three cousins, who taught him traditional Blue Ridge Mountain songs. He married as a young man and, when not working various odd jobs, played music for friends and neighbors. After hearing a Henry Whitter record and swearing he could do better, in 1924 he set off to New York to get a recording contract and prove it. His first single, "The Sinking of the Titanic," came out on the Okeh label later that year and became one of the biggest hits of the 1920s. At first he was accompanied only by his autoharp (his best-known instrument) and harmonica, but later switched to guitar; Stoneman was also adept at playing the Jew's harp and the clawhammer banjo. In 1926 he surrounded himself with a full string band, composed mostly of relatives and neighbors. His career reached its peak in 1927, when he became the top country artist at Victor and led the Bristol sessions, which helped the Carter Family and Jimmie Rodgers gain renown. Stoneman continued to record through 1929, setting down more than 200 songs.

When the Great Depression hit in the early '30s, Stoneman lost everything and moved his wife and nine children to Washington, DC. They remained there in desperate poverty while Stoneman worked odd jobs and tried to re-establish his career, finally finding work at a munitions plant. At the end of the 1940s, he and his talented clan began performing as the Stoneman Family. By 1956 he had earned the moniker "Pop" and appeared on the NBC television game show "The Big Surprise," where he won $10,000. Later, his children's band, the Blue Grass Champs, became the Stonemans, which Pop himself joined after retiring from the plant in the late '50s. He continued appearing with them and singing lead vocals through the early '60s. In 1965 the Stonemans signed with MGM in Nashville and hosted a syndicated TV show. In 1967 Stoneman's health began to deteriorate, but he continued recording and performing through the spring of 1968; he died in June. —*Sandra Brennan*

Old-Time Tunes of the South / 1957 / Folkways ✦✦✦✦

Cool Cowboy / 1959 / Capitol ✦✦✦

Pops Stoneman Memorial Album / 1969 / MGM ✦✦✦

● **Ernest Stoneman: 1928 Edison Recordings** / 1996 / County ✦✦✦✦
1928 Edison Recordings contains all 22 tracks that Ernest Stoneman recorded for Edison in 1928. On these sessions he was backed by a string band, which gave him and his autoharp a fuller sound; yet this music remains pure, direct, and rural. His versions of traditional numbers like "The Prisoner's Lament," "I Remember Cavalry," and "Fallen by the Wayside" are startling in their openness. —*Thom Owens*

Family and Friends / Old Homestead ✦✦✦
This music was recorded in the mid-'20s. —*AMG*

Ernest Stoneman (Blue Ridge Corn Shuckers) / Rounder ✦✦✦

Stonemans

Traditional Country, Nashville Sound/Countrypolitan
The Stonemans (or the Stoneman Family) ranked among country music's most famous family bands, and were closely associated with their legendary father, Ernest "Pop" Stoneman, who played with them for a number of years. The core of the band was six of Pop's 13 children: Patsy, Scotty, Donna, Jimmy, Roni, and Van. They were originally known as the Blue Grass Champs and got their start after winning on "Arthur Godfrey's Talent Scouts" in the mid-'50s. They soon added members and gained a following in Washington, DC, and the surrounding area. Eventually Pop joined them, and they added television appearances to their live performance schedule, eventually getting their own television show. They debuted on the Grand Ole Opry in 1962, and throughout the decade they toured the country, playing regularly at the Black Poodle in Nashville. They also hosted a syndicated television show, shown on about 50 stations nationwide. In 1966 they had their first country hit with "Tupelo Country Jail," which made it to the Top 40. The next year, they made it past the Top 30 with "The Five Little Johnson Girls." After Pop Stoneman's death in 1968, Patsy Stoneman joined the band. In 1968 they had their final chart hit with "Christopher Robin," which reached only the Top 50. They underwent several major personnel changes through the '70s and began recording less frequently, gradually easing into retirement. —*Sandra Brennan*

Big Ball in Monterey / 1964 / World Pacific ✦✦✦

White Lightning / 1965 / Starday ✦✦✦

Those Singin,' Swingin,' Stompin,' Sensational Stonemans / 1966 / MGM ✦✦✦✦

● **Stoneman's Country** / 1967 / MGM ✦✦✦✦

All in the Family / 1967 / MGM ✦✦✦✦

The Great Stonemans / 1968 / MGM ✦✦✦

Pop Stoneman Memorial Album / 1969 / MGM ✦✦✦

In All Honesty / 1970 / RCA ✦✦✦

The Stonemans / 1970 / MGM ✦✦

Stoney Lonesome

Country, Traditional Bluegrass
Stoney Lonesome consists of Kate MacKenzie (guitar, vocals), Chris Kaiser (mandolin, lead guitar, vocals), Kevin Barnes (banjo, dobro, vocals), Brian Wicklund (fiddle, vocals), and Patty Shove

(bass). The group first gained attention by appearing frequently on "Prairie Home Companion" during the '80s. In the early '90s, the quintet began releasing albums on Red House Records, starting with *Lonesome Tonight* in 1991 and followed by *Blue Heartache* the next year. —*John Bush*

Lonesome Tonight / 1991 / Red House ✦✦✦
Stoney Lonesome frequently appeared on the radio series "A Prairie Home Companion." This album includes originals, plus traditional music from Ola Belle Reed and the Stanley Brothers. —*AMG*

● **Blue Heartache** / 1992 / Red House ✦✦✦✦
On their second album *Blue Heartache*, Stoney Lonesome's music gelled, thanks in particular to Kate Mackenzie's powerful, emotional singing. The album is split between originals and covers of classic country and bluegrass songs; the originals often hold their own with the classics. —*Thom Owens*

Carl Story

b. May 29, 1916, Lenoir, NC, **d.** Mar. 30, 1995
Fiddle, Vocals / Traditional Bluegrass, Country Gospel
Fiddler Carl Story was a key figure in the development of gospel bluegrass music throughout his decades-long career. He was born to musically inclined parents, from whom he learned much about playing guitar and fiddle; though his parents played traditional and square dance music, young Story was most interested in the more modern sound of groups such as the Carolina Ramblers. In the early '30s, he moved to Lynchburg, VA, and began hosting a radio show. In 1935 he returned home, where he played with several musicians; eventually he and teenage banjoist Johnnie Whisnant moved to Spartanburg to play in the Lonesome Mountaineers. From there the two founded the Rambling Mountaineers, playing at various radio stations and making the occasional record until Story left to become a fiddler for Bill Monroe and his Blue Grass Boys. In 1943 he left Monroe to join the Navy.

After his discharge, Story reassembled the Rambling Mountaineers with Jack and Curley Shelton, Hoke Jenkins, and Claude Boone. As they moved from station to station, the membership changed and many of the members, such as Tater Tate and the Brewster Brothers, went on to become important bluegrass figures. Story and his group began recording secular and gospel songs for Mercury in 1947 and remained with the label until 1952. He moved to Columbia the following year and recorded more than a dozen singles. Although his music was close to bluegrass, Story and his band did not become full-fledged bluegrass players complete with banjo, mandolin, and dobro until 1957. Between the late '50s and the early '70s, they became fixtures on the bluegrass festival circuit. Story began recording less frequently during the '70s, but still continued touring. On occasion, he also worked as a deejay at WSEC in Greenville, SC. —*Sandra Brennan*

● **16 Greatest Hits** / Starday ✦✦✦✦

George Strait

b. May 18, 1952, Pearsall, TX
Guitar, Vocals / Contemporary Country, New Traditionalist, Western Swing Revival
Out of all the new country singers to emerge in the early '80s, George Strait stayed the closest to traditional country. Drawing from both the honky tonk and Western swing traditions, Strait didn't refashion the genres; instead, he revitalized them for a new decade. In the process, he became one of the most popular and influential singers of the decade, sparking a wave of neo-traditionalist singers from Randy Travis and Dwight Yoakam to Clint Black, Garth Brooks, and Alan Jackson.

Strait was born and raised in Texas, the son of a junior high school teacher who also owned and operated a ranch that had been in the Strait family for nearly 100 years. When George was a child, his mother left the family, taking her daughter but leaving her sons behind with their father. During his childhood, he would spend his weekdays in town and his weekends on the ranch. Strait began playing music as a teenager, joining a rock 'n' roll garage band.

George Strait

After his high school graduation in the late '60s, George enrolled in college but he soon dropped out and eloped with his high school sweetheart Norma. In 1971 Strait enlisted in the Army; two years later, he was stationed Hawaii. While in Hawaii, he began playing country music, initially with an Army-sponsored country band called Rambling Country. They played several dates off the base under the name Santee. Strait left the army in 1975, returning to Texas with the intent of completing his education. He enrolled in Southwest Texas State University at San Marcos, where he studied agriculture. While he was studying, he formed his own country band, Ace in the Hole.

Ace in the Hole made a few records for the independent Dallas-based label D in the late '70s, but they never went anywhere. Toward the end of the decade, Strait attempted to carve out a niche in Nashville, but he failed since he lacked any strong connections. In 1979 he became friends with Erv Woolsey, a Texas club owner who had formerly worked for MCA Records. Woolsey had several MCA executives come to Texas to hear Strait. His performance convinced the company to sign him in 1980.

"Unwound," George's first single, was released in the spring of 1981 and climbed into the Top Ten. The follow-up, "Down and Out," stalled at No. 16, but "If You're Thinking You Want a Stranger (There's One Coming Home)" reached NO. 3 in early 1982. The song sparked a remarkable string of Top Ten hits that ran well into the '90s. During that time he had an astonishing 31 No. 1 singles, beginning with 1982's "Fool Hearted Memory."

Throughout the '80s he dominated the country singles charts, and his albums consistently went platinum or gold. Strait rarely abandoned hardcore honky tonk and Western swing; toward the beginning of the '90s, his sound became a little slicker, but it was only a relative change. He was also one of the few '80s superstars to survive the generational shift of the early '90s that began with the phenomenal success of Garth Brooks. In 1992 he made his first movie, *Pure Country*, which featured him in the lead role. Strait released a four-disc box set career retrospective, *Strait Out of the Box*, in 1995. By the spring of 1996, it had become one of the five biggest selling box sets in popular music history. *Blue Clear Sky*, his 1996 album, debuted on the country charts at No. 1 and on the pop charts at No. 7. —*Stephen Thomas Erlewine*

Strait Country / 1981 / MCA ✦✦✦
The first is still fine. —*Mark A. Humphrey*

Strait from the Heart / 1982 / MCA ✦✦✦
Strait From the Heart contains the singer's first No 1 hit, "Fool Hearted Memory." —*Jason Ankeny*

Right or Wrong / 1983 / MCA ✦✦✦
The title track is vintage Bob Wills, and much here draws from similar swinging Southwestern roots. —*Mark A. Humphrey*

Strait Country/Strait from the Heart / 1983 / MCA ✦✦✦
Two early albums appear in one. The first and arguably the best of the '80s crop of Haggard-indebted hats, Strait has never much wavered from a Western-swing-tinged, honky tonk base. —*Mark A. Humphrey*

☆ **Does Fort Worth Ever Cross Your Mind** / 1984 / MCA ✦✦✦✦✦
Does Fort Worth Ever Cross Your Mind? is George Strait's first full-fledged masterpiece, signaling that his fusion of honky tonk, Western swing, and post-outlaw contemporary country had reached its fruition. Strait's performance is confident and assured, while producer Jimmy Bowen helps bring the music into focus, bringing subtle dynamic shades to a set of excellent swing numbers, ballads, and honky tonk ravers. The record includes several of Strait's best songs, includng "Honky Tonk Saturday Night," "Fireman," and the title track. —*Thom Owens*

Something Special / 1985 / MCA ✦✦✦✦
Something Special is another excellent George Strait record from the mid-'80s, featuring new traditionalist classics like "Left's Gone" and "The Chair." Occasionally, the album wanders into softer, more sentimental territory than Strait has explored in the past, yet that only makes the straight country more effective. —*Thom Owens*

★ **Greatest Hits** / 1986 / MCA ✦✦✦✦✦
A good overview of Strait's first round of MCA chartbusters from the early '80s, it includes "Right or Wrong," "Amarillo by Morning," "You Look So Good in Love," "Fool Hearted Memory," "A Fire I Can't Put Out," "Let's Fall to Pieces Together," and several other hits. —*Mark A. Humphrey*

Ocean Front Property / 1987 / MCA ✦✦✦✦

#7 / 1987 / MCA ✦✦✦
No frills 'n' fine. —*Mark A. Humphrey*

☆ **Greatest Hits, Vol. 2** / 1987 / MCA ✦✦✦✦✦
Greatest Hits, Vol. 2 picks up George Strait's string of hits in 1984 and includes ten of his biggest singles from the mid-'80s, including "Does Fort Worth Ever Cross Your Mind," "The Fireman," "The Chair," "Nobody in His Right Mind Would've Left Her," "It Ain't Cool to Be Crazy About You," "Ocean Front Property," and "All My Exs Live in Texas." —*Stephen Thomas Erlewine*

If You Ain't Lovin' (You Ain't Livin') / 1988 / MCA ✦✦✦
Included is a great cover of the old Faron Young title song, and other swingin' tonkers. —*Mark A. Humphrey*

Beyond the Blue Neon / Feb. 6, 1989 / MCA ✦✦✦
Beyond the Blue Neon doesn't really alter George Strait's formula at all, but it is remarkable for its consistent quality. Over the course of its ten tracks, nothing on the album rings false. Strait's voice is pure and gorgeous, while the material—particularly "Ace in the Hole," "Hollywood Squares," and "Baby's Gotten Good at Goodbye"—is first-rate. In short, it is one of his finest albums. —*Thom Owens*

Livin' It Up / May 15, 1990 / MCA ✦✦✦
It features "Amen," "Stranger in My Arms," "Lonesome Radio Cowboy," and others. —*AMG*

Chill of an Early Fall / 1991 / MCA ✦✦✦
Strait holds his own on this hit album, despite a plethora of new hats in the decade since his debut. —*Mark A. Humphrey*

Ten Strait Hits / 1991 / MCA ✦✦✦✦
Ten Strait Hits covers ten straight Top Ten singles (including eight No. 1 hits) that George Strait had between 1988 and 1990, all of which are presented in chronological order. Several of his most popular songs—including "Famous Last Words of a Fool," "Ace in the Hole," "Baby Blue," "Baby's Gotten Good at Goodbye," "I've Come to Expect It from You" and his biggest hit, "Love Without End, Amen"—are featured on this collection. Though Strait did make very good albums, his singles compilations remain excel-

lent albums in their own right, showcasing some of the very best country music made in the '80s and '90s. —*Thom Owens*

Pure Country / 1992 / MCA ✦✦✦
The soundtrack to the movie of the same name starring George Strait himself. The songs are a little larger than life if you are a Strait fan, but very nice nevertheless. Some were put together just for this movie. "Where the Sidewalk Ends" and "The King of Broken Hearts" stand out, but the version of "I Cross My Heart" recorded here is just one great song. —*Michael Erlewine*

Holding My Own / 1992 / MCA ✦✦✦
This features "Faults and All," "Here We Go Again," and "Gone As a Girl Can Get," among others. —*AMG*

Easy Come Easy Go / 1993 / MCA ✦✦✦

Lead On / Nov. 8, 1994 / MCA ✦✦✦

☆ **Strait out of the Box** / Sep. 12, 1995 / MCA ✦✦✦✦✦
George Strait was one of the few country singers of the '80s that kept hardcore country alive, whether it was honky tonk, Western swing, or his forte, balladry. *Strait out of the Box* is the definitive chronicle of his career, containing all 31 of his No. 1 singles, as well as 11 other hits, 19 album cuts, and 11 rare cuts. Over the course of the four discs, Strait proves that he defined the new traditionalist movement of the decade and left behind an impressive body of great recordings. For fans of both Strait and country music, *Strait out of the Box* is essential listening. —*Stephen Thomas Erlewine*

Blue Clear Sky / Apr. 1996 / MCA ✦✦✦✦
Country's most consistent traditionalist, George Strait, scores again with *Blue Clear Sky*, one of the best albums of his 15-year career. *Blue Clear Sky* shows off Strait's range with a well-chosen sweep of material. "Rockin' in the Arms of Your Memory" and "I'd Just as Soon Go" prove that well-written, mainstream adult ballads can carry an insinuating strength when performed with the subtle grace of a master. On "Need I Say More," Strait reveals, again, that he's also a wonderful jazz-tinged crooner. "I Ain't Never Seen No One like You" swings with the joyful ease of a youngster on a backyard set, and "Do the Right Thing" gives Strait the chance to show casually that he can navigate an eccentric meter, masking how difficult the inventive arrangement might have been for a lesser vocalist. Strait, an experienced calf-roping competitor, also includes "I Can Still Make Cheyenne." Instead of creating a deadly dramatic situation or joking about the macho manner of the lifestyle, the song uses a telephone call between a struggling rider and his lover to convey the dreams, the fears, the financial hardships, and the difficulties of life on the road that surround the sport. Just like the singer, the song relies on quietly reserved emotion to convey enormously important sentiments. —*Michael McCall*

Mel Street

b. Oct. 21, 1933, Grundy, WV, **d.** Oct. 21, 1978, Hendersonville, TN
Vocals / Traditional Country, Progressive Country, Honky Tonk
Singer-songwriter Mel Street had one of the great voices in contemporary country music; unfortunately, he was unable to withstand the pressures of fame, and his career ended in tragedy. He was born King Malachi Street near Grundy, VA, and got his start at age 16 on Cecil Surratt's radio show on stations WELC and WBRW out of Welch, WV. Street married and spent the next decade raising a family and living in various towns in Ohio, where he worked on radio transmission towers as an electrician. By 1960 the Streets had moved to Niagara Falls, where he began playing in nightclubs. It was there that he began learning the auto body trade, and three years later he moved to Bluefield, WV, to open his own body shop. He also began performing on the "Country Jamboree" on WHIS-TV, where he made his debut singing the Johnny Cash hit "Ring of Fire." From 1968-1972, Street had his own half-hour Saturday night show on the station.

He got his first shot at stardom when cable television company owners Jim and Jean Prater saw him perform and suggested he make a record. In 1970 he released his first single, "Borrowed Angel," which peaked on the Top 70 of the country charts. The song attracted the notice of Royal American Records, who licensed the master, reissued it, and helped it become a Top Ten hit. Street's follow-up, "Lovin' on Back Streets," became his biggest hit, making the Top Five. In 1973 Street had two Top 15 hits, and the next year he signed to GRT Records, where he had two Top 20 hits, including "Forbidden Angel."

Over the next two years, Street continued to make chart appearances and also began an intense touring schedule. In 1976 he had another Top Ten hit with "I Met a Friend of Yours Today." Afterward, he signed to a major label, Polydor, and scored a Top 20 hit with "Barbara Don't Let Me Be the Last to Know." In 1978 he had a Top Ten hit with "If I Had a Cheating Heart." He had one more Top 20 hit, and, after Polydor closed its Nashville division, moved to Mercury. However, the pressures of constant touring and recording, coupled with personal problems, began taking their toll; he began drinking heavily and lapsed into a deep depression. On October 21, 1978—his 45th birthday—Mel Street committed suicide. —*Sandra Brennan*

● **Greatest Hits** / 1976 / Deluxe ✦✦✦✦
This features "Bad Bad Leroy Brown," "Let's Put Out the Fire," "Borrowed Angel," and more. —*AMG*

The Very Best of Mel Street / 1980 / Sunbird ✦✦✦

Strength in Numbers

Progressive Bluegrass, Traditional Bluegrass
Strength in Numbers consists of Sam Bush (fiddle and mandolin), Jerry Douglas (dobro), Bela Fleck (guitar and banjo), Mark O'Connor (guitar and mandolin), and Edgar Meyer (bass). Each is recognized as a highly influential master of his instrument. After working together in various combinations through the '80s on each other's solo albums, they became known as the Telluride All Stars for their outstanding performances at the Telluride Bluegrass Festival in Telluride, CO. All the members are involved in other endeavors, and Strength in Numbers is essentially a side project. —*Chip Renner*

The Telluride Sessions / 1989 / MCA ✦✦✦✦
Telluride Sessions, the only album from the bluegrass supergroup Strength in Numbers, is an off-the-cuff set of newgrass that demonstrates the considerable instrumental skill of each member. Fluctuating between jazzy experiments and straightforward bluegrass, the music on *The Telluride Sessions* is adventurous and unpredictable, revealing more levels upon each listen. —*Thom Owens*

Stringbean (David Akeman)

Banjo / Traditional Bluegrass, Old-Time, Country Humor
Although Stringbean was best known as a country comedian, he was also an exceptional banjo player, credited with helping revive the instrument's use in both bluegrass and country music. He was born David Akeman in Jackson County, KY, surrounded by such distinguished musicians as Buell Kazee, Lily May Ledford, and B.F. Shelton. He made his first banjo out of a shoebox and thread, but by age 12 had begun playing a real one. As a teen, he won his first talent contest and then joined Asa Martin's band; during his debut, Martin forgot his new banjo player's name and introduced the lanky Akeman as "String Bean."

Stringbean got his break as a comedian when Martin's regular funnyman called in sick. Martin ordered Stringbean to sing and threatened to fire him if he didn't; fortunately, the youth turned out to be a natural. In the late '30s, Stringbean worked in several different Kentucky bands. He was discovered by Bill Monroe and remained with his group for three years, recording such notable songs as "Footprints in the Snow" and "True Life Blues." Stringbean then spent three years working with Lew Childre, appearing on the Opry and performing in tent shows. At the Opry he came under the tutelage of Uncle Dave Macon, who taught him classic jokes along with traditional banjo tunes and styles of playing.

By 1950, Stringbean was a nationally known performer, although he did not cut his first solo records for another decade; the first was a 1961 album for Starday, *Old Time Banjo Pickin' and Singin'*, followed two years later by *Salute to Uncle Dave Macon*. In 1969 he and longtime Opry cohort Grandpa Jones were among the first to join the cast of CBS' country variety show

"Hee Haw." On November 10, 1973, as Stringbean was at the apex of his popularity, he and his wife returned to their Nashville home and were murdered by burglars. —*Sandra Brennan*

● **Old Time Pickin' and Singin'** / 1961 / Starday ✦✦✦✦

Stringbean / 1962 / Starday ✦✦✦✦

Salute to Uncle Dave Macon / 1963 / Starday ✦✦✦

Way Back in the Hills of Old Kentucky / 1964 / Starday ✦✦✦✦

Marty Stuart

b. Sep. 30, 1958, Philadelphia, MS
Mandolin, Vocals / Traditional Bluegrass, Country-Rock, Contemporary Country, New Traditionalist
Fusing honky tonk with a gritty rockabilly backbeat and a fondness for bluegrass, Marty Stuart became one of the most popular country performers of the early '90s, as well known for his edgy music as he was for his flamboyant, glittery Nudie suits.

The Mississippi-born Stuart was a child prodigy on guitar and mandolin. By the age of 12 he had played with the Sullivans, and by 13, he had joined Lester Flatt's band as a guitarist. In 1973 Stuart became Flatt's mandolin player after Roland White left the band, and soon he was also singing lead vocals and harmonies. Stuart remained with Flatt until 1978, when the aging musician disbanded the group because of his failing health. Stuart then began working with Doc and Merle Watson. A year later he married Johnny Cash's daughter Cindy and was invited to join his father-in-law's band; he played with Johnny until 1985.

In 1982 Stuart released his first solo effort, *Busy Bee Cafe*, which featured an all-star lineup of backup musicians including Cash, Earl Scruggs, the Watsons, and Carl Jackson. Stuart left Cash's band for a full-time solo career in 1985 and released an eponymous solo album that yielded four minor hits, including the Top 20 "Arlene." Later in 1986 his marriage disintegrated, and he went back to Mississippi to rejoin the Sullivans. Stuart's first album for MCA, *Hillbilly Rock*, generated several hit singles, including "Don't Leave Her Lonely Too Long" and the title track, his first Top Ten hit. *Tempted* was his breakthrough album, producing Top Ten hit singles in "Little Things" and the title track. Late in 1991 Stuart duetted with Travis Tritt on the No. 2 hit "The Whiskey Ain't Working"; the next year, the two singers embarked on the popular "No Hats Tour." Also in 1992 Stuart released *This One's Gonna Hurt You* and had two Top Ten hits and three additional Top 20 singles. He joined the Grand Ole Opry in 1993 and then released a fourth album, *Love and Luck*. In 1995 he released the compilation *Marty Stuart Hit Pack*, followed in 1996 by *Honky Tonkin's What I Do Best*. —*Sandra Brennan*

Busy Bee Cafe / 1982 / Sugar Hill ✦✦✦
Busy Bee Cafe is a loose, jam-oriented record with guest appearances from Johnny Cash, Earl Scruggs, and Doc Watson. —*Jason Ankeny*

Let There Be Country / 1988 / Columbia ✦✦✦✦
This early recording gives a clear idea of just who Marty Stuart is. Without all the hype and overproduction of many of the MCA recordings, *Let There Be Country* displays Stuart's traditional hillbilly bent. Only his 1982 Sugar Hill debut, *Busy Bee Cafe*, defines him better. Self-produced, it is obvious that the artist knows what he is doing in terms of material and performance. The album includes only two original songs, but the rest of the tunes are strong statements by Stuart about country music. Merle Haggard's "Mirrors Don't Lie" is evidence of Stuart's affiliations. Also good is Bill Monroe's "Get Down on Your Knees and Pray." Marty's version of the Johnny Horton hit "One Woman Man" is priceless, and the sincere sweetness he reflects on the Harlan Howard-Max D. Barnes number "I'll Love You Forever (If You Want Me To)" is stunning. A worthy addition to any Stuart collection. —*Jana Pendragon*

● **Hillbilly Rock** / 1989 / MCA ✦✦✦✦
This first MCA project is the epitome of what the adult Marty Stuart is all about. With a new groove that runs just left of center, while still retaining a classic C&W bluegrass flair, *Hillbilly Rock* is a wild ride to what surely must be honky tonk heaven. On par with Dwight Yoakam's debut, *Hillbilly Rock* sets the tone for a

whole new faction of neotraditionalists. Opening with the title cut, an infectious romp that demands your attention, and ending on a high note with a love song, "Since I Don't Have You," crafted by Stuart and another tragically overlooked supernova, Mark Collie, this is one heck of an album. "Western Girls," a favorite of the numerous cowgirls who follow his career, and the Merle Killgore-Tillman Franks tune "The Wild One" all demonstrate how effective Marty Stuart is. "Cry, Cry, Cry," a Johnny Cash hit, is made new again. While this release displays more of Stuart's own songwriting skills, it also displays how deeply involved he is with the music he plays. —*Jana Pendragon*

Tempted / 1991 / MCA ✦✦✦✦
Equal in scope and purpose to Dwight Yoakam's sophomore release *Hillbilly Deluxe*, *Tempted* is still a wild and wonderful adventure into hillbilly territory. With a slight tempering of Stuart's sharp edge and abandon, there is still plenty here to rave about. Stuart kicks country-pop in its well-defined hindquarters with his take on the always popular Hank Sr.-Bill Monroe number "I'm Blue, I'm Lonesome." More than just infectious, this is one song you can't get enough of. "Little Things," "Burn Me Down," and "Paint the Town Tonight" all capture the spirit of the honky tonk. But Stuart is just as deadly when he slows things down and does a ballad. "'Til I Found You" and "I Want a Woman," written with Montana's most notable resident, Kostas, are a delight. Another winner from the man who said, "You can't really be in country music unless you've spent a few nights in the parking lot of the Palomino . . . ," (use your imagination). An experienced night owl, Stuart brings all those nights at the Pal and many other bars, dives, and dancehalls to good use here. Very authentic. —*Jana Pendragon*

Once upon a Time / 1992 / CMH ✦✦✦
This is certainly a special compilation that records the importance of Lester Flatt, Roland White, and the band the Nashville Grass to a budding 12-year-old who played a burning mandolin. That boy would grow up to be Marty Stuart. With performances featuring Stuart on mandolin and guitar, it is apparent from the start that Lester Flatt saw something special in Marty and made a place for him in his band. Mentoring is what it was called, it is not as common as it once was; but because of Flatt's interest, country and roots music has been doubly rewarded. Marty Stuart's connection to the past, his interest in the old timers who still play, and his own talent make him a true musical treasure. This release documents the early years and provides a glimpse into the development of an artist of character and quality. —*Jana Pendragon*

This One's Gonna Hurt You / 1992 / MCA ✦✦✦✦
With a snappy duet of the title with his buddy Travis Tritt, and an interesting prologue that explains how Stuart and Hank Sr. got together somewhere in outer space, this is a fun experience. "High on a Mountain Top" is outstanding, as is "Hey Baby." His paean to country music, "Now That's Country," explains why this is a gold album. But Stuart's edge is verging on the pedestrian in places. —*Jana Pendragon*

Marty Stuart / Aug. 18, 1992 / Columbia ✦✦
A former bluegrass picker and Johnny Cash sideman, Stuart burst on the scene with this largely rockabilly-flavored album. Not a great album, but made somewhat more interesting by some of the people appearing on the record and by the inclusion of two Steve Forbert songs. —*Jim Worbois*

Love and Luck / 1994 / MCA ✦✦✦✦
This is an album that has special moments throughout. However, there is a dulling of Stuart's edge that is all too obvious. Unsettling yes, but still Marty Stuart gives a good performance overall. His cover of the Hillman-Parsons classic "Wheels" is a standout emotionally, as is his version of Billy Joe Shaver's "If I Give My Soul." With more of his gentle side showing, Stuart writes with Harlan Howard and comes up with "I Ain't Giving Up on Love" and "Oh, What a Silent Night." He is still one of the best, even when he is not hitting every pitch out of the ballpark. —*Jana Pendragon*

● **Marty Party Hit Pack** / 1995 / MCA ✦✦✦✦
This is a hits package that shows off Marty Stuart's hard-earned success with tongue firmly planted in cheek. The man is a precious commodity. The songs presented here include his contribution to the Mercury tribute album to Elvis, *It's Now or Never*. "Don't Be Cruel" is handled expertly and given a little panache by the Don Was Band and the Jordanaires. The Staple Singers join Stuart for a gospel version of "The Weight," produced by Was. As for the known hits, they are all here including the Tritt-Stuart duet that appeared on Tritt's album of the same name, "This One's Gonna Hurt You (For a Long, Long Time)." Another classic from the man who also penned "The Whiskey Ain't Workin'" with Ronny Scaife. "Western Girls," "Hillbilly Rock," and two previously unreleased cuts, "If I Ain't Got You" and "The Likes of Me," round things out. —*Jana Pendragon*

Honky Tonkin's What I Do Best / Jun. 18, 1996 / MCA ✦✦✦
There is something missing here that is an important element of Marty Stuart's artistry—unadulterated enthusiasm. While we get a strong glimpse of it when he performs "The Mississippi Mud Cat and Sister Sheryl Crow," a song he wrote specifically for the pop diva, the only time it really takes control is on the title cut, another duet with Travis Tritt. *Honky Tonkin's What I Do Best* is not as much a honky tonk album as a reflection of lethargy. The production is often over the top or too soft and takes away from what we know is intrinsically Stuart. In a mellow mood, Stuart writes or co-writes all the tunes. He and Kostas come up with "You Can't Stop Love." Also included are "Shelter from the Storm," "Sweet Love," "Rocket Ship," and "Thanks to You." "Country Girls" is too much like an earlier tune that worked, "Western Girls," to really make a splash. Overall, this is not a good representation of the great talent that is Marty Stuart. Perhaps he's been in that factory town too long, working with too many of the same factory clones to continue to reach beyond that tiny pinpoint of light they consider to be country music. Stuart has always stood apart from this crowd. Perhaps it's time to get out, find a new stake of ground to honky tonk on and a new producer or two who won't fence him in. Travis did it when he broke away and came to California to work with Don Was, and so have many other successful Nashville acts seeking to move beyond the pop-shlock-country format that has been forced upon them. Stuart is in the same league as his mentors, Lester Flatt, Johnny Cash, and Merle Haggard. This 1996 release falls too far short to be placed among his other works. —*Jana Pendragon*

The Sullivan Family

Traditional Bluegrass, Country Gospel
The Sullivan Family, a bluegrass/gospel group who've played extensively on the festival circuit, were known for their distinctive, driving beat and the robust singing of Margie Sullivan. The trio was founded by Enoch and Emmett Sullivan, both of whom were born in the Tombigbee Valley in southern Alabama. The sons of a minister, the brothers grew up with a love of gospel music. They also liked string-band music and were influenced by Bill Monroe and Johnnie and Jack. Born in northern Louisiana, Margie also grew up influenced by the traditional bluegrass singers she heard on the radio. In addition to Monroe's music, she was influenced by such singers as Wilma Lee Cooper and Molly O'Day. After touring with evangelist Hazel Chain, she met Enoch at a revival in 1949. After they married, they bought a farm near St. Stephen, AL. As a group, the Sullivans started out playing in local churches and then appeared on a local radio station in Picayune, MS. In 1950 they moved to a station in Jackson, AL, and six years later moved to Thomasville. In 1959 they made their recording debut for Revival and later that year were befriended by Walter Bailes, on whose Loyal Records they recorded for many years. The Sullivans performed primarily at churches, on television, and on radio. Longtime friends of Bill Monroe, the Sullivans began playing at his various bluegrass festivals in 1968 and soon gained a whole new following. Over the years, the band has included other family members, including father Arthur, uncle Jerry, and Margie's youngest daughter Lisa. The band continued to

perform and record on different American and Canadian labels up to the mid-'90s. —*Sandra Brennan*

● **Get on Board** / Old Homestead ✦✦✦✦

Doug Supernaw

b. Sep. 26, 1960, Bryan, TX
Vocals / Contemporary Country, New Traditionalist
Doug Supernaw was a singer-songwriter from Houston, TX, who was influenced by Gene Watson, Vern Gosdin, Keith Whitley, and George Jones. Supernaw first attended college on a golf scholarship before playing throughout Texas in assorted clubs. He came to Nashville in the mid-'80s, eventually landing a contract as a writer at a music publishing company. He was dissatisfied with the situation, however, and decided to go back to Texas and perfect his act. He had a quick string of three hits from his 1993 debut album, *Red and Rio Grande,* including the chart-topping "I Don't Call Him Daddy." Supernaw broke his neck while surfing; shortly after his neck brace was removed, he was in a head-on auto collision. To compound matters, all of his band's gear was stolen in Ohio, and Supernaw nearly died from a case of food poisoning the morning after a performance in Roanoke, VA. Despite all of the catastrophes, Supernaw survived and continued to work on his career; in 1994 he released *Deep Thoughts from a Shallow Mind,* followed a year later by *You Still Got Me.* —*Sandra Brennan*

● **Red and Rio Grande** / Apr. 27, 1993 / BNA ✦✦✦✦
Included are his initial mainstream country hit, "Reno," and the anthem for divorced fathers, "I Don't Call Him Daddy." —*Michael McCall*

Deep Thoughts from a Shallow Mind / Sep. 13, 1994 / BNA ✦✦✦

You Still Got Me / Nov. 1995 / Giant ✦✦✦

Swampwater

Country-Rock, Cajun
Outside of Europe, where their music found a serious following, Swampwater remains best remembered as Linda Ronstadt's late 1960s backing group, her first post-Stone Poneys band. Formed by John Beland (guitar, dobro, piano), Gib Gilbeau (fiddle, guitar), Stan Pratt (drums), and Eric White (bass)—Clarence's brother, and an ex-member of the Kentucky Colonels—in 1969, Swampwater specialized in a then-unique Louisiana-based style of rock 'n' roll. Eric White left the lineup after their first national tour backing Ronstadt and was succeeded by Thad Maxwell, who had previously played with Beland in One Man's Family. Early in 1970 the group cut an album for Starday/King Records that was originally intended as a Gib Gilbeau solo vehicle, but it evolved into a group effort with a unique sound, not as smooth as Poco or Rick Nelson's Stone Canyon Band or as spaced out as the Flying Burrito Brothers. Their main influences—Gilbeau's country and Cajun roots and Beland's admiration of harmony-based acts such as the Byrds, the Beach Boys, and the Everly Brothers—were reflected in the 11 songs that were finished over a two-day period, and then went unreleased for 25 years.

Theirs was a brand of well-sung Cajun rock, straight out of the Louisiana bayou (except for the harmonies, which would've done credit to the Byrds). They had no prior equivalent in rock music, and the group's singing was considered so unusual that they got a fair amount of session work just singing backup to other acts, including Pete Seeger, Arlo Guthrie, Joan Baez, Country Joe McDonald, and Odetta. It was Guthrie who finally lured them away from Ronstadt in 1971. Her next backing band was the Eagles. Swampwater did a second self-titled album for RCA with Herb Pedersen added on guitar and vocals, and then went their separate ways. While the Eagles, Firefall, and other country-rock groups made regular runs up the charts and embedded themselves in the popular consciousness, Swampwater was largely forgotten except in Los Angeles and by dedicated early Ronstadt fans. After the breakup, Gilbeau joined the Burrito Brothers, and Beland performed on a number of session dates before going solo. Thad Maxwell played with Arlo Guthrie before hooking up

with Gilbeau again and Sneaky Pete Kleinow in a group called Sierra; he later played guitar with Mac Davis for some time before becoming a teacher. —*Bruce Eder*

Swampwater / 1970 / One Way ✦✦✦✦
No, not their RCA album, but the never-released Starday/King record from 1970, the loss of which for 25 years seems a real tragedy. As beautiful, lyrical, and unpretentious an album as ever surfaced from the Los Angeles country-rock scene. The sounds run the gamut from swamp-rock like "Workin' on a Tugboat" to almost elegant L.A.-type country-rock like "Louisiana Woman" and "Look out Your Window," resplendent in a lush mix of acoustic and electric guitars and dobro, and soaring harmonies. The Merle Haggard style "It's Your Game Mary Jane"; the Creedence Clearwater Revival-style "River People," not quite catchy as "Proud Mary" but more vivid and honest in its sentiments and details, and with a hotter beat; and even one Everly Bros. homage, "Desperation's Back Again," where Swampwater sounds more like Don and Phil than Don and Phil could've at the time, and with a song that is as good as anything the duo ever cut. The overall quality of the songs is extremely high—anything on here could've been a single at some point, and all of it is hummable, and a match for the best country-style albums of the Byrds, or the best work Poco ever issued. And it may just beat out the Burrito Bros., apart from their first three albums. It's a must-own body of work for anyone who likes the Byrds, Crazy Horse, the Burritos, or the Eagles. —*Bruce Eder*

Billy Swan

b. May 12, 1942, Cape Giradeau, MS
Guitar, Keyboards, Vocals / Rock & Roll, Country-Rock
One of rock's more interesting fringe characters, Billy Swan had been in the music business for more than a decade before he landed a surprise No. 1 neo-rockabilly hit in 1974 with "I Can Help." His composition "Lover Please" was a hit for Clyde McPhatter in the early '60s, and he spent the rest of the decade as a combination roadie, engineer's assistant, and songwriter, penning material for Conway Twitty, Waylon Jennings, and Mel Tillis. He played with Kris Kristofferson, Kinky Friedman, and Billy Joe Shaver in the '70s before the success of "I Can Help," whose swirling organ and classic '50s rockabilly arrangement anchored one of the best hit singles of the mid-'70s. Swan recorded a few albums as a solo act that were well received by critics, but he never hit the Top 40 again. Too eclectic to be characterized as a '50s revivalist, he actually mixed country, soul, and pop into his sound more frequently than out-and-out rockabilly. After a few years, Swan returned to Kristofferson's band, where he stayed until 1992. —*Richie Unterberger*

I Can Help / 1975 / Monument ✦✦✦✦

Billy Swan / 1975 / Monument ✦✦✦✦

Rock 'n' Roll Moon / 1976 / Monument ✦✦✦

Four / 1977 / Monument ✦✦✦

● **Billy Swan's Best** / 1993 / Red Baron ✦✦✦✦
Listeners expecting tuneful updated rockabilly along the lines of "I Can Help" (which leads off this collection) may be disappointed by this CD. There's nothing as instantly compelling as the big hit (only "Vanessa" approaches its energy), much of the material lies closer to country than rock, and there are a few tame covers of '50s oldies. Nonetheless, Swan ranks among the more interesting country-pop-rock hybrids, as you could guess from the song title "(You Just) Woman Handled My Mind," and his thin, wavering voice is oddly memorable. Most of the material on this best-of is written by Swan, with occasional assistance from notables Guy Clark, Buddy Emmons, and Kris Kristofferson. —*Richie Unterberger*

Sweethearts of the Rodeo

Contemporary Country
Drawing from country-rock, bluegrass, and pop, the harmony duo Sweethearts of the Rodeo—Janis Oliver Gill and Kristine Oliver Arnold—made a series of records in the late '80s and early '90s that received positive reviews and earned the group a cult follow-

ing. Janis and Kristine Oliver were both born and raised in Manhattan Beach, CA, and influenced by the Byrds and Poco. The sisters began performing country and bluegrass music in high school and played various clubs along the California coast. Kristine sang leads, while Janis harmonized and played guitar. In 1973 the sisters began calling themselves Sweethearts of the Rodeo after the Byrds album of the same name, and began moving their music toward county-rock. Emmylou Harris spotted the group at a Long Beach bluegrass festival and later invited them to sing at one of her shows. As a result, the Sweethearts began opening for acts like Willie Nelson, Poco, and Pure Prairie League.

In 1983 Janis and her husband, Vince Gill, moved to Nashville to began work on his career. Soon after he signed to RCA, producer Steve Buckingham encouraged Janis to continue with her own career. When Kristine and her husband, Blue Steel's Leonard Arnold, also moved to Nashville, the sisters resumed their act. In 1986 the duo scored a Top 30 hit with their debut single "Hey Doll Baby." Their second single, "Since I Found You," hit the Top Ten, and "Midnight Girl" hit the Top Five. The Sweethearts released their second album, *One Night, One Time,* in 1988 and had two Top Five hits, "Satisfy You" and "Blue to the Bone." In 1990 they released a third album, *Buffalo Zone,* which was followed two years later by *Sisters.* In 1993 they released *Rodeo Waltz; Beautiful Lies* appeared in 1996. *—Sandra Brennan*

● **Sweethearts of the Rodeo** / 1986 / Columbia ✦✦✦✦
These California sisters gone to Music City feature good vocal harmony on contemporary, rock-tinged country. *—Mark A. Humphrey*

One Time One Night / 1988 / Columbia ✦✦✦
One Time, One Night includes the group's hit remake of the Beatles' "I Feel Fine." *—Jason Ankeny*

Buffalo Zone / 1990 / Columbia ✦✦✦
More melancholy than the Sweethearts' earlier work, *Buffalo Zone* includes the hit "This Heart." *—Jason Ankeny*

Sisters / 1992 / Columbia ✦✦
Sisters is a subtle, sweet album of introspective folk-laced country, highlighted by the lovely harmonies of the Sweethearts of the Rodeo. *— Thom Owens*

Rodeo Waltz / 1993 / Sugar Hill ✦✦✦
This duos album is refreshingly open sounding. The soft Nashville production provides a fine background for the sweet vocal harmonies. "Jenny Dreamed of Trains," "Get Rhythm," and "Broken Arrow" are standout cuts. *—Richard Meyer*

Beautiful Lies / Aug. 20, 1996 / Sugar Hill ✦✦✦
Beautiful Lies is a typically engaging release from Sweethearts of the Rodeo. Throughout the album, the duo's harmonies border on the magical, even when the material borders on the mediocre. For fans, it's certainly is a worthwhile purchase, even if it won't win any new converts. *— Thom Owens*

Swinging Steaks

Roots-Rock
Paul Kochanski (vocals, bass) and Jamie Walker (vocals, guitar) first played together in the early '80s for a Boston-based band named the Drive. Local acclaim and a first-place finish on MTV's

"The Basement Tapes" didn't prevent the band from breaking up in 1989. The Swinging Steaks were formed soon after, when Kochanski and Walker recruited Tim Giovanniello (vocals, guitar) and Jim Gambino (vocals, piano, organ); they later picked up the Del Fuegos' drummer Joe Donnelly when that band folded. The group pursued a roots-rock style, using soul, honky tonk, gospel, and pop in addition to straight-ahead rock n' roll. After an album was released on the band's own Thrust label, 1992's *Suicide at the Wishing Well,* Capricorn signed the band and released *Southside of the Sky* (1993). *—John Bush*

Southside of the Sky / 1993 / Capricorn ✦✦✦

Sylvia (Sylvia Kirby Allen)

b. Dec. 9, 1956, Kokomo, IN
Vocals / Country-Pop, Urban Cowboy
Growing up in Kokomo, IN, Sylvia moved to Nashville around Christmas of 1975 with a definite gameplan: get a job as a secretary, get to know influential people in town, and build a career as a recording artist. The plan worked. She picked up a job as the receptionist for Pi-Gem Music, headed by record producer Tom Collins. She started singing on demo sessions, and Collins helped her secure a recording contract with RCA.

Since she'd never performed live before, Sylvia ended up learning to do concerts at the same time she was making hit records. With an engaging voice, a bubbly personality, and a beautiful appearance, Sylvia was practically a marketing dream; and Collins built her sound around catchy melodies and strong backbeats. Songs like "Drifter" (No. 1, 1981), "The Matador" (1981), "Nobody" (No. 1, 1982) and "Like Nothing Ever Happened" (1982) became big hits; "Nobody" even crossed over into the pop Top 40. The material was often lyrically shallow, however, and Sylvia grew increasingly frustrated. She left Collins and recorded a pair of albums with record producer Brent Maher. The second was never released. Instead, Sylvia was dropped by RCA in 1987.

She used the opportunity for personal growth (she toured almost constantly during the height of her career and was emotionally drained) and to develop as a songwriter. In 1992 she reemerged as a touring artist and pursued a recording deal with self-penned material that was inner-directed and uplifting. *— Tom Roland*

Drifter / 1981 / RCA ✦✦✦

Just Sylvia / 1982 / RCA ✦✦✦✦
Producer Tom Collins plays around with her vocals a lot, altering them electronically for effects that range from ever-so-slight to overbearing. But the material's predominantly sassy, and as catchy as a virus. The honesty in "You Can't Go Back Home" really hurts. *— Tom Roland*

Snapshot / 1983 / RCA ✦✦✦

Surprise / 1984 / RCA ✦✦

One Step Closer / 1985 / RCA ✦✦

● **Greatest Hits** / 1987 / RCA ✦✦✦✦
All of Sylvia's biggest hits, including her No. 1 singles "Drifter" and "Nobody," are compiled on the brief but entertaining *Greatest Hits. —Thom Owens*

T

Gid Tanner

Old-Time, String Band

This influential string band of the '20s and '30s featured three major figures of early country music: Gideon "Gid" Tanner, fiddler Clayton McMichen (1900-1970), and Blind Riley Puckett (1894-1946) on guitar. Tanner's band, the Skillet Lickers, featured fiddle breakdowns, folk material, and comedy skits dealing with moonshine. This high-spirited band broke up in 1934. —*David Vinopal*

Gid Tanner and His Skillet Lickers / 1973 / Rounder ✦✦✦✦

● **Kickapoo Medicine Show** / 1988 / Rounder ✦✦✦✦

A '20s string band, they play raucous and rippin' old-time music on this album. —*Mark A. Humphrey*

Tarnation

Alternative Country-Rock, Dream-pop

The country art band Tarnation was essentially a vehicle for Paula Frazer, a talented singer and songwriter who returned to roots music only after a successful foray into 1980s post-punk. Frazer was born and raised in Sautee Nacoochee, GA, a tiny community located in the foothills of the Smoky Mountains, where as a child she sang in her father's church choir, developing a remarkably adept soprano. When she was 14, the Frazers moved to Arkansas, where she began performing with local jazz groups.

After graduating from high school, Frazer relocated to San Francisco, where she followed a stint in a Bulgarian women's choir with tenures in a number of area punk groups, most notably the all-female Frightwig. In 1992 she formed Tarnation with former SF Seals members Lincoln Allen and Michelle Cernuto, along with steel guitarist Matt Sullivan. Setting their dark ballads and love songs against a stark, ominous backdrop dominated by reverb-soaked guitars, Tarnation debuted in 1993 with *I'll Give You Something to Cry About.* In 1995 they issued *Gentle Creatures*, their first LP for the arty British label 4AD. Shortly after the record's release, Allen, Cernuto, and Sullivan left the group and were replaced by guitarist Alex Oropeza, drummer Joe Byrnes, and bassist/lap steel player Bill Cuevas. —*Jason Ankeny*

● **Gentle Creatures** / 1995 / 4AD ✦✦✦✦

Given that Tarnation's frontwoman Paula Frazer is best known for her work with the post-punk band Frightwig—and since *Gentle Creatures* is, after all, a product of the arty 4AD label—the absolute-torch-and-twang authenticity that defines the record is a wonderful surprise; ethereal yet earthy, the album's strength derives from all of its seeming contradictions. Powered by Frazer's deft songwriting and smoky vocals, *Gentle Creatures* is melancholy and gorgeous, its love songs and ballads cloaked in reverb and gothic imagery. What Tarnation shares with its 4AD stablemates is an uncanny knack to build and maintain a rich, dense atmosphere; the record is dusky and otherworldly, haunted by the spirits of failed relationships, late-night radio transmissions, and other ghostly presences. —*Jason Ankeny*

Carmol Taylor

b. Sep. 5, 1931, Brilliant, AL, **d.** Dec. 5, 1986

Vocals / Traditional Country, Honky Tonk

Carmol Taylor was best known as a honky tonk songwriter, but he was also a talented performer. He was born in Brilliant, AL, and began playing professionally in his early teens. When he was about 15, Taylor teamed up with Billy Sherrill to form Carmol Taylor and the Country Pals. The group stayed together for more than 20 years, and between 1954 and 1974 played on a number of Southern radio stations. Taylor launched his recording career in 1955, and in the early '60s he and the Pals began hosting a television show out of Columbus, MS, where they performed for nine years.

Sherrill went on to become one of the most influential record producers in country music, and he helped Taylor break into professional songwriting by getting him a job at Al Gallico Music. In 1965 Charlie Walker had a Top Ten hit with Taylor's "Wild as a Wildcat." Soon after, Taylor began collaborating with Sherrill, Norro Wilson, and George Richey. Together they produced several hits during the 1970s, including "He Loves Me All the Way," "My Man," "The Grand Tour," and "There's a Song on the Jukebox." Although he had been recording since the mid-'50s, Taylor didn't appear on the charts until the mid-'70s, with such songs as "Play the Saddest Song on the Jukebox" and "I Really Had a Ball Last Night." In 1980 Taylor himself became a producer, and in 1985 he and Gary Lumpkin provided George Jones and Lacy J. Dalton with a Top 20 hit, "Size Seven Round (Made of Gold)." Taylor died of lung cancer the next year. —*Sandra Brennan*

● **Honky Tonk Two Steppin' Beer Drinkin' Saturday Nite** / 1987 / Password [UK] ✦✦✦✦

I Think They Call It Homesick / Country International ✦✦✦

Song Writer / Elektra ✦✦✦

Les Taylor

b. Dec. 27, 1948, Oneida, KY

Guitar, Vocals / Contemporary Country

Despite his attempts to forge a successful solo career, Les Taylor remained best known as the rhythm guitarist and occasional lead vocalist of the group Exile, with whom he played for ten years. A native of Oneida, KY, who started out as a weekend musician, Taylor had his first solo success with "Shoulda, Woulda, Coulda," a 1989 Top 50 single he co-wrote with Lonnie Wilson and Ron Moore. The next year he had another mid-range hit with "Knowin' You Were Leavin'," which appeared on his debut album *That Old Desire.* In 1991 he had two more mid-chart singles and released his second album, *Blue Kentucky Wind.* —*Sandra Brennan*

● **Blue Kentucky Wind** / 1991 / Epic ✦✦✦✦

"I Gotta Mind to Go Crazy" and "The Very First Lasting Love," a duet with Shelby Lynne, are the highlights of *Blue Kentucky Wind.* —*Jason Ankeny*

That Old Desire / Epic ✦✦✦

That Old Desire features the minor hits "Shoulda, Coulda, Woulda Loved You" and "Knowin' You Were Leavin." —*Jason Ankeny*

Tut Taylor (Robert Taylor)

b. 1923, Milledgeville, GA

Dobro / Traditional Bluegrass, Old-Time

A musician's musician, Tut Taylor never achieved widespread popularity, but he was highly respected and emulated by his peers. He was born in Milledgeville, GA, and started playing banjo as a child before learning mandolin. His lifelong passion for the dobro began at age 14, when he heard Brother Bashful Oswald play. After writing to Roy Acuff to learn the name of the instrument, he bought one and began teaching himself to play, using the same flat-picking style he used on his mandolin. In the early '60s, Taylor, Glen Campbell, and the Dillards formed the Folkswingers, and through 1964 released three albums, including *12 String Dobro!* Taylor made his debut solo album *Dobro Country* in 1964. In the late '60s he joined the Dixie Gentlemen, and in 1969 he and fiddler Vassar Clements became the core of John Hartford's backup band. In 1970 Taylor co-founded GTR, a noted instrument shop in Nashville, and recorded with such artists as David Bromberg. He didn't record another solo album until 1972's *Friar Tut;* he and Randy Wood then teamed up with Ginger Boatwright and Norman Blake to created the popular nightclub and music store the Old Time Pickin' Parlor, which became a favorite haunt of the Nashville elite. The next year he appeared on the album *Hank Wilson's Back.* Taylor released another solo effort in 1975, *The Old Post Office,* followed in 1976 by *Dobrolic Plectoral Society.* From the rest of the decade until his retirement, he also ran Tut Taylor's General Store in Nashville. *— Sandra Brennan*

12 String Dobro / 1964 / World Pacific ✦✦✦

Dobro Country / 1975 / United Artists ✦✦✦

The Old Post Office / 1976 / Flying Fish ✦✦✦
Here, Taylor plays old and new tunes on the dobro with guests Butch Robbins and Norman Blake. *—AMG*

Dobrolic Plectoral Society / 1976 / Takoma ✦✦

● **Friar Tut** / 197 / Rounder ✦✦✦✦

Gordon Terry

b. Oct. 7, 1931, Decatur, AL

Fiddle, Vocals / Traditional Bluegrass

Gordon Terry was one of the finest fiddlers in bluegrass. The Decatur, AL, native first gained national exposure when he joined the Grand Ole Opry at age 19. He remained there for eight years, and during that time recorded a few solo singles for different labels as well as playing with Bill Monroe's Blue Grass Boys. In 1957, he had his most popular single with "Wild Honey." He made his film debut in the Western *Hidden Guns*, and moved to Los Angeles in 1958 to continue his solo career. Terry also turned up on different television shows, including the "Sky King" series. He returned to Tennessee in the late '60s to do side and session work, and in 1977 he released *Disco Country.* In 1981 Terry issued *Rockin' Fiddle. —Sandra Brennan*

● **Lotta Women** / 1995 / Bear Family ✦✦✦✦
Bear Family's single-disc, 30-track *Lotta, Lotta Women* compilation showcases the bulk of Gordon Terry's early-'60s recordings, including "It Ain't Right," "Trouble on the Turnpike," "Queen of the Seasons," "Lonely Road," "For Old Time's Sake," "You Remembered Me," "Long Black Limousine," "Slow Down Old World," "I Don't Hurt Anymore," "All By My Lonesome" and the title track. *—Thom Owens*

Texas Instruments

Roots-Rock

A product of the same vibrant Austin roots-rock scene that produced the True Believers, the Reivers, and the Wild Seeds, the Texas Instruments were formed in 1983 by guitarist David Woody, bassist Ron Marks, and drummer Steve Chapman. Combining their mutual interest in punk with an affection for heartland music, the group issued their debut EP *More Texas Instruments!* in 1985; a self-titled full-length album appeared two years later.

After the release of 1988's *Sun Tunnels,* the Texas Instruments added second guitarist Clay Daniel to their lineup. In 1989 the group completed its third album, *Crammed into Infinity;* before the record's release, however, their longtime label Rabid Cat declared bankruptcy, and the disc spent many months in limbo, eventually seeing the light of day in 1990. *Magnetic Home* followed three years later. *—Jason Ankeny*

More Texas Instruments [EP] / 1985 / Longhead ✦✦✦
The Texas Instruments' debut EP offers a glimpse of the group's fusion of post-punk and electric roots music in its earliest stages of development. *—Jason Ankeny*

Texas Instruments / 1987 / Rabid Cat ✦✦✦

Sun Tunnels / 1988 / Dr. Dream ✦✦✦✦
The first of the Texas Instruments' records cut with noted underground producer Spot, this full-length debut offers heartfelt roots-rock blasted through with punk abandon; in addition to clear debts to country and garage rock, the band salutes its folk heritage by closing out the disc with covers of Woody Guthrie's "Do-Re-Mi" and Bob Dylan's "A Hard Rain's Gonna Fall." *—Jason Ankeny*

● **Crammed into Infinity** / 1990 / Dr. Dream ✦✦✦✦
The band's first album with newly added guitarist Clay Daniel, *Crammed into Infinity* marks the continued emergence of frontman David Woody's topical, world-weary lyrics, which range from the political ("Decade of Denial") to the deeply personal ("World's Gotten Smaller," "Over Before It Started"). *—Jason Ankeny*

Magnetic Home / Jan. 1993 / Doctor Dream ✦✦✦

The Texas Tornados

Tex-Mex, Roots-Rock, Americana

A spicy Tex-Mex quartet that fused Mexican polkas and folk music with '50s-style rock, doo wop, and blues, the Texas Tornados consisted of four quite seasoned players. The most famous of the four, '70s country star Freddy Fender, is joined by Augie Meyers, a veteran of the Sir Douglas Quintet; Doug Sahm, with whom Meyers played in Doug Sahm and the Texas Tornados in 1974; and legendary Southwestern accordion player Flaco Jimenez. During the '80s the careers of the individuals seemed to languish, but after they formed the Texas Tornados in 1989, they finally regained fame and popularity. The band signed with Reprise Records in 1990 and released their self-titled debut album later that year. Produced by the band with Bill Halverson, the album—available in both Spanish and English versions—made the Top 25 on the country charts. A second album, *Zone of Our Own,* followed in 1991, and one year later the Texas Tornados recorded their last and best album, *Hangin' On by a Thread.* After the LP's release, the individual Tornados resumed their solo careers. *—Sandra Brennan*

Texas Tornados / Aug. 1990 / Reprise ✦✦✦✦
Predictably, this debut album by a sort of Tex-Mex Traveling Wilburys is a delight. Forty percent of the Sir Douglas Quintet—Doug Sahm and Augie Meyers—is represented, along with Freddy Fender and accordionist Flaco Jimenez. The album reflects the differing strains that each brings to the music, from the more pop/country approach of Sahm and Meyers to Fender's bluesy singing and Jimenez' Mexican playing. An all-star project that brings out the best in its members, *Texas Tornados* is a landmark Tex-Mex album. (The track "Soy de San Luis" won the 1990 Grammy Award for Best Mexican/American Performance.) [*Texas Tornados* was also released in an all-Spanish edition.] *— William Ruhlmann*

Zone of Our Own / 1991 / Reprise ✦✦✦✦
Not quite as jubilant as the first album, but these guys are incapable of not being fun. (*Zone of Their Own* was nominated for a 1991 Grammy Award for Best Country Performance by a Duo or Group with Vocal.) *—Jeff Tamarkin*

Hangin' on by a Thread / 1992 / Reprise ✦✦✦
They lean more heavily on accordion-driven Tex-Mex fare than on the previous albums, probably because that's where the bulk of their sales were. Mostly light-hearted party music, except for a delicate cover of Dylan's "To Ramona." The thread on which they

were hanging unraveled shortly after the album's release, and this outstanding group went their separate ways. —*Michael McCall*

● **The Best of Texas Tornados** / Feb. 8, 1994 / Reprise ✦✦✦✦
Featuring material from all of their albums, *The Best of Texas Tornados* is a terrific compilation of one of the best Tex-Mex bands of the last two decades. —*AMG*

4 Aces / Jul. 9, 1996 / Reprise ✦✦✦
Despite a few good moments—like the rollicking "Clinging to You"—*4 Aces* is a bit too predicable of a good time from the Texas Tornados. Certainly, all of the ingredients that made their previous recordings delightful are present, but the problem is the album doesn't ever quite catch fire with the goofy fun that distinguished their best music. —*Thom Owens*

B.J Thomas (Billy Joe Thomas)

b. Aug. 7, 1942, Houston, TX
Vocals / Country-Pop, Soft Rock, Pop-Rock
B.J. Thomas (born Billy Joe Thomas) straddled the line between pop-rock and country, achieving success in both genres in the late '60s and '70s. At the beginning of his career, he leaned more heavily on rock 'n' roll, but by the mid-'70s, he had turned to country music, becoming one of the most successful country-pop stars of the decade.

Thomas began singing while he was a child, performing in church. In his teens, he joined the Houston-based band the Triumphs, who released a number of independent singles that failed to gain any attention. For the group's last single, Thomas and fellow Triumph member Mark Charron wrote "Billy and Sue," which was another flop. After "Billy and Sue," Thomas began a solo career, recording a version of Hank Williams' standard "I'm So Lonesome I Could Cry" with producer Huey P. Meaux. Released by Scepter Records in early 1966, the single became an immediate hit, catapulting to NO. 8 on the pop charts. Although he had a series of moderate follow-up hits, including a re-release of "Billy and Sue," Thomas failed to reenter the Top Ten until 1968, when "Hooked on a Feeling" became a No. 5, gold single. The next year, he scored his biggest hit with Burt Bacharach and Hal David's "Raindrops Keep Fallin' on My Head," taken from the hit film *Butch Cassidy and the Sundance Kid.* It was followed by a string of soft-rock hits in the next two years, including "Everybody's Out of Town," "I Just Can't Help Believing," "No Love at All," and "Rock and Roll Lullaby," which featured guitarist Duane Eddy and the vocal group the Blossoms.

After "Rock and Roll Lullaby," Scepter Records went out of business, and B.J. Thomas headed to Paramount Records. At Paramount, Thomas had no hits, prompting the singer to pursue a new country-pop direction at ABC Records. "(Hey Won't You Play) Another Somebody Done Somebody Wrong Song," his first single for ABC, became his second No. 1 record on the pop charts, as well as establishing a country career for the vocalist. For the next decade, he continued to have hits on the country charts, with a couple of songs—most notably "Don't Worry Baby"—crossing over into the pop charts. During this period, he switched record companies at a rapid pace, but it did nothing to slow the pace of his hits. Thomas hit his country peak in 1983 and 1984, when he had the No. 1 hits "Whatever Happened to Old Fashioned Love" and "New Looks from an Old Lover," as well as the Top Ten hits "The Whole World's in Love When You're Lonely" and "Two Car Garage." Throughout the '80s, B.J. Thomas recorded a number of hit gospel records for Myrrh concurrently with his country hits.

At the end of the '80s, the hits began to dry up for Thomas, but he continued to tour and put out the occasional country and gospel record in the '90s. —*Stephen Thomas Erlewine*

16 Greatest Hits / 1986 / Trip ✦✦✦
16 Greatest Hits offers a lackluster summation of Thomas' career; while "Raindrops Keep Fallin' on My Head" is here, none of his biggest country chart hits, including "(Hey Won't You Play) Another Somebody Done Somebody Wrong Song" and "Whatever Happened to Old Fashioned Love," are featured. —*Jason Ankeny*

● **Greatest Hits [Rhino]** / 1990 / Rhino ✦✦✦✦
A fine 18-song collection that features all of B.J. Thomas' greatest hits. From "I'm So Lonesome I Could Cry" through "Hooked on a

Feeling" to "(Hey Won't You Play) Another Somebody Done Somebody Wrong Song," *Greatest Hits* is the definitive retrospective of his career. —*Stephen Thomas Erlewine*

More Greatest Hits / Sep. 12, 1995 / Varèse Sarabande ✦✦✦✦
Picking up where Rhino's *Greatest Hits* collection left off, Varese's *More Greatest Hits* doesn't have any of the big hit singles, but it is ideal for those listeners who want to dig a little deeper into B.J. Thomas' extensive catalog. —*Thom Owens*

Hank Thompson (Henry William Thompson)

b. Sep. 3, 1925, Waco, TX
Guitar, Vocals / Traditional Country, Western Swing, Honky Tonk
Country Hall of Famer Hank Thompson has had chart hits in five different decades. Between Bob Wills and Asleep at the Wheel, there was Thompson with his Brazos Valley Boys, keeping the sound of Western swing alive. His swing music and well-written honky tonk songs produced 21 Top 20 charters from 1949 and 1958. His signature song, "The Wild Side of Life" (1952), was his biggest hit, prompting Miss Kitty Wells to defend bar-life females in "It Wasn't God Who Made Honky Tonk Angels." Much of his best music was set in the dim lights and thick smoke of the honky tonk, with such hits as "Hangover Tavern," "On Tap, in the Can, or in the Bottle," "Smokey the Bar," "A Six-Pack to Go," and "Honky-Tonk Girl." While music tastes changed during his career, he kept touring worldwide with his band, keeping true honky tonk and Western swing in the public's ear. He's often seen on Ralph Emery's "Nashville Now" TV show. —*David Vinopal*

A Six Pack to Go / 1961 / Capitol ✦✦✦✦
Beer-drinkin' music and honky tonk from the '50s, this features a great band, including Merle Travis on guitar on some cuts. —*George Bedard*

At the Golden Nugget / 1961 / Capitol ✦✦✦✦
At The Golden Nugget was not only the first live album ever recorded for commercial release by a single country artist, but it is arguably Hank Thompson's best album, representing his amalgam of honky-tonk and Western swing better than any other long-player in his history. Most country artists of his generation responded better to the enthusiasm of an audience than to the cold, usually tense, often retake-laden ambience of a studio, and Thompson had a very satisfied audience that night in March 1961. The record is made all the more alluring by the presence of Merle Travis (who had played on Thompson's recordings since 1953) on lead guitar, and two numbers out of Travis' repertory ("Nine Pound Hammer," "John Henry") are among the 13 songs here. The CD transfer, from 1995, is state-of-the-art, and the historical notes are an extra treat. Along with Capitol's 1996 *Vintage Collections* compilation, this is essential to own, and not just for country music fans—rock 'n' rollers (and not just Flying Burrito Bros. aficionados) can also learn a few things from Thompson. —*Bruce Eder*

The Best of Hank Thompson / 1963 / Capitol ✦✦✦
Several of his best beer-drinkin' tunes and novelty songs are included, many done with his Bob Wills-style big band at a time when Thompson was pretty much carrying the torch of Western swing alone. —*George Bedard*

Capitol Collector's Series / 1989 / Capitol ✦✦✦✦
Hank Thompson's *Capitol Collector's Series* contains a good cross-section of his big hits and lesser-known singles, making it an excellent single-disc introduction to one of the finest honky tonk vocalists of the late '40s and early '50s. —*Thom Owens*

Country Music Hall of Fame Series / 1992 / MCA ✦✦✦✦
These 1968-1978 recordings from Dot Records document a past-his-prime Thompson still capable of turning out good singles when the Nashville sound didn't smother him. —*Brian Mansfield*

● **Vintage** / 1996 / Capitol ✦✦✦✦
Twenty songs, containing nearly all of the essential items from Thompson's history with Capitol Records from 1947 through 1961, from "(I've Got A) Humpty Dumpty Heart" through "Oklahoma Hills." In addition to containing all of the expected hits, such as "The Wild Side of Life," there are a few nice bonus tracks, such as the Brazos Valley Boys' instrumental "Big Beaver," and excel-

lent notes, depicting Thompson's arrival at the label, the founding of the Brazos Valley Boys, the beginning of his long and profitable relationship with producer Ken Nelson, and the background on each song's recording and history. —*Bruce Eder & Thom Owens*

Hank Thompson & His Brazos Valley Boys (1946-1964) / 1996 / Bear Family ✦✦✦✦
"Massive" is the only word that can be used to describe *Hank Thompson and His Brazos Valley Boys (1946-1964)*. Spanning 14 years, 12 CDs, and nearly 320 songs, the set is overwhelming even to dedicated fans. Nevertheless, Thompson deserves a weighty retrospective such as this. As one of the primary musicians to fuse honky tonk and Western swing, he became one of the most popular and influential country musicians of the '50s. For most listeners, his importance can be conveyed through single-disc collections like *Vintage*, but this box set is a treasure for dedicated fans. It contains not only his entire output for Capitol Records, but his early sides for Globe and Bluebonnet, three complete live albums, and a handful of unreleased cuts. Nearly as impressive is the detailed packaging, which comes complete with a hardcover book that provides a comprehensive biography and sessionography. A box as extensive as this is necessary only for historians and dedicated fans, but those that want to invest money in the set will not be disappointed. —*Stephen Thomas Erlewine*

Best of Hank Thompson: 1966-79 / Oct. 22, 1996 / Varèse ✦✦✦✦
The Best of Hank Thompson: 1966-79 contains the great majority of his biggest hits from the latter half of his career. Drawing from his recordings for Warner and Dot, the 16-track compilation features singles like "On Tap, in the Can, or in the Bottle," "Next Time I Fall in Love (I Won't)," and "Smoky the Bar." A few hits are missing, but the compilation nevertheless draws a full portrait of Thompson's latter-day career. —*Stephen Thomas Erlewine*

20 Greatest Hits / Deluxe ✦✦
For the most part, *20 Greatest Hits* offers re-recordings of Thompson chestnuts like "Wild Side of Life," "A Six Pack to Go," and "Humpty Dumpty Heart." —*Jason Ankeny*

Hank Thompson and His Brazos Valley Boys / Country Routes ✦✦✦
The French LP *Hank Thompson and His Brazos Valley Boys* is a compilation of live radio performances Thompson and his band gave in 1952, just as his career was beginning to take off with the massive success of "The Wild Side of Life." Though neither that song nor any of his earlier, lesser hits, is included on this collection, the album doesn't suffer as a result. Thompson and the Brazos Valley Boys sound tough and inspired, bringing a considerable amount of grit to his swinging honky tonk. The record remains an item for collectors only, but for those willing to seek it out, it is an enjoyable and fascinating historical artifact. —*Stephen Thomas Erlewine*

Marsha Thornton

b. Oct. 22, 1964, Killen, AL
Vocals / Contemporary Country
Marsha Thornton was a part of the wave of Nashville-based New Traditionalist female singers in the late '80s. Her two MCA albums are 1989's *Marsha Thornton*, produced by the legendary Owen Bradley, and 1991's *Maybe the Moon Will Shine*. Like many of her contemporaries, Thornton is stylistically indebted to Emmylou Harris. —*Mark A. Humphrey*

● **Maybe the Moon Will Shine** / 1991 / MCA ✦✦✦✦
Featured are pleasant pipes and Emmylou Harris-style production. —*Mark A. Humphrey*

Marsha Thornton / MCA ✦✦✦

Thrasher Shiver

Contemporary Country
Thrasher Shriver is a modern country band led by Neil Thrasher and Kelly Shriver. The group released their self-titled debut album on Elektra/Asylum in the fall of 1996. —*Stephen Thomas Erlewine*

Thrasher Shiver / Sep. 9, 1996 / Elektra/Asylum ✦✦✦
Thrasher Shriver's eponymous debut album is polished but impassioned country-rock that touches on honky tonk, barroom weepers, and modern country barn-burners. Although the band sometimes suffers from trying too hard to avoid Nashville cliches, resulting in underdeveloped songs, they manage to create a classy, rootsy sound that gives their best songs a bracing directness that cuts quite deeply. Moments like "Goin' Goin' Gone" and "All the King's Horses" suggest that the band will be able to develop into something quite special, given just a little more time. —*Thom Owens*

Sonny Throckmorton

b. Apr. 2, 1941, Carlsbad, NM
Vocals / Traditional Country
Sonny Throckmorton started out as a performer, but he became one of the most successful songwriters in country music, with more than 1,000 of his songs recorded by such artists as Tanya Tucker, Dave and Sugar, Merle Haggard, Jerry Lee Lewis, the Oak Ridge Boys, Doug Stone, and even comedian George Burns.

He was born James Fron Sonny Throckmorton in Carlsbad, NM, and spent much of his childhood traveling the Southwest before his family finally settled in Wichita Falls, TX. After college, Throckmorton moved to San Francisco and played rock 'n' roll in area clubs. At the urging of guitarist and publisher Pete Drake, he switched to country music and moved to Nashville in 1964, working as a bass player for Carl and Pearl Butler for two years. He then wrote for and managed Drake's publishing company. In 1965 Bobby Lewis had a Top Five hit with Throckmorton's "How Long Has It Been." He remained in Nashville for a few more years as a song promoter and staff writer for different companies before landing a job as a staff writer for the prestigious Tree Publishing. Unfortunately, none of the young writer's songs became hits, and he was fired.

In 1975 Throckmorton moved to Texas, because he had promised himself that he would quit music if he didn't succeed by age 35. His fellow songwriters continued trying to sell Throckmorton's songs, however, and six months later he returned and was rehired by Tree. In nine months, more than 150 of his songs were recorded, including "Thinking of a Rendezvous," Johnny Duncan's first No. 1 hit. Another of his songs, "Knee Deep in Love with You," became a country standard. Between 1976 and 1980, a Throckmorton song appeared on the charts almost every week. His 1978 hit for Jerry Lee Lewis, "Middle Age Crazy," even became the basis of a major movie, and he was named Songwriter of the Year by the Nashville Songwriters Association three years in a row between 1978 and 1980.

In 1976 Throckmorton tried recording his own songs, first for Starcrest and then for Mercury, but the biggest hit he had, "Last Cheater's Waltz," reached only the Top 50. Fortunately, his stature as a major songwriter flourished. In 1987, with countless hits under his belt, Throckmorton was inducted by the Nashville Songwriters Hall of Fame. He recorded *Southern Train* for Warner in 1988 and then retired to his Texas farm to be with his family. —*Sandra Brennan*

● **The Last Cheater's Waltz** / 1978 / Mercury ✦✦✦✦
Southern Train / 1986 / Warner Brothers ✦✦✦✦

Mel Tillis

b. Aug. 8, 1932, Tampa, FL
Guitar, Vocals / Traditional Country, Country-Pop
In light of all the attention given Mel Tillis' infamous speech impediment—he even named his autobiography *Stutterin' Boy*—the polished, sincere vocal delivery and songwriting skills that first earned him fame were often lost in the shuffle; nonetheless, throughout the course of his many decades in country music, Tillis remained one of Nashville's most enduring personalities. Born Lonnie Melvin Tillis in Tampa, FL, on August 8, 1932, it is believed that his stuttering was the result of a bout with malaria at the age of three. As a child, he learned guitar, and in high school he studied both violin and drums. At the age of 16, he first performed publicly at a local talent show, and after graduation he

entered the military. While stationed in Okinawa, Japan, he formed a group called the Westerners, which played local clubs.

After exiting the service in 1955, Tillis went to college and held odd jobs until moving to Nashville 1956. He found little success as a writer or performer there, and soon returned to Florida; then, in 1957, Webb Pierce reached No. 3 with Tillis' composition "I'm Tired," earning the aspiring artist a songwriting contract with Pierce's Cedarwood Music. After playing with the likes of Minnie Pearl and Judy Lynn, Tillis cut his first single, a cover of the standard "It Takes a Worried Man to Sing a Worried Song," in 1957; the B-side, the self-penned "Honky Tonk Song," quickly became a chart-topper for Pierce. After a few excursions into rock 'n' roll territory, Tillis earned his first Top 40 hit with 1958's "The Violet and a Rose."

While Tillis continued to chart singles like 1959's "Finally" and a pair of duets with Bill Phillips, "Sawmill" and "Georgia Town Blues," his greatest success at the turn of the decade remained as a songwriter. He continued supplying Pierce with hit after hit, including the 1959 smashes "I Ain't Never" and "No Love Have I," along with 1962's "Crazy Wild Desire" and 1963's "Sawmill." Also covering Tillis' songs were Bobby Bare ("Detroit City"), Ray Price ("One More Time," "Burning Memories," "Heart Over Mind"), Stonewall Jackson ("Mary Don't You Weep"), and Little Jimmy Dickens ("The Violet and a Rose," also covered by Wanda Jackson). In 1962 Tillis released his first LP, *Heart Over Mind;* a year later, he teamed with Pierce for the hit "How Come Your Dog Don't Bite Nobody But Me."

In 1965 Tillis recorded his first Top 15 hit, "Wine." A string of successes followed, including 1966's "Stateside," "Life Turned Her That Way" (the title cut from his 1967 album), and his first Top Ten, 1968's "Who's Julie." At the same time, his stature as a songwriter continued to grow, thanks to hit covers of his "Ruby, Don't Take Your Love to Town" (by both Johnny Darrell and Kenny Rogers and the First Edition) and "Mental Revenge" (Waylon Jennings). At the end of the 1960s, Tillis and his esteemed new backing band the Statesiders came into their own as performers; after two 1969 Top Ten hits, "These Lonely Hands of Mine" and "She'll Be Hanging Around Somewhere," he scored back-to-back Top Five hits in 1970 with "Heart Over Mind" and "Heaven Everyday." In 1971 he began a successful string of duets with Sherry Bryce that included "Take My Hand" and "Living and Learning," and released the album *Live at the Sam Houston Coliseum.*

In 1972 "I Ain't Never" became his first chart-topper, and the remainder of the decade that followed was Tillis' most fertile period as an artist, as evidenced by a series of Top Five smashes like "Neon Rose," "Sawmill," "Midnight, Me and the Blues," "Stomp Them Grapes," and "Memory Maker." Between 1976 and 1980, he scored five more No. 1s—"Good Woman Blues," "Heart Healer," "I Believe in You," "Coca Cola Cowboy," and "Southern Rains." He also appeared in a number of films, including 1975's *W.W. and the Dancekings* (with Burt Reynolds and Jerry Reed), 1977's *The Villain* (starring Kirk Douglas and Arnold Schwarzenegger), Clint Eastwood's *Every Which Way But Loose* in 1979, and 1980's all-star *Smokey and the Bandit Part II.* Albums of the period included 1976's *Love Revival* and 1980's *M-M-Mel Live,* in addition to a series of hits compilations.

In 1981 Tillis recorded a duets album with Nancy Sinatra called *Mel and Nancy,* but like most of his work throughout the 1980s, it failed to repeat the success he had previously enjoyed. Although he continued to work in films (co-starring in both *Cannonball Run* pictures) and notch the occasional Top Ten hit (like 1981's "A Million Old Goodbyes" or 1983's "In the Middle of the Night,"), his days as a superstar were over. Still, he remained a popular songwriter, especially among younger artists; his "Honey (Open That Door)" and "Diggin' Up Bones" were No. 1 hits for, respectively, Ricky Skaggs and Randy Travis. Tillis also continued as a successful road act, and in the early 1990s, his daughter Pam became one of country's biggest stars. —*Jason Ankeny*

M-M-Mel Live / 1980 / MCA ◆◆◆

Tillis the showman heard working a crowd. —*Mark A. Humphrey*

Pam Tillis

Mel and Nancy / 1981 / Elektra ◆◆◆

Mel and Nancy is a collection of duets from Tillis and Nancy Sinatra. It includes the minor hits "Play Me or Trade Me" and "Where Would I Be." —*Jason Ankeny*

American Originals / 1989 / Columbia ◆◆◆◆

American Originals compiles material from Tillis' brief time at Columbia Records. He was with the label at the beginning of his career, and while he was there, he recorded primarily his own material. *American Originals*, though too brief at ten tracks, gives a good sense of his developing talents. —*Thom Owens*

Greatest Hits / 1991 / Curb ◆◆◆◆

Featuring a selection of his late '70s and early '80s hits—including the No. 1 "Coca Cola Cowboy," "Lying Time Again," "Southern Rains," "Your Body Is an Outlaw," "New Patches," and "Blind In Love"—Curb's *Greatest Hits* is a serviceable, but not thorough, retrospective that does work as an effective introduction to Tillis at the height of his popularity. —*Thom Owens*

● **Memory Maker** / 1995 / Mercury ◆◆◆◆

Although he reached his commercial peak in the latter half of the decade, Tillis hit his creative stride in the early 1970s, the period compiled on *The Memory Maker.* Leading off with "I Ain't Never," his first No. 1, the collection also features "Sawmill," "Mental Revenge," "Neon Rose," and "Midnight, Me and the Blues." —*Jason Ankeny*

The Best of Mel Tillis / MCA ◆◆◆◆

Fine '60s hard-country singer-songwriter with Ray Price shuffles, etc. —*Mark A. Humphrey*

Pam Tillis

b. 1957, Plant City, FL

Vocals / Country-Pop, Contemporary Country, Contemporary Country, Urban Cowboy

Like many children of famous fathers, Pam Tillis was forced to overcome several obstacles to establish herself as an individual artist and not simply the daughter of country vocalist Mel Tillis; eventually, she earned her own identity, which led to a string of country hits in the early '90s.

Though born in Plant City, FL, Tillis was raised in Nashville, where she made her debut on the Grand Ole Opry at the age of eight. As a child she took classical piano lessons, and she began playing guitar at age 12 by watching an instructional show on television. Tillis made her professional debut during a talent contest at Nashville's Last Chance Saloon when she was a teenager. Despite a natural affinity for country music, she also found herself drawn to other genres; she was a rebellious teen, partying too hard and running wild. At the age of 16, she suffered a nearly fatal car crash that left her face badly shattered, forcing her to undergo painful reconstructive surgery for the next five years. Tillis persevered, however, and while attending college she founded the High Country Swing band and performed in a folk duo with Ashley Cleveland. In 1976 she dropped out of school to become a songwriter, taking a job at her father's Sawgrass Music publishing house. Barbara Fairchild recorded one of her early tunes, "I'll Meet You on the Other Side of Morning."

Eventually, Tillis wanted to find her own musical identity, so she formed the Pam Tillis Band and moved to San Francisco. She soon changed the group's name to Freelight, and the band became an experimental free-form jazz and rock outfit. In 1978 she went back to Nashville, becoming a backup singer for her father and fronting her own R&B band. She also continued to write, providing pop singers like Gloria Gaynor and Chaka Khan with successful songs. Tillis made her own recording debut in 1983, releasing *Beyond the Doll of Cutey*. A year later, she had her first charting single with "Goodbye Highway," which inched its way to No. 71. It took another two years before she reappeared on the charts with the moderate hit "Those Memories of You." Throughout the latter half of the '80s, she had a string of minor country hits. During this time she also wrote commercial jingles, wrote songs for Tree Publishing and performed in Las Vegas.

For a brief time at the turn of the decade Tillis flirted with pop music, but she decided to return to her country roots in 1990, when she signed with Arista Records. "Don't Tell Me What to Do," her first single for the label, catapulted to No. 5, becoming her first genuine hit. For the next few years, she had a steady stream of hit singles, highlighted by "Maybe It Was Memphis," which reached No. 3 in early 1992. That same year she released *Homeward Looking Angel*, and in 1993 it, too, went gold. In 1994 her album *Sweetheart's Dance* reached the country Top Ten; in 1995, she released *All of This Love. —Sandra Brennan*

Put Yourself in My Place / 1991 / Arista ✦✦✦✦
The album that established Tillis as a performer in her own right has a traditional country base cut with bluegrass, folk, and rock. It all creates the same sort of mixed breed she sings about in "Melancholy Child": "You take a black Irish temper, some solemn Cherokee, a Southern sense of humor, and you got someone like me." Her characters are the awkward dancers of "I've Seen Enough to Know": bruised, tentative, and needing to be cajoled back to love. Even the throwaway songs are of a high standard; the best ones ("Maybe It Was Memphis," "Don't Tell Me What to Do") are truly enticing. —*Brian Mansfield*

Homeward Looking Angel / 1992 / Arista ✦✦✦
Tillis had an enviable challenge with *Homeward Looking Angel*—topping *Put Yourself in My Place*, which spawned four Top Ten singles, including "Don't Tell Me What to Do." Tillis' pure, full-bodied country voice can be both a boon and a burden. Some tracks on *Angel* reek with cliche, her twang exaggerated to the verge of annoyance, for instance, on the retro "Do You Know Where Your Man Is." Others work an original magic, including the sly and sexy "Shake the Sugar Tree" and the wry and telling "Cleopatra, Queen of Denial." These songs, along with "Let That Pony Run," had no trouble finding their way to the chart heights of their predecessors. —*Roch Parisien*

● **Pam Tillis Collection** / Feb. 1, 1994 / Warner Brothers ✦✦✦✦
Before hitting big with Arista Records and "Don't Tell Me What to Do," Tillis had recorded rock-influenced country for Warner Bros. She had minor success with the likes of "There Goes My Love" and "These Memories of You," but what makes *Collection* interesting is early versions of "One of Those Things" and "Maybe It Was Memphis" as well as a version of "Five Minutes," later a hit for Lorrie Morgan. —*Brian Mansfield*

Sweetheart's Dance / Apr. 26, 1994 / Arista ✦✦✦✦
Producing herself for the first time (along with Steve Fishell), Tillis found the magic blend of Nashville Sound, California country-rock and post-Beatles pop. She released the heady "Spilled Perfume" as her first single, but the riches of *Sweethearts Dance* go much deeper: the Bo Diddley/Tejano rhythms of "Mi Vida Loca (My Crazy Life)," the lilting waltz of "In Between Dances," and a playfully romantic title cut. A charming album without a bad cut, *Sweethearts Dance* ranks with the best of Trisha Yearwood, Wynonna Judd, and Carlene Carter. —*Brian Mansfield*

All of This Love / Nov. 7, 1995 / Arista ✦✦✦

Floyd Tillman

b. Dec. 8, 1914, Ryan, OK
Guitar, Vocals / Traditional Country, Honky Tonk
Floyd Tillman is probably best known for writing "It Makes No Difference Now," a country classic that he sold to Jimmie Davis for $300 in 1938, only to watch it become a hit for Davis, Bob Wills, Bing Crosby, and Gene Autry. Tillman was born in Ryan, OK, but raised in Post, TX. He began playing guitar and performing as a backup musician for local fiddlers while he was still a child. In 1933, at age 19, Tillman joined Adolph and Emil Hofner's house band at Gus' Palm Garden in San Antonio. Two years later he became the leader of the Blue Ridge Playboys. In 1936 he began singing and playing electric guitar, mandolin, and banjo with the Mark Clark Orchestra. He also wrote songs and occasionally sang them with the band. Tillman began a solo recording career in the late '30s and had his first No. 1 hit in 1944 with "They Took the Stars Out of Heaven," which he followed up with two Top Five hits, "G.I. Blues" and "Each Night at Nine," with his Favorite Playboys. In the late '40s he had more hits, "Slippin' Around" and "I Love You So Much It Hurts." His Western swing/honky tonk mixture and easy vocal delivery, with its distinctively bent notes, made Tillman a much-imitated performer, and he continued writing songs through the 1960s; his last solo success came in 1960 with "It Just Tears Me Up." —*David Vinopal & Sandra Brennan*

● **Country Music Hall of Fame Series** / 1991 / MCA ✦✦✦✦
Tillman had his biggest hits in the late '40s while recording for Columbia, but these World War II-era sides for Decca show him as a leader of a Texas dance band that's not afraid to mix it up with some jazz playing. Moon Mullican plays piano on a number of these sides. —*Brian Mansfield*

★ **Columbia Historic Edition** / Columbia ✦✦✦✦✦
The 11-track *Columbia Historic Edition* contains the bulk of Floyd Tillman's hits from the late '40s, including "Drivin' Nails in My Coffin," "I Love You So Much, It Hurts," and "Slippin' Around," plus a number of lesser-known songs that rival the hits in quality. Certain songs, like his Decca hits and "I'll Never Slip Around Again" and "I Gotta Have My Baby Back," aren't included but *Columbia Historic Edition* remains the best compilation of Tillman's peak. —*Stephen Thomas Erlewine*

The Best of Floyd Tillman / Columbia ✦✦✦✦
It contains his classics, such as "Slippin' Around" and "Gotta Have My Baby Back." Wait for this one; with Columbia reissuing much of its vintage country material, this stuff has got to appear on CD in some form. —*Richard Lieberson*

Aaron Tippin

b. 1958, Pensacola, FL
Vocals / Contemporary Country, New Traditionalist
Aaron Tippin was part of the 1990s' new traditionalist wave of honky tonk singers; although his music was among the rootsiest of the new traditionalists, he became massively popular—his singles regularly charted in the Top Ten, and his albums went platinum.

Born in Pensacola, FL, Tippin was raised on a 120-acre family farm in South Carolina; his chief influences included Jimmie Rodgers, Hank Thompson, and Lefty Frizzell. At age ten he began playing guitar and performing in local groups. At age 20 he was working as a commercial pilot, but he switched to music before obtaining his Airline Transport Rating. During the early '80s he wrote songs for various Nashville publishing outfits. In 1986 he moved to Nashville, where he eventually became a staff writer at Acuff-Rose. He also tried to land his own recording contract, with little success. Eventually, his demo tape arrived at RCA, which offered him a contract.

Tippin's debut single, "You've Got to Stand for Something," reached the Top Ten in 1991 and was followed by an album of the same name that spawned two other minor hit singles and peaked at No. 25 on the country charts. *Read Between the Lines*, his second album, was released in 1992 and contained his first No. 1 single, "There Ain't Nothing Wrong with the Radio." *Read Between the Lines* climbed to the Top Ten and crossed over to the Top 50 on the pop album charts; it went platinum in 1993 and produced two more hits, including the Top Five "I Wouldn't Have It Any Other Way." In 1993 Tippin released his third album, *Call of the Wild*, which went gold four months after its release. *Lookin' Back at Myself* appeared the next year, while *Tool Box*, his fifth album, was released in 1995. —*Sandra Brennan*

You've Got to Stand for Something / 1991 / RCA ✦✦✦✦
This exciting hardcore country comes from a man whose previous blue-collar experience as a farm hand, welder, pilot, and truck driver made him a publicist's dream. It includes the singles "You've Got to Stand for Something," "I Wonder How Far It Is over You," and "She Made a Memory Out of Me." —*Brian Mansfield*

Read Between the Lines / 1992 / RCA ✦✦✦✦
A good follow-up by this popular hatless hillbilly contains "There Ain't Nothin' Wrong with the Radio," "I Wouldn't Have It Any Other Way," "My Blue Angel," and more. —*Mark A. Humphrey*

Call of the Wild / Aug. 1993 / RCA ✦✦✦
Though he was still capable of singing up a storm and cranking out great grooves, some of Tippin's song choices were hillbilly silly. Of course, they were also the singles, which had names like "Honky Tonk Superman" and "Working Man's Ph.D." —*Brian Mansfield*

● **Lookin' Back at Myself** / Nov. 8, 1994 / RCA ✦✦✦✦
Lookin' Back At Myself has a good cross-section of Aaron Tippin's biggest hits and best songs, making it an excellent introduction. —*Thom Owens*

Tool Box / Nov. 21, 1995 / RCA ✦✦✦
Aaron Tippin's *Tool Box* ranks among his finest work, as the singer explores slightly new territory. In addition to his trademark honky tonk and barroom ravers, there are a number of soulful ballads that demonstrate the full range of Tippin's talents. —*Stephen Thomas Erlewine*

● **Greatest Hits and Then Some** / Mar. 25, 1997 / RCA ✦✦✦✦
Greatest Hits and Then Some contains all of Aaron Tippin's best-known songs and biggest hits from the early '90s, including "I Wouldn't Have It Any Other Way," "My Blue Angel," "Working Man's Ph.D.," "I Get It Honest," and the No. 1 singles "You've Got to Stand for Something" and "That's As Close As I'll Get to Loving You." —*Thom Owens*

Karen Tobin

Vocals / Alternative Country
Tobin worked in the Los Angeles-area country bars in the late '80s as half of the country duo Crazy Hearts (cf. Enigma's *A Town South of Bakersfield II* anthology) before signing a solo deal with Atlantic in 1991. Her debut album offers contemporary traditional-country tunes. —*Mark A. Humphrey*

Carolina Smokey Moon / 1991 / Atlantic ✦✦✦✦
Like Emmylou Harris, an obvious influence, Tobin possesses a clear, powerful voice, and her songs shun studio gloss in favor of old-timey authenticity. —*Jason Ankeny*

Tony Toliver

Piano, Vocals / Contemporary Country, New Traditionalist
Singer-songwriter/pianist Tony Toliver was best known as Dottie West's former bandleader. Raised in Texas, Toliver started out playing piano with his family's gospel group. He played both country and pop music in local clubs before coming to Nashville

and signing on to play piano in West's band. Soon he was promoted to bandleader, and West gave him solo shots during her shows. The crowds liked him, so West introduced him to performers like Merle Haggard and Larry Gatlin, who felt that Toliver had the right stuff to make it on his own and helped him land a solo deal. Toliver's eponymous 1991 debut album featured seven of his own songs, one written with Hank Cochran, and another with Dottie West, but did nothing on the charts. The follow-up, *Half Sinner, Half Saint*, did not appear until 1996. —*Sandra Brennan*

Tony Toliver / 1991 / Curb ✦✦✦

● **Half Saint Half Sinner** / Sep. 24, 1996 / ✦✦✦✦
Tony Toliver's third solo album *Half Saint Half Sinner* is a terrific set of rootsy contemporary country, driven by his pounding piano. —*Thom Owens*

Tractors

Country-Rock, Contemporary Country
The Tractors were one of the country-rock bands to benefit from the modern country boom of the early '90s. With their good-time boogie and rootsy country-rock, the Tractors were able to send their eponymous debut to platinum status.

Although based in Tulsa, all of the members of the Tractors—guitarist Steve Ripley, bassist Ron Getman, vocalist Casey Van Beek, keyboardist Walt Richmond, and drummer Jamie Oldaker—were well-known Nashville session musicians before they came to prominence in the early '90s. The group landed a contract with Arista Records and released their self-titled debut album in the summer of 1994. Supported by the hit single "Baby Likes to Rock It," the record became a Top Ten country hit, eventually selling over two million copies. Instead of following the debut with a standard second record, the band released a holiday album, *Have Yourself a Tractors Christmas*, in the fall of 1995. Like its predecessor, the Christmas record was a hit, although it didn't come close to replicating the chart status of *The Tractors*.

The band took most of 1996 off, spending time with their families and working on side projects, as lead songwriter Steve Ripley prepared material for their third album, scheduled for release in the spring of 1997. —*Stephen Thomas Erlewine*

● **Tractors** / 1994 / Arista ✦✦✦✦

Have Yourself a Tractors Christmas / Oct. 10, 1995 / Arista ✦✦✦
Country Christmas gets wrapped up boogie blues-rockin' style thanks to the Tractors' *Have Yourself a Tractors Christmas*. A little manipulative, perhaps, to redo their hit single "Baby Likes to Rock It" under the guise of "Santa Claus Is Comin' (In a Boogie Woogie Choo Choo Train)" but, with the exception of a couple of slow cookers, this blend of originals and trads rolls right on down the track. —*Roch Parisien*

Diana Trask

b. Jun. 23, 1940, Melbourne, Australia
Vocals / Traditional Country, Country-Pop
Australian singer Diana Trask was a popular performer in the US during the '60s and '70s. She was born in Warburton, a small logging town near Melbourne, to a musically talented family. She first gained attention in Australia at age 16 after winning a nationwide talent contest, and began playing on television. Later she was part of a pop group that opened for such American stars as Sammy Davis, Jr., who liked her music and suggested she come to the US. In 1959 Trask did, but she didn't find much success until she spent a week guesting on Don McNeil's "Breakfast Club," which led to a contract with Columbia and a regular spot on the TV show "Sing Along with Mitch." Both of her initial albums were pop-oriented.

After marrying in the early '60s, Trask returned to Australia, but by 1966 she and her family were living in New York, where she continued trying to further her pop career. After visiting the CMA DJ Convention in Nashville, she decided to focus on country music. She debuted on the country charts in 1968 with the low-ranked "Lock, Stock and Teardrops," but later that year she reached the Top 60 with "Hold What You've Got." In 1969 Trask released her debut album, *Miss Country Soul*, and she toured

Merle Travis

with Hank Williams, Jr. Although she continued to have modest hits, her popularity didn't take off until 1972, when she had a Top 30 hit with "We've Got to Work It Out Between Us." In 1973 she made the Top 20 twice with "Say When" and "It's a Man's World (If You Had a Man Like Mine)." The following year, she had a Top 15 crossover hit with "Lean on Me." She returned to Australia during the mid-'70s and earned a few gold records there. Trask returned to the US in 1981 to record a pair of singles, but then retired for the remainder of the decade. During the 1990s she again resumed performing. — *Sandra Brennan*

Diana Trask on TV / 1961 / Columbia ✦✦✦

● **Diana Trask's Greatest Hits** / 1974 / ABC/Dot ✦✦✦✦

The ABC Collection / 1977 / ABC ✦✦✦✦

Merle Travis

b. Nov. 29, 1917, Rosewood, KY, d. Oct. 20, 1983, Tahlequah, OK
Guitar, Vocals / Traditional Country, Instrumental Country, Country Boogie

Merle Travis was virtually without peer as a guitarist and songwriter. A unique stylist, he was respected and prominent enough to have an instrumental style ("Travis picking") named after him, and only Chet Atkins even comes close to the influence that Travis had on the way the guitar was understood and played in country music. (Indeed, Atkins was initially signed to RCA to be that label's Merle Travis.) As a songwriter, he wasn't far behind, with originals such as "Sixteen Tons" crossing over as popular standards in the hands of other artists. He even played two different vital and indirect roles in the development of rock 'n' roll, and was no slouch as a recording artist, with his own share of chart hits and novelty songs.

Merle Robert Travis was born Nov. 29, 1917, in Rosewood, KY. His father was a coal miner, and the family lived on the bare edge of poverty; eventually this experience, coupled with a phrase that Travis' father used to describe their lives, became the basis for the song "Sixteen Tons." His very first instrument was a five-string banjo, but when he was 12 years old his older brother gave him a homemade guitar. Travis was lucky enough to have as neighbors Ike Everly, later the father of Don and Phil, and Mose Rager, who played in a unique three-finger guitar style that had developed in that area of Kentucky. Travis learned this approach as a teenager and grew astonishingly proficient in a repertory that included

blues, ragtime, and popular tunes. It wasn't enough to earn a living, and he survived by working in the Civilian Conservation Corps as a teenager.

His first break came during a visit to his brother's home in Evansville, IN, in 1935, where his chance to entertain at a local dance resulted in membership in a couple of local bands and a chance to appear on a local radio station. By 1937 he was a member of Clayton McMichen's Georgia Wildcats, and a year later he'd moved on to the Drifting Pioneers, who found a permanent broadcasting gig at Cincinnati's WLW. The "Boone Country Jamboree" radio show kept the group busy until World War II came along and forced it to disband. While a member of the Drifting Pioneers, Travis acquired a national following and began playing with Grandpa Jones and the Delmore Brothers in a gospel quartet called the Brown's Ferry Four. He later teamed up with Jones as "The Shepherd Brothers," the first artists to record for the newly-founded King Records label in 1943. He and Jones even exchanged songs, and found the sources for a few songs together—it was while out with Jones one day at a Black church in Cincinnati that Travis heard the sermon that became the song "That's All."

Travis spent a short stint in the Marines, but he was quickly discharged and returned to Cincinnati. During the late winter of 1944, he headed for Los Angeles, where he began making appearances in Charles Starrett's Western movies and playing with Ray Whitley's Western swing band. With guidance from Tex Ritter and bassist Cliffie Stone, in 1946 he released the topical song "No Vacancy"—dealing with the displacement of returning veterans—along with "Cincinnati Lou," and earned a double-sided hit. His next major project was a concept album, *Folk Songs of the Hills*, which was intended to compete with Burl Ives' successful folk recordings. The record, released as a set of four 78 rpm discs, was a failure at the time it was released in 1947 (it wasn't even transferred to long-playing disc until nearly ten years later). However, it yielded several classics, among them the Travis originals "Sixteen Tons," "Dark As a Dungeon," and "Over By Number Nine," as well as introducing such standards as "Nine Pound Hammer"; it also became a unique document, depicting a beautiful all-acoustic solo guitar performance by this master virtuoso.

The initial failure of the folk album aside, 1947 began a boom period in Travis' career. In addition to writing the million-selling hit "Smoke! Smoke! Smoke!" for his friend Tex Williams, he had a half dozen Top Ten records himself, including "Divorce Me C.O.D.," "So Round, So Firm, So Fully Packed," and "Three Times Seven." Travis also devised the first solid body electric guitar, coming up with a model which, when perfected by Leo Fender, would become a key element in early rock 'n' roll. The string of hits didn't last, but Travis' career continued uninterrupted, with performances on stage, television, and record. In 1953 he landed a fairly visible movie role in one of the biggest films of the year, *From Here to Eternity*, where he performed "Re-Enlistment Blues." It was around that same time that he began playing on all of his friend Hank Thompson's records. In 1955 Tennessee Ernie Ford had his crossover hit with "Sixteen Tons," and it was around that same time that Travis acolytes such as Chet Atkins were making a major impact on music themselves. Scotty Moore, who'd first been influenced by Travis from his radio performances, had become Elvis Presley's lead guitarist, and a year after Elvis hit nationally, the Everly Brothers (themselves Chet Atkins disciples) started topping the charts.

Travis was one of those musical figures who was referred to constantly, either musically or literally, by dozens of major figures, but he was never able to ascend the charts himself again. Much of the problem lay in his personal life. Along with a reputation as one of country music's top axemen, Travis also became known as a wildman, especially when he drank. He was arrested more than once for public intoxication and drunk driving—on his motorcycle—and in 1956 there was a highly publicized report of police surrounding his home after he assaulted his wife. In the early 1960s he was hospitalized briefly after being arrested while driving under the influence of narcotics. He managed to pull his professional life together in the mid-1960s to do one new folkstyle album, *Songs of the Coal Mines*, which, like its predecessor

Folk Songs of the Hills, failed to sell on its original release. His other albums—mostly instrumental, such as *Walkin' the Strings*—proved much more significant and influential at the time as standard acquisitions for aspiring guitarists. He still played occasionally and became something of a star on the college folk circuit, teaming with Chet Atkins for the Grammy-winning *Atkins-Travis Traveling Show* in 1974. Travis finally seemed to settle down after he married his fourth wife, Dorothy—the former wife of his longtime friend Hank Thompson—and focused once again on music. He recorded tribute albums to the Georgia Wildcats and began working again with old associates like Grandpa Jones, and it looked as if Travis was to enjoy a resurgence of musical and public acclaim. At age 65, however, he suffered a massive heart attack and died the next morning. —*Bruce Eder*

Folk Songs of the Hills / Jun. 0, 1917 / Capitol ◆◆◆
Eight acoustic folk songs, including the original version of "Sixteen Tons." No need to look for this rare 78-rpm edition, as it's been reissued in its entirety, with five other cuts, on CD. —*Richie Unterberger*

Back Home / 1957 / Capitol ◆◆◆◆
A reissue of his eight-song 1947 album *Folk Songs of the Hills*, with four additional cuts from the Capitol *Electrical Transcription* series. The LP has been reissued in its entirety on the 1996 CD version of *Folk Songs of the Hills*, with the addition of a song that was previously unreleased in the US. —*Richie Unterberger*

Walkin' the Strings / 1960 / Capitol ◆◆◆◆
Although originally issued on LP in 1960 (it was reissued on CD in 1996), these 22 songs were actually recorded in the late '40s and early '50s for Capitol's *Electrical Transcription* series. This showcases Travis' fingerpicking abilities at their best, on unaccompanied acoustic vocal and instrumental numbers; most of the material is original, with a few standards by the likes of Stephen Foster and Georgia Tom Dorsey. —*Richie Unterberger*

Songs of the Coal Mines / 1963 / Capitol ◆◆◆◆
Travis recorded this concept album over a period of three days in March 1963. It consists of 12 originals dealing with the lives of coal miners, a subject that Travis knew well, as the only male member of his family to have escaped a livelihood earned underground. The material consists of folk and blues ("Pay Day Comes Too Slow" is one of the best pieces of White blues you'll ever hear, regardless of how many Eric Clapton albums you may own already), all very vivid in its textures and sensibilities, and it's a crying shame that the album never made the charts, as this was obviously a project very close to Travis' heart. The cover is also something of a classic, though it hardly emphasized this as a Travis album, consisting of drawings that might've come out of any miner's family album. —*Bruce Eder*

Great Songs of the Delmore Brothers / 1969 / Capitol ◆◆◆◆

Travis Pickin' / 1981 / CMH ◆◆◆◆
Until his Capitol Records instrumental recordings become available again, this is one for guitar buffs to go for. —*Richard Lieberson*

★ **The Merle Travis Story—24 Greatest Hits** / 1989 / CMH ◆◆◆◆◆
Although *The Merle Travis Story—24 Greatest Hits* consists of re-recordings from the late '70s, it gives a better sense of why Travis was important than Rhino's *The Best of Merle Travis*. Unlike Rhino's set, CMH concentrates on Travis' guitar playing, which is why he was an important musician. Therefore, it gives a far better sense of why the guitarist was a revered, influential artist than the vocal hits of Rhino's collection, even if the music was recorded late in his career. —*Thom Owens*

The Best of Merle Travis / 1990 / Rhino ◆◆◆◆
Rhino's *The Best of Merle Travis* may contain all of his big chart hits, but it's a misleading collection. Instead of focusing on Travis' revolutionary playing, the set runs through his hits and novelty songs, which all emphasize his vocals. Therefore, it isn't quite as comprehensive—or essential—as it initially appears. The album hints at his greatness, but it never shows why Travis' playing was so groundbreaking. —*Thom Owens*

The Radio Shows, 1945-1946 / 1990 / Country Routes ◆◆◆

☆ **Merle Travis 1944-49** / 1991 / Country Routes ◆◆◆◆◆
A dazzling collection of 22 radio recordings by Travis, some solo and some done backed up by the likes of Johnny Bond, done for such shows as "Hollywood Barn Dance," the "Melody Roundup" and "Dinner Bell Roundup," the Grand Ole Opry, "Country Barn Dance," and the "Cliffie Stone Western Party." The earliest of these sides date from immediately after Travis' 1944 discharge from the Marine Corps and show him establishing himself in Los Angeles, in association with producer/emcee Cliffie Stone, who later brought Travis to Capitol Records. The later stuff, from 1946 on, overlaps with Travis' early period at Capitol, including things like his Grand Ole Opry performance of "John Henry," which he had also cut for *Folksongs of the Hills*. Travis preferred the radio performances to his studio recordings because of radio's less formal requirements and easier-going approach to music-making, which allowed him to improvise as he pleased within the time available; you could joke around on radio in ways that no one was allowed to in the studio. Among the notable songs is Travis' cover of "Old Rattler," a dog song that he learned from Grandpa Jones during their period playing together in the Brown's Ferry Four; his cover of Jimmie Rodgers' "T For Texas"; and "Roll On Mississippi," an old Boswell Sisters harmony number played by Travis in a subordinate position to Johnny Bond. Some of the stuff is very short, but all of it is worth hearing by anyone who presumes to like Travis. The sound quality is uniformly good, and the notes are excellent. —*Bruce Eder*

Folk Songs of the Hills (Back Home/Songs of the Coal Mines) / 1993 / Bear Family ◆◆◆◆
This German import—which goes for about double the cost of the US CD *Folk Songs of the Hills*—contains not only *Folk Songs of the Hills/Back Home* (but *not* the previously unreleased "This World Is Not My Home"), but also an entire additional Travis album, the 1963 *Songs of the Coal Mines*, which deals with the lot and lives of coal miners. The songs include "Black Gold," "Harlan County Boys," "The Browder Explosion," and "Bloody Brethitt County," a song as savage as its title implies. The extra cost is worth it, in the absence of a separate US CD release of *Songs of the Coal Mines*. Travis completists will want it, and any folk or blues enthusiast (check out "Pay Day Comes Too Slow") should want it. —*Bruce Eder*

Folk Songs of the Hills [expanded] / 1996 / Capitol ◆◆◆◆
In 1946 Capitol approached Travis with the idea of cutting a folk album, and although he wasn't an especially folk-oriented artist, he agreed to give it a go. Although the resulting 1947 record (released as a 78-rpm album) didn't sell well, it was a respectable effort performed by Travis on solo acoustic guitar. Folksy introductions embellish the songs, which include standbys like "John Henry" and "Nine Pound Hammer." Travis added a few songs of his own penned in the folk style, and one of these, "Sixteen Tons," would prove to be his most famous composition, reaching No. 1 when it was covered by Tennessee Ernie Ford in the 1950s. The CD reissue combines the eight songs from the 1947 release with four songs from the Capitol *Electrical Transcription* series that were added to the batch when the album was reissued as *Back Home* in 1957. It also adds a song from the 1946 sessions that was previously unreleased in the US, "This World Is Not My Home." —*Richie Unterberger*

Unreleased Radio Transcriptions 1944-1949 / Rounder ◆◆◆
This album contains 22 tracks of performances originally broadcast on such shows as *Hollywood Barn Dance, Melody Roundup*, and The Grand Ole Opry, among others. —*AMG*

Randy Travis (Randy Traywick)

b. May 4, 1959, Marshville, NC
Guitar, Vocals / Contemporary Country, New Traditionalist
Like the Beatles in rock, Randy Travis marks a generational shift in country music. When his *Storms of Life* came out in 1986, country music was still wallowing in the post-*Urban Cowboy* recession, chasing elusive crossover dreams. Travis brought the music back to its basics, sounding like nothing so much as a perfect blend of George Jones and Merle Haggard. He became the dominant male voice in country until the rise of "hat acts" like

Garth Brooks and Clint Black, releasing seven consecutive No. 1 singles during one stretch. He won the CMA's Horizon Award in 1986 and was the association's Male Vocalist of the Year in 1987 and '88.

Randy Travis (born Randy Bruce Traywick, May 4, 1959, Marshville, NC) was born and raised in North Carolina, in a small town outside of Charlotte. Travis' father encouraged his children to pursue their musical inclinations, as he was a fan of honky tonkers like Hank Williams, George Jones, and Lefty Frizzell. Randy began playing guitar at the age of eight, and within two years, he and his brother Ricky had formed a duo called the Traywick Brothers. The duo played in local clubs and talent contests.

Each of the brothers had a wild streak, which resulted in Ricky's going to jail after a car chase and Randy's running away to Charlotte at the age of 16. While he was in Charlotte, he won a talent contest at Country City USA., a bar owned by Lib Hatcher. Hatcher was impressed by Travis and offered him a regular gig at her bar, as well as a job as a cook.

For several years, he sang and worked at Country City. He still had trouble with the law in his late teens. At his last run-in with the police, the judge told him if he saw Travis again, he should be prepared to go to jail for a long time. Randy was released into the care of Hatcher. In a short time, Hatcher became Travis' manager and the pair began to concentrate on his career. Joe Stampley helped Randy land a contract with Paula Records in 1978. The next year, Travis released two singles under his given name; one of them, "She's My Woman," scraped the bottom of the country charts.

In 1982 Travis and Hatcher moved to Nashville, where she managed the Nashville Palace nightclub while he sang and cooked. Within a couple of years, the pair independently released his debut album under the name Randy Ray; the record was called *Randy Ray Live* and sold primarily in the Nashville Palace.

Thanks to Hatcher's persistent efforts and the *Randy Ray Live* album, Warner Brothers signed him in 1985 and suggested that he change his performing name to Randy Travis. "On the Other Hand," his first single for the label, was released in the summer of that year and climbed to No. 67. Despite its lackluster performance, radio programmers were enthusiastic, as evidenced by the No. 6 placing of "1982," which was released late in the year. "1982" was followed by a re-release of "On the Other Hand" in the spring of 1986. This time, the song hit No. 1.

Storms of Life, Travis' full-fledged debut album, was released in the summer of 1986 and became a huge success, eventually selling more than three million copies. Travis was the first country artist to go multi-platinum; before his success, most country artists had difficulty achieving gold status. With his mass appeal, he set the stage for country music's crossover success in the early '90s. However, Travis dominated the late '80s. The last two singles from *Storms of Life,* "Diggin' Up Bones" and "No Place like Home," were No. 1 and 2, respectively. "Forever and Ever, Amen"—the first single from Randy's second album, 1987's *Always and Forever*—began a streak of seven straight No. 1 singles that ran through 1989. *Always and Forever* was more successful than his debut, reaching No. 19 on the pop charts and going quadruple platinum; it also earned him the CMA's award for Male Vocalist of the Year. *Old 8X10* (1988) and *No Holdin' Back* (1989) weren't quite as successful as their predecessors; but they still spawned No. 1 singles, and both went platinum.

Travis was still at the top of his form in the beginning of the '90s, starting the decade with his biggest hit, "Hard Rock Bottom of Your Heart." However, his hold at the top of the charts began to slip after Clint Black and, in particular, Garth Brooks. Nevertheless, Travis never fell away completely; his albums continued to gold and he usually could crack the Top Ten. *Wind in the Wire,* a soundtrack to his television special released in 1992, marked his first unsuccessful album; none of the singles broke the Top 40. *This Is Me,* released in 1994, was a successeul comeback to the top of the charts, featuring "Whisper My Name," his first No. 1 hit in two years. In 1996 Travis released *Full Circle. —Brian Mansfield & Stephen Thomas Erlewine*

☆ **Storms of Life** / 1986 / Warner Brothers ✦✦✦✦✦
His first and best album features astonishing Lefty Frizzell-style pipes, excellent material, and sympathetic production. Easily the most impressive country debut of the '80s, it includes "1982," "On the Other Hand," "Diggin' up Bones," and "No Place like Home." *—Mark A. Humphrey*

Always and Forever / 1987 / Warner Brothers ✦✦✦✦
This one stayed at the top of the country charts for 10 months and sold five million copies. Well, of course he was huge. If you had songs as good as "Forever and Ever, Amen," you'd be a star, too. *—Brian Mansfield*

Old 8x10 / 1988 / Warner Brothers ✦✦✦✦
Almost on a par with *Storms of Life, Old 8x10* lacks the monster hits of his debut but wears just as well. When Travis sings of love, he doesn't mean romance; there's a permanence in his voice that sounds like settling down. The album contains "Honky Tonk Moon," "Deeper than the Holler," and "Is It Still Over?" *—Brian Mansfield*

No Holdin' Back / 1989 / Warner Brothers ✦✦✦✦
Though it's essentially a formulaic album from Randy Travis, *No Holdin' Back* is nevertheless an exceptional formula record, demonstrating both the strengths of traditionalist country songwriting and Travis' classically honky tonk voice. *No Holdin' Back* is filled with remarkable songs and performances, highlighted by a version of Brook Benton's "It's Just a Matter of Time." Occasionally the lack of musical experimentation is a little frustrating, but there's no denying that the album offers many pleasures, particularly for listeners who thought the spirit of traditional country had died out in the late '80s. *—Thom Owens*

Old-Time Christmas / Aug. 29, 1989 / Warner Brothers ✦✦✦
Of these ten Christmas songs, some are old, some are new, and one is by Travis ("How Do I Wrap My Heart for Christmas," written with Paul Overstreet). "God Rest Ye Merry Gentlemen" is outstanding. *—Brian Mansfield*

Heroes and Friends / 1990 / Warner Brothers ✦✦✦
This duets album includes the obvious influences (George Jones, Conway Twitty, Tammy Wynette) as well as a few surprises (B.B. King, Clint Eastwood). The Jones song, "A Few Ole Country Boys," and the title track were hit singles. *—Brian Mansfield*

High Lonesome / 1991 / Warner Brothers ✦✦✦
With young whippersnappers like Clint Black and Garth Brooks breathing down his neck, Travis realized he needed to be more than just a pretty voice. On *High Lonesome* he proved he could write, too, helping pen five of the album's ten songs, including "Forever Together" for his manager-turned-wife Lib Hatcher, and the country-gospel "I'm Gonna Have a Little Talk," sung a cappella with Take 6. It also includes "Better Class of Losers," written with Alan Jackson. *—Brian Mansfield*

Wind in the Wire / 1992 / Warner Brothers ✦✦
This album of Western cowboy music, some old and some new, was made to go with a TV show of the same name. *—Brian Mansfield*

★ **Greatest Hits, Vol. 1** / Sep. 15, 1992 / Warner Brothers ✦✦✦✦✦
When Travis finally got around to releasing a greatest-hits collection, he realized he had almost enough material for two albums. So, adding two new songs to each, he put them out simultaneously. Volume one gets the edge for including those first two hits, "1982" and "On the Other Hand". The best of the new songs, "If I Didn't Have You" and the shattering "Reasons I Cheat," proved as early as 1986 that Travis could write 'em as well as sing 'em. *—Brian Mansfield*

☆ **Greatest Hits, Vol. 2** / Sep. 15, 1992 / Warner Brothers ✦✦✦✦✦
Eleven more Travis classics are included here, among them "Diggin' Up Bones," "Forever and Ever, Amen" and a fabulous remake of Brook Benton's "It's Just a Matter of Time." The new songs are "Look Heart, No Hands" and "Take Another Swing at Me." *—Brian Mansfield*

This Is Me / 1994 / Warner Brothers ✦✦✦✦
The vanity project *Wind in the Wire* excepted, Travis hadn't released an album of new music in three years, and some people

were wondering what had happened to the man who started the neo-traditionalist boom. *This Is Me,* which included the wildly funny "Before You Kill Us All" and a stunning song called "Whisper My Name" that synthesized countrypolitan with gospel, silenced most of the questioners and showed the young whippersnappers what all the fuss had been about in the first place. —*Brian Mansfield*

Forever and Ever...The Best of / 1995 / Warner Brothers ✦✦✦✦

Full Circle / Aug. 1996 / Warner Brothers ✦✦✦✦

Randy Travis' *Full Circle* is a return to form, of sorts. Although he never really left the country charts, his mid-'90s albums suffered from a tendency to sound a bit too similar too each other. *Full Circle* solves that problem by simultaneously reaching back into his hardcore honky tonk roots and moving toward more contemporary material, such as Mark Knopfler's "Are We in Trouble Now." Travis' exquisitely textured and weathered voice gives the new songs a gravity they might not have had if another vocalist had sung them. Furthermore, producer Kyle Lehning has once again assembled a top-notch backing band that manages to sound rootsy and professional simultaneously. With a fine band and an excellent set of material, Travis rises to the occasion with *Full Circle,* producing one of his finest albums of the '90s. —*Thom Owens*

Buck Trent (Charles Wilburn Trent)

b. Feb. 17, 1938, Spartanburg, SC
Banjo, Vocals / Traditional Country
Buck "Mr. Banjo" Trent was not only one of the finest players in country music, he was also the inventor of the electric banjo. Born Charles Wilburn Trent in Spartanburg, SC, he began playing steel guitar at age seven and debuted professionally on an Ashville, NC, television station at age 17. He joined the "Bill Carlisle Show" near the end of the 1950s and soon made his first appearance on the Grand Ole Opry. In 1962 he joined Porter Wagoner's Wagon Masters and designed the electric banjo, an instrument shaped something like a steel guitar that featured a mobile bridge used to change the pitch. Trent remained with Wagoner through 1973 and then spent the next seven years as the opening act for Roy Clark; he also appeared regularly as a featured musician on the long-running TV show "Hee Haw." He began recording in 1962, initially under the name Charles Trent; during the '70s, he recorded several albums, including *Bionic Banjo* (1976). He began recording on his own Buck Trent label in the 1980s and two years later recorded an eponymous album on MCA/Dot. During the 1990s he was a regular performer in Branson, MO. —*Sandra Brennan*

● **The Best of Buck Trent** / MCA ✦✦✦✦

Rick Trevino

b. May 16, 1971, Austin, TX
Vocals / Contemporary Country, Tex-Mex, Tejano
During the mid-'90s, Rick Trevino emerged as one of the first popular Hispanic singers in country music since the mid-'70s, when Freddy Fender and Johnny Rodriguez were having hits. Beginning with "She Can't Say I Didn't Cry" in 1994, Trevino racked up several hits over the next few years with his Garth Brooks-inspired blend of new country and album rock.

Rick Trevino was born into a musical family—his father was a member of a local Tejano group. Both of his parents fostered his musical interests, and as a child he listened to a variety of music, including Tejano, country, classical pianist Van Cliburn, and mainstream pop-rockers like Elton John and Billy Joel. Soon he was taking classical piano lessons and studying the clarinet. After graduating from high school, he was offered a baseball scholarship to Memphis State University, but he declined the offer to study music.

In 1993 he released his first album, the Spanish-language *Dos Mundos.* It was accompanied by a single release of "Just Enough Rope," which was released in English, Spanish, and a bilingual version; it was the first traditional country single to be released in both Spanish and English. The English version was a moderate hit, reaching No. 44. In 1994 Trevino released an eponymous album, which featured English versions of most of the songs from

Randy Travis

Dos Mundos, plus a few new cuts. *Rick Trevino* became a hit, producing the Top 40 "Honky Tonk Crowd" and the Top Ten singles "She Can't Say I Didn't Cry" and "Doctor Time."

Trevino's second album, *Looking for the Light,* was released in 1995; it was accompanied by a Spanish version. Like its predecessor, *Looking for the Light* was a hit, albeit not as big as the debut; it spawned only one Top 40 hit, the No. 6 "Bobbie Ann Mason." *Learning As You Go,* was Trevino's third album. —*Stephen Thomas Erlewine*

Dos Mundos / Sep. 1993 / Sony Discos ✦✦✦

Rick Trevino / 1994 / Columbia ✦✦✦✦

● **Looking for the Light** / 1995 / Columbia ✦✦✦✦

Un Rayo De Luz / 1995 / Sony ✦✦✦

Learning As You Go / 1996 / Columbia ✦✦✦

Learning As You Go, Rick Trevino's third English album, isn't quite as consistent as its two predecessors, but songs like "Learning As You Go" demonstrate that this is only a slight slump for the singer, not the end of the road. —*Thom Owens*

Trio

Traditional Country
This contemporary country superstar trio was comprised of Dolly Parton, Linda Ronstadt, and Emmylou Harris. In 1987 they recorded an album of country music and did a concert tour to support it. —*Bil Carpenter*

The Trio / 1987 / Warner Brothers ✦✦✦✦

Dolly Parton, Linda Ronstadt, and Emmylou Harris tried to make this album in 1978, but contractual problems (they all recorded for different labels), a lack of specific direction, and a shortage of time (they tried to make the album in ten days), kept it from occurring, although occasional tracks did emerge on Harris' solo albums. The wait was worth it—shimmering harmonics in a traditional acoustic package that emphasizes their very different vocal styles. —*Tom Roland*

Tony Trischka

b. Jan. 16, 1949, Syracuse, NY

Banjo / Progressive Bluegrass

The avant-garde banjo sylings of Tony Trischka inspired a whole generation of progressive bluegrass musicians; he was not only considered among the very best pickers, he was also one of the instrument's top teachers; he created numerous instructional books and teaching videotapes and cassettes.

A native of Syracuse, NY, Trischka's interest in banjo was sparked by the Kingston Trio's "Charlie and the MTA" in 1963. Two years later he joined the Down City Ramblers, where he remained through 1971. That year Trischka made his recording debut on *15 Bluegrass Instrumentals* with the band Country Cooking; at the same time, he was a member of Country Granola. In 1973 he began a two-year stint with Breakfast Special. Between 1974 and 1975 he recorded two solo albums, *Bluegrass Light* and *Heartlands*. After one more solo album in 1976, *Banjoland*, he went on to become musical leader for the Broadway show *The Robber Bridegroom*. Trischka toured with the show in 1978, the year he also played with the Monroe Doctrine.

Beginning in 1978 he also played with artists such as Peter Rowan, Richard Greene, and Stacy Phillips. In the early 1980s he began recording with his new group, Skyline, which recorded its first album in 1983. Subsequent albums included *Robot Plane Flies over Arkansas* (solo, 1983), *Stranded in the Moonlight* (with Skyline, 1984), and *Hill Country* (solo, 1985). In 1984 he performed in his first feature film, *Foxfire*. Three years later he worked on the soundtrack for *Driving Miss Daisy*. Trischka produced the Belgian group Gold Rush's *No More Angels* in 1988. The next year, Skyline recorded its final album, *Fire of Grace*. Trischka also recorded the theme song for "Books on the Air," a popular National Public Radio Show, and continued his affiliation with the network by appearing on Garrison Keillor's "Prairie Home Companion," "Mountain Stage," "From Our Front Porch," and other radio shows. —*Sandra Brennan*

Bluegrass Light / 1973 / Rounder ◆◆◆

Bluegrass Light is Tony Trischka's debut album and demonstrates how the banjoist pushed the boundaries of the genre by incorporating jazz, folk, and country elements. Though some of his ideas sound a little unformed, the album remains one of the most exciting records in his catalog. —*Thom Owens*

Heartlands / 1975 / Rounder ◆◆◆

Robot Plane Flies over Arkansas / 1983 / Rounder ◆◆◆

An early release that spotlights Trischka's banjo skills. A progressive album. —*Chip Renner*

Hill Country / 1985 / Rounder ◆◆◆

A traditional bluegrass album. —*Chip Renner*

Skyline Drive / 1986 / Flying Fish ◆◆◆◆

With *Skyline Drive*, Tony Trischka injects progressive bluegrass techniques into the smooth, post-Urban Cowboy country-pop. While Trischka isn't as technically skilled as Bela Fleck or Ricky Skaggs, he is more accessible to a mainstream country audience on this album. For most bluegrass fans, of both traditional and progressive persuasions, the pop concessions are a bit hard to swallow, but there are some very strong—mainly instrumental—songs that make it a worthwhile listen. —*Thom Owens*

● **Dust on the Needle** / 1988 / Rounder ◆◆◆◆

A good collection of Trischka's six Rounder albums, featuring Sam Bush, Marc O'Connor, and David Grisman. —*Chip Renner*

Fire of Grace / 1989 / Flying Fish ◆◆◆◆

Glory Shone Around: A Christmas Collection / Oct. 1995 / Rounder ◆◆◆

Traditional folk fans will want to snap up Tony Trischka's *Glory Shone Round*, a diverse, highly textural seasonal collection in which Trischka's acclaimed banjo work ranges from raw bluegrass to delicate classical, with such guests as Pete Seeger and the Turtle Island String Quartet. —*Roch Parisien*

Travis Tritt

b. 1963, Marietta, GA

Guitar, Vocals / Contemporary Country, New Traditionalist

Travis Tritt was one of the leading new country singers of the early '90s, holding his own against Garth Brooks, Clint Black, and Alan Jackson. He was the only one not to wear a hat and the only one to dip into bluesy Southern rock. Consequently, he developed a gutsy, outlaw image that distinguished him from the pack. Throughout the early '90s, he had a string of platinum albums and Top Ten singles, including three No. 1 hits.

Tritt fell in love with music as a child, teaching himself how to play guitar when he was eight and beginning to write songs when he was 14. Travis was determined to have a musical career, but his parents didn't encourage him to follow his instincts. His mother didn't mind that he wanted to perform, but she wanted him to sing gospel; his father was afraid there was no money in singing. When he was 18, he tried to settle down, work, and have a family, but he was unsuccessful; he was married and divorced twice before he was 22. He continued to play music while working various jobs, including one at an air-conditioning company. The company's vice-president was a guitarist who had given up hopes of a musical career, and he urged Tritt to follow his dreams. Travis quit his job and began pursuing a career full-time.

In 1982 Tritt began his pursuit by recording a demo tape at a private studio that was owned by Danny Davenport, who happened to be an executive at Warner Brothers. Davenport heard the vocalist's songs and was impressed, deciding to take Tritt under his wing. For the next several years the pair recorded demo tapes while Tritt played the honky tonk circuit. The singer was developing a distinctive sound, adding elements of country-rock and Southern rock to his honky tonk.

Partway through 1989, Warner Brothers' Nashville division signed Tritt; his debut album, *Country Club,* appeared in the stores in spring 1990. It was preceded by the Top Ten hit "Country Club." Upon the release of his debut album, Tritt entered the first ranks of new country singers. His next two singles, "Help Me Hold On" and "I'm Gonna Be Somebody," hit No. 1 and No. 2, respectively. "Put Some Drive in Your Country," which had a clear rock 'n' roll influence, stalled at No. 4, since radio programmers were reluctant to feature such blatantly rock-derived music.

Despite his success, the Nashville music industry was hesitant to embrace Tritt. His music and stage show owed too much to rock 'n' roll, and his image didn't conform to the behatted legions of new male singers. Nevertheless, Travis had a breakthrough success with his second album, 1991's *It's All About to Change*. Before its release, he had hired manager Ken Kragen, who also worked with Lionel Richie, Trisha Yearwood, Kenny Rogers, and We Are the World. Kragen helped market Tritt in a way that appealed to both country fans and a mass audience, sending *It's All About to Change* into multi-platinum territory.

T-R-O-U-B-L-E, Tritt's third album, was released in 1992. Although it didn't match the success of *It's All About to Change*, it had the No. 1 single "Can I Trust You With My Heart" and went gold. Travis bounced back in 1994 with *Ten Feet Tall and Bulletproof*, which went platinum, spawned the No. 1 single "Foolish Pride," and marked his highest position, No. 20, on the pop charts. His 1995 compilation *Greatest Hits—From the Beginning* went platinum within six months of its November release. —*Stephen Thomas Erlewine*

Country Club / 1990 / Warner Brothers ◆◆◆

Tritt proclaimed his influences early with "Put Some Drive in Your Country," which paid homage not only to Roy Acuff and George Jones but to Hank Williams, Jr., and Duane Allman. It was the lowest-charting single off Tritt's debut, but it sold him a ton of albums. Radio programmers preferred the ambitious "I'm Gonna Be Somebody" and the ballads "Help Me Hold On" and "Drift Off to Dream." —*Brian Mansfield*

It's All About to Change / 1991 / Warner Brothers ◆◆◆◆

Better production means ballads like "Anymore" sound bigger and rockers like "Bible Belt" (with Little Feat) and a cover of bluesman Buddy Guy's "Homesick" rock harder. Tritt brought in Marty Stuart for a duet on "The Whiskey Ain't Workin'" and revived "Here's a Quarter (Call Someone Who Cares)" as a catch-phrase. —*Brian Mansfield*

T-R-O-U-B-L-E / 1992 / Warner Brothers ✦✦✦
Tritt's covers of Buddy Guy ("Leave My Girl Alone") and Elvis Presley ("T-R-O-U-B-L-E") are nice touches and show deeper roots than the Gary Rossington cowrite ("Blue Collar Man") or the last album's Little Feat remake. Beyond that, *T-R-O-U-B-L-E* is almost indistinguishable from *It's About to Change:* a good novelty song masquerading as more, a couple of ballads with big flourishes, and a large helping of Southern. That's a good formula, granted, but it still sounds like a formula. —*Brian Mansfield*

A Travis Tritt Christmas—Loving Time of the Year / May 1992 / Warner Brothers ✦✦✦
The harder Tritt rocks on *Loving Time of the Year,* the better he sounds. His Southern-boogie versions of "Winter Wonderland" and "Silver Bells" make a perfect antidote to sleigh-bell burnout. When he tries to be an "interpretive singer" on "Have Yourself a Merry Little Christmas," he falls flat on his face. Elsewhere, Tritt writes the title track and covers two by Buck Owens and one by Sonny James. —*Brian Mansfield*

Ten Feet Tall and Bulletproof / 1994 / Warner Brothers ✦✦✦✦
Tritt's most personal album is the one in which he feels most comfortable with his Southern rock/outlaw mantle. ("Outlaws like Us," in fact, features the voices of Hank Williams Jr. and Waylon Jennings.) Tritt poked fun at his own foibles in the title track and co-wrote "Wishful Thinking" and "No Vacation from the Blues" with Lynyrd Skynyrd's Gary Rossington. "Wishful Thinking" and "Foolish Pride" are ballads that rival "Anymore" for power and Skynyrd and Bob Seger for production values. —*Brian Mansfield*

● **Greatest Hits—From the Beginning** / Sep. 12, 1995 / Warner Brothers ✦✦✦✦
Greatest Hits—From the Beginning features 15 of Travis Tritt's biggest hits, including "Country Club," "Help Me Hold On," "Here's a Quarter (Call Someone Who Cares)," and "Tell Me I Was Dreaming." Although a couple of hits are missing, nothing essential has been overlooked, and it's a first-rate introduction. —*Stephen Thomas Erlewine*

Restless Kind / Aug. 27, 1996 / Warner Brothers ✦✦✦✦
Under the direction of Don Was, Travis Tritt turns in one of his leanest and easily his grittiest country record yet. Cutting back the country-rock flourishes that have always distinguished his sound, Tritt opts for twangy guitars, wailing fiddles, dobros, and unaffected guts vocals. Mirroring the stripped-down instrumentation, the song selection is straightahead honky tonk, rockabilly, and traditional country. Tritt benefits immeasurably from this approach; he has never sounded so alive. Actually, he has never sounded so purely country. —*Thom Owens*

Greg Trooper

Singer-Songwriter, Folk, Americana
Trooper, who was born and raised in New Jersey, has had his songs recorded by the likes of Steve Earle, Rosanne Cash, and Vince Gill. In the early '70s, Trooper left the folk clubs of Greenwich Village for the music scene of Austin, TX, before moving to Lawrence, KS, where he entered college and continued to hone his guitar, singing, and songwriting skills. He returned to New York for the '80s and part of the '90s, where he recorded his first two records: *We Won't Dance* and the critically acclaimed *Everywhere.* The records caught the attention of Earle, who recorded Trooper's "Little Sister." In the early '90s, Trooper met fellow New Jerseyan and ex-E Street Band bassist Garry Tallent, who, like Trooper, would settle in Nashville. Tallent produced Trooper's 1996 album *Noises in the Hallway* and released it on his D'Ville Records. —*Jack Leaver*

We Won't Dance / 1986 / Wild Rags ✦✦✦

Noises in the Hallway / Jan. 30, 1996 / DVI ✦✦✦✦
Singer-songwriter Greg Trooper has been covered by artists as diverse as Billy Bragg, Steve Earle, and Maura O'Connell, which gives an idea of the wide range of styles on *Noises in the Hallway.* Working from a basic folk-rock base, Trooper adds stylistic

Travis Tritt

flourishes that makes the album compelling not only lyrically, but musically. —*Stephen Thomas Erlewine*

Ernest Tubb

Guitar, Vocals / Traditional Country, Honky Tonk
The incomparable Ernest Tubb ("E.T." to all who knew him) became a legend as much for what he was personally as for the half-century career that stretched from his first radio date in 1932 to his death in 1984. Though other singers with better voices and more raw musical talent have come and gone, none has inspired greater love from the fans over six decades. Along with such performers as Jimmie Rodgers, Roy Acuff, Bill Monroe, Hank Williams, Lefty Frizzell, and George Jones, E.T. is country music personified. Tubb was among the first of the honky tonk singers and the first to achieve national recognition. His first recording was "The Passing of Jimmie Rodgers," a tribute to his hero. His long association with Decca began with "Blue Eyed Elaine" in 1940. Three years later his self-penned "Walkin' the Floor Over You," a country classic, was a hit, leading to the Opry, movie roles, and stardom. In 1947 he opened his Nashville record store and began the "Midnight Jamboree," which followed the Opry on WSM and advertised the shop, while showcasing stars and those on the rise. By that time he had become one of the most recognizable musical stars in the world, bringing country music to the widest audience it had ever had. Over the years Tubb toured widely with his Texas Troubadours, pressing the flesh with fans after shows that featured his many hits, including "Slippin' Around," "Two Glasses Joe," "Tomorrow Never Comes," "Drivin' Nails in My Coffin," "Rainbow at Midnight," "Let's Say Goodbye like We Said Hello," and "Driftwood on the River." In 1975, after 35 years with Decca/MCA, he was let go, the allegiance of company executives not matching that of his multitude of fans. Because of a lung disease Ernest Tubb had to rest in pain on a cot between takes, ending his career just as his hero Jimmie Rodgers had 50 years earlier. Quoting one of his album titles, Tubb left a legend and a legacy.

The youngest of five children, Ernest Tubb was born in Ellis County, TX, but his farming parents moved across the state to Benjamin when he was six years old. By the time he was in his pre-adolescence, his parents had divorced, and he spent his teens traveling between his two parents, working odd jobs. Early in his adolescence, Tubb was attracted to the music of Jimmie Rodgers. By his late teens, Tubb had picked up the guitar on the advice of a friend and fellow guitarist named Merwyn Buffington. After Jimmie Rodgers' death in May 1933, Tubb decided that he wanted to pursue a musical career and emulate his idol. He moved to San Antonio, where he again hooked up with Buffington, who was playing with the Castleman Brothers on a local radio station. The guitarist convinced his employers to let Tubb sing as a guest vocalist, and soon ET had his own regular early-morning show.

At this point in his career, Tubb sounded very similiar to Jimmie Rodgers and was still obsessed with his idol. Eventually, he tracked down and met Rodgers' widow Carrie, who was quite taken with Ernest, lending him one of Jimmie's guitars and convincing RCA to sign the young singer. The first singles he recorded were quite similar to Rodgers' (including two tributes to the Singing Brakeman); but the records failed to sell, and he was quickly dropped from the label. Ernest continued to plow ahead, playing a variety of small clubs and radio stations without gaining much attention. A major point in Tubb's musical development was the removal of his tonsils in 1939. After that he could no longer yodel, which meant he developed his own distinctively twangy, nasal singing style. Decca Records agreed to record him in April 1940, and one of the resulting singles, "Blue Eyed Elaine," became a minor hit. Decca agreed to sign him to a longer contract by the end of the year, by which time he also had a regular radio show on a Fort Worth station, KGKO, sponsored by the flour company Gold Chain.

Early in 1941 he cut several new songs, this time backed by Fay "Smitty" Smith, a staff electric guitarist for KGKO. The first single released from these sessions was "Walking the Floor Over You." Over the next few months, the single became a massive hit, eventually selling more than a million copies. "Walking the Floor Over You" was the first honky tonk song, launching not only Tubb's career but also the musical genre itself. He sang the song in the Charles Starrett movie *Fighting Buckeroos* (1941), which led to another film appearence in Starrett's *Ridin' West* (1942). By the end of 1942 he was popular enough to gain a release from his Gold Chain contract, and he headed to Nashville. Upon his arrival in January 1943, he joined the Grand Ole Opry, and he became the first musician to use an electric guitar in the Opry.

Between 1942 and 1944 Tubb made no recordings because of a strike within the recorders' union, but he continued to tour, often with Pee Wee King and Roy Acuff. Tubb turned to recording in 1944, releasing the No. 2 "Try Me One More Time" early in the year, followed by his first No. 1 single, "Soldier's Last Letter," that summer. The two singles kicked off a nearly 15-year streak of virtually uninterrupted Top Ten singles (only four of his 54 singles of that era failed to crack the Top Ten, and even then they made the Top 15). In 1946 he began recording solely with his band, the Texas Troubadours, and he became one of the first country artists to record in Nashville. Between the end of 1945 and the conclusion of 1946, he had a number of huge hits, including "It's Been So Long Darling," "Rainbow at Midnight," "Filipino Baby," and "Drivin' Nails in My Coffin." The singles cemented his reputation in the US and won him new fans around the world.

Early in 1947 he opened the Ernest Tubb Record Shop in Nashville, which he promoted through the "Midnight Jamboree," a radio program he designed to fill the post-Opry slot on the radio. That year he became the first country star to play Carnegie Hall in New York, signaling how much he had done to increase country music's popularity across the United States; a few years before, it would have been unthinkable to have such rural music play in such an urban venue. During 1949 he hit the height of his popularity, charting an astonishing 13 hit singles, even more remarkable considering that the chart had only 15 positions each week. Most of those songs were classics, including "Have You Ever Been Lonely? (Have You Ever Been Blue)," "Let's Say Goodbye like We Said Hello," "I'm Biting My Fingernails and Thinking of You" (a collaboration with the Andrews Sisters), "Slipping Around" and "Blue Christmas." The next year, he had 11 hit singles, including "I Love You Because" and "Throw Your Love My Way," plus several hit duets with Red Foley, including "Tennessee Border No. 2" and the No. 1 "Goodnight Irene." Tubb also demonstrated his influence by helping Hank Snow appear on the Grand Ole Opry and supporting Hank Williams.

Throughout the '50s, Ernest Tubb recorded and toured relentlessly, racking up well over 30 hit singles, the majority of

which—including the classics "Driftwood on the River" (1951) and "The Yellow Rose of Texas" (1955)—reached the Top Ten. By the end of the decade his sales had dipped slightly, which only meant he wasn't reaching the Top Ten, only the Top 20, with regularity. Nevertheless, he stopped having big hits in the early '60s, as rock 'n' roll and newer, harder honky tonk singers cut into his audience. Even with the decline of his sales, Tubb was able to pack concert halls, and his television show was equally popular. While the quality of his recordings was rather uneven during this time, he still cut a number of classics, including "Thanks a Lot," "Pass the Booze," and "Waltz Across Texas." Beginning in 1964, Decca had him record a series of duets with Loretta Lynn, and over the next five years they made three albums and had four hit singles: "Mr. and Mrs. Used to Be," "Our Hearts Are Holding Hands," "Sweet Thang," and "Who's Gonna Take the Garbage Out."

In 1966 Tubb was diagnosed with emphysema. In spite of the doctors' warnings, he continued to tour and record actively into the early '70s. During that time, he continued to rack up a number of minor hits, as well as lifetime achievement awards. In 1965 he became the sixth member inducted by the Country Music Hall of Fame. In 1970 he was one of the first artists inducted by the Nashville Songwriters International Hall of Fame. Shortly after receiving the last reward, his hits slowed down drastically; over the next five years he had only one minor hit with 1973's "I've Got All the Heartaches I Can Handle." Decca and Tubb parted ways in 1975, and he signed with Pete Drake's First Generation label, where he had one minor hit, "Sometimes I Do," in early 1978. The next year, Drake developed an all-star tribute to Tubb, *The Legend and the Legacy*, which featured stars like Willie Nelson, Merle Haggard, Chet Atkins, and Charlie Daniels overdubbing their own work on original recordings Tubb had made. Released on Cachet Records, the album produced two minor hits with "Waltz Across Texas" and "Walkin' the Floor Over You" before being pulled from the market for contractual reasons.

The Legend and the Legacy would be the last time Tubb reached the charts. In the three years after its release, he continued to tour; but in late 1982 he was forced to retire because of his health. During the last days of his final tours, he had to take oxygen and rest on a cot between shows, eerily resembling the circumstances of Jimmie Rodgers' last recording sessions. Ernest Tubb succumbed to emphysema on September 6, 1984. —*David Vinopal*

The Ernest Tubb Story / 1958 / Decca ✦✦✦
These re-recordings of older material are well-done, but it would be better to have the originals. —*George Bedard*

The Importance of Being Ernest / 1959 / Decca ✦✦✦
A good album, it's representative of his later ('50s and '60s) sound, with above-average song selections. —*George Bedard*

Ernest Tubb's Golden Favorites / 1961 / Decca ✦✦✦
These re-recordings of older material are well-done, but it would be better to have the originals. —*George Bedard*

Family Bible / 1963 / Decca ✦✦✦✦
It contains the title track plus "Stand by Me," "The Wings of a Dove," "I Saw the Light," and others. —*AMG*

Honky Tonk Classics / 1983 / Rounder ✦✦✦✦
Honky Tonk Classics is a nice, LP-only compilation of 12 tracks that Ernest Tubb recorded for Decca between 1940 and 1954. The song selection may not consist entirely of hits, but the cuts that weren't hits are often better and more interesting—the very essence of honky tonk, in fact—than the hits, which makes *Honky Tonk Classics* one of the very best Tubb collections ever compiled. Too bad it's not available on compact disc. —*Stephen Thomas Erlewine*

★ **Country Music Hall of Fame** / 1987 / MCA ✦✦✦✦✦
Boasting 16 tracks, *Country Music Hall of Fame* is the most complete single-disc Ernest Tubb compilation available. All of the songs—which range from "Walking the Floor Over You" in 1941 to "Waltz Across Texas" in 1965—are the original hit versions, not the remakes that tend to flood the budget-line collections. That alone would make *Country Music Hall of Fame* a necessary purchase, but the compilers have also done an excellent job of whit-

tling down Tubb's extensive career to 16 tracks that show neo-phytes exactly how and why the vocalist was important. Not every one of Tubb's biggest hits are included, but many of the most important—"Soldier's Last Letter," "You Nearly Lose Your Mind," "Seaman's Blues," "It's Been So Long Darlin'," and "Letters Have No Arms"—are present, making the disc an essential addition to any basic country record collection. —*Stephen Thomas Erlewine*

Live 1965 / 1989 / Rhino ✦✦✦✦

Live 1965 wasn't intended to be a special show, but in a way that's why it is. The album was recorded in 1965 on one of Ernest Tubb's many concerts that year, and it captures him in his element, joking with the audience and running through a selection of his greatest hits. Though the performance certainly isn't rau cous, it's engaging, and the disc functions as a valuable historical document. —*Stephen Thomas Erlewine*

Let's Say Goodbye like We Said Hello / 1991 / Bear Family ✦✦✦✦

Let's Say Goodbye like We Said Hello is a mammoth five-disc box set featuring 115 songs Ernest Tubb recorded between 1947 and 1953. (Only five songs that Tubb recorded during that era are missing.) Though this music is historically important—indeed, these records formed the foundation of modern honky tonk—the box isn't necessarily an essential addition to every country music library. Musicologists and historians will find *Let's Goodbye like We Said Hello* a fascinating document, but most listeners will find the sheer comprehensiveness of the set rather tedious. Tubb, for all of his importance, wasn't versatile enough to make these five discs consistently engaging. There are some highlights that are available only here, such as his duets with Red Foley and a few forgotten rowdy honk tonk gems, but these are items that only dedicated listeners will treasure, not things that add considerable depth to Tubb's legacy. Granted, those are the kinds of consumers who will want to invest in a set as thorough as *Let's Goodbye like We Said Hello*, and in that sense, it is worthwhile. But for the casual country fan, a single-disc collection will tell you most of what you need to know about Tubb. —*Stephen Thomas Erlewine*

Yellow Rose of Texas / 1993 / Bear Family ✦✦✦✦

Beginning right where *Let's Say Goodbye like We Said Hello* ended, the five-disc set *Yellow Rose of Texas* begins. It contains 150 songs that Ernest Tubb recorded for Decca Records in the '50s, beginning in 1954 and finishing at the end of the decade. Though the set is ideal for a collector, the comprehensive nature of the box makes it difficult for anyone but diehard fans or historians to enjoy. —*Thom Owens*

Walking the Floor Over You [Box Set] / 1996 / Bear Family ✦✦✦✦

The eight-disc box set *Walking the Floor over You* covers the earliest recordings Tubb made for Decca Records, beginning in 1936 and ending in 1947, as well as his very rare transcriptions for World Records. The music on this set documents the birth of honky tonk music, as Tubb brought traditional country into the modern era. It's possible to hear that transformation on *Walking the Floor Over You*, since Tubb clearly moves from being a Jimmie Rodgers imitator to developing a style of his own with his first hit single, "Walking the Floor Over You." The rest of his early hits—"Try Me One More Time," "Soldier's Last Letter," "Yesterday's Tears," "Tomorrow Never Comes," "Careless Darlin'," It's Been So Long Darling," "Rainbow at Midnight," "Filipino Baby" and "Drivin' Nails in My Coffin" among them—are included on the set, as are a number of lesser-known songs and several alternate takes. In all, the set runs well over 200 songs. Though this set has immense historical value, it is not easy listening. The strict chronological session order of the sequencing and the similarity of Tubb's material means that the box is best digested in small doses. Therefore, only dedicated Tubb fans and musicologists should invest in *Walking the Floor Over You*, and casual listeners should stick with single-disc compilations, which present this material in a more digestible manner. —*Stephen Thomas Erlewine*

Ernest Tubb: Vol. 1 (1942-1949) / 1996 / Australian Import ✦✦✦✦

Ernest Tubb, Vol. 1 (1942-1949) is a 22-track disc that covers E.T.'s biggest early hits for Decca, including "Drivin' Nails in My Coffin," "Filipino Baby," and "Have You Ever Been Lonely." For listeners who want a more comprehensive single-disc introduction than the *Country Music Hall of Fame* collection, this Australian-only collection and its companion volume are worth tracking down, even though it is missing his signature song, "Walking the Floor Over You." —*Stephen Thomas Erlewine*

Ernest Tubb: Vol. 2 (1949-1951) / 1996 / Australian Import ✦✦✦✦

Ernest Tubb, Vol. 2 (1949-1951) is a 20-track disc that covers the second wave of hits that Tubb had for Decca in the late '40s and early '50s, including "I Love You Because," "My Filipino Rose," "Slipping Around," "Warm Red Wine," "Driftwood on the River," "Letters Have No Arms," and "I'm Biting My Fingernails and Thinking of You." For listeners who want a more comprehensive single-disc introduction than the *Country Music Hall of Fame* collection, this Australian-only collection and its companion volume are worth tracking down. —*Stephen Thomas Erlewine*

Best of Ernest Tubb / Oct. 29, 1996 / Curb ✦✦

The Best of Ernest Tubb contains re-recorded versions of several of Tubb's biggest hits, including "Walking the Floor Over You," "Soldier's Last Letter," and "It's Been So Long Darlin'." Though these versions aren't particularly bad, ET doesn't sound as strong as he did on the original recordings, so musically they offer no revelations. Historically, they're of no importance, since the original recordings were the groundbreaking work. In other words, this budget-priced *Best of* is no bargain and is most definitely not the place to start. —*Stephen Thomas Erlewine*

Retrospective, Vol. 1 / MCA ✦✦✦

Features "Filipino Baby," "Walking the Floor Over You," and "Blue Eyed Elaine." —*AMG*

Retrospective, Vol. 2 / MCA ✦✦✦

This second volume contains such favorites as "Mr. & Mrs. Used to Be," "Waltz Across Texas," "Too Old to Cut the Mustard," and others. —*AMG*

The Ernest Tubb Collection / Step One ✦

On this late-'70s all-star tribute, guests include Marty Robbins, Loretta Lynn, Merle Haggard, Willie Nelson, and Conway Twitty. It features the lean and likable Tubb's final strong vocal performance. —*Mark A. Humphrey*

Justin Tubb

b. Aug. 20, 1935, San Antonio, TX

Vocals / Traditional Country, Honky Tonk

A fixture on the Grand Ole Opry, singer-songwriter Justin Tubb, the eldest son of the legendary Ernest Tubb, had a style all his own; except for one duet version of "Blue Eyed Elaine" on his 1985 album *The Legend and Legacy*, he always recorded independently of his famous father.

Justin was born in San Antonio, TX, and spent most of his life in the Lone Star State with his mother Elaine, who separated from Ernest in 1948. He got his professional start in local clubs during college, and eventually moved to Nashville. At his father's suggestion, Tubb got a job working as a deejay in Gallatin, TN, where he occasionally performed some of the songs he had written. He made his recording debut in 1953 with "Ooh-La-La." Throughout the 1950s, Tubb recorded steadily, but he had only moderate success with his solo efforts. He did a little better singing novelty duets with Goldie Hill; in 1954, they reached the Top Five with their version of Jim Ed and Maxine Brown's "Looking Back to See," followed with the Top 15 "Sure Fire Kisses." In 1955 he joined the Opry, and in 1956 he had his first solo success with the Top Ten hit "I Gotta Go Get My Baby."

Tubb signed to Starday in the early '60s, released a few albums, and toured so much that he was temporarily dropped from the Opry for not appearing often enough. After 1963 he signed with RCA and released two duets with Lorene Mann, including "We've Gone Too Far Again." He had one more minor hit with "But Wait

There's More," his last chart appearance. He continued to record, tour, and appear on the Opry through the '70s. He also continued to write songs, and his "Lonesome 7-7203" was a No. 1 hit for Hawkshaw Hawkins, while "Be Glad" became a major hit for Del Reeves. Additionally, his "What's Wrong with the Way We're Doing It Now" became a popular song with fans of the traditional country sound. Tubb also wrote and recorded songs paying tribute to his father, including "Thanks, Troubadour, Thanks" and "Just You and Me, Daddy." —*Sandra Brennan*

● **The Best of Justin Tubb** / 1965 / Starday ✦✦✦✦

Tanya Tucker (Tanya Denise Tucker)

b. Oct. 10, 1958, Seminole, TX

Vocals / Country-Rock, Country-Pop, Contemporary Country

Tanya Tucker had her first country hit in 1972, when she was just 13 years old. Over the succeeding decades, Tucker became one of the few child performers to mature into adulthood without losing her audience, and during the course of her career, she notched a remarkable streak of Top Ten and Top 40 hits.

Born in Seminole, TX, much of Tucker's childhood was spent moving throughout the Southwest as her father pursued construction jobs. At the age of six, she began taking saxophone lessons; two years later, she decided she wanted to sing, and she made an auspicious debut with Mel Tillis. In 1969 Tucker and her family moved to Las Vegas, where she performed regularly. Eventually she recorded a demo tape that gained the attention of songwriter Dolores Fuller, who sent it to producer Billy Sherrill. At the time, Sherrill was the head of A&R at CBS Records, and he was so impressed with the demo tape that he signed the teenaged vocalist to Columbia Records. Sherrill initially planned to have Tucker record "The Happiest Girl in the Whole USA," but she passed on the tune, choosing "Delta Dawn," a song she'd heard Bette Milder sing on "The Tonight Show." Released in the spring of 1972, the song became an instant hit, peaking at No. 6 on the country charts and scraping the bottom of the pop charts.

At first, Columbia Records tried to downplay Tucker's age, but soon word leaked out, and she became a sensation; her second single, "Love's the Answer," also became a Top Ten hit later in 1972. Tucker's third single, "What's Your Mama's Name," became her first No. 1 hit in the spring of 1973. Two other No. 1s—"Blood Red and Goin' Down" and "Would You Lay with Me (In a Field of Stone)"—followed, establishing Tucker as a major star. In 1975 she signed with MCA Records, where she had a string of hit singles that ran into the late '70s. In 1978 she decided to radically change her image and cross over to rock with her *T.N.T.* album. Despite the controversy over the record and its sexy cover, it went gold the next year.

By the end of the '70s, her sales were declining; in 1980 she had only two hits. Also in 1980, she recorded a few singles with Glen Campbell, with whom she was romantically linked. In addition to recording, she made her feature film debut in *Hard Country*. She switched to Arista Records in 1982, where she had several hits, highlighted by the Top Ten "Feel Right." In 1984 and 1985 she had no hits and signed with Capitol Records. In early 1986 she returned with "One Love at a Time," which rocketed to No. 3. For the rest of the decade, she scored a constant stream of Top Ten singles, including four No. 1 hits. Her success continued in the early '90s, even though her sales began slumping as the decade wore on. —*Sandra Brennan*

Greatest Hits / 1975 / Columbia ✦✦✦✦

Greatest Hits collects the ten biggest hits Tanya Tucker had for Columbia Records in the early '70s, when she was just a teenager. Among the tracks are her debut single "Delta Dawn," "Love's the Answer," "The Man That Turned My Mama On," and the No. 1 hits "What's Your Mama's Name?," "Blood Red and Goin' Down," and "Would You Lay With Me (In a Field of Stone)." —*Stephen Thomas Erlewine*

Greatest Hits Encore / 1976 / Liberty ✦✦✦

This contains "The Jamestown Ferry," "Pecos Promenade," "Delta Dawn," "Here's Some Love," and other hits. —*AMG*

★ **Greatest Hits** / 1978 / MCA ✦✦✦✦✦

No matter how far Tucker's come the last 20 years, it all comes back to "Delta Dawn," "What's Your Mama's Name?," and the other hillbilly-Gothic hits of her youth. Producer Billy Sherrill is best known for his work with George Jones and Tammy Wynette, but how he turned an underage, waifish Southwest homegirl into a singer to make old boys sweat is surely his most notable, if unsettling, career achievement. —*Dan Cooper*

T.N.T. / 1978 / MCA ✦✦✦

Tucker rocks out on this steamy album. —*Mark A. Humphrey*

Greatest Hits / 1978 / MCA ✦✦✦

Featured are strong charters from 1975-1980. —*Mark A. Humphrey*

The Best of Tanya Tucker / 1982 / MCA ✦✦✦

Later '70s material for the blooming of a belter, honky tonk style. —*Mark A. Humphrey*

Girls like Me / 1986 / Capitol ✦✦✦

A bad girl tries to go good in the '80s on a new label. —*Mark A. Humphrey*

Love Me like You Used To / 1987 / Liberty ✦✦✦✦

This fully mature artist is uncompromisingly gritty in the sanitized new Nashville. —*Mark A. Humphrey*

Strong Enough to Bend / 1988 / Liberty ✦✦✦

More pop-country, but it's still Tanya. —*Mark A. Humphrey*

Greatest Hits [Liberty] / 1989 / Liberty ✦✦✦✦

Tanya, undergoing her second coming as a commercial country queen, appears here with her 1986-1991 hits. —*Mark A. Humphrey*

Tennessee Woman / 1990 / Liberty ✦✦✦

Here's one Tennessee singer who is more fiery than most Nashville divas. —*Mark A. Humphrey*

Greatest Country Hits / 1991 / Curb ✦✦✦✦

Greatest Country Hits includes Tucker favorites like "Just Another Love," "Lizzie and the Rainman," "Texas (When I Die)," and "I'll Come Back as Another Woman." —*Jason Ankeny*

What Do I Do with Me / 1991 / Liberty ✦✦✦

Ballads ("Down to My Last Teardrop," "Trail of Tears") are belted by the best female country singer of her generation. —*Mark A. Humphrey*

Can't Run from Yourself / Sep. 28, 1992 / Liberty ✦✦✦

Edgier and more consistent than *What Do I Do with Me, Can't Run from Yourself* runs the range of Tucker's abilities, from the slow-blues burn of Marshall Chapman's "Can't Run from Yourself" to the wistful melancholy of Hugh Prestwood's "Half the Moon." A rollicking duet with Delbert McClinton on "Tell Me About It" is matched by the fine romance of "Two Sparrows in a Hurricane"; which one you prefer is strictly personal. Switch one song on each side, and you've got a side of rockers and a side of ballads. —*Brian Mansfield*

Greatest Hits 1990-1992 / 1993 / Liberty ✦✦✦✦

As the title says, *Greatest Hits 1990-1992* contains all of the biggest hits Tanya Tucker had in the early '80s, including the No. 2 singles "Down to My Last Teardrop," "(Without You) What Do I Do with Me," "Some Kind of Trouble," and "Two Sparrows in a Hurricane," among others. —*Stephen Thomas Erlewine*

Greatest Hits [Capitol] / 1993 / Capitol Special Products ✦✦✦

Tanya Tucker returned to the top of the charts with her late '80s records for Capitol Records. Though it is a budget-line collection and, by nature, too brief, *Greatest Hits* nevertheless has several of her best songs from this era and is worth acquiring as a sampler. —*Thom Owens*

Soon / Oct. 11, 1993 / Liberty ✦✦

Soon dips into some average material and over-synthesized production. Fortunately, Tucker pulls out of the dive, thanks to two ballads—"Soon" and "Silence is King"—strong enough to rise above the treatment, and a pair of toothy tracks—"Sneaky Moon" and "A Blue Guitar"—that get back to the resonating riffs of the opener. —*Roch Parisien*

Love Songs / Aug. 20, 1996 / Capitol ✦✦✦
Love Songs is a budget-priced collection of Tanya Tucker's most popular love ballads from the late '80s and early '90s, as well as a few rarities ("I'm in Love and He's in Dallas" and "Your Love Amazes Me") that were previously included only on her eponymous box set. It's a nice collection, even if it is a little brief. However, it isn't a true hits compilation, so it's not as valuable or useful as some of her other collections. Casual fans should stick with the greatest hits sets, but for the budget-minded, *Love Songs* is a fun sampler. — *Stephen Thomas Erlewine*

Greatest Hits [Columbia] / Columbia ✦✦✦✦
Tanya Tucker's *Greatest Hits, 1973-1976* features her earliest hits, including "Delta Dawn," "Love's the Answer," "The Jamestown Ferry," "What's Your Mama's Name," "Blood Red and Goin' Down," "Would You Lay with Me (In a Field of Stone)," and "The Man That Turned My Mama On." Although a few singles Columbia released after Tucker left the label are missing, all of the highlights from her stint at the label are included here. — *Thom Owens*

The Tune Wranglers

Western Swing
During the 1930s, the Tune Wranglers were a very popular band in San Antonio, TX. Although the band recorded six sides between 1936 and 1938, its members were content to remain merely a local sensation, considering themselves cowboys first and musicians second. The Wranglers were founded in 1935 by guitarist/singer Buster Coward, banjo picker Eddie Fielding, and fiddler/singer Charlie Gregg. Fielding remained for less than a year and was replaced by Joe "Red Brown" Barnes. Like many Texas swing players of their era, the Wranglers played pop-flavored cowboy tunes and traditional country music. Their best-known recorded song was "Texas Sand," which was penned by Coward. — *Sandra Brennan*

The Tune Wranglers / Texas Rose ✦✦✦✦
● **1936-1938** / Texas Rose ✦✦✦✦
Featured are "El Rancho Grande," "Black-Eyed Susan," "Hawaiian Honeymoon," and others. — *AMG*

Shania Twain

b. Aug. 28, 1965, Timmins, Ontario, Canada
Vocals / Contemporary Country
Emerging in the mid-'90s, Shania Twain (pronounced shu-NYE-uh) became the most popular country music artist since Garth Brooks. Skillfully fusing mainstream AOR rock production with country-pop, Twain and her producer/husband Robert John "Mutt" Lange created a commercial juggernaut with her second album, *The Woman in Me*. The record became a multi-platinum phenomenon, peaking at No. 5 on the pop charts and eventually selling more than nine million copies in America alone. Twain might have sold a lot of records, but like other mega-selling acts before her, she earned few good reviews. Most critics accused her of diluting country with bland, anthemic hard rock techniques and with shamelessly selling her records with sexy videos. Fans ignored such complaints, mainly because her audience was comprised of many listeners who had grown accustomed to such marketing strategies by constant exposure to MTV. And Twain, in many ways, was the first country artist to fully exploit MTV's style. She created a sexy, video-oriented image—she didn't even tour during the year when *The Woman in Me* was on top of the country charts—that appealed not only to the country audience, but to pop fans. In turn, she became a country music phenomenon.

Shania Twain was born in Windsor, Ontario, and raised in the small, rural town of Timmins, Ontario. She learned to play guitar at an early age and would spend much of her time singing, writing, and playing. Early on in her musical development, her parents pushed her on stage, making her perform frequently around their little town; often, she would be pulled out of bed around one in the morning to sing at local bars, since as a child, she could appear in the clubs only after they had stopped serving alcohol. She also sang on local radio and television stations and at community events. When she was 21 years old, both of her parents died in an car crash, forcing her to take responsiblity for her four younger brothers. In order to pay the bills and keep food on the table, she took a job singing at a resort in Deerhurst. With the money she earned at the resort, she bought a house and had the family settle down.

At the resort, she sang showtunes from George Gershwin to Andrew Lloyd Webber, as well as a little country. Twain stayed there for three years, at the end of which all of her siblings had begun lives of their own. When she was finally independent again, she assembled a demo tape of her songs, and her manager set up a showcase concert in Canada. Twain caught the attention of a few insiders with the concert, and within a few months, Mercury Nashville had signed her to their roster. Her eponymous debut album was released in 1993; although it wasn't a major hit, it performed respectably in the United States, launching two minor hit singles, "What Made You Say That" and "Dance with the One That Brought You". In Europe the album was more successful, and Country Music Television Europe named her Rising Video Star of the Year.

Shortly after the release of *Shania Twain*, the singer met and fell in love with Robert John "Mutt" Lange, a hard rock producer known for his work with AC/DC, Def Leppard, Foreigner, and the Cars. Lange had been wanting to move into country music for a while, and after hearing Twain's debut album, he decided to get in contact with her with the intention of working on an album. By the end of the year, the pair had married and begun working on her second record. The two either wrote or co-wrote the material that eventually formed *The Woman in Me*.

The Woman in Me was released in the spring of 1995. Its first single, "Whose Bed Have Your Boots Been Under?" went to No. 11 early in the year, quickly followed by "Any Man of Mine," which became her first No. 1 single in the spring. The album's title track went to No. 14 in the fall, while the fourth single, "(If You're Not in It for Love) I'm Outta Here!," rocketed to No. 1 toward the end of the year. Early in 1996 "No One Needs to Know" became her third No. 1 hit. By the beginning of 1996, *The Woman in Me* had sold more than six million copies and broken the record for the most weeks spent at No. 1 on the country charts. During the course of 1996, it would rack up another three million in sales. — *Stephen Thomas Erlewine*

Shania Twain / Apr. 20, 1993 / Mercury ✦✦✦
Shania Twain's eponymous debut album was a bland set of contemporary country that demonstrated her considerable vocal abilities but none of the spark that informed her breakthrough, *The Woman in Me*. Part of the problem is that none of the songs is well constructed, and each leans towards soft-rock instead of country or country-rock. By and large, the songs lack strong melodies, so they have to rely on Twain's vocal skills; although she is impressive, she is too showy to make any of these mediocre songs stick. It's a promising debut, largely because it showcases her fine vocal skills, but it isn't engaging enough to be truly interesting outside of a historical context. — *Thom Owens*

● **The Woman in Me** / 1995 / Mercury ✦✦✦✦
Shania Twain's second album broke down the doors of stardom for the singer, selling more than four million copies by the beginning of 1996. Like many country artists of the mid-'90s, Twain's music combined country conventions with mainstream rock flourishes, creating a sound that appealed to both audiences. *The Woman in Me* isn't necessarily flawless product—the material is a bit inconsistent, and the music plays it a bit too safe—but it all sounds convincing, thanks to the dynamic charisma of Shania Twain. — *Stephen Thomas Erlewine*

Conway Twitty (Harold Lloyd Jenkins)

b. Sep. 1, 1933, Friars Point, MS, d. Jun. 5, 1993, Branson, MO
Guitar, Vocals / Traditional Country, Country-Pop, Rockabilly, Nashville Sound/Countrypolitan
Originally a '50s rock 'n' roll singer, Conway Twitty became the reigning country superstar of the '70s and '80s, racking up a record 40 No. 1 hits over the course of two decades. With his deep, resonant down-home voice, Twitty was one of the smoothest bal-

ladeers to work in Nashville during the country-pop era, but he was also one of the most adventurous. More than any other singer, he was responsible for selling country as "adult" music, slipping sexually suggestive lyrics into his lush productions, but never singing misogynist lyrics. By and large, his songs were sensitive and sensual, which is part of the reason he achieved such great success. After Twitty reached the top of the country charts in the late '60s, he stayed there for years on end, releasing a consistent stream of Top Ten hits that both defined and expanded the limitations of country-pop by adding subtle R&B, pop, and rock 'n' roll influences. Though he had some pop success, Twitty remained country to the core. Occasionally, his song titles were simply too corny, which was why he retained his popularity until his death in 1993.

The son of a riverboat captain, Conway Twitty was born in Mississippi and raised in Helena, AR, where he learned to love not only country, but blues and gospel. When he was ten years old, he joined his first group, the Phillips Country Ramblers, who occasionally performed on local radio. Despite his interest in music, he originally planned to become a professional baseball player. Jenkins was talented enough to be offered a contract by the Philadelphia Phillies, but he was unable to join the team, because he was drafted into the Army during the Korean War. While he was serving in the Far East, he sang with a country band called the Cimarrons. Returning to America in 1956, Jenkins still had an open offer to join the Phillies, but he decided to pursue a musical career after he heard Elvis Presley.

With dreams of recording for Sun Records, Harold Jenkins headed to Memphis, where Sam Phillips did indeed sign him to a recording contract, but none of the tracks he cut was ever released. Jenkins' biggest contribution to the label was writing "Rockhouse," a minor hit for Roy Orbison. Leaving Sun in late 1956, he set out on a rockabilly package tour, during which he invented the stage name of Conway Twitty by combining the names of Arkansas and Texas cities. At the beginning of 1957 he signed to Mercury Records, where he released a handful of singles that didn't make much of an impact, though "I Need Your Lovin'" scraped the very bottom of the pop charts. In 1958 he moved to MGM Records, where he finally achieved success with "It's Only Make Believe," a song he had written with Jack Nance. Recorded with vocal support by Presley's backup group the Jordanaires, "It's Only Make Believe" became a major hit, spending two weeks at No. 1 and going gold. Over the course of 1959 and 1960, Twitty released a number of singles, the most popular of which were the Top TEn "Danny Boy" and "Lonely Blue Boy," and he appeared in the B-movies *Sex Kittens Go to College, Platinum High School,* and *College Confidential.*

Twitty's rock 'n' roll fame arrived suddenly, and it went away just as quickly. By the beginning of 1961 his singles had stopped entering the Top 40. Nevertheless, he continued to tour; but soon MGM dropped him from their roster. Signing with ABC-Paramount, he began to add more country songs to his repertoire, but he was still recording primarily pop material. When Ray Price took Twitty's "Walk Me to the Door" to the country Top Ten, Conway decided he wanted to become a country singer, but he didn't actively pursue that avenue until 1965, when he walked out in the middle of a concert at a New Jersey nightclub. By the end of 1965 Twitty had begun a collaboration with record producer Owen Bradley, one of the cornerstones of the Nashville sound, and had signed to Decca Records. In the spring of the next year, he released his first country single, "Guess My Eyes Were Bigger than My Heart," which peaked at No. 18. For the next two years he had four minor hits, finally breaking into the Top Ten with "The Image of Me" in the spring of 1968, followed a few months later by his first No. 1 hit, "Next in Line." For the next four years, he had a string of 12 Top Five singles for Decca, eight of which—including "I Love You More Today," "To See My Angel Cry," "Hello Darlin'," "Fifteen Years Ago," and "How Much More She Can Stand"—were No. 1 hits.

In late 1970 he began a professional relationship with Loretta Lynn, releasing their first duet, "After the Fire Are Gone," early in 1971. The record became the first of five straight No. 1 country hits, which included "Lead Me On," "Louisana Woman, Mississippi

Man," "As Soon as I Hang Up the Phone," and "Feelin's." Over the course of the decade, Lynn and Twitty coninued to work together, releasing one album a year and racking up a total of 14 Top Ten hits; they also won four Duo of the Year awards from the Country Music Association, three Vocal Group of the Year honors from the Academy of Country Music, and one Grammy for Best Vocal Performance by a Group ("After the Fire Is Gone").

Twitty's solo career continued to thrive alongside his duets with Lynn. In 1973 Decca was absorbed by MCA Records, and all of his new records were released on MCA. The changeover in labels happened to coincide with an increased suggestiveness in much of his material, including the major hit single "You've Never Been This Far Before," which spent three weeks at No. 1 during the summer of 1973, despite having been banned by several radio stations. Not all of his songs were as explicitly sexual, but they all had an adult theme and the layered, string-laden production was designed for a more mature audience, who bought Twitty records in droves. Until 1983 he had a remarkably consistent string of Top Ten singles for Decca, most of which hit No. 1. Among his best-known hits from this era were "I See the Want To in Your Eyes," "Linda in My Mind," "Touch the Hand," "After All the Good is Gone," "I've Already Loved You in My Mind," "Happy Birthday Darlin'," "Tight Fittin' Jeans," and "Red Neckin' Love Makin' Night." As he continued to rule the charts, Twitty expanded into other business ventures, including banking, property, a booking agency, and a theme park called Twitty City. The size of his international popularity was confirmed when he re-recorded "Hello Darlin'" in Russian for a joint American/Soviet space mission.

In late 1981 he moved briefly to Elektra, where he released several hit singles, many of which were pop covers like the Pointer Sisters' "Slow Hand" and Bette Midler's "The Rose." Twitty signed with Elektra in 1983, where he had a string of hits over the next three years. Again, he covered several pop songs—the Eagles' "Heartache Tonight," the Commodores' "Three Times a Lady"—but he kept recording country songs, including the No. 1s "Somebody's Needin' Somebody," "I Don't Know a Thing About Love (The Moon Songs)," "Don't Call Him a Cowboy," and "Desperado Love," a 1986 chart-topper that proved to be his last No. 1.

Twitty returned to MCA in 1987, releasing the back-to-back No. 2 hits "Julia" and "I Want to Know You Before We Make Love." Though he continued to have Top Ten hits through the end of the decade, his success began to slip slightly in the early '90s, as "new country" forced older performers off the top of the charts. Nevertheless, he remained quite popular, selling both records and concert tickets, until his sudden death from an abdominal aneurysm in the summer of 1993. Immediately after his death, he was praised and mourned by all quarters of the public, not just country music fans, and his record of more than 40 No. 1 hits remains unlikely to be surpassed. —*Stephen Thomas Erlewine*

Conway Twitty's Greatest Hits / 1960 / MGM ♦♦♦

These are the songs that helped make Conway Twitty a household name (and inspire the character Conrad Birdie in the musical *Bye Bye Birdie*.) This stuff still holds a thrill more than 30 years later. Also, the liner notes, while not entirely accurate, are still a lot of fun. Check out Twitty's Vital Statistics. —*Jim Worbois*

Conway Twitty / 1965 / MGM ♦♦♦♦

One of early rock 'n' roll's most soulful and dramatic singers, he was inspired by Elvis Presley, but with a country-gospel edge all his own. This includes his biggest hits, the self-penned "It's Only Make Believe," along with "Lonely Blue Boy" and the great gospel-tinged "I'll Try." —*George Bedard*

Conway Twitty Sings / 1965 / Decca ♦♦♦

It includes his first country hit, Liz Anderson's "Guess My Eyes Were Bigger than My Heart," and a version of "Truck Drivin' Man" that could duke it out with Buck Owens' and win. —*George Bedard*

Look into My Teardrops / 1966 / Decca ♦♦♦

A great version of "Almost Persuaded" beats David Houston's No. 1 hit version all to hell. Twitty also cuts Webb Pierce with a searing "There Stands the Glass." Good covers of some George Jones songs are included, too. —*George Bedard*

Hello Darlin' / 1970 / Decca ✦✦✦✦
This is Twitty's finest hour as a country singer and songwriter. The great title track is included, plus "Up Comes the Bottle" and "I'm So Used to Loving You." He's at his C&W vocal peak on this one, and almost all of the material is good—even forgive the inclusion of "Rocky Top." —*George Bedard*

★ **Greatest Hits, Vol. 1** / 1972 / MCA ✦✦✦✦✦
Every one of these songs was a Top Ten hit, and this 1972 package goes a long way to explain Twitty's appeal. There's not a weak track on this record. Smaller hits like "I Wonder What She'll Think About Me Leaving?" and "Image of Me" are every bit as good as the monster hits. —*Jim Worbois*

You've Never Been This Far Before / 1973 / MCA ✦✦✦
When the title track was issued as a single in 1973, many stations banned it for being too suggestive. That aside, this is a fine album. Even the songs that have been done over and over (like "Seasons of My Heart" and "Above and Beyond") sound fresh. —*Jim Worbois*

Greatest Hits, Vol. 2 / 1976 / MCA ✦✦✦✦
Greatest Hits, Vol. 2 is a fine summation of Conway's early '70s hits, including "You've Never Been This Far Before," "There's a Honky Tonk Angel (Who'll Take Me Back In)," and "I See the Want To in Your Eyes," among others. —*Thom Owens*

The Very Best of Conway Twitty / 1978 / MCA ✦✦✦
Released in 1978, *The Very Best of Conway Twitty* contains several of his biggest hits from the early and mid-'70s, including "Hello Darlin'," and as such it is an enjoyable listen, but it has been supplanted by better, more comprehensive compilations such as *20 Greatest Hits*. —*Stephen Thomas Erlewine*

☆ **The Very Best of Conway & Loretta** / 1979 / MCA ✦✦✦✦
Lust and guilt and stunning soulful harmonizing by Twitty and Loretta Lynn from the early to mid-'70s. Featured is stupendous country vocalizing in a honky tonk vein. —*Mark A. Humphrey*

Crosswinds / 1979 / MCA ✦✦✦
Not a great Twitty album, it still has its moments. This album does feature two hits ("Don't Take It Away" and "Happy Birthday Darlin'"), as well as "Heavy Tears," a fine John Hiatt song that Hiatt has yet to release. —*Jim Worbois*

Number Ones [MCA] / 1982 / MCA ✦✦✦✦
After moving from rock 'n' roll to country, Twitty remained sensitive to criticism he might not be serious, rarely deviating from the standard three-chord country song for about his first decade in the format. This package, which selects material almost randomly from 1975-1981, does a good job of showing a Twitty more willing to experiment, particularly with the soulful "Don't Take It Away" and the dramatic "I May Never Get to Heaven." —*Tom Roland*

☆ **20 Greatest Hits** / 1987 / MCA ✦✦✦✦✦
20 Greatest Hits covers a large portion of Conway Twitty's biggest hits from the '70s and '80s, from "Hello Darlin'" to "Red Neckin' Love Makin' Night," making it an excellent retrospective and introduction to his long, prolific career. —*Stephen Thomas Erlewine*

Borderline / 1987 / MCA ✦✦
Borderline includes the hits "Julia," "I Want to Know You Before We Make Love," and "That's My Job." —*Jason Ankeny*

Still in Your Dreams / 1988 / MCA ✦✦✦
The Top Ten hits "Goodbye Time," "Saturday Night Special" (with harmonies by Vince Gill), and "I Wish I Was Still in Your Dreams" are among the featured cuts on *Still in Your Dreams*. —*Jason Ankeny*

Number Ones: The Warner Brothers Years / 1988 / Warner Brothers ✦✦✦
This greatest-hits set shows (with the exception of "The Rose") an artist in command of his own performance, with a clear grasp on quality material and a strong sense of powerful arrangements. —*Tom Roland*

Making Believe / 1988 / MCA ✦✦✦
A reunion of early '70s hitmakers (Twitty and Loretta Lynn) proves they're still in fine form. —*Mark A. Humphrey*

Conway Twitty

House on Old Lonesome Road / 1989 / MCA ✦✦
House on Old Lonesome Road leads off with "She's Got a Single Thing in Mind," the energizing hit that reaffirmed Twitty's standing among the era's country giants. —*Jason Ankeny*

Crazy in Love / 1990 / MCA ✦✦
Crazy in Love generated a pair of Top Three hits, "I Couldn't See You Leavin'" and the title cut. —*Jason Ankeny*

Greatest Hits, Vol. 3 / 1990 / MCA ✦✦✦
Greatest Hits, Vol. 3 runs through Conway Twitty's big hits from his second stint at MCA Records in the late '80s. The collection includes the Top Ten hits "Julia," "I Want to Know You Before We Make Love," "That's My Job," "Goodbye Time," "Saturday Night Special," "I Wish I Was Still in Your Dreams," and "She's Got a Single Thing in Mind." —*Stephen Thomas Erlewine*

☆ **Silver Anniversary Collection** / 1990 / MCA ✦✦✦✦
Twenty-five hits from Twitty's work for MCA and Warner Bros. are on this album, from "Guess My Eyes Were Bigger than My Heart" (1966) to "She's Got a Single Thing in Mind" (1989). It's an excellent introduction to one of the most popular singers in country music history. —*AMG*

The Best of Conway Twitty, Vol. 1: The Rockin' Years / 1991 / Polygram ✦✦✦✦
The Best of Conway Twitty, Vol. 1: The Rockin' Years contains all of the recordings he made for Mercury Records in the late '50s, when he was trying to follow in the footsteps of Elvis. Naturally, there's a lot of rockabilly on this collection—which he did very well—as well as some ballads that hint at his future country career. In between are some of his very best moments, including "It's Only Make Believe," "Mona Lisa," "Is A Bluebird Blue," and "Lonely Blue Boy." —*Stephen Thomas Erlewine*

Even Now / 1991 / MCA ✦✦✦
"She's Got a Man on Her Mind" and "Who Did They Think He Was" are the hits included on *Even Now*. —*Jason Ankeny*

Final Touches / 1993 / MCA ✦✦✦
Produced by Don Cook, *Final Touches* has its moments, but it seems a less fitting swan song for Twitty than his princely duet with Sam Moore on the *Rhythm Country and Blues* album. —*Dan Cooper*

Rockin' Conway: The MGM Years / Oct. 19, 1993 / Mercury ✦✦✦✦

At a mere ten songs, it's too brief, but it includes "It's Only Make Believe," a rocked-out version of "Danny Boy," and "Is a Blue Bird Blue?," the first major cut for songwriting legend Dan Penn. —*Dan Cooper*

☆ **The Conway Twitty Collection** / 1994 / MCA ✦✦✦✦✦

The Conway Twitty Collection is a stellar four-disc box set that contains every essential track he ever recorded. Beginning with some early recordings—including a cut from when he was a pre-teen—the set runs through every hit from 1958's "It's Only Make Believe" to 1993's "I'm the Only Thing (I'll Hold Against You)." Several rarities are scattered throughout, but the true treasure of the compilation is the simple fact that it contains the great major-ity of his Top Ten hits, including his duets with Loretta Lynn. It is a lasting testament to his considerable talents. —*Stephen Thomas Erlewine*

Country Classics / Oct. 15, 1996 / Critique ✦✦✦

Country Classics is a budget-priced collection that features a few of Conway Twitty's biggest hits—including "It's Only Make Believe" and "You've Never Been This Far Before"—plus a spe-cially written personalized tribute to Twitty himself, which is available only on this compilation. Though there are a few hits here, the fidelity isn't very good, the selection is scattershot and missing several big hits, and the packaging is a little cheap. In short, it's all right for the budget-minded, but there are far better collections on the market. —*Stephen Thomas Erlewine*

T. Texas Tyler (David Luke Myrick)

b. Jun. 20, 1916, Mena, AR, **d.** Jan. 28, 1972, Springfield, MO
Vocals / Traditional Country

Charismatic singer-songwriter T. Texas Tyler was a successful fig-ure from the late '40s through the mid-'50s, credited with popular-izing the "country narrative record." He was born David Luke Myrick in Mena, AR, and from childhood aspired to become a country performer. As a young man, Tyler moved to Rhode Island to live with his brother, who was stationed there while serving in the Navy. He got his start working on a local radio station during the early 1930s and then spent much of the decade touring and singing on other stations, creating his stage name by combining the names of movie cowboy crooners Tex Ritter and Tom Tyler. While performing in Charleston, WV, in 1939, Tyler teamed up with fiddler Clarence Clere to become Slim and Tex. They remained together playing radio stations in West Virginia until 1942, when Tyler enlisted. After his discharge, Tyler went to southern California and began appearing daily on the radio in Long Beach and Los Angeles. In 1946 he made the Top Five with "Filipino Boy," followed by "Remember Me" and "Oklahoma Hills."

Tyler had his biggest single in 1948 with the enormously popu-lar "talking song" "Deck of Cards," which peaked in the Top Three. He followed it with a recitation of Mary Jean Shurtz' "Daddy Gave My Dog Away." In 1949 he sang a song in the West-ern *Horsemen of the Sierras;* later that year, he had a Top Five hit with "My Bucket's Got a Hole in It." Tyler had two more major hits in 1953, including "Courtin' in the Rain," and then went into a personal and professional slump with the advent of rock 'n' roll. In 1957 he joined the Grand Ole Opry and signed with Hank Snow Promotions. The next year he became a gospel singer and Assembly of God minister. Tyler spent the bulk of the 1960s tour-ing and preaching; he also recorded a gospel album for Capitol, a regular country album for Starday, and three independently pro-duced gospel albums that he sold at his revivals. After the death of his first wife, Claudia, in 1968, Tyler remarried and settled down in Springfield, MO, where he preached to a local congrega-

tion and performed occasionally. T. Texas Tyler died in early 1972 of stomach cancer. —*Sandra Brennan*

● **The Hits of T. Texas Tyler** / 1965 / Capitol ✦✦✦✦

Ian Tyson

b. Sep. 25, 1933, Victoria, British Columbia, Canada
Guitar, Vocals / Cowboy, Contemporary Folk, Americana

Half of the early 1960s folk group Ian and Sylvia, Ian Tyson retreated from performing and recording after the duo disbanded in the mid-'70s to become a rancher in the foothills of Southern Alberta, Canada. He quietly returned to music-making in the 1980s, releasing a series of albums that focused on detailed songs about the concerns of the working cowboy.

Tyson was born in Victoria, British Columbia. As a child he was involved in rodeo, not music. He didn't learn to play the guitar until he was recovering from rodeo-related injuries. In the late '50s he began performing as a folk singer. In 1961 he met singer-songwriter Sylvia Fricker, and the two musicians began perform-ing together; they also married three years later. Ian and Sylvia and their band, Great Speckled Bird, became popular on the folk scene and released a self-titled debut album in 1962. In 1963 they released *Four Strong Winds;* the title track, written by Tyson, became a folk standard. Ian and Sylvia successfully recorded together through the mid-'70s. The duo also began hosting a tele-vision show, "Nashville North," which became the "Ian Tyson Show" when the couple split up in the middle of the decade.

After Ian and Sylvia's breakup, Tyson recorded *Ol'Oen.* He tem-porarily retired from recording in 1979 to work his ranch, but he returned with *Old Corrals and Sagebrush* in 1983. In 1984 he toured with Ricky Skaggs and released an eponymous album. Tyson released a third album, *Cowboyography,* two years later, and in 1991 he released another popular Canadian album, *And Stood There Amazed,* which contained the hits "Springtime in Alberta" and "Black Nights." —*Sandra Brennan and Michael McCall*

Ian Tyson / 1984 / Stony Plain ✦✦✦✦

Cowboyography / 1987 / CCS ✦✦✦

One of the few Ian Tyson albums to be released in the United States, *Cowboyography* is also one of his best records, demon-strating his skill for melding traditional Western musical and lyri-cal themes with contemporary arrangements, productions, and sensibilities. —*Thom Owens*

I Outgrew the Wagon / 1989 / Stony Plain ✦✦✦✦

This is the best of his series of homegrown albums— simple, unadorned songs affectionately yet unromantically examining rural life on the Canadian plains, as well as a couple of philosoph-ical offerings. —*Michael McCall*

And Stood There Amazed / Feb. 1991 / Stony Plain ✦✦✦

Eighteen Inches of Rain / 1994 / Vanguard ✦✦✦✦

Tyson emerges from Canada to record an album with producer Jim Rooney in Nashville. The basic charms and wise observations remain, but they are brought into focus without detracting from the raw appeal of Tyson's purposefully casual style. —*Michael McCall*

All the Good 'Uns / 1996 / Stony Plain ✦✦✦✦

Ian Tyson is the undisputed master of traditional cowboy culture music and *All the Good 'Uns,* drawn from his five *Cowboyogra-phy* releases, removes any possible excuse for those who even casually appreciate roots music from being converted. Nineteen distinctive narratives of wide-eyed wonder, love of the land, and sagebrush wisdom conveyed through good, honest songs per-formed with integral simplicity. —*Roch Parisien*

● **Greatest Hits, Vol. 1** / Vanguard ✦✦✦✦

Greatest Hits, Vol. 2 / Vanguard ✦✦✦✦

U

Uncle Tupelo

Alternative Pop-Rock, Indie Rock, Alternative Country-Rock

With the release of their 1990 debut LP *No Depression*, the Belleville, IL, trio Uncle Tupelo launched more than simply their own career; by fusing the simplicity and honesty of country music with the bracing fury of punk, they kick-started a revolution that reverberated throughout the American underground. Thanks to a successful on-line site and subsequent fanzine that adopted the album's name, the tag "No Depression" became a catch-all for the like-minded artists who, along with Tupelo, signaled alternative rock's return to its country roots—at much the same time, ironically, that Nashville was itself embracing the slick gloss associated with mainstream rock and pop.

Uncle Tupelo was led by singers/songwriters Jay Farrar and Jeff Tweedy, lifelong friends born in the same Belleville hospital in 1967. During high school, the pair formed a punk cover band called the Primitives, along with drummer Mike Heidorn and Farrar's older brother, Wade. After Wade enlisted in the Army, the Primitives broke up, but in 1987 the remaining trio reunited, changed their name to Uncle Tupelo, and began incorporating elements of country into their music as well as writing original material. Touring constantly throughout the Midwest, the band members eventually quit school as their music became more and more successful, and in 1989 they signed a contract with the small independent label Rockville.

Taking its name from the A.P. Carter gospel song covered therein, *No Depression* reflected the band's disparate influences, ranging from everyone from Hank Williams to bluesman Leadbelly through to the famed postpunk trio Hüsker Dü. The most rock-centric of Uncle Tupelo's releases, its songs were meditations on small-town, small-time life, candid snapshots of days spent working thankless jobs and nights spent in an alcoholic fog. After the release of "I Got Drunk," a brilliant single backed with a cover of the Flying Burrito Brothers' "Sin City," 1991's *Still Feel Gone* struck a finer balance between their rock and country aims. While Farrar's contributions—sung in his reedy, Neil Young-like voice—were often informed by a rootsy, scorched-earth mentality, Tweedy's, with their grittier vocals, delved deeper into the trio's punk origins, as typified by the song "D. Boon," a tribute to the late frontman of the legendary Minutemen.

A year later, Uncle Tupelo released *March 16-20, 1992*, an acoustic record that saw the group plunging fully into country and folk. Recorded live in the studio with producer Peter Buck (of the band R.E.M.), the album drew heavily on painstakingly authentic covers of standards like "Moonshiner" and "Satan, Your Kingdom Must Come Down" along with a fitting rendition of the Louvin Brothers' "The Great Atomic Power" and Farrar and Tweedy's originals, which maintained the record's spare, haunting ambience. Shortly after its release, Mike Heidorn left the group to devote time to his family; he was replaced by drummer Ken Coomer, formerly of the group Clockhammer. Multi-instrumentalists Max Johnston and John Stirratt also signed on as part-time members.

In 1992 Uncle Tupelo signed to major label Sire/Reprise, and in 1993 issued the LP *Anodyne*. Widely regarded as the group's definitive statement, it was a true country-rock hybrid that accented the power of both musical forms. The album even featured a cover of the song "Give Back the Key to My Heart" sung with its writer, roots-rock pioneer Doug Sahm. After a tour in support of the album, however, the long-standing relationship between Farrar and Tweedy dissolved in bitter acrimony, and Uncle Tupelo disbanded. Shortly thereafter, Tweedy recruited Coomer, Johnston, and Stirratt to form the band Wilco, while Farrar reunited with Heidorn in Son Volt. *—Jason Ankeny*

No Depression / 1990 / Gasatanka ♦♦♦♦
Uncle Tupelo's landmark opening salvo is the group's most rock-oriented album, steeped more in breakneck speed, punk crunch, and guitar dissonance than any of their subsequent efforts. Indeed, despite the presence of mandolins, fiddles, and banjos—as well as the inclusion of the title track, a faithful cover of the A.P. Carter classic—the trio's vaunted country leanings are less musical than thematic on *No Depression*, thanks in large part to singers/songwriters Jay Farrar and Jeff Tweedy's acute depictions of rural, blue-collar life. Like the Replacements—never more obvious an influence than on this LP—Uncle Tupelo's songs paint grim, unrelenting portraits of aimless Midwestern existence, split between days working on the opening cut's "Factory Belt" and nights spent blurry-eyed and wasted ("Whiskey Bottle," "Before I Break"). Still, for all of the record's doleful cynicism—virtually every cut nods towards dashed hopes, broken promises, and paralyzing fear—there's an undeniable electricity afoot as well; by channeling the mournful clarity of country into the crackling fury of punk, *No Depression* brings new life to both musical camps. *—Jason Ankeny*

Still Feel Gone / 1991 / Gasatanka ♦♦♦
Still Feel Gone is Tupelo's transitional record; while it goes far in fusing the band's rock origins with their country aspirations, the alliance is often uneasy, even schizophrenic. Writers Jay Farrar and Jeff Tweedy are rarely in synch; while the former's contributions embrace roots music wholeheartedly, Tweedy's songs journey more deeply into rock than ever before; his opening track, "Gun," is the most straightforward pop number the trio ever recorded, while "D. Boon," a tribute to the fallen leader of the legendary post-punk trio the Minutemen, borders on thrash. While *Still Feel Gone* lacks the consistency of its predecessor, *No Depression*, it's a more wide-ranging record, deeper in maturity, subtlety, and texture—clear evidence of things to come. *—Jason Ankeny*

March 16-20, 1992 / 1992 / Gasatanka ♦♦♦♦
Produced by R.E.M.'s Peter Buck, *March 16-20, 1992* represents Uncle Tupelo's full evolution into a true country unit; with the exception of the eerie squalls of guitar feedback that haunt Jeff Tweedy's mesmerizing "Wait Up," there's virtually no evidence of the trio's punk heritage. Instead, the all-acoustic album—a combination of Tupelo originals and well-chosen traditional songs—taps into the very essence of backwoods culture, with its music rooted in the darkest corners of Appalachian life. An inescapable sense of dread grips this collection, from the large-scale threat depicted in the stunning rendition of the Louvin Brothers' "The Great Atomic Power" to the fatalism of the worker anthems "Grindstone" and "Coalminers;" even the character studies, including a

revelatory "Moonshiner," are relentlessly grim. A vivid glimpse of the harsh realities of rural existence, *March 16-20, 1992* is a brilliant resurrection of a bygone era of American folk artistry. *—Jason Ankeny*

★ **Anodyne** / May 1993 / Sire ✦✦✦✦✦
Uncle Tupelo never struck a finer balance between rock and country than on *Anodyne,* their major-label debut and parting shot. For all of the ill will undoubtedly simmering throughout these sessions, Jay Farrar and Jeff Tweedy have never before been more attuned to each other musically. Where earlier records often found the band's twin forces moving in opposing directions, *Anodyne* bears the full fruits of their shared vision. Recorded live in the studio, the LP encompasses and reinterprets not only country-rock (evidenced by the group's pairing with Doug Sahm on his "Give Back the Key to My Heart") but traditional country (the tribute to the songwriting legacy of "Acuff-Rose"), rock (the churning "The Long Cut," "Chickamauga"), and folk ("New Madrid," "Steal

the Crumbs"), the band's reach never once exceeding its grasp. *—Jason Ankeny*

Uncle Walt's Band

Progressive Country, Contemporary Folk, Americana
Uncle Walt's Band pioneered a new form of progressive Southern folk music. It featured Walter Hyatt, David Ball, and Champ Hood. They combine complex harmonies and acoustic swing rhythm, producing a unique form of music. *—Chip Renner*

● **An American in Texas Revisited** / 1980 / Sugar Hill ✦✦✦✦
Compilation of *An American in Texas* (1980) and *Live* (1982). The band members are well suited to one another. Walter's vocals are great. *—Chip Renner*

The Girl on the Sunny Shore / 1980 / Sugar Hill ✦✦✦
This is a compilation of a 1975 release (*Uncle Walt's Band*) and a 1988 release (*6-26-79*). Very good. Features some great vocals and Champs' great fiddle. *—Chip Renner*

V

Joe Val

b. Jun. 25, 1926, Everett, MA, **d.** Jun. 11, 1985
Vocals / Bluegrass, Traditional Folk
Singer-songwriter Joe Val was a prominent traditional bluegrass musician and leader of the New England Bluegrass Boys. A native of Everett, MA, he was born Joseph Valiante, and his interest in bluegrass started in his early teens. He was influenced by fiddler Tex Logan, who had come north to study at M.I.T. and wound up giving the young performer his stage name. Val started out as a guitar player, but he also mastered the banjo and the mandolin. He got his professional start playing with the Radio Rangers and later joined the Berkshire Mountain Boys; with the progressive Charles River Valley Boys, Val recorded a distinguished album of bluegrass-adapted Beatles songs in 1967. Although Val played with progressive groups, he continued to favor a more traditional bluegrass sound; to this end, he founded the New England Bluegrass Boys in 1970 with guitarist Herb Applin, banjo player Bob French, and bass player Bob Tidwell. The next year, they made their debut album. Although the group underwent many personnel changes in the next decade, Val was able to produce a remarkably consistent sound over the course of numerous albums. Sadly, Joe Val was stricken with cancer in the 1980s just as his band was beginning to achieve wider recognition; his last performance was in late 1984, and he died June 11, 1985. — *Sandra Brennan*

● **Diamond Joe** / Oct. 17, 1995 / Rounder ♦♦♦♦
Joe Val's strong, penetrating tenor voice and hearty mandolin work is showcased on Rounder's recent album *Diamond Joe*, which compiles 25 recordings from the '70s and '80s (Val died in 1985) and serves as an excellent Joe Val primer. — *Kurt Wolff*

One Morn in May / 1996 / Rounder ♦♦♦

Leroy Van Dyke

b. Oct. 4, 1929, Spring Fork, MO
Vocals / Traditional Country, Country-Pop, Nashville Sound/ Countrypolitan
Singer-songwriter Leroy Van Dyke was best known for penning the country novelty standard "Auctioneer" and the country-pop smash "Walk On By," his biggest hit. Born in Missouri, Van Dyke originally wanted to be a farmer, and he earned a BS in agriculture at the University of Missouri, which was where he first began playing guitar. After graduation Van Dyke worked as a newspaper reporter and later as an auctioneer. While stationed in Korea, he began performing for his peers and wrote "Auctioneer," which was dedicated to his cousin. After military service, Van Dyke returned to journalism in Chicago. In 1956 he entered WGN Chicago's talent contest and sang "Auctioneer." Deejay Buddy Black signed up as Van Dyke's manager and slipped in a document giving him co-writing credits and half the royalties for the song, which made the pop charts later that year and appeared on the country charts in early 1957, where it climbed to the Top Ten. The next year, Van Dyke began appearing on Red Foley's *Ozark Jubilee* television show.

In 1961 Van Dyke went to Nashville and signed to Mercury, where he released "Walk On By." It went right to the top of the country charts and remained there for 19 weeks; it also crossed over to the Top Five on the pop charts. Its success was followed with another major crossover hit, "If a Woman Answers (Hang Up the Phone)," and the Top 40 "Black Cloud." In 1962 Van Dyke joined the Grand Ole Opry. His next few Mercury releases reached only the middle of the charts, and in 1965 he signed to Warner Brothers and had Top 40 success with "Roses from a Stranger." In 1967 Van Dyke appeared in the film *What Am I Bid?* He recorded throughout the decade but hit the charts only with "Louisville" in 1968. In 1977 he notched one final minor hit, "Texas Tea." Later that year he also released two albums, *Gospel Greats* and *Rock Relics*, both produced by old friend Shelby Singleton. In 1982 he resurfaced with a self-titled effort. — *Sandra Brennan*

Leroy Van Dyke's Greatest Hits / 1969 / Kapp ♦♦♦♦

Leroy Van Dyke: The Original Auctioneer / 1988 / Bear Family ♦♦♦♦

● **Hits and Misses** / 1994 / Bear Family ♦♦♦♦
While *The Auctioneer* contained the highlights of Leroy Van Dyke's '50s hits for Dot, *Walk on By* concentrates on his early '60s singles for Mercury, including "If a Woman Answers (Hang Up the Phone)," "Black Cloud," "Happy to Be Unhappy," and the title track, which spent an extraordinary 19 weeks at the top of the country charts. By and large, the material on *Walk on By* is stronger than that on *The Auctioneer*, making it an excellent introduction to this talented singer. — *Thom Owens*

Ricky Van Shelton

b. 1952, Danville, VA
Guitar, Vocals / Contemporary Country
Noted for his rich baritone voice, Ricky Van Shelton became an overnight country music sensation in the late '80s. Between 1987 and 1994, he had more than 13 No. 1 hits. Van Shelton was raised in Grit, VA, and grew up listening to gospel music. As a teen, he was interested in pop music and had little interest in country music until his brother convinced him to become the lead vocalist in his country band. After his wife got a job in Nashville, he moved there in the mid-'80s; shortly after his arrival, he began playing local clubs. In 1986 he signed with Columbia Records. Van Shelton's debut single, the title track from his album *Wild Eyed Dream*, hit the Top Ten, beginning a streak of Top Ten hits that ran for several years. During this time, he had No. 1 hits with "Somebody Lied" (1987), "I'll Leave This World Loving You" (1988), "From a Jack to a King" (1989), and "I've Cried My Last Tear for You" (1990). In 1991 he and Dolly Parton had a chart-topper with "Rockin' Years." Van Shelton's first four albums went platinum. By the mid-'90s, his popularity had slipped somewhat, however, and he had trouble cracking the country Top 40. Despite his declining record sales, he remained a popular concert attraction. — *Sandra Brennan*

Wild-Eyed Dream / 1987 / Columbia ♦♦♦
This debut from this country hunk balladeer, with occasional thumpin' at the hop, contains "Working Man's Blues," "Crime of Passion," and more. — *Mark A. Humphrey*

Loving Proof / 1988 / Columbia ✦✦✦✦
Here are stabs at rockabilly alongside the ballads at which Shelton excels. Some of the songs on the album are "From a Jack to a King," and "Hole in My Pocket." *–Mark A. Humphrey*

RVS 3 / 1990 / Columbia ✦✦✦
The third album puts out more sounds in the winning Shelton formula, such as "I Still Love You," "I've Cried My Last Tear for You," "Oh Pretty Woman," and more. *–Mark A. Humphrey*

Don't Overlook Salvation / Jun. 1990 / Columbia ✦✦
Featured are "The Old Rugged Cross, " "The Mansion in the Sky," "Just as I Am," and others. *–AMG*

Backroads / 1991 / Columbia ✦✦✦✦
When he's not trying to be Roy Orbison (as he did on 1990's *RVS 3*), it's easy to see that Van Shelton's a fine singer. And this is a fine record–so fine it's tempting to hunt for signs of listener manipulation. But Van Shelton balances the self-pity of songs like "After the Lights Go Out" with the uptempo punch of stuff like "Call Me Up." So even though Van Shelton recycles "Rockin' Years," the duet from Dolly Parton's *Eagle When She Flies*, just call it good taste, sit back, and enjoy. *–Brian Mansfield*

● **Greatest Hits Plus** / 1992 / Columbia ✦✦✦✦
Despite rocking hits like "Wild Man," and "I Am a Simple Man" (or even the new cover of Elvis Presley's Wear My Ring Around Your Neck"), Ricky Van Shelton's greatest-hits collection shows that he's made his best records as a balladeer raised on stone-country gospel. For proof, just listen to "Just As I Am," "I'll Leave This World Loving You," or "Keep It Between the Lines." *–Brian Mansfield*

Bridge I Didn't Burn / 1993 / Columbia ✦✦✦

Love and Honor / Nov. 1, 1994 / Columbia ✦✦✦

Super Hits / 1996 / Columbia ✦✦✦✦

Super Hits, Vol. 2 / Sony ✦✦✦✦
Super Hits, Vol. 2 is a nice budget-line collection that features six of Ricky Van Shelton's Top Five hits among its ten tracks, as well as rare covers of "Oh Pretty Woman," and "Wear My Ring Around Your Neck." For the very casual fan, *Super Hits, Vol. 2* may be satisfactory, but it'll leave many listeners craving more material. *–Thom Owens*

Townes Van Zandt

b. 1944, Fort Worth, TX, **d.** Jan. 1, 1997
Guitar, Vocals / Folk, Progressive Country, Country-Rock, Singer-Songwriter, Contemporary Folk, Americana
Townes Van Zandt's (b.March 7, 1944, Fort Worth, TX) music doesn't jump up and down, wear fancy clothes, or beat around the bush. Whether he's singing a quiet, introspective country-folk song or a driving, hungry blues, Van Zandt's lyrics and melodies are filled with the kind of haunting truth and beauty that you know instinctively. His music comes straight from his soul by way of a kind heart, an honest mind, and a keen ear for the gentle blend of words and melody. He can bring you down to a place so sad that you feel as if you're scraping bottom, but just as quickly he can lift your spirits and make you smile at the sparkle of a summer morning or a loved one's eyes–or raise a chuckle with a quick and funny talking blues. The magic of his songs is that they never leave you alone.

Despite his warm, dusty-sweet voice, as a singer Townes never had anything resembling a hit in his nearly 30-year recording career; he had a hard enough time simply keeping his records in print. Nonetheless he was widely respected and admired as one of the greatest country and folk artists of this generation. The long list of singers who've covered his songs includes Merle Haggard and Willie Nelson (who had a No. 1 country hit with "Pancho and Lefty" in 1983), Emmylou Harris, Jimmie Dale Gilmore, Nanci Griffith, Hoyt Axton, Bobby Bare, the Tindersticks, and the Cowboy Junkies.

Van Zandt was a Texan by birth and a traveler by nature. His father was in the oil business, and the family moved around a lot–Montana, Colorado, Minnesota, Illinois, among other places–which accounted for his sometimes vague answers to questions of where he "came from." Townes spent a couple of years in a military academy and a bit more time in college in Colorado before dropping out to become a folksinger. Van Zandt often returned to Colorado in subsequent years, spending entire summers, he said, alone in the mountains on horseback.)

Van Zandt moved to Houston and got his first paying gigs on the folk music circuit there in the mid-'60s. He played clubs like Sand Mountain and the Old Quarter (where in 1973 he recorded one of his finest albums, *Live at the Old Quarter*, released four years later), and he met singers such as Guy Clark (who became a lifelong friend and frequent road partner), Jerry Jeff Walker, and blues legend Lightnin' Hopkins, who had a large influence on Van Zandt's guitar playing in particular.

Another Texas songwriter, Mickey Newbury, saw Van Zandt in Houston one night and soon had him set up with a recording gig in Nashville (with Jack Clement producing). The sessions became Van Zandt's debut album, *For the Sake of the Song*, released in 1968 by Poppy Records. The next five years were the most prolific of his career, as Poppy released the albums *Our Mother the Mountain, Townes Van Zandt, Delta Mama Blues, High, Low and in-Between*, and *The Late, Great Townes Van Zandt*. These included such gems as "For the Sake of the Song," "To Live's to Fly," "Tecumseh Valley," "Pancho and Lefty," and many more that made him a legend in American and European songwriting circles.

Van Zandt moved to Nashville in 1976 at the urging of his new manager, John Lomax. He signed a new deal with Tomato Records and in 1977 released *Live at the Old Quarter*, a double album–and the first of several live recordings–that contained many of his finest songs. In 1978 Tomato released *Flyin' Shoes;* the long list of players on that album included Chips Moman and Spooner Oldham.

Van Zandt didn't record again for nearly a decade, but he continued to tour. He moved back to Texas briefly, returning again to Nashville in the mid-'80s. During the early '80s both "If I Needed You" and "Pancho and Lefty" became country radio hits. In 1987 Van Zandt was back in business with his eighth studio album, *At My Window*, which came out on his new label, Sugar Hill. By this time his voice had dropped to a lower register, but the weathered, somewhat road-weary edge to it was as pure and expressive as ever. Two years later Sugar Hill released *Live and Obscure* (recorded in a Nashville club in 1985), and two more live albums (*Rain on a Conga Drum* and *Rear View Mirror*) appeared on European labels in the early '90s. In 1990 Van Zandt toured with the Cowboy Junkies, and he wrote a song for them, "Cowboy Junkies Lament," that appeared on the group's *Black Eyed Man* (along with a song the Junkies wrote for him, "Townes Blues").

Sugar Hill released *Road Songs* in 1994, on which Van Zandt covered songs by Lightnin' Hopkins, Bruce Springsteen, the Rolling Stones, and others, all recorded off the sound board during concerts. At the end of that same year, Sugar Hill released *No Deeper Blue*, his first studio album since 1987. Van Zandt recorded it in Ireland with a group of Irish musicians. He sang every song but played guitar on only one. A year and a half after the release of *No Deeper Blue*, Townes Van Zandt died unexpectedly on January 1, 1997; he was 47 years old.

Van Zandt had re-recorded 60 of his songs for a planned career retrospective for Tomato Records. The collection, however, has yet to be released. *–Kurt Wolff*

For the Sake of the Song/First Album / 1968 / Poppy ✦✦✦
Produced by Jack Clement, Van Zandt's debut is unfortunately marred by inappropriate arrangements. Includes the first recordings of the title song and "Tecumseh Valley," along with obscure songs like "The Velvet Voices" and "Talkin' Karate Blues." Re-released by Rhino in 1993 as *First Album*. *–Kurt Wolff*

Our Mother the Mountain / 1969 / Tomato ✦✦✦✦
Weirdly heavy on the strings behind Van Zandt's sweet and smooth–but eternally haunted–voice, though in this case the arrangements work. Songs like "Kathleen," "St. John the Gambler," and the title track will last forever. *–Kurt Wolff*

Townes Van Zandt / 1969 / Tomato ✦✦✦✦
On his third album, Townes Van Zandt recut three crucial tracks from his debut album, "For the Sake of the Song," "Waiting Around to Die," and "I'll Be Here in the Morning." It was some

indication of the obscurity in which he remained enveloped, but no indication of the quality of his work. (Actually, Van Zandt re-recorded songs from his first album on his later ones because he disliked the earlier recordings.) As usual, his closely observed lyrics touched on desperate themes, notably in the mining ballad "Lungs," but they were still highly poetic, especially the album-closing "None but the Rain," which reflected on a failed relationship. Van Zandt's finger-picking was augmented by spare arrangements, usually featuring one added instrument, such as fiddle or flute, for color. (Originally released by Poppy Records in 1969, *Townes Van Zandt* was reissued by Tomato Records in 1989.) — *William Ruhlmann*

Delta Momma Blues / 1971 / Tomato ✦✦✦

Townes Van Zandt's dour viewpoint found more expression on his fourth album, its most characteristic song being "Come Tomorrow," on which he looked forward to how lonely life would be when his lover left. Even "Brand New Companion," which hailed the arrival of a lover, was done as a blues. "Here's to feeling good," he sang in "Only Him Or Me," then added, "Here's to feeling bad." But, as usual, what made Van Zandt so compelling was that in songs like "Rake" and "Nothin'," he painted despair so vividly. (Originally released by Poppy Records in 1970, *Delta Momma Blues* was reissued by Tomato Records in 1989.) — *William Ruhlmann*

High, Low and in Between / 1972 / Rhino ✦✦✦✦

Townes Van Zandt's fifth album was different from his first four, starting with the first few notes. Leadoff track "Two Hands" was an uptempo gospel number featuring piano and backup vocals. Van Zandt returned to religion in the country waltz "When He Offers His Hand," sang rock 'n' roll with a harmony vocal on "Standin'," tried a martial beat worthy of Johnny Cash on the gambling story song "Mr. Gold and Mr. Mudd," and even turned to comedy in "No Deal." The musical variety made *High, Low and in Between* a more interesting listen than Van Zandt's previous work, but what made it his best album since his debut was the quality of the songs, especially "You Are Not Needed Now" and "To Live Is to Fly." (Originally released by Poppy Records in 1971, *High Low and in Between* was reissued by Tomato Records in 1989.) — *William Ruhlmann*

The Late Great Townes Van Zandt / 1972 / Tomato ✦✦✦✦

On his sixth album in five years, Townes Van Zandt seemed to be getting less prolific, but his songwriting craft only improved. Van Zandt re-recorded yet another track from his debut album, "Sad Cinderella," and did three cover tunes, including one by main influence Hank Williams. But among the remaining seven new originals were "Pancho and Lefty," a sly Western story song about two outlaws, and "If I Needed You," among his most telling romantic statements. The two songs would become valuable copyrights for Van Zandt, and they made this oddly titled album one of his best, which was good since, as it happened, it would be his last release for five years. (Originally released by Poppy Records in 1972, *The Late, Great Townes Van Zandt* was reissued by Tomato Records in 1989.) — *William Ruhlmann*

★ **Live at the Old Quarter (Houston, Texas)** / 1977 / Tomato ✦✦✦✦✦

Townes Van Zandt is one of the most impressive songwriters to emerge in the 70s, and his extensive catalog is sufficiently consistent to be recommended in its entirety, once the listener has acquired a taste for his spare, dry delivery and gallows humor. The place to get that taste is on this live disc (originally a two-LP set), which features the best of Van Zandt's early songs, including "If I Needed You" and "Pancho and Lefty." — *William Ruhlmann*

Flyin' Shoes / 1978 / Rhino ✦✦✦

His songs are a bit overburdened by production, but the writing is still great. — *Richard Meyer*

At My Window / 1987 / Sugar Hill ✦✦✦✦

Van Zandt's first album after a long layoff found him in a more accessible musical setting, courtesy of producers Jack Clement and Jim Rooney, with his striking lyrical observations intact. Van Zandt's qualities are sometimes subtle, and this is an album that gets better every time it's listened to. — *William Ruhlmann*

Townes Van Zandt

Live and Obscure / 1989 / Sugar Hill ✦✦✦

Recorded live in Nashville in 1985, the sound quality is good, but the song choices are nothing new to Van Zandt fans. — *Kurt Wolff*

The Nashville Sessions / 1993 / Tomato ✦✦✦

When Poppy Records went bankrupt in 1973, it left Townes Van Zandt with two unreleased albums. One was *Live at the Old Quarter, Houston, Texas*, which was released by Tomato, Poppy's successor, in 1977. The other was a studio recording that languished for 20 years until being issued by Rhino/Tomato in 1993 under the title *The Nashville Sessions*. By that time, Van Zandt had put ten of its 12 songs on such albums as *Live at the Old Quarter*, *Flyin' Shoes*, *At My Window*, and *Live and Obscure*. Since six of them turned up on his next studio album, *Flyin' Shoes*, *The Nashville Sessions* acted as a kind of rough version of that album. Otherwise, one might have suspected that the songs came from before Van Zandt's sixth album, *The Late, Great Townes Van Zandt*, since they seemed to have more in common with his fifth album, *High, Low and in Between*. One of the two previously unheard songs, "Upon My Soul," was similar to the uptempo gospel tunes on that album. One also might have suspected that the songs could be outtakes from the fifth and sixth albums, since they were not quite up to the quality of those records. — *William Ruhlmann*

Rear View Mirror / 1993 / Sundown ✦✦✦

In 1990 Townes Van Zandt was working on a three-CD retrospective for which he was re-recording much of his repertoire. That album never appeared, but in 1993 the tiny Austin-based Sundown label released *Rear View Mirror*, a 17-track album running nearly 58 minutes and containing newly recorded versions of Van Zandt songs dating back to 1968. "Unique Instrumentation," a cover note read, though that seemed to consist of the occasional second guitar and a fiddle. (Sparse applause indicated the recording had been made in a club.) Many of Van Zandt's best-known songs were included—"Pancho and Lefty," "If I Needed You," "To Live Is to Fly," "Tecumseh Valley," and others—and while this was not the best set of recordings of those songs, the tendency of Van Zandt's albums to go out of print might mean this was the only one you would find in your nearest record bin, in which case the album was highly recommended. — *William Ruhlmann*

Roadsongs / 1994 / Sugar Hill ✦✦✦

An album of nothing but covers, recorded off the soundboards at various live dates. Includes "Ira Hayes," "Racing in the Streets," two Dylan songs, and four by Lightnin' Hopkins. — *Kurt Wolff*

No Deeper Blue / 1995 / Sugar Hill ✦✦✦
No Deeper Blue was Townes Van Zandt's first studio album of new material in seven years, and only his third in the 22 years since the release of his sixth album, *The Late, Great Townes Van Zandt*, in 1972. In that time, Van Zandt's subject matter had not changed much, as was apparent only a few lines into the leadoff track, "A Song For," when Van Zandt spoke-sang, "I'm weak and I'm weary of sorrow." In fact, he wasn't weary of enumerating the causes of sorrow, as was proved especially in "Marie," sung in the voice of a derelict whose life gets worse and worse until his pregnant girlfriend dies. Songs like that were typical of Van Zandt, but this time he also displayed an unusual range, from the scary, Calypso-like song of temptation, "The Hole" to the tall, weird tale of "Billy, Boney and Ma," in which a man and a skeleton turn to a life of crime. That song showed off Van Zandt's humorous side, as did "If I Was Washington," which would fit nicely into John Prine's repertoire. And Van Zandt even found room for two lullabies. Musically, the album, which was recorded in Ireland and produced by Philip Donnelly, who also played guitar, benefited from an unusually varied group of styles, from the Chicago blues of "Goin' Down to Memphis" to the Memphis rockabilly of "Gone Too Long," with a strong complement of Irish-flavored tunes played on such traditional instruments as Uileann pipes and tin whistle. The diverse musical styles made the album Van Zandt's most listenable, even when the lyrics were at their most desperate. By 1994, after a stream of live rerecordings of his older material, Van Zandt had begun to seem like a songwriter whose best songs, good as they were, were behind him. *No Deeper Blue* demonstrated that the muse was still with him. *— William Ruhlmann*

Rain on a Conga Drum: Live in Berlin / Nov. 7, 1995 / MMS ✦✦✦✦
This 18-track, 63-minute import disc was Townes Van Zandt's third live album, recorded in October 1990. It shared eight selections with his first, *Live at the Old Quarter, Houston, Texas*, and five with his second, *Live and Obscure*. Distinguishing this set were some interesting covers, including Lightnin' Hopkins' "Short-Haired Woman Blues" and the Rolling Stones' "Dead Flowers," a long, funny story concerning the composition of Van Zandt's most famous song, "Pancho and Lefty," and the otherwise unrecorded original "Catfish Song," a typically poetic and downcast Van Zandt composition. And, if you didn't have any of Van Zandt's other albums, discovering material like "If I Needed You," "To Live Is to Fly," and "Tecumseh Valley" would be a revelation. *— William Ruhlmann*

High, Low and in Between [EMI] / Sep. 1996 / EMI ✦✦✦✦
EMI's 1996 reissue of *High, Low and in Between*, although identically titled to the original 1972 release, is actually a two-fer combining *High, Low and in Between* and *The Late Great Townes Van Zandt* onto one disc. Be mindful of the difference between it and the original when shopping; by combining two of his most highly acclaimed albums, it's a considerably better bargain than the other vinyl or CD packages bearing the same title. *— Richie Unterberger*

The Vidalias

Alternative Country
One of the most promising bands of the insurgent country movement of the '90s, the Atlanta five-piece the Vidalias—named for Georgia's famous onions—blended country, rockabilly, bluesy rock, and occasional swing, deriving a sound that recalls the country-rock of the Flying Burrito Brothers and at times hints at the Western swing of Asleep at the Wheel. Led by the vocal, guitar, and songwriting talents of Charles Walston, the group included Henry Bruns on pedal steel guitar, bassist Jim Johnson, guitarist Page Waldrop, and David Michaelson—of the original Georgia Satellites—on drums. *— Jack Leaver*

Melodyland / 1995 / Upstart ✦✦✦✦
The debut album from this Georgia-born quintet manages to capture both the essence and spirit of classic country and the soulful rawness of early rock 'n' roll. Throughout the 11-song set, fun tunes like the catchy Western swing/rockabilly opener "Faking It" are mixed with sad ballads such as the second song, "Tokens of

Affliction." The latter begins with the lonesome wail of a harmonica and builds with the haunting and mournful cry of Henry Bruns' superb pedal steel guitar. When Charles Walston opens his mouth, it's a classic and earnest country delivery, reminiscent of Gram Parsons. Walston is a remarkable songwriting talent, able to indulge in wordplay without sounding trite and to supply melodies that sound instantly familiar, while remaining highly original. *— Jack Leaver*

● **Stayin' in the Doghouse** / Sep. 17, 1996 / Upstart ✦✦✦✦
The Vidalias' Charles Walston possesses a singing voice that bears an uncanny, almost frightening resemblance to his fellow Georgian Gram Parsons. At a time when it seems that everybody and his brother is dropping the country-rock pioneer's name as an influence, being saddled with the comparison could be considered more a curse than blessing. Walston and the other four Vidalias, however, need not worry. There's enough originality here to put to rest any notion that Walston and company are merely an imitation or a novelty. *Stayin' in the Doghouse*, the Vidalias' second album, is a 12-song collection continuing the great musicianship and first-rate songwriting of 1995's *Melodyland*. If anything, this record is slightly more consistent than that effort, with the band's sound more focused, due largely to the fact that Walston's songwriting has just gotten better. With a tip of the hat to country-era Byrds, the original Flying Burrito Brothers, and a straight-ahead roots-rock sensibility, *Stayin' in the Doghouse* is a pleasure throughout. Once again, pedal steel guitarist Henry Bruns demonstrates he's a force to be reckoned with, whether it be lightning-quick picking or weeping crescendos. Song highlights include the country-rockin' swagger of "Misery Loves Company," and the minor-keyed "Whose Side Are You On?" with Bruns copping a snippet of melody from the Western movie theme *The Good, the Bad and the Ugly* for effect. *— Jack Leaver*

Gene Vincent (Vincent Eugene Craddock)

b. Feb. 11, 1935, Norfolk, VA, **d.** Oct. 12, 1971, Los Angeles, CA
Vocals / Rock & Roll, Rockabilly
Gene Vincent had only one really big hit, "Be Bop a Lula," which epitomized rockabilly at its prime in 1956 with its sharp guitar breaks, spare snare drums, fluttering echo, and Vincent's breathless, sexy vocals. Yet his place as one of the great early rock 'n' roll singers is secure, backed up by a wealth of fine smaller hits and non-hits that rate among the best rockabilly of all time. The leather-clad, limping, greasy-haired singer was also one of rock's original bad boys, lionized by romanticists of past and present generations attracted to his primitive, sometimes savage style and indomitable spirit.

Vincent was bucking the odds by entering professional music in the first place. As a 20-year-old in the Navy, he suffered a severe motorcycle accident that almost resulted in the amputation of his leg and left him with a permanent limp and considerable chronic pain for the rest of his life. After the accident he began to concentrate on building a musical career, playing with country bands around Norfolk, VA. Demos cut at a local radio station, fronting a band assembled around him by his management, landed Gene Vincent and the Blue Caps a contract at Capitol, which hoped it had found competition for Elvis Presley.

Indeed it had, as by this time Vincent had plunged into all-out rockabilly, capable of both fast-paced exuberance and whispery, almost sensitive ballads. The Blue Caps were one of the greatest rock bands of the '50s, anchored at first by the stunning silvery, faster-than-light guitar leads of Cliff Gallup. The slap-back echo of "Be-Bop-a-Lula," combined with Vincent's swooping vocals, led many to mistake the singer for Elvis when the record first hit the airwaves in mid-1956, on its way to the Top Ten. The Elvis comparison wasn't entirely fair—Vincent had a gentler, less melodramatic style, capable of whipping up a storm or winding down to a hush.

Brilliant follow-ups like "Race with the Devil," "Bluejean Bop," and "B-I-Bickey, Bi, Bo-Bo-Go" failed to click in nearly as big a way, although these too are emblematic of rockabilly at its most exuberant and powerful. By the end of 1956 the Blue Caps were beginning to undergo the first of constant personnel changes that would continue throughout the '50s, the most crucial loss being the departure of Gallup. The 35 or so tracks he cut with the band—many of which showed up only on albums or B-sides—were unquestionably Vincent's greatest work, as his subsequent recordings would never again capture their pristine clarity and uninhibited spontaneity.

Vincent had his second and final Top 20 hit in 1957 with "Lotta Lovin'," which reflected his increasingly tamer approach to production and vocals, the wildness and live atmosphere toned down in favor of poppier material, more subdued guitars, and conventional-sounding backup singers. He recorded often for Capitol throughout the rest of the '50s, and it's unfair to dismiss those sides out of hand; they were respectable, occasionally exciting, rockabilly, a disappointment only in comparison with his earliest work. His act was captured for posterity in one of the best scenes of one of the first Hollywood films to feature rock 'n' roll stars, *The Girl Can't Help It*.

Live, Vincent continued to rock the house with reckless intensity and showmanship, and he became particularly popular overseas. A 1960 tour of Britain, though, brought tragedy when his friend Eddie Cochran, who shared the bill on Vincent's UK shows, died in a car accident in which Vincent was also involved. By the early '60s his recordings had become much more sporadic and lower in quality, and his chief audience was in Europe, particularly in England (where he lived for a while) and France.

His Capitol contract expired in 1963, and he spent the rest of his life recording for several other labels, none of which got him close to that comeback hit. Vincent never stopped trying to resurrect his career, appearing at a 1969 Toronto rock festival on the same bill as John Lennon, though his medical, drinking, and marital problems were making his life a mess, and diminishing his stage presence as well. He died at the age of 36 from a ruptured stomach ulcer, one of rock's first mythic figures. —*Richie Unterberger*

Bop That Just Won't Stop / 1974 / Capitol ✦✦✦✦
A good distillation of 12 of Vincent's best early tracks. Subsequent compilations have included this material and much more. But this is one of the most consistent of the lot, eliminating a lot of the average stuff and focusing exclusively on tracks cut with the band's first and best lineup (with guitarist Cliff Gallup). Beware of later editions of the LP that inexcusably eliminated a couple of the better songs. —*Richie Unterberger*

The Capitol Years 1956-63 / 1987 / Charly ✦✦✦✦
While Vincent recorded a fair number of overlooked gems during his prime, he also cut a greater number of uninspired tracks. This lavishly packaged and exhaustively annotated ten-album set inadvertently charts the rapidly plummeting quality of his recordings, even as it unearths worthy obscurities. It does manage to gather all of his classic 1956 sessions with guitarist Cliff Gallup, but Gene's subsequent efforts could easily have been boiled down to a supplementary disc or two. —*Richie Unterberger*

★ **Capitol Collectors Series** / 1990 / Capitol ✦✦✦✦✦
Breathless, unintelligible, and spirited rockabilly at its non-Sun best, this 21-track compilation covers Vincent's Capitol recordings (including "Be-Bop-a-Lula," "Race with the Devil," and "Lotta Lovin'") in admirable form. —*Hank Davis & Stephen Thomas Erlewine*

Greatest Hits / 1993 / Curb ✦✦
The bare bones of Vincent's best work, with ten tracks including "Be-Bop-a-Lula," "Lotta Lovin'," "Bluejean Bop," and "Race with the Devil." It gets a low rating not for the quality of the music (which is good), but its brevity. There's a much more thorough, slightly more expensive Gene Vincent best-of available (on Capitol) that can be found with a minimum of effort. —*Richie Unterberger*

Gene Vincent Box Set / 1994 / EMI ✦✦✦✦
Six CDs containing the complete Capitol and EMI-Columbia recordings by Vincent, from 1956 through 1964. The 151 tracks may seem excessive, but the sound glitters, and since most of the post-1962 material was never issued in the United States, this stuff could be revelatory to serious fans. The booklet is filled with detailed notes, sessionographies, and great photos. —*Bruce Eder*

★ **The Screaming End: Best of Gene Vincent** / Razor & Tie ✦✦✦✦✦
The Screaming End: The Best of Gene Vincent and His Blue Caps contains 20 of Gene Vincent's very best songs, including all of his hit singles ("Be Bop a Lula," "Race with the Devil," "Lotta Lovin'," "Wear My Ring," "Dance to the Bop") and several lesser-known but equally exciting singles and album tracks ("Bluejean Bop," "Crazy Legs," "Cruisin'," "Cat Man," "Who Slapped John," "Jump Back, Honey, Jump Back," "B-I-Bickey Bi, Bo-Bo Go," "Red Blue Jeans and a Ponytail"). *The Screaming End* may have one less song than *Capitol Collectors Series*, but it contains a stronger selection of material and the original mixes, plus a more infectious, listenable sequence, making it the definitive single-disc overview of this rock 'n' roll pioneer. —*Stephen Thomas Erlewine*

Rhonda Vincent

Fiddle, Mandolin, Vocals / Progressive Bluegrass
Vincent spent years working on the bluegrass and country circuit before she was signed to Rebel Records for three albums in the early '90s: *New Dreams and Sunshine, A Dream Come True*, and *Timeless and True Love*. She moved to Giant for 1993's *Written in the Stars*. —*John Bush*

Timeless and True Love / 1991 / Rebel ✦✦✦✦
Rhonda Vincent's vocals shine on this release, cementing her place as one of the finest vocalists in bluegrass. This CD features 12 solid cuts, and she is backed by Darrin Vincent, Bela Fleck, Alison Brown, Randy Kohrs, Scott Sanders, Kenny Malone, Sonny Louvin, and Hargus "Pig" Robbins. —*Chip Renner*

Written in the Stars / Oct. 26, 1993 / Giant ✦✦✦

● **Trouble Free** / 1996 / Giant ✦✦✦✦
Rhonda Vincent is a bluegrass prodigy who has been a favorite on the string-band festival circuit for years. Her 1994 album for Giant Records found her being pushed a little too forcibly toward the country mainstream; still, on occasion, the specialness of her hard-country twang shone through. With *Trouble Free*, she fulfills her promise with soaring beauty. Co-producer (and Giant Records chief) James Stroud backs off and allows Vincent to explore a traditional country terrain that encompasses the fierce, severe magnificence of bluegrass and the sorrowful whine of honky tonk heartbreak. Vincent excels at both, showing the same kind of hard, soulful splendor that Keith Whitley displayed when he evolved from bluegrass to traditional country. Vincent's guests pretty much define her tastes. She performs a duet with Randy Travis—in his best performance in years—and, elsewhere, enjoys harmony support from Alison Krauss and Dolly Parton. Vincent and Krauss have been linked for years (Vincent was once a runner-up in a bluegrass contest that Krauss won.) Krauss' recent commercial success certainly helped renew Giant's belief that Vincent, too, could attract a larger mainstream audience. But the two aren't that similar as vocalists. Where Krauss' voice is sweet and pure, Vincent's is twangy and aggressive. What they share is a commitment to musical integrity. With any luck, Vincent will become as celebrated in 1996 as Krauss was in 1995. —*Michael McCall*

New Dreams and Sunshine / Rebel ✦✦✦
New Dreams and Sunshine moves closer to the Nashville mainstream with its emphasis on country ballads and slicker production values. —*Jason Ankeny*

Dream Come True / Rebel ✦✦✦✦
A Dream Come True is Vincent's most authentic contemporary bluegrass effort. —*Jason Ankeny*

Bound for Gloryland / Rebel ✦✦✦

Rick Vincent

b. , San Bernadino, CA
Vocals / Bakersfield Sound, Alternative Country
A singer who came by his Bakersfield sound honestly, Vincent was born in San Bernadino, but raised in Bakersfield. —*Brian Mansfield*

A Wanted Man / 1993 / Capitol ✦✦✦✦
Vincent draws on the legacies of hometown heroes like Buck Owens and Merle Haggard without ever trying to sound just like them. He doesn't need to: Vincent, who wrote or co-wrote all ten of these songs, writes thoughtful and literate lyrics (he alludes to John Steinbeck and *Casablanca*). And whether he's shuffling into drunken despair in "Hello, She Lied" or comparing his marriage to an abandoned railway in "Ain't Been a Train Through Here in Years," he's got a voice as big and warm as the San Joaquin Valley. —*Brian Mansfield*

Volebeats

Roots-Rock, Alternative Country
Formed in the Motor City in 1988, the Volebeats shared boredom with and dislike of trendy bands and music. Lead guitarist/vocalist Matthew Smith and vocalist/guitarist Jeff Oakes began writing songs with Terry Rohm and Jeff's brother Al. With Keir McDonald (from Detroit's Medusa Cyclone) on drums, the Volebeats began performing on street corners throughout the Detroit suburbs. For the first few years of its existence, the band had a revolving group of musicians that included another Oakes brother, Brian, on upright bass, drummer Mike Murphy, and guitarist Mark Niemenski (both from the Detroit band Hysteric Narcotics), drummer Bill Peterson, and Rebecca Kaplan on fiddle. Fusing hardcore country and folk music with a melodic pop flair and rock 'n' roll sensibility, the Volebeats released their debut *Ain't No Joke* on Relapse Records in 1989, with current guitarist and songwriter Bob McCreedy—who had played with Oakes in the Frames in 1981—joining the group shortly thereafter. Over the next few years they recorded a single for Icon Records and could be found on various compilations. In 1994 the Volebeats signed with the Safe House label, releasing their second full-length, *Up North*, which garnered critical acclaim. A six-song EP, *Bittersweet* was released in 1995 and featured a cover of Barry White's "I'm Gonna Love You Just a Little More, Baby." With drummer Scott Michalski and bassist Russell Ledford joining the band, the Volebeats' lineup was solidified as the group entered the studio to record its 1997 release *The Sky and the Ocean*. —*Jack Leaver*

Ain't No Joke / Relapse ✦✦✦

Up North / 1994 / Safe House ✦✦✦✦
A folky, country record that's inviting and likable in its simple and uncomplicated presentation. Songs of longing, such as "Back in Your Heart," are driven with the locomotive shuffle of brushes on a snare, and garnished with the lonesome cry of a lap steel or Smith's single tremolo lead guitar lines. But what really elevates this record is songwriting that is ripe with memorable melodic content and an acute sense of lyrical phrasing. Just as important is the way in which the two principal writers and singers Jeff Oakes and Matthew Smith work off each other vocally. Whether in unison or tight harmony, together or in counterpart fashion, their voices, backed by low-key instrumentation, create a mood that captivates and brings these deceptively simple songs to life. —*Jack Leaver*

Bittersweet / 1995 / Third Gear ✦✦✦✦
A six-song EP, *Bittersweet* contains well-written and pleasing country/folk songs with Oakes and Smith's vocals delivering the same pure and unpretensious charm that made *Up North* such a great record. The arrangements are simple but affecting, and you get an intriguing and darkly seductive cover of Barry White's "I'm Gonna Love You Just a Little More, Baby." —*Jack Leaver*

● **The Sky and the Ocean** / Mar. 7, 1997 / Safe House ✦✦✦✦
Detroit's Volebeats' third full-length album is a standout effort, demonstrating that their songwriting chops just continue to improve with each album. Once again band members Jeff Oakes (vocals), Matthew Smith (lead guitar, vocals) and Bob McCreedy (guitar, vocals), serve up unforgettable melodic hooks with thoughtful lyrical content. The Volebeats' arrangements are uncluttered and the laid-back, acoustic-based country/folk grooves are embellished mainly by Smith's haunting Shadows-style lead guitar. And that style is particularly gripping on the stunning title track, underscoring artful lyrics with a eerie musical vibe that resembles a '60's movie theme. The band steps it up on an uncharacteristic, although fittingly welcome, rockabilly-tinged number "Warm Weather," which features some rollicking, ivory-tickling by one-time band member Keir McDonald. Although any of the group's records would be a worthwhile choice, *The Sky And The Ocean* showcases an extremely ear-pleasing and talented band that has hit its stride. —*Jack Leaver*

W

Waco Brothers

Alternative Country-Rock, Americana

The Waco Brothers were one of many projects spearheaded by Jon Langford, the frontman of the seminal British punk band the Mekons. An alternative country outfit based in Langford's adopted home of Chicago, the Waco Brothers essentially grew out of mid-1980s Mekons records like *Fear and Whiskey* and *The Mekons Honky-Tonkin',* which explored the group's interest in roots music. After the Mekons returned to a more straightforward, punk-flavored sound, the Waco Brothers emerged more than a decade later as a vehicle for Langford's long-dormant country leanings. Fusing honky tonk and rockabilly with Langford's typically political lyrics, they issued their debut *To the Last Cowboy* in 1995. *Cowboy in Flames* followed in 1997. *—Jason Ankeny*

● **To the Last Dead Cowboy** / Sep. 5, 1995 / Bloodshot ✦✦✦✦

Wagoneers

Alternative Country

The Wagoneers came out of Austin, TX, during the 1980s with a sound that quickly attracted a following among traditionalists as well as the rockabilly crowd. Made up of Austin favorite Monte Warden on lead vocals and rhythm guitar, Brent Wilson playing lead and contributing backing vocals, Craig Allan Pettigrew on bass, and drummer Thomas A. Lewis, Jr., the Wagoneers opened the floodgates for what was to be known as alternative country. Throwing a fist in the face of Nashville's manufactured hat act syndrome, the Wagoneers created a very loud buzz. With a first successful release on Herb Alpert's A&M Records, *Stout and High,* they filled a void that had been overlooked. After making a big splash, the Wagoneers followed up with a second CD that quickly vanished from memory. However, their contribution to the neverending search for real country music places them in the history books alongside bands like the Lonesome Strangers, the Georgia Satellites, the Derailers, and another Texas act, High Noon. The band eventually disintegrated, and Warden went on to a solo career that depended more on pop music than the traditional C&W that fit his vocal style so well. *—Jana Pendragon*

● **Stout and High** / 1988 / A&M ✦✦✦✦

An exceptional debut from this Austin-based quartet that combined edgy country and rockabilly. Led by lead singer and principal songwriter Monte Warden, the Wagoneers' sound borrowed heavily from the country leanings of Buddy Holly and his teenage collaboration with fellow Texan Bob Montgomery. Warden has a magnetism that jumps from the grooves, and lead guitarist Brent Wilson adds tight harmony and capably sings lead on his own "Lie and Say You Love Me." Aficionados of pedal steel guitar will delight in the understated but expressive playing by veteran Katon Roberts. There really isn't a weak cut here, and co-label head and legendary trumpet player Herb Alpert even lends his legendary trumpet—in a magnificent Tex-Mex solo flourish—at the intro of the title track, a story song about the historic fall of the Alamo. Although the band had a minor hit with "I Wanna Know Her Again," the band broke up after two albums. Warden went on to a solo career and followed more of a rootsy/pop muse,

but he sounds the most natural singing the country stuff. The Wagoneers were a precursor to kindred but more successful bands like the Mavericks. Produced by notable Nashville producer Emory Gordy, Jr., this record might have had a better commercial chance if it had been released three or four years later. *—Jack Leaver*

● **Good Fortune** / 1989 / A&M ✦✦

Coming on the heels of their premiere hit CD *Stout and High,* this second release is more than just disappointing. The band that had taken traditional C&W music by the boot straps and brought it back into the limelight failed miserably to repeat. While the talent is there, the energy and enthusiasm are not. At best, this is a third-rate recording that appears to have been done in a hurry with little or no concern for the end result. Sadly, the production is more in tune with pop music, and lead singer Monte Warden's leanings in that direction kill the original spirit of the Wagoneers. As if an omen of what was to come, the album starts off with a Warden-Palermo co-write that seemingly reflects Warden's plans for a solo career. Still, there are moments when the band comes around. Ahead of their time and making every cut count on *Stout and High,* they recapture their foresight on "Por Favor Senior," which foreshadows the early sound of future Nashville hit makers the Mavericks. An all-star lineup of talent makes the failure of this project all the more baffling. Sleepy LaBeef, Glen Duncan, Glen D. Hardin, and pedal steel provided by Kayton Roberts should add up to success. Warden, always the main songwriter, exhibits some of the old zest when he joins six-string bassist Craig Pettigrew in the writing of "Take Me." The predecessors of Big Sandy and His Fly-Rite Boys, High Noon, and the Lucky Stars will always be regarded as pioneers who pointed us back to tradition, substance, and real C&W music the way it's supposed to be done in spite of their drastic plunge into oblivion. *—Jana Pendragon*

Porter Wagoner

Vocals / Traditional Country, Country-Pop, Nashville Sound/ Countrypolitan

Porter Wagoner, the Thin Man from West Plains, MO, is an artist often ahead of his time who has always appeared hopelessly behind the times. He's among the most immediately recognizable figures in country music, largely due to his exploiting TV—and flashy costumes—a good 20 years before the video boom. And while he's forever perceived as the man who tried to hold Dolly Parton back from pop success, he was also responsible, in many ways, for putting her in a career position where the issue could even arise. As for his music, since signing with RCA in 1952 he has produced a wealth of superb hard country, and just as much of the most wretchedly oversentimentalized tripe you'll ever want to hear. The latter, of course, is half the reason we love him.

As he grew up, Wagoner fell in love with the country music he heard on the radio, teaching himself guitar so he could sing and play along. When he was a teenager, he landed a job at a local market, where he would frequently sing when business was slow. The owner believed that Wagoner's singing was helping the store's reputation, so he arranged to sponsor a local radio show that would feature the fledgling vocalist.

Throughout the late '40s, Wagoner was singing on the local West Plains radio station. Springfield radio station KWTO offered him a show in 1951. Around the same time, Red Foley was beginning his "Ozark Jamboree" program, which was based in Springfield and broadcast both on KWTO and national television. Foley brought Wagoner onto his show, which helped the young vocalist land a record contract with RCA Records in 1954. Later that year, his first single, "Company's Comin'," hit the Top Ten. It was followed in the spring of 1955 with "A Satisfied Mind," which stayed at No. 4 for four weeks. At the end of the year he released "Eat, Drink, and Be Merry (Tomorrow You'll Cry)," which climbed to No. 3 in early 1956. In 1957 he joined the Grand Ole Opry and moved to Nashville, where he formed his backing band, the Wagonmasters.

For the rest of the '50s, Porter continued to record, but he never broke the Top Ten again. It would take another television show for him to return to the top of the charts. In 1961 he began hosting his own television show, which was syndicated out of Nashville. It was the most popular country show of the '60s, growing from 18 stations in '61 to more than a hundred in the early '70s. Wagoner often sang with Norma Jean, a new female singer he introduced to the country audience, on these programs. The look of Wagoner's television show defined country music for much of America's general public during the '60s, although his music rarely departed from traditional country.

In 1967 Norma Jean was fired and replaced by Dolly Parton, who was then an unknown singer. Not only did exposure on Wagoner's program kick-start Parton's career, it provided a boost for Wagoner's as well. Parton was enormously popular on the show, and their first joint single, "The Last Thing on My Mind," rocketed to No. 7 at the beginning of 1968. The song launched a string of Top Ten hits that ran more or less uninterrupted until 1975, when the duo stopped working together. In 1968 the Country Music Assocaition named the duo the Vocal Group of the Year; the CMA would award them Vocal Duo of the Year in 1970 and 1971, as well.

Although the duo of Wagoner and Parton was successful, it wasn't stress-free. Wagoner continued to have solo hits during the late '60s and early '70s, though none of them was as big as his songs with Parton. Furthermore, he resented her attempts at a solo career; she felt musically restrained by him. The tensions culminated in late 1974, when they parted ways. RCA issued two singles in 1975 and 1976, and both of the songs—"Say Forever You'll Be Mine" and "Is Forever Longer Than Always"—hit the Top Ten. The pair would continue to duet sporadically over the next decade, highlighted by the No. 2 hit, "Making Plans," from 1980.

After Parton and Wagoner separated in 1975, Wagoner continued to film his TV show and to chart singles, but all of his hits were minor. In 1976 he retired from touring, choosing to concentrate on producing at his own studio, Fireside. Wagoner sued Parton in 1979 over various contractual problems; the suit was settled out of court the next year. For the first few years of the '80s, Wagoner had several minor hits, but he stopped recording in 1983. In 1981 his television show went off the air. Throughout the '80s and '90s, he earned his living through various businesses and investments, performing occasionally. —*Dan Cooper & Stephen Thomas Erlewine*

Satisfied Mind / 1956 / RCA Victor ✦✦✦✦
This is a common vinyl sampling of Porter's raw-boned early sound. The title cut, from 1955, was his first No. 1 hit. It also has "Company's Comin'," in which he makes the arrival of dinner guests sound as exciting as logging onto the Internet in the current context . —*Dan Cooper*

Slice of Life-Songs Happy 'n' Sad / 1963 / RCA Victor ✦✦✦✦

An Old Log Cabin for Sale / 1965 / RCA Camden ✦✦✦✦
Though it doesn't have any major hits, *An Old Log Cabin* contains several excellent performances from Porter Wagoner, including "Everything She Touches Gets the Blues," "Dear Lonesome," and the title track. —*Thom Owens*

● **The Best of Porter Wagoner** / 1966 / RCA Victor ✦✦✦✦
The Wagonmasters could drive as hard as any backup band of the day, and this set shows it on cuts like "Y'all Come (You All Come)." Meanwhile, good ol' Porter could be as morbid as any singer of his day. Witness "Misery Loves Company," "Green, Green Grass of Home," and "Skid Row Joe." —*Dan Cooper*

Confessions of a Broken Man / 1966 / RCA Victor ✦✦✦✦
Not the coolest of the cool among you can hear the aforementioned "Skid Row Joe" without a lump rising in your throat to interrupt your laughter. —*Dan Cooper*

Your Old Love Letters / 1966 / RCA Camden ✦✦✦
Your Old Love Letters features several excellent country ballads, including the title song and "Out of Sight, Out of Mind." It also has its share of filler, but there are enough fine moments to make the LP a worthwhile bargain-bin purchase. —*Thom Owens*

The Cold Hard Facts of Life / 1967 / RCA Victor ✦✦✦
Good, straightahead country is one reason to hunt for this LP. The other reason is the album cover—a near-consensus choice as the hillbilly graphics howler of all time. Write to your congressman to get this back in print as is. —*Dan Cooper*

The Thin Man from West Plains / 198 / Bear Family ✦✦✦✦
It seems a little snooty, this otherwise exemplary four-CD box set. One can't help noticing that it cuts off at approximately the same time Porter became famous for hawking laxative on TV. —*Dan Cooper*

● **Pure Gold** / 1991 / RCA ✦✦✦✦
This low-budget CD is the pick title until RCA sees fit to give him a legitimate reissue set. Actually, it's a pretty decent glimpse of the many moods of career-peak Wagoner. And yup, it's got "Skid Row Joe." —*Dan Cooper*

★ **The Essential Porter Wagoner and Dolly Parton** / Jun. 1996 / RCA ✦✦✦✦✦
The Essential Porter and Dolly contains all of Wagoner and Parton's Top Ten hits, including "The Last Thing on My Mind," "Holding On to Nothin'," "Just Someone I Used to Know," "If Teardrops Were Pennies," "Please Don't Stop," and "Say Forever You'll Be Mine." In addition to the hits, a handful of interesting obscurities are included, making this the definitive retrospective of Porter and Dolly's partnership. —*Thom Owens*

Sweet Harmony / Pair ✦✦
Another poor, budget excuse for a reissue, it's still better than it appears. The 20 tracks will give you a pretty strong sense of the weird tension that drove the duo's work and ultimately drove them apart. —*Dan Cooper*

Frank Wakefield

b. Jun. 26, 1934, Emory Gap, TN
Mandolin / Progressive Bluegrass, Traditional Bluegrass
One of the chief innovators on the mandolin, Frank Wakefield played straight bluegrass with a number of well-known bands, including Red Allen and the Greenbriar Boys. Born into a musical family in Emory Gap, TN, by age eight he knew how to play harmonica, guitar, and bass. In 1950 his family moved to Dayton, OH, and soon afterward he took up the mandolin and formed the gospel-oriented Wakefield Brothers with sibling Ralph, who played guitar. In 1951 the brothers made their first radio appearance in Dayton. After the duo split up, Frank teamed with Red Allen in 1952 to form Red Allen and Frank Wakefield and the Kentuckians. They remained partners through 1972, occasionally pursuing side projects, as well. It was with Allen that Wakefield mastered the banjo and dobro, and when he moved with Allen to Washington, DC, in 1960 he began offering private mandolin lessons; his star pupil was a young David Grisman. Wakefield joined the Greenbriar Boys in 1965 and remained with them through 1970. He also founded the Good Ol' Boys, and in 1971 recorded *The Frank Wakefield Band*. He cut *Pistol Packin' Mama* in 1974 with Don Reno, Jerry Garcia, Dave Nelson, and Chubby Wise. He also continued to teach and released an instructional video. —*Sandra Brennan & David Vinopal*

● **Frank Wakefield with Country Cooking** / Rounder ✦✦✦✦
A fine bluegrass album. Wakefield is backed by Country Cooking, featuring Peter Wernick, Tony Trischka, Russ Barenberg, and Kenny Kosek. —*Chip Renner*

Pistol Packin' Mama / Rounder ✦✦✦✦
Wakefield and David Nelson (New Riders) give a more San Francisco sound to this album, with Jerry Garcia producing "Ashes of Love," "Dim Lights, Thick Smoke," and "Glendale Train." All excellent. —*Chip Renner*

Jimmy Wakely

b. Feb. 16, 1914, Mineola, AR, **d.** Sep. 25, 1982, Mission Hills, CA
Guitar, Piano, Vocals / Cowboy

Jimmy Wakely was one of the last vocalists to make it in movies as a singing cowboy or transform a movie contract into a successful recording career. A protege and discovery of Gene Autry, he was never remotely as successful as Autry in movies, nor did his record sales approach those of his mentor; but Wakely was successful as a crossover act, his voice and repertory attractive enough to find favor with pop as well as country and Western audiences.

James Clarence Wakely was born in Arkansas on February 16, 1914, but he was raised in Oklahoma, where he spent much of his early life in a succession of odd jobs while he nursed his ambitions for a career in music. Eventually he joined up with Dick Reinhardt and Johnny Bond to form the Jimmy Wakely Trio in 1937. The group's main influence was the Sons of the Pioneers, and their singing and playing proved attractive enough to land them a regular broadcasting gig in Oklahoma City. Having achieved some recognition locally, they managed to parlay that into a meeting with Gene Autry when he toured Oklahoma in 1940, and the singer was impressed enough with their work to invite them to California. Wakely and company became regulars on Autry's "Melody Ranch" radio show and began appearing in his films for Republic Pictures. Strangely enough, despite Wakely's later success, in 1941 Johnny Bond was the first member of the trio to get a recording contract. Wakely got his own recording deal in 1942, shortly after he left the Autry fold, and had his first hit a year later with a cover of Elton Britt's wartime anthem "There's a Star-Spangled Banner Waving Somewhere."

Despite—or perhaps because of—the omnipresence of World War II in peoples' lives, the singing cowboy image movies that Gene Autry established were still thriving. The public on the homefront, especially the kids, liked them, and there was money to be made. Autry was serving in the US Army Air Force, but Roy Rogers and Tex Ritter both continued riding and singing their way through screen adventures, and other small studios were in the market for their own singing cowboys. Monogram Pictures, Republic's major competitor among B-movie studios, approached Wakely with a contract in 1944, and his first picture, *Song of the Range*, was a modest success, leading to a five-year stint in front of the cameras. Wakely was never as natural an actor as Autry or Roy Rogers, but his voice was attractive and his 28 Westerns were reasonably successful. Amid Wakely's work in B-Westerns, his recording career thrived, as he began recording a uniquely sophisticated array of country, cowboy, and pop songs. His string began with his own "Song of the Sierras," a richly atmospheric ballad that presented his voice in a deep, serious light. His first major crossover hit followed in 1948 with "One Has My Name (The Other Has My Heart)," a touching song about a tragic romantic triangle. It reached the top spot on the country and Western charts and the Top Ten on the pop charts. Wakely became closely associated with the music of honky tonk songwriter Floyd Tillman, and one cover, "I Love You So Much It Hurts," spent five weeks at No. 1 on the country charts in 1949.

It was producer Lee Gillette who thought of teaming Wakely with songstress Margaret Whiting in what proved to be a very successful partnership. Their first song together, the infidelity story "Slippin' Around," set the pattern for their partnership; the effervescent Whiting and the smooth, laid-back Wakely—who, by that time, was becoming known as the Bing Crosby of country-and-western music—balanced each other perfectly. "Slippin' Around" spent 17 weeks at No. 1 on the country charts and a

week at the No. 1 pop chart position, and the two had nine subsequent hits together, including "Wedding Bells" and "When You and I Were Young Maggie Blues." Despite this success, their relationship was uneasy, and Wakely was constantly concerned with being upstaged musically by his singing partner, by some accounts even counting the number of words that each one got to sing in their duets. In 1952 Wakely became the star of "The Jimmy Wakely Show" on CBS radio. After co-hosting the ABC television network series "Five Star Jubilee" in 1961 with Tex Ritter, he continued to record for his own Shasta Records label, which he founded as a mail order distribution company in the mid-1960s. He continued to perform live in an act that included his son and daughter, and remained popular during the 1970s, until age and health problems began taking their toll. Wakely died of emphysema in 1982. —*Bruce Eder*

● **Vintage Collection** / Aug. 7, 1996 / Capitol ✦✦✦✦
This 20-song collection is comprised of virtually all of the musical highlights of Wakely's seven-year stay with Capitol Records, with all of his solo hits and three of his best known duets with Margaret Whiting, as well as four previously unreleased outtakes. The latter include the extraordinary Western swing number "Don't Lay the Blame on Me" and Wakely's cover of the Jimmie Rodgers number "Roll Along, Kentucky Moon." The sound is excellent, and the notes are very thorough, with good session information as well as background material. —*Bruce Eder*

Dusty Wakeman

Bakersfield Sound, Alternative Country

Dusty Wakeman, born Donald Wakeman, came out of Texas with a full head of steam and headed for California in the mid-70s. Part of the baby-boomer generation, Wakeman had spent his school years playing bass in rock bands and absorbing the Texas culture that surrounded him. But after graduating from high school he figured his fortune lay in Los Angeles. He quickly established a 24-track studio in Venice and took on another Texan, Michael Dumas, as a partner. Working together, Wakeman and Dumas made Mad Dog Studios the top recording spot in town. Both were able to fit in other projects on the side. As a musician, Wakeman played with Jackson Browne, Rosie Flores, Michelle Shocked, and Jim Lauderdale.

As one of the top dogs in L.A., Wakeman was at the heart of many projects that promoted roots music. His firm but delicate touch was felt on the impressive 1990 *L.A. Ya Ya* compilation that presented the best of the local R&B scene. He was also instrumental in the success of the *A Town South of Bakersfield* project, which gleaned three volumes from the Los Angeles country community. Trusted and well-liked by the musicians and industry alike, Wakeman had the confidence and ear of Buck Owens and the respect of Dwight Yoakam, both of whom benefited from his expertise. A contributor to the health of the Bakersfield sound, Dusty Wakeman was responsible for getting the Lonesome Strangers back into the studio after their HighTone deal went south, producing their *Land of Opportunity*.

As a producer, co-producer, and engineer, Wakeman made contributions to Lucinda Williams and all of Dwight Yoakam's recordings and brought to light the talent of a new and successful alternative rock band called Reach Around. Other clients included Scott Joss, Steve Forbert, Somebody's Darling, Jim Lauderdale, Joy White, and Giant Sand. In 1995 Wakeman and Dumas relocated their Mad Dog Studios to Burbank, closer to the corporate offices of the record label they helped found, Little Dog Records. Concentrating on the studio, Wakeman, Dumas, and Szu Wang, Wakeman's wife, created a multifunctional, multimedia recording studio and sound stage. He also continued to be involved in all of Yoakam's projects. —*Jana Pendragon*

Walkabouts

Alternative Pop-Rock, Alternative Country-Rock

Despite their background (punk), geography (Seattle), and label affiliation (Sub Pop), the Walkabouts were anything but a grunge band; dark, haunting and elegaic, their work instead sprang forth from the storytelling traditions of American roots music and the kinetic excitement of rock 'n' roll. The Walkabouts were formed in 1984 by Chris Eckman and his brothers Curt and Grant, all of whom had previously played together in a number of punk/pop outfits, along with singer Carla Torgerson, a veteran of folk and street singing. The group's line-up proved fluid, although Chris Eckman and Torgerson remained the Walkabouts' driving forces; a later roster including bassist Michael Wells, multi-instrumentalist Glenn Slater, and drummer Terri Moeller did hang together for a number of years.

After issuing a self-titled cassette in 1984, the Walkabouts released the EP *22 Disasters* a year later. A full-length LP, *Weights and Rivers* was planned for 1987, but the record was never released—a harbinger of music industry problems to come. Instead, the group offered *See Beautiful Rattlesnake Garden* in 1988, which not only marked the continued maturity of Eckman and Torgerson's songwriting but earned the Walkabouts a contract with the fledgling Sub Pop label. The deal resulted in upgraded production values, as evidenced by 1989's *Cataract* and its follow-up, the next year's six-song EP *Rag & Bone*, which featured the keyboard work of the newly-added Slater.

Scavenger in 1991 proved to be the last Walkabouts record issued in their native land for some time, however; while the deal with Sub Pop's American division went sour, the label's Glitterhouse division in Europe, where their following had been steadily growing, hung on to the band. Between 1993 and 1995, the Walkabouts issued a staggering seven full-length records in Europe —three by the full band, a limited-edition live collection, and three more released by the duo of Chris and Carla. Finally in 1995 the three aforementioned Walkabouts albums—the double LP set *New West Motel*, the all-covers *Satisfied Mind*, and the more rock-oriented *Setting the Woods on Fire*—all appeared domestically. A year later the band issued two more albums, the all-new *Devil's Road* (recorded with the Warsaw Philharmonic Orchestra) and *Death Valley Days: Lost Songs and Rarities, 1985-1995*, a collection of odds and ends. In November 1996 Wells left the Walkabouts to devote himself to his side project, Pluto Boy; he was replaced by bassist Baker Saunders. —*Jason Ankeny*

22 Disasters [EP] / 1985 / Necessity ✦✦

See Beautiful Rattlesnake Gardens / 1987 / Pop Llama ✦✦✦
The band's sound is still in its embryonic stages; the focus is on jangly, electric folk-rock, with few traces of the country, blues, and roots music from which their later work would draw. Still, the songwriting of Chris Eckman and Carla Torgerson is already strong, and Torgerson's vocals are lovely. —*Jason Ankeny*

Cataract / 1989 / Sub Pop ✦✦✦
The band's first Sub Pop LP is a diverse affair sewn together from an ever-expanding array of influences and passions, highlighted by such haunting roots meditations as "Hell's Soup Kitchen," "Long Black Veil" (an original composition, and not the standard), and "Whiskey XXX." —*Jason Ankeny*

Rag and Bone / 1990 / Sub Pop ✦✦✦
The addition of keyboardist Glenn Slater fleshes out the Walkabouts' sound on the six-song *Rag and Bone* EP, texturing typically strong efforts like the honky tonk rave-up "The Anvil Song" and the gentle "Medicine Hat" with even greater color and dimension. —*Jason Ankeny*

Scavenger / Oct. 1990 / Sub Pop ✦✦✦
Like its predecessors, *Cataract* refines the Walkabouts' sound even as the band's scope broadens; the further afield their fascination with music's backroads takes them, the more remarkably assured they grow. —*Jason Ankeny*

● **Satisfied Mind** / 1993 / Creative Man ✦✦✦✦
Like Yo La Tengo's *Fakebook*, the Walkabouts' *Satisfied Mind* is a definitive artistic statement masquerading as a loose-knit collection of acoustic covers. Sometimes a group's selection of cover material, combined with their ability to make the songs their own, winds up revealing as much about their craft as their original music, and such is the case here; mining the work of diverse artists like the Carter Family, Gene Clark, Mary Margaret O'Hara, John Cale, and Nick Cave, *Satisfied Mind* represents the purest evocation to date of the Walkabouts' aesthetic and its standing at the crossroads of

country, rock, folk, and punk. By casting well-known songs in an entirely new light—Patti Smith's "Free Money" becomes an ominous waltz, while Charlie Rich's "Feel Like Going Home" is renewed as an epic dirge—the album makes explicit all of the implicit connections in the Walkabouts' work. By extension, it underlines the connections binding the spectrum of roots music as well; *Satisfied Mind* doesn't simply suggest that diverse sounds can co-exist together—it proves that they always have. —*Jason Ankeny*

New West Motel / 1993 / Glitterhouse ✦✦✦✦
The double-album *New West Motel* bears more than a passing similarity to the work of Neil Young (whose "Like a Hurricane" gets covered here), thanks to its edgy juxtaposition of blistering guitar workouts and plaintive acoustic cuts. —*Jason Ankeny*

Setting the Woods on Fire / 1994 / Cargo ✦✦✦✦
Despite taking its title from a Hank Williams song, *Setting the Woods on Fire* ranks among the Walkabouts' most rock-based efforts. A sweeping, stately record, it owes a great deal to the Stones' *Exile on Main St.*, particularly on the boogie shuffle "Old Crow" and the horn-powered, R&B-flavored "Hole in the Mountain." —*Jason Ankeny*

Devil's Road / 1996 / Virgin Schallplatten ✦✦✦✦
Half of the tracks comprising *Devil's Road* feature the string arrangements of the Warsaw Philharmonic Orchestra, giving greater depth to a sound that's already impossibly rich. Recorded in Berlin, the album is dark and soulful, the work of a band at the peak of its powers. —*Jason Ankeny*

Death Valley Days: Lost Songs and Rarities, 1985-1995 / Nov. 1996 / Glitterhouse ✦✦✦
Death Valley Days is a fragmentary collection reining in scattered tracks drawn from demos, B-sides, unreleased albums, compilations, and tribute records, along with a few covers left off the domestic reissue of *New West Motel*. —*Jason Ankeny*

Billy Walker

b. Jan. 14, 1929, Ralls, TX
Guitar, Vocals / Traditional Country, Western Swing, Honky Tonk
A native of West Texas active on the Grand Ole Opry to this day, Billy Walker emerged from the talent-rich Dallas scene of the late '40s and early '50s. After a brief stint on Capitol, he was signed to Columbia in 1951 at almost exactly the same time as Ray Price. For awhile Walker, Price, and Lefty Frizzell were all recording at the legendary Jim Beck studio in Dallas, which did for 1950s honky tonk what the Sun Studio in Memphis did for rockabilly. Nevertheless, Walker enjoyed his greatest success ten years later in Nashville, where the studio sound was perhaps more suited to his smooth tenor voice. —*Dan Cooper*

● **Billy Walker's Greatest Hits** / 1963 / Columbia ✦✦✦✦
Early-'60s Nashville Sound, though always with Walker's voice agreeably front and center, it contains "Charlie's Shoes" and a 1961 take on Willie Nelson's "Funny How Time Slips Away." —*Dan Cooper*

Cross the Brazos at Waco / 1993 / Bear Family ✦✦✦✦
Here's the usual exhaustive, prestigious, and expensive package (six CDs and a book) from Germany's Bear Family, the best roots music reissue company in the world. Covering the years 1949 to 1965, the set chronicles Walker's career from his initial, tentative Capitol cuts through his entire career on Columbia. —*Dan Cooper*

Clay Walker

b. Aug. 19, 1969, Beaumont, TX
Vocals / Contemporary Country, New Traditionalist
With his first two singles reaching No. 1 upon their release, Clay Walker immediately established himself as a commercial success. Unlike most of his new country contemporaries of the mid-'90s, he was able to sustain that success over a couple of years, racking up no less than five No. 1 singles in the first three years of his career.

Walker was born and raised on a farm in Beaumont, TX, the hometown of George Jones. Clay fell in love with country music at nine years old when his father gave him a guitar. After he graduated from high school, Clay pursued a musical career, playing concerts across the South, the Midwest, and Canada. For more than three years, he toured and went to school, taking courses about the music business. During this time, he acted as his own manager. Eventually, he became the house singer at the Neon Armadillo bar in Beaumont. While he was performing at the club, producer James Stroud heard Walker and offered to work with him. Stroud helped Walker secure a contract with Giant Records, and the pair began working on the vocalist's debut album.

"What's It to You" became a No. 1 hit upon its release in August 1993, with "Live Until I Die" following it into the pole position later that year. Both singles were featured on his debut album, *Clay Walker*, released in the fall of 1993. "Where Do I Fit in the Picture," the third single from the album, became a No. 11 hit in early 1994. "White Palace" was a flop, failing to crack the Top 40, but "Dreaming with My Eyes Open" became his third No. 1 hit in the summer of 1994, helping make his debut record a platinum album. *If I Could Make a Living* was not quite as successful as his debut, but it still yielded the No. 1 title track. *Hypnotize the Moon*, Walker's third album, appeared in the fall of 1995, preceded by the No. 2 single "Who Needs You Baby." — *Stephen Thomas Erlewine*

Clay Walker / 1993 / Giant ✦✦✦✦

Clay Walker is another country music product from Beaumont, TX, (others include George Jones, Mark Chestnut, Doug Supernaw, and Tracy Bird) who has broken into the Nashville music scene. Walker has a high-energy voice and a growl that reminds you of Conway Twitty. The highlights of his first album include "What's It to You?," his first No. 1 hit, and "Live Until I Die." Other featured songs include "The Silence Speaks for Itself" and "White Palace." — *Larry Powell*

● If I Could Make A Living / Sep. 27, 1994 / Giant ✦✦✦✦

Hypnotize the Moon / Oct. 17, 1995 / Giant ✦✦✦

Clay Walker's *Hypnotize the Moon* is his most assured, cohesive album to date. Walker shines on both polished, contemporary ballads and gritty traditional country, and his consistently excellent performance is what carries the album over the weak spots. — *Stephen Thomas Erlewine*

Self Portrait / Oct. 15, 1996 / Giant ✦✦✦

Self Portrait is a CD-ROM that is divided between interview footage of Clay Walker, music videos, and exclusive shots of Walker's Houston ranch. Most of Walker's hits—plus a previously unheard version of "Nobody's Darling"—are featured, but this is a disc designed for a fan of Clay Walker the personality, not Clay Walker the musician. Most of the information is trivial and unrelated to the construction of his music or progression of his career. Still, Walker fanatics will find certain segments of the ROM of use, even though the interface could have been a little more user-friendly. — *Thom Owens*

Jerry Jeff Walker (Ronald Clyde Crosby)

b. Mar. 16, 1942, Oneonta, NY

Guitar, Vocals / Progressive Country, Singer-Songwriter, Outlaw Country

Jerry Jeff Walker is best known as the writer of "Mr. Bojangles," an enduring pop classic he wrote at the beginning of his career after meeting a street singer named Bojangles in a New Orleans drunk tank. He's also strongly associated with the progressive ("outlaw") country scene that centered around Austin, TX, in the 1970s and included such figures as Willie Nelson, Guy Clark, and Townes Van Zandt.

Ironically, however, Walker is not a native Texan. He was born Ronald Clyde Crosby in upstate New York and recorded his first several albums while living in New York City. He didn't move to Austin until 1971, but he's remained a major figure in the area ever since.

Walker first recorded with the folk-rock group Circus Maximus for Vanguard in 1967. The band split after its second album, and Walker signed with Atco and released his first solo album, "Mr. Bojangles," in 1968. His version of "Bojangles" never hit it big, but the Nitty Gritty Dirt Band's rendition made the Top Ten of the pop charts in 1971.

Walker lived briefly in Key West, FL, in 1970 but soon found himself in Austin. In 1972 he signed with MCA and released a

Jerry Jeff Walker

self-titled album that included his version of Guy Clark's "L.A. Freeway." His best-known album, however, is *Viva Terlingua*, which he recorded in 1973 in the tiny Texas town of Luckenbach with the Lost Gonzo Band. The album went gold, and it's his biggest-selling album to date.

Walker was a hard partier throughout much of his career (his friends called him "Jacky Jack"), and this reputation became part of his identity. He's since cleaned up his act—in part thanks to his wife, Susan, whom he married in 1974—and he's continued to record steadily into the 1990s. He released a couple of albums on Elektra/Asylum in the late '70s, but remained mostly with MCA until his 1982 album *Cowboy Jazz*—a record that became his last for any major label. In 1985, however, he showed the industry he could live without their help and released *Gypsy Songman*, the first of a series of self-made cassettes, many of which he sold via a mailing list that has grown to more than 40,000. In 1987 Walker worked out a deal with Rykodisc to release his CDs, but he still sells the cassettes himself through his own company, Tried and True Music.

In 1991 and 1992 Walker hosted the weekly TV show "The Texas Connection" on TNN. In 1993 he returned to Luckenbach for an anniversary recording that became the album *Viva Luckenbach!* Walker's birthday is a major celebration in Austin every March, when he plays several shows in different local clubs and theaters. — *Kurt Wolff*

Circus Maximus with Jerry Jeff Walker / Aug. 1967 / Vanguard ✦✦✦

The style of this album has more to do with the sound of the Beau Brummels or Sagittarius than with the work of Jerry Jeff the solo artist or with country music. The songs are better than those on the first album, but this is definitely a product of its time. — *Jim Worbois*

Mr. Bojangles / 1968 / Rhino ✦✦✦✦

Walker's debut introduced his dry vocals and narrative songwriting style with support from many session musicians, the most notable of whom were Ron Carter and David Bromberg. The influence of Dylan and other singer-songwriters of the time is felt fairly strongly on this extremely low-key release (especially on the seven-minute "Desolation Row"-like "The Ballad Of the Hulk"), but Walker favored the country and folk side of folk-rock much more than the rock side. The title track, taken into the Top Ten by the Nitty Gritty Dirt Band, remains his most famous song. The CD reissue includes the original mono single version of "Mr. Bojangles" and its flip side, as well as liner notes with comments on the songs by Jerry Jeff himself. —*Richie Unterberger*

Driftin' Way of Life / 1969 / Vanguard ✦✦✦✦
A beautifully simple album of country-flavored original songs, mostly from the point of view of the sentimental roustabout, this great record sounds as though the players just went in, knocked it off, and hit the road. —*Richard Meyer*

Jerry Jeff Walker / 1969 / MCA ✦✦✦✦
This classic 1972 record set the stage for his monumental *Viva Terlingua*, which would follow a year later. But don't ignore this one. There are some fine songs on here, including two early Guy Clark songs. —*Jim Worbois*

Viva Terlingua / 1973 / MCA ✦✦✦✦
The Lost Gonzo spirit settles in. —*Robert Gordon*

Walker's Collectibles / 1974 / MCA ✦✦✦
How do you follow an album like *Viva Terlingua?* By doing something completely different. This record features rock ("Rock Me Roll Me"), a Dixieland-styled song ("First Showboat"), and a gospel quartet-type number as well as the usual things one would expect from Jerry Jeff. It doesn't always work, but at least he tries. —*Jim Worbois*

Ridin' High / 1975 / MCA ✦✦✦✦
This is progressive country at its most fun. —*Robert Gordon*

A Man Must Carry On / 1977 / MCA ✦✦✦
It's an interesting mix of live material, spoken word, studio recordings, and stereo chickens. —*Robert Gordon*

Jerry Jeff Walker / 1978 / Elektra ✦✦
This could easily be called *The Two Sides of Jerry Jeff.* The first side is the rough and rowdy Walker, with the best two performances being "Eastern Ave . . ." and "Lone Wolf." The second side reflects a kinder, gentler Walker who has taken refuge in the love of his woman. —*Jim Worbois*

Contrary to Ordinary / 1978 / MCA ✦✦✦
Though it didn't spawn any hit singles, *Contrary to Ordinary* is one of Jerry Jeff Walker's finest efforts, featuring a wonderful collection of songs by contemporary singer-songwriters like Susanna Clark, Bobby Charles, and Butch Hancock. Walker sings with warmth and a good-natured humor, selling the songs softly and welcoming the audience with his understated charm. It's an ingratiating, simple record that works because of its low, laidback energy. —*Thom Owens*

Too Old to Change / 1979 / Elektra ✦✦
Though he didn't write any of the songs on this record, his ear didn't fail him in selecting some fine songs. Many of the writers on this record were up-and-coming artists and writers of the period. Unfortunately, it sounds as though the old contractual obligation was taking its toll on Walker's voice and performances. Not to be missed is Carole King's duet on "I'll Be Your San Antonio Rose." Who would have thought she could do country too? —*Jim Worbois*

The Best of Jerry Jeff Walker / 1980 / MCA ✦✦✦✦
The Best of Jerry Jeff Walker is a concise, ten-track collection of tunes from his years on the MCA label. It includes all the Jerry Jeff favorites while never being anything more than a straightforward greatest-hits compilation, thereby making it a fine record for those wishing an overview of his career. —*James Chrispell*

Gypsy Songman / 1988 / Rykodisc ✦✦✦✦
Gypsy Songman is a very good 28-song overview of Jerry Jeff Walker's career, concentrating on his lesser-known songs. The compilation is divided between originals and eight covers, all of which are performed with his signature laidback style. —*Thom Owens*

Live from Gruene Hall / 1989 / Rykodisc ✦✦✦
Live from Gruene Hall is an excellent return to form from Jerry Jeff Walker. Running through a selection of new songs, Walker is accompanied by a tight version of the Lost Gonzo Band, who help turn these performances into little gems. The hit singles "I Feel Like Hank Williams Tonight," "The Pickup Song" and "Trashy Women" are only the tip of the iceberg. It may be a live album, but *Live from Gruene Hall* is arguably one of the best records Walker ever made. Of special note is a brief vocal cameo by Willie Nelson. —*Thom Owens*

● **Great Gonzos** / 1991 / MCA ✦✦✦✦
Great Gonzos is a good cross-section of 14 of Jerry Jeff Walker's best-known songs, including "Mr. Bojangles," "Old Five and Dimers like Me," "Desperados Waiting for the Train," and "Sangria Wine." It's not necessarily definitive—several of his actual charting hits did not make the collection, including "Jaded Lover," "It's a Good Night for Singing," and "Got Lucky Last Night"—but it cuts to the essence of Walker, making it an excellent introduction. —*Thom Owens*

Navajo Rug / Aug. 1991 / Rykodisc ✦✦✦
Navajo Rug offers Walker's tribute to aging athletes, "Nolan Ryan (He's a Hero to Us All)." —*Jason Ankeny*

Hill Country Rain / 1992 / Rykodisc ✦✦✦
Hill Country Rain has a handful of fine songs—"Rock & Roll My Baby" and "So Bad Last Night" roll along gently—but the album suffers from mediocre songwriting and merely competent performances. —*Thom Owens*

Man Must Carry On, Vol. 1 / Jan. 28, 1997 / MCA ✦✦✦✦
Man Must Carry On, Vol. 2 / Jan. 28, 1997 / MCA ✦✦✦✦

Chris Wall

Guitar, Harmonica, Vocals / Singer-Songwriter, Alternative Country, Americana
Any guy could put on a John Stetson hat and pretend he is a country singer, but Chris Wall is the real thing, a songwriter who knows about honky tonks and country clichés. He is alternately humorous ("Something to Shoot" from *Honky-Tonk Heart*) and personable, relating little stories that show Wall wearing his honky tonk heart on his sleeve. Born in Newport Beach, CA, Chris Wall was the son of a singer who collaborated with Sons of the Pioneers' Bob Nolan. Wall spent time at his uncle's cattle ranch, growing to love the country more than his usual surroundings. He later moved to Montana and began writing country songs. He met Guy Clark in 1987; and after the two swapped songs, Clark recommended the young singer to Jerry Jeff Walker, who caught his show in Jackson Hole, WY. Impressed by what he saw, Walker invited Chris Wall to Austin in 1988 to record with him. After a few sessions, he moved there and released his debut tape in mid-1989. Rykodisc signed the back-to-basics country guitarist after hearing the tape and seeing his support slot for Walker. Remixed and remastered, *Honky Tonk Heart* appeared in 1990. *No Sweat* was released the next year. —*John Bush & Dennis MacDonald*

● **Honky Tonk Heart** / 1991 / Rykodisc ✦✦✦✦
Though it could use a more distinguished instrumental backing, *Honky Tonk Heart* is a fine neo-traditional country album, demonstrating that Chris Wall is a vocalist of considerable promise. —*Thom Owens*

No Sweat / Sep. 27, 1991 / Rykodisc ✦✦✦

Don Walser

Vocals / Alternative Country, Americana
Don Walser, a country-roadhouse yodeler, first gained a national release in 1994, *Rolling Stone from Texas*. After appearances on NPR's "All Things Considered" and ABC's "PrimeTime Live," Watermelon Records released two volumes of *The Archive Series*, featuring Walser and his band (the Pure Texas Band) doing old favorites, some recorded before *Rolling Stone from Texas*. —*John Bush*

● **Rolling Stone From Texas** / 1994 / Watermelon ✦✦✦✦
The Archive Series, Vol. 1 / 1995 / Watermelon ✦✦✦✦
The Archive Series, Vol. 2 / 1995 / Watermelon ✦✦✦✦

Texas Top Hand / Mar. 19, 1996 / Watermelon ✦✦✦✦
After decades of playing Texas dancehalls, Don Walser enjoyed his first national recognition in 1994, thanks to the gleeful celebration of his unmistakable vocal talent in *Rolling Stone from*

Texas. Texas Top Hand finds him enjoying the fruits of his success by taking a few songs uptown. Working again with producer Ray Benson of Asleep at the Wheel, Walser again yodels with unabashed acrobatic delight and soars with nimble, full-throated joy through country classics and old-sounding new tunes. He sings with a robustly happy spirit, as his sky-high trills convey, and this time he occasionally leads a brassy big band with the same homespun clarity that he lends to steel-driven, peanut-shell dancehall tunes. *— Michael McCall*

Sings Pure Country / Bear Family ✦✦✦

Monte Warden

Vocals / Alternative Country, Americana

Monte Warden combines a rockabilly roots-rock with honky tonk and blue-eyed-soul ballads. When he was 15, Warden's trio Whoa Trigger! was named Best New Band in 1983 at an awards show in his native Austin, TX. Five years later his band, the Wagoneers, won the award again and became a "young country" favorite with two albums on A&M, *Stout and High* and *Good Fortune*. His first solo album (self-titled) appeared in July 1993, and the follow-up, *Here I Am*, was released in July 1995. His solo backing band, the Lonesharks, includes guitarist Brent Wilson (formerly of the Wagoneers), bassist Brad Fordham, and drummer/co-producer Mas Palermo. *— John Bush*

● **Monte Warden** / 1993 / Watermelon ✦✦✦✦
Imagine finding a long-lost Buddy Holly album—not outtakes, but the real thing. Then start playing *Monte Warden* just about anywhere—"Don't Know a Thing," "It's Amazing," "All I Want Is You," or even the ballad "Just to Hear Your Voice." You won't feel let down. *— Brian Mansfield*

Here I Am / 1995 / Watermelon ✦✦✦

Steve Wariner

b. Dec. 25, 1954, Noblesville, IN

Bass, Guitar, Vocals / Contemporary Country, Country-Folk, Neo-Traditionalist Country

One of country's most versatile performers, Wariner's gone seemingly unnoticed for each of his skills: as a vocalist, guitarist, and songwriter. Wariner grew up in suburban Indianapolis, interested in the Beatles on the radio, and Chet Atkins and George Jones, the artists his father listened to most frequently. He started playing in his dad's band, and by his high school years, he was playing local clubs. At age 17 Wariner caught the ear of Dottie West, who persuaded him to join her band; he ended up playing bass on her classic "Country Sunshine." Wariner moved on to work as a sideman for Bob Luman and signed with RCA Records in 1976. His career developed slowly; he didn't put out an album until 1982. In the beginning, the low-tuned guitars and wide range of his singles brought frequent comparisons to the early Glen Campbell hits. Gradually Wariner took more personal direction in his recording career, and his albums became progressively more guitar-oriented, more adventurous musically, and more insightful lyrically. *— Tom Roland*

● **Steve Wariner** / 1982 / RCA ✦✦✦✦
RCA waited until they had a veritable greatest-hits package before releasing Wariner's first album. Bright arrangements have lots of dovetailing instruments, and Wariner shows off a substantial vocal range. *— Tom Roland*

Life's Highway / 1985 / MCA ✦✦✦

One Good Night Deserves Another / 1985 / MCA ✦✦✦

It's a Crazy World / 1987 / MCA ✦✦✦✦
Wariner's in charge vocally and seems to glide through the album effortlessly. He's received more responsibility for his own direction, and—with one or two exceptions—has upgraded every aspect of his record, particularly in song selection and musicianship. *— Tom Roland*

Greatest Hits / Sep. 7, 1987 / MCA ✦✦✦✦
Many of Steve Wariner's his best moments were his singles, and *Greatest Hits* contains many of his best and biggest hits, includ-

ing the No. 1s "Some Fools Never Learn, "You Can Dream of Me," and "Life's Highway." *— Thom Owens*

I Should Be with You / Mar. 7, 1988 / MCA ✦✦✦

I Got Dreams / 1989 / MCA ✦✦✦

Laredo / 1990 / MCA ✦✦✦
After nine years and nine No. 1 singles, Wariner had basically established himself as Mr. Consistency. *Laredo* proved, again, that he could sing any type of country well—swing ("L-O-V-E, Love"), rock ("The Domino Theory"), and heartbreak ballads conveying genuine pain ("She's in Love," "There for Awhile"). *— Brian Mansfield*

Greatest Hits, Vol. 2 / 1991 / MCA ✦✦✦✦
This contains "Baby I'm Yours" and other Wariner favorites. *— AMG*

I Am Ready / 1991 / Arista ✦✦✦✦
Wariner, a master of the subtle touch, builds this album's impact quietly and methodically, with songs like Bill Anderson's "The Tips of My Fingers" and Wariner's own "Like a River to the Sea." "Leave Him out of This" is a masterpiece of smoldering intensity, its raging anger and pain barely held in check. The only time Wariner lets it loose is at the end, where he locks his guitar in mortal combat with Mark O'Connor's fiddle in the cathartic "Crash Course in the Blues." *— Brian Mansfield*

Drive / Jul. 27, 1993 / Arista ✦✦✦

No More Mr. Nice Guy / Mar. 12, 1996 / Arista ✦✦✦

Jamie Warren

Vocals / Contemporary Country

Jamie Warren is a contemporary country vocalist based in Canada. At the beginning of his career, the Canadian Country Music Association named him Outstanding New Artist in 1985. In the years after the award, he toured Canada frequently, in addition to releasing independent singles. By the mid-'90s, he had built up a strong following, and in 1995, he had two Top 20 hits in Canada—"Ready to Run" and "What Goes Around Comes Around." The next year he made his stateside debut with *Fallen Angel*, which was released on A&M Records. *— Stephen Thomas Erlewine*

Fallen Angel / Sep. 9, 1996 / A&M ✦✦✦✦
Fallen Angel, Jamie Warren's first American album, is an overproduced but engaging set of contemporary country that doesn't offer any original thrills, but it is so well-crafted and performed that its slight predictability doesn't matter. Warren is a charming, down-to-earth vocalist who can sell even mediocre songs, but *Fallen Angel* isn't burdened by weak material. Most of the album, from the single "One Step Back" to "What Goes Around Comes Around," is professional contemporary country that pushes all the right buttons without seeming calculating. Listening to *Fallen Angel*, it's easy to see why Warren was so popular in Canada for so long. *— Thom Owens*

Paul Warren

b. May 17, 1918, Lyles, Hickman County, TN, d. Jan. 12, 1978

Fiddle, Session Musician / Progressive Bluegrass, Traditional Bluegrass, Bluegrass

Paul Warren was an extraordinary bluegrass sideman who played fiddle on scores of radio and television shows and recording sessions; although he was in the music business more than 35 years, he never made a solo studio album. Warren was born and raised in Hickman County, TN; his earliest influences were his father, who played clawhammer banjo, and Fiddlin' Arthur Smith. He got his start playing high school dances with partner Emory Martin in the mid-'30s. In 1938 he joined Johnnie Wright's band; by 1940 they had become successful enough to abandon their day jobs and focus full-time on music. He remained with Wright and his Tennessee Hillbillies until entering the Army in 1942, where legend has it that he survived capture and two years in a German POW camp because he entertained the guards by playing "Under the Double Eagle" on fiddle. After his discharge, Warren returned to Wright's band. After Wright formed Johnnie and Jack with Jack

Anglin, Warren played behind them until 1953. He also spent a year playing on Kitty Wells recordings like "It Wasn't God Who Made Honky-Tonk Angels" and "Release Me." In 1954 he began his long association with Lester Flatt and Earl Scruggs when he replaced Benny Martin in their Foggy Mountain Boys; he appeared on all of their recordings between 1954 and 1969. When Flatt and Scruggs broke up in the late '60s, Warren played in Flatt's Nashville Grass through early 1977 when his health began to fail and he was forced to retire; he died the next year. Although he never recorded by himself, a collection of tunes featuring his work was posthumously gathered by Lance Le Roy, who released them on a tribute album in 1979. —*Sandra Brennan*

● **America's Greatest Breakdown Fiddle Player** / 1957 / CMH ✦✦✦✦

The Watson Family

Old-Time, Traditional Country, Traditional Folk
In the mid-'60s, the Watson and Carlton families were recorded, creating a storehouse of traditional mountain music. Though Doc Watson shines through (as expected), the resulting albums were by no means his showcase. Joining him are mother Annie, wife Rosa Lee, father-in-law Gaither Carlton, brother Arnold, and son Merle. This is as authentic as country music gets, folks. —*David Vinopal*

● **The Watson Family** / 1990 / Smithsonian/Folkways ✦✦✦✦
Watson Family Tradition / Rounder ✦✦✦

Dale Watson

b. Oct. 7, 1962
Guitar, Vocals / Alternative Country, Americana
Dale Watson is a singer/guitarist who writes and plays original material in the tradition of 1950s and '60s honky tonk, which makes him something of an outsider in the 1990s country music market. He was born in Alabama but moved with his family to Pasadena, TX, just outside of Houston, when he was a teenager, and considers Texas his home state. His early musical inspiration came from his father, a singer and guitarist, and his brother Jim, who gave him his first music lessons. Watson began writing songs at age 12, and recorded his first at age 14. By the time he graduated from high school, he was performing locally. He spent the next seven years playing the clubs and honky tonks around Pasadena.

In 1988 Watson moved to L.A., seeking the Bakersfield sound of Buck Owens and Merle Haggard, two of his major inspirations. His friend singer-songwriter Rosie Flores had encouraged him to relocate there. He soon landed a gig at L.A.'s Palomino Club, playing guitar in the house band at the club's weekly "barn dances." He also had a small role in the movie *Thing Called Love*, starring River Phoenix.

Watson recorded two singles for Curb, "One Tear at a Time" and "You Pour It On," which were released in 1990. He also contributed one track to volume three of the L.A. country compilation *A Town South of Bakersfield*, released in 1992. That same year he moved to Nashville, where he worked as a staff writer for Gary Morris Music, a publishing company. Eventually, however, he settled in Austin, TX. He landed a recording deal with HighTone Records, which released Watson's debut album, *Cheatin' Heart Attack*, in 1995. Watson and his band, Lone Star, released a follow-up, *Blessed or Damned*, in 1996. —*Kurt Wolff*

● **Cheatin' Heart Attack** / 1995 / Hightone ✦✦✦✦
Watson's hearty, down-to-earth honky tonk makes *Cheatin' Heart Attack* one of the most exciting country debuts this side of Junior Brown's *12 Shades of Brown*. Watson and his band Lone Star burn through 14 no-nonsense songs that prove the genre can be vital and fun at the same time. Watson's voice is pure, deep, and strong, and his songs feature guitar and pedal steel prominently. He's a veteran of the Texas honky tonk circuit, which shows in his sharp arrangements on songs like "List of Reasons," "Holes in the Wall," and "Nashville Rash"—the latter mixing heartfelt commentary on the current country market with a smart sense of humor. —*Kurt Wolff*

Blessed or Damned / 1996 / Hightone ✦✦✦
Blessed or Damned pretty much picks up where Watson's 1995 debut, *Cheatin' Heart Attack*, left off. He pines for "A Real Country Song" on modern radio, sings praises for his adopted state on "That's What I Like About Texas" (a good-natured duet with Johnny "Whiskey River" Bush), and wonders at the fate of his chosen musical genre on the moving title track. Watson may have no surprise ace in the hole on *Blessed or Damned*, but it's nonetheless a solid hand of fresh, invigorating material. —*Kurt Wolff*

Doc Watson (Arthel Watson)

b. Mar. 2, 1923, Deep Gap, NC
Banjo, Guitar, Vocals / Old-Time, Traditional Country, Traditional Folk
In this half of our century there have been three preeminently influential guitar players: Merle Travis, Chet Atkins, and Arthel "Doc" Watson, a flat-picking genius from Deep Gap, NC. Unlike the other two, Watson was in middle age before he gained any attention. Since 1960, though, when Watson was recorded with his family and friends in Folkways' *Old Time Music at Clarence Ashley's*, people have remained in awe of this gentle blind man who sings and picks with pure and emotional authenticity. The present generation, folkies and country pickers alike, including Ricky Skaggs, Vince Gill, the late Clarence White, Emmylou Harris, and literally hundreds of others, acknowledge their great debt to Watson. Watson has provided a further service to country/folk by his encyclopedic knowledge of many American traditional songs. While Merle Travis and Chet Atkins started on acoustic guitars and moved to electric, before Watson's "discovery" during the folk revival in the early '60s, he played electric in a local all-purpose band that played current rock, swing, country, and, of course, folk music. He gained recognition gradually, first from the *Clarence Ashley* album, which led to a performance at the Newport Folk Festival in 1963. Folkways soon recorded an album of Watson's, followed in 1964 by a series of albums by Vanguard, nearly one a year through the decade. No sooner had interest in folk music waned than Watson was back in great demand because of the three-disc *Will the Circle Be Unbroken*, a watershed album in 1972 that was created by the Nitty Gritty Dirt Band. It featured Watson, Travis, Roy Acuff, and a Who's Who of country greats. Watson's son Merle, a talent in his own right, began appearing with his father regularly. The result was good enough for them to win two Grammys for traditional music, in 1973 and 1974. Father and son played beautiful music together for more than 15 years, until Merle died on the family farm in 1985. Doc Watson continued his appearances, showcasing his beautiful voice, his great instrumental talent, and his mastery of traditional material.

Early in his childhood in Deep Gap, Watson was struck by an illness that restricted the bloodflow to his eyes, resulting in blindness at an early age. As a child he was surrounded by music and was given a new harmonica every Christmas. When he was ten, his father gave him a homemade fretless banjo, which Doc played consistently for the next three years. About the same time he picked up the banjo, Watson began attending the School for the Blind in Raleigh, NC. At the age of 13, Doc began playing guitar after being introduced to the instrument by his cousin. Six months after receiving his guitar, Doc and his older brother Linney began busking on street corners, singing traditional numbers. By his late teens, Watson had learned how to finger-pick from his neighbor Olin Miller.

In 1941 Watson joined a band that had a regular radio program in Lenoir, NC. It was on this show that he earned his nickname when one of the announcers referred to the guitarist as "Doc" during the broadcast. For the next six years he played around North Carolina. In 1947 he married Rosa Lee Carlton, the daughter of fiddler Gaither W. Carlton. Though his father-in-law taught him a number of traditional songs, Doc didn't play any traditional material publically during the '40s, preferring to concentrate on country. To pay the bills, he also worked as a piano tuner. Watson joined the supporting band of a local pianist and railroad worker named Jack Williams in 1953. With Williams, Doc played electric guitar and perfromed a variety of music, from country to rock and pop. After staying with Williams for eight years, Watson joined the Clarence Ashley String Band and travelled with the group to New York to appear at a Friends of Old-Time Music concert. His performance at the concert was a resounding success, and he was invited to perform at Gerde's Folk City in Greenwich Village.

The invitation to perform in New York was an indication that the folk boom of the early '60s was beginning to gain momentum, and Doc Watson became one of the major benefactors of the revival. College students began to follow his music, and he soon switched to acoustic guitar on the advice of Ralph Rinzler. In 1961 Watson made his recording debut on Clarence Ashley's *Old Time Music at Clarence Ashley's*, a performance that earned him considerable acclaim. Two years later his solo spot at the Newport Folk Festival stole the show; that same year he released his first solo album, *Doc Watson and Family*. In 1964 Doc began giving concerts accompanied by his son Merle on second guitar. From that point on, Doc and Merle were constant collaborators and popular performers on the folk and traditional music circuit. Even when the folk boom of the '60s died down toward the end of the decade, Watson retained his audience. When he was spotlighted on the Nitty Gritty Dirt Band's breakthrough 1972 album *Will the Circle Be Unbroken*, he earned another generation of new fans. In 1974 his album *Then and Now* won the Grammy for Best Ethnic or Traditional Recording; the next year, he and Merle took home the same award for their *Two Days in November*.

Doc and Merle continued to perform and record successfully during the early '80s, giving many successful concerts each year and earning many awards, including another Grammy in 1979 (Best Country Instrumental Performance for "Big Sandy/Leather Britches"). In 1985 Merle died in a tractor accident on his farm. After his son's death, Doc stopped performing for a short time, but he made a comeback supported by guitarist Jack Lawrence and bassist T. Michael Coleman, who had played with Watson since 1974. Throughout the '80s and '90s, Doc continued to perform and record to enthusiastic audiences. During that time he won two more Grammys—Best Traditional Folk Recording for both 1986's *Riding the Midnight Train* and 1990's *On Praying Ground*—as well as a North Carolina Award in Fine Arts. —*David Vinopal*

☆ **The Doc Watson Family** / 1963 / Smithsonian/Folkways ✦✦✦✦✦
Featuring musical support from such family members as fiddler Gaither Carlton, Doc Watson's debut album, *The Doc Watson Family*, boasts the most traditional performances of Watson—this is as authentic as country music gets. —*Mark A. Humphrey & David Vinopal*

☆ **Doc Watson** / 1964 / Vanguard ✦✦✦✦✦
His first Vanguard album, ca. 1964, features warm vocals, influential guitar, harmonica, and old-time banjo. —*Mark A. Humphrey*

Treasures Untold / 1964 / Vanguard ✦✦✦✦
Treasures Untold is comprised of unreleased performances recorded at the 1964 Newport Folk Festival. Doc Watson and his family were in fine form, breathing life into a number of old-timey songs ranging from ballads to folk songs to gospel. It's an exciting, affectionate performance, highlighted by four duets by Clarence White. —*Thom Owens*

☆ **Southbound** / 1966 / Vanguard ✦✦✦✦✦
Southbound was a pivotal record for Doc Watson. It demonstrated that Watson was capable of more than just dazzling interpretations of folk songs; he could also write excellent original material and rework new country songs in a fascinating manner. *Southbound* also marked the recorded debut of Merle Watson, Doc's astonishingly talented son. —*Thom Owens*

Ballads from Deep Gap / 1967 / Vanguard ✦✦✦
Featured are fine traditional songs, old ballads, and more. —*Mark A. Humphrey*

Old-Timey Concert / 1967 / Vanguard ✦✦✦
These wonderful performances feature Fred Price and Clint Howard. —*Mark A. Humphrey*

Doc Watson on Stage (Featuring Merle Watson) / 1971 / Vanguard ✦✦✦
A fine live album, it includes Watson's son Merle. —*Mark A. Humphrey*

Two Days in November / 1974 / Poppy ✦✦✦✦
The title of this record refers to the period of time over which it was recorded (Nov 1 & 2, 1973). That aside, there is nothing rushed about it. Watson made some of his best records while on the Poppy label, and this is no exception. —*Jim Worbois*

Memories / 1975 / Sugar Hill ✦✦✦✦
Doc Watson's musical influences were varied, and *Memories* demonstrates just how diverse those influences were. It features traditional country music from the Carter Family and Jimmie Rodgers, the bluegrass of Bill Monroe and the Country Gentlemen, the blues of Mississippi John Hurt, and the Texas swing of Bob Wills. It also features Doc a cappella and a cut with him on claw-hammer banjo. For those who enjoyed Doc's performances on the *Will the Circle* album, this would be a natural follow-up. —*Jim Worbois*

Red Rocking Chair / 1981 / Flying Fish ✦✦✦
This features such guest artists as Herb Pedersen, T. Michael Coleman, and more. —*AMG*

Doc and Merle Watson's Guitar Album / 1983 / Flying Fish ✦✦✦✦
Like *Pickin' the Blues*, *Guitar Album* features Doc and Merle Watson supported by a small band and playing blues. Both guitarists play with deft, nimble grace, spinning out surprisingly hard-edged lines that are simultaneously fluid and gritty. —*Thom Owens*

Riding the Midnight Train / 1984 / Sugar Hill ✦✦✦
This bluegrass album has Nashville super-pickers Sam Bush, Mark O'Connor, and Bela Fleck. These are the last recordings of Merle Watson. —*Mark A. Humphrey*

Down South / 1984 / Rykodisc ✦✦✦
More fine Vanguard tracks. —*Mark A. Humphrey*

Pickin' the Blues / 1985 / Flying Fish ✦✦✦✦
As the title says, *Pickin' the Blues* features Doc Watson playing the blues with his son Merle. The two guitarists are backed by a small band, which gives the two musicians the opportunity to stretch out. By the time of the album's 1984 release, Merle had already demonstrated that he was an exceptional blue guitarist, which makes the real revelation of the album Doc's hard, gritty playing. Rarely, if ever, had Doc sounded so tough, and that alone makes *Pickin' the Blues* a true delight. —*Thom Owens*

★ **The Essential Doc Watson** / 1986 / Vanguard ✦✦✦✦✦
Drawn from performances at the 1963 and 1964 Newport Folk Festival and featuring traditional country and folk songs, *The Essential Doc Watson* is a concise introduction to one of the greatest guitarists in country and folk music. —*Thom Owens*

Portrait / 1988 / Sugar Hill ✦✦✦
On this album, Watson is joined by such guest artists as Sam Bush and Mark O'Connor. —*AMG*

On Praying Ground / 1990 / Sugar Hill ✦✦✦
Down-home gospel. —*Mark A. Humphrey*

My Dear Old Southern Home / 1991 / Sugar Hill ✦✦✦
My Dear Old Southern Home is one of Doc Watson's best latter-day records, boasting an affectionate collection of old time and traditional country songs. Watson pays attention to the standards by the Carter Family and Jimmie Rodgers, but he also digs deep into the old timey songbook and comes up with gems from more obscure acts like the Delmore Brothers and Bonnie Dodd. For some fans, *My Dear Old Southern Home* will seem to lack Watson's signature guitar work, but it's a wonderful, warm listen. —*Thom Owens*

Remembering Merle / Jun. 1992 / Sugar Hill ✦✦✦✦
Remembering Merle is an affectionate tribute to Doc Watson's deceased son, featuring several songs, all recorded live between 1970 and 1976, that showcased his work. Doc and Merle touch on a number of different genres, from folk and blues to rockabilly, all the while demonstrating the younger Watson's considerable talent. —*Thom Owens*

Original Folkways Recordings / 1994 / Smithsonian/Folkways ✦✦✦

Vanguard Years / Nov. 14, 1995 / Vanguard ✦✦✦✦
Four-CD, 64-song collection drawn principally from Doc's Vanguard releases of the 1960s and early 1970s, tapping his solo LPs and performances at the 1963 and 1964 Newport Folk Festival. This was Doc's best period recording-wise, and certainly you couldn't hope for a better document of his virtuosity, as the guitarist covers all manner of American folk and blues styles over the course of the set. It's too much, however, for listeners who aren't big fans; Vanguard's *Essential Doc Watson* is a more economical survey. If you *are* a big fan, though, you'll be especially interested in the 16 previously unreleased performances. Comprising the whole of disc four, these are taken mostly from live duets with Merle Travis or Doc's son, Merle Watson. —*Richie Unterberger*

Watson Family Tradition / Rounder ✦✦✦✦
Featured are austere beauty, ancient ballads, and rough string-band sounds. Joining in are mother Annie Watson, wife Rosa Lee Watson, father-in-law Gaither Carlton, brother Arnold Watson, and son Merle Watson. The unpolished roots of Doc Watson. —*Mark A. Humphrey*

Lonesome Road / EMI America ✦✦
Doc does the country blues as well as anything else, and this record is filled with fine performances. From "Stone Wall" (on which Doc sings harmony with himself) to the hot picking on songs like "Minglewood Blues" and "I Ain't Going Honky Tonkin' Anymore," this is quite a good record. —*Jim Worbois*

Songs for Little Pickers / Sugar Hill ✦✦✦
Songs for Little Pickers is a wonderful live recording of Doc Watson performing family material that he remembers singing as a child in North Carolina. —*Thom Owens*

Gene Watson

b. Oct. 11, 1943, Palestine, TX
Guitar, Vocals / Traditional Country, Country-Pop, Honky Tonk
Though he can sing honky tonk, Gene Watson has made a reputation for soulful ballads in the classical country tradition. After working as an auto-body man, he had success with "Love in the Hot Afternoon," which did well in 1975 as a single and as his debut album. His hits have been steady since then, with "Farewell Party," "Got No Reason Now for Going Home," "Nothing Sure Looked Good on You," and "Memories to Burn." Watson is a vocal stylist of considerable talent. —*David Vinopal*

Greatest Hits [MCA] / 1986 / MCA ✦✦✦✦
MCA's *Greatest Hits* collection fills in the gaps left by Curb's *Greatest Hits* collection, featuring such '80s hit singles as "What She Don't Know Won't Hurt Her," "Fourteen Carat Mind," and "You're Out Doing What I'm Here Doing Without." —*Thom Owens*

Back in the Fire / 1989 / Warner Brothers ✦✦✦
Gene Watson's music was always traditionalist, so it is no suprise that his 1989 comeback album *Back in the Fire* fits directly within the new traditionalist movement that began to dominate country music at the time of the record's release. What separates Watson from the pack of singers that followed him is how closely he sticks to the roots—despite a relatively slick contemporary production, the album is straightforward, hard country, highlighted by a clutch of remarkable ballads. What distinguishes *Back in the Fire* is the first-rate song selection and the exceptional performances from Watson, who continually demonstrates his talent for pure, unaffected country singing. —*Thom Owens*

● **Greatest Hits [Curb]** / 1990 / Curb ✦✦✦✦
This is a solid collection of `70s hits by this unpretentious, terribly underrated country singer. The key track is "Farewell Party," a deceptive, near-trance-inducing honky tonk number that delivers an emotional knockout at precisely the moment many country songs wimp out. —*Dan Cooper*

Gillian Welch

Guitar, Vocals / Singer-Songwriter, Alternative Country, Americana
A young singer-songwriter armed with a voice and sensibility far beyond her years, Gillian Welch drew widespread acclaim for her

deft, evocative resurrection of the musical styles most commonly associated with the rural Appalachia of the early 20th century. Welch was born in 1968 in California and grew up in West Los Angeles, where her parents scored the music for "The Carol Burnett Show." As a child she became fascinated by bluegrass and early country music, in particular the work of the Stanley Brothers, the Delmore Brothers, and the Carter Family.

In the early 1990s Welch attended the Berklee School of Music in Boston. As part of a duo with fellow student David Rawlings she began performing her own material as well as traditional country and buegrass songs. After honing their skills in local open mike showcases, the duo began performing regularly throughout the country. While opening for Peter Rowan in Nashville, they were spotted by musician and producer T-Bone Burnett, who helped Welch and Rawlings land a record deal. With Burnett producing, they cut 1996's starkly beautiful *Revival*, an album split between bare-bones duo performances—some recorded in mono to capture a bygone sound—and more full-bodied cuts featuring legendary session-men like guitarist James Burton, upright bassist Roy Huskey, Jr., and drummers Buddy Harmon and Jim Keltner. —*Jason Ankeny*

● **Revival** / Apr. 1996 / Geffen ✦✦✦✦
Gillian Welch's debut album, *Revival*, looks to be one of the strongest artistic introductions of the year. Produced by T Bone Burnett, *Revival* could be lifted from some long-lost Depression Era folk recording. Welch sings with a focused austerity, bypassing any modern conceits to concentrate on songs about the rudiments of life: survival, heartbreak, struggle, honesty, natural beauty. The closest thing to decadence comes when a dying man asks that his still be burned down, turning to ash the bane of his life. The closest thing to optimism comes in a song about a fragile mountain flower's ability to endure the elements. Welch may be accused of losing herself in the styles of the past; her music evokes the primitive, yet aesthetically timeless, work of the Carter Family and the Stanley Brothers. But such an argument becomes empty when hearing the deep passion, and compassion, of Welch's songs. From the astringent quality of her voice to the bare beauty of her melodies to the resourceful moodiness of guitarist David Rawlings, Welch comes on like a rare and precious talent with a vision so set and strong that it can't be denied. You'll be hearing about her soon. —*Michael McCall*

Kevin Welch

b. Aug. 17, 1955, Long Beach, CA
Vocals / Singer-Songwriter, Alternative Country, Americana
Oklahoma singer-songwriter Kevin Welch made his name as a writer of hits for the Judds, Ricky Skaggs, Gary Morris, Moe Bandy, Don Williams, and others before bringing the fully realized characters of his songs to his own recordings in 1990. Though based in Nashville, Welch can claim kinship with the songwriting style of Texans like Joe Ely and Butch Hancock. —*Brian Mansfield*

● **Kevin Welch** / 1990 / Reprise ✦✦✦✦
Welch's songs sprawl out like great, open flatlands, mixing elements of folk, country, and rock in a captivating way. Welch himself—half-singing, half-speaking songs such as "Hello, I'm Gone" and "Some Kind of Paradise"—comes off as a cross between a renegade storyteller and a heartland romantic. —*Brian Mansfield*

Western Beat / 1991 / Reprise ✦✦✦
The title of *Western Beat* signals what kind of music Kevin Welch plays—it's Western music, but with a heavy, urban beat. It's a fresh, lively sound, supported by a number of first-rate songs, including "Sam's Town," "Train to Birmingham," and "Early Summer Rain." —*Thom Owens*

Life Down Here on Earth / 1995 / Dead Reckoning ✦✦

Freddy Weller

b. Sep. 9, 1947, Atlanta, GA
Guitar, Vocals / Country-Pop, Pop-Rock
Freddy Weller found success as a singer, musician, and songwriter in both pop and country. Born in Atlanta, he began playing banjo

and mandolin at age eight, and went on to learn guitar. As a songwriter, he was influenced at a young age by Hank Williams. Weller got his start as a performer on the "Georgia Jubilee" as a teen, where he played with Jerry Reed, Ray Stevens, Joe South and Billy Joe Royal. After playing on Royal's hit "Down in the Boondocks" in 1965, Weller joined his band; while on tour he met the pop group Paul Revere and the Raiders, and later joined them as lead guitarist.

His first songwriting success came in 1969 when he and Tommy Roe penned the pop hits "Dizzy" and "Jam Up Jell Tight." Later that year he made his solo recording debut with the Joe South tune "Games People Play." His next effort, "These Are Not My People," climbed to the Top Five. He continued recording as a solo act and touring with the Raiders through 1971, when he left the group and began to focus on a career in Nashville. In 1972 he wrote "Lonely Women Make Good Lovers," providing Bob Luman with a Top Five hit. That year he also had three hits of his own, the biggest being the Top 15 "She Loves Me (Right out of My Mind)."

Weller had his final Top Ten hit the next year with a cover of Chuck Berry's "Too Much Monkey Business." He then recorded a self-titled album, but it only provided two minor hits. Through the early '80s, Weller continued to reach the lower rungs of the chart, but major success eluded him; still, he continued to do well as a songwriter, penning successful songs for such big names as Reba McEntire ("They Asked About You"), John Michael Montgomery ("She Don't Need a Band to Dance"), and George Jones ("What I Do Best"). —Sandra Brennan

Games People Play/These Are Not My People / 1969 / Columbia ✦✦✦✦

The Promised Land / 1972 / Columbia ✦✦✦

● **Freddy Weller's Greatest Hits** / 1975 / Columbia ✦✦✦✦

Freddy Weller / 1975 / ABC/Dot ✦✦✦

Love Got in the Way / 1978 / Columbia ✦✦✦

Go for the Night / 1980 / Columbia ✦✦✦

Freddy Weller rides into the '80s with *Go for the Night*, a record that sounds like slick, countrified versions of songs Jimmy Buffett passed on. Nothing stands out as on his previous efforts, but there is a certain charm that pervades this release. Weller is too much a professional to make a bad record, but this isn't one of his best. —James Chrispell

Kitty Wells (Muriel Deason)

b. Aug. 30, 1918, Nashville, TN

Guitar, Vocals / Traditional Country, Honky Tonk, Nashville Sound/Countrypolitan

One of the few country stars born in Nashville, Kitty Wells (born Muriel Deason) had a string of hits from the '50s to the early '70s that earned her the title "Queen of Country Music." She made her radio debut on Nashville's WSIX, where she met her future husband, Johnnie Wright of Johnnie and Jack. She began touring as part of Johnnie and Jack's show; Wright gave her the stage name, taken from a folk song called "I'm A-Goin' to Marry Kitty Wells." Wells recorded unsuccessfully for RCA before switching to Decca, where she hit with 1952's "It Wasn't God Who Made Honky Tonk Angels," a response to Hank Thompson's "The Wild Side of Life." Its controversial pre-feminist lyrics, which blamed unfaithful men for creating unfaithful women, paved the way for Loretta Lynn and Tammy Wynette and established Wells as the first major female country star. Wells recorded a number of answer songs and remakes, but she has top-notch original material as well, including some of Harlan Howard's earliest hits.

Wells began singing as a child, learning guitar from her father. As a teenager, she sang with her sisters on a local radio station; they performed under the name the Deason Sisters. The group began singing on the station in 1936. The next year she married Johnny Wright. Shortly after their marriage, Wells and Wright began performing together, along with his sister, Louise Wright; they called themselves Johnny Wright and the Harmony Girls. Jack Anglin, Louise's husband, joined the group in 1939, and they

renamed the band the Tennessee Hillbillies, which would eventually evolve into the Tennessee Mountain Boys.

Anglin was drafted in 1942. After his departure, Wright and Wells performed as a duo; it was at this time that she adopted her stage name. When Anglin returned from the army, he and Wright formed a duo, Johnny and Jack. Kitty would tour with the duo, occasionally performing backup vocals. In 1946 and 1947 the duo had a regular spot at the Grand Ole Opry and Wells rarely performed with them. However, she did sing with the pair when they joined the "Louisiana Hayride" in 1948.

The "Louisiana Hayride" helped Johnny and Jack land a record contract with RCA Records in 1949. That same year, Kitty recorded some gospel tracks—featuring Johnny and Jack as instrumental support for RCA, but they were unsuccessful. After those recordings, Wells was more or less retired for the next few years. In 1952 Paul Cohen, an executive at Decca Records, approached her to record "It Wasn't God Who Made Honky Tonk Angels." It became a smash hit, reaching No. 1 in the summer and staying in that position for six weeks. Later in 1952 she joined the Grand Ole Opry.

"It Wasn't God Who Made Honky Tonk Angels" was followed by "Paying for That Back Street Affair," a response to Webb Pierce's "Back Street Affair." The single reached No. 6 in the spring of 1953, helping to establish a permanent place at the top of the charts for Wells. For the rest of the '50s, she hit the Top Ten with regularity, racking up a total of 23 Top Ten hits. In the early '60s her career dipped slightly, but she continued to have Top Ten hits frequently. During the late '60s and '70s Wells' streak of hits evaporated, but she managed to have a string of minor hits and remained a popular concert attraction.

In 1974 Wells was inducted into the Country Music Hall of Fame, and with good reason. Kitty Wells broke down the doors for female country singers, paving the way for artists like Patsy Cline, Tammy Wynette, and Loretta Lynn. During the '80s her activity slowed—in addition to running a museum outside of Nashville, she toured with her husband and frequently appeared on the Grand Ole Opry. In 1991 Kitty Wells was given a Lifetime Achievement Award from the Grammys. —Brian Mansfield & Stephen Thomas Erlewine

Dust on the Bible / 1959 / Decca ✦✦✦✦

Dust on the Bible is a moving set of country gospel performed with affection and honest by Kitty Wells. The material on the LP ranges from standards to contemporary classics like "The Great Speckled Bird," and not a single cut on the record fails to raise the hairs on the back of your neck. In the late '50s, country gospel albums didn't come much finer than *Dust on the Bible*. —Thom Owens

Seasons of My Heart / 1960 / Decca ✦✦✦✦

Seasons of My Heart is an excellent LP collection of country ballads highlighted by the title track, Hank Thompson's "Most of All," Marty Robbins' "The Hands You're Holding Now," Hank Locklin's "Send Me the Pillow You Dream On," John D. Loudermilk's "If I Had the Right to Do You Wrong," Kitty's original "I'll Be All Smiles Tonight," and the hit singles "Fickle Fun," "The Other Cheek" and "Amigo's Guitar." —Thom Owens

Kitty's Choice / 1960 / Decca ✦✦✦✦

Kitty's Choice is comprised almost entirely of contemporary country classics like "Sugartime," "Your Cheatin' Heart," "Half As Much," "Tennessee Waltz," "Jambalaya," and "My Happiness," adding a couple of obscurities for good measure. All of the songs are performed with gusto by Wells, making it one of her most enjoyable records of the early '60s. —Thom Owens

Kitty Wells' Golden Favorites / 1961 / Decca ✦✦✦✦

Despite the title, *Kitty Wells' Golden Favorites* isn't strictly a greatest hits collection. Though most of the LP is comprised of big hits—"Hey Joe," "(I'll Always Be Your) Fraulein," "Jealousy," "Mommy for a Day," "Amigo's Guitar," "Left to Right"—it is padded out by tracks that were either lesser hits ("All the Time") or songs that were never released as singles (an excellent version of Don Gibson's "I Can't Stop Loving You," "Your Wild Life's Gonna Get You Down"). All of the cuts that weren't hits are nearly equal in quality to the popular singles, making *Golden Favorites* one of Wells' best early-'60s records. — *Stephen Thomas Erlewine*

Queen of Country Music / 1962 / Decca ✦✦✦

It's ironic that an LP called *Queen of Country Music* would contain covers of pop songs like "Moody River" and "What Am I Living For," but it's a testament to Kitty's talent that she can make the songs sound like genuine country numbers. Furthermore, the rest of the record consists of excellent cuts like "Hello Walls," "Am I That Easy to Forget," and "Pick Me Up on Your Way Down," making the record a thoroughly enjoyable listen—even if it doesn't include any hit singles. — *Thom Owens*

~~**Singing on Sunday** / 1962 / Decca ✦✦✦~~

Relying on traditional gospel songs, ~~*Singing on Sunday* is an~~ enjoyable but unexceptional early-'60s gospel LP from Kitty Wells, highlighted by excellent takes on "The Wings of a Dove" and "That Glory Bound Train." — *Thom Owens*

The Kitty Wells Story / 1963 / Decca ✦✦✦✦

The Kitty Wells Story was the first vinyl collection of Kitty's biggest hits ("It Wasn't God Who Made Honky Tonk Angels," "Paying for That Back Street Affair," "Whose Shoulder Will You Cry On," "Makin' Believe") and it remains a strong compilation. Not all of her biggest hits are present on the set ,and it was later replaced with stronger collections; but the compilation remains entertaining, and it has a couple of gems that never found their way onto any other set (with the notable exception, of course, of Bear Family's gigantic, multi-disc box set). — *Thom Owens*

Especially for You / 1964 / Decca ✦✦✦

Though the production occasionally leans too heavily toward the pop direction and there are a few awkward covers such as "Busted," *Especially for You* remains an exceptional mid-'60s LP from Kitty Wells, highlighted by the hit singles "Unloved Unwanted," "Will Your Lawyer Talk to God," and "We Missed You," plus strong versions of "Act Naturally," "Make the World Go Away," and "Ring of Fire." — *Thom Owens*

Country Music Time / 1964 / Decca ✦✦✦

Despite a handful of undistinguished songs, *Country Music Time* remains a strong mid-'60s album from Kitty Wells, highlighted by the hit singles "This White Circle on My Finger," "Password," and "I've Thought of Leaving You." — *Thom Owens*

Burning Memories / 1965 / Decca ✦✦✦

Though it has a few strong tracks, particularly the hit single "I'll Repossess My Heart," the LP *Burning Memories* is too uneven in terms of material and is burdened by too many overdubbed vocal choruses and strings to be consistently enjoyable. — *Thom Owens*

The Kitty Wells Family Gospel Sing / 1965 / Decca ✦✦✦

The Kitty Wells Family Gospel Sing is a good, but unremarkable, country gospel LP from the mid-'60s, largely comprised of contemporary songs that fail to make a lasting impression. — *Thom Owens*

Lonesome, Sad and Blue / 1965 / Decca ✦✦✦

A loosely constructed concept LP about loneliness and heartbreak, *Lonesome, Sad and Blue* is a typically enjoyable set of country ballads and weepers from Kitty Wells. Though the production and song selection occasionally veer too close to country-pop territory (witness the version of Henry Mancini's "Dear Heart" and the Jordanaires' vocal accompaniment), Wells' powerful voice keeps the album's footing firmly in country, especially when she belts out "Oh, Lonesome Me," "The Race Is On," "Welcome to My World," "Cheatin' Is Catching," and "You're the Only World I Know." — *Thom Owens*

Lonely Street / 1965 / Decca ✦✦✦

Lonely Street is a slightly uneven but enjoyable mid-'60s LP that alternates between country-pop ballads and honky tonk. Among the highlights are "If Teardrops Were Pennies," "Sweeter Than the Flowers," "The Waltz of the Angels," and the title track. — *Thom Owens*

Country All the Way / 1966 / Decca ✦✦✦

Country All the Way is a strong mid-'60s LP from Kitty Wells, featuring supportive, not overbearing, vocal accompaniment from the Jordanaires, as well as an excellent selection of songs high-

lighted by the hit singles "A Woman Half My Age," "A Woman Never Forgets," and "Meanwhile Down at Joe's," plus excellent album cuts like "Too Many Rivers," "Together Again," "Cryin' Time," and "Nobody But a Fool (Would Love You)." — *Thom Owens*

The Kitty Wells Show / 1966 / Decca ✦✦

The Kitty Wells Show is an entertaining LP documenting a mid-'60s concert headlined by Wells. Kitty performs only four songs—"You Left Your Mark on Me," "It's All Over But the Crying," "Love's Enough for Me," and her trademark "It Wasn't God Who Made Honky Tonk Angels"—with the rest of the album taken over by her fellow country vocalists Bill Phillips, Bobby Wright, and Johnny Wright, plus instrumentalists Paul Yandell and Odell Martin. Though it would have been nice to hear a complete concert from Kitty, the record is fun; nevertheless, it isn't really the kind of album that holds up on repeat listens. — *Thom Owens*

Songs Made Famous by Jim Reeves / 1966 / Decca ✦✦✦

Songs Made Famous by Jim Reeves is an enjoyable LP collection of Kitty singing songs associated with Reeves including "Four Walls," "Billy Bayou," "She'll Have to Go," "Welcome to My World," and "Bimbo." — *Thom Owens*

Kitty Wells [Vocalion] / 1966 / Vocalion ✦✦✦

Released on Decca's Vocalion subsidary, *Kitty Wells* is a fitfully entertaining LP collection of odds and ends that ranges from sublime ("Thou Shalt Not Steal," "You'll Never Be Mine Again," "A Heartache for a Keepsake") to the merely average ("The Life They Live in Songs"). — *Thom Owens*

Love Makes the World Go Around / 1967 / Decca ✦✦✦

For most Kitty Wells fans, *Love Makes the World Go Around* is a bit of a frustrating listen. The LP does boast a handful of fine songs, particularly the Dallas Frazier covers "Baby's Coming Home" and "There Goes My Everything," but the production is too lush for Kitty's honky tonk roots, as the minor hit singles "Only Me and My Hairdresser Know" and "Love Makes the World Go Around" indicate. — *Thom Owens*

Queen of Honky Tonk Street / 1967 / Decca ✦✦✦

Though the material is slightly uneven and the album has only one hit single (in the form of the title track), *Queen of Honky Tonk Street* is still a very good late-'60s LP by Kitty Wells. Occasionally the production is a bit too heavy for Wells' honky tonk inclinations, but her gutsy voice always makes the songs worth hearing. — *Thom Owens*

Together Again / 1967 / Decca ✦✦✦

Together Again is a very entertaining reunion album from Kitty Wells and Red Foley. From the hit singles "Happiness Means You," "Hello Number One," and "Living As Strangers" to album tracks like "Together Again," "My Wall Came Tumblin' Down," "Have I Told You Lately That I Love You?" and "My Happiness," there isn't a weak song on the LP, and the two vocalists sound terrific together. — *Thom Owens*

Singin' 'em Country / 1970 / Decca ✦✦✦

Singin' 'Em Country is a slightly uneven but thoroughly enjoyable LP from 1970, boasting excellent versions of Felice Bryant's "We Could," Don Gibson's "Don't Take All Your Loving," and Carl Perkins' "Rise and Shine." — *Thom Owens*

Greatest Hits, Vol. 1 / 1989 / Step One ✦✦✦

Contrary to what the title suggests, Step One's *Greatest Hits, Vol. 1* does not contain the original hit versions of Kitty Wells' biggest hits. Instead, the album consists entirely of re-recordings from 1989; they are adequate, but they pale next to the originals. — *Thom Owens*

Greatest Hits, Vol. 2 / 1989 / Step One ✦✦✦

This second volume contains "I'll Get Over You" and other hits. — *AMG*

★ **Country Music Hall of Fame Series** / 1991 / MCA ✦✦✦✦✦

Country Music Hall of Fame contains 16 of Kitty Wells' best songs, giving a reasonably thorough overview of her career by combining big hits like "It Wasn't God Who Made Honky Tonk Angels" with minor hits like "A Woman Half My Age." The songs on this single disc were recorded for Decca Records between 1952 and 1965, so it naturally touches on many of the highlights from her artistic heyday, including "Release Me," "Making Believe," "I Can't Stop Loving You," "Mommy for a Day," and "Heartbreak, USA." It's an excellent retrospective, even though several important cuts—including most of her uptempo material—are missing. Nevertheless, it collects many of her most important songs and provides a terrific introduction to one of the most important vocalists in country music history. —*Stephen Thomas Erlewine*

Kitty Wells Duets / 1995 / Pair ♦♦♦

Honky Tonk Angel / 1996 / ♦♦♦♦
Honky Tonk Angel is a 19-track, single-disc import compilation of the majority of Kitty Wells' Top Ten hits from the '50s and the early '60s. Featuring such classic honky tonk hits as "Makin' Believe," "Release Me," "Heartbreak USA," "Jealousy," "Searching (For Someone Like You)" and "It Wasn't God Who Made Honky Tonk Angels," the disc is first-rate, but it doesn't offer enough material that is different from *Country Music Hall of Fame* to make it worth an extensive search. —*Stephen Thomas Erlewine*

Country Spotlight / K-Tel ♦
Country Spotlight does not feature the original, classic versions of Wells' greatest hits; it's full of decidedly inferior re-recordings. Besides that, it is woefully short, at 25 minutes, making this disc a complete ripoff. —*Stephen Thomas Erlewine*

Queen of Country [box set] / Bear Family ♦♦♦♦
The Queen of Country is an exhaustive four-disc box that covers all of Kitty Wells' recordings for RCA and Decca between 1949 and 1958. For the diehard fan, it's an essential collection, but the casual fan will find its thoroughness overwhelming. —*Stephen Thomas Erlewine*

Peter Wernick

Banjo / Progressive Bluegrass, Instrumental
Pete Wernick is a founding member and banjo player for Hot Rize, a progressive bluegrass group from Colorado. —*David Vinopal*

● **Dr. Banjo Steps Out** / 1978 / Flying Fish ♦♦♦♦
Wernick steps out on this one and explores new ground. Not a Hot Rize album. —*Chip Renner*

On a Roll / 1993 / Sugar Hill ♦♦♦

Dottie West

b. Oct. 11, 1932, McMinnville, TN, d. Sep. 4, 1991, Nashville?
Guitar, Vocals / Country-Pop, Nashville Sound/Countrypolitan
Dottie West was one of the most successful, and controversial, performers to rise to popularity during the Nashville Sound era; like her friend and mentor Patsy Cline, West's battles for identity and respect within the male-dominated country music hierarchy were instrumental in enabling other female artists to gain control over their careers. Born Dorothy Marie Walsh outside McMinnville, TN, she was the oldest of ten children; after her abusive, alcoholic father abandoned the family, her mother opened a small cafe. West began appearing on local radio just shy of her 13th birthday and went on to study music at Tennessee Tech, where she also sang in a band. The group's steel guitar player, Bill West, became her first husband in 1953.

After graduation, the Wests and their two children moved to Cleveland, OH; there, Dottie began appearing on the television program "Landmark Jamboree" as one half of a country-pop vocal duo called the Kay-Dots alongside partner Kathy Dee. At the same time, West made numerous trips to Nashville in hopes of landing a recording deal; in 1959, she and Bill auditioned for Starday's Don Pierce, and were offered a contract. Although the resulting singles West cut for the label proved unsuccessful, she nonetheless moved to Nashville in 1961. There, she and her husband fell in with a group of aspiring songwriters like Willie Nelson, Roger Miller, Hank Cochran, and Harlan Howard; they also became close friends with Patsy Cline and her husband, Charlie Dick.

West earned her first Top 40 hit in 1963 with "Let Me Off at the Corner," followed a year later by the Top Ten "Love Is No Excuse," a duet with Jim Reeves (who had scored a major success with her

Dottie West

"Is This Me?"). Also in 1964 she auditioned for producer Chet Atkins, the architect of the Nashville Sound, who agreed to produce her composition "Here Comes My Baby." The single made West the first female country artist to win a Grammy Award, leading to an invitation to join the Grand Ole Opry. In Atkins, West found the perfect producer for her plaintive vocals and heart-wrenching songs; after releasing the *Here Comes My Baby* LP in 1965, they reunited for the next year's *Suffer Time*, which generated her biggest hit yet in "Would You Hold It Against Me." In 1967 the West/Atkins pairing issued three separate albums— *With All My Heart and Soul* (featuring the smash "Paper Mansions"), *Dottie West Sings Sacred Ballads*, and *I'll Help You Forget Her*. She also appeared in a pair of films, *Second Fiddle to a Steel Guitar* and *There's a Still on the Hill*.

After the 1968 LP *Country Girl*, West teamed with Don Gibson for a record of duets, 1969's *Dottie and Don*, featuring the No. 2 hit "Rings of Gold." The album was her last with Chet Atkins, and she followed it with two 1970 releases, *Forever Yours* and *Country Boy and Country Girl*, a collection of pairings with Jimmy Dean. Around the time of 1971's *Have You Heard...Dottie West*, she left Bill West, and in 1972 she married drummer Bryan Metcalf, who was a dozen years her junior. Suddenly, West's image underwent a huge metamorphosis; the woman who once performed dressed in gingham dresses and refused to record Kris Kristofferson's "Help Me Make It Through the Night" because it was "too sexy" began appearing in skin-tight stage attire. As the sexual revolution peaked, so did West's career; after the 1973 success of the crossover smash "Country Sunshine," written for Coca-Cola, her material became far more provocative and, much to the chagrin of country purists, more commericially successful as well.

After the release of *House of Love* in 1974, West notched a number of Top 40 hits like "Last Time I Saw Him," "When It's Just You and Me," and "Tonight You Belong to Me." In 1977 she was recording the song "Every Time Two Fools Collide" when, according to legend, Kenny Rogers suddenly entered the studio and began singing along. Released as a duet, the single hit No. 1, West's first; the duo's 1979 "All I Ever Need Is You" and 1981 "What Are We Doin' in Love" topped the charts as well, and a 1979 duets album titled *Classics* also proved successful. As a solo artist, West notched a pair of No. 1s in 1980—"A Lesson in Leavin'" and "Are You Happy Baby?"

As the 1980s progressed, West's popularity began to slip; she appeared in a revealing photo spread in the men's magazine *Oui*, and toured with a production of the musical *The Best Little Whorehouse in Texas*. In 1983 she was married for the third time, to soundman Al Winters, who was some 23 years younger than she. A year later she appeared in the play *Bring It On Home*. Her last chart hit, "We Know Better Now," reached only No. 53 in 1985. Although she remained a popular touring act, West's financial problems mounted, and in 1990, after divorcing Winters, she declared bankruptcy, culminating in the foreclosure of her Nashville mansion. After a car accident and a public auction of her possessions, she began making plans for a comeback, including an album of duets and an autobiography. But en route to a September 4, 1991, appearance at Opryland, the car she was riding in flipped, and a few days later West died of her injuries. A made-for-television biography followed a few years later. —*Jason Ankeny*

A Legend in My Time / 1971 / RCA ✦✦✦✦
Sparse instrumentation on a 1970 reissue of sad ballads: "Don't You Ever Get Tired of Hurting Me" and "There Goes My Everything." —*Bil Carpenter*

Special Delivery / 1979 / United Artists ✦✦✦
With her career revitalized by the duets with Kenny Rogers, West takes a new tack. Her "Country Sunshine" is replaced with country-funk and a touch of melancholy. —*Tom Roland*

● **Essential Dottie West** / Jan. 30, 1996 / RCA ✦✦✦✦
Featuring 20 of her best songs, *The Essential Dottie West* lives up to its title. All of her biggest singles—not only solo hits like "Country Sunshine" and "Paper Mansions," but also her duets with Don Gibson ("Rings of Gold" and "There's a Story (Goin' Round)" and Jim Reeves ("Love Is No Excuse")—are included, making this the one definitive compilation. —*Stephen Thomas Erlewine*

Shelly West

b. 1958, Cleveland, OH
Vocals / Country-Pop, Urban Cowboy
Shelly West, daughter of the legendary Dottie West and her first husband, Bill, was a popular singer of pop-flavored country tunes during the 1980s.

She got her start at age 17 touring with her mother's show; she started out singing backup but was soon given lead vocal chores. While touring, she fell in love with her mother's lead guitarist, Allen Frizzell; they married and left the band in 1977 to move to California. Allen was the little brother of Lefty and David Frizzell, the latter of whom had a regular gig in a neighboring town. The newlyweds soon joined his band and played with him for a few months. They toured the Southwest, and upon their return, David began looking for a record label. A demo of the duet "Lovin' on Borrowed Time" featuring West and her brother-in-law impressed record producer Snuff Garrett, who signed them both to Casablanca West. Unfortunately, Polygram took over the label and dumped the duo, who unsuccessfully tried their luck in Nashville. Garrett still believed the two had potential and eventually played their song and its follow-up "You're the Reason God Made Oklahoma" to actor Clint Eastwood, who had just founded his own record label, Viva. Eastwood liked the latter song and added it to his film *Any Which Way You Can*, and the song hit No. 1 on the country charts in early 1981.

Their next four songs, beginning with the Top Ten hit "A Texas State of Mind," were also successful, and the duo's considerable success continued through 1985, when they split up. (They cited a lack of good duet songs as their main reason; the fact that West and her husband had just divorced may also have been a factor). West made her solo debut in 1983 with "Jose Cuervo," which hit No. 1 and provided a sales boost for the tequila company. Her solo follow-up, "Flight 309 to Tennessee," made the Top Five. Between 1984 and 1986 West had a string of solo successes that included "Somebody Buy This Cowgirl a Beer" and "Don't Make Me Wait on the Moon." Later that year she had one more mid-range hit, "Love Don't Come Any Better Than This," and then faded from the charts. She basically stopped recording after remarrying, but she did reunite with David Frizzell for a few shows in the late 1980s. —*Sandra Brennan*

Red Hot / 1983 / Viva ✦✦✦
● **West by West** / 1983 / Warner/Viva ✦✦✦✦
Don't Make Me Wait on the Moon / 1984 / Warner/Viva ✦✦✦

Speedy West

b. 1924, Springfield, MO
Pedal Steel Guitar / Traditional Country, Instrumental Country
One of the greatest virtuosos that country music has ever produced, Speedy West bridged the Western swing and rockabilly eras with eye-popping steel guitar. Besides contributing to literally thousands of country sessions, West cut many of his own instrumentals, as a solo act and with his guitarist partner Jimmy Bryant. Adept at boogie, blues, and Hawaiian ballads, West played with an infectious joy and daring improvisation that, at its most adventurous, could be downright experimental. It's doubtful that anyone could collect all of Speedy's solos under one roof, but it was his sessions of the 1950s and early 1960s—especially those with Jimmy Bryant—that found his genius at its most freewheeling and dazzling. —*Richie Unterberger*

Two Guitars Country Style / 1954 / Capitol ✦✦✦✦
West of Hawaii / 1958 / Capitol ✦✦✦
Steel Guitar / 1960 / Capitol ✦✦✦✦
A twin album to the set released by his partner Jimmy Bryant at the same time (*Country Cabin Jazz*), both featuring the same bands. Twelve virtuosic steel guitar showcases, ranging from frenetic boogie to Hawaiian-like tranquil moods. —*Richie Unterberger*

Guitar Spectacular / 1963 / Capitol ✦✦✦
Steel Guitar from Outer Space / 1989 / See For Miles ✦✦✦✦
Together with the 1960 *Steel Guitar* LP, this is West at his peak. This compilation gets the nod not because of superior quality, but because of sheer quantity—24 tracks, half from rare '50s singles, the other half comprising the entirety of his 1963 album *Guitar Spectacular*. The appeal of these skyrocketing boogies and swing tunes is not at all limited to country fans; even in the 1990s, it sounds quite advanced and cutting-edge. —*Richie Unterberger*

For the Last Time / 1990 / Step One ✦✦✦
Featured are "Wound Tight," "Boogie Man," "Lazy Guitar," "Moonlight Valley," and others. —*AMG*

● **Stratosphere Boogie** / 1995 / Razor & Tie ✦✦✦✦
The 16-track *Stratosphere Boogie: The Flaming Guitars of Speedy West and Jimmy Bryant* collects highlights from the duo's early '50s records, picking out selected album tracks and singles. It's an excellent retrospective, demonstrating the depth of their mind-bending instrumental genius. —*Thom Owens*

Johnny Western

b. Oct. 28, 1934, Twin Harbors, MN
Vocals / Cowboy
A lover of the Old West and its mythos from childhood, Johnny Western was one of the finest and most impassioned exponents of cowboy songs, a successor to both Gene Autry and Marty Robbins. His career paved the way for the work of Michael Martin Murphey, Ian Tyson, and the Riders in the Sky, all of whom owed him a debt for carrying cowboy music into and beyond the 1960s. He was born in Twin Harbors, MN, and raised at various Civilian Conservation Corps camps (where his father was an officer and instructor) and Indian reservations along the Canadian border. The turning point in his life came on his fifth birthday, when his parents took him to see a 1936 Western called *Guns and Guitars* starring Gene Autry; Johnny knew then and there that he wanted to be exactly like the man on the horse, strumming a guitar and singing a song.

For his twelfth birthday, Western was given a guitar; hardly a year had gone by when he was invited to turn professional. He'd been recorded at the local 4-H Club singing Gene Autry's "Riding Down the Canyon" and other songs, which resulted in an invitation to join a collegiate singing trio. He mostly played rhythm guitar but also got to sing, and when the group recorded an audition tape for KDHL in Faribault, MN, Johnny was asked to sing a solo.

He chose "(Ghost) Riders in the Sky" and ended up getting a weekly radio spot, which then became three days a week, and finally six days each week. In addition to singing, he acted as a deejay and host, introducing live and recorded country and western music. He also earned a mention in *Billboard* as the youngest deejay and singer on American radio. By the age of 16 he was playing on bills with his one-time idols the Sons of the Pioneers.

Soon after graduation, he made the jump from radio to television, becoming a singing cowboy on KMMT-TV, and landed a recording contract with a small Minnesota-based record label called JOCO. He and his fellow guitarist John Fields cut a handful of singles, including "The Violet and the Rose" and "Let Old Mother Nature Have Her Way," which received good airplay locally and in Iowa, Wisconsin, and the Dakotas. Johnny Western's television show, which allowed him to sing to his young audience before introducing the day's Western movie, lasted for two years. During this period, he got to play concerts with Western stars such as Rex Allen and Tex Ritter, and had them as guests on his show. In 1954, however, he gave up the progam, heading for Hollywood to pursue his real goal, to be a movie cowboy.

This was the hardest jump of all, because they weren't making many Westerns in Hollywood or looking for singing cowboys. It was years before he got to work in front of a movie camera; in the meantime, he earned a place in Gene Autry's band, replacing Johnny Bond as a guitarist and singer. After Autry retired from performing, Western did a pilot for a series called "Pony Express," which led to appearances in more than 30 other television shows (including "Gunsmoke") and several feature films, including *The Dalton Girls, Fort Bowie*, and *Gunfight at Dodge City*. In 1957 a new series called "Have Gun—Will Travel" went into production; Johnny was cast in a small role in one episode, and while working on the show he composed a song about the series' hero, Paladin. "The Ballad of Paladin" was adopted as the show's closing theme, and Johnny Western was signed to the CBS network's record division, Columbia Records.

He was soon either acting in or singing on the music tracks of several series, including "Pony Express," "Boots and Saddles," "Tales of Wells Fargo," and "Bat Masterson"; his performing and singing careers were suddenly revived. Under Columbia Records' producer Don Law (who also produced Johnny Cash), he recorded dozens of sides, including the singles "Only the Lonely" (1959), "Della's Gone" (1960), "Darling Corey" (1961), "Gunfighter" (1962), and "Kathy Come Home," along with an album, *Have Gun Will Travel* (1962). He was also asked by Johnny Cash to join his band as a singer-guitarist. He remained a member of Cash's band for six years, playing rhythm guitar on recordings such as "Johnny Yuma—The Rebel," "The Little Drummer Boy," and "Lorena," among many others. During his years at Columbia, Western was also befriended by Marty Robbins, who later participated in recordings of "(Ghost) Riders in the Sky" and the redone "Ballad of Paladin." When he wasn't on tour with Cash, Western was playing shows on his own and working with ex-members of Ernest Tubb's and Porter Wagoner's bands.

At the end of 1963 he left Columbia Records and moved to Philips, where he had a very brief, unsuccessful stay. Western was a popular draw in Las Vegas, however, and also began making the rounds of Western shows. He continued to record for various labels, including Hep ("The Violet and the Rose," 1967), and he made the acquaintance of Waylon Jennings, then a songwriter and aspiring country star. He recorded "The Streets of Dodge City" for the 1970 film *Dodge City, Kansas*, and wrote the music for a documentary film, *Rodeo—A Matter of Style*, released in 1976 as part of the country's Bicentennial celebration. Western also record numerous sides for Johnny Cash's House of Cash label, which became the basis for a restrospective album. During most of this period, he played 200 shows a year. In 1986 he resumed his radio career with a series in Wichita, KS. In 1993 Western began work on a new album, a sort of cowboy super-session with the Sons of the Pioneers (Rex Allen, Rex Allen Jr., Red Stegall, and Michael Martin Murphey), titled *Johnny Western and the Sons of the Pioneers and Friends*. Health problems intervened, however, when Western was incapacitated by a hypass operation, and the album went unreleased. —*Bruce Eder*

Have Gun, Will Travel / 1962 / Columbia ✦✦✦✦
Johnny Western's only album for a major label wasn't recorded until he'd been with Columbia Records for three years, so it's a fully mature work, resplendent in the lore and lure of the West. In addition to his third version of "The Ballad of Paladin," the album features "The Lonely Man," one of Western's finest and most introspective vocal performances, the gallows ballad "Hannah Lee," the standard "The Streets of Laredo" (done with a bit too much drama), Stan Jones' hauntingly beautiful "Cowpoke" and "The Searchers," and "The Last Round-Up." The production is fairly elaborate at times but, except for "The Streets of Laredo," never excessive, and Western's baritone sounded beautiful in those days. (out-of-print) —*Bruce Eder*

Johnny Western / 1980 / Bear Family ✦✦✦✦

The Gunfighter / 1981 / Bear Family ✦✦✦✦

● **Gunfight at O.K. Corral** / 1989 / Bear Family ✦✦✦✦
Johnny Western as he sounded in 1984, which is good—the voice is still a rich, enveloping baritone, rougher and not as flexible as it was in the early 1960s, but still pleasing and memorable. His rendition of "Gunfight at OK Corral" won't displace Frankie Laine's, but it has a drive and power all its own. Stan Jones' "Ghost Riders in the Sky" gets a beautiful workout, as flamboyant vocally as Johnny Cash's was instrumentally. Jones is also represented by "The Searchers," "Hannah Lee," "Lillies Grow High," and "Cheyenne." Bob Nolan's poignant "Song of the Bandit" (adapted from the English ballad "The Highwayman") is also here, sung with great affection, sincerity, and intensity. Western also covers his own "The Gunfighter," which he wrote for Marty Robbins, and Johnny Cash's "Don't Take Your Guns to Town." At this point in his career, Western's voice lacked the expressive range of Cash's. There are also lots of covers of television themes, including two very upbeat medleys of "Johnny Yuma—The Rebel" (originally a Johnny Cash song on which Western played rhythm guitar), "Bonanza," "The Ballad of Paladin," "Bat Masterson," "Wyatt Earp," and the theme from "Rawhide." The personnel include Billy Strange, Art Sparer, Jack Clement (who also produced), and Western on guitars. —*Bruce Eder*

☆ **Heroes and Cowboys** / 1993 / Bear Family ✦✦✦✦✦
This is as good as it gets for Johnny Western fans. And in the absence of a single-disc collection from Columbia or Rhino, it's also the only route to go to get any Johnny Western material other than "The Ballad of Paladin." The three-CD set with 200 minutes of music, which retails for a whopping $85, has everything that Western recorded from 1952 for JOCO up through his 1970s sides for House of Cash, and a ton of rare radio transcription recordings. It may seem like overkill to have five different versions of "The Ballad of Paladin" here, except that they are all genuinely different. Equally important are Western's early 1960s Columbia sides, including his original versions of "The Gunfighter," "Hannah Lee," "The Searchers," and "The Last Roundup." Disc one also contains some unreleased Columbia sides, Western's covers of Johnny Cash's "The Big Battle" and "Forty Shades of Green," one of the prettiest recordings he ever did, and the JOCO sides from 1952 and 1953, nicely restored, with John Field showing himself a great one-man Western combo with the use of overdubs, Les Paul style, especially on "Let Old Mother Nature Have Her Way," which, with a great vocal performance by Western, also could've passed for an early Gene Autry recording. Disc Two features more Columbia sides from the late 1950s and early 1960s, as well as Western's 1964 Philips sides and his songs cut for the Hep label in 1966. Among the highlights is the unissued 1959 side "Uh-Huh," which has hit written all over it, but which somehow didn't make it out before the public until 1981. The Columbia material includes Western's attempts to crack the folk market ("Willowgreen" etc.), which may not have succeeded commercially but are great listening anyway. The Hep sides are the most interesting, however, for the sheer restraint that they show—Western's later sides for Columbia and Philips showed a certain degree of excess on the production side, while the Hep sides, especially "Ruby, Don't Take Your Love to Town" and "I'll Try to Forget You If I Can," benefit from a slightly leaner, more delicate use of backup choruses, etc. The House of Cash recordings featured on

disc two also show off Western in a leaner setting, doing new performances of "Forty Shades of Green" and superb covers of material such as Waylon Jennings' "The Last Time I Saw Phoenix." Disc three consists of rare radio transcription performances done for the syndicated radio shows "Country Style, USA" and "Country Music Time," circa 1960, with Western doing sharp, lean renditions of numerous songs, backed by a band that included Marty Robbins on the piano. The material was a mix of country and folk standards, along with Western material that he was directly associated with, including "The Ballad of Paladin," "Lonely Street," "John Henry" (some high-velocity steel driving there), Stan Jones' "Rollin' Dust," "Cowpoke," and "Delia's Gone," and some fascinating covers such as Johnny Cash's "I Walk the Line." The sound has held up exceptionally well, and it is exclusive to the Bear Family release. *— Bruce Eder*

Billy Edd Wheeler

b. Dec. 9, 1932, Whitesville, WV

Vocals / Traditional Country, Country-Pop

One of the most versatile artists in Nashville, Billy Edd Wheeler was perhaps best known as a songwriter; his most memorable tune, "Jackson," was a major hit for June Carter and Johnny Cash in 1967. Not just a talented writer, though, Wheeler is also a singer, musician, poet, and actor.

Wheeler was born in Boone Country, WV. He attended Warren Wilson College in North Carolina and Berea College in Kentucky, where he earned a BA in 1955. After college, he worked as a magazine editor and then served two years as a Navy pilot. He taught at Berea College until 1961, when he played several folk songs at a concert with the Lexington Kentucky Symphony Orchestra. Spurred by the attention, he recorded a few songs on the Monitor label. Wheeler studied at the Yale Drama School for a year and then moved to New York, where he worked as a playwright. He also began writing songs, two of which ("The Reverend Mr. Black" and "Desert Pete") became pop hits for the folk-pop Kingston Trio.

In 1963 Wheeler began recording folk songs for Kapp Records. The next year he debuted on the charts with "Ode to the Little Brown Shack Out Back," which hit NO. 3. No more hits were forthcoming, however, though Johnny Cash and June Carter reached No. 2 in 1967 with a tale of unfaithfulness called "Jackson." Wheeler finally found his way back to the charts one year later, though "I Ain't the Worryin' Kind" stalled at NO. 63. He signed with United Artists in 1969 and had minor success with "West Virginia Woman" and "Fried Chicken and a Country Tune."

During the '70s he recorded for RCA Victor and Capitol but charted only occasionally. In 1980 he hit it big as a songwriter when he and Roger Bowling penned Kenny Rogers' smash hit "Coward of the County." It spent three weeks at NO. 1 on the country charts.

Wheeler is also a noted poet and published his first volume, *Song of a Woods Colt* in 1969. He has also written plays, including *Song of the Cumberland Gap.* Wheeler also writes comical stories from the Appalachians, continues to perform at festivals, holds workshops, and sometimes records for such independent labels as Flying Fish and Sagitarius. *— Sandra Brennan*

Billy Edd / 1961 / Monitor ♦♦♦

Bluegrass Too / 1962 / Monitor ♦♦♦♦

New Bag of Songs / 1964 / Kapp ♦♦♦

Memories of America/Ode to the Little Brown Shack Out Back / 1965 / Kapp ♦♦♦

Wheeler Man / 1965 / Dapp ♦♦♦

Goin' Town and Country / 1966 / Kapp ♦♦

Paper Birds / 1967 / Kapp ♦♦

I Ain't the Worryin' Kind / 1968 / Kapp ♦♦♦♦

● **Wild Mountain Flowers** / 1979 / Flying Fish ♦♦♦♦

Hits and songs come from this Southern singer-songwriter. *—AMG*

Some Mountain Tales About Jack / Spoken Arts ♦♦♦

Cheryl Wheeler

b. Jul. 10, 1951, Timonium, MD

Guitar, Vocals / Singer-Songwriter, Country-Folk, Contemporary Folk

Folk singer-songwriter Cheryl Wheeler was raised in Timonium, MD, and began playing the guitar and ukulele as a child. She first performed professionally at a local restaurant, but she soon graduated to clubs in the Baltimore and Washington, DC areas. Wheeler's self-titled debut LP bowed in 1986; appearances on a number of compilations followed, but she did not issue another full-length record until 1991, when she released both *Half a Book* and *Circles and Arrows.* Two years later, Wheeler followed with *Driving Home,* and *Mrs. Pinocci's Guitar* appeared in 1995. *—Jason Ankeny*

● **Cheryl Wheeler** / 1986 / North Star ♦♦♦♦

Her debut album features her hit "Addicted" and is more rock 'n' roll than her other albums. If you like the rest, you should add this to the collection. *—Chip Renner*

Circles and Arrows / 1990 / Capitol ♦♦♦♦

Wheeler shines on this CD. Guests include Mark O'Connor, Jerry Douglas, Jonathan Edwards, and Billy Joe Walker. Every song is a winner, especially "Northern Girl," "Aces," and "I Know This Town." *—Chip Renner*

Half a Book / 1991 / Cypress ♦♦♦

With guest Jonathan Edwards, this features a clean sound and "Emotional Response." *—Chip Renner*

Driving Home / 1993 / Philo ♦♦♦

On *Driving Home* Cheryl Wheeler has finally got the natural-sounding production that her material needs. Her melodies are highly ornamented and shine through. The distinctive nature of her voice is never overshadowed by synthesized sound as on previous albums. As in the past, the material is often humorous, ("Don't Forget the Guns"), commercially romantic ("Silver Lining"), and heart-warmingly beautiful ("Arrow"). This is an excellent album. *—Richard Meyer*

Mrs. Pinocci's Guitar / Oct. 17, 1995 / Philo ♦♦♦

Onie Wheeler

b. Nov. 10, 1921, Senath, MO, **d.** May 27, 1984

Vocals / Traditional Bluegrass, Traditional Country, Rockabilly

Onie Wheeler recorded traditional country, bluegrass, and rockabilly (for Sun) in a career that stretched from a small radio show in Missouri to the Grand Ole Opry. He played guitar and harmonica as a child but never performed professionally until after service in World War II. Beginning in 1945, he worked radio broadcasts in Missouri, Arkansas, Michigan, and Kentucky. Wheeler formed the Ozark Cowboys five years later with Ernest Thompson and brothers A.J. and Doyal Nelson. The Cowboys played clubs in Texas in 1952 and were encouraged by Little Jimmy Dickens to travel to Nashville.

After reaching Music City, Onie Wheeler and the Cowboys found a deal with Columbia. They recorded in 1953, and though the material wasn't successful, Lefty Frizzell reached the country Top Ten a year later with Wheeler's "Run 'em Off." By the mid-'50s Wheeler's repertoire began to lean toward rockabilly; he signed to Sun Records in 1957 and toured with Elvis Presley, Jerry Lee Lewis, and Carl Perkins. He spent some of the late '50s in California, but he returned to Nashville to record for Epic, Starday, United Artists, and Musicor during the '60s. Wheeler toured with the bands of George Jones and Roy Acuff, and he finally hit the charts himself when "John's Been Shucking My Corn" placed modestly in 1973. He even watched his daughter Karen place three singles on the charts during the mid-'70s. Wheeler owned and operated a guitar repair shop during the late '70s and early '80s, working occasionally with Acuff on the Grand Ole Opry. He was playing at the Opry with Rev. Jimmie Snow in May 1984 when he collapsed and died on stage. *— John Bush*

John's Been Shuckin' My Corn / 1973 / Onie ♦♦♦

● **Onie's Bop** / 1991 / Bear Family ✦✦✦✦
These rare mid-'50s country-rock sides from Columbia and Sun are proto-rockabilly. —*Hank Davis*

Onie's Country Boppers / Onie ✦✦✦✦
Similar coverage plus some obscure singles, it's available on import. —*Hank Davis*

Whiskeytown

Alternative Country-Rock, Americana
The alternative country quintet Whiskeytown emerged in the mid-1990s from the same North Carolina music scene best known for producing indie rock bands like Superchunk. The group was led by singer-songwriter Ryan Adams, who formed Whiskeytown after the breakup of his punk outfit, the Patty Duke Syndrome. Showcasing Adams' songwriting and Gram Parsons-like twang, *Angels*, the band's four-song debut EP, bowed in 1995. *Faithless Street*, their full-length follow-up, surfaced later in the year. —*Jason Ankeny*

Faithless Street / 1996 / Mood Food Records ✦✦✦
Faithless Street, mixes a rich, laidback country twang with the rough energy of garage-born rock 'n' roll. It's unabashedly similar musical territory to that covered by Uncle Tupelo, but with time the influences clear up and Whiskeytown's own personality begins to shine through. At times slow and delicately arranged, other times dirty and burned around the edges, "Faithless Street" is an album of earthbound songwriting that's got more honest "country" at its core than most of the video-friendly poseurs taking up space on TNN. —*Kurt Wolff*

The White Brothers

Progressive Bluegrass, Traditional Bluegrass
Guitar great Clarence White (b. 1944–d. 1973) and mandolinist Roland White played in the Country Boys band when Clarence was only 10 and Roland 16. In 1962 they became part of the Kentucky Colonels, a bluegrass band famous especially among young city audiences. Clarence White went on to become a much-in-demand session man; he was killed by a drunk driver in 1973. Roland White has continued performing with various groups, including the Nashville Bluegrass Band. —*David Vinopal*

Live in Sweden / Rounder ✦✦✦✦

Bryan White

Vocals / Contemporary Country
With his big voice, easy-going manner and streamlined mainstream country-pop, Bryan White easily fit into the post-Garth Brooks climate of the mid-'90s. His first album, *Bryan White*, began a string of No. 1 hits that ran into 1996.

White was born and raised in Oklahoma City, where he became involved in music at an early age. Both his parents were professional musicians, and when Bryan was five, his father taught him how to play drums. As a teenager he played drums in both his mother's and father's bands. His mom sang rock 'n' roll, his father country—which gave him broad musical knowledge and skill. Eventually he formed his own trio. At first, he only drummed but during a soundcheck his mother heard him sing "Stand By Me." After the song was over, his mother was in tears and she encouraged him to become a vocalist himself. In no time, he learned how to play guitar and began writing songs.

After his graduation from high school, White headed to Nashville, where he hooked up with Billy Joe Walker, Jr., a family friend who happened to be a session musician in the Music City. Over the next two years Walker helped White hone his act and helped him land a job as a demo singer. Eventually producer Kyle Lehning, who had worked with Randy Travis and Dan Seals, began working with Walker and White. The three crafted White's debut album and landed the singer a record contract with Asylum. The self-titled debut appeared in 1994.

The first two singles from the record—"Eugene You Genius" and "Look at Me Now"—didn't gather much attention, with the latter peaking at No. 24. However, in the spring of 1995 "Someone Else's Star" rocketed to No. 1, followed by "Rebecca Lynn" in the

fall. In the spring of 1996, his second album, *Between Now and Forever*, was released, accompanied by the No. 1 single "I'm Not Supposed to Love You Anymore." "So Much for Pretending" became his fourth No. 1 single in a row in the fall of 1996. Also in the fall, he won the Country Music Association's 1996 Horizon Award, as well as their award for Best New Touring Artist. —*Stephen Thomas Erlewine*

Bryan White / 1994 / Asylum ✦✦✦
● **Between Now and Forever** / Mar. 26, 1996 / Asylum ✦✦✦✦
Sounding like a cross between a young Bobby Vinton and early Johnny Tillotson, Bryan White could also be called a '90s Glen Campbell, someone he often refers to in his stage act. While not everything on *Between Now and Forever* is top notch, most songs are high-quality Nashville fare. Throughout the album, White brings us songs of experience with an air of undeniable cleanliness, and the result is a debut that is not bad at all. —*James Chrispell*

Clarence White

b. Jun. 7, 1944, Lewiston, ME, d. Jul. 14, 1973, Palmdale, CA
Guitar / Progressive Bluegrass, Traditional Bluegrass, Progressive Country, Country-Rock
Clarence White was a gifted guitarist who was one of the pioneers of country-rock in the late '60s. Although died young, his work with the Byrds and the Kentucky Colonels, among others, remained celebrated among country-rock and bluegrass aficionados in the decades after his death.

Born in Maine but raised in California, White began playing the guitar at an early age, joining his brothers' band, the Country Boys, when he was just ten years old. The band eventually evolved into the Kentucky Colonels. Clarence left the Colonels in the mid-'60s, becoming a session musician; he played electric guitar on many rock and pop albums. He also began playing with the duo of Gib Gilbeau and Gene Parsons in local California clubs. Gilbeau and Parsons frequently worked with the Gosdin Brothers, so the duo was able to land a cameo appearance for White on the *Gene Clark and the Gosdin Brothers* album. About the same time, Clarence recorded a solo album for Bakersfield International, which the label didn't release.

In 1968 White joined Nashville West, which also featured Gene Parsons, Gib Gilbeau, Sneaky Pete Kleinow, Glen D. Hardin, and Wayne Moore. Nashville West recorded an album for Sierra Records, but the record didn't appear until 1978. White was invited to join the Byrds in the fall of 1968. Roger McGuinn was rebuilding the Byrds' lineup after the departure of Chris Hillman and Gram Parsons, who went on to form the Flying Burrito Brothers. Clarence White fit into the revamped Byrds' country-rock direction. He played on the group's untitled album, which spawned the single "Chestnut Mare." While he was with the band, he continued to work as a session musician, playing on Randy Newman's *12 Songs* (1970), Joe Cocker's eponymous 1969 album, and the Everly Brothers' *Stories We Could Tell* (1971), among others.

When the Byrds disbanded in 1973, Clarence White continued his session work and joined Muleskinner, which also featured David Grisman, Peter Rowan, John Guerin, Bill Keith, John Kahn, and Richard Greene. Muleskinner released only one album, which appeared later in 1973.

After the Muleskinner record was finished, White played a few dates with the Kentucky Colonels and began working on a solo album. He had completed only four tracks when he was killed by a drunk driver while he was loading equipment onto a van; he died on July 14, 1973. After his death, several posthumous albums of his work with the Kentucky Colonels and the Byrds appeared, as did various albums that featured his playing, including Jackson Browne's *Late for the Sky* and Gene Parsons' *Kindling*. —*Stephen Thomas Erlewine*

● **And the Kentucky Colonels** / 1964 / Rounder ✦✦✦✦
Clarence White and the Kentucky Colonels includes 1964-1967 live performances that are musts for bluegrass guitar enthusiasts. White was a member of the Byrds and a session player for Linda Ronstadt and the Everly Brothers. —*Richard Lieberson*

Muleskinner / 1973 / Warner Brothers ✦✦✦✦

Kentucky Colonels: Live in Sweden (1973) / 1976 / Rounder ✦✦✦

A good live show. Clarence White is at his best, performing with the White Brothers. —*Chip Renner*

Nashville West / 1976 / Sierra ✦✦✦

Joy Lynn White

Vocals / Contemporary Country, Americana

Noted for her distinctive vibrato and rocking honky tonk, Joy Lynn White earned critical praise for her first two albums in the early '90s, but she never quite broke into the mainstream. White was born in Arkansas but raised in Mishawaka, IN. It was from her father, Nathan "Gene" White, that she inherited her love of music, particularly for artists like Emmylou Harris, Jimmie Rodgers, and Linda Ronstadt. White began performing in a band while still in high school. After graduation she moved to Nashville, where she worked at odd jobs and recorded her own demo tapes for a while. Her unique voice attracted notice, and she quickly became a popular demo singer. White made her debut album *Midnight and Hindsight* as Joy White for Columbia in 1992. The album produced several minor hits including "Little Tears" and "True Confessions," a song that made it to No. 45 on the country charts in 1993. Her second album, *Wild Love*, was released in 1994. —*Sandra Brennan*

Between Midnight and Hindsight / Apr. 1992 / Columbia ✦✦✦

White's rousing country-rocker singles "Little Tears" and the Marty Stuart-penned "True Confessions" didn't rip up the charts, but the accompanying videos and White's flaming red hair made her a cult favorite among those into pumped-up, hardcore honky tonk. White's wild vibrato added intensity to her ballad weepers, too. —*Brian Mansfield*

● **Wild Love** / 1994 / Columbia ✦✦✦✦

White added a middle name but didn't change her sound much. On the Springsteenian raveup "Wild Love," her hillbilly vibrato left the impression of passion about to spin out of control. Her version of the redneck-pride anthem "I Am Just a Rebel" (earlier recorded by Billy Hill, Dennis Robbins and Confederate Railroad) added toughness to her image (as though she needed it), and the likes of "Too Gone to Care" and "On and On and On" showed she could rock out even while singing hard country. —*Brian Mansfield*

Lari White

b. 1966, Dunedin, FL
Vocals / Contemporary Country

Most contestants on televised talent shows are never able to forge a lasting career, but Lari White is the exception that proves the rule. After winning on the Nashville Network's "You Can Be a Star," White went on to become one of the most popular female new country singers of the mid-'90s, breaking through into the big time in 1994.

Born and raised in Dunedin, FL, White began performing when she was a child, singing in a gospel group with her parents and brother. The group, called the White Family Singers, sang at local church and community gatherings. After a while, the children began working pop music into the act, most notably Elvis Presley. As a teenager, Lari sang show tunes at talent contests and sang with a local rock 'n' roll band. She earned a scholarship to the University of Miami, where she studied vocals and music engineering. She began writing her own songs, singing in local clubs at night, and taking professional singing jobs. Upon graduating from college, she traveled around the United States, looking at various local music scenes. In 1988 she decided to move to Nashville and try to become a professional.

Later in 1988 she appeared on the Nashville Network's "You Can Be a Star" and won the first prize. The award led to a record contract with Capitol. Before the end of the year she had released a single on Capitol, "Flying Above the Rain," which became a hit in the South but failed to break into the big time. Later that same year, she joined Ronnie Milsap's publishing house and began tak-

ing acting lessons. For the next few years White continued in this vein, choosing to hone her talent, sing in local dinner theaters, and wait for another break. That break arrived in 1991, after an ASCAP showcase revived interest in her talents. After the showcase, Rodney Crowell asked her to sing backup vocals in his live band. In 1992 Lari signed a record contract with RCA, and Crowell produced her debut album, *Lead Me Not*, which was released the following year.

Lead Me Not received strong reviews and produced three minor hit singles—"What a Woman Wants," "Lead Me Not," and "Lay Around and Love You." *Wishes*, White's second album, became her breakthrough release, producing the Top Ten singles "That's My Baby," "Now I Know" and "That's How You Know (When You're in Love)." *Don't Fence Me In*, White's third album, wasn't quite as successful as its predecessors, but it continued her success. —*Stephen Thomas Erlewine*

Lead Me Not / Apr. 27, 1993 / RCA ✦✦✦✦

White's amibitious debut covered a lot of musical territory, from straight country ("Where the Lights Are Low") to torch ballad ("Just Thinking"), from Latin-flavored pop ("Made to Be Broken") to fervid gospel ("Good Good Love"). The breadth of her talent turned out to be something of a problem. Since nobody could get a handle on her, none of the album's three singles ("What a Woman Wants," "Lead Me Not," and "Lay Around and Love on You") broke the Top 40. —*Brian Mansfield*

● **Wishes** / Jun. 1994 / RCA ✦✦✦✦

Produced by Garth Fundis (Trisha Yearwood, Keith Whitley), *Wishes* focused White's abilities into something more palatable to the country mainstream. The first single, "That's My Baby," sounded like a companion piece to Yearwood's breakthrough "She's in Love with the Boy." But where Yearwood turned her back on that kind of small-town, teen-passion song, White made a whole album of them. *Wishes* is filled with charm, playfulness, and nifty hooks, especially on "That's How You Know," a thrilling duet with Hal Ketchum. —*Brian Mansfield*

Don't Fence Me In / Feb. 13, 1996 / RCA ✦✦✦

● **Best of Lari White** / Jan. 28, 1997 / RCA ✦✦✦✦

Lari White didn't have that many big hits—she didn't begin having Top Ten singles until 1995—but that doesn't mean she didn't record a wealth of strong music, as *The Best of Lari White* proves. By selecting the highlights from her three albums, the compilation helps neophytes get up to speed with her past, but *Lead Me Not* and *Wishes* remain terrific albums in their own right. —*Thom Owens*

Tony Joe White

b. Jul. 23, 1943, Oak Grove, LA
Guitar, Vocals / Rock & Roll, Country-Rock, Country-Pop, Pop-Rock

Tony Joe White has parlayed his songwriting talent into a modestly successful country and rock career in Europe as well as America. White was born into a part-Cherokee family. He began working clubs in Texas during the mid-'60s and moved to Nashville by 1968. White's 1969 debut album for Monument, *Black and White*, featured his Top Ten pop hit "Polk Salad Annie" and another charting single, "Roosevelt and Ira Lee (Night of the Moccasin)." That same year Dusty Springfield reached the charts with his "Willie and Laura Mae Jones." Brook Benton recorded a version of White's "Rainy Night in Georgia" that hit No. 4 early in 1970; the song has since become a near-standard, with more than 100 credits. Tony Joe White's own "Groupie Girl" began his European success with a short stay on the British charts in 1970.

White moved to Warner Brothers in 1971, but success eluded him on his albums *Tony Joe White*, *The Train I'm On* and *Homemade Ice Cream*. Other stars, however, continued to keep his name on the charts during the '70s; Elvis charted with "For Ol' Times Sake" and "I've Got a Thing About You Baby" (Top Five on the country charts), and Hank Williams, Jr. took "A Rainy Night in Georgia" to No. 13 country. White himself recorded *Eyes* for 20th Century Fox in 1976, but then he disappeared for four years. He signed to Casablanca for 1980's *The Real Thang* but moved to

Columbia in 1983 for *Dangerous*, which included the modest country hits "The Lady in My Life" and "We Belong Together."

Tony Joe White was inactive through much of the '80s, but he worked with Tina Turner on her 1989 *Foreign Affair* album, writing four songs and playing guitar and harmonica. He released *Closer to the Truth* a year later for his own Swamp label and toured with Eric Clapton and Joe Cocker to very receptive French crowds. (*Closer to the Truth* has sold 100,000 copies in that country alone.) His 1993 album *Path of a Decent Groove* was released only in France, though Warner's *The Best of Tony Joe White* earned an American release the same year. —*John Bush*

● **Polk Salad Annie: The Best of Tony Joe White** / 1994 / Warner Archive ✦✦✦✦

Warner Archive's *Polk Salad Annie: The Best of Tony Joe White* contains all of his most familiar and best tracks from his time at Warner, making it a definitive single-disc retrospective of the songwriter's work. —*Thom Owens*

The Whites

Progressive Bluegrass, Traditional Bluegrass, Contemporary Country, Country Gospel

A part of country music for more than 30 years, the Whites started out in bluegrass, then adopted a contemporary country sound and later evolved into a gospel group. Buck White and his daughters Sharon and Cheryl comprise the core of the group, though other group members have included Ricky Skaggs on fiddle and guitar, Tim Crouch on fiddle, dobro player Jerry Douglas, drummer Neil Worf, and backup singers Rosie White, Pete Reniger, and Steve Thomas. Buck White was born in Oklahoma and raised in Wichita Falls, TX. His early influences included bluesmen Pete Johnson and Albert Ammons as well as country performers on the WLS "Barn Dance" and the Grand Ole Opry. By the time he was a teen, White was proficient on the piano and mandolin; he formed his first band in 1947 and then began playing on a Vernon, TX, radio station. During this time, he was most influenced by groups like the Callahan Brothers, the Blue Sky Boys, and the early bluegrass of Bill Monroe. In 1952 he joined the Blue Sage Boys and worked as a sideman, playing piano and mandolin.

White married Pat Goza in 1951; 11 years later they formed the Down Home Folks with Arnold and Peggy Johnston in Fort Smith, AR. Sharon and Cheryl White teamed up with Teddie and Eddie Johnston to form the Down Home Kids in the mid-'60s. In 1971 the Whites moved to Nashville, and the Down Home Folks were comprised of the entire White family. They recorded a self-titled debut bluegrass album in 1972 for County Records in a motel room. Pat retired from the group one year later, but Buck and his daughters continued with the band, recording *In Person/Live at the Old Time Picking Parlor* in 1975. Later that year they made *That Down Home Feelin'* for Ridge Runner, joined by Ricky Skaggs and Jerry Douglas. Although Buck White and His Down Home Folks recorded two more albums during the '70s, they didn't really get their big break until 1979, when they worked with Emmylou Harris on *Blue Kentucky Girl* and later toured with her.

By the early '80s, Buck had decided to focus on mandolin playing and became a highly respected player. Sharon married Ricky Skaggs in 1981; later that year they had a brief contract with Capitol and had their first chart success with "Send Me the Pillow You Dream On." After changing their name to the Whites, the group moved away from bluegrass music. In 1982 they made the Top Ten with "Holding My Baby Tonight" and "Give Me Back That Old Familiar Feeling." They had two more high-ranking hits the next year from their MCA/Curb album *Forever You*. All of their recordings during the early '80s, including Buck's 1980 solo album *More Pretty Girls than One* for Sugar Hill, were produced by Skaggs. After joining the Grand Ole Opry in 1984, the Whites produced the Top 30 single "It Should Have Been Easy," from their 1986 album *Whole New World*. The group moved toward gospel music in 1989 with *Doing It by the Book* on Canaan. They didn't record during the early '90s but continued to perform live and on the Opry. —*Sandra Brennan*

● **Greatest Hits** / 1987 / Curb ✦✦✦✦

This is early '80s sweet harmony from dad and his daughters. —*Mark A. Humphrey*

Doing It by the Book / 1988 / Word ✦✦✦

Poor Folks Pleasure / Nov. 17, 1995 / Koch ✦✦✦

Give a Little Back / Feb. 6, 1996 / Rock Bottom ✦✦✦

Keith Whitley

b. Apr. 1, 1955, Sandy Hook, KY, d. May 9, 1989, Nashville, TN
Guitar, Vocals / Progressive Bluegrass, Progressive Country, New Traditionalist

Keith Whitley's legacy loomed large over the country music landscape of the '90s. A talented new country singer and songwriter, Whitley was just beginning to emerge as a superstar at the time of his death in 1989. Throughout the next decade, his reputation as both a performer and writer continued to grow, as other artists had hits with his songs and posthumous recordings climbed into the Top Ten.

Born and raised in Kentucky, Whitley began singing as a child, winning a talent contest at the age of four. When he was eight years old, he learned how to play guitar and within a year he was singing on a Charleston, WV-based radio station. Whitley formed his first band at the age of 13, playing nothing but straight bluegrass. A few years later he formed the Lonesome Mountain Boys with his high school friend, Ricky Skaggs. The Lonesome Mountain Boys played primarily Stanley Brothers songs and soon became a popular attraction.

In the late '60s Ralph Stanley was looking to re-form his band after the death of his brother and partner, Carter. He was so impressed with Whitley and Skaggs that he asked them to join his Clinch Mountain Boys. The duo accepted the offer and began appearing with the band in 1970. Whitley stayed with the Clinch Mountain Boys for two years, recording a total of seven albums, including 1971's *Crying from the Cross*, which was named the Bluegrass Album of the Year.

In 1973 Whitley left the group. For two years he drifted through various bands, including acts that played country, not bluegrass. He returned to the Clinch Mountain Boys in 1975 and stayed with them for another two years. During his second tenure with the band, he made five albums. In 1978 Whitley joined J.D. Crowe's band, the New South. Whitley recorded three albums with the New South between 1978 and 1982; they vacillated between bluegrass and straight country.

Whitley began a full-fledged solo career after leaving the New South in 1982. Signing with RCA Records, he released his debut album, *Hard Act to Follow*, in 1984. A record of pure honky tonk, it didn't attract much of an audience. The next year he released *L.A. to Miami*, a more commercial affair that spawned the No. 14 single "Miami, My Amy." After that single peaked early in 1986, he had three back-to-back Top Ten hits—"Ten Feet Away," "Homecoming '63," and "Hard Livin'." Late in 1986

Although *L.A. to Miami* was a success, its slick production didn't please Whitley. In 1987 he recorded a follow-up that sounded exactly the same. Unsatisfied with the musical direction of his new effort, Whitley convinced RCA to shelve the completed album and have him work on another record with a new producer, Garth Fundis. *Don't Close Your Eyes* was the result. Released in the spring of 1988, the album solidified Whitley's commerical standing. The first three singles from *Don't Close Your Eyes*—"Don't Close Your Eyes," "When You Say Nothing at All," and "I'm No Stranger to the Rain"—were all No. 1 hits.

Things may have been going smoothly on the surface for Keith Whitley, but behind the scenes he was being torn apart by alcoholism. On May 9, 1989, he suffered a fatal case of alcohol poisoning; he was 34. Just before his death, he completed his fourth album, *I Wonder Do You Think of Me*. The record was released shortly after his death, and its first single, the title track, reached No. 1, as did its follow-up, "It Ain't Nothin." Another single from the album, "I'm Over You," reached No. 3 in 1990. During the '90s, RCA repackaged and re-released many of Whitley's recordings—including several unreleased songs—in various compilations. Lorrie Morgan recorded an electronic duet, "'Til a Tear

Becomes a Rose," with her late husband in 1990; it peaked at No. 13. In 1994 a tribute album to Whitley was released. —*Stephen Thomas Erlewine*

Hard Act to Follow / 1984 / RCA ✦✦

Whitley's first album has some hints of brilliance, but it suffers from uneven material and unfocused production. —*Thom Owens*

L.A. to Miami / 1985 / RCA ✦✦

Whitley's first mainstream country album is nice but not as strong as his later work. —*Mark A. Humphrey*

Don't Close Your Eyes / 1988 / RCA ✦✦✦✦

Don't Close Your Eyes was more successful than Keith Whitley's two previous albums, and it's easy to see why. Though the record still suffered from a handful of mediocre songs and slightly soft production, the overall album was leaner and more direct than Whitley's earlier solo work, showcasing his talent for heartfelt honky tonk singing and his skill for crafting excellent barroom ballads. "Don't Close Your Eyes," "When You Say Nothing at All," and "I'm No Stranger to the Rain" were the hits, but there's a wealth of excellent material here, including a haunting version of Lefty Frizzell's "I Never Go Around Mirrors." The sheer strength of the best numbers makes the handful of weaker songs perfectly excusable. After all, country in the late '80s rarely got better than *Don't Close Your Eyes* at its best. —*Thom Owens*

★ I Wonder Do You Think of Me / 1989 / RCA ✦✦✦✦✦

Though Keith Whitley displayed his immense talents on his previous albums, it was only in small measure. It wasn't until *I Wonder Do You Think of Me*, his fourth and final album, that he truly came into his own. The difference between this album and its predecessors is focus. The essential style remains the same, but Whitley has decided to concentrate on a heart-tugging, gritty honky tonk and to give the record an appropriately straightforward, simple production. The direct approach gives more weight to the sad tales of lost love and drinking, and when Whitley died shortly before the record's release, these songs gained even more gravity. *I Wonder Do You Think of Me* stands as an excellent testament—songs like "It Ain't Nothin'," "I'm Over You," and the title track only begin to suggest the depth and appeal of this album. —*Thom Owens*

☆ Greatest Hits / 1990 / RCA ✦✦✦✦✦

Assembled shortly after Keith Whitley's death, *Greatest Hits* contains nine of his biggest hits—including the Top Ten singles "Ten Feet Away," "Don't Close Your Eyes," "When You Say Nothing at All," "I'm No Stranger to the Rain," "I Wonder Do You Think of Me," "It Ain't Nothin'," and "I'm Over You"—plus two unreleased songs, a duet with wife Lorrie Morgan on "Til A Tear Becomes A Rose" and a demo of "Tell Lorrie I Love Her." It's an excellent compilation, but it is a bit unbalanced, drawing almost entirely from *Don't Close Your Eyes* and *I Wonder Do You Think of Me*. Granted, those are his two best albums, but it would have been nice to have collected the highlights from his uneven first two solo records as well as the obvious hits. Nevertheless, *Greatest Hits* is the perfect record for fans who want just the hits. —*Thom Owens*

Kentucky Bluebird / 1991 / RCA ✦✦✦

This is a posthumous collection of previously unreleased performances. —*Mark A. Humphrey*

● Essential Keith Whitley / Jun. 18, 1996 / RCA ✦✦✦✦

The Essential Keith Whitley is an excellent single-disc retrospective of the late country singer-songwriter, including such classic songs as "I Wonder Do You Think of Me," "If You Think I'm Crazy Now," "I'm Losing You All Over Again," and "Miami, My Amy." Although it concentrates on his earlier recordings, it is still the best, most comprehensive collection assembled on the tragically short-lived country star. —*Thom Owens*

Ray Whitley

b. Dec. 5, 1901, Atlanta, GA, d. Feb. 21, 1979, California
Vocals / Cowboy

Singer-songwriter Ray Whitley was one of Hollywood's first cowboy crooners. Unlike Gene Autry, he remained a supporting actor and never starred in his own series of feature films, although he

did make many musical short films during the mid-'30s; with Fred Rose, he co-penned some of Autry's best-loved songs, including "Back in the Saddle Again" and "Ages and Ages Ago." Whitley was born in Atlanta, GA, and played only occasionally at community gatherings until discovering Jimmie Rodgers in the late '20s. He finally turned to performing when the Depression forced him into prolonged unemployment; his first gigs were with the Range Ramblers, later renamed the Six Bar Cowboys, who played the World Championship Rodeo through the 1960s. Whitley made his recording debut in 1933 and finally came to Hollywood in 1936, where he made his feature film debut with William Boyd in *Hopalong Cassidy Returns*. Between 1938 and 1942 he made a series of short films for RKO and played the sidekick in a few Tim Holt films. He made his final film appearance playing the ranch manager in the James Dean classic *Giant*. During the 1950s he briefly managed the Sons of the Pioneers and Jimmy Wakely. Whitley recorded through the late '70s and was a popular performer at cowboy film festivals, where he sang and demonstrated his considerable prowess with a bullwhip. He died in 1979 on a fishing trip to Mexico. —*Sandra Brennan*

Ray Whitley Sings His Favorite Songs / Circle D Video ✦✦✦✦

Slim Whitman (Otis Dewey Whitman Jr)

b. Jan. 20, 1924, Tampa, FL
Guitar, Vocals / Traditional Country, Cowboy, Country-Pop, Folk-Pop

Once known as "America's Favorite Folksinger," Slim Whitman was more famous in Europe than in the United States for the majority of his career. Best remembered for his early '50s hit singles like "Love Song of the Waterfall," "Indian Love Call," and "Singing Hills," Whitman was an excellent yodeler known for singing mellow, romantic, and clean-cut songs.

As a child, Slim Whitman (born Otis Dewey Whitman, Jr.) became infatuated with music and learned to yodel listening to Montana Slim and Jimmie Rodgers records. At 17 he married 15-year-old Geraldine Crist, a preacher's daughter. The newlyweds moved to a 40-acre farm south of Jacksonville, FL, where Whitman worked as a meat packer. As he was working in the plant, he suffered an accident and lost two fingers on his left hand. After the accident, he worked in a Tampa shipyard. During World War II he served in the US Navy, where he learned to play guitar. After the war, he returned to the shipyard and joined the Plant City Berries, a Class C baseball team in the Orange Belt League. Whitman remained with the team through 1948 and then began building a singing career at several Tampa radio stations, eventually creating a backup band, the Variety Rhythm Boys.

Whitman got his first big break after Colonel Tom Parker—who was managing Eddy Arnold at the time— heard him singing on radio station WFLA. Parker landed Whitman a contract with RCA by the end of 1948. The label suggested he change his first name to "Slim," and Whitman reluctantly complied with their request. His first single, "I'm Casting My Lasso Towards the Sky," was released in early 1949 and eventually became his theme song. He made his national debut on the Mutual Network's "Smokey Mountain Hayride" in the summer of 1949, and the next year he joined the "Louisiana Hayride." Despite his national exposure, Whitman wasn't making much of an impact and he was forced to take a job as a part-time mailman.

In the early '50s he released a cover of Bob Nolan's "Love Song of the Waterfall," which became his breakthrough hit, peaking at No. 10 on the country charts; the follow-up single, "Indian Love Call," made him a star, peaking at No. 2 on the country charts and crossing over into the pop Top Ten. Both sides of his next single—"Keep It a Secret"/"My Heart Is Broken in Three"—were also major hits, and he continued to have a string of Top Ten hits into the mid-'50s. In 1955 his title song for the film *Rose-Marie* became a smash on both sides of the Atlantic; after its success, Whitman joined the Grand Ole Opry and then went to Britain in 1956 as the first country singer to play the London Palladium. Throughout the late '50s and early '60s, he had a string of British hits, including "Tumbling Tumbleweeds," "Unchain My Heart," and "I'll Take You Home Again Kathleen."

Although he was experiencing great success in the UK, Whitman's career was in neutral in the US. After 1954's "Singing Hills," he had only two Top 40 hits in the course of a decade. In 1965 he bounced back into the country Top Ten with "More Than Yesterday." For the next few years, he had a series of minor country hits, including "Rainbows Are Back in Style" (1968), "Happy Street" (1968), and "Tomorrow Never Comes" (1970). Throughout the early '70s he continued to have minor hits, but in 1974 he retired from active recording.

In 1979 Whitman filmed a television commercial to support Suffolk Marketing's release of a collection of his greatest hits. On the strength of the commercials, *All My Best* sold four million records, becoming the best-selling television-marketed album in history. After its success, the label released *Just for You* in 1980 and *The Best* in 1982. Between 1980 and 1984, Whitman had a small run of minor hits, highlighted by 1980's No. 15 hit, "When." In the late '80s he returned to television-marketed albums, releasing *Slim Whitman—Best Loved Favorites* in 1989 and *20 Precious Memories* in 1991. During the '90s, Whitman didn't record frequently, but he continued to tour successfully, particularly in Europe and Australia. *—Sandra Brennan*

The Best of Slim Whitman / 1960 / EMI America ✦✦✦✦
Featuring such hits as "Cattle Call", "The 12th of Never", "Rose Marie," and his classic rendition of "Indian Love Call," *The Best of Slim Whitman* contains just about every essential item Whitman ever recorded. *—James Chrispell*

● **The Best of Slim Whitman (1952-1972)** / 1990 / Rhino ✦✦✦✦
Over its 17 tracks, *The Best of Slim Whitman (1952-1972)* runs through all of his Top Ten hits—from "Love Song of the Waterfall" to "Something Beautiful (To Remember)"—adding significant hit singles like "Cattle Call," "The Twelfth of Never," and "Rainbows Are Back in Style." Out of all the Whitman collections, nothing surpasses this one for selection and sound—it's the definitive compilation. *—Thom Owens*

Rose Marie / 1996 / Bear Family ✦✦✦✦
Rose Marie is a six-disc, 162-track box set containing all of Slim Whitman's recordings between 1949 and 1959, including all of his early sides for RCA Victor and his classic singles ("Singing Hills," "Indian Love Call," "Rose-Marie," "Love Song of the Waterfall") for Imperial Records. For any dedicated Slim Whitman fan, this lovingly assembled collection is necessary, but the size of the collection may be a bit too much for the casual listener. The box stands as the most comprehensive set ever assembled on Whitman's heyday, and it is unlikely to be surpassed in terms of sheer quantity and comprehensiveness. *—Stephen Thomas Erlewine*

The Whitstein Brothers

Traditional Country, Close Harmony
The classic harmonies of the Whitstein Brothers gave even the most contemporary songs an old-fashioned twist. Robert and Charles Whitstein were born one year apart in Pineville, LA, to farmer R.C. Whitstein, who sang and played guitar on his own radio show in Alexandria. They appeared on the television show "Country Time" in the mid-'50s and won local talent shows. They made their first recordings in their early teens; their debut single, "Louisiana Woman," became a local hit in 1962. Its success inspired the Whitstein brothers to head for Nashville, where they billed themselves as the Whitt Brothers and toured with Faron Young, Porter Wagoner, and Little Jimmy Dickens. The Whitsteins were drafted in the early '60s; they returned home to record *The Whitstein Brothers Sing Gospel Songs of the Louvin Brothers*. They gained national recognition in the 1980s, when they recorded a series of albums for Rounder, including 1989's Grammy-nominated *Old Time Duets*. The brothers split up in the early '90s, and Charles Whitstein teamed up with Charlie Louvin in 1992 to record *Charlie Louvin and Charles Whitstein: Hoping That You're Hoping*, followed a year later by a live album recorded in Holland. In 1994 the Whitstein Brothers reunited and resumed recording together. *—Sandra Brennan*

★ **Rose of My Heart** / 1984 / Rounder ✦✦✦✦✦
The first album was heavily influenced by the Louvin Brothers. *—Charles S. Wolfe*

Trouble Ain't Nothin' but the Blues / 1987 / Rounder ✦✦✦
The second set has a more modern sound. *—Charles S. Wolfe*

☆ **Old Time Duets** / 1990 / Rounder ✦✦✦✦✦
On *Old Time Duets*, the Whitstein Brothers returned to pure traditional country, recording many songs that influenced them to begin playing country music. The Whitsteins play songs by the Louvin Brothers, the Blue Sky Boys, and the Delmore Brothers, bringing these classic songs to life. It's an album that firmly establishes the duo as heirs to the tradition of close-harmony brother duets. *—Thom Owens*

Charlie Louvin and Charles Whitstein: Hoping / 1992 / Copper Creek ✦✦✦

Sweet Harmony / Feb. 1996 / Rounder ✦✦✦✦
While no one can be expected to follow in the footsteps of the Louvin Brothers, arguably the greatest of country music's long history of brother acts (which also includes the Delmores, the Blue Sky Boys, and Charlie and Bill Monroe), the Whitstein Brothers are nonetheless keeping the tradition of harmonizing siblings very much alive—and creating wonderful music in the process. *Sweet Harmony* is Robert and Charles Whitstein's fifth album for Rounder Records, and it's a beautiful, acoustically-based mix of traditional (Roy Acuff, Louvin Brothers) and contemporary (David Olney, Paul Simon) material, lovingly rendered by the brothers' sweet, steady voices. *—Kurt Wolff*

The Wilburn Brothers

Traditional Country
As members of the larger Wilburn Family group (mother, father, elder brothers, sister), nine-year-old Teddy (b. 1931) and ten-year-old Doyle (1930-1982) appeared on the Opry in 1940; 13 years later they became part of the Opry's regular cast. With Jim and Jesse McReynolds and Bobby and Sonny Osborne, the Wilburns continued the tradition of brother duets in country music. Their wide choice of material is shown by the traditional "Knoxville Girl," a hit in 1959, and the more modern sound of "Hurt Her Once for Me" (1966). *—David Vinopal*

The Wonderful Osborne Brothers / 1961 / King ✦✦✦✦
It features "Way Down Under Blues," "Heart Please Be Still," and others. *—AMG*

Carefree Moments / 1962 / VL ✦✦✦
Their sometimes slick Nashville Sound recordings and tendency to double-track the vocals sometimes obscure the fact that these guys are one of the great brother duets in C&W. When they keep it straight, as in the rockabilly-esque "Cry Baby Cry" here, they can hold their own with anyone. *—George Bedard*

● **Retrospective** / MCA ✦✦✦✦
This nice overview of the Wilburn Brothers' smooth Decca hits of the '50s and '60s features 12 songs. *—Mark A. Humphrey*

Wilco

Alternative Pop-Rock, Alternative Country-Rock
The alternative country band Wilco rose from the ashes of the seminal roots rockers Uncle Tupelo, who disbanded in 1994. While Jay Farrar, one of the group's two singer-songwriters, went on to form the band Son Volt, his ex-partner Jeff Tweedy established Wilco with the remaining members of Tupelo's final incarnation, which included drummer Ken Coomer as well as part-time bandmates John Stirratt (bass) and Max Johnston (mandolin, banjo, fiddle and lap steel). Guitarist Jay Bennett rounded out the group, which in 1995 issued their debut album, *A.M.*, a collection of spry country-rock tunes that followed the course established in Tweedy's earlier work. Wilco's sophomore effort, 1996's two-disc set *Being There*, marked a radical transformation in the group's sound; while remaining steeped in the style that earned Tweedy his reputation, the songs took unexpected detours into psychedelia, power-pop, and soul, complete with orchestral touches and R&B horn flourishes. Shortly after the release of *Being There*, which most critics judged to be among the year's best releases, Johnston left the group to play with his sister, singer Michelle Shocked, and was replaced by guitarist Bob Egan of the band Freakwater. At the same time, while remaining full-time mem-

bers of Wilco, Stiratt, Bennett, and Coomer began performing together in the pop side project Courtesy Move. —*Jason Ankeny*

A.M. / 1995 / Sire/Reprise ✦✦✦

Not surprisingly, Wilco's debut album, *A.M.*, isn't a great departure from Uncle Tupelo. Wilco's music rocks in a more conventional way than Uncle Tupelo, rolling along with a loping beat that swings more than it rocks. "Casino Queen" is a shambling, bluesy honky tonk number that's boozier than anything Tupelo recorded, which is indicative of the major difference between the bands. Wilco wears its heart on its sleeve, writing songs that fit into the conventions of country-rock, not ones that rework the rules. "Box Full of Letters" doesn't deviate from the standard mid-tempo country-rock number, but it's done so well, it doesn't matter. Still, the opener, "I Must Be High"—a clever love song that subtly tweaks both lyrical and musical cliches, as well as featuring a killer melody—casts a shadow over *A.M.*, offering the knowledge that Wilco can subvert the genre without losing its accessibility. In its light, all the very good songs that follow seem somewhat disappointing. —*Stephen Thomas Erlewine*

● **Being There** / Oct. 29, 1996 / Sire/Reprise ✦✦✦✦
While Wilco's debut *A.M.* spread its wings in an expectedly country-rock fashion, their sophomore effort *Being There* is the group's great leap forward, a masterful, wildly eclectic collection shot through with ambitions and ideas. Although a few songs remain rooted in their signature sound, here Jeff Tweedy and band are as fascinated by their music's possibilities as its origins, and they push the songs that make up this sprawling two-disc set along consistently surprising paths and byways. For starters, the opener "Misunderstood" is majestic psychedelia, built on studio trickery and string flourishes, while "I Got You (At the End of the Century)" is virtual power-pop, right down to the handclaps. The lovely "Someone Else's Song" borrows heavily from the Beatles' "Norwegian Wood," while the R&B-influenced boogie of "Monday" wouldn't sound at all out of place on *Exile on Main St.;* and on and on. The remarkable thing is how fresh all of these seeming cliches sound when re-imagined with so much love and conviction; even the most traditional songs take unexpected twists and turns, never once sinking into mere imitation. "Music is my savior/I was named by rock 'n' roll/I was maimed by rock 'n' roll/I was tamed by rock 'n' roll/I got my name from rock 'n' roll," Tweedy sings on "Sunken Treasure," the opener of the second disc, and throughout the course of these 19 songs he explores rock as though he were tracing his family genealogy, fervently seeking to discover not only where he came from but also where he's going. With *Being There*, he finds what he's been looking for. —*Jason Ankeny*

Wild Rose

Contemporary Country, Neo-Traditionalist Country
The five-piece all-woman band Wild Rose was founded by multi-talented musician Wanda Vick, who got her start as a session player and side player for Lynn Anderson's group. Vick first teamed with drummer Nancy Given Prout in Right Combination, Porter Wagoner's all-female band. Later, Vick and Prout were joined by former New Coon Creek Girls Pamela Gadd and Pam Perry, who sang and played guitar. Bass guitarist and singer Kathy Mac, formerly of Tina Carroll and the Nashville Satins, rounded out the group. They first called themselves Miss Behavin', but changed to Wild Rose before signing with Universal Records in 1988. With the assistance of James Stroud, they produced one album, *Breakin' New Ground;* its title track reached the Top 20 the next year, just before the label folded. In 1990 Wild Rose appeared on the television special "Night of 100 Stars" and later that year signed to Capitol to work with producer Jimmy Bowen. Capitol reissued their debut album, and it made the Top 50 of the country album charts. The album produced one more Top 40 hit, "Go Down Swingin'." They made their first video that year for "Everything He Touches," from their second album *Straight and Narrow*. Shortly after releasing their third album, *Listen to Your Heart* (1991), the members of Wild Rose went their separate ways. —*Sandra Brennan*

● **Breaking New Ground** / Apr. 9, 1990 / Liberty ✦✦✦✦

Straight and Narrow / Sep. 24, 1990 / Liberty ✦✦✦

Listen to Your Heart / Sep. 2, 1991 / Liberty ✦✦✦

Honey Wilds

Vocals / Old-Time, Traditional Country, Country Humor
Revisionist history has largely erased the name of Honey Wilds from country music lore. His importance to the music's evolution remains unassailable: a Southern humorist and regular performer on the Grand Ole Opry between 1932 and 1952, Wilds was the creative force behind the Opry's first tent tours, which were instrumental in bringing rural music to mass audiences. His recorded legacy was less substantial, resulting in only a handful of songs. Regardless, the reason Wilds' name is frequently omitted from the official record is a simple—yet infinitely complex—one: he was a minstrel singer who performed in blackface for white audiences during the segregation era. Rather than serving as a painful reminder of America's past, he fell prey to the nation's notoriously selective memory and has essentially vanished.

Although many of the details of his life remain sketchy, it is known that Lee David Wilds was born into abject poverty in southeastern Texas in 1902. His father, the owner of a brickyard, died of pneumonia at the age of 32. Wilds grew up in a racially mixed community, learning to play the blues from the Black musicians who performed at a nearby theater. He also took up the ukelele. In the mid-1920s he joined a minstrel show, forming a duo with Lasses White, a blackface comedian and veteran of vaudeville. White, who had earned his nickname as a child because of his sweet tooth, was known for giving his partners complementary stage names, and so Honey Wilds was born.

Although music accounted for a large share of Lasses and Honey's act, the two were primarily comedians. They performed novelty songs, often parodies of current hits. Like Al Jolson and Emmett Miller before them, their act consisted of material appropriated from African-American culture, allowing white audiences the opportunity to experience, albeit second-hand, a form of entertainment that society at large otherwise deemed wholly inappropriate. (There also existed a parallel circuit where Black performers appeared in whiteface, again as a means of crossing color lines.) Most blackface performers insisted that their work sprang not from racism but from a deep admiration for Black popular culture; the validity of such statements is debatable, although in Wilds' case it appears to have been true, especially given his background and adult friendships with the likes of DeFord Bailey, one of country music's few Black acts.

In 1932 Lasses and Honey were offered a six-week contract to perform at the *Opry*. Wilds ended up staying for more than two decades, his tenure broken only by a brief 1939 foray into Hollywood. Although he soon returned to the Opry, both White and their mutual friend Chill Wills remained in California. Instead of going solo, Wilds formed another duo, Jam-Up and Honey, in 1940. After his return from the West Coast, he also began pondering methods of improving the existing touring network, which consisted typically of two or three acts hitting the road together. With the Opry's endorsement, he bought an 80-by-200 foot tent, assembled a road crew and a wide variety of entertainers, and began promoting the tour throughout the country. The Opry tent shows proved highly successful, running annually from early April to Labor Day between 1940 and 1949.

Despite close friendships with Hank Williams (according to legend, it was Wilds who nicknamed Hank Jr. "Bocephus"), Roy Acuff, Ernest Tubb, Red Foley, and other Opry staples, Wilds rarely wrote or recorded his own material, focusing instead on live performances. His few existing recordings include "Alabamy Bound," a traditional country blues, and "De Lion's Cage," an old Emmett Miller routine cut with producer Owen Bradley. In 1952 Jam-Up and Honey left the Opry to accept an offer in Knoxville; by that time, the duo no longer performed in blackface, and their act gradually fell out of favor. In 1957 the team split, and Wilds dropped out of music, running a service station until 1960, at which time he began hosting a local children's television program. By 1967 he had retired permanently, and he died several years later. —*Jason Ankeny*

Slim Willett
....

Vocals / Traditional Country

Slim Willet was best known for writing "Don't Let the Stars Get in Your Eyes," a smash hit not only for himself but also Skeets McDonald and Ray Price. He was born Winston Lee Moore in Texas and started out working in the aircraft industry in the late '40s. Near the decade's end, he became a regular on KRBC Abilene. In 1950 Willett founded the Hired Hands and made his recording debut with "Tool Pusher from Snyder." Before the year's end he had become a regular on WFAA Dallas' "Big D Jamboree"; he also joined Shreveport's "Louisiana Hayride" in 1951 and continued working on all three shows through the mid-'50s. Willet and his band debuted on the Grand Ole Opry in 1954, the year he launched his own label and released four singles, including "Old Light Waltz." By 1956 the band had split up, and Willett began working on KNIT Abilene, where he remained until 1964. Willet later purchased part of KCAD Abilene, where he worked until he died of heart failure in 1966. — *Sandra Brennan*

● **Slim Willett** / 1959 / Audio Lab ◆◆◆◆

Old Patch Songs / 1962 / Winston ◆◆◆

Don Williams
....

b. May 27, 1939, Floydada, TX

Guitar, Vocals / Traditional Country, Country-Pop

With his laidback, straightforward vocals and large, imposing build, Don Williams came to be known as "the Gentle Giant." That nickname was bestowed on him in the early '70s, when he began a string of countrypolitan hits that ran into the early '90s. Williams was never known as an innovator, but his ballads were immensely popular; in the course of his career, he had 17 No. 1 hits.

Williams began playing guitar when he was child, learning the instrument from his mother. As a teenager, he played in a variety of country, rockabilly, folk, and rock 'n' roll bands. After completing high school, he formed his first band with a friend, Lofton Kline. Williams and Kline recruited another singer, Susan Taylor, and formed the Pozo-Seco Singers, a folk-pop group, in 1964. The next year, the band signed a contract with Columbia Records. In 1966 the Pozo-Seco Singers had a pop hit with "Time," which climbed into the Top 50. For the next two years, they had a series of minor hits, highlighted by two Top 40 hits in late 1966, "I Can Make It with You" and "Look What You've Done." The group stayed together until 1971.

After the Pozo-Seco Singers disbanded, Williams decided to pursue a career as a songwriter in Nashville, since he wasn't convinced that he was suited for a solo career. He signed with Jack Clement's Jack Music, Inc., as a songwriter. By the end of 1972, he had signed with JMI as a solo artist, releasing "Don't You Believe" as his debut. The song went nowhere, but "The Shelter of Your Eyes" climbed to No. 14 at the beginning of 1973. For the next year, Williams scored a string of minor hits before he had his 1974 breakthrough, "We Should Be Together," which reached No. 5. The single led to a contract with ABC/Dot.

"I Wouldn't Want to Live If You Didn't Love Me," his first single for ABC/Dot, reached No. 1 in the summer 1974. The single launched a string of Top Ten hits that ran more or less uninterrupted until 1991—between 1974 and 1991, only four of his 46 charting singles didn't make the Top Ten. Instead of reaching the top of the charts with his original material, most of his big hits were covers of other songwriters, including John Prine, Bob McDill, Dave Loggins, and Wayland Holyfield.

During the '70s Don Williams became the most successful country artist in the world. His country-pop not only crossed over into the American pop mainstream, it also gained him a large following in England and Europe. In addition to his Top Ten hits, Williams won several country music awards, highlighted by the Country Music Association's naming him Male Vocalist of the Year in 1978, the same year his No. 1 single "Tulsa Time" was named Single of the Year. In the late '70s he began acting, appearing primarily in the films of his friend Burt Reynolds, including *W.W. and the Dixie Dancekings* and *Smokey and the Bandit II.*

In the early '80s Williams slowed down the pace of his career slightly, as he was suffering from back problems. Nevertheless, the hits continued to come and many of his singles reached No. 1. In 1986 he left MCA Records—who had acquired the ABC label while he was recording for it—and signed with Capitol. The change in labels didn't affect his career, as he continued to hit the Top Ten with regularity. In 1987 he underwent back surgery, which solved his problems.

Williams signed with RCA Records in 1989. Initially, he continued to have hits, but his streak came to an end in early 1992, after his last Top Ten single, "Lord Have Mercy on a Country Boy." Although he continued to perform in the mid-'90s, he had in effect retired to his Nashville farm. — *Stephen Thomas Erlewine*

Don Williams, Vol. 1 / 1973 / MCA ◆◆◆◆
Don Williams' first album as a country singer was originally released on Cowboy Jack Clement's JMI label before being snapped up by ABC-Dot the following year. There were four hits on this record, not a small feat for any artist, much less on the first try. Over the years Williams has made some fine records, but none better than this. — *Jim Worbois*

Don Williams, Vol. 2 / 1974 / JMI ◆◆◆

Don Williams, Vol. 3 / 1974 / MCA ◆◆◆
Williams continues in the vein of his first record, with lots of good stuff; still, it's not quite on par with the first album. — *Jim Worbois*

Greatest Hits, Vol. 1 / 1975 / MCA ◆◆◆◆
Greatest Hits, Vol. 1 contains 12 of Don Williams' biggest hits from the mid-'70s, including "Amanda," "Come Early Morning," "The Shelter of Your Eyes," "I Wouldn't Want to Live if You Didn't Love Me," "We Should Be Together," and "The Ties That Bind." In addition to the hits, the compilation contains first-rate album tracks like "Ghost Story" and "I Recall a Gypsy Woman," making it an excellent retrospective of Williams' early career. — *Thom Owens*

Greatest Country Hits / 1976 / Curb ◆◆◆
Greatest Country Hits covers only Williams' late-'80s chart successes like "Heartbeat in the Darkness," "Then It's Love," and "We've Got a Good Fire Goin'." — *Jason Ankeny*

Best of Don Williams, Vol. 2 / 1979 / MCA ◆◆◆◆
Best of Don Williams, Vol. 2 contains 11 of his late-'70s country hits, including the No. 1 hits "Tulsa Time," "(Turn Out the Light and) Love Me Tonight," "'Til the Rivers All Run Dry," "Say It Again," "Some Broken Hearts Never Mend," and "I'm Just a Country Boy." On the whole, this album is even better than the first volume of greatest hits, and it captures Williams' laidback style perfectly. — *Thom Owens*

I Believe in You / 1980 / MCA ◆◆◆◆
The title cut of *I Believe in You* is Williams' biggest hit; the LP also includes "Falling Again." — *Jason Ankeny*

Especially for You / 1981 / MCA ◆◆◆◆
Especially for You is highlighted by "If I Needed You," Williams' hit duet with Emmylou Harris. — *Jason Ankeny*

I Believe in You/Especially for You / 1981 / MCA ◆◆◆
Two early (1980-1981) collections for the price of one, including the gem "Lord, I Hope This Day Is Good." — *Hank Davis*

Prime Cuts / 1981 / Capitol ◆◆◆◆
Williams released four greatest-hits albums for MCA, so this is the fifth of his career. The R&B flavor of "Heartbeat in the Darkness" shakes up his approach. Much of the remainder is a thing of sparsely scored beauty. — *Tom Roland*

Best of Don Williams, Vol. 3 / 1984 / MCA ◆◆◆◆

Cafe Carolina / 1984 / MCA ◆◆◆
Williams has a very identifiable core sound, but occasional subtle differences can seem like major alterations. Here he recruits sax player Jim Horn, and while Horn doesn't play on every track, his mere presence provides a fresh change. — *Tom Roland*

Greatest Hits, Vol. 4 / 1985 / MCA ◆◆◆

★ **20 Greatest Hits** / 1987 / MCA ◆◆◆◆◆
The best thing about Don Williams is that it's so hard to peg him against this, that or the other country music era. Hits like

"Amanda," "You're My Best Friend," "I Believe in You," and "Good Ole Boys like Me," all present in this collection, are so understated it's as if they float on top of Nashville history. —*Dan Cooper*

One Good Well / 1989 / RCA ✦✦✦
"I've Been Loved by the Best" and "Just as Long as I Have You" are just two of the hits found on *One Good Well*. —*Jason Ankeny*

True Love / 1990 / RCA ✦✦✦
True Love includes the hits "Back in My Younger Days" and "Lord Have Mercy on a Country Boy." —*Jason Ankeny*

Currents / 1992 / RCA ✦✦✦✦
This contains such hits as "Catfish Bates," "The Old Trail," "Too Much Water," and more. —*AMG*

Hank Williams, Sr. (Hiriam King Williams)

b. Sep. 17, 1923, Mount Olive, AL, **d.** Jan. 1, 1953, Oak Hill, WV
Guitar, Vocals / Traditional Country, Honky Tonk
Hank Williams is the father of contemporary country music. Williams was a superstar by the age of 25; he was dead at the age of 29. In those four short years, he established the rules for all the country performers who followed him and, in the process, for much of popular music. Williams wrote a body of songs that became popular classics, and his direct, emotional lyrics and vocals became the standard for most popular performers. Hank lived a life as troubled and reckless as that depicted in his songs.

Hank Williams was born in Mount Olive, AL, on September 17, 1923. When he was eight years old, Williams was given a guitar by his mother. His musical education was provided by a local blues street singer, Rufus Payne, who was called Tee Tot. From Tee Tot, Williams learned how to play the guitar and sing the blues, which would come to provide a strong undercurrent in his songwriting. Williams began performing around the Georgiana and Greenville areas of Alabama in his early teens. His mother moved the family to Montgomery, AL, in 1937, where she opened a boarding house. In Montgomery, Hank formed a band called the Drifting Cowboys and landed a regular spot on the local radio station, WSFA, in 1941. During his shows, Williams would sing songs from his idol, Roy Acuff, and other country hits of the day. WSFA dubbed him the Singing Kid, and Williams stayed with the station for the rest of the decade.

Williams met Audrey Mae Sheppard, a farmgirl from Banks, AL, in 1943 while he was playing a medicine show. The next year, the couple married and moved into Lilly's boarding house. Audrey became Hank's manager just before the marriage. By 1946 Williams was a local celebrity, but he was unable to make much headway nationally. That year, Hank and Audrey visited Nashville with the intent of meeting songwriter/music publisher Fred Rose, one of the heads of Acuff-Rose Publishing. Rose liked Williams' songs and asked him to record two sessions for Sterling Records, which resulted in two singles. Both of the singles—"Never Again" in December 1946 and "Honky Tonkin'" in February 1947—were successful, and Hank signed a contract with MGM Records early in 1947. Rose became the singer's manager and record producer.

"Move It On Over," released later in 1947, became Hank Williams' first single for MGM. It was an immediate hit, climbing into the country Top Five. By the summer of 1948 he had joined the "Louisiana Hayride," appearing on its tours and radio programs. "Honky Tonkin'" was released in 1948, followed by "I'm a Long Gone Daddy." While neither song was as successful as "Move It On Over," they were popular, with the latter peaking in the Top Ten. Early in 1949 he recorded "Lovesick Blues," a Tin Pan Alley song initially recorded by Emmett Miller and made popular by Rex Griffin. The single became a huge hit in the spring of 1949, staying at No. 1 for 16 weeks and crossing over into the pop Top 25. Williams sang the song at the Grand Ole Opry, where he performed an unprecedented six encores. He had become a star.

Hank and Audrey had their first child, Randall Hank, in the spring of 1949. Also in the spring, Hank assembled the most famous edition of the Drifting Cowboys, featuring guitarist Bob McNett, bassist Hillous Butrum, fiddler Jerry Rivers, and steel guitarist Don Helms. Soon he and the band were earning $1,000 per concert and were selling out shows across the country. Williams

had no fewer than seven hits in 1949 after "Lovesick Blues," including the Top Fives "Wedding Bells," "Mind Your Own Business," "You're Gonna Change (Or I'm Gonna Leave)," and "My Bucket's Got a Hole in It." In addition to having a string of hit singles in 1950—including the No. 1s "Long Gone Lonesome Blues," "Why Don't You Love Me," and "Moanin' the Blues," as well as the Top Tens "I Just Don't Like This Kind of Livin'," "My Son Calls Another Man Daddy," "They'll Never Take Her Love from Me," "Why Should We Try," and "Nobody's Lonesome for Me." That same year Williams began recording a series of spiritual records under the name Luke the Drifter.

Williams continued to rack up hits in 1951, beginning with the Top Ten "Dear John" and its No. 1 flipside, "Cold Cold Heart." That same year, pop vocalist Tony Bennett recorded "Cold, Cold Heart" and had a hit, leading to a stream of covers from such mainstream artists as Jo Stafford, Guy Mitchell, Frankie Laine, Teresa Brewer, and several others. Hank had also begun to experience the fruits of crossover success, appearing on the Perry Como television show and being part of a package tour that also featured Bob Hope, Jack Benny, and Minnie Pearl. In addition to "Dear John" and "Cold, Cold Heart," Hank had several other hits in 1951, including the No. 1 "Hey, Good Lookin'" and "Howlin' at the Moon," "I Can't Help It (If I'm Still In Love With You)," "Crazy Heart," "Lonesome Whistle," and "Baby, We're Really in Love," which all charted in the Top Ten.

Though his professional career was soaring, Hank Williams' personal life was beginning to spin out of control. Before he became a star, he had a mild drinking problem, but it had been more or less controlled during his first few years of fame. However, as he began to earn large amounts of money and spend long times away from home, he began to drink frequently. Furthermore, Hank's marriage to Audrey was deteriorating. Not only were they fighting, resulting in occasional separations, but Audrey was trying to create her own recording career without any success. In the fall of 1951 Hank was hunting on his Tennessee farm when he tripped and fell, re-activating a dormant back injury. He began taking morphine and other pain killers for his back and quickly became addicted.

In January 1952 Hank and Audrey separated for a final time, and he headed back to Montgomery to live with his mother. The hits were still coming fast for Williams, with "Honky Tonk Blues" hitting No. 2 in the spring. In fact, he released five more singles in 1952—"Half as Much," "Jambalaya," "Settin' the Woods on Fire," "You Win Again," and "I'll Never Get Out of This World Alive"—which all went Top Ten. In spite of all his success, Hank turned completely reckless in 1952, spending nearly all of his waking hours drunk and taking drugs, while he was frequently destroying property and playing with guns.

Williams left his mother in early spring, moving in with Ray Price in Nashville. In May Audrey and Hank were officially divorced. She was awarded the house and their child, as well as half of his future royalties. Williams continued to play a large number of concerts, but he was either drunk during the show or missed the gig altogether. In August the Grand Ole Opry fired him for that very reason. He was told that he could return when he was sober. Instead of heeding the Opry's warning, he just sank deeper into his self-destructive behavior. Soon, his friends were leaving him, as the Drifting Cowboys began working with Ray Price, and Fred Rose no longer supported him. Williams was still playing the "Louisiana Hayride," but he was performing with local pickup bands and was earning reduced wages. That fall, he met Billie Jean Jones Eshlimar, the 19-year old daughter of a Louisiana policeman. By October they were married. Hank also signed an agreement to support the baby—who had yet to be delivered—of one of his other girlfriends, Bobbie Jett, in October. By the end of the year, Williams was having heart problems, and Toby Marshall, a con-man doctor, was giving him various prescription drugs to help soothe the pain.

Williams was scheduled to play a concert in Canton, OH, on January 1, 1953. He was scheduled to fly out of Knoxville, TN, on New Year's Eve, but the weather was so bad he had to hire a chauffeur to drive him to Ohio in his new Cadillac. Before they left for Ohio, Williams was injected with two shots of the vitamin

B-12 and morphine by a doctor. Williams got into the backseat of the Cadillac with a bottle of whiskey, and the teenage chauffeur headed out for Canton. When the driver was stopped for speeding, the policeman noticed that Williams looked like a dead man. Williams was taken to a West Virginian hospital, and he was declared dead at 7 AM on January 1, 1953. The last single released in his lifetime was "I'll Never Get Out of This World Alive."

Hank Williams was buried in Montgomery, AL, three days later. His funeral drew a record crowd, larger than any since Jefferson Davis was inaugurated as president of the Confederacy in 1861. Dozens of country music stars attended, as did Audrey Williams, Billie Jean Jones, and Bobbie Jett, who happened to give birth to a daughter three days later. "I'll Never Get Out of This World Alive" reached No. 1 immediately after his death, and it was followed by a number of hit records throughout 1953, including the number ones "Your Cheatin' Heart," "Kaw-Liga," and "Take These Chains from My Heart."

After his death, MGM wanted to keep issuing Hank Williams records, so it took some of his original demos and overdubbed bands onto the original recordings. The first of these, "Weary Blues from Waitin'," was a hit, but the others weren't quite as successful. In 1961 Hank Williams was one of the first inductees to the Country Music Hall of Fame. Throughout the '60s, Williams' records were released in overdubbed versions featuring heavy strings, as well as reprocessed stereo. For years, these bastardized versions were the only records in print; only in the '80s, when his music was released on compact disc, was his catalog restored to its original form. Even during those years when only overdubbed versions of his hits existed, Hank Williams' impact never diminished. His songs have become classics, his recordings have stood the test of time, and his life story is legendary. — *Stephen Thomas Erlewine*

24 of Hank Williams' Greatest Hits / 1970 / MGM ◆◆◆◆
24 of Hank Williams' Greatest Hits was originally released as a set of overdubbed recordings, where the spare original recordings were augmented by a fuller band and, occasionally, strings. In the '80s, Mercury reissued the album with the original, undubbed versions of the songs, and this version stands as an excellent retrospective of Williams' finest moments, containing a wealth of tremendous, timeless songs like "Your Cheatin' Heart," "I'm So Lonesome I Could Cry," "Honky Tonk Blues," "Cold, Cold Heart," "Mind Your Own Business," "Hey Good Lookin'," and "Jambalaya," among others. It's an excellent introduction, but *40 Greatest Hits* offers a deeper selection and, therefore, is an even better starting point. — *Stephen Thomas Erlewine*

24 Greatest Hits, Vol. 2 / 1976 / Polygram ◆◆◆◆
When compared with *40 Greatest Hits* (which came out the next year), this record is light on both tracks and liner notes. Adding insult to injury, these tracks are also offered in simulated stereo. There are better packages. — *Jim Worbois*

24 Greatest / 1976 / Mercury ◆◆◆◆
24 Greatest Hits might feature a significant portion of Hank Williams' greatest songs, but it isn't all it appears to be. The album contains overdubbed versions of the original recordings, which dilutes the power of his material. These songs should be heard in their original version, not in this form. [*24 Greatest* was later reissued on compact disc, featuring the songs in their original recorded versions.] — *Stephen Thomas Erlewine*

★ **40 Greatest Hits** / 1978 / Polydor ◆◆◆◆◆
Over the course of two CDs, *40 Greatest Hits* runs through all of Hank Williams' essential songs, presented in their original, undubbed versions. It is the perfect place to start listening to Williams. — *Stephen Thomas Erlewine*

☆ **I Ain't Got Nothin' But Time (December 1946—April 1947): Vol. I** / Jan. 1985 / Polydor ◆◆◆◆◆
I Ain't Got Nothin' But Time (December 1946—April 1947): Vol. 1 kicked off Polydor's eight-volume reissue series of Hank Williams' complete recorded works. Though the series did eventually leave several demos, radio performances, and live tracks in the can, those were later issued in a variety of other formats. The eight-volume series did contain all of Williams' studio recordings, plus the bulk of his home recordings and live tracks. What makes the

series especially interesting is how his great songs are placed in context with the large variety of material Hank also performed. For instance, on *I Ain't Got Nothin' But Time*, "Honky Tonkin'," "Move It On Over," and "I Saw the Light" sit next to a batch of gospel recordings ("Battle of Armageddon," "Wealth Won't Save Your Soul") as well as home versions of Western and Western swing songs ("Cool Water," "Roly Poly"). It's an endlessly fascinating listen, especially for Hank fans who know only *40 Greatest Hits*, or even *The Complete Singles Collection*. A wealth of hidden gems, as well as several lesser, but still enjoyable, songs are on each volume, and each collection is essential for any serious Williams fan, or any country music historian. Since it contains his very first recordings, *I Ain't Got Nothin' But Time* is sparse and direct, which gives the songs—largely comprised of gospel numbers—more weight. Highlights include "Calling You," "My Love for You Has Turned to Hate," "(Last Night) I Heard You Crying In Your Sleep," and the non-session "Alone and Forsaken" in addition to the aforementioned hits. — *Stephen Thomas Erlewine*

☆ **Lovesick Blues (August 1947—December 1948): Vol. II** / Feb. 1985 / Polydor ◆◆◆◆◆
Among the material on *Lovesick Blues (August 1947—December 1948): Vol. 2*, the second volume of Polydor's series of Hank Williams' complete recorded works, is "Lovesick Blues," the single that made him a star. That song illustrates the difference between this volume and its predecessor, *I Ain't Got Nothin' But Time*. By and large, the secular music on *Lovesick Blues* is lighter than the gospel that dominated the first volume. The majority of the songs are pure honky tonk, whether it's the rollicking boogie of "Rootie Tootie" and "Fly Trouble," the gritty "Honky Tonkin'" and "I'm a Long Gone Daddy," or the wrenching ballad "A Mansion on the Hill." Among the other highlights of a disc filled with uniformly excellent songs are the session recordings "I'm Satisfied with You" and "I'll Be a Bachelor 'til I Die," the overdubbed no-session recording "We Live in Two Different Worlds," and the non-session recordings "Please Don't Let Me Love You" and "Weary Blues from Waitin'." — *Stephen Thomas Erlewine*

☆ **Lost Highway (December 1948—March 1949): Vol. III** / Jan. 1986 / Polygram ◆◆◆◆◆
Though "Lovesick Blues" made Hank Williams into a star, it didn't become successful until March 1949, which means the material that comprises *Lost Highway (December 1948—March 1949): Vol. 3* was all recorded before he knew it was a hit. As a result, the music on *Lost Highway* is a bit uneven, since the future of Hank's recording career was uncertain; he wasn't sure whether his records would sell, and he consequently performed a couple of his most unfocused sessions. The session recordings on *Lost Highway* do contain several classics—"Honky Tonk Blues" (presented in a rocking alternate take), "Mind Your Own Business" and the title track—but there are also several awkward duets with his wife Audrey ("Lost on the River," "I Heard My Mother Praying for Me"). The true gems on *Lost Highway* arrive in the non-session recordings. The overdubbed non-session recordings contain the excellent "A Teardrop on a Rose," "I'm Going Home," and "The Angel of Death," while the undubbed non-session recordings contain "Singing Waterfall," "I'm Free at Last," and "Alabama Waltz." — *Stephen Thomas Erlewine*

☆ **I'm So Lonesome I Could Cry (March 1949—August 1949): Vol. IV** / Feb. 1986 / Polydor ◆◆◆◆◆
With much of the material on *I'm So Lonesome I Could Cry (March 1949—August 1949): Vol. 4*, Hank Williams began to reveal his personal demons through his songs—"I'm So Lonesome I Could Cry," "I Just Don't Like This Kind of Living," "You're Gonna Change (Or I'm Gonna Leave)," "A House Without Love" and the initial, non-hit version of "My Son Calls Another Man Daddy" all cut close to the bone. Ironically, his career was riding high at the time, with songs like "Wedding Bells," "You're Gonna Change (Or I'm Gonna Leave)" and "My Bucket's Got a Hole in It" peaking in the upper reaches of the country Top Ten. The aforementioned songs comprise the bulk of the session recordings on *I'm So Lonesome I Could Cry*, and the non-session recordings are just as strong as the official recordings. Most of the overdubbed non-session songs on the compilation are first-rate gospel ("Are

You Building a Temple in Heaven," "How Can You Refuse Him Now"), while the undubbed tracks contain such gems as a demo of "Fool About You," "No One Will Ever Know," "If You'll Be a Baby (To Me)," and "We're Getting Closer to the Grave Each Day." *—Stephen Thomas Erlewine*

☆ **Long Gone Lonesome Blues (August 1949—December 1950): Vol. V** / Jan. 1987 / Polydor ♦♦♦♦♦
Among the highlights of the studio recordings on *Long Gone Lonesome Blues (August 1949—December 1950): Vol. V* are the hit singles "Long Gone Lonesome Blues," "Why Don't You Love Me?," "My Son Calls Another Man Daddy," "They'll Never Take Her Love from Me," "Nobody's Lonesome for Me," "Moanin' the Blues," and "Cold, Cold Heart"—in fact, out of the eight studio sessions on the collection, only "Why Should We Try Anymore?" failed to chart. The rest of the compilation consists of a handful of overdubbed non-session recordings and live tracks, as well as several excellent undubbed non-session songs ("Low Down Blues," "It Just Don't Matter Now," "There's No Room in My Heart for the Blues," "Last Night I Dreamed of Heaven), and the first Luke the Drifter recordings (including "Too Many Parties and Too Many Pals," "The Funeral," and "Everything's Okay"). *—Stephen Thomas Erlewine*

☆ **Hey, Good Lookin' (December 1950—July 1951): Vol. VI** / Feb. 1987 / Polydor ♦♦♦♦♦
Out of the ten studio recordings on *Hey, Good Lookin' (December 1950—July 1951): Vol. VI,* no less than six—"Dear John," "I Can't Help It (If I'm Still in Love with You)," "Howlin' at the Moon," "Hey Good Lookin'," "(I Heard That) Lonesome Whistle," and "Crazy Heart"—were hits, while two of the four remaining cuts ("My Heart Would Know," "I'd Still Want You") were nearly as strong as the well-known songs. The other two, "The Pale Horse and His Rider" and "A Home in Heaven," were duets with Hank's wife Audrey, and while they were better than most of their collaborations, her voice remains tuneless and painful. The pair of live tracks are engaging, but the undubbed non-session recordings are the real hidden gems; all three songs ("The Angel of Death," "I Can't Escape from You," "Message to My Mother") are haunting and evocative. The remainder of *Hey, Good Lookin'* is comprised of six Luke the Drifter recordings, and while they are strong (particularly "Ramblin' Man," "A Picture from Life's Other Side" and "I've Been Down That Road Before"), they pale slightly compared to the rest of the compilation. *—Stephen Thomas Erlewine*

☆ **Let's Turn Back the Years (July 1951—June 1952): Vol. VII** / Mar. 1987 / Polydor ♦♦♦♦♦
Hank Williams' life was beginning to unravel during the time he recorded the material on *Let's Turn Back the Years (July 1951—June 1952): Vol. VII,* but that didn't mean his music suffered. In fact, much of *Let's Turn Back the Years* ranks among his best work. Among the hits on the ten studio tracks on the disc are "Crazy Heart," "Half As Much," "Baby, We're Really in Love," "Honky Tonk Blues," "Jambalaya (On the Bayou)," and I'll Never Get Out of This World Alive." The studio tracks include the fine "I'm Sorry for You, My Friend," "Window Shopping," and the title track. While the overdubbed and group non-session recordings are good gospel, the true gems of the non-session material arrive in the undubbed recordings, which include such simple and affecting performances as "Thank God," "Someday You'll Call My Name," "How Can You Refuse Him Now?," "When You're Tired of Breaking Other Hearts," and "A Teardrop on a Rose." *—Stephen Thomas Erlewine*

☆ **I Won't Be Home No More (June 1952—September 1952): Vol. VIII)** / Apr. 1987 / Polydor ♦♦♦♦♦
The music on *I Won't be Home No More (June 1952—September 1952)* is the last that Hank Williams recorded, and his inner demons and personal traumas are evident throughout the compilation. There are a couple of light-hearted songs on *I Won't Be Home No More,* namely "Settin' the Woods on Fire" and "Kaw-Liga," and they stand out among the unflinching despair and sorrow that comprise the remainder of the collection. In addition to the two previously mentioned songs, the studio recordings feature "You Win Again," "I Won't Be Home No More," "I Could Never Be Ashamed of You," "Your Cheatin' Heart" and "Take These Chains

from My Heart." While the studio tracks are all chilling in their emotional immediacy, the remaining live cuts, Luke the Drifter sides, and non-session recordings are even more haunting, with "Mother Is Gone," "A House of Gold," "Ready to Go Home," and "Why Don't You Make Up Your Mind" ranking as some of the highlights. *I Won't Be Home No More* is supremely affecting, containing some of the finest music Hank Williams ever recorded. *—Stephen Thomas Erlewine*

☆ **The Collectors' Edition** / 1987 / Mercury ♦♦♦♦♦
After completing an excellent, comprehensive reissue of every recording Hank Williams made during his life, Polygram and Mercury packaged the eight discs in the indespensable box set, *The Collector's Edition.* Since it is difficult to buy one installment in the series without wanting the remaining volumes, the box is the best way to purchase the series. However, during the mid-'90s, *The Collector's Edition* became difficult to find, since Polygram/Mercury inexplicably took the set, as well as the eight individual discs, off the general market. The record company made a deal with Tower Records, and the chain became the only retailer to sell Williams' complete recordings as of the mid-'90s. And Tower sells the eight discs only as *The Collector's Edition* box, which means that the set is the only way to purchase the complete recordings of country music's most important artist. It may take a little time to track it down, but for any serious country fan, *The Collector's Edition* is worth the effort. *—Stephen Thomas Erlewine*

Rare Demos: First to Last / 1990 / Country Music Foundation ♦♦♦♦
Rare Demos: First to Last compiles all 24 publisher's demos that the Country Music Foundation originally released as *The First Recordings* and *Just Me and My Guitar.* These are stark, moving recordings that cut to the core of each song. Though the master takes are masterpieces in their own right, the demo versions are equally essential for dedicated fans, since they offer new insights to Williams' songwriting, as well as his performance technique. *—Stephen Thomas Erlewine*

☆ **Original Singles Collection...Plus** / 1992 / Polydor ♦♦♦♦♦
The title of *The Original Singles Collection...Plus* is slightly misleading. Although PolyGram marketed the three-disc, 84-song set as a complete collection, it doesn't feature all of the singles Hank Williams released during his lifetime. Several singles Williams released under the pseudonym "Luke the Drifter," as well as all of the duets he cut with Audrey Williams, are missing. Everything else is included in original, undubbed versions and is presented in the best sound possible. For a fan who wants all the essential songs without springing for the eight-disc series of complete recordings, *The Original Singles* collection is invaluable. *—Stephen Thomas Erlewine*

Health and Happiness Shows / 1993 / Mercury ♦♦♦♦
The double-disc set *Health and Happinesss Shows* collects eight complete radio shows that Hank Williams recorded in 1949, when his career was just taking off. Throughout the collection, Williams sounds energetic and vibrant, even during his between-song stage patter, which is nearly fascinating as the music. It's a set designed for collectors, but even casual Williams fans will find much to treasure on the *Health and Happiness Shows. —Stephen Thomas Erlewine*

American Legends #18 / Apr. 1996 / LaserLight ♦♦
You have to read the small print on the cover of this CD to realize that it is a various-artists album, not one made up entirely of Hank Williams recordings. Actually, Williams is heard on four of the 13 tracks, along with three each by Rose Maddox and Molly O'Day, two by the Osborne Brothers, and one by Tompall and the Glaser Brothers (whose name is misspelled on the album jacket). Williams' renditions of songs like "Why Don't You Love Me?" and "You Win Again" are classic, of course; the rest are mediocre. At a running time of 33 minutes, the album's brevity more than justifies the discount price. But even sold cheaply, this isn't a good way to get a sense of Hank Williams. *—William Ruhlmann*

Low Down Blues / Aug. 20, 1996 / Polygram ♦♦
Low Down Blues is a mid-priced compilation of Hank Williams' bluesiest material. The 16-track collection features classics like

"Honky Tonk Blues," "Lovesick Blues," "Moanin' the Blues," and "Long Gone Lonesome Blues," as well as five demo recordings. As a sampler, *Low Down Blues* is fine—it offers a different perspective on Hank than most other collections and it was thoughtfully compiled—but serious collectors will want to stick with the more complete compilations, and casual fans will be better served by either *40 Greatest Hits* or *24 Greatest Hits*. And that means *Low Down Blues* essentially doesn't have an audience. It's a nice collection, but its essentially purposeless. Only collectors who enjoying hearing the subtle differences in different sequencing will find *Low Down Blues* essential. —*Stephen Thomas Erlewine*

Lonesome Blues / Spm ✦✦✦

The music on *Lonesome Blues* is certainly first-rate, but the budget packaging leaves a lot to be desired. Featuring a skimpy track selection and liner notes, the disc is useful only for the extremely budget-conscious. Those looking for an introduction to Williams' work should stick with *40 Greatest Hits*. —*Stephen Thomas Erlewine*

There's Nothing As Sweet As My Baby / Mount Olive ✦✦✦

There's Nothing As Sweet As My Baby is a documentation of a 1951 radio transcription that features rowdy, exciting takes of several country classics, as well as Hank's versions of contemporary songs. There might not be many of his big hits, but listeners buying this album aren't looking for hits, they're looking for revelations; *There's Nothing As Sweet As My Baby* is full of them. Williams turns in terrific versions of "Cherokee Boogie," "Blue Eyes Crying in the Rain," "Lonely Tombs," and "I Can't Help It (If I'm Still in Love with You)," and there is a brief interview, as well as a song, by his wife, Audrey Williams. It's an excellent addition to a comprehensive Hank Williams collection, and perfect for fans of the double-disc set *Health and Happiness Shows*. —*Stephen Thomas Erlewine*

Hank Williams, Jr.

Hank Williams, Jr. (Randall Hank Williams)

b. May 26, 1949, Shreveport, LA
Guitar, Vocals / Traditional Country, Country-Rock, Southern Rock, Outlaw Country, Urban Cowboy
The offspring of famous musicians often have a hard time creating a career for themselves, but Hank Williams, Jr. is one of the few to develop a career that is not only successful, but markedly different from his legendary father. Originally, Hank Jr. simply copied and played his father's music, but as he grew older, he began to carve out his own niche, and it was one that owed as much to country-rock as it did to honky tonk. In the late '70s, he retooled his image to appeal both to outlaw country fans and rowdy Southern rockers. His makeover worked, resulting in a string of Top Ten singles—including the No. 1 hits "Texas Women," "Dixie on My Mind," "All My Rowdy Friends (Have Settled Down)," "Honky Tonkin'," and "Born to Boogie"—that ran into the late '80s. Hank Jr. never was above capitalizing on his father's name, but his tributes and name-dropping often seemed affectionate, not crass. Also, Bocephus—as his father nicknamed him when he was a child—was a passionate cheerleader for patriotic American values; he even wrote a pro-Gulf War song during 1991. All of these actions helped make him an American superstar during the '80s, becoming one of the most recognizable popular culture figures of the era. As new country took over the airwaves in the '90s, Williams slowly disappeared from the charts; his concerts stopped selling as well as they did ten years earlier, but he retained a devoted core audience throughout the decade.

The son of Hank and Audrey Williams, Hank Williams, Jr. was born in Shreveport, LA, in 1949. Less than four years later, his father died. When Hank Jr. was eight years old, Audrey decided to push him into the spotlight, positioning him as the rightful heir to his father's legacy. Dressed in a white Nudie suit, he would sing Hank Sr.'s biggest hits on package tours, and by the time he was 11, he had made his first appearance on the Grand Ole Opry. After a few years of touring, Hank Jr.'s voice broke in 1963. As soon as his voice changed, Audrey had her son sign a contract with MGM Records. Hank Jr. recorded his father's "Long Gone Lonesome Blues" as his debut single, and the record was a hit upon its early 1964 release, climbing to No. 5. Later that year, he

sang all the material for the Hank Williams, Sr. biopic, *Your Cheatin' Heart*, and starred in the film *A Time to Sing*. Though he immediately had a hit, he wasn't able to follow it up with another Top Ten hit until 1966, when his self-penned "Standing in the Shadows" reached No. 5. By that time, he had begun to grow tired of his reputation as a Hank Williams imitator and was trying to create his own style, as "Standing in the Shadows" proved. Following that single, he began to explore rock 'n' roll somewhat, occasionally performing under the name Rockin' Randall.

Despite his half-hearted rock 'n' roll attempts, Williams continued to concentrate on country music, turning out a string of hit singles, including the No. 1 "All for the Love of Sunshine" and a number of inspirational cuts released under the name "Luke the Drifter, Jr.," a reference to his father's alter-ego. Though his career was doing well, Hank Jr. began falling into drug and alcohol abuse after he turned 18 years old. His personal life became progressively more complicated, culminating in a suicide attempt in 1974. After the attempt, Williams moved to Alabama where he not only got his life together, but changed his musical direction, as well. Hooking up with Southern-rockers like Charlie Daniels, Marshall Tucker, and Toy Caldwell, he recorded *Hank Williams Jr. and Friends*, which fused hardcore country with rock 'n' roll. Though he wasn't scoring as many hits as he had in the early '70s, his music was becoming more original and focused.

Just as his career was being revived, tragedy befell Williams. While he was climbing a mountain in Montana in 1975, he fell 442 feet. His injuries were serious—his skull was split and his face was crushed—but he survived. After extensive reconstructive cosmetic surgery, he had to relearn how to speak and sing. Williams' recovery period lasted a full two years. When he re-emerged in 1977, he aligned himself with the outlaw country movement, as Waylon Jennings produced Hank Jr.'s comeback effort, *The New South*. It took several years before Williams began to have hits again—his biggest hit in the late '70s was a cover of Bobby Fuller's "I Fought the Law," which reached No. 15—but in the final six months of 1979, he had two Top Ten singles, "Family Tradition" and "Whiskey Bent and Hell Bound," which began a virtually uninterrupted streak of 29 Top Ten hits that ran into 1988.

Throughout the '80s, Hank Williams, Jr. was one of the most popular, and controversial, figures in country music. After his image makeover, he appealed primarily to young and rowdy crowds with his hell-raising anthems and jingoistic ballads. Though he had established his own distinctive style, he continued to name-check and pay tribute to his father, and these salutes became as much a part of his act as his redneck rockers. Both the wild music and the party-ready atmosphere of his concerts made Hank Jr. an immensely popular musician and helped him cross over into the rock 'n' roll audience. Williams' career really began to take off in 1981, when he had three No 1 hits—"Texas Women," "Dixie on My Mind," and "All My Rowdy Friends (Have Settled Down)." *Rowdy* began a streak of 15 gold or platinum albums that ran until 1990. He won several awards, including back-to-back Country Music Association Entertainer of the Year in 1987 and 1988.

By the end of the decade, Hank Jr.'s persona was becoming a little tired, especially in light of the new breed of clean-cut new country singers who had taken over Nashville. Williams could still have a hit—such as "There's a Tear in My Beer," which was an electronic duet between him and his father—but by the end of 1990, he was no longer hitting the Top Ten. By the middle of the decade he had trouble reaching the Top 40. Despite his declining record sales, Hank Jr. remained a popular concert draw into the latter half of the '90s. —*Stephen Thomas Erlewine*

Living Proof: The MGM Recordings 1963-1975 / 1974 / Mercury ✦✦✦✦
Living Proof is a double-disc set that chronicles Hank Williams Jr.'s recordings between 1964 and 1975. During this time he was still developing his own style and began moving out of his father's shadow. Nearly all of the worthwhile tracks he recorded in this period are included on this set, and while they aren't as forceful as his later, rowdier hits, many of the songs are almost as memorable. —*Thom Owens*

☆ **Hank Williams Jr. and Friends** / 1975 / Polydor ✦✦✦✦✦
The breakthrough record of Williams' career. On his first mature record (made in his mid-20s), Williams teamed with Southern rockers Charlie Daniels, Toy Caldwell (Marshall Tucker Band), and Chuck Leavell (Allman Brothers Band), among others, for a session that opened his musical vistas to folk, blues, and rock, and incidentally introduced his mature persona in songs like "Stoned at the Jukebox" and "Living Proof." —*William Ruhlmann*

14 Greatest Hits / 1976 / Polydor ✦✦✦✦
Williams was a good, if conventional, country singer during the early years covered in this anthology (1966-1974). It includes 11 of his first 12 Top Ten hits, among them the No. 1s "Eleven Roses" and "All for the Love of Someone." —*William Ruhlmann*

Family Tradition / 1979 / Warner Brothers ✦✦✦
After the successful artistic makeover of *The New South*, Hank Williams Jr. made his commercial comeback with the equally excellent *Family Tradition*. A tough fusion of rock 'n' roll attitude and roadhouse honky tonk, the album is filled with first-rate songs, both covers ("To Love Somebody," "I Fought the Law," "Only Daddy That'll Walk the Line") and originals ("I've Got Rights," "Family Tradition," "Paying on Time"). *Family Tradition* set the template for Hank Jr.'s albums of the '80s, and though he got close to equalling it, he never bettered it. —*Thom Owens*

Habits Old and New / 1980 / Warner Brothers ✦✦
Habits Old and New is a standard Hank Williams Jr. album from the early '80s, containing several covers of his father's classics ("Kaw-Liga," "Move It On Over"), a tribute to his father (Kris Kristofferson's "If You Don't Like Hank Williams"), plus several rabble-rousing redneck rockers ("All in Alabama," "American Way"). —*Thom Owens*

The Pressure Is On / 1981 / Warner Brothers ✦✦
The Pressure Is On includes the Bocephus perennials "A Country Boy Can Survive" and "All My Rowdy Friends (Have Settled Down)." —*Jason Ankeny*

Rowdy / 1981 / Warner Brothers ✦✦✦
In 1981 Hank Williams Jr. was one of the hottest acts in country music, starting the year with this album, which spawned the No. 1

hits "Texas Women" and "Dixie on My Mind" and the striking "Are You Sure Hank Done It This Way." —*William Ruhlmann*

High Notes / 1982 / Warner Brothers ✦✦
Containing his hit cover of his father's "Honky Tonkin'" as well as an intriguing version of the Beatles' "Norwegian Wood," *High Notes* is a typically entertaining early-'80s record from Hank Williams Jr., featuring a handful of excellent redneck country-rockers—"Whiskey on Ice," "Heaven Ain't a Lot Like Dixie," "South's Gonna Rattle Again"—mixed with a little filler and the odd soul-searching cut like "If You Wanna Get to Heaven." —*Thom Owens*

★ **Hank Williams Jr.'s Greatest Hits** / 1982 / Warner Brothers ✦✦✦✦✦
Hank Williams Jr. established himself as a country superstar in the late '70s and early '80s with a fusion of outlaw country and Southern rock. *Hank Williams Jr.'s Greatest Hits* contains his ten biggest hits from that era, including "Family Tradition," "Whiskey Bent and Hell Bound," "Women I've Never Had," "Texas Women," "Dixie on My Mind," "A Country Boy Can Survive," and "All My Rowdy Friends (Have Settled Down)." It's not only some of the best music Williams ever made, but it's some of the definitive work of the era. —*Thom Owens*

Man of Steel / 1983 / Warner Brothers ✦✦✦
Man of Steel features a pair of Top Five hits, "Queen of Hearts" and the title tune. —*Jason Ankeny*

Major Moves / 1984 / Warner Brothers ✦✦✦
Williams topped the country charts with this album, largely on the strength of the raucous "All My Rowdy Friends Are Coming Over Tonight," though the title track and the caustic "Attitude Adjustment" were also hits. —*William Ruhlmann*

Greatest Hits, Vol. 2 / 1985 / Warner Brothers ✦✦✦✦
A well-chosen hits collection covering 1983 to 1985, including "Leave Them Boys Alone" and "All My Rowdy Friends Are Coming Over Tonight." —*William Ruhlmann*

Five-O-Five / 1985 / Warner Brothers ✦✦
The chart-topping "I'm for Love" and the frenetic "I Really Like Girls" are the high points of *Five-O.* —*Jason Ankeny*

Greatest Hits, Vol. 3 / 1989 / Warner Brothers ✦✦✦✦
This chronicles Williams' ongoing '80s success, 1985-1989, featuring the No. 1 hits "I'm for Love," "Ain't Misbehavin'," "Mind Your Own Business," and "Born to Boogie." —*William Ruhlmann*

America (The Way I See It) / 1990 / Warner Brothers ✦✦✦
Williams plays political commentator on this, a collection of his best revenge fantasies, reasons for America's problems, and the theme from Monday Night Football. The album includes the survivalist anthem "A Country Boy Can Survive" and "Don't Give Us a Reason," an open letter to Saddam Hussein. —*Brian Mansfield*

Lone Wolf / 1990 / Warner Brothers ✦✦✦
It features "Man to Man," "Big Mamou," and other hits. —*AMG*

Pure Hank / 1991 / Warner Brothers ✦✦✦
Pure Hank generated two minor hits, "If It Will It Will" and "Angels Are Hard to Find." —*Jason Ankeny*

Maverick / Oct. 1991 / Capricorn ✦✦✦
Williams' first album for the revived Capricorn label rocks harder than usual, even while he's evangelizing for country music. A good chuck of *Maverick* sounds like a cross between a roaring drunk and a Penthouse letter. There's also a great ghost story ("Cut Bank, Montana") and a really dumb novelty song ("Fax Me a Beer"). There's probably not a soul on earth who could pull off "Come On Over to the Country" but Hank—it's corny and obvious about everything country music wishes it was. But every time the slide guitar kicks in, he makes it all come true. —*Brian Mansfield*

The Bocephus Box: Hank Williams Jr. Collection '79-92 / 1992 / Capricorn ✦✦✦✦
A box set covering much the same turf as the Warner Brothers greatest-hits volumes, it does have additional outtakes and live cuts for the completist to enjoy. —*Dan Cooper*

The Best of, Vol. 1: Roots and Branches / Aug. 4, 1992 / Mercury ✦✦✦✦
The title is a bit of a ringer here, as these are the songs Hank Jr. charted with through the mid-'60s to mid-'70s, before his reincar-

nation as Bocephus, the outlaw country-rocker, brought him mega-success. However, this 20-track compilation makes for interesting listening, showing how he evolved to his present style. — *Cub Koda*

Out of Left Field / 1993 / Warner Brothers ♦♦♦

Williams had been making the same rowdy records over and over again for so long that the aptly-titled, ballad-oriented *Out of Left Field* amounts to a small revelation. Not only does Williams turn down the guitars here, he turns down the Southern rebel persona as well; the songs are reflective and fairly sensitive, mournful ballads invested with real emotion. *Out of Left Field* doesn't completely toss out the rockers, but the quiet, melancholy hues make this Williams' best effort in quite some time. — *Jason Ankeny*

Greatest Hits, Vol. 1 / Sep. 21, 1993 / Curb ♦♦♦

Three Generations of Hank / Sep. 17, 1996 / Curb ♦♦

Hank Williams, Jr. has never been above tampering with his father's recorded works—an overdubbed version of "There's a Tear in My Beer" was a Top Ten hit in 1989—but there was no precedent for *Three Generations of Hank*, which features overdubbed, electronic trio recordings of Hank Sr., Hank Jr. and Hank Williams III. There might be a lot of wonderful songs on this record, but it's hard to get beyond the weird, morbid sensation of hearing these pieced-together electronic duets. Even though Hank Jr. is the blood heir to his father's legacy, *Three Generations of Hank* is one of the strangest and most unnecessary tributes to that legacy yet recorded. — *Thom Owens*

Lucinda Williams

b. Jan. 26, 1953, Lake Charles, LA

Guitar, Vocals / Singer-Songwriter, Folk-Rock, Alternative Country-Rock, Contemporary Folk, Americana

Lucinda Williams isn't the kind of artist who caves in easily. Faced with label executives and producers who want to shape her music into clean-cut, radio-friendly rock or country numbers—no doubt with someone like Bonnie Raitt in mind—Williams has time and again proven herself to be as stubborn (and most certainly for her own good) as she is talented. She's released a mere four albums (and one EP) since her debut on Folkways in 1979, partly because she's had such a hard time finding a label whose demands don't get in the way of the music as she hears it.

Raised under the intellectual nurture of her father—poet, critic, and English lit professor Miller Williams (a buddy of Tom T. Hall)—Lucinda spent her youth on the ramble from one college burg to another in the American South, as well as Mexico City and Santiago, Chile. She was already singing and playing by the time she was 12, when Dylan's *Highway 61 Revisited* had seeped into her psyche; she later found inspiration in the raw Delta blues of singers like Skip James, Bukka White, and Robert Johnson. By the early '70s she was playing shows of her own, mixing folk-inspired originals and traditional material. She traveled a bit before landing in Austin in 1974 at the height of the cosmic cowboy era. Next she tried Houston and became part of a folk scene there that included Nanci Griffith, Lyle Lovett, and Townes Van Zandt.

In 1978 she spent an afternoon in the Jackson, MS, R&B studio Malaco, and the result was her 1979 debut for Folkways, *Ramblin' on My Mind*, a collection of traditional blues and country standards. A year later she recorded "Happy Woman Blues" in Houston. This time all the songs were originals, and they featured a full band of acoustic guitar, fiddle, pedal steel, bass, and drums. Both albums have since been reissued on Smithsonian/Folkways.

It was eight years, however, until Williams' third album, *Lucinda Williams*, recorded for the indie-rock label Rough Trade. In the meantime she had lived back and forth between Houston and Austin before moving to Los Angeles in 1984. She's been courted by several labels but always held out for creative control. In the end she won it, and her Rough Trade album immediately stood out for its integration of traditional folk, country, and blues influences into a rock 'n' roll format. The album featured such stellar songs as "The Night's Too Long," "Passionate Kisses," and "Changed the Locks," and marked a new, more rock-oriented

direction for Williams. Her guitarist and co-producer on that album, Gurf Morlix, has also become a vital part of her music, recording and touring with her ever since. In 1989 Rough Trade released the EP *Passionate Kisses*, which included four additional songs, three of which were live radio broadcasts.

An ill-fated association with RCA followed, but again Williams was unhappy with the results, and left the label before releasing anything. Her next album, *Sweet Old World*, didn't emege until 1992, and again it was on an indie label, Chameleon. Well worth the wait, it was rich with Williams' hearty, twangy voice and solid, Southern-inflected rock 'n' roll originals. Once again, too, critics and fans found it irresistible, and practically thanked God that Williams had chosen to keep her artistic integrity intact.

Since then Williams has switched labels again, this time to American Recordings. A new album has been scheduled and resheduled several times; it's expected to finally see the light in late 1996. — *Kurt Wolff*

Ramblin' / Mar. 1978 / Folkways ♦♦

A collection of blues and country standards by Robert Johnson, Memphis Minnie, Hank Williams, and others. Williams is accompanied only by guitarist John Grimaudo. Re-released by Smithsonian/Folkways in 1991 as *Ramblin'*. — *Kurt Wolff*

● **Happy Woman Blues** / 1980 / Folkways ♦♦♦♦

Williams' first collection of original material—recorded with a full band—is stunning for its mixture of blues, folk, and country traditions with her captivating, complex, and visceral approach to writing and singing. Songs like "Lafayette," "King of Hearts," and "Sharp Cutting Wings" are classics, structurally solid and emotionally intense. A gutsy, refreshingly rootsy album. Re-released by Smithsonian/Folkways in 1990. — *Kurt Wolff*

Lucinda Williams / 1988 / Rough Trade ♦♦♦♦

Williams shows her rock 'n' roll colors here, mixing her rootsy Southern twang with big, burly production and arrangements and a full-on electric band that includes guitarist Gurf Morlix, who's collaborated with her ever since. Williams' writing skills continue to strengthen, the result being such indelible gems as "The Night's Too Long," "Side of the Road," and "Changed the Locks." This album revived Williams' career and cemented her reputation. — *Kurt Wolff*

Passionate Kisses / 1989 / Rough Trade ♦♦♦

The title track of this EP comes from Williams' 1988 album. Also included are four live acoustic cuts—"Side of the Road" and three blues covers. — *Kurt Wolff*

● **Sweet Old World** / 1992 / Chameleon ♦♦♦♦

A bright, lively, rock 'n' roll album that picks up where "Lucinda Williams" left off. The arrangements mix fiddle and dobro with the electric guitars, and while the production is big, the songs speak on a personal level and are wholly down-to-earth. The album contains a new slate of Williams' classics, including "He Never Got Enough Love," "Little Angel, Little Brother," and the knockout "Pineola." — *Kurt Wolff*

Robin and Linda Williams

Progressive Bluegrass, Bluegrass, Contemporary Folk

Singers/songwriters Robin and Linda Williams were regulars on Garrison Keillor's "A Prairie Home Companion" radio show. Some of their songs have been recorded by Emmylou Harris, Kathy Mattea, and Michael Martin Murphey. Their harmonies are smooth and well matched, and their musicianship is tight and well crafted. — *Chip Renner*

Harmony / 1981 / June Appal ♦♦♦♦

Very hard to find, but it should be in your collection. — *Chip Renner*

● **Close As We Can Get** / 1984 / Flying Fish ♦♦♦♦

Perfect in all ways. "The Leaving Train" is one of their best songs. As good as *All Broken Hearts*. — *Chip Renner*

Nine 'til Midnight / 1985 / Flying Fish ♦♦♦

A very good live album featuring gospel, traditional country, and contemporary songs. — *Chip Renner*

All Broken Hearts Are the Same / 1988 / Sugar Hill ✦✦✦✦
With top-notch songwriting and smooth vocals, this features Jerry Douglas, Stuart Duncan, and T. Michael Coleman. —*Chip Renner*

Rhythm of Love / 1990 / Sugar Hill ✦✦✦
These 12 songs are all good. Features guests Jerry Douglas and Stuart Duncan. —*Chip Renner*

Turn Toward Tomorrow / 1993 / Sugar Hill ✦✦✦
Produced by John Jennings, this collection of primarily Robin and Linda songs is held together by great economical band arrangements. Weepers like "When the Last Tear Falls" and "Chain of Pain" are given an uptempo treatment so we don't have to get too torn up about life's hardships. "Lying to the Moon" brings the CD to a peaceful close. —*Richard Meyer*

Robin and Linda Williams and Their Fine Group Live / 1994 / Sugar Hill ✦✦✦
Recorded while on tour in Holland, this album finds Robin and Linda Willams in a more basic band setting. It lets the strength of their vocals come through better than on some of their slicker studio records. The highpoint comes with "The Devil Is a Mighty Wind." —*Richard Meyer*

Sugar For Sugar / Apr. 1996 / Sugar Hill ✦✦✦

Close As We Can Get/Nine 'til Midnight / Flying Fish ✦✦✦✦

Tex Williams (Sol Williams)

b. Aug. 23, 1917, Ramsey, Fayette County, IL, **d.** Oct. 11, 1985
Guitar, Vocals / Western Swing

Although not nearly as well known as figures like Bob Wills, the Maddox Brothers, and Merle Travis, Tex Williams was an important Western swing performer. Like all of the aforementioned musicians, he helped develop country music from its rural, acoustic origins to a more danceable, citified, and electrified form with a much wider popular appeal. At his peak in the late 1940s, he also recorded some of the most enjoyable country swing of the time, distinguished by his talking-blues vocal delivery. Much of his style can be heard in the Western swing-influenced recordings of revivalists like Asleep at the Wheel, Commander Cody, and Dan Hicks.

The singer and guitarist caught his first big break after moving to Los Angeles in 1942. At that time California was populated by many former Texans and Oklahomans working in the defense industry, creating a need for Western swing entertainment in a region not noted for country music. One of the musicians on this circuit was fiddler Spade Cooley, who employed Jack Williams as his singer, nicknaming him "Tex" to ensure easy identification by the many Texans in their audiences. Several of Cooley's mid-'40s Columbia singles featured Tex on vocals.

Capitol offered a contact to Williams as a solo artist, which strained the relationship between Tex and the tempestuous Cooley to the breaking point. Cooley fired Williams in June 1946, a move which backfired badly, as most of Cooley's band opted to follow Tex rather than remain with their difficult boss. Cooley achieved his greatest subsequent notoriety when he was convicted of beating his wife to death in a drunken fit in 1961.

Tex's renamed backing band, the Texas Caravan, was one of the best units of its kind. Numbering about a dozen members, it attained an enviable level of fluid interplay between electric and steel guitars, fiddles, bass, accordion, trumpet, and other instruments (even the occasional harp). At first the group recorded polkas for Capitol, with limited success. They found their true calling when Williams' friend Merle Travis wrote most of "Smoke! Smoke! Smoke! (That Cigarette)" for him, emphasizing Tex's talking-blues delivery and heavier boogie elements. The song was a monstrous commercial success in 1947 and one of the biggest country hits of all time, making No. 1 on the pop charts.

That set the model for several of Williams' subsequent hits: hot Western swing backup, over which Tex would roll his deep, laconic, easygoing narratives of humorous, slightly ridiculous situations. As enjoyable as these were, they were just one facet of the Texas Caravan's talents. The outfit was also capable of generating quite a heat on boogie instrumentals and more straightforward

vocal numbers in which Williams actually sang rather than speaking.

Williams' commercial success began to peter out in the early 1950s, and he left Capitol in 1951. He continued to record often in the 1950s, mostly for Decca, without much success; in 1957, the Western Caravan disbanded. He pressed on, however, returning to Capitol in the early 1960s and recording a live album that included Glen Campbell on guitar. He had one final country hit, the memorably titled "The Night Miss Ann's Hotel for Single Girls Burned Down," which entered the Top 30 in 1971. —*Richie Unterberger*

★ **Vintage Collection Series** / Jan. 23, 1996 / Capitol ✦✦✦✦✦
Vintage collects most of Tex Wiliams' best and most popular Western swing hits, including "Smoke Smoke Smoke That Cigarette," making it a perfect introduction to one of the most innovative country artists of the late '40s. —*Stephen Thomas Erlewine*

Rompin' / Bear Family ✦✦✦✦

Victoria Williams

Guitar, Vocals / Singer-Songwriter, Folk-Rock, Alternative Country-Rock, Contemporary Folk
Despite a successful career as an idiosyncratic country-folk performer, Victoria Williams was perhaps best known as a songwriter—thanks, ironically enough, to a tribute album recorded in her honor. Born in Louisiana in 1959, Williams taught herself to play the guitar while still in her teens, and she soon began composing songs. In college she joined her first band, the G.W. Korners. After spending some time on the road, she ended up in California in 1979, where she was a regular at Los Angeles' famed Troubadour Club's "Hoot Nights." After returning to Louisiana with the intent of forming a band, she moved back to L.A., where she performed on Venice Beach and signed a recording contract that proved fruitless.

Soon after, Williams met musician Peter Case, formerly of the Plimsouls. Not only did they form an act together—a jugband-like trio named the Incredibly Strung Out Band—but they married. Williams made her solo recording debut in 1987 with *Happy Come Home*, a collection showcasing her vivid songcraft and her off-kilter, squeaky vocal style. After the record was released, Williams starred in a documentary by the filmmaker D.A. Pennebaker. In 1989 she and Case divorced; a follow-up record, *Swing the Statue!*, appeared in 1990.

In 1992, while opening for Neil Young, Williams began experiencing numbness in her hands which made it increasingly difficult to play her guitar. She was diagnosed with the degenerative neurological disorder multiple sclerosis. The medical bills quickly piled up, and like many musicians, she was not covered by health insurance. In response, her manager began assembling friends and fans to record Williams' songs for a benefit album; the result, 1993's *Sweet Relief: A Benefit for Victoria Williams*, featured Pearl Jam, Lou Reed, Matthew Sweet, the Jayhawks, and Soul Asylum, whose rendition of "Summer of Drugs" was the record's first single. Due to its all-star lineup, *Sweet Relief* far outsold any of Williams' own efforts, raising not only funds for her medical treatment, but her visibility within the musical community. The record's success enabled Williams to establish the Sweet Relief Fund to assist other musicians with health problems; in 1996, a second tribute record, honoring the paralyzed singer-songwriter Vic Chestnutt, was released.

In 1994 Williams issued *Loose*, a varied collection featuring duets with Soul Asylum's Dave Pirner and the Jayhawks' Mark Olson, Williams' second husband. A year later, she and her Loose Band released *This Moment in Toronto*, a live career overview which also offered a handful of standards ("Smoke Gets in Your Eyes," "Imagination") and one new song, "Graveyard." —*Jason Ankeny*

Happy Come Home / 1987 / Geffen ✦✦✦
This debut LP by Victoria Williams is as wonderful as it is eclectic. Van Dyke Parks' arrangements give the collection a carnival feel, while Anton Fier's pop productions never let this become anything close to an ordinary singer-songwriter album. But how could it, with Williams' elastic vocals and trippy lyrics? This is a

great record to play when anyone says that all L.A. pop albums are slick and sanitized. *—Richard Meyer*

● **Swing the Statue** / 1990 / Rough Trade ◆◆◆◆
Victoria Williams' second album was her most accomplished set of folk-rock, featuring the remarkable "Summer of Drugs." *—Stephen Thomas Erlewine*

Loose / 1994 / Mamoth ◆◆◆◆
What a great collection. Victoria Williams has put together a fine-tuned tight but loose band, as expressed in the title. Her folk-rock Carol Channing voice is perfectly suited to the arrangements, some of which were written by Van Dyke Parks. The group includes Greg Cohen, Peter Buck, and Don Heffinton. Her originals are quirky and beautiful. Wllliams' choice of covers is also refreshing. She does a heartbreaking take on "What a Wonderful World" and revives the psychedelic chestnut "Nature's Way," making it her own. *Loose* is a wonderful album, full of life. *—Richard Meyer*

This Moment: Live in Toronto / Nov. 7, 1995 / Atlantic ◆◆◆
Recorded on the *Loose* tour, Victoria Williams' live album *This Moment: Live in Toronto* demonstrates the depths of her songwriting talents. Performing with a sympathetic folk-rock supporting band, Williams runs through her catalog, playing nearly all of her fans' favorite songs. She is in fine voice, turning in an impassioned performance; but the best thing about the record is how all of the songs play off each other. Unlike her other records, there is no filler on *This Moment*, which makes the album a perfect introduction to her rich talents. *—Stephen Thomas Erlewine*

Foy Willing (Foy Willingham)

b. 1915, Bosque County, TX, **d.** Jun. 24, 1978
Vocals / Cowboy
Singer, songwriter, and actor Foy Willing was best known as the founder of the Riders of the Purple Sage, a popular cowboy band known for their close harmonies and appearances in low-budget Westerns from the '40s and '50s. Born Foy Willingham in Bosque County, TX, he began as a soloist and member of a gospel group on local radio. In 1933 he began appearing on a radio show in New York City, but he left in 1935 to work as a radio announcer back in Texas. In 1940 Willing moved to California, and a year later he founded the Riders of the Purple Sage. They were primarily a radio group, but in 1944 they made their feature film debut in *Cowboy from Lonesome River*, a Western featuring Charles Starrett. The next year, the band began appearing regularly on the "All Star Western Theater." They continued appearing in films through the decade and in 1948 became Roy Rogers' new backup band after the Sons of the Pioneers left. Over the years they had a few hits, including "Have I Told You Lately That I Love You," "No One to Cry To," and "Cool Water." The Riders of the Purple Sage disbanded in 1952, and Willing retired from active performing. During the late '50s and early '60s, the group occasionally reunited to record and perform, and Willing went on to appear at Western festivals during the 1970s. *—Sandra Brennan*

Riders of the Purple Sage / 1950 / Varsity ◆◆◆

● **Cowboy** / 1958 / Roulette ◆◆◆◆

The New Sound of American Folk / 1962 / Jubilee ◆◆◆

Kelly Willis

b. 1959, Annandale, VA
Vocals / Contemporary Country, New Traditionalist
Although the work of New Traditionalist singer-songwriter Kelly Willis earned widespread critical acclaim, she found little in the way of comparable commercial success; her sound, a smart hybrid of country and rock, simply assimilated both musical styles too well to gain acceptance in either camp. Born in Oklahoma and raised in the Washington, DC, area, she began performing in her boyfriend (and future husband) Mas Palermo's band at the age of 16. Her powerhouse vocals were so popular with club audiences that soon the group was renamed Kelly and the Fireballs. After Willis graduated from high school, the band moved to Austin, TX, only to break up six months later.

As a result, Willis began learning to play guitar while drummer Palermo honed his songwriting chops. The duo started a new band, Radio Ranch, with guitarist David Murray, steel player Michael Hardwick, and bassist Michael Foreman. One of Radio Ranch's performances so impressed singer Nanci Griffith that she began lobbying her label MCA to sign the group, leading to Willis' 1990 debut *Well-Travelled Love*. In an attempt to capitalize on Willis' stunning looks, she was marketed as a girl-next-door type, and despite the presence of the full band, only her name appeared on the album jacket. Despite the glowing reviews, the LP fared poorly, so for her 1991 sophomore effort *Bang Bang*, she was depicted as a coquettish pin-up. Again, however, the publicity the record received did not translate to radio airplay, let alone chart sales.

For her third album, comprised largely of her own songs, Willis joined forces with pop producer Don Was; the self-titled 1993 effort suffered the same fate as its predecessors, however, and she was dropped by MCA shortly after its release. After a few years of relative inactivity, she resurfaced in 1995, duetting with Son Volt's Jay Farrar on the *Red Hot and Bothered* compilation. After issuing a 1996 independent label EP, *Fading Fast*, she announced plans for a 1997 LP on A&M. In late 1996 she married fellow Austin musician Bruce Robison. *—Jason Ankeny*

Well Travelled Love / 1990 / MCA ◆◆◆
On her debut, this Austin country-rocker sings Texas-steel tunes and roisterous rockers with spirited assurance, but there's a natural tremble in her voice that makes her sound dangerous, yet vulnerable. Willis is one of the few country singers with the disarming beauty to become a true sex symbol, and if she's the feminine response to all the hat acts, that's fine. *—Brian Mansfield*

● **Bang Bang** / 1991 / MCA ◆◆◆◆
Willis' idea of country comes from female rockabillys like Janis Martin and Wanda Jackson and from the blues-influenced Texas crowd she runs with in Austin. *Bang Bang* reflects that influence in the blistering tempos of "Too Much to Ask" and "Standing by the River," the Tex-Mex groove of "The Heart That Love Forgot," and an absolutely incendiary version of Joe Ely's "Settle for Love." *—Brian Mansfield*

Kelly Willis / 1993 / MCA ◆◆◆◆
Where Willis' first two albums occasionally turned into showcases for her musicians, *Kelly Willis* emphasizes concise, twangy pop songs over barn-burners. Willis sings a mandolin-propelled cover of Marshall Crenshaw's "Whatever Way the Wind Blows" and blends her voice with two members of Jellyfish on "One More Night." She also dips into Nashville's back catalog with a version of the Kendalls' 1977 "Heaven's Just a Sin Away." *—Brian Mansfield*

Bob Wills (James Robert Wills)

b. Mar. 6, 1905, Kosse, TX, **d.** May 13, 1975
Fiddle, Vocals / Traditional Country, Western Swing
Bob Wills' name will forever be associated with Western swing. Although he did not invent the genre, he did popularize it and change its rules. In the process, he reinvented the rules of popular music. Bob Wills and his Texas Playboys were a dance band with a country string section that played pop songs as if they were jazz numbers. Their music expanded and erased boundaries between genres. It was also some of the most popular music of its era. Throughout the '40s, the band was one of the most popular groups in the country, and the musicians in the Playboys were among the finest of their era. As the popularity of Western swing declined, so did Wills' popularity, but his influence is immeasurable. From the first honky tonkers to Western swing revivalists, generations of country artists owe him a significant debt, as do certain rock and jazz musicians. Bob Wills was a maverick, and his spirit infused American popular music of the 20th century with a renegade, virtuosic flair.

Bob Wills was born outside of Kosse, TX, in 1905. From his father and grandfather, learned how to play mandolin, guitar, and, eventually, fiddle and he regularly played local dances in his teens. In 1929 he joined a medicine show in Fort Worth, where he played fiddle and did blackface comedy. At one performance he met guitarist Herman Arnspiger, and the duo formed the Wills Fiddle Band. Within a year they were playing dances and radio stations around Fort Worth. During one of the performances, the pair met vocalist Milton Brown, who joined the band. Soon Brown's guitarist brother Durwood joined the group, as did Clifton "Sleepy" Johnson, a tenor banjo player.

In early 1931 the band landed their own radio show, which was sponsored by the Burris Mill and Elevator Company, the manufacturers of Light Crust Flour. The group rechristened themselves the Light Crust Doughboys. Their show was broadcast throughout Texas, hosted and organized by W. Lee O'Daniel, the manager of Burris Mill. By 1932 the band had star status in Texas, but there was some trouble behind the scenes; O'Daniel wasn't allowing the band to play anything but the radio show. This led to the departure of Milton Brown; Wills eventually replaced Brown with Tommy Duncan, with whom he would work for the next 16 years. By late summer 1933, Wills, aggravated by a series of fights with O'Daniel, left the Light Crust Doughboys, and Duncan left with him.

Wills and Duncan relocated to Waco, TX, and formed the Playboys, which featured Wills on fiddle, Duncan on piano and vocals, rhythm guitarist June Whalin, tenor banjoist Johnny Lee Wills, and Kermit Whalin, who played steel guitar and bass. For the next year the Playboys moved through a number of radio stations, as O'Daniel tried to force them off the air. Finally the group settled in Tulsa, where they had a job at KVOO.

In Tulsa Bob Wills and the Texas Playboys began to refine their sound. Wills added an 18-year-old electric steel guitarist called Leon McAuliffe, pianist Al Stricklin, drummer Smokey Dacus, and a horn section to the band's lineup. Soon the Texas Playboys were the most popular band in Oklahoma and Texas. The band made their first record in 1935 for the American Recording Company, which would later become part of Columbia Records. At ARC they were produced by Uncle Art Satherley, who would wind up as Wills' producer for the next 12 years. They cut a number of tracks that were released on a series of 78s. The singles were successful enough that Wills could demand that steel guitarist Leon McAuliffe—who wasn't on the first sessions because ARC had an abundance of steel players under contract—was featured on the Playboys' next record, 1936's "Steel Guitar Rag." The song became a standard for steel guitar. Also released from that session was "Right or Wrong," which featured Tommy Duncan on lead vocals.

Toward the end of the decade, big bands were dominating popular music; Wills wanted a band capable of playing complex, jazz-inspired arrangements. To help him achieve his sound, he hired arranger and guitarist Eldon Shamblin, who wrote charts that fused country with big band music for the Texas Playboys. By 1940 he had replaced some of the weaker musicians in the lineup, winding up with a full 18-piece band. The Texas Playboys were breaking concert attendance records across the country, filling venues from Tulsa to California, and they had their first genuine national hit with "New San Antonio Rose," which climbed to No. 11 in 1940. Throughout 1941 and 1942, Bob Wills and the Texas Playboys continued to record and perform, and they were one of the most popular bands in the country. Their popularity was quickly derailed, however, by World War II. Tommy Duncan enlisted in the Army after Pearl Harbor, and Al Stricklen became a defense plant worker. Late in 1942 Leon McAuliffe and Eldon Shamblin both left the group. Wills enlisted in the Army late in 1942, but he was discharged as being unfit for service in the summer of 1943, primarily because he was out of shape and disagreeable. Duncan was discharged around the same time, and the pair moved to California by the end of 1943. Wills revamped the sound of the Texas Playboys after the war, cutting out the horn section and relying on amplified string instruments.

During the '40s, Art Satherley had moved from ARC to OKeh Records, and Wills followed him to the new label. His first single for OKeh was a new version of "New San Antonio Rose";it became a Top Ten hit early in 1944, crossing over into the Top 15 on the pop charts. Wills stayed with OKeh for about year, having several Top Ten hits, as well as the No. 1s "Smoke on the Water" and "Stars and Stripes on Iwo Jima." After he left OKeh, he signed

with Columbia Records, releasing his first single for the label, "Texas Playboy Rag," toward the end of 1945.

In 1946 the Texas Playboys began recording a series of transcriptions for Oakland's Tiffany Music Corporation. Tiffany's plan was to syndicate the transcriptions throught the Southwest, but their goal was never fufilled. Nevertheless, the Texas Playboys made a number of transcriptions in '46 and '47, and these are the only recordings of the band playing extended jams. Consequently, they are close approximations of the group's live sound. Though the Tiffany Transcriptions would turn out to be important historical items, the recordings that kept Wills and the Playboys in the charts were their singles for Columbia, which were consistently reaching the Top Five between 1945 and 1948; in the summer of 1946, they had their biggest hit, "New Spanish Two Step," which spent 16 weeks at No. 1.

Guitarist Eldon Shamblin returned to the Playboys in 1947, the last year Wills recorded for Columbia Records. Beginning in late '47, Wills was signed to MGM. His first single for the label, "Bubbles in My Beer," was a Top Ten hit early in 1948, as was its follow-up, "Keeper of My Heart." Though the Texas Playboys were one of the most popular bands in the nation, they were beginning to fight internally, mainly because Wills had developed a drinking problem that caused him to behave erratically. Furthermore, Wills came to believe Tommy Duncan was demanding too much attention and asking for too much money. By the end of 1948, he had fired the singer.

Duncan's departure couldn't have come at a worse time. Western swing was beginning to fall out of public favor, and Wills' recordings weren't as consistently successful as they had been before; he had no hits at all in 1949. That year he relocated to Oklahoma, beginning a 15-year stretch of frequent moves, all designed to find a thriving market for the band. In 1950 he had two Top Ten hits—"Ida Red Likes the Boogie" and "Faded Love," which would become a country standard; they would be his last hits for a decade. Throughout the '50s, he struggled with poor health and poor finances, but he continued to perform frequently. However, his audience continued to shrink. Wills moved throughout the Southwest during the decade, without ever finding a new home base. Audiences at dance halls plummeted with the advent of television and rock 'n' roll. The Texas Playboys made some records for Decca that went unnoticed in the mid-'50s. In 1959 Wills signed with Liberty Records, where he was produced by Tommy Allsup, a former Playboy. Before recording his first sessions with Liberty, Wills expanded the lineup of the band again and reunited with Tommy Duncan. The results were successful, with "Heart to Heart Talk" climbing into the Top Ten during the summer of 1960. Again, the Texas Playboys were drawing sizable crowds and selling a respectable number of records.

In 1962 Wills had a heart attack, but by 1963 he was making an album for Kapp records. The next year he had a second heart attack, which forced him to disband the Playboys. After that, he performed and recorded solo. His solo recordings for Kapp were made in Nashville with studio musicians and were generally ignored, though he continued to be successful in concert.

In 1968 the Country Music Hall of Fame inducted Bob Wills, and the next year the Texas State Legislature honored him for his contribution to American music. The day after he appeared in both houses of the Texas state government, Wills suffered a massive stroke, which paralyzed his right side. During his recovery, Merle Haggard—the most popular country singer of the late '60s—recorded an album dedicated to Bob Wills, *A Tribute to the Best Damn Fiddle Player*, which helped return Wills to public consciousness and spark a wide-spread Western swing revival. In 1972 Wills was well enough to accept a citation from ASCAP in Nashville, as well as appear at several Texas Playboy reunions, which were all very popular. In the fall of 1973 Wills and Haggard began planning a Texas Playboy reunion album, featuring Leon McAuliffe, Al Stricklin, Eldon Shamblin, and Smokey Dacus, among others. The first session was held December 3, 1973, with Wills leading the band from his wheelchair. That night, he suffered another massive stroke in his sleep; the stroke left him comatose. The Texas Playboys finished the album without him. Bob Wills never regained consciousnesss, and he died May 15,

1975, in a nursing home. Wills was buried in Tulsa, where his legend began. —*Stephen Thomas Erlewine*

★ **Bob Wills Anthology** / 1973 / Columbia ✦✦✦✦✦
This two-LP set gives listeners a very good overview of the highly influential recordings of Bob Wills and the Texas Playboys. Many of Wills' best-known recordings of his prime years are included among the 24 selections, with highlights including "Spanish Two Step," "Maiden's Prayer," "Steel Guitar Rag," "New San Antonio Rose," and "Twin Guitar Special." Programmed in loosely chronological order, the music is split fairly evenly between the 1935-38 and 1940-41 period, with two later performances wrapping up the two-fer. Wills was the most famous of the Western swing bandleaders, leading a very strong outfit that featured the steel guitar of Leon McAuliffe, guitarist Eldon Shamblin, fiddlers Jesse Ashlock and Louis Tierney, and vocalist Tommy Duncan. Some selections also include horns. Wills' band found the perfect blend between country music and swing-oriented jazz, and this set can serve as an excellent introduction to his enjoyable music. —*Scott Yanow*

For the Last Time / 1974 / United Artists ✦✦✦
Wills and the Texas Playboys reunited for the last swinging session of his life. Sitting in on fiddle and vocals is one of his biggest fans, Merle Haggard. —*Dan Cooper*

Columbia Historic Edition / 1982 / Columbia ✦✦✦
Columbia Historic Edition is a ten-track compilation of material Bob Wills and the Texas Playboys recorded for Columbia Records in the late '30s and '40s, with eight of the tracks dating before 1941. Many of Wills' greatest songs, such as "Right or Wrong" and "Cherokee Maiden," are included, as are a handful of lesser-known songs like "Lyla Lou" and the instrumental "Cowboy Stomp." Though there are several more-comprehensive collections available on the market, *Columbia Historic Edition* is a thoroughly entertaining and concise sampling of Wills' classic period. —*Stephen Thomas Erlewine*

Golden Era / 1987 / Columbia ✦✦✦
A perfect complement to *The Bob Wills Anthology*, this two-LP set from 1987 does not duplicate any of the earlier compilation's performances. Bob Wills' Texas Playboys was the most influential of all Western swing bands, setting the standard for other groups to follow. This very interesting collection has 32 lesser-known but rewarding performances, including 13 previously unissued selections (many of which are alternate takes). Drawn from Wills' prime years, the spirited renditions feature such top musicians as fiddlers Jesse Ashlock and Louis Tierney, the great steel guitarist Leon McAuliffe, and pianist Al Stricklin, in addition to singer Tommy Duncan and Wills himself on fiddle. Highly recommended, at least until Columbia gets around to having a more complete series on CD. —*Scott Yanow*

Fiddle / 1987 / Country Music Foundation ✦✦✦
As the title suggests, *Fiddle* concentrates on Bob Wills' sometimes neglected Western fiddle style. Over the course of 20 tracks recorded between 1935 and 1942, Wills and his colleagues—including Jesse Ashlock, Louis Tierney, Joe Holley, Clifton Johnson, and Art Haines—run through a number of styles, ranging from direct fiddle and guitar duets, to cajun and jazzy big band numbers. For dedicated fans, it's an excellent addition to a library, even if it is a bit specialized for some tastes. —*Stephen Thomas Erlewine*

★ **Anthology 1935-1973** / 1991 / Rhino ✦✦✦✦✦
The only comprehensive retrospective of Bob Wills and the Texas Playboys, the double-disc set *Anthology 1935-1973* contains material from every label the Playboys recorded for and features the hit version of each of Wills' most famous songs, including "Right or Wrong," "Time Changes Everything," "Corrine, Corrina," "New San Antonio Rose," "Take Me Back to Tulsa," "Cherokee Maiden," "Roly-Poly," "Stay A Little Longer," "Big Beaver," "Bubbles in My Beer," "Faded Love," and many others. It's the rare compilation that functions both as a definitive overview and an excellent introduction. —*Stephen Thomas Erlewine*

Country Music Hall of Fame Series / 1992 / MCA ✦✦✦✦
This set contains Western swing recordings made by Wills from 1955-1967, including such hits as "With Tears in My Eyes," "Cornball Rag," "Texas Two Step," and many more. —*AMG*

The Essential Bob Wills and His Texas Playboys / Aug. 25, 1992 / Columbia/Legacy ✦✦✦✦
A basic 20-track primer to some of the Western swing master's best sides. Acknowledged classics like "Steel Guitar Rag," "Take Me Back to Tulsa," and "Stay a Little Longer" are all here, with the players and arrangements that made Wills and his Texas Playboys legends in country music. —*Cub Koda*

Longhorn Recordings / 1993 / Bear Family ✦✦✦✦
These mid-'60s Dallas sessions feature Wills in both large-band and small-combo settings. —*Dan Cooper*

Classic Western Swing / 1994 / Rhino ✦✦✦
American Legends #13 / Apr. 1996 / LaserLight ✦✦✦
This miscellaneous sampler gets one of its three diamonds for its discount price; otherwise, it's a minimally acceptable compilation of Bob Wills' music. Typical for a LaserLight release, this licensed recording from Rod McKuen's Stanyan Records label is a skimpy collection of the artist's work, randomly mixing later stereo tracks with earlier mono performances (sound quality, as you might expect, varies), with no annotations to indicate the sources, dates, or personnel of the recordings. Versions of Wills' hits such as "New San Antonio Rose," "Stay a Little Longer," "Bubbles in My Beer," and "Keeper of My Heart" are included, but not necessarily the hit ones. And timing out at less than 31 minutes, this is hardly a generous set. Still, if you want to get an idea of what Wills' music was like without buying a full-scale (and full-price) compilation, this will serve. —*William Ruhlmann*

☆ **Tiffany Transcriptions, Vols. 1-9** / Rhino ✦✦✦✦✦
In 1946 Bob Wills and the Texas Playboys began recording a series of radio transcriptions for Oakland, CA's Tiffany Music Corporation. Tiffany's plan was to syndicate the transcriptions throught the Southwest, but their goal was never fufilled. Nevertheless, the Texas Playboys made a number of transcriptions in '46 and '47, and these are the only recordings of the band playing extended jams. Consequently, they are close approximations of the group's live sound. The Tiffany Transcriptions weren't released until the '80s, when the Kaleidoscope label issued a multi-volume set of all the sessions. These were later reissued by Rhino in the '90s. Available in nine individual volumes, every disc of the Tiffany Transcriptions illustrates the depth and breadth of the Texas Playboys. They are among the few recordings that capture all of the Playboys' eclectic talents intact. —*Stephen Thomas Erlewine*

Johnnie Lee Wills

b. 1912, Jewett, TX, d. 1984
Banjo, Fiddle / Traditional Country, Western Swing
Fiddler Johnnie Lee Wills led the most popular Western swing band around the Oklahoma area—that is, after older brother Bob moved his Texas Playboys to California in 1940. He was born in Jewett, TX, on September 2, 1912, the second of four musical sons and seven years behind Bob. Johnnie Lee learned about music from his father, and began playing banjo with Bob when the Texas Playboys moved to KVOO-Tulsa in 1934. He formed the Rhythmairs in 1939 but returned to the fold the next year when Bob split the Playboys into two groups. Johnnie Lee took over the second unit (switching from banjo to fiddle), with younger brother Luther Jay on bass. A few months later Bob moved to California and left Johnnie with his own band, christened Johnnie Lee Wills and His Boys. The brothers remained close, and when Bob needed a substitute leader, he called Johnnie.

Johnnie Lee Wills and His Boys signed with Decca in 1941 and recorded ten initial sides. The group played on another session when a recording ban was lifted after World War II, but they moved to Bullet Records in 1949. Wills' Bullet recordings proved to be the most popular of his career. Early in 1950 "Rag Mop" spent five weeks at the No. 2 spot in the country charts and crossed over to the popular Top Ten; a version by the Ames Brothers did even better. Later that year, "Peter Cotton Tail" also hit the country Top Ten. Wills moved to RCA Victor in 1952, but none of his recordings sold very well. Western swing's popularity was declining, though Wills' regional fame remained unchanged and he continued to appear regularly on KVOO until 1958.

Wills recorded several albums for Sims in the early '60s, but his band broke up in 1964. He continued to work occasional shows and dances, and he opened a Western clothing store in Tulsa with his son, John Thomas Wills. By the late '70s, the Western swing revival took notice of Johnnie Lee Wills, and releases of his early-'50s material appeared on Rounder and Bear Family. He also recorded reunion albums for Flying Fish and Delta, with many former Texas Playboys. —*John Bush*

Where There's a Wills, There's a Way / 1962 / Sims ✦✦✦

At the Tulsa Stampede / 1963 / Sims ✦✦✦

Tulsa Swing / 1978 / Rounder ✦✦✦
Tulsa Swing is culled from a variety of live radio transcriptions Johnnie Lee Wills and His Boys recorded between 1950 and 1951, during the group's heyday. Relying more on standards than on Wills' own hits "Rag Mop" and "Peter Cotton Tail," *Tulsa Swing* nevertheless offers a good idea of Wills' standard concert repertoire, as well as the band's loose, freewheeling sound, particularly that of fiddler Curley Lewis and vocalist Leon Huff. —*Stephen Thomas Erlewine*

● **Reunion** / 1978 / Flying Fish ✦✦✦✦
Bob Wills' brother remained in Tulsa in the '30s and led a band that became a training ground for dozens of Western swing sidemen; many of the best are reunited here, in what were to be his last recordings. —*Charles S. Wolfe*

Dance All Night / 1980 / Delta ✦✦✦

Rompin' Stompin' Singin' Swingin' / 1983 / Bear Family ✦✦✦✦

Jesse Winchester

b. May 17, 1944, Shreveport, LA
Guitar, Keyboards, Vocals / Singer-Songwriter, Contemporary Folk
Jesse Winchester was the music world's most prominent Vietnam War draft-evader, though his renown came from a body of wry, closely observed songs. After growing up in Memphis, Winchester received his draft notice in 1967 and moved to Montreal, Canada, rather than serve in the military. In 1969 he met Robbie Robertson of the Band, who helped launch his recording career. In the same way that James Taylor's history of mental instability and drug abuse served as a subtext for his early music, Winchester's exile lent real-life poignancy to songs like "Yankee Lady," which appeared on his debut album, *Jesse Winchester* (1970). He became a Canadian citizen in 1973. Despite critical acclaim, his inability to tour in the US prevented him from taking his place among the major singer-songwriters of the early '70s, but he made a series of impressive albums—*Third Down, 110 to Go* (August 1972), *Learn to Love It* (August 1974), *Let the Rough Side Drag* (June 1976), and *Nothing but a Breeze* (March 1977)—before President Jimmy Carter instituted an amnesty that finally allowed him to play in his homeland. By that time, the singer-songwriter boom had passed, though Winchester continued to record (*A Touch on the Rainy Side* [July 1978], *Talk Memphis* [February 1981], *Humour Me* [1988]) and even scored a Top 40 hit with "Say What" in 1981. His most prominently covered songs include "Yankee Lady" (Brewer and Shipley), "The Brand New Tennessee Waltz" (Joan Baez and Ian Matthews), "Biloxi" (Tom Rush and Jimmy Buffett), "Mississippi, You're on My Mind" (Jerry Jeff Walker and Stoney Edwards [for a Top 40 country hit]), "Defying Gravity" (Jimmy Buffett and Emmylou Harris), "Rhumba Girl" (Nicolette Larson [for a pop chart entry]), "Well-a-Wiggy" (the Weather Girls [for an R&B chart entry]), and "I'm Gonna Miss You, Girl" (Michael Martin Murphey [for a Top Ten country hit]). —*William Ruhlmann*

Jesse Winchester / 1970 / Rhino ✦✦✦✦
Jesse Winchester first gained notice as a protégé of the Band's Robbie Robertson, who produced and played guitar on his debut album and brought along bandmate Levon Helm to play drums and mandolin. The album had much of the rustic Southern charm and rollicking country-rock of the Band. Winchester's other immediate appeal was a certain sense of mystery. A Southern Ameri-

can expatriate living in Canada, he was unable to appear in the US to promote the album, which was released in a fold-out LP jacket that featured the same sepia-toned portrait (which looked like one of those austere Matthew Brady photos from the Civil War era) on each of its four sides. Winchester emphasized the dichotomy between his Southern origins and his Northern exile in songs like "Snow" (which Robertson co-wrote), "The Brand New Tennessee Waltz" ("I've a sadness too sad to be true"), and "Yankee Lady." *Jesse Winchester* was timely; it spoke to a disaffected American generation that sympathized with Winchester's pacifism. But it was also timeless. The songs revealed a powerful writing talent (recognized by the numerous artists who covered them), and Winchester's gentle vocals made a wonderful vehicle for delivering them. (Originally released by Ampex in 1970, *Jesse Winchester* was reissued by Bearsville Records in 1976 and again in 1988 by Rhino/ Bearsville). —*William Ruhlmann*

Third Down, 110 to Go / 1972 / Bearsville ✦✦✦✦
If Jesse Winchester's debut album was an auspicious introduction to a powerful new songwriting talent, his two-and-a-half-years-in-the-making follow-up was in some ways even more impressive. Without the influence of Robbie Robertson, Winchester, who produced most of the album himself (three tracks were handled by Todd Rundgren), gave it a homemade feel, using small collections of acoustic instruments, an appropriate setting for a group of short, intimate songs that expressed a deliberately positive worldview set against an acknowledgement of desperate times. Winchester found hope in religion and domesticity, but the key to his stance was a kind of good-humored accommodation. "If the wheel is fixed," he sang, "I would still take a chance. If we're skating on thin ice, then we might as well dance." The album was littered with such examples of aphoristic folk wisdom, adding up to a portrait of a man cut off from his very deep roots and yet determined to maintain his dignity with grace and even occasionally a goofy sense of humor. —*William Ruhlmann*

Learn to Love It / 1974 / Bearsville ✦✦✦
As the title suggests, making a virtue of necessity had always been a goal of Jesse Winchester's, and by the time of the release of his third album, the American expatriate had gone ahead and assumed Canadian citizenship. This seemed to free him to comment explicitly on his anti-war exile in "Pharaoh's Army" and especially a version of the old campaign song "Tell Me Why You Like Roosevelt" updated with new lyrics: "In the year of 1967, as a somewhat younger man, the call to bloody glory came, and I would not raise my hand." Elsewhere, Winchester continued to write love songs to his lost South ("L'Air de la Louisiane," "Mississippi, You're on My Mind") and, to a lesser extent, to pursue the wistful philosophizing found on *Third Down, 110 to Go* ("Defying Gravity"). The sense that he was repeating himself was inescapable, however, and with one third of the album written by others and two of the originals in French Canadian, it was also obvious that Winchester was straining to come up with material. Interestingly, the two Russell Smith songs included, "Third Rate Romance" (which Smith sang uncredited) and "The End Is Not in Sight," went on to become Top 40 country hits for Smith's group, the Amazing Rhythm Aces, in the next two years. Stoney Edwards took "Mississippi, You're on My Mind" into the country Top 40 in 1975. —*William Ruhlmann*

Let the Rough Side Drag / 1976 / Bearsville ✦✦✦
At his best, Jesse Winchester is an inspired songwriter with a unique worldview. But even at less than his best, he is a craftsman, capable of turning out an album's worth of well-written songs like those here that, now and then, suggest his personal viewpoint. The title track, another of Winchester's reflections on the importance of persevering under difficult circumstances, and "Damned If You Do," which suggests that you might as well follow your heart because you're in trouble either way, are up to his usual standard. But even slight songs like "Everybody Knows But Me" are clever and enjoyable, and overall, *Let the Rough Side Drag*, with its accomplished mixture of country and R&B, was Winchester's most accessible album so far, even if it was his least ambitious. —*William Ruhlmann*

Nothing But a Breeze / 1977 / Bearsville ✦✦✦

Jesse Winchester regularly took two years between record releases, but he brought in his fifth album, *Nothing But a Breeze*, a mere nine months after its predecessor, *Let the Rough Side Drag*. The impetus for such speed seems to have been the potential commercial bonanza to be gained by Winchester's first US appearances (thanks to President Jimmy Carter's amnesty programs) since he moved to Canada to avoid the draft in 1967. Winchester also used a real producer, Brian Ahern (known for his work with Emmylou Harris), for the first time and augmented his usual backup band with session stars such as Ricky Skags and James Burton, plus supporting vocalists like Harris and Anne Murray. The result was an Ahern-style country-pop album, but, perhaps predictably, a rather light effort for Winchester, who performed three covers among the ten tracks and included among the originals such comic trifles as "Twigs and Seeds" and "Rhumba Man." The title track, which became his first singles-chart entry, and "My Songbird," which Harris later covered, were effective songs; but the significance of *Nothing But a Breeze*, which enjoyed a media buzz and became Winchester's highest charting album (which isn't saying much), was in inverse proportion to the attention it received. — *William Ruhlmann*

A Touch on the Rainy Side / 1978 / Bearsville ✦✦✦

With American recording studios open to him for the first time, Jesse Winchester traveled to Nashville and enlisted producer Norbert Putnam, who assembled the elements of the Nashville Sound, with its strings and horns and backup choruses, to make an album that moved him more toward lush country and especially R&B. Winchester's flexible voice, capable of gliding into a sweet falsetto, made the latter more successful than might have been expected. What kept the album from being one of his better collections was not the slick production but the material. A year after a media blitz had failed to make him a star, Winchester was starting to show signs of strain. He led the album off with the title track, an explicit expression of devotion to his wife, whom he mentioned by name. This was followed by a sour on-the-road song, "A Showman's Life," and later there were tributes to driving and drinking. In fact, the most heartfelt song was "Little Glass of Wine," an alcoholic's love song. None of this was up to his songwriting standard. — *William Ruhlmann*

Talk Memphis / 1981 / Bearsville ✦✦✦

Having rushed to make *Nothing But a Breeze* and *A Touch on the Rainy Side* and getting his two least impressive albums for his trouble, Jesse Winchester spent two and a half years woodshedding before returning to the record racks with *Talk Memphis*. For the album, he returned to his hometown and worked with producer Willie Mitchell, best known for his Al Green records. That wasn't as unlikely a match as might be imagined; Winchester had always had a soulful, flexible voice as ready as Green's to take off into the upper registers to express emotion. And Memphis-style R&B had always been an element, along with country, folk, pop, and gospel, in Winchester's sound. On his early albums, his lighthearted style had been in the service of an embattled vision, but gradually that darkness gave way, to the point that he began to seem lightweight. *Talk Memphis* put his effervescence and musicality to good use, resulting in his first Top 40 hit, the catchy "Say What." The rest of the album was just as easy on the ears, with the title track providing a suitably gritty Memphis-soul sendoff. But that wasn't enough to break the album beyond the bottom rungs of the charts, and after seven albums in 11 years, Winchester left the world of major-label record-making. — *William Ruhlmann*

Humour Me / 1988 / Sugar Hill ✦✦✦

After seven years, Jesse Winchester returned to record stores with a well-crafted pop album made up of new originals in his familiar, winning style. He mixed elements of folk, rock, country, R&B, and gospel on the songs, employing a first-rate backup group featuring New Grass stars Sam Bush, Jerry Douglas, Bela Fleck, Edgar Meyer, and Mark O'Connor, plus saxophonist Jim Horn. These pros were able match Winchester's forays into light gospel ("Let's Make a Baby King") and R&B ("Well-a-Wiggy," which had been a hit for the Weather Girls), as well as the straightforward romantic pop songs that made up the bulk of the record. *Humour*

Me lacked the depth of Winchester's best work, but it was easily on a par with his substantial body of craftsmanlike music of the mid-'70s. His voice remained warm and supple, so that his own versions of the songs were effective, and the album also served as a demo for other singers in search of good pop material. — *William Ruhlmann*

● **The Best of Jesse Winchester** / 1989 / Rhino ✦✦✦✦

Jesse Winchester wrote and recorded more than enough great songs for Bearsville to fill a single-disc compilation, which means that some of them were bound to be left off. The trick was to balance the material from the brilliant first two albums with a careful selection from the subsequent five albums, each of which had its virtues. This 14-track album chooses four from *Jesse Winchester*, including the essential "Yankee Lady," "Biloxi," and "The Brand New Tennessee Waltz," and three from its follow-up, *Third Down, 110 to Go*. There are three from *Learn to Love It*, one each from *Nothing But a Breeze* and *A Touch on the Rainy Side*, and two from *Talk Memphis*. Lesser material such as "Tell Me Why You Like Roosevelt" and "Rhumba Man" could have been excised in favor of more from *Third Down*, but the selection is good enough to give a reasonable representation of Winchester's seven Bearsville albums, which contain some of the most impressive songwriting of the 1970s. — *William Ruhlmann*

Mac Wiseman

b. May 23, 1925, Waynesboro, VA

Guitar, Vocals / Traditional Bluegrass

Famed for his clear and mellow tenor voice, Mac Wiseman recorded with many great bluegrass bands, including those of Molly O'Day, Flatt and Scruggs, Bill Monroe, and the Osborne Brothers, and his command of traditional material made him much in demand by bluegrass and folk fans alike.

Wiseman was born in Cremora, VA, and grew up influenced by traditional and religious music and such radio stars as Montana Slim Carter. Wiseman started out working as a radio announcer in Harrisonburg in 1944. At the same time, he worked as a singer with Buddy Starcher. He later formed his own group and continued performing with others, including Molly O'Day and Flatt and Scruggs, through the '40s. In 1949 he recorded a single, "Travelin' Down This Lonesome Road," with Bill Monroe. By the 1950s, Wiseman was again leading his own band.

Possessing one of the best tenor voices in bluegrass, Wiseman differed from Monroe and Flatt and Scruggs in that he usually sang alone, with little or no harmonizing. His band also employed two fiddles to play contemporary songs such as Speedy Drise's "Goin' Like Wildfire," as well as adaptations of standards such as the Carter Family's "Wonder How the Old Folks Are at Home" and Mac and Bob's "'Tis Sweet to Be Remembered." With the Country Boys, a band that featured such pioneering musicians as Eddie Adcock and Scott Stoneman, Wiseman recorded many popular local singles. He had his first national Top Ten hit with his version of "The Ballad of Davy Crockett." The song's success steered Wiseman away from bluegrass and more toward pop and country. In 1957 Wiseman began recording for Dot; he had a few major successes for the label with such songs as "Jimmy Brown the Newsboy" before moving to Capitol in 1962, where he recorded both country and bluegrass tunes. He began working for Wheeling's WWVA "Jamboree" in 1965 and began to play at bluegrass festivals; over the next three decades, he became one of the most popular performers on the circuit.

Wiseman moved to Nashville in 1969 and signed with RCA Victor. His first—and only—hit for the label was the Top 40 novelty tune "If I Had Johnny's Cash and Charley's Pride." While at RCA he also recorded three well-received bluegrass albums with Lester Flatt. From the mid-'70s on, Wiseman concentrated on bluegrass, becoming a fixture at festivals and releasing a series of records on independent records that ran into the '90s. In 1992 Wiseman narrated the documentary "High Lonesome," a chronicle of bluegrass music, and in 1993 he was inducted into the Bluegrass Hall of Fame. — *Sandra Brennan & David Vinopal*

Songs that Made the Jukebox Play / 1974 / CMH ✦✦✦

A nice album. — *Chip Renner*

Country Music Memories / 1976 / CMH ✦✦✦
This has a slightly different sound than other albums; more country than bluegrass. —*Chip Renner*

The Mac Wiseman Story / 1976 / CMH ✦✦✦✦
The best of Mac Wiseman. A good place to start. —*Chip Renner*

Mac Wiseman Sings Gordon Lightfoot / 1979 / CMH ✦✦✦
Well done. Belongs in the collection of any Gordon Lightfoot fan. —*Chip Renner*

● **Essential Bluegrass Album** / 1979 / CMH ✦✦✦✦
The Essential Bluegrass Album features 24 of the finest songs Mac Wiseman and the Osborne Brothers recorded together in the '60s and '70s. Instead of adhering to the rigid traditionalism of Bill Monroe, the Osbornes and Wiseman open the music up, bringing in a drummer and elements of Western swing, Tex-Mex, and traditional country. It's an excellent collection, epitomizing the best of progressive bluegrass in the '60s and '70s. —*Thom Owens*

Classic Bluegrass / 1987 / Rebel ✦✦✦
Classic Bluegrass captures a 1976 recording session where Mac Wiseman re-recorded many of his earlier hits, plus a handful of new material. Instead of being tired retreads, these new versions nearly equal the original versions, since Wiseman's voice has matured and is rich with nuance. *Classic Bluegrass* may not be the definitive Mac Wiseman album, but it comes very close. —*Thom Owens*

Early Dot Recordings, Vol. 2 / 1988 / Rebel ✦✦✦✦
Early Dot Recordings, Vol. 2 picks up where the first volume left off, featuring some of the best early recordings Mac Wiseman made, including the hit "Jimmy Brown the Newsboy." —*Thom Owens*

Greatest Bluegrass Hits / 1989 / CMH ✦✦✦✦
A good collection. —*Chip Renner*

Grassroots to Bluegrass / 1990 / CMH ✦✦✦
Grassroots to Bluegrass is a 22-track album that features some outstanding vocals from Wiseman. A Grammy nominee.—*Mark Donkers*

Early Dot Recordings, Vol. 3 / 1992 / County ✦✦✦✦
Early Dot Recordings, Vol. 3 (the first two volumes were released only on vinyl) is a compilation of highlights that Mac Wiseman recorded for Dot Records in the early '50s, and it contains some of his finest performances. —*Thom Owens*

Rare Singles and Radio Transcriptions / 1992 / Cowgirlboy [Germany] ✦✦✦✦

Twenty Greatest / ✦✦✦
This features "Wabash Cannonball," "Poison Love," "Love Letters in the Sand," and other hits. —*AMG*

Jeff Wood

b. May 10, 1968, Oklahoma City, OK
Contemporary Country, Americana
A graduate of Oklahoma State University who also attended two years of law school, Jeff Wood knew megastar Garth Brooks from college and used to watch him perform at a Holiday Inn there. When Wood was thinking of moving to Nashville to pursue a music career, Brooks was the first one to show him around town. Getting his first publishing deal in 1994 with EMI Publishing, Wood wrote "Cowboy Love," which was cut by John Michael Montgomery. After a short-lived and fruitless deal with Liberty Records, Wood signed with Imprint Records and recorded his debut album in 1996. —*Jack Leaver*

● **Between the Earth and the Stars** / 1997 / Imprint ✦✦✦
Most of Jeff Wood's debut is of the '70s sensitive singer-songwriter fare, although a couple of cuts stand out and help to establish him as a viable country artist. The opening track, "You Call That a Mountain," is the strongest track in this collection and could almost sell the album on its own merit. Wood's style and delivery are worthwhile, and he co-writes five of the ten songs here. Also noteworthy is the Don Schlitz/Vince Gill contribution "You Just Get One," and Wood's uptempo "Long Way from OK." A mostly mellow set, heavy with pop-ish power ballads that should appeal

to fans of the Dave Loggins-meets-John Berry school of country-pop. —*Jack Leaver*

Wooden Leg

Alternative Country-Rock, Americana
After the breakup of the electric bluegrass band the Blood Oranges, the group's mandolinist Jim Ryan and guitarist Mark Spencer reunited to form the more rock-oriented Wooden Leg, which issued its self-titled debut LP in 1996. —*Jason Ankeny*

● **Wooden Leg** / Apr. 1996 / East Side Digital ✦✦✦✦
Blood Oranges founder Jimmy Ryan has come back around to rurally inspired rock 'n' roll with Wooden Leg, whose self-titled debut also features former Oranges guitarist Mark Spencer (now a regular in Freedy Johnston's band) and drummer Keith Levreault. Ryan's mandolin is placed up front in the mix, but this is not a bluegrass album. The guitars and rhythms keep the songs balanced. —*Kurt Wolff*

Bob Woodruff

b. Mar. 14, 1961
Country-Rock
Bob Woodruff played in rock 'n' roll bands as a kid growing up in New York City and New York State, but when he started writing songs, country music was where he found his vehicle for expression. While attending college in New York, Woodruff started writing country-oriented songs and formed a band called the Fields, which developed a loyal following regionally and was offered a recording contract with Restless Records. The Fields recorded a low-budget record, but Restless went bankrupt before the album could be released, and at that point Woodruff decided to pursue music as a solo act. He started playing gigs by himself, and as his songwriting became more country, his lawyer was sending tapes to Nashville. In the meantime, Restless solved its bankruptcy problems and offered Woodruff another deal, but he ended up signing with Asylum Records' Nashville division in late 1992. His debut album, *Dreams and Saturday Nights*, was released in 1994 to critical acclaim, but his melding of R&B, country, and rock didn't go over at country radio. Woodruff ended up parting ways with the label after one album. Woodruff found a new home for his music at Imprint Records and released his second album, *Desire Road*, in 1997. —*Jack Leaver*

● **Dreams and Saturday Nights** / 1994 / Asylum ✦✦✦✦
A wonderful but mostly overlooked debut from this talented native-New York singer and songwriter. The album's leadoff track, "Bayou Girl," garnered some airplay, but unfortunately it did very little to gain Woodruff any substantial audience in country music. Woodruff's songs deal with typical country music subject matter: failed romance, broken dreams, etc. But what make these stories and characters so believable are the yearning and the hint of vulnerability in his lyrics and vocal delivery. Whether it's a musician's dreams worn down by rejection ("Hard Liqour, Cold Women, Warm Beer") or the trapped feeling of becoming a father too soon ("Poisoned at the Well"), Woodruff's words paint unforgettable pictures of everyday longing and frustration. To convey a feeling, he's even willing to leave clever wordplay and convention at the door and simply wear his heart on his sleeve. Musically, *Dreams and Saturday Nights* is roots country with sharp rock 'n' roll sensibility; the lack of contemporary Nashville production slickness is refreshing. The legendary James Burton plays lead guitar on almost every cut, and an album highlight is a duet with Emmylou Harris on the lonesome ballad "I'm the Train." —*Jack Leaver*

Desire Road / 1997 / Imprint ✦✦✦✦
With a change of record labels, Woodruff returns with a strong follow-up to his 1994 debut *Dreams and Saturday Nights*. Taking a decidedly more roots-rock and pop approach in the production, these songs are still more country than most of the modern stuff, and *Desire Road* isn't likely to alienate anyone who was grabbed by Woodruff's excellent debut. Hook-laden melodies abound, driven along with jangly 12-string guitars that still have a lot of meat to them and merge a Beatles/Byrds melodic sense with a Creedence-like earthiness. In fact, the album kicks off with Fogerty's "Almost Saturday Night," in a country-rockified version

that doesn't have too far to stretch. Woodruff continues with potent original songs, such as "That Was Then," a song about an aging musician who just has to keep playing, which sounds like a continuation of the character he introduced with "Hard Liquor, Cold Women, Warm Beer," the unforgettable song from his first album. "All That Love Has Worn Away" takes a delicious guitar figure, a la British Invasion, and sets it off against a Spanish-sung chorus with an intoxicating melody that makes the song as wonderfully unusual as it is compelling. Throw in a couple of Arthur Alexander R&B gems (including "Everyday I Have to Cry" and "If It's Really Got to Be This Way") handled with loving care, and you have a record you'll want to visit again and again. —*Jack Leaver*

Sheb Wooley (Ben Colder)

b. Apr. 10, 1921, Erick, OK
Vocals / Novelty, Traditional Country, Cowboy, Country Humor
Sheb Wooley was the real article as far as his work with cowboy songs was concerned. A rodeo rider from the time that he was a boy, he was making a living on the circuit as a teenager before he turned to music; as an actor, he appeared in such Westerns as *High Noon* before he was well known as a singer. He later spent six seasons playing cowhand Pete Nolan on the television series "Rawhide" even as he pursued a career in country music. In addition to cowboy songs, his repertoire includes traditional country music and hillbilly tunes, but he also managed to score a No. 1 hit on the pop charts with 1950's comedy song "Purple People Eater." Later he developed a drunken comic performing persona named Ben Colder, whose success in satirizing various elements of country music, its audience, and its sensibilities threatened to eclipse Wooley's own identity.

Wooley was born in Erick, OK, on April 10, 1921. An avid rider from an early age, he was competing in local rodeos before he was ten years old, and by the time he was a teenager, he was one of the best young riders on the circuit. Music was also one of his interests, and Wooley got his first guitar when his father swapped a shotgun for the instrument. He led his own country band in high school, but after graduation he made his living for a time working the oil fields of Oklahoma as a welder. When World War II broke out, he found himself ineligible for military service because of injuries he'd suffered as a rodeo rider, and he spent much of the war working in defense plants.

In 1945 he made his first records and began appearing as a singer/guitarist on WLAC and WSM in Nashville. A year later he moved to Fort Worth, TX, and got a regular spot on radio there. In 1949 he decided to take the plunge and head for California. He was signed to the newly founded MGM Records label, and he took acting lessons in hopes of getting work on the screen. Wooley eventually appeared in small parts in 40 feature films, beginning with *Rocky Mountain*, Errol Flynn's final Western, in 1949. His most notable screen role came two years later in the classic *High Noon* (1952), in which he played Ben Miller, the leader of the outlaw gang gunning for town marshal Gary Cooper. He also played an important supporting role in the historical drama *Little Big Horn* (1951), and was seen in *The Man Without a Star* (1955), *Giant* (1956), and *Rio Bravo* (1959).

Amid all of his film work, Wooley continued recording and writing songs. It wasn't until 1958, however, that he had a hit of any consequence. Wooley had always displayed a gift for parody, and the song that reached the top of the pop charts was "Purple People Eater," a parody of various pop culture crazes including monster movies (some people at the time said that the teenagers vs. monster-on-the-loose classic *The Blob*, released at around the same time as Wooley's song, was virtually a film of the song). Wooley had to fight to get the song released, but it proved to be one of the biggest hit singles in the history of MGM. It wasn't until 1962 that he had another hit, this time a country chart-topper called "That's My Dad."

In 1958 Wooley was cast in the role of Pete Nolan in the television western "Rawhide," starring Eric Fleming and Clint Eastwood; he later wrote some scripts for the series as well. In 1959, in order to fulfill public demand for a recording of the series' title song, he recorded his own version of the "Rawhide" theme song and an entire album of Western songs, which failed to chart. He

later recorded an album of folk-style material that was released in the wake of the widescreen epic *How the West Was Won*, but this also failed to catch on with the public.

His film work continued during this time, and because of movie and television commitments he was unable to record the song "Don't Go Near the Indians." Instead, former movie cowboy/singer Rex Allen recorded it and had a hit. In response to his bad luck, Wooley cut a joke parody followup to the song, entitled "Don't Go Near the Eskimos," and created a new, inebriated comic persona to present it. "Ben Colder" was born with "Don't Go Near the Eskimos," and for the rest of his career Wooley—in a manner anticipating the lot of David Johansen/Buster Poindexter—split his time between appearances as "straight" country/cowboy singer Sheb Wooley and drunken comic Ben Colder. In 1969, when the country music showcase "Hee Haw" went on the air, Wooley became the show's resident songwriter, providing the series' comic musical numbers. "Ben Colder" went on to have several more hits, including "Almost Persuaded No. 2," and in 1968 the Colder persona was voted Comedian of the Year. Wooley continued recording under both guises into the 1980's, although his last chart single in either persona dated back to 1971. —*Bruce Eder*

Tales of How the West Was Won / 1963 / MGM ✦✦✦

● **The Very Best of Sheb Wooley** / 1965 / MGM ✦✦✦✦

Rawhide/How the West Was Won / Feb. 1996 / Bear Family ✦✦✦✦
This isn't an ideal compilation in the sense that none of the material on it was ever a hit, so the general public might not care for it. People looking for anything like "Purple People Eater" or the Ben Colder material will be disappointed. But Bear Family has gathered Wooley's two early-'60s country-western albums, and they're very fine, even including a few originals that are quite good. He does a good job with the *Rawhide* title song and with deeply evocative pieces like "Enchantment of the Prairie" and "The Story of Billy Burdell," backed by Earl Palmer on drums. *How the West Was Won* includes numbers such as "High Lonesome," "Plowin' in the New Ground," and the sentimental "Papa's Old Fiddle," all of which come off well, in the manner of Gene Autry/Johnny Western/Sons of the Pioneers-style Western songs. The backing musicians include Charlie McCoy on harmonica and Earl Palmer on drums. —*Bruce Eder*

Blue Guitar / Bear Family ✦✦✦✦

Curtis Wright

b. Jun. 6, 1955, Huntington, PA
Vocals / Contemporary Country
Pennsylvania native Curtis Wright was a member of the Super Grit Cowboy Band and sang backup for Vern Gosdin, but he probably made more money as the writer of hits like Shenandoah's "Next to You, Next to Me" and "Rock My Baby." He and frequent co-writer Robert Ellis Orrall formed Orrall and Wright in 1994. —*Brian Mansfield*

Curtis Wright / Jul. 6, 1992 / Liberty ✦✦✦✦
Wright's singles, the utterly charming "Hometown Radio" and "If I Could Stop Lovin' You," hardly dented the charts, but his only solo album did get heard; Clay Walker turned "What's It to You" into a No. 1 hit in 1993, and Daron Norwood recorded "Phonographic Memory" and "If I Ever Love Again." —*Brian Mansfield*

Johnny Wright

b. May 13, 1914, Mt. Juliet, TN
Vocals / Traditional Bluegrass, Traditional Country
Singer-songwriter Johnnie Wright spent much of his career working with Jack Anglin in the popular duo Jonnnie and Jack, and was also the husband of Kitty Wells. He was born in Mt. Juliet, TN, and first performed with Anglin in 1936. They teamed up full-time in the 1940s and, except for the time Anglin spent overseas during the war, remained together for more than two decades. In 1952 the duo and Wells were invited to join the Grand Ole Opry, where they remained for 15 years. After Anglin's death in 1963, Wright continued performing and making records. In 1964 he and his Tennessee Mountain Boys had a Top 25 hit with "Walkin', Talkin', Cryin',

Barely Beatin' Broken Heart." The next year he had success with "Hello Vietnam," a No. 1 hit. In 1968 he and Wells recorded an autobiographical duet, "We'll Stick Together," and continued playing live shows together through the early '80s, when they left music to run a souvenir shop. In 1992 the couple and their son Bobby began playing together again. —*Sandra Brennan*

Hello Viet Nam / 1965 / Decca ✦✦✦

Country Music Special / 1966 / Decca ✦✦✦

Country, the Wright Way / 1967 / Decca ✦✦✦

● **Johnny Wright Sings Country Favorites** / 1968 / Decca ✦✦✦✦

Michelle Wright

b. Jul. 1, 1961, Morpeth, Ontario, Canada
Vocals / Country-Pop, Contemporary Country
Canadian singer Michelle Wright was known for her rich, powerful voice and her R&B-tinged country songs. She was born in Morpeth, Ontario, where her father performed in a country band and her mother sang with the Reflections for more than a decade. Heavily influenced by Motown, Wright began singing as a child and joined her first band while she was attending college. She spent the next three years performing in a variety of bands and then founded her own group, which toured North America for five more years. In 1988 she released her debut album *Do Right by Me* in Canada and the next year won a contract with Arista Records in Nashville. In 1990 she released the single "A New Kind of Love," which cracked the Top 40, and in 1992 she had her first Top Ten success in the US with "Take It like a Man," which also provided her with her first No. 1 on the Canadian charts. Later that year she issued her third album, *Now and Then,* followed in 1996 by *For Me It's You.* —*Sandra Brennan*

Do Right by Me / 1988 / Savannah ✦✦✦

● **Michelle Wright** / 1990 / Arista ✦✦✦✦
With her husky, cigarette-deep voice, Wright sounds like nothing so much as a young Lacy J. Dalton on her American debut. There's some straight country here ("The Dust Ain't Settled Yet"), but more often than not, Wright's singing R&B material with steel guitars. Not only does she sing the stuff, but she knows how; drop her voice two octaves on "Not Enough Love to Go 'Round," and she's Barry White. —*Brian Mansfield*

Now and Then / 1992 / Arista ✦✦✦
Wright made a mainstream move with *Now and Then,* downplaying the R&B and remaking herself as a sleek, sultry version of Lorrie Morgan. It paid off, too; she had her first real hits in the US with "Take It like a Man" and "He Would Be 16," a tear-jerking ballad dealing with the regrets of giving up an illegitimate child for adoption. Her Nudie jackets and black bodysuits made her a video favorite, too. The music's not as distinctive here as on *Michelle Wright,* but the hits hold up nicely. —*Brian Mansfield*

For Me It's You / Aug. 27, 1996 / Arista ✦✦✦✦
For Me It's You continues Michelle Wright's streak of winning albums. Featuring songs from writers as gifted as Rodney Crowell and Pam Tillis, the album has a rich selection of material that is alternately gritty and soulful and always powerful. Wright blesses each song with her powerful pipes, singing the songs with conviction. Even when the songs border on lightweight country-pop, she sings them as if they were pure country. The result is a terrific little album, one that makes you wonder why Wright isn't a star in America as she is in her native Canada. —*Thom Owens*

New Kind of Love / Arista ✦✦✦

Wylie & the Wild West Show

Country-Rock, Western Swing, Alternative Country
After moving to Los Angeles from his native Montana, Wylie Gustafson formed the Wild West Show in 1989. Influenced by his father, a Montana rancher who also played guitar and sang cowboy songs, and an older brother, with whom he was once in a band, Wylie is an accomplished yodeler, who blends West Coast honky tonk with Western music. Landing in Nashville in 1992, Wylie and the Wild West Show have since released several videos that receive regular airplay on both CMT and TNN, and although

the tall, bespectacled redhead has yet to break ground on radio, he makes regular appearances at the Grand Ole Opry. The high-energy performer and his band also tour extensively, having played throughout the US, Australia, Canada, and Europe. Wylie and the Wild West Show have released three albums, and in 1996 they were signed to Rounder Records. —*Jack Leaver*

● **Wylie and the Wild West Show** / 1992 / Cross Three ✦✦✦✦
The jumpin' debut from the tall bespectacled redhead from Montana and his band. About as good as modern roots-rockin' country and Western swing can get, this is wild fun, with Wylie and his band supplying plenty of dance-inspiring tracks. Wylie has an encyclopedic ear for the aforementioned styles and is blessed with a golden voice that falls somewhere between his obvious hero, Marty Robbins, and maybe a young Merle Haggard. Lead guitarist Will Ray's string-bending is superb, as is Marty Rifkin's steel playing. Check out Wylie's masterful yodeling on "The Yodeling Fool" and "All Hat, No Cattle," a humorous indictment of "hat" singers. This is true-to-form stuff, with memorable songs that sound traditional without coming off as cheap retro knock-offs. And Wylie and company mix up the grooves enough to keep things interesting, as in the swampy "Talkin' About My Baby," and the blues-tinged "Wishful Thinking." —*Jack Leaver*

Get Wild / 1994 / Cross Three ✦✦✦
Evoking the spirit of the singing cowboy and mixing Bob Wills-style Western swing with traditional country and old fashion ed rock 'n' roll sensibility, Wylie's brand of music is as wide open as the northern plains of Montana, the state from which he hails. Fans of the late Marty Robbins will delight in the heartfelt homage Wylie pays his musical hero by including two of Robbins' classics: "Devil Woman" and "I'm Gonna Be a Cowboy." Wylie's original tunes are also shadowed by Robbins' influence. Check out the Spanish-flavored "Hey Maria." A guest spot by Merle Haggard on the humorous ode to rejection "Ugly Girl Blues" is lots of fun, and "Too Late," co-written by the Mavericks' Raul Malo, is truly great rockabilly. —*Jack Leaver*

Way Out West / 1996 / Two Medicine Music ✦✦✦✦
The third album from Wylie and the Wild West Show can do nothing but gain the lanky redhead more of an audience. *Way Out West* contains a little bit of everything that made his first two records so enjoyable: honky tonk shuffles, traditional swing country, great ballads, a yodel tune, and plain ol' rockin' roots country. Wylie and his band's ripping through the Del Reeves truckin' classic "Girl on the Billboard" is an album highlight. Wylie demonstrates his powerful falsetto, reinventing the much-covered pop standard "I Remember You" while also impressively yodeling his way through the Tex-Mex frolic of "Give Me a Pinto Pal." As with his other records, the musicianship is superb, making this album a must for anyone who appreciates traditional country styles injected with youthful verve. —*Jack Leaver*

Tammy Wynette (Virginia Wynette Pugh)

b. May 5, 1942, Itawamba County, MS
Guitar, Vocals / Traditional Country, Country-Pop, Honky Tonk, Nashville Sound/Countrypolitan
In many ways, Tammy Wynette deserves the title of the First Lady of Country Music. During the late '60s and early '70s, she dominated the country charts, scoring 17 No. 1 hits. Along with Loretta Lynn, she defined the role of female country vocalists in the '70s.

After her father, who was a musician, died when she was just eight months old, Wynette was raised at her grandparents' home in Mississippi; her mother moved to Birmingham, AL, to do military work. As a child, Tammy taught herself to play a variety of instruments left behind by her father. When she was a teenager, she moved to Birmingham to be with her mother. At 17, she married her first husband, Euple Byrd, and set to work as a hairdresser and beautician. The marriage was short-lived, but it produced three children within three years. By the time her third child was born, the couple were divorced. The third child had spinal meningitis, which meant there were expensive medical bills. In order to earn some extra money, Wynette began performing in clubs at night. In 1965 she landed a regular spot on the television program the "Country Boy Eddie Show," which led to appearances on Porter Wagoner's syndicated show. The next year she moved to Nashville, where she auditioned for several labels before producer Billy Sherrill signed her to Epic Records.

"Apartment No.9," Wynette's first single, was released late in 1966 and almost broke the country Top 40 early in 1967. It was followed by "Your Good Girl's Gonna Go Bad," which became a big hit, peaking at No. 3. The stone launched a string of Top Ten hits that ran until the end of the '70s, interrupted by three singles that didn't crack the Top Ten. After "Your Good Girl's Gonna Go Bad" was a success, "My Elusive Dreams" became her first No. 1 in the summer of 1967, followed by "I Don't Wanna Play House" later that year.

During 1968 and 1969, Wynette had five No. 1 hits: "Take Me to Your World," "D-I-V-O-R-C-E," "Stand by Your Man" (all 1968), "Singing My Song," and "The Ways to Love a Man" (both 1969). In 1968 she started a relationship with George Jones that would prove to be extremely stormy. Beginning in 1971, Wynette and Jones recorded a series of duets—the first was the Top Ten "Take Me"—that were as popular as their solo hits. However, the marriage was difficult, and the couple divorced in 1975; they continued to record sporadically over the next two decades.

Throughout the '70s, Tammy Wynette racked up No. 1 hits. In the early '80s, her career began to slow down. Although she still had hit singles, she didn't reach the Top Ten as easily as she had in the previous decade. That trend continued into the '90s. Even though she didn't have as many hits as in the past, Wynette remained a respected star and a popular concert attraction. —*Stephen Thomas Erlewine*

Your Good Girl's Gonna Go Bad / 1967 / Epic ♦♦♦♦
Her unmatched first album proves why she's the greatest female C&W "heart" singer. —*George Bedard*

Take Me to Your World / 1967 / Epic ♦♦♦♦

D-I-V-O-R-C-E / 1967 / Epic ♦♦♦♦

Stand by Your Man / 1968 / Epic ♦♦♦♦

☆ **Greatest Hits** / 1969 / Epic ♦♦♦♦♦
This follows Wynette's trail of tears right out of the chutes on classics like "Stand by Your Man" and "D-I-V-O-R-C-E." Producer Billy Sherrill's less-than-light touch never found a better instrument to work with than her voice. —*Dan Cooper*

Tammy's Touch / 1970 / Epic ♦♦♦

The World of Tammy Wynette / 1970 / Epic ♦♦♦

The First Lady / 1970 / Epic ♦♦♦

We Sure Can Love Each Other / 1971 / Epic ♦♦♦

Tammy's Greatest Hits, Vol. 2 / 1971 / Epic ♦♦♦♦

Bedtime Story / 1972 / Epic ♦♦♦

My Man / 1972 / Epic ♦♦

Kids Say the Darndest Things / 1973 / Epic ♦♦♦
Wynette and Sherrill join forces for a concept album, including "Listen, Spot," "My Daddy Doll," "Buy Me a Daddy," and "Too Many Daddies." Sound funny? It is. Except "Too Many Daddies" will still rip your heart out. —*Dan Cooper*

Greatest Hits, Vol. 3 / 1975 / Epic ♦♦♦
The best reason to include this package is that one greatest-hits album from Wynette just isn't enough. The lyrical and musical

Tammy Wynette

themes here are much the same as in the first package, but the quiet determination of "Til I Get It Right" and the pure celebration of "My Man (Understands)" help broaden the picture of Wynette just a little. —*Tom Roland*

★ **Anniversary: 20 Years of Hits** / 1987 / Epic ♦♦♦♦♦
"Stand by Your Man" and "D-I-V-O-R-C-E" speak for themselves. But not to be overlooked are "Apartment No. 9," written by Johnny Paycheck, and "Your Good Girl's Gonna Go Bad," in which her freedom (instead of little J-O-E's tears) are at stake. Also included are three duets with George Jones. —*Dan Cooper*

Tears of Fire: the 25th Anniversary Collection / Nov. 3, 1992 / Epic ♦♦♦♦
Tears of Fire: 25th Anniversary, a three-disc box set covering Wynette's entire career, contains most of her hits as well as rarities and oddities like her lead vocal on KLF's "Justified and Ancient." It's hard to fault a collection that includes such classics as "Stand by Your Man" and "D-I-V-O-R-C-E," but casual fans might want to stick with the single disc *Anniversary: 20 Years of Hits* collection. —*Thom Owens*

Super Hits / Mar. 19, 1996 / Epic ♦♦♦♦
A no-frills, ten-song disc running under 29 minutes, *Super Hits* should be purchased only at a discount price by a newcomer to Tammy Wynette who wants to get an idea of her music. The set contains her three biggest hits, "I Don't Wanna Play House," "D-I-V-O-R-C-E," and "Stand by Your Man"; five other No. 1 hits; and two more that made the country Top Ten between 1967 and 1976. Strictly speaking, these are not Wynette's ten biggest hits, but they constitute a good sampling of her most popular work. —*William Ruhlmann*

Y

Trisha Yearwood

b. Jun. 27, 1959, Monticello, GA
Vocals / Contemporary Country

The daughter of a prominent Georgia banker, Trisha Yearwood exploded onto the country scene in the early '90s with her chart-topping smash single "She's in Love with the Boy," which kick-started a string of hits and albums that established her as one of the most popular country performers of the '90s. Though born in Monticello, GA, Yearwood spent most of her childhood growing up on a 30-acre farm. As a teen, she idolized Elvis Presley, and in school she occasionally participated in talent shows and jammed with local club bands. She enrolled in college in 1985 to study the music business, and before graduating she did a two-year internship at MTM Records. She enjoyed the work and moved to Nashville in 1987, where she began hanging out with such developing artists as Garth Brooks. For a while Yearwood worked as a demo singer and then began singing backup for Brooks, who promised her that if he became successful, he would help her career. She also worked with Pat Alger, and while singing with him at a local bar she was discovered by producer Garth Fundis, who got her the showcase that led to her signing with MCA Records. Her debut single came out in 1990 and was followed by "That's What I Like About You," which appeared on her self-titled first album. She was later tapped to become Brooks' opening act, and her next two albums, *Hearts in Armor* (1992) and *The Song Remembers When* (1993), provided her with an impressive string of hits. In 1994 she again hit No. 1 with "XXXs and OOOs (An American Girl)" from the album *The Sweetest Gift*. In 1995 she released her fourth album, *Thinkin' About You,* followed a year later by *Everybody Knows.* —*Sandra Brennan*

Trisha Yearwood / 1991 / MCA ✦✦✦✦
This impressive debut brought everybody to lend a hand: Vince Gill, Mac McAnally, keyboardist Al Kooper, and more. Garth Brooks co-wrote two songs and helped sing one, the tentatively tender "Like We Never Had a Broken Heart." Yearwood's more at home with blue-collar romance than sweltering Texas nightlife, but her big Georgia range lets her sing just about anything, from the ballad "When Goodbye Was a Word" to Pat McLaughlin's saucy "That's What I Like About You." —*Brian Mansfield*

★ **Hearts in Armor** / Sep. 1, 1992 / MCA ✦✦✦✦✦
Take away the bluesy hit "Wrong Side of Memphis" and this is practically an emotional diary of Yearwood's divorce (which happened just as she hit the big time). In light of that event, "Nearest Distant Shore" and "Hearts in Armor" assume devastating significance, and the cover of Emmylou Harris' "Woman Walk the Line" couldn't be more appropriate. As before, she's got the big-name backup singers—Harris, Don Henley, Vince Gill, and Garth Brooks—but not one steals the spotlight. *Hearts in Armor* is strictly Yearwood's show, and she's marvelous in it. —*Brian Mansfield*

The Song Remembers When / 1993 / MCA ✦✦✦✦
Yearwood shares common ground with peers Nanci Griffith and Mary-Chapin Carpenter by walking the line between country, folk, and pop, appealing to those who elevate the song above cat-egory limitations. Yearwood doesn't write her own material, but she and producer Garth Fundis have impeccable taste, securing contributions from the likes of Rodney Crowell, Willie Nelson (both also guest on backing vocals), and Matraca Berg. Pure, sweet, sparsely rendered ballads like "One in a Row" and "Lying to the Moon" are Yearwood's forte. —*Roch Parisien*

Thinkin' About You / 1995 / MCA ✦✦✦
Though there are a couple of high points on *Thinkin' About You,* the record is weighed down with mediocre material and slick, commerically-oriented production. Occasionally Yearwood's vocals save the day, but there are times where she over-sings the songs, giving them emotion they don't deserve. In all, it's one of the few Trisha Yearwood albums that can be called a disappointment. —*Thom Owens*

Everybody Knows / Aug. 27, 1996 / MCA ✦✦✦
Trisha Yearwood firmly enters middle age with *Everybody Knows,* a collection of ballads and country-pop. Even when she kicks the tempo into high gear, Yearwood and her band lay back, easing the beat along instead of pushing it. Similarly, the country-pop is engaging and relaxed, gently winning you over. But the heart of the album lies in her ballads, which are appropriately theatrical and grandiose; it's big music with big melodies. The quality of the songs is a little uneven, but Yearwood continues to improve as a singer, which means she brings conviction even to the lackluster material on *Everybody Knows.* —*Thom Owens*

Dwight Yoakam

b. 1956, Pikeville, KY
Guitar, Vocals / Country-Rock, Bakersfield Sound, New Traditionalist, Alternative Country

With his stripped-down approach to traditional honky tonk and Bakersfield country, Dwight Yoakam helped return country music to its roots in the late '80s. Like his idols Buck Owens, Merle Haggard, and Hank Williams, Yoakam never played by Nashville's rules; consequently, he never dominated the charts like his contemporary Randy Travis. Then again, Travis never played around with the sound and style of country music like Yoakam. On each of his records, he twists around the form enough to make it seem that he doesn't respect all of country's traditions. Appropriately, his core audience was composed mainly of roots-rock and rock 'n' roll fans, not the mainstream country audience. Nevertheless, he was frequently able to chart in the country Top Ten, and he remained one of the most respected and adventurous recording country artists well into the '90s.

Born in Kentucky but raised in Ohio, Yoakam learned how to play guitar at the age of six. As a child, he listened to his mother's record collection, honing in on the traditional country of Hank Williams and Johnny Cash, as well as the Bakersfield honky tonk of Buck Owens. When he was in high school, Dwight played with a variety of bands, playing everything from country to rock 'n' roll. After completing high school, Yoakam briefly attended Ohio State University, but he dropped out and moved to Nashville in the late '70s with the intent of becoming a recording artist.

At the time he moved to Nashville, the town was in the throes of the pop-oriented Urban Cowboy movement and had no interest in his updated honky tonk. While in Nashville, he met guitarist Pete Anderson, who shared a similar taste in music. The pair moved out to Los Angeles, where they found a more appreciative audience than in Nashville. In L.A., Yoakam and Anderson played the same nightclubs that punk and post-punk rock bands like X, the Dead Kennedys, Los Lobos, the Blasters, and the Butthole Surfers did. They shared similar musical influences, drawing from '50s rock 'n' roll and country. In comparison to the polished music coming out of Nashville, Yoakam's stripped-down, direct revivalism seemed radical. The cowpunks, as they were called, who attended Yoakam's shows provided invaluable support for his fledgling career.

Yoakam released an independent EP, *A Town South of Bakersfield*, in 1984 that received substantial airplay on Los Angeles college and alternative radio stations. The EP also helped him land a record contract with Reprise Records. Yoakam's full-length debut album, *Guitars, Cadillacs, Etc., Etc.*, was released in 1986 and was an instant sensation. Rock and country critics praised it, and it earned airplay on college stations across America. More importantly, it was a hit on the country charts, as its first single, a cover of Johnny Horton's "Honky Tonk Man," climbed to No. 3 in the spring, followed by the No. 4 "Guitars, Cadillacs" in the summer. The album would eventually go platinum.

Hillbilly Deluxe, a 1987 followup, was equally successful, spawning four Top Ten hits—"Little Sister," "Little Ways," "Please, Please Baby," and "Always Late with Your Kisses." In 1988 Yoakam had his first No. 1 hit with "Streets of Bakersfield," a cover of a Buck Owens song recorded with Buck himself. It was the first single off his third album, *Buenas Noches from a Lonely Room*, which continued his streak of Top Ten hits. "I Sang Dixie," the album's second single, went to No. 1, and "I Got You" reached No. 5. In 1989 Yoakam released a compilation album, *Just Lookin' for a Hit*, that went gold. "Long White Cadillac," taken from the collection, stalled at No. 35 in the fall of 1989.

Although his 1990 album, *If There Was a Way*, didn't have as many Top Ten hits, it was a major success; it was his first album since the debut to go platinum. *This Time*, released in the spring of 1993, was an even bigger hit, spawning three No. 2 singles—"Ain't That Lonely Yet," "A Thousand Miles from Nowhere," and "Fast As You"—and going platinum. After its release, Yoakam was silent for two years, returning in the summer of 1995 with *Dwight Live*, which didn't set the charts on fire. In the fall of that year, he released his sixth album, *Gone*, which went gold by the spring of 1996, although it didn't produce any major country hits. *—Stephen Thomas Erlewine*

Guitars, Cadillacs, Etc., Etc. / 1986 / Reprise ✦✦✦✦
Who would have guessed when this album was released, with its uncompromisingly basic, honky tonk approach, that it would not only be a success but would help move the country music industry back from its crossover ways of the early '80s to a renaissance based on its most traditional sounds? Maybe Yoakam, who doggedly stuck to that approach and wrote a songs that fit in with covers like Johnny Horton's "Honky Tonk Man." *—William Ruhlmann*

Hillbilly Deluxe / 1987 / Reprise ✦✦✦
Hillbilly Deluxe essentially follows the same formula as *Guitars, Cadillacs, Etc., Etc.* and is just slightly less successful than Yoakam's breakthrough debut. The record is quite enjoyable—not only are updated honky tonk originals like "Little Ways" first-rate, but so are covers like Elvis Presley's "Little Sister" and Lefty Frizzell's "Always Late (With Your Kisses)." So the problem with the album lies in the fact that it doesn't move forward signficantly; it is just Yoakam treading water. It's an enjoyable record, but it ranks as a minor work in his canon. *—Thom Owens*

Buenos Noches from a Lonely Room / 1988 / Reprise ✦✦✦✦
The first five cuts constituted a cold-blooded cycle that ran from possessive love to murderous rage with alarming quickness. The rest was subsequently a letdown, but it still gave Yoakam a couple of big hits in "I Sang Dixie" and "Streets of Bakersfield," a duet with Buck Owens. *—Brian Mansfield*

Trisha Yearwood

★ **Just Lookin' for a Hit** / 1989 / Reprise ✦✦✦✦✦
A strong 10-track singles collection with a typically sarcastic title, paced by duets with K.D. Lang on Gram Parsons' "Sin City" and with Buck Owens (a match made in heaven) on "Streets of Bakersfield." *—William Ruhlmann*

☆ **If There Was a Way** / 1990 / Reprise ✦✦✦✦✦
Dwight Yoakam began a new decade with *If There Was a Way* and, along with it, a new approach to recording. Working from the foundation he laid with *Buenas Noches from a Lonely Room*, Yoakam lightens the tone somewhat without abandoning the gut-wrenching emotional impact or ambitious musical eclecticism. If anything, he's even more eclectic, bringing in touches of R&B and '50s rock 'n' roll that make his honky tonk tales of despair cut even deeper. Of particular note is the Dwight Yoakam and Roger Miller collaboration, "It Only Hurts When I Cry." *—Thom Owens*

La Croix D'Amour / 1992 / Reprise ✦✦✦✦
An international-only compilation, *La Croix D'Amour* is worth searching out for its rarities: two songs that appeared on other collections (Elvis Presley's "Suspicious Minds" and the Grateful Dead's "Truckin'") and four new tracks, among them covers of the Beatles' "Things We Said Today" and Them's "Here Comes the Night." *—Brian Mansfield*

☆ **This Time** / 1993 / Reprise ✦✦✦✦✦
Heartbroke fool that he is, Dwight Yoakam knows all the words for loneliness. He doesn't let up once he starts on the self-pity binge of *This Time*. He begins as the devastated lover and winds up 11 songs later the desolate loner. Musical traditionalist that he is, he knows all the styles, too, from Buck Owens' Bakersfield country ("This Time") to Gene Pitney's mini-soundtracks ("A Thousand Miles from Nowhere") to rock's spite fantasies ("Fast as You"). He knows so many that *This Time* sounds more like a collection of individual songs than the single-minded work that it is. He understands them, too; that's why Yoakam gets good mileage from campy gimmicks like the ooh-wah background vocals on "Pocket of a Clown." There's plenty of hardcore country here—"This Time," "Home for Sale," "Lonesome Road"—but the best stuff allows for Yoakam's pop roots, too. *—Brian Mansfield*

Dwight Live / May 23, 1995 / Reprise ✦✦
A straight presentation of Dwight Yoakam playing his greatest hits in concert, *Dwight Live* is a solid record, highlighted by a

Dwight Yoakam

long, intense take on "Suspicious Minds." Nevertheless, nothing on the album improves on the original recorded versions, making *Dwight Live* essential only for devoted fans. *—Stephen Thomas Erlewine*

Gone / Nov. 1995 / Reprise ✦✦✦

With *Gone*, Dwight Yoakam continued to push the boundaries of country music, adding elements of rock 'n' roll, Tex-Mex, Stax R&B, strings, and even sitar to his already eclectic Bakersfield country. However, what makes *Gone* distinctive is the directness of the songwriting. For the first time, Yoakam has written the majority of the album alone, and the results are riveting. He is able to fuse disperate elements into an emotional and daring whole. Ten years into his career, Dwight Yoakam remains one of country's most exciting and restless talents. *—Stephen Thomas Erlewine*

York Brothers

Traditional Country, Close Harmony
The York Brothers played together from the '30s through the '50s, developing a musical style that grew from traditional country into a more contemporary sound. Both George and Leslie York were born in Lawrence County, KY, and were heavily influenced by the Delmore Brothers. As a young man, George worked in coal mines and later began his music career in Denver, playing in local clubs and on the radio in the evenings. Leslie, who was seven years younger, got his start after winning a talent contest in Lexington, KY. Not long afterward, the brothers played together on a station in Portsmouth, OH. They then moved to Detroit, where their music caught fire with the Southern transplants who had come to work in the burgeoning auto industry.

The Yorks made their recording debut in 1939 and had success with "Going Home" and the controversial, slightly racy "Hamtramck Mama," which was banned in the Polish-American Detroit suburb of the same name. The notoriety got the brothers signed to Decca in 1941, where they released six singles, including "Speak to Me Little Darling." Just as they were becoming popular, World War II erupted, and both Yorks served in the Navy until the war's end. They then joined the Grand Ole Opry and began recording for King in 1947, where they found success with such outspoken tunes as "Let's Not Sleep Again" and "Mountain Rosa Lee." They also became interested in rhythm and blues, a musical style that influenced some of their later songs like "Tennessee Tango" and "River of Tears."

George and Leslie returned to Detroit in 1950, where they stayed until 1953, moving to Dallas to work on local television. They recorded on King until 1956 and then started their own label. Around this time, George began having problems with his voice, so Leslie took over the lead parts. Eventually, the York

Brothers went their separate ways; George ran a Dallas night club before his death in 1974, while Leslie worked different jobs until passing on a decade later. *—Sandra Brennan*

● **16 Great Country and Western Hits** / 1963 / King ✦✦✦✦

Rusty York

b. May 24, 1935, Harlan County, KY
Banjo, Vocals / Rock & Roll, Traditional Bluegrass, Traditional Country, Rockabilly
Rusty York was a rockabilly musician who was equally at home playing bluegrass. He was born in Harlan County, KY, where as a boy he learned about traditional Appalachian music and was heavily influenced by Earl Scruggs and his Foggy Mountain Boys, whom he saw live in 1951. He moved to Cincinnati at age 17 and bought his first new five-string banjo (he had learned to play on an old, converted tenor banjo). There he teamed up with Willard Hale and began working the local clubs in conjunction with such artists as Jimmie Skinner and Hylo Brown. When Elvis Presley became a national sensation, York decided to update his sound, and in 1957 he and Hale cut a version of Buddy Holly's "Peggy Sue" on the King label. The record led Syd Nathan, the head of King, to team York with singer Bonnie Lout to record rockabilly songs like "Lah de Dah." In 1959 he recorded two of his best-known rockers, "Red Rooster" and "Sugaree," which crossed over to the pop charts. During the '60s, York abandoned the rockabilly sound for bluegrass and country. He began cultivating an interest in the business end of country, and in 1961 started building a studio in his garage that later became Jewel Records, the home of such artists as J.D. Jarvis, Claude Ely, and Jimmie Logson. In 1971 York retired from active performing, although he did record an album with Ronnie Mack, *Dueling Banjos*, in 1973. *—Sandra Brennan*

Rusty York and the Kentucky Mountain Boys / 1960 / Blue Grass Special ✦✦✦

● **Dueling Banjos** / 1973 / Q.C.A. ✦✦✦✦

Rock 'n' Memories / 1981 / Jewel ✦✦✦

Faron Young

b. Feb. 25, 1932, Shreveport, LA, **d.** Dec. 18, 1996
Guitar, Vocals / Traditional Country, Country-Pop, Honky Tonk, Nashville Sound/Countrypolitan
Originally known as the "Hillbilly Heartthrob" and the "Singing Sheriff," Faron Young had one of the longest-running and most popular careers in country music history. Emerging in the early '50s, Young was one of the most popular honky tonkers to appear in the wake of Hank Williams' death, partially because he was able to smooth out some of the grittiest elements of his music. At first he balanced honky tonk with pop vocal phrasing and flourishes. This combination of grit and polish resulted in a streak of Top Ten hits—including "If You Ain't Lovin'," "Live Fast, Love Hard, Die Young," "Sweet Dreams," "Alone With You," and "Country Girl"—that ran throughout the '50s. During the '60s, Young gave himself over to country-pop, and while the hits weren't quite as big, they didn't stop coming until the early '80s. Through that time, he was a staple at the Grand Ole Opry and various television shows, including "Nashville Now," and he also founded the major country music magazine, *Music City News*. Most importantly, he continued to seek out new songwriters—including Don Gibson, Willie Nelson, and Kris Kristofferson—thereby cultivating a new generation of talent.

Faron Young was born and raised outside of Shrevport, LA. While he was growing up on his father's dairy farm, he was given a guitar, and by the time he entered high school, he had begun singing in a country band. After high school, he briefly attended college, but left school to join the "Louisiana Hayride" as a regular performer. While on the "Hayride" he met Webb Pierce, and soon the pair were touring throughout the South, singing as a duo in various nightclubs and honky tonks. In 1951 Young recorded "Have I Waited Too Long" and "Tattle Tale Tears" for the independent label Gotham. After hearing the singles, Capitol Records decided to buy Young's contract from Gotham in 1952. That same year he was invited to perform regularly on the Grand Ole Opry.

Just as his career was taking off, Young was drafted into the Army to serve in the Korean War. Assigned to the Special Services division, he sang for the troops in Asia and appeared on recruitment shows; while on leave, he recorded his Capitol debut, "Goin' Steady." Upon its early 1953 release, it climbed to No. 2 on the country charts, and it was followed in the summer by "I Can't Wait (For the Sun to Go Down)," which hit No. 5. Young was discharged from the Army in November 1954, releasing "If You Ain't Lovin'," his biggest hit to date, shortly after he returned. The single was quickly followed in the spring of 1955 by "Live Fast, Love Hard, Die Young," which became his first No. 1 hit, and the No. 2 single, "All Right."

As soon as he returned to the States, Faron Young began turning out singles at a very rapid pace, and most of them charted in the Top Ten. In addition to recording, he began appearing in films, starting with 1955's *Hidden Guns*. Over the next few years he was in no less than ten—including *Daniel Boone, Road to Nashville, Stampede, A Gun and a Gavel, That's Country* and *Raiders of Old California*—and was featured in many television shows. Upon his first fim appearance, Young earned the nickname the "Young Sheriff," which eventually metamorphasized into the "Singing Sheriff." Young's career truly began to hit its stride in 1956, as "I've Got Five Dollars and It's Saturday Night"/"You're Still Mine" reached No. 4 and No. 3, respectively, during the spring, followed by the No. 2 "Sweet Dreams" later that summer. "Sweet Dreams" not only was his biggest hit since "All Right," but it gave songwriter Don Gibson his first significant exposure. Soon Young developed a reputation for finding promising new songwriters, bringing Roy Drusky's "Alone with You" to the top of the charts in the summer of 1958 and taking Willie Nelson's "Hello Walls" to No. 1 in 1961; Young was one of the first artists to record a Nelson song.

Young continued to record for Capitol through 1962, when he switched labels and signed with Mercury. In general, Young's Mercury recordings were more pop-oriented than his Capitol work, possibly because "Hello Walls," his last No. 1 for Capitol, reached No. 12 on the pop charts. Throughout the early and mid-'60s, Young's music became more polished and produced, but his audience didn't decline dramatically—he may not have been hitting the top of the charts with the same frequency as he was during the '50s, but he was still a consistent hit-maker, and singles like "You'll Drive Me Back (Into Her Arms Again)," "Keeping Up with the Joneses," and "Walk Tall" climbed into the Top Ten.

Young left the Grand Ole Opry in 1965, deciding that it was more profitable for him to tour as a solo artist instead of being restricted to the Opry. He began to explore a number of different business ventures, including a Nashville-based racetrack and helping to run the country music publication *Music City News*, which he co-founded with Preston Temple in 1963. By the end of the decade, he began to return to honky tonk, most notably with the hit "Wine Me Up," which reached No. 2 upon its summer 1969 release. For nearly five years Young continued to reach the Top Ten with regularity, including such hits as "Your Time's Comin'," "If I Ever Fall in Love (With a Honky Tonk Girl), "Step Aside," and "It's Four in the Morning." Young continued to appear on television shows, and he made the occasional appearance on the Grand Ole Opry. During the late '70s, his hits gradually began to fade. In 1979 he left Mercury for MCA, but none of his singles for the new label reached the Top 40.

For most of the '80s, Young performed concerts, maintained his business interests, and appeared on television; in short, he was acting like the country music statesman he was. In 1988 he briefly returned to recording, signing with the small label Step One, and had two minor hits. After that brief burst of activity, he retreated to semi-retirement, occasionally making concert appearances.

During the '90s, Young was stricken with debilitating emphysema. Depressed by his poor health, he committed suicide in December 1996. Though he was underappreciated toward the end of his career, Faron Young was a groundbreaking vocalist

during the '50s, and he remained one of the finest honky tonkers of his time. —*Stephen Thomas Erlewine*

The All-Time Great Hits . . . / 1963 / Capitol ✦✦✦
An interesting chronological retrospective, it illustrates Young's transformation from a Hank Williams-inspired honky tonk singer into a "sophisticated balladeer." The two find a happy medium in "Hello Walls," a great song written by Willie Nelson. Young gives a fine performance on one of the best country records ever. The earlier stuff, like "Live Fast, Love Hard," is fun, too. —*George Bedard*

I'll Be Yours / 1968 / Pickwick ✦✦✦
Pickwick's *I'll Be Yours* is a reissue of an excellent original Capitol LP by Faron Young, featuring such definitive Young performances as "Just Married," "When It Rains It Pours," and "You're Still Mine." Though there are a couple of weak tracks, the album remains a thoroughly engaging listen. —*Thom Owens*

☆ **All-Time Greatest Hits** / 1990 / Curb ✦✦✦✦✦
Curb's *All-Time Greatest Hits* is a nice, but too brief, collection of Faron Young's biggest hits: "Hello Walls," "Live Fast, Love Hard, Die Young," "Alone with You," "Sweet Dreams," and "Goin' Steady." It's hardly a definitive collection—classic early hits like "If You Ain't Lovin' (You Ain't Livin')," "I've Got Five Dollars," and "All Right" aren't included—but it's a good sampler for the budget-conscious. It shouldn't, however, be thought of as a substitute for the more complete *Live Fast, Love Hard: Original Capitol Recordings, 1952-1962. —Stephen Thomas Erlewine*

★ **Live Fast, Love Hard: Original Capitol Recordings, 1952-1962** / Oct. 1995 / Country Music Foundation ✦✦✦✦✦
Faron Young was one of the most popular honky tonk stars of the '50s, and *Live Fast, Love Hard: Original Capitol Recordings, 1952-1962* is an excellent, 24-song overview of the peak of his career. Featuring his big hits like "If You Ain't Lovin' (You Ain't Livin')" as well as more obscure tracks (a radio transcription of "Three Days"), the album is the most thorough and listenable single-disc retrospective ever assembled on Young. For honky tonk fans, it's an essential listen. —*Stephen Thomas Erlewine*

The Classic Years 1952-62 / Bear Family ✦✦✦✦
Swashbuckling Louisiana honky tonk, much of Faron Young's early work on Capitol is marked by an undertone of grinning lasciviousness. That's not a bad thing, given how many of his industry pals completely hid their wolfishness behind apple-pie lyrics. In any case, Bear Family has here collected the entirety of Young's Capitol output on five CDs. Besides the swaggering stuff ("If You Ain't Lovin'," "Live Fast, Love Hard, Die Young," and the amazing "Alone with You") one can hear the hit version of "Sweet Dreams" he cut seven years before Patsy Cline's. It comes with a beautiful 48-page book. —*Dan Cooper*

Neil Young

b. Nov. 12, 1945, Toronto, Ontario, Canada
Guitar, Piano, Ukulele, Vocals / Rock & Roll, Country-Rock, Singer-Songwriter, Hard Rock, Folk-Rock
With the exception of Bob Dylan, Neil Young is the most acclaimed and accomplished singer-songwriter of his generation. Born in Toronto, Young learned to play ukulele and then guitar in his teens, and played in a variety of groups. He moved to Los Angeles with his friend bassist Bruce Palmer, and hooked up with Stephen Stills, Richie Furay, and Dewey Martin to form Buffalo Springfield in 1966. After the Springfield split in 1968, Young went solo, releasing his first album, *Neil Young*, an acoustic effort with strings, in January 1969. Characteristically, Young followed it only four months later with the hard rock *Everybody Knows This Is Nowhere*, backed by the electric three-piece band Crazy Horse; it became his first gold-selling album. Young joined Crosby, Stills and Nash in June 1969, and combined solo and group careers until the band split the next summer. His third solo album, *After the Gold Rush* (August 1970), reached the Top Ten and included his first Top 40 hit, "Only Love Can Break Your Heart." But Young's commercial peak came early in 1972, when he released the No. 1, three-million-selling album *Harvest*, which contained the chart-topping gold single "Heart of Gold."

Instead of following up such success, Young worked on the documentary film *Journey through the Past* (and its accompanying soundtrack album) for the rest of the year, then launched a concert tour in early 1973, by which time Crazy Horse's guitarist Danny Whitten had died of a heroin overdose. The tour was a ragged affair chronicled on the live album *Time Fades Away*. After it, Young recorded (but did not release) *Tonight's the Night*, which memorialized Whitten and Bruce Berry, a Young roadie who had also overdosed.

Young's first new studio album in 18 months, *On the Beach*, was released in the summer of 1974. Much of it was acoustic, and it expressed dire sentiments. He finally put out *Tonight's the Night* in the summer of 1975, and the hard-rocking *Zuma* in the autumn. In the spring of 1976 Young toured with Stephen Stills, and the two recorded the duo album *Long May You Run*. Young's next solo album was 1977's *American Stars 'n' Bars*, made up of studio tracks dating back three years. In the fall of 1977 he released *Decade*, a three-album (later two-CD) career retrospective. In 1978 he released *Comes a Time*, Young's most country-folk-oriented album since *Harvest*, and his first since *Harvest* to reach the Top Ten. In 1979 Young launched a tour with Crazy Horse under the banner *Rust Never Sleeps*, including a critically acclaimed album of the same name and, eventually, a tour film and a live album called *Live Rust*.

Young spent the better part of the '80s veering from one musical style to another, as his commercial fortunes declined. He turned to electronic music on *Trans*, to rockabilly on *Everybody's Rockin'*, to country on *Old Ways*, and to horn-backed R&B on *This Note's for You*. In 1989, however, Young returned to his more familiar folk and rock styles for *Freedom*, and was rewarded with critical hosannas and his first gold album in a decade. The hard-rocking *Ragged Glory* was even more rapturously received, topping the *Village Voice* critic's poll for Best Album of 1990. In late 1991 Young issued a double live album, *Weld*, as well as *Arc*, an album of instrumental guitar feedback. He was said to be working on a box set retrospective follow-up to *Decade*.

In 1992 Young was being hailed as "the Godfather of Grunge," as dozens of new rock 'n' roll bands from Pearl Jam to the Jayhawks were claiming him as an influence. Naturally, Young backed away from the hard, overdriven rock of *Weld* and *Ragged Glory*, releasing the quiet *Harvest Moon*, the sequel to his country-rock landmark, *Harvest*. In 1993 he released a live album (*Unplugged*) while he worked on his long-awaited box set; he released another album recorded with Crazy Horse, *Sleeps with Angels*, in late summer 1994. The next summer Young released *Mirror Ball*, which was recorded with Pearl Jam. In the summer of 1996 Young released *Broken Arrow*, which was recorded with Crazy Horse. *— William Ruhlmann*

Neil Young / Jan. 1969 / Reprise ♦♦♦

Young's debut, one of his most low-key efforts, went almost unnoticed at the time, but it did introduce many of the traits that would characterize much of his work: countryish ballads, medium-tempo rockers with searing lead guitar lines, tasteful strings and female backing vocals, and gentle but disquieting romantic ruminations. The material isn't strong enough to qualify this as one of his better albums, but it has a touching grace, embellished by Jack Nitzsche's elaborate production on a few tracks. The nine-and-a-half-minute closer, "The Last Trip to Tulsa," is Young's most long-winded and Dylanesque surrealist epic. *—Richie Unterberger*

☆ **Everybody Knows This Is Nowhere** / May 1969 / Reprise ♦♦♦♦♦

Young's breakthrough album is also the first one to feature the backup of Crazy Horse for a seminal rock session that produced the Young favorites "Cinnamon Girl," "Down by the River," and "Cowgirl in the Sand." *— William Ruhlmann*

☆ **After the Gold Rush** / Aug. 1970 / Reprise ♦♦♦♦♦

The years have been kind to what sounded like Young's best album when it was released. It's a mixture of his folkie ("Tell Me Why"), country ("Oh, Lonesome Me"), and hard-rocking ("Southern Man") selves, and there's also that mystical title track, which

remains Neil Young's definitive statement of purpose. *—William Ruhlmann*

Harvest / Feb. 1972 / Reprise ♦♦♦♦

Uneven, yes, perhaps due to the overambitiousness of the orchestral pieces, but this album, Young's biggest seller, still contains "Heart of Gold," the rocker "Alabama," and such telling ballads as "Old Man." *— William Ruhlmann*

Journey Through the Past / Nov. 1972 / Reprise ♦♦

Neil Young's unexpected followup to the million-selling *Harvest* was this two-LP soundtrack to his rarely seen film. It contains performances by Buffalo Springfield and Crosby, Stills, Nash, and Young, plus Young himself, all previously familiar, except for one minor new Young song, "Soldier." *— William Ruhlmann*

Time Fades Away / Oct. 1973 / Reprise ♦♦♦

The beginning of Young's mid-'70s descent into decadence, this is part of a trilogy including *Tonight's the Night* and *On the Beach* that explores drug addiction, desperation, and determination. The subject matter isn't expressed just in the lyrics; it's in the roughly played music and the strained vocals. The most gripping music of Young's career. *— William Ruhlmann*

☆ **On the Beach** / Jul. 1974 / Reprise ♦♦♦♦♦

After the 1973 *Time Fades Away* tour, which was haunted by the drug death of Crazy Horse guitarist Danny Whitten, and an abortive CSNY reunion that was coincident with the drug death of CSNY roadie Bruce Berry, Neil Young wrote and recorded an Irish wake of a record called *Tonight's the Night* and went on the road drunkenly playing its songs to uncomprehending listeners and hostile reviewers. Reprise rejected the record, and Young went right back into the studio and made *On the Beach*, which shares some of the ragged style of its two predecessors. But where *Time* was embattled and *Tonight* mournful, *On the Beach* was savage and, ultimately, triumphant. "I'm a vampire, babe," Young sang, and he proceeded to take bites out of various subjects, adopting a mad militia man's stance in "Revolution Blues" and threatening the lives of the stars who lived in L.A.'s Laurel Canyon (like, until recently, himself); answering Lynyrd Skynyrd, whose recently released "Sweet Home Alabama" had taken him to task for his criticisms of the South in "Southern Man" and "Alabama" ("they do their thing, I'll do mine," he noted in "Walk On"); and rejecting the critics (presumably both the press and his record company) as well as his manager, who had complained that CSNY were "just pissing in the wind" when they should be playing together ("Ambulance Blues"). But the barbs were mixed with humor and even affection (the album was dedicated to his manager), and, beginning with "Walk On" ("Sooner or later it all gets real") and ending with "Ambulance Blues" ("An ambulance can only go so fast / It's easy to get buried in the past / When you try to make a good thing last"), Young seemed to be emerging from the grief and self-abuse that had plagued him for two years. But the album was so spare and underproduced, with many songs in standard blues form and plodding along at slow tempos, and the lyrics were so harrowing, that it was easy to miss Young's conclusion, that he was saying goodbye to despair, not being overwhelmed by it. (As of mid-1996, *On the Beach* remained one of six Neil Young albums on Reprise not to have been reissued on CD.) *— William Ruhlmann*

☆ **Tonight's the Night** / Jun. 1975 / Reprise ♦♦♦♦♦

Written and recorded in 1973 shortly after the death of roadie Bruce Berry, Neil Young's second close associate to die of a heroin overdose in six months (the first was Crazy Horse guitarist Danny Whitten), *Tonight's the Night* was Young's musical expression of grief, combined with his rejection of the stardom he had achieved in the late '60s and early '70s. The title track, performed twice, was a direct narrative about Berry. "Bruce Berry was a working man / He used to load that Econoline van." Whitten was heard singing "Come On Baby Let's Go Downtown," a live track recorded years earlier. Elsewhere, Young frequently referred to drug use and used phrases that might have described his friends, such as the chorus of "Tired Eyes": "He tried to do his best, but he could not." Performing with the remains of Crazy Horse, bassist Billy Talbot and drummer Ralph Molina, along with Nils Lofgren (guitar and piano) and Ben Keith (steel guitar), Young sang in the ragged manner familiar from *Time Fades Away;* his voice was often hoarse, and he strained to reach high notes. The playing was loose, with mistakes and shifting tempos. But the style worked perfectly for the material, emphasizing the emotional tone of Young's mourning and contrasting with the polished sound of CSNY and *Harvest,* which Young also disparaged. He remained unimpressed with his commercial success, noting in "World on a String," "The world on a string / Doesn't mean anything." In "Roll Another Number," he said he was "a million miles away / From that helicopter day" when he and CSN had played Woodstock. And in "Albuquerque," he said he had been "starvin' to be alone, / Independent from the scene that I've known" and spoke of his desire to "find somewhere where they don't care who I am." Songs like "Speakin' Out" and "New Mama" seemed to find some hope in family life, but *Tonight's the Night* did not offer solutions to the personal and professional problems it posed. It was the work of a man trying to turn his torment into art and doing so unflinchingly. Depending on which story you believe, Reprise Records rejected it or Young withdrew it from its scheduled release at the start of 1974 after touring with the material in the US and Europe. In 1975, after a massive CSNY tour, Young at the last minute dumped a newly recorded album and finally put out *Tonight's the Night* instead. Though it did not become one of his bigger commercial successes, the album immediately was recognized as a unique masterpiece by critics, and it has continued to be ranked as one of the greatest rock 'n' roll albums ever made. — *William Ruhlmann*

Zuma / Nov. 1975 / Reprise ✦✦✦✦
Having apparently exorcised his demons by releasing the cathartic *Tonight's the Night,* Neil Young returned to his commercial strengths with *Zuma* (named after Zuma Beach in Los Angeles, where he now owned a house). Seven of the album's nine songs were recorded with the reunited Crazy Horse, in which rhythm guitarist Frank Sampedro had replaced the late Danny Whitten, but there were also nods to other popular Young styles in "Pardon My Heart," an acoustic song that would have fit on *Harvest,* his most popular album, and "Through My Sails," retrieved from one of Crosby, Stills, Nash, and Young's abortive recording sessions. Young had abandoned the ragged, first-take approach of his previous three albums, but Crazy Horse would never be a polished act, and the music had a lively sound well-suited to the songs, which were some of the most melodic, pop-oriented tunes Young had crafted in years, though they were played with an electric-guitar-drenched rock intensity. The overall theme concerned romantic conflict, with lyrics that lamented lost love and sometimes longed for a return ("Pardon My Heart" even found Young singing, "I don't believe this song"), though the overall conclusion, notably in such catchy songs as "Don't Cry No Tears" and "Lookin' for a Love," was to move on to the next relationship. But the album's standout track (apparently the only holdover from an early intention to present songs with historical subjects) was the seven-and-a-half-minute epic "Cortez the Killer," a commentary on the Spanish conqueror of Latin America that served as a platform for Young's most extensive guitar soloing since his work on *Everybody Knows This Is Nowhere.* — *William Ruhlmann*

Long May You Run / Sep. 1976 / Reprise ✦✦
Long May You Run is not a Neil Young solo album. It is credited to "The Stills-Young Band," which is to say, Stephen Stills and his band with Young added, and the two divide up the songwriting and lead vocals, five for Young, four for Stills. The pairing, though it proved short-lived and had, in fact, ended before this album was released, must have seemed commercially logical. Like Young, Stills had seen his record sales decline after the 1970 breakup of CSNY. So had erstwhile partners David Crosby and Graham Nash, but they had returned to Top Ten, gold-selling status in the fall of 1975 with their *Wind on the Water* duo album. Why couldn't Stills and Young do the same thing? Maybe they could have (and, actually, this was the first gold album for either in two years) if they had made a better record together. Young's songs were pleasant, newly written throwaways with the exception of the title track, a trunk song he had written as a tribute to an old car. Stills' compositions seemed more seriously intended but were still not substan-

tial. The playing, largely handled by the professional sessionman-types in Stills' band, was far smoother than what one was accustomed to in a Young album. The result was a listenable record, but not a compelling one, and thus well below Young's usual standard and Stills' best. (As of mid-1996, *Long May You Run* had not been released in the US on CD.) — *William Ruhlmann*

American Stars & Bars / Jun. 1977 / Reprise ✦✦✦
Neil Young made a point of listing the recording dates of the songs on *American Stars 'n' Bars;* the dates even appeared on the LP labels. They revealed that the songs had been cut at four different sessions dating back to 1974. But even without such documentation, it would have been easy to tell that the album was a stylistic hodge-podge, its first side consisting of country-tinged material featuring steel guitar and fiddle, plus backup vocals from Linda Ronstadt and the then-unknown Nicolette Larson, while the four songs on the second side varied from acoustic solo numbers like "Will to Love" to raging rockers such as "Like a Hurricane." Just as apparent was the album's unevenness: Side one consisted of lightweight compositions, while side two had more ambitious ones, with "Will to Love," for example, extending the romantic metaphor of a salmon swimming upstream across seven minutes. The album's saving grace was "Like a Hurricane," one of Young's classic hard rock songs and guitar workouts, a perennial concert favorite. Without it, *American Stars 'n' Bars* would have been one of Young's least memorable albums, and since it turned up the following year on the compilation *Decade,* the LP was rendered unessential. (As of mid-1996, *American Stars 'n' Bars* had not been released on CD in the US.) — *William Ruhlmann*

★ **Decade** / Nov. 1977 / Reprise ✦✦✦✦✦
Given the quirkiness of Neil Young's recording career, with its frequent cancellations of releases and last-minute rearrangements of material, it is some relief to report that this two-disc compilation (with a running time of two hours, 24 minutes) is so conventional and so satisfying. Knowing Young, it could easily have consisted entirely of unreleased material, but instead it proves to be a well-thought-out 35-track selection of the best of Young's work between 1966 and 1976, including songs performed by his groups Buffalo Springfield, Crosby, Stills, Nash, and Young, and the Stills/Young Band, as well as solo work. There are five unreleased songs, one, "Down to the Wire," from the Springfield era, though Young makes a point of noting that only he and Stephen Stills from the group appear on the recording, accompanied by session players. Of the four other newly issued tracks, the most notable is "Love Is a Rose," a romantic ballad earlier covered by Linda Ronstadt. The others are "Winterlong," "Deep Forbidden Lake," and "Campaigner," the last a song displaying some compassion for Richard Nixon, who was a subject of castigation in Young's "Ohio," a CSNY track also included. The previously released material includes such key tracks as the Springfield's "Mr. Soul," "Broken Arrow," and "I Am a Child"; "Sugar Mountain," a song that had appeared only as a single before; "The Loner" from *Neil Young;* "Cinnamon Girl," "Down by the River," and "Cowgirl in the Sand" from *Everybody Knows This Is Nowhere;* "Southern Man" and the title track from *After the Gold Rush;* and "Old Man" and the chart-topping "Heart of Gold" from *Harvest.* This is the material that built Young's reputation between 1966 and 1972, and heard together, it is surprisingly well-crafted. Maybe the surprise comes because, as the later material from albums like *Tonight's the Night* and *On the Beach* follows, it becomes clear that craftsmanship, at least in terms of recording technique, was only a phase for Young, albeit one to which he was willing to return on occasion. (In one of many revealing sleeve notes, Young writes that he gave up overdubbing his vocals after his second solo album.) Young is selective and somewhat idiosyncratic with the later material, including the blockbusters "Like a Hurricane" and "Cortez the Killer," but mixing in more of the unreleased recordings as the set draws to a close. He seems intent on making the album a listenable one that will appeal to a broad base of fans; and he succeeds, though some may wish he had included more of the harrowing work of 1973-1975. Nevertheless, the album is an ideal sampler for new listeners, and since there is no one-disc Young compilation covering any

significant portion of his career, this lengthy chronicle is the place to start. — *William Ruhlmann*

Comes a Time / Oct. 1978 / Reprise ✦✦✦✦

Six and a half years later, *Comes a Time* finally was the Neil Young album for the millions of fans who had loved *Harvest*, an acoustic-based record with country overtones and romantic, auto-biographical lyrics. Many of those fans returned to the fold, enough to make *Comes a Time* Young's first Top Ten album since *Harvest*. He signaled the album's direction with the leadoff track, "Goin' Back," its retrospective theme augmented by an orchestral backup and the deliberate beat familiar from his No. 1 hit "Heart of Gold." Of course Young remained sly about this retrenchment. "I feel like goin' back," he sang, but added, "Back where there's nowhere to stay." Doubtless he had no intention of staying with this style, but for the length of the album, melodies, love lyrics, lush arrangements, and steel guitar solos dominated, and Young's vocals were made more accessible by being paired with Nicolette Larson's harmonies. Larson's own version of Young's "Lotta Love," released shortly after the one heard here, became a Top Ten hit single. Other highlights included the reflective "Already One," which treats the unusual subject of the nature of a divorced family, the ironic "Field of Opportunity," and a cover of Ian Tyson's folk standard "Four Strong Winds" (a country Top Ten hit for Bobby Bare in 1965). — *William Ruhlmann*

☆ **Rust Never Sleeps** / Jul. 1979 / Reprise ✦✦✦✦✦

Rust Never Sleeps, its aphoristic title drawn from an intended advertising slogan, was an album of new songs, some of them recorded on Neil Young's 1978 concert tour, not a live album chronicling that tour or the soundtrack to the *Rust Never Sleeps* film that opened simultaneously with its release. (Young's next album, *Live Rust*, would be both those things.) Instead, it was his strongest collection of songs since *Tonight's the Night* and a far more varied and ambitious record than that narrowly focused effort. Its obvious antecedent was Bob Dylan's 1965 masterpiece, *Bringing It All Back Home*, and, as Dylan did, Young divided his record into acoustic and electric sides while filling his songs with wildly imaginative imagery. Especially on the folkish first side, Young sang highly poetic lyrics that ranged from the abstract to the particular, from Mars to the Alamo, often in the same song. The leadoff track, "My My, Hey Hey (Out of the Blue)" (repeated in an electric version at album's end as "Hey Hey, My My [In the Black]" with slightly altered lyrics), is the most concise and knowing description of the entertainment industry ever written; its lyrics should be memorized by every aspiring rock star before he ever leaves his bedroom for the local bar. It was followed by "Thrasher," which describes Young's parallel artistic quest in an extended metaphor that also reflected the album's overall theme: the inevitability of deterioration and the challenge of overcoming it. Young then spent the rest of the album demonstrating that his chief weapons against rusting were his imagination and his daring; who else would muse about sleeping with Pocahontas and talking to Marlon Brando about Hollywood ("Pocahontas") or toss in the comic relief of "Welfare Mothers," with its rousing chorus, "Welfare mothers make better lovers / DEE VORR CEE!"? And Young was just as effective when taking a traditional form, such as the narrative death ballad, and coming up with "Powderfinger," an apocalyptic drama with an irresistible guitar riff and a compelling melody. Several of the songs on *Rust Never Sleeps* dated back a few years, demonstrating the depth of Young's famous archives and making for an unusually consistent album that played more like a hits collection (especially for longtime fans) than a new set. But just as important was the force of the performances, especially Young's always explosive interaction with the crude rock of Crazy Horse. *Rust Never Sleeps* was an archetypal Neil Young album in the sense that it encapsulated his many styles on a single disc, but it was also a unique document that contained great songs unlike any Young had written before. Lacking a substantial hit single (though "Hey Hey, My My [Into the Black]" was a chart entry), the album nevertheless became Young's best-selling album since *Harvest* nine years before. — *William Ruhlmann*

Live Rust / Nov. 1979 / Reprise ✦✦✦✦

All the kudos Neil Young earned for *Rust Never Sleeps* he lost for *Live Rust*, the double-LP live album released four months later. *Live Rust* was the soundtrack to Young's concert film, *Rust Never Sleeps* (he had wanted to give it that title, but Reprise vetoed the idea, fearing confusion with the earlier album), and, like it, was recorded Oct. 22, 1978, at the Cow Palace in San Francisco. But much of the *Rust Never Sleeps* album had been recorded on the same tour, and *Live Rust* repeated four songs from that disc. Since Young had released the career retrospective *Decade* in 1977, critics felt he was unfairly recycling his older material and repeating his new material. In retrospect, however, *Live Rust*, now a single 74-minute CD, comes off as an excellent Neil Young live album and career summary, starting with the early song "Sugar Mountain" and running through then-new songs like "My My, Hey Hey (Out of the Blue)" and "Powderfinger." Young is effective in both his acoustic folksinger and hard-rocking Crazy Horse bandleader modes. The various distractions of the concert itself and the film, such as the pretentious props and cowled roadies, are absent, and what's left is a terrific Neil Young concert recording. — *William Ruhlmann*

Hawks & Doves / Nov. 1980 / Reprise ✦✦✦

Following the triumph of *Rust Never Sleeps, Hawks and Doves* benefited from the enormous critical goodwill Neil Young had amassed, though fans and critics nevertheless were baffled by its set of obscure acoustic and country-tinged songs. The seven-plus-minute "The Old Homestead" (copyright 1974) was interpreted by some as an allegory for Young's relationship to CSNY, perhaps because that was the only way to make any sense of the most mysterious Young lyric since "The Last Trip to Tulsa." In retrospect, now that we know Young was distracted by domestic medical concerns while working on the album, its theme of perseverance in the face of adversity, both in a personal context of family commitment ("Stayin' Power," "Coastline"), and in a national context of hard work and patriotism ("Union Man," "Comin' Apart at Every Nail," "Hawks and Doves") seems more apparent, as does the sense that Young may have been trying to fulfill his recording contract (even with the inclusion of trunk songs like "The Old Homestead," the album runs less than half an hour) while devoting a bare minimum of his time and attention to the effort. The result is correspondingly slight. (As of October 1996, *Hawks and Doves* still had not been issued on CD in the U.S.) — *William Ruhlmann*

Re-ac-tor / Nov. 1981 / Reprise ✦✦

Neil Young employs Crazy Horse to help him bash out a guitar-drenched hard rock set made up of thrown-together material. The group plays fiercely, as usual, but the lyrics are sketchy, seemingly improvised (the nadir is the nine-minute "T-Bone," which consists of the lines "Got mashed potato / Ain't got no t-bone" repeated over and over), and frequently cranky, as in "Motor City," which finds Young criticizing Japanese cars, and "Rapid Transit," which takes a belated swipe at new wave music while sounding like second-rate Talking Heads. For the second album in a row, Young seems to be just fulfilling his one-album-a-year record contract. The exception is the album-closing "Shots" (written by 1978), a more substantive and threatening song given a riveting performance. Later it would be revealed that Young was finding time for his music while giving most of his attention to caring for his disabled son. Still, he might have been better advised to have suspended record-making for a few years instead of turning out half-baked efforts like this one. — *William Ruhlmann*

Trans / Jan. 1983 / Geffen ✦✦

When it was released, *Trans* was Neil Young's most baffling album. He had employed a Vocoder to synthesize his voice on five of the album's nine tracks, resulting in disembodied singing, the lyrics nearly impossible to decipher without the lyric sheet. And even when you read the words, "Computer Age," "We R in Control," "Transformer Man," "Computer Cowboy," and "Sample and Hold" seemed like a vague mishmash of hi-tech jargon. Later Young would reveal that some of the songs expressed a theme of attempted communication with his disabled son, and in that context, lines like "I stand by you" and "So many things still left to do / But we haven't made it yet" seemed clearer. But the Vocoder, which robbed Young's voice of its dynamics and phrasing, still kept the songs from being as moving as they were intended to be. And despite the crisp dance beats and synthesizers, the music sounded less like new Kraftwerk than like old Devo. A few more conventional Young songs (left over from an earlier rejected album) seemed out of place. *Trans* had a few good songs, notably "Sample and Hold" (which seemed to be about a computer dating service for robots), a remake of "Mr. Soul," and "Like an Inca" (an intended cross between "Like a Hurricane" and "Cortez the Killer"?), but on the whole it was an idea that just didn't work. (*Trans* has been released in the US on CD. The European CD release replaces the original 5:09 take of "Sample and Hold" with the 8:04 alternate take later used on the *Lucky Thirteen* compilation.) *— William Ruhlmann*

Everybody's Rockin' / Aug. 1983 / Geffen ♦♦
By following the hi-tech *Trans* after only seven months with a rockabilly album, Neil Young baffled his audience. Just as he had followed the sales peak of *Harvest* in 1972 with a series of challenging, uncommercial albums, Young had now dissipated the commercial and critical acceptance he had enjoyed with 1979's *Rust Never Sleeps* with a series of mediocre albums and inexplicable genre exercises. *Everybody's Rockin',* credited to "Neil and the Shocking Pinks," represented the nadir of this attempted career suicide. Running less than 25 minutes, it found Young covering early rock evergreens like "Betty Lou's Got a New Pair of Shoes" and writing a few songs in the same vein ("Kinda Fonda Wanda"). If he had presented this as a mini-album at a discount price, it would have been easier to enjoy the joke Young seemed to intend. As it was, fans who already had their doubts about Young dropped off the radar screen. *Everybody's Rocking* was his lowest charting album since his 1969 solo debut, and he didn't release another album for two years (his longest break ever between records). *Everybody's Rockin'* has not been released on CD in the US, though it has appeared in other countries, including Canada. *— William Ruhlmann*

Old Ways / Aug. 1985 / Geffen ♦♦♦
After Neil Young moved to Geffen Records in 1982, he submitted to the label two albums that were rejected, *Island in the Sun* in 1982 and *Old Ways* in 1983, and two that were released, *Trans* (on which he altered his voice with a Vocoder) and *Everybody's Rockin'* (on which he played rockabilly covers and originals). Both of the albums sold in the range of their immediate predecessors, *Hawks and Doves* (1980) and *Re-ac-tor* (1981), but far below the typical sales Young's albums had enjoyed in the 1970s. In 1984 Geffen sued Young on the grounds that he had submitted uncharacteristic, uncommercial records to the label. By the time a settlement had been reached, Young had been on the road with a country band called the International Harvesters for a year and a half and recorded a revamped version of *Old Ways,* which Geffen released unenthusiastically and which went on to be Young's worst-selling album yet. It is in the style of *Harvest* and *Comes a Time,* but with a stronger country leaning. Young depends heavily on friends, especially for vocals—Waylon Jennings sings harmony on six out of the ten tracks, one of the others is a duet with Willie Nelson, and the others feature less famous singers along with Young. Though populated by cowboys and country references, Young's take on the genre is typically idiosyncratic, including a reworked version of his autobiography in "Get Back to the Country" (a Country Top 40 hit single), a cover of the 1956 Gogi Grant hit "Wayward Wind," and the uncategorizable "Misfits," which portrays astronauts watching Muhammad Ali fights on television in space. *Old Ways* is not a great Neil Young album, and at the time of its release it served to alienate him even further from his audience. But it has its moments. (Like most of Neil Young's 1980s albums, *Old Ways* was skipped over for CD reissue for a long time. Finally, more than a decade after its original release, it was licensed by the Mobile Fidelity audiophile label and appeared as a high-priced gold-plated Ultradisc CD on January 9, 1996.) *— William Ruhlmann*

Landing on Water / Jul. 1986 / Geffen ♦♦
Backed only by co-producer Danny Kortchmar on guitar and Steve Jordan on drums, with all three playing synthesizers, Neil

Young turns in an album that attempts to mix the raunchy rock thrust of his Crazy Horse-style music with contemporary trends in pop, especially the tendency to turn the drums way up in the mix. It's an uneasy combination in which Jordan's forceful drumming dominates the tracks, with Young's vocals nearly buried. But that only means that the production has ruined a group of songs, few of which were any good anyway. The only one that offers the promise of being one of Young's better efforts is "Hippie Dream," a sober criticism of what became of '60s idealism in general and Young's erstwhile bandmate David Crosby in particular. But if *Landing on Water* was not a good album, at least it seemed to point Young away from the stylistic dabbling of his last three albums and back toward the kind of rock he did best, and at least some of his fans returned as a result, giving him a slight uptick in sales. *— William Ruhlmann*

Life / Jul. 1987 / Geffen ♦♦♦
In the fall of 1978, Neil Young undertook a North American tour with Crazy Horse, then added overdubs to new songs recorded on the tour for one of his best albums, *Rust Never Sleeps.* In the fall 1986, he did the same thing, but *Life,* Young's first album with Crazy Horse since 1981's *Re-ac-tor,* was not one of his best albums. It was, however, better than most of the other albums he had made in the 1980s, and it was the first really interesting album he'd made in a long time. Despite the return to Crazy Horse, Young continued to use some of the production techniques from *Landing on Water,* especially the loud drums and the synthesizers. But he mixed things up, including acoustic-based songs such as "Long Walk Home" (which recalled "After the Gold Rush") and "Inca Queen" (the third in his series of long, atmospheric songs about the Incas) and rockers like "Prisoners of Rock 'n' Roll." The last, with its attacks on "record company clowns" and chorus "That's why we don't want to be good" seemed intended as the theme song for the *Rusted-Out Garage Tour* on which it was performed and served as a reminder that Young was still at odds with Geffen Records, which he left after releasing this album. Despite the criticism he had endured for his support of President Reagan's military build-up, Young had foreign policy on his mind in the action-movie-in-song "Mideast Vacation" and in "Long Walk Home," which addressed military misadventures from Vietnam to Beirut. It could be argued that Young was repeating himself on much of this material and that the album was typically uneven. But *Life* was an encouraging step back to the tried and true for an exploratory artist who finally seemed to have realized that he had experimented too much for his own good. *— William Ruhlmann*

This Note's for You / Apr. 1988 / Reprise ♦♦♦
This Note's for You was another installment in Neil Young's '80s tour of genres, recorded with a ten-piece, horn-driven blues band. In terms of style, it was merely another genre exercise, but the songs on the album were his strongest in several years, particularly the haunting "Coupe Deville," and began his late-'80s return to form. *— Stephen Thomas Erlewine*

Eldorado / 1989 / Reprise ♦♦♦
When this five-song, 25-minute EP was released in Japan in 1989, it served notice that Neil Young was capable of writing powerful songs and playing fierce rock 'n' roll again, a fact confirmed by the subsequent release of the *Freedom* album. Three of the songs on *Eldorado* turned up on that record ("Don't Cry" in a different version), but "Cocaine Eyes" and "Heavy Love" did not, making this disc a necessary purchase for Young completists. *— William Ruhlmann*

Freedom / Oct. 1989 / Reprise ♦♦♦♦
Neil Young is famous for scrapping completed albums and substituting hastily recorded ones in radically different styles. *Freedom,* which was a major critical and commercial comeback after a decade that had confused reviewers and fans, seemed to be a selection of the best tracks from several different unissued Young projects. First and foremost it was a hard-rock album like the material heard on Young's recent EP *Eldorado* (released only in the Far East), several of whose tracks were repeated on *Freedom.* On these songs—especially "Don't Cry," which sounded like a song about divorce, and a cover of the old Drifters hit "On Broadway" that he concluded by raving about crack—Young played dis-

torted electric guitar over a rhythm section in an even more rau-cous fashion than that heard on his Crazy Horse records. Second was a followup to Young's previous album, *This Note's for You,* which had featured a six-piece horn section. They were back on "Crime in the City" and "Someday," though these lengthy songs, each of which contained a series of seemingly unrelated, mood-setting verses, were more reminiscent of songs like Bob Dylan's "All Along the Watchtower" than of the soul standards that inspired the earlier album. Third, there were tracks that harked back to acoustic-based, country-tinged albums like *Harvest* and *Comes a Time,* including "Hangin' on a Limb" and "The Ways of Love," two songs on which Young duetted with Linda Ronstadt. There was even a trunk (or, more precisely, a drunk) song, "Too Far Gone," which dated from Young's inebriated *Stars 'n' Bars* period in the '70s. While one might argue that this variety meant few Young fans would be completely pleased with the album, what made it all work was that Young had once again written a great bunch of songs. The romantic numbers were carefully and sincerely written. The long imagistic songs were evocative with-out being obvious. And bookending the album were acoustic and electric versions of one of Young's great anthems, "Rockin' in the Free World," a song that went a long way toward restoring his political reputation (which had been badly damaged when he praised President Reagan's foreign policy) by taking on hopeless-ness with a sense of moral outrage and explicitly condemning President Bush's domestic policy. *Freedom* was the album Neil Young fans knew he was capable of making but feared he would never make again. — *William Ruhlmann*

☆ **Ragged Glory** / Oct. 11, 1990 / Reprise ◆◆◆◆◆

Having re-established his reputation with the musically varied, lyri-cally enraged *Freedom,* Neil Young returned to being the lead gui-tarist of Crazy Horse for the musically homogenous, lyrically hope-ful *Ragged Glory.* The album's dominant sound was made by Young's noisy guitar, which bordered on and sometimes slipped over into distortion, while Crazy Horse kept up the songs' bright tempos. Despite the volume, the tunes were catchy, with strong melodies and good choruses, and they were given over to love, humor, and warm reminiscence. They were also platforms for often extended guitar excursions: "Love to Burn" and "Love and Only Love" ran over ten minutes each, and the album as a whole lasted nearly 63 minutes with only ten songs. Much about the record had a retrospective feel; the first two tracks, "Country Home" and "White Line," were newly recorded versions of songs Young had played with Crazy Horse but never released in the '70s. "Mansion on the Hill," the album's most accessible track, celebrated a place where "psychedelic music fills the air" and "peace and love live there still." There was a cover of the Premiers' garage rock oldie "Farmer John," and "Days That Used to Be," in addition to its back-ward-looking theme, borrowed the melody from Bob Dylan's "My Back Pages" (by way of the Byrds' arrangement). "Mother Earth (Natural Anthem)" was the folk standard "The Water Is Wide" with new, environmentally aware lyrics. Young was not generally known as an artist who evoked the past this much, but if he could extend his creative rebirth with music this exhilarating, no one was likely to complain. — *William Ruhlmann*

Weld / Oct. 1991 / Reprise ◆◆◆◆

Weld, Neil Young's two-hour-plus double-CD chronicle of his 1991 Ragged Glory/Smell the Horse Tour with Crazy Horse, was received with only mild enthusiasm from Young's fans and rock critics, perhaps because it seemed redundant. Such warhorses as "Like a Hurricane" and "Cortez the Killer" were making their fourth appearances on a Young album, and the five songs from the *Ragged Glory* album were basically unchanged from their stu-dio versions. Containing only 16 tracks, the album's songs aver-aged over seven and a half minutes in length, and that length was given over to extended guitar improvisations, which often were filled with feedback and distortion. Where Young's previous dou-ble live album, *Live Rust,* which bore some similarities to this one, was a career retrospective including some acoustic numbers, *Weld* was all electric rock with Crazy Horse. The one previously unreleased song was a Gulf War-era cover of Bob Dylan's "Blowin' in the Wind," complete with gunshots and exploding bombs. In

retrospect, *Weld* seems like an excellent expression of one part of Young's musical persona, putting some of his best hard rock material onto one album. (Initially, *Weld* was released in a 25,000 copy limited edition called *Arc Weld* [Reprise 26746] containing a third disc made up of guitar feedback and called *Arc*.) — *William Ruhlmann*

Harvest Moon / Oct. 27, 1992 / Reprise ◆◆◆

After 20 years, Neil Young finally decided to release the sequel to *Harvest,* his most commercially successful album. *Harvest Moon* is a better album, lacking the orchestral bombast that stifled some of the songs on the first album and boasting a stronger overall selection of songs. *Harvest Moon* manages to be sentimental without being sappy, wistful without being nostalgic. The lovely "Unknown Legend," "From Hank to Hendrix" and the beautiful "Harvest Moon" are among Young's best songs. Only the overlong (11 minutes) and oversimplified "Natural Beauty" hurts a beauti-ful album that proudly displays scars, heartaches, and love. — *Stephen Thomas Erlewine*

Lucky Thirteen / 1993 / Geffen ◆◆◆

Geffen Records seems to have intended a straightforward "best of" compilation containing the singles released from Neil Young's five albums with the label between 1982 and 1987. Then Young himself became involved, and his version of a Geffen sampler naturally turned out to be more unusual. There were four songs never before released on a Young album: "Depression Blues" had been recorded for the first, rejected version of the countryish *Old Ways;* "Get Gone" (a soundalike to "Willie and the Hand Jive") and the bluesy "Don't Take Your Love Away from Me" were live recordings with the "Shocking Pinks" rockabilly band that made *Everybody's Rockin';* and "Ain't It the Truth" was a live recording from the Bluenotes tour that came just as Young was leaving Gef-fen. There were also an alternate version of "Sample and Hold" from *Trans* that ran an extra few minutes and a live take of "This Note's from You," the title song from Young's 1988 return to Reprise Records. None of these was revelatory, and Young's choices from the albums *Trans, Old Ways, Landing on Water,* and *Life* (there was nothing from *Everybody's Rockin'*) were not the best he could have made. (Among the missing: "Little Thing Called Love," "Like an Inca," "Get Back to the Country," "Are There Any More Real Cowboys?," "Weight of the World," "Inca Queen," and "Long Walk Home.") Given that Young veered wildly from synth-pop to rockabilly to country to rock during this period, assembling a coherent compilation was something of a challenge, and Young didn't even try, just picking his favorites and sequenc-ing them chronologically. There were some interesting songs here, to be sure, notably "Hippie Dream" (which ran an extra 15 seconds in this version) and "Mideast Vacation," but this sum-ming-up of Young's least impressive, most bizarre era, instead of rehabilitating that era, was itself bizarre and unimpressive. (*Lucky Thirteen* was Neil Young's first album since his debut not to reach the charts.) — *William Ruhlmann*

Unplugged / Jun. 15, 1993 / Reprise ◆◆◆◆

Like Paul McCartney's, Neil Young's *Unplugged* seems to be an attempt to thwart bootleggers by releasing the material before they get a chance. Young's album doesn't offer any revela-tions—it's just a solid, thoroughly enjoyable concert. Acoustic per-formances of "Mr. Soul," "World on a String," "Like a Hurricane," and especially the synthesized "Transformer Man" are essential for the serious Young collector. Fans of *Harvest, After the Gold Rush, Comes a Time,* and *Harvest Moon* will find that *this* is the live Neil Young they need in their collection; hardcore fans will realize that this is the acoustic equivalent of the stunning *Weld.* — *Stephen Thomas Erlewine*

Sleeps with Angels / Aug. 16, 1994 / Reprise ◆◆◆◆

Reportedly spurred by the death of Kurt Cobain (who quoted Young's line, "It's better to burn out than to fade away," in his sui-cide note), Young turns in an unusually low-key, elegiac effort, its songs worrying about depression, lack of communication, and drive-by shootings, its music (despite the presence of Crazy Horse) slow and meditative (except for the funny change-of-pace rocker "Piece of Crap"). The result is not as gloomy as *Tonight's the Night* (in which Young seemed past the point of caring and even managed a certain gallows humor), but it's extremely mournful, with only glimmers of hope. — *William Ruhlmann*

Mirror Ball / 1995 / Reprise ✦✦✦
Knocked out in about two weeks, Neil Young's collaboration with Pearl Jam is considerably different than *Sleeps with Angels;* the record sounds like a spiritual rebirth after its bleaker predecessor. Playing with the Seattle band has reinvigorated Young. In fact, it has reinvigorated him so much that he hasn't spent much time on the songs, preferring to let the music carry the record. Pearl Jam's grooves are more elastic than Crazy Horse, but new drummer Jack Irons reins in the group's tendency to meander, as does Young himself, who dominates the proceedings with his jerky, wailing guitar. A couple of stray, minute-long organ-and-voice fragments from the *Sleeps with Angels* album punctuate the second side, but the album isn't contemplative—it barrels ahead. —*Stephen Thomas Erlewine*

Dead Man / Feb. 27, 1996 / Vapor ✦✦
Even within the unpredictable Neil Young discography, this qualifies as one of his most unpredictable efforts. This soundtrack to the Jim Jarmusch film *Dead Man* is entirely instrumental, with the exception of some poetry read by Johnny Depp (who stars in the film) and a bit of dialogue. What's more, these untitled instrumental passages are dominated by subterranean guitar rumbles that manage to sound both grungy and subdued. Young also takes care to vary his approach a bit, switching occasionally to pump organ, detuned piano, and acoustic guitar. The results not only evoke the hostile, desolate landscapes of the film's Old West, but work on their own terms as ambient mood music for the non-new age crowd, creating an atmosphere of restless disturbance with subtlety and grace. It's not necessarily for the typical Neil Young fan (whoever that might be), but it's certainly one of his most successful experimental efforts. —*Richie Unterberger*

Broken Arrow / Jul. 2, 1996 / Reprise ✦✦✦
In many ways *Broken Arrow* follows the same path as Neil Young's other '90s albums with Crazy Horse. *Broken Arrow* floats on waves of lumbering guitars and cascading feedback, ebbing and flowing with winding solos and drifting melodies. In a typical display of artistic perversion, Young has front-loaded the album with three epics with a combined running time of just over 25 minutes. Following the three epic-length songs come four concise tunes that range from the country-rock stomp of "Changing Highways" to the reflective "Music Arcade." Like the three songs that preceded them, these are uneven, with hazy melodies and underdeveloped lyrics. Finally, a long live workout of Jimmy Reed's "Baby What You Want Me to Do"—which sounds as if it was taken from an audience recording—is tacked on to the end of the album. Although the song is a standout, it raises the question: What is the purpose of *Broken Arrow*? The album floats from song to song, with the guitars drowning out the sound of Young's voice. There are some fine songs buried amidst the long jams, but the album is directionless, and that lack of direction never manages to develop a consistent emotional tone. — *Stephen Thomas Erlewine*

Steve Young

b. Jul. 12, 1942, Newnan, GA
Guitar, Vocals / Progressive Country, Contemporary Country, Outlaw Country
A singer, tunesmith, and purveyor of what he dubbed "Southern music"—a brew of country, folk, rock, blues, gospel, and Celtic styles—Steve Young was a songwriter's songwriter, an acclaimed performer whose work found its greatest commercial success in the hands of other artists. Born in Alabama and raised throughout the South, by his teens Young was an established musician. In the early 1960s he moved to New York City and became affiliated with the burgeoning Greenwich Village folk music scene. After a brief return to Alabama, he settled in California in 1964. On the West Coast Young found work as a postal carrier while striking up friendships with the likes of Stephen Stills and Van Dyke Parks. A tenure with the psychedelic folk unit Stone Country yielded an eponymous 1968 LP, and a year later Young issued his solo debut *Rock Salt and Nails*, a country-rock excursion featuring cameos by Gram Parsons, Chris Hillman, and Gene Clark.

With the title track of 1971's *Seven Bridges Road*, he offered perhaps his best-known composition, popularized through a series of covers by artists like the Eagles, Joan Baez, Rita Coolidge, and Iain Matthews. He remained a prolific artist throughout the decade, releasing albums like 1975's *Honky Tonk Man*, 1976's *Renegade Picker*, and 1978's *No Place to Fall.*

Despite his success as a songwriter—"Lonesome, Orn'ry and Mean" became Waylon Jennings signature tune, while Hank Williams Jr. notched a hit with "Montgomery in the Rain"—Young flirted with the charts but never rose beyond a devoted cult following. Along with releasing records like 1982's *To Satisfy You* and 1987's *Look Homeward Angel*, he spent the majority of the 1980s touring the world, garnering a reputation as a standout live performer. The trend continued into the next decade, and in 1991 he issued his first concert recording, *Solo/Live*, an acoustic collection summarizing his career to date and including pop and soul covers like "You Don't Miss Your Water" and "Drift Away." The LP *Switchblades of Love* followed two years later. —*Jason Ankeny*

Rock Salt and Nails / 1969 / Canyon ✦✦✦
A Japanese import worth looking for, it showcases Young's lonesome vocals on tunes by Hank Williams and Johnny Horton, plus memorable originals. It also features Gram Parsons, Chris Hillman, and Gene Clark. —*Hank Davis & Chip Renner*

Seven Bridges Road / 1972 / Rounder ✦✦✦
The title tune is this folkie's best work. —*Hank Davis*

Honky Tonk Man / 1975 / Rounder ✦✦✦✦
These early sides are surrounded by stellar, largely acoustic backing. A good album—a four-year layoff helped him hone his trade. —*Hank Davis and Chip Renner*

Renegade Picker / 1976 / RCA ✦✦✦✦
A very good album featuring Tracy Nelson, Johnny Gimble, and Buddy Emmons. Features his hit "Tobacco Road." —*Chip Renner*

No Place to Fall / 1977 / RCA ✦✦✦✦
Critically acclaimed album—this one and *Renegade Picker* were forerunners of the progressive country movement. —*Chip Renner*

To Satisfy You / 1981 / Rounder ✦✦✦✦
Here Steve Young interprets songs by Jesse Winchester, Cat Stevens, Buddy Holly, Jagger/Richards, Waylon Jennings, and others. —*Chip Renner*

Old Memories / 1984 / Country Roads ✦✦✦
Compilation of his two RCA albums. Good! —*Chip Renner*

Look Homeward Angel / 1986 / ✦✦✦
This was recorded in Scandinavia. Synthesizers give it a new sound. —*Chip Renner*

Long Time Rider / 1990 / Voodoo ✦✦✦
Steve Young's sound deepens somewhat with *Long Time Rider*, as he moves toward a low-key, introspective acoustic territory, occasionally adding keyboards to the music. Though the songwriting is somewhat uneven, the very best songs here, such as "War of Ancient Days," are among his best work. —*Thom Owens*

Steve Young Live / 1991 / Watermelon ✦✦✦
A good collection of Young's music. The sound is rich, and the audience is into the show. —*Chip Renner*

● **Solo/Live** / Mar. 1991 / Watermelon ✦✦✦✦
In all likelihood, there will never be a Steve Young greatest-hits collection—all of his chart success has come courtesy of other artists' renditions of his material. In any case, at least there's *Solo/Live*, an intimate acoustic collection that serves as a fine overview of Young's career and a good introduction to his talents. Recorded in 1990 at Houston's Anderson Fair, the record includes most of his best-loved songs, including "Seven Bridges Road," "Montgomery in the Rain," and "Long Way to Hollywood." In addition, there are covers of "You Don't Miss Your Water," "Tobacco Road," and "Drift Away," as well as the traditional sea chanty "Go to Sea No More." —*Jason Ankeny*

Switchblades of Love / 1993 / Watermelon ✦✦✦
Switchblades of Love is a typically strong effort from Young, highlighted by the title cut. Among the guests: Van Dyke Parks and the Heartbreakers' Benmont Tench. —*Jason Ankeny*

VARIOUS ARTISTS

200 Years of American Heritage in Song: 100 Song Collection / CMH ✦✦✦
Released in 1975 to coincide with the bicentennial celebration, *200 Years of American Heritage in Song: 100 Song Collection* is a collection of 100 folk and country songs that are intended to tell the story of America in song. The selection combines traditional songs like "The Building of America" and "Westward Migration" with newer songs like "The Yellow Rose of Texas" and "John Henry," which have already become standards. Supported by an informative 45-page booklet by Norm Cohen, the collection is terrific conceptually, but the execution is somewhat faulty. In particular, it's sunk by the performances, which are merely perfunctory and never quite gripping. Nevertheless, as an educational piece, *200 Years of American Heritage in Song* is useful, even if it isn't something that will become compulsive listening. —*Stephen Thomas Erlewine*

☆ **24 Greatest Bluegrass Hits** / CMH ✦✦✦✦✦
Here are the bluegrass greats, ranging from Bill Monroe to Flatt and Scruggs and the Osborne Brothers. —*David Vinopal*

● **25 Years of Studio B Hits** / 1982 / CMF ✦✦✦✦
This album features Waylon Jennings' "Honky Tonk Heroes," Dolly Parton's "The Seeker," and other hits recorded at the studio that saw the emergence of the Nashville Sound. —*AMG*

50 Years of Bluegrass Hits / 1992 / CMH ✦✦✦
Included are 28 tracks of Buddy Spicher and others performing old-time swing and bluegrass music. —*AMG*

50 Years of Bluegrass Hits, Vol. 2 / CMH ✦✦✦
Twenty-five tracks by Jim & Jesse, Lester Flatt, and others—over 60 minutes' worth of music. —*AMG*

American Cowboy Songs / New World ✦✦✦✦
Back in the Saddle Again: American Cowboy Songs is a 28-track collection that follows the history of cowboy music from 1925 to 1980. The album features a great majority of the legendary Western songs and cowboy performers, including Gene Autry, Sons of the Pioneers, Rex Allen, Harry Jackson, Patsy Montana, and Riders in the Sky. As far as introductions to Western music go, there are few albums better than *Back in the Saddle Again*. —*Thom Owens*

And the Answer Is: Great Country Answer Discs from the '50s and '60s, Vol. 1 / 1994 / Bear Family ✦✦✦✦
Bear Family's three-volume *And the Answer Is: Great Answer Discs from the '50s and '60s* series documents the phenomenon of answer records, presenting both the original hit and the response to the single. These were songs designed to respond to hit singles, with the hopes that the second record would climb up the charts as well. Answer records were prevalent in pop and R&B as well as country, but on *And the Answer Is: Vols. 1 & 3*, Bear Family concentrates on country records. At their best, answer records became classics of their own—Kitty Wells' "It Wasn't God Who Made Honky Tonk Angels," her response to Hank Thompson's "Wild Side of Life," arguably became even more famous than the record it was answering—but most of the singles were simply novelties. Consequently, the music here is for fetishists and collectors—after all, the average fan doesn't need to hear Jim Reeves' "Mexican Joe" followed by Carolyn Bradshaw's "The Mar-

riage of Mexican Joe"—but for any country or pop music fan with an interest in the arcane and unusual, *And the Answer Is* is a very enjoyable series. Highlights of *Vol. 1* include Webb Pierce's "There Stands the Glass" / Betty Cody's "Please Throw Away the Glass," Hank Thompson's "Yesterday's Girl" / Goldie Hill's "I'm Yesterday's Girl," Skeets McDonald's "Don't Let the Stars Get in Your Eyes" / Goldie Hill's "I Let the Stars Get in My Eyes," Hank Williams' "Jambalaya" / Goldie Hill's "I'm Yvonne (From the Bayou)," and Hank Locklin's "Geisha Girl" / Skeeter Davis' "Lost to a Geisha Girl." —*Stephen Thomas Erlewine*

And the Answer Is: Great Pop Answer Discs from the '50s and '60s, Vol. 2 / 1995 / Bear Family ✦✦✦✦
Bear Family's three-volume *And the Answer Is: Great Answer Discs from the '50s and '60s* series documents the phenomenon of answer records, presenting both the original hit and the response to the single. These were songs designed to respond to hit singles, with the hopes that the second record would climb up the charts as well. Answer records were prevalent in country, pop, and R&B, but on *And the Answer Is: Vol. 2*, Bear Family concentrates on pop-rock records from the '60s. Pop-rock answer records never produced a classic on the level of Kitty Wells' "It Wasn't God Who Made Honky Tonk Angels," her response to Hank Thompson's "Wild Side of Life." Instead, most pop responses were simply novelties, which means *And the Answer Is: Great Answer Discs from the 50s and '60s, Vol. 2* is designed for fetishists and collectors with a taste for the arcane and unusual. Anyone who has a passing interest in the bizarre side roads of pop music will find the compilation very entertaining. Highlights of *Vol. 2* include Marcie Blane's "Bobby's Girl" / the Sherry Sisters' "Stay Away from Bobby," Jack Scott's "Burning Bridges" / Bobbie Jean's "You Burned the Bridges," Ray Peterson's "Tell Laura I Love Her" / Marilyn Michaels' "Tell Tommy I Need Him," Bobby Vee's "Please Don't Ask About Barbara" / Mike Regal's "Is It True What They Say About Barbara," Pat Boone's "Are You Lonesome Tonight" / Thelma Carpenter's "Yes, I'm Lonesome Tonight," and Barry Mann's "Who Put the Bomp" / Frankie Lymon's "I Put the Bomp." —*Stephen Thomas Erlewine*

And the Answer Is: Great Country Answer Discs from the '50s and '60s, Vol. 3 / 1994 / Bear Family ✦✦✦✦
Bear Family's three-volume *And the Answer Is: Great Answer Discs from the '50s and '60s* series documents the phenomenon of answer records, presenting both the original hit and the response to the single. These were songs designed to respond to hit singles, with the hopes that the second record would climb up the charts as well. Answer records were prevalent in pop and R&B as well as country, but on *And the Answer Is: Vols. 1 & 3*, Bear Family concentrates on country records. At their best, answer records became classics of their own but most of the singles were simply novelties. Consequently, the music here is for fetishists and collectors, but for any country or pop music fan with an interest in the arcane and unusual, *And the Answer Is* is a very enjoyable series. Highlights of *Vol. 3* include Johnny Cash's "Ballad of a Teenage Queen" / Tommy Tucker's "Return of the Teenage Queen," Jim Reeves' "He'll Have to Go" / Jeannie Black's "He'll Have to Stay," David Houston's "Almost Persuaded" / Donna Harris' "(He Was) Almost Persuaded," Kenny Rogers' "Ruby, Don't

Take Your Love to Town" / Geraldine Stevens' "Billy, I've Got to Go to Town," Hank Locklin's "Please Help Me, I'm Falling" / Skeeter Davis' "(I Can't Help You) I'm Fallin' Too," and Billy Walker's "Charlie Shoes" / Jonie Mosby & Johnny's "The Answer to 'Charlie's Shoes.'" —*Stephen Thomas Erlewine*

Anthology of Country Music: Early Country Harmony 1930s / ACM ✦✦✦✦

If you're talking close country harmony, the 1930s were a golden era, particularly as many of the country harmony acts were family or brother acts that had honed their skills over decades. This is an outstanding 20-cut compilation of rare vintage recordings, with two cuts apiece from famous artists (the Delmore Brothers, the Monroe Brothers, the Blue Sky Boys, the Dixon Brothers) and less celebrated ones (the Crowder Brothers, Karl and Harty, Lulu Belle and Scotty). Male (usually brother) acts were more heavily recorded than female harmonizers, so it's especially interesting to hear some women singers on this LP, such as the Girls of the Golden West. Country music doesn't get more down-home or heartfelt than this. The LP and its companion volume (which covers the 1940s) are now hard to find, but any serious country fan will want to locate them. The sound isn't quite state-of-the-art (likely it was dubbed from rare original copies), but it is quite listenable. —*Richie Unterberger*

Anthology of Country Music: Early Country Harmony 1940s / ACM ✦✦✦✦

Twenty rare gems of early country harmony, including selections from the Blue Sky Boys, the Louvin Brothers ("I Love God's Way of Living" is a stone classic), Johnny & Jack, the Carlisle Brothers, and names that are primarily known only to country scholars, like Molly O'Day & Lynn Davis, James & Martha, and Carl Butler. Four of the tracks were previously unissued, including a radio duet between Hank Williams & Little Jimmy Dickens. This is country music just down from the mountains, with a spiritual quality in both the gospel tunes and the secular ones. The only factors preventing this LP (and its companion volume covering the 1930s) from getting a five-star rating are the imperfect transfers from original copies (although the sound quality's fairly good), and the total lack of liner notes. Otherwise, they should be considered essential to any comprehensive collection of early country music. —*Richie Unterberger*

Are You from Dixie?: Great Country Brother Teams of the 1930s / 1988 / RCA ✦✦✦

The title is truth in advertising. Excellent sides and spellbinding harmony vocals from the Delmore Brothers, the Monroe Brothers, the Blue Sky Boys, the Dixon Brothers, the Allen Brothers, and the Lone Star Cowboys. —*Richie Unterberger*

Best of Austin City Limits: Country Music's Finest Hour / 1996 / Columbia/Legacy ✦✦✦

From its inception in the mid-'70s until the late '90s, *Austin City Limits* was the premier country music television show in America. What distinguished the show from its competition was its emphasis on performance–each show spotlighted one or two showcase artists, plus various guest artists, who were allowed to play whatever they wanted. The result was a freewheeling, eclectic, and passionate music show unlike any other. *The Best of Austin City Limits: Country Music's Finest Hour* collects 16 highlights from the show's long, illustrious history and, as expected, some of the biggest names in country music are involved. From Merle Haggard ("Silver Wings," 1978) and George Jones ("He Stopped Loving Her Today," 1985) to Asleep at the Wheel ("Boogie Back to Texas," 1987) and Alison Krauss ("Baby, Now That I've Found You," 1995), the album has a wide selection of first-rate artists and stellar performances that hint at the rich legacy of the show. In fact, if there's anything wrong with the disc, is the fact that it feels incomplete, even though it includes such luminaries as Willie Nelson, Tammy Wynette, Waylon Jennings, k.d. lang, Mary Chapin Carpenter, Dwight Yoakam, the Mavericks, the Judds, Charlie Daniels, and Patty Loveless. There's no fault with any of these selections, indeed, but after the disc is finished, you're waiting for the sequel. —*Thom Owens*

Best of Bluegrass / K-Tel ✦✦✦

Here are ten bluegrass classics performed by the legends who originally recorded them, such as Bill Monroe, the Country Gentlemen, the Osborne Brothers, Mac Wiseman, Lester Flatt & Earl Scruggs, and others. —*AMG*

☆ Best of Bluegrass, Vol. 1 / PolyGram ✦✦✦✦✦

The Best of Bluegrass, Vol. 1 is an excellent 22-track sampler of the genre, containing the majority of the most famous songs in bluegrass, including the Country Gentlemen's "Can't You Hear Me Calling?," the Lonesome Pine Fiddlers' "Blue Moon of Kentucky," Flatt & Scruggs' "Roll in My Sweet Baby's Arms" and "Foggy Mountain Breakdown," and the original version of "Duelin' Banjos," which appeared under the title "Feudin' Banjos" by Arthur Smith and Don Reno. As a one-stop introduction, it's hard to beat this collection. —*Stephen Thomas Erlewine*

The Beverly Hillbillies [TV Soundtrack] / 1993 / Columbia/Legacy ✦✦

The *Beverly Hillbillies* television series, which ran from 1962 to 1971, was a situation comedy, not a musical show, notwithstanding its famous Flatt & Scruggs theme song. Nevertheless, after three years on the air, the show spun off this album, in which members of the cast, prominently featuring Buddy Ebsen and Irene Ryan, sang songs based on their characters. The result is a novelty with a vengeance. Ebsen, a former musical comedy star, comes off fine, but even fans of the show may not be ready to hear Max Baer sing out about the foibles of life in Beverly Hills. Long out of print, the album was released on CD in 1993 in anticipation of the movie version of the show. —*William Ruhlmann*

Billboard Top Country Hits: 1959 / 1990 / Rhino ✦✦✦✦

Each volume of this series contains the Top Ten country hits of that year. This volume contains Johnny Cash's "Don't Take Your Love to Town," George Jones' "White Lightning," Johnny Horton's "The Battle of New Orleans," and more. —*AMG*

Billboard Top Country Hits: 1960 / 1990 / Rhino ✦✦✦✦

This features Jim Reeves' "He'll Have to Go," Marty Robbins' "El Paso," Hank Locklin's "Please Help Me, I'm Falling," and other hits. —*AMG*

Billboard Top Country Hits: 1961 / 1990 / Rhino ✦✦✦✦

This features Patsy Cline's "I Fall to Pieces," Jimmy Dean's "Big Bad John," and other Top Ten hits from 1961. —*AMG*

Billboard Top Country Hits: 1962 / 1990 / Rhino ✦✦✦✦

Featuring Patsy Cline's "She's Got You," Hank Snow's "I've Been Everywhere," Claude King's "Wolverton Mountain," and other top hits from 1962. —*AMG*

Billboard Top Country Hits: 1963 / 1990 / Rhino ✦✦✦✦

Included are Johnny Cash's "Ring of Fire," Buck Owens' "Act Naturally," and Ned Miller's "From a Jack to a King," among other early-'60s favorites. —*AMG*

Billboard Top Country Hits: 1964 / 1990 / Rhino ✦✦✦✦

This volume in the series contains George Jones' "The Race Is On" and Roger Miller's "Dang Me," among other hits. —*AMG*

Billboard Top Country Hits: 1965 / 1990 / Rhino ✦✦✦✦

Featured are Eddy Arnold's "Make the World Go Away" and Roger Miller's "King of the Road." —*AMG*

Billboard Top Country Hits: 1966 / 1990 / Rhino ✦✦✦✦

This volume includes David Houston's "Almost Persuaded," Loretta Lynn's "You Ain't Woman Enough," and Jack Greene's "There Goes My Everything." —*AMG*

Billboard Top Country Hits: 1967 / 1990 / Rhino ✦✦✦✦

This includes David Houston and Tammy Wynette's duet "My Elusive Dream" and Wynn Stewart's "It's Such a Pretty World." —*AMG*

Billboard Top Country Hits: 1968 / 1990 / Rhino ✦✦✦✦

This volume contains such hits from 1968 as Merle Haggard's "Mama Tried," Tammy Wynette's "Stand by Your Man," Jeanne C. Riley's "Harper Valley PTA," and Johnny Cash's "Folsom Prison Blues." —*AMG*

Billboard Top Country Hits: 1986 / 1986 / Rhino ✦✦✦✦

Rhino's most recent set of *Billboard* country anthologies begins with 1986 and shows through its lineup just how much things have changed since then in country circles. Ricky Skaggs, John Conlee, Lee Greenwood, T.G. Sheppard, and T. Graham Brown are not exactly factors in the 1990s, while Exile is hanging on for dear life. Both Tanya Tucker and Dan Seals have seen better days. Only Hank Williams, Jr. and Steve Wariner currently matter, and Wariner is doing better tunes now than "Life's Highway." *—Ron Wynn*

Billboard Top Country Hits: 1987 / 1987 / Rhino ✦✦✦✦
The 1990s have seen country continue to evolve, and the second volume in Rhino's latest anthology line demonstrates the changes once more. There are cuts from the Forester Sisters, O'Kanes (defunct), Highway 101 (now with a new lead vocalist), and hold-overs Hank Williams, Jr. and Steve Wariner. But the compilation also begins with Randy Travis' superb "Forever and Ever, Amen" and includes Rosanne Cash's sublime "This Is the Way We Make a Broken Heart." These compensate for another Exile song. *—Ron Wynn*

Billboard Top Country Hits: 1988 / 1988 / Rhino ✦✦✦✦
The third volume in Rhino's latest country series towers over the previous two, reflecting both improved songwriting and a higher performance level. Although Earl Thomas Conley's "What I'd Say" dips slightly, such songs as "Streets of Bakersfield" from the duo of Dwight Yoakam and Buck Owens, Keith Whitley's "When You Say Nothing at All," and Randy Travis' "I Told You So" and "Set 'Em Up Joe" are fabulous cuts, as is Tanya Tucker's "Strong Enough to Bend" and Highway 101's "Cry, Cry, Cry." *—Ron Wynn*

Billboard Top Country Hits: 1989 / 1989 / Rhino ✦✦✦✦
While country ranks as the number one radio format and is arguably the nation's most popular adult form, Rhino's anthology series of No. 1 hits certainly provides ample food for thought regarding what types of songs have been genuine hits: Eddie Rabbitt, Shenandoah, and Eddy Raven had No. 1 hits in 1989. The disc's saving grace comes from Patty Loveless, Randy Travis, Keith Whitley, Highway 101, and Steve Wariner, and is filled out by Ronnie Milsap and a decent Dolly Parton cut. *—Ron Wynn*

Billboard Top Country Hits: 1990 / 1990 / Rhino ✦✦✦✦
The fifth and final volume in the latest Rhino country anthology line concludes things in 1990. Once more, many of the No. 1s offer reason to stop and ponder the condition of contemporary country radio. Shenandoah, Paul Overstreet, Dan Seals, and Mike Reid are not bad, but all of them are as close to MOR and folk as country. Randy Travis, Patty Loveless, and Holly Dunn also scored No. 1 hits, as did Lorrie Morgan. Joe Diffie is a lot closer to country than many of these acts, and Alabama is almost hardcore honky-tonk next to Shenandoah. *—Ron Wynn*

Bluegrass Album / 1982 / Rounder ✦✦✦
The Bluegrass Album demonstrates the depth and richness of bluegrass, thanks to the talents of the musicians involved. Tony Rice, Doyle Lawson, J.D. Crowe, Bobby Hicks, and Todd Phillips play traditional bluegrass with a passion and invention that has rarely been matched; they also bring a gritty rootsiness to progressive numbers that keeps the songs from sinking into pretension. The result is one of the most compulsively listenable bluegrass albums not only of the '80s, but of the genre's entire history. *—Thom Owens*

Bluegrass Breakdown / 1992 / Vanguard ✦✦✦
This album, which features the work of such artists as Bill Monroe, the Stanley Brothers, the Dillards, and the Greenbriar Boys, was recorded at the Newport Folk Festival in 1963-1965. *—AMG*

Bluegrass Class of 1990 / 1990 / Rounder ✦✦✦
An excellent sampler, featuring Ricky Skaggs, Tony Rice, Alison Krauss, Lynn Morris, Sam Bush, and J. D. Crowe. *—Chip Renner*

Bluegrass Masters / 1996 / Vanguard ✦✦✦✦
The title doesn't lie—this disc has 21 tracks by three of the best acts in the field (Bill Monroe, Flatt & Scruggs, and Jim & Jesse McReynolds), recorded live at the 1965 and 1966 Newport Folk Festivals. The sound and performances are good, and each act presents some familiar favorites—the McReynolds offer "Dueling Banjos" and "Sugarfoot Rag," Monroe does "Shady Grove" and "Cotton-Eyed Joe," and Flatt & Scruggs play "Orange Blossom Special," "Foggy Mountain Chimes," and "The Ballad of Jed Clam-

pett." A youthful Peter Rowan, then a guitarist with Monroe, does a duet vocal with the bandleader on "Walls of Time." *—Richie Unterberger*

Bluegrass at Newport / Vanguard ✦✦✦✦
A gem of a CD featuring Flatt & Scruggs, Jim & Jesse, Mac Wiseman, Doc Watson, and the New Lost City Ramblers. *—Chip Renner*

Bonanza: Ponderosa Party Time! / 1962-1966 / Bear Family ✦✦✦✦
Under ordinary circumstances, the cast of *Bonanza* would not be listed in a country music guide, but Bear Family Records of Germany has made the matter academic by rereleasing the albums that they recorded in the early 1960s. Based loosely on the history of Virginia City, NV, and the aftermath of the nearby "Bonanza" silver strike, *Bonanza* was the quintessential epic Western television series. It told the story of the Cartwright family, led by patriarch Ben Cartwright (Lorne Greene), who had sired three sons by different wives—introspective, intellectual Adam (Pernell Roberts), hulking, good-natured Hoss (Dan Blocker), and volatile, handsome Little Joe (Michael Landon). Their adventures on their ranch, the Ponderosa, kept audiences glued to their sets and kept the series in the Top Ten programs on the air for 13 seasons, ending only with the sudden death of Blocker in 1972 and the NBC network's decision to move the show out of the Sunday night time slot where it had been unbeatable for more than a decade.

When *Bonanza* went on the air in 1959, it was common practice in the entertainment industry to get movie stars and the leading actors of major hit series to expand into other areas, especially music recording. This resulted in some genuine embarrassments (those William Shatner albums), a few interesting '60s artifacts (those Richard Harris/Jimmy Webb collaborative efforts), and a handful of genuine pop successes. Lorne Greene had more than his share of those. A Canadian native, he'd virtually created the whole notion of education in broadcasting in his own country, as well as being the "Voice of Canada" during World War II, when he'd broadcast the war news nightly for the Canadian Broadcasting Corporation, and became the only Canadian ever to win the NBC broadcasting award. Greene had come to Hollywood in the mid-1950s after a handful of successful performances on Broadway, and he was spotted by producer David Dortort while playing a role in the series *Wagon Train*, and picked for the part of Ben Cartwright in *Bonanza*.

With his warm persona and commanding voice and manner, Greene became one of the most popular actors on television during the 1960s, and something of a model father in the popular culture of the day. He began his recording career in the early 1960s on the RCA-Victor label, first with the cast of *Bonanza* in a couple of albums of old-style Western songs featuring the whole cast, and then with four more albums (*The Man, Portrait of the West, American West, Welcome to the Ponderosa*), and in 1964 had a No. 1 hit single with the song "Ringo," the story of an outlaw saved from death and brought back to health by a sheriff, who later had to gun him down. Essentially, Greene didn't "sing," but talked these songs in the manner of Rex Harrison, but his voice was resonant enough that the public loved it, and RCA kept recording him. (Greene made a major career out of personal appearances before conventions, sports gatherings, and other public events, in which he would do a song or two, give an inspirational talk about the West or patriotism, and close with a devotional piece.)

Pernell Roberts, born in Waycross, GA (the same hometown as Gram Parsons), had started a successful career on Broadway when he went to Hollywood. After a few film appearances in ever larger roles, he was picked for the role of Adam Cartwright. A perfectionist by nature, with a background in Shakespearean parts, he resented the glaring simplicity of the scripts he was given in *Bonanza* and left the series in the mid-1960s, but not before he recorded an album of folk songs. His *Come All Ye Fair and Tender Ladies* is a decent folk album, using mostly traditional or traditional-sounding material—he isn't the best singer in the world, but at the time neither were too many other people trying to make it with this music.

Dan Blocker, born in Texas, was a giant of a man, six foot four and 250 pounds. A one-time doctoral candidate in education and a Korean War veteran, Blocker came to theater by accident—with his great strength and stamina, he was needed by the drama club in his college to clear the "bodies" offstage for the denouement in *Arsenic and Old Lace*—but came to love it, and eventually he had most of his college's football team trying for theatrical roles. His size made him ideal to play villains, but producer David Dortort, spotting him in such a role in the series *The Restless Gun*, saw a gentleness in Blocker that he felt could be brought out on the screen, and gave him the part of Hoss Cartwright. Always popular on the series, Blocker became a major television star and moved into film acting in pictures such as the Frank Sinatra detective thriller *Lady in Cement* and, in his best part, *Something for a Lonely Man*, a serious Western. He died in 1972 from complications following routine surgery. Blocker's album *Our Heritage*, recorded with singer/actor John Mitchum, was an interesting story-and-song celebration of American history, with Blocker telling the stories and Mitchum singing. The perspective is doubly fascinating because Blocker was an unabashed liberal Democrat, a supporter of Robert Kennedy and other liberal and progressive political figures, yet he did this album with the kind of fervor one might've expected from John Wayne. If more liberals could've made the stretch as far as the symbolism, their ideology might've fared better over the ensuing 20-odd years. —*Bruce Eder*

☆ **The Bristol Sessions** / 1991 / Country Music Foundation ✦✦✦✦✦
It's common knowledge that Ralph Peer's open recording session in Bristol, TN, launched the careers of the Carter Family and Jimmie Rodgers, but as this double CD proves, they weren't the only worthwhile musicians to turn up. In fact, Peer recorded 21 other acts, including the Stoneman Family and Blind Alfred Reed in what turns out to be an amazing display of rural talent and the birth of country music. —*William Ruhlmann*

Cat'n Around / Krazy Kat ✦✦✦
Cat'n Around compiles a selection of country-boogie, proto-rockabilly, and honky tonk tracks recorded for the Houston-based Macy record label between 1949-1951. Featuring such artists as Bob Greene, Harry Choates, Ray Welch, Morris Mills, and Clint Small, *Cat'n Around* doesn't have a lot of big names, but it is filled with wonderful obscurities, making it an excellent purchase for hardcore honky tonk and hillbilly fans. —*Thom Owens*

Cattle Call: Early Cowboy Music and Its Roots / 1996 / Rounder ✦✦✦✦
The first of a four-volume history of cowboy music, this collection of 14 songs from 1925-60 was compiled with an eye for illustrating the roots of the style, as heard in songs from sources that date before the commercialization of the form. It covers a fair amount of territory, including stars like Jimmie Rodgers, Tex Ritter, Tex Owens, and the Sons of the Pioneers; early women performers in the style, Patsy Montana and the Girls of the Golden West; early cowboy film singers Ken Maynard and Ray Whitley; and even the Mexican sounds of Trio Los Pancho. Like the entire series, each track is annotated with thorough notes about the history of the songs and the performers. —*Richie Unterberger*

Classic Country Music, Vol. 2 / Smithsonian ✦✦✦✦
Classic Country Music, Vol. 2 has a good cross-section of honky tonk, cowboy, and traditional country cuts from the '50s, including tracks from Hank Williams, Kitty Wells, Webb Pierce, Al Dexter, Moon Mullican, Gene Autry, Hank Thompson, Floyd Tillman, and Lefty Frizzell. —*Thom Owens*

Classic Country Music: A Smithsonian Collection / 1991 / Smithsonian ✦✦✦✦

Classic Jamie Masters / 1995 / Bear Family ✦✦✦✦
The double-disc set *Classic Jamie Masters* contains a selection of highlights from the Jamie vaults, boasting 60 tracks from the late '50s and early '60s. Jamie didn't really have a signature sound, which means that *Classic Jamie Masters* is all over the place in terms of sound and style, flipping between rock 'n' roll, country, pop, and R&B in the blink of an eye. Furthermore, the set doesn't

contain many hit singles. While there are a number of famous names, only two of them—Duane Eddy and Barbara Lynn—are represented by big hits. Nevertheless, the set is quite entertaining, especially for listeners who are looking for rarities, obscurities, and arcane items from big names. *Classic Jamie Masters* contains tracks by Duane Eddy ("Rebel Rouser," "Because They're Young," "40 Miles of Bad Road"), Barbara Lynn ("You'll Lose a Good Thing," "(I Cried At) Laura's Wedding"), Titus Turner ("Sound Off"), Barbara Mason ("Yes I'm Ready"), Bruce Channel ("Going Back to Louisiana"), Johnny Rivers ("Hole in the Ground"), Mac Davis ("I'm a Poor Loser"), Danny & the Juniors ("Oh-La-La Limbo"), Neil Sedaka ("Ring a Rockin"), Maureen Gray ("Dancing the Strand"), Lee Hazlewood ("Words Mean Nothing"), Sanford Clark ("Son of a Gun"), Harold Melvin & the Blue Notes ("Get Out"), and Barbara Mason ("Oh How It Hurts"). —*Stephen Thomas Erlewine*

Cliffie Stone's Radio Transcriptions 1945-49 / Country Routes ✦✦✦✦
Cliffie Stone's Radio Transcriptions 1945-49 contains 19 performances from several of the biggest names in country music in the late '40s. Stone was one of the best known and most popular record producers and radio hosts in California during that era, and was responsible for helping to promote many of the best performers on the West Coast during that time, as this compilation proves. *Radio Transcriptions* boasts an impressive array of styles and talents, ranging from the country-boogie of Tennessee Ernie Ford with Merle Travis and the hillbilly duets of the Armstrong Twins, to the swinging guitarist Red Murrell and the smooth croons of Jimmy Wakely. It's an entertaining and informative portrait of West Coast country in the postwar years, and many die-hard country fans will find it very worthwhile. —*Stephen Thomas Erlewine*

☆ **Columbia Country Classics, Vol. 1: Golden Age** / Columbia ✦✦✦✦✦
This five-volume set contains 128 of the greatest country music recordings in Columbia's vaults, which span the genre from its beginnings. Each volume (available separately or as a set) contains major country artists. This first volume contains 27 landmark recordings by the artists that made them famous, such as the late Roy Acuff's "Wabash Cannonball" and the Carter Family's "Will the Circle Be Unbroken"—16 artists in all. —*AMG*

☆ **Columbia Country Classics, Vol. 2: Honky Tonk Heroes** / 1984 / Columbia ✦✦✦✦✦
The second volume in the series contains 27 songs performed by Stonewall Jackson, Floyd Tillman, Lefty Frizzell, Marty Robbins, Carl Butler, Carl Smith, and Little Jimmy Dickens—13 performers in all. —*AMG*

Columbia Country Classics, Vol. 3: Americana / Columbia ✦✦✦✦
Included are 18 artists—top country musicians like Billy Walker, Willie Nelson, the Statler Brothers, Johnny Cash, Jimmy Dean, the Highwaymen, and Merle Haggard—on 25 tracks. —*AMG*

Columbia Country Classics, Vol. 4: Nashville Sound / Columbia ✦✦✦✦
The fourth volume in the series contains hits from Tammy Wynette, Charlie Rich, Johnny Cash, Johnny Paycheck, June Carter, George Jones, and others. —*AMG*

Columbia Country Classics, Vol. 5: New Tradition / 1988 / Columbia ✦✦✦
The final volume in the set contains music from both established artists and up-and-coming ones, like Larry Gatlin, Asleep at the Wheel, Willie Nelson, Sweethearts of the Rodeo, the O'Kanes, and more. —*AMG*

Come Together/America Salutes the Beatles / 1995 / Liberty ✦✦
Come Together: America Salutes the Beatles is a collection of contemporary country artists covering the Beatles. Instead of sounding like honky tonk reinterpretations of Merseybeat, most of the songs wind up sounding like Eagles songs. Occasionally, that can sound fine, but frequently the album sounds unfocused and

bland, appealing neither to country fans nor Beatles aficionados.
—*Stephen Thomas Erlewine*

Common Ground: Country Songs of Faith, Love & Inspiration / Oct. 17, 1995 / Sony ✦✦✦

Common Ground—Country Songs of Faith, Love & Inspiration combines older tracks by the likes of Ricky Skaggs, Shenandoah, and Doug Stone with newer recordings by Patty Loveless, Rick Trevino, and Ricky Van Shelton. All of the songs are polished contemporary country inspirational material, delivered with style and conviction. Though the music will be too slick for some tastes, fans of CCM and modern country will find this ten-song collection enjoyable. —*Thom Owens*

Common Thread: The Songs of the Eagles / 1994 / Warner Brothers ✦✦

In a benefit album for Don Henley's pet project, Walden Pond, a number of the biggest stars in contemporary country music came together to pay tribute to the influence the Eagles had on country and rock. Ironically, all of the interpretations on *Common Thread* are more pop-rock-oriented than the original versions, making the album a well-intentioned but pointless exercise. —*AMG*

Conmemorativo: A Tribute to Gram Parsons / 1993 / Rhino ✦✦✦✦

In his short recording career Gram Parsons attempted to bridge the gap between country and rock music. Arguably the founder of country-rock, Parson's timeless influence on music is undeniable, and that is perhaps why this tribute works so remarkably well. A diverse group of artists is included, with interpretations that range from reverent note-perfect readings, like the Musical Kings' (featuring Kevin Kinney and R.E.M.'s Peter Buck) version of the Flying Burrito Brothers' "Cody, Cody" to renditions that rework the songs, as in Finger's cover of "Still Feeling Blue," which takes straight honky tonk country and gives it a rockin' Rolling Stones' feel. And although he recorded a number of cover versions, every song on this tribute was either written or co-written by Gram. Every phase of his career is also represented in the 17 tracks: from his folkie days in the mid-'60s—"November Nights" (Coal Porters)—to his final recording session in 1973—"Return of the Grievous Angel" (Joey Burns and Victoria Williams). Noteworthy is the inclusion of Polly Parsons (Gram's daughter) & Eden performing "The New Soft Shoe." All in all, there really isn't a bad song here, and some of them are superb, such as Uncle Tupelo's "Blue Eyes," Steve Wynn's "Christine's Tune," and Stephen McCarthy's "One Hundred Years from Now." —*Jack Leaver*

Country All-Stars: Jazz from the Hills / 1994 / Bear Family ✦✦✦

Formed in the mid-'60s, the Country All-Stars is a supergroup comprised of in-demand Nashville session musicians. The group's *Jazz from the Hills* is an appropriately swinging set of country standards and original material. While the playing is tasteful and frequently engaging, it is a bit too slick for hardcore country fans, but fans of collegiate jazz and mainstream country-pop will find *Jazz from the Hills* entertaining. —*Thom Owens*

Country Music Classics, Vol. 1 (1950s) / 1990 / K-Tel ✦✦

How can you account for a whole decade on one disc? It's not easy, and K-Tel didn't quite do it. There are some classics on this disc, like Patsy Cline ("Walking After Midnight"), Kitty Wells ("It Wasn't God Who Made Honky Tonk Angels"), and Hank Williams ("Jambalaya"). Overall, this isn't a bad disc, it's just that it was too much time to cover on one disc. —*Jim Worbois*

Country Music Classics, Vol. 2 (1960-65) / K-Tel ✦✦

Solid, if somewhat short (ten tracks), compilation of country hits from the early '60s. This stuff still holds up very well after 30 years. Artists featured include Faron Young ("Hello Walls"), Patsy Cline ("I Fall to Pieces"), and Dave Dudley ("Six Days on the Road"). No surprises here. Just top country hits. —*Jim Worbois*

Country Music Classics, Vol. 3 (1965-70) / 1984 / K-Tel ✦✦

If you fondly remember country music before it went "uptown" in the '70s, this disc is one you'll enjoy. Some of the highlights include Tammy Wynette's classic "Stand by Your Man," David Houston's "Almost Persuaded," and Leon Ashley's original version of "Laura (What's He Got That I Ain't Got)," later done by Marty

Robbins. Not all the tracks are classics, but there are no duds here either. —*Jim Worbois*

Country Music Classics, Vol. 4 (1970-75) / K-Tel ✦✦

When Conway Twitty released "You've Never Been This Far Before" in the early '70s, country radio was more than a little nervous. Twenty years later, it's one of the highlights of this disc, which also includes the Ray Price monster hit "For the Good Times" (written by Kris Kristofferson), the somewhat sultry version of "Help Me Make It Through the Night" by Sammi Smith (another Kristofferson tune), and Tanya Tucker's "Delta Dawn." This is one of the better discs in this series. —*Jim Worbois*

Country Music Classics, Vol. 5 (1975-80) / 1988 / K-Tel ✦✦

These songs aren't strictly country when you look at the fact that "When You Needed Me" (Anne Murray), "Don't It Make My Brown Eyes Blue" (Crystal Gayle), and "Rhinestone Cowboy" (Glen Campbell) were all pop hits. Nor when you take into account that there probably isn't one person in North America who doesn't know at least part of "Take This Job and Shove It," no matter what their musical preference. The title is a bit of a misnomer, but if you long for the hits of the '70s, there are worse choices. —*Jim Worbois*

Country Music Classics, Vol. 6 (1980-1985) / 1992 / K-Tel ✦✦

These songs are a little too new to be classics but there is something on this disc for everyone, even if you know little about country music. Eddie Rabbitt is here with "I Love a Rainy Night," Willie Nelson with "Always on My Mind," and Lee Greenwood with "God Bless the USA." If Bette Midler's version of "Wind Beneath My Wings" was a little too much for you, check out this one by Gary Morris. —*Jim Worbois*

Country Music Classics, Vol. 7 (Late '70s) / 1991 / K-Tel ✦✦✦

Country Music Classics, Vol. 8 (1985-1990) / 1991 / K-Tel ✦✦✦

Country Music Classics, Vol. 9 (Mid-'60s) / 1990 / K-Tel ✦✦

While this disc tends to lean more toward comedy material (with the inclusion of Little Jimmy Dickens' "May the Bird of Paradise" and one or two others), there are some real classics here. One of several discs made up entirely of tracks from the vaults of Columbia Records and its subsidiaries. —*Jim Worbois*

Country Music Classics, Vol. 10 (1975-1980) / May 1993 / K-Tel ✦✦✦✦

With monster hits by Willie Nelson, Waylon Jennings, and Freddie Fender, and the crossover hit by Dolly Parton, this seems to be one of the stronger discs in this series covering the '70s and the '80s. —*Jim Worbois*

Country Music Classics, Vol. 11 (Early '70s) / Jun. 1993 / K-Tel ✦✦✦✦

George Jones came back strong in the early '80s with his classic "He Stopped Loving Her Today," which is one of the high points of this disc. The other high point is the inclusion of the original, and still the best, version of "I Will Always Love You" by its writer, Dolly Parton. Overall, not a bad disc. —*Jim Worbois*

Country Classics, Vol. 12 (Mid-'70s) / 1991 / K-Tel ✦✦✦

There are a couple classics on this one, but it's not quite up to the quality of some of the earlier discs. The standout cut is George Jones' "Grand Tour," followed not so closely by Lynn Anderson ("What a Man My Man Is") and a Marty Robbins title that harkens back to his gunfighter albums, "El Paso City." This is one of several discs made up entirely of tracks from the vaults of Columbia Records and its subsidiaries. —*Jim Worbois*

Country Music Classics, Vol. 13 (Late '70s) / 1991 / K-Tel ✦✦✦✦

This disc is certainly representative of what was happening in country music in the late '70s, but I don't know if anyone would call any of these tracks "classics." Okay for what it is. —*Jim Worbois*

Country Music Classics, Vol. 14 (1940's) / 1993 / K-Tel ✦✦✦✦

While this is a nice disc, it is by no means a complete representation of the entire decade, though it does show what diverse styles the term country music covered in the '40s. There is Western swing from Bob Wills, cowboy music from The Sons of the Pioneers, bluegrass from Bill Monroe, and Merle Travis doing music from the hills of Kentucky. There's something for everyone on this disc. —*Jim Worbois*

Country Music Classics, Vol. 15 (1950-55) / 1993 / K-Tel ✦✦✦✦
This disc does, in fact, contain some fine moments in country music. It could be a nice place to start if you're just getting into country music. —*Jim Worbois*

1955-60, Vol. 16 / 1993 / K-Tel ✦✦✦✦
Overall, a pleasing disc with many of country music's biggest names from the period represented. —*Jim Worbois*

Country Music Classics, Vol. 17 (1960-1965) / 1993 / K-Tel ✦✦✦✦
Aside from the fact that "The Race Is On" is not the hit version but one George Jones remade at a later date, there are some nice things on this disc, including the hit versions of two Willie Nelson originals (Patsy Cline's "Crazy," and "Night Life" by Ray Price). —*Jim Worbois*

Country Music Classics, Vol. 18 (1965-70) / 1993 / K-Tel ✦✦✦✦
This short but satisfying disc includes some of the biggest-selling country artists of the time, such as Buck Owens, Johnny Cash, and Loretta Lynn. Also of note, this disc contains one of the earliest Jimmy Webb songs Glen Campbell covered, "Galveston." Campbell is one artist who has consistently made use of the wealth of material Webb has created over the years. —*Jim Worbois*

Cowboy Hymns & Prayers / Jul. 29, 1996 / Warner Brothers ✦✦✦
Cowboy Hymns & Prayers features a good cross-section of contemporary cowboy singer-songwriters contributing originals and covers of Christian sprituals and inpirational songs. All of the material is drawn from the Warner Western vaults, with all but two of the tracks (Waddie Mitchell's "Cowboy Prayer" and Mark O'Connor's "Amazing Grace") featured on the label's official albums. Like many various artists collections, *Cowboy Hymns & Prayers* is slightly uneven, but the best of the songs on the record are moving, heartfelt, and rustically poetic, as only real cowboys can be. —*Stephen Thomas Erlewine*

Cowboy Way / 1994 / 550 Music/Epic ✦✦
In keeping with the cowboys-in-New-York theme of the movie, this collection of 11 songs from the soundtrack of *The Cowboy Way* features a number of country and Southern rock artists, notably Travis Tritt, the Allman Brothers Band, and Emmylou Harris. But there's also miscellaneous hard rock (Bon Jovi, Jeff Beck, and Paul Rodgers), alternative (Cracker, Blind Melon), and even R&B (En Vogue), meaning that this is another of those random roundups of rejects that pass for movie soundtracks these days. —*William Ruhlmann*

Dead Reckoners: Night of Reckoning / Mar. 11, 1997 / Dead Reckoning ✦✦✦✦
A label that's owned by the artists on its roster, Dead Reckoning releases music that is uncompromised in its vision. *Night of Reckoning* is a concept album, taking its title from a traveling revue that features Dead Reckoning artists and co-owners Kieran Kane, Kevin Welch, Tammy Rogers, Mike Henderson, and Harry Stinson backing each other musically and calling themselves the Dead Reckoners. A condensed studio-recorded version of the show, *Night of Reckoning* also features the playing of bassist Alison Prestwood and accordianist/fiddler/steel guitarist Fats Kaplan. The 12 tracks included here are inspired and showcase the excellent quality of artistry on this fine label. —*Jack Leaver*

Don't Fence Me In: Western Music's Early Golden Era / Feb. 1996 / Rounder ✦✦✦✦
The second volume of Rounder's cowboy music retrospective documents the form's coming of age in the late '30s and '40s, when the genre became part of the popular mainstream via both commercial recordings and films. The music was becoming more commercial via slicker arrangements and harmonies, but retained links to country and folk sources even as it widened its popular appeal. These 14 cuts include classics by some of the leading cowboy singers, including Gene Autry, the Sons of the Pioneers, Tex Ritter, and Roy Rogers, as well as relative lesser-knowns like Louise Massey and Ray Whiteley, and a track in the cowboy style by Western swing king Bob Wills. —*Richie Unterberger*

Early Mandolin Classics, Vol. 1 / 1989 / Rounder ✦✦✦✦
This fascinating glimpse into multi-ethnic mandolin music of the '20s and '30s features recordings ranging from ragtime and blues to Ukrainian bands and, of course, hillbilly music. —*Mark A. Humphrey*

Early Roanoke Country Radio / ✦✦✦✦
This features music recorded between 1920 and 1959 from early country radio broadcasts. The collection was compiled by the Blue Ridge Institute. —*AMG*

Fifty Years of Country Music from Mercury / Nov. 1995 / Mercury ✦✦✦

For a Life of Sin: A Compilation of Insurgent Chicago Country / 1994 / Bloodshot ✦✦✦
This is the first in a series of compilations featuring artists performing country and American roots music who are uncompromising in their dedication to each individual musical vision. The term "Insurgent Country" has been used to describe a growing faction of artists who reach back to traditional foundations, bringing them forward and injecting their own personal feel. The first volume primarily focuses upon an already-established Chicago country and roots community dating back to the 1920s, when the WLS *National Barn Dance* began its reign. Although the first volume is the weakest of the three, it's definitely worth a listen, with a good cross-section of the current alternative country scene, including strong tracks by Robbie Fulks ("Cigarette State") and Freakwater ("Drunk Friend"), as well as the legendary Chicago stalwarts the Sundowners ("Rockin' Spot"). —*Jack Leaver*

★ **Guitar Player Presents Legends of Guitar: Country, Vol. 1** / Rhino ✦✦✦✦✦
Part one of an astutely compiled pair, it showcases the kings of country guitar from the '30s to the '70s and includes work from Jimmy Bryant, Speedy West, Chet Atkins, and Joe Maphis. Good liner notes on both sets. —*John Floyd*

☆ **Guitar Player Presents Legends of Guitar: Country, Vol. 2** / 1991 / Rhino ✦✦✦✦✦
Guitar Player Presents Country, Vol. 2 is a terrific sampling of some of the finest guitarists in country music history, including not only solo musicians like Merle Travis, but also sidemen like Buck Owens, Don Rich, and several exceptionally talented studio musicians. It's a stunning collection, not only for guitarists, but for country fans in general. —*Thom Owens*

Hank Williams Songbook / Oct. 29, 1991 / Columbia ✦✦✦✦
The material on *The Hank Williams Songbook* is comprised entirely of 20 Williams covers by Columbia recording artists. Most of this material was released while Hank was still alive, which means that the music tends to be looser and less reverent than many of the Williams tributes that have been recorded in the years since his death. Several big names—including Ray Price, Johnny Cash, Roy Acuff, Carl Smith, and Marty Robbins—are featured here, but so are lesser-known artists like Curley Williams and the Cumberland Mountain Folk. While some of this touches on the haunting qualities of Hank's most desperate moments, much of the album is simply fun, and it's a worthwhile purchase for dedicated fans of '50s country music. —*Thom Owens*

Hillbilly Boogie / 1994 / Legacy/Columbia ✦✦✦✦

★ **Hillbilly Fever, Vol. 1: Legends of Western Swing** / 1995 / Rhino ✦✦✦✦✦
Whereas most country various artists collections are designed with dollars, not sense, in mind, Rhino's five-disc series *Hillbilly Fever* was thoughtfully compiled and intelligently executed. *Hillbilly Fever* concentrates on the classic era of recorded country music, running from 1933 to 1975, spotlighting nearly every important artist (usually with one of their best-known songs) along the way. This first volume of the series, *Legends of Western Swing*, is an 18-track compilation that encapsulates the genre. Featuring cuts by the Fort Worth Doughboys, Milton Brown, the Light Crust Doughboys, Cliff Bruner, Johnnie Lee Wills, Bob Wills, Spade Cooley, Tex Williams, Leon McAuliffe, and Hank Thompson, this disc contains all of the most important musicians in the genre, as well as a handful of terrific obscurities. As a result, *Legends of Western Swing* functions as a definitive, essential intro-

duction to one of the most infectious genres in country music. [None of the five discs in the *Hillbilly Fever* series sold in its initial release, probably because its title was too smug to appeal to either hardcore record collectors or casual country fans. A year after the release of *Hillbilly Fever*, Rhino reissued the entire series under the title *Heroes of Country Music*. Unfortunately, the second time around, they pulled several essential tracks from each disc, but even in its edited form the series is worth getting.] —*Stephen Thomas Erlewine*

★ **Hillbilly Fever, Vol. 2: Legends of Honky Tonk** / 1995 / Rhino ✦✦✦✦✦

Hillbilly Fever, Vol. 2: Legends of Honky Tonk is an essential primer in country music's most enduring genre, boasting 17 of the greatest bar-room tunes ever recorded. Beginning in 1937 with Al Dexter's "Honky Tonk Blues" and ending 30 years later with Jim Edward Brown's "Pop a Top," the disc contains 18 definitive honky tonk cuts from nearly all of the genre's major players, including Rex Griffin ("The Last Letter"), Ernest Tubb ("Walking the Floor Over You"), Floyd Tillman ("Drivin' Nails in My Coffin"), Hank Williams ("Honky Tonkin'"), Leon Payne ("I Love You Because"), Hank Thompson ("The Wild Side of Life"), Lefty Frizzell ("Just Can't Live That Fast [Any More]"), and George Jones ("A Girl I Used to Know"). Though there are several songs and artists that could have been included, *Legends of Honky Tonk* nevertheless is an essential overview and introduction to country's defining genre. [None of the five discs in the *Hillbilly Fever* series sold in its initial release, probably because its title was too smug to appeal to either hardcore record collectors or casual country fans. A year after the release of *Hillbilly Fever*, Rhino reissued the entire series under the title *Heroes of Country Music*. Unfortunately, the second time around, they pulled several essential tracks from each disc, but even in its edited form the series is worth getting.] —*Stephen Thomas Erlewine*

★ **Hillbilly Fever, Vol. 3: Legends of Nashville** / 1995 / Rhino ✦✦✦✦✦

"The Nashville Sound" is commonly known as the lushly orchestrated country-pop sound called countrypolitan that came to prominence in the late '50s, but *Hillbilly Fever, Vol. 3: Legends of Nashville* bypasses that era, choosing to concentrate on the classic days of the Grand Ole Opry. As a result, *Legends of Nashville* has a wide range of styles, from honky tonk to country-pop, but it all sounds unified because it captures the essence of pre-rock 'n' roll country music (1945-1956). Though it doesn't have a story to tell like its two predecessors, *Legends of Nashville* is just as essential to any comprehensive country collection, simply because of the number of classics available on the disc: Eddy Arnold's "Bouquet of Roses," Ernest Tubb's "It's Been So Long Darling," Pee Wee King's "Tennessee Waltz," Hank Williams' "Lovesick Blues," George Morgan's "Room Full of Roses," Webb Pierce's "Wondering," Slim Whitman's "Indian Love Call," Kitty Wells' "It Wasn't God Who Made Honky Tonk Angels," Faron Young's "If You Ain't Lovin (You Ain't Livin')," the Louvin Brothers' "I Don't Believe You've Met My Baby," Ray Price's "Crazy Arms," Marty Robbins' "Singing the Blues," and Patsy Cline's "Walkin' After Midnight." [None of the five discs in the *Hillbilly Fever* series sold in its initial release, probably because its title was too smug to appeal to either hardcore record collectors or casual country fans. A year after the release of *Hillbilly Fever*, Rhino reissued the entire series under the title *Heroes of Country Music*. Unfortunately, the second time around, they pulled several essential tracks from each disc, but even in its edited form the series is worth getting.] —*Stephen Thomas Erlewine*

★ **Hillbilly Fever, Vol. 4: Legends of the West Coast** / 1995 / Rhino ✦✦✦✦✦

Hillbilly Fever, Vol. 4: Legends of the West Coast doesn't just cover the Bakersfield sound of the late '50s and early '60s, but it traces its development through the late '40s and '50s. The disc begins with a selection of cowboy songs (Jack Guthrie's "Oklahoma Hills," Gene Autry's "You Are My Sunshine," Sons of the Pioneers' "Cool Water") before moving toward Western swing (Al Dexter's "Too Late to Worry," Spade Cooley's "Shame on You") and coun-

try-boogie (Tennessee Ernie Ford's "Mule Train"). By the end of the disc—after Skeets McDonald's "Don't Let the Stars Get in Your Eyes," Jimmy Wakely's "One Has My Name (The Other Has My Heart)," Tex Ritter's "High Noon (Do Not Forsake Me)," and Joe Maphis & Rose Lee's "Dim Lights, Thick Smoke (And Loud, Loud Music)" have been heard—the electrified honky tonk of Bakersfield begins to emerge in the form of Jean Shepard ("A Dear John Letter"), Tommy Collins ("You Better Not Do That"), Ferlin Husky ("Gone"), Wynn Stewart ("Wishful Thinking"), Buck Owens ("Second Fiddle"), and Merle Haggard ("Sing a Sad Song"). Since it covers so many different styles, *Legends of the West Coast* is a little inconsistent. Nevertheless, it tells its story well and contains a wealth of classics, making it another essential addition to any comprehensive country library. [None of the five discs in the *Hillbilly Fever* series sold in its initial release, probably because its title was too smug to appeal to either hardcore record collectors or casual country fans. A year after the release of *Hillbilly Fever*, Rhino reissued the entire series under the title *Heroes of Country Music*. Unfortunately, the second time around, they pulled several essential tracks from each disc, but even in its edited form the series is worth getting.] —*Stephen Thomas Erlewine*

★ **Hillbilly Fever, Vol. 5: Legends of Country Rock** / 1995 / Rhino ✦✦✦✦

If you're a big country-rock fan, you're probably familiar with most of the work on this compilation. But if you're not, it's a good introductory survey of the genre; or, if you are, but aren't passionate enough about the style to actively collect country-rock recordings, it may satisfy more basic needs. Focusing exclusively on the music from country-rock's heyday in the late '60s and early '70s, this has cuts by most of the leading lights of the scene, including the Flying Burrito Brothers, the International Submarine Band, the Byrds, the Everly Brothers, Poco, the Nitty Gritty Dirt Band, Michael Nesmith, and New Riders of the Purple Sage. It also ventures into the mid-'70s (briefly) with Pure Prairie League and Marshall Tucker. There are also off-the-beaten tracks by Linda Ronstadt and Bob Dylan, as well as country-rock outings by name acts who weren't primarily affiliated with the style, such as the Lovin' Spoonful, the Youngbloods, and Delaney & Bonnie. It's a good mix of the familiar and the unfamiliar, though it doesn't include important work in the field by Buffalo Springfield, the Grateful Dead, the Beau Brummels, and Rick Nelson, mostly because of licensing restrictions. —*Richie Unterberger*

☆ **Hillbilly Music: Thank God!, Vol. 1** / 1989 / Bug ✦✦✦✦✦

Hillbilly Music . . . Thank God!, Vol. 1 is a 24-track, double-LP/single-disc collection of proto-Bakersfield, hillbilly, and honky tonk music from the Capitol Records vaults. All of the material on the compilation was recorded between the late '40s and the mid-'50s, and most of these artists are from the West Coast, which means this music has a different flavor than the Nashville-based honky tonk of the same era. *Hillbilly Music* is also filled with rarities from the likes of Buck Owens, Tommy Collins, Tennessee Ernie Ford, Hank Thompson, Jean Shepard, Merle Travis, Rose Maddox, and Tex Ritter. *Hillbilly Music* is a historical document of the best kind—it's entertaining and educational. —*Thom Owens*

Home on the Range / 1992 / Pavilion ✦✦✦✦

It's sort of embarrassing that a collection of early cowboy songs as good as this has to come out of England. Gene Autry is represented by his stripped-down, mournful 1930 ballad "No One to Call Me Darling," the delightful 1938 "I've Got the Jailhouse Blues," the equally bluesy "I'll Always Be a Rambler," and two other seldom reissued numbers. Roy Rogers is here with "Colorado Sunset," but the really good material comes from the other side of the tradition, in the guise of Jimmie Rodgers and "Round up Time Out West," "I've Only Loved Three Women," and "Any Old Time." The rarities here include superb tracks by the little-known Hillbillies (including a version of "Home on the Range" with a delightful trilling banjo), and Carson Robison and His Pioneers, doing the sentimental "There's a Bridle Hangin' on a Wall" and the more upbeat "Blue River Train." The sound is very good, with most of the material drawn from British sources (especially EMI's Regal Zonophone label) pressed in the 1930s. —*Bruce Eder*

Honky Tonk Super Hits / Mar. 19, 1996 / Epic ✦✦✦
In case there was any doubt that drinking and hanging around in bars continues to be a preoccupation in country music, this ten-song compilation should dispel it. From George Jones and James Taylor's 1978 hit "Bartender's Blues" to Rick Trevino's 1994 chart single "Honky Tonk Crowd," these singers proclaim the wonders of the nightlife and the joy of crying in your beer. The most successful songs are from Doug Stone, whose "A Jukebox with a Country Song" topped the charts in 1992 by lamenting that the local watering hole had turned into a fern bar, and Vern Gosdin, who went to No. 1 in 1988 with "Set 'Em Up Joe." But all these night owls have something to howl about. — *William Ruhlmann*

Hot Swing Fiddle Classics 1936-1943 / 1936-1943 / Folk Lyric ✦✦✦✦
When one thinks of swing violin, the names Joe Venuti and Stephane Grappelli come immediately to mind. However this LP from Arhoolie's subsidiary Folklyric features three other talented violinists from the 1930s. Stuff Smith, heard on five songs with his 1936 sextet that co-starred trumpeter Jonah Jones, received a certain amount of fame, but Svend Asmussen (because he remained in Europe throughout his career) is lesser known, and Emilio Caceres (heard on four of the six titles recorded at his only early session as a leader) is completely forgotten. Caceres (featured in a trio with his brother Ernie on clarinet and vocals along with guitarist Johnny Gomez) holds his own with Smith and Asmussen on this consistently enjoyable album. — *Scott Yanow*

How the West Was Won / 1997 / Rhino ✦✦✦✦
This double CD has generally superior sound to the 1992 Sony Music release, but its more than two hours of music may be a classic case of overkill. The essential problem is that *How the West Was Won* is rooted in two separate bodies of music, the Alfred Newman instrumental and orchestral material (including the rousing main title theme), spiced with a few traditional (i.e. folk) and traditional-style tunes; and the songs sung by Debbie Reynolds in her various set pieces as an entertainer, principally "Home in the Meadow" (adapted from "Greensleeves"). The Alfred Newman material generally recalls Aaron Copland's musical Americana (especially the Lincoln Portrait) at its best and most accessible, and the folk songs handled by the choir or Dave Guard's Whiskeyhill Singers come off well—but then there are those numbers done by Reynolds, which sort of break the spell. It's not that she's a bad singer, but just that her voice doesn't fit within the surrounding musical settings. One guesses the producers had no choice but to give full play to this part of the score, but one wishes there'd been a way around it. The annotation is very thorough, and the photographs (including some behind-the-scenes shots of co-director John Ford) are a nice treat, and anyone who likes the movie or Newman's music is sure to enjoy this. — *Bruce Eder*

I'm a Honky Tonk Daddy / Flyright ✦✦✦✦
I'm a Honky Tonk Daddy is a 20-track collection that features a good cross-section of material recorded for Flyright during the '50s. The compilation does feature Lefty Frizzell, but most of it is dedicated to obscure performers. For hardcore honky tonk fans, the very rarity of these artists makes *I'm a Honky Tonk Daddy* worthwhile, but for most country fans, the music on this collection will only be of passing interest. — *Thom Owens*

Insurgent Country, Vol. 2 / 1995 / Bloodshot ✦✦✦
With the second volume of the *Insurgent Country* series, Bloodshot Records broadens their scope to include bands from all over the country. The results give an inkling of just how many great country and roots artists exist—ones that are making remarkable music out there with minimal, or no, radio exposure. The quality of the performances are more even here than on the first volume and of the 17 artists and songs represented, there are many strong tracks. Once again, Chicago's country singer-songwriter Robbie Fulks highlights the set with "She Took a Lot of Pills (And Died)." Detroit's best-kept secret the Volebeats turn in a typical low-key, but memorable, song, "One I Love," and Dallas' Old 97's contribute the rowdy, bluegrass-tinged raveup "Por Favor." One of the collection's other standout tracks, "22," from San Francisco's Richard Buckner, is also the darkest. In chilling literary detail, Buckner's

song character describes his suicide from unrequited love, casting a long but compelling shadow on the collection. — *Jack Leaver*

● **Insurgent Country, Vol. 3: Nashville—The Other Side of the Alley** / 1996 / Bloodshot ✦✦✦✦
The best and most consistent of the lot so far, *Volume 3* concentrates on alternative country and roots acts based in and around Nashville. A wonderful way to get a good sampling of this exciting and growing music scene. Highlights of the 18-song set include Tim Carroll's "Open Flame," mainstay forefathers Jason & The Scorchers' "One Last Question," Kristi Rose & The Handsome Strangers' "Rise & Shine," and the Wilco offshoot Courtesy Move's "Those I'll Provide." — *Jack Leaver*

Johnny Gimble's Texas Honky-Tonk Hits / CMH ✦✦✦
Johnny Gimble's Texas Honky-Tonk Hits is a two-album compilation of the fiddler's finest moments. The album does feature solo cuts from Gimble, but the real meat of the collection lies in the wonderful selection of songs that he recorded with other artists. Featuring tracks by the Wills Brothers, Mac Wiseman, Carl Butler, Johnny Bond, Rose Lee Maphis, and Stuart Hamblen, all of the music on *Texas Honk-Tonk Hits* swings with the best of Western swing and tugs at the heart like the best honky tonk, and throughout it all, Gimble's fiddle soars. More than anything, *Texas Honky-Tonk Hits* offers convincing evidence that Johnny Gimble was the finest country fiddler to ever record. — *Thom Owens*

☆ **The King-Federal Rockabillys** / Deluxe ✦✦✦✦✦
This album features such artists as Charlie Feathers, Hank Mizell, Mac Curtis, and others on rare cuts originally recorded for the Federal and King labels during the '50s. — *AMG*

The Kings of Country Music / Oct. 1995 / Ranwood ✦✦✦
Twenty big country hits (some of which were rock 'n' roll hits as well) from the 1950s, including smashes by Johnny Cash, Carl Perkins, Hank Williams, Hank Snow, Jim Reeves, George Jones, Don Gibson, Marty Robbins, Ernest Tubb, and Tennessee Ernie Ford. Nothing here is rare, but for those who are just looking for a decent sampler of popular male-sung country from the 1950s, this will do fine. — *Richie Unterberger*

Legendary Songs of the Old West / Columbia Special Products ✦✦✦✦
Legendary Songs of the Old West is a four-LP set of classic country, Western, cowboy and Western swing songs from the likes of the Sons of the Pioneers, Bob Wills, Gene Autry, Tex Ritter, Patsy Montana and Roy Rogers. Most of the genre's best-known songs and standards—including "Cool Water," "The Yellow Rose of Texas," "Back in the Saddle Again," and "Home on the Range"—are included on this excellent 40-song set. For anyone wanting a concise overview of the classic days of cowboy and Country & Western music, *Legendary Songs of the Old West* is an excellent, even essential, primer. — *Thom Owens*

Memphis Ramble: Sun Country Collection, Vol. 1 / 1990 / Rhino ✦✦✦✦
Memphis Ramble: Sun Country Collection is an excellent, single-disc cross-section of hits and obscurities from the vaults of Sun Records, including prime cuts from the likes of Johnny Cash, Warren Smith, and Jerry Lee Lewis. — *Thom Owens*

Not Fade Away (Remembering Buddy Holly) / Feb. 1996 / Decca ✦✦✦
Not Fade Away (Remembering Buddy Holly) is a decidedly uneven tribute to the late, great rock 'n' roller. Though it is clear the artists on the tribute are sincere in their affection for Holly, their covers add nothing to the original versions. Few of the selections attempt a reinterpretation of the song, and those that do aren't successful. When the cover is close to the original, it doesn't sound as fresh as Holly's version. Consequently, the best way to keep Holly's memory alive is to replay his records, not this collection. — *Stephen Thomas Erlewine*

The Okeh Western Swing / Nov. 14, 1927-Jul. 30, 1950 / Epic ✦✦✦✦
The beginnings and evolution of Western swing are explored in colorful fashion on this definitive two-LP set. The 28 selections (programmed loosely in chronological order) start out with a couple of country-oriented singers performing in jazz settings (Al

Bernard and Emmett Miller during 1927-28) before moving to the mid-'30s and performances by Roy Newman, the Blue Ridge Playboys, the Range Riders, W. Lee O'Daniel & His Hillbilly Boys and the Crystal Springs Ramblers. Seven selections from Bob Wills' Texas Playboys (dating from 1935-41) are followed by numbers from the Saddle Tramps, the Sons of the Pioneers, the Light Crust Doughboys, the Hi Neighbor Boys, Hank Penny, the Swift Jewel Cowboys, and the Sweet Violet Boys. Side four covers 1941-42 with cuts by Ocie Stockard's Wanderers, the Hi-Flyers, Sons of the West, Adolf Hofner, and Slim Harbert before concluding with a 1946 performance by Spade Cooley and an obscurity from Leon McAuliffe in 1950. This two-fer serves as a perfect introduction to listeners (from both the country and jazz worlds) who are not that familiar with the joyous country/jazz fusion from the Depression years known as Western swing. Recommended. —*Scott Yanow*

The Original Skeets McDonald's "Tattooed Lady" plus Seven Other Sizzlers / Fortune ✦✦✦✦

Original Skeets McDonald's "Tattooed Lady" plus Seven Other Sizzlers is a raunchy, old-fashioned hillbilly humor record, featuring 12 bawdy honky tonk classics, including McDonald's "Birthday Cake Boogie" and Johnny Bucket's "Let Me Play with Your Poodle." —*Thom Owens*

Outlaws—Super Hits / 1996 / Columbia ✦✦✦

Outlaws—Super Hits is a budget-line collection that does an adequate job of summing up the attitude, if not the actual sound, of late-'70s outlaw country. Part of the problem is that the album concentrates solely on artists that recorded for Columbia and its affiliated labels. Therefore, a few major outlaw artists—including Billy Joe Shaver and Tompall Glaser—aren't included at all, while others, like Waylon Jennings, have a misrepresentative number of tracks. Furthermore, several artists that have only a tangential relationship with outlaw—such as Johnny Cash and Merle Haggard, who were more responsible for inspiring the movement than actually being part of it—are given numerous tracks. Still, *Outlaws—Super Hits* is enjoyable for what it is—a brief, cheap ten-track sampler with a few good songs. Certain songs are stone-cold outlaw classics—such as Willlie Nelson's "Blue Eyes Crying in the Rain," David Allan Coe's "Long Haired Redneck," and Haggard & Nelson's duet, "Pancho and Lefty—while others are just classics (Johnny Paycheck's "Take This Job and Shove It," Johnny Cash's "Ring of Fire" and "Folsom Prison Blues"). And that just means that although *Outlaws—Super Hits* isn't a definitive outlaw compilation, it's still an enjoyable listen. —*Stephen Thomas Erlewine*

☆ Ragged but Right / Mar. 29, 1934-Jan. 27, 1938 / RCA ✦✦✦✦✦

The little-known performances on this very interesting CD features four separate quartets comprised of strings (including violin, banjo, guitar, mandolin, and/or bass) and smaller collaborations from the same dates. There are selections from the final recording sessions of Gid Tanner and His Skillet Lickers and numbers from the Prairie Ramblers (a top Western swing group), the pioneer bluegrass group J.E. Mainer's Mountaineers, and Ade Mainer's similar Sons of the Mountaineers. While one thinks of the 1930s as the big-band era, clearly there was a great deal of other music being performed at the same time and this CD sampler should greatly interest collectors of early country and Southern roots music. —*Scott Yanow*

Real: A Tribute to Tom T. Hall / 1997 / Delmore ✦✦✦✦

Tom T. Hall is boundless in his artistry as a storyteller. The title of this project was inspired by a quote Steve Earle gave in an interview with *No Depression* magazine, where he stated that no categorization is necessary when you're dealing with real music. Because of the diversity of artists, this project bypasses the mundane material that most tributes display. Moving from folk to rock to country and bluegrass artists, *Real* serves to reinforce the notion that Tom T. Hall has influenced the many genres of American music. There are many highlights on this double-length album, beginning with the incomparable Johnny Cash and his acoustic rendition of "I Washed My Face in the Morning Dew." Calexico performs a dour Tex-Mex version of "Tulsa Telephone Book," giving an uncommon edge that captures the solitude of the original Hall composition. Richard Buckner emotes the sad-

ness of "When Love Is Gone," in his stark reading, and legendary bluegrass great Ralph Stanley and his son Ralph Jr. resurrect "The Water Lily." Also, the Mary Janes' cover of "I'm Not Ready Yet" would set comfortably on any country jukebox, and Syd Straw turns in a humorous tongue-in-cheek twist on the multi-million seller "Harper Valley, P.T.A.," while being backed spiritedly by the Skeletons. While this record has a dark aura that defies Hall's distinctively cheerful image, it works extremely well. A worthy tribute that not only fulfills its sincere intentions, but also spotlights the innovative songwriting talent that is Tom T. Hall. —*Jack Leaver*

Rig Rock Deluxe: A Musical Salute to American Truck Drivers / Sep. 3, 1996 / Upstart ✦✦✦✦

Rig Rock Deluxe is a salute to the American truck driver, as performed by a number of country-rockers and honky tonkers. No Depression upstarts like Son Volt sit comfortably with new traditionalists like Steve Earle and Marty Stuart and outlaws like Billy Joe Shaver, as well as Buck Owens, Kelly Willis, and Nick Lowe. This is hard-driving, raw country—all of the contributors sound vibrant, ripping through their songs with energy. It's one of those rare various artists compilations that stands as an entertaining, cohesive listen. —*Thom Owens*

Saddle Up! The Cowboy Renaissance / Apr. 1996 / Rounder ✦✦✦✦

This 14-song collection covers some familiar territory, but it also includes one of Bob Nolan's very last recordings ("Wandering"), making this worthwhile by itself, not to mention superb singing by the Reinsmen and the usual excellence of the Riders in the Sky, as well as contributions by Michael Martin Murphey, Ian Tyson, and Rex Allen, Jr. —*Bruce Eder*

Silver Screen Cowboys / 1994 / Sony Music ✦✦✦✦

From Ken Maynard ("Home on the Range") and Gene Autry ("Back in the Saddle Again") to Rex Allen ("Don't Go Near the Indians"), an above-average compilation, despite its being limited to a dozen songs. The familiar songs are rounded out by a pair of genuine rarities, a comic song by Smiley Burnette ("Mama Don't Like Music"), and a short tall-tale told by Gabby Hayes. —*Bruce Eder*

The Singing Cowboys / 1992 / CEMA ✦✦✦✦

This CEMA (Capitol-EMI) collection covers a lot of territory from the pop side of the cowboy genre, from Roy Rogers' delightful 1972 "Candy Kisses" and "Tennessee Waltz" and Tex Ritter's throaty "I've Got Spurs That Jingle Jangle Jingle" to Marty Robbins' beautifully played and sung cover of Bob Nolan's "Song of the Bandit." Slim Whitman puts in an appearance with the yodel song "Cattle Call," and Rex Allen Sr. contributes the hauntingly beautiful "Twilight on the Trail" and "The Last Roundup." —*Bruce Eder*

The Singing Cowboys / 1994 / K-Tel ✦✦✦

This collection covers the most obvious bases as a survey of Western songs, including the Sons of the Pioneers' version of "I'm an Old Cowhand (From the Rio Grande)," Autry's "Back in the Saddle Again" (in a later version than the original), Marty Robbins' "Big Iron," Tennessee Ernie Ford's "Mule Train," Tex Ritter's "High Noon," and Roy Rogers' and Dale Evans' "Happy Trails." None of this is rare, but it is a good-sounding start for anyone trying to get the most familiar classics in the genre all in one place. —*Bruce Eder*

Small Screen Cowboy Heroes / 1994 / Sony ✦✦✦✦

The 1950s saw a revival of Western songwriting in a popular vein, mostly sparked by the popularity of the Western on television, where it was the dominant genre during the years 1957-1963 (at one point there were over two dozen Western series running each week on the three networks, in addition to syndicated series). This 12-song collection draws from some of the most popular of them (Johnny Western's "The Ballad of Paladin," Frankie Laine's "Rawhide," Johnny Cash's "The Rebel-Johnny Yuma," Roy Rogers' "Happy Trails,") and a number of rarities, such as Gail Davis (TV's Annie Oakley) singing "I'm Female Thru and Thru" and Robert Horton, star of the mid-1960s series *A Man Called Shenandoah* (precursor to *The Lazarus Man*) singing "Shenandoah." —*Bruce Eder*

☆ **Son of Rounder Banjo** / 1992 / Rounder ✦✦✦✦✦
Like the first *Rounder Banjo, Son of Rounder Banjo* is an hour-long sampler of the best banjoists to have recorded for Rounder Records. Encompassing both traditional and progressive blue-grass, the disc features cuts by Bela Fleck, Alison Brown, John Hickman, John Hartford, the Johnson Mountain Boys, Alan Munde, and Herb Pedersen, among many others, offering a good overview of not only the label, but bluegrass banjo in general. —*Thom Owens*

Songs of the West / 1993 / Rhino ✦✦✦✦
This "definitive collection of cowboy songs" covers both famous and obscure odes to the high lonesome plains by Gene Autry, Roy Rogers, Tex Ritter, Marty Robbins, Slim Pickens, Bob Wills, and others. Spanning the 1930s to the present, the 72-track, four-CD collection is broken into four separate thematic discs. Vol. 1 features "Cowboy Classics" like "Back in the Saddle Again," "Mule Train," and "Happy Trails." The real find here has to be the ultradramatic narrative by Walter Brennan describing the "Gunfight at the O.K. Corral." Vol. 2, "Silver Screen Cowboys," features tunes from Hollywood Westerns; Vol. 3 is devoted exclusively to performances by the kingpins of the genre, Gene Autry and Roy Rogers. The final disc is perhaps the most fun of the batch, presenting movie and television themes like "Bonanza," "Gunsmoke," "The Good, the Bad, and the Ugly," and "Rawhide." The box comes with a 60-page color booklet that includes detailed essays, photos, and reproductions of movie posters. —*Richie Unterberger*

Stampede! Western Music's Late Golden Era / 1996 / Rounder ✦✦✦✦
The third installment of Rounder's four-volume cowboy music series contains the songs most likely to be familiar to the general listener: Tex Ritter's "High Noon," Vaughn Monroe's "Riders in the Sky," Marty Robbins' "El Paso," Johnny Western's "The Ballad of Paladin," Eddy Arnold's "Cattle Call." Spanning the years 1945-1960, it presents the form at its most pop-oriented, but it's not less enjoyable for that. Filling out the 14-track set are numbers by the likes of Elton Britt, Jimmy Wakely, and the Sons of the Pioneers (one of whose tracks is the theme to one of the definitive cowboy Western films, *The Searchers*). —*Richie Unterberger*

★ **The Sun Country Years: 1950-1959** / Bear Family ✦✦✦✦✦
This collection, available only as ten LPs, contains classic performances from the beginning of rock 'n' roll, many of which are now available for the first time. Among the artists on the set are Hardrock Gunther, Jerry Lee Lewis, Charlie Feathers, Johnny Cash, Warren Smith, Jack Clement, Carl Perkins, and others. A 128-page booklet accompanies the set. —*AMG*

Super Hits of 1994 / Oct. 31, 1995 / Sony ✦✦✦✦
Super Hits of 1994 compiles ten of Columbia and Epic's biggest country hits of 1994, including Joe Diffie's "Third Rock from the Sun," Mary-Chapin Carpenter's "Shut Up and Kiss Me," and Collin Raye's "Little Rock." It's an entertaining listen, and is a fairly good representation of what was popular in 1994, even if it only relies on one label. In short, it's a good budget-priced collection. —*Thom Owens*

Super Hits of 1995 / Mar. 19, 1996 / Epic ✦✦✦
Actually, 1995 was not that good a year in country music for the Epic and Columbia labels of Sony Music, and some of the labels' biggest hits, such as Collin Raye's "One Boy, One Girl," are not included in this ten-song compilation. But some of the best country hits of the year, among them Joe Diffie's "Pickup Man," James House's "This Is Me Missing You," Rick Trevino's "Bobbie Ann Mason," Mary-Chapin Carpenter's "House of Cards," and Ty Herndon's "What Mattered Most" are included, which makes this a reasonable sampler of the year, at least from one major label's perspective. —*William Ruhlmann*

Texas Sand: Anthology of Western Swing / Rambler ✦✦✦✦
This wide-ranging LP sampler launched Mutual Music's Rambler subsidiary in the early '80s, a label dedicated to reissuing previously rare Western swing recordings. Although it skips around

quite a bit chronologically (and would certainly not be the first choice of completists), the performances are quite enjoyable; a special bonus is that three of the more obscure selections are from the late '40s, when Western swing was considered to be somewhat passé but (as shown here) could still be quite viable. There are hot performances on this album by the Tune Wranglers, Roy Newman, the legendary Milton Brown ("Ida"), Cliff Bruner, the Prairie Ramblers, Jimmie Revard's Oklahoma Playboys, Johnny Tyler's Riders of the Rio Grande, Curly Williams' Georgia Peach Pickers, the Sunshine Boys, Jesse Ashlock and "T" Texas Tyler's Oklahoma Melody Boys. —*Scott Yanow*

Texas Super Hits / Aug. 27, 1996 / Sony ✦✦✦
You would think that *Texas Super Hits* would be a cross section of songs recorded by some of the most famous natives of the Lone Star State. Instead, this brief budget-priced compilation has songs from Texans and songs *about* Texas from non-Texans like Merle Haggard, George Jones, and Johnny Cash. It's an enjoyable collection, but most of the songs on *Texas Super Hits* were technically not hits and only beloved standards. Still, it's an enjoyable, if slightly unnecessary, compilation for the budget-minded consumer. —*Thom Owens*

Top of the Hill Bluegrass / Nov. 21, 1995 / Sugar Hill ✦✦✦
Top of the Hill Bluegrass is an introduction to artists from the Sugar Hill label's roster; contributions come from Doc Watson, Ricky Skaggs, Peter Rowan, and others. —*Jason Ankeny*

Town South of Bakersfield, Vol. 3 / Mar. 18, 1992 / Restless ✦✦✦✦
Not as generous as the first disc, it's still worth the price. This disc features more of the music and artists that may not otherwise have been heard but deserve to be. Let's hope there are more to follow. —*Jim Worbois*

☆ **Town South of Bakersfield, Vols. 1 & 2** / Restless ✦✦✦✦✦
Thanks to the likes of Buck Owens and Merle Haggard, Bakersfield has long played an important part in country music. This disc features some of the new generation. A few of the artists (like Rosie Flores and Katy Moffatt) have been around for a long time but have never received the recognition they deserve. The variety of styles on this disc ensure that there is something for everyone. —*Jim Worbois*

Tulare Dust: Tribute to Merle Haggard / 1994 / Hightone ✦✦✦✦
This tribute to Merle Haggard is just great. Any fan of contemporary singer-songwriters will want this CD because the lineup includes Peter Case, Iris DeMent, Barance Whitfield, Katy Moffatt, Dave Alvin, and Marshall Crenshaw, not to mention producer Tom Russell. All the songs are presented straight, and they all jump out of the speakers as wonderful examples of from-the-heart, rough-and-ready songwriting. Also, as with all good tunes, you'll find yourself humming along. —*Richard Meyer*

Twisted Willie / Jan. 30, 1996 / Justice ✦✦
Like most tribute albums, *Twisted Willie* is a decidedly uneven covers collection. This time, Willie Nelson is the subject, and the musicians paying tribute are alternative rock stars, including Dinosaur Jr., Mudhoney, and members of Nirvana, Alice In Chains, the Breeders, and Soundgarden. At times, they perform duets with country outlaws Waylon Jennings, Johnny Cash, and Kris Kristofferson. Perhaps with such a diverse lineup, it makes sense that the album isn't consistently enjoyable, or even listenable, but it does provide some entertaining tracks for fans of the featured artists, even if it doesn't offer a new perspective on Nelson's catalogue. —*Stephen Thomas Erlewine*

☆ **Uncle Art Satherly: American Originals** / Columbia ✦✦✦✦✦
This pioneering A&R man recollects the recordings of several early country standards, making this a fine best-of '30s and '40s vintage Columbia label country. Included is "San Antonio Rose" by Bob Wills and "I Want to Be a Cowboy's Sweetheart" by Patsy Montana, among others. —*Mark A. Humphrey*

Under the Double Eagle: Great Western Swing Bands / Apr. 4, 1934-Aug. 12, 1935 / RCA ✦✦✦✦
This single CD has nine selections apiece from two of the earliest and finest Western swing bands. Milton Brown and His Musical Brownies was the first group in the idiom to record and it could

actually hold its own against most jazz bands of the time despite not having any horns. Brown's cheerful and easy-to-understand vocals were always enjoyable and his group included such fine players as violinist Cecil Brower, pianist Fred "Papa" Calhoun, and banjoist Ocie Stockard; "Brownie's Stomp," "Where You Been So Long, Corrine," and "Just Sitting on Top of the World" are highlights. (A very definitive five-CD set from Texas Rose containing all of Milton Brown's recordings is also currently available.) The other band on this CD, Bill Boyd's Cowboy Ramblers, ranged from a quartet to a sextet and benefited greatly from the contributions of Boyd on guitar, violinist Art Davis (who doubled on mandolin), and the vocals of several bandmembers. But actually the highpoint of their nine songs are two stirring instrumentals: "Under the Double Eagle" and "The Train Song." This 1990 CD is a fine sampler but unfortunately *Vol. 2* has yet to appear! —*Scott Yanow*

Urban Cowboy 2 / 1981 / Epic ✦✦✦✦

☆ **Urban Cowboy [O.S.T.]** / 1980 / Asylum ✦✦✦✦✦
This includes Joe Walsh, Bob Seger, Boz Scaggs, and Dan Fogelberg, so it's obviously not strictly a country album. But the soundtrack is important because it symbolizes the country trend that grew, then faded, in the early '80s (a case can be made that J.R. Ewing had a lot more influence on the fad than the film *Urban Cowboy*). Most of the country tracks here lean toward MOR. —*Tom Roland*

Wanted! The Outlaws / 1996 / RCA ✦✦✦✦
The term "outlaw" had been bandied about after Jennings' 1972 hit "Ladies Love Outlaws," but it didn't permanently gel until the release of the album *Wanted! The Outlaws* in 1976. The songs in this packaged product weren't new—the album contained previously released material by Nelson, Jennings, Glaser, and Jennings' wife, Jessie Colter (who had hit the charts a year earlier with "I'm Not Lisa"). But it marked the industry's recognition of the changing times, and as the centerpoint of a campaign to publicize Nashville's new "progressive" breed, it worked like a charm. It quickly became the first country album to sell more than a million copies, and it boosted the careers of all involved. In 1996, RCA reissued *Wanted! The Outlaws* on CD for the first time, adding one new Waylon and Willie recording (a lively reading of Steve Earle's "Nowhere Road") and nine "lost" tracks. But "lost" isn't really correct: Like the original 11 selections, such songs as Waylon's "Slow Movin' Outlaws" and Willie's "Healing Hands of Time" have been previously released. They do, however, sweeten the package, making this 20th anniversary edition a decent (though by no means definitive) sampler of outlaw country. —*Kurt Wolff*

Western Swing on the Radio / Country Routes ✦✦✦✦
Western Swing on the Radio is a 20-song compilation of Western swing from the '30s, '40s, and '50s, including terrific cuts from bandleaders like Bob Wills, Wesley Tuttle, Hank Thompson, Leon McAuliffe, Tex Williams, and Cecil Brower. What makes the compilation quite interesting, for both casual fans and collectors, is how it spotlights lesser-known artists, not just the King of Western Swing, Bob Wills. In doing so, it provides an excellent service, demonstrating the richness of the music, as well as its surprising variety. Since *Western Swing on the Radio* is comprised largely of radio transcriptions, it isn't necessarily an essential item, yet it remains a terrific, low-key way of exploring one of the most popular genres in country music. —*Thom Owens*

● **Western Swing, Vol. 1** / Old Timey ✦✦✦✦
Ths includes such artists as Bob Wills, Harry Choates, Bill Boyd, Milton Brown, and the Light Crust Doughboys, among others. —*AMG*

Western Swing, Vol. 2 / Old Timey ✦✦✦✦
This second volume features Jimmie Revard, the Tune Wranglers, W. Lee O'Daniel, and others, including several artists who appeared on the first album. —*AMG*

Western Swing, Vol. 3 / Old Timey ✦✦✦✦
This album features several artists who appeared in the preceding volumes, plus such additions as the Modern Mountaineers, Brown's Brownies, and Spade Cooley. —*AMG*

Western Swing, Vol. 4 / Old Timey ✦✦✦✦
This member of the series features Ted Daffan, Milton Brown, the Washboard Wonders, Jimmie Revard, Hank Penny, the Crystal Ramblers, Claude Casey, Shelly Lee Alley, and several other artists old and new to the series. —*AMG*

Western Swing, Vol. 5 / Old Timey ✦✦✦✦
This album features music recorded during the '30s by the Universal Cowboys, Buddy Jones, Bob Skyles, Ocie Stockard, the Farr Brothers, the Nite Owls, and others. —*AMG*

Western Swing, Vol. 6 / Old Timey ✦✦✦✦
This features Buddy Duhon & Harry Choates, Johnny Tyler, Don Churchill, Johnnie Lee Wills, T. Texas Tyler, Pee Wee King, Jerry Irby, Easy Adams, Webb Pierce, and other '40s and '50s stars. —*AMG*

Western Swing, Vol. 7 / Old Timey ✦✦✦✦
This volume also features music recorded between 1940 and 1960, this time by such artists as Ole Rasmussen, Hoyle Nix, T. Texas Tyler, Bob Wills, Arkie Shibley, Tommy Mooney, Glynn Duncan, Tommy Duncan, Tex Williams, Rocky Billy Ford, and others. —*AMG*

Western Swing, Vol. 8 / Old Timey ✦✦✦✦
More from the '40s and '50s, this time by Jimmy Walker, Jack Rhodes & Al Petty, the Maddox Brothers & Rose, Hawkshaw Hawkins, T. Texas Tyler, Big Jim DeNoone, Tommy Duncan, and others. —*AMG*

☆ **When I Was a Cowboy, Vol. 1** / 1996 / Yazoo ✦✦✦✦✦
These are the records that gave everyone from Gene Autry through Marty Robbins the basis for their careers, bridging the gap between nineteenth century reality and twentieth century nostalgia. These 23 songs are the real article from the mid-to-late 1920s, a time when the singers had ridden the range, and the events they sung of were often within living memory. This material is the White equivalent of recordings by Blind Lemon Jefferson, Papa Charlie Jackson, et al., and anyone owning their records—even if they don't like cowboy songs—ought to own this as well; J.D. Farley's "Bill Was a Texas Lad" could even pass for blues. Alas, there is no information included about Farley, the Cartwright Brothers, Harry McClintock ("Sam Bass"), Edward L. Crain ("Bandit Cole Younger"), the Crowder Brothers, Taylor's Kentucky Boys ("The Dixie Cowboy"), Carl Sprague ("The Last Longhorn"), Billie Maxwell, Watts & Wilson, Lonesome Luke & His Farm Hands (who give us an authentic square dance), or Patt Patterson & His Champion Rep Riders, and the only name that will be recognizable to modern listeners is rider-actor Ken Maynard, whose "Lone Star Trail" is one of the best things here. All of it is stripped down, sometimes with no more than a guitar accompaniment; the singing is raw and unaffected, but some of it displays surprising virtuosity, most notably the Arkansas Woodchopper's dexterous guitar playing on "I'm a Texas Cowboy" and "Texas Ranger" by the Cartwright Brothers, with a droning fiddle accompaniment that emphasizes the British origins of the melodies behind some of these songs. The sound is also unusually good. —*Bruce Eder*

☆ **When I Was a Cowboy, Vol. 2** / 1996 / Yazoo ✦✦✦✦✦
Yazoo Records' second cowboy compilation has some of the same artists and a few others, like the Crockett Family ("Buffalo Gals Medley"), Paul Hamblin ("The Strawberry Roan"), Buell Kazee, and McGinty's Oklahoma Cowboy Band ("Cowboy's Dream"). The material is equally strong, and much of it, including Harry McClintock's "Jesse James," is absolutely priceless. As with the first volume, there's no biographical material on any of the artists, but the music speaks well for itself—Jules Allen's "The Girl I Left Behind Me" seems pretty much the basis for every version that has followed since, Rowdy Wright's "I'm a Wandering Bronco Rider" and "I'm a Jolly Cowboy" both have delightfully raw energy, and the Delmore Brothers' exquisitely harmonized "The Fugitive's Lament" is the thematic precursor to every record the Everly Brothers ever cut, especially "Take a Message to Mary." The real find, however, may be Buell Kazee's soaring, banjo-driven "The Cowboy Trail," sung in a haunting nasal twang, which is one of the most honest *and* dramatic pieces among the 23 songs here.

The sound is generally excellent, apart from distortion in the opening bars of "The Burial of Wild Bill" by Frank Jenkins & His Pilot Mountaineers, and some unavoidable surface noise evident on Dick Devall's otherwise gorgeous a capella "Tom Sherman's Barroom." —*Bruce Eder*

White Mansions / 1978 / A&M ✦✦✦✦
A historical country-folk concept album featuring such diverse talents as Waylon Jennings, the Eagles' Bernie Leadon, and Eric Clapton. The result is a rather lovely blending of folk, blues, and country. Not central to a collection, but well made. See also *Songs of the Civil War.* —*Bruce Eder*

Wild Wild Country / May 7, 1992 / Priority ✦✦✦
Wild Wild Country is an enjoyable collection of '80s outlaws, but it doesn't offer enough material to make it a definitive disc. —*Stephen Thomas Erlewine*

Young Country: Country Dynamite / 1995 / Priority ✦✦✦
The *Country Dynamite* disc is an installment of Priority's *Young Country* series, featuring a selection of the biggest hits from some of the '90s' most popular artists. *Country Dynamite* features tracks from Sawyer Brown, Confederate Railroad, Shenandoah, and Brother Phelps, among others. —*Stephen Thomas Erlewine*

Young Country: Kings of Country / 1995 / Priority ✦✦✦
The *Kings of Country* disc is an installment of Priority's *Young Country* series, featuring a selection of the biggest hits from some of the '90s' most popular artists. *Kings of Country* features tracks from Randy Travis, Vince Gill, Alan Jackson, Mark O'Connor, Marty Stuart, and several others. —*Stephen Thomas Erlewine*

Young Country: Queens of Country / 1995 / Priority ✦✦✦
The *Queens of Country* disc is an installment of Priority's *Young Country* series, featuring a selection of the biggest hits from some of the '90s' most popular artists. *Queens of Country* features tracks from Pam Tillis, Suzy Bogguss, Lorrie Morgan, Michelle Wright, and the Judds, among others. —*Stephen Thomas Erlewine*

ESSAYS

Old-Time Traditional Country

For some, the mention of "old-time traditional" country music evokes images of mountain string bands and singers ranging somewhere from quaint and prosaic to stereotypical and cartoonish; for others, it is the ground floor of the music at its purest and most unsullied. A genre rich in oral tradition and untainted by commercial restrictions, it exists within a clear time frame (the mountain music passed around by early American settlers in Tennessee and Virginia from the late 1800s through the early 1920s, when it was first recorded). It abruptly changed into country music's next phase with the rise of the radio and recording star (better known as the singing cowboy phenomenon) in the late 1920s and early '30s. That it has survived into the present time is genuinely to be admired, mainly due to the work of a dedicated band of preservationists. Yet its very name implies its self-imposed limitations, and thus ultimately mummifies its creative progress; its traditional designs are revered for what they are, yet allowed to progress no further creatively, lest they coalesce into something else entirely. Still, the music's roots have survived, and they remain very deep roots indeed.

The history of country music stretches much further back than its beginnings in the United States; it is in the ballads of the British Isles that we find the music's true roots. Sometimes reaching as far back as the 17th century for their point of origin, ballads such as "The Cruelty of Barbary Allen" and "The Gypsy Lad" coalesced over time into traditional folk songs better known as "Barbara Allen" and "Black Jack David," respectively. The derivatives (and *their* subsequent derivations and spinoffs) of these songs served double duty, not only as topical entertainment based on the grisliest of current events but as extensions of the oral tradition from town to village. The song would consequently develop and change, taking new shape as each singer added verse and stanza before passing it on to the next songster, ultimately making it to its best known version. "Black Jack David" had gone through at least a half dozen title and lyrical variants, with its eventual American sobriquet having ties to both Scottish and English dialects of that period; while a love ballad like "The Lass of Loch Royal" had reached an interminable 35-verse length in its English incarnation before it was eventually trimmed to a mere three-verse stanza by its arrival on American shores as "Who's Gonna Shoe Your Pretty Little Feet." Sometimes nothing more was needed in translation between cultures than a change in town for an English murder ballad like "The Wexford Girl" to assume similar American mythic folk song proportions as "The Knoxville Girl." But songs that were full of death, regret, and recrimination were more than commonplace, and survived into the New World seemingly intact.

The old-timey genre comprises many sounds and styles. While the music of the Appalachian mountains—with its high, lonesome tenor vocal stylings (later the identifying aural fingerprint of bluegrass)—played its obvious role, equally pivotal were the styles of the medicine shows of Tennessee and Mississippi, the cowboy singers of Texas, and the regional variations provided by the singers and instrumentalists of Virginia, North Carolina, Louisiana, and Georgia. In the early days, performances were of a strictly family nature, for the sole enjoyment of the musician and those within immediate earshot. Songs were sung inside the home as the day's chores were being done, and this simple, unreconstructed a cappella singing brought with it countless regional variations.

The fiddle was the dominant—and only—instrument from its arrival on American shores in the 1600s, and the fiddler and singer soon became one, keeping their own highly rhythmic beat and accompaniment going between shouted verses with no other support behind them. By the mid-1800s, the fiddle was joined by the newly popular banjo; an instrument of entirely African-American derivation, it was cheap and easy to make, and in the 1800s was played almost exclusively by slaves and minstrel show performers. But before long it was being mainstreamed into the mountain regions and the South, where white musicians quickly adapted to it. Initially, guitars had no place within the music's confines; yet that quickly changed with the invention of the steel string around the turn of the century. The guitars being built by Martin and Gibson offered stronger bracing to accommodate the added string tension, and the suddenly louder and brighter instrument could now keep up with a flailing banjo and a fiddle. Performers now embraced the instrument in droves, and by the 1920s, the guitar—along with its smaller stylistic cousin, the mandolin—had arrived.

For a music with such a long pedigree, it still took a very long time to be documented on records, at least in its pure, unadulterated form. Recordings of songs popularized by "hill country musicians" had been going on since the turn of the century ("Soldier's Joy," a staple fiddler's piece, was recorded by the Victor Military band, for example), but these were versions bleached of all unvarnished regional eccentricities in order to appeal to a mainstream audience. Traditional country was considered "fringe" music of an uneducated people, and in the social climate of the Roaring Twenties, it was believed to have almost no commercial appeal. But the twin factors of a downturned economy and the coming of radio made the recording industry start looking for new markets to peddle their wares to. Jazz was emerging, and the first blues recordings were taking place; it wasn't long before country music became the third new market to be courted by the major labels.

In 1922, Texas fiddlers Eck Robinson and Henry Gilliland strong-armed their way into a Victor recording audition in New York. More to be rid of them than anything else, the Victor engineer recorded a handful of duets and solo sides on Robinson before dispatching the duo and filing the masters away. The following year, the label reluctantly released one of the duets, "Turkey in the Straw," as a single. Meanwhile, Okeh Records had recorded the Atlanta musician Fiddlin' John Carson, who sang along with his fiddle playing, making him the first country singer ever recorded (although the producer of the session thought his voice was horrendous). His first single, "The Little Log Cabin in the Lane," was released without a catalog number, as the label considered it to be little more than a vanity pressing. Soon, however, both the Robinson-Gilliland duet and the Carson single had racked up impressive sales, and suddenly there was a mad scram-

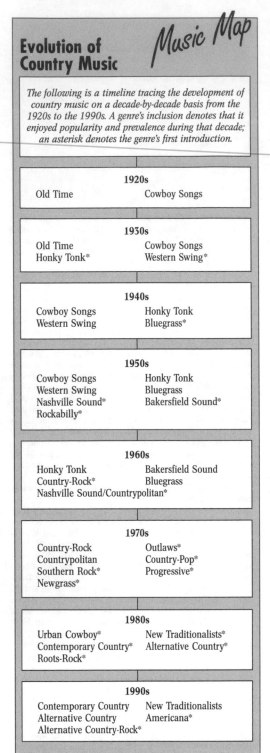

Evolution of Country Music

Music Map

The following is a timeline tracing the development of country music on a decade-by-decade basis from the 1920s to the 1990s. A genre's inclusion denotes that it enjoyed popularity and prevalence during that decade; an asterisk denotes the genre's first introduction.

1920s
Old Time	Cowboy Songs

1930s
Old Time	Cowboy Songs
Honky Tonk*	Western Swing*

1940s
Cowboy Songs	Honky Tonk
Western Swing	Bluegrass*

1950s
Cowboy Songs	Honky Tonk
Western Swing	Bluegrass
Nashville Sound*	Bakersfield Sound*
Rockabilly*	

1960s
Honky Tonk	Bakersfield Sound
Country-Rock*	Bluegrass
Nashville Sound/Countrypolitan*	

1970s
Country-Rock	Outlaws*
Countrypolitan	Country-Pop*
Southern Rock*	Progressive*
Newgrass*	

1980s
Urban Cowboy*	New Traditionalists*
Contemporary Country*	Alternative Country*
Roots-Rock*	

1990s
Contemporary Country	New Traditionalists
Alternative Country	Americana*
Alternative Country-Rock*	

fiddlers and string band practitioners, a large chunk of the music's history went unrecorded. It would take folklorists working for the Library of Congress (like Alan Lomax) another decade before solo vocal and fiddle performances were documented, with the form just a hair's breadth away from extinction. But that same year, Victor sent recording supervisor (a forerunner to today's record producer) Ralph Peer down to the border town of Bristol, TN. Armed with gigantic "portable" recording equipment and two engineers, his early flyers broadcasting his impending arrival stood him in excellent stead as far as attracting new talent.

The resulting applicants for audition came from as far afield as West Virginia, and in a space of two weeks—recording literally around the clock—Peer had amassed over 76 masters from various participants. Some, like Ernest Stoneman, the Alcoa Quartet and the Johnson Brothers, had minimal experience in recording and were considered at least semi-professional musicians; others showed up just for the opportunity to cut a record and make a little pocket money. This brace of masters has gone down in country music history as "the Bristol Sessions," the first major label documenting of old time country in a wide variety of regional strains. Although much fine music (and invaluable historical documentation) came from these recordings, there was still no defined "star" system. Artists like Macon, Vernon Dalhart, and Robinson & Carson all sold records in large quantities, but it could honestly be said that the song started the artist, and not the other way around. But with the pivotal Bristol sessions, two new acts emerged that would change the face of country music forever: A.P. Carter and the Carter Family, and the Singing Brakeman, Jimmie Rodgers.

These two new recording acts—both contemporaries of each other—attacked the new music's equations from entirely different perspectives. The Carter Family were unreconstructed Appalachian hill people solidly rooted in rural church music, shape note singing, and a traditional family-style presentation. With A.P. (Alvin Pleasant) as bass singer and leader, his wife Sara on autoharp and lead vocals, and the tenor vocals and guitar of sister-in-law Maybelle entwining together in song, their somewhat nasal voices nonetheless established the basic outlines of country music harmonies. A.P. was also a master at taking traditional material and adapting it into new pieces, and the Carters' first hits ("Wildwood Flower," "Keep on the Sunny Side," "Bury Me Beneath the Willow," "The Storms Are on the Ocean," "Will the Circle Be Unbroken") clearly reflect how the traditional sounds and songs were mainstreamed into easily digestible performances that would fit onto one side of a phonograph record. Provincial in both their musical and performing demeanor, their live performance posters (declaring that "this show is morally good") solidified their image as the first great country music family act, a point not lost on similar units who came in their wake.

But it was the rise of Jimmie Rodgers that brought old time traditional country to its zenith in popularity. Where the Carters projected an image of rigid stoicism, Rodgers was jaunty, frolicsome, and quick with a slang expression, and while the Carter Family sang hymns, Jimmie Rodgers sang the blues with gusto, abandon, and a high-pitched yodel that quickly became his vocal trademark (although the practice itself had roots that were centuries old). He made his show business pull recasting himself as "The Singing Brakeman," a jaunty tip of the cap to both his railroading roots and the exotic, colorful image it represented to mainstream America at the time. But once success quickly came with the release of his first recordings, Rodgers just as quickly shucked the railroader's dungarees (with the rare exception of a one-reel movie short made in 1929, the only filmed record of him) and took to wearing straw hats and fancy suits. He cut records—110 of them in six years—as if nothing could possibly contain him or his irrepressible spirit, and became the biggest country star of his day, maintaining strong roots in old-time traditional music while recasting it—and his image—in a way that was new and advanced for the time. In other words, Rodgers was the first artist to consciously promote the idea of a country singer as being something more urbane than the buffoonish image of the barefoot hick, the rube ready for the taking.

There's no telling how big a star Jimmie Rodgers would have ultimately become if he hadn't been dying of tuberculosis, a dis-

ble within the industry to record this new, strange music. By 1927, labels were regularly sending field units down south to record the best singers and instrumentalists, issuing the results almost as fast as they could. But in the major labels' rush to record the best ease totally incurable during his lifetime. Knowing he was on borrowed time with an audience that *knew* he was on borrowed time, Rodgers fortified himself with the old show business determination to keep plugging along, damn the consequences. In a final defiant gesture—equal parts bravado, financial insurance, sentimentalism, and hillbilly senselessness—he traveled to New York to record one last session. Racked with pain but determined to leave something behind for his family, Rodgers returned to his original style: just himself and his simply picked guitar accompaniment. A cot was kept in the studio so he could lie down and rest between takes, and according to legend, there was also a bucket next to him to spit blood into. Two days later, Jimmie Rodgers died from a severe internal hemorrhage. In the wake of his death, the first country tribute records appeared, all of them solemnly intoning the sadness everyone felt over "The Death of Jimmie Rodgers"; within a couple of years, the "Singing Cowboy" was the rage in country music. By the time the first country music shows started appearing on radio in the mid-1930s, the music of the Appalachian mountains was already being described as "old timey" and "traditional"—the sound of a bygone age, forever preserved.

—Cub Koda

The Grand Ole Opry

The longest-running broadcast in radio history, nothing is more tied to the image of country music than the institution known as the Grand Ole Opry. For the last 70-plus years, the highest aspiration of all country singers has been to play the Grand Ole Opry. It is country music's ultimate prestige gig; to be invited to stand on its stage and sing and pick means you have arrived—only the best get to play the Opry. For years, its alumni were the very best the genre had to offer, and to be asked to become a member was the highest honor anyone in country music could achieve. Its Saturday night broadcasts brought a rural nation together, imparting a commonality of both community and language; it gave its audience a sense of belonging. Long before cable, car phones, and faxes entered our lives, the Grand Ole Opry radio show let a whole rural nation know that they weren't alone.

The Opry started both as an accident and a knockoff of another—more successful—show. In October of 1925, radio station WSM began broadcasting in Nashville. WSM was owned by National Life and Accident Insurance Company, whose slogan "We Shield Millions" became the station's call letters. WLS in Chicago had had great success with their *National Barn Dance*, and WSM had lured George D. Hay from WLS to become their station director. The Opry had its genesis on the night of November 28, 1925, when a preacher missed his regular broadcast and Hay grabbed a local fiddler named Uncle Jimmy Thompson to fill in the dead air time. The response from listeners was swift, immediate, and overwhelmingly positive. By December 26, the show was a regular feature of the WSM lineup, featuring Hay as emcee, with Thompson and Uncle Dave Macon on banjo as its nominal cast.

The show progressed mightily in the next year, adding local musicians like the Crook Brothers, Humphrey Bate's Possum Hunters, and the African-American harmonica wizard DeFord Bailey to the regular lineup. For the first year or so of its radio life, it went by the not-so-original handle of the *WSM Barn Dance*, but one night in 1927 (following a national radio hookup of classical music and grand opera) Hay coined the name Grand Ole Opry and suddenly the show had a whole new outlook that distanced them from the competition. By the early 1930s, WSM had boosted its AM signal to a whopping 50,000 watts, which, on their nightly broadcasts, beamed them into 30 of the 48 states and sections of Canada. While shows like the *National Barn Dance* and Shreveport's *Louisiana Hayride* (both precursors to the Opry) continued on successfully, suddenly the Opry—and Nashville—became the hot spot for country music. The show got larger and more varied by the decade's end, with the Delmore Brothers, Pee Wee King

and His Golden West Cowboys, Bill Monroe, and Minnie Pearl all becoming regular cast members.

But no one defined the image of the Opry, country music, and Nashville more than Roy Acuff. Joining the show in 1938 (a year before Monroe and two years before Minnie Pearl), Acuff was a superb athlete, his baseball-playing skills earning him a spring-training tryout with the New York Yankees. But a severe bout with sunstroke in 1929 put those aspirations to rest. He concentrated on fiddling, learning his trade as part of a medicine show that traveled the Smoky Mountains (where he was born and raised). It was show business training you couldn't buy for a million dollars and Acuff soaked it up like a sponge; he learned how to work a crowd, how to do train whistle imitations, and how to balance his fiddle on his nose. All this showmanship led to his first radio spot, on Knoxville's WROL. His backup combo was called the Tennessee Crackerjacks, but Acuff's unbridled enthusiasm with the group caused the station announcer to re-dub them "Roy Acuff and his Crazy Tennesseans." When they inherited a song called "The Great Speckled Bird," Acuff's emotionally charged performance was strong enough to nail them a recording contract and a chance to audition for the Opry. The response from the radio audience was overwhelming, and Acuff and his band—with their new, Opry-applied name, the Smoky Mountain Boys—quickly became synonymous with the image of the show.

Acuff's tenacity in keeping his music mountain-influenced and down-to-earth cost him several band members, but it proved to be the perfect forum for him when the show began national broadcasting over NBC in 1939. At a time when everybody wanted to be either a cowboy singer or in a Western swing band, Acuff was already an anachronism, with an audience that mirrored his beliefs every note of the way. He was the first modern-day star of country music, with hit records under his belt ("Wabash Cannonball," "Wreck on the Highway," "Fireball Mail," The Precious Jewel), crowds of adoring fans at his personal appearances, and an overall popularity—especially with American servicemen during World War II—commensurate with pop performers like Frank Sinatra. He continued to influence and shape country music both as a music publisher (one of Nashville's first and most successful) and defender of older styles and their practitioners. His constant presence on the Opry assured the audience that as long as Roy Acuff was still there, certain traditions would always be in place.

The Grand Ole Opry grew bigger and more popular during the wartime years of the 1940s, eventually overtaking WLS' *National Barn Dance* in popularity as *the* country music program of choice. It stayed traditional, allowing neither drums nor references to liquor on its stage. It also moved with the times, bringing such new stars into the fold as Ernest Tubb, Eddy Arnold, and, by the decade's end, the biggest of them all, Hank Williams. In early 1943 the show took up residence at the Ryman Auditorium, a huge tabernacle located in downtown Nashville. The inside of the place suited the music and the down-home image of the show perfectly. It was a big old church and virtually no attempts were made to renovate it, so its past was kept alive as well. It was cold and drafty in the winter and hot as hell in the summer. It was unprepossessing and charming all at once—or, as one performer put it, "not so big, just so famous." Soon the old church would be welcoming Little Jimmy Dickens, Hank Snow, Moon Mullican, and comic Rod Brasfield to the show's roster.

Since WSM (and National Life) knew they had a good thing going with this enterprise, they protected their interests by having its cast members booked through the station's Artist Service bureau. One of the strictest enforcements by the Opry was that cast members appear a set number of Saturdays a year, giving up lucrative show dates for union scale. The first artist to leave the fold (others had been fired for missing radio broadcasts) was Eddy Arnold, who bucked the system and went on to even greater success. Although artists like Cowboy Copas, Carl Smith, and Porter Wagoner were early 1950s stars seemingly tailor-made for the show's musical makeup, the face of the Opry was changing. New Opry managers Jim Denny and Jack Stapp wrested control of the show away from George D. Hay, as the "Solemn Old Judge" was in failing health by the early 1950s. They planned to modernize the show (less mountain-style string bands, more Nudie-suited recording star singers) while clinging tenaciously to the program's etched-in-stone conservative values (no references to alcohol onstage and no drums). The older stars had their traditional spots, with old-timers like Acuff and Hank Snow boosted up to hosting their own segments of the three-hour radio broadcast. The "give the public what they want" modernization only went so far and the two managers missed the boat completely when rockabilly and rock 'n' roll—themselves both clear outgrowths of country music—came to prominence in the mid-1950s. The story of Denny telling Elvis to go back to driving a truck after his lone Opry appearance is legendary, and while shows like the *Louisiana Hayride* welcomed the new music (and its upstart practitioners), when Carl Perkins sat atop all three music charts with "Blue Suede Shoes," his Opry appearance left his drummer sitting in the car, listening to the show on the radio. It would be decades before a drum set was unpacked and set up on the stage of Ryman Auditorium.

But the Opry was now on a more youth-oriented kick, adding artists like Stonewall Jackson, Roy Drusky, Jimmie C. Newman, Charlie Louvin, Bobby Helms, Jean Shepard, and Don Gibson to its already burgeoning roster. By the late '60s the youth movement was even more pronounced with the additions of Bill Anderson, David Houston (himself a former rockabilly), George Jones, Connie Smith, Jack Greene, and the woman who would become the queen of country crossover, Dolly Parton. With a fresh stable of artists and its staid traditions still firmly in place, the radio show went out every Saturday night like clockwork, establishing Nashville as country music's world headquarters and drawing tourists by the Grey Line busfuls. While this massive influx of tourism boded well for the city and the industry, it spelled the end for the Ryman Auditorium. The old church—with its straight church pews for seating still in place—was simply not equipped for this many people, either in the cast or in the audience. Sometime in the late 1960s, National Life stepped in and started making plans for the Opry to be moved to a bigger facility, the centerpiece of an amusement park to be called Opryland. The final Grand Ole Opry show in the Ryman was held on March 9, 1974, and without missing a beat, the inaugural broadcast from Opryland was on the air the following week. But the following decades saw the Opry diminish in importance, with the onslaught of country-pop crossover artists and rock 'n' roll's unflagging influence infiltrating its ranks. No longer was the Grand Ole Opry the only game in town or the only way a country artist could truly become a big name; by the end of the 1960s, the chart-topping success of West Coast stars like Buck Owens and Merle Haggard had already proven that point.

Though its popularity stayed as high as ever and tourists still flocked to Opryland from around the world, the Opry went from cream-of-the-crop cutting-edge country to its current incarnation as a solid standard-bearer of country's rich traditions. Finally coming to terms with its old nemesis rock 'n' roll, the show has also dropped its restrictive booking practices, making Opry cast members out of many of today's superstars, with the requirement of so many appearances a year no longer preventing artists from joining the show. Its very traditionalism has oddly enough attracted many of the new breed to its fold as a matter of pride and validation, and its current membership includes Vince Gill, Ricky Skaggs, Randy Travis, Alison Krauss, and Alan Jackson, with new members joining every day. Although you can now make your fortune in country music by other means and routes, the Grand Ole Opry is *still* the ultimate prestige gig.

—Cub Koda

Singing Cowboys

Strictly speaking, cowboy songs—the "western" part of Country & Western music—should stand on their own, separate from country music. They come from a tradition far older than the commercial country music, and derive from origins unique in the history of the United States. Apart from the power of their melodies and words, much of their original appeal lay in their nostalgic connection with a specific era in American history that had long since

passed. Western songs have been grouped with country music mainly because the original instrumentation of the two genres was similar (acoustic guitars, fiddles, harmonicas, upright bass and concertinas), the sentiments and orientations of both were distinctly rural (or, at least, non-urban), and some of the same people who played cowboy songs also played country songs.

The music's roots lay in the expansion of the United States, especially the migration of the white European-spawned population beyond the boundaries of the original 13 states. Before any songs surfaced that would take a lasting hold on the imagination, there were stories, legends, and folktales, some of them quite grisly. When the country moved west, the songs that people knew went west with them. The basic problem for anyone traveling west was the open spaces beyond the Mississippi and Missouri Rivers; getting anywhere took months. Mostly, Western music was conceived to overcome loneliness—to fight the monotony, families would sing together to break up their days' unyielding routine. A song might spread one farm or ranch at a time, town by town or county by county, from saloon to saloon, getting altered along the way by bad memories and the better-or-worse musical talents that were applied to playing them. Other than that most common of instruments, the human voice, the usual means of playing this material were the most portable of instruments: guitar, banjo, harmonica, fiddle, and concertina. In the early days, spinets and upright pianos were a rarity in saloons, and anything larger than that was virtually unknown.

Cowboys constituted virtually a separate society unto themselves. Most were drifters, and they came mostly from the East or the South (after the Civil War, they even included a significant number of freed black men). They brought the music they knew with them, and it became the raw material around which the new songs of the West were built, reflecting the new surroundings and environment in which the singers were working and living. It was only with the dawn of the twentieth century that the idea came to collect and write down the tunes. It was a cowboy, N. Howard Thorp, who printed a 23-song collection called *Songs of the Cowboys* in 1908. This was followed two years later by *Cowboy Songs and Other Frontier Ballads*, edited by John A. Lomax—the same man who was to discover Leadbelly some 20 years later—a much more ambitious work containing 122 songs.

The Thorp and Lomax books sold well, but not in enormous numbers. There was little new interest in the music of the West at the time, but public fascination did grow. Ironically, all of this activity was taking place just at the time that the reality behind the songs was passing into history; by the turn of the century, the cowboy had begun to slowly fade from the West, though he never disappeared entirely. As early as 1925, Western songs had become a mainstay of radio; among the singers who recorded cowboy songs during this era were Carl T. Sprague, Harry "Mac" McLintock, Goebel Reeves (aka The Texas Drifter), and Jules Van Allen. Sprague's "When the Work's All Done This Fall" became an enormous hit in 1925, selling 900,000 copies; in 1927, McLintock's "The Old Chisholm Trail" also sold in the hundreds of thousands. California was an especially fertile land for Western groups, including Len Nash and His Country Boys, which included future Sons of the Pioneers Hugh and Karl Farr; Sheriff Loyal Underwood's Arizona Wranglers; and Jack LeFevre and His Texas Outlaws. In 1929, a young Texan named Gene Autry came to New York to try his hand at a recording career; in 1931, he had his first major hit with "That Silver-Haired Daddy of Mine."

In Hollywood, Westerns had long been a staple of the film industry, and in 1933 producer Nat Levine of Mascot Pictures began producing features starring the former silent cowboy actor Ken Maynard. In Maynard's earlier movies, the actor had sung a song or two that seemed to go over well—not only did the songs break up the tension and add variety to the movies' tempos, but the audiences seemed to like the movies better. Maynard was no singer, and Levine reasoned that if he could make a song work, then a professional singer might make even more of a difference in the popularity of a film. After a screen test, Autry and another ARC artist, comic-singer-songwriter Smiley Burnette, were brought out to Hollywood to appear in a barn dance sequence in the Maynard movie *In Old Santa Fe.*

Autry and Burnette only appeared in one scene in the film, but they proved the most popular elements in the movie. The next step was for Levine to try and build an entire film around Autry. These Westerns proved to be a gold mine—Autry's singing, coupled with his personality in front of the cameras, drew people by the millions into theaters to see his movies, which further helped his record sales. By 1936, he was virtually unrivaled as a Western film star and had no peer as a recording artist. In the meantime, every small studio wanted to release its own series of B-Westerns. Columbia signed up ex-football star Charles Starrett as "The Durango Kid," but Starrett didn't sing, so the studio signed up the highly popular Sons of the Pioneers to appear in his films and provide the music. The fledgling Grand National studios got Tex Ritter, and even John Wayne, still making his way in B-pictures, was pressed into service in the part of the lawman "Singin' Sandy," his voice dubbed by a professional. In 1937, Autry and Republic Pictures found themselves at loggerheads over a contract dispute, and the singer failed to report for the shooting of his next scheduled film. The studio began looking for a substitute, and found one in Leonard Slye, a founding member of the Sons of the Pioneers, who made his debut as Gene Autry's replacement in *Under Western Stars* (1937) with his new screen name, Roy Rogers. Autry's dispute with the company was settled soon after, but Republic Records now had two Western stars on its roster.

During World War II, Rogers continued making Westerns, while Autry joined the armed forces. By the end of the war, Rogers was the undisputed king of the movie cowboys, and Autry returned from military service to resume his career. At the same time, a new generation of singing cowboys had come along, led by Jimmy Wakely and Rex Allen, who began their own series of B-westerns spiced with songs. The days of the B-Western were numbered, however, by change in the population and the way that it looked at entertainment. World War II had cost Autry and Rogers much of the adult portion of their audience—the country came out of the war a lot less rural than it had gone in, and without the problems of the Great Depression to send millions of people looking for simple stories and solutions in movie theaters for a few hours at a time.

And then came television. As soon as audiences were able to stay home on Saturdays and see action films for free on TV, the attendance for B-Westerns, serials, and other low-budget film entertainment declined rapidly. Autry and Rogers, who owned their own properties (Rogers had taken legal ownership of the Roy Rogers name and all merchandising rights associated with it during the early 1940s), saw the handwriting on the wall and, by the end of the 1940s, had shifted their activities to the new medium. It was here that the Western song was preserved in popular culture. While there were no singing cowboys on television after Autry's and Rogers' respective retirements in the mid-1950s, there were lots of cowboy songs around. It seemed like every late 1950s adult Western had to have a title song, and while few of these songs were hits in commercial release, all were well known enough to keep the cowboy song alive in popular culture.

The following decades saw the deaths of many of the most important original singers of cowboy songs from the first commercial wave, including most of the founding Sons of the Pioneers. Others, however, picked up the tradition. Apart from the newer generation of the Sons of the Pioneers, and veteran singer-songwriters such as Johnny Western and Rex Allen Sr., younger solo artists such as ex-folk singer Ian Tyson, cosmic cowboy songster Michael Martin Murphey, established country stars like Emmylou Harris, and even Allen's son, Rex Allen Jr. carried on, and groups such as the Riders in the Sky and the Sons of the San Joachin have made entire careers singing about the West.

—Bruce Eder

Recommended Recordings:

Various Artists, *When I Was a Cowboy, Vol. 1* (Yazoo)
Various Artists, *When I Was a Cowboy, Vol. 2* (Yazoo)
Various Artists, *Saddle Up!* (Rounder)

Various Artists, *The Singing Cowboys* (K-Tel)
Various Artists, *The Singing Cowboys* (CEMA)
Various Artists, *Home on the Range* (Pavilion)
Various Artists, *Silver Screen Cowboys* (Sony Music)
Various Artists, *Small Screen Cowboy Heroes* (Sony Music)
Various Artists, *Songs of the West* (Rhino)
Gene Autry, *Back in the Saddle Again* (Sony Music)
Sons of the Pioneers, *Country Music Hall of Fame Series* (MCA)
Marty Robbins, *Gunfighter Ballads* (Sony Music)
Johnny Western, *Gunfight at the O.K. Corral* (Bear Family)

Western Swing

Western swing is a genre of country music where string band sounds mesh with jazz stylings to produce a unique new form. A diverse and interesting amalgam, its form draws on everything from blues to pop tunes (complete with crooner style vocals reminiscent of Bing Crosby) to fiddle breakdowns to jazz standards, with a big band swing beat underpinning it all. Completely Southwestern in its derivation—coming from the twin musical and geographical wellsprings of Texas and Oklahoma—the beginnings of the style can be traced back to a single source.

The group generally credited for giving the style its first creative forum was the Fort Worth-based Wills Fiddle band, later to become the Aladdin Laddies, who even later became the Light Crust Doughboys. Not unlike bluesman Muddy Waters' famous first electric blues band—loaded with brand-name players like Little Walter who went on to stardom of their own—the Doughboys featured the twin fountainheads of this new music, fiddler Bob Wills and vocalist Milton Brown. Originally a trio (with guitarist Herman Arspiger as the third member), the group started broadcasting over WBAP in 1930, changing their name every time they changed sponsors. They also started experimenting with the music early on, especially when they played dances at the Crystal Springs Pavilion on the edge of town. The development of this musical hybrid was directly tied to the patrons' tastes and what they wanted to hear. Although old-time fiddle tunes expertly played were still great crowd pleasers, folks in a modern-thinking metropolis like Fort Worth liked to dance to hot jazz, the style then in vogue. Wills and Brown adjusted their set list to accommodate this stylistic addition, and soon started bringing more musicians into the group with similar eclectic tastes. The seeds of a distinct style were being planted with an audience that was responding to it, thus shaping it as well.

But the next pivotal move in the music's development came when the station management at WBAP handed down the edict that the Doughboys had to give up their appearances at Crystal Springs. Milton Brown resigned from both band and station, immediately starting up his own outfit, Milton Brown and His Musical Brownies. He landed a noontime slot on rival station KTAT and moved into the Doughboys' old slot with his new band, playing at Crystal Springs four nights a week. Brown's vision for the music was more cutting-edge—at least at first—than Wills', and he was the first to get on record, cutting an eight-song session for Bluebird in 1934. Whereas Bob Wills was content to take older fiddle breakdowns and the like and jazz them up with the new beat, Brown would take the current hits of the day and do them up in the new hybrid string band style. Although Milton did not play an instrument, his smooth, honey-toned vocals—equal parts Bing Crosby, Cab Calloway, and Emmett Miller—were also highly influential with other country singers.

While both bands featured the twin fiddle sound that would become the connecting thread of Western swing, the Brownies' true secret weapon was Bob Dunn. Dunn brought the first amplified steel guitar into the genre and although the instrument was crude by modern standards (a cheap Mexican guitar with a warped neck and a homemade pickup stuck on it), it was state-of-the-art for the time and the sounds he produced on it changed country music forever. Dunn's jazzy, hornlike leads, combined with a jagged dissonance in his approach, were featured front and center on all of the Brownies' records for the next year. It was a sound that sent shock waves throughout country music, and soon

Western Swing

Music Map

```
                        ┌─────────────────────────────┐
                        │         Influences          │
                        │  Jig-Dancing, Itinerant Music │
                        │     (early 20th century)     │
                        └─────────────────────────────┘

                        ┌─────────────────────────────┐
                        │       Old Time Music        │
                        │ Jimmie Rodgers, The Carter Family │
                        │       (1920s – 1930s)       │
                        └─────────────────────────────┘

┌──────────────────┐    ┌─────────────────────────────┐
│  Big Band Jazz   │    │      Early Development      │
│     (1930s)      │    │    Light Crust Doughboys    │
└──────────────────┘    │       (1930 – 1934)         │
                        └─────────────────────────────┘

                        ┌─────────────────────────────┐
                        │ First Inclusion of Amplified Steel Guitar │
                        │ Milton Brown and His Musical Brownies │
                        │  Bob Wills and the Texas Playboys │
                        │       (1934 – 1935)         │
                        └─────────────────────────────┘

                        ┌─────────────────────────────┐
                        │      Early Recordings       │
                        │   Bob Wills, Art Satherly   │
                        │     (1935 – WWII era)       │
                        └─────────────────────────────┘

                        ┌─────────────────────────────┐
                        │       California Era        │
                        │ Bob Wills, Spade Cooley, Hank Penny │
                        │  (mid-1940s – mid-1950s)    │
                        └─────────────────────────────┘

                        ┌─────────────────────────────┐
                        │       Swing Revival         │
                        │ Merle Haggard, Asleep at the Wheel, Dan Hicks and His Hot Licks, │
                        │  Big Sandy and His Fly-Rite Boys │
                        │     (late '60s – present)   │
                        └─────────────────────────────┘
```

Bob Wills was ordering up an amplified steel for his guitarist Leon McAuliffe. The Brownies were seminal in the creation of several imitation bands, and their influence spread as far as Louisiana Cajun country and Alabama. The future for the band was looking extremely bright when Brown was killed in a car accident in April 1936. His younger brother assumed leadership of the band, but soon its key players scattered to several territory bands (primarily Cliff Bruner's Texas Wanderers and Dunn's Vagabonds), spelling an end to the innovative outfit. Meanwhile, up in Tulsa, OK (after moving from Fort Worth to Waco to Oklahoma City), Bob Wills had settled in at Cain's Ballroom and spent all of 1934 and 1935 almost single-handedly redefining the new form while simultaneously stretching the boundaries of acceptable country instrumentation. By now the new aggregation was called Bob Wills and His Texas Playboys and by 1934 the group featured two fiddles, two guitars, banjo, piano, string bass and the vocals of Tommy Duncan, a holdover from the Light Crust Doughboys. Wills hired violinist Jesse Ashlock away from Milton Brown, letting Ashlock (a disciple of jazz great Joe Venuti) play all the "hot" breaks, while he did the traditional breakdowns. Adding a trumpet, trombone, and a saxophone to this string band lineup, Wills further instructed his musicians to play jazz lines as much as possible, trying to imitate the horn section of Fletcher Henderson's

band on stringed instruments. Realizing he needed a bigger beat to go with this bigger sound, Wills broke with convention (again) and became the first country band to have a drummer in it, a former Dixieland player named Smokey Dacus.

Above all, Wills was simply a superb bandleader, with a keen eye for talent and how to best utilize it. While a tough taskmaker with definite ideas about how he wanted his music played and presented, he promoted a family atmosphere within the ranks, making him someone you wanted to play your heart out for. Above all, he prized music loaded with feel, and would let mistakes slide if the groove was right. When the Texas Playboys locked into the right spirit of the selection, Wills would start shouting encouragement, usually capped off with his trademark holler of "a-ha!". He never assigned solo spots, merely pointing his fiddle bow at whomever he wanted to take it or hollering out their name a scant moment or two before they were to start. While Tommy Duncan is to be commended for keeping a straight face while Wills constantly interjected nonsensical patter between his vocal lines, a quick listen to the group's *Tiffany Transcription* recording of "Are You from Texas?" proves that this wasn't always the case: no one could ever accuse the Bob Wills band of being boring or too somber in its approach.

By 1935, he had assembled his first great version of the Texas

Playboys and was ready to record. At their first session, the producer—Arthur Satherly, who had cut hits with everyone from Ma Rainey to Gene Autry—admonished Wills for hollering too much, claiming it was drowning out the music. Wills was ready to yank the band out of the studio right then and there, and when Satherly tried to placate him he was promptly told, "You want Bob Wills, you get Bob Wills, and Bob Wills hollers anytime he wants." Satherly let Wills follow his muse and by the second session in Chicago the following year was fully converted, letting the band play and yell their heads off. The big hit from this session was "Steel Guitar Rag," a modern style swing tune that featured Wills' admonition, "Ah, take it away, Leon" with McAuliffe providing the rest of the fireworks. Wills kept adding more horns to the band in the late 1930s and brought aboard Eldon Shamblin as electric lead guitarist and occasional arranger. The 1940s brought Wills his greatest successes on records with hits like "San Antonio Rose," "Time Changes Everything," "Corrine, Corrina," "Take Me Back to Tulsa," "Cherokee Maiden" and "Stay a Little Longer."

World War II broke up this configuration of the band, the draft leaving only Wills and Tommy Duncan behind. Wills reorganized the unit and moved it to California, finding an enthusiastic audience of transplanted Texans and Okies who had moved there to work in the defense plants. This proved to be the last great hurrah for Bob and the Texas Playboys and for the Western swing movement as well. Hollywood had been co-opting the style for a spate of low budget cowboy movies, using the more modern-sounding genre to "upscale" the music behind their sometimes nominal stars. Even singing cowboys like Gene Autry were augmenting their old-timey string bands with trumpet and accordions. In the wake of Wills' coming to California, territory bands started springing up like wildfire, kicking off the entire California country movement, which reached its commercial and creative apex with the Bakersfield sound of the 1960s. The most successful of these was led by Spade Cooley (himself a transplanted Oklahoman), whose band featured vocalist Tex Williams, who would later go on to a successful solo career of his own. Wills stripped his horn section down to a single trumpet, hired the jazzy guitar of Junior Barnard and the electric mandolin of Tiny Moore and scored his final hit in 1950 with the classic "Faded Love."

By the mid-1950s, the heyday of Western swing was over. Mirroring its decline in popularity was the decline in health and success of Bob Wills himself. The crowds got smaller, Wills kept drinking, the band got smaller, Wills kept drinking, the record companies got smaller, and Wills kept drinking until he drank himself into two heart attacks by 1962 and 1964. Five years later, he suffered a massive stroke, and spent his remaining days confined to a wheelchair. His final session, reuniting him with several of the original Texas Playboys, was organized by longtime fan Merle Haggard with Wills still cueing the soloists and hollering "a-ha!" from his wheelchair.

The music went through a renaissance of sorts in the '70s through the hippie revivalist efforts of bands like Commander Cody and His Lost Planet Airmen, Dan Hicks and His Hot Licks and most notably Asleep at the Wheel. Led by visionary Ray Benson, the group's sound and spirit is much more than mere revivalism, and has survived numerous personnel changes to become part of the country music firmament itself. In mainstream country, the sound reverberates as well in the music of Junior Brown, George Strait, Merle Haggard, and Willie Nelson, making Western swing accessible to yet another generation of fans.

—Cub Koda

Recommended Recordings:

Bob Wills, *Anthology* (Rhino)

Milton Brown and His Musical Brownies, *Pioneer Western Swing Band* (MCA)

Cliff Bruner, *Cliff Bruner's Texas Wanderers* (Texas Rose)

Spade Cooley, *Spadella!: The Essential Spade Cooley* (Columbia Legacy)

Tex Williams, *Capitol's Collector Series* (Capitol)

Merle Haggard, *A Tribute to the Best Damn Fiddle Player in the World (Or My Salute to Bob Wills)* (Capitol/Koch International)

Asleep at the Wheel, *Texas Gold* (Capitol)

Various Artists, *Hillbilly Fever, Vol 1.: Legends of Western Swing* (Rhino)

Honky Tonk

One of the most enduring of all of country's myriad genres, the history of honky tonk music boasts several anomalies that make it unique. For one, the form—unlike bluegrass—is one of the few in country music that doesn't come from a "folk" background, its sound and style being almost fully a by-product of rural people living in the city (Southern cities though they may be). Two, while other trends have briefly dominated country music with great commercial success (countrypolitan, Western swing, etc.)—only to be swept aside when public favor waned—as long as there's been a country band playing in a bar somewhere, honky tonk music has survived and, in many ways, developed and prospered.

While the first documented instance of the term being used goes back to a newspaper article published in 1891, the terminology didn't enter the country music vocabulary until the mid-1930s. The man responsible for naming the genre was singer-songwriter Al Dexter. Dexter had operated a honky tonk in Texas since the early 1930s (although he always referred to it as a tavern), but his friend and fellow songwriter James Paris turned him on to the phrase—one describing "those beer joints up and down the road"—and the two of them parlayed it into the genre's first hit, "Honky Tonk Blues." From the very beginning, the style celebrated both the good times inherent in the Friday payday-night kick-up-your-heels experience and the wages of sin and guilt extracted from those good times. There was no such thing in country as "cry-in-your-beer music" until honky tonk came along.

The years preceding World War II led to the growth and development of honky tonk music. The mood in the country, especially among rural Southerners who had rafts of family and loved ones fighting overseas, was perfectly suited to the twin themes of celebration and sin that were part and parcel of the music. Here was a country that had every reason to celebrate—if only to cast off their wartime woes—yet couldn't really commit to wholesale revelry because of the religion-tinged guilt and despair that came as a consequence of partying too hard and too loosely.

If honky tonk didn't develop lyrically beyond those two themes it was because it really didn't have to. There was gold a-plenty in those two ideas and—not unlike the axiom that there's always a new way to say "I love you" in a song—a million lyrical twists and turns to be derived from them. Whether it was just an uptempo celebration of a hillbilly Saturday night, dancing a sprightly jig while getting loaded on cheap liquor, or the poor average Joe with a cold one in hand lamenting his sorry lot in life, the form was elastic as all get-out. Not only did honky tonk music change the face of country music, but perhaps its greatest contribution is how it changed the face of country songwriting forever. No longer were songs about trains, dead dogs, and Mama going to get the job done anymore.

The sound of honky tonk was a break with country music's past as well. The main reason for this change in the sound was electricity, and the different, more highly evolved type of player that embraced that change. Electric instruments, still a quite new phenomena on the music scene, started creeping into country bands, and soon the sound of the amplified steel guitar became the linchpin of the honky tonk style. Bob Dunn, of Milton Brown and His Musical Brownies, was country music's first amplified steel player, and his jagged, swooping jazz-inspired lines set the pace on the new instrument. When Brown was killed in an automobile accident in 1936, the band leadership role fell to a 20-year-old Texas fiddler named Cliff Bruner. Starting his own band, Bruner's Texas Wanderers, he soon enlisted the services of Dunn on steel guitar and pianist-singer-songwriter Moon Mullican. The Texas Wanderers took honky tonk even further uptown, featuring numerous electric instruments in the band (including an amplified mandola, a descendant of the mandolin family) and a syn-

Honky Tonk

Music Map

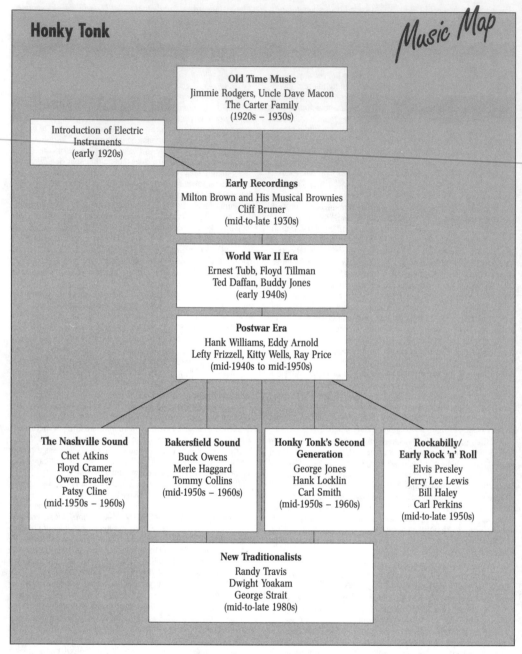

Old Time Music
Jimmie Rodgers, Uncle Dave Macon
The Carter Family
(1920s – 1930s)

Introduction of Electric Instruments
(early 1920s)

Early Recordings
Milton Brown and His Musical Brownies
Cliff Bruner
(mid-to-late 1930s)

World War II Era
Ernest Tubb, Floyd Tillman
Ted Daffan, Buddy Jones
(early 1940s)

Postwar Era
Hank Williams, Eddy Arnold
Lefty Frizzell, Kitty Wells, Ray Price
(mid-1940s to mid-1950s)

The Nashville Sound
Chet Atkins
Floyd Cramer
Owen Bradley
Patsy Cline
(mid-1950s – 1960s)

Bakersfield Sound
Buck Owens
Merle Haggard
Tommy Collins
(mid-1950s – 1960s)

Honky Tonk's Second Generation
George Jones
Hank Locklin
Carl Smith
(mid-1950s – 1960s)

Rockabilly/ Early Rock 'n' Roll
Elvis Presley
Jerry Lee Lewis
Bill Haley
Carl Perkins
(mid-to-late 1950s)

New Traditionalists
Randy Travis
Dwight Yoakam
George Strait
(mid-to-late 1980s)

ergy with other Texas bands that led to further developments in the style.

Above all, they had great songs, and on September 13, 1938, the band committed to wax (literally, as magnetic tape hadn't been invented yet) the first great classic of the honky tonk genre, "It Makes No Difference Now." The tune was written by Floyd Tillman, one of country music's most successful songwriters, himself at the time a member of the Blue Ridge Playboys, another Texas band that worked the circuit with Bruner's outfit. Sung by the Texas Wanderers' guitarist Dickie McBride, the song and performance were astounding in their simplicity and directness, tapping a raw nerve of emotion hitherto unexplored in country music. Songwriting royalties being in the state they were in back then, Tillman sold the song outright for $300 to singer Jimmie

Davis, who would later turn his back on honky tonk and "lewd music" when he ran for governor of Louisiana, making his mawkish "You Are My Sunshine" his theme song. Following the megasuccess of "It Makes No Difference Now" (it was the first song to be listed at No. 1 on *Billboard*'s new country charts), Tillman left the Playboys and struck out on his own, eventually becoming a one-man hit-writing machine in the Nashville firmament.

But Nashville aside, the music in its formative years was almost entirely of Texas invention and derivation, with a few notable exceptions. Singer Buddy Jones and steel guitarist Ted Daffan called Louisiana home, but both made notable contributions to the music. Jones' songs were full of the honky tonk, wild side of life spirit, and while Daffan was no match for Dunn's inventive steel work, his enduring classic "Born to Lose" ensured his name in the history books forever. Mirroring the despair of wartime thoughts, "Born to Lose" was a massive hit, even during wartime shellac rationing. The only country record that outsold it in 1943-1944 was Al Dexter's "Pistol Packin' Mama," a hammy piece of lighthearted honky tonk that became a huge crossover pop hit and the first of its kind to be featured on *Your Hit Parade*, the weekly radio (later TV) show that presented a fixed troupe of singers doing the popular songs of the day.

But no one brought a more Texas-sized sensibility to the music or moved the form into its next phase as much as Ernest Tubb. Originally a Jimmie Rodgers clone of the highest order, Tubb quickly found his own voice and recast it in the new sound of the Texas honky tonks. His band, the Texas Troubadours, became the model honky tonk combo, spawning several solo careers over the years. Tubb's plodding, ordinary sounding voice became the standard that the drunk at the bar could always claim he could sing better while simultaneously shoveling nickels into the jukebox to play one Ernest Tubb record after another to make his point. His style never really altered or changed, and by the time of his death in 1982, he was ensconced as one of country music's most noble and gentle figures, a true legend.

But it was the music of Hank Williams, Sr., that finally gave honky tonk its true voice. One critic has opined that if it were not for Williams' volume of classic songs, the sound of honky tonk bands (with everyone taking a shot at "Your Cheatin' Heart" sooner or later) would have stopped decades ago. Certainly Hank's music—and his legend—is the ghost that still hangs over country music, held up as the icon of everything that is "pure" about the style. His music—with his band, the Drifting Cowboys, doing much to establish the integral role of each band member within the style's framework—was equal parts religious guilt and torment, self-pity and recrimination, with the other side of the coin mirroring the best Saturday night party anyone could ever attend. Love, true love, was something ever elusive, something that was always just along the way, and the ache of it—and for it—would last a lifetime, until your dying day. Or you could just jump in your old jalopy with your honey, go into town and order up two bowls of chili, as was his description of the hillbilly highlife in "Settin' the Woods on Fire." Either way, Hank Williams raised the level of honky tonk music—all of country songwriting, for that matter—to new artistic heights. To call his stark, lyrical work poetry would not be laying it on too thick.

Of all the honky tonkers who followed after Hank's death on New Year's Eve, 1953, no one defined it better than Lefty Frizzell. Possessing a clear, melodic voice in stark contrast to the rough nasality of Williams and Tubb, the best of Frizzell's music ("If You've Got the Money, I've Got the Time," "Always Late [With Your Kisses]") freezes a moment in time of the style's creative peak. Others contributing classics to the genre included Webb Pierce ("Slowly," "There Stands the Glass," "Back Street Affair"), Hank Thompson ("The Wild Side of Life," "A Six Pack to Go"), and Ray Price, whose rough-edged turns on tunes like "Release Me" and "Crazy Arms" would later seem at odds with his eventual move to pop crossover material.

It was George Jones who brought honky tonk into its next glorious phase, once again reinventing country music in the process. No country singer has ever possessed a greater voice, a better interpretation of commonplace lyrics, or a more effective means of putting those sentiments over while making the hair on the back of your neck stand up. From his early Texas sides to his later, overblown Nashville sides (with Billy Sherrill burying him under a sea of strings and ooh-wahing choruses), no amount of alcohol, less-than-stellar backup, mundane tunes or overwrought production could dilute his message. That he is revered today as country music's last pure singer is testimony enough to his art.

Meanwhile in Bakersfield, CA, a new strain of honky tonk was developing, raucous and more electric (and more tied to rock 'n' roll, '50s style), primarily pioneered by singer Wynn Stewart. Stewart would help launch the careers of Buck Owens and Merle Haggard, Bakersfield's two greatest exports of the 60s honky tonk sound. Both racked up hit after hit, and the guitar work of Don Rich with Buck's Buckaroos and Roy Nichols with Haggard's Strangers popularized the trebly Fender Telecaster as the must-

have sound on any honky tonk record or bandstand. Also a note-worthy contributor to the form was the late 1960s comeback of rocker Jerry Lee Lewis, whose run of hits on the country charts were distilled from the purest of honky tonk essence.

One of the goals of the batch of new traditionalists that invaded country in the 1980s was a determination to restore the music to its rootsier and rougher side. Part of that return fully embraced honky tonk's sound and pioneers. You could hear the new breed's nod to their heroes in their style and sound and draw straight lines back to the original source points: Randy Travis (George Jones), Dwight Yoakam (Buck Owens), George Strait (Jones and Hank Williams), and Junior Brown (Ernest Tubb). Bluegrass musi-cian-turned-roadhouse rocker Marty Stuart has successfully brought the form even further into a contemporary groove while sacrificing none of the basic elements of the genre. The chart-top-ping successes of Alan Jackson's "Don't Rock the Jukebox" and Stuart's "Honky Tonkin's What I Do Best" prove once again that there's always another great honky tonk song in the making and best of all, that the form is alive and well, headed for the 21st cen-tury.

—Cub Koda

Recommended Recordings:

Milton Brown and His Musical Brownies, *Pioneer Western Swing Band* (MCA)

Cliff Bruner, *Cliff Bruner's Texas Wanderers* (Texas Rose)

Floyd Tillman, *Country Music Hall of Fame* (MCA)

Jimmie Davis, *Country Music Hall of Fame* (MCA)

Ernest Tubb, *Country Music Hall of Fame* (MCA)

Kitty Wells, *Country Music Hall of Fame* (MCA)

Loretta Lynn, *Country Music Hall of Fame* (MCA)

Webb Pierce, *King of the Honky-Tonk: from the Original Master Tapes* (Country Music Foundation)

Hank Williams, *40 Greatest Hits* (Polydor)

Lefty Frizzell, *Best of Lefty Frizzell* (Rhino)

George Jones, *Cup of Loneliness* (Mercury)

Jerry Lee Lewis, *The Mercury Years, Vol. 1* (Mercury)

Hank Thompson, *Vintage* (Capitol)

Faron Young, *Live Fast, Love Hard: Original Capitol Recordings, 1952-1962* (Country Music Foundation)

Hank Locklin, *Send Me the Pillow You Dream On* (Bear Family)

Various Artists, *Hillbilly Fever, Vol. 2: Legends of Honky Tonk* (Rhino)

Country Duos/Close Harmonies

The tradition of duet singing in country music, in all likelihood, extends back far beyond the birth of country styles. Before the dawn of the 20th century, American families would gather in their parlors, or in their churches, to sing both secular and reli-gious tunes. This was musical family values in the purest sense, an expression of deep blood bonds, community recreation, and religious devotion.

When country music began to be recorded for commercial audiences in the 1920s and 1930s, it made sense that many of the best harmony teams tended to be from the same family. Genetics ensured that the vocal blends between brother and brother, sister and sister, brother and sister, and so forth would be more pleasing and natural than it would between singers without common ancestry. Just as crucially, many harmony teams from the same family had been singing together since they were children. This gave their harmonies a deep-seated telepathy, ironed and per-fected over years of experience, that would be almost impossible to develop between singers that had been raised in different households.

Not all of the great early country harmony teams were duets. The Carter Family, perhaps the most influential of all, was a trio; they were indeed all family, but they weren't even siblings. It was

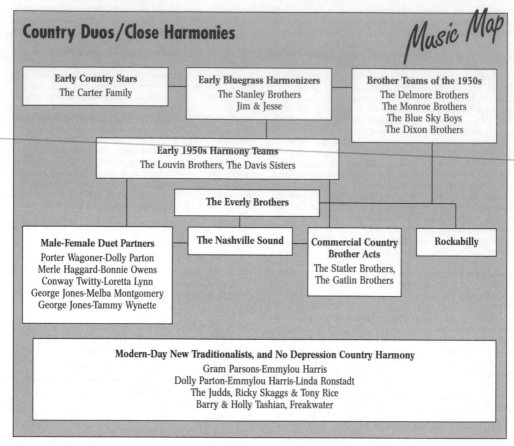

Country Duos/Close Harmonies

Music Map

Early Country Stars
The Carter Family

Early Bluegrass Harmonizers
The Stanley Brothers
Jim & Jesse

Brother Teams of the 1930s
The Delmore Brothers
The Monroe Brothers
The Blue Sky Boys
The Dixon Brothers

Early 1950s Harmony Teams
The Louvin Brothers, The Davis Sisters

The Everly Brothers

Male-Female Duet Partners
Porter Wagoner-Dolly Parton
Merle Haggard-Bonnie Owens
Conway Twitty-Loretta Lynn
George Jones-Melba Montgomery
George Jones-Tammy Wynette

The Nashville Sound

Commercial Country Brother Acts
The Statler Brothers,
The Gatlin Brothers

Rockabilly

Modern-Day New Traditionalists, and No Depression Country Harmony
Gram Parsons-Emmylou Harris
Dolly Parton-Emmylou Harris-Linda Ronstadt
The Judds, Ricky Skaggs & Tony Rice
Barry & Holly Tashian, Freakwater

the Carters who would, to a large degree, be responsible for synthesizing old-time Appalachian music, gospel, and pop into early country music with wide commercial appeal. Indeed, along with Jimmie Rodgers, they were vital in the transformation of commercial country music into a vocal product, as opposed to an instrumental one.

As the commercial country market began to develop in the 1930s, brother teams in particular became popular items. It's not hard to divine the reasons for their appeal; close, tight harmonies more than doubled the impact of hearing a singer on his own, and many of the choices in their repertoire would be familiar to their audiences as traditional hymns or folk tunes. As Billy Altman writes in his liner notes to *Are You from Dixie: Great Country Brother Teams of the 1930s*, "Certainly in no place and at no time was the country duet ever more prominent than in the Southeastern United States in the 1930s. Spurred on at the close of the previous decade by both the national recording successes of the Carter Family and Jimmie Rodgers as well as the enormous rise in demand for live radio performers, countless numbers of home-trained brother teams who previously never envisioned themselves as anything more than, at best, local celebrities suddenly found themselves before far-ranging audiences."

The most notable of the brother teams to make an impact in this period were the Dixon Brothers, the Delmore Brothers, the Monroe Brothers, and the Blue Sky Boys (the last of whom comprised the brothers Bill and Earl Bolick). These duet teams were notable not just for their singing, but wide repertoires that encompassed gospel, sacred hymns, folk, and even blues. What's more, most of them were talented and prolific songwriters, able to draw on all of these influences to come up with something more original and slightly more modern. Backed only with guitars and other simple string instruments, the basic arrangements ensured

that the emotional qualities of their singing would be at the forefront of the records. The homespun, gut-level sincerity of the harmonies—whether celebrating simple pleasures, mourning tragedies, or offering supplications to loved ones or the Almighty—have ensured that the recordings continue to appeal to contemporary listeners, despite the relatively primitive fidelity of the performances.

Two of these brother acts would have an influence that extended well beyond pre-World War II popular music. The Delmore Brothers would take the blues influence to further extremes between the mid-'40s and early '50s by adding boogie beats, harmonica, and thumping rhythms. This new kind of hillbilly music helped pave the way for the fusion of blues and country that became rockabilly, though the Delmores' contribution in this area is still underappreciated. Whether singing proto-rockabilly or sacred hymns, the Delmores always featured great harmony singing. Alton and Rabon Delmore were rarities in country music for switching high and low harmony parts from song to song, or even within the same tune.

One of the Monroe Brothers was Bill Monroe, who would become known as the father of bluegrass after World War II. In the 1930s, however, he recorded over 50 tracks with his brother Charlie before the siblings split to form separate bands in 1938. Whether or not one views bluegrass as central to the mainstream country tradition, it would be hard to argue that bluegrass helped the duet/close harmony style survive in the 1940s and 1950s, as the focus of country music shifted toward solo singers and Western swing bands.

Bluegrass owes much of its famed "high and lonesome" qualities to the harmonic blends of the vocals, which hadn't changed much since the family recordings of the 1930s, except that now they were more professionally recorded. The most notable of these acts happened, again, to be brother teams. The Stanley Brothers were one of the most tradition-based bluegrass acts, though their instrumental approach was influenced by the more modern vision of Bill Monroe. Jim and Jesse, usually billed without any last names given, were brothers Jim and Jesse McReynolds. As Bill Malone writes in *Country Music USA,* "If Jesse was the instrumental mainstay of the duo, Jim was the key to their heralded vocal blend. His smooth and deceptively effortless tenor was sometimes reminiscent of Ira Louvin, but without the latter's sharp edge. He was probably the least strident of bluegrass singers, and on some slow songs his voice assumed a plaintiveness that recalled the singing of Bill Bolick. Jim and Jesse brought a mellow, soft tone to bluegrass singing, and a receptivity to songs from other genres, that gave them an audience which extended well beyond the borders of their adopted musical field.

Duet harmonies weren't ghettoized to the country field. The Louvin Brothers, Charlie and Ira, owed a lot to gospel and bluegrass traditions. But they also made some effort to make their material more palatable to wider country and pop audiences, even employing Chet Atkins as electric guitarist for some sides. Johnnie & Jack (who were not relatives) also did their part to link old-time music with more modern elements.

Perhaps the most notable of the relatively few female harmony teams were the Davis Sisters, who had one huge hit, "I Forgot More Than You'll Ever Know," before Betty Jack Davis died in a car crash in 1953. Actually, the Davis Sisters were not sisters, but close friends, one of whom was actually named Mary Frances Penick. Penick changed her name to Skeeter Davis for professional services, and, after the death of Betty Jack, attempted to keep the act going for a while with Betty Jack's sister, Georgie. Skeeter would eventually find success as a solo act. The Davis Sisters' recordings owed less to old-time music or bluegrass than the more traditional, older acts that had begun recording in the 1930s did. Some of their sides feature a young Chet Atkins, and their most boisterous material anticipates rockabilly. Their material continues to interest listeners as early showcases for harmony singing within a relatively modern country music format.

It could be said that the brothers in the most influential country duet team weren't country singers at all. Phil and Don Everly were raised with old-time country music; their father was a respected country guitarist, and the brothers started performing professionally before their teens. Their first recordings (in 1955) were straight country music, but when they started to cut hits in 1957, they were rock 'n' rollers. The country influence was always strong in their peerless soaring harmony vocals, though, which essentially modernized the best of Appalachian/old-time country duet singing for the pop-rock market.

The Everlys could thus be seen as the link in the chain that finally brought the magic of country harmony singing to a wide international pop audience. In the process they weren't playing country music anymore, although you could hardly say they sold out, given that they made some of the finest rock and pop records of the late '50s and early '60s. Their influence was immense on the Beatles, the Hollies, Simon & Garfunkel, and many other rock and pop acts of the last several decades that built their sound around close harmonies.

Within mainstream country music itself, duet harmony acts, family or otherwise, were becoming less prevalent. Perhaps that's due, in part, to social changes in the 20th century that were eroding the sort of family structures in which close harmony singing thrived. After World War II, families didn't gather in the parlor that often (if they had a parlor at all) to sing together. There were other distractions for providing entertainment, like television and other mass media. Instead of creating music themselves, families could turn on their radios and record players. And increased mobility meant that families were moving around more frequently and staying together for shorter periods of time, if they were staying together at all.

The duet/close harmony tradition survived, most frequently, via collaborations between male and female stars. These are too numerous to mention in a paragraph or two, but some of the most prominent of these would be Porter Wagoner-Dolly Parton, Merle Haggard-Bonnie Owens, and Conway Twitty-Loretta Lynn.

George Jones likes to record duet albums, perhaps as a boost to his apparent quest to release more material than any other popular singer. His most celebrated partnerships, however, have been with Melba Montgomery and ex-wife Tammy Wynette (he also recorded little-noticed duets with pop-rock singer Gene Pitney in the mid-'60s). Male-male duets were not unknown either; Willie Nelson recorded albums with Waylon Jennings, Merle Haggard, Webb Pierce, Kris Kristofferson, and Hank Snow, though most fans would agree that Nelson's forte is solo singing, not harmonizing.

But by and large, these duets were not permanent, or even long-running, partnerships. They were side projects of celebrities whose individual careers were far more important concerns than building inspiring artistic collaborations. It would not be fair to dismiss them entirely as marketing gimmicks, but they could also not be truly compared to the decades-long relationships, musical and otherwise, that had built up with the best pre-1960 duet harmony teams. Some brother acts (the Statler Brothers, the Gatlin Brothers) built long-running careers, but shed some of the purity of their gospel-country roots by absorbing middle-of-the-road country/pop influences.

Close harmonies haven't been entirely neglected by the commercial country market in the '80s and '90s. The Judds put a twist into the family blend by offering a mother-daughter duo (as opposed to a sibling one). They weren't a duo, but Dolly Parton, Emmylou Harris, and Linda Ronstadt came up with an interesting side project on their 1987 *Trio* album that emphasized tight harmonies.

The best close harmony recordings of recent teams have tended to originate from outside the country mainstream. Gram Parsons and Emmylou Harris began a promising vocal partnership in 1973 on Parsons' *G.P.* and *Grievous Angel* albums. Unfortunately, Parsons died in late 1973, before the collaboration could be taken any further. In hindsight, it seems doubtful that Harris would have delayed her solo career for long, but she did do enough duets with various partners to generate an entire compilation of them in 1990. While moving from bluegrass stardom to mainstream country success, Ricky Skaggs took the time to do some old-school country harmonies with Tony Rice on *Skaggs and Rice.* Of course the high and lonesome harmonic sound survives in innumerable contemporary bluegrass recordings.

For the most outstanding close harmony act of the alternative rock-influenced No Depression movement, check out the female harmonies of Freakwater, who reach back into the spirit of Appalachia for their brand of country-folk. Its appeal to an underground rock audience seems to indicate that the beauty of sparsely adorned close harmony singing will always retain its appeal. Its acceptance by listeners seeking a cutting edge also seems to indicate that the more things change, the more they remain the same.

–Richie Unterberger

Recommended Recordings:

The Carter Family, *Country Music Hall of Fame* (MCA)

Various Artists, *Are You from Dixie?: Great Country Brother Teams of the 1930s* (RCA)

Various Artists, *Something Got a Hold of Me: A Treasury of Sacred Music* (RCA)

Various Artists, *Anthology of Country Music: Early Country Harmony 1930s* (ACM)

Various Artists, *Anthology of Country Music: Early Country Harmony 1940s* (ACM)

The Blue Sky Boys, *There'll Come a Time/Can't You Hear That Nightbird* (Blue Tone)

The Delmore Brothers, *Sand Mountain Blues* (County)

The Stanley Brothers, *Complete Columbia Recordings* (Columbia/Legacy)

Jim and Jesse, *1952-1955* (Bear Family)

The Louvin Brothers, *When I Stop Dreaming: The Best of the Louvin Brothers* (Razor & Tie)

The Davis Sisters, *Memories* (Bear Family)

The Everly Brothers, *Cadence Classics: Their 20 Greatest Hits* (Rhino)

George Jones & Melba Montgomery, *Vintage Collection Series* (Capitol)

Porter Wagoner & Dolly Parton, *The Essential Porter Wagoner and Dolly Parton* (RCA)

Gram Parsons, *G.P./Grievous Angel* (Reprise)

Ricky Skaggs & Tony Rice, *Skaggs and Rice* (Sugar Hill)

Dolly Parton, Linda Ronstadt, & Emmylou Harris, *Trio* (Warner Bros.)

The Judds, *Greatest Hits* (RCA)

Emmylou Harris, *Duets* (Reprise)

Freakwater, *Dancing Under Water* (Amoeba)

Country Comedy

Probably no form of humor has been as enduring—and as constantly defiled by highbrow critics—as what is collectively known as country comedy. It covers as wide of a field of genres—and the similar development of those genres—as any strain of the music itself. From gentle, homespun storytellers to outrageous cartoonish characters playing the "rube" to Southern stand-up comics hip enough to work north of the Mason-Dixon line, it is readily apparent that comedy has been at the core of country music almost from its inception.

Comedy has always been part of the presentation in a live country appearance, whether it is a few well-placed jokes by the star of the show, a straight comedy act added to the bill to provide laughs, or a baggy pants, toothless bass player in the star's backup band doing a stand-up turn. It is also a style of humor that is profoundly Southern in derivation and outlook. Country comedy was never originally intended to play to any other audience than the one that came out to country music live performances or that tuned into country radio shows. Its broadness, ruralness, and folksiness was perfectly grooved for the white Southerners who listened and laughed. The audience at a typical country music show was generally straightlaced, conservative church-going folk who would titter at the wheeziest old punch lines, seemingly unable to distinguish between good comedy and bad. Indeed one of the charges leveled against country comedy by its detractors is that the genre is little more than bad vaudeville jokes told with a hillbilly accent. But to be fair, that same audience in question has never been quite as square—or stupid—as its critics have made it out to be.

However, certain social and show business proprieties had to be observed if country comedians were going to work on the same show, where the cast would "gather 'round the microphone and sing an old-time hymn." George Burns once asked veteran country standup Pat Buttram how he got away for years with essentially ribald material in front of audiences generally acknowledged to be living on the buckle of the Bible Belt. Buttram's answer not only gets to the essence of what fuels the genre, but provides an excellent example of it as well: "We could do anything we wanted with animals, crops, fields, outhouses, as long as we stayed out of the bedroom. Once I told the story about a husband and wife who were invited to a masquerade party. They looked around the farmhouse and found some skin and horns, so she dressed as a cow and he dressed as a bull. On the way to this party their car broke down and they decided to cut across an open pasture. They got halfway across when this old bull started charging down the hill towards them. Well, this husband and wife were really scared, and the wife said, 'What'll we do, what'll we do?' 'Well, honey,' the husband said, 'I'm gonna munch grass. You better brace yourself.'"

This folksy, good old boy approach obviously had much milder beginnings and only changed marginally over the years as social mores loosened a bit. Its documentation on record goes back to the turn of the century with Cal Stewart's very successful "Uncle Josh" series of 78s, early Southern storytelling at its best. It was

certainly a broad characterization that Stewart employed, but its general easygoing style set the stage for almost everything that came afterward.

Certainly, incorporating bits of comedy into your act was the mark of a well-rounded performer, and most everybody took a stab at it at one time or another. But for those fans and historians with a taste for the surreal mixed in with their early country, they would do well to check out the comedy skit recordings of Jimmie Rodgers with the Carter Family, neither of them exactly noted for the mirth-inducing qualities of their respective musical styles. A stretch to say the least, honestly mirrored in their clumsy and wooden delivery of even the most mundane of lines, but an important indicator of comedy's integral role in country music's makeup, even back then.

The rise of radio brought country music into homes nationwide, and with it, a new spate of country comics. With national broadcasts like the *National Barn Dance* on WLS and WSM's *Grand Ole Opry*, country comedy entered its first popular phase. *Lum and Abner* was one of the new medium's most popular early series, paving the way for later movie and television "hillbilly family" comedies. Jam Up and Honey were a popular blackface duo working the Opry and the Southern vaudeville circuit while the aforementioned Pat Buttram regaled audiences both onstage and on radio. The Hoosier Hot Shots, with their appearances on the *Uncle Ezra* show and *National Barn Dance*, also broke new ground by proving that the music itself could be played and sung in a wild and humorous way. Dorothy Shay, known as "The Park Avenue Hillbilly," played slow-drawling comedic foils on a number of radio shows with hit recordings into the mid-'40s.

And of course, the movies played a substantial role in showcasing country comedy to a wider audience. Westerns were a staple of the so-called "poverty row" studios, who ground them out like sausage for Depression-era audiences starved for any form of escapism. It seemed as if every Western movie cowboy of the 1930s and 1940s had to have a funny sidekick. The best of the lot were undoubtedly Gene Autry's Smiley Burnette and ventriloquist Max Terhune. A great female country comic of the period who scored big with audiences was Judy Canova, whose movie career took off with a series of country corn films for Republic Pictures, home to low-budget John Wayne Westerns and the like. Meanwhile on the radio, the *National Barn Dance* on WLS found a goldmine in the duo of Homer & Jethro, whose broad musical satires of pop tunes would keep their careers prospering well into the late 1960s.

Novelty material was always big with country audiences, and this niche was easily filled on the Opry with loud, exciting acts like Little Jimmy Dickens (Skeets McDonald also mined similar turf with tunes like "The Tattooed Lady"), Grandpa Jones, and Lonzo and Oscar. Lonzo and Oscar's secret weapon was the instrumental comedy work of their steel guitar player, Cousin Jody, who had just come from a tenure with Roy Acuff. He looked funny, he acted funny, and most interestingly of all, he *played* funny. While the Grand Ole Opry was host to some of country music's best pickers, a player like Cousin Jody was worth his weight in comedic gold. Having a player in your band who could do comedy was a distinct plus for any traveling outfit, and this role usually fell on the shoulders of the string bass player. Besides doing the standard schtick of riding the instrument like a horse, it became comedy protocol for the bassman to don the most ridiculous "rube" outfit available, black out their teeth if necessary, and make with the corn. Every major band seemed to have one of these and certainly nobody was better at it than "Speck" Rhodes, who started in Memphis in his brother Slim's band, moving on to national prominence later with Porter Wagoner.

Meanwhile, a new batch of stand-ups were making their presence felt on WSM's airwaves, most notably the "gal from Grinder's Switch," Minnie Pearl. Her talents were voluminous, and Minnie could be plugged in anywhere the show needed her; she could sing, do monologues, work with another comic or singer (usually her favorite foil in two-person skits was Sad Sack comedian Rod Brasfield), and even emcee the whole proceedings if need be. Another comic who hit paydirt on the Opry was Whitey Ford, who told old-time folksy one-liners as "The Duke of Pad-

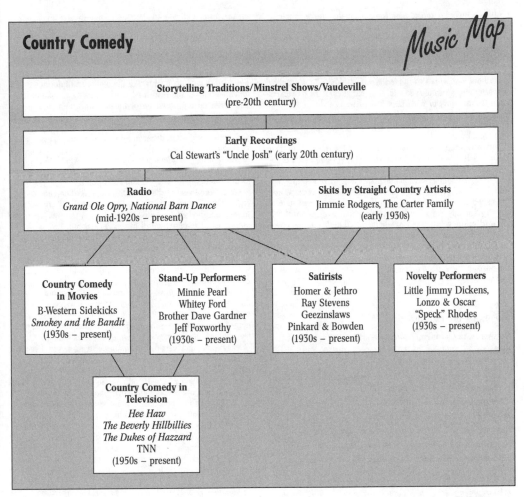

Country Comedy

Music Map

Storytelling Traditions/Minstrel Shows/Vaudeville
(pre-20th century)

Early Recordings
Cal Stewart's "Uncle Josh" (early 20th century)

Radio
Grand Ole Opry, National Barn Dance
(mid-1920s – present)

Skits by Straight Country Artists
Jimmie Rodgers, The Carter Family
(early 1930s)

Country Comedy in Movies
B-Western Sidekicks
Smokey and the Bandit
(1930s – present)

Stand-Up Performers
Minnie Pearl
Whitey Ford
Brother Dave Gardner
Jeff Foxworthy
(1930s – present)

Satirists
Homer & Jethro
Ray Stevens
Geezinslaws
Pinkard & Bowden
(1930s – present)

Novelty Performers
Little Jimmy Dickens,
Lonzo & Oscar
"Speck" Rhodes
(1930s – present)

Country Comedy in Television
Hee Haw
The Beverly Hillbillies
The Dukes of Hazzard
TNN
(1950s – present)

ucah," always closing with his trademark line, "I'm going back to the wagon, boys, these shoes are killin' me!"

While it's hard to imagine television legend Andy Griffith making his show business entry as a country stand-up, that's exactly what happened in the early '50s. Griffith came to national prominence with a spate of recorded stand-up routines, including the big hit, "What It Was, Was Football." The success of his comedy recordings secured him film work and guest shots on TV. When he portrayed a country sheriff named Andy Taylor on an episode of *The Danny Thomas Show*, his future was secured.

Probably the most important and influential country comedian of the late 1950s was Brother Dave Gardner. He started as a singing drummer and, as time went on, started peppering his stage routine with more and more bits until the drums were relegated to a solo spot in his show if they were needed at all. Brother Dave's comedic approach was equal parts jazz hipster and hell and brimstone radio preacher, wed to the then-current crop of '50s "sick" comics. His albums were extremely successful and the early '60s found him making the rounds of all the big TV variety and talk shows. While the Duke of Paducah and his ilk worked the gymnasiums and country fairs down South, Gardner—because of his hipness—was one of the few country comedy artists (Homer and Jethro being the other) that could work to a Northern audience with no dilution or change to his act. His influence was almost incalculable; one line from a Brother Dave routine would resurface years later as a complete Ray Stevens song! But for all of Gardner's new-breed hipness, America still liked its country humor as broad and as corny as it could get it. The ongo-

ing mega-success of TV sitcoms like *The Beverly Hillbillies* and *Green Acres* (with veteran Pat Buttram playing a central role as Mr. Haney) drove that point home as only successful television ratings can. There was still plenty of room in country comedy for the same "rube" characterizations and good old boys one-liners, proven by the multi-decade success of the country music-comedy show *Hee Haw*. Not only did the show make national stars out of its hosts Buck Owens and Roy Clark, but it brought new life to the careers of veterans Minnie Pearl, Grandpa Jones, George "Goober" Lindsay and Archie Campbell, as well as up-and-comers like Junior Samples and rotundo singer-comedian Kenny Price.

As the '70s and '80s brought a new awareness of country music to the general public, new stand-up comedians emerged on the scene. Jerry Clower, an ordained minister from Louisiana, brought a proud-to-be-country aspect to his stories and found an audience for it that effortlessly bridged the gap between young and old. Working a similar track was Justin Wilson, noted for his "Cajun Cooker" TV shows, whose impenetrable Louisiana accent made Northern audiences sometimes wish he came with subtitles.

If every comic wants to play Shakespeare, then perhaps there beats a comedian in many country singers as well. Autry Inman, who had cut several chart singles for Decca, issued no less than three albums of straight stand-up. Sheb Wooley—who had played on the TV Western *Rawhide* and had a '50s novelty hit with "The Purple People Eater"—found an alter ego for himself in the personage of "Ben Colder," doing tipsy drunk parodies of country hits while the Statler Brothers' parody of a less-than-marginally-talented country band (Lester Moran, "the Old Roadhog," and his

Cadillac Cowboys) spread their tonal mayhem over a couple of albums and the occasional television appearance.

Ray Stevens started in rock 'n' roll but over the years gravitated toward the country field, where his numerous Brother Dave Gardner-meets-Spike Jones-inspired takeoffs upped the ante in the novelty record sweepstakes. Pinkard & Bowden have also carved out a niche in this still fertile turf with their Cousin Bubba character and a run of successful song parodies based on current country hits. Novelty material still does well in the genre—witness the work of the Geezinslaw Brothers or the one-off success of Elmo and Patsy with the Christmas perennial, "Grandma Got Run Over by a Reindeer."

Virtually impossible to categorize despite the rigidness of their format, Riders in the Sky's presentation stands right on the precipice between satire and loving tribute. Certainly comedy is a large part of their stage persona, but their rhythmic drive and fine harmonies reveal serious musicianship underneath the chaps and ten gallon hats. And of course, no mention of the current state of country comedy would be complete without a mention of Jeff Foxworthy, the young stand-up who parlayed his "you might be a redneck if" routine into a national catchphrase. Foxworthy has logged in a series of best selling albums and videos, culminating with an NBC self-titled sitcom. With a new century looming on the horizon, the state of country comedy remains very much alive and well.

—Cub Koda

Recommended Recordings:

Brother Dave Gardner, *Motorcycle Story*

Little Jimmy Dickens, *I'm Little but I'm Loud: The Little Jimmy Dickens Collection* (Razor & Tie)

Homer & Jethro, *America's Favorite Song Butchers: The Weird World of Homer & Jethro* (Razor & Tie)

Grandpa Jones, *Hall of Fame Series* (MCA)

Minnie Pearl, *The Best of Minnie Pearl*

Ray Stevens, *His All-Time Greatest Comic Hits* (Curb)

Riders in the Sky, *Best of the West Rides Again* (Rounder)

Jeff Foxworthy, *You Might Be a Redneck If . . .* (Warner)

Bluegrass

For those who value popular music at its most authentic, it may appear on the surface that no style could serve their needs as well as bluegrass. Relying mostly or entirely upon acoustic instruments, it reaches back centuries into Appalachian and Anglo-Celtic traditions for the foundations of its sound. The vocals place a high premium upon harmony and emotional expressiveness. The lyrics are usually as down-to-earth as they come, celebrating family, the land, and the simple pleasures of life. There is also a strong religious/spiritual thread running through most of the material, even among bluegrass bands that most likely don't go to church every Sunday.

Yet upon closer examination, it's a bit of a stretch, if not ridiculous, to characterize bluegrass as an "authentic" music. Like all strains of pop music, it's drawn and bastardized from a multitude of genres. Although it's often associated with rural life and generations-old mountain traditions, in fact it's only been in existence since about World War II, and is not even the oldest country-related subgenre. Though it acts as a bastion of traditional musical values, it's changed and evolved over the years like everything else in modern times.

Anyone who tries to master this supposedly "simple" music knows that it can demand as much in the way of instrumental virtuosity, complex harmonics, and tricky time signatures as the most intricate jazz. At times it's spilled onto the pop charts, and indeed pop culture, whether in the incidental music to *The Beverly Hillbillies*, or the obligatory bluegrass soundtrack for B-movie car chase scenes. It's never been the most profitable sector of country music, but it's maintained a strong degree of influence

on the form, and even made a noticeable impact upon rock 'n' roll.

The roots of bluegrass were bred in (but not exclusively limited to) the Appalachian Mountains, which stretch over 1,500 miles from Quebec to Alabama. Here, even more than other areas of the South, music was a vital family and social activity. It was dominated by string instruments like the banjo, and informed by the folk traditions of the British Isles, where many of the musicians had ancestral roots. On top of the old-time "mountain music" styles came the early country music of giants like the Carter Family, the gospel music of the churches in this most religious region, and the early duos and harmony acts of country music, which were often composed of brother teams. As radio and records began to bring the region into closer contact with external influences, the musicians also became exposed to early jazz, Western swing, country blues, and Tin Pan Alley pop.

It's difficult to detect the exact origins of most pop and country styles. Not so, however, with bluegrass, in which it's easy not only to pinpoint the first bluegrass performer, but the way the music got named. The source of all bluegrass that followed, of course, was Bill Monroe, who earned the title of "father of bluegrass," and whose backup band, the Blue Grass Boys, soon gave the style a monicker of its own. Monroe made his first few records—quite a few of them, in fact—as half of one of the best brother teams in country music in the 1930s, with his brother Charlie. By 1938 he was working on his own, and he made his first recordings with the Blue Grass Boys in 1940. Over the next few years he would cultivate and popularize the style known as bluegrass. As the name implies, it was to some degree a combination of rural country and the blues, but it was a bit more complex than that.

Monroe not only established the basic string-driven, five-piece format of the bluegrass ensemble, but also made sure his bands escaped from the limited formats—namely, the C, D, and G keys—that dominated most traditional country music. The fast, rhythmic drive of his mandolin playing was clearly influenced by urban forms of jazz and blues; he made sure his bands were as disciplined as any ensemble in country, or *any* kind of music. He helped set the prototype for the "high, lonesome" sound that typified bluegrass vocals. That particular "high, lonesome" phrase may have become a cliche, but it does ring true to a large extent. Bluegrass singers usually need a wide range; it's hard to imagine, for instance, Johnny Cash or Kris Kristofferson tackling the music successfully.

As James Rooney writes in his biography of Monroe in the book *Bossmen*, "His singing was high and clear as a bell, his mandolin cut through on solos and supplied a driving beat behind the others, the fiddle would swing into its breaks like a frightened deer, and when they all sang together on gospel numbers, the harmonies with Bill way on top gave people the shivers. This was not just another old-time band. It was driving and together. It brought the audience up to a new level of musical experience. They instinctively recognized a special musical excellence that was part of their culture, that was theirs to share. They realized that there was more to their music than a few laughs and a whoop. It said something to them stronger and deeper than music had before. This new mixture of lonesome, blue, old-time, jazzy, religious music hit country people inside."

As Mark Humphrey observes in his liner notes to Rhino's *Appalachian Stomp* collection, when Monroe began recording for Columbia, "The old-time string-band music of Appalachia was radically streamlined; it attained a tighter ensemble sound and a newly improvisational character that demanded high levels of musicianship. Complex vocal harmonies and piercing high-register leads (the high, lonesome sound) likewise became trademarks of this new music, and its effect was electrifying. In short order, hosts of Southern bands enthusiastically followed Monroe's lead."

Monroe's band is also vastly important for another reason, though it's not one that gave him much satisfaction at the time. After Monroe had established himself as a country star in the mid-'40s, two of his best sidemen—mandolinist Lester Flatt and banjo player Earl Scruggs—split to form their own phenomenally successful act. Scruggs pioneered a three-finger form of banjo playing that began to get picked up by other acts, such as Ralph

Bluegrass

Music Map

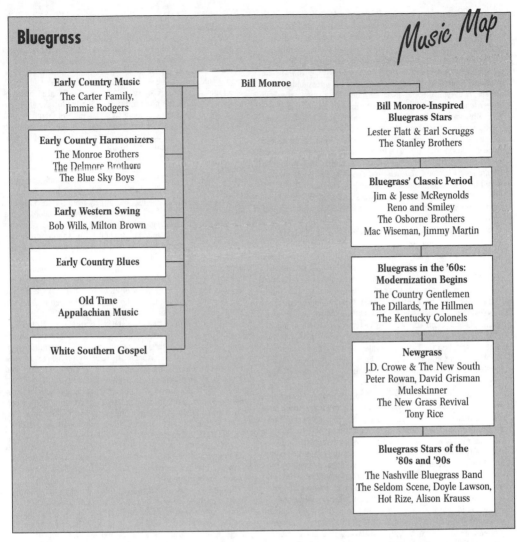

Early Country Music
The Carter Family,
Jimmie Rodgers

Bill Monroe

Early Country Harmonizers
The Monroe Brothers
The Delmore Brothers
The Blue Sky Boys

Early Western Swing
Bob Wills, Milton Brown

Early Country Blues

**Old Time
Appalachian Music**

White Southern Gospel

**Bill Monroe-Inspired
Bluegrass Stars**
Lester Flatt & Earl Scruggs
The Stanley Brothers

Bluegrass' Classic Period
Jim & Jesse McReynolds
Reno and Smiley
The Osborne Brothers
Mac Wiseman, Jimmy Martin

**Bluegrass in the '60s:
Modernization Begins**
The Country Gentlemen
The Dillards, The Hillmen
The Kentucky Colonels

Newgrass
J.D. Crowe & The New South
Peter Rowan, David Grisman
Muleskinner
The New Grass Revival
Tony Rice

**Bluegrass Stars of the
'80s and '90s**
The Nashville Bluegrass Band
The Seldom Scene, Doyle Lawson,
Hot Rize, Alison Krauss

Stanley, who switched from a clawhammer style to three-fingered playing after hearing Scruggs. Monroe, it seems, was unaware of just how influential his work had been; in his eyes, imitators were trying to muscle in on his territory. When Columbia signed the Stanley Brothers at the end of the 1940s, Bill was upset enough to leave for another company.

Yet by 1950, bluegrass music had gathered such a head of steam that its format was starting to become codified. In the words of Frank and Marty Godbey, writing in *The Blackwell Guide to Recorded Country Music:* "Bluegrass is an ensemble music, generally played by five or six people, using guitar, five-string banjo, mandolin, fiddle, and bass, although dobro (a raised-string resonator guitar noted with a steel bar) and multiple fiddles are sometimes included, and an electric bass guitar occasionally replaces the acoustic bass. The delimiting characteristic of bluegrass, however, is not instrumentation but 'timing,' in which the downbeat of guitar and bass is balanced by the offbeat mandolin 'chop' and the driving roll of three-finger-style banjo. Lead singing in bluegrass is often 'high lonesome,' but varies according to the range of the singer; two or three voices combine in bluegrass harmony, usually on choruses, but frequently throughout an entire song. In bluegrass quartets, primarily of a religious nature, a vocal bass line is added. Topics of bluegrass songs may be nostalgic (home and mother, idyllic life), personalized statements

(love lost, love found, regret for past actions), sentimentality (death of child, sweetheart, or other loved one, broken heart), or reworking of 'murder ballads' and traditional songs."

Bluegrass would never be the majority taste of the country audience, however. More than most styles, it staunchly resisted radical modernization, which made it sound somewhat passé to some ears and radio programmers as country slowly became more urbanized in the '50s and '60s. The widespread popularity of rock 'n' roll was another obstacle to consistent chart success for bluegrass acts, though the speed and drive of rockabilly owed a certain something to the bluegrass pioneers. The B-side of Elvis Presley's first single, in fact, was a rockabilly cover of one of Bill Monroe's biggest hits, "Blue Moon of Kentucky." Monroe was sparked by the success of this young upstart to record a rockabilly-influenced remake of the tune just a couple of months after Elvis' version had appeared on Sun Records. For the most widely known close mating between bluegrass and rockabilly, check out the Fendermen's one-shot hit version of "Mule Skinner Blues" from 1960, which was as wild as rock got during a year that found rock's very existence threatened by the onslaught of teen idols. Bluegrass's evolution over the past five decades has been slow and subtle, but the form did begin to modify from the 1950s onward. Jesse McReynolds, of the duo Jim & Jesse, developed a "cross-picking" banjo style that approximated the style of Earl

Scruggs using a flat pick. Mac Wiseman established himself as bluegrass's most renowned solo singer; the Stanley Brothers built a body of original material that sounded, as much as we hate to use the word, as "authentic" as any traditional mountain tune.

The Osborne Brothers helped introduce changes in bluegrass harmonizing that gave the style more flexibility. As Bill Malone explains in his *Country Music USA*, "Most bluegrass and country groups had typically put their harmony lines above the lead singer who sang the melody. In bluegrass trio singing, for example, someone usually sang a tenor just above the lead, and another voice either sang a baritone just below the lead or went up above the tenor into what was called a high baritone. The Osborne Brothers, on the other hand, put the two harmony voices below Bobby's high lead. They made this change in order to take advantage of Bobby's unusual tenor range and to make singing with him more comfortable for Sonny [Osborne] and Red Allen. Other bluegrass groups, though, were charmed by the style's uniqueness and found that it permitted a wider range of vocal arrangements and choice of keys."

By the 1960s, faced with the twin assaults of the Nashville sound and rock, bluegrass was becoming a pretty specialized market—a niche that, with occasional exceptions, it still occupies today. At the same time, however, the early '60s folk revival welcomed bluegrass masters onto the folk circuit, throwing out a lifeline that enabled the genre's practitioners to survive and sometimes thrive when their records weren't selling in huge quantities. There were occasional fluke bluegrass hits, like Flatt and Scruggs' "Ballad of Jed Clampett," or Eric Weissberg & Steve Mandell's "Dueling Banjos," although these usually had to ride onto the radio airwaves on the back of massive television/movie exposure ("Ballad of Jed Clampett" was the theme for *The Beverly Hillbillies*, "Dueling Banjos" was used in the popular 1972 movie *Deliverance*).

In pure musical terms, bluegrass had the image of being the most conservative of styles, yet in some respects it was more progressive than any other country microgenre. Bands like the Country Gentlemen were opening up the bluegrass repertoire beyond old-time and country songs. The Country Gentlemen, the Dillards, and the Hillmen were among the first acts of *any* sort to cover Bob Dylan material, at a time when mainstream country acts wouldn't touch him (with the exception of Johnny Cash). The Hillmen's young mandolin prodigy, Chris Hillman, became the bassist for the Byrds; eventually, Kentucky Colonels guitarist Clarence White would join the same group. Buffalo Springfield drummer Dewey Martin had served a short stint in the Dillards. You could occasionally hear bits of bluegrass in straight rock bands, such as the tunes Hillman penned for the Byrds' 1967 *Younger Than Yesterday* album, "Time Between" and "The Girl with No Name." More unlikely examples include the Beatles' "I've Just Seen a Face," Buffalo Springfield's "Bluebird," and the Doors' bizarre bluegrass-soul concoction, "Runnin' Blue." There was even a bit of movement in the other direction, when the Dillards broadened their repertoire to such an extent that it became difficult to tag them as a bluegrass group. *Wheatstraw Suite* (1968) was certainly a triumph in illustrating just how much a bluegrass group could change with the times, although ultimately the album is much more suitably categorized as a country-rock album than as a bluegrass one.

Rock music would eventually have a hand in the creation of progressive bluegrass, or "newgrass," in the 1970s; but not so much in actual sound as in approach. Musicians such as Peter Rowan and David Grisman—who had once played together in the Boston psychedelic band Earth Opera—were not so much interested in creating a bluegrass-rock fusion as making bluegrass itself more open and diverse. These musicians were not dilettantes, even though they may have outraged purists; Rowan, for instance, had served an apprenticeship in Bill Monroe's band before broadening his scope. What "newgrass" meant was an increased tolerance for electric instruments, bluegrass covers of material from rock, blues, jazz, and other outside sources, some jam-like sense of instrumental improvi-

sation, and the freedom to collaborate with musicians who didn't have strict traditional backgrounds.

Rowan, Grisman, and Clarence White brought the rock "supersession" vibe to their collaboration in Muleskinner, although Muleskinner's album was far more disciplined and respectful of tradition than any all-star counterpoint in the rock world. Grisman would collaborate with Jerry Garcia of the Grateful Dead, and espouse a form of "dawg" music, a jazz-influenced brand of bluegrass that, as the name implies, didn't try to take itself too seriously. A newgrass ensemble that was more influential upon the straight country scene was J.D. Crowe and the New South, a breeding ground for budding solo acts. The two most famous members of this group were Ricky Skaggs and the late Keith Whitley, who both went on to stardom in the straight country market. Not all Crowe alumni went in this direction; Tony Rice, for instance, has stuck to largely acoustic sounds, and teamed up with fellow Crowe vet Skaggs for a well-received duet album.

In recent decades, bluegrass has largely been confined to independent labels, college and noncommercial radio stations, and a thriving live circuit that includes several major festivals. Bluegrass is to some degree an insular culture of its own, with devotees planning vacations around festivals, and aspiring musicians hanging around parking lots at bluegrass events for impromptu jam sessions and workshops where they might pick up a few pointers. The increased level of instrumental virtuosity in the bluegrass community has led to a proliferation of ensembles that have taken the musicianship to a more intense level: this can be seen in the Nashville Bluegrass Band, the New Grass Revival, and Hot Rize.

It's a fact that most bluegrass doesn't stake out much territory beyond the tried and true. If diversity and adventurousness are your prime musical targets, you're better off concentrating on another field. Old-time gospel music remains a large part of most bands' repertoires, some groups (such as Doyle Lawson and Quicksilver) emphasizing this feature more than others. Other acts with broad tastes sometimes craft gospel/spiritual-only albums to attract a particular market or concentrate upon a certain aspect of their set. Stylistic bluegrass radicals, like mandolinist Niles Hokkanen—who would insert licks from Jimi Hendrix's "Purple Haze" into a cover of "Orange Blossom Special," played in a band called the Flaming Grassholes, wrote tunes like "Help I'm Married to a Houseplant," and once described his wilder work as sounding like a cross between Dan Hicks, Syd Barrett, and Nick Drake—are rare indeed.

Bluegrass's very conservatism, however, gives it a sturdier foundation than other minority tastes, which has enabled it to survive, albeit with a low commercial profile, more readily than most other styles. It's an exciting music to watch live, for one thing, which guarantees a lot of concert work for the many ensembles that sell only a few thousand records. In the 1990s, bluegrass-bred innovators like fiddler Mark O'Connor and banjoman Bela Fleck have brought bluegrass sensibilities into other fields. Fleck in particular has become a gadfly, moving into jazz and new acoustic music without ever entirely shedding his bluegrass roots. The mid-1990s, to the surprise of many, saw the first bluegrass-pop crossover in many a moon when fiddler Alison Krauss went into the Top Ten with *Now That I've Found You*. Though her most commercial recordings may owe as much to pop and country as bluegrass, her success is a doubly important milestone for bluegrass as a whole, as she's both one of the few performers to achieve pop stardom in the style, and one of the few female performers in a pretty male-dominated field.

—Richie Unterberger

Recommended Recordings:

Various Artists, *Appalachian Stomp: Bluegrass Classics* (Rhino)

Bill Monroe, *The Essential Bill Monroe (1945-1949)* (Columbia/ Legacy)

Bill Monroe, *Country Music Hall of Fame* (MCA)

Flatt and Scruggs, *The Complete Mercury Sessions* (Mercury)

The Stanley Brothers, *Complete Columbia Recordings* (Columbia/Legacy)

Jim and Jesse, *1952-1955* (Bear Family)

Mac Wiseman, *The Mac Wiseman Story* (CMH)

The Osborne Brothers, *The Osborne Brothers* (Rounder)

The Country Gentlemen, *Country Songs Old and New* (Smithsonian/Folkways)

The Dillards, *There Is a Time (1963-70)* (Vanguard)

The Kentucky Colonels, *Appalachian Swing!* (Rounder)

Muleskinner, *Muleskinner* (Warner Brothers)

J.D. Crowe & the New South, *J.D. Crowe & the New South* (Rounder)

David Grisman, *The David Grisman Quintet* (Rhino)

The New Grass Revival, *Best of New Grass Revival* (Liberty)

Alison Krauss, *Now That I've Found You: A Collection* (Rounder)

The Nashville Sound

For some country fans, the rise of the Nashville Sound in the mid-1950s signaled the end of country music's first golden age. With its sweet choruses and string sections sanding off all the rough edges in an effort to reach a crossover pop audience, the Nashville Sound can also be seen as country music's first acknowledgment of the existence of a world outside of its own. The attempts to fuse pop music sensibilities to a country lilt—sometimes only the most tenuous connection to its roots was present—brought the music for the first time to audiences who had previously viewed the genre as little more than a joke. While it's commonplace nowadays to see a Garth Brooks album on top of the pop charts, this separation of marketplaces was no more in evidence than in the early 1950s.

At this stage of the game, there was no such thing as crossover music; if a pop audience was going to hear Hank Williams' latest hit (which had already sold thousands of copies in the country market), they were going to hear a crooner like Tony Bennett or Frankie Laine sing it. You didn't hear "Sixteen Tons" by Merle Travis on pop radio, you heard Tennessee Ernie Ford's pop version of it. Not unlike the rhythm and blues field, country music was denied access to the big national audience (and the big money to be made from it); conversely its traditionalism became even more trenchant as it continued preaching to the converted.

But by the mid-1950s, country music was in a bit of a tailspin. The undeniable influence of rock 'n' roll—led by Elvis Presley, a man kicked off the stage of the Grand Ole Opry—had made several inroads into its core audience. Suddenly the younger generation country audience wanted something newer and more uptown. Some artists like Marty Robbins and Webb Pierce took a stab at the new music while others waited for it all to blow over. But something happened in the meantime that changed the course of country music forever in how it was presented and how it was played: crossover, handed over to country music via the success of Presley, had arrived.

Although this broader basing of the audience had its seeds in the work of Eddy Arnold and the genre-bending recordings of Les Paul and Mary Ford, 1957 and 1958 were banner years in the roots of country-pop fusion. Johnny Cash's "Ballad of a Teenage Queen," Ferlin Husky's "Gone," George Hamilton IV's "A Rose and a Baby Ruth," and Marty Robbins' "A White Sport Coat" all catered to the teenage market and met with far more success than the hardcore honky tonk sounds that were still topping the country charts. By the late 1950s, the sound of a fiddle sawing away or the keening wail of a steel guitar could barely be heard on mainstream country records. If an "authentic" country record was going to crash the upper regions of the pop charts, it would be more on the order of novelty tunes like Johnny Horton's "Battle of New Orleans" or Stonewall Jackson's "Waterloo," hillbilly sing-alongs fortified with a big beat. In the meantime, the sound of country records was becoming more and more homogeneous.

This pasteurization of the music had a lot to do with Nashville's emergence as the center of the country music universe. All of the major labels had offices there, all of the important studios, producers, and song publishers were there, and the Grand Ole Opry

was still an omnipresent figure in dictating the pecking order in the genre's star system. It was also where the session player rose to prominence, musicians who didn't tour with regular bands and seldom recorded under their own name. By the mid-'50s there was a solid core of reliable players who were used on almost every session, regardless of label affiliation or stylistic diversions. A great many of these players possessed talents that were far beyond the scope of what they were laying down behind country artists, and several of them indeed had inclinations toward jazz and smoother sounds. If Nashville was going to become a part of the big mainstream music picture, somebody was going to have to do something.

One picker that *was* in a position to do something was guitarist Chet Atkins. A guitarist with chops to spare and a wide range of musical tastes running from the Carter Family to jazz to classical, Chet had risen to prominence both as a session player and as a solo recording artist. By 1957, his profile as a link to these musicians and as a forward-thinking individual led to his installation as chief of RCA Victor's country division in Nashville. Atkins set out to create a style that would still preserve some elements of country music while simultaneously removing all lyrical references to rural life and any hard twang still present in the sound. Working with a group of players whom he would often jam with in Printer's Alley—Floyd Cramer on piano, Buddy Harman on drums, Bob Moore on bass, and Boots Randolph on tenor saxophone—this collection of pickers would end up on the majority of sessions cut in what was now beginning to be known as "Music City, USA." Also moving things along in a similar direction was the work of producer-studio owner Owen Bradley. Working almost exclusively with Decca artists, Bradley's sharp ear for sonics, great players (guitarists Hank Garland, Grady Martin, Ray Edenton, and pianist Hargus "Pig" Robbins were first-call regulars on his sessions) and commercial sounds helped to move country into this new style. The ultimate in sweetening came with the vocal choruses added to so many of these sessions by groups like the Anita Kerr Singers and the Jordanaires, who edged the music closer to mainstream pop with every breath.

Both Atkins and Bradley found that this new synthesis was just the ticket in reaping a bigger market share for the music, and many RCA Victor and Decca artists were plugged into the machine. But the Nashville Sound was only accessible to singers who could adapt to the sound; Atkins brought pop success to singers like Don Gibson ("Oh Lonesome Me" and "I Can't Stop Loving You"), Skeeter Davis ("The End of the World"), the Browns ("Three Bells"), and most significantly Jim Reeves, who managed to hit the inside corner of the plate with every release and simultaneously appealed to both pop and country audiences. Owen Bradley was making similar inroads with his recasting of big-voiced honky tonk singer Patsy Cline into a pop hit-making machine, changing the role of women in country music forever. Another artist eminently qualified to take on the new music was Marty Robbins, whose countrypolitan stylings served him in good stead right until his death in 1983.

But not everyone in Nashville approved of these stylistic changes. There was a backlash in the country community—both with its core audience and the older performers—and the battle lines were drawn. While a former honky tonker like Ray Price was now standing in front of an orchestra with a string section, older artists like Porter Wagoner made only marginal concessions to the style, seeing the Nashville Sound as an artistic compromise necessary for making records. Meanwhile, the Texas-California contingent—which had moved the music forward in the previous decade with the birth of Western swing—was developing its own strain of honky tonk music that would soon signal the line where hard country started and countrypolitan ended. Honky tonker Buck Owens issued a publicity-grabbing proclamation in the mid-1960s to try to get authentic genre artists to declare that they "will not sing a song that is not a country song," even as his twangy guitar and big beat driven-Bakersfield Sound was making country far more accessible to rock 'n' rollers than the music now coming out of Nashville.

By the late 1960s and early 1970s all recordings coming out of Music City were dubbed as having "that Nashville sound." The

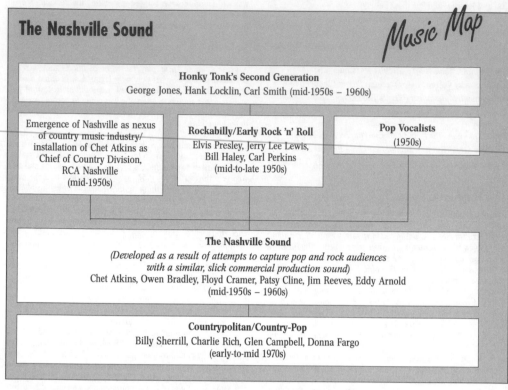

The Nashville Sound

Music Map

Honky Tonk's Second Generation
George Jones, Hank Locklin, Carl Smith (mid-1950s – 1960s)

Emergence of Nashville as nexus
of country music industry/
installation of Chet Atkins as
Chief of Country Division,
RCA Nashville
(mid-1950s)

Rockabilly/Early Rock 'n' Roll
Elvis Presley, Jerry Lee Lewis,
Bill Haley, Carl Perkins
(mid-to-late 1950s)

Pop Vocalists
(1950s)

The Nashville Sound
*(Developed as a result of attempts to capture pop and rock audiences
with a similar, slick commercial production sound)*
Chet Atkins, Owen Bradley, Floyd Cramer, Patsy Cline, Jim Reeves, Eddy Arnold
(mid-1950s – 1960s)

Countrypolitan/Country-Pop
Billy Sherrill, Charlie Rich, Glen Campbell, Donna Fargo
(early-to-mid 1970s)

next backlash against the style came with the rise of "outlaw music," a return to rougher sounds led by Willie Nelson and Waylon Jennings, themselves Nashville artists dissatisfied with the system and its one-sound-fits-all production values. Mainstream country took another sock in the jaw in the mid-1980s—some point to this period as the true end of the Nashville Sound—with the rise in popularity of several youth-oriented performers with strong stylistic ties to country's past. Singers like Randy Travis and George Strait recalled the glory of George Jones, and Dwight Yoakam recast Buck Owens' Bakersfield sound in a move that looked forward and backward at the same time. Hank Williams, Jr. came up with his own rocking hybrid that married the honky tonk sound to the more rocked out sensibilities of Southern rock bands like Lynyrd Skynyrd. But a new audience was coming to country music, one that grew up on rock 'n' roll, and it turned to younger and more rock-oriented country acts like Garth Brooks when it no longer heard music on rock stations that it could identify with.

But in the end, country will evolve once again and, in an odd way, the genre has the rise of the Nashville Sound to thank for it. Its success, while alternately broadening and dividing its fan base, has provided the music with its essential stylistic yin and yang. There couldn't have been any radical movements in the music ('60s honky tonk, outlaw music, neo-traditionalism) or conservative bastions clinging to older styles if the Nashville Sound had not created the center from which these alternatives sprang.

—Cub Koda

Recommended Recordings:

Jim Reeves, *Welcome to My World: The Essential Jim Reeves Collection* (RCA)

Patsy Cline, *12 Greatest Hits* (MCA)

Don Gibson, *A Legend in His Time* (Bear Family)

Marty Robbins, *The Essential Marty Robbins: 1951-1982* (Columbia Legacy)

The Browns, *20 of the Best* (RCA)

Skeeter Davis, *The Essential Skeeter Davis* (RCA)

Ray Price, *The Essential Ray Price (1951-1962)* (Columbia Legacy)

Porter Wagoner, *The Thin Man from West Plains* (Bear Family)

Porter Wagoner & Dolly Parton, *The Essential* (RCA)

Rockabilly

If rock 'n' roll can be called the child of rhythm and blues and Country & Western music, no style is a purer blend than rockabilly. The first form of rock 'n' roll performed by white musicians, its period of mass popularity was brief, but the best of it remains among the most exciting and frenetic rock 'n' roll ever waxed.

Even in the segregated American South of the early 20th century, blacks and whites often had cause to interact with each other on a daily basis. The interaction carried over to music, and white hillbilly country performers have reflected the influence of the blues and other African-American music since they began recording, as a listen to Jimmie Rodgers will attest. Just as blues became jazzier, faster, and more electric throughout the 1940s and early '50s, so did country, through swing bands like Bob Wills and the Maddox Brothers. The Delmore Brothers, starting as a more traditional hillbilly harmony act, anticipated much of rockabilly's mania when they added a thumping country boogie beat to the equation on their finest recordings in the late '40s. Nearly forgotten performers like Arthur Smith and Hardrock Gunter laid down country boogie sides that brought the guitar to the forefront.

Considering that most rockabilly musicians of importance came from the South, it's ironic that the first records that could be termed as honest-to-god rockabilly were issued by a Northerner, Bill Haley. The Philadelphian had been pursuing a hillbilly career with generally dismal results until 1951, when he covered Jackie Brenston's "Rocket 88" (which is often cited as one of the very first

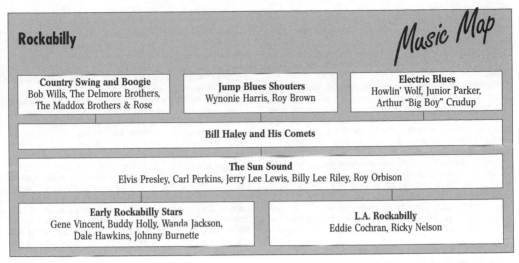

rock 'n' roll records). Although they aren't nearly as well known as his huge rock 'n' roll hits like "Rock Around the Clock," the sides he cut for the small Essex label between 1951 and 1954 are groundbreaking early rockabilly; the 1952 single "Rock the Joint," in fact, is almost identical in melody and arrangement to "Rock Around the Clock." Haley was no Elvis vocally, and the steel guitars and jump beats of his Comets betrayed lingering influences of hillbilly and swing music. But he was undoubtedly the first to bring together R&B and C&W with such force, although nobody knew quite what to call the music at the time.

There were certainly numerous musicians in the South experimenting with primitive rockabilly-like sounds by mid-1954. Sam Phillips and his Memphis record label, Sun Records, were chiefly responsible for honing the sound and capturing it on vinyl. Often quoted as having said that he could make a fortune with a white singer who sounded black (though he has denied saying this in such explicit terms), Phillips found the perfect vehicle for doing so with Elvis Presley, who recorded five singles for Sun between mid-1954 and the end of 1955. Supported by guitarist Scotty Moore and bassist Bill Black, this was rockabilly, if not rock 'n' roll, at its best and purest; as great as his subsequent achievements were, by critical consensus this handful of 45s ranks as Elvis' finest work.

As has already been noted by some conscientious historians, it would be inaccurate to say that Elvis simply whitewashed the blues for the mass market. Look at the Sun singles themselves: they usually pair a blues/R&B cover with a rocked-up rendition of a country tune. "Blue Moon of Kentucky," the flipside of his debut 45 "That's All Right Mama," was a cover of a Bill Monroe composition. "You're a Heartbreaker," "I'm Left, You're Right, She's Gone," and "I Forget to Remember to Forget"—these are all, essentially, country songs given a rockabilly treatment. Also, in his Sun days, Elvis was really thought of as a country, or hillbilly, performer—the term "rock 'n' roll" had hardly been applied to any white performers yet, for one thing. Elvis played the country circuit in the South, where he shared the stage with such mainstream country stars as Hank Snow, and was signed to a management deal with Colonel Tom Parker, who had worked with Snow and Eddy Arnold. When his records began to chart, first locally and then nationally, they were on the country listings, not the pop ones. Before Elvis had ever dented the pop charts, "Baby Let's Play House" and "I Forgot to Remember to Forget" were nationwide country hits, the latter making No. 1 in 1955.

Presley didn't set off a mass wave of imitators right away; he was primarily a regional sensation until his contract was bought by RCA. Sam Phillips used the money from the sale to develop his own formidable stable of rockabilly performers. Carl Perkins' "Blue Suede Shoes" almost beat Elvis' "Heartbreak Hotel" to the top of the charts, and although Perkins was never able to dupli-

cate Elvis' success, Sun generated a wealth of great rockabilly hits and misses over the next few years by Jerry Lee Lewis, Billy Lee Riley, Sonny Burgess, Carl Mann, and Roy Orbison. The Sun Sound—echo-chamber vocals, crisp electric guitar leads, and slapback bass—became the standard of rockabilly excellence, often imitated, never recaptured.

Almost all of the rockabilly singers had been playing country music before they caught the rockabilly fever, whether or not they recorded before the rockabilly explosion. (There were a few black rockabilly singles here and there, such as the Jerry Lee Lewis-like outings of Big Al Downing from Oklahoma, but these were quite rare.) Listen, for instance, to the early Sun outtakes of Elvis Presley, which show a far tamer, more countrified vocalist (not to mention one who was also considerably influenced by pop ballads). Carl Perkins, prior to recording "Blue Suede Shoes," laid down some pure country with "Tennessee," complete with fiddle. Even some rockabilly stars who made their recording debuts after 1955 would sometimes ooze pure country, as on Jerry Lee Lewis' debut single "Crazy Arms" (a cover of a Ray Price song), or Gene Vincent's delicately crooned "Important Words."

But rockabilly, and Elvis Presley in particular, was so exciting—and commercially viable—that many young country singers didn't need much prodding to change their style. Bob Luman, who would make both rockabilly and country records, described an early Elvis Presley show in Paul Hemphill's Nashville Sound: "This cat came out in red pants and a green coat and a pink shirt and socks, and he had this sneer on his face and he stood behind the mike for five minutes, I'll bet, before he made a move. Then he hit his guitar a lick, and he broke two strings. I'd been playing ten years, and I hadn't broken a total of two strings. So there he was, these two strings dangling, and he hadn't done anything yet, and these high school girls were screaming and fainting and running up to the stage, and then he started to move his hips real slow like he had a thing for his guitar.

"That was Elvis Presley when he was about nineteen, playing Kilgore, Texas. He made chills run up my back, man, like when your hair starts grabbing at your collar. For the next nine days he played one-nighters around Kilgore, and after school every day me and my girl would get in the car and go wherever he was playing that night. That's the last time I tried to sing like Webb Pierce and Lefty Frizzell."

By 1956, even such old-school country stars as Webb Pierce would be jumping onto the rockabilly bandwagon, either to keep up with trends or to try and revive flagging careers. George Jones, Rose Maddox, the Delmore Brothers, Patsy Cline, Marty Robbins, Tex Williams, and Buck Owens—all of these artists are thought of as country giants, not rock singers. Yet all of them recorded rockabilly in the 1950s, sometimes quite well, and sometimes (as with Marty Robbins' cover of "That's All Right Mama") with some commercial success. George Jones was so reluctant to sing the music that he recorded some rockabilly under the pseudonym of Thumper Jones. Johnny Cash probably would have been just as happy not to do any rockabilly at all, but as he was recording for Sam Phillips at Sun, hits like "I Walk the Line" bore just enough traces of the slap-back echoed beat to bleed into the rockabilly margins.

Presleymania overran the country in 1956, instigating a wave of rockabilly recordings, nationally and (more often) regionally distributed, that was similar in some respects to the garage band explosion of a decade later. Hundreds of performers found their way into studios in Tennessee, Texas, California, and other locales, embracing the new sound with a hepped-up enthusiasm that often bordered on mania. The singles were usually crudely recorded, extremely basic and derivative, their not inconsiderable saving grace being their infectious energy.

While the Sun Sound was the pinnacle of rockabilly, several performers became legends outside of Sam Phillips' studio. Gene Vincent's 1956 sides, featuring his breathy vocals and the speed-of-light guitar of Cliff Gallup (from Vincent's backing band the Blue Caps), were usually brilliant. Eddie Cochran brought a sophisticated brand of teenage rebellion to his rockabilly hits, which helped pioneer the use of overdubbed guitars and vocals. Ricky Nelson recorded first-class rockabilly pop in Hollywood with the help of ace guitarist James Burton. Johnny Burnette and his trio recorded some of the raunchiest Elvis-derived rock 'n' roll of the time, including the first rock version of "The Train Kept A-Rollin.'" Dale Hawkins cut a crackling classic with "Suzy Q.," and Wanda Jackson's raspy rockabilly sides rank as the finest rock 'n' roll recorded by a female singer in the 1950s.

Rockabilly began to fade as a commercial force around 1958, not just because of fickle popular taste, but because of the rapid evolution of rock 'n' roll itself. One of the greatest rockabilly singers, Buddy Holly's facility for melodic invention branched into all forms of pop-rock, and had a far-reaching influence on all of pop that extended to the British Invasion. Along with the Everly Brothers and Ricky Nelson, he began gravitating toward a more gentle, melodic sound that was less structurally limited, if not as energetic, as pure rockabilly. Elvis himself was moving toward more straightforward rock material, and then toward pop after his hitch in the Army.

Those performers that stuck with the basic rockabilly sound faced diminishing returns. Some, like Gene Vincent, simply vanished from the charts, although they maintained loyal audiences, especially overseas. Roy Orbison, never comfortable as a rockabilly singer in the first place, reinvented himself as a masterful crooner of pop-rock ballads. Jerry Lee Lewis' career was crippled by scandal. Eventually he would find success in the Country & Western mainstream, a path followed by many other singers who had achieved limited success with rockabilly.

The list of those who "returned" to Country & Western from rockabilly is substantial, though it varied in degrees. Wanda Jackson, Brenda Lee, Conway Twitty, and quite a few other rockabilly artists did mostly country after the early '60s. The Everly Brothers and Ricky Nelson tried to have their cake and eat it too by helping pioneer country-rock in the late '60s. Most of the first wave of rockabilly singers—Carl Perkins, Roy Orbison, and Elvis Presley himself—would occasionally sing quite a bit of straight country on their recordings, without ever redefining themselves as country artists. Sometimes these singers reverted to country music as a matter of personal choice, and at any rate, having grown up with country music, they could have been expected to always maintain a country influence.

But often it was also a matter of survival. Rockabilly was passé after the 1950s, and all-country radio formats were becoming increasingly common. Some felt compelled to record country records in order to get airplay, which was necessary to keep the live work coming. In many cases, country music may have represented the best (or only) option. It's also true that some artists who dallied in rockabilly, such as George Jones, Jack Scott, Marty Robbins, and Waylon Jennings, were at heart country artists all along.

Rockabilly never returned to the charts in a significant way after the '50s, though several acts have scored big hits in the style,

such as Billy Swan and the Stray Cats. Some obscure rockabilly singers from the old days, like Ronnie Dawson, Sleepy LaBeef, and Ray Campi, enjoyed a considerably more widespread following in later decades as part of mini-rockabilly revivals. Others who weren't around for the first wave of rockabilly have carved a career for themselves as rockabilly artists playing for small and specialized audiences, such as Shakin' Stevens in Britain, and, much more recently, Big Sandy.

A huge influence on the early Beatles, Creedence Clearwater Revival, and others, rockabilly was instrumental in establishing the focus of rock 'n' roll on the electric guitar-bass-drums combination, doing so with a simple joy and force that has helped inspire generations of musicians. The influence of rockabilly upon country itself is harder to ascertain, however. Ex-rockabillys like Jerry Lee Lewis and Charlie Rich always kept some hell-raising tunes in the wings, whether for album tracks or live gigs. Some of the more frenetic straight country singers, like Lewis' cousin Mickey Gilley, have a trace of muted rockabilly in some of their material. Sometimes a big country star will drag out an old rockabilly-related tune (as Alan Jackson did on his hit treatment of Eddie Cochran's "Summertime Blues"), although the results usually have a lot more to do with standard Nashville pop than real rockabilly.

Of the country stars of the 1990s, Marty Stuart may be the only one whose style bears the most visible influence of rockabilly, although Stuart has really not gone into rockabilly in an all-out way.

If rockabilly's a part of contemporary country music, it's by and large kept in the closet. There are a few artists that approach rockabilly from a country footing (as opposed to a rock one), though outings such as Doc Watson's mid-'90s rockabilly album (*Docabilly*) are relatively rare. The best of these mavericks may be Rosie Flores, who brought it all home by recording some material with rockabilly queen Wanda Jackson, who has come back to the music herself, making her first all-rockabilly tour of the United States in the mid-1990s.

–Richie Unterberger

Recommended Recordings:

Elvis Presley, *King of Rock'n'Roll: Complete '50s Masters* (RCA)

Buddy Holly, *Buddy Holly Collection* (MCA)

Gene Vincent, *Capitol Collectors Series* (Capitol)

Carl Perkins, *Original Sun Greatest Hits* (Rhino)

Jerry Lee Lewis, *18 Original Sun Greatest Hits* (Rhino)

Johnny Burnette, *Tear It Up* (Solid Smoke)

Eddie Cochran, *Legendary Masters* (EMI)

Ricky Nelson, *Legendary Masters* (EMI)

Wanda Jackson, *Rockin' with Wanda* (Capitol)

The Collins Kids, *Introducing Larry and Laurie* (Epic)

Bill Haley and His Comets, *Rock the Joint!* (School Kids')

Various Artists, *Rock This Town Vol. 1 & 2* (Rhino)

Books:

Good Rockin' Tonight: Sun Records and the Birth of Rock 'n' Roll, by Colin Escott with Martin Hawkins (St. Martin's, 1991)

Last Train to Memphis, by Peter Guralnick (Little, Brown & Co., 1994)

Elvis: The Illustrated Record, by Roy Carr & Mick Farren (Harmony, 1982)

Remembering Buddy: The Definitive Biography of Buddy Holly, by John Goldrosen and John Beecher (Da Capo, 1996)

The Day the World Turned Blue: A Biography of Gene Vincent, by Britt Hagarty (Blandford Press, UK, 1984)

Ricky Nelson: Idol for a Generation, by Joel Selvin (Contemporary, 1990)

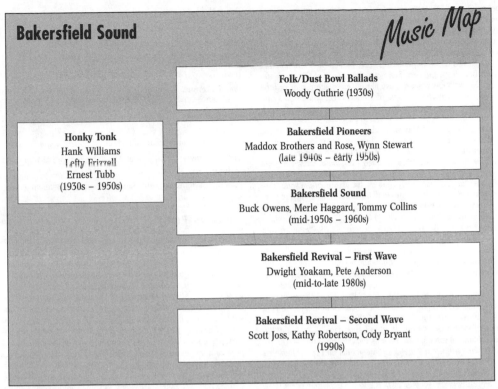

Bakersfield Sound

Music Map

Folk/Dust Bowl Ballads
Woody Guthrie (1930s)

Honky Tonk
Hank Williams
Lefty Frizzell
Ernest Tubb
(1930s – 1950s)

Bakersfield Pioneers
Maddox Brothers and Rose, Wynn Stewart
(late 1940s – early 1950s)

Bakersfield Sound
Buck Owens, Merle Haggard, Tommy Collins
(mid-1950s – 1960s)

Bakersfield Revival – First Wave
Dwight Yoakam, Pete Anderson
(mid-to-late 1980s)

Bakersfield Revival – Second Wave
Scott Joss, Kathy Robertson, Cody Bryant
(1990s)

The Bakersfield Sound

Because Nashville has long been uncontested as the home of country music, the idea of the working-class town of Bakersfield, CA, being a country music hot spot was a surprise, to say the least—and likely, at least in the minds of more than a few Music Row executives, sacrilege. In the late 1950s and '60s, the development of the Nashville Sound meant that the majority of charting hits were softer, smoother, and easier to swallow. So for a bona fide blue-collar, hard-country movement to spring up some 2,000 miles west—and for several of these West Coast artists to eventually be recognized by the establishment and played on country radio—was something close to a revolution, albeit short-lived.

The so-called Bakersfield Sound probably wouldn't be remembered—or even exist as such—if not for the huge and lasting success of two specific artists: Merle Haggard and Buck Owens. But it's also likely that those two country singers might not be the superstars they are today if not for the rich music scene that thrived in the city during the 1950s and '60s. The development of Bakersfield's honky-tonk style is indirectly tied to the region's natural resources. Located at the southern end of California's San Joaquin Valley and 100 miles northeast of Los Angeles, Bakersfield became a boom town in the mid-to-late 1800s thanks first to gold (in Kern River Canyon) and, more significantly, to oil. It also grew into a major regional market and distribution center for all sorts of agricultural goods. Thanks to the Dust Bowl, the Depression, and World War II, Bakersfield saw a huge influx of Okies in the 1930s, '40s, and '50s. Coming to pick California's fruit and cotton and to work its oil fields, these rural transplants brought their love of country music, and turned Bakersfield into a musical boom town as well. The city's growing number of dance halls, bars, and honky tonks became, then, fertile ground for performers who understood the hard-edged, traditionally rooted dancing and drinking music these working people craved every weekend ("loud music that plays until all hours," as Bakersfield singer Wynn Stewart tells it in his song "How the Other Half Lives").

A series of bars and clubs actually sprouted all up and down the state, creating a California country music circuit that would feed the careers of many West Coast-based singers as well as countless touring acts. But it was Bakersfield, the biggest city in the southern San Joaquin, that became the hub for cultural life in the region. It was here that, in the 1950s, country artists such as Tommy Collins, Johnny Bond, and Ferlin Husky, the Maddox Brothers and Rose, and bandleaders like Bill Woods and Billy Mize played regularly and earned reputations as solid acts with large draws.

While the music in nearby Los Angeles was often urban and swanky, Bakersfield was home to a less sophisticated crowd. Attempting to erase the working-class angst of the weekend revelers in the area honky-tonks, the Bakersfield Sound is marked by the sharp, loud, high-end sound of the electric and steel guitars, fiddles, and lead and harmony vocals—influenced by rock 'n' roll and rockabilly as well as traditional country. It was simple in structure and designed to be heard over the din of the average honky-tonk. This was a direct contrast with the production style of the Nashville Sound, at the time filling the country airwaves with crooning voices, lush string arrangements, and background choruses.

If anyone deserves to be called the king of Bakersfield, it's Buck Owens. Though born in Texas and raised in Arizona, Owens and his family moved to Bakersfield in 1951 because there was work to be had in the city's nightclubs. He played in a house band at the Blackboard with bandleader Bill Woods, and soon landed session work at Capitol Records with Tommy Collins, Wanda Jackson, Gene Vincent, and others. Owens' style was influenced by rock 'n' roll as well as traditional country, and his guitar playing (on his Fender Telecaster) stood out for its sharp, punchy sound. Soon Owens was signed to Capitol himself, and his 1960 version of his friend Harlan Howard's song "Above and Beyond" catapulted him into the national spotlight. Like most of his numerous hits, it's an immediately bright and lively song, sharp, upbeat, and cut to be noticed.

One of Nashville's top songwriters, Howard got his start while living in L.A. in the 1950s. His songs are loosely tied to the Bakersfield crowd via Owens and, to a lesser degree, Wynn Stewart, who recorded a version of "Above and Beyond" six months before Owens. Stewart's version failed to catch on; other songs of his ("How the Other Half Lives," a duet with Howard's wife Jan, and the superb "Wishful Thinking") also failed to make Stewart much of a household name, yet today they stand out as some of the classic recordings of the era. "Wishful Thinking" in particular is a clear-minded, hard-driving song packed with energy that grabs hold from the very first notes. Like much of Owens' material, Stewart's records were usually far more aggressive in tone and approach than the work of crooners like Jim Reeves and Patsy Cline—even more so than the honky tonk being made back East at the time by Ray Price and George Jones.

Stewart was a mainstay and highly successful performer on the region's club circuit. He was also responsible for giving a job to another upstart musician, Merle Haggard, who played in his band for a year. In 1963, Haggard recorded a version of Stewart's "Sing a Sad Song" for the Bakersfield-based Tally label, and it became his first charting record; his 1964 hit, the Liz Anderson song "(My Friends Are Gonna Be) Strangers," led to his being signed to Capitol. (Anderson, who lived for a while in California, also penned the Haggard hit "I'm a Lonesome Fugitive.")

Haggard was the only artist associated with Bakersfield who was actually born there. His style matured into something far more personal and individualistic than his honky-tonk surroundings, yet his San Joaquin roots remained in his soul, and he's never forgotten them. He wrote a song paying tribute to his friend, Bakersfield mainstay Tommy Collins ("Leonard"), and covered that artist's material many times ("High on a Hilltop," "Carolyn"). Haggard's album *Someday We'll Look Back* recalls the field work of his youth (his parents were Okie migrants), and includes the Dallas Frazier song "California Cotton Fields," probably the best picture of the migrant workers' life ever written in song.

Frazier grew up in Bakersfield and got his start in the business thanks to Ferlin Husky, who was a regular on the region's club circuit in the 1950s. Frazier soon moved to Nashville, however, where he became another of Music Row's top songwriters from the 1960s onward. (His song "Elvira" was a smash for the Oak Ridge Boys.) Collins (born Leonard Raymond Sipes) worked in and out of Bakersfield's live music circuit in the 1950s and '60s. Collins also got help from Husky—in this case for a Capitol recording contract. Collins' cutesy 1952 song "You Better Not Do That" (with Owens on lead guitar) was his biggest hit, but he had others. Haggard wasn't the only artist to have recorded Collins' material over the years; his song "If You Ain't Lovin'," for instance, was a hit for Faron Young in 1955 and George Strait in 1988. The national success of Bakersfield's artists owes significant thanks to Los Angeles-based Capitol Records. Owens, Haggard, Husky, Collins, and Stewart were all members of the Capitol roster at one time or another, signed and produced by Ken Nelson, who was head of the label's country music division from the mid-1950s through the '70s. (Capitol, a major player in the country music industry, was also home to Hank Thompson, Jean Shepard, Faron Young, Wanda Jackson, Freddie Hart, and many others.)

The strength of Bakersfield's country music scene eventually tapered off as Owens and Haggard shifted their focus in other directions, and as the town's economy began to falter. Today, few reminders of the old club scene remain in Bakersfield, and Southern California's country music community is based in and around Los Angeles, with Dwight Yoakam being the figurehead. Yoakam—whose hard-edged, rocked-up approach is the closest today to the once-proud Bakersfield sound—deliberately moved to California instead of Nashville because it was home to individualists like Owens. He even brought his idol out of retirement to cut a duet version of Owens' 1972 song "The Streets of Bakersfield," which in 1988 hit No. 1.

—Kurt Wolff

Recommended Recordings:

Tommy Collins, *Words and Music Country Style* (Capitol)

Tommy Collins, *Leonard* (Bear Family)

Dallas Frazier, *Singing My Songs* (RCA)

Ferlin Husky, *Gone* (Capitol)

Ferlin Husky, *Vintage* (Capitol)

Merle Haggard, *Someday We'll Look Back* (Capitol)

Merle Haggard, *Down Every Road* (box set) (Capitol)

Buck Owens, *The Buck Owens Collection, 1959-1990* (Rhino)

Buck Owens, *Buck Owens Sings Harlan Howard* (Capitol)

Wynn Stewart, *California Country: The Best of the Challenge Masters* (AVI)

Various Artists, *A Town South of Bakersfield, Vol. I and II* (Restless)

Dwight Yoakam, *Buenas Noches from a Lonely Room* (Reprise)

Various Artists, *Hillbilly Fever, Vol. 4: Legends of the West Coast* (Rhino)

Jean Shepard, *Honky Tonk Heroine* (Country Music Foundation)

Country-Pop

If Chet Atkins' countrypolitan was *the* sound of mainstream country during the '60s, Billy Sherrill's lush, string-laden productions defined the country-pop of the '70s. Though Atkins and Sherrill appeared to work the same ground, Sherrill's approach was considerably different. Sherrill produced country records as if they were pop-rock singles, adapting Phil Spector's "Wall of Sound" for the genre. Instead of relying on standard country instruments like steel guitars and fiddles, he recorded with string sections and vocal choruses, often overdubbing parts to give the music a grandiose, epic sound. Some critics complained that his style wasn't pure country, yet there is no denying that he helped bring country music to a wider pop audience during the late '60s and '70s with the recordings he made with George Jones, Tammy Wynette, Charlie Rich, and Johnny Paycheck, as well as many others. In his wake, numerous other producers—including Nashville Sound predecessors like Owen Bradley—adapted Sherrill's sweeping, melodic technique, often bringing in even more overt rock 'n' roll influences in order to make the records appealing to mainstream, AM pop radio.

Initially a rock 'n' roll and R&B musician, Sherrill became interested in country music in 1962 when an unknown Nashville country artist cut one of his songs. Encouraged by the unannounced royalty check, he moved to Nashville. Upon his arrival, Sherrill was hired by Sam Phillips to oversee Sun Records' Nashville studios. After Sun and Phillips went bankrupt the following year, Epic Records' Nashville division hired him as an in-house producer, and he was assigned to record any artist that all of the label's other producers had already rejected. At that time, he was unfamiliar with many of country music's production techniques and musical conventions. Instead of heeding the advice of the studio musicians he was working with, Sherrill forged ahead and created his own style, telling the professional musicians what to play. Basing his sound on the work of Phil Spector, Don Law, Owen Bradley, and Chet Atkins, he began pushing the boundaries of the Nashville Sound of the '50s and early '60s by making productions bigger and grander. Sherrill also decided to select the songs that his artists would record, often co-writing the songs to suit the singer's style and his own production.

Sherrill's first major hit arrived in 1965, when David Houston took Sherrill's song "Livin' in a House Full of Love" to No. 3 late that year. The following year, Houston recorded the Sherrill/Glenn Sutton song "Almost Persuaded," which spent nine weeks at No. 1. "Almost Persuaded" quickly became a standard, becoming the subject of cover versions by artists as diverse as Louis Armstrong, Louis Prima, and Etta James. The success of "Almost Persuaded" launched Sherrill's career as much as it did Houston's, and Sherrill found his first superstar the following year when he discovered Tammy Wynette, an Alabama hairdresser and waitress. Wynette had previously approached several other record labels but had been rejected. Sherrill signed her, co-writing "Your Good Girl's Gonna Go Bad" with Sutton with her specifically in

Country Rock

Music Map

Early Country Rock
The International Submarine Band, The Byrds, Bob Dylan, Hearts & Flowers

Late '60s Country Rock
The Beau Brummels, The Everly Brothers, Ian & Sylvia

Southern California Country Rock
The Flying Burrito Brothers, Poco, Rick Nelson & The Stone Canyon Band, Mike Nesmith, Gene Clark, The Dillards

'70s Southern Country Rock
Pure Prairie League, Charlie Daniels

L.A. Country Rock-Influenced Superstars
The Eagles, Linda Ronstadt

Texas Cult Country Rock
The Flatlanders, Joe Ely, Butch Hancock, Jimmie Dale Gilmore

mind. The single became a hit upon its early 1967 release, launching a very successful career for Wynette.

By 1968, Sherrill had begun to develop a distinctive sound that was highlighted by his detailed production; nevertheless, he hadn't yet hit upon his unique, near-operatic blend of orchestration and sound effects. In fact, he kept fairly close to the honky tonk roots of Wynette, while letting Charlie Rich explore his idiosyncratic fusion of jazz, blues, R&B, and country. Over the next two years, he slowly pushed Tammy toward string-laden country-pop arrangements, the kind he explored on Barbara Mandrell's early Columbia records.

By the early '70s, it became apparent that Sherrill's sleek, urban production was catching on, as AM pop radio embraced hits that sounded quite similar to his own productions. Simultaneously, artists like B.J. Thomas and Glen Campbell were carving out a country-pop sound that was simpler and more direct than Sherrill's. Both musicians had extensive backgrounds in pop, rock, and folk, and their recordings reflected their past endeavors. Soon, a number of singers developed a compromise between the sound of Campbell and Sherrill, and these records—Donna Fargo's "The Happiest Girl in the Whole USA," Lynn Anderson's "Rose Garden"—began receiving heavy airplay on AM pop radio. Before long, Sherrill and his artists were having crossover hits, most notably in the form of Charlie Rich's "Behind Closed Doors" and "The Most Beautiful Girl" in 1973.

For the remainder of the '70s, this lush, pop-ready form of country-pop dominated mainstream country music. By the middle of the decade, pop had turned away from the style, yet many country artists continued to record singles in this vein. George Jones, who began recording with Sherrill in 1971, made some of his very best recordings during this era, as did Conway Twitty, who recorded with Owen Bradley. Toward the end of the decade, country-pop had lost much of its appeal, and major artists like Jones and Twitty were beginning to expand its boundaries. Still, the sound of country-pop remained popular until the beginning of the '80s, when urban cowboy and its more pronounced soft rock influences came along. Urban cowboy smoothed out the remaining edges in country-pop, making it more appealing to the emerging adult contemporary radio format, while co-opting the outlaw image to create a pop culture sensation. In its wake, country-pop began to fade, yet there were several artists that pursued the distinctively lush Nashville Sound during the '80s.
—*Stephen Thomas Erlewine*

Recommended Recordings:

George Jones, *Anniversary* (Epic)
Conway Twitty, *20 Greatest Hits* (MCA)
Charlie Rich, *Behind Closed Doors* (Epic)
Loretta Lynn, *20 Greatest Hits* (MCA)

Don Williams, *20 Greatest Hits* (MCA)
Tammy Wynette, *Anniversary* (Epic)
Glen Campbell, *The Essential Glen Campbell* (Razor & Tie)
B.J. Thomas, *The Best of B.J. Thomas* (Rhino)
Donna Fargo, *Best of Donna Fargo* (Varese)

Country-Rock

Country-rock is one of the hardest rock 'n' roll styles to map and define. Country music, of course, was integral to the birth of rock 'n' roll, and has continued to exert a huge influence on rock. You can find innumerable examples of rock 'n' roll performers that are heavily soaked with country, from Elvis Presley to Elvis Costello. As a label and as a movement, however, country-rock is primarily identified with a school of bands in the late '60s and early '70s that brought the modern and irreverent qualities of rock to the more traditional musical values of country music.

There are many antecedents to country-rock; the close harmonies and acoustic guitars on much of the Everly Brothers' material foreshadow much of it. In the mid-'60s, Del Shannon recorded an entire album of Hank Williams tunes, George Jones and Gene Pitney teamed up for an LP of duets, and the trashy British R&B/punk band the Downliners Sect recorded a bizarre straight country album that was unnoticed commercially and unsuccessful artistically. Several of the '60s' top groups dallied successfully with countrified rock 'n' roll at times, such as the Beatles (especially around the *Beatles for Sale* period, on tracks like "I Don't Want to Spoil the Party"), the early Byrds ("Satisfied Mind," "Mr. Spaceman," "Time Between"), and Buffalo Springfield ("Go and Say Goodbye," "Kind Woman"); all of these bands placed a premium on close harmonies, and could incorporate country signatures into their sound with natural ease when the spirit moved them. The term "country-rock" actually began to get used and thrown around in 1968, when most of the major rock acts were retreating from their psychedelic experiments into a "back to basics" approach. Bob Dylan, who had never embraced psychedelia in the first place, led the way with his *John Wesley Harding* album. Dylan had recorded in Nashville before, but this early 1968 effort was far more basic in instrumentation and far more country in tone. In 1969, he would largely eschew his inscrutable wordplay for basic homilies on *Nashville Skyline*, as well as recording an entire unreleased LP with one of his chief mentors, Johnny Cash.

The true god of country-rock, though, was guitarist and singer Gram Parsons. As the leader of the International Submarine Band, he recorded an album in 1967, *Safe at Home*, that prominently used pedal steel guitar. The LP is seen by some scholars as the first true country-rock record, although it was little noticed upon its release. Shortly afterwards, Parsons joined the Byrds, and was almost single-handedly responsible for altering the band's focus from folk-rock to country-rock. Byrds leader Roger McGuinn had been entertaining the idea of an ambitious double album with heavy use of electronics, but the project was scuppered in favor of *Sweetheart of the Rodeo*. The 1968 release is almost universally hailed as one of the first and best country-rock efforts. The Byrds' country-rock era was short; Parsons left the band after a year. Longtime Byrds bassist Chris Hillman left the group around the same time, and the pair quickly teamed to form the nucleus of the Flying Burrito Brothers. Parsons only stayed with the band for a couple albums, but these works, also prominently featuring Sneaky Pete Kleinow on pedal steel, are the purest and most influential country-rock hybrids, and among the few major country-rock recordings that are not in reality closer to rock than country.

Country music may have sprung from the Southern states, but country-rock primarily flourished in Southern California. Other country-rock acts of note in the late '60s included the little-known Hearts & Flowers—who actually surfaced before 1968, but were classified as folk-rock at the time—and Poco, featuring former Buffalo Springfield members Richie Furay and Jim Messina. In Northern California, the New Riders of the Purple Sage established themselves as a more countrified and laidback cousin of the Grateful Dead in the early '70s.

Some veteran acts primarily associated with other forms of rock and folk became country-rockers for a time in the late '60s. Folk-rock pioneers the Beau Brummels went to Nashville to record *Bradley's Barn* at the legendary studio of the same name; the Everly Brothers' *Roots* was their most critically acclaimed post-early-'60s work; Ian & Sylvia moved from contemporary folk to country as a duo and leaders of the band Great Speckled Bird; Rick Nelson had an artistic renaissance while fronting the Stone Canyon Band, which featured future Eagle Randy Meisner. Former Byrd Gene Clark recorded country-rock on his own and as part of Dillard & Clark. The Dillards themselves, primarily known as a bluegrass act before the late '60s, had already acted as important figures in folk-rock by helping teach the Byrds harmony vocals, and employing Dewey Martin on drums before he left to join Buffalo Springfield. On 1968's *Wheatstraw Suite*, they became one of the few noted country-rock performers to move into the style from country rather than rock.

Country-rock wasn't big commercially, and may have made its greatest impact as an influence on other performers. The Band, the Grateful Dead, Creedence Clearwater Revival, and George Harrison, for instance, could not be called country-rock performers by any means, but all recorded some impressive country-rock material on their late-'60s and early-'70s albums. Gram Parsons was a big influence on the Rolling Stones around this time, and on Keith Richards in particular, though it should be pointed out that the Stones had fused country and rock as far back as 1966 on "High and Dry." Still, their *Let It Bleed* and *Sticky Fingers* albums had quite a few country licks, most famously on "Wild Horses" (which appeared as a cover by the Flying Burrito Brothers before the Stones released their own version).

Country-rock hasn't gotten much attention as a movement since the early '70s. Commercially, it found its greatest success in the mid-'70s on hits by the Eagles (who featured ex-members of the Burritos, Poco, and the Stone Canyon Band) and Linda Ronstadt, who absorbed country-rock into their brands of soft rock and pop. Southern bands like Pure Prairie League and Charlie Daniels had some success with more southern-fried sounds, and southern rock bands like the Allman Brothers, the Ozark Mountain Daredevils, and Lynyrd Skynyrd recorded some country-influenced material, although their focus remained blues-rock and hard rock. (In the 1980s and 1990s, it could be argued that Nashville has been a lot more successful in borrowing from rock than the other way around.) Country-rock arguably never recovered from the death of Gram Parsons in 1973, but it's remained alive and kicking, if hardly omnipresent. Elvis Costello made an all-out country album, albeit a commercial flop, in 1981 with *Almost Blue;* country music informs much of Neil Young's work, in whatever decade he's working in; alternative rockers like the Meat Puppets and the Jayhawks have leaned heavily on country-rock at times. Texas eccentrics Joe Ely, Butch Hancock, and Jim-

mie Dale Gilmore (all of whom have played with each other at some point) have formed a sort of extended family for their brand of maverick country-rock. Once in a while a country-rock band will get a big push, like Lone Justice, but the hybrid seems to resist huge commercial success.

–Richie Unterberger

Recommended Recordings:

The Byrds, *Sweetheart of the Rodeo* (Columbia)

The Flying Burrito Brothers, *Farther Along: The Best of the Flying Burrito Brothers* (A&M)

The International Submarine Band, *Safe at Home* (Rhino)

Hearts & Flowers, *Now Is the Time / Of Horses, Kids, and Forgotten Women* (Edsel, UK)

The Beau Brummels, *Bradley's Barn* (Edsel, UK)

Poco, *Pickin' up the Pieces* (Epic)

The Everly Brothers, *Roots* (Warner)

The Dillards, *Wheatstraw Suite* (Elektra)

Bob Dylan, *John Wesley Harding* (Columbia)

Various Artists, *Hillbilly Fever, Vol. 5* (Rhino)

The Flatlanders, *More a Legend than a Band* (Rounder)

Neil Young, *Harvest Moon* (Reprise)

Books:

Gram Parsons: A Music Biography, by Sid Griffin (Sierra, 1985)
Hickory Wind: The Gram Parsons Story, by Ben Fong-Torres

The Outlaws

While country music is full of outlaws—many who have done real jail time—the term "outlaw" also refers to a period during the early- to mid-1970s. It was a time when the '60s generation began to have its effect on the Nashville establishment, and the long reign of the staid, crooner-oriented Nashville Sound finally came to an end.

The term "outlaw" began as a nickname for the music (and lifestyles) of Waylon Jennings, Tompall Glaser, Willie Nelson, and their compatriots and hangers-on, but it soon became a marketing and publicity tool that helped RCA and other major labels cross over into the rock 'n' roll market and sell more albums than the country industry ever had before. Nonetheless, the work these artists produced during this period is some of the freshest and most viscerally exciting in modern country music history.

The origin of the name more or less originated with a song by Lee Clayton, "Ladies Love Outlaws," that became the title track of a 1972 Waylon Jennings album. Jennings soon after grew a beard, his hair got longer, and coupled with his penchant for denim and leather clothes, he certainly looked the part. Journalists picked up on the catchy name, and publicist Hazel Smith also used the term to promote the Glaser Brothers.

To many Music Row executives, "outlaw" meant an unwanted infusion of self-important long-haired singers—roughnecks who mixed dope with their drink and wore biker gear instead of Nudie suits—into the comfortably conservative establishment. But as record sales quickly showed, singers like Jennings, Nelson, Glaser, Kris Kristofferson, and Billy Joe Shaver were loaded with talent, and they possessed exactly the kind of youthful energy the stiff-collared industry needed. These and others of the outlaw ilk not only reinforced the bridge that was beginning to appear between country and rock 'n' roll audiences—magazines like *Rolling Stone* began paying serious attention to Nashville for the first time—but showed an honest love and reverence for country music's history. Despite their ragged lifestyles and rock and roll associations, the music these artists created was far more traditional—more "country"—than almost anything that had come out of Nashville during the previous decade.

That's because the outlaw movement wasn't about long hair and cheap drugs, it was about creative control for the artists in the

The Outlaws

Music Map

Honky Tonk's Second Generation
George Jones, Hank Locklin, Carl Smith (mid-1950s – 1960s)

The Nashville Sound	**Bakersfield Sound**	**Country-Rock**
Chet Atkins, Floyd Cramer, Owen Bradley, Patsy Cline (mid-1950s – 1960s)	Buck Owens, Merle Haggard, Tommy Collins (mid-1950s – 1960s)	Gram Parsons, The Byrds, Flying Burrito Brothers (late 1960s – early 1970s)

The Outlaws
Developed out of Honky Tonk, the Bakersfield Sound and Country-Rock, but also as a direct reaction to the slick, commercial Nashville Sound.
Waylon Jennings, Willie Nelson, David Allen Coe, Tompall Glaser, Jessi Colter, Billy Joe Shaver (1970s)

---

recording studio. This was fairly standard practice for rock musicians, but in the world of country music, under the guidelines of the Nashville Sound, producers were in the driver's seat; they hired the band and picked most of the songs. All a singer needed was his or her voice, which was often shaved of its rough edges, to fit the mold of the smooth, pop-oriented countrypolitan sound that was the radio-friendly norm of the time. So when Waylon Jennings, fed up with being told what to play and how to play it, argued for the right to choose his own producers and bring his road band into the studio, he was attacking an entire industry standard.

He struck, though, at the right time. Not only was the industry ripe for a shake-up, but Waylon himself was a successful singer—he'd been so since the mid-1960s. He was also becoming more and more outspoken about his beliefs, so rather than lose this lucrative artist (and probably also to shut him up), his longtime label RCA eventually met his demands. His 1973 album *Lonesome, Orn'ry and Mean* was the first featuring his own production work (the title track, written by Steve Young, became something of a theme song for the genre), and it's marked by bigger beats, an absence of background choruses, and arrangements that feel loose and raw.

However, it's really the following collection, *Honky Tonk Heroes*, that is Waylon's landmark "outlaw" album. Featuring nine out of ten songs written by up-and-coming Texas songwriter Billy Joe Shaver, the record's informal production and spare, simple arrangments brought the lyrics and melodies out into the open air in a way that country fans had rarely heard in well over a decade. (The album cover, which featured Jennings, Shaver, and their shaggy cohorts in the studio, also caused a stir.) The catchy, rock-inflected song "Are You Sure Hank Done It This Way?" on Waylon's 1975 album *Dreaming My Dreams*—the second masterpiece of his career, co-produced by the legendary Jack Clement (who founded the first independent recording studio in Nashville)—is as clear a statement as any he made of his struggle to break free of the industry's countrypolitan confines.

Thanks to the critical acclaim of *Honky Tonk Heroes*, as well as the support of his friend Kris Kristofferson, Billy Joe Shaver got the chance to record his first album, *Old Five and Dimers Like Me*, in 1973 for Kristofferson's label, Monument. Shaver, for various reasons, never saw the financial success of his contemporaries—a rambling cowboy by nature, he wasn't so good at self-promotion—but his records remain classics of the genre. Kristofferson himself was never really an "outlaw" by name, but when he took the podium in long hair and jeans to receive his songwriter's award from the Country Music Association in 1970

for "Sunday Mornin' Comin' Down," he signaled Music Row that the new generation's musical revolution was underway.

Willie Nelson was in a bind similar to Jennings'. He'd been a hugely successful songwriter since the early '60s ("Night Life," "Crazy"), but as a singer, his career had failed to take off. While it's hard to comprehend that a man who's today considered one of country music's finest singers would have such trouble getting attention, the blame again goes to the era's production methods, which downplayed the personality of his dusty-sweet baritone voice.

As a performer, though, Nelson, a native Texan, always did well in his home state. His eventual move in 1971 from the Nashville area to a ranch outside of Austin was another signal to the establishment that change was in the air. Fate had played a hand here: Nelson's Nashville house had burned down a few months earlier, and his second wife, Shirley, had left him. Combined with the seeming lack of support for his singing career, Nelson decided to move to where he was better appreciated. What he found in Austin—an audience of both longhaired hippies and rednecked cowboys who were wild for the kind of rock- and folk-influenced country that became known as "progressive" (Jerry Jeff Walker, Michael Martin Murphey, Commander Cody)—reinvigorated him.

In 1972, Nelson put together the first of several infamous outdoor music showcases in Dripping Springs, TX, which mixed young and old country singers and fans. These Woodstock-like Fourth of July picnics also served as grass-roots promotion machines for Willie and his pal Waylon's brand of country music, showcases for countrified rockers like Leon Russell, and launching pads for singer-songwriters like Shaver.

RCA finally dropped Nelson in 1972, but soon after he was signed to Atlantic's new country division by legendary R&B producer Jerry Wexler. The results included the albums *Shotgun Willie* and *Phases and Stages*, two of the finest works of his career and the beginning of the turnaround of his sales figures. In 1975, he switched to Columbia Records and released *The Red-Headed Stranger*. This became his landmark album for two reasons: first, he argued for creative control to keep the mostly acoustic arrangements sparse and quiet, and he got it; second, it sold massively, and turned out two No. 1 hits.

It's ironic that the most outgoing outlaw of them all, Tompall Glaser, is the least remembered today. Not only was he a successful singer and songwriter at the time, but the studio he ran with his brothers, Chuck and Jim—dubbed "Hillbilly Central"—became the meeting hall and focal point for all things "outlaw" in Nashville. Several years earlier, the brothers had caused a stir by forming their own publishing company; Nashville's old boy network got a hearty shake when one of their songs, John Hartford's "Gentle on My Mind," became a smash hit. Now, the Glasers had their own fortress.

When the Glaser Studios opened in 1969, Tompall had been the lead voice in the folk/country singing group Tompall and the Glaser Brothers for more than a decade. When the brothers split up in the early 1970s, Tompall began recording as a solo artist, and "outlaw" became his badge of honor. He, too, had been fed up with Nashville's old-fashioned attitudes and old-boy networks. His way of fighting was to take a businessman's angle and start his own production company, a tactic that worked wonders for him financially and allowed him the creative control he desired. Tompall made several excellent albums in the 1970s, but his first, *Charlie* (1973), is his undisputed best, deserving a history-book spot alongside *Honky Tonk Heroes* and *The Red-Headed Stranger.*

Ex-con singer David Allan Coe didn't wait for an invitation to jump onto the outlaw bandwagon, even writing a song called "Willie, Waylon and Me." Many of Coe's ragged, rocked-up songs, however, deserve greater recognition. Johnny Paycheck also joined the club when he grew a beard and renamed himself "John Austin Paycheck" on his 1976 album *11 Months and 29 Days.*

Other singers and songwriters associated to varying degrees with the era include Guy Clark, Sammi Smith (her version of Kristofferson's "Help Me Make It Through the Night" was a major hit in 1970), Kinky Friedman, Johnny Rodriguez, and even Jimmy Buffett. Two other songwriters-turned-singers, Mickey Newbury and Tom T. Hall, may have been clean-cut Music Row favorites for the hits they'd written, but they associated aesthetically and philosophically with what the outlaw movement stood for.

The movement culminated in the 1976 album *Wanted! The Outlaws,* which compiled previously recorded material by Waylon, Willie, Jessi Colter (Waylon's wife and the voice behind the hit "I'm Not Lisa"), and Tompall. Waylon's record company (RCA) had decided the time was right to exploit the outlaw moniker, and they were right: less than a musical landmark, the album is best remembered for being the first country album to sell over a million copies. After the success of *Wanted! The Outlaws,* however, "outlaw" quickly became an overused label. And when Jennings was arrested in 1977 for cocaine possession, he reacted by recording the song "Don't You Think This Outlaw Bit Done Got Out of Hand?" The party, it seemed, was finally winding down.

—*Kurt Wolff*

Recommended Recordings:

David Allan Coe, *The Mysterious Rhinestone Cowboy* (Columbia)

Jack Clement, *All I Want to Do in Life* (Elektra)

Tompall Glaser, *Charlie* (MGM)

Kris Kristofferson, *Kristofferson* (Monument)

Waylon Jennings, *Dreamin' My Dreams* (RCA)

Waylon Jennings, *Honky Tonk Heroes* (RCA)

Willie Nelson, *A Classic and Unreleased Collection* (box set) (Rhino)

Willie Nelson, *Red-Headed Stranger* (Columbia)

Billy Joe Shaver, *Old Fiver and Dimers Like Me* (Monument)

Sammi Smith, *Help Me Make It Through the Night* (Mega)

Steve Young, *Renegade Picker* (RCA)

Various Artists, *Wanted! The Outlaws: Twentieth Anniversary Edition*

The Lubbock Country Scene

It's one of the great ironies of country music that one of the most conservative regions of America has been responsible for some of the most progressive country sounds of the late 20th century. Lubbock, TX, 300 miles west of Dallas, is so far into the western region of the state that it's just an hour or two drive away from New Mexico. It's still a "dry" county where liquor is hard to come by, with more churches per capita than any other mid-size city in the US. As recently as 1928, a city ordinance was passed that prevented residents with more than one-tenth of African-American blood from living west of Avenue D.

Yet this is also the city that gave the world Buddy Holly, who makes anyone's list as one of the three or four most important pioneers of early rock 'n' roll. In the late '50s, a young Waylon Jennings had a show on a radio station here. He was touring with Holly's band in early 1959 when Buddy died in a plane crash; if the Big Bopper hadn't convinced Waylon to give up his seat and take the bus instead, Jennings himself would have been on that plane as well. Not that the city itself was too proud of its prodigal sons, refusing to serve Holly's Puerto Rican wife at a local diner, and not erecting a statue in Buddy's memory until about 20 years after his death.

Much less well known than Holly are the maverick country singer-songwriters that emerged from the city in the 1970s and 1980s. If Joe Ely, Jimmie Dale Gilmore, Butch Hancock, and Terry Allen are influenced by Holly, it's more a matter of attitude than actual sound. All of the aforementioned Lubbockites are stone-cold country, even if their records and arrangements bear some rock and folk influences. They're too stone-cold country, actually, for either Nashville or most of the mainstream country audience. And their lyrics are way too eccentric for either pop or country listeners. It's been no coincidence that Lubbock's major country talents have established themselves outside of Lubbock, usually in the more liberal and tolerant musical and political climates of the state capital, Austin.

It was the tension between the endlessly flat West Texas landscape and these performers' fiery imaginations that fueled the innovations of their music. As Terry Allen once wrote in the notes to a Texas Tech Museum exhibit called *Nothin' Else to Do,* "Lubbock is so flat in every direction that if you grew up in it (and are blessed with any curiosity at all), your attention just naturally runs to the horizon, the edge . . . I don't think the music comes so much from 'nothin' else to do' as really from just nothin' better to be done."

Any discussion of modern-day Lubbock country music must begin with the Flatlanders, a Lubbock supergroup of sorts that recorded one album, *More a Legend Than a Band,* in 1972. At the time, the appellation "supergroup" was most inappropriate. The band's three singer-songwriter-guitarists—Butch Hancock, Joe Ely, and Jimmie Dale Gilmore—were unknown, and would largely remain so for years. The record was released on a tiny independent label (it has now been reissued), and would be the outfit's sole recorded legacy before they scattered to solo careers. Yet these three performers, individually and collectively, were almost solely responsible for carving a mini-genre of their own within country music.

Gilmore and Ely had been working toward a fusion of country music and rock sensibilities since the mid-'60s. When the Flatlanders finally got around to recording, however, the music owed more to country/folk than psychedelic rock. There was no drummer; the guitars were supported by fiddle, dobro, and Steve Wesson's strange musical saw. From contemporary rock, the group borrowed a willingness to play by their own rules, addressing eerily personal concerns without heed for commercial success. In the *Rolling Stone Album Guide,* David McGee wrote that it was "beholden on one hand to the entire sweep of country and mountain folk music of an Appalachian nature, on the other to nothing save the sort of brutal honesty that cuts into souls in the dark heart of a lonesome night . . . . real outlaw music, years ahead of its time and years behind; it is the first blow of the new traditionalist movement, sharper and more penetrating than the anguished (and justly acclaimed) sides the late Gram Parsons produced in 1973."

Joe Ely was the first of the trio to taste solo success. He is also the most rock-influenced of the three, though much of his solo output could be more aptly categorized as modern honky-tonk music. The influence of his former colleagues was not just symbolic; Ely popularized several Hancock and Gilmore compositions at a time when those guys were without record deals. He also utilized the talents of two musicians, Lloyd Maines (pedal steel) and Ponty Bone (accordion), whose rootsy touches are now identified with the Lubbock/progressive Texas sound as a whole. Ely never found great commercial success, but he did make inroads into the rock audience when the Clash, to the surprise of many onlookers, tapped him as an opening act on one of their tours.

Hancock is simultaneously the most tradition-bound of the trio, and the most eccentric. His very earliest solo recordings are a goldmine for those who love very early Bob Dylan; like the early '60s Dylan, he updates the Woody Guthrie aesthetic with close-to-the-bone original folk tunes, featuring guitar and harmonica. These solo albums, which started appearing in the late '70s on his own Rainlight label, suffered from such microscopic distribution that they were almost unknown outside of Austin, unless you happened to catch one of Butch's gigs. By the mid-'80s he had several albums under his belt, but was, perversely, far more appreciated in England, where he was able to tour to critical acclaim. In his homeland, he was not as much neglected as unfound; even top specialist record stores didn't carry his releases. In time his albums became more slickly produced, though for Butch, as is usually the case with such talents, less is definitely more. Getting the word out about Hancock remains a problem to this day, as most of his catalog is still only available on his tiny Rainlight label (sometimes on cassette only), although Sugar Hill has picked up some material for wider distribution.

Ultimately, however, it was Jimmie Dale Gilmore who would fare best in the critical sweepstakes. While Ely and Hancock were beginning to build their catalog, Gilmore was missing in action, forgoing professional music to live in Colorado and study metaphysics. In the 1980s he moved to Austin, always a sympathetic climate for roots-music oddballs. He finally made his solo debut in 1988, moving to a major label and year-end placings in poprock critic polls by the 1990s, inspiring purple prose usually reserved for the likes of Neil Young and R.E.M. *The Spin Alternative Record Guide,* for instance, hails his "encompassing spirituality" and "reconfiguration of rural music's tug between sin and salvation that speaks not of a judging god but of connections between people, the flexibility of time and space, the relative triteness of the ego." Maybe so. For many listeners, however, the chief pleasure of Gilmore's records is his voice, which delivers some of the most expressive pure country singing of recent times.

Even by Lubbock standards, singer-songwriter Terry Allen is very much a cult figure, and perhaps the weirdest of the lot. Actually, this renaissance man has experienced far greater success as an internationally acclaimed artist than as a musician. His resume includes NEA grants and a Guggenheim fellowship; he's worked in painting, film, sculpture, poetry, theater, and video. He wrote songs for David Byrne's *True Stories* soundtrack and Little Feat, and wrote a new national anthem with Gilmore, Ely, and Hancock. But Allen is also a recording artist whose material is perhaps the most sociopolitical and left-leaning to be found in all of country; he crafts concept albums that affectionately satirize small-town life, or assembles a set of songs (as on *Juarez*) reflecting images of Mexico. He is not afraid to mince words, make fun of the "hats" dominating Nashville, or tackle tough topics like teenage runaways. Indeed, part of the reward of listening to Allen is the sheer pleasure of finding a country performer who not only has genuinely left-of-center politics, but makes no bones about expressing them within the songs themselves—a true rarity in contemporary country music.

That also means that those with more centrist beliefs, and more mainstream musical tastes, will have no truck with the likes of Allen or his Lubbock buddies. As some critics quip, the Lubbock sound is too country in orientation to even get played on country radio. That's why much, and perhaps most, of the audience for Lubbock country music is found not in traditional country circles, but in alternative rock or folk ones. The Lubbockites certainly have a greater affinity with the contemporary No Depression country-rock bands than with the average Nashville star (or Nashville songwriter). In the mid-1990s Richard Buckner, a singer-songwriter with a rock-oriented background, even went to the extent of recording his solo debut in Lubbock. With Lloyd Maines—who has worked with Hancock,

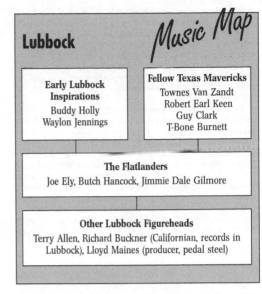

Lubbock *Music Map*

Early Lubbock Inspirations
Buddy Holly
Waylon Jennings

Fellow Texas Mavericks
Townes Van Zandt
Robert Earl Keen
Guy Clark
T-Bone Burnett

The Flatlanders
Joe Ely, Butch Hancock, Jimmie Dale Gilmore

Other Lubbock Figureheads
Terry Allen, Richard Buckner (Californian, records in Lubbock), Lloyd Maines (producer, pedal steel)

Ely, Gilmore, and Allen—producing, the resulting effort sounded as authentically Lubbock as anything by Buckner's obvious inspirations.

The Lubbock sound's influence within country itself, however, has not been negligible. Certainly other progressive country musicians in Texas seemed to have been influenced by the Lubbock performers, including Guy Clark, Townes Van Zandt, Nanci Griffith, Robert Earl Keen, Lyle Lovett, and T-Bone Burnett (though it's fair to point out that the interchange went both ways). It would seem to be a longshot that Lubbock can consistently produce more first-rate talent, especially as its major figureheads are well into middle age. For the time being, though, it functions as a repository of a sort for the best of the new traditionalism.

—Richie Unterberger

Recommended Recordings:

The Flatlanders, *More a Legend Than a Band* (Rounder)
Joe Ely, *Honky Tonk Masquerade* (MCA)
Butch Hancock, *Own and Own* (Sugar Hill)
Terry Allen, *Lubbock on Everything* (Sugar Hill)
Jimmie Dale Gilmore, *After Awhile* (Elektra/Nonesuch)
Richard Buckner, *Bloomed* (Dejadisc)

Austin in the '70s

Located three hours south of Dallas and 80 miles north of The Alamo, with LBJ's ranch to the west and numerous dry towns to the east, Austin, TX, has long enjoyed a reputation as an oasis for free thinkers in a state known for its conservative politics, strict religious practices, and traditional values. Like any city, Austin—which straddles a river called the Colorado (different from the one that runs through the Grand Canyon)—has its ghettos, its downtown traffic, and its suburban housing developments. But it's also grown into a cultural crossroads that thrives on its diversity. The town's liberal attitude is in large part due to the university located here that each year brings a new roster of young, eager, and largely open minds. And with the city's diverse cultural background comes all sorts of music, drifting in from every direction—Cajun, conjunto, and German oom-pah music; honky tonk, blues, folk, and R&B; and all sorts of cowboy country and ribald rock 'n' roll.

Over the last few decades, Austin has drifted in and out of fashion as a musical mecca. In the 1970s, the city found itself in the national spotlight thanks to the success of singers like Willie Nelson, Jerry Jeff Walker, and Michael Murphey; and since the mid-

1980s, it gets pounced on each spring by thousands of fans, bands, and music industry reps who fill up on Shiner beer, greasy enchiladas, and late-night concerts during the annual South by Southwest Music Conference. But whether they're "hip" in the eyes of the visiting press or not, Austin's residents have continued to nurture and enjoy their town's reputation as a lively, friendly, and creative place for musicians and fans—individualistic folks who like their culture outside the mainstream—to get together, hang out, and grow.

Austin was always a good town for all sorts of music, but in the 1970s, it became known for a country-rock mixture called "progressive country" (thanks to radio station KOKE) or sometimes "redneck rock" (from the title of a book by Jan Reid, *The Improbable Rise of Redneck Rock*). It was a country-fried sound that mixed West Coast psychedelic-rock influences with traditional cowboy ballads and honky-tonk numbers, and put ropers and dopers in the same room at the same time, grooving to the same music.

This inter-generational convergence had been happening for at least a decade previously at Threadgill's, a former gas station on Austin's north side that was converted to a bar and makeshift music venue in 1933 by country singer Kenneth Threadgill. By the 1960s, university students were mixing regularly with the country-folks at Threadgill's shows, which often featured traditional country acts but also nurtured the talents of young unknown singers, including the club's most famous discovery, Janis Joplin. In the 1970s, Threadgill became regarded as the patriarch of the town's burgeoning music community.

Radio station KOKE may have coined and then publicized the moniker "progressive country," but the centerpoint (though not the only point) of much of this convergence was the Armadillo World Headquarters, a converted national guard armory that opened in 1970 as a rock 'n' roll venue and haven for the town's hippie community. It was large enough to attract big-name national acts that might otherwise have passed Austin by—and soon became a favorite stop on the tour circuit—yet it was also the principal base for the town's homegrown music. The armadillo itself—a creature of the western desert landscape—was a clear example of how the local counterculture had successfully adopted cowboy and western imagery as its identity.

The country-rock scene was already swinging in Austin when Willie Nelson moved there in 1971. An established songwriter in Nashville but a frustrated performer, Nelson had met some bad luck that year when his house burned down. It was time to collect his thoughts, and so the Fort Worth native moved back home to Texas, a place where his concerts had always been met with enthusiasm. He quickly became the town's star attraction, and his local performances probably brought more cowboys and long-hairs together than ever before; on one hand he was a traditional country singer, on the other a casually dressed, shaggy-haired friend of the counterculture. It was Willie's concerts—his appearances at the Armadillo or his numerous outdoor "picnics" in Dripping Springs (where singers like Roy Acuff, Tom T. Hall, Billy Joe Shaver, and Leon Russell often shared the bill)—that gave us the colorful stories of wide-eyed, gray-haired ranch couples dancing side-by-side with freaky youngsters and encountering pot smoke for the first time.

Another of Austin's famous residents is Jerry Jeff Walker, a hard-partying folksinger best known for his song "Mr. Bojangles." Despite his strong Texas identity, however, Walker was no native; he was born in upstate New York, recorded his first several albums in New York City, and didn't move to Austin until 1971. He's remained a major figure in the area ever since, though, helping confirm the "progressive country" movement with his informal folk-inspired albums and loose, party-friendly performances, which frequently turned into "drunken clown shows," as writer John Morthland once put it. (He's long since cleaned up his act, however.)

Walker used to write nearly all his songs, but in Austin he began championing the work of up-and-coming writers like Guy Clark and Ray Wylie Hubbard. In 1972, Walker recorded two of Clark's songs—"L.A. Freeway" and "That Old Time Feeling"—on his self-titled MCA album. On Walker's best-known record, "Viva

Terlingua," which he recorded in 1973 in the tiny Texas town of Luckenbach (turning the place into a tourist attraction in the process), he created a loud-mouthed hippie anthem out of Hubbard's good-natured but sharp-edged "Up Against the Wall, Redneck Mothers." It became an answer song of sorts to Merle Haggard's "Okie from Muskogee."

Walker knew Clark and fellow singer-songwriter Townes Van Zandt from years before in Houston. Clark was never technically an Austin artist—he moved to California and then Nashville—but his songs are frequently associated with the scene there. He was born in west Texas, and many of his best songs center around his days growing up there. After years playing live around the state, Clark's excellent debut album, *Old No. 1*, was finally released by RCA in 1975. He's since become a successful songwriter deeply respected by his peers. Like Clark, Van Zandt drifted in and out of Texas over the years (a young Jimmie Dale Gilmore once picked him up hitchhiking), becoming one of Austin's favorite singer-songwriting figures and an influence on many generations of musicians yet to come.

Hubbard tried to turn the success of "Redneck Mothers" into a viable solo career, but with more than one record company, he encountered many of the same difficulties (overproduction and a refusal to allow his road band, the Cowboy Twinkies, in the studio) that had plagued Waylon Jennings and other Nashville artists for years, and had been the basis for the "outlaw" movement. Hubbard's best album just might be his 1994 comeback, *Loco Gringo's Lament*, an acoustic collection of country-folk material. Michael Murphey, meanwhile, was the town's "cosmic cowboy" folksinger. He was a Dallas native who'd moved to California and earned a career as a successful songwriter ("Calico Silver" for the First Edition, among others), but like so many others he tired of the city grind and eventually moved back home, landing in Austin. He was soon a star of the local scene. Early albums of his such as *Geronimo's Cadillac* are loose country-rock affairs, but by the time his song "Wildfire" became a huge national hit in 1975, Murphey's music had turned far too precious.

Kinky Friedman was the infamous self-dubbed "Texas Jewboy" whose shows brimmed over with his satirical songs (though he also showed his penchant for serious observation when he wrote one of the best fallen-cowboy songs of the modern era, "Sold American"), while Asleep at the Wheel brought the region's Western swing history back to life when they moved to Austin from Berkeley in 1974. Other singers and songwriters associated with the local cowboy-folk-rock scene include B.W. Stevenson, Willis Alan Ramsey, Gary Nunn, Steve Fromholz, Bill and Bonnie Hearne, and Bobby Bridger. Some made albums of their own, and most had songs recorded by Walker, Murphey, and other compatriots. Some of the best performances, though, of these and other Texas artists were captured on time-capsule compilations like *Texas Folk and Outlaw Music*, which features live performances at the nearby Kerrville Folk Festival from 1972 to 1976.

If Willie Nelson is the country embodiment of Austin's musical mish-mash and Jerry Jeff Walker its most famous folkie, then Doug Sahm is the blustery rock 'n' roller. He's also the artist who best embodies the city's (and the state's) wide range of musical influences, from blues and rock to conjunto, R&B, and hardcore honky tonk. A San Antonio native, Sahm achieved fame in the 1960s as leader of the Sir Douglas Quintet. The band was based in San Francisco during the Haight-Ashbury heyday, but in the early '70s, Sahm got tired of the hippie trip and moved back home to Texas to rediscover his roots, recording *The Return of Doug Saldana* with the Quintet. This and subsequent albums like 1976's *Texas Rock for Country Rollers* are some of the most country-oriented—and best—albums of Sahm's career. In 1973, producer Jerry Wexler snatched him up, and Sahm recorded a rootsy album with a famous guest list (*Doug Sahm and Friends*). Sahm's career, however, never took off like Wexler hoped, and by the end of the decade, restless as ever, he was shifting labels and heading off in new musical directions.

Like any scene, Austin eventually got over-hyped, and national attention shifted elsewhere. But the music never stopped in the town's numerous clubs, and by the mid-1980s and '90s, the city's reputation for solid, individualistic performers (non-mainstream)

was back on track—thanks in large part, certainly, to the South by Southwest Music Conference. Jimmie Dale Gilmore, Joe Ely, and Butch Hancock are some of the stars of this latest generation (and Lucinda Williams, whenever she's in town), and Junior Brown, Robert Earl Keen, Dale Watson, and Jo Carol Pierce are also country favorites who are loaded with talent. But some things never change. The names Walker and Nelson have never left the vernacular (Walker's birthday concerts are still some of the town's most popular events), and Threadgill's has expanded into a thriving restaurant business, still home to regular music shows.

—Kurt Wolff

Recommended Recordings:

Asleep at the Wheel, *Texas Gold* (Capitol)

Guy Clark, *Old No. 1* (RCA)

Joe Ely, *Joe Ely* (MCA)

Kinky Friedman, *Sold American* (Vanguard)

Butch Hancock, *West Texas Waltzes and Dust-Blown Tractor Tunes* (Rainlight)

Michael Murphey, *Geronimo's Cadillac* (A&M)

Willie Nelson, *Shotgun Willie* (Atlantic)

Doug Sahm, *Texas Rock for Country Rollers* (ABC/Dot)

Various Artists, *Texas Folk and Outlaw Music* (Adelphi Records)

Jerry Jeff Walker, *A Man Must Carry On* (MCA)

Urban Cowboy

Urban cowboy was the (perhaps) inevitable culmination of the two most popular country genres of the '70s—polished Nashville country-pop and outlaw country. For most of the decade, country had been moving closer into the mainstream, with country-pop making inroads on pop radio stations and outlaw singers winning the hearts of rock 'n' roll fans. Urban cowboy fused those two audiences, taking the hooks of country-pop and crossing it with the working class, down-to-earth image of outlaw country. Urban cowboy was considerably slicker than outlaw, but it was designed to appeal to an audience that had been reluctant to embrace country—urban professionals and soft rock fans. As the '80s progressed, the sound of urban cowboy gravitated toward adult contemporary pop, as the grittier stance and sound of outlaw was adopted by both roots-rockers and new traditionalists. However, the sound and style of urban cowboy—with its slick productions, light rock flourishes and hummable melodies—set the pace for mainstream country music for the remainder of the decade.

The sound of urban cowboy had been evolving since the mid-'70s, when honky tonkers like Mickey Gilley began injecting touches of country-pop and rock 'n' roll into their sound. Nevertheless, the style didn't emerge as a full-fledged musical genre until 1980, when the music was packaged as the soundtrack to the hit John Travolta film *Urban Cowboy*. Based on an 1979 *Esquire* article about a group of Houston oil workers who spent their free time in roadhouse nightclubs like Gilley's, the film sparked a pop culture sensation. Not only was the film a blockbuster, but it inspired numerous other films about contemporary country life (*Honeysuckle Rose, Coal Miner's Daughter*) and provided the basis for the popular television series *Dukes of Hazzard.* The movie popularized various country dances and fashion, as well as the pastime of riding mechanical bulls.

What the pop culture phenomenon signaled was how country music had adapted itself to the modern age; it was no longer rural music, but it was music for big-city dwellers, as well, no matter if they were blue or white collar workers. And nowhere was this more evident than on the soundtrack to *Urban Cowboy* itself. Comprised of material from country-pop crooners like Kenny Rogers, watered-down honky tonk from Mickey Gilley and Johnny Lee, country-rock from the Eagles and Linda Ronstadt & J.D. Souther, southern rock from the Charlie Daniels Band, and straightahead rock 'n' roll from Bob Seger, Bonnie Raitt and Joe

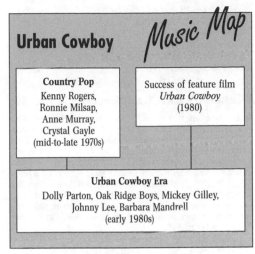

Urban Cowboy *Music Map*

Country Pop
Kenny Rogers,
Ronnie Milsap,
Anne Murray,
Crystal Gayle
(mid-to-late 1970s)

Success of feature film
Urban Cowboy
(1980)

Urban Cowboy Era
Dolly Parton, Oak Ridge Boys, Mickey Gilley,
Johnny Lee, Barbara Mandrell
(early 1980s)

Walsh, the album blurred the lines between country and rock 'n' roll, opening up a whole new audience for country music in the process. For rock 'n' roll fans, country music no longer seemed like the province of rednecks; for country fans, the lexicon of rock 'n' roll began to inch its way into their music, slowly beginning to undermine its traditions. For instance, before *Urban Cowboy*, the Eagles were considered a straight rock 'n' roll act, but a decade after the album's release, the group had influenced more country singers than rock bands.

During the '80s, the impact of urban cowboy became apparent. Between 1980 and 1983, country was a dominant force in the American pop marketplace. Rock 'n' roll artists continued to comprise the bulk of the album charts, but country-pop had completely infiltrated the upper reaches of the pop Top 40, with singers like Kenny Rogers, Dolly Parton, Barbara Mandrell, Juice Newton, and Charlie Daniels all scoring significant pop hits. Perhaps more importantly, the country industry—which has always been driven by fads and product—devoted itself to the pursuit of crossover hits. During the '70s, Billy Sherrill's grandiose, string-laden productions had received criticism for their over-the-top orchestrations, but those seemed like pure honky tonk compared to the sound of post-urban cowboy country music. By 1983, the tempos in country-pop had become quite slow, the productions were slick and smooth, filled with synthesizers, and there was no difference between pop-oriented country and adult contemporary AM pop—Kenny Rogers and Dolly Parton had the biggest single of their respective careers with their duet "Islands in the Stream," a song written by the Bee Gees and produced by Barry Gibb.

During 1983, country-pop was swept off mainstream pop radio by the twin forces of MTV-sponsored new wave and Michael Jackson's *Thriller*, but the sound of mainstream country didn't change at all. Over the next five years, country-pop was ruled by the polished sounds of post-urban cowboy country-pop. A few performers, such as George Strait, Ricky Skaggs, and Randy Travis, broke through with their hard-edged, updated take on traditional country, but the appeal of urban cowboy didn't fade until the late '80s. During the latter half of the decade, a wave of new traditionalists inspired by Strait and Skaggs captured the attention of the country audience, bringing country back closer to its roots. Yet urban cowboy hadn't completely left the consciousness of many country audiences, and a fusion of its slick, pop-oriented sensibilities and the hard-edged music of new traditionalists dubbed new country enjoyed crossover success in the early '90s, ten years after urban cowboy conquered the pop charts.

—Stephen Thomas Erlewine

Recommended Recordings:

Urban Cowboy soundtrack (Asylum)

Urban Cowboy II soundtrack (Asylum)

Kenny Rogers, *25 Greatest Hits* (Liberty)
Alabama, *Greatest Hits* (RCA)
Mickey Gilley, *Ten Years of Hits* (Epic)
Barbara Mandrell, *The Best of Barbara Mandrell* (MCA)
Charlie Daniels Band, *A Decade of Hits* (Epic)
Dolly Parton, *Greatest Hits* (RCA)

Nashville's New Traditionalists in the '80s

At the same time that outlaw fever was sweeping Nashville in the mid-1970s, another trend was stirring feathers among the city's traditionalists—an infiltration into Music City by pop singers like Olivia Newton-John, Linda Ronstadt, and John Denver. Not only were these lightweight vocalists hitting the tops of the country charts, but they were winning Country Music Association awards. (When, in 1975, presenter Charlie Rich opened the envelope containing the name of the CMA's Entertainer of the Year and found the winner was John Denver, he burned the envelope right then and there—a moment that may have been shameful at the time, but is now legendary.)

By the close of the decade, outlaw chic was pretty much played out—and it was clear that, as strong as the back-to-the-basics music of Waylon Jennings and Willie Nelson had been, it wasn't going to eradicate the country music industry's interest in playing footsie with the pop music market. Rising superstar Kenny Rogers showed the powerful crossover potential of watered-down country when "The Gambler" hit in 1978. Dolly Parton had had her first big crossover hit, "Here You Come Again," a year earlier, and seemed to be giving up the traditional country she'd grown up singing (her partnership with Porter Wagoner "broke up" a couple of years later). By the turn of the decade, names like Mac Davis, Anne Murray, the Little River Band, and Barbara Mandrell were appearing on the country charts more and more often.

This was also the era when country went Hollywood. Nelson, Parton, and Kris Kristofferson enjoyed prominent movie roles, and Mandrell had a glitzy "uptown" TV show that had little to do with country music's hillbilly past (which had been ghettoized on *Hee Haw*). But it was *Urban Cowboy* in 1980 that marked the peak of the industry's love affair with soft-country gaudiness—and the point of market saturation. Greed for bigger and bigger pop hits had been rampant, and now it was clear that national sales figures were not keeping up with industry spending. The pop-country infatuation was headed for a fall.

Which is why it was so refreshing to hear the plain, unadorned voice of Texan George Strait hit the airwaves in 1981 with "Unwound." As a singer, Strait hardly matches someone like George Jones, but there's a sincerity in his voice that is immediately refreshing. And his music had nothing to do with pop—it was a back-to-basics, neo-traditional approach in arrangements and instrumentation that had hardly been heard since the Outlaw days. Instead of trying to hide his music's hillbilly roots, Strait celebrated them—he had no crossover aspirations. Some of Strait's most enduring songs released throughout the mid-1980s include "Amarillo by Morning," "Right or Wrong," and "Does Fort Worth Ever Cross Your Mind." (Strait's big cowboy hat may at the time have been a genuine mark of his rural background, but some ten years down the road it would inspire the "hat act" look and become an overused prop among a whole new breed of male country stylists.)

Another singer making his mark at the time was John Anderson, a Florida native who'd come to Nashville in 1971 and recorded his first single in 1974. He didn't, though, get major attention until early in the following decade with the release of "1959" and "I'm Just an Old Chunk of Coal." The latter was a Billy Joe Shaver song from the '70s, which helps connect the dots between the two decades. Anderson has lots of Lefty Frizzell in his voice, and like Strait, his music was at the opposite (traditional) end of the musical spectrum from someone like Mandrell (who was CMA's Entertainer of the Year in 1980 and '81, the years of Anderson's and Strait's breakthroughs). In 1982, Anderson had his first No. 1 with "Wild and Blue," a great, punchy song that speaks franky of sexual tension and is becoming something of a

modern classic (the Mekons even recorded a version of it); a year later, Anderson's popularity was cemented by the huge success of "Swingin.'"

Ricky Skaggs was perhaps the most "traditional" of this slowly-forming group of "new traditionalist" singers. A mandolin prodigy in his early childhood—though also skilled on fiddle and guitar—Skaggs played for several years with bluegrass legend Ralph Stanley (joining when he was 15), and later with Emmylou Harris' Hot Band. So it was natural that his solo country records would feature an exciting mix of traditional bluegrass and country. His debut album, *Waitin' for the Sun to Shine* (1981), produced several hit songs, and Skaggs became one of the most popular country artists of the early 1980s. The Judds were a mother-daughter duo (Naomi and Wynonna) from Ashland, KY, who started by making early-morning appearances on Ralph Emery's radio show, and ended up one of the most popular country acts of the decade. Their music was simple and had mass appeal, but it was far more traditional than anything on Dolly Parton's records at the time. They released their first single in 1983, and the following year won a Grammy for "Mama He's Crazy."

It's hard to say what exactly makes the doors in Nashville open a bit wider every once in a while—allowing individualists and oddballs a chance they otherwise might never get—but that's exactly what happened in the mid-1980s. Perhaps it was the popularity of people like Strait, Anderson, and Skaggs, but whatever the cause, record contracts (and substantial promotion to boot) were suddenly available for artists like Steve Earle, the O'Kanes, and Lyle Lovett, superb talents that spiced up the "straight" world of country music considerably. The year 1986 turned out to be a magic one, as Earle, Lovett, Dwight Yoakam, and Randy Travis each released their debut albums. Unlike the outlaws a decade earlier, each of these artists came from different musical (and geographical) directions and worked independently of the others; there was no clique or scene—no "Hillbilly Central"—to hang out in.

Earle has proven himself the rocker of the bunch, perhaps the closest in spirit to the classic work of Waylon Jennings. Earle looked rather clean cut on his debut, *Guitar Town*—as hard and up-front a country album as any to have come out of Nashville in years, and much more aggressive than anything George Strait ever recorded—but he soon showed his true ragged-glory colors with *Copperhead Road* two years later. That album's title track did have a twangy mandolin intro, but once it got going, it almost felt like heavy metal. Lovett's music is strongly rooted in Texas folk and country, especially on his self-titled debut (which featured the classic "This Old Porch," co-written with his buddy Robert Earl Keen). But as later albums have shown, the world of country music couldn't contain this diverse talent. His third release (*Lyle Lovett and His Large Band*) was marked by arrangements that had been jazzed up considerably, including a snazzy, big-band-style cover of "Stand by Your Man." By this point, Lovett had moved away from traditional country and was off in new, refreshing directions.

Travis' 1986 debut album, *Storms of Life*, was a beautiful showcase for his strong, versatile, George Jones-inspired vocal work, and contained great catchy songs like "Digging Up Bones" and "1982." He quickly turned into one of the most popular country stars of the decade (his follow-up album, 1987's *Always and Forever*, stayed on top of the country charts for nearly a year). Yoakam was something of an outsider, having settled in L.A. instead of Nashville. On the West Coast, he hooked into the rockabilly-revival and punk-rock communities, and his debut album, *Guitars, Cadillacs, Etc., Etc.*—with its hard, honky-tonk sound and Yoakam's pure, strong voice—was immediately popular with rock 'n' rollers as well as a large number of the country crowd. Yoakam's later association with Buck Owens showed his affinity for the Bakersfield Sound. Another group that released their debut album in 1986 was the O'Kanes, a catchy country duo comprised of Jamie O'Hara and Kieren Kane (the latter of whom would go on to found the Dead Reckoning record label a decade later). Their music was based around spare, folk-inspired melo-

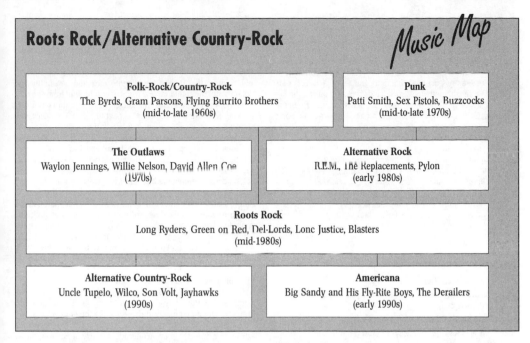

Roots Rock/Alternative Country-Rock — Music Map

Folk-Rock/Country-Rock
The Byrds, Gram Parsons, Flying Burrito Brothers
(mid-to-late 1960s)

Punk
Patti Smith, Sex Pistols, Buzzcocks
(mid-to-late 1970s)

The Outlaws
Waylon Jennings, Willie Nelson, David Allen Coe
(1970s)

Alternative Rock
R.E.M., The Replacements, Pylon
(early 1980s)

Roots Rock
Long Ryders, Green on Red, Del-Lords, Lone Justice, Blasters
(mid-1980s)

Alternative Country-Rock
Uncle Tupelo, Wilco, Son Volt, Jayhawks
(1990s)

Americana
Big Sandy and His Fly-Rite Boys, The Derailers
(early 1990s)

dies and arrangements that featured fiddle, mandolin, and accordion—and gentle, pleasant harmonies.

Toward the end of the decade, more names had cropped up that were associated with "new traditionalism," which was now more visible as a genre. Ricky Van Shelton was one of the most prominent, a guy who inspired the "hunk" look of the 1990s but also had a penchant for material that was more or less traditionally based. He even recorded a gospel album. Keith Whitley (a pal of Ricky Skaggs) died at an early age, but his mark as a strong, distinct vocalist and modern honky-tonk stylist has proved indelible. And Kentucky native Patty Loveless, who emerged in the late 1980s, has proven herself not just one of the strongest female solo artists of the era (though that title probably should go to Reba McEntire based on popularity and hard work alone), but someone who truly feels the soul in country's roots. By the 1990s, however, "new traditionalist" had become an all-too-common buzzword, as such labels inevitably do. And the accoutrements that went with this back-to-basics music—big hats and hunky, fresh-faced singers in clean white T-shirts—were images that contributed to the big new boom in country music's popularity. It's likely, though, that it's because of the success of artists like George Strait, Randy Travis, and even Steve Earle that we get singers like Alan Jackson and Marty Stuart at the top of the charts today.

—*Kurt Wolff*

Recommended Recordings:

John Anderson, *Wild & Blue* (Warner Brothers)
Rosanne Cash, *King's Record Shop* (Columbia)
Steve Earle, *Guitar Town* (MCA)
The Judds, *The Greatest Hits* (RCA)
Patty Loveless, *If My Heart Had Windows* (MCA)
Lyle Lovett, *Lyle Lovett* (MCA/Curb)
The O'Kanes, *The O'Kanes* (Columbia)
Ricky Skaggs, *Waitin' for the Sun to Shine* (Epic)
George Strait, *Does Fort Worth Ever Cross Your Mind* (MCA)
Randy Travis, *Storms of Life* (Warner Brothers)
Keith Whitley, *I Wonder Do You Think of Me* (RCA)
Dwight Yoakam, *Guitars, Cadillacs, Etc. Etc.* (Reprise)

Roots-Rock

Roots-rock was one of the more curious trends of the '80s. In the previous two decades, there were always back-to-basics movements in rock 'n' roll, whether it was the periodic rockabilly revivals or the punk explosion of the late '70s, but roots-rock was a different beast entirely. Growing out of the tangled web of post-punk in the early '80s, roots-rock was as equally indebted to underground, American indie-rock as it was to country-rock. It functioned outside of the mainstream of the industry, building up a cult following through constant touring and a steady stream of records. Roots-rock occasionally roared with punk energy, but its sensibilities came out of the country-rock movement of the late '60s and early '70s. No roots-rock band ever broke into the mainstream—the Del Fuegos came the closest, but that was only in the form of a beer commercial—but they laid the groundwork for the Americana and alternative country/country-rock boom of the '90s. Indeed, many of its alumni were still active in Americana or alternative country during the '90s.

While most roots-rock bands were heavily influenced by the raunchy swagger of the Rolling Stones and the hard twang of Gram Parsons, it is unlikely that many of them would have existed without R.E.M. Though the Athens-based band only occasionally delved into country-rock, R.E.M. ushered in an era of simple, garage-based pop and rock in the mid-'80s. By wiping out the synth-pop of new wave and the arty post-punk experiments of the early '80s, the group allowed both neo-psychedelic rockers and roots-rockers to grab the spotlight. Before R.E.M., the Los Angeles-based Blasters had played an edgy variation of roots-rock and punk, while X had flirted with rockabilly (the Stray Cats had a couple of new wave pop hits with their kitschy rockabilly revival as well), but roots-rockers did not appear until after R.E.M.

Once the roots-rockers appeared, they quickly divided themselves into two camps: edgy "cow-punk" bands like Jason & the Scorchers and the Beat Farmers, and straightforward country-rockers like the Long Ryders and the Del Fuegos. Over the course of the mid-'80s, the groups steadily built up strong followings. Country audiences paid no mind to the bands, but alternative country artists like Dwight Yoakam and k.d. lang came to prominence through this movement; both musicians adhered to country traditions more than even the Gram Parsons-devoted Long

Ryders, but the conservative Nashville establishment ignored them, leaving the roots-rock circuit as their only option.

During the late '80s, roots-rock began to splinter. None of the bands had sold many records, and the climate of American indie rock was beginning to change. No longer were rootsy garage rockers and jangling guitar-pop bands like R.E.M. hip currency, as grunge and artsy post-punk bands began to earn larger audiences. As a result, many roots-rock bands broke up during the last three years of the '80s. Most musicians left the industry. Some, like Syd Griffin, worked behind the scenes as journalists. Some kept performing, eventually carving out their own niche as singer-songwriters on such labels as Hightone Records.

Many roots-rockers got a second chance in the '90s, when alternative country-rock became a hip underground movement. Bands like Jason & the Scorchers re-formed, while the leaders of other bands carved out solo careers. Much of the alternative country movement was inspired by the original roots-rockers. Though roots-rock rarely offered any sonic innovations, it kept the spirit of the music alive during an era when hard country had virtually disappeared.

—Thom Owens

Recommended Recordings:

R.E.M., *Reckoning* (IRS)

Jason & the Scorchers, *Essential, Vol. 1 (Are You Ready for the Country)* (Capitol)

The Blasters, *The Blasters Collection* (Slash)

The Beat Farmers, *Tales of the New West* (Rhino)

Lone Justice, *Lone Justice* (Geffen)

The Long Ryders, *Two-Fisted Tales* (Island)

The Del-Lords, *Johnny Comes Marching Home* (EMI)

Green on Red, *Gas Food Lodging* (Enigma)

The Del Fuegos, *The Longest Day* (Slash)

True Believers, *True Believers* (EMI)

The Silos, *Cuba* (Record Collect/Watermelon)

New Country

The unprecedented crossover success of Garth Brooks in the early '90s was the sign that new country had come into its own. A blend of new traditionalist sensibilities and the slick, pop-savvy crossover potential of urban cowboy, new country not only appealed to fans of hard-edged, honky tonk-derived traditional country, but also a wide variety of urban pop fans—including both teenagers and maturing baby boomers. The music owed as much to the mainstream arena rock of the '70s as it did to country music—Brooks himself was an avowed fan of not only George Strait, but also the Eagles, KISS, and Billy Joel—which gave it a crossover appeal unmatched even by urban cowboy. Depending on the artist, new country either sounded like an updated version of country-boogie or twangy power ballads, which meant that it appealed to both rock and country audiences equally. New country had an even more powerful impact on the country audience than urban cowboy did in the previous decade—by the mid-'90s, new country artists ruled the airwaves completely, leaving older artists in the dust.

Given the ultimate result of new country, it is somewhat ironic that its roots lay in the revival of traditional country values represented by such singers as George Strait and Randy Travis. During the mid-'80s, Strait and Travis—along with singers like Dwight Yoakam and k.d. lang, who both functioned outside of Nashville's mainstream—were part of only a handful of new vocalists that refused to bend to the pop inclinations of post-urban cowboy country radio, instead choosing to adhere to the traditions of George Jones, Merle Haggard, and Lefty Frizzell. Both Strait and Travis were considerably successful, which led the industry to believe that there was an audience for harder-edged country.

For a while, new traditionalists dominated the country charts during the latter half of the '80s, signaling that the genre was experiencing a kind of artistic rebirth. But it wasn't until the early '90s that this burgeoning movement broke through into the mainstream, in the guise of new country singers like Clint Black, Travis Tritt and, of course, Garth Brooks. None of these three vocalists were traditionalists like Strait and Travis—they adopted the rootsy tendencies of their immediate predecessors, melding them into a sound that demonstrated more rock and pop influences. Not only did the sound of new country crib heavily from the rock industry, so did the image. No longer was the country industry working from rural roots, doing its best to hide the redneck past of its artists. Instead, it groomed a breed of attractive, good-looking vocalists who on the surface had very little to do with either the down-home appeal of George Jones and Hank Williams, or the rugged redneck image of outlaw singers like Waylon Jennings and Hank Williams, Jr. New country singers were clean, well-groomed and non-threatening—ideal for crossover success.

That crossover success happened when Garth Brooks' *No Fences* gained momentum in 1991. Brooks had enough cowboy in him to appeal to the new traditionalists, but also enough pop savvy to appeal to a generation of baby boomers weaned on the Californian country-rock of the Eagles and Linda Ronstadt. As a result, he became a pop music phenomenon—*No Fences* went platinum 13 times over, while its successor, 1991's *Ropin' the Wind,* spent 18 weeks at the top of the pop charts and sold over 11 million albums; in the process, it ushered in a whole new generation of country singers to the charts. There were both one-hit wonders like Billy Ray Cyrus and more substantial acts like Brooks & Dunn that followed Brooks to the top of the charts.

During the first half of the '90s, the new country boom was extraordinary. In the previous decade, country artists were lucky if they went gold, but during the '90s, they regularly went multi-platinum. As a result, country radio changed its format according to its new audience. Since there were so many new listeners to country radio unfamiliar and impatient with such older stars as George Jones, Dolly Parton, Willie Nelson, Johnny Cash, and Merle Haggard, the older artists were removed from the playlists in favor of newer musicians. Soon, veteran artists were not heard on the radio at all, and their record sales dried up. In no time, "fringe" country artists were phased out of rotation as well.

By the middle of the decade, new country completely dominated the country charts and radio, and while it was harder than the post-urban country music, it nevertheless owed more to pop than country. Shania Twain, the biggest star of the mid-'90s, was produced by Robert "Mutt" Lange—who made his name by working with heavy metal acts like AC/DC and Def Leppard, as well as new wave rockers like the Cars—and her music appropriately resembled slightly rootsy AOR pop-rock. Though Twain's *The Woman in Me* sold eight million copies, it was the last of the country blockbusters. In 1996, the country audience declined drastically, partially because the music was becoming too similar, and partially because its fans had found other genres to listen to. True country fans listened to the edgy sound of alternative country-rock, while baby boomers found themselves leaning toward the adult alternative sounds of pop radio. By the end of 1996, the sales of country albums was approaching the levels of the pre-Garth days. It remains to be seen how the country industry will sort itself out.

—Stephen Thomas Erlewine & Thom Owens

Recommended Recordings:

Garth Brooks, *Ropin' the Wind* (Liberty)

Garth Brooks, *The Hits* (Liberty)

Brooks & Dunn, *Brand New Man* (Arista)

Clint Black, *Greatest Hits* (RCA)

Shania Twain, *The Woman in Me* (Mercury)

Alan Jackson, *Greatest Hits Collection* (Arista)

Vince Gill, *Souvenirs* (MCA)

Reba McEntire, *Greatest Hits, Vol. 2* (MCA)

Wynonna Judd, *Greatest Hits* (MCA/Curb)

Travis Tritt, *Greatest Hits—From the Beginning* (Warner Bros.)

Lorrie Morgan, *Greatest Hits* (BNA)

Tim McGraw, *All I Want* (Curb)

John Michael Montgomery, *John Michael Montgomery* (Atlantic)
Trisha Yearwood, *Thinkin' About You* (MCA)

Alternative Country in the '90s

In 1990, a band called Uncle Tupelo from Belleville, IL—a small town just north of East St. Louis—released their debut album. Titled *No Depression*, it featured a rough but captivating mixture of raucous punk-rock songs, but it also added something different: several toned-down, acoustic ballads that had a distinct country flavor. And the title track itself was even a cover of a Carter Family song from the 1930s.

A few years later, when Uncle Tupelo's music began catching on among indie rockers with a taste for old time country, that simple little song and album title became the name of an internet fan club and chat group. But it didn't stop there: in 1995, a magazine of the same name went into publication, and "No Depression" soon became the leading moniker for the burgeoning alternative country movement. Other names include "insurgent country" (coined by Chicago label Bloodshot, which put out a couple of acclaimed "alternative country" compilations), "Americana," or simply "alt.country," the latter reminding us of the role the internet has played in the growth and publicity of this movement (a development that is distinctly separate from the growth of the music itself).

For the most part, No Depression or alt.country bands aren't much of a threat to the sales figures of mainstream Nashville country artists. But the speed with which this music (and its various nicknames) has caught on has shown that a substantial number of people are fed up with the overproduced pop trends of 1990s mainstream country music, and the limited range of styles and sounds that are typically played on country radio stations. When today's average rock fans think country, they think Garth Brooks; this, says No Depression fans, is a crime and a damn shame.

Alternative music in any genre is nothing new. As long as there's been a mainstream, there have been other, less obvious artists struggling to get their brand of music noticed. In country music's recent past, names like Gram Parsons, Waylon Jennings, and Willie Nelson—and practically anything that came out of Austin, TX—are frequently cited examples of people who struggled for the chance just to play music the way they wanted. In addition, the blending of country and rock music is as old as Elvis Presley's recording of Bill Monroe's "Blue Moon of Kentucky" in 1954. Johnny Cash and Bob Dylan helped tear down the walls between the two genres with their famous collaborations in the 1960s; Gram Parsons took the Byrds all the way to the Grand Ole Opry; Waylon Jennings covered Rolling Stones songs and got a standing ovation opening for the Grateful Dead in the 1970s; and Neil Young got hippies singing "Are You Ready for the Country" while Merle Haggard's "Okie from Muskogee" was still fresh in most Americans' minds. Jennings may be a favorite of many No Depression fans, but it's Parsons who is considered the patron saint of this movement—a guy who grew up a rocker but always had a love of pure, traditional country music. He was an outsider looking in, while "outlaw" Jennings was an established country singer trying to make more room for himself in a claustrophobic industry.

But there is something about this No Depression movement that's genuinely distinct from past country-rock trends. Maybe it's the fact that a good number of its fans grew up on punk rock, and have come to realize that many of the old-time country outfits are musically untrained and express a similar do-it-yourself philosophy to the one shared by many punk bands (as well as a penchant for fast rhythms, rough-edged guitar licks, and unadorned lyrics). Or maybe these same punks simply got tired of loud, brash rock bands. Or maybe it's the fact that people are finally realizing that country music is a big, wide world unto itself that has much more to offer than Top 40 radio stations and the industry bigwigs on Music Row would have the average person believe. Many of the artists at the top of the No Depression and insurgent country rosters are bands who play in rock 'n' roll clubs, not at county fairs. The fact that they can get young punk-rock fans bobbing their heads to straight-up covers of songs by Tom T Hall or the Louvin Brothers—a group few would know by name—is proof enough

that this music is able to reach beyond the traditional boundaries of the country and rock genres. While Uncle Tupelo and its offshoot bands, Wilco and Son Volt—both formed in the wake of UT's breakup—are the centerpieces of the No Depression movement, to say that the '90s alternative country scene began with this single Uncle Tupelo album isn't really correct. The music itself already existed—it simply didn't have such a visible umbrella under which to fall.

The country roots of L.A. punk legends X, for instance, began showing up in their later albums, and they even recorded a full-on country album in 1985 under the name the Knitters. Southern California, long a haven for individualistic country artists (Merle Haggard, for instance), even spawned an entire "cowpunk" crowd (Rank and File, Lone Justice), not to mention a rockabilly revival scene (the Blasters, Big Sandy) that's remained strong into the 1990s. Jason & the Scorchers' debut album *Lost and Found* (1985) was an electrified inspiration to many rock fans who liked their twang on the loud side. And the raucous British punk group the Mekons became, on later albums, more and more fixated on American roots music; singer Jon Langford now fronts a far more countrified side project called the Waco Brothers.

Souled American was a late-'80s Chicago band that mixed country and folk influences into their quirky rock songs. On their third album, *Around the Horn*, the twang got thicker and deeper, and they twisted the country genre in their own way by taking the rhythms down to a slow, mesmerizing crawl. Unfortunately, Souled American has never gotten the recognition it deserves (partly because the band's label, Rough Trade, went bankrupt). The Blood Oranges spiked their excellent albums with country-inspired ballads (often featuring the beautiful voice of Cheri Knight) and heavy doses of bluegrass. Go to Blazes play barroom rock 'n' roll laced with country and blues (and a few choice Charlie Rich and Hank Williams, Jr. covers). Freakwater is an acoustic group inspired by Carter Family songs and other old-time mountain folk ballads, and despite being fronted by two women who grew up in the punk scene of Louisville, KY, they're one of the most "traditional" country acts of the 1990s. Lambchop is a lush, arty Nashville band that claims '70s pop producer and songwriter Billy Sherrill as its idol.

Rock is certainly the background of most No Depression fans and artists, but the community has also become extremely fond of artists like Merle Haggard and George Jones, country music legends who are more and more finding themselves shunned by an industry (one with an shockingly short memory) that's become obsessed with sales figures and a flurry of young, fresh-scrubbed singers. Steve Earle was once one of those fresh faces himself (though not too well scrubbed), but his confrontational, "bad boy" attitude has kept him at a distance from Nashville almost since his debut *Guitar Town*. In 1996 he graced the cover of *No Depression* magazine, and has been an alt.country hero ever since. Another favorite is Dale Watson, a straight-up honky tonker based in Austin, TX, who's one of the strongest country artists working today, yet is on a West Coast indie label, Hightone, and like his idols (Haggard, Buck Owens, Johnny Paycheck), is virtually ignored by Nashville. Acclaimed singer-songwriters like Townes Van Zandt, Guy Clark, Lucinda Williams, Billy Joe Shaver, and Jimmie Dale Gilmore—many of them Texas artists, showing that Austin's colorful, off-center musical history has much in common with the No Depression scene as well—also are icons of the alt.country genre. And all sorts of musicians and fans continue to go back further still for inspiration, to artists like the Louvin Brothers, Bill Monroe, Rose Maddox, and the Carter Family.

—*Kurt Wolff*

Recommended Recordings:

Dave Alvin, *Blue Blvd.* (Hightone)

The Blood Oranges, *The Crying Tree* (East Side Digital)

Steve Earle, *I Feel Alright* (E-Squared)

Freakwater, *Old Paint* (Thrill Jockey)

Geraldine Fibbers, *Lost Somewhere Between the Earth and My Home* (Virgin)

Jimmie Dale Gilmore, *After Awhile* (Elektra Nonesuch/American Explorer)

Go to Blazes, *Waiting Around for the Crash* (East Side Digital)

Joe Henry, *Short Man's Room* (Mammoth)

The Jayhawks, *Blue Earth* (Twin Tone)

Lambchop, *How I Quit Smoking* (Merge)

The Palace Brothers, *There Is No-One What Will Take Care of You* (Drag City)

The Scud Mountain Boys, *Massachusetts* (Sub Pop)

Shaver, *Tramp on Your Street* (Zoo/Praxis)

Son Volt, *Trace* (Warner Bros.)

Souled American, *Around the Horn* (Rough Trade)

Uncle Tupelo, *Anodyne* (Reprise)

Townes Van Zandt, *Live at the Old Quarter, Houston, Texas* (Tomato)

Dale Watson, *Cheatin' Heart Attack* (Hightone)

Wilco, *Being There* (Reprise)

Lucinda Williams, *Lucinda Williams* (Rough Trade)

The Bakersfield Revival

There are those who continue to claim that only Nashville can be the home of Country & Western music. In fact, the West Coast was recording and promoting Country & Western music a full decade before Nashville caught on. It was out in the wilds of the West that Western swing, honky tonk, bluegrass, mountain music, hillbilly and C&W were first given a foothold beyond the clutches of the Big Apple. Los Angeles was the place, and due to its thriving movie industry, entertainments of all kinds were sought out. A hearty percentage of the population of California was comprised of immigrants from Arkansas, Oklahoma, Missouri, Kentucky, and yes, even Tennessee and Texas. They brought with them their culture and, more importantly, their music.

It was only natural that as the 20th century progressed through two world wars, a dust bowl and a depression, something had to give. In California's San Joaquin Valley it was the music, where a sound was starting to take shape that was distinctly a melding of all the different musics that had come together in this region. Carried upon the shoulders of Missouri fiddle players and Dust Bowl Okies who made their daily bread as migrant farm workers, day laborers and, later, as factory workers, the music settled in and took root in the fertile soil of Bakersfield. Once an agricultural crossroads that had also found affluence in oil and gold mining the century before, Bakersfield was suddenly a cultural axis that captured the imaginations of players, writers, singers, and fun seekers, all craving the hard-edged, wild, and loud honky tonk sound.

Prior to the boom years of the 1950s and '60s, Bakersfield had something boiling beneath its surface. Bill Woods and His Orange Blossom Playboys were playing at the infamous Blackboard as the house band before Buck Owens even set foot within Bakersfield city limits. Tommy Collins and Billy Mize were already making waves before the 1950s brought attention to Bakersfield and Capitol Records decided to take a chance on the hillbillies who were creating such a revolutionary sound. The boom years saw Bakersfield cement its reputation as the center of all West Coast C&W music activity. Recording, performing, and access to Los Angeles were all in its favor, as was the local population. Famed guitarist and songwriter Roy Nichols came from Fresno just as the Maddox Brothers and Sister Rose moved south from Modesto. Others, like Buck and Bonnie Owens, came from Arizona, while some made their way from Texas and other points east, north, and south.

Ferlin Husky, Jean Shepard, Harlan Howard, Dallas Frazier, Jan Howard, Wynn Stewart, and Lefty Frizzell all owe Bakersfield a debt of gratitude. Others who found their way there and made names for themselves include Ralph Mooney, Tom Bramley, Don Rich, Norm Hamlin, Jim Shaw, Henry Sharp, Don Markham, Doyle Holly, and Roy Hays. Bonnie Owens, sometimes referred to

as "the Queen of Bakersfield," and songwriter Red Simpson created a niche for themselves after taking up residence in Bakersfield. It was the working class who paved the way to the Bakersfield Sound. Those who worked a five- or six-day week at minimum wage with no future found sustenance within the music and a form of communication that defined their lives and their own emotions. Almost mythical in proportion, the sound and the scene fueled a whole new generation of traditionalists beyond its glory years. Dwight Yoakam makes no bones about the fact that he was a disciple of the Bakersfield Sound, even though he grew up in Ohio and Kentucky, where his grandparents exposed him to the hillbilly culture so many others had taken with them on their quest for a better life in California.

Today the boom town may be gone, but the sound remains. Its expansion into Los Angeles, the San Fernando Valley, Orange County and beyond allowed the Bakersfield Sound to continue to prevail between the 1970s and the mid-'80s explosion generated by the compilation project *A Town South of Bakersfield*. Kept alive by the rebel bands that found a camaraderie with Don Rich, the '70s was a time for the meshing together of country and rootsrock, the result being the New Riders of the Purple Sage, Commander Cody and His Lost Planet Airmen, the Flying Burrito Brothers, Poco, and the Eagles.

The success of *A Town South of Bakersfield* generated a renewed interest in the C&W music coming from the West Coast. The major label interest given to Dwight Yoakam added fuel to the fire as the Lonesome Strangers, Syd Straw, the Neon Angels, the Plowboys, Sid Griffin, Kathy Robertson, Rosie Flores, Larry Dean, Katy Moffatt, Dale Watson, Patty Booker, James Intveld, Dave Alvin, Ronnie Mack, and a slew of other talent took up the cause. L.A. sought out the energy and tradition of their musical heritage and because of their foresight, a quiet Bakersfield Renaissance began to unfold as the mid-'90s rolled around.

By 1996 the renaissance was catching on in Texas, Chicago, Portland, and North Carolina, and even Nashville was beginning to feel the force that was once again rising out of the West. Artists and bands like the Derailers, Junior Brown, Robbie Fulks, the Backsliders, BR5-49, and Rebecca Kilgore found the Bakersfield spirit alive and well within their own music. Bakersfield band Big House was signed by MCA, and another hometown outfit, the Wichitas, continued to move forward with their contribution to the Bakersfield Sound in the recording studio.

The evidence was mounting. Herb Pedersen and Chris Hillman recorded the tribute *Bakersfield Bound*, which featured exceptional versions of classic tunes including "Playboy." Former Haggard apprentice Scott Joss, who was just a teenager when he began his career as a member of the Strangers, released his first solo effort, *Souvenirs*, which honored Bakersfield and Joss's mentors Tiny Moore, Roy Nichols, and Merle Haggard. And too, there are those who have carefully nurtured the sound, passing it on to the next generation. Larry Dean, who came from Idaho because he heard the call of Bakersfield almost 20 years ago, was mentored by Nichols and in turn is mentoring newcomer Michael Dart. Cody Bryant and Kathy Robertson count Red Simpson as their teacher and friend, and Bonnie Owens has always reached out to younger players and singers in the hopes of giving them a hand. The next generation includes the many who come to sit at Red's feet on any given Monday night when he holds court at Trout's.

With an influx of pilgrims comes an increase in business and the need for venues. This brought about the opening of Buck Owens' Crystal Palace Museum and Theatre. Other venues are being remodeled, restored, and reopened. The grand old Fox Theatre is in the midst of a five-year reconstruction project. Trout's remains the old lady of distinction, and it continues to support local musicians as well as welcome the many who make the two-hour drive from Los Angeles. Some of the clubs in L.A. are jumping on the bandwagon and giving the Bakersfield Revolution a push. The Foothill Club, just south of L.A., is still operating and booking more C&W acts. Thrown to the punk crowd in the '70s and '80s, this legendary honky tonk is looking to the future and feeling optimistic. It is the place that the real honky tonkers want to play when they come to the City of Angels. Just as important, the Bakersfield Revolution has spread to non-country clubs; Jacks Sugar Shack, once known for blues and rock, now seeks out country and roots music.

As we come nearer to the end of the 20th century it is interesting to note that our great-grandparents, grandparents, and parents, who trudged out from the Ozarks, the Appalachians, and the Dust Bowl, set into motion a cultural phenomenon that is still vibrant and meaningful 70 and 80 years later. This is their legacy and ours as we look towards a future filled with unknowns. Those who continue to be purveyors of the Bakersfield Sound carry with them the strength of a past they are deeply connected to and the seeds that will be planted once again in a still farther off, distant future. Because they are the Bakersfield bards whose perseverance in the face of greed and convention has no limits, no one will ever forget what took place in the little town north of Los Angeles. In fact, people will more than likely seek out the Bakersfield Sound time and time again, hunting for the joy and sustenance that their forbears found in that special music when the initial strains of fiddle, guitar, and pedal steel joined together in perfect harmony, ringing through the starry Western night, calling out to the faithful.

—Jana Pendragon

Recommended Recordings:

Tommy Collins, *Words and Music Country Style* (Capitol)

Dallas Frazier, *Singing My Songs* (RCA)

Ferlin Husky, *Gone* (Capitol)

Billy Mize, *This Time and Place* (Imperial)

Merle Haggard, *The Lonesome Fugitive: the Anthology (1963-1977)* (Razor & Tie)

Buck Owens, *The Buck Owens Collection, 1959-1990* (Rhino)

Wynn Stewart, *The Best of the Challenge Masters* (AVI)

Various Artists, *A Town South of Bakersfield, Vols. 1&2* (Restless)

Various Artists, *Hillbilly Fever; Vol. 4: Legends of the West Coast* (Rhino)

Jean Shepard, *Classic Capitol Recordings, 1952-1964* (CMF)

Hank Penny, *Rompin', Stompin', Swingin'* (Bear Family)

Joe and Rose Lee Maphis, *Dim Lights, Thick Smoke* (CMH)

Lefty Frizzell, *Lefty Frizzell* (Columbia)

Molly Bee, *Good Golly Ms. Molly* (Granite)

Freddie Hart, *The Best of Freddie Hart* (Harmony)

Johnny Bond, *That Wild, Wicked but Wonderful West* (Starday)

Larry Dean, *Outside Chance* (USA Music Group)

Dwight Yoakam, *Guitars, Cadillacs, Etc., Etc.* (Reprise)

Desert Rose Band, *Running* (MCA/Curb)

Rick Shea, *Buffalo Show* (Major Label Records)

Kathy Robertson, *At the Cantina* (Kitty LA Tour)

Cody Bryant, *Big Dose of Country* (Wagon Wheel)

Mark Insley, *Good Country Junk* (Country Town Records)

James Intveld, *James Intveld* (Bear Family)

Neil Mooney, *Ranchdressing* (Strawdog)

Scott Joss, *Souvenirs* (Little Dog)

The Lonesome Strangers, *The Lonesome Strangers* (Hightone)

Chris Gaffney, *Loser's Paradise* (Hightone)

Country Albums by Rock Artists

Country music has always gotten a lot of lip service from rock musicians, whether it's to praise the vocals of George Jones and the songwriting of Hank Williams, or just enthuse wildly over artists like the Carter Family and Tammy Wynette. It's relatively rare, however, that artists who define themselves as rock musicians will take their admiration into action by recording an entire country album. To do so means alienating a good many of their fans, for one thing. More importantly, liking a music and playing it are

two entirely separate things. Making a detour into country music is a risky venture that has led to extremely erratic results, ranging from inspired fusions and landmark albums to ill-advised experiments that are best forgotten.

Country music was a big part of the chemical equation that gave birth to rock 'n' roll, and naturally its influence has been felt, to small and large degrees, within rock music for the past 40 years. The first generation of rockabilly singers mostly came from straight country backgrounds. Many of them would record country tunes at roughly the same time they were getting established as rockers; see Jerry Lee Lewis' "Crazy Arms," Carl Perkins' "Tennessee," and much of Wanda Jackson's early Capitol output for easy reference. And many rockabilly singers would redefine themselves as country singers after rockabilly passed out of fashion in the 1960s.

In this essay, however, we're concerned not with artists who have balanced rockabilly and country music (see the separate piece on rockabilly for a more in-depth discussion of those), but with musicians who dallied with country after firmly establishing themselves as rock performers. The first of them to do so on a large scale was Ray Charles, who surprised audiences with his *Modern Sounds in Country & Western Music* album in early 1962. Charles had only recently established himself as a pop star, after a decade or so of gospel-infused R&B hits that were instrumental to the birth of soul. Now the voice behind "I Got a Woman" and "What'd I Say" was covering songs identified with white country singers like Hank Williams, Eddy Arnold, and Don Gibson. Add to this the MOR flavor of some of the strings and backing singers, and it seemed that Charles ran a great risk of alienating his constituency.

The record, however, became a huge commercial success, reaching No. 1 on the LP charts and yielding two massive hit singles, "I Can't Stop Loving You" and "You Don't Know Me." Almost as successful was *Modern Sounds in Country & Western Music Vol. 2*, released at the end of 1962. Charles' move to country sounds is more understandable when considering the eclecticism of his career as a whole. He may have been principally known as an R&B/rock singer, but before 1960 he had also played straight jazz and, at the very beginning, straight pop. He did not think of himself so much as an R&B singer as a singer, period, who could handle a wide repertoire. Like many Americans, he had developed an appreciation for country music by listening to the Grand Ole Opry while growing up.

The crossover success of the *Modern Sounds* albums, however, was probably due to the fact that they were at least as much pop as country. Indeed, they weren't entirely successful on pure aesthetic grounds; Ray's vocals were perennially soulful, but the arrangements were often quite mushy exercises that would have found a more comfortable home with Ray *Conniff*. Charles never went to the extent of identifying himself as a country singer, though he has continued to insert country items into his repertoire ever since the early '60s. Nor did his country outings inspire other black soul singers to do the same. Charles' talents were perhaps too singular to generate an imitative trend, though it's worth noting that in the early 1980s B.B. King did an MOR country album, *Love Me Tender*. Many fans judge this to be the worst mistake of his career, despite the disingenuous sleeve note, in which B.B. himself claims that this is the album he's always wanted to make.

Prior to the inception of country-rock in the late '60s, there were a few odd attempts by rock singers to work in the country idiom that stick out more as curiosities than innovations. Gene Pitney and George Jones teamed up for a bunch of duets in the mid-'60s that, despite some decent tracks, wouldn't rate among the highlights of either man's career. Pitney also did some recording with one of Jones' *other* duet partners, country singer Melba Montgomery. Pitney, Jones, and Montgomery happened to all record for the same label (Musicor), leading some historians to suspect that the Pitney duets might have been more of a convenient marketing exercise than an experimental artistic enterprise.

Around the time that Pitney was cutting his country duets, Del Shannon paid tribute to one of country's legends with *Del Shannon Sings Hank Williams*. It's hard to figure exactly who this would have been pitched to: not the fans that bought his hard-driving rock singles like "Keep on Searchin'," one would think, nor the somewhat older straight country fans, who might not have been familiar with Shannon in the first place. The album was not as interesting as you might guess. It sounds, well, exactly like you would think Shannon would sound singing Hank Williams tunes, with competent but unexciting interpretations that neither add much to the originals, nor stretch Shannon's vocals in unexpected directions. Another Hank Williams tribute album was offered by Charlie Rich, who in the mid-'60s had yet to firmly identify himself as a country artist, playing the field with rock and soul at least as often. Considering his enormous interpretive gifts, Rich's *Sings the Songs of Hank Williams* is also a disappointment, relying far more upon predictably reverent, lukewarm covers than canny reinvention.

Prior to the late '60s, self-contained rock groups—who had become the pacesetters of rock music since the Beatles achieved international stardom in 1964—made very few serious nods in the direction of country. There were some very interesting individual tracks by top rock groups that fairly stank of country pie: the Beatles' own "I Don't Want to Spoil the Party" and "Baby's in Black," for instance, or "I've Just Seen a Face," which can be rearranged into a bluegrass cover with very little effort. The Rolling Stones covered Hank Williams' "I'm Movin' On," and wrote a down-home country tune of sorts for *Aftermath*, "High and Dry." On "Go and Say Goodbye" and especially "Kind Woman," Buffalo Springfield put folk-rock harmonies and arrangements to material that was country to the core. But there were no entire country albums by rock groups, save for the Downliners Sect's bizarre *The Sect Sing Country Songs*, by a little-known mid-'60s British group. The Downliners Sect were much more noted for sloppy punk/R&B in the mold of the Rolling Stones and the Pretty Things; their country LP, which suffered from poor execution, is best considered as a novelty rather than a groundbreaking creative endeavor. (Even more of a novelty was Nancy Sinatra's *Country My Way,* which did little to enhance her career in either the country or pop markets.)

Nineteen sixty-eight was a sort of "back to basics" year for rock, and Bob Dylan's predominantly acoustic *John Wesley Harding* helped point the compass toward country sounds as well. *John Wesley Harding* was recorded (as much of *Blonde on Blonde* was) in Nashville, and the last cut in particular, "I'll Be Your Baby Tonight," was straight country, complete with steel guitar. The album still featured much of Dylan's oblique wordplay, but that was largely discarded on his follow-up, *Nashville Skyline,* on which Bob for the first time could be said to be more of a country artist than a folk or rock one. The record still sold well, partly because of its hit single ("Lay Lady Lay"), and partly because Dylan had such a large, adoring group of listeners willing to follow him into unexpected waters. Much of Dylan's audience, though, was disappointed with the record overall, not necessarily because of the country textures, but because the record itself was rather uninspired, and because Dylan had substituted country clichés for ambitious poetry. Dylan would never immerse himself as deeply in country again.

Several major rock groups helped ignite country-rock in 1968 by recording country albums, most notably the Byrds. Their *Sweetheart of the Rodeo* is often acclaimed as one of the greatest country-rock records, and introduced Gram Parsons to a wide audience. The Byrds' country phase was not entirely unexpected, given that back in 1966 they had covered a Porter Wagoner song ("A Satisfied Mind"), that bassist Chris Hillman had originally been a bluegrass musician, and that some of their best originals had a strong country feel ("Mr. Spaceman," "Time Between"). It was quite a switch from their electric folk-rock era, and they even played the Grand Ole Opry before Gram Parsons, who had only been in the band for about six months, left, eventually forming the Flying Burrito Brothers with Hillman. The Byrds had always been about change, and nothing else they did was as pure country as *Sweetheart.*

Nineteen sixty-eight also saw interesting country albums by the Beau Brummels (*Bradley's Barn*) and the Everly Brothers (*Roots*). The Everlys had always maintained strong ties to country

in their vocal style, and their late '50s album *Songs Our Daddy Taught Us* could even be considered a country record if you stretched things (though it might be more appropriately classified as a folk disc). The Everlys weren't the only early rock 'n' roll stars to dabble in country. In the late '60s, Rick Nelson made country-flavored albums with the Stone Canyon Band, although these records are perhaps more notable for the musicians (including future members of the Eagles, Little Feat, and the Desert Rose Band) than the music. There were also a host of acts that played country-rock from the start, like the Flying Burrito Brothers, Michael Nesmith, Poco, Hearts & Flowers, and former Byrd Gene Clark. As they always considered country a main staple rather than a side dish, they are described in more depth in a separate country-rock essay (as are latter-day country-rockers such as Son Volt and Uncle Tupelo, who are covered as part of the No Depression movement).

By the early '70s the influence of country-rock had spread to rock acts who would never be principally identified as country-rock musicians. The Rolling Stones, probably as a result of their friendship with Gram Parsons, recorded some countryish material in the late '60s and early '70s, with "Wild Horses" being the most successful and famous example. There was too much folk, blues, and muted psychedelia in the Grateful Dead's *American Beauty* and *Workingman's Dead* for those to be considered country-rock albums, but there was a great deal of country in the songwriting, musicianship, and especially the harmonies. George Harrison made some relatively little-noticed forays into country on the *All Things Must Pass* cuts "Behind That Locked Door" and "If Not for You," which featured ace pedal steel player Pete Drake. Less successful was Ringo Starr's *Beaucoups of Blues*, cut in Nashville with some of the city's session men, including Drake, whose publishing company also supplied the ex-Beatle with material for the record.

Of the California-based singer-songwriters who appropriated some of country-rock's laid-back feel, Neil Young has delved into country with the greatest depth. Country and folk influences pepper all of his acoustic-oriented (and some of his electric) work. They truly came to the forefront on 1972's *Harvest*, which went to No. 1 and netted him a No. 1 pop single, "Heart of Gold," that featured a weepy steel guitar. It was his most countrified album for quite some time, until he decided in the mid-'80s to go the whole nine yards with *Old Ways*, which could be safely considered a *country* album, as opposed to a country-influenced rock record. Waylon Jennings and Willie Nelson contributed guest vocals, just in case anyone doubted that Young was serious.

Young had always flip-flopped between musical styles (and political viewpoints), and at the time he implied that he would be happy to leave the rock world completely and pursue country music full-time. That didn't happen, of course; by 1990 he was making eardrums bleed again with *Ragged Glory*. Just to keep everyone on their toes, *Harvest Moon* (1992) was another right turn into a predominantly country-folk mood, although Young's lyrics (and his image) are too eccentric to find their way onto country playlists or the collections of mainstream country listeners.

When the country-rock trend began to die down after the early '70s, such unabashedly countryish outings became rarer. The punk/new wave movement of the late '70s made them rarer still. The musical conservatism of much country music, and its frequent reflection of mainstream, family-oriented values, were among the last things that interested the safety-pin-and-torn-T-shirts crowd. Elvis Costello, who owed much of his success to that crowd, tried to defy audience expectations by releasing an album of country covers in the early '80s, *Almost Blue*. Recorded in Nashville, it may be the most notorious example of a rock star turning into a country singer with little or no notice.

Actually, Costello's country experiment would not have been a surprise for those paying extremely close attention to his career. Before he made records, Elvis had occasionally sung in bar bands that played country music; he also penned enthusiastic liner notes for a George Jones reissue. *Almost Blue*, however, sold poorly and was panned by most critics, and not just because they might have been too close-minded to give it a chance. No one can doubt that

Costello's affection for country music was (and is) sincere. Whether he actually had the ability to make good country music himself, despite his obvious desire to do so, was another question entirely; the opinion was near-universal that Costello was a major rock/new wave artist, and a non-event as a country vocalist.

Generally, the same disparity in results afflicts other rock artists who decide to make an all-out country album. If they were *really* meant to sing country, we can reasonably ask, why have they been singing rock for all these years instead? Marianne Faithfull may claim to have been deeply influenced by Waylon Jennings, but she sounded ill-suited for outlaw territory on her *Faithless* country album, recorded just before she reoriented herself to the new wave crowd with *Broken English*. Jonathan Richman, who has adapted doo-wop and Spanish music to his own idiosyncratic child-rock weltanschauung, did the same with *Jonathan Goes Country*, which was more colored by the naïveté of Richman himself than the time-honored traditions of C&W. Better left unexamined is the *Rhythm Country & Blues* compilation, which paired a bunch of well-known country and soul singers for an album of celebrity duets. But it looked more like a marketing exercise to the adult contemporary audience than a convincing aesethetic project.

In the mid-1990s, The The, much more noted for dark modern English rock than anything rootsy, tore a page out of the Del Shannon songbook by recording a tribute album to Hank Williams. It attracted more notice than some of The The's original material had in the States, though the results weren't as strange as one might have anticipated. The point seemed to be that Matt Johnson (who is, essentially, the core of The The) was able to make Hank Williams songs sound like fodder for modern rock playlists—which, in the eyes of many music fans, is not so much making a point as being pointless. In the *All Music Guide to Rock*, Stephen Thomas Erlewine aptly summarized, "Strangely enough, it works better than several The The records, since Hank Williams is a better songwriter than Matt Johnson."

One way to get around the thorny issue of trying to sell country albums to a rock following is for rock musicians to release country records as side projects, particularly within the alternative world, where there's generally more freedom for flexibility in this regard. John Doe and Exene Cervenka of X, with assistance from Dave Alvin, formed the Knitters to offer country-flavored music on *Poor Little Critter on the Road*, which was still poorly received, but at least didn't alienate X fans who wanted brittle underground rock. Janet Bean, drummer/singer of the fairly straightforward alternative rock band Eleventh Dream Day, formed an acoustic band, Freakwater (in which she sings and plays guitar), for the purposes of playing country folk music. Ironically, the Appalachian-flavored musings of Freakwater may well prove to be more enduring than those of the rock band from which Bean sprung.

Then there's the approach that purists may find most offensive—to treat the whole issue of rock artists slumming in country as something of a joke. The Mekons, a long-lived British alternative band of considerable eclecticism, often offer a brand of cowpunk that seems equal parts reverence and iconoclastic satire. More blatantly satirical is Eugene Chadbourne, the avant-rock guitarist, who often uses C&W forms to advocate adamantly left-wing politics that will find no comfortable home on Music Row. On 1980's *There'll Be No Tears Tonight*, he devoted the whole set to avant-garde interpretations of country standards. And if you want to make sure there's Country & Western in the house to offend anyone regardless of political orientation, there's Ween's *12 Golden Country Greats*, in which the most successful comedy rock group of the 1990s marries its juvenile wit to straight MOR country backing.

—Richie Unterberger

Recommended Recordings:

Ray Charles, *Modern Sounds in Country & Western Music* (Rhino)

Bob Dylan, *Nashville Skyline* (Columbia)

The Byrds, *Sweetheart of the Rodeo* (Columbia)

The Everly Brothers, *Roots* (Warner Brothers)

The Beau Brummels, *Bradley's Barn* (Edsel)

The Grateful Dead, *American Beauty* (Warner Brothers)

Elvis Costello, *Almost Blue* (Rykodisc)

Neil Young, *Old Ways* (Geffen)

The The, *Hanky Panky* (550 Music/Epic)

RESOURCES

Books

Country Music, Bob Millard, 1993, Harper Perennial, US
Bob Millard's *Country Music* is a unique and useful approach to the evolution of country music; instead of a collection of essays or biographies, it's compiled as a year-by-year historical overview. In addition to lists of milestones–key births, deaths, awards, and the like–the individual annual surveys also offer more in-depth essays exploring industry trends, popular artists, landmark debuts, and essential recordings. *–Jason Ankeny*

Country on Compact Disc, Paul Kingsbury, editor, 1993, Grove Music, US
As a consumer guide to country music, *Country on Compact Disc* is an engaging effort; well-written and insightful, it offers a comprehensive look at the best (and worst) the CD format has to offer, as well as brief biographies of the performers. The problem, however, is that so far the book has never been updated beyond its initial 1993 publication; since then not only have thousands of new releases appeared, but thousands of older recordings have been reissued on compact disc. At the same time, many of the records listed in *Country on Compact Disc* have subsequently gone out of print. Still, the book offers a good overview of essential albums, along with a helpful index listing No. 1 singles and where they appear on CD; even out of date, it's a worthwhile purchase. *–Jason Ankeny*

Country: The Music and the Musicians, Country Music Foundation, 1988, Abbeville Press, US
Compiled by the Country Music Foundation, the hefty *Country: The Music and the Musicians* is a lavishly illustrated volume that offers a superior overview of the music's evolution. A collection of lengthy, insightful essays that chronologically detail the rise of country from a backwoods, rural sensation to a mainstream phenomenon, the book is stuffed with information, using sidebars and photo captions to flesh out the big picture. *–Jason Ankeny*

Definitive Country: The Ultimate Encyclopedia of Country Music and Its Performers, Barry McCloud, July 1995, Perigee, USA
Published in 1995, *Barry McCloud's Definitive Country* doesn't live up to its lofty title, but it is nonetheless one of the better and more comprehensive country volumes on the market. The product of nearly a decade of research, *Definitive Country's* primary function is as a source of biographical and anecdotal information; McCloud based much of his work on interviews with his subjects, and as a result delivers a more detailed overview of artists' lives and careers than many other similar guides. However, coverage of performers outside of the country mainstream is rare, and at times, McCloud's enthusiasm for the music gets the better of him; his homey, conversational writing lacks critical distance and objectivity, and the book is littered with factual errors, including incorrect record release dates and chart information. The biggest downfall of the book, however, is the focus on the musicians rather than the music itself: artistic appraisal within the context of the individual biographies is slim, and in lieu of any in-depth reviews of an artist's oeuvre, a brief "recommended albums" list is appended to the entry. Still, as a beginner's guide to country music, it gets the job done. *–Jason Ankeny*

Giants of Country Music, Neil Haislop et. al., 1995, Billboard Books, US
Published by Billboard magazine, *Giants of Country Music* is a slight volume that fails to offer anything new or different from other similar references. Its focus is, of course, on country's best-selling stars, and while biographies of all the big names are included, the book doesn't take into account the many fringe artists who never charted but whose music was highly influential. Given that *Giants* is a *Billboard* publication, its chart information is surprisingly scant; best-selling albums and singles are noted in charts accompanying each entry, but taken out of context, the information is not very helpful. Joel Whitburn's *Billboard* chart books are a more valuable resource. *–Jason Ankeny*

Goldmine Country Western Record & CD Price Guide, Fred Heggeness, 1996, Krause Publications, US
Published by Goldmine magazine, Fred Heggeness' *Country Western Record & CD Price Guide* is an informative look at the hobby of collecting rare country recordings. It also includes country artists' discographies and label affiliations; while most guides cover only a performer's hits, essential recordings and prominent releases, Heggeness delves into obscurities and rarities, and assigns them monetary values for the collector's market. *–Jason Ankeny*

The Big Book of Country Music, Richard Carlin, 1995, Penguin, US
While Richard Carlin's *Big Book of Country Music* is far from being the most comprehensive volume of its kind, it does offer its own distinct critical identity, a quality most similar biographical guides lack. Carlin is an outspoken writer unafraid to take shots at artists and musical styles that don't suit his tastes, and he also strives to include performers outside of the Nashville mainstream: Steve Young, Lucinda Williams, and Michelle Shocked are just three of the acts who appear here but rarely make the cut in most country guides. Another worthwhile feature of the book is its brief but informative overviews of different country movements and genres. Unfortunately, Carlin's brevity extends to the rest of the book, and his short biographical entries pale in comparison to the competition; similarly, discographies, when they appear at all, consist typically of one or two entries, and lack in-depth critical appraisal beyond the author's initial judgments. As a result, *The Big Book of Country Music* makes for a lively read, but not an enlightening one. *–Jason Ankeny*

♦♦♦♦ The Blackwell Guide to Recorded Country Music, editor Bob Allen, 1994, Blackwell, US
This may be the most useful book in the Blackwell music reference series, simply because there isn't as much competition in the country field as there is in the other genres they've covered (blues, jazz, soul). The format remains the same: ten chapters divided into various genres/styles/eras (honky tonk, bluegrass, Western

music, etc.), with a main essay covering the principal performers/ events, and 400 recommended albums, many with succinct capsule reviews. There are some excellent contributors here, particularly editor Bob Allen (also editor of *Country Music Magazine*), Nick Tosches, and Charles Wolfe. Every major movement is covered, from early country recordings through Nashville, countrypolitan, and the hat period. Refreshingly, there is a large chapter devoted to "alternative country" that covers mavericks like Butch Hancock, Townes Van Zandt, and outlaws that often elude coverage by the country mainstream. Unusually, there is also a chapter on Irish country, a subgenre you won't find covered in many other sources, although unfortunately this section is not compellingly written. The book is not all-encompassing; some important performers, such as Hank Locklin, Tex Williams, and Terry Allen, are barely mentioned or omitted. On the whole, however, it's a valuable volume, especially considering the relatively poor standards of the average country music reference title. —*Richie Unterberger*

The Comprehensive Country Music Encyclopedia, Editors, Country Music, 1994, Times Books, US

Compiled by the editors of *Country Music* magazine, *The Comprehensive Country Music Encyclopedia* is an extensive volume filled with concise and informative biographical entries, including several fringe acts. The book also covers creative movements within the music, and touches on outside forums like radio shows, television programs, and popular clubs that proved instrumental in the development and rise of country music. Well-written and authoritative, it's among the best volumes of its kind. —*Jason Ankeny*

Top Country Singles 1944-1993, Joel Whitburn, 1994, Record Research Inc., US

Like all of Joel Whitburn's *Billboard* chart books, *Top Country Singles 1944-1993* is meticulously researched and an invaluable resource for students of the country music industry. The format is a simple one: all singles hitting the *Billboard* Country Music Top 100 charts between the chart's January 8, 1944, introduction (when the list was comprised of "Juke Box Folk Records") and the book's 1993 cutoff date are included, as is brief biographical information about the recording artists and rankings of their biggest hits. In addition, the book indexes the songs alphabetically according to their titles, offers lists of No. 1 hits and other worthy chart feats, and even includes a ranking of country's 400 most historically successful chart acts. —*Jason Ankeny*

Magazines

Country Music

Country may be the most popular music in the land bar rock, but the quality of the journalistic coverage and criticism of the music is surprisingly poor. *Country Music* is, by a wide margin, the best national publication devoted to the style. In fact, it is the only country magazine worth recommending, and the only one to offer intelligent, knowledgeable criticism. Adhering mostly to the standard feature/interview/review format, it covers the entire spectrum of country; the Nashville superstars, of course, get a bigger chunk than anyone else, but there's also a good amount of space for more rootsy and acoustic-based performers, independent label releases, vintage reissues, and hillbilly. It also includes regular contributions from nationally renowned writers like Rich Kienzle and John Morthland. (329 Riverside Ave., Westport, CT 06880) —*Richie Unterberger*

Dirty Linen

The leading American magazine devoted to "folk, electric folk, traditional and world music," by a longshot, this bimonthly has plenty of features, oodles of CD, tape, video, concert, and book reviews, roundups of neglected genres and old recordings, listings of new releases, and lots of miscellaneous news. It also offers tour information via several online services. Not as glossy, well-written, or wide-ranging as *Folk Roots*, but almost as informative, *Dirty Linen* complements that British magazine's coverage well.

(P.O. Box 66600, Baltimore, MD 21239-6600) —*Richie Unterberger*

Discoveries

Discoveries, like *Goldmine*, is a tabloid-sized magazine (published monthly) devoted to record collectors and record collecting. Also like *Goldmine*, it is filled with articles (and discographies) on artists and groups that will interest non-collectors. The two magazines differ somewhat in the music and styles they cover. *Goldmine* is geared toward rock'n'roll, blues, and R&B, both on vinyl and CDs, while *Discoveries* is oriented more toward vinyl, focusing on earlier rock, country, jazz, blues, and even some traditional popular music. In addition, *Discoveries* encourages readers to communicate with each other through the magazine's mailbox regarding music trivia and record questions. Discoveries can be reached at P.O. Box 255, Port Townsend, WA 98368; 206-385-1200.—*JME*

Goldmine

Published since 1974, *Goldmine* is just that—a goldmine of discographical information, extended articles, and great album reviews. Nowhere else will you find such in-depth articles on individual artists and groups. And almost every article is accompanied by a complete discography. *Goldmine* is geared to the record collector; a good part of each issue is filled with collectors' ads. Reading through these is an experience in itself, as those of us who aren't collectors may have little idea of the amount of activity in out-of-print and hard-to-find albums. Thanks to these folks, it is possible to obtain almost any hard-to-find album.

Goldmine has some of the best writers in the business, and almost every major freelance writer has written for them at one time or another. It is a tabloid-sized magazine of about 170 pages, published biweekly. There is a lot of information here. If you have never browsed through a copy, you have an experience in store for you. It's an eye-opener. Write to them and mention the *AMG* and you will receive a free sample issue. *Goldmine* can be reached at 700 E. State St., Iola, WI 54990; 715-445-2214.—*JME*

ICE

Although steeply priced ($3.95 for each 20-page issue), this newsletter is extremely useful for the hard-bitten record collector, as well as for those involved in the music industry at almost any level. It includes a very comprehensive schedule of upcoming releases, both new and reissues; lots of news about in-the-works projects and reissue packages; items about hard-to-find imports; a column devoted to complaints about inadequate CD remastering, track selection, or packaging, featuring responses from the labels themselves; and listings (with brief comments) of CD bootlegs. Most interesting are the feature stories about major reissues, box sets, or new releases, which often highlight in-depth, inside scoops from the label, compilers, or artists themselves. Mostly rock-oriented, with some coverage of jazz, country, blues, and other genres. (P.O. Box 3043, Santa Monica, CA 90408) —*Richie Unterberger*

Mojo

This is a fat, glossy general interest British monthly rock magazine with much more of a historical perspective than most. Coverage is about equally divided between current acts and artists from the past, with a bit (not much) of a bias toward "classic rock" performers. The in-depth interviews, historical surveys, and eyewitness recollections of all sorts of interesting stars and cult rock icons of the past are often fascinating, and usually considerably more well-written and less oriented toward collector details than those that appear in *Goldmine*. Also includes record and book reviews, news bits, and other interesting columns. (Tower House, Lathkill Street, Sovereign Park, Market Harborough, LE 16 9EF, UK) —*Richie Unterberger*

Musician

Perhaps the most intelligent and well-written mainstream US music publication, with an emphasis on long (but not exhausting) features and interviews, *Musician* leans a bit toward the classic rock side of the coin, or new performers in the classic rock mold, but there's reasonable coverage of alternative rock, as well as some jazz and other music (hip-hop and Black pop gets a pretty thin slice). The magazine also contains a fair amount of technology info, including equipment reviews and details of specific musicians' instruments, along with comments from the artists themselves. — *Richie Unterberger*

No Depression

No Depression magazine can lay claim to a rare distinction: not only did the publication's coverage of the 1990s alternative country scene help give rise to the music's popularity, but over time, the name *No Depression* even emerged as a catch-all description for the genre. Founded by co-editors Grant Alden and Peter Blackstock, it began not as a print journal but as an online message board for fans of the influential band Uncle Tupelo. Taking its name from the title of the group's first album (which, in turn, borrowed its name from the A.P. Carter song covered therein), *No Depression* quickly evolved into an America Online discussion forum for fans of left-of-center country music before becoming a true print magazine in 1995. Originally published on a quarterly basis, the publication's success allowed it to go bimonthly the following year. — *Jason Ankeny*

Option

The production values have gotten steadily slicker in the decade since this bimonthly started, and the coverage of widely known, major label acts has expanded, with a corresponding (but slighter) decrease in the articles about total unknowns. Still, it's the leading international publication devoted to alternative and indie music of all kinds, and there's still plenty of space for way-underground acts in both the features and reviews sections. *Option* reviews about 200 releases, mostly independent, in every issue, and contains columns devoted to alternative music industry trends and developments, other media, and miscellaneous news. — *Richie Unterberger*

Q

This glossy British monthly is probably the best general interest rock and pop music publication. The review section of each issue covers literally hundreds of new releases, including a lot of British imports and reissues. Also included are in-depth features on major performers covering the entire rock and pop spectrum, departments for up-and-coming bands and gossip, book and movie reviews, cool "where are they now?" reports, and eyewitness recollections of major moments in rock history. The writing is much more straightforward and accessible to Yankee readers than the more whimsical and personality-oriented British rock weeklies. Expensive, but worth it, and widely distributed in the US (Tower Publishing Services Ltd., Tower House, Lathkill Street, Sovercign Park, Market Harborough LE16 9EF, UK) — *Richie Unterberger*

Online Sites

Country Music Online

For an art form legendary for clinging to traditional values and beliefs, country music has proven surprisingly willing to embrace modern technology, as evidenced by the ever-increasing number of internet sites devoted to the music and its performers. Computer-savvy country aficionados have applied their online skills to take fandom to its next level; thanks to the efforts of their followers, virtually every act, from chart-topping superstars to fringe-dwelling cult artists, now has a website and homepage—some authorized, some not. Similarly, most record labels have created their own websites to promote talent, offering sound and video clips as well as biographical information. The Web has also proven to be an increasingly vital forum for country news and debate. *No Depression* (http://www.nodepression.net/), which began as a discussion board for fans of the alternative country trio Uncle Tupelo, was so well-received that it ultimately became a respected bimonthly print magazine; the publication's name even became a catch-all tag for bands within the burgeoning alt-

country movement. Other fine sources for country news, interviews, and reviews include:

Twangin'! (http://www.well.com./user/cline/twangin.html)
Country Music Time (http://www1.usa1.com/—CST.html)
Cybergrass: The Internet Bluegrass Music Magazine (http://www.banjo.com/BG/)
Music City News (http://www.hsv.tis.net/mcn/)
and, of course, our own AMG site (http://www.allmusic.com).
—*Jason Ankeny*

Mail Order

Elderly Instruments

This free 100-page catalog features folk, blues, bluegrass, traditional and old-time country, children's, all manner of international music, and more. Aside from new CDs, LPs, and cassettes, Elderly Instruments also has a fair trade-in allowance for used CDs and LPs. They stock musical instruments as well. A reliable company. For more information, write to:

Elderly Instruments
1100 N. Washington
P.O. Box 14210
Lansing, MI 48910
(517) 372-7890
(517) 372-5155 —*Michael Erlewine*

Smithsonian Recordings

There are two different companies that share a legitimate tie to the Smithsonian; Smithsonian Recordings is the first. You won't see these recordings in stores (though you may get a flyer in the mail if you have used your credit card lately); they are, for the most part, box sets (CDs and albums) on different music genres—folk, country, jazz, big band, classical, and others. Many of these sets are well conceived and serve as good introductions to a particular kind of music.—*JME*

Smithsonian/Folkways Recordings

Folkways Recordings, started by Moses Asch and Marian Distler in 1947, introduced baby boomers to real folk music. Folkways was the folk/world label back in the '60s. With 2,100-plus albums in their catalog, Folkways is the way many of us first heard the likes of the New Lost City Ramblers, the Country Gentlemen, Woody Guthrie, Cisco Houston, Leadbelly, and others, not to mention a wealth of indigenous world music. But for a while, it looked like Folkways (a real national treasure) would be gone forever. However, thanks to a special arrangement with Rounder Records in 1987, every original Folkways album is once again available under a new company called Smithsonian/Folkways. New and priceless recordings from the archives have been added to the catalog.—*JME*
The complete Folkways catalog is available by writing to:

Smithsonian/Folkways Recordings
Center for Folklife Programs
955 l'Enfant Plaza, Suite 2600
Smithsonian Institution
Washington, D.C. 20560

Time-Life Series

The Time-Life Series is available only by mail order. You will find it advertised everywhere—on TV and in many magazines. Time-Life offers sets of recordings on R&B, country, the music of the '70s, Hit Parades ('40s and '50s hits), classic rock 'n' roll, the rock 'n' roll era, and others. Each set consists of many separate albums, each one containing the big hits for a particular year. In the case of rock, there are often second and third albums for a given year featuring additional minor hits.

The bad news is that these CDs are expensive. By the time you pay the shipping and handling, each one costs about $20 a shot, which is just too much. For this reason, I wish I could suggest that you ignore the Time-Life Series, that they were poorly done or that there was some other reason not to buy them. But the truth is that these CDs are, for the most part, well conceived and well executed. No other hits collection series is nearly as comprehensive. Perhaps some of the early albums in the rock series are a little weak, but they are worth having.

Typically, there are from 20 to 24 hits per disc, with good liner notes (and complete discographies!) written by well-known music writers. I am not alone in this opinion: after talking with some of the other editors of the *AMG,* the word is that this series is expensive but a real value. The R&B series is especially nice.—*JME*

Label Addresses

BEAR FAMILY RECORDS
P.O. Box 1154
D-27727 Hambergen, Germany
Phone: (0 47 94) 13 99
Fax: (0 47 94) 15 74

BLOODSHOT RECORDS
912 W. Addison
Chicago, IL 60613-4339
Phone: (773) 248-8709
Fax: (773) 248-8702
E-mail: bludshot@mcs.com
Homepage: http://www.narl.com/bloodshot

COLLECTORS' CHOICE MUSIC
P.O. Box 838
Itasca, IL 60143-0838
(800) 923-1122

COUNTRY MUSIC HALL OF FAME MAIL ORDER
4 Music Square East
Nashville, TN 37203
800-255-2357

COUNTY SALES
P.O. Box 191
Floyd, VA 24091
(703) 745-2001

DEJADISC, INC.
821 Porter Road
Nashville, TN 37206
Phone: (615) 262-9680
Fax: (615) 650-2957
E-mail: dejadisc@eden.com

DIESEL ONLY RECORDS
100 North 6th Street
Brooklyn, NY 11211
E-mail: DieselOnly@aol.com

DOWN HOME MUSIC
10341 San Pablo Avenue
El Cerrito, CA 94530
(415) 525-1494

DRAG CITY RECORDS
P.O. Box 476867
Chicago, IL 60647

DUTCH EAST INDIA TRADING
P.O. Box 738
Syosset, NY 11791
E-mail: info@dutch-east.com

ELDERLY INSTRUMENTS
1100 North Washington
Lansing, MI 48901
(517) 372-7890

HIGHTONE RECORDS
220 4th Street No.101
Oakland, CA 94607
Phone: (510) 763-8500 (sorry, no phone orders)
Fax: (510) 763-8558

MUSIC CITY NEWS
P.O. Box 22975
Nashville, TN 37202-2975
Phone: (615) 329-2200
Homepage: http://www.hsv.tis.net/mcn

RAZOR AND TIE RECORDS
P.O. Box 585
Cooper Station, NY 10276

REBEL
P.O. Box 3057
Roanoke, VA 24015
(540) 343-5476

ROUNDER RECORDS
One Camp Street
Cambridge, MA 02140-1194
Phone: 800-44-DISCS (1-800-443-4727)
Fax: (617) 868-8769
Homepage: http://www.rounder.com/

SAFE HOUSE
P.O. Box 5349
W. Lebanon, NH 03784
Phone: (802) 295-1269
Fax: (802) 295-4930

SUB POP RECORDS
1928 Second Avenue
Seattle, WA 98101
Phone: 1-800-SUB-POP1
Homepage: http://shiva.subpop.com/

VINYL VENDORS
1800 South Robertson Boulevard No.279
Los Angeles, CA 90035
Phone: (310) 275-1444
Fax: (310) 275-8444
E-mail: paul@vinylvendors.com
Homepage: http://www2.vinylvendors.com/VinylVendors/

INDEX

When it comes to music, we wrote the book

All Music Guide to Rock
The Best CDs, Albums & Tapes—Rock, Pop, Soul, R&B, and Rap

Edited by Michael Erlewine, Chris Woodstra and Vladimir Bogdanov

This is the ultimate guide to rock recordings. For 15,500 CDs, albums and tapes by 2,500 artists—everything from doo-wop to hip-hop—you get concise reviews, expert ratings and revealing career profiles, plus historical music maps and dozens of essays on rock styles and influences.

Softcover, 970pp, 6-1/8 x 9-1/4, ISBN 0-87930-376-X, $24.95

All Music Guide
The Best CDs, Albums & Tapes—Third Edition

Edited by Michael Erlewine, Chris Woodstra and Vladimir Bogdanov

This fascinating reference leads readers to the best recordings of 4,000-plus artists and groups. From rock to rap, classical to country and everything in between, more than 21,000 recordings in 20 categories are reviewed and rated by 150 top music critics. Includes artist bios, music timelines, and more.

Softcover, 1,500pp, 6-1/8 x 9-1/4, ISBN 0-87930-423-5, $27.95

All Music Guide to The Blues
The Experts' Guide to the Best Blues Recordings

Edited by Michael Erlewine, Chris Woodstra, Vladimir Bogdanov, and Cub Koda

This comprehensive, easy-to-use and fun-to-browse book is a crucial companion for anyone who listens to the blues. It features reviews and ratings of over 2,600 recordings and profiles of over 560 musicians.

Softcover, 432pp, 6-1/8 x 9-1/4, ISBN 0-87930-424-3, $17.95

All Music Guide to Jazz
The Best CDs, Albums & Tapes—Second Edition

Edited by Michael Erlewine, Chris Woodstra, Vladimir Bogdanov, and Scott Yanow

The essential reference for starting, expanding, or fine-tuning a prime jazz collection. Noted jazz critics profile the lives and work of 1,400 key artists, and review and rate each one's superior recordings—more than 13,000 in all.

Softcover, 900pp, 6-1/8 x 9-1/4, ISBN 0-87930-407-3, $24.95

All Music Book of Hit Albums
The Top 10 US & UK Album Charts from 1960 to the Present Day

Compiled by Dave McAleer

From the birth of album charts in 1960, this unique book lists the Top 10 albums in both the US and the UK through the present. Also filled with photos and fascinating trivia.

Softcover, 352pp, 8 x 8-1/2, ISBN 0-87930-393-X, $22.95

All Music Book of Hit Singles
Top Twenty Charts from 1954 to the Present Day • Second Edition

Compiled by Dave McAleer

This musical time capsule compares U.S. and U.K. Top 20 charts for the past 40 years. The book is studded with photos, trivia and chartfacts featuring the stars and styles of pop music.

Softcover, 432pp, 8 x 8-1/2, ISBN 0-87930-425-1, $22.95

The Musician's Guide to Reading & Writing Music

By Dave Stewart

For the brand new rocker, the seasoned player or the pro who could use new problem-solving methods, this is a clear and practical guide to learning written music notation. "Essential reading for hitherto lazy rock musicians!" —*Keyboard*

Softcover, 112pp, 6 x 9, ISBN 0-87930-273-9, $9.95

The Musician's Home Recording Handbook
Practical Techniques for Recording Great Music at Home

By Ted Greenwald

This easy-to-follow, practical guide to setting up a home recording studio will help any musician who wants to get the best results from the equipment already at hand.

Softcover, 176pp, 8-1/2 x 11, ISBN 0-87930-237-2, $19.95

Making Music Your Business
A Guide for Young Musicians

By David Ellefson

This book is designed to help young musicians understand how to manage the business side of their career. Professional electric bassist David Ellefson, bassist for Megadeath, draws on nearly 20 years of recording and touring experience to share his hands-on knowledge about how the music industry works—from the musician's perspective.

Softcover, 144pp, 6 x 9-1/4, ISBN 0-87930-460-X, $14.95

The Hammond Organ
Beauty in the B

By Mark Vail

This book celebrates the rich history of the Hammond B-3 tonewheel organ; its right-hand man, the whirling Leslie speaker; and their combined influence on gospel, blues, jazz, and rock since the '50s. It also covers other famous Hammond models, and includes photos and performance tips from B-3 stars, plus tips on buying and maintaining a B-3.

Softcover, 240pp, 8-1/2 x 11, 200 photos, ISBN 0-87930-459-6, $24.95

Piano
A Photographic History of the World's Most Celebrated Instrument • By David Crombie

A stunning full-color showcase of how the piano has evolved over the past 300 years, transforming the world of music like no other instrument. This book reveals the grace and beauty of the piano's design, its tremendous musical heritage, and the technics of its inner workings that render tones uniquely sweet, rich, and versatile.

Hardcover, 112pp, 200 color photos, 10 x 12-3/4, ISBN 0-87930-372-7, $35.00

Rock Hardware
40 Years of Rock Instrumentation

By Tony Bacon

This richly illustrated book chronicles the development of the great instruments of rock, how they are used, and how they shape the sound of popular music. It covers guitars, keyboards, synthesizers, drums, brass, recording gear, and more.

Softcover, 144pp, 8-1/2 x 11, 200 color photos, ISBN 0-87930-428-6, $24.95

When it comes to music, we wrote the book

When it comes to music, we wrote the book

The Ukulele
A Visual History • By Jim Beloff

The humble ukulele has left its mark on popular music and culture not only in Hawaii but throughout the world. This book provides a colorful look at the past and present of this intriguing, diminutive musical instrument. It's packed with photos of rare and unusual ukuleles, and memorabilia such as whimsical sheet music covers and witty advertisements.

Softcover, 112pp, 200 color photos, 7-3/8 x 9-1/4, ISBN 0-87930-454-5, $24.95

Secrets from the Masters
40 Great Guitar Players

Edited by Don Menn

Featuring the most influential guitarists of the past 25 years: Jimi Hendrix, Les Paul, Eric Clapton, Eddie Van Halen, Chuck Berry, Andrés Segovia, Pete Townshend and more. Combines personal biography, career history, and playing techniques.

Softcover, 300 pp, 8-1/2 x 11, ISBN 0-87930-260-7, $19.95

Blues Guitar • The Men Who Made the Music
—Second Edition • Edited by Jas Obrecht

Readers get a look inside the lives and music of thirty great bluesmen, through interviews, articles, discographies, and rare photographs. Covers Buddy Guy, Robert Johnson, John Lee Hooker, Albert King, B.B. King, Muddy Waters, and more.

Softcover, 278pp, 8-1/2 x 11, ISBN 0-87930-292-5, $22.95

Bass Heroes
Styles, Stories & Secrets of 30 Great Bass Players • Edited by Tom Mulhern

Thirty of the world's greatest bass players in rock, jazz, studio/pop, and blues & funk share their musical influences, playing techniques, and opinions. Includes Jack Bruce, Stanley Clarke, James Jamerson, Paul McCartney, and more.

Softcover, 208pp, 8-1/2 x 11, ISBN 0-87930-274-7, $19.95

The Fender Amp Book
A Complete History of Fender Amplifiers

By John Morrish

Before Fender electric guitars became household words, Fender amplifiers were already making the scene. Here is the absorbing tale of how Fender fame spread via one of the company's most important product lines.

Hardcover, 96pp, 4-1/2 x 9-1/8, ISBN 0-87930-345-X, $17.95

How to Play Guitar
The Basics & Beyond—Chords, Scales, Tunes & Tips

By the Editors of Guitar Player

For anyone learning to play acoustic or electric guitar, this book and CD set is packed with music, licks, and lessons from the pros. The CD guides readers through nine lessons.

Softcover, 80 pp, 8-1/2 x 11, ISBN 0-87930-399-9, $14.95

Hot Guitar
Rock Soloing, Blues Power, Rapid-Fire Rockabilly, Slick Turnarounds, and Cool Licks • By Arlen Roth

This collection of hot techniques and cool licks includes detailed instruction and hundreds of musical examples. This book covers string bending, slides, picking and fingering techniques, soloing, and rock, blues, and country licks.

Softcover, 130pp, 8-1/2 x 11, ISBN 0-87930-276-3, $19.95

Picks! The Colorful Saga of Vintage Celluloid Guitar Plectrums • By Will Hoover

An eye-catching look back at the vast variety and fascinating history of vintage celluloid guitar picks. "Will Hoover has taken what you might imagine to be a mundane subject and made it fascinating." —Billboard

Softcover, 107pp, 6-1/2 x 6-1/2, ISBN 0-87930-377-8, $12.95

Jaco • The Extraordinary and Tragic Life of Jaco Pastorius, "The World's Greatest Bass Player"
By Bill Milkowski

This is a fitting tribute to the talented but tormented genius who revolutionized the electric bass and single-handedly fused jazz, classical, R&B, rock, reggae, pop, and punk—all before the age of 35, when he met his tragic death.

Softcover with CD 264pp, 6 x 9, ISBN 0-87930-426-X, $14.95

Guitar Player Repair Guide
How to Set Up, Maintain, and Repair Electrics and Acoustics —Second Edition

By Dan Erlewine

Whether you're a player, collector, or repairperson, this hands-on guide provides all the essential information on caring for guitars and electric basses. Includes hundreds of photos and drawings detailing techniques for guitar care and repair.

Softcover, 309pp, 8-1/2 x 11, ISBN 0-87930-291-7, $22.95

Do-It-Yourself Projects for Guitarists
35 Useful, Inexpensive Electronic Projects to Help Unlock Your Instrument's Potential

By Craig Anderton

A step-by-step guide for electric guitarists who want to create maximum personalized sound with minimum electronic problems, and get the satisfaction of achieving all this themselves.

Softcover, 171pp, 7-3/8 x 10-7/8, ISBN 0-87930-359-X, $19.95

The Bass Book
A Complete Illustrated History of Bass Guitars

By Tony Bacon and Barry Moorhouse

Celebrating the electric bass and its revolutionary impact on popular music worldwide, this richly colorful history features rare, classic and modern basses, plus exclusive quotes from Paul McCartney, Stanley Clarke, and other bass greats.

Hardcover, 108pp, 7-1/2 x 9-3/4, ISBN 0-87930-368-9, $22.95

The Chinery Collection
150 Years of American Guitars

By Scott Chinery and Tony Bacon

Scott Chinery's fantastic collection can at last be seen in this beautifully illustrated book, documenting the designs, technology, and art of the greatest guitars of recent times. It tells the full story of the American guitar, from the 1800s to today.

Hardcover & slipcase, 132 pp, 500 color photos, 10 x 12-3/4, ISBN 0-87930-482-0, $75.00

Gibson's Fabulous Flat-Top Guitars
By Eldon Whitford, David Vinopal, and Dan Erlewine

250 photos and detailed text illustrate the development of Gibson's flat-tops, showing why these guitars have been the choice of so many great musicians over the decades. Includes detailed specs on historic and modern Gibson flat-tops.

Softcover, 207pp, 8-1/2 x 11, ISBN 0-87930-297-6, $22.95

Stand By Your Music